# BREWER'S DICTIONARY of PHRASE & FABLE

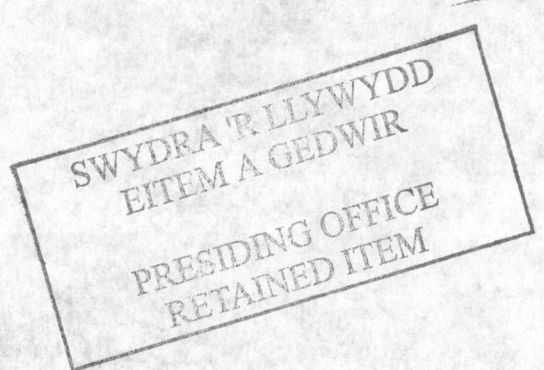

# BREWER'S DICTIONARY *of* PHRASE & FABLE

## MILLENNIUM EDITION

Revised by Adrian Room

CASSELL

**Cassell & Co**
Wellington House
125 Strand,
London WC2R OBB



First published 1870
Millennium edition 1999

Reprinted 2000 (twice)

Reprinted with corrections 2001

Reprinted 2001 (twice), 2002 (three times)

**British Library Cataloguing in Publication Data**
A catalogue record for this book is available from the British Library

ISBN 0–304–35096–6 (hbk)
ISBN 0–304–35873 (pbk)

Typeset in Plantin and Imprint by
Gem Graphics, Trenance, Cornwall
Printed in Finland by WS Bookwell Ltd

# CONTENTS

# FOREWORD

## BY TERRY PRATCHETT

I was a Brewer's boy. I first grasped the spine of my second-hand copy when I was twelve. It's still in amazing condition, considering the work I've made it do.

It was my introduction to mythology and ancient history and a lot more, too, because Brewer's is a serendipitous (see page 1063) book. In other words, you might not find what you're looking for, but you *will* find three completely unexpected things that are probably more interesting. Reading one item in Brewer's is like eating one peanut. It's practically impossible. There are plenty of other useful books. But you *start* with Brewer's.

Nevertheless, the book is hard to describe. You could call it a compendium (I didn't find this in my ancient edition, but I did find 'Complutensian Polyglot', so the effort was not wasted) of myth, legend, quotation, historical byways and slang, but that would still miss out quite a lot of it. A better description would be 'an education', in the truest sense. Brewer's flowered in those pre-*Trivial Pursuit* days when people believed that if you patiently accumulated a knowledge of small things a knowledge of big things would automatically evolve, and you would become a better person.

Brewer's has been updated for this Millennium Edition. It includes Gandalf as well as Attila the Hun (and why shouldn't it?) Some of the duller nymphs and more obscure Classical items have been dropped to make way for such additions to the language as 'hit the ground running' and 'all dressed up and nowhere to go'. To be considered obscure by a Brewer's editor is a real badge of obscurity, and it is sad to see them go; the serious Brewerite can only hope that Cassell might one day be persuaded to release a 'preservation' edition, so that this detritus of myth and legend is not forever lost.

But today is tomorrow's past. One day the Fab Four (ask your dad) will be one with ... oh, some of the things that no one cares about any more. Given the speed of change, they're already well on the way. It's an education in itself, seeing them take their place with old Roman senators and mythological fauna, and watching the dust settle. We're the next millennium's ancients...

*Brewer's Dictionary of Phrase and Fable* is the first book to turn to when questions arise and the final desperate volume when all the lesser reference books have failed. No bookshelf, no WORLD is complete without it. It's as simple as that.

# FROM THE PREFACE TO THE 1ST EDITION OF 1870

'What has this babbler to say?' is substantially the question of every one to whom a new book is offered. For ourselves, it will be difficult to furnish an answer in a sentence equally terse and explicit; yet our book has a definite scope and distinct speciality, which we will proceed to unfold. We call it a 'Dictionary of Phrase and Fable', a title wide enough, no doubt, to satisfy a very lofty ambition, yet not sufficiently wide to describe the miscellaneous contents of this 'alms-basket of words'. As the Gargantuan course of studies included everything known to man and something more, so this sweep-net of a book encloses anything that comes within its reach. It draws in curious or novel etymologies, pseudonyms and popular titles, local traditions and literary blunders, biographical and historical trifles too insignificant to find a place in books of higher pretension, but not too worthless to be worth knowing. Sometimes a criticism is adventured, sometimes an exposition. Vulgar errors, of course, form an item; for the prescience of the ant in laying up a store for winter, the wisdom of the bee in the peculiar shape of its honey-comb, the disinterestedness of the jackal, the poisonous nature of the upas tree, and the striding of the Rhodian Colossos, if not of the nature of fable, are certain 'more strange than true' ...

In a word, from a mass of material in manuscript, fully thrice the size of the present volume, we have selected some 20,000 examples of what we have thought to be the best suited for popular purposes. Much has been culled, of necessity, from the thousand and one sources of such lore, in English, German or French, and more is entirely new. We cannot even hope that all our explanations will pass the ordeal of critics unscathed. It is the bread and cheese of some to 'pick holes in a' our coats'; and the lighting on weak places carries with it something of the ferret's or huntman's 'passion'. What is fair game will, of course, be run hard; and some of our statements must of necessity be mere matters of opinion, in more than one instance modified even while these pages have been passing through the press; but we doubt not that most of them are correct, and are bold to believe that we have in many cases succeeded, where others have wholly or partially failed. The labour has been the willing labour of an enthusiast, who has been for twenty years a 'snapper-up of unconsidered trifles'.

# PREFACE TO THE MILLENNIUM EDITION

This new, Millennium Edition of Dr Brewer's *Dictionary of Phrase and Fable*, following the 15th edition of 1995, sees changes on four fronts. First, a number of new entries have been added. These range, as before, from the 'golden oldies' to the modern and new-fangled, and from the general to the specialised. Long-established words and phrases that slipped through the net before but that now form part of the corpus include *Alarums and excursions*, *Bedside manner*, *Black eye*, *Country dance*, *Dilly-dally*, *Early bird*, *Garden party*, *Lo and behold* and *Old retainer.* Modern additions include *Ants in one's pants*, *Barbie doll*, *Couch potato*, *Essex girl*, *Full monty*, *Honey trap*, *Mockney*, *Paparazzi* and *Trick or treat*. Names of historical and fictional characters that now appear for the first time include *Canute*, *David Copperfield*, *Gulliver*, *Hannibal*, *Marie Antoinette*, *Naomi*, *Robespierre*, *Trilby*, *Yorick* and *Zacchaeus*. Some personal names have more of a tale to tell in their origin than their identity, and typical of them are *Baby Bunting*, *Godzilla*, *Gretchen*, *Nemo*, *Sharon* and *Tracy*. In the area of specialised entries there was a perceptible lacuna in the field of literary terms, so the reader will now find, among others, *Anacoluthon*, *Anadiplosis*, *Catachresis*, *Hendiadys*, *Hypallage*, *Prolepsis* and *Wellerism*. New 'general' entries, dealing with a particular area of words or names, are *Chambersisms*, *Hurricane names*, *Literary place-names*, *Lovers' acronyms*, *Mispronounced words*, *Romany names of towns and countries*, *Titled trains* and *Verlan*. This last, a type of French jargon, may seem to verge on the esoteric, but esotericism has always been an essential element of *Brewer*, and the entry is thus accompanied by such bedfellows as *Beau ténébreux*, *Croque-monsieur*, *Drunken forest*, *Scapulimancy* and *Technogamia*.

The second front also involves additions, but this time in the area of sub-entries, where readers will find more examples of phrases involving a particular word. The third area is in that of quotations. Many new quotations have been added, and a few existing ones replaced by more recent or more appropriate citations. One of the pleasures of a dictionary are the examples of actual usage accompanying a particular word or phrase, and *Brewer* aims to provide a more generous offer here than before. Finally, a few entries that had been retained in the 15th edition appeared increasingly obscure or irrelevant, so have been quietly dropped. Their loss should not be mourned, and has been more than compensated for by the greater number of new entries. It goes without saying that errors noted in the 15th edition have now been corrected and the factual information updated where necessary. Thanks are due to correspondents who pointed out such errors and who also wrote to suggest new entries.

In short, this new edition of *Brewer* has a blend of 'the mixture as before' and 'the new and improved', as is perhaps nicely exemplified by the revised and expanded entry *Millennium* and the entirely new entry *Millennium bug*, both agreeably apt for the edition's designation.

ADRIAN ROOM

# INTRODUCTION

## BY JOHN BUCHANAN-BROWN

A reference book that has flourished for over a hundred years is clearly something exceptional. Its original compiler needs to hit upon not so much a new area of information of wide and permanent interest as a way of presenting that material and of providing access to it that satisfies and attracts generation after generation of readers. Equally, such a compiler needs to place his book with publishers sensitive to changing tastes and aware of the need periodically to give the work that face-lift needed to attract fresh generations of readers to the mass of information within. Both these conditions have been satisfied in the case of *Brewer's Dictionary of Phrase and Fable.* That this is a fresh revision – the Millennium Edition – speaks loudly enough for the publishers' keeping their side of the bargain. Hence it is the purpose of this short introduction to set the original edition in the context of 1870 and to show how skilfully the compiler was able to make available to a wider and predominantly self-educated working-class public some of the more specialized results of 19th-century scholarship.

But what of the compiler himself? What sort of man was Dr E. Cobham Brewer? Some clue was given in the brief Memoir of Dr Brewer with which his grandson, Captain P.M.C. Hayman, introduced the Centenary Edition, spicing the plain facts of biography with childhood memories of his grandfather. (After the death of his wife in 1878, Dr Brewer had come to live with his eldest daughter, Captain Hayman's mother, and her husband, Canon H.T. Hayman, Vicar of Edwinstowe in Nottinghamshire.)

'Dr Brewer', Captain Hayman wrote, 'must have been nearly 80 years of age when I was old enough to remember him at the Vicarage. He had an upstairs room furnished as a bed-sitting-room, for he used to work far into the night, often until three or four in the morning. He always declared that he did his best work then – but he was always down to breakfast dead on time at nine o'clock.

'The walls of this room were papered with a plain white paper, upon which he used to write in pencil stray memoranda and the names of any particularly interesting visitors and the dates on which they came to see him. These names included that of the Duchess of Portland, then one of the most beautiful women in the country. She insisted on going upstairs to my grandfather's own room and carried on a long conversation with him, sitting on his bed, a highly informal proceeding in those days, which particularly pleased the old gentleman!

'He had a wonderful way with children and would put aside whatever he was doing to amuse the children of the house before they went to bed. He was a great hand at cutting out, drawing, telling stories, showing his "treasures" which he had collected in various countries and relating his experiences in France and at the Court of Napoleon III and his Empress. But it was his sense of humour, which he could adapt to the childish mind, which made Dr Brewer in his old age such a very delightful companion to the youngest of his grandchildren.

'He was also quite fearless. On one occasion the Vicarage odd-job-man – not remarkable for either intelligence or courage – came up to the house to announce that a rough-looking man was asleep in the stable. Before my father, a county cricketer and a noted sportsman, could move, Dr Brewer had seized a stick and, when the Vicar arrived at the stable, he found the old gentleman belabouring the trespasser, a hulking tramp, and exclaiming, "Be off, you scoundrel!" This onslaught was too much for the tramp, who made off as hard as he could go.'

However vivid and photographic a child's memories of a fascinating and much-loved figure, these memories, like the photograph, capture only a fleeting moment in a very long life. This is the patriarchal figure of the portrait by his younger daughter, which was reproduced as a frontispiece to the Centenary Edition. But what of his youth and middle age? Here the information is tantalizingly scanty.

Ebenezer Cobham Brewer was born on 2 May 1810, the son of a Norwich schoolmaster. In 1832 he went up to Trinity Hall, Cambridge, to read for a degree in Law. At the age of 22, he was considerably older than most undergraduates: Thackeray, a year his junior, had departed from neighbouring Trinity College, prematurely, it is true, a couple of years earlier. Brewer's university career was, however, the antithesis of the novelist's. So, far from leaving after a year and heavily in debt, Brewer, according to his grandson, worked his way through college and crowned his achievement by graduating with first-class honours in 1836. Undoubtedly he then hoped for a college fellowship for, such posts then being confined to clergy of the Church of England, he was ordained deacon in 1836 and priest two years later. Equally clearly, he was disappointed in his ambition, for he next appears as assistant and then as successor to his father in their school, Mile End House, Norwich.

One is bound to wonder just how much of a living the school provided for Brewer and his father. It is, perhaps, indicative of financial stringency that Brewer went up to Cambridge so much later than the average undergraduate and that he had to support himself while at the university. Moreover, it is still more suggestive that we next find him in the early 1850s settled in Paris, for throughout the century the

Continent was the refuge of those English suffering financial embarrassment. I am not hinting at anything dishonourable, but if Dr Brewer had had to give up his school through financial pressure, the Continent was the ideal place in which to recuperate. Living was cheap, and, above all, there was no need to keep up those middle-class appearances so essential in one's native land.

How Brewer earned his living during those years it is impossible to say. The fact that in later life he was editor of *The Morning Chronicle* would point to journalism, and his familiarity with French Imperial circles would seem to confirm this, since a foreign correspondent would have easy access to Napoleon III and his ministers. At the same time the list of his published books (all educational) shows that he continued in the vein he had first explored while still a Norwich schoolmaster. Around 1841 he had written his most successful *Guide to Science* for the Norwich printers and publishers, Jarrolds, which became his principal publishers thereafter. Turning, however, from speculation to known fact, we find that by 1856 Brewer had become well enough established to return to England, marry and settle at Lavant in West Sussex.

In the early 1860s he became associated with Messrs Cassell, Petter and Galpin, to whom his facility as an educational writer and experience as a schoolmaster were particular recommendations. The publishing house that John Cassell had founded in 1848 and that George William Petter and Thomas Dixon Galpin had rescued in 1855 when success overstrained the founder's resources was built upon those twin pillars of Victorian stability, religion and self-improvement, with a strong flavour of total abstinence, for John Cassell had started out as a temperance lecturer. His major contribution to the field of adult education was his *Popular Educator,* launched in 1850 as a penny weekly part-issue and designed to enable the working man to educate himself to university entrance standards in a wide variety of subjects. This was followed by more specialized courses, and it is interesting to note that what have become the mainstays of the Cassell list for so many years – the foreign-language dictionaries – started life as major elements in integrated language-teaching series. In 1853 French, German and Latin dictionaries began to be issued in threepenny numbers, along with the appropriate grammars, readers and exercises (for which keys were provided), all parts of complete 'teach yourself' courses.

But if adult education had been the dominant strain in the first half of the century, by the 1850s the focus of concern had shifted to primary schooling. In 1858 a Royal Commission on popular education was appointed and although it was not until 1870 that the new school boards were empowered to make education compulsory in England and Wales if they so wished, the trend was apparent far earlier. Cassell was therefore moving with this tide when it widened its horizons to include the children as well as their fathers in *Child Educator* of 1855 and the later series, *My first book of* ... . Of this, the first six titles were published in 1864 (the year before John Cassell died) and another six followed in 1868. All twelve were written by Dr E.C. Brewer.

While the tradition in the family is that Dr Brewer occupied a senior editorial post at Cassell at this time, the evidence from the diary of another employee, Bonavia Hunt, which Simon Nowell-Smith quotes in *The House of Cassell* (1958), points to the conclusion that Brewer had simply been provided with an office at the firm's headquarters at La Belle Sauvage where he compiled his books for them. Very probably he was engaged in other projects, since the period of two years covered by the diary falls midway between the publication of the two batches of *My first book of…* . Nor, I fear, did the middle-aged Dr Brewer make such a favourable impression on his young colleague as he was to make upon his grandson in old age. 'What a fussy old gentleman Dr Brewer is!' Hunt wrote. 'I find it very tedious to humour and be affable to him, he is so insufferably inquisitive and such an old gossip.' However trying it may have been to the young editor, this inquisitiveness is surely the sustaining virtue of Dr Brewer's enduring contribution to the fortunes of the house of Cassell, his *Dictionary of Phrase and Fable*.

From the compiler's own account it is not absolutely certain whether Cassell was offered the finished manuscript of the *Dictionary of Phrase and Fable* for publication or whether it commissioned it from him on the basis of sample material that he had already collected. The latter seems the more probable for, as he himself wrote:

> the popularity of this book *[A Guide to Science]* brought me in a large number of questions on all imaginary matters. I kept these questions and their answers till they grew into a large book, when I sorted them and made the nucleus of the *Dictionary of Phrase and Fable*. I consulted the Editor of *The Despatch,* to whom I was well known, but it was his opinion that the book would have no sale as it would be wholly impossible to exhaust the subject.

Fortunately Cassell thought differently and despite expressing doubt 'whether the book would pay the expense of printing' – a typical ploy when it comes to negotiating with an author – the *Dictionary* was an undoubted success. By 1886, that is, within 16 years of its first publication, it had been reprinted 18 times, and with the first printing of the second edition of 1894–5 the publishers could claim that 100,000 copies of the book had been produced.

The *Dictionary* undoubtedly owed its popularity to the way in which its subject matter, whether by intuition or by conscious design, responded to the needs of a reading public created by 19th-century conditions. From the rapidly growing towns and cities emerged a class of reader, literate if not educated in the academic sense, that looked beyond the pure entertainment of novels and poetry, the utility of self-education and the moral uplift of religious books to the satisfaction of simple intellectual curiosity. This is that spirit of enquiry that at one end of the scale leads to pure scholarship and at the other to the acquisition of what some would stigmatize as totally useless information. It was that lower end of the scale that turned to the compilations of John Timbs (1801–75), sometime editor of *The Mirror* and *The Illustrated London News*. Using Dr Brewer's method of scissors, paste and pigeon-holes, he abstracted the curiosities of science, history and human behaviour that came his way in the course of his editorial duties and rehashed them in such books as *Things not Generally Known, Curiosities of London* and *Curiosities of History,* all of which enjoyed considerable popularity in the mid-1850s.

Certainly there is an element of Timbs in some of the subjects included in the *Dictionary,* but Brewer gives them a permanent rather than an ephemeral value because he presents them for information rather than entertainment. More important is that the mere quirks of history are subordinated to the popularization of a very important segment of 19th-century scholarship – the investigation of the language, customs and belief of the common people, all part and parcel of what may be loosely termed the Romantic Movement away from the Classicism that had dominated Europe since the Renaissance.

In England the trend had become apparent in the 18th century in the cult of the Gothic exemplified by Horace Walpole's villa at Strawberry Hill, in the interest in Norse and Celtic mythology evinced, for example, by Gray's poems and Macpherson's *Ossian,* in such collections of folk-custom and belief as the Newcastle antiquary, John Brand's *Observations of Popular Antiquities,* first published in 1777 and reprinted throughout the 19th century, and in Frederick Grose's *Classical Dictionary of the Vulgar Tongue* (1785). However, and as in so many other fields, German scholarship took the lead in the early years of the 19th century. *Grimm's Fairy Tales* has become one of the most popular of children's books, but the tales originated as a scholarly collection by those great philologists, the Brothers Grimm. Indeed, philology and folklore go hand in hand and by 1839 we can find the specialist publisher, John Russell Smith, including in his list not merely a new edition of Grose's *Glossary of Provincial and Local Words* but a whole series of similar vocabularies devoted to different parts of England and to stories and poems written in dialect. Again, while Joseph Jacobs's two classic collections of English fairy tales were not to appear until the last decade of the century, they are in some sense the culmination of the work of many others in the field. Thomas Crofton Croker, for example, had been collecting such material in the south of Ireland in the 1820s and the wider general interest in such lore is typified by the publication in 1850 of Thomas Keightley's wide-ranging *Fairy Mythology*.

Folk-customs and belief, and Celtic and Norse mythology are important elements in Dr Brewer's compilation, but the philological is, perhaps, the most striking in the early editions. The century saw the publication of important etymological dictionaries by Wedgwood and Skeat, the whole brought together in the

Philological Society's great work, *The New English Dictionary.* Better known by its current name of *The Oxford English Dictionary,* the first volume had been published in 1884, and it is very probably to this that Dr Brewer referred in the Preface to the second edition of 1894–5 as principal among those researches into English philology in the previous 25 years that enabled him to make so many corrections and additions in this field. For the great feature of both the editions that Brewer himself prepared is the wealth of philological and etymological information with which they responded to the wide interest among the public at large in the meaning and derivation of English words. This may perhaps be best exemplified by the success of Archbishop Trench's *The Study of Words.* Originating as lectures to the Winchester Diocesan Training School, the book was first published in 1851 and had by 1904 achieved a (posthumous) 27th edition.

Thus we can see how the *Dictionary of Phrase and Fable* was conceived in the mainstream of 19th-century philological and antiquarian research, but no consideration of the genesis of the book would be complete without mention of the work that, I would suggest, inspired Dr Brewer to his masterpiece. This was *Noted Names of Fiction,* originally contributed as a supplement to the 1864 edition of *Webster's Dictionary* by William Adolphus Wheeler (1833–74) and subsequently enlarged and published as a separate book. Wheeler, who later helped to produce various abridgements of *Webster* and was employed in the Boston Public Library, also included in his work 'familiar pseudonyms, surnames bestowed on eminent men, and analogous popular appellations often referred to in literature and conversation'. Comparison between his book and Brewer's shows beyond any shadow of doubt that his was a source, and a very substantial source, of material for fields of common interest. Yet it was precisely what was *not* in *Noted Names* that very probably prompted Brewer's undertaking, for Wheeler wrote in his Preface that:

> The introduction of appellative or generic names, such as *abbot of unreason, lord of misrule, kobold,* etc., as well as the explanation of celebrated customs and phrases, such as *flap-dragon, nine-men's morrice, philosophy of the Porch, to send to Coventry, to carry coals to Newcastle,* etc., would open too vast a field of enquiry; and besides, there are copious special treatises on these subjects already before the public.

If Brewer really did take this hint, it is surely to his credit that he was undaunted by the vastness of the field and shrewd enough to realize that although there might be treatises before the public, his public, Cassell's working- and lower middle-class public, would either be unaware of or overawed by them. So when he came to compile his *Dictionary,* it was not only Wheeler's noted names that went into the mixing-bowl, but all those words and phrases that Wheeler had specifically declined – and many more like them – as well as generous helpings of philology, etymology, folklore, mythology and those curiosities that Timbs had collected before him. Thus, if its ingredients were drawn from common stock, the recipe was all Brewer's very own.

And what a successful recipe it has proved to be. Of course tastes have changed in the ensuing hundred years and more. Modern English dictionaries cater for the etymologies of words; we no longer feel the need to know the names of all the characters in Sir Walter Scott's novels or the *dramatis personae* of long-forgotten 18th-century comedies, but we still want to know the story of 'words that have a tale to tell' – this is what makes *Brewer's* such a splendid book for browsing.

In paying tribute to the compiler, let us not forget the publishers. Cassell had created something new in dictionaries, but it seems to have realized that it needed to speak with a special accent to each succeeding generation of users. Accordingly, it invited Dr Brewer himself to revise, correct and expand a new edition in 1894–5, exactly 25 years from the date of the first *Brewer's*. This edition ran up to and beyond the First World War and in 1923 Lawrence H. Dawson edited the revised and up-dated version, which was to carry *Brewer's* through the years of slump and depression and the horrors of the Second World War. Once again it was time to bring *Brewer's* up to date and a new edition of the *Dictionary of Phrase and Fable* was among the top priorities of the post-war publishing programme. The then Chairman of Cassell, Dr Desmond Flower, M.C., made it his especial concern, and a new and revised edition duly appeared in 1952. Dr Flower was again the moving spirit behind the Centenary Edition and was especially fortunate in his choice of editor for that task. Ivor H. Evans not only prepared this edition for publication in 1970 but was to act as trustee of *Brewer's* fortunes for the next 19 years. He was responsible for the revised editions first published in 1981 and 1989 and for the corrected reprints that appeared in the interim. In a very real sense he helped to keep *Brewer's* alive and handed to his successor a reference work that continues to be a household name.

# GUIDE TO THE USE OF THE DICTIONARY

Entries are arranged in strict alphabetical order on a letter by letter basis. Thus, for example, *D notice* appears after *djinn*, and *arm-in-arm* comes after *armed to the teeth*. As has always been the case with *Brewer's*, words that are linguistically related are grouped together, which means that the entries on *tarpaulin* and *tarred and feathered* can be found under the main entry *tar*, and *first fruits* is discussed under the main entry *first*.

Phrases and expressions appear for the most part under the first word they contain. *Just the thing*, for instance, appears under *just*, and *blow one's top* comes under *blow*. However, expressions that begin with a very common word, such as *make, have, be, in* and *on*, generally appear under the next main word they contain, so that the entry for *have one's cake and eat it* will be found under *cake*, and *make head or tail of* will be found under *head*.

Words and phrases that appear after a main headword are arranged in two alphabetical sequences. The first is made up of those terms that commence with the main word; the second consists of expressions in which the main word appears later on. The sequence of entries at *rain*, for example, begins with *rain cats and dogs* and *rain check* and ends with *it never rains but it pours* and *put something by for a rainy day*.

To help readers find their way around the dictionary, and to draw their attention to articles that are either directly or tangentially related, a large number of cross-references have been included. These are indicated by the use of SMALL CAPITALS.

Abbreviations

| | | | |
|---|---|---|---|
| AD | Anno Domini (year of Our Lord) | e.g. | *exempli gratia* (for example) |
| | | *fl.* | *floruit* (flourished) |
| b. | born | i.e. | *id est* (that is) |
| BC | before Christ | No. | number |
| Bk | book | Pt | part |
| *c.* | *circa* (about) | r. | reigned |
| ch | chapter | Rev. | reverend |
| d. | died | Vol | volume |

# THE DICTIONARY

# A

**A.** This letter evolved from the Hebrew and Phoenician character known as *aleph*, 'ox', supposedly because it originally represented an ox head. However, as now it was probably simply a conventional symbol. *See also* SCARLET LETTER.

**A1.** 'First class'. In LLOYD'S *Register of Shipping* the state of a ship's hull is designated by letters and that of her equipment by figures. A1 thus generally means 'excellent'.

**A or ab** (Latin, 'from').

**Ab ovo** (Latin, 'from the egg'). The reference is to one of the twin eggs of LEDA and the Swan (ZEUS) from which HELEN was born. Had Leda not laid this egg, Helen would never have been born, therefore PARIS could not have eloped with her, therefore there would have been no TROJAN WAR and so on. The English use of the phrase probably derives either from the line in Horace's *De Arte Poetica* (1st century BC):

> Nec gemino bellum Troianum orditur ab ovo.
> (It is not from the twin egg that the Trojan War begins.)

or from another phrase from Horace's *Satires* (1st century BC):

> Ab ovo jusque ad mala
> (From the egg to the apples)

referring to the Roman repast, which began with an egg and concluded with apples.

**A mensa et thoro.** *See* A VINCULO MATRIMONII.

**A posteriori** (Latin, 'from the latter'). An *a posteriori* argument proves the cause from the effect. Thus if we see a watch, we conclude that there must have been a watchmaker. Robinson CRUSOE inferred that there was another human being on the desert island because he saw a human footprint in the wet sand. It is thus that the existence and character of God are inferred from his works. *See also* A PRIORI.

**A priori** (Latin, 'from the previous'). An *a priori* argument is one in which a fact is deduced from something occurring or existing before it, so that certain effects can be inferred from particular causes. Mathematical proofs are of this kind, whereas judgements in the law courts are usually A POSTERIORI.

**A vinculo matrimonii** (Latin, 'from the bond of matrimony'). A divorce or dissolution of marriage. A divorce *a mensa et thoro* ('from board and bed'), the equivalent of a modern decree of judicial separation, was formerly granted by the church courts until the Matrimonial Causes Act of 1857 transferred this jurisdiction to the king's court.

**Aaron.** The first high priest of the Israelites and the brother of MOSES (Exodus 4:14). The origin of his name is uncertain. It may come from Hebrew *harōn*, 'mountainous', or from *arōn*, 'coffer', 'cupboard'. More likely, it is of Egyptian origin and of unknown meaning.

**Aaron's beard.** The popular name of the flowering plant ROSE OF SHARON (*Hypericum calycinum*). The reference is to Psalm 133:2.

**Aaron's rod.** The name given (with reference to Numbers 17:8) to various tall flowering plants, but especially the great mullein (*Verbascum thapsus*). It is also a name for the DIVINING ROD.

**Aaru, Field of.** *See under* FIELD.

**Aarvak** (Old Norse, 'early waker'). In Scandinavian mythology the horse that draws the Sun's chariot, driven by the maiden SOL.

**Aback, To be taken.** To be startled or disconcerted. The expression comes from the nautical term describing a ship that has the wind blowing against her so that she cannot make any forward progress.

**Abacus.** A counting device that traditionally consists of a frame holding rods on which ten beads can slide. One rod represents units, the next tens, the next hundreds and so on. The abacus is still in regular use in eastern countries, and in China it is known as *hsüan pan*, 'computing tray'. Its English name comes from Greek *abax*, a term for a board covered with sand on which calculations could be traced, itself from Hebrew *ābhāk*, 'dust'. The multiplication table invented by PYTHAGORAS is called Abacus Pythagoricus. *See also* NAPIER'S BONES.

**Abaddon** (Hebrew *avaddōn*, 'destruction'). The angel of the bottomless pit (Revelation 9:11). In rabbinical literature the word is used for HELL. Milton used the name for the pit itself:

> In all her gates Abaddon rues
> Thy bold attempt.
> *Paradise Regained*, iv (1671)

**Abaris.** A mythical priest of APOLLO mentioned by Herodotus, Pindar and others, and surnamed 'the Hyperborean'. Apollo gave him a magic arrow (the 'dart of Abaris'), which rendered him invisible and on which he rode through the air. He cured diseases and spoke oracles. Abaris gave the dart to PYTHAGORAS.

**Abbasids.** A dynasty of caliphs who ruled the Muslim Empire from 750 until destroyed by the Mongol invasion in 1258, and who claimed descent from al-Abbas (d.653), uncle of the Prophet MOHAMMED. Haroun al-Raschid (b.765; r.786–808) was one of their number.

**Abbot. Abbot of Misrule.** *See* KING OF MISRULE.

**Abbots Bromley horn dance.** One of England's oldest traditional dances, dating back to pre-Christian times. It takes place at Abbots Bromley, Staffordshire, on the Monday after 4 September, but if this is a Sunday, the dance is a week later, on 12 September. The twelve male dancers include six Deermen wearing reindeer antlers, a hobbyhorse, a 'maid' (a man dressed as a woman), two boys, one with a triangle, the other with a crossbow, and two musicians. At certain junctures the bowman pretends to shoot at the Deermen. The dance is probably based on ancient hunting or fertility rites.

**ABC.** The ALPHABET. To 'know one's ABC' is thus to know the rudiments of a subject. An ABC was formerly a child's reading primer.

**Abd.** In Arabic names this represents *'abd*, 'slave', 'servant', so that ABDIEL and ABDULLAH mean 'servant of God', Abd-el-Kader means 'servant of the powerful one', Abd-el-Latif is 'servant of the gracious one' and so on.

**Abdera.** A Greek city on the coast of Thrace, founded in the 7th century BC and supposedly named by HERCULES in memory of ABDERUS. The inhabitants were proverbial for their stupidity, but among them were the philosopher DEMOCRITUS, the SOPHIST Protagoras, and the lyric poet ANACREON.

**Abderus.** A friend of HERCULES, who was devoured by the horses of DIOMEDES while guarding them.

**Abdication Crisis.** The constitutional upheaval in which Edward VIII (1894–1972) renounced the throne in order to marry Mrs Wallis Simpson (1896–1986), an American divorcee.

Edward became king on 20 January 1936 amid rumours of an existing romantic attachment. In the autumn came the news that the king intended to marry Mrs Simpson, who in 1927 had divorced her first husband, a US navy officer, and that same year married a London stockbroker, Ernest Simpson. The national objection to any marriage was not that Mrs Simpson was an American, nor that she was a commoner, but that she was a divorcee, which would seriously put in question Edward's relationship with the ESTABLISHED CHURCH, which officially censured the whole idea of divorce. But events took their course, and on 27 October 1936 Mrs Simpson was granted a *decree nisi*. The king was now faced with four options: (1) he could marry Mrs Simpson and make her queen; (2) he could contract a MORGANATIC MARRIAGE, so that neither Mrs Simpson nor any children of the marriage would share royal status or property; (3) he could abdicate and then marry; (4) he could abandon Mrs Simpson. He chose the third option, and by the Declaration of Abdication Act, 10 December 1936, Edward VIII renounced the throne and was succeeded by his brother, George VI, who created him Duke of Windsor. The marriage took place in France on 3 June 1937.

Edward VIII thus had the shortest reign of any British monarch except that of his namesake, Edward V (1470–83), one of the PRINCES IN THE TOWER.

**Abdiel** (Arabic *'abd īēl*, 'servant of God', from *'abd*, 'servant', and *el*, 'God'). In Milton's *Paradise Lost* (1667), the faithful seraph who withstood SATAN when he urged the angels to revolt.

**Abdullah** (Arabic *'abd allāh*, 'servant of God', from *'abd*, 'servant', and *Allāh*, 'God'). The father of MOHAMMED. Like ISAAC, he is said to have been offered by his father as a sacrifice to the gods. He was saved at the last minute, however, when the gods accepted a hundred camels in his place. He died while on a trading journey shortly before his son was born.

**Abe, Old.** *See under* OLD.

**Abecedarian, An.** A teacher or learner of the ABC or rudiments.

**Abecedarian hymns.** Hymns whose lines or divisions begin with the letters of the ALPHABET in order. Psalm 119 is abecedarian, and its 176 verses are divided into groups of eight, each beginning with (and headed by) a different letter of the Hebrew alphabet. *See also* ACROSTIC POETRY.

**Abel** (perhaps Hebrew *hevel*, 'breath'). In the Old Testament, the younger son of ADAM and EVE, who was murdered out of jealousy by his brother CAIN (Genesis 4:1–8). The Christian church regards him as a pre-Christian martyr, and Jesus specifically spoke of him as 'righteous' (Matthew 23:35). His murder is the first in the Bible and may be taken to imply that blood must be shed before peace can come. His name suggests that his life was cut short to this end.

**Abelard and Héloïse.** Peter Abelard (1079–1142), an eminent scholar, theologian and philosopher, studied under Guillaume de Champeaux (*c.*1070–1171) and Anselm of Laon (1033–1109), and founded an internationally famous school of theology in Paris. At the age of 36 he became tutor to Héloïse, the beautiful

17-year-old niece of Canon Fulbert of Notre Dame. They fell in love, a son was born, and they were secretly married, but Héloïse soon disavowed the marriage so as not to hinder Abelard's preferment. Fulbert, enraged at her husband's apparent connivance, had him castrated. Abelard entered the monastery of Saint-Denis, while Héloïse became a nun at Argenteuil. Abelard continued his controversial teaching and later founded another school near Nogent-sur-Seine called PARACLETE, which, after his departure to become abbot of the remote Breton monastery of St Gildas, was given to a sisterhood under Héloïse. His stormy career ended in 1142, and Héloïse was laid by his side in 1164. Their remains were transferred from Paraclete and reburied in the PÈRE LACHAISE cemetery, Paris, in 1817.

**Aberdovey, The Bells of.** *See under* BELL.

**Abhidhamma** (Sanskrit, 'special doctrine'). The third *pitaka* ('basket') of the three texts (TRIPITAKA), which together form the sacred canon of the Buddhists. It is arranged in seven books and deals with such subjects as ethics, psychology and epistemology. The texts are not regarded as representing the words of the BUDDHA himself but are nevertheless highly venerated.

**Abhorrers.** *See* PETITIONERS AND ABHORRERS.

**Abif.** *See* HIRAM ABIF.

**Abigail** (Hebrew *avīgáil*, 'whose father rejoices', from *av*, 'father', and *gīl*, 'to rejoice'). Abigail (1 Samuel 25:24–8) repeatedly called herself DAVID's handmaid, with the result that her name came to be used for a lady's maid in general. In *The Scornful Lady* (1616) Francis Beaumont and John Fletcher called the 'waiting gentlewoman' by this name, and it was used by Jonathan Swift, Henry Fielding and others. The general sense was further popularized by Lady Abigail Masham (d.1734), woman of the bedchamber to Queen ANNE and a royal favourite.

**Abimelech** (Hebrew, 'father of the king').

(1) A title of the king of the ancient PHILISTINES.

(2) The natural son of GIDEON. He murdered his 70 brothers (except the youngest, Jothar, who escaped) and became king of Shechem. Jothar's protest about Abimelech's action forms the first parable in the Bible (Judges 9).

**Abiogenesis** (Greek *a-*, 'without', *bios*, 'life', and *genesis*, 'birth'). A term applied by T.H. Huxley in 1870 to the old theory that non-living matter could produce living. An example is found in Virgil's *Georgics* (iv (1st century BC)) when the shepherd Aristaeus, son of APOLLO and CYRENE, having lost his bees through disease and famine, killed four bulls on his mother's orders. On the ninth morning bees swarmed forth from the decomposing corpses.

**Abner, Li'l.** *See under* LI'L.

**Abo.** A derogative colloquial abbreviation of Aborigine or Aboriginal, used in Australia.

**Abolitionists.** Supporters of the abolition of the slave trade, as in Britain in the early 19th century or in the mid-19th century in the USA. The former campaign, which was led by William Wilberforce, resulted in the ending of slavery in the British colonies in 1833. The latter culminated in the Emancipation Proclamation, which was made in 1863 and ratified in 1865.

**Abominable Snowman.** The popular name for the yeti, a large manlike or apelike animal said to inhabit the Himalayas. The phrase translates the Tibetan *metohkangmi*, from *metoh*, 'foul', and *kangmi*, 'snowman'. *See also* BIGFOOT.

**About. About one's ears.** Causing trouble. The allusion is to a hornet's nest buzzing about one's head.

**About the size of it.** How matters stand, approximately the facts of the case.

**Above. Above board.** In the open, without dishonesty or fraud. According to Dr Johnson, the expression was 'borrowed from gamesters, who, when they put their hands under the table, are changing their cards'.

**Above oneself, To be.** To be presumptuous or conceited.

**Above par.** *See* PAR.

**Abracadabra.** A magical word, used in certain GNOSTIC writings, which is probably related to the Greek word ABRAXAS. The word was written on parchment as shown below and hung from the neck by a linen thread.

A B R A C A D A B R A<br>
A B R A C A D A B R<br>
A B R A C A D A B<br>
A B R A C A D A<br>
A B R A C A D<br>
A B R A C A<br>
A B R A C<br>
A B R A<br>
A B R<br>
A B<br>
A

**Abraham** (according to Genesis 17:5 from Hebrew *av hamon goyim*, 'father of a multitude of nations'). The first of the Jewish patriarchs, who at the age of 75 entered into a covenant with God that his descendants should possess the land of Canaan (Genesis 12:1–7). In addition to the Bible stories about him, Muslim legend adds the following. His parents were Prince Azar and his wife Adna. As King NIMROD had been told that one shortly to be born would dethrone him, he proclaimed a 'massacre of the innocents'. Adna retired to a cave where Abraham was born and was nourished by sucking two of her fingers, one giving milk and the other honey. By the age of 15 months the boy was the size of a boy 15 years old and he was so wise that Azar introduced him to Nimrod's court. Abraham and his son 'Ismail' are also said to have rebuilt the KAABA for the fourth time.

**Abrahamic Covenant.** The promise given by God to ABRAHAM because he left his father's house to live in a strange land as God told him, and interpreted to mean that the MESSIAH should spring from Abraham's seed (Genesis 12:1–3 and 17).

**Abraham** or **Abram man.** One of a number of beggars in the 16th and 17th centuries who pretended to be maniacs and so gain alms. Genuine inmates of BEDLAM who were not dangerous were occasionally allowed out of the 'Abraham ward', where they were kept, and given the opportunity to beg on the streets. The impostors caught on to the custom and capitalized on it. Hence TO SHAM ABRAHAM.

**Abraham's bosom.** The place where the just repose in death:

> The sons of Edward sleep in Abraham's bosom.
> SHAKESPEARE: *Richard III*, IV, iii (1592)

The allusion is to the ancient custom of allowing a dear friend to recline on one's bosom, as John did on the bosom of Jesus (Luke 16:22).

**Call of Abraham, The.** *See under* CALL.

**Plains of Abraham.** *See under* PLAIN.

**Sham Abraham, To.** *See under* SHAM.

**Abraxas.** A word used by the GNOSTICS to personify a deity, the source of 365 emanations. This figure is not only the number of days in the year but the sum of the numbers represented by the word's Greek letters, as follows: A (A) = 1 + B (B) = 2 + R (P) = 100 + A (A) = 1 + X (X) = 60 + A (A) = 1 + S (Σ) = 200 = 365. The word itself is perhaps of cabbalistic origin and is said to derive from Hebrew *arba' kesa*, 'hide the four' (meaning God, and alluding to the TETRAGRAMMATON). If the first word of this is reversed, the result is *'abra kesa*. The word was often engraved on gems used as TALISMANS. *See also* ABRACADABRA; MITHRA.

**Abroad, The schoolmaster is.** *See under* SCHOOL.

**Absalom** (Hebrew *avshalōm*, 'father of peace', from *av*, 'father', and *shalōm*, 'peace'). The third son of DAVID, remarkable for his good looks, who rose in rebellion against his father, aided by AHITHOPHEL. In his flight after defeat, Absalom was trapped in the branches of a tree and slain by JOAB, the king's general. David's great sorrow is expressed thus (2 Samuel 18:33):

> O my son Absalom, my son, my son Absalom! would God I had died for thee, O Absalom my son, my son!

In John Dryden's *Absalom and Achitophel* (1681), Absalom represents the Duke of Monmouth.

**Absent. Absence makes the heart grow fonder.** A line from the song 'The Isle of Beauty' by T. Haynes Bayly (1797–1839) but found much earlier in Francis Davison's *Poetical Rhapsody* (1602).

**Absent are always wrong, The.** From the French proverb, *Les absents ont toujours tort*. It implies that it is always easy to blame those not present, who cannot defend themselves.

**Absinthe.** A liqueur, technically a gin, that originally was highly flavoured with WORMWOOD (*Artemisia absinthium*). It appears frequently in accounts of the life of French literary and artistic circles at the end of the 19th century and in the early 20th century, and it was first popularized by being prescribed as a febrifuge to French troops during the Algerian War (1830–47). *L'Absinthe* (1876) is the title by which the painting *Au Café* by Edgar Degas is better known. Émile Zola vividly described the horrors of absinthe poisoning in *L'Assommoir* ('The Dram Shop') (1877). Its sale and manufacture have been illegal in France since 1915.

**Absolute zero.** The point at which it would be impossible to get any colder, calculated as –273.15°C (–460°F). *See also* ZERO.

**Abstinence.** Ecclesiastically Days of Abstinence are those when the eating of meat is not permitted, as distinct from Fast Days, when only one full meal is allowed in 24 hours. In modern Roman Catholic practice, however, fasting generally means one main meal at midday and a small 'collation' in the morning and evening. The two obligatory Fast Days for Roman Catholics are ASH WEDNESDAY and GOOD FRIDAY.

**Abstract.** Things are said to be 'taken in the abstract' when they are considered absolutely without relation to specific circumstances or to practical experience.

**Abstract number.** A number that may be considered without reference to anything else, e.g. 1, 2, 3. The converse is a concrete number, which refers to a particular object or objects, e.g. one house, two feet, three men.

**Abstract of title.** A legal phrase for a summary of the ownership of land.

**Abu Bakr** (Arabic *abū bakr*, 'father of Bakr', from *ab*, 'father', and *bakr*, a name literally meaning 'young camel'). The closest adviser and companion (AD 573–634) of MOHAMMED. He was the father of Mohammed's wife AYESHA and succeeded him as first caliph of Islam.

**Abu Hassan** ('son of Hassan'). A rich merchant in the ARABIAN NIGHTS ENTERTAINMENTS ('The Sleeper Awakened'), who while asleep was transferred to the bed of the Caliph Haroun al-Raschid. Next morning he was treated as the Caliph and every effort was made to make him forget his original identity. The same trick was played on Christopher SLY in the Induction of Shakespeare's *The Taming of the Shrew* (1593), and according to Richard Burton (*Anatomy of Melancholy* (1621)) by Philip the Good, Duke of Burgundy, on a drunken rustic, the subject of *The Frolicsome Duke, or the Tinker's Good Fortune* found in PERCY'S RELIQUES.

**Abundant number.** A number with divisors that add up to more than itself. An example is 12, because its divisors, 1, 2, 3, 4 and 6, add up to 16, which is greater than 12.

**Abyla.** *See* PILLARS OF HERCULES.

**Abyssinian Christians.** A branch of the Coptic Church. *See also* COPTS.

**Academy.** Originally a garden near Athens where PLATO taught, named after the legendary hero *Akadēmos*. Hence the philosophical school of Plato, and later a society or institution for the advancement of literature, art or science.

The teaching of Plato and his early followers came to be known as the Old Academy, the modified Platonic system founded by Arcesilaus (*c*.224 BC) as the Middle, and the half-sceptical school founded by Carneades (*c*.155 BC) as the New. Plato's followers were known as Academics. As well as referring to an academy, the adjective academic has come to mean theoretical, scholarly, abstract or unpractical. *See also* PLATONISM.

**Academic year.** The school or university year, usually beginning in the autumn.

**Royal Academy.** *See under* ROYAL.

**Acadia** (American Indian *akadi*, 'fertile land'). A former French settlement (also known as Acadie) in North America, founded in 1604 in what is now Nova Scotia, Canada. It was ceded to Britain under the Treaty of Utrecht in 1713, and in 1755 many Acadians were deported for refusing to take an oath of loyalty to Britain. This deportation provided the subject for Henry Wadsworth Longfellow's narrative poem *Evangeline* (1847).

**Acanthus** (Greek *akantha*, 'thorn', 'spine'). The representation of the leaf of *Acanthus spinosus* used to decorate the capitals of CORINTHIAN and Composite columns. The story is that an acanthus sprang up around a basket of flowers that Callimachus had placed on his daughter's grave. This so struck the fancy of the architect that he introduced the design into his buildings.

**Accent, Oxford.** *See under* OXFORD.

**Accessory after the fact.** A former legal term for a person who, knowing that a felony had been committed, received, relieved, comforted or assisted the felon, or helped him to escape. A classic example is a receiver of stolen goods. An accessory before the fact was a person who directly or indirectly procured a felony but who was not actually present when it was committed. The terms became obsolete in 1967 when the distinction between a felony and a misdemeanour was abolished.

**Accident.** In logic, an accident is some quality or property that an object possesses but that is not essential to it, such as the height of a person, the whiteness of paper or the redness of a brick. *See also* TRANSUBSTANTIATION.

**Accidental colour.** A colour that is seen on a white ground after looking for some time at a bright object such as the sun. The accidental colour of red is bluish-green, that of orange is dark blue, that of violet is yellow, and vice versa.

**Accident waiting to happen, An.** A disaster that, with hindsight, one can see was likely or even inevitable. The expression often relates to public safety standards or their lack.

**Chapter of accidents.** *See under* CHAPTER.

**Accius Naevius.** A legendary Roman augur who forbade Tarquin the Elder (616–579 BC) to increase the number of centuries (divisions of an army) instituted by ROMULUS without consulting the augurs. Tarquin asked him if, according to the augurs, the thought then in his mind was feasible of accomplishment. 'Undoubtedly,' said Accius, after consultation. 'Then cut through this whetstone with the razor in your hand.' The priest gave a bold cut and the block fell in two (Livy, *Historia*, i (1st century AD)). *See also* AUGURY.

**According. According to Cocker.** Reliably, correctly. Edward Cocker (1631–75) published his *Arithmetick*, which ran through over a hundred editions. The phrase was popularized by Arthur Murphy in his farce, *The Apprentice* (1756).

> 'So you ought to be, according to Cocker, spending all your time in sick rooms.'
> 'According to who?'
> 'According to Cocker.'
> 'Who is Cocker?'
> 'Oh, I don't know; some old fellow who wrote the rules of arithmetic, I believe; it's only a bit of slang.'
>
> THOMAS HUGHES: *Tom Brown at Oxford*, ch xxxii (1861)

**According to Gunter.** Carefully and correctly done, with no chance of a mistake. Surveyors traditionally used 'Gunter's chain', 66 feet long and divided into 100 links. Edmund Gunter (1581–1626) was its inventor. The expression is the American counterpart of the British ACCORDING TO COCKER.

**According to Hoyle.** According to the best usage; on the greatest authority. Edmund Hoyle (1671–1769) was the author of *A Short Treatise* *on the Game of Whist* (1742), long the standard authority on the game.

**Account. Call someone to account, To.** *See under* CALL.

**Cast accounts, To.** *See under* CAST.

**Doctor an account, To.** *See under* DOCTOR.

**Give a good account of oneself, To.** *See under* GOOD.

**Salt an account, To.** *See under* SALT.

**Square accounts with someone, To.** *See under* SQUARE.

**Ace.** The unit of cards or dice, from *as*, the Latin unit of weight. In the First World War the French word *as*, applied to an airman who had brought down ten enemy aeroplanes, was imported in its English equivalent ace, then extended to any specially expert flier, golfer or the like.

**Have an ace in the hole, To.** To have a secret or powerful advantage. The reference is to the game of stud poker, in which an ace is turned face down on the table. Only the player who holds it knows of his secret power.

**Have an ace up one's sleeve, To.** To have a surprise or secret weapon. Here the allusion is to the cardsharp, who would slip the high-ranking ace up his sleeve ready for use at the crucial moment.

**Aceldama** (purportedly Aramaic *haqal*, 'field', and *demā*, 'blood'). The name is figuratively used for any place of great slaughter. It was the POTTER'S FIELD near Jerusalem bought to bury strangers in (*see* Matthew 27:7–8 and Acts 1:18–19), and it was used by Christians during the CRUSADES and as late as the 17th century.

**Acestes, Arrow of.** *See under* ARROW.

**Achemon.** According to Greek legend Achemon and his brother Basalas were two Cercopes (a people of Ephesus) forever quarrelling. One day they saw HERCULES asleep under a tree and insulted him, so he tied them by their feet to his club and walked off with them, heads downwards. Everyone laughed at the sight, and a proverbial cry among the Greeks, when two men were seen quarrelling, was 'Look out for Melampygos!' This name, translating from the Greek as 'Black Buttocks', referred to Hercules' hirsute rump, which the Cercopes were faced with when hanging from his club.

**Acheron.** The 'woeful river' of HADES over which the souls of the dead were ferried by CHARON. Its name is popularly derived from Greek *o akhea rheōn*, 'the river of woe'. *See also* STYX.

**Acherontian Books.** *See* TAGES.

**Acherusia.** A cavern on the borders of Pontus, through which HERCULES dragged CERBERUS from the infernal regions to earth.

**Acheulean.** The name given to stages of PALAEOLITHIC hand axe culture, typified by the tools found at St Acheul, near Amiens, France. In Africa the name is used of every stage of hand axe development.

**Achillea.** A genus of 85 species of perennial, including yarrow (*Achillea millefolium*), so called from ACHILLES. The tale is that the Greeks, on the way to TROY, landed in Mysia and were opposed by Telephus, son of HERCULES. Dionysus (BACCHUS) caused Telephus to stumble and he was wounded by Achilles with his spear. Told by the ORACLE that Achilles would be the healer, Telephus sought out the Greek leader, promising to lead him to Troy in return for his help. Achilles agreed, scraped some rust from his spear, the plant yarrow sprang from it, and this healed the wound. Shakespeare and Chaucer allude to the dual power of Achilles' spear:

> Whose smile and frown, like to Achilles's spear,
> Is able with the change to kill and cure.
>
> SHAKESPEARE: *Henry VI, Pt II*, V, i (1590)

> And of Achilles with his marvellous spear,
> Able to heal no less than it could shear.
>
> CHAUCER: *Canterbury Tales*, 'The Squire's Tale' (*c*.1387) (modern translation by Nevill Coghill, 1951)

**Achilles** (traditionally from Greek *a*-, copulative prefix, and *kheilos*, 'lip', so 'with beautiful lips'). The great hero of the ILIAD, the son of PELEUS, king of the MYRMIDONS in Thessaly, and grandson of Aeacus. Brave and relentless, his quarrel with AGAMEMNON, the Greek commander-in-chief, caused him to withdraw from the struggle. The Trojans prevailed and Achilles allowed PATROCLUS to lead the Myrmidons back. Patroclus was killed by HECTOR. Achilles then returned, routed the Trojans and slew Hector. According to later poems, Achilles was killed by PARIS at the Scaean gate. *See also* ACHILLES' TENDON.

**Achilles and the tortoise.** The expression alludes to a paradox by ZENO OF ELEA. In a race, Achilles, who can run ten times as fast as a tortoise, gives the latter 100 yards start. He cannot win the race, however, because while he is running the first 100 yards, the tortoise runs ten, and while he runs that ten, the tortoise runs one, and while he runs that one, the tortoise runs one-tenth of a yard, and so on. The tortoise will always be ahead, even if infinitesimally so.

**Achilles' heel.** *See* ACHILLES' TENDON.

**Achilles' horses.** BALIOS and XANTHUS.

**Achilles' mistress in Troy.** Hippodamia, surnamed BRISEIS.

**Achilles of England.** The Duke of Wellington (1769–1852).

**Achilles of Germany.** Albert III, Elector of Brandenburg (1414–86).

**Achilles of Lombardy.** In Tasso's JERUSALEM DELIVERED the brother of Sforza and PALAMEDES in the allied army of Godfrey. He was slain by Corinna.

**Achilles of Rome.** Sicinius Dentatus, Roman general (d.*c*.450 BC), also called the Second Achilles.

**Achilles of the North.** BEOWULF.

**Achilles of the West.** ROLAND the PALADIN, also called the Christian THESEUS.

**Achilles' tendon** (*tendo Achillis*). A strong sinew connecting the heel and calf, which is frequently strained by athletes. The tale is that THETIS took her son ACHILLES by the heel, and dipped him in the River STYX to make him invulnerable, but the heel in her hand remained dry. The hero was slain by an arrow wound in the heel, his one weak spot. Hence the phrase 'Achilles' heel' is used for a person's small but potentially damaging weakness.

**Achilles' tutors.** PHOENIX, who taught him the arts of war and rhetoric, and CHIRON, the CENTAUR, who taught him the art of healing.

**Achilles' wife.** DEIDAMIA.

**English Achilles, The.** John Talbot, 1st Earl of Shrewsbury (*c*.1388–1453).

**Achitophel.** *See* AHITHOPHEL.

**Achor.** According to Pliny the deity prayed to by the Cyreneans for the averting of insect pests. *See also* GOD OF FLIES.

**Acid. Acid test.** Gold is not attacked by most acids but will dissolve in AQUA REGIA, a 3–1 mixture of concentrated hydrochloric acid and concentrated nitric acid (AQUA FORTIS). Hence the use of the phrase for a vital test.

**Put on the acid, To.** To put pressure on someone when asking for a favour. An expression used mainly in Australia and New Zealand, and perhaps derived from ACID TEST.

**Acis.** The son of FAUNUS, in love with GALATEA, crushed to death with a rock by his rival, POLYPHEMUS the CYCLOPS, and changed into the River Acis (Ovid, *Metamorphoses*, xiii, 750–968 (1st century AD)).

**Ack Ack.** Slang from the First and Second World Wars meaning 'anti-aircraft', especially for ack-ack guns. From 'ack', letter A in the phonetic alphabet. *See also* PIP EMMA.

**Acknowledge the corn, To.** An American expression, meaning to confess or acknowledge a charge or a failure. In a Congressional debate in 1828, one of the states claiming to export corn admitted that the corn was used to feed hogs, and exported in that form.

> I hope he will give up the argument, or to use a familiar phrase, acknowledge the corn.
>
> Mr Speight of Mississippi, speaking in the US Senate (1846)

**Acme** (Greek *akmē*, 'point'). The highest pitch of perfection. Old medical writers divided the progress of a disease into the 'arche', or beginning, the 'anabasis', or increase, the 'acme' or crisis, and the 'paracme' or decline.

**Aconite.** The herb monkshood or wolfsbane, *Aconitum*. According to classic fable, when HERCULES, at the command of Eurystheus, dragged CERBERUS from the infernal regions, the poisonous aconite grew from the foam that dropped from his many mouths.

**Acquaintance. Nodding acquaintance, A.** *See under* NOD.

**Scrape acquaintance with.** *See under* SCRAPE.

**Acrasia** (Greek *akrasia*, 'lack of self-control'). The personification of intemperance. In Edmund Spenser's *The Faerie Queene* (II, xii (1590)) Acrasia, an enchantress, mistress of the Bower of Bliss, transformed her lovers into monstrous shapes and kept them captive. Sir Guyon destroyed her bower, freed her victims and sent her in chains to the Faerie Queene.

**Acre** (Old English *æcer*, 'field', related to Latin *ager*).

**Acre-fight.** A good example of a GHOST WORD. It was wrongly explained by John Cowell in *The Interpreter* (1607) as a duel in the open field on the Scottish border fought with sword and lance by single combatants. It is actually a transliteration from the Medieval Latin phrase *acram committere*, where *acram* (for *pugnam*) is a poor translation of Old English *camp*, 'combat', which was confused with Latin *campus*, 'field', French *champ*, and so with English 'acre'. It is found only in Cowell and some later dictionaries that perpetuated the error.

**Acres of Diamonds.** A lecture said to have been given over 6000 times by the American Baptist minister, R.H. Conwell (1843–1925), in which he urged the acquisition of riches as a social duty. His assertion that 3900 of the then 4500 American millionaires were self-made men led to the growth of the 'success story' in American magazines.

**Bob Acres.** A coward is sometimes called 'a regular Bob Acres' after the character in Richard Brinsley Sheridan's comedy *The Rivals* (1775), whose courage always 'oozed out at his fingers' ends'.

**God's acre.** *See under* GOD.

**Pedlar's Acre.** *See under* PEDLAR.

**Three acres and a cow.** *See under* THREE.

**Across. Across the board.** Generally; applying to everyone or eveything. The allusion is to the board displaying odds in a horse race. A bet staked 'across the board' will bring results if the horse wins (comes in first), places (comes in second) or shows (comes in third).

**Get across someone, To.** To quarrel with or annoy a person.

**Get** or **put across something, To.** To make a point well and be readily understood. The expression may come from the theatre, where actors must reach their audience across the footlights.

**Acrostic** (Greek *akros*, 'extreme', and *stikhos*, 'line of verse'). Verse in which the first letters of each line read downwards to form a word. If the final letters also form a word it is a double acrostic. If the middle letters do likewise, it is a triple acrostic. The term was first applied to the obscure prophecies of the Erythraean SIBYL written on loose leaves, which made a word when sorted into order. The following alliterative acrostic spells out the name of the popular singer Kitty Stephens, later Countess of Essex (1794–1882):

> She sings so soft, so sweet, so soothing still
> That to the tone ten thousand thoughts there thrill;
> Elysian ecstasies enchant each ear –
> Pleasure's pure pinions poise – prince, peasant, peer,
> Hushing high hymns, Heaven hears her harmony, –
> Earth's envy ends; enthralled each ear, each eye;
> Numbers need ninefold nerve, or nearly name,
> Soul-stirring Stephens' skill, sure seraphs sing the same.

**Acrostic poetry.** Among the Hebrews this consisted of 22 lines or stanzas beginning with the letters of the ALPHABET in succession. *See also* ABECEDARIAN HYMNS.

**Act. Act of God.** A term applied by lawyers to happenings indisputably outside human control, for which there is no legal redress (e.g. losses caused by flood, storm, earthquake etc).

**Act of Grace.** A pardon, a general pardon granted by Act of Parliament, especially that of 1690, when William III pardoned political offenders, and that of 1784, when the estates forfeited for high treason in connection with the FORTY-FIVE were restored.

**Act of Parliament.** A law or statute made by PARLIAMENT. Introduced as a BILL, it becomes an Act when passed, after it has received the ROYAL ASSENT. *See also* REGNAL YEAR.

**Act of truth.** An event which, following a solemn oath, was held to prove or disprove its truth as in trial by ORDEAL.

**Act of Union, The.** Specifically the Act of Union of 1707 declaring that on and after 1 May 1707 England and Scotland 'for ever after be united into One Kingdom by the Name of Great Britain'. It provided for one Parliament for both countries. There had been a common sovereign since 1603.

The term also applies to the Act of 1536, incorporating Wales with England, and the Act of 1800, which united the Kingdoms of Great Britain and Ireland on and after 1 January 1801, a union that came to an end in 1922.

**Acts of Pilate, The.** An apocryphal work, probably of the 4th century, recounting the trial, death and resurrection of Christ. In combination with another treatise on the *Descent of Christ into Hades*, the two are known as the GOSPEL OF NICODEMUS. *See also* APOCRYPHA.

**Act or play the giddy goat, To.** To fool around. Goats are noted for their capriciousness. The literal sense of giddy is 'possessed by a god'. *See also* CUT A CAPER.

**Bubble Act, The.** *See under* BUBBLE.

**Conventicle Act.** *See under* CONVENTICLE.

**Get one's act together, To.** To get organized; to plan systematically. The expression seems to hint at a theatrical origin.

**Intolerable Acts.** *See under* INTOLERABLE.

**Six Acts, The.** *See under* SIX.

**Test Acts.** *See under* TEST.

**Thellusson Act.** *See under* THELLUSSON.

**University Tests Act, The.** *See under* UNIVERSITY.

**Actaeon** (Greek *aktaios*, 'coastal'). In Greek mythology a huntsman who, having surprised DIANA bathing naked with her nymphs (or, according to Euripides, boasted of his superiority in the chase), was changed into a stag and then torn to pieces by his own hounds. Thus, as a stag, he became representative of men whose wives are unfaithful. *See also* CUCKOLD; WEAR THE HORNS.

**Actian games.** The games that were celebrated at Actium in honour of APOLLO. They were renewed by AUGUSTUS after his naval victory over Antony off Actium (31 BC).

**Action. Action sermon.** In the Scottish Presbyterian Church, the sermon sometimes preached before administering the Communion. John Calvin (*see* CALVINISM) used the expression *action de grâces* for the thanksgiving that followed Communion, and it was probably from this use that John Knox took it as a name for the whole service. The sermon has now become less important than the prayers preceding the Communion, and it is frequently omitted.

**Direct action.** *See under* DIRECT.

**Industrial action.** *See under* INDUSTRIAL.

**Actresses.** Thomas Coryate says: 'When I went to a theatre [in Venice] I observed certain things that I never saw before; for I saw women act ... I have heard that it hath sometimes been used in London' (Coryate's *Crudities* (1611)). Female parts on the English stage were always taken by boys until the RESTORATION. The name of the first English actress is unknown. There are many claimants, but whoever she was, she played Desdemona in Shakespeare's *Othello* (1604) at a theatre in Clare Market, London (8 December 1660).

**As the bishop said to the actress.** *See under* AS.

**Acupuncture** (Latin *acus*, 'needle', and English 'puncture'). Modern acupuncture developed from the technique for relieving pain developed in China some time before 2500 BC, which itself arose from the ancient dualistic theory of YIN AND YANG. The theory is that disease is caused by an imbalance of these two forces in the body, so that acupuncture aims to restore the person to health by bringing yin and yang back in balance with each other again. The imbalance itself results in an obstruction of the *ch'i*, or life force, which flows through 12 meridians or pathways in the body, each connected with a major internal organ, such as the liver, kidneys etc.

Acupuncture involves the insertion of needles at hundreds of points on the body, both along the 12 basic meridians and over certain other meridians. The needles may then be manipulated or linked to a low-voltage electric current. The way in which they actually relieve the pain has not yet been conclusively determined, and it is uncertain to what extent the relief is physically produced and to what extent psychologically. It is certain that the procedure has been beneficial in some cases.

**Ad** (Latin, 'to'). Of the many Latin expressions beginning with this word, the following are among the commonest.

**Ad calendas graecas** ('at the Greek calends'). Never, as the Greeks had no CALENDS.

**Ad hoc** ('to this'). For a specific 'one-off' purpose, as an 'ad hoc' arrangement.

**Ad hominem** ('to the man'). Related to, or associated with, a particular person. An 'ad hominem' argument is one that appeals to the emotions rather than to reason.

**Ad infinitum** ('to infinity'). Without limit, extending indefinitely.

So, naturalists observe, a flea
Hath smaller fleas that on him prey;
And these have smaller still to bite 'em;
And so proceed *ad infinitum*.
JONATHAN SWIFT: *On Poetry. A Rhapsody* (1733)

**Ad libitum** ('according to pleasure'). Without restraint, freely . To 'ad lib' is to depart from one's given script or music and to improvise.

**Ad nauseam** ('to sickness'). To an excessive degree, to a disgusting extent.

**Ad rem** ('to the matter'). To the point, to the purpose. The expression contrasts with AD HOMINEM. A debater who argues 'ad rem' addresses the matter at issue to score points; one who argues 'ad hominem' attacks an opponent to gain an advantage.

**Ad valorem** ('according to the value'). A term used in imposing customs and stamp duty, the duty increasing according to the value of the transaction or goods involved.

**Adam** (perhaps Hebrew *adama*, 'earth', or *adom*, 'red').

(1) The first man, whose rib was used by God to make EVE, the first woman (*see* ADAM'S RIB), and who lived in the Garden of EDEN until he ate the fruit of the TREE OF KNOWLEDGE and was driven out to live a life of work and pain (Genesis 1–4). The Talmudists say that Adam lived in Paradise for only 12 hours before he was thrust out. Muslim legend relates as follows.

God sent GABRIEL, MICHAEL and ISRAFEL in turn to fetch seven handfuls of earth from different depths and of different colours for the creation of Adam (hence the varying colours of mankind), but they returned empty handed because Earth foresaw that the creature to be made from her would rebel against God and draw down his curse on her. AZRAEL was then sent. He fulfilled the task and so was appointed to separate the souls from the bodies, thus becoming the Angel of Death. The earth he fetched was taken to Arabia to a place between MECCA and Tayef (now At-Taif), kneaded by angels, fashioned into human form by God and left to dry for either 40 days or 40 years. The tradition holds that Adam was buried on a mountain in Arabia. *See also* TALMUD.

(2) The name 'Adam' is also applied to the elegant neoclassical style of architecture and interior decoration created by the brothers Adam, especially Robert Adam (1728–92). *See also* ADELPHI.

**Adam Bell.** *See* CLYM OF THE CLOUGH.

**Adam Cupid.** The archer CUPID, probably alluding to Adam Bell (*see* CLYM OF THE CLOUGH). In all early editions the line in Shakespeare's *Romeo and Juliet* (II, i, 13 (1594)) 'Young Adam Cupid, he that shot so trim', reads 'Young Abraham Cupid'. The emendation was suggested by George Stevens (1736–1800).

**Adamites.** One of a number of small Christian sects, which aimed to revert to man's primitive state in the Garden of EDEN by adopting nudity. Adamites are mentioned in James Shirley's comedy *Hyde Park* (II, iv (1632)) and in the *Guardian*, No. 134 (1713). *See also* ADAM.

**Adam's ale.** Water, first man's only drink, sometimes called Adam's wine in Scotland. *See also* ADAM.

**Adam's apple.** The visible projection of the thyroid cartilage of the larynx at the front of the neck, so called from the supposition that a piece of the FORBIDDEN FRUIT stuck in ADAM's throat.

**Adam's bridge.** *See* RAMA.

**Adam's needle.** A name given chiefly to the yucca, especially *Yucca filamentosa*, with its needle-like spines. The allusion is presumably to Genesis 3:7, which tells how ADAM and EVE 'sewed fig leaves together'.

**Adam's Peak.** A mountain in Sri Lanka where, according to Muslim legend, ADAM, after his expulsion from Paradise, expiated his crime by standing on one foot for 1000 years until GABRIEL took him to Mount Ararat, where he found EVE. In the granite there is a large impression resembling a human foot. Hindus assert that it was made by BUDDHA when he ascended into heaven.

**Adam's profession.** Gardening or agriculture. *See* Genesis 2:15 and 3:23.

> There is no ancient gentlemen but gardeners, ditchers, and grave-makers; they hold up Adam's profession.
>
> SHAKESPEARE: *Hamlet*, V, i (1600)

*See also* ADAM.

**Adam's rib.** While ADAM slept, God took one of his ribs and from it made the first woman (Genesis 2:21–22). Adam innately sensed the unity of her body with his own, saying that she 'shall be called Woman, because she was taken out of Man' (Genesis 2:23). The play on words happens to work as well in English as it does in the original Hebrew, which has *ish*, 'man', and *ishah*, 'woman'. The whole story is an Eastern parable, and the parable itself is a paradigm of the Christian view of marriage.

**As old as Adam.** *See under* AS.

**Curse of Adam, The.** *See under* CURSE.

**Not to know someone from Adam.** *See under* KNOW.

**Old Adam, The.** *See under* OLD.

**Parson Adams.** A leading character in Henry Fielding's *Joseph Andrews* (1742), often taken as the type of the good-natured, hard-working and learned country curate who is totally ignorant of 'the ways of the world'. He was based on Fielding's friend, the Rev. William Young (1702–57), who edited Robert Ainsworth's *Latin Dictionary* (1752). Young was so absent-minded that he was reputed to have once written a letter to himself, and while an army chaplain, to have strolled, Aeschylus in hand, into the hands of the enemy, who considerately directed him back to his regiment.

**Second Adam, A.** *See under* SECOND.

**When Adam delved.** *See under* WHEN.

**Adamastor** (Latin and Greek *adamas*, 'steel'). The spirit of the CAPE OF STORMS (the Cape of Good Hope), described by Luis de Camoëns (1524–80) in the LUSIADS, who appeared to Vasco da Gama and foretold that disaster would befall all attempting the voyage to India. Adamastor also features in the novels of Rabelais.

**Adams, Jack.** *See under* JACK.

**Add. Add fuel to the fire** or **flames, To.** To say or do something that increases the emotion of a person.

**Add insult to injury, To.** To wound by word or deed someone who has already suffered an act of violence or injustice. PHAEDRUS quotes the fable of AESOP about a bald man who, in attempting to kill a fly that had bitten him on the head, missed and dealt himself a sharp smack. Whereupon the fly said: 'You wished to kill me for a mere touch. What will you do to yourself since you have added insult to injury?'

**It doesn't add up.** No sensible answer can be arrived at from the known facts, it does not make sense. A phrase derived from simple arithmetic.

**Addams Family, The.** A macabre family in the cartoons of the American artist Charles Addams, whose work first appeared in the *New Yorker* in 1935. A television series of the mid-1960s starred the gruesome group, with John Astin playing Gomez Addams, Carolyn Jones as Morticia and an ageing Jackie Coogan in the role of Uncle Fester.

**Adder, As deaf as an.** *See under* AS.

**Addison. Addisonian termination.** The name given by Richard Hurd, bishop of Worcester (1720–1808), to the construction, frequently employed by the essayist Joseph Addison (1672–1719), which closes a sentence with a preposition, e.g. 'which the prophet took a distinct view of'.

**Addison of the North.** Henry Mackenzie (1745–1831), author of *The Man of Feeling* (1771), literary leader in Edinburgh. So called by Sir Walter Scott.

**Addle, To** (Old English *adela*, 'filth'). To make anything rotten or putrid. Hence an addled egg is a rotten egg, and the word is used figuratively in addle-brained, addle-pated, of anyone or anything confused or muddled.

**Addled Parliament** (5 April to 7 June 1614). So called for its sterility, being dissolved by James I without passing a single Act. It refused to grant supplies unless the king abandoned IMPOSITIONS.

**Address. Farewell Address.** *See under* FAREWELL.

**Gettysburg Address.** *See under* GETTYSBURG.

**Adelphi, The.** A small district in London, between the STRAND and the THAMES, designed by Robert ADAM and his three brothers in 1768. (*Adelphoi* is Greek for 'brothers'.) Originally the site of the bishop of Durham's palace, it is rich in literary and historical associations, having accommodated the Savage Club, David Garrick, Thomas Rowlandson, Thomas Hardy, James Barrie and others. The arches upon which the streets were built, known as the Shades, became of ill repute. John Adam Street still accommodates the Royal Society of Arts, but most of the Adelphi has been replaced by modern buildings.

**Adieu** (French *à Dieu*, 'to God'). An elliptical form for 'I commend you to God'. *See also* GOODBYE.

**Adirondack country.** The northeastern region of New York State, the picturesque locale of the Adirondack Mountains, amid a host of gorges, waterfalls, lakes and swamps. The whole area is a popular tourist and holiday centre for New Yorkers and other East Coast Americans, and the healthy climate and in places spectacular scenery has encouraged the growth of resort villages and sanatoriums.

**Aditi.** The great earth mother of Hindu mythology, sometimes an abstract concept of limitless space and time. She is variously described as the mother, wife and daughter of VISHNU, and her name means 'infinity'.

**Adityas.** In the VEDAS, the divine sons of ADITI, the chief being VARUNA, sustainer of the moral law.

**Admass.** A term coined by J.B. Priestley in *Journey Down a Rainbow* (1955) to describe the vast mid-20th-century proliferation of commercial advertising and high-pressure salesmanship, especially in the USA. The dated word came to denote the vast mass of the general public to which advertisers addressed their publicity.

**Administration, Letters of.** *See under* LETTER.

**Admirable, The.** A title used of Abraham ben Meir ibn Ezra (1092–1167), a celebrated Spanish Jew. He was a noted mathematician, philologist, poet, astronomer and commentator on the Bible, and he was the Rabbi Ben Ezra of Robert Browning's poem of that name (1864).

**Admirable Crichton, The.** *See under* CRICHTON.

**Admirable Doctor, The.** Roger Bacon (*c*.1220–92), the great English philosopher. He was also known as Doctor Mirabilis ('The Wonderful Doctor').

**Admiral** (from Arabic *amīr*, 'emir', 'commander', as in the phrase *amīr-al-bahr*, 'commander of the sea', subsequently influenced by Latin *admirabilis*, 'admirable'). Milton, speaking of SATAN, uses an early form of the word for a ship:

> His spear – to equal which the tallest pine
> Hewn on Norwegian hills, to be the mast
> Of some great ammiral, were but a wand –
> He walked with.
> *Paradise Lost*, i (1667)

In the Royal Navy there are now four ranks of admiral: admiral of the fleet, admiral, vice admiral and rear admiral, their army equivalents being respectively field marshal, general, lieutenant general and major general.

**Red admiral.** *See under* RED.

**White admiral.** *See under* WHITE.

**Adonai** (Hebrew *adonay*, plural of *adōn*, 'lord'). A Hebraic name of God, used instead of Yahweh (JEHOVAH), 'the ineffable name', wherever it occurs. In Latin and Greek versions of the Bible it is always translated respectively by *Dominus* and *Kurios*, and in English versions it thus appears as 'Lord', e.g. in Isaiah 6:1. *See also* TETRAGRAMMATON.

**Adonists.** Those Hebraists who maintain that the vowels of the word ADONAI are not those necessary to make the TETRAGRAMMATON J H V H into the name of the Deity. *See also* JEHOVAH.

**Adonais.** The name given by Percy Bysshe Shelley to John Keats in his elegy *Adonais* (1821), lamenting the latter's death, probably in allusion to the mourning for ADONIS. Shelley is said to have based his poem on the *Lament for Adonis* (2nd century BC) by the Greek pastoral poet Bion. This describes the distress of APHRODITE as news of the gory death of the Assyrian hunter is spread abroad.

**Adonia.** An eight-day feast of ADONIS, celebrated in Assyria, Alexandria, Egypt, Judaea, Persia, Cyprus, Greece and Rome. The women first lamented the death of Adonis, then wildly rejoiced at his resurrection. The custom is referred to in the Bible (Ezekiel 8:14), where Adonis appears under his Phoenician name of Tammuz. *See also* THAMMUZ.

**Adonis** (Phoenician and Hebrew *adōn*, 'lord'). In classical mythology this beautiful youth was the son of MYRRHA (or Smyrna). He was born from a myrrh tree, loved by APHRODITE (VENUS) and died young, killed by a boar while hunting. The name is thus applied to any handsome young man. Both John and Leigh Hunt were sent to prison for libelling the Prince Regent by calling him 'a corpulent Adonis of fifty' (*Examiner*, 1813). The Akkadian name of Adonis was THAMMUZ.

**Adonis flower.** A name for a number of plants of the family Ranunculaceae, of which the most common is the species known as pheasant's eye (*Adonis annua*). ADONIS was killed by a wild boar, and APHRODITE was so sorrowful at his loss that she made the red flower spring up from the blood he shed at his death.

**Adoption. Adoption by arms.** An ancient custom of giving arms to a person of merit, which put them under the obligation of being one's champion and defender.

**Adoption by baptism.** Being godfather or godmother to a child.

**Adoption by hair.** Boso, king of Provence (r.879–889), is said to have cut off his hair and given it to Pope John VIII (r.872–882) as a sign that the latter had adopted him.

**Adoption of children.** In English law adoption is effected by a court order that vests parental responsibility for a child to the adopter or adopters and extinguishes the parental responsibility of the birth parents. The effect of an adoption order is thus that the child is treated as if born as a child of the marriage of his or her adoptive parents and not as the child of anyone else. The requirements for making adoption orders are set out in the Adoption Act 1976.

**Adoptive emperors.** A collective name for the five Roman emperors – Nerva, TRAJAN, Hadrian, Antoninus Pius and Marcus Aurelius – each of whom (except Nerva, who was elected by the Senate) was the adopted son of his predecessor.

Their period (96–180) is said to have been the most stable in Roman history.

**Adrammelech** (Babylonian *Adar-malik*, 'Adar is prince'). An Assyrian deity to whom infants were burned in sacrifice (2 Kings 17:31). He may have been the sun-god worshipped at Sippar (Sepharvaim). *See also* ASSYRIA.

**Adrastus** (Greek *adrastos*, 'immobile', 'not fleeing').

(1) A mythical Greek king of Argos, leader of the expedition of the SEVEN AGAINST THEBES.

(2) An Indian prince, slain by RINALDO (in Tasso's JERUSALEM DELIVERED, xx (1580)), who aided the king of Egypt against the crusaders.

**Adriatic.** *See* BRIDE OF THE SEA.

**Adrift** (*a*, 'on', 'in', and *drift*). At the mercy of wind and tide, floating or being carried aimlessly. In colloquial naval usage 'to be adrift' is to be late, overdue from leave or absent from one's place of duty.

**All adrift.** *See under* ALL.

**Adullamites.** A group of some thirty Liberals led by Robert Lowe, 1st Viscount Sherbrooke (1811–92), who withdrew from the party in opposition to Lord Russell's Reform Bill in 1866. They were likened by John Bright to the malcontents who joined DAVID when he escaped to the cave of Adullam (1 Samuel 22:1–2).

**Adulterous Bible, The.** *See* WICKED BIBLE *under* BIBLE..

**Advantage, To set off something to.** *See under* SET.

**Advent** (Latin *adventus*, 'arrival'). The four weeks before CHRISTMAS, beginning on St ANDREW'S Day (30 November) or the Sunday nearest to it, and commemorating the first and SECOND COMING of Christ: the first to redeem (as he did in the past) and the second to judge the world (as he will in the future). Advent was formerly kept as LENT, but with less strictness.

**Adventists.** A Christian group holding that the SECOND COMING of Christ is imminent. They originated in the USA as MILLERITES. *See also* MILLENARIANS; SECOND ADVENTISTS; SEVENTH-DAY ADVENTISTS.

**Advent Sunday.** The first Sunday in Advent, the traditional beginning of the church year, except in the GREEK CHURCH where it begins in the middle of November.

**Adversary, The.** SATAN or the DEVIL (from 1 Peter 5:8).

**Adverse, Anthony.** The hero of the historical novel that bears his name (1934) by the American writer Hervey Allen. He has a number of picaresque adventures in early 19th-century Europe and America. As his name implies, some of them are more misadventures. The book was a phenomenal bestseller in its day, selling half a million copies in the first two years and rivalling Margaret Mitchell's *Gone with the Wind* (1936).

**Adversity Hume.** The MP Joseph Hume (1777–1855) was so called through his prediction of a national disaster in the mid-1820s. *See also* PROSPERITY ROBINSON *under* ROBINSON.

**Advice, Letter of.** *See under* LETTER.

**Advocate. Advocates' Library, The.** A well-known library founded in Edinburgh by Sir George Mackenzie, dean of the Faculty of Advocates (i.e. members of the Scottish bar), and opening in 1689. In 1925 it became the National Library of Scotland and has received a copy of all books published since the Copyright Act of 1709. *See also* LIBRARY.

**Devil's advocate.** *See under* DEVIL.

**Advowson** (Latin *advocatio*, 'summoning'). In ecclesiastical law, the right of presentation to a church BENEFICE. It is so named because the patron was the advocate or defender of the living and of the claims of his candidate. There are two kinds of advowson: 'collative', when the bishop of the diocese is the patron, and 'presentative', when the patron is some other person ('patron').

**Adytum** (Greek *aduton*, 'not to be entered'). The HOLY OF HOLIES in Greek and Roman temples, into which the public was not admitted. Hence, generally, any sanctum.

**Aegeon.** *See* BRIAREUS.

**Aegeus** (perhaps from a pre-Hellenic word *aiges*, 'waves'). A mythical king of Attica, who sent his son THESEUS to Crete to deliver Athens from the yearly tribute of seven boys and seven girls exacted by MINOS. If successful, Theseus was to hoist white sails (in place of black mourning sails) on his return, as a signal of his safety. He forgot to do so, however, and Aegeus, thinking that his son was lost, threw himself into the sea, which was henceforth known as the Aegean Sea. The story is repeated in the tale of TRISTRAM and YSOLDE.

**Aeginetan sculptures.** Two groups of figures from the east and west pediments of the temple of Aphaia, on the island of Aegina, representing exploits of the Greek heroes at TROY. They date from *c*.500 BC, and are preserved in the Glyptothek, Munich.

**Aegir** (Old Norse *ægir*, 'sea', 'ocean'). In Norse mythology, the god of the ocean, linked with the goddess Ran. They had nine daughters (the billows), who wore white robes and veils.

**Aegis** (Greek *aigis*, perhaps related to *aix, aigos*, 'goat'). The shield of ZEUS, which was made by Hephaestus (*see* VULCAN), the god of fire, and covered with the skin of the goat AMALTHEA, who had suckled the infant Zeus. By shaking his aegis, Zeus produced storms and thunder. It was also carried by Zeus' daughter ATHENE, when it is usually represented as a cloak fringed with serpents and with the GORGON's head in the centre. It is symbolic of divine protection, hence 'under the aegis of', meaning 'under the protection of'.

**Aegisthus.** The son of THYESTES, who raped CLYTEMNESTRA, wife of his cousin AGAMEMNON, and then murdered Agamemnon himself, only to be killed in turn by ORESTES. The fearful chain of events forms the theme of Aeschylus' trilogy, the *Oresteia* (5th century BC), and of plays by Sophocles and Euripides.

**Aegyptus.** In Greek legend, a son of Belus and twin brother of Danaus. He was king of that part of Africa named after him (Egypt).

**AEIOU.** The device adopted by Frederick V, Archduke of Austria, on becoming the Emperor Frederick III in 1440. The letters, used by his predecessor, Albert II, stood for:

> Albertus Electus Imperator Optimus Vivat.
> (Long live Albert, the best elected emperor.)

Frederick interpreted them thus:

> Archidux Electus Imperator Optime Vivat.
> (Long live the Archduke, elected emperor for the best.)

Among other versions are:

> Austriae Est Imperare Orbi Universo.
> (It is given to Austria to rule the whole world.)
> Alles Erdreich Ist Oesterreich Unterthan.
> (All earth is subject to Austria.)

To which wags added after the defeat of Prussia in 1866:

> Austria's Empire Is Ousted Utterly.

Frederick the Great of Prussia (1712–86) is said to have translated the motto thus:

> Austria Erit In Orbe Ultima.
> (Austria will be the world's last survivor.)

**Aemilian law.** The Roman praetor Aemilius Mamercus made a law in the 5th century BC empowering the eldest praetor to drive a nail in the CAPITOL on the IDES of September, with the supposition that it would stop pestilence or avert a calamity. It is mentioned by Livy (1st century AD).

**Aeneas** (perhaps from Greek *aineō*, 'I praise', or *ainos*, 'praise'). In Greek mythology the son of ANCHISES, king of DARDANUS, and APHRODITE. According to Homer he fought in the TROJAN WAR, and after the sack of TROY withdrew to Mount IDA and reigned in the Troad. The post-Homeric legends are largely embodied in the AENEID (1st century BC).

**Aeneid.** VIRGIL's epic poem (1st century BC) in 12 books, accounting for the settlement of AENEAS in Italy and thus claiming Trojan origins for the Roman state. The story tells how Aeneas escaped from the flames of TROY, carrying his father ANCHISES to Mount IDA. With his Trojan followers he sailed to Crete but learned in a vision that he was destined for Italy, and eventually reached Sicily where his father died. Heading for the mainland, he was wrecked on the coast of Carthage. He left secretly, at JUPITER'S behest, whereupon the lovelorn Queen DIDO of Carthage killed herself. Reaching Latium, he was betrothed to Lavinia, daughter of King LATINUS, but war arose with Turnus, king of the Rutulians, who also wished to marry Lavinia. Turnus was finally killed by Aeneas.

**Aeolian. Aeolian harp.** A musical instrument taking its name from AEOLUS and consisting of a wooden resonating box with strings of different thickness tuned to the same deep note. When they are exposed to the wind, the strings vibrate producing a chord, rising and falling up and down the harmonic series as the wind speed varies. The Aeolian harp has been known since at least the 17th century, and it is mentioned in the poetry of S.T. Coleridge and Percy Bysshe Shelley.

> 'Tis the deep music of the rolling world,
> Kindling within the strings of the waved air
> Æolian modulations.
> P.B. SHELLEY: *Prometheus Unbound*, IV, i (1818).

**Aeolian mode.** In music one of the four 'church modes' added to the existing eight by Henricus Glareanus (Heinrich Glarian) in 1547, the range being from A to A, with final on A. The other three new modes were the Hypoaeolian (E to E, with final on A), Ionian (C to C), and Hypoionian (G to G), the last two with finals on C.

**Aeolian rocks.** Those rocks that have been deposited or eroded largely by the wind.

**Aeolus** (Greek *aiolos*, 'mobile', 'agitated', 'swift'). In Homeric legend, the ruler of the winds. He was appointed by ZEUS and lived on his island of Aeolia.

**Aeon** (Greek *aiōn*, 'infinitely long time'). An age of the universe, an infinite length of time. Also the personification of an age, a god or any being or thing that is eternal.

**Aeschylus** (Greek *aiskhos*, 'shame'). The father of Greek tragic drama (525–456 BC). Only 7 plays of his remain from a known total of over 80 titles. According to legend he was killed when an eagle dropped a tortoise onto his head, mistaking it for a stone on which the shell could be broken.

**Aesculapius** (perhaps from Greek *skalops*, 'mole', or *skallō*, 'I hollow out'). The Latin form of the Greek Asklepios, god of medicine and of healing, son of APOLLO and father of HYGEIA. His attribute was a serpent entwined around a staff. The usual offering to him was a cock, hence to 'sacrifice a cock to Aesculapius' means to give thanks (or pay the doctor's bill) after recovery from an illness.

> When men a dangerous disease did scape,
> Of old, they gave a cock to Aesculape.
> BEN JONSON: *Epigrams* (1616)

**Aesir** or **Asir** (Old Norse *æsir*, 'gods'). The collective name of the 12 mythical gods of Scandinavia, who lived in ASGARD. Their composition varies according to the source, but one listing includes: (1) ODIN, the chief, (2) THOR, (3) TIU, (4) BALDER, (5) Brag, god of poetry, (6) VIDAR, god of silence, (7) Hoder the blind (slayer of Balder), (8) Hermoder, Odin's son and messenger, (9) Hoenir, a minor god, (10) Odnir, husband of FREYJA, (11) LOKI, (12) Vali, Odin's youngest son.

**Aesop** (perhaps from Greek *aisa*, 'lot', 'destiny'). A deformed Phrygian slave (*c*.620–560 BC) who is the traditional author of a collection of popular animal FABLES. Many of the fables predate him, however, and are found on Egyptian papyri dating almost 1000 years earlier. SOCRATES, in prison, began committing them to verse. A collection made in choliambics by BABRIUS (early 3rd century AD), was found in a monastery on Mount Athos in 1844. *See also* PHAEDRUS.

**Aesop of England, The.** John Gay (1685–1732), poet and playwright.

**Aesop of France, The.** Jean de LA FONTAINE (1621–95).

**Aesop of Germany, The.** Gotthold Ephraim Lessing (1729–81), playwright and man of letters.

**Aetherius.** In 1954 His Eminence Sir George King (b.1919) claimed to have been contacted by the Master Aetherius, a power from the planet Venus, who told him to become the Voice of Interplanetary Parliament. The result was the formation of the Aetherius Society, which now has branches worldwide. King, whose titles have not been verified, maintains he has met Jesus Christ, the Buddha and St Peter, who all now speak to him and through him. The Society teaches that a race of wise fish on the distant planet Garouche are trying to suck the air away from Earth, so killing all terrestrial life except marine creatures, which supposedly obtain their oxygen from the water. Members of the Society charge up devices known as spiritual batteries by spending a fixed number of hours in prayer.

**Aetion.** One of the characters in Edmund Spenser's *Colin Clout's Come Home Againe* (1595) who represents Michael Drayton, the poet. *See also* COLIN CLOUT.

**Aetites** (Greek *aetos*, 'eagle'). Eagle stones, which according to fable are found in eagle's nests and possess magical and medical properties.

> The stone in question is big with another inside it, which rattles, as if in a jar when you shake it.
> PLINY: *Natural History*, x (1st century AD)

**Affair. Affair of honour, An.** A dispute to be settled by a duel.

Duels were generally provoked by offences against the arbitrary rules of courtesy and etiquette, not recognized at law and thus to be settled by private combat. *See also* LAWS OF HONOUR.

**Affair of the Diamond Necklace, The.** A notorious scandal in French history (1784–6) centring on Queen Marie Antoinette, Cardinal de Rohan, an ambitious and dissolute prelate, and an adventuress, Jeanne, Countess de la Motte. The countess tricked Rohan by pretending to conduct a correspondence with the queen in his name. She persuaded him to purchase for the queen (for 1,600,000 livres) a diamond necklace originally made for Louis XV's mistress, Madame du Barry. The cardinal did so and gave it to the countess, who said she would pass it to the queen. She actually sold it to an English jeweller and kept the money. When the original jewellers, Boehmer and Bassenge of Paris, claimed payment, the queen denied all knowledge of the matter. The arrest of Rohan and Jeanne de la Motte followed. After a sensational trial, the cardinal was acquitted and exiled to the abbey of La Chaise-Dieu, and the countess was branded as a thief and consigned to the Salpêtrière but subsequently escaped.

**Sacheverell Affair, The.** *See under* SACHEVERELL.

**Settle one's affairs, To.** *See under* SETTLE.

**Affection, Starved of.** *See under* STARVE.

**Affinity Bible, The.** *See under* BIBLE.

**Affluent society, The.** A phrase, in vogue from the 1950s, denoting the overall growth in material prosperity of British society as evidenced by the growingly widespread ownership of cars, televisions, washing machines, refrigerators and the like. The term was popularized by the title of J.K. Galbraith's book *The Affluent Society* (1958).

**Afraid. Not afraid with any amazement.** A phrase occurring as the final words of the marriage service in the BOOK OF COMMON PRAYER, as a quotation from 1 Peter 3:6. The meaning is 'not distracted or tempted aside', i.e. from doing God's bidding. Shakespeare uses 'amazement' in the same sense.

> Behold, destruction, frenzy, and amazement,
> Like witless antics, one another meet.
> *Troilus and Cressida*, V, iii (1601)

**Afreet** or **Afrit** (Arabic *'ifrīt*). In Muslim mythology the second most powerful of the five classes of JINN OR DEVILS. They were of gigantic stature, malicious and inspired great dread.

**Africa. African Sisters, The.** The HESPERIDES, who dwelt in Africa.

**Black Africa.** *See under* BLACK.

**Horn of Africa.** *See under* HORN.

**Semper aliquid novi Africam adferre.** *See under* SEMPER.

**Union of South Africa.** *See under* UNION.

**Afrikaner Bond.** The first South African political party, founded in 1883 with the aim of protecting Afrikaner interests in the Cape Colony. The Bond joined with other Afrikaner parties in 1910 and was wound up in 1911.

**Aft.** *See* FORE AND AFT.

**After. After meat, mustard.** Expressive of the sentiment that something that would have been welcome a little earlier has arrived too late and is no longer wanted.

**After one's own heart.** Just what one likes; exactly as one would have wished.

**Against the grain.** Against one's natural inclination. The allusion is to wood which cannot be properly planed the wrong way of the grain.

> Your minds,
> Pre-occupied with what you rather must do
> Than what you should, made you against the grain
> To voice him consul.
>
> SHAKESPEARE: *Coriolanus*, II, iii (1607)

**Aga Khan.** The hereditary title of the imam, or spiritual leader, of the Nizari Ismaili sect of Shi'ite Muslims. It is of Turkish origin and means 'master ruler'. The first imam to bear the title, Aga Khan I (1800–81), was born Hasan Ali Shah. He was succeeded by his son Aga Khan II (d.1885), born Ali Shah, and the latter's son in turn, Aga Khan III (1877–1957), originally Sultan Sir Mohammed Shah, famous for his racing interests. This last's grandson, Aga Khan IV (b.1936), originally Karim Al-Hussain Shah, became known for his business interests and continued the family's racehorse breeding activities.

**Agamemnon** (perhaps Greek *aga-*, intensive prefix, and *memnōn*, 'resolute'). In Greek legend the king of Mycenae, son of ATREUS, grandson of PELOPS, brother of MENELAUS, and leader of the Greeks at the siege of TROY. He married CLYTEMNESTRA. ORESTES was their son. Their daughters were IPHIGENIA and/or Iphianassa, Laodice (in later legend ELECTRA), and Chrysothemis. He returned from Troy with CASSANDRA, the daughter of King PRIAM, and both were murdered by his wife Clytemnestra and her lover AEGISTHUS. The guilty pair were killed by Orestes.

**Aganippe** (perhaps Greek *aga-*, intensive prefix, and *hippos*, 'horse'). In Greek legend a fountain of BOEOTIA at the foot of Mount HELICON, dedicated to the MUSES because it imparted poetic inspiration. The name is also that of the NYMPH of this fountain.

**Agape** (Greek *agapē*, 'love'). A love feast. The early Christians held a love feast in conjunction with the LORD'S SUPPER at which the rich provided food for the poor. Eventually they became a scandal and were condemned by the Council of Carthage (397). There has however been some interest in restoring the agape in recent times, and in 1949 it was revived in the Norfolk parish of Hilgay in an attempt to bring Anglicans and Methodists together. Agape was also the mother of Priamond, Diamond and Triamond in Edmund Spenser's *The Faerie Queene* (IV, ii (1596)). The word is pronounced in three syllables.

**Agapemone** (Greek *agapē*, 'love', and *monē*, 'dwelling'). A fanatical sect of men and women, followers of the Rev. Henry James Prince (1811–99), curate of Charlynch, Somerset, and his rector Samuel Starky (hence their alternative name of Starkyites). They founded a communal 'abode of love' at Spaxton, Somerset, in 1849, but their licentious conduct led to trouble with authority. In the early 1890s the movement revived in Clapton, London, as the Children of the Resurrection under the Rev. John Hugh Smyth-Pigott, who proclaimed himself to be Christ. He was unfrocked in 1909.

**Agapetae** (Greek *agapētos*, 'beloved'). A group of 3rd-century ascetic women who, under vows of virginity, contracted spiritual marriage with monks and attended to their wants. The practice became widespread, and the consequent scandals led to their condemnation in the 4th century and suppression by the LATERAN COUNCIL of 1139.

**Agate.** The form of quartz is so called, says Pliny (*Natural History*, xxxvii (1st century AD)), from the River Achates or Gagates, in Sicily, near which it is found in abundance. It was supposed to render a person invisible and to turn the sword of foes against themselves.

**Agatha** (Greek *agathē*, feminine of *agathos*, 'good'). The saint of this name was tortured and murdered at Catania in Sicily, possibly during the Decian persecution of 250–253. She is sometimes represented holding a salver containing her severed breasts and the shears or pincers with which she was mutilated. Her feast-day is 5 February.

**Agave** (Greek *agauē*, feminine of *agauos*, 'illustrious'). According to classical mythology the plant is named from Agave, daughter of CADMUS and Harmonia. The agave is native to tropical America and is related to the gigantic American ALOE or maguey of Mexico, mistakenly called the century plant, in the belief that it takes 100 years to flower.

**Age.** A word used in mythology, geology, archaeology, history and the like to denote a period of time marked by particular characteristics, e.g. Atomic Age, AUGUSTAN AGE, DARK AGES,

Elizabethan Age, GOLDEN AGE, ICE AGE, Machine Age, MIDDLE AGES, STONE AGE.

Hesiod (8th century BC) names five ages: the Golden or patriarchal; the SILVER AGE or voluptuous; the Brazen, warlike and violent; the Heroic or renaissant; and the IRON AGE or present, an age of misery and crime when justice and piety have vanished.

Lucretius (*c*.94–55 BC) distinguishes three ages, stone, bronze and iron, according to the material from which implements were made.

Varro (116–27 BC) recognizes three ages: from the beginning of mankind to the DELUGE; from the Deluge to the first OLYMPIAD, called the mythical period; from the first Olympiad to his own time, called the historic period (*Fragments* (1623)).

Ovid (43 BC–AD 18) describes four ages: Golden, Silver, Bronze and Iron (*Metamorphoses*, i (1st century AD)).

Thomas Heywood (*c*.1572–1650) has a series of plays based on classical mythology called *The Golden Age* (1611), *The Silver Age* (1613), *The Brazen Age* (1613) and *The Iron Age* (1632), while more recently the historian Eric Hobsbawm published a trilogy *The Age of Revolution, 1789–1848* (1962), *The Age of Capital, 1848–1875* (1975) and *The Age of Empire, 1875–1914* (1987). A subsequent volume was *The Age of Extremes* (1994).

Shakespeare's SEVEN AGES OF MAN are described in *As You Like It*, II, vii (1599). They are the infant, the schoolboy, the lover, the soldier, the justice, the 'lean and slipper'd pantaloon' and finally 'second childishness and mere oblivion'.

**Age before beauty.** Age has precedence over youth. The expression is often used trivially or playfully when holding a door open for someone. Even so, courtesy has long traditionally demanded that an older person should go through a door before a younger.

**Age of animals.** According to an old Celtic rhyme:

Thrice the age of a dog is that of a horse;
Thrice the age of a horse is that of a man;
Thrice the age of a man is that of a deer;
Thrice the age of a deer is that of an eagle.

**Age of Aquarius.** In NEW AGE terminology the period beginning in the 1960s when peace, freedom, brotherhood and the conquest of space all seemed feasible.

When the moon is in the seventh house
And Jupiter aligns with Mars,
Then peace will guide the planets,
And love will steer the stars;
This is the dawning of the age of Aquarius,
The age of Aquarius.

JAMES RADO AND GEROME RAGNI: *Hair* (1966)

**Age of consent.** The age at which a girl's consent to sexual intercourse or marriage is legal. In English and Scottish law the age is 16. There is also a homosexual age of consent in private, which was 21 in 1967 and 18 in 1994. A Government vote in favour of a further lowering of the age to 16 was overturned in 1998 by the HOUSE OF LORDS but again passed on a second reading in 1999.

**Age of discretion.** In English law, a child of 14 years is deemed to have sufficient discretion to be prosecuted for an offence.

**Age of puberty.** In English law the age at which puberty begins is usually reckoned as 14 in boys and 12 in girls.

**Age of reason.** For Roman Catholics, the end of the seventh year, when a child is old enough to distinguish between right and wrong and to assume moral responsibility for his or her actions.

The 18th century is also called the Age of Reason as a period of ENLIGHTENMENT when philosophy was in vogue throughout Europe.

**Alexandrine age.** *See under* ALEXANDRINE.
**Augustan age.** *See under* AUGUSTAN.
**Awkward age, The.** *See under* AWKWARD.
**Brazen Age, The.** *See under* BRAZEN.
**Canonical age.** *See under* CANON.
**Dark Ages, The.** *See under* DARK.
**Eolithic Age.** *See under* EOLITHIC.
**Golden Age.** *See under* GOLDEN.
**Heroic age.** *See under* HEROIC.
**Ice Age.** *See under* ICE.
**Iron Age.** *See under* IRON.
**Light of the Age, The.** *See under* LIGHT.
**Middle Ages.** *See under* MIDDLE.
**Neolithic Age.** *See under* NEOLITHIC.
**New Age.** *See under* NEW.
**Palaeolithic Age.** *See under* PALAEOLITHIC.
**Rock of Ages.** *See under* ROCK.
**Seven ages of man, The.** *See under* SEVEN.
**Silver Age, The.** *See under* SILVER.
**Steam age.** *See under* STEAM.
**Stone Age.** *See under* STONE.
**Third age.** *See under* THIRD.

**Age hoc** (Latin, 'attend to this'). In sacrifice the Roman crier perpetually repeated these words to arouse attention. Somewhat similar is the use of the exhortation OYEZ! OYEZ! OYEZ!

**Agenor** (Greek *agēnōr*, 'manly', 'brave'). King of Tyre, son of POSEIDON (NEPTUNE). His descendants Europa, CADMUS, PHOENIX, Cilix and others, are known as Agenorides.

**Agent. Agent orange.** A type of herbicide containing a deadly toxin (dioxin), notorious from its use by the US forces in the Vietnam War (1954–75) in order to defoliate trees. The substance affects not only plant life but human (although the users were not aware of this at the time), as a result of which much of Vietnam's agricultural economy was ruined and infant birth defects subsequently appeared, both in Vietnam and back in the United States among military families.

**Agent provocateur** (French, 'provocative agent'). A person employed as a secret agent with the aim of provoking suspected persons to commit illegal acts and so be disclosed or punished.

**Indian agent.** *See under* INDIAN.

**Aggie Weston's** or **Aggies.** The Sailors' Rests, Christian social clubs which offered food and accommodation, set up by Dame Agnes E. Weston (1840–1918) as an alternative to pubs in her crusade against intemperance in the navy. The first were at Devonport (1879) and Portsmouth (1881).

**Aglaia** (Greek *aglaia*, 'clearness', 'beauty'). One of the THREE GRACES.

**Agnes** (Greek *agnos*, 'pure', influenced by Latin *agnus*, 'lamb'). The patron saint of young virgins, said to have been martyred in the Diocletian persecution (*c.*304) at the age of 13. There are conflicting accounts of the manner of her death. Some say she was burned at the stake, others that she was beheaded or stabbed in the throat. She refused offers of marriage because she was dedicated to Christ. Her festival is on 21 January. Upon St Agnes' night, says John Aubrey in his *Miscellanies* (1696), you take a row of pins and pull out each one, one at a time. Say a PATERNOSTER, stick a pin in your sleeve and you will dream of the one you will marry. In *The Eve of St Agnes* (1820) John Keats tells how:

> Young virgins might have visions of delight,
> And soft adorings from their loves receive
> Upon the honey'd middle of the night,
> If ceremonies due they did aright;
> As, supperless to bed they must retire,
> And couch supine their beauties, lilly white.

Tennyson also has a poem *St Agnes' Eve* (1842).

**Black Agnes.** *See under* BLACK.

**Agnoetae** (Greek *agnoeō*, 'I am ignorant'). A group of 4th-century Eunomian heretics, who maintained that God was not completely omniscient. The name was also used of a group of 6th-century MONOPHYSITES, who maintained that Christ, by the limitations of his human nature, had incomplete knowledge of both present and future.

**Agnostic** (Greek *a-*, 'not', and *gnostic*, 'knowing'). A term coined by T.H. Huxley in 1869 (with allusion to St PAUL'S mention of an altar 'To the Unknown God' in Acts 17:23) to denote a person who holds that knowledge of a Supreme Being is impossible. An atheist denies the existence of God. An agnostic says that it is impossible to know whether God exists or not. *See also* GNOSTICS; THEIST.

**Agnus. Agnus Bell.** *See* AGNUS DEI (4).

**Agnus Dei** (Latin, 'Lamb of God').

(1) A title of Jesus.

(2) The figure of a lamb bearing a cross or flag, the symbol of Christ.

(3) A cake of wax or dough bearing this imprint, distributed by the pope on the Sunday after EASTER, as a relic of the ancient custom of distributing the wax of the Paschal candle, which was stamped with the lamb.

(4) The part of the MASS that is introduced by the ringing of the Agnus bell, beginning with the words, *Agnus Dei, qui tollis peccata mundi* ('O Lamb of God, that takest away the sins of the world'); also part of the Gloria in the English Communion service.

**Agonistes** (Greek *agōnistēs*, 'combatant', 'champion'). The title of Milton's last poem, *Samson Agonistes* (1671), means 'Samson the Champion'. Similarly *Sweeney Agonistes* (1932), a poetic drama by T.S. Eliot.

**Agony. Agony aunt.** A person, traditionally a woman, who conducts an advice column or page in newspapers or magazines (especially women's) answering correspondents who seek help with their problems. Many of the letters are from female readers and are concerned with such matters as family relationships, marital problems, sex and boyfriends. The male equivalent is an 'agony uncle'. *See also* LONELY-HEART.

> [Former MP] Ron Brown, self-styled man of the people, yesterday embarked on his new job as an agony uncle.
> *The Times* (17 October 1998)

**Agony column.** A magazine or newspaper feature run by an AGONY AUNT. Also a part of a newspaper that contains advertisements for lost relatives, personal messages and the like.

**Agramant, The Ring of.** *See under* RING.

**Agreement. Gentleman's agreement.** *See under* GENTLEMAN.

**Sweetheart agreement.** *See under* SWEET.

**Aguecheek.** Sir Andrew Aguecheek, in Shakespeare's *Twelfth Night* (1599), is a timid, foolish but amusing country squire. His name suggests that he is thin and wan.

**Aguilar, Alonzo of.** *See under* ALONZO.

**Ahab.** The husband of JEZEBEL and a king of Israel who displayed more wickedness before God than any other king. He harassed the prophets, especially ELIJAH, and when he was finally killed in battle in Samaria, the dogs licked up his blood (1 Kings 22:38).

**Ahasuerus** (Hebrew *ahashwerōsh*). Under this name the Emperor XERXES (r.485–465 BC), husband first of VASHTI, then of ESTHER, appears in the biblical books of Ezra and Esther. The Ahasuerus of the Book of Daniel has not been identified. The name is also traditionally that of the WANDERING JEW.

**Ahaz, Dial of.** *See under* DIAL.

**Ahead of one's time.** Having ideas too advanced to be accepted by one's contemporaries.

**Ahithophel.** A treacherous friend and adviser. Ahithophel was the traitorous counsellor of King DAVID, who deserted to ABSALOM but hanged himself when Absalom overruled his advice (2 Samuel 15:12–17:23). In John Dryden's poem *Absalom and Achitophel* (1681), Achitophel (Ahithophel) represents Lord Shaftesbury.

**Ahmed** (Arabic *aḥmad*, 'very glorious'). Prince Ahmed, in the ARABIAN NIGHTS ENTERTAINMENTS, is noted for the tent given him by the fairy Paribanou, which can cover a whole army but also be carried in one's pocket, and also for the apple of Samarkand (*see* PRINCE AHMED'S APPLE), which would cure all diseases. Similar qualities to those of the tent are common to many legends. *See also* BAYARD; MAGIC CARPET; SKIDBLADNIR.

**Ahriman.** The spirit of evil in the dualism of later Zoroastrianism (*see* ZOROASTRIANS). His name is a Persian form of *Angra-Mainyu* ('enemy spirit'), and he is in eternal conflict with Ahura Mazda or ORMUZD.

**Ahura Mazda.** *See* ORMUZD.

**Aid, First.** *See under* FIRST.

**Aïda.** The heroine of Giuseppe Verdi's popular opera of the same name (1871). She is an Ethiopian princess who is taken as a slave-girl in Egypt during the time of the pharaohs. She hides in the crypt where her lover, Radamès, is to be buried alive, and at the end of the opera dies in his arms. Her name suggests not only Arabic *aida*, 'benefit', but also French *aider*, 'to save', and Greek *aidōs*, 'modesty', 'reverence'.

**Aidan** (diminutive of Irish *aodh*, 'fire'). St Aidan was a monk of Iona who was chosen by King Oswald in 635 to spread and rekindle Christianity in Northumbria. He established a monastery on the island of Lindisfarne (HOLY ISLAND) and founded many churches and schools on the mainland. He died at Bamburgh in Northumberland in 651. His feast-day is 31 August.

**Aide. Aide-mémoire** (French *aider*, 'to help', and *mémoire*, 'memory'). Anything serving as a reminder or 'memory-jogger'. In diplomatic parlance, the term is used for a memorandum or summary of an agreement sent from one country to another.

**Aide-toi, le Ciel t'aidera.** A line from LA FONTAINE (*Fables*, vi, 18 (1668–94)), often rendered in English as 'heaven helps those who help themselves'. It is the motto of the Massie family of Coddington, Cheshire.

**Air.** Held by Anaxagoras (*c.*500–*c.*428 BC) to be the primary form of matter and, by EMPEDOCLES and ARISTOTLE, to be one of the four ELEMENTS.

'To take the air' is to go out of doors for a walk or stroll.

**Airhead.** A silly or foolish person, who has 'nothing up top'.

**Airlift.** An organized manoeuvre to transport troops or stores to a destination by air. The Berlin airlift, to victual the British and American zones of the city after the Russian embargo on all land transport, began 26 June 1948 and ended 12 May 1949, after 195,530 flights carrying 1,414,000 tons of food, coal and other stores.

**Airline.** An organization or company that provides scheduled air transport over a regular route. In American use, an airline can also be the equivalent of an English BEELINE.

**As free as air.** *See under* AS.

**Beat the air, To.** *See under* BEAT.

**Castle in the air.** *See under* CASTLE.

**Change of air, A.** *See under* CHANGE.

**Clear the air, To.** *See under* CLEAR.

**Hot air.** *See under* HOT.

**Walk on air, To.** *See under* WALK.

**Aisha.** *See* AYESHA.

**Aisle.** The aisle in a church is one of the two parts parallel to the nave, from which it is usually separated by a row of pillars. The word comes from Latin *ala*, 'wing', but has somehow become associated with 'isle'. It is sometimes wrongly taken to be the nave itself, as in: 'The bride walked up the aisle.' But the bride walks up the nave, not one of the aisles.

**Rolling in the aisles.** *See under* ROLL.

**Aitchbone.** The rump bone in cattle or a cut of beef from it or including it. The word evolved from 'a nache bone', misdivided as 'an ache-bone'. *Nache* means 'buttock', ultimately from Latin *natis* in this sense. For examples of similarly misdivided words *see* APRON; NICKNAME.

**Ajax** (perhaps from Greek *aia*, 'earth', or *aianēs*, 'eternal').

**Ajax the Greater.** A hero of the TROJAN WAR, the son of Telamon and king of Salamis. He was a man of giant stature, daring but slow-witted. In the ODYSSEY, when the armour of ACHILLES was awarded to Odysseus (ULYSSES), as the champion, Ajax killed himself.

**Ajax the Lesser.** In HOMER the son of Oileus, king of Locris, and a man of small stature. As a consequence of raping PRIAM's daughter CASSANDRA he was drowned by POSEIDON after being shipwrecked.

**Akbar** (Arabic, 'greater', 'bigger'). An Arabic title, applied especially to Abu-ul-Fath Jalal-ud-Din Muhammad Akbar, known in English as Akbar the Great (1542–1605), the Mogul emperor of India from 1556 to his death. Among his ancestors were TAMBERLANE and GENGHIS KHAN.

**Akhenaten.** The name assumed by AMENHOTEP IV

when he encouraged the worship of ATEN. It means 'He who pleases Aten'.

**Akhoond** or **Akond.** King and high priest of the Swat (northwestern provinces of India). The title means 'teacher'.

> Who, or why, or which, or what,
> Is the Akond of Swat?
> EDWARD LEAR: 'The Akond of Swat' (1888)

**Alabama claims.** The claims made by the USA against Britain for losses caused during the CIVIL WAR (1861–5) by British-built Confederate raiders and notably the cruiser *Alabama*, which captured or sank 68 ships. In 1872 an international tribunal awarded the USA $15.5 million in gold.

**Aladdin** (Arabic *'ālā' ad-dīn*, 'excellence of the faith', from *ālā*, 'raised up', *al*, 'the', and *dīn*, 'faith', 'religion'). The poor youth in the ARABIAN NIGHTS ENTERTAINMENTS who obtains a magic lamp and a ring and has a splendid palace built by the genie of the lamp. He marries the daughter of the sultan of China and his palace is transported to Africa. He subsequently returns with wife and palace to China to live happily for many years.

**Alamo** (Spanish *álamo*, 'poplar', 'cottonwood'). The name of a Franciscan mission at San Antonio, Texas, which stood in a grove of cottonwood trees but which, by the end of the 18th century, was used as a fort. In the Texan War of Independence (1836) a garrison of about 155 Texans and Americans, including David CROCKETT, was wiped out by a large force of Mexicans under Santa Anna, after a 13-day siege. 'Remember the Alamo' became the war cry with which Sam Houston led the Texans to victory. Alamo is sometimes called the THERMOPYLAE of America, and the buildings are now preserved as a national monument.

**Alans.** Large hunting dogs introduced to Britain from Spain, where they are said to have been brought in the early 5th century by the Alani, a barbarian tribe. Chaucer in 'The Knight's Tale' (*c*.1387) describes LYCURGUS on his throne guarded by 'alaunts, twenty and mo, as grete as any steer'. Sir Walter Scott mentions them in *The Talisman* (ch vi (1825)). *See also* RACHE.

**Al Araf** (Arabic, 'the partition'). In the Koran a region between Paradise and Jahannam (HELL), for those who are neither morally good nor bad, such as infants and the mentally disturbed. It serves as a kind of LIMBO, where those whose good and bad deeds are equally balanced can await their eventual admission to heaven.

**Alarm. Beat an alarm, To.** *See under* BEAT.

**Call alarm, A.** *See under* CALL.

**False alarm.** *See under* FALSE.

**Alarums and excursions.** Confused noise and bustle. The expression was a stage direction in Elizabethan drama for appropriate sounds and cries to be made offstage to indicate a skirmish or other flurry of martial activity. 'Alarums' represents an old spelling of 'alarm'. The direction appears in slightly varying forms in Shakespeare, for example at the beginning of *Henry VI, Pt 3* (V, ii (1593)).

**Alasnam.** In the ARABIAN NIGHTS ENTERTAINMENTS Alasnam had eight magnificent golden statues, but he was required to find a ninth more precious still. He found it in the person of a beautiful woman, who became his wife.

**Alastor** (Greek *a-*, 'not', and *lanthanomai*, 'I forget'). The Greek name of the Avenging Deity, literally 'he who does not forget'. Percy Bysshe Shelley has a visionary poem entitled *Alastor; or the Spirit of Solitude* (1816).

**Alauda** (Latin, 'lark'). A Roman legion raised by Julius CAESAR in GAUL, so called from the lark's tuft on the soldiers' helmets.

**Alban** (perhaps Latin *Albanus*, 'person from Alba', or Celtic *alp*, 'rock', 'crag'). Britain's first martyr (Latin, *Protomartyr Anglorum*), who was beheaded *c*.305 at Verulamium (modern St Albans) during the Diocletian persecution, or possibly earlier, for harbouring a Christian priest. The present abbey stands near (although probably not on) the site of his execution, and his shrine is to be found there. His feast-day is on 20 June (17 June in the Book of Common Prayer). Like many other saints he is sometimes represented carrying his head to signify death by beheading.

**Albany** (perhaps Celtic *alp*, 'rock, 'crag'). An ancient name applied to the northern part of Scotland, inhabited by PICTS, and called CALEDONIA by the Romans. The name survives in that of Breadalbane ('neck of Elbyn'), an area of the Grampians in western Perthshire. *See also* ALBION.

In London, the name is that of a block of bachelors' chambers converted from the Duke of York's house in 1803 and adjoining Burlington House, PICCADILLY, where Macaulay wrote his *History of England* (1849, 1855). The block is no longer exclusively restricted to bachelors.

**Albatross** (Portuguese *alcatraz*, 'pelican', from Arabic *al-ghattās*, 'the white-tailed sea-eagle', influenced by Latin *albus*, 'white'). A large oceanic bird, noted for its powerful gliding flight. It was called the Cape Sheep by sailors from its frequenting the Cape of Good Hope, and it was said to sleep in the air. Sailors have long believed that to shoot one brings bad luck. *See also* ANCIENT MARINER.

More generally, an albatross is a constant burden or handicap. In golf, the word is used for a score of three strokes under par.

**Alberich** (Germanic *alfi*, 'elf', and *rik*, 'powerful'). In Scandinavian mythology the all-powerful king of the DWARFS. In Wagner's version

(1869–76) of the 13th-century NIBELUNGENLIED he appears as a hideous GNOME and steals the magic gold guarded by the Rhine Maidens, but he is later captured by the gods and forced to give up all he has in return for freedom. *See also* OBERON.

**Albert, An.** A watch-chain across the waistcoat from one pocket to another or to a buttonhole, so called from Albert (1819–61), Prince Consort, who set the fashion. He was presented with such a chain by the jewellers of Birmingham, when visiting the town in 1849.

**Albert the Bad.** Landgrave of Thuringia and Margrave of Meissen (d.1314).

**Albert the Good.** Prince Consort to Queen Victoria (1819–61).

> Beyond all titles, and a household name,
> Hereafter, thro' all times, Albert the Good.
>
> ALFRED, LORD TENNYSON: Dedication to *Idylls of the King* (1891)

**Albert the Great.** Albertus Magnus (*c.*1206–80), Albert of Cologne, renowned DOMINICAN scholastic philosopher, also called *Doctor universalis*.

Also the nickname, given by analogy with Albert the Good, of Albert Chevalier (1861–1923), 'the coster's Laureate' and a favourite of the MUSIC HALLS. Among the best known of his COCKNEY songs are 'Knock'd 'em in the Old Kent Road' and 'MY OLD DUTCH' (*see under* DUTCH).

**Albigenses.** A name for various MANICHEAN sects in southern France and northern Italy from the 11th to the 13th century. They are so named from the city of Albi, Languedoc, where their persecution began. They were violent opponents of the CATHOLIC CHURCH and were subjected to a crusade by Innocent III in 1208. They were eventually exterminated by the end of the 14th century.

**Albino** (Latin *albus*, 'white'). A term denoting congenital absence of pigmentation in the skin, eyes and hair. The word is occasionally used figuratively. Thus Oliver Wendell Holmes, in the AUTOCRAT OF THE BREAKFAST-TABLE (ch viii (1857–8)), speaks of Kirke White as one of the 'sweet albino poets', whose 'plaintive song' he admires, apparently implying some deficiency of virility while possibly playing upon the name.

**Albion.** An ancient and poetic name for Britain, perhaps from the white (Latin *albus*) cliffs that face GAUL, but possibly from Celtic *alp*, 'rock', 'crag'. Albion or ALBANY originally may have been the Celtic name of all Britain.

One legend is that a giant son of NEPTUNE, named Albion, discovered the country and ruled over it for 44 years. Another story tells how 50 daughters of the king of Syria (the eldest of whom was named Albia) were all married on the same day and murdered their husbands on their wedding night. They were set adrift in a ship as punishment and eventually reached this western isle where they duly married natives.

**New Albion.** *See under* NEW.

**Perfidious Albion.** *See under* PERFIDIOUS.

**Al Borak.** *See* BORAK.

**Alcaic verse** or **Alcaics.** A Greek and Latin lyrical metre, so called from Alcaeus (7th century BC) who supposedly invented it. It consists of a strophe of four lines, each having four feet. A.C. Swinburne, Tennyson and R.L. Stevenson experimented with the metre in English poems. A well-known example is the following, the opening lines of Tennyson's 16-line poem on Milton:

> O mighty-mouthed inventor of harmonies,
> O skilled to sing of Time or Eternity,
> God-gifted organ-voice of England,
> Milton, a name to resound for ages.
>
> *Milton: Alcaics* (1863)

**Al Capone.** *See under* CAPONE.

**Alcatraz** (Spanish *Isla de los Alcatraces*, 'island of the pelicans'). A notorious American prison on the rocky island of the same name in San Francisco Bay. It was originally a place of detention for military offenders in 1868 but later accommodated civilian prisoners. From 1934 it housed the most dangerous civilian criminals, its inmates including such figures of infamy as Al Capone, George 'Machine Gun' Kelly and Robert Stroud, the 'Birdman of Alcatraz'. Shortage of water eventually led to the abandonment of the penitentiary in 1963. Following subsequent abortive Sioux Indian claims on the island, it became part of the Golden Gate National Recreation Area in 1972 and is now open to visitors.

**Alcestis** (Greek *alkē*, 'power', 'courage'). In Greek legend the daughter of Pelias and wife of Admetus, king of Thessaly, to whom the FATES agreed to grant deliverance from death if his mother, father or wife would die for him instead. Alcestis thus sacrificed her life but was restored to her husband from HADES by HERCULES.

**Alchemilla.** A genus of plants of the rose family, so called because alchemists collected the dew of its leaves for their operations. The species *Alchemilla mollis* is also called lady's mantle, from the Virgin MARY.

**Alchemy** (Arabic *al-kīmiyā'*, 'the transmutation'). The pseudoscientific predecessor of chemistry sought to find a way of transmuting base metals into gold by means of the PHILOSOPHER'S STONE, a universal solvent or ALKAHEST, a PANACEA and an ELIXIR OF LIFE. Ben Jonson wrote a play called *The Alchemist* (1610).

**Alcina** (Greek *alkē*, 'power'). In Ariosto's ORLANDO FURIOSO (1516), the personification of carnal pleasure, otherwise the CIRCE of fable and Labe of the Arabians. Handel's opera *Alcina* appeared in 1735.

**Alcmena** (Greek *alkē*, 'power', and *mēnis*, 'anger'). In Greek mythology the daughter of Electryon, king of Mycenae, wife of AMPHITRYON, and mother (by ZEUS, who came to her in the guise of her husband) of HERCULES.

**Alcofribas Nasier.** The anagrammatic pseudonym used by François Rabelais, under which the first two books of GARGANTUA (1535) and PANTAGRUEL (1532) appeared.

**Aldebaran** (Arabic *al-dabarān*, 'the follower', i.e. of the PLEIADES). A binary star, one component of which is a red giant,  Tauri, representing the bull's eye in the constellation of TAURUS.

**Aldine editions.** The internationally famous editions of the Greek and Latin classics printed and published at Venice by the firm founded by Aldus Manutius (*c*.1450–1515) in 1490. The type called italics, once called Aldine, was devised by his type designer, Francesco Griffo. The founder's grandson, Aldus the Younger (1547–97), closed the business on taking charge of the Vatican press in 1590.

**Ale** (Old English *alu* or *ealu*, related to Old Norse *ǫl*). A beverage made from barley is mentioned by Tacitus (*c*.55–*c*.120) and even Herodotus (5th century BC). Ale in Britain is of pre-Roman origin and was a malt brew without hops. Hopped or bitter beer was introduced by the Flemings in the 15th century. Ale and beer are now largely synonymous terms, although the word ale is not used for the thick black beers (STOUT and porter) that became popular in the 18th century. In some areas ale is used for the stronger malt liquors and beer for the weaker, in others the terms are reversed. *See also* AUDIT ALE; CHURCH-ALE.

**Ale stake** or **pole.** The pole set up before an alehouse by way of a sign, often surmounted by a bush or garland. Thus, Chaucer says of the Sumpner (Summoner):

> He wore a garland set upon his head
> Large as the holly-bush upon a stake
> Outside an ale-house.
> *Canterbury Tales*, 'Prologue' (*c*.1387) (modern translation by Nevill Coghill, 1951)

**Alewife.** The landlady of an alehouse. In America, a fish of the herring family, possibly from French *alose*, 'shad', but influenced by alewife, from the fish's plump appearance, like that of a stout landlady.

**Adam's ale.** *See under* ADAM.

**Audit ale.** *See under* AUDIT.

**Cakes and ale.** *See under* CAKE.

**Whitsun ale.** *See under* WHITSUN.

**Alec, Smart.** *See under* SMART.

**Alecto** (Greek *alēktos*, 'ceaseless', 'unending'). In Greek mythology, one of the three ERINYES, the goddesses of vengeance, the equivalent of the Roman FURIES.

**Alectorian stone** (Greek *alektōr*, 'cock'). A stone, fabled to be of talismanic power, found in the stomach of cocks. Those who possess one are strong, brave and wealthy. MILO of Crotona is said to have owed his strength to one.

**Alectryomancy** (Greek *alektōr*, 'cock', and *manteia*, 'divination'). DIVINATION by means of a cock. Draw a circle, and write in succession round it the letters of the alphabet, laying a grain of corn on each. Then put a cock in the centre of the circle, and watch what grains he pecks up. The letters will prognosticate the answer. Libanus and Jamblicus thus discovered who was to succeed the Emperor Valens. The cock ate the grains over the letters T, H, E, O, D, signifying Theodorus.

**Alexander.** So PARIS, son of PRIAM, was called by the shepherds who brought him up.

**Alexander and the robber.** The pirate Diomedes, having been captured, was asked by Alexander the Great how he dared to molest the seas. 'How darest thou molest the earth?' was the reply. 'Because I am the master of a single galley I am termed a robber; but you who oppress the world with huge squadrons are called king.' Alexander was so struck by this reasoning that he made Diomedes a rich prince and a dispenser of justice. *See also* GESTA ROMANORUM, cxlvi (13th century).

**Alexander of the North.** The war-loving Charles XII of Sweden (1682–1718), whose army was annihilated by Peter the Great at Poltava (1709).

**Alexander's beard.** A beardless, smooth chin, otherwise an AMAZONIAN CHIN.

> I like this trustie glass of Steele ...
> Wherein I see a Sampson's grim regarde
> Disgraced yet with Alexander's bearde.
> GEORGE GASCOIGNE: *The Steele Glas* (1576)

**Alexander the Corrector.** The self-assumed nickname of Alexander Cruden (1701–70), bookseller and compiler of the *Complete Concordance to the Holy Scriptures* (1737). He was several times confined to a lunatic asylum, but his activities as a corrector of morals were many and varied. He carried a damped sponge to wipe out the graffiti found on walls and buildings.

**Alexander the Great.** Alexander III of Macedon (356–323 BC).

**Continence of Alexander, The.** *See under* CONTINENCE.

**Only two Alexanders.** *See under* ONLY.

**You think of Parmenio and I of Alexander.** *See under* THINK.

**Alexandra. Alexandra limp.** In the 1860s Queen Alexandra (then Princess of Wales), after a painful attack of rheumatism in the knee, developed a limp, which was imitated in sycophantic fashion by many women about the court. Hence the 'Alexandra limp'.

**Alexandra Rose Day.** A day in June when rose emblems are sold for the hospital fund inaugurated in 1912 by Queen Alexandra (1844–1925), Danish consort of Edward VII, to celebrate the 50th year of her residence in England.

**Alexandrian.** Anything from the East was so called by the old writers because Alexandria was the depot from which Eastern goods reached Europe. Thus ARIOSTO says:

Reclined on Alexandrian [i.e. Persian] carpets.
*Orlando Furioso*, x (1532)

**Alexandrian codex.** A Greek manuscript of the Scriptures, probably of the 5th century, written in UNCIALS on parchment and said to have originated at Alexandria. It was presented to Charles I in 1628 by the Patriarch of Constantinople and was placed in the British Museum on its foundation.

**Alexandrian school.** An academy of learning founded about 310 BC at Alexandria by Ptolemy I (SOTER) and Demetrius of Phaleron, especially noted for its literary scholars and mathematicians. Its most noted scholars were Aristarchus (*c.*217–145 BC), Eratosthenes (*c.*275–194 BC) and Harpocration (2nd century AD). Its mathematicians included EUCLID (*fl.c.*300 BC), author of the *Elements*, the celebrated treatise on geometry, and the astronomer Ptolemy (2nd century AD). Alexandria remained a centre of learning until 640 AD when the library was, supposedly, finally destroyed.

**Catherine of Alexandria.** *See under* CATHERINE.

**Pleiad of Alexandria, The.** *See under* PLEIADES.

**Alexandrine.** In prosody, an IAMBIC or trochaic line of twelve syllables or six feet with, usually, a caesura (break) at the sixth syllable. It is perhaps so called from the 12th-century French *Roman d'Alexandre*, a collection of romances about the adventures of Alexander the Great. It has been the standard metre of French poetry since the 16th century, especially in dramatic form. English poets who have used it include Michael Drayton, Robert Browning and Robert Bridges. Alexander Pope also used it, even when deriding it, as in the second line of the following:

A needless Alexandrine ends the song
That, like a wounded snake, drags its slow length along.
*Essay on Criticism*, ii (1709)

**Alexandrine age.** The age when the ALEXANDRIAN SCHOOL was the centre of literature, science and philosophy.

**Alexandrine philosophy.** A school of philosophy that developed at Alexandria in the early centuries of the Christian era. It gave rise to Gnosticism and neo-Platonism and attempted to reconcile Christianity and Greek philosophy. *See also* GNOSTICS.

**Alexis** (Greek *aleksō*, 'I ward off'). The patron saint of hermits and beggars. According to the story in the GESTA ROMANORUM (xv (13th century)) he lived on his father's estate as a hermit until he died but was never recognized. He may, in fact, have never existed. His feast-day is 17 July.

**Alfadir** (Old Norse, 'father of all'). In Scandinavian mythology, one of the epithets of ODIN.

**Alfana** ('mare'). The horse of Gradasso in ORLANDO FURIOSO.

**Alfar** (Old Norse, 'elves'). The elves of northern mythology. In German legend the *Döckalfar* frequent dark underground caverns and mines. *See also* ELF.

**Alf Garnett.** *See under* GARNETT.

**Alfred. Alfred the Great.** King of WESSEX (849–899), especially noted for his resistance to the Danish invaders, who, in the winter of 877–878, occupied much of Wessex. Alfred withdrew to his base at Athelney (near Taunton, Somerset), and it is to this period that the story of Alfred and the cakes belongs, with the first known version probably dating from the 11th or 12th century. The story is that the king, unrecognized, took refuge in a cowherd's hut. While seated by the fire attending to his equipment, he allowed the housewife's loaves to burn, for which he was vigorously scolded. The story is not found in Asser's *Life of Alfred* (written in 893) and is first recorded only in the 11th century. After the defeat of the Danes, Alfred commanded that a monastery be built at Athelney. *See also* ATHELING.

Alfred (or Ælfræd) was the son of Æthelwulf, also king of Wessex (839–855), and in the Anglo-Saxon manner his name alliterates with that of his father and those of his brothers, Æthelbeald, Æthelbeorht and Æthelræd.

**Alfred Crowquill.** *See under* CROWQUILL.

**Alhambra** (Arabic *al-hamrā'*, 'the red [house]'). The citadel and palace built at Granada in Spain by the Moorish kings in the 13th century. Also the name of a formerly famous theatre and music hall in Leicester Square, London, built in Moorish style. *See also* PANOPTICON.

**Ali** (Arabic *'alā*, 'to be high'). MOHAMMED's cousin and son-in-law, famed among Persians for the beauty of his eyes, hence *Ayn Hali* ('eyes of Ali') as the highest expression for beauty.

**Ali Baba** (Arabic *'alā*, 'to be high', and *bābā*, 'father', 'papa'). A poor woodcutter who is the hero of a story in the ARABIAN NIGHTS ENTERTAINMENTS. He sees a band of robbers enter a cave by means of the magic password OPEN SESAME! When they have gone away he enters the cave, loads his ass with treasure and returns home. The 40 thieves discover that Ali Baba has learned their secret and resolve to kill him, but they are finally outwitted by the slave-girl MORGIANA.

**Alias** (Latin, 'otherwise', 'at another time'). 'You have as many aliases as Robin of Bagshot' is a phrase formerly said to one who passes under many names. It is from Gay's *Beggar's Opera* (1728), in which Robin of Bagshot, one of Macheath's gang, was alias Gordon, alias Bluff Bob, alias Carbuncle, alias Bob Booty. He was meant to represent Sir Robert Walpole.

**Alibi** (Latin, 'elsewhere'). A plea of having been elsewhere at a time that an offence is alleged to have been committed. A clock that strikes a different time on the hour from that shown by the hands has been humorously called 'an alibi clock'. In modern usage, the word is used generally for an excuse or pretext.

**Aliboron** (perhaps from the name of the Arab scholar Al-Biruni (973–1048)). The name of a jackass in LA FONTAINE's *Fables* (1668–94) and earlier that of a DEVIL in the Middle Ages. In the trial of Gilles de Rais (1440), Maistre Aliborum was used as a title for the Devil. The name probably passed to the jackass from Jean-François Sarrasin's *Le Testament de Goula* (1656), in which the author makes the following punning remark:

> Ma sotane est pour Maistre Aliboron, car la sotane à sot ane appartient.
> (My cassock is for Master Aliboron, for the cassock [sotane] belongs to the foolish ass [sot ane].)

In 1910, at the Salon des Indépendants in Paris, a picture titled *Coucher du soleil sur l'Adriatique* ('Sunset over the Adriatic') was presented, the artist being one Raphaël-Joachim Boronali. No one realized that Boronali was simply an anagram of Aliboron. The picture, which was highly praised, had in fact been painted, under the supervision of an official, with a donkey's tail serving as a paint brush.

**Alice.** The short name of Alice Springs in Northern Territory, Australia, 'the capital of the centre'. It was named from Lady Alice Todd, wife of Sir Charles Todd, who supervised the building of the Overland Telegraph Line in the early 1870s. It was formerly called Stuart after the explorer John McDouall Stuart (1815–66).

> It's railhead, of course, for trucking cattle down to Adelaide – that's one thing. But it's a go-ahead place is Alice; all sorts of things go on there.
> NEVIL SHUTE: *A Town Like Alice*, ch vi (1950)

**Alice in Wonderland.** *Alice's Adventures in Wonderland* (1865) and *Through the Looking-Glass* (1871), widely-read children's classics, originally illustrated by Sir John Tenniel, were written by C.L. Dodgson, an Oxford mathematician, under the pseudonym of Lewis Carroll. The original of Alice was Alice Liddell, daughter of Dean Liddell, famous as co-editor, with Robert Scott, of the *Greek-English Lexicon* (1843). The Alice stories are noted for their whimsical humour and the 'nonsense' verse that they include. *Through the Looking-Glass* concludes with an ACROSTIC poem, one of Carroll's best, with the lines spelling out Alice Pleasance Liddell's full name.

'Alice in Wonderland' schemes and ideas are those that are unreal or totally impractical:

> A £1,500 council house is costing my city over £6,000. This is an Alice in Wonderland situation.
> *Guardian* (21 March 1961)

*See also* CLOUD-CUCKOO-LAND; LOOKING-GLASS.

**Alien priory.** A priory that was dependent upon a monastery in a foreign country.

**Alifanfaron** (blend of ALI and FANFARON). Don QUIXOTE attacked a flock of sheep, and declared them to be the army of the giant Alifanfaron. The story is similar to that of AJAX, who, in a fit of madness, fell upon a flock of sheep, mistaking them for the sons of ATREUS.

**Alive. Alive and kicking.** Active and in good health. The expression probably refers to a healthy baby either in the womb or just after birth.

**Look alive!** *See under* LOOK.

**Al Kadr** (Arabic, 'the divine decree'). A particular night in the month of RAMADAN when Muslims say that angels descend to earth and GABRIEL reveals to man the decrees of God (Koran, ch xcvii).

**Alkahest.** A sham Arabic word attributed to PARACELSUS, used for the universal solvent sought by alchemists. *See also* ALCHEMY.

**All. All adrift.** In figurative use, mentally aimless and confused.

**All along the line.** At every stage; in every detail, as: 'The accuracy of the statement is contested all along the line by the witnesses.'

**All and sundry.** Everyone and everything. 'Sundry' is related to 'sunder' and properly refers to distinctive individuals. The expression as a whole thus refers to a collective group and its individual members.

**All at sea.** See AT SEA.

**All Blacks, The.** The New Zealand's Rugby XV, which first played in England in 1905. They are so named from their black playing strip.

**All cats love fish but fear to wet their paws.** An old adage said of a person who is anxious to obtain something of value but does not want to incur the necessary trouble or risk. It is to this saying that Shakespeare referred in *Macbeth* (I, vii (1605)):

> Letting 'I dare not' wait upon 'I would',
> Like the poor cat i' the adage.

**All dressed up and nowhere to go.** Ready for action but not required. The source of the line is the title of a song by Silvio Hein and Benjamin Burt dating from 1912, 'When You're All Dressed Up and No Place to Go'.

**All ears.** All attention. The original phrase was 'all ear'.

> I was all ear,
> And took in strains that might create a soul
> Under the ribs of Death.
> MILTON: *Comus* (1637)

**All eyes.** Watching closely; very attentive.

**All fingers and thumbs.** Awkward, clumsy. The expression is probably a corruption of 'All my fingers are thumbs', since all people have fingers and thumbs anyway.

**All Fools' Day.** 1 April. *See* APRIL FOOL.

**All fours.** A game of cards, so called from the points at stake: High, Low, Jack and Game.

**All girls together.** Women on terms of close friendship with one another, especially when engaged in a collective enterprise that for each individually would seem unlikely.

**All go.** A constant state of activity or busyness, as: 'It's all go this week.'

**All Greek to me.** Quite unintelligible; a foreign language. Shakespeare's Casca says: 'For mine own part, it was Greek to me' (*Julius Caesar*, I, ii (1599)).

**All Hallows Day.** Another name for All Saints' Day (1 November), 'hallows' deriving from Old English *hālig*, 'holy'. Pope Boniface IV converted the PANTHEON at Rome into a Christian church, dedicated to all the martyrs, in 610. The festival of All Saints, originally held on 1 May, was changed to 1 November in 834.

**All Hallows Eve.** *See* HALLOWEEN.

**All Hallows summer.** Another name for St MARTIN'S SUMMER or an INDIAN SUMMER, so called because it is set about All Hallows. Similarly there is a St LUKE'S SUMMER (from 18 October).

> Farewell, thou latter spring! farewell, All-hallown Summer!
> SHAKESPEARE: *Henry IV, Pt I*, I, ii (1597)

**All hands.** In nautical parlance, the whole crew, as: 'All hands on deck.'

**All hands and the cook.** A phrase, originating in the western USA, denoting a state of emergency when the herds were so restless that everyone, including the cook, had to ride to quieten them down.

**Allheal.** A name of various plants said to have healing properties, and especially valerian, also called Hercules' woundwort, because HERCULES is supposed to have learned its virtues from CHIRON. Spikenard (*Nardostachys grandiflora*), mentioned in the Bible (Mark 14:3), and extracted from a Himalayan member of the family, was used in perfumes by the ancient Egyptians, Greeks and Romans.

**All hell broke loose.** There was chaos and confusion, bedlam and babel.

**All he touches turns to gold.** All his ventures succeed; he is always lucky. The allusion is to MIDAS.

**All in.** Completely exhausted. The expression probably derives from Stock Market jargon. Dealers would cry 'All in!' meaning that all stock should be held in, when prices were falling and the market was depressed, and conversely 'All out!' when they were rising and the market buoyant.

**All in good time.** In due course; when conditions are right.

**All in the day's work.** Something that is unusual or unexpected but that can be accommodated as part of the normal routine. The expression was common by the 18th century but its origins are uncertain. A character in Sir Walter Scott's novel *The Monastery* (1820) says: 'That will cost me a farther ride ... but it is all in the day's work.'

**All in the same boat.** We are in this together; we all take the same risks. The reference is to the perils faced by people in a small boat at sea.

**All leather or prunella.** Nothing of any importance; mere dross. The expression arose through a misunderstanding of the lines by Pope, who was drawing a distinction between the work of a cobbler and that of a parson.

> Worth makes the man, and want of it the fellow;
> The rest is all but leather or prunella.
> ALEXANDER POPE: *Essay on Man*, iv (1733)

Prunella is a worsted stuff, formerly used for clergymen's gowns and for the uppers of ladies' boots. It was probably so called because it was the colour of a plum (French *prune*).

**All Lombard Street to a China orange.** An old saying, implying very long odds, Lombard Street being the great centre of banking and mercantile transactions. To stake the wealth of London against an orange is to stake great wealth against a trifle.

> 'It is Lombard Street to a China orange,' quoth Uncle Jack.
> EDWARD BULWER-LYTTON: *The Caxtons*, IV, iii (1849)

**All my eye and Betty Martin.** All nonsense, BOSH, rubbish. A curious expression of uncertain origin. A popular explanation was that it was a British soldiers' or sailors' rendering of *O mihi, beate Martine*, an invocation to St MARTIN heard abroad. 'All my eye' is the older saying:

> That's all my eye, the King only can pardon, as the law says.
> OLIVER GOLDSMITH: *The Good Natur'd Man* (1767)

**All of.** Quite as much or possibly more than, for example: 'It is all of fifty miles from London to Brighton.'

**All one's geese are swans.** To overestimate; to see things in too rosy a light; to paint too rosy a picture. All one's children are paragons, and whatever one does is, in one's own eyes, superfluous.

**All one's swans are geese.** All one's fine promises or expectations have proved fallacious. 'Hope told a flattering tale.'

**All over bar the shouting.** Success is so certain that only the applause is lacking. The phrase perhaps derives from boxing, the 'shouting' being the noisy appeal against the referee's decision.

**All-overish.** Not at one's best; beset with weariness and indifference, as before the onset of an illness.

**All over the shop.** Scattered in every direction; all over the place.

**All roads lead to Rome.** All efforts of thought converge in a common centre. As from the centre of the Roman world roads radiated to every part of the empire, so any road, if followed to its source, must lead to the great capital city, Rome.

**All Saints Day.** *See* ALL HALLOWS DAY.

**All serene** (Spanish *al sereno*, 'in the open'). Spanish *sereno*, meaning 'calm', 'clear', was called out by night watchmen and came to be the word for a night watchman himself. It meant that the weather was fine and was equivalent to our 'All's well'. It was a popular catchphrase from the late 19th century.

**All set.** All ready to begin. The expression probably dates from the days of sailing ships, when a ship set her sails before leaving harbour.

**All shipshape and Bristol fashion.** With everything stowed and the ship fully ready for sea; hence organized and ready in general. The expression derives from the port of Bristol's reputation for efficiency in the days of sail.

**All-singing, all-dancing.** Spectacularly impressive. The phrase is of immediate military origin but subsequently came to apply to a fulsome business presentation or marketing promotion. The ultimate reference is to a lavishly staged musical number.

**All Sir Garnet.** Originally an army phrase of the late 19th century, meaning 'everything is as it should be'. It originally referred to the successful military expeditions of Sir Garnet Wolseley (1833–1913), especially in Egypt.

**All Souls College.** An Oxford college founded in 1438 by Henry Chichele, archbishop of Canterbury, with Henry VI a co-founder. It was intended as a CHANTRY, whose members were to study and pray for the souls of Henry V and Henry VI, and for those killed or who might be killed in their French wars. It has a warden and 50 fellows, few of whom are in residence, and was unique, until the new foundations of the 1960s, in having no undergraduates.

**All Souls' Day.** 2 November, the day following ALL HALLOWS DAY, which Roman Catholics devote to prayer and almsgiving on behalf of the faithful departed. According to tradition a certain pilgrim returning from the Holy Land took refuge on a rocky island during a storm. There he met a hermit, who told him that among the cliffs was an opening to the infernal regions, through which flames ascended, and where the groans of the tormented were distinctly audible. The pilgrim told Odilo, abbot of Cluny, who appointed the day following (2 November 998) to be set apart for the benefit of those souls in PURGATORY. In England it was formerly observed by ringing the soul bell or PASSING BELL, by making and distributing SOUL CAKES, by blessing beans and so on.

**All Souls' Parish Magazine.** *The Times* was so nicknamed during the editorship (1923–41) of G.G. Dawson, fellow of All Souls. He and some of his associates, who were also fellows of the college, frequently met there for discussions.

**All Stuarts are not sib** (Old English *sibb*, 'related'). An old Scottish proverb rebuking those who, sharing a surname with a famous person (in this case the royal Stuarts), advance false claims of kinship to inflate their self-esteem.

**All tarred with the same brush.** All alike to blame; all having the same faults; all sheep of the same flock. The allusion is to the former treatment of sores and the like on sheep, with a brush dipped in tar.

**All that glitters is not gold.** Do not be deceived by appearances. A saying most familiar from Shakespeare: 'All that glisters is not gold; Often have you heard that told' (*Merchant of Venice*, II, vii (1596)). As he implies, the proverb dates from earlier times, and was familiar to Chaucer:

> However, all that glitters is not gold,
> And that's the truth as we're so often told
> *Canterbury Tales*, 'Canon's Yeoman's Tale' (*c.*1387) (modern translation by Nevill Coghill, 1951)

**All the best.** Best wishes, a form of greeting.

**All the go.** All the fashion; all the rage; quite in VOGUE.

**All the Talents.** The unsuitable name given to Lord Grenville's ministry (1806–7), formed on the death of the Pitt the Younger. It was an attempt at a broadly based administration but largely consisted of the followers of Charles James Fox, who was Foreign Secretary. Its one great measure was the abolition of the slave trade in 1807.

**All the world and his wife.** Everyone without exception.

**All thumbs.** Clumsy; to be ALL FINGERS AND THUMBS.

**All tickety-boo.** Everything is in order, everything is fine and as it should be. An expression of uncertain origin, possibly from 'ticket' as in THAT'S THE TICKET (*see under* TICKET).

**All-time high, An.** A record. An expression of American origin.

**All to break.** 'And a certain woman cast a piece of a millstone upon ABIMELECH's head, and all to brake his skull' (Judges 9:53). This does not mean that she did so with the sole aim of breaking his skull but that she wholly smashed it. The 'to' is used intensively, like the inseparable verbal prefix *zer-* in German, with 'all' added naturally.

**All to the good.** Satisfactory; tending towards a desirable outcome. 'Good' here refers to a plus balance in accounting, denoting a profit.

**Cap it all, To.** *See under* CAP.

**Dash it all.** *See under* DASH.

**End it all, To.** *See under* END.

**Go on all fours, To.** *See under* GO.

**Put** or **have all one's eggs in one basket, To.** To stake everything on a single speculation or enterprise.

**Allah** (Arabic *allah*, 'the god', from *al*, 'the', and *ilah*, 'god'). The chief Muslim name for God. The Muslim war cry *Allah il Allah* is a form of *la illah illa allah* ('there is no God but the God'), the first clause of the Islamic confession of faith. *Allah akbar* means 'God is most mighty'. All the suras (chapters) of the KORAN, with the exception of the ninth, begin with the formula: *bismi llah ar-raḥman ar-raḥīm* ('In the name of God the Merciful and Compassionate').

Muslim scholars have related that Allah has 3000 names. One thousand are known only by the angels, 300 are in the TORAH, 300 in Zabur (Psalms of David), 300 in the New Testament, and 99 in the KORAN. One name that has been hidden by Allah is Ism Allah al-a'zam, 'The Greatest name of Allah'.

The 99 'most beautiful names' of Allah, as given in Shems Friedlander's *Ninety-Nine Names of Allah* (1993), are as follows:

ar-Rahman ('the Beneficent'),
ar-Rahim ('the Merciful'),
al-Malik ('the Sovereign Lord'),
al-Quddus ('the Holy'),
as-Salam ('the Source of Peace')
al-Mu'min ('the Guardian of Faith')
al-Muhaymin ('the Protector')
al-'Aziz ('the Mighty')
al-Jabbar ('the Compeller')
al-Mutakabbir ('the Majestic')
al-Khaliq ('the Creator')
al-Bari' ('the Evolver')
al-Musawwir ('the Fashioner')
al-Ghaffar ('the Forgiver')
al-Qahhar ('the Subduer')
al-Wahhab ('the Bestower')
ar-Razzaq ('the Provider')
al-Fattah ('the Opener')
al-'Alim ('the All-Knowing')
al-Qabid ('the Constrictor')
al-Basit ('the Expander')
al-Khafid ('the Abaser')
ar-Rafi' ('the Exalter')
al-Mu'izz ('the Honourer')
al-Muzill ('the Dishonourer')
as-Sami' ('the All-Hearing')
al-Basir ('the All-Seeing')
al-Hakam ('the Judge')
al-'Adl ('the Just')
al-Latif ('the Subtle One')
al-Khabir ('the Aware')
al-Halim ('the Forbearing One')
al-'Azim ('the Great One')
al-Ghafur ('the All-Forgiving')
ash-Shakur ('the Appreciative')
al-'Ali ('the Most High')
al-Kabir ('the Most Great')
al-Hafiz ('the Preserver')
al-Muqit ('the Maintainer')
al-Hasib ('the Reckoner')
al-Jalil ('the Sublime One')
al-Karim ('the Generous One')
ar-Raqib ('the Watchful')
al-Mujib ('the Responsive')
al-Wasi' ('the All-Embracing')
al-Hakim ('the Wise')
al-Wadud ('the Loving')
al-Majid ('the Most Glorious One')
al-Ba'ith ('the Resurrector')
ash-Shahid ('the Witness')
al-Haqq ('the Truth')
al-Wakil ('the Trustee')
al-Qawi ('the Most Strong')
al-Matin ('the Firm One')
al-Wali ('the Protecting Friend')
al-Hamid ('the Praiseworthy')
al-Muhsi ('the Reckoner')
al-Mubdi ('the Originator')
al-Mu'id ('the Restorer')
al-Muhyi ('the Giver of Life')
al-Mumit ('the Creator of Death')
al-Hayy ('the Alive')
al-Qayyum ('the Self-Subsisting')
al-Wajid ('the Finder')
al-Majid ('the Noble')
al-Wahid ('the Unique')
al-Ahad ('the One')
as-Samad ('the Eternal')
al-Qadir ('the Able')
al-Muqtadir ('the Powerful')
al-Muqaddim ('the Expeditor')
al-Mu'akhkhir ('the Delayer')
al-Awwal ('the First')
al-Akhir ('the Last')
az-Zahir ('the Manifest')
al-Batin ('the Hidden')
al-Wali ('the Governor')
al-Muta'ali ('the Most Exalted')
al-Barr ('the Source of All Goodness')
at-Tawwab ('the Accepter of Repentance')
al-Muntaqim ('the Avenger')
al-'Afuw ('the Pardoner')
ar-Ra'uf ('the Compassionate')
Malik-ul-Mulk ('the Eternal Owner of Sovereignty')

Dhul-Jalal-wal-Ikram ('the Lord of Majesty and Bounty')
al-Muqsit ('the Equitable')
al-Jame' ('the Gatherer')
al-Ghani ('the Self-Sufficient')
al-Mughni ('the Enricher')
al-Mani' ('the Preventer')
ad-Darr ('the Distresser')
an-Nafi' ('the Propitious')
an-Nur ('the Light')
al-Hadi ('the Guide')
al-Badi' ('the Incomparable')
al-Baqi ('the Everlasting')
al-Warith ('the Supreme Inheritor')
ar-Rashid ('the Guide to the Right Path')
as-Sabur ('the Patient')

**Allan-a-Dale.** A minstrel in the ROBIN HOOD ballads who also appears in Sir Walter Scott's *Ivanhoe* (1819). Robin Hood helped him to carry off his bride when she was on the point of being married against her will to a rich old knight.

**Alleluiah.** *See* HALLELUJAH.

**Allen, Barbara.** The heroine of an old ballad given in PERCY'S RELIQUES (1765) called 'Barbara Allen's Cruelty'. She died of remorse after showing no pity for the young man who was dying of love for her.

> Farewell, she sayd, ye virgins all,
> And shun the fault I fell in:
> Henceforth take warning by the fall
> Of cruel Barbara Allen.

**Alley** or **Ally.** A choice, large playing marble made of stone or alabaster, from which it takes its name. The alley tor (taw) beloved of Master Bardell in Dickens' *Pickwick Papers* (ch xxxiv (1836–7)) was a special alley that had won many taws or games. In Australia the word is also used for a group of gamblers or their den.

**Alley, The.** An old name for Change Alley in the City of London, where dealings in the public funds used to take place.

**Alley cat.** A cat that roams in back streets, or a person who leads an existence like one, such as a RAGAMUFFIN or a prostitute.

**Blind alley.** *See under* BLIND.

**Tin Pan Alley.** *See under* TIN.

**Alliance. Grand Alliance.** *See under* GRAND.

**Holy Alliance.** *See under* HOLY.

**Alliensis, Dies.** *See under* DIES.

**Alligator.** When the Spaniards first saw this reptile in the New World, they called it *el lagarto,* 'the lizard'. In American slang, alligator has several figurative meanings, among them 'a Mississippi River keel-boat sailor', derived from the real or supposed battles of early boatmen with alligators. Hence it is a symbol of manliness. A common parting pleasantry in the 1950s and 1960s, especially among teenagers, was 'See you later, alligator,' to which the regular response was 'In a while, crocodile'. The phrase was popularized by a Bill Haley hit in the film *Rock Around the Clock* (1956).

**Alligator pear.** The name given to the fruit of the West Indian tree, *Persea americana*, more commonly known as the avocado. Both these names derives from Spanish *aguacate*, which itself is a corruption of Nahuatl *ahuacatl*, 'testicle', alluding to the shape of the fruit.

**Alliteration.** The rhetorical device of commencing adjacent accented syllables with the same letter or sound, as ridiculed by Quince:

> Whereat, with blade, with bloody blameful blade,
> He bravely broach'd his boiling bloody breast.
>
> SHAKESPEARE: *A Midsummer Night's Dream*, V, i (1595)

Alliteration was an essential feature of Old and Middle English poetry, but it is often used in more modern poetry with great effect, as in:

> The fair breeze blew, the white foam flew,
> The furrow followed free.
>
> S.T. COLERIDGE: 'The Rime of the Ancient Mariner' (1798)

Many fantastic examples of excessive alliteration are extant (*see also* AMPHIGORY).

Thomas Tusser (1524–80) has a rhyming poem of 12 lines, every word of which begins with t; and in the 1890s a serenade of 28 lines was published 'sung in M flat by Major Marmaduke Muttinhead to Mademoiselle Madeline Mendoza Marriott', which contained only one word not beginning with m, in the line 'Meet me by moonlight, marry me'. The alliterative alphabetic poem beginning:

> An Austrian army, awfully arrayed
> Boldly, by battery, besieged Belgrade;
> Cossack commanders cannonading come,
> Dealing destruction's devastating doom;

was published in *The Trifler* (7 May 1817), ascribed to the Rev. B. Poulter. It was later revised by Alaric A. Watts (1797–1864).

Alliterative tongue-twisters have always been popular with children, as the following:

> Betty Botter bought some butter,
> But, she said, the butter's bitter;
> If I put it in my batter
> It will make my batter bitter,
> But a bit of better butter,
> That would make my batter better.

**Ally. Ally Pally.** A familiar name for Alexandra Palace, north London, first opened in 1863 but burned down and rebuilt in 1873. A popular amusement centre, like the CRYSTAL PALACE, and partly used as a radio and television centre, it was badly damaged by another fire in 1980 but was restored and reopened in 1988.

**Ally Sloper.** A bulbous-nosed, impecunious hero of Victorian comic strips. He first appeared, with his friend Ikey Mo, in the pages of *Judy* magazine in 1867. He was the creation of

Charles Henry Ross, although he became famous only under the hand of William G. Baxter. It was the latter who drew the characters for *Ally Sloper's Half-Holiday*, a penny comic that enjoyed an extraordinary popularity in the 1880s. Ally Sloper's name became a household word, and the market teemed with Ally Sloper umbrellas, walking sticks, pipes, toys, sweets and other domestic paraphernalia.

**Alma** (Italian, 'soul', 'spirit'). In Matthew Prior's poem 'Alma, or The Progress of the Mind' (1718), the name typifies the mind or guiding principles of man. Alma is queen of 'Body Castle', and is beset by a rabble rout of evil desires, foul imaginations and silly conceits for seven years. In Edmund Spenser's *The Faerie Queene* (II, ix (1590)), Alma typifies the soul. She is mistress of the House of Temperance, and there entertains Prince Arthur and Sir Guyon.

**Alma Mater** (Latin, 'bountiful mother'). A name or title for one's school, college, or other 'fostering mother'.

> You might divert yourself, too, with Alma Mater, the Church.
>
> HORACE WALPOLE: *Letters* (1778)

**Almack's** (1) A gambling club opened in Pall Mall, London, in 1762 by William Almack, a Scotsman, with the support of regular young gamesters from WHITE'S. In 1764 the club split into two others which became known as BOODLE'S and BROOKS'S. *See also* CLUB.

(2) A suite of assembly rooms in King Street, St James's, Westminster, opened in 1765 by William Almack, founder of the above-named gambling club. Success came early and weekly subscription balls, presided over by ladies of the highest rank, were held there during the LONDON SEASON for more than 75 years. To be admitted was regarded as being almost as great a distinction as being presented at Court. On Almack's death in 1781 the establishment passed to his niece, Mrs Willis. In 1893 part of the premises was taken over by auctioneers and the rest let as shops. The building was bombed in the Second World War, and in 1949–50 a block of offices known as Almack House was built on the site.

**Almagest.** The English form of the Arabic name, *al-majisti* (from Greek *megistē*, 'greatest'), given to Ptolemy's *Mathematikē Suntaxis*, his classic astronomical treatise in 13 books, of the mid-2nd century. An Arabic translation was made about 820. In the third book the length of the year was first fixed at 365 days. His geocentric astronomy lasted until the introduction of the COPERNICAN SYSTEM.

**Almanac.** A medieval Latin word of obscure origin for a calendar of days and months with astronomical data and the like.

> A calendar, a calendar! look in the almanack; find out moonshine, find out moonshine.
>
> SHAKESPEARE: *A Midsummer Night's Dream*, III, i (1595)

Some early almanacs before the invention of printing were by:

| | |
|---|---|
| Solomon Jarchi in and after | 1150 |
| Peter de Dacia about | 1307 |
| Walter de Elvendene | 1327 |
| John Somers, Oxford | 1380 |
| Nicholas de Lynna | 1386 |
| Georg von Peuerbach | 1457–61 |

Examples after the invention of printing were by:

| | |
|---|---|
| Regiomontanus at Nuremberg | 1474 |
| Andreas Zainer at Ulm | 1478 |
| Richard Pynson (Shepeheard's Kalendar) | 1497 |
| Johann Stöffler at Venice | 1499 |
| Poor Robin's Almanack | 1652 |
| Francis Moore's Almanack | 1698–1713 |
| POOR RICHARD'S ALMANACK (USA) | 1732–57 |
| Almanach de Gotha (successively suppressed by Hitler, Stalin and Adenauer) | 1764–1944 |
| Whitaker's Almanack from 1868 | |

**Clog almanac.** *See under* CLOG.

**Almanzor** (Arabic *al-manṣūr*, 'the victorious'). The title was adopted by several Muslim rulers, notably Abu Amir al-Mansur (938–1002), who was famous for his victories over the Christians in Spain.

One of the characters in John Dryden's *Conquest of Granada* (1672) is an almanzor, and it is also the name of one of the lackeys in Molière's *Les Précieuses Ridicules* (1659).

**Almesbury.** It was in a SANCTUARY at Almesbury (otherwise Amesbury, Wiltshire) that Queen GUINEVERE, according to Malory, took refuge after her adulterous passion for LANCELOT OF THE LAKE was revealed to King ARTHUR. Here also she died, but her body was buried at GLASTONBURY. Tennyson celebrated the incident in his *Idylls of the King*:

> Queen Guinevere had fled the court, and sat
> There in the holy house at Almesbury
> Weeping, none with her save a little maid.
>
> 'Guinevere' (1859)

**Almighty dollar, The.** An expressive term emphasizing the power of money. Washington Irving seems to have first used this expression:

> The almighty dollar, that great object of universal devotion throughout our land.
>
> *Wolfert's Roost*, 'The Creole Village' (1855)

**Almond, Jordan.** *See under* JORDAN.

**Almonry.** The place where the almoner resides. In monasteries, one-tenth of the income was distributed to the poor by the almoner. Almonry is from Late Latin *eleemosynarium*, 'place for alms', but the word became confused with AMBRY.

> The place wherein this chapel or almshouse stands was called the 'Elemosinary' or Almonry, now corrupted into Ambrey, for that the almis of the Abbey are there distributed to the poor.
> JOHN STOW: *Survey of London* (1598)

**Alms** (Old English *ælmysse*, from Late Latin *eleemosyna*, from Greek *eleēmosunē*, 'pity'). Gifts to the poor. It is a singular word which, like 'riches' (from French *richesse*), has by usage become plural. The Bible has '(he) asked an alms' (Acts 3:3), but Dryden writes 'alms are but the vehicles of prayer' (*The Hind and the Panther*, iii, 106 (1687)).

**Almshouse.** A house or group of dwellings built and endowed for the accommodation of the poor and aged. There are essentially two kinds, the first being a house founded by charity, the second a house belonging to a monastery where alms and hospitality were dispensed. Almshouses are often an architectural attraction in a town, although some were rebuilt in the 19th century in a revived Gothic style. A number are named 'Hospital', such as St Mary's Hospital, Chichester, the Fishermen's Hospital, Great Yarmouth, and Browne's Hospital, Stamford. *See also* CALAIS.

**Almsman** or **almswoman.** A person who gives or (more usually) receives alms.

**Plough alms.** *See under* PLOUGH.

**Alnaschar's dream.** An example of counting one's chickens before they are hatched. In the ARABIAN NIGHTS ENTERTAINMENTS Alnaschar, the Talkative Barber's fifth (and deaf) brother, spent all his money on a basket of glassware, on which he was to make a profit that was to be invested to make more, and so on until he grew rich enough to marry the vizier's daughter. Being angry with his imaginary wife he gave a kick, overturned his basket and broke all his wares.

**Aloe** (Greek). A genus of very bitter plants of the family Liliaceae. Hence the line in Juvenal's sixth satire (181), *Plus aloes quam mellis habet* ('He has in him more bitters than sweets'), said of a writer with a sarcastic pen. The aloes of the Bible are not a bitter herb but a fragrant spice used as a perfume and on the linen wrapped round a corpse.

> I have perfumed my bed with myrrh, aloes, and cinnamon.
> Proverbs 7:17

**ALOE.** These initials represent A Lady Of England, the pseudonym of Charlotte Maria Tucker (1821–93), the author of evangelical tales and allegories for children. The suggestion of the bitter plant name appears to be simply coincidental.

> This Aloe is not at all in keeping with her cognomen, for she has produced upwards of fifty pieces, or volumes, since 1854, under the above initials, and we commend them to the reader as of exceeding beauty.
> OLPHAR HAMST: *Handbook of Fictitious Names* (1868)

**Aloha.** A Hawaiian word meaning 'love', used in the United States and elsewhere to express affection or kind wishes as a greeting or farewell. Hawaii is itself the Aloha State, and an 'aloha party' is one held on the occasion of an arrival or departure. The spirit of the word can also be visually, if vulgarly, expressed in an 'aloha shirt', a loose and brightly coloured sports shirt.

**Alonzo of Aguilar.** When Fernando, king of Aragon, was laying siege to Granada in 1501, he asked who would undertake to plant his banner on the heights. Alonzo, 'the lowmost of the dons', undertook the task but was cut down by the MOORS. His body was exposed in the wood of Oxijera, and the Moorish damsels, struck with its beauty, buried it near the brook of Alpuxarra. There are several Spanish ballads on the subject.

**À l'outrance.** To the uttermost, to the death. An incorrect English form of the French *à outrance*.

**Alpha.** 'I am Alpha and Omega, the first and the last' (Revelation 1:11). *Alpha* (A) is the first and *Omega* (Ω) the last letter of the Greek alphabet. *See also* TAU.

**Alphabet.** The word goes back to Greek *alphabētos*, combining *alpha* and *beta*, the first two letters of the Greek alphabet. A sentence that contains all the letters of the alphabet is known as a pangram. A near example is Ezra 7:21, although it misses the letter j. An old popular typing test is the 33-letter pangram 'The quick brown fox jumps over a lazy fox'. It is difficult to compose a pangram of exactly 26 letters, but the following is offered in Tony Augarde's *The Oxford Guide to Word Games* (1984): 'Vext cwm fly zing jabs Kurd qoph'. This can be understood: 'An annoyed fly in a valley vigorously stings a qoph (the 19th letter of the Hebrew alphabet) carried by a Kurd.'

The number of letters in an alphabet varies in different languages. Although the English alphabet is capable of innumerable combinations and permutations, there are no means of differentiating the vowel sounds. For example, a sounds differently in fate, fat, Thames, war, orange, ware, abide, calm, swan. So with e, as in era, the, there, prey, met, England, sew, herb, clerk. The other vowels are equally variable. *See also* LETTER. *See also table on page 30*.

**Cyrillic alphabet.** *See under* CYRILLIC.

**Roman alphabet.** *See under* ROMAN.

**Alpheus and Arethusa.** Greek legend says that the river-god Alpheus fell in love with the nymph Arethusa, who fled from him in fright to Ortygia, an island near Syracuse, where ARTEMIS changed her into a fountain. Alpheus flowed under the sea

| SEMITIC | | | | GREEK | | | | | ETRUSCAN | LATIN | | MODERN ROMAN |
|---|---|---|---|---|---|---|---|---|---|---|---|---|
| Phoenician | Classical and Modern Hebrew | Name | Transliteration | Early | Classical | Name | Transliteration Classical | Transliteration Modern | | Early | Classical | English |
| 𐤀 | א | 'aleph ('ox') | ' | A | A α | alpha | a | a | 𐌀 | A ᐱ | A | A a |
| 𐤁 | ב | bēth ('house') | b, v | B | B β | beta | b | v | 𐌁 | B | B | B b |
| 𐤂 | ג | gimel ('camel') | g | Γ | Γ γ | gamma | g | gh, y | 𐌂 | < | C | C c |
| 𐤃 | ד | dāleth ('door') | d | Δ | Δ δ | delta | d | dh | 𐌃 | D | D | D d |
| 𐤄 | ה | hē ('lattice window') | h | E | E ε | epsilon | e | e | 𐌄 | E | E | E e |
| 𐤅 | ו | waw, vav† ('hook') | w | Ϝ | | | | | 𐌅 | F | F | F f |
| | | | | | | | | | | | G‡ | G g |
| 𐤆 | ז | zayin ('weapon') | z | I | Z ζ | zeta | z | z | 𐌆 | | | |
| 𐤇 | ח | heth | ḥ | ⊟ | H η | eta | ē | i | 𐌇 | H | H | H h |
| 𐤈 | ט | teth | ṭ | ⊗ | Θ θ | theta | th | th | 𐌈 | | | |
| 𐤉 | י | yod, yodh ('arm') | y | ϟ | I ι | iota | i | i | 𐌉 | | I | I i |
| | | | | | | | | | | | J | J j |
| 𐤊 | כ ך* | kāph ('hand') | k | K | K κ | kappa | k | k | 𐌊 | K | K | K k |
| 𐤋 | ל | lāmedh ('ox goad') | l | | Λ λ | lambda | l | l | 𐌋 | L | L | L l |
| 𐤌 | מ ם* | mēm ('water') | m | M | M μ | mu | m | m | 𐌌 | M | M | M m |
| 𐤍 | נ ן* | nūn ('fish') | n | N | N ν | nu | n | n | 𐌍 | N | N | N n |
| 𐤎 | ס | samekh ('support') | s | | Ξ ξ | xi | x | x, ks | | | | |
| 𐤏 | ע | 'ayin ('eye') | ʻ | O | O o | omicron | o | o | 𐌏 | O | O | O o |
| 𐤐 | פ ף* | pē ('mouth') | p | Π | Π π | pi | p | p | 𐌐 | P | P | P p |
| 𐤑 | צ ץ* | ṣadhē | ts, tz | | | | | | | | | |
| 𐤒 | ק | qōph ('eye of needle') | q | | | | | | | Q | Q | Q q |
| 𐤓 | ר | rēsh ('head') | r | P | P ρ | rho | r, rh | r | 𐌓 | R | R | R r |
| 𐤔 | ש | shin, sin ('tooth') | sh, s | Σ | Σ σ, ς | sigma | s | s | 𐌔 | S | S | S s |
| 𐤕 | ת | tāw, tāv ('mark') | t | T | T τ | tau | t | t | 𐌕 | T | T | T t |
| | | | | | | | | | | | | U¶ u |
| | | | | Y | Υ υ | upsilon | y, u | i | 𐌖 | V | V | V¶ v |
| | | | | | | | | | | | | W¶ w |
| | | | | | Φ φ | phi | ph | f | | | | |
| | | | | X | X χ | chi | ch | h, kh | | X | X | X x |
| | | | | | | | | | | | Y | Y¶ y |
| | | | | | | | | | | | Z | Z z |
| | | | | Ψ | Ψ ψ | psi | ps | ps | | | | |
| | | | | Θ | Ω ω | omega | ō | o | | | | |

* Form on left is used when letter occurs at the end of word.
† Split by the Greeks into *digamma* (form survives in modern F) and *upsilon*.
‡ Derived from C. ¶ Derived from Greek *upsilon*.

**Development of the alphabet**

from Peloponnesus to rise in Ortygia and so unite with his beloved. The myth seems to derive from the fact that the Alpheus, in places, flows underground. Alpheus may get his name from Greek *alphos*, 'white', and Arethusa hers from Greek *ardō*, 'I water'.

**Alpine race.** Another name for the broadheaded CELTIC race, because of its distribution in the mountainous regions from Armenia to the Pyrenees. They were a midway race between the Scandinavian Nordics and the dark Mediterranean folk. The La TÈNE period, from about the 5th century to the 1st BC, witnessed the zenith of their culture.

**Alsatia.** The name formerly applied to a 'rogues' republic' in the Whitefriars district of London. It probably alluded to Alsace, the debatable land between France and Germany. The district had a right to grant sanctuary to fugitives even after the dissolution of the monasteries (1536–9), and it became a haunt of thieves, debtors and vagabonds, much in the same way as the sanctuary of Westminster Abbey. The district is described in Thomas Shadwell's *The Squire of Alsatia* (1688), from which Sir Walter Scott borrowed freely when describing this precinct in *The Fortunes of Nigel* (1822), as did Leigh Hunt in *The Town* (1848). *See also* RIGHT OF SANCTUARY.

**Al-Sirat** (Arabic, 'the path'). In Muslim mythology, the bridge leading to Paradise, a bridge over a mid-HELL, no wider than the edge of a sword, across which all who enter heaven must pass.

**Also ran, An.** In horseracing, a runner who fails to come in among the first three. Hence an unsuccessful person, a 'loser'.

**Alsvid** or **Alswider** (Old Norse, 'all-swift'). The horse that draws the chariot of the moon in Norse mythology.

**Altar** (Latin *altus*, 'high'). The block or table used for religious sacrifice. In many Christian churches the term is applied to the Communion Table.

**Gospel side of the altar, The.** *See under* GOSPEL.

**High altar.** *See under* HIGH.

**Lead to the altar, To.** *See under* LEAD.

**Alter ego** (Latin, 'other I', 'other self'). One's double, one's intimate and thoroughly trusted friend; a person who has full power to act for another. *See also* SECOND SELF.

**Alternative.** A word fairly consistently in vogue from the late 1960s to express some cultural or other value that differs from the norm. It had its roots in the 'alternative society', associated with the world of the hippies, which was dubbed 'counterculture' by academics but the 'underground' by the media. 'Alternative medicine' also appeared at this time, favouring such procedures and remedies as homoeopathy and ACUPUNCTURE, and today having its devotees among those who have become disillusioned with traditional medicine.

The 1980s saw the evolution of both 'alternative comedy' and 'alternative therapy'. The former, involving the satirical as well as the surreal, has been popularized on television by such performers as Dawn French and Jennifer Saunders or Vic Reeves and Bob Mortimer. The latter, a progression of alternative medicine, involves special psychiatric (or quasi-psychiatric) techniques, such as rebirthing, group counselling and other practices based on simplified Freudian theories and applications. In the 1990s 'alt.' as an abbreviation for 'alternative' became familiar from Internet addresses containing 'alt.music', 'alt.tv' and the like, the main pornography conduit being 'alt.binaries.pictures.erotica'.

> Where would we be without 'family values', political manifestos based upon 'family values', and the spin doctors who conceive them? Where would we be? In an alternative culture?
>
> STEVEN DALY AND NATHANIEL WICE: *alt. culture* (1995)

**Alternative Services Book.** *See* BOOK OF COMMON PRAYER.

**Althaea** (Greek *althainein*, 'to heal'). In Greek mythology, the daughter of Thestius, king of Aetolia, and mother of MELEAGER, Gorge and DEIANEIRA. At the moment Meleager was born, the FATES told Althaea that he would live just a long as a log of wood, then on the fire, remained unconsumed. Althaea therefore immediately snatched it from the flames. Years later, to avenge her brothers, whom Meleager had slain, she threw the brand into the fire, and her son died as it was consumed (Ovid, *Metamorphoses*, viii (1st century AD)). 'Althaea's brand' thus came to be used of any urgent or fatal contingency.

> As did the fatal brand Althaea burned.
>
> SHAKESPEARE: *Henry VI, Pt II*, I, i (1590)

**Althea** (Greek *althainein*, 'to heal'). The 'divine Althea' of Richard Lovelace (1618–58) was Lucy Sacheverell, also called Lucasta by the poet.

> When love with unconfinèd wings
> Hovers within my gates;
> And my divine Althea brings
> To whisper at my grates:
> When I lie tangled in her hair,
> And fettered to her eye;
> The gods, that wanton in the air
> Know no such liberty.
> 'To Althea, from Prison' (1649)

Lovelace was imprisoned in the Gatehouse, Westminster, by the LONG PARLIAMENT for his royalist activities. Hence the 'grates' (railings) referred to.

**Altis.** The sacred precinct of ZEUS at OLYMPIA,

combining the altar of Zeus, the temples of Zeus and HERA, and the Pelopion (grave of PELOPS). It was connected by an arched passage with the stadium, where the games were held.

**Altmark, The.** In the Royal Navy an opprobrious synonym for a ship or an establishment with a reputation for very strict discipline. It derives from a naval exploit of February 1940, when Captain (later Admiral of the Fleet) Philip Vian, commanding the destroyer HMS *Cossack*, entered Norwegian territorial waters to effect the release of 299 British prisoners of war from the German supply ship *Altmark*, which had taken refuge in Jossingfjord.

**Alto relievo** (Italian, 'high relief'). A term used for sculptures so cut as to project more than one half their thickness from the background. The ELGIN MARBLES are notable examples. *See also* BAS-RELIEF.

**Always behind, like a cow's tail.** A proverbial saying of ancient date.

**Alzire.** A daughter of MONTEZUMA, invented by VOLTAIRE and the central character of his play *Alzire* (1736), which is set in Peru instead of Mexico.

**Amadis. Amadis of Gaul.** The hero of the prose romance *Amadís de Gaula*. The oldest extant edition (1508) is in Spanish by Garcia de Montalvo but is probably an adaptation of a 14th-century Portuguese or Spanish original with his own additions. Many details derive from Arthurian legend, and subsequent writers increased the romance to 14 books by adding other exploits. It long enjoyed popularity and exerted a wide influence on literature.

Amadis, called the Lion Knight, from the device on his shield, and Beltenebros ('darkly beautiful'), was a love child of Perion, king of Gaula (Wales), and Elizena, princess of Brittany. He was cast away at birth and became known as the Child of the Sun. After many adventures he secured the hand of ORIANA. He is represented as a poet and musician, a linguist and a gallant, a knight errant and a king, the very model of CHIVALRY.

Further names by which Amadis was known include the Knight of the Green Sword and the Knight of the Dwarf. *See also* ARTHURIAN ROMANCES; BEAU TÉNÉBREUX.

**Amadis of Greece.** A supplemental part of the romance *Amadis of Gaul*, supposedly added by the Spaniard Feliciano de Silva in 1530.

**Amaimon.** A DEVIL, king of the eastern portion of HELL in medieval demonology. He might be bound or restrained from doing hurt from the third hour till noon, and from the ninth hour till evening. ASMODEUS is his chief officer. *See also* BARBASON; LUCIFER.

> Amaimon sounds well; Lucifer well; Barbason well; yet they are devils' additions, the names of fiends.
>
> SHAKESPEARE: *The Merry Wives of Windsor*, II, ii (1600)

**Amalfitan Code.** The oldest existing collection of maritime law, compiled in the 11th century at Amalfi, then an important Italian trading centre.

**Amalthea** (perhaps Greek *amaltheus*, 'generous'). In Greek mythology a NYMPH, the nurse of ZEUS, or the she-goat that suckled him. In Roman legend she is a SIBYL of Cumae who offered the SIBYLLINE BOOKS to Tarquin II.

**Amalthea's horn.** The cornucopia or HORN OF PLENTY. The infant ZEUS was fed with goat's milk by Amalthea, daughter of Melisseus, king of Crete. In gratitude, Zeus broke off one of the goat's horns and gave it to Amalthea, promising that the possessor should always have in abundance everything desired. *See also* AEGIS.

> When Amalthea's horn
> O'er hill and dale the rose-crowned flora pours,
> And scatters corn and wine, and fruits and flowers.
>
> LUIS DE CAMOËNS: *Lusiads*, ii (1572)

**Amaranth** (Greek *amarantos*, 'unfading'). In Pliny the name of some real or imaginary fadeless flower. Clement of Alexandria (*c*.150–*c*.215 AD) says:

> Amarantus flos, symbolum est immortalitatis.
> (The amaranth flower is the symbol of immortality.)

It is so called because its flowers retain to the last much of their deep blood-red colour. Two of the best known species are LOVE-LIES-BLEEDING (*Amaranthus caudatus*) and tampala or Chinese spinach (*Amaranthus tricolor*). William Wordsworth has a poem called 'Love lies Bleeding' (1842) and Milton refers to 'Immortal amarant' in *Paradise Lost* (iii (1667)). Edmund Spenser has 'sad Amaranthus' (*The Faerie Queene*, III, vi (1590)), one of the flowers 'to which sad lovers were transformed of yore', but there is no known legendary basis for this assertion.

**Amaryllis** (Greek *amarussō*, 'I sparkle', so 'running stream'). A rustic sweetheart, from a shepherdess in the pastorals of THEOCRITUS and VIRGIL.

> To sport with Amaryllis in the shade.
>
> MILTON: *Lycidas* (1638)

In Edmund Spenser's *Colin Clout's Come Home Againe* (1595), Amaryllis represents Alice Spenser, Countess of Derby.

**Amasis, Ring of.** *See under* RING.

**Amaterasu.** The sun-goddess who is the central figure of SHINTOISM and the ancestral deity of the Japanese imperial house. She was born from the left eye of the primordial god Izanagi, and according to mythology is obliged to join her brother, Susano-Wo, in order to survive. The centre of her cult is the Ise Naiku ('inner') shrine, southern Honshu, which is visited by about five million devotees every year. She also takes pride of place in every family shrine. Her full name is Amaterasu Omikami, meaning 'great goddess of the shining sky'.

**Amati.** A first-rate violin, properly one made by Andrea Amati (*c.*1505–80) or his sons Antonio (*c.*1538–95) and Girolamo (1561–1630), or by Girolamo's son Nicolò (1596–1684) at CREMONA in the 16th and 17th centuries. *See also* STRAD.

**Amaurote** (Greek *amauros*, 'dark', 'gloomy', 'unknown'). The chief city of Sir Thomas More's *Utopia* (1516). Rabelais introduces UTOPIA and 'the great city of the Amaurots' into his *Pantagruel* (Bk II, ch xxiii (1532)).

**Amazement, Not afraid with any.** *See under* AFRAID.

**Amazon** (popularly derived from Greek *a-*, 'not', and *mastos*, 'breast'). In Greek mythology a race of female warriors who were said to 'pinch out' or 'cauterize' the right breast so as to facilitate their throwing of the javelin. There were no men in the nation, and any sons born of their union with their neighbours were killed or sent to their fathers. Indeed, Amazons existed in order to be fought, and ultimately killed, by men. The *Iliad* tells how BELLEROPHON killed them in Lycia, and the ninth labour of HERCULES was to fetch the girdle of HIPPOLYTA, the Amazon queen. No real etymology is known for their name. The word is now used of any tall, strong or aggressive woman.

> Never, perhaps, has the alchemy of Greek genius been more potent than in the matter of the Amazonian myth.
>
> GUY CADOGAN ROTHERY: *The Amazons* (1910)

**Amazonia.** An old name for the regions about the River Amazon in South America, which was so called by the early Spanish explorers under Francisco do ORELLANA (*c.*1500–49) who claimed to have seen female warriors on its banks.

**Amazonian chin.** A beardless chin like that of a woman warrior.

> When with his Amazonian chin he drove
> The bristled lips before him.
>
> SHAKESPEARE: *Coriolanus*, II, ii (1607)

**Amber** (Arabic *'anbar*, 'ambergris'). A hard, yellow, translucent fossil resin. It is derived from extinct coniferous trees and often contains trapped insects. Legend says that amber is a concretion of the tears of birds who were the sisters of MELEAGER and who never ceased weeping for the death of their brother (Ovid, *Metamorphoses*, viii (1st century AD)).

**Ambree, Mary.** An English heroine who is said to have fought in the siege of Ghent of 1584 to avenge her lover's death. She is frequently mentioned in old ballads, including that named for her in PERCY'S RELIQUES:

> When captaines couragious, whom death cold not daunte,
> Did march to the siege of the citty of Gaunt,
> They mustred their souldiers by two and by three,
> And the formost in battle was Mary Ambree.

Her name was proverbial for a woman of heroic spirit or a virago.

> My daughter will be valiant
> And prove a very Mary Ambry in the business.
>
> BEN JONSON: *Tale of a Tub*, I, ii (1633)

**Ambrose** (Latin *ambrosia*). The saint (*c.*340–397) who became bishop of Milan in 374. He was noted for the penance he imposed on the Eastern Emperor Theodosius for the massacre of the Thessalonians, and also for his victory over the ARIANS at the synod of Aquileia (381) and for his organization of church music. The Ambrosian Chant was used until the GREGORIAN CHANT became the basis of church music two centuries later. His feast-day is 7 December. His emblems are (1) a beehive, alluding to the legend that a swarm of bees settled on his mouth when he was lying in his cradle (a favourable omen), and (2) a scourge, by which he expelled the Arians from Italy.

**Ambrosia** (Greek *a-*, 'not', and *brotos*, 'mortal'). The food of the gods, so called because it made them immortal. Hence anything delicious to the taste. *See also* NECTAR.

**Ambrosian Library.** A library founded in Milan (1609) by Cardinal Borromeo, archbishop of Milan, and named in honour of St AMBROSE. Its collection of manuscripts includes a 4th-century codex of HOMER, the earliest known.

**Ambrosian Nights.** John Wilson (Christopher North), James Hogg and other literary figures would forgather at Ambrose's Tavern, Edinburgh, of an evening for convivial conversation. Their talk was reproduced by North (with embellishments) as a series of papers on literary and topical subjects in the form of dialogues. These *Noctes Ambrosianae* (1822–35) were published in *Blackwood's Magazine*. *See also* BANNATYNE CLUB.

**Ambrosius Aurelianus.** A shadowy 5th-century figure who, according to GILDAS, was the last of the Roman nation in Britain. Under his leadership the Britons rallied to resist the SAXON invaders.

**Ambry** (Latin *armarium*, 'cupboard', 'chest'). A cupboard, wall press or locker. In a church an ambry is a closed recess for keeping books, vestments, sacramental plates, consecrated oil and the like. There are several variant forms such as aumbry, awmry and almery, the last of which causes confusion with ALMONRY.

**Ambsace** or **amesace** (Old French *ambes as*, 'both

aces'). Two aces, the lowest throw at dice, or figuratively, bad luck.

> I had rather be in this choice than throw amesace for my life.
>
> SHAKESPEARE: *All's Well that Ends Well*, II, iii (1602)

**AMDG.** An abbreviation for Latin *ad majorem Dei gloriam*, 'to the greater glory of God', the Jesuit motto.

**Ameer** or **amir** (Arabic, 'commander'). Ruler of Afghanistan, Sind, and the title of certain other Muslim princes. *See also* EMIR.

**Amelia** (Germanic *amal*, 'work'). A model of conjugal affection in Henry Fielding's last novel, *Amelia* (1751). It is known that the character was intended for his own wife, Charlotte. The fictional Amelia is represented as having suffered an injury to her nose, as had Fielding's wife, and this impaired her popularity among her readers. Thackeray, however, considered her 'the most charming character in English fiction', and Amelia Sedley is 'one of the best and dearest creatures' in his own *Vanity Fair* (1847–8).

**Princess Amelia.** The fifteenth and youngest child of George III. She was sickly from birth (1783) and died young, aged 27. On her deathbed she had a mourning ring made for her father, consisting of a lock of her hair set round with diamonds. Saying 'Remember me', she herself pressed it on his finger, thereby throwing him into such a paroxysm of grief that he passed into the final condition of madness from which he was never restored.

**Amen Corner.** A site at the west end of PATERNOSTER ROW, London, where the monks finished the PATERNOSTER on CORPUS CHRISTI Day as they went in procession to St Paul's Cathedral. They began in Paternoster Row with the Lord's Prayer in Latin, which was continued to the end of the street, then they said Amen at the corner of the Row. On turning down Ave Maria Lane, they began chanting the Hail Mary, then, crossing LUDGATE, they entered Creed Lane chanting the CREDO. Paternoster Row, Amen Corner and much of Ave Maria Lane were destroyed in an air raid on 28 December 1940.

**Amende honorable** (French, 'honorable compensation'). An anglicized French phrase for a full and public apology. In medieval France the term was applied to the degrading punishment inflicted on traitors, parricides and the sacrilegious, who were brought into court with a rope around their necks, stripped to their undershirt and made to beg pardon of God, the king and the court.

**Amenhotep.** The name of four pharaohs. The best known is Amenhotep IV (*fl.*14th century BC), who married NEFERTITI and who encouraged the worship of ATEN. In doing so, he changed his name from Amenhotep ('Ammon is satisfied') to AKHENATEN and founded a new city called Akhetaten ('place of Aten's power').

**Amen-Ra** or **Amon-Ra.** The sun-god and principal of the gods during the ancient Egyptian Empire, a development from Amon ('the hidden one'), patron of Thebes. He was usually represented as human-headed, with two long ostrich plumes rising above his head, but sometimes appears with a ram's head. The ram was sacred to him and his oracle was at the oasis of JUPITER AMMON. The Greeks identified him with ZEUS.

**America.** The name of the continent is usually derived from that of the Italian navigator Amerigo Vespucci (1451–1512), who sailed to the New World in 1499 with the Spanish cavalier Alonso de Ojeda. Vespucci parted company with Ojeda before land was sighted, heading his ship south to discover and explore the mouth of the Amazon. He then cruised the northern shore of South America before returning to Spain in 1500. In 1507 the German geographer Martin Waldseemüller published his *Cosmographiae Introductio*, containing a map of the world in 12 sheets, and applied Vespucci's name to South America and the West Indies. From there it subsequently spread to the whole continent.

A rival source for the name has been advanced in the person of Richard Ameryk, sheriff of Bristol, who financed John Cabot's voyage to America in 1497, five years after Columbus. Cabot is said to have applied his patron's name to the new land, either in gratitude or as part of a financial negotiation. This explanation is decried by many but has its academic advocates and is the preferred etymology in *The Chambers Dictionary* (1998). *See also* UNITED STATES OF AMERICA.

> Strange that broad America was to wear the name of a thief! Amerigo Vespucci, the pickle-dealer at Seville, who went out in 1499, a subaltern with Hojeda, and whose highest rank was boatswain's mate, in an expedition that never sailed, managed in this lying world to supplant Columbus, and baptize half the earth with his name!
>
> RALPH WALDO EMERSON: *English Traits* (1856)

**American dream, The.** The concept that the American social, economic and political system makes success possible for every American.

> It has been a dream of being able to grow to fullest development as man and woman, unhampered by the barriers which had slowly been erected in older civilizations, unrepressed by social orders which had developed for the benefit of classes rather than for the simple human being of any and every class.
>
> J.T. ADAMS: *The Epic of America*, Epilogue (1938)

**American Fabius.** *See under* FABIUS.

**American Indians.** When Columbus left Spain in 1492 he set out to reach India and China by sailing west. When he reached the Bahamas the natives were called Indians in the belief that he had reached the fringes of the East. Hence the later name West Indies. *See also* AMERINDIAN.

**American Standard Version.** *See under* BIBLE.

**American workhouse, The.** A name given by taxi drivers to the Park Lane Hotel, London, because of its popularity with affluent Americans, and hence in general a hotel offering luxurious accommodation.

**Avenue of the Americas.** *See under* AVENUE.

**Daughters of the American Revolution.** *See under* DAUGHTER.

**Latin America.** *See under* LATIN.

**United States of America.** *See under* UNITED.

**When good Americans die they go to Paris.** *See under* WHEN.

**Amerindian.** A PORTMANTEAU WORD combining American and Indian applied to indigenous peoples of the NEW WORLD as distinct from those of India and the East Indies.

**Amesace.** *See* AMBSACE.

**Amethyst** (Greek *a-* 'not', and *methuein*, 'to intoxicate'). A violet-blue variety of quartz supposed by the ancients to prevent intoxication. Cups and goblets of amethyst were a charm against inebriety, and the stone was especially cherished by Roman matrons from the belief that it would preserve inviolate the affection of their husbands. *See also* PRECIOUS STONES.

**Amicable numbers.** Any two numbers either of which is the sum of the divisors of the other, e.g. 220 and 284. The divisors of 220 are 1, 2, 4, 5, 10, 11, 20, 22, 44, 55, 110, the sum of which is 284, while the divisors of 284 are 1, 2, 4, 71, 142, the sum of which is 220. *See also* NUMBERS.

**Amiel** (perhaps Hebrew *'ammī el*, 'my people is God'). In Dryden's *Absalom and Achitophel* (1681) this name is meant for Sir Edward Seymour, Speaker of the House of Commons. It is popularly explained as an anagram of Eliam ('God is kinsman'). Eliam, in 2 Samuel 23:34, is the son of AHITHOPHEL the Gilonite, and one of DAVID's heroes. In 2 Samuel 11:3 the name appears as that of BATHSHEBA's father, which in 1 Chronicles 3:5 is given as Ammiel.

**Am I my brother's keeper?** CAIN's rhetorical question to God when, following Cain's murder of ABEL, the Lord asked him where his brother was (Genesis 4:9). The response has a modern ring and is typical of a person who resents any responsibility for the safety or welfare of another.

**Amis et Amiles.** *See* AMYS AND AMYLION.

**Amish, The.** A strictly conservative religious sect, the followers of Jakob Amen (*c.*1645–*c.*1730), a Swiss MENNONITE preacher. They separated from the Mennonites in the late 17th century. They first appeared in Pennsylvania *c.*1714 and settlements in other parts of America followed. They reject the 'evil' world outside and are conspicuous for their customs, industry and frugality. They effectively live in a time-warp, without cars, telephone, electricity, radio or television. They still use the German language, wear old-fashioned dress and beards without moustaches, use hooks and eyes instead of buttons, till the land with mule-drawn ploughs and for transport rely on horse-buggies. The name of their sect is usually pronounced to rhyme with 'famish'.

**Ammon** or **Hammon.** The Greek form of the name of the Libyan and Egyptian god Amun or Amon. *See also* AMEN-RA.

**Jupiter Ammon.** *See under* JUPITER.

**Son of Ammon.** *See under* SON.

**Ammonites.** Fossil molluscs allied to the nautilus and cuttlefish. They are so called because they resemble the horn on the ancient statues of JUPITER AMMON.

The name also applies to the children of Ammon, the descendants of Ben-ammi, the son of Lot by his younger daughter (Genesis 19:38). They were a constant enemy of the Israelites.

**Amon-Ra.** *See* AMEN-RA.

**Amoret** (Old French *amorete*, diminutive of *amour*, 'love'). A character in Spenser's *The Faerie Queene* (III (1590)), the twin sister of BELPHOEBE. She is a personification of female loveliness: young, handsome, merry, witty and good. She is as soft as a rose, as sweet as a violet, as chaste as a lily and as gentle as a dove; she loves everybody and is loved by all.

An amoret is also a general word for a love song, love knot, love look, love affair or any personification of love.

> He will be in his amorets, and his canzonets, his pastorals and his madrigals.
>
> THOMAS HEYWOOD: *Loves Maistresse* (1633)

**Amorous, The.** Philip I of France (1060–1108). He deserted his wife Bertha and carried off Bertrada, the wife of Fulk of Anjou.

**Amos.** The third of the Minor Prophets. He was a herdsman who prophesied the downfall of Israel as a consequence of its greed and oppression of the poor.

**Amos and Andy.** A pair of BLACKFACE clowns, Amos Jones and Andy Brown, who appeared in a popular American radio series, *Amos 'n' Andy*, from the 1920s to the 1940s. The white comedians who played the two were Freeman S. Gosden and Charles V. Correll respectively. The characters appeared for a few years on television in the early 1950s, but by then their material was regarded as offensive, even though the pair were actually played by black actors.

**Amour-propre** (French, 'self love'). One's self-respect or awareness of what is right and proper for oneself. To wound a person's amour-propre is to gall their good opinion of themselves.

**Ampersand.** The character '&' for 'and'. In the old HORNBOOKS, after giving the 26 letters, the character & was added (... x, y, z, &), and was called 'Ampersand', a corruption of 'and per se and', i.e. the symbol & by itself represents 'and'. The symbol is an adaptation of *et* (Latin 'and'), as can be better seen in the italic ampersand (*&*), where the e and the cross of the t are clearly recognizable. *See also* TIRONIAN.

**Amphialus.** In Philip Sidney's *Arcadia* (1580–90), the valiant and virtuous son of the wicked Cecropia, who always had the misfortune to injure those he loves. He ultimately married Queen Helen of Corinth.

**Amphictyonic Council** (Greek *amphiktiones*, 'dwellers round about'). In Greek history the council of the Amphictyonic League, which consisted of the deputies of the 12 member tribes, who met twice a year at either DELPHI or THERMOPYLAE. At Delphi the council administered the sanctuary of the Pythian APOLLO and also conducted the PYTHIAN GAMES. It was named after its supposed founder, Amphictyon, son of DEUCALION.

**Amphigory** (of uncertain origin, but derived by some from Greek *amphi*, 'about', and *guros*, 'circle', or *-agoria*, 'speech', as in *allegory*). Verses that, while sounding well, contain no meaning. A good example is A.C. Swinburne's 'Nephelidia' (1880), a well-known alliterative parody of his own style, which begins:

> From the depth of the dreamy decline of the dawn
> through a notable nimbus of nebulous moonshine,
> Pallid and pink as the palm of the flag-flower that
> flickers with fear of the flies as they float,
> Are they looks of our lovers that lustrously lean
> from a marvel of mystic miraculous moonshine?

**Amphion.** The son of ZEUS and Antiope who, according to Greek legend, built Thebes by the music of his lute, which was so melodious that the stones danced into walls and houses of their own accord.

**Amphisbaena** (Greek *amphis*, 'both ways', and *bainein*, 'to go'). A fabulous venomous serpent with a head at each end and able to move forwards or backwards. A genus of South American lizards is also so named, for their head is so much like their tail that it is difficult to distinguish one from the other.

**Amphitrite** (Greek *amphi*, 'about', and *Tritōn*, 'Triton'). In classical mythology the goddess of the sea, wife of POSEIDON, daughter of NEREUS and Doris. Her name can be understood as 'she who surrounds the world', since she is like the ocean, where TRITON reigns.

**Amphitryon** (Greek *amphi*, 'around', and *truos*, 'distress', 'labour'). In Greek mythology, the son of Alcaeus and the husband of ALCMENA.

> Le véritable Amphitryon
> Est l'Amphitryon où l'on dîne.
> MOLIÈRE: *Amphitryon* (1668)

That is, the person who provides the feast (whether master or mistress of the house or not) is the real host. The tale is that ZEUS assumed the likeness of Amphitryon in order to visit Alcmena and gave a banquet to this end. However, Amphitryon came home and claimed the honour of being master of the house. As far as the servants and guests were concerned, 'he who gave the feast was to them the host'.

**Amram** (Hebrew *'amram*, 'parent of the exalted'). The father of MOSES and AARON (Exodus 6:18–20). Milton's reference in *Paradise Lost*, i, 338–40 (1667) is to the time when Moses 'stretched forth his rod over the land of Egypt' (Exodus 10:13):

> As when the potent rod
> Of Amram's son, in Egypt's evil day,
> Waved round the coast.

**Amrita** (Sanskrit *amṛta*, 'immortal'). In Hindu mythology, the elixir of immortality, corresponding to the AMBROSIA of classical mythology.

**Amulet** (Latin *amuletum*). A trinket or piece of jewellery worn, usually round the neck, as a preventive charm. The word was formerly connected with the Arabic *himalah*, the name given to the cord that secured the KORAN to the person.

The early Christians wore amulets called ICHTHYS. *See also* TALISMAN.

**Amun** or **Amon.** *See* AMEN-RA.

**Amyclaean silence.** Amyclae in the south of Sparta was so often alarmed by false rumours of the approach of the SPARTANS that a decree was issued forbidding mention of the subject. When the Spartans actually came, no one dared give warning and the town was taken. Hence the proverb 'to be more silent than Amyclae'. CASTOR AND POLLUX were born in Amyclae and are hence sometimes called the Amyclaean brothers. The town itself was said to be ruled by the mythical Tyndareus.

**Amys and Amylion** or **Amis et Amiles.** A late 12th-century French romance telling the story of the friendship of two knights in the reign of CHARLEMAGNE. At the end of the story Amylion slays his children to cure his friend of leprosy.

**Anabaptists** (Greek *anabaptizein*, 'to baptize again'). At the time of the REFORMATION this was the name given to various sects that did not believe in infant baptism and that were noted for their extremist views, especially those groups based at Zwickau and Münster in Germany. On coming to years of discretion, members of the sects were rebaptized. In 17th-century England Baptists and others who rejected Anglican doctrine and 'holy orders' were often abusively called Anabaptists.

**Anacharsis** (perhaps Greek *an-*, 'not', and *akharis*, 'without grace', 'unpleasant'). A Scythian philosopher (*c*.600 BC) and admirer of Greek civilization. He studied at Athens and became acquainted with SOLON.

In 1787 the Abbé Barthélemy published *Le Voyage du Jeune Anacharsis en Grèce*, an account of Greek customs and antiquities, on the composition of which he spent 30 years. It became a popular work, and was the imaginary narrative of a descendant of the Scythian philosopher.

**Anacharsis Cloots.** *See under* CLOOTS.

**Anachronism** (Greek *anakhronizein*, 'to err in a time reference'). Something wrongly dated and so in the wrong chronological relationship with other things and events. Anachronisms are most commonly found in imaginative works in an historical setting. Thus in Shakespeare's *Henry IV, Pt I* (II, i (1597)) the carrier complains 'The turkeys in my pannier are quite starved', but turkeys were introduced from America, which was not discovered until nearly a century after Henry IV's time. In *Julius Caesar* (II, i (1599)) the clock strikes and Cassius says 'The clock has stricken three', yet striking clocks were not invented until 1400, years after the days of Caesar. Medieval romances abound with anachronisms. In more recent times, G.B. Shaw perpetrated an anachronism in his play *Androcles and the Lion* (1912) by referring to the emperor as DEFENDER OF THE FAITH.

**Anacoluthon** (Greek, 'lacking sequence'). A sentence that lacks grammatical sequence, most commonly seen when it begins one way and continues or ends in another. The break is often indicated by a dash, as: You know what I – but let's leave it there.' Shakespeare has several examples, as the following, when King LEAR fulminates against REGAN and GONERIL:

> I will have such revenges on you both
> That all the world shall – I will do such things, –
> What they are yet I know not.
> *King Lear*, II, iv (1605)

**Anacreon** (Greek *ana*, 'again', and *Kreōn*, 'Creon'). A Greek lyric poet (*c*.572–*c*.488 BC) who wrote chiefly in praise of love (heterosexual and homosexual) and wine. Hence Anacreontics as a name for this kind of verse or the metrical form in which it was written.

The *Anacreontea* or *Anacreontics* proper are a collection of 62 short Greek poems in metres derived from Anacreon. Their main subjects, as his, are wine and love. They were first published in 1554 and acclaimed as Anacreon's work but by the early 19th century it was clear to scholars that the poems all date from long after his time. There are not many examples of anacreontic verse in English literature, but in 1800 Thomas Moore published a version of Anacreon's poems called *Odes of Anacreon*. Ode 50 (of 79) begins:

> When I drink, I feel, I feel,
> Visions of poetic zeal!
> Warm with the goblet's freshening dews,
> My heart invokes the heavenly Muse.

**Anacreon Moore.** *See under* MOORE.

**Anacreon of Painters, The.** Francesco Albano (1578–1660), a painter of beautiful women.

**Anacreon of the Guillotine, The.** Bertrand Barère de Vieuzac (1755–1841), one of the Committee of Public Safety, so called from the flowery language and convivial jests directed towards his wretched victims.

**Anacreon of the Temple, The.** Abbé Guillaume Amfrye de Chaulieu (1639–1720), poet and wit and member of the LIBERTINE circle of the TEMPLE, which influenced VOLTAIRE.

**Anacreon of the Twelfth Century, The.** Walter Map or Mapes, ecclesiastic (1140–1210), the 'jovial archdeacon', was unsuitably so called. He is perhaps best known for the verse that became the well-known drinking-song *Meum est propositum in taberna mori* ('It is my intention to die in an inn').

**French Anacreon, The.** Pontus de Thiard or Tyard (1521–1605), one of the FRENCH PLÉIADE poets.

**German Anacreon, The.** Paul Fleming (1609–40), a German writer of lyric and religious verse.

**Persian Anacreon, The.** Hafiz of Shiraz (*c*.1320–89), whose *Divan* of over 500 poems revealed him to be the greatest Persian lyric poet.

**Scotch Anacreon, The.** Alexander Scott, poet (*c*.1520–85).

**Sicilian Anacreon, The.** Giovanni Meli (1740–1825).

**Anadiplosis** (Greek, 'doubling'). The use of repetition to gain a special effect. The following is an example:

> I seek
> This unfrequented place to find some ease,
> Ease to the body some, none to the mind
> From restless thoughts.
> JOHN MILTON: *Samson Agonistes* (1671)

**Anagram** (New Latin *anagramma*, a shortened form of Greek *anagrammatismos*, from *ana-*, 'back', and *gramma*, 'letter'). A word or phrase formed by transposing the letters of another word or phrase. Some well-known examples are:

> Western Union = no wire unsent
> circumstantial evidence = can ruin a selected victim
> funeral = real fun
> the Morse Code = here come dots

Victoria, England's Queen = governs a nice quiet land
schoolmaster = the classroom
teacher = cheater
mother-in-law = Hitler-woman

The formation of apt anagrams from a famous person's name has long been a pastime of the ingenious. Lewis Carroll composed two on the name of William Ewart Gladstone: *A wild man will go at trees* and *Wild agitator! Means well*. A century on, another prime minister, Tony Blair, inspired more subtle compilations, such as *Brainy lot*, alluding to the new cabinet, and *Not by rail*, a comment on travel by train under Labour's administration.

The following form interchangeable pairs of words:

Alcuinus and Calvinus
Amor and Roma
Eros and Rose
Evil and Live
God and Dog

Some anagrams form whole sets of words, as this chain of ten:

Carest, Carets, Cartes, Caster, Caters, Crates, Cresta, Reacts, Recast, Traces

*See also* HONORIFICABILITUDINITATIBUS.

**Ananias.** In the New Testament (Acts 5) a Christian convert who, with his wife Sapphira, sold his possessions but gave only part of the proceeds to the APOSTLES. Upon being rebuked by PETER, he fell down dead. Ignorant of his deception, Sapphira came home three hours later, practising the same deception and, on discovery, also fell down lifeless.

**Anaphora** (Greek, 'carrying back'). A rhetorical device involving the repetition of a word or group of words in successive clauses. It is commonly found in ballad and song, as well as in oratory. The following is a fine example:

> Said Sir Ector ... Sir Launcelot ... thou wert never matched of earthly knight's hand; and thou wert the courteoust knight that ever bare shield; and thou wert the truest friend to thy lover that ever bestrad horse; and thou wert the truest lover of a sinful man that ever loved woman; and thou wert the kindest man that ever struck with sword; and thou wert the goodliest person that ever came among press of knights; and thou wert the meekest man and the gentlest that ever ate in hall among ladies; and thou wert the sternest knight to thy mortal foe that ever put spear in the rest.
>
> THOMAS MALORY: *Le Morte d'Arthur* (1485)

**Anastasia** (Greek *anastasis*, 'rising up', 'resurrection'). A Roman saint and matron said to have been beheaded with St Basilissa for having buried the bodies of St PETER and St PAUL. Her feast-day is 25 December. Anastasia was also widely known as the youngest daughter of the Russian tsar Nicholas II. In 1918, aged 17, she was executed by the Bolsheviks together with other members of the royal Romanov family, but many believed she had survived. Some even claimed to be her, such as 'Anna Anderson' from the Black Forest, who in 1968 went to the USA and married a former history lecturer, Dr John Manahan. In 1994, however, a Russian government report confirmed that Anastasia had indeed shared her family's fate.

**Anaesthetic, General.** *See under* GENERAL.

**Anathema** (Greek, 'dedicated', i.e. to evil). A denunciation or curse. The original Greek word, *anathema*, was subsequently taken as *anathēma*, 'offering', literally 'thing set up', i.e. to the gods. Thus Gordius (*see* GORDIAN KNOT) hung up his yoke and beam, the shipwrecked hung up their wet clothes, retired workmen hung up their tools, cripples their crutches and so on. Later an anathema was a thing devoted to evil, since animals offered up were destined for death, upon which they were also hung up in the butcher's yard.

In the Catholic and Calvinistic Churches the word came to denote a more extreme form of denunciation than EXCOMMUNICATION.

**Anatomy.** In some former uses, a mere skeleton, a very thin person, like one whose flesh has been anatomized or cut off.

> They brought one Pinch; a hungry lean-faced villain,
> A mere anatomy, a mountebank.
>
> SHAKESPEARE: *The Comedy of Errors*, V, i (1592)

Shakespeare also uses 'atomy' as a synonym. Thus Quickly calls the Beadle 'Thou atomy, thou!' in *Henry IV, Pt II* (V, iv (1597)).

**Ancaeus.** The helmsman of the ship ARGO, after the death of TIPHYS. He was told by a hard-pressed slave that he would never live to taste the wine of his vineyards, and when wine, made from his own grapes, was set before him, he sent for the slave to laugh at such absurd prognostications. The slave, however, answered: THERE'S MANY A SLIP 'TWIXT CUP AND LIP (*see under* SLIP). At this very instant a messenger informed Ancaeus that the CALYDONIAN BOAR was devastating his vineyard, whereupon he set down his cup, went out to see off the boar and was slain in the encounter.

**Anchises** (perhaps from Greek *ankhi*, 'near', 'close by'). In Greek mythology, the ruler of DARDANUS. APHRODITE fell for his fine features and bore him AENEAS, the Trojan hero. According to one legend Anchises was blinded or killed by lightning for identifying his son's mother.

**Anchor.** In Christian symbolism the anchor is the sign of hope, in allusion to Hebrews 6:19: 'Which hope we have as an anchor of the soul.' It also symbolizes security. In art it is an attribute of St CLEMENT, Pope Clement I, who was said to have been martyred by being tied to an anchor and cast into the sea (1st century), and also of St Nicholas of Bari, the patron saint of sailors. The emblem of an anchor entwined by a dolphin was used by the Venetian printer Aldus Manutius. *See also* ALDINE EDITIONS.

**Anchor light.** A white light visible all round the horizon, shown from the forepart of an anchored vessel. Vessels over 150ft (45.7m) in length must carry two, one forward, the other aft.

**Anchorman** or **anchorwoman.** A person who coordinates activities, especially in a radio or television broadcast. The term is also used in sport for a person at the back of a tug-of-war team or the last runner in a relay race.

**Anchor watch.** A watch kept when a vessel is anchored as a precaution lest the anchor be dragged.

**Cast anchor, To.** *See under* CAST.

**Foul anchor.** *See under* FOUL.

**Swallow the anchor, To.** *See under* SWALLOW.

**Weigh anchor, To.** *See under* WEIGH.

**Ancien. Ancien Régime** (French, 'old regime'). The old way of doing things. The phrase was used during the French Revolution for the political and social system, with all its evils and shortcomings, that previously existed under the BOURBON monarchy.

**Anciens crapauds prendront Sara, Les** (French, 'The old toads will take Sara'). One of the cryptic prophecies of NOSTRADAMUS (1503–66). 'Sara' is 'Aras' reversed, and when in 1640 the French under Louis XIII took Arras from the Spanish, this verse was remembered.

**Ancient.** In the now obsolete sense of a flag or standard, or a standard-bearer, the word is a corruption of 'ensign'. Pistol was FALSTAFF's ancient and Iago was Othello's.

> 'Tis one Iago, ancient to the general.
> SHAKESPEARE: *Othello*, II, i (1604)

> My whole charge consists of Ancients, corporals, lieutenants, gentlemen of companies.
> SHAKESPEARE: *Henry IV, Pt I*, IV, ii (1597)

**Ancient lights.** These words, found formerly on notice boards in England, mean that for at least 20 years uninterruptedly a certain building has enjoyed light, and no structure may be erected that will substantially deprive it of such light.

**Ancient Mariner.** Having shot an ALBATROSS, the Ancient Mariner and his companions were subjected to fearful penalties. On repentance he was forgiven, and on reaching land told his story to a hermit. At times, however, distress of mind drove him from land to land, and wherever he stayed he told his tale of woe, to warn against cruelty and to persuade men to love God's creatures. This story in S.T. Coleridge's 'The Rime of the Ancient Mariner' (1798) is partly based on a dream told by his friend George Cruikshank, and partly gathered from his reading. William Wordsworth told him the story of the privateer George Shelvocke, who shot an albatross while rounding Cape Horn in 1720, and was dogged by bad weather. Other suggested sources are Thomas James' *Strange and Dangerous Voyage* (1683) and the *Letter of St Paulinus to Macarius, In Which He Relates Astounding Wonders Concerning the Shipwreck of an Old Man* (1618). A full examination of the possible sources is to be found in *The Road to Xanadu* (1927) by J.L. Lowes.

**Ancient monument.** A building or site of special architectural, historical or archaeological interest that is protected by Act of Parliament from damage or destruction. In England such monuments are cared for by English Heritage, in Scotland by Historic Scotland, and in Wales by Cadw. There are around 18,000 scheduled sites in England alone, plus a further 370,000 or so listed buildings. It is forbidden by law to demolish, extend or alter the character of the latter without prior consent from the local planning authority, although in some cases permission may be given retrospectively.

**Ancient of Days.** A scriptural name given to God (Daniel 7:9), familiar from the first verse of Robert Grant's hymn (1833), a paraphrase of Psalm 104:

> O worship the King, all-glorious above;
> O gratefully sing his power and his love:
> Our Shield and Defender, the Ancient of Days,
> Pavilioned in splendour, and girded with praise.

The grandiloquent name is in fact simply a rendering of a Hebrew phrase meaning 'old man'.

**Royal and Ancient.** *See under* ROYAL.

**Ancile** (Latin). The PALLADIUM of Rome, the sacred shield of the ancient Romans, said to have fallen from heaven in the reign of Numa. To prevent its being stolen, as the safety of the state depended on it, Numa had 11 others made, exactly similar, and entrusted them to 12 priests called SALII.

**Ancren Riwle** or **Ancrene Wisse** (old English, 'rule of anchoresses'). An early 13th-century book of devotional and practical advice written for the guidance of women who were trying to live the strict religious lives of anchoresses. Among the counsels given them is to work hard, to avoid gossiping and to limit their pets to 'but one cat'. The author may have been an Augustinian priest.

**And. And how.** That's for certain. The American expression probably came into English from German *und wie*, although it is also found in other languages, such as French *et comment* and Italian *e come*.

**And I don't mean maybe.** I am not fooling; I mean it.

Yes sir, That's my Baby;
No sir, Don't mean maybe;
Yes sir, that's my Baby now.
GUS KAHN: 'Yes Sir, That's My Baby' (song) 1925

**And so to bed.** That's all; the day's work is over. The phrase frequently occurs as the final words of the daily entries in Samuel Pepys' *Diary* (1660–69).

**And thereby hangs a tale.** There is an interesting or intriguing story behind that. The words are from Shakespeare:

And so, from hour to hour we ripe and ripe,
And then from hour to hour we rot and rot,
And thereby hangs a tale.
*As You Like It*, II, vii (1599)

**Andaman marble.** An exceptionally hard timber grown in the Andaman Islands, of the same family as ebony.

**Anderson. Anderson shelter.** The small prefabricated air-raid shelter became a familiar sight in many gardens during the Second World War. It took the form of a curved steel hut that was partly buried in the ground and covered with 2–3ft (60–90cm) of earth to protect the occupants against explosions. The shelters were the invention of a Scottish engineer, William Paterson, and took their name from Sir John Anderson, Home Secretary in the opening years of the war (1939–40). *See also* MORRISON SHELTER.

**John Anderson, my Jo.** *See under* JOHN.

**Andiron.** A firedog, that is, one of a pair of short, horizontal iron bars, with legs or a supporting stand, for holding the ends of logs in an open fireplace. The word is from the Old French *andier*, of unknown origin, and has nothing to do with iron.

**Andrea Ferrara.** A sword, also called an Andrew and a Ferrara, after the famous 16th-century sword maker of this name.

Here's old tough Andrew.
JOHN FLETCHER: *The Chances* (1618)

**Andrew** (Greek *anēr*, *andros*, 'man'). A name used in old plays for a valet or manservant. *See also* ABIGAIL; MERRY ANDREW.

**Andrew, The.** This old nickname for the Royal Navy derives from the time of the French Revolutionary and Napoleonic Wars when one Andrew Miller acquired such a reputation in Portsmouth as a PRESS-GANG operator that it came to be said that his victims had been snatched into 'the Andrew'. In the 19th century 'Andrew Miller' was also used to mean 'warship' or 'government authority'.

**St Andrew.** The saint who was a fisherman and brother of St PETER, depicted in Christian art as an old man with long, white hair and beard, holding the Gospel in his right hand, and leaning on a St Andrew's cross. His day is 30 November. It is said that he was crucified in Patrae (*c.* AD 70) on a *crux decussata*. He is also the patron saint of Russia and Scotland. *See also* CONSTANTINE'S CROSS; CROSS AS A MYSTIC EMBLEM; RULE.

**Androcles and the lion.** Androcles was a runaway slave who took refuge in a cavern. A lion entered and, instead of tearing him to pieces, lifted up its forepaw in a plea for Androcles to extract a thorn from it. The slave, when subsequently captured, was doomed to fight with a lion in the Roman arena. By chance the same lion was led out against him and, recognizing his benefactor, showed him every demonstration of love and gratitude.

The tale is told by Aulus Gellius (*c.* AD 130–180), and similar stories are found in the fables of AESOP (6th century BC) and the GESTA ROMANORUM (13th century AD). G.B. Shaw's play *Androcles and the Lion* (1912) is based on the story.

**Android** (Greek *andro-*, 'man', and *-eidēs*, '-like'). A former name for an automaton figure resembling a human. In more recent times the word has come to be used of a robot in science fiction.

PHILIP K. DICK: *Do Androids Dream of Electric Sheep?* (book title) (1968)

**Andromache** (Greek *andromakhos*, 'fighting against men', from *anēr*, *andros*, 'man', and *makhē*, 'battle', 'combat'). In Greek legend the wife of HECTOR, on whose death she was given to Pyrrhus (Neoptolemus). The latter was killed by ORESTES and she became the wife of Helenus, Hector's brother. Her name is the title of a play (5th century BC) by Euripides.

**Andromeda** (Greek *anēr*, *andros*, 'man', and *medō*, 'I rule'). The daughter of CEPHEUS and CASSIOPEIA. Her mother boasted that her beauty surpassed that of the NEREIDS, so the latter induced NEPTUNE to send a sea monster to destroy the land, which could be placated only by the sacrifice of Andromeda. She was thus chained to a rock but was rescued by PERSEUS, who married her and turned PHINEUS, another suitor, to stone. After death she was placed as a constellation among the stars.

**Andy.** *See* AMOS AND ANDY.

**Andy Capp.** *See under* CAPP.

**Andy Pandy.** A popular puppet, in a blue and white striped suit and matching floppy hat, which first appeared in the 1950s on the children's television programme *Watch with Mother*. He was alone at first, but was later joined by a teddy bear and a rag doll called Looby Loo, with whom he shared a basket. Only 26 programmes were made, but they were repeated right up to the 1970s.

**Angel.** (1) In post-canonical and apocalyptic literature angels are grouped in different orders. The commonly used hierarchy of nine orders is that popularized by the Pseudo-Areopagite or Pseudo-Dionysius (early 5th century) in his *De Hierarchia Celesti*, which arranges them in three triads: SERAPHIM, cherubim (*see* CHERUBS) and THRONES in the first circle; DOMINIONS, Virtues and Powers in the second circle; PRINCIPALITIES, ARCHANGELS and Angels in the third circle. The names are taken from the OLD TESTAMENT and Colossians 1:16.

The seven holy angels, or archangels, are MICHAEL, GABRIEL, RAPHAEL, URIEL, Chamuel, Jophiel and ZADKIEL. Michael and Gabriel are mentioned in the Bible, Raphael in the APOCRYPHA, and all appear in the non-canonical first Book of Enoch (8:2). *See also* PSEUDEPIGRAPHA.

In *Paradise Lost* (i, 392 (1667)) Milton gives a list of the fallen angels, beginning with MOLOCH.

Muslims say that angels were created from pure bright gems, the genii from fire and man from clay.

(2) An English gold coin copied from the French *ange* and minted from 1465 to the reign of Charles I. It was to replace the NOBLE and was at first called 'angel noble'. Valued at 6s 8d and later at 10s, it bore the figure of the archangel Michael slaying the dragon, and was the coin presented to persons touched for the KING'S EVIL.

(3) In modern theatrical parlance an angel is the financial backer of a play. In more general terms the word is used for a helpful or beautiful person. Romeo, looking up at Juliet at her window, says:

> O! speak again, bright angel; for thou art
> As glorious to this night, being o'er my head,
> As is a winged messenger of heaven.
> SHAKESPEARE: *Romeo and Juliet*, II, ii (1594)

(4) In RAF slang, a height of 1000ft (300m). The word usually occurs in the plural, as in the title of the film *Angels One Five* (1952) about the BATTLE OF BRITAIN.

(5) A popular name for a public house. *See also* PUBLIC HOUSE SIGNS.

**Angel cake.** A very light sponge cake made without egg yolks.

**Angel dust.** A nickname for the hallucinogenic drug phencyclidine hydrochloride.

**Angelic Doctor.** St THOMAS AQUINAS (*c*.1225–74) was so called because of the purity and excellence of his teaching. His exposition of the most recondite problems of theology and philosophy was judged to be the fruit of almost superhuman intelligence, and in 1879 Pope Leo XIII directed that his teachings should be the basis of theology. His *Summa Theologiæ* is the culmination of SCHOLASTICISM. *See also* DUMB OX.

**Angelic Hymn, The.** The hymn, also known as the GLORIA IN EXCELSIS, beginning 'Glory to God in the highest' (Luke 2:14). It is so called because the first part of it was sung by the angel host that appeared to the shepherds of Bethlehem.

**Angelic Salutation, The.** The AVE MARIA.

**Angel of the North.** A huge sculpture of an angel with outstretched wings erected on a hillside near Gateshead in the northeast of England in 1998. It proclaims the steel and manufacturing ambition of the region and also denotes the boundary of a different country, the lands of the VENERABLE BEDE and St COLUMBA on the one hand and the largest shopping complex in Britain on the other. Its creator was Anthony Gormley (b.1950).

**Angel of the Schools, The.** St THOMAS AQUINAS. *See also* ANGELIC DOCTOR.

**Angels of Mons, The.** The 3rd and 4th Divisions of the OLD CONTEMPTIBLES, under the command of General H.L. Smith-Dorrien were hard pressed in their retreat from Mons (26–27 August 1914). On 29 September that year the *London Evening News* published a story by Arthur Machen crediting their preservation to St GEORGE and the angels, who, clad in white, held back the might of the German First Army by wielding longbows and raining arrows on the enemy. For some, the imaginary became a reality, and the 'Angels of Mons' became a legendary phrase.

**Angels on horseback.** A savoury dish of oysters wrapped in bacon slices and served on slivers of toast. It is not quite the same as DEVILS ON HORSEBACK.

**Angel visits.** Delightful encounters, of short duration and rare occurrence.

> Like angel visits, few and far between.
> THOMAS CAMPBELL: *Pleasures of Hope*, ii (1799)

**Angel water.** An old Spanish cosmetic, made of roses, trefoil and lavender, but originally mainly from ANGELICA, hence the name.

> Angel-water was the worst scent about her.
> CHARLES SEDLEY: *Bellamira, or the Mistress* (1687)

**Entertain angels unawares, To.** *See under* ENTERTAIN.

**Fallen angels.** *See under* FALL.

**Fools rush in where angels fear to tread.** *See under* FOOL.

**Flying angel, A.** *See under* FLY.

**Hell's Angels.** *See under* HELL.

**On the side of the angels.** *See under* SIDE.

**Angelica** (Latin, 'angelic'). A beautiful but fickle young woman who was the heroine of Matteo Boiardo's ORLANDO INNAMORATO (1487) and Ariosto's ORLANDO FURIOSO (1532). Orlando's unrequited love for her drove him mad. The name was also used by William Congreve for the principal character in *Love for Love* (1695) and by George Farquhar in *The Constant Couple* (1699) and *Sir Harry Wildair* (1701).

It is likewise the name of a plant (*Angelica archangelica*), cultivated for its aromatic stalks, which are candied and used in decorating cakes and confectionery. The plant, called the angelic herb from a belief in its medicinal virtues, especially against plague and pestilence, was also used as an ingredient of ABSINTHE, of gin and of Benedictine.

**Angelico, Fra** (Italian, 'Brother Angelic'). The name by which Giovanni da Fiesole (*c*.1400–55), famed for the spiritual quality of his paintings, is better known. The art historian Vasari particularly associated the name with Giovanni's *Coronation of the Virgin*, formerly in the Convent of San Domenico, Fiesole, and now in the Louvre, Paris.

> The whole colouring of that work appears to be by the hand of a saint or an angel ... wherefore it was with very good reason that this excellent monk was ever called Fra Giovanni Angelico.
>
> GIORGIO VASARI: *Lives of the Painters, Sculptors and Architects* (1550)

**Angelus, The.** A Roman Catholic devotion in honour of the ANNUNCIATION. It begins with the words *Angelus Domini nuntiavit Mariae* ('The angel of the Lord brought tidings to Mary'). It is recited three times daily, usually at 6 am, noon and 6 pm at the sound of the Angelus bell.

**Angevin kings** (French *Angevin*, 'of Anjou'). A name for the PLANTAGENET kings from Henry II to John. Henry II (r.1154–89) was the son of Matilda (daughter of Henry I) and Geoffrey Plantagenet, Count of Anjou.

**Angle. Angle, To.** To try to get something by an indirect or devious method, like a fisher trying to catch a fish. Thus if you angle for an invitation to a party, you ingratiate yourself to this end. A similar approach is to FISH FOR COMPLIMENTS.

**Angle of dip.** *See* DIP.

**Dead angle.** *See under* DEAD.

**Father of Angling, The.** Izaak Walton (1593–1683).

**Angles. Non Angli, sed angeli** (Latin, 'not Angles, but angels'). According to legend when Pope GREGORY THE GREAT (540–604) saw some fair-haired youths in the slave market, he asked whence they had come. He was told that they were Angles and also heathen. 'Not Angles, but angels' was his comment, and on becoming pope he sent St AUGUSTINE to convert them.

**Anglican Church.** *See* CHURCH OF ENGLAND.

**Anglo. Anglo-Catholic.** A more formal term for the HIGH CHURCH section of the CHURCH OF ENGLAND, based on a blend of 'Anglican' and Catholic.

**Anglo-Saxon Chronicle.** The basic source for the history of Anglo-Saxon England, and the first history in English to use the dating system ANNO DOMINI. It is written in Old English and was probably begun in the reign of ALFRED THE GREAT (871–899). There are seven manuscript versions extant, which substantially deal with events from the time of Julius Caesar to 1154. Four of these are usually regarded as distinct chronicles: the Parker Chronicle (named after Archbishop Parker), the Abingdon Chronicles, the Worcester Chronicle and the Laud Chronicle (named after Archbishop Laud).

**Angra Mainyu.** *See* AHRIMAN.

**Angry Young Men.** A name applied to certain modern British writers, and in particular to John Osborne (1929–94), from whose play *Look Back in Anger* (first performed 1956) the term was derived. They were typically young and of provincial lower-middle class or working-class origin, and gained notoriety for their satirical treatment and criticism of the ESTABLISHMENT, with its false or outmoded social, moral, political and intellectual values. The name is also sometimes applied to some American writers of protest.

**Angurvadel** (Old Norse, 'stream of anguish'). FRITHIOF's sword, inscribed with runic letters, which blazed in time of war, but gleamed with a dim light in time of peace.

**Animal. Animal Farm.** A satire in fable form by George ORWELL, published in 1945, and depicting a totalitarian regime like that of Russia under STALIN. The story describes how the pigs, by cunning, treachery and ruthlessness, come to dominate the more honest, gullible and hard-working animals. Their ultimate slogan is: 'All animals are equal, but some animals are more equal than others.' The leader of the pigs is Napoleon, representing Stalin.

**Animals in Christian art.** Some animals are appropriated to certain saints, as the calf or ox to St LUKE, the cock to St PETER, the eagle to St JOHN the Divine, the lion to St MARK and St JEROME, and the raven to St Benedict. *See also* SYMBOLS OF SAINTS *under* SAINT.

**Animals in heaven.** According to Muslim legend the following ten animals have been allowed to enter Paradise:

JONAH's whale
SOLOMON's ant
The ram caught by ABRAHAM and sacrificed instead of ISAAC
The lapwing of BALKIS
The camel of the prophet Saleh
BALAAM's ass
The ox of MOSES
The dog KRATIM of the SEVEN SLEEPERS
MOHAMMED's steed Al BORAK
NOAH's dove

**Animals in symbolism.**

Ant: diligence, patience, humility and foresight
Antelope: grace, speed and clarity of vision
Ape: vice, malice, lust and cunning
Ass: stupidity
Badger: slyness
Bantam: pluckiness and priggishness
Bat: blindness and madness
Bear: brute force, ill temper and uncouthness
Bee: diligence, sociabiliity and wisdom
Beetle: blindness
Boar: strength, aggression and courage
Buffalo: peaceable power
Bull: strength, potency and fecundity
Bulldog: pertinacity
Butterfly: lightmindedness and immortality
Calf: purity in sacrifice and prosperity
Camel: sobriety and dignified obedience
Carp: courage, virility and scholastic success
Cat: stealthy cunning, clairvoyance and agility
Chameleon: changeability
Cicada: immortality
Cock: vigilance, courage, virility and reliability
Cow: maternal nourishment
Crane: vigilance, longevity, wisdom and fidelity
Cricket: happiness and good fortune
Crocodile: voracity and hypocrisy
Crow: war, death, solitude and bad luck
Cuckoo: jealousy and opportunism
Deer: purity, creativity and spirituality
Dog: loyalty, vigilance and contempt
Dolphin: salvation, transformation and love
Dove: peace, purity, love, tenderness and hope
Dragon: primordial power
Dragonfly: lightness and elegance
Duck: happiness and fidelity
Eagle: majesty, domination, victory and valour
Eel: deviousness and fertility
Elephant: strength, sagacity and longevity
Ermine: purity and chastity
Falcon: asipiration, light and liberty
Fly: evil and pestilence
Fox: guile, malice and hypocrisy
Frog: fecundity
Goat: virility, lust, cunning and destructiveness
Goose: vigilance, loquaciousness and love
Grasshopper: fertility
Gull: gullibility
Hare: fertility, guile and magic
Hawk: rapacity and belligerence
Hedgehog: pugnacity and gluttony
Hen: maternal care
Heron: inquisitiveness
Hippopotamus: brute force and destructiveness
Hog: gluttony, lust and impurity
Horse: vitality, velocity and beauty
Hyena: greed and hypocrisy
Jackdaw: vanity and conceit
Jaguar: divination and sorcery
Jay: garrulousness
Kingfisher: fidelity and peace
Kitten: playfulness
Lamb: purity, self-sacrifice and innocence
Lark: cheerfulness
Leopard: ferocity, courage and pride
Lion: royal authority, strength and wisdom
Lynx: acuity and vigilance
Magpie: joy, married bliss and mischievousness
Mole: blindness and obtuseness
Monkey: malice, lust and greed
Mouse: timidity
Mule: obstinacy
Nightingale: pain, anguish and loss
Ostrich: stupidity
Otter: fertility
Owl: wisdom, death and prophecy
Ox: patience, strength and submissiveness
Parrot: mockery and verbosity
Partridge: fecundity and love
Peacock: pride and immortality
Pelican: self-sacrificial love
Pig: obstinacy, gluttony, filth and lust
Pigeon: peace, purity, love and hope
Puppy: conceit
Quail: ardour and courage
Rabbit: fecundity
Ram: ardour, virility and obstinacy
Rat: destructiveness, avarice and foresight
Raven: death, loss and war
Robin: trust
Salmon: fecundity, courage and wisdom
Scorpion: death, retribution and treachery
Sheep: meekness and stupidity
Sparrow: lasciviousness
Spider: divination and ensnarement
Squirrel: voraciousness
Stag: lasciviousness
Stork: longevity and filial devotion
Swallow: renewal
Swan: light, death, beauty and melancholy
Tiger: ferocity, power, beauty and speed
Toad: death and lust
Tortoise: patience, fecundity and longevity
Turkey: fertility
Vulture: greed
Whale: regeneration
Wolf: cruelty, ferocity, cunning and evil
Worm: self-abasement and mortality
Wren: happiness

The lamb, the pelican and the unicorn are symbols of Christ; the dragon, serpent and swine symbolize SATAN and his crew.

**Animals sacred to special deities.**

AESCULAPIUS: the serpent
APOLLO: the wolf, the griffon and the crow
BACCHUS: the dragon and the panther
DIANA: the stag
HERCULES: the deer
ISIS: the heifer
JUNO: the peacock and the lamb
JUPITER: the eagle
MARS: the horse and the vulture
MERCURY: the cock
MINERVA: the owl
NEPTUNE: the bull
TETHYS: the halcyon
VENUS: the dove, the swan and the sparrow
VULCAN: the lion

**Age of animals.** *See under* AGE.
**Clean and unclean animals.** *See under* CLEAN.
**Cries of animals.** *See under* CRY.

**Anima mundi** (Latin, 'the soul of the world'). An expression that the earliest philosophers used to mean 'the source of life'. PLATO used it to mean 'the animating principle of matter', inferior to pure spirit, while the STOICS gave it the sense 'the whole vital force of the universe'.

**Animula, vagula.** The opening of a poem to his soul, ascribed to the dying Emperor Hadrian (AD 76–138):

Animula, vagula, blandula,
Hospes comesque corporis;
Quae nunc abibis in loca,
Pallidula, rigida, nudula,
Nec, ut soles, dabis jocos?

Byron rendered this as follows:

Ah! gentle, fleeting, wav'ring sprite,
Friend and associate of this clay!
To what unknown region borne,
Wilt thou now wing thy distant flight?
No more with wonted humour gay,
But pallid, cheerless, and forlorn.
'Adrian's Address to His Soul When Dying' (1804)

**Anjou, The Fair Maid of.** *See under* FAIR.

**Ankh** (Egyptian, 'life', 'soul'). The ancient Egyptian symbol of eternal life, in the form of a cross with a loop at the top. It represented eternity when placed in the hands of deities, and was used in rituals, especially those involving royal cults. Its geometrical shape can be read as the rising sun, as the union of male and female principles, and as a key to esoteric knowledge and the afterworld of the spirit. It experienced a revival in NEW AGE ritualism and has enjoyed commercialized exploitation as an ornament or latter-day AMULET.

**Ann, Mother.** *See under* MOTHER.

**Anna Karenina.** *See under* KARENINA.

**Annals of the Four Masters, The.** A chronicle of Irish history from antiquity to 1616, published (1636) as *Annála Ríoghachta Éireann*, or *Annals of the Kingdom of Ireland*. The Four Masters (authors or compilers) were Michael O'Clery (1575–1643), Conaire his brother, his cousin Cucoigriche O'Clery (d.1664) and Fearfeasa O'Mulconry.

**Annapurna.** A Hindu goddess venerated for her power to provide food. Her name, which derives from Sanskrit *anna*, 'food', and *purna*, 'abundant', indicates this attribute. She gave the name of Annapurna, the Himalayan massif in Nepal, whose mountains are regarded as favouring agriculture in the valleys below.

**Annates** (Latin *annus*, 'year'). In the Roman Catholic Church on the appointment of a bishop or other ecclesiastic, payments, also called FIRST FRUITS, of a year's income of the SEE OF BENEFICE, were made to the pope. In England these payments were finally stopped in 1534 and transferred to the crown. *See also* QUEEN ANNE'S BOUNTY *under* ANNE.

**Anne. Anne Boleyn.** *See* BOLEYN, ANNE.

**Anne Frank.** *See under* FRANK.

**Anne's Great Captain.** The Duke of Marlborough (1650–1722).

**Queen Anne.** Daughter of James II and his first wife Anne Hyde. Her reign extended from 1702 to 1714 and her name is still used in certain phrases.

**Queen Anne is dead.** A slighting retort made to a teller of stale news.

**Queen Anne's Bounty.** A fund established by Queen Anne in 1704 for the relief of the poorer clergy of the CHURCH OF ENGLAND. It was created out of the FIRST FRUITS and TENTHS, formerly given to the papacy, which were annexed to the crown by Henry VIII. In 1809 there were 860 incumbents still getting less than £50 per annum, and the fund was increased by parliamentary grants (1809–20). Queen Anne's Bounty was merged with the Ecclesiastical Commission in 1948 to form the Church Commissioners. *See also* ANNATES.

**Queen Anne's fan.** *See* COCK A SNOOK.

**Queen Anne's footstool.** A name given to St John's Church, Smith Square, Westminster, a fine specimen of baroque architecture by Thomas Archer, completed in 1728. There is an apocryphal story that Queen Anne, when interviewing the architect, kicked over her footstool and said 'Make it like that', the four upturned legs representing the towers. In reality, the building began to settle during construction and to stabilize it a tower and lantern turret were added at each corner. Lord Chesterfield likened the church to an elephant thrown on its back with its four feet erect. It was burned out in 1742 and again in 1941, after which it was reopened in 1969 as a concert and lecture hall.

**Queen Anne style.** The style in buildings, decoration, furniture, silverware and the like, characteristic of her period.

**Annie. Annie Laurie.** *See under* LAURIE.

**Annie Oakley.** *See under* OAKLEY.

**Anniversaries, Wedding.** *See under* WED.

**Anno Domini** (Latin, 'in the year of our Lord'). This system of dating from the Nativity of Christ was introduced by the monk Dionysius Exiguus, who lived in the first half of the 6th century. 'Anno Domini' is also used colloquially as a synonym for old age, as: 'He is beginning to feel the effects of Anno Domini.' The phrase is invariably abbreviated AD in dates. *See also* ANGLO-SAXON CHRONICLE.

**Annunciation. Feast of the Annunciation, The.** *See under* FEAST.

**Order of the Annunciation.** *See under* ORDER.

**Sisters of the Annunciation.** *See* FRANCISCANS.

**Annus. Annus horribilis** (Latin, 'horrible year'). Any disastrous or unpleasant year. Such for the Royal Family was 1992, which saw the divorce of the Princess Royal, the separation of the Duke and Duchess of York, newspaper photographs of the latter topless, and a fearful fire at Windsor Castle. The Queen used the phrase in a speech to guests at a banquet in the Guildhall that year.

**Annus luctus** (Latin, 'year of mourning'). The period during which a widow is supposed to remain unmarried. If she marries within about nine months from the death of her husband and a child is born, a doubt might arise as to its paternity. Such a marriage is not illegal.

**Annus mirabilis** (Latin, 'wonderful year'). Such a year was 1666, memorable for the GREAT FIRE OF LONDON and the successes of English arms over the Dutch, commemorated in Dryden's poem titled *Annus Mirabilis* (1667). The year 1809 is also considered an *annus mirabilis*, seeing the birth of Charles Darwin, Abraham Lincoln, Alfred, Lord Tennyson, Edgar Allan Poe, Felix Mendelssohn, W.E. Gladstone, Fanny Kemble and Kit Carson, among others.

**Annwn** or **Annwfn** (Welsh, 'underworld', 'hell'). In Welsh legend the land of the departed, the Celtic HADES.

**Anodyne necklace, An.** An anodyne relieves pain. An anodyne necklace was an AMULET supposedly efficacious against suffering. Samuel Johnson's *Idler*, No. 40 (1758) says:

> The true pathos of advertisements must have sunk deep into the heart of every man that remembers the zeal shown by the seller of the anodyne necklace, for the ease and safety of poor soothing infants.

The term then came to be applied to a hangman's noose:

> May I die by an anodyne necklace, but I had rather be an under-turnkey than an usher in a boarding school.
> OLIVER GOLDSMITH: *The Vicar of Wakefield*, ch x (1766)

**Anon** (Old English *on āne*, literally 'in one'). The present meaning of the word as 'soon', 'in a little while', is a misuse of the earlier meaning, 'immediately', 'straight away'. Mark 1:30 (Authorized Version) gives an instance of the old meaning:

> But Simon's wife's mother lay sick of a fever, and anon they tell him of her.

The Revised Version gives 'straightway'. William Wordsworth in *The White Doe of Rylstone* (i, 31 (1815)) exemplifies the later meaning:

> Fast the churchyard fills; – anon
> Look again, and they are all gone.

The word was also used by servants, tapsters and others as a response meaning 'Coming, sir!'

**Anorak.** A word of Greenland Inuit (Eskimo) origin for a type of waterproof jacket with a hood, as originally worn in polar regions. The garment's popularity, practicality and relative cheapness caused it to be widely adopted for a number of outdoor uses, from walking to train-spotting. The latter pastime in particular gave it a 'nerdish' image and as a result the word passed to denote a boring person or SQUARE, especially one with solitary interests.

**Another. Another course would have done it.** A little more would have completed the job. It is said that the inhabitants of a Yorkshire village tried to wall in a cuckoo in order to enjoy an eternal spring. They built a wall round the bird, and the cuckoo just skimmed over it. 'Ah!' said one of the peasants, 'another carse would 'a' done it.'

**Another man's shoes.** 'To stand in another man's shoes' is to occupy the place of another. Among the Vikings, when a man adopted a son, the person adopted put on the shoes of the adopter.

In REYNARD THE FOX, Reynard, having turned the tables on Sir Bruin the Bear, asked the queen to let him have the shoes of the disgraced minister; so Bruin's shoes were torn off and put upon the new favourite.

**Another Richmond in the field.** Said when another unexpected adversary turns up. The reference is to Shakespeare's *Richard III* (V, iv (1592)), where the king, speaking of Henry of Richmond (afterwards Henry VII), says:

> I think there be six Richmonds in the field;
> Five have I slain to-day, instead of him.

**Anschluss, The.** In a historical context, this German word, meaning 'junction', 'union', refers to the annexation of Austria by NAZI Germany in March 1938.

**Answer. Answer is in the negative, The.** A formal or pompous circumlocution for 'No'.

**Answer's a lemon, The.** Nothing doing. The phrase is a suitable answer to an unreasonable or ridiculous request or question. The expression originated in the USA at the beginning of the 20th century. The fruit, with its acid juice, was taken to represent a tart response to an unreasonable request.

**Answer to a maiden's prayer, The.** An eligible bachelor, ideally young, handsome and wealthy, or generally anything which exactly meets requirements.

> You're the answer to a maiden's prayer, dear heart. No need for you to do a stroke of work, you can marry money and live the life of a gentleman.
> JOAN FLEMING: *Maiden's Prayer* (1957)

**Dusty answer.** *See under* DUST.

**Know all the answers, To.** *See under* KNOW.

**Not to take no for an answer.** To persist, despite setbacks or refusals. Paul Gallico's story *The Small Miracle* (1951), about a small boy who goes to Rome to get permission from the pope to take his sick donkey to be blessed, was turned into a film called *Never Take No for an Answer*, alluding to the boy's pertinacity in his bid to see the Holy Father.

**Soft answer.** *See under* SOFT.

**Ant.** For many centuries the ant has been a symbol of thrift and industry. The Bible says 'Go to the ant, thou sluggard; consider her ways and be wise' (Proverbs 6:6). AESOP has a fable on the 'Ant and the Grasshopper' in which the indolent grasshopper, in the winter, went to the busy little ants to beg for food.

**Ants in one's pants.** Excessively restless or eager. The expression was popularized by Hugh S. Johnson, the colourful former American Army general, who headed the National Recovery Administration in 1933–4. Pants here has the American sense of trousers.

**Antaeus** (Greek *antaios*, 'situated opposite'). In Greek mythology a gigantic wrestler, son of Earth and Sea (GAIA and POSEIDON), who became stronger whenever he touched the earth. HERCULES lifted him from the ground and slew him.

**Antediluvian** (Latin *ante*, 'before', and *diluvium*, 'flood'). Before the DELUGE. A word colloquially used for anything hopelessly outdated.

**Anthem, National.** *See under* NATIONAL.

**Anthology** (Greek *anthos*, 'flower', and *legein*, 'to collect'). A collection of poems or prose extracts, regarded as a collection of flowers or a 'nosegay'. In 1944 Field Marshal Wavell, the Middle East army commander, published an anthology of favourite poems by other poets entitled *Other Men's Flowers*.

**Greek Anthology, The.** *See under* GREEK.

**Anthony. Anthony Adverse.** *See under* ADVERSE.

**Anthony Eden.** A popular name for the style of black felt homburg hat worn by Sir Anthony Eden (Lord Avon) when Foreign Secretary in the 1930s, which was fashionable in WHITEHALL circles.

**Anthony of Egypt.** The patron saint (*c*.250–356) of herdsmen and hermit of Upper Egypt, also the father of Christian monasticism. The story of his temptations by the DEVIL was a popular subject in literature and art. His feast-day is 17 January.

**Anthony of Padua.** The saint (1195–1231) who was a rigorous follower of St FRANCIS of Assisi and a renowned preacher. He was canonized in 1232 by Pope Gregory IX. His feast-day is 13 June.

**St Anthony's cross.** The TAU CROSS T, called a lace.

**St Anthony's fire.** In medieval times a pestilential disease, so called from the belief that those who sought the intercession of ST ANTHONY OF EGYPT recovered from this epidemic or sacred fire. It was commonly supposed to be erysipelas (Greek, 'red skin') or the rose (from its colour) but in fact could have been ergotism (French *ergot*, 'cockspur'), a poisoning due to eating rye bread with fungal infection. *See also* VITUS' DANCE.

**St Anthony's pig.** A pet pig, the smallest of the litter, also called the TANTONY PIG.

**Anthroposophus.** The nickname of Thomas Vaughan (1622–66), cleric and alchemist and twin brother of Henry Vaughan the SILURIST. He was so called from his book *Anthroposophia Theomagica* (1650), which dealt with the condition of man after death.

**Anthroposophy** (Greek *anthrōpos*, 'man', and *sophia*, 'wisdom'). The name given to the 'spiritual science' developed by the Austrian philosopher Rudolf Steiner (1861–1925), a former theosophist. *See also* THEOSOPHY.

**Antic hay.** The hay, a word of uncertain origin, was an old English country dance, somewhat of the nature of a reel, with winding movements around other dancers, bushes and the like, when danced in the open.

> My men, like satyrs grazing on the lawns,
> Shall with their goat feet dance an antic hay.
>
> CHRISTOPHER MARLOWE: *Edward II*, I, i (1593)

Aldous Huxley wrote a novel (1923) of this title.

**Antichrist.** The MAN OF SIN, due to appear at the end of time, is mentioned in 1 John 2:18–22 and is derived from Hebrew teachings. The belief that the arrival of Antichrist was to precede the second advent is chiefly founded on 2 Thessalonians 2:1–12, and Revelation 13. In the early Christian church the Roman Empire and its rulers were frequently referred to as Antichrist, and later the title was bestowed on the Emperor Frederick II and various popes. With the REFORMATION, the PROTESTANT conception of the papacy as Antichrist became widespread, and its later use is largely as an abusive term. It has been applied even to Napoleon Bonaparte and William II of Germany. The Muslims have a legend that Christ will slay the Antichrist at the gate of the church at Lydda, in Palestine. *See also* NUMBER OF THE BEAST.

**Anticlea.** The daughter of AUTOLYCUS. SISYPHUS raped her in order to avenge her father's theft of his cattle. Pregnant by him, she was married off by her father to LAERTES, and bore Odysseus (ULYSSES) to him. She died of grief while Odysseus was fighting at TROY or, according to another version of the story, killed herself on hearing a false report of his death. Her own story is told in the *Odyssey* (8th century BC).

**Antigone** (Greek *anti*, 'opposite', 'instead of', and *gonē*, 'childbirth'). The subject of a tragedy (5th century BC) by Sophocles. She was the daughter of OEDIPUS by his mother, Jocasta. She killed herself to avoid being buried alive for disobeying an edict of CREON. She was famed for her devotion to her brother Polynices. Hence the Duchess of Angoulême (1778–1851) was called the Modern Antigone for her attachment to her brother Louis XVII.

**Antimony** (Medieval Latin *antimonium*). The name of the silvery-white metal is of uncertain origin. Samuel Johnson's *Dictionary* (1755) derives it erroneously from a Greek word *antimonakhos*, which he interprets as 'bad for monks'. The explanation for this was from the story of a prior who gave some of the mineral to his convent pigs. They thrived on it and became very fat. The prior next tried it on the monks, who died from its effects.

**Antinomian** (Greek *anti*, 'against', and *nomos*, 'law'). A name for one who believes that Christians are not bound to observe the 'law of God', but 'may continue in sin that grace may abound'. The term was first applied to John Agricola (1492–1566) by Martin Luther (1483–1546), and was given to a sect that appeared in Germany about 1535. It was put forward as an excuse for immorality by extremist sects from early Christian times and appeared in England during the COMMONWEALTH period.

**Antinous** (Greek *anti*, 'opposing', and *noos*, 'intelligence').

(1) In Greek mythology the most prominent of PENELOPE's suitors, killed by Odysseus (ULYSSES) on his return home.

(2) In history Antinous was the favourite and companion of the Roman Emperor Hadrian. His head was stamped on coins, and many museums of Roman antiquities have a statue or bust of this handsome, soft-looking boy. He drowned in the Nile when he was about 20 years old.

**Antipope.** A usurping or rival pontiff set up in opposition to one canonically elected. Of the 39 antipopes, those residing at Avignon during the GREAT SCHISM (1378–1417) are perhaps best known. When John XXIII (a schismatic) summoned the Council of Constance (1414) to end the schism, there were three rival popes. John and Benedict XIII were deposed as schismatics, Gregory XIII resigned, and a new pope, Martin V, was elected in 1417. The last of the antipopes was Felix V (r.1439–49).

**Antisthenes** (Greek *anti*, 'opposite', and *sthenos*, 'force'). An Athenian philosopher (*c*.455–*c*.360 BC), the founder of the CYNIC School. He wore a ragged cloak and carried a wallet and staff like a beggar. SOCRATES, whose pupil he was, wittily said he could 'see rank pride peering through the holes of Antisthenes' rags'.

**Antithesis** (Greek, 'opposition'). A literary device in which contrasting ideas are sharpened by the use of opposite meanings. The following lines are a classic example:

> Rais'd in extremes, and in extremes decri'd,
> With Oaths affirm'd, with dying Vows deni'd,
> Not weigh'd or winnow'd by the Multitude,
> But swallow'd in the Mass, unchewed and crude.
> Some Truth there was, but dashed and brew'd with
> Lies;
> To please the Fools, and puzzle all the Wise.
> Succeeding Times did equal Folly call
> Believing nothing or believing all.
>
> JOHN MILTON: *Absalom and Achitophel* (1681)

**Antonine. Antonine Column.** *See* COLUMN OF MARCUS AURELIUS.

**Antonine Heresy.** A religious protest of the early 18th century in the Bantu kingdom of Kongo in Angola, then a Portuguese colonial possession with an active force of CAPUCHIN missionaries. In 1703 a young woman named Beatrice (originally Kimpa Vita), claiming to be a reincarnation of St ANTHONY OF PADUA, begged the local ruler, Pedro IV, to return to the ancient capital of Mbanza Kongo (Portuguese São Salvador). When he failed to do so, she led the return herself, taking up residence by the ruined cathedral. She conducted services there, charging the missionaries with concealing the Congolese origin of Jesus Christ, the Virgin Mary and St Francis. Her fellow proselytes, known as Lesser Anthonies, adopted the names of Christian martyrs and arrogated the duties of the missionaries, baptizing children and remitting sins. In early 1706 Beatrice was seized by the Bakongo authorities, tried for heresy and on 1 July burned at the stake on the orders of the Portuguese priest Bernaldo da Gala. Her death led to open insurrection. The local ruler was assassinated in Soyo in 1708 and the Capuchin monastery destroyed. The stand was finally broken in early 1709.

**Antonine Wall, The.** A turf wall fronted by a deep ditch with forts at intervals stretching across southern Scotland from Carriden, on the Forth, to Old Kilpatrick on the Clyde (about 36 miles/58km). It was built between 140 and 142 by Lollius Urbicus, governor of Britain under the Emperor Antoninus Pius, for whom it is named. It was abandoned before the end of the 2nd century. *See also* HADRIAN'S WALL.

**Antwerp, Giles of.** *See under* GILES.

**Anu.** The chief god of the Sumerians and Babylonians, king of heaven and ruler of destiny. The centre of his cult was at Erech, mentioned in Genesis 10:10 as part of Nimrod's kingdom.

**Anubis** (origin unknown). An Egyptian god similar to HERMES of Greece, with whom he was sometimes identified. His office was to take the souls of the dead before the judge of the infernal regions. The son of OSIRIS, the judge, he was represented with a human body and a jackal's head.

**Any port in a storm.** Said when one is in a difficulty

and has to take whatever refuge, literal or metaphorical, offers itself.

**Anzac.** A word coined in 1915 from the initials of the Australian and New Zealand Army Corps. It was also applied to the cove and beach in Gallipoli where they landed. *See also* DIGGER.

**Anzac Day.** 25 April, commemorating the landing of the Anzacs in Gallipoli in 1915.

**Anzac Pact, The.** The agreement reached between Australia and New Zealand in 1944 to cooperate in their policies with regard to armistices with the AXIS powers, the post-war settlement, and in certain other matters.

**A-OK.** Excellent; in good order. An American space age expression, allegedly standing for all systems OK.

**Aonian.** Poetical, pertaining to the MUSES. According to Greek mythology the Muses dwelt in Aonia, that part of BOEOTIA which contains Mount HELICON and the Muses' fountain. Milton speaks of 'the Aonian mount' (*Paradise Lost*, i (1667)), and James Thomson calls the fraternity of poets:

> The Aonian hive
> Who praised are, and starve right merrily,
> *Castle of Indolence*, ii (1748)

**À outrance.** *See* À L'OUTRANCE.

**Apache** (from Mexican Spanish, probably from Zuñi *Apachu*, 'enemy'). The name of a group of tribes of North American Indians, given to (or adopted by) the hooligans of Paris about the end of the 19th century (in this sense pronounced 'a pash'). This usage has a close parallel in the MOHOCKS of the 18th century.

**Apache State.** Arizona, the land of the Apache Indians. *See also* UNITED STATES OF AMERICA.

**Apart, Poles.** *See under* POLE.

**Apartheid** (Afrikaans, 'separateness'). A policy adopted by the Afrikaner National Party in 1948 to ensure the dominance of the white minority. It divided South Africa into separate areas for whites and blacks, causing the country's withdrawal from the British Commonwealth in 1961 and leading to rioting, repression and isolation from other nations. Limited constitutional rights were granted to non-whites in 1985, and the remaining apartheid laws were repealed in 1991.

**Ape, To.** To copy, to imitate.

> He keeps them, like an ape, in the corner of his jaw; first mouthed, to be last swallowed.
> SHAKESPEARE: *Hamlet*, IV, ii (1600)

Most of the OLD WORLD monkeys have cheek pouches, used as receptacles for food.

**Buffoon Ape, The.** *See under* BUFFOON.

**Go ape, To.** To become agitated, violent or sexually aggressive, an expression of American origin.

**Lead apes in hell, To.** *See under* LEAD.

**Naked ape.** *See under* NAKED.

**Play the ape, To.** *See under* PLAY.

**Play the sedulous ape, To.** *See under* PLAY.

**Apelles.** The Greek painter and contemporary of Alexander the Great, born at Colophon on the coast of Asia Minor in the first half of the 4th century BC and famous for his portrait APHRODITE ANADYOMENE and for his painting *Calumny* copied by Botticelli. He was known as the 'Chian Painter'. Chian means 'of Chios', although Apelles was, in fact, associated with Cos, and died on that island.

> The Chian Peincter, when he was requirde
> To pourtraict *Venus* in her perfect hew,
> To make his worke more absolute, desird
> Of all the fairest Maides to haue the vew.
> EDMUND SPENSER: *Dedicatory Sonnets*, 'To all the gratious and beautifull Ladies in the Court' (1590)

**Aphrodite** (popularly from Greek *aphros*, 'foam', and *dineō*, 'I whirl', or *duō*, 'I dive', but perhaps really from Sanskrit *abhradatta*, 'cloud-given', from *abhra*, 'cloud', and *datta*, 'given'). The Greek VENUS, so called because she sprang from the foam of the sea. In HOMER she is the daughter of ZEUS and DIONE.

**Aphrodite Anadyomene.** VENUS rising from the sea, accompanied by dolphins. The Greek word means literally 'rising up', referring to the way in which Venus sprang full grown from the sea foam. The name is given to the famous lost painting by APELLES, which he is said to have made after seeing PHRYNE on the sea-shore naked and with dishevelled hair. Sandro Botticelli's painting *The Birth of Venus* (*c.*1483–4), in the Uffizi Gallery at Florence, is devoted to the same subject. *See also* VENUS ON THE HALF SHELL.

**Aphrodite Callipyge** (Greek, 'with the beautiful buttocks'). The name given to the Graeco-Roman copy of a Hellenistic statue in the Museo Nazionale at Naples. It shows a young woman raising her robe to expose her legs and buttocks and turning to admire them. There is no real ground for connecting the statue with VENUS.

**Aphrodite's girdle.** The CESTUS.

**Apicius.** A GOURMAND, from the name of three famous Roman gourmands. Marcus Gavius Apicius, of the time of AUGUSTUS and Tiberius, whose income was reduced by luxurious living, committed suicide to avoid the misery of a plain diet.

**Apis** (origin unknown). In Egyptian mythology, the bull of Memphis, sacred to PTAH (later associated and identified with OSIRIS) of whose soul it was supposed to be the image. SERAPIS was the dead Apis. The sacred bull had to be black with special markings. Sometimes it was not granted to live more than 25 years, when it was sacrificed and embalmed with great ceremony. Cambyses, king of Persia (529–521 BC), and conqueror of Egypt, slew the bull of Memphis and is said to have been punished with madness.

**Apocalypse. Apocalyptic number.** The mysterious number 666 (Revelation 13:15). *See also* NUMBER OF THE BEAST.

**Four Horsemen of the Apocalypse, The.** *See under* FOUR.

**Apocrypha** (Late Latin *apocrypha scripta*, 'hidden writings', from Greek *apokruptein*, 'to hide away'). The word came to apply to any text that was 'withheld from general circulation' (for various reasons), and therefore regarded as of doubtful origin, false or spurious. In the early 5th century JEROME inappropriately applied the word to the non-canonical books of the Old Testament found in the SEPTUAGINT and VULGATE and not usually included in PROTESTANT Bibles. The Apocrypha was included in the AUTHORIZED VERSION of 1611. The Apocrypha proper consists of:

1 and 2 Esdras, TOBIT, Judith, the rest of ESTHER, the WISDOM OF SOLOMON, ECCLESIASTICUS, BARUCH, with the Epistle of Jeremiah, the SONG OF THE THREE HOLY CHILDREN, the History of Susanna, Bel and the Dragon, the Prayer of Manasses, 1 and 2 Maccabees.

The books of the Apocrypha are called deuterocanonical ('second-level') by Roman Catholics, to distinguish them from protocanonical ('first-level') books, but they are regarded as authoritative and are included within the body of the Old Testament.

Apart from other Old Testament Apocryphal books there are numerous New Testament Apocryphal Gospels, Acts and Teachings of the Apostles, Epistles and Apocalypses. *See also* ACTS OF PILATE; PROTEVANGELIUM; PSEUDEPIGRAPHA.

**Apocryphal.** Applied to a story or anecdote, especially one concerning a celebrity or well-known person to indicate that it is typical or in character but probably fictitious.

**Apollinarians.** A heretical 4th-century sect formed by followers of Apollinaris, bishop of Laodicea, a vigorous opponent of Arianism. They held that body, soul and spirit coexist in man but that Christ, although having a human body and soul, had no human spirit. The spirit was thus replaced by the Divine *Logos*. This heresy was condemned at the Council of Constantinople (381).

**Apollo** (perhaps from an Indoeuropean root element *abol*, 'apple', or from Semitic *ap olen*, 'universal father'). In Greek mythology the son of ZEUS and LETO (LATONA), sometimes identified with HELIOS the sun-god. He was the brother of Artemis (DIANA), half-brother of HERMES and father of AESCULAPIUS. He was the god of music, poetry, archery, prophecy and the healing art. His plant was the LAUREL and he is represented as the perfection of youthful manhood.

'A perfect Apollo' is a model of male handsomeness, referring to the APOLLO BELVEDERE.

**Apollo Belvedere.** An ancient statue of Apollo, so called from the Belvedere Gallery in the Vatican, where it stands. It is said to be a copy of a bronze votive statue of DELPHI commemorating the repulse of an attack by the Gauls on his shrine in 279 BC. It was discovered at Antium (Anzio) in 1485. It depicts the god as a beardless youth, with his cloak thrown back to display his naked perfection.

**Apollo of Portugal.** Luis de Camoëns (1524–80), author of the LUSIADS, so called for the beauty of his poetry.

**Apollonius of Tyana.** A Pythagorean philosopher (b.*c*.4 BC), accredited with exceptional powers of magic. It was he who discovered that the Phoenician woman whom Menippus Lycius intended to marry was in fact a serpent or LAMIA. This story was noted by Robert Burton in his *Anatomy of Melancholy* (1621). It also forms the subject of John Keats' *Lamia* (1820).

**Apollyon.** The Greek name of ABADDON, king of HELL. It is used by Bunyan in *The Pilgrim's Progress* (1678, 1684).

**Aposiopesis.** *See* QUOS EGO.

**Apostate, Julian the.** *See under* JULIAN.

**Apostle** (Greek *apostolos*, 'messenger', from *apostellein*, 'to send forth'). The word was specially applied to the 12 Disciples of Christ as those sent forth to preach the gospel. They are named in Matthew 10:1–4, Mark 3:14–19, Luke 6:13–16, and Acts 1:13. The original list was PETER, ANDREW, JAMES and JOHN (the sons of Zebedee), PHILIP, BARTHOLOMEW, THOMAS, MATTHEW, James (the son of Alphaeus), Judas or JUDE, SIMON and JUDAS ISCARIOT. Matthew and Mark give Thaddaeus in place of Jude, and John 21:1–2 has Nathanael, who by some has been identified with Bartholomew. JAMES THE LESS has also been identified, somewhat dubiously, with James, the son of Alphaeus. MATTHIAS and PAUL were subsequent additions. The badges or symbols of the 14 apostles (i.e. the original 12 with Matthias and Paul) are as follows:

Andrew: an X-shaped cross, because he was crucified on one

Bartholomew: a knife, because he was flayed with one

JAMES THE GREAT: a scallop shell, a pilgrim's staff, or a gourd bottle, because he is the patron saint of pilgrims

James the Less: a fuller's pole, because he was killed by a blow on the head with one, dealt him by SIMEON the fuller

John: a cup with a winged serpent flying out of it, in allusion to the tradition about Aristodemos, priest of DIANA, who challenged John to drink a cup of poison; John made the sign of a cross on the cup, Satan like a dragon fled from it, and John then drank the cup, which was quite innocuous
Judas Iscariot: a bag, because he 'had the bag and bare what was put therein' (John 12:6)
Jude: a club, because he was martyred with one
Matthew: a hatchet or halberd, because he was slain at Nadabar with one
Matthias: a battleaxe, because after being first stoned he was beheaded with one
Paul: a sword, because his head was cut off with one; the convent of La Lisla in Spain claims to possess the very instrument
Peter: a bunch of keys, because Christ gave him 'the keys of the kingdom of heaven' (Matthew 16:19); a cock, because he went out and wept bitterly when he heard the cock crow (Matthew 26:75)
Philip: a long staff surmounted with a cross, because he suffered death by being suspended by the neck from a tall pillar
Simon: a saw, because he was sawn to death, according to tradition
Thomas: a lance, because he was pierced through the body with one, at Mylapore

The traditional burial sites of the Apostles are:

Andrew: at Amalfi (Naples)
Bartholomew: at Rome, in the church of Bartholomew, on the Tiber Island
James the Great: at Santiago de Compostela, in Spain
James the Less: at Rome, in the church of SS Philip and James
John: at Ephesus
Jude: at Rome
Luke the Evangelist: at Padua
Mark the Evangelist: at Venice
Matthew: at Salerno (Naples)
Matthias: at Rome, in the church of St Peter
Paul: at Rome, in the church of San Paolo fuori le Mura
Peter: at Rome, in the church of St Peter
Philip: at Rome
Simon or Simeon: at Rome
Thomas: at Ortona (Naples) or, according to another tradition, at Mylapore, near Madras

*See also* EVANGELISTS; SYMBOLS OF SAINTS *under* SAINT.

**Apostle of Free Trade, The.** Richard Cobden (1804–65), the principal founder of the Anti-Corn Law League in 1838.

**Apostle of Temperance, The.** MATTHEW.

**Apostles** or **Apostles Society, The.** *See* CAMBRIDGE APOSTLES.

**Apostles' Creed.** A Christian creed claiming to encapsulate the doctrine taught by the Apostles. It was received into the LATIN CHURCH, in its present form, in the 11th century, but a formula somewhat like it existed in the 2nd century. Items were added in the 4th and 5th centuries, and verbal alterations were made much later. *See also* ATHANASIAN CREED; NICENE CREED.

**Apostles in history.** A number of individuals, including some of the original Apostles, have earned or been given the title Apostle of (the) ... Among them:

Abyssinians: St Frumentius (*c*.300–*c*.360)
Alps: Felix Neff (1798–1829)
American Indians: Bartolomé de Las Casas (1474–1566); John Eliot (1604–90)
Andalusia: Juan de Avila (1500–69)
Ardennes: St HUBERT (d.727)
Armenians: Gregory the Illuminator (*c*.257–*c*.337)
Brazil: José de Anchieta, Jesuit missionary (1533–97)
East Indies: St Francis Xavier (1506–52)
English: St AUGUSTINE (d.604); St GEORGE (d.*c*.300)
Free Trade: Richard Cobden (1804–65)
French: St Denis (? 3rd century)
Frisians: St Willibrod (*c*.657–738)
Gauls: St Irenaeus (*c*.130–*c*.200); St MARTIN OF TOURS (*c*.316–400)
Gentiles: St PAUL (d.67)
Germany: St BONIFACE (680–754)
Highlanders: St Columba (521–597)
Hungary: St STEPHEN (975–1038), the Apostle King
Infidelity: VOLTAIRE (1694–1778)
Ireland: St PATRICK (*c*.389–461)
North: St Ansgar or Anscarius (801–65), missionary to Scandinavia; Bernard Gilpin (1517–83), archdeacon of Durham, evangelist of the Scottish border
Peru: Alonso de Barcena, Jesuit, missionary (1528–98)
Picts: St Ninian (? 5th century)
Rome: St Philip Neri (1515–95) for his good works there; *see also* ORATORIANS
Scottish Reformers: John Knox (1505–72)
Slavs: St Cyril (827–869)
Spain: St JAMES THE GREAT (d.44)
Sword: MOHAMMED (*c*.570–632)
Temperance: Father MATHEW (1790–1856)
Yorkshire: Paulinus, archbishop of York (d.644)
Wales: St DAVID (*c*.500–*c*.600)

**Apostle spoons.** Silver spoons, formerly given at a christening, that have figure of an APOSTLE at the top of the handle. Sometimes 12 spoons were given, representing the 12 apostles, sometimes four, representing the four EVANGELISTS, and sometimes only one. Occasionally a set included an additional Master Spoon and Lady Spoon. Silver spoons were given to children of the wealthier classes, hence the saying to be BORN WITH A SILVER SPOON IN ONE'S MOUTH.

**Apostolic Constitutions.** A comprehensive rule in eight books concerning church doctrines and customs. They are of unknown authorship, are probably of Syrian origin and date from about the 4th century.

**Apostolic Fathers.** A term for Christian writers who were born in the 1st century and were supposedly in contact with the original APOSTLES. POLYCARP, the last of the Apostolic Fathers, born about 69, was believed to be the disciple of St

John the Apostle. CLEMENT of Rome died *c*.101, IGNATIUS *c*.120 and Polycarp *c*.155. Others are BARNABAS, Hermas (author of *The Shepherd* (2nd century)) and Papias (a bishop of Hierapolis, mentioned by Eusebius).

**Apostolic Majesty.** A title borne by the emperor of Austria, as king of Hungary, first conferred by Pope Sylvester II on King Stephen of Hungary in 1001.

**Apostolic succession.** The doctrine that the mission given to the APOSTLES by Christ (Matthew 28:19) must extend to their legitimate successors in an unbroken line. Thus the only valid ministry is that of clergy ordained by properly consecrated bishops.

**Cambridge Apostles, The.** *See under* CAMBRIDGE.

**Catholic and Apostolic Church.** *See under* CATHOLIC.

**Prince of the Apostles.** St PETER (Matthew 16:18–19).

**Vicar apostolic.** *See under* VICAR.

**Apostrophe** (Greek, 'turning away'). A figure of speech in which a thing, place, abstract quality, idea or a dead or absent person is addressed as if present and capable of understanding. The following are two classic examples:

> Sweet Auburn, loveliest village of the plain.
> OLIVER GOLDSMITH: *The Deserted Vilage* (1770)

> Milton! Thou shouldst be living at this hour:
> England hath need of thee.
> WILLIAM WORDSWORTH: *Poems Dedicated to National Independence and Liberty*, I, xiv, 'London, 1802' (1807)

**Apparel** (Old French *apareiller*, 'to make ready'). One meaning of this word used to be 'ornament' or 'embellishment', especially when applied to orphreys, the embroidered borders of ecclesiastical vestments, and in particular to the ornamental parts of the alb, at the lower edge and at the wrists.

> The albe should be made with apparels worked in silk or gold, embroidered with ornaments.
> A.W.N. PUGIN: *Glossary of Ecclesiastical Ornament* (1844)

**Apparent, Heir.** *See under* HEIR.

**Appeal. Appeal to arms, To.** To decide an issue by resorting to the test of war.

**Appeal to the country, An.** An invitation to the nation to express its opinion on some particular issue or issues by dissolving Parliament and holding a GENERAL ELECTION.

**Court of Appeal.** *See under* COURT.

**Appearances, Save.** *See under* SAVE.

**Appiades.** Five divinities whose temple stood near the Appian aqueduct in Rome. Their names are VENUS, ATHENE, Concord, Peace and VESTA. They were represented on horseback, like AMAZONS. The name also came to apply to the prostitutes of this locality.

**Appian Way.** The 'queen of long-distance roads', leading from Rome to Brundisium (Brindisi), a length of 363 miles (582km). This most famous Roman road was begun by the censor Appius Claudius Caecus about 312 BC. *See also* DOMINE, QUO VADIS?

**Apple.** The apple has a related name in many languages, such as German *Apfel*, Russian *yabloko*, Welsh *afal* and Irish *úll* (earlier *abhall*), and the Roman town of Abella (now Avella) in Campania, Italy, was said by Virgil to be so named because it looked over apple trees (*et quos maliferae despectant moinia Abellae*) (*Aeneid*, vii, 740 (1st century BC)). The apple also appears more than once in Greek legend. *See also* ADAM'S APPLE; APPLE OF DISCORD; ATALANTA; AVALON; BIG APPLE; HESPERIDES.

There is no mention of an apple in the Bible story of EVE's temptation. She took 'the fruit of the tree which is in the midst of the garden' (Genesis 3:3).

For the story of William Tell and the apple *see under* TELL.

**Apple a day keeps the doctor away, An.** A popular notion that the inclusion of an apple in one's daily diet will ensure good health. The proverb is of 19th-century origin and has no particular medical backing. On the other hand, apples provide vitamins and fibre and certainly do the metabolism no harm.

**Apple charlotte.** A hot pudding made of fruit, typically apple, baked in a case of bread, sponge cake or the like, usually in a deep round mould. It was probably named after Queen Charlotte (1744–1818), wife of George III, who was a keen patron of apple growers. *See also* CHARLOTTE RUSSE.

**Apple Islanders, The.** A nickname for the inhabitants of Tasmania, who are also known as Tassies. Tasmania is popularly known as an apple-growing region.

**Applejack.** An apple turnover is sometimes so called in East Anglia. In the USA the name is that of a drink distilled from fermented apple juice, something like French Calvados.

**Apple-john.** An apple so called from its being mature about 24 June, St JOHN THE BAPTIST'S Day. The French call it *Pomme de Saint Jean*. Apple-johns are said to keep for two years, and to be at their best when shrivelled.

> I am withered like an old apple-john.
> SHAKESPEARE: *Henry IV, Pt I*, III, iii (1597)

**Apple of discord.** A cause of dispute, or bone of contention. At the marriage of THETIS and PELEUS, where all the gods and goddesses assembled, Discord (Eris), who had not been invited, threw on the table a golden apple inscribed 'For the Fairest'. HERA (JUNO), ATHENE (MINERVA) and APHRODITE (VENUS) put in their claims, and PARIS, as referee, gave judgement in favour of Aphrodite. This brought him the vengeance of Hera and Athene, so beginning a chain of events that led to the fall of TROY.

**Apple of one's eye, The.** The pupil, because it was formerly believed to be a round, solid ball like an apple. The phrase came to apply generally to any very precious or much loved person or thing.

> He kept him as the apple of his eye.
> Deuteronomy 32:10

**Apple-pie bed.** A bed in which the sheets are so folded that a person cannot lie at full length in it. The phrase is popularly derived from French *nappe pliée*, 'folded cloth'.

**Apple-pie order.** Perfect order. The origin of the phrase is uncertain. It has been popularly derived from *cap-à-pie*, 'head to foot', used of a person correctly dressed or armed.

**Apple-polishing.** An attempt to win favour by gifts or flattery. From the practice of American schoolchildren bringing shiny red apples to their teachers.

**Apples and pears.** RHYMING SLANG for 'stairs'.

**Apples of Iduna.** *See* IDUNA.

**Apples of Paradise.** According to tradition apples in the Garden of EDEN had a bite on one side, to commemorate that taken by EVE.

**Apples of perpetual youth.** *See* IDUNA.

**Apples of Sodom.** Possibly the *madar* or *oschur* (*Caloptris procera*). The fruit of trees reputed to grow on the shores of the DEAD SEA 'which bear lovely fruit, but within are full of ashes'. JOSEPHUS, Strabo and Tacitus refer to them.

**Apple Tree Gang.** The name given to John Reid and his Scottish friends, who introduced golf into the USA in 1888, at Yonkers, New York. The name was coined in 1892 when they moved to their third 'course' at Yonkers, a 34-acre (13.75-hectare) orchard which yielded six holes.

**Adam's apple.** *See under* ADAM.

**As sure as God made little apples.** *See* AS.

**Big Apple, The.** *See under* BIG.

**Bob for apples, To.** *See under* BOB.

**Devil's apple.** *See under* DEVIL.

**Golden apple.** *See under* GOLDEN.

**Isle of Apples.** *See* AVALON.

**Love apple.** *See under* LOVE.

**Newton and the apple.** *See under* NEWTON.

**Prince Ahmed's apple.** *See under* PRINCE.

**Punic apple.** *See under* PUNIC.

**Upset the applecart, To.** *See under* UPSET.

**Appointment, By.** *See under* BY.

**Après moi le déluge** (French, 'After me the deluge'). Madame de Pompadour (1721–64), mistress of Louis XV, is reputed to have remarked to her lover, *Après nous le déluge*, following the defeat of the French and Austrian armies by Frederick the Great in the Battle of Rossbach (1757). Metternich (1773–1859), the Austrian statesman, also used the expression, meaning that the existing order would collapse when his guiding hand was removed.

**April** (popularly from Latin *aperire*, 'to open', but probably of Etruscan origin). The month when trees unfold and the earth opens with new life. Its Old English name was *Eastermōnath*, 'EASTER month'. In the FRENCH REVOLUTIONARY CALENDAR it largely coincided with Germinal, the time of germinating or budding (22 March to 20 April).

**April fool.** A person fooled or tricked on All Fools' Day (1 April), called in France *un poisson d'avril*, and in Scotland a *gowk* (cuckoo). In India similar tricks are played at the Holi Festival (31 March), so that it cannot refer to the uncertainty of the weather nor yet to a mockery of the trial of Christ, as two popular explanations claim. A better solution is that, as 25 March used to be NEW YEAR'S DAY, 1 April was its octave, when its festivities climaxed and concluded.

Another account refers to the Roman CEREALIA, held at the beginning of April. The story is that PROSERPINA was sporting in the Elysian meadows and had just filled her lap with daffodils, when PLUTO carried her off to the lower world. Her mother, CERES, heard the echo of her screams, and went in search of the echo. Her search, however, was a fool's errand.

In modern times the fooling itself has ranged from homely pranks such as telling someone a shoelace is undone to elaborate impersonations and spurious announcements in the news media. Children generally accept that their licence to play tricks expires at noon, but adults take the whole day and may mark the occasion by arranging the delivery of a kissogram or some similar embarrassment.

**Apron** (Old French *naperon*, 'little cloth'). The word was originally 'napron' in English, and it is representative of many words that have either lost or gained an n through a misapplication of the indefinite article 'a' or 'an'. 'A napron' thus became 'an apron'. Other examples are 'an adder' for 'a nadder', 'an auger' for 'a nauger' and 'an umpire' for 'a numpire'. The opposite formation may be seen in 'a newt' for 'an ewt', 'a nickname' for 'an ekename', and the obsolete 'nuncle' for 'mine uncle'. *See also* NICKNAME; NONCE.

**Tied to one's mother's apron strings, To be.** *See under* TIE.

**Aqua. Aqua fortis** (Latin, 'strong water'). Nitric acid.

**Aqua Libra** (Latin, 'water balance'). The proprietary name for a soft drink based on a mixture of mineral water and fruit juices with herbal and other flavourings. It was first sold in the 1980s and is promoted as an aid to good digestion and alkaline balance.

**Aqua regia** (Latin, 'royal water'). A mixture usually of one part concentrated nitric acid with three parts concentrated hydrochloric acid, so called because it dissolves GOLD, the king of metals.

**Aqua tofana.** A poisonous liquid containing arsenic, much used in Italy in the 18th century by young wives who wanted to get rid of their husbands. It was invented about 1690 by a Greek woman named Tofana, who called it the MANNA of St Nicholas of Bari, from a popular notion that an oil of miraculous efficacy flowed from the tomb of that saint.

**Aqua vitae** (Latin, 'water of life'). Brandy or distilled spirits. Aquavit, EAU DE VIE, whisky and the Irish USQUEBAUGH have the same meaning. The name was also used for certain ardent spirits employed by alchemists. Ben Jonson calls a vendor of one such an 'acquavitae man' (*Alchemist*, I, i (1612)). The ELIXIR OF LIFE was made from distilled spirits.

**Aquarius** (Latin, 'water carrier'). The eleventh sign of the ZODIAC (21 January to 18 February). Its symbol is a man pouring water from a vessel, its sign ≈ representing a stream of water.

**Age of Aquarius.** *See under* AGE.

**Aquiline** ('like an eagle'). Raymond's steed, bred on the banks of the Tagus (Tasso, *Jerusalem Delivered* (1580)).

**Aquinas, St Thomas.** *See under* THOMAS.

**Aquinian Sage, The.** Juvenal is so called because he was born at Aquinum, a town of the Volscians, in Latium.

**Arab, Street.** *See under* STREET.

**Arabesque** (Italian *arabesco*, 'in the Arabic style'). A term used in ballet, music and the arts. In ballet it denotes a classical position in which the dancer has one leg raised to the rear and both arms stretched out in a conventional pose. In music it is a piece with an ornamental or decorated melody. In art it is a curvilinear decoration with an intricate design.

The original Moorish Arabesque (now usually called Moresque, Alhambresque or Saracenic) did not permit the representation of natural objects.

**Arabia.** It was Ptolemy who devised the threefold division of the land into Arabia Petraea ('Rocky Arabia'), for the northwestern part, including the Sinai Peninsula, Arabia Felix ('Fruitful Arabia'), for the main part of the Arabian Peninsula, and Arabia Deserta ('Desert Arabia'), for the northern part between Syria and MESOPOTAMIA.

**Arabian bird, The.** The PHOENIX, and hence, figuratively, a marvellous or unique person.

> All of her that is out of door most rich!
> If she be furnish'd with a mind so rare,
> She is alone the Arabian bird.
> SHAKESPEARE: *Cymbeline*, I, vi (1609)

**Arabian Nights Entertainments** or **Thousand and One Nights, The.** These ancient Oriental tales were first introduced into western Europe in a French translation by Antoine Galland (12 volumes, 1704–17), derived from an Egyptian text probably of 14th- or 15th-century origin. English translations based on Galland were made by R. Heron (1792) and W. Beloe (1795). The later English translations by Henry Torrens (1838), E.W. Lane (1839–41), John Payne (1882–4), and Sir Richard Burton's unexpurgated edition published at Benares (16 volumes, 1885–8) are based on a late 18th-century Egyptian text. The standard French translation (1899–1904) by J.-C.-V. Mardrus has been severely criticized.

The basis of the tales is that they were told nightly by SCHEHERAZADE, bride of Sultan Schahriah, to stave off her execution. *See also* ALADDIN; ALI BABA; SINBAD THE SAILOR.

**Arabic numerals.** The numbers 0, 1, 2, 3, 4 etc, so called because they were introduced to Europe by the Arabs, who brought them from India. They were familiar in Europe by the 12th century but did not generally supersede the Roman numerals (I, II, III, IV etc) until the 16th century. The cipher or nought was an immensely valuable gain, and the introduction of place value made possible a decimal system, with the numbers to the left of the point increasing by tens and those to the right decreasing correspondingly. *See also* NUMBERS.

**Darley Arabian.** *See under* DARLEY.

**Saudi Arabia.** *See under* SAUDI.

**Street Arab.** *See under* STREET.

**Arachne** (Greek *arakhnē*, 'spider'). The story is that Arachne, a young Lydian girl, challenged ATHENE to a weaving contest and hanged herself when the goddess destroyed what she had woven. Athene then changed her into a spider. Hence Arachnida, the scientific name for the class including spiders, scorpions, ticks, mites and harvestmen. 'Arachne's labours' are those of spinning and weaving.

**Aragon, Catherine of.** *See under* CATHERINE.

**Aram, Eugene.** A schoolmaster (1704–59) of considerable learning who, while at Knaresborough in Yorkshire, was involved with one Daniel Clark in a series of frauds. He murdered Clark in 1745 but was not found out until 1758, when he was teaching at King's Lynn. He was executed on 6 August 1759. A competent scholar in Latin, Greek, Hebrew and other languages, his story is told in Thomas Hood's poem *The Dream of Eugene Aram* (1831), and Lord Lytton's novel *Eugene Aram* (1832).

**Arawn.** King of ANNWN.

**Arbor Day** (Latin *arbor*, 'tree'). A day set apart in Canada, the United States and New Zealand for planting trees, first observed in 1872 in Nebraska, where it became a legal holiday in 1885. The date varies according to the locality. In Nebraska it is usually 22 April.

**Arcades ambo.** A phrase from Virgil's seventh ECLOGUE: *Ambo florentes aetatibus, Arcades ambo* ('Both in the flower of youth, Arcadians both'), meaning 'both poets or musicians', now extended to two persons having tastes or habits in common. Byron gave the phrase a whimsical turn:

> Each pulled different ways with many an oath,
> 'Arcades ambo' – *id est*, blackguards both.
> *Don Juan*, iv (1819–24)

*See also* ARCADIA.

**Arcadia.** A district of the Peloponnesus named after Arcas, son of JUPITER, chiefly inhabited by shepherds. It is also the abode of PAN. According to Virgil it was the home of pastoral simplicity and happiness. The name was used by Sir Philip Sidney for the title of his prose romance (1590) and it soon became a byword for rustic bliss.

**Et in Arcadia ego.** *See under* ET.

**Arcas.** *See* CALLISTO AND ARCAS.

**Arch. Arch of Titus, The.** The arch built in ROME in commemoration of the capture of JERUSALEM (AD 70) by Titus and his father Vespasian. Titus became emperor in AD 79. The arch is richly sculptured, and the trophies taken at the destruction of the temple are shown in relief.

**Court of Arches.** *See under* COURT.

**Dean of the Arches.** *See under* DEAN.

**Marble Arch.** *See under* MARBLE.

**Trajan's Arch.** *See under* TRAJAN.

**Archangel.** In Christian stories the title is usually given to MICHAEL, the chief opponent of SATAN and his angels, and to GABRIEL, RAPHAEL, URIEL, Chamuel, Jophiel and ZADKIEL. *See also* ANGEL.

According to the Koran there are four archangels: Gabriel, the angel of revelations, who writes down the divine decrees; Michael, the champion, who fights the battle of faith; AZRAEL, the angel of death; and ISRAFEL, who is commissioned to sound the trumpet of the resurrection.

**Archbishop Parker's table.** The table of prohibited degrees within which marriage was forbidden, published in 1563 and to be found as the Table of Kindred and Affinity in the BOOK OF COMMON PRAYER. Matthew Parker was archbishop of Canterbury from 1559 to 1575. *See also* NAG'S HEAD CONSECRATION; VESTIARIAN CONTROVERSY.

**Archers.** The best known archers in British legend are ROBIN HOOD and his two companions LITTLE JOHN and Will SCARLET.

The famous archers of Henry II were Tepus, his bowman of the guards, Gilbert of the white hind, Hubert of Suffolk and Clifton of Hampshire. Nearly equal to these were Egbert of Kent, William of Southampton and CLYM OF THE CLOUGH.

The Roman Emperor Domitian was said to be able to shoot four arrows between the spread of the fingers of a man's hand.

The story of William TELL reproduces the Scandinavian tale of EGIL, who at the command of King Nidung performed a precisely similar feat.

**Archeus** (Greek *arkhaios*, 'original'). According to PARACELSUS the immaterial principle that energizes all living substances. There were supposed to be numerous *archei*, with the chief one residing in the stomach.

**Archies.** In the First World War anti-aircraft guns and batteries were thus nicknamed, probably from the popular MUSIC HALL song 'Archibald, certainly not' (1909).

**Archilochian bitterness.** Ill-natured satire or bitter mockery, so named from Archilochus, a Greek satirical poet (*fl.*7th century BC).

**Archimago** (pseudo-Italian, 'chief magician'). The great enchanter in Edmund Spenser's *The Faerie Queene* (I and II (1590)), typifying hypocrisy.

**Archimedes. Archimedes' principle.** The apparent loss in weight of a body immersed in liquid will equal the weight of the displaced liquid. This discovery was made by Archimedes of Syracuse (*c.*287–212 BC). *See also* EUREKA.

**Archimedes' screw.** A flexible tube twisted spirally round an axis, said to have been invented by Archimedes while in Egypt, as a method of irrigation. A carpenter's auger is designed on the same principle. Later it became a spiral screw contained in a close-fitting cylindrical case.

**Architecture. Flamboyant architecture.** *See under* FLAMBOYANT.

**Gothic architecture.** *See under* GOTHIC.

**Roman architecture.** *See under* ROMAN.

**Romanesque architecture.** *See under* ROMANESQUE.

**Archon** (Greek *arkhōn*, 'ruler'). Chief of the nine magistrates of ancient ATHENS. The next in rank was called Basileus.

**Arcite.** A Theban knight made captive by Duke THESEUS, and imprisoned with Palamon at ATHENS. Both captives fell in love with Emily, the duke's sister (or daughter in some versions), and she, having secured their release, was promised by the duke to whichever should be the victor in a tournament. Arcite won, but was thrown from his horse and killed when riding to receive his prize. Emily thus became the bride of Palamon. Chaucer, in 'The Knight's Tale' (*c*.1387), borrowed the story from Boccaccio's *Teseide* (1341), and it is told by John Fletcher in his *Two Noble Kinsmen* (1634) and by John Dryden in his *Fables* (1699).

**Arcos barbs.** War steeds of Arcos, in Andalusia, often mentioned in Spanish ballads. *See also* BARB.

**Arctic** (Greek *arktikos*, 'northern'). The Greek word that gave the name of the northern polar region itself derives from *arktos*, 'bear', referring to the constellation of the GREAT BEAR (URSA MAJOR), which lies over it. The same word lies behind the name of the star Arcturus (Greek *arktos*, 'bear', and *ouros*, 'keeper'). This, the brightest star in the constellation BOÖTES and one of the most magnificent in the northern hemisphere, can be found by following the curve of the Great Bear's tail. In the Bible, Arcturus is used for the Great Bear itself.

> Canst thou bring forth Mazzaroth in his season? or canst thou guide Arcturus with his sons?
> Job 38:32

The Antarctic (Greek *anti*, 'opposite', and *arktikos*, 'northern') is thus the southern polar region, opposite the Arctic.

**Arden. Arden of Feversham.** A play (printed in 1592) once attributed to Shakespeare and possibly written by Thomas Kyd (1558–94), based on the murder in 1551 of Thomas Arden, mayor of Faversham, Kent. Alice Arden plans the murder with the aid of two ruffians, who rush in on the signal 'Now I take you', when her husband and her lover, Mosbie (or Mosby), are playing draughts.

George Lillo's play of this name was completed after his death (1736) by Dr John Hoadly and acted in 1759.

**Enoch Arden.** The story in Tennyson's poem of this name (1864), of a husband who mysteriously and unwillingly disappears and returns years later to find that his wife (who still treasures his memory) is married to another, is not an uncommon theme. It is reminiscent of Crabbe's 'The Parting Hour' (No. 2 in *Tales in Verse* (1812)), and a similar story appeared in Adelaide Anne Procter's 'Homeward Bound' (in her *Legends and Lyrics*, 1858).

**Forest of Arden.** *See under* FOREST.

**Ardennes, The wild boar of the.** *See under* WILD.

**Ard Ri** (Irish, 'high king'). The seat of the Ard Ri (high kings) of Ireland was at Tara in County Meath. According to the ancient lists, Slaigne the Firbolg was the first high king, and from the time of his accession until AD 1 there were 107 high kings, including 9 Firbolg, 9 Dé Danaan and 80 MILESIANS. From AD 1 there were 83 high kings, the first being Conaire Mór and the last Ruaraidh Ó CONCHOBAR (1161–98).

**Area, Grey.** *See under* GREY.

**Areopagus** (Greek *Areios pagos*, 'hill of Ares'). A hill to the northwest of the Acropolis in ATHENS, the seat of a famous tribunal. It is so called from the tradition that MARS (ARES) was tried there for causing the death of NEPTUNE's son Halirrhothius, who had raped Ares' daughter at this spot.

**Ares** (perhaps Greek *arrēn*, 'male'). The Greek god of war, son of ZEUS and HERA and identified with the Roman MARS.

**Arethusa.** *See* ALPHEUS AND ARETHUSA.

**Aretinian syllables.** Ut, re, mi, fa, sol and la, which were used by Guido d'Arezzo or Aretino in the 11th century for his hexachord or scale of six notes. These names were taken from a Latin hymn by Paulus Diaconus, addressed to St JOHN THE BAPTIST, which Guido used in teaching singing:

> Ut queant laxis resonare fibris,
> Mira gestorum famuli tuorum,
> Solve polluti labii reatum.
> (Uttered by the wondrous story,
> Reprehensive though I be,
> Me make mindful of thy glory,
> Famous son of Zacharee;
> Solace to my spirit bring,
> Labouring thy praise to sing.)
> E.C. BREWER

Si was added in the 16th century, and do or doh (perhaps from *dominus*, 'lord') took the place of ut in the 17th century. In England te replaced si in the 19th century. In the USA either ti or si is used. *See also* GAMUT; TONIC SOL-FA.

**Argan** (perhaps from Greek *arguros*, 'silver', 'money', French *argent*). The principal character in Molière's *Le Malade Imaginaire* (1673), a hypochondriac, uncertain whether to think more of his ailments or of his purse.

**Argentina** or **Argentine, The** (Spanish *argento*, 'silver'). This South American republic, the 'Silver Republic', takes its name from the silver ornaments worn by the indigenous inhabitants at the time of its exploration by the Italian-born Spanish navigator Sebastian Cabot in 1526. They lived along the banks of a great river, which Cabot accordingly named Rio de la Plata, 'river of silver'. The 'river' subsequently turned out to be the estuary of the Paraná and the Uruguay.

**Argo** (Greek *argos*, 'swift'). The galley of JASON in which he sailed in search of the GOLDEN FLEECE and finally succeeded with the help of MEDEA. Hence a sailing ship on any particularly adventurous voyage.

The name is also that of a southern constellation (the Ship).

**Argonauts.** The sailors of the ship ARGO, who sailed from Iolcos to Colchis in quest of the Golden Fleece. Apollonius of Rhodes wrote an epic poem, *Argonautica* (3rd century BC), on the subject. The name is also given to the paper nautilus, the cephalopod mollusc *Argonauta argo*.

**Argosy.** A merchant ship. The word is a corruption of Italian *Ragusea nave*, 'ship of Ragusa'. Large merchant ships were built and sailed from Ragusa in Dalmatia (now Dubrovnik in Croatia).

> He hath an argosy bound to Tripolis, another to the Indies ... a third at Mexico, a fourth for England.
> SHAKESPEARE: *The Merchant of Venice*, I, iii (1596)

**Argue. Argue the toss, To.** To dispute a decision already made. Once the coin has been tossed, with the result for all to see, there is no point in disputing the throw.

**Argument of silence, The** (Latin *argumentum e silentio*). The conclusion that, if the works of an author omit all reference to a particular subject, the writer was unaware of it.

**Sledgehammer argument, A.** *See under* SLEDGEHAMMER.

**Argus** (probably Greek *argos*, 'shining', 'white'). According to Grecian fable the giant Argus had 100 eyes, and JUNO set him to watch IO, of whom she was jealous. MERCURY, however, charmed him to sleep with his lyre and slew him. Juno then set the eyes of Argus on the peacock's tail. *See also* PEACOCK'S FEATHER.

**Argus-eyed, To be.** To be be keen-sighted or vigilant.

**Argyle, God bless the Duke of.** *See under* GOD.

**Ariadne** (Greek *ari-*, intensive prefix, and *adnos*, 'holy'). In Greek mythology daughter of the Cretan king, MINOS. She helped THESEUS to escape from the LABYRINTH and later went with him to Naxos where he deserted her. Here, Dionysus found her and married her.

**Arians.** The followers of Arius, a presbyter of the church of Alexandria in the 4th century. He maintained that: (1) the Father and Son are distinct beings; (2) the Son, though divine, is not equal to the Father; (3) the Son had a state of existence prior to His appearance on earth, but not from eternity; and (4) the MESSIAH was not real man, but a divine being in a veil of flesh. The heresy was condemned by the COUNCIL OF NICAEA (325), which upheld the orthodox view of Athanasius that the Son was 'of the same substance' with the Father.

**Ariel** (Hebrew *ari'el*, 'lion of God'). In Isaiah 29: 1–7 the name is applied to JERUSALEM. In astronomy Ariel is a satellite of URANUS. In demonology and literature he is a spirit. Thus Ariel is one of the seven angelic 'princes' in Thomas Heywood's *Hierarchie of the Blessed Angels* (1635), one of the rebel angels in Milton's *Paradise Lost* (vi (1667)) and a SYLPH, the guardian of Belinda, in Alexander Pope's *The Rape of the Lock* (1712). The name is best known, however, as that of 'an ayrie spirit' in Shakespeare's *The Tempest* (1611). According to the play Ariel was enslaved to the witch Sycorax (I, ii) who overtasked him, and by way of punishment for not doing what was beyond his power, shut him up in the cleft of a pine tree for 12 years. On the death of Sycorax, Ariel became the slave of CALIBAN, who tortured him most cruelly. PROSPERO liberated him and was gratefully served by the fairy until he set Ariel free.

**Aries** (Latin, 'ram'). The RAM, as the first sign of the ZODIAC in which the sun is from 21 March to 19 April. The legend is that the ram with the GOLDEN FLEECE, which bore Phrixus and Helle on its back, was finally sacrificed to ZEUS, who set it in the heavens as a constellation.

**Arimanes.** Another form of AHRIMAN. Byron introduces him under this name in *Manfred* (1817), seated 'on a Globe of Fire, surrounded by the Spirits'.

**Arimaspians** (Greek *Arimaspoi*, according to Herodotus from Scythian *arima*, 'one', and *spou*, 'eye'). A one-eyed people of Scythia constantly at war with the GRIFFINS who guarded a hoard of gold. They are mentioned by Lucan (*Pharsalia*, iii (1st century AD)), Herodotus (*Histories*, iii; iv (5th century BC)), Pliny, Strabo and other writers. Rabelais (*Gargantua*, Bk IV, ch lvi (1548), and *Pantagruel*, Bk V, ch xxix (1562)) so names the peoples of northern Europe who had accepted the REFORMATION, the suggestion being that they had lost one eye: that of faith.

> As when a gryphon through the wilderness
> With winged course, o'er hill or moory dale,
> Pursues the Arimaspian, who by stealth
> Had from his wakeful custody purloin'd
> The guarded gold.
> MILTON: *Paradise Lost*, ii (1667)

**Arimathea, St Joseph of.** *See under* JOSEPH.

**Arioch.** The name, which means 'a fierce lion', was used for one of the fallen angels in *Paradise Lost* (vi (1667)). Milton took it from Daniel 2:14, where it is the name of the captain of the guard.

**Arion** (perhaps from Greek *Arēs*, 'Ares', or Hebrew *arī*, 'lion').

(1) A Greek poet and musician (7th century BC) reputed to have been cast into the sea by mariners but carried to Taenaros on a dolphin's back.

(2) HERCULES' horse, given to ADRASTUS. It earlier belonged to NEPTUNE, who brought it out of the ground by striking it with his trident. Its right feet were those of a man. It spoke with a human voice and ran with incredible swiftness.

**Ariosto. Ariosto of the North, The.** So Byron called Sir Walter Scott (*Childe Harold*, iv, 40 (1818)).

**Ludovico Ariosto.** Italian poet (1474–1533), the author of ORLANDO FURIOSO.

**Aristides** (Greek *aristos*, 'best', and *-idēs*, 'descendant of'). An Athenian statesman and general, surnamed 'the Just' (*c*.520–*c*.468 BC), who took part in the Battles of MARATHON and Salamis, and was in command at Plataea.

**British Aristides, The.** Andrew Marvell (1621–78), poet and satirist.

**French Aristides, The.** Jules Grévy (1807–91), president of the THIRD REPUBLIC (1879–87), a barrister by profession.

**Aristophanes** (Greek *aristos*, 'best', and *phainō*, 'I bring to light', 'I make appear'). The great Athenian comic dramatist (*c*.450–*c*.385 BC).

**English** or **Modern Aristophanes, The.** Samuel Foote (1722–77), the author of *The Mayor of Garret* (1764).

**French Aristophanes, The.** MOLIÈRE (Jean Baptiste Poquelin) (1622–73).

**Aristotle** (Greek *aristos*, 'best', and *telos*, 'aim', 'end'). The great Greek philosopher (384–222 BC), pupil of PLATO and founder of the PERIPATETIC SCHOOL.

**Aristotelian philosophy.** Aristotle maintained that four separate causes are necessary before anything exists: the formal cause, the material cause, the moving cause and the final cause. The first is the essence and heart of existence, causing any thing to be what it is. The second is matter and its subordinate, that from which the thing arises. The third is that which moves the thing or causes it to assume a particular form. The fourth cause is that for which a thing exists.

**Aristotelian unities.** *See* DRAMATIC UNITIES.

**Ark. Ark of the Covenant, The.** The sacred box made of shittim wood covered with gold that was borne by the Hebrews in their journey in the desert. Its lid, the 'mercy seat', was of solid gold and had two cherubs with outstretched wings. It contained the tablets of the Law (Deuteronomy 10:2), a pot of MANNA and Aaron's rod (Hebrews 9:4), and was the focal point of the presence of God. It was kept at Shiloh until it was captured by the PHILISTINES and set up in their temple at Ashdod. It eventually found a resting-place in the TEMPLE OF SOLOMON, where it remained until the fall of JERUSALEM, when (2 Maccabees 2) Jeremiah hid it in a cave until God should gather his people again. By New Testament times it no longer existed (Hebrews 9:4–5).

**Noah's ark.** *See under* NOAH.

**Arlington Cemetery.** The Arlington National Cemetery, named after the suburb of Washington, D.C., in which it is located, is essentially the official cemetery of the USA and the resting place of outstanding military leaders and statesmen. The first soldier buried here, in 1864, was a Confederate prisoner who had died in a local hospital. Famous figures to be interred in the cemetery include General Pershing, Admiral Byrd, Senator Taft, President John F. Kennedy and Senator Robert F. Kennedy. The Tomb of the Unknown Soldier is also located here. *See also* UNKNOWN WARRIOR.

**Arm** or **arms.** This word can mean either the limb (from Old English *arm*) or the weapon (from Latin plural *arma*). It is almost always used in the plural when denoting weapons and also in heraldic usage. Some of the better known phrases are:

**Arm and a leg, An.** A large sum of money, as if worth two of one's four limbs.

**Armed to the teeth.** So fully armed, that one is even carrying a weapon in one's teeth.

**Arm in arm.** With one arm interlinked with that of a person beside one, thereby indicating affection.

**Arm of the sea.** A narrow inlet.

**Adoption by arms.** *See under* ADOPTION.

**Appeal to arms, To.** *See under* APPEAL.

**As long as your arm.** *See under* AS.

**At arm's length.** *See under* AT.

**Babe in arms, A.** *See under* BABE.

**Bear arms, To.** *See under* BEAR.

**Call to arms, To.** *See under* CALL.

**Canting arms.** *See under* CANT.

**Chance one's arm, To.** *See under* CHANCE.

**Coat of arms.** *See under* COAT.

**King of Arms.** *See* HERALD.

**Lay down arms, To.** *See under* LAY.

**Long arm of the law, The.** *See under* LONG.

**Make a long arm, To.** *See under* LONG.

**Right to bear arms, The.** *See under* RIGHT.

**Royal Arms of England, The.** *See under* ROYAL.

**Secular arm.** *See under* SECULAR.

**Shot in the arm, A.** *See under* SHOT.

**Small arms.** *See under* SMALL.

**To arms!** *See under* TO.

**Twist someone's arm, To.** *See under* TWIST.

**Under arms.** *See under* UNDER.

**Up in arms.** *See under* UP.

**Within arm's reach.** *See under* WITHIN.

**With open arms.** *See under* WITH.

**Armageddon** (Hebrew *har meggidōn*, 'mountain district of Megiddo'). The name given in the APOCALYPSE (Revelation 16:16) to the site of the last great 'battle of that great day of God almighty' between the forces of good and evil. Megiddo, in northern Palestine, is the site of various battles described in the Old Testament. Hence any great battle or scene of slaughter.

**Armchair critic.** A person who expresses critical views from the comfort of an armchair, especially when taking no active part in the matter concerned, or having no firsthand knowledge of it. A BACK-SEAT DRIVER is somewhat similar. *See also* STOP-WATCH CRITICS.

**Armenteers, Mademoiselle from.** *See under* MADEMOISELLE.

**Armida.** An enchantress in Tasso's JERUSALEM DELIVERED (1580–8). RINALDO became enslaved by her and wasted much time in voluptuous pleasure with her. When he finally escaped from her, Armida followed him, but being unable to lure him back, set fire to her palace, rushed into combat and was slain. Armida's palace and gardens were so luxurious and splendid that the gardens of Armida became a synonym for gorgeous luxury.

In 1806 Frederick William III of Prussia declared war on Napoleon, and his young queen rode about in military costume to arouse popular enthusiasm. When Napoleon was told of it, he said: 'She is Armida, in her distraction setting fire to her own palace.'

**Arminians.** Followers of Jacobus Hermansen or Arminius (1560–1609), anti-Calvinist theologian and professor at Leiden. They asserted that God bestows forgiveness and eternal life on all who repent and believe, that He wills all men to be saved and that His predestination is founded on His foreknowledge. His Dutch followers came to be called Remonstrants after their 'remonstrance' of 1610 embodying their five points of difference from orthodox CALVINISM. In England the name was applied to the supporters of William Laud, archbishop of Canterbury (1633–45).

**Armistice Day.** 11 November, the day set aside to commemorate the fallen in the First World War, marked by a TWO-MINUTE SILENCE at 11 am and religious ceremonies. The armistice ending the war came into effect at 11 am on 11 November 1918. In 1946 the name was changed to REMEMBRANCE DAY. In the USA and Canada 11 November is a legal holiday, its name being changed to Veterans' Day in 1954. *See also* AT THE ELEVENTH HOUR.

**Armoises, Jehanne des.** A Frenchwoman who from 1436 to 1439 claimed to be JOAN OF ARC (1412–31), assuming, as many did, that the latter had not actually been burned at the stake. She was the wife of Robert des Armoises (or des Harmoises or des Ermoises), Seigneur of Tichimont, whose noble family bore as its device the plant artemisia (French *armoise*). Her claim seems implausible, if only because it is unlikely that a nobleman should marry an adventuress of this kind. However, she was acknowledged to be the Maid of Orleans by so many members of the contemporary aristocracy that any imposture on her part would have been hard to sustain.

The descendants of a collateral branch of her family exist today under the name de Sermoise, which is the same name but with a break before the first s instead of after.

**Armory.** The old name for HERALDRY, the word originally used to describe arms, military equipment and their employment.

**Armoury** or **armory.** The place where armour and arms are kept. It may also mean armour collectively, as in *Paradise Lost* (iv (1667)):

> but nigh at hand
> Celestial armoury, shields, helms, and spears,
> Hung high with diamond flaming and with gold.

**Army. Army marches on its stomach, An.** The troops need to be well provisioned if they are to be fighting fit. The saying has been attributed to Napoleon and Frederick the Great, among others.

**Barmy army.** *See under* BARMY.
**Church Army.** *See under* CHURCH.
**Dad's Army.** *See under* DAD.
**New Model Army.** *See under* NEW.
**Popski's Private Army.** *See under* POPSKI.
**Red Army.** *See under* RED.
**Sally Army.** *See* SALVATION ARMY.
**Salvation Army.** *See under* SALVATION.
**Tartan army.** *See under* TARTAN.

**Arnhem, Mary of.** *See under* MARY.

**Arnold of Rugby.** Dr Thomas Arnold (1795–1842), father of the poet Matthew Arnold, and famous headmaster and reformer of Rugby, portrayed as 'The Doctor' in *Tom Brown's Schooldays* (1857) by Thomas Hughes. His avowed aim in education was 'if possible to form Christian men, for Christian boys I can scarcely hope to make'.

> A shudder ran through the whole form, and the Doctor's wrath fairly boiled over; he made three steps up to the construer, and gave him a good box on the ear.
>
> Pt I, ch viii

**Aroint thee.** Get ye gone, be off. The phrase occurs in Shakespeare's *Macbeth* (I, iii (1605)) and *King Lear* (III, iv (1605)), on both occasions in connection with witches. The origin of 'aroint' is unknown. The Brownings used the word in their poetry: Elizabeth Barrett Browning in 'To Flush' (1850) – 'Whiskered cats arointed flee' – and Robert Browning in 'The Two Poets of Croisic' (1878) – 'That Humbug, whom thy soul aroints'.

**Arondight.** The sword of Sir LANCELOT OF THE LAKE.

**Arras.** A tapestry, so called from Arras in Artois, once famed for its manufacture. When rooms were hung with tapestry it was easy for a person to hide behind it. It was thus that Hubert hid the two villains who were to put out Arthur's eyes (Shakespeare, *King John*, IV, i (1596)). POLONIUS was slain by Hamlet while concealed behind the arras (*Hamlet*, III, iv (1600)), and FALSTAFF hid behind it in Ford's house (*The Merry Wives of Windsor*, III, iii (1600)).

**Arrière. Arrière-ban.** *See under* LEVER.

**Arrière-pensée** (French, 'behind thought'). An unrevealed thought, or a hidden or reserved motive.

**Arrow. Arrow of Acestes.** In a trial of skill Acestes, the Sicilian, shot his arrow with such force that it took fire (*Aeneid*, v (1st century BC)).

**Broad arrow.** *See under* BROAD.

**Devil's Arrows, The.** *See under* DEVIL.

**Elf arrows.** *See under* ELF.

**Golden Arrow.** *See under* GOLDEN.

**Arse. Duck's arse.** *See under* DUCK.

**Kiss my arse.** *See under* KISS.

**Art. Art deco.** A decorative style in painting, glass, pottery, silverware, furniture, architecture and the like, at its height in the 1930s. It is distinguished by bold colours, geometrical shapes, stylized natural forms and symmetrical designs. The name is a shortened form of French *art décoratif*, 'decorative art', from the *Exposition des arts décoratifs* held in Paris in 1925.

**Art nouveau** (French, 'new art'). A decorative style of art and architecture of the 1890s, characterized by stylized natural forms, such as flowers and leaves, and by the use of swelling, sinuous curves.

**Art trouvé** (French, 'found art'). Art that is not the direct creation of the artist but adapted from 'found' or natural objects, which have been primarily shaped by circumstances, nature and the elements. Items found on the seashore, such as shells, are ready examples of the raw material of *art trouvé*.

**Art Union.** Originally, in Europe and Britain, an association formed to promote art by purchasing paintings and other works of art and dispersing them among the membership by lottery. In Australia and New Zealand, after a while, all kinds of prizes were offered and consequently the name came to be applied to a lottery with money prizes.

**Black art, The.** *See under* BLACK.

**Byzantine art.** *See under* BYZANTINE.

**Degrees in Arts.** *See under* DEGREE.

**Fine arts, The.** *See under* FINE.

**Artaxerxes** (Old Persian *artakhshtrā*, 'powerful ruler', from *arta*, 'powerful', and *khshtrā*, 'ruler', 'king'). The younger son of XERXES and king of the Persians (465–425 BC). He was called the long-handed (*Longimanus*) because his right hand was longer than his left. He is mentioned in the Bible in connection with his part in the restoration of Jerusalem after the Captivity (Ezra 4, 6, 7 and Nehemiah 2, 5, 8).

**Artegal** or **Arthegal, Sir.** The hero of Bk V of Edmund Spenser's *The Faerie Queene* (1596), lover of BRITOMART, to whom he was made known by means of a magic mirror. He is emblematic of Justice and in many of his deeds, such as the rescue of Irena (Ireland) from Grantorto, is based on Arthur, 14th Lord Grey de Wilton, who became lord deputy of Ireland in 1580 and Spenser's patron. *See also* ELIDURE.

**Artemis.** The Greek goddess identified by the Romans with the Italian goddess DIANA. She was said to be the daughter of ZEUS and LETO and the twin sister of APOLLO. She was a virgin huntress, associated with uncultivated places and wild animals, and was also a primitive birth-goddess. She brought natural death with her arrows. The biblical reference to the Temple of Diana of the Ephesians (Acts 19) is really to the Artemisium at Ephesus, one of the SEVEN WONDERS of the Ancient World. A statue of her there was covered all over with breasts to mark her connection with childbirth. Her name has been associated with Greek *artemia*, 'safety', 'soundness', alluding to her virginity.

**Artemus Ward.** *See under* WARD.

**Artesian State, The.** South Dakota, better known as the Coyote State. *See also* UNITED STATES OF AMERICA.

**Artful Dodger.** A young thief, adept in villainy and up to every sort of wicked dodge. Such was the character of Jack Dawkins, a member of FAGIN's gang, in Dickens' *Oliver Twist* (1837–8).

**Arthegal.** *See* ARTEGAL.

**Arthur** (probably from Celtic *art*, 'bear'). As a shadowy 'historical' figure, King Arthur is first mentioned under the Latin name Artorius in the late 7th-century *Historia Britonum* (usually known by the name of Nennius, its 9th-century editor). Arthur, as *Dux Bellorum*, not king, is said to have led the Britons against the Saxons in 12 great battles culminating in the great victory of *Mons Badonicus* (fought between 493 and 516). He is mentioned again by WILLIAM OF MALMESBURY (early 12th century), but ARTHURIAN ROMANCES owe most to Geoffrey of Monmouth.

A slate with a Latin inscription unearthed at TINTAGEL in 1998 was taken by some to prove Arthur's historicity. The wording was *Pater Coliavificit Artognov*, 'Artognou, father of a descendant of Coll, made this'. 'Artognou', probably pronounced 'Arthnou', was judged close enough to 'Arthur' to refer to the legendary warrior king. *See also* CAMELOT.

**Arthurian Romances.** The stories that have King Arthur as their central figure appear as early as 1136 in Geoffrey of Monmouth's mainly fabulous *Historia Regum Britanniae*, which purported to be a translation (in Latin) of an ancient Celtic history of Britain, lent to him by

Walter Map, archdeacon of Oxford. Geoffrey's *Historia* was dedicated to Robert, Earl of Gloucester, a natural son of Henry I. This was versified in French in Wace's *Roman de Brut* or *Brut d'Angleterre* (1155), which is the first to mention the ROUND TABLE. These were used by Layamon, the Worcestershire priest, whose BRUT (in English) was completed in about 1205, with additions such as the story of the fairies at Arthur's birth, who transported him to AVALON at his death. In France, in the late 12th century, Robert de Borron introduced the legend of the HOLY GRAIL and gave prominence to MERLIN. Chrétien de Troyes brought in the tale of ENID and GERAINT, the tragic loves of LANCELOT OF THE LAKE and GUINEVERE, the story of PERCEVAL and other material, which was probably drawn from Welsh sources including the MABINOGION. Thus Map and the Arthurian writers introduced the romantic spirit of CHIVALRY and courtly manners into European literature and King Arthur became the embodiment of the ideal Christian knight. Many other Welsh and Breton ballads, lays and romances popularized the legend. The whole corpus was collected and edited by Sir Thomas Malory (d.1471), whose great prose romance *Le Morte d'Arthur* was produced by Caxton in 1485. Tennyson's *Morte d'Arthur* (1842) and *Idylls of the King* (1855–85) were based on it. *See also* ALMESBURY; ARONDIGHT; ASTOLAT; BALIN; BAN; BATTLE OF CAMLAN; BEDIVERE; CAMELOT; DAGONET; DIAMOND JOUSTS; ELAINE; EXCALIBUR; GLASTONBURY; LAUNFAL; LYONESSE; MODRED; MORGAN LE FAY; TRISTRAM; YSOLDE.

**Arthur's Seat.** A hill overlooking Edinburgh from the East. The name is said to be a corruption of the Gaelic *Ard-na-said*, 'height of the arrows', from its suitability as a shooting ground. On the other hand, it may simply be a romantic invention, similar to 'Castle of Maidens' for Edinburgh Castle.

**Artichoke, Jerusalem.** *See under* JERUSALEM.

**Article. Five Articles of Perth, The.** *See under* FIVE.

**Leading article.** *See under* LEAD.

**Six Articles, The.** *See under* SIX.

**Thirty-nine Articles, The.** *See under* THIRTY.

**Arundel** (Old French *arondel*, 'swallow'). The horse of BEVIS OF HAMPTON, so named for its swiftness.

**Arundel marbles.** A collection of ancient sculptures made by Thomas Howard, 14th Earl of Arundel (1585–1646), and presented to Oxford University in 1667 by his grandson Henry, 6th Duke of Norfolk. They are in the ASHMOLEAN MUSEUM and include the *Marmor Chronicon* or *Parian Chronicle* (said to have been executed in the island of Paros *c.*263 BC), which recorded events in Greek history from 1582 to 264 BC, although now incomplete and ending at 354 BC.

**Arval brothers** (Latin *arvum*, 'ploughed field'). An ancient Roman college of priests, Fratres Arvales, revived by AUGUSTUS. It consisted of 12 priests (including the emperor), whose sole duty was to preside at the festival of Dea Dia in May. Ceremonies took place in Rome and in the grove of the goddess, who seems to be identical with Acca Larentia, goddess of cornfields. The priests were so called from the public sacrifices that they offered for the fertility of the fields.

**Aryans** (Sanskrit *ārya*, 'of noble birth'). A former name for the peoples supposedly descended from speakers of INDOEUROPEAN languages, especially speakers of an Iranian or Indic language in ancient times. Anti-Semitism prostituted the word, and it was used by the German NAZIS to denote any CAUCASIAN of non-Jewish descent, especially those of Nordic type.

**As. As a bear has no tail, for a lion he'll fail.** The same as *Ne sutor supra crepidam* ('let not the cobbler aspire above his last'). Robert Dudley, Earl of Leicester, a descendant of the Warwick family, is said to have changed his own crest (a green lion with two tails) for the Warwick bear and ragged staff. Given command of the expedition to the Netherlands (1585), he was suspected of wider ambitions when the Netherlanders granted him 'absolute authority' (1586). Because the lion is monarch among beasts, some wit wrote under his crest set up in public, *Ursa caret cauda non queat esse leo*, in other words:

> Your bear for lion needs must fail,
> Because your true bears have no tail.

**As a matter of course.** In the normal nature of things; as a regular part of the proceedings.

**As bald as a coot.** Completely bald. The common coot, a water bird, has a white bill and frontal shield which give the impression of baldness.

**As black as a crow.** Among the many similes used to denote blackness are: as black as a crow, a RAVEN, a raven's wing, ink, HELL, HADES, death, the grave, your hat, thunder, midnight, pitch, soot, tar.

**As black as your hat.** Quite black, black being a common colour for hats.

**As blind as a bat, beetle, mole or owl.** Blind, with very poor sight. None of these creatures is actually blind. The phrase is often used sarcastically of someone who cannot see what is under their nose.

**As bold as brass.** Impudent or immodest. A similar expression is BRAZEN-FACED.

**As bright as a button.** Alert; mentally quick. The origin was probably in the days when buttons were made of metal and, when new, were thus bright and conspicuous.

**As brown as a berry**. Said of a dark-skinned or tanned person or a brown-coated animal. The comparison is found in Chaucer:

> His palfrey was as brown as is a berry.
> *Canterbury Tales*, 'Prologue' (*c*.1387) (modern translation by Nevill Coghill, 1951)

**As busy as a bee**. Bees are noted for their industry. *See also* BUSY BEE.

**As clean as a whistle.** Very clean; untarnished. An earlier form of the phrase was 'as clear as a whistle', and this suggests the origin. But a whistle must even so be clean to sound a pure note.

**As clever** etc. **as they come.** The cleverest etc. there is.

**As cold as a paddock.** A paddock is a toad or frog.

> Here a little child I stand,
> Heaving up my either hand;
> Cold as paddocks though they be,
> Here I lift them up to Thee,
> For a benison to fall
> On our meat, and on us all. Amen.
> ROBERT HERRICK: 'Another Grace for a Child' (1647)

**As cold as charity.** An ironic expression, or a realistic one for the charity one expects but does not receive. In the past some charities gave aid grudgingly to the 'undeserving' poor without the warmth and compassion of Christian charity.

**As common as muck** or **as dirt.** Said disparagingly of a person regarded as lacking finesse or style.

**As cool as a cucumber.** Perfectly composed; not in the least angry or agitated. Cucumbers, with their high water content, are traditionally served in the summer as an antidote to the dryness and heat.

**As cross as a bear with a sore head** or **as two sticks.** Very cross or angry. A bear with a sore head will be very grumpy, and two sticks can be laid to form a cross.

**As daft as a brush.** Completely crazy; quite mad. The expression is said to have been adapted from the northern phrase 'as soft as a brush' by the comedian Ken Platt when entertaining troops in the Second World War.

**As dead as a dodo.** Long since dead and forgotten. The dodo was extinct by 1681.

**As dead as a doornail.** A doornail is either one of the heavy-headed nails with which large, outer doors used to be studded, or the knob on which the knocker strikes. As this is frequently knocked on the head, it cannot be supposed to have much life left in it. The expression is found in PIERS PLOWMAN (*c*.1367–70). Other well-known similes are 'as dead as the nail in a coffin' and Chaucer's 'as dead as stone'.

**As dead as mutton.** Absolutely dead. The reference is to mutton on the butcher's slab.

**As deaf as a beetle.** This does not refer to the insect but to the heavy wooden mallet used to level paving-stones or drive in stakes.

**As deaf as an adder.** 'Like the deaf adder that stoppeth her ear; which will not hearken to the voice of charmers, charming never so wisely' (Psalm 58:4–5). In the East if a viper entered the house, the charmer was sent for to entice the snake and put it into a bag. According to tradition the viper tried to stop its ears when the charmer uttered his incantation, by putting one ear to the ground and twisting its tail into the other.

**As deaf as a post.** Quite deaf, or so inattentive as not to hear what is said. One might as well speak to a doorpost or log of wood.

**As deaf as a white cat.** It is said that white cats are deaf and stupid.

**As different as chalk and cheese.** Quite unalike; differing completely, especially in essentials. Chalk and cheese may outwardly look alike but underneath they are entirely different. *See also* KNOW CHALK FROM CHEESE.

**As drunk as a lord.** The nobility of bygone days could afford to indulge in excessive drinking if they were so inclined. In the 18th and 19th centuries gross intoxication was common, and many men of fashion prided themselves on the number of bottles of wine they could consume at a sitting.

**As drunk as Davy's sow.** According to Francis Grose's *Classical Dictionary of the Vulgar Tongue* (1785), one David Lloyd, a Welshman who kept an alehouse at Hereford, had a sow with six legs, which was an object of great curiosity. One day David's wife, having indulged too freely, lay down in the sty to sleep, and a group came to see the sow. David led them to the sty saying as usual, 'There is a sow for you! Did you ever see the like?' One of the visitors replied: 'Well, it is the drunkenest sow I ever beheld.' The woman was ever after called 'Davy's sow'.

**As dull as ditchwater.** Boring and uninteresting, as applied to a person or activity. The allusion is to the dull and muddy water in ditches, with an implied contrast to the 'bright and clear' water of a running stream.

**As dry as a bone.** Quite dry, when expected to be damp or wet. It is hard to credit that dry bones once formed the framework of a living body composed largely of fluid.

**As dry as dust.** Dull and uninteresting. The phrase evokes the dusty pages of unread books.

**As easy as falling off a log.** Uncomplicated; readily done. It is hard to keep one's balance on a log.

**As easy as pie.** Agreeably uncomplicated. The reference is hardly to the making of a pie, which is not easy, but to the eating of one. A similar metaphor is a PIECE OF CAKE.

**As every schoolboy knows.** Said, often condescendingly or as a 'put-down', of something that is common knowledge, or that the speaker considers should be such. The expression is particularly associated with Macaulay, although recorded earlier.

> Every schoolboy knows who imprisoned
> Montezuma, and who strangled Atahualpa.
>
> THOMAS BABINGTON MACAULAY: 'Lord Clive' (1840)

**As fit as a fiddle.** In a very healthy condition; in excellent physical form. The allusion is probably to a street fiddler, who sways and swings about as he saws energetically with his bow.

**As flat as a pancake.** Quite flat.

**As free as air.** Quite free; without any hindrance. The image is of a bird flying free.

**As fresh as a daisy.** Bright and cheerful; reinvigorated. A daisy closes its petals at night but flowers anew every morning in the sun.

**As fussy as a hen with one chick.** Overanxious about small matters; overfussy. A hen with one chick is for ever clucking round it and never leaves it alone.

**As game as Ned Kelly.** The phrase refers to the noted Australian desperado and BUSHRANGER, Ned Kelly (1855–80), who, after a legendary career of crime, was captured in a suit of armour of his own making and hanged at Melbourne. He died bravely, his last words being: 'Such is life.'

**As generous as Hatim.** An Arabian expression. Hatim was a Bedouin chief famous for his warlike deeds and boundless generosity. His son was a contemporary of MOHAMMED.

> Let Zal and Rustum bluster as they will,
> Or Hatim call to supper – heed not you.
>
> EDWARD FITZGERALD: *Rubáiyát of Omar Khayyám*, x (1859)

**As good as.** Almost, virtually, as: 'We've as good as won already.'

**As good as gold.** Very good, very well behaved.

**As good as one's word.** Doing what one has promised to do. *See also* OF ONE'S WORD *under* WORD.

**As green as grass.** Naive; gullible; inexperienced. The alliterative words are in fact etymologically related.

**As happy as a sandboy.** Very happy. An old-established expression from the days when sandboys (or men) drove their donkeys through the streets hawking bags of sand, usually obtained from beaches. The sand was used by people for their gardens, by builders and by publicans for sanding their floors. The happiness of sandboys was due to their habit of indulging in liquor with their takings.

**As happy as Larry.** Very happy. An Australian expression. It is suggested that the original Larry may have been Larry Foley (1847–1917), the noted boxer, but the word may actually relate to LARRIKIN.

**As hard as nails.** Stern, hard-hearted, unsympathetic; in other words, able to stand hard blows like nails. The phrase is used in both a physical and a figurative sense, since a man in perfect training is 'as hard as nails', and bigotry and cynicism make people 'as hard as nails'.

**As high as a kite.** Drunk. The comparison is with the child's toy. 'High' in its sense of intoxicated alludes to the 'lift' given.

**As honest as the day is long.** Utterly dependable and reliable. The implication is that a person is always unfailingly honest.

**As hungry as a hunter.** Very hungry; famished. A hunter catches animals for food.

**As innocent as a lamb.** Naive; free of responsibility. A gambolling lamb seems to have not a care in the world and is ignorant of the fate the farmer has in store for it.

**As keen as mustard.** Very keen and enthusiastic. Mustard gives an 'edge' to the food it accompanies.

**As large as life.** Of the same size as the object represented; life-size, in person, in the flesh. The phrase is sometimes jocularly extended to 'As large as life and twice as natural'.

**As light as a feather.** Of little weight or pressure. A feather is one of the lightest natural objects, associated with flight.

**As like as two peas.** Very similar; almost identical. Individual peas are hard to tell apart.

**As long as your arm.** Very long.

**As loose as a goose.** Very relaxed; perfectly easy. The phrase owes as much to the rhyme as anything, but could also allude to the notion that a goose has loose bowels.

**As luck would have it.** As it agreeably turned out; as it favourably happened.

**As mad as a hatter.** A phrase popularized by Lewis Carroll in *Alice in Wonderland* (1865). It is found in W.M. Thackeray's *Pendennis* (1850) and is recorded in America in 1836. Mercurous nitrate was used in the making of felt hats, and its effects can produce St VITUS' DANCE or lesser tremulous manifestations, hence the likely origin of the phrase. It has also been suggested that the original 'mad hatter' was Robert Crab, a 17th-century eccentric living at Chesham, who gave all his goods to the poor and lived on dock leaves and grass.

Carroll himself is said to have based his character of the name on one Theophilus Carter, a furniture dealer, who was known locally as 'the Mad Hatter', partly because he wore a top hat and partly because of his eccentric notions. An example of the latter was his invention of an 'alarm clock bed' that woke the sleeper by tipping him onto the floor. (Hence perhaps the Mad Hatter's obsession with time and his keenness to stir the sleepy dormouse.)

**As mad as a March hare.** Hares are unusually shy and wild in March, which is their rutting season.

> The March Hare will be much the most interesting, and perhaps, as this is May, it won't be raving mad – at least not so mad as it was in March.
>
> LEWIS CARROLL: *Alice in Wonderland*, ch vi (1865)

**As merry as a cricket.** *See under* GRIG.

**As near as damn it.** As near as it is possible to get.

**As neat as a new pin.** Very neat and tidy, as if fastened with a newly bought pin.

**As old as Adam.** Well known long ago.

**As old as Methuselah.** Very old indeed, almost incredibly old. He is the oldest man mentioned in the Bible, which states (Genesis 5:27) that he died at the age of 969.

**As old as the hills.** Very old indeed. Hills are one of the oldest natural features of the landscape.

**As one makes one's bed, so one must lie on it.** Everyone must bear the consequences of their actions.

**As one man.** All together, unanimously. The expression is biblical.

> And all the people arose as one man, saying, We will not any of us go to his tent.
>
> Judges 20:8

**As plain as a pikestaff.** Quite clear, obvious, unmistakable. The earlier form of the phrase (mid-16th century) was 'as plain as a packstaff', i.e. the staff on which a pedlar carried his pack, which was worn plain and smooth.

**As plain as the nose on your face.** Extremely obvious, patent to all. The nose is the sole salient feature of the face.

**As pleased as a dog with two tails.** Visibly delighted or elated.

**As pleased as Punch.** Greatly delighted. Mr Punch is always gloating with self-satisfaction at the success of his evil actions. *See also* PUNCH AND JUDY.

**As poor as a church mouse.** In a church there is no cupboard or pantry where a mouse may take his food, and he thus has an extremely lean time.

**As poor as Job.** The allusion is to JOB being deprived by SATAN of everything he possessed.

**As poor as Lazarus.** This is the beggar LAZARUS, full of sores, who was laid at the rich man's gate and desired to be fed with crumbs that fell from DIVES' table (Luke 16:19–31).

**As pretty as a picture.** Said of a good-looking or attractively dressed person, or of an agreeable scene generally.

**As pure as the driven snow.** Spotless; immaculate.

**As quiet as a mouse or as mice.** Very quiet. Said sometimes of well-behaved children. A former longer form of the phrase was 'As quiet as a mouse in cheese'.

**As quick as a flash.** Very speedily. The reference is to a flash of lightning.

**As rich as Croesus.** Croesus, the last king of Lydia (560–546 BC), was so rich and powerful that his name became proverbial for wealth. Many of the wise men of Greece were drawn to his court, including AESOP and SOLON. He was overthrown by CYRUS of Persia. *See also* ORACLE.

**As right as a trivet.** Quite right; in an excellent state. The trivet was originally a three-legged stand or tripod, and the allusion is to it standing firmly on its three legs.

**As right as ninepence.** Perfectly well, in perfect condition. The expression is said to relate to silver ninepenny pieces formerly given as love tokens.

**As right as rain.** Perfectly fit and well, especially after an illness. Rain is good for growth.

**As round as Giotto's O.** Said of work that is perfect and complete, but done with little effort. *See also* GIOTTO'S O.

**As safe as houses.** Secure and reliable. Houses are built to withstand the daily disturbances and motions of their occupants.

**As scarce as hen's teeth.** Very rare. Hens have no teeth.

**As seen on TV.** A stock advertising recommendation for a product that has appeared in a television commercial or documentary programme.

**As sick as a cat.** Cats are prone to vomiting. Hence a person who vomits is said 'to cat' or 'to shoot the cat'.

**As sick as a dog.** Very sick. A similar phrase is AS SICK AS A CAT. The Bible speaks of dogs returning to their vomit (Proverbs 26:11; 2 Peter 2:22).

**As silent as the grave.** Dead quiet.

**As slippery as an eel.** Elusive; devious.

**As smart as paint.** Quick-witted and enterprising. A coat of fresh paint will always smarten an object's appearance.

**As snug as a bug in a rug.** Cosy and comfortable. A whimsical but expressive comparison that dates from the 18th century.

**As sober as a judge.** Completely sober. Judges are popularly regarded as pedantically ponderous and lacking in levity.

**As soft as butter.** Easily swayed; responding readily to an emotional appeal.

**As sound as a bell.** Quite sound; in perfect condition. A cracked bell is useless.

**As steady as a rock.** Firm and dependable.

**As stiff as a poker.** Straight and unbending.

**As straight as a die.** Entirely honest; morally upright. The reference is to the engineer's die used to cut the thread down the outside of a metal rod. The die must be straight-running and true if the thread is to engage properly with the groove cut into the female receiver.

**As strong as a horse.** Very strong. Horse is often used with intensive effect, as 'to work like a horse' or 'to eat like a horse'.

**As sure as eggs is eggs.** Very sure; certain in fact. It has been suggested that this is a corruption of the logician's formula '*x* is *x*'.

**As sure as God made little apples.** A phrase for anything certain, or intended to be so.

> I'll tie you up and give you fifty for yourself, as sure as God made little apples.
>
> MARCUS CLARKE: *His Natural Life* (1874)

**As sure as God's in Gloucestershire.** A strong asseveration, as a less common equivalent of AS SURE AS GOD MADE LITTLE APPLES.

**As the bell clinks, so the fool thinks** or **As the fool thinks, so the bell clinks.** A foolish person believes what he desires. The tale says that when Dick WHITTINGTON ran away from his master, and had got as far as Highgate Hill, he was hungry, tired and wished to return. Bow bells began to ring, and Whittington fancied they said: 'Turn again, Whittington, lord mayor of London.' The bells clinked in response to the boy's thoughts.

**As the bishop said to the actress.** A response to an unintentional DOUBLE ENTENDRE. The phrase dates from the music hall era, when stand-up comedy abounded in 'bishop and actress' jokes. The association of the two types is either so unlikely or so potentially scandalous that the interpretation of a remark will be either innocuous or indecent. The rejoinder is often prompted by an entirely innocent reference, as: 'I've never seen one like that before' ('As the bishop said to the actress'). *See also* TOM SWIFTIES; WELLERISM.

**As the crow flies.** As directly as possible; by the shortest route. It is actually the rook that flies straight to its destination, rather than the crow, but the two black birds are often popularly identified with each other. *See also* AIRLINE; BEELINE.

**As the Devil loves holy water.** Not at all. HOLY WATER drives away the DEVIL.

**As thick as thieves.** Intimate; very friendly. Thieves notoriously plot privately together.

**As thick as two short planks.** Very obtuse. Two short planks laid together are twice as thick as one long one.

**As thin as a rake.** Said of a thin person or animal. Unlike many other implements, a rake has a thin and angular head. The phrase dates from at least the time of Chaucer.

**As tough as old boots.** Tough and resilient, like the leather of well-worn boots.

**As true as Troilus.** TROILUS is intended by Shakespeare to represent constancy, and CRESSIDA female inconstancy.

> 'As true as Troilus' shall crown up the verse.
> And sanctify the numbers.
>
> *Troilus and Cressida*, III, ii (1601)

**As ugly as sin.** Very ugly.

**As warm as toast.** Warm and comfortable, especially after being cold.

**As weak as water.** Feeble; lacking strength or vitality. The allusion is to a drink without 'spirit'.

**As well be hanged for a sheep as a lamb.** Don't stop at half measures; IN FOR A PENNY, IN FOR A POUND (*see under* PENNY).

**As white as a sheet.** Very pale.

**As you pipe, I must dance.** I must accommodate myself to your wishes; HE WHO PAYS THE PIPER CALLS THE TUNE (*see under* PAY).

**Asaph** (Hebrew, 'collector').

(1) In the Bible a famous musician in DAVID's time (1 Chronicles 16:5 and 25:1–2). He is supposed to be the founder of the choir in the Second Temple (Ezra 3:10–11 and Nehemiah 7:44). Psalms 50 and 73–83 are ascribed to Asaph. Nahum Tate lauds Dryden under this name in *Absalom and Achitophel*, Pt ii, 1063 (1681).

> While Judah's throne and Sion's rock stand fast,
> The song of Asaph and the fame shall last.

(2) A 6th-century Welsh saint, abbot and first Welsh bishop of the see of Llanelwy, which came to be called St Asaph in the 12th century.

**Ascalaphus.** In Greek mythology a son of ACHERON who said that PROSERPINA had partaken of a pomegranate when PLUTO had given her permission to return to the upper world if she had eaten nothing. In revenge Proserpina turned him into an owl by sprinkling him with the water of PHLEGETHON. Another source says he was placed under a heavy stone in Hades.

**Ascendant.** In ASTROLOGY the ascendant is a point on the ECLIPTIC, or degree of the ZODIAC, which is just rising above the eastern horizon at a particular moment, for example at the birth of a child, and which changes as the earth rotates on its axis. The house of the ascendant includes 5 degrees of the zodiac above this point and 25 degrees below it. The lord of the ascendant is any planet within the house. Both house and lord are said by astrologers to exercise great influence on the future life of the child. Hence 'in the ascendant' is said of someone or something gaining in influence or prosperity.

**Ascension Day.** The day set apart by the Christian churches to commemorate the ascent of Christ from earth to heaven. It is the fortieth day after EASTER and is also known as HOLY THURSDAY. *See also* BEAT THE BOUNDS.

**Asclepiad** or **Asclepiadic metre.** A Greek and Latin verse form, possibly invented by Asclepiades (3rd century BC) consisting of one spondee, two or three choriambs, and one iamb, usually with a caesura in the middle. It was used for lyric and tragic verse and was highly favoured by Horace:

> Quodsi me lyricis vatibus inseres,
> Sublimi feriam sidera vertice.
> *Odes*, Bk I, i (1st century BC)

These two lines have been translated into English by Dr Brewer in the same metre:

> My name, if to the lyre haply you chance to wed,
> Pride would high as the stars lift my exalted head.

**Asclepius.** The Greek hero and god of healing, known to the Romans as AESCULAPIUS. According to Homer (8th century BC), he was mortal and had been taught medicine by the centaur CHIRON. In later mythology he is said to be the son of APOLLO and CORONIS. Each shrine of his widespread cult had sacred snakes, and artistic representations of him usually show him holding a staff entwined with a snake.

**Ascot, Royal.** *See under* ROYAL.

**Asgard** (Old Norse *Ásgarthr*, from *áss*, 'god', and *garthr*, 'enclosure'). The realm of the AESIR or the Northern gods; the OLYMPUS of Scandinavian mythology. It is said to be situated in the centre of the universe and to be accessible only by the rainbow bridge, BIFROST. It contains many regions, and mansions such as Gladsheim and VALHALLA.

**Ash. Ashes, The.** The mythical prize contended for in the CRICKET test matches between England and Australia. When England was beaten at the OVAL in 1882 a mock obituary of English cricket appeared in the *Sporting Times*:

> In Affectionate Remembrance of English Cricket,
> Which died at the Oval on 29th August, 1882.
> Deeeply lamented by a large circle of sorrowing friends and acquaintances.
> R.I.P.
> N.B. – The body will be cremated and the ashes taken to Australia.

The ashes of a burned cricket stump were subsequently placed in an urn and given to the English team when it next won.

**Ashes to ashes, dust to dust.** A phrase from the English burial service, used sometimes to denote total finality. It is based on scriptural texts such as 'Dust thou art, and unto dust thou shalt return' (Genesis 3:19), and 'I will bring thee to ashes upon the earth in the sight of all them that behold thee' (Ezekiel 27:18).

> Ashes to ashes and dust to dust,
> If God won't have him the Devil must.

According to Sir Walter Scott (see his edition of Swift's *Journal to Stella*, 25 March 1710–11) this was the form of burial service given by the sexton to the body of the French spy Guiscard, who, in 1711, had attempted to murder Robert Harley.

**Ash tree** or **Tree of the Universe.** *See* YGGDRASIL.

**Ash Wednesday.** The first day of LENT, so called from the Roman Catholic custom of sprinkling on the heads of penitents the consecrated ashes of palms remaining from the previous PALM SUNDAY. The custom is of uncertain date but is commonly held to have been introduced by Pope GREGORY THE GREAT (r.590–604). *See also* ABSTINENCE.

**Dust and ashes.** *See under* DUST.

**Oak before the ash.** *See under* OAK.

**Wear sackcloth and ashes, To.** *See under* WEAR.

**Ashmolean Museum.** The first public museum in England, opened at the University of Oxford in 1683 from a collection presented in 1677 by the antiquarian Elias Ashmole (1617–92).

**Ashtaroth** or **Astoreth** (Hebrew *'ashtarōt*). The goddess of fertility and reproduction among the Canaanites and PHOENICIANS, called by the Babylonians ISHTAR (VENUS) and by the Greeks ASTARTE. She is referred to in 1 Samuel 21:10, 1 Kings 11:5, and 2 Kings 23:13, and she may be the 'queen of heaven' mentioned in Jeremiah 7:18 and 44:17, 25. She was formerly supposed to be a moon goddess. Hence Milton's reference in 'The Hymn' from his 'On the Morning of Christ's Nativity' (1645):

> And moonèd Ashtaroth,
> Heaven's Queen and Mother both.
> xxii

**Ashur.** *See* ASSHUR.

**Asia. The Light of.** *See under* LIGHT.

**Asir.** *See* AESIR.

**Ask. Ask for it, To.** To invite trouble; to provoke.

**Ask for** or **get one's cards, To.** To resign one's job or to be dismissed from it. The reference is to the National Insurance cards kept by a person's employer. Similarly 'to be given one's cards' means to be dismissed or sacked.

**Ask me another.** I do not know; I cannot answer your question.

**Ask the hand of someone, To.** To ask for a person's hand in marriage.

**For the asking.** Free; obtainable simply by asking.

**If you ask me.** In my opinion (which I will give you whether you ask me for it or not).

**Askance at, To look.** *See under* LOOK.

**Aslan.** The great lion who is a central character in the NARNIA children's books by C.S. Lewis (1898–1963). His death and resurrection in the first book identify him as a deific or even specifically Christ-like figure. His name, which is the

Turkish word for 'lion', is said to have come from Lewis' reading of the ARABIAN NIGHTS ENTERTAINMENTS.

**Asleep at the switch, To be.** To fail to attend to one's duty; to be unvigilant. An American expression derived from the railroads. 'To switch a train' is to transfer it to another set of rails by operating a switch. Failure to do this according to schedule might well lead to a catastrophe.

**Asmodeus.** The evil demon who appears in the Apocryphal Book of TOBIT and is derived from the Persian Aeshma. In the Book of Tobit Asmodeus falls in love with Sara, daughter of Raguel, and causes the death of seven husbands in succession, each on his bridal night. He was finally driven into Egypt through a charm made by Tobias of the heart and liver of a fish burned on perfumed ashes, as described by Milton in *Paradise Lost* (iv (1667)). Hence Asmodeus often figures as the spirit of matrimonial jealousy or unhappiness. Alain Le Sage gave the name to the companion of Don Cleophas in his *Le Diable Boiteux* (1707).

**Asmodeus flight.** Don Cleophas, catching hold of his companion's cloak, is perched on the steeple of St Salvador, Madrid. Here the foul fiend stretches out his hand, and the roofs of all the houses open in a moment, to show the Don what is going on privately in each respective dwelling.

> Could the reader take an Asmodeus-flight, and, waving open all roofs and privacies, look down from the roof of Notre Dame, what a Paris were it!
>
> THOMAS CARLYLE: *French Revolution*, Bk II, ch vi, (1837)

**Asoka** (Sanskrit *ásoka*, 'without flame', 'causing no hurt'). The emperor of India (*c*.274–232 BC) who was converted to BUDDHISM by a miracle and became its 'nursing father', as Constantine was of Christianity.

**Aspasia** (Greek *aspasios*, 'welcomed'). A Greek courtesan, the most celebrated of the Hetaerae. She lived at Athens as mistress of Pericles and after his death (429 BC) with Lysicles, the democratic leader.

**Aspatia.** A character in Francis Beaumont and John Fletcher's *The Maid's Tragedy* (1619). She is noted for her deep sorrows, her great resignation and the pathos of her speeches. Amintor deserts her, women point at her with scorn, she is the jest and byword of everyone, but she bears all with patience.

**Aspen** or **trembling poplar.** The aspen leaf is said to tremble, from shame and horror, because Christ's cross was made of this wood. In fact, owing to the shape of the leaf and its long, flexible stalk, it is liable to move with the slightest breath of air.

**Asphaltic Lake.** The DEAD SEA, where asphalt abounds both on the surface of the water and on the banks.

**Asphodel** (Greek *asphodelos*). A plant genus of the lily family, particularly associated with death and the underworld in Greek legend. It was planted on graves, and the departed lived their phantom life in the Plain of Asphodel. The name DAFFODIL is a corruption of asphodel.

**Aspidistra.** A very hardy member of the lily family, with broad, lance-shaped leaves and small, inconspicuous flowers borne at soil level. It was a popular house plant from late Victorian times until the 1920s because of its ability to survive in gas-lit rooms, and it became a symbol of lower middle-class philistinism and dull respectability. George ORWELL wrote a novel called *Keep the Aspidistra Flying* (1936).

**Ass.** According to tradition the dark stripe running down the back of an ass, crossed by another at the shoulders, was the cross communicated to the creature when Christ rode on the back of this animal in His triumphant entry into Jerusalem. The ass is now more usually called the donkey, although the name is still found in older literary texts, proverbs and the like. One reason for the word's demise is that, in American use, ass means 'arse'.

'To make an ass of oneself' is to behave absurdly or foolishly.

**Ass-eared.** MIDAS had the ears of an ass. The tale says APOLLO and PAN had a contest and chose Midas to decide which was the better musician. Midas decided in favour of Pan, and Apollo, in disgust, changed his ears into those of an ass.

> Avarice is as deaf to the voice of virtue, as the ass to the voice of Apollo.
>
> LUDOVICO ARIOSTO: *Orlando Furioso* (1532)

**Asses as well as pitchers have ears.** Children and even the densest minds hear and understand many a word and hint that the speaker supposed would pass unheeded. *See also* WALLS HAVE EARS.

**Asses' bridge.** *See* PONS ASINORUM.

**Ass in a lion's skin, An.** A coward who hectors; a fool that apes a wise man. The allusion is to the fable of an ass that put on a lion's skin but was betrayed by its braying.

**Ass is deaf to music, The.** The tradition that the ass is tone deaf arose from the hideous noise made by asses when braying. *See also* ASS-EARED.

**Ass with two panniers, An.** A man out walking with a lady on each arm. The expression is from the French *faire le panier à deux anses* ('to make a basket with two handles').

**Balaam's ass.** *See under* BALAAM.

**Buridan's ass.** *See under* BURIDAN.

**Feast of asses.** *See* FEAST OF FOOLS.

**Golden Ass, The.** *See under* GOLDEN.

**Law is an ass, The.** *See under* LAW.

**Wrangle for an ass's shadow, To.** *See under* WRANGLE.

**Assassins** (Arabic *hashāshshīn*, plural of *hashshāsh*, 'hashish eater'). Violent murderers, especially of important political figures. The original Assassins were a sect of Muslim fanatics founded in Persia, *c.*1090, by Hasan-e Sabbah (d.1124). Their terrorism was mainly directed against the SELJUK authority. From Persia and Iraq they extended their activities to Syria in the early 12th century. Their power was broken by 1273 through the attacks of the Mongols and the MAMELUKE Sultan Bibars. Their name is derived from their reputed habit of dosing themselves with hashish prior to their murderous assaults.

**Assay** or **essay** (from Old French *essai*, from Latin *exagium*, 'weighing'). The assay of a metal or a coin is its chemical analysis, the aim being to determine its degree of purity. The word was also formerly used for the tasting of food or drink before it was offered to a monarch. Hence, 'to take the assay' is to taste wine to prove it is not poisoned.

The aphetic form of the word, say, was common until the 17th century. Thus Edmund in *King Lear* (V, iii (1605)), says to Edgar, 'Thy tongue some say of breeding breathes', i.e. your speech gives indication of good breeding.

Assay can also mean a test or trial in general:

> (He) makes vow before his uncle never more
> To give the assay of arms against your majesty.
> SHAKESPEARE: *Hamlet*, II, ii (1600)

The usual spelling of the word is now essay (from French), with assay kept for the special use of testing metals.

**Assaye Regiment.** *See* REGIMENTAL AND DIVISIONAL NICKNAMES.

**Assemblage, Nouns of.** *See under* NOUNS.

**Assembly. Assembly of Notables, The.** In French history an assembly of persons of distinction and political weight summoned by the VALOIS kings at their pleasure instead of convening the STATES GENERAL. It was the only concession made to consulting the will of the nation. They were called together by Richelieu in 1626–7 and not again until 1787, when Louis XVI was harassed by impending financial collapse. The last time they met was 6 November 1788. *See also* PARLIAMENT.

**Constituent Assembly.** *See under* CONSTITUENT.

**Westminster Assembly.** *See under* WESTMINSTER.

**Assent, Royal.** *See under* ROYAL.

**Asset, Fixed.** *See under* FIX.

**Asshur** or **Assur.** Originally the local god of Asshur, the capital of ASSYRIA, he became the chief god of the kingdom. His symbol was the winged sun disc enclosing a male figure wearing a horned cap, often with a bow in his hand. His name was frequently linked with the goddess ISHTAR of Nineveh. *See also* ASHTAROTH.

**Assisi, St Francis of.** *See under* FRANCIS.

**Assizes, Bloody.** *See under* BLOODY.

**Association, Free.** *See under* FREE.

**Assumption, The.** In full the Assumption of the Blessed Virgin Mary, one of the FEASTS OF OBLIGATION in the ROMAN CATHOLIC CHURCH. It is celebrated on 15 August and commemorates the death of the Virgin MARY and the assumption (taking up) of her body into HEAVEN when it was reunited to her soul. It can be traced back to the 6th century. In 1950 Pius XII declared it as a matter of divinely revealed dogma that the Virgin *expleto terrestris vitae cursu, fuisse corpore et anima ad caelestem gloriam assumptam* ('having completed her earthly course was in body and soul assumed into heavenly glory').

**Assur.** *See* ASSHUR.

**Assurance.** In insurance parlance assurance is applied to life policies only.

**Make assurance doubly sure, To.** To make security doubly sure or secure.

> But yet I'll make assurance double sure
> And take a bond of fate.
> SHAKESPEARE: *Macbeth*, IV, i (1605)

**Assyria.** An ancient land located in what is now northeastern Iraq, and taking its name from the small settlement of Assur, on the west bank of the Tigris. It grew into the greatest empire in the world, becoming independent of Babylon in the 17th century BC. Its capital was Nineveh, and one of its best known rulers was SENNACHERIB. On the death of its ruler Essarhaddon, in the 7th century BC, the empire was divided, and an alliance of Medes and Babylonians stormed and destroyed Nineveh, finally overthrowing the Assyrian Empire in 612 BC. The key episodes of its rise and fall are chronicled in the Old Testament.

**Astarte** (Old Persian *Ashtart* or *Ishtar*, from *stara*, 'star'). The Greek and Roman name for the supreme goddess of the PHOENICIANS, ASHTAROTH.

Byron gave the name to the lady beloved by Manfred in his drama, *Manfred* (1817). It has been suggested that Astarte was drawn from the poet's half-sister, Augusta Leigh.

**Asterix.** The comic French cartoon hero who first appeared in 1959 as the creation of writer René Goscinny and artist Albert Uderzo. He is a pint-sized, moustachioed, xenophobic Gaul who lives in Armorica (Brittany) and does his best to keep the Romans at bay. His friends include the obtuse Obelix and the Druid Getafix. First appearing in a weekly comic, he has since featured in a number of books and animated cartoons. His name (properly *Astérix*) is based on French *astérisque*, 'asterisk', with a final *-rix* found in typical Gaulish names such as VERCINGETORIX.

**Astley's.** The popular name for an enterprising and much patronized place of entertainment from 1770 to 1862, opened and developed by Philip Astley (1742–1814). After service as a Sergeant-Major in the Dragoons under General Eliott during the SEVEN YEARS' WAR, Astley, with his charger Gibraltar, opened a theatre with an unroofed circus at Lambeth in 1770 for equestrian displays. Eventually called the Royal Grove Theatre, it was burned down in 1794 and rebuilt as the Royal Amphitheatre, when it was patronized by the Prince of Wales and the Duke of York, among other notables. It grew in repute as a centre for equestrian and circus entertainment under Astley's pioneering management. He was the best horse-tamer of his day. Astley's was destroyed again by fire in 1803 but was reopened in 1804. Astley was eventually succeeded by his son who died seven years after his father, when the venture passed into other hands. *See also* SADLER'S WELLS.

**Astolat.** This town, mentioned in the ARTHURIAN ROMANCES, is generally identified with Guildford, in Surrey. Another form of the name gave that of the LADY OF SHALOTT.

**Lily maid of Astolat, The.** ELAINE.

**Aston University.** The Birmingham university was formed from a college of advanced technology in 1966 and was so named to be distinguished from the existing University of Birmingham, founded in 1901. It is not actually in Aston, a district 2 miles (3.2km) to the north, but in Gosta Green, near the city centre, and it took the name so as to be at the top of the alphabetical list of new universities and so readily catch the eye of the University Grants Committee.

**Astoreth.** *See* ASHTAROTH.

**Astraea** (Greek *astron*, 'star'). During the GOLDEN AGE this goddess dwelt on earth, but when sin began to prevail, she reluctantly left it and was metamorphosed into the constellation VIRGO.

**Astral. Astral body** (Greek *astron*, 'star'). In theosophical parlance the phantasmal or spiritual appearance of the physical human form, which exists both before and after the death of the material body, although during life it is not usually separated from it. To certain gifted individuals, a person's astral body is discernible, if not actually visible, as an aura.

**Astral spirits.** The spirits animating the stars. According to occultists each star had its special spirit, and PARACELSUS maintained that every man had his attendant star, which received him at death and took charge of him until the great resurrection.

**Astray, To lead someone.** *See under* LEAD.

**Astrea, The Divine.** *See under* DIVINE.

**Astrology.** The pseudoscience of the ancient and medieval world, concerned chiefly with DIVINATION. Natural astrology, which dealt with the movements and positions of the planets, the sun and the moon, as well as with tides, eclipses, the fixing of EASTER and the like, was the forerunner of the science of astronomy. Judicial astrology dealt with what is now known as astrology, the influence of the stars upon human affairs. *See also* ALCHEMY; ASCENDANT; HOROSCOPE; MICROCOSM; STAR.

**Astrological houses.** In judicial astrology the whole heaven is divided into 12 portions by means of great circles crossing the north and south points of the horizon, through which the heavenly bodies pass every 24 hours. Each of these divisions is called a house, and in casting a HOROSCOPE the whole is divided into two parts (beginning from the east), six above and six below the horizon. The eastern ones are called the ASCENDANT, because they are about to rise. The other six are the descendant, because they have already passed the ZENITH. The 12 houses each have their special functions: (1) the house of life; (2) fortune and riches; (3) brethren; (4) parents and relatives; (5) children; (6) health; (7) marriage; (8) death; (9) religion; (10) dignities; (11) friends and benefactors; and (12) mystery and uncertainty.

Three houses were assigned to each of the four ages of the person whose horoscope was to be cast, and his or her lot in life was governed by the ascendancy of these at the various periods and by the stars that ruled in the particular 'houses'.

**Astronaut** (Greek *astron*, 'star', and *nautēs*, 'sailor'). A voyager in interstellar space. This word, first used in 1929, gained popular acceptance after the first manned space flight by Major Yuri Gagarin (1934–68) of the USSR on 12 April 1961. He landed safely after orbiting the earth in 108 minutes at altitudes reaching a maximum of 203 miles (327km). *See also* COSMONAUT.

**Astronomer Royal.** The honorary title awarded to an eminent British astronomer. Until 1972 the Astronomer Royal was also director of the Royal Greenwich Observatory. Astronomers Royal to date have been (with year of appointment):

John Flamsteed (1675)
Edmund Halley (1720)
James Bradley (1742)
Nathaniel Bliss (1762)
Nevil Maskelyne (1765)
John Pond (1811)
Sir George Airy (1835)
Sir William Christie (1881)

Sir Frank Dyson (1910)
Sir Harold Jones (1933)
Sir Richard Woolley (1955)
Sir Martin Ryle (1972)
Sir Francis Graham-Smith (1982)
Sir Arnold Wolfendale (1991)
Sir Martin Rees (1995)

**Astrophel.** Sir Philip Sidney (1554–86). The poet took Phil. Sid., an abbreviated form of his own name, as a contraction of Greek *philos*, 'loving', and Latin *sidus*, 'star'. He then translated Latin *sidus* to its Greek equivalent, *astron*, reversed the words (as *astron philos*), and blended them to get Astrophel. The meaning is thus 'star lover'. The 'star' was Penelope Rich, whom he called Stella (Latin, 'star') in his collection of sonnets known as *Astrophel and Stella* (*c.*1582). Edmund Spenser wrote a pastoral called *Astrophel* (*c.*1591–5) to the memory of his friend and patron, who fell at Zutphen.

**Asur.** *See* ASSHUR.

**Asurbanipal.** *See* SARDANAPALUS.

**Asynja.** The goddesses of ASGARD, the feminine counterparts of the AESIR.

**At. At all events.** In any case; regardless of circumstances.

**At a loose end, To be.** Without anything to do; uncertain what to do next. The loose ends of any agreement or transaction are the final details requiring settlement, and 'to tie up the loose ends' is to settle the outstanding points of detail. The original reference was probably to weaving or the making of nets.

**At a loss, To be.** To be unable to decide; to be puzzled or embarrassed.

**At a loss for words, To be.** Not to know what to say.

**At a pinch.** If hard pressed; if absolutely essential. There are things that one cannot do in the ordinary way, but that one may manage 'at a pinch'.

**At a rate of knots.** Very fast, as: 'He drove off at a rate of knots.'

**At arm's length.** As far as an arm can reach; far enough to avoid familiarity.

**At a round pace.** Briskly, rapidly, smartly.

**At best** or **at the very best.** Regarded in the most favourable light; making every allowance.

**At bottom.** Radically; in reality.

**At close quarters.** Engaged in hand-to-hand combat or generally in close proximity.

**At crack of dawn.** Very early in the morning; as soon as it gets light or the sun rises.

**At cross purposes, To be.** Misunderstanding or conflicting with one another.

**At daggers drawn, To be.** To be fiercely opposed; at great enmity.

> Boffins at daggers drawn in corridors of power.
> *The Times* (headline) (8 April 1965)

**At death's door, To be.** On the point of death; very dangerously ill.

**At ease, To be.** Resting, without pain or anxiety.

**At fault, To be.** Not on the right track. Hounds are at fault when they have lost the scent, for example because the fox has jumped over a wall, swum a river, run through a flock of sheep or doubled like a hare.

**At first blush.** At first sight; when first noticed. The reference is to the rosy light of dawn.

> At the first blush we thought they had been shippes come from France.
> RICHARD HAKLUYT: *Principal Navigations*, iii (1589)

**At first hand.** From one's own knowledge or personal observation.

**At first sight.** On first being seen; on an initial impression.

**At full tilt.** At full speed. From the encounter at full gallop of knights in a tilt. *See also* TILTING AT THE QUINTAIN.

**At hand.** Conveniently near. 'Near at hand' means quite close by.

**At heart.** At bottom; basically; deep down.

**At home.** In the proper sense of the term, at one's own home and prepared to receive visitors. An 'at home' promises a lunch, drinks or a dinner party. It may not be literally 'at home' but at a restaurant, hotel or club. Experts on etiquette point out that 'at homes' should strictly speaking be held only by women. The expression 'not at home' was at one time a euphemism for 'not prepared to receive visitors'. It did not necessarily mean that the person was out.

In a metaphorical sense, 'to be at home with a subject' is to be quite conversant with it.

**At issue.** Under dispute.

**At large, To be.** At liberty. The phrase is of French origin, and *prendre le large* is to sail out to sea so as to be free to move.

**At loggerheads, To be.** To be in a state of disagreement or dispute with someone. A loggerhead, as an old word for a stupid person, is probably from the dialect word 'logger', a heavy block of wood, plus 'head'.

**At odds, To be.** At variance.

**At one blow.** At one stroke.

**At one's best, To be.** On top form in all respects.

**At one's elbow.** Close at hand; within easy reach.

**At one's fingertips.** Readily available. To have something at one's fingertips is to be entirely familiar with it. The allusion may be to a game in which manual dexterity plays an important part.

**At one's little games again** or **at the same old game, To be.** To be at one's old tricks; to revert to one's bad old ways.

**At one's wits' end, To be.** At a complete loss as to what to say or do; desperate to know how to proceed.

**At pains, To be.** To take trouble; to make a positive effort.

**At sea** or **all at sea, To be.** Wide of the mark; in a state of uncertainty or error, like someone at sea who has lost their bearings.

**At sixes and sevens, To be.** Higgledy-piggledy; in a state of confusion; or, of persons, unable to come to an agreement, AT LOGGERHEADS. The phrase comes from dicing. Nicholas Udall, in *Erasmus' Apothegmes* (1542) says: 'There is a proverb *Omnem jacere aleam*, to cast all dice by which is signified to set all on six and seven ... assaying the wild chance of fortune, be it good, be it bad.'

However, it is also traditionally held that the expression arose out of a dispute between two of the great LIVERY COMPANIES, the Merchant Taylors and the Skinners as to which was sixth and which seventh in the order of the companies going in processions in the City of London, both companies having been chartered in 1327 within a few days of each other. In 1484 they submitted the matter to the judgement of the then mayor, Sir Robert Billesden, and the aldermen. The award was that the master and wardens of both companies entertain each other to dinner annually and that the Skinners were to precede the Taylors in that year's procession. The next year the Taylors were to take the sixth place and this alternation was to continue 'ever more'.

> Lat not this wreched wo thyne herte gnawe,
> But manly, set the world on six and sevene,
> And if thou deye a martyr, go to hevene.
> CHAUCER: *Troilus and Criseyde*, iv (c.1386)

**At someone's hands.** From them, as: 'She recalled the acts of kindness at their hands.'

**At the back of one's mind.** In one's subconscious thoughts.

**At the best of times.** Even in the most favourable circumstances.

**At the bottom of, To be.** To be behind; to be the ultimate cause of.

**At the double.** In military parlance, at twice the marching speed. The phrase is also used as an order to do something quickly or immediately. *See also* DOUBLE-QUICK.

**At the drop of a hat.** On a signal; instantly; without delay. The expression alludes to the American frontier practice of dropping a hat as a signal for a fight to begin, usually the only formality observed. Races are sometimes started by the downward sweep of a hat.

**At the eleventh hour.** Just in time; at the last moment. The allusion is to the parable of the labourers hired for the vineyard, in which those starting to work 'about the eleventh hour', i.e., about 5 pm, were paid the same as those who had 'borne the burden and heat of the day' (Matthew 20:1–16). The armistice ending the First World War came into effect at the 11th hour (11 am) of the 11th day of the 11th month (November). *See also* ARMISTICE DAY.

**At the end of one's tether.** At the end of one's resources or endurance. The reference is to a tethered animal that can graze only as far as the rope allows. Horace calls the end of life *ultima linea rerum*, the final goal, referring to the white chalk mark at the end of a racecourse. *See also* TO THE BITTER END.

**At the end of the day.** When all's said and done; in the final analysis. The phrase is modern but has an almost medieval ring, as if alluding to the close of a day in the field.

**At the sharp end.** Directly involved in the action; up where the competition or danger is greatest. The allusion is not to the point of a sword, but to the bows of a ship, which first approach the enemy and any engagement.

**At the top of the tree.** At the highest position attainable in one's profession or calling.

**At this moment in time.** Now. A wordy circumlocution favoured by self-important politicians and others.

**At will.** As and when one pleases.

**Atalanta** (Greek *atalantos*, 'equal in weight'). In Greek myth the daughter of Iasus or of Schoeneus. She took part in the hunt of the CALYDONIAN BOAR and, being very swift of foot, refused to marry unless the suitor should first defeat her in a race. Melanion (or HIPPOMENES) outran her by dropping at intervals during the race three golden apples, the gift of VENUS. Atalanta stopped to pick them up, lost the race and became his wife.

**Atargatis.** The Syrian Mother Goddess, worshipped at Askalon as a mermaid under the name Derketo. Her Syrian name is said to be a compound of ASTARTE and the Phoenician-Canaanite goddess Anat, whose functions she took over, especially those relating to fertilty.

**Atatürk** (Turkish, 'father of the Turks', from *ata*, 'father', and *Türk*, 'Turks'). A surname adopted in 1934 by Mustapha Kemal (1881–1938), the maker of modern Turkey, when all Turks were made to assume surnames. In the First World War he held the Dardanelles and subsequently ruthlessly set out to westernize the republic he had established in 1923. European dress was imposed, polygamy abolished, women enfranchised and the Latin script replaced the Arabic.

**Ate.** In Greek mythology, the goddess of vengeance and mischief. She was cast down to earth by ZEUS.

> And Caesar's spirit, ranging for revenge,
> With Ate by his side come hot from hell.
> SHAKESPEARE: *Julius Caesar*, III, i (1599)

In Edmund Spenser's *The Faerie Queene* (1590, 1596) the name is given to a lying and slanderous hag, the companion of Duessa.

**Atellane** or **Atellan farces.** Coarse improvised interludes in the Roman theatres introduced from Atella, in Campania. The characters of Maccus, 'the clown', and Bucco, 'the fool', are the forerunners of the English Mr Punch (*see* PUNCH AND JUDY) and CLOWN. There were also Dossenus, 'the glutton', the ogre Manducus, 'the chewer' (perhaps an alternative name for Dossenus) and Pappus, the 'old gaffer'.

**Aten** (Egyptian *itn*, 'sun-disc'). The Egyptian creator sun-god, represented as the disc of the sun and worshipped at Thebes, HELIOPOLIS, Memphis, el-Amarna and other sanctuaries in the Nile valley. His cult at Heliopolis was initiated by Amenhotep III, and AMENHOTEP IV renamed himself AKHENATEN in his honour. When Akhenaten died in 1335 BC, el-Amarna fell victim to the many enemies of the new god, and Aten was banished.

**Athanasian Creed.** One of the three creeds accepted by the Roman and Anglican Churches, so called because it embodies the opinions of Athanasius (*c*.298–373) respecting the TRINITY. It is of unknown authorship. *See also* APOSTLES' CREED; NICENE CREED.

**Atheists.** During the Second World War the Rev. W.T. Cummings, an American army chaplain in Bataan, declared in one of his sermons, 'There are no atheists in the foxholes', meaning that no one can deny the existence of God in the face of imminent death. *See also* THEIST.

**Atheling** (Old English *æthele*, 'noble', 'famous'). In Anglo-Saxon England a title of distinction to those of noble family, but subsequently restricted to royal princes or the heirs apparent. The Isle of Athelney, a marsh near Taunton, Somerset, has a name meaning 'princes' island'. It is the place where ALFRED THE GREAT took refuge from the Danes (878–879) and is said to have burned the cakes.

**Athena.** *See* ATHENE.

**Athenaeum.** (1) A temple in Athens which became a meeting place of learned men.

(2) A famous academy in Rome founded by Hadrian *c*.135 AD.

**Athenaeum, The.** The leading intellectual CLUB in London, in PALL MALL, was founded in 1824 in the apartments of the ROYAL SOCIETY at SOMERSET HOUSE. It was originally known as The Society, but changed its name on moving to its present premises in 1830. An older club of the same name in Liverpool, famous for its proprietary library, was founded in 1797. (Its full members, limited to 100, are actually known as 'proprietors'.) The literary review called *The Athenaeum* was founded by James Silk Buckingham in 1828 and was incorporated with *The Nation* in 1921, which merged with the *New Statesman* in 1931 (which merged with *New Society* in 1988).

**Athene** or **Pallas Athene** (Greek *a*-, 'not', and perhaps *thnētos*, 'mortal', or *tithēnē*, 'nurse'). The patron goddess of ATHENS and patroness of arts and crafts, the goddess of wisdom and subsequently identified with MINERVA by the Romans (and therefore sometimes called Pallas Minerva). Her name can thus perhaps be interpreted as either 'immortal' or 'born without a nurse', the latter referring to the fact that she sprang, fully armed, from the head of ZEUS (JUPITER). Her mother was Metis. Another suggestion is that the epithet Pallas derived from that of Pallas, a giant, whom she flayed, using his skin as a covering.

**Athenian Bee, The.** PLATO (*c*.429–347 BC), a native of ATHENS, was so called from the tradition that a swarm of bees alighted on his mouth when he was in his cradle, so that thereafter his words flowed with the sweetness of honey. The same tale is told of St AMBROSE, among others. *See also* BEE.

Xenophon (*c*.430–*c*.354 BC) was also called the Athenian Bee or Bee of Athens. *See also* ATTIC BEE.

**Athens.** When ATHENE and POSEIDON disputed for the honour of being the city's patron, the goddess of wisdom produced an olive branch, the symbol of peace and prosperity, and the sea-god created a horse, symbolic of war. The gods deemed the olive the better boon, and the city was called Athens.

**Athens of Ireland.** Belfast.

**Athens of the New World.** Boston, Massachusetts.

**Athens of the North.** Edinburgh. An unfinished PARTHENON stands on Calton Hill, and at the foot of the hill lies the Royal High School, modelled on the Temple of Theseus at Athens.

**Athens of the West.** Cordoba, in Spain, was so called in the Middle Ages.

**Maid of Athens.** *See under* MAID.

**Timon of Athens.** *See under* TIMON.

**Atholl Brose.** A mixture of honey, oatmeal, water and whisky, left to ferment before it is consumed. It is named from *Atholl*, a district in Perthshire, and *brose*, a Scots word related to English *broth*.

> Charm'd with a drink which Highlanders compose,
> A German traveller exclaim'd with glee, –
> Potztausend! sare, if dis is Athol Brose,
> How goot dere Athol Boetry must be!
> THOMAS HOOD (1799–1845)

**Atkins, Tommy.** *See under* TOM.

**Atlantean shoulders.** Shoulders able to bear a great weight, like those of ATLAS.

> Sage he stood,
> With Atlantean shoulders fit to bear
> The weight of mightiest monarchies.
> MILTON: *Paradise Lost*, ii (1667)

**Atlantes.** Figures of men, used in architecture as pillars. So called from ATLAS. Female figures are called CARYATIDES. *See also* TELAMONES.

**Atlantic. Atlantic Charter.** During the Second World War President Roosevelt and Prime Minister Winston Churchill met at sea (14 August 1941) and made this eight-point declaration of the principles on which peace was to be based, consequent upon Allied victory. It can be compared with President Wilson's FOURTEEN POINTS.

**Atlantic Ocean, The.** The world's second-largest ocean is named after either the Atlas Mountains, North Africa, or the mythical ATLANTIS.

**Atlantic Wall.** The name given by the Germans in the Second World War to their defences along the Atlantic coast of Europe, built to resist invasion.

**Battle of the Atlantic, The.** *See under* BATTLE.

**Atlantis.** According to ancient myth an extensive island in the Atlantic Ocean, mentioned by PLATO in the *Timaeus* (4th century BC) and the *Critias* (4th century BC). It was said to have been a powerful kingdom before it was overwhelmed by the sea. The story was brought from Egypt by Solon. In the 16th century it was suggested that America was Atlantis, and there have been a number of other implausible identifications. More recently, and more likely, the work of archaeologists and scientists has placed it in the Mediterranean. The centre of the former island of Strongyle (Stromboli) collapsed after catastrophic volcanic action and was submerged (*c*.1500 BC). The civilization of the island was Minoan, and the Minoan Empire suffered overwhelming disaster at this time. The general conclusion equates Atlantis with Strongyle and Minoan Crete. *See also* LEMURIA; LYONESSE; NEW ATLANTIS.

**Atlas** (perhaps Greek *a-*, euphonious prefix, and *tlēnai*, 'to bear', or *athlos*, 'contest', or Berber *adrar*, 'mountain'). In Greek mythology one of the TITANS, condemned by ZEUS for his part in the war of the Titans to bear the heavens on his shoulders. His abode became the Atlas Mountains in North Africa, which accorded with the legend that they supported the heavens.

A book of maps is so called because the figure of Atlas with the world on his back was put on the title page by Mercator when he published his father's maps in 1595. In the paper trade before metrication, atlas was a standard size of drawing paper, 26 × 34in (660 × 864mm).

**Atman** (Sanskrit *ātman*, 'breath'). In Buddhist philosophy the personal soul or self, the thinking principle as it manifests itself in consciousness. In the UPANISHADS the Atman is regarded as the Universal Soul, the great Self or Person that dwells in the entire created order.

**Atomic theory.** From the 5th century BC atomic theories were held by Greek philosophers, notably EMPEDOCLES, Leucippus, DEMOCRITUS and EPICURUS. Matter was said to consist of minute, indivisible and indestructible particles. Modern atomic theory largely begins with John Dalton (1766–1844), who first wrote on the subject in 1803. His hypotheses still remain of real value in chemistry and to a lesser extent in physics as well, but the indivisibility of the atom was disproved (it was first split by Lord Rutherford in 1919) and fresh concepts of the structure of atoms resulted from the discovery of the electron and the nucleus. *See also* CORPUSCULAR PHILOSOPHY.

**Atomy.** *See* ANATOMY.

**Atonement** ('at-one-ment'). Reconciliation; expiation; the making of amends. In Christian usage the Atonement denotes the reconciliation of God and man through the life, sufferings and crucifixion of Jesus Christ. It presupposes man's alienation from God through sin.

**Day of Atonement.** *See under* DAY.

**Atossa.** Sarah, Duchess of Marlborough (1660–1744), is said to be intended under this name by Alexander Pope (*Moral Essays*, ii (1731–5)). Her friend, Lady Mary Wortley Montagu, is called SAPPHO. The Duchess of Buckingham has also been suggested for Atossa. The name was originally that of the daughter of CYRUS, king of Persia, in the 6th century BC. She was successively the wife of her brother Cambyses, of the Magdian Smerdis, and of DARIUS the Great, by whom she bore XERXES.

**Atreus.** The king of Mycenae who was the son of PELOPS, father of AGAMEMNON and MENELAUS, and husband of Aerope. The last was raped by Atreus' brother, THYESTES, and in revenge for the violation, Atreus served up the flesh of the incestuously conceived children to Thyestes, at which the sun turned back in its course in horror. The details of the grim tale are variously told and embellished.

**Atropos** (Greek, 'not turning', 'unchangeable'). In Greek mythology the eldest of the three FATES, and the one who severs the thread of life.

**Attaboy** (perhaps from 'That's the boy!'). An exclamation of enthusiastic approval or encouragement, originating in America and widely used in the 1930s by young people in the English-speaking world. 'Attagirl' also exists when the one encouraged is female.

> 'Look at that little mite with *Attaboy*
> Printed across her paper sailor hat.
> Disgusting, isn't it? Who *can* they be,

Her parents, to allow such forwardness?'
JOHN BETJEMAN: *Selected Poems*, 'Beside the Seaside' (1948)

**Attainder, Bill of.** *See under* BILL.

**Attendant, Care.** *See under* CARE.

**Attic.** Of ATHENS or Attica.

**Attic bee, The.** Sophocles (*c*.496–406 BC), the Athenian tragic poet, so called from the sweetness of his compositions. *See also* ATHENIAN BEE.

**Attic bird, The.** The NIGHTINGALE, so called either because Philomel was the daughter of the king of Athens, or because there was an abundance of nightingales in Attica.

**Attic boy, The.** Cephalus, beloved by AURORA or the Dawn and passionately fond of hunting.

Thus, Night, oft see me in thy pale career,
Till civil-suited Morn appear,
Not tricked and frounced, as she was wont
With the Attic boy to hunt,
But kerchieft in a comely cloud.
MILTON: 'Il Penseroso' (1645)

**Attic faith.** Inviolable faith, the very opposite of PUNIC FAITH.

**Attic Hercules, The.** THESEUS, who went about like Hercules, destroying robbers and achieving wondrous exploits.

**Attic muse, The.** Xenophon (*c*.430–*c*.354 BC), the historian, a native of Athens, so called because the style of his composition is a model of elegance. *See also* ATHENIAN BEE.

**Attic salt.** Elegant and delicate wit. Salt, both in Latin and Greek, was a common term for wit, or sparkling thought well expressed. Thus CICERO says, *Scipio omnes sale superabat* ('Scipio surpassed all in wit'). The Athenians were noted for their wit and elegant turns of thought.

**Atticus.** An elegant Roman scholar and master of Greek, publisher and patron of the arts (110–32 BC). His taste and judgement were so highly thought of that even CICERO submitted several of his treatises to him.

**Christian Atticus, The.** Reginald Heber (1783–1826), bishop of Calcutta, a great hymn writer.

**English Atticus, The.** Joseph Addison (1672–1719), so called by Alexander Pope (*Epistle to Dr Arbuthnot*, 1735) because of his refined taste and philosophical mind.

**Irish Atticus, The.** George Faulkner (1700–75), bookseller, publisher and friend of Jonathan Swift, so called by Lord Chesterfield when Lord Lieutenant of Ireland.

**Attila the Hun.** Known as the 'Scourge of God' for the widespread destruction caused by his armies, Attila (*c*.406–453), king of the Huns, held sway over a dominion that extended from the Rhine to the frontiers of China. He devastated all the territories between the Black Sea and the Mediterranean and in 451 invaded Gaul, but was driven back by the Roman commander Aetius and by Theodoric I, king of the Visigoths. He retreated to Hungary but then rallied to make inroads into Italy, laying waste several cities. Only the personal mediation of Leo I saved Rome itself. Attila, whose name is Gothic for 'little father', appears in the NIBELUNGENLIED as Etzel. *See also* HUN.

**Attis.** *See* ATYS.

**Attitude, To strike an.** *See under* STRIKE.

**Attorney** (Old French *atourner*, 'to direct to'). One who acts for another in business and especially legal matters. Solicitors practised in the courts of equity and attorneys in the courts of common law until the Judicature Act of 1873 declared that 'all persons admitted as solicitors, attorneys or proctors ... shall be called Solicitors of the Supreme Court'. In the USA an attorney-at-law possesses the functions of both BARRISTER and solicitor.

**Attorney-General, The.** The chief law officer of the crown, the chief legal adviser to the government and head of the BAR. Since the Revolution of 1688 the Attorney-General has sat in the HOUSE OF COMMONS.

In the USA the Attorney-General is the chief law officer of the Federal Government, with an office dating from 1789. Initially giving legal advice to the government and conducting government cases in the Supreme Court, he became head of the new Department of Justice in 1870 with control over federal district attorneys and marshals. Many of his duties are now administrative. He is also a member of the CABINET. There is also a law officer in each state usually designated attorney-general.

**Power of attorney.** *See under* POWER.

**Attrition, War of.** *See under* WAR.

**Atys** or **Attis** (of unknown origin). A youth beloved by Agdistis (CYBELE). Driven mad by her jealousy, he castrated himself with a sharp stone. According to Ovid's *Metamorphoses* (1st century AD), Cybele changed him into a pine tree as he was about to commit suicide.

**Au. Au courant** (French, 'in the current'). To be *au courant* is to be up-to-date, especially in current affairs.

**Au fait** (French, 'to the point'). Fully informed; conversant with.

**Au fond** (French, 'at the bottom'). Fundamentally; basically.

**Au pair** (French, 'on an equal footing'). A young foreigner, usually a girl, who joins a family to take on housework and help with young children in exchange for board and lodging and a modest weekly wage. She usually does so to learn the language or to improve her knowledge of it.

**Au pied de la lettre** (French 'to the foot of the letter'). Exactly; literally.

> Arthur is but a boy, and a wild and enthusiastic young fellow, whose opinions one must not take *au pied de la lettre*.
>
> W.M. THACKERAY: *Pendennis*, ch xi (1848–50)

**Au revoir** (French, 'to the seeing again'). Goodbye. *See also* AUF WIEDERSEHEN.

**Aubry's dog** or **Dog of Montargis, The.** Aubry of Montdidier was murdered in 1371 in the forest of Bondy. His dog, Dragon, excited suspicion of Richard of MACAIRE by always snarling and flying at his throat whenever he appeared. Richard, condemned to a judicial combat with the dog, was killed and, in his dying moments, confessed the crime.

**Auburn.** The word is regularly applied to reddish-brown hair. Its original meaning, however, was yellowish or white, since it ultimately derives from Latin *albus*, 'white'. In the 17th century the word was often spelt *abrune* or *abroun*, and so became associated with 'brown'. The hamlet of Auburn described by Goldsmith in *The Deserted Village* (1770) was long thought to be Lissoy, County Westmeath, Ireland, where the poet spent his childhood, but it is now believed to be a composite depiction.

**AUC.** An abbreviation of Latin *Ab urbe condita* or *Anno urbis conditae* ('from the foundation of the city' (i.e. Rome), 'in the year of the city's foundation'). It is the starting point of the Roman system of dating and corresponds to 753 BC.

**Auction, Dutch.** *See under* DUTCH.

**Audit ale.** A strong ALE that was brewed at some of the Oxford and Cambridge colleges and originally broached on audit day, when college accounts had to be paid up by the students. Whether this was intended as a consolation to the students or a mild form of celebration by the college authorities is uncertain.

**Audrey.** In Shakespeare's *As You Like It* (1599), an awkward country wench who jilted William for Touchstone. *See also* TAWDRY.

**Auf Wiedersehen** (German, 'to the seeing again'). Goodbye. The exact equivalent of the French AU REVOIR. When concluding a telephone conversation, Germans say *Auf Wiederhören* ('to the hearing again').

**Augean stables.** The stables of Augeas, the mythological king of Elis, in Greece, which housed his great herd of oxen. They were never cleaned, and it was one of the labours of HERCULES to cleanse them, which he did by diverting the course of a river through them. Hence 'to cleanse the Augean stables' means to clear away an accumulated mass of rubbish or corruption, physical, moral, religious or legal.

**Augsburg Confession.** The historical confession of faith compiled by MELANCHTHON in consultation with Luther and presented to Charles V at the Diet of Augsburg in 1530.

**Augury** (perhaps from Latin *augere*, 'to increase'). Properly, the function of an augur, a Roman religious official. The duty of members of the college of augurs was to pronounce, by the observation of signs called AUSPICES, whether the gods favoured or disfavoured a proposed course of action. Augurs were regularly consulted before any important public action. *See also* DIVINATION; INAUGURATE; OMENS; SINISTER.

**August.** Formerly called Sextilis in the Roman calendar, as the sixth month from March, when the year began. The name was changed to Augustus in 8 BC in honour of AUGUSTUS (63 BC–AD 14), the first Roman emperor, whose 'lucky month' it was. It was the month in which he began his first consulship, celebrated three TRIUMPHS, received the allegiance of the legions on the Janiculum, reduced Egypt and ended the civil wars. *See also* JULY.

The Old English name for August was *Wēodmōnath*, 'weed month', *wēod* meaning 'grass', 'herbs'. In the FRENCH REVOLUTIONARY CALENDAR the equivalent month was THERMIDOR ('gift of heat'), which lasted from 20 July to 18 August.

**Augusta.** A name given to many Roman provincial towns. London was given the honorific Roman title of Augusta some time in the early 4th century AD.

**Augustan age.** The GOLDEN AGE of Latin literature, so called from the Emperor AUGUSTUS, in whose reign (27 BC–AD 14) HORACE, Ovid, VIRGIL, Livy, Propertius and Tibullus, among others, flourished.

**Augustan age of English literature.** The period of the classical writers of the time of Queen Anne and George I, or to interpret it more widely, from John Dryden to Samuel Johnson.

**Augustan age of French literature.** The period of Pierre Corneille (1606–84), MOLIÈRE (1622–73) and Jean Racine (1639–99).

**Augustan History.** A series of biographies of the Roman emperors from Hadrian to Carinus (AD 117–284), purporting to be the work of six authors, but possibly written as propaganda during the reign of JULIAN THE APOSTATE (361–363).

**Augustine** (Latin *augustinus*, diminutive of *augustus*, 'sacred', 'great'). Saint (354–430), bishop of Hippo, DOCTOR OF THE CHURCH and the greatest of the Latin fathers. He was baptized in 387 after an earlier life of self-indulgence and in due course (396) became bishop of Hippo in North Africa. He is distinguished by his zealous opposition to the heresies of his time and by his prolific writings, his best known works being his *Confessions* and *De Civitate Dei* ('The City of God').

**Augustine of Canterbury.** Saint (d.604), APOSTLE of the English and first archbishop of

Canterbury. He was sent from Rome by Pope GREGORY THE GREAT with a band of 40 monks to convert the English. They first landed on the Isle of Thanet, gained the support of King Aethelbert of Kent and established themselves at Canterbury in 597 when Aethelbert was baptized. Differences with the older British church became apparent before Augustine's death.

**Augustinian canons.** Regular CANONS who adopted the Rule of St AUGUSTINE in the 11th century. Also called Austin canons, their first house in England was established at Colchester between 1093 and 1099. Like the monks, they took religious vows, but they made clerical and parochial duties their principal obligation.

**Augustinian** or **Austin friars.** The fourth of the MENDICANT ORDERS, which first came to England in 1248. They are also known as the Augustinian Hermits, from whom they were formed (1243–56).

**Second Augustine, The.** *See under* SECOND.

**Augustus.** A title, meaning 'venerable', bestowed upon Gaius Julius Caesar Octavianus, the first Roman emperor, in 27 BC, and borne by all successive Roman emperors except Vitellius.

Augustus was also the name given to Philip II of France (r.1180–1223) and to Sigismund II of Poland (r.1520–7), both of whom were born in August.

**Auld. Auld Clootie.** OLD NICK. The Scots call a cloven hoof a 'cloot', so that Auld Clootie is 'Old Cloven-foot'.

> O thou! whatever title suit thee,
> Auld Hornie, Satan, Nick, or Clootie.
> ROBERT BURNS: 'Address to the Deil' (1786)

**Auld Hornie.** After the establishment of Christianity, the heathen deities were degraded by the church into fallen angels, and PAN, with his horns, crooked nose, goat's beard, pointed ears and goat's feet, was transformed to his satanic majesty, and called Old Hornie. *See also* AULD CLOOTIE.

**Auld Kirk, The.** The CHURCH OF SCOTLAND.

**Auld lang syne** (Scottish, 'old long since'). Times past. The song, commonly sung at the conclusion of dances and revelries, particularly in the Christmas and New Year season, and usually attributed to Robert Burns, is really a new version by Burns of a much older song. In Watson's *Collection* (1711), it is attributed to Francis Sempill (d.1682), but it is probably even older. Burns wrote in a letter to Thomson: 'It is the old song of the olden times, which has never been in print. [...] I took it down from an old man's singing.' And in another letter: 'Light be on the turf of the heaven-inspired poet who composed this glorious fragment.'

> Should auld acquaintance be forgot,
> And never brought to min'?
> Should auld acquaintance be forgot,
> And auld lang syne?
> ROBERT BURNS: 'Auld Lang Syne' (1796)

**Auld Reekie** (Scottish, 'old smoky'). Edinburgh, so called from the pall of smoke that formerly hung over it.

**Auld Robin Gray.** A ballad by Lady Anne Lindsay, daughter of the Earl of Balcarres, and afterwards Lady Barnard, written (1771) to an old Scottish tune called 'The bridegroom grat when the sun gaed down'. Auld Robin Gray was the herdsman of her father. When Lady Anne had written a part, she called her younger sister for advice. She said, 'I am writing a ballad of virtuous distress in humble life. I have oppressed my heroine with sundry troubles. For example, I have sent her Jamie to sea, broken her father's arm, made her mother sick, given her Auld Robin Gray for a lover, and want a fifth sorrow. Can you help me find one?' 'Steal the cow, sister Anne,' said the little Elizabeth. So the cow was stolen awa', and the song completed. Lady Anne later wrote a sequel in which Auld Robin Gray died, Jeannie married Jamie, and all turned to a happy ending.

**Aulis.** The port in BOEOTIA where the Greek fleet assembled before sailing against TROY. The fleet was becalmed here, and AGAMEMNON was forced by his troops to sacrifice his daughter IPHIGENIA in order to appease Artemis (DIANA). This is the subject of Gluck's opera *Iphigénie en Aulide* (1774), based on Racine's *Iphigénie* (1675).

**Aunt.** The word 'aunt' was formerly applied to any old woman.

**Aunt Edna.** A typical theatre-goer of conservative taste. The playwright Terence Rattigan (1911–77) introduced the character in the preface to the second volume of his *Collected Works* (1953), describing her as an average middle-class attender of matinées whom playwrights must take into account. Critics subsequently adopted the invention when complaining about the middle-class, middle-brow nature of his own plays.

**Aunt Emma.** In croquet, an unenterprising player.

**Auntie.** The BBC, regarded as a conservative or 'nannyish' organization. The BBC has itself accepted the nickname and exploited it punningly in such programme titles as *Auntie's Bloomers*, a selection of mishaps during filming.

**Aunt Sally.** A game in which sticks or cudgels are thrown at a a figure of an old woman's head mounted on a pole, the object being to hit its nose, or break the pipe stuck in its mouth. An 'Aunt Sally' is now a term for anyone or anything that is an object of ridicule or a target of abuse.

**Agony aunt.** *See under* AGONY.

**Charley's Aunt.** *See under* CHARLES.

**My Aunt Fanny.** A phrase used to express disbelief or negation.

She's got no more idea how to run this house than my Aunt Fanny.
MONICA DICKENS: *Thursday Afternoons*, ch i (1945)

**Aura.** The glow or 'field' that, according to a NEW AGE theory, surrounds all humans. Invisible to all but gifted psychics, it is of variable size and colour, the latter being particularly important. Pink, for example, signifies affection, bright red anger, dark red passion, yellow intellectuality, orange pride, brown greed and blue devotion, while green has many interpretations. *See also* AUREOLE.

**Aureole** (Medieval Latin *aureola corona*, 'golden crown'). A luminous radiance surrounding the whole figure in paintings of Christ and sometimes of the saints. The French historian Charles du Cange (1610–88) writes that the aureole of nuns is white, of martyrs red and of doctors green. *See also* AURA; HALO; NIMBUS; VESICA PISCIS.

**Aurignacian.** An upper PALAEOLITHIC culture characterized by the extensive use of flint scrapers, blade flakes and bone tools, probably originating in Palestine. It is the period of CRO-MAGNON man, famous for cave paintings like those of Altamira in Spain. The name refers to Aurignac, France, in the Pyrenees, near which is the cave where the remains of this culture were discovered.

**Aurora** (Latin, 'dawn'). Early morning. According to Greek mythology the dawn goddess EOS, the Roman Aurora, sets out before the sun to proclaim the coming of day.

**Aurora borealis.** Bands, curtains, or streamers of light seen in the sky round the North Pole, hence the alternative name Northern Lights. The similar phenomenon in the southern polar regions is the Aurora australis. Both are caused by collisions between air molecules and charged particles from the sun that have become trapped in the earth's magnetic field. *See also* MERRY DANCERS.

**Aurora's tears.** The morning dew.

**Ausonia.** An ancient name of Italy, so called from Auson, son of Odysseus (ULYSSES), and father of the Ausones.

**Auspices** (Latin *avis*, 'bird', and *specere*, 'to look'). In ancient Rome the name for the interpreters of signs from birds, animals and other phenomena, who were later called augurs. Only a chief commander was allowed to take the auspices of war, so that if a subordinate gained a victory he won it 'under the auspices' of his superior. *See also* AUGURY; DIVINATION.

**Aussie.** A familiar name for an Australian, first in use among Australian soldiers in the First World War. Their own colloquial name for themselves was DIGGER.

**Auster** (Latin). A poetic name for the south wind, regarded by classical writers as pernicious to flowers and health. Its modern equivalent is the Italian sirocco, a hot, dry and dusty wind.

**Austin friars.** *See* AUGUSTINE FRIARS.

**Australia.** The states of Australia have their colloquial names, not always complimentary:

New South Wales: Ma State
Northern Territory: Top End, White Elephant
Queensland: Banana State
South Australia: Wheat State
Victoria: Cabbage Patch
Western Australia: Westralia, Groperland

Among the cities, Perth is called the Swan City, Adelaide, the City of Churches, and Melbourne, City of the Cabbage Garden.

**Australia Day.** 26 January, commemorating the first landing at Sydney Cove in 1788. The Monday following has been a national holiday since the establishment of the Commonwealth of Australia in 1901. It began in New South Wales in 1818 and was originally called Foundation or Commemoration Day.

**Australian Capital Territory.** The name given to an area in New South Wales, of 939 square miles (2431 sq km), which is a Federal Territory, containing Canberra, the Federal Capital and seat of government. The Territory was created so that Australia's capital would not be constructed in either Victoria or New South Wales.

**Austrian lip.** A characteristic of the royal family of HABSBURGS, one of the most famous cases of hereditary physical deformity, said to have been derived through marriage with a daughter of the Polish princely house of Jagellon. Motley (*The Rise of the Dutch Republic* (1855)), describing the Emperor Charles V, at the age of 55, says: 'the lower jaw protruding so far beyond the upper, that it was impossible for him to bring together the few fragments of teeth which still remained, or to speak a whole sentence in an intelligible voice.' Of Philip II of Spain, he says: 'he had the same heavy, hanging lip, with a vast mouth, and monstrously protruding lower jaw.' Macaulay (*History of England* (1849, 1855)) says of Charles II, the last of the Spanish Habsburgs: 'the malformation of the jaw, characteristic of his family, was so serious that he could not masticate his food.'

**Aut Caesar aut nullus** (Latin, 'either Caesar or no one'). All or nothing; either first or nowhere. Caesar used to say that 'he would sooner be first in a village than second at Rome'. The phrase was used as a motto by Pope Alexander VI's natural son, Cesare Borgia (1476–1507).

**Authentic Doctor.** A title bestowed on the scholastic philosopher, Gregory of Rimini (d.1358).

**Authorized Version, The.** *See under* BIBLE.

**Autocrat of the Breakfast-Table, The.** A name given to Oliver Wendell Holmes (1809–94), who wrote a series of essays under this title first published in the *Atlantic Monthly* in 1857.

**Auto-da-fé** (Portuguese, 'act of faith'). The ceremonial procedure of the Spanish INQUISITION when sentences against heretics were read. Persistent heretics were subsequently delivered to the secular arm for punishment. The victims were burned because inquisitors were forbidden to 'shed blood'. This perverse procedure was based on the axiom of the ROMAN CATHOLIC CHURCH, *Ecclesia non novit sanguinem* ('The church is untainted with blood').

> 'For once we'll be gay, a Grand *Auto-da-fé*
> Is much better fun than a ball or a play!'
>
> R.H. BARHAM: *Ingoldsby Legends*, 'The Auto-da-Fé' (1840)

**Autolycus** (Greek, 'the wolf itself', from *autos*, 'oneself', and *lukos*, 'wolf'). In Greek mythology, the son of MERCURY, and the craftiest of thieves. He stole his neighbours' flocks and altered their marks, but SISYPHUS outwitted him by marking his sheep under their feet. Delighted with this device, Autolycus became friends with Sisyphus. Shakespeare uses his name for a rascally pedlar in *The Winter's Tale* (IV, ii (1610)).

> My father named me Autolycus; who being, as I am, littered under Mercury, was likewise a snapper-up of unconsidered trifles.

**Automedon** (Greek, 'the king himself', from *autos*, 'oneself', and *medōn*, 'ruler', 'king'). In Greek mythology, the charioteer of ACHILLES.

**Auto State, The.** A nickname of Michigan, in which Detroit is situated, this being the city where Henry Ford (1863–1947) originally made his automobiles. *See also* UNITED STATES OF AMERICA.

**Autumn.** The third season of the year, in the northern hemisphere August or September, October and November, astronomically from the September equinox to the December SOLSTICE. It is figuratively a season of maturity or decay as in Percy Bysshe Shelley's *Alastor* (1816):

> And now his limbs were lean; his scattered hair,
> Sered by the autumn of strange suffering,
> Sung dirges in the wind.

**Avalokiteshvara.** One of the most important deities of the MAHAYANA sect of BUDDHISM, and in LAMAISM the tutelary god of Tibet. He is the equivalent of VISHNU in HINDUISM, and in cosmic mythology is a creator deity. Many forms of him exist, and he can have up to eleven heads, sometimes arranged in pyramid shape. One of his main attributes is a blue lotus, and his attendant animal is a lion. It is to him that the Tibetan mantra OM MANI PADME HUM ('Hail to the jewel in the lotus') is addressed. His name means 'the god who watches' (i.e. keeps guard over the human race), from Sanskrit *avalokita*, 'watch', 'observation', and *ishvara*, 'supreme god'.

**Avalon.** A Celtic name traditionally interpreted as 'island of apples', and in Celtic mythology the Island of Blessed Souls. In the ARTHURIAN ROMANCES it is the abode and burial place of Arthur, who was carried there by MORGAN LE FAY. Its identification with GLASTONBURY is due to etymological error. (Avalon had come to be associated with the paradisal 'Glass Island' of Celtic legend that itself was identified with *Ineswytrin*, the Welsh name of Glastonbury, which was popularly translated as 'island of glass'.) OGIER THE DANE and OBERON also held their courts at Avalon.

**Avant-garde** (French, 'vanguard'). The advanced guard of an army, otherwise the vanguard. The term is also applied to artists, writers, musicians and the like whose techniques or ideas are markedly experimental or ultra-modern.

**Avars.** *See* BANAT.

**Avatar** (Sanskrit *avatāra*, 'descent'). In Hindu mythology the advent to earth of a deity in a visible form. The ten avatars of VISHNU are the most celebrated. He appeared as: (1) Matsya ('fish'), (2) Kurma ('tortoise'), (3) Varaha ('boar'), (4) Narasimha ('man-lion'), (5) Vamana ('dwarf'), (6) Parasurama ('RAMA with the axe'), (7) Rama (again), (8) KRISHNA and (9) BUDDHA. The tenth advent is to occur at the end of the four ages and will be as Kalki ('white horse'), to destroy the earth.

The word is used metaphorically to denote a manifestation or embodiment of some idea or phrase:

> I would take the last years of Queen Anne's reign as the zenith, or palmy state of Whiggism, in its divinest avatar of common sense.
>
> S.T. COLERIDGE: *Table Talk* (1836)

**Ave** (Latin for 'Hail!').

**Ave atque vale.** Hail and farewell! The words of Catullus at his brother's tomb.

> Multas per gentes et multa per aequora vectus
> Advenio has miseras, frater, ad inferias,
> Ut te postremo donarem munere mortis
> Et mutam nequiquam alloquerer cinerem.
> Quandoquidem fortuna mihi tete abstulit ipsum,
> Heu miser indigne frater adempte mihi,
> Nunc tamen interea haec prisco quae more parentum
> Tradita sunt tristi munere ad inferias,
> Accipe fraterno multum manantia fletu,
> Atque in perpetuum, frater, ave atque vale.
> (By many lands and over many a wave
> I come, my brother, to your piteous grave,
> To bring you the last offering in death
> And o'er dumb dust expend an idle breath;
> For fate has torn your living self from me,

And snatched you, brother, O, how cruelly!
Yet take these gifts, brought as our fathers bade
For sorrow's tribute to the passing shade;
A brother's tears have wet them o'er and o'er;
And so, my brother, hail, and farewell evermore!)
CATULLUS: *Carmina*, No. 101 (1st century BC)
(translation by Sir William Marris)

**Ave Maria** (Medieval Latin, 'Hail, Mary!'). The first two words of the Latin prayer to the Virgin MARY used in the ROMAN CATHOLIC CHURCH (Luke 1:28). The phrase is applied to the smaller beads of a ROSARY, the larger ones being termed PATERNOSTERS.

**Avenger of Blood, The.** In ancient Israel, the man who had the right to avenge the death of one of his kinsmen (Joshua 20:5). The Avenger in Hebrew is called GOEL.

CITIES OF REFUGE were appointed for the protection of homicides, and of those who had caused another's death by accident (Numbers 35:12). The Koran sanctions the Jewish custom.

**Avenue. Avenue of the Americas.** The official name given in the 1940s to Sixth Avenue, New York, to honour the Latin American countries. Few New Yorkers use the appellation, preferring the briefer numerical name. The street runs from Canal Street in the south to CENTRAL PARK in the north, and for many years its length was followed by an elevated 'subway' or 'el' train.

**Fifth Avenue.** *See under* FIFTH.

**Averages, Law of.** *See under* LAW.

**Avernus** (Greek *a*-, 'without', and *ornis*, 'bird'). A lake in Campania, Italy, so called from the belief that its sulphurous exhalations caused any bird that attempted to fly over it to fall into its waters. Latin mythology made it the entrance to HELL. Hence Virgil's lines:

Facilis descensus Averno:
Noctes atque dies patet atri ianua Ditis;
Sed revocare gradum superasque evadere ad auras,
Hoc opus, hic labor est.
*Aeneid*, vi (1st century BC)

This is rendered in John Dryden's *Virgil* (1697) as:

Smooth the descent and easy is the way
(The Gates of Hell stand open night and day);
But to return and view the cheerful skies,
In this the task and mighty labour lies.

**Avesta** (Pahlavi, 'original text'). The sacred writings of ZOROASTER, sometimes called ZEND-AVESTA. The present Avesta was compiled under the SASSANIDES, using earlier sources from the time of Zoroaster onwards and adding to them. It essentially consists of: (1) the Yasna, the chief liturgical portion including the Gathas or hymns; (2) the Visp-rat, a lesser liturgical work; (3) the Vendidad, containing the laws, like the Christian PENTATEUCH; (4) the Yashts, 21 hymns to various gods and ancient heroes; and (5) the Khurda Avesta (Little Avesta), containing minor texts, hymns and short prayers.

**Aveyron, The wild boy of.** *See under* WILD.

**Avianus.** A Roman fabulist whose work was a popular medieval schoolbook. His material is largely based on BABRIUS.

**Avicenna** or **Ibn Sina.** A great Muslim philosopher, mathematician, astronomer and physician (980–1037). About 100 treatises are attributed to him, and his *Canon of Medicine* remained a standard textbook into the 17th century. He wrote mostly in Arabic, although his native language was Persian. His full name was Abu Ali al-Husayn ibn Abd Allah ibn Sina ('father of Ali Hussein, son of Abdullah, son of Sina').

**Avignon popes.** In 1309 Pope Clement V (r.1305–14), a Gascon, under pressure from Philip the Fair of France, transferred the papal court to Avignon, where it remained until 1377. This BABYLONIAN CAPTIVITY weakened the papacy and led to the GREAT SCHISM.

Other Avignon popes were:

| | | | |
|---|---|---|---|
| John XXII | 1316–34 | Innocent VI | 1352–62 |
| Benedict XII | 1334–42 | Urban V | 1362–70 |
| Clement VI | 1342–52 | Gregory XI | 1370–78 |

**Avila, St Teresa of.** *See under* TERESA.

**Avoid extremes.** A traditional wise saw of Pittacus of Mytilene (*c*.650–570 BC).

**Avon, The Swan of.** *See under* SWAN.

**Awkward. Awkward age, The.** Adolescence, when one is no longer a child but not yet fully an adult. Henry James has a novel of this title (1899) about a young woman's emergence into an understanding of the world.

**Awkward squad, The.** Military recruits not yet trained to take their place in the ranks.

**Axe. Get the axe, To.** To be dismissed from one's place of work. A similar expression is 'to get the chop'. *See also* GET THE SACK *under* SACK.

**Have an axe to grind, To.** To have an ulterior motive or grievance. Benjamin Franklin tells of a man who wanted to grind his axe but had no time to turn the grindstone. Going to the yard where he saw young Franklin, he asked the boy to show him how the machine worked, kept praising him till his axe was ground and then laughed at him for his pains.

**Put the axe in the helve, To.** To solve a problem; to HIT THE NAIL ON THE HEAD.

**Send the axe after the helve, To.** *See* THROW THE HELVE AFTER THE HATCHET.

**Axinomancy.** DIVINATION by the axe, practised by the ancient Greeks with a view to discovering crime. An agate or piece of jet was placed on a red-hot axe, which then indicated the guilty person by its motion.

**Axis.** The alliance of NAZI Germany, FASCIST Italy and Japan, established in 1936 and lasting until the defeat of these countries in the Second World War.

**Axle grease.** Money, as an Australian colloquial expression. Money makes life run more smoothly, as axle grease helps the wheels to turn.

**Ayesha** or **Aisha** (Arabic, 'flourishing'). The third and favourite wife (*c*.613–678) of MOHAMMED, daughter of ABU-BEKR. He married her when she was only a child, soon after the HEGIRA, and ultimately died in her arms, leaving her a childless widow of 18. Rider Haggard used the name for the heroine of his novel *She* (1887) and for the title of its sequel (1905).

**Aymon, The Four Sons of.** *See under* FOUR.

**Ayrshire poet, The.** Robert Burns (1759–96), who was born at Alloway in Ayrshire.

**Azazel** (Hebrew *'azāzel*, perhaps 'power of God'). Leviticus 16:8 tells how AARON, as an atonement, was to cast lots on two goats: 'one lot for the Lord, and the other lot for the scapegoat.' 'Scapegoat' is here a mistranslation of Azazel, who was actually the demonic being to whom the scapegoat was to be sent.

Milton uses the name for the standard bearer of the rebel angels (*Paradise Lost*, i). In Muslim demonology Azazel is the counterpart of the DEVIL, cast out of heaven for refusing to worship ADAM. His name was changed to EBLIS (Iblis), which means 'despair'.

**Azaziel.** In Byron's *Heaven and Earth* (1822), a seraph who fell in love with Anah, a granddaughter of CAIN. When the flood came, he carried her under his wing to another planet.

**Azilian.** A MESOLITHIC culture of the transitional period between PALAEOLITHIC and NEOLITHIC. It is named from the bone and flint implements found in the cave at Mas d'Azil in the French Pyrenees.

**Azoth** (Arabic *az-zā'ūq*, 'the mercury'). The alchemists' name for mercury, also the PANACEA or universal remedy of PARACELSUS. In Robert Browning's *Paracelsus* (v (1835)), it is the name of Paracelsus' sword:

> Last, my good sword; ah, trusty Azoth, leapest
> Beneath thy master's grasp for the last time?

**Azrael.** The Muslim ANGEL of death, one of the four closest to ALLAH. He has four faces and four thousand wings, and his whole body consists of eyes and tongues, the number of which corresponds to the number of people inhabiting the earth. He will be the last to die, but will do so at the second trump of the ARCHANGEL. *See also* ADAM.

> The bitter cold stole into the cottages, marking the old and feeble with the touch of Azrael.
>
> MRS HUMPHRY WARD: *Marcella*, II, i (1894)

**Wings of Azrael, The.** *See under* WINGS.

**Azrafil.** *See* ADAM; ISRAFEL.

**Aztec State, The.** One of the names by which Arizona has been known. It is also called the Apache State, the Grand Canyon State and the Valentine State, the latter because it was admitted as a state of the USA on St VALENTINE'S day (14 February) 1912. *See also* UNITED STATES OF AMERICA.

**Azure** (Arabic *lāzaward*, 'lapis lazuli'). The heraldic term for the colour blue, represented in royal arms by the planet JUPITER, and in noblemen's by the sapphire. The ground of the old shield of France was azure. In heraldic devices azure is represented by horizontal lines. The word is also a poetic synonym for the clear blue sky.

# B

**B.** The form of the Roman capital B can be traced through early Greek to Phoenician and Egyptian hieratic. The small b is derived from the cursive form of the capital. In Hebrew the letter is called *beth* ('house'), but it never graphically represented a house.

B in Roman notation stands for 300. With a line above, it denotes 3000.

**Know B from a battledore, Not to.** *See under* KNOW.

**Marked with a B, To be.** *See under* MARK.

**Ba.** The SOUL, which, according to early primitive Egyptian belief, roamed the burial places at night. Later belief held that it became the manifested form of a god. The bull APIS is the Ba of OSIRIS and the star SIRIUS the Ba of ISIS.

**Baal** (Hebrew *bá'al*, 'lord', 'master'). The chief SEMITIC fertility god and in Phoenician mythology the sun-god and supreme national deity. There were also local Baals, such as those established in Canaan when the Israelites arrived. The latter adopted many rites of the Canaanites and grafted them to their own worship of Yahweh (JEHOVAH), who thus tended to become merely the national Baal. It was this form of worship that HOSEA and other prophets denounced as heathenism. BEL is the Assyrian form of the name. *See also* ASSYRIA; BEELZEBUB; BELPHEGOR.

**Baal** or **Bale fires.** Fires lighted on the highest moorland hilltops on Midsummer Eve. The custom still survives in Cornwall. *See also* BELTANE.

**Baalbek.** *See* CHILMINAR AND BAALBEK.

**Baba, Ali.** *See under* ALI.

**Babar.** The elegantly dressed African elephant in the books for young children by the French writer and illustrator Jean de Brunhoff, first published in French in 1931. Babar has inspired works in unexpected quarters, including a sequence of piano pieces by Francis Poulenc (1899–1963) and a study by the Marxist critic Ariel Dorfman entitled *The Empire's Old Clothes* (1983). His name, perversely enough, appears to derive from Hindi *babar*, 'lion'.

**Baba Yaga** (Russian *baba*, 'old woman', and a word probably related to Old Icelandic *ekki*, 'pain', 'grief'). A cannibalistic ogress of Russian folklore who stole young children and ate them. She lived in the remote forest, sailed through the air in an iron cauldron, raising tempests on her way, and swept with a broom all traces of her passing. She bears a strong resemblance to BERCHTA, a goddess of south German folklore.

**Babbitt.** The leading character in Sinclair Lewis' novel of this name (1922). He is a prosperous 'realtor' or estate agent in the western city of Zenith, a simple, likeable fellow, with faint aspirations to culture that are forever smothered in the froth and futile hustle of American business life. Drive (which takes him nowhere), hustle (by which he saves no time) and efficiency (which does not enable him to do anything) are the keynotes of his life. Babbitt came to typify the business man of orthodox outlook and virtues, with no interest in cultural values. *See also* MAIN STREET.

**Babe. Babe in arms, A.** One too young to walk and so one that has to be carried.

**Babes in the wood.** The phrase has been humorously applied to: (1) simple trustful folks, who are never suspicious and are easily fooled; (2) Irish insurrectionaries who infested the mountains of Wicklow and the woods of Enniscorthy towards the close of the 18th century; and (3) men in the stocks or the PILLORY. *See also* CHILDREN IN THE WOOD.

**Babel** (Akkadian *Bāb-ilu*, 'gate of God'). A confusion of noises or voices; a hubbub. The allusion is to the CONFUSION OF TONGUES during the building of the Tower of Babel (Genesis 11).

**Babrius.** An ancient fabulist, probably a Hellenized Roman of the early 3rd century, who may have lived in Syria. *See also* AESOP; AVIANUS; FABLES.

**Baby. Babies in the eyes.** Love in the look of the eyes. Love is the baby CUPID, represented by the tiny image of a person that can be seen in the pupil of another person's eyes.

> She clung about his neck, gave him ten kisses.
> Toyed with his locks, looked babies in his eyes.
> THOMAS HEYWOOD: *Love's Maistresse* (1633)

**Baby boom.** A sudden increase in the birth rate. A noted baby boom followed the Second World War, when husbands and fathers returned home. A person born at this time is sometimes known as a 'baby boomer'.

**Baby bunting.** A nursery nurse's term of affection for a young baby. The second word simply means 'chubby one'. A well-known nursery rhyme contains the name.

Bye, baby bunting,
Daddy's gone a-hunting,
Gone to get a rabbit skin
To wrap the baby bunting in.

**Baby snatcher.** *See* CRADLE SNATCHER.
**Baby teeth.** *See* MILK TEETH.
**Blue baby.** *See under* BLUE.
**Deities protecting babies.** *See under* DEITIES.
**Left holding the baby, To be.** *See under* LEAVE.
**Throw the baby out with the bath water, To.** *See under* THROW.
**War baby.** *See under* WAR.
**Warming-pan baby, The.** *See under* WARM.
**Wet the baby's head, To.** *See under* WET.

**Babylon** (Akkadian *Bāb-ilān*, 'gate of the gods'). The chief city of ancient MESOPOTAMIA, first settled about 3000 BC.

**Babylonian captivity.** The period beginning from 597 BC, when the Jews became captives in Babylon after the attacks by NEBUCHADNEZZAR, until their return (from 538 BC) after their release by CYRUS, following his conquest of Babylon.

**Babylonian captivity of the papacy.** *See* AVIGNON POPES.

**Hanging Gardens of Babylon, The.** *See under* HANG.

**Whore of Babylon, The.** *See under* WHORE.

**Baca, The Valley of.** *See under* VALLEY.

**Bacbuc** (Hebrew *baqbūq*, 'pitcher', 'cruse'). Rabelais' personification of the 'Holy Bottle'. PANURGE consulted the Holy Bottle on the question whether or not he ought to marry, and it answered with a click, like the noise made by glass snapping. Bacbuc told Panurge the noise meant *trinc* ('drink'), and that was the response, the most direct and positive it had ever given. Panurge might interpret it as he liked. The Holy Bottle's own name is similar and represents the sound of a bottle being poured or emptied. The 'cruse' in 1 Kings 14:3 is this word in the original Hebrew.

**Bacchanalia.** Roman festivals in honour of BACCHUS, the equivalent of the Greek Dionysia, characterized by drunkenness and licentiousness (although it must be noted that Greek drama had its origins in the Dionysia). Hence 'Bacchanalian orgy' for any wild and drunken revelry.

**Bacchanals, Bacchants** or **Bacchantes.** Priests and priestesses, or male and female votaries of BACCHUS and hence drunken roisterers. *See also* BAG O'NAILS *under* PUBLIC HOUSE SIGNS.

**Bacchus** (perhaps of Thracian or Lydian origin). In Roman mythology, the god of wine, the Dionysus of the Greeks, son of ZEUS and SEMELE. The name was originally merely an epithet of Dionysus. At first represented as a bearded man, he later appears as a handsome youth with black eyes and flowing locks, crowned with vine and ivy. In peace his robe was purple, in war it was a panther's skin. According to some accounts he married ARIADNE after her desertion by THESEUS. The Romans seem to have confused this god with the ancient Italic deity *Liber Pater*, god of wine.

Bacchus, in the LUSIADS, is the evil demon or antagonist of JUPITER, the lord of destiny. As MARS is the guardian power of Christianity, Bacchus is the guardian power of Islam.

**Bacchus sprang from the thigh of Zeus.** The tale is that SEMELE, at the suggestion of JUNO, asked JUPITER to appear before her in all his glory, but the foolish request proved her death. Jupiter saved the child, which was prematurely born, by sewing it up in his thigh till it came to maturity.

**Priest or son of Bacchus, A.** *See under* PRIEST.

**Bach** or **batch.** In Australia, a holiday house or 'weekender', especially one at the beach, so named as associated with a single occupant or BACHELOR.

**Bachelor.** A man who has not been married. The word is from Old French *bacheler*, itself from Vulgar Latin *baccalaris*, 'farm worker', in turn perhaps related to Latin *vacca*, 'cow'. The word was applied to aspirants to knighthood, and KNIGHTS of the lowest rank were known as knights bachelor, those too young to display their own banners.

With him ther was his sone, a yong *Squyer*
A lovyere, and a lusty bacheler.
CHAUCER: *Canterbury Tales*, 'Prologue' (*c*.1387)

**Bachelor girl.** A now somewhat dated expression for an independent unmarried young woman, the erstwhile 'modern miss'.

**Bachelor of Arts, Science, Medicine etc.** In most British and American universities, one who has taken his first degree in the appropriate faculty. Originally the degrees of 'master' and 'doctor' were for those further qualified to teach at the university.

**Bachelor's buttons.** Buttons similar in principle to press-studs used in dress-making and affixed without the need of sewing. Hence the name, for bachelors are traditionally limited in their domestic accomplishments.

Various button-shaped flowers are also so called: red bachelor's buttons (double red campion), yellow (the upright crowfoot and buttercup and *Kerria japonica*), white (white ranunculus and white campion). Rustics were wont to put them in their pockets and their growth was an indication that they would find favour with their sweethearts. Maidens wore them under their aprons.

**Bachelor seal, A.** A young male seal, especially one that has not yet mated.

**Bachelor's fare.** Bread and cheese and kisses.

**Bachelor's porch, A.** An old name for the north door of a church. Menservants and old men used to sit on benches down the north aisle, and maidservants and poor women on the south side. After the service the men formed one line and the women another, through which the clergy and gentry passed.

**Bachelor's wife, A.** A hypothetical ideal or perfect wife.

> Bachelers wiues, and maides children be well tought.
>
> JOHN HEYWOOD: *Proverbs* (1562)

**Back. Back, To.** To support with money, influence or encouragement. To lay money on a horse or any other participant in a race or contest.

As a commercial term the meaning is to endorse. When a merchant backs or endorses a bill he guarantees its value. Falstaff says to the Prince:

> You care not who sees your back: call you that backing of your friends? A plague upon such backing!
>
> SHAKESPEARE: *Henry IV, Pt I*, II, iv (1597)

**Back and fill, To.** A nautical phrase meaning to fill and empty the sails of wind alternately in order to manoeuvre in a narrow channel. Metaphorically, to be irresolute or vacillate.

**Back and forth.** To and fro.

**Backbencher, A.** An ordinary member of the House of Commons in the British Parliament, who does not hold office and occupies the back benches. *See also* FRONT BENCH.

**Back burner, The.** The back burners or rings on a cooking stove are used for keeping saucepans simmering, while the front burners are usually the hottest and are used for cooking or heating quickly. Figuratively, when something is put on the back burner, it is put to one side for the time being, to be kept in reserve for use when necessary.

**Back door, The.** The rear entrance to a building. The expression 'to get in by the back door' means to gain irregular entry to a job, position or the like, for example by 'string-pulling'. *See also* PULL STRINGS.

**Back down, To.** To yield a point; to withdraw an earlier claim.

**Back end, The.** Autumn. A north of England phrase, in full 'the back end of the year'.

**Back-handed compliment, A.** A double-edged one. Also, shortened, a backhander.

**Backhander, A.** A blow with the back of the hand. Also a bribe, especially one made surreptitiously.

**Back list, A.** A publisher's list of books that were previously published and that are still available.

**Back number, To be a.** To be superseded, relegated or out of the swim; to be a person with outdated ideas. The reference is to old back issues of newspapers, with news that is no longer topical or of interest. Figuratively, a back number is an old-fashioned person or 'has-been'.

**Back of beyond, The.** A phrase originating in Australia to describe the vast spaces of the interior, the great OUTBACK. The term 'back-block' is found in 1850, referring to those territories divided up by the government into blocks for settlement.

**Back off, To.** To draw back; to retreat.

**Back out, To.** To withdraw from an engagement, commitment or the like; to retreat from a difficult position.

**Back passage.** A euphemism for the rectum.

**Backroom boys.** A name given to the unpublicized scientists and technicians in the Second World War who contributed much to the development of scientific warfare and war production, and since applied generally to such anonymous laboratory workers. The phrase comes from a speech by Lord Beaverbrook on war production (24 March 1941):

> Now who is responsible for this work of development on which so much depends? To whom must the praise be given? To the boys in the back rooms. They do not sit in the limelight. But they are the men who do all the work. Many of them are Civil Servants.

**Backs, The.** In Cambridge the beautiful gardens that lie to the rear of certain colleges in the centre of the city and that run down to the River Cam.

**Backscratcher, A.** In a figurative sense a person who provides money or a service for someone else with the aim of receiving a similar payment or service in return. The principle is summarized in the saying: 'You scratch my back and I'll scratch yours.' Physically, the back is the one part of the body that one cannot scratch oneself. Someone else is therefore needed.

**Back seat, A.** Used figuratively to mean a relatively obscure position compared with the one previously occupied. To 'take a back seat' can also mean to submit to humiliation.

**Back-seat driver, A.** One who gives a car driver advice and instructions from the back seat. The meaning is similar to ARMCHAIR CRITIC.

**Back slang.** A form of slang that consists in pronouncing a word near enough backwards. It was formerly much used by 'flash' COCKNEYS, costermongers, thieves and the like, and mainly centres on words for different coins, vegetables, fruit, police court terms and the like. Thus 'cool' is look, 'dunop' a pound, 'elrig' a girl, 'eno' one, 'genitraf' a farthing, 'nam' a man, 'nammow' a woman, 'nig' gin, 'rape' a pear, 'shif' fish, 'slop' a policeman, 'storrac' carrots, 'spinsrap' parsnips, 'tenip' a pint, 'yannep' a penny and 'yob' a boy. This last has passed into everyday speech.

**Backstairs influence.** Private or unrecognized influence, especially at court. Royal palaces have more than one staircase, and the backstairs would be used by those who sought the sovereign upon private matters. It was, therefore, highly desirable to win over the officials in charge of the 'backstairs'. Hence backstairs gossip is tittle-tattle obtained from servants, and backstairs plots or politics are underground or clandestine intrigue.

**Backstreet, A.** A street in a town that is remote from the main streets. Hence an illicit activity that could take place in such a street, such as a backstreet abortion.

**Back the field, To.** To bet on all the horses except one, the favourite.

**Back the wrong horse, To.** To make an error of judgement. A phrase from the TURF.

**Back to basics.** A return to 'ground rules' and traditional values. The phrase became a catch-all political slogan of the CONSERVATIVE Party in the 1990s. It rang somewhat hollow following a series of sex scandals.

> The message from this Conference is clear and simple. We must go back to basics.
> JOHN MAJOR: Speech at Conservative Party Conference (8 October 1993)

**Back to nature.** Returning to a primitive or natural state.

**Back to square one.** Back to where one started. The expression apparently gained currency from the early days of broadcast commentaries on football matches when, in order to make the course of the game easier to follow, a diagram of the pitch, divided into numbered squares, was printed in radio programmes. The idea may have been derived from earlier board games such as SNAKES AND LADDERS.

**Back to the drawing board.** Back to begin again, especially after the aborting of an enterprise. The implication is that the venture was not properly or adequately planned. The expression may have originated with aircraft designers in the Second World War, when tests revealed faults in some models.

> Disney sends Elton's rock'n'roll Aida back to the drawing board.
> *Sunday Times* (headline) (13 December 1998)

**Back to the wall.** To have one's back to the wall is to be in a defensive or desperate situation. When threatened or attacked, it is best to get one's back against a wall so as to have protection in the rear.

**Back up, To.** To uphold or support, as someone who stands at another person's back to support him or her. In CRICKET the non-striking BATSMAN backs up by beginning to advance down the pitch in order to take a quick run if he sees that the striker has the chance to do so.

**Backwardation.** A former STOCK EXCHANGE term for the postponement of delivery by a seller of securities until the next settlement period. This mostly occurred when the price of a stock or commodity was lower than the cash or spot price. *See also* CONTANGO.

**Backward blessing, A.** A curse. To say the Lord's Prayer backwards was to invoke the DEVIL.

**Backwards in coming forwards, To be.** To be self-effacing, shy or reluctant to draw attention to oneself.

**Backwater, A.** Properly, a pool or stretch of water fed by the backflow of a stream or river. Figuratively, to be in a backwater is to be isolated from the active flow of life.

**Back water, To.** To row backwards in order to reverse or stay a boat's motion, hence, to go easy, to retrace one's steps, to retreat.

**Backwoodsman, A.** Someone from the back-woods, a remote and sparsely populated place. Hence an uncouth person or 'hick'. In British politics, a backwoodsman is a peer who rarely or never attends the HOUSE OF LORDS.

**At the back of one's mind.** *See under* AT.

**Behind one's back.** *See under* BEHIND.

**Break one's back, To.** *See under* BREAK.

**Break the back of, To.** *See under* BREAK.

**Cast back, To.** *See under* CAST.

**Double back, To.** *See under* DOUBLE.

**Flat on one's back, To be.** *See under* FLAT.

**Get off someone's back, To.** *See under* GET.

**Get someone's back up, To.** *See under* GET.

**Go back on a person, To.** *See under* GO.

**Go back on one's word, To.** *See under* GO.

**Hogs Back.** *See under* HOG.

**Make a rod for one's own back, To.** *See under* ROD.

**Men stand with their backs to the fire.** *See under* MAN.

**On the back of.** Resulting from; following as a consequence. An expression often associated with the business world.

> Share prices rallied in London on the back of the overnight rebound on Wall Street. But it was a half-hearted affair, lacking conviction.
> *The Times* (3 September 1998)

**See the back of, To.** *See under* SEE.

**Small of the back, The.** *See under* SMALL.

**Turn one's back on, To.** *See under* TURN.

**Backwards, To bend over.** *See under* BEND.

**Bacon. Bring home the bacon, To.** *See under* BRING.

**Save one's bacon, To.** *See under* SAVE.

**Baconian philosophy.** Inductive philosophy as

formulated by Francis Bacon (1561–1626) in the second book of the *Novum Organum* (1620). He did not invent it but gave it a new importance.

**Baconian theory.** *See* SHAKESPEARE, WILLIAM.

**Bactrian Sage, The.** Zoroaster or Zarathustra, founder of the ancient Persian religion, who was probably either a Bactrian or a Mede. *See also* ZOROASTRIANS.

**Bad. Bad, The.** Among rulers called 'the Bad' are:

Albert, Landgrave of Thuringia and Margrave of Meissen (d.1314)
Charles II, king of Navarre (r.1349–87)
William I, king of Sicily (r.1154–66)

**Bad Bible, The.** *See under* BIBLE.

**Bad blood.** Vindictiveness, ill-feeling. Hence 'to make bad blood' is to create or renew ill-feeling.

**Bad company.** An unsuitable circle of friends or acquaintances.

**Bad debt.** A debt unlikely to be paid.

**Bad egg, A.** A disreputable character.

**Bad excuse is better than none, A.** An adage first appearing in Nicholas Udall's RALPH ROISTER DOISTER, the first English comedy, performed *c.*1553.

**Bad form.** An offence against social convention, something 'not done'.

**Bad hat, A.** A rascal or good-for-nothing. In America also applied to a bad actor.

**Bad job.** A regrettable state of affairs.

**Bad Lands, The.** The *Mauvaises Terres*, the extensive tracts of sterile, rocky and desolate hill-country that early French trappers encountered in the west of South Dakota.

**Bad lot, A.** A morally or commercially unsound person, or a commercial project or stock that is worthless. The expression has its origin in auctioneering, meaning a lot for which no one will bid.

**Bad news.** Colloquially, someone or something that is undesirable, that one could do without.

**Bad patch, A.** A difficult time or troubled period, as: 'She went through a bad patch.'

**Bad quarter of an hour, A.** A brief unpleasant experience. The expression translates the French *un mauvais quart d'heure*.

**Bad shot, A.** A wrong guess. A sporting phrase for a shot that misses the mark.

**Bad with the good.** 'To take the bad with the good' is to accept the disadvantages; the drawbacks as well as the gains.

**Feel bad about, To.** *See under* FEEL.

**Go from bad to worse, To.** To deteriorate even further.

**Go to the bad, To.** To become ruined or depraved.

**In a bad way.** Gravely ill; in trouble.

**Not bad.** Quite good.

**Not half bad.** *See under* HALF.

**Not so bad.** Fairly good.

**Too bad.** Said of a regrettable situation that one can no longer rectify.

**To the bad.** *See under* TO.

**Badge, Rogue's.** *See under* ROGUE.

**Badinguet.** A nickname given to NAPOLEON III, reputedly the name of the workman whose clothes he wore when he escaped from the fortress of Ham in 1846. His adherents were known as Badingueux.

> If Badinguet and Bismarck have a row together let them settle it between them with their fists.
> ÉMILE ZOLA: *The Downfall*, ch ii (1892)

**Badminton.** The Gloucestershire seat of the Dukes of Beaufort, which has given its name to a CLARET CUP and also to the game played with rackets and shuttlecock. In pugilistic parlance, blood, which is sometimes called claret, from the colour, was also formerly called 'badminton'.

**Badoura** (Arabic *badr al-budūr*, 'full moon of full moons', a phrase denoting outstanding beauty). 'The most beautiful woman ever seen upon earth', as the heroine of the tale of Camaralzaman and Badoura in the ARABIAN NIGHTS ENTERTAINMENTS. Their story is the proverbial one of 'love at first sight'.

**Baedeker.** Karl Baedeker (1801–59) published the first of the famous series of guidebooks, modelled on John Murray's *Handbooks*, at Coblenz in 1839. They were noted for their reliability and thoroughness and were widely used by tourists the world over. Baedeker inaugurated the practice of marking with one or more stars objects and places of interest according to their historic or aesthetic importance.

**Baedeker raids.** A phrase originating in 1942 to describe German air attacks on historic or culturally important British cities, like those listed in Baedeker, such as Bath, Canterbury and Norwich. The raids were made in reprisal for British raids on Cologne and Lübeck.

**Baffle.** Originally the punishment or public disgracing of an errant KNIGHT, taking the form of hanging him or his effigy by the heels from a tree.

> He by the heeles him hung vpon a tree
> And baffuld so, that all which passed by,
> The picture of his punishment might see.
> EDMUND SPENSER: *The Faerie Queene*, VI, vii (1596)

**Bag. Bag, To.** To secure for oneself; to purloin. Probably from sporting or poaching use, meaning to put into one's bag what one has shot or trapped. Hence, a good bag is a big catch of game or fish.

**Bag and baggage.** In entirety. Originally a military phrase signifying the soldier with all his belongings or the whole of the equipment and stores of an army. Hence W.E. Gladstone's bag and baggage policy with regard to the Middle East, which implied that the Turks must be completely cleared out of the Balkans. *See also* BAGGAGE; LOCK, STOCK AND BARREL.

**Bag lady, A.** A homeless woman who wanders the streets carrying all her possessions in shopping bags. The phrase originated in the USA.

**Bagman, A.** A travelling salesman, from the bag of samples that he carries. Formerly the horses of commercial travellers often bore outsize saddlebags. In modern use, a bagman is a person who collects and distributes money obtained by racketeering and other dishonest means.

The term bagmen (or Leadenhallers) also denoted those who dealt in bag-foxes, which were regularly traded at Leadenhall Market. From the late 18th until the mid-19th century, foxes were brought in (mainly from France) to overcome the scarcity created by the destruction of foxes by gamekeepers and farmers. The fox was released from the bag at the time of the hunt.

**Bag of bones.** A lean or emaciated person.

**Bag of nerves.** A tense or agitated person.

**Bag of tricks** or **Whole bag of tricks, The.** The whole lot; every possible device. An allusion to the conjuror's bag, in which he carried his equipment for performing tricks.

**Bag o'Nails.** *See under* PUBLIC HOUSE SIGNS.

**Bags.** Slang for 'trousers', which may be taken as the bags of the body. *See also* OXFORD BAGS.

**Bags I.** Schoolboy slang assertion of a claim. *See also* FAINS.

**Bags of mystery.** Dated slang for sausages and saveloys. The allusion is to the unknown contents.

**Bags under the eyes.** Puffy bulges under the eyes, regarded as a sign of dissipation.

**Body bag.** *See under* BODY.

**Bottom of the bag, The.** *See under* BOTTOM.

**Diplomatic bag.** *See under* DIPLOMAT.

**Doggy bag.** *See under* DOG.

**Empty the bag, To.** *See under* EMPTY.

**Gladstone bag.** *See under* GLADSTONE.

**In the bag.** As good as certain. In horse-racing parlance in Australia it means that the horse referred to will not be running.

**Lawyers' bags.** *See under* LAWYER.

**Left holding the bag, To be.** *See under* LEFT.

**Let the cat out of the bag, To.** *See under* LET.

**Old bag, An.** *See under* OLD.

**Oxford bags.** *See under* OXFORD.

**Pack one's bags, To.** *See under* PACK.

**Baggage.** As applied to an immoral or flirtatious woman, this word dates from the days when soldiers' wives, taken on foreign service with the regiment, travelled with the regimental stores and baggage.

**Bag and baggage.** *See under* BAG.

**Baggins, Bilbo.** The hero of J.R.R. Tolkien's children's novel, *The* HOBBIT (1937). He is a small, hairy-footed being who, accompanied by the wizard GANDALF and a dozen 'dwarves', helps slay a dragon and recover a lost treasure. He reappears in *The* LORD OF THE RINGS (1954–5). *See also* FRODO.

**Bail, To jump.** *See under* JUMP.

**Bailey** (Old French *baille*, 'enclosed court'). The external wall of a medieval castle, also the outer court, i.e. the space immediately within the outer wall. When there were two courts they were distinguished as the inner and outer bailey. Subsequently the word was attached to the buildings, as the OLD BAILEY, London. The paved surround at the back of a house is still called 'the bailey' in South Wales.

**Bailey bridge.** A bridge made of prefabricated steel parts that can be erected speedily, which was invented by the British engineer Sir Donald Coleman Bailey (1901–85). In the Second World War they were a major factor in the rapidity of Allied advances, especially in northwestern Europe.

**Bailiff.** *See* BUMBAILIFF.

**Bailiff of Bedford, The.** The overflowing of the River Ouse in former days was so called, possibly because it turned people out of their homes.

**Bailiff of the Marshland, The.** A feverish shivering fit to which newcomers to Fenland were supposed to be prone. It is mentioned in Thomas Fuller's *The History of the Worthies of England*, published posthumously in 1662.

**Bailiff's Daughter of Islington, The.** A ballad given in PERCY'S RELIQUES (1765) on the popular theme of a pair of lovers, a squire's son and a bailiff's daughter, separated by differences of social rank. The Islington concerned is the one near King's Lynn in Norfolk. It has appeared in the American versions of the story as 'Ireland Town' and 'Hazelington Town'.

**Bailiwick.** A district under the jurisdiction of a BAILIFF. The term is particularly associated with the CHANNEL ISLANDS, which for administrative purposes are grouped into the two bailiwicks of Jersey and Guernsey.

**Baily's beads.** When, in an ECLIPSE, the disc of the moon has reduced that of the sun to a thin crescent, the crescent assumes a resemblance to a string of beads. This phenomenon, caused by the sun shining through the depressions between the lunar mountains, was first accurately described in 1836 by the English astronomer Francis Baily (1774–1867). Hence the name.

**Bairam** (Turkish). The name given to two Muslim festivals. The Lesser Bairam begins on the new moon of the month Shawwal, immediately after the feast of RAMADAN, and lasts for three days. The Greater, 70 days after the Lesser, also lasts for three days, beginning on the tenth day of the twelfth month, and it forms the concluding ceremony of the pilgrimage to MECCA.

**Bajadere.** *See* BAYADERE.

**Bajan** or **Bajanella.** *See* BEJAN.

**Bajazet** (Arabic *abū yazīd*, 'father of Yazid', a name meaning 'more', 'addition'). The name of various Ottoman SULTANS. Bajazet (or Bayezid) I, who was sultan from 1389 to 1403, was a great warrior, noted for his victories especially against the Hungarians and their allies at Nicopolis in 1396. He was overwhelmed by TAMBERLANE (Timur) at Ankara in 1402 and held prisoner until his death. There is no evidence for the story, popularized by the dramatists Christopher Marlowe and Nicholas Rowe, that Tamberlane carried him about in an iron cage.

**Bake. Baked meats** or **bake meats.** Meat pies.

> The funeral bak'd meats
> Did coldly furnish forth the marriage tables.
> SHAKESPEARE: *Hamlet*, I, ii (1600)

Hamlet's words mean that the hot meat pies, served at the funeral and not eaten, were served cold at the marriage banquet, so short was the interval between the death of Gertrude's husband (Hamlet's father) and her remarriage to Claudius.

**Baker. Baker, The.** Louis XVI (r.1774–93) was so called, with his queen (MARIE ANTOINETTE) 'the baker's wife' and their son, the Dauphin, the 'shop boy', because they gave bread to the starving men and women who came to VERSAILLES on 6 October 1789.

> The return of the baker, his wife, and the shop-boy to Paris had not the expected effect. Flour and bread were still scarce.
> A. DUMAS: *The Countess de Charny*, ch ix (1853–5)

**Baker's cyst.** A firm, fluid-filled lump the size of a walnut behind the knee. It is caused by increased pressure within the knee joint due to a build-up of fluid. Baker's cyst is so named in recognition of its first description by the eminent surgeon W.M. Baker (1839–96) of St Bartholomew's Hospital, London.

**Baker's dozen, A.** Thirteen for twelve. In earlier times when a heavy penalty was inflicted for short weight, bakers used to give an extra number of loaves, called the inbread, to avoid all risk of incurring a fine. The thirteenth was the 'vantage loaf'.

**Baksheesh** (Persian *bakhshīsh*, 'gift'). A tip or gratuity. Such gifts are traditionally demanded in the Middle East by beggars, servants and others, more as a right than a gratuity.

> I was to give the men, too, a 'baksheish', that is, a present of money, which is usually made upon the conclusion of any sort of treaty.
> ALEXANDER KINGLAKE: *Eōthen* (1844)

**Balaam** (Hebrew *bil'am*, perhaps 'non-people'). A misleading prophet or ally, as Balaam was in Numbers 22–4. In John Dryden's *Absalom and Achitophel* (1574) Balaam represents the Earl of Huntingdon. The 'citizen of sober fame' called Balaam in Alexander Pope's *Moral Essays* (iii (1731–5)) is partly based on DIAMOND PITT.

The word also formerly denoted matter kept in type for filling up odd spaces in periodicals, alluding to a person who talks like BALAAM'S ASS (Numbers 22:30). John Lockhart writes in his *Memoirs of the Life of Sir Walter Scott* (ch lxx (1837–8)):

> Balaam is the cant name for asinine paragraphs about monstrous productions of nature and the like, kept standing in type to be used whenever the real news of the day leaves an awkward space that must be used up somehow.

Hence Balaam basket or box, the printer's slang for the receptacle for such matter, and also (in the USA) for the place where stereotyped 'fill-ups' are or were kept.

**Balaamite.** One who makes a profession of religion for profit or gain, as did Balaam.

**Balaam's ass.** The following tale is related in Numbers 22:21–35. BALAAM one day rode his ass towards MOAB, where Balak wanted him to curse the Israelites, against the will of God. On the way the angel of the Lord appeared. Only the ass saw him and turned aside. Her master hit her. She turned aside again, wedging Balaam's foot against a wall. He hit her again. She lay down, and her master belaboured her a third time. At that point God gave her the power of speech, and she asked her master why he had hit her three times. He replied that he was ready to kill her for mocking him. She answered: 'Am I not thine ass, upon which thou hast ridden ever since I was thine unto this day? Was I ever wont to do so unto thee?' The angel then became visible to Balaam, telling him that if the ass had not turned away, he, not the ass, would have been killed. When Balaam reached the Israelites, he blessed them instead of cursing them. The story expresses God's anger against those who do not listen to Him.

**Balaclava.** *See* CARDIGAN.

**Balafré, Le** (French, 'the gashed'). Francis, 2nd Duke of Guise (1519–63), who in the siege of Boulogne (1545) received a sword cut that left a fearful scar on his face. At Dormans (1575), his son Henri, 3rd Duke of Guise (1550–88), earned the same title. It was also given by Sir Walter Scott (in *Quentin Durward* (1823)) to Ludovic Lesly, an archer of the Scottish Guard.

**Balan.** A strong and courageous giant in many old romances. In FIERABRAS he is the 'Sowdan of Babylon', father of Fierabras, ultimately conquered by CHARLEMAGNE. In the ARTHURIAN ROMANCES he is the brother of BALIN.

**Balance, The.** LIBRA, an ancient zodiacal constellation between VIRGO and SCORPIO representing a pair of scales, the seventh sign of the ZODIAC, which the sun enters a few days before the autumnal equinox. *See also* ASTROLOGY.

According to Persian mythology at the LAST DAY there will be a huge balance as big as the vault of HEAVEN. The two scale pans will be called that of light and that of darkness. In the former all good will be placed, in the latter all evil, and everyone will be rewarded according to the verdict of the balance.

**Balance of nature, The.** An ecological equilibrium, produced by the interaction of living organisms.

**Balance of payments, The.** The difference over a given period between a nation's gross receipts from other countries and its gross payments to them, the result being adverse or favourable.

**Balance of power, The.** The distribution of power among sovereign states in such a way that no state has a preponderance over any of the others.

**Balance of terror, A.** A balance of power produced by the equal possession of nuclear weapons.

**Balance of trade, The.** The difference in value between the exports and imports of a nation.

**Hang in the balance, To.** *See under* HANG.

**In the balance.** Uncertain; at a critical stage.

**On balance.** All things considered.

**Strike a balance, To.** *See under* STRIKE.

**Tip the balance, To.** *See under* TIP.

**Weighed in the balance and found wanting.** *See under* WEIGH.

**Balclutha.** A fortified town on the banks of the Clutha (i.e. the Clyde) mentioned in *Carthon*, one of the OSSIAN poems. It was captured and burned by Comhal, father of FINGAL, in one of his forays against the Britons.

**Bald. Baldfaced Stag.** Common among old PUBLIC HOUSE SIGNS. 'Baldfaced' was applied to horses and other animals with a white strip down the forehead. *See also* BLAZE.

**As bald as a coot.** *See under* AS.

**Charles le Chauve.** Charles II of France (823–877), son of Louis the Pious or the DEBONAIR (le Débonnaire), was nicknamed 'the Bald'.

**Go for someone baldheaded, To.** To act impetuously, without regard for the consequences. The expression is of American origin and is said to date from the days when men wore wigs, and any energetic action or fray required that the wig should be thrown aside. Some authorities refer the phrase to a cavalry charge at Warburg (1760) led bareheaded by the Marquis of GRANBY. *See also* PUBLIC HOUSE SIGNS.

**Balder** (Old Norse *baldr*, 'bold'). A Scandinavian god of light, the son of ODIN and FRIGG, noted for his handsomeness and gentle nature. He dwelt at Breidhablik, one of the mansions of ASGARD. One legend says that Frigg took oaths from all things not to harm him, but accidentally omitted MISTLETOE, with a twig of which he was slain. Another tells that he was slain by his rival, the blind god Hod, while fighting for the beautiful Nanna. His death was the final prelude to the overthrow of the gods.

**Baldwin** (Germanic *bald*, 'brave', and *wine*, 'friend').

(1) In the CHARLEMAGNE romances, the nephew of ROLAND and the youngest and fairest of Charlemagne's PALADINS.

(2) The first king of Jerusalem (r.1100–18), brother of Godfrey of Bouillon, the previous ruler, who declined the title of king. He figures in Tasso's JERUSALEM DELIVERED (1580–1) as the restless and ambitious Duke of Bologna, leader of 1200 horsemen in the allied Christian army.

**Bale out, To.** To remove water from a boat with buckets or other receptacles. In air force usage it means to parachute from an aircraft in an emergency, and in army usage it means to escape quickly from a tank or other vehicle when it is hit.

**Balfour. Balfour's Poodle.** The HOUSE OF LORDS. From 1906 the CONSERVATIVE leader Arthur Balfour (1848–1930) exploited his party's majority in the House of Lords to block the legislation of the LIBERAL government, which had an overwhelming majority in the Commons. When the Lords rejected the Licensing Bill of 1908, Henry Chaplin MP claimed that the House of Lords was the 'watchdog of the constitution', to which Lloyd George replied: 'You mean it is Mr Balfour's poodle! It fetches and carries for him. It barks for him. It bites anybody that he sets it on to!' *See also* BLOODY BALFOUR.

**Blasphemous Balfour.** *See under* BLASPHEMOUS.

**Bloody Balfour.** *See under* BLOODY.

**Bali.** A demonic Hindu god. In the second world age he ruled over all three worlds but had to yield sovereignty over earth and heaven to VISHNU. He has ruled the underworld ever since. According to the MAHABHARATA he lives in the form of an ass in a tumbledown hut. *See also* HINDUISM.

**Balin.** The devoted brother of BALAN in the ARTHURIAN ROMANCES. The two men accidentally slew each other in ignorance of each other's identity and were buried in one grave by MERLIN. The story is told by Sir Thomas Malory in *Le Morte d'Arthur* (1485), and an altered version appears in Tennyson's *Idylls of the King* (1859).

**Balios** (Greek, 'spotted', 'dappled'). One of the horses given by NEPTUNE to PELEUS. It afterwards belonged to ACHILLES. Like XANTHUS, its sire was the west wind, and its dam Swift-foot the HARPY.

**Balisarda.** ROGERO's sword, made by a sorceress.

**Balk** (Old English *balca*, 'ridge', 'bank'). The word came to apply to the ridge between two furrows left in ploughing (in the old OPEN-FIELD SYSTEM of agriculture the cultivated strips were divided by unploughed turf balks). More generally, it was used of any obstacle, stumbling-block or check on one's actions. Thus in billiards, the baulk or balk is the part of the table behind the line where the cue balls are placed at the start of a game, and from which one has to play when one's freedom is checked. So 'to balk' is to stop suddenly at an obstacle in one's way.

**Balk of timber, A.** A large, roughly squared piece of timber.

**Balkis.** The Muslim name of the queen of SHEBA, who visited SOLOMON. She appears in the Bible (1 Kings 10) but is not mentioned by name. According to the Koran she had hairy legs but concealed them under a long dress. On her visit to Solomon, the king decided to see if this rumour was true, and arranged that she should approach his palace over a courtyard with a mirror floor. Thinking it was a pool, Balkis raised the hem of her dress and revealed her secret.

**Ball.** (1) A spherical body; an Old Norse word.

(2) A dance; from Old French *baller*, 'to dance', from Late Latin *ballare*.

**Ball is in your court, The.** It is your turn now; the responsibility passes to you; you must make the next move.

**Ball lightning.** A slow-moving luminous ball that is occasionally seen in a thunderstorm.

**Ball of fortune, A.** A person tossed like a ball, FROM PILLAR TO POST; one who has experienced many vicissitudes of fortune.

**Belle of the ball.** *See under* BELLE.

**Catch** or **take the ball before the bound, To.** *See under* CATCH.

**Cross and ball.** *See under* CROSS.

**Have the ball at one's feet, To.** To have an opportunity; a metaphor from football.

**Keep one's eye on the ball, To.** To be alert.

**Keep the ball rolling, To.** To maintain progress; to keep the fun, conversation or activity going. A metaphor from ball games.

**On the ball.** Alert; well informed.

**Open the ball, To.** *See under* OPEN.

**Play ball, To.** *See under* PLAY.

**Start** or **set the ball rolling, To.** *See under* START.

**Three golden balls.** *See under* THREE.

**Whole ball of wax, The.** *See under* WHOLE.

**Witch balls.** *See under* WITCH.

**Ballad** (Old French *balade*, from Late Latin *ballare*, 'to dance'). Originally a song accompanying a dance.

**Bon Gaultier Ballads.** *See under* BON.

**Ballet.** A theatrical representation combining PANTOMIME, music and dancing, introduced into France from Italy by Catherine de Medici when she married Henry II in 1533. She later invited to her house an Italian arranger of dances known as Balthasar Beaujoyeux, and in 1581 he made his name with the first ballet of importance, *Le Balet comique de la Royne*.

**Balliol College.** The Oxford college was founded *c.*1263 by John de Balliol, lord of Barnard Castle, as a penance for insulting the bishop of Durham. On his death in 1269, his widow, Devorguilla, took on the role of patroness. In the 19th century a Balliol scholarship became a much coveted distinction. Benjamin Jowett, the college's best known Master, was in office from 1870 to 1893.

> I know I'd sooner win two School House matches running than get the Balliol scholarship any day.
>
> THOMAS HUGHES: *Tom Brown's Schooldays*, Pt I, ch vi (1857)

**Balloon. Pilot balloon, A.** *See under* PILOT.

**When the balloon goes up.** *See under* WHEN.

**Ballot** (Italian *ballotta*, 'little ball'). This method of voting was common in ancient Greece and Rome. The name comes from the use of small balls put secretly in a box. Although it was one of the six points of CHARTISM, voting by ballot was not adopted in Britain until the Ballot Act of 1872 and not until after 1884 in the USA. *See also* BEANS.

**Ballyhoo.** The word is popularly associated with Ballyhooly, a village in County Cork, Ireland, but in its sense of a noisy demonstration to attract attention, or extravagant advertising or publicity, it originates from the USA.

**Balm** (Old French *basme*, from Latin *balsamum*, 'balsam'). An aromatic gum exuded from certain trees and used in perfumery and medicine.

**Is there no balm in Gilead?** (Jeremiah 8:22) Is there no remedy, no consolation? 'Balm' here is the GENEVA BIBLE's (*see under* BIBLE) translation of Hebrew *sori*, which probably means 'mastic', the resin yielded by the mastic tree, *Pistacia lentiscus*. In WYCLIF'S BIBLE (*see under* BIBLE) the word is translated 'gumme' and in Coverdale's 'triacle'. *See also* TREACLE BIBLE *under* BIBLE.

The fragrant gold-coloured resin now known as 'Balm of Gilead' is that from the tree *Commiphora opabalsamum* of Africa and western Asia.

**Balmoral bonnet** or **bluebonnet, A.** A Scottish brimless hat, often of blue wool, with a cockade and a plume on one side.

**Balmung.** One of the swords of SIEGFRIED made by Wieland.

**Balmy.** *See* BARMY.

**Balnibarbi.** A land occupied by projectors in Jonathan Swift's *Gulliver's Travels* (1726).

**Baloney.** *See* BOLONEY.

**Balthazar** (Babylonian *Bēlu-sharu-uṣur*, 'Bel protect the king'). One of the THREE KINGS OF COLOGNE. *See also* MAGI.

**Baltic, The.** The familiar name of the Baltic Mercantile and Shipping Exchange in the City of London, which was founded in the 18th century. It originated from meetings, at the Baltic COFFEE House, of merchants concerned with the Baltic trade, and it is now at St Mary Axe as a commodity and freight-chartering market. Membership largely consists of shipowners, shipbrokers and merchants. *See also* LLOYD'S.

**Bamberg Bible, The.** *See* THIRTY-SIX-LINE BIBLE *under* BIBLE.

**Bambi.** A young deer who lives in a German forest. He originated as the creation of Felix Salten (real name Sigmund Salzmann) in his gentle children's novel *Bambi* (1926), which is a more or less realistic depiction of forest life. Bambi gained his greatest fame, however, from the Walt Disney feature-length cartoon named after him, released in 1942. His name is a shortening of Italian *bambino*, 'baby'.

> Walt Disney made no more drastic or mistaken change than when he showed Bambi as a cute, lisping celluloid puppet titupping through a rainbow-hued landscape. A child who came to the book after seeing Disney's cartoon would find it hard to believe that Salten's young deer was the same character.
>
> MARGERY FISHER: *Who's Who in Children's Books* (1975)

**Bambocciades.** Grotesque pictures of scenes in low life, such as country WAKES, PENNY WEDDINGS and so on. They take their name from Italian *bamboccio*, 'child', 'puppet', a nickname given to Pieter van Laar (1592–*c*.1675), a noted Dutch painter of such scenes.

**Bamboo.** The tall treelike plant, with its hollow woody-walled stems, has earned a reputation in the Far East for its versatility, hence its nickname 'the friend of China'. It has come to be used for the manufacture of a variety of articles, notably household furniture, and its cane was for a long time the instrument for flogging criminals in China and beating schoolboys in England. Bamboo shoots are still sometimes given to nursing mothers in China to increase their flow of milk, while in European cuisine they are regarded as a delicacy, as a sort of oriental equivalent of asparagus.

**Bamboo Curtain, The.** Formed by analogy with IRON CURTAIN to denote the veil of secrecy and mistrust drawn between the Chinese Communist bloc and the non-Communist nations. *See also* GARLIC WALL.

**Bampton Lectures.** Founded by the Rev. John Bampton, minor CANON of Salisbury, who in 1751 left £120 per annum to the University of Oxford, to pay for eight divinity lectures on given subjects to be preached yearly at Great St Mary's and for their subsequent publication. Only MAs of Oxford and Cambridge are eligible as lecturers and the same person may not be chosen twice. The first lecture was given in 1780. Since 1895 they have been delivered biennially.

**Ban** (Old English *bannan*, 'to proclaim'). Originally meaning to summon, the verb came to mean to anathematize or imprecate, and the noun was applied specifically to an ecclesiastical curse, a formal prohibition or a sentence of outlawry. Banish and BANNS OF MARRIAGE are from the same root.

**Ban the bomb.** A slogan first current in the 1950s, when it was publicly promoted by the Campaign for Nuclear Disarmament.

**Lever le ban et l'arrière-ban.** *See under* LEVER.

**Ban, King.** In the ARTHURIAN ROMANCES, the father of Sir LANCELOT OF THE LAKE. He died of grief when his castle was taken and burned through the treachery of his seneschal.

**Banagher, That beats.** *See under* BEAT.

**Banana. Banana oil.** A phrase used colloquially in Australia and America for 'nonsense' or 'insincere talk'.

**Banana republic.** A small state, especially one in Central America, whose economy centres solely on the export of bananas. In consequence, the country is heavily dependent on foreign capital. The expression has a pejorative ring.

**Banana skin.** A cause of upset and humiliation. Fake banana skins are stock devices in pantomime for causing a 'pratfall'.

> The man who slips on the cunningly placed banana-skin does not laugh so soon as those who set the harmless trap and so, from the first, observe the whole scene.
>
> JOHN RUSSELL BROWN: *Shakespeare's Plays in Performance*, ch x (1966)

**Go bananas, To.** To go crazy or mad with anger, frustration, excitement or the like. The allusion is to monkeys and apes, who like bananas and will frantically try to seize them when they are proffered. *See also* GO APE *under* APE.

**Second banana.** *See under* SECOND.

**Top banana.** *See under* TOP.

**Banat.** A territory governed by a *ban* (Persian, 'lord'), particularly certain districts of Hungary and Croatia. The word was imported to Europe by the Avars, who ruled in Slavonic countries subject to Hungary.

**Banbury.** A town in Oxfordshire, proverbially known for its PURITANS, its 'cheese-paring', its cakes and its cross. Hence a 'Banbury man' is a

Puritan or bigot. Zeal-of-the-land Busy in Ben Jonson's *Bartholomew Fair* (1614) is described as a Banbury man.

> In my progress travelling Northward,
> Taking my farewell o'th Southward,
> To Banbery came I, O prophane one!
> Where I saw a Puritane-one,
> Hanging of his cat on Monday,
> For killing of a Mouse on Sunday.
> RICHARD BRATHWAITE: *Barnabee's Journal* (1638)

**Banbury cake.** A kind of spiced pastry cake with a criss-cross pattern on the top, once made exclusively at Banbury.

**Banbury Cross.** The cross of nursery rhyme fame was removed from Banbury by the PURITANS as a heathenish memorial in 1646. A new cross was erected on the site in 1858.

**Shepherd of Banbury, The.** *See under* SHEPHERD.

**Banco.** A commercial term denoting bank MONEY OF ACCOUNT as distinguished from currency. The term was used in exchange business when current money had depreciated from its former value.

**Bancus Communium Placitorum.** The Bench of COMMON PLEAS.

**Bancus Regius** or **Bancus Reginae.** The KING'S BENCH or Queen's Bench.

**In banco.** *See under* IN.

**Band. Band of Hope.** The name given (1847) to children's temperance societies in the United Kingdom. The movement grew steadily and the Band of Hope Union was founded in 1855.

**Beat the band, To.** *See under* BEAT.

**Bandbox. Bandbox Plot, The.** In his *Histoire d'Angleterre* (1724) Paul de Rapin (1661–1725) relates that in Queen ANNE's reign a bandbox was sent to the Lord Treasurer containing three pistols charged and cocked, their triggers tied to a thread fastened to the lid. When the lid was lifted, the pistols would go off and shoot the person who opened it. Dean Swift happened to be at hand when the box arrived and, seeing the thread, cut it, thus saving the life of the Lord Treasurer.

**Look as if one came out of a bandbox, To.** *See under* LOOK.

**Bandicoot.** A small Australian marsupial of the family Peramelidae, which ravages garden and farm produce.

**Bandit, One-armed.** *See under* ONE.

**B and S.** Brandy and soda. *See also* G AND T.

**Bands.** Clerical bands are a relic of the ancient amice, a square linen tippet tied about the neck of priests during the saying of MASS. ANGLICAN clergy abandoned their use in the late 19th century, although they have partially come back into fashion of late and are also worn by PRESBYTERIAN ministers and continental clergy.

**Geneva bands.** *See under* GENEVA.

**Legal bands.** *See under* LEGAL.

**Bandwagon, To climb on the.** *See under* CLIMB.

**Bandy words, To.** To wrangle; to argue heatedly. The metaphor is from the Irish game bandy (the precursor of hockey), in which each player has a stick with a crook at the end. The ball is bandied from side to side, each party trying to beat it home to the opposite goal. It was earlier a term in tennis, as is shown by the line in John Webster's *The White Devil* (IV, iv (1612)):

> That while he had been bandying at tennis.

**Bang. Bang on.** Absolutely accurate; spot on.

**Bang on about, To.** To talk tediously and lengthily about something.

**Bang** or **run one's head against a brick wall, To.** To make fruitless endeavours against insuperable difficulties.

**Bang their heads together, To.** To make two arguing people see sense.

**Bang up.** SWELL, fine, first-rate. Current as colloquial English by the end of the 18th century. A second meaning, now obsolete, was 'overcoat'.

> A green coat cut round in jockey fashion, and over it a white bang-up.
> C.J. LEVER: *Jack Hinton, the Guardsman* (1843)

**Big Bang.** *See under* BIG.

**Whole bang shoot** or **whole shooting match, The.** *See under* WHOLE.

**Bank.** (1) Originally meaning 'bench' or 'shelf', in Italy the word BANCO was applied specially to a tradesman's counter, and hence to a money-changer's bench or table. It is from this that the modern meaning of an establishment dealing with money is derived.

(2) The bank of a river. If you stand facing downstream, that is, with your back to the river's source, the left bank is on your left and the right bank on your right. The artistic quarter of Paris, the *rive gauche* or Left Bank, is thus the south bank of the Seine, whereas London's BANKSIDE and South Bank arts complex are on the right bank of the Thames, though rarely referred to as such.

**Bank holidays.** Properly, days when banks are legally closed. In 1830 Bank of England closures were limited from more than 40 to 18 and in 1834 to just four. By the Bank Holiday Act of 1871 days were again fixed for England, Wales, Ireland and, with a slight variation, Scotland. These Bank Holidays soon became general public holidays. Alterations have taken place from 1967, so that by 1999 there were nine Bank Holidays for England and Wales, 11 for Scotland, and 13 for Northern Ireland.

**Bankrupt** (Italian *banca rotta*, 'broken bench'). In Italy, when a money-lender was unable to continue business, his bench or counter was broken up, so that he was literally quite 'bankrupt'.

**Bankside.** A historic part of the borough of SOUTHWARK on the right bank of the Thames between Blackfriars Bridge and LONDON BRIDGE. At one end stood the CLINK prison and the church of St Mary OVERY (now Southwark Cathedral). The district was also famed in Shakespeare's time for BULL-BAITING and the GLOBE THEATRE and notorious for its brothels and ruffians.

The adjacent upstream site between Westminster Bridge and Blackfriars Bridge is known as the South Bank. The Festival of Britain was held here in 1951 and the area is now a complex of theatres, concert halls (including the Royal Festival Hall) and art galleries.

**Bottle bank.** *See under* BOTTLE.

**Break the bank, To.** *See under* BREAK.

**Clearing bank.** *See under* CLEAR.

**Banks's horse.** A horse called Marocco, belonging to one Banks about the end of Queen Elizabeth I's reign, and trained to do all manner of tricks. One of its exploits is said to have been the ascent of St Paul's steeple. A favourite story of the time is of an apprentice who called his master to see the spectacle. 'Away, you fool,' said the shopkeeper, 'why need I go to see a horse on the top when I can see so many horses at the bottom!' The horse is mentioned by Sir Walter Ralegh, Gayton, Kenelm Digby, Ben Jonson and others.

**Bannatyne Club.** The literary club founded by Sir Walter Scott, Archibald Constable and others in 1823 and named after George Bannatyne (*c.*1545–1608), to whose manuscript (now in the ADVOCATES' LIBRARY) is due the preservation of much 15th- and early 16th-century Scottish poetry. The club had convivial meetings and printed 116 rare works of Scottish history and literature. It was dissolved in 1861. *See also* MAITLAND CLUB; ROXBURGHE CLUB.

**Banner. Banner of the Prophet, The.** The original standard of MOHAMMED is said to be preserved in the Eyab Mosque of Istanbul. It is 12ft (3.6m) long and made of four layers of silk, the topmost being green, embroidered with gold. In times of peace it is kept in the hall of the 'noble vestment', as the Prophet's garb is styled, with his stirrup, sabre, bow and other relics.

**Banners in churches.** These are suspended as thank offerings to God. Those in St George's Chapel, Windsor, Henry VII's Chapel, WESTMINSTER, and elsewhere, are to indicate that the KNIGHT whose banner is hung up avows himself devoted to God's service.

**Banner State, The.** In the USA the state that, in a presidential election, gives the victor the biggest majority or vote. The adjective is used in other contexts to mean 'leading' or 'foremost'. *See also* UNITED STATES OF AMERICA.

**Sacred Banner of France, The.** The ORIFLAMME.

**Star-spangled Banner, The.** *See under* STAR.

**Banneret.** One who leads his VASSALS to battle under his own banner. Also an order of knighthood conferred on the field of battle for deeds of valour by tearing off the points of the recipient's pennon. This medieval order lapsed after the reign of Elizabeth I and was last properly conferred by CHARLES I in 1642 on Colonel John Smith for his recovery of the Royal Standard at Edgehill.

**Banns. Banns of marriage.** The publication in the parish church for three successive Sundays of an intended marriage. It is made after the second lesson of the morning service or of the evening service if there is no morning service. The word is from the same root as BAN.

**Bid the banns, To.** *See under* BID.

**Forbid the banns, To.** *See under* FORBID.

**Banquet** (Italian *banchetto*, 'little table'). In addition to its present meaning, the word also formerly meant 'dessert'. Thus in the *Pennyles Pilgrimage* (1618), John Taylor, the WATER POET, writes:

> Our first and second course being three-score dishes at one boord, and after that, always a banquet.

**Banshee** (Irish *bean sídhe*, 'woman of the fairy mound'). In Irish folklore, a female spirit who announces her presence by shrieking and wailing under the windows of a house when one of its occupants is close to death.

**Bantam.** A breed of small domestic fowl. Figuratively, a plucky little person who will not be bullied by someone bigger than himself. The bantam cock will take on a dunghill cock five times its own weight, and is therefore said to 'have a great soul in a little body'. The bantam originally came from the village of Bantam in Java.

**Banyan.** The tree of tropical Asia, remarkable for its size and shape, is so called from the banyan or banian, a Hindu trader and merchant who wore a particular dress, was strict in his observance of fasts and abstained from eating any kind of flesh, the word itself deriving from Gujarati *vāniyo*, 'man of the trading caste', from Sanskrit *vānija*, 'merchant'. A group of these traders set up a small pagoda under a banyan tree near Gombroon (now Bandar-e 'Abbas) on the Persian Gulf, in what is now southern Iran. Europeans in the locality applied the word to the particular tree, whence it was extended to become the English name of all such trees.

The tree itself is of the fig genus and exists in two species, *Ficus benghalensis* and *Ficus religiosa*. The latter is also known as the bo tree or peepul.

*Ficus benghalensis* begins its life as an epiphyte, growing on the branches of some other tree, to which its seeds have been borne by birds. It develops aerial roots, which drop rapidly downwards and take hold in the ground to become a tangle of new roots while thickening as accessory trunks. The crown of the tree meanwhile spreads laterally, so that a single seed eventually produces what looks like a dense thicket but what in reality is just one tree. A 150-year-old banyan in the botanical gardens at Calcutta had a crown almost 1000ft (300m) in circumference with over 300 accessory trunks. *Ficus religiosa* is similar but not usually an epiphyte. As its name indicates, it is sacred to the Hindus, and it is said to be the tree under which the BUDDHA received enlightenment.

**Baobab.** Nicknamed the 'upside-down tree' because its branches, when devoid of leaves, look like roots, the baobab (*Adansonia digitata*) is native to Africa but has been introduced elsewhere in warm climates as a curiosity. Its large white blossoms open at night to give off a strong musk-like scent, attracting the BUSH-BABY, which feeds on its nectar and so fertilizes it. Its long, pulpy fruit is regularly eaten by monkeys, giving it the additional nickname of 'monkey tree'. It grows to a height of around 60ft (18m) and has a huge trunk, some 30ft (9m) in diameter. Certain tribes in Sudan bathe their newborn baby boys in a broth made from its bark in a custom that, it is believed, will make them grow up strong and healthy.

**Baptism.** This SACRAMENT of the Christian church dates back in one form or another to pre-apostolic times.

**Baptism for the dead, The.** Formerly a kind of vicarious baptism of a living person for the sake of one dead, regarded by the early Christians as a heretical and superstitious custom.

> Else what shall they do which are baptized for the dead, if the dead rise not at all? why are they then baptized for the dead?
> 1 Corinthians 15:29

**Baptism of blood, A.** Martyrdom for the sake of Christ, which took the place of baptism if the martyr was unbaptized.

**Baptism of desire, The.** The grace or virtue of baptism acquired by one who earnestly desires baptism by water but dies before receiving it.

**Baptism of fire, A.** Properly martyrdom, but the phrase more generally refers to a soldier's first experience of battle and hence any first experience of something difficult or dangerous.

**Baptists.** English Baptists are of 16th-century origin. Their first independent church, however, was founded from a group of separatists under John Smythe at Amsterdam in 1609, from where an offshoot returned to London in 1612 to form the General Baptists. Their Arminianism (*see* ARMINIANS) led to the growth of the Strict, Particular or Calvinistic Baptists in the 1630s. In the 18th century many General Baptists became UNITARIANS, while the more orthodox members formed the New Connection in 1770. The Baptist Union (1832) eventually led to closer cooperation, and the Strict Baptists joined forces with the New Connection in 1891. Church government is congregational and baptism by total immersion is only for believers. *See also* CONGREGATIONALISTS; PRESBYTERIANS; SEVENTH-DAY BAPTISTS.

**Adoption by baptism.** *See under* ADOPTION.

**Bush Baptist.** *See under* BUSH.

**St John the Baptist.** *See under* JOHN.

**Bar.** (1) The whole body of BARRISTERS. The bar, in the INNS OF COURT, is the partition separating the benchers from the rest of the hall.

(2) Excepting. In the language of the TURF, 'two to one, bar one' means betting two to one against any horse in the field with one exception. Hence also 'bar none', without exception.

(3) In HERALDRY, a horizontal band across the shield taking up not more than one fifth of the field.

**Barring out.** In former days, a schoolboys' practice of barricading masters out of the classroom or the school. In 1818 soldiers were called in to deal with a rebellious outbreak at Winchester College.

**Bar sinister.** A heraldic term popularly mistaken as an indication of bastardy, correctly denoted by a baton sinister. *See also* BEND SINISTER.

**All over bar the shouting.** *See under* ALL.

**Behind bars.** *See under* BEHIND.

**Colour bar.** *See under* COLOUR.

**Called to the bar, To be.** *See under* CALL.

**Called within the bar, To be.** *See under* CALL.

**Crush bar.** *See under* CRUSH.

**Hershey bar.** *See under* HERSHEY.

**Prisoner at the bar, The.** *See under* PRISONER.

**Stars and Bars, The.** *See under* STAR.

**Temple Bar.** *See under* TEMPLE.

**Tommy bar.** *See under* TOM.

**Trial at bar.** *See under* TRIAL.

**Barabbas.** At the trial of Jesus, the crowds were asked to choose between Him and Barabbas, under sentence of death for murder, as the prisoner to whom PILATE would grant amnesty in honour of the PASSOVER. The crowd chose Barabbas (John 18:40), obliging Pilate to release a guilty man and condemn an innocent. The episode is regarded by some biblical scholars as a fabrication. It may not be a coincidence that the name of Barabbas means 'son of the father', a title of Jesus.

**Barataria** (Spanish *barato*, 'cheap'). SANCHO PANZA's island city, in *Don* QUIXOTE (1605), over which he was appointed governor. The table was presided over by Doctor Pedro Rezio de Aguero, who caused every dish set upon the board to be removed without being tasted, some because they heated the blood, and others because they chilled it, some for one ill effect, and some for another, so that Sancho was allowed to eat nothing. *See also* BARMECIDE.

**Barathrum** or **Barathron** (Greek, 'gulf', 'pit'). A deep ditch behind the Acropolis of Athens into which malefactors were thrown, rather in the same way that criminals at Rome were cast from the TARPEIAN ROCK. The word was sometimes used figuratively, as in Philip Massinger's *A New Way to Pay Old Debts* (1633) where Sir Giles Overreach calls Greedy a 'barathrum of the shambles' (III, ii), meaning that he was a sink into which any kind of food or offal could be thrown.

> *Carion*: Barathrum? What's Barathrum?
> *Mercury*: Why, Barathrum is Pluto's boggards [privy]: you must all be thrown into Barathrum.
> THOMAS RANDOLPH: *Hey for Honesty*, V, i (*c*.1630)

**Barb.** (1) Used in early times in England for the beard of a man (from Latin *barba*, 'beard') and thus for the feathers under the beak of a HAWK ('beard feathers'). Its first English use was for a curved instrument such as a fish-hook. The barb of an arrow had two iron 'feathers' or hooks near the point to hinder extraction.

(2) A Barbary horse (from Italian *barbero*, 'of Barbary') noted for docility, speed, endurance and spirit. *See also* ARCOS BARBS; BARBARY ROAN.

**Barbara** (Latin, 'barbarian', 'foreign').

**Barbara Allen.** *See under* ALLEN.

**St Barbara.** Saint and virgin martyr (reputedly *c*.4th century). Her father, a fanatical heathen, delivered her up to Martian, governor of Nicomedia, for being a Christian. After she had been subjected to cruel tortures, her father was about to strike off her head, when a lightning flash laid him dead at her feet. Hence she is invoked against lightning and is the patron saint of arsenals and artillery. Her actual existence is in some doubt.

**Barbarian.** The Greeks and Romans called all foreigners 'barbarians' since they were 'babblers', speaking a language not understood by them. The word is thus imitative of unintelligible speech. The extension of meaning to imply 'uncivilized' or 'uncultured' is a natural consequence.

> Therefore if I know not the meaning of the voice, I shall be unto him that speaketh a barbarian, and he that speaketh shall be a barbarian unto me.
> 1 Corinthians 14:11

**Barbarossa** (Italian *barba rossa*, 'red beard'). The byname of Frederick I (1122–90), Holy Roman Emperor. He was drowned during the Third CRUSADE. The name was also applied by the Christians to a family of Turkish sea rovers, the best known being the pirate Khair ed-Din (*c*.1465–1546), who became bey of Algiers in 1518 and high admiral of the Turkish fleet in 1537.

**Barbary. Barbary Coast, The.** The Mediterranean coast of North Africa, which was infested by Muslim sea rovers from the 16th century until the early 19th century. The Berbers here derive their name from the Roman habit of referring to indigenous peoples as *barbari*.

**Barbary roan.** The favourite horse of Richard II. As the Groom of the Stable says to the king:

> O! how it yearn'd my heart, when I beheld
> In London streets, that coronation day,
> When Bolingbroke rode on roan Barbary,
> That horse that thou so often hast bestrid,
> That horse that I so carefully have dress'd.
> SHAKESPEARE: *Richard II*, V, v (1585)

**Barbason.** A fiend mentioned by Shakespeare in *The Merry Wives of Windsor* (II, ii (1600)):

> Amaimon sounds well; Lucifer, well; Barbason, well; yet they are devils' additions, the names of fiends.

The name seems to have been taken from Reginald Scot's *The Discoverie of Witchcraft* (1584).

**Barbecue** (American Spanish *barbacoa*, 'frame made of sticks'). A West Indian term formerly used in America for a wooden bedstead, and also for a large gridiron upon which an animal could be roasted whole. Hence an animal, such as a pig, so cooked, and the feast at which it is roasted and eaten. The word is now familiar for a meal cooked out of doors on an open fire, or for a party or picnic centring on such a meal.

> Oldfield with more than harpy throat endued,
> Cries, 'Send me, gods, a whole hog barbecued!'
> ALEXANDER POPE: *Satires and Epistles of Horace Imitated*, II, ii (1734)

**Barbed steed.** A horse in armour. 'Barbed' should properly be 'barded', as the word is from Old French *barde*, 'caparison'. Horses' 'bards' were the metal coverings for the breast and flanks.

> And now, – instead of mounting barbed steeds,
> To fright the souls of fearful adversaries, –
> He capers nimbly in a lady's chamber
> To the lascivious pleasing of a lute.
> SHAKESPEARE: *Richard III*, I, i (1592)

**Barber** (ultimately from Latin *barba*, 'beard'). A person who cuts men's hair and shaves or trims beards; a hairdresser. Originally barbers also practised dentistry and surgery. The Company of Barber Surgeons in London was first incorporated in 1461, and in 1540 it became the Company of Barbers and Surgeons, limited (other than in its proper functions) to drawing teeth. In 1745 it was renamed the Barbers Company, and is still one of the London LIVERY COMPANIES.

From ancient Roman times the barber's shop has been a centre for the dissemination of scandal, and the talk of the town.

**Barber of Seville, The.** The comedy of this name (*Le Barbier de Séville*) was written by Pierre Beaumarchais and produced in Paris in 1775. The character of FIGARO appeared in it as the barber. Paisiello's opera appeared in 1782 but was eclipsed by Rossini's *Il Barbiere di Siviglia*, with libretto by Sterbini. The latter work was hissed on its first performance in 1816 under the title *Almaviva*.

**Barber Poet, The.** Jacques Jasmin (1798–1864), a Provençal poet, who was also known as 'the last of the TROUBADOURS'. He was a barber by trade, and a poet by inclination.

**Barbershop.** A term used to denote a style of close harmony four-part singing by male quartets. Informal music-making existed in barber shops in the 16th and 17th centuries in Britain as well as Europe. It lapsed in the 18th century but continued in the USA, where the barbershop quartet came into being. Its romantic and sentimental songs were popular in the 1920s and 1930s.

**Barber's pole.** This pole, painted spirally with two stripes of red and white and displayed outside barbers' shops, derives from the days when barbers also practised phlebotomy. The pole represents the staff gripped by persons in venesection, which was painted red since it was usually stained with blood. The white spiral represents the bandage that was twisted round the arm before blood-letting began. The gilt knob at the end of the pole represents the brass basin, which was sometimes actually suspended from it. The basin, which had a notch in it to fit the throat, was used for lathering customers before shaving.

**Greenwich barbers.** *See under* GREENWICH.

**Barbican.** The word is most familiar as the proper name of the London Barbican, a complex of high-rise apartment blocks grouped around the Barbican Centre, a large and brutish building opened in 1982 as a major cultural and exhibition centre. The complex takes its name from a former street, which was itself named after a watchtower in the city walls. The word represents Medieval Latin *barbacana*, but the origin of this is unknown.

**Barbie doll.** A small doll originating in the USA in 1959. With sleek body and long blond hair, she is designed to represent a conventionally attractive young woman but in some circles has come to typify a mindless 'bimbo', an association perhaps partly suggested by her name, with its echoes of 'baby doll'.

**Barchester.** A fictional cathedral city (modelled on Salisbury or Winchester or a blend of both) in the county of Barsetshire. It is the setting of Anthony Trollope's 'Barchester Novels': *The Warden* (1855), *Barchester Towers* (1857), *Doctor Thorne* (1858), *Framley Parsonage* (1861), *The Small House at Allington* (1864) and *The Last Chronicle of Barset* (1867). Angela Thirkell (1890–1961) also used Barsetshire and Barchester as a setting for some of her novels, the first of which (though not intended as such) was *High Rising* (1933).

**Bar Cochba** or **Bar Kokhba** (Aramaic, 'son of a star'). The byname of Simeon, leader of the second Jewish revolt against the Romans, who is reputed to have claimed to be the 'Star out of Jacob' mentioned in Numbers 24:17. He took Jerusalem in 132 and was acclaimed by some as the MESSIAH. He was overwhelmed and slain by the forces of Julius Severus in 135.

**Bard.** The minstrel of the ancient Celtic peoples, the Gauls, British, Welsh, Irish and Scots. Bards celebrated the deeds of the gods and heroes, incited to battle, acted as heralds and sang at festivities. The oldest extant bardic compositions are of the 5th century. *See also* EISTEDDFOD.

**Bard of Avon, The.** William Shakespeare (1564–1616), who was born and buried at Stratford-upon-Avon.

**Bard of Ayrshire, The.** Robert Burns (1759–96), a native of Ayrshire.

**Bard of Democracy, The.** Walt Whitman (1819–92), the American poet who wrote *The Democratic Review* (1841–5) and published *Democratic Vistas* (1871).

**Bard of Erin, The.** Thomas Moore (1779–1852). Born in Dublin, writer of *Irish Melodies* (1807–34), *Lalla Rookh* (1817) and other works. He spent most of his life in England.

**Bard of Hope, The.** Thomas Campbell (1777–1844), author of *The Pleasures of Hope* (1799).

**Bard of Mulla's Silver Stream, The.** Edmund Spenser (*c.*1552–99) was so called by William Shenstone (1714–63), because at one time his home in Ireland was on the banks of the Mulla, or Awbeg, a tributary of the Blackwater.

**Bard of Olney, The.** William Cowper (1731–1800), who for many years lived at Olney, Buckinghamshire.

**Bard of Prose, The.** Giovanni Boccaccio (1313–75), author of the DECAMERON.

**Bard of Rydal Mount, The.** William Wordsworth (1770–1850), who from 1813 to the end of his life lived at Rydal Mount, Grasmere.

**Bard of the Imagination, The.** Mark Akenside (1721–70), author of *The Pleasures of the Imagination* (1744, rewritten 1757).

**Bard of the Silvery Tay, The.** William McGonagall (1825–1902), the Scottish poetaster whose best known poem is 'The Tay Bridge Disaster' (1880). His poems were uniformly bad. The one cited here, from which his byname is taken, begins thus:

Beautiful Bridge of the Silv'ry Tay!
Alas, I am very sorry to say
That ninety lives have been taken away
On the last Sabbath day of 1879,
Which will be remembered for a very long time.

**Bard of Twickenham, The.** Alexander Pope (1688–1744), who lived there for 25 years. Contemporaries sometimes called him the Wasp of Twickenham because of his acerbity.

**Bardolph.** One of FALSTAFF's inferior officers. Falstaff calls him 'the knight of the burning lamp', because his nose was so red, and his face 'so full of meteors'. He is a low-bred, drunken swaggerer, without any principles, and AS POOR AS A CHURCH MOUSE (*Henry IV, Pts I* and *II* (1597); *Henry V* (1598); *The Merry Wives of Windsor* (1600)).

**Bare. Bareback.** On an unsaddled horse or donkey.

**Bare bones, The.** The essentials of something.

**Barebones Parliament.** The Nominated or Little Parliament (4 July to 11 December 1653) of 140 'godly' members approved by Cromwell and the officers and derisively named after one of its members, Praise-God Barebon.

**Barefaced.** Open or shameless. A clean-shaven face cannot hide its expression.

**Barefoot.** The traditional state of certain friars and nuns (some of whom wear sandals instead of shoes), especially the reformed section of the CARMELITES (White Friars) founded by St TERESA OF AVILA in the 16th century, known as the Discalced Carmelites (Latin *calceus*, 'shoe'). The practice is defended by the command of Christ to His disciples: 'Carry neither purse, nor scrip, nor shoes' (Luke 10:4). The Jews and Romans used to take off their shoes in mourning and at the time of public calamities, by way of humiliation.

**Barefoot doctor.** A paramedical worker with basic medical training, especially in China. The phrase translated the original Chinese.

**Bargain. Bargain basement.** The basement of a shop or store where bargains are displayed for sale.

**Best of a bad bargain, The.** *See under* BEST.

**Drive a hard bargain, To.** *See under* DRIVE.

**Dutch bargain.** *See under* DUTCH.

**Gatepost bargain.** *See under* GATE.

**Into the bargain.** *See under* INTO.

**Strike a bargain, To.** *See under* STRIKE.

**Bargepole, To touch with a.** *See under* TOUCH.

**Barisal guns.** The name given to mysterious booming sounds, which occur at Barisal (Bangladesh) and which seem to come from the sea. Similar phenomena at Seneca Lake, New York, are called 'Lake guns'; on the coast of Holland and Belgium they are *mistpoeffers*; and at certain coastal sites in Italy they are known as *bombiti* or *baturlio marina*.

**Bark.** Dogs in their wild state never bark, but howl, whine and growl. Barking is an acquired habit.

**Bark** or **bay at the moon, To.** To agitate uselessly, especially those in high places, as a dog attempts to frighten the moon by baying at it. There is a superstition that when a dog does this it portends death or ill-luck.

I had rather be a dog, and bay the moon,
Than such a Roman.
SHAKESPEARE: *Julius Caesar*, IV, iii (1599)

**Barker, A.** A person who stands at the entrance to a show, fair booth or the like, or by a market stall, shouting to attract custom. In the USA a barker is also a baseball coach.

**Bark up the wrong tree, To.** To waste energy; to be on the wrong scent. The phrase comes from racoon hunting, which takes place in the dark. The dogs have been trained to mark the tree where the racoon has fled, but they can mistake the tree in the dark and bark up the wrong one.

**Go between the bark and the tree, To.** To instigate a quarrel between closely related people.

**His bark is worse than his bite.** He is bad-tempered and irritable, but he never harms anyone.

**Peruvian bark.** *See under* PERU.

**Barkis is willin'.** The message sent by the carrier Barkis to Clara Peggotty through David Copperfield, in Charles Dickens's novel (1849–50), expressing his desire to marry. It became a proverbial expression indicating willingness.

**Bar Kokhba.** *See* BAR COCHBA.

**Barlaam and Josaphat.** An Indian romance telling how Barlaam, an ascetic of the desert of Sinai, converted Josaphat, a Hindu prince, to Christianity. It had probably been translated into Greek by the 6th century, and was put into its final form by St JOHN DAMASCENE, a Syrian monk of the 8th century. Some parts of it correspond closely with the legendary story of BUDDHA's youth, and it became widely popular as a medieval romance. The Story of the Three Caskets was used by Shakespeare in *The Merchant of Venice* (1596).

**Barley. Barley-bree.** ALE; malt liquor brewed from barley, also called barley-broth.

The cock may craw, the day may daw,
And aye we'll taste the barley-bree.
ROBERT BURNS: 'Willie Brew'd a Peck o' Maut' (1790)

**Barley mow.** A heap or stack of barley. *See also* MOW.

**Barley sugar.** A brittle, amber-coloured sweet, a

traditional remedy for travel sickness. It was originally made from a barley extract.

**Barley water.** A drink made from an infusion of barley and usually flavoured with lemon or orange.

**Cry barley, To.** *See under* CRY.

**John Barleycorn.** *See under* JOHN.

**Barm, Beggar's.** *See under* BEG.

**Barmecide** (Arabic *barmok*, 'high priest'). In the ARABIAN NIGHTS ENTERTAINMENTS, a prince of the priestly Barmecide family in Baghdad, desirous of sport, asked Schacabac, a poor starving wretch, to dinner. Having set before him a series of empty plates, the merchant asked, 'How do you like your soup?' 'Excellently well,' replied Schacabac. 'Did you ever see whiter bread?' 'Never, honourable sir,' was the civil answer. Illusory wine was later offered, but Schacabac excused himself by pretending to be drunk already, and knocked the Barmecide down. The latter saw the humour of the situation, forgave Schacabac and provided him with food to his heart's content. Hence 'Barmecide' is used of something sham, illusory or disappointing because it did not materialize.

**Bar Mitzvah** (Hebrew, 'son of the law'). The ceremony celebrating the arrival of a Jewish boy at the age of full religious obligations, 13 years. The equivalent for a Jewish girl, at age 12, is the Bat Mitzvah ('daughter of the law').

**Barmy** or **balmy.** Mad, crazy; literally 'full of barm'. Hence, in prison slang, 'to put on the barmy stick' is to feign insanity. There is a popular misconception that the word comes from Barming, near Maidstone, Kent, because the county lunatic asylum was at Barming Heath.

**Barmy army.** A phrase used of enthusiastic sports spectators, especially at cricket and football matches. Rowdy cricket fans were nicknamed the 'Barmy Army' on the ASHES tour of Australia in 1994–5. A Scottish equivalent is the TARTAN ARMY.

> As tension mounted and the drinks flowed, a huge man wearing a Union Jack T-shirt stepped forward: 'Barmy Army! Barmy Army!' he cried, immediately joined in this chorus by several hundred voices.
> *The Times* (4 July 1998)

**Barn. Barnburners.** Destroyers, who like the Dutch in history, would burn down their barns to rid themselves of the rats. In the USA the term was applied to the radical section of the Democratic party in New York State in the presidential election of 1844 by their conservative opponents, who were called Hunkers. The Barnburners finally joined the Republican party in the 1850s to further the anti-slavery cause.

**Barn of Scullabogue, The.** In the Irish rebellion of 1798, which largely degenerated into a war between CATHOLICS and PROTESTANTS, revenge was taken after the repulse of the rebels at New Ross. The barn at Scullabogue, containing over 180 Protestant loyalists, was set on fire, and all those in it perished.

**Barnstormer.** A strolling player, and hence any second-rate actor, especially one whose style is of an exaggerated declamatory kind. The reference is to the itinerant actors who performed in village barns.

In the USA the term has also been applied to a stunt air pilot touring country districts or offering flights for a fee, as well as to a person carrying out speaking tours in rural areas.

**Dutch barn.** *See under* DUTCH.

**Barnabas** or **Barnaby. Barnabites.** An order of regular clerks of St PAUL, recognized by Pope Clement VII in 1533, and probably so called from the church of St Barnabas in Milan, which became their centre.

**Barnaby Bright.** An old provincial name for St BARNABAS' DAY (11 June). Before the reform of the calendar in England and Wales in 1752 it was the longest day, hence the jingle in John Ray's *Collection of English Proverbs* (1670):

> Barnaby bright! Barnaby bright!
> The longest day and the shortest night.

**Barnaby Lecturers.** In the University of Cambridge, four lecturers elected annually on St BARNABAS' DAY, to lecture on mathematics, philosophy, rhetoric and logic.

**Barnaby Rudge.** This novel by Charles Dickens, published in 1841, centres round the Gordon anti-popery riots of 1780, and he drew upon the memories of survivors of these times. Barnaby was a half-witted lad whose companion was Grip, the raven.

**St Barnabas' Day.** 11 June. St Barnabas was a fellow labourer of St PAUL. His symbol is a rake, because 11 June is about the time when haymaking begins.

**Barnacle.** A species of wild goose, *Branta leucopsis*, allied to the brent goose. Also the popular name of the *Cirripedia*, the marine crustaceans that live attached to rocks, submerged wooden structures, ship bottoms and the like. In medieval times it was held that the goose developed from the shellfish as a frog does from a tadpole.

**Barnardos.** For many years familiar as Dr Barnardo's Homes, the charity for orphans and deprived children was founded in 1867 by the Dublin-born philanthropist of Spanish ancestry, Thomas John Barnardo (1845–1905). His title of Dr was strictly speaking honorary, as he had no medical qualifications.

**Barnard's Inn.** One of the old Inns of CHANCERY, formerly situated on the south side of Holborn, London, and once known as Mackworth's Inn, because Dean Mackworth of Lincoln (d.1454) lived there. Its present name is from the man, one Barnard, who subsequently owned the inn.

**Barney.** A dispute or noisy argument. As a proper name, Barney is a contraction of BARNABAS. It was a fairly common name among Irish settlers in the 19th century, and the present sense of the word is popularly said to allude to their reputed temperament and behaviour.

**Barnwell, George.** The subject of the 17th-century ballad in PERCY'S RELIQUES (1765), which formed the basis of George Lillo's prose tragedy *The London Merchant, or the History of George Barnwell*, produced in 1731. Barnwell was a London apprentice, who fell in with a licentious woman in SHOREDITCH, named Sarah Millwood, to whom he gave £200 of his master's money in return for her favours. He next robbed his uncle, a rich grazier at Ludlow, and beat out his brains. Having spent the money, Sarah turned him out. Each informed against the other and both were hanged.

**Baron** (Old French, from a word related to Germanic *baro*, 'freeman'). After the Norman Conquest of England in 1066, the man or VASSAL of a great noble, especially the king. By the 13th century the distinction between greater and lesser barons was well established. The greater barons came to be summoned to the GREAT COUNCIL by individual writs and the term baronage became equated to peerage. It is now the lowest order of nobility.

In colloquial speech the word is the equivalent to 'magnate', as in 'press baron'. *See also* COURTESY TITLES; PEERS OF THE REALM.

**Baron Münchausen.** *See under* MÜNCHAUSEN.

**Baron of beef, A.** A double SIRLOIN, left uncut at the backbone, and of great size, roasted at special festivities. Jocosely, but wrongly, the name is said to pun on 'baron' and 'sir loin'.

**Barons of the Cinque Ports.** The name given to the representatives of the CINQUE PORTS in the HOUSE OF COMMONS until the Reform Act of 1832.

**Barons' War, The.** The name applied to the civil war (1264–7) fought between the baronial supporters of Simon de Montfort and the supporters of Henry III. Michael Drayton's poem *The Barrons Warres* appeared in 1603.

**Court baron.** *See under* COURT.

**Last of the Barons, The.** *See under* LAST.

**Tobacco baron.** *See under* TOBACCO.

**Baronet.** The lowest hereditary title of honour, below a BARON. It was instituted by James I in 1611, and the sale of the honours was to provide funds for the defence of the plantation of Ulster. The RED HAND of Ulster became the badge of Baronets of England, of Great Britain, of the United Kingdom and of Ireland (instituted in 1619). Baronets of Scotland and Nova Scotia were created from 1625. Nova Scotian patents ceased in 1638, after the colony had fallen to the French; Scottish creations ceased in 1707, and Irish creations from 1801, consequent upon the respective ACTS OF UNION.

**Barrack. Barrack, To.** To jeer at, shout against or interrupt with rude comments, particularly sports players. In Australia, where the word came into use during the 1880s, it is nearly always used in the opposite sense meaning to cheer or support a team. It is popularly said to allude to the supporters of the Victoria Barracks army team at South Melbourne cricket ground, who were greeted with shouts of 'Here come the barrackers'. It is more likely, however, to derive from Northern Ireland dialect *barrack*, 'to brag', though some favour an origin in the Aboriginal word *borak*, 'banter'. Barracking was probably introduced into England by Australian cricketers and their supporters. That it acquired an opposite meaning is understandable.

**Barrack-room lawyer, A.** A person, originally a soldier, who uses professed knowledge of regulations to make complaints against authority. An American equivalent is a latrine lawyer.

**Barrel. Barrel-chested.** Having a large rounded chest.

**Barrel of fun** or **of laughs, A.** A source of much fun or merriment. The expression is mostly found in the negative, as: 'It wasn't exactly a barrel of laughs.' A barrel contains beer, which is conducive to merriment.

> Roll out the barrel,
> We'll have a barrel of fun!
>
> JAROMIR VEYVODA, WLADIMIR TIMM and LEW BROWN: 'The Beer Barrel Polka' (song) (1939)

**Barrel roll.** An acrobatic manoeuvre in which an aircraft describes a single turn of a spiral while rolling once about its longitudinal axis.

**Lock, stock and barrel.** *See under* LOCK.

**Over a barrel.** *See under* OVER.

**Pork barrel.** *See under* PORK.

**Scrape the barrel, To.** *See under* SCRAPE.

**Barrell's Blues.** *See under* REGIMENTAL AND DIVISIONAL NICKNAMES.

**Barrier, Crush.** *See under* CRUSH.

**Barricade.** To block or bar a street, building or the like against attack. The term arose in France in 1588, when Henri of Guise returned to Paris in defiance of Henry III. The king called out the SWISS GUARD, and the Parisians tore up the pavements, threw chains across the streets and piled up barrels (French *barriques*) filled with earth and stones, from behind which they shot down the Swiss.

**Day of the Barricades, The.** *See under* DAY.

**Barrister.** A lawyer who has been called to the BAR, and is thereafter entitled to plead in any court, having received a brief from a solicitor. Formerly called 'outer' or 'UTTER' barristers, after ten years as junior counsel they may apply to take SILK to become KING'S COUNSEL or Queen's Counsel (KC or QC). Until 1877 there was a superior third group called SERJEANTS-AT-LAW. Every barrister must be a member of one of the four INNS OF COURT. The KC or QC is a senior barrister and is entitled to wear a silk gown and full-bottomed wig. Other barristers wear a stuff gown and short wig.

**Barrister's bags.** *See* LAWYER'S BAGS.

**Revising barrister.** *See under* REVISE.

**Utter and inner barristers.** *See under* UTTER.

**Barry, Cornwall.** *See under* CORNWALL.

**Bartholomew** (Aramaic *bar-talmay*, 'son of Talmay'). The symbol of this saint is a knife, in allusion to the one with which he was flayed alive, reputedly in AD 44. His day is 24 August.

**Bartholomew fair.** A FAIR opened annually at SMITHFIELD on St Bartholomew's Day (24 August) from 1133 to 1752. After the reform of the calendar it began on 3 September. It was removed to Islington in 1840 and was last held in 1855 (*see* CALEDONIAN MARKET). It was one of the great national fairs, with a variety of amusements and entertainments, and long held its place as a centre of London life. The PURITANS failed to suppress it. Ben Jonson's *Bartholomew Fair*, a comedy of manners, was first acted in 1614.

> Here's that will challenge all the fairs,
> Come buy my nuts and damsons and Burgamy pears!
> Here's the *Woman of Babylon, the Devil and the Pope*.
> And here's the little girl just going on the rope!
> Here's *Dives and Lazarus*, and the *World's Creation;*
> Here's the Tall Dutchwoman, the like's not in the nation.
> Here is the booths where the high Dutch maid is,
> Here are the bears that dance like any ladies;
> Tat, tat, tat, tat, says little penny trumpet;
> Here's Jacob Hall, that does so jump it, jump it;
> Sound trumpet, sound, for silver spoon and fork.
> Come, here's your dainty pig and pork!
> *Wit and Drollery* (1682)

**Bartholomew pig.** A fat person. At BARTHOLOMEW FAIR one of the chief attractions was a pig, roasted whole and sold piping hot. Doll Tearsheet calls Falstaff:

> Thou whoreson little tidy Bartholomew boar-pig.
> SHAKESPEARE: Henry *IV, Pt II*, II, iv (1597)

**St Bartholomew's Day Massacre.** The slaughter of the French HUGUENOTS, which began on St Bartholomew's Day, 24 August 1572, in Paris and the provinces, at the instigation of Catherine de Médicis, mother of Charles IX. Estimates of those who perished range from 2000 to 70,000, while modern writers put the number at 3000 in Paris alone.

**Baruch.** In the Old Testament, the faithful secretary of JEREMIAH. He wrote his master's prophecies on a scroll and took it to the Temple, where it was confiscated and taken to King Jehoiakim, who destroyed it as it was read out to him. Baruch's name has been attached to a number of works, one of which is included in the APOCRYPHA. The Book of Baruch is a hotchpotch of a letter supposedly written by Jeremiah himself, a prophecy of a return to Jerusalem from the Captivity in Babylon, and an assortment of prophecies and pearls of wisdom. Baruch as a name represents the Hebrew word for 'blessed', and it is the Hebrew phrase *barruk habba* ('blessed be he that cometh (in the name of the Lord)') (Psalm 118:26), occurring frequently in the Jewish liturgy, that gave modern French and English 'brouhaha'.

**Bas. Bas bleu.** *See* BLUE STOCKING.

**Bas-relief** (French, 'low relief'). Sculpture in low relief, with the outlines projecting slightly from the background but never completely detached from it. It is typically found in architectural ornamentation and on tombstones, memorial plaques, coins and medals. It is also known by the Italian equivalent, *basso relievo*. Its converse is ALTO RELIEVO. *See also* CAVO RELIEVO.

**Basement, bargain.** *See under* BARGAIN.

**Base tenure.** Originally tenure not by military, but by base service, such as a serf or VILLAIN might give. Later, villein tenure became COPYHOLD tenure.

**Bashan, To roar like a bull of.** *See under* ROAR.

**Bashibazouk** (Turkish *başibozuk*, 'irregular soldier', literally, 'one with head turned', from *baş*, 'head', and *bozuk*, 'turned', 'corrupt'). A savage and brutal ruffian. The word was applied in Turkey to non-uniformed irregular soldiers who made up in plunder what they did not get in pay. The term came into prominence at the time of the Crimean War (1854–6) and again through the Bulgarian atrocities of 1876.

**Basic. Basic English.** A fundamental selection of 850 English words designed in the 1920s by C.K. Ogden as a common first step in the teaching of English and as an auxiliary language. The name comes from the initials of the words British, American, Scientific, International, Commercial. In computer programming Basic is a language that uses common English terms and stands for Beginner's all-purpose symbolic instruction code. *See also* ESPERANTO; INTERLINGUA; VOLAPÜK.

**Back to basics.** *See under* BACK.

**Basilica** (Greek *basilikos*, 'royal'). Originally a royal palace, but afterwards, in Rome, a large building with nave, aisles and an apse at one end, which was used as a court of justice and for public meetings. Some were adapted by the early Christians, and many churches were modelled on them. Constantine built the great basilicas of St Peter (rebuilt in the 16th century), St Paul and St John Lateran.

**Basilisk** (Greek *basiliskos*, 'royal child'). The fabulous king of SERPENTS, also called a COCKATRICE and alleged to be hatched by a serpent from a cock's egg. It was reputed to be capable of 'looking anyone dead on whom it fixed its eyes'.

It is also the name given to a genus of Central American lizard and to a brass cannon of Tudor times.

**Basingstoke.** A respectable town in Hampshire whose name for some reason has come to be regarded as droll or even irresistibly amusing, placing it on a par with towns such as Chipping Sodbury, Godalming, SCUNTHORPE, Wigan and Surbiton.

> *Mad Margaret*: When I am lying awake at night ... strange fancies crowd upon my poor mad brain, and I sometimes think that if we could hit upon some word for you to use whenever I am about to relapse – some word that teems with hidden meaning – like 'Basingstoke' – it might recall me to my saner self.
> W.S. GILBERT: *Ruddigore*, II (1887)

**Basin Street.** A street in the RED LIGHT DISTRICT of the French quarter of New Orleans which is possibly the original home of American JAZZ music. The well-known 'Basin Street Blues' was composed by Spencer Williams in 1928.

**Basket. Basket case, A.** Originally, a soldier who had lost all four limbs. Hence, generally, a person who is mentally unstable or unable to cope emotionally. By extension, the phrase is also sometimes used of a bankrupt country. The image is of someone unable to support himself physically.

**Basket clause, A.** An all-inclusive or comprehensive clause in a contract.

**Left in the basket, To be.** *See under* LEFT.

**Put all your eggs in one basket, To.** *See under* ALL.

**Bast.** *See* BUBASTIS.

**Bastard.** An illegitimate child, said to be from Old French *fils de bast*, 'son of the packsaddle', referring to a child born to a muleteer or other traveller, who used his animal's saddle as a pillow. *See also* BATMAN.

Also an old name for a sweetened Spanish wine made from the bastard muscadine grape.

> I will pledge you willingly in a cup of bastard.
> SIR WALTER SCOTT: *Kenilworth*, ch iii (1821)

**Bass, Ground.** *See under* GROUND.

**Baste, To.** To beat thoroughly; to thrash. The word is of uncertain origin but may derive from the fact that lazy scullions and turnspits were sometimes beaten by the enraged cook with the basting-stick, a long-handled wooden spoon ending in a funnel, which was used for basting the joint of meat on the spit with hot fat from the dripping pan beneath.

**Bastille** (Old French *bastir*, now *bâtir*, 'to build'). A fortress, but specifically the state prison in Paris built as a royal castle by Charles V between 1370 and 1383, and seized and sacked by the mob on 14 July 1789, at the beginning of the French Revolution. As used generally of a building or establishment, the word implied prison-like qualities, the equivalent of the modern COLDITZ. *See also* ALTMARK; INVENTORS.

**Bat.** Five bats are sometimes seen on Chinese plates. They stand for the five blessings (*wu fu*): longevity, wealth, MENS SANA IN CORPORE SANO, the love of virtue and a peaceful end. The creature was adopted for this symbolism since the Chinese character meaning 'bat' is identical in sound with that for 'blessing'.

**Batman** (1) (Old French *bat*, 'packsaddle'). Originally a soldier in charge of a bat-horse (packhorse) and its load of officer's baggage. The word came to denote an army officer's servant in the First World War through its inaccurate use by non-regular wartime officers. *See also* BASTARD.

**Batman.** (2) The costumed superhero of American comics, in popular regard almost as famous as SUPERMAN himself. He first appeared in 1939, conceived and drawn by Bob Kane for *Detective Comics*. His real name is Bruce Wayne, and in day-to-day life he is a Gotham City socialite, but dons his special bat suit, with cape and mask, in order to unmask villains incognito. His assistant is Robin, the Boy Wonder, alias Dick Grayson. He has appeared in most popular media, including books, films and television, and has inspired a female equivalent, Batgirl, alias Babs Gordon, who made her debut in *Detective Comics* in 1967. Batman can be said to have classical antecedents in heroes such as HERCULES and Odysseus (ULYSSES).

**Bats in the belfry.** 'To have bats in the belfry' means to be crazy, bats here being the nocturnal kind. The 'belfry' is the human head.

**Batsman.** As well as the term for a cricketer who is 'in', i.e. batting at the wicket, the word also denotes the signaller on an airfield or aircraft carrier who uses a pair of lightweight bats to guide the pilot of an aircraft when taking off or landing.

**Batty.** Crazy; to have BATS IN THE BELFRY.

**As blind as a bat.** *See under* AS.

**Carry one's bat, To.** *See under* CARRY.

**Dead bat.** *See under* DEAD.

**Go at a fair bat, To.** To go at a good pace or speed.

**Like a bat out of hell.** *See under* LIKE.

**Off one's own bat.** *See under* OFF.

**Parliament of Bats, The.** *See* CLUB PARLIAMENT.

**Without batting an eyelid.** *See under* WITHOUT.

**Bath. Bath brick.** A scouring brick made at Bridgwater, Somerset, used for cleaning polished metal, made from sand and clay taken from the River Parrett, which runs through the town. It is said to be so called either from one Bath, who originally manufactured it, or more likely from its resemblance to BATH STONE.

**Bath bun.** A sweet bun, containing spices and dried fruit, originally made at Bath.

**Bath chair.** An invalid wheelchair, first used at Bath, frequented by the sick on account of its hot springs.

**Bath chap.** The lower part of the cheek of a pig, usually eaten cold. The connection with the town of Bath is not clear, although the dish does seem to have WEST COUNTRY associations. *See also* CHOP.

**Bath King of Arms.** *See* HERALD.

**Bath metal.** An alloy like PINCHBECK consisting of copper, zinc, lead and tin.

**Bath Oliver.** A kind of unsweetened biscuit, invented by (or named after) Dr William Oliver (1695–1764), founder of the Royal Mineral Water Hospital, Bath, and an authority on GOUT. He left his biscuit recipe to his coachman, Atkins.

**Bath stone.** An attractive but not very durable limestone, quarried near Bath.

**King of Bath.** Richard NASH (1674–1762), commonly called Beau Nash, for 56 years the celebrated master of ceremonies at Bath.

**Knights of the Bath.** *See under* KNIGHT.

**Turkish baths.** *See under* TURK.

**Bathia.** The name given in the TALMUD to the daughter of the pharaoh who found MOSES in the ark of bulrushes.

**Bathos** (Greek, 'depth'). First used by Alexander Pope in the sense of a ludicrous descent from grandiloquence to the commonplace.

> And thou, Dalhousie, the great god of war,
> Lieutenant-general to the Earl of Mar.
> *Bathos*, ix (1727)

**Bathsheba.** The wife of URIAH THE HITTITE. DAVID spied her bathing from his rooftop and instantly lusted after her. He discovered the identity of her husband and sent Uriah into the front line of battle so that he was killed. He married the widow and they had a son. God was angered at David's deed, however, and made the child die. They had a second child, who was SOLOMON. The story of David and Bathsheba's initial sin is told with austere brevity in 2 Samuel 11. Psalm 51 was subsequently attributed to David as his repentance 'after he had gone in to Bathsheba'.

**Bathyllus.** A beautiful boy of Samos, who was greatly loved by Polycrates the tyrant and by the poet ANACREON (Horace, *Epistle*, xiv (1st century BC)).

**Bat-Kol** (Hebrew, 'daughter of the voice'). A heavenly or divine voice announcing the will of God. It existed in the time of the Jewish prophets but was also heard in post-prophetic times. 'Daughter of a voice' means a small voice, so differentiating it from the normal voice. Bat-Kol also denoted a kind of OMEN or AUGURY. After an appeal to Bat-Kol the first words heard were considered oracular.

**Bat Mitzvah.** *See* BAR MITZVAH.

**Batrachomyomachia.** A STORM IN A TEACUP, much ado about nothing. The word means 'The Battle of the Frogs and Mice' (perhaps 5th century BC) and is the name of a mock-heroic Greek epic once attributed to Homer but probably by Pigres of Caria.

**Battels** (perhaps from obsolete *battle*, 'to feed'). At Oxford University, the accounts for board, provisions and other college expenses, and more loosely for total college expenses for the term, including tuition fees. The word has also been used for the provisions or rations themselves.

**Batten down the hatches, To.** To prepare for trouble. A ship's hatches, providing the entry to the hold where the cargo is stored, are firmly clamped down before a storm.

**Battersea.** A Thames-side region of southwest London famous for Battersea Park, with its sculptures by Henry Moore, Battersea Dogs' Home (which also takes cats) and its unique landmark, Battersea Power Station, opened in 1933 and closed in 1983. In 1993 it was sold to a firm of Hong Kong property developers who were hoping to turn it into a theme park when their business collapsed.

**Battle. Battle above the Clouds, The.** A name given to the Battle of Lookout Mountain, part of the Battle of Chattanooga, fought during the American Civil War (1861–5), on 24 November 1863. The Union forces defeated the Confederates and part of the fighting took place in a heavy mist on the mountains, hence the name.

**Battle of Britain, The.** The attempt of the German Luftwaffe by their prolonged attack on southeastern England (August to October 1940) to defeat the RAF, as a prelude to invasion. RAF Fighter Command gained the victory and won universal admiration. The name arose from Sir Winston Churchill's speech (18 June 1940): 'What General Weygand called the "Battle of France" is over. I expect that the Battle of Britain is about to begin.'

**Battle of Camlan, The.** In ARTHURIAN ROMANCES the battle that put an end to the KNIGHTS OF THE ROUND TABLE, and at which ARTHUR received his death wound from the hand of his nephew MODRED, who was also slain. The site of the battle is traditionally placed at Slaughterbridge on the River Camel in Cornwall.

**Battle of Hastings.** *See* HAROLD GODWINSSON.

**Battle of the Atlantic, The.** The continuous struggle for control of the sea routes around the British Isles in the Second World War.

**Battle of the Books, The.** A satire by Swift (written 1697, published 1704) on the current literary dispute as to the relative merits of ancient and modern authors. In the battle, ancient and modern books assail each other in St James's Library.

**Battle of the Bulge, The.** The final chief German counteroffensive in the Second World War, when the Allied forces were pushed back into Belgium in 1944. The Germans were repulsed by the end of January 1945. The expression is also in colloquial use for a struggle to lose weight, a 'fight against flab'.

**Battle of the Frogs and Mice, The.** *See* BATRACHOMYOMACHIA.

**Battle of the Giants, The.** A name given to the Battle of Marignano, 10 miles (16km) southeast of Milan, where on 13–14 September 1515, after a fierce contest, the French defeated the Swiss mercenaries defending Milan.

**Battle of the Herrings, The.** That of 12 February 1429 during the HUNDRED YEARS' WAR. Sir John Fastolf was conveying provisions to the English besiegers of Orleans and was unsuccessfully attacked by superior French forces seeking to intercept the supplies. The English used the barrels of herrings with which their wagons were loaded as a defence.

**Battle of the Nations, The.** A name given to the Battle of Leipzig (16–19 October 1813), which led to the first overthrow of NAPOLEON BONAPARTE. Prussians, Russians, Austrians and Swedes took part against the French.

**Battle of the Poets, The.** A satirical poem (1725) by John Sheffield, Duke of Buckingham, in which the versifiers of the time are brought into the battlefield.

**Battle of the Saints, The.** Admiral Rodney's victory, on 12 April 1782, over the French fleet during the American War of Independence, which restored British supremacy in the West Indies. It was fought off the islands of Les Saintes near Guadeloupe.

**Battle of the Spurs, The.** A name given to: (1) the Battle of Courtrai (11 July 1302), when the French were defeated by the Flemings, so called from the thousands of spurs collected as trophies after the battle; (2) the Battle of Guinegate (1513), when the French spurred away from their vanquishers, the forces of Henry VIII of England and the Emperor Maximilian.

**Battle of the Standard, The.** The battle between the English and Scots at Cowton Moor, near Northallerton (22 August 1138). Here David I, fighting on behalf of Matilda, was defeated by King Stephen's army under Thurstan, archbishop of York, and Raoul, bishop of Durham. It received its name from the mast (erected on a wagon) carrying the banners of St Peter of York, St JOHN OF BEVERLEY and St WILFRID of Ripon, surmounted by a PYX containing the Host. It was this occasion which introduced the word 'standard' into the English language.

**Battle of the Standards, The.** The nickname given to the presidential election contest of 1896. The Republican candidate, William McKinley, upheld the single GOLD STANDARD, and the Democratic candidate, William Jennings Bryan, fought for the free and unrestricted coinage of silver. The latter was defeated by a comparatively small margin. It was regarded as a victory for 'big property'.

**Battle of the Three Emperors, The.** The Battle of Austerlitz (2 December 1805), when the French Emperor NAPOLEON BONAPARTE routed the Emperors of Austria and Russia, all three being personally present on the field.

**Battle royal, A.** In COCKFIGHTING a certain number of birds are pitted together and left to fight until there is one survivor, the victor of the battle royal. Metaphorically the term is applied to any contest of wits or general mêlée. *See also* WELSH MAIN.

**Close battle, A.** *See under* CLOSE.

**Do battle, To.** *See under* DO.

**Half the battle.** *See* FIRST BLOW IS HALF THE BATTLE.

**Line of battle.** *See under* LINE.

**Michelangelo of battle scenes, The.** *See under* MICHELANGELO.

**Ordeal of battle.** *See under* ORDEAL.

**Order of battle.** *See under* ORDER.

**Pitched battle.** *See under* PITCH.

**Battledore, Not to know B from a.** *See under* KNOW.

**Baturlio marina.** *See* BARISAL GUNS.

**Baubee.** *See* BAWBEE.

**Bauble** (Old French *baubel*, 'plaything'). A showy toy or trinket of little value. The word was originally used for the short stick, ornamented with ass's ears, carried by licensed fools. Oliver Cromwell contemptuously indicated the MACE of the House of Commons with the words 'Take away that fool's bauble' when dismissing the RUMP on 20 April 1653.

**Baucis.** *See* PHILEMON AND BAUCIS.

**Bauld Willie.** *See* BELTED WILL.

**Baulk.** *See* BALK.

**Baviad, The.** A merciless satire by William Gifford

on the DELLA CRUSCAN poetry, published in 1794, and republished with *The Maeviad* in 1795. Bavius and Maevius were two minor poets who were pilloried by Virgil (*Eclogue*, iii (1st century BC)).

**Bavieca** (Spanish *babieca*, 'blockhead', 'dolt'). The CID's horse. He survived his master for two and a half years, during which time no one was allowed to ride him. He was buried in front of the monastery gates at Valencia and two elms were planted to mark his grave.

**Bavius.** *See* BAVIAD.

**Bawbee** or **baubee.** A Scottish small coin or halfpenny first issued in 1541. The name comes from Alexander Orok of Sillebawby, who was mint master from 1538.

**Bawn, Colleen.** *See under* COLLEEN.

**Bay.** (1) A shrub of the Lauraceae family, *Laurus nobilis*, which is used for flavouring, was the bay of the ancients. As the LAUREL tree of APOLLO (*see also* DAPHNE) it was held to be a safeguard against thunder and lightning. Hence, according to Pliny, Tiberius and other Roman emperors wore a wreath of bay as an AMULET.

(2) The word also means a reddish-brown colour, and it is generally used of horses. The word is Old French *bai*, from Latin *badius*, a term used by Varro in his list of colours appropriate to horses. Thus BAYARD means 'bay-coloured'.

**Bay at the moon, To.** *See under* BARK.

**Bay Psalm Book** or **Whole Booke of Psalmes, The.** A translation for colonial churches by Thomas Welde, Richard Mather and John Eliot. It was the first book published in NEW ENGLAND, printed by Stephen Daye and his family at Cambridge, Massachusetts, in 1640. Only eleven copies are known to have survived, and it is now highly prized.

**Bay rum.** An aromatic liquid used by perfumers, originally made from rum in which bay leaves had been steeped.

**Bay State, The.** Massachusetts. Originally the Colony of Massachusetts Bay. *See also* UNITED STATES OF AMERICA.

**Bay Street.** The financial centre of Toronto, in which Canada's main stock exchange is located.

**Bay window.** An old nickname for a round, fat belly, which sticks out, as a bay window does from the front of a house.

**Botany Bay.** *See under* BOTANY.

**Crowned with bays.** *See under* CROWN.

**Flourish like a green bay tree, To.** *See under* FLOURISH.

**Queen's Bays, The.** *See under* REGIMENTAL AND DIVISIONAL NICKNAMES.

**Bayadere** or **bajadere** (Portuguese *bailadeira*, 'dancing girl', from *bailar*, 'to dance'). A Hindu professional dancing girl or nautch girl, employed for religious dances and private entertainment. *La Bayadère* (1877) is a ballet by the Austrian composer Léon Minkus.

**Bayard.** A horse of incredible swiftness, given by CHARLEMAGNE to the FOUR SONS OF AYMON. If only one of the sons mounted, the horse was of ordinary size, but if all four mounted, his body extended to the requisite length. He appears in Boiardo's ORLANDO INNAMORATO, Ariosto's ORLANDO FURIOSO and Tasso's RINALDO. The name, which is also that of Fitz-James' horse in Sir Walter Scott's *The Lady of the Lake* (1810), is used generally for any valuable or wonderful horse. *See also* BAY.

**Bayard of the Confederate Army, The.** Robert E. Lee (1807–70).

**Bayard of the East** or **of the Indian Army, The.** Sir James Outram (1803–63).

**Bayard's Leap.** Three stones, about 30 yards (27m) apart, 5 miles (8km) northwest of Sleaford, Lincolnshire. According to legend a horse named BAYARD made a mighty leap here to escape from a witch. The stones are said to represent the three horseshoes that he lost in the leap.

**British Bayard, The.** Sir Philip Sidney (1554–86), the pride of Elizabeth I's court, who was mortally wounded at the Battle of Zutphen (1586).

**Chevalier de Bayard, Le.** *See under* CHEVALIER.

**Polish Bayard, The.** Prince Józef Poniatowski (1763–1813), who served with the greatest distinction under NAPOLEON BONAPARTE.

**Bayardo.** The steed of RINALDO, which once belonged to AMADIS OF GAUL. *See also* BAYARD.

**Bayeux Tapestry.** A remarkable visual record of the Norman Conquest, culminating in the death of HAROLD GODWINSSON in 1066. It is properly not a tapestry but an embroidery, some 230ft (70m) long and about 20in (50cm) high, worked in coloured wools on coarse linen, and it presents events in the form of a sequence of 79 vignettes with a Latin running commentary. It was produced for Bishop Odo of Bayeux, half-brother of WILLIAM THE CONQUEROR, and is now generally believed to have been made in England, probably in Kent. It long hung in the cathedral at Bayeux in Normandy and is now in the Musée de la Tapisserie de la Reine Mathilde there.

**Bayonets.** A former synonym of RANK AND FILE, that is, privates and corporals of infantry, for example, 'the number of bayonets was 25,000'. The strength of a cavalry force was indicated similarly by 'sabres'.

**Bayou State, The.** The state of Mississippi, so called from its numerous bayous. A bayou is a creek or sluggish and marshy offshoot of a river or lake. The word is of Choctaw origin. *See also* UNITED STATES OF AMERICA.

**Bazooka.** (1) A trombone-like instrument invented by the American comedian Bob Burns (1896–1956). The name is perhaps modelled on 'bazoo' or 'kazoo', a once popular submarine-shaped toy producing sounds of the 'comb and paper' variety.

(2) A portable tubular rocket-launcher used as an anti-tank weapon in the Second World War.

**Bazooka'd, To be.** To be in a tank struck by such a weapon and thus metaphorically to be 'scuppered' or put out of action.

**BC.** In dating, an abbreviation for Before Christ, before the Christian era.

**Marked with BC, To be.** *See under* MARK.

**Be. Be good!** A friendly exhortation not to misbehave, usually said on parting. It is sometimes expanded to: 'If you can't be good, be careful!' An alternative is: 'Don't do anything I wouldn't do!'

**Be my guest.** Do as you wish; help yourself. The expression may have arisen as a form of hotel welcome.

**Be prepared.** The motto of the BOY SCOUTS and GIRL GUIDES, taken from the initials of the movements's founder, Sir Robert Baden-Powell, known familiarly as 'B.P.'

**Be that as it may.** Given that it may be so. An expression said when one wishes to continue a discussion, often because one would rather not talk about a point or be side-tracked by it.

> Rose kissed me to-day.
> Will she kiss me to-morrow?
> Let it be as it may,
> Rose kissed me to-day.
>
> HENRY AUSTIN DOBSON: *Rose-Leaves* (1885)

**Beach, On the.** *See under* ON.

**Beachcomber.** A person who subsists on what FLOTSAM AND JETSAM he can find on the seashore. The word originated in New Zealand, where it is found in print in 1845. An earlier form was 'beach ranger' (1827), analogous to BUSHRANGER.

**Beachy Head.** The chalk headland on the Sussex coast southwest of Eastbourne has a name that misleadingly suggests 'beach'. It actually represents Old French *beau chef*, 'beautiful headland', a name given by the Normans, who must have regarded it as a distinctive landmark when approaching England across the Channel. Its attractiveness has been marred by its sad reputation as a 'Cape Farewell' for suicides, who throw or drive themselves over its clifftop to the beach 500ft (152m) below.

**Beacon, Belisha.** *See under* BELISHA.

**Bead** (Old English *bedu*, 'prayer'). Prayers were originally 'told' (i.e. counted as having being said) on a PATERNOSTER OR ROSARY. The word thus came to be transferred to the small globular object which, threaded on a string, was used for such 'telling'.

**Beadhouse.** An ALMSHOUSE for BEADSMEN.

**Beadsman** or **Bedesman.** Properly, one who prays, and hence an inmate of an ALMSHOUSE, since most of these charities, under the terms of their foundation, required the inmates to pray for the soul of the founder.

**Baily's beads.** *See under* BAILY'S.

**Bid one's beads, To.** *See under* BID.

**Draw a bead on, To.** *See under* DRAW.

**St Cuthbert's beads.** *See under* CUTHBERT.

**St Martin's beads.** *See under* MARTIN.

**Beadle.** One whose duty it is to bid or cite persons to appear in a court, also a church servant, whose duty it was to act as an usher and keep order. The word is related to Germanic *butil*, 'bailiff'. *See also* BEDEL.

**Beak.** A slang word for a judge, a magistrate, a headmaster or a schoolmaster. The word was originally thieves' jargon.

> As a former beak I cannot help thinking that your headline today, 'Teachers face ban on sex with pupils', is of the 'Bishops face ban on wife-swapping' or 'Old Etonians face ban on living in council estates' variety: a trifle unnecessary.
>
> *The Times* (Letter to the Editor) (26 June 1998)

**Beam.** In nautical usage, the part of the ship's side between the bows and quarter and also the extreme breadth of a ship. Thus 'on the port beam' means away on the left-hand side of the ship when facing the bows, and 'on the starboard beam' is similarly away on the right-hand side. 'On the weather beam' is the side of the ship from which the wind is blowing.

**On one's beam ends, To be.** To be virtually destitute. The beams of a wooden ship are the transverse timbers, which support the decks and retain the sides, and a vessel is said to be on her beam ends when heeling over through an angle of 90 degrees.

**On the beam, To be.** To be on the right course or track. A modern phrase coming from the directing of aircraft by means of a radio beam.

**Bean. Beanfeast.** Much the same as WAYZGOOSE. It was properly an annual dinner given by an employer to his employees, and so called because beans and bacon were an indispensable feature of the meal. The word is now applied to various annual outings and jollifications or 'beanos'.

**Bean king, The.** *Rey de Habas*, the child appointed to play king on TWELFTH NIGHT, the bean king's festival. He is the one who has found the bean in the Twelfth Night cake.

**Beans.** Slang for property, money, and also formerly for a sovereign and a GUINEA. PYTHAGORAS forbade the use of beans to his disciples, not as a food, but the use of beans for political elections. Magistrates and other public officers were elected by beans cast by the voters into a helmet, and what Pythagoras advised was that his disciples should not interfere with politics or 'love beans' (i.e. office). According to ARISTOTLE the word bean implied venery, and the prohibition 'to abstain from beans' meant 'to keep the body chaste'.

**Blue beans.** *See under* BLUE.

**Full of beans.** *See under* FULL.

**How many beans make five?** *See under* HOW.

**Jack and the Beanstalk.** *See under* JACK.

**Jumping bean.** *See under* JUMP.

**Not worth a bean.** *See under* WORTH.

**Old bean.** *See under* OLD.

**Spill the beans, To.** *See under* SPILL.

**Bear** (noun). In STOCK EXCHANGE parlance, a speculator for a fall in the price of shares. Thus 'to operate for a bear' or 'to bear the market', is to use every effort to depress prices so as to buy cheap and profit on the rise. Such a transaction is known as a bear account. The term was current at least as early as the SOUTH SEA BUBBLE and probably derives from the proverb to SELL THE SKIN BEFORE ONE HAS CAUGHT THE BEAR. One who sold stocks in this way was formerly called a bearskin jobber. *See also* BACKWARDATION; BULL.

**Bear, The.** Albert (Albrecht), Margrave of Brandenburg (*c.*1100–70).

**Bear and ragged staff, The.** Crest of the Nevilles and later, Earls of Warwick, attracting particular note through the activities of the Earl of Warwick, the KINGMAKER, and used as a PUBLIC HOUSE SIGN.

> Now by my father's badge, Old Nevil's crest,
> The rampant bear chain'd to the ragged staff.
> SHAKESPEARE: *Henry VI, Pt II*, V, i (1590)

Legend has it that the first earl was Arthgal, a KNIGHT OF THE ROUND TABLE, whose cognizance was a bear because he had strangled one. Morvid, the second earl, slew a giant with a club made of a young tree stripped of its branches. To commemorate this victory he added the 'ragged staff'.

**Bear Bible, The.** *See under* BIBLE.

**Bear garden, A.** A place of tumult and disorder. In Tudor and Stuart times the gardens where bears were kept and baited for public amusement were notorious for noise and riotous disorder.

**Bear hug, A.** A wrestling hold, in which the arms tightly lock the opponent's body and arms. More generally, any similar tight embrace, whether in combat or affection.

**Bear leader, A.** In the 18th century, the tutor who conducted a young nobleman or youth of wealth and fashion on the GRAND TOUR. The reference is to the old custom of leading muzzled bears about the streets and making them show off to attract notice and money. (This practice was made illegal only in 1925.)

**Bear sucking his paws, A.** It was once held that when a bear was deprived of food it sustained life by sucking its paws. The same was said of the badger. The phrase is applied to industrious idleness.

**As a bear has no tail, for a lion he'll fail.** *See under* AS.

**As cross as a bear with a sore head.** *See under* AS.

**Bloody bear, The.** *See under* BLOODY.

**Bridled bear, A.** *See under* BRIDLED.

**Chicago Bears.** *See under* CHICAGO.

**Congleton Bears.** *See under* CONGLETON.

**Great Bear and Little Bear, The.** *See under* GREAT.

**Northern Bear, The.** *See under* NORTH.

**Rupert Bear.** *See under* RUPERT.

**Take the bear by the tooth, To.** To place one's head into the lion's mouth; to run a needless risk.

**Teddy bear.** *See under* TED.

**Yogi Bear.** *See under* YOGI.

**Bear** (verb). **Bear a charmed life, To.** To escape accidents or danger with amazing good luck.

**Bear a hand, To.** To give assistance.

**Bear arms, To.** To do military service; to be entitled to heraldic COAT OF ARMS and crest.

**Bear away, To.** A nautical expression meaning the same as to BEAR UP, but applied to the ship instead of the helm.

**Bear down on, To.** To approach in a threatening manner or (nautical) from windward.

**Bear fruit, To.** To produce results.

**Bear in mind, To.** To remember for consideration.

**Bear one company, To.** To be someone's companion.

> His faithful dog shall bear him company.
> ALEXANDER POPE: *Essay on Man*, i (1733–4)

**Bear one's cross, To.** To carry one's own burden or troubles. The allusion is to the practice of the person condemned to crucifixion being made to carry his cross to the place of execution. Hence the cross that appears on the robes of some monastic orders, which is also 'borne'. *See also* CRUTCHED FRIARS.

> But on his brest a bloudie Crosse he bore,
> The deare remembrance of his dying Lord.
> EDMUND SPENSER: *The Faerie Queene*, I, ii (1590)

**Bear out, To.** To corroborate; to confirm.

**Bear** or **carry away the bell, To.** To take first prize; to be the best. The reference is to the BELLWETHER, which leads the herd, but the allusion has been confused with an old custom of presenting a little gold or silver bell to the winners of certain contests or races.

**Bear the brunt, To.** To bear the main force of the blow or shock. The 'brunt of the battle' is the hottest part of the fight. Brunt is of uncertain origin.

**Bear the palm, To.** To be the best. The allusion is to the Roman custom of giving the victorious GLADIATOR a branch of the palm tree.

**Bear up, To.** To endure cheerfully, to keep the spirits up. In nautical language, to keep further away from the wind by putting the helm up. *See also* BEAR AWAY.

**Bear with me.** Please wait. A phrase frequently used by an employee when requested by a member of the public for something not immediately to hand.

**Bring to bear, To.** *See under* BRING.

**Grin and bear it, To.** *See under* GRIN.

**Right to bear arms.** *See under* RIGHT.

**Beard.** Among the Jews, Turks, Persians and many other peoples, the beard has long been a sign of manly dignity, and to cut it off wilfully is a deadly insult. Muslims swore by the beard of the Prophet and to swear by one's beard was an assurance of good faith. To pluck or touch a man's beard was an extreme affront, hence 'to beard' is to oppose boldly or impertinently.

**Bearded, The.** A byname (*Pogonatus*) given to Constantine IV, Byzantine emperor (668–685), also to Baldwin IV, Count of Flanders (988–1036). Fidel Castro (b.1927) is known as *El Barbudo*, 'the bearded one'.

**Bearded Master, The.** So Persius styled SOCRATES, under the notion that the beard is a symbol of wisdom.

**Beard the lion in his den, To.** To challenge someone personally or have it out FACE TO FACE. The imagery is partly of seizing the lion's beard, partly of taking the beard to stand for the whole face, as in the old expression 'to one's beard', meaning to one's face.

> Thy servant kept his father's sheep, and there came a lion, and a bear, and took a lamb out of the flock: And I went out after him, and smote him, and when he arose against me, I caught him by his beard, and smote him, and slew him.
>
> 1 Samuel 17:34–35

**Aaron's beard.** *See under* AARON.

**Alexander's beard.** *See under* ALEXANDER.

**Lie in one's beard, To.** *See under* LIE.

**Old man's beard.** *See under* OLD.

**Singeing the king of Spain's beard.** *See under* SINGE.

**Tax upon beards.** *See under* TAX.

**Vandyke beard.** *See under* VANDYKE.

**Bearings. Find** or **get one's bearings, To.** *See under* FIND.

**Lose one's bearings, To.** *See under* LOSE.

**Béarnais, Le.** Henry IV of France (1553–1610). So called from Le Béarn, his native province.

**Beast. Beast of Belsen, The.** In the Second World War the name given to Josef Kramer (1906–45), commandant of the infamous Belsen concentration camp.

**Beast of Bodmin, The.** The nickname for a wild animal, possibly a black panther, that has attacked sheep and calves on farms in the region of Bodmin Moor, Cornwall, since the early 1980s. It was first sighted in 1983 but has still not been captured or even fully identified. A legendary beast of Dartmoor forms the subject of Sir Arthur Conan Doyle's tale *The Hound of the Baskervilles* (1902).

**Beast of Bolsover, The.** The Labour MP Dennis Skinner (b.1932), famous for his forthrightness, so nicknamed from his constituency.

**Beast of burden, A.** An animal used for carrying loads, especially a mule.

**Beasts of heraldry.** In English HERALDRY all manner of creatures (many derived from BESTIARIES) have been borne as charges or as crests, notably the bear, boar, bull, cat, EAGLE, griffin, LEOPARD, lion, PELICAN, stag, swallow (called a martlet), UNICORN and WYVERN. The attitude or position of the animal is thus described:

> couchant: lying down with head erect
> dormant: sleeping, with head lowered
> passant: walking
> passant gardant: walking but looking at the beholder
> rampant: on its hind legs
> rampant combattant: two beasts rampant facing one another
> rampant endorsed: two beasts rampant back to back

If a beast is 'proper', it is emblazoned in its natural colour. If it is 'naissant', it has only its forepart shown above a horizontal division of the shield. If it is 'erased', it has a head or limb missing from its body.

**Beauty and the Beast.** *See under* BEAUTY.

**Blatant beast.** *See under* BLATANT.

**Mark of the beast, The.** *See under* MARK.

**Number of the Beast, The.** *See under* NUMBER.

**Beat** (Old English *bēatan*). The first sense of the word was that of striking. That of overcoming or defeating developed from this. As a noun, a beat is a track, range or walk, trodden or beaten by the feet, as the 'beat of a policeman'.

**Beat about, To.** A nautical phrase meaning to tack against the wind.

**Beat about the bush, To.** To approach a matter cautiously, in a roundabout way; to SHILLY-SHALLY. The reference is probably to the hunting of birds by night when they are resting or roosting. The bushes are beaten, the birds are disturbed and fly out, and they are then netted or stunned as they try to escape.

**Beat an alarm, To.** To give notice of danger by beat of a drum. To beat to arms and to beat a charge are likewise military orders by drum beat.

**Beat a retreat, To.** To withdraw from or abandon a position or undertaking.

**Beat down, To.** To force or persuade a seller to accept a lower price.

**Beaten at the post.** Defeated at the last moment. The allusion is to a race, where an apparent winner approaching the finish is overtaken by another from behind. A similar expression is PIPPED AT THE POST.

**Beat Generation, The.** The post-war generation of the 1950s, who rejected traditional Western values by turning to drugs, living communally, and generally adopting an anarchic attitude towards society. More specifically, the name refers to a group of American writers at this time, among the most notable of whom were Jack Kerouac (1922–69), Allen Ginsberg (1926–97) and William Burroughs (1914–97). The use of 'beat' in this sense was probably coined by Kerouac, who related it to 'beatitude'. Recent authorities, however, claim it was the creation of the writer and drug addict Herbert Huncke (1916–96). He was the template for Elmer Hassel in Kerouac's *On the Road* (1957), for an 'angel-headed hipster' in Ginsberg's *Howl* (1956) and for Herman in Burroughs' *Junkie* (1953).

**Beat it, To.** To go away, to clear off.

**Beat one's breast, To.** To display one's guilt or remorse publicly.

**Beat retreat, To.** Originally, in the military sense, to summon men by drum beat to withdraw to camp or behind the lines when hostilities temporarily ceased at the approach of darkness. It was also to give warning to the guards to collect and be posted for the night.

The drums were later augmented by fifes and more recently, with the advent of military bands, beating retreat became an impressive ceremonial display.

**Beat someone hollow, To.** To beat someone utterly or thoroughly. Hollow here is perhaps a corruption of 'wholly'.

**Beat someone's brains out, To.** To kill a person by beating or hitting them about the head.

**Beat the air, To.** To strike out at nothing as pugilists do before a fight; to toil without profit; to work to no purpose.

**Beat the band, To.** To excel, to exceed or surpass, from the idea of making more noise than the band.

**Beat the bounds, To.** An old custom, still observed in a few English parishes, of going round the parish boundaries on ASCENSION DAY. The schoolchildren, accompanied by the clergymen and parish officers, walk round the boundaries, which the boys 'beat' with peeled willow-wands. The boys were originally themselves sometimes 'beaten' at the limits of the boundaries to make them remember the place. *See also* RIDE THE MARCHES.

**Beat the bush while another takes the bird, To.** To allow another to profit by one's exertions, often with the sense that the workman does the work while the master makes the money. The allusion is to beaters who start the game from the bushes for a shooting party, and the phrase 'to beat the bush while another takes the hare' is an alternative.

**Beat the clock, To.** To complete a task within a stated time. The phrase was popularized in the 1950s by the television game show *Beat the Clock*.

**Beat the Devil's tattoo, To.** To drum on the table with one's fingers a wearisome number of times, or to tap on the floor with one's foot similarly.

**Beat the drum for, To.** To publicize or promote someone or something.

**Beat the Dutch, To.** To 'draw a very long bow'; to say something incredible.

**Beat time, To.** To indicate time in music by beating or moving the hands, feet or a baton.

**Beat up, To.** To assault someone brutally, often with repeated blows.

**Can you beat it?** Can you believe that? An exclamation used to express surprise or amazement.

**Dead beat.** *See under* DEAD.

**It beats me.** I do not understand it.

**Not in my beat.** Not in my line; not in the range of my talents or inclination.

**That beats Banagher.** That surpasses everything, that beats the lot. Banagher is a town in County Offaly, Ireland. It formerly sent two members to Parliament and was a notorious POCKET BOROUGH. When a member spoke of a family borough where every voter was a man employed by the owner, it was not unusual to reply, 'Well, that beats Banagher.'

**Beatification.** In the ROMAN CATHOLIC CHURCH a solemn act by which a deceased person is formally declared by the pope to be one of the blessed departed and therefore a proper subject for a MASS and Office in his or her honour, generally with some local restriction. Beatification is usually, though not necessarily, a step to CANONIZATION.

**Beatific vision.** The sight of God or of the blessed in the realms of HEAVEN, especially that granted to the SOUL at the instant of death. *See* Isaiah 6:1–3 and Acts 7:55–6.

**Beatitude.** Blessedness, perfect felicity.

**Beatitudes, The.** The eight blessings pronounced by Christ at the opening of the SERMON ON THE MOUNT. As cited by Matthew 5:3–10, blessed are:

(1) the poor in spirit: for theirs is the kingdom of heaven;
(2) they that mourn: for they shall be comforted;

(3) the meek: for they shall inherit the earth;
(4) they which do hunger and thirst after righteousness: for they shall be filled;
(5) the merciful: for they shall obtain mercy;
(6) the pure in heart: for they shall see God;
(7) the peacemakers: for they shall be called the children of God;
(8) they which are persecuted for righteousness' sake: for theirs is the kingdom of heaven.

**Beatles, The.** Probably the world's most famous pop group, formed in 1959 by four young Liverpool musicians: Paul McCartney, John Lennon (murdered 1980), George Harrison and Ringo Starr (real name Richard Starkey). They broke up in 1970, but the demand for their music has continued unabated. In their day they were worshipped by the young, respected by the not so young and even compared by one music critic (William Mann, of *The Times*) to Schubert.

> The easiest way to account for the lasting impact of the ... Beatles is to praise the genius of their music, and, in particular, their songwriting. This scarcely needs reiterating.
> *Sunday Times* (15 January 1995)

**Beatnik**. A member of the BEAT GENERATION, or loosely, any person with long hair and scruffy clothes. The Yiddish suffix *-nik* is of Russian origin, as for SPUTNIK.

**Beatrice.** *See* DANTE AND BEATRICE.

**Beau** (French, 'fine', 'beautiful', 'handsome'). A lover or sweetheart, or a man who escorts a woman or girl. The word was formerly prefixed to the name of a DANDY or leader of fashion, such as Beau BRUMMELL, Beau Didapper (in Fielding's *Joseph Andrews* (1742)), Beau D'ORSAY, Beau FEILDING, Beau GESTE, Beau NASH and Beau Tibbs (in Goldsmith's *Citizen of the World* (1762)).

**Beauclerc** (French, 'fine scholar'). A byname given to Henry I, king of England (r.1100–35), for his scholarly accomplishments.

**Beau idéal** (French, 'ideal beauty'). A phrase used in English to mean perfect beauty or excellence.

**Beau monde** (French, 'fine world'). The world of fashion and society.

**Beau of Leadenhall Street.** *See* DIRTY DICK'S.

**Beau Sabreur, Le** (French, 'the handsome swordsman'). Joachim Murat (1767–1815), a renowned French cavalry officer, the brother-in-law of NAPOLEON BONAPARTE, and king of Naples. Hence generally any dashing adventurer. P.C. Wren's novel *Beau Sabreur* (1926), a sequel to *Beau* GESTE, centres on the adventures of John Geste, Beau Geste's sole surviving brother.

**Beau ténébreux, Le** (French, 'the handsome dark one'). A term for a saturnine young man, especially one who is both grave and taciturn. The epithet was originally applied to AMADIS OF GAUL.

**Beaumontage** or **Beaumontague.** A filling compound used in joinery and metalwork, said to be named after the French geologist Élie de Beaumont (1798–1874). As it can be used for disguising bad workmanship, it has the added meanings of literary padding and bad work generally.

**Beauty. Beautiful Parricide, The.** Beatrice Cenci (1577–99), daughter of Francesco Cenci, a dissolute Roman nobleman. Because of her father's cruelties to the family, she and two of her brothers contrived his murder (in 1598). She was executed a year later at the age of 22. Their story has been a favourite theme in literature and art. Percy Bysshe Shelley's tragedy on the subject, *The Cenci* (1819), is well known, and there is a painting of Beatrice by Guido Reni (1575–1642) in the Barberini Palace, Rome.

**Beauty and the Beast.** A beautiful woman with an unlovely male companion. The names are familiar as those of the heroine and hero of the fairy tale in which Beauty saves the life of her father by consenting to live with the Beast. The Beast, set free of his spell by Beauty's love, becomes a handsome prince and marries her. The story is found in Straparola's *Le Piacevoli Notti* (1550), and this is probably the source of Mme Marie Leprince de Beaumont's popular French version (1756). It is the basis of Grétry's opera *Zémire et Azor* (1771) and, in a different art form, of Jean Cocteau's film *La Belle et la Bête* (1945). The story is of great antiquity and takes various forms. *See also* LOATHLY LADY.

**Beauty is only skin deep.** Beauty or handsomeness is no guide to a person's true inner nature.

> O formose puer, nimium ne crede colori.
> (O beautiful boy, trust not too much to your pretty looks.)
> VIRGIL: *Bucolics*, Eclogue, ii (1st century BC)

**Beauty of Buttermere, The.** *See* MAID OF BUTTERMERE.

**Beauty queen.** A woman judged the most beautiful in a competition.

**Beauty sleep.** Sleep before midnight. Those who habitually go to bed after midnight, especially during youth, are said to become pale and haggard.

**Beauty spot.** Formerly, a small dark-coloured patch that a lady wore on her face as an intriguing adornment. Hence a nickname for a mole, which may serve similarly. The phrase is otherwise in general use for an attractive rural site, especially one with a fine view.

> One of the best known beauty-spots of the South-East, Box Hill [in Surrey] rises to nearly 600ft above sea-level.
> *New Shell Guide to England* (1981)

**Age before beauty.** *See under* AGE.

**Black Beauty.** *See under* BLACK.
**England, home and beauty.** *See under* ENGLAND.
**Line of beauty.** *See under* LINE.
**Sleeping Beauty, The.** *See under* SLEEP.
**Small is beautiful.** *See under* SMALL.

**Beaux. Beaux esprits** (French, 'fine wits'). Witty or clever people. The singular is *bel esprit*.

**Beaux yeux** (French, 'beautiful eyes'). Attractive looks. 'I will do it for your *beaux yeux'* means that I will do it because you are so pretty or attractive.

**Beaver.** (1) The lower and movable part of a helmet, so called from Old French *baviere*, 'bib', from *baver*, 'to dribble', from its resemblance to this child's garment.

> *Hamlet*: Then you saw not his face?
> *Horatio*: O yes, my lord; he wore his beaver up.
> SHAKESPEARE: *Hamlet*, I, ii (1600)

(2) Also the former name for a man's hat, because some hats were made of beaver fur. In the 1920s the word was popularly applied to anyone wearing a beard.

**Beaver, The.** Name given in journalistic circles to Lord Beaverbrook (William Maxwell Aitken, 1879–1964), Canadian-born politician and newspaper magnate. He served in a number of capacities in the First World War and as Minister of Aircraft Production in the Second World War.

**Beavers.** Young boys, aged from six to eight years, who are members of the youngest group in the Scout Association. The group was inaugurated in 1971 in Canada, a country where beavers are well known and where they were formerly exploited for their fur. *See also* BOY SCOUTS; EAGER BEAVER.

**Because.** The present single word represents an earlier 'by cause', in turn based on French *par cause de*, 'by reason of'. A modern colloquial form in speech and writing is 'cos or coz, and 'cause' alone is found in dialect speech from the 16th century. In St Andrew's Church, Ipplepen, Devon, there is an inscribed floor-stone to the memory of two infants who died in 1683:

> Mourn not for vs dear Relatiues Caus We
> So earely left this Vale of Misery.
> Blesst Infants soonest to their port arriue,
> The aged longer with the stormes do striue.

**Bed. Bed and breakfast.** Overnight accommodation. In STOCK EXCHANGE parlance, 'to bed and breakfast' shares is to sell them after hours one evening and buy them back as soon as the market opens the following morning. The procedure establishes a loss for tax purposes.

**Bedchamber Crisis** or **Question, The.** In May 1839, Lord Melbourne's insecure WHIG ministry resigned, and when Sir Robert Peel accepted office he requested that some of the Whig ladies of the bedchamber be replaced by TORIES. Queen Victoria refused and Peel resigned, whereupon Melbourne was recalled to office. The question was resolved, with the intervention of Albert, the Prince Consort, before Melbourne's resignation in 1841.

**Bed of nails, A.** A situation of great anxiety and apprehension.

**Bed of roses, A.** A situation of ease or comfort.

**Bed out, To.** To transfer plants that have been raised in pots or a greenhouse out into the open ground.

**Bedroom eyes.** Eyes expressing a sensual or sexual invitation.

> With his beefy arms, gym-toned physique, bedroom eyes and maniacal energy, Britain's most sought-after chef is like a bad-boy Jilly Cooper hero made flesh.
> *Sunday Times* (6 September 1998)

**Bedroom farce.** A play depicting an absurd situation resulting from extramarital relations. The characters typically frolic in a bed or bedroom, cavort in nightclothes or indulge in similarly suggestive antics.

**Bedside manner.** The professional approach of a doctor visiting a patient in bed.

> The ordinary notion is that a good bedside manner consists of suavity carried to the verge of civility.
> *British Medical Journal* (28 December 1907)

**And so to bed.** *See under* AND.
**Apple-pie bed.** *See under* APPLE.
**As one makes one's bed, so one must lie on it.** *See under* AS.
**Between you and me and the bedpost.** *See under* BETWEEN.
**Devil's bedpost, The.** *See under* DEVIL.
**Flying bedstead.** *See under* FLY.
**Get out of bed on the wrong side, To.** *See under* GET.
**Great Bed of Ware, The.** *See under* GREAT.
**Lazy bed.** *See under* LAZY.

**Make the bed, To.** To arrange the bedding ready for use.

**Procrustes' bed.** *See under* PROCRUSTES.

**Put to bed, To.** To complete work on a printed publication, such as a newspaper, so that it is ready to go to press.

**Take to one's bed, To.** To stay in bed because of sickness or physical incapacity.

**Beddgelert.** A village in Caernarvonshire (now part of Gwynedd), North Wales, with a name popularly said to mean 'grave of Gelert', from Welsh *bedd*, 'grave'. According to local legend Prince Llewelyn returned to his castle to find his dog Gelert's jaws dripping with blood. His son had been left in Gelert's care but the baby was not to be found. In his distress, Llewelyn slew the faithful hound and found his son, close to the body of a wolf, which the hound had killed. This story is not peculiar to Wales, however, and it appears that the 'legend' was introduced here in the 18th century by an enterprising local innkeeper, David Prichard, in order to attract custom.

**Bede. Cuthbert Bede.** *See under* CUTHBERT.

**Venerable Bede, The.** *See under* VENERABLE.

**Bedel** or **Bedell.** Old forms of the word BEADLE, still used at Oxford and Cambridge universities for the officer who carries the mace before the vice-chancellor and performs certain other duties. At Oxford there are four bedels, of Divinity, Law, Medicine and Arts, each of whom carries the appropriate staff.

**Bedell's Bible.** *See under* BIBLE.

**Bedesman.** *See* BEADSMAN.

**Bedford.** The name has London associations that derive only indirectly from the county town. Bedford Park, Chiswick, the earliest planned GARDEN SUBURB in England, is named after Tubbs Bedford, a local landowner at the turn of the 18th century. The Earls of Bedford (the Russell family) held land here, but their connection with the area ceased in the 17th century. Bedford College, part of London University, was founded in 1849 as a women's college and takes its name from its original site in Bedford Square, itself named for the Dukes of Bedford (of the same Russell family). The college merged in 1985 with the Royal Holloway College to become the Royal Holloway and Bedford New College (now simply Royal Holloway).

**Bailiff of Bedford, The.** *See under* BAILIFF.

**Bedivere, Sir.** In the ARTHURIAN ROMANCES, a KNIGHT OF THE ROUND TABLE, the butler and staunch adherent of King ARTHUR. It was he who, at the request of the dying king, threw EXCALIBUR into the lake, and afterwards bore his body to the ladies in the barge that was to carry him to AVALON.

**Bedlam** (form of bethlem, a contraction of Bethlehem). Originally, a lunatic asylum or madhouse, and hence a place of hubbub and confusion. The priory of St Mary of Bethlehem outside Bishopsgate, London, was founded in 1247 and began to receive lunatics in 1377. It was given to the City of London as a hospital for lunatics by Henry VIII in 1547. In 1675 it was transferred to Moorfields and became one of the sights of London, where for a few pence, anyone might gaze at the poor wretches and bait them. It was a place for assignations and one of the disgraces of 17th-century London. In 1800 it moved to Lambeth and in 1930 to Aldington, Surrey. The present Bethlehem Royal Hospital is at Beckenham, Kent. See also ABRAHAM MAN.

**Bedlamite.** A madman, a fool, an inmate of Bedlam.

**Tom o'Bedlam.** *See under* TOM.

**Bedouin** (Old French *beduin*, from Arabic *badāwi*, from *badw*, 'desert'). The name of the nomadic tribes of Arabs inhabiting the deserts of Arabia, Jordan and Syria. Hence also formerly a general term for a person leading a wandering or homeless existence. *See also* STREET ARAB.

**Bedrock.** The end of one's resources, one's 'bottom dollar'. Bedrock is the geological term for the solid rock that lies beneath the loose surface deposits.

**Bee.** Legend has it that JUPITER was nourished by bees, and that PINDAR was fed by bees with honey (instead of milk). The Greeks consecrated bees to the MOON. With the Romans a flight of bees was considered a bad OMEN. Appian (*Civil War*, ii (2nd century AD)) says a swarm of bees lighted on the altar and prognosticated the fatal issue of the Battle of PHARSALIA. *See also* AMBROSE; ATHENIAN BEE; ATTIC BEE.

As the bee is a social insect, the word bee has been given to a social gathering for some purpose, such as a SPELLING BEE. *See also* ANIMALS IN SYMBOLISM.

**Beeline, A.** The shortest distance between two given points, such as a bee is supposed to take in making for its hive. *See also* AIRLINE.

**Bee's knees, The.** Said of someone who is outstanding in some way or who claims to be so. The term, in the singular, was earlier used of something small or insignificant. The reference may be to the pollen containers on a bee's legs. The process of removing the pollen involves much bending of the bee's knees and is performed with great precision.

**Beeswing.** A crust or film of tartar that forms in port and other wines after long keeping in the bottle, so named from its filmy, veined appearance, like a bee's wing.

**Athenian Bee, The.** *See under* ATHENIAN.

**Attic bee, The.** *See under* ATTIC.

**Birds and the bees, The.** *See under* BIRD.

**Busy bee, A.** *See under* BUSY.

**Have a bee in one's bonnet, To.** To be obsessed with a particular idea or notion, as if mentally all 'abuzz'. The earlier expression was 'to have bees in the head'. *See also* MAGGOT.

**Queen bee.** *See under* QUEEN.

**Spelling bee.** *See under* SPELL.

**Beeb, The.** A colloquial term for the BBC.

**Beecham's Pills.** A long-famous patent medicine, 'worth a guinea a box'. The pills were the proprietary preparation of Thomas Beecham (1820–1907), a Wigan chemist who first sold his product in 1850. A box cost 1s 1d, the cost of production was half a farthing, and the ingredients were aloes, ginger and soap. Beecham's grandson was the orchestral conductor Sir Thomas Beecham (1879–1961).

**Beef** (Old French *boef*, 'ox'). Like mutton (Old

French *moton*, 'sheep'), the word is a reminder of the period after the Norman Conquest when the Saxon was the servant of the conquerors. The Saxon was the herdsman and used the word for the beast under his charge, the Normans had the cooked meat and used the appropriate French name for it.

**Beefcake.** A colloquial term for pictures or photographs of men displayed for their muscular bodies or 'hunkiness'. *See also* CHEESECAKE.

**Beefeaters.** The popular name of the Yeomen of the Guard, first formed as a royal bodyguard at Henry VII's coronation in 1485. The name is also that of the Yeomen Extraordinary of the Guard, who were appointed as Warders of the TOWER OF LONDON by Edward VI and who wear the same Tudor costume. The name was probably first specifically applied to the Yeomen of the Guard about the middle of the 17th century.

The literal meaning is 'eaters of beef', and the word does not derive from French *buffetier*, as popularly supposed.

> Those goodly Juments of the guard would fight
> (As they eat beef) after six stone a day.
> WILLIAM CARTWRIGHT: *The Ordinary* (*c*.1635)

**Beefsteak Club.** The original CLUB, frequented by the wits, where refreshment was limited to steaks and beer or wine, was established in London in 1709, with a gridiron as its badge. In 1735 the Sublime Society of Steaks was inaugurated when Lord Peterborough supped with John Rich, manager of the COVENT GARDEN Theatre. His lordship was so delighted with the steak provided that he proposed to repeat the entertainment every Saturday. The Sublime Society continued to meet there until the fire of 1808, when it moved to other premises. The 'Steaks' included many famous actors until its cessation in 1867. The modern Beefsteak Club was founded in 1876.

**Baron of beef.** *See under* BARON.

**Bully beef.** *See under* BULL.

**Jerked beef.** *See under* JERK.

**Where's the beef?** *See under* WHERE.

**Beelzebub.** A god of the PHILISTINES (2 Kings 1:3), referred to in Matthew 12:24 and elsewhere as 'the prince of the Devils'. His original Phoenician name was *ba'al zebūl*, 'lord of the seat'. But the Jews interpreted the name perversely as *ba'al zevel*, 'lord of the dungheap' or *ba'al zevūv*, 'lord of the flies', because his statue, which was constantly covered in blood, attracted flies. Milton places him next in rank to SATAN.

> One next himself in power, and next in crime,
> Long after known in Palestine, and named
> Beelzebub.
> *Paradise Lost*, i (1667)

William Golding's novel *Lord of the Flies* (1954) has the translated name as its allegorical title.

**Beer.** *See* ALE.

**Beer and sandwiches.** Informal negotiations. The phrase became associated with last-ditch talks between trade unionists and politicians at No. 10 DOWNING STREET when a strike or stoppage was in the offing, as frequently happened in the 1960s and 1970s. The named fare is regarded as typical of the negotiators, as a sort of working man's equivalent of CHAMPAGNE AND CHICKEN.

**Beer belly.** A stomach that protrudes as a result of the excessive consumption of beer. It is also known as a 'beer gut'.

**Beer money.** An allowance of 1d (one penny) per day paid to British soldiers and NCOs between 1800 and 1823 instead of an issue of beer. The expressions is now sometimes used to denote 'spending money' for refreshment or pleasure.

**Life is not all beer and skittles.** *See under* LIFE.

**Small beer.** *See under* SMALL.

**Spruce beer.** *See under* SPRUCE.

**Beersheeba, From Dan to.** *See under* FROM.

**Beetle. Beetle, To.** To overhang, to threaten, to jut over. The word seems to have been first used by Shakespeare:

> Or to the dreadful summit of the cliff
> That beetles o'er his base into the sea.
> *Hamlet*, i, iv (1600)

He may have formed the verb from the adjective beetle-browed, used of someone with prominent or shaggy eyebrows. The origin of beetle in this use is uncertain, but it may refer to the tufted antennae which, in some beetles, stand straight out from the head.

**As blind** or **deaf as a beetle.** *See under* AS.

**Deathwatch beetle.** *See under* DEATH.

**Beeton, Mrs.** *The Book of Household Management*, a classic mid-Victorian work on 'domestic economy', was written by Mrs Isabella Beeton (1836–65) and first published in 1861. The bulk of its contents consisted of some 4000 recipes, and it readily established itself as the best known of all English cookery books. The name of Mrs Beeton became synonymous with this book, although she compiled other lesser ones during her short life. It still exists in revised editions. Mrs Beeton was doubtless familiar with the books written by the French cook Alexis Soyer (1809–58), who came to England after the French Revolution of July 1830. See also GLASSE, MRS HANNAH

**Befana** (corruption of Italian *epifania*, 'EPIPHANY'). The good fairy of Italian children, who is supposed to fill their stockings with toys when they go to bed on TWELFTH NIGHT. Someone enters the children's bedroom for the purpose and the wakeful youngsters cry out, *Ecco la Befana*.

According to legend Befana was too busy with household affairs to look after the MAGI when they went out to offer their gifts and said she would wait to see them on their return. But they went by another route, and Befana, every Twelfth Night, watches for them.

**Before. Before the cat can lick its ear.** Never; before the GREEK CALENDS. No cat can lick its ear. (It licks its paw and uses that to wash its ear.) *See also* NEVER.

**Before you can say Jack Robinson.** Immediately; instantly. Francis Grose, in the 1811 edition of his *Dictionary of the Vulgar Tongue*, says that the saying has its origin 'from a very volatile gentleman of that appellation, who would call on his neighbours, and be gone before his name could be announced'. James Halliwell, in his *Dictionary of Archaic and Provincial Words* (1846), a remarkable work for a young man of only 26, says that the following lines from 'an old play' are elsewhere given as the original phrase:

> A warke it ys as easie to be done.
> As tys to saye Jacke! robys on.

However, the 'old play' has never been identified. The phrase was in use in the 18th century, and it is to be found in Fanny Burney's *Evelina* (1778). The dramatist Richard Brinsley Sheridan (1751–1816), who became an MP in 1780, when attacking government bribery, retorted in response to shouts of 'Name, Name', looking directly at John Robinson, Secretary of the Treasury, 'Yes, I could name him as soon as I could say Jack Robinson'. Thomas Hudson's ditty 'Jack Robinson' was immensely popular in the early 19th century. It tells how the sailor Jack Robinson returned to find his lady married to another man.

**Beg,** or **Beggar. Beggar description, To.** To be so extraordinary or unusual that it is difficult or impossible to describe.

**Beggar-my-neighbour.** A card game in which one player tries to win the cards of the other.

**Beggars, The.** *See* GUEUX.

**Beggars' barm.** The yeast-like scum that collects on the surface of ponds, brooks and the like at the point where the current is dammed or slowed. It is thus not proper yeast, but only a froth, suitable for beggars.

**Beggars' bullets.** Stones.

**Beggars cannot be choosers.** Beggars must take what is given to them and be grateful, for they are not in a position to pick and choose or dictate terms to the giver.

**Beggars of the sea, The.** *See* GUEUX.

**Beggar's Opera, The.** A popular comic opera by John Gay, first staged in 1728. The hero is a highwayman, MacHeath, and it centres around NEWGATE. The topical satire was produced by John Rich (*see* BEEFSTEAK CLUB), and was said to have made Gay rich and Rich gay. The music was made up of traditional ballads and popular tunes of the day arranged by the German composer Johann Pepusch (1667–1752). The beggar of the title has only a speaking role.

**Begging friars.** *See* MENDICANT ORDERS.

**Begging letter, A.** A letter sent to a rich person by a stranger asking for money. Football pools and lottery winners are frequent recipients of such letters.

**Beg the question, To.** To take for granted or to assume the truth of the matter in question. The phrase is now commonly used to mean simply to raise the question, to invite the obvious question, as in: 'Most people live in towns, which begs the question whether country life has the advantages claimed for it.'

**Go begging, To.** To be untaken or unwanted, as: 'There's an apple here going begging.'

**King of the Beggars, The.** *See under* KING.

**Beghards.** Monastic fraternities, which first arose in the Low Countries in the late 12th century, named after the BÉGUINES. They took no vows and were free to leave the society at will. In the 17th century, those who survived papal persecution joined the TERTIARIES of the FRANCISCANS. The name may have caused the spelling of 'beggar', where 'begger' would be expected. *See also* LOLLARDS; ORATORIANS.

**Begin. Begin at, To.** To start from.

> To begin at the beginning: It is spring, moonless night in the small town, starless and bible-black.
> DYLAN THOMAS: *Under Milk Wood* (1954)

**Beginner's luck.** Good fortune or success at the start of an enterprise. Beginners are not expected to have immediate success since they obviously lack experience.

**Beginning of the end, The.** The first clear signs of a final outcome.

> Now this is not the end. It is not even the beginning of the end. But it is, perhaps, the end of the beginning.
> SIR WINSTON CHURCHILL: Speech at the Mansion House, London (10 November 1942)

**To begin with.** In the first place; as the first thing. Used when considering a sequence of events, as: 'He should never have been there to begin with.'

**Beguine** (French *béguin*, 'flirtation'). A popular Martinique and South American dance, or music for this dance in bolero rhythm. It inspired Cole Porter's popular song 'Begin the Beguine' (1935).

**Béguines.** A sisterhood founded in the late 12th century by Lambert le Bègue ('the stammerer'), a priest of Liège. They were free to leave the cloister and to marry, and the order formerly flourished in the Low Countries, Germany,

France, Switzerland and Italy. There are still communities in Belgium. The cap called a *béguin* was named from this sisterhood. *See also* BEGHARDS.

**Begum** (Urdu, from Eastern Turkish *begim*, 'my lady', related to BEY). A queen, princess or lady of high rank in India.

**Behemoth** (Hebrew *behemōt*, apparently the plural of *behema*, 'big beast', itself perhaps from Egyptian *pā-eḥ-mū*, 'the water ox'). The animal described under this name in Job 40:15–24 is probably the hippopotamus. The poet James Thomson seems to have taken it to be a rhinoceros.

> The flood disparts: behold! in plaited mail,
> Behemoth rears his head.
> *The Seasons:* 'Summer' (1727)

**Behind. Behind bars.** In prison.

**Behind one's back.** Secretly or deceitfully; without one's knowledge.

**Behind the eight ball.** In a dangerous position from which it is impossible to escape. The phrase comes from the game of pool, in one variety of which all the balls must be pocketed in a certain order, except the black ball, numbered eight. If another ball touches the eight ball, the player is penalized. Therefore, if the eight ball is in front of the one which he intends to pocket, he is in a hazardous position.

**Behind the scenes.** Off stage; out of public view; secretly. The expression comes from the theatre. Many 'dastardly deeds' such as murders are not represented directly on the stage but take place off it, to be reported by a breathless messenger or shocked witness.

**Behind the times.** Outmoded or antiquated.

**Come from behind, To.** *See under* COME.

**Put behind one, To.** To try to forget; to move on following an unhappy experience, as in: 'She put the divorce behind her.'

**Behistun.** A village in western Iran, by the old road from Ecbatana to Babylon. A nearby cliff bears CUNEIFORM inscriptions in Old Persian, Elamite and Babylonian, describing the enthronement of Darius I. By 1846 Henry Rawlinson had succeeded in translating the Persian, thus providing the key for the subsequent translation of the Elamite and Babylonian, and laying the foundations of scientific Assyriology. *See also* ROSETTA STONE.

**Behram.** The most holy kind of fire, according to the PARSEES.

**Beijing.** *See* PEKING.

**Bejan** or **bajan.** A freshman at the Scottish universities of St Andrews and Aberdeen. A woman student is called a 'bajanella' or 'bejanella'. The word is a corruption of French *bec jaune*, 'yellow beak', with allusion to a fledgling or young bird, and was used in the University of Paris and elsewhere. In France *béjaune* is still the name for the meal that a freshman in theory provides for his new companions. The word also means 'ignorant young man'.

**Bel** (Akkadian *Bēlu*, 'lord'). The name of the Sumerian god Enlil, the god of winds and agriculture, having the same meaning as BAAL. The story of Bel and the Dragon, which tells how DANIEL convinced the king that Bel was not an actual living deity but only an image, was formerly part of the Book of Daniel, but is now relegated to the APOCRYPHA.

**Bel esprit.** *See* BEAUX ESPRITS.

**Belch, Sir Toby.** A reckless, roistering knight in Shakespeare's *Twelfth Night* (1599).

**Belcher.** A blue neckerchief with large white spots, each containing a dark blue spot, popular in the 19th century. It was so called from the pugilist Jim Belcher (1781–1811), who sported it, as did many of his supporters.

**Belfast Regiment, The.** *See under* REGIMENTAL AND DIVISIONAL NICKNAMES.

**Belfry** (Old French *berfrei*, of Germanic origin). Historically, a movable tower used in sieges from which the attackers threw missiles. The term was then used for a watch tower or bell tower, where an alarm could be sounded. Hence the modern church bell tower, with the word coming to be popularly associated with 'bell'.

**Bats in the belfry.** *See under* BAT.

**Belgravia.** A fashionable district of London centred on Belgrave Square, itself named for the Belgrave estate in Cheshire, the property of the Dukes of Westminster, who also owned much of modern Belgravia. The Cheshire estate was originally Merdegrave, an Old English name meaning 'marten grove', since these animals frequented the place. But it was taken to be Old French for 'dung grove', so was changed to Belgrave, a more salubrious name, meaning 'beautiful grove'.

**Belial** (Hebrew *belī ya'al*, 'without worth'). In Old Testament usage the word has the meaning of worthlessness or wickedness, but it later came to be used as a proper noun for the Devil or SATAN.

> What concord hath Christ with Belial?
> 2 Corinthians 6:15

Milton uses it as a proper name:

> Belial came last – than whom a spirit more lewd
> Fell not from heaven, or more gross to love
> Vice for itself.
> *Paradise Lost*, i (1667)

**Sons of Belial, The.** *See under* SON.

**Believe. Believe it or not.** Said of something that seems incredible but that is actually true. The American illustrator Robert Ripley (1893–1949) gained considerable popularity with his syndicated newspaper features entitled *Believe It or Not!* His first cartoon appeared in the New York *Globe* of 19 December 1918 and portrayed nine oddities from the world of athletics.

**Make believe, To.** To pretend, to play a game at. Make-believe is also a noun meaning 'pretence'.

> Oh had our simple Eve
> Seen through the make-believe!
> Had she but known the
> Pretender he was!
> RALPH HODGSON: *Poems*, 'Eve' (1917)

**Old Believers.** *See under* OLD.

**Would you believe it?** Can you credit it? Is it possible?

**Belisarius** (perhaps from the name of the Celtic goddess Belisama). The greatest of Justinian's generals (*c*.505–565), who was accused of conspiring against the emperor and imprisoned in 562, but restored to favour after six months. The later story that his eyes were put out and that he was reduced to asking passers-by to 'Give an obolus to Belisarius' is without foundation.

**Belisha beacon.** A flashing light in an amber-coloured globe mounted on a black and white banded pole, the sign of a pedestrian crossing. It is named after Leslie Hore-Belisha (1893–1957), Minister of Transport from 1934 to 1937, who introduced it.

**Bell. Bell, book and candle.** The popular phrase for ceremonial EXCOMMUNICATION in the ROMAN CATHOLIC CHURCH. The ceremony traditionally concluded with the words, 'Doe to the book, quench the candle, ring the bell!', whereupon the officiating cleric closed his book, quenched the candle by throwing it to the ground and tolled the bell as for one who has died. The book symbolizes the BOOK OF LIFE, and the candle that the soul is removed from the sight of God as the candle is from the sight of man.

**Bell-bottoms.** Trousers with a marked flare below the knee, traditionally part of a sailor's uniform. The allusion is to a bell-mouth. Alma Cogan, 'the girl with the laugh in her voice', made her breakthrough as a singer in 1954 with the novelty hit 'Bell Bottom Blues'.

**Bellboy.** A hotel page boy or 'bellhop', who answers a bell rung by a guest. The term was earlier used for a ship's boy.

> 'Who art thou, boy?' 'Bell-boy, sir; ship's-crier. Ding, dong, ding!'
> HERMAN MELVILLE: *Moby-Dick*, III, xxxix (1851)

**Bell Harry.** The splendid late 15th-century central tower of Canterbury Cathedral is so called after the single bell 'Harry' that it houses. It replaced the square Norman tower of Lanfranc's day known as the Angel Tower.

**Bellman.** *See* TOWN CRIER.

**Bells and smells.** Anglo-Catholic or HIGH CHURCH. The allusion is to the use of altar bells and incense in the service of the Eucharist, in the Roman Catholic manner.

**Bells and whistles.** In computing jargon, additional attractive features, gimmicks or 'gizmos'. The allusion is to a fairground organ with its multiplicity of bells and whistles. *See also* ALL-SINGING, ALL-DANCING.

> You don't need to spend any more than this on a computer ... £700 will get you on the way, £1,000 will add bells and whistles and £1,500 will buy you a state-of-the-art machine.
> *The Times* (18 November 1998)

**Bell Savage.** *See* BELLE SAUVAGE.

**Bells of Aberdovey, The.** A Welsh folksong first published in *Ancient National Airs of Gwent and Morgannwg* (1844) by Maria Jane Williams. Because the tune had appeared in various English collections before this year, it has been wrongly ascribed to Charles Dibdin. Aberdovey (Aberdyfi) is a port and resort on the west coast of Wales. The song has been counter-claimed by Swansea on the grounds that the title really relates to Abertawe, the Welsh name of Swansea (*see* WALES). The bells are popularly said to be those of the mythical land of Cantre'r Gwaelod ('The Lowland Hundred'), which according to legend was drowned in what is now Cardigan Bay.

**Bells of Shandon, The.** Those of St Anne's Church, Shandon, Cork, made famous in the lines of 'Father Prout' (F.S. Mahony) (1804–66):

> 'Tis the bells of Shandon
> That sound so grand on
> The pleasant waters
> Of the River Lee.

The old church was destroyed in the siege of 1690 and rebuilt (1722–6).

**Bell-the-Cat.** Archibald Douglas, 5th Earl of Angus (*c*.1449–1514), was so called. James III made favourites of architects and masons, Robert Cochrane, a mason, being created Earl of Mar. The Scottish nobles held a council in the church of Lauder for the purpose of putting down these upstarts, when Lord Gray asked 'Who will bell the cat?' 'I shall,' said Douglas, and he fearlessly put the obnoxious minions to death, in the king's presence.

**Bell the cat, To.** To undertake a dangerous mission. The allusion is to the fable of the cunning old mouse (given in *Piers Plowman* (*c*.1367–70) and elsewhere), who suggested that they should hang a bell on the cat's neck to give notice to all mice of her approach. 'Excellent', said a wise young mouse, 'but who will bell the cat?'

**Bellwether.** A sheep that leads the herd, often with a bell fastened to its neck. Hence any setter of a standard, pattern or trend, especially in finance or industry.

> Marks & Spencer, for years seen as the bellwether of British retailing, is understood to be heading for its first profits downturn in living memory.
> *The Times* (18 September 1998)

**As sound as a bell.** *See under* AS.
**As the bell clinks, so the fool thinks** or **As the fool thinks, so the bell clinks.** *See under* AS.
**Bear** or **carry away the bell, To.** *See under* BEAR.
**Canterbury bell.** *See under* CANTERBURY.
**Cap and bells.** *See under* CAP.
**City of Bells, The.** *See under* CITY.
**Gabriel Bell.** *See under* GABRIEL.
**Give someone a bell, To.** To telephone them.
**Liberty Bell.** *See under* LIBERTY.
**One bell in the last dog watch.** *See under* ONE.
**Pardon bell.** *See under* PARDON.
**Passing bell.** *See under* PASS.
**Ring a bell, To.** *See under* RING.
**Ring of bells, A.** *See under* RING.
**Ring the bells backwards, To.** *See under* RING.
**Sacring bell.** *See under* SACRING.
**Sanctus bell.** *See* SACRING BELL.
**Three bells, five bells.** *See under* THREE.
**Warm the bell, To.** *See under* WARM.
**Warwick shakes his bells.** *See under* WARWICK.

**Belladonna** (Italian *bella donna*, 'beautiful lady'). The deadly nightshade (*Atropa belladonna*). Its power of dilating the pupils is said to have been exploited by women as a means of allurement.

**Bellarmine.** A large Flemish gotch, or stone beer jug, originally made in Flanders in ridicule of Cardinal Bellarmine (1542–1621), a great defender of the ROMAN CATHOLIC CHURCH. It carried a bearded mask as a rough representation of the Cardinal. *See also* DEMIJOHN; GREYBEARD.

**Belle** (French, 'beautiful'). A beautiful girl or woman, especially one who has dressed or prepared herself to present her looks and figure to their best advantage.

**Belle époque** (French, 'fine period'). The period of comfortable living that existed before the First World War.

**Belle Gabrielle, La.** *See under* GABRIELLE.

**Belle laide** (French, 'beautiful ugly one'). An intriguingly unattractive woman.

**Belle of the ball, The.** The most beautiful woman in the room or in the company.

**Belle Sauvage, La.** The site on the north side of Ludgate Hill, London, occupied by the House of Cassell from 1852 until 11 May 1941, when the whole area was demolished in an air raid. The name is a corruption of 'Savage's Bell Inn' and the French form appears to have been first used by Joseph Addison (1672–1719) in *The Spectator* (No. 82). There seems to have been an inn on the site from about the 14th century, originally called the Bell on the Hope, the 'Hope' or 'Hoop' being the garlanded ivy bush. From its position just outside Ludgate, its yard became a rendezvous for bear baiting, play acting and the like, and from the 17th until the mid-19th century it was a departure point for coaches. The inn licence was not renewed after 1857. *La Belle Sauvage* translates from French as 'the beautiful wild girl', and a representation of her (as a half-kneeling skin-clad POCAHONTAS with bow and arrows) was originally Cassell's COLOPHON.

**Belles-lettres** (French, 'fine letters'). Literary works, typically essays and poetry, that are valued more for their aesthetic appeal than their content.

**Bellerophon** (Greek, 'killer of Belleros'). The JOSEPH of Greek mythology, Antaea, wife of Proetus, being the POTIPHAR'S WIFE who tempted him and afterwards falsely accused him. Proetus sent Bellerophon with a letter to Iobates, king of Lycia, his wife's father, describing the charge, and requesting that the bearer might be put to death. Iobates, reluctant to slay Bellerophon himself, gave him many hazardous tasks, including the killing of the CHIMERA, but as he succeeded in all of them, Iobates made him his heir. Later, Bellerophon attempted to fly to heaven on PEGASUS, but ZEUS sent a gadfly to sting the horse, and the rider was thrown.

This was also the name of the 74-gun ship of the Royal Navy that took part in the Battles of the Nile (1798) and Trafalgar (1805) and to whose captain NAPOLEON BONAPARTE finally surrendered after Waterloo. The name was corrupted by sailors to 'Bully Ruffian' and similar perversions.

**Bellerus.** A Cornish giant introduced by Milton in his *Lycidas* (1637) to account for Belerium, the Roman name for Land's End.

> Or whether thou, to our moist vows denied,
> Sleep'st by the fable of Bellerus old.

**Bellona** (Latin *bellum*, 'war'). The Roman goddess of war, the wife (or sometimes sister) of MARS.

**Belly. Belly button** or **tummy button.** The navel.

**Belly dance.** A sensuous and provocative dance of Middle Eastern origin, performed by women, and involving sinuous movements of the lower torso and hips. The belly (or midriff) is usually visible.

**Belly landing.** A crash landing of an aircraft on the underside of the fuselage, made when the undercarriage is not lowered.

**Belly laugh.** A loud and usually unrestrained laugh.

**Beer belly.** *See under* BEER.
**Go belly up, To.** To become bankrupt; to die.
**Pot belly.** *See under* POT.

**Belomancy** (Greek *belos*, 'dart', and *manteia*, 'divination'). DIVINATION by arrows. Labels are attached to a given number of arrows, the archers shoot them, and the advice on the label of the arrow that flies farthest is accepted. It was anciently practised by the Babylonians and Scythians, among others. Sir Thomas Browne describes it in *Pseudodoxia Epidemica* (v, 23 (1646)) and it is also mentioned in Ezekiel 21:21.

**Beloved. Beloved Disciple, The.** St JOHN THE EVANGELIST (John 13:23).

**Beloved Physician, The.** St LUKE (Colossians 4:14).

**Below. Below par.** *See* PAR.

**Below stairs.** In the basement among the servants. In most of the town houses built from the end of the 18th century for the well-to-do, the kitchens and servants' daytime quarters were in the basement, hence the phrase. 'Above stairs' has the opposite implications and associations.

**Below the belt.** Unfairly, unscrupulously. It is prohibited in the QUEENSBERRY RULES of prize-fighting to hit below the waist belt.

**Below the gangway.** In the HOUSE OF COMMONS, below the cross-passage about halfway down the chamber which leads to the back benches on either side and which separates the Government and leaders of the OPPOSITION from the rest of the members. Thus 'to sit below the gangway' is to sit among the members in general. *See also* BACKBENCHER.

**Belphegor.** The Assyrian form of Baal-Peor (*see* BAAL), the Moabitish god to whom the Israelites became attached in Shittim (Numbers 25:3), which was associated with licentious orgies (Hosea 9:10).

The name was given in medieval Latin legend to a demon sent into the world by his fellows to test rumours concerning the happiness of married life on earth. After a thorough trial, he fled to the happy regions where female companionship was non-existent. Hence the name is applied to a misanthrope and to any unpleasant or licentious fellow. The story is found in MACHIAVELLI, occurs in English in Barnabe Rich's *Farewell to the Militarie Profession* (1581), and is used in *Grim, The Collier of Croyden* (1600), Ben Jonson's *The Divell is an Asse* (1616), and John Wilson's *Belphegor, or the Marriage of the Devil* (1691).

**Belphoebe** (French *belle*, 'beautiful', and PHOEBE). The goddess of the hunt in Spenser's *The Faerie Queene* (1590, 1596), daughter of Chrysogone and sister of AMORET, typifies Queen Elizabeth I as a model of chastity. She was like DIANA and MINERVA, cold as an icicle, passionless, immovable and, like a moonbeam, light without being warm.

**Belsen, The Beast of.** *See under* BEAST.

**Belshazzar.** A co-regent of Babylon in the 6th century BC, described as king and son of NEBUCHADNEZZAR in the Old Testament (Daniel 5:1, 17, 8:1). Belshazzar was feasting when a mysterious human hand appeared and wrote on the wall MENE, MENE, TEKEL, UPHARSIN, interpreted by Daniel to mean 'You have been weighed in the balance and found wanting'. That night, Belshazzar was slain and his land was conquered by his enemies. The Aramaic words, literally meaning 'numbered, weighed, divisions', are the original WRITING ON THE WALL.

**Belt. Belt and braces.** Doubly safe. The expression is usually said of a policy offering twofold secuity. Trousers kept up by both belt and braces are hardly likely to collapse.

**Belted earl or knight.** A reference to the belt and spurs with which KNIGHTS were invested. In American usage, a 'belted earl' is a person who claims noble birth.

**Belted Will.** Lord William Howard (1563–1640), third son of Thomas, 4th Duke of Norfolk. Scott gives him this name in *The Lay of the Last Minstrel* (IV, vi (1805)), and also makes him warden of the western marches, but he was known to contemporaries as Bauld ('bold') Willie. He carried out an enlightened policy in restoring order and civilization to the border districts. His wife was called 'Bessie with the braid [broad] apron' from her ample dowry.

**Belt out, To.** To sing loudly and vigorously.

**Belt up, To.** To become silent, usually when forced to do so.

**Below the belt.** *See under* BELOW.

**Black belt.** *See under* BLACK.

**Black Belt, The.** *See under* BLACK.

**Chastity belt.** *See under* CHASTITY.

**Green belt.** *See under* GREEN.

**Hit below the belt, To.** *See under* HIT.

**Sam Browne belt.** *See under* SAM.

**Stockbroker belt.** *See under* STOCK.

**Sun Belt, The.** *See* SUNBELT.

**Tighten one's belt, To.** *See under* TIGHTEN.

**Under one's belt.** *See under* UNDER.

**Beltane** (Scottish Gaelic *bealltainn*). An ancient Celtic festival with a sacrificial fire on MAY DAY. The derivation is uncertain, but the name is not connected with BAAL. Fires were lit on the hill tops, and cattle were driven between the flames, either to protect them from disease or as a preparation for sacrifice. Animal guisering, familiar from the hobby horse (*see* HOBBY), derives from Beltane animal sacrifices, and a person born 'between the Beltanes', i.e. in the week beginning on May Day, is said to have power and influence over all living things.

**Belvedere. Apollo Belvedere.** *See under* APOLLO.

**Torso Belvedere, The.** *See under* TORSO.

**Ben. Big Ben.** *See under* BIG.

**Rare Ben.** *See under* RARE.

**Benares.** The holy city of the Hindus, the equivalent of MECCA for Muslims. It contains many temples, including the Golden Temple of SIVA, and is much frequented by pilgrims. It is of great antiquity and was for centuries a Buddhist centre. It is now more usually known as Varanasi.

**Bench.** Originally the same word as BANK, a bench is properly a long wooden seat. Hence the official seat of judges or magistrates in court, bishops in the HOUSE OF LORDS, and the like, and so by extension the judges and bishops themselves, or the dignity of their office.

**Bench and Bar.** Judges and barristers. *See* BAR; BARRISTER.

**Benchers.** Senior members who administer the INNS OF COURT and call students to the BAR. They also exercise powers of expulsion.

**Bench mark.** A surveyor's mark cut in some lasting material such as a rock or the wall of a building to act as a reference point when determining the elevation of an area. In Britain it consists of cuts in the shape of a broad arrow with a horizontal incision across its tip. When making the reading, an angle iron was inserted in the incision to form the bench on which the levelling staff was rested. Hence the name.

**Front bench, The.** *See under* FRONT.

**King's** or **Queen's Bench.** *See under* KING.

**On the bench.** Appointed a judge or magistrate. In sports jargon, a player 'on the bench' is a substitute or reserve ready behind the touchline to come on the field if required.

**Raised to the bench, To be.** *See under* RAISE.

**Raised to the episcopal bench, To be.** *See under* RAISE.

**Bend.** In HERALDRY, an ORDINARY formed between the two parallel lines drawn across the shield from the DEXTER chief (i.e. the top left-hand corner when looking at the shield) to the SINISTER base (the opposite corner). It is said to represent the sword belt.

**Bend over backwards, To.** To make exceptional efforts to please or appease. One normally bends over forwards. To bend over backwards is thus to take a special stance.

**Bend sinister.** A diagonal line bisecting a shield from the SINISTER chief, i.e. from top right to bottom left. It is occasionally an indication of bastardy, although a 'baton sinister' is more often used. *See also* BAR SINISTER.

**Bend someone's ear, To.** To importune an unwilling listener at length, especially to tell them one's troubles. The phrase may also mean simply to have a word with someone.

**Bends, The.** Decompression sickness, especially in divers. The reference is to the sufferer being bent double in pain or to the slight easing of pain gained by flexing a joint.

**Bend the rules, To.** To change the rules to suit one's own convenience.

**Caught bending, To be.** *See under* CATCH.

**Grecian bend.** *See under* GRECIAN.

**Round the bend.** *See under* ROUND.

**Benedicite** (Latin, 'bless ye'). A grace or a blessing, many of which began with this word. In the BOOK OF COMMON PRAYER it is the name of the canticle beginning 'O all ye works of the Lord, bless ye the Lord', translating the Latin *Benedicite, omnia opera Domini, Domino*, and originating in Daniel 3:57. The word has also been used as an expression of astonishment.

> The God of Love! Ah! *Benedicite*!
> How mighty and how great a lord is he!
> CHAUCER: *Canterbury Tales*, 'The Knight's Tale' (*c*.1387) (modern translation by Nevill Coghill, 1951)

**Benedick** or **Benedict.** A confirmed bachelor caught in the snares of matrimony. The reference is to Benedick in Shakespeare's *Much Ado about Nothing* (1598), who marries Beatrice at the end of the play.

**Benedict.** A saint (*c*.480–*c*.547), who is sometimes known as the founder of monasticism. St Benedict's sister Scholastica (d.*c*.543) is regarded as the founder of the Benedictine nuns.

**Benedictine.** A liqueur still made on the site of the Benedictine abbey at Fécamp, and based on the original early 16th-century recipe of Brother Vincelli. *See also* BENEDICTINES.

**Benedictines.** Monks who follow the rule of St Benedict, also known as the Black Monks. Monte Cassino in Italy became their chief centre and they were renowned for their learning. Apart from their religious exercises, the monks were to be employed in study, teaching and manual labour. The Benedictines were a great civilizing influence in western Europe.

**Benefice.** Under the Romans certain grants of land made to veteran soldiers were called *beneficia*, and in early feudal times an estate held for life, in return for military service, was called a benefice. The term came to be applied to the possessions of the church held by individuals as a recompense for their services. Hence a church 'living'.

**Benefit. Benefit of clergy.** Formerly, the privilege enjoyed by the English clergy of trial in an ecclesiastical court, where punishments were less harsh than in the secular courts and where bishops could not impose the death penalty. By an Act of Henry IV's reign, no woman was to suffer death for circumstances in which a man could 'plead his clergy', and a blind man could avoid the rope if able to speak Latin 'congruously'. Benefit of clergy was steadily curtailed from the time of Henry VII and by the end of the 17th century most of the serious crimes were excluded, but it was not finally abolished until 1827.

**Benefit society.** *See* FRIENDLY SOCIETY.

**Fringe benefits.** *See under* FRINGE.

**Benevolence.** A royal expedient for raising money without parliamentary consent. It was first so called in 1473, when Edward IV raised such a forced loan from his nobility and subjects as a mark of goodwill towards his reign. It was last levied by James I in 1622, and was declared illegal by the BILL OF RIGHTS, 1689.

**Bengal Tigers, The.** *See under* REGIMENTAL AND DIVISIONAL NICKNAMES.

**Benin.** The West African state known until 1975 as Dahomey. Its name comes from its original indigenous people, the Bini, who are now more usually linked with Nigeria (hence Benin City in that country). Their own name is probably related to Arabic *banī*, 'sons'. The name of Dahomey represents the former kingdom here of Dan Homé, traditionally interpreted as 'on the stomach of Dan'. The reference is said to be to the palace of King Aho, built on the spot where his rival Dan was buried, but it may actually represent Agbomi, 'inside the fort', from *agbo*, 'strength', 'rampart' (literally 'buffalo'), and *mi*, 'inside'.

**Benjamin** (Hebrew *binyamīn*, 'son of my right [hand]'). A former nickname for the pet or youngest member of a family, in allusion to Benjamin, the youngest son of Jacob (Genesis 35:18).

**Benjamin bush** or **tree.** The tree *Lindera benzoin* that yields benzoin, of which the name is a corruption. Its leaves are used to make a tea and the fruits as a substitute for allspice.

> Taste, smell; I assure you, sir, pure benjamin, the only spirited scent that ever awaked a Neapolitan nostril.
>
> BEN JONSON: *Cynthia's Revels*, V, ii (1600)

**Benjamin's mess.** The largest share. The allusion is to the banquet given by Joseph, viceroy of Egypt, to his brethren. 'Benjamin's mess was five times so much as any of theirs' (Genesis 43:34).

**Ben trovato** (Italian, 'well found'). The equivalent of French *bien trouvé*. The full Italian saying *Se non è vero, è molto ben trovato* means 'If it is not true, it is very well invented'.

**Beowulf** (perhaps Old English *beadu*, 'war', and *wulf*, 'wolf'). The hero of the Old English epic poem of the same name, of unknown date and authorship but certainly originally written before the Saxons came to England and modified subsequent to the introduction of Christianity. In its present form, it probably dates from the 8th century. It is the oldest epic in English and also in the whole Germanic group of languages.

The scene is laid in Denmark or Sweden. The hall of HROTHGAR is raided nightly by the monster GRENDEL, whom Beowulf mortally wounds after a fierce fight. Next night Grendel's mother comes to avenge his death. Beowulf pursues her to her lair under the water and slays her with a magic sword. He eventually becomes king and 50 years later is killed in combat with a DRAGON, which had ravished the land.

**Bequest, The Chantrey.** *See under* CHANTREY.

**Berchta.** A goddess of south German mythology akin to the HULDA of north Germany, but after the introduction of Christianity she was degraded into a BOGY to frighten children. In her current form she is the personification of the night before EPIPHANY, and in Alpine districts gifts are placed for her on the roof on this day, which is named after her as *Perchtentag*.

**Berchtesgaden.** A charmingly situated resort in southeastern Bavaria, Germany, known for its salt mines, royal castle and abbey. It was the site of Adolf Hitler's fortified mountain retreat, which could be entered only by a lift and a tunnel through the rock.

**Berenice** (interpreted as from Greek *Pherenikē*, 'bringer of victory', but actually Egyptian in origin). The wife of Ptolemy III Euergetes (246–221 BC). She vowed to sacrifice her hair to the gods if her husband returned home the vanquisher of Asia. She hung up her tresses in the temple, but they were stolen the first night and Conon of Samos told the king that the winds had wafted them to heaven, where they still form the seven stars near the tail of LEO, called Coma Berenices.

**Bergomask.** A rustic dance (*see A Midsummer Night's Dream*, V, i (1595)), so called from Bergamo, a Venetian province, whose inhabitants were noted for their clownishness. The word has also been used for a CLOWN.

**Berlin.** A four-wheeled, two-seated, covered carriage, popular in the 18th century. It was introduced into England by a German officer from Berlin about 1670.

**Bermoothes.** The name of the island in *The Tempest* (1611), pretended by Shakespeare to be enchanted and inhabited by witches and DEVILS. He almost certainly had the newly discovered Bermudas in mind.

**Bermuda. Bermuda rig.** A type of sailing boat rig with a tall mainsail (Bermudian mainsail) tapering to a point.

**Bermuda shorts.** Close-fitting shorts that come down to the knee, perhaps first fashionable among yacht crews. *See also* BERMUDA RIG.

**Bermuda Triangle, The.** The triangular sea area between Bermuda, Florida and Puerto Rico, said to be a region of profound danger for anyone venturing into it. The story began in December 1944 when five bombers of the US Navy were lost while on a routine training mission from the Fort Lauderdale air base. A sensational book by Charles Berlitz, *The Bermuda Triangle* (1974), brought this to the attention of the public. A number of ships and other aircraft were subsequently said to have vanished in the area. However, these either did not exist, or sank or capsized elsewhere, or simply went down from natural causes, such as the violent storms and rough seas for which the Bermuda Triangle is notorious.

**Bernadette, St.** *See* LOURDES.

**Bernard.** Saint and abbot of Clairvaux (1090–1153). He was renowned for his wisdom and abilities, did much to promote the growth of the CISTERCIAN Order and exercised great influence in church matters. He was nicknamed the 'Mellifluous Doctor' for the sweetness of his writings.

**Bernardine.** A monk of the Order of St BERNARD of Clairvaux, a strict branch of the CISTERCIAN Order.

**St Bernard Passes.** Two Alpine passes into Italy, the Great St Bernard from Switzerland, the Little St Bernard from France. On the former is the hospice founded by St Bernard of Menthon (d.*c*.1081), served by the AUGUSTINIAN CANONS. From early days they have succoured pilgrims and others crossing the pass, for this purpose breeding the large and handsome St Bernard dog, trained to track and aid travellers lost in the snow. In May 1800 NAPOLEON BONAPARTE made his famous passage of the Alps across the Great St Bernard pass with 30,000 men, the only track then being a bridle path.

**St Bernard's soup.** *See* STONE SOUP.

**Bernardo del Carpio.** A semi-mythical Spanish hero of the 9th century and a favourite subject of minstrels. Lope de Vega (1562–1635) wrote several plays around his exploits. He is credited with having defeated ROLAND at Roncesvalles.

**Bernesque poetry.** Seriocomic poetry, so called from Francesco Berni (*c*.1497–1536), the Italian cleric and poet who greatly excelled in it. Lord Byron's *Beppo* (1818) is a good example of English bernesque.

**Berry, As brown as a.** *See under* AS.

**Berserk** (Icelandic *berserkr*, from *björn*, 'bear', and *serkr*, 'shirt'). In Scandinavian mythology, a fierce warrior, who wore a bearskin shirt or coat. Hence the present use of the word to mean frenziedly violent, especially in the expression 'to go berserk'.

**Berth. Give a wide berth to, To.** *See under* WIDE.

**Bertha, Big.** *See under* BIG.

**Berthe au Grand Pied** (French, 'Bertha of the big foot'). The mother of CHARLEMAGNE and great-granddaughter of Charles MARTEL. She had a club foot and died in AD 783.

**Bertie. Bertie Wooster.** *See under* WOOSTER.

**Burlington Bertie.** *See under* BURLINGTON.

**Bertram. Bertram, Count of Roussillon.** The hero of Shakespeare's *All's Well that Ends Well* (1602), beloved by Helena.

**Bertram Mills.** *See under* MILLS.

**Berwick.** The Northumberland town of Berwick-upon-Tweed lies close to the Scottish border and was at one time Scotland's most effective and richest port. The border-line itself was long unstable and the town a regular subject of dispute between Scots and English. It thus changed hands no fewer than 13 times until it was finally surrendered to England in 1482. Even so, it continued to be exposed to the aggression of both countries until 1551, when it was made a free town by treaty between Edward VI and Mary, Queen of Scots. It retained this status until 1885, when by Act of Parliament Queen Victoria again included it in England.

**Besant.** *See* BEZANT.

**Beside. Beside oneself.** Frantic with worry or some strong emotion. The idea is that one is out of one's normal mental condition. A similar concept is expressed by ECSTASY.

**Beside the mark.** Not to the point. A phrase from archery, in which the mark was the target.

**Beside the point.** Irrelevant. An expression that possibly evolved from BESIDE THE MARK. The reference would be to gunnery, in which the target is more of a point than in archery.

**Besom, To jump the.** *See under* JUMP.

**Bess. Bessie Bell and Mary Gray.** A ballad relating how two young women of Perth, to avoid the plague of 1666, retired to a rural retreat called the Burnbraes, near Lynedock, the residence of Mary Gray. A young man, in love with both, carried them provisions, and they all died of the plague and were buried at Dornock Hough.

**Bessie with the braid apron.** *See* BELTED WILL.

**Bess o'Bedlam.** A female lunatic vagrant. *See also* BEDLAM; TOM O'BEDLAM.

**Bess of Hardwick.** Elizabeth Talbot, Countess of Shrewsbury (1518–1608), to whose husband's charge Mary, Queen of Scots was committed in 1569. The countess treated the captive queen harshly, through real or feigned jealousy of her husband. The daughter of John Hardwick of Derbyshire, she married four times: Robert Barlow (when she was 14), Sir William Cavendish, Sir William St Loe and lastly George Talbot, 6th Earl of Shrewsbury. She was known as 'building Bess of Hardwick', and in a district straddling the Nottinghamshire–Derbyshire border built Hardwick Hall and mansions at

Oldcotes and Worksop, as well as restoring Bolsover Castle and completing Chatsworth.

**Black Bess.** *See under* BLACK.

**Good Queen Bess.** *See under* GOOD.

**Best. Best bib and tucker.** *See* TUCKER.

**Best boy.** In filming, the assistant to the senior electrician or 'key grip'.

**Best buy.** The purchase that gives the best value in proportion to its price, otherwise a bargain.

**Best end of neck.** The rib end of a neck of lamb, regarded as the best for cooking and eating. The opposite end is the 'scrag end'.

**Best foot forward.** To put one's best foot forward is to get a move on; to hurry. Also, to try to do one's best.

**Best friend.** One's favourite friend.

**Best girl.** A man's favourite female companion.

**Best man.** The bridegroom's chosen friend, who attends him at his wedding as the bridesmaids attend the bride.

**Best of a bad bargain, The.** The best of a matter in which one has lost or come off worst, usually heard in the expression 'to make the best of a bad bargain'. Similarly, 'to make the best of it' or 'to make the best of a bad job' means to do the best one can in unfavourable circumstances.

**Best of both worlds, The.** The benefits of two contrasting ways of life or views on life.

**Best of British luck, The.** An ironic expression of encouragement, implying that the required luck may not materialize. The expression is an elaborated form of 'the best of luck'.

**Best part of, The.** Most of.

**Best-seller.** A book or other item that has sold in large numbers. A novel winning a literary award such as the BOOKER PRIZE may becomes a best-seller, as more generally does crime fiction.

> A story of a murder in London's Inns of Court, it [P.D. James's *A Certain Justice*] went straight onto the bestseller lists.
>
> *Britannica Book of the Year* (1998)

**Best somebody, To.** To get the better of them.

**All the best.** *See under* ALL.

**At best or at the very best.** *See under* AT.

**At one's best.** *See under* AT.

**At the best of times.** *See under* AT.

**Do one's best, To.** *See under* DO.

**For the best.** *See under* FOR.

**Six of the best.** *See under* SIX.

**With the best of them.** *See under* WITH.

**Bestiaries.** Books that had a great vogue between the 11th and 14th centuries, describing the supposed habits and peculiarities of animals both real and fabled, with much legendary lore and moral symbolism. They ultimately derived from the Greek *Physiologus*, compiled by an unknown author before the middle of the 2nd century AD, while those in English were mostly translations of continental originals. Among the most popular were those of Philippe de Thaun, Guillaume le Clerc and Richard de Fournival, the latter's 14th-century *Bestiaire d'Amour* applying the allegory to love.

**Bet. Bet one's boots, To.** To be certain.

**Bet one's bottom dollar on, To.** To be absolutely sure about, to wager. The reference is to the pile of dollar coins on an American poker table which the confident player will push to the centre, including the dollar at the bottom of the pile.

**You bet.** You may be sure; you can take that for granted.

**Bête noire** (French, 'black beast'). A pet aversion; the thing one dislikes or fears. Black animals are often regarded with ill favour. A BLACK SHEEP is an unwelcome oddity, and a black cat crossing one's path brings bad luck. Black generally is also the colour of the Devil.

**Bethel** (Hebrew, 'house of God'). A hallowed place where God is worshipped (Genesis 28:18–19). The name has frequently been given to Nonconformist chapels, especially in Wales, and also to religious meeting houses for seamen. They were sometimes referred to by ANGLICANS, somewhat disparagingly, as 'little Bethels'.

**Bethesda.** In the New Testament (John 5), the pool at the Sheep's Gate of JERUSALEM whose waters healed the sick. Christ restored the sight of a blind man there. As for BETHEL, the name came to be adopted for Nonconformist chapels, and it was around one such chapel that the slate-mining town of Bethesda in North Wales arose.

> On coming to a town, lighted up and thronged with people, I asked one of a group of young fellows its name.
>
> 'Bethesda,' he replied.
>
> 'A scriptural name,' said I.
>
> 'Is it?' said he; 'well, if its name is scriptural the manners of its people are by no means so'.
>
> GEORGE BORROW: *Wild Wales*, ch xvi (1862)

**Bethlehem. Bethlehemites.** (1) A monastic order existing at Cambridge in 1257. Members wore a red star on the breast in memory of the STAR OF BETHLEHEM.

(2) A military order instituted by Pius II in 1459 against the Turks.

(3) A religious society for tending the sick, founded in Guatemala, *c*.1659, by Pierre de Bethencourt, a native of the Canaries. Innocent XI approved of the order in 1687.

(4) Followers of John Huss (*c*.1369–1415), so called from the fact that he used to preach in the church of Bethlehem in Prague.

(5) An order of monks and nuns founded in France in 1976 and since spreading to other countries.

Only the last of these survives.

**Star of Bethlehem.** *See under* STAR.

**Betsy Ross.** *See under* ROSS.

**Better. Better feelings.** One's conscience.

**Better half.** One's wife, or less often husband, a facetious phrase.

**Better late than never.** An excuse for not being on time or said as a civility by a person who has been kept waiting. The phrase is an old one.

And you that use it, master your desire
Lest you lose all; for better late than never.
Long is the ruin that can last for ever!

CHAUCER: *Canterbury Tales*, 'The Canon's Yeoman's Tale' (*c*.1387) (modern translation by Nevill Coghill, 1951)

**Better off.** In easier circumstances financially.

**Better 'ole, A.** Old Bill, a walrus-moustached, disillusioned old soldier, in the First World War, portrayed by Captain Bruce Bairnsfather (1887–1959), artist and journalist, in his publications *Old Bill* and *The Better 'Ole*. Cowering in a wet and muddy shell hole in the midst of a withering bombardment, he says to his grousing pal Bert, 'If you knows of a better 'ole, go to it.' The joke and Old Bill struck the public fancy, and Old Bill became the embodiment of a familiar type of simple, cynical, long-suffering, honest old grouser.

It is probably from this that the 'Old Bill', or simply the 'Bill', became a nickname for the police, and the Metropolitan Police in particular. The precise connection is uncertain, but it may be either because many ex-servicemen took employment with the Metropolitan Police after the war, or because such servicemen were recruited by posters showing Bairnsfather's Old Bill in a Special Constable's uniform.

**Better part of, The.** Most of, a large part of.

**Better red than dead.** Better to live under Communist domination than be exterminated. The phrase arose among nuclear disarmers in the 1950s.

**Better safe than sorry.** Do not take a risk, for you may regret it; err on the side of caution.

**Better than one's word, To be.** To do more than originally promised.

**For better, for worse.** *See under* FOR.

**Get the better of, To.** To defeat or outwit.

**Go one better, To.** *See under* GO.

**Kiss it better.** *See under* KISS.

**Know better than to, To.** *See under* KNOW.

**No better than one should be, To be.** *See under* NO.

**Think better of, To.** *See under* THINK.

**Bettina.** Elisabeth von Arnim (1785–1859), German writer and wife of the poet Ludwig Achim von Arnim. Her first book, *Letters to a Child* (1835), was based on her (largely fictitious) correspondence with Goethe, with whom she was infatuated.

**Betty Boop.** *See under* BOOP.

**Between. Between a rock and a hard place.** In a dilemma. The expression has a biblical ring but is of modern and American origin.

**Between Scylla and Charybdis.** Between equal dangers. *See also* CHARYBDIS; HOBSON'S CHOICE; SCYLLA.

**Between the Devil and the deep (blue) sea.** Between SCYLLA and CHARYBDIS; between two evils or alternatives, so that one is in a hazardous or precarious position. The expression may be of nautical origin, the devil being a seam in the hull of a ship that ran along the waterline. *See also* DEVIL TO PAY AND NO PITCH HOT.

**Between wind and water.** In a most dangerous spot. The phrase refers to that part of a sailing ship's hull around the waterline, which is alternately wet and dry according to the motion of both ship and waves. This is a dangerous place for a ship to be holed.

**Between you and me** or **between ourselves** or **between you and me and the gatepost** or **bedpost** or **lamppost.** In confidence; secretly. The phrase often indicates that a piece of gossip or tittle-tattle is to follow. All three objects mentioned are inanimate, so will not pass on the private information.

**Fall between two stools, To.** *See under* FALL.

**Betwixt and between.** Neither one thing nor the other, but somewhere between the two. Thus, grey is neither white nor black, but betwixt and between.

**Beulah.** *See* LAND OF BEULAH.

**Beverley, St John of.** *See under* JOHN.

**Beverly Hills.** A fashionable district of Los Angeles, near HOLLYWOOD, famous for its individualistic or extrovertly eccentric residences, the homes of film and television stars and of millionaires of all kinds. Its opulent mansions and winding drives form an elegant oasis of some 31,000 residents, cocooned from the hurly-burly of downtown Los Angeles, which completely surrounds it. It adopted its present name in 1911, before which it was simply Beverly. The name comes from Beverly Farms, where in 1906 a newspaper report claimed President Taft was staying.

**Bevin Boys.** A nickname for the young men directed to work in coal mines in the Second World War instead of doing military service. The name comes from that of Ernest Bevin (1881–1951), Minister of Labour and National Service, who devised the scheme. Some 21,000 were conscripted, the figure at the end of their call-up number determining their selection as miners rather than military men. The nearest they thus got to a uniform was the miner's helmet and safety lamp, and they were denied the protection of the buttonhole badge that identified members of the Merchant Navy. Although literally out of the public eye, their contribution to the war effort was fully recognized by Winston Churchill:

> One will say: 'I was a fighter pilot'; another will say: 'I was in the Submarine Service'; another: 'I marched with the Eighth Army'; a fourth will say: 'None of you could have lived without the convoys and the Merchant seamen'; and you, in your turn, will say, with equal pride and with equal right: 'We cut the coal.'
>
> Report (22 April 1943)

**Bevis.** In Sir Walter Scott's *Marmion* (1808), Lord Marmion's red-roan charger. The name is also that of the boy who is the central character of Richard Jefferies' wonderful evocation of country childhood, *Bevis, the Story of a Boy* (1882). A note to the Everyman edition of the latter work, published in 1930, explains that the name should be pronounced with a short 'e'.

**Bevis of Hampton.** The hero and title of a popular English medieval romance, in places bearing some similarity to the CHARLEMAGNE cycle. Bevis sought to avenge his father's death, which had been contrived by his mother. As a result he was sold to heathen merchants, and after many adventures he married Josian, daughter of King Ermyn, eventually returning to England to avenge his father. Hampton is usually interpreted as Southampton. The English version (14th century) is based on an earlier French version, but it is possible that the story had previous English origins. Michael Drayton tells the story in his *Polyolbion* (Song ii (1612–13)).

**Bevy.** A throng or company of girls, women, roebucks, quails or larks. The word has been popularly derived from Old French *bevee*, 'drink', as if the reference were to a group of animals drinking together or to a social gathering at which drinks were served, but its precise origin is unknown. It is now common in the alliterative phrase 'bevy of beauties'. Group names of this type are often of unconventional or uncertain origin. *See also* NOUNS OF ASSEMBLAGE.

**Beware the Ides of March.** Said as a warning of impending and certain danger. The allusion is to the warning received by Julius CAESAR before his assassination:

> What is still more extraordinary, many report that a certain soothsayer forewarned him of a great danger which threatened him on the ides of March, and that when the day was come, as he was going to the senate-house, he called to the soothsayer, and said, laughing, 'The ides of March are come'; to which he answered, softly, 'Yes; but they are not gone.'
>
> PLUTARCH: *Julius Caesar* (Langhorne translation) (2nd century AD)

**Bey** (Turkish, 'lord'). In the Turkish Empire a superior military officer or the governor of a minor province or sanjak.

**Beyond. Beyond measure** or **out of all measure.** Beyond all reasonable degree; exceedingly; excessively.

**Beyond question.** Beyond doubt, as: 'His honesty is beyond all question.'

**Beyond the veil.** The unknown state of those who have departed this life.

**Back of beyond.** *See under* BACK.

**Bezant** or **besant** (Medieval Latin *Byzantinus*, 'of Byzantium'). A gold coin of varying value struck by the Byzantine emperors and current in England until the time of Edward III. In HERALDRY the name is given to a plain gold ROUNDEL on the shield.

**Bezoar.** A stone from the stomach or gall bladder of an animal, especially a goat or antelope, set as a jewel and believed to be an antidote against poison. The word derives from Persian *bādzahr*, from *bād*, 'against', and *zahr*, 'poison'.

**B flat.** A former humorous euphemism for a bedbug (*Cimex lectularius*), characterized by its flatness.

**Bhagavadgita** (Sanskrit, 'Song of the Blessed One', from *bhaga*, 'blessing', and *gītā*, 'song'). One of the great religious and philosophical poems of India which occurs in the sixth book of the MAHABHARATA. In it, KRISHNA, in the form of a charioteer, instructs the warrior Arjuna in his duties and elaborates his ethical and pantheistic philosophy, finally revealing himself as the Supreme Being.

**Bianchi** (Italian, 'Whites'). In 1300 the Guelph family in Florence split into two rival factions, 'Whites' and 'Blacks' (Neri). The Bianchi, among whom Dante was prominent, allied with their Ghibelline opponents. After the triumph of the Neri in 1301, Dante was exiled from Florence. *See also* GUELPHS AND GHIBELLINES.

**Bib. Best bib and tucker.** *See* TUCKER.

**Biberius Caldius Mero.** The punning nickname of the Roman Emperor Tiberius Claudius NERO (ruled 14–37). Biberius (for Tiberius) means 'bibulous', 'drink-loving', and Caldius Mero (for Claudius Nero), represents *calidus mero* ('hot with undiluted wine').

**Bible.** The word is derived, through Medieval Latin *biblia*, from Greek *ta biblia*, 'the books'.

**Bible-basher.** An aggressive evangelical preacher, so called from his blows on his Bible as he rams home his text. Alternative names are Bible-thumper and Bible-puncher.

**Bible Belt, The.** In the USA the south central Midwest, south of the MASON AND DIXON LINE, reputedly associated with Puritanism and religious FUNDAMENTALISM.

**Bible Christians.** An EVANGELICAL sect founded in 1815 by William O'Bryan, a Cornish METHODIST. Hence their alternative name of Bryanites. The movement grew steadily, beginning in the fishing and farming districts of Devon and

Cornwall. They joined the United Methodist Church in 1907.

**Bible clerk.** A student at Oxford or Cambridge who formerly got pecuniary advantages for reading the Bible in chapel.

**Giants of the Bible.** *See under* GIANTS.

**Picture Bible.** Another name for the BIBLIA PAUPERUM.

**Statistics of the Bible.** The following statistics are those given in the *Introduction to the Critical Study and Knowledge of the Bible*, by Thomas Hartwell Horne, DD, first published in 1818. They apply to the English AUTHORIZED VERSION.

| | *O.T.* | *N.T.* | *Total* | *Apocrypha* |
|---|---|---|---|---|
| Books | 39 | 27 | 66 | 14 |
| Chapters | 929 | 260 | 1189 | 183 |
| Verses | 23,214 | 7959 | 31,173 | 6031 |
| Words | 593,493 | 181,253 | 774,746 | 125,185 |
| Letters | 2,728,100 | 838,380 | 3,566,480 | 1,063,876 |

| | *O.T.* | *N.T.* |
|---|---|---|
| Middle book | Proverbs 2 | Thessalonians |
| Middle chapter | Job 19 | Romans 13 and 14 |
| Middle verse | 2 Chronicles 20:17–18 | Acts 17:17 |
| Shortest verse | 1 Chronicles 1:25 | John 11:35 |
| Shortest chapter | Psalm 117 | |
| Longest chapter | Psalm 119 | |

Ezra 7:21 contains all the letters of the alphabet except j.

2 Kings 19 and Isaiah 37 are exactly the same.

The last two verses of 2 Chronicles and the opening verses of Ezra are similar.

Ezra 2 and Nehemiah 7 are similar.

The word *and* occurs in the Old Testament 35,543 times, and in the New Testament 10,684 times.

The word 'Jehovah' occurs 6855 times, and 'Lord' 1855 times.

About 30 books are mentioned in the Bible, but not included in the canon.

In addition it is noteworthy that by the end of 1994 the Bible had been translated into 2009 languages. *See also* APOCRYPHA; DEAD SEA SCROLLS; NEW TESTAMENT; OLD TESTAMENT; PENTATEUCH; PSALMS; PSEUDEPIGRAPHA; 'Q'; SEPTUAGINT; VULGATE.

**Words italicized in the Bible.** *See under* WORD.

BIBLE: PRINCIPAL ENGLISH VERSIONS

**American Standard Version, The.** A modification (1901) of the REVISED VERSION of 1881 to meet American preferences.

**Authorized Version, The.** This version, still in general use in England, was produced by some 47 scholars, working at the command of King James I, and was a by-product of the Hampton Court Conference (1604). It was begun in 1607 and published in 1611, and was based on the BISHOPS' BIBLE, but TYNDALE's, MATTHEW's, COVERDALE's and the GENEVA BIBLES were followed where they gave more accurate renderings. Since 1984 it has been published as the Authorized King James's Version.

**Bishops' Bible, The.** A revision of the GREAT BIBLE to counter the growing popularity of the GENEVA BIBLE. It was organized by Archbishop Matthew Parker and appeared in 1568. A number of the abler bishops took part in the work. It reached its 18th edition by 1602 and was the basis of the AUTHORIZED VERSION. *See also* TREACLE BIBLE.

**Coverdale's Bible.** This first printed edition of a complete English Bible appeared in 1535, translated 'out of Douche (German) and Latyn', by Miles Coverdale (1488–1568). It was based on Luther, the ZÜRICH BIBLE, the VULGATE, the Latin version of Pagninus and Tyndale. The first edition was probably printed at Zürich, the second was printed by Nicolson at Southwark in 1537 (the first Bible printed in England). *See also* BUG BIBLE.

**Cranmer's Bible.** The name given to the 1540 edition of the GREAT BIBLE. It and later issues contained a prologue by Cranmer, and, on the woodcut title page by Holbein, Henry VIII is shown seated handing copies to Cranmer and Cromwell. Its Psalter is still incorporated in the BOOK OF COMMON PRAYER.

**Cromwell's Bible.** The GREAT BIBLE of 1539. The title page includes a portrait of Thomas Cromwell, under whose direction the Bible was commissioned.

**Douai Bible, The.** A translation of the VULGATE by English Roman Catholics. The New Testament was published at the English College at Rheims in 1582, and the Old Testament at Douai in 1609. It was hence called the Rheims-Douai Bible. *See also* ROSIN BIBLE.

**Geneva Bible, The.** An important revision in the development of the English Bible, undertaken by English exiles in Geneva during the Marian persecutions, first published in 1560. It was largely the work of William Whittingham, assisted by Anthony Gilby and Thomas Sampson. Whittingham had previously (1557) published a translation of the New Testament. It was based on earlier versions, such as the GREAT BIBLE and MATTHEW'S BIBLE, and was the first English Bible to be printed in roman type instead of black letter (i.e. Gothic type), in quarto size, and the first in which the chapters were divided into verses (on the model of Robert Stephen's Greek-Latin Testament of 1537). It was immensely popular, and from 1560 to 1616 no year passed without a new edition. *See also* BREECHES BIBLE; GOOSE BIBLE; PLACEMAKERS' BIBLE.

**Good News Bible, The.** An illustrated version, produced by the American Bible Society, designed to be easily understood, including by those whose first language is not English. The New Testament was published in 1966 and the complete Bible in 1976. It follows the traditional numbering of chapter and verse.

**Great Bible, The.** Published by Grafton and Whitchurch in 1539 as an authorized Bible sponsored by Cranmer and Cromwell, being a revision by Coverdale substantially based on MATTHEW'S BIBLE. It went through seven editions and it was made compulsory for all parish churches to possess a copy. *See also* CRANMER'S BIBLE; CROMWELL'S BIBLE.

**Jerusalem Bible, The.** A new translation of the Bible, prepared from the ancient originals by Roman Catholic scholars, and largely in contemporary English. It was first published in 1966, and derives its notes and introduction from the French *La Bible de Jérusalem* produced under the editorship of Père Roland de Vaux in 1956. Yahweh replaces the traditional JEHOVAH.

**King James's Bible.** The AUTHORIZED VERSION.

**Knox Version, The.** A new Roman Catholic translation of the VULGATE by Monsignor R.A. Knox (1888–1957). The New Testament was authorized in 1945, and the Old Testament (for private use only) in 1949.

**Matthew Parker's Bible.** *See* BISHOPS' BIBLE.

**Matthew's Bible.** Printed in Antwerp in 1537 as the translation of Thomas Matthew, most probably an alias of John Rogers, an assistant of Tyndale. It is essentially made up from the work of Tyndale and Coverdale. Like Coverdale's third edition it appeared under the king's licence, but was soon superseded by the GREAT BIBLE. It is important as a basis of the approved editions, which culminated in the AUTHORIZED VERSION. *See also* BUG BIBLE.

**Moffatt's Translation.** A revised edition of the Bible by James Moffatt (New Testament, 1913, Old Testament, 1924, complete edition, 1935).

**New English Bible, The.** A translation into contemporary English first proposed by the CHURCH OF SCOTLAND and directed by a joint committee of the PROTESTANT Churches of Great Britain and Ireland. The New Testament appeared in 1961 and the translations of the Old Testament and the APOCRYPHA were finished in 1966. The complete Bible was published in 1970.

**New International Version, The.** A new translation, the work of an Anglo-American team seeking to present a modernized version in good English. It was first published by the New York Bible Society in 1978, with a British edition following in 1979.

**New Jerusalem Bible, The.** A revision of the JERUSALEM BIBLE, published in 1985 and incorporating the results of recent biblical scholarship.

**New Revised Standard Version, The.** A revision of the REVISED STANDARD VERSION, published in 1989. It is regarded as one of the most successful modern versions, and was the fruit of over 15 years' work by a team of Christian and Jewish scholars. The translation uses 'gender-inclusive' language where the original text refers to men and women, but references to God, Kingdom and the Son remain unchanged.

**New Testament in Modern English, The.** A translation by J.B. Phillips, aiming at clarity of expression, first published in 1958 with a revised version in 1973.

**New Testament in Modern Speech, The.** A new translation (1903) from the Greek by R.F. Weymouth.

**Revised English Bible, The.** A radical revision of the NEW ENGLISH BIBLE, published in 1989. It is generally more satisfactory for public reading and eliminates 'sexist' words such as man, sons, brothers and the like.

**Revised Standard Version, The.** The work of American scholars issued between 1946 and 1952. It was to embody the results of modern scholarship 'and to be in the diction of the simple classic English style of the King James's version'. The APOCRYPHA was published in 1957.

**Revised Standard Version Common Bible, The.** This version, published in 1973, was based on both the Protestant and Roman Catholic (1966) editions of the REVISED STANDARD VERSION, and was intended for interdenominational use. It has been accepted by the PROTESTANT churches generally as well as by the ROMAN CATHOLIC and EASTERN CHURCHES.

**Revised Version, The.** This revision of the AUTHORIZED VERSION resulted from a resolution passed by Houses of Convocation in 1870. It was the work of two companies of English scholars, with American cooperation. The New Testament appeared in 1881, the Old Testament in 1885 and the APOCRYPHA in 1895.

**Taverner's Bible.** A revision of MATTHEW'S BIBLE by Richard Taverner printed in 1539. It had little influence on subsequent translations but is notable for its idiomatic English.

**Tyndale's Bible.** This consists of the New Testament printed at Cologne in 1525 (revisions 1534 and 1535); the PENTATEUCH, printed at Marburg, 1530; the Book of Jonah, 1531; Epistles of the Old Testament (after the Use of Salisbury), 1534; and a manuscript translation of the Old Testament to the end of Chronicles, which was afterwards used in MATTHEW'S BIBLE. His work was chiefly based on Greek originals, while making use of the Greek and Latin versions of the New Testament by Erasmus, Luther's Bible and the VULGATE. His work fixed the language and style of subsequent English versions, which were more often revisions of his work rather than independent translations.

**Wyclif's** or **Wycliffe's Bible.** The name given to two translations of the VULGATE. The earlier one, completed *c.*1384, is the first complete English Bible, although there were renderings of parts of the Scriptures from Anglo-Saxon times. Wyclif may have translated parts of it and one of his circle, Nicholas of Hereford, is known to have contributed. The second and improved version, probably written between 1395 and 1397, is considered to owe much to John Purvey, a LOLLARD scholar. As a whole it remained unprinted until a monumental edition of both versions, prepared by Forshall and Madden, appeared in 1850.

BIBLE: SOME SPECIALLY NAMED EDITIONS

**Adulterous Bible, The.** The WICKED BIBLE.

**Affinity Bible, The.** A version of 1923 which contains a table of affinity with the error, 'A man may not marry his grandmother's wife'.

**Bad Bible, The.** A printing of 1653 with a deliberate perversion of Acts 6:6, whereby the ordination of deacons was ascribed to the disciples and not to the apostles.

**Bamberg Bible, The.** The THIRTY-SIX-LINE BIBLE.

**Bear Bible, The.** The Spanish Protestant version printed at Basle in 1569, and so called because the woodcut device on the title page is of a bear.

**Bedell's Bible.** An Irish translation of the Old Testament carried out under the direction of Bishop William Bedell (1571–1642). The Irish New Testament was published in 1601.

**Breeches Bible, The.** The popular name for the GENEVA BIBLE, because in it Genesis 3:7 was rendered, 'and they sowed figge-tree leaves together, and made themselves breeches'.

**Brothers' Bible, The.** The KRALITZ BIBLE.

**Bug Bible, The.** COVERDALE'S BIBLE of 1535 is so called because Psalm 91:5 is translated: 'Thou shalt not nede to be afrayed for eny bugges by night.' The same occurs in MATTHEW'S BIBLE and its reprints. Both the AUTHORIZED VERSION and REVISED VERSION read 'terror'.

**Camel's Bible, The.** A version of 1823 in which Genesis 24:61 reads: 'And Rebekah arose, and her camels' (instead of 'damsels').

**Complutensian Polyglot, The.** A version published between 1514 and 1517 at Alcalá (formerly Complutum), near Madrid, at the expense of Cardinal Ximenes. It was in six FOLIO volumes, containing the Hebrew and Greek texts, the SEPTUAGINT, the VULGATE, and the Chaldee paraphrase of the PENTATEUCH with a Latin translation, together with Greek and Hebrew grammars and a Hebrew dictionary.

**Denial Bible, The.** Printed at Oxford in 1792. In Luke 22:34 the name Philip is substituted for Peter, as the apostle who would deny Jesus.

**Discharge Bible, The.** An edition of 1806 containing 'discharge' for 'charge' in 1 Timothy 5:21: 'I discharge thee before God ... that thou observe these things.'

**Ears to Ear Bible, The.** An edition of 1810, in which Matthew 13:43 reads: 'Who hath ears to ear, let him hear' (instead of 'hear').

**Ferrara Bible, The.** The first Spanish edition of the Old Testament (1553) for the use of Spanish Jews. A second edition for Christians was published in the same year.

**Fool Bible, The.** An edition of Charles I's reign in which Psalm 14:1 reads: 'The fool hath said in his heart there is a God' (instead of 'no god'). The printers were fined £3000 and all copies were suppressed.

**Forgotten Sins Bible, The.** A version of 1638 in which Luke 7:47 reads: 'Her sins which are many, are forgotten' (instead of 'forgiven').

**Forty-two-line Bible, The.** The MAZARIN BIBLE.

**Goose Bible, The.** The editions of the GENEVA BIBLE printed at Dort, where the press had a goose for its device.

**Gutenberg Bible, The.** The MAZARIN BIBLE.

**He Bible, The.** In the first of the two editions of the AUTHORIZED VERSION in 1611, known as 'the He Bible', Ruth 3:15 reads: 'and he went into the city.' The other, and nearly all modern editions (except the REVISED VERSION), have 'she'. 'He' is the correct translation of the Hebrew.

**Idle Bible, The.** An edition of 1809, in which 'the idol shepherd' (Zechariah 11:17) is printed 'the idle shepherd'. In the REVISED VERSION the translation is 'the worthless shepherd'.

**Incunabula Bible, The.** The date on the title page reads 1495 instead of 1594. *See also* INCUNABULA.

**Indian Bible, The.** The first complete Bible printed in America, translated into the dialect of the Indians of Massachusetts by the Rev. John Eliot and published by Samuel Green and Marmaduke Johnson in 1663.

**Judas Bible, The.** Published in 1611. Matthew 26:36 has 'Judas' instead of 'Jesus'.

**Kralitz Bible, The.** A version, also called the Brothers' Bible, which was published by the United Brethren of Moravia at Kralitz, 1579–93.

**Large Family Bible, The.** An Oxford edition of 1820 has 'cease' for 'cause' in Isaiah 66:9: 'Shall I bring to the birth and not cease to bring forth?'

**Leda Bible, The.** The third edition (second folio) of the BISHOPS' BIBLE, published in 1572, and so called from the decoration of the initial at the Epistle to the Hebrews, which is a startling and incongruous woodcut of JUPITER visiting LEDA in the guise of a swan. This and other decorations in the New Testament were from an edition of Ovid's *Metamorphoses*. Such was the protest that they were never used again.

**Leopolita Bible, The.** A Polish translation of the VULGATE by John of Lemberg (Jan Nicz of Lwów) published at Cracow in 1561. So called from the Latin name, Leopolis, of his birthplace.

**Lions Bible, The.** A Bible issued in 1804 that contained many printers' errors such as: 'The murderer shall surely be put together' (instead of 'to death') (Numbers 25:18), 'But thy son that shall come forth out of thy lions' (for 'loins') (1 Kings 8:19), and 'For the flesh lusteth after the Spirit' (for 'against the Spirit') (Galatians 5:17).

**Mazarin Bible, The.** The first known book to be printed from movable type, probably by Fust and Schöffer at Mainz, who took over most of Gutenberg's presses in 1455. This edition of the VULGATE was on sale in 1456 and owes its name to the copy discovered in the MAZARIN LIBRARY in Paris in 1760. A copy of Volume I fetched a record price of £21,000 at a London auction in 1947. It was for long credited to Gutenberg and is frequently called the Gutenberg Bible. It is usually known to bibliographers as the Forty-two-line Bible (for its 42 lines to the column) to differentiate it from the THIRTY-SIX-LINE BIBLE.

**More Sea Bible, The.** An edition of 1641. Revelation 21:1 reads: 'and there was more sea' (instead of 'no more sea').

**Murderers' Bible, The.** An edition of 1801 in which Jude 16 reads: 'These are murderers' (for 'murmurers').

**Old Cracow Bible, The.** The LEOPOLITA BIBLE.

**Ostrog Bible, The.** The first complete Slavonic edition, printed at Ostrog, Volhynia, Russia, in 1581.

**Pfister's Bible, The.** The THIRTY-SIX-LINE BIBLE.

**Placemakers' Bible, The.** The second edition of the GENEVA BIBLE, 1562. Matthew 5:9 reads: 'Blessed are the placemakers' (for 'peacemakers'). It has also been called the WHIG BIBLE.

**Printers' Bible, The.** An edition of about 1702 in which David, in Psalm 119:161, complains that 'printers have persecuted me without a cause' (instead of 'princes').

**Proof Bible, The.** The revised version of the first impression of Luther's German Bible. A final revision appeared in 1892.

**Rosin Bible, The.** The DOUAI BIBLE (1609), is so called because it has in Jeremiah 8:22: 'Is there noe rosin in Galaad?' The AUTHORIZED VERSION translates the word by 'balm', but gives 'rosin' in the margin as an alternative. *See also* TREACLE BIBLE.

**Sacy's Bible.** A French translation by the JANSENIST Louis Isaac le Maistre de Sacy, director of PORT-ROYAL (1650–79). He began his work when imprisoned in the BASTILLE.

**Schelhorn's Bible.** The THIRTY-SIX-LINE BIBLE.

**September Bible, The.** Luther's German translation of the New Testament, published anonymously at Wittenberg in September 1522.

**She Bible, The.** *See* HE BIBLE.

**'Sin on' Bible, The.** The first version printed in Ireland was dated 1716. John 5:14 reads: 'sin on more' (instead of 'sin no more'). The fatal inversion was not discovered until 8000 copies had been printed and bound.

**Standing Fishes Bible, The.** An edition of 1806 in which Ezekiel 47:10, reads: 'And it shall come to pass that the fishes shall stand upon it' (instead of 'fishers').

**Sting Bible, The.** A version published in 1746, in which Mark 7:35 has 'the sting of his tongue' (instead of 'string').

**Thirty-six-line Bible, The.** A Latin Bible of 36 lines to the column, probably printed by A. Pfister at Bamberg in 1460. It is also known as the Bamberg, or Pfister's, Bible and sometimes as Schelhorn's, as it was first described by the German bibliographer J.G. Schelhorn in 1760.

**'To remain' Bible, The.** In a Bible printed at Cambridge in 1805 Galatians 4:29 reads: 'persecuted him that was born after the spirit to remain, even so it is now.' The words 'to remain' were added in error by the printer. The editor had answered a proofreader's query regarding the comma after 'spirit' with the pencilled reply in the margin, 'to remain'. The mistake was repeated in the Bible Society's first octavo (8vo) edition (1805) and their duodecimo (12vo) edition of 1819.

**Treacle Bible, The.** A popular name for the BISHOPS' BIBLE of 1568, because Jeremiah 8:22 reads: 'is there no tryacle in Gilead, is there no phisition there?' 'Tryacle' is also given for 'balm' in Jeremiah 46:11 and Ezekiel 27:17. COVERDALE'S BIBLE also uses the word 'triacle'. *See also* ROSIN BIBLE.

**Unrighteous Bible, The.** A Cambridge printing of 1653 contains: 'Know ye not that the unrighteous shall inherit the Kingdom of God?', instead of 'shall not inherit' (1 Corinthians 6:9). In Romans 6:13 it has: 'Neither yield ye your members as instruments of righteousness unto sin' (in place of 'unrighteousness'). This edition is also sometimes known as the WICKED BIBLE.

**Vinegar Bible, The.** An Oxford printing of 1717 in which part of the chapter heading to Luke 20 reads: 'The parable of the Vinegar' (for 'Vineyard').

**Whig Bible, The.** Another name for the PLACEMAKERS' BIBLE. Many Whigs were PLACEMEN.

**Wicked Bible, The.** So called because the word 'not' was omitted in the seventh commandment (Exodus 20:14) making it: 'Thou shalt commit adultery.' It was printed by Barker and Lucas, the king's printers at Blackfriars in 1631. The fine of £300 ruined the printer. It is also called the Adulterous Bible. *See also* UNRIGHTEOUS BIBLE.

**Wife-hater Bible, The.** An 1810 edition gives Luke 14:26: 'If any man come to me, and hate not his father, and mother ... yea, and his own wife also' (instead of 'life').

**Wuyck's Bible.** An authorized Polish translation by the Jesuit, Jacub Wuyck (or Wujek), printed at Cracow in 1599.

**Zürich Bible, The.** A German version of 1530 composed of Luther's translation of the New Testament and portions of the Old, with the remainder and the APOCRYPHA by other translators.

**Biblia Pauperum** (Latin, 'poor man's Bible'). A misnomer coined long after the first appearance in the 1460s of the late medieval block books. They contain a series of New Testament scenes from the life of Christ, each surrounded by their Old Testament antitypes, and with a brief text engraved in the same block below the illustration. Despite their name, the *Biblia Pauperum* can hardly have been intended for the illiterate, their iconography and text being replete with allegory and symbol, and must rather have served itinerant preachers and the lower orders of clergy. *See also* SPECULUM HUMANAE SALVATIONIS.

**Bibliomancy.** DIVINATION by means of the Bible. *See also* SORTES.

**Bibliomania.** A love of books, sometimes pursued to the point of unreason or madness. One Don Vicente, a Spanish scholar, is reputed to have committed murder to obtain a supposedly unique book.

**Bibliophilia.** A devotion to books and book collecting.

Sir Thomas Phillipps (1792–1872) is an especially notable example of a bibliophile whose manuscript collection surpassed all other private hoards. His obsession bordered on BIBLIOMANIA and kept him constantly on the edge of bankruptcy.

**Bickerstaff, Isaac.** A name assumed by Dean Swift (1667–1745) in a satirical pamphlet against Partridge, the ALMANAC-maker. So diverting was the ensuing paper war that Steele issued the *Tatler* under the editorial name of 'Isaac Bickerstaff, Esq., Astrologer' (1709). An actual Isaac Bickerstaffe, playwright, was born in Ireland in 1735.

**Bicorn** (Latin *bicornis*, 'two-horned'). A mythical beast, fabled by the early French romancers to grow fat through living on good and tolerant husbands. It was the anti-type of CHICHEVACHE. The name alludes to the horned CUCKOLD.

**Bicycle, Safety.** *See* PENNY FARTHING.

**Bid.** The modern verb 'to bid' may be from either of two Old English verbs: (1) *bēodan*, 'to offer', 'to announce', 'to command', or (2) *biddan*, 'to ask', 'to entreat', 'to demand'. The two words have now become confused. The following four examples are from (1) *bēodan*:

**Bid against, To.** To offer a higher price than someone else for an article at auction.

**Bid defiance, To.** To resist boldly.

**Bidding prayer.** In the CHURCH OF ENGLAND this term is now commonly applied to a prayer for the souls of benefactors said before the sermon, in cathedrals, university churches and on special occasions. It stems from the PRE-REFORMATION vernacular prayer of the 'bidding of the beads'. 'Bidding' was here used in the sense of 'praying' and the priest told the people what to remember in their prayers. By the time of Elizabeth I the 'bidding of prayers' came to mean the 'directing' or 'enjoining' of prayers, hence the modern meaning.

**Bid fair, To.** To seem likely or probable; to give good promise, to indicate future success, as: 'He bids fair to be a good negotiator.'

The following examples are from (2) *biddan*.

**Bid for, To.** To promise to support certain measures in Parliament in order to obtain votes.

**Bid good night, To.** To wish. So also 'to bid good day' etc.

**Bid one's beads, To.** To tell off one's prayers by beads. *See also* ROSARY.

**Bid the banns, To.** To ask if anyone objects to the marriage of the persons named. *See also* SI QUIS.

**Take-over bid, A.** *See under* TAKE.

**Biddy.** A pet form of Bridget as a former generic name for an Irish servant girl, as Mike is for an Irish labourer. Such names were once common. Others were Tom Tug for a waterman, Jack Pudding for a buffoon, JACK TAR for a sailor and TOMMY Atkins for a soldier. *See also* NICKNAME.

Biddy also denotes a hen, sometimes in the form chick-a-biddy. The word is that used for calling chickens, so does not properly represent the name.

**Old Biddy.** *See under* OLD.

**Red Biddy.** *See under* RED.

**Bideford Postman, The.** Edward Capern (1819–94), the DEVONSHIRE POET, so called from his former occupation and abode.

**Bier, Ordeal of the.** *See under* ORDEAL.

**Bifrost** (Icelandic *bifa*, 'to shake', and *rost*, 'path'). In Scandinavian mythology, the bridge between heaven and earth, ASGARD and MIDGARD. The rainbow may be considered to be this bridge, and its various colours are the reflections of its precious stones. HEIMDALL is its keeper.

**Big. Big Apple, The.** New York City. The name was first popularized in the 1920s by John J. FitzGerald, a reporter for the *Morning Telegraph*, who used it to refer to the city's racetracks and who claimed to have heard it used by black stable-hands in New Orleans in 1921. Black jazz musicians in the 1930s took up the name to refer to the city (and especially HARLEM) as the jazz capital of the world. The nickname then faded from use but was revived in 1971 as part of a publicity campaign by Charles Gillett, president of the New York Convention and Visitors Bureau. The general allusion is to a city that is the 'big apple' or (punningly) 'apple core' sought as an ultimate prize by anyone after world fame. There are also classical allusions. *See* ATALANTA.

**Big Bang.** In cosmology a theory explaining the origin of the universe. It postulates that a small, superdense mass exploded, hurling matter in all directions in a cataclysmic explosion. As the fragments slowed down, the stars and galaxies formed, although the universe is still expanding.

The major modernization of the STOCK EXCHANGE, in the City of London, which took place on 27 October 1986, was also known as the Big Bang. The distinction between a stockjobber and a STOCKBROKER was abolished, and operations became fully computerized. The aim was to maintain London's position as a leading international financial centre.

**Big Ben.** Properly, the bell in the Clock Tower (St Stephen's Tower) of the Houses of Parliament, so called after Sir Benjamin Hall, who was Chief Commissioner of Works when it was cast in 1856. The first casting, weighing some 15 tons, developed serious cracks when being tested in Palace Yard and was scrapped. The new bell, weighing about 13 tons, was installed in October 1858. This also developed a crack, but of a less serious nature. There are also four quarter bells whose weight varies between about 4 tons and 1 ton. The clock and tower as a whole are now generally known as 'Big Ben'.

**Big Bertha.** The name given by the French to the large howitzers used by the Germans against Liège and Namur in 1914. They were made at the Škoda works, but were mistakenly assumed to be manufactured by Krupp, the German armament firm. Hence the allusion to Bertha Krupp (1886–1957), great-granddaughter of the firm's founder, Friedrich Krupp (1787–1826), to whom control of the works had passed on her father's death in 1902. In 1918 Paris was shelled from a range of 76 miles (122km) by the 142-ton 'Paris' gun, to which the name Big Bertha was again applied.

**Big Board, The.** A nickname for the New York Stock Exchange.

**Big Brother.** A person or organization that exercises dictatorial control, supposedly for one's own welfare and in one's best interests. The name is that of the invisible state machinery in George ORWELL's *Nineteen Eighty-Four* (1949), representing the real-life political leader of the USSR:

> On each landing, opposite the lift shaft, the poster with the enormous face gazed from the wall. It was one of those pictures which are so contrived that the eyes follow you about when you move. BIG BROTHER IS WATCHING YOU, the caption beneath it ran.
>
> ch i

**Big bug.** An important or conceited person; a BIGWIG.

**Big C, The.** Cancer, which one is reluctant to name in full.

**Big cheese.** The boss or someone in an important position.

**Big deal!** An ironic exclamation belittling a supposedly fine offer or proposal.

**Big dipper.** In Britain, a term for a fairground switchback at a fairground. In the USA, an alternative name for the GREAT BEAR.

**Big-endians.** In Jonathan Swift's *Gulliver's Travels* (1726), a party in the empire of Lilliput who made it a matter of conscience to break their eggs at the big end. They were looked on as heretics by the orthodox party, who broke theirs at the little end. The Big-endians represent the CATHOLICS and the Little-endians the PROTESTANTS.

**Big Five, The.** The five countries regarded as the most important or influential after the Second World War: USA, Britain, the former USSR, China and France.

**Bigfoot.** A supposed YETI-like animal of the northwestern USA and western Canada, also known as Sasquatch, from a Salish word meaning 'wild men'. It is so named from its big footprints, some measuring up to 24in (60cm) in length and 8in (20cm) in width. Its discovery in 1811 is usually credited to the British explorer David Thompson, but many modern scientists deny its existence. A short piece of film made in 1967 by Roger Patterson at Bluff Creek, California, appears to show a female of the species walking away from the camera. *See also* ABOMINABLE SNOWMAN.

**Big game.** Large animals hunted for 'sport'.

**Bigger and better.** Superior to anything of its kind that has gone before. An advertiser's phrase. Bigger does not of course necessarily means better. *See also* SMALL IS BEAUTIFUL.

**Bighead.** A conceited person.

**Big-hearted.** Generous. 'Big-hearted Arthur' was the self-promoted nickname of the British comedian Arthur Askey (1900–82).

**Big house, The.** The main house in a village.

**Big idea.** An important scheme or action. The phrase is usually encountered ironically, typically in the question 'What's the big idea?'

**Big league.** A top league in a professional sport, especially baseball.

**Big lie.** An intentional distortion of the facts or disinformation, especially by a politician.

**Big Mac.** A proprietary name for the largest hamburger in the range served by McDonald's fast-food outlets.

**Bigmouth.** A noisy or indiscreet person.

**Big noise.** *See* BIGWIG.

**Big one, The.** Something promoted to be BIGGER AND BETTER than any of its kind before.

**Big pot, A.** An important person. The phrase is also descriptive of a big belly. *See also* POT BELLY.

**Big shot, A.** An important person. A development of the 19th-century 'great gun' or 'big bug'.

**Big Smoke, The.** One of the nicknames of London, more commonly 'the Smoke'. It has also been applied to other large cities, such as Sydney, Australia. *See also* AULD REEKIE.

**Big stick diplomacy.** The backing of negotiations with the threat of military force. The term was popularized by Theodore Roosevelt's declaration in 1900 that he had always been fond of the West African proverb 'speak softly and carry a big stick'. He used such tactics successfully (1902–4) in the Alaskan boundary dispute and the second Venezuelan crisis.

**Big time, The.** Success in a profession, especially show business.

**Big top, The.** The great circus tent in which the main performance takes place.

**Big triangle, The.** A former nautical term denoting the round trip frequently made by sailing ships from a British port to Australia, thence with New South Wales coal to South America, and back home with a cargo of nitrates.

**Big wheel.** A FERRIS WHEEL. Also another term for a BIGWIG.

**Big white chief, The.** An important person, or the head or leader of an organization.

**Bigwig.** An important person. The term alludes to the large wigs that in the 17th and 18th centuries encumbered the head and shoulders of the aristocracy of England and France. They are still worn by the LORD CHANCELLOR, judges and the SPEAKER of the HOUSE OF COMMONS. Bishops continued to wear them in the HOUSE OF LORDS until 1880.

**Give someone a big hand, To.** To applaud a person.

**In a big way.** On a large scale; with great enthusiasm, as: 'She goes in for home-baking in a big way.'

**Look big, To.** *See under* LOOK.

**Talk big, To.** *See under* TALK.

**That's big of you.** An ironic reaction to a supposedly generous offer.

**Too big for one's boots, To be.** *See under* TOO.

**Biggles.** The best known aviator in boys' fiction was the creation of Captain W.E. Johns (1893–1968), who drew on memories of his experiences in the Royal Flying Corps during the First World War. His hero's full name is James Bigglesworth, DSO, DFC, MC, and he made his bow in magazine stories of the early 1930s. He also starts his flying career in the First World War and eventually becomes commander of a flying squadron. In the Second World War he plays a major role in the BATTLE OF BRITAIN. His gung-ho exploits continued until his creator's death.

**Bikini.** This atoll in the Marshall Islands, the scene of US nuclear weapon testing in 1946 (and 1954), gave its name to a scanty two-piece swimming costume worn by women. The allusion is supposedly to the devastation of the atom-bomb test and the 'explosive' effect caused by a woman wearing such a costume. The 'bi-' of bikini was later popularly understood to mean 'two', with reference to the two parts of the costume, so that a one-piece or topless swimsuit (the lower half of a bikini) was called a monokini.

**Bilbo.** A rapier or sword. So called from Bilbao, in Spain, once famous for its finely tempered blades. *See also* ANDREA FERRARA; TOLEDO.

**Bilbo Baggins.** *See under* BAGGINS.

**Bile.** According to ancient theory bile is a HUMOUR of the body. Black bile was believed to cause melancholy, and yellow bile anger. The word is generally used to denote irritability or peevishness.

**Bilge water.** The filthy water that collects in a ship's bilge, this being the part of the hull where the sides curve inwards to form the bottom. Hence 'bilge' to mean nonsense or rubbish.

**Bilk.** Originally a term in cribbage meaning to spoil your opponent's score, to BALK him. The two words are probably variants of each other. It now usually means to cheat; to obtain goods and depart without paying.

> He cannot drink five bottles, bilk the score,
> Then kill a constable, and drink five more.
>
> WILLIAM COWPER: 'Progress of Error' (1782)

**Bill.** The mouthpart of a bird, also called the beak. The word has also passed into topographical use for a headland or narrow promontory, such as Portland Bill in Dorset or Selsey Bill in Sussex.

**Bill, A.** The draft of an ACT OF PARLIAMENT. When a Bill is passed and receives the ROYAL ASSENT it becomes an Act. *See also* PRIVATE BILL; PRIVATE MEMBER'S BILL; PUBLIC BILL.

**Bill, The.** A nickname for the police. It is probably a shortening of Old Bill. *See also* BETTER 'OLE.

**Bill of Attainder.** This was a legislative Act that

found people guilty, without trial, of felony or treason and attainted them, or deprived them of their civil rights on being sentenced to death or outlawry. Bills of Attainder were used for arbitrarily destroying political enemies of the government, or for criminal offences against the state and public peace, with Parliament acting as both judge and jury. The Bill was introduced in 1549, and the last Bill of Attainder was passed against Lord Edward Fitzgerald, Irish rebel leader, in 1798.

**Bill of Divorcement.** A term from former days of divorce procedure. Before the Matrimonial Causes Act, 1857, 'divorce', or in effect judicial separation, could be granted only by the ecclesiastical courts, but remarriage was prohibited except when a special bill was promoted and passed in Parliament for either of the parties. Few could afford such an expensive process. *See also* A VINCULO MATRIMONII.

**Bill of exchange.** An order transferring a named sum of money at a given date from the debtor (drawee) to the creditor (drawer). The drawee, on signing the bill, becomes the 'acceptor', and the document is then negotiable in commercial circles just like money itself.

**Bill of fare.** A list of dishes provided in a restaurant, otherwise a menu.

**Bill of health.** A document given to the master of a ship by the consul of the port from which he comes, certifying that when the ship sailed no infectious disorder existed in the place. This is 'a clean bill of health', and the term is often used figuratively. A 'foul bill of health' means that the place from which the vessel sailed was infected. *See also* YELLOW JACK.

**Bill of lading.** A document signed by the master of a ship in acknowledgement of goods laden in his vessel. In this document he binds himself to deliver the articles in good condition to the persons named, subject to certain circumstances. These bills are generally in triplicate: one for the shipper, one for the consignee and one for the master of the vessel.

**Bill of Peace, A.** A bill intended to secure relief from perpetual litigation. It is brought by a person who wishes to establish and perpetuate a right which he claims, but which, from its nature, is controversial.

**Bill of Rights.** A constitutional enactment (October 1689) of fundamental importance consolidating the GLORIOUS REVOLUTION of 1688. It asserted the liberties and rights of the nation, declared William and Mary king and queen, and settled the succession.

A Bill of Rights, designed to guarantee civil liberties, was embodied in the American Constitution in 1791. It consists of the first ten amendments, proposed in 1789.

**Bill of sale.** When a person borrows money and delivers goods as security, they give the lender a 'bill of sale', i.e. permission to sell the goods if the money is not returned on the stated day.

**Bill Sikes.** *See under* SIKES.

**Block a bill, To.** *See under* BLOCK.

**Fill the bill, To.** *See under* FILL.

**Foot the bill, To.** *See under* FOOT.

**Omnibus bill.** *See under* OMNIBUS.

**Pecos Bill.** *See under* PECOS.

**Private Bill.** *See under* PRIVATE.

**Private Member's Bill.** *See under* PRIVATE.

**Public Bill.** *See under* PUBLIC.

**Treasury bills.** *See under* TREASURY.

**Billabong.** In Australia, a backwater channel that forms a pool, or the branch of a river that runs to a dead end. The word is from Wiradhuri *billa*, 'river', and *bong*, 'dead'. *See also* WALTZING MATILDA.

**Billet.** As a soldier's lodging place, the word derives from Old French *billette*, a diminutive of *bulle*, 'document', referring to the official note that required the addressee to provide accommodation for its bearer. *See also* EVERY BULLET HAS ITS BILLET.

**Billet-doux** (French, 'sweet letter'). In humorous use, a love letter.

**Billingsgate.** The largest fish market in London, formerly on the site of an important Thames-side wharf. Its porters were notorious for their foul and abusive language. Hence Billingsgate as a term for such language.

**Billy.** (1) In North American use a policeman's truncheon. The word probably comes from the personal name Billy.

(2) In Australia and New Zealand, a metal pot or can for boiling water over a campfire. Here the word is perhaps of Aborigine origin, from *billa*, 'water'. *See also* BILLABONG.

**Billy boy.** Formerly, a bluff-bowed north country coaster of river-barge build.

**Billy Bunter.** *See under* BUNTER.

**Billycock hat.** A round, low-crowned, hard felt hat with a wide brim, something like a BOWLER HAT. It apparently takes (or took) its name from William (Billy) Coke, nephew of the Earl of Leicester, for whom it was first made in about 1850. Old-established hatters in London's West End used to call them Coke hats. *See also* COKE'S CLIPPINGS.

**Billy goat.** A male goat. From this came the formerly common term for a tufted beard, a billy or goatee.

**Billy the Kid.** William H. Bonney (1859–81), American outlaw and baby-faced killer, who committed his first murder at the age of 12. He was prominent in the Lincoln County cattle war in New Mexico and boasted that he had killed a man for every year of his life. He was finally shot, at the age of 21, by Sheriff Pat Garrett.

**Billy Williams' Cabbage Patch.** The English RUGBY Football Union's ground at Twickenham, the headquarters of the game, also known as Twickers. It is popularly so called after William (Billy) Williams (1860–1951), who discovered the site and who was instrumental in acquiring the ground in 1907. The latter part of the nickname refers to the ground's former partial use as a market garden. The first match was played there on 2 October 1909. The nearby Railway Tavern changed its name to the Cabbage Patch in the early 1970s.

**Blue Billy.** *See under* BLUE.

**Like billyo** or **billyoh.** *See under* LIKE.

**Silly Billy.** *See under* SILLY.

**Bimetallism.** The use of two metals, silver and gold, for fixing the relative values of currency. Both metals are used for standard money or LEGAL TENDER.

**Bimini.** A legendary island of the Bahamas where the FOUNTAIN OF YOUTH gave everlasting life to all who drank from it. The name also appeared on early maps for the peninsula of Florida and in the 16th century was sometimes associated with Mexico. The mythical island gave the name of the two small islands of Bimini in the Bahamas, and a particular pattern of rock discovered off their coast in 1968 led some to claim discovery of a road built on the site of the lost ATLANTIS. The 'road', however, is in fact the former coastline of one of the islands and is made of 'beach rock', a concretion of shells and other debris.

**Binary notation.** A number notation in which the base is 2 instead of 10, a method suggested for certain uses by Gottfried Leibnitz (1646–1716). The value of any position in a binary number increases by powers of 2 (i.e. doubles) with each move from right to left (1, 2, 4, 8, 16, and so on). The binary number 1011 is thus the equivalent of 11, since the respective digits reading from left to right denote $(1 \times 8) + (0 \times 4) + (1 \times 2) + (1 \times 1)$, giving $8 + 0 + 2 + 1 = 11$. The zero thus indicates a power that is omitted. Most computers work on this system, since the 0 and the 1 can be electrically represented as 'off' and 'on'. *See also* BIT.

**Bing Boys.** The nickname of the Canadian troops in the First World War, from the name of their commanding officer, Lord Byng of Vimy (1862–1935). The name was also popularized by the revue, *The Bing Boys Are Here*, which opened at the ALHAMBRA in 1915.

**Bingham's Dandies.** *See under* REGIMENTAL AND DIVISIONAL NICKNAMES.

**Bingo.** A lastingly popular gambling game, played typically by pensioners in bingo halls converted from cinemas. The game is simple: players have a card printed with a selection of numbers, and they cover the numbers as they are announced at random by a caller. The player who first covers all the numbers on his or her card calls 'Bingo' (or 'House') and wins a prize. The allure of the game is in its conviviality and in the caller's patter, which has traditional rhymes for the various numbers, such as 'legs eleven' for 11, 'dinkie doos' for 22 and 'all the threes' for 33. The usual call at the start of the game is 'Eyes down, look in!' The word bingo itself probably imitates the 'ping' of a bell formerly rung to announce a win.

**Birch. John Birch Society.** *See under* JOHN.

**Bird.** The word has evolved from Old English *brid*, which was the general name for a young bird or nestling. The word that is now 'fowl' was formerly used to mean 'bird' generally.

The word was also used to mean 'girl', 'young woman', though it lacked the disparaging overtones that it now sometimes has in this sense. It can also be used of any person, especially with an adjective. An 'odd bird' is thus a strange person, a 'wily bird' a cunning person, a 'tough old bird' a resilient elderly person and so on.

'To get the bird' is to be hissed or given a hostile reception, a term used of public performers. Of an employee, the expression means to get the SACK.

**Bird-brained.** Silly, stupid. Birds have small heads and are therefore presumed to have small brains.

**Birdcage Walk.** The walk, in St James's Park, Westminster, London, is said to be named from the aviary kept there by Charles II (r.1660–85).

**Bird Catchers, The.** *See under* REGIMENTAL AND DIVISIONAL NICKNAMES.

**Bird has flown, The.** The person sought has left or escaped.

**Birdie.** A hole at golf which the player has completed in one stroke less than par (the standard for the course). Two strokes less is an eagle. Three strokes less is an albatross.

The story goes that one day in 1903 A.B. ('Ab') Smith was enjoying a game of golf in Atlantic City, USA. Endeavouring to improve his already good game, he made a shot that enabled him to sink his ball one under par. The success prompted his cry of delight, 'That's a bird of a shot!' The term caught on and in due course became affectionately known as a 'birdie'. The eagle and the albatross followed logically, since a stroke two under par is rare, like the eagle, and one three under par even rarer, like the albatross.

**Bird in the hand is worth two in the bush, A.** Possession is better than expectation.

This proverb exists in several languages:

Italian: *È meglio oggi l'uovo, che domani la gallina.*
(Better the egg today than the hen tomorrow.)

French: *Un 'tiens' vaut mieux que deux 'tu l'auras'.* (One 'here you are' is worth more than two 'you'll get it'.)

German: *Ein Vogel in der Hand ist besser als zehn über Land.* (One bird in the hand is better than ten flying over the land.) *Besser ein Spatz in der Hand, als eine Taube auf dem Dache.* (Better a sparrow in the hand than a pigeon on the roof.)

Russian: *Ne suli zhuravlya v nebe, a day sinitsu v ruki.* (Don't promise the crane in the sky, but give the tit in your hand.)

Latin: *Certa amittimus dum incerta petimus* (Plautus). (We lose what is certain while seeking that which is uncertain.)

**Bird of Freedom** or **of Washington, The.** The bald or white-headed EAGLE, the emblematic bird of the USA.

**Bird of ill omen, A.** One who is regarded as unlucky or who is in the habit of bringing bad news. The phrase comes from the custom of AUGURY, and even today owls, crows and RAVENS are often regarded as unlucky birds, while swallows and STORKS are lucky. Ravens by their acute sense of smell can often locate dead and decaying bodies at a great distance hence, perhaps, they indicate death. Owls screech when bad weather is at hand and, as foul weather often precedes sickness, so the owl is looked on as a funeral bird.

**Bird of Jove, The.** The EAGLE.

**Bird of Juno, The.** The peacock. MINERVA's bird is either the cock or the owl, while that of VENUS is the DOVE.

**Bird of passage, A.** A person who shifts from place to place, like a migrant bird such as a CUCKOO, swallow or swift.

**Birds and the bees, The.** A euphemism for sexual activity or reproduction, alluding to the fanciful stories told to young children on the subject.

Birds do it, bees do it,
Even educated fleas do it,
Let's do it, let's fall in love.
COLE PORTER: 'Let's Do It' (1954)

**Bird's-eye view.** A general or overall view, or more specifically a mode of perspective drawing in which the artist is felt to be above the objects drawn, so that they appear as a bird in the air would see them.

**Bird's nest soup.** The Chinese delicacy is actually made from the outer parts of the gelatinous nests of the swallow *Hirundo esculenta*, the nests themselves being fabricated from a kind of seaweed.

**Birds of a feather flock together.** Those of similar character, taste or status associate together. The saying is based on the observation that birds in a group on the ground or in flight are often all of the same species.

**Bird strike.** A collision between a flying bird or group of birds and an aircraft.

**Bird walking weather.** A flying expression of American origin, indicating CEILING ZERO, coined from the phrase: 'The weather is so bad, even the birds are walking.'

**Arabian bird, The.** The PHOENIX.

**Attic bird, The.** *See under* ATTIC.

**Beat the bush while another takes the bird, To.** *See under* BEAT.

**Blue bird of happiness.** *See under* BLUE.

**Call bird, To.** *See under* CALL.

**Colly bird.** *See under* COLLY.

**Devil's bird.** *See under* DEVIL.

**Do bird, To.** *See under* DO.

**Dolly bird.** *See under* DOLLY.

**Downy bird.** *See under* DOWNY.

**Early bird, An.** *See under* EARLY.

**Fine feathers make fine birds.** *See under* FINE.

**Following bird.** *See under* FOLLOW.

**Give someone the bird, To.** To tell them to clear off.

**Kill two birds with one stone, To.** *See under* KILL.

**Little bird told me, A.** *See under* LITTLE.

**Oozlum bird.** *See under* OOZLUM.

**Phaeton's bird.** *See under* PHAETON.

**Phasian bird.** *See under* PHASIAN.

**Roman birds.** *See under* ROMAN.

**St Martin's bird.** *See under* MARTIN.

**Sir Boyle Roche's bird.** *See under* ROCHE.

**Strictly for the birds.** *See under* STRICTLY.

**Stymphalian Birds.** *See under* STYMPHALIAN.

**Watch the birdie, To.** *See under* WATCH.

**White bird.** *See under* WHITE.

BIRDS PROTECTED BY SUPERSTITIONS

**Chough, The.** Protected in Cornwall because the soul of King ARTHUR was fabled to have migrated into one. The arms of Cornwall contain 'over the crest on a wreath Argent and Azure a chough proper resting the dexter claw upon a ducal coronet Or'.

**Falcon, The.** Held sacred by the Egyptians because it was the form assumed by RA and HORUS.

**Ibis, The.** Held sacred by the Egyptians because the god THOTH escaped from the pursuit of TYPHOEUS disguised as an Ibis.

**Mother Carey's chickens** or **Storm petrels.** Protected by sailors from a superstition that they are the living embodiment of the souls of dead mariners. *See also* MOTHER CAREY'S CHICKENS.

**Robin, The.** Protected on account of Christian tradition and nursery legend. *See also* ROBIN REDBREAST.

**Stork, The.** Held sacred in Sweden, from the legend that it flew round the cross crying, 'Styrka, Styrka!' when Jesus was crucified. *See also* STORK.

**Swan, The.** Protected in Ireland from the legend of FIONNUALA (daughter of King LIR) who was metamorphosed into a swan and condemned to wander the waters until the coming of Christianity. Moore wrote a poem on the subject:

When shall the swan, her death-note singing,
Sleep, with wings in darkness furl'd?
When will heaven, its sweet bells ringing,
Call my spirit from this stormy world?

THOMAS MOORE: *Irish Melodies*, 'The Song of Fionnuala' (1807)

**Birmingham. Birmingham Poet, The.** John Freeth, who died at the age of 78 in 1808. He was a wit, a poet and a publican, who not only wrote the words and tunes of songs but also sang them.

**To Birmingham by way of Beachy Head.** *See under* TO.

**Birth, Virgin.** *See under* VIRGIN.

**Birthday. Birthday honours.** The honours awarded on the date that is the sovereign's official birthday (as distinct from the actual one). For Elizabeth II, this is a Saturday in June. Most of the honours, in the form of peerages, knighthoods, military and civilian awards, are made from a list drawn up by the Prime Minister, which includes about 50 individuals recommended 'for political services'. The vast majority of those honoured, however, receive an OBE (Order of the British Empire). The BEM (British Empire Medal) was also awarded until 1993, when it was discontinued. Only the highest honours are received personally from the sovereign, and the junior award is presented by royal representatives. A similar system operates for the New Year honours.

**Birthday suit.** A state of nakedness, as when born. The expression was originally used for the magnificent suit of clothes specially ordered by courtiers to be worn on the sovereign's birthday.

The Sun himself, on this auspicious Day,
Shines, like a Beau in a new Birth-day Suit.

HENRY FIELDING: *Tom Thumb the Great*, I, i (1731)

**Happy birthday!** *See under* HAPPY.

**Bis** (Latin, 'twice'). French and Italian audiences use this as English audiences use ENCORE.

**Bis dat, qui cito dat** (Latin, 'He gives twice who gives promptly'). An instant payment or contribution will do as much good as twice the sum later.

**Biscuit. Garibaldi biscuit.** *See under* GARIBALDI.

**Take the biscuit, To.** To beat everything for effrontery or outrageousness. Biscuits and cakes containing special spices were formerly regarded as representing certain desirable attributes and were given as rewards in a variety of competitions. *See also* TAKE THE CAKE *under* CAKE.

**Bishop** (Old English *biscop*, from Late Latin *episcopus*, from Greek *episkopos*, 'overseer'). A high-ranking Christian priest who has spiritual and administrative powers over a diocese.

The name is given to one of the men in CHESS and to a drink made by pouring red wine, such as CLARET or burgundy, either hot or cold, on ripe bitter oranges, the liquor being sugared and spiced to taste. Similarly a 'cardinal' is made by using white wine instead of red and a 'pope' by using tokay. *See also* BOY BISHOP.

**Bishop, To.** Formerly, to confirm, to admit into the church. There are two other verbs 'to bishop', both from proper names. One is obsolete and meant to murder by drowning, from the name of a man who drowned a little boy in Bethnal Green and sold the body to the surgeons for dissection. The other means to make a horse look younger than it really is by filing or otherwise tampering with its teeth.

**Bishop has put his foot in it, The.** Said of milk or porridge that is burned, or of meat over-roasted. Tyndale says, 'If the porage be burned to, or the meate over rosted we saye the byshope hath put his fote in the potte', explaining that this is so 'because the bishopes burnt who they lust'. Such food is also said to be bishopped.

**Bishop of Fleet Street.** A nickname given to Hannen Swaffer (1879–1962) by his fellow journalists because of his pronouncements on public morality and his sombre, stylized mode of attire.

**Bishops' Bible, The.** *See under* BIBLE.

**Bishops' Wars, The.** The name given to the two short wars waged by CHARLES I in 1639–40 against the Scots when they renounced EPISCOPACY. The wars ended with his defeat and caused the summoning of the LONG PARLIAMENT.

**As the bishop said to the actress.** *See under* AS.

**Boy Bishop.** *See under* BOY.

**Seven Bishops, The.** *See under* SEVEN.

**Titular bishops.** *See under* TITULAR.

**Tulchan bishops.** *See under* TULCHAN.

**Bissextile.** Relating to a LEAP YEAR, when a day is added to FEBRUARY. The Romans added a day after 24 February every fourth year, and called it *dies bissextus,* 'twice sixth day', referring to the (repeated) sixth day before the CALENDS of 1 MARCH.

**Bistro.** A small restaurant. The word may come from Russian *bystro*, 'quick', 'fast', and date from the Allied occupation of France in 1815, when Russian soldiers would enter a café and demand food and drink with the command 'Bystro, bystro!' Others, however, take the word from French *bistouille,* a local word for a drink of coffee and brandy, itself apparently from *bis*, 'twice', and *touiller*, 'to stir'.

**Bit.** A piece, a morsel, and basically the same word as 'bite', meaning a piece bitten off. French *morceau*, 'bit', 'piece', is similarly related to *mordre*, 'to bite'. The word was also formerly used for a piece of money, as a 'threepenny bit', 'two-shilling bit'. In the USA a bit is an eighth of a DOLLAR, so two bits are a QUARTER. In computer jargon a bit is the term for a choice between 0 and 1 in BINARY NOTATION. Here the origin is in a shortened form of 'binary digit'.

**Bit between** or **in one's teeth, The.** To have the bit between one's teeth is to be determined, to rebel. When a horse has a mind to run away, he catches the bit between his teeth and the driver or rider no longer has control over him.

**Bit of all right, A.** A pleasant person or thing.

**Bit of fluff** or **skirt** or **stuff, A.** An attractive girl or woman. Fluff is the light, downy, soft stuff. The terms are regarded by many as offensive.

**Bit of rough, A.** A male sexual partner whose lack of sophistication is part of his attraction.

**Bit on the side, A.** An extramarital affair or the person with whom one is having such an affair.

**Bits and pieces** or **bobs**. Odds and ends; a diffuse assortment of small items. Weather forecasters sometimes refer to 'bits and bobs of rain' meaning simply scattered showers.

**Devil's bit.** *See under* DEVIL.

**Do one's bit, To.** *See under* DO.

**Not a bit of it.** Not at all. A phrase also sometimes said as an alternative to 'You're welcome' in response to thanks.

**Two bits.** *See under* TWO.

**Bitch, Son of a.** *See under* SON.

**Bite. Bite off more than one can chew, To.** To undertake more than one is capable of doing or completing.

**Bite off someone's head, To.** To respond unnecessarily angrily, for example after mild criticism.

**Bite** or **snap off someone's nose, To.** To speak snappishly. To pull (or wring) the nose is to affront by an act of indignity, to snap someone's nose is to affront by speech. Snarling dogs snap at each other's noses.

**Bite one's lip, To.** To express vexation and annoyance; to suppress an emotion such as anger or laughter, in some cases by literally biting one's lip.

**Bite one's thumb at, To.** Formerly, to insult or defy someone by putting the thumbnail into the mouth and clicking it against the teeth. A similar gesture is still current in Italy (which is where the quotation below is set).

> *Gregory*: I will frown as I pass by; and let them take it as they list.
> *Sampson*: Nay, as they dare. I will bite my thumb at them: which is a disgrace to them, if they bear it.
> SHAKESPEARE: *Romeo and Juliet*, I, i (1584)

**Bite one's tongue, To.** To repress one's speech; to remain silent under provocation.

**Bite on the bridle, To.** To suffer great hardship. Horses bite on the bridle when trying to get their own way.

**Bite on** or **bite the bullet, To.** To endure pain courageously; to face trouble or adversity with fortitude; to behave stoically. The expression probably originated in field surgery in the days before anaesthesia. A surgeon about to operate on a wounded soldier would give him a bullet to bite on to distract him from the pain and reduce his ability to scream, which would in turn distract the surgeon.

**Biter, A.** Formerly, a cheater or a sharper. The sense remains in the biter bit, meaning that the cheater has had a dose of his own medicine. The moral is illustrated by AESOP's fable the VIPER AND THE FILE.

**Bite the dust, To.** To fall down dead, as if falling from one's horse. The catchphrase 'Another redskin bit the dust' derives from WILD WEST stories, and was current in the Second World War, especially in the RAF. The phrase is now often heard in the form 'Another one bites the dust' following the achievement of some kind of feat or success.

**Bite the hand that feeds one, To.** To repay kindness or generosity with ingratitude. The image is of a dog, which may on occasion round on its owner and feeder.

**His bark is worse than his bite.** *See under* BARK.

**Once bitten, twice shy.** *See under* ONCE.

**Two bites of a cherry.** *See under* TWO.

**Bitter. Bitter pill to swallow, A.** Something unpleasant that must be endured.

**Archilochian bitterness.** *See under* ARCHILOCHIAN.

**Gall of bitterness, The.** *See under* GALL.

**To the bitter end.** *See under* TO.

**Black.** *See under* COLOURS for its symbolism. Its use for MOURNING was a Roman custom (Juvenal, *Satires*, x, 245 (2nd century AD)), borrowed from the Egyptians. At funerals mutes who wore black cloaks were sometimes known as the blacks, and sometimes as Black Guards (*see* BLACKGUARD).

> I do pray ye
> To give me leave to live a little longer.
> You stand about me like my Blacks.
> FRANCIS BEAUMONT and JOHN FLETCHER: *Monsieur Thomas*, III, i (1613)

**Black Africa.** Africa south of the Sahara, where black people predominate.

**Black Agnes.** A palfrey of Mary, Queen of Scots, given by her brother Moray and named after Agnes of Dunbar.

**Black and blue.** With the skin badly bruised, as after a severe beating.

**Black and Tans.** The name of a pack of hounds in County Limerick, applied to the specially recruited auxiliary force sent to Ireland by the British government in 1921 to supplement the Royal Irish Constabulary. This force was so called from the colour of their uniforms.

**Black art, The.** BLACK MAGIC; NECROMANCY. The name seems to have derived from Medieval Latin *nigromantia* used erroneously for Greek *nekromanteia*. The DEVIL was also portrayed as black.

**Blackball, To.** To vote against; to exclude from a particular group. In the BALLOT those who accepted a candidate dropped a red or white ball into the box, those rejecting dropped a black one.

**Black Beauty.** The horse who is the hero of Anna Sewell's children's classic of the same name, published in 1877. He suffers much at first, but eventually finds a happy home.

**Black belt.** In judo and karate, a belt worn by an instructor or expert in the dan grades.

**Black Belt, The.** The region of the southern USA that extends from Georgia across Alabama and Mississippi. It not only has a high black population but has rich, black soil.

**Black Bess.** Dick TURPIN's mythical but celebrated mare, created by Harrison Ainsworth in his romance *Rookwood* (1834), and particularly known for Dick's ride to York.

**Blackboard jungle, The.** Schools in which delinquency is rife and discipline difficult to impose. The name is taken from the title of a novel by Evan Hunter published in 1954 and filmed in 1955. It was based on a New York school and was a savage indictment of certain aspects of the American state educational system.

**Black Book.** Some historic publications with this title are: (1) *The Black Book of the Admiralty*, a 14th-century collection of maritime law; (2) *The Black Book of the Exchequer*, an official account of royal revenues, payments, perquisites and the like, in the reign of Henry II; (3) *The Black Book of the Household*, purporting to deal with court customs of the reign of Edward III; (4) *The Black Books*, as the earliest records of LINCOLN'S INN (dating from 1422); (5) *The Black Book*, as a collective title for the reports presented to Parliament in 1536 prior to the dissolution of the monasteries; and (6) *The Black Book* (1820) and the *Extraordinary Black Book* (1831), which set out to expose the abuses in church and state of those times. There are also two notable Welsh manuscripts of this name: (1) *The Black Book of Carmarthen*, a 12th-century collection of Welsh poetry containing references to King ARTHUR; and (2) *The Black Book of Chirk*, a codex of Welsh law in the Welsh language (probably 12th century).

To be in someone's black books is to be out of favour, in disgrace. A black book is one recording the names of those who are in disgrace or have merited punishment. Amhurst, in his *Terrae Filius, or the Secret History of the University of Oxford* (1726), speaks of the PROCTOR's black book and says that no person whose name is found there can proceed to a degree.

**Black bottom.** A popular dance of the 1920s, of American origin. It involved a sinuous rotation of the hips ('bottom').

**Black box.** An aircraft's flight data recorder, today usually orange in colour, not black.

**Black bun.** In Scotland, a type of rich dark fruitcake.

**Black Canons.** The AUGUSTINIANS, from their black cloaks.

**Black cap.** A small square of black cloth. In Britain it was worn by a judge when passing the death sentence. It is part of a judge's full dress and is also worn on 9 November, when the new lord mayor of London takes the oath at the Law Courts. Covering the head was a sign of mourning among the Israelites, Greeks, Romans and Anglo-Saxons.

> And David went up by the ascent of mount Olivet, and wept as he went up, and had his head covered, and he went barefoot.
> 2 Samuel 15:30

**Black Country, The.** The dense and heavily industrialized region of the West Midlands, with Dudley as the geographical centre. The collieries, blast furnaces, foundries and metal industries grimed and blackened the area with smoke. Hence the name.

**Black Death, The.** The plague, both pneumonic and bubonic, that came from Asia and ravaged Europe between 1348 and 1351. It reached England in 1348 where it probably carried off one-eighth of the population, the clergy being particularly badly hit. The name does not appear before the 16th century and may refer to the devastating nature of the visitation. It is more likely, however, to have been prompted by the dark discoloration of the skin (ecchymosis). Coughing and sneezing were doubtless accompanying symptoms, hence the somewhat improbable suggestion that the nursery rhyme:

> Ring-a-ring o'roses,
> A pocket full of posies,
> A-tishoo! A-tishoo!
> We all fall down.

was some form of folk memory of the Black Death. The pandemic appeared in 1361–2 and 1379, and there were periodic epidemics until the GREAT PLAGUE.

**Black diamonds.** Coal. Coal and diamonds are both forms of carbon.

**Black Dick.** Richard, Earl Howe (1726–99), British admiral and victor of the Battle of the First of June (1794), so called from his swarthy complexion.

**Black dog.** An early 18th-century name for a counterfeit SHILLING or other 'silver' coin made of pewter. Also another name for the BLUES. *See also* BLACK DOG HAS WALKED OVER HIM.

**Black dog has walked over him, A.** Said of a sullen person. Horace writes that the sight of a black dog with its pups was an unlucky omen, and the DEVIL has been frequently symbolized by a black dog.

**Black Douglas.** Sir James Douglas (1286–1330), or 'Good Sir James', champion of Robert BRUCE, was called 'Black Douglas' by the English of the Border to whom he became a figure of dread. He twice took Douglas Castle from its English occupants. The story is told in Sir Walter Scott's *Castle Dangerous* (1831).

**Black dwarf, A.** A GNOME of the most malignant character, once held by the dalesmen of the BORDER as the author of all the mischief that befell their flocks and herds. In Sir Walter Scott's novel of this title (1816), the name is given to Sir Edward Mauley, alias Elshander, the recluse, Cannie Elshie, and the Wise Wight of Mucklestane Moor.

**Black earth.** The rich black soil found in the grasslands of Russia. The name translates its geological Russian-based designation of *chernozem*.

**Black economy.** The part of a country's income that remains illegally undeclared, often as a means of avoiding tax.

**Black eye.** Bruised skin around the eye caused by a blow.

> Two lovely black eyes,
> Oh, what a surprise!
> Only for telling a man he was wrong.
> Two lovely black eyes!
> CHARLES COBORN: 'Two Lovely Black Eyes' (1886)

**Blackface.** A white performer made up to look like a black, traditionally by applying burnt cork to the face. The name is also that of a breed of sheep with a dark-coloured face.

**Black flag.** The emblem of piracy or JOLLY ROGER; the emblem of no QUARTER. A black flag was formerly hoisted over a prison immediately after an execution, and in the Second World War submarines, on returning to base, sometimes hoisted a black flag to indicate a 'kill'.

Chinese mercenaries who opposed the French in Tonkin in the 1880s were known as the Black Flags, as also were the troops of the caliph of Baghdad, because his banner, that of the ABASSIDS, was black. It is said that the black curtain that hung before the door of AYESHA was taken for a national flag.

**Blackfoot.** The popular name of a group of North American Indian peoples, speaking an Algonquian language. The name translates their own name for themselves, *Siksika*.

**Black Forest gateau.** A chocolate sponge with layers of morello cherries or cherry jam and whipped cream and topped with chocolate icing. So called as it originated in southern Germany, where the Black Forest is.

**Black Friars.** The DOMINICAN Friars, from their black mantle. The London district of Blackfriars is on the site of the former Dominican monastery.

**Black Friday.** Among the most notable days so called are: (1) 6 December 1745, the day on which the news arrived in London that the YOUNG PRETENDER had reached Derby; (2) 11 May 1866, when the failure of the London bankers Overend, Gurney & Co. caused widespread panic; and (3) in the USA, 24 September 1869, when many speculators were ruined by the Government's release of gold into the open market in order to bring down the price, which had been forced up by stock manipulators. *See also* RED FRIDAY.

**Black frost.** A frost less severe than one with snow or rime, so called as it blackens plants.

**Blackguard.** The origin of this term, long applied to rogues and scoundrels, is uncertain. In the 16th and 17th centuries it was applied to lowest menials in great houses, scullions, camp followers and the like. It was also given to the linkboys and torchbearers at funerals.

**Black Hand.** The popular name of the Slav secret society largely responsible for contriving the assassination of the Archduke Franz Ferdinand in Sarajevo on 28 June 1914. This was the event which precipitated the First World War. The name was also that of a group of Sicilian blackmailers and terrorists operating in the USA in the early 20th century.

**Blackheath.** A district of southeast London that was once the haunt of footpads and highwaymen. The followers of Wat Tyler in 1381 and Jack Cade in 1450 assembled there. Here also the Londoners welcomed Henry V after Agincourt and Charles II met the army on his way to London in 1660. *See also* JACK CADE LEGISLATION.

**Black hole.** In astronomy a hypothetical region of space that results from the gravitational collapse of a star when its nuclear fuel has been exhausted.

**Black Hole of Calcutta, The.** Siraj-ud-Dawlah, Nawab of Bengal, reputedly confined (on 20–21 June 1756) 146 British prisoners, including one woman, in the small prison – 18ft × 14ft 10in (5.5 × 4.5m) – of the East India Company's Fort William, after its capture. Only 22 men and the woman escaped suffocation. A military punishment cell or guardroom is often nicknamed the Black Hole, and dark, stuffy places are sometimes said to be 'like the Black Hole of Calcutta'.

**Black Horse, The.** *See under* REGIMENTAL AND DIVISIONAL NICKNAMES.

**Black ice.** Thin, hard ice, especially when transparent and invisible on a road surface.

If the steering feels light, this may indicate black ice and your vehicle losing its grip on the road.
*The Highway Code* (1996)

**Black in the face.** Angry, with great exertion, so that the face is darkly flushed.

**Blackjack.** (1) A large leather gotch, or can for beer, so called from the outside being tarred; (2) in North America, a truncheon of leather-covered lead; (3) a dark variety of the mineral sphalerite, rich in iron, so named by Cornish miners; (4) pontoon, or some other card game; (5) a small American oak, *Quercus marilandica*, so named for its blackish bark.

Black Jack was also the nickname of the American General J.A. Logan (1826–86), on account of his dark complexion and hair, and of General Pershing (1860–1948) who commanded the Americans in the First World War.

**Blacklead.** *See* MISNOMERS.

**Blackleg.** An old name for a swindler, especially at cards or races. The word is now used for a non-union member who acts against the interest of a TRADE UNION, or who works during a strike.

**Black letter.** Gothic or German type which in the early days of printing was the most commonly used. It is so named because of its heavy black appearance in comparison with ROMAN TYPE.

**Black-letter day.** An inauspicious or unlucky day. The allusion is to the old liturgical calendars in which major saints' days and festivals were distinguished by being printed in red. Black was used for holy days of less importance. *See also* RED-LETTER DAY.

The Romans marked the unlucky days with a piece of charcoal and their lucky ones with white chalk.

**Blacklist.** A list of those in disgrace, or who have incurred censure or punishment, or who are regarded as untrustworthy or disloyal.

**Black looks.** Looks of displeasure.

**Black magic.** Magic used for evil purposes, invoking the power of the DEVIL. *See also* NECROMANCY; WHITE MAGIC.

**Blackmail.** Mail here is the old Scottish word for a rent or tax payment. Blackmail was originally a tribute paid by the BORDER farmers to FREEBOOTERS in return for protection or immunity from harassment. Hence the modern sense of the word, for payment extorted by intimidation or threat, or a threat that some harmful or embarrassing action will be taken if a condition is not met.

**Black Maria.** The police van used for the conveyance of prisoners. It is suggested that the name is derived from that of Maria Lee, the black owner of a lodging-house in Boston. She was so tall and strong that when the police required help they sent for 'Black Maria', who soon collared the refractory men and helped the police escort them to the jail. The term is known to have been in use in Boston in the 1840s.

**Black market.** The illegal buying and selling of goods or currencies. *See also* UNDER THE COUNTER.

**Black Mass.** A blasphemous MASS in which the DEVIL is invoked in place of God and various obscene rites are performed in mockery of the proper ceremony. *See also* HELLFIRE CLUB.

The term is also used for a REQUIEM Mass, from the black vestments worn.

**Black Monday.** (1) The supposed nickname of Easter Monday, 14 April 1360, when Edward III was besieging Paris. The day was so dark, windy and bitterly cold that many men and horses died. In fact 14 April that year fell on the Tuesday of the week after Easter. The Monday after Easter Monday is called Black Monday in allusion to this fateful day. (2) In Melbourne, Australia, 27 February 1865 was so called from a fearful north wind which caused much damage between Sandhurst and Castlemaine. (3) On the London STOCK EXCHANGE, 19 October 1987, when share prices on world stock markets fell dramatically.

**Black money.** *See* BLACK DOG.

**Black Monks, The.** The BENEDICTINES.

**Black Muslims.** A political and religious movement of black people in the USA. They are followers of ISLAM and aim to establish a new black nation.

**Black Nell.** Wild Bill HICKOK's mare.

**Blackout.** The term was first used in the theatre, when the lighting was extinguished to darken the whole stage. It is now mainly associated with its use in the Second World War as an air raid precaution. From the outbreak of war (3 September 1939) until 23 April 1945 (coastal areas, 11 May), it was obligatory throughout Britain to cover all windows, skylights and the like before dark so that no gleam of light could be seen from outside. Moving vehicles were allowed only the dimmest of lights. A blackout is also a loss of consciousness.

**Black Panthers.** A group of extremists in the USA set up to fight for the rights of black people. The organization was founded in 1966 in Oakland, California, by Huey Newton and Bobby Seale.

**Black Parliament.** A name given to the REFORMATION Parliament (1529–36), which effected the breach with ROME.

**Black pigeons of Dodona, The.** According to classical legend two black pigeons took their flight from Thebes, in Egypt. One flew to Libya and the other to Dodona. On the spot where the former alighted, the temple of JUPITER AMMON was erected. In the place where the other settled, the ORACLE of Jupiter was established, and responses there were made by the black pigeons that inhabited the surrounding groves. The fable is possibly based on a pun upon the word *peleiai*, which usually meant 'old women' but in the dialect of the Epirots signified pigeons or doves.

**Blackpool.** The Lancashire resort's earthy name derives from a peaty pool that existed here before the present town arose in the 19th century. In some ways it evokes the down-to-earth pleasures and entertainments that are on offer. They include golden sands for bathing, the Blackpool Tower, a scaled-down version of the Eiffel Tower, housing a zoo, a circus, a ballroom and a large organ, and a promenade, the Golden Mile, thronged with holidaymakers and trundling trams by day and illuminated by strings of gaudy lights at night. Blackpool is in many ways the Brighton of the north, a bright, extrovert town in which to indulge in the transient joys of life. On the business side, it shares with Brighton the honour of hosting major political and trade union conferences.

> The tom-toms from Blackpool this week may beat out a familiar war cry, but the British working classes are a tribe in retreat. Bury their heart on the Golden Mile.
> *The Times* (15 September 1998)

**Black Pope, The.** The General of the JESUITS.

**Black Power.** An emotive concept originating among certain sections of Negro opinion in the USA since 1966, whose advocates aim at redressing racial injustice by militant black nationalism that allows for violence and race war.

**Black Prince, The.** Edward, Prince of Wales (1330–76), the eldest son of Edward III. He is popularly supposed to be so named from his black armour. The name does not appear to have been used before the latter part of the 16th century and first appeared in writing in 1569.

> Brave Gaunt, thy father and myself
> Rescued the Black Prince, that young Mars of men,
> From forth the ranks of many thousand French.
> SHAKESPEARE: *Richard II*, II, iii (1585)

**Black Rod.** The short title of the Gentleman Usher of the Black Rod, named from his staff of office, a black wand surmounted by a gold lion. He is responsible for maintaining order in the HOUSE OF LORDS and for summoning the Commons at the opening and proroguing of Parliament. He is also chief gentleman usher to the sovereign and usher to the order of the GARTER.

**Black Russia.** Central and southern Russia, perhaps so named from the region's black soil.

**Blacks, The.** *See* BIANCHI; BLACK HORSE, *under* REGIMENTAL AND DIVISIONAL NICKNAMES.

**Black Saladin.** Warwick's coal-black horse. Its sire was Malech, and according to tradition, when the race of Malech failed, the race of Warwick would fail also. And thus it was.

**Black Sash.** In South Africa an organization of women opposed to APARTHEID.

**Black Saturday.** In Scotland, 4 August 1621, on which day a violent storm occurred at the very moment the Parliament was sitting to force EPISCOPACY upon the people.

**Black Sea, The.** Formerly called the EUXINE SEA and probably given its present name from its dangers and lack of shelter rather than from the colour of its waters.

**Black September.** A Palestinian terrorist group formed when the Palestine Liberation Organization was driven from Jordan in September 1970.

**Black sheep** or **Black sheep of the family, The.** A ne'er-do-well; a person regarded as a disgrace to the family or community, or as a failure in it. Black sheep are not as valuable as white, and in times of superstition were looked on as bearing the Devil's mark. A black sheep in a white flock is the ODD MAN OUT. *See also* BÊTE NOIRE.

**Blackshirts.** Mussolini's Italian FASCISTS, who wore black shirts, as did their English imitators. The name was also used in NAZI Germany for Himmler's SS, in contrast with the Brownshirts of the SA.

**Black spot.** A place on a road where accidents often occur, such as a bend or crossing.

**Blackstone.** The short title of the lawyers' bible, William Blackstone's *Commentaries on the Laws of England* (1765–9), encapsulating the sometimes convoluted tenets of the British constitution.

**Black Stone, The.** The stone kissed by every pilgrim to the KAABA at MECCA. Muslims say that it was white when it fell from heaven but that it turned black because of the sins of mankind. The stone was worshipped centuries before MOHAMMED. In Persian legend it was an emblem of SATURN.

**Black Swan.** *See* RARA AVIS.

**Blackthorn winter.** A period of cold weather, which frequently occurs when the blackthorn is in blossom. *See also* ICE SAINTS.

**Black Thursday.** 24 October 1929, the day of the spectacular WALL STREET crash, when almost 13 million shares changed hands.

**Black tie.** A conventional indication on an invitation that a dinner jacket is to be worn.

**Black Tom.** The 10th Earl of Ormonde (1532–1614), Lord High Treasurer of Ireland, from his ungracious ways and BLACK LOOKS.

**Black velvet.** A drink of CHAMPAGNE and GUINNESS in equal parts. It was the favourite drink of Bismarck, the IRON CHANCELLOR.

**Black Watch, The.** The Royal Highland Regiment, so nicknamed from their dark tartan. They are distinguished by the red hackle (small group of red feathers) on their bonnets. *See also* REGIMENTAL AND DIVISIONAL NICKNAMES.

**Black Wednesday.** 16 September 1992, when Britain pulled out of the Exchange Rate Mechanism (ERM), allowing sterling to float. The Chancellor of the day, Norman Lamont, raised interest rates by 2% and then by 3%, but without improving sterling's value.

**Black widow.** A venomous American spider, *Latrodectus mactans*. It is black with red markings and the female eats its mate. Hence widow.

**All Blacks, The.** *See under* ALL.

**As black as a crow.** *See under* AS.

**As black as your hat.** *See under* AS.

**Devil is not so black as he is painted, The.** *See under* DEVIL.

**In black and white.** In writing or printing, the paper being white and the ink black.

**Not as black as one is painted.** Not as bad or disreputable as one is said to be.

**Penny Black.** *See under* PENNY.

**Pot calling the kettle black, The.** *See under* POT.

**Swear black and blue, To.** *See under* SWEAR.

**Swear black is white, To.** *See under* SWEAR.

**Blacksmith.** A smith who works in black metal, such as iron.

**Harmonious Blacksmith, The.** *See under* HARMONIOUS.

**Learned Blacksmith, The.** *See under* LEARN.

**Blade.** A former name for a dashing or swaggering young man. He was probably so called from the blade of the sword that he usually wore.

**Bladud.** A mythical English king, the father of King LEAR. According to Geoffrey of Monmouth he built Bath and dedicated the medicinal springs to MINERVA, studied magic and was dashed to pieces when he fell into the temple of APOLLO while trying to fly.

**Blaise, Modesty.** The strip cartoon adventuress created by Peter O'Donnell took her maiden bow in the London *Evening Standard* in 1963. She is popularly regarded as a sort of female James BOND, and she rose to fame in the 1960s, when spy fiction was all the rage. She 'wrote' a number of novels (the author was actually O'Donnell), the first of which, *Modesty Blaise*, appeared in 1965.

**Blake, Sexton.** A detective hero of boys' stories, in many ways the equivalent of Sherlock HOLMES. He first appeared in Hal Meredith's story 'The Missing Millionaire', published in Harmsworth's *Halfpenny Marvel* in 1893. He later transferred to another Harmsworth magazine, the *Union Jack*, and it was there that he made his name. He has a boy assistant called Tinker and a landlady called Mrs Bardell, a 'treasure' in the best domestic tradition. Like Holmes, he has rooms in Baker Street, from which he sallies forth to solve all kinds of mysteries. Unlike Holmes, however, he uses brawn rather than brain. His adventures have been written by around 200 different authors.

**Blanch, To.** A method of testing the quality of money paid in taxes to the king, used by Roger of Salisbury in the reign of Henry I. A total of 44 shillings' worth of silver coin was taken from the amount being paid in, a pound's weight of it was melted down, and the impurities were skimmed off. If it were then found to be light, the taxpayer had to throw in enough pennies to balance the scale.

**Blanchefleur** (French, 'white flower'). The heroine of the Old French metrical romance *Flore et Blanchefleur*, used by Giovanni Boccaccio for his prose romance, *Il Filocolo* (*c*.1334–40). It is substantially the same as that of Dianora and Ansaldo in the DECAMERON (1349–51) and that of Dorigen and Aurelius in Chaucer. The tale is of a young Christian prince who is in love with the SARACEN slave-girl with whom he has been brought up. They are parted, but after many adventures he rescues her unharmed from the harem of the emir of Babylon.

**Blanco White.** In the British army the popular designation of personnel named White. It derives from the tradename Blanco for the preparation which replaced pipeclay as the universal substance for whitening the webbing in a soldier's equipment. It was made by a Sheffield firm called Pickering from about 1881 until the 1960s. Khaki Blanco was also used.

**Blank. Blank cartridge.** Cartridge with powder only, without shot, bullet or ball, used in battle practice or as a signal.

**Blank cheque.** A signed cheque, leaving the amount to be filled in by the payee. To give a blank cheque is thus to give CARTE BLANCHE.

**Blank verse.** Rhymeless verse in IAMBIC PENTAMETERS, first used in English by the Earl of Surrey about 1540 in his version of Books ii and iv of the *Aeneid* (1st century BC). Blank verse was also used by James Thomson in *The Seasons* (1726–30), by Edward Young in *Night Thoughts* (1742), and by William Cowper in *The Task* (1785). William Wordsworth and S.T. Coleridge also favoured it. All the Romantic poets used blank verse extensively, as did many great 19th-century poets.

**Draw a blank, To.** *See under* DRAW.

**Blanket. Blanketeers.** The starving handloom weavers and spinners who assembled in St Peter's Field, Manchester, 10 March 1817, each with a blanket for their march to London to petition the Prime Regent. Few reached Macclesfield after intimidation from the authorities, and none got beyond Derby.

**Born on the wrong side of the blanket, To be.** *See under* BORN.

**Wet blanket, A.** *See under* WET.

**Blarney.** Flattering talk, often with wheedling or flowery turns of phrase. The term comes from the BLARNEY STONE.

**Blarney Stone, The.** A block of rough limestone measuring 4ft (1.2m) by 1ft (30cm) in the wall of Blarney Castle, near Cork, set 83 ft (25m) high in the battlements. The tradition is to kiss it, which can be done only by lying on one's back and leaning out over a sheer drop, with a pair of strong arms gripping one's shins. This feat, it is believed, will give the gift of cajolery.

The legend surrounding the stone is said to date from 1602, when the smooth-talking Lord of Blarney, Cormac MacDermot MacCarthy, was asked by George Carew, Queen Elizabeth's deputy in Ireland, to give up the tradition by which Irish clans elected their chiefs and to transfer his allegiance to the English crown. MacCarthy constantly procrastinated with blandishments, until the Queen finally exploded: 'Blarney! Blarney! What he says he never means! It's the usual Blarney!' Blarney thus became the laughing stock of the Queen's ministers. The tradition of kissing the stone dates from the 18th century, when the Blarney Castle estate was developed by the Jefferyes family.

**Blasphemous Balfour.** Sir James Balfour (*c.*1525–83), Scottish judge, was so called for his apostasy. He 'served with all parties, deserted all, and yet profited by all'.

**Blast. Like the blast of Roland's horn.** *See under* LIKE.

**Blatant beast.** In Spenser's *The Faerie Queene* (V, VI (1596)) 'a dreadful feend of gods and men ydrad', typifying calumny or slander. He was born of CERBERUS and CHIMERA, and had a thousand tongues and a sting. With his tongues he speaks things 'most shameful, most unrighteous, most untrue', and with his sting 'steeps them in poison'. Sir CALIDORE muzzled him and drew him with a chain to Fairyland but the beast escaped. The word 'blatant' was probably coined by Spenser himself and seems to be based on Latin *blatire*, 'to babble'.

**Blayney's Bloodhounds.** *See under* REGIMENTAL AND DIVISIONAL NICKNAMES.

**Blaze** (probably from Middle Low German *bles*, 'white mark', related to English 'blemish'). A white marking on the forehead of a horse, also called a star. Similarly, a white mark made on a tree by chipping off a piece of bark. Hence to blaze a trail by marking trees in this way to mark a route, especially when exploring or pioneering.

**Blazer.** Originally a brightly coloured jacket used in boating, cricket and other sports. This is now often called a sports blazer to distinguish it from the more sober blazer worn as part of school uniform or the like.

> A blazer is the red flannel boating jacket worn by the Lady Margaret, St John's College, Cambridge, Boat Club.
>
> *Daily News* (22 August 1889)

The jacket was so called from its bright, 'blazing' colours.

**Blazes, Go to.** Go to HELL.

**Bleed. Bleeder.** A derogatory term for a despicable person, or for a person generally, especially when preceded by an adjective, as lucky bleeder.

**Bleeding of the nose.** According to some this is a sign that one is in love. Francis Grose (1731–91) says if it bleeds one drop only it forebodes sickness, if three drops the omen is still worse. In his *Astrologaster* (1620), John Melton says: 'If a man's nose bleeds one drop at the left nostril it is a sign of good luck, and vice versa.' There are dozens of popular remedies for curing a nose bleed, ranging from pressing a finger across the upper lip to placing cold coins on the forehead or dropping a key down the back. The best treatment is in fact to pinch the lower part of the nostrils for a time, breathing through the mouth, until the flow of blood eases.

**Bleed someone white, To.** To extort a person's last penny. Money is the life-blood of commerce.

**My heart bleeds for you.** *See under* HEART.

**Blefuscu.** An island off LILLIPUT in Jonathan Swift's *Gulliver's Travels* (1726). In describing it he satirized France.

**Blenheim Palace.** This mansion, at Woodstock, Oxfordshire, was given to the Duke of Marlborough for his great victory over the French at Blenheim (1704). It has given its name to the Blenheim spaniel and to a golden-coloured apple, the Blenheim orange.

**Bless. Blessing.** A blessing with three fingers in Christian churches is symbolic of the TRINITY.

**Blessing in disguise, A.** An apparent misfortune that turns out to be favourable. The expression arose in the 18th century with a specific religious reference.

> Ev'n Crosses from his sov'reign Hand
> Are Blessings in Disguise.
>
> JAMES HERVEY: *Reflections on a Flower-Garden*, 'Since all the downward tracts of time' (hymn) (1746).

**Bless me!** or **Bless my soul!** or **God bless my soul!** An exclamation of surprise.

**Bless you!** Said to someone who has sneezed.

The words to some extent echo the sound of the SNEEZE itself.

> 'Bless you, my dear!' he said, and 'bless you, bless you!' at the second and third sneeze.
> APULEIUS: *The Golden Ass* (2nd century AD) (translated by Robert Graves)

**Backward blessing, A.** *See under* BACK.

**Count one's blessings, To.** *See under* COUNT.

**I'll be blessed if I'll do it.** I will certainly not do it. A EUPHEMISM for damned.

**Islands of the Blest.** *See* FORTUNATE ISLANDS.

**Not to have a penny to bless oneself with.** *See under* PENNY.

**Out of God's blessing into the warm sun.** *See under* OUT.

**Seraphic Blessing.** *See under* SERAPHIC.

**Bligh, Captain.** *See* MUTINY ON THE BOUNTY.

**Blighty.** A colloquial name for England used by soldiers serving abroad in the First World War but originating among those who had served in India some years before. It represents Urdu *bilāyatī*, 'foreign land', from Arabic *wilāyat*, 'country'. Three popular songs during the First World War were: 'There's a ship that's bound for Blighty', 'We wish we were in Blighty' and 'Take me back to dear old Blighty, put me on the train for London town'.

**Blimp** (apparently a coinage based on limp, perhaps from the code name Type B-limp). A word originally applied to an observation balloon in the First World War. 'Colonel Blimp' was created after the war by the cartoonist David Low as a plump, pompous ex-officer who was rigidly and blindly opposed to anything new. Hence Colonel Blimp or blimp as a now rather dated term for a military officer, or any person with stuffy or reactionary views.

> He [Tony Blair] must also be the first party leader since Neville Chamberlain ... to have the whole-hearted support of Colonel Blimp. What can one hear the old boy saying? 'Gad sir, it's good to have a public school man back at the helm.'
> WILLIAM REES-MOGG in *The Times* (29 August 1994)

**Blind, A.** Something serving to conceal the truth. The metaphor is from window blinds, which prevent outsiders from seeing in.

**Blind alley.** A cul-de-sac. It is blind because it has no 'eye' or passage through it. It is also a term for a situation in which no further progress can be made.

**Blind corner.** One that is concealed and cannot be readily seen.

**Blind date.** A hopefully romantic meeting between a man and a woman who have not met before; also a person so met.

**Blind drunk.** Very drunk; so drunk as to be unable to distinguish things clearly.

**Blind Half-hundred, The.** *See under* REGIMENTAL AND DIVISIONAL NICKNAMES.

**Blind Harper, The.** John Parry (*c.*1710–82). He lived with the Williams-Wynn family at Wynnstay, Ruabon, played at concerts in London, Oxford and Dublin, and published three collections of Welsh music.

**Blind leading the blind, The.** Those who give advice to others or who take the lead but who are unfitted to do so. The allusion is biblical.

> Let them alone: they be blind leaders of the blind. And if the blind lead the blind, both shall fall into the ditch.
> Matthew 15:14

**Blind Magistrate, The.** Sir John Fielding (1722–80), Bow Street magistrate, blinded in his youth, was reputed to know countless thieves by their voices.

**Blind man's buff.** A game in which a blindfolded person tries to catch and identify the other players. The buff is the tap on the shoulder that was originally given to the identified person.

**Blind spot.** A small area on the retina where the optic nerve enters the eye and where vision is not experienced. The term is used figuratively to denote some area in one's understanding where judgement and perception are regularly lacking.

**Blind with science, To.** To impress or overawe a person with a display of knowledge, usually spurious.

**Blindworms.** *See* MISNOMERS.

**As blind as a bat, beetle, mole or owl.** *See under* AS.

**Colour blindness.** *See under* COLOUR.

**Fly blind, To.** *See under* FLY.

**Go it blind, To.** To enter upon a project without sufficient forethought, inquiry or preparation. In poker, if a player chooses to 'go it blind', he doubles the ante before looking at his cards.

**Love is blind.** *See under* LOVE.

**Swear blind.** *See under* SWEAR.

**Turn a blind eye, To.** *See under* TURN.

**Blitz, The.** The name (an abbreviation of BLITZKRIEG) given to the intensive German air raids on London in 1940 and 1941 which resulted in the destruction of many buildings and the death of over 15,000 people. *See also* BATTLE OF BRITAIN; BLACKOUT.

**Blitzkrieg** (German, 'lightning war'). A concentrated military offensive designed to produce a knock-out blow. The term was particularly applied to the attacks by Hitler's Germany on various European countries between 1939 and 1941. In 1940 in western Europe the Germans captured Copenhagen on 9 April, Oslo on 10 April, The Hague on 14 May, Brussels on 17 May and Paris on 14 June, resulting in the British withdrawal at DUNKIRK. *See also* D-DAY.

**Have a blitz on, To.** To make a real attack on something, especially a long overdue task. An expression often used when a thorough clean-up or clear-out is undertaken.

**Block. Block a bill, To.** In parliamentary language, to postpone or prevent the passage of a bill by giving notice of opposition, thus preventing its being taken after ten o'clock at night.

**Blockbuster.** Anything of great power or size, such as an epic film or a BESTSELLER. The term derives from the heavy high-explosive bombs dropped in the Second World War, which were capable of destroying a whole block of buildings.

**Block capitals.** Letters printed without serifs, or written with each letter separate and in capitals. Those filling out forms are often asked to enter information in this form for the sake of legibility. See also UPPER CASE.

**Blockhead.** A stupid person. The allusion is to a wooden head for hats or wigs.

> Nay, your wit will not so soon out as another man's will – 'tis strongly wedged up in a blockhead.
> SHAKESPEARE: *Coriolanus*, II, iii (1607)

**Blockhouse.** The defensive building of this name is not so called because it was originally made of blocks of wood but because it was designed to block the passage of the enemy at a strategic site such as a mountain pass or bridge. In modern usage, a blockhouse is a reinforced concrete building near a rocket-launching site that is designed to protect personnel and equipment during launching.

**Blockship.** A ship used to block a channel, usually for strategic reasons.

**Block system.** On a railway, a system by which no train may enter a section that is not clear, the section itself being known as the block section. The system is controlled by signals and was introduced in the era of semaphore signals. A block train is nothing to do with this but is a freight train carrying a complete load of a single commodity such as oil, stone or fertilizers between terminals and private sidings. A special type of block train is the MERRY-GO-ROUND.

**Block vote.** A vote by a delegate at a conference, counted as the number of people he or she represents.

**Chip off the old block, A.** *See under* CHIP.

**Halftone block.** *See under* HALF.

**Stumbling block, A.** *See under* STUMBLING.

**Writer's block.** *See under* WRITE.

**Bloggs, Joe.** *See under* JOE.

**Blonde, Dumb.** *See under* DUMB.

**Blondie.** The heroine of the American cartoon strip of the same name by Chic Young, first published in 1930. She began as the flapper Blondie Boopadoop, but subsequently became the wife of the ineffectual Dagwood Bumstead and mother of the precocious Baby Dumpling. Her domestic dramas burgeoned into a series of over 20 films with Blondie in the title, such as *Blondie Brings up Baby* (1939). The last was *Blondie's Hero* (1950), after which she moved to television.

**Blondin.** One of the best known acrobats of all time, born at St Omer, France, in 1824, and dying at Ealing, near London, in 1897. His real name was Jean François Gravelet. His greatest feat was in 1859, when he crossed the Niagara Falls on a tightrope, embroidering the performance by repeating it blindfold, wheeling a barrow, twirling an umbrella and carrying a man on his back. He made a fortune by this act and soon after settled in England, where he gave performances until old age forced him to retire. His adopted name came from his tutor in the art, Jean Ravel Blondin.

**Blood.** In figurative use, the word came to denote members of the same family or race, then family descent generally, then a person having (or claiming) noble ancestry, and so finally a BUCK or dashing young man. In this last sense the term also had associations of 'hot blood', otherwise temper or mettle. The 'blood' also denotes royalty, as in an expression such as a 'prince of the blood'.

**Blood and Guts** or **Old Blood and Guts.** Nickname given by the soldiers in the Second World War to the American General George Smith Patton (1885–1945), with reference to his ungovernable temper. His career ended when he struck an enlisted man. Blood and Guts is also a disrespectful term for the red ensign.

**Blood and thunder.** A term describing a melodramatic adventure story. It is sometimes humorously perverted as 'thud and blunder'.

**Blood brother.** A brother by birth or by the ceremonial mingling of blood.

**Blood group.** A classification of blood according to the two types of antigens, known as A and B, on the surface of blood cells. According to whether a person's blood contains one or other of the two types or both or neither, it is classified as type A, B, AB or O. In Britain the most common group is A, followed by O, then B and finally AB.

**Blood heat.** The normal body temperature of a healthy human being, about 98.4°F (37°C).

**Blood horse.** A thoroughbred or horse of good parentage or stock.

**Bloodhound.** A detective, whether amateur or professional. The reference is to the breed of dog, formerly much used in tracking and police work.

**Blood is thicker than water.** Family ties and obligations are stronger than any other. The allusion is to blood in the sense of 'ancestry'.

**Bloodless Revolution.** An alternative name for the GLORIOUS REVOLUTION.

**Blood money.** Money paid to a person for giving information that will lead to the conviction of a murderer or other criminal. The expression is also used for money paid to a hired murderer or traitor, as it was to JUDAS ISCARIOT for his betrayal of Jesus. The term also applies to money paid as compensation to the relatives of a murdered person, usually to induce them to forgo any right of revenge or seeking of 'blood for blood'.

**Blood orange.** An orange with red or red-streaked pulp.

**Blood-red wedding, The.** The marriage of Henry of Navarre and Margaret of Valois (18 August 1572), which was followed a week later by the St BARTHOLOMEW'S DAY MASSACRE.

**Blood relation** or **relative.** A person related to another by birth, as distinct from one related by marriage.

**Blood sport.** An event involving the killing of animals. The three traditional blood sports are HUNTING, SHOOTING AND FISHING, and the allusion is to the shedding of blood. Opponents of the exercise claim that 'sport', with its connotation of fair play, is a sad misnomer.

**Bloodstone.** *See* HELIOTROPE.

**Bloodsucker.** Any animal or insect that sucks blood, such as a leech or mosquito. Hence a sponger, parasite or extortioner.

**Blood, toil, tears and sweat.** The words used by Sir Winston Churchill in his speech to the HOUSE OF COMMONS, on becoming Prime Minister, 13 May 1940. 'I would say to the House, as I have said to those who have joined this Government: I have nothing to offer but blood, toil, tears and sweat.' In *An Anatomy of the World* (1611), John Donne says, 'Mollify it with thy tears, or sweat, or blood', and Lord Byron has:

> Year after year they voted cent per cent,
> Blood, sweat, and tear-wrung millions – why? for rent!
>
> *The Age of Bronze*, xiv, 621 (1823)

Churchill alluded to his promise of blood, toil, tears and sweat in subsequent speeches of 8 October 1940, 7 May and 2 December 1941 and 10 November 1942.

**Avenger of Blood, The.** *See under* AVENGER.

**Bad blood.** *See under* BAD.

**Baptism of blood, A.** *See under* BAPTISM.

**Blue blood.** *See under* BLUE.

**Dragon's blood.** *See under* DRAGON.

**Field of Blood, The.** *See under* FIELD.

**First blood.** *See under* FIRST.

**Flesh and blood.** *See under* FLESH.

**Get one's blood up, To.** To be the cause of anger or annoyance.

**Have blood on one's hands, To.** To be guilty of murder or injury, or to be responsible for it.

**In cold blood.** *See under* COLD.

**Laws written in blood.** *See under* LAW.

**Make one's blood boil, To.** To make one very angry or indignant.

**Make one's blood run cold, To.** To 'chill' with horror.

**Myrtle which dropped blood, The.** *See under* MYRTLE.

**Nelson's blood.** *See under* NELSON.

**New, fresh** or **young blood.** *See under* NEW.

**Sweat blood, To.** *See under* SWEAT.

**Bloody.** Several fanciful derivations are suggested for this expletive, for example that it is a corruption of By our Lady, or associated with aristocratic rowdies (*see* BLOOD). The common meaning of the word, however, with its unpleasant and lurid associations, is a sufficient explanation of its origin and its use as an intensive.

> It was bloody hot walking today.
>
> JONATHAN SWIFT: *Journal to Stella*, letter xxii (1710–13)

As a title the adjective has been bestowed on Otto II, Holy Roman Emperor (r.973–983), and Queen Mary Tudor (r.1553–8) was called BLOODY MARY.

**Bloody Assizes.** The Assizes conducted in the western circuit under Judge Jeffreys after MONMOUTH'S REBELLION, 1685. The name refers to the brutality, severity and unfairness of the proceedings.

**Bloody Balfour.** In 1887, when Arthur Balfour (1848–1930) became Chief Secretary for Ireland, the police fired on a riotous meeting at Mitchelstown, County Cork, occasioned by the prosecution of a nationalist leader, William O'Brien. Three people were killed. As a consequence of Balfour's resolute support of authority the nickname Bloody Balfour soon became current in Ireland. The meeting in Trafalgar Square on BLOODY SUNDAY was held to protest against O'Brien's imprisonment. *See also* BALFOUR'S POODLE.

**Bloody bear, The.** In John Dryden's *The Hind and the Panther* (1687), the INDEPENDENTS.

**Bloody Butcher, The.** The Duke of Cumberland (1721–65), second son of George II, so called for his ruthless suppression of the Highlanders after the rising under the YOUNG PRETENDER. *See also* JACOBITES.

**Bloody but unbowed.** Wounded but undefeated. The expression has an almost medieval ring but dates from relatively recent times.

> In the fell clutch of circumstance,
> I have not winced nor cried aloud;
> Under the bludgeonings of chance
> My head is bloody, but unbowed.
>
> W.E. HENLEY: *Echoes* (1888)

**Bloody Eleventh, The.** *See under* REGIMENTAL AND DIVISIONAL NICKNAMES.

**Bloody Friday.** 21 July 1972, when 11 people were killed and 130 injured by IRA bombs in Belfast.

**Bloody hand.** A term in Old Forest Law denoting a man whose hand was bloody, and who was therefore presumed to be guilty of killing a deer. In HERALDRY it is the badge of a BARONET and the armorial device of Ulster. *See also* RED HAND.

**Bloody Mary.** Queen Mary Tudor (b.1516, r.1553–8) was so called for her persecution of PROTESTANTS. Some 300 suffered death, including, in 1556, Thomas Cranmer, archbishop of Canterbury. The name is also that of a cocktail made from vodka and tomato juice.

**Bloody Saturday.** 15 August 1998, when an IRA splinter group planted a bomb that killed 29 and injured more than 200 in Omagh, Northern Ireland.

**Bloody Sunday.** (1) 13 November 1887. The dispersal of a socialist demonstration in Trafalgar Square, which had been prohibited by the Commissioner of Police, led to baton charges, the summoning of Footguards and Life Guards, and the arrest of two Scottish MPs, Robert Cunninghame Graham and John Burns. Two of the crowd died of injuries. (2) 22 January 1905. A deputation of workers led by Father Gapon marched to the Winter Palace in St Petersburg to present a petition to the Tsar. After giving warnings to disperse, the troops fired into the crowd. Over 100 people were killed and many hundreds more wounded. (3) 30 January 1972. Paratroops of the British army opened fire on a banned civil rights march in Londonderry, killing 13. BLOODY FRIDAY followed six months later.

**Bloody Tower, The.** Built as the Garden Tower, this addition to the TOWER OF LONDON dates from the reign of Richard II (1377–99). It had won its present name by 1597 from the belief that it witnessed the murder of the PRINCES IN THE TOWER. It subsequently housed such famous prisoners as Sir Walter RALEIGH, Archbishop Laud and Judge Jeffreys.

**Dark and bloody ground.** *See under* DARK.

**Bloomer.** An error, a mistake, as a BLOOMING error.

**Bloomers.** Originally a female costume consisting of jacket, skirt and Turkish trousers gathered closely round the ankles, introduced in about 1849 by the American social reformer Amelia Jenks Bloomer (1818–94). The outfit initially met with little success, mainly because of its association with the 'women's rights' movement. The word is now loosely used for women's or girls' baggy knickers.

> The tireless search for something else has paused for a moment to put matching bloomers or shorts under the skirt.
> *Observer* (30 April 1967)

**Bombay bloomers.** *See under* BOMBAY.

**Blooming.** A EUPHEMISM for BLOODY. There is perhaps an association with flowers in full bloom, since the adjective is an intensive.

> You asks me no bloomin' imper'int questions, an I tells yer no bloomin' lies.
> *Scotsman* (20 August 1885)

**Bloomingdales.** A fashionable department store that is one of New York's minor institutions. It was founded by Lyman G. Bloomingdale and his brother Joseph in 1872 on Third Avenue, and is usually full of shoppers seeking gifts of style and quality. If 'Bloomies' hasn't got what you want, it probably doesn't exist.

> *Diane Keaton*: Sometimes I wonder how I would stand up to torture.
> *Woody Allen*: You? The Gestapo would take away your Bloomingdale's charge card and you'd tell them everything.
> WOODY ALLEN and MARSHALL BRICKMAN: *Annie Hall* (film) (1977)

**Bloomsbury. Bloomsbury Gang.** In the 1760s the WHIG party faction adhering to the Duke of Bedford was so called. Bedford House was in Bloomsbury, the duke's London property.

**Bloomsbury Group.** The name given to a group of writers, artists and intellectuals, who lived and worked in Bloomsbury from about 1907 to 1930. They included Leonard and Virginia Woolf, Clive and Vanessa Bell, Roger Fry, E.M. Forster, Lytton Strachey, Duncan Grant and John Maynard Keynes. They saw themselves as advocates of a new rational, civilized society and many of them had Cambridge links. They were considerably influenced by G.E. Moore's *Principia Ethica* (1903).

**Blossom, Orange.** *See under* ORANGE.

**Blot. Blot one's copybook, To.** To make a serious blunder; to make some error or gaffe that spoils one's hitherto good record.

**Blot on one's escutcheon, A.** A stain on one's character or reputation. An escutcheon is a shield bearing a coat of arms. *See also* BLOT ONE'S COPYBOOK.

> The banishment of Ovid was a blot in his escutcheon.
> JOHN DRYDEN: *Virgil*, ii, Dedication (1697)

**Blouzelinda.** A country girl in John Gay's set of pastorals *The Shepherd's Week* (1714). She is not the usual simple rustic maiden but a stolid farm worker, milking the cows, feeding the pigs and doing other equally unromantic things. Her name is probably influenced by that of DOWSABELL but more directly derives from 'blowze' as a word for 'a ruddy, fat-faced young woman' (*Chambers Dictionary*, 1998).

> We fair fine ladies, who park out our lives
> From common sheep-paths, cannot help the crows
> From flying over,—we're as natural still
> As Blowsalinda.
>
> ELIZABETH BARRETT BROWNING: *Aurora Leigh*, Bk III (1857)

**Blow.** (1) To move as a current of air, to send a current of air from the mouth or some other source, from Old English *blāwan*, related to modern German *blähen*, 'to blow up', 'to swell', and Latin *flare*, 'to blow'.

(2) To blossom, to flourish, from Old English *blōwan*, related to English bloom, also to German *blühen* and Latin *florere*, both meaning 'to bloom'.

(3) A stroke with the fist, probably of Germanic origin.

**Blow a kiss, To.** To kiss one's fingers and then move the hand away from the mouth in the direction of the person or people for whom the kiss is intended.

**Blow a raspberry, To.** A 20th-century slang expression for showing contempt of someone. In action, to blow a raspberry is to put one's tongue between closed lips and expel air forcibly with a resulting rude noise. It is otherwise known as a BRONX CHEER. Raspberry here is short for 'raspberry tart', RHYMING SLANG for fart. *See also* COCK A SNOOK.

**Blow away the cobwebs, To.** To clear one's mind by taking fresh air; to freshen oneself up.

**Blow great guns, To.** Of a wind, to blow so violently that its noise resembles the roar of artillery.

**Blow hot and cold, To.** To be inconsistent; to vacillate. The allusion is to the fable of a traveller who was entertained by a SATYR. The traveller blew on his cold fingers to warm them and afterwards on his hot broth to cool it. The indignant satyr turned him out of doors, because he blew both hot and cold with the same breath.

**Blowing Stone, The.** A rough block of red sarsen at Kingston Lisle, Oxfordshire, in the Vale of WHITE HORSE. It is about 3ft 6in (1m) high and is perforated with two or three holes, which, if blown properly, produce a wailing or moaning sound.

> 'Um do say, sir,' says mine host, rising purple-faced, while the moan is still coming out of the Stwun, 'as they used in old times to warn the countryside, by blawing the Stwun when the enemy was a-comin' – and as how folks could make un heered then for seven mile round'.
>
> THOMAS HUGHES: *Tom Brown's Schooldays*, Pt I, ch i (1857)

**Blow it!** An exclamation of annoyance or frustration.

**Blow me down** or **I'll be blowed!** Exclamations of surprise, admiration and the like, perhaps ultimately of nautical origin, as in the sea shanty 'Blow the man down'.

**Blow me tight!** An old expression of surprised wonder, incredulity or the like.

> 'If there's a soul will give me food, or find me in employ,
> By day or night, then blow me tight!' (he was a vulgar Boy).
>
> R.H. BARHAM: *Ingoldsby Legends*, 'Misadventures at Margate' (1840)

**Blow one's brains out, To.** To kill oneself by shooting oneself in the head.

**Blow one's horn, To.** In North America the equivalent of BLOW ONE'S OWN TRUMPET.

**Blow one's mind, To.** To alter one's mental state, as if by drugs.

**Blow one's own trumpet, To.** To boast about oneself; to sing one's own praises. The allusion is to HERALDS, who used to announce the knights who entered a list with a flourish of trumpets.

**Blow one's socks off, To.** *See* KNOCK ONE'S SOCKS OFF.

**Blow one's top, To.** To lose one's temper excessively; to lose all self-control. The allusion is probably to an oil well that blows as a gusher.

**Blowout.** A 'tuck-in' or feast, which swells the stomach; also a sudden burst in a tyre.

**Blow over, To.** To cease to be talked about, as a gale blows over or ceases.

**Blow someone up, To.** To give them a good scolding. The metaphor is from blasting by gunpowder.

**Blow the gaff, To.** To let out a secret, to inform against a companion. In carnival slang, a gaff is a concealed device that makes it impossible for the customer to win. To blow the gaff is thus to reveal the device's hidden mechanism, as if exposing a conjuror's trick.

**Blow the whistle on, To.** To inform on someone; to bring a stop to something. The allusion is either to the policeman's whistle or to that of the referee in a football match.

**At one blow.** *See under* AT.

**Body blow.** *See under* BODY.

**Come to blows, To.** *See under* COME.

**First blow is half the battle, The.** *See under* FIRST.

**Without striking a blow.** *See under* WITHOUT.

**Blue.** AZURE. *See under* COLOURS for its symbolisms.

The COVENANTERS wore blue as their badge in opposition to the scarlet of royalty. They based their choice on Numbers 15:38:

> Speak unto the children of Israel, and bid them that they make them fringes in the borders of their garments throughout their generations, and that they put upon the fringe of the borders a ribband of blue.

It was one of the traditional WHIG colours and is

now that of the CONSERVATIVES. It was also the colour of the Unionists in the American Civil War (1861–5); the colour of the CONFEDERATE STATES was grey. At Oxford and Cambridge, a blue is a student representing the university in rowing, cricket or some other sport.

**Blue baby.** A baby with a blue complexion resulting from a lack of oxygen in the blood. The cause is usually a congenital defect of the heart or the major blood vessels.

**Blue beans.** Lead shot.

**Bluebeard.** A BOGY; a murderous tyrant in Charles Perrault's *Contes du Temps* (1697). In this version Bluebeard goes on a journey leaving his new wife the keys of his castle, but forbidding her to enter one room. Curiosity overcomes her, and she opens the door to find the bodies of all Bluebeard's former wives. On his return he finds a blood spot on the key, which tells him of his wife's disobedience. He is about to cut off her head when her two brothers rush in and kill him. The tale is of an internationally widespread and ancient type. Gilles de Rais (1404–40), who fought alongside JOAN OF ARC, is usually regarded as the historical Bluebeard who tortured and murdered over 140 children, his nickname coming from his glossy black beard.

**Blue Billy.** A nickname of Admiral Sir William Cornwallis (1744–1819).

**Blue bird of happiness, The.** A visionary concept elaborated from Maurice Maeterlinck's play of this name, first produced in London in 1910. It tells the story of a boy and girl seeking 'the blue bird', which typifies happiness.

**Blue blood.** High or noble birth or descent. The expression translates Spanish *sangre azul*. The veins of the pure-blooded Spanish aristocrat, whose race had suffered no Moorish admixture, were believed to be more blue than those of mixed ancestry.

**Blue Boar.** A cognizance of Richard, Duke of York, father of Edward IV. The cognizance of Richard III was a white boar. After his defeat at Bosworth in 1485, White Boars were changed to Blue Boars.

**Blue Bonnets** or **Blue Caps.** The Highlanders of Scotland, or the Scots generally, from the blue woollen cap formerly in general use in Scotland.

**Blue book.** In Britain a parliamentary publication with a stiff blue paper cover. It is usually the report of a royal commission or a committee, but short ACTS OF PARLIAMENT, even without a wrapper, come under the same designation. *See also* WHITE PAPER.

**Bluebottle.** A policeman; also formerly an almsman or anyone else whose distinctive dress was blue. Shakespeare makes Doll Tearsheet denounce the BEADLE as a 'blue-bottle rogue'. The large buzzing fly of this name, *Calliphoria vomitoria*, has a metallic-blue body.

**Blue Caps.** *See* BLUE BONNETS.

**Blue cheese.** Cheese containing a blue mould, such as Stilton or Danish Blue.

**Bluecoat School.** Christ's Hospital is so called because the boys there wear a long blue coat with clerical bands and saffron-coloured socks. It was founded in the City of London in 1552, but moved to Horsham, West Sussex, in 1902. There were other charity schools so named.

**Blue-collar worker.** A manual industrial worker, who traditionally wears blue overalls. *See also* WHITE-COLLAR WORKER.

**Blue devils.** *See* BLUES.

**Blue Ensign.** The flag flown by auxiliary vessels of the Royal Navy. It is blue, with the UNION JACK in the corner. *See also* WHITE ENSIGN.

**Blue-eyed boy.** A favourite or 'darling'; a person highly thought of and given preference.

**Blue Flag.** An award given a seaside resort that meets international standards of cleanliness, especially on its beaches and in bathing areas.

**Blue for a boy.** Blue is a colour popularly associated with a boy, and pink with a girl. Blue has a link with the sky and with heaven, and hence in some cultures with males, who are or were regarded more highly than females. Pink, on the other hand, has more down-to-earth associations of flesh, warmth and gentleness, and as such has been linked with motherhood. The two colours are also complementary, representing the natural division of the sexes. The Huntington Art Gallery, San Marino, California, has complementary portraits of two 12-year-olds in Thomas Gainsborough's *Blue Boy* (1770), Jonathan Buttall, and Sir Thomas Lawrence's *Pinkie* (1795), Sarah Barrett Moulton. The paintings face each other in the Main Gallery.

**Blue funk.** *See under* FUNK.

**Blue Hen's Chickens.** The inhabitants of the state of Delaware. It is said that in the Revolutionary War (1775–83) one Captain Caldwell, commander of an efficient Delaware regiment, used to say that no cock could be truly game whose mother was not a blue hen. Hence his regiment became known as Blue Hen's Chickens, and the name was transferred to the inhabitants generally.

**Blue in the face.** Exhausted after a prolonged effort. The expression is common in a form such as: 'I tried until I was blue in the face.'

**Bluejackets.** Sailors in the navy, from the colour of their jackets (worn 1857–90 and subsequently replaced by jumpers). *See also* TARPAULIN.

**Blue John.** A bluish-purple fluorspar, found in the Blue John Mine near Castleton, Derbyshire, so called to distinguish it from BLACK JACK. John is said to refer to John Kirk, the miner who first noticed it.

**Blue laws.** In the USA laws such as SUMPTUARY LAWS and those regulating personal morals or interfering with personal freedom.

**Bluemantle.** One of the four English PURSUIVANTS attached to the College of Arms or Heralds' College, so called from his official robe.

**Blue movie.** A pornographic film. The name is fancifully derived from the custom of Chinese brothels being painted blue externally.

**Blue murder.** *See under* SCREAM.

**Bluenoses.** A nickname for the inhabitants of Nova Scotia.

> 'Pray Sir,' said one of my fellow-passengers, 'can you tell me the reason why the Nova Scotians are called Blue-noses?'
>
> 'It is the name of a potato,' said I, 'which they produce in the greatest perfection, and boast to be the best in the world. The Americans have, in consequence, given them the nickname of Blue Noses.'
>
> THOMAS HALIBURTON: *Sam Slick* (1836)

**Blue pencil.** The mark of editing or censorship. The term presumably relates to 'blue' in the sense 'obscene'.

**Blue Peter.** A blue flag with a white square in the centre, hoisted as a signal that a ship is about to sail. Peter is the personal name, standing for letter P in the former phonetic alphabet, and indicated by this flag in the International Code of Signals. *Blue Peter* is also the name of a popular children's television programme, first broadcast in 1958. It was so called because it aimed to set sail with its young viewers on a voyage of discovery.

**Blue plaque.** A blue ceramic plaque set into the façade of a building in London where a distinguished person lived, giving the relevant dates and details. The first was placed by the London County Council in 1903 on the house, Holly Lodge, Kensington, in which Thomas Macaulay died. In recent years plaques have commemorated events as well as lives. One set on an EAST END railway bridge in 1988 reads: 'The first Flying Bomb on London fell here, 13 June 1944.'

**Blueprint.** Strictly, a photographic print of a detailed plan, technical drawing or the like, in white lines on a blue background. The word is now used generally for any project, scheme or design.

**Blue Riband.** The liner gaining the record for the fastest Atlantic crossing was said to hold the Blue Riband of the Atlantic, and from 1907 to 1929 it was held by Cunard liner *Mauretania*. It then passed to the *Europa* (1930) and *Bremen* (1933) of Germany, to the *Rex* of Italy (1933), and to the French liner *Normandie* in 1935. After that it was held by the *Queen Mary* of Britain from 1938 until its capture by the American-owned *United States* in 1952. A trophy offered in 1935 by H.K. Hales (1868–1942) was first accepted by the United States Lines in 1952. *See also* BLUE RIBBON.

**Blue Ribbon.** The blue ribbon is the MOST NOBLE ORDER OF THE GARTER, the most coveted Order of Knighthood in the gift of the British Crown. The term is thus used to denote the highest honour attainable in any profession or walk of life. *See also* CORDON BLEU.

**Blue Ribbon Army.** A TEETOTAL society founded in the USA and extending to Britain by 1878, whose members wore a piece of narrow blue ribbon as a badge. It became the Gospel Temperance Union in 1883. The phrase came to be applied to teetotallers generally.

**Blue Ribbon of the Turf.** The DERBY STAKES. Lord George Bentinck sold his stud and found to his vexation that one of the horses sold won the Derby a few months later. Bewailing his ill luck, he said to Disraeli, 'Ah! You don't know what the Derby is.' 'Yes, I do,' replied Disraeli, 'it is the blue ribbon of the turf.'

**Blue-rinse brigade, The.** A derogatory group term for elderly and conservative women, who sometimes use a special rinse to give their grey or white hair a temporary blue tint.

**Blues.** A traditional form of American folk-song expressive of the unhappiness of black men and women in the DEEP SOUTH. The usual subject matter is love, the troubles that beset the singer or a nostalgic longing for home, coupled with an acceptance of life as it is. Blues usually consist of 12 bars made up of three 4-bar phrases in 4/4 time. They can be vocal or instrumental and have had more influence on JAZZ than on RAGTIME.

**Blues, The.** A mood of depression or dejection. The expression is short for the blue devils. *See also* OXFORD BLUES *under* REGIMENTAL AND DIVISIONAL NICKNAMES.

**Blueshirts.** An Irish FASCIST organization under General Eoin O'Duffy, former Commissioner of the Garda, which developed from the Army Comrades Association in the early 1930s. A Blueshirt battalion led by O'Duffy fought for General Franco in the Spanish Civil War (1936–9).

**Blue Sky Laws.** In the USA laws passed to protect the inexperienced buyer of stocks and bonds against fraud. The name is said to have its origin in a phrase used by one of the supporters of the earliest of these laws, who said that certain business operators were trying to capitalize 'the blue skies'.

**Blue stocking.** A now disparaging nickname for a scholarly or intellectual woman. In 1400 a society of men and women was formed in Venice, distinguished by the colour of their stockings and called *della calza*. A similar society appeared in Paris in 1590 and was the rage among lady *savants*. The name is derived directly from such a society, founded in about 1750 by Elizabeth Montagu, née Robinson (1720–1800), from the fact that a prominent member, Benjamin Stillingfleet (1702–71), wore blue worsted stockings in place of the usual black silk. The last of the clique was Miss Monckton, afterwards Countess of Cork, who died in 1840. Mrs Montagu is also said to have deliberately adopted the badge of the French *Bas bleu* club.

**Black and blue.** *See under* BLACK.

**Bolt from the blue, A.** *See under* BOLT.

**Boys in blue, The.** *See under* BOY.

**Dark blue.** *See under* DARK.

**Into the blue.** *See under* INTO.

**Light blue.** *See under* LIGHT.

**Look or feel blue, To.** *See under* LOOK.

**Once in a blue moon.** *See under* ONCE.

**Out of the blue.** *See under* OUT.

**Oxford blue.** *See under* OXFORD.

**Oxford Blues, The.** *See under* REGIMENTAL AND DIVISIONAL NICKNAMES.

**Prooshan blue.** *See under* PROOSHAN.

**Prussian blue.** *See under* PRUSSIAN.

**Queen of the Blues, The.** *See under* QUEEN.

**Scream, shout** or **yell blue murder, To.** *See under* SCREAM.

**True blue.** *See under* TRUE.

**Bluff.** In card games, a stake on a bad hand, as a ruse to lead an adversary to throw up his cards and forfeit his stake rather than risk them against the one who is bluffing. To bluff is thus generally to deceive by pretence.

**Bluff King Hal.** Henry VIII (r.1509–47), so nicknamed from his bluff, hearty manner.

**Call someone's bluff, To.** *See under* CALL.

**Double bluff.** *See under* DOUBLE.

**Blunderbore.** A nursery tale giant, the brother of CORMORAN, who put JACK THE GIANT-KILLER to bed and intended to kill him. Jack put a block of wood into the bed and crept under it. Blunderbore came with his club and broke the block to pieces. The next morning he was amazed to see Jack at breakfast. He asked Jack how he had slept. 'Pretty well,' said the Cornish hero, 'but once or twice I fancied a mouse tickled me with its tail.' This increased the giant's surprise. When hasty pudding was provided for breakfast, Jack stowed away such a bulk in a bag concealed under his clothes that the giant could not keep up with him. Jack cut the bag open to relieve his 'gorge' and the giant, to gain similar relief, plunged his knife into his stomach and so killed himself.

**Blurb.** A publisher's promotional description on the dustjacket or cover of a book. The word is said to have originated from the name 'Miss Blinda Blurb', coined in 1907 by the American humorist Gelett Burgess for the figure of a pulchritudinous young lady on a comic book jacket. Burgess later defined the word as follows:

> 1. A flamboyant advertisement; an inspired testimonial. 2. Fulsome praise; a sound like a publisher.
> *Burgess Unabridged* (1914)

**Blush, At first.** *See under* AT.

**Boa.** Pliny (*Natural History*, VIII, xiv (1st century AD)) fancifully says the word is from Latin *bos* ('cow'), from the belief that the snake sucked the milk of cows.

**Boadicea** or **Boudicca** (Celtic, 'victor'). The British warrior queen, wife of Prasutagus, king of the Iceni, a tribe inhabiting what is now Norfolk and Suffolk. On her husband's death (AD 60) the Romans seized the territory of the Iceni. The widow was scourged for her opposition and her two daughters raped. Boudicca raised a revolt of the Iceni and Trinovantes and burned Camulodunum (Colchester), Londinium (London) and Verulamium (St Albans). When finally routed by the Roman governor Suetonius Paulinus, she took poison. She is the subject of poems by William Cowper and Tennyson.

**Boanerges** (Hebrew *benī regesh*, 'sons of tumult'). A name given to James and John, the sons of Zebedee, because they wanted to call down 'fire from heaven' to consume the Samaritans for not 'receiving' Christ. The name is interpreted in the Bible as 'sons of thunder' (Mark 3:17).

**Boar. Boar, The.** Richard III. *See* BLUE BOAR.

**Boar's head.** The English custom of serving this as a Christmas dish is said to derive from Norse mythology. FREYR, the god of peace and plenty, rode the boar Gullinbursti. His festival was held at Yuletide, when a boar was sacrificed to his honour. The English custom is described in Washington Irving's *Sketch Book* ('The Christmas Dinner') (1819–20). The Boar's Head was brought in ceremoniously to a flourish of trumpets and a carol was sung. The following is the first verse of that sung before Prince Henry at St John's College, Oxford, at Christmas, 1607:

> The Boar is dead
> So, here is his head;
> What man could have done more
> Than his head off to strike,
> Meleager like
> And bring it as I do before?

**Boar's Head Tavern, The.** An inn immortalized by Shakespeare and Prince Hal, and formerly standing in Eastcheap. It was destroyed in the GREAT FIRE OF LONDON, but was rebuilt. Annual Shakespeare Dinners were held there until 1784. It was demolished in 1831. Washington Irving has an essay, 'The Boar's Head Tavern, Eastcheap', in his *Sketch Book* (1819–20).

**Blue Boar.** *See under* BLUE.

**Buddha and the boar.** *See under* BUDDHA.

**Calydonian boar, The.** *See under* CALYDONIAN.

**Wild boar of the Ardennes, The.** *See under* WILD.

**Board.** In all its many senses the word derives from Old English *bord*, related to Old Norse *borth*, 'ship's side', 'table'. The verb 'to board', meaning to enter a ship by force, was influenced by French *aborder*, 'to board', 'to land', from the same word *bord*, meaning the side of a ship, as in STARBOARD AND LARBOARD, inboard, overboard etc. In sailing, to make a board is to make a distance, leg or tack when working to windward.

To take something on board is to accept or understand instructions, a new situation or the like.

**Board.** A council that sits at a board or table, such as a board of directors, school board, the BOARD OF TRADE and so forth.

**Board, To.** To feed and lodge. The reference is to the board as a table.

**Boarding school.** A school where the pupils are fed and lodged as well as being taught. The term is sometimes euphemistically applied to prison.

**Board of Green Cloth, The.** So called from the green-covered table at which the board originally sat under the Lord Steward. It examined all the accounts of the English Royal Household and formerly dealt with all offenders within the verge of the palace, which extended 200 yards (about 60m) from the palace gate. Its powers were curtailed in 1782, and it is now concerned with the royal domestic arrangements under the Master of the Household.

In modern slang the board of green cloth is the card table or the billiard table.

**Board of Trade, The.** A government department concerned with the various aspects of trade, first set up in 1786. It developed from the various PRIVY COUNCIL Committees of Trade appointed from 1622 onwards, which were then much concerned with colonial matters. In 1970 it merged with the Ministry of Technology to form the Department of Trade and Industry (DTI). Michael Heseltine then revived the old title of President of the Board of Trade when he took charge of the DTI in 1992, and it was initially retained by his Labour successor in 1997. It was dropped in 1998, however, after a CABINET reshuffle.

**Above board.** *See under* ABOVE.

**Across the board.** *See under* ACROSS.

**Back to the drawing board.** *See under* BACK.

**Big Board.** *See under* BIG.

**Board school.** *See* SCHOOLBOARDS.

**Bristol board.** *See under* BRISTOL.

**Full board.** *See under* FULL.

**Go by the board, To.** To go for good; to be completely destroyed or lost. When a ship's mast is carried away it is said 'to go by the board', board meaning the ship's side.

**Half board.** *See under* HALF.

**Sweep the board, To.** *See under* SWEEP.

**Trade board.** *See under* TRADE.

**Tread the boards, To.** *See under* TREAD.

**Walk the boards, To.** *See under* WALK.

**Boast of England, The.** A name given to TOM THUMB by Richard Johnson, who in 1599 published a 'history of this ever-renowned soldier, the Red Rose Knight, surnamed The Boast of England'.

**Boat. Boater.** A flat-topped, shallow-crowned straw hat, usually trimmed with a band of ribbon, popular in late Victorian and EDWARDIAN England and seen until the early 1930s at cricket matches, picnics and boating parties (hence the name). It is the established headgear of Harrow School and was formerly much favoured by butchers and fishmongers, some of whom still sport it.

> Surprisingly large numbers of schools still want straw boaters for summer, though some leave it as an option.
>
> *The Times* (3 September 1994)

**Boatswain.** Lord Byron's favourite dog, buried at Newstead Abbey. His master wrote a 26-line epitaph, concluding:

> To mark a friend's remains these stones arise;
> I never knew but one, – and here he lies.
>
> 'Inscription on the Monument of a Newfoundland Dog' (30 November 1808)

**All in the same boat.** *See under* ALL.

**Burn one's boats, To.** *See under* BURN.

**Jolly boat.** *See under* JOLLY.

**Liberty boat.** *See under* LIBERTY.

**Miss the boat, To.** *See under* MISS.

**Push the boat out, To.** *See under* PUSH.

**Rock the boat, To.** *See under* ROCK.

**Wade's boat.** *See under* WADE.

**Boaz.** The wealthy landowner from Bethlehem who was the husband of RUTH, a Moabitess. He first encountered her when she was gleaning in his fields (Ruth 2:5) and was impressed by her goodness and loyalty to her mother-in-law, Naomi. Their son Obed was the father of Jesse who was the father of DAVID, so that the royal line of the Jews was rooted in both Bethlehem and Moab.

**Jachin and Boaz.** *See under* JACHIN.

**Bob.** Slang for the old SHILLING. This use, of unknown origin, dates from about 1800. It is also a term used in campanology denoting certain changes in the long peals. A bob minor is rung on six bells, a bob triple on seven, a bob major on eight, a bob royal on ten, and a bob maximus on twelve.

**Bob acres.** *See under* ACRE.

**Bob-a-Job Week.** A fund-raising week instituted by the BOY SCOUTS in 1949. All kinds of jobs were undertaken, some for their publicity value, for the payment of one shilling. It became an annual effort but with the declining value of the 'bob' and the advent of DECIMAL CURRENCY, Scout Job Week took its place in 1972.

**Bobbed hair.** Hair that has been cut short or docked like a bobtailed horse.

**Bob for apples** or **cherries, To.** To try and catch them in the mouth while they float about in a bucket of water or swing backwards and forwards, suspended on a string.

**Bob's Own.** *See under* REGIMENTAL AND DIVISIONAL NICKNAMES.

**Bob's your uncle.** There you are; it's that simple. The phrase is said to have been occasioned by A.J. Balfour's promotion by his uncle Robert Arthur Talbot Gascoyne-Cecil, 3rd Marquis of Salisbury, the TORY Prime Minister, to the post of Chief Secretary for Ireland. Balfour had previously been made President of the Local Government Board in 1886, then Secretary for Scotland with a seat in the CABINET. The suggestion of nepotism was difficult to ignore. *See also* BALFOUR'S POODLE; BLOODY BALFOUR.

**Dry bob.** *See under* DRY.

**Ragtag and bobtail.** *See under* RAG.

**Wet bob.** *See under* WET.

**Bobadil, Captain.** A character in Ben Jonson's *Every Man in his Humour* (1598), a military braggart of the first water. His name was probably derived from that of Boabdil, the last Moorish king of Granada (1482–3, 1486–92), whose own name is a corruption of Arabic *abū 'abd allah* ('father of the servant of God'). *See also* ABDULLAH.

**Bobbery.** A noisy commotion or shindy. The word, which was much used in India, comes from Hindi *bāp re*, 'Oh, father!' a common exclamation of surprise.

**Bobby.** A policeman, from Sir Robert Peel, Home Secretary, who established the Metropolitan Police in 1829. *See also* PEELER.

**Bobby-dazzler.** Something showy, striking or exciting to look at, especially an attractive girl.

**Bobby socks.** White ankle-length socks commonly worn by teenage girls in the USA in the early 1940s. Hence bobbysoxers for the adolescent girls who wore such socks, especially as fans of popular singers.

**Bocland** or **bookland.** A term denoting land of inheritance granted from folkland (common land) in Anglo-Saxon England by the king and the Witan by written charter or book. It was at first given to the church, but also to lay subjects. The place-name Buckland is derived from this.

**Bodice, Liberty.** *See under* LIBERTY.

**Bodkin.** Originally a small dagger, but in Elizabeth I's reign the word was applied to the stiletto pin worn by ladies in their hair. Shakespeare probably used it in this sense. It later came to denote the blunt, large-eyed needle used for drawing tape through openwork. The word itself is probably Celtic in origin.

**Bodleian Library, The.** The famous Oxford library, named from Sir Thomas Bodley (1545–1613), who restored it in 1598. It is rich in manuscript collections, is second in importance in England only to the BRITISH LIBRARY and receives copies of all publications under the Copyright Acts. *See also* COPYRIGHT LIBRARY.

**Bodmin, The Beast of.** *See under* BEAST.

**Body. Body bag.** A bag for carrying a corpse from the scene of warfare or an accident, such as a plane crash.

**Body blow.** In boxing a punch to the body; figuratively, therefore, a shattering blow, a severe setback or shock.

**Body building.** The carrying out of regular exercises with the aim of developing an obviously muscular body.

**Body colour.** Opaque paint containing 'body' or density.

**Body corporate.** A legal term for a group of individuals united into a corporation for a particular enterprise.

**Body language.** The use of movements of the body, or gestures, mostly unconsciously, to convey a meaning or information. Thus, a nod of the head means 'yes' and a shake of the head means 'no'. Different races have differing body languages.

**Body-line bowling.** In CRICKET fast bowling aimed at the batsman's body rather than the wicket with the intention of forcing him to give a catch while defending his person. The accurate but dangerous bowling of Harold Larwood and Bill Voce won the ASHES for England in 1932–3 but aroused a storm of indignation in Australia and caused a modification in the laws of cricket.

**Body piercing.** The piercing of holes in parts of the body other than the ear lobes, a fashion among young people in the 1990s.

**Body politic.** A whole nation considered as a political corporation, otherwise the state.

**Body search.** A search, especially by customs officials or the police, of a person's body for illicit weapons, drugs, and the like.

**Body-snatcher.** Formerly, a person who stole newly buried corpses to sell them for dissection. *See also* BURKE; RESURRECTIONISTS.

By a play on the words, a BUMBAILIFF was so called, because his duty was to snatch or capture a delinquent.

**Body stocking.** A woman's undergarment covering the trunk and legs. It is similar to a bodysuit, or body, a close-fitting one-piece garment worn for sports and exercising.

**Astral body.** *See under* ASTRAL.

**Heavenly body.** *See under* HEAVENLY.

**Keep body and soul together, To.** To survive; from the notion that the SOUL gives life. Latin *anima* and Greek *psukhē* mean both 'soul' and 'life'. According to Homeric mythology and the common theory of 'ghosts', the departed soul retains the shape and semblance of the body. *See also* ASTRAL BODY.

**Over my dead body.** *See under* OVER.

**Seven bodies, The.** *See under* SEVEN.

**Boeotia.** The ancient name for a district in central Greece, popularly said to be so called from its abundance of cattle. The fable is that CADMUS was conducted thence by an ox (Greek *bous*) to the spot where he built Thebes. *See also* AULIS.

**Boeotian.** Rude and unlettered. The ancient Boeotians were an agricultural and pastoral people, and the Athenians used to say that they were as dull and thick as their own atmosphere. However, Hesiod, PINDAR, Corinna, Plutarch, Pelopidas and Epaminondas were Boeotians.

**Boethius.** Roman philosopher and writer (*c.*AD 475–*c.*525). His manuals and translations from the Greek were widely used in the Middle Ages. Both ALFRED THE GREAT and Chaucer translated his *De Consolatione Philosophiae*.

**B of BK.** Mysterious initials applied to himself in Arthur Orton's diary (*see* TICHBORNE CASE). They were said to denote 'Baronet of British Kingdom' and were for some time popularly applied to anyone who put on airs.

**Boffin.** A nickname used by the RAF in the Second World War for a research scientist, one of the BACKROOM BOYS. It passed into general use in the 1940s. Its origin is uncertain. One theory derives it from an obsolete torpedo bomber, the Blackburn Baffin, itself named after the navigator William Baffin (*c.*1584–1622), discoverer in 1616 of Baffin Bay in the North Atlantic. The word has now passed into school slang to mean a studious person or 'swot'.

> Although boffin isn't really an offensive name, it sounds bad and makes us feel like we're not human – believe me, we are! So even though we may get ten out of ten at school, please treat us normally. OK?!
> *The Times* (letter from 11-year-old reader of children's section *meg@*) (16 January 1999)

**Bog, The Serbonian.** *See under* SERBONIAN.

**Bogey.** In golf the number of strokes a scratch player should need for the course or for a single hole. The number is settled by the committee of the particular club and is generally taken to be the lowest that a good average player could do it in. It is usually the same as par at a hole, but among American players is often one stroke above par.

The term is first recorded in the 1890s and may relate to a BOGY as an imaginary opponent, the precise origin perhaps being in 'The Bogey Man', a popular song then current. The story goes that in 1890 Dr Thomas Browne, RN, honorary secretary of the Great Yarmouth club, was playing against a Major Wellman, the match being against the 'ground score', as the name of the scratch value of each hole. This system was new to the major, and he exclaimed, thinking of the song, that his invisible and apparently invincible opponent was a regular 'bogey man'. The expression caught on in Great Yarmouth and was subsequently taken up by other golfers. *See also* COLONEL BOGEY.

**Boggard** or **boggart** (perhaps from a form of 'bug'). A north of England name for a GOBLIN or spectre, especially one haunting a particular place. It is the same as a BROWNIE OR KOBOLD and the Scottish 'bogle'. When a horse took fright it was said to have seen a boggart. In the ISLE OF MAN a buggane was an evil creature with a great head and body, with long teeth and nails. *See also* BOGY; BUG.

**Bogomils.** Members of a heretical sect that arose in Bulgaria in the 10th century. Most historians are agreed that their name comes from Bogomil, the priest who founded the heresy, his own Slavic name meaning 'beloved of God'. Their philosophy centred on the duality of the world and the constant struggle between Good and Evil. In their view, the material world and the human body were the work of the Devil, while heaven and the human soul were manifestations of Good.

**Bogtrotter.** A derogatory nickname for an Irishman, especially a peasant. The reference is to the skill of the rural Irish in making their way across bogs by trotting from tussock to tussock.

**Bogy.** A HOBGOBLIN, a person or object of terror, a bugbear. The word first appeared in the 19th century and is perhaps connected with the Scottish 'bogle' and so with the obsolete BUG. There was also an evil creature in Manx folklore called a buggane. *See also* BOGEY; BOGGARD.

**Bohemia. Bohemian.** A term applied to artists, writers and others who lead an unconventional life. Originally the name was applied to a GYPSY, from the belief that Bohemia was the home of the gypsies, or because the first to arrive in France, in the 15th century, came by way of Bohemia.

**Bohemian Brethren.** A religious sect formed from the HUSSITES which arose in Prague in the 15th century. They were the forerunners of the MORAVIANS.

**Queen of Bohemia, The.** *See under* QUEEN.

**Boil. Boiled shirt, A.** A white shirt or, more usually, a dress shirt.

**Boiling point, To be at.** To be very angry or seething with rage. Boiling point is properly the point at which water under ordinary conditions boils (100°C/212°F).

**Ordeal of boiling water.** *See under* ORDEAL.

**Bold. As bold as brass.** *See under* AS.

**Make bold, To.** To take the liberty; to venture.

**Put a bold face on the matter, To.** To make the best of a bad matter; to bear up under something disagreeable.

**Boleyn, Anne.** The beautiful but thoughtless young woman (1501–36) who became the second wife of Henry VIII in 1533 following his divorce from CATHERINE OF ARAGON. When she failed to bear him a son, Henry charged her with adultery, divorced her in turn and had her beheaded. She is the subject of numerous plays and historical novels.

**Bollywood.** A nickname for the Indian popular film industry, which is based in Bombay. The word is a blend of 'Bombay' and HOLLYWOOD. The standard product of such companies as Bombay Talkies Ltd was originally garish imitation of Hollywood entertainment.

**Bolognese. Bolognese school.** There were three periods to the Bolognese school in painting: the Early, the Roman and the ECLECTIC. The first was founded by Marco Zoppo in the 15th century, and its best exponent was Francesco Francia (*c*.1450– *c*.1517). The second was founded in the 16th century by Bagnacavallo, its main exponents being Francesco Primaticcio (1504–70), Pellegrino Tibaldi (1527–96) and Niccolò dell'Abbate (*c*.1512–71). The third was founded by Carracci at the close of the 16th century, with its best masters Domenico Domenichino (1581–1641), Giovanni Lanfranco (1582–1647), Il Guercino (1591–1666) and Francesco Albani (1578–1660).

**Spaghetti bolognese.** *See under* SPAGHETTI.

**Boloney** or **baloney.** Nonsense, rubbish. Also a Bologna sausage. The former sense may derive from the latter, since the sausage is traditionally stuffed with odds and ends from slaughter.

**Bolshevik.** Properly a member of the Russian revolutionary party under LENIN, which seized power in 1917, aiming at the establishment of the supreme power of the proletariat and declaring war on capitalism. The Bolsheviks were so called from the fact that at the party conferences of 1902–3 the Leninists were the majority group (Russian *bol'she*, 'more'). The defeated minority were called MENSHEVIKS.

**Bolshie** or **Bolshy.** A contraction of BOLSHEVIK, used to denote a person with left-wing tendencies, or a rebellious or 'difficult' person.

**Bolsover, Beast of.** *See under* BEAST.

**Bolt.** The word was originally used for a short, thick arrow with a blunt head, as fired from a crossbow. It then came to be applied to the door lock, in which the bar is of similar shape.

**Bolt, To.** Of a horse, to shoot off like a bolt or arrow.

**Bolt from the blue, A.** A sudden and wholly unexpected event or catastrophe, like a thunderbolt from the blue sky, or a flash of lightning without warning. Here bolt is used for lightning, although strictly a meteorite is a thunderbolt.

**Bolt in tun.** In HERALDRY a bird-bolt, in pale, piercing through a tun, often used as a PUBLIC HOUSE SIGN. The punning crest of Serjeant Bolton, who died in 1787, was 'on a wreath a tun erect proper, transpierced by an arrow fesseways or'. Such punning signs or REBUSES were quite common for names such as Luton, Hatton or Ashton.

**Bolt one's food, To.** To swallow it quickly without waiting to chew it.

**Bolt upright.** Straight as an arrow shot from a crossbow.

> Skittish she was, and jolly as a colt,
> Tall as a mast and upright as a bolt.
>
> CHAUCER: *Canterbury Tales*, 'The Miller's Tale' (*c*.1387) (modern translation by Nevill Coghill, 1951)

**Fool's bolt is soon shot** or **spent, A.** *See under* FOOL.

**Nuts and bolts.** *See under* NUT.

**Shoot one's bolt, To.** *See under* SHOOT.

**Bomb.** A metal shell filled with an explosive. The word comes from Greek *bombos*, of imitative origin, and thus akin to English boom.

**Bomb-happy.** An expression current in the Second World War to describe someone in a state of near-hysteria induced by bombing, which often took the form of irrational euphoria. A similar expression is trigger-happy, as applied to someone liable to shoot at any time. *See also* SLAP-HAPPY.

**Ban the bomb.** *See under* BAN.

**Brown Bomber.** *See under* BROWN.

**Carpet bombing.** *See under* CARPET.

**Drop a bombshell, To.** *See under* DROP.

**King Bomba.** A nickname given to Ferdinand II (1810–59) king of Naples (r. from 1830), for his heavy bombardment of Sicilian cities in 1848 to suppress a revolution. His son Francis II was called Bomba II, or Bombalino ('Little Bomba'), for his bombardment of Palermo in 1860.

**Like a bomb.** *See under* LIKE.

**Bombast.** Literally the produce of the bombyx or silkworm (Greek *bombux*). The word was formerly applied to material used for padding and hence to 'padded' or inflated language.

**Bombay. Bombay bloomers.** An old nickname for army shorts.

**Bombay duck.** A fish, the bummalo, which is dried and eaten with curries. The name is partly a corruption of bummalo itself, partly from

Bombay, the port in India from which it was exported.

**Bombiti.** *See* BARISAL GUNS.

**Bon. Bon accord** (French, 'good agreement'). The motto of Aberdeen, Scotland, gained after 1308, when the party of Robert BRUCE ejected Edward I's garrison of English soldiers.

**Bon Gaultier Ballads.** Parodies of contemporary poetry by W.E. Aytoun and Sir Theodore Martin. They first appeared in *Tait's*, *Fraser's* and *Blackwood's Magazines* in the 1840s, and in volume form in 1885. The two writers took their pseudonym from Rabelais, who uses *Bon Gaultier* (literally 'good Walter') in the Prologue to GARGANTUA (1534) in the general sense of 'good fellow'.

**Bon mot** (French, 'good word'). A clever or apt remark.

**Bon ton** (French, 'good tone'). Sophisticated manners or the world of fashionable society in general.

**Bon vivant** (French, 'good living'). A person who enjoys good living, especially good food and drink.

**Bon viveur** (French, 'good liver'). A person who is seen and known to enjoy good food and drink and a comfortable or self-indulgent life generally. The expression is not genuine French.

**Bon voyage** (French, 'good journey'). An expression wishing a pleasant journey to a departing traveller, used because the English, though inveterate travellers, have no native phrase to convey this thought.

**Bona. Bona dea** (Latin, 'good goddess'). A Roman goddess supposed to preside over the earth and all its blessings. She was worshipped by the Vestals as the goddess of chastity and fertility. Her festival was 1 May, and no men were allowed to be present at the celebration.

**Bona fide** (Latin, 'with good faith'). Real, genuine. In law, *bona fides* (Latin, 'good faith') is used with reference to credentials, to a proof of identity or to the ability to perform what one professes to perform.

**Bonanza** (Spanish, literally 'calm sea', from Latin *bonus*, 'good', and *malacia*, 'dead calm'). The term was applied in the mining areas of the USA to the discovery of a rich vein or pocket, when the mine was said to be 'in bonanza'. The word is now generally used for an unexpected source of wealth or success. The 'calm sea' of the original sense is one that brings smooth sailing and hence a fortunate passage.

**Bond. Afrikaner Bond.** *See under* AFRIKANER.

**English bond.** *See under* ENGLISH.

**James Bond.** The ultimate superspy, famous from the novels by Ian Fleming (1908–64) and from the gripping films based on them. He is intelligent and resourceful, a technological adept, a lover of fast cars and a wily seducer. Wherever his adventures and misadventures take him, he is always ultimately the victor and the avenger. He first appears in *Casino Royale* (1953). His persona is an amalgam of some of the men whom Fleming met when he was serving in British Naval Intelligence in the Second World War. His name, more prosaically, was taken from that of James Bond, an ornithologist and writer on birds who was one of Fleming's neighbours in Jamaica.

**Treasury bonds.** *See under* TREASURY.

**Bonduca.** Another form of BOADICEA or Boudicca. John Fletcher wrote a tragedy of this name, which was first performed in 1613–14.

**Bone. Bone, To.** To steal. Shakespeare (*Henry VI, Pt II*, I, iii (1590)) says, 'By these ten bones, my lords,' meaning the fingers, and calls the ten fingers 'pickers and stealers' (*Hamlet*, III, ii (1600)).

**Bonehead.** A stupid or unintelligent person.

**Bone idle.** Extremely lazy.

**Bone of contention.** A disputed point; a point not yet settled. The metaphor is taken from two dogs fighting for a bone.

**Boneshaker.** An old type of bicycle of the days before pneumatic tyres, or any 'old crock' of a vehicle.

**Bone up on, To.** To study intensively; to gain information on. The expression suggests a stiffening of one's knowledge, as a strip of whalebone strengthens a corset, but there may also be an influence from the classical translations published by Henry Bohn (1796–1884) and in demand among 19th-century students when 'cramming' for an examination.

**As dry as a bone.** *See under* AS.

**Bag of bones.** *See under* BAG.

**Bare bones, The.** *See under* BARE.

**Barebones Parliament, The.** *See under* BARE.

**Bred in the bone.** *See under* BRED.

**Crazy bone.** *See under* CRAZY.

**Devil's bones.** *See under* DEVIL.

**Feel in one's bones, To.** *See under* FEEL.

**Funny bone.** *See under* FUNNY.

**Have a bone in one's leg, To.** An excuse given to children for not moving from one's seat. Similarly 'to have a bone in one's arm' is to be excused from using it for the present.

**Have a bone in one's throat, To.** To be unable to talk; to be unable to answer a question.

**Have a bone to pick, To.** To have a bone to pick with someone is to have a cause for dispute with them. This is another allusion to the kennel: two dogs and one bone invariably form a basis for a fight.

**Make no bones about, To.** To be direct and candid. Dice are called bones, and the French *flatter le dé*, 'to slide the dice', is the opposite of the English expression.

**Napier's bones.** *See under* NAPIER.

**Near** or **close to the bone.** *See under* NEAR.

**Old bones.** *See under* OLD.

**Skin and bones, To be.** *See under* SKIN.

**Work one's fingers to the bone, To.** *See under* WORK.

**Boney.** A slang name for NAPOLEON BONAPARTE. 'If you aren't a good boy Boney will catch you,' was an old threat from a children's nurse or harassed parent. Napoleon's threatened invasion of England was a real threat in the early years of the 19th century.

**Bonfire.** Originally a bone fire, that is, a fire made of bones, especially a ceremonial one in MIDSUMMER.

> I have heard of another Custom that is practised in some Parts of Lincolnshire, where, on some peculiar Nights, they make great Fires in the publick Streets of their Towns with Bones of Oxen, Sheep, &c. which are heaped together for some time before. I am apt to believe this Custom was continued in memory of burning their Dead, and that from hence came the original of Bonefires.
>
> JOHN BAGFORD: Introduction to John Leland's *Collectanea*, vol i (1700)

**Bonhomme.** *See* JACQUES.

**Boniface** (Latin *Bonifatius*, from *bonum fatum*, 'good fate'). The patron saint of Germany, a west Saxon saint, whose original name was Wynfrith (680–754). He was archbishop of Mainz from 746. His feast-day is 5 June.

**Bonne bouche** (French, 'good mouthful'). A tasty morsel or titbit.

**Bonnet.** In old slang a player at a gaming table or an accomplice at auctions, who lures others to play or bid. The person is so called because he blinded the eyes of his dupes, just as if he had 'bonneted them' or pulled their hats down over their eyes.

**Bonnet monkey.** An Indian macaque, which has a bonnet-like tuft of hair.

**Bonnet piece.** A gold coin of James V of Scotland, on which the king's head is depicted wearing a bonnet.

**Bonnet rouge** (French, 'red cap'). The red LIBERTY CAP worn by the leaders of the French Revolution in 1789.

**Balmoral bonnet** or **bluebonnet.** *See under* BALMORAL.

**Blue Bonnets.** *See under* BLUE.

**Cast one's bonnet over a windmill, To.** *See under* CAST.

**Glengarry bonnet.** *See under* GLENGARRY.

**Have a bee in one's bonnet, To.** *See under* BEE.

**Poke bonnet.** *See under* POKE.

**Bonnie Dundee.** John Graham of Claverhouse, Viscount Dundee (1649–89), a noted supporter of the Stuart cause and a relative of Montrose. He was killed at the Battle of Killiecrankie.

**Booby.** An ignorant or foolish person, or the losing player in a game.

> Ye bread-and-butter rogues, do ye run from me?
> An my side would give me leave, I would so hunt ye,
> Ye porridge-gutted slaves, ye real-broth boobies!
>
> FRANCIS BEAUMONT and JOHN FLETCHER: *The Humorous Lieutenant*, III, vii (1619)

A species of gannet (*Sula piscator*) is called a booby, from its apparent stupidity.

**Booby hatch.** An American slang expression for a psychiatric hospital.

**Booby prize.** A prize, often of a humorous or worthless kind, given to the person who has the lowest score in a game or contest or who has given the worst performance.

**Booby trap.** A trap for an unsuspecting victim, such an object balanced on top of a door to fall down on to the person who opens it. More deadly booby traps are the hidden explosive devices used in warfare.

**Boodle's.** A London CLUB founded in 1762 by Edward Boodle. It was originally in PALL MALL, but in 1783 it moved to its present premises in St James's Street. Its members are chiefly country gentlemen in London on business. Past members include Pitt the Elder and Pitt the Younger, Edward Gibbon, William Wilberforce, Beau BRUMMELL and the Duke of Wellington.

**Boogie-woogie.** A style of piano JAZZ in which the left hand maintains a heavy repetitive pattern of eight beats to the bar while the right hand improvises. It was probably developed in the Middle West early in the 20th century. The name seems to have originated in Clarence 'Pinetop' Smith's 'Pinetop's Boogie-Woogie' (1928). Boogie already existed as a slang word for a party. Its origin is uncertain. Woogie was added as a rhyming element. *See also* BLUES; RAGTIME; SWING.

**Boojum.** *See* SNARK.

**Book** (Old English *bōc*, related to modern 'beech'). The bark of beech trees was originally used as a writing surface.

In betting the book is the record of people's bets on the various horses made by the bookmaker.

In WHIST, bridge and other card games, the book is the first six tricks taken by either side.

**Book a ticket** or **seat, To.** To reserve or buy a ticket or seat, as for a train journey or a theatre performance. In coaching days and in the early days of railways, tickets sold at booking offices were written out and entered up in the books by clerks.

**Booked, To be.** To have a previous commitment or engagement and so to be unavailable. Also, to have something entered in writing against one and so to be caught or penalized. The reference is to the policeman's or referee's notebook in which the offence is recorded.

**Booked up, To be.** To be fully taken or reserved, so that no further appointments can be offered or reservations accepted.

**Book-keeping.** A system of keeping debtor and creditor accounts in books provided for the purpose, either by single or by DOUBLE ENTRY. In the former each debit or credit is entered only once in the ledger, either as a debit or credit item, under the customer's or salesman's name. In double entry, each item is entered twice in the ledger, once on the debit and once on the credit. The daily debits and credits are entered in the day book, and these are ultimately 'posted' in the ledger. In the waste book each transaction is entered as it occurs.

**Bookland.** *See* BOCLAND.

**Bookmaker** or **bookie.** A person who makes a professional living by taking bets, usually on horse races, and who pays out to winning betters.

**Book of Books, The.** The Bible, also called simply 'the Book', or 'the good Book'.

**Book of Canons, The.** A collection of 178 canons enacted by the councils of Nicaea, Ancyra, Neocaesarea, Laodicea, Gangra, Antioch, Constantinople, Ephesus and Chalcedon. It was first published in 1610 and is probably of late 4th- or early 5th-century origin.

**Book of Changes, The.** The *I Ching*, an ancient Chinese book of DIVINATION. Answers to questions are obtained by reading the text that accompanies one of 64 hexagrams, selected at random.

**Book of Common Prayer, The.** The official liturgy of the CHURCH OF ENGLAND first issued in 1549 under Cranmer. It was modified in 1552, 1559 and 1604, revised after the RESTORATION and reissued in 1662. The amended Prayer Books of 1927 and 1928 were approved by Convocation but rejected by Parliament.

Since the 1960s the Book of Common Prayer has been increasingly displaced by alternative forms of service commonly known as Series 1, Series 2 and Series 3. The Alternative Service Book of 1980 contains three alternative forms of Communion Service, namely, revised versions of Series 1 and 2 (largely based on the Book of Common Prayer), and the more controversial Series 3 (Revised) in modern English. The other services are all in the Series 3 idiom, those for the Visitation and Communion of the Sick being dropped. None of the readings (formerly called lessons) is from the AUTHORIZED VERSION (*see under* BIBLE).

**Book of Hours.** A book of devotions for private use, especially during the CANONICAL HOURS. Such books in the later Middle Ages were often beautifully and lavishly illuminated, and they have a particular importance in the history of the arts.

**Book of Kells, The.** Kells, an ancient town in County Meath, Ireland, was the see of a bishop until the 13th century. Among its antiquities, and now preserved in the Library of Trinity College, Dublin, is the 8th-century *Book of Kells*, one of the finest extant illuminated manuscripts of the Gospels in Latin.

**Book of life** or **of fate, The.** In biblical language, a register of the names of those who are to inherit eternal life (Philemon 4:3; Revelation 20:12).

**Book of Mormon, The.** *See* MORMONS.

**Book of Numbers.** In the Old Testament the Fourth Book of Moses, so named from the 'numbering' of the Israelites in chapters 3 and 26.

**Book of the Dead, The.** A collection of ancient Egyptian texts, both religious and magical, concerned with guidance for the safe conduct of the soul through Amenti (the Egyptian HADES). The Egyptians called it *The Book of Going Forth by Day*, and copies, or parts of it, were buried with the mummy. There is a variety of texts.

**Book of the Dun Cow, The.** An early 12th-century manuscript account of earlier Irish romance. It derives its name from the story that it is a copy of those written down on the hide of a cow by St Kieran of Clonmacnoise in the 6th century. *See also* DUN COW.

**Book of words.** A libretto or the script of a play.

**Books of Discipline.** The books which formed the basis of the constitution and procedure of the CHURCH OF SCOTLAND after the REFORMATION. The first was drawn up under John Knox in 1566, and the second, which amplified the first, between 1575 and 1578.

**Bookworm.** Someone who is always poring over books, so called in allusion to the maggot that eats holes in books, and lives in and on their pages.

**Battle of the Books, The.** *See under* BATTLE.

**Bell, book and candle.** *See under* BELL.

**Black Book.** *See under* BLACK.

**Blue book.** *See under* BLUE.

**Bring to book, To.** *See under* BRING.

**Closed book, A.** *See under* CLOSE.

**Close the books, To.** *See under* CLOSE.

**Coffee-table book.** *See under* COFFEE.

**Cook the books, To.** *See under* COOK.

**Devil's books.** *See under* DEVIL.

**Domesday Book.** *See under* DOMESDAY.

**Exeter Book, The.** *See under* EXETER.

**In my book.** In my way of seeing things. So similarly, 'not in my book', not in my way of doing things.

**In someone's good** or **bad books, To be.** *See under* GOOD.

**In the book.** In the telephone directory or phone book.

**Keep the books, To.** To keep a record of an organization's financial transactions. *See also* BOOK-KEEPING.
**King's Book, The.** *See under* KING.
**Kiss the book, To.** *See under* KISS.
**Make a book, To.** To arrange or take bets on a particular event or occurrence.
**On the books.** On the list of a club, on the list of candidates, or any official or members' list. Conversely, 'to take one's name off the books' is to withdraw from a club, organization or register.
**Open book, An.** *See under* OPEN.
**Penguin Books.** *See under* PENGUIN.
**Read someone like a book, To.** *See under* READ.
**Red Book.** *See under* RED.
**Red Book of Hergest, The.** *See under* RED.
**Red Book of the Exchequer.** *See under* RED.
**Sibylline books, The.** *See under* SIBYL.
**Take a leaf out of someone's book, To.** *See under* LEAF.
**Throw the book at, To.** *See under* THROW.
**Turn-up for the books, A.** *See under* TURN.
**Yellow books.** *See under* YELLOW.
**Yellow Book, The.** *See under* YELLOW.

**Booker Prize.** The leading British annual literary prize, launched in 1968 by the firm of Booker McConnell and in 1998 worth £20,000. It is for a novel first published between 1 October and 30 September in the year of the award, and since 1981 it has been presented live on television. Winning novels sometimes experience a marked increase in sales. Some awards have been controversial, however.

**Boom, Baby.** *See under* BABY.

**Boomerang.** A curved wooden missile developed by the Australian Aborigines, varying from 2ft (60cm) to 2ft 9in (84cm) in length. When it is thrown, it describes a wide arc and returns to, or near to, the thrower.

Metaphorically a boomerang is a scheme or proposal that recoils on its originator.

**Boon companion.** A convivial or congenial companion, from Old French *bon*, 'good'.

**Boondoggle, To.** In North American usage to do useless or futile work. The word is of uncertain origin. According to one account it was invented in the 1930s by an American scoutmaster, Robert H. Link, for a type of braided lanyard. This took time or trouble to make, hence the word passed to a futile task in general.

**Boone, Daniel.** The American pioneer and frontiersman (1733–1820) renowned for his prowess and exploits. He became a hunter when only 12 years old and at one time was captured and adopted by the Shawnees. He is now part of American folklore.

**Boop, Betty.** A supposedly sexy star of short cartoon films produced by Max Fleischer (1883–1972) in the 1920s and 1930s. She had big sparkling eyes, a button nose and a squeaky voice, and often appeared in various degrees of undress. Her tagline was 'Boop-Boop-a-Doop'. She was the first cartoon character to be censored, and by the mid-1930s had abandoned her provocative garter, short skirt and *décolletage*.

**Boot. Boot and saddle.** The order to cavalry to get packed and ready to go. It is a corruption of French *boute selle*, 'place saddle', and has nothing to do with boots.
**Bootie** or **bootneck.** A nickname for a Royal MARINE, so called from the leather tab with which they close their tunic collars.
**Boot is on the other foot, The.** The situation is now reversed; you and I have changed places, and circumstances have altered now.
**Bootjack.** An appliance for pulling off boots by inserting the heel in a V-shaped opening.
**Bootlegger.** One who traffics illegally in alcoholic liquor. The expression derives from the smuggling of flasks of liquor in boot legs.
**Bootless errand.** An unprofitable or futile errand. *See also* TO BOOT.

> I sent him
> Bootless home and weather-beaten back.
> SHAKESPEARE: *Henry IV, Pt I*, III, i (1597)

**Bootlicker.** A TOADY or creep. *See also* LICK SOMEONE'S BOOTS.
**Boots.** An inn or hotel servant whose duty it was to clean the boots. Dickens has a *Christmas Tale* (1855) called 'The Boots of the Holly-tree Inn'.

The bishop with the shortest period of service in the HOUSE OF LORDS, whose duty it is to read prayers, is colloquially known as the 'Boots'. The name is also applied to the youngest officer in a regimental mess.

**Bootstrap.** A loop at the back of a boot to pull it on. To pull oneself up by one's own bootstraps is to better oneself by one's own efforts.
**As tough as old boots.** *See under* AS.
**Bet one's boots, To.** *See under* BET.
**Die with one's boots on, To.** *See under* DIE.
**Have one's heart in one's boots, To.** *See under* HEART.
**Lick someone's boots, To.** *See under* LICK.
**Like old boots.** *See under* LIKE.
**Order of the boot, The.** *See under* ORDER.
**Puss in Boots.** *See under* PUSS.
**Put the boot in, To.** To kick someone when they are down; to complete a task brutally.
**Seven-leagued boots.** *See under* SEVEN.
**To boot.** *See under* TO.
**Too big for one's boots, To be.** *See under* TOO.

**Boötes.** Greek for 'the ploughman', as the name of the constellation, which contains the bright star, Arcturus (*see* ARCTIC). According to ancient mythology Boötes invented the plough, to which he yoked two oxen, and at death was taken to heaven with his plough and oxen and made a constellation. Homer calls it 'the wagoner', i.e. the wagoner of CHARLES'S WAIN, the GREAT BEAR.

**Bootsie and Snudge.** An army private and his irascible sergeant, played by Alfie Bass and Bill Fraser in the popular television series *The Army Game* (1957–62). The pair also appeared in the film *I Only Arsked* (1958) and made sporadic returns subsequently. Their humour was very much in the mould of the *Carry On* films.

**Booze, To.** To drink steadily and/or excessively. Though a slang word, its origin is in Middle Dutch *būsen*, 'to drink heavily'. Edmund Spenser uses the word in his description of Gluttony:

> Still as he rode, he somewhat still did eat,
> And in his hand did beare a bouzing can,
> Of which he supt so oft, that on his seat
> His dronken corse he scarse vpholden can.
> *The Faerie Queene*, I, iv (1590)

**Bor.** An East Anglian form of address to a boy or young man, e.g. 'Well, bor, I saw the mauther you spoke of' ('Well, boy, I saw the girl you mentioned'). It is apparently from Old English *gebūr*, 'neighbour'.

**Borak** or **Al Borak** (Arabic, 'the lightning'). The animal brought by GABRIEL to carry MOHAMMED to the seventh heaven, and itself received into Paradise. It had the face of a man but the cheeks of a horse; its eyes were like jacinths, but brilliant as the stars; it had the wings of an eagle, spoke with the voice of a man, and glittered all over with radiant light. *See also* SEVEN HEAVENS.

**Border, The.** The frontier of England and Scotland, which from the 11th to the 15th century was a field of constant forays. Hence Borders as the name of the modern Scottish administrative region bordering England.

**Border Minstrel, The.** Sir Walter Scott (1771–1832), because he wrote of the BORDER.

**Border States, The.** The five 'slave' states (Delaware, Maryland, Virginia, Kentucky and Missouri), which lay next to the 'free' states. So called in the American Civil War (1861–5). *See also* UNITED STATES OF AMERICA.

**Border terrier.** A small terrier originating in the Cheviot Hills, near the BORDER.

**King of the Border, The.** *See under* KING.

**Boreas** (perhaps related to Sanskrit *giri* or Slavic *gora*, 'mountain'). In Greek mythology the god of the north wind and the wind itself. He was the son of Astraeus, a TITAN, and EOS, the morning, and he lived in a cave of Haemus in Thrace.

**Borgias, A glass of wine with the.** *See under* GLASS.

**Born. Born again.** Converted, especially to a type of evangelical Christianity. The allusion is biblical.

> Verily, verily, I say unto thee, Except a man be born again, he cannot see the kingdom of God.
> John 3:3

**Born and bred.** By birth and upbringing.

**Born in the gutter, To be.** To be of lowly origins; a child of beggars or vagrants.

**Born in the purple, To be.** *See* PORPHYROGENITUS.

**Born on the wrong side of the blanket, To be.** To be illegitimate.

**Born to be hanged.** 'He that is born to be hanged shall never be drowned.' An old proverb.

**Born under a lucky** or **unlucky planet, To be.** According to ASTROLOGY some planet, at the birth of every individual, presides over their destiny. Some of the planets, like JUPITER, are lucky; others, like SATURN, are unlucky. *See also* ASTROLOGICAL HOUSES.

**Born with a silver spoon in one's mouth, To be.** To be born to good luck or with hereditary wealth. The reference is to the usual gift of a silver spoon by the godparents; *see also* APOSTLE SPOONS. The lucky child does not need to wait for the gift for it inherits it at birth. A phrase with a similar meaning is 'born under a lucky star'. The allusion is to ASTROLOGY.

**Born within sound of Bow Bells, To be.** Said of a true COCKNEY. St Mary-le-Bow, Cheapside, long had one of the most celebrated bell-peals in London, until an air raid destroyed the bells and the interior of the church in 1941. John Dun, mercer, in 1472 gave two tenements to maintain the ringing of Bow Bell every night at nine o'clock, to direct travellers on the road to town. In 1520 William Copland gave a bigger bell for 'sounding a retreat from work'. It is said that the sound of these bells, which seemed to say 'Turn again, Whittington, lord mayor of London', encouraged the young Dick WHITTINGTON to return to the City and try his luck again.

**In all one's born days.** As far as this point in one's life or experience.

**Not born yesterday.** Not inexperienced and gullible; not easily duped or fooled.

**Poets are born, not made.** *See under* POET.

**To the manner born.** *See under* TO.

**Borough** or **burgh.** Originally, a corporate town with privileges granted by royal charter. By the Local Government Act of 1888 many large towns became county boroughs with the same governing powers as a county, but they were abolished by an Act of 1972. By the same Act non-county boroughs lost their status except in the Greater London Council area set up by the London Government Act of 1963. Subsequently various district councils have been granted the title of borough by royal charter, thus enabling their chairmen to become mayors. The word borough has lost its historic meaning since being granted to rural districts. Burgh is in many respects the Scottish equivalent.

**Borough, The.** SOUTHWARK, a district rich in

historic and literary associations. The TABARD INN, BANKSIDE and the MARSHALSEA are some examples.

*The Borough* (1810) is also the title of a collection of poetical tales by George Crabbe about the Suffolk borough of Aldeburgh, one of which forms the theme of Benjamin Britten's opera *Peter Grimes* (1945).

**Borough English.** A custom abolished in 1925 by which real estate passed to the youngest son instead of the eldest. It was of English origin and was so called to distinguish it from Norman custom. If there were no son, the youngest daughter was sole heiress. Failing a daughter, the youngest brother was the heir. Failing him, the youngest sister and so on. Land held by Borough English was sometimes termed 'Cradle-holding' or 'Cradle-land'. It was found in Kent, Middlesex, Surrey, Sussex and Somerset. *See also* GAVELKIND.

**Five Boroughs, The.** *See under* FIVE.

**Parliamentary borough.** *See under* PARLIAMENT.

**Rotten** or **pocket borough.** *See under* ROTTEN.

**Borrow.** Originally a noun meaning a pledge or security. The modern sense of the verb depended originally on the actual pledging of something as security for the loan. Even today the idea that a loan is the property of the lender and must be returned some day is always present. The noun sense is seen in the old oath 'St George to borowe', which is short for 'I take St George as pledge'.

**Borrowed** or **borrowing days.** The last three days of MARCH are said to be 'borrowed from APRIL', as is shown by the proverb in John Ray's *Collection of English Proverbs* (1670): 'March borrows three days of April, and they are ill.'

In Scotland, FEBRUARY also has its 'borrowed days', the 12th, 13th and 14th, which are said to be borrowed from JANUARY. If these prove stormy, the year will be one of good weather; if fine, the year will be foul. They are called *Faoilteach.*

**Borrowed time.** An unexpected extension of the time allowed for something, particularly with regard to a person's life. To live on borrowed time is thus to continue living against the odds, especially during a serious illness. The time is borrowed from Death.

**Borstal.** A prison or detention centre for young male offenders, since 1982 officially designated a youth custody centre and subsequently a young offender institution. The centres took their name from the location of the first, which opened at Borstal, near Rochester, Kent, in 1902. By a curious linguistic coincidence, the place-name Borstal means 'security place'. Brendan Behan's *Borstal Boy* (1958) gives a vivid fictionalized autobiographical account of life in a borstal.

**Boru, Brian.** *See under* BRIAN.

**Bosh** (Turkish *boş*, 'empty'). Empty talk, nonsense. The word was popularized by James Morier in his novel *Ayesha* (1834) and other Eastern romances.

**Bosom. Bosom friend, pal** or **buddy.** A dear friend. NATHAN's 'one little EWE LAMB' grew up with him and 'lay in his bosom, and was unto him as a daughter' (2 Samuel 12:3). St JOHN THE EVANGELIST is represented in the New Testament similarly:

> Now there was leaning on Jesus' bosom one of his disciples, whom Jesus loved.
> John 13:23

**Abraham's bosom.** *See under* ABRAHAM.

**Bosporus** or **Bosphorus.** A Greek compound popularly translated as 'ox ford'. The Thracian Bosporus unites the Sea of Marmora with the EUXINE OR BLACK SEA. Greek legend says that ZEUS, enamoured of IO, changed her into a white heifer from fear of HERA, to flee from whom Io swam across the strait, which was thence called *boos poros*, 'ford of the cow'. Hera discovered the trick and sent a gadfly to torment Io, who was made to wander, in a state of frenzy, from land to land, ultimately finding rest on the banks of the Nile. The wanderings of the Argive princess were a favourite theme among ancient writers.

**Boss.** (1) The word, which derives from the Dutch *baas*, 'master', has come to mean any person in charge, and in the USA has come to be used specifically for a political leader or senior figure. Hence to boss someone about is to be overbearing towards them, making them do what one wants.

(2) Derived from the Old French *boce*, the word here means a protuberance, such as a raised ornament on a shield or a ceiling.

**Boss-eyed.** Having a squint. This comes from boss as a dialect word, meaning to miss or bungle a shot at a target. Hence a boss-shot, that misses the target.

**Boston.** From colonial days until after the Civil War (1861–5), this American city was the intellectual, social and literary capital of the country, and was known as 'the Hub'.

> And this is good old Boston,
> The home of the bean and the cod,
> Where the Lowells talk to the Cabots,
> And the Cabots talk only to God.
> J.C. BOSSIDY: 'Toast, Holy Cross Alumni Dinner' (1910)

**Boston Strangler, The.** Albert de Salvo (1933–73), who strangled 13 women in Boston, Massachusetts, in the early 1960s. He was jailed for life and stabbed to death by a fellow prisoner.

**Boston Tea Party, The.** An incident (1773) serving to worsen the relations between Britain and its American colonies. By the Tea Act of 1773 the East India Company was enabled to ship its surplus stocks of tea direct to America to the disadvantage of American merchants. At Boston patriots disguised as Indians boarded the tea ships and dumped all the tea into the harbour. In consequence the British Parliament passed the INTOLERABLE ACTS.

**Botanomancy** (Greek *botanē*, 'plant', and *manteia*, 'divination'). DIVINATION by leaves. One method was to write sentences on leaves, which were exposed to the wind, the answer being gathered from those that were not blown away. Another was through the crackling made by leaves of various plants when thrown on the fire or crushed in the hands.

**Botany. Botany Bay.** An inlet in the coast of New South Wales, 5 miles (8km) south of Sydney, which was discovered by Captain Cook in April 1770 and so named by him on account of the great variety of new plants observed there. Although the first convicts landed there in 1788, the settlement was established at Port Jackson, now part of Sydney Harbour. At one time Botany Bay was an alternative name for New South Wales, and to be sent to Botany Bay meant to be transported to Australia.

> One of the great difficulties in Botany Bay is to find proper employment for the great mass of convicts who are sent out.
>
> SYDNEY SMITH: 'Botany Bay' *Edinburgh Review* (July 1819)

**Botany wool.** A fine wool made from merino sheep, and so called because Australian woollens were first made at BOTANY BAY by Simeon Lord in 1815.

**Bothy** (perhaps related to booth). A humble cottage or hut, and in particular the one-room farm servants' dwelling in the northeast of Scotland, which was often part of the stabling. The bothy system was formerly widespread, and the unmarried men were crowded into these sparsely furnished habitations, often preparing their own food.

**Bo tree.** An alternative name for the BANYAN, especially the *Ficus religiosa*.

**Bottle.** The accepted commercial size of a wine bottle is one holding 75 centilitres (25.36 fluid ounces). The numbers of ordinary bottles held by large bottles are:

| | |
|---|---|
| Magnum: | 2 |
| Double-magnum or Jeroboam: | 4 |
| Rehoboam: | 6 |
| Methuselah: | 8 |
| Salmanazar: | 12 |
| Balthazar: | 16 |
| Nebuchadnezzar: | 20 |

A 'nip' is ¼ of a bottle, a 'baby' is ⅛.

**Bottle and jug.** A once common name for a public house bar where beer was sold in bottles and draught beer could be collected in jugs for consumption off the premises. The words can still be found engraved in the windows of some pubs.

**Bottle bank.** A large metal container in which empty bottles are deposited (as if in a bank) by the public so that the glass can be recycled.

**Bottled moonshine.** An impractical social or benevolent scheme, such as UTOPIA or S.T. Coleridge's PANTISOCRACY.

> Godwin! Hazlitt! Coleridge! Where now are their 'novel philosophies and systems'? Bottled moonshine, which does not improve with keeping.
>
> AUGUSTINE BIRRELL: *Obiter Dicta* (1885)

**Bottleneck.** A narrow stretch of road where the smooth flow of traffic is impeded; any impediment that holds up production or trade.

**Bottlenose.** A swollen nose, especially one produced by drinking.

**Bottle out, To.** The same as to LOSE ONE'S BOTTLE.

**Bottle party.** A party to which guests are expected to bring a bottle of wine or some similar drinkable contribution.

**Bottle up, To.** To suppress or not express, as of a strong emotion.

**Bottle-washer.** A menial servant or general factotum. The full phrase, which is often applied more or less ironically, is 'chief cook and bottle-washer'.

**Brought up on the bottle.** *See under* BRING.

**Cock and Bottle.** *See under* COCK.

**Crack a bottle, To.** *See under* CRACK.

**Crush a bottle, To.** *See under* CRUSH.

**Lose one's bottle, To.** *See under* LOSE.

**New wine in old bottles.** *See under* NEW.

**Oracle of the Holy Bottle, The.** *See under* ORACLE.

**Bottom.** Of a ship, the lower part of the hull, usually below the waterline. Hence the hull itself or the whole ship. A vessel is said to have a full bottom when the hull construction allows large stowage, and a sharp bottom when it is capable of speed.

To get to the bottom of something is to discover the actual truth about it.

**Bottom drawer.** The most capacious drawer in a chest is usually at the bottom, and when a young woman who is engaged starts collecting articles for setting up her future home, she is said to be putting them in her bottom drawer.

> As soon as a girl passed her fifteenth birthday she began to sew for the 'bottom drawer'.
>
> ARNOLD BENNETT: *Anna of the Five Towns*, ch xiii (1902)

*See also* TOP DRAWER.

**Bottomless Pit, The.** Hell is so called in Revelation 20:1. *See also* ABADDON. William Pitt, the younger (1759–1806), was humorously called the Bottomless Pitt, in allusion to his thinness.

**Bottom line, The.** The basic truth; the ultimate criterion. The reference is to the line at the bottom of a financial statement, which reveals how a business fared over a particular period in terms of the difference between income and expenditure.

**Bottom of the bag, The.** The last expedient, after having emptied one's bag of all others. A TRUMP CARD held in reserve.

**Bottom out, To.** To reach a low level and remain at it, without sinking any lower, so that a rise may even be expected. The term is frequently used in economics.

**Bottoms up!** A call to drain one's glass, so that the bottom is uppermost.

**Bottom the Weaver.** A man who fancies he can do everything and do it better than anyone else. Shakespeare has portrayed him as a profoundly ignorant, brawny, mock hero, with a superabundance of conceit. At one point in *A Midsummer Night's Dream* (1585) he is represented with an ass's head, and under a spell TITANIA, the queen of the fairies, caresses him as an ADONIS.

The name is appropriate, since one meaning of the word 'bottom' is a ball of thread used in weaving.

**At bottom.** *See under* AT.

**At the bottom of, To be.** *See under* AT.

**Bell-bottoms.** *See under* BELL.

**Bet one's bottom dollar on, To.** *See under* BET.

**Black bottom.** *See under* BLACK.

**Foggy Bottom.** *See under* FOGGY.

**From the bottom of one's heart.** *See under* FROM.

**Get to the bottom of, To.** *See under* GET.

**Knock the bottom out of, To.** *See under* KNOCK.

**Rock bottom.** *See under* ROCK.

**Touch bottom, To.** *See under* TOUCH.

**Boudicca.** Nowadays the preferred form of BOADICEA.

**Bought.** *See under* BUY.

**Bouillabaisse** (Provençal *bouiabaisso*, 'to boil down'). A rich soup made of fish boiled with herbs in water or white wine.

> This Bouillabaisse a noble dish is –
> A sort of soup, or broth, or brew
> Or hotchpotch of all sorts of fishes
> That Greenwich never could outdo:
> Green herbs, red peppers, mussels, saffron,
> Soles, onions, garlic, roach and dace;
> All these you eat at Terre's tavern,
> In that one dish of Bouillabaisse.
>
> W.M. THACKERAY: 'The Ballad of Bouillabaisse' (1855)

**Boule** or **boulle.** A kind of marquetry in which brass, gold or enamelled metal is inlaid into wood or tortoiseshell. It is named after André Charles Boulle (1642–1732), a gifted cabinet-maker who worked for Louis XIV on the decorations and furniture at VERSAILLES. With English furniture dealers 'buhl' (a German form of the name, and now the regular American spelling) came to denote inlay work of this sort, however inferior or cheap.

**Boulevard, Sunset.** *See under* SUNSET.

**Boulogne, Column at.** *See under* COLUMN.

**Bounds, To beat the.** *See under* BEAT.

**Bountiful, Lady.** *See under* LADY.

**Bounty. Mutiny on the Bounty.** *See under* MUTINY.

**Queen Anne's Bounty.** *See under* ANNE.

**Royal Bounty.** *See under* ROYAL.

**Bourbon.** The family name of the kings of France from 1589 to 1793 (Henry IV, Louis XIII, XIV, XV and XVI) and from 1815 to 1830 (Louis XVIII, Charles X), derived from the seigniory of Bourbon, in the Bourbonnais in central France. The family is a branch of the house of CAPET. Bourbons also ruled in Spain, Naples and Sicily, and later in Lucca, Parma and Piacenza, as a result of the accession of Philip of Anjou (grandson of Louis XIV) to the Spanish throne in 1700.

It was said of the restored Bourbons that they had learned nothing and forgotten nothing. Hence in the USA the name Bourbon was applied to the Democratic Party leaders of the southern states, with the implication that they were guided by a pre-Civil War outlook.

In the USA the word 'bourbon' is also used for a whisky made from Indian corn, sometimes with rye or malt added. The first Kentucky whisky was made by a BAPTIST clergyman named Elijah Craig at Royal Spring, near Georgetown, in 1789. Georgetown (now county seat of Scott County) was then in Bourbon County.

**Boustrapa.** A nickname of NAPOLEON III, in allusion to his unsuccessful attempts at a COUP D'ÉTAT at Boulogne (1840) and Strasbourg (1836) and the successful one at Paris (1851).

**Boustrophedon** (Greek *bous*, 'ox', and *strophē*, 'turning'). A method of writing found in early Greek inscriptions in which the lines run alternately from right to left, and left to right, like the path of oxen in ploughing.

**Bovril.** A concentrated beef extract used as a flavouring, a stock or a drink. It was the invention in 1887 of John Lawson Johnston and took its name from a combination of Latin *bos, bovis*, 'ox', and Vril, a substance described in Lord Lytton's novel *The Coming Race* (1871) as an 'electric fluid … capable of being raised and disciplined into the mightiest agency of all forms of matter'. This name itself suggests Latin *virilis*, 'manly', so that the overall name implies 'beefiness'.

**Bow** (noun). **Bow Street Runners.** The first regular police and detective force in London, organized in the mid-18th century under the chief magistrate at Bow Street, near COVENT GARDEN. They were eventually superseded by the Metropolitan Police. *See also* BOBBY; PEELER.

**Born within sound of Bow Bells.** *See under* BORN.

**Draw a bow at a venture, To.** *See under* DRAW.

**Have more than one string to one's bow, To.** *See under* STRING.

**Ulysses' bow.** *See under* ULYSSES.

**Bow** (verb and noun). **Bow down in the house of Rimmon, To.** To compromise one's conscience, to do that which one knows to be wrong so as to save one's face. The allusion is to Naaman obtaining ELISHA's permission to worship the god when with his master:

> In this thing the Lord pardon thy servant, that when my master goeth into the house of Rimmon to worship there, and he leaneth on my hand, and I bow myself in the house of Rimmon: when I bow down myself in the house of Rimmon, the Lord pardon thy servant in this thing.
> 2 Kings 5:18

*See also* RIMMON.

**Bow out, To.** To make one's exit; to retire gracefully. The allusion is to an actor acknowledging applause before leaving the stage, perhaps for the last time.

**Take a bow, To.** To acknowledge applause; to show one's appreciation of praise or thanks.

**Bow.** The forward end of a boat or ship.

**Cross someone's bows, To.** *See under* CROSS.

**On the port** or **starboard bow.** *See under* PORT.

**Send a shot across someone's bows, To.** *See under* SEND.

**Bowdlerize, To.** To expurgate. In 1818 the editor Thomas Bowdler (1754–1825) published a ten-volume edition of Shakespeare's works 'in which nothing is added to the original text; but those words are omitted which cannot with propriety be read aloud in a family'. He thus cut Juliet's speech of longing for Romeo from 30 lines to 15, together with many of the Nurse's comments, and in King Lear's speech of madness, beginning 'Ay, every inch a king', he cut 22 lines to seven. He removed the character of Doll Tearsheet altogether.

**Bowels of mercy.** Compassion, sympathy. The affections were once supposed to be the outcome of certain secretions or organs. The head was regarded as the seat of understanding, the heart was the seat of affection and memory (hence 'learning by heart'), the bowels were the seat of mercy, and the spleen was the seat of passion or anger. *See also* HUMOUR.

**Bowery, The.** A densely populated street in lower Manhattan, New York City. It takes its name from *bowerij*, the Dutch word for farm, because in the 17th century it was a farming area north of the city. In 1651 Governor Peter Stuyvesant (1592–1672) bought much of the land there. It is noted for its many cheap hotels and bars and from the 19th century was frequented by vagrants and drunks as an archetypal SKID ROW. It was also the haunt of the notorious ruffians called the Bowery Boys.

> The Bowery, the Bowery!
> They say such things and they do such things
> On the Bowery, the Bowery!
> I'll never go there any more!
> CHARLES M. HOYT: 'The Bowery' (song) (1892)

**Bowie knife.** James Bowie (1790–1836) was a Southerner who for some years from 1818 smuggled in black slaves with the pirate Jean Laffitte. In 1827 he was present at a duel on a sandbar in Mississippi near Natchez, which ended in a general mêlée. Six of the seconds and spectators were killed and 15 wounded. Bowie killed one Major Norris Wright with a knife fashioned from a blacksmith's rasp. It was some 10–15in (25–38cm) long, with one sharp edge curving to the point, and it attracted such attention that Bowie sent it to a cutler in Philadelphia who sold copies as the Bowie knife. Bowie was with Davy CROCKETT at the fall of the ALAMO on 6 March 1836.

**Bowl** (noun). **Golden bowl is broken, The.** *See under* GOLDEN.

**Bowl** (verb). **Bowled out, To be.** A metaphor from CRICKET, meaning to be defeated in argument or detected in a falsehood. *See also* CLEAN BOWLED.

**Bowled over.** Physically knocked down; figuratively, suddenly overcome by some strong emotion.

**Body-line bowling.** *See under* BODY.

**Clean bowled.** *See under* CLEAN.

**Collar the bowling, To.** *See under* COLLAR.

**Bowler hat.** A hard felt hat, known in the USA as a DERBY hat. Like the BILLYCOCK HAT it is said to have been introduced by the Norfolk landowner, William Coke. Because he found his tall riding hat frequently swept off by overhanging branches, in 1850 he asked Locks, the well-known hatters of St James's, to design him a hat with a lower crown. The first 'Coke' or bowler is said to have been made from felt supplied by Thomas and William Bowler. However, according to another account, the name comes from the hatter who designed it, John Bowler. *See also* COKE'S CLIPPINGS.

**Bowler-hatted, To be.** To be discharged from the armed forces with a gratuity before the normal termination of one's commission, a bowler hat being the (former) emblem of CIVVY STREET. *See also* GOLDEN HANDSHAKE.

**Bow-wow.** A word in imitation of the sound of a

dog's bark. Hence the bow-wow theory as one of the speculative theories concerning the origin of language. It claims that human speech arose from the imitation of animal sounds. The term was first used by Max Müller (1823–1900). *See also* ONOMATOPOEIA.

**Box.** There are three words box in English. The container is so called from Latin *pyxis*, itself from Greek *puxos* (*see* PYX), which gave the name of the tree, as the second word. The pugilistic sport has a name of uncertain origin, although some authorities see it as a figurative use of the word for the container, perhaps in allusion to the shape of the ring.

**Box, The.** One of the colloquial names for television.

**Box and Cox.** By turns, turn and turn about or alternately. The phrase derives from the story in which Mrs Bouncer, a deceitful lodging-house landlady, lets the same room to two men, Box and Cox. Unknown to each other they occupy it alternately, one being out at work all day, the other all night. The story itself is staged in J.M. Morton's farce *Box and Cox* (1847), adapted from two French vaudevilles.

**Box camera.** A simple box-shaped camera. A popular camera of this type was the Kodak BROWNIE.

**Boxcar.** In North America a closed freight car or goods wagon on the railway.

**Box clever, To.** To act in a clever or effective way, like an experienced boxer.

**Box days.** A custom established in the Scottish COURT OF SESSION in 1690, providing two days in spring and autumn, and one at Christmas (during vacation) on which pleadings could be filed. Informations were to be placed in a box for each judge and examined in private.

**Boxing Day.** *See* CHRISTMAS BOX.

**Box junction.** An area at a road junction marked out with a yellow grid. Drivers are supposed to enter the box only if their exit is clear. However, a driver may enter if intending to turn right and prevented from doing so only by oncoming traffic or by other vehicles waiting to turn right.

**Box number.** A number by which replies are made to a private advertisement in a newspaper. Such replies were originally placed in a box or 'pigeonhole' in the newspaper's office.

**Box office.** An office for reserving seats and buying tickets at a theatre, cinema or other entertainment. The term is extended to apply to the commercial success or otherwise of a production.

**Box spanner.** A spanner with a box-shaped end to fit over the head of a nut.

**Box the compass, To.** In nautical parlance to name the 32 points of the compass in their correct order. Hence a wind is said to box the compass when it blows from every quarter in rapid succession. Hence also, figuratively, to revert to one's original standpoint after changing to the opposite view, as in politics.

**Black box.** *See under* BLACK.

**Call box.** *See under* CALL.

**Christmas box.** *See under* CHRISTMAS.

**Dead letter box.** *See under* DEAD.

**In the wrong box.** *See under* WRONG.

**Omnibus box.** *See under* OMNIBUS.

**Pandora's box.** *See under* PANDORA.

**Boxers.** Members of a nationalistic Chinese secret society, which took a prominent part in the rising against foreigners in 1900 and which was suppressed by joint European action. Their Chinese name was *Yì Hé Quán*, 'righteous harmony fists', and it was the last word of this that gave their English name of Boxers.

**Boy.** In a number of connections 'boy' has no reference to age. It is a common term for a 'native' servant or labourer of any age, and a ship's boy is the lowest category among mariners, being essentially a GREENHORN. An OLD BOY can be a former member of a particular school or an elderly man, and 'old boy' is used as a form of address by some men.

**Boy, The.** CHAMPAGNE. The name is said to take its origin from a shooting-party at which a boy with an iced bucket of wine was in attendance. When he was Prince of Wales and needed a drink, Edward VII used to shout, 'Where's the boy?', and thence the phrase passed into fashionable parlance.

> He will say that port and sherry his nice palate always cloy;
> He'll nothing drink but 'B. and S.' and big magnums of 'the Boy'.
> *Punch* (11 February 1882)

**Boy Bishop.** St NICHOLAS of Bari was called the Boy Bishop because from his cradle he manifested marvellous indications of piety.

The custom of choosing a boy from the cathedral or parish choir on his day (6 December), as a mock bishop, is ancient. It was also the custom in schools and colleges such as St Paul's, Eton, Winchester, King's College, Cambridge and elsewhere. The boy held office for three weeks and the rest of the choir were his prebendaries. If he died in office he was buried in his episcopal robes. Probably the reference is to the boy Jesus sitting in the temple among the doctors. The custom survives in modern times in the enthronement of a boy bishop on the Sunday nearest St Nicholas' day at Mendlesham, Suffolk, and on the day itself at Edwinstowe, Nottinghamshire.

**Boyfriend.** A person's regular male companion or lover, more likely to be a man than an actual boy. The same holds for a girlfriend, as the female equivalent.

> Some people like the idea of having a boyfriend or girlfriend more than the actuality of it. They want intimacy without commitment.
> *Sunday Times* (28 June 1998)

**Boy meets girl.** A phrase descriptive of a conventional love match or story. *See also* GIRL MEETS BOY.

**Boyo.** A boy or young man, especially a Welsh one.

**Boy Scouts** or **Scouts.** A popular youth movement started by General Sir Robert Baden-Powell (Lord Baden-Powell of Gilwell) in 1908. The aim was to train boys to be good citizens with high ideals of honour, service to others, cleanliness and self-reliance, based essentially on training in an outdoor setting. The movement became worldwide. There are four branches: Beaver Scouts (aged 6 to 8), Cub Scouts, formerly Wolf Cubs (8 to 10½), Scouts (10½ to15½) and Venture Scouts, formerly Rover Scouts (15½ to 20). About one-third of Venture Scouts are now girls, and in 1990 younger girls were admitted to the Scouts. *See also* BEAVERS; BE PREPARED; GIRL GUIDES.

**Boys in blue, The.** The police, from the colour of their uniforms.

**Boys will be boys.** Youthful exuberance or indiscretions must be tolerated. A retort to the expression by one less tolerant is sometimes 'Boys will be men'.

**Attic boy, The.** *See under* ATTIC.

**Backroom boys.** *See under* BACK.

**Best boy.** *See under* BEST.

**Bevin Boys.** *See under* BEVIN.

**Billy boy.** *See under* BILLY.

**Bing Boys.** *See under* BING.

**Blue-eyed boy.** *See under* BLUE.

**Blue for a boy.** *See under* BLUE.

**Bristol Boy.** *See under* BRISTOL.

**Fair-haired boy.** *See under* FAIR.

**Gazelle Boy, The.** *See under* GAZELLE.

**Give the boys a holiday.** A phrase attributed to Anaxagoras (*see under* FAMOUS LAST WORDS). The old custom of so marking a noteworthy event has always been popular with pupils, but the unexpected holiday is less readily given now that most schools are subject to closer bureaucratic regulations.

**Golden boys.** *See under* GOLDEN.

**Green Mountain Boys.** *See under* GREEN.

**Jobs for the boys.** *See under* JOBS.

**Naked boy.** *See under* NAKED.

**Naked Boy courts.** *See under* NAKED.

**Nancy boy.** *See under* NANCY.

**Oak boys.** *See under* OAK.

**Old boy.** *See under* OLD.

**Old boy network.** *See under* OLD.

**One of the boys.** *See under* ONE.

**Peep-o'Day Boys.** *See under* PEEP.

**Principal boy.** *See under* PRINCIPAL.

**Roaring boys.** *See under* ROAR.

**Slip of a boy.** *See under* SLIP.

**Yellow boy.** *See under* YELLOW.

**Whipping boy.** *See under* WHIP.

**White-haired boy.** *See under* WHITE.

**Wild boy of Aveyron, The.** *See under* WILD.

**Boycott, To.** To refuse to have any dealings with a person or group of people, as a means of protest or coercion. The term dates from 1880, when such methods were used by the Irish LAND LEAGUE against Captain C.C. Boycott (1832–97), a land agent in County Mayo, as a means of coercing him to reduce rents. *See also* SEND TO COVENTRY.

**Boz.** Charles Dickens (1812–70). 'Boz, my signature in the *Morning Chronicle*,' he explained, 'was the nickname of a pet child, a younger brother, whom I had dubbed Moses, in honour of the Vicar of Wakefield, which being pronounced Boses, got shortened into Boz.' Dickens used the name for the title of an early collections of writings on life and manners, *Sketches by Boz* (1836–7).

**Bozzy.** James Boswell (1740–95), the biographer of Dr Johnson.

**Brabançonne, La.** The national anthem of Belgium, composed by François van Campenhout in the revolution of 1830, and so named from Brabant, of which Brussels is the chief city.

**Braces, Belt and.** *See under* BELT.

**Bradamante** (Italian *brada*, 'wild', 'untamed', and *amante*, 'loving'). The sister of RINALDO in ORLANDO FURIOSO (1532) and ORLANDO INNAMORATO (1487). She is represented as a Christian AMAZON, possessed of an irresistible spear, which unhorsed every knight it struck.

**Bradbury.** A £1 note, as issued by the Treasury in 1914–28, bearing the signature of J.S. Bradbury (1st Baron Bradbury), who launched the issue as Joint Permanent Secretary to the Treasury.

**Bradshaw.** A famous British railway guide, first printed in Manchester in 1839 by George Bradshaw (1801–53). The 'Monthly Guide' was first issued in December 1841, and consisted of 32 pages, giving tables of 43 railway lines. Publication ceased in 1961.

> 'There is a train at half-past nine', said I, glancing over my Bradshaw. 'It is due at Winchester at 11:30.' 'That will do very nicely.'
> SIR ARTHUR CONAN DOYLE: *Adventures of Sherlock Holmes*, 'The Adventure of the Copper Beeches' (1892)

**Braggadocio.** A braggart, a boaster. The word comes from Braggadocchio, a boastful character in Edmund Spenser's *The Faerie Queene* (1590, 1596). His own name is probably a combination of braggart and the Italian augmentative suffix -*occhio*, meaning overall 'big boaster'. It is thought that Spenser had the Duke of Alençon, a suitor of Queen Elizabeth I, in mind when he drew this character.

**Bragi** (Old Norse *bragr*, 'poem', 'melody'). In Norse mythology the god of poetry and eloquence, son of ODIN and husband of IDUNA. He welcomes the slain heroes who arrive in VALHALLA.

**Brahma** (Sanskrit, 'the Absolute'). In HINDUISM, the Creator, the god who with VISHNU, the Preserver, and SIVA, the Destroyer, forms the triad known as the TRIMURTI ('three forms'). The BRAHMANS claim Brahma as their founder.

**Brahmans** or **Brahmins.** Worshipper of BRAHMA, the highest or priestly CASTE in the Hindu caste system.

**Braid St Catherine's tresses, To.** To live one's life as a virgin. The reference is to St CATHERINE OF ALEXANDRIA, virgin martyr.

> Here is Baptiste Leblanc, the notary's son, who has loved thee
> Many a tedious year; come, give him thy hand and be happy!
> Thou art too fair to be left to braid St Catherine's tresses.
>
> H.W. LONGFELLOW, *Evangeline* (1847)

**Braille.** A system of writing made up of varying combinations of raised dots enabling the blind to read by touch, invented in 1829 by the Frenchman Louis Braille (1809–52). It has been likened to a domino block, as it consists of different groups of one to six raised points. Braille devised his system after becoming acquainted with a 12-dot system invented by Captain Charles Barbier for passing messages at night. Braille accidentally blinded himself in one eye as a child of three and soon lost his sight completely. In 1819, at the age of ten, he was put in the Institution Nationale des Aveugles at Paris, where he later became a teacher and organ player and modified his system for reading music.

**Brain. Brainchild.** An idea or plan produced by creative thought as the product of an individual's brain.

**Brain drain.** A phrase used to denote the drift abroad, which occurred from the early 1960s, of British-trained scientists, technologists, doctors and university teachers (especially to the USA), attracted by higher salaries and often better facilities for their work.

**Brainstorm, A.** A sudden and violent upheaval in the brain, causing temporary loss of control or even madness.

**Brains Trust.** The name was originally applied by James M. Kieran of the *New York Times* to the advisers of F.D. Roosevelt (1882–1945) in his election campaign. Later it was used for the group of college professors who advised him in administering the NEW DEAL. In Britain it became the name of a popular BBC programme, first broadcast in 1942, in which public figures aired their views on questions submitted by listeners. The term is now in general use for any such panel of experts or team which answers questions.

**Brainwashing.** The subjection of someone to an intensive course of indoctrination in order to transform his or her opinions and political loyalties.

**Brain wave.** A sudden inspiration; 'a happy thought'.

**Beat someone's brains out, To.** *See under* BEAT.

**Blow one's brains out, To.** *See under* BLOW.

**Cudgel one's brains, To.** *See under* CUDGEL.

**Pick someone's brains, To.** *See under* PICK.

**Rack one's brains, To.** *See under* RACK.

**Softening of the brain.** *See under* SOFT.

**Bran.** FINGAL's dog. The expression 'If not Bran, it is Bran's brother' means that even if it is not the real thing, it is just as good. The saying stems from the fact that Bran was a great favourite with Fingal.

**Branch, Root and.** *See under* ROOT.

**Brandenburg Confession.** A formulary of faith drawn up in the city of Brandenburg in 1610, by order of the elector, with the view of reconciling the tenets of Luther with those of Calvin and putting an end to the disputes occasioned by the AUGSBURG CONFESSION.

**Brand-new** or **bran-new.** Absolutely new, as if just branded, like newly forged iron, fresh from the furnace. Shakespeare uses 'fire-new' in the same sense.

**Brandy Nan.** Queen ANNE, who was partial to brandy. On her statue in St Paul's churchyard a wit once wrote:

> Brandy Nan, Brandy Nan, left in the lurch,
> Her face to the gin-shop, her back to the church.

A 'gin palace' used to stand at the southwest corner of St Paul's churchyard. *See also* EST-IL POSSIBLE.

**Brasenose College.** The Oxford college takes its name from the bronze nose, or sanctuary knocker, first recorded in a document of 1279, that at one time was attached to the main gate of Brasenose Hall. The original knocker was taken in the 1330s to Stamford, Lincolnshire, to which town students had migrated in search of a more peaceful site for academic studies, Oxford then being torn by north-south divisions and TOWN-AND-GOWN disputes. The knocker remained on Brasenose House in Stamford until 1890, when the college bought the house to recover the knocker, which now hangs in the college hall.

**Brass.** A slang term for money. Also an engraved brass memorial tablet set in the wall or floor of a church. The earliest complete specimen, dating from the late 13th century, is in Stoke d'Abernon Church, Surrey. There are about 8000 brasses in English churches, about half of them depicting human figures, and the rest engraved with heraldic devices. Their number was formerly much greater, but thousands were destroyed by both sides in the Civil War (1642–9).

**Brassed off.** Fed up; disgruntled.

**Brass hat.** A service term for an officer of high rank. It dates from the first Boer War (1880–1), and refers to the braid on the brim of senior officers' caps, sometimes nicknamed 'scrambled egg'. Officers of the highest rank are called 'top brass' or simply 'brass'.

**Brass monkey.** In expressions such as 'cold enough to freeze the balls off a brass monkey', the reference is to a type of brass rack or 'monkey' in which cannon balls were stored and which contracted in cold weather, so ejecting the balls.

**Brass rubbing.** The taking of impressions of brasses, usually by rubbing heelball over paper. The pastime is popular among those interested in local history.

**As bold as brass.** *See under* AS.

**Corinthian brass.** *See under* CORINTH.

**Drake brass plate, The.** *See under* FAKES.

**Get down to brass tacks, To.** *See under* GET.

**Man of Brass, The.** *See under* MAN.

**Not worth a brass farthing.** *See under* WORTH.

**Top brass.** *See under* TOP.

**Where there's muck, there's brass.** *See under* WHERE.

**Brave.** A fighting man among the AMERICAN INDIANS was so called.

Alphonso IV of Portugal (1290–1357) was called 'the Brave'.

**Brave the elements, To.** To venture out into the weather; to defy adverse weather conditions. The elements here are the atmospheric forces, such as wind, rain and cold.

**Bravest of the Brave.** Marshal Ney (1769–1815) was so nicknamed on account of his great bravery at the Battle of Borodino (1812) in the Napoleonic Wars. NAPOLEON BONAPARTE said of him: 'That man is a lion.'

**Fortune favours the brave.** *See under* FORTUNE.

**Bray, The Vicar of.** *See under* VICAR.

**Brazen. Brazen Age, The.** The age of war and violence. It followed the SILVER AGE.

**Brazen bull.** An instrument of torture. *See also* INVENTORS.

**Brazen-faced.** Shameless, impudent. *See also* AS BOLD AS BRASS.

> What a brazen-faced varlet art thou!
> SHAKESPEARE: *King Lear*, II, ii (1605)

**Brazen head.** The legend of the wonderful head of brass that could speak and was omniscient, found in early romances, is of Eastern origin. Ferragus in VALENTINE AND ORSON is an example. The best known example in English legend is that fabled to have been made by the great scholar Roger Bacon (*c*.1220–92). It was said if Bacon heard it speak he would succeed in his projects, but if not, he would fail. His familiar, Miles, was set to watch, and while Bacon slept the Head spoke thrice: 'Time is.' Half an hour later it said, 'Time was.' In another half-hour it said, 'Time's past,' fell down and was broken to pieces. *See also* SPEAKING HEADS.

**Brazen horse, The.** A magic horse given to CAMBUSCAN by the king of Arabia and India. If it was given instructions and a pin in its ear was turned, it would carry its rider anywhere.

**Brazen it out, To.** To stick to an assertion knowing it to be wrong; to outface in a shameless manner; to disregard public opinion.

**Breach. Breach of promise.** A contract to marry was as binding in English law as any other contract, and the man or woman who broke an engagement was liable in law. The plaintiff was entitled to recover any pecuniary loss due to outlay in anticipation of marriage, and a woman might be awarded substantial damages in certain circumstances. If the man was the injured party he was advised to seek consolation or compensation other than in a court of law. Breach of promise was abolished for England and Wales in 1970.

**Breach of the peace.** An offence against public order caused by behaviour harming, or likely to harm, a person or, in his presence, his property. All citizens have the COMMON LAW power of arrest for breach of the peace.

**Breaches.** As used of creeks or small bays, the word is to be found in Judges 5:17. DEBORAH, complaining of the tribes who refused to assist her in her war with Sisera, says that Asher 'continued on the sea shore, and abode in his breaches'. Such bays are so called as they form a breach or break in the coast.

**Bread. Bread and butter.** One's livelihood or basic means of subsistence. A bread-and-butter letter is a letter of thanks for hospitality, since one's host has provided one's subsistence.

**Bread and cheese.** Food generally, but usually with the sense of a frugal nature. CHARTISM has often been referred to as a 'bread and cheese question', meaning it was largely caused by want and hunger, in this case lack of bread and cheese.

**Bread and circuses.** Free food and entertainment. *Panem et circenses* were, according to Juvenal's *Satires* (2nd century AD), the two things the Roman populace desired. The circus here is the stadium, where the Romans watched chariot races or public games.

**Bread and salt.** To take bread and salt is to take

an oath. In Eastern lands bread and salt were once eaten when an oath was taken.

**Bread and scrape.** Bread and thinly spread butter.

**Bread-basket.** The stomach.

**Bread is the staff of life.** A 17th-century proverb. Bread has long been important in religion, and is mentioned in many contexts in the Bible.

> And Jesus said unto them, I am the bread of life: he that cometh to me shall never hunger.
> John 6:35

*See also* STAFF OF LIFE.

**Breadline, The.** Subsistence level. To be on the breadline is to have barely enough to live on. A breadline was originally a queue of poor people waiting to be given bread or some other food as charity.

**Bread never falls but on its buttered side.** An old north country proverb.

**Breadwinner.** The person whose work provides the income for a family or household, traditionally the husband but now increasingly the wife or female partner, working at home. Bread has long been a staple of the human diet. *See also* HOUSE HUSBAND.

**Breaking of bread, The.** *See under* BREAK.

**Butter one's bread on both sides.** *See under* BUTTER.

**Cast one's bread upon the waters, To.** *See under* CAST.

**French bread.** *See under* FRENCH.

**Know which side one's bread is buttered, To.** *See under* KNOW.

**Sad bread.** *See under* SAD.

**Singing bread.** *See under* SING.

**Take the bread out of someone's mouth, To.** To deprive them of their livelihood.

**Break.** In addition to the phrases below, the expressions 'to get a break' and 'to make a break' are used colloquially in different ways. To get a break means to be offered an unexpected chance or to have an opportunity of advancing oneself. To make a break can mean either to make a complete change in one's life, either temporarily (as from a holiday) or more permanently (as through a change in occupation), or to run up a score in billiards or snooker.

**Break, To.** To bankrupt. Hence broke to mean penniless.

Also, of a boy's voice, to 'crack' or alter at puberty. The reference here may be to a bell, whose 'voice' alters if it is cracked.

**Break a butterfly on a wheel, To.** To employ great effort in the accomplishment of a small matter.

> Satire or sense, alas! can Sporus feel?
> Who breaks a butterfly upon the wheel?
> ALEXANDER POPE: *Epistle to Dr Arbuthnot* (1735)

**Break a flag, To.** To hoist it rolled up and to 'break' it, or let it fly, by pulling the halyard to release the hitch that holds it together.

**Break a journey, To.** To stop before the journey is accomplished, with the intention of completing it later.

**Break a leg!** A traditional wish of good luck in the theatre. The expression is said to relate to the assassination of Abraham Lincoln in his private box at Ford's Theatre, Washington, D.C., on 14 April 1865. The murderer, John Wilkes Booth, a Shakespearean actor of some repute, made good his escape after firing the shot by leaping down onto the stage, breaking his leg. 'Break a leg' subsequently arose as an example of black humour.

**Break a promise, To.** To go back on one's word.

**Break away, To.** To escape; to go off abruptly.

**Break camp, To.** To pack up camping equipment and leave.

**Break cover, To.** To emerge suddenly from a hiding place; of a hunted animal or person, to come out of a covert or hiding place. The den of a fox is usually blocked the night before a hunt so that it is obliged to seek some other cover. When it leaves that cover, the hunt is on.

**Break down, To.** To cease to function; to collapse. A nervous breakdown is a mental illness in which the patient ceases to function properly.

**Breakers ahead.** Hidden danger is at hand. Breakers in an open sea are a sign of sunken rocks, sandbanks or other submerged obstacles.

**Break even, To.** To reach the point in a financial activity, whether gambling or commercial, at which one makes neither profit nor loss.

**Break in, To.** To interrupt a conversation with a remark of one's own; to accustom a person or animal to a particular way of life or routine; to enter a building with the aim of stealing or committing some other crime. Breaking and entering was the former legal term for the act of doing this.

**Breaking of bread, The.** The EUCHARIST. In scriptural language to break bread is to share food with others.

**Break new ground, To.** To do something that has not been done before. The allusion is probably to digging a new trench in a siege operation or to commence a new project, as a settler does in a new country.

**Break of day.** Dawn.

**Break off, To.** To stop working; to conclude a conversation; to end an engagement or friendship.

**Break one's back, To.** To overwork or work very hard. The metaphor is from carrying burdens on the back.

**Break one's duck, To.** To score one's first run in a CRICKET match. *See also* DUCK'S EGG.

**Break one's fast, To.** To take food after long abstinence. Hence breakfast after the night's fast.

**Break one's heart, To.** To pine away or die of disappointment. To be brokenhearted is to be overwhelmed by grief or disappointment. It is possible to die 'of a broken heart'.

**Break one's neck, To.** To dislocate the bones of one's neck; to do something energetically at great speed; to be in a great and possibly dangerous hurry.

**Break one's word, To.** To fail to do what one has promised.

**Break on the wheel, To.** To torture a person by lying them on their back on a horizontally placed wheel, binding their arms and legs to the spokes or the rim and smashing their limbs with an iron bar. A COUP DE GRÂCE was then usually delivered to the stomach. St CATHERINE OF ALEXANDRIA was tortured on a revolving wheel.

**Break out, To.** To escape from prison; to throw off restraint.

**Break point.** In tennis, a point which would win the game for the player receiving service.

**Break ship, To.** Of a sailor, to fail to return to one's ship on the expiration of leave.

**Break someone's heart, To.** To make someone grieve or feel acute distress, especially through love. *See also* BREAK ONE'S HEART.

**Break step, To.** To get out of step when marching.

**Break the back of, To.** To complete the greatest or hardest part of a difficult task.

**Break the bank, To.** To ruin financially, especially through a successful gambling move.

**Break the ice, To.** To be the first to do something; to dispel the stiffness and reserve of a first meeting or conversation. The allusion is to the breaking of a path in the ice to enable a ship to proceed.

**Break the mould, To.** To change from one's usual habits. In former times an artist would break the mould of a high-quality cast so that it could not be replicated by others.

**Break the news, To.** To be the first to give it to someone, often delicately or tactfully.

**Break through, To.** To force a passage; to overcome major obstacles, especially in the field of scientific or technical progress.

**Break up, To.** To break into pieces; to smash; to finish classes at the end of term and go home; to separate or disperse.

**Break wind, To.** To release gas from the anus.

**Break with, To.** To end an association or relationship. A break with tradition is a change from customary procedure.

**Broken** or **bruised reed, A.** Something not to be trusted for support; a weak adherent. Egypt is called a broken reed, in which HEZEKIAH could not trust if the Assyrians made war on Jerusalem (2 Kings 18:21; Isaiah 36:6).

**All to break.** *See under* ALL.

**Clean break.** *See under* CLEAN.

**Even break.** *See under* EVEN.

**Go for broke, To.** To risk everything one has in a venture, as when staking all one's money in gambling.

**Leg break.** *See under* LEG.

**Lucky break.** *See under* LUCK.

**Make and break.** *See under* MAKE.

**Make or break.** *See under* MAKE.

**Breakfast. Bed and breakfast.** *See under* BED.

**Dog's breakfast.** *See* DOG'S DINNER.

**Donkey's breakfast.** *See under* DONKEY.

**Wedding breakfast.** *See under* WED.

**Breast. Beat one's breast, To.** *See under* BEAT.

**Make a clean breast of, To.** *See under* CLEAN.

**Pigeon breast.** *See under* PIGEON.

**Breath. Breath of fresh air, A.** Figuratively, a refreshing change, as: 'The new minister's policies were a breath of fresh air.'

**Catch one's breath, To.** *See under* CATCH.

**Hold one's breath, To.** *See under* HOLD.

**In the same breath.** Almost at the same time. Often applied to a person who says one thing then, a moment later, contradicts it.

**Keep** or **save one's breath to cool one's porridge, To.** *See under* SAVE.

**Out of breath.** *See under* OUT.

**Take breath, To.** To cease from exertion for a time in order to recover one's breath.

**Take one's breath away, To.** To astound, causing one to hold one's breath.

**Under one's breath.** *See under* UNDER.

**Breathe. Breathe again, To.** To feel relief after tension, as if breathing normally after holding one's breath.

**Breathe down someone's neck, To.** To stand close to someone in order to see (or oversee) what they are doing.

**Breathe fire and brimstone, To.** To be threatening or wrathful.

**Breathe one's last, To.** To die.

**Heavy breather.** *See under* HEAVY.

**Not to breathe a word.** To say absolutely nothing about; to keep entirely to oneself.

**Bred in the bone.** Inherent; part of one's nature. 'What's bred in the bone will come out in the flesh': a natural propensity cannot be repressed.

**Breeches. Breeches Bible, The.** *See under* BIBLE.

**Dutchman's breeches.** *See under* DUTCH.

**Too big for one's breeches, To be.** *See under* TOO.

**Breeze, Gentle.** *See under* GENTLE.

**Brendan, St.** A semi-legendary Irish saint, said to have been born at Tralee in 484. He founded the abbey of Clonfert and died in 577. The Rule of St Brendan was dictated to him by an angel and he is said to have presided over 3000 monks in the various houses of his foundation.

He is best known for the medieval legend, widespread throughout Europe, of his seven-year voyage in search of the Land of the Saints, the Isle of St Brendan, reputed to be in mid-Atlantic. The very birds and beasts he encountered observed the Christian fasts and festivals. The earliest surviving version of the story is the *Navigatio Brendani* (11th century). *See also* VOYAGE OF MAELDUIN.

**Bren gun.** The lightweight quick-firing machine-gun made its first appearance in the years immediately preceding the Second World War. It was originally made in Brno, Czechoslovakia, then in Enfield, England. Bren is a blend of Brno and Enfield. *See also* STEN GUN.

**Brer Fox and Brer Rabbit.** The chief characters in stories by the American writer Joel Chandler Harris (1848–1908). Written in a Negro dialect, these animal stories, which began to appear in 1879, were supposedly told to a plantation owner's little boy by Uncle Remus, a kindly old Negro. Brer means 'Brother'.

**Brethren. Bohemian Brethren.** *See under* BOHEMIA.

**Elder Brethren.** *See* CORPORATION OF TRINITY HOUSE.

**Plymouth Brethren.** *See under* PLYMOUTH.

**Bretwalda.** The title given in the ANGLO-SAXON CHRONICLE to Egbert of Wessex (802–839) and seven earlier English kings, who exercised some sort of supremacy over other English kings south of the River Humber. The title probably means 'overlord of the Brets (Britons)' and was sometimes assumed by later kings. *See also* HEPTARCHY.

**Breviary.** A book containing the ordinary and daily services of the ROMAN CATHOLIC CHURCH, which those in orders are bound to recite. It omits the EUCHARIST, which is contained in the MISSAL, and the special services (marriage, ordination etc), which are found in the Ritual or Pontifical. It is called a breviary because it is an abridged version, in the sense that it contains prayers, hymns, lessons and so on, in a single volume, so obviating the need to use a separate hymn book and Bible.

**Brew up, To.** To make tea, especially when out of doors or in a work break.

**Brian Boru.** This great Irish chieftain (*c.*941–1014) became king of Munster in 978 and chief king of all Ireland in 1002. On Good Friday 1014 his forces defeated an alliance of Norsemen and Leinstermen at the Battle of Clontarf, but Brian, too old to fight, was killed in his tent by the axe of a fleeing Norseman.

**Briareus** (Greek *briaros*, 'strong', 'powerful') or **Aegeon** (Greek *aiks, aigos*, 'goat'). A giant with fifty heads and a hundred hands. Homer says the gods called him Briareus, but men called him Aegeon (*Iliad*, i (8th century BC)). He was the offspring of Heaven and Earth and was one of the race of TITANS, with whom he fought in their war with ZEUS, although there is another tradition that has him fighting with the Olympians against the Titans.

**Briareus of languages, The.** Cardinal Mezzofanti (1774–1849), who is said to have spoken 58 different tongues. Byron called him 'a walking polyglot; a monster of languages; a Briareus of parts of speech'.

**Bric-à-brac.** Odds and ends; a miscellany of small curiosities. The word is probably a jingling reduplication of French *bric*, 'piece'.

**Brick.** A now somewhat dated term for a generous or reliable person, a 'good sort'.

> 'What a brick, not to give us even twenty lines to learn!' said the Tadpole, as they reached their bedroom.
>
> THOMAS HUGHES: *Tom Brown's Schooldays*, Pt I, ch vii (1857)

**Brickdusts, The.** *See under* REGIMENTAL AND DIVISIONAL NICKNAMES.

**Bricks without straw.** To make bricks without straw is to attempt to do something without actually having the necessary materials. The allusion is to the Israelites in Egypt, who were commanded by their taskmasters to undertake this (Exodus 5:7).

**Brick tea.** The inferior leaves of the plant mixed with a glutinous substance (sometimes bullock's or sheep's blood), pressed into cubes and dried. In this form it was sent overland from China to Russia and the blocks were frequently used as a medium of exchange in central Asia.

**Bang one's head against a brick wall, To.** *See under* BANG.

**Bath brick.** *See under* BATH.

**Come down on someone like a ton of bricks, To.** *See under* COME.

**Drop a brick, To.** *See under* DROP.

**Gold brick, A.** *See under* GOLD.

**Bride. Bride-ale.** *See* CHURCH-ALE. This word, a noun, gave the adjective 'bridal'.

**Bride cake.** A relic of the Roman *confarreatio*, a mode of marriage practised by the highest class in Rome. It was performed by the *Pontifex Maximus* before ten witnesses, and the contracting parties mutually partook of a cake of salt, water and flour (*far*). Only those born in such wedlock were eligible for the high sacred offices.

**Bridegroom.** In Old English this word was *brȳdguma*, the latter element from *guma*, 'man'. This became 'bridegroom' in the 16th century, *guma* being confused with Middle English *grom*, 'manservant'.

**Bride of the Sea, The.** Venice. The Italian city is so called from the ancient ceremony of the wedding of the sea, when the DOGE threw a ring into the Adriatic saying: 'We wed thee, O sea, in token of perpetual domination.' This took place annually on ASCENSION DAY, and the custom was enjoined upon the Venetians in 1177 by Pope Alexander III, who gave the Doge a gold ring from his own finger in token of the Venetian fleet's victory over Frederick BARBAROSSA, in defence of the pope's quarrel. At the same time his Holiness desired the event to be commemorated each year. *See also* BUCENTAUR.

**GI bride.** *See under* GI.

**War bride.** *See under* WAR.

**Bridewell.** A former generic term for a HOUSE OF CORRECTION, or a prison, so called from the City Bridewell, Blackfriars, formerly a royal palace built over the holy well of St Bride. After the REFORMATION Edward VI made it a penitentiary for unruly apprentices and vagrants. It was demolished in 1863, although much of the palace had already been destroyed in the GREAT FIRE OF LONDON.

**Bridge. Bridge of Asses.** *See* PONS ASINORUM.

**Bridge of Gold.** According to a German tradition in seasons of plenty CHARLEMAGNE's spirit crosses the Rhine on a golden bridge at Bingen to bless the vineyards and cornfields.

**Bridge of Jehennam.** Another name for AL-SIRAT.

**Bridge of Sighs.** Over this bridge, which connects the DOGE's palace with the state prisons of Venice, prisoners were conveyed from the judgement hall to the place of execution. The passageway which used to connect New York's Tombs prison (formally the Manhattan House of Detention for Men) with the criminal court was so dubbed for similar reasons.

A bridge over the Cam at St John's College, Cambridge, which resembles the Venetian original, is called by the same name, as also is a similar bridge at Oxford, linking the two parts of Hertford College.

Waterloo Bridge, London, was also called the Bridge of Sighs when suicides were frequent there.

**Bridge roll.** A soft, finger-shaped bread roll, perhaps so called as originally eaten for tea during a bridge party.

**Bailey bridge.** *See under* BAILEY.

**Cross a bridge when one comes to it, To.** *See under* CROSS.

**Devil's Bridge.** *See under* DEVIL.

**London Bridge.** *See under* LONDON.

**Water under the bridge.** *See under* WATER.

**Bridget, St.** The second patron saint of Ireland (453–523), whose feast-day is 1 February. She was a nun renowned for her piety and founded an abbey at Kildare, the first for women in Ireland.

**Fifteen O's of St Bridget.** *See under* FIFTEEN.

**Bridle. Bridle at, To.** To show anger or indignation at something. The metaphor is from a horse being pulled up suddenly and sharply.

**Bridled bear, A.** A young nobleman under the control of a travelling tutor. *See also* BEAR LEADER.

**Bridle path.** A path suitable for riding or leading a horse.

**Bite on the bridle, To.** *See under* BITE.

**Scold's bridle, A.** *See under* SCOLD.

**Brief. Dock brief.** *See under* DOCK.

**Watching brief.** *See under* WATCH.

**Brigade. Brigade of Guards.** *See* HOUSEHOLD TROOPS.

**Blue-rinse brigade.** *See under* BLUE.

**Household Brigade.** *See* HOUSEHOLD TROOPS.

**Red Brigades.** *See under* RED.

**Brigadore** or **Brigliadore** (Italian *briglia d'oro*, 'golden bridle'). Sir Guyon's horse in Edmund Spenser's *The Faerie Queene* (1590, 1596). It had a distinguishing black spot on its mouth, like a horseshoe. ORLANDO's charger, second only to BAYARDO in swiftness and wonderful powers, was similarly called Brigliadoro.

**Brigand** (Old Italian *brigante*, 'fighter', from *brigare*, 'to fight'). The 14th-century 'Free Companies' of France, as in Sir Arthur Conan Doyle's story *The White Company* (1891), were brigands or irregular troops addicted to marauding. Hence also brig, brigandine and brigantine for a pirate ship and, later, for a more general type of sailing vessel. Brigade and brigadier are also derivatives.

**Bright. Bright and early.** Very early in the morning.

**Bright-eyed and bushy-tailed.** Alert and sprightly. The image is of a squirrel sitting on its haunches looking about for food or keeping an eye open for possible danger.

**Bright lights, The.** The glamour and glitter of a city.

**Bright spark.** A witty or intelligent person.

**As bright as a button.** *See under* AS.

**Barnaby Bright.** *See under* BARNABAS.

**Look on the bright side, To.** *See under* LOOK.

**Brighton, Dr.** Brighton, Sussex, from its popularity as a health resort. Its earlier name, Brighthelmstone, was 'smoothed' to Brighton in the early 19th century. Dr Richard Russell drew attention to its possibilities as a watering-place in the 1750s, and it rapidly gained in favour after the Prince Regent (later GEORGE IV) first spent a holiday there in 1782. Subsequently he built the Royal Pavilion, in which he resided on his annual visits, thereby making the town fashionable. This NICKNAME seems to have come into being about the end of the REGENCY.

**Brilliant.** A form of cutting of precious stones introduced by Vincenzo Peruzzi at Venice in the late 17th century. Most diamonds are now brilliant cut, and the word 'brilliant' commonly means a diamond cut in this way. In a perfect brilliant there are 58 facets.

**Brilliant Madman** or **Madman of the North, The.** Charles XII of Sweden (b.1682, r.1697–1718).

**Brimstone. Breathe fire and brimstone, To.** *See under* BREATHE.

**Fire and brimstone.** *See under* FIRE.

**Bring. Bring about, To.** To make something happen.

**Bring-and-buy sale.** A charity sale to which one brings items to sell and at which one buys items brought by others.

**Bring down the house, To.** To cause loud and long applause in a theatre.

**Bring forth, To.** To give birth.

**Bring forward, To.** In BOOK-KEEPING to transfer the total of figures at the bottom of one column or page to the top of the next.

**Bring home the bacon, To.** To bring back the prize; to succeed. The expression may refer to the DUNMOW FLITCH or to the sport of catching a greased pig at country fairs.

**Bring home to, To.** To convince a person of something; to blame someone for a thing.

**Bring in, To.** To introduce; to pronounce a verdict.

**Bring into line, To.** To make someone conform.

**Bring into play, To.** To cause to act; to set in motion.

**Bring off, To.** To achieve successfully.

**Bring on, To.** To cause an event or speed it up.

**Bring out, To.** To publish; to reveal something hidden; to encourage a person to be less shy or reserved.

**Bring round, To.** To restore to consciousness or health.

**Bring someone to their knees, To.** To force a person into submission.

**Bring someone to their senses, To.** To cure them of folly; to make them see reason.

**Bring something home to someone, To.** To make a matter clear to a person.

**Bring to, To.** To restore to consciousness; to resuscitate.

**Bring to bear, To.** To apply oneself to; to focus one's efforts or attention upon, as guns or searchlights are trained on a target; to bring into operation or effect.

**Bring to book, To.** To reprimand someone, or make them explain their conduct.

**Bring to light, To.** To discover and expose; to reveal.

**Bring to mind, To.** To recall.

**Bring to pass, To.** To cause to happen.

**Bring under, To.** To bring into subjection.

**Bring up, To.** To rear from birth or an early age; to moor or anchor a ship; to raise a matter; to vomit.

**Bring upon oneself, To.** To be responsible for something that one suffers, as: 'He brought it on himself.'

**Brought up on the bottle.** Of a baby, artificially fed and not breast-fed.

**Brinkmanship.** A term coined by Adlai Stevenson (1900–65) in 1956 (although he disclaimed originality), with especial reference to the policy of J. Foster Dulles as leading to the brink of war.

**Brinvilliers, Marquise de.** A notorious French poisoner (*c.*1630–76). She married the Marquis in 1651 and in 1659 became the mistress of a friend of her husband, J.-B. Godin de Sainte-Croix. Her father secured the latter's consignment to the BASTILLE in 1663 by LETTRE DE CACHET, where he learned the use of poison. The two together plotted revenge. She poisoned her father in 1666 and her two brothers in 1670, but an attempt on her husband failed. Her crimes were discovered when Sainte-Croix died of accidental poisoning in 1672. She was duly beheaded four years later. *See also* CHAMBRE ARDENTE.

**Briny, The.** The sea, which is salt like brine.

**Brioche.** A kind of soft roll or loaf, made from a light dough. The French phrase *Qu'ils mangent de la brioche*, popularly translated as 'Let them eat cake', has been commonly, but apocryphally, attributed to Queen Marie Antoinette. The remark was said to have been occasioned at the time of the bread riots at Paris (October 1789), when she was told that the starving populace could not afford bread. The saying in various forms has also been attributed to Yolande, Duchesse de Polignac, to the Princess Victoire, to Queen Maria Theresa and others, but seems to have a considerably earlier ancestry. It is said that Princess Charlotte (1796–1817), daughter of the then Prince Regent (later GEORGE IV), avowed that she would for her part 'rather eat beef than starve' and wondered why the people wanted bread when it was so scarce.

**Briseis.** The patronymic of Hippodamia, daughter of Briseus. She was the cause of the quarrel between AGAMEMNON and ACHILLES, and when the former stole her from the latter, Achilles withdrew from battle and the Greeks lost ground daily. Ultimately, Achilles sent his friend PATROCLUS to supply his place. He was killed, and Achilles, towering with rage, rushed into battle and slew HECTOR. TROY fell subsequently.

**Bristol. Bristol board.** A stiff drawing paper or

fine cardboard, said to have been first made at Bristol.

**Bristol Boy, The.** Thomas Chatterton (1752–70), who was born at Bristol and there composed his ROWLEY POEMS (*see under* FAKE).

**Bristol Cream.** A fine rich brand of SHERRY. The name is a proprietary one of Harvey's of Bristol. *See also* BRISTOL MILK.

**Bristol fashion.** *See* ALL SHIPSHAPE AND BRISTOL FASHION.

**Bristol milk.** Sherry. The nickname arose in the 17th century when sherry SACK was a major import at Bristol. *See also* JEREZ.

**Bristols.** A slang word for a woman's breasts. It derives from Bristol City (alluding to Bristol City Football Club) as RHYMING SLANG for titty. There may also be a punning reference to BRISTOL MILK. The words 'Bristol' and 'breast' are similar in any case.

**Britain.** An anglicized form of Britannia, the Roman name for what is now England, Wales and Scotland. In the 4th century BC the inhabitants were known as Prettanoi, and under the Roman occupation they were known as Brittani.

The name Great Britain was first officially used in 1604, when James I was proclaimed 'King of Great Britain'. It had been used earlier by some writers, however, to distinguish Britain from Britannia Minor, or Brittany, in France.

**Battle of Britain, The.** *See under* BATTLE.

**Little Britain.** *See under* LITTLE.

**Britannia.** The earliest figure of Britannia as a female figure reclining on a shield is on a Roman coin of Antoninus Pius, who died in AD 161. The figure reappeared on English copper coins in 1665, in the reign of Charles II. The model was Frances Stewart, afterwards Duchess of Richmond. The engraver was Philip Roetier.

> The king's new medall, where, in little, there is Mrs Stewart's face ... and a pretty thing it is, that he should choose her face to represent Britannia by.
>
> SAMUEL PEPYS: *Diary* (25 February 1667)

**Cool Britannia.** *See under* COOL.

**Pax Britannica.** *See under* PAX.

**Rule, Britannia.** *See under* RULE.

**British. British bulldog.** A team game popular among boys. Members of one team dash across a field and attempt to break through a line formed by the other team, who in turn attempt to catch them. A caught player is hoisted off the ground with the cry 'British bulldog!' and then joins the opposing team.

**British disease, The.** An uncomplimentary term used abroad with reference to the prevalence of strikes and INDUSTRIAL ACTION in Britain during the 1970s.

**British Legion.** An organization for promoting the welfare of ex-service personnel, especially the aged, sick and disabled. It was founded in 1921 largely through the exertions of Field Marshal Earl Haig (1861–1928), and it became the Royal British Legion in 1971. There are many local branches, and much of the money is raised by the sale of artificial poppies. *See also* ARMISTICE DAY; REMEMBRANCE DAY.

**British Library, The.** The British national library, formed in 1973 from the BRITISH MUSEUM library. It opened in new premises at St Pancras, London, in 1998. *See also* COPYRIGHT LIBRARY.

**British Lion, The.** The pugnacity of the British nation, as opposed to JOHN BULL, who symbolizes its solidity and obstinacy.

**British Museum, The.** This famous institution began in Montague House, Great Russell Street. It resulted from an Act of 1753, and its first collections were purchased from the proceeds of a public lottery.

**British warm, A.** A thick short overcoat worn by army officers.

**Britomart.** In Spenser's *The Faerie Queene* (1590, 1596), a female knight, the daughter of King Ryence of Wales. She is the personification of chastity and purity, encounters the 'savage, fierce bandit mountaineer' without injury, and although assailed by 'hag and unlaid ghost, goblin and swart fairy of the mine', she 'dashes their brute violence into sudden adoration and blank awe'. She finally marries ARTEGAL.

Spenser got the name from Britomartis (traditionally, 'sweet maid'), a Cretan NYMPH of Greek mythology, who was fond of the chase. King MINOS fell in love with her, and persisted in his advances for nine months, after which she threw herself into the sea.

**Briton, North.** *See under* NORTH.

**Brittany. Damsel of Brittany, The.** *See under* DAMSEL.

**Eagle of Brittany, The.** *See under* EAGLE.

**Fair Maid of Brittany, The.** *See under* FAIR.

**Broach a subject, To.** To open up a subject or to start a topic in conversation. The allusion is to beer barrels, which are tapped by means of a peg called a broach.

**Broad. Broad arrow.** The mark designating British government property, formerly also used on convicts' clothing. There are various explanations of its origin, but in 1698 an Act was passed imposing heavy penalties on anyone found in possession of naval stores or other goods marked with the broad arrow. *See also* ROGUE'S YARN.

**Broad Church.** A group within the CHURCH OF ENGLAND favouring theological liberalism and tolerance, typified by the writers of *Essays and Reviews* (1860). The name dates from the mid-19th century and the party had certain affinities with the LATITUDINARIANS of former times. They were the forerunners of the Modernists. *See also* HIGH CHURCH; LOW CHURCH; MODERNISM.

**Broads, The.** The Broads, or Norfolk Broads, are an area of lakes, rivers and cuts in Norfolk (and partly in Suffolk) that are famous for their boating and their bird and plant sanctuaries. Although largely manmade, they originated as the water-filled pits left by turf cutters in ancient times. Only coastal defences prevent them from being flooded.

Their name alludes to the width of many of the waterways, as against the restricted channels of rivers and canals. The Broads were designated a national park in 1988.

**Broad Scotch (Braid Scots).** The vernacular of the lowlands of Scotland, which is different from the speech of Edinburgh and from the individuality of the Glasgow dialect.

**Broadside.** In naval language, the whole side of a ship. Hence to fire a broadside is to discharge all the guns on one side simultaneously. The word later came into general use for a verbal onslaught. It is also another name for a broadsheet, a large sheet of paper printed on one side, once a popular form of selling printed ballads.

**Broadway.** Extending 17 miles (27km) through Manhattan and a further 4 miles (6km) through the BRONX, New York's Broadway is a virtual synonym for the theatre world, as the American equivalent of London's WEST END, although by the late 1980s only one 'legitimate' theatre, the Palace, was actually on Broadway itself, all the others having moved up to TIMES SQUARE. *See also* GREAT WHITE WAY; OFF-BROADWAY.

**Brobdingnag.** In Jonathan Swift's *Gulliver's Travels* (1726), the country of the giants, to whom GULLIVER was a pygmy. Hence the adjective, 'brobdingnagian', used of anything very big. In his novel *Lothair* (1870), Benjamin Disraeli wrote of 'a bran-new brobdingnagian hotel'. The name itself is said by some scholars to be an anagram of 'grand big noble' minus the last two letters.

**Brocken, Spectre of the.** *See under* SPECTRE.

**Broken.** *See under* BREAK.

**Broker.** This word originally meant a man who broached wine and then sold it. Hence it came to designate a person who buys to sell again or an agent of some kind. The word is formed in the same way as tapster, one who taps a cask. The word is often preceded by the naming of a particular commodity, as in pawnbroker, shipbroker or STOCKBROKER.

**Bromide.** A dull or boring person, or a trite saying made by such a person. The term was first used in this sense by the American humorist Gelett Burgess in his essay *Are You a Bromide?* (1906). Bromide is properly a dose of sodium, given as a sedative.

**Brontes.** A blacksmith personified, and in Greek mythology, one of the CYCLOPS. The name represents Greek *brontē*, 'thunder'.

**Brontë sisters, The.** The three sisters Charlotte (1816–55), Emily (1818–48) and Anne (1820–49) Brontë, all born at Thornton, Yorkshire, the daughters of an Irish-born clergyman who had changed his name from Brunty. In 1846 they published *Poems by Currer, Ellis and Acton Bell*, choosing these names to disguise their sex. Their novels include two masterpieces: Charlotte's *Jane Eyre* (1847) and Emily's *Wuthering Heights* (1847). Anne's achievement is generally regarded as more modest. The sisters' religious upbringing and intellectual gifts, combined with their emotional and spiritual qualities, place them above most of their contemporaries, and the disparity between what is lofty and what is basic in life is implicit in the name of Charlotte's heroine, evoking air, and that of her anti-heroine, Bertha, Mr Rochester's wife, evoking earth.

> Averse to publicity, we veiled our own names under those of Currer, Ellis, and Acton Bell; the ambiguous choice being dictated by a sort of conscientious scruple of assuming Christian names positively masculine, while we did not declare ourselves women, because – without at the time suspecting that our mode of writing and thinking was not what is called 'feminine,' – we had a vague impression that authoresses are liable to be looked on with prejudice.
>
> MRS GASKELL: *The Life of Charlotte Brontë* (1857)

**Bronx, The.** The residential area of New York, to the north of Manhattan, derives its name from Jonas Bronck, a Swedish sea captain from the Netherlands, who settled here in 1639 in what was then Dutch territory. It was subsequently occupied by religious dissenters and settlers from New England. It is famous for the Bronx Zoo, which opened here in 1899. It is infamous for the BRONX CHEER.

**Bronx cheer.** A mainly American term for a derisive or contemptuous sound, imitating the breaking of wind, made with the tongue between the lips. The British produce the same effect when they BLOW A RASPBERRY.

**Brooklyn.** The largest and most densely populated region of New York, to the southwest of Manhattan, with which it is connected by three bridges. The best known of these is Brooklyn Bridge, a magnificent suspension bridge over the East River whose reputation, however, is marred by the fact that several lives were lost during its construction (1869–93) and that it is a favoured site for suicides. Brooklyn's name reflects its origin as a region of Dutch settlement. It originated as Breuckelen, so called by the Dutch farmer Joris Jansen de Rapalje in 1646 after his native village near Amsterdam. The accent known as Brooklynese is typified by the voice of the cartoon rabbit BUGS BUNNY.

**Brooks's.** This LIBERAL and social CLUB was originally a gambling club, previously ALMACK'S, which had acquired the former reputation of WHITE'S for the high stakes laid by its members. In the late 18th century it led the fashion in hazard and faro. The WHIG statesman Charles James Fox was a patron, as was the Prince Regent (later GEORGE IV). The younger Pitt was a member at one time but subsequently withdrew to White's. It later became a leading Whig club.

**Broom.** (1) The small wild shrub with yellow flowers (Latin *planta genista*) from which the English royal dynasty unhistorically called PLANTAGENETS were named. The founder of the dynasty, Geoffrey of Anjou (father of Henry II), was nicknamed Plantagenet because he wore a sprig of broom in his hat, but it was not until about 1448 that the name was assumed by Richard, Duke of York (father of Edward IV) as a surname. It is more correct to refer to ANGEVIN, LANCASTRIAN and YORKIST kings.

(2) A broom hung at the masthead of a ship indicated that it was for sale or to be 'swept away'. The idea is popularly taken to be an allusion to Admiral Van Tromp (*see* PENDANT). It is more probably due to the custom of hanging up something special to attract notice, as a bush meant wine for sale, an old piece of carpet outside a window meant furniture for sale, a wisp of straw meant oysters for sale and so on.

**Broomstick.** The long handle of a broom, as supposedly ridden through the air by witches.

**Jump over the broomstick, To.** *See under* JUMP.

**New brooms sweep clean.** *See under* NEW.

**Brother.** When used with another noun, this word can denote a fellow member of the same calling, order, corporation or the like. Apart from the more regular instances, such as brother workers, former designations of this type included brother birch for a fellow schoolmaster, brother blade for a fellow soldier or companion in arms, brother brush for a fellow painter, brother bung for a fellow innkeeper, brother Crispin for a fellow shoemaker, brother mason for a fellow freemason, and brother string for a fellow violinist.

**Brother Jonathan.** It is said that when George Washington was in want of ammunition, he called a council of officers, but no practical suggestion was forthcoming. 'We must consult brother Jonathan,' said the general, meaning His Excellency Jonathan Trumbull, state governor of Connecticut. This was done and the difficulty was remedied. Hence the former phrase 'To consult Brother Jonathan', with Brother Jonathan himself becoming the JOHN BULL of the United States until replaced by UNCLE SAM. However, the name may originally have been inspired by 2 Samuel 1:26: 'I am distressed for thee, my brother Jonathan.'

**Brothers' Bible, The.** *See* KRALITZ BIBLE *under* BIBLE.

**Brothers Dromio, The.** *See under* DROMIO.

**Am I my brother's keeper?** *See under* AM.

**Arval borthers.** *See under* ARVAL.

**Big Brother.** *See under* BIG.

**Blood brother.** *See under* BLOOD.

**Bush Brotherhood.** *See under* BUSH.

**Christian Brothers.** *See under* CHRISTIAN.

**City of Brotherly Love, The.** *See under* CITY.

**Pre-Raphaelite Brotherhood.** *See under* PRE-RAPHAELITE.

**Brougham.** A closed four-wheel carriage drawn by one horse, similar to the old GROWLERS. It was named after Lord Brougham (1778–1868), a prominent WHIG politician and former LORD CHANCELLOR.

**Brought.** *See under* BRING.

**Browbeat, To.** To discourage or frighten with threats. The reference is to the scowl or frown that can intimidate when making such a threat.

**Brown.** A former name for a penny or any copper coin, so called from its colour. *See also* YELLOW BOY.

**Brown Bomber.** Joe Louis (1914–81), undefeated heavyweight champion of the world from 1937 until his retirement in 1949. On his return in 1950 he was defeated by Ezzard Charles. He began his career in 1934, winning 27 fights, all but four by knock-outs. The phrase comes from his being black and from the great power of his punches.

**Browned off.** Fed up, disgruntled, disheartened. The slang phrase became popular in the Second World War. The reference is probably to a dish that has been overcooked. Cheesed off is a similar expression. *See also* COOKING.

**Brownie.** The home spirit in Scottish superstition, in England he is called ROBIN GOODFELLOW. At night he is supposed to busy himself on helpful chores for the family over which he presides. Brownies are brown or tawny spirits, and farms are their favourite abode. *See also* GIRL GUIDES.

Brownie was also the name of a make of BOX CAMERA manufactured by Kodak. The first model was introduced in 1900 and was named by George Eastman, the founder of Kodak, from the 'Brownies', the miniature humanoids who populated the children's books of the Canadian-born writer and illustrator Palmer Cox (1840–1928). Eastman's camera was cheap, simple and easy to operate and was especially aimed at children. Hence the appropriate name.

**Brownie points.** Notional credit for something done to please or win favour. The expression probably relates to to BROWN-NOSE but has become popularly associated with the Brownies (*see* GIRL GUIDES), and is thus often spelt with a capital letter.

**Brown, Jones and Robinson.** *See* TOM, DICK AND HARRY.

**Brown-nose, To.** To curry favour; to behave sycophantically. The term relates to 'arse-licking'. *See also* BROWNIE POINTS.

**Brownshirts.** *See* SA.

**Brown study.** A mood of brooding or of thoughtfulness. At one time brown meant 'gloomy', and the meaning has survived in this expression.

> Tom was in a brown study, brooding, like a young William Tell, upon the wrongs of fags in general, and his own in particular.
>
> THOMAS HUGHES: *Tom Brown's Schooldays*, Pt I, ch viii (1857)

**As brown as a berry.** *See under* AS.

**Capability Brown.** Lancelot Brown (1715–83), landscape gardener and architect, who was patronized by most of the rich men of taste. He set their great country houses in a surround of parkland and informal pastoral charm. He was given this nickname because he habitually assured prospective employers that their land held 'great capabilities'.

**Father Brown.** The priest and detective who appears in the short stories by G.K. Chesterton (1874–1936), which were collected in *The Innocence of Father Brown* (1911) and other books. Although outwardly meek and modest, he has a shrewd understanding of the criminal mind. His most fearsome adversary is the French thief Flambeau. His most powerful assistant is his God. Chesterton based him on the Irish priest Monsignor John O'Connor (1870–1952), a well-known figure in Catholic literary circles and the author's lifelong friend.

**John Brown.** *See under* JOHN.

**War of the Brown Bull.** *See under* WAR.

**Bruce, Robert.** In 1306 Robert Bruce (1274–1329) began a resistance to Edward I's domination of Scotland and was crowned king at Scone. The story is that, when in hiding in the island of Rathlin, he noticed a spider try six times to fix its web on a beam in the ceiling. 'Now shall this spider (said Bruce) teach me what I am to do, for I also have failed six times.' The spider made a seventh effort and succeeded. Bruce thereupon left the island (1307), with 300 followers, landed at Carrick, and at midnight surprised the English garrison in Turnberry Castle. His successes steadily grew until, in 1314, he routed the English at Bannockburn. *See also* BON ACCORD.

**Bruderhof** (German, 'band of brothers'). A Christian sect founded in Germany in 1921 with beliefs similar to the MENNONITES. They journeyed to Gloucestershire in England in 1937 when driven out by the NAZIS, but to avoid internment in the Second World War left for Paraguay in 1941. They re-established themselves in Sussex in 1971. The men wore beards and dark trousers with braces, the women were clad in long skirts and headscarves or caps.

They supported themselves by making quality wooden toys in community workshops, and the children first left the community at the secondary school stage. They later became known simply as the Christian Community. There are four other groups in the eastern USA and these are linked with the Hutterian ANABAPTISTS in the western USA and Canada. *See also* KIBBUTZ.

**Bruin** (Dutch, 'brown'). The name of the bear in several children's tales, and originally in the medieval beast epic REYNARD THE FOX.

**Brumaire.** In the FRENCH REVOLUTIONARY CALENDAR, the month from 23 October to 21 November; named from *brume*, 'mist' (Latin *bruma*, 'winter'). The celebrated COUP D'ÉTAT of 18 Brumaire (9 November 1799) was when NAPOLEON BONAPARTE overthrew the DIRECTORY and established the Consulate.

**Brumby.** In Australia, a wild horse, especially one descended from runaway stock. The origin of the word is obscure.

**Brummagem.** Worthless or inferior metal articles, made in imitation of genuine ones. The word is a local form, influenced by gem, of the name Birmingham, a town formerly noted for its manufacture of cheap trinkets, toys, imitation jewellery and the like.

> A work-table ... inlaid with brass ... in that peculiar taste which is vulgarly called Brummagem.
>
> E. BULWER-LYTTON: *My Novel* (1853)

From this comes Brummie as a nickname for an inhabitant of Birmingham, and Brum as a colloquial name for the city itself. On road signs the name is usually abbreviated as B'ham.

**Brummell, George Bryan.** Known as Beau Brummell (1778–1840), a personal friend of the Prince Regent, later GEORGE IV.

**Brunhild** or **Brünnhilde** (Germanic *brun*, 'armour', and *hild*, 'battle'). The daughter of the king of Islant, a powerful virgin warrior loved by GUNTHER, one of the two great chieftains in the NIBELUNGENLIED. She was to be won by strength, which SIEGFRIED achieved, although she never forgave him his treachery.

**Brunt, To bear the.** *See under* BEAR.

**Brush.** The tail of a fox or a squirrel, which is bushy and brush-like.

**Brush aside, To.** To sweep out of the way; to dismiss or disregard.

**Brush by, To.** To touch someone slightly in passing. Hence 'brush' as a brief encounter or skirmish.

**Brush up, To.** To renovate or revive; to refresh one's knowledge of something. In a literal sense, 'to wash and brush up' is to wash one's hands and brush one's clothes or hair after a journey.

**As daft as a brush.** *See under* AS.

**Get the brush-off, To.** To be given a curt rebuff; to be dismissed or ignored.

**Brut.** A rhyming chronicle of British history beginning with the mythical BRUTUS and so named from him. Wace's *Le Roman de Brut* or *Geste des Bretons* (1155) is a rhythmic translation of Geoffrey of Monmouth's *Historia Regum Britanniae* (*c*.1136), with additional legends. Wace's work formed the basis of Layamon's *Brut* (early 13th century), a versified history of England from the fall of TROY to AD 698. *See also* ARTHURIAN ROMANCES.

**Brutum fulmen** (Latin, 'senseless thunderbolt'). A mere noise, an ineffectual act or empty threat. The phrase is from Pliny's *Natural History* (II, xliii, 113 (1st century AD)): *Bruta fulmina et vana, ut quae nulla veniant ratione naturae* ('Thunderbolts that strike blindly and harmlessly, being traceable to no natural cause').

> No legal aid certificate in a limited form could be issued for such a limitation would be *brutum fulmen*.
> *The Times* (8 March 1963)

**Brutus** (Latin, 'heavy', 'stupid'). In the mythological history of Britain the first king and legendary progenitor of the British people, the son of Sylvius (grandson of Ascanius and great-grandson of AENEAS). Having inadvertently killed his father, he first took refuge in Greece, and then in Britain. In remembrance of TROY he called the capital of his kingdom Troy Novant, now London. After the death of Brutus, according to Geoffrey of Monmouth, his kingdom was divided into three parts among his three sons. LOCRINUS received the land called LOEGRIA (England), Camber was granted CAMBRIA (Wales) and Albanactus was given Albania (Scotland) (*see* ALBANY). *See also* MARCUS BRUTUS *under* MARCUS.

**Et tu Brute.** 'Thou, too, Brutus!' Julius CAESAR's exclamation when he saw that his old friend was one of his assassins. 'Does my old friend raise his hand against me?'

**Junius Brutus.** *See under* JUNIUS.

**Marcus Brutus.** *See under* MARCUS.

**Spanish Brutus, The.** Alphonso Pérez de Guzmán (1258–1320). While he was governor, Castile was besieged by Don Juan who had revolted against his brother Sancho IV. Juan threatened to cut the throat of Guzmán's son, whom he held captive, unless Guzmán surrendered the city. Guzmán replied, 'Sooner than be a traitor, I would myself lend you a sword to slay him,' and he threw a sword over the city wall. With this the son was slain before his father's eyes.

**Bryanites.** *See* BIBLE CHRISTIANS.

**Bubastis.** The ancient capital of Lower Egypt, named after Bast, the local cat-headed goddess. The Greeks identified her with ARTEMIS and the cat was sacred to her.

**Bubble.** An unreliable scheme or enterprise, which may at any time burst, like a bubble. *See also* MISSISSIPPI BUBBLE; SOUTH SEA BUBBLE.

**Bubble Act, The.** An Act of 1719 which was designed to check the formation of 'bubble' companies or schemes. It proved to be ineffectual and was repealed in 1825.

**Bubble and squeak.** Cold boiled potatoes and greens fried up together (sometimes with meat). They first bubble in water when boiled and afterwards hiss or squeak in the frying pan.

**Bubbles.** The name given to the portrait of a young curly-headed boy, clad in velvet, with pipe and bowl, blowing bubbles. It was painted by Sir John Millais in 1886 and became widely familiar when used as an advertisement for Pears' Soap. The boy concerned came to be Admiral Sir William James (1881–1973), affectionately known in the Royal Navy as 'Bubbles James'.

**Bubbly.** Sparkling CHAMPAGNE. Until well into the 18th century champagne was fashionable as a still drink.

**Mississippi Bubble.** *See under* MISSISSIPPI.

**Soap bubble.** *See under* SOAP.

**South Sea Bubble.** *See under* SOUTH.

**Buccaneer.** This name was particularly applied to the PROTESTANT sea rovers and pirates of England, France and the Netherlands who haunted the Caribbean in the 17th century. It is derived through French *boucanier* from Old French *boucan*, a word of Tupi origin used for a frame for smoking meat. The adventurers learned how to prepare smoked meat from the indigenous inhabitants of Hispaniola, and came to combine this trade with their regular piracy. Hence the general use of the word to denote a pirate.

**Bucentaur** (Italian *bucentoro*, popularly derived from Greek *bous*, 'ox', and *kentauros*, 'Centaur'). The name of the Venetian state galley used by the DOGE on ASCENSION DAY when Venice was made BRIDE OF THE SEA. The original galley is said to have been ornamented with a man-headed ox. The third and last Bucentaur was destroyed by the French in 1798.

**Bucephalus** (Greek *boukephalos*, 'ox-headed', from *bous*, 'ox', 'bullock', and *kephalē*, 'head'). The charger of Alexander the Great, which, like other Greek horses of the day, was branded with a bull's head.

**Buchan's weather periods.** Alexander Buchan (1829–1907) was secretary of the Scottish Meteorological Society, which, under his influence, built an observatory on Ben Nevis. After many years' observation of weather and temperatures he worked out a curve of recurrent periods, six cold and two warm, in the year. The cold periods are 7–10 February, 11–14 April, 9–14 May, 29 June–4 July, 6–11 August and 6–12 November. The warm periods are 12–15 July and 12–15 August. It should be noted that these dates are the average of many observations and do not predict the probable weather every year.

**Buchis.** The sacred bull of the ancient town of Hermonthis in Egypt, an incarnation of Menthu, a personification of the heat of the sun. He changed colour every hour of the day.

**Buchmanism.** *See* OXFORD GROUP.

**Buck.** A former name for a spirited young man or DANDY.

> A most tremendous buck he was, as he sat there serene, in state, driving his greys.
>
> W.M. THACKERAY: *Vanity Fair*, ch vi (1847)

The word is also American slang for a DOLLAR, perhaps in allusion to the time when skins were classified as 'bucks' and 'does', the former being the more valuable.

**Buckboard.** An open, four-wheeled, horse-drawn vehicle formerly used in North America. It was named from the 'bucking' motion endured by the occupants due to the springy structure of the floorboards.

**Buckeye State.** Ohio, from the abundance of buckeyes or horse chestnut trees that grow there. A Buckeye is a native of Ohio. *See also* UNITED STATES OF AMERICA.

**Buckhorse, A.** Formerly a severe blow or slap on the face, from an 18th-century pugilist, John Smith, whose nickname was Buckhorse. For a small sum he would allow anyone to strike him heavily on the side of the face.

**Buck's fizz.** A cocktail made of CHAMPAGNE and orange juice. It takes its name from its purported place of origin, Buck's Club, where it is said to have been the invention of the club's first barman. The club opened in 1919 and took its name from its founder, Captain Herbert Buckmaster. A cocktail of this type was known in Paris long before this, however.

**Buck tooth.** A projecting upper front tooth.

**Pass the buck, To.** *See under* PASS.

**Bucket. Bucket along, To.** To go fast. Originally the phrase was used when riding a horse fast, so 'pumping' him or taking it out of him 'by the bucket'.

**Bucket shop.** An unofficial or unregistered firm of stockbrokers, which engages in shady dealings with the funds of its clients. The word is also used for any small business that is not entirely reliable, especially one that sells cheap airline tickets. The expression probably alludes to getting something cheap, 'by the bucketful'.

**Kick the bucket, To.** *See under* KICK.

**Buckle down, To.** To get down to work; to apply oneself with determination. The allusion is to buckling on armour before a battle.

**Buckler.** *See* SHIELD.

**Sword and buckler.** *See under* SWORD.

**Bucklersbury.** A street in east central London at one time noted for druggists and herbalists. Hence Falstaff says:

> I cannot cog, and say thou art this and that, like a many of these lisping hawthorn buds, that come like women in men's apparel, and smell like Bucklersbury in simple-time.
>
> SHAKESPEARE: *The Merry Wives of Windsor*, III, iii (1600)

**Buckley's chance.** A phrase used in Australia and New Zealand for an extremely remote chance. One explanation of the phrase is that it comes from a convict named William Buckley (1780–1856) who escaped in 1803 and lived for more than 30 years with Aborigines in southern Victoria. Another derives it from the Melbourne business house of Buckley and Nunn. This produced the pun: 'There are just two chances, Buckley's or None.'

**Buckmaster's Light Infantry.** *See under* REGIMENTAL AND DIVISIONAL NICKNAMES.

**Buckram.** A strong, coarse kind of cloth. It is probably so named as it originally came from Bukhara, in Uzbekistan.

**Buckshee.** Free; gratis. A military slang word derived from BAKSHEESH.

**Buckskin.** A Virginian.

**Bud, To nip in the.** *See under* NIP.

**Buddha** (Sanskrit, 'the Enlightened'). The title given to Prince Siddhartha or GAUTAMA (*c*.563–483 BC), the founder of BUDDHISM. He is also called Sakyamuni from the name of the Sakyas, the warrior tribe into which he was born. This title means 'Sakya sage'.

**Buddha and the boar.** A Hindu legend relates that BUDDHA died from eating dried boar's flesh. The third AVATAR of VISHNU was in the form of a boar, and in the legend 'dried boar's flesh' probably typifies ESOTERIC knowledge prepared for popular use. None but Buddha himself must take the responsibility of giving out occult secrets, and he died while preparing for the general esoteric knowledge.

**Buddhism.** A religion inaugurated by BUDDHA in India in the 6th century BC. It holds that the way to enlightenment consists in knowledge of the Four Noble Truths:

(1) That existence is suffering
(2) That this suffering has a cause
(3) That it can be suppressed
(4) That there is a way to accomplish this, the Noble Eightfold Path: right understanding, right thought, right speech, right action, right livelihood, right effort, right mindfulness and right concentration

**Esoteric Buddhism.** *See* THEOSOPHY.

**Budget** (Old French *bougette*, 'little bag'). The present meaning of the annual estimate of revenue and expenditure and statement on financial policy, which the CHANCELLOR OF THE EXCHEQUER lays before the HOUSE OF COMMONS, arose from the custom of bringing the relevant papers to the House in a leather bag and laying them on the table. Hence to budget is to estimate or to make proper provision for meeting one's expenses. The modern equivalent of the bag is the battered red despatch box which the Chancellor formerly held up outside the door of No. 11 Downing Street, before departing to the House of Commons to make his Budget statement. This was first used to carry the Budget Speech to the House by William Ewart Gladstone in about 1860. It was replaced by a brand-new case in 1997 when Labour came to power.

**Buff.** Properly, soft stout leather prepared from the skin of a buffalo, and hence any light-coloured leather or, figuratively, the bare skin.

**Buffs, The.** *See under* REGIMENTAL AND DIVISIONAL NICKNAMES.

**Blind man's buff.** *See under* BLIND.

**In the buff.** Without clothing; nude.

> The girls call themselves the Groupies and claim they recorded their song in the buff.
> *Rolling Stone* (28 June 1969)

**Buffalo Bill.** William Frederick Cody (1847–1917) earned this name from hunting the buffalo to provide meat for the labourers constructing the Kansas Pacific Railway in 1876–8. He is held to have killed 4280 buffalo in 18 months. He was born in Iowa and, when little more than a boy, was a rider of the PONY EXPRESS. In 1861 he became a scout for the US Army and fought in the Civil War (1861–5). Later on he was fighting once more in the Indian wars and single-handed killed Yellowhand, the Cheyenne chief. In 1883 he organized his WILD WEST Show, which he brought to Europe for the first time in 1887. He paid various subsequent visits and toured the Continent in 1910. His show, with its Indians, cowboys, sharpshooters and rough-riders, was a sell-out.

**Buffer.** An old fogy; a bumbling old man. In Middle English the word was used for a stammerer.

**Buffer state.** A small state between two larger neighbours acting as a shock absorber between the two.

**Buffet, Finger.** *See under* FINGER.

**Buffoon Ape, The.** In John Dryden's *The Hind and the Panther* (i (1687)), the Freethinkers.

> Next her, the *Buffoon Ape*, as Atheists use,
> Mimick'd all Sects and had his own to chuse.

**Bug.** An old word for GOBLIN, sprite (*see* SPIRIT), BOGY and the like, probably from Middle Welsh *bwg*, 'ghost'. The word is used in the BUG BIBLE (*see under* BIBLE), and survives in 'bogle', 'bogy' and in 'bugaboo', a monster or goblin, and 'bugbear', a scarecrow or sort of HOBGOBLIN in the form of a bear.

In common usage the word 'bug' is applied to almost any kind of insect or germ, especially an insect of the 'creepy-crawly' sort, and notably the bed bug. Also it is colloquially used to refer to anyone 'bitten' with a particular craze or obsession, such as money bug, video bug. *See also* BUGHOUSE.

**Bugbear.** *See* BUG.

**Bug Bible, The.** *See under* BIBLE.

**Bug-eyed monster.** A creature from outer space, formerly popular in science fiction, from American slang bug-eyed, having bulging eyes.

**Bughouse.** In American slang, an offensive word for a psychiatric hospital. Hence, as an adjective, 'crazy', 'insane'. In British use the word was applied to a cheap cinema, a 'fleapit'.

**As snug as a bug in the rug.** *See under* AS.

**Big bug.** *See under* BIG.

**Firebug.** *See under* FIRE.

**Jitterbug.** *See under* JITTER.

**Litterbug.** *See under* LITTERBUG.

**Buggane.** *See* BOGGARD.

**Buggins' turn.** The principle of awarding promotion by rotation rather than on individual merit. Buggins is a supposedly common surname, but there were only two in the 1980 London telephone directory. The name itself is familiar in another context from 'Grandma Buggins', a tiresome old lady played by Mabel Constanduros in a radio series that ran from 1925 to the late 1940s.

**Bugs Bunny.** The cartoon rabbit made his first appearance in a Warner Brothers animated short in 1938. He went on to star in comics and on television. His catchphrase, 'What's up, Doc?', was used for the title of a comedy film of 1972. He was to have been called Jack Rabbit, but in the end was named after the infamous West Coast mobster, Bugsy Siegel (1906–47).

**Buhl.** A form of BOULE.

**Building, Body.** *See under* BODY.

**Bulge, The Battle of the.** *See under* BATTLE.

**Bull.** The word has, or had, a number of different senses, some of which are given here.

(1) A blunder, or inadvertent contradiction of terms, for which the Irish are alleged to be proverbial. *The British Apollo* (No. 22 (1708)) says the term derives from one Obadiah Bull, an Irish lawyer of London in the reign of Henry VII, whose blundering in this way was notorious, but this story lacks corroboration. Another explanation is that it is suggested by the contradiction in a PAPAL BULL in which the pope humbly styles himself 'servant of servants' while asserting complete authority.

(2) Formerly, a five-shilling piece. Half a bull was half a crown (2s 6d). Thomas Hood, in one of his comic sketches, speaks of a rogue who, being apprehended, 'swallowed three hogs [shillings] and a bull'.

(3) A short form of BULL'S EYE.

(4) A short form of 'bullshit', army slang for excessive spit and polish and the unnecessary cleaning of equipment. The word is used generally for anything useless or unnecessary, or any foolish talk or nonsense. *See also* COCK AND BULL STORY.

(5) In STOCK EXCHANGE language a bull is a speculative purchase for a rise or the buyer who makes such a purchase. In this sense it is the opposite of a BEAR. A bull account is a speculation made in the hope that the stock purchased will rise before the day of settlement. Since the early 18th century the terms bull and bear have been broadly used on the Stock Exchange to describe an optimist or pessimist in share dealing.

(6) In astronomy the Bull is the English name of the northern constellation TAURUS, which contains ALDEBARAN and the PLEIADES. Hence also the sign of the ZODIAC, which the sun enters about 22 April.

**Bull and Gate** or **Bull and Mouth.** Two possibly related PUBLIC HOUSE SIGNS, said to be a corruption of Boulogne Gate or Boulogne Mouth, adopted out of compliment to Henry VIII, who took Boulogne in 1544. In his 1749 novel, Henry Fielding's Tom Jones stayed at the Bull and Gate in HOLBORN, where there is still a public house of that name.

**Bull-baiting.** The baiting of bulls and bears was a popular sport in Tudor and Stuart England. The beasts were usually tethered and set upon by dogs. Bull-baiting was made illegal in 1835.

**Bulldog.** A determined or tenacious person is sometimes so called. The bulldog itself is so called since it was formerly used for BULL-BAITING. At Oxford University the bulldogs or bullers are the officials who accompany the proctors on ceremonial occasions. *See also* BRITISH BULLDOG.

**Bulldog clip.** A strong metal clip for holding papers together, or on a clipboard.

**Bulldog Drummond.** The manly hero of a popular series of thrillers by 'Sapper' (H.C. McNeile), beginning in 1920 with the one that bears his name. He is a young ex-army officer with a spirit of adventure, and invariably becomes embroiled with a variety of crooks, spies and other sinister individuals. As his nickname implies (he is really Hugh Drummond), he is true 'Empire breed', and his actions and attitudes are thus hopelessly racist, protofascist and anti-Semitic. At the same time, he was undoubtedly the inspiration for James BOND. He was based on the soldier and writer Gerard Fairlie (*c.*1900–83), but his character also displays traits of 'Sapper' himself.

**Bulldozer.** The origin of the word is in the verb to bulldoze, which originally meant to intimidate by violence, probably from bull (the animal) and an altered form of 'dose'. Coercion by physical means, such as whipping, is tantamount to dosing a bull. A bulldozer was a person who threatened in this way, and the term then passed to the powerful machine used for levelling. The word is thus not a corruption of 'bullnoser', as sometimes supposed.

**Bull in a china shop, A.** A clumsy person. The metaphor is obvious.

**Bullring.** In Spain the arena where bullfights take place, and in England, formerly, the place where bulls used to be baited. The name survives in many English towns, as in Birmingham. *See also* MAYOR OF THE BULLRING.

**Bullroarer.** A flat piece of wood, about 8in (20cm) long, attached to a cord and whirled above the head, producing a moaning or humming sound. It was used by the primitive peoples of Australia and North America in rain-making, as well as in initiation and fertility ceremonies.

**Bull run.** A Spanish 'sport' of running through streets before bulls. The best known bull run is that held annually in Pamplona on 7 July, the feast-day of San Fermín, the city's first bishop. The festival lasts nine days, with daily bull fights preceded each morning by the *encierro* (enclosing) of the bulls, which are then driven through the streets behind crowds of men and boys. The runners risk serious injury as they dodge the frantic beasts. The event is vividly described in Ernest Hemingway's novel *The Sun Also Rises* (1926), published in Britain under the title *Fiesta*. Bull runs have also been introduced in some American towns of the old WILD WEST.

**Bull session.** In the USA and Canada this phrase is used for an informal discussion among men only, whether about life in general or some particular problem.

**Bull's eye.** The innermost disc or centre of a target, which in archery and shooting has the highest score. The name is also familiar as that of a black and white streaked peppermint-flavoured sweet. It is also the term for a thick disc or boss of glass, such as one set into a ship's deck to admit light. Hence a bull's-eye lantern, also called a bull's-eye.

**Brazen bull.** *See under* BRAZEN.

**British bulldog.** *See under* BRITISH.

**Charge like a bull at a gate, To.** *See under* CHARGE.

**Cock and bull story.** *See under* COCK.

**Farnese Bull, The.** *See under* FARNESE.

**Ferdinand the Bull.** *See under* FERDINAND.

**Golden Bull, The.** *See under* GOLDEN.

**John Bull.** *See under* JOHN.

**Like a bull at a gate.** *See under* LIKE.

**Not to know B from a bull's foot.** *See under* KNOW.

**Papal bull.** *See under* PAPAL.

**Perillus and the brazen bull.** *See under* INVENTORS.

**Roar like a bull of Bashan, To.** *See under* ROAR.

**Score a bull, To.** *See* BULL'S EYE.

**Sitting Bull.** *See under* SIT.

**Take the bull by the horns, To.** To face danger or a challenge boldly. The allusion is to a form of bullfight in which the matador first tires and weakens the bull then seizes it by the horns in an effort to wrest it to the ground. The metaphor is found in other languages, as French *prendre le taureau par les cornes*, Spanish *coger el toro por los cuernos*, German *den Stier bei den Hörnern packen* and Russian *vzyat' byka za roga*.

**War of the Brown Bull.** *See under* WAR.

**Bullet. Beggars' bullets.** *See under* BEG.

**Bite on or bite the bullet, To.** *See under* BITE.

**Every bullet has its billet.** *See under* EVERY.

**Get the bullet, To.** To be dismissed; to get the sack.

**Bulletin.** An official report of a public event or public news, or an announcement from medical attendants on the health of public personages. The word comes from Italian *bullettino*, a theatre or lottery ticket, from *bulla* (*see* PAPAL BULL), because of their authentication by an official *bulla* or seal.

**Bullions, St Martin of.** *See under* MARTIN.

**Bully.** A person who harms, hurts or threatens weaker people. The original meaning of the noun was 'sweetheart' as in:

> I kiss his dirty shoe, and from my heart-strings
> I love the lovely bully.
>
> SHAKESPEARE: *Henry V*, IV, i (1598)

Its origin is probably in Middle Dutch *boele*, 'lover'. The sense development seems to have gone as follows: (1) lover, (2) fine fellow, (3) blusterer, (4) bully. A lover may still bully a rival.

**Bully beef.** Tinned corned beef. The origin is in French *bœuf bouilli*, 'boiled beef'.

**Bullyboy.** A hired ruffian. Bullyboy tactics are those that put the pressure on.

**Bully off, To.** To start a game of HOCKEY. Two players, one from each side, stand facing each other, with the ball on the ground between them. With their sticks, they then alternately tap the ground and each other's stick three times, after which each tries to be the first to obtain the ball. Bully here may have come from the word for a scrum in Eton football. *See also* WALL GAME.

**Bullyrag, To.** To intimidate or bully, especially by means of cruel practical jokes. The origin of 'rag' is uncertain.

**Rhodian bully.** *See under* RHODIAN.

**Bum.** The word has two distinct uses, of different origins. To the British, the word is first and foremost used for the buttocks or posterior. To Americans, it is a term for a vagrant, and hence any worthless person or thing. The first sense is of uncertain origin. The second is probably from German *bummeln*, 'to loaf'.

**Bumbailiff.** Formerly an official who collected debts and arrested debtors for non-payment. He was so called because he followed close behind the debtors, on their tail.

**Bumboat.** A small boat used to carry provisions to vessels lying off shore. The source of the word may be Dutch *boomschip*, 'canoe', literally 'tree boat', although some derive it from bum (buttocks) in a special use for a scavenger's boat that removed refuse from ships. 'The Bumboat Woman's Story', one of W.S. Gilbert's *Bab Ballads* (1869), has Poll Pineapple of Portsmouth as the narrator:

> A bumboat woman was I, and I faithfully served the ships
> With apples and cakes, and fowls, and beer, and halfpenny dips,
> And beef for the generous mess, where the officers dine at nights,
> And fine fresh peppermint drops for the rollicking midshipmites.

**Bumfreezer.** An Eton jacket, which is short and does not cover the buttocks. The word has also been used for similar jackets for men. *See also* MONKEY JACKET.

**Bumble.** A BEADLE. So called from the officious, overbearing beadle in Dickens' *Oliver Twist* (1839). Hence 'bumbledom', self-importance in a minor office.

**Bummaree.** A former name for a dealer at BILLINGSGATE Market or a porter at SMITHFIELD Market. The word is of uncertain origin. It has been suggested that it could be a corruption of French *bonne marée*, 'good fresh seafish'.

**Bump. Bump and grind, To.** To dance erotically by rotating the pelvis, evoking the motions of a sexual coupling.

**Bumping races** or **Bumps.** Rowing contests held annually at Oxford and Cambridge between the colleges, where the boats try to bump one another, not to overtake.

**Bump into, To.** To meet someone by chance; to run into them.

**Bump off, To.** To murder, a EUPHEMISM deriving from to TAKE SOMEONE FOR A RIDE (*see under* RIDE).

**Bumps, The.** A light-hearted custom of marking a person's birthday. The celebrant is lifted by the arms and legs and 'bumped' (let down to the ground) the same number of times as the age. A similar tradition obtains in other initiation rites. Boys entering the choir at Salisbury Cathedral are admitted by their seniors with an eight-bump ritual. The singer is held upside down and his head bumped gently on a special stone in the cathedral, the bumps falling on the accented syllables of the following, with one for luck: 'We bump you a chorister of Salisbury Cathedral according to ancient custom (bump).'

**Bump suppers.** Festivities that follow the BUMPING RACES, traditionally accompanied by rowdy behaviour from the undergraduates.

**Bump up, To.** To increase prices or charges.

**Bun.** HOT CROSS BUNS on GOOD FRIDAY were supposed to be made of the dough kneaded for the HOST, and were marked with a cross accordingly. As they are said to keep for 12 months without turning mouldy, some people still hang up one or more in their house as a 'charm against evil'.

The Greeks offered cakes with 'horns' on them to APOLLO, DIANA, HECATE and the MOON. Such a cake was called a *bous*, and they also, it is said, never grew mouldy. The round bun represented the full moon, and the cross symbolized the four quarters.

A bun is also a woman's hair gathered in a bun shape at the back of the head.

**Bun fight.** A tea party, or an official party or function.

**Bun in the oven, A.** To have a bun in the oven is to be pregnant.

**Bun penny.** An old penny showing Queen Victoria with her hair in a bun on the obverse. They were issued between 1860 and 1894.

**Bath bun.** *See under* BATH.

**Black bun.** *See under* BLACK.

**Bunch of fives.** Slang for the hand or fist.

**Bundle. Bundle of nerves, A.** A 'jittery' or apprehensive state, or a person in such a state.

**Bundle up, To.** To dress warmly or snugly; to tie things up in a bundle.

**Farthing Bundles.** *See under* FARTHING.

**Go a bundle on, To.** To be very fond of.

**Bungalow** (Hindi *banglā* 'of Bengal'). Originally, the house of a European in India, generally of one storey only with a veranda all round it, and the roof thatched to keep off the hot rays of the sun. The word may have been influenced by 'low', since most houses are of two storeys. In Dr Brewer's 1894 edition of this Dictionary, he mentions that: 'There are English bungalows at Birchington [in Kent] and on the Norfolk coast near Cromer.'

**Bungay, Friar.** Thomas de Bungay of Suffolk, a FRANCISCAN who lectured at Oxford and Cambridge in the 13th century, whose story is much overlaid with legend. He came to be portrayed as a magician and necromancer. In the old prose romance, *The Famous History of Friar Bacon*, and in Robert Greene's *Honourable History of Friar Bacon and Friar Bungay* (acted 1594), he appears as the assistant to Roger Bacon (*c*.1220–92). He also features anachronistically in Bulwer-Lytton's *Last of the Barons* (1843).

**Bunkum.** Empty talk; nonsense. Now more commonly shortened to bunk. The word arose in about 1820 in the USA, when Felix Walker, Congressional representative for the district of Buncombe, North Carolina, made a long, dull and irrelevant speech, when other members of the House of Representatives wanted to conclude the debate on the Missouri Question. He replied that he was not addressing the House: 'I'm talking to Buncombe.'

**Bunny.** A rabbit. It is so called from Scottish Gaelic *bun*, 'tail', 'scut'.

**Bunny girl.** A night-club hostess whose somewhat skimpy costume includes a rabbit-like tail and a head-dress with long ears, like those of a rabbit. They were introduced by Hugh Hefner in his Playboy Club, the perception presumably being that they provided men with an evening's chase.

> Hugh Hefner might never have made it to the big time if he had called his girls *rabbits* instead of *bunnies*. He probably chose *bunny* because he wanted something close to, but not quite so obvious as, *kitten* or *cat* — the all-time winners for connotating female sexuality.
>
> ALLEEN PACE NILSEN: *Sexism and Language* (1977)

**Bunny hug.** A type of dance in RAGTIME rhythm, popular in America in the early 20th century.

**Bugs Bunny.** *See under* BUGS.

**Bunter, Billy.** A fat or greedy boy or man. The name is that of the fat and greedy schoolboy in the stories by 'Frank Richards' (Charles Hamilton) published between 1908 and 1961.

**Bunting, Baby.** *See under* BABY.

**Bunyan, Paul.** A legendary hero of the lumber camps of the northwestern USA. His feats, such as cutting the Grand Canyon of the Colorado by dragging his pick behind him, are told and retold with embellishments by the lumbermen.

**Bunyip.** According to Australian Aboriginal lore this is a man-eating bellowing monster that drags its victims down to the bottom of the lake or swamp that it inhabits. Its name comes from a native Australian language.

**Burble.** To talk quickly and incoherently. The word is probably of imitative origin, but it gained popularity from its use by Lewis Carroll in *Through the Looking Glass* (1872):

> The Jabberwock, with eyes of flame,
> Came whiffling through the tulgy wood
> And burbled as it came.

**Burden.** A line of words repeated at the end of each verse of a ballad or other song, in other words a type of chorus or refrain. It is nothing to do with the burden that is a load, but derives from Old French *bourdon*, 'bass horn', 'droning sound', itself of imitative origin.

**Burden of proof, The.** In law, the obligation to provide evidence that will convince the court or jury of the truth of one's argument.

**Bureaucracy** (French *bureau*, 'desk', 'office'). A system of government in which business is carried on in bureaux or departments. Hence bureaucrat, the head of a department in a bureaucracy; now used to imply an official who rigidly or unfeelingly sticks to the rules.

**Burgh.** *See* BOROUGH.

**Burglary.** A term that in English law used to mean breaking into a house by night with intent to commit a felony, and by the Larceny Act of 1861 'night' was limited to the hours between 9 pm and 6 am. At other times such an offence became housebreaking. The 1861 Act has been repealed and burglary, as defined by the Theft Act of 1968, is no longer restricted to particular hours and includes the damaging of premises entered and infliction of 'grievous bodily harm'.

**Cat burglar.** *See under* CAT.

**Buridan's ass.** An indecisive person, who cannot make up his mind which of two alternatives to take. Jean Buridan was a 14th-century French philosopher who is spuriously said to have posed the following dilemma:

> If a hungry ass were placed exactly between two haystacks in every respect equal, it would starve to death, because there would be no motive why it should go to one rather than to the other.

**Burke.** (1) To murder by smothering, or by some other method that leaves no mark on the body. The allusion is to William Burke (1792–1829), an Irish murderer and body-snatcher, who with his accomplice, William Hare, suffocated his victims and sold the bodies to Dr Robert Knox, an Edinburgh surgeon. With the aid of their wives they lured 15 people to their deaths before being discovered. Hare turned King's Evidence and Burke was hanged. *See also* RESURRECTIONISTS.

(2) The short name of John Burke's *Peerage, Baronetage and Knightage*, which since 1826 has been a recognized authority on Britain's titled classes with their family pedigrees. 'To be in Burke' is thus to belong to an aristocratic family. *See also* DEBRETT.

**Burlington Bertie.** A would-be elegant 'man-about-town' or 'masher', personified by Vesta Tilley in a popular song of this name by Harry B. Norris (1900). The song below is a parody, written by William Hargreaves for his wife, the male impersonator Ella Shields.

> I'm Burlington Bertie:
> I rise at ten thirty
> And saunter along
> Like a toff;
> I walk down the Strand
> With my gloves on my hand,
> And I walk down again
> With them off.
>
> WILLIAM HARGREAVES: 'Burlington Bertie from Bow' (song) (1915)

**Burma Road.** The route that was made in 1937–9 to open up the western interior of China by communication with the sea and that ran from Lashio to Kunming in Yunnan, a distance of 770 miles (1240km). It was the chief highway for supplies to China during the Second World War until the Japanese cut it in 1941. It was recaptured in 1945.

**Burn. Burn a hole in one's pocket, To.** Of money, to be readily and easily spent.

**Burn** or **hang in effigy, To.** To burn or hang the dummy or representation of someone in order to show dislike or contempt. From earliest times it has been believed that magic was worked by treating an effigy as one would wish to treat the original. In France the public executioner used to hang the criminal in effigy when the criminal could not be found. The word effigy derives from Latin *effingere*, 'to form', 'to portray'.

**Burning bush, The.** The bush, traditionally a blossoming green thornbush, in the centre of which MOSES saw flames when he came to 'Horeb, the mountain of God' (perhaps Mount Sinai). As he watched, 'the bush was burning, yet it was not consumed' (Exodus 3:2). However one explains the phenomenon, the event was the first of a series of appearances of God to mankind that occur in the Book of Exodus, and the presence of God made the spot become 'holy ground'.

**Burning fiery furnace, The.** The test of faith imposed by King NEBUCHADNEZZAR on Shadrach, Meshach and Abednego, the three Jewish friends of DAVID. The king ordered them to worship a golden statue or else be thrown into a fiery furnace. They chose the latter, telling Nebuchadnezzar that their God had the power to save them. The three walked together unscathed inside the furnace, accompanied by a fourth figure, a protecting angel. The king was so impressed that he called the men out and blessed their God for saving them. The story is told in Daniel 4, and is an object lesson about the value of trust in God.

**Burning of the Clavie, The.** An annual ceremony held on HOGMANAY in the village of Burghead, Scotland, on the Moray Firth northwest of Elgin. The clavie is a sort of bonfire made of casks split up. One of the casks is split into two parts of different sizes, and an important part of the ceremony is to join these parts together with a huge nail made for the purpose. Hence perhaps the name, from Latin *clavus*, 'nail'. The ceremony may be a relic of DRUID worship, with the two unequal divisions of the cask symbolizing the unequal parts of the old and new year.

**Burning question, The.** A question under hot discussion; the vital question.

**Burn one's boats, To.** To take an irrevocable step; to commit oneself to an action from which there is no turning back. When invading forces burned their boats they were impelled to conquer or die, and there was no returning. *See also* RUBICON.

**Burn one's fingers, To.** To suffer from having meddled or taken a risk. The allusion is to taking chestnuts from the fire.

**Burned child dreads the fire, A.** Once bitten twice shy.

**Burn the candle at both ends, To.** To exhaust oneself by getting up early and going to bed late. The expression can imply either overwork or a life of dissipation, or even both.

**Burn the midnight oil, To.** To sit up late; to work or study late into the night.

**Back burner, The.** *See under* BACK.

**Chinese burn.** *See under* CHINESE.

**Go for the burn, To.** To undertake vigorous physical exercise. The burn is the hot, painful sensation in a muscle after exertion.

**Money to burn.** *See under* MONEY.

**Third-degree burn.** *See under* THIRD.

**Burns' Night.** The evening of 25 January, the birthday of the Scottish poet Robert Burns (1759–96). In Scotland it is a celebration accompanied by feasting and drinking, the HAGGIS being a prominent dish of the meal. *See also* AULD LANG SYNE.

**Burst. Burst a blood vessel, To.** To make a great effort; to strain to the utmost.

**Bursting to do something.** Keen or anxious to do it, so that one feels one may burst if one cannot.

**Burst into tears, To.** To begin to cry suddenly and copiously.

**Burst one's buttons, To.** To overeat.

**Burst out laughing, To.** To laugh suddenly and loudly.

**Burton, Gone for a.** Of a person or a thing, absent, missing or lost, and of a person alone, dead or presumed dead. The expression was common among service personnel in the Second World War. Its origin is uncertain. One account claims that it refers to the training of RAF wireless operators in Burton's clothing store at Blackpool. Those who failed their tests were said to have gone for a Burton and it was subsequently applied to those who were killed. Another popular explanation relates to Burton beer, so that an absent person is presumed to have gone off for a pint. Another suggestion is that when George Cadbury was standing for Birmingham Council in 1878 and supporting the temperance interest, his opponent, Dr Burton, was openly backed by the licensed victuallers. The *Birmingham Post* (22 July) says: 'During the whole of the polling day men were seen coming from Dr. Burton's committee room, and, parading Steward St. with jugs of beer in their hands, on which were painted papers "Vote for Burton".' There are other alleged origins.

**Bury. Burial in woollen.** Under Acts of 1666 and 1678 corpses were not to be buried 'in any shirt, shift, sheet, or shroud' other than of wool nor was the coffin to be lined with any other material. It was intended to encourage English wool manufacturers and was eventually repealed in 1814, after it had largely fallen into abeyance. It had long been ignored by those able and willing to pay the fines for its non-observance:

> 'Odious! in woollen! 'twould a saint provoke!'
> (Were the last words that poor Narcissa spoke).
> 'No! let a charming chintz and Brussels lace
> Wrap my cold limbs, and shade my lifeless face.
> One would not, sure, be frightful when one's dead;
> And – Betty – give this cheek a little red.'
>
> ALEXANDER POPE: *Moral Essays*, Epistle I, iii (1733)

**Bury one's head in the sand, To.** To shirk facing realities. Ostriches were popularly reputed to hide their head in the sand when pursued, since by not seeing their pursuer they thought that they themselves could not be seen.

**Bury the hatchet, To.** To be reconciled after hostility; to let bygones be bygones. The Great Spirit commanded the North AMERICAN INDIANS, when they smoked their CALUMET or peace pipe, to bury their hatchets, scalping knives and war clubs so that all sign of hostility might be put out of sight.

> Buried was the bloody hatchet,
> Buried was the dreadful war-club,
> Buried were all warlike weapons,
> And the war-cry was forgotten.
> There was peace among the nations.
>
> H.W. LONGFELLOW: *The Song of Hiawatha*, xiii (1855)

**Let the dead bury their dead.** *See under* LET.

**Bus.** A contraction of omnibus. A colloquial term for any favourite vehicle, such as an old car or van.

**Busboy.** A person who clears the dirty dishes from tables in a restaurant or café, so called from his 'bus' or trolley.

**Busman's holiday.** There is a story that in the old days of horse-drawn buses a driver spent his holiday travelling about on a bus driven by one of his mates. Hence the phrase, which means a holiday or free time spent doing the same sort of thing that one does at work, so that it is a holiday in name only.

**Miss the bus, To.** *See under* MISS.

**Bush.** An Australian term for wild, wooded and sparsely populated country, derived from Dutch *bosch* and imported from South Africa before the early 19th century. It has given rise to several expressions, some of which follow.

**Bush-baby.** A small, nocturnal, tree-dwelling, lemur-like animal native to Africa, so called from its habitat and its large, baby-like eyes. It is also known as the galago.

**Bush Baptist.** A person of dubious religious convictions.

**Bush Brotherhood.** An association formed to take the Christian religion to the OUTBACK and remote cattle stations. Its members sacrifice their own personal and domestic comforts in so doing.

**Bush carpenter.** A clumsy, inept joiner.

**Bushed.** In Australian use, lost, confused. In British use, however, the word means tired, exhausted; and in Canadian use it means mentally disturbed as the result of living in isolation, especially in the north.

**Bush lawyer.** A person who gives opinions freely but is not qualified to do so.

**Bush oyster.** A EUPHEMISM for a bull's testicle as an item of food.

**Bushranger.** A word originally used for an escaped convict or robber in Australia who lived in the bush to avoid recapture. The word is now used for someone who takes advantage of others by sharp practice or crime. *See also* AS GAME AS NED KELLY.

**Bush telegraph.** In early Australian slang a person who informed escaped convicts about police movements. The word is now used to indicate any rapid and informal spreading of information, or the network by which this takes place.

> Our 'bush telegraphs' were safe to let us know when the 'traps' were closing in on us, and then – why the coach would be 'stuck up' a hundred miles away, in a different direction, within twenty-four hours.
>
> ROLF BOLDREWOOD: *Robbery Under Arms*, ch i (1888)

**Bushwhacker.** In Australia, a person who lives in the bush, especially an axeman engaged in clearing scrub. Hence generally any unsophisticated person or 'hick'. In the USA the word was used for a deserter in the Civil War (1861–5), who looted behind the lines. Pulling a boat along by means of bushes growing on the river banks was also known as bushwhacking.

**Beat about the bush, To.** *See under* BEAT.

**Beat the bush while another takes the bird, To.** *See under* BEAT.

**Benjamin bush.** *See under* BENJAMIN.

**Bright-eyed and bushy-tailed.** *See under* BRIGHT.

**Burning bush.** *See under* BURN.

**Good wine needs no bush.** *See under* GOOD.

**Bushel, To hide one's light under a.** *See under* HIDE.

**Bushido** (Japanese *bushi*, 'warrior', and *dō*, 'way'). The code of conduct of the SAMURAI of Japan. Courage, self-discipline, courtesy, gentleness and honouring one's word were among the virtues enjoined. *See also* CHIVALRY.

**Business.** In theatrical parlance, 'business' is used for some incidental action, such as an actor lighting a cigarette, or Hamlet toying with Ophelia's fan. The business is usually created by the actor who plays the part, but it can be handed down to actors who subsequently play the same part.

> Some scholars have argued that Shakespeare's plays should be performed with the minimum of business; but the text often invites unspecified gestures and movements, and we know that in Shakespeare's own day these were important elements of performance.
>
> JOHN RUSSELL BROWN: *Shakespeare's Plays in Performance*, ch iii (1966)

**Business as usual.** A phrase indicating that normal business carries on as best it can under difficult circumstances. The expression became familiar in the Second World War when shops and businesses aimed to keep going in bomb-damaged premises. The term is something of a hyperbole, since conditions were hardly usual.

> The maxim of the British people is 'Business as usual'.
>
> WINSTON CHURCHILL: Speech at Guildhall, London (9 November 1914)

**Business end, The.** The end or part of the tool or weapon that does the job, as distinct from the handle. The business end of a chisel is the cutting edge, of a rifle the barrel.

**Funny business.** *See under* FUNNY.

**Have no business to, To.** To have no right to, as in: 'She has no business to keep sticking her nose in like that.'

**Land office business.** *See under* LAND.

**Like nobody's business.** *See under* LIKE.

**Mind one's own business, To.** *See under* MIND.

**Send someone about their business, To.** *See under* SEND.

**Busiris.** A mythical king of Egypt who, in order to avert a famine, sacrificed to the gods all strangers who set foot on his shores. HERCULES was captured by him and nearly became a victim. He broke his chain, however, and killed the inhospitable king. The king's name is directly related to that of OSIRIS.

**Busker.** A person who makes money by singing, dancing, acting and the like in a public place, typically by a theatre queue or in a passage of the London Underground. The word may come from French *busquer*, 'to seek'.

**Bust.** Originally a dialect pronunciation of BURST. There are two common senses: (1) A raid, search, or arrest by the police; (2) Having no money, 'broke'. Hence to go bust, meaning to become bankrupt.

**Buster.** Anyone or anything big and powerful, able to bust. The word is also used as a nickname or term of address for a boy or man.

> If you go on accusing me of attacking you lot, buster, you'll have the police to answer to.
> PAT ARROWSMITH: *Jericho*, ch xix (1965)

**Busy bee, A.** An active or industrious person, one who has many things to do. *See also* AS BUSY AS A BEE.

> How doth the little busy bee
> Improve each shining hour,
> And gather honey all the day
> From every opening flower!
> ISAAC WATTS: *Divine Songs for Children* (1715)

**Butcher.** A title given to many soldiers and others noted for their bloodthirstiness. The Duke of Cumberland, second son of George II, was so called for his defeat of the Jacobites with great slaughter at CULLODEN.

**Butcher of Lyons, The.** Klaus Barbie (1913–91), head of the GESTAPO in Lyons from 1942 to 1944, was so nicknamed because of his alleged cruelty, torture and murder of French Resistance fighters and others.

**Bloody Butcher, The.** *See under* BLOODY.

**Royalist Butcher, The.** *See under* ROYALIST.

**Butlin's.** The popular holiday camps of this name were the enterprise of Sir William ('Billy') Butlin (1899–1980), who opened the first on the site of a former sugar-beet field near Skegness, Lincolnshire, on Easter Saturday, 11 April 1936. The camps evolved into modern holiday centres, with a variety of amenities and entertainments on tap for both residents and visitors. The original at Skegness is now 'Butlins Funcoast World'.

**Butter. Buttercup.** The yellow flower, of the genus *Ranunculus*, is probably so called because its colour suggests the butter that is produced from the cows that commonly graze where it grows. The plants are, in fact, poisonous to cattle.

**Butterfingers.** Someone who drops things, or lets things slip through their fingers.

> I never was a butter-fingers, though a bad batter.
> HENRY KINGSLEY: *Silcote of Silcotes*, III, vii (1867)

**Butter one's bread on both sides, To.** To be wastefully extravagant and luxurious; to gain advantages from two sides at once.

**Butter up, To.** To flatter a person with smooth talk, as one spreads butter on bread to make it palatable.

**As soft as butter.** *See under* AS.

**Bread and butter.** *See under* BREAD.

**Bread never falls but on its buttered side.** *See under* BREAD.

**Fine words butter no parsnips.** *See under* FINE.

**Know which side one's bread is buttered, To.** *See under* KNOW.

**Look as if butter would not melt in one's mouth, To.** *See under* LOOK.

**Butterfly.** Figuratively, a person who can never settle on anything for long, but who flits from one interest or pleasure to another.

**Butterfly kiss.** A 'kiss' given by lightly brushing a person's cheek with one's flickering eyelashes.

**Butterfly stroke.** A stroke in swimming, in which the arms are raised simultaneously and brought forward above the water, like the wings of a butterfly. The legs perform an undulating motion from the hips.

**Break a butterfly on a wheel, To.** *See under* BREAK.

**Have butterflies in one's stomach, To.** To experience a fluttering sensation in one's stomach before a formidable venture.

> 'I always have butterflies when I open Parliament', she [Queen Elizabeth II] remarked.
> *Sunday Times* (25 January 1959)

**Madame Butterfly.** In John Luther Long's story (1897) named after her, Cio-Cio-San, a naïve Japanese GEISHA, who falls in love with the American naval officer B.F. Pinkerton only to be deserted by him when she is pregnant. When he returns to Japan married to an American she commits HARA-KIRI. Her story is familiar from David Belasco's play (1900) and above all from Puccini's opera version (1904).

**Buttermere, The Maid of.** *See under* MAID.

**Button. Buttonhole, A.** A flower or nosegay worn in the coat buttonhole.

**Buttonhole, To.** To detain a person in conversation. The allusion is to a former habit of holding a person by the button or buttonhole while in conversation. The French have the same expression: *Serrer le bouton* (*à quelqu'un*).

**Button one's lip, To.** To keep quiet, to stop talking.

**As bright as a button.** *See under* AS.

**Bachelor's buttons.** *See under* BACHELOR.

**Belly button.** *See under* BELLY.

**Burst one's buttons, To.** *See under* BURST.

**Red Button.** *See under* RED.

**Buxom.** The word literally means 'bowsome', and originally applied to a person who was meek and compliant. Since plump women are often comely and good-natured, the term subsequently passed to them.

> Doctors are calling for more images of 'buxom wenches' in the media after fears that waif-like models may be contributing to an increase in anorexia.
> *The Times* (9 July 1998)

**Buy. Bought it.** Killed. One has paid for death with one's life.

**Buy in, To.** To collect stock by purchase; to buy back something offered at auction because the bidding has not reached the reserve price. On the STOCK EXCHANGE the phrase means to buy securities from a defaulting seller, charging that seller with the market differences. *See also* SELLING OUT.

**Buy off, To.** To give a person money or some form of reward to drop a claim, not press a charge or the like.

**Buy out, To.** To purchase the control of a company; to obtain the release of a person from the armed services by a payment of money.

**Buy time, To.** To delay an undertaking temporarily.

**Buy up, To.** To purchase all stock, or as much as possible, in order to obtain a virtual monopoly, and thus command the market. *See also* CORNER.

**Best buy.** *See under* BEST.

**Buzfuz.** Sergeant Buzfuz was the windy, grandiloquent counsel for Mrs Bardell in the BREACH OF PROMISE trial in Dickens's *Pickwick Papers* (1836–7). He represented a type of barrister of the early 19th century, seeking to gain his case by abuse of the other side and a distortion of the true facts.

**By. By a long chalk.** By far; easily. The allusion is to the custom of making merit marks with chalk, before lead pencils were common. *See also* NOT BY A LONG CHALK *under* LONG.

**By and by.** Soon, eventually. The earlier meaning of the phrase was 'instantly', 'immediately'.

> When tribulation or persecution ariseth because of the word, by and by he is offended.
> Matthew 13:21

However, this can be compared with a corresponding passage:

> When affliction or persecution ariseth for the word's sake, immediately they are offended.
> Mark 4:17

**By and large.** Generally speaking; on the whole. This is a nautical phrase. To sail by and large is to sail close to the wind and slightly off it, so making it easier for the helmsman to steer and less likely for the vessel to be taken ABACK.

> Taking it 'by and large', as the sailors say, we had a pleasant ten days run from New York to the Azores islands.
> MARK TWAIN: *The Innocents Abroad*, ch v (1869)

**By Appointment.** The words displayed by the tradesmen and firms that are holders of the Royal Warrant, denoting that they are recognized as regular suppliers of goods and services to the royal households. In the 1990s, there were 850 royal warrant holders, with around 1000 warrants between them. Warrants at this time have been granted only by the Queen, the Duke of Edinburgh, the Queen Mother and the Prince of Wales. Royal warrants are awarded for 10 years, and the holder is entitled to display the appropriate royal coat of arms. The appointment dates from medieval times, when the royal patronage of favoured merchants was first practised.

**By ear.** To sing or play by ear is to sing or play without reading the music, relying on the ear alone.

**By fair means.** Straightforwardly, without deception or compulsion.

**By Gad.** A minced form of God, occurring also in Gadzooks, Begad and Egad.

> How he still cries 'Gad!' and talks of popery coming in, as all fanatiques do.
> SAMUEL PEPYS: *Diary* (24 November 1662)

**By George.** An oath or exclamation. 'St George' was the battle cry of English soldiers, and from this arose such expressions as 'before George', 'fore George'. In American usage it is 'George' that has additional meanings, one of which, applied to any person or thing, has the same significance as the CAT'S PYJAMAS.

**By halves.** Not thoroughly or properly. The expression is normally used with a negative, as, 'He doesn't do things by halves,' meaning that he does them fully and completely.

**By hand.** Without the aid of machinery or an intermediate agent. A letter sent 'by hand' is one delivered by a personal messenger, not sent through the post. But a child brought up 'by hand' is one BROUGHT UP ON THE BOTTLE (*see under* BRING).

**By hook or by crook.** By any means, one way or another. The expression perhaps derives from an old manorial custom, which authorized tenants to take as much firewood as could be reached down by a shepherd's crook and cut down with a billhook.

> His tyreling iade he fiercely forth did push,
> Through thicke and thin, both ouer banke and bush
> In hope her to attaine by hooke or crooke
> EDMUND SPENSER: *The Faerie Queene*, III, i (1590)

**Bylaw** or **bye-law.** A law made by a local authority to apply to the area or district that it governs. The word derives from Old Norse *býr*, 'town', but became associated with 'by' in the sense of something subsidiary. *See also* BY THE BY.

**Byline.** A journalist's signature. A newspaper reporter who progresses from being anonymous to having signed contributions has been given a byline.

**By numbers.** Following simple instructions. The reference is to a procedure where the directions are numbered. A particular example is 'painting by numbers', in which blank areas of an outline drawing are numbered according to the colour to be applied.

**By return of post.** By the next mail in the opposite direction. Originally the phrase referred to the messenger, or 'post', who brought the dispatch and could return with the answer.

**By the by.** Incidentally. 'By-' can often denote something subsidiary or secondary, such as: by-election, an election in a single constituency; byplay, the secondary action in a play; by-product, a subsidiary product; and byroad, a minor road.

**By the dozen.** In large quantities, not necessarily in multiples of 12.

**By the rood** or **by the holy rood.** Old expletives used by way of asseveration. In Shakespeare's *Hamlet* (1600), when the Queen asks Hamlet if he has forgotten her, he answers 'No, by the rood, not so' (III, iv).

**By the skin of one's teeth.** Only just, by a mere hair's breadth. The phrase is biblical:

> My bone cleaveth to my skin, and to my flesh, and I am escaped with the skin of my teeth.
> Job 19:20

**By word of mouth.** Orally, as, 'the message was passed by word of mouth', i.e. spoken, not written.

**Bye, Leg.** *See under* LEG.

**Byerly Turk.** *See* DARLEY ARABIAN.

**Byron.** Lord George Gordon Byron (1788–1824), the great English poet, much admired by his European contemporaries, who died at Missolonghi, serving the cause of Greek independence.

**Polish Byron, The.** Adam Mickiewicz (1798–1855), Polish orator and national poet, buried among the Polish kings in Wawel Cathedral, Cracow.

**Russian Byron, The.** Alexander Sergeyevich Pushkin (1799–1837). The affinity was also attributed to other Russian poets of the age.

> No, I'm not Byron, it's my role
> To be an undiscovered wonder,
> Like him, a persecuted wand'rer,
> But furnished with a Russian soul.
> MIKHAIL LERMONTOV: 'No, I'm not Byron' (1832)
> (translated by Alan Myers)

**Byzantine.** Another name for the BEZANT.

**Byzantine art** (of Byzantium, modern Istanbul, or of the Byzantine Empire). A blend of Roman and Eastern influence and Christian symbolism by the early Greek or Byzantine artists. Its chief features are the circle, dome and round arch, and its chief symbols are the lily, the cross, the vesica and the NIMBUS. Santa SOPHIA at Istanbul and St Mark at Venice are fine examples of Byzantine architecture and decoration. Westminster Cathedral, the Roman Catholic cathedral in London, first used in 1904, is a modern example of Early Byzantine style. It was designed in 1894 by J.F. Bentley (1839–1902).

**Byzantine Empire.** The Eastern or Greek Empire, which lasted from the separation of the eastern and western Roman Empires on the death of Theodosius in AD 395 until the capture of Constantinople by the Turks in 1453.

**Byzantium.** The ancient Greek city on the BOSPORUS, which was founded *c.*660 BC, was rebuilt by Constantine I in AD 330 and called Constantinople. It is now Istanbul.

# C

**C.** The form of the letter is a rounding of the Greek *gamma* (Γ), which was a modification of the Phoenician sign for *gimel*, 'camel', although not actually representing this animal. It originally corresponded with the Greek *gamma*, as its place in the alphabet indicates.

C in Roman notation stands for *centum*, 100. Hence the French and American cent and similar coinages. When the French *c* has a cedilla under it, thus, ç, it is pronounced as an s.

There are poems written in which every word begins with C. Henry Harder composed one of 100 lines in Latin hexameters called *Canum cum Catis certamen carmine compositum currente calamo C. Catulli Caninii* ('A Singing Contest of Dogs and Cats Composed by the Cursive Pen of C. Catullus Caninius'). The opening line is 'Cattorum canimus certamina clara canumque' ('We chant the clear contests of cats and canines').

In music, C begins the only major scale that has no sharps or flats and that is played solely on the white keys on a piano.

It is also the designation of a physical weakling or something of third-rate quality. It is the lowest category in the medical examination for service in the armed forces. *See also* A1.

**Cab.** A contraction of cabriolet, a small one-horse carriage, from French *cabriole*, 'goat-like leap'. The reference is to the lightness of the carriage, which seemed to 'caper' by comparison with its lumbering predecessors. Cabs were introduced into London in the 19th century.

**Cabal.** A JUNTA; a council of intriguers. The word does not come from the Cabal (1667–73) of Charles II's reign, as the group of ministers whose initials (Clifford, Ashley, Buckingham, Arlington, Lauderdale) happened to spell it. It was often applied in the 17th century to the king's inner group of advisers. *See also* CABBALA.

**Cabala, Cabalist.** *See* CABBALA.

**Cabbage. Billy Williams' Cabbage Patch.** *See under* BILLY.

**Cabbala** (Hebrew *qabbālāh*, 'tradition'). A Jewish mystical system of theology and metaphysics, dating from the 11th and 12th centuries, but with much older antecedents in the teachings of, among others, the neo-Platonists and neo-Pythagoreans. Its aim was to relate the finite and the infinite, which was brought about by emanations from the Absolute Being. Passages from the Old Testament were treated as symbolic, and interpretation was based on the significance of numbers. The most important Cabbalistic work is the *Zohar*, written in the 13th century but based on earlier material. English CABAL is from Cabbala.

**Cabbalist.** From the later Middle Ages the main occupation of the cabbalists lay in the devising and decoding of charms, mystical anagrams and the like by means of combinations of letters, words and numbers, in searching for the PHILOSOPHER'S STONE, in prognostications and in attempted or pretended relations with the dead and similar fantasies.

**Cabin, Log.** *See under* LOG.

**Cabinet, The.** In Britain the inner committee of ministers, headed by the Prime Minister, who hold the highest executive offices and largely determine national policy. The Prime Minister chooses the ministers and decides the composition of the cabinet, which has varied in size over the years but usually numbers about 20. Those included in 1998, apart from the Prime Minister himself, who is also traditionally First Lord of the Treasury and Minister for the Civil Service, were: the LORD CHANCELLOR, the CHANCELLOR OF THE EXCHEQUER, the HOME SECRETARY, the Lord Privy Seal, the President of the Council, the CHANCELLOR OF THE DUCHY OF LANCASTER, the Chief Secretary to the Treasury, Secretaries of State for Foreign and Commonwealth Affairs, for the Environment, Transport and the Regions, for Defence, for Health, for Culture, Media and Sport, for Education and Employment, for Social Security, for Scotland, for Northern Ireland, for Wales, for International Development, for Trade and Industry, and Ministers for the Cabinet Office, for Women, and of Agriculture, Fisheries and Food. A Minister for Transport was not a member of the cabinet but was authorized to attend cabinet meetings. Some of the posts were combined, such as Minister for the Cabinet Office and Chancellor of the Duchy of Lancaster. *See also* BOARD OF TRADE. The cabinet is collectively responsible to PARLIAMENT, and its decisions are binding on all members of the government.

The word 'cabinet' originally meant a small room, and it came to apply to the group of politicians who met in the room. The cabinet has its real origins in the reign of Charles II (1660–85). It developed steadily from Hanoverian times with the growth of the Prime Minister's influence, and by the latter part of the 18th century its ministerial responsibility was well established.

In the USA the cabinet consists of the heads of the major departments of state, who are appointed by the President and serve as his advisers. In 1997 these departments were Agriculture, Commerce, Defense, Education, Energy, Health and Human Services, Housing and Urban Development, Interior, Labor, State, Transportation, Treasury, and Veterans' Affairs. Also in the cabinet were: Administrator, Environmental Protection Agency, Ambassador to the United Nations, Director, Office of Management and Budget, National Security Adviser, Trade Representative, and White House Chief of Staff. Unlike their British counterparts, these are not members of the legislature and cannot take part in debates. A new cabinet post must be authorized by an Act of Congress. The President is more independent of his cabinet's advice than is the British Prime Minister.

**Kitchen cabinet.** *See under* KITCHEN.

**Shadow cabinet.** *See under* SHADOW.

**Cabiri** (perhaps from Greek *kaiein*, 'to burn', or Hebrew *gibbōr*, 'powerful'). Certain deities, probably of PHRYGIAN origin, worshipped in Asia Minor, Greece and the islands. Samothrace was the centre of their worship, which involved scandalous obscenities. The traditional four deities are Axierus, Axiocersa, Axiocersus and Cadmilus, who promoted fertility and safeguarded mariners.

**Cable.** In nautical usage the word commonly denotes the rope or chain to which the anchor is secured. Ship's cable is measured in shackles, a shackle being 12 fathoms.

**Cable's length.** A nautical unit of length that has various values. In the USA it is usually taken as 120 fathoms (720ft/220m), while in Britain it is normally one-tenth of a nautical mile (608ft/185m). It is also sometimes taken as 100 fathoms (600ft/183m).

**Slip the cable, To.** *See under* SLIP.

**Veer cable, To.** *See under* VEER.

**Caboched** (Old French *caboche*, 'head'). A term in HERALDRY to denote that a beast's head is borne full face, without any part of the neck.

**Caboodle, The whole.** *See under* WHOLE.

**Ca'canny.** A Scots expression meaning 'go easy', 'don't exert yourself', much the same as 'go slow'. In trade union parlance it means to WORK TO RULE, i.e. to restrict output so as to exert pressure on employers. The expression represents 'call canny', 'to drive gently'.

**Cache.** A French word, from *cacher*, to hide, used in the designations of objects that conceal the thing named by the second word.

**Cache-peigne** ('comb-hider'). An ornament worn at the back of a woman's hat.

**Cache-pot** ('pot-hider'). An ornamental container for a flower pot.

**Cache-sexe** ('sex-hider'). A covering for the genitals, as worn by a model or striptease artist.

**Cache-torchons** ('rag-hider'). A receptacle for keeping cleaning rags out of sight.

**Cachet** (French, 'seal'). A distinguishing mark; a stamp of individuality.

**Lettres de cachet.** *See under* LETTRES.

**Cacique.** *See* CAZIQUE.

**Cackle, To cut the.** *See under* CUT.

**Cacodaemon** (Greek *kakos daimōn*, 'evil spirit'). Astrologers gave this name to the Twelfth House of Heaven, from which only evil prognostics proceed.

> Hie thee to hell for shame, and leave this world,
> Thou cacodemon.
> SHAKESPEARE: *Richard III*, I, iii (1592)

**Cacoethes** (Greek *kakoēthēs*, 'of an evil disposition'). An irresistible or uncontrollable urge, especially to do something harmful.

> Such is the malady and cacoethes of your pen, that it beginneth to bark, before it hath learned well to write.
> JOHN FOXE: *Actes and Monuments* (1563)

**Cacoethes loquendi** (Latin). A passion for making speeches or talking.

**Cacoethes scribendi** (Latin). The love of rushing into print, a mania for being published.

> Tenet insanabile multos
> Scribendi cacoethes.
> (The incurable itch for scribbling affects many.)
> JUVENAL: *Satires*, vii (2nd century AD)

**Cacus** (Greek *kakos*, 'bad', 'evil'). In classical mythology a robber, the son of VULCAN, represented as three-headed and vomiting flames. He lived in Italy and was strangled by HERCULES for stealing some of his cattle. The curate of La Mancha says of Lord Rinaldo and his friends: 'They are greater thieves than Cacus' (Cervantes, *Don Quixote* (1605)).

**Cad** (short form of CADDIE). A man who is 'not a gentleman', especially in his behaviour to others. The word is now old-fashioned, and much less offensive than formerly.

> Bigamist married to three wives at the same time is branded a cad by judge.
> *The Times* (headline) (10 September 1994)

**Caddie.** This word is now solely used for the person who carries a golfer's clubs on the links. In the 17th century it was the term for a gentleman who learned the military profession by serving in the army without a commission. Hence, from the 18th century, it came to be applied in Scottish use to a person looking for employment, and was also a word for an errand-boy. Its origin is in the French word that gave English CADET.

**Cade. Jack Cade legislation.** *See under* JACK.

**Cadency, Marks of.** *See* DIFFERENCE.

**Cader Idris.** A mountainous ridge near Dolgellau in North Wales. It derives its name from Welsh *cadair*, 'chair', and IDRIS, a semi-historical Welsh king. Its central peak and summit is known as Pen y Gadair, 'head of the chair'. The legend is that anyone who passes the night in this 'chair' will be either a poet or a madman.

**Cadet.** Younger branches of noble families are called cadet from the identical French word meaning 'little head', a diminutive ultimately from Latin *caput*, 'head'. Their armorial shields bore the marks of cadency (Latin *cadere*, 'to fall'). *See also* DIFFERENCE.

The word is now generally used to denote certain junior categories of military personnel, especially those training to become officers.

**Cadger.** A SPONGER; one who sets out to obtain things from others without payment, otherwise a scrounger. The word was earlier used for an itinerant dealer in butter, eggs and the like who visited remote farmhouses and made what extra he could by begging. The word is of uncertain origin but is possibly connected with 'catch'.

**Cadmus** (Phoenician). In Greek mythology the son of AGENOR, king of Phoenicia, and of Telephassa. He was the founder of THEBES in BOEOTIA and the introducer of the alphabet into Greece. Legend says that he killed the dragon that guarded the fountain of Dirce, in Boeotia, and sowed its teeth, from which sprang a number of armed men intent on killing him. By the counsel of ATHENE, he threw a precious stone among them. The warriors started killing each other in the struggle to gain it, until only five remained to help him build the city. *See also* JASON.

**Cadmean letters.** The 16 simple Greek letters that CADMUS is supposed to have introduced from Phoenicia. *See also* PALAMEDES.

**Cadmean victory.** A victory purchased with great loss. The allusion is to the armed men who sprang from the dragon's teeth sown by CADMUS.

**Caduceus** (Doric Greek *karukeion*, from *karux*, 'herald'). A white wand carried by Roman heralds when they went to treat for peace. It was carried by MERCURY, the herald of the gods, who used it to give sleep to any person he chose. It is generally pictured with two serpents twined about it, a symbol thought to have originated in Egypt. It was adopted as the badge of the Royal Army Medical Corps, with reference to the serpents of AESCULAPIUS.

**Caedmon.** An Anglo-Saxon poet and monk (d.680) famed for his *Hymn of Creation*, which is preserved in Bede's Latin. All his other work is lost. The VENERABLE BEDE says he was an ignorant man, knowing nothing of poetry, who was commanded in a dream, by an angel, to sing the Creation, which he immediately did. On waking he remembered his verses and composed more. He was received into the monastery at Whitby, where he spent his life praising God in poetry. He has been called the 'Father of English Song'.

**Caerleon.** A town, the Isca of the Romans, on the River Usk near Newport in South Wales. It is the traditional residence of King ARTHUR, where he lived in splendid state, surrounded by hundreds of knights, 12 of whom he selected to be KNIGHTS OF THE ROUND TABLE. *See also* CAMELOT; ROUND TABLE.

Caerleon's present name evolved from its alternative popular Roman name, *Castra Legionis*, 'camp of the legion'.

**Caesar.** The cognomen of Caius Julius Caesar, assumed by his male successors, and by the heir apparent to the imperial throne. The origin of the name is uncertain. It was traditionally explained by the ancients as deriving from Latin *caesus*, 'cut', as Caesar was cut from his mother's womb at birth (the original CAESARIAN SECTION). Pliny related the name to Latin *caesaries*, 'hair', since the emperor is said to have been born with a full head of hair. But these are almost certainly folk etymologies, and the name may really be of Etruscan origin. The titles KAISER and TSAR or Czar derive from the name. *See also* AUGUSTUS.

**Caesarian section.** The delivery of a child from the womb through an incision in the abdomen. The operation is said to be so called because Julius CAESAR was thus brought into the world, but a better derivation is from Latin *caesus*, '(having been) cut'.

**Caesar's wife must be above suspicion.** When Pompeia, CAESAR's wife, was accused of adultery with Publius Clodius, Caesar divorced her, not because he believed her guilty but because the wife of Caesar must not be even suspected of crime and her name must be untainted.

**Aut Caesar aut nullus.** *See under* AUT.

**Café Royal.** The Regent Street restaurant developed from that opened in Glasshouse Street in 1865 by a French wine merchant, Daniel Thévenon. From the 1890s to the 1920s it was a famous and fashionable meeting-place for writers and artists, among them Walter Sickert, Augustus John, Oscar Wilde, Aubrey Beardsley and Max Beerbohm. In more recent times its patrons have also been BBC people.

**Cage, Gilded.** *See under* GILD.

**Cagliostro.** Count Alessandro di Cagliostro was the assumed name of the Italian adventurer and impostor Giuseppe Balsamo (1743–95), of Palermo. He played a prominent part in the AFFAIR OF THE DIAMOND NECKLACE, and among his many frauds was the offer of everlasting youth to all who would pay him for his secret.

**Cagmag.** A northern dialect word for anything shoddy or of poor quality. It originally denoted tough goose meat or bad meat or offal in general. Its derivation is uncertain.

**Cagoulards.** Members of a secret right-wing organization in France in the 1930s were so called because they wore a garment like a *cagoule* or monk's cowl. The English adopted the French word for a lightweight type of anorak, especially one that comes down to the knees. The garment is familiarly known as a cag.

**Cahoots, In.** In collusion. The origin of the word is uncertain. Some claim a derivation in French *cahute*, 'cabin'.

**Caiaphas.** The high priest in Jerusalem whose term of office included the trial of Jesus (Matthew 26:57). He was the son-in-law of the high priest Annas. According to Dante's *Inferno* (*c*.1309–*c*.1320) both he and Annas were crucified in a ditch together with all the members of the SANHEDRIN.

**Cain.** The first son of ADAM and EVE, and a tiller of the soil. Cain and his brother, ABEL, a shepherd, made a gift to God of their produce. God accepted Abel's gift but not Cain's. Cain then killed Abel and, when challenged by God regarding Abel's whereabouts, replied 'AM I MY BROTHER'S KEEPER?' (Genesis 4:9). God then cursed Cain and condemned him to a life of labour and vagrancy. But He also 'set a mark upon Cain' (Genesis 4:15) so that nobody would kill him. Cain moved to the LAND OF NOD, east of EDEN, where his wife bore him a son, Enoch. According to tradition, Cain met his death in a hunting accident.

> Had Cain been Scot, God would have changed his doom
> Nor forced him wander, but confined him home.
> JOHN CLEVELAND: 'The Rebel Scot' (1647)

**Cainites.** A heretical sect of the 2nd century AD, so named because they held that Cain was made by an almighty power and ABEL by a weak one. They renounced the New Testament in favour of the 'Gospel of Judas', which justified the false disciple and the crucifixion of Jesus, and held that the way to salvation was to yield to every lust.

**Curse of Cain, The.** *See under* CURSE.

**Raise Cain, To.** *See under* RAISE.

**Ça ira** (French, 'Things will work out', literally 'It will go'). The name and refrain of a popular French patriotic song, which became the musical banner of the French Revolution. It went to the tune of the *Carillon National*, which Marie Antoinette liked to strum on her harpsichord.

As a rallying cry it was borrowed from Benjamin Franklin, who used to say, in reference to the American Revolution, '*Ah! ah! ça ira, ça ira!*' The refrain of the French revolutionary version was:

> Ah! ça ira, ça ira, ça ira,
> Les aristocrates à la lanterne.
> (Oh, we'll get by, we'll get by, we'll get by,
> String up the nobs on the lamp-post high.)

**Caius College.** The Cambridge college, properly Gonville and Caius, was founded by Edmund Gonville in 1348 as a hall. In 1558 it was raised to the status of a college by Dr John Caius, of Norwich. He was first physician to Edward VI, Mary Tudor and Elizabeth I and wrote treatises on various subjects, including one on the antiquity of Cambridge University, which, he asserted, was founded by Cantaber in 394 BC.

**Cake. Cakes and ale.** A good time. The phrase 'life is not all cakes and ale' means that life is not all pleasure or all 'beer and skittles'. In Shakespeare's *Twelfth Night* (1601) the roistering Sir Toby Belch says to the puritanical Malvolio, who seeks to quell a rowdy party: 'Dost thou think, because thou art virtuous, there shall be no more cakes and ale?' (II, iii). W. Somerset Maugham has a novel *Cakes and Ale* (1930).

**Cakewalk.** A dance based on a march with intricate steps, originally danced by blacks in the southern states of America. The prize for the best dancer was a cake. Hence the fairground attraction known as the cakewalk, a series of platforms or gangways moved by machinery along which one does one's best to walk.

**Angel cake.** *See under* ANGEL.

**Banbury cake.** *See under* BANBURY.

**Bride cake.** *See under* BRIDE.

**Fairy cake.** *See under* FAIRY.

**Go** or **sell like hot cakes, To.** To be a great success; to sell well.

**Have one's cake and eat it, To.** To enjoy each of two equally desirable things. Mostly one cannot do this, so that it is more common to hear: 'You can't have your cake and eat it.'

**Land of Cakes, The.** *See under* LAND.

**Piece of cake, A.** *See under* PIECE.

**Pontefract cakes.** *See under* PONTEFRACT.

**Simnel cakes.** *See under* SIMNEL.

**Soul cakes.** *See under* SOUL.

**Take the cake, To.** To carry off the honours; to beat all others in absurdity. The reference is to the CAKEWALK, the prize for which was a cake. In ancient Greece, a cake was the award to the toper who held out longest, and in Ireland the best dancer in a dancing competition was rewarded, at one time, by a cake. *See also* TAKE THE BISCUIT *under* BISCUIT.

**Welsh cake.** *See under* WELSH.

**Calainos.** The hero of an old Spanish ballad. Calainos the Moor asked a maid to marry him. She agreed on condition that he bring her the heads of the three PALADINS of CHARLEMAGNE: RINALDO, ROLAND and OLIVER. Calainos went to Paris and challenged them. Sir BALDWIN, the youngest knight, accepted the challenge and was overthrown, but his uncle Roland then opposed the Moor and slew him.

**Calais.** This city and port on the English Channel in northern France was in English hands for over 200 years. It was won by Edward III following his victory at CRÉCY in 1347 and returned to the French only in 1558, when it was retaken by Francis I, 2nd Duke de Guise. Its loss was a bitter blow to BLOODY MARY. In medieval times the name of Calais was written and pronounced Callis, and this is believed to have given callis as a local word for an ALMSHOUSE in certain towns associated with the wool staple at Calais, such as St Peter's Callis and Williamson's Callis at Stamford, Lincolnshire. Callis sand was similarly a type of fine white sand used for blotting ink, scouring and the like. It was got from the sand dunes at Calais, a favourite location for duels in the 17th century.

> When I am dead and opened, you shall find 'Calais' lying in my heart.
>
> MARY TUDOR: *Holinshed's Chronicles*, IV (1808)

**Calamity Jane.** The popular name of Martha Jane Burke, *née* Cannary (*c*.1852–1903), American frontierswoman famed for her skill at riding and shooting, particularly during the Gold Rush days in the Black Hills of Dakota. It is claimed that she threatened 'calamity' to any man who tried to woo her, but she did, in fact, marry.

**Calceolaria.** The slipperwort, so named from its speckled, slipper-shaped flowers, from Latin *calceolus*, 'little shoe'.

**Calchas.** A Greek soothsayer in the TROJAN WAR. He told the Greeks that the aid of ACHILLES was essential for the taking of the city, that IPHIGENIA must be sacrificed before the fleet could sail from AULIS and that the siege would take ten years. He is said to have died of disappointment after being beaten in a trial of skill by the prophet Mopsus.

**Calculate, To.** The verb is from Latin *calculus*, 'pebble', referring to the small stones used by the Romans for counters. In the ABACUS the round balls were called calculi. The Greeks voted by pebbles dropped into an urn, a method adopted both in ancient Egypt and Syria. To count these pebbles was to calculate the number of voters.

**Calculator, The.** Among those of unusual mathematical prowess who have been awarded this title are:

- Alfragan, the Arabian astronomer (d.830)
- Jedediah Buxton (1705–72) of Elmton, Derbyshire, a farm labourer of little education, who exhibited in London in 1754
- George Bidder (1806–78) of Moretonhampstead, Devon, and Zerah Colburn (1804–40) of Vermont, USA, who as young boys both publicly performed astonishing mathematical feats
- Jacques Inaudi (1867–1950), an Italian who exhibited 'his astounding powers of calculating' at Paris in 1880; his additions and subtractions, contrary to the usual procedure, were from left to right

*See also* TRACHTENBERG SYSTEM.

**Calcutta, The Black Hole of.** *See under* BLACK.

**Caleb.** In the Old Testament (Joshua 14–15), a spy sent by MOSES into the PROMISED LAND. He and his close companion, JOSHUA, are the only Israelites to cross both the RED SEA out of Egypt and the Jordan.

**Caledonia.** The Roman name for Scotland but now used only in poetry and in a few commercial or geographical connections, such as the Caledonian Hotel or the Caledonian Canal.

**Caledonian Market.** Until its closure at the outbreak of the Second World War, this Islington cattle and general market was especially noted for miscellaneous second-hand goods and was much frequented by bargain hunters. Dubbed the 'thieves' market', it was partially a relic of London's BARTHOLOMEW FAIR, which ceased in 1855, the year in which the Caledonian Market opened. A legacy of the original survives, however, in the New Caledonian Market, a weekly antiques market or 'rag fair' in Bermondsey Street.

**Calendar.** The word comes from Medieval Latin *kalendarium*, 'account book', itself from *Kalendae*, CALENDS, the day when interest on debts became due in the ROMAN CALENDAR. *See also* FRENCH REVOLUTIONARY; GREGORIAN; JEWISH; JULIAN; MUSLIM; NEWGATE.

**Calender** (Persian *kalandar*). A member of a begging order of dervishes founded in the 13th century by Qalander Yusuf al-Andalusi, a native of Spain. They took a vow of perpetual wandering and feature in the story of 'The Three Calenders' in the ARABIAN NIGHTS ENTERTAINMENTS.

**Calends** (Latin *calare*, 'to proclaim'). The first day of each month in the ROMAN CALENDAR. Varro says the term originated in the practice of calling the people together on the first day of the month, when the pontifex informed them of the time of the new moon, the day of the NONES and the festivals and sacred days to be observed. *See also* GREEK CALENDS.

**Calepin, A.** A dictionary. Ambrogio Calepino (*c*.1440–1510) of Calepio in Italy was the author of a Latin–Italian dictionary (1502), and the expression 'my Calepin' was used in earlier days as 'my EUCLID', 'my Liddell and Scott', 'my Lewis and Short', 'my Hillard and Botting', 'my Kennedy' and so on became common later.

Whom doe you prefer,
For the best linguist? And I seelily
Said, that I thought Calepines Dictionarie.
JOHN DONNE: *Satyre* iv (1594)

**Calf. Calf love.** A youthful infatuation; immature love as opposed to lasting attachment.

**Calf's- or calves'-foot jelly.** A jelly made from the stock of boiled calves' feet, formerly given as an easily digestible food to invalids.

**Calfskin.** Fools and jesters used to wear a calfskin coat buttoned down the back. In Shakespeare's *King John* (III, i (1596)), Constance says scathingly to the Archduke of Austria:

Thou wear a lion's hide! Doff it for shame,
And hang a calf's skin on those recreant limbs!

**Calves.** The inhabitants of the Isle of Wight were sometimes so called from a tradition that a calf once got its head firmly wedged in a wooden pale, and instead of breaking up the pale, the farmhand cut off the calf's head.

**Kill the fatted calf, To.** *See under* KILL.

**Worship the golden calf, To.** *See under* WORSHIP.

**Caliban.** A brutish man. The allusion is to Shakespeare's Caliban in *The Tempest* (1611), the deformed half-human son of a demon and a witch, slave to PROSPERO. His name is thought to be a near-anagram of cannibal, although it could also be Romany *kaliban*, 'blackener'. At one point in the play (V, i) he is referred to as a 'thing of darkness'.

**Caliburn.** A poetic variant of EXCALIBUR, King ARTHUR's well-known sword.

And onward Arthur paced, with hand
On Caliburn's resistless brand.
SIR WALTER SCOTT: *Bridal of Triermain*, xv (1813)

**Calidore, Sir.** In Edmund Spenser's *The Faerie Queene* (VI (1596)) the archetype of courtesy and the lover of 'fair Pastorella'. He is described as the most courteous of all knights and is referred to as the 'all-beloved'. He probably represents Sir Philip Sidney or the Earl of Essex.

**Calif.** *See* CALIPH.

**Caligula.** A notorious Roman emperor (AD 12–41), so named because, when with the army as a boy, he wore military sandals called *caligae*, which had no upper leather and were used only by the common soldiers.

Caligula's cruelties and excesses amounted almost to madness. He built a temple to himself, committed incest with his sisters, fed animals luxuriously in his palace as if they were human and made his horse, INCITATUS, a consul. He was assassinated.

**Calipash** and **calipee.** These exotic terms describe choice portions of the turtle. Calipash is the fatty, dull greenish substance of the upper shell, and calipee is the light yellow fatty stuff belonging to the lower. The origin of the words is uncertain, but the first, at least, appears to derive from carapace, the word for the turtle's upper shell.

Cut off the bottom shell, then cut off the meat that grows to it (which is the callepy or fowl).
MRS RAFFALD: *English Housekeeping* (1769)

**Caliph** or **calif** (Arabic *khalifa*, 'successor'). A title given to the successors of MOHAMMED in temporal and spiritual affairs. After the first four successors, the caliphate passed to the Omayyad dynasty (661), thence to the ABBASSIDS (670–1538). The caliphate of Baghdad reached its highest splendour under Haroun al-Raschid (786–809). From the 13th century the titles of caliph, sultan and imam came to be used indiscriminately, but in the 19th century Ottoman sultans sought to revive their claim to the title, especially Abdul Hamid II (1876–1908). In 1924 the Turks declared the abolition of the caliphate.

**Call, A.** A summons; an invitation felt to be divine, as a call to the ministry.

**Call alarm, A.** An electronic alarm used to summon help by an elderly or disabled person living alone.

**Call a person names, To.** To insult a person through the use of derogatory nicknames; to hurl opprobrious epithets at someone.

Sticks and stones
May break my bones
But words can never hurt me.
Old rhyme

**Call a spade a spade, To.** To be outspoken or blunt, even to the point of rudeness; to call things by their proper names without any beating about the bush. The ancient Greeks had a similar expression, and Menander (1st century BC) has a character say: 'I call a fig a fig, a spade a spade.'

**Call bird, A.** Originally a bird trained as a decoy. Hence, in commercial parlance, a cheap article displayed in a shop to attract custom. Those enticed by it may be persuaded to buy more expensive items.

**Call box, A.** A public telephone booth.

**Callboy, A.** A boy or man employed in theatres to call or summon actors in time for them to appear on the stage.

**Called to the bar, To be.** To be admitted a BARRISTER. Students having attained the necessary standing used to be called from the body of the hall to the bar. To disbar means to expel a barrister from his profession. *See also* BAR.

**Called within the bar, To be.** To be appointed KING'S COUNSEL or Queen's Counsel, i.e. to be admitted within the bar that separate the members of the court from the prisoners, junior counsel and the public. KCs and QCs are thus of the inner bar.

**Call girl, A.** A prostitute whom potential clients can call by telephone.

**Call God to witness, To.** To declare solemnly that what one states is true.

**Call in, To.** To visit someone when in their locality. To summon a professional person, such as a specialist, to give advice. In banking, to call in is to take coins or notes out of circulation.

**Call in** or **into question, To.** To dispute; to doubt the truth of a statement.

**Call it a day, To.** To give in; to give up; to stop work.

**Call it quits, To.** To agree that matters are now even; to call a truce in a dispute or disagreement. 'Quit' here may be an abbreviation of medieval Latin *quittus*, from Latin *quietus*, 'quiet'.

**Call letters.** The CALL SIGN of an American radio station.

**Call loan, A.** A loan repayable on demand.

**Call me stupid.** A phrase, usually followed by 'but', used to point out a truth that others seem to have overlooked. The speaker implies that the adjective, although at other times perhaps applicable, is not so in this instance.

> Call me old-fashioned, but it seems to me that one of the great things to be said for being married is the combination of company and privacy.
> LIBBY PURVES in *The Times* (12 January 1999)

**Call of Abraham, The.** The invitation or command of God to ABRAHAM to leave his idolatrous country, under the promise of becoming father of a great nation (Genesis 12:1–2).

**Call off, To.** To cancel a forthcoming event; to withdraw from a deal.

**Call off the dogs, To.** To desist from some pursuit or inquiry, to break up a disagreeable conversation. In the chase the huntsman calls off the dogs if they are on the wrong track.

**Call of God, The.** An invitation, exhortation or warning by the dispensations of Providence (Isaiah 22:12), or, more generally, divine influence to do or avoid something (Hebrews 3:1).

**Call of nature, A.** A need to urinate or defecate.

**Call out, To.** To summon a person outside his or her normal working hours, as one calls out a plumber in an emergency. Also, to order workers to strike.

> An electrician told me that the previous evening his firm had been called out to change a light bulb in the judges' lodgings at a cost (to the taxpayer) of £25.
> *The Times* (28 September 1994)

**Call** or **haul over the coals, To.** To bring to task; to reprimand. At one time Jews were 'bled' whenever the kings or barons wanted money. One common torture, if they resisted, was to haul them over the coals of a slow fire so as to give them a 'roasting'. In Sir Walter Scott's *Ivanhoe* (1819) Front-de-Boeuf threatens to haul Isaac over the coals.

**Call sign.** The group of letters and numbers that identifies a (usually amateur) radio station.

**Call someone's bluff, To.** To challenge someone to prove their claims. A poker player sometimes bluffs by exaggerating the strength of his hand, betting large sums on it in the hope that others will withdraw. At some stage, however, an opponent matching his stake has the right to call on him to show his hand.

**Call someone to account, To.** To rebuke a person; to insist on an explanation for a person's actions.

**Call the shots, To.** To have control over a situation; to be the one who is in charge. The allusion is to a game of pool, in which the player nominates which ball must go into which pocket, so avoiding fluke scores.

**Call to arms, To.** To summon; to prepare for battle.

**Call to mind, To.** To recollect; to remember.

**Call to order, To.** To request to be orderly; to declare a meeting open.

**Call up, To.** To summon for military service.

**Close call.** *See under* CLOSE.

**Cold call.** *See under* COLD.

**Curtain call.** *See under* CURTAIN.

**House of call.** *See under* HOUSE.

**Trunk call.** *See under* TRUNK.

**Caller herrings.** Fresh herrings. The adjective is also applied in Scotland to fresh air, water and the like, if it is cool. The word is a form of 'calver', an old word specifically applied to fresh fish. 'Caller Herrin'' is the title of a poem, written *c.*1821, to fit the tune of a piece by Nathaniel Gow (1766–1831). Scottish fishwives would cry:

> Wha'll buy ma caller herrin'?
> They're bonnie fish an' halesome farin'.

**Calliope** (Greek *kalliopē*, 'beautiful voice', from *kallos*, 'beauty', and *ops*, 'voice'). The Muse of epic or heroic poetry, and of poetic inspiration and eloquence. *See also* MUSES.

The name is also applied to a type of steam organ.

**Callippic period.** A correction of the METONIC CYCLE by Callippus, the Greek astronomer of the 4th century BC. To remedy the defect in the Metonic cycle, Callippus quadrupled the period of Meton, making his cycle one of 76 years, and deducted a day at the end of it, by which means he calculated that the new and full moons would be brought round to the same day and hour. His calculation, however, is not absolutely accurate, as one whole day is lost every 553 years.

**Callisto and Arcas.** Callisto (Greek *kallistos*, 'the most beautiful') was an Arcadian NYMPH metamorphosed into a she-bear by JUPITER. Her son Arcas (Greek *arktos*, 'bear') met her when hunting and would have killed her, but Jupiter converted him into a he-bear, and placed them both in the heavens, where they are recognized as the GREAT BEAR and Little Bear. *See also* ARCTIC.

**Calomel.** A type of whitish medicinal powder consisting mainly of mercurous chloride. Robert Hooper's *Compendious Medical Dictionary* (1798) says the following:

> This name, which means 'beautiful black', was originally given to the Aethiop's mineral, or black sulphuret of mercury. It was afterwards applied in joke by Sir Theodore Mayerne to the chloride of mercury, in honour of a favourite negro servant whom he employed to prepare it. As calomel is a white powder, the name is merely a jocular misnomer.

However, this is almost certainly a folk etymology. The name does mean 'beautiful black', from Greek *kalos*, 'beautiful', and *melas*, 'black', but this is probably because the substance was sublimed from a black mixture of mercury and mercuric chloride.

**Calpe.** The ancient name of (the Rock of) Gibraltar and in Greek mythology one of the PILLARS OF HERCULES. The other, the opposite promontory in Morocco, is Jebel Musa, originally called Abyla. According to one account these two were originally one mountain, which HERCULES tore asunder.

**Caltrop** or **caltrap.** A medieval four-spiked iron ball, or four joined spikes, placed on the ground to lame the horses of the attacking cavalry. The name is originally that of a tropical plant with spiny burs or bracts. It derives from Medieval Latin *calcatrippa*, probably meaning 'heel trap', from *calx*, 'heel', and *trippa*, 'trap'. One form of the English word to evolve was chevaltrap, as if from French *cheval*, 'horse', and trap. There is a modern equivalent in the 'stinger', a device of metal spikes used to puncture pneumatic tyres.

**Calumet.** The 'pipe of peace' of the North American Indians. The word is of French Canadian origin, from the Norman dialect word meaning 'straw', ultimately from Latin *calamus*, 'reed'. It was the name they gave to certain plants used by the natives as pipe stems, and hence to the pipe itself. The calumet is about 2ft 6in (76cm) long, the stem is reed and the bowl is of highly polished red marble. To present the calumet to a stranger is a mark of hospitality and goodwill, and to refuse such an offer is an act of hostility. *See also* MATÉ.

> Gitche Manito, the mighty,
> Smoked the calumet, the Peace-Pipe,
> As a signal to the nations.
>
> H.W. LONGFELLOW: *Song of Hiawatha*, i (1855)

**Calvary.** The name given to the place of Christ's crucifixion represents Late Latin *Calvaria*, a translation of Greek *kranion*, 'skull', itself a translation of Aramaic *gulgulta*, which gave the alternative name of the place, GOLGOTHA. Legend has it that the skull of ADAM was preserved here, but the name is probably due to a fancied resemblance of the configuration of the ground to the shape of a skull.

The actual site may be that occupied by the church of the Holy Sepulchre, or possibly an eminence above the grotto of Jeremiah not far from the Damascus Gate.

**Calvary, A.** A representation of the successive scenes of the PASSION of Christ in a series of pictures or the like in a church, or else the shrine containing such representations. Wayside calvaries or crosses, representing the crucifixion, are common in parts of Europe and some notable examples are to be found in Brittany.

**Calvary clover.** A common trefoil, *Medicago echinus*, said to have sprung up in the track made by PILATE when he went to the cross to see his 'title affixed' ('Jesus of Nazareth, King of the Jews'). Each of the three leaves has a carmine spot in the centre. In the daytime they form a sort of cross, and in the flowering season the plant bears a small yellow flower, like a 'crown of thorns'. Julian the Apostate (332–363) writes that each of the three leaves had in his time a white cross in the centre, and that the centre cross remains visible longer than the others.

**Calvary cross, A.** A Latin CROSS mounted on three steps.

**Calvinism.** The doctrines of the reformer Jean Calvin (1509–64), particularly as expressed in his *Institutio Religionis Christianae* (1536). Some chief points of his teaching are: (1) the transcendence of God; (2) the total depravity of natural man, who can achieve nothing without God; (3) the predestination of certain men for salvation through Christ, made by God before the world began; (4) the sole authority of the scriptures and the Holy Spirit; and (5) the enforcement of the church's public discipline by the community.

**Calydon.** In classical geography a city in Aetolia, near the forest that was the scene of the legendary hunt of the CALYDONIAN BOAR. Also, in ARTHURIAN ROMANCE, the name given to a forest in northern England.

**Calydonian boar, The.** In Greek legend Oeneus, king of Calydon in Aetolia, having neglected the sacrifices to ARTEMIS, was punished by the goddess sending a ferocious boar to ravage his lands. A band of princes collected to hunt the boar, which was wounded by ATALANTA and killed by MELEAGER.

**Calypso** (Greek, 'the hidden one', from *kaluptō*, 'I cover', 'I hide').

(1) In classical mythology the queen of the island of Ogygia on which Odysseus (ULYSSES) was wrecked. She kept him there for seven years and promised him perpetual youth and immortality if he would remain with her for ever. She bore him two sons and was inconsolable when he left. Ogygia is generally identified with Gozo, near Malta.

(2) A type of popular West Indian song or ballad, especially one from Trinidad, improvised on topical subjects. It apparently takes its name from the first meaning of the word.

**Camacho.** A rich but unfortunate man in one of the stories in Cervantes' *Don* QUIXOTE (1605) who is cheated of his bride just when he has prepared a feast for the wedding. Hence the phrase 'Camacho's wedding' to describe anything involving useless show and expenditure.

**Cam and Isis.** The universities of Cambridge and Oxford, so called from the rivers on which they respectively stand.

> May you, my Cam and Isis, preach it long,
> The right divine of kings to govern wrong.
> ALEXANDER POPE: *Dunciad*, iv (1728)

**Camarina.** A lake in Sicily, which was a source of malaria to the inhabitants, who, when they consulted APOLLO about draining it, received the reply: *Ne moveas Camarinam* ('Don't provoke Camarina'). They drained it, however, and before long the enemy marched over its dry bed and plundered the city. The proverb is apt for those who remove one evil only to release another that is greater. In other words, 'leave well alone'.

**Cambalo's ring.** Cambalo was the second son of CAMBUSCAN and the brother of Algarsife in Chaucer's unfinished 'The Squire's Tale' (*c*.1387). He is introduced as Cambel in Spenser's *The Faerie Queene* (1590, 1596). The ring, which was given him by his sister Canace, had the power to heal wounds.

**Camber.** In British legend, the second son of BRUTE. Wales fell to him and hence (in popular mythology) received its name of CAMBRIA.

**Cambria.** The ancient name of Wales, the land of the Cymry.

**Cambridge Apostles, The.** An exclusive debating society founded at Cambridge in 1826 by John Sterling (1806–44), which included dons and undergraduates, many of whom later attained celebrity. Among them were Frederick Denison Maurice, Richard Chenevix-Trench, John Kemble, James Spedding, Richard Monckton Milnes, Alfred, Lord Tennyson and A.H. Hallam. More recent members include Henry Sidgwick, Roger Fry, Bertrand Russell, G.E. Moore, Desmond MacCarthy, Lytton Strachey, Leonard Woolf, J.M. Keynes and Lowes Dickinson. The Apostles have been discredited by such members as the traitors Anthony Blunt, Guy Burgess and Donald Maclean.

**Cambuscan.** In Chaucer's unfinished 'The Squire's Tale' (*c*.1387), Cambuscan is the king of Sarra, in Tartary, the archetype of all royal virtues. His wife was Elfeta, his two sons were Algarsife and Cambalo, and his daughter was Canace. Milton famously praised the tale. See *also* CAMBALO'S RING.

> Or call up him that left half-told
> The story of Cambuscan bold,
> Of Camball, and of Algarsife,
> And who had Canace to wife,
> That owned the virtuous ring and glass.
> JOHN MILTON: *Il Penseroso* (1632)

**Cambuscan's mirror.** Sent to Cambuscan by the king of Araby and Ind, the mirror warned of the approach of ill fortune and told if love was returned (Chaucer, *Canterbury Tales*, 'The Squire's Tale' (*c*.1387)).

**Camden Society.** A historical society founded in 1838 for the publication of early historical texts and documents, named after William Camden (1551–1623), schoolmaster, antiquary and author of *Britannia* (1586), a survey of the British Isles. In 1897 it amalgamated with the Royal Historical Society, and its long series of publications was transferred to that body.

**Camel.** MOHAMMED's favourite camel was Al KASWA, and the mosque at Koba (modern Aqaba) covers the spot where it knelt when he fled from MECCA. Mohammed considered the kneeling of the camel as a sign sent by God, and he remained at Koba in safety for four days. The swiftest of his camels was Al Adha, who is fabled to have performed the whole journey from Jerusalem to Mecca in four bounds, thereby gaining a place in heaven along with BORAK, BALAAM'S ASS, TOBIT's dog and KRATIM, the dog of the SEVEN SLEEPERS.

**Camel's Bible, The.** *See under* BIBLE.

**It is easier for a camel to go through the eye of a needle, than for a rich man to enter into the Kingdom of God.** A saying of Jesus found twice in the New Testament (Matthew 19:24, Mark 10:25). The Koran has a similar locution: 'The impious shall find the gates of heaven shut, nor shall he enter till a camel shall pass through the eye of a needle.' The meaning of the passage is reinforced by Mark 10:24: 'How hard is it for them that trust in riches to enter into the Kingdom of God!' In the Rabbinical writings there is a variant of the expression: 'Perhaps thou art one of the Pampedithians, who can make an elephant pass through the eye of a needle.'

**Strain at a gnat and swallow a camel, To.** *See under* STRAIN.

**Camelot** (probably from Celtic *cant*, 'circle', 'edge'). In British fable this was the legendary spot where King ARTHUR held his court. It has been tentatively located at CAERLEON, at the hill fort known as Cadbury Castle in Somerset and at Camelford in Cornwall, where the Duke of Cornwall resided in his castle of TINTAGEL. The Cadbury site is the most probable, although recent claims have also been made for Colchester, Essex, partly on the grounds that this city's Roman name, *Camulodunum*, is similar to Camelot and partly because Geoffrey of Monmouth's description of the Camelot countryside in *Historia Regum Britanniae* (*c*.1136) fits north Essex better than any of the WEST COUNTRY sites. Camelot is mentioned in Shakespeare's *King Lear* (II, ii (1605)) and in Tennyson's *Idylls of the King* (1859), among other works. *See also* KNIGHTS OF THE ROUND TABLE.

> On either side the river lie
> Long fields of barley and of rye,
> That clothe the wold and meet the sky;
> And throu' the field the road runs by
> To many-tower'd Camelot.
>
> ALFRED, LORD TENNYSON: *The Lady of Shalott*, i (1832)

**Camera. Box camera.** *See under* BOX.

**Candid camera.** *See under* CANDID.

**Cameron Highlanders.** The 79th Foot, raised by Alan Cameron of Erracht in 1793. In 1961, by amalgamation, it became the Queen's Own Highlanders (Seaforth and Camerons).

**Cameronian. Cameronian Regiment.** The 26th Infantry, which had its origin in a body of CAMERONIANS in the Revolution of 1688, called the Cameronians (Scottish Rifles) from 1881. In 1969 the regiment opted for disbandment rather than amalgamation.

**Cameronians.** Members of a religious body also known as the Reformed PRESBYTERIANS. They were organized by the strict COVENANTER and religious reformer Richard Cameron (1648–80), who was killed in battle at Aird's Moss. He objected to the alliance of church and state under Charles II and seceded from the Kirk. His followers refused to take the Oath of Allegiance and thus deprived themselves of some of the privileges of citizenship. In 1876 the majority of Cameronians united with the FREE CHURCH.

**Camford.** A name, made up as a PORTMANTEAU WORD from Cambridge and Oxford, which has never acquired the same currency as OXBRIDGE. *See also* REDBRICK.

> He was a Camford man and very nearly got the English Prize Poem; it was said.
>
> W.M. THACKERAY: *Pendennis*, ch iii (1848–50)

**Camilla** (perhaps from Latin *camilla*, feminine of *camillus*, 'child acolyte'). In Roman legend, a virgin queen of the Volscians, who helped Turnus against AENEAS. Virgil (*Aeneid*, vii (1st century BC)) says she was so swift that she could run over a field of corn without bending a single blade or make her way over the sea without wetting her feet.

> Not so, when swift Camilla scours the plain,
> Flies o'er the unbending corn, and skims along the main.
>
> ALEXANDER POPE: *Essay on Criticism* (1711)

**Camillo, Don.** The tough rural priest in a series of humorous stories by the Italian writer Giovanni Guareschi (1908–68). His adversary is Peppone, the local Communist mayor. The stories first appeared in the Italian magazine *Candido* in the late 1940s and were subsequently collected in a number of books. The first of these in English translation was *The Little World of Don Camillo* (1950), and film and television versions have followed.

**Camillus.** A Roman soldier and statesman who came to be revered as the second founder of Rome after the sack of the city by the Gauls in *c*.390 BC. His exploits were subsequently embellished by Livy, Plutarch and others. He died in 365 BC.

**Camisado** or **camisade** (Old Spanish *camisada*, from *camisa*, 'shirt'). A night attack, so called because the attacking party wore a shirt over their armour, both to conceal it and to recognize one another in the dark.

**Camisards.** In French history the PROTESTANT insurgents of the Cévennes, who resisted the violence of the DRAGONNADES occasioned by the Revocation of the EDICT OF NANTES in 1685 and carried on a fierce war of reprisals with Louis XIV's forces until finally suppressed in 1705. Their leader was Jean Cavalier (1681–1740), afterwards governor of Jersey and later of the Isle of Wight. They were so called from the blouse (Provençal *camisa*) worn by the peasants.

**Camlan, The Battle of.** *See under* BATTLE.

**Camlet** (Old French *camelot*, perhaps from Arabic *hamlat*, 'plush fabric'). A soft woollen fabric, used in Asia in the Middle Ages, made of silk and camel's hair. In modern times the word has come to apply to a kind of tough, waterproof cloth.

> After dinner I put on my new camelott suit, the best that I ever wore in my life, the suit costing me above £24.
>
> SAMUEL PEPYS: *Diary* (1 June 1664)

**Camorra.** A lawless secret society of the 19th century, run on gangster lines, which terrorized Naples. It started in about 1820 among prisoners in the jails and exacted tribute from traders and brothel-keepers alike. From 1848 it began to intervene in politics and continued to be a menace until 1911, when severe judicial action led to its extinction. The name is probably from Spanish *camorra*, 'quarrel', and is now used for any similar clandestine group. *See also* MAFIA.

**Camp. Camp David.** The rural retreat of American Presidents, in Catoctin Mountain Park, Maryland, some 70 miles (112km) from Washington, D.C. It was established under the name SHANGRI LA in 1942 by F.D. Roosevelt and was made an official retreat by Harry S Truman in 1945. In 1953 Dwight D. Eisenhower renamed it Camp David after his grandson (b.1947), who grew up to marry Richard M. Nixon's younger daughter Julie (b.1948).

**Camp followers.** A trail or group of civilians who follow an army with the aim of providing various services, such as washerwomen, prostitutes and sellers of liquor.

> In the moment of failure (at Bannockburn) the sight of a body of camp-followers, whom they mistook for reinforcements to the enemy, spread panic through the English host.
>
> J.R. GREEN: *A Short History of the English People*, ch iv (1874)

*See also* BAGGAGE.

**Camp it up, To.** To draw attention to oneself by ostentatious parading or overacting in a camp manner:

> Look at that fellow who scored such a hit in the late-night show as Actaeon's mother, camping it up like mad.
>
> JUVENAL: *Satires*, vi (2nd century AD) (translation by Peter Green, 1967)

The origin of camp in its application to homosexuality or effeminacy is uncertain, although French *se camper* means to adopt an audacious or authoritarian attitude. The reference is not likely to be to soldiers who in the 19th century clandestinely served as male prostitutes while camped out in Regent's Park, London, as sometimes explained.

**Break camp, To.** *See under* BREAK.

**High camp.** *See under* HIGH.

**Strike camp, To.** *See under* STRIKE.

**Campaign. Smear campaign.** *See under* SMEAR.

**Whispering campaign.** *See under* WHISPER.

**Campania** (Latin, 'plain'). The ancient geographical name for the fertile district of south-western Italy containing the towns of Cumae, Capua, Baiae, Puteoli, Herculaneum, Pompeii and other historic sites. The name is now that of a much larger region in this part of the country.

**Campaspe.** A beautiful concubine, the favourite of Alexander the Great. He handed her over to APELLES, who is said to have modelled his APHRODITE ANADYOMENE on her.

> Cupid and my Campaspe play'd
> At cards for kisses – Cupid paid.
>
> JOHN LYLY: *Campaspe* (1584)

**Campbell. Campbellites.** The followers of John McLeod Campbell (1800–72), who taught the universality of the atonement, for which he was ejected from the CHURCH OF SCOTLAND in 1831.

In the USA the name is sometimes given to the Disciples of Christ, a body founded in 1809 by Thomas (1763–1854) and Alexander Campbell (1788–1866) of Pennsylvania. They reject creeds, practise baptism by immersion and weekly communion and uphold Christian union on the foundation of the Bible alone. They are also known simply as Christians.

**Campbells are Coming, The.** This stirring song is said to have been composed in 1715 when John Campbell, Duke of Argyll, defeated the Earl of Mar and the JACOBITES. It subsequently became the regimental march of the Sutherland Highlanders (93rd Regiment) and after 1881 of the Argyll and Sutherland Highlanders when the two regiments merged.

At the second relief of Lucknow in November 1857 the besieged in the Residency became aware of the approach of Sir Colin Campbell and the Sutherland Highlanders when they heard the distant sound of bagpipes playing 'The Campbells are Coming'.

**Campeador.** The CID.

**Can. Can of worms.** A complicated matter that is likely to cause problems or even scandal. The image is of opening a tin of food and finding inside a mass of writhing maggots that will have to be dealt with. A similar concept is that of PANDORA'S BOX.

**Carry the can, To.** *See under* CARRY.

**Jerry can.** *See under* JERRY.

**Canaan.** In the Old Testament (Genesis 9), the son of HAM and the reputed ancestor of the Canaanites who confronted ABRAHAM coming from the valley of the Euphrates and, later, the Israelites leaving Egypt under the leadership of MOSES and JOSHUA. The land of Canaan is sometimes identified with the geographical ISRAEL.

**Canard** (French, 'duck'). A hoax; an extravagant false report. The French lexicographer Emile Littré (1801–81) says that the term comes from an old expression, *vendre un canard à moitié*, 'to half-sell a duck'. As this was no sale at all, it came to mean 'to take in', 'to make a fool of'. Another explanation is that a certain Cornelissen, to try the gullibility of the public, reported in the papers that he had 20 ducks, one of which he cut up and threw to the 19, who devoured it greedily. He then cut up another, then a third, and so on until the nineteenth was gobbled up by the survivor.

**Canard Enchaîné, Le** ('The Fettered Duck'). A French satirical weekly, first published in 1915, when it arose from an anti-militarist tract of troops in the trenches. It is well known for its exposés of scandals and abuses of power and is the BÊTE NOIRE of the authorities, who bugged its new offices in the 1970s. Its name alludes to its beleaguerment, with CANARD in the sense above.

**Canary.** Wine from the Canary Islands was popular in the 16th and 17th centuries.

> Farewell, my hearts, I will to my honest knight Falstaff, and drink canary with him.
> SHAKESPEARE: *The Merry Wives of Windsor*, III, ii (1600)

The word was also at one time slang for a GUINEA or SOVEREIGN, from its yellow colour.

**Cancan.** A fast, high-kicking dance performed by a female chorus line, originating in the 19th century in the casinos of Paris. The best known example is in Offenbach's opera *Orpheus in the Underworld* (1858). The origin of the name is uncertain. It is popularly derived from Latin *quamquam*, 'although', allegedly from the frequent use of this word in a noisy scholastic debate.

> They were going through a quadrille with all those supplementary gestures introduced by the great Rigolboche, a notorious *danseuse*, to whom the notorious cancan owes its origin.
> A. EGMONT HAKE: *Paris Originals* (1878)

**Cancer** (Latin, 'crab'). One of the 12 signs of the ZODIAC, the Crab. It appears when the sun has reached its highest northern limit and begins to go backward to the south. Like a crab, however, it makes its return sideways (21 June to 22 July).

According to fable JUNO sent Cancer against HERCULES when he fought the HYDRA of Lerna. It bit the hero's foot, but Hercules killed the creature and Juno took it up to heaven.

**Candace.** A title of the queens of Meroe in Upper Nubia. The Candace mentioned in the Bible (Acts 8:27) ruled in Ethiopia in the time of Paul and the evangelist Philip, who converted and baptised her eunuch.

**Candaules.** King of Lydia (*c.*710–668 BC). Legend relates that he exposed the charms of his wife to GYGES, whereupon she compelled the latter to assassinate her husband, after which she married the murderer. Plato's version is that Gyges obtained possession of the queen by using the ring that made him invisible.

**Candidate** (Latin *candidatus*, 'clothed in white'). A person who seeks nomination for a position or who applies for official acceptance in some way, as by an interview or an examination. Those who solicited a high office among the Romans, such as that of consul, dressed themselves in a loose white robe. It was loose so that they could show the people their scars and white as a token of fidelity and humility.

**Candid camera.** An unseen camera which is used to photograph an unsuspecting subject. Candid camera shots have long been used in pictorial journalism. In the 1950s an American television series of the name, later taken up in Britain, set up scenes putting people in an embarrassing situation and then filming their reaction. In one classic example a car without an engine was 'driven' to a garage with a request for a repair to be carried out.

**Candide** (Latin *candidus*, 'white'). The hero of VOLTAIRE's philosophical novel, *Candide, ou l'Optimisme* (1759). All sorts of misfortunes are heaped upon him, which he bears philosophically. It was written at the time of the Lisbon earthquake to satirize philosophical optimism.

**Candle. Candlemas Day.** 2 February, formerly the Feast of the Purification of the Virgin MARY, now called the Presentation of Christ. One of the QUARTER DAYS in Scotland. In Roman Catholic churches all the candles that will be needed in the church throughout the year are consecrated on this day. They symbolize Jesus Christ, 'the light of the world' and 'a light to lighten the Gentiles'. The ancient Romans had a custom of burning candles to scare away evil spirits.

> If Candlemas Day be dry and fair,
> The half o'winter's come and mair;
> If Candlemas Day be wet and foul,
> The half o'winter was gone at Youl.
> Scottish proverb

**Candlewick.** The name given to a type of embroidery with tufts of soft cotton yarn, used mainly to decorate bedspreads. It is said that snippets of the thick yarn used for the wicks of candles were put to decorative use on the borders of the dust covers for beds by the thrifty wives of the early settlers in America.

**Bell, book, and candle.** *See under* BELL.

**Burn the candle at both ends, To.** *See under* BURN.

**Corpse candle.** *See under* CORPSE.

**Devil's candle, The.** *See under* DEVIL.

**Devil's candlestick, The.** *See under* DEVIL.

**Hold a candle to, To.** *See under* HOLD.

**Not worth the candle.** *See under* WORTH.

**Roman candle.** *See under* ROMAN.

**Sell by the candle, To.** *See under* SELL.

**Vow a candle to the Devil, To.** *See under* VOW.

**What is the Latin for candle?** *See* TACE IS LATIN FOR CANDLE.

**Candour, Mrs.** In *The School for Scandal* (1777) Richard Brinsley Sheridan drew the perfect type of backbiter, concealing her venom under an affectation of frank amiability.

**Canephorus** (Greek *kanēphoros*, 'basket-bearing' from *kaneon*, 'basket', and *pherein*, 'to bear'). A sculptured figure of a young woman bearing a basket on her head. In ancient Athens the *canephori* bore the sacred things necessary at the feasts of the gods.

**Canicular** (Latin *canicula*, diminutive of *canis*, 'dog').

**Canicular days.** The DOG DAYS.

**Canicular period.** The ancient Egyptian cycle of 1461 years or 1460 JULIAN YEARS, also called a SOTHIC PERIOD, during which it was supposed that any given day had passed through all the seasons of the years.

**Canicular year.** The ancient Egyptian year computed from one helical rising of the DOG STAR to the next.

**Canker.** An ulceration of part of an animal's body, such as the ear of a dog or the mouth of a bird. The word is also used of a disease of plants or of a caterpillar that destroys plants, and at one time it was a name for the DOG ROSE (*Rosa canina*).

> To put down Richard, that sweet lovely rose,
> And plant this thorn, this canker, Bolingbroke.
> SHAKESPEARE: *Henry IV, Pt I*, I, iii (1597)

**Canmore.** *See* GREAT HEAD.

**Cannae.** The place where Hannibal defeated the Romans under Varro and Aemilius with great slaughter in 216 BC. Hence any fatal battle that is the turning point of a military leader's success. Moscow was thus the Cannae of NAPOLEON BONAPARTE.

**Canned. Canned laughter.** Pre-recorded laughter that is dubbed on to radio and television comedy programmes. It is the modern equivalent of the claques who were hired to clap and cheer at theatre performances and is a device of American origin. It was first heard in Britain in the American television comedy show *I Love Lucy*, starring Lucille Ball, screened when ITV opened on 22 September 1955.

> The trend in TV has been to the canned laugh, a laugh reproduced by recording from some previous happy crowd, or synthetically manufactured.
> VANCE PACKARD: *The Hidden Persuaders*, ch xviii (1957)

**Canned music.** Music that is recorded and reproduced, as opposed to LIVE MUSIC, which is played by musicians present in person. The comparison is with canned foods, since such music can be stored and used whenever it is required.

**Cannon.** A cannon is a stroke in billiards in which the cue ball contacts one of the other balls in such a way that it glances off it and strikes another ball. A North American equivalent for the term is carom, which is short for carambole, as if this were carom ball. Its own origin is from Spanish *carambola*, the name of a sour greenish fruit. It is not clear why this particular word should have been adopted.

**Cannon fodder.** Soldiers regarded simply as expendable material in battle. The phrase translates German *Kanonenfutter* and echoes Falstaff's words before the battle of Shrewsbury:

> Tut. tut; good enough to toss; food for powder, food for powder; they'll fill a pit as well as better: tush, man, mortal men, mortal men.
> SHAKESPEARE: *Henry IV, Pt I*, IV, ii (1597)

**Cannon into, To.** To collide with someone, especially when in a hurry.

**Nursery cannons.** *See under* NURSERY.

**Canny.** *See* CA'CANNY.

**Canoe.** A Caribbean word, brought to Europe by the Spanish and used for a boat hollowed out of a tree trunk.

**Paddle one's own canoe, To.** *See under* PADDLE.

**Canon.** The word comes ultimately from Greek *kanōn*, 'measuring rule'. Hence its modern sense for a general rule or standard. Hence also the various senses outlined below.

(1) The church dignitary known as a canon is a capitular member of a cathedral or COLLEGIATE CHURCH, usually living in the precincts and observing the rule or canon of the body to which he is attached. The canons, with the DEAN or provost at their head, constitute the governing body or CHAPTER of the cathedral. These are the canons residentiary. There are also honorary canons who have no share in the cathedral government and receive no emoluments. Minor canons are mainly concerned with the singing of the services and have no part in the decisions of the chapter.

The title once had a much wider application and was used to designate most of the diocesan clergy. When its use came to be limited to the SECULAR CLERGY of a cathedral, they were called secular canons as distinct from the canons regular such as the Austin or AUGUSTINIAN CANONS.

(2) A canon in music is a composition written strictly to rule for two or three voices. They each sing exactly the same melody, one a few beats after the other, either at the same or at a different pitch. Simple forms of the canon are the catch and the round, such as 'Three Blind Mice' and 'London's Burning'. A London choral club was founded in 1843 called the Round, Catch and Canon Club.

**Canon, The.** The body of books in the Bible that are accepted by the Christian church generally as genuine and inspired, otherwise the whole Bible from Genesis to Revelation, excluding the APOCRYPHA.

The CHURCH OF ENGLAND 'Book of Canons' was adopted in 1604 as the basis of ecclesiastical law. A Book of Canons for the Scottish Church was drawn up under CHARLES I's command and issued in 1636. It mainly helped to precipitate religious strife in Scotland.

**Canoness.** The title was given to certain women living under rule, less strict than that of nuns, in the Frankish Empire from the late 8th century. Like their male counterparts, they came to be divided into canonesses regular and secular.

**Canonical age.** An age fixed by CANON LAW when an individual may undertake various functions or duties. In the CHURCH OF ENGLAND a man may become a deacon at 23, a priest at 24 and a bishop at 30. In the ROMAN CATHOLIC CHURCH a novice must be 16, a deacon 22 and a bishop 30. FASTING begins at the age of 21.

**Canonical dress.** The distinctive or appropriate costume worn by the clergy according to the direction of the canon. BISHOPS, DEANS and archdeacons, for instance, wear canonical hats. This distinctive dress is sometimes called simply canonicals.

The same name is given also to the special parts of such robes, such as the pouch on the gown of an MD, originally designed for carrying drugs, the lambskin on some BA hoods, in imitation of the TOGA CANDIDA of the Romans, the tippet on a BARRISTER's gown, originally a wallet to carry briefs in, and the PROCTORS' and proproctors' tippet for papers.

**Canonical epistles.** The seven CATHOLIC EPISTLES, as distinct from those of St PAUL, which were addressed to particular churches or individuals.

**Canonical hours.** The different parts of the DIVINE OFFICE, which follow the hours of the day and are named after them. They are seven: matins, prime, tierce, sext, NONES, VESPERS and COMPLINE. Prime, tierce, sext and nones are the first, third, sixth and ninth hours of the day, counting from 6 am. There are seven because DAVID says, 'Seven times a day do I praise thee' (Psalm 119:164). *See also* BREVIARY.

In general legal use, the canonical hours are those within which persons can be legally married: from 8 am to 6 pm.

**Canonical obedience.** The obedience due by the inferior to the superior clergy. Thus bishops owe canonical obedience to the archbishop of the same province.

**Canonization.** The solemn act by which the pope proclaims the sanctity of a person, subsequent to the lesser act of BEATIFICATION, whereupon he or she is worthy to be honoured as a saint and is put upon the Canon or Catalogue of Saints of the Church.

**Canon law.** A collection of ecclesiastical laws that serve as the rule of church government. Specialists in canon law are called canonists.

**Canons of the Mass.** The fixed form of consecratory prayer used in the GREEK CHURCH and ROMAN CATHOLIC CHURCH, from the Sanctus to the PATERNOSTER.

**Augustine canons.** *See under* AUGUSTINE.

**Black Canons.** *See under* BLACK.

**Book of Canons, The.** *See under* BOOK.

**Crab canon.** *See under* CRAB.

**White Canons.** *See* PREMONSTRATENSIAN.

**Canopus.** Alpha Argus or Canopus, in the constellation Carina (originally Argo Navis), is the brightest star in the night sky after SIRIUS. It takes its name from Canopus, the pilot of MENELAUS, king of Sparta, in Greek mythology.

**Canopy.** The word derives from Medieval Latin *canopeum*, 'mosquito net', which is itself from Greek *kōnōpeion*, 'bed with mosquito curtains', from *kōnōps*, 'mosquito'. Herodotus describes (*Histories*, ii (5th century BC)) how the fishermen of the Nile used to raise their nets on a pole and so form a sort of primitive tent under which they slept undisturbed, because mosquitoes will not pass through the meshes of a net.

**Canossa.** Canossa, in the duchy of Modena, is where the Holy Roman Emperor Henry IV humbled himself to Pope Gregory VII (HILDEBRAND) by standing for three days barefoot in the courtyard of the palace in the garb of a penitent (January 1077). This was during the INVESTITURE CONTROVERSY.

Hence, to go to Canossa is to undergo humiliation; to EAT HUMBLE PIE. During Bismarck's quarrel with Pope Pius IX at the time of the KULTURKAMPF, he said in the Reichstag (14 May 1872): *Nach Canossa gehen wir nicht* ('We shall not go to Canossa').

**Cant.** The specialized vocabulary of a particular group of people, such as thieves, lawyers, or journalists. The word probably derives from Latin *cantare*, 'to sing', and thus originally applied, in a disparaging sense, to the chanting in medieval religious services. The term later came to be applied to the whining speech of beggars, who were known as the CANTING CREW. In Harman's *Caveat, or Warning for Common Cursetors, Vulgarly Called Vagabonds* (1567) the following occurs:

> As far as I can learne or understand by the examination of a number of them, their language – which they term peddelars Frenche or Canting – began within these xxx yeeres.

He goes on to give an example of canting:

> Bene Lightmans to thy quarromes, in what tipken hast thou lypped in this darkemans, whether in a lybbege or in the strummel?
> (Good morrow to thy body, in what house hast thou lain all night, whether in a bed or in the straw?)

In a more general sense, the word is now used of any insincere talk, especially with regard to religion or morals.

**Canting arms.** In heraldry a COAT OF ARMS that makes a visual punning reference to the surname or title of its owner. For example, the Duke of Arundel has a swallow (Old French *arondel*) on his arms, and Anne Boleyn, second wife of Henry VIII, came from a family whose coat of arms depicted a bull's head. Civic coats of arms are also frequently canting, such as that of Oxford, which shows an ox crossing a ford, or that of Magdeburg, Germany, which has a maiden (German *Magd*) over a castle (*Burg*). Baden, in Austria, has a man and woman taking a bath (German *Bad*) in a tub. The arms additionally allude to the fact that Baden is a spa. *See also* REBUS.

**Canting crew.** Beggars, gypsies, thieves and vagabonds, who use CANT. In *c*.1690 'B.E., Gent.' (no further identification has ever been offered) published the first English slang dictionary with the title *A New Dictionary of the Terms, Ancient and Modern, of the Canting Crew in its Several Tribes*.

**Cantate Sunday.** Rogation Sunday, the fifth Sunday after EASTER, so called from the first word of the introit of the MASS: *Cantate Domino*, 'O, sing unto the Lord'. Similarly LAETARE SUNDAY, the fourth in LENT, is so called from the first word of the introit of the mass. *See also* QUASIMODO SUNDAY; ROGATION DAYS.

**Canter.** An easy gallop, originally called a Canterbury trot, from the supposed gait adopted by mounted pilgrims to the shrine of St Thomas à Becket at Canterbury.

**Preliminary canter, A.** *See under* PRELIMINARY.

**Canterbury. Canterbury bell.** The cultivated campanula (*Campanula medium*), named after the bells on the horses of the pilgrims riding to Canterbury, as described by Chaucer in his CANTERBURY TALES.

**Canterbury Tales.** In his tales (*c*.1387), Chaucer imagined that he was with a party of around thirty pilgrims setting out from the TABARD INN at SOUTHWARK to pay their devotions to the shrine of St Thomas à Becket at Canterbury. According to the *Prologue,* he intended each pilgrim should tell two tales on the way there and two on the way back. Whoever told the best tales was to be treated with a supper on the homeward journey. The work is incomplete, however, and there are none of the tales told on the way back.

**Augustine of Canterbury.** *See under* AUGUSTINE.

**Canuck.** The name given to Canadians generally, but in Canada to Canadians of French descent. The name is of uncertain origin. One account derives it from Connate, a name originally applied by the French Canadians to Irish immigrants.

**Canute** or **Cnut.** Sometimes known as the Great, Canute (*c*.995–1035) was the younger son of Sweyn Forkbeard and king of England (from 1016), Denmark (from 1019) and Norway (from 1028). His rule of England was largely peaceful. Canute's chief claim to fame is his supposed attempt to turn back the tide. Henry of Huntingdon, the 12th-century chronicler who first recounted the incident, gives no location, but it is traditionally said to have occurred at the inland port of Gainsborough, Lincolnshire, where Canute's father died and where the Trent is noted for its bore or eagre during the spring tides. The story has been entirely misinterpreted, since Canute was actually trying to demonstrate to his courtiers that only God could control the tide, not man.

**Canvas.** Properly, cloth made of hemp (Latin *cannabis*).

**Canvass, To.** To solicit votes, as before an election. The word perhaps derives from an obsolete sense of canvas, which was to toss someone in a canvas sheet. Hence to harass or criticize someone generally, and so to solicit support for one's own point of view. At an election, one often votes against a candidate or a party as much as for one.

**Carry too much canvas, To.** *See under* CARRY.

**Under canvas.** *See under* UNDER.

**Caora.** A river described in Richard Hakluyt's *Voyages* (1589) on the banks of which lived a people whose heads grew beneath their shoulders. Their eyes were in their shoulders, and their mouths in the middle of their breasts. Walter Ralegh, in his *Discoverie of Guiana* (1596) gives a similar account of a race of men.

**Cap.** The word is used figuratively by Shakespeare for 'top, 'summit', 'peak', as in 'A very riband in the cap of youth' (*Hamlet*, IV, vii (1600)), or 'Thou art the cap of all the fools alive' (*Timon of Athens*, IV, iii (1607)).

**Cap, To.** To take off or touch one's cap to, in token of respect; to outdo or excel, as when one caps a person's story by telling a better one.

**Cap and bells.** The insignia of a professional fool or jester.

**Cap and gown.** The full academic costume of a university student, tutor or graduate, worn on formal occasions.

> Is it a cap and gown affair?
>
> 'CUTHBERT BEDE': *The Adventures of Mr Verdant Green* (1853–7)

**Cap and Stocking.** A Leicester public house whose name and sign commemorates the importance of these articles to the town's industry, especially the making of STATUTE CAPS. *See also* PUBLIC HOUSE SIGNS.

**Capful of wind.** Olaus Magnus tells how Eric, king of Sweden, was said to be so familiar with evil spirits that the wind would blow whichever way he turned his cap, and for this he was called Windy Cap. The Laplanders had a profitable trade in selling winds, and even as recently as 1814 Bessie Millie of Pomona (Orkney) used to sell favourable winds to mariners for the small sum of sixpence.

**Cap in hand.** Submissively or humbly, like a servant.

**Cap it all, To.** To surpass what has gone before; to make things even worse.

**Cap of liberty.** *See* LIBERTY CAP.

**Cap of maintenance.** A ceremonial cap or hat, worn or carried as a symbol of office. Examples are the fur cap of the lord mayor of London, worn on days of state, and the cap carried before the British sovereigns at their coronation. The significance of maintenance here is uncertain, but the cap was an emblem of great honour, for it was conferred by the pope three times on Henry VII and once on Henry VIII. It is borne in the COAT OF ARMS of certain old families, either as a charge or in place of the wreath.

**Capped, To be.** A player who has represented England, Scotland, Ireland or Wales in an international match at any of the major field sports may wear a cap bearing the national emblem. 'He was capped for England' thus means that he represented England in a national sport.

**Cap verses, To.** To add a line of verse to one given, beginning it with the final letter of the previous line. For example:

> The way was long, the wind was cold (D)
> Dogs with their tongues their wounds do heal (L)
> Like words congealed in northern air (R)
> Regions Caesar never knew (W)
> With all a poet's ecstasy (Y)
> You may decide my awkward pace (E) etc.

There are parlour games of capping names, proverbs, and the like, in the same way. For example, with names: Plato, Otway, Young, Goldsmith etc, or with proverbs: 'Handsome is as handsome does', 'Silence is golden', 'Noblesse oblige', 'Enough is as good as a feast', 'Time is money' and so forth.

**Black cap.** *See under* BLACK.

**Cater cap.** *See under* CATER.

**Cloth cap.** *See under* CLOTH.

**College cap.** *See under* COLLEGE.

**Dunce's cap.** *See under* DUNCE.

**Dutch cap.** *See under* DUTCH.

**Feather in one's cap, A.** *See under* FEATHER.

**Fool's cap.** *See under* FOOL.

**Forked cap.** *See under* FORK.

**If the cap fits, wear it.** *See under* IF.

**John Knox cap.** *See under* JOHN.

**Liberty cap.** *See under* LIBERTY.

**Phrygian cap.** A LIBERTY CAP.

**Scotch cap.** *See under* SCOTCH.

**Send the cap round, To.** *See under* SEND.

**Set one's cap at, To.** *See under* SET.

**Square cap.** A TRENCHER CAP or MORTARBOARD.

**Statute cap.** *See under* STATUTE.

**Thinking cap.** *See under* THINK.

**Trencher cap.** *See under* TRENCHER.

**Wear the cap and bells, To.** *See under* WEAR.

**Capability Brown.** *See under* BROWN.

**Cap-à-pie** (Old French). From head to foot, usually with reference to arming or accoutring.

> Armed at all points exactly cap-a-pie.
> SHAKESPEARE: *Hamlet*, II, i (1600)

**Cape. Cape, The.** The Cape of Good Hope (originally known as the CAPE OF STORMS), Cape Province, South Africa.

**Cape Cod turkey.** Salt fish, a product of the Cape Cod fisheries, Massachusetts. *See also* BOMBAY DUCK; CAPON.

**Cape Coloured.** A term for the mixed white and non-white population of Cape Province, South Africa.

**Cape doctor, The.** A bracing southeast wind blowing at the Cape of Good Hope, especially in the summer. It is so named from the time when the British in India used the Cape as a health resort, to recuperate from the more exacting climate of India. Hill stations were later used for the same purpose.

**Cape Dutch.** An old name for Afrikaans, current in the days when the language was regarded as a dialect of Dutch.

**Cape gooseberry.** The strawberry tomato, *Physalis peruviana*, a plant with small, edible, yellow berries. It takes its name from the Cape of Good Hope but is of South American origin.

**Cape Horn.** The southern extremity of South America, so named by Willem Schouten (*c*.1580–1625), a Dutch mariner, who first rounded it (1616). He named the cape after his native town of Hoorn in northern Holland. To seamen it was simply known as 'the Horn'.

**Cape of Good Hope, The.** *See* CAPE OF STORMS.

**Cape of Storms, The.** Bartholomew Diaz thus named the southernmost point on the Cape Peninsula, southwestern Africa in 1486, but John II of Portugal (1455–95) changed this unpropitious name to the more promising Cape of Good Hope.

**Double a cape, To.** *See under* DOUBLE.

**Spirit of the Cape, The.** *See* ADAMASTOR.

**Capel Court.** A lane that, until 1973, led to the London STOCK EXCHANGE, where dealers congregated to do business. It is so called from Sir William Capel, lord mayor in 1504. Hence, formerly, a name for the Stock Exchange itself, and hence also 'Capel Courtier', a humorous term for a professional stockdealer.

**Caper, To cut a.** *See under* CUT.

**Capet.** Hugh Capet (AD 938–996), the founder of the Capetian dynasty of France, is said to have been named from the cape, or monk's hood, which he wore as a lay abbot of St Martin de Tours. The Capetians of the direct line ruled from 987 till 1328, when they were succeeded by the collateral house of VALOIS and by that of

BOURBON in 1589 (Henry of Navarre). Louis XVI was arraigned before the National Convention under the name of 'Louis Capet'. *See also* CONVENTION PARLIAMENT.

**Capital.** Money or money's worth available for production.

**Capital cross.** In HERALDRY a Greek CROSS with terminations similar to the architectural capital of the TUSCAN ORDER. It is also called brick-axed because the ends resembled a mason's brick axe.

**Capital gain.** The amount by which the selling price of an asset exceeds its cost.

**Capital goods.** Goods that are used in the production of other goods rather than being sold to consumers.

**Capital levy.** A tax on capital or property, as distinct from a tax on income. It was first proposed in the British House of Commons in 1914, and a capital gains tax was introduced in 1965. *See also* CAPITAL GAIN.

**Capital punishment.** The imposition of the death penalty for crime (from Latin *caput*, 'head').

**Capital ship.** Warships of the largest class, like the now obsolete battleship of which the DREADNOUGHT was the prototype.

**Active capital.** *See under* ACTIVE.

**Block capitals.** *See under* BLOCK.

**Make capital out of, To.** To turn to account. In politics one party is always ready to make political capital out of the errors or misfortunes of another.

**With a capital A.** *See under* WITH.

**Capitol, The.** The meeting-place of the United States Congress in Washington, D.C. It opened for the first Congress in 1800 and took its name from the temple in ancient Rome, which was itself so called from the Capitoline Hill on which it stood. The designation is used in the USA generally for the statehouse in various state capitals, the oldest being at Williamsburg, formerly capital of Virginia. The similarity between 'Capitol' and 'capital' is purely coincidental.

**Geese save the Capitol, The.** *See under* GOOSE.

**Capitulary.** A collection of ordinances or laws, especially those of the Frankish kings. The laws were known as capitulars, from their being arranged in chapters (Medieval Latin *capitularius*). *See also* CHAPTER.

**Capon.** Properly, a castrated cock, fattened for eating. However, the name has been given to various fish, perhaps originally by humorous friars who wished to avoid the Friday fast and so eased their consciences by changing the name of the fish and calling a chicken a fish out of the coop. Examples of such fish are GLASGOW CAPON and NORFOLK CAPON.

Capon is also an obsolete term for a love letter, from French *poulet*, which means not only 'chicken' but also formerly 'love letter'. Thus Henry IV of France (1553–1610), consulting with Sully about his marriage, says: 'My niece of Guise would please me best, though report says maliciously that she loves poulets in paper better than in fricassee.'

**Glasgow capon.** *See under* GLASGOW.

**Capone, Al.** A notorious Chicago gangster and racketeer of Sicilian origin (1899–1947). He rose to power in the heyday of the BOOTLEGGERS in the 1920s and made himself master of the rackets in the city by organizing the killing of most of the rival gunmen. After the St Valentine's Day Massacre of 1929, when seven rival gangster leaders were gunned down, he was left in supreme control of the protection racket, speakeasies, brothels and so on. The suburb of Cicero was completely dominated by him. *See also* MAFIA.

**Capp, Andy.** The cloth-capped working man from the northeast of England who is the lazy and loutish anti-hero of the popular comic newspaper strip by Reg Smythe (1917–98). He and his nagging wife, Flo, first appeared in the *Daily Mirror* in 1957. He survives today, but in a rather more POLITICALLY CORRECT form, so that, for example, a cigarette no longer dangles from his lower lip. But he still keeps his cap on indoors, even when snoozing on the sofa. His name is an obvious pun on 'handicap', a racing word instantly appreciated by his gambling cronies.

**Capricorn.** At one time the winter SOLSTICE occurred on the entry of the sun into Capricorn (the Goat), but as the stars have since moved a whole sign to the east, the winter now falls at the sun's entrance into SAGITTARIUS (the Archer). Capricorn is the tenth, or strictly, the eleventh sign of the ZODIAC (21 December to 20 January). The name derives from Latin *Capricornus*, translating Greek *aigokēros*, 'goat-horned', from *caper*, 'goat', and *cornu*, 'horn'.

In classical mythology Capricorn was PAN, who, from fear of the great TYPHOEUS, changed himself into a goat, and was made by JUPITER into one of the signs of the Zodiac.

**Captain. Captain Bligh.** *See* MUTINY ON THE BOUNTY.

**Captain Bobadil.** *See under* BOBADIL.

**Captain Cauf's Tail.** In Yorkshire, the chief MUMMER who led his following from house to house on PLOUGH MONDAY. He was fantastically dressed, with a cockade and many coloured ribbons, and he always had a genuine calf's (cauf's) tail fixed behind him.

**Captain Cooker.** A popular name for the wild boar of New Zealand, descended from those introduced by Captain Cook (1728–79), the explorer.

**Captain Fracasse.** *See under* FRACASSE.
**Captain Marvel.** *See under* MARVEL.
**Captain Moonlight.** *See under* MOONLIGHT.
**Captain of industry.** An influential businessman. 'Captains of Industry' is a chapter title in Thomas Carlyle's *Past and Present*, pt IV, ch iv (1843).
**Captain of the heads.** In naval ships, the rating in charge of the heads or lavatories. The ship's latrines are so called from their original position, forward at the head of the vessel.
**Captain Swing.** *See under* SWING.
**Flag captain.** *See under* FLAG.
**Great Captain, The.** *See* GRAN CAPITÁN.

**Capuchin.** A friar of the strict group of FRANCISCANS that arose about 1520. The name refers to the pointed cowl (French *capuche*) that they wear. They became a separate order in 1619. *See also* ANTONINE HERESY.

**Capulet.** A noble house in Verona, the rival of that of Montague. In Shakespeare's ROMEO AND JULIET (1594) Juliet is a Capulet, and Romeo a Montague. Hence Juliet's plea (II, ii) to the night air:

> O Romeo, Romeo! wherefore art thou Romeo?
> Deny thy father and refuse thy name:
> Or, if thou wilt not, be but sworn my love,
> And I'll no longer be a Capulet.

**Caput mortuum** (Latin, 'dead head'). An alchemist's term for the residuum left after exhaustive distillation or sublimation; hence anything from which all that made it valuable has been removed. Thus an athlete who has been paralysed is a *caput mortuum* of his or her former self. The French DIRECTORY, towards its close, was a mere *caput mortuum* of a government.

**Car. Club car.** *See under* CLUB.
**Jim Crow cars.** *See under* JIM CROW.
**Stock car.** *See under* STOCK.

**Carabineer** or **carabinier.** *See* CARBINEER.

**Caracalla.** Marcus Aurelius Antoninus (AD 188–217), Roman emperor from 211 to 217, was so called because instead of the Roman TOGA he adopted the Gaulish *caracalla*. This was a long, close-fitting, hooded mantle, which came down to the heels and was slit up to the waist in front and to the rear.

**Caradoc.** A KNIGHT OF THE ROUND TABLE, noted for being the husband of the only lady in the queen's train who could wear 'the mantle of matrimonial fidelity'. He appears as Craddocke in the old ballad 'The Boy and the Mantle' in PERCY'S RELIQUES (1756).

In history Caradoc was also the British king better known as Caractacus, whom the Romans took captive to Rome in AD 51.

**Caran d'Ache.** A Russian-born French caricaturist and illustrator, with military subjects as his speciality. His real name was Emmanuel Poiré (1858–1909), and he took his pen-name from a Gallic respelling of *karandash*, the Russian word for 'pencil'.

**Carat.** A measure of weight for precious stones, previously defined as 3.17 grains, but now standardized internationally as 0.20 grams. For gold it is a ratio or proportional measure of $\frac{1}{24}$th. Thus 22 carats of gold means 22 parts gold, 2 parts alloy. The word comes from Arabic *qīrāt*, 'weight of four grains', from Greek *keration*, 'little horn'.

**Caraway.** Caraway seeds were formerly popular for flavouring cakes, which were then known as seedcake, or formerly, simply caraway.

> Nay, you shall see my orchard, where in an arbour, we will eat a last year's pippin of my own graffing, with a dish of caraways.
> SHAKESPEARE: *Henry IV, Pt II*, V, iii (1597)

**Carbineer, carabineer** or **carabinier.** This was originally the word for a cavalryman armed with a carabin, a light, short-barrelled shoulder rifle. Later, it was a soldier armed with a short rifle called a carbine. The 9th Horse (subsequently the 6th Dragoon Guards) were named the Carabiniers by William III in 1692. Louis XIV's Royal Carabiniers were so named in 1693. In 1939 the 3rd and 6th Dragoon Guards amalgamated to form the 3rd Carabiniers. Together with the Greys, the Carabiniers now form part of the Royal Scots Dragoon Guards in the Royal Armoured Corps.

**Carbonado** (Spanish *carbonada*, from *carbón*, 'charcoal'). Grilled meat or fish. Strictly speaking, a carbonado is a piece of meat cut crosswise for the gridiron.

**Carbonari.** The Italian name, which means charcoal burners, was adopted by a political secret society in Naples formed about 1808 with the aim of overthrowing despotic and foreign government. Their meeting-place was called a 'hut', the inside 'the place of selling charcoal', the outside 'the forest', their opponents 'wolves' and so on. Much of their ritual was drawn from FREEMASONRY, and kindred societies grew up throughout Italy and also France. The Italian Carbonari were largely merged into YOUNG ITALY in the 1830s. BYRON and Giuseppe Mazzini were members, and NAPOLEON III was associated with the movement in his earlier days.

**Card.** A witty or eccentric person, a 'character'. Arnold Bennett has a novel called *The Card* (1911), in which 'Denry' (Edward Henry) Machin is the amiable title character. The word is now much less common, but it was formerly often preceded by a stock adjective, such as a knowing card, an old card, a rum card, a queer card and the like.

You're a shaky old card; and you can't be in love with this Lizzie.

DICKENS: *Our Mutual Friend*, Bk III, ch i (1864–5)

The term itself was perhaps suggested by a phrase such as sure card, meaning a winning card that a player has in his hand. Alternatively, there may be a pun on Latin *carduus* meaning thistle, as an instrument for combing and teasing cloth to raise its nap. The role of a card is similar.

**Cards on the table.** To put or lay one's cards on the table is to declare one's intentions openly.

**Ask for** or **get one's cards, To.** *See under* ASK.

**Charge card.** *See under* CHARGE.

**Christmas cards.** *See under* CHRISTMAS.

**Court cards.** *See under* COURT.

**Face card.** *See under* FACE.

**Have a card up one's sleeve, To.** To have resources unsuspected by one's opponents; to have a plan in reserve. The reference is to cheating at cards, but there is no implication of dishonesty in the figurative use.

**House of cards.** *See under* HOUSE.

**Leading card.** *See under* LEAD.

**On the cards.** Likely to happen. The expression is probably derived from fortune-telling by cards but could also be an allusion to a racing programme or card. The American equivalent is usually 'in the cards'.

**Play one's cards close to one's chest, To.** *See under* PLAY.

**Play one's cards right, To.** *See under* PLAY.

**Play one's trump card, To.** *See under* PLAY.

**Red card.** *See under* RED.

**Trump card.** *See under* TRUMP.

**Wild card.** *See under* WILD.

**Yellow card.** *See under* YELLOW.

**Cardi.** A native of Cardiganshire, Wales. 'Cardis' are popularly reputed to be clannish, parsimonious and excessively thrifty. Thus, among Welsh people, 'an old Cardi' denotes one reluctant to pay for a round of drinks or a stingy person.

**Cardigan.** A knitted jacket or sweater with buttons up the front, named after the 7th Earl of Cardigan (1797–1868), who led the Light Brigade in the charge of Balaclava (1854). It appears to have been first worn by the British to protect themselves from the bitter cold of the Crimean winter. The Balaclava helmet or cap, a knitted woollen covering for the head and neck, has a similar origin. *See also* NOBLE YACHTSMAN.

**Cardinal** (Latin *cardinalis*, 'relating to a hinge', from *cardo, cardinis*, 'hinge'). The literal sense has been taken up figuratively in English and other languages to mean 'that on which something turns like a hinge', hence 'principal', 'chief'. In Rome, a cardinal church was a parish church, as distinct from an oratory attached to it, and the word was next applied to the senior priest of such a church. From the mid-8th century the word denoted urban as distinct from rural clergy, and subsequently the clergy of a diocesan town and its cathedral. It was later restricted, however, to the cardinals of the Roman see. In 1567 Pius V formally reserved the title for members of the pope's council, the COLLEGE OF CARDINALS.

The Cardinal's red hat was made part of the official vestments by Innocent IV in 1245. This 30-tasselled hat (not worn) was abolished in 1969. *See also* BISHOP.

**Cardinal humours.** An obsolete medical term for the four principal HUMOURS of the body.

**Cardinal numbers.** The natural basic numbers, which denote quantity, such as 1, 2, 3, 4 and 5. 1st, 2nd, 3rd etc are ordinal numbers, since they denote order.

**Cardinal points.** The four main points of the compass, north, south, east and west, so called because they are the points on which the intermediate ones (northeast, northwest, north-northeast and so on) hinge. The poles, being the points on which the earth turns, were called in Latin *cardines* (*see* CARDINAL). The cardinal points are those that lie in the direction of the poles and of sunrise and sunset. Thus the winds that blow due north, east, west and south are called cardinal winds. It is probably from the fact that there are four cardinal points that there are four CARDINAL HUMOURS, CARDINAL VIRTUES and other objects.

**Cardinal signs.** In the ZODIAC these are the two equinoctial signs, ARIES and LIBRA, and two solstitial signs, CANCER and CAPRICORN.

**Cardinal virtues.** The most important moral qualities, traditionally the four virtues of justice, prudence, temperance and fortitude, on which all other virtues hang or depend. The term was introduced by the SCHOOLMEN to distinguish the 'natural' virtues from the 'theological' virtues (faith, hope and charity).

**College of Cardinals** or **Sacred College.** *See under* COLLEGE.

**Care. Care attendant.** A person who is paid to look after physically or mentally handicapped people in day centres and residential homes.

**Care killed the cat.** It is said that a cat has nine lives, but care would wear them all out.

Hang sorrow! care'll kill a cat.

BEN JONSON: *Every Man in his Humour*, I, iii (1598)

**Care Sunday.** The fifth Sunday in LENT. Care here means 'trouble', 'suffering', so that Care Sunday is an alternative name for JUDICA SUNDAY (Passion Sunday). Care Sunday is also known as Carle Sunday or Carling Sunday. It was an old custom, especially in the north, to eat dried peas fried in butter on this day, and these were called 'carlings', this word itself presumably evolving from 'care'.

**For all I care.** *See under* FOR.

**Have a care.** Take care; be careful.

**I couldn't care less.** I am quite indifferent to what you say. Americans usually say 'I could care less'.

**In care.** Said of a child taken into care by a local authority.

**Not to care a fig.** Not to care at all. Here 'fig' is either an example of something of little value or alternatively the fig of Spain or FICO. The word is used in many expressions denoting something of little or no value, such as 'not worth a fig', i.e. worth nothing.

**Take care.** Now a general wish on concluding a conversation or a letter.

**Take care of the pence and the pounds will take care of themselves.** A sound piece of advice, which Lord Chesterfield records in his letter to his son (5 February 1750) as having been given by 'old Mr Lowndes, the famous Secretary of the Treasury, in the reigns of King William, Queen Anne and George I'. The saying is parodied in the Duchess's words of advice in Lewis Carroll's *Alice in Wonderland* (1865): 'Take care of the sense, and the sounds will take care of themselves.'

**Carey. Carey Street.** To be in Carey Street is to be bankrupt. Carey Street is in the City of London, off Chancery Lane, and the Bankruptcy Court is situated here, behind the Law Courts.

**Mother Carey's chickens.** *See under* MOTHER.

**Mother Carey's goose.** *See under* MOTHER.

**Carfax.** A crossroads in the centre of Oxford, at the meeting-point of four streets that formerly ran from the city's north, south, east and west gates. The name is a corruption of Latin *quadrifurcus*, 'four-forked'. At one time there was a crossroads of the same name in Exeter, and there is still a Carfax in Horsham, East Sussex.

**Carle** or **Carling Sunday.** *See* CARE SUNDAY.

**Carlists.** Don Carlos (1788–1855), the second son of Charles IV of Spain, would have become king on the death of his brother Ferdinand VII, had not the SALIC LAW been set aside in favour of Ferdinand's daughter, Isabella. Don Carlos was supported by the church, and the Carlist Wars ensued (1833–40), but Isabella's supporters triumphed. Carlist intrigues continued until the death of Don Carlos II in 1909. In 1937 the Carlists supported General Franco's FALANGE, maintaining Carlos Hugo de Borbón-Parma as claimant to the throne. On General Franco's death in 1975, Alphonso XIII's grandson became king of Spain as Juan Carlos I, his succession having been accepted by Franco in 1969.

**Carlovingians.** *See* CAROLINGIANS.

**Carmagnole.** This was originally the name of a workman's jacket introduced into France from Carmagnola in Piedmont and adopted by French revolutionaries, who wore it with black trousers, a red LIBERTY CAP and a tricoloured sash. Thus the name came to be applied to them, to the soldiers of the Republic and to a widely popular song and dance that invariably accompanied the executions of 1792 and 1793. The first verse of the song is:

> Madame Veto avait promis
> De faire égorger tout Paris,
> Madame Veto avait promis
> De faire égorger tout Paris,
> Mais son coup a manqué.
> Dansons la carmagnole,
> Vive le son, vive le son,
> Dansons la carmagnole,
> Vive le son du canon.
> (Madame Veto had promised to have all Paris massacred, but she failed. Let us dance the carmagnole, long live the cannon's sound.)

Madame VETO was their name for Marie Antoinette, as she was believed to have instigated the king's unfortunate use of the veto. Carmagnole was subsequently applied to other revolutionary songs such as ÇA IRA, the MARSEILLAISE and the CHANT DU DÉPART, also to the speeches in favour of the execution of Louis XVI, called by the revolutionary Bertrand Barère *Carmagnoles*.

**Carman.** The Chevalier BAYARD's horse, given to him by the Duke of Lorraine. It was a Persian horse from Kerman or Carmen (Laristan).

**Carmel, Mount.** The mountain in Israel where, in biblical times, ELIJAH summoned Israel to choose between God and Baal as the place of retreat for Elijah and ELISHA (1 and 2 Kings). Its Hebrew name means 'garden' and in turn gave the name of the CARMELITES.

**Carmelites.** A mendicant order of friars of 12th-century origin, taking its name from Mount CARMEL and with a mythical history associating the order with the prophet ELIJAH. They are also called White Friars from the white mantle worn over a brown habit. One of their houses, founded in London on the south side of Fleet Street in 1241, gave its name to the district called Whitefriars or ALSATIA, which was long a sanctuary. *See also* BAREFOOTED; RIGHT OF SANCTUARY.

**Carmen.** The beautiful but fickle gypsy girl who is the heroine of Bizet's opera of the same name (1875). Arrested after a fight, she is assigned to the custody of Don José, a corporal, who becomes besotted with her and allows her to escape. She is sought out by the glamorous toreador, Escamillo, and when attending a bullfight with him is joined by José who begs her to start a new life with him. She refuses, and at the very moment of Escamillo's triumph in the ring, is stabbed to death by José in his jealousy. The libretto is based on Prosper Mérimée's tale

*Carmen* (1847). The heroine's name comes from Latin *carmen*, 'song', 'charm', 'prediction'.

**Carmen Sylva.** The pseudonym of Queen Elizabeth of Romania (1843–1916). She was a musician, painter and writer of poems and stories. The queen's pen-name reflected her love of singing and of walking in the forest, and represents Latin *carmen*, 'song', and *silva*, 'wood'.

**Carnaby Street.** In the 1960s the much publicized clothing centre for fashion-conscious young people, east of London's Regent Street. It became associated with trendy unisex costumes and was somewhat showily refurbished by Westminster City Council in 1973, but its popularity had declined by 1975 when boutiques in the King's Road, Chelsea, began to attract this type of custom. *See also* MONMOUTH STREET.

**Carnegie.** A name associated with American philanthropy. It is that of Andrew Carnegie (1835–1919), a Scottish-born steel magnate. He built and owned the Carnegie Hall, the New York concert hall that opened in 1891, and founded many charitable trusts.

**Carnival.** The season immediately preceding LENT, ending on SHROVE TUESDAY, and a period in many Roman Catholic countries devoted to amusement. Hence the use of the word for a festive occasion or a travelling fair. It derives from Italian *carnevale,* going back ultimately to Medieval Latin *carnelevamen*, 'raising flesh', from Latin *caro, carnis*, 'flesh', and *levare*, 'to raise'. To 'raise flesh' is to abstain from meat, which is the regime that Lent strictly entails.

**Carol** (Old French *carole*, perhaps from Latin *choraula*, 'flute player', but influenced by Latin *corona*, 'garland', 'circle'). The earliest use of the word in English was for a round dance, then later it came to denote a light and joyous hymn, especially one associated with the Nativity. An account of the festivities on TWELFTH NIGHT in 1487 says:

> At the Table in the Medell of the Hall sat the Deane and thoos of the kings Chapell, which incontynently after the Kings furst Course sange a Carall.

The first printed collection of carols came from the press of Wynkyn de Worde in 1521. It included the Boar's Head Carol, which is still sung at Queen's College, Oxford. *See also* BOAR'S HEAD.

**Carolingians** or **Carlovingians.** The dynasty named from Carolus Magnus or CHARLEMAGNE. The Carolingians were descended from Arnulf, a 7th-century bishop of Metz, and ruled in France (751–987), Germany (752–911) and Italy (744–887).

**Carolus.** A gold coin of the reign of CHARLES I. It was at first worth 20s, later 23s.

**Carpathian Wizard, The.** PROTEUS, who lived in the island of Carpathus (now Scarpanto), between Rhodes and Crete, and who could transform himself into any shape he pleased. He is represented as carrying a sort of crook in his hand, because he was an ocean shepherd and had to manage a flock of sea calves.

**Carpe diem** (Latin, 'seize the day'). Enjoy yourself while you have the chance.

> Carpe diem, quam minimum credula postero.
> (Seize the day, put no trust in the future.)
> HORACE: *Odes*, Bk I, xi (1st century BC)

The same sentiment has been expressed by later poets, such as Robert Herrick's injunction to maidens to forsake their virginity and make the most of life:

> Gather ye rosebuds while ye may,
> Old Time is still a-flying:
> And this same flower that smiles to-day,
> To-morrow will be dying.
> 'To the Virgins, to Make Much of Time' (1648)

**Carpenter, Bush.** *See under* BUSH.

**Carpet. Carpetbagger.** The name given in the USA to the northern political adventurers who sought a career in the southern states after the Civil War ended in 1865. Their only 'property qualification' was a 'carpet bag' of personal belongings, and they were regarded by the southerners as parasites and exploiters. The southern state governments of this time are called carpetbagger governments from the presence of these Republican office holders from the north.

The word subsequently came to be used generally of an unscrupulous opportunist, especially in politics or the financial market. Its particular application to building society members dates from 1995, when it was adopted by Peter Robinson, a former building society executive, to describe speculators who joined a society purely in the hope of a 'windfall' payment made when it converted from a mutual organization to a bank.

> Societies may have more than enough carpetbaggers to defeat loyalists who favour remaining as mutuals owned by their members, rather than by shareholders.
> *Financial Times* (16 January 1999)

**Carpetbiter.** A person subject to violent fits of rage. Chewing and biting of this kind has always been a sign of uncontrolled temper, and there are many accounts of this type of behaviour among the notoriously violent-tempered, from the ANGEVIN KINGS to Adolf Hitler.

**Carpet bombing.** The systematic intensive bombing of an area. Hence, in less serious vein, the delivery by the postman of unsolicited advertising matter or 'junk mail'.

**Carpet knight.** A knight dubbed at court by favour, not having won his spurs by military service in the field. The expression may have arisen from the fact that non-military knighthoods were conferred 'on the carpet', rather than 'in the field', or else allude to the attachment shown to the carpeted drawing room by non-martial knights. By extension the term came to apply disparagingly to any soldier who spends his life away from battle or to any idler in general.

> You are women
> Or, at the best, loose carpet-knights.
> PHILIP MASSINGER: *Maid of Honour*, II, v (*c*.1620)

**Carpet slippers.** The indoor slippers are so called not because they are worn for use on carpets but because they were originally made with woollen uppers resembling carpeting.

**Magic carpet, The.** *See under* MAGIC.

**On the carpet** or **carpeted, To be.** To be reprimanded; to be 'called over the coals'.

**Red carpet.** *See under* RED.

**Sweep under the carpet, To.** *See under* SWEEP.

**Carriage.** This word was originally used to mean things carried, i.e. luggage.

> And after those days we took up our carriages, and went up to Jerusalem.
> Acts 21:15

**Carriage clock.** A portable clock, usually in a rectangular case with a handle on top. Such clocks were originally used by travellers.

**Carriage dog.** A former name for the dalmatian. This breed of dog was originally intended to guard mail coaches, but it soon became fashionable for any smart carriage to have one or two dalmatians as an escort, either running alongside, next to the wheels, or with their noses to the back axle.

**Carriage return key.** A key pressed to return the carriage of an electric typewriter to a fixed position, an operation in many cases involving a resounding crash.

**Carriage trade.** Trade from the wealthier section of society, who formerly travelled by carriage.

**Carronade.** A now obsolete naval gun of short barrel and large bore, like a mortar. It was first made in 1779 at the Carron iron foundry in Scotland. Hence its name. Carronades were fastened to their carriages by a loop underneath, and they were chiefly used on ships to enable heavy shot to be thrown at close quarters.

**Carry. Carried out feet foremost, To be.** To be dead.

**Carry all before one, To.** To win unanimous support or approval for oneself.

**Carry arms! Carry swords!** Military commands directing that the rifle or drawn sword is to be held in a vertical position in the right hand and against the right shoulder.

**Carry a torch for someone, To.** To suffer unrequited love for them, the torch being the torch of love. A torch singer is a female who sings sentimental ditties of such love.

**Carry coals to Newcastle, To.** To do what is superfluous; to take something where it is already plentiful. The French say, *porter de l'eau à la rivière* ('to carry water to the river'). The Germans say, *Eulen nach Athen tragen* ('to carry owls to Athens'). Russians say, *yekhat' v Tulu so svoim samovarom* ('to go to Tula with one's own samovar').

**Carry fire in one hand and water in the other, To.** To say one thing and mean another; to flatter; to deceive.

**Carry forward, To.** In BOOK-KEEPING, to transfer a balance to the next page.

**Carry it off, To.** To do well under difficulties.

**Carry on, To.** To continue an activity from the point already reached; to make a scene or cause a fuss. The title of the popular *Carry On* films puns on both meanings, as well as on 'carrying on' in its sense of questionable or flirtatious behaviour.

**Carry one's bat, To.** Of a cricketer, to go in first and be not out at the close of the innings. Hence, figuratively, to outlast one's opponents, to see through an undertaking.

**Carry one's point, To.** To succeed against opposition; to overrule; to win. Candidates in Rome were balloted for and the votes marked on a tablet by points. Hence, *omne punctum ferre* meant 'to be carried *nem con*' or to gain every vote, and 'to carry one's point' is to carry off the points at which one aimed.

**Carry on with someone, To.** To have an affair with them.

**Carry out** or **through, To.** To continue a project to its completion.

**Carry over, To.** In BOOK-KEEPING, to transfer an item to the following year's account instead of writing it off against profit and loss.

**Carry the can, To.** To take the responsibility for the mistakes or misdeeds of others. The phrase may refer to the performance of menial tasks, carried out for the benefit of others.

**Carry the day, To.** To win a contest, to succeed.

**Carry too much canvas, To.** To attempt something beyond one's resources. A ship carrying too much canvas has spread more sail than she can safely carry.

**Carry water to the river, To.** To CARRY COALS TO NEWCASTLE.

**Carry weight, To.** To have influence. In horse-racing, to equalize the weight of two or more riders by adding to the lighter ones.

> He carries weight! he rides a race!
> 'Tis for a thousand pounds.
> WILLIAM COWPER: 'John Gilpin' (1785)

**Dot and carry one.** *See under* DOT.

**Fetch and carry, To.** *See under* FETCH.

**Carson, Kit.** The US trapper and explorer (1809–68) who took part in the conquest of California and who fought Native American tribes that sided with the Confederacy in the Civil War. He came to be regarded as the quintessential frontiersman. Carson City, the capital of Nevada, is named after him.

**Cart. In the cart.** In trouble, in difficulty.

**Put the cart before the horse, To.** To reverse the right or natural order of things.

> This methinks is playnely to sett the carte before the horse.
>
> *The Babees Book* (Early English Tract Society, p. 23) (*c*.1475)

Other languages have their equivalents, in some cases meaning 'to put the plough before the oxen':

French: *Mettre la charrue devant les bœufs*
German: *Die Pferde hinter den Wagen spannen*
Greek: HYSTERON PROTERON
Italian: *Mettere il carro innanzi ai buoi*
Latin: *Currus bovem trahit praepostere*
Spanish: *Echar el carro antes de los bueyes*

**Carta, Magna.** *See under* MAGNA.

**Carte. Carte blanche** (French, 'blank paper'). Literally, a paper with only the signature written on it, so that the recipient may write his own terms upon it, knowing they will be accepted. The expression is of military origin, referring to unconditional surrender, but it is now used solely in a figurative sense, so that to give someone carte blanche is to grant them absolute freedom of action. *See also* BLANK CHEQUE.

**Carte de visite** (French, 'visiting card'). A photographic likeness on a card, originally intended to be used as a visiting card. The idea was proposed in 1857 but never caught on, although it made the small size of photograph popular.

**Carte du jour** (French, 'card of the day'). A menu listing dishes available on a particular day.

**Cartesian philosophy.** The philosophical system of René Descartes (1596–1650), often called the father of modern philosophy. The basis of his system is *Cogito, ergo sum*, 'I think, therefore I am', the reasoning being that 'I think' presupposes the existence of 'I'.

Thought must proceed from SOUL and therefore man is not wholly material. Soul must be from some Being that is not material, and that Being is God. As for physical phenomena, they must be the result of motion excited by God. These motions Descartes termed vortices, to explain the movement of heavenly bodies.

Descartes' reasoning has been criticized by later philosophers, such as the biologist T.H. Huxley:

> He [Descartes] stopped at the famous formula, 'I think, therefore I am.' Yet a little consideration will show this formula to be full of snares and verbal entanglements. In the first place, the 'therefore' has no business there. The 'I am' is assumed in the 'I think', which is simply another way of saying 'I am thinking'. And, in the second place, 'I think' is not one simple proposition, but three distinct assertions rolled into one. The first of these is 'something called I exists'; the second is 'something called thought exists'; and the third is 'the thought is the result of the action of the I'.
>
> Now it will be obvious to you, that the only one of these three propositions which can stand the Cartesian test of certainty is the second.
>
> 'On Descartes' *Discourse on Method*' (1870)

**Carthage of the North.** This name was given to Lübeck when it was the head of the HANSEATIC LEAGUE.

**Carthaginem esse delendam.** *See* DELENDA EST CARTHAGO.

**Carthaginian faith.** Treachery. *See also* PUNIC FAITH.

**Carthusians.** An order of monks founded *c*.1084 by St Bruno of Cologne, who with six companions retired to the solitude of Chatrousse, a village northeast of Grenoble, and there built the monastery known as La Grande Chartreuse. (Many dictionaries say that their name derives from the latter, but the name of the monastery really comes from that of their order, itself evolving from the Latin name of the village, Catorissium.) It is here they make the liqueur called CHARTREUSE. In 1902 monks were evicted by order of the French government and most of them found refuge in Spain. In 1940 they returned to La Grande Chartreuse. *See also* CHARTERHOUSE.

**Cartridge, Blank.** *See under* BLANK.

**Carvilia.** *See* MORGAN LE FAY.

**Caryatides** or **caryatids.** Figures of women in Greek costume, used in architecture to support entablatures. Caryae, in Laconia, sided with the Persians at THERMOPYLAE, as a result of which the Greeks destroyed the city, slew the men and made the women slaves. Praxiteles, to perpetuate the disgrace, employed figures of these women instead of columns. *See also* ATLANTES; CANEPHORUS; TELAMONES.

**Casabianca.** At the Battle of the Nile (1798), Louis Casabianca, captain of the French flagship *L'Orient* (120 guns), gallantly fought his ship to the end, although the admiral had been killed. His 13-year-old son, Giacomo Jocante, refused to leave him and perished with his father. This is the historical background to the well-known lines:

> The boy stood on the burning deck
> Whence all but he had fled;
> The flame that lit the battle's wreck

Shone round him o'er the dead.
FELICIA HEMANS: 'Casabianca' (1849)

**Casanova.** To be regarded as a Casanova is to have a reputation for amorous adventures, in allusion to Giovanni Jacopo Casanova de Seingalt (1725–98), who secured his own reputation as a sexual entrepreneur by writing his lengthy *Mémoires*. Following his expulsion from a Venetian seminary on the grounds of immoral conduct, he wandered the capitals of Europe, mixing with aristocratic and wealthy society, posing as alchemist, preacher, gambler and diplomatist among others, and generally leading a lubricious life. He was also a knight of the papal order of the Golden Spur and was acquainted with both Stanislaus Poniatowski and Frederick the Great, but he soon exhausted the goodwill of those around him.

**Case. Case, To.** To skin an animal, thus depriving it of its 'case'. *See also* FIRST CATCH YOUR HARE.

**Case a joint, To.** To inspect a building carefully with the aim of robbing it. The expression originated among American criminal society.

**Case-hardened.** Without any sense of honour or shame; callous. The allusion is to steel that has been hardened by having a surface layer of high carbon content added to its surface.

**Case history.** The record of a person's background and medical history, especially with regard to proposed treatment.

**Case is altered, The.** This PUBLIC HOUSE SIGN may derive simply from the fact that the circumstances of a particular inn have altered substantially, but there are several other suggested origins of the sign. One is that it is from PLOWDEN's use of the expression. Another (as in the Harrow district) is that it is a corruption of *Casa Alta* (Spanish 'High House'), which was said to be adopted as a name when soldiers of the 57th Foot returned to Middlesex after the Peninsular War.

**Basket case.** *See under* BASKET.

**Leading case.** *See under* LEAD.

**Lower case.** *See under* LOW.

**Open-and-shut case.** *See under* OPEN.

**Upper case.** *See under* UPPER.

**Cash. Hard cash.** *See under* HARD.

**Spot cash.** *See* READY MONEY.

**Casket.** A small chest or box.

**Casket Homer, The.** An edition corrected by ARISTOTLE, which Alexander the Great always carried about with him and laid under his pillow at night together with his sword. After the Battle of Arbela (331 BC), a golden casket richly studded with gems was found in the tent of DARIUS, and Alexander, when asked to what purpose it should be put, replied, 'There is but one thing in the world worthy of so costly a depository,' whereupon he placed in it his edition of Homer.

**Casket Letters, The.** Letters supposed to have been written between Mary, Queen of Scots and Bothwell, at least one of which was held to prove the complicity of the queen in the murder of Darnley, her husband. They were kept in a casket, which fell into the hands of the Earl of Morton in 1567. They were examined in England and used as evidence (although denounced as forgeries by the queen, who was never allowed to see them), and they disappeared after the execution of the Earl of Gowrie (1584), into whose possession they had passed on Morton's execution in 1581. Their authenticity is still in dispute.

**Children of the Casket.** *See under* CHILD.

**Cassandra** (perhaps a feminine form of Greek *Alexandros*, 'Alexander'). In Greek legend the daughter of PRIAM and HECUBA, who was gifted with the power of prophecy. She refused APOLLO's advances, and he arranged it that no one believed her predictions, although they were invariably correct. She appears in Shakespeare's *Troilus and Cressida* (1602). In the figurative sense the name is usually applied to a prophet of doom.

**Cassation, Court of.** *See under* COURT.

**Cassibelan.** The uncle of Cymbeline, mentioned in Shakespeare's *Cymbeline* (1611). He is the historical Cassivellaunus, a British king who ruled over the Catuvellauni (in southern Britain), *c.*50 BC, and was conquered by CAESAR. *See* CUNOBELIN.

**Cassidy, Hopalong.** *See under* HOP.

**Cassiopeia.** In Greek mythology the wife of CEPHEUS, king of Ethiopia, and mother of ANDROMEDA. Through boasting of her beauty, she was sent to the heavens as the constellation Cassiopeia, the chief stars of which form the outline of a woman sitting in a chair and holding up both arms in supplication.

**Cassiterides.** The tin islands, generally supposed to be the Scilly Isles and Cornwall, but possibly the isles in Vigo Bay (off northwest Spain) are meant. It is said that the Veneti procured tin from Cornwall and carried it to these islands, keeping its source a profound secret. The Phoenicians were the chief customers of the Veneti.

**Cassius.** In full Gaius Cassius Longinus (d.42 BC), one of the principal assassins of CAESAR.

**Cast.** As applied to the eye, a squint. One meaning of the verb 'cast' is 'to twist' or 'to warp'. When a fabric warps, it is thus said to 'cast'. There is also a CASTING VOTE.

**Cast about, To.** To search visually or mentally. This is a sporting phrase. When hounds lose the scent they 'cast' for it, by spreading out and searching in different directions to find it again.

**Cast accounts, To.** To balance or keep accounts.

To cast up a line of figures is to add them together and set down the sum they produce.

**Cast anchor, To.** To throw out the anchor in order to bring the vessel to a standstill.

**Castaway.** The word was at first an adjective meaning rejected, then a noun meaning a reprobate. It occurs once in the Bible in the latter sense (1 Corinthians 9:27). The use of the word for a shipwrecked person comes from William Cowper's poem *The Castaway* (1799). Based on an incident in Baron Anson's *Voyage Around the World* (1748), it describes the fate of a seaman washed overboard while manning the shrouds.

**Cast back, To.** To turn one's mind or thoughts back to the past.

**Cast down.** Dejected; depressed.

**Casting vote.** The vote of the presiding officer or chairman when the votes of the assembly are equal. The final vote 'casts' or turns the issue one way or the other.

**Cast in someone's teeth, To.** To throw reproof at someone. The allusion is to knocking someone's teeth out by stones.

> All his faults observ'd,
> Set in a notebook, learn'd and conn'd by rote,
> To cast into my teeth.
> SHAKESPEARE: *Julius Caesar*, IV, iii (1599)

**Cast** or **draw lots, To.** To obtain a decision by casting or drawing from a set of objects selected for the purpose was an old form of DIVINATION and an established practice in WITCHCRAFT. Lots were used in ancient Israel in deciding the division of property, appointing to office, the discovering of culprits and the like (*see* Leviticus 16:7–10) with the presupposition of divine influence affecting the result.

> The lot is cast into the lap; but the whole disposing thereof is of the Lord.
> Proverbs 16:33

**Cast not a clout till May is out.** An old warning not to shed winter clothing too early in the year. 'Clout' here is a rag or patch, hence a piece of clothing. May is also another name for hawthorn, which blossoms in May. Thus some hold that the proverb means 'do not discard clothing until the hawthorn blossoms', but more likely it means 'wait until the end of May'. F.K. Robinson's *Whitby Glossary* (1855) has:

> The wind at North and East
> Was never good for man nor beast,
> So never think to cast a clout
> Until the month of May be out.

**Cast off, To.** To remove the mooring lines that tie a ship to the dock or a boat to the shore. To knit a final row of stitches in completing a piece of knitting. *See also* CAST ON.

**Cast on, To.** To form the first row of stitches in knitting. *See also* CAST OFF.

**Cast one's bonnet over a windmill, To.** To throw caution to the winds; to decide on a risky course of action.

**Cast one's bread upon the waters, To.** To do good without expecting thanks or recognition. The implication is that one so doing will in due course be rewarded. The source of the expression is biblical, but the precise allusion remains uncertain. One explanation is that seed cast on flooded land will take root and profit the sower when the waters recede, bread here meaning 'corn' or 'seed'.

> Cast thy bread upon the waters: for thou shalt find it after many days.
> Ecclesiastes 11:1

**Cast one's eye over, To.** To look at something with the aim of assessing it.

**Cast pearls before swine, To.** To offer something of a quality that the uncultured PHILISTINE is unable to appreciate; to offer one's 'pearls of wisdom' to an unappreciative audience.

> Give not that which is holy unto the dogs, neither cast ye your pearls before swine, lest they trample them under their feet.
> Matthew 7:6

**Cast the first stone, To.** To take the lead in criticizing, fault-finding, quarrelling or the like. The phrase is from John 8:7:

> He that is without sin among you, let him first cast a stone at her.

**Die is cast, The.** *See under* DIE.

**Castaly.** A fountain of PARNASSUS sacred to the MUSES. Its waters had the power of inspiring with the gift of poetry those who drank of them.

**Caste** (Portuguese *casta*, 'race', 'breed'). One of the hereditary classes of society among Hindus, and hence any hereditary or exclusive class. The four Hindu castes are Brahmans or Brahmins (the priestly order), Kshatriya (soldiers and rulers), Vaisya (husbandmen and merchants) and Sudra (agricultural labourers and artisans). The first issued from the mouth of BRAHMA, the second from his arms, the third from his thighs, and the fourth from his feet. Below this come 36 inferior classes, to whom the VEDAS are sealed and who are held cursed in this world and without hope in the next.

**Castle. Castle in the air** or **in Spain, A.** A visionary project or daydream. Fairy tales have such castles, which vanish as fast as they are built, like that built for ALADDIN by the genie of the lamp. The French equivalent is regularly *château en Espagne*, 'castle in Spain', a country that borders France and that was long the nearest Moorish country to Christendom.

**Castle of Indolence, The.** In James Thomson's poem of this name (1748) the Castle is situated in the land of Drowsiness, where every sense is steeped in enervating delights. The owner was an enchanter, who deprived all who entered his domains of their energy and free will.

**Castle Terabil** or **Terrible.** In ARTHURIAN ROMANCE a castle that stood in Launceston, Cornwall. It had a steep keep surrounded by a triple wall. It is also known as Dunheved Castle.

**Doubting Castle.** *See under* DOUBTING.

**Elephant and Castle.** *See under* ELEPHANT.

**King of the castle.** *See under* KING.

**Maiden Castle.** *See under* MAIDEN.

**Perilous Castle.** *See under* PERILOUS.

**Castor and Pollux.** In classical mythology, the twin sons of JUPITER and LEDA, also known as the Dioscuri. They had many adventures, including sailing with JASON in quest of the GOLDEN FLEECE. They were worshipped as gods, and were finally placed among the constellations as the GEMINI. Their names used to be given by sailors to ST ELMO'S FIRE or CORPOSANT. If only one flame showed itself, the Romans called it Helen's fire and said that the worst of the storm was yet to come. Two or more luminous flames they called Castor and Pollux and said that they foretold the end of the storm.

**Casus belli** (Latin, 'occasion of war'). An event or incident that justifies war or hostilities.

**Cat.** The cat is called a FAMILIAR from the medieval superstition that Satan's favourite form was a black cat. Hence witches were said to have a cat as their familiars. The superstition may have arisen from the classical legend of Galenthias, who was turned into a cat and became a priestess of HECATE.

In ancient Rome the cat was a symbol of liberty, and the goddess of Liberty was represented with a cat at her feet. No animal is as averse to confinement as a cat.

In ancient Egypt the cat was held sacred. The goddess Bast (*see* BUBASTIS), representative of the life-giving solar heat, was portrayed as having the head of a cat, probably because that animal likes to bask in the sun. Diodorus wrote that in Egypt whoever killed a cat, even by accident, was to be punished by death. According to tradition DIANA assumed the form of a cat and thus excited the fury of the Giants.

The male, or Tom, cat in Scotland is sometimes called a gib, while the female is a doe. Cat is also a term for a spiteful woman, so that a spiteful remark is said to be 'catty'.

**Cat among the pigeons, The.** To put or set the cat among the pigeons is to stir up trouble; to cause alarm. The allusion is obvious.

> Professor Stephen Hawking put the cat among the pigeons last week with his cheery remarks about comet Machholz-2, which some astronomers believe could be heading our way.
>
> *The Times* (19 September 1994)

**Cat-and-dog.** Said of a quarrelsome relationship.

**Cat and Fiddle.** There are several fanciful derivations for this PUBLIC HOUSE SIGN, such as a supposed corruption of French *Catherine la Fidèle*, Catherine the Faithful, alluding to the wife of Peter the Great, but it most probably comes from the nursery rhyme:

> Heigh diddle diddle
> The cat and the fiddle.

There is a possible reference to the once popular game of tipcat, with the fiddle representing the dancing that would attract customers to the inn. The second highest English inn is the Cat and Fiddle near Buxton, Derbyshire.

**Cat and Kittens.** A PUBLIC HOUSE SIGN alluding to the large and small pewter pots in which beer was served. Stealing these pots was called 'cat and kitten sneaking'.

**Cat and Mouse Act, The.** The popular name for the Prisoners (Temporary Discharge for Ill Health) Act of 1913, which was passed during the SUFFRAGETTE disturbances to avoid the imprisoned lawbreakers from achieving martyrdom through hunger strikes. They were released on licence when necessary, subject to re-arrest if need arose. To play cat and mouse with someone is to treat them cruelly or teasingly before a final act of cruelty or unkindness.

**Cat burglar.** A burglar who enters buildings stealthily by climbing in through a window or skylight after dark, like a cat.

**Catcall.** A kind of shrill whistle used by audiences or at public gatherings to express displeasure or impatience.

> I was very much surprised with the great Consort of Cat-calls ... to see so many Persons of Quality of both Sexes assembled together at a kind of Catterwawling.
>
> JOSEPH ADDISON: *Spectator*, No. 361 (1712)

**Catflap.** A small, two-way flap built in the bottom of a door to enable a cat to go outside and come indoors at will.

**Catgut.** A strong cord made from the intestines of animals (usually sheep, but never cats), used for the strings of musical instruments and sports rackets. The name has never been satisfactorily explained, but it may be a corruption of kitgut, kit being an old word for a small fiddle. In modern use the word is often shortened to gut.

> Here's a tune indeed! pish,
> I had rather hear one ballad sung i' the nose now
> Than all these simpering tunes played upon cat's guts
> And sung by little kitling.
>
> THOMAS MIDDLETON: *Women Beware Women*, III, ii (1657)

Shakespeare, however, gives catgut its probable true origin:

> Now divine air! Now is his soul ravished! Is it not strange that Sheep's guts should hale souls out of men's bodies? Well, a horn for my money when all's done.
> *Much Ado about Nothing*, II, iii (1598)

**Cat has nine lives, A.** A cat is more tenacious of life than many animals. It is wary and hardy and after a fall generally lands upon its feet without injury, its feet and toes being well padded.

> *Tybalt*: What wouldst thou have with me?
> *Mercutio*: Good king of cats, nothing but one of your nine lives.
> SHAKESPEARE: *Romeo and Juliet*, III, i (1594)

**Cat in hell's chance, A.** No chance at all.

**Cat i' the adage.** *See* ALL CATS LOVE FISH BUT FEAR TO WET THEIR PAWS.

**Catlick.** A perfunctory wash.

**Cat may look at a king, A.** An impertinent remark by an inferior to a superior, meaning 'I am as good as you.' There was a political pamphlet published with this title in 1652.

**Catnap.** A short sleep or doze, such as a cat takes.

**Cat o'mountain** or **catamount.** A name used for various wildcats, such as the puma or lynx.

**Cat-o'-nine-tails.** A whip with nine lashes used for punishing offenders, in short known as the cat. It was at one time used for flogging in the armed services and was not formally abolished as a civil punishment for crimes of violence until 1948. Popular superstition says that there were nine tails because flogging by 'a trinity of trinities' would be both more efficient and more efficacious. *See also* ROOM TO SWING A CAT.

**Cats' chorus** or **concert.** A discordant din, like the caterwauling of cats at night.

**Cat's cradle.** A game played by making complex patterns with a length of string looped over the fingers. It has been suggested that the name is a corruption of cratch-cradle, referring to the manger-cradle in which the infant Jesus was laid (cratch is French *crèche*, 'rack', 'manger'). However, this is probably a folk etymology.

**Cat's eye.** A gem which possesses a changeable lustre. The true or precious cat's eye is a variety of chrysoberyl. The semi-precious kind is a form of quartz.

Catseye is also the proprietary name of a reflective stud set in a rubber pad in the road as a guide to drivers when it is dark or foggy. The studs were the invention in 1934 of Percy Shaw (1889–1975), when 50 were laid at Brightlington crossroads, a notorious BLACK SPOT near Bradford, Yorkshire.

**Cat's paw.** A pattern of ripples on a surface of water, caused by a light wind. In nautical parlance, a cat's paw is a hitch in the form of two loops in the bight of a line, used to attach it to a hook.

To make a cat's paw of someone is to use them as a tool; to get them to do one's dirty work. The allusion is said to be to the fable of the monkey who wanted to get some roasted chestnuts from the fire, and used the paw of his friend the cat for the purpose.

**Cat's pyjamas, The.** Something excellent or praiseworthy. A colloquialism of American origin. The CAT'S WHISKERS or the BEE'S KNEES have a similar sense.

**Catsuit.** A one-piece, close-fitting trouser suit, so called from its resemblance to the costume worn by a pantomime cat.

**Cat's whisker.** In the old 'crystal' wireless sets or radio receivers, this was the name given to the fine pointed wire that made contact with the crystal.

**Cat's whiskers.** An excellent person or thing. There is a real allusion to the whiskers of a cat, since their extreme sensitivity enable it to pass through narrow spaces in total darkness.

**Catwalk.** A narrow pathway or gangway over a theatre stage or along a bridge. Also an extended stage at a fashion show. Cats are able to walk safely along a raised narrow surface such as the top of a wall.

> The uncompromising catwalk statement is 'long with flat'.
> *Financial Times* (4 July 1998)

**All cats love fish but fear to wet their paws.** *See under* ALL.

**Alley cat.** *See under* ALLEY.

**As deaf as a white cat.** *See under* AS.

**As sick as a cat.** *See under* AS.

**Before the cat can lick its ear.** *See under* BEFORE.

**Bell the cat, To.** *See under* BELL.

**Care killed the cat.** *See under* CARE.

**Dick Whittington and his cat.** *See under* WHITTINGTON.

**Doctor a cat, To.** *See under* DOCTOR.

**Fat cat.** *See under* FAT.

**Felix the Cat.** *See under* FELIX.

**Fight like Kilkenny cats, To.** *See under* FIGHT.

**Gib cat.** *See under* GIB.

**Grin like a Cheshire cat, To.** *See under* GRIN.

**Have no room to swing a cat, To.** *See under* ROOM.

**Lead a cat and dog life, To.** *See under* LEAD.

**Let the cat out of the bag, To.** *See under* LET.

**Like a cat on a hot tin roof.** *See under* LIKE.

**Like something the cat brought in.** *See under* LIKE.

**Manx cat.** *See under* MANX.

**Play cat and mouse, To.** *See* CAT AND MOUSE ACT.

**Rain cats and dogs, To.** *See under* RAIN.

**Rat, cat and dog.** *See under* RAT.

**See how** or **which way the cat jumps, To.** *See under* SEE.

**Touch not the cat.** *See under* TOUCH.

**When the cat's away the mice will play.** *See under* WHEN.

**Catachresis** (Greek, 'misuse'). The misapplication of a word, especially in a MIXED METAPHOR. Milton has a well-known example:

> Blind mouths! that scarce themselves know how to hold
> A sheep-hook, or have learned aught else the least
> That to the faithful herdsman's art belongs!
> *Lycidas* (1637)

**Catacomb.** A subterranean gallery for the burial of the dead, especially one of those at Rome. The origin of the name is unknown, but the cemetery under the basilica of St SEBASTIAN on the APPIAN WAY was called the Catacumbas. This was perhaps a place-name which in the course of time came to be applied to similar cemeteries. Their extensive development in Rome took place in the 3rd and 4th centuries and was due to the spread of Christianity. At times they were used by the Christians for their meetings. They suffered much destruction from the GOTHS and Lombards and eventually came to be forgotten until rediscovered in 1578 following a landslip.

**Catalogue raisonné** (French, 'methodical catalogue'). A catalogue of paintings or other works of art, classed according to their subjects and with explanatory notes or comments.

**Catamaran.** A colloquial term for a quarrelsome old woman, so called from a pun on cat. It properly means a raft consisting of logs lashed together with ropes, as used on the coasts of India, with its derivation in Tamil *kattumaram*, 'tied timber'. In modern use the word applies to a sailing vessel with twin hulls linked in parallel. A vessel that has two hulls flanking the main hull is a trimaran.

> No, you old catamaran, though you pretend you never read novels.
> W.M. THACKERAY: *Lovel the Widower*, ch i (1860)

**Catastrophe** (Greek *katastrephein*, 'to overturn'). The term was originally used of the denouement of a classical tragedy, which is usually an 'overturning' of the beginning of the plot.

> All the actors must enter to complete and make up the catastrophe of this great piece.
> SIR THOMAS BROWNE: *Religio Medici* (1642)

**Catch. Catch a crab, To.** In rowing to fail to put one's oar deep enough into the water, so that one loses one's balance and falls backwards or even overboard. A crab can be scooped out of the water with an oar.

**Catch, get** or **cop a packet, To.** To be injured suddenly; to undergo an unpleasant experience.

**Catch-as-catch-can.** Using any available method or opportunity to get what one wants. In wrestling the name is that of a style in which holds are allowed on any part of the body.

**Catch** or **clutch at a straw, To.** *See* DROWNING MEN CLUTCH AT STRAWS.

**Catch crop.** A quick-growing crop between the rows of a main crop or a substitute for one that has failed. A catch crop is often used by market gardeners to increase the productivity of a plot of land.

**Catch it, To.** To be reprimanded or punished. The phrase is often heard in the form 'you'll catch it', said (not unsympathetically) to a person who has committed some misdemeanour or is in the act of doing so or is about to do so.

**Catch me.** You may be sure I shall never do that; I shall certainly not do what you say.

**Catch on, To.** To grasp mentally; to become popular, of a song, fashion or the like.

**Catch one's breath, To.** To rest from exertion for a moment in order to resume one's normal breathing.

**Catch one's death of cold, To.** To contract a bad cold.

**Catchpenny.** Designed to have instant appeal, so as to 'catch the pennies' and be sold quickly.

**Catchphrase.** A phrase that has caught on and is repeated by all and sundry. It is virtually the same as CATCHWORD.

**Catchpole.** In medieval England a SHERIFF's officer whose business it was to apprehend criminals. The word is nothing to do with a pole or staff, or with poll (the head); it comes from Medieval Latin *cacepollus*, literally 'chicken catcher', with *cace-* an early form of 'catch', and *pollus* from Latin *pullus*, 'chick'.

**Catchpole, Margaret.** An almost legendary Suffolk character (1773–1841). She was the daughter of a farm labourer and eventually a servant of John Cobbold, the Ipswich brewer. According to the Rev. Richard Cobbold's *The History of Margaret Catchpole* (1845), she twice saved the lives of her employer's children but subsequently stole one of his horses and, dressed as a man, rode to London in ten hours. She intended to meet her lover, William Laud, a local sailor turned smuggler, but was captured and sentenced to death. Fortunately this was commuted to seven years' imprisonment. While interned, she managed to escape to join Laud by scaling a 22ft (7m) wall with the aid of a clothes line. Laud was shot dead in self-defence by one of their pursuers, Margaret was caught and again sentenced to death but reprieved and transported to BOTANY BAY. There she established herself as a trusted and respectable character and by strange chance met up with John Barry, son of a Suffolk miller, now a prosperous and influential settler, whose proposal of marriage she had formerly rejected, thus causing him to emigrate. They wed in 1812.

**Catch someone's eye, To.** To attract their attention, as of a waiter in a restaurant.

**Catch someone with their trousers** or **pants down, To.** A metaphor of American origin meaning to catch someone at a disadvantage. There is often a ring at the door when one is otherwise engaged in the smallest room.

**Catch** or **take the ball before the bound, To.** To anticipate an opportunity; to be over-hasty. A metaphor from CRICKET.

**Catch the Speaker's eye, To.** The rule in the HOUSE OF COMMONS is that the member whose rising to address the House is first observed by the SPEAKER is allowed precedence.

**Catch the sun, To.** To be slightly sunburned; to have a gentle tan.

**Catch-22.** A 'no-win' situation: whichever alternative you choose, you will lose or be in trouble. *Catch-22* is the title of Joseph Heller's novel, published in 1961. The story centres on Captain Yossarian of the 256th United States (Army) bombing squadron in the Second World War, whose main aim is to avoid being killed.

> There was only one catch and that was Catch-22, which specified that a concern for one's own safety in the face of dangers that were real and immediate was the process of a rational mind. Orr was crazy and could be grounded. All he had to do was to ask; and as soon as he did, he would no longer be crazy and would have to fly more missions.
> ch v

**Catchweight.** A term in racing, wrestling or boxing, meaning without restrictions as to weight.

**Catchword.** A popular cry, a word or CATCHPHRASE, particularly adopted as a political slogan. 'THREE ACRES AND A COW', 'CHINESE SLAVERY', 'Scholarships not battleships', 'the NEW MORALITY' and 'the AFFLUENT SOCIETY' are examples.

In printing, the first word on a page, which was formerly printed at the foot of the preceding page, is known as the catchword. The first printer to employ catchwords may be either Balthazar Azoguidus of Bologna (in his Italian and Latin editions of Antoninus' *Confessionale* (1472)) or Vindelinus de Spira of Venice (in his undated editions of Philelphus' *Epistolae*, and Tacitus' *Opera* printed before 1474).

Printers also use the name for the headwords in a dictionary, i.e. those at the head of each article, printed in bold type so as to catch the eye, such as 'Catchword' at the head of this entry.

In the theatre, the cue (the last word or so of an actor's lines) is also called the catchword.

**Caught bending, To be.** To be caught at a disadvantage. If you are bending you are vulnerable, partly because you have to straighten yourself to deal with a situation, partly because you invite a smack on the posterior. In about 1903 one of George Robey's songs declared:

> My word! If I catch you bending!

*See also* CATCH SOMEONE WITH THEIR TROUSERS DOWN.

**Caught flat-footed, To be.** To be caught off one's guard, as a football player who is tackled by an opponent before he has been able to advance.

**Caught napping, To be.** To suffer some disadvantage while off one's guard. Pheasants, hares and other animals are sometimes surprised 'napping'.

**Caught out, To be.** To be unmasked in a lie or subterfuge. The expression may derive from CRICKET, in which the batsman is out when he hits a ball that is caught by a fielder.

**Caught short.** Having a sudden need to urinate or defecate, short of a lavatory.

**First catch your hare.** *See under* FIRST.

**Lie at the catch, To.** *See under* LIE.

**Catechism, Shorter.** *See under* SHORT.

**Catechumen** (Greek *katēkhoumenos*, 'one being verbally instructed', from *katēkhein*, 'to instruct orally', literally 'to shout down', from *kata-*, 'down', and *ēkhein*, 'to sound'). In the early church, the word was used for a person undergoing instruction before being baptized. The instruction involved a catechism, or series of questions and answers.

**Caterans.** Scottish Highland brigands and marauders, otherwise FREEBOOTERS. The word probably derives from Scottish Gaelic *ceathairneach*, 'robber'.

**Cater cap** (French *quartier*, 'quarter'). A square cap or MORTARBOARD.

**Cater-cornered.** Placed diagonally, as of a badly parked car in a parking space. Cater is an old word for the four dots on dice, which form diagonals, from French *quatre*, four. Other spellings of the term are catty-cornered and kitty-cornered, as if somehow to do with cats.

**Cater-cousin.** An archaic word for an intimate friend or remote kinsman. The word probably refers to persons being catered for together, so that they eat together. The same idea lies behind foster brother, in which foster derives from Old English *fōstor*, 'food'.

> His master and he, saving your worship's reverence, are scarce cater-cousins.
> SHAKESPEARE: *The Merchant of Venice*, II, ii (1596)

**Caterpillar Club.** An unofficial club started by the Irvin Parachute Company during the Second World War. The caterpillar is that of the silkworm, which supplied the material from which parachutes were formerly made. The company presented a small gold caterpillar pin to any RAF airman who had baled out in action, on his supplying the number of the parachute that had saved his life. Similarly the Goldfish Club existed for those who had been forced to resort to their rubber dinghies. Since then, similar clubs have been formed to encourage the wearing of protective clothing by industrial workers.

**Catharine.** *See* CATHERINE.

**Cathay.** The name used by Marco Polo for what roughly corresponds to northern China, and the name for that part of China that the 16th-century navigators sought to discover via a NORTH-EAST or a NORTHWEST PASSAGE. The word comes from Medieval Latin *Cataya*, a name of Turkic origin applied to a Manchurian Tartar kingdom of the 10th century and, less specifically, to China in general. The modern Russian name for China, *Kitay*, preserves this origin. *See also* MANGI.

> Paulus Venetus, who dwelt many yeres in Cataia, affirmed that he sayled 1500 miles upon the coastes of Mangia, and Anian, towards the Northeast: always finding the open seas before him.
>
> SIR HUMPHREY GILBERT: *Discourse to Prove a Passage by the Northwest to Cataya, etc* (printed 1576)

An English Cathay Company was founded by Michael Lok in 1577 to develop Sir Martin Frobisher's discoveries. In more modern times the name has remained in English poetic usage.

> Thro' the shadow of the globe we sweep into the
> younger day:
> Better fifty years of Europe than a cycle of Cathay.
>
> ALFRED, LORD TENNYSON: *Locksley Hall* (1842)

**Cathedrals of the Old Foundation.** A collective name for the ancient cathedrals that existed in England before Henry VIII founded and endowed new cathedrals out of some of the revenues obtained from the dissolution of the monasteries. The latter, known as Cathedrals of the New Foundation, are Chester, Gloucester, Peterborough, Bristol and Oxford.

**Catherine. Catherine of Alexandria.** Saint and virgin martyr of noble birth (supposedly in the 4th century) in Alexandria. She adroitly defended the Christian faith at a public disputation with certain heathen philosophers at the command of the Emperor Maximinus, for which she was put on a spiked wheel. Legend says that as soon as the wheel turned, her bonds were miraculously broken (hence the CATHERINE WHEEL) and she was instead beheaded. She is the patron saint of craftsmen whose work is based on the wheel, such as wheelwrights, spinners and millers, as well as of young women, students and nurses (because milk, not blood, flowed from her severed head). However, she has no ancient cult, is not mentioned in early martyrologies and is not depicted in early works of art. Such negative evidence thus casts positive doubt on her actual existence. Her feast-day is 25 November. Her name is popularly derived from Greek *katharos*, pure, but is actually of uncertain origin.

**Catherine of Aragon.** The youngest daughter (1485–1536) of Ferdinand and Isabella of Spain, and the first wife of Henry VIII (1509). Henry's infidelities and desire for a son and heir soured the marriage and in 1527 he began proceedings for a divorce in order to marry Anne BOLEYN. In 1534 the pope pronounced Catherine's marriage valid, provoking Henry's final break with Rome and bringing about the establishment of the CHURCH OF ENGLAND.

**Catherine of Siena.** A patron saint of Italy (1347–80). She was canonized in 1461 and in 1970 became the second woman to be made a DOCTOR OF THE CHURCH. As well as serving the poor she was instrumental in bringing about the return of the pope from Avignon to Rome. Her feast-day is 29 April. *See also* AVIGNON POPES; GREAT SCHISM.

**Catherine Théot.** *See under* THÉOT.

**Catherine wheel.** A kind of firework in the form of a wheel, which rotates rapidly as a result of the recoil from the explosion of the various squibs of which it is composed. It is named after St CATHERINE OF ALEXANDRIA.

**Catherine wheel window.** A wheel window, sometimes called a rose window, with ribs radiating from the centre.

**Braid St Catherine's tresses, To.** *See under* BRAID.

**Order of St Catherine, The.** *See under* ORDER.

**Catholic.** The word (Greek *katholikos*) means 'general', 'universal', 'comprehensive'. It is used in this sense in the following extract:

> Creed and test
> Vanish before the unreserved embrace
> Of Catholic humanity.
>
> WILLIAM WORDSWORTH: *Ecclesiastical Sonnets*, III, xxxvi (1822)

From the viewpoint of the church it thus distinguishes (1) the whole body of Christians as apart from 'Jews, heretics and infidels'; (2) a member of a church which claims the APOSTOLIC SUCCESSION and direct descent from the earliest body of Christians; (3) the ROMAN CATHOLIC CHURCH, i.e. the Western or Latin branch of the ancient catholic or universal church.

Alphonso I, king of the Asturias, 739–757, was surnamed 'the Catholic' on account of his zeal in erecting and endowing monasteries and churches.

A person of 'catholic tastes' is one who is interested in a wide variety of subjects.

**Catholic and Apostolic Church.** The name given to the followers of Edward Irving

(1792–1834) and to the church founded in 1835, after his death (also called IRVINGITES). He was a former member of the CHURCH OF SCOTLAND from which he was expelled for heresy in 1833.

**Catholic Church.** The whole body of Christians, as distinct from the churches and sects into which they are divided. The Latin Church called itself Catholic after the separation from the Eastern or ORTHODOX CHURCH. At the REFORMATION, the Reformers called the Western Church under papal jurisdiction the ROMAN CATHOLIC CHURCH as opposed to their own Reformed or PROTESTANT churches. Members of the CHURCH OF ENGLAND hold themselves to be Catholics but in popular usage Catholic usually means Roman Catholic.

> I believe in ... the holy Catholic Church.
> Book of Common Prayer: Apostles' Creed

**Catholic Epistles.** Those epistles in the New Testament that are not addressed to any particular church or individual, i.e. the epistles of James, 1 and 2 Peter, 1 John and Jude. 2 John is addressed to 'the elect lady and her children', and 3 John to Gaius, but they are usually included. They are so called because they are 'general', i.e. universal or catholic.

**Catholic League.** (1) The party headed by the Guise faction in France (1584) in alliance with Philip II of Spain, whose objects were to prevent the succession of Henry of Navarre to the French crown and to place the Cardinal of Bourbon on the throne on the death of Henry III. (2) A Catholic confederacy formed in Germany in 1609 to counterbalance the Protestant Union of 1608. These rival groupings resulted in the THIRTY YEARS' WAR (1618–48).

**Catholicon.** A PANACEA, a universal remedy, from Greek *katholikos*, 'universal', 'all-embracing' (*see* CATHOLIC). The word is also the name of a comprehensive work of the encyclopedic dictionary type. A famous edition of the 13th-century *Catholicon* (the first so called) of Johannes Balbus of Genoa was printed by Gutenberg at Mainz in 1460. An English–Latin dictionary compiled about 1483, called *Catholicon Anglicanum,* was published by the Early English Text Society in 1881, and a Breton–Latin–French dictionary called the *Catholicon* was printed in 1499.

**Catholicos.** A title borne by the head of the Assyrian Church of the East (NESTORIANS) and the Patriarchs of the Armenian and Georgian Churches.

**Catholic roll.** A document that Roman Catholics were obliged to sign on taking their seats as Members of Parliament. It was abolished when a single oath was prescribed to all members by an Act of 1866.

**His Catholic Majesty.** A title given by Pope Innocent VIII to Ferdinand of Aragon and Isabella of Castile, and confirmed by Pope Alexander VI, for their conquest of the Moors in 1492 and subsequent expulsion of the Jews. Those who remained and became nominal Christians were called Moriscos. The title was thereafter used as a traditional title of the kings of Spain.

**Old Catholics.** *See under* OLD.

**Roman Catholic Church.** *See under* ROMAN.

**Catiline's Conspiracy.** Lucius Sergius Catilina conspired with a number of dissolute young nobles (65 BC) to plunder the Roman treasury, destroy the senate and fire the city as part of a political revolution. CICERO, who was consul, gained full information of the plot and delivered his first Oration against Catiline (8 November 63 BC), whereupon Catiline left Rome. Next day Cicero delivered his second Oration, and several of the conspirators were arrested. His third Oration regarding the punishment to be accorded was made on 4 December and, after his fourth Oration the following day, sentence of death was passed. Catiline was killed together with his supporters near Pistoria in Etruria (early January 62).

**Cato.** To be a Cato is to be a person of simple life, self-denying habits, strict justice, brusque manners, blunt of speech, like the Roman censor Marcus Porcius Cato (234–149 BC).

**Cato Street Conspiracy.** A plot by Arthur Thistlewood (1770–1820) and his associates to murder Castlereagh and other members of the cabinet while they were dining with the Earl of Harrowby (23 February 1820), set fire to London, seize the Bank and Mansion House (the official residence of the lord mayor of London) and form a provisional government. The conspirators met in a loft in Cato Street, a small mews near the Edgware Road, where some were arrested following a tip-off to the police from one of the conspirators. Thistlewood and others escaped, but he was caught the following morning. Five, including Thistlewood, were hanged, and five others transported for life.

**Cattle. Chillingham cattle.** *See under* CHILLINGHAM.

**Store cattle.** *See under* STORE.

**Caucasian.** The white or light complexioned race is so called. The term originated with J.F. Blumenbach (1752–1840), who in 1775 selected a Georgian skull as the perfect type of Indoeuropean. His views are no longer held, but the word has been used with certain qualifications by later anthropologists.

**Caucus.** An American word, first recorded as having been used in Boston about 1750 and popularized in England by Joseph Chamberlain

(1836–1914) about 1878 in Birmingham. In America it means a closed meeting of some division of a political or legislative body for the purpose of agreeing upon a united course of action in the main assembly. In England it is applied opprobriously to an inner group that seeks to manipulate affairs behind the backs of its party. The word is probably of Algonquin origin and related to *caucauasu*, 'adviser'.

> In all these places is a severall commander, which they call *Werowance*, except the *Chickhamanians*, who are governed by the priests and their Assistants, or their Elders, called *cawcawwassoughes*.
> CAPTAIN JOHN SMITH: *Travels in Virginia*, 6th voyage (1606)

**Caudillo.** The title adopted by General Franco, head of the Falangist government in Spain, in imitation of Mussolini's DUCE and Hitler's FÜHRER. Like them it means 'leader'. *See also* FALANGE.

**Caudine Forks.** A narrow pass in the mountains near Capua, now called the Valley of Arpaia. It was here that the Roman army fell into the hands of the Caudini Samnites (321 BC), and were made to PASS UNDER THE YOKE.

**Caudle** (Latin *calidus*, 'warm'). A hot spiced wine made with gruel, formerly given as a medicine to women in childbed, as well as to the 'gossips' who visited them to see the baby.

**Caudle lecture.** A CURTAIN LECTURE. The term is derived from a series of papers by Douglas Jerrold, *Mrs Caudle's Curtain Lectures*, which were published in *Punch* (1846). These papers represent Job Caudle as a patient sufferer of the lectures of his nagging wife after they had gone to bed and the curtains were drawn.

**Cauf. Captain Cauf's Tail.** *See under* CAPTAIN.

**Caught.** *See under* CATCH.

**Caul.** The word was formerly used for a net, now called a SNOOD, in which women enclosed their hair.

> Her head with ringlets of her hair is crowned,
> And in a golden caul the curls are bound.
> JOHN DRYDEN: *Aeneid*, vii (1697)

It was also used for a membrane that enclosed any part of the intestines.

> And thou shalt take all the fat that covereth the inwards, and the caul that is above the liver.
> Exodus 29:13

The membrane (a portion of the amniotic sac) that sometimes covers the head of newborn infants is the caul and is held to be a charm, especially against death by drowning. They were once advertised for sale and frequently sought after by mariners. To be born with a caul was with the Romans tantamount to being 'born with a silver spoon in the mouth'.

> You were born with a caul on your head.
> BEN JONSON: *Alchemist*, I, i (1610)

**Cauliflower ear.** An ear permanently thickened and deformed by boxing injuries. It bears a fanciful resemblance to a cauliflower head.

**Caurus.** The Latin name for the northwest wind:

> The ground by piercing Caurus seared.
> JAMES THOMSON: *The Castle of Indolence*, ii, 78 (1748)

**Cause.** For the four Aristotelian causes *see* ARISTOTELIAN PHILOSOPHY.

**Cause** or **Good Old Cause, The.** As a noun, the word 'cause' has general reference to the ideals or aims of a group or organization. In the 17th century it was used with particular reference to the PURITAN cause, and the phrase 'the cause' or 'the good cause' was commonly used by the supporters of the Puritan Revolution in Cromwellian times and afterwards.

> The army, resolute as it still remained for the maintenance of 'the cause', was deceived by Monk's declarations of loyalty to it.
> J.R. GREEN: *A Short History of the English People*, ch viii (1874)

**Cause a flutter in the dovecot, To.** To alarm, disturb, or cause confusion among those conventionally minded or settled in their ways, as would a bird of prey in a dovecot. *See also* CAT AMONG THE PIGEONS.

**Cause célèbre** (French, 'famous case'). Any well-known lawsuit or trial, such as the TICHBORNE CASE.

**First cause.** *See under* FIRST.

**Causeway, Giant's.** *See under* GIANT.

**Caution.** An amusing or surprising person or thing. The use of the word in this sense is American in origin:

> The way the icy blast would come down the bleak shore was a caution.
> C.F. HOFFMAN: *Winter West* (1835)

> His wife was what the Yankees call a Caution.
> MORTIMER COLLINS: *Vivien*, III, ii (1870)

A caution is also a formal warning given by a police officer to someone suspected of an offence. The warning in use from the 1960s was: 'You do not have to say anything unless you wish to do so but what you say may be given in evidence.' In 1995 a modified version was introduced: 'You do not have to say anything. But it may harm your defence if you do not mention when questioned something which you later rely on in court. Anything you do say may be given in evidence.'

**Caution money.** A sum deposited with college authorities, at an INN OF COURT and at certain other establishments, as a safeguard against misbehaviour. Some colleges retain a portion of the sum at the end of a student's course as a 'gift' to augment their revenues.

**Cavalier** (Italian *cavaliere*, ultimately from Latin *caballus*, 'horse'). A horseman, whence a knight, a gentleman.

**Cavalier, The.** This was applied as an honorary title or nickname to the following:

Charles de Beaumont d'Éon (*Chevalier d'Éon*) (1728–1810), French diplomat and secret agent, who in 1755 stayed at the court of the Russian Princess Elizabeth dressed as a woman; hence eonism as an alternative name for transvestism.
Charles Breydel (1677–1744), Flemish landscape painter
Francesco Cairo (*Cavaliere del Cairo*) (1598–1674), Italian historical and portrait painter
Jean le Clerc (*le chevalier*) (1587–1633), French painter
Giovanni Battista Marini (*Il Cavaliere*) (1569–1625), Italian poet
Andrew Michael Ramsay (1686–1734), Scottish-French writer

**Cavalier of** or **Chevalier de St George.** James Francis Edward Stuart, called the Pretender or the OLD PRETENDER (1688–1766). *See also* WARMING-PAN BABY.

**Cavalier Parliament.** The first Parliament (1661–79) of Charles II after the RESTORATION, and thus named from its Royalist majority. It was also called the PENSIONER PARLIAMENT or LONG PARLIAMENT of Charles II.

**Cavaliers.** The Royalists or adherents of CHARLES I at the time of the English Civil War (1642–6). Their opponents were called ROUNDHEADS.

**Laughing Cavalier, The.** *See under* LAUGH.

**Mad Cavalier, The.** *See under* MAD.

**Young Cavalier** or **Bonnie Chevalier, The.** *See* YOUNG PRETENDER.

**Cave** or **cavern. Cave in, To.** To subside or collapse. The expression was originally 'to calve in', perhaps as a dialect rendering of Flemish *inkalven*, meaning to collapse inwards. This in turn could be seen as the converse of *uitkalven*, literally 'to calve out', said of a calf falling out from its mother at birth. Whatever the case, the word later became associated with English 'cave'.

**Cave of Adullam.** *See* ADULLAMITES.

**Cave of the Nativity, The.** The Cave of the Nativity at Bethlehem, discovered, according to Eusebius, by St HELENA, is under the chancel of the basilica of the Church of the Nativity. It is a hollow scraped out of rock, and there is a stone slab above the ground with a star cut in it to mark the spot where Jesus is said to have been laid. There are no grounds for connecting the Nativity with a cave.

**Corycian cave.** *See under* CORYCIAN.

**Fingal's Cave.** *See under* FINGAL.

**Kent's Cavern.** *See under* KENT.

**King's Cave.** *See under* KING.

**Mammoth Cave.** *See under* MAMMOTH.

**Cave!** (Latin, 'beware!'). A traditional schoolboy's warning on the approach of a master. The word is usually pronounced in two syllables. The presence of a watchdog in a Roman household was often advised by the written warning *Cave canem*, 'Beware of the dog'.

**Caveat** (Latin, 'let him beware'). A legal notice directing the recipient to refrain from some act pending the decision of the court. Hence, to give legal notice that the opponent is not to proceed with the suit in hand until the party giving notice has been heard. In general use, a caveat is a warning or caution.

**Caveat emptor** (Latin, 'let the buyer beware'). A purchaser is responsible for the quality of the goods bought unless they are covered by the vendor's guarantee or warranty.

**Caviare.** Sturgeon's roe, pickled, salted and used as a savoury or HORS D'OEUVRE. Caviare is usually appreciated only by those who have acquired a taste for it. Hence Shakespeare's 'caviare to the general' (*Hamlet*, II, ii (1600)), which has been adopted as a catchphrase to mean something that is too good to appeal to popular taste.

In the days of Tsarist Russia, certain matter in imported periodicals was censored by being heavily blacked out with a patterned ink stamp. Such matter came to be known as 'caviare' because its appearance was reminiscent of black, salted caviare on a slice of bread.

**Cavo relievo** or **cavo rilievo** (Italian, 'hollow relief'). A relief sculpture whose highest point in the carving is lower than the level of the original surface. *See also* ALTO RELIEVO; BAS-RELIEF.

**Caxton, William.** The father of English printing, whose name has come to be applied to branded articles in the printing and paper trades. He was born *c.*1422 in Kent and learned his printing in Cologne and Bruges. He set up shop at the sign of the Red Pole in the shadow of Westminster Abbey in about 1476 and died in 1491, by which time he had printed about a hundred books. He was printer, publisher, retailer and translator.

**Cayuse.** A small American Indian pony used by cowboys. The Cayuses were a RED INDIAN tribe.

**Cazique** or **Cacique** (Arawak, 'chief'). A native prince of the ancient Peruvians, Cubans, Mexicans and others, also applied to chiefs of Indian tribes in South America and the West Indies.

**Cean Poet, The.** Simonides of Ceos (*c.*556–468 BC).

**Cecilia.** The patron saint of the blind and patroness of music, especially church music. She was born in Rome and is traditionally said to have been martyred in AD 230, but the date is uncertain. She was blind and, according to some, was the inventor of the organ. An angel fell in love with her on account of her musical skill. Her husband VALERIAN saw the heavenly visitor, who gave to both of them a crown of martyrdom, which he brought from Paradise. Her day is 22 November, on which the Worshipful Company of Musicians, a LIVERY COMPANY of the City of London, meets and goes in procession for divine service in St Paul's Cathedral. Both John Dryden and Alexander Pope wrote odes in her honour.

> At length divine Cecilia came,
> Inventress of the vocal frame.
> JOHN DRYDEN: *Alexander's Feast* (1697)

**Cecil's fast.** A dinner of fish. William Cecil, Lord Burghley (1520–98), for nearly 40 years chief minister to Queen Elizabeth I, introduced a law to require fish to be eaten on certain days in order to promote the fishing industry.

**Ceiling.** The term is figuratively applied to the maximum height to which an aircraft can rise under certain conditions, or to an upper limit for prices or wages. In meteorology, the ceiling is the highest level from which the earth's surface can be seen, which is effectively the height of the cloud base above ground level.

**Ceiling zero.** An expression meaning that the clouds or mist are down to ground level.

**Glass ceiling.** *See under* GLASS.

**Celer** (Latin, 'swift'). The horse of the Roman Emperor Lucius Versus. It was fed on almonds and raisins, covered with royal purple and stalled in the imperial palace.

**Celeste, Mary.** *See under* MARY.

**Celestial. Celestial City.** Heaven is so called by John Bunyan in his PILGRIM'S PROGRESS (1678, 1684).

**Celestial Empire, The.** China, as a translation of the Chinese *tiāncháo*, literally 'heavenly dynasty', alluding to the belief that the old emperors were in direct descent from the gods. Hence the Chinese have sometimes been called Celestials.

**Celestines.** An order of reformed BENEDICTINES founded *c.*1260 by Pietro da Morrone (1215–96), who became Pope Celestine V in 1294.

**Celt.** A piece of stone, ground artificially into a wedge-like shape with a cutting edge, used for axes, chisels and the like. The term is also loosely applied to metal axe-heads, especially of bronze.

**Celtic.** A name used both for the languages of that branch of the Indoeuropean family that includes Irish, Manx, Welsh, Cornish, Breton and Scottish Gaelic, and for the people who speak these languages. The term was formerly applied by the Greeks and Romans to the peoples of western Europe generally, but when CAESAR wrote of the Celtae he referred to the people of middle GAUL only. The word Celt may mean 'warrior'. Fable accounts for it by the story of Celtina, daughter of Britannus, who had a son by HERCULES, named Celtus, who was the progenitor of the Celts.

**Celtic fringe.** A sometimes derogatory name for those parts of Britain whose population is predominantly of Celtic stock, namely Wales, Cornwall, Scotland and Ireland.

**Celtic Sea.** This area is formally defined as 'that part of the continental shelf lying between the 200 fathom contour, southern Ireland, the southwestern tip of Wales, Land's End and Ushant'. The term derives from the surrounding Celtic areas, i.e. Brittany, Cornwall, Wales and Ireland, and was first used by E.W.L. Holt in 1921.

**Celtic twilight.** The title used by W.B. Yeats for his collection of stories (1893) based on Irish folk-tales. Hence the term's sometimes disparaging use for Irish folklore in general.

**Cemetery.** The proper sense of the word is 'sleeping place', from Greek *koimētērion*, 'dormitory'. The Persians call their cemeteries 'the cities of the silent'.

**Arlington Cemetery.** *See under* ARLINGTON.

**Cenci.** *See* BEAUTIFUL PARRICIDE.

**Ce n'est que le premier pas qui coûte** (French, 'It is only the first step that costs anything'). An observation made by Mme du Deffand (1697–1780) on hearing Cardinal de Polignac's description of the miraculous walk of St DENYS after decapitation. PYTHAGORAS used to say: 'The beginning is half the whole.'

**Cenimagni.** The name given to the inhabitants of East Anglia by Caesar in his *Commentaries* (1st century BC). Modern scholars believe the name to be a corrupt form of *Iceni magni*, 'strong Iceni', as this British people occupied much of East Anglia, were a powerful force when BOADICEA rebelled, and of the five tribes which submitted to Caesar are the only one known to history from other texts.

**Cenobites.** *See* COENOBITES.

**Cenotaph** (Greek *kenotaphion*, from *kenos*, 'empty', and *taphos*, 'tomb'). A monument raised to the memory of a person or persons buried elsewhere. By far the most noteworthy to all of British race is that in Whitehall, designed by Sir Edwin Lutyens, which was dedicated on 11 November 1920 to those who fell in the First World War. It has since been adapted to commemorate the fallen of the Second World War.

**Cent, Not a red.** *See under* RED.

**Centaur.** In Greek mythology a creature with the head, arms and torso of a man and the lower body and legs of a horse. Centaurs are said to have dwelt in ancient Thessaly, so that the origin of the myth is probably to be found in the expert horsemanship of this region's inhabitants. The Thessalian centaurs were invited to a marriage feast, and one of their number attempted to abduct the bride, whereupon conflict ensued and the centaurs were driven out of the country by the LAPITHS. The origin of the word is unknown. *See also* IXION.

**Cent Nouvelles Nouvelles** (French, 'a hundred new tales'). The collection of stories of this name first appeared in a manuscript dated 1456. It is on much the same lines as the DECAMERON, and tells in French some of the tales already made familiar by the Italian novelists. Nicolas de Troyes produced his *Paragon des Nouvelles Nouvelles* in 1535, containing tales of his own and drawing others from the GESTA ROMANORUM (13th century) and the *Decameron* (1349–51).

**Cento** (Latin, 'patchwork'). Poetry made up of lines borrowed from established authors, an art freely practised in the decadent days of Greece and Rome. Ausonius (4th century BC), who has a nuptial idyll composed from verses selected from Virgil, made rules for their composition. An example of a stanza from a modern cento, with lines taken from 19th-century poets, is the following:

> I only knew she came and went (Lowell)
> Like troutlets in a pool; (Hood)
> She was a phantom of delight (Wordsworth)
> And I was like a fool. (Eastman)

**Central Park.** New York's largest public park, and one of the first to be architecturally landscaped, by Frederick Law Olmsted. It opened on a former slum site in 1876. It has numerous footpaths and cycle tracks, which afford views and vistas at almost every point. It contains the Metropolitan Museum of Modern Art, CLEOPATRA'S NEEDLE, and New York's oldest zoo. By day Central Park is a popular resort for New York City dwellers, among them cyclists, joggers, rollerskaters, softball players and nature lovers. By night it can be rather less salubrious, and has known robbery and murder. The rape by a gang of youths of a 28-year-old banker out jogging there on the evening of 19 April 1989 gained notoriety for its randomness and brutality.

**Centre. Centrefold.** A printed and usually illustrated sheet that has been folded to form the centre spread of a magazine. The term was extended to the model, usually naked or at best skimpily clad, whose photograph features there. This sense became specifically associated with Hugh Hefner's *Playboy*, where the spread first appeared in February 1954, the subject being Margaret Scott.

> The concept of the centerfold became world famous and added a new word to the language. 'Centerfold' became another way of referring to a picture of a beautiful girl, just as 'pin-up' had the decade before.
>
> HUGH HEFNER: *The Playmate Book*, Introduction (1996)

**Centre party.** In politics, the party occupying a place between two extremes: the left centre is the more radical wing, and the right centre is the more conservative. In the French Revolution the Centre of the Legislative Assembly included the friends of order.

**Dead centre.** *See under* DEAD.

**Left, right and centre.** *See under* LEFT.

**Centurion** (Latin *centum*, 'hundred'). A Roman officer who had the command of a century (100 men). There were 60 centurions, of varying ranks, to a legion, the chief being the first centurion of the first maniple of the first cohort, whose title was *Primus pilus prior* or *Primipilus*. The centurion's emblem of office was a vine-staff.

**Century. Century of the Common Man, The.** The 20th century, the age of democracy. *The Century of the Common Man* (1940) was the title of a book by Henry A. Wallace, Vice President of the United States (1941–5) under F.D. Roosevelt. The phrase speedily became popular on both sides of the Atlantic and was much favoured by Nancy, Viscountess Astor.

**Magdeburg Centuries.** *See under* MAGDEBURG.

**Cephalus and Procris.** Cephalus was the husband of Procris, who deserted him through jealousy. He went in search of her and rested for a while under a tree. Procris crept through some bushes to discover if a rival was with him, and Cephalus, hearing the noise and thinking it was made by some wild beast, hurled his javelin into the bushes and slew Procris. When he discovered what he had done he killed himself with the same javelin. The story is the subject of a painting by Piero di Cosimo (*c.*1500) in the National Gallery, London, in which poignancy is added by the large brown dog seated mournfully at the feet of the dead Procris.

**Cepheus.** A constellation of the northern skies, named from Cepheus, king of Ethiopia or Palestine, husband of CASSIOPEIA, and father of ANDROMEDA.

**Cerberus.** According to classical mythology Cerberus was the three-headed dog that guarded the entrance to HADES. HERCULES dragged the monster to earth and let him go again. ORPHEUS lulled Cerberus to sleep with his lyre, and the SIBYL who conducted AENEAS through the Inferno also threw the dog into a profound sleep with a cake seasoned with poppies and honey. The origin of the fable of Cerberus may lie in the ancient Egyptian custom of guarding graves with dogs. *See also* ACONITE; SOP TO CERBERUS.

**Cerealia.** Festivals in honour of CERES, celebrated by the Romans and originally held in April. A second festival was introduced by CICERO in August.

**Ceremonious, The.** Pedro IV of Aragon (1336–87) was so named.

**Ceremony** (Latin *caerimonia*, 'that which is sacred'). By way of accounting for this word, whose ultimate origin is uncertain, Livy writes that when the Romans fled before Brennus, one Albinus, who was carrying his wife and children in a cart to a place of safety, overtook at Janiculum the VESTAL VIRGINS bending under their load. He took them up and conveyed them to Caere in Etruria, where they remained and continued to perform their sacred rites, which were consequently called *Caeremonia*.

**Ceremony of the Keys, The.** When the gates of the TOWER OF LONDON are locked at 10 pm each night by the Chief Yeoman Warder and his escort, the party is challenged on its return by the sentry with the words: 'Halt, who goes there?' The chief warder answers: 'The Keys.' The sentry asks: 'Whose keys?' 'Queen Elizabeth's keys', is the reply. The guard presents arms and the chief warder removes his bonnet and calls 'God preserve Queen Elizabeth!' to which the whole guard replies, 'Amen.' The keys are then deposited in the Queen's House. *See also* BEEFEATERS.

**Master of ceremonies.** *See under* MASTER.

**Stand on ceremony.** *See under* STAND.

**Ceres** (perhaps from Latin *crescere*, 'to grow'). The Roman name of MOTHER EARTH, the protectress of agriculture and of all the fruits of the earth. She is the corn goddess, who had a daughter by JUPITER, called PROSERPINA. She is identified with the Greek DEMETER.

**Ceridwen** (Welsh *cerdd*, 'poem', 'poetry', and *gwyn*, 'white'). The Welsh goddess of poetic inspiration. She is the mother of TALIESIN and is depicted as the hag aspect of the mother goddess. She is said to have prepared the cauldron of knowledge.

**Cerus** (Greek *kēros*, 'of the heart'). The horse of ADRASTUS, which was swifter than the wind.

**Cess** (short for assessment). A special tax, such as a land tax in Scotland. In Ireland the word is used to mean 'luck', especially in the imprecation, 'Bad cess to you!'

> The poor jade is wrung in the withers out of all cess.
> SHAKESPEARE: *Henry IV, Pt I*, II, i (1597)

**Cesspool, To have a mind like a.** *See under* MIND.

**C'est magnifique, mais ce n'est pas la guerre.** (French, 'it is magnificent, but it is not war'). The criticism of the charge of the Light Brigade at Balaclava, 25 October 1854, made on the field at the time by the French General Pierre Bosquet to Sir Austen Henry Layard. Some modern wit remarked about the Church of La Madeleine in Paris, *C'est magnifique, mais ce n'est pas la gare* ('It is magnificent, but it is not the station').

**Cestus** (Greek *kestos*, 'belt'). The girdle of VENUS, made by her husband VULCAN, which had the power to cause amorousness. According to a poetic fiction, all women of irresistible attraction are said to wear the cestus. *See also* CHASTITY BELT.

The word is also used for the Roman boxing glove composed of leather thongs wound round the hand and wrist and sometimes loaded with iron. In this case the origin is from Latin *caestus*, probably from *caedere*, 'to strike', 'to kill'.

**Ceteris paribus** (Latin). Other things being equal.

**Chacun à son goût** (French, 'everyone to his taste'). The phrase is sometimes thought of by English speakers as *chacun a son goût* ('everyone has his taste'), but this is a misinterpretation of the French, who themselves equally say *à chacun son goût*.

**Chad** (Old English *Ceadda*). A Northumbrian by birth and a pupil of St AIDAN, he subsequently became bishop of MERCIA with Lichfield as his see. He died in 672 and was the patron saint of springs. The New River, which was once London's main water supply, has its source in Chad's Well Springs between Hertford and Ware. There was also a spa at King's Cross, opened early in the reign of George III, called St Chad's Well.

**Chad** or **Mr Chad.** A character whose bald head and large nose were depicted appearing over a wall and inquiring, 'Wot, no [word filled in to suit the circumstances]?', as a comment on a shortage of some commodity during and after the Second World War. Chad was particularly popular among the forces and offered scope for light relief in many a difficult situation. He was the creation in 1938 of the cartoonist 'Chat' (George Edward Chatterton). *See also* GRAFFITI; KILROY.

**Chaff.** The word is regularly used for the husks and the like that are separated from seeds during threshing. Hence 'to separate the wheat from the chaff' is to pick out what is valuable from what is worthless. A modern use of the word 'chaff' is for the thin strips of metallic foil that are released into the atmosphere from aircraft to deflect radar signals and prevent detection. This usage arose in the USA in the Second World War.

**Chaff, To.** To tease. The word may have arisen as a slang form of chafe, but it was probably influenced by the other chaff. The banter involved in chaffing someone is as light and trivial as the husks of grain are.

**Separate the wheat from the chaff, To.** *See under* SEPARATE.

**Chagan.** The chief of the Avars. *See also* BANAT.

**Chain. Chain lightning.** Two or more flashes of lightning, repeated without intermission.

**Chain letter.** A letter, frequently anonymous,

that the recipient is asked to copy and send to a stated number of friends or associates, requesting that they do the same, the aim being to secure a large sum of money or some other favour. Some chain letters threaten the recipient with bad news if they fail to sign. The notorious St JUDE chain letter is said to have been circulating worldwide since 1903.

**Chain smoker.** A person who smokes addictively and continually, lighting a new cigarette from the stub of the last one.

**Daisy chain.** *See under* DAISY.

**Gunter's chain.** *See under* GUNTER.

**Chair, The.** The person in authority or the president of an assembly or meeting whose decisions, like those of the SPEAKER of the HOUSE OF COMMONS, are final in all points of doubt. When debaters call out 'Chair', they mean that the chairman or chairwoman is not being sufficiently heeded and properly supported.

A university professorship is also called a chair, as 'the chair of Italian at Oxford'.

**Chair of St Peter.** The office of the pope of Rome, founded by St PETER, the apostle. However, St Peter's Chair means the Catholic festival held in commemoration of the two episcopates founded by the apostle, one at Rome (18 January) and the other at Antioch (22 February). The reputed chair itself in St Peter's at Rome is kept locked away and exhibited only once every century. It is of wood with ivory carvings, the wood being much decayed. It is probably 6th-century Byzantine work.

**Bath chair.** *See under* BATH.

**Groaning chair.** *See under* GROANING.

**Sedan chair.** *See under* SEDAN.

**Take the chair, To.** To be the chairman or chairwoman of a meeting or assembly of some kind. Colloquially, 'to be in the chair' means to act as host or to be the one paying for the round of drinks.

**Chalice, Poisoned.** *See under* POISON.

**Chalk. Chalk and talk.** A sometimes derogatory term given to the traditional or formal method of teaching using a blackboard and the teacher's voice. *See also* CHALKFACE.

**Chalkface.** The art or act of teaching, especially 'nitty gritty' classroom teaching or CHALK AND TALK, as distinct from administration or supervision.

**Chalk it up, To.** To credit a payment to an account or to put it on the SLATE.

**Chalktalk.** In North America an informal lecture using a blackboard to make relevant points.

**As different as chalk and cheese.** *See under* AS.

**By a long chalk.** *See under* BY.

**Not by a long chalk** *See under* LONG.

**Not to know chalk from cheese.** *See under* KNOW.

**Walk the chalk, To.** *See under* WALK.

**Walk your chalk.** *See under* WALK.

**Challenge** (Old French *chalenge*, from Latin *calumnia*, 'calumny'). The original meaning of the word was 'accusation' or 'charge', and only secondarily 'claim', 'questioning', as now.

**Challenge a jury, To.** To object to a person who has been summoned to serve as a juror. This may be a 'challenge to the array', in which the objection is to the whole jury on the grounds that the person responsible for summoning the jurors is biased or has acted improperly, or a challenge to one or more individual jurors on the grounds that they are ineligible or suspected of being biased. It was formerly possible to challenge a juror without giving any reason. The number of such challenges was reduced to three in 1977 and abolished altogether in 1988.

**Cham.** Formerly, the title of the sovereign prince of Tartary, now written 'khan'.

> Fetch you a hair off the great Cham's beard.
>
> SHAKESPEARE: *Much Ado about Nothing*, II, i (1598)

**Great Cham of Literature, The.** *See under* GREAT.

**Chamber. Chamber of Horrors.** *See* MADAME TUSSAUD'S.

**Jerusalem Chamber.** *See under* JERUSALEM.

**Second Chamber.** *See under* SECOND.

**Star Chamber.** *See under* STAR.

**Chambersisms.** Such may be called the idiosyncratic definitions that have regularly appeared in the various editions of *Chambers Dictionary* since its original publication in 1901. Their number has declined over the years, presumably under the constraints of POLITICAL CORRECTNESS or simply on grounds of accuracy, but the following remain in the 1998 edition:

- double-locked: locked by two turns of the key, as in some locks and many novels
- éclair: a cake, long in shape but short in duration
- he-man: a man of exaggerated or extreme virility, or what some women consider to be virility
- Japanese cedar: a tall Japanese conifer (*Cryptomeria japonica*), often dwarfed by Japanese gardeners
- jaywalker: a careless pedestrian whom motorists are expected to avoid running down
- middle-aged: between youth and old age, variously reckoned to suit the reckoner
- Pict: one of a dwarfish race of underground dwellers, to whom (with the Romans, the Druids and Cromwell) ancient monuments are generally attributed
- picture restorer: a person who cleans and tries to restore old pictures
- sea serpent: an enormous marine animal of serpent-like form frequently seen and described by credulous sailors, imaginative landsmen and common liars

**Chambré** (French *chambre*, 'room'). Used of wine that has been warmed to raise it from the cellar temperature to the temperature of the room in which it is to be served, which for red wine is often ideal.

**Chambre. Chambre ardente** (French, 'burning chamber'). In French history the name given to certain courts of justice held under the ANCIEN RÉGIME for trying exceptional cases such as charges of heresy or poisoning. They were usually held at night and were lit by torches both then and also when held in daytime. The courts were devised by the Cardinal of Lorraine and first used by Francis I in 1535. Louis XIV used a Chambre Ardente in 1679 to investigate suspected poisoners as a result of the scare caused by the trial of the Marquise de BRINVILLIERS. These courts were abolished in 1682.

**Chambre introuvable** (French, 'chamber not to be found again'). The French Chamber of Deputies, which met in 1815 after the second return of Louis XVIII, was so named by the king for its fervent royalist sympathies. It was afterwards used to denote any ultra-royalist assembly.

**Chameleon.** Figuratively, a fickle or inconstant person, like a VICAR OF BRAY, shifting according to the opinions of others, just as a chameleon can change its colour to blend with its background.

> Would they [poets] ever change their hue
> As the light chameleons do,
> Suiting it to every ray
> Twenty times a day?
>
> PERCY BYSSHE SHELLEY: *An Exhortation* (1819)

**Champagne.** The sparkling wine is named for Champagne, the district of its production in northeastern France, the district name itself coming from Latin *campus*, 'plain'. The name is applied outside France generically, but with certain restrictions, to many white and rosé wines, which are usually designated by their place of origin. Similar wines from Spain and elsewhere are usually called 'champagne-style'. It is the standard celebratory wine, and has accrued a number of aristocratic associations and a variety of nicknames, among them 'champers', 'fizz', BUBBLY, the BOY and the WIDOW. *See also* BLACK VELVET.

> Champagne certainly gives one werry gentlemanly ideas, but for a continuance, I don't know but I should prefer mild hale.
>
> R.S. SURTEES, *Jorrocks' Jaunts and Jollities*, ch ix (1838)

**Champagne and chicken.** Fare symbolic of a socially desirable engagement. The literary beauty Lady Mary Wortley Montagu mentions a meeting 'with champagne and a chicken at last' in her *Six Town Eclogues*, 'The Lover' (1747). *See also* BEER AND SANDWICHES.

**Champagne Charlie.** The nickname has been given to various individuals, usually with an allusion to opulence. They include:

- Charles Townshend (1725–67), son of the 3rd Viscount Townshend, who was so nicknamed by the Americans when he described their protest over taxes as 'perfect nonsense'
- Charles Morton (1819–1904), who owned a vast empire of music halls
- George Leybourne (real name Joseph Saunders) (1822–84), who first sang the popular song 'Champagne Charlie' in 1866 dressed as a man about town, and who was said to have always drunk champagne
- Charles Philip Yorke, 5th Earl of Hardwicke (1836–97), Comptroller of the Royal Household and prominent in the social circle around the Prince of Wales
- Henry Waysford Charles Plantagenet Rawdon, 4th and last Marquis of Hastings (1841–67) (*see also* PLUNGER)
- Charles Edward Maurice Spencer, 9th Earl Spencer (b.1964), brother of the late Diana, Princess of Wales

The nickname itself is said to have originated from a wine merchant who was generous in his gifts of champagne to friends.

**Champagne socialism.** The practising and advocacy of socialist beliefs by those who are patently seen to be consumers of the best things in life. The writer John Mortimer (b.1923), the Labour MP Barbara Follett (b.1942) and the newspaper tycoon Robert Maxwell (1923–91) are examples of champagne socialists cited in the media. The term came to be more generally associated with the 'New Labour' image fostered by Tony Blair following the 1997 GENERAL ELECTION.

> In a time which has given bachelors a bad name, he [Labour MP Frank Field] has preserved his good one. In a party of champagne socialists, he is the champagne monk.
>
> *The Times* (31 July 1998)

**Champ de Mars.** The prominent park in Paris, by the Seine, was laid out in 1765 as a parade ground for the nearby École Militaire; hence its name, referring to MARS, the Roman god of war. The name was adopted from that of the Campus Martius, in Rome, which was the exercise ground for Roman armies between the Capitol and the River Tiber. St Petersburg also has a 'Field of Mars' (Russian *Marsovo Pole*) laid out by Peter the Great in the 18th century.

In French history, the Champ de Mars Affair was one of the most important days in the Revolution. On 17 July 1791, the CORDELIERS placed on the Altar of the Fatherland, in the Champs de Mars, a petition objecting to the deposing of Louis XVI, who had returned from Varennes, and to the setting up of a republic. The mayor of Paris, Bailly, proclaimed a state of martial law, and the resulting confrontation between the troops and the petitioners cost the lives of around 50 of the latter.

NAPOLEON BONAPARTE gave the name of Champ de Mai to the assembly he called together on 26 May 1815. In fact, it was actually held on the Champ de Mars on 1 June, when he signed the liberal *Acte additionnel*.

**Champion. Champion of England** or **King's** or **Queen's Champion.** A person whose office it was to ride up Westminster Hall on a Coronation Day and challenge anyone who disputed the right of succession. The office was established by William the Conqueror and given to Robert de Marmion and his male descendants with the manor of Scrivelsby, near Horncastle, Lincolnshire, the home of the Dymoke family. De Ludlow received the office and manor through the female line, and at the coronation of Richard II Sir John Dymoke succeeded, also through the female line. Since then the office has continued in the Dymoke family, but the custom of the challenge was last observed at the coronation of George IV, since when the Champion has borne the sovereign's standard at the coronation and, at the coronations of 1937 (George VI) and 1953 (Elizabeth II), the UNION JACK instead.

**Seven Champions, The.** *See under* SEVEN.

**Chamuel.** *See* ARCHANGEL.

**Chan, Charlie.** The Chinese-American detective, an assiduous solver of murder mysteries, was created by the American writer Earl D. Biggers (1884–1933), who featured him in six novels, beginning with *The House Without a Key* (1925). The detective went on to appear in a number of popular films and was memorably played by the Swedish actor Warner Oland. His adventures on British television in the 1950s were rather less successful.

**Chance. Chance one's arm** or **luck, To.** To run a risk in the hope of succeeding and obtaining a profit or advantage. The former phrase is perhaps of army origin. A non-commissioned officer who offends against service regulations risks demotion and the loss of a stripe from his sleeve.

**Buckley's chance.** *See under* BUCKLEY'S.

**Cat in hell's chance.** *See under* CAT.

**Fat chance.** *See under* FAT.

**Ghost of a chance, The.** *See under* GHOST.

**Main chance, The.** *See under* MAIN.

**Stand a chance, To.** *See under* STAND.

**Chancel** (Latin *cancelli*, 'lattice'). In the Roman law courts the lawyers were cut off from the public by a latticed screen. The chancel of a church is the part at the eastern end, which contains the altar, sanctuary and choir, and is often separated from the nave and transepts by a screen of wood or iron latticework.

**Chancellor** (Late Latin *cancellarius*, 'porter', 'secretary'). Originally the title of the official in the Roman law courts who was stationed at the CHANCEL as usher of the court. In the Eastern Empire, he was a secretary or notary, subsequently invested with judicial functions. The name has been used in most European countries for an officer of state with varying powers and functions. In England the office of Chancellor was introduced by EDWARD THE CONFESSOR and under the Normans the Chancellor became the chief secretary in charge of all important legal documents, head of the CHANCERY and keeper of the GREAT SEAL. In France the Chancellor was the royal notary, president of the councils and keeper of the Great Seal. Bismarck was made Chancellor of the newly created German Empire in 1871, and the title is still that of the head of the government (corresponding to the British PRIME MINISTER) in some European countries, notably Austria and Germany.

There are also diocesan chancellors who preside over the bishop's court, chancellors of cathedrals, academic chancellors who are usually the titular heads of universities, and other posts of this title.

**Chancellor of the Duchy of Lancaster, The.** A minister of the crown, nominally appointed as a representative of the sovereign as Duke (or Duchess) of Lancaster. In practice he is chiefly employed on parliamentary work determined by the PRIME MINISTER.

**Chancellor of the Exchequer, The.** The minister of finance in the British CABINET. *See also* EXCHEQUER.

**Chancery.** One of the three divisions of the High Court of Justice. It is mainly concerned with equity, bankruptcy and probate business, and it is presided over by the LORD CHANCELLOR. Not all its work is done in London. There is also a Chancery Court in Manchester, such jurisdiction having existed in the COUNTY PALATINE of Lancashire since the end of the 15th century. The word is shortened from Chancellery.

**Dancing Chancellor, The.** *See under* DANCE.

**In chancery.** In wrestling or boxing a competitor's head is said to be in chancery if it is held or locked under an opponent's arm. The allusion is probably to the long and exhausting suits for which the Court of Chancery was once notorious.

> When I can perform my mile in eight minutes or a little less, then I feel as if I had old Time's head in chancery.
>
> OLIVER WENDELL HOLMES: *Autocrat of the Breakfast-Table*, ch vii (1857–8)

**Iron Chancellor.** *See under* IRON.

**Lord Chancellor** or **Lord High Chancellor, The.** *See under* LORD.

**Change. Change hands, To.** To pass from one possessor to another.

**Change of air, A.** A change of climate; variety.
**Change of heart, A.** A reversal of one's opinions or attitude.
**Change of scene, A.** A change of job or a move to different surroundings, especially through travel. The allusion is to the frequent changes of scenery in the theatre.
**Change one's feet, To.** An informal way of saying to change one's shoes.
**Change one's mind, To.** To revise one's plans; to alter one's opinion.
**Change one's skin, To.** To undergo an impossible change of character or attitude. The allusion is biblical.

> Can the Ethiopian change his skin, or the leopard his spots?
> Jeremiah 13:23

**Change one's tune, To.** To alter one's behaviour or one's account of an event.
**Change the subject, To.** To start talking about something else, especially in order to avoid embarrassment.
**Book of Changes, The.** *See under* BOOK.
**Ring the changes, To.** *See under* RING.
**Sea change, A.** *See under* SEA.
**Small change.** *See under* SMALL.
**Wind of change.** *See under* WIND.

**Changeling.** A peevish, sickly child. The notion used to be that the fairies took a healthy child, and left in its place one of their starveling elves, which never thrived. The word literally means 'changed person'.

> Your precious babe is hence convey'd,
> And in its place a changeling laid.
> JOHN GAY: *Fables* (1727)

**Channel Islands.** The islands of Jersey, Guernsey, Alderney, Sark and lesser islets, off the north-west coast of France, enjoy a unique status as the only portions of the Dukedom of Normandy that still belong to the British crown, by which they have been held since the Conquest. Uniquely also, they were the only British territory to come under German occupation in the Second World War. The four main islands have their own legislative assemblies and systems of local administration, as well as their own courts, and they are grouped for this purpose into the two BAILIWICKS of Jersey and Guernsey. They are a lure for tourists on account of their mild, maritime climate and are a tax haven for residents. Jersey and Guernsey enjoy a tax of only 20p in the £ and there is no tax of any kind in Sark.

**Chansons de geste** (French, 'songs of deeds'). Narrative poems dealing with the heroic families of French history and legend and composed at various times between the 11th and 15th centuries. The *Chanson de Roland* is generally regarded as the finest. *See also* ROLAND.

**Chant, Gregorian.** *See under* GREGORIAN.

**Chantage.** BLACKMAIL or the extortion of money by threatening to expose a scandal or the like. The word is French in origin and is explained by the French lexicographer Émile Littré as 'the action of making someone sing [*chanter*]'. *See also* CHEQUEBOOK JOURNALISM.

> No one proposes that the laws which protect women from insult and outrage should be relaxed because they may be abused for the purpose of *chantage*.
> *Law Times* (29 November 1884)

**Chant du départ** (French, 'song of departure'). After the MARSEILLAISE, this was the most celebrated song of the French Revolution. It was written by Marie-Joseph Chénier for a public festival in 1794 to commemorate the fifth anniversary of the storming of the BASTILLE. The music is by Étienne Méhul. A mother, an old man, a child, a wife, a girl and three warriors sing a verse in turn, and the sentiment of each is, 'We give up our claims on the men of France for the good of the Republic.' *See also* CARMAGNOLE.

> La république nous appelle,
> Sachons vaincre ou sachons périr:
> Un Français doit vivre pour elle,
> Pour elle un Français doit mourir.
> (The republic calls us,
> We must conquer or perish:
> A Frenchman must live for her,
> A Frenchman must die for her.)

**Chanticleer** (Old French *chanter cler*, 'to sing clearly'). The cock in the tale of REYNARD THE FOX and in Chaucer's 'The Nun's Priest's Tale' (*c*.1387). He is also in Edmond Rostand's play *Chantecler*, produced in Paris in 1910.

**Chantrey Bequest, The.** When the sculptor Sir Francis Legatt Chantrey (1781–1841) died, he left a sum yielding £3000 a year to the Royal Academy, of which the president was to receive £300 and the secretary £50, with the remainder to be devoted to the purchase for the nation of works of art executed in Britain. Many of the works so bought are in the Tate Gallery, London.

**Chantry.** A religious, often charitable endowment that is usually connected with a chapel (often part of the parish church) and that is intended mainly to provide for the chanting of masses for the founder. Their spoliation was begun by Henry VIII in 1545 and completed under Edward VI in 1547. Little of the proceeds was used for charitable or educational purposes.

**Chap.** The informal word for a man or boy arose as a shortening of chapman, from Old English *cēapman*, 'trader', 'merchant' (modern 'cheap'). A good chapman was regarded favourably, hence the modern 'good chap', 'clever chap' and so on. An analogous converse phrase is an 'awkward customer'. *See also* QUEER CUSTOMER; UGLY CUSTOMER.

**Chapbook.** A cheap little book containing tales, ballads and the like, sold by chapmen.

**Chapess.** A colloquial word for a woman, especially in the phrase 'chaps and chapesses' as a demotic equivalent of ladies and gentlemen.

**Chaps.** Wide leather leggings worn by Amerian COWBOYS to protect their legs from injury. The word is a colloquial abbreviation of Mexican Spanish *chaparejos*. The pronunciation is both 'chaps' and 'shaps'.

**Bath chap.** *See under* BATH.

**Chapel.** The word originally denoted a chest containing relics or the shrine of such relics, which was so called from the *capella* (Latin, 'little cloak') of St MARTIN, preserved by the Frankish kings as a sacred relic. The place in which it was kept when not in the field was called the *chapele*, and its keeper the *chapelain*. Hence the name came to be attached to a sanctuary or a private place of worship other than a parish or cathedral church. It is also used for a place of worship belonging to the FREE CHURCHES, as a METHODIST chapel or BAPTIST chapel, or for a separately dedicated oratory within a church.

Among printers a chapel is a collective name for the members of a trade union, with the shop steward known as the father of the chapel. This use of the word apparently derives from the earliest days of English printing, when presses were set up in chapels attached to abbeys. *See also* CAXTON.

**Chapelle ardente** (French, 'burning chapel'). The chapel or resting place of kings or exalted personages when lying in state, so called from the many candles that were lit around the catafalque, a custom at least dating from the funeral rites of Dagobert, king of the Franks in 638. The term is now also applied to other mortuary chapels.

**Chapel of ease.** A place of worship for the use of parishioners residing at a distance from the parish church.

**Chapel of rest.** A euphemism for a mortuary on an undertaker's premises.

**Chapel of the Rolls.** Formerly the Chapel of the House of the Converts, in Chancery Lane, founded by Henry III in 1232 for the reception of Jewish converts to Christianity. Edward I expelled the Jews, and by 1377 the House of the Converts was allocated to the Keeper of the Rolls of CHANCERY, who was an ecclesiastic. The chapel remained a place of worship but was also increasingly used for storing records. Most of the documents were transferred to the adjoining and newly built Public Record Office in 1856, subsequently replaced by the Museum of the Public Record Office. The name derives from the practice of keeping parchment documents in rolls for convenience of storing.

**Chapel Royal.** A private chapel attached to a royal court. The present Chapels Royal are St James's Palace, HAMPTON COURT, the Chapels Royal of St John the Evangelist and ST PETER AD VINCULA (*see under* PETER) in the Tower of London, and the Queen's Chapel of the SAVOY.

**Lady Chapel.** *See under* LADY.

**Old Chapel, The.** *See under* OLD.

**Sistine Chapel.** *See under* SISTINE.

**Chaperon** or **chaperone.** A married or mature woman who escorted a young unmarried woman in public places and acted as adviser and protector. The word comes from Old French *chaperon*, 'little hood', the analogy apparently being that the chaperon protected her charge as a hood protects the face.

**Chappaquiddick.** A tiny island off the Massachusetts coast that gained worldwide notoriety on 18 July 1969, when Senator Edward Kennedy, brother of the late President John F. Kennedy, was involved in an accident in which a 28-year-old woman, Mary Jo Kopechne, was trapped and drowned when a car he was driving ran off a small bridge. After an initial attempt to conceal the whole incident, Kennedy was eventually exonerated, despite a legal ruling that he had probably been driving negligently and had thus contributed to Miss Kopechne's death. Popular opinion claimed that Kennedy had escaped penalty through his social standing and political power, and the whole episode left a bitter taste in the mouth of the American public.

**Chapter** (Latin *capitulum*, 'little head'). The chapter of a cathedral, composed of the CANONS and presided over by the DEAN or provost, is so called from the ancient practice of the canons and monks reading at their meetings a chapter of their rule or of scripture. *Ire ad capitulum* meant to go to the meeting for the reading of the chapter, hence to the meeting, hence to the body that made up the meeting.

**Chapter and verse.** The exact authority for an action or statement. The original reference was to a chapter and verse in the Bible, as a precise authority. Biblical chapters and verses were invented for convenience at quite a late date. The Jewish Masoretes of the 6th to 10th centuries divided the books into verses. The New Testament was divided into chapters by Archbishop Langton (d.1228), and verses were introduced in the Greek and Latin editions of the New Testament of Robert Stephanus of Geneva and reproduced in the GENEVA BIBLE (*see under* BIBLE).

**Chapter of accidents.** A series of misfortunes or unforeseen events. 'A Chapter of Accidents' is the heading of Pt 1, ch ix of Thomas Hughes' *Tom Brown's Schooldays* (1857).

**Chapter of Myton, The.** The Battle of Myton (1319) in Yorkshire was so called when the clergy led out their flocks to repel the Scottish invaders. Many were slain, and the Scots devastated the area.

**Char.** This is an abbreviation for 'charwoman', a woman who cleans in a house or office, working by the hour or day. The word derives from Old English *cerr*, 'turn', referring to the time worked. Another form of the same word is 'chore', meaning a dull, routine task.

The colloquial word char meaning 'tea' derives from Chinese *chá*, and tea itself ultimately comes also from this.

**Character.** An odd, eccentric or unusual person, whether real or fictional. Dickens's Sam Weller is a character, so is his Mr Pickwick.

**In character.** Typical of a person's habitual nature or behaviour.

**Out of character.** *See under* OUT.

**Shady character.** *See under* SHADE.

**Charades** (French *charade*, 'entertainment'). A popular party game that had its heyday in the inter-war years but that is still played today. The aim is to 'act' syllables of words, using words whose spoken syllables enable them to be regarded as individual words. An example is 'poor' and 'puss' to form 'porpoise'. One team chooses a word outside the room, then enters and 'acts' its first syllable, then its second syllable and finally the whole word. The opposition has to guess it. The whole affair can be made more or less sophisticated, with puns and riddles, according to taste.

**Charge. Charge, To.** To make an attack or onset; to accuse a person of a crime or misdemeanour.

**Charge card.** A credit card for which the account must be paid in full when a statement is issued.

**Charge hand, A.** A workman who has a position of authority just below that of foreman.

**Charge like a bull at a gate, To.** To tackle something precipitately, without due forethought.

**Charge nurse, A.** A nurse in charge of a ward in a hospital, the male equivalent of sister.

**Charge oneself with, To.** To take the responsibility for something onto oneself.

**Charge sheet, A.** A document on which a police officer sets out in correct language the specific charges that an accused person has to answer.

**Give in charge, To.** To hand over a person to the charge of a police officer.

**In charge.** In command; in control; having authority.

**In charge of.** Responsible for; looking after or caring for.

**Lay a charge at someone's door.** *See under* LAY.

**Lay to one's charge, To.** *See under* LAY.

**On a charge.** In the services, entered as a defaulter and brought before the appropriate officer for a hearing. If the charge is held proven, punishment is awarded in accordance with service regulations.

> Patrick trembles with fear and relief when he thinks of Mr Fergusson who first put him on a charge.
>
> MURIEL SPARK: *The Bachelors*, ch x (1960)

**Return to the charge, To.** *See under* RETURN.

**Charing Cross.** The original Charing Cross was erected in the centre of the ancient village of Charing, which stood midway between the cities of London and Westminster, by Edward I to commemorate his queen, Eleanor. It was the spot at which her coffin was halted for the last time on its way from Harby, Nottinghamshire, to Westminster (*see* ELEANOR CROSSES). The cross was sited where the statue of King CHARLES I now stands on the south side of Trafalgar Square, but it was destroyed by the PURITANS in 1647. The present Gothic cross in the courtyard of Charing Cross Station was designed by Edward Middleton Barry and erected in 1865.

The name of Charing Cross is popularly derived from French *chère reine*, 'dear queen', as if an endearing tribute from Edward to his wife. It actually comes from Old English *cerring*, meaning a bend in the road. The old Roman road here may have turned in a bend to the west at this point, or the name could even refer to a bend in the Thames.

**Chariot** (Old French, 'large car'). According to Greek mythology the chariot was invented by ERICHTHONIUS to conceal his feet, which were those of a dragon.

Mythological characters were drawn in their chariots or cars by the following:

Admetus by lions and wild boars
BACCHUS by panthers
CERES by winged dragons
CYBELE by lions
DIANA by stags
JUNO by peacocks
NEPTUNE by sea horses
PLUTO by black horses
The sun by seven horses (the seven days of the week)
VENUS by doves

**Charity. Charity begins at home.** A saying that has its biblical counterpart: 'But if any widow have children or nephews, let them learn first to shew piety at home' (1 Timothy 5:4).

**As cold as charity.** *See under* AS.

**Charivari** (Late Latin *caribaria*, 'headache', from Greek *karē*, 'head', and *barus*, 'heavy'). A French term for an uproar caused by banging pans and kettles and accompanied by hissing, shouting and the like to express disapproval, especially at an unpopular wedding. The name *Charivari* was adopted for a satirical paper in Paris in 1832 and

*The London Charivari* was the subtitle of *Punch*, which derided the shortcomings of society, politicians and others. *See also* PUNCH AND JUDY; SHIVAREE; ROUGH MUSIC.

**Charlatan** (Italian *ciarlare*, 'to prattle'). A person who claims knowledge or skill that they do not possess, otherwise a MOUNTEBANK. The term was particularly applied to vendors of quack remedies, who covered their ignorance with high-sounding, often meaningless words.

There have been many noted charlatans of history. A modern charlatan was 'Sequoia', a white man posing as RED INDIAN, who in the late 19th century toured Britain in a coach with attendant 'Redskins' and a brass band, drawing teeth 'painlessly' (all cries drowned by the band) and supplying an 'Indian oil' to cure all manner of aches and pains. Another was Psalmanazar (*see under* FAKES).

**Charlemagne** (Latin *Carolus Magnus*, 'Charles the Great'). Charlemagne (742–814) became sole king of the Franks in 771 and the first Holy Roman Emperor in 800. He ruled over most of western Europe and was noted as a law-giver, administrator, protector of the church and promoter of education. He was married nine times.

Charlemagne and his PALADINS are the centre of a great series of chivalric romances. They tell how he was 8ft (2.4m) tall and of enormous strength and could bend three horseshoes together in his hands. He was buried at Aix-la-Chapelle (Aachen), but according to legend he waits, crowned and armed, in Oldenburg, Lower Saxony, for the day when ANTICHRIST appears. He will then go forth to battle and rescue Christendom. Another legend says that in years of plenty he crosses the Rhine on a BRIDGE OF GOLD, to bless the cornfields and vineyards.

**Charlemagne's Pleiad.** The group of scholars with which the emperor surrounded himself: Charlemagne (who, in this circle, was known as 'David'), Alcuin ('Albinus'), Adelard ('Augustine'), Angilbert ('Homer'), Riculfe ('Damaetas'), Varnefrid and Eginhard. *See also* FRENCH PLÉIADE.

**Charles.** Many rulers bearing this name have been afflicted with misfortune:

England:

- CHARLES I was beheaded by the Cromwellians (1649)
- Charles II lived long in exile; *see also* CHARLES AND THE OAK
- Charles Edward Stuart, the YOUNG PRETENDER, died in poverty in Rome in 1788

France:

- Charles II, the Fat, reigned wretchedly, was deposed in 877 and died in poverty in 888
- Charles III, the Simple, died a prisoner in the castle of Péronne in 929
- Charles IV, the Fair, reigned six years (1322–8), married three times and outlived all his children except one daughter, who was forbidden by the SALIC LAW to succeed to the crown
- Charles VI, the Foolish (r.1380–1422), went mad in 1392
- Charles VII (r.1422–61) starved himself to death, partly through fear of being poisoned and partly because of a painful and incurable abscess in the mouth
- Charles VIII, the Affable (r.1483–98), accidentally smashed his head against the lintel of a doorway in the Château d'Amboise and died in agony at the age of 28, leaving no issue
- Charles IX died at the age of 24 (1574), stricken with remorse for the part he had taken in the St BARTHOLOMEW'S DAY MASSACRE
- Charles X spent a quarter of a century in exile, and after less than six years on the throne, fled for his life and died in exile (1836)
- Charles the Bold, of Burgundy, lost his life at Nancy in 1477, when he was routed by the Swiss

Naples:

- Charles I (r.1266–85) lost Sicily as a result of the SICILIAN VESPERS and experienced many disasters
- Charles II, the Lame (r.1285–1309), was in captivity at the time of his father's death
- Charles III, his great-grandson, was assassinated (1386) at the age of 41

**Charles and the oak.** When Charles II fled from the Parliamentary army after the Battle of Worcester (3 September 1651) he took refuge in Boscobel House near Shifnal in Shropshire, but it was unsafe to remain there, and he hid in an oak tree. According to the antiquary William Stukeley, this tree 'stood just by a horse-track passing through the wood, and the king, with Colonel Carlos, climbed into it by means of the hen-roost ladder. The family reached them victuals with a nuthook' (*Itinerarium Curiosum*, ii (1724)). *See also* OAK-APPLE DAY.

**Charles I.** When Bernini's bust of Charles I of England was brought home, the king was sitting in the garden of Whitehall Palace. He ordered the bust to be uncovered, and at that moment a hawk with a bird in its beak flew by, and a drop of blood fell on the throat of the bust. The bust was ultimately destroyed when the palace was burned down.

The bronze statue of Charles I in Whitehall was modelled by Le Sueur and cast in 1633 for the Earl of Portland for his home in Roehampton. The earl died before the statue was finished, and it was stored in the crypt of St Paul's Covent Garden, until it was sold for scrap by the Parliamentarians in 1650. John Revett, the purchaser, did a flourishing trade in cutlery 'made from the statue', which was in fact hidden away. It was recovered by the Earl of Portland's son at the RESTORATION and erected on the present site, roughly the old position of CHARING CROSS, in 1674. Wreaths are still laid on the statue, on each anniversary of the king's execution, by the JACOBITES of today. *See also* REMEMBER.

**Charles le Chauve.** *See under* BALD.

**Charles's Wain.** An old popular name for the seven bright stars of the GREAT BEAR. The constellation forms the rough outline of a wheelbarrow or rustic wagon, and according to some the name is a corruption of churl's wain ('peasant's cart'). However, it almost certainly derives from CHARLEMAGNE's wain. It is also called the Wagon, the Plough and the Dipper, and, by the Romans, the Septentriones ('seven ploughing oxen'). *See also* SEPTENTRIONAL SIGNS.

**Charleys** or **Charlies.** The old night WATCH, before the police force was organized in 1829. The name may derive from CHARLES I, under whom London's watch system was reorganized in 1640.

**Charley's Aunt.** In Brandon Thomas's play so named (1892), the eccentric aunt whose support is needed for a young man's marriage. She is humorously impersonated by Charley's male friend Babs and tells how she is from Brazil, 'where the nuts come from'.

**Charlie.** The name has gained wide use as a slang term for a particular type of person or object. Among them are: (1) a silly or stupid person (a 'proper Charlie'); (2) in American military slang, a member of the Vietcong, from Victor Charlie, communications code for VC (Vietcong); (3) in black slang, a white man; (4) the drug cocaine; (5) (charlies) a woman's breasts. The first sense here may well owe something to the unfortunate reputation of the many kings named CHARLES. In his play *Saint Joan* (1924), G.B. Shaw makes Joan address the spoilt French dauphin Charles VII (1403–61) as 'Charlie'.

**Charlie Chan.** *See under* CHAN.

**Bonnie Prince Charlie.** *See* YOUNG PRETENDER.

**Champagne Charlie.** *See under* CHAMPAGNE.

**King Charles's head.** *See under* KING.

**King Charles spaniel.** *See under* KING.

**Sir Charles Grandison.** *See under* GRANDISON.

**Tail-end Charlie.** *See under* TAIL.

**Charleston.** A FOXTROT that was popular in the 1920s, originating as a back-kicking dance among the American Negroes. Charleston is the main seaport in South Carolina, much of whose population is black.

**Charlotte. Charlotte russe.** A pudding similar to an APPLE CHARLOTTE but cold and with custard instead of fruit. It was supposedly invented in 1802 by the French chef Antonin Carême, who first called it *charlotte à la parisienne*, after the earlier dish, but then renamed it in honour of his employer, Tsar Alexander I of Russia.

> They soon play'd the deuce
> With a large *Charlotte Russe*;
> More than one of the party despatch'd his plate twice
> With 'I'm really ashamed, but—another small slice!
> Your dishes from Russia are really *so* nice!'
>
> R.H. BARHAM: *Ingoldsby Legends*, 'The Blasphemer's Warning' (1840)

**Apple charlotte.** *See under* APPLE.

**Charm** (Latin *carmen*, 'song', 'verse'). An incantation that is alleged to work magic or a small object (lucky charm) that brings good luck. A charm or chirm is also a word for a flock of finches or other birds. Hence the punning title of Viscount Grey of Falloden's ornithological reminiscences *The Charm of Birds* (1927).

**Charm offensive.** The deliberate use of personal charm, willing cooperation, generous gifts and so on to achieve a particular goal.

**Bear a charmed life, To.** *See under* BEAR.

**Like a charm.** Perfectly, wonderfully, as if by a magic charm. as in: 'It worked like a charm.'

**Music hath charms.** *See under* MUSIC.

**Prince Charming.** *See under* PRINCE.

**Snake charmer.** *See under* SNAKE.

**Charon.** In Greek mythology, the son of EREBUS and Nox, the old man who ferried the spirits of the dead over the Rivers STYX and ACHERON for the fare of an *obolus*.

**Charon's toll.** A coin placed in the mouth or hand of the dead by the ancient Greeks to pay CHARON for ferrying the spirit across the rivers of the underworld to ELYSIUM.

**Charter, Atlantic.** *See under* ATLANTIC.

**Charterhouse.** A CARTHUSIAN monastery. The word evolved from CHARTREUSE, or more precisely from French *maison Chartreuse*, 'Carthusian house', influenced by the English word 'house'. The first English Charterhouse was founded by Sir Walter de Menny at London in 1371, and the Carthusians were among the staunchest opponents of Henry VIII at the time of the dissolution of the monasteries. In 1883 the Carthusians were re-established in the Charterhouse near Partridge Green, West Sussex.

Charterhouse public school, near Godalming, Surrey, was founded in 1611 on the site of a Carthusian monastery in what is still called Charterhouse Square in the City of London. It moved to its present location in 1872.

**Chartism.** A working-class movement, beginning in 1837, which embodied its agreed demands in the People's Charter of 1838. Its six points were: manhood suffrage, vote by ballot, annual Parliaments, payment of MPs, equal constituencies and the abolition of the property qualification for MPs. The movement collapsed after the failure of the Chartists' petition to Parliament in 1848.

**Chartreuse.** A greenish or yellowish liqueur made of brandy and various aromatic herbs. It is made at La Grande Chartreuse by the CARTHUSIANS, now as a commercial operation. Originally the money was spent on the maintenance of the Carthusian houses and mostly on charity. *See also* CHARTERHOUSE.

**Charybdis.** A whirlpool on the coast of Sicily. SCYLLA and Charybdis are employed to signify two equal dangers. Thus Horace says an author trying to avoid Scylla drifts into Charybdis, in other words, in seeking to avoid one fault, he falls into another.

The Homeric account says that Charybdis dwelt under an immense fig tree on the rock, and that three times a day he swallowed the waters of the sea and three times threw them up again. Later writers say that he stole the oxen of HERCULES, was killed by lightning and changed into the gulf.

**Chase** (Old French *chacier*, from Latin *captare*, 'to chase after').

(1) A small unenclosed deer forest, held mainly by private individuals and protected only by COMMON LAW. Forests were royal prerogatives and protected by the Forest Laws.

(2) Another type of chase is the iron frame used by printers for holding type. Here the origin is in French *châsse*, 'frame', related to *chassis*, ultimately from Latin *capsa*, 'case'.

**Chase the dragon, To.** To smoke opium or HEROIN. The drug is placed on a folded piece of tinfoil, which is heated with a taper. As the fumes are inhaled, they waft up and down the tinfoil with movements resembling the undulating tail of a CHINESE DRAGON. Hence the term.

**Chevy Chase.** *See under* CHEVY.

**Wild-goose chase.** *See under* WILD.

**Chasidim.** *See* HASIDEAN.

**Chastity belt.** In medieval times this was a type of padded metal belt that a man could fasten round his wife in such a way as to prevent her having sexual intercourse during his prolonged absence. It is said to have come into vogue at the time of the CRUSADES when such protracted absence was common. One or two examples exist in museums. *See also* CESTUS.

**Chasuble** (Late Latin *casubla*, 'garment with a hood', from Latin *casula*, 'cloak', literally 'little house'). The principal vestment worn by the priests in celebrating MASS. It is a roughly rectangular, sleeveless garment, with a hole for the head in the middle, thus hanging down both back and front. It is usually richly decorated with embroidery, and medieval chasubles were finely ornamented with gold wire and gilded silver, this form of work being known throughout Europe as OPUS ANGLICANUM. The City of London was the home of some of the best work of the 12th and 13th centuries. The chasuble is said to represent the seamless coat of Christ.

**Château** (French, 'castle', 'mansion', 'country seat'). The wines of various districts of France, especially Bordeaux, are named after the château of the estate from which they are produced and in some cases where they are also bottled. Château-Lapompe, or Castle Pump, is a punning name for water drunk with a Frenchman's meal with or instead of wine.

**Château en Espagne.** A CASTLE IN THE AIR.

**Chatelaine** (French). Originally, the mistress of a CHÂTEAU. The word later came to be used for a chain or clasp that women wore at the waist for the purpose of carrying keys, scissors, a handkerchief and the like. These represented the objects the mistress of a castle was likely to use.

**Chats, Fireside.** *See under* FIRE.

**Chattanooga.** A Tennessee city famous as the headquarters of the Tennessee Valley Authority and historically noted for a battle (1863) in the American Civil War (1861–5), which contributed to victory for the North. It is popularly associated with its railroads, which arrived in the 1840s and 1850s, and which include the mountain railway up nearby Lookout Mountain. It is the Indian name of this mountain, meaning 'rock rising to a point', that gave the city its own name.

> Pardon me boy, is that the Chattanooga Choo-Choo,
> Track twenty-nine,
> Boy you can gimme a shine.
>
> MACK GORDON: 'Chattanooga Choo-Choo' (song) (1930)

**Chattels, Goods and.** *See under* GOODS.

**Chattering classes, The.** A term for newspaper journalists and broadcasters, whose job it is to 'chatter' in print about matters of topical interest.

> Who are these 'chattering classes'? ... This phrase, like 'PC', is now common in Australia – used by the lazy and arrogant to abuse people and ideas they don't like without having to justify their contempt.
>
> *Times Literary Supplement* (Letter to the Editor) (15 January 1999)

**Chautauqua.** In the USA this was formerly the name given to an assembly for educational purposes with lectures, entertainments and so on, held in the summer out of doors. It took its name from the Chautauqua Assembly, which was first held in 1874 at the village and summer resort on Lake Chautauqua, New York, and which developed into the Chautauqua Literary and Scientific Circle in 1878 to promote home reading and study.

**Chauvinism.** Fanatical patriotism similar to JINGOISM. Nicolas Chauvin was a soldier of the French Republic and Empire, well known by contemporaries for his blind devotion to NAPOLEON BONAPARTE. He was introduced as a type of exaggerated bellicose patriotism into a number of contemporary plays, and his name was quickly adopted on both sides of the Channel.

**Cheap. Cheapjack.** A vendor of small wares who is usually ready to 'cheapen' his goods, i.e. take less for them than the price he first named.

**Cheapside.** The London street originally ran along the south side of the Cheap (Old English *cēap*), the main market of medieval London.

**Cheapskate.** A miserly person. Skate is an old word for a mean or contemptible person.

**Dirt** or **dog cheap.** *See under* DIRT.

**Cheater.** Such a person was originally an escheator, or officer of the king's EXCHEQUER appointed to receive dues and taxes. The present general meaning shows how these officers were wont to fleece people. *See also* PUBLICANS.

**Windcheater.** *See under* WIND.

**Cheat the Devil, To.** To mince an oath; to do evil for gain and give part of the profits to the church or charity. It is not unusual in monkish traditions. Thus the DEVIL'S BRIDGE, over the Fall of Reuss in Switzerland, is a single arch over a cataract. It is said that Satan knocked down several bridges but promised the abbot, Giraldus of Einsiedeln, to let this one stand, provided he would give him the first living thing that crossed it:

> The Abbot, standing at its head,
> Threw across it a loaf of bread,
> Which a hungry dog sprang after,
> And the rocks re-echoed with peals of laughter
> To see the Devil thus defeated!
> H.W. LONGFELLOW: *Golden Legend*, v (1851)

**Check.** A sudden stop or hindrance; a control. The word comes from CHESS, in which a threat to the king is a check. *See also* CHECKMATE.

**Check in, To.** To register on arrival at a hotel, a conference, an airport or the like.

**Checkmate.** A term in CHESS for the situation in which an opponent's king is threatened but unable to escape. This wins the game. Figuratively, to checkmate is to thwart someone, or make them powerless. The word comes from Arabic *shāh māt*, 'the king is dead', as if from Persian *māta*, to die, instead of *mat*, to be perplexed. The true origin is thus in Persian *shāh mat*, the king is perplexed, i.e. the king is defeated. *See also* CHECK.

**Check off, To.** To mark with a tick.

**Check out, To.** To settle one's account at a hotel on leaving, to register one's departure.

**Check up on, To.** To investigate a person, especially when one's suspicions have been aroused.

**Hand in one's checks, To.** *See under* HAND.

**In check.** Under restraint.

**Rain check.** *See under* RAIN.

**Spot check.** *See under* SPOT.

**Cheek. Cheek, To.** To be insolent; to be disrespectful.

**Cheek by jowl.** Side by side, close together.

> I'll go with thee, cheek by jowl.
> SHAKESPEARE: *A Midsummer Night's Dream*, III, ii (1595)

**Cheek to cheek.** With one's cheek touching that of one's partner in ballroom dancing, an intimate pose that was popular in the 1920s.

**Have the cheek, To.** To have the face or assurance or presumption. 'He hadn't the cheek to ask for more.'

**None of your cheek.** None of your insolence. A cheeky person is one who is saucy and presumptuous.

**Turn the other cheek, To.** *See under* TURN.

**With one's tongue in one's cheek.** *See under* WITH.

**Cheer. Bronx cheer.** *See under* BRONX.

**Three cheers.** *See under* THREE.

**Cheese.** In his *Five Hundred Points of Good Husbandry* (1573) Thomas Tusser says that a cheese to be perfect should be: (1) not like Gehazi, i.e. dead white like a leper, (2) not like Lot's wife, all salt, (3) not like Argus, full of eyes, (4) not like Tom Piper, 'hoven and puffed' like the cheeks of a piper, (5) not like Crispin, leathery, (6) not like LAZARUS, poor, (7) not like ESAU, hairy, (8) not like MARY MAGDALENE, full of whey or maudlin, (9) not like the Gentiles, full of MAGGOTS or gentils, and (10) not like a bishop, made of burned milk. This last is a reference to the old phrase, the BISHOP HAS PUT HIS FOOT IN IT.

**Cheesecake.** Pictures or photographs of women displayed for their sex appeal. *See also* BEEFCAKE. A literal cheesecake is a type of rich tart, filled with a mixture of cream cheese, cream, sugar, and sometimes fruit, with or without a fruit topping.

**Cheesed off.** Fed up, disgusted, disgruntled, like milk that has gone sour in the process of becoming cheese.

**Cheese it!** Stop it! Stow it! Also, in thieves' slang, clear off, make oneself scarce.

**Cheesemongers, The.** *See under* REGIMENTAL AND DIVISIONAL NICKNAMES.

**Cheeseparer.** A skinflint or mean person; literally someone who pares off the rind or mould of cheese so as to waste the minimum amount. Hence cheeseparing, stinginess.

**As different as chalk and cheese.** *See under* AS.

**Big cheese.** *See under* BIG.

**Blue cheese.** *See under* BLUE.

**Bread and cheese.** *See under* BREAD.

**Cottage cheese.** *See under* COTTAGE.

**Devil's Cheesewring, The.** *See under* DEVIL.

**Green cheese.** *See under* GREEN.

**Hard cheese.** *See under* HARD.

**Not to know chalk from cheese, Not to.** *See under* KNOW.

**Say cheese!** *See under* SAY.

**Chef.** *See* ARM SHRINES.

**Chef d'oeuvre** (French, 'chief [piece] of work'). A masterpiece.

**Chellean.** An early Palaeolithic stone-tool culture named by the French archaeologist Gabriel de Mortillet (1821–98) from the site at Chelles-sur-Marne, north central France, where the remains were found. The term is no longer in technical use, and Abbevillian is preferred instead, from Abbeville in northern France, where stone hand axes were discovered.

**Chelsea. Chelsea Pensioner.** The popular name for an inmate of the Chelsea Royal Hospital for old or disabled soldiers, founded by Charles II at the instigation of Sir Stephen Fox, the Paymaster General of the Forces. It was opened in 1692. The legend that Nell GWYN suggested the foundation is apparently imaginary.

**Sage of Chelsea.** *See under* SAGE.

**Chemistry, The Father of.** *See under* FATHER.

**Chemosh.** The national god of the Moabites, mentioned in 1 Kings 11:7. Little is known of his cult, but human beings were sacrificed to him in times of crisis.

> Next Chemos, th' obscene dread of Moab's sons,
> From Aroer to Nebo and the wild
> Of southmost Abarim.
>
> MILTON: *Paradise Lost*, i (1667)

**Cheque. Chequebook journalism.** A phrase first current in the 1960s for the practice of securing exclusive rights to newspaper stories by offering large sums of money to anyone who can provide them, with scant regard for any ethical or moral considerations.

> Newspapers ... should ... come to a self-denying ordinance to abandon the chequebook journalism of confession stories by criminals, prominent divorcees and others who have won notoriety.
>
> *New Statesman* (24 May 1963)

**Blank cheque.** *See under* BLANK.

**Chequers.** A PUBLIC HOUSE SIGN. The arms of the Fitzwarren family, whose head licensed alehouses in the reign of Edward IV (1461–83), probably helped to popularize this sign, but it is of much older origin. It has been found on houses in Pompeii and probably referred to some game like draughts being played on the premises.

One explanation is that in medieval times some innkeepers were also money-changers and used an 'exchequer board' as a sign of their calling. In addition, certain public houses were used by the parish authorities for the payment of doles, and a chequerboard was provided for that purpose and likewise adopted as a sign.

Chequers, the official country residence of the Prime Minister, near Princes Risborough in Buckinghamshire, was presented to the nation for this purpose by Sir Arthur and Lady Lee (Lord and Lady Lee of Fareham) in 1917 and first officially used by Lloyd George in 1921.

**Cherish a serpent in one's bosom, To.** To show kindness to someone who proves ungrateful. The Greeks say that a husbandman found a frozen serpent, which he put into his bosom. The snake, revived by the warmth, stung its benefactor.

**Cheroots.** *See* CIGARS.

**Cherry. Cherry picker.** A colloquial term for a hydraulic crane with a railed platform at the top, used to raise and lower people working on lofty locations such as overhead lighting, electric cables, high windows and the like.

**Cherry-pickers.** *See under* REGIMENTAL AND DIVISIONAL NICKNAMES.

**Cherry trees and the cuckoo.** The cherry tree is associated with the CUCKOO in many stories, because of the tradition that the cuckoo must eat three good meals of cherries before it is allowed to cease singing.

> Cuckoo, cuckoo, cherry-tree,
> Good bird, prithee, tell to me
> How many years I am to see.

The answer is gathered from the number of times the cuckoo repeats its cry.

**Two bites of a cherry.** *See under* TWO.

**Cherubims.** *See under* REGIMENTAL AND DIVISIONAL NICKNAMES.

**Cherubs.** Celestial winged beings of Jewish, Christian and Islamic literature, their name properly cherubim in the plural, from an Akkadian word meaning 'to pray' or 'to bless'. In the Old Testament they are chiefly the throne bearers of God, and gold cherubs form the two ends of the mercy seat of the ARK OF THE COVENANT (Exodus 25: 18–20). In Christianity, cherubs rank among the higher order of angels, and continually praise God as His celestial attendants. In art they are usually depicted as a child's head with one or more pairs of wings.

> The Lord is King, be the people never so impatient: he sitteth among the cherubims, be the earth never so unquiet.
>
> Psalm 99:1

**Che sarà, sarà** (Italian, 'what will be, will be'). The motto of the Dukes of Bedford and the Russell family. Its Spanish equivalent, *Ché será, será*, became familiar from a popular song of the 1950s sung by Doris Day.

**Cheshire cat, To grin like a.** *See under* GRIN.

**Chess.** 'The game of kings' derives its name from Old French *esches*, the plural of *eschec*, CHECK. Its name has the same origin in many languages, and Persian *shāh*, 'king', can be seen behind modern

French *échecs*, German *Schach*, Italian *scacchi*, Russian *shakhmaty* and Hungarian *sakk*. However, the terms for the game in Persian (*chatrang*) and Sanskrit (*chaturanga*) mean 'four members of an army', these being elephants, horses, chariots and foot soldiers, and this gave the name in other languages, such as Arabic *shṭranj*, Turkish *satranç*, Spanish *ajedrez* and Portuguese *xadrez*. *See also* CHECKMATE.

**Chestnut.** A stale joke. The term is said to have been popularized in America by a Boston actor named Warren, who, on a certain apposite occasion, quoted from *The Broken Sword*, a forgotten melodrama by William Dimond, first produced at COVENT GARDEN in 1816, in which one of the characters, Captain Xavier, is forever telling the same jokes with variations, one of which concerned his exploits with a cork tree. He is corrected by Pablo, who says: 'A chestnut. I have heard you tell the joke twenty-seven times, and I am sure it was a chestnut.'

**Pull the chestnuts out of the fire, To.** *See under* PULL.

**Cheval** (French, 'horse').

**Cheval de bataille** (French, 'horse of battle'). A person's strong argument or favourite subject.

**Cheval de frise** (French, 'horse from Friesland'). A device consisting of a bar carrying rows of pointed stakes, set up so that the bar can revolve, and used in warfare as a defence against enemy cavalry. It is so called from its first use by the Frisians (who had few if any horses) in the siege of Groningen, Friesland, in 1594. A somewhat similar instrument had been used before. In German it is *ein spanischer Reiter* ('a Spanish horseman').

**Cheval glass.** A full-length swinging mirror, long enough to reflect the whole of the figure, and so called from the 'horse' or framework that supports it.

**Chevalier. Chevalier de Bayard, Le.** Pierre du Terrail (*c*.1473–1524), a celebrated French knight and national hero, distinguished in the Italian campaigns of Charles VIII, Louis XII and Francis I. *Le bon chevalier* ('the good knight') and *Le chevalier sans peur et sans reproche* ('the fearless and irreproachable knight') were two names bestowed upon him. *See also* CRICHTON, ADMIRABLE.

**Chevalier de St George.** *See under* CAVALIER.

**Chevalier d'industrie** (French, 'knight of industry'). A man who lives by his wits and calls himself a gentleman, otherwise an adventurer or swindler.

> Be cautiously upon your guard against the infinite number of fine-dressed and fine-spoken *chevaliers d'industrie* and *aventuriers*, which swarm at Paris.
> LORD CHESTERFIELD: *Letters to His Son* (26 April 1750)

**Chevalier sans peur et sans reproche, Le.** *See* CHEVALIER DE BAYARD.

**Young Chevalier.** *See* YOUNG PRETENDER.

**Chevy Chase.** The name is historically famous from the Battle of Chevy Chase, which took place near Otterburn, Northumberland, in 1388, and in which the Scots, under Earl Douglas, defeated Henry Percy. There had long been a rivalry between the families of Percy and Douglas, which showed itself by incessant raids into each other's territory. Percy once vowed he would hunt for three days in the Scottish border, without condescending to ask leave of Douglas. The Scots warden said in his anger, 'Tell this vaunter he shall find one day more than sufficient.' 'The Ballad of Chevy Chase', dating from the 15th century, has as its subject the rivalry mentioned. It is quoted with notes by Addison in the *Spectator*, Nos 21 and 25 (1711), and is given in PERCY'S RELIQUES (1765). Another ballad, 'The Battle of Otterbourne', recounts the battle itself, and is also in Percy's *Reliques*. Chevy Chase itself is a former hunting ground, which derives its name from a hill in the locality. Its own name may relate to the Cheviots, some dozen miles to the north.

Chevy Chase is also the name, adopted from the ballad, of a suburb of Washington, D.C. The suburb in turn gave the screen name of the American actor Chevy Chase (b.1943), his original name being Cornelius Crane Chase.

**Chew. Chew the cud, To.** To reflect; to ruminate.

**Chew the fat, To.** An old colloquialism meaning to argue over a point. Also, less commonly, to gossip. The allusion may be to chewing through fat or gristle, in which the mouth goes through motions similar to that in heated argument *See also* JAW.

**Chew the rag, To.** To grouse; to grumble. In the USA the expression means simply to chat. The tongue is sometimes known as the 'red rag'.

**Bite off more than one can chew, To.** *See under* BITE.

**Chian Painter, The.** APELLES.

**Chiantishire.** A media name for the area of Tuscany in Italy where Chianti wine is produced, especially in its role as a holiday resort for the English middle classes, who may even purchase homes there.

> These Nimrods of the New Forest are surely on their mettle. Summoned from the slopes of Chiantishire, they should don the pink and take down the horn.
> *The Times* (12 August 1998)

**Chiasmus** (Greek, 'a placing crosswise'). An inversion in the second of two parallel phrases of the order followed in the first. An example is the last line of Shakespeare's *Sonnet* 154 (1609): 'Love's fire heats water, water cools not love.'

**Chicago Bears.** A former record-breaking professional American football team, with a home base at Wrigley Field, Chicago. They held the record for the greatest number of consecutive wins, 18 (twice), in the National Football League, and their star player, George Blanda, played in a record 340 games in a record 26 seasons between 1949 and 1958.

**Chicane.** A term used in bridge or whist for a hand containing no trumps. Its general meaning is the use of petty subterfuge, especially in legal dodges and quibbles. It is a French word of uncertain origin, derived by some authorities from Late Greek *tzykanion*, 'game of mall' (*see* PALL MALL), in turn from Persian *tchugagan*, 'crooked mallet'.

On a motor-racing circuit, a chicane is a short section of sharp bends formed by barriers, designed to serve as a test of driving skill.

**Chichevache.** A fabulous monster that lives only on patient wives and that was, therefore, all skin and bone, because its food was so scarce. It was thus the opposite of BICORN. Chaucer apparently introduced the word and changed it from French *chichefache* or *chicheface* ('thin face', 'ugly face') into *chichevache* ('lean cow', 'ugly cow').

> O noble wives, in highest prudence bred,
> Allow no such humility to nail
> Your tongues, or give a scholar cause to shed
> Such light on you as this astounding tale
> Sheds on Griselda, patient still and kind,
> Lest Chichevache engulf you like a whale.
>
> CHAUCER: *Canterbury Tales*, 'The Clerk's Tale' (*c*.1387) (modern translation by Nevill Coghill, 1951)

**Chicken. Chicken feed.** A trivial amount of money, SMALL BEER, from the fact that chicken corn usually consists of the smaller, cheaper grains.

**Chicken-hearted** or **chicken-livered.** Cowardly. Young chickens are remarkably timid and run to the mother hen at the slightest alarm.

**Chicken or the egg, The.** A phrase used of an unresolved question about which of two things caused the other. A problem of this kind is thus a 'chicken-and-egg problem'.

**Chicken out, To.** To back out from doing something through fear or failure of nerve, as a CHICKEN-HEARTED person does.

**Blue Hen's Chickens.** *See under* BLUE.

**Champagne and chicken.** *See under* CHAMPAGNE.

**Count one's chickens before they are hatched, To.** *See under* COUNT.

**Curses, like chickens, come home to roost.** *See under* CURSE.

**Hen and chickens.** *See under* HEN.

**Mother Carey's chickens.** *See under* MOTHER.

**No chicken** or **no spring chicken.** No longer young, said of a person who has reached an age when they are no longer a chick. A spring chicken is a young fowl ready for eating, which was originally in the spring.

**Pharaoh's chicken.** *See under* PHARAOH.

**Play chicken, To.** *See under* PLAY.

**Why did the chicken cross the road?** *See under* WHY.

**Child.** At one time this was a provincial term for a female infant, and was the opposite of boy.

> Mercy on's, a bairn; a very pretty bairn! A boy or a child, I wonder?
>
> SHAKESPEARE: *The Winter's Tale*, III, iii (1610)

**Childe.** In CHILDE HAROLD, CHILDE ROLAND and the like childe is a title of honour, something like Spanish *infante*. In the days of CHIVALRY a noble youth who was a candidate for knighthood, during his time of probation, was called infans, valet, damoysel, bachelier and childe.

**Childe Harold.** BYRON's poem depicts a world-weary man who roams from place to place to escape from himself. The 'Childe' may have been Byron himself, who was only 21 when he began the poem, and 28 when he finished it. In Canto i (1809), he visited Portugal and Spain, in Canto ii (1810) Turkey in Europe, in Canto iii (1816) Belgium and Switzerland, and in Canto iv (1817) Venice, Rome and Florence.

**Childermas.** An old name for the feast of the HOLY INNOCENTS (28 December).

**Childe Roland.** The youngest brother of the 'fair burd Helen' in the old Scottish ballad. Guided by MERLIN, he successfully undertook to bring his sister from Elfland, where the fairies had taken her.

> Child Rowland to the dark tower came;
> His word was still 'Fie, foh, and fum,
> I smell the blood of a British man.'
>
> SHAKESPEARE: *King Lear*, III, iv (1605)

Browning's poem, 'Child Roland to the Dark Tower Came' (1855), is not connected, other than by the first line, with the old ballad.

**Child of God.** In the CHURCH OF ENGLAND and the ROMAN CATHOLIC CHURCH, a person who has been baptized. Some consider the phrase to mean one converted by special grace and adopted into the holy family of God's church.

> QUESTION: Who gave you this Name?
> ANSWER: My Godfathers and Godmothers in my baptism; wherein I was made a member of Christ, the child of God, and an inheritor of the kingdom of heaven.
>
> Book of Common Prayer, Catechism

**Child of nature.** An innocent or naïve person, sometimes one attractively so.

> Dear Child of Nature, let them rail!
> —There is a nest in a green dale,

A harbour and a hold;
Where thou, a Wife and Friend, shalt see
Thy own heart-stirring days, and be
A light to young and old.

WILLIAM WORDSWORTH: 'To a Young Lady, Who Had Been Reproached for Taking Long Walks in the Country' (1802).

**Children** or **Babes in the Wood, The.** The story is that the master of Wayland Hall, Norfolk, left a little son and daughter to the care of his wife's brother. Both were to have money, but if the children died first the uncle was to inherit. After 12 months the uncle hired two ruffians to murder the babes. One of the men relented and killed the other, leaving the children in a wood. They died during the night, and ROBIN REDBREAST covered them with leaves. All now went wrong for the wicked uncle: his sons died, his barns were fired, his cattle perished, and he himself finally died in gaol. After seven years the ruffian was arrested for highway robbery and confessed the whole affair.

The ballad 'The Children in the Wood' appears in PERCY'S RELIQUES and also in a crude MELODRAMA, which was printed in 1601 and attributed on the title page to Rob Yarington, called *Two Lamentable Tragedies; the one of the murder of Maister Beech, a chandler in Thames-streete, etc. The other of a young child murthered in a wood by two ruffians, with the consent of his unkle.* It is uncertain which is earlier, the play or the ballad. *See also* BABES IN THE WOOD.

**Children of the Casket.** Between 1728 and 1751 the Mississippi Company sent regular shipments of respectable middle-class girls to New Orleans to provide wives for the French settlers in Louisiana. Each was presented on her departure with a casket of suitable clothing. They were known as *filles à la cassette*, to distinguish them from the women of bad character shipped out from the Salpêtrière prison during the same period. Louisiana families like to claim descent from a casket girl as New Englanders do from a MAYFLOWER pilgrim.

**Children's Crusade, The.** A crusade of 1212 that was the result of misguided zeal. There were two main expeditions. Some 40,000 German children, led by one Nicholas, set off over the Alps for Italy. Only a few reached Genoa and Rome, where Innocent III ordered them home. Some hundreds possibly sailed from Brindisi to disappear from history. Another 30,000 French children, under Stephen of Cloyes, set out for Marseilles, and about 5000 were eventually offered passage by scoundrelly shipmasters only to be wrecked or sold as slaves to the Muslims. *See also* PIED PIPER OF HAMELIN.

**Child's play.** Something easy or simple.

It is no child's play
Choosing a wife. It needs consideration.

CHAUCER: *Canterbury Tales*, 'The Merchant's Tale' (*c.*1387) (modern translation by Nevill Coghill, 1951)

**Adoption of children.** *See under* ADOPTION.
**Burned child dreads the fire, A.** *See under* BURN.
**Eagle and Child, The.** *See under* EAGLE.
**Love child.** *See under* LOVE.
**Natural child.** *See under* NATURAL.
**Second childhood.** *See under* SECOND.
**Tub of naked children.** *See under* TUB.
**Wild child.** *See under* WILD.

**Chiliasts** (Greek *khilioi*, 'thousand'). Members of a sect also called MILLENARIANS, who believe that Christ will return to this earth and reign a thousand years in the midst of his saints. Chiliasm was originally a Judaistic theory, but became a heresy in the early Christian church. It was condemned by St Damasus, who was pope from 366 to 384, but was not abolished. Article 41 of the English Church further condemned Chiliasm in 1553. This Article was omitted in 1562.

**Chillingham cattle.** A breed of cattle preserved in the grounds of Chillingham Castle, the Northumberland home of the Earl of Tankerville. They are reputed to be a remnant of the wild oxen of Britain.

**Chillon, Prisoner of.** *See under* PRISONER.

**Chilminar and Baalbek.** According to legend, two cities built by the Genii, acting under the orders of Jinn bin Jann, who governed the world long before ADAM. Chilminar, or the 'Forty Towers', is PERSEPOLIS. The cities were intended as hiding places for the Genii.

**Chilo.** One of the WISE MEN OF GREECE or the seven sages of Greece.

**Chiltern Hundreds.** The three HUNDREDS of Stoke, Desborough and Burnham, in Buckinghamshire, over which a steward was originally appointed to suppress the robbers who frequented the thickly wooded Chiltern Hills. The necessity has long since ceased, but the office remains. As a consequence of the Succession Act of 1701 and later Acts, the holding of most non-political offices of profit under the crown meant resignation from the HOUSE OF COMMONS, and after 1750 application for the stewardship of the Chiltern Hundreds was used as a means of relinquishing membership of Parliament (since members cannot resign directly). The stewardships of Old Shoreham (Sussex), East Hendred (Oxfordshire), Hempholme (Yorkshire), Poynings (Sussex) and Northstead (Yorkshire) were also used for this purpose, as were (until 1838) the escheatorships of Munster and Ulster, in Ireland. By the House of Commons Disqualification Act (1957) the stewardship of the

Chiltern Hundreds and the Manor of Northstead were retained for this use and their gift remains with the CHANCELLOR OF THE EXCHEQUER.

**Chime in, To.** To join in or interrupt a conversation already in progress, often in an unwelcome manner. The allusion is to the chiming of bells, or more precisely to bellringers who remain silent except when they enter with a particular note in the sequence of changes.

**Chimera** (Greek *khimaira*, 'she-goat'). A fabulous monster in Greek mythology. According to Homer it has a lion's head, a goat's body and a dragon's tail. It was born in Lycia and slain by BELLEROPHON. Hence the use of the name in English for a wild, unrealistic fancy or notion.

**Chimney, The Devil's.** *See under* DEVIL.

**Chin. Amazonian chin.** *See under* AMAZONIA.

**Double chin.** *See under* DOUBLE.

**Lead with one's chin, To.** *See under* LEAD.

**Take it on the chin, To.** *See under* TAKE.

**China.** *See* MISNOMERS.

**Chinaman.** A cricketing term (not to be confused with GOOGLY) denoting an offbreak bowled by a left-handed bowler to a right-handed batsman. It is said that the name derives from the bowler Ellis Achong, who, although he played for the West Indies, was actually Chinese and who practised this kind of bowling, although not the first to do so.

**Chinatown.** The part of any city that forms the Chinese quarter, especially in the USA. New York's Chinatown, in lower Manhattan, is particularly well known, and evolved rapidly from the mid-19th century. London's Chinatown, between Shaftesbury Avenue and Leicester Square, has been the focus of the capital's Chinese community since the 1960s and now has an impressive array of CHINESE RESTAURANTS. Moscow also has a Chinatown, but the name of the medieval quarter is an English mistranslation of Russian *Kitay-gorod*, deriving from *kita*, a type of earth-filled woven basket used to strengthen the original wall.

**Bull in a china shop, A.** *See under* BULL.

**From China to Peru.** *See under* FROM.

**Dresden china.** *See under* DRESDEN.

**Not for all the tea in China.** *See under* TEA.

**Chin-chin.** Now used in English as a term for both greeting and departure, as well as by way of a toast, the phrase has its origin in Chinese *ch'ing-ch'ing*, literally 'please-please'. *See also* NAPOO.

> Chin-chin, Effie my dear, and all the best for Xmas!
>
> J.B. PRIESTLEY: *The Good Companions*, II, vii (1929)

**Chindit.** The word is a corruption of Burmese *chinthe*, the lion-headed dragon gracing the outside of Burmese pagodas. It was adopted as the device of the troops under Major-General Orde Wingate operating in Burma behind the Japanese lines (1943–5). Wingate himself was killed in an aircrash in March 1944.

**Chinese. Chinese burn.** A form of 'torture' practised among schoolchildren, in which the victim's wrist is seized and twisted in opposite directions in the hands of the perpetrator.

**Chinese dragon, The.** In China, a five-clawed dragon is introduced into pictures and embroidered on dresses as an AMULET.

**Chinese Gordon.** General Charles Gordon (1833–85), who in 1863 was placed in command of the 'Ever-victorious Army' of Chinese soldiers under European and American officers, and after 33 engagements succeeded in suppressing the formidable TAIPING rebellion by 1864.

**Chinese restaurant.** A restaurant specializing in Chinese TAKEAWAY dishes, a regular outlet on the British High Street. The first Chinese restaurant in Europe opened in London in 1908, when Chung Koon, a Chinese ship's cook, left his vessel and, marrying an English girl, set up an eating establishment in Piccadilly Circus. The restaurant, the Cathay, catered mainly for old colonial types who had returned to England from the Orient. Its popularity increased in the Second World War, when American GIs began taking their girlfriends there. Other family-run restaurants started to open elsewhere in London and in cities such as Liverpool and Manchester, their chief clientele after the war being British soldiers who had returned from the Far East. The aroma of CHOP SUEY and CHOW MEIN is now familiar in even the smallest market town.

**Chinese slavery.** Effective slavery in the form of much hard work for negligible rewards. The phrase became widely used as a political slogan by the Liberals from 1903, when Balfour's Conservative government (1902–5) introduced coolies from China to combat the shortage of Kaffir labour in the Rand gold mines after the dislocation caused by the South African War. They were kept in compounds and allowed out only under permit.

**Chinese wall.** On the STOCK EXCHANGE a ban on the passing or leak of confidential financial information from one department to another, especially when detrimental to a client. The allusion is to the GREAT WALL OF CHINA.

> The Law Lords have ruled that there can be no guarantee that Chinese walls constructed on an ad hoc basis are leak proof. That will pose problems at dozens of institutions where Chinese walls owe more to jerry building techniques than brilliant architecture.
>
> *The Times* (19 December 1998)

**Chinese water torture.** A form of torture in which water drips steadily onto a bound victim's forehead with the aim of driving him insane. *See also* WATER TORTURE.

**Chinese whispers.** Mistakes caused by faulty communication. The reference is to the party game in which a message is passed in a whisper to all the participants in turn. By the time it reaches the last player, it is so distorted that it might as well be in Chinese. A well-known example is the military message 'Send reinforcements, we are going to advance', which emerged as 'Send three and fourpence, we are going to a dance'.

**Chinook.** A warm, dry, southwesterly wind, which blows down the east side of the Rocky Mountains in winter causing rapid rises in temperature and sudden thawing of snow. It is a cooling wind in the summer and takes its name from the Chinook Indians of the Columbia River area.

**Chintz.** A plural word that has erroneously become singular. Hindi *chīnt* (from Sanskrit *chitra*, 'variegated') was the name given in the 17th century to the painted and stained calico imported from the East. However, as the plural chints was more common in commercial use, it came to be taken for the singular and was written chince or chinse and, finally, chintz. Chintzy is thus used for a style associated with chintz soft furnishings, and hence for anything gaudy or garish.

> And 'Tea!' she said in a tiny voice
> 'Wake up! It's nearly *five*'.
> Oh! Chintzy, chintzy cheeriness,
> Half dead and half alive!
> JOHN BETJEMAN: *Mount Zion*, 'Death in Leamington' (1932)

**Chios, The Man of.** HOMER

**Chip. Chip in, To.** (1) To make a contribution. (2) To interrupt. The first of these meanings derives from the game of poker, in which the chips, representing money, are placed by the players in the 'pot'. The second may be from the same source.

**Chip off the old block, A.** A person whose behaviour is similar to that of his or her mother or father. A chip is of the same wood as the block from which it comes. The expression was earlier 'chip of the old block'.

> He's my son, and he's a chip off the old block, and I'm proud of him.
> H.E. BATES: *Seven Tales and Alexander* (1929)

**Chippy.** (1) A fish-and-chip shop; (2) a carpenter; (3) a chipmunk; (4) in the USA, a prostitute or promiscuous woman.

**Chips, Mr.** The archetypal bachelor public schoolmaster, who devotes his life to his school and his boys, and is fondly regarded by all. His real name is Arthur Chipping, and he was the creation of James Hilton (1900–54), who introduced him in the sentimental story *Goodbye, Mr Chips* (1934), in which his life is told in flashback. He is an amalgam of Hilton's own headmaster father and a housemaster at the Leys School, Cambridge, which Hilton had attended. He is memorably played by Robert Donat in a classic film version (1939).

**Have a chip on one's shoulder, To.** To be quarrelsome; to parade or have a grievance. The expression is of 19th-century American origin, and alludes to a form of challenge in which a man or boy dares another to dislodge the chip (piece of wood) he carries on his shoulder.

**Have had one's chips, To.** To be defeated, condemned to death, killed or otherwise 'finished'. The expression probably comes from the game of poker. When the chips have been staked and lost, there is no way of replacing them.

**When the chips are down.** *See under* WHEN.

**Chiromancy.** *See* PALMISTRY.

**Chiron** (perhaps from Greek *kheiro-n*, 'inferior', or *kheir*, 'hand'). The wise and kind CENTAUR who taught ACHILLES and many other heroes in their youth. JUPITER placed him in heaven among the stars as SAGITTARIUS.

In the *Inferno* Dante gives the name to the keeper of the lake of boiling blood, in the seventh circle of hell.

**Chisel** or **chizzle, To.** To cheat or obtain by cheating. Hence schoolboy slang chiz or chizz for a cheat or swindle.

**Cold chisel.** *See under* COLD.

**Chivalry.** A general term for all that pertains to the romance of the old days of knighthood. The word is of the same origin as 'cavalry' and 'chevalier'. Chivalry embodied the medieval concept of the ideal, with valour, courtesy, generosity and dexterity in arms the peak of any man's attainment.

A great literature arose out of chivalry, notably the ROLAND epics, those of CHARLEMAGNE and those of ARTHUR. It was, perhaps, prophetic of the fate of chivalry itself that in every case these great epics end in tragedy. Thus the PALADINS of Charlemagne were all scattered by the Battle of Roncesvalles, the champions of Dietrich were all assassinated at the instigation of Chriemhild (KRIEMHILD), the bride of ATTILA THE HUN, and the KNIGHTS OF THE ROUND TABLE were all destroyed in the fatal BATTLE OF CAMLAN.

**Flower of chivalry, The.** *See under* FLOWER.

**Chivy** or **chivvy, To.** To chase or urge someone on. The word is probably a variant of 'chevy', from CHEVY CHASE. At one time 'chivy' was a hunting cry.

> When you are ready, I am … with a Hey Ho Chivey, and likewise with a Hark Forward, Tantivy.
> DICKENS: *Our Mutual Friend*, Pt III, ch x (1864)

**Chizzle.** *See* CHISEL.

**Chloe** (Greek *khloē*, 'green shoot'). The shepherdess beloved by DAPHNIS in the Greek pastoral romance of Longus called *Daphnis and Chloe*, and hence a generic name in literature for a rustic maiden.

In Alexander Pope's *Moral Essays* (ii (1731–5)) Chloe represents Lady Suffolk, mistress of George II, 'content to dwell in decencies for ever', and the poet Matthew Prior (1664–1721) uses the name for the dramatist and actress Susannah Centlivre (1669–1723).

**Chock-full** or **chock-a-block.** Completely full. The chock has a different origin in these expressions. In chock-full it is a form of choke. In chock-a-block it is from chock in its use for a nautical block (through which a line or rope passes), so that the sense is essentially 'block against block'. However, chock-a-block was probably influenced by chock-full, as a much older word.

**Chocolate.** The produce of the cocoa bean (cacao seed) was introduced into England from Central America in the early 16th century as a drink. It was sold in London coffee houses from the middle of the 17th century. The Cocoa Tree Chocolate House, in Pall Mall, London, was one of the best known coffee houses of the early 18th century. The origin of the word is in Nahuatl *chocolatl*, from *xococ*, 'bitter', and *atl*, 'water'. *See also* COFFEE.

**Choice. Hercules' choice.** *See under* HERCULES.

**Hobson's choice.** *See under* HOBSON'S.

**Spoilt for choice.** *See under* SPOILT.

**Choir. Three Choirs Festival.** *See under* THREE.

**Choke.** In ancient times people accused of robbery had a piece of barley bread given to them over which Mass had been said. They put the bread in their mouths saying the words, 'May this piece of bread choke me, if what I say is not true', and if they were then able to swallow it without being choked they were pronounced innocent. Tradition ascribes the death of Earl Godwin in 1053 to choking with a piece of bread after this solemn appeal. *See also* CORSNED.

**Choose. Beggars cannot be choosers.** *See under* BEG.

**Pick and choose, To.** *See under* PICK.

**Chop.** The word has four different origins.

(1) To chop, meaning to cut something off with an axe or knife. From 'chap', as applied to a crack in the skin ('chapped lips'). Hence 'chop' as a slice of meat, 'chophouse' as a restaurant specializing in steaks and grills, and 'choppy' (earlier 'chopping'), describing rough water, which is full of 'cracks'.

(2) To chop and change, meaning, to fluctuate or alter continuously. From Old English *cēapian*, 'to barter', which also gave 'cheap' and CHAP ('fellow'). 'Choplogic', in its sense of fallacious reasoning, is also of this origin.

(3) Chops, in the sense of jaws, jowls, mouth, as when one licks one's chops, is of uncertain origin. The word was also spelt 'chap', hence BATH CHAP, and 'chapfallen' (or 'chopfallen'), for someone who is dejected or CRESTFALLEN.

(4) Some forms of chop are of oriental origin, as the next three entries.

**Chop chop.** PIDGIN ENGLISH for 'quickly'. From a Chinese dialect phrase related to Cantonese *kap kap*.

**Chopsticks.** Two thin sticks of wood or ivory that the Chinese, Japanese and Koreans use to eat with. From PIDGIN ENGLISH 'chop' (as for CHOP CHOP) and English 'stick'. The Chinese name for them is *kuài tse*, 'quick ones'.

**Chop suey.** A Chinese-style dish of meat, bean sprouts and the like, served with rice. From Chinese *tsap sui*, 'mixed bits'.

**Lick one's chops, To.** *See under* LICK.

**Choragus** (Greek *khoragos*). The leader of the chorus in the ancient Athenian drama.

**Choral, Vicar.** *See under* VICAR.

**Choriambus** or **choriamb** (Greek *khoriambos*, 'chorus iamb'). This was a metrical foot in classical verse that consisted of four syllables: two long or stressed ones enclosing two short or unstressed, otherwise long-short-short-long, as in English 'pieces of eight'. It was particularly associated with HORACE.

**Chorus, Cat's.** *See under* CAT.

**Chosen People, The.** The Israelites, the Jews.

**Chouans.** French peasant bands in Brittany, under the leadership of Jean Cottereau (1757–94), who rose in revolt in 1793 and joined the royalists of La Vendée. Chouan (from *chat-huant*, 'screech owl') was the nickname given to Cottereau, who imitated the screech of the owl to warn his companions of danger, and the name was extended to his followers. Georges Cadoudal (1771–1804) was their leader after 1794. The movement reappeared in 1814–15 and again during the JULY REVOLUTION of 1830. *See also* COMPANIONS OF JEHU.

**Choughs.** *See under* BIRDS PROTECTED BY SUPERSTITIONS.

**Chow mein.** A Chinese-style dish of fried noodles with shredded meat or shrimps and vegetables. The name represents Chinese *chao miàn*, 'fried flour'.

**Chrism** or **chrisom** (Greek *khrisma*, 'anointing', 'unction'). The mixture of oil and balm consecrated for use in baptism, confirmation and other sacramental rites. Originally 'chrisom' was merely a variant of 'chrism' resulting from a frequent form of pronunciation but later differentiated from the latter when it came to designate the white cloth or robe worn at baptism. This was used as a shroud if the child died within the ensuing month. As late as 1726 such infants were called 'chrisoms'.

> 'A made a finer end, and went away, an it had been any chrisom child.
> SHAKESPEARE: *Henry V*, II, iii (1598)

**Christ. Christ Church.** The Oxford college was founded in 1546 and was at first called Cardinal College, after Cardinal Wolsey, who had established it in 1524. In 1546, however, Henry VIII designated the former priory church here as Christ Church cathedral and as the college chapel. Hence its name. A noted resident was Lewis Carroll, who gained fame from the stories he told to the young daughter of the college dean, H.G. Liddell (*see* ALICE IN WONDERLAND). In the works of Thomas Hardy, Christ Church appears under its original name of Cardinal College, while Oxford itself is Christminster.

**Christ-cross.** *See* CRISS-CROSS.

**Christ's cross me speed.** A formula said before beginning the alphabet and later, generally, before beginning any work.

> Christes crosse be my speede, in all vertue to proceede,
> A, b, c, d, e, f, g,
> h, i, k, l, m, n, o, p,
> q, r, s, & t, double w, v,
> x with y, ezod, & per se,
> con per se tittle tittle est Amen
> When you haue done, begin againe, begin againe.
> THOMAS MORLEY: *A Plaine and Easie Introduction to Practicall Musicke* (1597)

This formula has been adopted by some families and institutions as a motto, often with a MALTESE CROSS in place of the first two words. ✠ *me spede* is thus the motto of Stamford School (for boys, founded 1532), Lincolnshire, and its sister foundation, Stamford High (for girls, founded 1877). *See also* CRISS-CROSS.

**Tear Christ's body, To.** *See under* TEAR.

**Vicar of Christ, The.** *See under* VICAR.

**Christadelphians** (Greek *Khristos*, 'Christ', and *adelphos*, 'brother'). Members of a Christian sect sometimes called Thomasites after their founder Dr John Thomas (1805–71), who migrated from London to Brooklyn and formed the sect *c*.1848. They believe in 'conditional immortality' for the faithful (only the just will enter eternal life) and the full inspiration of the Bible and look for the return of Christ to reign on the earth.

**Christendom.** A collective term for all Christians, and formerly a synonym for Christianity.

> By my christendom,
> So I were out of prison, and kept sheep,
> I should be as merry as the day is long.
> SHAKESPEARE: *King John*, IV, i (1596)

**Christian.** A follower of Christ. According to the Bible, Christians were first so called at Antioch (Acts 11:26). Christian is also the hero of Bunyan's PILGRIM'S PROGRESS (1678, 1684) who fled from the CITY OF DESTRUCTION and journeyed to the CELESTIAL CITY. He started with a heavy burden on his back, which fell off when he stood at the foot of the cross.

**Christian Brothers.** A secret society formed in London in the early 16th century to distribute the New Testament in English. The name is now better known as that of the Roman Catholic teaching congregation of laymen, founded in France by the Abbé de la Salle in 1684. It still exists in France, Britain and elsewhere.

**Christian Science.** The religion founded at Boston by Mrs Mary Baker Eddy (1821–1910) in 1879, as 'the scientific system of divine healing'. Her views were put forward in her book *Science and Health, with Key to the Scriptures*, which was first published in 1875. Christian Science is founded on the Bible but distinguishes between what is taught in the New Testament and what is taught in the creeds and later dogma. It emphasizes spiritual healing and the unreality of matter. It now has a considerable following and is not limited, as is popularly assumed, to the healing of those who are ill. Its churches are called First (Second etc) Church of Christ, Scientist.

**Father of Christian Monasticism, The.** St ANTHONY OF EGYPT (*c*.250–356). *See also* FATHERS OF THE DESERT.

**Most Christian King, The.** *See under* MOST.

**Rice Christians.** *See under* RICE.

**Christiana.** The wife of CHRISTIAN in Part II (1684) of Bunyan's PILGRIM'S PROGRESS who journeyed with her children and Mercy from the CITY OF DESTRUCTION some time after her husband.

**Christianity, Muscular.** *See under* MUSCULAR.

**Christmas.** 25 December is Christmas Day although almost certainly not the day on which Christ was born, as is popularly supposed. The date was eventually fixed by the church in AD 440, and is the day of the winter SOLSTICE, which had anciently been a time of festival among heathen peoples. In Anglo-Saxon England, the year began on 25 December, but from the late 12th century until the adoption of the GREGORIAN CALENDAR in 1752 the year began on LADY DAY, 25 March. Christmas Day has the advantage of being exactly nine months after Lady Day, the traditional length of a human pregnancy. *See also* GREGORIAN YEAR; OLD STYLE.

**Christmas box.** A gratuity or present formerly given on Boxing Day (the day after Christmas Day), St STEPHEN's Day. Boxes placed in churches for casual offerings used to be opened on Christmas Day, and the contents, called the 'dole of the Christmas box' or the 'box money', were distributed next day by priests. Apprentices also used to carry a box around to their masters' customers for small gratuities. Postmen received such gifts until after the Second World War. *See also* HANDSEL.

**Christmas cards.** This popular form of seasonal greeting is of comparatively recent origin. W.C.T. Dobson, RA, is usually regarded as having sent the first such card in 1844. Sir Henry Cole and J.C. Horsley produced the first commercial Christmas card in 1846, although it was condemned by temperance enthusiasts because members of the family group in the centre piece were cheerfully drinking wine. They first came widely into fashion when commercial firms began printing them in the 1870s.

**Christmas Day in the Workhouse.** This is the popular title of the much parodied long narrative poem (21 verses) properly entitled *In the Workhouse: Christmas Day* (1879) by George R. Sims. It was frequently burlesqued in the days of the MUSIC HALL and subsequently. Its first verse originally ran as follows:

It is Christmas Day in the Workhouse,
And the cold bare walls are bright
With garlands of green and holly,
And the place is a pleasant sight:
For with clean-washed hands and faces,
In a long and hungry line,
The paupers sit at the tables,
For this is the hour they dine.

**Christmas decorations.** The Roman festival of SATURN was held in December and the temples were decorated with greenery. The DRUIDS are associated with MISTLETOE, and the Saxons used HOLLY and IVY. These customs have been transferred to the Christian festival. The holly (popularly associated with 'holy') is called 'Christ's thorn' in Germany and Scandinavia, from its use in church decorations and its berries, which are borne about Christmas time. The early Christians gave an emblematic turn to the custom, referring to the 'righteous branch', and justifying it from Isaiah 60:13: 'The glory of Lebanon shall come unto thee, the fir tree, the pine tree, and the box together, to beautify the place of my sanctuary.'

The decorated Christmas tree was in use among the Romans and was introduced to Britain from Germany soon after Queen Victoria's marriage with Prince Albert of Saxe-Coburg-Gotha in 1840. SANTA CLAUS and his reindeer came to Britain at the same time.

**White Christmas.** *See under* WHITE.

**Christopher.** Legend relates that St Christopher was a giant who one day carried a child over a brook, and said, 'Chylde, thou hast put me in gret peryll. I might bere no greater burden.' To which the child answered, 'Marvel thou nothing, for thou hast borne all the world upon thee, and its sins likewise.' This is an allegory: Christopher (Greek *Khristophoros*) means 'Christ-bearer', the child was Christ, and the river was the river of death.

**Christopher Robin.** The little boy who shares adventures with WINNIE-THE-POOH and other animal friends in the stories and poems by A.A. Milne. He represents Milne's son, Christopher Robin Milne (1920–96), who was also the model for E.H. Shepard's illustrations. In his autobiography *The Enchanted Places* (1974) the original Christopher Robin tells how he grew up to wish his name were Charles Robert.

**Christopher Sly.** *See under* SLY.

**Christy Minstrels.** In 1846 the public of New York was first entertained by a troupe of BLACKFACED minstrels organized by the American minstrel Edwin P. Christy (1815–62). To an accompaniment of various stock Negro antics they sang plantation songs and cracked jokes with characters such as Bones, Sambo and others. Stephen Foster (1826–64) provided their best songs, of which 'Beautiful Dreamer' is one of the most famous. The company disbanded in 1854, but the name was purloined by two members of the troupe who took a Christy Minstrel show to London, opening in 1857. Various other troupes also got in on the act, so that there were Christy Minstrel shows in both England and America into the 20th century.

**Chronicle. Anglo-Saxon Chronicle.** *See under* ANGLO.

**Parian chronicle.** *See under* PARIAN.

**Chronogram** (Greek, 'time writing'). A sentence or inscription in which certain letters stand for a date or epoch. In the following English chronogram, commemorating the death of Queen Elizabeth, the capital letters, if rearranged, give the year 1603 in Roman numerals:

My Day Is Closed In Immortality = MDCIII = 1603

In the following Latin chronogram, with U serving as V, the capitals give the year 1627:

ChrIstVs DuX ergo triVMphVs (Christ the Leader, therefore triumphant) = MDCXVVVII =1627

On the title page of a work called *Hugo Grotius his Sophompaneas,* published in 1652, the date is not printed in the usual form but is indicated by the author's name, serving as a chronogram:

FranCIs GoLDsMIth = MDCLII = 1652

**Chrononhotonthologos.** A burlesque of contemporary drama by Henry Carey (*c.*1690–1743), 'the Most Tragical Tragedy that was ever Tragediz'd by any Company of Tragedians', first performed in 1734. Chrononhotonthologos is king of Queerummania, and two of the other characters are Aldiborontiphoscophornia and

Rigdum-Funnidos. The king's name, which suggests a Greek-derived blend of *chronos*, 'time', *onthos*, 'dung' and *logos*, 'word', has sometimes been used to apply to any bombastic person.

**Chrysaor** ('sword as good as gold'). ARTEGAL's sword in Edmund Spenser's *The Faerie Queene* (1590, 1596).

**Chrysostom, St John.** *See under* JOHN.

**Chum.** A close friend; a 'mate'. The word is Oxford University slang and arose as a short form of 'chamber fellow'. Its Cambridge equivalent is 'crony', which has more or less the same meaning but a different origin. It comes from Greek *khronios*, 'of long duration', from *khronos*, 'time'.

**Church.** The word has its origin in Old English *cirice*. This came from Late Greek *kurikon*, in turn from Greek *kuriakon dōma*, 'the Lord's house'. It can denote either the whole body of Christians, or a particular sect or group of Christians, or a place of worship. It can also denote the clergy, as distinct from the laity, or the established religion of a country, as a political or social force that is distinct from the state.

**Church, To.** To bring a woman to church after childbirth for the appointed service of thanksgiving.

**Church-ale.** A former church festivity akin to the WAKES, when specially brewed ale was sold to the people and money was collected for church purposes. The word ale in such composite terms as bride-ale, church-ale, clerk-ale, LAMB-ALE, Midsummer-ale and Scot-ale means 'revelry', 'feast', since ale was the chief liquor provided. There was an unsuccessful attempt to ban church-ales in 1603 but they effectively came to an end during the INTERREGNUM.

**Church Army.** A CHURCH OF ENGLAND evangelical body founded by the Rev. Wilson Carlile in 1882. It began its work among the poor of London on somewhat similar lines to those of the SALVATION ARMY.

**Church Commissioners.** *See* ECCLESIASTICAL COMMISSIONERS; QUEEN ANNE'S BOUNTY *under* ANNE.

**Church Invisible.** Those who are known to God alone as his sons and daughters by adoption and grace. *See also* CHURCH VISIBLE.

> There is ... a Church visible and a Church invisible; the latter consists of those spiritual persons who fulfil the notion of the Ideal Church – the former is the Church as it exists in any particular age, embracing within it all who profess Christianity.
>
> F.W. ROBERTSON: *Sermons* (1855–63)

**Church in Wales.** Following lengthy agitation, an Act of 1914 finally disestablished the Church in Wales, and this took effect in 1920, when a separate province was created.

**Church Militant.** The church or whole body of believers who are said to be 'waging the war of faith' against 'the world, the flesh and the Devil'. It is therefore militant or in warfare.

**Church of England.** The Church of England first severed its connection with Rome in 1534 under Henry VIII. Doctrinal changes were largely effected in the reign of Edward VI (1547–53) and embodied in the BOOK OF COMMON PRAYER of 1549 and the more obviously PROTESTANT version of 1552.

**Church of Ireland.** The Church of Ireland became PROTESTANT in the same way as the Church of England and, although most of the Irish remained ROMAN CATHOLIC, it was not disestablished until 1869, when it was largely disendowed.

**Church of North America.** The Protestant Episcopalian Church in North America was established in November 1784, when Bishop Seabury (1729–96), chosen by the churches of Connecticut, was consecrated in Scotland. The first convention was held at Philadelphia in 1787.

**Church of Scotland.** The reformed Church of Scotland became PRESBYTERIAN in 1560, but EPISCOPACY was cautiously restored by King James VI and I from 1599. It was finally rejected, however, in 1638. It is an ESTABLISHED CHURCH.

**Church Triumphant.** Those who are dead and gone to their rest. Having fought the fight and triumphed, they belong to the Church Triumphant in heaven.

**Church Visible.** All ostensible Christians, or those who profess to be Christians, or those who have been baptized and admitted into the communion of the church. *See also* CHURCH INVISIBLE.

**Churchwarden.** A long-stemmed clay pipe, such as churchwardens were supposed to smoke when they met together in the parish tavern, after they had made up their accounts in the VESTRY or had been elected to office at the EASTER meeting.

**Churchyard cough.** A deep, chesty cough, which possibly presages a permanent removal to the churchyard.

**Anglican Church.** *See* CHURCH OF ENGLAND.

**Banners in churches.** *See under* BANNER.

**Broad Church.** *See under* BROAD.

**Catholic Church.** *See under* CATHOLIC.

**Christ Church.** *See under* CHRIST.

**Collegiate church.** *See under* COLLEGIATE.

**Doctors of the Church.** *See under* DOCTOR.

**Eastern Church, The.** The ORTHODOX CHURCH. *See also* GREEK CHURCH.

**Established Church.** *See under* ESTABLISHED.

**Fathers of the church.** *See under* FATHER.

**Free Churches.** *See under* FREE.

**Free Church of Scotland.** *See under* FREE.

**Go into the church, To.** *See under* GO.
**Greek Church.** *See under* GREEK.
**High Church.** *See under* HIGH.
**Latin Church.** *See under* LATIN.
**Low Church.** *See under* LOW.
**Notes of the church.** *See under* NOTE.
**Orthodox Church.** *See under* ORTHODOX.
**Pentecostal churches.** *See under* PENTECOST.
**Roman Catholic Church.** *See under* ROMAN.
**Seven churches of Asia, The.** *See under* SEVEN.
**Uniat Churches.** *See under* UNIAT.
**United Reformed Church.** *See under* UNITED.
**Western Church, The.** The ROMAN CATHOLIC CHURCH.

**Churlish, Reply.** *See under* REPLY.

**Churn supper.** *See* MELL SUPPER.

**Churrigueresque.** A highly ornate style of baroque architecture in Spain in the late 17th and early 18th centuries. It takes its name from José Churriguera (1665–1725), a Spanish architect and sculptor.

**Cicero.** Marcus Tullius Cicero (106–43 BC), the great Roman orator, philosopher and statesman, formerly known to English students of the classics as Tully. He is said by Plutarch to have been called Cicero, from Latin *cicer*, 'chickpea', 'wart', because he had 'a flat excrescence on the tip of his nose'. Other sources claim that he inherited the name from his father, who had such a wart.

**Cicerone.** A guide who conducts sightseers and points out objects of interest to them. The eloquence and erudition of such guides was regarded as rivalling that of the great orator CICERO.

**Cicero of France, The.** Jean Baptiste Massillon (1663–1742), a noted pulpit orator.

**Cicero of Germany, The.** John, Elector of Brandenburg (ruled 1486–99).

**Cicero of the British Senate, The.** George Canning (1770–1827).

**Bouche de Cicéron, La.** Philippe Pot, chief minister of Louis XI of France (1428–94).

**British Cicero, The.** William Pitt, Earl of Chatham (1708–78).

**Christian Cicero, The.** Lucius Coelius Lactantius or Lactantius Firmianus, a Christian Father (*c*.260–*c*.340).

**German Cicero, The.** Johannes Sturm (1507–89), printer and scholar.

**Cicisbeo.** The escort or lover of a married woman, especially in 18th-century Italy. At that time it was unfashionable for a husband to associate with his wife in society or in public and she was therefore accompanied by her cicisbeo. The word is Italian, but of uncertain origin.

> English ladies are not attended by their cicisbys yet; nor would any English husband suffer it.
>
> JOHN WESLEY: *Works* (1782)

**Cid.** A corruption of Arabic *sayyid*, 'lord', as the title given to Rodrigo Diaz de Vivar (*c*.1043–99), the national hero of Spain and champion of Christianity against the Moors. His exploits, real and legendary, form the basis of many Spanish romances and chronicles, as well as Corneille's tragedy *Le Cid* (1636).

**Ci-devant** (French, 'heretofore'). A word used to mean 'former', 'recent', especially of an office holder, so that a ci-devant governor was once a governor but is now no longer so. In the time of the first French Republic the word was used as a noun meaning a nobleman of the ANCIEN RÉGIME.

> Much they marvelled to see the wealth of the ci-devant blacksmith.
>
> H.W. LONGFELLOW: *Evangeline*, II, iii (1847)

**Cigars, cigarettes** and **cheroots.** The word cigar comes from Spanish *cigarro*, perhaps itself from Mayan *sicar*, 'to smoke'. The natives of Cuba were already smoking tobacco in this form when Europeans first arrived. Cigars as we know them were introduced into the USA by General Putnam in 1762, on his return from the capture of Havana by the Earl of Albermarle.

Cigarettes have a name of French origin, as a diminutive of *cigare*. They are thus 'little cigars'. Cigarettes were originally rolled individually by the smoker and were not sold ready made in packets until the late 19th century.

Cheroots, made from tobacco grown in Southern India, Burma or the Philippines, are merely cigars with both ends cut square. The name comes from Tamil *curuttu*, 'curl', 'roll'.

**Cimmerian.** The word is used of a dense darkness or gloom. Homer (possibly from some story about the Arctic night) supposes the Cimmerians to dwell in a land 'beyond the ocean stream', where the sun never shone (*Odyssey*, xi (8th century BC)). Spenser refers to 'Cymerian shades' in *Virgil's Gnat* (1591) and Milton to 'Cimmerian desert' in 'L'Allegro' (1645).

The Cimmerians were known in post-Homeric times as a historical people on the shores of the BLACK SEA, whence (perhaps) the name Crimea.

**Cinch.** A certainty. A word of American origin derived from the Mexican saddle girth (Spanish *cincha*), which was strong, tight and safe.

**Cinchona.** The medicinal bark, which yields quinine, is so named from the Countess of Chinchón (1576–1639), vicereine of Peru, who was cured of a tertian fever by its use. Linneus erroneously named it 'Cinchona' instead of 'Chinchona'. *See also* PERUVIAN BARK.

**Cincinnatus** (Latin, 'curly-haired'). Lucius Quinctius Cincinnatus, a Roman general and statesman of *c*.519–438 BC, who was twice taken from his plough to be dictator. After he had conquered the Aequians and delivered his country from danger, he laid down his office and returned to his farm.

**Cincinnati, The.** Members of a society of officers of the American Army after the peace of 1783 'to perpetuate friendship, and to raise a fund for relieving the widows and orphans of those who have fallen during the war'. On their badge was a figure of CINCINNATUS.

The Ohio city of Cincinnati, formerly Losantiville, was renamed in 1790 in honour of General St Clair, governor of the North West Territory, who was president of the Cincinnati.

**Cincinnatus of the Americans, The.** George Washington (1732–99).

**Cinderella** (French *Cendrillon*, 'Little Cinders'). The heroine of a fairy tale of ancient, probably Eastern, origin, found in German literature in the 16th century and popularized by Perrault's *Contes de ma mère l'oye* (1697). Cinderella is drudge of the house, while her elder sisters go to beautiful balls. At length, a fairy enables her to go to the prince's ball. The prince falls in love with her and traces her by means of a glass slipper, which she drops but which will fit no foot but her own.

The glass slipper has been conjectured as a fur or sable slipper, supposedly from *pantoufle de vair* ('fur') not *de verre* ('glass'). Perrault's text has *de verre*, which is more in keeping with the story.

**Cinquecento.** The Italian name for the 16th century, applied as an epithet to art and literature with much the same significance as RENAISSANCE or Elizabethan. It was the revival of the classical or antique, but is also understood as a derogatory term, implying debased or inferior art. The word is a shortening of Italian *milcinquecento*, '1500', as the first year of the 16th century.

**Cinque Ports** (Old French *cink porz*, 'five ports'). The original collective name from the 12th century of the five Kent and Sussex seaports of Hastings, Sandwich, Dover, Romney and Hythe, which were granted special privileges through their provision of ships and men for the defence of the Channel. Winchelsea and Rye were subsequently added and there were ultimately 32 lesser members. Their privileges were largely surrendered in 1685. The Duke of Wellington and Sir Winston Churchill are among those who have held the office of Lord Warden of the Cinque Ports. In 1965 Sir Robert Menzies, Prime Minister of Australia, was given this appointment. Queen Elizabeth, the Queen Mother, was made Lord Warden in 1978.

**Barons of the Cinque Ports.** *See under* BARON.

**Circe** (Greek *kirkos*, 'falcon'). A sorceress in Greek mythology, who lived on the island of Aeaea. When Odysseus (ULYSSES) landed there Circe turned his companions into swine, but Ulysses resisted this metamorphosis by virtue of a herb called MOLY, given to him by MERCURY.

> Who knows not Circe,
> The daughter of the Sun, whose charmed cup
> Whoever tasted, lost his upright shape,
> And downward fell into a grovelling swine?
>
> MILTON: *Comus* (1637)

**Circle. Circle of Ulloa.** A white rainbow or luminous ring sometimes seen in Alpine regions opposite the sun in foggy weather. The phenomenon is named from Antonio de Ulloa (1716–95), a Spanish naval officer, who founded the observatory at Cadiz and initiated many scientific enterprises.

**Crop circles.** *See under* CROP.

**Druid's circles.** *See under* DRUID.

**Great circle.** *See under* GREAT.

**Square the circle, To.** *See under* SQUARE.

**Vicious circle.** *See under* VICIOUS.

**Wheel is come full circle, The.** *See under* WHEEL.

**Circuit, Judicial.** *See under* JUDICIAL.

**Circular, Court.** *See under* COURT.

**Circumlocution Office.** A term applied in ridicule by Charles Dickens in *Little Dorrit* (1855–7) to government departments, where everybody tries to relegate every matter needing action to someone else. Before any action can be taken the matter thus passes through so many departments and suffers so many delays that it is hardly worth raising it in the first place.

> Whatever was required to be done, the Circumlocution Office was beforehand with all the public departments in the art of perceiving – How not to do it.
>
> ch x

**Circus. Bread and circuses.** *See under* BREAD.

**Flying circus.** *See under* FLY.

**Sanger's Circus.** *See under* CIRCUS.

**Three-ring circus.** *See under* THREE.

**Cist** (Latin *cista*, 'box', 'chest', from Greek *kiste-*). A box-shaped burial chamber, made from flat stones placed on edge with another stone as a lid and usually covered by a round barrow. The Greek and Roman cist was a deep cylindrical basket made of wickerwork. The basket into which voters cast their tablets was also called a cist, but the mystic cist used in the rites of CERES was later made of bronze. *See also* KIST OF WHISTLES.

**Cistercians.** A monastic order, founded in 1098 at Cistercium (modern Cîteaux, near Dijon) by Robert, abbot of Molesme, as strict BENEDICTINES. They are also known as Grey or White Monks from their habits and as Bernadines from St BERNARD of Clairvaux, who with 30 companions joined the abbey of Cîteaux in 1113. They were noted agriculturists and in medieval England became great producers of wool.

**Citizen. Citizen King, The.** Louis Philippe of France. So called because he was elected king of the French (1830–48), not king of France, after the downfall of Charles X. He was the son of PHILIPPE ÉGALITÉ.

**Citizen of the world, A.** One who is cosmopolitan and at home anywhere. The phrase goes back to Cicero, who in *De Legibus* Bk I, ch xxiii (1st century BC) wrote of *civem totius mundi*. Later, Francis Bacon wrote: 'If a man be gracious and courteous to strangers, it shows he is a citizen of the world' (*Essays*, 'Of Goodness, and Goodness of Nature' (1625)).

**City.** Strictly, a town incorporated by charter, although any large town is so called in ordinary speech, especially if it has a cathedral. In England, the term is of historical and ceremonial rather than administrative significance. In the Bible it sometimes means a town having walls and gates, although in some instances 'city' is used for a place that was really just a small settlement. This is the case, for example, in the following: 'And Joseph also went up from Galilee, out of the city of Nazareth' (Luke 2:4). Although now a major Arab city, the Nazareth of biblical times was merely an insignificant village.

**Cities of Refuge.** Six walled cities, three on each side of the Jordan, set aside under Mosaic Law as a refuge for those who committed accidental homicide. Such refuges were necessitated by the primitive law which exacted blood vengeance by next of kin. All seeking asylum were tried, and if found guilty of murder right of asylum was withdrawn. The cities were Ramoth, Kedesh, Bezer, Shechem, Hebron and Golan (Joshua 20:7–8). In Numbers 35 and elsewhere, the choice of cities is attributed to MOSES, but in Joshua 20 Joshua is said to have nominated them.

Among Muslims MEDINA, where MOHAMMED took refuge when driven by conspirators from MECCA, is known as 'the City of Refuge'. He entered it, not as a fugitive, but in triumph (AD 622). Through him it is also called the City of the Prophet.

**Cities of the Plain, The.** SODOM AND GOMORRAH (Genesis 13:12).

**City, The.** The City of London within its historic boundaries, as distinct from other London boroughs. 'The City' is also a general term for the business and financial interests of the City of London.

> Mobile phone operators set right tone for the City.
> *The Times* (headline) (3 July 1998)

**City College, The.** An old ironic name for NEWGATE PRISON.

**City of a Hundred Towers, The.** Pavia, in Italy, famous for its towers and steeples.

**City of Bells, The.** Strasbourg.

> He was a Strasburgher, and in that city of bells had been a medical practitioner.
> MAYNE REID: *The Scalp Hunters*, ch xxv (1851)

**City of Brotherly Love, The.** PHILADELPHIA. A somewhat ironical but quite etymological nickname for this city (Greek *philadelphia*, 'brotherly love').

**City of David, The.** JERUSALEM. So called in compliment to King DAVID (2 Samuel 5:7–9).

**City of Destruction, The.** In Bunyan's PILGRIM'S PROGRESS (1678, 1684), the world of the unconverted.

**City of Dreadful Knights, The.** Cardiff. After the First World War, Lloyd George, Prime Minister in the coalition government, made lavish grants of honours in a cynical and blatant fashion. In 1922 Lord Salisbury opened an attack and it was alleged that the government had fixed prices for the sale of titles, the money being put into party political funds. The Conservatives profited, as did Lloyd George's private party chest. As a consequence, a Royal Commission was set up in 1922 to recommend future procedure. Three people connected with prominent South Wales newspapers were among the recipients of these honours, hence Cardiff was dubbed the 'City of Dreadful Knights', a punning allusion to James Thomson's poem 'The City of Dreadful Night' (1874).

**City of Dreaming Spires, The.** Oxford. A name derived from Matthew Arnold's 'Thyrsis' (1866): 'And that sweet City with her dreaming spires'.

**City of Elms, The.** New Haven, Connecticut.

**City of Firsts, The.** Kokomo, Indiana, which was the first city to introduce the mechanical corn-picker, the push-button car radio, the commercially built car and canned tomato juice.

**City of Five Flags, The.** Mobile, Alabama, which historically has been in territory under France, Spain, Britain, the CONFEDERATE STATES and the United States.

**City of God, The.** The church, or whole body of believers; also, the Kingdom of Christ, as distinct from the CITY OF DESTRUCTION. The phrase is from St Augustine's *De Civitate Dei* (413–427).

**City of Isms, The.** Syracuse, New York, which early in its history was a meeting-place of abolitionists and reformers.

**City of Kind Hearts, The.** Boston, Massachusetts, was so called by Helen Keller because her teacher, Anne Mansfield Sullivan, came from there as did many others who helped and inspired her.

**City of Lanterns, The.** An imaginary city in Lucian's *Verae Historiae* (2nd century AD), situated somewhere beyond the ZODIAC.

**City of Legions, The.** CAERLEON, where King ARTHUR held his court.

**City of Light, The.** Paris, *la 'Ville-Lumière'*.

**City of Lilies, The.** Florence, which has lilies in its coat-of-arms.

**City of Magnificent Distances, The.** Washington, D.C., famous for its wide avenues and splendid vistas.

**City of Palaces, The.** Agrippa, in the reign of AUGUSTUS, converted Rome from 'a city of brick huts to one of marble palaces'. Calcutta is also called the City of Palaces.

**City of St Michael, The.** Dumfries, whose patron saint is MICHAEL.

**City of Saints, The.** Montreal is so called because many of its streets are named after saints. Salt Lake City, Utah, is also so called, from its MORMON inhabitants.

**City of the Golden Gate, The.** San Francisco. *See also* GOLDEN GATE.

**City of the Prophet, The.** MEDINA. *See also* CITIES OF REFUGE.

**City of the Seven Hills, The.** Rome, which was built on seven hills (*Urbs Septacollis*). The hills are the Aventine, Caelian, Capitoline, Esquiline, Palatine, Quirinal and Viminal.

Aventine Hill: named for the River Aven and given to the people for settlement in 456 BC. It was deemed unlucky because Remus was slain here. It was also called *Collis Dianae*, from the temple of DIANA which stood there.

Caelian Hill: given to Caelius Vibenna, the Etruscan adventurer, who came to the help of the Romans in the Sabine war.

Capitoline Hill: on which stood the great castle or citadel of Rome, was the most important of the seven. It is said to take its name from Latin *caput Oli*, 'head of Olus', referring to a mythological giant whose skull is said to have been discovered here. It contained the Temple of Jupiter Capitolinus.

Esquiline Hill: on the eastern side of the city, was given by AUGUSTUS to MAECENAS, who built here a magnificent mansion which he bequeathed to Augustus. The name literally means 'outer settlement', from *exquilinus*, a conjectural word deriving from *ex*, 'out', and *colere*, 'to inhabit'.

Palatine Hill: the largest of the seven. Here Romulus traditionally held his court. The derivation of the name is thus in *palatium*, 'palace'. (English palace comes from this.)

Quirinal Hill: takes its name from Quirinus, the Sabine god identified with Romulus. The people known as the Quirites settled here as Rome's earliest inhabitants. The hill was also called Cabalinus, from two marble statues of a horse (Latin *caballus*), one of which was the work of Phidias, the other of Praxiteles.

Viminal Hill: so called from the number of osiers (*vimines*) which grew there. It contained the Temple of Jupiter Viminalis.

**City of the Sun, The.** Baalbek, Rhodes and Heliopolis, which had the sun for their god, were so called. It is also the name of a treatise on the Ideal Republic by the Dominican Friar Campanella (1568–1639), similar to Plato's *Republic* (4th century BC), Sir Thomas More's UTOPIA (1516), and Francis Bacon's NEW ATLANTIS (1626).

**City of the Three Kings, The.** Cologne, the reputed burial place of the MAGI.

**City of the Tribes, The.** Galway, because it was the home of the thirteen 'tribes' or chief families, who settled there in 1232 with Richard de Burgh.

**City of the Violated Treaty, The.** Limerick, Ireland, because of the way the Pacification of Limerick (1691) was broken by England.

**City of the Violet Crown, The.** Athens is so called by Aristophanes. Macaulay refers to Athens as the 'violet-crowned city'. Ion (Greek *ion*, 'violet') was a legendary king of Athens, whose four sons gave names to the four Athenian tribes, and Greece in Asia Minor was called Ionia. Athens was the city of 'Ion crowned its king' or 'of the Violet crowned'.

**City of Witches, The.** SALEM, Massachusetts, where 19 women were executed for WITCHCRAFT in 1692. *See also* WITCHES OF SALEM.

**Celestial City.** *See under* CELESTIAL.

**Crescent City.** *See under* CRESCENT.

**Empire City, The.** *See under* EMPIRE.

**Eternal City, The.** *See under* ETERNAL.

**Forbidden City.** *See under* FORBID.

**Forest City.** *See under* FOREST.

**Garden city.** *See under* GARDEN.

**Granite City.** *See under* GRANITE.

**Holy City.** *See under* HOLY.

**Inner city.** *See under* INNER.

**Monumental City.** *See under* MONUMENT.

**Queen City.** *See under* QUEEN.

**Rose-red City.** *See under* ROSE.

**Sacred City, The.** *See* HOLY CITY.

**Sea-born city, The.** *See under* SEA.

**Vatican City State, The.** *See under* VATICAN.

**Windy City.** *See under* WIND.

**Civil. Civil liberty.** Freedom from arbitrary restraint in the citizen's conduct of his own affairs, limited only by the laws established on behalf of the community.

**Civil List.** The annual grant to the crown and royal family, voted by Parliament for royal expenditure from the CONSOLIDATED FUND. It was so named in the early 18th century because the salaries of civil servants, judges and others were paid from it (until 1831). It originated in the reign of William III. George III gave up most of the hereditary revenues in 1760 in return for an annual grant. In 1952 it was fixed at £475,000, but by the Civil List Act 1972 was increased that year to £980,000. In 1983 it was £3,710,000, but in 1991 it was again fixed, this time at £7,900,000, a figure held until 2000. The various Civil List Acts provide for annuities to other members of the royal family, but from 1993 the Queen has reimbursed all such annuities except those paid to herself, to Queen Elizabeth the Queen Mother, and to the Duke of Edinburgh. The Prince of Wales does not receive an annuity but derives his income from the revenues of the Duchy of Cornwall. *See also* ROYAL BOUNTY.

**Civil service.** This name, for all those employed in administering the civil business of the state, was originally used by the English East India Company to distinguish its civilian employees from its soldiers.

**Civil service estimates.** The annual parliamentary grant to cover the expenses of the diplomatic service, the Home Office, the prison service, education, the collection of the revenue and various other expenses pertaining neither to the sovereign nor to the armed services.

**Civil war.** War between citizens of the same state. In English history the term is particularly applied to the war between CHARLES I and Parliament, but the BARONS' WAR and the WARS OF THE ROSES were also civil wars. The USA was confronted with a costly civil war between 1861 and 1865, when the eleven CONFEDERATE STATES sought to secede from the Union. Other major wars of this type were the Russian Civil War (1917–22), between Revolutionaries (Reds) and Counter-Revolutionaries (Whites), and the Spanish Civil War (1936–9), between Republicans and Nationalists.

**Keep a civil tongue in one's head, To.** To avoid rudeness; to make a point of being polite.

**Civilization, Push-button.** *See under* PUSH.

**Civis Romanus sum.** 'I am a Roman citizen', a plea that in ancient Rome sufficed to stop arbitrary condemnation, bonds and scourging. No Roman citizen could be condemned unheard, by the Valerian Law he could not be bound, and by the Sempronian Law it was forbidden to scourge him or beat him with rods. When the chief captain commanded that PAUL 'should be examined by scourging', Paul asked a centurion: 'Is it lawful for you to scourge a man that is a Roman, and uncondemned?' (Acts 22:24–5).

**Civvies.** Civilians or civilian clothes as opposed to military uniform. *See also* MUFTI.

**Civvy Street.** The name by which members of the armed services refer to civilian life, especially during a war or conflict.

> Dick was in splendid shape, sampling every delight Civvy Street had to offer.
>
> JOHN BRAINE: *The Vodi*, ch viii (1959)

**Clack dish.** A dish or basin with a movable lid. Beggars would formerly proclaim their need by clacking the lid of a wooden dish.

> Can you think I get my living by a bell and clack-dish?
> By a bell and a clack-dish? how's that?
> Why, by begging, sir.
>
> THOMAS MIDDLETON: *The Family of Love* (1608)

**Claims, Alabama.** *See under* ALABAMA.

**Clam.** A bivalve mollusc like an oyster, which burrows in sand or mud. In America, especially, clams are esteemed a delicacy. Hence the 'clambake' or picnic by the sea, at which clams are baked.

**Clam up, To.** To refuse to speak, to keep information secret when asked to give it.

**Clameur de haro.** To cry out haro to anyone, haro being in Old French an exclamation or a call for help. This cry is an ancient practice in the CHANNEL ISLANDS, usually as a form of protest against trespass, which must then cease until the matter is settled in court. It dates from the time of the 1st Duke of Normandy. The cry, 'Haro, to my aid, my prince, wrong is being done to me,' was raised in the Guernsey Parliament in January 1966 by a government employee seeking redress.

**Clan.** The word is ultimately from Latin *planta*, 'sprout', 'plant'. The popular idea that the Scottish Highland clan consisted of the chief of a family and his followers, related by ties of kinship and bearing his name, is erroneous. It comprised the chief and his followers irrespective of descent, and only in its narrowest sense applies to the chief, his family and kindred. The legal power and hereditary jurisdiction of the head of a clan was abolished in 1747 after the '45 Rebellion.

**Clan-na-Gael** (Irish, 'children of the Irish'). An Irish FENIAN organization founded in Philadelphia in 1881 and known as the 'United Brotherhood'. Its object was to secure 'the complete and absolute independence of Ireland from Great Britain, and the complete severance of all political connexion between the two countries, to be effected by unceasing preparation for armed insurrection in Ireland'.

**Gathering of the clans, A.** *See under* GATHER.

**Clang of shields, The.** When a Celtic chief doomed a man to death, he struck his shield with the blunt end of his spear as a means of giving notice to the royal bard to begin his death song.

**Clapham. Clapham Sect.** The name given by the Rev. Sydney Smith to a group of EVANGELICALS with common social and political interests, most of whom lived in Clapham in the late 18th and early 19th centuries. William Wilberforce the ABOLITIONIST was their leader. Henry Thornton the banker, Zachary Macaulay, John Venn and James Stephen were among his close associates. Their opponents derisively called them 'the Saints'.

**Man on the Clapham omnibus, The.** *See under* MAN.

**Claptrap.** In the 18th century claptrap was something contrived to bring applause, otherwise a trap to make people clap. After a magician has performed a trick, his nubile assistant will spread her arms as a signal that the feat is finished and as a cue for the audience to clap. The word is now simply empty talk or pretentious 'waffle'.

**Claque** (French *claquer*, 'to clap'). A body of hired applauders, as at a theatre. The device is said to have been first organized in 1820 by a M. Sauton, who set up an office in Paris in that year to ensure the success of dramatic performances. The manager ordered the required number of *claqueurs* and divided them into groups. There were the *commissaires*, who committed the play to memory and noisily pointed out its merits, the *rieurs*, who laughed uproariously at the puns and jokes, the *pleureurs*, mainly women, who held their handkerchiefs to their eyes during the emotional scenes, the *chatouilleurs*, who kept the audience in good humour with their quips and gestures (French *chatouiller*, 'to tickle'), and the *bisseurs*, who cried BIS (encore). 'Claque' is also French for an opera hat:

> A gentleman in black with ringlets and a tuft stood gazing fiercely about him, with one hand in the armhole of his waistcoat and the other holding his claque.
>
> W.M. THACKERAY: *Pendennis*, ch xxv (1848–50)

**Clare, Order of St.** *See under* ORDER.

**Clarenceux King of Arms.** The second of the three English Kings of Arms, under the head of the College of Arms, having jurisdiction over the counties east, west and south of the Trent. The office was instituted by the Duke of Clarence, third son of Edward III. *See also* HERALDRY.

**Clarendon. Clarendon Code, The.** The four acts passed by the CAVALIER PARLIAMENT, named after the king's minister, the Earl of Clarendon, although he was not their originator. They are: the Corporation Act (1661), the Act of Uniformity (1662), the CONVENTICLE ACT (1664), and the FIVE MILE ACT (1665). They were directed against the NONCONFORMISTS.

**Clarendon Press, The.** The name of the Oxford University Press when housed in the Clarendon Building, and subsequently its academic imprint. Edward Hyde, Earl of Clarendon (1609–74), bequeathed the copyright of his *History of the Rebellion* to the university, and the profits from its publication (1702–4) were used to build a new printing house named after him, and the home of the Press until 1830. In 1998 Oxford University Press announced that it had decided to 'phase out' the Clarendon Press imprint on the grounds that it was anachronistic.

**Clarendon type.** A boldface condensed type, such as that used for a CATCHWORD or words. It is named after the CLARENDON PRESS, which introduced it.

**Constitutions of Clarendon, The.** *See under* CONSTITUTIONS.

**Claret.** The English name for the red wines of Bordeaux, originally the yellowish or light red wines as distinguished from the white. The name, which is not used in France, derives from Old French *vin claret*, 'clear wine'. The purplish-red colour known as claret took its name from the wine.

**Claret cup.** An iced drink made of claret, brandy, lemon, sugar and sometimes other ingredients. *See also* BADMINTON.

**Riddle of claret, A.** *See under* RIDDLE.

**Claribel.** The pen-name of Mrs Charlotte Alington-Barnard (1830–69), writer of many once popular ballads, the best known being 'Come back to Erin'. Her pseudonym may have been borrowed from the Spenserian character, the bride of Phaon in *The Faerie Queene* (1590, 1596), but could equally have been formed from letters of her own name. It can be understood as a combination of Latin *clarus*, 'bright', and *bellus*, 'fair' (or of French *clair* and *bel* with the same meanings).

**Claridge's.** The London hotel, associated with the rich and the royal, has its origins in a small hotel in Brook Street, which was bought in the mid-19th century by William Claridge, a butler in a royal household. In 1855 he acquired the neighbouring Mivart's Hotel, and this, in rebuilt and extended form, was the physical building from which sprang the present grand edifice.

**Clark, Nobby.** Nobby Clark is the popular name among service personnel for any man surnamed Clark or Clarke. It originated in the dressy or NOBBY attire affected by clerks and other BLACK-COATED WORKERS of the early 19th century. *See also* NICKNAME.

**Clary water.** A cordial of bygone days made from an infusion of the flowers of wild sage or clary in brandy, flavoured with cinnamon.

**Classes, Chattering.** *See under* CHATTER.

**Classic. Classical Latin.** The Latin of the best authors centred around the Golden or AUGUSTAN AGE, as Livy and Cicero in prose or Horace, Virigil and Ovid as poets.

**Classic races.** The five chief horse races in England, all for three-year-olds: the One Thousand Guineas (fillies), the Two Thousand Guineas (fillies and colts), the OAKS, the DERBY and the St LEGER. *See also* RACES.

**Classics.** The best authors. The Romans were divided by Servius into five classes. Any citizen who belonged to the highest class was called *classicus*; all the rest were said to be *infra classem* (unclassed). From this the best authors were termed *classici auctores* (classic authors), i.e.

authors of the best or first class. The high esteem in which Greek and Latin authors were held at the RENAISSANCE obtained the name of classic for these authors. When other first-rate works are intended, some distinctive name is added, such as the English classics or French classics.

**Claude Lorrain** or **Lorraine.** This form is generally used in both English and French for the name of Claude Gellée (1600–82), the French landscape painter, born at Chamagne in Lorraine.

**Claudia.** A Christian woman of Rome mentioned once in the Bible (2 Timothy 4:21), when together with Eubulus, Pudens and Linus she sends greetings through Paul to Timothy. Her identity is obscured in a web of mystery, but she may well have been the mother of Linus. The wife of PILATE is also said to have been called Claudia and to have been a secret follower of Jesus, on the strength of which she was canonized by the ORTHODOX CHURCH and assigned 27 October as her feast-day.

**Claudius.** The Roman Emperor Tiberius Claudius Nero Germanicus (10 BC–AD 54) suffered from some physical disability and was also generally regarded as being mentally deficient. He took part in the invasion of Britain in AD 43 and was present at the capture of Camulodunum (Colchester). In 48 he divorced his first wife, MESSALINA, and married his niece, Agrippina, who is popularly held to have been responsible for his death, poisoned by a dish of mushrooms. His name appears to represent Latin *claudus*, 'lame', doubtless with regard to his disability. Robert Graves's novel *I, Claudius* (1934) and its sequel *Claudius the God* (1934) portray him as a spastic and epileptic.

**Claus, Santa.** *See under* SANTA.

**Clause. Basket clause.** *See under* BASKET.

**Conscience clause.** *See under* CONSCIENCE.

**Clavie, The Burning of the.** *See under* BURN.

**Claw, The Devil's.** *See under* DEVIL.

**Clay, To have feet of.** *See under* FOOT.

**Clean. Clean and unclean animals.** Among the Hebrews of the Old Testament those animals that chew the cud and 'divide the hoof' (as ungulates) were clean and might be eaten. Hares and rabbits could not be eaten because, although they chew the cud, they do not divide the hoof. Pigs and camels were unclean, because, although they divide the hoof, they do not chew the cud. Birds of prey were accounted unclean. Fish with fins and scales were accounted fit food for man. Details of all that is clean and unclean are to be found in Leviticus 11.

According to PYTHAGORAS, who taught the doctrine of the TRANSMIGRATION OF SOULS, it was lawful for man to eat only those animals into which the human soul never entered, the others being held unclean. This notion existed long before the time of Pythagoras, who learned it in Egypt.

**Clean bill of health.** *See under* BILL OF HEALTH.

**Clean bowled.** In CRICKET, bowled by a ball that hits the wicket without first hitting the batsman or his bat. *See also* BOWLED OUT.

**Clean break, A.** A quick and final separation, as at the end of a marriage or relationship.

**Clean down, To.** To wash down; to swill down.

**Clean hands.** Freedom from guilt. A person innocent of some accusation may say: 'My hands are clean.' *See also* HAVE CLEAN HANDS *below*.

**Clean-limbed.** Having well-proportioned limbs, as of an athlete or a horse.

**Cleanliness is next to godliness.** An old saying, quoted by John Wesley (*Sermon* lxxxviii, 'On Dress' (1791)) and others. The origin is said to be found in the writings of Phinehas ben Yair, an ancient rabbi.

**Clean-living.** Upright in character.

**Clean out, To.** To purify; to make tidy. Also, to impoverish, by 'cleaning out' a person's pocket or purse. The analogy may be with gutting a fish or removing the viscera from a bird or animal before cooking them.

**Clean-shaven.** Without beard, whiskers or moustache.

**Clean sheet.** A record without any blemishes, or one cleared of any past offence or charge.

**Clean slate.** A freeing from accusations or imputations; a fresh start. Essentially the same as a CLEAN SHEET. The reference is to the slate blackboards formerly used in schools and the small writing slates used earlier by individual pupils.

**Clean up, To.** To wash up; to put in order. In North America, to make a big profit. In the American goldfields, to clean up was to wash the pieces of gold sifted from silt and mud.

**As clean as a whistle.** *See under* AS.

**Come clean, To.** *See under* COME.

**Good clean fun.** *See under* GOOD.

**Have clean hands, To.** To be quite clear of some stated evil. Hence to keep one's hands clean, not to be involved in wrongdoing.

**Keep a clean tongue, To.** To refrain from abusive language or swearing.

**Keep one's nose clean, To.** *See under* NOSE.

**Make a clean breast of it, To.** To make a full and unreserved confession, concealing nothing.

**Make a clean job of it, To.** To do something thoroughly.

**Make a clean sweep, To.** To make a complete change; to dispose of anyone or anything regarded as obsolete or harmful.

**New brooms sweep clean.** *See under* NEW.

**Show a clean pair of heels, To.** *See under* SHOW.

**Spring cleaning.** *See under* SPRING.

**Squeaky clean.** *See under* SQUEAK.

**Take to the cleaners, To.** To defraud or rob; also to criticize. If one robs a person of all their money, they are 'cleaned out'. The advent of the dry cleaning establishment brought this variant of the older expression. *See also* CLEAN OUT.

**Clear. Clearances, The.** *See* HIGHLAND CLEARANCES.

**Clear away, To.** To remove.

**Clear conscience, A.** An easy mind; a knowledge that one is right and cannot be blamed.

**Clearing bank.** Any bank that makes use of the central CLEARING HOUSE in London. The original nucleus of British clearing banks has in recent years been joined by building societies converting to banks.

**Clearing house.** An institution which 'clears' or cancels the amounts owed between banks (as a result of various cheques drawn on their accounts) so that only one sum need be paid by one bank to another. This system avoids individual transactions for each cheque since it simply produces a net debit or credit at the end of each day after all the different cheques have been taken into account. In London, the clearing house has been in Lombard Street since about 1770. 'Clearing house' is also used for any central agency that collects and distributes information, for example the Universities and Colleges Admission Service (UCAS), which handles applications from potential university students.

**Clear off, To.** To make oneself scarce; to remove oneself or something.

**Clear one's throat, To.** To cough slightly in order to make one's voice clear.

**Clear out, To.** To empty out; to make tidy.

**Clear round, A.** In showjumping, a round made without any fences being knocked down or any points lost.

**Clear the air, To.** To remove misunderstandings or ambiguities in a situation or argument. In a literal sense, the sun and wind usually clear the air after a thunderstorm.

**Clear the court, To.** To remove all strangers or persons not officially concerned in the case.

**Clear the decks, To.** To remove everything not required, especially when making ready for action. The allusion is to a sailing ship preparing for battle, when anything that was in the way of firing the guns was removed from the usually cluttered decks.

**Clear the land, To.** In nautical parlance, to have good 'sea room' or to escape from the land.

**Clear the room, To.** To remove from it every thing or person not required.

**Clear the table, To.** To remove what has been placed on it.

**Clear the way, To.** To remove obstacles.

**Clear up, To.** To become fine after rain or cloudy weather; to elucidate what was obscure; to tidy up.

**Clear winner, A.** An obvious winner; one who has won easily.

**Coast is clear, The.** *See under* COAST.

**In the clear.** Free of suspicion or blame; not guilty.

**Cleave.** This verb has two quite distinct meanings: on the one hand, 'to stick to', and on the other, 'to split apart'. An example of the former is: 'Therefore shall a man leave his father and his mother, and shall cleave unto his wife' (Genesis 2:24). An example of the latter is: 'Thou didst cleave the earth with rivers' (Habakkuk 3:9).

**Cleft stick, In a.** In a dilemma; in a situation in which one can go neither forwards nor backwards. The form of torture inflicted on ARIEL by the witch Sycorax in Shakespeare's *The Tempest* (I, ii (1611)) was to confine him in the trunk of a cleft pine tree.

**Clement.** The patron saint of tanners, and himself a tanner. His feast-day is 23 November, and his symbol is an anchor, because he is said to have been martyred by being thrown into the sea tied to one.

**Cleopatra** (Greek *Kleopatros*, 'born of a famous father'). Queen of Egypt (69–30 BC), as joint ruler with, and wife of, her brother Ptolemy Dionysius. In 48 she was driven from the throne, but was reinstated in 47 by Julius Caesar, by whom she had a son. In 41 Mark Antony fell under her spell and abandoned his wife Octavia. When he was defeated at Actium by Octavian, he committed suicide, and Cleopatra is said to have killed herself in turn by the bite of an asp on her breast in order to avoid being captured by Octavian.

**Cleopatra and her pearl.** It is said that Cleopatra gave a banquet for Antony at Alexandria, the cost of which aroused his astonishment. When Antony expressed his surprise she took a pearl eardrop and dissolved it in her drink in order to impress him even more.

A similar story is told about Sir Thomas Gresham when Queen Elizabeth I visited the ROYAL EXCHANGE. He is said to have drunk her health in a cup of wine in which a precious stone worth £15,000 had been crushed.

> Here fifteen thousand pounds at one clap goes
> Instead of sugar; Gresham drinks the pearl
> Unto his queen and mistress.
>
> THOMAS HEYWOOD: *If You Know Not Me You Know Nobody* (1604)

**Cleopatra's Needle.** The OBELISK so called, now on the Thames Embankment, was brought from Alexandria in 1878, where it and its fellow (now in CENTRAL PARK, New York) had been moved from Heliopolis by Augustus *c.*14 BC. It has no connection with Cleopatra other than having been in her capital, Alexandria, and was originally set up by Thothmes III *c.*1500 BC.

**Cleopatra's nose.** Blaise Pascal wrote, *Le nez de Cléopâtre: s'il eût été plus court, toute la face de la terre aurait changé*, 'Had the nose of Cleopatra been shorter, the whole face of the earth would have changed' (*Pensées*, ii, 162 (1670)). The allusion is to the momentous consequences that resulted from her conquest, through her charm and beauty, of both Julius Caesar and Mark Antony.

**Clergy.** The word derives ultimately from Greek *klēros*, 'heritage', with reference to the Levites, the priestly tribe of Levi whose inheritance was the Lord (Deuteronomy 10:9 and elsewhere).

**Clergyman's throat.** Chronic inflammation of the pharynx, to which clergymen and others who are habitually liable to overstrain the vocal organs were at one time frequently prone.

**Clerical titles.**

Clerk: in former times the clergyman or cleric (Ecclesiastical Latin *clericus*) was usually one of the few who could read and write. Hence clerk in general use as a word for a person whose business is writing, keeping records and the like. Clerk still has its ecclesiastical sense in the title clerk in holy orders for an ordained minister.

Curate: properly and originally, a clergyman who has the cure or care of souls in a parish. The word is now used, however, as a clergyman who assists a parish priest.

Parson: the same word as person, originally applied to a parish priest who held an ecclesiastical benefice, i.e. who was the same as a rector. The term is now used for any clergyman.

Rector: formerly, a parish priest entitled to the whole of the TITHES, as distinct from a VICAR. The word derives from Latin *rector*, 'director', 'ruler', meaning the priest who ruled and guided the parish.

Vicar: originally, a parish priest who did not receive tithes but a stipend, and who acted in place of the rector. His post as deputy was thus a vicarious one. The term is now used for a parish priest in general. In France the *vicaire* is the assistant in a parish, and the equivalent of the English curate, while the *curé* corresponds to the vicar.

**Clerical vestments.** There are five liturgical colours for clerical vestments and other liturgical objects, such as altar cloths, depending on the season of the ecclesiastical year.

White: the colour of purity, worn on all feasts, saints' days and many sacramental occasions.

Red: the colour of blood and of fire, worn on the feasts of apostles and martyrs, and (paradoxically) on Whit Sunday, when the HOLY GHOST came down like tongues of fire. Since 1970 it has also been used on PALM SUNDAY and GOOD FRIDAY.

Green: worn on Sundays and ferial days (neither feasts nor fasts) between EPIPHANY and LENT and between TRINITY SUNDAY and ADVENT.

Purple: the colour of mourning, worn in Advent and Lent, and sometimes for funerals.

Black: worn when masses are said for the dead, and until 1969 on Good Friday.

**Benefit of clergy.** *See under* BENEFIT.

**Secular clergy.** *See under* SECULAR.

**Clerihew.** The name given to a particular kind of humorous verse invented by E. Clerihew Bentley (1875–1956). It is usually satirical and often biographical, consisting of four rhymed lines of uneven length. A classic example is:

Sir Christopher Wren  
Said 'I am going to dine with some men.  
If anybody calls,  
Say I'm designing St Paul's.'

A more recent clerihew, not by Bentley, is:

Prime Minister John Major  
Was hardly an old stager;  
He cut little ice  
By simply being nice.  
A.R.

**Clerk. Clerk-ale.** *See* CHURCH-ALE.

**Clerk in holy orders.** The official title of a clergyman. *See also* CLERGY.

**Clerk of the Closet.** The title of the sovereign's principal chaplain. The office, now usually held by a diocesan bishop, arose in the 15th century and originated with a junior cleric who was responsible for the 'stuf of the closet', i.e. the material needs of the royal chapels (*see* CHAPEL ROYAL).

**Clerk of the course.** The secretary of the judges in horse or motor racing.

**Clerk of the House.** A senior official of the HOUSE OF COMMONS who reads whatever is required to be read in the House, who endorses bills sent or returned to the HOUSE OF LORDS, and who has custody of all records and other documents in the House.

**Clerk of the Peace.** Formerly, an official who kept county records and assisted JUSTICES OF THE PEACE in QUARTER SESSIONS. The post was abolished in 1972.

**Clerk of the weather.** A humorous personification of whatever forces govern the weather.

**Clerk of the works.** A person who supervises building work or the maintenance of existing buildings.

**Clerk to the Justices.** A lawyer who acts as adviser to the lay magistrates in a court.

**Parson and clerk.** *See under* PARSON.

**St Nicholas' clerks.** *See under* NICHOLAS.

**Clerkenwell.** This district of London takes its name from the well where clerks (in medieval terms, students) were accustomed to gather.

**Clever. Clever clogs.** A CLEVER DICK.

**Clever Dick.** A know-all, a SMART ALEC.

**As clever as they come.** *See under* AS.

**Box clever, To.** *See under* BOX.

**Clicquot.** A nickname of Frederick William IV of Prussia (1795–1861), so called from his fondness for champagne, in allusion to the well-known brand Veuve Clicquot. *See also* WIDOW.

**Cliff. Cliffhanger.** Figuratively, a state of affairs producing anxiety. The term derives from early American serialized adventure films, in which the hero or heroine was left in a perilous plight at the end of an episode in order to whet the audience's appetite for the next instalment. A classic exponent of the art was Pearl White, the star of *The Perils of Pauline* (1914), who frequently finished up dangling from the Palisades over the Hudson River. The suspense, in both senses of the word, ensured that the audience returned.

> There are enough cliffhangers this week to fill a wardrobe as Grant and Tiffany lurch from one marital crisis to another.
> *Radio Times* (12–18 September 1998)

**White cliffs of Dover, The.** *See under* WHITE.

**Climacteric.** It was once believed by astrologers that the seventh and ninth years, with their multiples, especially the odd multiples (21, 27, 35, 45, 49, 63 and 81), were critical points in life. These were called the climacteric years and were presided over by SATURN, the malevolent planet. Sixty-three, which is produced by multiplying 7 and 9 together, was termed the grand climacteric, which at one time few persons succeeded in outliving.

> When do the reasoning Powers decline?
> The Ancients said at Forty-Nine.
> At Forty-Nine behoves it then
> To quit the Inkhorn and the Pen.
> AUSTIN DOBSON: 'The Climacteric' (1889)

**Climb on the bandwagon, To.** To show support for a popular movement or trend with intent to profit or to reap easy material benefit. It was customary in the USA, particularly in southern states, for a band to play on a wagon through the streets to advertise a forthcoming meeting, political or otherwise. At election time local leaders would show their support of a candidate by climbing on the wagon and riding with the band.

**Clink.** A slang word for a prison, derived from the gaol, the Clink in SOUTHWARK, destroyed in the Gordon Riots of 1780. The prison itself may have been so called because its gates clinked shut on the prisoner.

**Clio** (Greek *kleos*, 'fame', 'glory'). One of the nine MUSES, the inventress of historical and heroic poetry, the Muse of history. Hence the old pun, 'Can Clio do more than amuse?'

Addison adopted the name as a pseudonym, and many of his papers in the *Spectator* are signed by one of the four letters in this word, allegedly the initial letters of the places where they were written: Chelsea, London, Islington or the Office. *See also* NOTARIKON.

**Clip. Clip joint.** A night club or place of entertainment where patrons are grossly overcharged or 'clipped'. The word alludes to the former practice of clipping gold and silver coins before passing them on.

**Clippie.** A nickname for a bus or tram conductress during and after the Second World War, from the fact that she clipped or punched the tickets.

**Clip someone's wings, To.** To reduce a person's conceit; to hamper their freedom of action. Birds with clipped wings cannot fly.

**Bulldog clip.** *See under* BULL.

**Coke's clippings.** *See under* COKE.

**Clipper.** A fast sailing ship, of a type first built at Baltimore in about 1830. Smyth's *Sailor's Word-Book* (1867) describes the word as 'formerly chiefly applied to the sharp-built raking schooners of America, and latterly to Australian passenger-ships'. The ship was so called because it clipped, or moved swiftly. In the 1930s the word came to be applied to a transatlantic flying boat. *See also* CUTTY SARK.

**Cliveden set, The.** The name given to the right-wing politicians and journalists who gathered for weekend parties in the late 1930s at Cliveden, the country home of Lord and Lady Astor in Buckinghamshire. They were alleged to favour the appeasement of NAZI Germany.

**Cloacina** (Latin *cloaca*, 'sewer'). The goddess of sewers.

> Then Cloacina, goddess of the tide,
> Whose sable streams beneath the city glide,
> Indulged the modish flame: the town she roved,
> A mortal scavenger she saw, she loved.
> JOHN GAY: *Trivia*, II (1716)

**Cloak and dagger plays.** Swashbuckling plays, full of fighting and adventure. The name comes from the *comedias de capa y espada*, literally, 'comedies of cloak and sword', as typified by the Spanish dramatists, Lope de Vega (1562–1635) and Calderón (1600–81). In France a comedy of this type was known as a *comédie de cape et d'épée*, and this is the direct source of the English phrase. Hence, the phrase 'cloak and dagger' has come to be used for any operation involving intrigue and espionage.

**Clock.** The word was originally used for a church bell. Hence the related word for 'bell' in other languages, such as French *cloche* and German *Glocke*.

The tale about Paul's clock striking 13 is given in Mackenzie Walcott's *Memorials of Westminster* (1849), and refers to John Hatfield, a soldier of William III's reign who died in 1770, aged 102. Accused before a court martial of falling asleep on duty on Windsor Terrace, he asserted in proof of his innocence that he heard St Paul's strike 13. His statement was confirmed by several witnesses.

Another incident is related concerning BIG BEN. On the morning of Thursday, 14 March 1861, 'the inhabitants of Westminster were roused by repeated strokes of the new great bell, and most persons supposed it was for the death of a member of the royal family. It proved, however, to be due to some derangement of the clock, for at four and five o'clock ten and twelve strokes were struck instead of the proper number.' Within 24 hours of this the Duchess of Kent (Queen Victoria's mother) was declared to be dying, and early on 16 March she was dead.

**Clock golf.** A form of putting on a green marked like a clock dial. The player putts from the position of each hour figure to the hole in or near the centre. *See also* CRAZY GOLF.

**Clock off** or **out, To.** To leave one's workplace, especially by registering the time of one's departure by inserting a card in a clock-based machine.

**Clock on, To.** To check in at one's workplace, especially by registering the time of one's arrival by entering a card in a clock-based machine.

**Clock-watch, To.** To watch the clock anxiously as one works with the aim of not exceeding minimum working hours.

**Beat the clock, To.** *See under* BEAT.

**Carriage clock.** *See under* CARRIAGE.

**Cuckoo clock.** *See under* CUCKOO.

**Grandfather clock.** *See under* GRANDFATHER.

**Put the clock back, To.** To revert to an earlier practice or way of life; also to put back the hands of a clock at the end of Summer Time. *See also* GREENWICH TIME; STANDARD TIME; SUMMER TIME.

**Put the clock on, To.** To put forward the hands of a clock, particularly at the beginning of Summer Time. *See also* GREENWICH TIME; STANDARD TIME; SUMMER TIME.

**Round the clock.** All day and (usually) all night.

> We're gonna rock around the clock tonight,
> We're gonna rock, rock, rock, 'til broad daylight,
> We're gonna rock, gonna rock around the clock
> tonight.
>
> MAX C. FREEMAN and JIMMY DE KNIGHT: 'Rock Around the Clock' (song) (1953).

**Run** or **go like clockwork, To.** *See under* RUN.

**Clog. Clog almanac.** A primitive almanac or calendar, originally made of a foursquare 'clog' or log of wood. Notches divided each of the sharp edges into three months each, every week being marked by a bigger notch. The faces contained the saints' days, the festivals, the phases of the moon and so on, sometimes in Runic characters, and for this reason the clog was also called a 'Runic Staff'. They are not uncommon and specimens may be seen in the British Museum, the Bodleian Library, the Ashmolean Museum and elsewhere. *See also* RUNE.

**Clog dance.** A rustic dance performed in clogs, associated in particular with Ireland and Lancashire. It is sometimes found in ballet, a noted example being the dance by Mother Simone in Frederick Ashton's production of *La Fille Mal Gardée* (1960).

**Clever clogs.** *See under* CLEVER.

**Cloister** (Medieval Latin *claustrum*, 'monastic cell', from Latin *claudere*, 'to close'). Most monasteries had a cloister or covered walk, which generally occupied three sides of a quadrangle. Hence 'cloistered' is applied to a secluded existence or way of life.

**Clootie, Auld.** *See under* AULD.

**Cloots, Anacharsis.** The adopted pseudonym of Jean-Baptiste du Val-de-Grâce, baron de Cloots (or Clootz) (1755–94), self-titled Orator of the Human Race, a Prussian nobleman of Dutch origin, who became a supporter of the French Revolution. He travelled Europe as a young man and was a member of the Convention. His name punningly mocked his aristocratic ancestry, as Greek *anacharsis* means 'graceless'. He was guillotined by Robespierre, who accused him of being a foreign agent.

**Close. Close battle.** Originally a naval engagement at close quarters, in which opposing ships engage each other alongside.

**Close call.** A narrow escape. The term is of American origin and may come from baseball, in which a decision called by an umpire could have gone either way, i.e. it was close.

**Closed book, A.** A person or thing that cannot be understood. 'Computers are a closed book to me,' means that I cannot understand anything about them.

**Close down, To.** To cease operations or activities, often permanently.

**Closed shop.** A term, first used in the USA, to characterize a workplace where all employees must belong to an agreed trade union.

**Close harmony.** A type of singing in which all the parts except the bass lie close together. *See also* BARBERSHOP.

**Close-hauled.** In nautical parlance, sailing with the sails flat, so as to follow a course as close to the wind as possible.

**Close in, To.** To begin to surround. When the evening closes in it begins to get darker, announcing the approach of night. When the days close in they begin to get shorter, announcing the approach of winter.

**Close one's eyes to, To.** To ignore deliberately.

**Close ranks, To.** To give one another mutual support in the face of an expected attack.

**Close season.** *See* SPORTING SEASONS IN ENGLAND.

**Close seasons for marriage.** These were formerly: from ADVENT to St Hilary's Day (13 January), SEPTUAGESIMA SUNDAY to LOW SUNDAY,

Rogation Sunday to TRINITY SUNDAY. They continued to be upheld in the English Church after the REFORMATION, but lapsed during the COMMONWEALTH.

The ROMAN CATHOLIC CHURCH does not allow nuptial MASS during what is left of the 'close season', i.e. between the first Sunday of Advent and the Octave of the EPIPHANY, and from ASH WEDNESDAY to Low Sunday.

**Close shave.** A narrow escape. The allusion is to the small margin between a smooth, closely shaven skin and a painful gash. A CLOSE CALL is synonymous.

**Close the books, To.** In BOOK-KEEPING, to balance acounts before preparing a statement.

**Closing time.** The time at which a pub must legally close.

**At close quarters.** *See under* AT.

**Sail close to the wind, To.** *See under* SAIL.

**Closet. Closet drama.** Plays that are better suited for reading rather than acting. Seneca wrote such plays in classical times, and many verse plays of the 19th century, such as those by Alfred de Musset and Tennyson, were written to be read. Several of the latter have, in fact, been staged with some success.

**Clerk of the Closet.** *See under* CLERK.

**Come out of the closet, To.** *See under* COME.

**Closure.** The ending of a HOUSE OF COMMONS debate by a member rising and saying, 'I beg to move that the question be now put.' The chair is not bound to accept the motion. The procedure was introduced in 1881 after Charles Stewart Parnell, leader of the Irish parliamentary party, conducted a deliberate policy of obstructing parliamentary business. As a result of his tactics, one sitting in February that year lasted from 4 pm on a Monday until 9.30 am the following Wednesday. *See also* FILIBUSTER; GUILLOTINE; KANGAROO.

**Cloth, The.** The word formerly applied to the customary clothes of any calling and was similar in usage to the word LIVERY. In the 17th century, however, it became restricted to the CLERGY and the clerical office. Hence 'respect for the cloth' and similar expressions.

**Cloth or flat cap.** A flat woollen cap with a stiff peak, a symbol of working-class origins or attitudes.

**Cloth-eared.** Deaf, in the sense of not hearing what is said to one.

**Field of the Cloth of Gold, The.** *See under* FIELD.

**Hickory cloth.** *See under* HICKORY.

**Clotho** (Greek *klōthein*, 'to draw thread', 'to spin'). One of the three FATES in classic mythology. She presided over birth and drew from her distaff the thread of life. *See also* ATROPOS; LACHESIS.

**Cloud. Cloud-Cuckoo-Land.** The *Nephelokokkygia* of *The Birds* by Aristophanes (*c*.450–*c*.385 BC), an imaginary city built in the air by the birds to separate the gods from humans. Hence the use of the name for any fantastic or impractical scheme.

**Battle above the Clouds, The.** *See under* BATTLE.

**Every cloud has a silver lining.** *See under* EVERY.

**In the clouds.** Out of touch with reality; unaware of the realities.

**On cloud nine.** Elated; very happy. The expression derives from terminology used by the US Weather Bureau. Clouds are divided into classes, and each class into nine types. Cloud nine is cumulonimbus, a cumulus cloud of great vertical extent, topped with shapes of mountains or towers.

**Under a cloud.** *See under* UNDER.

**War cloud.** *See under* WAR.

**With one's head in the clouds.** *See under* WITH.

**Cloudeslie, William of.** *See under* WILLIAM.

**Clough, Clym of the.** *See under* CLYM.

**Clout. Cast not a clout till May is out.** *See under* CAST.

**Colin Clout.** *See under* COLIN.

**Cloven hoof.** The mark or symbol of SATAN, represented with the legs and feet of a goat. However he disguised himself, he could never conceal his cloven feet. *See also* AULD CLOOTIE.

**Clover. Calvary clover.** *See under* CALVARY.

**Four-leaved clover.** *See under* FOUR.

**In clover.** In luck; in a state of ease or luxury. The allusion is to cattle feeding luxuriously in fields of clover.

**Pigs in clover.** *See under* PIG.

**Clovis.** The first king of the Franks and founder of the MEROVINGIAN DYNASTY (*c*.466–511). He succeeded his father at the age of 16 and matured to be a bold but prudent bandit and assassin, defeating the Alemanni, Burgundians, Visigoths and other peoples, and so gaining authority of the greater part of Gaul. He married Clotilda, a Christian princess, and was baptized a Christian himself. It was Clovis who selected Paris as the Gallic capital.

**Clown.** The clown of circus and PANTOMIME, in his baggy costume, whitened face, grotesque red lips and odd tuft of black hair is probably a relic of the DEVIL as he appeared in medieval miracle plays. He is the descendant of many court fools and jesters. Famous clowns have included Joseph GRIMALDI (1779–1837), 'Grock', the Swiss clown Adrien Wettach (1880–1959), and 'Coco', the Russian-born English clown, Nikolai Poliakov (1900–74). *See also* HARLEQUIN.

**Club.** In Britain the club has played an important part in social life. John Aubrey (1626–97) says 'we now used the word clubbe for a sodality in a taverne'. Some were political, such as the Rota, the October, the Green Ribbon and the eccentric Calves' Head Club. Others have been more riotous, like the MOHOCKS and the HELLFIRE CLUB. Clubs came into vogue in the reign of Queen Anne, as is evidenced by the *Tatler* and *Spectator*. Samuel Johnson's Ivy Lane Club (1749) and the Literary Club (1764), which he founded with Sir Joshua Reynolds, set a new standard in social clubs where like-minded men of culture could meet and converse. The latter included Edmund Burke, David Garrick, Oliver Goldsmith and James Boswell among its members. For many years clubs met in taverns and COFFEE houses and did not begin to occupy their own premises until the REGENCY. Many more sprang up in the early 19th century, with some, such as CROCKFORD'S (1828–44), being solely gaming clubs. The first exclusive modern ladies' club was the Alexandra (1883), to which no man was allowed admittance. Among the principal London clubs still flourishing in the late 1990s (with the dates of their foundation) are the following:

| | |
|---|---|
| Army and Navy: 1837 | Lansdowne: 1934 |
| ATHENAEUM: 1824 | National Liberal: 1882 |
| BEEFSTEAK: 1876 | Pratt's: 1841 |
| BOODLE'S: 1762 | Reform: 1836 |
| BROOKS'S: 1764 | Savage: 1857 |
| Buck's: 1919 | Savile: 1868 |
| Carlton: 1832 | Travellers': 1819 |
| GARRICK: 1831 | WHITE'S: 1693 |
| Groucho: 1985 | |

Some well-known clubs have merged. In 1976 the Guards Club moved to the home of the Cavalry Club to form the Cavalry and Guards Club. The United Service Club and the Royal Aero Club merged with the Naval and Military in 1976, retaining the name of the latter (*see* IN AND OUT). Others have closed.

Among the well-known clubs associated with sport are:

| | |
|---|---|
| MCC: 1787 | Royal Automobile: 1897 |
| Roehampton: 1901 | Turf: 1868 |

**Club-bearer, The.** In Greek mythology Periphetes, the robber of Argolis, is so called because he murdered his victims with an iron club.

**Club car.** A railway coach furnished as a lounge, often with a refreshment bar. Club cars, reserved for passengers paying a premium over the season ticket rate, were formerly provided on so-called club trains, long-distance commuter trains operating until the Second World War between Manchester and the North Wales coast, Manchester and the Fylde coast and Manchester and the Lake District, among other routes.

**Clubhouse.** The premises of a sports club, especially a golf club.

**Clubland.** That part of the West End of London centred around PALL MALL, where the principal clubs are situated.

**Club Parliament** or **Parliament of Bats, The.** A Parliament held at Northampton in 1426, during the quarrel between the Duke of Gloucester and Cardinal Beaufort. Forbidden to bear arms by the Regent Bedford, the members came armed with clubs or 'bats'.

**Club sandwich.** An American term for a 'three decker' sandwich of meat (especially chicken and bacon), tomato, lettuce and mayonnaise, usually with two layers of filling between the three layers of bread (or toast).

**Bannatyne Club.** *See under* BANNATYNE.

**Beefsteak Club.** *See under* BEEF.

**Caterpillar Club.** *See under* CATERPILLAR.

**Cordeliers Club.** *See under* CORDELIER.

**Darby and Joan club.** *See under* DARBY.

**Goldfish Club.** *See* CATERPILLAR CLUB.

**Hampden clubs.** *See under* HAMPDEN.

**Hellfire Club.** *See under* HELL.

**In and Out, The.** *See under* IN.

**Indian club.** *See under* INDIAN.

**In the club.** Pregnant.

**Jack of clubs.** *See under* JACK.

**Jockey Club.** *See under* JOCKEY.

**Kit-Cat Club.** *See under* KIT-CAT.

**Lions Clubs.** *See under* LION.

**Maitland club.** *See under* MAITLAND.

**Monday Club.** *See under* MONDAY.

**October Club.** *See under* OCTOBER.

**On the club.** Off work sick, especially when receiving sickness benefit.

**Other Club.** *See under* OTHER.

**Rotary Club.** *See under* ROTARY.

**Roxburghe Club.** *See under* ROXBURGHE.

**Slate club.** *See under* SLATE.

**Clue.** A 'clue' was originally a 'clew', i.e. a ball of thread. The only way of finding the way out of the Cretan LABYRINTH was by following a skein of thread.

**Not to have a clue.** To have no idea, to be completely baffled.

> 'Sorry, old boy,' he said. 'I haven't a clue.'
>
> EDWARD HYAMS: *Sylvester*, ch ix (1951)

**Cluniacs.** In 10th-century France discipline in the BENEDICTINE abbeys had declined almost completely and wealth and luxury predominated. At Cluny, northwest of Mâcon, a reformed abbey was established in 910, and in due course many abbeys adopted the monks' rigid rule. By the end of the 12th century there were over 300 European monasteries linked with Cluny, and some 30 or so Cluniac houses in England, including those of Bermondsey, Reading and Faversham. As with the Benedictines, wealth and laxity took over and the next major revival was that of the CISTERCIANS.

**Cluricaune** (Irish *clúracán*). An ELF in Irish folklore. He is of evil disposition and usually appears as a wrinkled old man. He has a knowledge of hidden treasure and is the fairies' shoemaker. Another name for him is LEPRECHAUN.

**Clutch** or **catch at straws, To.** *See* DROWNING MEN CLUTCH AT STRAWS.

**Clydesdale horses.** *See* SHIRE HORSES.

**Clydesiders, The.** A loose association of left-wing MPs representing Glasgow and Clydeside constituencies, who enlivened British politics and Parliament from 1922 until they were much diminished in numbers following the 1931 election. Notable among them were John Wheatley, of Housing Act fame, Campbell Stephen, Emanuel Shinwell and, best known of all, James Maxton, who became chairman of the INDEPENDENT LABOUR PARTY. They acted as a GINGER GROUP for the Labour Party and were notable champions of the poor and unemployed.

**Clym of the Clough.** A noted archer and outlaw, who forms the subject of a ballad in PERCY'S RELIQUES, together with Adam Bell and WILLIAM OF CLOUDESLIE. The three became as famous in the north of England as did ROBIN HOOD and LITTLE JOHN in the Midlands. They were presumed to have lived before Robin Hood and to have made their home in Englewood Forest, near Carlisle. The name means Clement of the Cliff.

**Clytemnestra** (Greek *Klutaimnēstra*, from *klutos*, 'famous', and *mnēstēr*, 'wooer'). In Greek legend the wife of AGAMEMNON, whom she killed on his return from the TROJAN WAR. She was a daughter of Tyndarus and LEDA. *See also* ELECTRA.

**Clytie.** In classical mythology an ocean NYMPH, in love with APOLLO. She was deserted by him and changed into the heliotrope or sunflower, which, traditionally, still turns to the sun, following him through his daily course. A painting of the subject by Lord Leighton is in the Fitzwilliam Museum, Cambridge.

**Cnidian Venus, The.** *See* VENUS OF CNIDUS.

**Cnut.** *See* CANUTE.

**Coach.** When railways replaced horse-drawn road transport in the 1830s and 1840s they took over the old coaching terms as the steamship did from the days of sail. Carriage, coach, driver, guard and passenger are all reminiscent of former coaching days. By the 1990s, however, with modernization and commercialization, many such terms had been superseded, as in 1988 all British Rail passengers became 'customers' while guards on InterCity trains were 'conductors' or 'senior conductors'. The original horse-drawn coach got its name from Hungarian *kocsi szekér*, 'wagon of Kocs', this being the village in Hungary where coaches were first made.

The coach who is a private tutor or sports trainer is probably so called because he 'carries' his pupils.

**Devil's coach-horse.** *See under* DEVIL.

**Devil's coach-wheel.** *See under* DEVIL.

**Drive a coach and horses through, To.** *See under* DRIVE.

**Coade stone.** An artificial stone of great durability and firmness of outline, much used from the 1770s until the 1830s for statues and ornamentations for buildings (CARYATIDES, keystone masks, friezes, vases etc). It was made from a kind of frost-resistant terracotta and was produced in Mrs Eleanor Coade's factory at Lambeth (later the firm of Coade and Sealy). The huge red lion, for long a familiar figure on London's South Bank from 1837, is an example of its use. The secret of its manufacture has been lost.

**Coal. Call** or **haul over the coals, To.** *See under* CALL.

**Carry coals to Newcastle, To.** *See under* CARRY.

**Heap coals of fire on, To.** *See under* HEAP.

**White coal.** *See under* WHITE.

**Coalition government.** A government formed of normally opposed parties, usually in times of crisis, when party differences are set aside. Examples are those of Fox and North (1783), of WHIGS and PEELITES under Aberdeen (1852–5), of CONSERVATIVES and LIBERAL UNIONISTS under Salisbury (1895–1902), of LIBERALS, UNIONISTS and LABOUR under Asquith (1915–16) (reformed under Lloyd George, 1916–22), Macdonald's NATIONAL GOVERNMENT (1931–5) and Winston Churchill's Coalition Government (1940–5).

**Coast. Coastal Command.** The RAF command that operated over the sea from coastal bases in Britain in the Second World War.

**Coaster.** A vessel engaged in coastal trade. The word also came to apply to a travelling container, often on castors or wheels, for passing food and drink (such as cheese, wine and beer) along large tables. They were commonly used in England in the 18th and early 19th centuries, and some were elaborate representations of carts and other wheeled vehicles. Hence the much more modest coaster that is now simply a mat for a glass.

**Coast is clear, The.** There is no likelihood of interference. The expression was originally a smuggling term, implying that no coastguards were about.

**Coast to coast.** Across an island or continent, from one coast to the other.

**Barbary Coast, The.** *See under* BARBARY.

**Pearl Coast, The.** *See under* PEARL.

**Slave Coast, The.** *See under* SLAVE.

**Coat. Coat card.** *See* COURT CARDS.

**Coat of arms** or **coat armour.** Originally a linen or silken surcoat worn by a knight to protect his armour from the sun's heat, dirt and the like, with the wearer's arms embroidered upon it as a distinguishing device. The use of coats of arms probably began in the 12th century. In HERALDRY the coat of arms is made up of the shield, helmet, crest, mantling and supporters. The shield is the central part.

**Coat of mail.** In medieval times, a protective garment made of mail (linked metal rings) or of overlapping metal plates.

**Coat of many colours.** *See under* JOSEPH.

**Cut one's coat according to one's cloth, To.** *See under* CUT.

**Doggett's Coat and Badge.** *See under* DOGGETT.

**Holy Coat.** *See under* HOLY.

**Trail one's coat, To.** *See under* TRAIL.

**Cob.** A short-legged, stout variety of horse, rather larger than a pony, from 13 to nearly 15 HANDS high (a hand is 4in/10cm). The word cob is of uncertain origin, but it is often used of something big and stout or hard and round. Hence cobble, cob loaf and cobnut.

**Cobalt** (German *Kobalt*, from Middle High German *kobolt*, 'goblin'). This metal, from which a deep blue pigment is made, was so called by miners partly because it was thought to be useless and partly because the arsenic and sulphur, with which it was found in combination, had bad effects on their health and on the silver ores. They therefore named it after the malicious mine demon who they believed had put it there.

**Cobb & Co.** A legendary Australian mail and passenger coach company, founded by Freeman Cobb and three other Americans in 1854, during the Ballarat gold rush, and providing reliable and comfortable transport between Melbourne and Bendigo in American-built coaches. Later, under the ownership of James Rutherford, another American, the company absorbed or eclipsed rival firms and secured a monopoly throughout Victoria, New South Wales and Queensland. At the height of its prosperity the company covered 28,000 miles (45,000km) a week, but the growth of railway and motor transport brought inevitable decline, although the last run was made as late as 1924. Tales of the exploits of Cobb & Co's crack drivers are as exciting as those of WELLS FARGO.

> Behind six foaming horses, and lit by flashing lamps,
> Old Cobb and Co., in royal state, went dashing past the camps.
>
> HENRY LAWSON: *The Roaring Days* (1889)

**Cobber.** An Australian colloquial word for a friend or companion, probably from an old dialect verb to cob, meaning to form a friendship.

**Cobbler.** An iced drink, typically made of sherry, sugar and lemon.

> This wonderful invention, sir ... is called a cobbler: Sherry cobbler, when you name it long, cobbler when you name it short.
>
> DICKENS: *Martin Chuzzlewit*, ch xvii (1843–4)

The name is also that of a hot fruit pie with no bottom crust and a top crust resembling scone or plain cake dough. It may have come to be so called from the resemblance of the uneven surface of the top crust to cobble stones.

**Cobbler Poet, The.** Hans Sachs of Nuremberg (1494–1576), prince of the MEISTERSINGER of Germany, who was trained as a cobbler.

**Cobblers.** A slang word for nonsense or rubbish. It is a shortened form of 'cobblers' awls', RHYMING SLANG for balls.

> Geno Washington says Grapefruit's recent attack on the Maryland Club, Glasgow, was 'a load of cobblers'. They are one of the best audiences in Britain, says Geno.
>
> *Melody Maker* (5 October 1968)

**Cobbler should stick to his last, A.** Each person should confine himself to his own affairs and not meddle in matters of which he is ignorant.

There is the story of a cobbler who detected a fault in a shoe latchet in a painting by APELLES. The artist rectified the fault. The cobbler then ventured to criticize the legs, but Apelles answered: 'Keep to your trade: you understand about shoes, but not about anatomy.'

**Cobham's Plot.** *See* MAIN PLOT.

**Coburg loaf.** A type of round loaf with a cross cut in the top, said to have been named in honour of the marriage of Prince Albert of Saxe-Coburg-Gotha to Queen Victoria in 1840.

**Cobwebs, To blow away the.** *See under* BLOW.

**Coca-Cola.** The carbonated drink was the invention in 1886 of John S. Pemberton, an American pharmacist. It is uncertain how he concocted the blend of ingedients that first went into the product, but his book-keeper, Frank Robinson, devised a name that indicated the source of two of the extracts: coca leaves and the cola nut. Coca leaves yield cocaine, a form of which was originally present in Coca-Cola. Hence the curative claims initially made for it, so that people took it for dyspepsia, headaches and similar malaises. The drink came to be nicknamed Coke, and the manufacturers registered this as an alternative name in 1920 as their exclusive property. Thus, while cola can be used as a general name for any carbonated drink made from cola nuts, Coca-Cola and Coke cannot.

**Cock.** In classical mythology the cock was dedicated to APOLLO because it announces the sunrise. It was also dedicated to MERCURY, because it summons people to business by its crowing, and to AESCULAPIUS, because 'early to bed and early to rise makes a man healthy'.

Muslim legend says that the Prophet found in the first heaven a cock of such enormous size that its crest touched the second heaven. The crowing of this celestial bird arouses every living creature except man. When this cock ceases to crow, the DAY OF RECKONING (Day of Judgement) will be at hand.

The WEATHERCOCK is a very old symbol of vigilance. As the cock heralds the coming of day, so does the weathercock tell what the weather is likely to be.

**Cock-a-doodle-doo.** The traditional English rendering of a cock crowing. In France they go *cocorico*, in Germany *kikeriki*, in Italy *chicchirichì*, in Spain *quiquiriquí* and in Russia *kukareku*. The English word has been influenced by 'cock' itself.

**Cock-a-hoop.** Jubilant, exultant, in high spirits. The expression may derive from the phrase to set the cock a hoop, meaning to live luxuriously, from literally putting a cock (the bird) on a hoop or full measure of grain. Equally, the word could derive from the fact that when the spigot or cock is removed from the beer barrel and laid on a hoop of the barrel, the beer flows freely.

**Cock-a-leekie.** A traditional Scottish soup made with boiling fowl ('cock') and leeks.

**Cockalorum.** A self-important little man, or the boasting ('crowing') of such a man. The word seems to be a combination of cock and the Latin genitive plural ending *-orum*, as if overall meaning 'cock of cocks'.

> 'Dies mies!—Hocus pocus—
> Adsis Demon! non est jokus!
> Hi Cocolorum—don't provoke us!
> Adesto! Presto! Put forth your best toe!'
> R.H. BARHAM: *Ingoldsby Legends*, 'The Lord of Thoulouse' (1840)

**Cock and Bottle** and **Cock and Pie.** Both are PUBLIC HOUSE SIGNS. The latter is probably The Cock and Magpie and the former probably means that draught and bottled beer are sold on the premises, with cock here meaning 'tap'.

**Cock and bull story.** A highly coloured or unbelievable story; a CANARD; a tale devised to serve as an excuse. The phrase possibly derives from old fables in which cocks and bulls and other animals conversed. Richard Bentley's *Boyle Lecture* (1692) has:

> That cocks and bulls might discourse, and hinds and panthers hold conferences about religion.

The 'hind and panther' allusion is an obvious reference to John Dryden's poem *The Hind and the Panther* (1687), and 'cocks and bulls' probably had a familiar meaning at the time. The final words in Laurence Sterne's *Tristram Shandy* (1759–67) are:

> L—d! said my mother, what is all this story about?—
> A Cock and a Bull, said Yorick – And one of the best of its kind, I ever heard.

The Cock and Bull inn sign is found in the 17th century and both Cock and Bull as separate signs were always popular. There is a story at Stony Stratford, Buckinghamshire, that in the coaching days the London coach changed horses at the Bull Inn and the Birmingham coach at the Cock. From the exchange of jests and stories between the waiting passengers of both coaches the 'Cock and Bull' story is said to have originated.

Today both 'cock' and 'bull' are used individually to denote an unlikely story, although 'bull' is of a different origin and 'cock' has come to be popularly (if erroneously) associated with the coarse sense of the word.

> I've never heard such cock in all my life.
> NEVIL SHUTE: *No Highway* (1948)

**Cock an eye, To.** To shut one eye and look with the other in a cheeky or furtive manner, to glance at questioningly. *See also* COCKEYE.

**Cock a snook, To.** To put the thumb to the nose and spread out the fingers. A rude gesture also sometimes known as Queen Anne's fan.

**Cockboat.** A small boat; any very light or frail craft. The word perhaps comes ultimately from Late Latin *caudica*, 'dug-out canoe', itself from Latin *caudex*, 'tree trunk'. An alternative form of the name is cockleboat.

**Cockcrow.** In biblical times the Hebrews divided the night into four WATCHES: (1) the 'beginning of the watches' or 'even' (Lamentations 2:19), (2) the 'middle watch' or 'midnight' (Judges 7:19), (3) the 'cockcrowing' (Mark 13:35), and (4) the 'morning watch' or 'dawning' (Exodus 14:24).

> Watch ye therefore: for ye know not when the master of the house cometh, at even, or at midnight, or at the cockcrowing, or in the morning.
> Mark 13:35

The Romans divided the day into 16 parts, each one hour and a half, beginning at midnight. The third of these divisions (beginning at 3 am) they called *gallicinium*, the time when cocks begin to crow (Latin *gallus*, 'cock'). The next division was *conticinium*, when they ceased to crow (*conticescere*, 'to become silent'), and the fifth was *diluculum*, 'dawn'.

If the Romans sounded the hour on a trumpet three times it would explain the diversity of the Gospels: 'The cock shall not crow, till thou hast denied me thrice' (John 13:38), 'The cock shall not crow this day, before that thou shalt thrice deny that thou knowest me' (Luke 22:34), 'This night, before the cock crow, thou shalt deny me thrice' (Matthew 26:34) and 'In this night, before the cock crow twice, thou shalt deny me thrice' (Mark 14:30).

According to a Christian superstition, apparitions vanish at cockcrow. Hence the cock as the watch-bird on church spires. *See also* WEATHERCOCK.

> The morning cock crew loud,
> And at the sound it [the Ghost] shrunk in haste away,
> And vanish'd from our sight.
> SHAKESPEARE: *Hamlet*, I, ii (1600)

**Cocked hat.** A hat with its brims turned up and brought together to give either two points (a bicorn) or, more commonly, three points (a tricorn). The second of these is traditionally worn as part of full dress by diplomats and naval and army officers. Cocked here means 'turned up'. *See also* KNOCK INTO A COCKED HAT.

**Cockeye.** An eye that squints.

**Cockeyed.** Having a squint; cross-eyed. It may mean that such an eye has to be cocked, as the trigger of a gun is cocked, before it can do its work effectively or it may be from the verb 'to cock' in the sense of 'to turn up' as in to COCK THE EARS. Cockeyed also means not straight, out of the true, as well as absurd or nonsensical.

> When it's Summer in the north, it's Winter in the south. Completely cockeyed.
> ARTHUR KOESTLER: *Twilight Bar* (1945)

**Cockfighting.** A favourite sport with both Greeks and Romans, cockfighting was introduced into Britain by the Romans. From the 12th to the 19th century cockfighting and throwing objects at cocks was the sport of schoolboys on SHROVE TUESDAY, and the triumphant boy, holding the winning bird in his hands, was sometimes carried aloft by some of his companions. This may be the origin of the old schoolboy phrase 'cock of the school'. The COCKPIT at WHITEHALL was added by Henry VIII and the 'royal diversion' was very popular with James I and Charles II. Cockfighting was made illegal in Britain in 1849. *See also* BATTLE ROYAL; WELSH MAIN.

**Cock Lane Ghost.** A phrase formerly used for a tale of imagined terrors. In 1762 mysterious knockings were heard at 33 Cock Lane, Smithfield, which William Parsons, the owner, said came from the ghost of his sister-in-law, Fanny Kent, who had recently died of smallpox. Parsons, with the hope of blackmail, wished people to think that she had been poisoned by her husband. All London was agog with the story. Royalty and the nobility made up parties to go to Cock Lane to hear the ghost. Dr Johnson and other learned people investigated the alleged phenomena. Eventually it was found that the knockings were made by Parsons' 11-year-old daughter rapping on a board that she took into her bed. Parsons was condemned to the pillory. *See also* STOCKWELL GHOST.

**Cock of hay** or **haycock** (perhaps of Scandinavian origin, as Norwegian *kok*, 'heap'). A small heap of hay thrown up temporarily.

**Cock of the North.** George, 5th Duke of Gordon (1770–1836), who raised the Gordon Highlanders in 1795, is so called on a monument erected to his honour at Fochabers in Morayshire.

**Cock of the walk.** The leader of a gang or clique, especially someone who pompously asserts himself. The place where barn-door fowls are fed is the walk, and if there is more than one cock, they will fight for the supremacy of this domain.

**Cock one's head, an arm, a leg etc, To.** To raise or turn up some part of the body, often cheekily or jauntily. The allusion is to a cock stretching its neck when crowing, or to its erect crest or tail. When a dog cocks a leg it raises a hind leg at an angle to urinate.

> 'Dessert?' asked the waitress, cocking one hip and resting a hand on it.
> LISA ALTHER: *Other Women*, II, ch vi (1984)

**Cockpit.** The arena in which gamecocks were set to fight, also the name of a theatre built *c.*1618 on the site of a cockpit in DRURY LANE. The word was also used for the after part of the orlop deck of an old man-of-war (formerly used as quarters for junior officers and as a sickbay in battle). Hence the modern use of cockpit for the area near the stern of a small yacht where the helmsman sits, the driver's compartment in a racing car and the pilot's compartment in an aircraft.

**Cockpit of Europe, The.** Belgium is so called because it has so frequently been the battleground of Europe, as is evidenced by Ramillies (1706), Oudenarde (1708), Fontenoy (1745), Fleurus (1794), Jemmapes (1792), Ligny, Quatre Bras and Waterloo (1815), Mons, Ypres and the continuous battles of the First World War (1914–18) and the German invasion of 1940.

**Cock Robin.** A nickname for the robin, strictly, the male bird only. Cock is applied to other birds similarly, such as cock sparrow.

**Cockscomb.** *See* COXCOMB.

**Cockshy.** A throw or 'go' at something. The allusion is to the once popular SHROVE TUESDAY 'sport' of throwing stones or sticks at a cock, which was given as a prize to the person who hit it. The phrase was popular in military circles in the Second World War for an ill-judged or ill-prepared attempt at something.

**Cocksure.** Assertively certain; overconfident. The term is of uncertain origin. The first part of the word may originally have been 'God', but it became associated with 'cock', as if meaning 'with all the assurance of a gamecock' or 'as certain as the cock is to crow in the morning'.

**Cock the ears, To.** To prick up the ears, as a horse or dog does when it hears a strange sound.

**Cock-up.** An error; a 'bungle'. The term may derive from printers' jargon for a letter that 'cocks up', or rises above the level of other letters in a line of print.

**Knock into a cocked hat, To.** *See under* KNOCK.

**Ride a cockhorse, To.** *See under* RIDE.

**Cockade** (earlier *cockard*, from obsolete French *cocard*, 'arrogant', 'strutting', from *coq*, 'cock'). A badge, feather or ribbon worn on certain military or royal headwear. The English cockade is black and circular in shape with a projecting fan at the top, except for naval officers, for whom the shape is oval without the fan. This form was introduced from Hanover by George I. Under Charles I the cockade was scarlet, but Charles II changed it to white. Thus the white cockade became the badge of the House of Stuart. William III (as Prince of Orange) adopted an orange cockade.

**White Cockade.** *See under* WHITE.

**Cockaigne.** An imaginary land of idleness and luxury, famous in medieval story. George Ellis in his *Early English Poets* (1803) gives an early translation of a 13th-century French poem called *The Land of Cockaign* in which 'the houses were made of barley sugar cakes, the streets were paved with pastry and the shops supplied goods for nothing'. The name derives from Old French *cocaigne*, from Middle Low German *kokenje*, 'little cake'. London has been so called, with punning reference to COCKNEY. Hence Elgar's concert overture *Cockaigne* (1900), subtitled 'In London Town'. Scotland is called the LAND OF CAKES.

**Cockatrice.** A fabulous and heraldic monster with the wings of a fowl, the tail of a DRAGON and the head of a cock. It is otherwise known as a BASILISK. Figuratively, a cockatrice is an insidious or treacherous person. The origin of the word is in Medieval Latin *cockatrix*, from Late Latin *calcatrix*, 'trampler', 'tracker', translating Greek *ikhneumon*, ICHNEUMON.

> And the sucking child shall play on the hole of the asp, and the weaned child shall put his hand on the cockatrice' den.
>
> Isaiah 11:8

**Cocker, According to.** *See under* ACCORDING.

**Cockle. Cockleboat.** *See* COCKBOAT.

**Cockle hat.** A pilgrim's hat. Pilgrims used to wear cockleshells on their hats as the symbol of St JAMES THE GREAT of COMPOSTELA. The polished side of the shell was scratched with some crude drawing of the Virgin, the crucifixion or some other object related to the pilgrimage. When blessed by the priest, the shells were considered amulets against spiritual foes and could also be used as drinking vessels.

> How should I your true love know
> From another one?
> By his cockle hat and staff,
> And his sandal shoon.
>
> SHAKESPEARE: *Hamlet*, IV, v (1600)

**Cockleshell.** A small boat or frail craft. The film *Cockleshell Heroes* (1955) told how a group of marines in the Second World War went by canoe to Bordeaux to fix limpet mines to German ships. *See also* COCKLE HAT.

**Hot cockles.** *See under* HOT.

**Warm the cockles of one's heart, To.** *See under* WARM.

**Cockney.** The word represents an earlier spelling *cokeney*, literally 'cock's egg', used as a nickname for the small, malformed egg occasionally laid by young hens, as distinct from a genuine 'hen's egg'. This then came to be applied by country folk to townsfolk generally for their reputed ignorance of country life and customs. Its restriction to working-class Londoners, particularly those born within the sound of Bow bells, dates from the 17th century. Cockney is also used to denote the characteristic London dialect or accent, with its RHYMING SLANG, dropped h's ("Arry') and th pronounced as v ('bruvver'). *See also* MOCKNEY.

**Cockney School, The.** A nickname given by Lockhart to a group of writers including Leigh Hunt, William Hazlitt, Percy Bysshe Shelley and John Keats. It was used derogatorily on account of the kind of rhymes they used in their verse, which smacked too much of everyday life instead of the classic purity preferred by the critics.

> If I may be permitted to have the honour of christening it, it may be henceforth referred to by the designation of the 'Cockney School'.
>
> JOHN LOCKHART: *Blackwood's Magazine* (October 1817)

**King of Cockneys, The.** *See under* KING.

**Cocktail.** An aperitif, or short drink taken before a meal, normally consisting of spirits, bitters and fruit juice or other flavourings. There are many varieties. The origin of the name is uncertain, but suggestions vary from 'a tail that cocks up' to the name of an Aztec princess Xochitl, who is supposed to have given a drink to the king with romantic results. It may simply be a drink that makes you feel perky, like a cock's tail. Coquetel, a mixed drink from the wine-growing district of the Gironde, has also been suggested as a possible source. The term first emerged in American society in the early 19th century.

The name also applies to a horse with a docked tail which 'cocks up', as well as to a halfbreed horse. The reference is to the custom of docking stagecoach horses and hunters, which were normally not thoroughbreds.

The social side to cocktails has led to a number of associated terms. A cocktail dress is a short evening dress worn at such parties. A cocktail stick is a small pointed stick used either for spearing an olive or cherry in a cocktail or for eating a very small sausage. A cocktail lounge is a room in a hotel or restaurant where cocktails and other drinks are served. The cocktail party phenomenon is the ability to listen to what two or more people are saying at once.

The only reason for a cocktail party
For a gluttonous old woman like me
Is a really nice tit-bit.

T.S. ELIOT: *The Cocktail Party*, I (1950)

**Coconut, Milk in the.** *See under* MILK.

**Cocytus.** One of the five rivers of hell, which flows into the ACHERON. The name derives from Greek *kōkuein*, 'to weep', 'to lament'. The unburied were doomed to wander about its banks for 100 years. *See also* CHARON; STYX.

**Cod, To.** To tease or deceive. The word may have evolved as a short form of 'codger', a term for an old or eccentric person, itself perhaps a variant of CADGER. *See also* OLD CODGER.

**Code. Code Napoléon.** The code of laws prepared (1800–4), under the direction of NAPOLEON BONAPARTE and based on work begun by a committee of the Convention and so called in 1807. It forms the basis of modern French law and is only second in importance to the code of Justinian. Equality in the eyes of the law, justice and common sense are its keynotes.

**Amalfitan Code.** *See under* AMALFITAN.

**Clarendon Code.** *See under* CLARENDON.

**Colour code.** *See under* COLOUR.

**Green Cross Code.** *See under* GREEN.

**Highway Code, The.** *See under* HIGHWAY.

**Codex, Alexandrian.** *See under* ALEXANDRIAN.

**Codger, Old.** *See under* OLD.

**Codswallop.** Nonsense. The word is of uncertain origin, but the following story is sometimes offered to account for it. In 1875 Hiram Codd patented a mineral water bottle with a marble stopper. Wallop is a slang term for beer. Thus Codd's wallop is said to have become a disparaging term among beer drinkers for mineral waters and weak drinks and in due course gained a more general application.

All that stuff about mutual respect between police and criminal was a load of old codswallop.

ALLAN PRIOR: *The Operators*, ch vi (1966)

**Coenobites** or **Cenobites** (Greek *koinobion*, 'convent', from *koinos*, 'common', and *bios*, 'life'). Monks who live in common, as distinct from hermits or anchorites.

**Coeur de Lion** (French, 'lion heart'). Richard I of England (r.1189–99) was so nicknamed for his valour in the Third CRUSADE.

**Coffee** (ultimately from Arabic *qahwah*, 'coffee', 'wine'). The first coffee house in England opened at Oxford in 1650 and the first in London *c.*1652. They soon became centres for social and political gossip and meeting-places for the wits and literary men of the day. *See also* BALTIC; CHOCOLATE; CLUB; LLOYD'S; TOM'S; WHITE'S.

**Coffee morning.** A social event at which morning coffee is served, the aim being to raise money for charity or some other cause.

**Coffee-table book.** A large, well-produced, well-illustrated book, designed more to be looked at than read, and traditionally kept on a coffee table, a long, low table on which newspapers can be placed and coffee served.

**Great Piazza Coffee House.** *See under* GREAT.

**Grecian Coffee House.** *See under* GRECIAN.

**Rose Coffee House, The.** *See under* ROSE.

**Will's Coffee House.** *See under* WILL.

**Coffin nail.** A cigarette. An expression in use long before the association between cigarette smoking and lung cancer was recognized but probably connected with the risk to health from cigarettes. *See also* NAIL IN SOMEONE'S COFFIN.

**Coggeshall job, A.** Something foolish. It is said that the Coggeshall (Essex) folk wanted to divert the current of a stream, and so fixed hurdles in its bed. Another tale is that a mad dog bit a wheelbarrow, and the people, fearing the wheelbarrow's madness, chained it up in a shed. *See also* WISE MEN OF GOTHAM.

**Cogito, ergo sum.** *See* CARTESIAN PHILOSOPHY.

**Cognoscenti** (through Italian from Latin *cognoscere*, 'to know'). People with a critical, expert and thorough knowledge of a subject, especially in literature, music and the fine arts; in other words, connoisseurs.

**Coin** (Old French *coin*, 'corner', 'stamping die', from Latin *cuneus*, 'wedge'). The die for stamping out money was often wedge-shaped and so came to be known as a coin. The word then passed to the money itself. *See also* ANGEL; BAWBEE; CAROLUS; CROSS AND PILE; DECIMAL CURRENCY; DOLLAR; FARTHING; FLORIN; GROAT; GUINEA; MANCUS; PENNY; PIECES OF EIGHT; SHILLING; SOVEREIGN.

**Coin a phrase, To.** To invent a phrase, which if it is apt or imaginative may gain currency, and become popular generally. Today this phrase is mostly used ironically to accompany a banal remark or cliché.

Who, to coin a phrase, would have thought of meeting you?

NGAIO MARSH: *Hand in Glove*, ch iv (1962)

**Corpse coins.** *See under* CORPSE.

**Crown in English coinage, The.** *See under* CROWN.

**Kufic coins.** *See under* KUFIC.

**Pay someone (back) in their own coin, To.** *See under* PAY.

**Sweat a coin.** *See under* SWEAT.

**Coke.** Slang for cocaine. *See also* COCA-COLA.

**Coke's clippings.** The colloquial name for the sheep-shearing gatherings held at Holkham, Norfolk, from 1778, by Thomas William Coke, Earl of Leicester (1752–1842), renowned for his pioneering work in agriculture. That of 1818 lasted a week, during which time he kept open house for some 600 people from all ranks of society, including foreign visitors. As many as 7000 people attended annually. Mornings were spent inspecting the land and stock, and after a three o'clock dinner the remainder of the day was taken up with discussions, toasts and speeches on farming topics. Similar gatherings were instituted by the Duke of Bedford at Woburn, Lord Egremont at Petworth and so on.

**Colcannon.** A dish of Irish origin made of potatoes and cabbage, pounded together and then fried in butter. The word represents Irish *cál ceannan*, 'white-headed cabbage'. *See also* BUBBLE AND SQUEAK.

**Colcannon night.** HALLOWEEN in parts of northeast Canada, when it is traditional to eat this dish.

**Cold. Cold Bath Fields.** A district of CLERKENWELL, London, so called from the cold baths established there in 1697 for the cure of rheumatism, convulsions and other nervous disorders. The Fields were renowned for the prison that was opened there in 1794 and closed in 1877. Leigh Hunt's brother, John, was an inmate from 1813 to 1815, for his part in an article ridiculing the Prince Regent. *See also* ADONIS.

**Cold-blooded.** Of animals, all except birds and mammals. Of people, unemotional, pitiless.

**Cold call.** An unsolicited call at the door or by telephone made by a salesperson to a potential customer.

**Cold chisel.** A steel chisel that has been toughened so that it will cut cold metal when struck with a hammer.

**Cold comfort.** Little or no consolation. Cold comfort is little comfort to the recipient.

**Cold Comfort Farm.** A phrase sometimes used to imply that a place of residence is untidy and comfortless. It is from a humorous novel of this title by Stella Gibbons.

> If she intended to tidy up life at Cold Comfort, she would find herself opposed at every turn by the influence of Aunt Ada ... Persons of Aunt Ada's temperament were not fond of a tidy life.
>
> STELLA GIBBONS: *Cold Comfort Farm*, ch v (1932)

**Cold feet.** A state of fear or apprehension; a 'funk'.

**Cold fish.** An unemotional, impassive person.

**Cold shoulder, The.** A show of intentional indifference; a deliberate slight. The expression is said to relate to medieval times, when a host offered an unwelcome guest a meal of cold shoulder of mutton, this being the normal fare for the servants of a household.

**Cold steel.** Bayonets, swords, knives and the like as weapons, as distinct from 'hot' weapons, such as guns and rifles.

**Cold sweat.** A chilly or moist skin caused by fear or nervousness.

**Cold turkey.** A way of curing drug addiction by abruptly discontinuing all doses or supplies. The allusion is to the unpleasant after-effects, which usually include COLD SWEAT and 'goose flesh', like the skin of an uncooked turkey. There is also an implied contrast with warm cooked turkey, with its pleasant taste and smell.

**Cold war.** A state of tension, distrust and mutual hostility between states or groups of countries, without recourse to actual warfare.

**Cold-water ordeal.** A former method of testing guilt or innocence. The accused person was tied under the arms and thrown into a river. If he sank, he was held guiltless and pulled out by the rope. If he floated, the water rejected him because of his guilt. *See also* WITCH-HUNTING.

**As cold as a paddock.** *See under* AS.

**As cold as charity.** *See under* AS.

**Blow hot and cold.** *See under* BLOW.

**Diplomatic cold.** *See under* DIPLOMAT.

**From cold.** *See under* FROM.

**In cold blood.** Showing no emotion; deliberately or calculatedly; not in the excitement of passion or battle. The allusion is to the old notion that the temperature of the blood ruled the emotions.

**Leave one cold, To.** *See under* LEAVE.

**Ordeal by cold water.** *See under* ORDEAL.

**Out in the cold.** *See under* OUT.

**Throw** or **pour cold water on, To.** *See under* THROW.

**Colditz.** A byword for a bleak prison or for any generally forbidding or unwelcoming edifice. Colditz Castle, in the town of this name about 30 miles (48km) from Leipzig, Germany, was a notorious prisoner-of-war camp in the Second World War and the site of many daring escape bids by Allied officers. The building and its name became widely known to the post-war generation from the highly popular television series *Colditz* (1972–4). Its 28 episodes were based on the books by Major Pat Reid and retold the ruses devised by British officers to effect a breakout.

**Coldstream Guards.** One of the five regiments of Foot Guards, historically General Monk's Regiment, which crossed the border at Coldstream in Berwickshire to effect the RESTORATION of Charles II in 1660. It became the 2nd

Regiment of Footguards in 1661, and in 1670 was officially called the Coldstream Guards.

**Cole, Old King.** *See under* OLD.

**Colettines.** *See* FRANCISCANS.

**Colin Clout.** A name which Spenser assumes as a shepherd's boy in *The Shepheardes Calender* (1579) and again in the pastoral *Colin Clout's Come Home Againe* (1595), which represents his return from a visit to Sir Walter Ralegh, 'the Shepherd of the Ocean'. John Skelton had previously (*c*.1520) used the name (in the form *Collyn Clout*) as a title of a satire directed against the abuses of the church. 'Clout' was formerly used for a clod of earth.

**Coliseum.** *See* COLOSSEUM.

**Collar. Collar, To.** To seize (a person) by the collar; to steal; to appropriate.

**Collar the bowling, To.** In CRICKET to hit the bowling all over the field so that it becomes easier to score, since the bowlers lose their length.

**Dog collar.** *See under* DOG.

**Get hot under the collar, To.** *See under* HOT.

**Spit and rub collar.** *See under* SPIT.

**White-collar workers.** *See under* WHITE.

**Colleen Bawn** (Irish *cailín bán*, 'fair maid'). An Anglo-Irish term for a marriageable young Irish girl. She was individualized in literature as the 'poor but honest' girl who is the heroine of Dion Boucicault's melodrama, *The Colleen Bawn* (1860). She is Eily O'Connor, secretly married to Hardress Cregan, who needs to marry the heiress Anne Chute in order to save his family's fortunes. He instructs his servant to kill Eily, but the attempt is frustrated by the vagabond Myles-na-Coppaleen, who loves Eily and is content to see her restored to her repentant husband. The play was based on Gerald Griffin's 'true-life' crime novel *The Collegians* (1829).

**College** (Latin *collegium*, 'company, 'society', i.e. 'band of colleagues'). In English the word has a wide range, as College of Surgeons, Heralds' College, College of Justice and College of Preceptors. It is most commonly used for a separate foundation of teachers and scholars within a university and for a wide range of educational institutions, including many schools, e.g. Eton College, Winchester College and Cheltenham Ladies' College.

In old slang a prison was known as a college, and the prisoners as collegiates. NEWGATE was 'City College' or 'New College' and to take one's final degree at New College was to be hanged. The King's Bench Prison was 'King's College' and so on.

**College cap.** A TRENCHER CAP, like the caps worn at the English universities.

**College of Cardinals** or **Sacred College.** This was originally formed from the clergy of the see of Rome. It now contains members from many nations who take their titles, as has always been customary, from a Roman parish. It consists of cardinal bishops, cardinal priests and cardinal deacons (the latter possibly deriving from the seven deacons appointed by St PETER), but these terms are essentially of historical significance only, as all cardinals are now consecrated bishops. The number of cardinals was fixed at 70 by Sixtus V in 1586. John XXIII (r.1958–63) raised it to 87, and there is now no upper limit. In 1994 there were 143 cardinals. The pope is elected by and from the College of Cardinals.

**College port.** The vintage port laid down in university college cellars for the special use of the Senior Common Room. The excellence of this is a source of college pride.

**College pudding.** A small baked or steamed suet pudding with dried fruit. The name may be an abbreviation of New College Pudding.

**All Souls College.** *See under* ALL.

**Brasenose College.** *See under* BRASENOSE.

**Caius College.** *See under* CAIUS.

**City College, The.** *See under* CITY.

**Corpus Christi College.** *See under* CORPUS.

**Dean of the Sacred College.** *See under* DEAN.

**Exeter College.** *See under* EXETER.

**Magdalen** and **Magdalene Colleges.** *See under* MAGDALENE.

**Queen's** and **Queens' Colleges.** *See under* QUEEN.

**Collegiate church.** A church that has a college or chapter of CANONS or prebends under a DEAN. There were many such churches in medieval England, but they were mainly suppressed during the reign of Edward VI (1547–53). St George's Chapel, Windsor and Westminster Abbey are surviving examples. Some of them eventually became cathedrals of new dioceses, for example at Manchester and Ripon.

**Collins.** A word formerly applied to the 'thank you letter' one writes after staying at another person's house. In Jane Austen's *Pride and Prejudice* (1813) Mr Collins appears as a bore and a snob. After a protracted and unwanted stay with the Bennets his parting words are: 'Depend upon it, you will speedily receive from me a letter of thanks for this, as for every mark of your regard during my stay in Hertfordshire' (ch xxi).

**John Collins.** *See under* JOHN.

**Tom Collins.** *See* JOHN COLLINS.

**Colly bird.** An old popular name for a blackbird. Colly is a dialect word for coal dust, from Old English *col*, 'coal'. The traditional song 'The Twelve Days of Christmas' has:

> The Fourth day of Christmas my true love sent to me,
> Four colly birds, Three French hens, Two turtle doves,
> And a partridge in a pear tree.

Modern versions of this Christmas carol have substituted 'calling birds' for 'colly birds'.

**Cologne. Eau de Cologne.** *See under* EAU.

**Three Kings of Cologne, The.** *See under* THREE.

**Colonel.** When an officer in the British Army is promoted to the rank of colonel he loses his regimental identity and becomes a member of the Staff Corps. The titular head of a regiment is also called the colonel and is usually a distinguished serving or retired General. The titular head of a Territorial Army regiment is called the Honorary Colonel.

**Colonel Bogey.** A name given in golf to an imaginary player whose score for each hole is settled by the committee of the particular club and is supposed to be the lowest that a good average player could do it in. It is usually the same as par at a hole, but among American players is often one stroke above par. To beat the bogey or the colonel is to play the hole in a lesser number of strokes. Colonel Bogey is also the name of a well-known military march tune (1913) by K.J. Alford.

**Colophon** (Greek *kolophōn*, 'finishing stroke'). Originally, as the name implies, the tail-piece at the end of a book giving the printer's name, the date and place of printing and so on, sometimes with laudatory remarks designed to promote sales. It survives in the brief information usually given on the recto (front) or verso (back) of the title page. The term is now applied to a printer's or publisher's house device, such as the penguin on PENGUIN BOOKS or La BELLE SAUVAGE formerly on the title pages of books published by Cassell.

The Ionian city of Colophon was famed for its horsemen, who were always reputed to turn the tide of battle by their last charge. Hence, in popular etymology, this name for the final part of the book.

**Colorado.** The North American river, and hence the American state, was so named by the Spanish explorers from its coloured appearance, from Spanish *colorado*, 'red'.

**Colosseum.** The great Flavian amphitheatre of ancient Rome, said to be named from the colossal statue of NERO that stood close by in the Via Sacra. It was begun by Vespasian in AD 72, and for 400 years was the scene of gladiatorial contests. The name has since been applied to other amphitheatres and places of amusement, sometimes in the form of the Coliseum. *See also* PALLADIUM.

**Colossus** (Latin, from Greek *kolossos*, 'giant statue'). The bronze colossus of Rhodes, completed by Chares about 280 BC, was a representation of the sun god HELIOS, and the statue commemorated the successful defence of Rhodes (305–304) against Demetrius Poliorcetes. It was one of the SEVEN WONDERS OF THE WORLD and probably stood some 100ft (30m) high. It was destroyed by an earthquake in 224. The story that it was built astride the entrance to the harbour and that ships could pass between its legs is of 16th-century origin and is not found in Strabo's or Pliny's descriptions.

**Colour or colours. Colour bar.** The discrimination by people of one colour against those of another, usually that shown by whites against blacks.

**Colour blindness.** A term introduced by Sir David Brewster (1781–1868), the inventor of the kaleidoscope, to denote the various forms of defective colour vision or perception. It is also known as Daltonism after the scientist John Dalton (1766–1844), who first described it in 1794 and who also suffered from it. Inability to perceive any colours as such is called total colour blindness. Complete partial colour blindness is where some bright colours are confused, as opposed to incomplete partial colour blindness, where composite and neutral shades are not recognized.

**Colour code.** A method of indicating different items or objects in a set by the use of colour, for example in electrical wiring.

**Colour of one's money, The.** The amount one has and that can be paid.

**Colour sergeant.** The sergeant who carries the REGIMENTAL COLOURS or other colours in a parade or ceremony.

**Colours in symbolism.**

Black:

- In blazonry: sable, denoting prudence, wisdom and constancy
- In art: denoting evil, falsehood and error
- In church decoration: denoting a funeral, and formerly, GOOD FRIDAY
- As a mortuary colour: denoting grief, despair, death; in the Roman Catholic Church violet may be substituted for black
- In metals: represented by lead
- In precious stones: represented by the DIAMOND
- In planets: stands for SATURN

Blue:

- Hope, the love of divine works, and (in dresses) divine contemplation, piety, sincerity
- In blazonry: azure, denoting chastity, loyalty, fidelity
- In art: (as an angel's robe) denoting fidelity and faith; (as the robe of the Virgin Mary) modesty; (in the Roman Catholic Church) humility and expiation
- In church decoration: blue and green were used equally for ordinary Sundays in the pre-Reformation Church
- As a mortuary colour: denotes eternity (applied to a deity), immortality (applied to man)
- In metals: represented by tin
- In precious stones: represented by sapphire
- In planets: stands for JUPITER

Pale blue:

- Peace, Christian prudence, love of good works, a serene conscience

Green:
Faith, gladness, immortality, the resurrection of the just, and (in dresses) the gladness of the faithful
In blazonry: vert, denoting love, joy, abundance
In art: denotes hope, joy, youth, spirit; among the Greeks and Moors it denotes victory
In church decoration: denotes God's bounty, mirth, gladness, the resurrection, and is used for weekdays and Sundays after TRINITY
In metals: represented by COPPER
In precious stones: represented by the emerald
In planets: stands for VENUS

Pale green:
Baptism

Purple:
Justice, royalty
In blazonry: purpure, denoting temperance
In art: denotes royalty
In church decoration: used for ASH WEDNESDAY and Holy Saturday
In metals: represented by quicksilver
In precious stones: represented by AMETHYST
In planets: stands for MERCURY

Red:
Martyrdom for faith, charity, and (in dresses) divine love
In blazonry: gules; blood red is called sanguine; the former denotes magnanimity, the latter fortitude
In church decoration: used for martyrs and for Whit Sunday
In metals: represented by iron (the metal of war)
In precious stones: represented by the ruby
In planets: stands for MARS

Violet, brown or grey:
In church decoration: used for ADVENT and LENT; in other symbolism violet usually stands for penitence, and grey for tribulation

White:
In blazonry: argent, denoting purity, truth, innocence
In art: priests, MAGI and DRUIDS are arrayed in white; Jesus after the resurrection is usually draped in white
In church decoration: used for festivals of our Lord, for MAUNDY THURSDAY and for all saints except martyrs
As a mortuary colour: indicates hope
In metals: represented by silver
In precious stones: represented by the pearl
In planets: stands for DIANA or the moon

Yellow:
In blazonry: or, denoting faith, constancy, wisdom, glory
In modern art: denoting jealousy, inconstancy, moral laxity; in France the doors of traitors used to be daubed with yellow, and in some countries Jews were obliged to dress in yellow; in Spain the executioner is dressed in red and yellow
In Christian art: JUDAS ISCARIOT is arrayed in yellow; but St PETER is also arrayed in golden yellow
In metals: represented by gold
In precious stones: represented by the topaz
In planets: stands for APOLLO or the sun

**Colour up, To.** To go red in the face; to flush; to blush.

**Accidental colour.** *See under* ACCIDENTAL.

**Body colour.** *See under* BODY.

**Cape Coloured.** *See under* CAPE.

**Complementary colour.** *See under* COMPLEMENTARY.

**Desert one's colours, To.** *See under* DESERT.

**Fast colour.** *See under* FAST.

**Fundamental colour.** *See under* FUNDAMENTAL.

**Get one's colours, To.** To be rewarded for prowess in sport by the privilege of wearing school, college or university colours on the appropriate garment. *See also* CAPPED; FLANNELLED FOOLS.

**Horse of a different colour, A.** *See under* HORSE.

**King's or Queen's Colour, The.** *See under* KING.

**Nail one's colours to the mast, To.** *See under* NAIL.

**Off colour.** *See under* OFF.

**Primary colour.** *See under* PRIMARY.

**Regimental colours.** *See under* REGIMENTAL.

**Sail under false colours, To.** *See under* SAIL.

**Secondary colour.** *See under* SECONDARY.

**See things in their true colours, To.** *See under* SEE.

**Show one's true colours, To.** *See under* SHOW.

**Take on a different colour, To.** *See under* DIFFERENT.

**Trooping the Colour.** *See under* TROOPING.

**Under colour of.** *See under* UNDER.

**University colours.** *See under* UNIVERSITY.

**Wear someone's colours, To.** *See under* WEAR.

**With flying colours.** *See under* WITH.

**With the colours.** *See under* WITH.

**Colporteur.** Formerly, a hawker or PEDLAR, especially of Bibles and religious books. The word probably comes from Old French *comporter*, 'to carry', but it was popularly interpreted as *porter à col*, 'to carry on the neck', since colporteurs carried their baskets or packs in this way.

**Colt.** The word basically applies to a young male horse under the age of four. Hence its use for a young male, especially an awkward one, or a person who needs to be 'broken in'. In sport a colt is either a young and inexperienced player or a member of a junior team. With a capital letter, a Colt is a type of revolver invented by the American firearms manufacturer Samuel Colt in 1835.

**Shoe the wild colt, To.** *See under* SHOE.

**Columbine.** A stock character in old Italian comedy from *c.*1560 and transferred to English PANTOMIME. She was the daughter of Pantaloon and the sweetheart of HARLEQUIN, and, like him, was supposed to be invisible to mortal eyes. *Columbina* in Italian is a pet name for a 'lady love', and means 'dove-like'. *See also* PANTALOONS.

**Columbo.** The dishevelled, one-eyed Italian-American police lieutenant in the television series of the 1970s named after him, played by Peter Falk. His trademarks are his shabby raincoat and his trick of talking inconsequentially about his dragon wife, then turning back at the door to ask one final, vital question.

**Columbus.** Born in Genoa and working for Spain, Christopher Columbus (1451–1506) set sail on 3 August 1492 on a journey that led to his momentous discovery of the NEW WORLD. Legend tells how he was the only person who believed the world was round, although this view was by then widely accepted. Another story is that he secured funds for his voyage through a romantic involvement with Queen Isabella of Spain. His name is borne by many places, including the Canadian province of British Columbia, the South American state of Colombia and the city of Columbus, capital of Ohio. The Italians know him as Cristoforo Colombo and the Spanish as Cristóbal Colón.

**Columbus' egg.** An easy task once one knows the trick. The story is that COLUMBUS, in reply to a suggestion that other pioneers might have discovered America had he not done so, is said to have challenged the guests at a banquet in his honour to make an egg stand on end. When none succeeded, he flattened one end of the egg by tapping it against the table and so stood it up, thus indicating that others might follow but that he had discovered the way.

**Columbus of the Skies, The.** Sir William Herschel (1738–1822), German-born discoverer of the planet URANUS, was so called. The name has also been applied to others, notably Galileo (1564–1642), Tycho Brahe (1546–1601) and Sir Isaac Newton (1642–1727).

**Knights of Columbus.** *See under* KNIGHT.

**Column. Column at Boulogne** or **Column of the Grand Army, The.** A marble DORIC column 176ft (54m) high carrying a bronze statue of NAPOLEON BONAPARTE, to commemorate the camp that was formed at Boulogne in 1804 in preparation for the invasion of England.

**Column of July, The.** The column erected in Paris in 1840 on the site of the BASTILLE to commemorate the July Revolution of 1830 when Charles X abdicated. It is a bronze column 154ft (47m) high, surmounted by a gilded statue of Liberty.

**Column of Marcus Aurelius** or **Antonine Column, The.** The column erected at Rome in honour of the Emperor Marcus Aurelius Antoninus (AD 121–180), covered like that of TRAJAN with spiral bas-reliefs representing the emperor's wars. It is a Roman DORIC column of marble 95ft (29m) high on a square pedestal. Pope Sixtus V ordered the original statue on this column to be replaced by a figure of St PAUL in 1589.

**Column of the Place Vendôme, The.** A column erected in Paris (1806–10) in honour of Napoleon I. It is made of marble encased with bronze, and the spiral outside in bas-relief represents his battles, ending with Austerlitz (1805). This imitation of TRAJAN'S COLUMN is 142ft (43m) high. The statue of NAPOLEON BONAPARTE at the top was hurled down by the COMMUNARDS in 1871 but replaced in 1874.

**Columns** or **Pillars of Hercules.** *See under* PILLAR.

**Agony column.** *See under* AGONY.

**Dodge the column, To.** *See under* DODGE.

**Duke of York's Column, The.** *See under* DUKE.

**Fifth column.** *See under* FIFTH.

**Infernal column.** *See under* INFERNAL.

**London's Column.** *See* MONUMENT.

**Nelson's Column.** *See under* NELSON.

**Trajan's Column.** *See under* TRAJAN.

**Coma Berenices.** *See* BERENICE.

**Comb. Fine-tooth comb.** *See under* FINE.

**Reynard's wonderful comb.** *See under* REYNARD.

**Combe, Duke.** *See under* DUKE.

**Combinations.** A type of underwear that varies according to the sex and age of the wearer. For men it is usually a garment that covers both legs and body, as a sort of 'long johns'. For women and children it can be any garment that combines two normally separate pieces, typically chemise and knickers, but also bodice and petticoat or knickers and petticoat. It first came into vogue in the 1880s. Its American equivalent is the 'union suit'. Like most intimate garments it has its pet name, usually combies or combs (or coms).

**Come. Come a cropper, To.** To fall heavily or fail badly. The origin probably lies in 'neck and crop', meaning 'altogether', 'completely'.

**Come again?** What did you say?

**Come-all-ye.** A type of ballad or folk-song consisting of a strong, simple narrative with little dialogue and usually ending with a moral reflection. Double ballad metre is the traditional form, and a typical first line is: 'Come all ye young maidens.'

**Come along, To.** To progress; to hurry up.

**Come and go, To.** To pass to and fro; to be transitory.

> In the room the women come and go
> Talking of Michelangelo.
>
> T.S. ELIOT: *Love Song of J. Alfred Prufrock* (1917)

**Come back to, To.** To return to; to reply after a delay.

**Come back** or **down to earth, To.** To abandon fantasy for reality.

**Come by, To.** To acquire, often implying that the action may have been 'accidental-on-purpose'.

**Come clean, To.** To tell the whole truth; to make a frank admission; to reveal everything.

**Come, come.** An expression of annoyance or impatience.

**Comedown, A.** A loss of prestige or position; a disappointment.

**Come down, To.** To leave a university at the end of a term or finally.

**Come down on, To.** To reproach, to punish.

**Come down on someone like a ton of bricks, To.** To punish or reprimand them severely.

**Come February, Christmas, Sunday etc.** When February etc comes. A colloquialism popular with radio and television weather forecasters.

> Come Lammas-eve at night shall she be fourteen.
> SHAKESPEARE: *Romeo and Juliet*, I, iii (1594)

**Come forward, To.** To offer one's help or services.

**Come from behind, To.** To win after lagging or trailing.

**Come good, To.** To recover; to turn out well in the end, possibly after a poor start.

**Come hell or high water.** Come what may. The expression may be a fanciful variant of BETWEEN THE DEVIL AND THE DEEP (BLUE) SEA.

**Come-hither look.** An enticing or seductive look, as of a woman to a man.

**Come home to roost, To.** Usually said of a lie, fault, misdeed or the like, which eventually rebounds on its perpetrator.

**Come into one's own, To.** To become fulfilled; to enter one's element.

**Come it over, To.** To try to impose on someone. Other words are frequently used in place of it, such as to COME THE OLD SOLDIER OVER.

> I'm not proposing to let any bimbo come the man of chilled steel over me just because I happen to kiss an old friend.
> P.G. WODEHOUSE: *The Luck of the Bodkins*, ch xi (1935)

**Come it strong, To.** To LAY IT ON THICK; to exaggerate or overdo.

**Come of, To.** To result from.

**Come off, To.** To occur; to succeed.

**Come off it!** Stop exaggerating; I don't believe that. The person so addressed is being figuratively advised to dismount from his lofty steed. *See* ON ONE'S HIGH HORSE *under* HIGH.

**Come on, To.** To improve; to hurry.

**Come-on, A.** A lure or enticement.

**Come out, To.** To make one's debut in society. The phrase was formerly used of a young woman after she had been presented at Court. The verb can also mean to come out on strike. *See also* COME OUT OF THE CLOSET.

> Like all rituals of initiation, 'coming out' creates its own bonding. Which for today's young career-minded female ... means cultivating a flurry of contacts.
> *Sunday Times* (18 September 1994)

**Come out of one's shell, To.** To cease to be shy and withdrawn; to become friendly and communicative. The allusion is to a tortoise rather than to a snail.

**Come out of the closet** or **come out, To.** To reveal publicly that one is homosexual. Clandestine homosexuals are sometimes referred to as 'closet queens'.

**Come over, To.** To experience a particular sensation, as in 'to come over all hot'.

**Come over all queer, To.** To feel suddenly giddy, faint, 'poorly' or the like.

**Come rain or shine.** Whatever the weather.

**Come round, To.** To recover consciousness; to change one's view or opinion.

**Come the old soldier over, To.** To dictate peremptorily and profess superiority of knowledge and experience, to impose.

> But you needn't try to come the old soldier over me, I'm not quite such a fool as that.
> THOMAS HUGHES: *Tom Brown at Oxford*, Pt II, ch xvii (1861)

**Come to, To.** To amount to; to regain consciousness.

**Come to a head, To.** To reach a crisis. The allusion is to the ripening, or coming to a head, of a boil or ulcer.

**Come to a sticky end, To.** To suffer an unpleasant death.

**Come to blows, To.** To turn a quarrel or argument into a physical assault or fight.

**Come to grief, To.** To meet with disaster; to be ruined.

**Come to hand, To.** To be received; to come within reach; to turn up.

**Come to life, To.** To become animate or conscious; to appear realistically.

**Come to light, To.** To be discovered or disclosed.

**Come to nothing, To.** To result in failure; to fail to materialize.

**Come to one's senses, To.** To regain consciousness; to be sensible after being foolish.

**Come to pass, To.** To happen; to come about. A literary phrase, common in the biblical usage, 'And it came to pass'.

**Come to stay, To.** To come as a guest; to come and remain permanently.

**Come to terms, To.** To make an agreement with; to reach an acceptance.

**Come to that.** If that is so.

**Come to the fore, To.** To come into notice; to distinguish oneself.

**Come to the point, To.** To speak out plainly; to avoid circumlocution; to get to the nub of the matter.

**Come under, To.** To be classified under.

**Come** or **go under the hammer, To.** To be sold at auction. The reference is to the rap of the auctioneer's hammer indicating that a lot is sold.

**Come up, To.** To start one's first term at a university.

**Come up against, To.** To encounter opposition.

**Come up smiling, To.** To laugh at one's misfortune; to 'bounce back'.

**Come up to, To.** To equal; to amount to the same quantity.

**Come up to scratch, To.** To be ready or good enough in any test; to make the grade. Under the London Prize Ring Rules, introduced in 1839, a round in a prize fight ended when one of the fighters was knocked down. After a 30-second interval, this fighter was allowed eight seconds in which to make his way unaided to a mark scratched in the centre of the ring. If he failed to do so, he 'had not come up to scratch' and was declared beaten.

**Come up with, To.** To produce.

**Come what may.** Whatever happens.

**Backwards in coming forwards, To be.** *See under* BACK.

**Get one's comeuppance, To.** To get one's deserved fate or punishment.

**How come?** *See under* HOW.

**If it comes to that.** *See under* IF.

**If the worst comes to the worst.** *See under* IF.

**It will all come out in the wash.** *See under* WASH.

**Make** or **stage a comeback, To.** To return successfully to one's former position or status after withdrawing from it.

**Marry come up.** *See under* MARRY.

**Second Coming, The.** *See under* SECOND.

**You've come to the wrong shop.** I can't help you; I can't give you the information you require.

**Comedy** (Greek *kōmōidia*, from *kōmos*, 'village festival', and *aeidein*, 'to sing'). Greek comedy appears to have originated from village revels, with certain elements of the festivities connected with the worship of Dionysus (*see* BACCHUS). The chorus probably derives from the practice of Attic revellers masquerading as birds, frogs, fishes and the like. *See also* TRAGEDY.

**Ealing comedies.** *See under* EALING.

**Father of Comedy, The.** Aristophanes (*c*.450–385 BC), the Athenian dramatist.

**Light comedian.** *See under* LIGHT.

**Low comedy.** *See under* LOW.

**Comfort. Cold comfort.** *See under* COLD.

**Cold Comfort Farm.** *See under* COLD.

**Creature comforts.** *See under* CREATURE.

**Dutch comfort.** *See under* DUTCH.

**Job's comforter.** *See under* JOB.

**Comic strip** or **cartoon.** A series or strip of drawings in a newspaper, telling a story, usually one episode per issue.

**Commander of the Faithful.** The CALIPH was so called by Muslims.

**Commandment. Eleventh commandment, The.** *See under* ELEVENTH.

**Ten Commandments.** *See under* TEN.

**Ten commandments, The.** *See under* TEN.

**Commando** (Afrikaans *kommando*, from Dutch *commando*, 'command'). Originally, an armed unit of Boer horsemen on military service. They were particularly active in the Kaffir or Frontier Wars (1779–1877), although the term was in South African use long after that.

In the Second World War the name was adopted for a member of the specially trained British assault troops formed from volunteers to undertake particularly hazardous tasks and originally, in 1940, to repel a German invasion of England.

> Plans should be studied to land secretly by night on the islands and kill or capture the invaders. This is exactly one of the exploits for which the Commandos would be suited.
>
> WINSTON CHURCHILL: *The Second World War*, ii (1948: these words written in 1940)

**Comme il faut** (French, 'as it should be'). Correct(ly), proper(ly); according to etiquette.

**Commemoration.** *See* ENCAENIA.

**Commissioners, The Ecclesiastical.** *See under* ECCLESIASTICAL.

**Committee. Committee of the Whole House.** In parliamentary parlance, all the MPs in the Chamber, regarded as a committee formed to examine three types of BILL: one that is uncontroversial, one that is urgent, or one that is constitutionally crucial, such as a Bill to reform the HOUSE OF LORDS. The SPEAKER leaves the chair, the mace is placed under the table, and the chair is taken by the chairman of the COMMITTEE OF WAYS AND MEANS. Any member may speak more than once.

**Committee of Ways and Means, The.** The name given in the HOUSE OF COMMONS to a COMMITTEE OF THE WHOLE HOUSE, which authorizes the Government to raise money for the upkeep of public services and approves new, altered or revised forms of taxation.

In addition, it also authorizes payments from the CONSOLIDATED FUND for these purposes. The uses to which the money is put are controlled by the Committee of Supply. The chairman of Ways and Means is the Chairman of Committees, the Deputy SPEAKER.

**Joint committee.** *See under* JOINT.

**L-committee.** *See* L-COMMITTEE.

**Select committee.** *See under* SELECT.
**Standing committee.** *See under* STAND.
**Steering committee.** *See under* STEER.
**Vigilance committee.** *See under* VIGILANCE.

**Commodore** (probably from Dutch *commandeur*). A naval officer ranking above a captain and below a rear admiral; of equivalent rank to a brigadier in the army. By courtesy, the title is given to the senior captain when two or more ships are in company. A commodore is also the title of the president of a yacht club.

The title was abolished in the United States Navy in 1899, except as a retiring rank for captains.

**Common.** Short for common land, which cannot be enclosed without an ACT OF PARLIAMENT. The enclosure of common land was a source of friction and discontent over the centuries and was not halted until the Commons Preservation Act of 1876. *See also* MANOR; OPEN-FIELD SYSTEM.

**Common law.** Originally the unwritten law of custom of the king's courts (except of Equity). From the late 15th century precedent began to be accepted, and it gradually superseded local customs until the 19th century, when precedent and case-made law predominated. *See also* STATUTE.

**Common-law wife.** A term applied to a woman cohabiting with a man as in a marriage relationship but based on mutual agreement and not on any civil or religious rite. Her partner has to maintain their children but she has no legal status under COMMON LAW.

> A judge objected to the use of the phrase 'Common Law Wife' by a barrister at a trial at Southend Crown Court yesterday ... 'Nowadays there is no stigma about unmarried people living together.'
> *Daily Telegraph* (4 December 1974)

**Common Market.** The former popular name for the European Economic Community (from 1993 European Union), the economic association set up by the Treaty of Rome in 1957 and consisting of Belgium, France, West Germany, Italy, Luxembourg and the Netherlands. It was joined by Britain, Denmark and Ireland in 1973, by Greece in 1981, by Spain and Portugal in 1986, by the former East Germany in 1990 and by Austria, Sweden and Finland in 1995. A Single Market came into effect in 1993 to overcome barriers to trade between individual member countries. A single European currency is planned for 2002 with a complete replacement of national currencies by the EURO.

**Common or garden.** Ordinary. The term is a mock-botanical formula.

**Common sense.** Ordinary good and practical judgement. The expression formerly denoted a supposed internal sense held to be common to all the senses, or one that acted as a link between them. *See also* SEVEN SENSES.

**As common as muck.** *See under* AS.
**Book of Common Prayer, The.** *See under* BOOK.
**Century of the Common Man, The.** *See under* CENTURY.
**Greenham Common.** *See under* GREENHAM.
**Rights of common.** *See under* RIGHT.

**Commoner.** A member of the ordinary people, below the rank of peer, and hence a member of the HOUSE OF COMMONS. The title is also used for a person with RIGHTS OF COMMON and, at some universities and colleges, for a student not on a scholarship.

**Great Commoner, The.** *See under* GREAT.

**Commons. Doctors' Commons.** *See under* DOCTOR.
**House of Commons.** *See under* HOUSE.
**Short commons.** *See under* SHORT.

**Commonwealth, The.** A term specifically applied to England in 1649 by the RUMP, the remnant of the LONG PARLIAMENT, after it had abolished the HOUSE OF LORDS and the monarchy and established the Council of State. Oliver Cromwell was styled LORD PROTECTOR OF THE COMMONWEALTH in 1653, and the period of his rule is usually called the Protectorate.

The term is currently applied to the British Commonwealth, the free association of most of the nations of the former British Empire.

**Ideal commonwealths.** *See under* IDEAL.
**Lord Protector of the Commonwealth, The.** *See under* LORD.

**Communards** (French, from *commune*, 'unit of local government'). After the Franco-Prussian War (1870–1) and the fall of NAPOLEON III, bitter political divisions arose between the people of Paris and the government at Versailles under Adolphe Thiers. Radicals, revolutionaries, socialists and workmen of the Paris Commune, adopting the name Communards, took control of the city in March 1871. They were ruthlessly suppressed by 29 May, with heavy loss of life, especially at the PÈRE LACHAISE cemetery.

**Communism.** In the general sense of a society or community based on common ownership of property and common labour with all sharing the common product, communism has been practised in many primitive societies and particular groups, for example the DIGGERS. Since the time of Plato's *Republic* (4th century BC) various forms of communism have been elaborated, but in current usage it derives from the theories of Karl Marx (1818–83) and Friedrich Engels (1820–95), as set out in the *Communist Manifesto* (1848) and in the former's *Capital* (1867–94). *See also* MARXISM; MATERIALISM.

The distinguishing feature of Communism is not the abolition of property generally, but the abolition of bourgeois property.
*Communist Manifesto*, ii

**Fifth-Amendment Communist.** *See under* FIFTH.

**Community, The Oneida.** *See* PERFECTIONISTS.

**Compact, Mayflower.** *See under* MAYFLOWER.

**Companion. Companions of Jehu.** The CHOUANS were so called, from a fanciful analogy between their self-imposed task and that given to Jehu when anointed king over Israel. Jehu was to cut off AHAB and JEZEBEL, with all their house (2 Kings 9:6–8). The Chouans were to cut off all who murdered Louis XVI, and to place his brother Louis XVIII ('Jehu') on the throne.

**Boon companion.** *See under* BOON.

**Company. Bad company.** *See under* BAD.

**Bear on company, To.** *See under* BEAR.

**Free companies.** *See under* FREE.

**Honourable Artillery Company.** *See under* HONOURABLE.

**In good company.** With companions who have done the same as oneself. The phrase often applies to a situation that could or should have been avoided, as: 'So you missed the train? You're in good company'.

**John Company.** *See under* JOHN.

**Keep company with, To.** To be regularly with, perhaps as a prelude to courtship.

**Keep someone company, To.** To accompany them; to act sociably towards them, especially if they are on their own.

**Part company, To.** *See under* PART.

**White Company.** *See under* WHITE.

**Compare. Compare notes, To.** To exchange opinions or observations with someone else on a particular matter or subject. The reference is to a written note.

**Comparisons are odorous.** So says DOGBERRY (Shakespeare, *Much Ado About Nothing*, III, v (1598)) (a blunder for 'odious').

We own your verses are melodious,
But then comparisons are odious.
JONATHAN SWIFT: 'Answer to Sheridan's Simile' (1725)

**Compass. Box the compass, To.** *See under* BOX.

**Goat and Compasses.** *See under* GOAT.

**Mariner's compass.** *See under* MARINER.

**Complementary colour.** A colour which when mixed with a given colour produces white or black. Thus orange and blue produce white.

**Complex.** A combination of memories, ideas and wishes that exercises an influence on the personality. *See also* OEDIPUS.

**Have a complex, To.** To have an obsession or irrational fear about something.

**Inferiority complex.** *See under* INFERIORITY.

**Oedipus complex.** *See under* OEDIPUS.

**Complexion, That schoolgirl.** *See under* SCHOOL.

**Compliment. Back-handed compliment.** *See under* BACK.

**Fish for compliments, To.** *See under* FISH.

**Left-handed compliment, A.** *See under* LEFT.

**Compline** (Medieval Latin *hora completa*, 'completed hour'). The last of the CANONICAL HOURS, said about 8 or 9 pm, and so called because it completes the series of the daily prayers or hours.

**Complutensian Polyglot, The.** *See under* BIBLE.

**Compos mentis.** *See* NON COMPOS MENTIS.

**Compostela.** Santiago de Compostela, the city in Spain where the relics of St JAMES THE GREAT are said to be preserved. Compostela is of uncertain origin. Some derive it from Latin *Campus Stellae*, 'field of the star', referring to the legend that the tomb containing the remains of St James was revealed by a bright star shining over it. Others take it from *compos stellae*, 'possessing the star', denoting the possession of the shrine by the city. Others again regard it as a corruption of Italian *Giacomo apostolo*, 'James the Apostle'. *See also* COCKLE HAT.

**Comstockery.** The rigid suppression of books, plays and other literature deemed to be salacious or corrupting, as advocated by the New York Society for the Suppression of Vice, whose moving spirit was the moral crusader Anthony Comstock (1844–1915). The word was coined in 1905 by G.B. Shaw. *See also* BOWDLERIZE.

**Comus** (Greek *kōmos*, 'revelry'). In Milton's masque of this name, the god of sensual pleasure, the son of BACCHUS and CIRCE.

In the masque, the First Brother represents 11-year-old Viscount Brackley, the Second Brother is nine-year-old Thomas Egerton, and the Lady is 15-year-old Lady Alice Egerton, children of the Earl of Bridgewater, at whose castle in Ludlow it was first performed in 1634, with the children actually taking these parts. *See also* SABRINA.

**Comyn, Red.** *See under* RED.

**Con. Con amore.** (Italian, 'with love'). In music a direction to play or sing lovingly. The phrase has also come to be used more generally for something said or done 'from the heart'.

An excellent account of reclamation on Exmoor Forest, a book written *con amore* as he was deeply interested both in land reclamation and in Exmoor.
*The Times* (1 July 1955)

**Con brio** (Italian, 'with spirit'). In music a direction to perform in a forceful or spirited manner.

**Con spirito** (Italian, 'with spirit'). In music a direction to perform in a lively or spirited manner.

**Conan** (Celtic *cuno*, 'high'). In the literature of

OSSIAN, 'a kind of Thersites, but brave even to rashness'.

**Conception. Feast of the Immaculate Conception, The.** *See under* FEAST.

**Immaculate Conception.** *See under* IMMACULATE.

**Conceptionists.** *See* FRANCISCANS.

**Concert. Concert pitch.** The pitch, internationally agreed in 1939, to which musical instruments are usually tuned, a frequency of 440 hertz (vibrations per second) for the A above middle C. Figuratively, therefore, 'concert pitch' is a state of alertness or keen readiness.

**Dutch concert.** *See under* DUTCH.

**Promenade concert.** *See under* PROMENADE.

**Conchie** or **conchy.** *See* CONSCIENTIOUS OBJECTOR.

**Conchobar.** In Irish legend the son of Nessa and king of ULSTER at the opening of the Christian era. He was uncle and guardian of CUCHULAIN and, as an old man, lusted after the young DEIRDRE, forcing her to marry him. He is also known as King Conor.

**Concierge.** The doorkeeper or porter of a block of flats in France, traditionally a middle-aged or elderly woman who makes it her business to know every detail of her residents' private lives and who marks every coming and going.

> Scowl at the concierge and your life will become a harassment; letters will be lost; parcels will be delayed; visitors will be told you are at home; a thousand little vexations will occur. The concierge in short is a rod which, you will observe, it is well to kiss.
>
> E.V. LUCAS: *A Wanderer in Paris* (1909)

**Conclamatio** (Latin, 'shouting by many together'). Among the Romans this was the loud cry raised by those standing round a deathbed at the moment of death. It probably had its origin in the idea of recalling the departed spirit and was similar to the Irish keening. 'One not howled over' (*corpus nondum clamatum*) meant a person at the point of death, and 'one howled for' was one given up for dead or actually deceased. Virgil makes the palace ring with lamentations when DIDO burns herself to death.

> Lamentis, gemituque, et femineo ululato,
> Texta fremunt.
> (The tapestries murmur with weeping and sighing and women's wailing.)
>
> *Aeneid*, iv (1st century BC)

**Conclave** (Latin *conclave*, 'place that can be locked up', from *con-*, 'with' and *clavis*, 'key'). Literally, a room or set of rooms that can be opened by only one key. The word is applied to small cells erected for the CARDINALS who meet, after the death of a pope, to elect a successor. Hence, by extension, the word came to denote the assembly of cardinals themselves and so, in general, to any private assembly for discussion. The conclave of cardinals dates from 1274, when it was introduced to hasten an election that had already been in progress for almost three years without a result. Those cardinals assembled in the Vatican are secluded in the conclave apartments, and votes are taken morning and evening until one candidate has secured a two-thirds majority. He is then declared pope.

**Conclusion. Foregone conclusion.** *See under* FORE.

**Jump to conclusions, To.** *See under* JUMP.

**Concordat.** An agreement, especially between a secular ruler and the pope, such as the Germanic Concordat of 1448 between the Emperor Frederick III and Nicholas V, the Concordat of 1516 between Francis I of France and Leo X to abolish the PRAGMATIC SANCTION, or the Concordat of 1801 between NAPOLEON BONAPARTE and Pius VII. In 1929 a concordat between the papacy and the Italian Government established the VATICAN CITY STATE.

**Concrete number.** *See* ABSTRACT NUMBER.

**Condé, Le Grand.** *See under* GRAND.

**Condottieri** (Italian *condotto*, 'hired', 'led'). A name applied to the leaders of bands of FREEBOOTERS, mercenaries or military adventurers of the 14th and 15th centuries. Notable among them were Sir John Hawkwood at Florence, Francesco of Carmagnola and Francesco Sforza. Italy was particularly plagued by them. The singular is condottiere.

**Conduct. Letter of safe conduct.** *See under* LETTER.

**Safe conduct.** *See under* SAFE.

**Conductor, Lightning.** *See under* LIGHTNING.

**Confederate States.** The eleven southern states that seceded from the Union in 1861 at the start of the American Civil War (1861–5), namely Alabama, Arkansas, North and South Carolina, Georgia, Florida, Louisiana, Mississippi, Tennessee, Texas and Virginia. *See also* UNITED STATES OF AMERICA.

**Confederation of the Rhine.** The 16 German states that allied themselves with France in 1806. The confederation was dissolved in 1813.

**Conference. Hampton Court Conference.** *See under* HAMPTON.

**Imperial Conference.** *See under* IMPERIAL.

**Lambeth conferences.** *See under* LAMBETH.

**Round table conference.** *See under* ROUND.

**Savoy Conference, The.** *See under* SAVOY.

**Confession. Augsburg Confession.** *See under* AUGSBURG.

**Brandenburg Confession.** *See under* BRANDENBURG.

**Seal of confession.** *See under* SEAL.

**Westminster Confession.** *See under* WESTMINSTER.

**Confetti.** The practice of throwing confetti over

the bridal pair after their wedding is a substitute for the old custom of throwing corn and, later, rice. It derives from an ancient fertility rite the intent of which was to ensure prosperity and fruitfulness. The word represents Italian *confetti*, 'bonbons', with reference to the little sweets, or imitations of them, thrown at carnivals in Italy. The English words 'comfit' and 'confectionery' are related.

**Confidence trick.** A swindle usually involving money, in which the swindler aims to gain the confidence of the victim. Hence con, as a short form of this, and con man for the swindler.

**Confucianism.** The religious philosophy of the Chinese sage Confucius (K'ung Tzu) (551–479 BC) centres on two tenets: the belief that the origin of things lies in the union of the passive and active principles of YIN AND YANG; and the ordering of human relationships on a patriarchal basis. Until 1912 Chinese political government, social organization and individual behaviour were governed by Confucianism, and the emperor of China was regarded as the father of his people, appointed to rule by heaven. The chief virtue was filial piety. Much of this was abandoned after the Revolution, although Confucianism continued to be practised in modified form under Communism.

**Confusion. Confusion of tongues.** According to the Bible (Genesis 11:1–9) the people of the earth originally spoke one language and lived together. They built a city and a tower as a rallying point, but God, seeing this as the beginning of ambition, 'did confound the language of all the earth' and scattered them abroad and hence the town was called BABEL. This was taken as an explanation of the diversity of languages and the dispersal of mankind and of the origin of the name BABYLON.

**Confusion worse confounded.** Disorder redoubled, a mix-up that has gone from bad to worse. The phrase is found in Milton:

> With ruin upon ruin, rout on rout,
> Confusion worse confounded.
> *Paradise Lost*, II (1667)

**Year of Confusion.** *See under* YEAR.

**Congé** (French, from Latin *commeatus*, 'leave of absence'). Formal permission to depart or formal dismissal. To give a person their congé is to dismiss them from one's service. To take one's congé is to give notice to friends or associates of one's departure by leaving a card inscribed PPC (*pour prendre congé*, 'to take leave') in the left-hand corner.

**Congé d'élire** (French, 'leave to elect'). A royal writ given to a CHAPTER to elect a named priest to a vacant see. Its use dates from 1533.

**Congleton Bears.** Men of Congleton, or Beartowners. Congleton in Cheshire was a noted north of England bear-baiting centre in the 16th and 17th centuries. Tradition has it that at some time in the 16th century the town bear died just before the annual WAKES. Money intended to purchase a Bible was diverted to purchase a bear, hence Congleton came to be called Bear Town and its inhabitants Congleton Bears. In the words of the jingle:

> Congleton rare, Congleton rare,
> Sold the Bible to buy a bear.

**Congregationalists.** The body of PROTESTANT DISSENTERS who maintained that each congregation was independent, with a right to govern its own affairs and choose its own minister. They evolved from the Brownists and BARROWISTS of Elizabeth I's reign. The Congregational Union was formed in 1832. *See also* UNITED REFORMED CHURCH.

**Congreve. Congreve rocket.** A rocket for use in war invented in 1808 by Sir William Congreve (1772–1828). It was used (not very successfully) at the Battle of Leipzig in 1813. He was Comptroller of the Royal Laboratory at Woolwich.

> But vaccination certainly has been
> A kind antithesis to Congreve's rockets.
> BYRON: *Don Juan*, I, cxxix (1819–24)

**Congreves.** Predecessors of the LUCIFER MATCH, said to have been invented by Sir William Congreve but more likely by the inventor John Walker (*c*.1781–1859). The splints were dipped in sulphur then tipped with chlorate of potash paste, in which gum was substituted for sugar, then a small quantity of sulphide of antimony was added. The match was ignited by being pulled smartly through a strip of folded sandpaper. *See also* PROMETHEAN.

**Conjure. Name to conjure with, A.** *See under* NAME.

**Conker.** A children's name for a horse chestnut, derived from the identical dialect word meaning a snail shell (related to conch) but popularly associated with 'conquer'. A chestnut (originally, a snail shell) is threaded on a string knotted at one end and used to strike an opponent's similarly strung conker until one or other breaks from the string. Conk, as a slang word for a nose, may be related in that it probably derives from conch.

**Old Conky.** *See under* OLD.

**Conk out, To.** To fail or stop running suddenly, as of an engine or motor. The word conk here is of uncertain origin. It may be simply onomatopoeic.

The verb also means to collapse suddenly, as from exhaustion, or even to die. The actor John Le Mesurier, familiar as Sergeant Wilson in the popular DAD'S ARMY television series, arranged for the following announcement to be placed in

*The Times* on his death (in 1983): 'John Le Mesurier wishes it to be known that he conked out on November 15th. He sadly misses family and friends.'

**Conn.** The great Irish hero, Conn of the Hundred Battles, high king of Ireland, who, according to the royal lists, reigned from AD 177 to 212. One day Conn and his followers were enshrouded in a thick mist and a man appeared, hurling missiles at them. On being warned that he was in the presence of the high king, he invited the company to his house. There Conn met the Sovranty of Ireland, a beautiful girl seated on a crystal chair and wearing a golden crown. The god Lugh was also there, and he prophesied that Conn's descendants would rule over Ireland.

**Connecticut.** The American state is called after the river of the same name. Its own name represents the American Indian word *kuenihtekot*, meaning 'long river'. The present spelling of the name has apparently been influenced by 'connect'. *See also* NUTMEG STATE.

**Conqueror.** The title has been applied to the following:

Alexander the Great, 'the conqueror of the world' (356–323 BC)
Afonso I of Portugal (*c*.1109–85)
Aurungzebe (Aurangzeb), fifth Mogul emperor of India (1618–1707)
James I of Aragon (1208–76)
Mohammed II, sultan of Turkey (1432–81)
Othman or Osman I, founder of the Ottoman dynasty in Turkey (1258–*c*.1326)
Francisco Pizarro, conqueror of Peru (*c*.1475–1541)
William, Duke of Normandy, conqueror of England (*c*.1028–87)

**Conqueror's nose.** A prominent straight nose, rising at the bridge. CHARLEMAGNE had such a nose, so had Henry the Fowler of Germany, Rudolf I of Germany, Frederick I of Hohenzollern, the IRON CHANCELLOR (Bismarck) and others. *See also* OLD CONKY.

**Conquest, The.** Duke William of Normandy's conquest of England (1066).

**William the Conqueror.** *See under* WILLIAM.

**Consecration, Nag's head.** *See under* NAG.

**Conscience. Conscience clause.** A clause in an ACT OF PARLIAMENT to relieve persons with moral scruples from certain requirements, usually of a religious character. It acquired a wider significance in connection with the Compulsory Vaccination Act of 1898.

**Conscience money.** Money paid anonymously to the government by persons who have defrauded the revenue, often by understating their income tax liabilities. The sum is advertised in the LONDON GAZETTE. The expression is also used generally to apply to any voluntary repayment made to ease one's conscience.

**Conscientious objector.** One who takes advantage of a CONSCIENCE CLAUSE and so evades some particular legal requirement. The term was at one time specially applied to those who had a conscientious objection to vaccination, but since the First World War it has come to mean a person who obtains exemption from military service on grounds of conscience. Colloquial names for a conscientious objector are 'CO' or (sometimes disparagingly) 'conchie' (or 'conchy').

**Court of conscience.** *See under* COURT.

**Clear conscience.** *See under* CLEAR.

**In all conscience.** In fairness; in accord with what one's conscience would allow.

**On one's conscience.** Causing feelings of guilt or remorse.

**Prick of conscience, The.** *See under* PRICK.

**Consciousness, Stream of.** *See under* STREAM.

**Conscript fathers** (Latin *patres conscripti*, standing for *patres et conscripti*, 'the heads of families and the newly elected'). The Roman Senate. ROMULUS is said to have instituted a senate of 100 elders called *patres* ('fathers'). After the SABINES joined the state, another 100 were added. Tarquinius Priscus, the fifth king, added a third 100, called *patres minorum gentium* ('heads of the lesser families'). When Tarquinius Superbus, the seventh and last king of Rome, was banished, several of the senate followed him and the vacancies were filled by JUNIUS BRUTUS, the first consul. The new members were enrolled in the senatorial register and so called *conscripti*. The entire body was then addressed as *patres et conscripti*. *See also* TARQUIN.

**Consent. Age of consent.** *See under* AGE.

**Silence gives consent.** *See under* SILENCE.

**Consentes dii.** The twelve chief Roman deities, six male and six female, the same as the Athenian twelve gods: JUPITER, APOLLO, NEPTUNE, MARS, MERCURY, VULCAN, JUNO, DIANA, MINERVA, VENUS, CERES and VESTA.

Ennius (239–169 BC) puts them into two hexameter lines:

Juno, Vesta, Minerva, Ceres, Diana, Venus, Mars,
Mercurius, Jovi', Neptunus, Vulcanus, Apollo.

The origin of *consentes* is obscure. According to Varro, the gods (*dii*) were so called

Quia in consilium Jovis adhibebantur.
(Because they were summoned to consult with Jupiter.)
*De Lingua Latina*, vii (1st century BC)

**Consenting stars.** Stars forming configurations for good or evil. Judges 5:20 tells how 'the stars in their courses fought against Sisera', i.e. formed unlucky or malignant configurations.

**Conservative.** One who believes in amending existing institutions cautiously, who opposes radical change and who favours the conservation of what is best in society and moral values. The name came to be applied to the TORY party from the 1830s after its use by J.W. Croker in the *Quarterly Review* of January 1830 (p. 276): 'We have always been conscientiously attached to what is called Tory, and which might with more propriety be called the Conservative Party'.

**Conservator of the Peace.** The predecessor of the JUSTICE OF THE PEACE and usually a function of the KNIGHT OF THE SHIRE.

**Consistory** (Medieval Latin *consistorium*, 'ecclesiastical tribunal'). The ecclesiastical court in the Church of Rome, that is, the assembly in council of the pope and cardinals. In England it is a diocesan court, presided over by the chancellor of the diocese.

**Consolidated fund.** A fund into which tax revenue is paid, held in the exchequer account at the Bank of England. The fund, which dates from 1787, is set aside for meeting the interest and management costs of the NATIONAL DEBT, CIVIL LIST and the like.

**Consols.** A contraction of consolidated stock, government securities that pay a fixed but low rate of interest.

**Consort. Prince consort.** *See under* PRINCE.

**Queen consort.** *See under* QUEEN.

**Conspiracy. Catiline's Conspiracy.** *See under* CATILINE.

**Cato Street Conspiracy.** *See under* CATO.

**Constable** (Latin *comes stabuli*, 'officer of the stables'). In the BYZANTINE EMPIRE the constable was master of the imperial stables and a great officer of state, hence the use of the name for an official of a royal household or a military commander. It was adopted by the Frankish kings, and the office grew steadily more important under their successors. *See also* CONSTABLE OF FRANCE.

Constable is also the term for a governor of a fortress, as the Constable of the TOWER OF LONDON. From Tudor times it became the designation of a parish officer, and later a policeman, as officers appointed to keep the peace. In England a 'special constable' is one enrolled to help the regular constabulary in time of pressure or emergency.

**Constable Country.** The pleasant pastoral and wooded country by the River Stour in Suffolk, preserved in the paintings of John Constable (1776–1837), who was born here at East Bergholt. Much of the landscape is identifiably what it was in the artist's day.

**Constable of England** or **Lord High Constable, The.** A royal official, first identifiable in Henry I's reign (1100–35), but since 1521 appointed for coronation days only.

**Constable of France, The.** Originally, the title of a great household official, judge of all matters pertaining to CHIVALRY and, from the 14th century, commander-in-chief of the army. The office was suppressed by Louis XIII in 1627 but temporarily revived by NAPOLEON BONAPARTE.

**Drink the constable, To.** *See* MOROCCO.

**Lord High Constable of Scotland, The.** *See under* LORD.

**Constantine. Constantine Dolmen, The.** A noteworthy DOLMEN in the village of this name southwest of Falmouth, Cornwall. It is known locally as the Tolmen.

> The Tolmen is a mass of granite, 33ft long, and weighing 450 tons. It was thrown down in 1870 from its former position upon two other stones. Persons could formerly pass beneath it.
>
> *Cassell's Gazetteer of Great Britain and Ireland*, ii (1895)

**Constantine's cross.** It is said that on his march to Rome Constantine saw a luminous cross in the sky with the motto *In hoc vinces*, 'by this [sign] conquer'. On the night before the Battle of Saxa Rubra (AD 312) he was commanded in a vision to inscribe the cross and motto on the shields of his soldiers. He obeyed the voice and was victorious. The LABARUM of Constantine was not really in the form of a cross but a monogram (XPI) formed of the first three letters of the word 'Christ' in Greek. The legend of the DANNEBROG is similar, and there are others. The Scots are said to have adopted St ANDREW's cross because it appeared in the heavens the night before Achaius, king of the Scots, and Hungus, king of the Picts, defeated Athelstan.

**Constituent Assembly.** The first of the National Assemblies of the French Revolution, which sat from July 1789 until 1791, so called from its main objective of drawing up a new constitution.

After the Second World War a National Constituent Assembly of 522 deputies was elected in France, according to the constitution promulgated in October 1945. In 1997 there were 577 deputies, 555 for Metropolitan France and 22 for the overseas departments and territories.

**Constitution.** The fundamental law or body of custom by which a state is organized and governed, or in other words, constituted.

**Constitution Hill.** A pleasant tree-lined road that runs up a slight incline from Buckingham Palace to Hyde Park Corner. It is said to be so named because Charles II took 'constitutional' walks there. It was the scene of three attempts on the life of Queen Victoria (in 1840, 1842 and 1849), and in 1850 Sir Robert Peel was fatally injured there after being thrown from his horse by the wicket gate into Green Park after calling at the Palace.

**Constitutions of Clarendon, The.** Laws made by Henry II at a council held at Clarendon in

Wiltshire in 1164, to check the power of the church and to restrain the prerogatives of ecclesiastics. These 16 ordinances defined the limits of the patronage and jurisdiction of the pope in England.

**Apostolic Constitutions.** *See under* APOSTLE.

**Fathers of the Constitution.** *See under* FATHER.

**Contact, Eye.** *See under* EYE.

**Contango.** In STOCK EXCHANGE parlance, the sum formerly paid by the purchaser of stock to the seller, for the privilege of deferring the completion of the bargain until the next settling day. The origin of the word is uncertain. It may be intended to express the idea 'I make contingent'. *See also* BACKWARDATION.

**Contemplate, To.** To meditate or reflect on; to consider attentively. The word derives from Latin *contemplare*, from *con-*, 'with', and *templum*, 'temple'. In AUGURY the templum was an open space marked out by the augur to observe the heavens. This observation was thus 'contemplation'.

**Contempt. Contempt of court.** A term of wide coverage, which, briefly defined, consists of conduct that interferes with the administration of justice or impedes or perverts the course of justice. Offenders can be anyone involved in a court case.

**Contempt of Parliament.** An offence against the authority or dignity of either of the Houses of Parliament or of one of its members. A breach of parliamentary PRIVILEGE is a contempt.

**Contemptibles, The Old.** *See under* OLD.

**Familiarity breeds contempt.** *See under* FAMILIAR.

**Contention, Bone of.** *See under* BONE.

**Contest of Wartburg.** A poetical contest of MINNESINGER, sometimes called the Battle of the Minstrels, held in 1207 at the Wartburg, a castle in Thuringia. The best of the contestants was Walther von der Vogelweide. The contest is commemorated in Wagner's TANNHÄUSER.

**Continence. Continence of Alexander, The.** Having won the Battle of Issus (333 BC), the family of Darius III, king of Persia, became the property of Alexander the Great. However, the victor treated the women with the greatest decorum. His continence drew respect from Darius.

**Continence of a Scipio.** It is said that a beautiful princess fell into the hands of Scipio Africanus, a man of strict moral integrity, and that he refused to see her, 'lest he should be tempted to forget his principles'. Similar stories are told of many historical characters including CYRUS the Great and Alexander the Great.

**Continent. Continental system.** The name given to NAPOLEON BONAPARTE's plan to cripple Britain by economic warfare when the invasion plan had failed. The Berlin Decrees of 21 November 1806 excluded all British goods from the ports of France and her allies and declared the British Isles in a state of blockade.

**Dark Continent, The.** *See under* DARK.

**Not worth a continental.** *See under* WORTH.

**Continuity girl** or **man.** The technique of cinematography allows a scenario or script to be filmed in scenes that are not necessarily in sequence, and each scene may also be shot several times. It is the task of the continuity girl or man to ensure that all details of costume, make-up, scenery and the like are correctly and consistently repeated each time.

**Contra** (Latin, 'against'). The word occurs in the phrase 'pro and contra' or, more commonly, pros and cons, meaning the points for and against a thing, its advantages and disadvantages. In BOOKKEEPING a contra is an entry on the right-hand or credit side of the ledger. *See also* PER CONTRA.

In Nicaraguan politics, the Contras were the forces opposing the Sandinista government. The word is short for Spanish *contrarrevolucionario*, 'counter-revolutionary'.

**Contra bonos mores** (Latin, 'contrary to good manners'). Not COMME IL FAUT.

**Contra ius gentium** (Latin, 'against the law of nations'). A term applied to usages in war that are contrary to the laws or customs of civilized peoples.

**Contra mundum** (Latin, 'against the world'). A phrase used of an innovator or reformer who sets his opinion against that of everyone else, especially as applied to Athanasius in his vehement opposition to the ARIANS.

**Contretemps** (French, literally 'against time'). A mishap; a minor but embarrassing disagreement.

**Control, Ground.** *See under* GROUND.

**Controversy. Filioque controversy.** *See under* FILIOQUE.

**Investiture controversy.** *See under* INVESTITURE.

**Marprelate controversy.** *See under* MARPRELATE.

**Vestiarian controversy.** *See under* VESTIARIAN.

**Convenience, Flag of.** *See under* FLAG.

**Conventicle** (Latin *conventiculum*, 'meeting'). The word was applied by the early Christians to their meeting-places, and it inevitably acquired the derogatory sense of a clandestine meeting. With the advent of Protestantism in England it came to be applied to the meetings and meeting-places of DISSENTERS.

**Conventicle Act.** In 1593 an Act of this name was passed containing severe penalties against those attending religious conventicles. The better known Act of 1664 forbade religious conventicles of more than five people except in accordance with the BOOK OF COMMON PRAYER. It was repealed in 1812.

**Convention. Convention Parliament.** Two Parliaments were so called. The first, in 1660, was so named because it was not summoned by the king but was convened by General Monk to effect the RESTORATION of Charles II. The second was the one authorized by William of Orange in January 1689, which offered the throne to William and Mary as joint sovereigns.

In 1787 the Constitution of the USA was drawn up by a convention at Philadelphia. In the USA National Party Conventions elect the official candidates for the Presidency and Vice Presidency.

In the French Revolution the National Convention succeeded the Legislative Assembly (21 September 1792), proclaimed the Republic (22 September) and governed France until October 1795, when it was succeeded by the DIRECTORY.

**Geneva Convention.** *See under* GENEVA.

**National convention.** *See under* NATIONAL.

**Cooing and billing, like Philip and Mary on a shilling.** The reference is to coins struck in 1555, in which Mary Tudor (r.1553–8) and her consort, Philip II (king of Spain, r.1556–98), are placed face to face, and not cheek by jowl, the usual way.

> Still amorous, and fond, and billing,
> Like Philip and Mary on a shilling.
> SAMUEL BUTLER: *Hudibras*, III, i (1680)

**Cook** or **cooking.** Terms belonging to cuisine can be applied to human beings in different ways. We can 'boil' with rage, be 'baked' by the heat and 'burn' with love or jealousy. We can be 'buttered up', 'cut up', or 'devoured' with greed. We may be 'eaten up' with grief. It is possible to COOK SOMEONE'S GOOSE, and we may well make a goose of ourselves. We can make a 'hash', get into 'hot water', find ourselves in a 'mess' or a 'pickle' or be in a 'stew'. An awkward person is often best left to 'stew in his own juice'. Someone may try to make 'mincemeat' of us or give us a 'roasting'. A foolish or stupid person is HALF-BAKED. To falsify accounts is to COOK THE BOOKS, wit is ATTIC SALT, and an exaggerated statement must be taken WITH A PINCH OF SALT.

A pert young person is 'saucy', old-fashioned lovers would 'spoon', we may have to 'fork out' when we pay, and when we are exhausted we can be 'dished'.

Some people are AS COOL AS A CUCUMBER; others are 'peppery'. A chubby child or short plump person is a 'dumpling' or 'pudding'. An eccentric or mentally deranged person is a 'fruitcake' or a 'nutter'. A dull or boring person is a 'prune'. A pregnant woman has a BUN IN THE OVEN. A sexually attractive woman or girl is a 'cookie', a 'crumpet', or a bit of 'crackling'. Such women are pictured as CHEESECAKE, while hunky men are BEEFCAKE. To indulge in sexual activity is 'to get one's greens'.

In RHYMING SLANG one's head is one's 'loaf', one's eyes are MINCE PIES, and one's feet are PLATES OF MEAT. *See also* BLOW A RASPBERRY; SAUSAGE.

Side whiskers may be MUTTONCHOPS. A greedy person is a 'pig', and a guilty or embarrassed person may look 'sheepish'. A coward is CHICKEN-HEARTED, a cross person is 'crusty', and an aristocrat belongs to the UPPER CRUST. Yeomen of the Guard are BEEFEATERS. An American soldier is a DOUGHBOY. A walking advertiser between two boards is a SANDWICH MAN. Two exactly similar people are AS LIKE AS TWO PEAS. Anything unexpectedly easy is a PIECE OF CAKE, while something audacious will TAKE THE BISCUIT (*see under* BISCUIT).

**Cook someone's goose, To.** To spoil their plans; to ruin their chances. The reference is perhaps to a goose that is being fattened for the table but that is killed and eaten early, so that there is none for the proper occasion.

**Cook the books, To.** To falsify a financial account or reckoning so as to make it more acceptable or palatable, as if by cooking.

**Cook up, To.** To invent; to concoct.

**That's the way the cookie crumbles.** That's the way it is; that's life for you. A cookie or biscuit may disintegrate in unpredictable directions as one breaks or bites it.

**What's cooking?** *See under* WHAT.

**Cooker, Captain.** *See* CAPTAIN COOKER.

**Cookie, Fortune.** *See under* FORTUNE.

**Cook's tour.** Any rapid but extensive tour or excursion. The name is that of Thomas Cook (1808–92), who began his career as a travel agent in 1841 by arranging for a special train to run between Leicester and Loughborough for a temperance meeting. In 1855 he conducted excursions to France for the Paris Exposition, and the following year led his first GRAND TOUR of Europe.

**Cool.** The early metaphorical sense of calm, unexcited, came to be applied in the 1940s to a style of jazz that was relaxed and the converse of 'hot' and hence to anyone or anything of which one approved.

> What such 'trendsetters' don't realise is that being outrageously uncool is just about the coolest thing you can do.
> *The Times* (15 August 1998)

**Cool Britannia.** A vogue phrase, punning on RULE, BRITANNIA, for the revitalized Britain that many saw emerging in 1997 on the election of a LABOUR PARTY government under Tony Blair. The watchword was 'new' by contrast with the staleness and paleness of John Major's earlier CONSERVATIVE administration.

> '[Britain and China] are two old and arrogant powers who know each other only too well', said one diplomat. 'It will take a lot more than Blair's New Labour and Cool Britannia to change fundamentally such a long, complex and often acrimonious relationship.'
> *The Times* (5 October 1998)

**Cooler.** A slang term, of American origin, for a prison or prison cell, especially one for solitary confinement. An inmate cools down there after the heat of the crime.

**Cool hundred, thousand, million etc, A.** The full amount stated. The expression may have originally referred to the calm deliberation with which the sum was counted out. *See also* COOL.

> He had lost a cool hundred, and would play no longer.
> HENRY FIELDING: *Tom Jones*, Bk VIII, ch xii (1749)

**Cooling-off period.** A period in which two sides in a dispute consider their position before resuming negotiations or discussions. The term is also used for the period of 14 days in which the signatory to a contract or agreement has the right to cancel.

**Cool it.** Relax, calm down. An injunction to someone who has become overheated.

**Cool one's heels, To.** To be kept waiting a long time, as for an appointment. The metaphor may allude to a horse who, tired after a long journey, stands in the stream from which it drinks.

**As cool as a cucumber.** *See under* AS.

**Lose one's cool, To.** *See under* LOSE.

**Coon.** Short for raccoon, a small North American arboreal animal, about the size of a fox, valued for its fur. The animal was adopted as a badge by the old WHIG party in the United States *c.*1840. The word is also derogatory slang for a Negro or an Australian Aborigine.

**Gone coon, A.** A person in a fix or on the verge of ruin. The coon being hunted for its fur is a 'gone coon' when it is treed and so has no escape from its pursuers.

**Coot, As bald as a.** *See under* AS.

**Cop. Cop, To.** To catch, lay hold of or capture. To get copped is to get caught, especially by the police, whence cop and COPPER for a policeman. The word is probably ultimately connected with Latin *capere*, 'to take'.

**Cop it, To.** To suffer the consequences, especially when a punishment is meted out.

**Cop out, To.** To avoid responsibility or commitment.

**Fair cop, A.** *See under* FAIR.

**Not much cop.** Of little value or use.

**Cope, Johnnie.** *See under* JOHNNIE.

**Copenhagen.** The chestnut horse ridden by the Duke of Wellington at Waterloo. The name commemorates the duke's part in the Copenhagen expedition of 1807. Copenhagen was pensioned off at Stratfield Saye and lived to the age of 27.

**Copernican system, Copernicanism.** The heliocentric or sun-centred theory of the universe postulated by Nicolaus Copernicus (1473–1543) in his book *De Revolutionibus Orbium Coelestium*. This superseded the PTOLEMAIC SYSTEM in which the sun is supposed to move round the earth. The idea was not entirely new and was vaguely held by the School of PYTHAGORAS. Pope Gregory XIII used *De Revolutionibus* when constructing his CALENDAR, but the book was placed on the INDEX in 1616. *See also* ALMAGEST.

**Cophetua.** An imaginary king of Africa who fell in love with a beggar maid 'all in gray' named Penelophon (Shakespeare's Zenelophon in *Love's Labour's Lost*, IV, i (1594)) and married her. They lived happily and were widely lamented at death. The story is given in the ballad 'King Cophetua and the Beggar-Maid' in PERCY'S RELIQUES (1765) and is referred to in Shakespeare's *Romeo and Juliet* (II, i (1594)) and *Richard II* (V, iii (1595)). A fine artistic representation may be seen in Sir Edward Burne-Jones's painting *King Cophetua and the Beggar Maid* (1884) at the Tate Gallery. This was itself based on Tennyson's poem 'The Beggar Maid' (1842).

**Copper.** A name for the large boiler, formerly used for laundry or cooking, which was originally made of copper but later of iron. Coppers are also coins of the lowest value. They were once minted of copper but from 1860 were issued in bronze.

In colloquial terms a copper is a policeman, so called because he will COP offenders. A corrupt police officer is colloquially known as a 'bent copper', punning on a damaged coin.

**Copperheads.** Secret foes. Copperheads are North American poisonous snakes which attack without warning. The name was applied by the early colonists to the Indians, then to the Dutch (*see* Washington Irving's *History of New York* (1809)). In the American Civil War (1861–5) it was given to those Northerners who were against the coercion of the CONFEDERATE STATES of the South. Copperhead badges were devised from one-cent copper pieces, and some Copperheads engaged in subversive activities, joining secret societies such as the Knights of the Golden Circle.

**Copper Nose.** A nickname for Oliver Cromwell (1599–1658), who was also called 'Ruby Nose', 'Nosey' and 'Nose Almighty'. The reference was no doubt to the *acne rosacea* from which he suffered and which gave him a red nose.

**Copper-nose Harry.** A nickname for Henry VIII (r.1509–47), who was notorious for his debasement of the coinage (from 1526). The copper content in the so-called 'silver' coins soon showed itself on the more prominent parts, especially the nose. Hence the king came to be called 'Old Copper Nose' or 'Copper-nose Harry'.

**Copper's nark.** *See* NARK.

**Copperfield, David.** The young hero of Charles Dickens's novel named after him (1849). After a wretched and unhappy childhood, he throws himself on the mercy of his aunt, Betsey Trotwood, who sends him to a new school. He eventually becomes a writer and finds happiness. He is generally seen as the author's thinly disguised self-portrait.

**Copts.** Christian descendants of the ancient Egyptians who became MONOPHYSITES and JACOBITES and who have retained the patriarchal chair of Alexandria since the Council of Chalcedon in 451, which still has nominal jurisdiction over the Ethiopian Church. Coptic ceased to be a living language in the 16th or early 17th century, but it is still used in their liturgy. The word is derived from Greek *Aiguptos*, 'Egypt', which became *qubt* after the 7th-century Arab invasion.

**Copy. Copybook.** A book in which specimen entries of handwriting, letters and figures are printed with blank spaces for the learner to imitate or copy them. Such exercise books were used in schools until the present century.

> Fair as a text B in a copy-book.
>
> SHAKESPEARE: *Love's Labour's Lost*, V, ii (1594)

**Copybook maxims.** Commonplace moral precepts of the sort found in copybooks. Actual examples are:

> All good subjects love their country.
> Your aim in life should be a noble one.
> Britannia must ever rule the waves.

**Copyhold.** Formerly, a tenure of land less than FREEHOLD held by possession of a copy made by the steward of a manor from its court roll. Copyhold tenure was abolished in 1922, and existing copyholds were enfranchised.

**Copyright.** The right to produce copies of a literary, musical or artistic work. Such right exists during the writer's (musician's, artist's) lifetime and for 70 years (until 1995, 50 years) after, when the work will be out of copyright.

**Copyright Library.** One of the six libraries entitled to receive a free copy of every book published in the United Kingdom. They are the BRITISH LIBRARY, the BODLEIAN LIBRARY in Oxford, Cambridge University Library, and the National Libraries of Scotland and Wales. Trinity College Library in Dublin is also a Copyright Library. *See also* LIBRARY.

**Blot one's copybook, To.** *See under* BLOT.

**Hard copy.** *See under* HARD.

**Corah.** In Dryden's *Absalom and Achitophel* (1681), the character of this name represents Titus Oates, notorious for his part in devising the POPISH PLOT (1678). The reference is to the rebellion against Moses and Aaron led by Korah (Numbers 16).

**Coral.** The Romans used to hang beads of red coral on the cradles and round the necks of babies as a charm against sickness and other ills, and soothsayers held that it was a charm against lightning, whirlwind, shipwreck and fire. PARACELSUS similarly advocated its use 'against fits, sorcery, charms and poison'. The bells on a baby's coral were a Roman Catholic addition to frighten away evil spirits.

> The corrall preserveth such as beare it from fascination or bewitching, and in this respect they are hanged about children's necks. But from whence that superstition is derived, and who invented the lie, I know not: but I see how readie the people are to give credit thereunto, by the multitude of corrals that waie emploied.
>
> REGINALD SCOT: *The Discoverie of Witchcraft*, ch xiii (1584)

**Coram. Coram judice** (Latin, 'in the presence of the judge'). In legal parlance, before a properly constituted court.

**Coram populo** (Latin, 'in the presence of the people'). Publicly.

**Cordelia.** The youngest of King LEAR's three daughters, and the only one that loved him. *See also* GONERIL; REGAN.

**Cordelia's gift.** 'Her voice was ever soft, gentle and low, an excellent thing in woman' (*King Lear*, V, iii (1605)).

**Cordelier** (French, 'cord-wearer'). FRANCISCAN Observantists or 'brethren of more strict observance' are called Cordeliers in France on account of their girdles of knotted cord. The story is that when these Minorites repulsed an army of infidels, St LOUIS of France (Louis IX, 1226–70) is reputed to have asked who those *gens de cordeliés* ('corded people') were. They received their name from this.

**Cordeliers' Club.** A French Revolutionary political club of the extreme left founded in 1790 by Georges Danton, Jean-Paul Marat and Camille Desmoulins, which met originally in the old convent of the Cordeliers. They were also called the Society of the Friends of the Rights of Man and of the Citizen, and nicknamed the Pandemonium. They were ahead of their rivals, the JACOBINS, in demanding the abolition of the monarchy but rapidly declined after the execution of its leaders in March and April 1794.

**Cordon** (Old French, 'little cord'). A line of sentries or military posts encircling some position, and hence an encircling line generally. The word is also specifically used for the ribbon of an order of chivalry or for one worn as the insignia of some honour.

**Cordon bleu** (French, 'blue ribbon'). The term originally applied in France to a knight of the ORDER OF THE HOLY GHOST (Saint-Esprit), from the fact that the insignia was suspended on a blue ribbon. The Commandeur de Souvé, Comte d'Olonne and other *cordons bleus* (knights of this order) met together as a sort of club and were noted for their excellent dinners. Hence *un repas de cordon bleu* was a well-cooked and well-appointed dinner, and the modern cordon bleu chef is one who prepares food to a high standard.

**Cordon noir** (French, 'black ribbon'). A knight of the Order of St MICHAEL, distinguished by a black ribbon.

**Cordon rouge** (French, 'red ribbon'). A chevalier of the Order of St LOUIS, distinguished by a red ribbon.

**Cordon sanitaire** (French, 'sanitary line'). A barrier line enclosing an infected area or, more generally, a line of buffer states, especially when protecting a particular country from attack.

**Corduroy.** A corded fabric, originally made of silk, and in modern times a heavy ribbed cotton material, capable of withstanding hard wear. Hence corduroys (or cords) as a name for trousers made of such material. The word is popularly derived from French *corde du roi*, 'king's cord', but no such phrase exists in French. The true origin may be in English 'cord' in the sense ribbed fabric and *duroy*, an obsolete name for a coarse woollen cloth.

**Corduroy road.** Roads formed of tree trunks sawn in two lengthwise and laid transversely, thus presenting a ribbed appearance like corduroy.

**Core, Hard.** *See under* HARD.

**Corineus.** A mythical hero who was the ally of BRUTE and who conquered the giant GOEMAGOT, for which achievement the whole western peninsula of England was allotted to him. He called it Corinea, and the people Corineans, after himself. This is the legendary explanation of the name of CORNWALL. *See also* BELLERUS.

> In meed of these great conquests by them got,
> *Corineus* had that Prouince vtmost west
> To him assigned for his worthy lot,
> Which of his name and memorable gest,
> He called *Cornewaile*, yet so called best.
>
> EDMUND SPENSER: *The Faerie Queene*, II, x (1590)

**Corinth** or **Corinthian.** The loose living of Corinth was proverbial both in Greece and Rome.

Hence, in the REGENCY period in England the term Corinthian was applied to a hard-living group of sportsmen devoted to pugilism and horse-racing. The sporting rake in Pierce Egan's *Life in London* (1821) was known as 'Corinthian Tom'. In Shakespeare's day a 'Corinthian' was the 'fast man' of the period. The term survives in the Royal Corinthian Yacht Club.

**Corinthian brass.** An alloy made of a variety of metals (said to be gold, silver and copper) melted at the conflagration of Corinth in 146 BC, when the city was burned to the ground by the consul Mummius. Vases and other ornaments, made of this metal by the Romans, were more highly prized than if they had been of silver and gold.

> I think it may be of 'Corinthian Brass',
> Which was a mixture of all metals, but
> The brazen uppermost.
>
> LORD BYRON: *Don Juan*, VI, lvi (1819–24)

**Corinthian order.** The most richly decorated of the five orders of Greek architecture. The shaft is fluted, and the capital is bell-shaped and adorned with ACANTHUS leaves. *See also* DORIC ORDER; IONIC ORDER; TUSCAN ORDER.

**Coriolanus.** Gnaeus Marcius Coriolanus, a great legendary hero of Rome. He won fame and his name (cognomen) from the capture of the Volscian town of Corioli, reportedly in 493 BC. On being exiled on charges of tyranny, he withdrew to his former enemies and led them against Rome but was persuaded to turn back by his mother, Veturia, and his wife, Volumnia. He subsequently either lived to a great old age or was assassinated. Shakespeare's play *Coriolanus* (1607) is based on a life by Plutarch.

**Corked.** Of wine, tainted through reacting with the tannin in the cork of the bottle. The term is sometimes erroneously taken to refer to a glass of wine containing crumbs of cork.

**Corker.** Anything outstanding, especially something that is the greatest yet experienced, such as a story, a problem, a hit in CRICKET etc. The idea is of something so good that it settles a dispute and one can 'put a cork in it'.

> 'You really enjoy watching fights?' 'I know what you mean,' I said. 'Nine times out of ten they're absolute washouts, of course. But this one was a corker.'
>
> P.G. WODEHOUSE: *Laughing Gas*, ch ii (1936)

**Cormoran.** A Cornish giant, who in the nursery tale fell into a pit dug by JACK THE GIANT-KILLER. For this fine achievement Jack received a belt from King ARTHUR with the following inscription:

> This is the valiant Cornish man
> That slew the giant Cormoran.

**Corn. Corn circles.** *See* CROP CIRCLES.

**Corn dolly.** Customarily, when the last load of the corn harvest was carried home, a Corn Dolly (called in some areas a Kern Baby or Mel Doll) was made from the last sheaf and carried by someone riding on top of the load. This female symbol of the Corn Spirit was hung in the farm kitchen until the next harvest. *See also* CRYING THE NECK; HARVEST HOME; MELL SUPPER.

**Corn-law Rhymer, The.** Ebenezer Elliott (1781–1849) denounced the CORN LAWS by portraying the sufferings and miseries of the poor in popular verse. His *Corn-Law Rhymes* appeared in 1831.

Ye coop us up and tax our bread,
And wonder why we pine;
But ye are fat, and round and red,
And filled with tax-bought wine.
'Caged Rats'

**Corn Laws.** Enactments, beginning in 1360, which were designed to regulate the export of grain and subsequently its import. The Corn Law of 1815 was particularly unpopular, since it forbade the import of foreign wheat until the domestic price reached 80s per quarter. This kept the price of bread unduly high in times of bad harvests, so increasing the hardships of the poor. A sliding scale was introduced in 1828, and this was further modified in 1842. In 1839 the Anti-Corn Law League was founded in Manchester, and in 1846 Sir Robert Peel secured the virtual repeal of the duties. A nominal duty of 1s per quarter remained until 1869.

**Acknowledge the corn, To.** *See under* ACKNOWLEDGE.

**Phantom corn.** *See under* PHANTOM.

**Pharaoh's corn.** *See under* PHARAOH.

**There's corn in Egypt.** There is abundance, there is a plentiful supply. The reference is to the Old Testament story of Joseph in Egypt.

And it came to pass, when they had eaten up the corn which they had brought out of Egypt, their father said unto them, Go again, buy us a little food.
Genesis 43:2

**Tread on someone's corns, To.** *See under* TREAD.

**Cornelia, Mother of the Gracchi.** The model of Roman matronly virtue. She was the second daughter of Scipio Africanus. On the death in 154 BC of her husband, Tiberius Sempronius Gracchus, she refused to remarry and devoted herself to the education of her three surviving children, Tiberius, Gaius and Sempronia. When asked to show her jewels, Cornelia produced her two sons, saying: 'These are the only jewels of which I can boast.' *See also* GRACCHI; LAWRENCE.

**Corner, To.** To BUY UP the whole of any stock in the market; to buy up the available stocks of a commodity so as to secure a virtual monopoly and thus raise the price. The idea is that the goods are piled and hidden in a corner out of sight.

The price of bread rose like a rocket, and speculators wished to corner what little wheat there was.
*New York Weekly Times* (13 June 1894)

To 'make a corner' is to combine with another person or group in order to control the price of a given article, and thus secure greater profits.

**Cornerstone.** A large square stone laid at the base of a building to strengthen the two walls where they meet at a right angle. In figurative use, Christ is called the chief cornerstone (Ephesians 2:20) because he united the Jews and Gentiles into one family, and daughters are called cornerstones (Psalm 144:12) because, as wives and mothers, they unite two families.

**Amen corner.** *See under* AMEN.

**Blind corner.** *See under* BLIND.

**Cut corners, To.** *See under* CUT.

**Driven into a corner, To be.** *See under* DRIVE.

**Four corners of the earth.** *See under* FOUR.

**Hell's Corner.** *See under* HELL.

**Poet's Corner.** *See under* POET.

**Puss in the corner.** *See under* PUSS.

**Rainbow Corner.** *See under* RAINBOW.

**Turn the corner, To.** *See under* TURN.

**Cornish. Cornish hug.** A special grip in wrestling. Cornish men were noted wrestlers and tried to throttle their antagonist with a particular grip or embrace called the Cornish hug.

The Cornish are Masters of the Art of Wrestling ... Their Hugg is a cunning close with their fellow combatant; the fruits whereof is his fair fall, or foil at the least. It is figuratively appliable to the deceitful dealing of such who secretly design their overthrow, whom they openly embrace.
THOMAS FULLER: *The History of the Worthies of England* (1662)

**Cornish language.** A member of the Brythonic branch of the Celtic family of languages, spoken mainly in Cornwall. It is supposed that Dolly Pentreath (Dorothy Jeffery, 1685–1778) was the last to speak Cornish as a native language, although it has enjoyed something of a revival since the 1950s.

**Cornish names.**

By Tre, Pol, and Pen
You shall know the Cornishmen.

Thus Tre ('farmstead', 'hamlet') gives Trebilcock, Tredinnick, Tregaskis, Tregenza, Trelawny, Treloar, Tremayne, Trenowth, Treseder and so on; Pol ('pool') gives Polglase, Polkinghorne, Polmear, Polwhele and the like; and Pen ('head', 'top') gives such names as Penberthy, Pengelly, Penhale, Penprase, Penrose and Penruddock. There are countless similarly formed place-names.

**Cornish Wonder, The.** John Opie (1761–1807), the Cornish painter. Peter PINDAR (John Wolcot) gave him this name.

**Cornubian shore, The.** Cornwall, formerly famous for its tin mines.

'Tis heard where England's eastern glory shines,
And in the gulphs of her Cornubian mines.
WILLIAM COWPER: *Poems*, 'Hope' (1782)

**Cornucopia.** *See* AMALTHEA'S HORN.

**Cornwall** (Cornish, *Kernow*). The name goes back to the tribal name Cornovii, meaning 'horn people', referring to the long peninsula that Cornwall is. The first part of the name was adopted by the Anglo-Saxons, who called the Britons who lived here *Cornwalas*, 'Corn-foreigners'. This eventually became modern Cornwall. See *also* CORINEUS; LAND'S END; WALES.

**Barry Cornwall.** The pseudonym of Bryan Waller Procter (1787–1874), based on an approximate anagram of his name. He began his career as a barrister, but went on to publish poems, songs and memoirs of Edmund Kean and Charles Lamb, among other works. He was popular with poets and other writers of his day, including Scott, Tennyson, Macaulay, Dickens and Thackeray, although Keats and Shelley were less enthusiastic.

**Coronation. Coronation Chair.** *See* STONE OF SCONE.

**Coronation Street.** An enduringly popular television 'soap opera' about working-class life in a North Country mill town, first screened on 9 December 1960. The locale is the street so named, and most of the action takes place in a pub, the Rover's Return, at one end and a corner shop at the other. The cast and the characters they play have become household names, and the series has been lauded by prime ministers (Harold Wilson) and poets (John Betjeman).

**Coronet.** A crown inferior to the royal crown. The coronet of the Prince of Wales has one arch fewer than the royal crown, and those of other princes have no arches. A duke's coronet is adorned with STRAWBERRY LEAVES above the band, that of a MARQUESS with strawberry leaves alternating with pearls, that of an EARL with pearls elevated on stalks, alternating with strawberry leaves above the band, that of a VISCOUNT with a string of pearls above the band, but no leaves, and that of a BARON with only six pearls.

*King*

*Duke*

*Marquess*

*Earl*

*Viscount*

*Baron*

**Coronis.** The mother of AESCULAPIUS by APOLLO, who slew her for her infidelity. The name is also that of the daughter of Coronaeus, king of Phocis, who was changed by ATHENE into a crow to enable her to escape from NEPTUNE.

**Corporal. Corporal Violet.** *See under* VIOLET.

**Lance corporal.** *See under* LANCE.

**Little Corporal.** *See under* LITTLE.

**Corporate, Body.** *See under* BODY.

**Corporation.** A body or succession of persons having legal existence, rights and duties, as distinct from the individuals that form it. In Britain the usual application of the term is to the body of individuals elected for the local government of a city or town. In America it commonly applies to a company. The word corporation is also facetiously given to a fat paunch, from the (former) tendency of civic bodies to indulge in rich feasts, so that members gained generous figures.

**Corporation of Trinity House.** The chief pilotage authority of the United Kingdom, which controls the lighting and marking of British coastal waters and certain maritime charities. Its headquarters are at Tower Hill, London, and its work is controlled by Elder Brethren, consisting of master mariners who have had long experience of command in the Royal Navy or merchant navy, together with individuals from the world of commerce and a Secretary. It developed from the guild of mariners and lodesmen of Deptford Strond, Kent, who obtained a charter from Henry VIII in 1514, and it acquired the Lord High Admiral's rights of buoyage and beaconage in 1594. Private lighthouses were acquired under an Act of 1836.

**Corposant.** The ball of fire which is (or was) sometimes seen playing around the masts of ships in a storm, so called from Portuguese *corpo santo*, 'holy body'. To the Romans the phenomenon was known as CASTOR AND POLLUX, and it is also known as St ELMO'S FIRE or St Helen's fire.

> Upon the main top-gallant masthead was a ball of light, which the sailors name a corposant (corpus sancti).
>
> R.H. DANA: *Two Years Before the Mast*, ch xxiv (1840)

**Corps. Corps de ballet** (French, 'body of ballet'). The group members of a ballet company, as distinct from the solo dancers. The term originally designated the whole body of dancers, and is still used in this sense at the Paris Opéra.

**Corps d'élite** (French, 'select body'). A select group of some kind, a picked company.

**Corps diplomatique** (French, 'diplomatic body'). The diplomatic corps in a capital, made up of the diplomatic representatives of the various foreign states.

**Corps législatif** (French, 'legislative body'). At various times in modern French history this name has been used for the lower house of the legislature. In 1799 NAPOLEON BONAPARTE substituted a *Corps législatif* and a tribunal for the two councils of the DIRECTORY. In 1807 there was a *corps législatif* and a *conseil d'état* (council of state). In 1849 a *corps législatif* was formed with 750 deputies, and under NAPOLEON III the legislative power was vested in the emperor, the Senate and the *corps législatif*.

**Honourable Corps of Gentlemen at Arms, The.** *See under* HONOURABLE.

**Peace Corps.** *See under* PEACE.

**Corpse. Corpse candle.** The IGNIS FATUUS is so called by the Welsh because it was supposed to forbode death and to show the road the corpse would take. The large candle used at LICH WAKES was similarly named.

> When any Christian is drowned in the river Dee, there will appear over the water where the corpse is, a light, by which means they do find the body: and it is therefore called the Holy Dee.
>
> JOHN AUBREY: *Miscellanies* (1721)

**Corpse coins.** An old name for the pennies placed on the eyelids of dead persons to keep them closed. In the New England states a half-dollar was traditionally used for the same purpose.

**Corpus** (Latin, 'body'). The whole body or substance of something, especially the complete collection of writings on one subject or by one person. The word is also the short name of CORPUS CHRISTI COLLEGE.

**Corpus Christi** (Latin, 'Body of Christ'). A church festival kept on the Thursday after TRINITY SUNDAY, in honour of the Blessed Sacrament. It was instituted by Pope Urban IV in 1264. It was the regular time for the performance of religious dramas by the trade guilds and, in England, many of the Corpus Christi plays of York, Coventry and Chester are extant. Since 1970 the Roman Catholic Church has called the festival *Festum Corporis et Sanguinis Christi*, Feast of the Body and Blood of Christ, to emphasize that both of the sacred elements are honoured, the shorter title wrongly implying that only one is.

**Corpus Christi College.** The Cambridge college was founded in 1352, and the college of the same name at Oxford in 1517.

**Corpus delicti** (New Latin, 'body of the offence'). The material thing in respect of which a crime has been committed. Thus a murdered body or some stolen property would be a 'corpus delicti'.

**Corpus juris** (Late Latin, 'body of law'). The particular laws of a nation or state.

**Corpuscular philosophy.** The theory promulgated by Robert Boyle which sought to account for all natural phenomena by the position and motion of corpuscles. *See also* ATOMIC THEORY.

**Correct. Alexander the Corrector.** *See under* ALEXANDER.

**House of correction.** *See under* HOUSE.

**Political correctness.** *See under* POLITICS.

**Corridor. Corridors of power.** A collective term for the ministries in WHITEHALL with their top-ranking civil servants. The phrase was popularized (but not invented) by C.P. Snow in his novel *Homecomings* (1956) and gained wide acceptance. He later used it for the title of the novel *Corridors of Power* (1964).

> Boffins at daggers drawn in corridors of power.
>
> *The Times* (headline) (8 April 1965)

**Polish Corridor, The.** *See under* POLAND.

**Corroboree.** A dance practised by Australian Aborigines on festal or warlike occasions. Hence any roistering or slightly riotous assembly. The word is an Aborigine one, from Dharuk *garabari*, a style of dancing.

> He roared, stamped, and danced corrobory, like any blackfellow.
>
> CHARLES KINGSLEY: *The Water-Babies*, ch viii (1862–3)

**Corrouge.** The sword of the PALADIN Otuel.

**Corsican.** An epithet applied to NAPOLEON BONAPARTE, who was born in Corsica, which became a French possession in 1768. He was often referred to as 'the Corsican upstart'.

**Corsned** (Old English *cor*, 'choice', 'trial', and *snǣd*, 'bit, 'piece'). The piece of bread, 'consecrated for exorcism', formerly given to a person to swallow as a test of his guilt, a form of trial by ORDEAL. The words of 'consecration' were: 'May this morsel cause convulsions and find no passage if the accused is guilty, but turn to wholesome nourishment if he is innocent.' *See also* CHOKE.

**Corvinus.** Matthias I, king of Hungary (1458–90), younger son of John (Janos) Hunyadi, was so called from the raven (Latin *corvus*) on his shield. He was one of the greatest of all book collectors, and some of the earliest European gilt-tooled bindings were executed for his library. They may be recognized by the raven stamped in the centre of the covers.

**Corvus, Marcus Valerius.** The Roman general (*c*.370–270 BC) was reputedly so called because while in combat with a gigantic Gaul in 349 he was helped by a raven (Latin *corvus*), which flew at the Gaul's face. The bird may in reality have been an emblem on his opponent's helmet.

**Corybantes** (Greek *Korubas*, probably of Phrygian origin). The Phrygian priests of CYBELE, whose worship was celebrated with orgiastic dances and loud, wild music. Hence a wild, unrestrained dancer is sometimes called a corybant. In 1890 T.H. Huxley referred to the members of the SALVATION ARMY as being 'militant missionaries of a somewhat corybantic Christianity'.

**Corycian cave.** A cave on Mount PARNASSUS named after the NYMPH Corycia. The MUSES are sometimes in poetry called Corycides or the Corycian Nymphs.

**Corydon.** A conventional name for a rustic or shepherd or for a mindless, lovesick youth. The name, which is that of the shepherd in Virgil's *Eclogue* (vii (1st century BC)), may derive from Greek *korudon*, 'crested lark'.

**Coryphaeus** (Greek *koruphaios*, 'leader'). The leader and speaker of the chorus in Greek dramas. Hence, figuratively, the leader generally; the most active member of a board, company, expedition or the like. At Oxford University the assistant of the CHORAGUS was so called. The offices of Choragus and Coryphaeus have long since disappeared.

> In the year 1626, William Heather, desirous to ensure the study and practice of music at Oxford in future ages, established the offices of Professor, Choragus, and Coryphaeus, and endowed them with modest stipends.
>
> GEORGE GROVE: *Dictionary of Music* (1879–89)

**Coryphaeus of German Literature, The.** Goethe, Prince of German Poets (1749–1832).

**Coryphaeus of Grammarians, The.** Aristarches of Samothrace (2nd century BC), an outstanding grammarian and critic.

**Coryphaeus of Learning, The.** Richard Porson (1759–1801), renowned for his knowledge of Greek.

**Coryphée** (French, 'coryphaeus'). A term for a minor solo ballet dancer. The French word is sometimes wrongly taken in English to refer solely to a female dancer.

**Cosmonaut** (Russian *kosmonavt*, from Russian *kosmos*, 'space', and Greek *nautēs*, 'sailor'). A Soviet ASTRONAUT. The word was first popularized in the late 1950s, when the USSR and the USA began their rivalry for space, and continued to be used for Russian astronauts in the post-Soviet era.

> Russia's endangered space programme was rescued yesterday by the skill of one of its cosmonauts.
>
> *The Times* (3 September 1994)

**Cost, To count the.** *See under* COUNT.

**Costard** (Old French *coste*, 'rib'). A large ribbed apple, and colloquially, a person's head. *See also* COSTERMONGER.

Shakespeare gives the name to a clown in *Love's Labour's Lost* (1594). He imitates the court wit of the period but misuses words in a manner similar to that of Mrs MALAPROP.

**Costermonger.** A now rare term for a street vendor of fruit, vegetables and the like. The word properly denotes an apple seller, from COSTARD and monger, a dealer or trader (Old English *mangian*, 'to trade'), as in ironmonger or fishmonger. The word came to be particularly associated with London 'barrow boys' and COCKNEY dealers. *See also* PEARLY KING.

**Cost the earth, To.** To be very expensive.

**Cotillion** or **Cotillon** (Old French, 'petticoat'). The word originally applied in the 18th century to a type of French formation dance for four or eight persons, in which the ladies held up their gowns and showed their petticoats. In later American usage the word came to denote a formal ball or 'coming-out' dance, as well as a complicated and energetic dance in which dancers frequently change partners. The French equivalent for PETTICOAT GOVERNMENT is *régime du cotillon*.

> Well – on a yacht, he met her; then at a ball – he met her; then at a cotillion – he met her; then at a dinner – he met her.
>
> PAUL L. FORD: *Tattle-Tales of Cupid* (1898)

**Cotset.** A word occurring in the DOMESDAY BOOK to denote one of the lowliest types of feudal bondsmen, from Old English *cot-sǣta*, 'cottage-dweller'.

**Cottage. Cottage cheese.** A type of soft white cheese made from curds of skimmed milk. The name alludes to the cheese's origins in the kitchens of farm cottages.

**Cottage Countess, The.** Sarah Hoggins of Shropshire, daughter of a small farmer, who in 1791 married Henry Cecil, nephew and heir presumptive of the 9th Earl of Exeter, Lord of Burleigh. He was living under the name of John Jones at the time and separated from his wife (Emma Vernon), who eloped with a clergyman. He subsequently obtained a divorce to legitimize the children of his second wife. Sarah was 17 at the time of her marriage at Bolas Magna (now Great Bolas), Shropshire, and 'John Jones' was 30. They lived there for two years until his succession to the peerage made her a countess. She died in 1797. Tennyson has a poem on the subject, called 'The Lord Burleigh' (1842).

**Cottage flat.** One of four flats, each formed from half the floor of a two-storey house.

**Cottage garden.** An informal garden well stocked with colourful hardy plants. Such gardens were popular subjects with Victorian watercolourists such as Helen Allingham (1848–1926), Myles Birket Foster (1825–99) and

William Stephen Coleman (1829–1904).

**Cottage hospital.** A small hospital in a rural location or at the edge of a town. It is often designed to resemble a cottage and so look homely and welcoming.

> There is nothing like a dear old cottage hospital, let's be honest, for arousing affectionate and therefore very fierce protective instincts in people.
>
> CLAIRE RAYNER in *New Statesman* (11 September 1998)

**Cottage industry.** An industry in which employees work in their own homes, using their own equipment.

**Cottage loaf.** A loaf of bread in two round lumps, the smaller being on top, and baked with a good crust. It was the traditional product of 'home baking' and the shape purely decorative.

**Cottage orné** (French *orné*, 'adorned'). A picturesque country cottage or small house designed for the well-to-do.

**Cottage piano.** A small upright pianoforte.

**Cottage pie.** Another name for shepherd's pie, made with minced meat topped with mashed potato.

**Love in a cottage.** *See under* LOVE.

**Cottingley fairies, The.** *See under* FAKES.

**Cotton. Cotton king.** A former nickname for a rich Lancashire or Manchester cotton manufacturer. Sir Robert Peel (1750–1830), the father of the Prime Minister of the same name, could be so designated.

**Cotton kingdom.** In the USA, the agricultural states of the South, where cotton production expanded rapidly from the close of the 18th century and stimulated the support for slavery. *See also* KING COTTON.

**Cotton on, To.** To catch on, to grasp a line of thought. The allusion is to cotton fibres that catch on to clothing.

**Cottonopolis.** Manchester, long famous for its textile trade, and especially for its cotton, which was Great Britain's largest single export during the 19th century.

**Cotton snobs.** In the USA a name applied in the 19th century to the slave-owning cotton magnates of the South, reputed to be pompous and overbearing and lacking the merits of an older aristocracy.

**Cotton to, To.** To begin to like; to come to admire. The Americanism alludes to a thread of cotton that attaches itself and sticks close.

**King Cotton.** *See under* KING.

**Sea-island cotton.** *See under* SEA.

**Cottonian Library.** A rich library of state papers and other manuscripts founded by the antiquary Sir Robert Cotton (1571–1631) and augmented by his son and grandson. It was secured for the nation in 1700 and transferred first to Essex House and then to Ashburnham House, Westminster, in 1730. A disastrous fire in 1731 destroyed over 100 volumes of irreplaceable manuscripts, and the remainder (some 800 volumes) were moved to Westminster School and finally lodged in the BRITISH MUSEUM in 1753.

**Cottus.** One of the hundred-handed giants, the son of URANUS (Heaven) and GAIA (Earth). His two brothers were BRIAREUS and Gyes.

**Cotytto.** The Thracian goddess of immodesty and debauchery, worshipped at Athens with licentious rites.

**Couchant.** *See* LEVANT AND COUCHANT.

**Couch potato.** A person who prefers lounging at home watching television to engaging in any purposeful activity, especially if it involves any physical effort. The expression is of American origin and appears to pun on 'boob-tube' as a slang term for a television, the potato being a plant tuber.

> The interactive potential of the new medium is the kiss of death for the couch potato. Your [digital] television will no longer be just a 'dumb instrument' dealing out whatever the programme planners have on their set menus.
>
> *Sunday Times* (4 October 1998)

**Couéism.** A form of psychotherapy by autosuggestion, propagated by Emile Coué (1857–1926), a French pharmacist and psychotherapist. The key phrase of his system was: 'Every day, and in every way, I am getting better and better' (in the original French, *Tous les jours, à tous points de vue, je vais de mieux en mieux*). This mantra was introduced in his work *De la suggestion et de ses applications* (1915), in which he recommended that it be said between 15 and 20 times daily, morning and evening.

**Cough, Churchyard.** *See under* CHURCH.

**Council. Council of Nicaea, The.** The first ECUMENICAL COUNCIL of the Christian church held under Constantine the Great in 325 at Nicaea in Bithynia, Asia Minor, primarily to deal with the ARIAN heresy, which it condemned. The second Council of Nicaea (787), the seventh General Council of the Church, was summoned by the Empress Irene to end the Iconoclastic Controversy.

**Council of Ten, The.** A secret tribunal exercising unlimited powers in the old Venetian republic. It was instituted in 1310 with ten members. The number was then increased to 17 and it continued in active existence until the fall of the republic in 1797.

**Council of war.** An assembly of officers called in a special emergency. Also, more generally, any meeting held in response to an emergency.

**Amphictyonic Council.** *See under* AMPHICTYONIC.

**Ecumenical councils.** *See under* ECUMENICAL.

**Great Council.** *See under* GREAT.

**Lateran Council.** *See under* LATERAN.
**Orders in Council.** *See under* ORDER.
**Privy Council.** *See under* PRIVY.
**Vatican Council.** *See under* VATICAN.

**Counsel. Counsel of despair.** An action to be taken when all else fails.

**Counsel of perfection.** Advice that is ideal but impracticable, or that guides towards moral perfection.

> Jesus said unto him, If thou wilt be perfect, go and sell that thou hast, and give to the poor, and thou shalt have treasure in heaven.
> Matthew 19:21

**Darken counsel, To.** *See under* DARK.
**King's** or **Queen's Counsel.** *See under* KING.
**Leading counsel.** *See under* LEAD.

**Count** (Old French *conte*, from Latin *comes*, *comitis*, 'companion', literally 'one who goes with'). The continental equivalent of the English EARL, of which 'countess' remains as the feminine equivalent.

**Count of the Saxon Shore.** *Comes Litoris Saxonici*, the Roman general in charge of the coastline of Britain from the Wash to the Solent, whose task it was to combat Saxon and Frankish raiders. In the later 4th century his jurisdiction was extended to the Yorkshire coast. *See also* SAXON SHORE.

**Count, To** (Old French *conter*, from Latin *computare*, 'to compute', 'to reckon').

**Count down, To.** To count backwards to zero, typically before a rocket launch.

**Counted out, To be.** Of a floored boxer, to fail to rise during the ten seconds counted out loud by the referee.

**Count kin with someone, To.** A Scots expression meaning to compare one's pedigree with that of another.

**Count me out.** Leave me out of this.

**Count noses, To.** A horse dealer counts horses by the nose, as cattle are counted by the head. Hence the expression is sometimes ironically used of numbering votes, as in the division lobbies.

**Count on, To.** To rely or depend on.

**Count one's blessings, To.** To be grateful for what one has. Edith Temple and Reginald Morgan's song 'Count Your Blessings One by One' became a hit in the late 1940s through such popular singers as Josef Locke and Harry Secombe.

**Count one's chickens before they are hatched, To.** To take as certain something that is not yet certain; to act as if one already had what one hopes to have but does not yet actually have. *See also* ALNASCHAR'S DREAM; BIRD IN THE HAND IS WORTH TWO IN THE BUSH.

**Count out the House, To.** Formerly, to adjourn a sitting of the HOUSE OF COMMONS when there was not a QUORUM. A member would rise and draw the attention of the SPEAKER to the fact that there were fewer than 40 members present. The Speaker would then say: 'Notice having been taken that 40 members are not present, strangers will withdraw.' The division bells would ring, and unless 40 members were in the Chamber at the end of eight minutes, the House would immediately adjourn. This procedure was abolished in 1971, but a quorum of 40 is still necessary for the business of the House to proceed. If there are fewer than 40 present, the particular business must be held over until the next sitting, and the House passes to the next matter.

**Count the cost, To.** To consider the risks before taking action, or to calculate the damage done afterwards.

**Lose count, To.** *See under* LOSE.

**Out for the count.** In boxing, defeated by being COUNTED OUT. Said also of someone demoralized or simply soundly asleep.

**Countenance, To.** To sanction; to support. Approval or disapproval is shown by the expression on the face or countenance.

**Keep one's countenance, To.** To keep one's composure, so that one's expression does not reveal one's thoughts.

**Out of countenance.** *See under* OUT.

**Counter. Counter-jumper.** A former derogatory nickname for a shop assistant, who was thought of as having to jump over the counter to go from one part of the shop to another.

**Counter-Reformation, The.** A name given by historians to the movement for reform within the Church of Rome (much stimulated by the REFORMATION) and the measures taken to combat the spread of Protestantism and to regain lost ground. It is usually reckoned to extend from the mid-16th century, when the Council of Trent (1545–63) strengthened and reawakened the life and discipline of the church, to the time of the THIRTY YEARS' WAR (1618–48).

**Under the counter.** *See under* UNDER.

**Countess.** *See* COTTAGE COUNTESS; COUNT.

**Country. Country cousin.** A derogative term for someone with a countrified appearance or manners, a 'hick'.

**Country dance.** A dance in which couples face each other in long lines. When during the REGENCY the dance was introduced to France from England, its name was corrupted there to *contre-danse*, literally 'dance opposite', referring to the positions of the dancers. However, the English form of the name is the original one. Even so, the French word was borrowed back into English (as contre-dance or contra-dance or some similar form) to refer to the Continental version of the English dance.

**Country house.** A large and often historic or architecturally interesting house in the country, especially one that is or was the seat of a COUNTY FAMILY. *See also* STATELY HOME.

**Appeal to the country, An.** *See under* APPEAL.

**Black Country, The.** *See under* BLACK.

**Constable Country.** *See under* CONSTABLE.

**Father of his Country, The.** *See under* FATHER.

**Go to the country, To.** To dissolve Parliament in order to ascertain the wishes of the country by a general election.

**In the country.** In cricket, far from the wickets, in the deep field.

**Line of country.** *See under* LINE.

**Low Countries.** *See under* LOW.

**Old country.** *See under* OLD.

**Ozark country.** *See under* OZARK.

**West Country.** *See under* WEST.

**Unknown country** or **territory.** *See under* UNKNOWN.

**Up country.** *See under* UP.

**County** (Old French *conté*, 'land belonging to a count'). A SHIRE. After the Local Government Act of 1888 and until 1972, certain of the larger towns had county status as county BOROUGHS. *See also* HUNDRED.

**County family.** A family belonging to the nobility or gentry with an ancestral seat in the county.

**County Palatine** or **Palatinate** (Latin *palatinus*, 'of the palace'). Properly, a COUNTY over which an EARL or other lord had quasi-royal jurisdiction. Cheshire, Shropshire, Durham and Kent became Counties Palatine after the Norman Conquest as frontier districts; Lancaster became one in 1351. At one time Pembroke, Hexhamshire and the Isle of Ely were also so designated, but only Cheshire, Durham and Lancaster still retain the title, and the CHANCELLOR OF THE DUCHY OF LANCASTER is a member of the Government. Their jurisdictions are now vested in the crown. *See also* PALATINATE.

**Home Counties.** *See under* HOME.

**King's** or **Queen's County, The.** *See under* KING.

**Six Counties, The.** *See under* SIX.

**Coup** (French, 'blow', 'stroke'). The word is used in English for a successful move or stroke in certain games (chess, billiards), for a stroke of policy or a sudden and successful act, and for an illegal attempt to overthrow an established government. *See also* COUP D'ÉTAT.

**Coup d'essai** ('blow of trial'). A piece of work serving as practice for the real thing; a first attempt.

**Coup d'état** ('blow of state'). A sudden illegal or violent seizure of power in a country, as by a military force. The *coup d'état* by which Louis Napoleon (NAPOLEON III) seized power occurred on 2 December 1851. *See also* MAN OF DECEMBER.

**Coup de foudre** ('stroke of lightning'). A sudden amazing incident or event. The phrase is sometimes used for 'love at first sight'.

**Coup de grâce** ('stroke of mercy'). A final fatal blow, such as one given to a prisoner under torture to put him out of his misery.

**Coup de main** ('stroke of hand'). In military parlance, a surprise attack.

> It appears more like a line of march than a body intended for a *coup de main*, as there are with it bullocks and baggage of different kinds.
>
> DUKE OF WELLINGTON: *Dispatches*, i (1799–1818)

**Coup d'oeil** ('stroke of eye'). A quick glance; a general view.

**Coup de pied de l'âne** ('kick from a donkey's foot'). Figuratively, a blow given to a conquered or fallen person; otherwise a cowardly blow or an insult given to someone who has no power to return it. The allusion is to the fable of the sick lion kicked by the ass.

**Coup de soleil** ('stroke of sun'). Sunstroke or any illness produced by exposure to the sun.

**Coup de théâtre** ('stroke of theatre'). An unforeseen or unexpected turn in a drama producing a sensational effect. An example is Burke's throwing down of the dagger in the HOUSE OF COMMONS. *See also* DAGGER SCENE.

**Coup manqué** ('missed stroke'). A miss, a failure.

> Shoot dead, or don't aim at all; but never make a coup manqué.
>
> OUIDA: *Under Two Flags*, ch xx (1867)

**Couple. In a couple of shakes.** In a moment; as soon as one can shake the dicebox twice.

**Coupon** (Old French *colpon*, 'piece cut off'). In commercial usage, a detachable ticket cut off a bond entitling the owner to payment of interest. The word is more commonly used for any part of a ticket or advertisement that can be detached or cut out for special use, mainly to buy or obtain something at a discount. In the Second World War coupons were cut out of ration books to buy particular types of food.

> They found his father checking sweet coupons when they entered.
>
> JOHN BRAINE: *The Vodi*, ch vii (1959)

**Coupon Election.** During the general election of 1918 Prime Minister David Lloyd George and Chancellor of the Exchequer Bonar Law sent a certificate or coupon to all candidates supporting the Coalition. The coupon was not accepted by the Asquith LIBERALS nor by the LABOUR Party. A 'couponeer' was a politician who accepted the coupon.

**Courage. Dutch courage.** *See under* DUTCH.

**Screw up one's courage, To.** *See under* SCREW.

**Course. Another course would have done it.** *See under* ANOTHER.

**As a matter of course.** *See under* AS.
**Clerk of the course.** *See under* CLERK.
**Horses for courses.** *See under* HORSE.
**In due course.** In due time.
**In the course of nature.** In the ordinary course of events.
**Run** or **take its course, To.** *See under* RUN.
**Stay the course, To.** *See under* STAY.

**Court** (Old French, from Latin *cohors, cohortis*, 'yard', 'company of soldiers'). The yard was the central point of a farm and of the buildings that grew up round it. Hence it became the central point of any building or group of buildings, such as a town, a fort and, eventually, a royal palace, with the word at every stage also serving for the people who lived and worked in or round it.

**Court baron.** A civil court dealing with matters concerning the duties and services relating to a MANOR, in which the freeholders were the judges. *See also* COURT LEET; HUNDRED.

**Court cards.** The king, queen, knave (jack) and ace in a pack of cards. Court is a corruption of 'coat' because, apart from the ace, the cards represent a clothed or coated figure. Court cards are not so called because the king, queen and knave belonged to a court.

The king of clubs may originally have represented the arms of the pope, the king of spades, the king of France, the king of diamonds, the king of Spain, and the king of hearts, the king of England. The kings on French cards are called David (spades), Alexander (clubs), Caesar (diamonds) and Charles (hearts), representing the Jewish, Greek, Roman and Frankish empires. The queens or dames are Argine, an anagram of *Regina* (Latin, 'queen') (hearts), Judith (clubs), Rachel (diamonds) and Pallas (spades), representing royalty, fortitude, piety and wisdom. They are likenesses of Maria d'Anjou, the queen of Charles VII, of Isabeau de Bavière, the queen mother, of Agnès Sorel, the royal mistress, and of JOAN OF ARC. The knaves or jacks are OGIER THE DANE (spades), LANCELOT OF THE LAKE (clubs), Hector de Gallard (or the hero of Troy) (diamonds), and Lahire, the companion of Joan of Arc (hearts). The double heads on court cards was an English invention. Earlier cards had a single figure.

**Court circular.** Daily information concerning the official engagements of royalty, currently published in *The Times*, the *Daily Telegraph*, and the *Scotsman*. George III introduced the custom in 1803 to prevent inaccuracies in the reports of royal activities.

**Court cupboard.** A wooden stand with two or three tiers, used in the 17th and 18th centuries to display flagons, cans, cups and beakers.

**Court dress.** The formal dress worn at court.

**Court fools.** From medieval times until the 17th century, licensed fools or jesters were commonly kept at court and were frequently in the retinue of wealthy nobles. Holbein painted Sir Thomas More's jester, Patison, in his picture of the Chancellor. The Earl of Morton, Scottish Regent (executed 1581), had a fool called Patrick Bonny, and as late as 1728 Swift wrote an epitaph on Dickie Pierce, the Earl of Suffolk's fool, who is buried in Berkeley churchyard, Gloucestershire. *See also* DAGONET.

Among the most celebrated court fools are:

Archie Armstrong and Thomas Derrie, of James I
Jenny Colquhoun and James Geddes, of Mary, Queen of Scots
Robert Grene, of Queen Elizabeth I
Muckle John, of CHARLES I, who was probably also the last court fool in England
Patch, of Elizabeth, wife of Henry VII
Rahère (founder of St Bartholomew's Hospital), of Henry I (according to a tradition)
John Scogan, of Edward IV
Will Somers, of Henry VIII

Fools in French courts include:

L'Angély, of Louis XIII and Louis XIV
Brusquet, of Henri II
Guillaume Louel, of Charles VII
Haincelin Coq, of Charles VI
Miton and Thévenin de St Léger, of Charles V
Sibilot and Chicot, of Henri III and IV
Triboulet, of Louis XII and Francis I

In chess the French name for the 'bishop' is *fou* ('fool'), and the piece was formerly represented in a fool's dress.

**Court hand.** A cursive form of handwriting, which developed in England by the late 12th century as the legal script used to write the king's business and the law courts. It was abolished in the reign of George II.

**Court leet.** A court of record granted by the crown to a HUNDRED, lordship, MANOR, BOROUGH etc. It took account of FRANKPLEDGE and dealt with minor criminal offences and a variety of administrative work. In its early days it was substantially the same as the COURT BARON.

**Court martial.** A court convened to try a person subject to military law. In Britain such courts resulted from the Mutiny Act of 1689.

**Court of Appeal.** A branch of the Supreme Court of Judicature that hears appeals from the HIGH COURT.

**Court of Arches.** The ecclesiastical court of appeal for the province of Canterbury, which was formerly held in the church of St Mary-le-Bow (*Sancta Maria de Arcubus*, St Mary of the Arches), Cheapside, London.

**Court of Cassation** (Late Latin *cassare*, 'to cancel'). In France the Court of Cassation is the highest Court of Appeal, the court that can quash the judgement of other courts.

**Court of conscience.** Courts of the recovery of small debts, established at London and various other commercial centres, and eventually superseded by county courts.

**Court of honour.** A military court set up to investigate matters of honour.

**Court of love.** A judicial court for deciding affairs of the heart, established in Provence during the days of the TROUBADOURS. The following is a case submitted to their judgement: a lady listened to one admirer, squeezed the hand of another and touched with her toe the foot of a third. Query: which of these three was the favoured suitor?

**Court of Peculiars.** In particular, a branch of the COURT OF ARCHES, which had jurisdiction over the PECULIARS of the archbishop of Canterbury.

**Court of Piepowder.** A court of justice formerly held at fairs to deal with disputes between buyers and sellers. The literal meaning is 'wayfarer's court', piepowder being from French *pied-poudreux*, 'dusty-footed', 'vagabond'.

**Court of record.** A court where proceedings are officially recorded and can be produced as evidence. The Supreme Court is a superior court of record.

**Court of requests.** A minor court of equity hearing poor men's causes, which fell into disuse during the 17th century.

**Court of Session.** The supreme civil court in Scotland, first established in 1532, and originally modelled on the PARLEMENT of Paris.

**Court of St James's.** The British court to which foreign ambassadors are officially credited. St James's Palace, PALL MALL, stands on the site of a medieval leper hospital dedicated to St JAMES THE LESS. The palace was begun by Henry VIII in 1532 and was used as a residence by various monarchs and their children. After the burning of WHITEHALL in 1697, it came to be used for state ceremonies, hence the Court of St James's. It ceased to be a royal residence in 1837, but was used for LEVEES and other official functions. The office of the BOARD OF GREEN CLOTH was at St James's.

**Court order.** An order or direction issued by a court or judge requiring a person to do something or not to do it.

**Court plaster.** Sticking plaster, so called from the fashion at court of ladies patching their faces with fanciful shapes cut out from such plaster. This fashion was in vogue in the reign of Charles I and in Queen Anne's time was employed as a political badge.

**Court shoes.** Low-cut shoes for women, without laces or straps, and so called from their use as part of court dress.

> 'Elfine, *whatever* you do, always wear court shoes. Remember – c-o-u-r-t.'
>
> STELLA GIBBONS: *Cold Comfort Farm*, ch xi (1932)

**Ball is in your court, The.** *See under* BALL.

**Capel Court.** *See under* CAPEL.

**Clear the court, To.** *See under* CLEAR.

**Contempt of court.** *See under* CONTEMPT.

**Crown Court.** *See under* CROWN.

**Drumhead court martial.** *See under* DRUM.

**Friend at court.** *See under* FRIEND.

**Friend of the court.** *See under* FRIEND.

**Hampton Court.** *See under* HAMPTON.

**High Court.** *See under* HIGH.

**Hold court, To.** *See under* HOLD.

**Inns of Court.** *See under* INN.

**Kangaroo court.** *See under* KANGAROO.

**Laugh out of court, To.** *See under* LAUGH.

**Out of court.** *See under* OUT.

**Palm court.** *See under* PALM.

**Pay court to, To.** *See under* PAY.

**Prize court.** *See under* PRIZE.

**Settle out of court, To.** *See under* SETTLE.

**Small claims court.** *See under* SMALL.

**Courtain** ('short sword'). One of the swords of OGIER THE DANE; Sauvagine was the other, and they both took Munifican three years to make.

**Courteous, The retort.** *See under* RETORT.

**Courtesy.** Civility, politeness. It was at court that those in attendance practised the refinements of the age. The word originally meant the manners of the court.

**Courtesy light.** The interior light in a motor vehicle, which usually switches itself on when one of the doors is opened.

**Courtesy titles.** Titles assumed or granted by social custom, without legal status. The courtesy title of the eldest son of a peer is normally one of his father's inferior titles, usually his second, but sometimes lower ones are used. Younger sons of DUKES and MARQUESSES have the courtesy title LORD. The daughters of dukes, marquesses and EARLS are styled LADY. The younger sons of earls and all sons of VISCOUNTS and BARONS are entitled 'The Honourable', as are daughters of viscounts and barons. Courtesy titles are allowed to the eldest son of courtesy marquesses and earls. None of these titles carries the right to sit in the HOUSE OF LORDS. *See also* PEERS OF THE REALM.

**Father of Courtesy, The.** Richard de Beauchamp, Earl of Warwick (1382–1439).

**Cousin.** A person's cousin (as full cousin or first cousin) is the child of their aunt or uncle. A person's second cousin is the child of one of their parents' first cousins. A person's third cousin is the child of one of their parents' second cousins. A person's first cousin once removed is the child of their first cousin.

Sir William Blackstone (1723–80) says that Henry IV, being related or allied to every EARL in the kingdom, artfully and constantly acknowledged this connection in all public acts. The usage has descended to his successors, and in royal writs and commissions an earl is addressed 'Our right trusty and well-beloved cousin', a MARQUESS 'Our right trusty and entirely beloved cousin', and a DUKE 'Our right trusty and right-entirely-beloved cousin'.

**Cousin-german.** A person's full COUSIN or first cousin.

**Country cousin.** *See under* COUNTRY.

**Dutch cousin.** *See under* DUTCH.

**Kissing cousin.** *See under* KISS.

**Cove.** A now dated slang word for a man, approximating to fellow or chap. It was often preceded by a stock adjective, such as flash cove (a swell), rum cove (an eccentric person or 'queer fish'), downy cove (a knowing or wily person) etc. The word is old thieves' CANT and probably derives from Romany *kova*, 'thing', 'person'. It is still current in Australian use.

**Covenant. Covenanters.** A term applied to those Scottish PRESBYTERIANS subscribing to various bonds or covenants for the security and advancement of their cause. The first was entered into by the Lords of the Congregation in 1557 and another was made by ordinance of James VI in 1581. In 1638 the National Covenant was directed against the Laudian prayer book imposed by CHARLES I. In 1643 a SOLEMN LEAGUE AND COVENANT pledged the Scots and their English Parliamentarian allies to preserve Presbyterianism in Scotland and to establish it in England and Ireland.

The name Covenanter is particularly applied to those who adhered to the Covenants after they were declared unlawful in 1662. Between the RESTORATION and the Revolution of 1688 they were harried and proscribed but exhibited a brave and often fanatical resistance. *See* CAMERONIANS.

**Covenant of salt, A.** A covenant that could not be broken. As salt was a symbol of incorruption, it symbolized perpetuity.

> It is a covenant of salt for ever before the Lord unto thee and to thy seed with thee.
> Numbers 18:19

**Abrahamic Covenant, The.** *See under* ABRAHAM.

**Ark of the Covenant, The.** *See under* ARK.

**Covent Garden.** A corruption of Convent Garden, as the garden and burial ground attached to Westminster Abbey. On the dissolution of the monasteries it was granted to the Duke of Somerset. On his attainder in 1552 it then passed to the Earl of Bedford, in whose family it remained until 1910.

The fruit, flower and vegetable market developed from the 17th century, when the square became popular with stallholders. The nucleus of the existing market buildings dates from 1850 but the market itself moved to Nine Elms, Battersea, in 1974. In the 17th and 18th centuries the area was the stamping ground of the MOHOCKS and other semi-fashionable ruffians, and its COFFEE houses, bagnios (brothels) and taverns were the favourite resorts of poets, actors and artists.

Covent Garden Theatre was opened by John Rich, the Prince of Harlequins, in 1732 but was burned down in 1808 and again in 1856. It became the Royal Italian Opera House in 1847 and the new opera house was opened in 1858. *See also* BOW STREET RUNNER; WILL'S COFFEE HOUSE.

**Coventry. Coventry Mysteries.** Miracle plays supposed to have been acted at CORPUS CHRISTI at Coventry until 1591. Although they were called 'Ludus Coventriae' by Sir Robert Bruce, Cotton's librarian in the time of James I, their special connection with Coventry or Corpus Christi is doubtful. However, there are two such plays extant: the play of the Shearman and Tailors, and the play of the Weavers. *See also* MYSTERY.

**Send to Coventry, To.** *See under* SEND.

**Cover. Cover girl.** A glamorous girl whose photograph appears on the cover of a magazine or newspaper.

**Cover note.** A document issued by an insurance company to confirm that a policy is effective. The note covers the period between the commencement date of the policy and that of its actual issue.

**Cover one's tracks, To.** To conceal or obliterate the evidence of what one has done.

**Cover-up.** The concealment or attempted concealment of a crime or misdeed of some kind.

**Cover version.** A version of a previously recorded song by a different artist. The aim is to take advantage of the original's success.

**Break cover, To.** *See under* BREAK.

**First-day cover.** *See under* FIRST.

**From cover to cover.** *See under* FROM.

**Under cover.** *See under* UNDER.

**Coverdale's Bible.** *See under* BIBLE.

**Coverings, Day of.** *See* DAY OF ATONEMENT.

**Coverley, Sir Roger de.** A member of an imaginary club in the *Spectator*, 'who lived in Soho Square when he was in town'. Sir Roger, who was created by Richard Steele, represents a simple, good, lovable country English squire in the reign of Queen Anne. He was supposed to write for the *Spectator*, but was essentially portrayed by Joseph Addison. The country dance of this name was well known before Addison's time, but, he claims, it was invented by his great-grandfather. Coverley represents Cowley, now a suburb of Oxford.

**Cow.** The cow that nourished YMIR with four streams of milk was called Audhumla ('Nourisher'). She took her own nourishment by licking salt rocks covered in rime.

**Cowboy.** The term used for the cattlemen of the American West, much romanticized in popular ballad and story. Their 'ten gallon' hats, leather CHAPS and high-heeled boots, were characteristic dress in the great days of the Cattle Kingdom. The name was also applied during the Revolutionary Wars to TORY partisans of New York State, notorious for their harsh treatment of their opponents. In colloquial usage the term cowboy is applied to unscrupulous or unqualified business operators, reckless lorry drivers and the like. The disparaging use of the word probably developed from the cowboy's reputation as a tough horseman and rough-and-ready rustler, and may owe something to his portrayal as such in westerns. *See also* WILD WEST.

**Cowcatcher.** In North America a metal frame on the front of railway locomotives to clear the track of animals.

**Cowlick.** A tuft of hair on the forehead, especially one that does not lie in the same direction as the rest of the hair.

> This term must have been adopted from a comparison with that part of a ... cow's hide where the hairs, having different directions, meet and form a projecting ridge, supposed to be occasioned by the animals licking themselves.
>
> J. BROCKETT: *Glossary of North Country Words* (1825)

**Cowpuncher.** A COWBOY, derived from the metal-tipped pole with which cattle are driven when being loaded on rail wagons.

**Always behind, like a cow's tail.** *See under* ALWAYS.

**Dun cow.** *See under* DUN.

**How now, brown cow?** *See under* HOW.

**Sacred cow.** *See under* SACRED.

**Strip a cow, To.** *See under* STRIP.

**Till the cows come home.** *See under* TILL.

**Tune the old cow died of, The.** *See under* TUNE.

**Coward.** The word perhaps comes ultimately from Latin *cauda*, 'tail', either because an animal 'turns tail' when frightened or because it has its tail between its legs. In HERALDRY a beast cowarded is one with its tail between its legs.

**Cowl** or **hood does not make the monk, The.** *See under* HOOD.

**Cox, Box and.** *See under* BOX.

**Coxcomb.** An empty-headed fop or dandy, who struts around like a cock with a prominent comb. Jesters of old were so called because they wore a hat like a cock's comb.

**Coxswain** or **cox.** The helmsman of a boat, who was originally the swain or man in charge of the COCKBOAT. The word was formerly spelt cockswain.

**Cozen, To.** To cheat or trick. This is a CANT word that is perhaps the same as cousin, so that a person who cozened someone lived on them as though a cousin. Some authorities trace the word back through Italian to Latin *cocio*, 'dealer'.

**Crab. Crab canon.** In music, a canon in which the imitating voice repeats the notes of the theme in reverse order. The name derives from the old mistaken belief that crabs walked backwards.

**Catch a crab, To.** *See under* CATCH.

**Diogenes crab.** *See under* DIOGENES.

**Crack.** First-rate, excellent, as 'a crack regiment' or 'a crack shot'. Formerly the word was used as a noun for a lively young fellow, a WAG.

> Indeed, La! 'tis a noble child; a crack, madam.
>
> SHAKESPEARE: *Coriolanus*, I, iii (1607)

A crack or wisecrack is now a sharp, witty, or humorous saying, often at someone's expense. *See also* CRACK UP.

**Crack a bottle, To.** To open and drink a bottle.

> You'll crack a quart together, ha! will you not, Master Bardolph.
>
> SHAKESPEARE: *Henry IV, Pt II*, V, iii (1597)

**Crack a crib, To.** To break into a house and steal; hence, 'cracksman', a burglar. *See also* CRIB.

**Crackbrained.** Eccentric, crazy.

**Crack down on, To.** To take strict action about; to punish severely.

**Cracking pace, A.** Very fast.

**Crack of doom.** The last trump, the signal for the final judgement. Doomsday, the end of the world, the LAST JUDGEMENT.

**Crackpot.** An eccentric person.

**Crack up, To.** (1) To praise highly, to present or describe in glowing terms. The expression is often encountered in the negative and passive form, as: 'He's not what he's cracked up to be'. (2) To break down in health or mind.

**At crack of dawn.** *See under* AT.

**Fair crack of the whip, A.** *See under* FAIR.

**Get cracking, To.** A popular expression, meaning to get moving or going; to start something promptly and energetically.

**Have a crack at, To.** To attempt.

**Paper over the cracks, To.** *See under* PAPER.

**Cracker. Cracker-barrel philosophy.** Roughly the same as homespun philosophy. In America the barrels in which crackers (biscuits) used to be kept were often used as seats in the country stores by local folk who met there and exchanged views on topics of the day. *See also* CROSSROADS.

**Crackerjack.** An excellent or first-class person or thing; originally a 'crack' (excellent) 'jack' (man).

**Crackers.** In colloquial usage, the same as CRACKBRAINED.

**Cradle. Cradle crown.** In medieval England, a fine paid by a priest (in lieu of penance) for fathering a child in his house and keeping a concubine. *See also* SIN RENT.

**Cradle snatcher** or **baby snatcher.** Someone who marries or has an affair with a much younger person.

**Cat's cradle.** *See under* CAT.

**From the cradle to the grave.** *See under* FROM.

**Hand that rocks the cradle rules the world, The.** *See under* HAND.

**Craft. Craft, The.** A name given to FREEMASONRY by its members.

**Gentle craft, The.** *See under* GENTLE.

**Crag, Salisbury.** *See under* SALISBURY.

**Crambo.** A once popular form of CHARADES in which one side chooses a word and gives a member of the other side a word to rhyme with it. The guesser runs through a range of rhyming words but must describe them, not say them. For example, the team chooses 'cat' and gives the guesser the word 'mat'. He might then ask, 'Does it hit a ball?', to which the first team reply, 'No, it is not bat'. He then tries, 'Is it the opposite of thin?', to which they answer, 'No, it is not fat.' And so on until he scores a hit. The word is said to come from Latin *crambe repetita*, 'cabbage repeated'.

> Get the maids to crambo of an evening and learn the knack of rhyming.
>
> WILLIAM CONGREVE: *Love for Love*, I, i (1695)

**Dumb crambo.** *See under* DUMB.

**Crammer.** A type of private (independent) secondary school that concentrates on preparing its students for examinations and university entry. They are so called since they 'cram' their fee-paying candidates with the appropriate subject knowledge and the 'tricks of the trade'. They are less in evidence now than they once were, but are by no means defunct, since there are always schools where pupils are poorly taught and always pupils who lack application or intellect.

**Cramp. Cramp rings.** Rings blessed by English sovereigns and distributed on GOOD FRIDAY, supposed to cure cramp and 'falling sickness' (epilepsy). The custom grew up after the time of EDWARD THE CONFESSOR, who was said to have been given such a ring by a pilgrim, and was continued until the reign of Queen Mary Tudor. *See also* KING'S EVIL.

> The superstitious use of cramp-rings, as a preservative against fits, is not entirely abandoned; instances occur where nine young men of a parish each subscribe a crooked sixpence, to be moulded into a ring for a young woman afflicted with this malady.
>
> JOHN ROKEWODE: *The Hundred of Thingoe* (Suffolk), Introduction (1838)

**Writer's cramp.** *See under* WRITE.

**Cranmer's Bible.** *See under* BIBLE.

**Crapaud.** *See under* JOHNNY.

**Anciens crapauds prendront Sara, Les.** *See under* ANCIEN.

**Craps.** The American term for dice, a most popular form of gambling in the USA. The name has been explained as follows. About 1800, when New Orleans was a French city, Bernard Marigny introduced dice-playing from France. He was a CREOLE and known as Johnny CRAPAUD, thus dice-playing, or Johnny Crapaud's game, became shortened into 'craps'. Burgundy Street in the Vieux Carré of New Orleans was, until 1860, known as Craps Street, after Marigny. However, it is more likely that the name derives from 'crabs', a term for the lowest throw in dice, perhaps alluding to the small and sour crab apple.

**Cravat.** The neckscarf takes its name from the neckcloth worn by Croat soldiers serving in the French army in the THIRTY YEARS' WAR (1618–48). The French adopted the style, and from there it spread to England. The word thus came into English, through French, from Serbo-Croat *Hrvat*, 'Croat'.

**Craven.** The word probably derives from Old French *crevant*, 'bursting', from *crever*, 'to burst', 'to die'. When controversies were decided by a challenge to battle, the combatants fought with batons, and if the accused could either kill his adversary or maintain the fight till sundown he was acquitted. If he wished to call off, he cried out 'Craven!' and was held disgraced. Hence the former phrase 'to cry craven', meaning to acknowledge oneself vanquished.

**Crazy. Crazy bone.** The American equivalent of the FUNNY BONE.

**Crazy Gang, The.** The lunatic outfit so named first formed in 1932 for a performance of the revue *Crazy Month* at the London Palladium. It consisted of three pairs of already famous comics: Flanagan and Allen, otherwise Bud Flanagan (Robert Wintrop, originally Reuben Weintrop) (1896–1968) and Chesney Allen (1894–1982), Nervo and Knox, i.e. Jimmy Nervo (James Henry Holloway) (1897–1975) and Teddy Knox (1896–1974), and the Scots pair Naughton and Gold, i.e. Charlie Naughton (1887–1976) and Jimmy Gold (James McGonigal) (1886–1967). They remained together until 1960.

**Crazy golf.** A form of putting in which balls have to negotiate a number of obstacles such as humps, tunnels, bends and bridges in order to reach the hole. *See also* CLOCK GOLF.

> Until recently crazy golf was regarded as a quaint relic of the 1950s: now, with a glut in conventional

18-hole courses, long-nurtured plans for wilder alternatives are beginning to emerge.
*Sunday Times* (26 July 1998)

**Crazy paving.** Paving composed of irregularly shaped stone or concrete slabs, used for ornamental effect on terraces, garden paths and the like.

**Creaking doors hang the longest.** Delicate persons often outlive the more robust.

**Cream, Bristol.** *See under* BRISTOL.

**Creation, The Lord of.** *See under* LORD.

**Creature.** That which is created, whether animate or inanimate. Thus living things are sometimes known as 'God's creatures', and the Communion Service in the BOOK OF COMMON PRAYER has 'these thy creatures of bread and wine'.

**Creature comforts.** Food and other material things necessary for the comfort of the body. A human being is supposed to consist of body and soul, so the body is the creature.

A very strong smell of brandy and water forewarned the visitor that Mr Squeers had been seeking in creature comforts a temporary forgetfulness of his unpleasant situation.
DICKENS: *Nicholas Nickleby*, ch lx (1838–9)

**Crécy.** The battle of this name between the French and English took place near the village of Crécy in northeast France on 26 August 1346. Each side began with a force of 14,000 to 20,000, the English under the command of Edward III, the French led by Philip VI. The superiority of the English archers, whose arrows could reach 300 paces, resulted in the resounding defeat of the French and the loss of about 1500 of their men-at-arms. This first great victory of the English in the HUNDRED YEARS' WAR enabled them to take CALAIS and use it as their main continental base.

**Credence. Credence table.** The table near the altar on which the bread and wine are placed before they are consecrated. In former times food was placed on a credence table to be tasted before being set before the guests. They were thus reassured that the meat was not poisoned. The word ultimately derives from Latin *credentia*, 'trust'.

**Letter of credence.** *See under* LETTER.

**Credibility gap.** The disparity that can exist between a claim or statement on the one hand and the reality of the situation on the other. If this is constantly experienced, it results in a loss of confidence in those making such statements. President Nixon created a credibility gap in the 1960s when he asked black Americans 'to judge him by his deeds and not his words'. They did, and were disappointed.

**Street cred.** *See under* STREET.

**Credit. Letter of credit.** *See under* LETTER.

**Paper credit.** *See under* PAPER.

**Credo** (Latin, 'I believe'). A statement of belief. The word represents the opening of the Apostles' and Nicene Creeds in Latin: *Credo in Deum* ('I believe in God').

**Credo quia impossibile** (Latin, 'I believe it because it is impossible'). A paradox ascribed to St AUGUSTINE, but founded on a passage in Tertullian. An alternative version is: *Credo quia absurdum est* ('I believe it because it is unreasonable'). The statement is a justification of faith on the grounds that there is no need to understand. Faith in the supernatural does not require an explanation.

**Creed. Apostles' Creed.** *See under* APOSTLE.

**Athanasian Creed.** *See under* ATHANASIAN.

**Nicene Creed.** *See under* NICENE.

**Creeping to the Cross.** The GOOD FRIDAY ceremony of the Veneration of the Cross was commonly so called in England, when priest and people kneel and kiss the cross on the sanctuary steps. The custom derives from the veneration of the True Cross at Jerusalem. *See also* INVENTION OF THE CROSS.

**Crème de la crème** (French, 'cream of the cream'). The very best; the choicest of what is already choice.

**Cremona.** A town in Lombardy famous for its violin makers. The best known were Nicolò AMATI (1596–1684), teacher of Andrea GUARNERI (*c*.1626–98) and Antonio Stradivari (1644–1737). The term is loosely applied to any good instrument. *See also* STRAD.

The organ stop known as the cremona is a corruption of German *Krummhorn*, 'crooked horn'. It is a reed stop like a clarinet stop.

**Cremorne Gardens.** Famous London pleasure gardens, opened in 1845 to rival VAUXHALL GARDENS on the land of Chelsea Farm, the former property of Thomas Dawson, Viscount Cremorne. They were a popular venue for fêtes and entertainments, but their clientèle degenerated and they were closed in 1877 after many local complaints. Lots Road Electric Power Station, on the left bank of the Thames near Battersea Bridge, occupies much of the former site. *See also* ROSHERVILLE GARDENS.

**Creole.** Originally a person of Spanish parentage born in the West Indies as against those of mixed blood, Negroes, new immigrants and Aboriginals. The name is often wrongly used to denote those of mixed blood, but its usage varies in different places: in the West Indies it implies European descent; in Louisiana, the French-speaking whites; in Mexico, whites of Spanish blood. Non-whites are called Negro Creoles, but in Mauritius, Réunion and elsewhere Creole is usually applied to Negroes. The Empress Josephine was a Creole from Martinique, and the liberated slaves of Liberia called themselves Creoles. The word came into English through

French and Spanish, and probably derives from Portuguese *crioulo*. This was a word used for a slave born in one's household or for a person of European parentage born in the colonies. The ultimate source is probably in Portuguese *criar*, 'to bring up'.

**Creon.** The name, meaning 'ruler' or 'prince', is that of several characters in Greek legend. They are mostly minor, but two of the more memorable are Creon, brother of Jocasta and successor to OEDIPUS at Thebes, and Creon, king of Corinth, who features in various stories about JASON and MEDEA.

**Crescent.** Tradition says that Philip of Macedon, the father of Alexander the Great, met with great difficulties in the siege of Byzantium so set the workmen to undermine the walls. However, a crescent moon illuminated the scene, and the plan miscarried. As a result the Byzantines erected a statue to DIANA, goddess of the moon, and the crescent became the symbol of the state.

Another legend is that Othman, the sultan, saw in a vision a crescent moon, which kept increasing till its horns extended from east to west. He thus adopted the crescent of his dream for his standard, adding the motto, *Donec repleat orbem*, 'Until it fills the world'.

The crescent as a symbol was used by the Seljuk sultan Ala-ud-Din in the mid-13th century, and it was reputedly adopted from this source by Osman, who founded the Ottoman dynasty in about 1281. It is also said that the crescent was placed on the Turkish flag by Mohammed II, after the capture of Constantinople in 1453.

**Crescent City.** A popular name in the USA for New Orleans, with reference to the location of the city on a sharp bend of the Mississippi.

**Red Crescent.** *See under* RED.

**Cresset.** A beacon light. The original cresset was an open metal cup at the top of a pole, the cup being filled with burning grease or oil. Hence the name, from Old French *craisset* (modern French *graisse*), 'grease'.

**Cressida** or **Cressid.** The daughter of CALCHAS, a priest, beloved by TROILUS. The two vowed eternal fidelity and as pledges Troilus gave the maiden a sleeve, while she gave the Trojan prince a glove. Scarcely had the vow been made when an exchange of prisoners was agreed. DIOMEDES gave up three Trojan princes, and in return was offered Cressida, who vowed to remain constant. Troilus swore to rescue her. She was led off to the Grecian's tent and soon gave all her affections to Diomedes, even bidding him wear the sleeve that Troilus had given her in token of his love.

> When they have said 'as false
> As air, as water, wind, or sandy earth,
> As fox to lamb, as wolf to heifer's calf,
> Pard to the hind, or stepdame to her son;'
> Yea, let them say, to stick the heart of falsehood,
> 'As false as Cressid.'
>
> SHAKESPEARE: *Troilus and Cressida*, III, ii (1601)

The origin of Cressida's name is complex. The name Briseis occurs in the *Iliad* (8th century BC) for a captive Greek girl. Benoît de Sainte-Maure, a 12th-century poet, adopted this name in the form Briseida for his great *Roman de Troie* (*c*.1160). Boccaccio, in the 14th century, altered the name to Criseida, basing it on the name of another Greek captive girl, Chryseis, the daughter of Chryses. Chaucer then altered this to Criseyde and Shakespeare finally gave the name its present form of Cressida.

**Cresswell, Madam.** A notorious bawd and procuress who flourished in London between about 1670 and 1684 and who was much patronized by RESTORATION courtiers and politicians. She wintered in CLERKENWELL and kept house in Camberwell in the summer. 'Old Mother Cresswell' was not married, although Sir Thomas Player went by the nickname of Sir Thomas Cresswell. In her old age she became religiously inclined and bequeathed £10 for a funeral sermon, in which nothing ill should be said of her. Sir Walter Scott attributes the sermon to the Duke of Buckingham:

> 'Why,' said the Duke, 'I had caused the little Quodling to go through his oration thus – That whatever evil reports had passed current during the lifetime of the worthy matron whom they had restored to dust that day, malice itself could not deny that she was born well, married well, lived well, and died well; since she was born in Shadwell, married to Cresswell, lived in Camberwell, and died in Bridewell.'
>
> *Peveril of the Peak*, ch xliv (1823)

**Cresta Run.** The tobogganing course of this name, famous for its dangerously winding, steeply banked channel of ice, is built each year at St Moritz, Switzerland. Competitors race on light toboggans, typically in a head-first position. The first run was built in 1884 and the name is now sometimes applied to hazardous downhill sections of other sporting 'runs', whether on toboggans or not.

> A phalanx of young male athletes came hurtling down the hill and past. They were, incredibly, running full tilt down this sludge-coloured Cresta Run.
>
> *The Times* (18 January 1999)

**Crestfallen.** Dejected or depressed. The allusion is to fighting cocks, whose crests fall in defeat and rise rigid and deep red in victory.

**Crete. Cretan labyrinth.** *See* LABYRINTH.

**Dictys Cretensis.** *See under* DICTYS.

**Hound of Crete, The.** *See under* HOUND.

**Infamy of Crete, The.** *See under* INFAMY.

**Cretinism.** Mental imbecility accompanied by

dwarfism and goitre, so called from the *Crétins* of the Swiss Alps. The word is a corruption of Swiss French *Crestin* ('Christian'), because of the kindness and gentleness of such people. Similarly, idiots are called innocents.

**Crew. Crew cut.** A form of haircut popularized by US athletes, particularly college rowing crews at Harvard and Yale universities, in the decade following the Second World War. The hair is closely cropped and brushed upright.

**Crew neck.** A close-fitting round neckline on a sweater. Its origin is similar to that of the CREW CUT.

**Canting crew.** *See under* CANT.

**Scratch crew.** *See under* SCRATCH.

**Creweian oration.** A Latin oration delivered in alternate years by the Public Orator and Professor of Poetry at the ENCAENIA of Oxford University, essentially to commemorate the benefactions of Nathaniel, 3rd Baron Crewe (1633–1721), bishop of Oxford and later of Durham. He was a notorious sycophant and a favourite of the Duke of York, afterwards James II. From 1688 he was in disgrace, and his benefactions may be regarded as belated attempts to restore his name. The oration is essentially a record of the year's outstanding events at the University. Until 1972 it was delivered in Latin, but that year Roy Fuller, then Professor of Poetry, introduced the practice of delivering the oration in English.

**Crewel garters.** Garters made of worsted or yarn. The resemblance in sound between 'crewel' (the derivation of which is unknown) and 'cruel' gave rise to many puns.

> Ha, ha! he wears cruel garters.
>
> SHAKESPEARE: *King Lear*, II, iv (1605)

**Crib.** The word has a variety of meanings, from a child's bed to a student's illicit translation of a foreign text. Yet all the senses are connected, and developed as follows: (1) a fodder rack or manger for animals; (2) a wickerwork basket similar to such a manger; (3) a child's bed with barred sides, also resembling a manger; (4) (as a verb, and thieves' slang) to steal something out of a basket; (5) to take or copy something from elsewhere and use it as if one had produced it in the first place.

**Crack a crib, To.** *See under* CRACK.

**Crichton, The Admirable.** James Crichton (1560–85), Scottish traveller, scholar and swordsman. So called by Sir Thomas Urquhart in *The Jewel* (1652):

> The admirable Crichtoun ... did ... present himself to epilogate this his almost extemporanean Comedie.

Hence a name for anyone excelling in studies or pursuits, or generally talented. Harrison Ainsworth was much indebted to Urquhart for his novel *The Admirable Crichton* (1837). J.M. Barrie's play of the same name about a perfect butler appeared in 1902.

**Cricket.** The name of the game apparently derives from Old French *criquet*, 'goal post', 'wicket'. It is first recorded in an English text only in the 16th century. Strutt in his *Sports and Pastimes of the People of England* (1801) suggests that cricket originated from the medieval game of club ball. John Derrick of Guildford in 1598, when he was about 59, states that as a boy at 'the Free schoole of Guldeford ... hee and several of his fellowes did runne and play there at Crekett and other plaies'. An earlier reference to 'criquet' has been traced to 15th-century Flanders. The game was certainly played at Winchester College before the Civil War (1642–51). It began to come into its own in the 18th century and owed much to the Hambledon Club matches on Broad Halfpenny Down, Hampshire, which came to an end in 1793. The Marylebone Cricket Club (MCC), which is regarded as the governing body of the game, was founded in 1787, and the present LORD'S Cricket Ground was opened in 1814.

Single and double wicket was played from early on, and the dimensions of the wicket and other essentials for the game varied considerably. At the beginning of the 18th century two stumps, 12in (30cm) high and 24in (60cm) apart, were used. In the rules made in 1774 the stumps were to be 22in (56cm) high with a bail of 6in (15cm). The third stump was added by the Hambledon Club in 1775 and the height of the stump raised from 27 to 28in (68.5 to 71cm) in 1929. *See also* CHINAMAN; GOOGLY; TEST MATCH.

> Who would think that a little bit of leather, and two pieces of wood, had such a delightful and delighting power?
>
> MISS MITFORD: *Our Village* ('A Country Cricket-Match') (1832)

**As merry as a cricket.** *See* GRIG.

**French cricket.** *See under* FRENCH.

**Not cricket.** Not fair, not sporting.

**Crime, Queen of.** *See under* QUEEN.

**Cripplegate.** The origin of the name for this street in the City of London is uncertain. It has been popularly associated with the cripples who begged at the gate here in medieval times. However, early forms of the name suggest that it may actually derive from Old English *crypel*, 'narrow passage', referring to an underpass or tunnel that perhaps connected the gate with the Barbican. The gate was demolished in 1760 so that the street could be widened.

**Crisis** (Latin, 'decision', from Greek *krinein*, 'to decide'). The earliest sense of the word in English (in the 16th century) was with regard to the decisive turning point in a disease, when the sick person began either to recover or to decline. HIPPOCRATES said that all diseases had their periods, when the HUMOURS of the body ebbed and flowed like the tide of the sea. These tidal days he called critical days, and the tide itself a crisis, because it was on these days the physician could determine whether the disorder was taking a good or bad turn. The seventh and all its multiples were critical days of a favourable character.

**Abdication Crisis.** *See under* ABDICATION.

**Bedchamber Crisis.** *See under* BED.

**Crispin and Crispinian.** Shoemakers who became patron saints of their craft. It is said that the two brothers, born at Rome, went to Soissons in France to propagate the Christian religion, maintaining themselves wholly by making and mending shoes. They were martyred *c.*286.

**St Crispin's Day.** 25 October, the day of the Battle of Agincourt. Shakespeare makes Crispin Crispian one person, and not two brothers. Hence Henry V says to his soldiers:

> And Crispin Crispian shall ne'er go by –
> But we in it shall be remembered.
> *Henry V*, IV, iii (1598)

**St Crispin's holiday.** Every Monday, so formerly named by those who began the working week on Tuesday, such as butchers and fishmongers etc. Monday was also a non-working day with shoemakers. Hence the name.

**St Crispin's lance.** A shoemaker's awl.

**Criss-cross.** Although often thought of as a reduplicated form of cross, the word actually evolved from Christ-cross, i.e. 'Christ's cross'. This was originally a cross, something like the MALTESE CROSS, that was placed before the alphabet in a HORNBOOK. The Christ-cross row was thus the alphabet. *See also* CHRIST'S CROSS ME SPEED.

> *Sir Ralph*: I wonder, wench, how I thy name might know.
> *Mall*: Why you may find it, sir, in th' Christcross row.
> PORTER: *Two Angry Women of Abington*, V, i (1599)

The word has also been spelt as chriss-cross. Shakespeare shortened it to cross-row:

> He hearkens after prophecies and dreams;
> And from the cross-row plucks the letter G,
> And says a wizard told him that by G
> His issue disinherited should be;
> And, for my name of George begins with G,
> It follows in his thought that I am he.
> *Richard III*, I, i (1592)

As the Maltese cross was also sometimes used in place of XII to mark that hour on clocks, criss-cross has occasionally been used for noon:

> The feskewe of the Diall is upon the Chriss-cross of Noone.
> ANON: *The Puritan Widow*, IV, ii (1607)

**Critic.** A judge, an arbiter. A captious, malignant critic is called a ZOILUS.

**Armchair critic.** *See under* ARMCHAIR.

**High criticism.** *See under* HIGH.

**Prince of Critics, The.** *See under* PRINCE.

**Stop-watch critics.** *See under* STOP.

**Croak, To.** In slang this means to die, the term probably coming from the hoarse death rattle or croak of the expiring breath. A HEDGE doctor or wandering QUACK was known as a Crocus, or someone who made his patients croak.

**Croaker.** A raven, so called from its croak, and also a grumbling person, or one who takes a despondent view of things. Oliver Goldsmith, in his *Good-natured Man* (1768), has a character so named.

**Croakumshire.** A name given to the county of Northumberland, whose inhabitants were alleged to speak with a peculiar croak. It was said to be particularly noticeable in Newcastle and Morpeth, where the people were believed to be born with a burr in their throats that prevented their voicing the letter r.

**Crockett, Davy.** An American folk hero (1786–1836) famed as a marksman, bear hunter and fighter. He served under Andrew Jackson in the Creek War (1813–14). His popularity led him to Congress where his natural wit and homespun stories made him a noted character. He was killed at the ALAMO in 1836.

**Crockford.** The popular name for *Crockford's Clerical Directory*, published since 1838 and first compiled by John Crockford. It is a reference book of all the clergy of the CHURCH OF ENGLAND and of the other churches in communion with the see of Canterbury.

**Crockford's.** Originally an exclusive gambling club established at 50 St James's Street in 1828 by William Crockford (1775–1844), the son of a fishmonger. It became the favourite haunt of the world of fashion, and fortunes were staked there. Crockford became a millionaire before he retired in 1840. Crockford's closed down in about 1848 in consequence of a change in the Gaming Laws. A new Crockford's opened at 21 Hertford Street in 1928, essentially as a bridge club, subsequently moving to sumptuous premises at Carlton House Terrace. It is now at 30 Curzon Street. The new Betting and Gaming Act of 1960, permitting the revival of games of chance, enabled it to acquire a leading position, with *chemin de fer* as its main game.

**Crocodile.** A symbol of deity among the Egyptians, because, says Plutarch, it is the only aquatic animal which has its eyes covered with a thin transparent membrane, by reason of which it sees and is not seen, as God sees all, Himself not being seen. To this he adds: 'The Egyptians worship God symbolically in the crocodile, that being the only animal without a tongue, like the Divine Logos, which standeth not in need of speech' (*De Iside et Osiride*, vol ii (2nd century AD)).

Achilles Tatius (2nd century AD) says: 'The number of its teeth equals the number of days in a year.' Another tradition is that, during the seven days held sacred to APIS, the crocodile will harm no one.

**Crocodile tears.** Hypocritical tears. The tale is that crocodiles moan and sigh like a person in deep distress in order to allure travellers to them and shed tears over their prey while devouring it or in sorrow after devouring it. Crocodiles do 'moan' (the sound has been described as something between a bark and a roar) and they do shed tears, but the latter result from a gland in the top of the mouth which is activated during feeding.

> As the mournful crocodile
> With sorrow snares relenting passengers.
> SHAKESPEARE: *Henry VI, Pt II*, III, i (1590)

**Croesus, As rich as.** *See under* AS.

**Crofters.** Smallholders in the Highlands of Scotland and the Western Isles, holding their land by a variety of ancient tenures. A cottar is somewhat similar to a crofter.

**Cro-Magnon man.** An early type of modern man, named after the Cro-Magnon cave near Les Eyzies in the Dordogne, France, where four of their skeletons were discovered in 1868. Cro-Magnon man is associated with the AURIGNACIAN culture. His skull was long and narrow and larger than that of the average European of today.

**Cromlech.** A name formerly used by British archaeologists for a NEOLITHIC AGE monument consisting of a large flat stone resting on top of two or more others, like a table (Welsh *crom*, 'bent', and *llech*, 'flat stone'). They appear to be the uncovered remains of burial chambers or cairns. The French name DOLMEN is now more commonly used. WAYLAND SMITH's Cave, Berkshire, Trethevy Quoit, Cornwall, KIT'S COTY HOUSE, Kent, and the 'killing-stone' at Louth, Ireland, are examples.

**Crompton's mule** or **spinning mule.** Invented by Samuel Crompton (1753–1827) in 1779. His invention was pirated at the outset and he derived little financial benefit from his efforts. It was so called because it was:

> a kind of mixture of machinery between the warp-machine of Mr Arkwright and the woof-machine or hand-jenny of Mr Hargrave.
> *Encyclopaedia Britannica* (1797)

**Cromwell. Cromwell's Bible.** *See under* BIBLE.

**Grandison Cromwell.** *See under* GRANDISON.

**Cronos** or **Cronus.** *See* KRONUS.

**Crony.** *See* CHUM.

**Crook.** A dishonest person is so called because he is crooked or 'bent'. The word first came into general use from American slang in the 19th century. Much earlier than this, crook was a word for a crooked deed or piece of trickery.

**Crook the elbow** or **finger, To.** This phrase occurs in England before the mid-1780s. It is the American equivalent of ELBOW-LIFTING. More recently in England to crook the finger means to drink from a tea or coffee cup with the little finger crooked. This is sometimes regarded as a mark of gentility.

**By hook or by crook.** *See under* BY.

**Crooning.** A sentimental type of humming or singing in a low subdued voice that began in the USA in the 1920s and that soon became popular.

> The principle of crooning is to use as little voice as possible and instead to make a sentimental appeal by prolonged moaning somewhere near the written notes, but preferably never actually on those notes.
> ERIC BLOM: *Everyman's Dictionary of Music* (1947)

**Crop. Crop circles.** Also known as corn circles, these are circular areas of standing crops that have been neatly but mysteriously flattened, apparently by some kind of scything motion or vortex. They first appeared in the early 1980s in the south of England and have baffled scientists. They have been ascribed to the action of fungi, to supernatural forces, and to the orchestrated handiwork of hoaxers, but no explanation for their appearance has been fully convincing or conclusive. Some 200 such circles were reported annually in the 1990s.

> If crop circle investigator Paul Vigay is right, the mysterious force which creates intricate patterns in fields doesn't just flatten corn — it genetically improves it.
> *The Times* (12 August 1998)

**Crop up, To.** To occur or arise, especially unexpectedly. The verb originates from mining, in which a stratum or vein that comes up to the surface is said to crop up. If it comes out of the side of a slope it is said to crop out. The former verb is now common in figurative use, but the latter is rare.

**Catch crop.** *See under* CATCH.

**Come a cropper, To.** *See under* COME.

**Eton crop.** *See under* ETON.

**Neck and crop.** *See under* NECK.

**Croque-mitaine** (French, literally 'glove-muncher'). A HOBGOBLIN, a bogeyman or ugly monster, used by French nurses and parents to frighten children into good behaviour. In 1863 Ernest L'Épine published a romance with this title, telling the story of a god-daughter of

CHARLEMAGNE whom he called 'Mitaine'. It was translated by Tom Hood. Some authorities derive the second word of the name not from French *mitaine*, answering to English 'mitten', but from Dutch *metjien*, 'little girl', the equivalent of German *Mädchen*.

**Croque-monsieur** (French, literally 'sir-muncher'). The French equivalent of a toasted cheese and ham sandwich. When served with a fried egg on top, it is known as a *croque-madame*. It is said to have first appeared in the early 20th century in a café on the Boulevard des Capucines in Paris. The name itself may have arisen as a whimsical variant of CROQUE-MITAINE.

**Croquet.** The garden game probably takes its name from a French dialect variant of *crochet*, 'little hook', because the early croquet mallets were shaped like hockey sticks. It is probably descended from the earlier game of pell mell or PALL MALL and became popular in England from the 1850s.

**Crosier** or **crozier** (Old French *crossier*, 'staff bearer', from *crosse*, 'pastoral staff', literally 'hooked stick'). The pastoral staff of an abbot or bishop, and sometimes applied to an archbishop's staff, which terminates in a cross and not in a crook as does the bishop's crosier. The word originally applied to the bearer of the staff, then passed to the staff itself.

A bishop turns his staff outwards to denote his wider authority. An abbot turns it inwards to show that his authority is limited to his own religious house. The abbot covers his staff with a veil when walking in the presence of a bishop, his superior.

**Cross.** The cross is not solely a Christian symbol originating with the crucifixion. In Carthage it was used for ornamental purposes. Runic crosses were set up by the Scandinavians as boundary marks and were also erected over the graves of kings and heroes. Cicero writes (*De Divinatione*, ii (1st century BC)) that the augur's staff that marked out the heaven was a cross. The Egyptians employed it as a sacred symbol, and two buns marked with a cross were discovered at Herculaneum. It was also a sacred symbol among the Aztecs. In Cozumel it was an object of worship, and at Tabasco it symbolized the god of rain. It was one of the emblems of QUETZALCOATL, as lord of the four cardinal points, and the four winds that blow from them.

The cross of the crucifixion is said to have been made of palm, cedar, olive and cypress, to signify the four quarters of the globe. Robert Curzon in *A Visit to the Monasteries of the Levant* (1848) gives the legend that SOLOMON cut down a cedar and buried it on the spot where the Pool of Bethesda stood later. A few days before the crucifixion, the cedar floated to the surface of the pool and was used as the upright of Christ's cross.

**Cross a bridge when one comes to it, To.** To deal with matters as and when they arise.

**Cross and ball.** The orb of royalty is a sphere or ball surmounted by a cross, an emblem of empire introduced in representations of Christ. The cross stands above the ball, to signify that the spiritual power is above the temporal.

**Cross and pile.** A former phrase for the obverse and reverse sides of a coin, otherwise head and tail, hence money generally and the game of PITCH AND TOSS in particular, to which Edward II was said to be partial. Coins were in former times stamped with a cross on one side. *Pile* (Latin *pila*) is French for the reverse of a coin. It is probably the same word as English 'pile', as used for a column of timber or concrete. The reference is to the small iron pillar on top of which the metal or coin was laid to be stamped. *See also* HEADS OR TAILS.

> Marriage is worse than cross I win, pile you lose.
> THOMAS SHADWELL: *Epsom Wells* (1672)

**Cross as a mystic emblem, The.** There are four basic types:

> The Greek cross, found on Assyrian tablets, Egyptian and Persian monuments, and on Etruscan pottery.
> The *crux decussata*, generally called St ANDREW'S cross, an X-shaped cross, found fairly commonly in ancient sculpture.
> The Latin cross or *crux immissa*. This symbol is found on coins, monuments and medals long before the Christian era.
> The tau cross or *crux commissa*. A very old cross. It is also the cross of St ANTHONY OF EGYPT.

The tau cross with a handle, or *crux ansata*, is common to several Egyptian deities, such as ISIS and OSIRIS, and it is the emblem of immortality and life generally. The circle on the top signifies the eternal preserver of the world, and the T is the monogram of THOTH, the Egyptian MERCURY, meaning wisdom. Tau derives from Hebrew *tav*, the last letter of the Hebrew alphabet, transliterated as t.

**Crossbelts, The.** *See under* REGIMENTAL AND DIVISIONAL NICKNAMES.

**Cross-benches.** Seats set at right angles to the rest of the seats in the HOUSE OF COMMONS and the HOUSE OF LORDS, on which independent members sit. Hence a cross-bencher is an independent.

**Crossbill.** The red plumage and curious crossing of the upper and lower bill-tips of this bird are explained by a medieval fable, which says that these distinctive marks were bestowed on it by Christ at the crucifixion, as a reward for its having attempted to pull the nails from the cross with its beak. The fable is best known to English readers through H.W. Longfellow's 'Legend of the Crossbill', a translation from the German of Julius Mosen.

**Crossbones.** *See* SKULL AND CROSSBONES.

**Cross-dressing.** The practice of wearing the clothes of the opposite sex; transvestism.

**Cross-grained.** Bad-tempered, perverse. Wood works smoothly only with the grain. When the grain crosses there is often a knot or curling, which is hard to work.

**Crossing the line.** Sailing across the equator. Advantage is usually taken of this for ceremonial practical joking aboard ship. Those who have not previously crossed the line are summoned to the court of NEPTUNE for trial, and are usually ducked by 'bears', sometimes lathered and roughly shaved, given 'soap pills' to swallow and so on. As at present practised the whole affair constitutes a good-humoured and amusing interlude, but in former days some of the buffoonery and horseplay was decidedly rough. Such performances have a long history and may have begun as propitiatory rites to the deities of the ocean. At one time similar ceremonies were performed when a ship crossed the 39th parallel (about the latitude of Lisbon) and also when passing through the Straits of Gibraltar and rounding the Cape of Good Hope.

**Cross in heraldry, The.** As many as 285 varieties of cross have been recognized, but the twelve in ordinary use, from which the others are derived, are:

(1) the ordinary cross
(2) the cross humetté or couped
(3) the cross urdé or pointed
(4) the CROSS POTENT
(5) the cross crosslet
(6) the cross botonné or treflé
(7) the cross moline
(8) the cross potence
(9) the cross fleury
(10) the cross patté
(11) the Maltese or eight-pointed cross
(12) the cross cleché and fitché

**Cross Keys, The.** The emblem of St PETER and also of St Servatius, St Hippolytus, St GENEVIÈVE, St Petronilla, St Osyth, St MARTHA and St Germanus of Paris. They also form the arms of the archbishop of York. The bishop of Winchester bears two keys and a sword in saltire, and the bishops of St Asaph, Gloucester, Exeter and Peterborough bear two keys in saltire. The Cross Keys are also used as a PUBLIC HOUSE SIGN.

**Cross-legged knights.** Crusaders were generally represented on their tombs with crossed legs.

> From him descended cross-legg'd knights,
> Fam'd for their faith and warlike fights.
> SAMUEL BUTLER: *Hudibras*, I, i (1662)

**Cross off** or **out, To.** To cancel by running a line through; to delete.

**Cross of Lorraine.** This cross, with two bars, was adopted as the emblem of the Free French during the Second World War. It is the patriarchal cross.

**Cross one's fingers** or **keep one's fingers crossed, To.** To hope for good luck. The words are often accompanied by the physical gesture of crossing one's first two fingers.

**Cross one's heart, To.** To promise or pledge. The words are often accompanied by a sign of the cross made over the heart.

> 'Let's both swear.' 'Cross my heart and hope to die. Now what about bed?'
> ROSE MACAULAY: *Crewe Train*, ch x (1926)

**Cross one's mind, To.** To occur to one briefly.

**Cross potent.** An heraldic cross, each limb of which has an additional cross-piece like the head of an old-fashioned crutch. It is so called from French *potence*, 'crutch'. It is also known as a Jerusalem cross and a Teutonic cross.

**Cross questions and crooked answers.** An old parlour game which consists in giving ludicrous or irrelevant answers to straightforward questions. The phrase is thus used of someone who is 'hedging' or trying to conceal the truth when questioned.

**Crossroads.** In the USA, when used as an adjective, the word implies a rural or unsophisticated quality. The reference is to the general stores at crossroads, which in thinly populated areas became meeting-places for gossip. *See also* CRACKER-BARREL PHILOSOPHY.

All people excluded from holy rites, such as criminals and suicides, were at one time buried at crossroads. Ancient Germanic peoples used such places for sacrifices and thus, by association, crossroads came to be places of execution. *See also* DIRTY WORK AT THE CROSSROADS.

**Crossroads of the Pacific.** A nickname for Honolulu, from its central position on sea and air routes.

**Cross someone's bows, To.** To annoy someone and incur their displeasure. The phrase is of nautical origin. It is a breach of good manners for a junior ship to cross the bows of a senior.

**Cross someone's path, To.** To meet or thwart someone.

**Cross swords, To.** To fight a duel; metaphorically, to argue.

**Cross the floor, To.** In parliamentary usage to change parties. Government and OPPOSITION benches are on opposite sides of the floor of the HOUSE OF COMMONS.

**Cross the great divide, To.** To die.

**Cross the hand** or **palm, To.** Gypsy fortune-tellers traditionally ask that one should 'cross their hand with a bit of silver'. This, they say, is

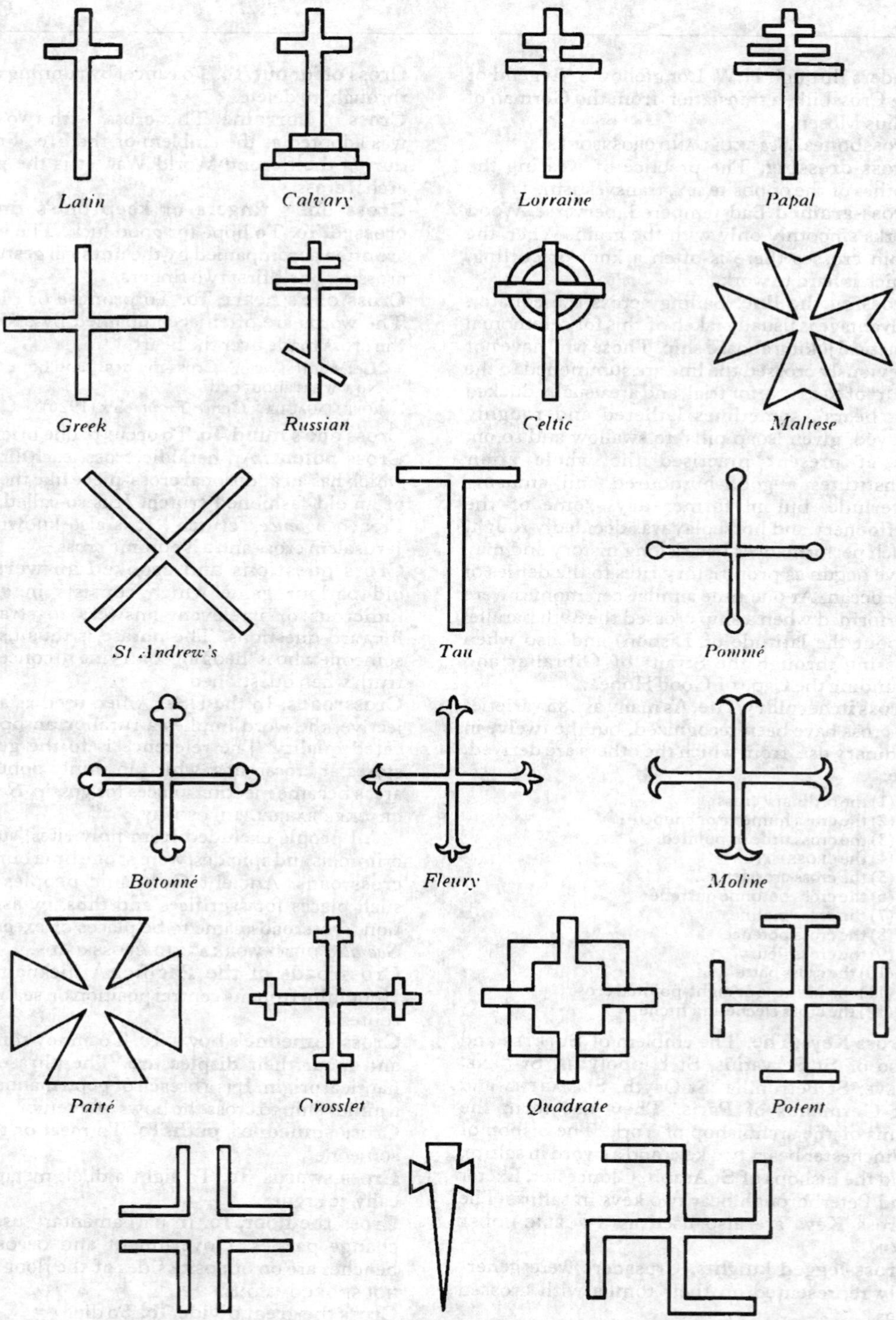
Latin
Calvary
Lorraine
Papal
Greek
Russian
Celtic
Maltese
St Andrew's
Tau
Pommé
Botonné
Fleury
Moline
Patté
Crosslet
Quadrate
Potent
Voided and Couped
Patté Fitché
Fylfot, Swastika

**Types of cross**

for luck. The coin remains with the owner of the crossed hand. The sign of the cross warded off witches and all other evil spirits, and as fortune-telling belongs to the black arts, the palm is signed with a cross to keep off the wiles of the Devil. To cross the palm of someone is also to give them money, often as an inducement or bribe.

**Cross the Rubicon, To.** To take an irrevocable step, as when the Germans crossed the Belgian frontier in August 1914, which led to war with Great Britain. The Rubicon was a small river (possibly the present-day Fiumicino) which separated ancient Italy from Cisalpine Gaul, the province allotted to Julius CAESAR. When Caesar crossed this stream in 49 BC he passed beyond the limits of his province and became an invader in Italy, thus precipitating war with Pompey and the Senate.

**Crossword.** The popular pastime or obsession has its origins in the puzzle devised in 1913 by the British-born American editor Arthur Wynne for the Christmas issue of the 'Fun' supplement to the *New York Sunday World*. It appeared on 21 December as a diamond-shaped device with 31 words to be entered and straightforward clues such as 'What bargain hunters enjoy' ('sales'). The First World War hampered the spread of the new craze, but it was taken up soon after in Britain and continental Europe, and on 1 February 1930 *The Times* published its 'Crossword Puzzle No. 1', compiled by the rural novelist Adrian Bell, who was paid 3 guineas a puzzle. Its clues were rather more sophisticated, one being 'The final crack' ('doom') and another 'Retunes (anag.)' ('tureens').

Cryptic clues soon became a regular feature of most British crosswords, based on the compiler's classic principle, 'I need not mean what I say, but I must say what I mean', a tenet first propounded by 'Afrit' (A.F. Ritchie). An example of such a clue, in *The Times* crossword No. 21,009 for 25 January 1999, is 'Map produced by husband in light vehicle', in which 'h', short for 'husband', goes in 'light vehicle', i.e. in 'cart', to produce 'chart', defined as 'map'. Crosswords that have become institutions include the cryptic 'Everyman' and harder 'Mephisto' in *The Sunday Times*, and the notoriously difficult *Listener* crossword, published weekly in *The Times* after that journal's demise in 1991.

**At cross purposes.** *See under* AT.
**Banbury Cross.** *See under* BANBURY.
**Bear one's cross, To.** *See under* BEAR.
**Calvary cross, A.** *See under* CALVARY.
**Capital cross.** *See under* CAPITAL.
**Charing Cross.** *See under* CHARING.
**Constantine's cross.** *See under* CONSTANTINE.
**Creeping to the Cross.** *See under* CREEP.
**Dine with cross-legged knights, To.** *See under* DINE.
**Dirty work at the crossroads.** *See under* DIRTY.
**Eleanor crosses.** *See under* ELEANOR.
**Exaltation of the Cross.** *See under* EXALTATION.
**Fiery cross.** *See under* FIERY.
**Fingers crossed.** *See under* FINGER.
**George Cross.** *See under* GEORGE.
**Get one's wires crossed, To.** *See under* GET.
**Grade crossing.** *See under* GRADE.
**Hot cross buns.** *See* BUN.
**Invention of the Cross, The.** *See under* INVENTION.
**Iron Cross, The.** *See under* IRON.
**Jerusalem cross.** A CROSS POTENT.
**Judgement of the Cross, The.** *See under* JUDGEMENT.
**Long cross.** *See* DAGGER.
**Maltese cross.** *See under* MALTA.
**Market cross.** *See under* MARKET.
**On the cross.** Not 'on the square', not straightforward. To get something 'on the cross' is to get it fraudulently.
**Ordeal of the cross.** *See under* ORDEAL.
**Paul's cross.** *See under* PAUL.
**Pelican crossing.** *See under* PELICAN.
**Red Cross, The.** *See under* RED.
**Red Cross Knight, The.** *See under* RED.
**St George's cross.** *See under* GEORGE.
**St John of the Cross.** *See under* JOHN.
**St Patrick's cross.** *See under* PATRICK.
**Stations of the Cross, The.** *See under* STATION.
**Take the cross, To.** In medieval times, to take the pledge to become a crusader. *See also* CRUSADES.
**Teutonic Cross.** *See* CROSS POTENT.
**True Cross.** *See* INVENTION OF THE CROSS.
**Veneration of the Cross.** *See* CREEPING TO THE CROSS.
**Victoria Cross.** *See under* VICTORIA.
**Way of the Cross, The.** *See* STATIONS OF THE CROSS.
**Weeping cross.** *See under* WEEP.

**Cross.** Irritable, bad-tempered.

**Crosspatch.** A moody, ill-tempered person. PATCH is an old name for a fool, and with the meaning 'fellow' is found in Shakespeare, as a 'scurvy patch'.

**As cross as a bear with a sore head** or **as two sticks.** *See under* AS.

**Crotona's Sage.** PYTHAGORAS, who was so called because he established his chief school of philosophy at Crotona in Italy (*c.*530 BC). Such success followed his teaching that the whole town soon became more moral and decorous.

**Crouchmas.** An old name for the festival of the INVENTION OF THE CROSS, also for Rogation Sunday and Rogation week. Crouch here comes from Latin *crux*, 'cross'. *See also* ROGATION DAYS.

**Croud.** *See* CROWD.

**Crow.** A crow symbolizes contention or discord.

**Crow-eaters.** A nickname for the inhabitants of South Australia.

**Crow over, To.** To exult, especially over a vanquished or humiliated person. The allusion is to cocks who crow when victorious.

**Crow's feet.** The wrinkles at the outer corner of a person's eye, somewhat resembling the feet of a crow. To some they suggest a happy character or a sunny disposition, but they can be removed by cosmetic surgery.

> Maggie is asking for the works. 'When I do *this*,' she complains, squinting and showing off her not-all-that-bad crow's feet, 'I can store quarters.'
> *Time* (13 July 1998)

**Crow's nest.** A barrel or cylindrical box fitted to the crosstrees of the maintop mast of a sailing ship for the lookout.

**As black as a crow.** *See under* AS.

**As the crow flies.** *See under* AS.

**Eat crow, To.** *See under* EAT.

**Jim Crow.** *See under* JIM.

**Stone the crows.** *See under* STONE.

**Crowd, Croud** or **Cruth** (Welsh *crwth*). A medieval rectangular instrument with from three to six strings, played with a bow. Hence 'crowder', a player of the crowd. It lingered on in Wales much longer than elsewhere. John Morgan, who died in 1720, was a noted player, and the Welsh *crwth* survived until the end of the 18th century.

> Harke how the Minstrels gin to shrill aloud
> Their merry Musick that resounds from far,
> The pipe, the tabor, and the trembling Croud,
> That well agree withouten breach or iar.
> EDMUND SPENSER: *Epithalamion* (1595)

**Far from the madding crowd.** *See under* FAR.

**Crown.** In HERALDRY nine crowns are recognized: the oriental, the triumphal or imperial, the DIADEM, the obsidional crown, the civic, the crown vallary, the mural crown, the naval, and the crown celestial.

Among the Romans of the Republic and Empire, crowns of various patterns formed marks of distinction for different services; the principal ones were:

- Blockade crown (*corona obsidionalis* or *graminea*): given to the general who liberated a beleaguered army. This was made of grass and wild flowers gathered from the spot.
- Camp crown (*corona castrensis*): given to the first to force his way into the enemy's camp. It was made of gold, and decorated with palisades.
- Civic crown (*corona civica*): awarded to anyone who saved a *civis* (Roman citizen) in battle. It was of oak leaves and bore the inscription H.O.C.S. (*Hostem Occidit, Civem Servavit*, 'He killed a foe, he saved a citizen').
- Mural crown (*corona muralis* or *vallaris*): given to the first man to scale the wall of a besieged town. It was made of gold and decorated with battlements.
- Naval crown (*corona navalis* or *classica* or *rostrata*): of gold and decorated with a ship's prow, given to a naval victor.
- Gold crown (*corona aurea*): given to those who distinguished themselves in an act of general gallantry.
- Ovation crown (*corona ovatis*): made of myrtle and given to the general who won a lesser victory.
- Triumphal crown (*corona triumphalis*): given to the general granted a triumph. It was made of LAUREL or bay leaves. Sometimes a massive gold crown was given to the victorious general.

**Crown Court.** The main criminal court for England and Wales, set up in 1971, when it superseded the assize courts and quarter sessions. It deals with the most serious offences, such as murder, manslaughter, rape and robbery, amounting to some 3 per cent of all criminal cases, and is presided over by a judge sitting with a jury. Lesser offences, such as burglary and some assaults, are tried by magistrates. In the late 1990s the Crown Court was sitting at about 90 centres. *See also* JUDICIAL CIRCUIT.

**Crowned with bays.** A reward of victory, from the ancient Roman custom of so crowning a victorious general.

**Crown in English coinage, The.** When first minted (1526), the crown was valued at 4s 6d and called the crown of the rose, but in the same year it was replaced by one worth 5s. It was a gold coin and did not disappear as such until the reign of Charles II. Silver crowns were struck from 1551. The name derives from the French gold coin (*couronne*) first issued by Philip of Valois in 1339, which bore a crown on the obverse.

In the paper trade, crown was a standard size of printing paper measuring 15 × 20in (before metrication). It was so called from an ancient watermark.

**Crown Jewels, The.** The crown and regalia worn by the monarch at coronations and certain other important occasions, such as the State Opening of Parliament. The priceless gems include the First and Second Stars of Africa, as the largest and third largest diamonds in the world, and the KOH-I-NOOR, the oldest known major diamond, and they are on public display in the Jewel House at the TOWER OF LONDON.

**Crown of St Stephen, The.** The crown of Hungary, this St Stephen (975–1038) being the first king of Hungary. He became a Christian in 985 and set out to convert his country. He was canonized in 1083 and his day is 16 August. The existing crown is probably of 13th-century origin. It was taken to the USA in 1944.

**Crown of the East.** Antioch, ancient capital of Syria, which consisted of four walled cities, encircled by a common rampart that 'enrounded them like a coronet'.

**Crown of Thorns, The.** That with which our

Saviour was crowned in mockery (Matthew 27:29), hence sometimes used of a very special affliction with which one is unjustly burdened.

According to tradition the original was broken up into many pieces and there are now many places claiming to possess one or more of the thorns. *See also* GLASTONBURY.

**Crown of Wild Olive.** The satisfaction of having performed a worthwhile task for its own sake rather than for gain. This crown was the only prize awarded to victors in the ancient OLYMPIC GAMES, the wild olive being held sacred from its having been first planted by HERCULES. John Ruskin published a book of this title in 1866, which contained four essays or lectures on work, traffic, war and the future of England.

**Crown prince.** The title of the heir apparent to the throne in some countries, as Sweden, Denmark and Japan (formerly also in Germany).

**Crowns of Egypt.** In ancient Egypt there were many crowns worn by kings and gods. As rulers of Upper Egypt and Lower Egypt the kings wore the double crown (*pschent*) made up of the red crown (*deshret*) of Lower Egypt and the white crown (*hedjet*) of Upper Egypt. The *khepresh*, sometimes erroneously called the 'war crown' of the PHARAOHS, was blue with gold discs. Each of the many crowns had its particular significance and symbolism, and the gods wore crowns that indicated their attributes.

**City of the Violet Crown, The.** *See under* CITY.

**Cradle crown.** *See under* CRADLE.

**Iron Crown of Lombardy, The.** *See under* IRON.

**Crowquill, Alfred.** This was the name used by Alfred Henry Forrester (1805–72), the black-and-white artist of *Punch* and the *Illustrated London News*. He was famous in his day as the illustrator of Dr SYNTAX (1809–21), the BON GAULTIER BALLADS (1845), Baron MÜNCHAUSEN (1785) and other popular works. A crow quill, so called as originally made from crows' quills, is a special type of artist's pen that can draw very fine lines.

**Crozier.** *See* CROSIER.

**Crucial.** Final or decisive; very important. The allusion is to Francis Bacon's phrase *instantia crucis* ('being present at the cross'), metaphorically referring to a signpost at the bifurcation of a road, when a decision must be made to go one way or the other. According to his theory, two different diseases might run in parallel for a time but would ultimately cross each other. For example, the plague might for a time resemble other diseases, but when the *bubo* or boil appeared, the plague would assume its special character. Hence a crucial test, crucial experiment, crucial question and so on. *See also* CRUX.

**Cruel, The.** Pedro, king of Castile and León (1334–69) was so called for the murders he perpetrated. He was finally defeated and slain in Bertrand du Guesclin's tent by his brother Henry of Trastámara (Henry II of Castile) (1333–79).

**Cruel garters.** *See* CREWEL.

**Cruella De Vil.** *See under* DE VIL.

**Cruft's.** The usual name for the internationally known Cruft's Dog Show, now held at the National Exhibition Centre, Birmingham (until 1991 at Olympia, London), and founded by Charles Cruft in 1891. Some years after his death in 1938 the show was taken over by the Kennel Club. Cruft's interest in dogs largely arose from his apprenticeship to James Spratt in 1876. Spratt had recently started a 'dog cake' business in Holborn, having got the idea from America.

**Crumble. That's the way the cookie crumbles.** *See under* COOK.

**Crummy.** The colloquial word was formerly used of something desirable, as 'that's crummy', 'that's good'. It also means 'plump', 'well developed', as 'she's a crummy woman'. It comes from crumb, being the soft or fleshy part of the bread (as distinct from the crust). Among soldiers the word came to mean 'lousy', initially in the literal sense, i.e. infested with lice. Hence the present sense of 'poor', 'inferior', 'unwell'. The reference was doubtless to the eggs of a louse, like crumbs of bread. *See also* CRUSTY.

**Crumpets.** *See* MUFFINS.

**Crusades.** Wars undertaken by Christians in the late Middle Ages to secure the right of Christian pilgrims to visit the HOLY SEPULCHRE and to recover the HOLY LAND from its Muslim conquerors. The name is derived from the cross that the Crusaders wore on their dress. Ideas of CHIVALRY as well as hopes of material gain were prominent. According to Matthew Paris, each nation had its special colour, which was red for France, white for England, green for Flanders, blue or azure for Italy, and gules (red) for Spain. Scotland had a St Andrew's cross, and the Knights TEMPLAR, red on white. *See also* TAKE THE CROSS *under* CROSS; PALMER.

There were eight principal crusades:

(1) Proclaimed by Urban II in 1095. The futile expeditions under PETER THE HERMIT and Walter the Penniless (Gautier Sans Avoir) were destroyed by the Turks, but the main expedition (1096–9) under Raymond of Toulouse, Robert of Normandy and Godfrey of Bouillon, ended with the capture of Jerusalem. The Latin Kingdom of Jerusalem was set up in 1100 under Baldwin I.

(2) After the loss of Edessa an unsuccessful expedition (1147–9) was promoted by St BERNARD under the leadership of the Emperor Conrad III and Louis VII of France.

(3) Inspired by the fall of Jerusalem in 1187 and led by Frederick Barbarossa, Philip Augustus of

France and Richard I of England. Begun in 1188, it reached a stalemate in 1192.
(4) Promoted by Innocent III in 1202 and led by Thibaut of Champagne and Baldwin of Flanders, it was diverted, in spite of the pope's prohibitions, into an attack on Constantinople. Baldwin became the first Latin emperor of Constantinople in 1204.
(5) Proclaimed by Innocent III for 1217 to recover Jerusalem. The main force was directed against Egypt. Damietta was taken but given up in 1221.
(6) The Emperor Frederick II obtained Nazareth, Bethlehem and Jerusalem by negotiation (1222–9), although under excommunication at the time, but was absolved on his return.
(7) Followed the loss of Jerusalem in 1244. It was organized and led by St LOUIS (Louis IX) of France in 1248. The main expedition against Egypt led to his capture in 1250. After his release he made fruitless efforts to recover the Holy Land and returned home in 1254.
(8) The Last Crusade. Undertaken by St Louis, Charles of Anjou and Prince Edward of England. St Louis died of the plague at Tunis in 1270 and the enterprise petered out in 1272.

**Children's Crusade, The.** *See under* CHILD.

**Cruse, Widow's.** *See under* WIDOW.

**Crush. Crush a bottle, To.** A former phrase meaning to drink a bottle. Milton has 'crush't the sweet poison' (*Comus* (1637)). The idea is that of crushing grapes. Shakespeare also has burst a glass in the same sense (Induction of *The Taming of the Shrew* (1593)). *See also* CRACK A BOTTLE.

Come and crush a cup of wine.
SHAKESPEARE: *Romeo and Juliet*, I, ii (1594)

**Crush a fly on a wheel, To.** An allusion to the absurdity of taking a wheel used for torturing criminals and heretics in order to kill a fly. *See also* BREAK A BUTTERFLY ON A WHEEL; USE A SLEDGEHAMMER TO CRACK A NUT.

**Crush bar.** A bar in a theatre where drinks are served in the interval, so named from the crush or crowd of people.

**Crush barrier.** A barrier, usually temporary, to restrain a crowd.

**Crushed strawberry.** A crimson red colour of dullish hue.

**Have a crush on, To.** To be infatuated with. The expression is traditionally associated with schoolgirls but is not restricted to them.

**Crusoe, Robinson.** The castaway hero of Defoe's novel named after him (1719) was suggested by the adventures of Alexander Selkirk (1676–1721). Crusoe's Island was not Más a Tierra, one of the Juan Fernández islets in the South Pacific, where Selkirk was put ashore in 1704, but an imaginary island near Trinidad. Defoe's description most closely fits Tobago.

**Crust. Crusted port.** When port is first bottled its fermentation is not complete. In time it precipitates argol (potassium hydrogen tartrate) on the sides of the bottle, where it forms a crust. Crusted port, therefore, is port that has completed its fermentation.

**Crusting.** An American hunting term for taking big game in winter when the ice of ponds, rivers and lakes will bear the weight of a human being but not that of a moose or deer.

**Crusty.** Ill-tempered, apt to take offence, cross, irritable, peevish. ACHILLES addresses the bitter THERSITES with:

Thou crusty batch of nature, what's the news?
SHAKESPEARE: *Troilus and Cressida*, V, i (1601)

**Upper crust, The.** *See under* UP.

**Crutched Friars.** 'Crutched' is a form of 'crouched', literally 'crossed', referring to the cross worn on the friars' habits. They were a mendicant order established in Italy by 1169 and followed an Augustinian rule. They arrived in England in 1244 but the order was suppressed by the pope in 1656. Hence Crutched Friars as a street in the City of London.

**Crux** (Latin, 'cross'). A vital or decisive point or stage; the nub of the matter. The word does not refer to the cross as an instrument of punishment, but to the crossing of two lines, called a node or knot, and hence meaning a trouble or difficulty. *See also* CRUCIAL.

**Crux ansata.** *See* CROSS AS A MYSTIC EMBLEM.

**Crux decussata.** *See* CROSS AS A MYSTIC EMBLEM.

**Crux pectoralis** (Latin *pectus*, 'breast'). A pectoral cross, i.e. one suspended over the breast, as usually worn by bishops, abbots and cardinals.

**Cry. Cries of animals.** A special word is used for the cry, call or sound of many animals, and it would be wrong or even ludicrous to use these words indiscriminately. Thus, a dog does not 'buzz' and a bee does not 'bark'. The following are appropriate words for each:

Apes gibber
Asses bray
Bears growl
Bees hum
Beetles drone
Bitterns boom
Blackbirds and thrushes whistle
Bulls bellow
Calves bleat
Cats mew, purr, swear and caterwaul
Chaffinches chirp and pink
Chicks cheep
Cocks crow
Cows low
Crows caw
Cuckoos cuckoo
Deer bell
Dogs bark, bay, howl, whine and yelp
Doves coo
Ducks quack
Eagles, vultures and peacocks scream
Falcons chant
Flies buzz

Foxes bark and yelp
Frogs croak
Geese cackle and hiss
Grasshoppers chirp
Guinea pigs and hares squeak
Hawks scream
Hens cackle and cluck
Horses neigh and whinny
Hyenas laugh
Jays and magpies chatter
Kittens mew
Linnets chuckle
Lions and tigers roar and growl
Mice squeak and squeal
Monkeys chatter and gibber
Nightingales pipe and warble
Owls hoot and screech
Oxen low and bellow
Parrots talk
Pigs grunt, squeak and squeal
Pigeons coo
Ravens croak
Rooks caw
Screech owls screech or shriek
Sheep and lambs bleat
Snakes hiss
Sparrows chirp
Stags bellow and call
Swallows twitter
Swans cry and sing just before death
Turkeys gobble
Wolves howl

For some animals there are also words to imitate the cry, call or sound itself. Thus:

Cats go 'miaow'
Cocks go 'cock-a-doodle-doo'
Cows go 'moo'
Dogs go 'woof''
Donkeys go 'hee-haw'
Guinea fowls go 'come back'
Nightingales go 'jug jug'
Owls go 'to-whit to-whoo'
Pigs go 'oink'
Sheep and lambs go 'baa'
Yellowhammers go 'a little bit of bread and no cheese'

**Cry barley, To.** An old country game similar to prisoners' base, having a 'home' which was called 'hell'. The game itself was known as barley-break. Barley, a corruption of parley, was a cry for truce in rough games.

> Since we were boys together,
> And play'd at barley-break.
> ROBERT SOUTHEY: *Wat Tyler* (1794)

**Cry down, To.** To condemn; to belittle.

**Cry for the moon, To.** To crave for what is unattainable. The allusion is to foolish children who 'cry for the moon to play with'. The French say *Il veut prendre la lune avec les dents* ('He wants to take the moon between his teeth').

**Cry from the heart.** A passionate appeal. It is not quite the same as the French *cri de cœur*, which is really an appeal in distress.

**Cry from the housetop, To.** To announce something in the most public manner possible. Jewish houses had flat roofs, where their owners often slept and held gatherings and from which public announcements were made.

> That which ye have spoken in the ear in closets shall be proclaimed upon the housetops.
> Luke 12:3

**Cry havoc, To.** *See* HAVOC.

**Crying the mare.** *See* CRYING THE NECK.

**Crying the neck.** Formerly, at the end of the harvest, especially in the north and west of England, the last sheaf of corn, the 'neck' (or the 'mare') was held aloft by the leader or Harvest Lord, who shouted 'I have it! I have it! I have it!' The harvesters around him cried 'What have 'ee? What have 'ee? What have 'ee?' The leader shouted back, 'A neck! A neck! A neck!' The noise made it plain that the harvest on that particular farm was complete. There were numerous regional variants of these proceedings. *See also* CORN DOLLY; HARVEST HOME; MELL SUPPER.

**Cry off, To.** To withdraw from a promise or agreement. In the USA, to sell by auction.

**Cry one's eyes out, To.** To cry immoderately or excessively. The image is of weeping so copiously that one washes one's eyes out of their sockets.

**Cry out for, To.** To demand self-evidently; to be obviously in need of, as: 'This fence is crying out for a new coat of paint.'

**Cry over spilt milk, To.** To bemoan an irremediable or irredeemable loss or error. The expression is mostly employed negatively: 'It's no use crying over spilt milk'.

**Cry peccavi, To.** To acknowledge oneself in the wrong. Sir Charles Napier, in 1843, allegedly sent a despatch to Lord Ellenborough with the single word 'Peccavi', Latin for 'I have sinned', i.e. punningly 'I have Sindh', announcing his conquest of that region, now a province of Pakistan. He was not the author of the witticism, however, which was the work of the hymnwriter Catherine Winkworth (1827–78), translator from the German of such familiar hymns as 'Now thank we all our God'. One day at school she remarked to her teacher that since Napier had been criticized in Parliament for his ruthless campaign, his despatch should have read 'Peccavi'. She sent her pun to *Punch*, which printed it in its edition of 18 May 1844 as a factual report, with the result that it came to be credited to Napier. The fourth edition of the *Oxford Dictionary of Quotations* (1996) attributes the saying correctly.

**Cry quarter, To.** To beg for mercy.

**Cry stinking fish, To.** To belittle or disparage one's own endeavours or offerings. 'To cry' here is to offer for sale by shouting one's wares in the street.

**Cry up, To.** To praise highly.

**Cry wolf, To.** To give a false alarm. The allusion is to the fable of the shepherd lad who so often called 'Wolf!' merely to make fun of the neighbours, that when at last the wolf came no one would believe him. This fable appears in almost every nation of the world.

**Don't cry** or **halloo till you are out of the wood.** Do not rejoice for having escaped danger until the danger has passed away.

**Far cry, A.** *See under* FAR.

**For crying out loud.** *See under* FOR.

**Great cry and little wool.** *See under* GREAT.

**Hue and cry.** *See under* HUE.

**In full cry.** *See under* FULL.

**Shoulder to cry on, A.** *See under* SHOULDER.

**Town crier.** *See under* TOWN.

**War cry.** *See under* WAR.

**Crystal. Crystal gazing.** An ancient form of DIVINATION. It was held that those who had the gift, by gazing fixedly and deeply into a polished crystal ball, could see what would happen in the future or what was actually happening elsewhere. To gaze into the crystal ball is to see into the future, to seek inspiration to answer questions. *See also* CRYSTALLOMANCY.

**Crystalline sphere, The.** According to Ptolemy, the ninth orb, identified by some with 'the waters which were above the firmament' (Genesis 1:7). It was placed between the PRIMUM MOBILE and the firmament, or sphere, of the fixed stars, and was held to have a shivering movement that interfered with the regular motion of the stars.

> They pass the planets seven, and pass the fixed,
> And that crystalline sphere whose balance weighs
> The trepidation talked, and that first moved.
> MILTON: *Paradise Lost*, iii (1667)

**Crystallomancy.** DIVINATION by means of transparent bodies such as a crystal globe, polished quartz and precious stones, especially a beryl. *See also* CRYSTAL GAZING.

**Crystal Palace.** One of the glories of the Victorian era. The huge building was designed entirely of glass and iron by Joseph Paxton (1801–65), a former head gardener to the Duke of Devonshire at Chatsworth House, to house the GREAT EXHIBITION of 1851 or, to give it its full name, the Great Exhibition of the Works of Industry of All Nations. It was originally erected in Hyde Park but moved to Sydenham in 1854 with some alterations, including the addition of two towers, and was used as an exhibition, entertainment and recreational centre. It became national property in 1911 but was destroyed by fire in 1936.

**Cub.** Properly the young of a fox, wolf, bear and certain other animals. Figuratively the word is used for a young or inexperienced person, often in a particular trade or occupation, such as 'cub reporter'. *See also* LICK INTO SHAPE.

**Cubbing** or **cub-hunting.** Preliminary training for young foxhounds. Fox cubs have neither the cunning nor the staying power of the grown fox and thus offer better 'sport' for young hounds.

**Wolf Cub.** *See under* WOLF.

**Cuba** (Latin *cubare*, 'to lie in bed'). The Roman deity who guarded infants in their cribs and sent them to sleep. *See also* DEITIES PROTECTING BABIES.

**Cube, Rubik's.** *See under* RUBIK.

**Cubism.** The style of an early 20th-century school of painters who depicted surfaces, figures, tints, light and shade, and so on, by means of a multiplicity of shapes of a cubical and geometrical character. The name was introduced in 1908 by the art critic Louis Vauxcelles, who took up a remark of Matisse's about Braque's 'little cubes'. It was essentially abstract and divorced from realism. It rejected any attempt to depict actual appearances and turned its back on traditional canons of art. It paved the way for much of modern art subsequently. Its chief exponents were Georges Braque, André Derain, Fernand Léger and, notably, Pablo Picasso. *See also* DADAISM; FAUVISM; FUTURISM; IMPRESSIONISM; ORPHISM; SURREALISM; SYNCHROMISM; VORTICISM.

**Cubit** (Latin *cubitum*, 'elbow'). An ancient measurement of length from the elbow to the tip of the longest finger. The Roman cubit was approximately 17in (44cm), the Egyptian about 21in (53cm), which was divided into seven palms, and that of the Hebrews about 22in (56cm). The English cubit was 18in (46cm).

> Which of you by taking thought can add one cubit unto his stature?
> Matthew 6:27

**Cuchulain** or **Cú Chulainn.** A legendary Irish hero, called the 'Hound of Culann' (Irish *cú*, 'dog') because, having accidentally slain the watchdog of the smith, Culann, he had to take the animal's place in penance. He was brought up in the court of King CONCHOBAR of Ulster, whose kingdom he defended single-handed against the queen of Connaught. He is called Cuthullin by OSSIAN.

**Cucking stool.** A kind of DUCKING STOOL formerly used for punishing disorderly women by plunging them into a pond. Cucking is from the old verb cuck, 'to defecate', and the stool used was often a close-stool (one containing a chamber pot).

> Now, if one cucking-stool was for each scold,
> Some towns, I fear, would not their numbers hold.
> *Poor Robin* (1746)

**Cuckold.** The husband of an adulterous wife, so called from the CUCKOO, whose chief characteristic is to deposit its eggs in other birds' nests.

The cuckoo then, on every tree,
Mocks married men, for thus sings he,
Cuckoo;
Cuckoo, cuckoo: O, word of fear,
Unpleasing to a married ear!

SHAKESPEARE: *Love's Labour's Lost*, V, ii (1594)

*See also* ACTAEON; WEAR THE HORNS.

**Cuckold's Point.** A spot on the south bank of the Thames in Limehouse Reach by Nelson Dockyard, Southwark, so called from a tradition that King John successfully courted a labourer's wife there.

**Cuckoo.** Folklore and superstitions abound with regard to this bird and often betoken its popularity as a herald of spring. One old rhyme runs:

In April the cuckoo shows his bill;
In May he sings all day;
In June he alters his tune;
In July away he'll fly;
In August go he must.

**Cuckoo clock.** A clock resembling a Swiss chalet that sounds the hour with a call like that of the cuckoo. A toy cuckoo usually pops out of a door and bobs to accompany each note.

**Cuckoo flowers.** There are many folk flower names associated with the cuckoo. Some examples are: the cuckoo flower or lady's smock (*Cardamine pratensis*), the cuckoo's joy or marsh marigold (*Caltha palustris*), the cuckoo pint or LORDS AND LADIES or priest in the pulpit (*Arum maculatum*), and the cuckoo bread or wood sorrel (*Oxalis acetosella*). The pint of the cuckoo pint was earlier pintle, from Old English *pintel*, 'penis'.

**Cuckoo spit** or **frog spit.** A frothy exudation deposited on plants by certain insects, especially the froghopper, of the family Cercopidae, for the purpose of protecting the larvae.

Cicades are bred out of cuccow spittle or Woodsear; that is, that spumous, frothy dew or exudation or both, found upon Plants, especially about the joints of Lavender and Rosemary, observable with us about the latter end of May.

SIR THOMAS BROWNE: *Pseudodoxia Epidemica*, v (1646)

**Cherry trees and the cuckoo.** *See under* CHERRY.

**Cloud-Cuckoo-Land.** *See under* CLOUD.

**Cucullus non facit monachum** (Latin, 'The cowl does not make the monk'). A person should not be judged by external appearances. An old proverb, quoted by Shakespeare in *Twelfth Night*, I, v (1599).

**Cucumber, As cool as a.** *See under* AS.

**Cud, To chew the.** *See under* CHEW.

**Cuddy.** A pet form of the name Cuthbert, and the North Country and Scottish familiar name for a donkey, which is elsewhere called NEDDY or Jack.

**Cudgel. Cudgel one's brains, To.** To think hard about a problem. The metaphor refers to beating a dull boy on the grounds that his dullness is the result of wilfulness or inattention.

Cudgel thy brains no more about it; for your dull ass will not mend his pace with beating.

SHAKESPEARE: *Hamlet*, V, i (1600)

**Take up the cudgels, To.** To maintain an argument or position; to fight, as with a cudgel, for one's own or another person's rights.

**Cuff, Off the.** *See under* OFF.

**Cui bono?** (Latin, 'For whose benefit?'). The phrase is sometimes wrongly used to mean, 'What good will it do?' or 'For what good purpose?' It was a question attributed by Cicero to the Roman judge Lucius Cassius Longinus Ravilla.

Cato, that great and grave philosopher, did commonly demand, when any new project was propounded unto him, *cui bono*, what good will ensue in case the same is effected?

THOMAS FULLER: *History of the Worthies of England*, 'The Design' (1662)

**Culdees.** A religious order in Ireland and Scotland from about the 8th century to the 13th, although they continued in Ireland until the REFORMATION. They are so called from Old Irish *céle dé*, 'servant of God'. They seem to have originated as independent communities of hermits or anchorites and latterly were essentially secular CANONS.

**Cullinan Diamond.** The largest known DIAMOND, named after Sir Thomas Major Cullinan (1862–1936), chairman of the Premier Diamond Mine, Johannesburg, where it was found in 1905. Its uncut weight was 3025Ɔ carats (about 1lb 6oz or 624g). It was presented to King Edward VII by the South African Government and was cut into a number of stones (the largest weighing some 516 carats), which now form part of the CROWN JEWELS.

**Culloden.** The Scottish moor near Inverness where in 1746 Bonnie Prince Charlie was defeated and with him the Highland clans, thus effectively ending both Stuart claims to the throne and all attempts at Scottish independence. *See also* YOUNG PRETENDER.

**Culross girdles.** The thin plate of iron on which oat cakes, scones and the like are cooked is called a girdle in Scotland and is similar in use to the Welsh bakestone. There are thus girdle cakes and bakestone cakes. Culross was formerly famous for its iron girdles.

Locks and bars, plough-graith and harrow-teeth! and why not grates and fireprongs, and Culross girdles?

SIR WALTER SCOTT: *Fair Maid of Perth*, ch ii (1828)

**Cultivate one's garden, To.** To attend to one's own affairs. The expression comes from a line in Voltaire's *Candide* (1759): *Il faut cultiver notre jardin* ('We must cultivate our garden').

**Cultures, The Two.** *See under* TWO.

**Culver.** A former or poetic name for a dove or pigeon, from Old English *culfre*, ultimately from Latin *columba*, 'dove'. Pigeons formed a very useful addition to the table in former times, and culver houses were maintained by manorial lords, monasteries and parish clergy. There were some thousands still in use in 17th-century England.

> Lyke as the Culuer on the bared bough,
> Sits mourning for the absence of her mate.
> EDMUND SPENSER: *Amoretti*: Sonnet lxxxix (1595)

**Culverkeys.** An old popular name for such plants as the bluebell, columbine and squill, the flowers of which have some resemblance to a bunch of keys.

**Cumberland. Cumberland Poets.** *See* LAKE SCHOOL.

**Cumberland Presbyterians.** A separatist group formed in Cumberland, Kentucky, in 1810, following a dispute with the Kentucky Synod of the American PRESBYTERIAN Church over the formal requirements for the ministry. Those of the Cumberland presbytery unsuccessfully urged the need to dispense with the usual high educational standards in a frontier environment.

**Cum grano salis** (Latin, 'with a grain of salt'). Not too literally. The English equivalent is usually 'with a pinch of salt', said when something is believed only with reservations.

**Cumquat** (Cantonese *kam kwat*, representing Mandarin Chinese *jīn jú*, 'golden orange'). The cumquat or kumquat is a kind of small Chinese orange with a sweet rind used for making preserves and various confections. The Chinese name is used metaphorically to mean 'dear one', 'darling', rather in the manner of French *chou*, 'cabbage', to which word it bears a coincidental resemblance.

**Cunctator** (Latin, 'delayer'). A nickname of the Roman general and statesman Quintus Fabius Maximus. He gained the epithet as an abusive title for his delaying tactics against Hannibal and his avoidance of pitched battles, but subsequent events, such as Hannibal's great victory at CANNAE (216 BC), seemed to justify his policy, and what began as a slur ended as an honour. Bertrand du Guesclin (*c*.1320–80) used similar tactics successfully against the English during the HUNDRED YEARS' WAR. *See also* FABIUS.

**Cuneiform.** A name for the writing of various languages of ancient Mesopotamia and Persia, which was made up of wedge-shaped impressions, representing letters, made on soft clay; the characters are also called arrow-headed (Latin, *cuneus*, 'wedge'). Cuneiform script was used from *c*.3800 BC until the early years of the Christian era. The first to decipher the letters was the German philologist Georg Friedrich Grotefend in 1802.

**Cunning.** A word with several meanings related to Old English *cunnan*, 'to know', as do 'ken' and 'can'. For 'the tree of knowledge of good and evil' (Genesis 2:9), WYCLIF'S BIBLE has:

> A tree of kunnynge of good and euil.

By extension of this came the meaning of 'skill':

> If I forget thee, O Jerusalem, let my right hand forget her cunning.
> Psalm 137:5

The word had already begun to imply a knowledge of occult and evil matters:

> We take cunning for a sinister, or crooked wisdom.
> FRANCIS BACON: *Of Cunning* (1612)

A 'cunning man' or 'cunning woman' was merely another name for a WIZARD OR WITCH.

> A cunning man did calculate my birth,
> And told me that by *Water* I should die.
> SHAKESPEARE: *Henry VI, Pt II*, IV, i (1590)

Hence the usual present meaning of 'sly', 'crafty'.

The American usage to mean 'charming', 'pretty', 'engaging', 'clever' was customary by the mid-19th century.

> Tea and coffee arrived (with sweet preserves, and cunning teacakes in its train).
> DICKENS: *Martin Chuzzlewit*, ch xvii (1844)

**Cunobelin.** Cunobelinus, king of the Catuvellauni (d.*c*.AD 42), and the father of Caractacus (CARADOC). His name is preserved in modified form in Shakespeare's *Cymbeline* (1609), in 'Cunobelin's Gold Mines', the local name for the dene holes (underground shafts) in the chalk beds of Little Thurrock, Essex, and in 'Cymbeline's Castle', the motte-and-bailey earthwork at Great Kimble, Buckinghamshire. However, this last is almost certainly a folk etymology, arising from early spellings of the name Kimble itself, such as Cynebellinga in the 10th century.

**Cup.** A mixture of strong ale with sugar, spice and a lemon, properly served up hot in a silver cup. Sometimes a roasted orange takes the place of a lemon. *See also* BISHOP.

**Cup Final.** The final round of a football or other contest, on the result of which a championship cup is awarded. In England the most popular is for the Football Association Cup, played at Wembley. In Scotland the equivalent is the Scottish Cup, played at Hampden Park, Glasgow. An engraved cup, usually of silver, is a common form of trophy for many sporting events.

**Cup of vows, The.** In ancient Scandinavia it was customary at feasts to drink from cups of mead and vow to perform some great deed worthy of the song of the *skald* (bard or minstrel), There were four cups: one to ODIN, for victory, one to FREYJA, for a good year, one to NIORD, for peace, and one to BRAGI, for celebration of the dead in poetry.

**Cup that cheers but not inebriates, The.** Tea. A quotation from William Cowper:

> And, while the bubbling and loud-hissing urn
> Throws up a steamy column, and the cups,
> That cheer but not inebriate, wait on each.
> *The Task*, iv, 36 (1785)

**Cider cup, claret cup** etc. Drinks made of these beverages, with sugar, fruit and herbs.

**Diogenes cup.** *See under* DIOGENES.

**Divination by cup.** *See under* DIVINATION.

**Drink the cup of sorrow, To.** *See under* DRINK.

**Grace Cup.** *See* LOVING CUP.

**In one's cups.** Drunk.

**Let this cup pass from me.** *See under* LET.

**Loving Cup.** *See under* LOVE.

**My cup runneth over.** My blessings overflow. Here cup means portion or blessing.

> My cup runneth over. Surely goodness and mercy shall follow me all the days of my life.
> Psalm 23:5–6

**Not my cup of tea.** Not what suits me; not to my taste.

**Stirrup cup.** *See under* STIRRUP.

**There's many a slip 'twixt cup and lip.** *See under* SLIP.

**Waterloo Cup, The.** *See under* WATERLOO.

**Cupboard. Cupboard love.** A show of love from self-interest or hope of gain. The allusion is to the pretence of love shown by children to an indulgent person who gives them tasty things from the cupboard.

**Court cupboard.** *See under* COURT.

**Skeleton in the cupboard, A.** *See under* SKELETON.

**Cupid** (Latin *cupido*, 'desire'). The Roman god of love, identified with the Greek EROS. He is usually represented as a pretty winged boy with a bow and arrow. There are varying legends of his parentage.

**Cupid and Psyche.** The story is told in the GOLDEN ASS of Apuleius. *See also* PSYCHE.

**Cupid's golden arrow.** Virtuous love.

**Cupid's leaden arrow.** Sensual passion.

**Adam Cupid.** *See under* ADAM.

**Jeune Cupidon, Le.** *See under* JEUNE.

**Curate.** *See* CLERICAL TITLES.

**Curate's egg.** Among the catchphrases that *Punch* (*see* PUNCH AND JUDY) has introduced into the language, 'Good in parts, like the curate's egg' is proverbial. The cartoon shows a timid young curate at his bishop's breakfast table.

> I'm afraid you've got a bad egg, Mr Jones.
>
> Oh no, my Lord, I assure you! Parts of it are excellent!
> (8 November 1895)

**Curé de Meudon.** A nickname of Rabelais (*c.*1495–1553), who was first a monk, then a physician, then a canon of St Maur and, lastly (1550), non-resident curé of Meudon.

**Curfew.** The ringing of a bell every evening as a signal to put out fires and go to bed; also the hour for this and the bell itself. The word is from Old French *cuevrefeu*, literally 'cover fire'. WILLIAM THE CONQUEROR instituted the curfew in England, in 1068, at the hour of 8 pm. The word is now extended to mean the period commonly ordered by occupying armies or government authorities in time of war or civil commotion when civilians must stay indoors.

> The curfew tolls the knell of parting day.
> THOMAS GRAY: *Elegy Written in a Country Churchyard* (1751)

**Curl. Curl one's lip, To.** To express contempt or disgust with the mouth.

**Get someone by the short and curlies, To.** *See under* SHORT.

**Kiss curl.** *See under* KISS.

**Repenter curls.** *See under* REPENTER.

**Curmudgeon.** A surly or miserly person. The word is of unknown origin. In his *Dictionary* (1755) Dr Johnson explains its derivation as follows: 'It is a vitious manner of pronouncing *cœur méchant*, Fr. an unknown correspondent', meaning that this suggestion was supplied by some informant unknown. By an absurd blunder, the Rev. John Ash copied Johnson's comment into his *New and Complete Dictionary of the English Language* (1775) to give an etymology 'from Fr. *cœur*, unknown, *méchant*, correspondent'.

**Currant.** The word evolved as a shortening of *rayson de Corannte*, 'raison of Corinth', since it was from this Greek port that currants were imported.

**Currency. Decimal currency.** *See under* DECIMAL.

**Hard currency.** *See under* HARD.

**Single currency.** *See under* SINGLE.

**Current. Devil's current.** *See under* DEVIL.

**Drift of the current, The.** *See under* DRIFT.

**Setting of the current, The.** *See under* SET.

**Curry favour, To.** The phrase was originally 'to curry favel' ('to groom the fallow horse'), the latter word being related to French *fauve* and English 'fallow' itself. The fallow horse was used in medieval allegories as a symbol of cunning, fraud or deceit, perhaps because of its indefinite colour. Since 'favel' was a word not familiar to English speakers, it was altered to a more meaningful 'favour', so that the expression came to refer specifically to ingratiation with a superior.

**Curse. Curse of Adam, The.** The necessity of working for a living. 'In the sweat of thy face shalt thou eat bread, till thou return unto the ground' (Genesis 2:19). In the story of the Creation, ADAM and EVE were driven from the Garden of EDEN for disobedience and God cursed the earth, which had hitherto borne only plants 'pleasant to the sight and good for food' (Genesis 2:9) so that it now put forth 'thorns also and thistles' (Genesis 3:18).

**Curse of Cain, The.** A person who is always on the move and has no abiding place is said to be 'cursed with the curse of Cain'. The allusion is to God's judgement on CAIN after he had killed his brother ABEL.

> And now art thou cursed from the earth … a fugitive and a vagabond shalt thou be in the earth.
> Genesis 4:11–12

**Curse of Scotland, The.** The nine of diamonds. The phrase seems to be first recorded in the early 18th century, for Houston's *Memoirs* (1715–47) tell how Lord Justice Clerk Ormistone became universally hated in Scotland and was called the Curse of Scotland. As a result, when ladies encountered the nine of diamonds at cards they called it Justice Clerk. Among the suggested origins of the phrase are:

(1) It may refer to the arms of Dalrymple, Earl of Stair, that is, *or* on a saltire azure, nine lozenges of the first. The earl was justly held in abhorrence for his share in the massacre of Glencoe.
(2) The nine of diamonds in the game of Pope JOAN is called the pope, the ANTICHRIST of the Scottish reformers.
(3) In the game of comette, introduced by Queen Mary, it was the main winning card, and the game was the curse of Scotland because it was the ruin of many.
(4) The word curse is a corruption of cross, and the nine of diamonds is so arranged as to form a St Andrew's cross (but so are the other nines).
(5) It was the card on which the BLOODY BUTCHER, the Duke of Cumberland, wrote his cruel order after the Battle of CULLODEN (1746). The term was, however, apparently already current then.
(6) Francis Grose, in his *Dictionary of the Vulgar Tongue* (1811) has the following alternative propositions: 'Diamonds, it is said, imply royalty, being ornaments to the imperial crown; and every ninth king of Scotland has been observed for many ages, to be a tyrant and a curse to that country. Others say it is from its similarity to the arms of Argyle; the Duke of Argyle having been very instrumental in bringing about the union, which, by some Scotch patriots, has been considered as detrimental to their country.'

**Curse of Tutankhamun, The.** A legend arising from the death in 1923 of the Egyptologist, the 5th Earl of Carnarvon, during the excavations at Tutankhamun's tomb. He died from pneumonia after an infection from a mosquito bite, but Sir Arthur Conan Doyle, a convinced spiritualist, suggested that the death might be attributed to elementals created by the priests of Tutankhamun. Coincidentally there was a power failure at Cairo when Carnarvon died, and his dog in England expired at the same time. Howard Carter, who excavated the tomb, survived until 1939. *See also* VALLEY OF THE KINGS.

**Curses, like chickens, come home to roost.** Curses rebound on the curser, just as chickens which stray during the day return to their roost at night.

**Cursing by bell, book and candle.** *See* BELL, BOOK AND CANDLE.

**Not to give a tinker's curse** or **cuss.** *See under* TINKER.

**Cursitors.** The 24 junior clerks who wrote out in COURT HAND the formal common form (*de cursu*) CHANCERY writs in their office in Chancery Lane, London, adjoining Cursitor Street. The growth of printed forms led to their abolition in 1835.

**Cursor Mundi** (Latin, literally 'the runner of the world'). An early 14th-century English poem of some 24,000 lines in northern dialect. It describes the 'Course of the World' from the Creation until Doomsday. It is essentially scriptural and designed to edify and to supplant chivalric romance. The author wrote in English so that those who lacked the more fashionable French might understand it. It is a valuable source of legend.

**Curtain. Curtain call.** An invitation to an actor or actress to appear in front of the curtain and receive the applause of the audience.

**Curtain lecture.** The nagging by a wife when she and her husband are in bed, originally behind bed curtains. *See also* CAUDLE LECTURE.

**Curtain raiser.** *See* LEVER DE RIDEAU.

**Bamboo curtain.** *See under* BAMBOO.

**Iron Curtain, The.** *See under* IRON.

**Ring down the curtain, To.** *See under* RING.

**Ring up the curtain, To.** *See under* RING.

**Curtal friar.** A curtal was a horse with its tail docked, hence the application to other things that were cut down or shortened. A curtal friar was one who wore a short cloak. In later use, especially by Sir Walter Scott, it acquired a vaguely derisory or belittling significance.

**Curtana.** The sword of mercy borne before kings and queens of England at their coronation. It has no point and is therefore shortened. Hence its name, from Old French *Cortain*, the name of ROLAND's sword, which was broken at the point. Its own name ultimately goes back to Latin *curtus*, 'short'. The curtana is also called the sword of EDWARD THE CONFESSOR, which, having no point, was the emblem of mercy.

But when *Curtana* will not doe the deed,
You lay that pointless clergy-weapon by,
And to the laws, your sword of justice fly.
JOHN DRYDEN: *The Hind and the Panther*, ii (1687)

**Curthose.** Robert II, Duke of Normandy (1087–1134), eldest son of WILLIAM THE CONQUEROR, was so nicknamed from his short stature, from Old French *curte-hose*, 'short boot'. He was also called 'Short-thigh', as in Michael Drayton's *The Tragicall Legend of Robert, Duke of Normandy, Surnamed Short-thigh* (1596).

**Curtmantle.** The byname of Henry II (1133–89), who introduced the Anjou mantle, which was shorter than the robe worn by his predecessors. *See also* CARACALLA.

**Curule.** In ancient Rome the term applied to the highest civil officials, literally those who were entitled to use the curule chair. This was an upholstered, folding seat with curved legs, so named from Latin *currus*, 'chariot', because it was originally a chariot chair.

**Cushion. Cushion dance.** A lively dance, popular in early Stuart times, in which kissing while kneeling on a cushion was a major feature.

In our court in Queen Elizabeth's time, gravity and state was kept up; in King James's time things were pretty well; but in King Charles's time there has been nothing but Trench-more and the cushion dance, omnium gatherum, tolly polly, hoyte cum toyte.
JOHN SELDEN: *Table Talk (King of England)* (1689)

It survived quite late in rural districts. John Clare (1793–1864), the PEASANT POET of Northamptonshire, mentions it in his 'May-Day Ballad' (1820):

And then comes the cushion, the girls they all shriek,
And fly to the door from the old fiddler's squeak:
But the doors they are fastened, so all must kneel down,
And take the rude kiss from th' unmannerly clown.

**Whoopee cushion.** *See under* WHOOPEE.

**Custer's Last Stand.** In America in the late 19th century this event was as favourite a subject for paintings and engravings as the 'Relief of Ladysmith' became in England. General George A. Custer (1839–76) was a dashing cavalry man with a popular reputation. The annihilation of his force of over 200 men by some 2000 Indian warriors under SITTING BULL at the Battle of Little Big Horn, Montana (25 June 1876), made a tremendous impact, and the episode became part of the national epic. Custer's body was spared mutilation, unlike most of the others.

**Custom-built** or **custom-made.** The American equivalent of 'made to measure', first applied to tailored clothes, then generally to any object made to the specifications of the customer. Hence, from the 1960s, customized cars.

**Customer. Queer** or **rum customer, A.** *See under* QUEER.

**Ugly customer, An.** *See under* UGLY.

**Custos Rotulorum** (Latin, 'keeper of the rolls'). The officer charged with keeping the records of the courts in a county. The LORD LIEUTENANT is now the Custos Rotulorum, and the work is done by his deputy.

**Cut. Cut** or **cut dead, To.** To ignore or snub an acquaintance. There are four kinds of cut, made as follows:

Cut direct: by staring an acquaintance in the face and pretending not to know him or her
Cut indirect: looking in another direction and pretending not to see a person
Cut sublime: admiring the top of some tall building or the clouds in the sky until the acquaintance has passed by
Cut infernal: stooping to adjust your shoes until the acquaintance has gone by

**Cut above the rest, A.** Markedly superior to the others.

**Cut a caper, To.** To skip or leap about playfully. 'Caper' here is probably from Italian *capreolo*, 'roebuck', itself ultimately from Latin *caper*, 'goat'. Goats are noted for their leaping and prancing. *See also* ACT THE GIDDY GOAT.

**Cut across, To.** To run counter to; to be contrary to, as of procedure.

**Cut a dash, To.** To make a show; to get oneself looked at and talked about through one's stylish or striking appearance.

**Cut along, To.** To hurry along; to clear off.

**Cut and come again.** Take a cut from the joint, and come for another if you like it. The expression is used by Swift in his *Polite Conversation* (ii (1738)).

**Cut and dried.** All ready or arranged in advance. The allusion is to timber that has been cut and dried and is now ready for use.

**Cut and run, To.** To escape in a hurry; to quit. In the days when a ship's anchor cable was made of hemp the cable was cut, if the occasion demanded it, and the vessel allowed to run before the wind. A classic example of this was when the Spanish Armada was anchored off Calais. Most of the captains cut their cables on the approach of Howard's fireships.

**Cut and thrust.** A lively argument or spirited discussion. The allusion is to fencing.

**Cut a pretty** or **a sorry figure, To.** To give a poor impression.

**Cut both ways, To.** To work both to the good and to the bad.

**Cut corners, To.** To do something the easiest and quickest way, in the process lowering standards.

**Cut** or **cut up didoes, To.** To frivol and frolic; to behave extravagantly. The phrase appears as early as 1807 in the autobiographical work

*A Narrative of the Life and Travels of John Robert Shaw, the Well-Digger*. Its source is uncertain. It may have originated from British sailors' slang and be connected in some way with the corvette *Dido*. A classical allusion, however, may be preferable. Legend says that after the death of her husband, Sychaeus, DIDO fled to Libya, where she was permitted to buy only as much land as could be covered by a bull's hide. Undaunted by the challenge, she imaginatively cut the hide into thin ribbons so that it enclosed several acres, upon which she founded Carthage. Hence the expression.

**Cut down to size, To.** To reduce in importance, to decrease a person's conceit.

**Cut it fine, To.** To allow little margin.

**Cut it out!** Stop it! Don't do that!

**Cut it short!** Don't be so prolix; come to the point; CUT THE CACKLE. Said to a speaker who goes round and round the subject.

**Cut it short, To.** To bring something to an abrupt end.

**Cut little** or **no ice, To.** To be of little or no account; to make a negligible impression. The reference may be to figure skating.

**Cut loose, To.** To break free; to break away from conventional restraints.

**Cutoff.** The American equivalent of the English short cut, as a more direct route.

**Cut off one's nose to spite one's face, To.** To act out of pique in such a way as to harm oneself.

**Cut off with a shilling.** Disinherited. To be left a shilling meant that the testator had not forgotten a person, but had deliberately disinherited them by bequeathing a trifling sum.

**Cut of someone's jib.** A person's appearance, attitude or manner. 'I don't like the cut of his jib' means 'I don't like the look of him'. The phrase is of nautical origin. Jib here is the triangular foresail. Sailors used to recognize a vessel at sea by the cut of her jib.

**Cut one's coat according to one's cloth, To.** To restrict one's expenditure or outgoings to the amount of one's income; to live within one's means.

**Cut one's eye teeth, To.** To acquire wordly wisdom; 'to have cut one's eye teeth' is to be 'wide awake' or to have acquired wordly wisdom or to be quite sophisticated. The eye teeth are cut late, the first set at about 16 months, the second set at 12 years. *See also* WISDOM TOOTH.

**Cut one's own throat, To.** Figuratively, to adopt a policy, or take action that ruins one's own chances, plans or the like.

**Cut one's teeth on, To.** To gain early experience of.

**Cut one's wisdom teeth, To.** To reach the years of discretion. *See also* WISDOM TOOTH.

**Cut out, To be.** To be left in the lurch or superseded. When there are too many for a game of cards, such as whist or bridge, it is customary for the players to cut out after a rubber, in order that another may have a turn. The players cut the cards on the table and the lowest turn-up gives place to a newcomer.

**Cut out for, To be.** To be naturally suited for. The allusion is to cutting out cloth for specific purposes.

**Cut short, To.** To shorten; to silence by interruption.

**Cut the cackle, To.** To stop talking aimlessly and come to the point. To behead a chicken for the pot is to silence its ceaseless clucking.

**Cut the ground from under** or **from under someone's feet, To.** To leave an adversary no ground to stand on, by disproving or forestalling all their arguments; to anticipate what someone is going to do or say and so negate or invalidate his or her deeds.

**Cut the knot, To.** To solve a problem in an unconventional but effective way. The reference is to the GORDIAN KNOT.

**Cut the mustard, To.** To do something well and efficiently, especially when it is suspected that one may lack the ability. The expression derives from 'mustard' as a slang word for a thing that is the best, and O. Henry has a character in *Cabbages and Kings* (1894) say: 'I'm not head-lined in the bills, but I'm the mustard in the salad just the same.' The 'cutting' refers to the act of harvesting the plant, i.e. garnering the best.

> Perhaps I could get a job as a maid in somebody's house … Idden convinced me I would never cut the mustard at this occupation.
>
> JESSICA MITFORD: *Hons and Rebels*, ch ix (1960)

**Cut the painter, To.** To sever connections or links, as a boat is set adrift if the painter is cut which holds it fast to the mooring post. The phrase was much used in the 19th century with reference to possible severance between Britain and her colonies.

**Cut to the quick.** Figuratively, deeply hurt. The reference here is to the sensitive flesh below the nails or skin, hence the seat of feeling.

**Cut up rough, To.** To become angry or quarrelsome.

**Crew cut.** *See under* CREW.

**Diamond cut diamond.** *See under* DIAMOND.

**Have one's work cut out, To.** *See under* WORK.

**Short cut is often the longest way round, The.** *See under* SHORT.

**Cuthbert.** A name coined by 'Poy' (Percy Hutton Fearon) (1874–1945), cartoonist of the London *Evening News* from 1913, for the fit men who avoided military service in the First World War by securing a post in a Government office or in the Civil Service. He depicted them as frightened-looking rabbits.

**Cuthbert Bede.** The pen-name of the Rev. Edward Bradley (1827–89), author of *The Adventures of Mr* VERDANT GREEN and other humorous works. He took the name from St Cuthbert and the Venerable Bede, the two patron saints of Durham, whose university he attended.

**St Cuthbert's beads.** Single joints of the articulated stems of encrinites (fossil crinoids), also called stone lilies. They are perforated in the centre and bear a fanciful resemblance to a cross. Hence their former use for ROSARIES. Legend relates that the 7th-century St Cuthbert sits at night on a rock in HOLY ISLAND and uses the opposite rock as an anvil while he forges the beads.

**St Cuthbert's duck.** The eider duck, so called because it breeds in the Farne Islands, where St Cuthbert made his base.

**Cutpurse.** An old word for a pickpocket. When purses were worn suspended from a girdle, thieves cut the strings by which the purse was attached. When purses came to be kept in pockets the cutpurse became a pickpocket.

> To have an open ear, a quick eye, and a nimble hand, is necessary for a cutpurse.
> SHAKESPEARE: *The Winter's Tale*, IV, ii (1610)

**Moll Cutpurse.** The familiar name of Mary Frith (*c*.1585–1660), a woman of masculine vigour who often dressed as a man. In 1611 she was sentenced to do public penance by the COURT OF ARCHES for parading about Fleet Street and the Strand in male costume. She was a notorious thief and once attacked General Fairfax on Hounslow Heath, for which she was sent to NEWGATE PRISON. She escaped by bribery and finally died of dropsy. Middleton and Dekker's comedy *The Roaring Girle* (1611) is based on her exploits.

**Cutty.** A Scottish and northern English word meaning 'short', as for a cutty pipe (a short clay pipe), a cutty gun (a popgun) or simply a cutty (a dumpy girl or a woman of dubious character). The word is an adjective formed from the verb cut. *See also* CUTTY SARK.

**Cutty sark.** A Scottish term for a short petticoat or short-tailed shirt, made famous by the *Cutty Sark*, the clipper built at Dumbarton in 1869 for Captain John Willis, shipowner and master mariner. After a long career, mainly in the China tea trade and in shipping wool from Australia, she became a Portuguese trader in 1895 and was renamed the *Ferreira*. She was purchased by Captain Dowman in 1922, and restored at Falmouth as a boys' training ship. In 1928 she was towed round to the Thames in London and in 1953 was taken over by the Cutty Sark Preservation Society as the last survivor of the clippers. The name is taken from Burns' poem 'Tam O'Shanter' (1791), which was illustrated on the carvings round the ship's bows, but the figurehead was of a woman in flowing garments with outstretched arm. The accompanying 'witches' round the bows were naked. At one stage in the ship's career a short shirt emblem was flown at the mainmast.

> Her cutty sark, o' Paisley harn [coarse linen],
> That while a lassie she had worn,
> In longitude tho' sorely scanty,
> It was her best, and she was vauntie [proud].
> 'Tam O'Shanter'

**Cutty stool.** A short-legged wooden stool, and in Scotland the familiar name for the STOOL OF REPENTANCE.

**Cwt.** The abbreviation for hundredweight, from the Roman numeral C (100) and weight. *See also* DWT.

**Cyanean rocks, The.** Two rocky islands at the entrance of the EUXINE SEA, where the breakers make the passage very hazardous. It was at one time believed that they floated and closed together to crush a vessel when it attempted to sail between them.

**Cybele.** The mother goddess of Phrygia and the goddess of fertility and of the mountains, commonly identified with Agdistis. Her favourite was ATYS, and her priests were called CORYBANTES. She is also associated with DEMETER.

**Cycle.** A period or series of events or numbers that recur everlastingly in the same order.

**Cycle of the moon.** The METONIC CYCLE, so named from its discoverer Meton of Athens (5th century BC). It is a period of 19 years, at the end of which the phases of the moon repeat themselves on the same days as they did 19 years previously. *See also* CALLIPPIC PERIOD.

**Cycle of the sun.** A period of 28 years, at the end of which the days of the month fall on the same days of the week as they did 28 years previously.

**Cyclic number.** A number whose square ends in the same digit as itself. Examples are 5 (25) and 6 (36).

**Cyclic poets.** Post-Homeric epic poets who wrote continuations, illustrations or additions to Homer's poems. These poets, who were active between 800 and 550 BC, were called cyclic because they confined themselves to the cycle of the TROJAN WAR. The chief ones were Agias, Arctinus, Eugammon, Lesches and Stasinus.

**Fairy cycle.** *See under* FAIRY.

**Platonic Cycle** or **Great Year, The.** *See under* PLATO.

**Cyclops** (Greek, 'round eye', from *kuklos*, 'circle', and *ōps*, 'eye'). One of a group or race of giants. They had only one eye each and that in the centre of the forehead, and their work was to forge iron for VULCAN. Hesiod limits their number to three:

Arges, Steropes and BRONTES. *See also* ARIMASPIANS.

**Cygnus.** *See* PHAETON'S BIRD.

**Cyllaros.** A celebrated horse of CASTOR AND POLLUX, named from Cylla in Troas.

**Cylleneius.** A name for MERCURY, from Mount Cyllene, in Peloponnesus, where he was born.

**Cymbeline.** *See* CASSIBELAN; CUNOBELIN.

**Cymodoce.** One of the NEREIDS, a companion of VENUS in Virgil's *Georgics* (1st century BC) and AENEID (1st century BC). In Edmund Spenser's *The Faerie Queene* (1590, 1596) she is a daughter of NEREUS and mother of Marinell by Dumarin. She frees Florimell from the power of PROTEUS. The word means 'wave-receiving', from Greek *kuma*, 'wave', and *dekhomai*, 'to receive'.

**Garden of Cymodoce, The.** *See under* GARDEN.

**Cynic.** The ancient school of Greek philosophers known as the Cynics was founded by ANTISTHENES and made famous by his pupil DIOGENES. They were ostentatiously contemptuous of ease, luxury or wealth and of convention. The name is derived either from their dog-like, slovenly and uncouth habits or from the fact that Antisthenes held his school in the Gymnasium called Cynosarges ('white dog'), from an incident when a white dog carried away part of a victim that was being offered to HERCULES.

**Cynic tub.** The tub from which Diogenes lectured. Similarly the 'porch' in STOIC philosophy, the 'garden' in Epicurean philosophy, the ACADEMY in Platonic philosophy and the 'colonnade' in ARISTOTELIAN PHILOSOPHY. *See also* PERIPATETIC SCHOOL.

**Cynosure.** The Pole Star and hence the observed of all observers. The word is Greek for dog's tail, from *kuōn*, 'dog', and *oura*, 'tail', and it was given as a name to the constellation called URSA MINOR. Because mariners guided their ships by the north star and observed it as well, the word 'cynosure' came to be used for anything that strongly attracts attention, as 'the cynosure of neighbouring eyes' (Milton, 'L'Allegro' (1645)), especially for guidance in some matter.

**Cynthia.** The moon, as a byname of Artemis or DIANA, who represented the moon and was called Cynthia from Mount Cynthus in Delos, where she was born. The name was one of many applied to Elizabeth I by contemporary poets.

**Cypress.** A funeral tree, dedicated by the Romans to PLUTO, because when once cut it never grows again. It is said that its wood was at one time used for making coffins. Hence Shakespeare's 'In sad cypress let me be laid' (*Twelfth Night*, II, iv (1599)). The Greeks and Romans put cypress twigs in the coffins of the dead, and the tree is associated with cemeteries. It was also traditionally the wood from which CUPID's arrows were made.

**Cyprian.** Cyprus was formerly famous for the worship of VENUS. Hence the former application of the adjective to lewd and profligate persons and prostitutes.

> A Night Charge at Bow Street Office; with other matters worth knowing, respecting the unfortunate Cyprian, the feeling Coachman, and the generous Magistrate.
>
> PIERCE EGAN: *Life in London*, Bk II, ii (1820)

**Cyrano de Bergerac.** The hero of Edmond Rostand's play named after him (1897), Savinien Cyrano de Bergerac (1619–55) was a historical character who fought over 1000 duels in his youth, mostly on account of his grotesque nose. His fictional persona is an embodiment of theatrical romance, but his passionate love for his cousin, Roxanne, is long unrequited and she only recognizes his devotion as he finally duels with Death itself.

**Cyrene.** A Thessalian nymph, the daughter or granddaughter of the river-god Peneus. She was carried off by APOLLO to the country that came to be called Cyrenaica, where she bore him a son named Aristaeus. *See* ABIOGENESIS.

**Cyrillic alphabet.** The alphabet traditionally used by the Slav peoples, as now primarily found in Russian, Bulgarian and the Serbian dialect of Serbo-Croat. It is a form of the Greek alphabet invented by two brothers, the apostles of the Slavs, Constantine (827–869) and Methodius (*c*.825–885) of Thessalonica. Constantine was more popularly known by his religious name of Cyril.

**Cyrus.** The founder of the Persian Empire (559–529 BC) and the 'Cyrus king of Persia' of the Old Testament (2 Chronicles 36:22). He extended his conquests to Lydia, Babylonia, Assyria, Syria and Palestine, where he was mostly welcomed as a liberator and was looked on by the Greeks as a model ruler. There are various stories of his premature death, one being that he was defeated and killed by the Scythian queen, Tomyris, who soaked his head in a pot full of his blood and mutilated his body. Xenophon's *Cyropaedia* (4th century BC) tells of his career.

**Cyst, Baker's.** *See under* BAKER.

**Czar.** *See* TSAR.

# D

**D.** This letter is the outline of a rude archway or door. It is called in Phoenician and Hebrew *daleth* ('door') and in Greek *delta*. In the latter language it has a triangular shape (Δ). In Egyptian hieroglyphics it is represented by a hand.

**D or d.** The initial of the Latin DENARIUS is used to indicate a pre-decimal penny or pence. As a Roman numeral D stands for 500 and represents the second half of CIↃ, the ancient Tuscan sign for one thousand. D̄ stands for 5000.

**Dab.** Clever or skilled, as commonly in the phrase 'a dab hand'. The word probably comes from dab in the sense 'touch lightly'.

> [Love is] such a Dab at his Bow and Arrows.
> *Athenian Mercury*, IV, No. 3 (1691)

**Da capo** (Italian, literally 'from the head'). A musical direction to repeat all or part of the piece from the beginning. It is often abbreviated to DC.

**Dactyls** (Greek *daktulos*, 'finger'). Mythical beings connected with the worship of CYBELE in Crete, supposed to be the discoverers of iron and copper. They are also called Idaean Dactyls ('fingers of IDA') after their mountain home. Their number is given as ten or more but was originally three: the Smelter, the Hammer and the Anvil.

In prosody a dactyl is a foot of three syllables, one long and two short, as in the word 'harmony', again from the similarity to the joints of a finger.

**Dad** or **Daddy.** A child's word for 'father', common to many languages, for example: Irish *daid*, *daidí*, Welsh *tad*, Cornish *tat*, Latin *tata*, Greek *atta*, *tetta* (used by young people to their elders), Sanskrit *tata*, Lapp *dadda* and so on. Sometimes a related word has passed to another member of the family, as in Russian, which has *ded*, 'grandfather', *dyadya*, 'uncle' and *tyotya*, 'aunt'.

**Daddy-long-legs.** A name for the crane fly; also for the harvestman (a long-legged spider).

**Dad's Army.** A nickname for the HOME GUARD, many of whose members were middle-aged fathers. The name was popularized by the enjoyably nostalgic television comedy series so titled, first broadcast from 1968 to 1977 and repeated many times since.

**Sugar daddy.** *See under* SUGAR.

**Dadaism.** An anarchic and iconoclastic art movement, which began at Zürich in 1916 and arose from indignation and despair at the catastrophe of the First World War. Its supporters, writers and painters, sought to free themselves from all artistic conventions and what they considered cultural shams. Dadaism was influenced by CUBISM and FUTURISM, and after about 1922 it was succeeded by SURREALISM. The origin of the name is surrounded in confusion, but one of the more plausible accounts tells how the German poets Hugo Ball and Richard Huelsenbeck were leafing through a German-French dictionary when they came across the French word *dada*, meaning 'hobbyhorse'. Partly because of its nonsensical sound and partly through its associations with the freedom of childhood, they decided to adopt it. Jean Arp (1888–1966), Max Ernst (1891–1976) and Marcel Janco (1895–1984) were among their number. There was a similar wave in New York at the same time associated with Marcel Duchamp (1887–1968), Francis Picabia (1879–1953) and Man Ray (1890–1977). A plaque showing a human navel was unveiled at Zürich in February 1966 to commemorate the fiftieth anniversary of the movement. *See also* FAUVISM; IMPRESSIONISM; ORPHISM; SYNCHROMISM; VORTICISM.

**Daedalus** (Greek *daidalos*, 'cunningly made'). A legendary Athenian, father of ICARUS, who formed the Cretan LABYRINTH and made wings, by means of which he flew from Crete across the archipelago. He is said to have invented various tools, such as the saw, the axe and the gimlet, and his name is perpetuated in English *daedal* or *dedal*, 'skilful'.

**Daffodil.** Legend says that the daffodil or LENT LILY was white before but Persephone (PROSERPINA), who had wreathed her head with them and fallen asleep in the meadow, was captured by PLUTO and carried off in his chariot. She let fall some of the lilies, and they turned to a golden yellow. Theophilus and Pliny write that they grow on the banks of ACHERON and that the spirits of the dead delight in the flower, called by them the ASPHODEL. In England in the 16th century it was called both 'daffodil' and 'affodil'. It has also been called by the poetic name of 'daffodilly' or 'daffadilly' and, as a playful extension of this, 'daffodowndilly' or 'daffadowndilly'. The origin of the name may be in Dutch *de affodil*, 'the asphodel'.

In the 20th century it became an alternative to the LEEK as a Welsh emblem, since some regarded this vegetable as vulgar.

O Proserpina!
For the flowers now that frighted thou let'st fall
From Dis's waggon! daffodils,
That come before the swallow dares, and take
The winds of March with beauty.
SHAKESPEARE: *The Winter's Tale*, IV, iii (1610)

**Daft as a brush, As.** *See under* AS.

**Dagger.** The printed sign (†), also called obelisk, is conventionally used for reference to a note after the asterisk (*) has already been used for this purpose. It originally appeared in church books, prayers of EXORCISM, at benedictions and so on, to remind the priest where to make the sign of the cross.

In the arms of the City of London the dagger supposedly commemorates Sir William Walworth's dagger, with which he slew Wat Tyler in 1381. Before this time the cognizance of the City was the sword of St PAUL. The inscription below Sir William's statue in Fishmongers' Hall announced:

Brave Walworth Knyght Lord Mayor that slew
Rebellious Tyler in his alarmes –
The king therefore did give in lieu
The Dagger to the Cytyes armes.

**Dagger scene.** During the French Revolution Edmund Burke threw down a dagger on the floor of the House, exclaiming as he did so: 'There's French fraternity for you! Such is the weapon which French Jacobins would plunge into the heart of our beloved king.' Sheridan spoilt the dramatic effect and set the House in a roar by his remark: 'The gentleman, I see, has brought his knife with him, but where is his fork?' *See also* COUP DE THÉÂTRE.

**At daggers drawn, To be.** *See under* AT.

**Cloak and dagger plays.** *See under* CLOAK.

**Look daggers, To.** *See under* LOOK.

**Dagobert, King.** *See under* KING.

**Dagon** (Phoenician *Dagan*, perhaps a diminutive of *dag*, 'fish'). A god worshipped by the PHILISTINES after their arrival in Canaan and supposedly symbolized as half-man and half-fish. Samson's vengeance on the Philistines occurred after their riotous celebrations to Dagon (Judges 16:23–30).

Dagon his name, sea-monster, upward man
And downward fish; yet had his temple high
Reared in Azotus, dreaded through the coast
Of Palestine, in Gath and Ascalon,
And Accaron and Gaza's frontier bounds.
MILTON: *Paradise Lost*, i (1667)

**Dagonet, Sir.** In the ARTHURIAN ROMANCES the fool of King Arthur, knighted by the king himself.

**Daikoku** (Japanese *dai*, 'big', and *koku*, 'black'). One of the seven Japanese gods of luck. He is god of wealth and good fortune and is represented sitting on bags of rice.

**Daisy.** An emblem of deceit. Robert Greene, in *A Quip for an Upstart Courtier* (1592), speaks of the 'dissembling daisie'. 'Light of love wenches' are warned by it 'not to trust every fair promise that such amorous bachelors make them'. In Shakespeare's *Hamlet* (1600), Ophelia gives the queen a daisy to signify 'that her light and fickle love ought not to expect constancy in her husband'.

The word is really 'day's eye', from Old English *dægesēge*, and the flower is so called because it closes its pink 'lashes' when the sun sets, but in the morning opens its petals to the light. *See also* VIOLET.

That well by reason men call it maie,
The daisie, or else the eie of daie.
CHAUCER: *The Legend of Good Women*, Prologue (*c*.1387)

**Daisy chain.** A garland or necklace of daisies, made by children, who thread the stalks together.

**Daisy-cutter.** In CRICKET a ball that rolls along the ground to the batsman when bowled; in tennis a service that drives the ball similarly. In the 19th century a horse that lifted its feet very little above the ground was so described, and more recently it was applied colloquially by the RAF to a perfect landing.

**Daisy roots.** Legend says that these, like the berries of dwarf elder, stunt the growth, a superstition that probably arose from the notion that everything had the property of bestowing its own speciality on others.

She robbed dwarf-elders of their fragrant fruit
And fed him early with the daisy root,
Whence through his veins the powerful juices ran,
And formed the beauteous miniature of man.
THOMAS TICKELL: *Kensington Gardens* (1722)

**Daisywheel.** A typewriter or printer wheel, whose many spokes, each with different characters on the end, resemble the petals of a daisy.

**As fresh as a daisy.** *See under* AS.

**Darling Daisy.** *See under* DARLING.

**Gert and Daisy.** *See under* GERT.

**Lazy daisy stitch.** *See under* LAZY.

**Push up the daisies, To.** *See under* PUSH.

**Dalai Lama.** *See* LAMAISM.

**Daleks.** The tin robots, resembling pepperpots on wheels, in the children's television series *Doctor* WHO, made their first appearance in 1963. They were the invention of the scriptwriter Terry Nation, who denied a claim that their name came arbitrarily from an encyclopedia volume titled DAL–LEK. They were famed for their threatening vocalization 'Exterminate! Exterminate!' and their ability to floor a foe with a ray beamed from their antennae.

**Daltonism.** *See* COLOUR BLINDNESS.

**Dam, The Devil and his.** *See under* DEVIL.

**Damascene, St John.** *See under* JOHN.

**Dame. Dame Durden.** *See under* DURDEN.

**Dame Partington and her mop.** A taunt against those who try to withstand progress or the inevitable. Sidney Smith, speaking at Taunton in October 1831, on the rejection of the Reform Bill by the House of Lords, compared them to Dame Partington, who, during a great storm at Sidmouth in 1824, tried to push back the Atlantic with her mop. 'She was excellent at a slop, or a puddle,' he said, 'but she should not have meddled with a tempest. Gentlemen, be at your ease, be quiet and steady. You will beat Mrs Partington.'

The American humorist Benjamin P. Shillaber published *The Life and Sayings of Mrs Partington* (1854), the old lady, like Mrs MALAPROP, constantly misusing words.

**Squire of dames.** *See under* SQUIRE.

**Damiens' ordeal.** Robert François Damiens (1715–57), a deranged French farmhand, managed to stab Louis XV as the latter was entering his carriage at Versailles. By way of punishment his chest, arms, thighs and calves were burned with pincers, his right hand, holding the knife with which he had attempted the assassination, was burned in sulphur, and the resulting wounds were dressed with molten lead, boiling wax, oil and resin. He was finally quartered by whip-goaded horses. The ordeal was unwillingly witnessed by CASANOVA and the affair regarded a shameful scandal.

**Damn.** A mild exclamation of annoyance, deriving ultimately from the Latin *damnum*, 'loss', 'injury'. 'Not to give a damn' is to be unconcerned or uninterested.

> I wish I could care what you do or where you go but I can't ... My dear, I don't give a damn.
>
> MARGARET MITCHELL: *Gone with the Wind*, ch lvii (1936)

**Damn with faint praise, To.** To praise in such restrained terms as to deprive the praise of any value.

> Damn with faint praise, assent with civil leer,
> And, without sneering teach the rest to sneer.
>
> ALEXANDER POPE: *Epistle to Dr Arbuthnot* (1735)

**As near as damn it.** *See under* AS.

**Not worth a damn.** *See under* WORTH.

**Damocles, The Sword of.** *See under* SWORD.

**Damon** (Greek *dēmos*, 'land', 'people'). The name of a goatherd in Virgil's *Eclogues* (1st century BC) and hence used by pastoral poets for rustic swains. *See also* CORYDON.

**Damon and Pythias.** Models of devoted friendship and mutual loyalty. In the 4th century BC Pythias (more correctly Phintias) was condemned to death for treason by Dionysius, the tyrant of Syracuse, but obtained leave to go home to arrange his affairs after his friend Damon had agreed to take his place and be executed should he not return. He did return in time to save Damon and Dionysius was so struck by this loyal friendship that he pardoned both of them.

**Damp squib, A.** Said of an enterprise, joke or the like, that fails to come off or to satisfy the expectations aroused, in just the same way as a damp squib disappointingly fails to explode. *See also* SQUIB.

**Damsel.** A maiden or young unmarried woman; a waiting maid or attendant. The word comes from Old French *damoisele*, the feminine of *damoisel*, 'squire'. This in turn is from Medieval Latin *domnicellus*, a contracted form of *dominicellus*, the diminutive of *dominus*, 'lord' (*see also* DONZEL). In medieval France the *domnicellus* or *damoiseau* was the son of a king, prince, KNIGHT or lord before he entered the order of knighthood. The king's bodyguards were called his *damoiseaux* or *damsels*. The chronicler Jean Froissart styles Richard II (d.1027) *le jeune damoisel Richart*, and Louis VII (Le Jeune) (1120–80) was called the 'royal damsel'.

**Damsel in distress, A.** A girl or woman in difficulty or in an embarrassing situation. She may be rescued by a KNIGHT IN SHINING ARMOUR. The archetypal damsel in distress is the one held captive by a DRAGON and freed by St GEORGE.

**Damsel of Brittany, The.** Eleanor (1185–1241), the daughter of Geoffrey, second son of Henry II of England, and Constance, daughter of Conan IV of Brittany. On the death in 1203 of Prince Arthur, grandson of Henry II and claimant to the throne, she became heiress to the English throne, but King John imprisoned her in Bristol Castle, where she died.

**Dan.** A title meaning 'sir' or 'master' (Latin *dominus*, related to Spanish *Don*), which is common with the old poets, as Dan Phoebus, Dan Cupid, Dan Chaucer and so on. *See also* DOM.

> Dan *Chaucer*, well of English vndefyled,
> On Fames eternall beadroll worthie to be fyled.
>
> EDMUND SPENSER: *The Faerie Queene*, IV, ii (1596)

**Dan.** One of the 12 sons of JACOB and thus a progenitor of one of the 12 tribes of Israel. His mother was Bilhah, the servant of RACHEL. His tribal territory was in the extreme north of the PROMISED LAND, hence the expression FROM DAN TO BEERSHEBA to denote the whole of Israel or any other territory.

**Dan Dare.** The space pilot in the boys' comic *Eagle* from 1950 to 1967. He serves as a colonel in the Interplanetary Space Fleet, and has adventures on Venus and beyond. His great enemy is the dome-headed MEKON. The cartoon strips featuring him were the work of Frank Hampson. Attempts to revive Dan Dare in comics of the 1970s and 1980s proved disappointing.

**Desperate Dan.** *See under* DESPERATE.

**From Dan to Beersheba.** *See under* FROM.

**Danace.** An ancient Persian coin, worth rather more than the Greek OBOLUS and sometimes placed by the Greeks in the mouth of the dead to pay CHARON'S TOLL.

**Danaë.** The daughter of Acrisius, king of Argos. He was told that his daughter's son would put him to death and thus determined that Danaë should never marry. She was accordingly locked up in an inaccessible tower. ZEUS foiled the king by changing himself into a shower of gold, under which guise he readily found access to the fair prisoner, and in this way she became the mother of PERSEUS.

**Danaides.** The 50 daughters of Danaus, king of Argos. They married 50 sons of AEGYPTUS, but at the command of their father all but HYPERMNESTRA, wife of LYNCEUS, murdered their husbands on their wedding night. They were punished in HADES by having to draw water everlastingly in sieves from a deep well.

**Dance. Dance and pay the piper, To.** To work hard to entertain; to take all the trouble and bear the expense as well. The allusion is to Matthew 11:17: 'We have piped unto you, and ye have not danced.'

**Dance attendance on, To.** To wait obsequiously on; to be constantly at someone's beck and call. It was a former custom at weddings for the bride, no matter how tired she was, to dance with every guest.

> They had parted so much honesty among 'em
> (At least, good manners) as not thus to suffer
> A man of his place, and so near our favour,
> To dance attendance on their lordships'
> pleasures.
>
> SHAKESPEARE: *Henry VIII*, V, ii (1612)

**Dance of Death** or **Danse Macabre.** An allegorical representation of Death (usually a dancing skeleton or corpse) leading people to the grave in order of social precedence. It is first found in the 14th century, and there is a series of woodcuts on the subject by Hans Holbein the Younger (1497–1543). In the cloister of Old St Paul's a 'Dance of Death' called the 'Dance of St Paul's' was painted at the cost of John Carpenter, town clerk of London (15th century), with translations of French verses by John Lydgate (*c.*1370–1451). There is a copy in the LAMBETH PALACE library. W.H. Auden's musical play *The Dance of Death* was published in 1933.

**Dances of the ancient world.**

Astronomical dances: invented by the Egyptians and designed to represent the movements of the heavenly bodies

Bacchic dances: grave (like the minuet), gay (like the gavotte) and a mixture of grave and gay

Children's dances: in Lacedaemonia, in honour of DIANA; the children were naked, and their movements were grave, modest and graceful

Corybantic dances: in honour of BACCHUS and accompanied with timbrels, fifes, flutes and a tumultuous noise produced by the clashing of swords and spears against brazen bucklers

Danse champêtre: invented by PAN and quick and lively; the dancers (in the open air) wore wreaths of oak and garlands of flowers

Funeral dances: in Athens, slow and solemn dances in which the priests took part; the performers wore long, white robes and carried cypress slips in their hands

Hymeneal dances: lively and joyous; the dancers were crowned with flowers

Jewish dances: DAVID danced in certain religious processions (2 Samuel 6:14); the people sang and danced before the golden calf (Exodus 32:19); Psalm 150:4 exhorts: 'Praise him with the timbrel and dance'; Miriam, the sister of Moses, after the passage of the Red Sea, was followed by all the women with timbrels and dances (Exodus 15:20)

Lapithae (invented by Pirithous): performed after some famous victory and designed to imitate the combats of the CENTAURS and LAPITHS; both difficult and dangerous

MAY DAY dances at Rome: at daybreak lads and lasses went out to gather 'may' and other flowers for themselves and their elders, and the day was spent in dances and festivities

Military dances: the oldest of all dances, executed with swords, javelins and bucklers, and said to have been invented by MINERVA to celebrate the victory of the gods over the TITANS

Nuptial dances: a Roman pantomimic performance representing the dances of HARLEQUIN and COLUMBINE

PYRRHIC DANCES

Salic dances: instituted by Numa Pompilius in honour of MARS, executed by 12 priests selected from the highest of the nobility and performed in the temple while sacrifices were being made and hymns sung

**Dance upon nothing, To.** To be hanged.

**Dancing around the maypole.** *See* MAYPOLE.

**Dancing Chancellor, The.** Sir Christopher Hatton (1540–91) was so called, because he first attracted Queen Elizabeth I's notice by his graceful dancing in a masque at court. He was LORD CHANCELLOR from 1587 till his death.

> His bushy beard and shoestrings green,
> His high-crowned hat and satin doublet,
> Moved the stout heart of England's queen,
> Though Pope and Spaniard could not trouble it.
>
> THOMAS GRAY: *A Long Story* (1750)

**Dancing dervishes.** *See* WHIRLING.

**Dancing girl.** A professional female dancer who dances to entertain patrons of a club or the like. *See also* BAYADERE; GEISHA.

**Dancing water.** A magic elixir, common to many fairy tales, which beautifies ladies, rejuvenates them and enriches them. In the Comtesse d'Aulnoy's *Contes des Fées* (1697) it fell in a cascade in the Burning Forest and could be reached only by an underground passage. Prince Chery fetched a bottle of it for his beloved Fairstar, but was aided by a dove.

**Abbots Bromley horn dance.** *See under* ABBOT.

**As you pipe, I must dance.** *See under* AS.

**Belly dance.** *See under* BELLY.

**Clog dance.** *See under* CLOG.

**Country dance.** *See under* COUNTRY.

**Cushion dance.** *See under* CUSHION.

**Fan dance.** *See under* FAN.

**Floral dance.** *See* FURRY DANCE.

**Giants' Dance, The.** *See under* GIANT.

**Horn dance.** *See* ABBOTS BROMLEY HORN DANCE.

**Ice dancing.** *See under* ICE.

**Lead one the Devil's own dance, To.** *See under* LEAD.

**Lead someone a dance, To.** *See under* LEAD.

**Merry dancers.** *See under* MERRY.

**Morris dance.** *See under* MORRIS.

**National dances.** *See under* NATIONAL.

**Nutters' dance.** *See under* NUT.

**Old-time dance.** *See under* OLD.

**Pyrrhic dance.** *See under* PYRRHIC.

**St Vitus' Dance.** *See under* VITUS.

**Song and dance.** *See under* SONG.

**Spot dance.** *See under* SPOT.

**Sword dance.** *See under* SWORD.

**War dance.** *See under* WAR.

**Dander. Get someone's dander up, To.** To annoy or anger someone. This is generally considered to be an Americanism, but 'dander', as a synonym for 'anger', has been a common dialect word in several English counties. It may well represent a colloquial form of 'dandruff'.

> He was as spunky as thunder, and when a Quaker gets his dander up, it's like a Northwester.
>
> SEBA SMITH: *Letters of Major Jack Downing* (1830)

**Dandiprat.** A small coin issued in the 16th century, with a value of three halfpence. The term is also applied to a DWARF, to a pageboy and to a conceited little fellow. Stanyhurst calls CUPID a 'dandiprat' in his translation of Virgil's *Aeneid* (i (1582)). The origin of the name is unknown.

**Dando.** A former name for a person who frequents hotels, restaurants and the like, satisfies his appetite and decamps without payment. The term comes from Dando, the hero of many popular songs in the early 19th century, who was well known for this.

**Dandy.** A COXCOMB or fop. The word is of late 18th-century Scottish origin and may derive from someone who has been spoilt by an excess of dandying or from the name Andrew, or it may be a shortened form of DANDIPRAT or JACK-A-DANDY.

**Dandy King, The.** Joachim Murat (1767–1815), NAPOLEON BONAPARTE's dashing cavalry leader, made king of Naples in 1808, was so nicknamed from his fondness for personal adornment. Napoleon is reputed to have called him *un roi de théâtre* ('a player king').

**Dandy roller.** A light roller used in paper-making to produce watermarks.

**Last of the Dandies, The.** *See under* LAST.

**Dane. Danegeld.** The geld (tax) on land originally raised to buy peace from the Danes in the time of Ethelred II (978–1016) and continued as a tax long after it was needed for its original purpose. The word also more generally means appeasement by bribery.

> And that is called paying the Dane-geld;
> But we've proved it again and again,
> That if once you have paid him the Dane-geld
> You never get rid of the Dane.
>
> RUDYARD KIPLING: 'Dane-Geld' (1911)

**Danelaw** (Late Old English *Dena lagu*, 'law of the Danes'). That part of north and east England, roughly bounded by a line from London to Chester, to which ALFRED THE GREAT (r.871–899) succeeded in containing the Danes and where Danish law was thus in force. The term was not used until the reign of King CANUTE (1016–35).

**Danesblood** or **Danewort.** Dwarf elder (*Sambucus ebulus*). It is called Danesblood from a belief that it was supposed to flourish in places where there had been battles against the Danes, and Danewort because it is believed to have been introduced by the Danes.

**Dane's skin.** A freckled skin. Red hair and a freckled skin were regarded as the traditional characteristics of Danish blood.

**Havelock the Dane.** *See under* HAVELOCK.

**Ogier the Dane.** *See under* OGIER.

**Danebrog** or **Dannebrog.** The national flag of Denmark. *Brog* is said to be Old Danish for 'cloth'. The tradition is that Waldemar II of Denmark saw a fiery cross in the heavens, which betokened his victory over the Estonians (1219). *See also* CONSTANTINE'S CROSS.

**Order of Danebrog, The.** *See under* ORDER.

**Daniel.** A prophet and wise man of the Jews during the BABYLONIAN CAPTIVITY. He became the chief administrator of the kingdom through his successful interpretation of the dreams of NEBUCHADNEZZAR (Daniel 2:4). He also correctly interpreted the WRITING ON THE WALL at BELSHAZZAR's feast, predicting Belshazzar's downfall (Daniel 5:17). When he continued to pray to God, in violation of a decree by King DARIUS, he was thrown into the lions' den, but God sent an angel to protect him (Daniel 6:16). According to some authorities, he is the judge who recognizes

Susanna's innocence in the apocryphal story of Susanna and the Elders.

**Daniel Boone.** *See under* BOONE.

**Daniel come to judgement, A.** A person who displays wisdom beyond his years. In Shakespeare's *The Merchant of Venice* (IV, i (1596)) Shylock says:

A Daniel come to judgement! yea, a Daniel!
O wise young judge, how I do honour thee!

The History of Susanna in the APOCRYPHA tells how Susanna rejected the advances of two elders, was falsely accused by them and condemned to death. They claimed to have seen her lying under a tree with a young man. Her innocence was established by the youthful Daniel, who asked the accusers separately under what kind of tree the adultery took place. Each named a different tree: one a 'mastick', the other a 'holm'.

**Dansker.** A Dane, from Danish *dansk*, 'Danish'. Hence POLONIUS says to Reynaldo:

Inquire me first what Danskers are in Paris.
SHAKESPEARE: *Hamlet*, II, i (1600)

**Dante and Beatrice.** Beatrice Portinari was only eight years old when Dante, who was still a boy, first saw her. The poet's love for her was as pure as it was tender. Beatrice married a nobleman, Simone de Bardi, in 1287 and she died in 1290 (not yet 24). A few years later Dante married Gemma Donati. Beatrice is celebrated and idealized in Dante's *Vita Nuova* (*c.*1292) and *Divina Commedia* (*c.*1309–*c.*1320). In the latter work the poet is conducted through HELL and PURGATORY first by VIRGIL (who represents human reason), then by the spirit of Beatrice (who represents the wisdom of faith) and finally by St BERNARD (who represents the wisdom from on high).

In *Vita Nuova* Dante makes much of the association of Beatrice with the number NINE. He meets her when she is in her ninth year, and she died at 9 o'clock on 9 June, 1290. He also declared her to have been herself 'a nine', or a symbol of perfection.

**Dantesque.** Dante-like, in the sense of vividly representing horrors, whether by words, as in the poem, or in visual form, as in Gustave Doré's illustrations (1861) of the *Inferno*.

**Danton, Georges Jacques.** A leader in the French Revolution, Danton (1759–94) is credited with initiating the REIGN OF TERROR, during which he was himself executed for treason. He came to be variously portrayed in literature, typically as the common man's hero, the egotistical tyrant, the misunderstood intellectual or the uncompromising idealist.

**Daphne** (Greek, 'laurel'). The daughter of the river-god Peneus in Thessaly. She was beloved by APOLLO but, because she had resolved to spend her life in perpetual virginity, she fled from him. On seeking the protection of the gods, she was changed by them into a LAUREL or BAY tree. Apollo declared that henceforth he would wear bay leaves instead of oak and that all who sought his favour should follow his example.

**Daphnis** (Greek *daphnē*, 'laurel'). In Greek mythology a Sicilian shepherd who invented pastoral poetry. He was a son of MERCURY and a Sicilian nymph, and he was protected by DIANA and taught by PAN and the MUSES. Daphnis was also the lover of CHLOE. He was the model for Allan Ramsay's *Gentle Shepherd* (1725), and the tale is the basis of Bernardin de St-Pierre's *Paul et Virginie* (1788).

**Dapple.** The name given in Tobias Smollett's translation (1755) of *Don* QUIXOTE to SANCHO PANZA's donkey (in the original it has no name). The word, whose origin is uncertain, means 'blotched', 'speckled in patches'. A dapple grey horse is one of a light grey shaded with a deeper hue, and a dapple bay is of a light bay spotted with a bay of deeper colour.

I had a little pony,
His name was Dapple Gray;
I lent him to a lady
To ride a mile away.
Nursery rhyme

**Darbies.** Handcuffs. The phrase 'father Derbies bands' for handcuffs is found in George Gascoigne's *Steel Glas* (1576). Father Derby (or Darby) may have been a usurer, and his 'bands' (or bonds) the strict agreement he held with his client.

An hark ye! Jem Clink will fetch you the darbies.
SIR WALTER SCOTT: *Peveril of the Peak*, ch xxxiii (1823)

**Darby and Joan.** An ideal elderly, loving, harmonious couple. The names belong to a ballad written by Henry Woodfall, first published in the *Gentleman's Magazine* in 1735. The characters are said to be John Darby, of Bartholomew Close, who died in 1730, and his wife Joan, described as: 'chaste as a picture cut in alabaster. You might sooner move a Scythian rock than shoot fire into her bosom.' Woodfall served his apprenticeship to John Darby. Another account, however, locates the couple in the West Riding of Yorkshire. The French equivalent is *St* ROCH ET SON CHIEN.

**Darby and Joan club.** A social club for elderly men and women. *See* DARBY AND JOAN.

**Darbyites.** A name sometimes given to the PLYMOUTH BRETHREN, from John Nelson Darby (1800–82), their founder.

**Dardanus.** A son of ZEUS and ELECTRA and the legendary founder of the royal house of TROY.

He eventually married Batea, daughter of King TEUCER, who gave him land near Abydos, where he established the town of Dardania or Dardanus. Hence, popularly, the name Dardanelles for what was once called the HELLESPONT.

**Dare, Dan.** *See under* DAN.

**Daric.** An ancient Persian gold coin, probably so called from King DARIUS I of Persia. There was also a silver daric, worth one-twentieth of the gold coin.

**Darius.** The name comes from Greek *Dareios*, from Old Persian *dārayavaush* or *dārayavush* ('I hold fast the good'). Darius the Great, son of Hystaspes (Vishtaspa), governor of Persia, assumed the name when he became king in 521 BC. As 'Darius, king of Persia', he is mentioned in the Bible (Ezra 4:5).

Legend relates that he conspired with six other Persian nobles to overthrow Smerdis, the usurper, and that they agreed that he whose horse neighed first should be king. The horse of Darius was the first to neigh. His exploits are recorded on the rock of BEHISTUN.

It is said that Darius III (Codommanus), the last king of the Persian Empire, who was conquered by Alexander the Great (331 BC), sent for the tribute of golden eggs on Alexander's accession. The Macedonian replied: 'The bird which laid them is flown to the other world, where Darius must seek them.' The Persian king then sent him a bat and ball, mocking his youth, but Alexander told the messengers that with the bat he would beat the ball of power from their master's hand. Lastly, Darius sent him a bitter melon as a symbol of the grief in store for him, but the Macedonian declared that he would make the Persian eat his own fruit.

**Dark. Dark Ages, The.** A term applied to the period of history between the end of the Roman Empire in AD 476 and the year 800, or more generally to the period between about 500 and 1000. The name is sometimes said to refer to the lack of historical knowledge about this period, although many take it as alluding to a period of intellectual darkness and barbarity. Part of the Dark Ages overlapped with the MIDDLE AGES.

**Dark and bloody ground.** Kentucky. So called by the American Indians because of the fierce wars waged in the forests and later so known by the whites for the same reason in their struggle against the indigenous people.

**Dark blue.** Relating to Oxford or Harrow.

**Dark Continent, The.** Africa, a continent about which the world was long 'in the dark' and much of which was an unknown land of mystery. It is also the land of dark-skinned races. H.M. Stanley's *Through the Dark Continent* appeared in 1878, *In Darkest Africa* in 1890 and *My Dark Companions and their Strange Stories* in 1893.

**Darken counsel, To.** To confuse an issue by introducing irrelevant or ill-founded considerations.

> Who is this that darkeneth counsel by words without knowledge?
> Job 38:2

**Darken someone's door, To.** To cross their threshold. The expression is typically used in an exhortation such as: 'Don't you dare darken my door again!' The door is darkened by one's shadow.

**Darkest hour is that before the dawn, The.** When things are at their worst, they can only get better.

> This is a terrible hour, but it is often that darkest point which precedes the rise of day.
> CHARLOTTE BRONTË: *Shirley*, ch xx (1849)

**Dark horse, A.** A racing term for a horse of possible promise, but about which nothing is known. The allusion is not to a dark-coloured horse but to one about which the public has been 'kept in the dark'. The phrase is also applied to a person whose abilities or possible course of action are unknown, or to a person who reveals unsuspected talent.

**Darkie.** An offensive colloquial name for an American Negro, found as early as 1775.

**Darkie Day.** A traditional event in Padstow, Cornwall, in which fishermen and their wives black up their faces and sing slave songs on Boxing Day and New Year's Day. The custom is said to date from an incident in the 17th century when a slave ship sheltered in the port en route to Bristol and its human cargo escaped to chant and caper on the quayside. The event has been criticized in modern times for its apparent lack of POLITICAL CORRECTNESS.

**Darkies, The.** A popular name for the former ADELPHI arches.

**Dark Lady of the Sonnets, The.** The woman about whom Shakespeare wrote the sonnets numbered cxxvii–clii. Her precise identity is still uncertain, but among the candidates favoured by the critics are Mary Fitton, Penelope Rich and Mrs Davenant, wife of an Oxford innkeeper. Dr Leslie Hotson claimed her to be Black Lucy or Luce, alias Lucy Negro, née Morgan, married to one Parker. This lady, a gentlewoman to Queen Elizabeth I, became a notorious bawd and brothel keeper at CLERKENWELL. More convincingly, Dr A.L. Rowse, with considerable supporting evidence, has identified her as Emilia Lanier, née Bassano, the illegitimate daughter of a Venetian court musician. She married Alfonso Lanier, another court musician, in 1592, at the end of which year the affair with Shakespeare probably began. She had previously been a mistress of Lord Hunsdon, the Lord Chamberlain.

**Dark lantern, A.** A lantern with a panel or shutter to dim the light.

**Dark star, A.** In astronomy a star that emits little or no visible light but is known to exist through observation of its spectrum or gravitational effect.

**In the dark.** In a state of ignorance.

**Keep it dark, To.** To keep something a dead secret, so as not to enlighten anyone about it.

**Leap in the dark, A.** *See under* LEAP.

**Shot in the dark, A.** *See under* SHOT.

**Whistle in the dark, To.** *See under* WHISTLE.

**Darley Arabian.** In 1704 Thomas Darley sent from Aleppo to his father Richard Darley, of Aldby Park, Yorkshire, an Arab horse of the best Maneghi breed. From this thoroughbred stallion came a famous breed of racehorses, including ECLIPSE.

All thoroughbred racehorses throughout the world are descended from three Arabs, of which the Darley Arabian was one. The others were the Byerly Turk, the charger of Colonel Byerly at the Battle of the Boyne (1690), and the Godolphin Arabian, brought to England in 1730 by Edward Coke, from whom it passed into the possession of the Earl of Godolphin.

**Darling. Darling Daisy.** Frances Evelyn Greville, Countess of Warwick (1861–1938), adulterous wife of the 5th Earl of Warwick and for nine years mistress of Edward VII, whom he often addressed in his letters to her as 'My Darling Daisy wife'. In 1914 she sought to make money by threatening to publish her memoirs, which would include the late king's letters. This was prevented by three prominent courtiers acting on behalf of George V. Her entry in the *Dictionary of National Biography* makes no mention of her infidelity, preferring instead to praise her beauty, her interest in socialism and her love of birds and animals.

**Duke or darling.** *See under* DUKE.

**Grace Darling.** An English heroine (1815–42) of almost legendary fame, the daughter of William Darling, keeper of the Longstone lighthouse on the Farne Islands, Northumberland. She and her father attempted the rescue of survivors of the wrecked *Forfarshire* in 1838. They launched their small boat in perilous seas and brought back five survivors to the lighthouse. Darling made a second trip with two of the *Forfarshire*'s crew and saved four more, 43 being drowned. She died of consumption.

**Darnex.** *See* DORNICK.

**D'Artagnan.** The swashbuckling hero of Dumas *père*'s popular novel *The* THREE MUSKETEERS (1844). He was apparently based on a real Sieur d'Artagnan who served Louis XIV as a captain of musketeers and who perished in battle in 1673. The fictional D'Artagnan and his three musketeer friends, Athos, Porthos and Aramis, reappear in two sequels: *Twenty Years After* (1845) and *The Vicomte de Bragelonne* (1847). He has been played by various well-known actors in filmed versions of the stories, including Douglas Fairbanks, Don Ameche and Gene Kelly.

**Dartmoor.** An extensive moorland in Devon, some 400 square miles (1035 sq km) in area, particularly noted for its tors, hut circles, stone rows, barrows, pounds and stannaries and synonymous with the prison at Princetown. This was founded in 1809 to house French prisoners during the Napoleonic Wars and was first used for criminals in 1850. Dartmoor is famous in literature as the setting of Sir Arthur Conan Doyle's dark tale *The Hound of the Baskervilles* (1902), with several passages evoking the wild allure of the region.

**Darts, Fairy.** *See under* FAIRY.

**Darwinian theory.** The theory of evolution as put forward by Charles Darwin, notably in his book *The Origin of Species by Natural Selection* (1859), summed up by Herbert Spencer as 'the survival of the fittest'. Evolution was not a new idea to science, but the shock to established science and orthodox Christian belief was profound.

**Dash. Dash it all, dash my wig, dash my buttons.** In these expressions 'dash' is a EUPHEMISM for 'damn'. Wig, buttons and so on are the relics of a fashion adopted by fops and dandies in the late 19th century of 'swearing' without using profane or obscene language.

**Cut a dash, To.** *See under* CUT.

**Date.** The Romans expressed the date of a letter as in the following example: *Dabam Romae prid. Kal. Apr.* ('I gave (this) at Rome on 31 March'). The opening words of this formula were later altered to *Data Romae*, 'given at Rome', and *data* (the feminine singular or neuter plural of *datus*, 'given') was adopted, through French, to give English 'date'.

**Date, A.** A social appointment, especially with someone of the opposite sex. A date rape is one of a girl or woman made during such a meeting.

**Date Line, The.** In full, the International Date Line, an imaginary line running from the North Pole to the South Pole through the Pacific Ocean, mainly along the 180th meridian of longitude, i.e. that furthest from GREENWICH. The date to the east of it is a day earlier than it is to the west.

**Blind date.** *See under* BLIND.

**Out of date.** *See under* OUT.

**Radiocarbon dating.** *See under* RADIOCARBON.

**Sell-by date.** *See under* SELL.

**To date.** *See under* TO.

**Up to date.** *See under* UP.

**Datum line.** A term used in surveying and engineering to describe the horizontal line from which all heights and depths are measured. The datum line upon which the ORDNANCE SURVEY maps of Britain were based until 1921 was the mean sea level at Liverpool. Since 1921 it has been the mean sea level at Newlyn, Cornwall.

**Daughter. Daughter of Peneus, The.** The bay tree was so called because it grew in greatest perfection on the banks of the River Peneus. *See also* BAY; DAPHNE.

**Daughter of Zion.** JERUSALEM or its people.

**Daughters of the American Revolution.** A patriotic American society founded in 1890 for the direct lineal descendants of soldiers of the Revolutionary period who helped the cause of Independence. Candidates must be 18 or over and 'personally acceptable' to the society. By the early 1980s there were around 200,000 members organized in over 3000 'chapters' throughout the USA and elsewhere in the world.

**Bailiff's Daughter of Islington.** *See under* BAILIFF.

**Devil's daughter.** *See under* DEVIL.

**Devil's daughter's portion, The.** *See under* DEVIL.

**Duke of Exeter's daughter.** *See under* DUKE.

**Kiss the gunner's daughter.** *See under* KISS.

**Long Meg and Her Daughters.** *See under* LONG.

**Owl was a baker's daughter, The.** *See under* OWL.

**Scavenger's daughter, The.** *See under* SCAVENGER.

**Dauphin.** The heir to the French throne under the VALOIS and BOURBON dynasties. Guy IX, Count of Vienne, was the first so styled, and he wore a dolphin as his cognizance. The title descended in the family until 1349, when Humbert III sold his seigneurie, the dauphiné, to Philippe VI (de Valois), one condition being that the heir of France assumed the title of *le Dauphin*. The first French prince so called was Jean, who succeeded Philippe, and the last was the Duc d'Angoulême, son of Charles X, who renounced the title in 1830.

The dauphinate of Auvergne appeared as a title in the 13th century, was joined to the French royal family by marriage in 1428 and was annexed to the crown in 1693. The heir to the French monarchy was called the 'king dauphin' and the dauphin of Auvergne the 'prince dauphin'.

**Grand Dauphin.** *See under* GRAND.

**Second** or **Little Dauphin.** *See under* SECOND.

**Davenport.** Two different articles of furniture bear this name, which is probably that of some forgotten craftsman or of the person who commissioned the piece. One is a tall, narrow desk with drawers at each side, the other is a large upholstered sofa or settee.

**Davenport trick.** A trick by which a person can break free when bound round and tied with rope. The term derives from the Davenport Brothers, Ira (1839–1911) and William (1841–77), two American impostors who claimed that spirits would untie them when they bound themselves with cords. Their fraud was exposed time and again by leading conjurers. *See also* HOUDINI.

**David** (Hebrew *dawid*, 'loved one'). The youngest son of Jesse and the slayer of GOLIATH. He temporarily rose in favour through comforting SAUL by his skill as a harpist. Saul's eventual jealousy led to David's flight, effected with the aid of his wife Michal and her brother JONATHAN, both children of Saul. After many vicissitudes David eventually became king of Israel (1 Samuel 16–31, 2 Samuel, 1 Kings 1–2). The Davidic authorship of the Psalms has largely been discounted. In Dryden's *Absalom and Achitophel* (1681), David represents Charles II. *See also* ABSALOM; ADULLAMITES.

**David and Jonathan.** An ideal pair of inseparable friends. *See also* BROTHER JONATHAN; DAMON AND PYTHIAS; PYLADES AND ORESTES.

> I am distressed for thee, my brother Jonathan: very pleasant hast thou been unto me: thy love to me was wonderful, passing the love of women.
>
> 2 Samuel 1:26

**David Copperfield.** *See under* COPPERFIELD.

**Camp David.** *See under* CAMP.

**City of David, The.** *See under* CITY.

**Star of David** or **Shield of David, The.** *See under* STAR.

**St David** or **Dewi.** The patron saint of WALES, whose day is 1 March. Historical information about him is scanty. He lived in the 6th century, dying *c.*600, and as the chief bishop of South Wales he moved the ecclesiastical centre from CAERLEON to MENEVIA (St David's). Legend is far more prolific and says that he was the son of Xantus, prince of Ceretícu (Cardiganshire) and that he became an ascetic in the Isle of Wight, visited Jerusalem, confuted Pelagius and was preferred to the see of Caerleon. Geoffrey of Monmouth makes him the uncle of King ARTHUR.

**Davidians, Davists.** *See* FAMILISTS.

**Davy. Davy Crockett.** *See under* CROCKETT.

**Davy Jones.** An 18th-century sailor's term for the evil spirit of the sea. Of the many conjectures as to its derivation the most plausible are that Davy is a corruption of the West Indian *duppy* ('devil') and that Jones is a corruption of JONAH, or that Davy Jones was a pirate.

**Davy Jones' locker.** The sea, especially as the grave of drowned sailors.

**As drunk as Davy's sow.** *See under* AS.

**Dawn. At crack of dawn.** *See under* AT.

**False dawn.** *See under* FALSE.

**Dawson, Jemmy.** The hero of William Shenstone's ballad of this name given in PERCY'S RELIQUES (1765). James Dawson (1717–46) joined the YOUNG PRETENDER and was one of the Manchester rebels who were hanged, drawn and quartered for high treason on Kennington Common in 1746. His betrothed, Katherine Norton, a young lady of good family and handsome fortune, died of a broken heart after witnessing his execution.

**Day.** Day begins at different times for different peoples, as follows:

(1) At sunset: for the Jews in their 'sacred year' and the Christian church, hence the eve of feast-days. Tacitus writes that the ancient Britons *non dierum numerum, ut nos, sed noctium computant* ('do not reckon by days, like us, but by nights') hence sennight ('seven nights', a former word for a week) and fortnight ('fourteen nights' or two weeks). The ancient Greeks, Chinese, Muslims and others also began the day at sunset.

(2) At sunrise: for the Babylonians, Syrians, Persians and modern Greeks.

(3) At noon: for the ancient Egyptians and modern astronomers.

(4) At midnight: for the Romans and most modern races.

**Day in, day out.** Constantly; routinely.

**Daylight.** In drinking toasts, daylight is the light seen between the wine and the rim of the glass when the wineglass is not full. Toastmasters used to cry out: 'Gentlemen, no daylights nor heeltaps.' *See also* HEELTAP.

**Daylight robbery.** A blatantly excessive charge. The analogy is with a robbery committed in broad daylight, with no attempt at concealment or subterfuge.

**Daylights.** Pugilists' slang for eyes.

**Daylight saving.** *See* SUMMER TIME.

**Day of Atonement, Day of Coverings** or **Yom Kippur** (Hebrew *yōm*, 'day', and *kipūr*, 'atonement'). The great Jewish fast day held on the tenth day of Tishri, the seventh month (September–October). The day is one of prayer, confession and repentance, and the closing service of this most sacred day ends with the sounding of the SHOFAR. The ceremonies are described in Leviticus 16:29:

> And this shall be a statute for ever unto you: that in the seventh month, on the tenth day of the month, ye shall afflict your souls, and do no work at all, whether it be one of your own country, or a stranger that sojourneth among you.

**Day of reckoning.** Settlement day, when one has to pay up one's account or fulfil one's obligation. The expression is also used of the Day of Judgement.

**Day of rest.** The SABBATH. The allusion is biblical.

> Six days may work be done; but in the seventh is the sabbath of rest, holy to the Lord.
>
> Exodus 31:17

**Day of the ..., The.** A popular formula for a novel title, especially when indicating some sinister person or force. Examples are Nathanael West's *The Day of the Locust* (1930), John Wyndham's *The Day of the Triffids* (1951), Paul Scott's *The Day of the Scorpion* (1968) and Frederick Forsyth's *The Day of the Jackal* (1971).

**Day of the Barricades, The.**

12 May 1588, when the people forced Henry III to flee from Paris
5 August 1648, the beginning of the Frondes
27 July 1830, the first day of *la grande semaine*, which resulted in the abdication of Charles X
24 February 1848, when Louis Philippe abdicated
25 June 1848, when the archbishop of Paris was shot in attempting to quell the insurrection following the closure of the national workshops
2 December 1851, the day of NAPOLEON III's *coup d'état*, when the radicals attempted resistance

In spite of Napoleon III's street widening in Paris, partly to prevent the successful erection of barricades, the Communards made further use of them during the second siege of Paris in 1871.

**Day of the Dupes, The.** In French history, 10 November 1630, when Marie de Medici, the queen mother, and others sought the overthrow of Louis XIII's minister, Cardinal Richelieu. The cardinal's friends interviewed Louis at Versailles later in the day and by the evening Richelieu was reassured of the royal favour. This was the *journée des Dupes* for those who reckoned on the minister's fall.

**Days fatal to kings.** Certain days were superstitiously held to be fatal to the sovereigns of Britain, although this is scarcely borne out by the facts. Of those who have died since 1066, Sunday has been the last day of the reign of seven, Monday, Tuesday and Thursday that of six each, Friday and Wednesday of five and Saturday of four.

Sunday: Henry I, Edward III, Henry VI, James I, William III, Anne, George I
Monday: Stephen, Richard II, Henry IV, Henry V, Richard III, George V
Tuesday: Richard I, Edward II, Charles I, James II, William IV, Victoria
Wednesday: John, Henry III, Edward IV, Edward V, George VI
Thursday: William I, William II, Henry II, Edward VI, Mary I, Elizabeth I
Friday: Edward I, Henry VIII, Charles II, Mary II, Edward VII
Saturday: Henry VII, George II, George III, George IV

**Days marked with a white stone.** Days to be remembered with gratification. The Romans used a white stone or chalk to mark their lucky days on the calendar. Unlucky days were marked with charcoal. *See also* RED-LETTER DAY.

**Days of grace.** Days allowed for making a payment or doing some other act after the time limit for that purpose has expired. Three days of grace were allowed for the payment of a bill of exchange but this was abolished by the Banking and Financial Dealings Act 1971.

**Days of the week.** The names of these days are of Anglo-Saxon origin while those of the months are derived from the Romans. See the individual entries for SUNDAY, MONDAY and so on, and also for JANUARY, FEBRUARY etc.

**Dayspring.** The dawn.

> The dayspring from on high hath visited us.
> Luke 1:78

**Daystar.** The morning star, and hence a symbol of hope and better prospects.

> Again o'er the vine-covered regions of France,
> See the day-star of Liberty rise.
> JOHN WILSON: *Noctes Ambrosianae* (January 1831)

**Alexandra Rose Day.** *See under* ALEXANDRA.
**All in the day's work.** *See under* ALL.
**All Souls' Day.** *See under* ALL.
**Ancient of Days.** *See under* ANCIENT.
**Anzac Day.** *See under* ANZAC.
**Arbor Day.** *See under* ARBOR.
**Armistice Day.** *See under* ARMISTICE.
**Ascension Day.** *See under* ASCENSION.
**As honest as the day is long.** *See under* AS.
**At the end of the day.** *See under* AT.
**Australia Day.** *See under* AUSTRALIA.
**Black-letter day.** *See under* BLACK.
**Borrowed days.** *See under* BORROW.
**Box days.** *See under* BOX.
**Break of day.** *See under* BREAK.
**Call it a day, To.** *See under* CALL.
**Candlemas Day.** *See under* CANDLE.
**Carry the day, To.** *See under* CARRY.
**Darkie Day.** *See under* DARK.
**Decoration Day.** *See* MEMORIAL DAY.
**Derby Day.** *See under* DERBY.
**Dog days.** *See under* DOG.
**Dog-whipping Day.** *See under* DOG.
**Early days.** *See under* EARLY.
**Egyptian days.** *See under* EGYPT.
**Ember days.** *See under* EMBER.
**Empire Day.** *See under* EMPIRE.
**Every dog has its day.** *See under* EVERY.
**Eye of the day, The.** *See under* EYE.
**Father's Day.** *See under* FATHER.
**Field day.** *See under* FIELD.
**Fish day.** *See under* FISH.
**Flag day.** *See under* FLAG.
**Gang day.** *See* ROGATION DAYS.
**Green Ribbon Day.** *See under* GREEN.
**Groundhog Day.** *See under* GROUND.
**Halcyon days.** *See under* HALCYON.

**Have had one's day, To.** To be past one's prime of life.

> 'Old Joe, Sir,' said the Major, 'was a bit of a favourite ... once. But Joe has had his day.'
> DICKENS: *Dombey and Son*, ch xx (1847–8)

**Heat of the day, The.** *See under* HEAT.
**High days and holidays.** *See under* HIGH.
**Holy Cross Day.** *See under* HOLY.
**Holy Rood Day.** *See* HOLY CROSS DAY.
**Hundred Days, The.** *See under* HUNDRED.
**Independence Day.** *See under* INDEPENDENCE.
**Labor Day.** *See under* LABOUR.
**Lady Day.** *See under* LADY.
**Lammas Day.** *See under* LAMMAS.
**Last Day.** *See under* LAST.
**Lose the day, To.** *See under* LOSE.
**Make a day of it, To.** To make an activity last the whole day.
**Memorial Day.** *See under* MEMORY.
**Mother's Day.** *See* MOTHERING SUNDAY.
**Mumping day.** *See under* MUMPING.
**Name the day, To.** *See under* NAME.
**New Year's Day.** *See under* NEW.
**No day without a line.** *See under* NO.
**Not one's day.** A day when nothing seems to go right, at the end of which one might say: 'It's not been my day today.'
**Oak-apple Day.** *See under* OAK.
**Off day.** *See under* OFF.
**One of these days.** Some time soon; before very long.
**One of those days.** A day when things are going badly.
**One's days are numbered.** One's days are drawing to a close; one is near to death.
**Orders of the day, The.** *See under* ORDER.
**Other day, The.** *See under* OTHER.
**Palmy days.** *See under* PALM.
**Patriots' Day.** *See under* PATRIOTS.
**Primrose Day.** *See under* PRIMROSE.
**Queen's Day.** *See under* QUEEN.
**Red-letter day.** *See under* RED.
**Remembrance Day.** *See under* REMEMBRANCE.
**Rogation Days.** *See under* ROGATION.
**Rome was not built in a day.** *See under* ROME.
**St Crispin's Day.** *See under* CRISPIN.
**St Distaff's Day.** *See under* DISTAFF.
**St Lambert's Day.** *See under* LAMBERT.
**St Partridge's Day.** *See under* PARTRIDGE.
**Salad days.** *See under* SALAD.
**Scare the living daylights out of, To.** *See under* SCARE.
**Speech day.** *See under* SPEECH.
**Tag day.** *See under* TAG.
**Thanksgiving Day.** *See under* THANKSGIVING.

**That will be the day.** That will never happen, as it will never be the day.

**This day and age.** The present time.

**Three Kings' Day.** *See under* THREE.

**Today a man, tomorrow a mouse.** *See under* TODAY.

**VE Day.** *See under* VE DAY.

**Veteran's Day.** *See* ARMISTICE DAY.

**VJ Day.** *See under* VJ DAY.

**Waitangi Day.** *See under* WAITANGI.

**Whip-dog Day.** *See under* WHIP.

**Win the day, To.** *See under* WIN.

**Wrenning Day.** *See under* WREN.

**DC.** *See* DA CAPO.

**D-Day.** In the Second World War the day appointed for the Allied invasion of Europe and the opening of the long-awaited second front. It was eventually fixed for 5 June 1944, but owing to impossible weather conditions, it was postponed at the last moment until 6 June. D simply stands for Day. *See also* OVERLORD.

**De. De facto** (Latin, 'in fact'). Actually, in reality; as opposed to *de jure* ('in law'), legally or rightfully. Thus, John was *de facto* king, but Arthur was so *de jure*.

**De gustibus non est disputandum** (Latin, 'about tastes there is no disputing'). There is no accounting for tastes. A similar English proverb is: 'One man's meat is another man's poison.' *See also* CHACUN À SON GOÛT.

**De haut en bas** (French, 'from high to low'). Condescendingly; with affected superiority.

**De jure.** *See* DE FACTO.

**De luxe** (French, 'of luxury'). Luxurious; of a superior kind.

**De mortuis nil nisi bonum** (Latin, 'of the dead, [speak] nothing but good'). Speak favourably about the dead or not at all. 'Speak not evil of the dead' was one of the maxims of CHILO.

**De nos jours** (French, 'of our days'). Of the present time.

**De nouveau** (French, 'anew'). Starting again.

**De novo** (Latin, 'anew'). Afresh; over again from the beginning.

**De profundis** (Latin, 'from the depths'). Out of the deep, hence a bitter cry of wretchedness. Psalm 130 is so called from the first two words in the Latin version. It forms part of the Roman Catholic burial service. These words were chosen as the title of Oscar Wilde's apologia, published posthumously in 1905.

**De règle** (French, 'of rule'). Customary; proper.

**De rigueur** (French, 'of strictness'). Required by strict etiquette or custom.

**De trop** (French, 'of too much'). Not wanted; superfluous. When a person's presence is not wished for, that person is *de trop*.

**Deacons, The Seven.** *See under* SEVEN.

**Dead. Dead-and-alive.** Dull, monotonous, as a dreary town or a boring person.

**Dead angle.** A term applied in old books on fortification to the ground in front of an angle in a wall that can be neither seen nor defended from the parapet.

**Dead bat.** In cricket, a bat held loosely so that the ball 'drops dead' when struck.

**Dead beat.** Completely exhausted; absolutely 'whacked', like a dead person who can no longer fight. A 'deadbeat' is a useless or socially undesirable person.

**Dead centre.** The exact centre.

**Dead cert.** An absolute certainty.

**Dead dog, A.** Something utterly worthless.

> After whom is the king of Israel come out? after whom dost thou pursue? after a dead dog, after a flea.
>
> 1 Samuel 24:14

*See also* IS THY SERVANT A DOG *under* SERVANT.

**Dead drunk.** So drunk as to be totally incapable or senseless.

**Dead duck.** Figuratively, something of no further use or interest.

> At the last election Britain's relationship with Europe was a dead duck.
>
> *The Times* (17 June 1966)

**Dead end kids.** Children from poverty-stricken back streets for whom the future seems to hold little promise. The Dead End Kids were a popular group of young American film actors who first appeared as 'hooligans' in *Dead End* (1937). This was set in New York's EAST SIDE, where slum kids and gangsters lived next to a luxury apartment block. They went on to appear in such films as *Angels with Dirty Faces* (1938) and *On Dress Parade* (1939). They subsequently split up into the Little Tough Guys, the East Side Kids and the Bowery Boys. The original Dead End Kids were Billy Halop, Leo Gorcey, Bernard Punsley, Huntz Hall, Bobby Jordan and Gabriel Dell.

**Deadeye.** A wooden block with three holes in it and a groove running around it, used in pairs or threes for the setting up of shrouds in sailing ships. The holes are the eyes. In the USA an expert marksman is known as a deadeye.

**Dead fire.** CORPOSANT, believed at one time to presage death.

**Dead from the neck up.** Stupid, 'thick'.

**Dead hand.** An oppressive influence, especially that of a deceased person.

**Deadhead.** A person who makes use of a free ticket for a theatre, cinema, train or the like.

**Dead Heart, The.** The remote interior of Australia. The phrase comes from the title of J.W. Gregory's book *The Dead Heart of Australia* (1906).

**Dead heat, A.** A tie, when two or more competitors in a race cross the line together.

**Dead language.** A language that is no longer spoken, such as Latin.

**Dead letter.** A law or regulation no longer acted upon. A letter which the post office has been unable to deliver either because of an incorrect address or because the person addressed is untraceable.

**Dead letter box** or **drop.** In espionage, a place where messages can be left by one person for another without either of them meeting.

**Deadlights.** Formerly strong wooden shutters to darken or protect the cabin windows of a ship. In a modern vessel they are steel plates fitted over the scuttles of portholes to strengthen the ship's side and to prevent the internal lighting showing outboard. 'To ship the deadlights' was to shut or fasten them in position. They are now usually closed.

**Deadline.** The final date or time when a task or assignment must be completed. This sense of strict demarcation derives from the 'deadline' round a military prison camp. The phrase was coined in the notorious Confederate prisoner-of-war camp, Andersonville, during the American Civil War (1861–5). Some distance from the peripheral wire fence a line was marked out and any prisoner crossing this line was shot on sight.

**Deadlock.** A lock that has no spring catch. Metaphorically, a state of things so entangled that there seems to be no solution.

**Dead loss.** A useless person or thing; a complete loss.

**Dead man's hand.** In the western states of the USA, a combination of aces and eights in poker, so called because when Sheriff Wild Bill HICKOK was shot in the back at Deadwood, South Dakota, he held such cards in his hand.

It is said that carrying a dead man's hand will provide a dead sleep. Another superstition is that a lighted candle placed in the hand of a dead man gives no light to anyone except the person who carries the severed hand. *See also* HAND OF GLORY.

**Dead man's handle.** A handle on the controls of an electric train, so designed that it cuts off the current and applies the brakes if the driver releases his pressure from illness or some other cause. It is now officially called a driver's safety device, and is usually in the form of a plate depressed by the foot. It was invented in 1902 by the American Frank J. Sprague.

**Dead march.** A funeral march. A well-known example is the dead march in Handel's oratorio *Saul* (1739), which is used on state occasions such as the funeral of a sovereign.

**Dead marines.** Empty bottles. *See also* MARINE.

**Dead men.** Empty bottles. When the 'spirit' is out of the bottle it is dead. In the USA 'dead soldiers' has the same meaning. *See also* DOWN AMONG THE DEAD MEN.

**Dead men's fingers.** (1) *Alcyonium digitatum*, a form of soft coral found attached to rocks and seaweed, so called from the appearance of its polyps when out of the water. (2) The early purple orchid (*Orchis mascula*), which has tuberous roots somewhat resembling distorted hands.

**Dead on.** Exactly right.

**Deadpan.** Emotionless, expressionless, of a person's face or manner. 'Pan' here is a colloquial word meaning 'face'.

**Dead reckoning.** A method of calculating a ship's position by plotting on from the last fix, or observed position, the speed made good through the water along the compass course steered.

**Dead right.** Entirely right.

**Dead ringer.** *See* RINGER.

**Dead ropes.** Those that are fixed or do not run on blocks.

**Dead Sea, The.** The Palestinian Salt Sea or Sea of the Plain of the Old Testament, in the ancient Vale of Siddim, called by the Romans *Mare Mortuum*. It is about 50 miles (80km) long and 11 miles (18km) wide, and it is fed by the River Jordan from the north but has apparently no outlet. The water is a bluish-green colour and its surface is about 1312ft (400m) below the level of the Mediterranean. The northern end is some 1300ft (396m) deep, and its salt content is 25 per cent, as compared to that of normal sea water, which is usually between 3 and 4 per cent. It supports no life other than microbes and a few very low organisms.

**Dead Sea fruit.** *See* APPLES OF SODOM.

**Dead Sea scrolls, The.** In 1947 a Bedouin goatherd made the first scroll discoveries in a cave at the northwest end of the DEAD SEA, since when some hundreds more have been found. The scrolls are in Hebrew and Aramaic, and most scholars accept them as originating from the monastery of the Jewish sect of the ESSENES at Qumran. There is still much controversy over their interpretation. According to radiocarbon tests made in 1991, most of the scrolls date to the last two centuries BC, so that they are the earliest extant manuscripts of the OLD TESTAMENT and APOCRYPHA.

**Dead set against.** Firmly against. The opposite is 'dead set on', firmly for or in favour of. The allusion is probably to a dog standing motionless and pointing with its muzzle to indicate game.

**Dead shot.** A person who shoots extremely accurately. A legendary example is William TELL.

**Dead soldiers.** *See* DEAD MEN.

**Dead spit of someone, The.** The exact counterpart. The equivalent of SPITTING IMAGE.

**Deadstock.** Farm machinery, as distinct from livestock.

**Dead to the world.** In a deep sleep or a state of exhaustion or intoxication, so that one is totally unconscious of one's surroundings.

**Dead water.** Eddying water that closes around a ship's stern as it passes through the water.

**Dead weight.** The weight of something without life. An oppressive thing or person.

**Dead wood.** Useless people or things.

**As dead as a dodo, a doornail** or **mutton.** *See under* AS.

**Baptism for the dead, The.** *See under* BAPTISM.

**Book of the Dead, The.** *See under* BOOK.

**Cut dead, To.** *See under* CUT.

**Down among the dead men let me lie.** *See under* DOWN.

**Drop dead!** *See under* DROP.

**Flog a dead horse, To.** *See under* FLOG.

**Let the dead bury their dead.** *See under* LET.

**Not to be seen dead in** or **with.** *See under* SEE.

**Over my dead body.** *See under* OVER.

**Seven deadly sins, The.** *See under* SEVEN.

**Deaf. As deaf as an adder, beetle, post** or **white cat.** *See under* AS.

**Ass is deaf to music, The.** *See under* ASS.

**There are none so deaf as those who will not hear.** The saying has its equivalent in other languages. The French say: *Il n'y a de pire sourd que celui qui ne veut pas entendre*. The Italians: *Gran sordo è quello che non vuol udire*. The Germans: *Es gibt keine ärgeren Tauben, als die nicht hören wollen*. The Romans also knew it: *Deterior surdus eo nullus qui renuit audire*.

**Turn a deaf ear, To.** *See under* TURN.

**Deal. Big deal.** *See under* BIG.

**New deal.** *See under* NEW.

**Package deal.** *See under* PACK.

**Raw deal.** *See under* RAW.

**Round dealing.** *See under* ROUND.

**Square deal.** *See under* SQUARE.

**Dean** (Late Latin *decanus*, 'one set over ten'). The ecclesiastical dignitary who presides over the CHAPTER of a cathedral or COLLEGIATE CHURCH, this having formerly consisted of ten canons. In the more recent foundations decanal functions are carried out by a provost. The bishop of London is an *ex officio* 'Dean of the Province of Canterbury' and summons the bishops of the Southern Province to meet in Convocation under a mandate from the Archbishop of Canterbury. The dean of CHRIST CHURCH, Oxford, is head of the college and also dean of the cathedral.

In the colleges of Oxford and Cambridge, the resident don responsible for undergraduate discipline, or in charge of the chapel, is called a dean.

In Scottish and most modern English universities the title is given to the head of a faculty, as in America, where it is applied to certain other college and administrative officers. *See also* DOYEN.

**Dean of Faculty.** In Scotland the barrister who presides over the Faculty of Advocates.

**Dean of Guild.** One who formerly decided mercantile and maritime causes in a Scottish burgh, but more recently largely concerned with regulations affecting buildings.

**Dean of the Arches.** The judge presiding over the COURT OF ARCHES, formerly at Bow Church, once a PECULIAR.

**Dean of the Sacred College.** The senior CARDINAL bishop who is given the title of bishop of Ostia and Velletri. He ranks next to the POPE in the hierarchy.

**Deans of Peculiars.** Once numerous and including those of COLLEGIATE CHURCHES such as Westminster and Windsor; surviving examples are those of Battle, Bocking and Stamford. *See also* PECULIARS.

**Rural dean.** *See under* RURAL.

**Dear. Dear John.** A letter ending a personal relationship. The expression dates from the Second World War, when American servicemen were separated from their partners, who then wrote to terminate the relationship. The words, a typical opening, have served as the title of various American and British comedies in which a hapless husband arrives home to find such a letter awaiting his return.

> 'Dear John', the letter began. 'I have found someone else whom I think the world of. I think the only way out is for us to get a divorce,' it said. They usually began like that, those letters that told of infidelity on the part of the wives of servicemen.
>
> *Democrat and Chronicle* (Rochester, New York) (17 August 1945)

**For dear life.** *See under* FOR.

**My dearest enemy.** As my dearest friend is my greatest friend, so my dearest foe is my greatest enemy.

> Would I had met my dearest foe in heaven,
> Or ever I had seen that day, Horatio!
>
> SHAKESPEARE: *Hamlet*, I, ii (1600)

**Nearest and dearest.** *See under* NEAR.

**Oh dear!** *See under* OH.

**Old dear.** *See under* OLD.

**Death. Death duty.** A tax on property inheritance, introduced in Britain in 1894. Estates worth between £100 and £500 were taxed at 1 per cent, while those over £1 million were subject to 8 per cent tax. It was replaced by capital transfer tax in 1975 and by inheritance tax in 1986.

**Death from unusual causes.**

AESCHYLUS (*c*.525–*c*.456 BC): killed by a tortoise that was dropped on his bald head by an eagle

(Valerius Maximus, *Facta et dicta memorabilia*, IX, xii (1st century AD) and Pliny, *Natural History*, VII, vii (1st century AD))

ANACREON (*c*.572–*c*.488 BC): choked by a grape pip (Pliny, *Natural History*, VII, vii (1st century AD))

Francis Bacon (1561–1626): died of a cold contracted when stuffing a fowl with snow as an experiment in refrigeration

Robert Burton (1577–1640), author of *The Anatomy of Melancholy* (1621): died on the very day that he had astrologically predicted

CALCHAS, a soothsayer in Greek mythology: died of laughter at the thought of having outlived the predicted hour of his death

Charles VIII of France (1470–98): showing his queen into a tennis court, he struck his head against the lintel, which caused his death

FABIUS (*fl*.2nd century BC), the Roman praetor: choked by the presence of a single goat hair in the milk he was drinking (Pliny, *Natural History*, VII, vii (1st century AD))

Frederick Louis, Prince of Wales (1707–51) son of George II: struck by a tennis ball

George, Duke of Clarence (1449–78) brother of Edward IV: drowned in a butt of MALMSEY

King John (1167–1216): traditionally said to have died from a surfeit of lampreys but more probably from dysentery resulting from excessive fatigue and indulgence in food and drink

Jean-Baptiste Lully (1632–87), the composer: when beating time by tapping the floor with his staff while directing a performance (1687) before Louis XIV of his monumental *Te Deum*, pierced his foot and subsequently died from gangrene

Thomas Otway (1652–85), the poet: while living in penury he was given a guinea with which he bought a loaf of bread and died while swallowing the first mouthful

William III (1650–1702): died after falling from his horse, which stumbled over a molehill

*See also* INVENTORS.

**Death in the pot.** During a dearth in Gilgal, there was made for the sons of the prophets a potage of wild herbs, some of which were poisonous. When they tasted the potage, they cried out 'there is death in the pot'. ELISHA put some meal into it and the poisonous qualities were counteracted (2 Kings 4:40).

**Death knell.** Literally, the tolling of a bell to mark a person's death. Figuratively a death knell is an event that heralds the end or destruction of something.

**Death or Glory Boys, The.** *See under* REGIMENTAL AND DIVISIONAL NICKNAMES.

**Death row.** In the USA a prison block or section for prisoners sentenced to death.

**Death's head.** A skull. Prostitutes and procuresses used to wear a ring bearing the impression of a death's head in the time of Queen Elizabeth I (1558–1603).

**Death's-head moth.** The largest British hawk moth, *Acherontia atropos*, so called from the markings on the back of the thorax, which resemble a skull. Its scientific name continues the theme of death. *See also* ACHERON; ATROPOS.

**Death trap.** An object that could potentially cause someone's death, such as an unsafe building or a poorly maintained car.

**Death Valley.** A desert valley in eastern California and western Nevada, the lowest, hottest and driest region of the USA. Its name, echoing the biblical 'valley of the shadow of death' (Psalm 23:4), relates to the severe conditions experienced by a party of immigrants when crossing it in 1849.

**Death warrant.** An official authority to carry out an execution. To sign one's own death warrant is to perform some act that potentially causes one's own destruction.

**Deathwatch beetle.** The beetle *Xestobium rufovillosum*, whose larvae bore through wood. The adult makes a sound like a watch ticking, which at one time was supposed to presage death.

**Death wish.** A wish, often unconscious, for a person's death, either that of oneself or of another.

**Angel of Death.** *See* AZRAEL.

**At death's door.** *See under* AT.

**Black Death, The.** *See under* BLACK.

**Catch one's death of cold, To.** *See under* CATCH.

**Dance of Death.** *See under* DANCE.

**Dogs howl at death.** *See under* DOG.

**Do to death, To.** *See under* DO.

**Fate worse than death, A.** *See under* FATE.

**Feel** or **look like death warmed up, To.** *See under* FEEL.

**Flog to death, To.** *See under* FLOG.

**In at the death.** *See under* IN.

**Hang on like grim death, To.** *See under* HANG.

**Kiss of death.** *See under* KISS.

**Like grim death.** *See under* LIKE.

**Living death.** *See under* LIVE.

**Matter of life and death.** *See under* MATTER.

**Till death us do part.** *See* DEPART.

**Wall of death.** *See under* WALL.

**Wheel of death.** *See under* WHEEL.

**Debonair** (Le Débonnaire). The byname of Louis I of France (778–840), son and successor of CHARLEMAGNE as Holy Roman Emperor. He was also called the PIOUS.

**Deborah.** There are two women of this name in the Old Testament. One is nurse to REBECCA (Genesis 35); the other is a prophetess and judge who leads the Israelites in revolt against Sisera (Judges 4). One of the gems of Jewish poetry is the 'Song of Deborah' (Judges 5), with its account of the gruesome murder of Sisera by JAEL.

> She put her hand to the nail, and her right hand to the workmen's hammer; and with the hammer she smote Sisera, she smote off his head, when she had pierced and stricken through his temples.
>
> Judges 5:26

**Debrett.** To be 'in Debrett' is to be included in

*Debrett's Peerage, Baronetage, Knightage and Companionage,* i.e. to be of an aristocratic or titled family. *Debrett's Peerage* was originally composed by John Debrett (*c*.1750–1822) and first published in 1802. It was followed by *Debrett's Baronetage* in 1808. *See also* BURKE.

**Debt. Debt of nature, The.** To pay the debt of nature is to die. Life is a loan and the debt is paid off by one's death.

**Debts of honour.** Debts contracted by betting or gambling, so called because these debts are not legally recoverable.

**Bad debt.** *See under* BAD.

**In someone's debt.** Under an obligation to them.

**National debt.** *See under* NATIONAL.

**Write off a debt, To.** *See under* WRITE.

**Decabrists** or **Dekabrists.** *See* DECEMBRISTS.

**Decalogue** (Greek *deka logos*, 'ten words'). The name given by the Greek Fathers to the TEN COMMANDMENTS referred to in Exodus 34:28 and elsewhere. They have sometimes been divided into those that define our duty to God and those that state our duty to others. The 'classic' version occurs in Exodus 20:2–17. Another is found in Deuteronomy 5:6–21. The form adopted by the CHURCH OF ENGLAND and most Protestant churches is that which JOSEPHUS says was used by his Jewish contemporaries.

**Decameron.** The collection of 100 tales by Boccaccio, completed *c*.1353, represented as having been told in ten days (Greek *deka*, 'ten', and *hēmera*, 'day') during the plague at Florence in 1348, seven ladies and three gentlemen each telling a tale daily. *See also* CANTERBURY TALES; HEPTAMERON.

**Decathlon** (Greek *deka*, 'ten', and *athlon*, 'contest'). An athletic contest in the modern OLYMPIC GAMES consisting of ten events: 100 metres race, long jump, shot put, high jump, 400 metres race, 110 metres hurdles, discus, pole vault, javelin and 1500 metres race.

**Deceiver, A gay.** *See under* GAY.

**Decem, Scriptores.** *See under* SCRIPTORES.

**December** (Latin, 'tenth month'). December was the tenth month in the Roman calendar when the year began in MARCH with the vernal equinox. The Old English name was *ǣrra gēola*, 'earlier YULE'. In the FRENCH REVOLUTIONARY CALENDAR it was Frimaire ('hoarfrost month'), from 22 November to 21 December.

**Decembrists.** Conspirators in the Russian army who made an unsuccessful attempt to overthrow Tsar Nicholas I in an uprising in Senate Square, St Petersburg, on 14 December 1825. The martyrdom of the revolutionaries was a source of inspiration to later generations of Russian dissidents.

**Man of December, The.** *See under* MAN.

**Decimal currency.** This was introduced in Britain on 15 February 1971, the new POUND consisting of 100 pence. The new coins were the seven-sided 50p piece, the 10p piece (the same size as the former FLORIN), the 5p piece (the same size as the former SHILLING), the 2p piece, the 1p piece and the ½p piece. The first three coins were silver in colour and the remainder copper-coloured. The introduction of a decimal currency was first mooted in 1816 by the Tory MP John Croker. The idea was again put forward in Parliament in 1824, 1847, 1853 and 1855.

**Deck.** A pack of cards, or that part of the pack left after the hands have been dealt. The term was current in England until the 19th century and is now regularly used in the USA.

> But, while he thought to steal the single ten,
> The king was slyly finger'd from the deck.
> SHAKESPEARE: *Henry VI, Pt III*, V, i (1590)

**Clear the decks, To.** *See under* CLEAR.

**Hit the deck, To.** *See under* HIT.

**Lower deck.** *See under* LOW.

**Sweep the deck, To.** *See under* SWEEP.

**Declare. Declaration of Independence, The.** The document that declared the USA to be independent of the British Crown. It was largely written by Thomas Jefferson (1743–1826) and was adopted by Congress on 4 July 1776.

> We, therefore, the Representatives of the United States of America, in General Congress, Assembled, appealing to the Supreme Judge of the world for the rectitude of our intentions, do, in the Name, and by the Authority of the good People of these Colonies, solemnly publish and declare, That these United Colonies are, and of Right ought to be Free and Independent States; that they are Absolved from all Allegiance to the British Crown, and that all political connection between them and the State of Great Britain, is and ought to be totally dissolved.
> *Declaration of Independence* (opening clauses of concluding statement)

**Declaration of Rights, The.** An instrument submitted to William and Mary, after the GLORIOUS REVOLUTION, and accepted by them (13 February 1689). It sought to remove the specific grievances arising from the arbitrary acts of James II, such as the use of the dispensing and suspending power, the maintenance of a standing army in time of peace, taxation without parliamentary consent, freedom of elections and so on. The Declaration, together with a settlement of the succession and so forth, was passed into law (October) as the BILL OF RIGHTS. It emphasized the importance of PARLIAMENT in the constitution, which no king subsequently dared to question. *See also* RIGHTS OF MAN.

**Declaration of the Rights of Man, The.** A manifesto of the French National Assembly (August 1789) embodying the 'principles' of the revolution. Thus, all citizens are born equal and are equal in the eyes of the law, with rights of liberty, property and security, and the right to resist tyranny, the nation is sovereign and laws are the expression of the general will, and every citizen has the right to freedom of opinion, speech, writing and so on. These rights were not, of course, honoured in practice, as the REIGN OF TERROR was to make manifest.

**Declarations of Indulgence.** Declarations issued by Charles II (1662 and 1672) and James II (1687 and 1688) suspending the penal laws against DISSENTERS and Roman Catholics. Except for that of 1662, they were issued under royal prerogative. The Declaration of 1688 led to the trial of the SEVEN BISHOPS.

**Declare one's interest, To.** To make known one's financial or other interests in an undertaking before it is discussed.

**Decoration. Decoration Day.** *See* MEMORIAL DAY.

**Christmas decorations.** *See under* CHRISTMAS.

**Decree nisi** (Latin *nisi*, 'unless'). A provisional order for divorce, made absolute in due course unless cause to the contrary is shown in the meantime. Every decree of divorce is, in the first instance, a decree nisi.

**Decuman gate.** The *porta decumana* or main entrance to a Roman camp, sited on the farthest side from the enemy; so called because it was guarded by the 10th cohort of each legion (Latin *decimus*, 'tenth').

**Dee, Dr.** John Dee (1527–1608), mathematician, alchemist and astrologer, was patronized by Queen Elizabeth I, but eventually died a pauper at Mortlake, where he was buried. He was one of the most inventive scholars of his day, writing 79 treatises on a variety of subjects. In 1563 he published the controversial *Monas Hieroglyphia* on the mystic science of numerology. It was written in his own code and only those in his confidence were able to decipher the text. Dee's magic crystal, through which he claimed to have been granted interviews with angels, is now in the British Museum.

**Deed poll.** A deed made by one party and so called because it was written on parchment with a polled or straight edge as opposed to an INDENTURE, which had an indented or wavy edge.

**Deemster, Dempster** or **Doomster.** The two judges of the ISLE OF MAN are called Deemsters, and they take an oath to execute the laws 'as indifferently as the herring backbone doth lie in the midst of the fish'. Hall Caine's once popular romance *The Deemster* appeared in 1887. In Scotland a Dempster or Doomster was formerly appointed to recite the sentence after it had been pronounced by the court. He combined this office with that of executioner. *See also* DOOM.

**Deep. Deep South, The.** The region of the United States that contains the southeastern states which were associated with a slave economy before the American Civil War (1861–5), that is, South Carolina, Tennessee, Louisiana, Mississippi, Alabama and Georgia.

**Deep space.** The regions beyond the solar system or the earth's atmosphere.

**Deep therapy.** Curative treatment with short-wave X-rays of high penetrative power.

**Drink deep, To.** *See under* DRINK.

**Go off the deep end, To.** *See under* GO.

**In at the deep end.** In a new situation or job without any preparation.

**In deep water.** In trouble or difficulty.

**Deer.** These animals were supposed by poets to shed tears. The drops, however, which fall from their eyes are not tears but an oily secretion from the so-called tear pits.

> A poor sequester'd stag ...
> Did come to languish ... and the big round tears
> Cours'd one another down his innocent nose
> In piteous chase.
>
> SHAKESPEARE: *As You Like It*, II, i (1599)

**Deerstalker.** A soft cloth cap with peaks in front and behind and ear flaps that are often joined at the top. It is so called as traditionally worn by sportsmen stalking deer. It is popularly regarded as an essential part of the habiliment of Sherlock HOLMES, an association mostly due to his illustrators and in particular to the *Strand* artist Sidney Paget (1860–1908).

**Small deer.** *See under* SMALL.

**Default, Judgement by.** *See under* JUDGEMENT.

**Defence, Dock.** *See under* DOCK.

**Defender. Defender of the Faith** (Latin *Fidei Defensor*). A title given to Henry VIII by Pope Leo X (11 October 1521) for his treatise *Assertio Septem Sacramentorum* attacking Luther's teachings. The initials 'F.D.' have continuously appeared on British coinage from the reign of George I (1714–27).

**Defenders.** An association of Irish Catholics (1784–98), formed in Northern IRELAND in opposition to the PEEP-O'-DAY BOYS. In 1795 a pitched battle was fought between the two and the Defenders suffered severe losses.

**Defenestration of Prague.** An incident in Bohemia in 1618 prior to the outbreak of the THIRTY YEARS' WAR when the two leading Roman Catholic members of the Bohemian National Council were thrown out of a window of the castle of Prague by the PROTESTANT members. They landed in the moat and sustained only minor injuries.

**Defiance. Bid defiance, To.** *See under* BID.

**Schythian defiance.** *See under* SCYTHIAN.

**Deficient number.** A number whose divisors add up to a total less than itself. An example is 10, the divisors of which are 1, 2 and 5. The sum of these is 8, which is less than 10. *See also* ABUNDANT NUMBER.

**Déficit, Madame.** Marie Antoinette, because she was always in need of money. She was noted for her extravagance and popularly regarded as being responsible for the nation's bankruptcy. *See also* BAKER.

**Degree. Degrees in Arts.** In the medieval universities the seven liberal arts consisted of the TRIVIUM (grammar, logic and rhetoric) and the QUADRIVIUM (arithmetic, geometry, music and astronomy).

In medieval England the Master of Arts was the person qualified to be the master of the students in arts, as the Doctor was in theology, law or medicine.

**Lambeth degrees.** *See under* LAMBETH.

**Pass degree.** *See under* PASS.

**Third degree.** *See under* THIRD.

**Deianeira.** The wife of HERCULES and the unwitting cause of his death. Nessus, the CENTAUR, having carried her across a river, attempted to rape her and was shot by Hercules with a poisoned arrow. The dying centaur gave Deianeira his tunic, steeped in blood, telling her that it would reclaim her husband from illicit loves. When she had occasion to give it to Hercules, the poisoned blood brought about his death. *See also* SHIRT OF NESSUS.

**Deidamia.** The daughter of Lycomedes, king of Scyros. ACHILLES, when staying there disguised as a woman, became the father of her son Pyrrhus (Neoptolemus).

**Dei Gratia** (Latin, 'by the grace of God'). This royal style is recorded as early as about AD 690, when 'I, Ine, by God's grace king of the West Saxons' is found. It also occurs in an ordinance of William I: *Willelmus gratia Dei Rex Anglorum*. It was first used on the GREAT SEAL by William II and all Great Seals from the reign of Edward I. It long appeared on British coins, where it was originally introduced on the gold coins of Edward III in 1344. It is now found on coins in the abbreviated form 'D.G.' *See also* GRACELESS FLORIN.

The style was also sometimes used by the archbishops of Canterbury and York down to the 17th century and is still so used by bishops of the Roman Catholic Church.

**Deiphobus.** The third husband of HELEN of Troy, whom she married after the death of his brother PARIS. Helen betrayed Deiphobus to her first husband, MENELAUS, who killed his rival.

**Deirdre.** In Irish romance the daughter of the king of Ulster's storyteller. At her birth it was prophesied that she would bring ruin to Ireland. King CONCHOBAR brought her up and planned to marry her, but she fell in love with Naoise, the eldest of the three SONS OF USNECH. She escaped to Scotland with the three brothers but they were lured back by Conchobar with false promises. The jealous king killed the three young men. One version of the story says that Deirdre killed herself, while another relates that she died the following year after living unhappily with Conchobar. Deirdre is the subject and title of a play (1907) by W.B. Yeats, and J.M. Synge also dramatized the legend in his *Deirdre of the Sorrows* (1910). The meaning of the name is uncertain.

**Deist.** *See* THEIST.

**Deities.** The more important classical, Germanic and Scandinavian deities have their own entries. The list below aims to include certain collective names as well as some of the better known gods and mythical characters associated with particular localities and functions.

Air: ARIEL, Elves (*see* ELF)
Caves or caverns: HILL FOLK or hill people, PIXIES
Corn: CERES (Greek DEMETER)
Domestic life: VESTA
Eloquence: MERCURY (Greek HERMES)
Evening: Vesper
Fairies: *See* FAIRY
FATES: NORNS
Fire: VULCAN (Greek Hephaestus), Vesta, MULCIBER
FURIES: (Greek EUMENIDES), ERINYES
Gardens: PRIAPUS, VERTUMNUS, POMONA
GRACES: Greek Charites
HADES: PLUTO with his wife PROSERPINA (Greek Aides and Persephone)
Hills: Pixies, TROLLS; also wood trolls and water trolls
Home spirits: LARES AND PENATES
Hunting: DIANA (Greek ARTEMIS)
Justice: THEMIS, ASTRAEA, NEMESIS
Love: VENUS (Greek APHRODITE), CUPID (Greek EROS)
Marriage: HYMEN
Medicine: AESCULAPIUS
Morning: AURORA (Greek EOS)
Mountains: OREADS, trolls
Ocean: OCEANIDS; *see also* SEA
Poetry and music: APOLLO, the nine MUSES
Rainbow: IRIS
Riches: PLUTUS
Rivers and streams: Fluviales (Greek Potameides, NAIADS, Nymphs)
Sea: NEPTUNE (Greek POSEIDON), TRITON, Nixies, MERMAIDS, NEREIDS
Shepherds and their flocks: PAN, the SATYRS
Springs, lakes, brooks etc: Nereids, Naiads; *see also* RIVERS
Time: SATURN (Greek Kronos)
Trees: *See* WOODS
War: MARS (Greek ARES), BELLONA, THOR
Water nymphs: NAIADS, UNDINE
Winds: AEOLUS
Wine: BACCHUS (Greek Dionysus)
Wisdom: MINERVA (Greek ATHENE)
Woods: DRYADS (a Hamadryad presides over some particular trees), wood trolls
Youth: HEBE

**Deities protecting babies.** According to Varro (116–27 BC), Roman infants were looked after by Vagitanus, the god who caused them to utter their first cry; by FABULINUS, who presided over their speech; by CUBA, who protected them in their cots; and by Domiduca, who brought young children safely home and guarded them when out of their parents' sight. In the Christian church St NICHOLAS is the patron saint of children.

**Sea deities.** *See under* SEA.

**Dekko, To take a.** To glance at; to have a look at. This is one of the many phrases brought back from India by the British Army. In Hindi *dekho* means 'look!'.

**Delectable Mountains.** In Bunyan's PILGRIM'S PROGRESS (1678, 1684), a range of mountains from which the CELESTIAL CITY may be seen.

**Delenda est Carthago** (Latin, 'Carthage must be destroyed'). The words with which Cato the Elder concluded every speech in the Senate after his visit to Carthage in 157 BC, when he saw in the city's revived prosperity a lasting threat to Rome. The phrase is now proverbial and means: 'Whatever stands in the way of our greatness must be removed at all costs.'

**Delhi Spearmen, The.** *See under* REGIMENTAL AND DIVISIONAL NICKNAMES.

**Delicious, Golden.** *See under* GOLDEN.

**Delight, Turkish.** *See under* TURK.

**Delilah, A.** A beautiful but treacherous woman, from the story of SAMSON and Delilah (Judges 16).

**Delinquents.** A term applied to the royalists by their opponents during the English Civil War (1642–5). Charles I was called the 'chief delinquent'.

**Delirium.** The Latin noun comes from the verb *delirare*, literally 'to swerve from the furrow', from *lira*, 'ridge', 'furrow'. A 'delirus' was thus a person who could not plough straight and was, therefore, crazy. Modern colloquial English has a similar notion in 'off one's trolley'. *See also* DTS; PREVARICATION.

**Deliver. Deliver the goods, To.** To perform as expected; to carry out one's part of the agreement.

**Jerusalem Delivered.** *See under* JERUSALEM.

**Stand and deliver!** *See under* STAND.

**Della Cruscans** or **Della Cruscan school.** A group of poets led by Robert Merry (1755–98) in Florence in the latter part of the 18th century. Their sentimental affectations, which appeared in *The World* and *The Oracle*, created a temporary stir but were mercilessly pilloried by William Gifford in *The* BAVIAD (1791) and, to a lesser extent, *The Maeviad* (1795). The clique took its name from the Accademia della Crusca ('academy of chaff'), which was founded in Florence in 1582 with the object of purifying the Italian language by sifting away its 'chaff' and which in 1611 published an important dictionary.

**Delos.** The smallest island of the Cyclades, sacred to APOLLO. Its name comes from Greek *dēlos*, 'visible', 'clear', by popular association with the legend that it appeared when called out of the deep by POSEIDON. It remained a floating island until ZEUS chained it to the bottom of the sea. It was the legendary birthplace of Apollo and Artemis (DIANA).

**Delphi.** An ancient town of Phocis at the foot of Mount PARNASSUS, famous for a temple of APOLLO and for its celebrated ORACLE, which was silenced only in the 4th century by the Emperor Theodosius. Delphi was regarded as the 'navel of the earth', and in the temple there was a white stone bound with a red ribbon to represent the navel and umbilical cord. The site of Delphi was occupied by the modern village of Kastri until 1890, when the village was moved to a nearby site and renamed Delphi.

In *The Winter's Tale* (1610), the same play in which he gives Bohemia a sea coast, Shakespeare makes 'Delphos' an island.

**Delphic utterance, A.** One that has the ambiguity associated with the words of the ORACLE.

**Deluge.** The biblical story of the flood (Genesis 6, 7, 8) has its counterpart in a variety of mythologies. In Babylonia it appears in the 11th tablet of the GILGAMESH EPIC, but on a higher level of civilization, since UTNAPISHTIM takes both craftsmen and treasure into his ark.

Apollodorus tells the story of DEUCALION AND PYRRHA, in some versions of which Deucalion is replaced by Ogyges (*see* OGYGIAN DELUGE). The account is also found in Ovid's *Metamorphoses* (i (1st century AD)).

In India one legend tells how MANU was warned by a fish of the approaching flood, and the fish subsequently towed his vessel to safety.

**Ogygian deluge.** *See under* OGYGIA.

**Delusion, A snare and a.** *See under* SNARE.

**Demesne.** *See* MANOR.

**Demeter.** The corn goddess of Greek legend, identified with the Roman CERES. She was the mother of Persephone (PROSERPINA) and the goddess of fruit, crops and vegetation. Her name has been derived from Greek *da*, 'O earth', an old vocative of *gē*, 'earth', and *mētēr*, 'mother', so that she is the 'Earth Mother' (or 'Mother Earth').

**Demi. Demijohn.** A glass or stoneware vessel with a large body and a small neck enclosed in wickerwork and containing more than a bottle. A common capacity is 5 gallons (about 23 litres). The word is probably from French *dame-jeanne*, 'Lady Jane'. *See also* BELLARMINE.

**Demimonde** (French, literally 'half world'). As

*le beau monde* is society, *le demimonde* denotes that class of women whose social standing is only half acknowledged, in particular because of their sexual promiscuity. The term was first used by Dumas *fils* for the title of his play *Le Demimonde* (1855), and has sometimes been incorrectly applied to fashionable courtesans.

**Demirep** (contraction of *demi-reputable*). A woman of bad repute, especially a prostitute.

> He had yet no knowledge of that character which is vulgarly called a demirep, that is to say, a woman that intrigues with every man she likes, under the name and appearance of virtue.
>
> HENRY FIELDING: *Tom Jones*, ch xv (1749)

**Demitasse** (French, 'half cup'). A small cup for serving coffee after a meal.

> You may tempt the upper classes
> With your villainous demitasses,
> But heaven will protect the Working Girl.
>
> EDGAR SMITH: 'Heaven will Protect the Working Girl' (song) (1910)

**Demi-vierge** (French, literally 'half virgin'). A woman who engages in sexual activity but who does not lose her virginity.

> 'I hope, Connie, you won't let circumstances force you into being a demi-vierge.'
>
> D.H. LAWRENCE: *Lady Chatterley's Lover*, ch ii (1928)

**Demiurge** (Greek *dēmiourgos*, 'artisan', literally 'one who works for the people', from *dēmos*, 'people', and *ergon*, 'work'). In the philosophy of PLATO, the mysterious agent that made the world and all that it contains. Among the GNOSTICS, the Demiurge is also creator of the universe, but a being that is subordinate to the Supreme Being. *See also* MARCIONITE.

Certain officials in some of the ancient Greek states were called *demiourgoi*.

**Democritus** (Greek, 'people's choice', from *dēmos*, 'people', and *kritos*, 'chosen'). The Greek philosopher (*c*.460–370 BC) was a follower of Leucippus and head of the school of ABDERA in Thrace. It is said that he put out his eyes that he might think the more deeply. A tradition among Latin writers represented him as 'the laughing philosopher', from his alleged inability to restrain his mirth at the prospect of human life. In many ways he is to be ranked with PLATO and ARISTOTLE.

> Si foret in terris, rideret Democritus.
> (If he were on earth, Democritus would laugh at the sight.)
>
> HORACE: *Epistles*, II, i (1st century BC)

**Democritus Junior.** The name under which Robert Burton (1577–1640) initially published *The Anatomy of Melancholy* (1621).

**Dine with Democritus, To.** *See under* DINE.

**Demogorgon.** A terrible deity, whose very name was capable of producing the most horrible effects. He is first mentioned by the 4th-century Christian writer, Lactantius, who in doing so broke with the superstition that the very reference to Demogorgon by name brought death and disaster. As it stands, his name appears to mean 'GORGON of the people', but it may have arisen from a scribe's miscopying of DEMIURGE.

> Must I call your master to my aid,
> At whose dread name the trembling furies quake,
> Hell stands abashed, and earth's foundations shake?
>
> NICHOLAS ROWE: Lucan's *Pharsalia*, vi (1718)

Milton speaks of 'the dreaded name of Demogorgon' (*Paradise Lost*, ii (1667)). According to Ariosto, Demogorgon was king of the elves and fays who lived on the Himalayas, and once in every five years summoned all his subjects before him to give an account of their stewardship. Edmund Spenser (*The Faerie Queene*, IV, ii (1596)) says that he dwells 'down in the bottom of the deep abyss' with the three fatal sisters. In John Dryden's *The Flower and the Leaf* (1690) he appears as 'cruel Demogorgon' and in Percy Bysshe Shelley's *Prometheus Unbound* (1820) he is the eternal principle that ousts false gods.

**Demons, Prince of.** *See under* PRINCE.

**Demos, King.** *See under* KING.

**Demosthenes.** One of the greatest of Greek orators (384–322 BC), who according to legend learned to speak well by placing pebbles in his mouth. He headed a fruitless endeavour to throw off the Macedonian yoke and, under sentence of death, fled to the island of Calauria where he took poison.

**Dempster.** *See under* DEEMSTER.

**Den, The Devil's.** *See under* DEVIL.

**Denarius.** A Roman silver coin, originally equal to ten asses (Latin *deni*, 'ten each'). The word was used in France and England for the inferior coins whether of silver or copper and for ready money generally. The initial d for PENNY in the old £sd is from *denarius*.

**Denarii Sancti Petri.** *See* PETER'S PENCE.

**Denarius Dei** (Latin, 'God's penny'). A token part of a bargain, which was given to the church or poor.

**Denial Bible, The.** *See under* BIBLE.

**Denims.** Coloured twilled cotton material used for overalls and, especially, jeans. Its name is a contraction of French *serge de Nîmes* ('serge of Nîmes'), from the town in the south of France where it was originally made.

**Denis.** *See* DENYS.

**Denmark.** According to the *Roman de la Rose* (*c*.1230), Denmark means 'country of Danaus', with reference to the king of Argos, who is said to have settled there after the siege of TROY, as BRUTE is similarly said to have settled in Britain.

In his *Gesta Danorum* SAXO GRAMMATICUS (*c*.1150–*c*.1206), with equal fancifulness, explains the name by making Dan, the son of Humble, the first king. His work is largely a collection of myths and oral tradition dealing with kings, heroes and national gods.

**Something is rotten in the state of Denmark.** *See under* SOMETHING.

**Dennis the Menace.** There are two cartoon characters of this name and title, one British, one American. The British Dennis has featured in the *Beano* comic since 1951 and was the creation of cartoonist David Law. He has a shock of black hair, wears a red striped jersey and is accompanied by a fearsome dog called Gnasher. His female counterpart is Beryl the Peril. His American namesake was created the same year by artist Hank Ketcham as a four-year-old brat. He has appeared in various cartoon stories, including a televised version in the early 1960s.

**Denys, Denis** or **Dionysius.** The apostle to the Gauls and a traditional patron saint of France, said to have been beheaded at Paris in 272. According to legend, after martyrdom he carried his head in his hands for 2 miles (3.2km) and laid it on the spot where the cathedral stands that now bears his name. The tale may have arisen from an ancient painting of his martyrdom in which the artist placed the head between the hands so that the subject might be identified. *See also* CE N'EST QUE LE PREMIER PAS QUI COÛTE.

**Montjoie St Denis.** *See under* MONTJOIE.

**St George he was for England, St Denis was for France.** *See under* GEORGE.

**Deo. Deo gratias** (Latin). Thanks to God. *See also* DEI GRATIA.

**Deo juvante** or **adjuvante** (Latin). With God's help.

**Deo volente** (Latin). God willing. The phrase is usually contracted to DV.

**Deoch-an-dorius.** *See* DOCH-AN-DORIS.

**Deodand.** Literally, something that should be given to God (Latin, *Deo dandum*). In former English law a personal possession that was responsible for the death of an individual was forfeited to the crown for some pious use. For example, if a man met his death from the fall of a ladder or the kick of a horse, the cause of death (the ladder or the horse) was sold and the proceeds given to the church. It originated from the idea that, as the victim met his death without the sacrament of extreme unction, the money could serve to pay for masses for his repose. Deodands were abolished in 1862.

**Depart.** Literally, to part thoroughly; to separate effectually. The marriage service in the old prayerbooks had 'till death us depart', which has been corrupted into 'till death us do part'.

> 'Depart' is sound English for 'part asunder', which was altered to 'do part' in 1661, at the pressing request of the Puritans, who knew as little of the history of their national language as they did of that of their national Church.
>
> J.H. BLUNT: *Annotated Book of Common Prayer* (1866)

**Derby.** The American name (pronounced as spelt) for the headgear known as the BOWLER HAT in Britain. The Brown Derby is a well-known Hollywood restaurant, shaped like a hat and frequented by film people.

**Derby, The.** The DERBY STAKES. (The name is pronounced as if 'Darby'.)

**Derby Day.** The day when the DERBY STAKES are run during the great Epsom Summer Meeting, formerly on the first Wednesday in June but from 1995 on the first or second Saturday.

**Derby dog.** A stray dog that wanders onto the racecourse on Epsom Downs as soon as it has been cleared for the main race. A general term for something that inevitably 'turns up'.

**Derby Stakes.** One of the CLASSIC RACES, also called the BLUE RIBBON OF THE TURF. It was instituted by the 12th Earl of Derby in 1780, one year after he established the OAKS. The Derby is for three-year-old colts and fillies only; therefore no horse can win it twice. *See also* EPSOM RACES; HERMIT'S DERBY.

**Donkey derby.** *See under* DONKEY.

**Hermit's Derby.** *See under* HERMIT.

**Kiplingcotes Derby.** *See under* KIPLINGCOTES.

**Derrick.** A contrivance or form of crane used for hoisting heavy objects, so called from Derrick, the TYBURN hangman of the early 17th century. The name was first applied to the gibbet and, from its similarity, to the crane.

> He rides circuit with the devil, and Derrick must be his host, and Tyborne the inn at which he will light.
>
> THOMAS DEKKER: *Bellman of London* (1608)

**Dervish.** *See* WHIRLING DERVISHES.

**Description, To beggar.** *See under* BEG.

**Desdemona.** The gentle and innocent heroine of Shakespeare's *Othello* (1604). She is a beautiful young Venetian noblewoman, who marries OTHELLO against her father's wishes and goes with him to the wars in Cyprus. She is ensnared in Iago's plot against Othello and Cassio and is made to seem to be having an affair with the latter, for which Othello kills her, traditionally doing so in stage versions by suffocating her with a pillow in her bed. Her name represents Greek *dusdaimōn*, 'ill-fated'.

**Deseret.** Deseret is a word that appears in the Book of MORMON (Ether 2:3) with the meaning 'honeybee', and it was the Mormons' original name for the state of Utah. The association was with a select and remote valley. The name remains as that of a town in Utah.

**Desert. Desert Fathers.** *See* FATHERS OF THE DESERT.

**Desert Island Discs.** The enduringly popular radio programme was created by Roy Plomley in 1942 and had its 2000th 'castaway' (the actor John Thaw) in 1990. Each celebrity is allowed to choose eight gramophone records and a single luxury and book (except the Bible or Shakespeare) that they would wish to have on their desert island. The first subject was the comedian Vic Oliver, and the only celebrity to be 'shipwrecked' four times was the comedian Arthur Askey. Plomley himself presented the programme until his death in 1985.

**Desert Rats, The.** *See under* REGIMENTAL AND DIVISIONAL NICKNAMES.

**Ship of the desert.** *See under* SHIP.

**Desert one's colours, To.** To become a TURNCOAT; to turn tail. The allusion is to the military flag.

**Desire, Baptism of.** *See under* BAPTISM.

**Despair. Counsel of despair.** *See under* COUNSEL.

**Giant Despair.** *See under* GIANT.

**Desperate Dan.** The brawny, stubble-chinned westerner who has appeared in the *Dandy* comic (which his name matches) since 1937. His favourite dish is cow pie, which he eats with the horns protruding from the pastry. He was the creation of the artist Dudley D. Watkins.

**Despond, Slough of.** *See under* SLOUGH.

**Destiny. Man of Destiny, The.** *See under* MAN.

**Stone of Destiny, The.** *See* STONE OF SCONE.

**Thread of Destiny, The.** *See under* THREAD.

**Destruction, The City of.** *See under* CITY.

**Desultory.** Roman circus riders who used to leap from one horse to another were called 'desultores', from Latin *desilire*, 'to jump down'. Hence the use of 'desultory' in English to denote someone who figuratively jumps about or flits from one thing to another.

**Deucalion and Pyrrha.** Deucalion (the Greek counterpart of NOAH) was a son of PROMETHEUS and the husband of Pyrrha, daughter of Epimetheus. He was king of part of Thessaly. When ZEUS, angered at the evils of the Bronze Age, caused the DELUGE, Deucalion built an ark to save himself and his wife, which came to rest on Mount PARNASSUS. Told by the ORACLE of THEMIS that to restore the human race they must cast the bones of their mother behind them (which they interpreted as the stones of Mother Earth), he and his wife obeyed the direction. The stones thrown by Deucalion became men and those thrown by Pyrrha became women.

> And men themselues, the which at first were framed
> Of earthly mould, and form'd of flesh and bone,
> Are now transformed into hardest stone:
> Such as behind their backs (so backward bred)
> Were throwne by *Pyrrha* and *Deucalione*.
>
> EDMUND SPENSER: *The Faerie Queene*, V, *Introduction*, ii (1596)

**Deuce.** The two in games with cards or dice as well as a score of 40 all in tennis, from Old French *deus*, 'two'. The tennis score is so called as two consecutive points are needed to win, the first being an 'advantage'. The word 'deuce' used as a EUPHEMISM for 'Devil' probably comes from the two at dice being an unlucky throw. The three in cards and dice is called 'trey', from Old French *treis*.

**Deuce-ace.** A throw of two dice, one showing one spot and the other showing two, and hence exceptionally bad luck.

**Deus. Deus ex machina** (Latin, 'god out of a machine'). The intervention of some unlikely or providential event just in time to extricate one from difficulties or to save a situation, especially as contrived in a novel or a play. The reference is to the god who was introduced into an ancient Greek or Roman play to resolve the plot. He appeared on a machine (Greek *makhana*, 'pulley'), a device suspended over the stage.

**Deus vult** (Latin, 'God wills it'). The war cry of the First CRUSADE, enjoined by Pope Urban II because these words were spontaneously used by the crowd in response to his address at Clermont in 1095.

**Deuteronomy.** The fifth book of the Old Testament has a name of Greek origin meaning 'second law'. It is so called because it contains a repetition of the DECALOGUE and parts of EXODUS. The name, however, is actually based on a mistranslation into Greek (*to deuteronomion touto*, 'this second law') of the Hebrew phrase in the SEPTUAGINT, *mishneh hattorah hazzoth*, 'a copy of this law'.

**Deva.** The Roman legionary fortress on the site of the present Chester. The name is that of the River Dee.

> Nor yet where Deva spreads her wizard stream.
>
> MILTON: *Lycidas* (1638)

**Development, Ribbon.** *See under* RIBBON.

**De Vil, Cruella.** The wicked heroine of Dodie Smith's children's novel *One Hundred and One Dalmatians* (1956), who kidnaps puppies with the aim of turning their fur into coats for humans. Her name, subsequently a byword for female heartlessness, implies that she is a cruel villainess or cruel deviless. The story was made into a popular Disney cartoon film of 1961.

**Devil, The.** The Devil is represented with a cloven foot because he is called *seirizzim* ('goat') by the Rabbinical writers. As the goat is a type of uncleanness, the prince of unclean spirits is aptly represented under this emblem. As the Prince of Evil he is also called SATAN.

In legal parlance a counsel who prepares a brief for another is called a 'devil' and the process is called 'devilling'. It is also applied when one counsel transfers his brief to another to represent him in court.

**Devil among the tailors, The.** Said when a slanging match is in progress. The phrase is also the name of a game in which a top (the 'devil') is spun among a number of wooden men (the 'tailors') with the aim of knocking down as many as possible. The phrase is said to have originated from a fracas made at a benefit performance *c.*1830 for the actor William Dowton (1764–1851). The piece was a burlesque called *The Tailors: a Tragedy for Warm Weather*, and the row was made outside the Haymarket Theatre by a large crowd of tailors, who considered the play a slur on their trade.

**Devil and bag o'nails.** *See* BAG O'NAILS *under* PUBLIC HOUSE SIGNS.

**Devil and his dam, The.** The Devil and something worse. 'Dam' here may mean either 'mother' or 'wife'. Rabbinical tradition relates that LILITH was the wife of ADAM, but was such a vixen that Adam could not live with her, and she became the Devil's dam. In many mythologies the Devil is typified by an animal, and in such cases 'dam' for 'mother' is not inappropriate.

**Devil a one.** Not even one.

**Devil Dick.** A nickname of Richard Porson (1759–1808), Regius Professor of Greek at the University of Cambridge and an outstanding Greek scholar.

**Devil dodger.** A sly hypocrite; a ranting preacher; a parson.

**Devil is not so black as he is painted, The.** Said in extenuation or mitigation, especially when it seems that exaggerated criticism or censure has been made.

**Devil looking over Lincoln, The.** Said of a vitriolic critic or a backbiter. Thomas Fuller in *The History of the Worthies of England* (1662) (under Oxford), says the phrase may allude either to the 'stone picture of the Devil which doth or lately did, overlook Lincoln College', or to a grotesque sculpture at Lincoln Cathedral. *See also* LINCOLN IMP.

**Devil-may-care.** Cheerfully reckless.

**Devil on two sticks.** *See* DIABOLO. This is also the English name of Alain-René Lesage's novel *Le Diable boiteux* (1707) in which ASMODEUS features.

**Devil rides on a fiddlestick, The.** Much ado about nothing. Beaumont and Fletcher, Shakespeare and others use the phrase 'Fiddlesticks!' as an exclamation meaning 'nonsense', 'rubbish'. When the prince and his companions are at the Boar's Head, first Bardolph rushes in to warn them that the sheriff's officers are at hand, then the hostess enters to warn her guests. But the prince says:

> Heigh, heigh! the devil rides upon a fiddlestick: what's the matter?
> *Henry IV, Pt I*, II, iv (1597)

**Devil's advocate.** A person who advocates an opposing or unpopular view, from Latin *Advocatus Diaboli* ('Devil's Advocate'). In the Roman Catholic Church this was the popular name given to the official appointed to put the case against a proposed BEATIFICATION or CANONIZATION. The supporter was (until 1983) called *Advocatus Dei* ('God's Advocate').

**Devil's apple, The.** The MANDRAKE and also the thorn apple.

**Devil's Arrows, The.** Three remarkable DRUID monoliths near Boroughbridge, North Yorkshire.

**Devil's bedpost. The.** In card games, the four of clubs. *See also* DEVIL'S FOUR-POSTER.

**Devils' Beef Tub.** A huge semicircular hollow in the hills north of Moffat, Scotland.

**Devil's Bible, The.** *See* DEVIL'S BOOKS.

**Devil's bird, The.** A Scottish name for the yellow bunting, from its note, 'deil'.

**Devil's bit.** A species of scabious, *Succisa pratensis*, the root of which ends abruptly and is said to have been bitten off by the Devil to destroy its usefulness.

**Devil's bones.** Dice, which were made of bones and led to ruin.

**Devil's books** or **Devil's picture book, The.** Playing cards. A PRESBYTERIAN phrase, used in reproof of the name King's Books, applied to a pack of cards, from French *livre des quatre rois* ('book of the four kings'). Also called the Devil's Bible.

**Devil's Bridge.** A popular name in mountainous areas for bridges built over ravines and chasms. There is a notable one over the Reuss in the Swiss canton of Uri. The village of this name in Ceredigion (Cardiganshire), central Wales is so called from the bridge across the gorge of the Mynach. The lower or Monk's Bridge was built by the monks of Strata Florida in the 12th century and the upper tiers in the 18th and 20th centuries. *See also* CHEAT THE DEVIL.

**Devil's candle, The.** So the Arabs call the MANDRAKE from its shining appearance at night.

**Devil's candlestick, The.** The common stinkhorn fungus (*Phallus impudicus*), also called the devil's horn and the devil's stinkpot.

**Devil's Cheesewring, The.** A mass of eight stones rising to a height of 32ft (9.8m) in the Valley of Rocks, Lynton, Devon, so called because it looks like a gigantic cheese-press.

**Devil's Chimney, The.** An outcrop of rock on the west side of Leckhampton Hill, south of Cheltenham, Gloucestershire.

**Devil's claw.** The herb *Physoplexis comosa*, often grown in rock gardens.

**Devil's coach-horse.** The large black beetle, *Staphylinus olens*, noted for its large jaws and aggressive attitude. It is also called the devil's cow.

**Devil's coach-wheel.** The corn crowfoot.

**Devil's Coits.** *See* HACKELL'S COIT.

**Devil's current.** Part of the current of the BOSPORUS is so called from its great rapidity.

**Devil's dancing-hour, The.** Midnight.

**Devil's darning needle, The.** The dragonfly or damselfly, also the climbing plant *Clematis virginiana*.

**Devil's daughter.** A shrew. *See also* DEVIL'S DAUGHTER'S PORTION.

**Devil's daughter's portion, The.** The saying is:

> Deal, Dover and Harwich,
> The Devil gave with his daughter in marriage.

The reference is to the scandalous impositions once practised in these ports on sailors and casual visitors.

**Devil's Den, The.** A CROMLECH near Marlborough, Wiltshire.

**Devil's door, The.** A small door in the north wall of some old churches, which used to be opened at baptisms and communions to 'let the Devil out'. The north used to be known as 'the Devil's side', where SATAN and his legion lurked to catch the unwary.

**Devil's dozen.** Thirteen, i.e. twelve and one for the Devil. *See also* BAKER'S DOZEN.

**Devil's dung.** An old pharmaceutical nickname for the asafoetida, an evil-smelling resinous gum.

**Devil's dust.** Flock and shoddy made from old rags torn up by a machine called a 'devil'.

> Does it beseem thee to weave cloth of devil's dust instead of true wool?
>
> THOMAS CARLYLE: *Miscellanies, IV: Dr Francis* (1843)

**Devil's Dyke.** (1) An ancient military earthwork in Cambridgeshire stretching from Reach across Newmarket Heath to Wood Ditton, south of Newmarket. On the eastern side it is 18ft (5.5m) high. (2) A ravine in the South Downs above the village of Poynings, Sussex, northwest of Brighton. The legend is that St Cuthman, priding himself on having christianized the area and having built a nunnery where the dykehouse was later built, was confronted by the Devil and told that all his labour was vain for he would swamp the whole country before morning. St Cuthman went to the nunnery and told the abbess to keep the sisters in prayer until after midnight and then to illuminate the windows. The Devil came at sunset with mattock and spade and began cutting a dyke into the sea, but was seized with rheumatic pains all over his body. He flung down his tools, and the cocks, mistaking the illuminated windows for sunrise, began to crow, whereupon the Devil fled in alarm, leaving his work unfinished. (3) *See* GRIMSDYKE.

> The Devil's Dyke [(1)], as this barrier is called, is clearly a work of defence against enemies advancing from the Fens; and as a defence to the East Anglians it was of priceless value, for, stretching as it did from a point where the country became fenny and impassable to a point where the woods equally forbade all access, it covered the only entrance to the country they had won.
>
> J.R. GREEN: *The Making of England* (1882)

**Devil's Elbow, The.** A double hairpin bend (now bypassed) south of Cairnwell Pass on the road from Braemar to Spittal of Glenshee, Scotland.

**Devil's fingers.** The starfish, also belemnites.

**Devil's four-poster.** A hand of cards containing four clubs. It is said that there never was a good hand at WHIST containing four clubs. *See also* DEVIL'S BEDPOST.

**Devil's Frying Pan, The.** A curious rock basin filled by the sea at high tide, situated near the village of Cadgwith, east of Lizard Point, Cornwall.

**Devil's guts.** The long, thin, red stems of the leafless, parasitic dodder plant, *Cuscuta epithymum* (also known as hellweed), and also a name for the creeping buttercup (*Ranunculus repens*).

**Devil's Hole, The.** A name of the Peak Cavern in Derbyshire.

**Devil's horn.** *See* DEVIL'S CANDLESTICK.

**Devil sick would be a monk, The.**

> When the Devil was sick, the Devil a monk would be;
> When the Devil got well, the Devil a monk was he.

An expression said of people who make pious resolutions in times of sickness or danger but forget them when danger is past and health recovered.

**Devil's Island.** A small island off the coast of French Guiana, formerly used as a convict settlement. Captain Alfred Dreyfus was confined there. *See also* DREYFUSARD.

**Devil's Kitchen.** A fissure in the rock face on the north side of Glyder Fawr, North Wales.

**Devil's Lake.** A lake in North Dakota, USA, and also the name of a city on its shore.

**Devil's livery.** Black and yellow: black for death, yellow for quarantine.

**Devil's luck.** Very good luck. People who enjoy very good luck were thought at one time to have compounded with the Devil.

**Devil's Mass.** Swearing at everybody and everything.

**Devil's milk.** The sun spurge (*Euphorbia helioscopia*), from its poisonous milky juice.

**Devil's Missionary, The.** A nickname given to VOLTAIRE (1694–1778).

**Devil's Nostrils, The.** Two vast caverns separated by a huge pillar of natural rock on Mainland, Shetland.

**Devils on horseback.** A savoury snack of prunes wrapped in bacon slices and served on toast. *See also* ANGELS ON HORSEBACK.

**Devil's Own, The.** *See under* REGIMENTAL AND DIVISIONAL NICKNAMES.

**Devil's paintbrush.** The hawkweed (*Pilosella aurantiaca*), which bears orange-red flowers.

**Devil's Parliament.** The Parliament that met at Coventry in 1459 and passed Acts of Attainder against the YORKIST leaders.

**Devil's Point.** A peak in the Cairngorms at the southeast end of Cairn Toul.

**Devil's Punch Bowl.** A deep dell on the southwest side of Hindhead Hill, Surrey, scene of the murder of an unknown sailor in 1786. His assassins, Lonagan, Casey and Marshall, were hanged in chains on nearby Hindhead Common. A similar dell in Mangerton Mountain, near Killarney, Ireland, has the same name.

**Devil's shoestrings, The.** Goat's rue (*Tephrosia virginiana*), so named from its tough, thin roots.

**Devil's snuffbox, The.** A puffball of the genus *Lycoperdon*, a fungus full of dust.

**Devil's stinkpot, The.** *See* DEVIL'S CANDLESTICK.

**Devil's stones.** The field gromwell (*Buglossoides arvensis*), probably so called from its hard twin fruits, like testicles. The plant is reputed to have contraceptive qualities.

**Devil's Throat, The.** Cromer Bay, Norfolk, so called from the danger to navigation.

**Devil's tongue.** The snake palm (*Amorphophallus rivieri*). The name refers to its long, funnel-shaped spathe.

**Devil's Tower, The.** A natural tower of volcanic rock some 600ft (183m) high on the Belle Fourche River, Wyoming, USA.

**Devil's walking-stick.** The spiny shrub *Aralia spinosa*, also known as the Hercules club or American angelica tree.

**Devil take the hindmost, The.** A phrase from late medieval magic, now denoting selfish competition. The Devil was said to have had a school at Toledo (or Salamanca) where the students, after making certain progress in their mystic studies, were obliged to run through an underground hall. The last man was seized by the Devil and became his imp. *See also* SCHLEMIHL; SHADOW.

**Devil to pay, The.** Trouble in store. *See also* DEVIL TO PAY AND NO PITCH HOT.

**Devil to pay and no pitch hot, The.** There will be serious trouble arising from this. The 'devil' was the seam between the outboard plank and the waterways of a ship and very awkward to reach. It also needed more pitch when caulking and 'paying' (covering with pitch), hence 'the devil'. *See also* PAY.

Rabelais (*Pantagruel*, Bk IV, ch xlvi (1532)) says that a farmer once bargained with the Devil for each to have on alternate years what grew under and over the soil. The canny farmer sowed carrots and turnips when it was his turn to have the underground share, and wheat and barley the year following.

**As the Devil loves holy water.** *See under* AS.

**Beat the Devil's tattoo, To.** *See under* BEAT.

**Between the Devil and the deep (blue) sea.** *See under* BETWEEN.

**Cheat the Devil, To.** *See under* CHEAT.

**French Devil, The.** *See under* FRENCH.

**Give the Devil his due.** Give even a bad person the credit they deserve.

**Go to the Devil.** Go to ruin. In the 17th century wits used to make a play on the applicability of the phrase to the Devil Tavern, TEMPLE BAR, a favoured rendezvous among lawyers and writers. The sign showed St DUNSTAN pulling the Devil's nose.

> *Bloodhound*: As you come by Temple Bar make a step to the Devil.
> *Tim*: To the Devil, father?
> *Sim*: My master means the sign of the devil, and he cannot hurt you, fool; there's a saint holds him by the nose.
>
> W. ROWLEY: *A Match at Midnight* (1633)

**Lead one the Devil's own dance, To.** *See under* LEAD.

**Like the Devil.** With great energy.

**Needs must when the Devil drives.** *See* NEEDS MUST.

**Play the very Devil with something, To.** *See under* PLAY.

**Printer's devil.** *See under* PRINT.

**Pull Devil, pull baker.** *See under* PULL.

**Raise the Devil, To.** *See under* RAISE.

**Robert the Devil.** *See under* ROBERT.

**Son of the Devil.** *See under* SON.

**Talk of the Devil.** *See under* TALK.

**Tell the truth and shame the Devil.** *See under* TELL.

**Very Devil, The.** A great difficulty or nuisance.

**Vow a candle to the Devil, To.** *See under* VOW.

**When the Devil is blind.** *See under* WHEN.

**White Devil.** *See under* WHITE.

**White Devil of Wallachia.** *See under* WHITE.

**Why should the Devil have all the good tunes?** *See under* WHY.

**World, the flesh and the Devil.** *See under* WORLD.

**Devonshire.** The name is derived from the early CELTIC inhabitants, the Dumnonii, whose own name may mean 'deep ones', in that they were valley dwellers. According to legend it is from Debon, one of the heroes who came with BRUTE from TROY and who was allotted this part of ALBION which was thus 'Debon's share'.

**Devonshire Poet, The.** O. Jones, a journeyman woolcomber, writer of *Poetic Attempts* (1786). Other Devonshire poets are John Gay (1685–1732) of Barnstaple and Edward Capern (1819–94), the postman poet of Bideford. The bell that Capern carried on his rounds still hangs in a niche on his tombstone at Heanton Punchardon.

**Dew. Dewclaw.** A rudimentary inner toe found on some dogs. It is perhaps so called because it only brushes the dewy surface of the grass as the dog walks, whereas the other claws press firmly into the soil.

**Dew ponds.** Artificial ponds or pools on the heights of the chalk downs of southern England and elsewhere, which very rarely dry out, even in the most severe drought. They formerly collected rainwater for sheep and are known locally as 'sheep ponds'. The notion that they were intended to collect dew springs from the romantic imagination of the early Victorians. Some dew ponds go back to the NEOLITHIC AGE, but most are no older than the 17th century or even later. Many are now simply circular grassy declivities.

> We have no waters to delight
> Our broad and brookless vales –
> Only the dewpond on the height
> Unfed, that never fails.
> RUDYARD KIPLING: 'Sussex' (1903)

**Dewan.** *See* DIWAN.

**Dewi.** *See* St DAVID.

**Dexter.** A Latin word meaning 'to the right-hand side', hence dextrous originally meant 'right-handed'. In HERALDRY the term 'dexter' is applied to that side of the shield to the right of the person holding it, hence it is the left side of the shield as seen by the viewer.

**Dey** (Turkish *dayi*, literally 'maternal uncle'). Governor of Algiers before it was annexed to France in 1830; also the 16th-century rulers of Tunis and Tripoli.

**Dharma** (Sanskrit, 'habit', 'usage'). The doctrine of universal truth common to all individuals, as proclaimed by the BUDDHA. Dharma, the Buddha himself, and the sangha (community of believers) make up the triratna ('three jewels') as the prime statement of Buddhist belief. In Hinduism, the dharma is the moral and religious law that governs individual conduct. It is one of the four ends of life, to be followed according to one's class, status and position in life.

**Diable, Le** (French, 'the Devil'). Olivier le Dain, the tool of Louis XI and once the king's barber. Much feared and even more disliked, he was hanged in 1484, after the king's death.

> Olivier le Dain, called sometimes Oliver le Mauvais, and sometimes Oliver le Diable, epithets derived from the unscrupulous cunning with which he assisted in the execution of the schemes of his master's tortuous policy.
> SIR WALTER SCOTT: *Quentin Durward*, ch viii (1823)

**Que diable allait-il faire dans cette galère?** *See under* GALÈRE.

**Diabolo** (Italian, 'Devil'). A modern name for an old toy formerly called the 'devil on two sticks'. The 'devil' is a hollow, turned piece of wood, roughly the shape of two cones joined at the points. The player places the 'devil' on a cord, held loosely between two sticks, and it is then made to spin by manipulating the sticks.

**Diadem** (Greek *diadein*, 'to bind round'). In ancient times, the headband or fillet worn by kings as a badge of royalty. It was made of silk, linen or wool and was tied at the back, with the ends falling on the neck. The diadem of BACCHUS was a broad band, which might be unfolded to make a veil. The diadem eventually became a flexible band of gold, and its development and decoration became largely inseparable from that of the CROWN.

> All hail the power of Jesus' Name;
> Let Angels prostrate fall;
> Bring forth the royal diadem
> To crown Him Lord of all.
> EDWARD PERRONET: 'On the Resurrection: The Lord is King' (1780)

**Dial.** An old term for a clock.

**Dial of Ahaz.** The only time-measuring device mentioned in the Bible. Probably a form of sun clock, its introduction by Ahaz may have been due to his contacts with the Assyrians. It is referred to in 2 Kings 20:9–11 and Isaiah 38:8.

> And he brought the shadow ten degrees backward, by which it had gone down in the dial of Ahaz.
> 2 Kings 20:11.

**Seven Dials.** *See under* SEVEN.

**Dialect, Doric.** *See under* DORIAN.

**Dialectic** or **dialectics** (Greek *dialektikē tekhnē*, 'the art of argument'). A word commonly used to mean abstract discussion, logic in general or the investigation of truth by analysis, although it has various technical implications in the language of philosophy. Under SOCRATES, dialectic became a search for definition by the systematic use of question and answer, and for PLATO the method of the highest kind of speculation. For ARISTOTLE a dialectic proof was a probable deduction as opposed to a scientific or demonstrative proof. From the time of the STOICS until the end of the medieval period dialectic was synonymous with logic.

Hegel gave dialectic a new meaning: the action and reaction between opposites (thesis and antithesis), out of which the new or higher synthesis emerges.

**Dialectical materialism.** The Marxist adaptation of the Hegelian DIALECTIC to describe the way in which phenomena have interacted and developed and will therefore continue to do so, as the general laws that govern the evolution of nature and society. Every stage of history contains the germs of its own destruction, the thesis provokes its opposite or antithesis, and from the clash a new synthesis arises, which preserves the best of both thesis and antithesis. The process then repeats itself. This conflict of opposites takes place gradually until a certain point, when quantitative change becomes qualitative change. By such processes is the classless society to be reached. It should be noted that ideas and institutions are the reflection of material conditions, the reverse of the Hegelian approach. *See also* MARXISM.

**Diamond** (Medieval Latin *diamas*, a form of Latin *adamas*, 'hardest steel').

(1) The gemstone is so called because the diamond, which cuts other substances, can be cut or polished only by one of its kind. *See also* CULLINAN DIAMOND; GLAUCUS; HOPE DIAMOND; KOH-I-NOOR; PITT DIAMOND; STAR OF SOUTH AFRICA.

(2) In baseball, either the whole playing field generally, or more precisely the square formed by the four bases.

(3) In cards, the suit marked with red diamond shapes.

**Diamond.** Sir Isaac Newton's little dog which, according to legend, one winter's morning upset a candle on his master's desk causing the destruction of the records of many years' experiments. On perceiving this disaster, Newton exclaimed: 'Oh, Diamond, Diamond, thou little knowest the mischief thou hast done!' and at once set to work to repair the loss. However, the story is a fiction. There was no dog, and the story was invented to explain Newton's nervous breakdown in 1693.

**Diamond cut diamond.** A meeting or match between two equally able people. A diamond is so hard that it can only be ground by diamond dust or by rubbing one against another.

> He had been conducting a difficult negotiation all day of the diamond-cut-diamond order, and was tired out and disgusted by the amount of knowledge of books which even a gentleman may possess.
>
> MRS HUMPHRY WARD: *David Grieve*, Bk II, ch ii (1892)

**Diamond Jim.** Jim Brady, or more correctly James Buchanan Brady (1856–1917), American speculator and philanthropist, who started life as a bellboy in a New York hotel. A well-known character in the night life of Broadway, he attracted attention and gained this nickname from the valuable and varied diamond ornaments with which he adorned his person.

**Diamond Jousts, The.** Jousts instituted by King ARTHUR 'who by that name had named them, since a diamond was the prize'. The story as embroidered by Tennyson in his *Lancelot and Elaine* (1870) is that Arthur once picked nine diamonds from the crown of a slain knight, and when he became king he offered them as a prize for nine successive annual jousts, all of which were won by Sir LANCELOT OF THE LAKE. The knight attempted to present them to Queen GUINEVERE but she flung them out of the window into the river below, through jealousy of ELAINE.

**Diamond Jubilee.** *See* WEDDING ANNIVERSARIES.

**Diamond Lil.** A nickname of the American film actress Mae West (1892–1980), from her play thus titled (1928) in which she took the main role. The heroine is so called because of the large amount of 'ice' (jewellery) her pimp has lavished on her.

**Diamond of the first water.** An especially fine diamond, one of the greatest value for its size. The degree of brilliance of a diamond is called its water. Hence 'of the first water' to denote an extreme of some kind, whether good or bad, e.g. 'genius of the first water', 'rogue of the first water'.

**Diamond Pitt.** Thomas Pitt (1653–1726), East India merchant and owner of the PITT DIAMOND and grandfather of the 1st Earl of Chatham.

**Diamond Sculls, The.** An annual race for amateur single scullers at the Henley Royal Regatta, first rowed in 1844. The prize is a pair of crossed silver sculls nearly 12in (30cm) long, surmounted by an imitation wreath of LAUREL and having a pendant of diamonds. The trophy passes from winner to winner but each winner retains a silver cup.

**Acres of Diamonds.** *See under* ACRE.

**Affair of the Diamond Necklace, The.** *See under* AFFAIR.

**Black diamonds.** *See under* BLACK.

**Cullinan Diamond.** *See under* CULLINAN.

**Florentine Diamond.** *See under* FLORENTINE.

**Hope Diamond.** *See under* HOPE.

**Koh-i-Noor Diamond.** *See under* KOH-I-NOOR.

**Pitt Diamond.** *See under* PITT.

**Rough diamond, A.** *See under* ROUGH.

**Sancy Diamond, The.** *See under* SANCY.

**Diana** (old form of *Diviana*, from Latin *divius*, 'divine'). An ancient Italian goddess identified with ARTEMIS. She was commonly regarded as a moon goddess and was also more specifically the goddess of hunting and the woodlands. She was associated with fertility and was thus largely worshipped by women. She was invoked by the Romans under her three aspects. *See also* SELENE.

Queen and huntress, chaste and fair,
Now the sun is laid to sleep,
Seated in thy silver chair,
State in wonted manner keep.
BEN JONSON: *Cynthia's Revels*, V, iii (1600)

**Diana of Ephesus.** A statue that purportedly fell from heaven. She is represented with many breasts and with trunk and legs enclosed in an ornamental sheath. The temple of Diana of Ephesus was one of the SEVEN WONDERS OF THE WORLD, with a roof supported by 127 columns. It was set on fire by Eratostratus for the sake of perpetuating his name. *See also* GREAT IS DIANA OF THE EPHESIANS.

And when the townclerk had appeased the people, he said, Ye men of Ephesus, what man is there that knoweth not how that the city of the Ephesians is a worshipper of the great goddess Diana, and of the image which fell down from Jupiter?
Acts 19:35

**Great is Diana of the Ephesians.** *See under* GREAT.

**Diana's tree.** *See* PHILOSOPHER'S TREE.

**Mirror of Diana, The.** *See under* MIRROR.

**Diapason.** A word of Greek origin, from *hē dia pasōn khordōn sumphōnia* ('concord through all the notes'). It is used for the compass or whole range of an instrument or voice and formerly denoted harmony in general. According to the Pythagorean system (*see* PYTHAGORAS), the world is a piece of harmony and man the full chord.

From Harmony, from heavenly Harmony
This universal Frame began:
From Harmony to Harmony
Through all the Compass of the Notes it ran,
The Diapason closing full in Man.
JOHN DRYDEN: *A Song for St Cecilia's Day* (1687)

**Diaries, The Hitler.** *See under* FAKES.

**Diavolo.** Another form of DIABOLO.

**Diavolo, Fra** (Italian, 'Brother Devil'). Michele Pozza (1771–1806), an Italian brigand and enemy of the French occupation, renowned for his atrocities. He features in Auber's light opera of this name (1831).

**Dice** (representing *dies*, plural of *die*). Dice are said to have been invented in China by Chen Su-Wang in the 3rd century AD. Chinese dice differ from western dice in that the ace (one) and four are usually red, while the other points are black. The ace is the highest throw, unlike the western six. It is uncertain why the four should have been so coloured, but the following story is told. The Emperor Hsuan Tsung of the Tang dynasty was one day playing a game with a favourite concubine and required three fours to win. As the dice rolled out of the pot, one settled to four but the other two kept on spinning. 'Four! Four!' cried his imperial majesty in great excitement, whereupon the dice immediately settled to display this number. A eunuch standing nearby suggested that this unusual event should be marked in some way, and the emperor gave an edict that four on dice should henceforth be painted red.

**No dice.** *See under* NO.

**Dick.** A slang word for a detective, from a shortened form of detective itself (like tec).

**Dick's hatband.** A popular reference to Richard Cromwell's 'crown' as in:

Dick's hatband was made of sand: his regal honours were a 'rope of sand'
As queer as Dick's hatband: few things have been more ridiculous than the exaltation and abdication of Oliver's son
As tight as Dick's hatband: the crown was too tight for him to wear with safety

**Dick Turpin.** *See under* TURPIN.

**Dick Whittington.** *See under* WHITTINGTON.

**Black Dick.** *See under* BLACK.

**Clever dick, A.** *See under* CLEVER.

**Devil Dick.** *See under* DEVIL.

**Dirty Dick's.** *See under* DIRTY.

**King Dick.** A scornful term for Richard Cromwell (1626–1712), who succeeded his father Oliver as Lord Protector in September 1658 and showed no capacity to govern. *See also* Queen DICK; TUMBLEDOWN DICK.

**Queen Dick.** Richard Cromwell (1626–1712), son of Oliver Cromwell, was sometimes so called, although he was also known as King DICK.

**Spotted dick.** *See under* SPOTTED.

**Tom, Dick and Harry.** *See under* TOM.

**Tumbledown Dick.** *See under* TUMBLEDOWN.

**Dickens, What the.** *See under* WHAT.

**Dickey.** A name for a male donkey, especially in East Anglia. It is a term of endearment, as a little bird is called a 'dicky bird'. The donkey is also called CUDDY, NEDDY and moke or mike.

**Dicky** or **Dickey.** In George III's time, a flannel petticoat.

A hundred instances I soon could pick ye –
Without a cap we view the fair,
The bosom heaving also bare,
The hips ashamed, forsooth, to wear a dicky.
PETER PINDAR: *Lord Auckland's Triumph* (1800)

The word was afterwards applied to what was called a false shirt, that is, a starched shirt front worn over another. It also came to be used for a woman's false blouse front, worn to fill the neck of a jacket or low-cut dress, as well as for a leather apron and a child's bib. Later, it was applied to the driver's seat in a carriage and the servant's seat behind. In the earlier 'two-seater' motor cars the dickey was the additional seating at the rear, where the occupants were exposed to the weather in the space corresponding to the boot of later models.

**Dictionary, Walking.** *See under* WALK.

**Dictys Cretensis** (Latin, 'Dictys of Crete'). A companion of IDOMENEUS at TROY and reputed author of an eyewitness account of the siege of Troy. The manuscript was probably written in the 2nd or 3rd century AD and translated into Latin in the 4th century. It is important as the chief source used by medieval writers on the Trojan legend.

**Didache** (Greek, 'teaching'). An early Christian treatise, also known as *The Teaching of the Twelve Apostles*, probably belonging to the late 1st or early 2nd century. It was discovered in the Patriarchal Library at Constantinople in 1875 and falls into two parts. The first is concerned with moral teachings and is based on an earlier document, seemingly of Jewish origin, called *The Two Ways*, with additions from the Sermon on the Mount and elsewhere. The second part is concerned with church ordinances.

**Dido.** The legendary daughter of Belus of Tyre and the founder queen of Carthage, after the murder of her husband Sichaeus by PYGMALION. According to Virgil's *Aeneid* (1st century BC) she fell in love with AENEAS, who was driven by a storm to her shores, and committed herself to the flames through grief at his departure. Older legend says that she did this to avoid marriage with the king of Libya. She is known in some accounts by the alternative name of Elissa.

Porson (*see* DEVIL DICK) said he could rhyme on any subject and when asked to rhyme on the three Latin gerunds, which appeared in the old Eton Latin grammar as -di, -do, -dum, created this couplet:

> When Dido found Aeneas would not come,
> She mourned in silence and was Di-do-dum(b).

**Cut or cut up didoes, To.** *See under* CUT.

**Didymus.** This Greek word for a twin, itself from the prefix *di-*, 'two', repeated twice, was applied to St THOMAS, as the name Thomas in Aramaic means 'twin'.

**Die** (noun). **Die is cast, The.** The step is taken and there is no drawing back. So said Julius CAESAR when he CROSSED THE RUBICON: *alea iacta est!* 'Die' here is probably from Latin *datum*, 'given'.

> I have set my life upon a cast,
> And I will stand the hazard of the die.
> SHAKESPEARE: *Richard III*, V, iv (1592)

**As straight as a die.** *See under* AS.

**Die** (verb). **Died for want of lobster sauce.** A phrase formerly said of a person who dies or suffers severely because of some trifling disappointment, pique or wounded vanity. At a grand feast given by the Great Condé to Louis XIV at Chantilly, Vatel, the chef, was told that the lobsters intended for sauce had not arrived, whereupon he retired to his room and ran his sword through his body, unable to survive the disgrace thus brought upon him.

**Diehards.** In political phraseology, those members of a party who refuse to abandon long-held theories and attitudes regardless of the changes that time and situation may bring. They would rather DIE IN THE LAST DITCH than give way.

**Diehards, The.** *See under* REGIMENTAL AND DIVISIONAL NICKNAMES.

**Die in harness, To.** To die working, while still in active employment or before retirement, like a draught horse that drops dead between the shafts of a cart, or the soldier who dies fighting in harness, i.e. armour.

> Blow, wind! come, wrack!
> At least we'll die with harness on our back.
> SHAKESPEARE: *Macbeth*, V, v (1605)

**Die in one's shoes, To.** To die a violent death, especially one on the scaffold. *See also* DIE IN HARNESS.

> And there is M'Fuze, and Lieutenant Tregooze;
> And there is Sir Carnaby Jenks, of the Blues,
> All come to see a man 'die in his shoes'!
> R.H. BARHAM: *Ingoldsby Legends*, 'The Execution' (1840)

**Die in the last ditch, To.** To fight to the death or last gasp.

> 'There is one certain means,' replied the Prince William of Orange, 'by which I can be sure never to see my country's ruin – I will die in the last ditch.'
> DAVID HUME: *History of England under the House of Tudor* (1759)

*See also* LAST-DITCH ATTEMPT.

**Die like a dog, To.** To have a shameful or miserable end.

**Die like Roland, To.** To die of starvation or thirst. One legend has it that ROLAND escaped the general slaughter in the defile of Roncesvalles and died of hunger and thirst in seeking to cross the Pyrenees. He was buried at Blayes, in the church of St Raymond, but his body was removed afterwards to Roncesvalles.

**Die with one's boots on, To.** To die a violent death, specifically by hanging.

> So I'm for drinking honestly, and dying in my boots.
> JOHN MASEFIELD: *Ballads* (1903)

**Do or die.** *See under* DO.

**Never say die.** *See under* NEVER.

**To die for.** Extremely good; so excellent or desirable that one is prepared to die for it.

**Dies** (Latin, 'day').

**Dies alliensis.** The day when the Romans were cut to pieces by the Gauls (390 BC) near the banks of the River Allia. It was ever after held to be a DIES NEFASTUS or unlucky day.

**Dies irae** (Latin, 'day of wrath'). A medieval

hymn on the LAST JUDGEMENT, probably the composition of Thomas of Celano (in the Abruzzi), who died in 1260. It is derived from the VULGATE version of Zephaniah 1:15 and is used by Roman Catholics in the MASS for the Dead and on ALL SOULS' DAY:

> Dies irae, dies illa,
> Solvet saeclum in favilla,
> Teste David cum Sibylla.
> (That day, the day of wrath,
> Will turn the universe to ashes,
> As David foretells and the Sibyl also.)

**Dies nefastus** (Latin, 'unlawful day'). An unlucky or inauspicious day. For the Romans *dies nefasti* were days on which no judgement could be pronounced nor any public business transacted. *See also* DIES ALLIENSIS.

**Dies non.** A non-business day, a contracted form of Latin *dies non juridicus*, 'non-judicial day', i.e. when the courts do not sit and legal business is not transacted. Such days are SUNDAYS, the Purification (CANDLEMAS) in HILARY TERM, the ASCENSION DAY in EASTER term and All Saints' Day (ALL HALLOWS DAY), with ALL SOULS' DAY in MICHAELMAS term.

**Dieu et mon droit** (French, 'God and my right'). The motto of Richard I at the Battle of Gisors (1198), meaning that he was no vassal of France but owed his royalty to God alone. The French were conclusively beaten, but the battle words do not seem to have been adopted as the royal motto of England until the time of Henry VI.

**Difference.** When Ophelia is distributing flowers (*Hamlet*, IV, v (1600)) and says: 'O! you must wear your rue with a difference', she is using the word in the heraldic sense, probably implying that she and the queen were 'to rue', she as the betrothed of Hamlet, eldest son of the late king, and the queen with 'a difference' as the wife of Claudius, the late king's brother, and so the cadet branch.

In HERALDRY, differences or marks of cadency indicate the various branches of a family. The eldest son, during the lifetime of his father, bears a label, i.e. a bar or fillet having three pendants, often now shaped like a dovetail. The second son bears a crescent; the third, a mullet (a star with five points); the fourth, a martlet (a footless bird); the fifth, an annulet; the sixth, a fleur-de-lis; the seventh, a rose; the eighth, a cross-moline (*see under* CROSSES IN HERALDRY); the ninth, a double quatrefoil.

**Split the difference, To.** *See under* SPLIT.

**Take on a different colour, To.** To look or appear different; to alter.

**Dig. Digger.** An Australian. The name was in use before 1850, consequent upon the discovery of gold, and was applied to ANZAC troops fighting (and digging in) in Flanders in the First World War and again in the Second World War.

> Burly, slouch-hatted, independent and profane, the Digger bestrides the battlefields of Gallipoli and the Western Front just as jauntily as his bronze monument looks down from Mont St Quentin above Péronne. It is integral to the Australian sense of nationhood and national character.
>
> *Times Literary Supplement* (review of Alistair Thomson, *Anzac Memories*) (16 September 1994)

**Diggers.** A small group of extreme radicals and social revolutionaries under Winstanley who began to dig the common at St George's Hill, Surrey in 1649. Their aim was to give back the land to the common people, but they were soon suppressed by the Cromwellian army leaders. *See also* LEVELLERS.

**Diggings** or **digs.** Lodgings, rooms. A word imported from California and its gold diggings.

> 'My friend here wants to take diggings; and as you were complaining that you could get no one to go halves with you, I thought that I had better bring you together.'
>
> SIR ARTHUR CONAN DOYLE: *A Study in Scarlet*, Pt I, ch i (1888)

**Dig in one's heels, To.** To be adamant; to stand one's ground.

**Dig oneself in, To.** To establish one's position, as if digging a defensive trench.

**Digest.** A compendium, synopsis, or summary, especially the Digest of Roman Law, or PANDECTS OF JUSTINIAN, compiled by Tribonian and his 16 assistants (AD 530–533) by order of Justinian.

**Digits** (Latin *digitus*, 'finger'). The first nine numerals are so called from the habit of counting as far as ten on the fingers.

**Dii penates** (Latin, literally 'gods in the store cupboard'). In Roman religion, household gods, who with the *lares* (*see* LARES AND PENATES) were regarded as protectors of the house. The expression has come to be used in modern times for specially prized household possessions.

**Dike.** *See* **Dyke.**

**Dildo.** An artificial substitute for an erect penis. The word may derive from Italian *diletto*, 'delight'.

**Dilemma, The horns of a.** *See under* HORN.

**Diligence.** A four-wheeled stagecoach common in France before the days of the railway. The word meant 'speed', 'dispatch', 'promptitude', as in Shakespeare's 'If your diligence be not speedy I shall be there before you' (*King Lear*, I, v (1605)).

**Dilly-dally, To.** To dawdle; to vacillate. The word is a jingle on 'dally'. A verb of similar meaning is SHILLY-SHALLY. *See also* REDUPLICATED WORDS.

> My old man said, 'Follow the van,
> Don't dilly-dally on the way!'
> Off went the cart with the home packed in it,

> I walked behind with my old cock linnet.
> But I dillied and dallied, dallied and dillied,
> Lost the van and don't know where to roam.
>
> CHARLES COLLINS and FRED W. LEIGH: 'Don't Dilly-Dally on the Way' (song) (1919)

**Dime.** An American ten-cent piece, taking its name from Old French *disme*, 'tithe'.

**Dime novel.** A cheap and lurid publication, formerly obtainable for a dime in the USA. *See also* PENNY-DREADFUL.

**Dimensions.** *See* FOURTH DIMENSION.

**Diminishing Returns, The Law of.** *See under* LAW.

**Dimissory** (Latin *dimittere*, 'to send round'). 'Letters dimissory' are a licence issued by the bishop of one diocese to the bishop of another authorizing the latter to ordain a candidate for holy orders when he himself finds it difficult or imposible to do so. The ordaining bishop must require the candidate to produce such letters.

**Dimity.** A light, strong cotton cloth woven with raised patterns. It is popularly said to be so called because it was originally made in Damietta, in Egypt; in reality, however, the word comes from Greek *dimiton*, 'double thread'. *See also* SAMITE; TWEED.

**Dimsie.** A fictional schoolgirl of the traditional 'jolly hockey sticks' type. She loves games and forms an 'Anti-Soppist Society' opposed to love, sentimentality and the use of cosmetics. She appeared in a lengthy series of stories by Dorita Fairlie Bruce, beginning with *The Senior Prefect* (1921) and was very popular among schoolgirl readers in the 1920s and 30s. Her full name is Dorothy Maitland.

**Dinah.** In the Old Testament (Genesis 34), a daughter of JACOB. When she is raped by a son of Hamor, Jacob's sons pretend to agree to her marriage and peace if Hamor's men will be circumcised. Then, 'when they were sore' (Genesis 34:25), her brothers attacked and killed them all.

**Dine. Dine with Democritus, To.** To be cheated out of one's dinner. DEMOCRITUS was the derider, or philosopher, who laughed at men's folly.

**Dine with Duke Humphrey, To.** To go dinnerless; to have no dinner to go to. The GOOD DUKE HUMPHREY was renowned for his hospitality. On his death it was reported that a monument would be erected to him in St Paul's, but he was buried in St Albans. The tomb of Sir John Beauchamp (d.1358), on the south side of the nave of old St Paul's, was popularly supposed to be that of the duke, and when the promenaders left for dinner, the poor stay-behinds who had no dinner to go to or who feared arrest for debt if they left the precincts, used to say, when asked by the revellers if they were going, that they would 'dine with Duke Humphrey' that day.

The expression was at one time quite common, as was the similar one 'To sup with Sir Thomas Gresham', the Exchange built by Sir Thomas being a common lounge.

> Though little coin thy purseless pocket line,
> Yet with great company thou art taken up;
> For often with Duke Humphrey thou dost dine,
> And often with Sir Thomas Gresham sup.
>
> ROBERT HAYMAN: *Quodlibets*, 'Epigram on a Loafer' (1628)

**Dine with Mohammed, To.** To die and dine in Paradise.

**Dine with the cross-legged knights, To.** To have no dinner at all. The knights referred to are the stone effigies of the TEMPLE church where lawyers once met their clients and where vagabonds loitered in the hope of being hired as witnesses. *See also* CROSS-LEGGED KNIGHTS; DINE WITH DUKE HUMPHREY.

**Dingbat.** A North American and Australian term for a stupid or eccentric person. The origin may be in 'ding' in the sense 'to beat' with 'bat' subsequently associated with BATTY. The word has also been used for various rather vaguely specified objects. In printing and computer jargon dingbats are special characters and symbols, i.e. those that differ from the standard letters and numerals.

**Ding-dong.** A ding-dong battle. A fight in good earnest. 'Ding-dong' is an onomatopoeic word reproducing the sound of a bell. The blows in such a fight fall regularly and steadily, like the hammer strokes of a bell.

**Dinkum.** A word of Australian origin meaning 'genuine', 'sincere', 'honest'. It probably derives from English country dialect, although its origin is unknown. It is often preceded by fair, as: 'a fair dinkum idea'.

**Dinmont.** *See* SHEEP.

**Dinna fash yersel'!** *See under* FASH.

**Dinner, A dog's.** *See under* DOG.

**Dinos** (Greek, 'whirl'). DIOMEDES' horse.

**Dinosaur.** Figuratively, an antiquated system that has not moved with the times, or the chance survivor of a type characteristic of past times. The dinosaurs proper, as reptiles of the Mesozoic era, became extinct some 65 million years ago. Scientists are still debating the cause of their demise. The most widely accepted explanation is that mountains arose in the lowland areas they inhabited, causing changes in the climate that affected the plants on which they fed. A more recent theory is that a comet or asteroid hit the Earth, causing a huge dust cloud. This blocked the sunlight so that photosynthesis was impossible. The plants died out, resulting in a collapse of the food chain. A third school holds that plumes of hot lava rose up from the Earth's centre, causing greenhouse gases to spew into the atmosphere. The creatures could have escaped the lava flows but were unable to survive the changing climate. The name dinosaur represents the Greek for 'terrible lizard' and refers to the gigantic size and fearful appearance of some of the beasts.

**Dint.** In such phrases as 'by dint of argument' or 'by dint of hard work', 'dint' means 'blow', 'striking' (Old English *dynt*). The more concrete 'dent' is of the same origin.

**Diogenes** (Greek, 'born of ZEUS', from *Dios*, genitive of *Zeus*, and *genos*, 'birth', 'origin'). The Greek philosopher (*c*.412–*c*.325 BC) was the founder of the CYNIC sect at Athens and, according to Seneca, lived in a tub in order to show his contempt for the amenities of life. Alexander the Great so admired him that he said: 'If I were not Alexander I would wish to be Diogenes.'

> The whole world was not half so wide
> To Alexander, when he cry'd
> Because he had but one to subdue
> As was a paltry narrow tub to
> Diogenes.
> SAMUEL BUTLER: *Hudibras*, I, iii (1662)

**Diogenes crab.** A West Indian hermit crab, which lives in another creature's shell, like DIOGENES in his tub.

**Diogenes cup.** The cup-like hollow formed by the palm of the hand with closed fingers bent upward. An allusion to the philosopher's simple mode of life, in which he drank by using his hollowed hand as a cup.

**Diomedes** or **Diomed** (Greek, 'thought of ZEUS', from *Dios*, genitive of *Zeus*, and *mēdos*, 'thought'). In Greek legend, a hero of the siege of TROY, second only to ACHILLES in bravery. With ULYSSES he removed the PALLADIUM from Troy. He appears as the lover of CRESSIDA in Boccaccio's *Filostrato* (*c*.1345) and later works.

The name was also that of a king in Thrace, the son of ARES, who fed his horses on human flesh. One of the labours of HERCULES was to destroy Diomedes, and his body was thrown to his own horses to be devoured.

**Diomedean exchange.** One in which all the benefit is on one side. The expression is founded on an incident related in the *Iliad*. GLAUCUS recognizes Diomedes on the battlefield, and the friends change armour:

> For Diomed's brass arms, of mean device,
> For which nine oxen paid (a vulgar price),
> He gave his own, of gold divinely wrought,
> An hundred beeves the shining purchase bought.
> ALEXANDER POPE: *Iliad*, vi (1715–20)

**Dione** (Greek *dios*, 'divine'). The daughter of OCEANUS and TETHYS and mother by JUPITER of VENUS. The name is also applied to Venus herself. Julius CAESAR, who claimed descent from her, was sometimes called Dionoeus Caesar.

> So young Dione, nursed beneath the waves,
> And rocked by Nereids in their coral caves …
> Lisped her sweet tones, and tried her tender smiles.
> ERASMUS DARWIN: *Economy of Vegetation*, ii (1791)

**Dionysia.** *See* BACCHANALIA.

**Dionysius.** *See* DENYS.

**Dionysius' ear.** A large, ear-shaped, underground cave cut in a rock and connected in such a way that Dionysius, the tyrant of Syracuse (431–367 BC), could overhear the conversation of his prisoners from another chamber. A similar whispering gallery exists in the underground passages beneath the remains of Hastings Castle, cut from the solid rock. The listening post is shaped like an ear.

**Dionysus.** *See* BACCHUS.

**Dioscuri** (Greek, 'boys of ZEUS', from *Dios*, genitive of *Zeus*, and *koros*, 'boy'). *See* CASTOR AND POLLUX.

**Horses of the Dioscuri, The.** *See under* HORSE.

**Dip. Dip** or **angle of dip.** The angle between a freely suspended needle and the horizontal. It is zero at the magnetic equator, where the needle rests horizontal, and 90° at the magnetic poles. In geology it is the angle between the horizontal and the line of greatest slope of a stratum.

**Dip a flag, To.** To haul down a flag to a half-mast position and then rehoist it. This is the usual salute between ships at sea. A flag is also flown at the dip as a sign of mourning.

**Dip of the horizon, The.** The apparent slope of the horizon as seen by an observer standing above sea level. This slope is due to the convexity of the earth.

**Dip one's toe in, To.** To start something new; to embark on something unfamiliar. The image is of a bather testing the water by dipping a toe in.

**Dipped in the Shannon, To be.** One who has been dipped in the Shannon, Ireland's longest river, is said to lose all bashfulness.

**Dip snuff, To.** A once prevalent habit in the southern states of the USA of dipping a stick into snuff and smearing it on the teeth and gums.

**Dip the headlights, To.** To lower or dim the headlights of a car, usually when meeting oncoming traffic.

**Farthing dip, A.** *See under* FARTHING.

**Go for** or **have a dip, To.** To go for a brief swim.

**Lucky dip, A.** *See under* LUCKY.

**Diphtheria** (Greek *diphthera*, 'leather'). An infectious disease of the throat, so called from its tendency to form a false membrane.

**Diplomat.** Literally, a person provided with a diploma or letter authorizing them to represent their government abroad. Latin *diploma* literally means 'letter folded double', i.e. in such a way that its contents are kept secret.

**Diplomatic bag.** A bag or other container in which official mail is sent to and from an embassy or consulate. It is not subject to customs inspection.

**Diplomatic cold, illness etc.** An indisposition exploited as a tactful excuse for avoiding a meeting or engagement that one does not wish to attend, ostensibly for diplomatic reasons.

**Diplomatic immunity.** The immunity from arrest, taxation, local jurisdiction (e.g. parking restrictions) and the like, granted to diplomats in a foreign country.

**Diplomatic Revolution.** A phrase applied to the reversal of alliances in 1756 under which Austria, France, Prussia and Britain had fought the War of the Austrian Succession, with the result that, in the ensuing SEVEN YEARS' WAR, France and her former enemy Austria fought against Britain and her former enemy Prussia.

**Diplomatics.** The study of the official sources of history, such as characters, treaties, statutes and registers, as opposed to literary and other sources. The term comes from a special use of the Latin word *diploma* for a historical document. As a modern study it was largely established by the French Benedictine monk Jean Mabillon (1632–1707) in his *De re diplomatica* (1681). His work was extended by Charles-François Toustain and René-Prosper Tassin in their six-volume *Nouveau Traité de Diplomatique* (1750–65).

**Diplomatic service, The.** The division of the CIVIL SERVICE that provides diplomats to represent the United Kingdom abroad.

**Dollar diplomacy.** *See under* DOLLAR.

**Gunboat diplomacy.** *See under* GUN.

**Open diplomacy.** *See under* OPEN.

**Dipper, The.** An old name for the seven principal stars of the constellation URSA MAJOR, the Great Bear, also known as the Plough or CHARLES'S WAIN. The name is derived from the supposed resemblance to the kitchen utensil of this name, a pan with a long handle.

**Big dipper.** *See under* BIG.

**Dircaean Swan.** PINDAR (518–438 BC), so called from the fountain of Dirce near Thebes, the poet's birthplace. Dirce was changed into a fountain by the gods, out of pity for the sufferings inflicted upon her by the sons of Antiope, who were avenging torments she had imposed on their mother.

**Direct. Direct action.** Action such as strikes or civil disobedience, used to attain industrial or political ends, as opposed to industrial or political negotiation and agitation.

**Direct tax.** Taxation such as income tax or land tax collected directly from the individual liable for such tax. Indirect taxes are those, such as VAT (Value Added Tax), which are levied on marketable commodities and services and are thus paid by the citizen indirectly.

**Directory, The.** The French constitution of 4 BRUMAIRE (26 October) 1795, at the end of the CONVENTION PARLIAMENT. It vested the executive authority in five Directors: Paul Barras (1755–1829), Jean-François Rewbell or Reubell (1747–1807), Emmanuel Joseph Sieyès (1748–1836), Louis François Letourneur (1751–1817) and Louis-Marie de la Révellière-Lépeaux (1753–1824). Sieyès retired at the outset and was replaced by Lazare Nicolas Marguerite Carnot (le Grand Carnot) (1753–1823). Its rule was ended by NAPOLEON BONAPARTE's *coup d'état* of 18 Brumaire (9 November) 1799, and the Consulate was established in its place.

**Dirt** (Old Norse *drit*, 'excrement'). The word has extended its sense to include filth generally, soil, dust and the like, as well as obscenity of any kind, especially language.

**Dirt cheap.** At a very low price; as cheap as dirt.

**Dirt-track racing.** Motorcycle racing on a track of cinders or similar material, introduced to England from Australia in 1928.

**Dirty Dick's.** A tavern in Bishopsgate, London, the interior of which is festooned with cobwebs and grimed with dirt. The name was taken from the once famous Dirty Warehouse in Leadenhall Street, owned by Nathaniel Bentley (*c.*1735–1809). He was brought up in easy circumstances and became known as the Beau of Leadenhall Street, but suddenly his mode of life altered completely to one of miserly squalor and he came to be called 'Dirty Dick'. His hardware store became famous for its dirt and decay, which increased with the years, and after his death some of its contents were bought by the tavern keeper to attract custom. His change from a man of fashion to one of slovenliness was reputedly the consequence of a broken engagement.

**Dirty dog, A.** A morally corrupt person, a CAD, a rotter. In the East the dog is still the scavenger of the streets. 'Him that dieth of Jeroboam in the city shall the dogs eat' (1 Kings 14:11).

**Dirty Half-hundred, The.** *See under* REGIMENTAL AND DIVISIONAL NICKNAMES.

**Dirty joke** or **story, A.** A smutty one.

**Dirty look, A.** A look of disapproval, annoyance or disgust.

**Dirty money.** Money acquired by dishonest or disreputable means. Such money can decriminalized by 'laundering' it through a legitimate business such as a bank.

> Lawyers in at least 60 firms are suspected by detectives and customs officers of laundering millions of pounds of dirty money for criminals.
>
> *The Times* (7 December 1998)

**Dirty old man.** A lecherous one, not necessarily old.

**Dirty protest.** A form of protest by prisoners in Northern Ireland in the 1970s. They refused to wash and fouled their cells with the aim of gaining political, as opposed to criminal, status.

**Dirty Shirts, The.** *See under* REGIMENTAL AND DIVISIONAL NICKNAMES.

**Dirty trick.** A malicious and underhand action. The Department of Dirty Tricks is the plans division of the American CIA, so named for its covert intelligence operations.

**Dirty weather.** Bad weather, especially when stormy at sea.

**Dirty weekend.** A weekend of illicit sex.

**Dirty word.** An obscene word, or specifically a person or thing that has become unpopular or suspect, often through unmerited criticism and denigration or from being out of line with current trends.

> To young people compromise is a dirty word.
> DAVID KARP: *Leave me Alone*, ch xx (1957)

**Dirty work at the crossroads.** Foul play; illegal activity. The expression may have arisen from the association with burial at CROSSROADS or from the fact that crossroads were often the scene of foul play.

**Dish the dirt on, To.** *See under* DISH.

**Do the dirty on, To.** *See under* DO.

**Eat dirt, To.** *See under* EAT.

**Pay dirt.** *See under* PAY.

**Treat someone like dirt, To.** *See under* TREAT.

**Wash one's dirty linen in public, To.** *See under* WASH.

**Disastrous Peace, The** (*La Paix Malheureuse*). The Treaty of Cateau-Cambrésis (3 April 1559), essentially between France and Spain. It recognized Spanish supremacy in Italy and involved the renunciation of the VALOIS claims there.

**Disc. Desert Island Discs.** *See under* DESERT.

**Gold disc.** *See under* GOLD.

**Discalced.** *See* BAREFOOTED.

**Discharge Bible, The.** *See under* BIBLE.

**Disciples.** The word is used many times in the New Testament (but only in the Gospels and Acts) both for the 12 apostles, who were the original followers of Jesus, and for a wide range of later followers. The word is from Latin *discipulus*, 'pupil', meaning that those so designated were the 'students' of Jesus. The 12 are listed by name in three of the Gospels (Mark 3, Matthew 10, Luke 6), and although the lists do not entirely agree, in either the names or their order, they are generally held to be as follows: St PETER; St JAMES (THE GREAT) and St JOHN (THE EVANGELIST), the sons of Zebedee; St ANDREW; St PHILIP; St BARTHOLOMEW; St MATTHEW; St THOMAS; St JAMES (THE LESS), the son of Alphaeus; St JUDE (also known as Thaddaeus or Judas), the son or brother of James; St SIMON the Cananaean or Zealot; and JUDAS ISCARIOT. Judas Iscariot was replaced by St MATTHIAS.

**Disciples of Christ.** *See* CAMPBELLITES.

**Discipline.** A scourge used for penitential purposes.

> Before the cross and altar, ... a lamp was still burning, ... and on the floor lay a discipline, or penitential scourge of small cord and wire, the lashes of which were stained with recent blood.
> SIR WALTER SCOTT: *Talisman*, ch iv (1825)

This is a transferred sense of one of the ecclesiastical uses of the word: the mortification of the flesh by penance.

**Books of Discipline.** *See under* BOOK.

**Discord.** Literally, 'severance of hearts', from Latin *discordia*. It is the opposite of 'concord', the coming together of hearts. In music it means disagreement of sounds, as when a note is followed by or played with another that is disagreeable to a musical ear.

**Apple of discord.** *See under* APPLE.

**Discretion, Age of.** *See under* AGE.

**Disease. British disease.** *See under* BRITISH.

**Dutch elm disease.** *See under* DUTCH.

**Foot-and-mouth disease.** *See under* FOOT.

**Legionnaires' disease.** *See under* LEGION.

**Disguise, A blessing in.** *See under* BLESS.

**Dish. Dished.** Exhausted or defeated. The allusion is to food which, when it is quite done, is dished up. *See also* COOK.

**Dish out, To.** To distribute carelessly or indiscriminately.

**Dish the dirt on, To.** To spread gossip about someone or something. The allusion is to gold-mining, in which the prospector swirls the dirt about in his pan to separate out the particles of gold. It is the latter precious metal that is the juicy gossip.

**Dish up, To.** To serve food; to prepare or arrange something attractively. The score of Percy Grainger's popular piece 'Handel in the Strand', originally composed for piano and strings (1911–12), has a note explaining that it was 'dished-up for piano solo' on 25 March 1930 in Denton, Texas.

**Dishy.** Attractive sexually. The notion is that the person is 'tasty' or 'good enough to eat'.

**Clack dish.** *See under* CLACK.

**Disjecta membra** (Latin, 'scattered limbs'). A term used for scattered fragments, as of extracts from different writings. The phrase is an alteration of Horace's *disjecti membra poetae*, 'limbs of a dismembered poet' (*Satires*, Bk I, iv (1st century BC)).

**Dismal science, The.** Economics, so named by Carlyle:

> The social science – not a 'gay science', but a rueful – which finds the secret of this Universe in 'supply

> and demand' what we might call, by way of eminence, the dismal science.
>
> THOMAS CARLYLE: 'On the Nigger Question' (1849)

**Dismas** (Greek *dusmē*, 'sinking', 'dying'). The traditional name of the Penitent Thief, who suffered with Christ at the crucifixion. His relics are claimed by Bologna and in the Roman Martyrology he is commemorated on 25 March. In the apocryphal GOSPEL OF NICODEMUS he is called Dimas (and elsewhere Titus), while the Impenitent Thief is Gestas.

In H.W. Longfellow's *The Golden Legend* (*The Nativity*, v (1851)), Dumachus (Dismas) and Titus both belonged to a band of robbers who harassed the HOLY FAMILY on their flight into Egypt.

**Disorderly house, A.** A brothel.

**Dispatches, Hatches, matches and.** *See under* HATCHES.

**Dispensation** (Latin *dispensatio*, from *dispendere*, 'to weigh out'). The system that God chooses to dispense or establish between himself and man. The dispensation of ADAM was between Adam and God. The dispensation of ABRAHAM and that of MOSES were those imparted to these men. The GOSPEL dispensation is that explained in the Gospels.

**Papal dispensation, A.** *See under* PAPAL.

**Displaced persons.** A phrase applied to the millions of homeless and uprooted people in Europe, India and Asia whose misfortunes resulted from the havoc produced by the Second World War and subsequent events. They were colloquially referred to as DPs.

**Dissenters.** In England, another name for the NONCONFORMISTS, commonly used from the RESTORATION until the 19th century, when it gradually fell into disuse.

**Distaff.** The staff from which the flax was drawn in spinning. Hence, figuratively, woman's work and a woman herself, in allusion to what was women's common daily task. *See also* SPINSTER.

**Distaff side, The.** The female side of a family, or a branch descended from the female side. *See also* SPINDLE SIDE.

**St Distaff's Day.** 7 January. So called because the Christmas festival terminated on TWELFTH NIGHT, and on the day following the women returned to their distaffs or daily occupations. *See also* PLOUGH MONDAY.

> Give S. Distaffe all the right,
> Then bid Christmas sport good night,
>
> ROBERT HERRICK: *Hesperides*, 'St Distaff's Day' (1648)

**Distance. City of Magnificent Distances, The.** *See under* CITY.

**Spitting distance.** *See under* SPIT.

**Distrain, To** (Latin *distringere*, 'to pull asunder', 'to draw tight'). To seize goods for non-payment, to coerce by exacting fines or the like.

**Distraint of knighthood.** The compelling of persons with lands of certain value and tenants of KNIGHTS' fees to become knights and to assume the obligations and liabilities of that rank. It was introduced in the reign of Henry III (1216–72). The fines levied by Charles I on those who neglected this obligation angered many of the gentry. It was abolished by the LONG PARLIAMENT in 1641.

**Distress. Damsel in distress, A.** *See under* DAMSEL.

**Flag of distress.** *See under* FLAG.

**District. Lake District.** *See under* LAKE.

**Peak District.** *See under* PEAK.

**Red-light district.** *See under* RED.

**Ditch. As dull as ditchwater.** *See under* AS.

**Die in the last ditch, To.** *See under* DIE.

**Dithyramb** (Greek *dithurambos*, 'choric hymn'). Dithyrambic poetry was originally a wild, impetuous kind of DORIAN lyric in honour of BACCHUS, traditionally ascribed to the invention of ARION of Lesbos who gave it a more definite form (*c.*600 BC) and who has hence been called the Father of Dithyrambic Poetry.

**Dittany.** The plant *Origanum dictamnus*, perhaps so named from the mountain of Dicte (Díkti) in Crete, where it grew in profusion. It was anciently credited with many medicinal virtues, especially in enabling arrows to be drawn from wounds and in curing such wounds. Godfrey is healed in this way in Tasso's JERUSALEM DELIVERED (Bk ix (1580–1)).

> Stags and hinds, when deeply wounded with darts, arrows and bolts, if they do but meet the herb called dittany, which is common in Candia, and eat a little of it, presently the shafts come out, and all is well again; even as kind Venus cured her beloved by-blow Aeneas.
>
> URQUHART and MOTTEUX: *Rabelais' Works*, Bk IV, ch lxii (1708)

**Ditto** (Italian *detto*, 'said'). That which has been said before, the same or a similar thing. In writing the word is often contracted to 'do'.

**Say ditto, To.** *See under* SAY.

**Divan** (Turkish, from Persian). The word has had various meanings, probably in the following order: (1) a collection of written pages or sheets; (2) a collection of poems; (3) a roll or register of soldiers or the like; (4) a military paybook; (5) a general account book; (6), a counting-house or customs house (whence French *douane*); (7) a tribunal or court; (8) a council chamber; (9) a long seat covered with cushions in such a chamber. The last sense here is the one that survived in English for a backless sofa or couch, or a bed similar to such a couch.

**Divan of the Sublime Porte.** The former

council of the Turkish Empire presided over by the Grand VIZIER.

**Dives.** The name popularly given to the rich man (Latin *dives*) in the parable of the rich man and LAZARUS (Luke 16:19).

**Divide.** When the members in the British HOUSE OF COMMONS interrupt a speaker by crying out 'Divide', they are calling for the debate to be brought to an end and the motion to be put to the vote, i.e. let the ayes divide from the noes, one group going into one LOBBY, and the others into the other. Hence 'Division' as the term for voting in Parliament.

**Divide and rule** (Latin *divide et impera*). Divide a nation into parties or set people at loggerheads, so that you can have your own way or exercise control. The old political maxim was adopted by MACHIAVELLI.

**Cross the great divide, To.** *See under* CROSS.

**Divination.** There are numerous forms of divination. The following appear in the BIBLE: ASTROLOGY (judicial) (Daniel 2:2); CASTING LOTS (*see under* CAST) (Joshua 18:6); HEPATOSCOPY (Ezekiel 21:21); ONEIROMANCY (Genesis 37:5–11); NECROMANCY (1 Samuel 28:7–14); RHABDOMANCY (Hosea 4:12); TERAPHIM (Genesis 31, Zechariah 10:2); and WITCHCRAFT (1 Samuel 28).

There are various other references including divination by fire, air and water, thunder, lightning, meteors etc. For example: Genesis 40 and 41, 2 Kings 27:17, 2 Chronicles 33:6, Proverbs 16:33, Hosea 3:4. *See also* ALECTRYOMANCY; AUGURY; AXINOMANCY; BELOMANCY; BIBLIOMANCY; BOTANOMANCY; CRYSTALLOMANCY; DIVINATION BY CUP; EMPYROMANCY; EXTISPICY; GEOMANCY; GYROMANCY; HARUSPEX; NECROMANCY; OMENS; ORACLE; PALMISTRY; PYROMANCY; RUNE; SCAPULIMANCY; SIEVE AND SHEARS; SORTES; XYLOMANCY.

**Divination by cup.** An ancient method of divination by floating certain articles on a cup of water and reading the signs. The practice survives in fortune-telling with a cup of tea: after the last of the tea is drunk, the pattern of the tea leaves is examined for signs.

> The girls themselves had their omens ... true love-knots lurked in the bottom of every tea-cup.
>
> OLIVER GOLDSMITH: *The Vicar of Wakefield*, ch x (1766)

**Divining rod.** A forked branch of hazel or willow also called *virgula divina*, AARON'S ROD or the wand of Mercury. When manipulated by the diviner or dowser, it bends towards the place where a concealed spring or a metallic lode is to be found. The Romans used the *virgula divina* in AUGURY, and the forked twig, or *virgula furcata*, was introduced into the Cornish mines from Germany in the reign of Elizabeth I. With the decline of mining in the southwest of England, dowsing is now confined to the finding of water.

**Divine, The.** Theophrastus (*c*.372–*c*.287 BC), the philosopher pupil of PLATO; his name means 'one who talks about God', from Greek *Theos*, 'God', and *phrazein*, 'to declare', 'to explain', and he is said to have changed his name from Tyrtamus when this epithet was given him by ARISTOTLE.

The following have also been so called:

Ludovico Ariosto (1474–1533), the Italian poet
Fernando de Herrera (1534–97), the Spanish lyric poet
Hypatia (*c*.370–415), daughter of Theon, who presided over the neo-Platonic school at Alexandria, was known as the Divine Pagan
Michelangelo (1475–1564) was called the Divine Madman
Luis de Morales (*c*.1509–86), the Spanish religious painter
Raphael (1483–1520)
Jean de Ruysbroeck (1293–1381), the ECSTATIC DOCTOR, was also called the Divine Doctor

*See also* St JOHN THE EVANGELIST.

**Divine Astrea, The.** Aphra Behn (1640–89), playwright and novelist, author of *Oroonoko* (*c*.1688), one of the first great English novels written by a woman.

> The stage how loosely does Astrea tread,
> Who fairly puts all characters to bed!
>
> ALEXANDER POPE: *Imitations of Horace*, I, ii (1737)

**Divine Office, The.** The obligatory prayers of the church, said by priests and the religious. The Divine Office (*horae canonicae*) of the Roman Catholic Church is contained in the BREVIARY.

**Divine plant, The.** VERVAIN, *Verbena officinalis*. *See also* HERBA SACRA.

**Divine Right of Kings, The.** The theory, of medieval origin, that kings reign by divine ordination, was first formulated in a rudimentary way during the struggle between the papacy and the empire. It was developed more fully to strengthen the European monarchies when they were later threatened by the activities of religious extremists and others. Monarchy based on primogeniture was held to be divinely anointed, and unquestioning obedience could therefore be demanded from subjects. Monarchs were responsible to God alone and their model was the patriarchal rule portrayed in the Old Testament. The theory was expounded fully by James I in his *True Law of Free Monarchies* (1598) and in Sir Robert Filmer's *Patriarcha* (1642, published 1680). Divine Right was destroyed in Great Britain by the GLORIOUS REVOLUTION of 1688.

> May you, may Cam and Isis, preach it long!
> The Right Divine of kings to govern wrong.
>
> ALEXANDER POPE: *Dunciad*, iv (1728)

**Divine Sarah, The.** Sarah Bernhardt (1844–1923), a French actress of international repute.

Her original name was Henriette-Rosine Bernard.

**Division.** (1) The sign ÷ for division was introduced by John Pell (1611–85), the noted Cambridge mathematician, who became professor of mathematics at Amsterdam in 1643. (2) In the military sense, a division (originated by NAPOLEON BONAPARTE) is the largest formation in an army, so designed as to be self-contained and capable of operating independently. It normally contains infantry, mechanized units, engineers, signals etc. There are also specialized armoured divisions. (3) For division as a parliamentary term, *see* DIVIDE.

**Division of labour.** The division of an employment or manufacture into particular parts so that each individual is concerned with one part or process of the whole. Adam Smith in his *Wealth of Nations* (1776) argued strongly in its favour.

**Divisions.** In the Royal Navy the formal morning parade of officers and ship's company is so called, the custom being introduced by Richard Kempenfelt (1718–82) in 1780. The name derives from the fact that the ship's complement is customarily divided or organized into parts of ship or divisions, usually Quarterdeck, Maintop, Foretop and Forecastle. Divisions are subdivided into WATCHES.

**Divisionist technique.** *See* POINTILLISM.

**Divorcement, Bill of.** *See under* BILL.

**Divot.** *See* FEAL AND DIVOT.

**Divus** (Latin, 'divine'). After the Augustan period this term was conferred as an epithet on deceased Roman emperors proclaiming them 'of blessed memory' rather than enrolling them among the gods.

**Diwali** (Sanskrit *dipavali*, 'row of lights'). A major Hindu festival, held over a five-day period from the 13th day of the 'dark' half of the month Asvina to the 2nd day of the 'light' half of Karttika, corresponding to a period in October in the Gregorian calendar. Lighted oil lamps are placed in rows along the parapets of houses and floated on rivers and streams. The festival commemorates the victory of Lord RAMA over the demon Ravana, who stole Rama's wife, Sita, and Rama's return to Ayodha after 14 years in exile. In Britain, Diwali brings thousands of Hindus to Neasden, Greater London, where one of Europe's leading Hindu temples is located.

> For a Hindu to ignore Diwali ... is equivalent to the rest of us failing to send cards at Christmas.
> *The Times* (17 October 1998)

**Diwan** or **Dewan** (Hindi, from Persian *dēvan*, 'register'). The prime minister or finance minister of an Indian state. *See also* DIVAN.

**Dix.** Former American slang for a ten-dollar bill, apparently derived from the fact that a bank in New Orleans used to issue such bills with the French word *dix* ('ten') printed on the back.

**Dixie** or **Dixieland.** A popular name for the southern states of the USA, south of the MASON-DIXON LINE. One suggestion is that the name originated from DIX. Another is that it derives from Dixieland, the estate of a kind slave-owner, one Dixie, on Manhattan Island, whose slaves lamented him when transferred south. Dixieland also denotes the type of JAZZ played in New Orleans about 1910.

**Dixie.** An army cooking pot. It derives its name from Hindi *degcī*, from Persian *degcā*, a diminutive of *deg*, 'pot'. Its naval counterpart is a 'fanny'.

**Dizzy.** A nickname of Benjamin Disraeli, 1st Earl of Beaconsfield (1804–81), Queen Victoria's favourite Prime Minister. *See also* PRIMROSE DAY.

**Djinn.** *See* JINN.

**Djinnestan.** The realms of the JINNS or genii of Oriental mythology.

**D notice.** An official notice sent to newspapers and the media generally forbidding them from publishing or broadcasting particular security information. D is the initial of the Defence, Press and Broadcasting Committee, the government body that sends out the notice. There were suspicions in the 1980s that the security in question might be that of the government rather than that of the nation.

**Do.** *See* DITTO; DOH.

**Do. Do, A.** A swindle, a fraud; a party, a 'session' of something.

**Do, To.** A verb that forms part of countless phrases and has equally numerous uses. Some modern senses are:

(1) To put, as in 'to do to death'; to bestow, as 'it did him no harm', 'do a good turn'; to perform, to effect, as 'to do one's work', 'Thou shalt do no murder', 'All is done and finished'; to visit as a tourist, as 'to do the cathedral'.

(2) To exert actively, to fare, to suffice, as: 'Let us do or die', 'I have done with you', 'How do you do?' 'Didn't she do well?' 'That will do.'

(3) Used instead of a preceding verb, as: 'He plays as well as you do.' Used as an auxiliary verb, also for the sake of emphasis, euphony or clarity: 'I do wish you would leave me alone', 'Not a word did he say', 'Solving a crossword does pass the time', 'Do you like rock music?' 'I do not wish to say', 'Do tell me where you have been!' 'Don't stop!'

**Do as you would be done by.** The GOLDEN RULE: Behave to others as you would have them behave to you.

**Do away with, To.** To abolish; to put an end to; to destroy entirely.

**Do battle, to.** To enter combat.

**Do bird, To.** To spend a spell in prison. 'Bird' is short for 'birdlime', RHYMING SLANG for 'time'.
**Do down, To.** To cheat or windle; to get the better of.
**Do for, To.** To act for or manage for. A landlady traditionally 'does' for her guests. Also to ruin, to destroy, to wear out. 'I'll do for him' means 'I'll ruin him' or even 'I'll kill him'. 'This heater is about done for' means 'it is nearly worn out'.
**Do it, To.** To do what everyone else is doing; to have sex.

> Everybody's doing it.
> IRVING BERLIN: song title (1911)

**Do-it-yourself.** A post-Second World War phrase applied primarily to the efforts of the amateur house repairer, home improver and the like, but also more widely applied to many forms of self-help. A do-it-yourself (DIY) shop is one that caters for the needs of people who like making and repairing things themselves rather than having someone else do it for them.
**Done for.** Dead, or in serious difficulty.
**Done in.** Physically exhausted.
**Done thing, The.** That which is recognized as socially acceptable and proper. The proper thing to do, as: 'It's not the done thing to make fun of the handicapped.' *See also* POLITICAL CORRECTNESS; U AND NON-U.
**Done to a turn.** Cooked exactly right; another turn on the spit would be too much.
**Do one's best, To.** To do all one can. The call of a WOLF CUB leader to the assembled pack was 'Dyb, dyb, dyb, dyb!', standing for 'Do your best'. The chanted reply was 'We'll dob, dob, dob, dob!' ('Do our best').
**Do one's bit, To.** To make one's contribution.
**Do oneself proud, To.** To give oneself a treat.
**Do one's head in, To.** To harass; to aggravate; to get on one's nerves.
**Do one's homework, To.** To make adequate preparation for the task facing one, especially to acquaint oneself thoroughly with the relevant material for a discussion, debate or speech, as a school pupil is expected to do work at home for the following day or later in the week.
**Do one's level best, To.** To do one's utmost. The expression is said to originate in the Californian gold rush.
**Do one's nut, To.** To fly into a rage or frenzy; to be worked up about something.
**Do one's own thing, To.** To assert one's individuality in one's day-to-day life.
**Do one's stuff, To.** To do what one has to do.
**Do or die, To.** To make a final supreme effort; to try hard until one either wins or loses.

> Their's not to make reply,
> Their's not to reason why,
> Their's but to do and die.
> ALFRED, LORD TENNYSON: 'The Charge of the Light Brigade' (1854)

**Do out of, To.** To cheat or trick, so that a person is deprived of something.
**Do over, To.** To restore or renovate. Also, to attack or beat up.
**Do porridge, To.** A slang expression for serving time in prison. It probably alludes punningly to the earlier slang name 'stir', perhaps with implied reference to prison fare.
**Dos and don'ts.** Recommendations of what to do and not do.
**Do someone in, To.** To kill them.
**Do someone out of, To.** To deprive them unjustly of; to swindle them out of.
**Do someone over, To.** To beat them up.
**Do someone proud, To.** To make much of someone, to treat them in a generous and hospitable way.
**Do something for, To.** To enhance the appearance or quality of something, as: 'That carpet does something for this room'.
**Do something in style, To.** To do it splendidly, regardless of expense.
**Do the dirty on, To.** To be mean or unkindly towards.
**Do the honours, To.** To render necessary civilities; to look after guests, as at a reception or entertainment.
**Do the trick, To.** To achieve the desired result.
**Do to death, To.** To repeat or overuse a joke or similar, so that it no longer has any effect.
**Do up, To.** To repair; to put in order; to renovate. 'This room wants doing up' means that it needs redecorating. Also to fasten a shoelace, a parcel, a button etc.
**Do well for oneself, To.** To prosper.
**Do with, To.** To be glad to have. The phrase is mostly preceded by 'could', as: 'I could do with a break.'
**Do without, To.** To deny oneself something, to manage without it. Preceded by 'can' or 'could' the phrase has the sense of wishing oneself free of the person or thing mentioned, as: 'I can do without their phone calls.'
**Have done, To.** To finish, as in the expression 'Have you done?'
**Have done with, To.** To end relations with.
**Have to do with, To.** To have dealings with; to be connected with. 'That has nothing to do with it' means 'it is irrelevant'.
**How do you do?** A polite enquiry when being introduced to someone. The words are properly repeated by way of a response.

> If anyone greets you with 'How do you do?', the

reply is 'How d'you do?' and not 'I'm very well, thank you' or words to that effect.
GUY EGMONT: *The Art of Egmontese* (1961)

**Make do, To.** To manage; to get by; to improvise.
**Nothing doing.** *See under* NOTHING.
**That's done it.** An exclamation of satisfaction ('That's finished it') or annoyance ('That's torn it').

**Dobbin.** A steady old horse, a child's horse. The name is a form of Robin, itself a pet form of Robert.

**Docetes** (Greek *Dokētai*, from *dokein*, 'to seem', 'to appear'). An early GNOSTIC sect, which maintained that Jesus Christ was divine only and that his visible form, involving the crucifixion and resurrection, were merely illusions. Christ had no real body on earth, they said, but only a phantom body.

**Doch-an-doris** (Gaelic *deoch-an-doruis*, 'drink at the door'). A Scottish term for a STIRRUP CUP or a final drink before departing, made familiar in England by one of Sir Harry Lauder's songs.

After the lord keeper, the Master, and the domestics, had drunk doch-an-dorroch, or the stirrup cup ... the cavalcade resumed its progress.
SIR WALTER SCOTT: *The Bride of Lammermoor*, ch xviii (1819)

**Dock. Dock brief.** When a prisoner in the dock pleads inability to employ counsel, the presiding judge can instruct a BARRISTER present in court to undertake the defence, a fee for this being paid by the court.
**Dock defence.** The instruction of counsel by a prisoner in the dock without the aid of a solicitor.
**In the dock.** On trial; under criticism or attack.

[Tony] Blair in the dock over 'cronyism'
*The Times* (headline) (9 July 1998)

**Docklands.** London's dockland region has changed dramatically since the flourishing trade of the 18th and 19th centuries, when the British Empire was expanding and the Thames was full of cargo vessels of all types, with the enclosed docks handling hundreds of ships a year. The docks were originally in private hands, but were taken over by the Port of London Authority in 1909. By the end of the 1960s the docks began to close, partly as a result of the demise of the empire, but also because of competition from other ports, labour troubles and other adverse factors. In the mid-1970s it was proposed to redevelop the dockland site for commercial and residential use, and in 1981 the London Docklands Development Corporation was set up to oversee this. By 1990 areas such as the Surrey Commercial Docks and Isle of Dogs had been transformed, as had Canary Wharf, now a massive office development. The area is served by the Docklands Light Railway, which opened in 1987 and links with the main Underground system. The whole enterprise has not been without its financial fiascos, exacerbated by the recession of the early 1990s, and some developers were unable to sell their completed schemes.

**Doctor** (Latin, 'teacher', 'instructor'). One who has obtained the highest university degree (a doctorate) in any faculty, such as arts, science, law or medicine. In common parlance a doctor is a medical practitioner, whether or not in possession of a doctorate. Because the doctor of medicine was most widely known, the title came to be applied generally to members of the medical profession.

'Now, if you are dying and call in some Dr So-and-so, you may find him a young fellow of three or four and twenty. As likely as not only an M.B. in reality, who has arrogated to himself the title of Doctor. For I hear some of them do it.'
MRS HENRY WOOD: *Johnny Ludlow* (4th Series) *Roger Bevere*, ii (1880)

To doctor a substance is to treat it in a way that makes it seem better or stronger than it is, or that alters its effect.
**Doctor a cat, To.** To neuter it, i.e. to 'cut' or castrate it.
**Doctor an account, To.** To falsify it.
**Dr Brighton.** *See under* BRIGHTON.
**Dr Dee.** *See under* DEE.
**Dr Dolittle.** *See under* DOLITTLE.
**Dr Fell.** *See under* FELL.
**Dr Jekyll and Mr Hyde.** *See under* JEKYLL.
**Dr Pangloss.** *See under* PANGLOSS.
**Dr Sangrado.** *See under* SANGRADO.
**Doctors' Commons.** The colloquial name for the College of Advocates and Doctors of Law, formerly situated near St Paul's Cathedral, London. From 1572 it housed the ecclesiastical and Admiralty courts, and the name arose from the fact that the doctors had to dine there four days in each term. The College ceased to function in the mid-19th century, and the buildings were demolished in 1867.
**Doctors of the Church.** Certain early Christian Fathers and other saints whose doctrinal writings gained special acceptance and authority.
In the Eastern Church they were:

St Athanasius, who defended the divinity of Christ against the ARIANS
St Basil the Great
St Gregory of Nazianzus
St JOHN CHRYSOSTOM

In the Western Church they were:

St Alphonsus Liguore
St AMBROSE
St Anselm of Canterbury
St AUGUSTINE of Hippo
St BERNARD of Clairvaux
St Bonaventura

St Francis de Sales
St GREGORY THE GREAT
St Hilary
St JEROME
St THOMAS AQUINAS

**Dr Syntax.** *See under* SYNTAX.
**Doctor Who.** *See under* WHO.
**Admirable Doctor.** *See under* ADMIRABLE.
**Angelic Doctor.** *See under* ANGEL.
**Apple a day keeps the doctor away, An.** *See under* APPLE.
**Authentic Doctor.** *See under* AUTHENTIC.
**Barefoot doctor.** *See under* BARE.
**Cape doctor, The.** *See under* CAPE.
**Ecstatic Doctor, The.** *See under* ECSTASY.
**Just what the doctor ordered.** *See under* JUST.
**Nicknamed doctors.** *See under* NICKNAME.
**Resolute Doctor, The.** *See under* RESOLUTE.
**Seraphic Doctor, The.** *See under* SERAPHIC.
**Spin doctor.** *See under* SPIN.
**Subtle Doctor, The.** *See under* SUBTLE.
**Wonderful Doctor, The.** *See under* WONDER.
**You're the doctor.** It is for you to say; the decision is yours.

**Dodge. Dodge the column, To.** To avoid one's duties or allotted tasks. The expression originated as army slang. A soldier may be counted as present when mustered for a task but then slope off unobserved as the column leaves the parade ground.

**Artful Dodger.** *See under* ARTFUL.
**Devil dodger.** *See under* DEVIL.

**Dodo** (Portuguese *doudo*, 'silly'). *Raphus cucullatus*, a large, flightless bird about the size of a turkey and related to the pigeon, which was last known to exist in Mauritius in the 1680s.

**As dead as the dodo.** *See under* AS.

**Dodona.** The site of a most ancient ORACLE of Epirus, dedicated to ZEUS. The oracles were delivered from the tops of oak trees, the rustling of the leaves being interpreted by the priests. The cooing of the sacred pigeons and the clanging of brass plates suspended in the trees when the wind blew gave further signs to the priests and priestesses. The Greek phrase *khalkos Dōdōnēs*, 'brass of Dodona', meaning a babbler, probably stems from this.

**Black pigeons of Dodona, The.** *See under* BLACK.

**Doe. John Doe and Richard Roe.** Any plaintiff and defendant in a former action of ejectment (brought by a wrongfully dispossessed owner seeking to recover possession of his land). They were sham names used to save certain 'niceties of law'. This legal fiction was abolished by the Common Law Procedure Act, 1852. The names JOHN-A-NOKES and John-a-Stiles were similarly used.

**Dog.** In addition to its literal sense, as in dog biscuit, dog is used in combination to denote the male of certain animals, as dog ape, dog fox and dog otter; to denote inferior plants or those that are worthless as food, as dog briar, dog cabbage, DOG GRASS, dog leek, dog lichen, dog's mercury, dog parsley, DOG ROSE, dog violets (scentless) and dog wheat; or to express spuriousness or some mongrel quality, as dog's logic and DOG LATIN.

**Dog, The.** DIOGENES (412–323 BC). When Alexander the Great of Macedon went to see Diogenes he introduced himself with these words: 'I am Alexander, surnamed the Great.' To which the philosopher replied: 'And I am Diogenes, surnamed the Dog.' The Athenians raised to his memory a pillar of Parian marble, surmounted by a dog. *See also* CYNIC.

**Dogcart.** A light one-horse trap, popular for informal country use in Victorian and Edwardian times, originally designed for carrying sportsmen's dogs. Also the name of a small cart drawn by dogs.

**Dog cheap.** Extremely cheap; DIRT CHEAP.

**Dog collar.** As well as its literal meaning, this is the popular name for a clergyman's 'back to front' collar. Also the ornamental band or collar worn close to the throat by women.

**Dog days.** Days of great heat. The Romans called the hottest weeks of the summer *caniculares dies*. Their theory was that the DOG STAR, rising with the sun, added to its heat and that the dog days (about 3 July to 11 August) bore the combined heat of both.

**Dog-ears.** The corners of pages crumpled and folded down. Dog-eared pages are so crumpled, like the turned-down ears of many dogs.

**Dog eat dog.** Ruthless competition.

**Dog-end.** A cigarette end.

**Dogfight.** Apart from the literal sense, the word came to apply to a close quarters combat between fighter aircraft. It can also be used generally for any 'scrap'.

**Doggone.** An American EUPHEMISM for God damn.

> But when that choir got up to sing.
> I couldn't catch a word;
> They sang the most doggonest thing
> A body ever heard!
>
> WILLIAM CARLETON: *Farm Ballads* (1873)

**Dog grass.** Couch grass (*Triticum repens*), which is eaten by dogs when they have lost their appetite. It acts as an emetic and purgative.

**Doggy bag.** A bag into which the remains of a meal are put, ostensibly to give to a dog but usually for the eater's own consumption.

**Doghouse, The.** To be in the doghouse is to be in disgrace, as a dog is confined to his kennel. The phrase is traditionally applied to a husband who has been misbehaving or has displeased his wife and is thus in disgrace or trouble. In J.M. Barrie's

PETER PAN (1904) Mr Darling lived in the dog kennel until his children returned, as a penance for his treatment of NANA.

**Dog in the manger, A.** A mean-spirited individual who will not use what is wanted by another, nor yet let the other have it to use; a person who prevents another enjoying something but does not enjoy it himself. The allusion is to the fable of the dog that made his home in a manger. He would not allow the ox to come near the hay but would not eat it himself.

**Dog in the night-time, A.** An unconscious conniver; an unwitting party to a crime. The reference is to the dog in Sir Arthur Conan Doyle's story *Silver Blaze* (1892), which did not bark in the night because it knew the man who took the horse from the stables. The exchange between Sherlock Holmes and Inspector Gregory is famous:

> 'Is there any point to which you would wish to draw my attention?'
> 'To the curious incident of the dog in the night-time.'
> 'The dog did nothing in the night-time'.
> 'That was the curious incident', remarked Sherlock Holmes.

**Dog Latin.** Spurious or 'mongrel' Latin, in which English words are treated like Latin, and Latin words like English, with sometimes embarrassing results.

> 'Nescio quid est materia cum me' [I don't know what is the matter with me], Sterne writes to one of his friends (in dog-Latin, and very sad dog-Latin too).
>
> W.M. THACKERAY: *English Humourists of the Eighteenth Century*, ch vi (1851)

**Dogleg.** A sharp bend like that in a dog's hind leg.

**Dog of God, The.** So the Laplanders call the bear, which 'has the strength of ten men and the wit of twelve'.

**Dog of Montargis, The.** *See* AUBRY'S DOG.

**Dog** or **doggy paddle.** A simple swimming stroke in which the swimmer paddles his hands like the front legs of a swimming dog.

**Dog rose.** The common wild rose (*Rosa canina*, Pliny's *kunorrodon*), so called because its root was believed by the ancient Greeks to cure the bite of mad dogs.

**Dogsbody.** A drudge; one who is generally exploited and used as a menial.

**Dog's dinner** or **breakfast, A.** A mess or muddle.

**Dogs howl at death.** A widespread superstition.

> In the Rabbinical Book, it saith
> The dogs howl, when with icy breath
> Great Sammaël, the Angel of Death,
> Takes through the town his flight!
>
> H.W. LONGFELLOW: *Golden Legend*, III, viii (1851)

**Dogs in classics and legend.** Among the better known dogs of myth and legend are:

Arctophonos (Greek, 'bear killer') and Ptoöphagos ('glutton of Ptous', a young man about whom little is known): the dogs of ORION
Argos (Greek, 'shining', 'bright'): the dog of Odysseus (ULYSSES), which recognized his master after his return from TROY and died of joy
Bran: FINGAL's dog
Cavall (Celtic, 'horse'): King ARTHUR's favourite hound
Dragon: AUBRY'S DOG
Gargittios (perhaps from Greek *gorgos*, 'fearful') and the two-headed Orthos ('straight'): GERYON's dogs, both of which were slain by HERCULES
Gelert: Llewelyn's greyhound; *see also* BEDDGELERT
Hodain or Leon ('lion'): TRISTRAM's dog
KRATIM (Katmir): the dog of the SEVEN SLEEPERS which, according to Muslim tradition, was admitted to Paradise
Laelaps (Greek *lailaps*, 'whirlwind'): Procris' dog
Luath (Irish, 'swift'): CUCHULAIN's hound
Mauthe dog: *see* MODDEY DHOO
Moera (Greek *marmareos*, 'sparkling', 'glistening'): ICARIUS' dog
Theron (perhaps Greek *thēr*, 'wild beast'): the dog of RODERICK the Goth

**Dogs in effigy.** In funeral monuments a dog in effigy is usually a memento of the dead person's pet and has no symbolical significance. However, where an effigy rests its feet on an animal, a lion usually indicates a man and a dog a woman.

**Dogs in medieval art.** Dogs frequently symbolize fidelity in medieval art. A dog is represented as lying at the feet of St BERNARD, St Benignus and St Wendelon, as licking the wounds of St ROCH and as carrying a lighted torch in representations of St DOMINIC. *See also* CEPHALUS AND PROCRIS.

**Dog sleep.** A pretended sleep, or a light, easily broken sleep. Dogs seem to sleep with 'one eye open'.

**Dog's life, A.** A miserable existence.

**Dog's nose.** Gin and beer, or some other mixture of alcohol.

> 'Dog's-nose, which your committee find upon inquiry, to be compounded of warm porter, moist sugar, gin and nutmeg.'
>
> DICKENS: *Pickwick Papers*, ch xxxiii (1836–7)

**Dogs of noted people and in literature.**

BOATSWAIN: Byron's favourite dog
Bounce: Alexander Pope's dog
Boy: Prince Rupert's dog, killed at the Battle of Marston Moor (1664)
Brutus: Landseer's greyhound, jocularly called 'The Invader of the Larder'
Dash: Charles Lamb's dog; also, the much-loved spaniel of the young Queen Victoria
DIAMOND: Sir Isaac Newton's dog
Flush: Elizabeth Barrett Browning's dog
Geist (German, 'ghost', 'spirit'): one of Matthew Arnold's dachshunds; he wrote the poem 'Geist's Grave' (1881) in its memory
Giallo (Italian, 'yellow'): Walter Savage Landor's dog
GREYFRIARS BOBBY
Hamlet: Sir Walter Scott's black greyhound

Kaiser: another of Matthew Arnold's dachshunds, commemorated in his last poem, 'Kaiser Dead' (1887); *see also* GEIST *above*
Luath (Gaelic, 'swift', 'nimble'): the favourite of Robert Burns
Lufra (perhaps Gaelic *lùthmhor*, 'strong', 'agile'): the hound of Douglas in Sir Walter Scott's *The Lady of the Lake* (1810)
MAIDA: Sir Walter Scott's favourite deerhound
Mathe ('Matthew'): Richard II's greyhound which left him in favour of Bolingbroke
NANA: Mr and Mrs Darling's dog, which is the children's nurse (nana) in J.M. Barrie's PETER PAN (1904)
Rufus: Sir Winston Churchill's poodle
St Bernard dogs: *see* BERNARD PASSES
TOBY: Mr Punch's famous dog

**Dogs of war, The.** The horrors of war, especially fire, sword and famine.

> Cry 'Havoc!' and let slip the dogs of war.
> SHAKESPEARE: *Julius Caesar*, III, i (1599)

**Dog star.** SIRIUS, the brightest star in the firmament in the constellation of the Big Dog, Alpha Canis Majoris. *See also* DOG DAYS.

**Dog tags.** Identity discs of members of the US armed forces in the Second World War.

**Dog-tired.** Exhausted, usually after exercise or hard manual labour, and wanting only to curl up like a dog and go to sleep.

**Dogtrot.** A gentle jog or trot.

**Dogwatch.** Two-hour watches (4–6 pm and 6–8 pm) instead of the usual four-hour watches introduced to enable seamen to vary their daily watch-keeping rota. Among various suggested origins are that it is a 'docked' or shortened watch or a corruption of 'dodge' watch. *See also* WATCH.

**Dog whipper.** A minor church officer of the days when sheepdogs, turnspits and others accompanied their owners to church. His job was to keep order among the canine congregation, to eject the badly behaved and to exclude troublesome dogs generally. Whips and dog-tongs were used. The office became redundant in the 19th century, but even as late as 1856 John Pickard was appointed dog whipper in Exeter Cathedral.

**Dog-whipping Day.** 18 October (St LUKE's Day). It is said that a dog once swallowed a consecrated wafer on this day.

**As pleased as a dog with two tails.** *See under* AS.

**As sick as a dog.** *See under* AS.

**Black dog.** *See under* BLACK.

**Black dog has walked over him, A.** *See under* BLACK.

**Aubry's dog.** *See under* AUBRY.

**Call off the dogs, To.** *See under* CALL.

**Carriage dog.** *See under* CARRIAGE.

**Dead dog, A.** *See under* DEAD.

**Derby dog.** *See under* DERBY.

**Die like a dog, To.** *See under* DIE.

**Dirty dog.** *See under* DIRTY.

**Every dog has his day.** *See under* EVERY.

**Gay dog, A.** *See under* GAY.

**Give a dog a bad name and hang him.** If you smear a person's reputation they are as good as condemned.

**Go to the dogs, To.** To go to ruin, morally or materially. Food unsuitable for human consumption used to be given to the dogs.

**Gun dog.** *See under* GUN.

**Hair of the dog that bit you, The.** *See under* HAIR.

**Help a lame dog over a stile, To.** *See under* HELP.

**Hot dog.** *See under* HOT.

**Hunt's dog.** *See under* HUNT.

**I am his Highness' dog at Kew; Pray tell me sir, whose dog are you?** Frederick Louis, Prince of Wales (1707–51), had a dog given him by Alexander Pope, and these words are said to have been engraved on his collar. They are sometimes quoted with reference to an overbearing, bumptious person.

**Isle of Dogs, The.** *See under* ISLE.

**Is thy servant a dog?** *See under* SERVANT.

**Keep a dog and bark oneself, To.** To do something that one has engaged another person to do. The expression is more common in the negative: 'I don't keep a dog and bark myself' means 'I am not going to do what I am paying someone else to do.'

> 'What time is it?' There was a clock right opposite him on the dining-room wall but Dover didn't believe in keeping a dog and barking himself. 'Just gone nine, sir.'
> JOYCE PORTER: *Dover Two*, ch xi (1965)

**Lazy dog.** *See under* LAZY.

**Lead a cat and dog life, To.** *See under* LEAD.

**Lead a dog's life, To.** *See under* LEAD.

**Let sleeping dogs lie.** *See under* LET.

**Lie doggo, To.** *See under* LIE.

**Like a dog with two tails.** *See under* LIKE.

**Lovell the Dog.** *See* RAT, CAT AND DOG.

**Love me, love my dog.** *See under* LOVE.

**More I see of men the more I love dogs, The.** *See under* MORE.

**Not a dog's chance, A.** No chance at all.

**Put on the dog, To.** To behave pretentiously.

**Rain cats and dogs, To.** *See under* RAIN.

**Sea dog.** *See under* SEA.

**See a man about a dog, To.** *See under* SEE.

**Shaggy dog story.** *See under* SHAGGY.

**Spotted dog.** *See under* SPOT.

**Surly dog, A.** *See under* SURLY.

**Tail wags the dog, The.** *See under* TAIL.

**Throw it to the dogs.** *See under* THROW.

**Top dog.** *See under* TOP.

**Yellow dog contracts.** *See under* YELLOW.

**You can't teach an old dog new tricks.** *See under* TEACH.

**You're a sly dog.** *See under* SLY.

**Dogberry.** An officious and ignorant JACK-IN-OFFICE. The allusion is to the ignorant, self-satisfied, overbearing but good-natured night constable of this name in Shakespeare's *Much Ado about Nothing* (1598).

**Doge** (Venetian dialect, ultimately from Latin *dux*, 'leader'). The chief magistrate of the Venetian Republic (*c*.700–1797). The first doge, according to tradition, was Paoluccio Anafesto (d.717), and the last Ludovico Manin (d.1797). *See also* BRIDE OF THE SEA.

The chief magistrate of Genoa was also called a doge. The first was Simone Boccanegra (1339), the last Giacomo Durazzo (1805).

**Doggett's Coat and Badge.** The prize given in an annual rowing match for Thames watermen held under the auspices of the Fishmongers' Company in July. It is so called from Thomas Doggett (1670–1721), a comic actor of DRURY LANE, who marked the accession of George I by instituting the race in 1715. It is from the Swan Steps at London Bridge to Cadogan Pier at Chelsea, a distance of 4½ miles (7.2km). The coat is an orange-coloured livery jacket.

**Dogie.** In the western USA the term for a neglected calf. At round-up time all motherless calves were called dough-guts, which became contracted into dogie. The original name refers to the flour and water paste with which they were fed.

> Whoopee ti yi yo, git along, little dogies,
> It's your misfortune and none of my own,
> Whoopee ti yi yo, git along, little dogies,
> For you know Wyoming will be your new home.
> Anonymous cowboy song

**Doh** or **Do.** The first or tonic note of the solfeggio system of music. *See also* ARETINIAN SYLLABLES; TONIC SOL-FA.

**Doily, doyly** or **doyley.** A small ornamental mat of lace or lace-like paper, laid on or under cake plates and the like. In the 17th century the word denoted a kind of woollen material, so that John Dryden, in *The Kind Keeper* (IV, i (1678)), speaks of 'Doily Petticoats', and Joseph Addison in No. 102 of the *Guardian* (1713) writes of his 'Doily suit'. The Doyleys, from which the stuff was named, were linen drapers in the Strand, London, from the time of Queen Anne until 1850. Doilies are now regarded as rather 'genteel'.

> Beg pardon, I'm soiling the doileys
> With afternoon tea-cakes and scones.
> JOHN BETJEMAN: 'How to get on in Society' (1954)

**Doister, Ralph Roister.** *See under* RALPH.

**Dolce. Dolce far niente** (Italian, 'sweet doing nothing'). Blissful idleness.

**Dolce vita** (Italian, 'sweet life'). A life of luxury and self-indulgence. The expression became familiar following Fellini's successful film *La Dolce Vita* (1960), centring on modern Roman high society.

**Doldrums, The.** A condition of depression, slackness or inactivity. The word was applied by sailors to regions where ships were likely to be becalmed and especially those parts of the ocean near the equator that are noted for calms and light winds. The word seems to have originated in Old English *dol*, 'dull', influenced by tantrum.

**Dole** (Old English *dāl*, 'share'). A portion allotted; a charitable gift; alms. From Saxon times the strips of land, especially of common meadow, distributed annually were called doles. Since the National Insurance Act of 1911, it has become the everyday term for unemployment benefit. A person 'on the dole' is one receiving this state payment.

**Tichborne dole.** *See under* TICHBORNE.

**Dolittle, Dr.** The genial and eccentric doctor who is the central character of the stories by Hugh Lofting (1886–1947). He has the special gift of speaking the language of most animals and eventually gives up his human practice to become an 'animal doctor'.

**Doll. Barbie Doll.** *See under* BARBIE.

**Corn dolly.** *See under* CORN.

**Dollar.** The sign $ is possibly a modification of the figure 8 as it appeared on the old Spanish 'pieces of eight', which were of the same value as the dollar. However, various other derivations have been proposed, most notably that it is the U of the United States superimposed on the S.

In pre-metric colloquial English a dollar was a CROWN or five shilling piece and half a dollar was a half crown and sometimes a two shilling piece.

The word is a variant of 'thaler' (Low German *daler*) and means 'valley' (English 'dale'). At the close of the 15th century the Counts of Schlick coined pieces from the silver extracted from the mines at Joachimsthal ('Joachim's valley', now Jáchymov, in the Czech Republic). These pieces, called 'Joachimsthaler', gained such repute that they became standard coin. Other coins made like them came to be called thalers.

Bank of England dollars were struck as bank tokens in 1797 and subsequently. Dollars were first coined in the USA in 1794.

**Dollar diplomacy.** A term applied to governmental support and furtherance of commercial interest abroad for both political and economic ends. The phrase, popular with critics of American policy, stems from the Taft administration (1909–13), which fostered such policies in the Far East and Latin America. Their intention was to control as well as to promote enterprise abroad by substituting dollars for bullets and lending 'all proper support to every legitimate and beneficial American enterprise abroad'.

**Almighty dollar, The.** *See under* ALMIGHTY.

**Bet one's bottom dollar on, To.** *See under* BET.
**Sword dollar.** *See under* SWORD.
**Trade dollar.** *See under* TRADE.

**Dolly. Dolly bird.** An attractive and stylish young woman.

**Dolly drop.** In CRICKET a full toss bowled in a slow high arc, so called because it is easy to hit. A dolly is also an easy catch.

**Dolly mixture.** A mixture of tiny, coloured sweets, such as a doll might eat.

**Dolly tub.** A wash-tub, the predecessor of the modern washing machine, so named for the dolly or revolving wooden disc with projecting dowels that stirred up its contents and was manually operated.

**Dolly Varden.** A woman's large-brimmed hat trimmed with flowers, so named after the character in Charles Dickens' *Barnaby Rudge* (1841), who wore one.

> As to Dolly, there she was again ... in a smart little cherry-coloured mantle, with a hood of the same drawn over her head, and ... a little straw hat trimmed with cherry-coloured ribbons.
> ch xix

**Dolmen.** A word of Celtic origin meaning literally 'stone table', the equivalent of the Welsh CROMLECH. The name is particularly used in Brittany. They are often called Devils' tables, fairies' tables and the like.

**Constantine Dolmen, The.** *See under* CONSTANTINE.

**Dolphin.** The dolphin in medieval art symbolizes social love. *See also* DAUPHIN.

**Dom** (Latin *dominus*, 'lord'). A title applied in the Middle Ages to the pope and later to other church dignitaries. It is now largely restricted to monks of the BENEDICTINE and CARTHUSIAN Orders. The Spanish word *Don* is of the same origin.

**DOM.** An abbreviation of Latin *Deo Optimo Maximo*, 'To God the best the greatest', or of *Datur omnibus mori*, 'It is allotted to all to die.' In the former sense it is inscribed on bottles of BENEDICTINE.

**Domboc.** *See* DOOM.

**Domdaniel.** A fabled abode of evil spirits, GNOMES and enchanters 'under the roots of the ocean' off Tunis, or elsewhere. It first appears in Chaves and Gazotte's *Continuation of the Arabian Nights* (1788–93), was introduced by Robert Southey into his *Thalaba the Destroyer* (1801) and used by Thomas Carlyle as synonymous with a den of iniquity. The word is made up from Latin *domus*, 'house', and *Danielis*, 'of Daniel', the latter being taken as a magician.

**Domesday Book.** The record of a survey of England begun in 1085 by order of WILLIAM THE CONQUEROR. It is written in Latin and originally consisted of two volumes: one (Great Domesday) containing most of England, the other (Little Domesday) only Essex, Suffolk and Norfolk, but in greater detail. The counties of Northumberland, Cumberland, Westmorland and Durham were omitted, and neither London nor Winchester is included. In 1986 the two volumes were redivided into five for ease of accessibility. Domesday Book was formerly kept in the EXCHEQUER, but is now housed in the Public Record Office.

Details of the ownership, extent, value, population, stock and so on of all holdings are given for the time of Edward the Confessor (1042–66) and also at the time of the survey. The value is also given for the time of the Conquest. The record was long used for taxation purposes and as a general governmental reference book. Domesday Book was published in a definitive English translation in 35 volumes by Phillimore, a specialist local history publisher, over the ten years from 1975. The title of the work refers to the fact that the record was regarded as a final and irrevocable authority, against which there was no appeal any more than there was against Doomsday.

The following is a manorial description of St Kew, Cornwall, from Great Domesday:

> ST KEW. 5 h[ides], but it paid for tax 2 h. Land for 22 ploughs; in lordship 1 h; 2 ploughs; 8 slaves. 59 villagers and 26 smallholders with 20 ploughs & 4 h. Meadow, 1 acre; pasture 40 acres; woodland, 1 league long and 3 f[urlongs] wide. It pays £6 weighed and assayed. 9 cattle; 120 sheep. Two manors, POUNDSTOCK and ST GENNYS, have been taken from this manor. 1½ h. Land for 12 ploughs. Iovin holds them from the Count of Mortain. Formerly 60s; value now 40s.

*See also* EXON DOMESDAY.

**Dominations.** *See* DOMINIONS.

**Domine, quo vadis?** (Latin, 'Master, whither goest thou?'). According to tradition, when St PETER was fleeing from NERO's persecution in Rome, he met Christ on the APPIAN WAY and greeted him with these words. The reply, *Venio Romam, iterum crucifigi* ('I am coming to Rome to be crucified again'), so shamed the apostle that he returned to martyrdom in Rome. The meeting is commemorated by a church on the Appian Way. He is said to have requested to be crucified head downwards and to have given this account when nailed upon the cross. The story is found in the Gnostic Acts and other texts and is featured in a historical novel by Henryk Sienkiewicz, *Quo Vadis?* (1896).

**Dominic.** The saint's original name was Domingo de Guzmán (1170–1221). He was the founder of the Dominican Order, or Preaching Friars, and was noted for his vehemence against the ALBIGENSES. He was canonized by Gregory IX. He is represented with a sparrow at his side and a dog carrying in its mouth a burning torch. It is said that the Devil appeared to him in the form of a sparrow. The dog refers to his mother's dream, during her pregnancy, that she had given birth to a dog that lighted the world with a burning torch.

**Dominicans.** The order of preaching friars founded by St DOMINIC in 1215, their rule being based on that of St AUGUSTINE. Their first home in England was at Oxford (1221). They gained the name of BLACK FRIARS and in France they were called JACOBINS. They were also called *Domini canes*, 'Hounds of the Lord'. Albertus Magnus, St THOMAS AQUINAS and Savonarola were representatives of an order notable for its intellectual distinction.

**Dominical letters** or **Sunday letters.** The first seven letters of the alphabet used in calendars, almanacs and the like to mark the Sundays throughout the year (Latin *Dominica Dies*, 'the Lord's Day', 'Sunday'). If 1 January is a Sunday, the Dominical letter for the year will be A, if 2 January is a Sunday it will be B and so on. Dominical letters are used for finding on what day of the week any day of the month falls in any particular year and thus for determining EASTER. Tables and instructions are found in prayer books, breviaries and similar manuals of devotion.

**Dominions.** The sixth of the nine orders in the medieval hierarchy of angels, also known as Dominations and symbolized in art by an ensign. *See also* ANGEL.

From the formation of the Dominion of Canada (1867) the word also came to be applied to the self-governing units of the British Empire as they were formed and their relations with the mother country were handled by the Dominions Office. As the word 'empire' came to be replaced by that of COMMONWEALTH, the Dominions Office became the Commonwealth Relations Office in 1947 and the Commonwealth Office in 1966, which was combined with the Foreign Office in 1968.

**Old Dominion, The.** *See under* OLD.

**Domino.** The word originally applied to a hooded clerical cloak and subsequently to a hooded garment worn at masquerades, then a hood only and finally a half-mask covering an inch or two above and below the eyes, worn as a disguise. The black ebony pieces used in the game of dominoes may have derived their name from some allusion to the black domino cloak or the black mask with the eyes showing through as the white pips. On the other hand, the origin could lie in the Italian word *domino!*, 'master!', called by the winner. The name of the cloak ultimately comes from Latin *dominus*, 'lord', presumably through some religious association.

**Don** (Latin *dominus*, 'lord'). A Spanish gentleman; any Spaniard; an aristocrat; a man of mark; a university tutor or fellow.

**Don Camillo.** *See under* CAMILLO.

**Don Juan.** *See under* JUAN.

**Don Pacifico.** *See under* PACIFICO.

**Don Quixote.** *See* KNIGHT OF LA MANCHA; QUIXOTE.

**Donald Duck.** The ill-tempered cartoon duck in a sailor suit, second in fame only to MICKEY MOUSE, was created by the Walt Disney studios in 1934, his first appearance being in the *Silly Symphony* cartoon *The Wise Little Hen*. His popularity was due in no small measure to his distinctive quacking voice, the creation of Clarence Nash.

**Donation. Donation of Constantine, The.** The presumed grant by the Emperor Constantine (r.306–337) to Pope Sylvester (d.335) and his successors in perpetuity, consequent upon his baptism of Constantine in 326, of the temporal jurisdiction over Rome and Italy. The document is now accepted as an 8th-century forgery.

**Donation of Pepin, The.** When PEPIN THE SHORT, king of the Franks, conquered Aistulf the Lombard king, the exarchate of Ravenna fell into his hands (756). Pepin gave it with the surrounding country and the Republic of Rome to Pope Stephen II, thus founding the Papal States and the temporal power of the papacy.

With the exception of the city of Rome, the Papal States were incorporated in the Kingdom of Italy in 1860, and when Rome was made the Italian capital in 1870 the pope declared himself a 'prisoner' in the VATICAN. This seclusion was ended by the Concordat with Mussolini's government in 1929.

**Donatists.** Schismatic followers of Donatus, a Numidian bishop of the 4th century who, on puritanical grounds, opposed the election of Caecilianus to the bishopric of Carthage (311). Their chief dogma was that the church was a society of holy people and that mortal sinners were to be excluded. St AUGUSTINE of Hippo vigorously combated their heresies.

**Doncaster.** The 'fort on the River Don'. Sigebert, monk of Gemblours, in 1100, derived the name from *Thong-ceaster* ('the castle of the thong'), and says that HENGIST AND HORSA purchased from the British king as much as they could encompass with a leather thong, which they cut into strips and so encompassed the land occupied by the city.

**Done.** *See* DO.

**Donkey.** An ass. The word is first found in the later 18th century and is perhaps derived from dun with reference to its colour, or else from the personal name Duncan. *See also* CUDDY; DOBBIN; NEDDY. For the story concerning the cross on the donkey's back, *see* ASS.

**Donkey derby.** A race in which contestants ride donkeys, as a scaled-down version of the DERBY.

**Donkey engine.** A small auxiliary engine used for subsidiary work, just as the horse does more important work than the donkey.

**Donkey jacket.** A thick jacket, usually blue in colour, worn by manual workers as protection against the weather. The allusion of the name is to the donkey as a working animal.

**Donkey's breakfast.** A merchant navy term for a straw-filled mattress.

**Donkey's years.** A long time. The expression probably derives from the pronunciation of ears as years, helped by an association with the length of a donkey's ears. Donkeys also can live to a great age.

**Donkey-work.** Groundwork or drudgery.

**Talk the hind leg off a donkey, To.** *See under* TALK.

**Two more and up goes the donkey.** *See under* TWO.

**Who stole the donkey?** *See under* WHO.

**Donnybrook Fair.** This fair, held in August from the time of King John until 1855, was noted for its bacchanalian routs and light-hearted rioting. Hence it is proverbial for a disorderly gathering or regular rumpus. The village is now a south-eastern suburb of Dublin.

**Donzel.** A SQUIRE or young man of good birth not yet knighted. The word comes from Italian *donzello*, from Late Latin *domnicellus*, a diminutive of Latin *dominus*, 'lord'. *See also* DAMSEL.

> He is Esquire to a Knight-Errant, donzel to the damsels.
>
> SAMUEL BUTLER: 'Characters' (1680)

**Doolally.** An army expression for an unbalanced state of mind or mental derangement. Formerly, time-expired soldiers in India were sent to Deolali, a town near Bombay to await passage home. There were often long, frustrating delays, when boredom and the climate may have led to some odd behaviour, which caused some of them to become 'doolally'. The full phrase was 'doolally tap', the latter word being of East Indian origin and meaning malarial fever.

**Doom** (Old English *dōm*). The original meaning was 'law' or 'judgement', and a 'doomsman' was a judge. The book of laws compiled by King Alfred was called the Domboc. *See also* DEEMSTER.

**Doomsday Book.** *See* DOMESDAY BOOK.

**Doomsday Sedgwick.** A Puritan zealot (*c*.1610–69) during the COMMONWEALTH. He claimed to have had it revealed to him in a vision that doomsday was at hand, and going to the house of Sir Francis Russell, in Cambridgeshire, he called upon a party of gentlemen playing at bowls to leave off and prepare for the approaching dissolution.

**Crack of doom.** *See under* CRACK.

**Doomster.** *See* DEEMSTER.

**Doones, The.** Outlaws and desperadoes who are said to have settled in the Badgworthy area of Exmoor, Devon, in about 1620. They lived by highway robbery and the plundering of farmsteads. They also abducted women. Numerous murders were attributed to them. When, *c*.1699, they killed a child and seized the mother, the people of the district stormed their stronghold, and those who were not destroyed fled. Some stories claim them to be of Scottish origin, but the legends vary. In romanticized guise, they form the subject of R.D. Blackmore's novel *Lorna Doone* (1869).

**Door** (Old English *duru*). The word is similar in many languages, thus: Danish *dør*, Icelandic *dyrr*, Greek *thura*, Latin *fores*, German *Tür* (also *Tor*, 'gate'), Russian *dver'*, Albanian *dera*.

**Doormat, A.** A person who lets others treat him with contempt, or 'walk over' him.

**Door must be either shut or open, The.** A thing must be one way or the other. The words are from de Brueys and Palaprat's comedy, *Le Grondeur* ('The Scolder') (1691). The master scolds his servant for leaving the door open. The servant says that he was scolded the last time for shutting it and adds: 'Do you wish it shut?' 'No.' 'Do you wish it open?' 'No.' 'Why,' says the man, 'it must be either shut or open.' Alfred de Musset has a comedy *Il faut qu'une porte soit ouverte ou fermée* ('A door must be either open or shut') (1845) in which from time to time one or other of the two speakers, a *comte* and a *marquise,* opens the door or leaves the room in disgust. The play ends with the two admitting their love for each other and leaving the room together.

**Doors of perception, The.** The senses, or the greatly increased sensitivity achieved by the taking of certain drugs, as described by Aldous Huxley in his book of that title (1954).

**Doorstep, A.** A thick slice of bread.

**As dead as a doornail.** *See under* AS.

**At death's door**. *See under* AT.

**Back door, The.** *See under* BACK.

**Creaking doors hang the longest.** *See under* CREAK.

**Darken someone's door, To.** *See under* DARK.

**Devil's door, The.** *See under* DEVIL.

**Foot in the door.** *See under* FOOT.

**Holy Door.** *See under* HOLY.

**Keep the wolf from the door, To.** *See under* WOLF.

**Lay a charge at someone's door, To.** *See under* LAY.

**Meet behind closed doors, To.** *See under* MEET.

**Open door.** *See under* OPEN.

**Open the door to, To.** *See under* OPEN.

**Outdoors** or **out of doors.** *See under* OUT.

**Show someone the door, To.** *See under* SHOW.
**Shut the door in someone's face, To.** *See under* SHUT.

**Dora.** The popular name of the Defence of the Realm Acts (DORA), which imposed many temporary restrictions. Their application to munitions factories and the drink trade caused particular irritation. The name passed into common speech after being used in the Law courts by Mr Justice Scrutton (1856–1934). In numerous newspaper cartoons Dora was portrayed as a long-nosed elderly female, the personification of restriction. There have been countless similar coinages since the Second World War, and their derivation is usually, but not always, obvious. One of the best known is ERNIE.

**Dorado, El.** *See* EL DORADO.

**Dorcas Society.** A woman's circle making clothing for charitable purposes. So called from Dorcas in Acts 9:39, who made 'coats and garments' for widows.

**Dorian** and **Doric.** Pertaining to Doris, a district of ancient Greece, or to the Doric or Dorian race, one of the four main divisions of the ancient Greeks, the others being the Aeolians, the Ionians and the Achaeans. The Dorians maintained some of the characteristics of a simple-living, pastoral people, and they were dominant in the southern and western Peloponnesus, including Sparta, Megara, Corinth, Argos, Halicarnassus, Rhodes, Syracuse and Crete.

**Dorian mode.** The scale represented by the white keys on a piano, beginning with D. It produces a simple, solemn form of music and is the first of the authentic church modes.

**Doric dialect.** The broad, hard dialect spoken by the natives of Doris in Greece. Hence any broad rustic dialect, especially that of Scotland, of which Robert Burns' verses are a notable example.

**Doric land, The.** Greece, of which Doris forms a part.

**Doric order.** The oldest, strongest and simplest of the Grecian orders of architecture. The Greek Doric is simpler than the Roman imitation. A characteristic of the Grecian is that the column stands directly on the pavement, whereas the Roman is placed on a plinth. *See also* CORINTHIAN ORDER; IONIC ORDER; TUSCAN ORDER.

**Doris.** *See* NEREIDS.

**Dornick.** Stout figured linen for tablecloths and the like, so called from Doornik, the Flemish name of Tournai, Belgium, where it was originally made. The word has various spellings, including Dornock and Darnex, and is sometimes wrongly connected with Dornoch in Scotland.

> I have got ... a fair Darnex carpet of my own
> Laid cross for the more state.
> JOHN FLETCHER: *The Noble Gentleman*, V, i (1625)

**Dorothea.** A saint and virgin martyr under Diocletian in about 300. She is represented with a rose branch in her hand, a wreath of roses on her head and roses with fruit by her side. The legend is that Theophilus, the judge's secretary, scoffingly said to her as she was going to execution: 'Send me some fruit and roses, Dorothea, when you get to Paradise.' Immediately after her execution, a young angel brought him a basket of apples and roses, saying 'From Dorothea in Paradise', and vanished. Theophilus was a convert from that moment. The story forms the basis of Philip Massinger and Thomas Dekker's tragedy, *The Virgin Martir* (1622). Her day is 6 February.

**d'Orsay, Beau.** Count d'Orsay (1801–52). *See also* JEUNE CUPIDON.

**Dorset.** The name of the county means 'dwellers around Dorn', from Old English *sǣte*, 'dwellers', 'settlers' and the short name of *Dornwaraceaster*, modern Dorchester. It is not certain what the first part of this name means, although it is Celtic in origin.

**Dorsetshire Novelist, The.** *See* NOVELIST OF WESSEX.

**Dorsetshire Poet, The.** William Barnes (1800–86), a clergyman who was born and lived in Dorset and who wrote much poetry in the local dialect. *See also* LINDEN.

**Dory, John.** *See under* JOHN.

**Dose. Take a dose of one's own medicine, To.** To be treated in the way one usually treats others.

**Dot. Dot and carry one.** An infant just beginning to toddle, a person who limps or someone who has one leg longer than the other.

**Dot the i's and cross the t's, To.** To be meticulous; to give most careful attention to detail; to finalize the details of an agreement. These two letters are not correctly written unless respectively dotted and crossed.

**On the dot.** Precisely on time. The expression is probably a reference to the minute hand of the clock being exactly over the dot marking the given minute on the dial.

**Year dot, The.** *See under* YEAR.

**Dotheboys Hall.** A private boarding school in Dickens' *Nicholas Nickleby* (1838–9), where boys were taken in and 'done for' (hence the name) by Mr Wackford Squeers, a brutish, ignorant, overbearing fellow, who starved them and taught them nothing. The ruthless exposure of this kind of school led to the closing or reformation of many.

**Douai Bible, The.** *See under* BIBLE.

**Double** (Latin *duplus*, 'twofold'). One's double is one's *alter ego*. The word is applied to such pairs as the DROMIO brothers.

**Double a cape, To.** To sail around a cape to the other side.

**Double act.** An act involving two people, who

'play off' each other. There are many well-known comic double acts, such as Abbott and Costello, Flanagan and Allen, Laurel and Hardy, Morecambe and Wise and the like.

> The traditional double-act, featuring the cross-talk beween low comedian and straight man, is a direct derivative from the earliest comic drama with its ironist and impostor, knave and fool, Belch and Aguecheek combination.
>
> JOHN FISHER: *Funny Way To Be a Hero*, ch iv (1973)

**Double agent.** An agent who appears to be spying for one country while actually working for another.

**Double and twist, To.** To prevaricate; to act evasively; to try to extract oneself from a difficulty by tortuous means. The phrase is taken from coursing. A hare 'doubles and twists' in seeking to escape the hounds.

**Double a part, To.** Of an actor, to play two parts in the same piece.

**Double back, To.** To turn back on one's course.

**Double-barrelled.** A double-barrelled gun is one with two barrels. A double-barrelled name is a hyphenated surname. A double-barrelled remark is an ambiguous one.

**Double bluff.** An action or statement that appears to be a bluff but that in actual fact is genuine.

**Double chin.** A fold of loose flesh under the chin.

**Double-cross, To.** Properly, to cheat or cross each of two parties, to betray both sides, but now commonly used to mean to betray just one person or side.

**Double-dealing.** Deceit or duplicity; professing one thing and practising another.

**Double-decker.** Anything with two decks or layers, such as a bus or a sandwich.

**Double-declutch, To.** To change to a lower gear in a motor vehicle by a particular operation. The driver first puts the gear lever into the neutral position, then engages the required gear while simultaneously releasing the clutch pedal and revving the engine.

**Double Dutch.** Gibberish or jargon, as of babies' prattle or a foreign tongue not understood by the hearer. Dutch is a synonym for 'foreign' here, and double implies to an excessive degree.

**Double-dyed.** Deeply stricken with guilt.

**Double-edged.** Able to cut either way. The phrase is used metaphorically of an argument that works for and against the person employing it, or of a compliment or statement with a double meaning.

> Your *Delphick* sword, the *Panther* then reply'd,
> Is double-edg'd, and cuts on either side.
>
> JOHN DRYDEN: *The Hind and the Panther*, iii (1687)

**Double entendre.** A corrupt English version of the French *double entente*, used of a word or phrase with a double meaning, one of which is usually coarse or indelicate.

> A woman walks into a pub and askes the barman for a double entendre. So he gives her one. This isn't very funny, but it's satisfying. ... In fact, all good double entendres are satisfying. They preserve the genteel status quo – there could, after all be a cocktail called a double entendre and that could be what the barman gives the woman. But the gentility is preserved at a cost – we are forced to consider the possibility that he had sex with her.
>
> BRYAN APPLEYARD in *Sunday Times* (26 July 1998)

**Double entry.** In BOOK-KEEPING the entering of a transaction as a credit in one account and a debit in another.

**Double exposure.** The repeated exposure of a photographic plate, either deliberately or by accident.

**Double-faced** or **two-faced, To be.** To be hypocritical; to say one thing and do another.

**Double first.** Formerly, a first-class degree in both of the classical and mathematical triposes at Cambridge. Now, a first class in any two final examinations.

**Double-headed eagle.** *See* TWO-HEADED EAGLE.

**Double-jointed.** Having joints of the body that are unusually flexible.

**Double negative.** A negative statement containing two negative elements, regarded as ungrammatical in standard English. An example is 'I ain't seen no one'.

> We don't need no education,
> We don't need no thought control.
>
> PINK FLOYD: 'Another Brick in the Wall' (single) (1979)

**Double or quits.** The winner stakes his stake, and the loser promises to pay twice the stake if he loses again. If, however, he wins the second throw, his loss is cancelled and no money changes hands.

**Double-park, To.** To park a motor vehicle alongside another already parked by the roadside, so causing an obstruction.

**Double pneumonia.** Pneumonia in both lungs.

**Double-quick.** In military usage, double quick-step or double time, the quickest step next to a run. *See also* AT THE DOUBLE; DOUBLE UP.

**Doublespeak.** Talk that is deliberately ambigious or obscure. *See also* LOOKING-GLASS.

**Double Summer Time.** *See* SUMMER TIME.

**Double take.** An actor's trick. It is to look away from the person who has addressed a remark to you and then to look back at him quickly when the purport of the remark sinks in. The phrase is also used for a second look prompted by surprise or admiration.

I said, 'Ah!' Then I did a quick double-take, and added, 'What reporter?'

ANGUS WILSON: *The Old Men at the Zoo*, ch i (1961)

**Doublethink.** A term used by George ORWELL in *Nineteen Eighty-four* (1949) to describe what unscrupulous propagandists achieved by NEWSPEAK, a kind of DOUBLESPEAK. It denoted the mental ability to hold simultaneously two entirely conflicting views or beliefs, a state achieved by political indoctrination.

**Double time.** As a military expression, the same as DOUBLE-QUICK.

**Double-tongued.** Making contrary declarations on the same subject at different times; deceitful; insincere.

Likewise must the deacons be grave, not double-tongued.

1 Timothy 3:8

**Double up, To.** To bend in two, as a person in pain may do or when laughing. Also, to share a room or accommodation that is designed for one person or family.

**Double whammy.** A double blow or setback. Whammy comes from 'wham', a blow.

**At the double.** *See under* AT.

**Doubting Castle.** In Bunyan's PILGRIM'S PROGRESS (1678, 1684), the castle of the giant Despair and his wife Diffidence, in which CHRISTIAN and Hopeful were incarcerated, but from which they escaped by means of the key called Promise.

**Doubting Thomas.** St THOMAS.

**Dough. Doughboy.** Originally a dough cake baked for sailors, but from the late 1840s the name came to be given to American soldiers until the Second World War, when GI generally took its place. The common explanation is that the large brass buttons of the soldier's uniform resembled a dough cake.

**Doughface.** In the USA an inhabitant of the northern states who was in favour of maintaining slavery in the South.

**Douglas.** The Scottish family name is from the River Douglas, south of Lanark, which itself means 'black stream', from Gaelic *dubh*, 'black', and *glais*, 'stream'. The small town of Douglas on the Douglas Water is the place of origin of the powerful Douglas family and their retainers, and nearby Douglas Castle, now ruined, was the original of Sir Walter Scott's 'Castle Dangerous'. The river name is found elsewhere in Scotland, as well as in Ireland and the Isle of Man. Legend explains the surname by the story that in 770 an unknown chief came to the assistance of a Scottish king. After the battle the king asked who was the 'Duglass' chieftain, his deliverer, and was given for answer 'Sholto Du-glas', which means 'Behold the dark grey man'.

The complexion of the day is congenial with the original derivation of the name of the country, and the description of the chiefs to whom it belonged – Sholto Dhu Glass – (See yon dark grey man).

SIR WALTER SCOTT: *Castle Dangerous*, ch iii (1831)

**Douglas larder, The.** On PALM SUNDAY 1307 Sir James Douglas regained his castle by a ruse and, knowing that he could not hold it, caused all the provisions to be heaped together in the cellar along with the bodies of the slain prisoners and dead horses. Drink was then poured over all and salt cast on it. The castle was then fired. This cellar is known as the Douglas larder.

**Black Douglas.** *See under* BLACK.

**Douse** or **dowse, To.** To douse a sail is to lower it hastily. Otherwise the word usually means to drench; to extinguish (a light or flame). The origin of the word is uncertain. Its original meaning, now obsolete, was to strike. *See also* DOWSE.

**Douse the glim.** Put out the candle, put out the light.

'What though he has his humours, and made my eye dowse the glim in his fancies and frolics.'

SIR WALTER SCOTT: *The Pirate*, ch xxiv (1821)

**Dove.** The name of the bird has been related to dive, perhaps referring to its habit of ducking its head. However this may be, it is curious that the bird's Latin name, *columba*, is similar to Greek *kolumbis*, 'diver' (the sea bird) and *kolumbos*, 'diver' (the person). It is more likely that the name imitates the bird's call, as is often the case. This is better seen in its Scottish name of *doo*, which could well represent its gentle cooing note.

In Christian art the dove symbolizes the HOLY GHOST, and the seven rays proceeding from it the SEVEN GIFTS OF THE SPIRIT or Holy Ghost. It also symbolizes the SOUL and as such is sometimes represented coming out of the mouth of saints at death. A dove bearing a ring is an attribute of St AGNES, and St DAVID is shown with a dove on his shoulder, St DUNSTAN and St GREGORY the Great with one at the ear, St Enurchus with one on his head, and St REMIGIUS with a dove bringing him holy chrism.

The clergy of the CHURCH OF ENGLAND are allegorized as doves in John Dryden's *The Hind and the Panther* (iii (1687)).

The dove is also the symbol of peace, tenderness, innocence and love. Billing doves are popularly seen as a courting couple, and 'lovey-dovey' also relates to a show of affection.

**Cause a flutter in the dovecot, To.** *See under* CAUSE.

**Hawks and doves.** *See under* HAWK.

**Rock dove.** *See under* ROCK.

**Stock dove.** *See under* STOCK.

**Dover.** In the jargon of English cooks a resurrection

pie or any *réchauffé* is called a dover – 'do over' again.

**Jack of Dover, A.** *See under* JACK.

**When Dover and Calais meet.** *See* NEVER.

**White cliffs of Dover, The.** *See under* WHITE.

**Dovercourt.** A former term for a confused gabble or babel. According to legend, Dovercourt church in Essex once possessed a cross that spoke, and John Foxe says that the crowd in the church was so great 'that no man could shut the door'. Dovercourt also seems to have been noted for its scolds and chattering women.

> And now the rood of Dovercourt did speak.
> Confirming his opinions to be true.
> *Grim, the Collier of Croydon* (1600)

**Dowager, Queen.** *See under* QUEEN.

**Dow–Jones index, The.** The figure, based on the average price of selected stocks, that indicates the relative price of shares on the New York Stock Exchange. It evolved from a stock bulletin first published in 1882 by the financial journalists Charles H. Dow (1851–1902) and Edward D. Jones (1856–1920). The term is sometimes used metaphorically for any 'barometer'.

> I'm young, employed, healthy, ambitious,
> Sound, solvent, self-made, self-possessed.
> But all my symptoms are pernicious.
> The Dow-Jones of my heart's depressed.
> VIKRAM SETH: *The Golden Gate*, I (1986)

**Dowlas, Mr.** A former generic name for a linen-draper, who sold dowlas, a coarse linen cloth (so called from Daoulas, east of Brest, in Brittany, where it was made).

> *Mrs Quickly*: I bought you a dozen of shirts to your back.
> *Falstaff*: Dowlas, filthy dowlas: I have given them away to bakers' wives, and they have made bolters [strainers] of them.
> *Mrs Quickly*: Now, as I am a true woman, holland of eight shillings an ell.
> SHAKESPEARE: *Henry IV, Pt I*, III, iii (1597)

**Down. Down among the dead men let me lie.** Let me get so drunk that I slip from my chair and lie under the table with the empty bottles.

**Down and out.** At the end of one's resources with no apparent chance of recovery. Homeless vagrants are sometimes termed down-and-outs. The allusion is to boxing. George Orwell wrote of his experiences as a beggar in *Down and Out in Paris and London* (1933).

**Down at heel.** In decayed circumstances, of which worn-down heels are a sign.

> A good man's fortune may grow out at heels
> SHAKESPEARE: *King Lear*, II, ii (1605)

**Down in the dumps.** Out of spirits, depressed.

> Why, how now, daughter Katharine! in your dumps?
> SHAKESPEARE: *The Taming of the Shrew*, II, i (1593)

**Down in the mouth.** Out of spirits, disheartened. When persons are sad and low-spirited, the corners of the mouth droop.

**Down on, To be.** To have a low opinion of or grudge against someone.

**Down on one's luck.** In adverse circumstances; short of cash and credit.

**Down on** or **on one's uppers.** Impoverished, as typified by the worn-out condition of one's footwear. *See also* DOWN AT HEEL.

**Down there** or **down below.** A maidenish euphemism for the genital region.

> A programme devoted to problems 'down there' was too shy for anything but innuendo.
> *Radio Times* (letter) (12–18 September 1998)

**Down time.** The time during which a computer is out of action or unavailable.

**Down to earth.** Forthright and plain spoken.

**Down tools, To.** To lay one's tools aside and stop work; to come out on strike.

**Downtown.** The business district of an American city, so called from New York, where financial houses are concentrated on the southern tip of Manhattan Island. The opposite is uptown, the residential district, away from the city centre.

**Down train, The.** The train away from London or the local centre, as distinct from the up train, which goes to it. The down platform is similar. A well-known SPOONERISM allegedly addressed by the Rev. W.A. Spooner to a student runs: 'You have hissed my mystery lectures; you have tasted a whole worm. You will leave Oxford on the next town drain.'

**Down under.** At the Antipodes, in Australia or New Zealand, which are on the other side of the globe, down under the feet of those in Britain.

> Down under may be the place to make money, but up over is the place to spend it!
> *Time* (14 June 1971)

**Down with.** A cry of disapproval or rejection of the thing or person stated, like French *à bas*. The opposite is UP WITH (*see under* UP).

**Back down, To.** *See under* BACK.

**Go down, To.** *See under* GO.

**Hold down, To.** *See under* HOLD.

**Run down, To.** *See under* RUN.

**Run down, To be.** *See under* RUN.

**Run someone down, To.** *See under* RUN.

**Sent down, To be.** *See under* SEND.

**Suit one down to the ground, To.** *See under* SUIT.

**Touch down.** *See under* TOUCH.

**Ups and downs.** *See under* UP.

**Downing Street.** A short street leading off WHITEHALL as a synonym for the British Government.

No. 10 was given in 1725 by George II to Sir Robert Walpole as the official residence of the

PRIME MINISTER and it is there that CABINET meetings are usually held. No. 11 is the official residence of the CHANCELLOR OF THE EXCHEQUER. No. 12 is the Government WHIP's Office. The street was named after Sir George Downing (*c*.1623–84), a noted parliamentarian and ambassador, who served under both Cromwell and Charles II and who owned property there.

**Downy bird, A.** A knowing or cunning fellow up to or, as formerly, down to every dodge. In Vaux's *Flash Dictionary* (1812) 'down' is given as a synonym for 'awake'. But there is probably a punning allusion to a young chick, who is artful though not yet fully fledged.

> Hilda, you're the downiest bird – I beg your pardon, the cleverest woman I ever met with.
>
> MARY ELIZABETH BRADDON: *Strangers and Pilgrims*, Bk III, v (1873)

**Dowsabell.** A common name in 16th-century poetry for a sweetheart, especially a simple country girl. It is a form of the name Dulcibella, popularly interpreted as French *douce et belle*, 'sweet and beautiful'. *See also* BLOUZELINDA.

> He had, as antique stories tell,
> A daughter cleaped [called] Dowsabel,
> A mayden fayre and free.
>
> MICHAEL DRAYTON: *Eclogues* (1593)

**Dowse, To.** To search for water, minerals and so on underground with a DIVINING ROD or dowsing rod. *See also* DOUSE.

**Doxology** (Greek *doxologos*, 'uttering praise', i.e. to God). The Greater Doxology is the hymn *Gloria in Excelsis Deo* ('Glory to God in the highest') at the EUCHARIST. The Lesser Doxology is the *Gloria Patri* ('Glory be to the Father') sung or said at the end of each psalm in the liturgy. Bishop Ken's hymn 'Praise God from whom all blessings flow' is also known as the Doxology.

**Doyen** (French, 'DEAN', from Late Latin *decanus*, 'leader of a group of ten'). The title of the senior accredited ambassador in a capital, but if there is a papal nuncio then he is automatically the doyen. The word is also applied to the senior member of a profession, group or society. The female equivalent is a doyenne.

> Miss Elsie Fogerty, the doyenne of The Central School of Dramatic Art.
>
> PETER BULL: *I Know the Face, but*..., ch i (1959)

**Doyley** or **doyley.** *See* DOILY.

**Dozen.** TWELVE. The word is derived from Old French *douzaine*, itself from Latin *duodecim*.

**Baker's dozen.** *See under* BAKER.

**By the dozen.** *See under* BY.

**Devil's dozen.** *See under* DEVIL.

**Long dozen, A.** *See under* LONG.

**Talk nineteen to the dozen, To.** *See under* TALK.

**Drachenfels** (German, 'dragon's rock'). The German mountain on the right bank of the Rhine, southeast of Bonn, a legendary haunt of the DRAGON that SIEGFRIED slew. He bathed in its blood and so became invulnerable except in one spot on which a linden leaf had fallen. *See also* NIBELUNGENLIED.

> The castled crag of Drachenfels
> Frowns o'er the wide and winding Rhine,
> Whose breast of waters broadly swells
> Between the banks which bear the vine.
>
> LORD BYRON: *Childe Harold's Pilgrimage*, III, lv (1816)

**Draconian Code.** A very severe code. Draco was an Athenian of the 7th century BC who drew up a code of laws noted for their severity. As nearly every violation of his laws was a capital offence, Demades, the orator, said that Draco's code was written in blood.

**Dracula.** *See* VAMPIRE.

**Drag.** Female dress worn by men; transvestite clothes.

> You would never have the fag
> Of dressing up in drag,
> You'd be a woman at the weekend.
>
> JOHN OSBORNE: *The World of Paul Slickey*, II, x (1959)

**Draggle-tail** or **daggle-tail.** A slovenly woman or slut, whose skirts are wet and bedraggled or whose dress trails in the dirt.

**Dragon.** The Greek word *drakōn* is related to *drakos*, 'eye', and in classical legend the idea of watching is retained in the story of the dragon who guards the golden apples in the Garden of the HESPERIDES, and in the story of CADMUS. In medieval romance captive ladies were often guarded by dragons.

A dragon is a fabulous winged crocodile, usually represented as of large size, with a serpent's tail, so that dragon and SERPENT are sometimes interchangeable. In the Middle Ages the word was the symbol of sin in general and paganism in particular, the metaphor being derived from Revelation 12:9, where SATAN is termed both 'the great dragon' and 'that old serpent', and from Psalm 91:13, where it is said 'the dragon shalt thou trample under feet'. Hence, in Christian art it has the same significance.

Among the many saints usually pictured as dragon-slayers are St MICHAEL, St GEORGE, St MARGARET, St Samson, archbishop of Dol, St Clement of Metz, St Romain of Rouen, destroyer of the huge dragon La GARGOUILLE, which ravaged the Seine, St PHILIP the Apostle, St MARTHA, slayer of the terrible dragon Tarasque (associated with Tarascon, the saint's patronal city), St Florent, who killed a dragon which haunted the Loire, St Cado, St Maudet and St Pol, who performed similar feats in Brittany, and St KEYNE of Cornwall.

Among the ancient Britons and the Welsh the dragon was the national symbol on the war standard. Hence the term PENDRAGON for the *dux bellorum*, or leader in war. *See also* RED DRAGON.

**Dragon Hill.** A site southeast of Faringdon, Oxfordshire (formerly Berkshire), where local legend claims St GEORGE killed the dragon.

> The well-known tradition, recorded as far back as 1738 by Wise, is that Dragon Hill is where St George slew the Dragon, and the patch of bare chalk on the knoll is where the blood issued from the Dragon's wound, poisoning the ground so that no grass has ever grown there since. This bare patch is just as plain now as it was two hundred years ago.
>
> L.V. GRINSELL: *White Horse Hill and the Surrounding Country* (1939)

**Dragon of Wantley, The.** An old story, preserved in PERCY'S RELIQUES (1765), tells of this monster who was slain by More of More Hall. He procured a suit of armour studded with spikes and kicked the DRAGON in the backside, where alone it was vulnerable. Percy says the Dragon stands for a greedy renter of the TITHES of the Wortley family who attempted to take the tithes in kind from the parishioners and More was the man who conducted the suit against him. There are other theories. Wantley is Wharncliffe near Sheffield.

**Dragon's blood.** An old name in pharmacy for the resin from certain plants, formerly used in certain preparations. The East Indian palm (*Calamus draco*) is used as a colouring matter for artists' varnishes.

In German legend, when SIEGFRIED was told to bathe in the blood of a dragon in order to make him immune from injury, a linden leaf fell on him and the place it covered remained vulnerable. There is a possible connection between this story and the term 'dragon's blood' applied to a powder used in printing which, applied to a block for processing, prevents the etching of that portion covered.

**Dragon's teeth.** A colloquial term for anti-tank obstacles resembling upward-pointing teeth.

**Chase the dragon, To.** *See under* CHASE.

**Chinese dragon, The.** *See under* CHINESE.

**Flying dragon, A.** *See under* FLY.

**Red dragon.** *See under* RED.

**Sow dragon's teeth, To.** *See under* SOW.

**Dragonnades.** The name given to Louis XIV's persecutions of the HUGUENOTS from 1681, until after the Revocation of the EDICT OF NANTES in 1685. The name arises from the billeting of DRAGOONS on those Protestants who refused to renounced their 'heresy'. The soldiery were given a free hand with the obvious results.

**Dragoon.** The name was originally that of a mounted infantryman, hence its inclusion in the present names of certain cavalry regiments, such as The Royal Scots Dragoon Guards. It is taken from the carbine called a 'dragon', which breathed forth fire like the fabulous beast of this name.

**Dragoon, To.** To force or coerce. The derivation is from the above. 'They dragooned him into it' means that they coerced him into it.

**Drain. Brain drain.** *See under* BRAIN.

**Down the drain.** Lost; wasted.

**Laugh like a drain, To.** *See under* LAUGH.

**Pour down the drain, To.** *See under* POUR.

**Drake. Drake brass plate, The.** *See under* FAKES.

**Drake's drum.** Sir Francis Drake's drum of legendary fame.

> Take my drum to England, hang et by the shore.
> Strike et when your powder's runnin' low;
> If the Dons sight Devon, I'll quit the port o'
> Heaven.
> An' drum them up the Channel as we drummed
> them long ago.
>
> SIR HENRY NEWBOLT: *Drake's Drum* (1897)

**Ducks and Drakes.** *See under* DUCK.

**Drama. Dramatic unities.** The three dramatic unities, the rules governing the so-called 'classical' dramas, are founded on RENAISSANCE misconceptions of passages in ARISTOTLE'S *Poetics* and are hence often, though very incorrectly, styled the Aristotelian Unities. They are (1) Unity of Action, (2) Unity of Time and (3) Unity of Place. Aristotle lays stress on the first, the second was deduced by Castelvetro (1505–71), the Italian scholar and critic, from an incidental reference to it by Aristotle, and the third followed almost inevitably.

The convention of the three unities was adopted in France, especially after the triumph of Corneille's *Le Cid* (1636) but met with little success in England. Shakespeare, like Aristotle, was concerned only with the Unity of Action, but the three unities were purposely adhered to in Ben Jonson's *Alchemist* (1610).

**Dramatis personae** (Latin, 'persons of the drama'). The characters of a play, novel or, by extension, of an actual transaction.

**Closet drama.** *See under* CLOSET.

**Father of Danish Drama, The.** *See under* FATHER.

**Father of French Drama, The.** *See under* FATHER.

**Father of Greek Drama, The.** *See under* FATHER.

**Father of Modern German Drama, The.** *See under* FATHER.

**Father of Spanish Drama, The.** *See under* FATHER.

**Kitchen sink drama.** *See under* KITCHEN.

**Drapier's Letters.** A series of letters written by Dean Swift to the people of Ireland, appearing in 1724 under the signature of M.B. Drapier, rousing them against the copper coinage called WOOD'S HALFPENCE.

**Drappie, Wee.** *See under* WEE.

**Drat.** A variant of 'Od rot!', 'Od' being a form of 'God', and the vowel showing the same modifications as in 'Gad!' or 'Gadzooks!' *See also* OD's.

**Draupnir** (Old Norse, 'dropper'). ODIN's magic ring, from which every ninth night dropped eight rings equal in size and beauty to itself. It was made by the DWARFS.

**Draw.** A tied game, contest or the like, in which neither side can claim a victory. The origin may be in a battle in which the troops withdraw on both sides when no decision seems possible.

**Draw a bead on, To.** To take aim at with a firearm. The bead referred to is the foresight.

**Draw a blank, To.** To meet with failure in a search. The allusion is either to sportsmen 'drawing' a covert and finding no game or to a lottery in which all the tickets except the winning ones are blank.

**Draw a bow at a venture, To.** To take a pot shot; to make a random remark, which may hit the truth. 'At a venture' is properly 'at adventure', i.e. at random, since the original meaning of 'adventure' was chance, luck.

> And a certain man drew a bow at a venture, and smote the king of Israel between the joints of the harness.
> 1 Kings 22:34

**Draw a veil over, To.** To say no more about a matter; to conceal something from the knowledge of others as a veil conceals a woman's face.

**Draw Dun out of the mire, To.** To lend a helping hand to someone in distress; to assist when things are at a standstill. The allusion is to an old English parlour game, in which a log of wood, called Dun, is brought into the parlour and placed in the middle. The cry goes up, 'Dun's in the mire!', i.e. the dun horse is stuck in the mud. Two of the players then try to drag it out. If they fail, others join them one at a time. This makes for an enjoyable rough-and-tumble, in which the log frequently falls on someone's toes.

> 'Dun's in the mire!' he said. 'Behold King Log;
> For love of money drag him from his bog!'
> CHAUCER: *Canterbury Tales*, Prologue to 'The Manciple's Tale' (*c*.1387) (modern translation by Nevill Coghill, 1951)

**Drawing down the moon.** A WITCH's ceremony held on or near 12 December, when the magic of the moon is invoked in drinking and dancing. The rite is dedicated to BACCHUS, the god of wine and fertility.

**Draw or pull in one's horns, To.** To retrench; to cut back on one's expenditure; to suppress or check one's emotions. The allusion is to the snail, which draws in its horns when sensing danger.

**Draw it mild!** Don't exaggerate! Don't make your remarks (or actions) stronger than necessary. The allusion is to the drawing of ALE. The expression is now dated.

**Drawn from life.** Drawn or described from some real person or object.

**Drawn from the wood.** Said of beer and wines served directly from the cask. Beer barrels have now largely been supplanted by metal containers and their contents dispensed through pressurized beer-engines, a matter of regret to connoisseurs of good ALE.

**Draw one's sword against, To.** To attack.

**Draw rations** or **kit, To.** In military parlance, to go to the place of issue and collect the named object.

**Draw rein, To.** To tighten the reins and hence to slacken pace; to stop.

**Draw someone out, To.** To entice or persuade them to speak; to encourage a shy person to talk, often with the aim of obtaining information.

**Draw someone's fire, To.** To attract hostility or criticism away from a more important target.

**Draw stumps, To.** At the end of a game of CRICKET the bails are removed from the wicket and the stumps drawn out of the ground.

**Draw the line at, To.** To refuse to go further than a certain point, as: 'I don't mind visiting her but I draw the line at staying overnight.'

**Draw the short straw, To.** To be chosen by lot for a disagreeable task. The choice is properly made by someone holding a handful of straws of which all but one are long. The person drawing the short straw loses out. *See also* STRAW.

**At daggers drawn.** *See under* AT.

**Back to the drawing board.** *See under* BACK.

**Hanged, drawn and quartered.** *See under* HANG.

**Luck of the draw, The.** *See under* LUCK.

**Teeth are drawn.** *See under* TOOTH.

**Drawcansir.** A bustling braggart, from the burlesque tyrant in George Buckingham's *The Rehearsal* (1671). He was a caricature of Dryden's ALMANZOR (1670). His name may pun on drawing a can of ale, with allusion to his capacity for drink. Drawcansir's opening speech (he has only three) is:

> He that dares drink, and for that drink dares die,
> And knowing this, dare yet drink on, am I.
> *The Rehearsal*, IV, i

which parodies Almanzor's:

> He who dares love, and for that love must die,
> And, knowing this, dare yet love on, am I.
> *Almanzor*, IV, iii

*See also* BOBADIL.

**Drawer. Bottom drawer.** *See under* BOTTOM.

**Top drawer.** *See under* TOP.

**Drawing room.** Originally the 'withdrawing room' to which the ladies retired after dinner leaving the men to continue their drinking and 'men's talk'.

**Drawing room of Europe, The.** So NAPOLEON BONAPARTE called St Mark's Square in Venice.

**Dreadnought.** The name given to the 17,900-ton turbine-engined, big-gun battleship completed in 1906, the first of a famous class, which greatly influenced subsequent naval construction. The first ship of this name was in use in the reign of Queen Elizabeth I.

The Seamen's Hospital at Greenwich, known as the Dreadnought Hospital, takes its name from the seventh Dreadnought, which was first in action in 1809, and from 1857 was anchored off Greenwich as a seamen's hospital. It was broken up in 1875.

**Dream. Alnaschar's dream.** *See under* ALNASCHAR.

**American dream, The.** *See under* AMERICA.

**Gates of dreams.** *See under* GATE.

**Immortal Dreamer, The.** *See under* IMMORTAL.

**Like a dream.** *See under* LIKE.

**Pipe dream.** *See under* PIPE.

**Dresden china.** The fine, hard porcelain so called, attaining high repute from the 18th century, was made from about 1709 at Meissen, some 12 miles (19km) from Dresden. Among the many figurines produced there, the Dresden shepherdess has remained a favourite for daintiness and grace. The factory was established by Augustus II, king of Poland and elector of Saxony (1670–1733), and its success was the result of the discovery of kaolin (china clay) at Aue. Every effort was made to retain the process of manufacture: the kaolin was dispatched from Aue in casks sealed by mute persons and the workmen at Meissen were sworn to secrecy, but by 1718 the secret was known in Vienna. In the 1750s beautifully ornamented 'table services' were selling at prices between 100 and 1000 guineas.

**Dress. Dress down, To.** To dress informally. Dressing down at work or in the office on Fridays arose as an American innovation, the idea being that the wearing of casual clothes would improve staff morale and increase productivity. Psychologists deny any connection, however, and for many employees, especially the more mature, obligatory dressing down may seem an imposition. The practice is sometimes coupled with a fund-raising effort for charity, and school students may also have the occasional 'non-uniform' day set aside for this purpose. To dress down in this sense is thus essentially the converse of to DRESS UP.

**Dressed to kill.** Dressed very smartly or in the height of fashion. The idea is from that of dressing so as to make a conquest or 'kill' of one of the opposite sex.

**Dressed up to the nines.** Dressed elaborately or even overdressed. The origin of the expression remains uncertain. 'Nines' is said by some to be a corruption of *eyne*, the Old English word for 'eyes'. However, the phrase has not been recorded earlier than the 18th century. Other authorities claim that 'nine' indicates a high degree of excellence, perfection itself being 'ten'.

**Dress rehearsal.** The final rehearsal of a play before its first performance, with each member of the cast dressed in the appropriate costume.

**Dress someone down, To.** To reprimand or scold them. The expression may derive from butchers' jargon, alluding to the initial cut into a carcass on a beam. A more likely reference is to builders' talk, in which to dress a brick down is to scour its front face to make it seem bright and new.

**Dress up, To.** To dress elaborately for a particular occasion; to dress in FANCY DRESS.

> Some women are born to dress up. They enter the world with fully formed credit cards and a homing instinct that leads directly to John Galliano.
> *The Times* (14 December 1998)

**All dressed up and nowhere to go.** *See under* ALL.

**Canonical dress.** *See under* CANON.

**Court dress.** *See under* COURT.

**Fancy dress.** *See under* FANCY.

**French dressing.** *See under* FRENCH.

**Full dress.** *See under* FULL.

**Window dressing.** *See under* WINDOW.

**Walking-out dress.** *See under* WALK.

**Dreyfusard.** An advocate of the innocence of Captain Alfred Dreyfus (1859–1935), a French artillery officer of Jewish descent who was convicted in 1894 on a charge of betraying military secrets to Germany and sent to DEVIL'S ISLAND. In 1898 Georges Clemenceau and Émile Zola took up his case and Zola wrote his open letter *J'accuse*. In 1899 Dreyfus was retried, again condemned, but shortly afterwards pardoned. In 1906 the proceedings were finally quashed. The whole affair reflected the greatest discredit on the French military hierarchy of the time.

**Drift of the current, The.** The rate per hour at which the current runs.

**Drink.** In colloquial English, the 'drink' is the sea or water.

**Drink deep, To.** To take a deep draught; to drink heavily.

> A little learning is a dangerous thing;
> Drink deep, or taste not the Pierian spring.
> ALEXANDER POPE: *Essay on Criticism*, ii (1711)

Shakespeare uses the expression metaphorically, as in *Henry V* (I, i (1598)):

> *Cant*: If it pass against us,
> We lose the better half of our possession …
> And to the coffers of the king, beside,
> A thousand pounds by the year: thus runs the bill.
> *Ely*: This would drink deep.
> *Cant*: 'Twould drink the cup and all.

**Drink in, To.** To listen closely or eagerly.

**Drinking of healths.** *See* GABBARA; HEALTHS.

**Drinking-up time.** The short time allowed for those in a pub to finish off their drinks before it closes. *See also* TIME, GENTLEMEN, PLEASE!

**Drink like a fish, To.** To drink abundantly or excessively. Many fish swim open-mouthed, thus appearing to be continually drinking. The idiom is found in Beaumont and Fletcher.

**Drink someone under the table, To.** To continue drinking and remain comparatively sober after everyone one else has succumbed to the effects of alcohol.

**Drink the cup of sorrow, To.** To undergo affliction; to suffer one's share of sorrow. 'To drink the cup' is used in the sense of 'to be allotted one's portion'.

**Drink to, To.** To toast; to wish success to. Agreeing with a particular sentiment, one may say: 'I'll drink to that'.

**Drive one to drink, To.** *See under* DRIVE.

**Eat, drink and be merry, for tomorrow we die.** *See under* EAT.

**I could use a drink.** *See under* USE.

**Meat and drink.** *See under* MEAT.

**Spike a drink, To.** *See under* SPIKE.

**Drive. Drive a coach and horses through, To.** To find a way of flagrantly ignoring or evading a law, ruling or the like, so making it an absurdity and effectively nullifying it. The phrase was commonly used with reference to an Act of Parliament.

**Drive a hard bargain, To.** To exact more than is quite reasonable.

**Drive a point home, To.** To stress a point with the utmost persistence; to ensure the acceptance of one's point and to make sure that it is understood. The allusion is to hammering a nail fully home.

**Drive a ship, To.** In nautical parlance, to sail or command a ship.

> As 'driving' a ship or plane in the Royal Navy is forbidden to colour-blind people, should not the same ruling be so for those in driving seats upon our roads?
>
> *The Times* (Letter to the Editor) (30 September 1994)

**Driven into a corner, To be.** To be placed in a situation from which there is no escape or let-out.

**Drive one to drink, To.** To exasperate or madden one, so that one considers taking refuge from the annoyance in drink.

**Drive someone up the wall, To.** To madden or exasperate them.

**Drive to the wall, To.** To push to extremity, to break or crush.

**Back-seat driver.** *See under* BACK.

**Sunday driver.** *See under* SUNDAY.

**What are you driving at?** *See under* WHAT.

**Droit. Droit de fauteuil.** *See* RIGHT OF TABOURET.

**Droit de tabouret.** *See* RIGHT OF TABOURET.

**Droit du seigneur.** *See* JUS PRIMAE NOCTIS.

**Dromio, The Brothers.** Two brothers who were exactly alike, who served two brothers who were exactly alike. The mistakes of masters and men form the fun of Shakespeare's *Comedy of Errors* (1592), based on Plautus' *Menaechmi* (2nd century BC).

**Drone.** The male of the honey bee which does no work but lives on the labour of the worker bees, hence a sluggard, an idler, a parasite, whether genteel or not.

> In the heart of London's clubland there stands a tall and grimly forbidding edifice known to taxi-drivers and the elegant young men who frequent its precincts as the Drones Club. Yet its somewhat austere exterior belies the atmosphere of cheerful optimism and bonhomie that prevails within. For here it is that young gallants of Mayfair forgather for the pre-luncheon bracer and to touch lightly on the topics of the day.
>
> P.G. WODEHOUSE: *Eggs, Beans, and Crumpets* (1940)

The three lower pipes of a bagpipe are called the drones because they produce a monotonous bass humming like that of a bee.

> I am as melancholy as a gib-cat … or the drone of a Lincolnshire bagpipe.
>
> SHAKESPEARE: *Henry IV, Pt I,* I, ii (1597)

**Drop.** In colloquial English a 'drop' is a euphemistic term for an alcoholic drink.

**Drop a bombshell, To.** To deliver or release suddenly some shattering or surprising news. *See also* BOLT FROM THE BLUE.

**Drop a brick, To.** To make an indiscreet or embarrassing remark. The expression is said to relate to a group of builders in Cambridge who dropped their bricks in surprise on seeing an extraordinarily inept column of student volunteers on the march one day in 1905. The actor and playwright Robert Morley edited an entertaining collection of verbal gaffes in *Robert Morley's Book of Bricks* (1978).

**Drop a curtsy, To.** To make a curtsy, dropping the body while doing so.

**Drop a stitch, To.** To let a stitch fall off the end of the needle while knitting.

**Drop dead!** An expression of irritation or contempt, and short for 'Why don't you drop dead!'

**Drop-dead.** Stunningly beautiful; excellent. The term is most frequently encountered with the adjective 'gorgeous'. The effect is enough to make one drop dead.

**Drop in, To.** To make a casual call or informal visit.

**Drop in one's eye, A.** Not exactly intoxicated, but having had quite enough.

We are na fou, we're no that fou,
But just a drappie in our ee!
ROBERT BURNS: 'Willie Brew'd a Peck o' Maut' (1788)

**Drop in the ocean, A.** A negligible or tiny quantity; something that makes little difference.

**Drop it!** Stop that!

**Drop off, To.** To fall asleep, especially from weariness.

**Drop-out.** A student who fails to complete a college or university course, or more generally a person who has 'opted out' of conventional society.

An international gathering of misfits and drop-outs, smoking pot and meditating in the Buddhist temples.
*New Statesman* (15 December 1967)

**Dropping fire.** Irregular fire from small arms, machine guns etc.

**Drop scone.** A small pancake made by dropping batter into a frying pan.

**Drop someone, To.** To allow an acquaintanceship or friendship to lapse.

**Drop someone a line, To.** To write to them.

**Drop someone in it, To.** To get someone into trouble. 'It' is a EUPHEMISM for 'the shit'.

**Drop the pilot, To.** To let a ship's pilot leave after he has completed his task of guiding the vessel through a channel. Figuratively, to dismiss a tried and trusted leader. The phrase was popularized (in the wording 'Dropping the pilot') by John Tenniel's *Punch* cartoon (29 March 1890) showing Count von Bismarck, wearing pilot's uniform, being dismissed by Kaiser Wilhelm II.

**At the drop of a hat.** *See under* AT.

**Dolly drop.** *See under* DOLLY.

**Penny dropped, The.** *See under* PENNY.

**Prince Rupert's drops.** *See under* PRINCE.

**You could have heard a pin drop.** *See under* PIN.

**Drown. Drowning men clutch** or **catch at straws.** People in acute danger or desperate circumstances cling in hope to trifles.

**Like a drowned rat.** *See under* LIKE.

**Drows.** DWARFS of Orkney and Shetland mythology.

**Drug. Drug on the market, A.** Something no one wants, something for which there is little or no demand, especially from there being a surfeit of the particular product in question.

**Nicknames of drugs.** *See under* NICKNAME.

**Truth drug.** *See under* TRUTH.

**Druids.** The ancient order of priestly officials in pre-Roman Gaul, pre-Roman Britain and Ireland. They seem to have combined priestly, judicial and political functions. The Druidic cult presents many obscurities, and the chief literacy sources on them are Pliny and CAESAR's *Commentaries on the Gallic War*. These tell how their rites were conducted in oak groves, that human sacrifices were offered up and that they regarded the OAK and MISTLETOE with particular veneration. It has been suggested that the name Druid is linked with some word meaning 'oak', such as Greek *drus* or Welsh *derw*, but a connection with Irish *draoi*, 'magician' seems more likely. They practised DIVINATION and ASTROLOGY and taught that the soul at death was transferred to another body. Their distinguishing badge was a serpent's egg. *See also* DRUID'S EGG.

In the 18th and 19th centuries there was a considerable revival of interest in Druidism and a new romantic and unhistorical cult grew up associated with the Welsh Eisteddfodau. This is usually termed Neo-Druidism. These are the 'Druids' who today gather together to greet the sunrise on Midsummer Day at STONEHENGE. *See also* EISTEDDFOD.

**Druid's circles.** A popular name for circles of standing stones, of which STONEHENGE is the best known example.

**Druid's egg, The.** According to Pliny, who claimed to possess one, this wonderful egg was hatched by the joint labour of several serpents and was buoyed in the air by their hissing. The person who caught it had to escape at full speed to avoid being stung to death, but the possessor was sure to prevail in every contest and to be courted by those in power.

**United Ancient Order of Druids.** *See under* UNITED.

**Drum.** A popular name in the 18th century and later for a crowded evening party, so called from its resemblance in noise to the drumming up of recruits. The more riotous of these parties were called drum-majors. *See also* HURRICANE; ROUT.

This is a riotous assembly of fashionable people of both sexes, at a private house, consisting of some hundred, not unaptly stiled a drum, from the noise and emptiness.
TOBIAS SMOLLETT: *Advice, a Satire* (1746)

**Drumhead court martial.** One held in haste in the field to punish on the spot, so named from the former custom of holding the court round the big drum.

**Drum major.** A non-commissioned officer, usually of warrant officer rank, who commands the corps of drums of a military band and who is in charge of both drums and band when they parade together.

**Drum majorette.** A girl or young woman who marches at the head of a procession, twirling and tossing a baton. Her uniform and commanding position to some extent mirror those of a DRUM MAJOR.

**Drummed out, To be.** To be expelled ignominiously, as a soldier in disgrace was dismissed from the regiment to the accompaniment of drum beats.

**Drum something into someone, To.** To drive it into their mind by constant repetition, as if by the beat of a drum.

**Drumsticks.** Legs, especially thin ones. A drumstick is also the lower joint of the leg of a dressed or cooked chicken.

**Drum up.** To gather or canvass, as when one 'drums up support'.

**Beat the drum for, To.** *See under* BEAT.

**Drake's drum.** *See under* DRAKE.

**Drummond. Drummond light.** An old term for LIMELIGHT.

**Bulldog Drummond.** *See under* BULL.

**Drunk. Drunken forest.** A forest in which the trees are bent or twisted and in which they are tilted in one direction or in different directions. The cause is a shift in the underlying soil while the trees are still growing. Such forests are a feature of parts of Russia, notably where they have been caused by landslides, as along the right bank of the Middle Volga, by the Black Sea coast of the Caucasus and along the southern shore of the Crimea.

**Drunken helot, A.** The Spartans used to make a helot (slave) drunk as an object lesson to youth of the evils of intemperance. Dr Johnson said of one of his old acquaintances:

> He is a man of good principles; and there would be no danger that a young gentleman should catch his manner; for it is so very bad, that it must be avoided. In that respect he would be like the drunken Helot.
> BOSWELL'S *Life* (2 April 1779)

**Drunken Parliament, The.** The Parliament assembled at Edinburgh in January 1661, of which Burnet says the members 'were almost perpetually drunk'.

**As drunk as a lord** or **Davy's sow.** *See under* AS.

**Blind drunk.** *See under* BLIND.

**Dead drunk.** *See under* DEAD.

**Punch drunk, To be.** *See under* PUNCH.

**Roaring drunk.** *See under* ROAR.

**Rolling drunk.** *See under* ROLL.

**Drury Lane.** The famous London thoroughfare and its theatre is named after Drury House, built by Sir William Drury in the 16th century.

The parent of the present Drury Lane Theatre was opened in 1663 but was burned down nine years later. Its successor was designed by Christopher Wren but replaced by a new structure in 1794. This was destroyed by fire in 1809. The present theatre, designed by Benjamin Dean Wyatt, was opened in 1812. Many well-known actors have appeared at Drury Lane, including Garrick, Kemble and Kean. Since the Second World War it has been noted for its musicals. Its official name is Theatre Royal, Drury Lane.

**Sweet Nell of Old Drury.** Nell GWYN.

**Druses.** A people and sect of Syria, Lebanon and Israel, of 11th-century origin. Their faith is a mixture of the PENTATEUCH, the Gospel, the KORAN and Sufism. They worship in both mosques and churches, but have their own SCRIPTURES. Their name is derived from their founder, the Muslim leader Ismail ad-Darazi ('Ismail the Tailor').

**Dry. Dry bob.** A boy at Eton College who plays cricket and football instead of rowing. *See also* WET BOB.

**Dry nurse.** A nurse for young children who is not required to breastfeed, as distinct from a WET NURSE.

**Dry out, To.** To undergo treatment for alcoholism.

**Dry run.** A test or rehearsal; a 'dummy run'. The allusion may be to the reconnoitring by bootleggers of the route they plan to use before transporting their illicit goods along it.

**Dry shave.** A shave without lathering the face. To give someone a dry shave is to rub their cheeks with one's own bristly face.

> I'll shave her, like a punished soldier, dry.
> PETER PINDAR: *The Lousiad*, ii (1785–95)

**Dry up, To.** To stop talking, either because one has nothing further to say or because one is talking too much.

**Dry wine.** As opposed to sweet. In sweet wine some of the sugar is not yet decomposed, whereas in dry wine all the sugar has been converted into alcohol.

**As dry as a bone** or **dust.** *See under* AS.

**Cut and dried.** *See under* CUT.

**High and dry.** *See under* HIGH.

**Home and dry.** *See under* HOME.

**Keep one's powder dry, To.** *See under* POWDER.

**Dryad.** In classical mythology, a tree NYMPH (Greek *drus*, 'oak', originally 'tree'). Hamadryads (Greek *hama*, 'together with') were tree nymphs whose life depended on that of their tree. When it died, they did. EURYDICE, the wife of ORPHEUS, was a dryad.

**Dryasdust.** The name given by Sir Walter Scott to the fictitious 'reverend doctor', a learned pundit to whom he addressed some of his prefaces, hence a heavy, plodding author, very prosy and dull, even if also very learned.

**DTs.** A contraction of *delirium tremens* (New Latin, 'trembling delirium'), a severe psychotic condition occurring in some alcoholics, marked by DELIRIUM and trembling.

**Dual** (Latin *dualis*, 'concerning two').

**Dualism.** A system of philosophy that refers all things that exist to two ultimate principles, such as Descartes' Thought (*res cogitans*) and Extension (*res extensa*), or, in the theological sense, good and evil. In modern philosophy it is opposed to MONISM and insists that creator and creation, mind and body, are distinct entities. *See also* MANICHEANS.

**Dual monarchy.** The situation when two states share the same monarchy but remain politically separate, as in the case of England and Scotland from 1603. The Stuart kings reigned in both countries which, however, remained politically independent of each other until the ACT OF UNION of 1707.

Historically the phrase is specifically applied to Austria-Hungary from the time of the *Ausgleich*, or Compromise, of 1867, until the collapse of 1918. During this period Francis Joseph was emperor of Austria and king of Hungary.

**Dual personality.** Used of someone who, on different occasions, reveals two quite different characters.

**Dub.** The original meaning (from Old English *dubbian*, 'to equip with arms') was to confer knighthood by a stroke of a sword. Hence its use for 'investing' a thing or person with a name or title.

**Dub up, To.** To put down the money; to 'fork out'. Dub here may be another form of dup, i.e. 'do up' or open (one's purse, pocket etc).

**Dubglas.** *See* DUGLAS.

**Ducat.** A coin first minted in 1140 by Roger II of Sicily as duke of the duchy (*ducato*) of Apulia. In 1284 the Venetians struck a gold coin bearing the legend *Sit tibi, Christe, datus, quem tu regis, iste ducatus* ('May this duchy which thou rulest be devoted to thee, O Christ') and through this the name ducat gained wider use.

**Duce** (Italian, 'leader'). The title adopted by Benito Mussolini (1883–1945), the FASCIST dictator of Italy from 1922 to 1943.

**Duchess, Flying.** *See under* FLY.

**Duck.** *See* DUCK'S EGG.

**Ducking stool.** A specially made chair in which the culprit was bound and publicly 'ducked' or immersed in the water. It was commonly used until the early 18th century, but its last recorded use in England was at Leominster, Herefordshire, in 1809, when Jenny Pipes was ducked. *See also* CUCKING STOOL.

**Ducks and drakes.** The ricocheting or rebounding of a flat stone thrown to skim across the surface of a pond or the like. The allusion is to the passage of the named birds over water.

> What figured slates are best to make
> On watery surface duck and drake.
> SAMUEL BUTLER: *Hudibras*, II, iii (1663)

**Duck's arse** or **DA.** A men's hairstyle in which the hair is swept back to a point at the nape of the neck, so that it looks like a duck's tail. The style was popular in the 1960s.

**Duck's egg.** Now always used in the shortened form of 'a duck', meaning in CRICKET no score at all. It arose from the resemblance of '0' on the scoreboard to a duck's egg. In American usage goose egg is used for no score at all in a game. *See also* LAY AN EGG.

**Duck soup.** Something easy to do, a 'doddle' or 'cinch'. The allusion may be to a 'sitting duck' as an easy target. The expression is American in origin. The Marx Brothers' film *Duck Soup* (1933) is one of their best.

**Bombay duck.** *See under* BOMBAY.

**Break one's duck, To.** *See under* BREAK.

**Dead duck, A.** *See under* DEAD.

**Donald Duck.** *See under* DONALD.

**Lame duck, A.** *See under* LAME.

**Like a duck to water.** *See under* LIKE.

**Like a dying duck in a thunderstorm.** *See under* LIKE.

**Like water off a duck's back.** *See under* LIKE.

**St Cuthbert's duck.** *See under* CUTHBERT.

**Ugly duckling.** *See under* UGLY.

**Dude.** Originally, a fop or dandy. Later, a city dweller, especially one holidaying on a ranch. The word suddenly became fashionable in New York early in 1883. Its origin is unknown.

**Dude ranch, A.** In the Western USA, a ranch specially organized as a holiday camp for inexperienced riders.

**Duff.** A type of boiled pudding, as plum duff. The word, a northern English form of DOUGH, probably gave the slang sense worthless, useless, since anything stodgy is dull, heavy and potentially unproductive.

**Duff up, To.** To beat; to thrash. The origin is probably in duffer, as a word for a foolish or useless person, who deserves beating.

**Up the duff.** Pregnant. The notion may be of having a BUN IN THE OVEN.

> Shaznay was reportedly none too happy that Melanie had got up the duff in the most important year of their career.
> *The Times* (8 January 1999)

**Duglas.** According to the 9th-century *Historia Britonum* by Nennius, King ARTHUR fought twelve great battles against the Saxons. 'The second, third, fourth and fifth, were on another river, by the Britons called Duglas in the region Linius.' The topography is vague and the whereabouts of the River Duglas (or Dubglas) is open to conjecture. *See also* DOUGLAS.

**Duke** (Latin *dux*, 'leader'). The title of the highest rank of nobility in Great Britain. The first English dukedom to be created was that bestowed by Edward III on his eldest son the BLACK PRINCE in 1338, when he was raised from Earl of Cornwall to Duke of Cornwall. The title is very rarely conferred except for royal dukes, and since 1874 (when Hugh Lupus Grosvenor, 3rd Marquis of Westminster, was made Duke of Westminster), it has been conferred only on the Earl of Fife, who was created Duke of Fife on his marriage with Princess Louise in 1889. On his death in 1912, his daughter, Princess Arthur of Connaught, became Duchess of Fife in her own right, by special remainder. Prince Philip was created Duke of Edinburgh in 1947. Other than royal dukes there are 24 noble dukedoms, the oldest being that of Norfolk, created in 1483. *See also* COURTESY TITLES; PEERS OF THE REALM.

**Duke Combe.** William Combe (1741–1823), also called Count Combe, author of *The Tour of Dr Syntax* etc, was so called from the splendour of his dress, the profusion of his table and the magnificence of his deportment, in the days of his prosperity. Having spent all his money he turned author, but passed much of his life in the King's Bench Prison. He died at Lambeth. *See also* SYNTAX.

**Duke Humphrey.** *See* DINE WITH DUKE HUMPHREY.

**Duke of Exeter's daughter, The.** The rack. It was introduced into England in 1447, when the Duke of Exeter was Constable of the TOWER OF LONDON. Hence the name.

**Duke of Shoreditch, The.** *See under* SHOREDITCH.

**Duke of Wellington's Bodyguard, The.** *See under* REGIMENTAL AND DIVISIONAL NICKNAMES.

**Duke of York's Column, The.** A noted column in London, at the top of Waterloo Steps leading from Waterloo Place into the Mall. It was completed in 1833 in memory of Frederick, Duke of York, George III's second son, who died in 1827. It is of the TUSCAN ORDER, designed by Benjamin Wyatt, and is made of Aberdeen granite, surmounted by a statue of the duke by Sir Richard Westmacott. It contains a winding staircase to the platform and is 124ft (38m) high. The duke faces the War Office (now part of the Ministry of Defence) in WHITEHALL. *See also* NOBLE DUKE OF YORK.

**Duke or darling.** Heads or tails. When the scandals about the Duke of York (1763–1827) and his mistress, Mrs Mary Anne Clarke, were the talk of the town, boys in the street quite often used to cry 'Duke or darling' instead of 'Heads or tails'.

**Dukeries.** That part of Nottinghamshire so called from the number of ducal residences established in the area from the 1680s, including Welbeck Abbey (Duke of Portland), Clumber (Duke of Newcastle), Thoresby (Duke of Kingston till 1773) and Worksop Manor (formerly Duke of Norfolk). The land was previously part of the Royal Forest of Sherwood.

**Dine with Duke Humphrey, To.** *See under* DINE.

**God bless the Duke of Argyle.** *See under* GOD.

**Good Duke Humphrey.** *See under* GOOD.

**Great Duke, The.** *See under* GREAT.

**Iron Duke.** *See* GREAT DUKE.

**Dulce. Dulce domum.** A school holiday song originating at Winchester College. The Latin words mean 'the sweet [sound of the word] home', not as often interpreted 'sweet home'. It is said to have been written by a boy detained, during the Whitsun holidays, for misconduct 'as report says, tied to a pillar'. According to tradition he pined away and died. On the evening preceding the Whitsun holidays, the masters, scholars and choristers still walk in procession round the pillar, chanting the six stanzas of the song. The music is by John Reading (d.1692), organist of Winchester Cathedral and of the college. *See also* HOME, SWEET HOME.

> Dulce domum resonemus.
> (Let us make the sweet sound of home resound.)

**Dulce et decorum est pro patria mori.** (Latin, 'It is sweet and becoming to die for one's country'; Horace, *Odes*, Bk III, ii (1st century BC)). The war poet Wilfred Owen referred to this as 'The old lie'.

**Dulcinea.** A former name for a man's sweetheart or 'ladylove', taken from the name of Don QUIXOTE's mistress. Her real name was Aldonza Lorenzo, but the knight dubbed her *Dulcinea del Toboso*, 'Dulcinea of El Toboso', from her birthplace in Toledo. Her name Dulcinea is based on Spanish *dulce*, 'sweet'.

**Dull. As dull as ditchwater.** *See under* AS.

**Dum. Dum sola** (Latin, 'while single'). A legal term applied to an unmarried woman. Similar terms are *Dum casta vixerit*, 'While she lives chastely', and *Dum fuit infra aetatem*, 'While he was within age'.

**Dum spiro spero** (Latin, 'While I breathe, I hope'). A motto of many British families and also of South California. Variations on it are *Dum cresco spero*, 'While I grow, I hope', motto of the Borough of Bromley, and *Dum spiro servo*, 'While I breathe, I serve', motto of the Chitty family.

**Dum vivimus vivamus** (Latin, 'While we live, let us live', i.e. let us enjoy life). This was the motto of the Epicureans (*see* EPICURUS). Catullus has a similar theme: *Vivamus, mea Lesbia, atque amemus*, 'Lesbia mine, let us live and love'. The motto was adopted on Dr Doddridge's coat of arms and converted into the following epigram:

> 'Live, while you live,' the epicure would say,
> 'And seize the pleasures of the present day.'
> 'Live, while you live,' the sacred preacher cries,
> 'And give to God each moment as it flies.'
> Lord, in my views, let each united be;
> I live in pleasure, when I live to thee.

**Dumb. Dumb blonde.** This now rather dated expression for a conspicuously attractive but stupid young blonde woman, the 'bimbo' of today, seems a contradiction in terms, since the lady is not normally noted for her silence. The first word of the phrase has probably been influenced by German *dumm*, 'stupid'.

**Dumb crambo.** A somewhat similar game to CRAMBO in which rhymes of the given word are pantomimed or acted in dumb show until they are guessed. *See also* CHARADES.

**Dumb down, To.** To reduce to a lower level of understanding. Dumbing down was perceived by some in the 1990s as increasingly pervasive in the media, in which 'serious' newspapers represented their material in a more populist fashion, while the more subtle points of television dramas and documentaries were demotically 'spelt out' for the benefit of the hedonistic viewer.

> Dumbing down, levelling down, politically correct, progressive – one word summarises the history many children are being taught: bunk.
>
> *The Times* (25 August 1998)

**Dumb Ox, The.** St THOMAS AQUINAS (1224–74), known afterwards as the ANGELIC DOCTOR, or Angel of the Schools. Albertus Magnus, his tutor, said of him: 'The dumb ox will one day fill the world with his lowing.' He was so nicknamed from his great bulk and his taciturnity.

**Dumbwaiter.** An 18th-century English contribution to the amenities of the DRAWING ROOM. The mahogany dumbwaiter introduced in the 1730s consisted of two or three circular trays of graduated sizes pivoted on a central stem, the legs of which were on castors. The trays usually contained food and wine, thus obviating the need for servants to be in close attendance on social occasions. In the days when servants were noted for making improper use of overheard confidences, the dumbwaiter was a notable asset.

**Dumdum.** A half-covered steel-cased bullet, which expands on impact and inflicts severe laceration. It is so called from the arsenal at Dum-Dum, near Calcutta, where they were first made in the 1890s. Their use was proscribed by the Second Hague Conference in 1899. At the time of the INDIAN MUTINY (1857), Dum-Dum was the scene of the first protests against the 'greased cartridges'.

**Dummy, Sell the.** *See under* SELL.

**Dumps, Down in the.** *See under* DOWN.

**Dun.** A person, especially a hired agent, who importunes someone for payment of a debt. The tradition is that the word refers to Joe Dun, a bailiff of Lincoln in the reign of Henry VII. The *British Apollo* (1708) said he was so active and dextrous in collecting bad debts that when anyone became 'slow to pay' the neighbours used to say to the creditors, 'Dun him', i.e. 'Send Dun after him'.

**Dun cow.** The savage beast slain by GUY OF WARWICK. A huge tusk, probably that of an elephant, is still shown at Warwick Castle as one of the horns of the dun cow. The fable is that it belonged to a giant and was kept on Mitchell Fold, Shropshire. Its milk was inexhaustible, but one day an old woman who had filled her pail wanted to fill her sieve also. This so enraged the cow that she broke loose from the fold and wandered to Dunsmore Heath, where she was slain.

> On Dunsmore heath I alsoe slewe
> A monstrous wyld and cruell beast,
> Calld the Dun-cow of Dunsmore heath;
> Which many people had opprest.
> Some of her bones in Warwicke yett
> Still for a monument doe lye.
>
> PERCY: *Reliques*, 'The Legend of Sir Guy' (1765)

**Book of the Dun Cow, The.** *See under* BOOK.

**Draw Dun out of the mire, To.** *See under* DRAW.

**Old Dun Cow, The.** *See under* OLD.

**Dunce.** A dolt or stupid person. The word is taken from John Duns Scotus (*c*.1265–1308), the SCHOOLMAN so called from his birthplace, Duns, west of BERWICK, in Scotland. His followers were called Dunses or SCOTISTS. Tyndal says that when they saw that their hair-splitting divinity was giving way to modern theology, 'the old barking curs raged in every pulpit' against the CLASSICS and new notions, so that the name indicated an opponent to progress and learning and hence a dunce. Duns Scotus was buried at Cologne. His epitaph reads:

> Scotia me genuit, Anglia me suscepit, Gallia me docuit, Colonia me tenet.
> (Scotland bore me, England took me, France taught me, Cologne holds me.)

**Dunce's cap.** A conical cap worn by the class 'dunce' as a symbol of disgrace and stupidity.

**Dunciad, The.** The 'dunce epic', a satire by Alexander Pope, first published anonymously in 1728 with Theobald featuring as the Poet Laureate of the realm of Dullness, but republished with an added fourth part in 1741 with Colley Cibber in that role. Many contemporary writers who were pilloried in this poem would have otherwise been unnoticed by posterity.

**King of the Dunces.** *See under* KING.

**Parliament of Dunces, The.** *See under* PARLIAMENT.

**Dundas, Starvation.** *See under* STARVE.

**Dundee, Bonnie.** *See under* BONNIE.

**Dundreary whiskers.** Lord Dundreary was the chief character in Tom Taylor's *Our American Cousin* (1858), the personification of a good-natured, indolent, blundering, empty-headed 'swell'. E.A. Sothern created the character by the brilliance of his acting and the liberties he took with the original text. The theatrical make-up for the part included long side whiskers, which set a fashion among the young men about town.

**Dunedin.** *See* EDINBURGH.

**Dung, Devil's.** *See under* DEVIL.
**Dunheved Castle.** *See* CASTLE TERABIL.
**Dunkers** or **Dunkards.** *See* TUNKERS.
**Dunkirk.** This once notorious haunt of pirates and privateers in northern France has acquired fresh associations since the Second World War. The name is now used figuratively to denote a forced military evacuation by sea to avoid disaster, a speedy and complete withdrawal, an entire abandonment of a position. The allusion is to the heroic evacuation of the main British expeditionary force (26 May to 4 June 1940), in the face of imminent disaster, by Vice-Admiral Ramsay's motley force of destroyers, yachts and other craft, with essential air cover from RAF Fighter Command. The phrase 'Dunkirk spirit' or 'spirit of Dunkirk' gained general currency to describe any sudden confrontation or crisis, especially one that is handled by 'rising to the occasion'.

> The Dunkirk spirit of only starting to try hard when it becomes really necessary is deeply engrained in the British character.
> *Listener* (19 October 1961)

**Dunmow flitch.** The expression 'eating Dunmow bacon' was formerly used of happily married couples, especially those who had lived long together and never quarrelled. The allusion is to a custom said to have been instituted by Lady Juga Baynard in 1104 and restored by Robert Fitzwalter in 1244. It was that any person going to Dunmow, in Essex, and humbly kneeling on two sharp stones at the church door, might claim a flitch (side) of bacon if he could swear that for 12 months and a day he had never had a household brawl or wished himself unmarried.

Allusions to the tradition are frequent in literature from the 17th century and the custom was revived in the second half of the 19th century. Today the Flitch Trials are held at Little Dunmow in mid-June every LEAP YEAR.

**Duns Scotus.** *See* DUNCE.
**Dunstable.** The lexicographer Nathan Bailey (d. 1742) gives the etymology of the name of this Bedfordshire town as follows: 'of Dunus, a Robber in the Time of King Henry I, who made it dangerous for Travellers, by his continual Robberies'. The name actually means 'Duna's boundary post', from *Duna*, an Anglo-Saxon here at some time, and Old English *stapol*, 'post', 'pillar'.

**Dunstable larks.** Once a highly prized dish, in the same way as Whitstable oysters. Famed from the 17th century, they were served as a speciality in the local inns, which were much patronized by the visiting gentry.

**Dunstan.** Archbishop of Canterbury (*c*.909–988) and patron saint of goldsmiths, himself a noted worker in gold. He is represented in pontifical robes and carrying a pair of pincers in his right hand. The latter refers to the legend that on one occasion he seized the Devil by the nose with a pair of red hot tongs and refused to release him till he promised never to tempt Dunstan again. *See also* HORSESHOES.

**Duodecimo.** A book whose sheets are folded into 12 leaves each (Latin *duodecim*, 12), often called 'twelvemo', from the contraction 12mo. The book is naturally a small one, hence the expression has been sometimes applied to other things or persons of small size.

**Dupes, Day of the.** *See under* DAY.
**Durandal** or **Durindana.** *See* ROLAND.
**Durden, Dame.** A former generic name for a housewife. In the old song she kept five serving girls to carry the milking pails and five serving men to use the flail and spade. Naturally, the men fall for the maids.

**Dust. Dust and ashes.** In Old Testament times, a person sprinkled earth, dust and ashes over the head as a sign of mourning. Dust and ashes was expressive of one's deep humiliation, insignificance and worthlessness. *See also* WEAR SACKCLOTH AND ASHES.

> And Abraham answered and said, Behold now, I have taken upon me to speak unto the Lord, which am but dust and ashes.
> Genesis 18:27

**Dust down, To.** To reprimand.

**Dust-up.** A row, a fight, a bit of a SHEMOZZLE or a SHINDIG.

**Dusty answer.** An unsatisfactory or peremptory reply.

> Ah, what a dusty answer gets the soul
> When hot for certainties in this our life!
> GEORGE MEREDITH, *Modern Love* (1862)

Rosamond Lehmann's first novel, *Dusty Answer* (1927), was a *succès de scandale*.

**Dusty Miller.** A common NICKNAME, particularly in the Royal Navy, for all those with the surname Miller, just as all Clarks are called NOBBY and Bells 'Daisy' or 'Dinger'. Its origin is obvious and appropriate. The auricula is also known as 'Dusty Miller' from the white mealiness of its leaves.

**Angel dust.** *See under* ANGEL.
**As dry as dust.** *See under* AS.
**Ashes to ashes, dust to dust.** *See under* ASH.
**Bite the dust, To.** *See under* BITE.
**Devil's dust.** *See under* DEVIL.
**Jack Dusty.** *See under* JACK.
**Kiss the dust, To.** *See under* KISS.
**Not so dusty.** Not too bad, fairly well. The phrase is mostly said in response to the enquiry, 'How are you?' Here dusty means soiled, bad, worthless.
**Raise** or **kick up a dust, To.** *See under* RAISE.
**Red duster.** *See under* RED.

**Shake the dust from one's feet, To.** *See under* SHAKE.

**Throw dust in someone's eyes, To.** *See under* THROW.

**When the dust settles.** *See under* WHEN.

**Dutch.** This word, properly relating to the Netherlands or Holland, is directly related to German *Deutsch*, 'German', and was formerly used in English to denote the people of Germany or of Teutonic stock, not merely the Netherlanders. The derogatory implications of some of the phrases below derive from the Anglo-Dutch wars of the 17th century. *See also* PENNSYLVANIA DUTCH.

**Dutch auction.** An auction in which the auctioneer offers the goods at gradually decreasing prices, the first bidder to accept becoming the purchaser. The process is the reverse of a normal auction. There is a Dutch auction daily at 6.30 am in the fish market at Hastings, when the day's catch is sold thus.

**Dutch bargain.** A one-sided bargain.

**Dutch barn.** A barn for hay or the like that consists simply of a roof set upon poles, without any walls. Such barns were common in Holland.

**Dutch cap.** A contraceptive device for women, so named because the shape it assumes when in position bears some resemblance to the cap with triangular flaps that forms part of Dutch women's national dress.

**Dutch clocks.** *See* MISNOMERS.

**Dutch comfort.** Cold comfort, implying that things might have been worse.

**Dutch concert.** A concert in which singers sing their different songs at the same time, or in which each person sings a verse of any song they like between bursts of a familiar chorus. Hence any great noise and uproar, like that made by a party of drunken Dutchmen, with singing, arguing and the like.

**Dutch courage.** The courage exerted by drink. The Dutch were considered heavy drinkers. *See also* DUTCH BARGAIN.

**Dutch cousins.** Close friends, a pun on COUSINS-GERMAN.

**Dutch elm disease.** A fungoid disease of elm trees, in which the foliage withers and the tree eventually dies. It was first discovered in Holland in about 1920.

**Dutch gold.** 'German' gold, an alloy of copper and zinc, yellow in colour, which easily tarnishes unless lacquered. Imitation gold leaf is made from it, hence the name Dutch leaf. It is also called Dutch metal.

**Dutchman's breeches.** The opening of two patches of blue in a stormy sky giving the promise of better weather, i.e. enough blue sky to make a Dutchman a pair of breeches. A nautical phrase.

The plant *Dicentra cucullaria* is also called Dutchman's breeches from its two-spurred flowers.

**Dutch talent.** That which is not done in true nautical and shipshape fashion, more the result of brawn than brain.

**Dutch treat.** A meal, entertainment or the like at which each person pays for himself. 'To go Dutch' has the same meaning.

**Dutch uncle.** A person who criticizes sharply or reproves severely. The Dutch were noted for their discipline.

**Dutch wife.** An open frame constructed of cane, originally used in the Dutch East Indies (modern Indonesia) and other hot countries to support the uppermost knee in bed when lying on one's side. A bolster is used for the same purpose.

**Beat the Dutch, To.** *See under* BEAT.

**Cape Dutch.** *See under* CAPE.

**Double Dutch.** *See under* DOUBLE.

**Flying Dutchman.** *See under* FLY.

**Go Dutch, To.** *See under* DUTCH TREAT.

**I'm a Dutchman.** An expression used to strengthen an affirmation or assertion. For example: 'If that's not Fred over there, then I'm a Dutchman.' I am obviously not a Dutchman, therefore it must be Fred.

**My old Dutch.** Here the word is a contraction of duchess and is nothing to do with Holland. It is a colloquial term for one's wife, especially the wife of a coster.

> There ain't a lady livin' in the land
> As I'd swop for my dear old Dutch!
>
> ALBERT CHEVALIER: 'My Old Dutch' (song) (1901)

**Pennsylvania Dutch.** *See under* PENNSYLVANIA.

**Duty. Death duty.** *See under* DEATH.

**Line of duty.** *See under* LINE.

**Point duty.** *See under* POINT.

**DV.** *See* DEO VOLENTE.

**Dwarf.** Dwarfs have figured in the legends and mythology of nearly every people, and the success of Walt Disney's children's classic *Snow White and the Seven Dwarfs* (1938) is evidence of their enduring appeal. Pliny gives particulars of whole races of them, possibly following travellers' tales of African pygmies. They are prominent in Germanic and Scandinavian legend and generally dwelt in rocks and caves and recesses of the earth. They were guardians of mineral wealth and precious stones and very skilful at their work. They were not unfriendly to man, but could, on occasions, be vindictive and mischievous.

In England dwarfs or midgets were popular down to the 18th century as court favourites or household pets. In later times they were often exhibited as curiosities at circuses or 'freak shows'.

Among those recorded in legend or history (with their reputed heights) the following are the best known:

ALBERICH: the dwarf of the NIBELUNGENLIED
Andromeda and Conopas: each 2ft 4in (71cm), the dwarfs of Julia, niece of Augustus
Bébé or Nicholas Ferry (1714–37): 2ft 9in (84cm), a native of France; he had a brother and sister, both dwarfs
Count Joseph Boruwlaski (d.1837): 3ft 3in (99cm)
Che-Mah: 2ft 1in (64cm) and 52lb (23.5kg), a Chinaman who exhibited in London in 1880
Colobri, Prince of Sleswig: 2ft 1in (64cm) and 25lb (11.3kg) at the age of 25 in 1851
Coppernin: the dwarf of the Princess of Wales, mother of George III; the last court dwarf in England
Caroline Crachami (1814–24): 1ft 8in (51cm), born at Palermo; exhibited in Bond Street, London, 1824
John Decker or Ducker (*fl.*1610): 2ft 6in (76cm), an Englishman
'The Fairy Queen': 1ft 4in (41cm) and 4lb (1.8kg), exhibited in Regent Street, London, 1850; her feet were less than 2in (5cm) long
Richard Gibson (1615–90): a good portrait painter; his wife's maiden name was Anne Shepherd; each measured 3ft 10in (117cm), and Waller sang their praises:

Design or chance makes others wive,
But Nature did this match contrive.

Harry Hopkins (1737–54): 2ft 7in (79cm), born at Llantrisant, Glamorgan; weighed 19lb (8.6kg) at age of 7, 13lb (5.9kg) at the time of his death
Sir Jeffrey HUDSON (1619–82): born at Oakham, Rutland; 3ft 9in (114cm) at the age of 30; he figures in Sir Walter Scott's *Peveril of the Peak* (1823)
William E. Jackson (1864–1900): 2ft 3in (69cm), born at Dunedin, New Zealand, and commonly known as Major Mite
John Jarvis (1508–56): 2ft (61cm), page of honour to Queen Mary
Mrs Catherine Kelly (1756–85): 2ft 10in (86cm), 'The Irish Fairy'
Wybrand Lolkes: 2ft 3in (69cm) and 57lb (25.8kg); exhibited at ASTLEY's in 1790
Lucius: 2ft (61cm) and 17lb (7.7kg), the dwarf of the Emperor Augustus
Count Primo Magri: 2ft 8in (81cm); *see* Lavinia WARREN *below*
Lizzie Marine: 2ft 9in (84cm) and 45lb (20.4kg)
Matjus and Bela Matina (b.1903, *fl.*1935): twins, each 2ft 6in (76cm), born in Budapest, Hungary
Pauline Musters (1876–95): 1ft 9½in (55cm) and 3lb 5oz (1.5kg) at the age of 9, full grown height exactly 2ft (61cm), born at Ossendrecht, the Netherlands; known as 'Princess Pauline'
Commodore Nutt: *see* TOM THUMB
Simon Paap: 2ft 4in (71cm) and 27lb (12.2kg); a Dutch dwarf
A.L. Sawyer: 2ft 6½in (77cm) and 39lb (17.7kg); editor in 1833 of the *Democrat*, a paper of considerable repute in Florida
C.H. Stoberin: 2ft 1in (64cm) at the age of 20; from Nuremberg
Nannette Stocker: 2ft 9in (84cm); exhibited in London in 1815
Strasse Davit family: man 1ft 8in (51cm), woman, 1ft 6in (46cm), child at age 17 only 6in (15cm)
Madame Teresia: 2ft 10in (86cm) and 27lb (12.2kg), a Corsican, exhibited in London in 1773
General TOM THUMB (1838–83): real name Charles S. Stratton, born at Bridgeport, Connecticut; exhibited first in London in 1844; in 1863 married Lavinia WARREN (*see below*) and was then 2ft 7in (79cm), she being 2ft 8in (81cm) and 21 years old; they visited England the following year with their dwarf son, Commodore Nutt
Lucy Wanmer: 2ft 6in (76cm) and 45lb (20.4kg); exhibited in London 1801, at the age of 45
Lavinia Warren (1841–1919): *see* TOM THUMB; in 1884 she married another dwarf, Count Primo Magri
John Wormberg (Hanoverian period): 2ft 7in (79cm) at the age of 38
Xit: the dwarf of Edward VI
Lucia Zarate (1863–89): 1ft 8in (51cm) and 4¾lb (2.15kg) at the age of 18; exhibited with her younger sister, who was a little taller, as 'The Midgets'; seen in London in 1881

*See also* GIANTS; HEAVIEST MEN.

**Black Dwarf, The.** *See under* BLACK.

**Seven Dwarfs, The.** *See under* SEVEN.

**Dwt.** Formerly, pennyweight, with D from Latin *denarius*, 'penny'. *See also* CWT.

**Dye. Dyed-in-the-wool.** Wool dyed in its original natural or 'raw' state retains a dye more thoroughly than when it has been treated and made up into a garment. Hence the phrase is used to mean through and through, genuine or out and out, as 'a dyed-in-the-wool teetotaller', a firm and definite abstainer.

**Villain of the deepest dye, A.** *See under* VILLAIN.

**Dying sayings.** *See* FAMOUS LAST WORDS.

**Dyke** or **dike.** The colloquial term for a lesbian, especially one of mannish appearance, is of uncertain origin and much debated. It may be a shortening of dialect 'morphodyke', representing a pronunciation of 'hermaphrodite', perhaps influenced by 'dick' in the sense of penis.

**Devil's Dyke.** *See under* DEVIL.

**Offa's Dyke.** *See under* OFFA.

**Dymoke.** The name of the family which has held the office of CHAMPION OF ENGLAND since the coronation of Richard II (1377).

**Dymphna** or **Dympna.** The patron saint of the insane. She is said to have been the daughter of a 7th-century Irish chieftain, who fled to Gheel in Belgium to escape her father's incestuous attentions and devoted herself to charitable works. She was eventually murdered by her father. In art she is shown dragging away a Devil. Gheel (Geel) has long been a centre for the treatment of the mentally afflicted. St Dymphna's day is 15 May.

**Dynasty, Merovingian.** *See under* MEROVINGIAN.

# E

**E.** This letter is derived from the Egyptian hieroglyph ⏍, and the Phoenician and Hebrew sign called *he*.

The following legend is sometimes found in churches under the two tables of the TEN COMMANDMENTS:

> PRSVR Y PRFCT MN
> VR KP THS PRCPTS TN
> The vowel E
> Supplies the key.

**Eager beaver.** An American expression in the Second World War for an over-zealous recruit whose keenness was marked by volunteering on every possible occasion. It was subsequently applied in civilian life to any glutton for work. The beaver is noted for its industry and hard work, but not specifically for its eagerness.

> It would be futile to play that game against Republican Earl Warren, one of the foremost spokesmen of the eager-beaver West.
> *Time* (5 July 1948)

*See also* BEAVERS.

**Eagle.** In mythology the eagle commonly represents the sun, but in Scandinavian myth the bird is usually associated with storm and gloom. It is also emblematic of courage, immortality and other fine or desirable attributes. In Christian art it is the symbol of St JOHN THE EVANGELIST (hence its use on church lecterns), St AUGUSTINE, St GREGORY THE GREAT and St PRISCA. Emblematically or in HERALDRY the eagle is a charge of great honour. It was called the Bird of JOVE by the Romans and was borne on their military standards. They used to let an eagle fly from the funeral pile of a deceased emperor, symbolizing the reception of his soul among the gods. John Dryden alludes to this custom in the opening stanza of his poem on the death of Oliver Cromwell:

> Like eager *Romans* e'er all Rites were past,
> Did let too soon the sacred Eagle fly.
> *Heroique Stanza's* (1658)

An eagle is also a former American gold 10-dollar piece, issued in 1795 and withdrawn from circulation in 1935. In golf an eagle is a score of two strokes under par.

**Eagle and Child, The.** The crest of the Stanley family and Earls of Derby, and a well-known PUBLIC HOUSE SIGN. The legend is that Sir Thomas Latham, an ancestor of the house, caused his illegitimate son to be placed under the foot of a tree in which an eagle had built its nest. When out walking with his wife, they 'accidentally' found the child, which he persuaded her to adopt as their heir. Later he changed his mind and left most of his wealth to his daughter, and the family altered the eagle crest to that of an eagle preying upon a child.

**Eagle eye.** An eye with keen and piercing sight. The expression is figuratively used of acute intellectual vision.

**Eagle of Brittany, The.** Bertrand du Guesclin (*c*.1320–80), CONSTABLE OF FRANCE.

**Eagle of Meaux, The.** Jacques Bénigne Bossuet (1627–1704), bishop of Meaux, the great pulpit orator, theologian and historian.

**Eagle of the Divines, The.** St THOMAS AQUINAS (*c*.1225–74).

**Eagle of the Doctors of France, The.** Pierre d'Ailly (1350–1420), French cardinal and SCHOOLMAN, who helped to end the papal schism.

**Eagle of the North, The.** Count Axel Oxenstierna (1583–1654), the Swedish statesman.

**Eagle stones.** *See* AETITES.

**Golden eagle, The.** *See under* GOLDEN.

**Grand eagle.** *See under* GRAND.

**Land of the White Eagle, The.** *See under* LAND.

**Spread-eagled.** *See under* SPREAD.

**Thy youth is renewed like the eagle's.** *See under* YOUTH.

**Two-headed eagle.** *See under* TWO.

**Ealing comedies.** Comedy films produced by the Ealing Studios, west London, from the late 1940s. They typically feature a downtrodden group rebelling against authority and are regarded as quintessentially 'English'. Among the best are *Whisky Galore* (1948), in which a ship with a cargo of whisky is wrecked on a small Scottish island, *The Lavender Hill Mob* (1951), centring on a timid clerk who plans and executes a bullion robbery, and *The Titfield Thunderbolt* (1952), telling how villagers take over a railway branch line when it is faced with closure.

**Ear.** If your ears burn, someone is talking about you. This is a very old superstition. Pliny says:

'When our ears do glow and tingle, some do talk of us in our absence.' In Shakespeare's *Much Ado About Nothing* (III, i (1598)), Beatrice says, when Ursula and Hero had been talking of her: 'What fire is in mine ears?' Sir Thomas Browne (1605–82) ascribes the conceit to guardian angels, who touch the right ear if the talk is favourable and the left if otherwise. This is done to cheer or warn.

> One ear tingles; some there be
> That are snarling now at me.
> ROBERT HERRICK: *Hesperides* (1648)

**Earful.** A ticking-off; a dressing-down; a 'piece of one's mind', especially when delivered at length.

> [The driving instructor] used to put a bottle on the seat, and if it rolled off when the pupil let his clutch out, he got an earful.
> *The Times* (11 February 1964)

**Earmarked.** Marked so as to be recognized. Figuratively, allocated or set aside for a special purpose. The allusion is to owner's marks on the ears of cattle and sheep.

**Ears to Ear Bible, The.** *See under* BIBLE.

**Ear to the ground.** Alert and well informed of what is taking place; alive to any possible developments. A figure derived from woodcraft.

**Earwig** (Old English *ēarwicga*, 'ear beetle'). The insect is so called from the erroneous notion that it can enter the ears and penetrate the brain.

**About one's ears.** *See under* ABOUT.

**All ears.** *See under* ALL.

**Ass-eared.** *See under* ASS.

**Asses as well as pitchers have ears.** *See under* ASS.

**Bend someone's ear, To.** *See under* BEND.

**By ear.** *See under* BY.

**Cauliflower ear.** *See under* CAULIFLOWER.

**Cock the ears, To.** *See under* COCK.

**Dionysius' ear.** *See under* DIONYSIUS.

**Fall on deaf ears, To.** *See under* FALL.

**Give ear to, To.** To listen to, to pay attention to.

**Have itching ears, To.** *See under* ITCH.

**In one ear and out the other.** *See under* IN.

**Jenkins' Ear.** *See under* JENKINS.

**Jew's ear.** *See under* JEW.

**Judas' ear.** *See* JEW'S EAR.

**Lend me your ears.** *See under* LEND.

**Little pitchers have long ears.** *See under* LITTLE.

**Make a silk purse out of a sow's ear, To.** *See under* SILK.

**Out on one's ear.** *See under* OUT.

**Pig's ear, A.** *See under* PIG.

**Play it by ear, To.** *See under* PLAY.

**Prick up one's ears, To.** *See under* PRICK.

**Sent off with a flea in one's ear, To be.** *See under* SENT.

**Thick ear, A.** *See under* THICK.

**Turn a deaf ear, To.** *See under* TURN.

**Up to one's ears.** *See under* UP.

**Walls have ears.** *See under* WALL.

**Wet behind the ears.** *See under* WET.

**Within earshot.** *See under* WITHIN.

**Earl** (Old English *eorl*, a man of position, as opposed to a *ceorl* or churl). The third in dignity in the British peerage, ranking next below MARQUESS. In later Anglo-Saxon England earls became important administrative officers commanding the MILITIA of their areas, and their growing political power is exemplified by that of Earl Godwin. WILLIAM THE CONQUEROR tried to introduce the name COUNT unsuccessfully, but the wife of an earl is still called a countess. *See also* COURTESY TITLES; PEERS OF THE REALM; VISCOUNT.

> The sheriff is called in Latin vice-comes, as being the deputy of an earl or comes, to whom the custody of a shire is said to have been committed.
> WILLIAM BLACKSTONE: *Commentaries on the Laws of England*, Bk I, ch ix (1765–9)

**Earl Grey.** A superior type of oriental tea flavoured and scented with oil of bergamot. The story goes that the recipe for it was given in the 1830s to Charles Grey, 2nd Earl Grey (1764–1845) by a grateful Chinese mandarin whose life had been saved by a British diplomat. The blend was then taken up commercially.

**Earl Marshal.** The officer of state who presides over the College of Arms, grants armorial bearings and is responsible for the arrangements of the sovereign's coronation, the state funeral of the sovereign and other state occasions, such as the state opening of Parliament. Since 1672 the office has been hereditary in the line of the Dukes of Norfolk. *See also* MARSHAL.

**Earl of Mar's Grey-breeks, The.** *See under* REGIMENTAL AND DIVISIONAL NICKNAMES.

**Belted earl.** *See under* BELT.

**Early. Early bird, An.** A person who rises early, arrives early, starts work early, and so on. The allusion is the proverb 'The early bird catches the worm', meaning that the person who acts promptly is the one to achieve an objective.

**Early days.** Too soon for something to happen or be realized. A typical form of the phrase is, 'It's early days yet,' said of a lengthy process that has only just started.

**Early grave, An.** An untimely or premature death.

**Early hours, The.** The very early morning, often before dawn.

**Early music.** Music from the earliest times up to and including the Baroque period, especially as revived in modern times and played on 'authentic' or period instruments. There are now many 'early music' ensembles, and the performance and recording of early music has become a significant feature of the classical music industry. A periodical devoted to the subject, *Early Music*, was founded in 1973.

**Early night, An.** An occasion on which one goes to bed earlier than usual. The term is subjective, as is the statement, 'I don't like to go to bed too late', which simply means 'I don't like to go to bed later than I like to go'.

**Early retirement.** Retirement from one's occupation earlier than the statutory age. From the 1980s many have been able to retire early on advantageous financial terms.

**Early warning.** Advance warning of a problem or, more seriously, of a nuclear attack, for which some countries have evolved a special so-called 'early warning system'.

**Bright and early.** *See under* BRIGHT.

**Earn the wages of sin, To.** To be hanged or condemned to death.

> The wages of sin is death.
> Romans 6:23

**Earth. Earthly Paradise, The.** It was a popular medieval belief that Paradise, a land or island where everything was beautiful and restful, and where death and decay were unknown, still existed somewhere on earth. It was usually located far away to the East, and in 9th-century maps it is shown in China. The fictitious letter of PRESTER JOHN to the Emperor Emmanuel Comnenus states that it was within three days' journey of his own territory, a 'fact' that is corroborated by Sir John MANDEVILLE. The Hereford *Mappa Mundi* (13th century) shows it as a circular island near India.

William Morris' poem of this title (1868–70) tells how a band of Norsemen seek vainly for this Paradise and return in old age to a nameless city where the gods of ancient Greece are still worshipped.

**Earth Mother** or **Goddess.** A general name often given to a primitive female deity who appears in mythologies around the world as the fundamental mother from whom all human beings and the earth itself are descended. The concept of an Earth Mother is bound up with basic femininity as well as primitive practices. Sir James Frazer in *The Golden Bough* (1890) describes human sacrifices made among the Dravidian races of Bengal to the Earth Goddess Tari Pennu. *See also* MOTHER EARTH.

**Earthquakes.** According to Indian mythology the world rests on the head of a great elephant, 'Muha-pudma', and when, for the sake of rest, the huge monster refreshes itself by moving its head, an earthquake is produced.

The lamas say that the earth is placed on the back of a gigantic frog, and when it moves its limbs or its head it shakes the earth. Other Eastern myths place the earth on the back of a tortoise.

Greek and Roman mythologists ascribe earthquakes to the restlessness of the giants whom JUPITER buried under high mountains. Thus Virgil (*Aeneid*, iii (1st century BC)) ascribes the eruption of Etna to the fiery breath of the giant ENCELADUS.

**Black earth.** *See under* BLACK.

**Come back** or **down to earth, To.** *See under* COME.

**Cost the earth, To.** *See under* COST.

**Down to earth.** *See under* DOWN.

**Ends of the earth, The.** *See under* END.

**Friends of the Earth.** *See under* FRIEND.

**Gone to earth.** Gone into hiding. A term derived from fox-hunting. *See also* GO TO GROUND *under* GROUND; RUN TO EARTH.

> They crouched and shuddered like beaten dogs as the terrible cry once more roused the shivering echoes!
> 'Gone to earth! Gone to earth!'
> MARY WEBB: *Gone to Earth*, ch xxxvi (1917)

**Heaven cannot support two suns, nor earth two masters.** *See under* HEAVEN.

**Run to earth, To.** *See under* RUN.

**Salt of the earth.** *See under* SALT.

**Scorched earth policy.** *See under* SCORCHED.

**What on earth?** *See under* WHAT.

**Ease** or **easy. Ease oneself** or **ease nature, To.** To urinate or, more commonly, defecate.

**Ease the helm, To.** In sailing to relieve the pressure of the water on the rudder by bringing the bow into the wind.

**Easy come, easy go.** What is easily gained is easily lost or spent.

**Easy does it.** Go carefully; don't rush it.

**Easy money.** Money obtained with little effort; MONEY FOR JAM.

**Easy on the eye** or **ear.** Pleasant to look at or to listen to.

**Easy-peasy.** Very simple. The second word is simply a rhyming jingle.

> But do I hear our ludic masochist asking for more? Univocalics? Easy. Lipograms? Peasy.
> DAVID CRYSTAL: *Language Play*, ch iii (1998)

**Easy Street.** Affluence; comfortable circumstances.

**Easy touch, An.** A gullible person.

**As easy as falling off a log** or **pie.** *See under* AS.

**At ease.** *See under* AT.

**Chapel of ease.** *See under* CHAPEL.

**Free and easy.** *See under* FREE.

**Go easy, To.** To be sparing or cautious, as: 'Go easy on the vegetables.'

**Ill at ease.** *See under* ILL.

**Stand at ease!** *See under* STAND.

**Stand easy!** *See under* STAND.

**Take it easy, To.** *See under* TAKE.

**East.** Christian churches are usually built 'east and west', and the altar is placed at the east end of the church to remind the congregation of Christ and the resurrection. The custom of turning to the east when the creed is repeated is to express the belief that Christ is the 'dayspring' and 'Sun of Righteousness'. The early Christians were accustomed to turn to the east in their devotions, just as the Jews turned their faces to Jerusalem when they prayed. People are often buried with their feet to the east to signify that they died in hope of the Resurrection. More recently it has been suggested that because so many churches were built on pagan sites, the eastern orientation reflects the pagan practice of praying towards the sunrise. It is significant that the very word orientation relates to orient, the east, itself from Latin *oriri*, to rise.

The ancient Greeks always buried their dead with the face upwards, looking towards heaven, while their feet were turned to the east, or the rising sun, indicating that the deceased were on their way to ELYSIUM and not to the region of night.

**East End, The.** Specifically the inner London boroughs east of the City of London itself, at one time essentially working-class areas, the inhabitants of which are known as East Enders. *See also* COCKNEY; WEST END.

**Eastern Church, The.** The ORTHODOX CHURCH. *See also* GREEK CHURCH.

**Eastern Empire, The.** The East Roman or BYZANTINE EMPIRE.

**Eastern Question, The.** As a historical term this essentially refers to the decay and disintegration of the Turkish Empire in southeastern Europe and the Near East from the time of the Greek revolt in 1821 until the establishment of the Turkish Republic in 1923.

**East is East and West is West.** A phrase from Rudyard Kipling emphasizing the divergence of views on ethics and life in general between the Oriental and Western peoples.

> Oh, East is East, and West is West, and never the twain shall meet,
> Till Earth and Sky stand presently at God's great Judgement Seat.
> 'The Ballad of East and West' (1892)

**East Side.** The region of Manhattan Island, New York, that extends from East River almost to the middle of Manhattan and from Brooklyn Bridge to 14th Street. It was the main place of settlement for immigrants and has retained much of its 'ethnic' character, with individual parts associated with particular races. The best known is CHINATOWN, with its many restaurants.

**Crown of the East.** *See under* CROWN.

**Far East, The.** *See under* FAR.

**Middle East, The.** *See under* MIDDLE.

**Easter.** The name was adopted for the Christian Paschal festival from Old English *ēastre*, a heathen festival held at the vernal equinox in honour of Eastre, a Germanic goddess of the dawn. Her own name relates to EAST.

Easter Day is the first Sunday after the Paschal full moon, i.e. the full moon that occurs on the day of the vernal equinox (21 March) or on any of the next 28 days. Thus Easter Sunday cannot be earlier than 22 March or later than 25 April, as laid down by the COUNCIL OF NICAEA in 325. The ORTHODOX CHURCH still celebrates Easter independently. In 1963 the VATICAN COUNCIL declared itself in favour of fixing the date of Easter when agreement with other churches could be reached.

It was formerly a common belief that the sun danced on Easter Day.

> But oh, she dances such a way,
> No sun upon an Easter day
> Is half so fine a sight.
> SIR JOHN SUCKLING: 'Ballad upon a Wedding' (1646)

Sir Thomas Browne combats the superstition:

> We shall not, I hope, disparage the Resurrection of our Redeemer, if we say the Sun doth not dance on Easter day. And though we would willingly assent unto any sympathetical exultation, yet cannot conceive therein any more than a Tropical expression.
> *Pseudodoxia Epidemica*, V, xxii (1646)

**Easter-ale.** *See* CHURCH-ALE.

**Easter eggs.** The egg as a symbol of fertility and renewal of life derives from the ancient world, as did the practice of colouring and eating eggs at the spring festival. The custom of eating eggs on Easter Sunday and of making gifts of Easter eggs to children probably derives from the Easter payment of eggs by the villein to his overlord. The idea of the egg as a symbol of new life was adopted to symbolize the Resurrection. Easter eggs are also known as 'pasch eggs' or 'pace eggs', from Old French *pasche*, ultimately from Hebrew *pesakh* (*see* PASSOVER). This name came to be used for the hard-boiled, hand-coloured eggs that were rolled down slopes as one of the Easter games, a practice surviving in the yearly egg-rolling held on the lawn of the WHITE HOUSE in Washington. *See also* PASCH.

**Easter Rising, The.** A rebellion that began on Easter Monday, 24 April 1916, in which Irish nationalists led by Patrick Pearse and James Connolly seized buildings in Dublin and issued a proclamation of Irish independence from Britain. The Rising was crushed by British forces within five days, the ensuing execution of fifteen of its leaders fuelling the growth of nationalist sentiment in Ireland. The timing of the Rising, originally intended to commence on Easter Day itself, was intended by Pearse to emphasize his notion of a blood-sacrifice in the cause of Irish freedom. W.B. Yeats wrote a poem inspired by the Rising entitled 'Easter 1916':

> All changed, changed utterly:
> A terrible beauty is born.
>
> W.B. YEATS: *Michael Robartes and the Dancer*, 'Easter 1916' (1921)

**Eat.** To eat together was, in the East, a sure pledge of protection. There is a story of a Persian grandee who gave the remainder of a peach he was eating to a man who implored his protection, only to find that his own son had been slain by this man. The nobleman would not allow the murderer to be punished, but said, 'We have eaten together: go in peace.' *See also* CALUMET; EAT SALT WITH SOMEONE.

**Eat crow, To.** In North American usage to be forced to do something humiliating or distasteful. The expression is said to derive from an incident during an armistice of the Anglo-American War of 1812–14. A New Englander unwittingly crossed the British lines while hunting and brought down a crow. An unarmed British officer heard the shot and resolved to punish the offender. He gained hold of the American's gun by praising his marksmanship and asking to see his weapon. The Britisher then told the American he was guilty of trespass and forced him at the point of the gun to take a bite out of the crow. When the officer returned the gun, the American in his turn covered the soldier and compelled him to eat the remainder of the crow.

**Eat dirt, To.** To put up with insults and mortification.

**Eat, drink and be merry, for tomorrow we die.** A popular variant of the biblical words: 'Let us eat and drink; for to morrow we shall die' (Isaiah 22:13). This was a traditional saying of the Egyptians who, at their banquets, exhibited a skeleton to the guests to remind them of the brevity of life.

**Eat humble pie, To.** To be humbled or humiliated. Here 'humble' is a pun on 'umble', the umbles being the heart, liver and entrails of the deer, the huntsmen's perquisites. When the lord and his family dined off venison at high table, the huntsman and his fellows took lower seats and partook of the umbles made into a pie.

**Eat no fish, To.** In the time of Elizabeth I the expression 'he eats no fish' was a way of saying that a person was an honest man and one to be trusted, because he was not a Papist. Roman Catholics were suspect at this time, and Protestants refused to adopt their custom of eating fish on Fridays. *See also* FISH DAY.

> I do profess to be no less than I seem; to serve him truly that will put me in trust; to love him that is honest; to converse with him that is wise, and says little; to fear judgement; to fight when I cannot choose; and to eat no fish.
>
> SHAKESPEARE: *King Lear*, I, iv (1605)

**Eat one's hat, To.** To be very surprised if one is proved wrong. Said when making a statement that one firmly believes to be true, as: 'If he ever arrives on time, I'll eat my hat.' A hat is typical of something undigestible.

**Eat one's heart out, To.** To fret or worry; to pine, brood or be jealous. The expression is often used frivolously, as a taunt to a person one has bettered, or supposedly bettered, in some way. Thus someone who has had a first short story published might say, 'Eat your heart out, Barbara Cartland!' (or some other popular writer).

**Eat one's words, To.** To withdraw what one has said; to admit one has been wrong.

**Eat out, To.** To dine at a restaurant.

**Eat out of someone's hand, To.** To be submissive and compliant to someone, as a tame animal will eat from a human hand.

**Eat salt with someone, To.** To be their guest; to partake of their hospitality. Among the Arabs, to eat a man's salt was to create a sacred bond between host and guest. No one who has eaten of another's salt should speak ill of him or do him an ill turn.

> Why dost thou shun the salt? that sacred pledge,
> Which, once partaken, blunts the sabre's edge,
> Makes even contending tribes in peace unite,
> And hated hosts seem brethren to the sight!
>
> LORD BYRON: *The Corsair*, II, iv (1814)

**Eat someone out of house and home, To.** Literally, to eat so much that the householder or host is ruined. A regular complaint of the mother of a growing family. Mistress Quickly in Shakespeare's *Henry IV, Pt II* (II, i (1597)), when the Lord Chief Justice asks her 'for what sum' she had caused Sir John Falstaff to be arrested, answers: 'He hath eaten me out of house and home; he hath put all my substance into that fat belly of his.'

**Eat the leek, To.** To be forced to eat one's own words or retract what one has said. Fluellen (in Shakespeare's *Henry V*, V, i (1598)) is taunted by Pistol for wearing a leek in his hat, but turns the tables by forcing him to eat it.

**Eat up, To.** To finish what is on one's plate, with the words often used as an exhortation to children. A car that eats up the miles is one that travels smoothly and quickly.

**Dog eat dog.** *See under* DOG.

**What's eating you?** *See under* WHAT.

**Eau. Eau de Cologne** (French, 'water of Cologne'). A perfumed spirit invented by an Italian chemist, Johann Maria Farina (1685–1766), who settled in Cologne in 1709. The usual recipe prescribes 12 drops of each of the essential oils, bergamot, citron, neroli, orange and rosemary, with one dram of Malabar cardamoms and a gallon of rectified spirits, which are distilled together.

**Eau de nil** (French, 'water of (the) Nile'). A pale greenish colour, supposedly that of the River Nile.

> The colour is not quite blue and not quite green but something in between: a shade of turquoise which I believe was all the rage in the 1950s, called *eau de nil*.
> *The Times* (4 October 1994)

**Eau de vie** (French, 'water of life'). Brandy. A translation of Latin AQUA VITAE. *See also* USQUEBAUGH.

**Eavesdropper.** Someone who secretly listens to other people's conversation. The eavesdrop or eavesdrip was the space of ground around the house that received the water dripping from the eaves. An eavesdropper was a person who took up a position in the eavesdrip to overhear what was said in the house.

> Under our tents I'll play the eavesdropper,
> To hear if any mean to shrink from me.
> SHAKESPEARE: *Richard III*, V, iii (1592)

**Ebenezer.** A name often adopted by NONCONFORMIST chapels from the Hebrew word meaning 'stone of help' (1 Samuel 7:12) and thus sometimes used as a symbol of Nonconformity. *See also* EXETER HALL.

**Eblis** (from Greek *diabolos*, 'Devil'). A JINN of Arabian mythology, the ruler of the evil genii, or fallen angels. Before his fall he was called AZAZEL. When ADAM was created, God commanded all the angels to worship him, but Eblis replied, 'Me thou hast created of smokeless fire, and shall I reverence a creature made of dust?' God turned the disobedient angel into a Shaitan (DEVIL, the same word as SATAN), and he became the father of Devils.

**E-boat.** In the Second World War an abbreviation for enemy torpedo boat, i.e. a German one.

**E-boat alley.** The name given to the coastal convoy route off the coast of East Anglia, which was the scene of much successful E-BOAT activity in the early years of the Second World War.

**Ebrew Jew.** A 'Hebrew Jew', i.e. a Jew of the purest stock. The phrase is an old expression of abuse, deriving from the days when Jews were subjected to constant persecution and were unpopular from their association with usury.

> You rogue, they were bound, every man of them; or I am a Jew else, an Ebrew Jew.
> SHAKESPEARE: *Henry IV, Pt I*, II, iv (1597)

**Ecce Homo** (Latin, 'Behold the man'). The name given to many paintings of Christ crowned with thorns and bound with ropes, as He was shown to the people by PILATE, who said to them, 'Ecce homo!' (John 19:5). Especially notable are those by Correggio, Titian, Guido Reni, Van Dyck, Rembrandt, Poussin and Albrecht Dürer. In 1865 Sir John Seeley published a study of Christ under this title.

**Ecclesiastes.** This book of the OLD TESTAMENT was formerly ascribed to SOLOMON, from its opening verse: 'The words of the Preacher, the son of David, king in Jerusalem.' It is now generally assigned to an unknown author of about the 3rd century BC.

**Ecclesiastical. Ecclesiastical Commissioners, The.** The administrators of the properties of the CHURCH OF ENGLAND. They were established in 1836 and consisted of the archbishops, bishops and deans of Canterbury, St Paul's and Westminster, together with certain judges and ministers of state and eleven eminent laymen. Essentially they administered surplus episcopal and cathedral endowments for relief of the poorer clergy and parochial ministries. In 1948 they merged with Queen ANNE'S BOUNTY as the Church Commissioners, basically to manage the ancient endowments of the church for the support of the ministry.

**Father of Ecclesiastical History, The.** *See under* FATHER.

**Ecclesiasticus.** The Latin name, properly meaning 'church book' (from its frequent use in the church), for the Book of Sirach, traditionally ascribed to Jesus, the son of Sira. It is perhaps the most important book of the APOCRYPHA of the OLD TESTAMENT, and both the German hymn *Nun danket alle Gott* ('Now thank we all our God') and the *Jubilee Rhythm* of St BERNARD of Clairvaux are taken from it. It has been much used by the Lutheran Church.

**Echidna** (Greek *ekhidna*, 'viper'). In classical mythology a celebrated monster, who is half-woman, half-SERPENT and is also mother of the CHIMERA, the two-headed dog ORTHOS, the hundred-headed DRAGON of the HESPERIDES, the Colchian dragon, the SPHINX, CERBERUS, SCYLLA, the GORGONS, the Lernean HYDRA, the vulture that ate the liver of PROMETHEUS and the NEMEAN LION. Edmund Spenser makes her the mother of the BLATANT BEAST in *The Faerie Queene* (VI, vi (1596)).

In zoology an echidna is a spine-covered anteater, allied to the platypus, found in Australia, Tasmania and New Guinea.

**Echo.** The Romans say that Echo was a NYMPH in love with NARCISSUS, but when her love was not returned, she pined away until only her voice remained.

> Sweet Echo, sweetest nymph, that liv'st unseen
> Within thy airy shell,
> By slow Meander's margent green,
> And in the violet-embroidered vale
> Where the love-lorn nightingale

Nightly to thee her sad song mourneth well:
Canst thou not tell me of a gentle pair
That likest thy Narcissus are?
MILTON: *Comus* (1637)

**Eckhardt.** In German legends Eckhardt appears on the evening of MAUNDY THURSDAY to warn all persons to go home in order to avoid being injured by the headless bodies and two-legged horses which traverse the streets on that night. He also sometimes appears as the companion of TANNHÄUSER.

**Eclectics.** The name given to those who do not attach themselves to any special school (especially philosophers and painters), but pick and choose from many (Greek *eklegein*, 'to select'). The name was first given to such a group of Greek philosophers of the 2nd and 1st centuries BC. The 17th-century Italian painters who followed the great masters are known as the Eclectic school.

**Eclipse.** (1) The total or partial obscuring of one celestial body by another. A solar eclipse occurs when the moon passes between the sun and the earth; a lunar eclipse when the earth passes between the sun and the moon. Total eclipses of the sun are of great importance to astronomers, for observations can be made then which cannot be made at any other time. Only two such eclipses were visible in England in the 20th century, the first on 29 June 1927, visible over part of northern England, the second on 11 August 1999, visible in Cornwall and part of Devon. The next total eclipse visible in England will be on 14 June 2051, visible in London.

Eclipses were considered by the Greeks and Romans as bad OMENS, and the Romans would never hold a public assembly during an eclipse. Some of their poets would say that an eclipse of the moon occurred when the moon was visiting ENDYMION.

A general notion among some races was that the sun or moon was devoured by some monster, hence the beating of drums and kettles to scare it away. The Chinese, Lapps and Persians call the evil beast a DRAGON. The East Indians say it is a black GRIFFIN. The ancient Mexicans thought that eclipses were caused by quarrels between sun and moon.

(2) One of the most famous of English race horses, the great-grandson of DARLEY ARABIAN, foaled on 1 April 1764, during a solar eclipse. He ran his first race on 3 May 1769, and from then until October 1770 ran in 18 races, never being beaten. His skeleton is preserved in the Royal Veterinary College, London. His fame gave rise to a saying applied to a person of outstanding ability who outstrips all rivals: 'Eclipse first, the rest nowhere.'

**Eclipse Stakes, The.** A race run at Sandown Park for horses of three years and upwards. It was inaugurated in 1884.

**Ecliptic.** In astronomy the great circle along the celestial sphere around which the sun has its apparent annual path. It lies in the middle of the ZODIAC and is an imaginary line produced by the earth's motion about the sun.

**Eclogue** (Greek *eklogē*, 'selection'). The word was originally used for Virgil's *Bucolics* (1st century BC) because they were selected poems. As they were all pastoral dialogues it came to denote such poems, and hence an eclogue is now a pastoral or idyllic dialogue in verse.

**Economy.** Literally, domestic management, from Greek *oikos*, 'house', and *nemein*, 'to manage'.

Sound economy includes the avoidance of waste, hence the sense of frugality that is illustrated by numerous proverbs: 'take care of the pence and the pounds will take care of themselves', 'many a mickle makes a muckle', 'a penny saved is a penny gained' and so on.

**Black economy.** *See under* BLACK.

**Grey economy.** *See under* GREY.

**Home economics.** *See under* HOME.

**Political economy.** *See under* POLITICAL.

**Ecstasy** (Greek *ekstasis*, 'displacement', literally 'causing to stand outside', from *ex-*, 'out', and *histanai*, 'to cause to stand'). Ecstasy is a state of enhanced delight or emotion in which one is 'beside oneself'. St PAUL refers to this when he says he was caught up to the third heaven and heard unutterable words, 'whether in the body, or out of the body, I cannot tell' (2 Corinthians 12:3). St JOHN THE EVANGELIST also says he was 'in the Spirit' (i.e. in a state of ecstasy) when he saw the apocalyptic vision (Revelation 1:10). The belief that the soul left the body at times was common in former ages, and there was a class of diviners among the ancient Greeks who used to lie in trances. When they came to, they gave strange accounts of what they had seen while they were 'out of the body'.

Ecstasy is also the name of a drug that acts as a stimulant and can cause hallucinations, as a state of supposed ecstasy. Its chemical name is methylenedioxymethamphetamine, usually abbreviated as MDMA.

**Ecstatic Doctor, The.** Jan van Ruysbroeck (1293–1381), the Dutch mystic.

**Ector, Sir.** In the ARTHURIAN ROMANCES, the foster-father of King ARTHUR.

**Ecumenical. Ecumenical Councils** (Greek *oikoumenikos*, 'the whole inhabited world', *gē*, 'earth', being understood). Ecclesiastical councils whose findings are, or were, recognized as binding on all Christians. The seven councils recognized in the East and West, which dealt with the heresies indicated, are:

Nicaea (325): Arianism
Constantinople (381): Apollinarianism
Ephesus (431): Nestorianism
Chalcedon (451): Eutychianism
Constantinople (533): Three Chapters Controversy
Constantinople (680–1): Monothelitism
Nicaea (787): Iconoclasm

The ROMAN CATHOLIC CHURCH also recognizes the following:

Constantinople (869–870)
Lateran I– IV (1123, 1139, 1179, 1215)
Lyons (1245, 1274)
Vienne (1311–12)
Constance (1414–18)
Ferrara-Florence (1438–9)
Lateran V (1512–17)
Trent (1545–63): protestantism and reform
Vatican I (1869–70): papal infallibility
Vatican II (1962–5)

The Second VATICAN COUNCIL was attended by observers from the CHURCH OF ENGLAND and 26 other denominations.

**Ecumenical movement.** The movement towards reuniting the various Christian churches, which has gathered strength in recent years, especially since the Second Vatican Council and the establishment of the World Council of Churches, inaugurated at Amsterdam in 1948, which includes most of the prominent Christian bodies.

**Edda.** This name, which may be from Icelandic *edda*, 'great-grandmother', or from Old Norse *odhr*, 'poetry', is given to two works or collections, *The Elder* or *Poetic Edda*, and *The Younger* or *Prose Edda*. The first-named was found in 1643 by an Icelandic bishop and consists of mythological and heroic Old Norse poetry dating from the 12th century. The *Younger Edda* by Snorri Sturluson (1178–1242) is in prose and verse and forms a guide to poets and poetry.

**Eddystone lighthouse.** *See* INVENTORS.

**Eden.** Paradise, the country and garden in which ADAM was placed by God (Genesis 2:15). The word is Hebrew in origin and means 'place of pleasure'. The Garden of Eden was traditionally said to be sited in Mesopotamia.

**Anthony Eden.** *See under* ANTHONY.

**Luck of Eden Hall, The.** *See under* LUCK.

**Edge. Edge away, To.** To move away very gradually, as a ship moves away from the edge of the shore.

**Have the edge on or over someone, To.** To have a slight advantage over a person.

**Live on a knife edge, To.** *See under* LIVE.

**On a razor's edge.** *See under* RAZOR.

**On edge.** Tense, nervously impatient.

**Set one's teeth on edge, To.** *See under* SET.

**Edict. Edict of Milan, The.** Proclaimed by Constantine after the conquest of Italy (313), to secure the Christians the restitution of their civil and religious rights.

**Edict of Nantes, The.** The decree of Henry IV of France, published from Nantes in 1598, giving guarantees to the HUGUENOTS and permitting them rights of worship. The edict was revoked by Louis XIV in 1685. *See also* DRAGONNADES.

**Edinburgh.** The name of Scotland's capital is traditionally interpreted as 'Edwin's burgh', supposedly because the fort here was built by Edwin, king of Northumbria (616–632). But the name was recorded before his time, in about AD 600, as Eidyn, so some other origin must be sought. This is probably in a Celtic phrase meaning 'fort on a slope', based on a word that is now Gaelic *dùn*, 'fort'. Old English *burh*, also meaning 'fort', was later added to this. The same Celtic root lies behind the city's poetic name of Dunedin. It was this name that was adopted by the Scottish PRESBYTERIANS who founded Dunedin, New Zealand, in 1848. Edinburgh is also called the Athens of the North. *See also* AULD REEKIE.

**Edinburgh Review, The.** An outstanding quarterly magazine founded at Edinburgh in 1802 by Francis Jeffrey (1773–1850), Sydney Smith (1771–1845) and Henry Brougham (1778–1868), and originally published in the buff and blue colours of the WHIG party by Constable. The first three numbers were edited by Smith, who then handed over the task to Jeffrey. Its brilliance and wit gave it great literary and political influence, especially in the earlier decades, but the unfairness and savagery of some of its reviews were particularly marked in the case of Wordsworth and Southey, and it provoked Byron's satire *English Bards and Scotch Reviewers* (1809). Its contributors included William Hazlitt, Lord Macaulay and Thomas Carlyle. It ceased publication in 1929.

**Edition. Aldine editions.** *See under* ALDINE.

**Variorum edition.** *See under* VARIORUM.

**Edmund.** King of East Anglia, St Edmund (*c*.841–870) met the Danes at Hoxne, Suffolk, when they invaded East Anglia and was defeated and killed. According to a traditional account, he was first tied to a tree when he refused to renounce his Christian faith, then shot to death with arrows by the pagan Danes. In 903 his remains were removed from Hoxne to Bury, now Bury St Edmunds.

**Edna. Edna Everage.** *See under* EVERAGE.

**Aunt Edna.** *See under* AUNT.

**Edom. Over Edom will I cast out my shoe.** *See under* OVER.

**Education, Higher.** *See under* HIGH.

**Edwardian.** Belonging to the reign of King Edward VII (1901–10). Edwardian style of dress was affected by many young men and youths in the 1950s, who soon came to be called teddy boys. They were notorious as much for their anti-social behaviour as for their distinctive costume. *See also* BEATNIK; MODS AND ROCKERS; MOHOCKS.

**Edward the Confessor.** The last Anglo-Saxon king (r.1042–66) of the old royal house, so called for his piety and monk-like virtues, although he was conspicuously deficient as a ruler. He was canonized in 1161 by Alexander III.

**Eel, As slippery as an.** *See under* AS.

**Effect, Greenhouse.** *See under* GREEN.

**Effigy. Burn** or **hang in effigy, To.** *See under* BURN.

**E.g.** (Latin *exempli gratia*, literally 'for sake of an example'). For example; for instance.

**Égalité.** Philippe, Duc d'Orléans (1747–93) (father of Louis-Philippe, king of the French) assumed this name when he renounced his title and voted for the death of Louis XVI. It is taken from the revolutionary motto *Liberté, Égalité, Fraternité* ('Liberty, Equality, Fraternity'). He was even so guillotined.

**Egeria.** The NYMPH who instructed Numa Pompilius, second king of Rome (753–673 BC), in his legislation. Hence the adoption of the name for a woman who advises or inspires. The name itself is probably of Etruscan or Sabine origin, but has been popularly derived from Latin *egerere*, 'to carry out', 'to bear away'.

> It is in these moments that we gaze upon the moon. It is in these moments that Nature becomes our Egeria.
>
> BENJAMIN DISRAELI: *Vivian Grey*, Bk III, ch vi (1826)

**Egg.** *See also* SHELL.

**Egg Feast** or **Egg Saturday.** The Saturday before SHROVE TUESDAY used to be so called, particularly in Oxfordshire, because the eating of eggs was forbidden during LENT.

**Egghead.** A 'brainy' or intellectual person. The term derives from the supposition that intellectuals are often bald. *See also* HIGHBROW.

**Egg on, To.** To incite or urge on, especially with regard to something foolish or dangerous. Here 'egg' is a form of 'edge', so that the meaning is to encourage someone to move gradually towards the edge.

**Eggshells.** Some people, after eating a boiled egg, break or crush the shell. This, according to Sir Thomas Browne:

> is but a superstitious relict … and the intent thereof was to prevent witchcraft; for lest witches should draw or pricke their names therein, and veneficiously mischiefe their persons, they broke the shell.
>
> *Pseudodoxia Epidemica*, V, xxiii (1646)

**As sure as eggs is eggs.** *See under* AS.

**Bad egg, A.** *See under* BAD.

**Chicken or the egg.** *See under* CHICKEN.

**Columbus' egg.** *See under* COLUMBUS.

**Curate's egg.** *See under* CURATE.

**Druid's egg, The.** *See under* DRUIDS.

**Duck's egg.** *See under* DUCK.

**Easter eggs.** *See under* EASTER.

**Golden eggs.** *See* GOLDEN GOOSE.

**Good egg, A.** *See under* GOOD.

**Lay an egg, To.** *See under* LAY.

**Mundane egg, The.** *See under* MUNDANE.

**Nest egg.** *See under* NEST.

**Orphic egg, The.** *See* MUNDANE EGG.

**Ostrich eggs.** *See under* OSTRICH.

**Philosopher's egg.** *See under* PHILOSOPHER.

**Put** or **have all one's eggs in one basket, To.** *See under* ALL.

**Scrambled eggs.** *See* BRASS HAT.

**Teach one's grandmother to suck eggs, To.** *See under* TEACH.

**Tread upon eggs, To.** *See under* TREAD.

**Wind egg.** *See under* WIND.

**With egg on one's face.** *See under* WITH.

**You can't make omelettes without breaking eggs.** *See under* OMELETTE.

**Egil.** The brother of WAYLAND SMITH, the VULCAN of northern mythology. He was a great archer and in the Saga of Thidrik there is a tale told of him exactly similar to that about William TELL and the apple.

**Ego** (Latin, 'I'). In various philosophical systems, 'ego' is used of the conscious thinking subject and 'non-ego' of the object. The term 'ego' was introduced into philosophy by Descartes, who employed it to denote the whole person, body and mind.

In psychoanalysis the ego is that part of the mind that perceives and takes cognizance of external reality and adjusts responses to it. In popular usage the 'ego' is one's image of oneself. Hence one can 'boost one's ego' or have an 'inflated ego'. *See also* ID; QUIS.

**Ego trip.** An action or experience indulged in with the aim of boosting one's image or drawing attention to oneself.

> All that travelling away from home and duty, staying in swanky hotels, ego-tripping, partying, generally overindulging.
>
> DAVID LODGE: *Small World*, Pt IV, ch iii (1984).

**Alter ego.** *See under* ALTER.

**Egremont Crab Fair.** A fair held in Egremont, Cumbria, on the third Saturday in September. The crabs are crab apples, now represented by a load of ordinary apples that are driven around the town and distributed to the crowd. Livestock is traded, while other attractions include wrestling, horse and bicycle racing and dog trailing. The fair's most popular draw, however, is 'gurning through a braffin', in which contestants poke their heads through a horse collar and pull as hideous and grotesque a face as possible. The event has won the title of World Gurning Championship.

**Egypt. Egyptian days.** Unlucky days; days on which no business should be undertaken. The Egyptian astrologers named two in each month, but the last Monday in APRIL, the second Monday of AUGUST and the third Monday of DECEMBER seem to have been specially baneful. *See also* DIES NEFASTUS.

**Anthony of Egypt.** *See under* EGYPT.

**Crowns of Egypt.** *See under* CROWN.

**Plagues of Egypt.** *See under* PLAGUE.

**There's corn in Egypt.** *See under* CORN.

**Eheu fugaces.** An expression of regret at the rapid passing of time. The words are from Horace:

> Eheu fugaces, Postume, Postume,
> Labuntur anni.
> (Alas, Postumus, Postumus, the years are slipping by.)
> *Odes*, Bk 2, No. 14 (1st century BC)

**Eight. Eights Week.** The end of the academic year at Oxford, in late May, a time of parties, dances and the rowing races between the Eights (hence the name) of the individual colleges.

**Behind the eight ball.** *See under* BEHIND.

**Figure of eight.** *See under* FIGURE.

**One over the eight.** *See under* ONE.

**Pieces of eight.** *See under* PIECE.

**Eikon Basilike** (Greek, 'royal image'). *Eikon Basilike: The Pourtraicture of His Sacred Majestie in His Solitudes and Sufferings* appeared in 1649 very soon after the execution of Charles I. It purported to be his own account of his reflections and feelings during, and before, his imprisonment. It greatly strengthened royalist sentiment and led to Milton's less influential *Eikonoklastes* ('image breakers') (1649). Dr John Gauden (1605–62) afterwards claimed authorship at the time of his election to the bishopric of Worcester. It appears that he had edited the king's papers, and his version received the royal approval. His claim is discussed at length in F.F. Madan's *A New Bibliography of the Eikon Basilike* (1950).

**Eisteddfod** (Welsh, 'session', from *eistedd*, 'to sit'). Eisteddfodau were held in medieval Wales and later, largely to regulate the admission of aspirants seeking to qualify as bards or minstrels. The revival of the Eisteddfodau was largely due to the romantic movement, and their modern development grew from the Corwen Eisteddfod of 1789, the druidic rites being introduced by Iolo Morgannwg in the early 19th century. They have been held annually since 1880, primarily for the encouragement of Welsh literature and music. The best known is the Royal National Eisteddfod of Wales, in which competitions are held in music, poetry, drama and the fine arts. It is held every summer on alternate sites in North and South Wales. *See also* DRUIDS.

**Elagabalus** or **Heliogabalus.** Varius Avitus Bassanius (203–222), who in 218 became Roman emperor as Marcus Aurelius Antonius, so called because he was passed off as an illegitimate son of CARACALLA. After a victory against Macrinus he became known by the name of the god Elagabalus, whose heritary priest he had been at Emesa. The name itself is a corruption of El Gebal, from *El*, 'god', and *Gebal*, 'mountain'. The form Heliogabalus arose under the influence of Greek *hēlios*, 'sun'. His brief reign was marked by deviant debaucheries and perverse practices. He and his mother were slain by the PRAETORIAN GUARD.

> Now Pompey's dead, Homer's read,
> Heliogabalus lost his head.
> EDITH SITWELL: *Façade* ('Popular Song') (1923)

**Elaine.** The Lily Maid of ASTOLAT, whose unrequited love for Sir LANCELOT OF THE LAKE caused her death. The story is told in Tennyson's 'Lancelot and Elaine' (1870) based on Malory and other sources of the ARTHURIAN ROMANCES. She loved him 'with that love which was her doom'. Sir Lancelot wore her favour at the ninth of the DIAMOND JOUSTS, thus arousing the jealousy of Queen GUINEVERE.

**Elbow. Elbowed out, To be.** To be replaced or ousted by a rival.

**Elbow grease.** Vigorous physical work, especially when rubbing, polishing, scrubbing etc. A time-honoured joke was to send the GREENHORN apprentice out to buy 'elbow grease'.

**Elbow-lifting.** Drinking. 'To lift the elbow' is to drink, and both expressions are used to indicate fondness of alcohol.

**Elbow one's way in, To.** To push one's way through a crowd; to get a place BY HOOK OR BY CROOK.

**Elbow room.** Sufficient space for the work in hand; literally, room to extend the elbows.

**At one's elbow.** *See under* AT.

**Crook the elbow, To.** *See under* CROOK.

**Devil's Elbow, The.** *See under* DEVIL.

**Give someone the elbow, The.** To send them away; to dismiss or reject them.

**More power to your elbow.** *See under* MORE.

**Out at elbow.** *See under* OUT.

**Up to one's elbows.** *See under* UP.

**Elder.** The importance of elders as people of authority in ancient communities was a natural development. In the Old Testament they appear as official authorities of a locality; and as the elders of the SYNAGOGUE they exercised religious discipline. The members of the SANHEDRIN were called elders. The name was also applied to officers of the early Christian church and is still used in this sense by the PRESBYTERIAN church.

**Elder Brethren.** *See* CORPORATION OF TRINITY HOUSE.

**Elder tree.** There are many popular traditions and superstitions associated with this tree. The cross of the crucifixion is supposed to have been made from its wood and, according to legend, JUDAS ISCARIOT hanged himself on an elder. Cup-shaped fungal excrescences on the bark are still sometimes known as Judas' (or Jew's) ears. *The Travels* (1356–7) of Sir John MANDEVILLE and Shakespeare, in *Love's Labour's Lost* (V, ii (1594)), say that Judas was hanged on an elder.

Warts are cured by being rubbed with elder and it is a protection against witchcraft. *See also* FIG TREE; JUDAS TREE.

**El Dorado** (Spanish, 'the gilded'). Originally the name given to the supposed king of the fabulous city of MANOA, believed to be on the Amazon. The king was said to be covered with oil and then periodically powdered with gold dust so that he was permanently, and literally, gilded. Expeditions from Spain and England (two of which were led by Sir Walter RALEIGH) tried to discover this territory. El Dorado and Manoa were used by the explorers as interchangeable names for the 'golden city'. Metaphorically, the name is applied to any place that offers opportunities of getting rich quickly or acquiring wealth easily.

**Eleanor crosses.** The crosses erected by Edward I (r.1272–1307) to commemorate his first wife Eleanor of Castile, who died at Harby in Nottinghamshire in 1290. She was buried in Westminster Abbey and crosses were set up at each of the 12 places where her body rested on its journey: Lincoln, Grantham, Stamford, Geddington, Hardingstone (now part of Northampton), Stony Stratford, Woburn, Dunstable, St Albans, Waltham (now Waltham Cross), West Cheap (Cheapside) and CHARING CROSS. Only those at Geddington, Hardingstone and Waltham survive.

**Elecampane.** The flowering plant *Inula helenium*, one of the Compositae family, allied to the aster. Its candied roots are used as a sweetmeat and were formerly held to confer immortality and to cure wounds. Pliny wrote that the plant sprang from HELEN'S tears, and Gerard embroiders the tale: 'It took the name Helenium of Helena, wife of Menelaus, who had her hands full of it when Paris stole her away into Phrygia.' It was much used in old medicines and herb remedies. The first part of the present name represents Latin *inula*, a form of its Greek name *helenion*, while the rest is probably Latin *campana*, 'of the fields'.

**Election. General election.** *See under* GENERAL.

**Coupon Election.** *See under* COUPON.

**Khaki Election.** *See under* KHAKI.

**Elector.** In the HOLY ROMAN EMPIRE those rulers who formed an electoral college to appoint the emperor were called 'electors'. Their number was eventually regularized by the GOLDEN BULL of 1356, and the seven electors were to be the archbishops of Mainz, Trier and Cologne, with the rulers of the Rhine Palatinate, Saxony, Brandenburg and Bohemia. The ruler of Bavaria gained admission during the THIRTY YEARS' WAR, and Hanover became an electorate in 1708. The office disappeared with the abolition of the Holy Roman Empire in 1806.

**Great Elector, The.** *See under* GREAT.

**Electra.** (1) One of the PLEIADES, mother of DARDANUS, the mythical ancestor of the Trojans. She is known as 'the Lost Pleiad', for she is said to have disappeared a little before the TROJAN WAR to avoid seeing the ruin of her beloved city. She showed herself occasionally to mortal eye but always in the guise of a comet. *See Odyssey* (v (8th century BC)) and *Iliad* (xviii (8th century BC)).

(2) A sister of ORESTES who features in the *Oresteia* (5th century BC) of Aeschylus and the two other dramas entitled *Electra* (5th century BC) by Sophocles and Euripides. The daughter of AGAMEMNON and CLYTEMNESTRA, she incited Orestes to kill their mother in revenge for the latter's murder of Agamemnon. In modern psychology an Electra complex is a girl's attraction towards her father accompanied by hostility towards her mother.

**Electricity** (Greek *ēlektron*, 'amber'). Thales of Miletus (600 BC) observed that when it was rubbed amber attracted small particles. From such observations of electrical phenomena the modern science of electricity has developed.

**Electuary** (Greek *ekleikhein*, 'to lick out'). A term applied in pharmacy to medicines sweetened with honey or syrup and originally meant to be licked off the spoon by the patient.

**Elegant Extracts, The.** *See under* REGIMENTAL AND DIVISIONAL NICKNAMES.

**Elegiacs.** Verse consisting of alternate hexameters and pentameters, so called because it was the usual metre in which Greek and Roman elegies were written. In Latin it was commonly used by Ovid, Catullus, Propertius, Tibullus and others. The following is a good specimen of English elegiacs:

> Man with inviolate caverns, impregnable holds in his nature,
> Depths no storm can pierce, pierced with a shaft of the sun:
> Man that is galled with his confines, and burdened yet more with his vastness,
> Born too great for his ends, never at peace with his goal.
>
> SIR WILLIAM WATSON: 'Hymn to the Sea' (1899)

**Element** (Latin *elementum*, 'first principle'). In ancient and medieval philosophy, earth, air, fire and water were the four elements from which all other substances were composed. This conception was introduced by EMPEDOCLES in the 5th century BC. Later a fifth immaterial element was added, called the QUINTESSENCE or *quinta essentia*, supposed by ARISTOTLE to permeate everything. The use of the word in chemistry to denote substances that resist analysis into simpler substances begins with Robert Boyle (1627–91).

To be 'in one's element' is to be in one's natural surroundings; doing what one does well; enjoying oneself thoroughly. The allusion is to the natural abode of any animals, as the air to birds, water to fish.

> God who created me
> Nimble and light of limb,
> In three elements free
> To run, to ride, to swim.
> H.C. BEECHING: *In a Garden and Other Poems*, ('Prayers') (1895)

*See also* MISNOMERS.

**Brave the elements, To.** *See under* BRAVE.

**War of the elements.** *See under* WAR.

**Elephant. Elephant and Castle.** The sign of a public house at Newington Butts that has given its name to an Underground station and to a district in south London. In ancient times, war elephants bore 'castles' (howdahs) on their backs containing bowmen and armed knights. A popular explanation is that the name is a corruption of Infanta de Castile, referring to Eleanor of Castile, wife of Edward I. The Elephant and Castle is the crest of the Cutlers' Company, which traded extensively in ivory.

**Elephant Man, The.** The nickname given to Joseph Carey Merrick (1862–90), a gravely disfigured person who was a professional 'freak' before he became a permanent patient of the London Hospital. His childhood was normal until about the age of five, when he began to show signs of the strange disorder that altered his whole appearance. His head became enormous, some 3ft (90cm) in circumference, with big bags of spongy brown skin hanging from the back of his head and across his face. His jaws were deformed, so that he could barely eat or talk, his right arm was discoloured and grotesque, and he was so lame that he could walk only with a stick. His disorder was long thought to be neurofibromatosis, but research in the late 20th century concluded that he had suffered from the extremely rare disease known as the Proteus syndrome. He died of accidental suffocation in hospital at the age of 27.

**Elephant paper.** Before metrication, a large-sized drawing paper measuring 23 × 28in (584 × 711mm). Double Elephant was a size of printing paper 27 × 40in (686 × 1016mm). The name is probably from an ancient watermark.

**Order of the Elephant, The.** *See under* ORDER.

**Pink elephants.** *See under* PINK.

**Rogue elephant, A.** *See under* ROGUE.

**See the elephant, To.** *See under* SEE.

**White elephant, A.** *See under* WHITE.

**Eleusinian mysteries.** The religious rites in honour of DEMETER OR CERES, originally an agrarian cult, performed at Eleusis in Attica but later taken over by the Athenian state and partly celebrated at Athens. The rites included sea bathing, processions and religious dramas, and the initiated obtained thus a happy life beyond the grave. Little is known about the chief rites, hence the figurative use of the phrase to mean something deeply mysterious. The Eleusinian mysteries were abolished by the Emperor Theodosius about the end of the 4th century AD.

**Elevation of the Host, The.** In the MASS, after the consecration, the raising of the Host and the Chalice by the celebrant to symbolize the offering to God and to show them for adoration.

**Eleven. Eleven-plus, The.** The name formerly given to the examination set to primary schoolchildren at the age of eleven or twelve and used as a means of judging their suitability for the various types of secondary education provided by the Education Act of 1944 (secondary modern, secondary technical, secondary grammar etc). The unreliability of testing children at this age and so determining the type of school to which they should be sent resulted in the 1976 Education Act, which compelled local authorities to draw up plans for comprehensive reorganization, although this was later repealed.

**Elevenses.** A popular name for a snack with tea or coffee at about 11 am.

**Eleventh commandment, The.** An ironical addition to the TEN COMMANDMENTS, usually interpreted as 'Thou shalt not be found out'. *See also* DECALOGUE.

**Eleven thousand virgins, The.** *See* URSULA.

**Eleven Years' Tyranny, The.** A name for the period from 1629 to 1640 when Charles I, with the support of Strafford and Laud, governed without summoning Parliament.

**At the eleventh hour.** *See under* AT.

**Give us back our eleven days.** When England adopted the GREGORIAN CALENDAR (by Chesterfield's Act of 1751) in place of the JULIAN CALENDAR, eleven days were dropped, 2 September 1752 being followed by 14 September. Many people thought that they were being cheated out of eleven days and also eleven days' pay. Hence the popular cry: 'Give us back our eleven days!'

**Legs eleven.** *See under* LEG.

**Elf** (Old English *ælf*, related to Middle Low German *alf*, 'incubus'). Originally a dwarfish being of Germanic mythology, possessed of magical powers which it used for the good or ill of mankind. Later the name was used for a malignant imp, and then for FAIRY creatures that dance on the grass in the full moon and so on.

> Every elf and fairy sprite
> Hop as light as bird from brier.
> SHAKESPEARE: *A Midsummer Night's Dream*, V, ii (1595)

**Elf arrows.** Arrowheads of the NEOLITHIC AGE. At one time they were supposed to be shot by elves at people and cattle out of malice or revenge.

**Elf-fire.** The IGNIS FATUUS.

**Elf-locks.** Tangled hair. It used to be said that one of the favourite amusements of Queen MAB was to tie people's hair in knots. When Edgar impersonates a madman in Shakespeare's *King Lear* (II, iii (1605)) he says that he will 'elf all my hair in knots'.

**Elf-marked.** Those born with a natural defect, according to Scottish superstition, are marked by the elves for mischief. Shakespeare makes Queen Margaret call Richard III:

> Thou elvish-mark'd, abortive, rooting hog!
> *Richard III*, I, iii (1592)

**Elf-shot.** Afflicted with some unknown disease, which was supposed to have been caused by an ELF ARROW.

**Elgin Marbles, The.** The 7th Earl of Elgin (1766–1841) was envoy to the Sublime PORTE from 1799 to 1803 and noticed that many of the classical sculptures at Athens were suffering from neglect and depredations. At his own expense he made a collection of statuary and sculpture, including the frieze from the PARTHENON and works of Phidias, and shipped them to England. He sold the 'Elgin Marbles' to the BRITISH MUSEUM in 1816 for £36,000, a good deal less than they had cost him. The Greek government has frequently requested that the Marbles be returned. Their official title in the British Museum is 'Parthenon Marbles'.

**Elia.** A *nom de plume* used by Charles Lamb (1775–1834), under which a series of essays appeared. The first of these, in the *London Magazine* (1820), was a description of the South Sea House, headquarters of the East India Company, with which he associated the name of Elia, an Italian clerk, a 'gay light-hearted foreigner', who was a fellow employee.

**Elidure.** A legendary king of Britain, who in some accounts was advanced to the throne in place of his brother, ARTEGAL or Arthgallo, supposed by him to be dead. Artegal, after a long exile, returned to his country, and Elidure resigned the throne. Wordsworth has a poem on the subject called 'Artegal and Elidure' (1820).

**Eligius.** *See* ELOI.

**Elijah.** The great Old Testament prophet who hears the 'still small voice' of God (1 Kings 19:12). He preaches against the wickedness of King AHAB and Queen JEZEBEL and for a while rids the kingdom of all idols. When driven into the wilderness, he is fed by ravens. At his death, he is taken into heaven in a chariot of fire. His story is told in 1 Kings 17–19 and 21, 2 Kings 1, and 2 Chronicles 21. *See also* MANTLE OF ELIJAH.

**Eliot, George.** The pseudonym of Mary Ann or Marian Evans (1819–80). Her first novel appearing under this name was *Scenes of Clerical Life* (1858). She also wrote *Adam Bede* (1859), *The Mill on the Floss* (1860), *Silas Marner* (1861), *Middlemarch* (1871–2) and other novels. She lived with George Henry Lewes from 1854 until his death in 1878, basing her pen name on that of her lover, and married her 'second' husband John Walter Cross as Mary Ann Evans Lewes.

**Eliott's Tailors.** *See under* REGIMENTAL AND DIVISIONAL NICKNAMES.

**Elisha.** The prophet and ploughman upon whom ELIJAH cast his mantle when he was guiding his oxen. He took over Elijah's task of anointing Hazael and Jehu as future kings in Syria, cured Naaman of his leprosy, miraculously refilled a window's cruse of oil and rewarded a Shunammite woman who had offered him board and lodging with a child even though her husband was old, bringing the child back to life when it died. His story is told in 1 Kings 19 and 2 Kings 2–9 and 13.

**Elissa.** An alternative name for DIDO, queen of Carthage.

**Elixir of life, The.** The supposed potion of the alchemists that would prolong life indefinitely. It was sometimes imagined as a powder, sometimes as a fluid. The origin of elixir is in Arabic *al iksīr*, 'the elixir', itself probably from Greek *xērion*, the term for a powder used for drying wounds (from *xēros*, 'dry'). The term elixir is now given to any sovereign remedy or panacea, or any special medicinal 'concoction', especially an exotic one.

> The elixir contains turtle blood, moth larvae and Korean ginseng root, among other curious substances.
> *The Times* (5 October 1994)

**Elizabeth.** The wife of Zacharias and mother of JOHN THE BAPTIST. The archangel Gabriel appeared to Zacharias in the Temple and promised that he and Elizabeth, though elderly, would have a son, a new ELIJAH. Later, Gabriel visited Elizabeth's cousin, MARY, and announced the birth of her forthcoming child, who was to be called Jesus. Mary went to visit Elizabeth and answered her greetings in the words that became known as the MAGNIFICAT. At the circumcision of Elizabeth's son everyone assumed that he would be called after his father, but Elizabeth said that he should be called John, and Zacharias, who had been struck dumb by Gabriel's message, confirmed this by writing the name on a tablet (Luke 1).

**Elizabeth of Hungary.** Patron saint (1207–31) of the Third Order of St FRANCIS of which she was a member. Her day is 19 November, and she was noted for her good works and love of the poor. She is commemorated in Charles Kingsley's blank verse drama *The Saint's Tragedy* (1846). The story is told that her husband Louis at first forbade her generous gifts to the poor. One day he saw her carrying away a bundle of bread and, asking what it contained, told her to open it. 'Only flowers, my lord,' said Elizabeth and, to save the lie, God changed the loaves into flowers and the king was faced with a mass of red roses. This miracle converted him.

**Queen Elizabeth's pocket pistol.** *See under* QUEEN.

**Ell.** An old measure of length, which, like FOOT, was taken from a part of the body (the forearm) and was originally 18in (45.5cm), as the approximate measurement from the elbow to the finger tips. The word is related to Latin *ulna*, now used as the name for the inner and longer of the two bones of the forearm. The measure varied at different times. The English ell of 45in (114cm) seems to have been introduced from France in the 16th century and was chiefly used as a measurement for cloth. The Scottish ell was 37in (94cm), the Flemish about 27in (68.5cm) and the French about 47in (119cm).

**Give him an inch and he'll taken an ell.** *See under* INCH.

**Elms, The City of.** *See under* CITY.

**Elmo's fire, St.** The luminous phenomenon also known as CORPOSANT that is sometimes observed round the masts of ships. Elmo, through Ermo, is an Italian corruption of Erasmus, the name of a 4th-century Syrian bishop who came to be regarded as the patron saint of seamen, and St Elmo's fire was attributed to him.

**Elohim.** A Hebrew word for God or gods, representing the plural form of *eloah*, itself an emphatic form of *el*, 'god'. The name had a magical property, which prevented devout Jews from pronouncing it outside a religious context or with their heads uncovered. When it was necessary to say it in such cases, as a vocabulary word, it was pronounced 'eloqim', the alteration of a single letter sufficing to 'sully' it and so deprive it of its magical power.

**Elohistic and Yahwistic sources.** The ascription of the authorship of the PENTATEUCH to MOSES is no longer held by biblical scholars, and the first six books of the Bible (the Hexateuch) are usually regarded as a literary entity compounded of a variety of sources. Among the evidence used to support this view is the use of the names ELOHIM and Yahweh. In some sections of the Hexateuch, Elohim is used, in others Yahweh, and in some the names are used indifferently, the general conclusion being that the various sources, written at different periods, were subsequently blended. *See also* ADONAI; JEHOVAH.

**Eloi** or **Eligius.** Patron saint (588–659) of goldsmiths and metal-workers, and apostle of Flanders. Trained as a goldsmith, he was treasurer to Dagobert I, the king of the Franks, and bishop of Noyon. *See also* KING DAGOBERT AND ST ELOI.

**Elysium.** In Greek mythology the abode of the blessed. Hence the Elysian Fields, the Paradise or 'happy land' in Greek poetry. Elysian Fields translates Greek *lusion pedion*, 'fields of the blessed'. The French have the Champs Élysées (Elysian Fields) as an imposing central thoroughfare of Paris. The Élysée Palace there is the official residence of the French head of state. Hence 'Élysée' as a synonym for the French government.

**Elzevir.** An edition of a classic author from the house of Elzevir, booksellers, printers and publishers, which made such works their chief concern. The firm was founded in 1580 by Louis, a Calvinist of Louvain, who settled at Leiden to escape persecution, and it continued in business until 1712. Members of the family established branches at The Hague, Utrecht and Amsterdam, and Isaak (1596–1651) was appointed printer to the University of Leiden in 1620. The firm was at its best in the first half of the 17th century and their DUODECIMO classics sold all over Europe. The Amsterdam branch closed in 1680, having published works of Bacon, Comenius, Descartes, Milton, Hobbes, Molière and Pascal. Elzevirs were cheap, soundly produced and recognized for the quality of their scholarship. The cult of collecting them reached its height during the 19th century.

**Em.** The traditional unit of measure in printing, the area taken up by the metal body of a capital M in whatever typeface is being used. For standard purposes the pica em is taken, measuring 12 points or 4.5mm ($\frac{1}{6}$in). The depth and width of a printed page was formerly measured in ems. An en is half an em, and is the average width of the letters in a fount.

**Embargo.** A ban or prohibition. The word comes from Spanish *embargar*, 'to detain', and is especially applied to an order prohibiting foreign ships from entering or leaving a port or from undertaking any commercial transaction.

**Embarras de richesse** (French, 'embarrassment of riches'). A perplexing amount of wealth or too great an abundance of a thing, so that selection is difficult. *L'Embarras des richesses* (1725) was the title of a comedy by the Abbé d'Allainval. An alternative is *embarras de choix*, 'embarrassment of choice'.

**Ember. Ember days.** The Wednesday, Friday and Saturday of the four EMBER WEEKS once observed as days of fasting and abstinence, the following Sundays being the days of Ordination. The name comes from Old English *ymbryne*, 'recurring period', from *ymb*, 'around', and *ryne*, 'course'. The four periods of Ember days recur like the rotation of the four seasons.

**Ember goose.** A name, not recognized by ornithologists, for the great northern diver (*Gavia immer*), called in Norway *emmer-gaas* because it appears on the coast about the time of EMBER DAYS in ADVENT. In Germany it is called *Adventsvogel*.

**Ember weeks.** The weeks next after the first Sunday in LENT, WHITSUNDAY, HOLY CROSS DAY (14 September) and St LUCY's Day (13 December). Uniformity of observance was fixed by the Council of Placentia in 1095, but they were introduced into Britain by AUGUSTINE OF CANTERBURY (d.604).

**Emblem.** A symbolic figure or representation, a pictorial design with an allusive meaning, which is inserted or 'cast into' the visible device (Greek *emballein*, 'to throw in'). Thus a 'balance' is an emblem of justice, 'white' of purity, a 'sceptre' of sovereignty. Some of the most common and simple emblems of the Christian church are:

A chalice: the EUCHARIST
The circle inscribed in an equilateral triangle or the triangle in a circle: the co-equality and co-eternity of the TRINITY
A cross: the Christian's life and conflict; the death of Christ for man's redemption
A crown: the reward of the perseverance of the saints
A dove: the HOLY GHOST
A hand from the clouds: God the Father
A lamb, fish or pelican: Jesus Christ
A phoenix: the Resurrection

**Emblematical poems.** Poems consisting of lines of different lengths so that the outline of the poem on the written page can be made to represent the object of the verse. Such poetry today is more commonly called concrete poetry. Thus, George Herbert in 'The Altar' (1633) wrote a poem that is shaped like an altar, and in 'Easter Wings' (1633) one in the shape of wings. George Puttenham in his *Arte of English Poesie* (1589) has a chapter on this form of word torture (which he calls 'Proportion in Figure'), giving examples of eggs, crosses, pillars, pyramids and the like. Samuel Butler had the following to say on the poet Edward Benlowes (*c.*1602–76):

> As for altars and pyramids in poetry, he has outdone all men that way; for he has made a gridiron and a frying-pan in verse, that, besides the likeness in shape, the very tone and sound of the words did perfectly represent the noise that is made by those utensils.
> *Characters* (1680)

**Emerald.** According to legend an emerald protected the chastity of the wearer. It also warded off evil spirits and epilepsy, cured dysentery and was supposed to aid weak eyesight.

**Emerald Isle, The.** Ireland, from its bright green vegetation. The term was first used by Dr William Drennan in his poem *Erin*.

> Nor one feeling of vengeance presume to defile
> The cause, or the men, of the Emerald Isle.
> WILLIAM DRENNAN: *Erin* (1795)

**Émigré** (French). An emigrant or refugee. The word originally applied to those royalists and members of the privileged classes who left France during the Revolution. Their cooperation with foreign powers led to severe laws against them. NAPOLEON BONAPARTE, as First Consul, proclaimed a general amnesty, when many returned to France. After the fall of the Empire they were rewarded with political favours by Louis XVIII but did not recover their estates and former privileges. In more recent times the term has been used in particular of political refugees.

> Dusty attics in Munich and Berlin inhabited in and around 1920 by displaced Balts and seedy Russian émigrés.
> *New Statesman* (30 April 1965)

**Éminence grise.** *See* GREY EMINENCE.

**Emir.** The independent chieftain of certain Arabian provinces as Bokhara, Nejd and elsewhere. A title also given to Arab chiefs who claim descent from MOHAMMED.

**Emma. Emma Peel.** *See under* PEEL.

**Aunt Emma.** *See under* AUNT.

**Pip emma.** *See under* PIP.

**Emmanuel** or **Immanuel** (Hebrew, 'God with us'). The name of the child whose birth was foretold by ISAIAH, and who was to be a sign from God to Ahaz (Isaiah 7:14). The name was later applied in the New Testament to the MESSIAH.

> Behold, a virgin shall be with child, and shall bring forth a son, and they shall call his name Emmanuel, which being interpreted is, God with us.
> Matthew 1:23

**Emmets and grockles.** A West Country expression applied to tourists and holidaymakers. 'Emmet' is an old word for an ant, and such insects swarm everywhere. The word 'grockle' is said to derive from the CLOWN Grock, implying someone to be laughed at. It arose in 1963 from comments made on holidaymakers at the Globe Inn, Brixham, and was used by Peter Draper in his film *The System* (1964), made at Brixham, Torquay and other parts of Devon.

**Empedocles.** Greek philosopher, statesman, and poet (*c*.493–*c*.433 BC). According to Lucian, he threw himself into the crater of ETNA, so that people would think he had returned to the gods, but Etna threw out his sandal and destroyed the illusion (Horace, *Ars Poetica* (1st century BC)).

> He who, to be deemed
> A god, leaped fondly into Aetna flames,
> Empedocles.
> MILTON: *Paradise Lost*, iii (1667)

Matthew Arnold published a dramatic poem with the title *Empedocles on Etna* (1852).

**Emperor** (Latin *imperator*, 'commander').

(1) This title, borne by certain monarchs as a mark of the highest regal dignity, derives from its use by the rulers of the Roman Empire. In the days of the Roman Republic, the title *imperator* was given to magistrates vested with *imperium*, the supreme administrative power, which included military command. It came to be applied as a title of honour to military commanders after a victory until the celebration of their triumph. Julius CAESAR was the first to use the title permanently, and it was adopted by Octavian as a praenomen (i.e. *imperator Caesar* not *Caesar imperator*). In due course it became the monarchical title of the head of the empire. Constantine XI, Palaeologus, the last of the emperors, fell in the siege of Constantinople in 1453.

CHARLEMAGNE was crowned Roman emperor in 800 but the first known use of the title HOLY ROMAN EMPIRE occurs in 1254. The so called Holy Roman Emperors, whose office was abandoned by Francis II in 1806, were at best rulers of Germany, Burgundy and northern Italy, and from 1556 the HABSBURG emperors were effectively no more than presidents of a loose Germanic federation.

In 1804 the Holy Roman Emperor Francis II assumed the hereditary title of emperor of Austria (as Francis I), a title last borne by Charles I (1916–18).

In 1804 NAPOLEON BONAPARTE crowned himself emperor of the French. The First Empire lasted until 1815. NAPOLEON III ruled the Second Empire from 1852 until 1870.

Peter the Great was proclaimed emperor of All Russia in 1721. The Russian Empire lasted until 1917.

In 1871 King William I of Prussia was proclaimed emperor of Germany at Versailles. William II, the last German emperor, abdicated in 1918.

King Victor Emmanuel III of Italy was declared emperor of Abyssinia in 1936, when Italian forces invaded the country and the rightful emperor, Haile Selassie I, went into exile until his return to his capital in 1941. Italy became a republic in 1946.

Queen Victoria assumed the title of Empress of India in 1876. The title was relinquished by British sovereigns in 1947.

Emperors ruled Brazil from 1822 to 1889, Mexico from 1822 to 1823 and 1864 to 1867 (the ill-fated Maximilian of Austria), Haiti from 1804 to 1806. The title has also been given to the mogul of India, and to the sovereigns of China, Japan, Ethiopia, among other countries.

(2) Before metrication, a standard size of drawing paper measuring 48 × 72in (1219 × 1829mm), the largest sheet made by hand.

**Emperor's Chambermaids, The.** *See under* REGIMENTAL AND DIVISIONAL NICKNAMES.

**Adoptive emperors.** *See under* ADOPTION.

**League of the Three Emperors.** *See under* LEAGUE.

**Purple emperor.** *See under* PURPLE.

**Empire. Empire City, The.** New York, the great commercial city of the United States, from its situation in the Empire State, the name given to New York State on account of its wealth and importance. Hence the name of the famous Empire State Building, the tallest building in the world until the 1970s.

**Empire Day.** Instituted by the Earl of Meath in 1902, after the end of the South African War, as a way to encourage schoolchildren to be aware of their duties and responsibilities as citizens of the British Empire. The day set aside was 24 May, Queen Victoria's birthday. In 1916 it was given official recognition in the United Kingdom, and it was renamed Commonwealth Day in 1958. Since 1977 this has been observed on the second Monday in March.

**Empire Loyalist.** *See* UNITED EMPIRE LOYALISTS.

**Empire on which the sun never sets, The.** This phrase, applied to the British Empire in the imperialist heyday, was not original. Thus in *Il Pastor Fido* (1590) Giovanni Guarini speaks of Philip II of Spain as 'that proud monarch to whom when it grows dark [elsewhere], the sun never sets', and Thomas Gage in his Epistle Dedicatory to his *A New Survey of the West India's* (1648) writes:

> It may be said of them [the Dutch], as of the Spaniards, That the Sunn never sets upon their Dominions.

**Empire Promenade, The.** A once famous feature of the former Empire Theatre, Leicester Square. This open space behind the dress circle was a regular parade of the 'ladies of the town'. In 1894 Mrs Laura Ormiston Chant of the London County Council directed a purity campaign against the MUSIC HALLS and sought to effect the closure of the Empire Promenade and its adjoining bars. This led to the erection of canvas screens between them, but these were soon demolished by a riotous crowd, a prominent member being the young Winston Churchill. Brick partitions were subsequently built.

**Empire style.** The style of architecture, furniture and costume that came into vogue in Napoleonic France, lasting from about 1800 until 1820. The empire style followed the pseudo-classical fervour of the Revolution, but was much influenced by NAPOLEON BONAPARTE'S wish to emulate the splendour of Imperial Rome, hence the imitation of Roman architecture. The Egyptian campaign led to the introduction of Egyptian embellishments, notably the SPHINX. There was much use of bronze appliqué ornament, mirrors and brocade, and court costume was rich and ornate. Women's fashions changed frequently, but the high-waisted Grecian style remained a constant motif.

**Byzantine Empire.** *See under* BYZANTINE.

**Celestial Empire, The.** *See under* CELESTIAL.

**Holy Roman Empire.** *See under* HOLY.

**Lower Empire.** *See under* LOW.

**Ottoman Empire.** *See under* OTTOMAN.

**Roman Empire.** *See under* ROMAN.

**Western Empire.** *See under* WEST.

**Empty the bag, To.** To tell everything and conceal nothing (French, *vider le sac*).

**Empyrean.** According to PTOLEMY, there are five heavens, the last of which is pure elemental fire and the seat of deity. This fifth heaven is called the empyrean (Greek *empuros*, 'fiery'). Hence in Christian angelology, the abode of God and the angels. *See also* HEAVEN.

> Now had the Almighty Father from above,
> From the pure empyrean where he sits
> High throned above all height, bent down his eye,
> His own works and their works at once to view.
>
> MILTON: *Paradise Lost*, iii (1667)

**Empyromancy.** An ancient method of DIVINATION by observing the behaviour of certain objects when placed on a sacrificial fire (Greek *empuros*, 'fiery'). Eggs, flour and incense were used for this purpose as well as a shoulder blade.

**En.** The French word, meaning 'in' or 'on', occurs in a number of phrases adopted by English.

**En attendant** ('in waiting'). Meanwhile.

**En bloc** ('in a block'). The whole lot together. *See also* EN MASSE.

**En brosse** ('in the manner of a brush'). With hair cut short so that it stands up like the bristles of a brush.

**En clair** ('in clear'). In ordinary language, not in clode or cipher. Said of a telegram, official message or the like.

**En famille** ('in a family'). In the privacy of one's own home.

**En fête** ('in festival'). Dressed as for a festival; in festive mood.

**En masse** ('in a mass'). As a whole; all together.

**En passant** ('in passing'). By the way. A remark made *en passant* is one made casually, almost as an aside.

**En pension** ('in lodgings'). Pension is payment for board and lodging. To live *en pension* is thus to live at a boarding-house or hotel for a charge that includes board and lodging.

**En rapport** ('in accord'). In harmony; in agreement.

**En route** ('on the road'). On the way; during the journey.

**En suite** ('in sequence'). As part of a set, forming a unit, such as a hotel room with bathroom *en suite*.

**Encaenia** (Late Latin, from Greek *enkainia*, 'commemoration'). At Oxford, the annual commemoration in June that concludes the academic year, held in the SHELDONIAN THEATRE. Benefactors are commemorated, honorary degrees conferred and prize compositions recited.

**Enceladus.** The most powerful of the hundred-armed giants, sons of URANUS and GAIA, who conspired against ZEUS. The king of gods and men cast him down at Phlegra, in Macedonia, and threw Mount ETNA over him. The poets say that the flames of the volcano arise from the breath of this giant.

**Enchantment, The Land of.** *See under* LAND.

**Encomium** (Greek *kōmos*, 'festivity'). In ancient Greece a eulogy or panegyric in honour of a victor in the games. Hence, praise in general, especially of a formal nature.

**Encore** (French, 'again'). A call for a performance or the like to be repeated. The French themselves call *bis*, 'twice', if they wish a repeat.

**Encratites.** In the early church, and especially among the GNOSTICS, a group of ascetics who condemned marriage, banned the eating of meat or drinking of wine, and rejected all the luxuries and comforts of life. The name is Greek, and means 'continent'.

**Encyclical** (Greek *enkuklios*, 'circular', 'general'). A pastoral letter issued by the pope and intended for extensive circulation among Roman Catholics worldwide. It deals with matters of doctrine as well as of moral, social or political concern, is not subject to discussion and is obligatory in its observance although not regarded as infallible. It is usually written in Latin and takes its title from the opening words, such as *Mater et magistra* ('Mother and mistress'), issued by John XXIII in 1961 to treat 'recent developments of the social question in the light of Christian teaching'.

A key encyclical of modern times was *Rerum novarum* ('Of new matters'), issued by Leo XIII on 15 May 1891 to apply to the new conditions created by the INDUSTRIAL REVOLUTION. It proclaimed private property a natural right, upheld wage settlements by free agreement, claimed the natural place of women to be in the home and emphasized the duty of the State to preserve justice and the responsibility of the Church in the moral aspects of employment. Pius XI ordered his encyclical *Mit brennender Sorge* ('With burning anxiety') to be read in all Roman Catholic pulpits on PALM SUNDAY, 21 March 1937. It expressed his belief that Nazism was fundamentally unchristian and attacked the idea of a German national church, which the Nazis wished to implement.

In 1979 Pope John-Paul II issued his first encyclical, *Redemptor hominis* ('Redeemer of man'), his vision of the Christian mission. Subsequent encyclicals included *Veritas splendor* ('The splendour of truth') in 1993, laying down a firm line on birth control and other moral dilemmas, *Ut unum sint* ('That they may be one') in 1995, dealing with ecumenity, and *Fides et ratio* ('Reason and faith') in 1998, on the relationship between modern philosophy and Christianity. This last was the Pope's 13th encyclical and marked the 20th anniversary of his election in 1978.

**Encyclopedia** or **encyclopaedia.** A book or books giving information on all branches of knowledge or on a particular subject, usually arranged alphabetically. The word represents New Latin *encyclopaedia*, from pseudo-Greek *enkuklopaideia*, an erroneous form of *enkuklios paideia*, literally 'encyclical education', referring to the circle of arts and sciences that the Greeks regarded as essential for an 'all-round' education.

The earliest encyclopedia extant is Pliny's *Naturalis historia* in 37 books (1st century AD). In *c.*1360 Bartholomew de Glanville, an English Franciscan friar, wrote *De proprietatibus rerum*, in 19 books, starting with an article on God and ending with a list of birds' eggs, but the first encyclopedia in English was that of John Harris, who in 1704 produced a *Lexicon technicum or an Universal English Dictionary of Arts and Sciences*. This was soon overshadowed by the work of Ephraim Chambers (*c.*1680–1740), who in 1728 brought out his *Cyclopaedia* in two volumes, the forerunner of *Chambers Encyclopaedia*, first published in 1859. The *Encyclopaedia Britannica* was first published at Edinburgh 'by a Society of Gentlemen in Scotland' in three volumes (1768–71). It was taken over by Constable in 1812, then by A. & C. Black, and in 1920 it passed into American hands. The 11th edition (1910–11), produced in 29 volumes, was issued by the Cambridge University Press. The 15th edition was published in 1974 as *Britannica 3*, a threefold arrangement of volumes, comprising the *Micropaedia* (Ready Reference), *Macropaedia* (Knowledge in Depth), and *Propaedia* (Outline of Knowledge). Since then a system of continuous revision has replaced the compilation of new editions.

The French *Encyclopédie* developed from a translation of Chambers' *Cyclopaedia*. The new work appeared in Paris between 1751 and 1772 in 28 volumes (including 11 volumes of plates) under the editorship of Denis Diderot, assisted by Jean d'Alembert, and many leading men of letters contributed to it. The Encyclopedists were exponents of sceptical, deistic and heretical opinions, and their attacks on the church and despotic government served the cause of revolution. Thus the name Encyclopedist designated a certain form of philosophy and gave their work conspicuous political importance, resulting in censorship and attempts at suppression.

**End. End for end.** In reverse position, as when turning a rope or plank so that each end occupies the opposite to its former position.

**Endgame.** The final stages of a game, especially chess, when few pieces remain. *End Game* is the English title of Samuel Beckett's French play *Fin de partie* (1957).

**End in** or **up in smoke, To.** To come to no practical result; to come to nothing.

**End is nigh, The.** The traditional slogan of placard-bearing religious fanatics announcing the END OF THE WORLD and the day of judgement. The apparently biblical phrase is not found in the exact words, although Joel 2: 1 has: 'The day of the Lord cometh, for it is nigh at hand'.

**End it all, To.** To commit suicide.

**End justifies the means, The.** A false doctrine, frequently condemned by various popes, which teaches that evil means may be employed to produce a good result.

> The End must justifie the means;
> He only sins who Ill intends;
> Since therefore 'tis to combat Evil;
> 'Tis lawful to employ the Devil.
>
> MATTHEW PRIOR: 'Hans Carvel' (1701)

**End of the line** or **road, The.** The furthest one can go; the limit of one's endurance.

**End of the world, The.** According to rabbinical legend, the world was to last 6000 years because:

(1) the name Yahweh contains six letters
(2) the Hebrew letter mem occurs 6000 times in the book of Genesis
(3) the patriarch Enoch, who was taken to heaven without dying, was the sixth generation from ADAM (Seth, Enos, Cainan, Mahalaleel, Jared, Enoch)
(4) God created the world in six days
(5) six contains three binaries: the first 2000 years were for the law of nature, the next 2000 the written law, and the last 2000 the law of grace

*See also* LAST TRUMP.

**Endpapers.** The two leaves at the front and back of a book, one of which is pasted down on to the inside of the cover and the other is free. They were formerly usually coloured or marbled. Sometimes maps, plans or illustrations are printed on them.

**Ends of the earth, The.** The remotest parts of the earth, the regions farthest from civilization.

> All the ends of the earth have seen the salvation of our God.
> Psalm 98:3

**End-stopped.** A term denoting that the sense of a line of verse is complete in that line and does not run over to the next. When the sense runs over to the next line, this is *enjambement* (French, 'straddling'). All the following lines are end-stopped, with both sense and meter pausing at the end of the line.

> All Nature is but art, unknown to thee;
> All chance, direction, which thou canst not see;
> All discord, harmony not understood;
> All partial evil, universal good.
> ALEXANDER POPE: *Essay on Man*, i (1733)

**At a loose end.** *See under* AT.

**At one's wits' end.** *See under* AT.

**At the end of one's tether, To be.** *See under* AT.

**At the end of the day.** *See under* AT.

**At the sharp end.** *See under* AT.

**Back end, The.** *See under* BACK.

**Beginning of the end, The.** *See under* BEGIN.

**Best end of neck.** *See under* BEST.

**Burn the candle at both ends, To.** *See under* BURN.

**Business end, The.** *See under* BUSINESS.

**Come to a sticky end, To.** *See under* COME.

**East End, The.** *See under* EAST.

**Fag end.** *See under* FAG.

**Feminine ending.** *See under* FEMININE.

**Go off the deep end, To.** *See under* GO.

**Happy ending.** *See under* HAPPY.

**In at the deep end.** *See under* DEEP.

**Keep one's end up, To.** To play one's part, despite difficulties. One's 'end' here is one's share or part in an undertaking or performance, which one strives to sustain.

**Land's End.** *See under* LAND.

**Make ends meet, To.** To spend no more money than is necessary; to manage to live without getting into debt. The 'ends' are probably the final figures on a balance sheet.

**Masculine ending.** *See under* MASCULINE.

**No end of.** An intensifying phrase. 'No end of work' is a lot of work; 'no end of complaints' is a large number of complaints.

**Odds and ends.** *See under* ODD.

**On end.** *See under* ON.

**Thin end of the wedge, The.** *See under* THIN.

**To the bitter end.** *See under* TO.

**West End, The.** *See under* WEST.

**Wrong end of the stick, The.** *See* GET HOLD OF THE WRONG END OF THE STICK.

**Endor, The Witch of.** *See under* WITCH.

**Endymion.** In Greek mythology, the shepherd son of Aethlius, loved by SELENE, the moon goddess who bore him fifty daughters. According to one story, ZEUS gave him eternal life and youth by allowing him to sleep perpetually on Mount Latmus, and Selene came down nightly to embrace him. This story is used by Keats in his *Endymion* (1818), and it forms the basis of John Lyly's comedy, *Endimion, the Man in the Moone* (1585).

> The moon sleeps with Endymion,
> And would not be awak'd.
> SHAKESPEARE: *The Merchant of Venice*, V, i (1596)

Benjamin Disraeli's novel *Endymion* was published in 1880.

**Enemy. How goes the enemy?** *See under* HOW.

**My dearest enemy.** *See under* DEAR.

**Enfant. Enfants Sans Souci.** A medieval French society of actors, mainly young men of good family, largely devoted to the production of the *Sotie*, a kind of political comedy in which public characters and the manners of the day were turned to ridicule. The head of the 'Care-for-Nothings' (*sans souci*) was called 'The Prince of Fools' (*Prince des Sots*), an office held for years by Pierre Gringoire (*c*.1475–1539).

**Enfant gâté** (French, 'spoilt child'). A person given undue flattery or attention.

**Enfant terrible** (French, 'terrible child'). An embarrassing person; one who says or does awkward things at the wrong moment; one who caused trouble by his unconventional behaviour. The sense arose from the untimely remarks made by a child.

**Engine. Donkey engine.** *See under* DONKEY.

**Pilot engine .** *See under* PILOT.

**England.** The name means literally 'land of the Angles', referring to the Germanic people who began to invade Britain in the late 5th century from the Baltic coast lands, Angeln at the southern end of the Danish peninsula being their chief centre.

**England expects that every man will do his duty.** Nelson's famous signal to his fleet before the Battle of Trafalgar. The intended signal was 'England confides (etc)', but the signal officer obtained permission to substitute 'expects' in order to save hoisting seven signal flags, as the word 'confides' was not in the signal book.

**England, home and beauty.** England as the Englishman's and Englishwoman's native land, especially as seen after a time abroad. The phrase comes from John Braham's patriotic poem, 'The Death of Nelson' (1812).

**Boast of England, The.** *See under* BOAST.

**Church of England.** *See under* CHURCH.
**Lady of England and Normandy.** *See under* LADY.
**Little Englander.** *See under* LITTLE.
**New England.** *See under* NEW.
**Young England.** *See under* YOUNG.

**English.** The language of the people of England. It is derived from the West Germanic branch of the Germanic division of the Indoeuropean family of languages. Historically it is divided into three main stages of development: Old English or Anglo-Saxon, from the invasion in the 5th century to *c.*1100, Middle English from *c.*1100 to *c.*1450, Modern English from *c.*1450. It is the most widely used language in the world.

**English as she is spoke.** Used of ungrammatical or unidiomatic English. The expression originated in an English edition of a book of selections from the French-Portuguese phrase-book *O Novo Guia da Conversação em Francês e Portuguêz* by José da Fonseca, published at Paris in 1836. In 1855 one Pedro Carolino added an English column of text to the original French and Portuguese. The English book, published by James Millington in 1883, took its title from a phrase in the section headed 'Familiar Dialogues'. The Portuguese proverb *Por dinheiro baila o perro*, literally 'The dog dances for money', appeared in English as 'Nothing some money nothing of Swiss' and the saying WALLS HAVE EARS was presented as 'The walls have hearsay'.

**English bond.** In bricklaying, a bond of brickwork arranged in alternate courses of stretchers, laid with their long side along the face of the wall, and headers, laid at right angles to the face.

**Englishman.** The national nickname of an Englishman is JOHN BULL. The old nickname for him in France was GODDAM.

**Englishman's home is his castle, An.** A saying generally used to mean that an Englishman is inviolable in his own home. Nowadays, it is less of a 'castle' than it was, as various public authorities have right of entry under certain conditions. The premises may even be taken over and destroyed as the result of a compulsory purchase order.

**English Pale, The.** The name given in the 14th century to that part of Ireland where English rule was effective as a result of the English settlement of Henry II's reign: Louth, Meath, Trim, Dublin, Kilkenny, Wexford, Waterford and Tipperary. By the latter 15th century it had shrunk to the four counties of Louth, Meath, Dublin and Kildare, and this shrinking continued until the reconquest of Ireland was effected by the Tudors.

The word is from Latin *palum*, 'stake', hence a fence, a territory with defined limits. Hence the phrase 'beyond the pale', pale here meaning 'the bounds of civilization' or 'civilized behaviour'.

There was also an English pale around Calais (1347–1558), and in Imperial Russia, from 1792, a notorious Pale or Settlement for the Jews.

**Englishry.** The differentiation between English and Normans or Anglo-Normans and Welsh. WILLIAM THE CONQUEROR introduced the 'murdrum', or fine for murder, to protect his fellow Normans. The fine was payable by the HUNDRED if the murderer could not be found. If it could be proved Englishry, i.e. that the corpse was English, the Hundred was exempt.

**English St Sebastian.** *See under* SEBASTIAN.
**Basic English.** *See under* BASIC.
**Borough English.** *See under* BOROUGH.
**Father of English Botany, The.** *See under* FATHER.
**Father of English History, The.** *See under* FATHER.
**Father of English Poetry, The.** *See under* FATHER.
**Father of English Song, The.** *See under* FATHER.
**Father of the English Novel, The.** *See under* FATHER.
**King's** or **Queen's English.** *See under* KING.
**Last of the English, The.** *See under* LAST.
**Luminary of the English Church, The.** *See under* LUMINARY.
**Oxford English.** *See under* OXFORD.
**Pidgin English.** *See under* PIDGIN.
**Plain English.** *See under* PLAIN.
**Put on English, To.** In the USA, to apply spin to the ball in billiards.
**Rock English.** *See under* ROCK.
**Wardour Street English.** *See under* WARDOUR.

**Engraving, Line.** *See under* LINE.

**Enid.** The daughter and only child of Yniol, and wife of Prince GERAINT, one of the KNIGHTS OF THE ROUND TABLE. Ladies called her Enid the Fair, but the people named her Enid the Good. Her story is told in Tennyson's 'Geraint and Enid' (1870).

**Enjambement.** *See* END-STOPPED.

**Enlightenment, The.** The name given to the general intellectual and literary trend in Europe between *c.*1690 and *c.*1790. In England it is more commonly known as the AGE OF REASON. It was characterized by steadily increasing philosophical and radical criticisms of the existing order. In the political sphere the writings of Locke, Montesquieu, Voltaire, Diderot and Rousseau are typical. It led to the growth of Deism (*see* THEIST), MATERIALISM and humanitarianism, as well as ideas of popular sovereignty and somewhat facile ideas of progress.

**Enniskillens.** *See* INNISKILLINGS.

**Ennius.** The Father of Roman Poetry (239–169 BC), noted for his dramas and epic poetry.

**English Ennius, The.** Layamon (*fl.c.*1200), who made a late Old English paraphrase of Wace's *Brut d'Angleterre*. Chaucer is also called the English Ennius.

**French Ennius, The.** Guillaume de Loris (*fl.*1230), author of the *Roman de la Rose*. Jean de Meung (*c.*1240–*c.*1305), who wrote a continuation of the romance, has also been so called.

**Spanish Ennius, The.** Juan de Mena (1411–56), Spanish poet and author of *El Laborinto de Fortuna*.

**Enoch Arden.** *See under* ARDEN.

**Ensa.** The Entertainments National Service Association, which in the Second World War provided concerts and shows for the British fighting forces on active service. Many famous figures in the entertainment and musical world took part, greatly helping to boost morale.

**Ensign. Blue Ensign.** *See under* BLUE.

**White Ensign.** *See under* WHITE.

**Entail.** An estate in which the rights of the owner are cut down (French *tailler*, 'to cut') by his or her being deprived of the right of the power of alienating them at pleasure and so depriving the rights of his or her issue. The term also applies to the settlement of an estate thus. 'Tail males' or 'tail females' were entails where the property passed exclusively to the males or females respectively.

**Entente. Entente cordiale** (French, 'cordial understanding'). A friendly understanding between nations, not amounting to an alliance but something more than a rapprochement. The term is particularly applied to the Anglo-French Entente of 1904, which settled outstanding colonial disputes. The phrase was used in the time of Louis-Philippe when Guizot was in power. He achieved a 'cordial understanding' with Lord Aberdeen in 1844.

**Little entente.** *See under* LITTLE.

**Enter. Enter a house right foot foremost, To.** A saying known to Petronius. It is unlucky to enter a house or to leave one's room left foot foremost. AUGUSTUS was very superstitious on this point. PYTHAGORAS taught that it is necessary to put the shoe on the right foot first.

**Enter the lists, To.** Figuratively, to enter any field of rivalry or controversy. The allusion is to the arrival of a challenger in the tilting-ground in medieval TOURNAMENTS.

**Double entry.** *See under* DOUBLE.

**Entertain angels unawares, To.** To meet and talk with someone famed for saintliness of life while unaware of their identity. Nowadays the expression is more usually applied to the entertainment of persons of note rather than of sanctity.

> Be not forgetful to entertain strangers: for thereby some have entertained angels unawares.
> Hebrews 13:2

*See also* PHILEMON AND BAUCIS.

**Enthusiasm.** The word represents Greek *enthousiasmos*, literally 'possessed by a god', from *en-*, 'in', and *theos*, 'god'. Inspiration is very similar, from Latin *inspirare*, literally 'to breathe in' (the god-like essence). In the 17th and 18th centuries the word enthusiasm was applied disparagingly to emotional religion.

**Entrée** (French, 'entry'). The word has a culinary sense and a legal one. For the cook or chef, the entrée is the dish served before the main course, or between the fish and the meat. It is so named because it was formerly served after an intermediate course called the *relevé*, 'remove'. In the legal sense, entrée is right of entry, so that 'to have entrée' is to have the right or privilege of entry or admission.

**Entre nous** (French, 'between us'). Between you and me; in confidence.

**Envelope. Mulready envelope.** *See under* MULREADY.

**Penalty envelopes.** *See under* PENALTY.

**Envy, Green with.** *See under* GREEN.

**Eolithic Age.** The name given to the earliest part of the STONE AGE, characterized by the rudest stone implements. The literal sense is 'dawn of stone', from Greek *ēōs*, 'dawn', and *lithos*, 'stone'.

**Eolus.** *See* AEOLUS.

**Eon.** *See* AEON.

**Eos.** The Greek goddess of the dawn, corresponding to the Roman AURORA. She was the daughter of HYPERION and Theia and the sister of HELIOS (the sun) and SELENE (the moon). She carried off many handsome young men, including TITHONUS, ORION, Cleitus and Cephalus. *See also* TEARS OF EOS.

**Epact** (Greek *epagein*, 'to bring in', 'to intercalate'). The difference in time between the solar year and the lunar year. The former consists of 365 days, the latter of 354, so that the difference is about 11 days. The epact of any year is the number of days from the last new moon of the old year to the first of the following January, and it is used in determining the date of EASTER. *See also* 'Table of Movable Feasts' at the beginning of the BOOK OF COMMON PRAYER.

**Epaulette.** A shoulder ornament worn by officers of the Royal Navy above the rank of sub-lieutenant, when in full dress. Epaulettes ceased to be worn in the army in 1855. Officers of the US Navy above the rank of ensign wear epaulettes, but since 1872, in the army, they have been worn by generals only.

**Ephebe** (Greek *hēbē*, 'young manhood'). A boy who has reached the age of puberty. In ancient Greece the term denoted a youth who had reached the age of 18 and who had to spend a year in military training and a second year on garrison duty. When fully trained, he was given his shield and spear. He also attended public functions and was immune from taxation.

The system was adopted throughout the Greek world and, during the Roman period, athletic, cultural and religious studies took the place of military training. Admission for ephebi was by selection.

**Ephesus, Diana of.** *See under* DIANA.

**Ephialtes.** A giant, the son of POSEIDON and brother of Otus. When they were nine years old, Ephialtes and Otus were nine fathoms tall and nine cubits broad. They were slain by APOLLO.

**Ephors.** In Sparta the five magistrates annually elected from the ruling caste. They exercised control over the king, the Gerousia (Council of Elders) and the Apella (Assembly).

**Epic poetry.** Narrative poetry of an elevated and dignified style dealing with heroic and historical events, real or fictitious and mythical. The ILIAD and ODYSSEY (both 8th century BC), Virgil's AENEID (1st century BC) and Milton's PARADISE LOST (1667) are good examples.

**Father of Epic Poetry, The.** HOMER.

**Epicurus.** The Greek philosopher (*c*.341–*c*.270 BC) who founded the Epicurean school and taught that 'pleasure' was the natural aim and highest good, but a pleasure that consisted of right living, which led to tranquillity of mind and body. The idea that 'good living' and luxury were the pleasures to be sought was a corruption of his teaching. Hence 'epicure' as a word for someone who cultivates a discriminating taste in food and drink, otherwise a gourmet. *See also* DUM VIVIMUS VIVAMUS; GOURMAND.

**Epigoni.** *See* SEVEN AGAINST THEBES.

**Epigram** (Greek *epigramma*, 'inscription'). A short piece of verse ending in a witty or ingenious thought, or more generally any short, pointed or witty saying. The original Greek verse epigrams were graceful lines for inscription on tombstones and elsewhere. The following are examples of epigrams in different styles.

> Treason doth never prosper; what's the reason?
> For if it prosper, none dare call it treason.
> SIR JOHN HARINGTON: *Epigrams*, Bk 4, No. 5 (1618)

> You beat your pate, and fancy wit will come:
> Knock as you please, there's nobody at home.
> ALEXANDER POPE: 'Epigram: You beat your pate' (1732)

> When I am dead, I hope it may be said:
> 'His sins were scarlet, but his books were read.'
> HILAIRE BELLOC: 'On His Books' (1923)

In more recent times epigrams have been composed in prose rather than verse. Examples are the following.

> The English country gentleman galloping after a fox — the unspeakable in full pursuit of the uneatable.
> OSCAR WILDE: *A Woman of No Importance*, i (1893)

> Youth, which is forgiven everything, forgives itself nothing: age, which forgives itself everything, is forgiven nothing.
> G.B. SHAW: *Man and Superman*, 'Maxims: Stray Sayings' (1903)

> The optimist proclaims that we live in the best of all possible worlds; and the pessimist fears this is true.
> J.B. CABELL: *The Silver Stallion*, IV, xxvi (1926)

**Epimenides.** A holy man of Crete (6th or 7th century BC). According to Pliny (*Natural History* (1st century AD)), he fell asleep in a cave as a shepherd boy and did not wake for 57 (or according to some accounts 40) years, when he sensed his powers as priest and poet. He is said to have purified Athens after a sacrilegious murder of friends of the nobleman Cylon and to have set up a shrine to the EUMENIDES. *See also* WINKLE, RIP VAN.

**Epiphany** (Greek *epiphaneia*, 'appearance', 'manifestation'). The manifestation of Christ to the Gentiles, i.e. to the Wise Men from the East, and 6 January is the feast of the Epiphany in commemoration of this. The Epiphany also marks the official ending of Christmas, as the twelfth day after 25 December. *See also* MAGI; TWELFTH NIGHT.

**Episcopacy** (Greek *episkopos*, 'overseer'). Church government by BISHOPS. Hence an episcopalian church is a church governed by bishops and its supporters are designated 'episcopalians'. Episcopacy in the CHURCH OF ENGLAND was contested early on by Calvinists, who advocated a PRESBYTERIAN system, and it was abolished by Parliament in 1643 but restored with the return of the Stuarts. *See also* ROOT AND BRANCH.

**Episcopal signatures.** It is the custom of BISHOPS of the CHURCH OF ENGLAND to sign themselves with their Christian name and name of their SEE. In some of the older dioceses the Latin form is used, conventionally abbreviated:

Cantuar: Canterbury
Carliol: Carlisle
Cestr: Chester
Cicestr: Chichester
Dunelm: Durham
Ebor: York
Exon: Exeter
Gloucestr: Gloucester
Londin: London
Norvic: Norwich
Oxon: Oxford
Petriburg: Peterborough
Roffen: Rochester
Sarum: Salisbury
Wigorn: Worcester
Winton: Winchester

**Episode** (Greek *epeisodion*, 'something added'). An episode, in Greek tragedy, was originally a dialogue between two choral odes. The term thus came to apply to a tale introduced into a main story, so that it was part of a greater whole while having its own identity. Hence the use of the word to apply to an incident in a course of events. In modern terms it is applied to a section in a serialized novel or to a radio or television programme that is part of a series.

**Epistle** (Greek *epistellein*, 'to send to'). This word, related in origin to APOSTLE, is particularly applied to the NEW TESTAMENT letters, from which extracts are read at the Communion service. There are thirteen from St PAUL, one from St JAMES, two from St PETER, three from St JOHN, one from St JUDE and the Epistle to the Hebrews, of unknown authorship, written to the various churches with which they were concerned.

**Epistles of Phalaris, The.** A series of 148 letters said to have been written by Phalaris, Tyrant of Agrigentum, Sicily, in the 6th century BC and edited by Charles Boyle in 1695. Boyle maintained them to be genuine, but Richard Bentley, applying methods of historical criticism, proved that they were forgeries, probably of the 2nd century AD.

**Canonical epistles.** *See under* CANON.

**Catholic Epistles.** *See under* CATHOLIC.

**Epitaph** (Greek *epitaphios*, 'over a tomb'). Strictly, an inscription on a tomb, but the term is often used to refer to any brief verses or apt commemoration of the departed.

> Here a pretty baby lies
> Sung asleep with lullabies;
> Pray be silent, and not stir
> Th' easy earth that covers her.
>
> ROBERT HERRICK: 'Upon a Child' (1648)

> Fuller's Earth.
>
> *Thomas Fuller's epitaph on himself* (1661)

> Life is a jest, and all things show it;
> I thought so once, and now I know it.
>
> *John Gay's epitaph on himself* (1732)

> Though I've always consider'd Sir Christopher
> Wren,
> As an architect, one of the greatest of men;
> And, talking of Epitaphs,— much I admire his,
> '*Circumspice si Monumentum requiris*';
> Which an erudite Verger translated to me,
> 'If you ask for his monument, *Sir-come-spy-see!*'
>
> R.H. BARHAM: *Ingoldsby Legends*, 'The Cynotaph' (1840)

**Epithalamium** (Greek *epithalamion*, 'outside the bridal chamber'). In ancient Greece, a song sung by youths and maidens outside the bridal chamber. The poets developed it as a special literary form, notably SAPPHO, ANACREON, Stesichorus and PINDAR. Edmund Spenser's *Epithalamion* (1595) is the most celebrated English poem of this kind. *See also* PROTHALAMION.

**E pluribus unum** (Latin, 'one out of many'). The motto on the Great Seal of the United States of America. The phrase is taken from *Moretum* ('The Salad'), a Latin poem formerly attributed to Virgil.

**Epoch** (Greek *epokhē*, 'cessation'). A definite point in time. The succession of events in the period following, and reckoned from an epoch, is called an ERA. In general usage epoch and era are treated as interchangeable terms.

**Gregorian epoch.** *See under* GREGORIAN.

**Epode** (Greek *epoidos*, 'aftersong'). A Greek ode, the part after the strophe and antistrophe. In the epode the chorus returned to their places and remained stationary. The term was also used for a form of lyric poetry invented by Archilochus in which a longer verse is followed by a shorter one. The *Epodes* of Horace (1st century BC) are the best known examples.

**Époque, Belle.** *See under* BELLE.

**Eppur si muove** (Italian, 'but it [the earth] does move [round the sun]'). The words are said to have been uttered by Galileo immediately after his recantation of belief in the COPERNICAN SYSTEM. He appeared before the INQUISITION at Rome in 1632. The saying is first recorded in Abbé Augustin Iraílh's *Querelles littéraires*, iii (1761).

**Epsom. Epsom races.** Horse races instituted in the reign of James I and held on Epsom Downs, Surrey (continuously from 1730, except during the First and Second World Wars). The races formerly took four days, beginning with DERBY DAY on the first Wednesday in June and ending with the OAKS on Saturday. From 1995, following falling attendances at the midweek Derby, the meeting was shortened to three days, with the OAKS on Friday, the Derby on Saturday and the final races on Sunday.

**Epsom salts.** Hydrated magnesium sulphate, used as a purgative and to reduce inflammation. It is so called because it was originally obtained by the evaporation of the water of a mineral spring at Epsom in Surrey. According to Thomas Fuller's *Worthies* (1662), the spring was discovered by a farmer in 1618, who noticed that, in spite of the drought, his cows refused to drink water from the spring. On analysis, it was found to contain the bitter purgative, sulphate of magnesia. Epsom Wells developed, like Tunbridge Wells, as a favourite London spa. Aubrey, Pepys, Nell GWYN and Queen Anne's consort were among its visitors. Thomas Shadwell's comedy *Epsom Wells* (1672) portrays the loose life of the spa in those times.

**Equal, Other things being.** *See under* OTHER.

**Equality.** The sign of equality in mathematics, two parallel lines (=), was invented by Robert Recorde, who died in 1558. As he said, nothing is more equal than parallel lines.

**Equinox** (Latin *aequus*, 'equal', and *nox*, 'night'). The day or date, falling twice a year, at which the sun crosses the celestial equator, when day and night are of equal length all over the world. In the northern hemisphere this occurs on about 22 September (autumnal equinox), officially the first day of autumn, and 20 March (vernal equinox), the first day of spring. *See also* SEASONS; SOLSTICE.

**Era.** A series of years beginning from some EPOCH or starting point as:

| *The Era of* | *BC* |
|---|---|
| Chinese | 2697 |
| Abraham (1 October) | 2016 |
| Greek Olympiads | 776 |
| Foundation of Rome | 753 |
| Nabonassar (Babylon) | 747 |
| Alexander the Great | 324 |
| Selucidae | 312 |
| Maccabees | 166 |
| Tyre (19 October) | 125 |
| Julian | 45 |
| Actium (1 January) | 30 |
| Augustus (27 June) | 27 |
| | *AD* |
| Diocletian (29 August) | 284 |
| Armenia (9 July) | 552 |
| Hegira (16 July) | 622 |
| Yezdegird (Persian) (16 June) | 632 |
| American Independence (4 July) | 1776 |
| French Republic (22 September) | 1792 |

The Christian Era begins theoretically from the birth of Christ, although the actual date of the Nativity is uncertain and was probably 6 or 7BC. The EPOCH of the Christian Era was fixed by the calculations of Dionysius Exiguus in AD 527 and was inexact.

**Era of Nabonassar, The.** An era that was in use for centuries by the Chaldean astronomers, and was generally followed by Hipparchus and PTOLEMY. It commenced at midday, Wednesday, 26 February 747 BC, the date of the accession of Nabonassar (d.733 BC) as king of Babylonia. The year consisted of 12 months of 30 days each, with 5 complementary days added at the end. As no INTERCALARY day was allowed for, the first day of the year fell one day earlier every four years than the JULIAN YEAR. Consequently, to transpose a date from one era to another it is necessary to know the exact day and month of the Nabonassarian date, and to remember that 1460 Julian years are equal to 1461 Babylonian.

**Erastianism.** A term derived from Thomas Erastus (1524–83), denoting the supremacy of the state in ecclesiastical affairs. Erastus (Greek *erastos*, 'beloved') was the name adopted by Thomas Lieber (Liebler, Lüber), professor of medicine at Heidelberg and at Basel, where he later held the chair of ethics. He was a follower of Zwingli, was noted for his opposition to Calvinistic claims and held that punishment for sin was the prerogative of the civil authority. The term was popularized in England after its use in the WESTMINSTER ASSEMBLY, and the CHURCH OF ENGLAND is sometimes called Erastian because in certain matters it is subject to state control. *See also* CONGÉ D'ÉLIRE.

**Erato** (Greek *eratos*, 'lovely'). One of the nine MUSES, and the Muse of love poetry, usually represented with a lyre.

**Erebus** (Greek *Erebos*, 'place of nether darkness'). In Greek mythology, the son of Chaos and brother of Night, hence darkness personified. His name was given to the gloomy underground cavern through which the Shades had to walk in their passage to HADES.

**Erewhon.** An ANAGRAM of 'Nowhere', the name of the IDEAL COMMONWEALTH in Samuel Butler's philosophical novel of the same name (1872).

**Erichthonius.** A mythical king of Athens, fathered by Hephaestus (VULCAN). ATHENE put him in a box and gave its charge to the daughters of Cecrops with strict orders not to open it, but they did so and were so frightened at what they saw (the child as a snake) that jumped off the Acropolis to their death. He was worshipped at Athens in the form of a snake and was set up as the constellation Auriga (Latin, 'charioteer').

**Erigone.** In Greek mythology an illegitimate daughter of CLYTEMNESTRA. Later the mistress of ORESTES, she brought him to trial for the murder of her mother and hanged herself when he was acquitted.

**Erin.** A poetic name for Ireland, from Irish *Éirinn*, the dative form of *Éire*, the country's Irish name.

> Erin! the tear and the smile in thine eyes
> Blend like the rainbow that hangs in thy skies!
> THOMAS MOORE: *Irish Melodies*, 'Erin! the Tear' (1807)

**Erin go bragh.** Ireland for ever. *See also* MAVOURNEEN.

**Erinyes.** In Greek mythology avengers of wrong, the Latin FURIES. *See also* EUMENIDES.

**Erlking.** In German legend a malevolent GOBLIN who haunts forests and lures people, especially children, to destruction. Goethe has a poem on him, set to music by Schubert. Erlking means 'king of the alders' but has popularly been understood to mean 'elf king'. This came about because Johann von Herder, Goethe's fellow poet, mistranslated Danish *elverkonge*, 'alder king', as 'elf king' (Danish *ellerkonge*).

**Ermine.** Another name for the stoat (*Mustela erminea*) but more usually used for its fur, which is brown in summer and white in winter. It is one of the furs used in HERALDRY and is represented by a white field flecked with black ermine tails. White tails on a black field is now called ermines. Other variants are erminois, a gold field with black tails, and erminites, the same as ermine but with a red hair on either side of each black tail. The name ermine itself evolved from Medieval Latin *Armenius mus*, 'Armenian mouse'.

**Ermine Street.** The name of this essentially Roman road from London to Lincoln (originally from a point near Pevensey, East Sussex, to York) arose after Roman times. It derives from the *Earningas* ('people of Earna'), a group of Anglo-Saxons who settled near part of its route through Cambridgeshire.

**ERNIE.** The Premium Bonds genius, more formally designated the electronic random number indicator equipment. ERNIE is thus not a computer, as is it sometimes described. The first prize was drawn in 1956, and ERNIE was still in high favour with 'investors' 40 years on, despite the competing allure of the National Lottery from 1994.

**Eros** (Greek, 'sexual love'). The Greek GOD OF LOVE, usually personified as a pretty young boy with bow and arrows, the equivalent of the Roman CUPID. It is also the popular name for the winged archer on the memorial fountain to the 7th Earl of Shaftesbury, in the centre of Piccadilly Circus, London, which was actually intended to represent the angel of Christian charity. It is the work of Sir Alfred Gilbert (1854–1934) and was unveiled in 1893.

**Errand. Bootless errand.** *See under* BOOT.

**Fool's errand.** *See under* FOOL.

**Erse.** The native language of the Highlands and Western Isles of Scotland. The word is a variant of Irish, the Scots coming originally from Ireland. It was formerly applied by the Lowlanders to the CELTIC tongue of the Highlanders. The language is now usually called GAELIC, while the word Erse is more usually applied to the native language of Ireland.

> Of the Earse language as I understand nothing, I cannot say more than I have been told. It is the rude speech of a barbarous people, who had few thoughts to express, and were content, as they conceived grossly, to be grossly understood.
>
> SAMUEL JOHNSON: *A Journey to the Western Islands of Scotland* (1775)

**Esau.** The twin brother of JACOB and the son of ISAAC and REBECCA. The conflict between the brothers represents the feud between the Edomites and Israelites. The struggle began in the womb, when Rebecca was told that she had conceived two nations and that the elder should serve the younger. The first born was Esau, who was followed by Jacob, clutching Esau's heel. Esau became a hunter, and Jacob a plainsman. Esau was his father's favourite, and Jacob his mother's. Later, faint and dying of hunger, Esau begged Jacob for food, which Jacob gave him in return for the sale of his birthright. Later still, old and blind, Isaac called Esau to give him his blessing. Learning of this, Rebecca told Jacob to kill two kids so that she could make a meal for Isaac that Jacob would give him. He would then bless Jacob instead of Esau. Jacob feared that Isaac would detect the deceit, as Esau was a hairy man, while he, Jacob, was smooth. Rebecca dressed Jacob in Esau's clothes and covered his head and neck with the kids' skins. The ruse succeeded, and Jacob received his father's blessing.

**Escorial** or **Escurial.** The royal palace, MAUSOLEUM and monastery built by Philip II of Spain (r.1556–98) some 27 miles (43km) northwest of Madrid. It was erected between 1563 and 1584 on a rocky altitude to commemorate his victory of St Lawrence's Day over the French at St Quentin (1557). It is generally believed that the shape of its plan represents the gridiron on which St LAWRENCE was martyred. It takes its name from the adjacent hamlet, which is itself apparently so called from the waste of local iron mines (Spanish *escorial*, 'slag heap').

**Escuage.** *See* SCUTAGE.

**Esculapius.** *See* AESCULAPIUS.

**Escutcheon.** In HERALDRY the shield on which armorial bearings are depicted. The word is from Old Northern French *escuchon*, ultimately from Latin *scutum* 'shield'.

**Blot one's escutcheon, To.** *See under* BLOT.

**Esoteric** (Greek *esōterō*, 'inner'). Secret; only for the initiated; those within, as opposed to 'exoteric', those without. The term originated with PYTHAGORAS, who stood behind a curtain when he gave his lectures. Those who were allowed to attend lectures, but not to see his face, he called his exoteric disciples; those who were allowed to enter the veil were his esoterics. ARISTOTLE adopted the same terms. Those who attended his evening lectures, which were of a popular character, he called his exoterics, while those who attended his more abstruse morning lectures, his esoterics.

**Esperanto.** An artificial international language first published in 1887 by Ludovik Lazarus Zamenhof, a Polish physician, which soon superseded VOLAPÜK. Its name means 'the hopeful one', the pseudonym of its inventor. It has a mainly Latin-Germanic vocabulary, is entirely phonetic, with one letter to one sound, has a single definite article, *la*, respective noun, adjective and adverb endings *-o*, *-a* and *-e*, and a verb that undergoes no change with regard to person or number. A sample follows:

> La inteligenta persono lernas la interlingvon Esperanto rapide kaj facile. Simpla, fleksebla, praktika solvo de la problemo de universala interkompreno, Esperanto meritas vian seriozan konsideron.

**Esprit** (French, 'spirit', 'mind', 'wit').

**Esprit de corps** (French, 'body spirit'). The spirit of awareness and pride in belonging to a particular group, with regard for its traditions and associations.

**Esprit de l'escalier** (French, 'staircase wit'). The rejoinder that comes too late; the witty retort that occurs to one after the moment has passed. The original reference was to the afterthought that occurred to a person when going downstairs from the salon to the street door.

> He prayed, as he followed the victorious young woman downstairs, that *l'esprit de l'escalier* might befall him.
>
> MAX BEERBOHM: *Zuleika Dobson*, ch xvi (1911)

**Beaux esprits.** *See under* BEAUX.

**Bel esprit.** *See* BEAUX ESPRITS.

**Esquire** (Old French *escuier* from Late Latin' *scutarius*, 'shield bearer'). A man who carried the shield of a KNIGHT and who ranked immediately below him. William Camden (1551–1623), the antiquary and one-time CLARENCEUX KING OF ARMS, defined four classes of esquire:

(1) The eldest sons of knights and their eldest sons in perpetual succession
(2) The eldest sons of the younger sons of peers and their eldest sons in perpetual succession
(3) Those created by the king's LETTERS PATENT or other investiture and their eldest sons
(4) Esquires by virtue of their offices, as JUSTICES OF THE PEACE, and others who bear any office of trust under the crown

Sir William Blackstone (1723–80) added to the list, but the title was loosely used before this time and the various attempts to define its use legally have met with little success. Esquires still feature in the 'Scale of General or Social Precedence', immediately before Gentlemen, the last on the list. In practice, it is mainly used in correspondence (abbreviated to 'Esq'), as an alternative to 'Mr', although even here it is increasingly rare.

> I am Robert Shallow, sir; a poor esquire of this county, and one of the King's justices of the peace.
>
> SHAKESPEARE: *Henry IV, Pt II*, III, ii (1597)

**Essays.** Francis Bacon's *Essayes* (1597–1625) were the first in English to bear this name. It had occurred earlier, however, as the title of Montaigne's *Essais* (1580).

**Essenes.** A Jewish fraternity, originating about the 2nd century BC, which lived a monastic kind of life and which rejected animal sacrifices. The Essenes were distinguished for their piety and virtue, and they were strict observers of the SABBATH. They were given to acts of charity and maintained themselves by manual labour (chiefly agriculture), lived in fellowship and held their goods in common. Their way of life was akin to that of Jesus and His disciples. *See also* DEAD SEA SCROLLS; HASIDEANS.

**Essex. Essex girl.** A type of unintelligent and materialistic young woman who emerged in the late 1980s as the female equivalent of ESSEX MAN and who became the butt of a variety of politically incorrect jokes. *See also* SHARON; TRACY.

**Essex man.** A type of socially ungraced CONSERVATIVE voter, typically a self-made businessman, who lives in Essex or London and southeast England and who in the late 1980s worshipped the consumer-oriented gospel of THATCHERISM. *See also* ESSEX GIRL.

**Established Church.** The church officially recognized and established by law and enjoying a privileged position. In England the established church is Episcopalian, while in Scotland it is PRESBYTERIAN. *See also* EPISCOPACY.

**Establishment, The.** A term long used to denote in particular the established CHURCH OF ENGLAND, but now a popular designation for the group or class of people who have authority within a society, especially, in Britain, those who control not only the Church of England but the Government, the CIVIL SERVICE and the armed forces. It has a somewhat derogatory significance associated with reaction, privilege and 'stuffiness'.

> By the 'Establishment' I do not mean only the centres of official power – though they are certainly part of it – but rather the whole matrix of official and social relations within which power is exercised.
>
> HENRY FAIRLIE in *Spectator* (23 September 1955)

**Estate** (Old French *estat*, from Latin *status*, 'condition', 'state').

**Estates General** (French *États généraux*). The French assembly, which was first summoned in 1302 as a consultative body consisting of clergy, nobility and the THIRD ESTATE. It did not meet again after 1614 until 1789, when the Revolution began. *See also* STATES GENERAL.

**Estates of the Realm.** Those classes, or orders, which have a recognized share or part in the body politic. In Britain the three estates are the LORDS SPIRITUAL, the LORDS TEMPORAL and the HOUSE OF COMMONS, although the term is now anachronistic.

**Fifth estate, The.** *See under* FIFTH.

**Fourth estate, The.** *See under* FOURTH.

**Third estate, The.** *See under* THIRD.

**Esther.** The wife of AHASUERUS, king of Persia, and the niece and adopted daughter of MORDECAI, a Jew. When the king discarded his disobedient wife, VASHTI, he ordered a search for young virgins. Esther was such, and the king made her his wife and queen. When Mordecai refused to bow down to the king's favourite, Haman, the latter planned to kill all Jews in revenge. At a banquet, Esther revealed to the king what he was planning, and Haman was hanged on the very gallows that he had prepared for Mordecai. The story is told in the Old Testament book that bears Esther's name and in the Rest of Esther in the APOCRYPHA.

**Est-il possible** (French, 'Is it possible?', 'Really?'). A nickname of Prince George of Denmark (1653–1708), the consort of Queen Anne. The story goes that when he was told of the abdication of his father-in-law, James II, all he did was to exclaim, 'Est-il possible?' and when told further of the various noblemen who had deserted him, could only add, 'Est-il possible?' *See also* BRANDY NAN.

**Estotiland.** An imaginary tract of land off the coast of Labrador in North America, said to have been discovered by John Scalve, a Pole. It appears on Ortelius' map of the New World (1570).

> The snow
> From cold Estotiland.
> MILTON: *Paradise Lost*, x (1667)

**E.T.** The gentle but rather grotesque creature from outer space which befriends the children of a Californian household in Steven Spielberg's film *E.T.: The Extra-Terrestrial* (1982). He comes to earth looking for plant specimens but is stranded. The children care for him, and he teaches them how to fly. He then devises equipment enabling him to phone home. He finally falls ill and apparently dies, but is reborn just before a spacecraft arrives to take him back. The sentimental story, which has a quasi-religious undertone, is curiously moving.

**État, c'est moi, L'** (French, 'I am the state'). The reply traditionally ascribed to Louis XIV when the president of the Parlement of Paris objected 'in the interests of the state' to the king's fiscal demands. This was in 1655, when Louis was only 17 years old. He acted on this principle with fair consistency throughout his long reign (1643–1715).

**Eternal, The.** God.

**Eternal City, The.** Rome. The epithet occurs in Ovid, Tibullus and other classical writers, and in many official documents of the empire. It has also been applied to the 'City of God'.

**Eternal Tables, The.** In Muslim legend a white pearl, extending from east to west and from heaven to earth, on which God has recorded every event, past, present and future.

**Eternal triangle, The.** The comic or tragic situation of the amorous involvement of one of a married couple with another member of the opposite sex. The phrase occurred as the title of a book review in the *Daily Chronicle* for 5 December 1907: 'Mrs. Dudeney's novel ... deals with the eternal triangle, which, in this case, consist of two men and one woman.'

**Etesian wind** (Greek *etēsios*, 'annual'). A Mediterranean wind, which rises annually about the DOG DAYS and blows mainly from the northwest for about 40 days. It is gentle and mild.

**Ethon** (Greek *aithōn*, 'fiery').

(1) One of the horses of HECTOR.

(2) The EAGLE or vulture that gnawed the liver of PROMETHEUS.

**Et in Arcadia ego** (Latin, 'And I too in Arcadia'). A tomb inscription often depicted in classical paintings. Its author is unknown, and its precise interpretation is disputed. It is possible that 'I' is Death. Poussin's painting so titled (1638) shows three young shepherds and a shepherdess making out the Latin words on a tomb and discussing their meaning. *See also* ARCADIA.

**Etna, Mount.** The highest active volcano in Europe. It stands over the Straits of Messina, about 10,900ft (3320m) high, covering an area of 460 square miles (1190 sq km). In Sicily Etna is known as Mongibello, probably representing Italian *monte bello*, 'beautiful mountain', influenced by Arabic *jabal*, 'mountain'. Many towns and villages live under its continual threat, and in 1983 an eruption lasting several months obliged the authorities to explode dynamite with the aim of diverting flows of lava. Virgil (*Aeneid*, iii (1st century BC)) ascribes its eruption to the restlessness of ENCELADUS, the most powerful of all the giants who plotted against JUPITER and who lies buried under the mountain. According to the Greek and Latin poets it is the site of the smithy of CYCLOPS and the forges of VULCAN. *See also* EARTHQUAKE.

**Eton crop.** A short boyish hairstyle, fairly popular among English women in the 1920s, called after the school for boys at Eton. The name was doubtless prompted by the Eton jacket, Eton collar and Eton suit, originally worn by the younger Eton boys but adopted and adapted for feminine wear before the First World War and returning to fashion after it.

> Sylvia was wearing Etons at Monckley's suggestion.
> COMPTON MACKENZIE: *Sylvia Scarlett*, I, ii (1918)

**Etrenne.** *See* STRENIA.

**Etruria.** A district of Stoke-on-Trent, northwest of the city centre, where Josiah Wedgwood established the Etruria pottery works in 1769. It is named after the ancient Etruria in Italy, the home of the celebrated Etruscan ware.

**Ettrick Shepherd, The.** The name given to James Hogg (1770–1835), the Scottish poet who was born at Ettrick, Selkirkshire, the son of a shepherd, and, for a time, a shepherd himself.

**Etzel.** *See* ATTILA THE HUN.

**Eucharist** (Greek *eukharistos*, 'thankful'). An ancient name for the Lord's Supper, Holy Communion or MASS, and also the consecrated Elements in the Communion. Christ gave thanks before giving the bread and wine to the disciples at the LAST SUPPER, and the church offers the Eucharist as a service of praise and thanksgiving. *See also* IMPANATION.

**Ordeal of the Eucharist.** *See under* ORDEAL.

**Euchre.** The most popular card game in the United States before it was replaced by auction bridge. A player is euchred when the side that makes the trumps fails to win three tricks. Hence, figuratively, 'to be euchred' is to be beaten or to be at a disadvantage. The name probably comes from German dialect *Juckerspiel*.

**Euclid.** Generations of schoolboys knew geometry only as 'Euclid', because the teaching of that branch of mathematics was based on the *Elements* of Eucleides, a Greek mathematician, who taught at Alexandria *c.*300 BC. Although many rival textbooks have been produced to supplant Euclid, few command the same respect.

**Eugene Aram.** *See under* ARAM.

**Euhemerus.** A Greek philosopher of the 4th century BC, who lived at the court of Cassander, king of Macedonia. In his *Sacred History* he maintained the theory that the gods were formerly kings and heroes of exceptional ability, reverenced after death and finally deified. Hence the term euhemerism for such explanations of primitive myth and the derivation of mythology from a historical basis.

**Eulalia** (Greek *eulalos*, 'speaking well'). The name of two 4th-century virgin martyrs, St Eulalia of Barcelona and St Eulalia of Merida, both presumed to have been put to death under Diocletian. Their ashes were scattered over a field upon which a pall of snow is said to have descended.

**Eulenspiegel, Till.** The name, rendered in English 'Owlglass', of a 14th-century villager of Brunswick who became the subject of a large number of popular tales of mischievous pranks and crude jests, first printed in 1515. The work was translated into many languages (first into English *c.*1560) and rapidly achieved wide popularity. Till Eulenspiegel is the subject of Charles de Coster's picaresque novel *Ulenspiegel* (1867), of various operas and of a tone poem by Richard Strauss, *Till Eulenspiegels Lustige Streiche* ('Till Eulenspiegel's Merry Pranks') (1895).

**Eumaeus.** The slave and swineherd of Odysseus (ULYSSES); hence a general name in literature for a swineherd.

**Eumenides** (Greek, 'benevolent ones'). The name given by the Greeks to the FURIES, as it would have been unpropitious to call them ERINYES ('moving ones'), their correct name.

**Eunuch** (Greek *eunoukhos*, 'attendant of the bedchamber', from *eunē*, 'bed', and *ekhein*, 'to keep'). A man who serves as a guard in a harem and who to this specific end has been castrated. Eunuchs were long in the services of the Chinese, and the emperor traditionally had some 3000 in all. Their use in China is said to date back to 1100 BC. Some have found a place in the history books, and in AD 190 a Chinese eunuch named Chang Jang actually kidnapped an emperor. In the early 15th century another eunuch, Cheng Ho, led a number of important expeditions, even reaching as far as Ceylon and the Persian Gulf. The collapse of the Ming dynasty in 1644 is ascribable to the influence of eunuchs in political affairs, and the succeeding Ching dynasty kept tight control over them in consequence. In 1869 the favourite eunuch of the future dowager empress, Kuang Hsu, was peremptorily executed for disorderly conduct in the province of Shantung, where he had gone to make purchases for his mistress.

**Euphemism** (Greek *euphēmismos*, 'speaking well'). A word or phrase substituted to soften an offensive expression. Examples are 'His Satanic Majesty' for the Devil, 'to pass away' for to die, 'Gosh' for God, 'to sleep with' for to have sexual intercourse with ('intercourse' itself being a euphemism for copulation). *See also* EUMENIDES; EUXINE SEA; FOUR-LETTER WORD.

**Euphuism.** An affected and artificial literary style, characterized by alliteration, ornate language, lengthy similes taken from myth and fable and the like, after the manner of John Lyly (1554–1606), author of *Euphues: the Anatomy of Wit* (1578) and *Euphues and his England* (1580). Euphues, the hero of Lyly's romance, has a Greek name meaning 'well-endowed by nature'. Euphuism was much imitated by Lyly's contemporaries, including Queen Elizabeth, Robert Greene and Thomas Lodge.

**Eureka** (Greek *heurēka*, 'I have found [it]'). An exclamation of delight at having made a discovery, originally that of Archimedes, the Syracusan philosopher, when he discovered how to test the purity of Hiero's crown. The story is that Hiero gave some gold to a smith to be made into a votive crown, but suspecting that the gold had been alloyed with an inferior metal, asked Archimedes to test it. The philosopher did not know how to proceed, but in getting into his bath, which was full, observed that some of the water ran over, and immediately concluded that a body must displace its own bulk of water when immersed. Silver is lighter than gold, therefore a pound weight of silver is bulkier than a pound weight of gold and would consequently displace more water. Thus he found that the crown was deficient in gold.

> When the idea flashed across his mind, the philosopher jumped out of the bath exclaiming,

'Heureka! heureka!' and, without waiting to dress himself, ran home to try the experiment.

VITRUVIUS POLLIO: *De Architectura*, Bk ix, preface (1st century BC) (translation in Dr Brewer's 1870 edition)

'Eureka!' is the motto of California, in allusion to the gold discovered there.

**Eureka Stockade, The.** A fortified stockade erected by the diggers in the Ballarat gold field, Australia, in 1854 after the arrest of three of their fellows. It was the climax to their protests against ill treatment by the police, lack of political representation, and the licence system. Troops took the stockade, 20 miners and two policemen being killed.

**Euro.** The name of the SINGLE CURRENCY that in 1999 began to circulate alongside the national currencies of 11 countries (but not Britain) in the European Union and that is due to replace those currencies in 2002. It was first minted as a coin by France in 1998. *See also* COMMON MARKET.

**Europa.** In Greek legend the sister of CADMUS, born on the Asian coast of the Mediterranean. ZEUS changed himself into a bull to seduce her and carried her on his back to Crete, where she bore him three sons and eventually married the king of Crete, Asterius. Europa's name is popularly linked with that of Europe, since it was there that Zeus had carried her.

**Europe. Cockpit of Europe, The.** *See under* COCK.

**Drawing room of Europe, The.** *See under* DRAWING.

**Sick Man of Europe, The.** *See under* SICK.

**Toyshop of Europe, The.** *See under* TOYSHOP.

**Young Europe.** *See under* YOUNG.

**Eurus.** The east wind, a name that is connected with Greek *ēōs* and Latin *aurora*, both meaning 'dawn'.

While southern gales or western oceans roll,
And Eurus steals his ice-winds from the pole.

ERASMUS DARWIN: *Economy of Vegetation*, vi (1791)

**Euryalus.** *See* NISUS AND EURYALUS.

**Eurycleia.** The old nurse of Odysseus (ULYSSES), who recognizes him on his return home from Troy by spotting a scar on his leg that had been made by the tusks of a wild boar when he had been a young man.

**Eurydice.** In Greek mythology the wife of ORPHEUS, killed by a serpent when fleeing from the attentions of Aristaeus. Orpheus sought her in HADES, charmed PLUTO by his music and was promised her return on condition that he did not look back until Eurydice had reached the upper world. Nearing the end of his journey he turned his head to see if Eurydice was following and she was instantly caught back into Hades.

**Eustace.** A martyr of unknown date and even uncertain existence, St Eustace is famous in legend as a Roman general who converted to Christianity when he saw a cross between a stag's antlers and who was roasted to death when he refused to sacrifice to the Roman gods. He is the patron of huntsmen and his day is 20 September.

**Euterpe** (Greek *euterpēs*, 'delightful', charming'). One of the nine MUSES, the daughter of JUPITER and MNEMOSYNE, the inventor of the double flute, the Muse of Dionysiac music, and the patroness of joy and pleasure.

**Euxine Sea.** The ancient Greek name for the BLACK SEA, meaning 'hospitable'. It was originally called Axeinos, 'inhospitable', because of its stormy waters and rocky shores, but the name was probably changed euphemistically to propitiate the powers supposedly controlling the elements. *See also* ERINYES; EUMENIDES.

**Evangelical.** From the time of the REFORMATION, Protestant churches were often called Evangelical churches from their insistence that their teachings were based on the evangel or Gospel (i.e. the Bible). Those known as Evangelicals in the CHURCH OF ENGLAND emerged at the same time as the METHODISTS, and they emphasized the importance of scriptural authority and salvation by faith in Christ. *See also* CLAPHAM SECT; LOW CHURCH.

**Evangelic Doctor, The.** John Wyclif (*c*.1320–84), 'the morning star of the Reformation'.

**Evangelists.** The four Evangelists, MATTHEW, MARK, LUKE and JOHN, are usually represented in art as follows:

Matthew: with pen in hand and scroll before him, looking over his left shoulder at an angel
Mark: seated writing, and by his side a couchant winged lion
Luke: with a pen, in deep thought, looking over a scroll, with a cow or ox nearby chewing the cud; he is also shown painting a picture, from the tradition that he painted a portrait of the Virgin
John: as a young man of great delicacy, with an EAGLE in the background to denote sublimity

The more ancient symbols were: for Matthew, a man's face; for Mark, a lion; for Luke, an ox; and for John, a flying eagle, in allusion to the four living creatures before the throne of God, described by St John:

And the first beast was like a lion, and the second beast was like a calf, and the third beast had a face as a man, and the fourth beast was like a flying eagle.

Revelation 4:7

The term evangelist was applied in the early church to preachers of the Gospel and is often used today to denote a revivalist preacher.

**St John the Evangelist.** *See under* JOHN.

**Evans Music-and-Supper Rooms.** In the 19th century one of the best known resorts of London night life, at 43 King Street, COVENT GARDEN. The premises, which were used by the National Sporting Club, were opened in 1773 as a family hotel, and in the 1830s they were occupied by the

Star Dinner and Coffee Room, which was much frequented by the nobility. The name Evans Music-and-Supper Rooms, by which the premises were known until their closure in 1880, derives from W.C. Evans, a member of the chorus of the Covent Garden Theatre, who was a former owner. He made it the most famous song and supper room in London giving entertainment of the 'blue' variety and allowing his patrons to outdo each other in dirty songs. John Greenmore ('Paddy Green') took over in 1844 and added a splendid new hall with a platform at one end. All the performers were male, and women were admitted only if they gave their names and addresses and even then were obliged to watch from behind a screen. The standard of entertainment under Green was outstanding, and Evans' song-and-supper room can be regarded as the precursor of the MUSIC HALL. The Prince of Wales (afterwards Edward VII) was a frequent visitor.

**Eve** (Hebrew *hawwah*, 'living'). The first woman, formed from one of the ribs of ADAM.

> And Adam called his wife's name Eve; because she was the mother of all living.
> Genesis 3:20

**Eve, St Mark's.** *See under* MARK.

**Even. Even break, An.** An equal chance. The expression may come from hare-coursing, in which the dogs are not handicapped but are released (allowed to break) at the same time.

**Even money.** Betting odds that offer the chance of winning the amount staked.

**Even stevens.** Quits; on a par. The term usually relates to a financial parity, which suggests that the second word may represents STIVER. *See also* EVEN MONEY.

**Even the worm will turn.** The most abject creature will turn on its tormentors if driven to extremity.

**Break even, To.** *See under* BREAK.

**Get even with someone, To.** To take one's revenge or settle one's score with them.

**Evening** or **sunset gun.** A gun fired at sunset or about 9 pm.

**Event. At all events.** *See under* AT.

**Field events.** *See under* FIELD.

**In the event.** As it turned out.

**In the event of.** If; in case of. 'In the event of a fire' means if there is one.

**Three-day event.** *See under* THREE.

**Wise after the event.** *See under* WISE.

**Ever. Ever and anon.** From time to time; every now and then. *See also* ANON.

**Ever-sworded 29th, The.** *See under* REGIMENTAL AND DIVISIONAL NICKNAMES.

**Everage, Edna.** Dame Edna Everage, a falsetto-voiced, larger-than-life Australian matron, with butterfly-winged spectacles, is the persona of the comedian Barry Humphries. She (he) first appeared on television in the 1970s, and shocked a delighted audience by the way she outrageously teased and insulted the star guests invited on to her show. Her sidekick is Madge Allsop, a little woman who is as dour and dumb as Edna is cheerful and chatty.

**Every. Every bullet has its billet.** Nothing happens by chance and no act is altogether without effect. The saying means that every bullet fired will find a lodging-place ('billet').

**Every cloud has a silver lining.** There is some redeeming brightness to be found in the darkest situation; while there is life there is hope. It is an old saying. Thus in Milton's *Comus* (i (1637)) the lady lost in the wood resolves to hope on, and says:

> Was I deceived, or did a sable cloud
> Turn forth her silver lining on the night?
> I did not err: there does a sable cloud
> Turn forth her silver lining on the night.

**Every dog has its day.** You may be enjoying luck or success now, but my turn will come in due course. A Latin equivalent is, *Hodie mihi, cras tibi,* 'Today to me, tomorrow to thee.'

> Let Hercules himself do what he may,
> The cat will mew, and dog will have his day.
> SHAKESPEARE: *Hamlet*, V, i (1600)

**Every Jack shall have his Jill.** Every man shall have a wife of his own. *See also* JACK AND JILL.

> Jack shall have Jill;
> Nought shall go ill;
> The man shall have his mare again,
> And all shall be well.
> SHAKESPEARE: *A Midsummer Night's Dream,* III, ii (1595)

**Everyman.** The central character in the famous anonymous English MORALITY PLAY (*c.*1509–19) drawn from a late 15th-century Dutch original. Everyman is summoned by Death and invites all his acquaintances (Kindred, Good Deeds, Goods, Knowledge, Beauty, Strength and others) to accompany him on his journey, but only Good Deeds will go with him. The following words, spoken by Knowledge, were the inspiration for the name of Everyman's Library, the popular standard edition of masterpieces of world literature founded by the publisher J.M. Dent in 1906:

> Everyman, I will go with thee, and be thy guide,
> In thy most need to go by thy side.

**Every man jack of you.** All of you, without exception.

**Everything but the kitchen sink.** Everything you could think of. The phrase is commonly applied to someone's excessive luggage or belongings when travelling.

**Everything in the garden is lovely.** All is well; the situation is perfect. The saying comes from

George Le Brunn and J.P. Harrington's song 'Everything in the garden's lovely' (1898) made popular by Marie Lloyd.

**Every which way.** In all directions; in a disorderly fashion. A term of American origin.

**Evidence.** In legal terms evidence, meaning testimony in proof or disproof of something, has a wide variety of classifications, as follows:

Circumstantial evidence: that based on relevant fact and circumstances to the fact in issue
Conclusive evidence: that which establishes proof beyond doubt
Derivative evidence: that which derives its force from some other source
Direct evidence: evidence of a fact in issue, that of an eyewitness
Documentary evidence: evidence supplied in written documents
Extrinsic evidence: that regarding the meaning of a document not found in the document itself
Hearsay evidence: that which is heard from another but not known to be true
Indirect evidence: evidence of a fact that then implies the fact at issue
Oral evidence: that made by witnesses in court
Original evidence: that which has an independent probative force of its own
Parol evidence: oral evidence
Prima facie evidence: that which seems likely unless it can be explained away
Primary evidence: original documentary evidence
Real evidence: that supplied by material objects produced for the inspection of the court
Secondary evidence: evidence other than original evidence, e.g. oral evidence of the contents of a lost document

**Evil. Evil eye.** An ancient and widespread belief that certain individuals had the power to harm or even kill with a glance. Various charms and gestures, many of an obscene kind, were employed to counteract it.

**Evil One, The.** The DEVIL.

**King's** or **Queen's evil, The.** *See under* KING.

**Ewe lamb.** A single, greatly prized possession, in allusion to Nathan's parable of the rich man and the poor man in 2 Samuel 12:1–14.

> But the poor man had nothing, save one little ewe lamb, which he had bought and nourished up: and it grew up together with him, and with his children; it did eat of his own meat, and drank of his own cup, and lay in his bosom, and was unto him as a daughter.

**Ex** (Latin, 'from', 'out of', 'after', 'by reason of'). A word that forms part of many adverbial phrases, of which some in common use in English are given below. As a prefix to the name of an office or dignity it denotes a former holder of that office, e.g. an ex-president, or the present holder's immediate predecessor, e.g. the ex-president.

**Ex cathedra** ('from the chair'). With authority. The pope speaking ex cathedra (from the papal throne) is said to speak with an infallible voice, as the successor and representative of St PETER. The phrase is applied to authoritative statements and ironically to dogmatic assertions.

**Ex gratia** ('out of kindness'). Given as a favour or gratuitously, such as a payment made when there is no legal obligation to make one.

**Ex hypothesi** ('from the hypothesis'). According to what is supposed or assumed, in consequence of an assumption.

**Ex libris** ('from the books'). A phrase written in books or on bookplates followed by the name of the owner (properly in the genitive). Hence, a bookplate is often called an 'ex libris'.

**Ex officio** ('from office'). By virtue of office. For example: 'The vicar will be ex officio one of the trustees.'

**Ex parte** ('from the party'). Proceeding only from one of the parties, so likely to be prejudiced. An ex-parte statement is a one-sided or partial statement, made by one side without modification from the other.

**Ex post facto** ('from [what is done] afterwards'). Having retrospective effect. An *ex post facto* law is one made to operate retrospectively.

**Ex silentio** ('from silence'). Said of a theory or assumption that is based on a lack of evidence to the contrary.

**Ex voto** ('from a vow'). In accordance with a vow or an offering made as fulfilment of a vow.

**Exaltation.** In ASTROLOGY a planet was said to be in its 'exaltation' when it was in that sign of the ZODIAC in which it was supposed to exercise its strongest influence. Thus the exaltation of VENUS is in Pisces, and her 'dejection' is in Virgo.

**Exaltation of the Cross, The.** A feast held in the ROMAN CATHOLIC CHURCH on 14 September (HOLY CROSS DAY), in commemoration of the restoration of the true cross to CALVARY in 629, after the victory of Heraclius over the Persians, into whose hands it had fallen in 614.

**Exarch** (Greek *exarkhos*, 'leader'). The title of a viceroy of the BYZANTINE EMPIRE, especially the Exarch of Ravenna, who was de facto governor of Italy.

**Excalibur.** The name of King ARTHUR's sword (Old French *Escalibor*), called by Geoffrey of Monmouth Caliburnus (as if from Latin *chalybs*, 'steel'). There was also a legendary Irish sword called Caladbolg ('hard belly'), so named as it was 'voracious' and capable of consuming anything.

According to Sir Thomas Malory's *Le Morte d'Arthur* (1470), Arthur was acclaimed king when he was the only person who could pull the sword from a great stone in which it had been magically fixed. Hence the title of T.H. White's story for children based on the legend, *The Sword in the Stone* (1938).

**Excelsior** (Latin, 'higher'). The motto of New

York State, popularized by H.W. Longfellow's poem of this name (1842):

> A youth who bore, 'mid snow and ice,
> A banner with the strange device,
> Excelsior!

The Latin word is properly an adjective, not an adverb, and according to a biography of Longfellow by his brother Samuel, published in 1886, the poet was unaware of his grammatical gaffe. When it was pointed out to him, he claimed that it could well have been an adjective extracted from a sentence such as *Scopus meus excelsior est* ('My sword is higher'). But this appears to be a rather lame excuse to absolve himself from the solecism.

**Exception. Exception proves the rule, The.** The very fact of an exception proves (i.e. tests) the rule. This saying is often misused, as if it meant that a particular exception proved the correctness of a rule, rather than putting it to the test.

**Take exception, To.** To feel offended; to find fault with; to object.

**Exchange. Bill of exchange.** *See under* BILL.

**Diomedean exchange.** *See under* DIOMEDES.

**Royal Exchange.** *See under* ROYAL.

**Stock Exchange.** *See under* STOCK.

**Exchequer.** The title derives from the chequered cloth used for calculations. The exchequer was originally the office or department that dealt with the crown's income and expenditure. It was in being by Henry I's reign (1100–35), and was presided over by the Treasurer until 1714, when the Treasury board took over. It was abolished in 1833.

**Chancellor of the Exchequer.** *See under* CHANCELLOR.

**Red Book of the Exchequer.** *See under* RED.

**Excommunication.** An ecclesiastical censure that excludes a person from the communion of the church and is sometimes accompanied by other deprivations. If the excommunicated person is a cleric, he is forbidden to administer the sacraments. As a form of discipline, it no doubt derives from the Jewish practice at the time of Christ, which involved exclusion from religious and social intercourse. It was a common punishment in medieval times and was on occasions applied to whole nations. Adrian IV used it against Rome in 1155, and Innocent III employed it against England in 1208. The practice was also adopted by PROTESTANT churches at the REFORMATION. Article XXXIII of the Articles of Religion in the Book of Common Prayer is headed, 'Of Excommunicate Persons, how they are to be avoided'. *See also* BELL, BOOK AND CANDLE; INTERDICT.

**Excursions.** *See* ALARUMS AND EXCURSIONS.

**Excuse. Bad excuse is better than none, A.** *See under* BAD.

**Executioners.** *See* HANGMEN AND EXECUTIONERS.

**Exercise, Five-finger.** *See under* FIVE.

**Exeter.** An episcopal see and county town of Devonshire called Isca Dumnoniorum by the Romans.

The Devonshire saying 'That's Exter, as the old woman said when she saw Kerton' means 'I thought my work was done, but I find there is still more to do.' The story is that the woman in question was going to Exeter and, seeing the fine old church of Kerton (Crediton), supposed it to be Exeter Cathedral. 'That's Exter', she said, 'and my journey is over', although she still had eight miles to walk.

**Exeter Book, The.** A manuscript collection of Old English poetry, presented (*c.*1060) by Bishop Leofric to Exeter Cathedral and still preserved in the cathedral library. It includes riddles, proverbs, poems and legal documents. Among them are *The Wanderer*, *The Seafarer*, *Deor*, *Widsith* and *The Ruin*, and longer religious poems such as *Guthlac*, *Christ*, *The Phoenix* and Cynewulf's *Juliana*. *Widsith* is thought to date from the 7th century and thus to be the earliest poem in Old English. It is named from its opening word, which means 'far traveller'. The Exeter OR EXON DOMESDAY is also sometimes called the Exeter Book.

**Exeter College.** The Oxford college was founded in 1314 by Walter de Stapeldon, bishop of Exeter, and was known as Stapeldon Hall until 1405. The *Oxford English Dictionary* associates the word 'twerp' with one T.W. Earp, an Exeter man matriculating in Michaelmas Term 1911.

**Exeter Hall.** A public hall opened in the Strand, London, in 1831 and largely used for the MAY MEETINGS of religious and philanthropic organizations. Their influence on colonial policy and in humanitarian causes was considerable, especially in the 1830s, and is generally known as 'the Exeter Hall influence'. The hall was acquired by the YMCA in 1880 and demolished in 1907, the site being used for the Strand Palace Hotel.

> Mr David has since had a 'serious call',
> He never drinks ale, wine, or spirits, at all,
> And they say he is going to Exeter Hall
> To make a grand speech, and to preach and to teach
> People that 'they can't brew their malt liquor too small'.
>
> R.H. BARHAM: *Ingoldsby Legends*, 'Patty Morgan the Milkmaid's Story' (1840)

**Duke of Exeter's daughter, The.** *See under* DUKE.

**Exhibition, The Great.** *See under* GREAT.

**Existence, A hand-to-mouth.** *See under* HAND.

**Existentialism.** A philosophical attitude owing much to the writings of Søren Kierkegaard (1813–55), which developed in Germany after the First World War and somewhat later in France and Italy. Atheistic existentialism was popularized in France by Jean-Paul Sartre (1905–80) during the Second World War. Existentialists emphasize the freedom and importance of individual 'existence' and personality and show a distrust of philosophical idealism. Much of their writing is characterized by disillusionment. The term is a translation of the German *Existenz-philosophie*.

**Exodus.** The second book of the Old Testament is so named from its account of the departure of the Israelites from Egypt under the leadership of MOSES.

**Exon.** One of the four officers in command of the Yeomen of the Guard (BEEFEATERS), who are exempt from regimental duties. The word is an anglicized pronunciation of French *exempt*, a former title of a junior officer who commanded in the absence of his superiors and who was exempt from ordinary duty.

**Exon Domesday.** A magnificent manuscript transcript of Great Domesday for the counties of Wiltshire, Dorset, Somerset, Devon and Cornwall, preserved in the muniments of Exeter Cathedral. It was published in 1816. Exon is the abbreviation of Exonia, the latinized name of Exeter. *See also* DOMESDAY BOOK.

**Exorcism.** The expelling of evil spirits by prayers and incantations. An ancient practice taken over by the Christian church, after the example of Christ and the Apostles who healed those possessed of evil spirits. The use of this rite in the ROMAN CATHOLIC CHURCH is now carefully regulated, but the practice itself has been sensationalized by stories and films of the supernatural, such as the horror movie *The Exorcist* (1973).

> And when he had called unto him his twelve disciples, he gave them power against unclean spirits, to cast them out.
> Matthew 10:1

**Exoteric.** *See* ESOTERIC.

**Expect. England expects that every man will do his duty.** *See under* ENGLAND.

**Shield of expectation.** *See under* SHIELD.

**Explosive, High.** *See under* HIGH.

**Exposure, Double.** *See under* DOUBLE.

**Express, Pony.** *See under* PONY.

**Expression. Hackneyed expression.** *See under* HACKNEY.

**Happy expression.** *See under* HAPPY.

**Extispicy.** The ancient practice of Roman soothsayers of DIVINATION by the inspection of the entrails of sacrificed animals, the same as HARUSPEX. The word represents Latin *extispex*, 'inspector of entrails', from *exta specere*, 'to look at entrails'.

**Extreme unction.** The last sacramental unction, the anointing with oil of a person who is seriously ill or dying, now usually called the Anointing of the Sick. It is one of the SEVEN SACRAMENTS of the ROMAN CATHOLIC CHURCH.

> Is there any sick among you? let him call for the elders of the church; and let them pray over him, anointing him with oil in the name of the Lord.
> James 5:14

**Eye. Eyeball to eyeball.** In close confrontation.

**Eye contact.** An exchange of glances; a direct look between two people, especially of strangers.

**Eye for an eye, An.** Punishment equal to the crime; retaliation in kind. A phrase from the Old Testament.

> Eye for eye, tooth for tooth, hand for hand, foot for foot.
> Exodus 21:24

Jesus took up the words in the New Testament and radically modified their message:

> Ye have heard that it hath been said, An eye for an eye, and a tooth for a tooth: But I say unto you, That ye resist not evil: but whosoever shall smite thee on thy right cheek, turn to him the other also.
> Matthew 5:38–9

**Eyeful, An.** A visually striking person or thing. Also, a long look or stare.

**Eye of day, The.** The sun. *See also* DAISY; MATA HARI.

> Never to have lived is best, ancient writers say;
> Never to have drawn the breath of life, never to
> have looked into the eye of day .
> W.B. YEATS: *The Tower*, 'From *Oedipus at Colonus*' (1928)

**Eye of Greece, The.** Athens.

> Athens, the eye of Greece, mother of arts.
> MILTON: *Paradise Regained*, iv (1671)

**Eye of the Baltic, The.** Gotland.

**Eye of the storm, The.** An opening in the storm clouds, or an area of low pressure and relative calm in the centre of a tornado. *See also* BULL'S EYE.

**Eye of the wind.** In nautical parlance the direction from which the wind is blowing.

**Eye-opener, An.** Something surprising or revealing. In American usage, an eye-opener is an alcoholic drink taken on waking.

**Eye rhyme.** A rhyme involving words that are similar in spelling but differ in pronunciation, such as come and home, or none and tone.

**Eyes and no eyes.** Unobservant. 'Eyes have they, but they see not' (Psalm 115:5).

**Eye service.** Unwilling service, of the sort only done when one's master is looking.

**Eyes front!** A military command to troops to look ahead. *See also* EYES LEFT; EYES RIGHT.

**Eyes left!** A military command to troops to look to the left, especially as a form of salute when marching.

**Eyesore.** Something very ugly, especially when contrasting with an otherwise pleasant scene.
**Eyes right!** A military command to troops to look to the right, especially as a form of salute when marching.
**Eye teeth.** The canine teeth, so called because they are located (in the upper and lower jaw) just under the eyes. 'To give one's eyeteeth for' means to go to any length for something or to make any sacrifice for it: 'I'd give my eyeteeth to have a camera like that.'
**Eyewash.** Nonsense; insincere talk. The allusion is to something that blinds one to the real state of affairs.
**All eyes.** *See under* ALL.
**All my eye and Betty Martin.** *See under* ALL.
**Apple of one's eye, The.** *See under* APPLE.
**Babies in the eyes.** *See under* BABY.
**Bags under the eyes.** *See under* BAG.
**Bedroom eyes.** *See under* BED.
**Black eye.** *See under* BLACK.
**Bull's eye.** *See under* BULL.
**Cast one's eye over, To.** *See under* CAST.
**Catch someone's eye, To.** *See under* CATCH.
**Catch the Speaker's eye, To.** *See under* CATCH.
**Cat's eye.** *See under* CAT.
**Close one's eyes, To.** *See under* CLOSE.
**Cock an eye, To.** *See under* COCK.
**Cry one's eyes out, To.** *See under* CRY.
**Cut one's eye teeth, To.** *See under* CUT.
**Drop in one's eye, A.** *See under* DROP.
**Eagle eye.** *See under* EAGLE.
**Evil eye.** *See under* EVIL.
**Get one's eye in, To.** To become adjusted to visual conditions in a game of cricket, billiards, golf, bowls and other sports in which 'sighting' is important.
**Give someone the glad eye, To.** *See under* GLAD.
**Green eye.** *See under* GREEN.
**Half an eye.** *See under* HALF.
**Have an eye for, To.** To have a sense of critical appreciation of something.
**Have an eye to, To.** To keep constantly in view; to act from motives of expediency.
**Have an eye to the main chance, To.** To keep self-advantage or profit constantly in view. *See also* MAIN CHANCE.
**In the twinkling of an eye.** *See under* TWINKLING.
**Jaundiced eye, A.** *See under* JAUNDICED.
**Keep an eye on, To.** To look after; to keep watch over someone or something.
**Keep an eye open, To.** To be on the lookout; to watch for.
**Keep one's eye on the ball, To.** *See under* BALL.
**Keep one's eyes skinned** or **peeled, To.** To be particularly watchful.
**Lazy eye.** *See under* LAZY.
**Make eyes at someone, To.** To ogle them; to look at them amorously. *See also* SHEEP'S EYES.
**Meet the eye, To.** *See under* MEET.
**Mind your eye.** *See under* MIND.
**More (to that) than meets the eye.** *See under* MORE.
**One-eyed.** *See under* ONE.
**One in the eye.** *See under* ONE.
**Open someone's eyes, To.** *See under* OPEN.
**Pope's eye.** *See under* POPE.
**Private eye.** *See under* PRIVATE.
**Public eye.** *See under* PUBLIC.
**Raise an eyebrow, To.** *See under* RAISE.
**Roving eye, A.** *See under* ROVE.
**Saucer eyes.** *See under* SAUCER.
**Scales fell from his eyes, The.** *See under* SCALES.
**See eye to eye, To.** *See under* SEE.
**Seeing Eye, The.** *See under* SEE.
**Set, lay or clap eyes on, To.** *See under* SET.
**Sheep's eyes.** *See under* SHEEP.
**Shut** or **close one's eyes to, To.** *See under* SHUT.
**Sight for sore eyes, A.** *See under* SIGHT.
**Third eye.** *See under* THIRD.
**Throw dust in someone's eyes, To.** *See under* THROW.
**Turn a blind eye to, To.** *See under* TURN.
**Up to one's eyes.** *See under* UP.
**Wipe someone's eye, To.** *See under* WIPE.
**With one's eyes open.** *See under* WITH.
**With one's eyes shut.** *See under* WITH.
**Without batting an eyelid.** *See under* WITHOUT.
**Worm's eye view.** *See under* WORM.

**Ezekiel.** The most unusual of the prophets, who flew through the air more than once and underwent periods of speechlessness and immobility. He experienced trances and had visions, one of these being of a valley of dry bones, which are reassembled and clothed with flesh. The symbolism of this is disputed, but it may represent the redemption and reunion of both Judah and Israel.

# F

**F.** The first letter in the Runic FUTHORC, but the sixth in the Phoenician and Latin alphabets and their derivatives. The Egyptian hieroglyph represented a horned asp and the Phoenician character a peg. Ph represents the same sound.

**Ff** or **ff.** As an initial in a few surnames, such as ffitch, ffolkes or ffrench (or Ffitch and so on), this is a mistaken use in print of the medieval capital F (*ff*) as it appeared written in official documents. In script, the old capital F looked very much like two small fs entwined. Its modern use is an affectation. The 1981 London telephone directory has 28 subscribers with names so spelt, including one ffennell.

**Three Fs, The.** *See under* THREE.

**Fab Four, The.** An early nickname of the BEATLES, 'fab' being a vogue form of 'fabulous'.

**Fabius.** Quintus Fabius Maximus (d.203 BC), surnamed CUNCTATOR. According to Ennius (*Annals* (xii, 2nd century)):

> Unus homo nobis cunctando restituit rem.
> (One man by delaying saved the state for us.)

**Fabian Society.** A society founded in 1884 by a small group of middle-class intellectuals with the aim of gradually working towards a democratic socialist state. They took their name from Quintus FABIUS Maximus, believing that 'long taking of counsel' was necessary before they could achieve their objective. Prominent members included George Bernard Shaw (1856–1950), Sidney Webb (1859–1947), Beatrice Webb (1858–1943) and Annie Besant (1847–1933).

**Fabian tactics.** Delaying tactics, masterly inactivity, 'winning by wearing out', in the manner of FABIUS called CUNCTATOR.

**American Fabius, The.** George Washington (1732–99), whose tactics as commander-in-chief in the American War of Independence (1775–83) were somewhat similar to those of FABIUS.

**Fables** (Latin *fabula*, 'narrative story', 'fable'). Although this name is applied in a general sense to fictitious tales, legends and myths, it is more particularly applied to didactic stories of which a moral forms an integral part. In this more restricted class, human thoughts and attributes are usually portrayed by particular animals and insects. *See also* AESOP; BABRIUS; LA FONTAINE; PHAEDRUS.

**Milesian fables.** *See under* MILESIANS.

**Fabliaux.** Medieval French metrical tales, mostly comical and satirical, and intended primarily for recitation by the TROUVÈRES, or early poets north of the Loire, and mostly of the period from the late 12th century to the second half of the 14th. They have little connection with the fable proper, beyond the name, and were usually in octosyllabic couplets. They were essentially to entertain the common people and were characterized by coarseness and by a satirical treatment of the weaknesses of the clergy, of feminine frailty and of the everyday incidents of life.

**Fabricius, Gaius Lusinus.** A Roman consul (d.*c*.270 BC) and hero of the war against Pyrrhus, renowned for his incorruptibility and honesty. Roman writers tell how he lived frugally on his farm, how he refused the bribes offered him by the Samnite ambassadors, and how, on his death, he was too poor to leave a portion for his daughters, so that the Senate was obliged to provide for them.

**Fabulinus** (Latin *fabulari*, 'to speak'). The god, mentioned by Varro, who taught Roman children to utter their first word. *See also* DEITIES PROTECTING BABIES.

**Face.** A colloquialism for impudence or effrontery, as: 'He has face enough for anything.' The use goes back to the 16th century. *See also* NECK.

Face is also a colloquial term for make-up, as: 'She took off her face before going to bed.'

**Face about, To.** To turn round and face the other way.

**Face-ache.** A colloquial term for an unpleasant-looking or miserable person.

**Face as long as a fiddle, A.** A miserable or gloomy expression.

**Face card.** In the USA, a COURT CARD.

**Face down, To.** To withstand with boldness and effrontery; to abash with a fixed stare.

**Face facts, To.** To admit the truth.

**Face it out, To.** To persist in an assertion that is not true; to maintain a bold front.

**Face-lift.** A method of enhancing looks or of concealing the marks of age by cosmetic surgery, which tightens the sagging skin of the face and smooths out the wrinkles. More generally, to give something a face-lift is to renovate it.

**Face off, To.** To adopt an attitude of confrontation, especially at the start of a fight or game.

**Face patches.** One of the more idiosyncratic fashions of the 17th and early 18th centuries was the wearing of face patches by women and sometimes by men. Round black patches were the most popular but diamonds and other shapes were also used, sometimes to hide blemishes but usually intended as an adornment.

**Face that launched a thousand ships, The.** The face of HELEN, the ships being the Greek fleet which sailed for TROY to avenge MENELAUS. The phrase is from Marlowe:

> Was this the face that launched a thousand ships,
> And burnt the topless towers of Ilium?
> *Doctor Faustus,* V, i (1604)

**Face the music, To.** To brave the consequences of one's actions or to put on a bold front in an unpleasant situation. The expression may derive from the stage, although some authorities take it from the military ceremony in which an officer being cashiered was required to face the drum squad while his charges were read out.

**Face to face.** Directly opposite each another, with no intermediary.

**Face up to something, To.** To meet one's difficulties bravely or resolutely.

**Face value.** A thing's apparent value. A currency note with a printed value may actually be worth less or more than the stated amount.

**Faceworker.** A miner who works at the coalface.

**Black in the face.** *See under* BLACK.

**Blue in the face.** *See under* BLUE.

**Fly in the face of, To.** *See under* FLY.

**In your face.** *See under* IN.

**Laugh in someone's face, To.** *See under* LAUGH.

**Laugh on the other side of one's face, To.** *See under* LAUGH.

**Let's face it.** *See under* LET.

**Long face, A.** *See under* LONG.

**Look someone in the face, To.** *See under* LOOK.

**Lose face, To.** *See under* LOSE.

**Make faces, To.** To grimace.

**M to represent the human face.** *See under* M.

**Pasty face, A.** *See under* PASTY.

**Poker face, A.** *See under* POKER.

**Pull a face, To.** *See under* PULL.

**Put a bold face on the matter, To.** *See under* BOLD.

**Save face, To.** *See under* SAVE.

**Set one's face against something, To.** *See under* SET.

**Show one's face, To.** *See under* SHOW.

**Shut the door in someone's face, To.** *See under* SHUT.

**Shut your face!** *See under* SHUT.

**Wry face, A.** *See under* WRY.

**Facile princeps** (Latin, 'easily first'). A phrase used of an obvious or acknowledged leader.

**Facilis descensus Averno.** *See* AVERNUS.

**Façon de parler** (French, 'manner of speaking'). An expression used of a mere phrase or formula.

**Fact. Facts of life, The.** The realities of a situation; information about sexual functions, especially as imparted to young people.

**Accessory after the fact.** *See under* ACCESSORY.

**Face facts, To.** *See under* FACE.

**Faction.** In Roman and Byzantine history the *factiones* were originally the companies into which the charioteers were divided, each group having its special colour. The original two factions at Rome were the white (*albata*) and red (*russata*), to which the green (*prasina*) and blue (*veneta*) were added when the number of competing chariots was increased from two to four. The political faction, as a small dissenting group within a larger one, is a modern development of this.

**Factory King, The.** The nickname given to Richard Oastler (1789–1861) for his strenuous and lifelong efforts to improve the lot of the factory workers, especially children. He initially drew public attention by writing to the Leeds press on 'Yorkshire Slavery', and he was the constant advocate of a ten-hour day.

**Factotum** (Latin *fac totum!*, 'do everything!'). A person who does all kinds of services for an employer. The term formerly meant a JACK OF ALL TRADES, and it was in this sense that Robert Greene (1558–92) used it in his reference to Shakespeare:

> There is an upstart Crow, beautified with our feathers, that with his *Tygers hart wrapt in a Players hyde*, supposes he is as well able to bombast out a blanke verse as the best of you: and beeing an absolute *Iohannes fac totum*, is in his owne conceit the onely Shake-scene in a countrey.
> *Greenes Groatsworth of Wit* (1592)

**Faculty, Dean of.** *See under* DEAN.

**Fadda** (Arabic, 'silver'). MOHAMMED's white mule.

**Fadge** (of uncertain origin, but perhaps a Scandinavian word, connected with *faga*, 'to suit'). An archaic word meaning to suit or fit together, as: 'It won't fadge.'

> How will this fadge?
> SHAKESPEARE: *Twelfth Night*, II, ii (1599)

**Faerie.** The land of the fairies; the dominions of OBERON. *See also* AVALON.

> The land of faery,
> Where nobody gets old and godly and grave,
> Where nobody gets old and crafty and wise,
> Where nobody gets old and bitter of tongue.
> W.B. YEATS: *The Land of Heart's Desire* (1894)

**Faerie Queene, The.** An allegorical romance of

CHIVALRY by Edmund Spenser, originally intended to have been in 12 books, each of which was to have portrayed one of the 12 moral virtues, but only six books were completed. The first three were published in 1590, and the second three in 1596. It details the adventures of various knights, who personify different virtues, so that Sir ARTEGAL is the Knight of Justice, and Sir CALIDORE the Knight of Courtesy. The knights belong to the court of GLORIANA, who sometimes typifies Queen Elizabeth I.

**Fafnir.** The dragon who guards the gold of the Nibelung and who is killed by SIEGFRIED (SIGURD). His story is told in the Volsung Saga and the NIBELUNGENLIED. The name means 'smith', from an Old Scandinavian word related to Latin *faber*. *See also* VOLSUNGS.

**Fag.** A schoolboy who performs (or performed) menial tasks for his seniors in certain boarding schools. The word is perhaps related to 'flag' in the sense of 'droop', or to 'fagged out', in the sense of 'very tired'.

> From supper until nine o'clock three fags taken in order stood in the passages, and answered any praeposter who called 'Fag', racing to the door, the last comer having to do the work ... And besides this night-work, each praeposter had three or four fags specially allotted to him, of whom he was supposed to be the guide, philosopher, and friend.
>
> THOMAS HUGHES: *Tom Brown's Schooldays*, Pt I, ch vii (1857)

**Fag.** A colloquial word for a cigarette, possibly connected with 'flag' in the sense 'droop', alluding to a cigarette dangling from the lips. *See also* COFFIN NAIL.

**Fag, To be a.** To be too much trouble or too much of an effort.

**Fag end.** Originally a term for the coarse end of a piece of cloth, and hence the remaining part of anything, as 'the fag end of a conversation'. It is also slang for a cigarette stub. *See also* FAG.

> The Kitchen and Gutters and other Offices of noise and drudgery are at the fag-end.
>
> *Howell's Familiar Letters* (20 May 1619)

**Fagged out.** Tired out; exhausted.

**Faggot.** (1) A bundle of sticks. In the days when heretics were burned at the stake, an embroidered representation of a faggot was worn on the arm by those who recanted, showing what they deserved but had narrowly escaped.

(2) The word faggot was also applied to a hireling who took the place of another at the muster of a regiment.

(3) A faggot is also a term for a male homosexual, but an 'old faggot' is a dreary old woman.

**Fagin.** The master and 'minder' of London pickpockets, including the ARTFUL DODGER and young Oliver TWIST, in Dickens' *Oliver Twist* (1838–9). He is the archetype of the villainous Jew and is said to have been based on Isaac 'Ikey' Solomons (*c*.1785–1850), a notorious London receiver of the 1820s, who was sentenced to 14 years' transportation for picking pockets.

**Fail. Words fail me.** *See under* WORD.

**Fainéants, Les Rois.** *See* ROIS FAINÉANTS.

**Fains.** A schoolchildren's term exempting the first to call it, as: 'Fains I go in goal' or 'Fains carry the bags back'. It is the opposite of BAGS I or 'Bags', by means of which a positive claim is asserted. The word is usually taken to be a corruption of fend, but Iona and Peter Opie, in *The Lore and Language of Schoolchildren* (1959), tell how Professor J.R.R. Tolkien advised them that the expression is of medieval origin and comes from French *se feindre*, 'to make excuses', 'to hang back' (originally used in battle).

**Faint heart never won fair lady.** An old proverb with an obvious meaning: go for it!

**Fair.** The following have been given this epithet, usually in the sense 'just', but sometimes meaning 'handsome':

Edwy or Eadwig, king of Wessex (r.955–959)
Philip the Fair, king of France, le Bel (r.1285–1314)
Charles IV, king of France, le Bel (r.1322–8), youngest son of Philip the Fair

**Fair and square.** Honestly; justly; with straightforwardness.

**Fair cop, A.** A discovery in the act of some transgression; an arrest by a police officer.

**Fair crack of the whip, A.** A fair chance or opportunity; a fair 'innings'. Whoever has the whip holds the reins, and is thus in charge.

**Fair do's.** Equal shares for all or an appeal for such shares.

**Fair enough.** An expression of (sometimes grudging) agreement.

**Fair game.** A person one may legitimately pursue or attack. The allusion is to game that may be hunted in the open season.

**Fair-haired, The.** Harold I, king of Norway (r.872–930).

**Fair-haired boy.** An American equivalent of a BLUE-EYED BOY.

**Fair Isle.** One of the Shetland Islands, where a special pattern of knitting is done, which is believed to be of Moorish origin and to have been derived from contacts with shipwrecked sailors from the Spanish Armada of 1588. The Duke of Medina Sidonia, admiral of the Armada, was wrecked on Fair Isle.

**Fair Maid of Anjou, The.** Lady Edith Plantagenet (*fl.*1200), a kinswoman of Richard I and an attendant on Queen Berengaria, who married David, Earl of Huntingdon, prince royal of Scotland. She is a central character in Sir Walter Scott's *The Talisman* (1825).

**Fair Maid of Brittany, The.** Eleanor (d.1241), granddaughter of Henry II and, after the death of her brother Arthur, the rightful sovereign of England. Her uncle, the usurper King John, imprisoned her in Bristol Castle, which she eventually left to enter a nunnery at Amesbury. Her father, Geoffrey, John's elder brother, was Count of Brittany.

**Fair maid of February, The.** A once popular name for the snowdrop.

**Fair maid of Ireland, The.** Another name for the IGNIS FATUUS.

**Fair Maid of Kent, The.** Joan (1328–85), Countess of Kent, wife of the BLACK PRINCE, and only daughter of Edmund Plantagenet, Earl of Kent. The prince was her second husband.

**Fair Maid of Norway, The.** Margaret (1283–90), daughter of Eric II of Norway, and granddaughter of Alexander III of Scotland. Acknowledged as heir to the throne of Scotland and engaged to Prince Edward, son of Edward I of England, she died in the Orkney Islands on her way to England.

**Fair Maid of Perth, The.** Katie Glover, heroine of Sir Walter Scott's novel of this name (1828), is said to have lived in the early 15th century, but she is not a definite historical character. The Fair Maid's House on Blackfriars Wynd in Perth is a rebuilt version of the one said to have been occupied by Simon Glover and his daughter. Bizet's opera, *La Jolie Fille de Perth* (1867), is based on the novel.

**Fair Maid of Ross, The.** Amy, the daughter of Captain Browne, the warden of Ross Castle, Killarney, was known as the Fair Maid of Ross. She attracted the attention of most of the young officers, especially Raymond Villiers, whom her father wanted her to marry, but she was already in love with Donough McCarthy, whose estates had been seized by the enemy. When the castle was besieged by the Cromwellians in 1652, Villiers, having been refused by Amy, resolved to betray Ross Castle to Ludlow, Cromwell's general, but when he was engaged on this mission Amy followed him and learned of his treason. When Villiers finally left the castle, Amy again followed him but was wounded by his pistol shot. In a subsequent skirmish McCarthy killed Villiers, and Captain Browne surrendered the castle on honourable terms. In due course McCarthy recovered his land and married Amy.

**Fair play.** Honest or straight dealing; fair or impartial treatment. A supposed traditional attribute of the British.

**Fair Rosamond, The.** Rosamund Clifford, who is generally believed to have died in 1176 and who was probably the mistress of Henry II in 1174. According to legend, Henry kept her in a house like a maze in Woodstock where only he could find her, but his queen, Eleanor of Aquitaine, traced her whereabouts by following a thread and 'so dealt with her that she lived not long after'. She was buried in the choir of Godstow Abbey near Oxford, and her remains were removed to the Chapter House there in about 1191.

The legend of her murder by Queen Eleanor first appears in the 14th century, and the story of the maze-like house even later. There is no evidence to support the stories that Fair Rosamond was the mother of WILLIAM LONGSWORD and Geoffrey, archbishop of York. A subterranean labyrinth in Blenheim Park, near Woodstock, is still pointed out as Rosamond's Bower.

**Fair sex, The.** Women. The phrase is modelled on the French *le beau sexe*.

**Fair's fair.** All concerned should act fairly.

**Fair-spoken.** Courteous.

**Fair to middling.** Moderately good; quite well.

**Fair-weather friends.** Those who are loyal when you are flourishing but desert as soon as your fortunes change.

**Fair words butter no parsnips.** *See* FINE WORDS BUTTER NO PARSNIPS.

**Bid fair, To.** *See under* BID.

**By fair means.** *See under* BY.

**Pretty fair.** *See under* PRETTY.

**Fair** (Old French *feire*, from Late Latin *feria*, 'holiday'). These great markets of former days were often held at the time of church festivals, but they came to be associated with side-shows, amusements and merrymaking. Although trade fairs or exhibitions are a link with the commercial aspect of the fairs of the past, the name is now largely associated with the travelling amusement fair. *See also* COURT OF PIEPOWDER.

**Bartholomew Fair.** *See under* BARTHOLOMEW.

**Donnybrook Fair.** *See under* DONNYBROOK.

**Egremont Crab Fair.** *See under* EGREMONT.

**Goose fair.** *See under* GOOSE.

**Hiring fair.** *See under* HIRING.

**Mop fair.** *See under* MOP.

**Paddington fair.** *See under* PADDINGTON.

**Statute fair.** *See under* STATUTE.

**Vanity Fair.** *See under* VANITY.

**Widecombe Fair.** *See under* WIDECOME.

**Fairy** or **fay.** In folklore and legend, a diminutive supernatural being of human shape, with magical powers. The names of the principal fairies and sprites known in fable and legend appear in this dictionary as individual entries. *See also* BROWNIE; DEITIES; DWARF; ELF; FAUNI; GNOME; GOBLIN; LEPRECHAUN; PIXIE.

Fairy is also a derogatory nickname for a male homosexual. The name may relate to the male actor in DRAG who traditionally plays the fairy godmother in pantomimes.

> Two girls stopped near our table and looked at us curiously. 'Come on,' said one to the other, 'we're wasting our time. They're only fairies.'
> EVELYN WAUGH: *Brideshead Revisited*, I, ch v (1945)

**Fairy cake.** A small individual cake, usually iced and decorated,

**Fairy cycle.** A child's bicycle.

**Fairy darts.** Flint arrowheads. *See also* ELF ARROWS.

**Fairy godmother, A.** A benefactress.

**Fairy lights.** Small coloured lights for decorating a Christmas tree, especially out of doors.

**Fairy loaves** or **stones.** Fossil sea urchins, said to be made by the fairies.

**Fairy money.** Found money, said to be placed by some good fairy at the spot where it is picked up. Also in legend, money given by the fairies, which turned into 'leaves' or other worthless forms.

**Fairy of the mine.** A malevolent GNOME, supposed to live in mines, who busied himself cutting ore, turning the windlass and the like.

> No goblin or swart faëry of the mine
> Hath hurtful power o'er true virginity.
> MILTON: *Comus* (1637)

**Fairy ring.** A circle of dark green grass, often found in lawns and meadows and popularly supposed to be produced by fairies dancing. The rings are caused by the growth of certain fungi below the surface of the earth. The spawn radiates from the centre at a similar rate annually, and the darker colour is due to the increased nitrogen produced by the action of the fungus. Mushrooms appear seasonally around the ring.

> You demi-puppets, that
> By moonshine do the green sour ringlets make
> Whereof the ewe not bites; and you, whose pastime
> Is to make midnight mushrooms.
> SHAKESPEARE: *The Tempest*, V, i (1611)

**Fairy tale.** A story about fairies, as told to young children. Hence something joyful and happy, such as a fairy-tale wedding, but also something improbable, such as a person's fairy-tale account of their encounters or achievements.

**Cottingley fairies, The.** *See under* FAKES.

**Fait accompli** (French, 'accomplished fact'). A thing that has already been done and that cannot be altered.

> I pointed out to Herr von Jagow that this *fait accompli* of the violation of the Belgian frontier rendered, as he would readily understand, the situation exceedingly grave.
> Sir Edward Goschen, Ambassador in Berlin, to Sir Edward Grey (8 August 1914)

**Faith. Faith healing.** Healing though faith and prayer, as opposed to conventional medicine.

**Act of faith.** *See* AUTO-DA-FÉ.

**Attic faith.** *See under* ATTIC.

**Defender of the Faith.** *See under* DEFENDER.

**In good faith.** *See under* GOOD.

**Punic faith.** *See under* PUNIC.

**Faithful.** The active supporters of any cult or party are often known as the faithful.

**Commander of the Faithful.** *See under* COMMANDER.

**Father of the Faithful, The.** *See under* FATHER.

**Fakes** (obsolete English *feak*, 'to thrash', from German *fegen*, 'to sweep', 'to thrash'). The difference between a fake and a forgery is a fine one. Generally speaking a fake is a thing that is not genuine, whether its creator or perpetrator intended to deceive or not, whereas a forgery is an attempt to pass off as genuine some piece of spurious work or writing with the intent to deceive or defraud. Among the notable examples given here, the ROWLEY POEMS are essentially fakes rather than forgeries. *See also* OSSIAN.

**Cottingley fairies, The.** In 1917 two little girls living at Bingley, Yorkshire, Elsie Wright and her cousin Frances, claimed they had seen fairies in nearby Cottingley Dell and said they had even taken photographs of them. The story came to the attention of Sir Arthur Conan Doyle, by then a convert to spiritualism. He believed the girls and vouched for the veracity of the photographs, even taking lantern slides made from them to America as part of a lecture tour. In 1983 Frances Griffiths, now aged 76, admitted that the pictures had been faked by photographing cut-outs of fairies from *Princess Mary's Gift Book*, a popular children's book.

**Drake brass plate, The.** Sir Francis Drake, during his voyage of circumnavigation (1577–80), anchored off the Californian coast in 1579 and set up a brass plate naming the territory New Albion and claiming it in the name of Queen Elizabeth. In 1936 the plate was said to have been found near San Francisco and the inscription seemed to be reasonably authentic, although some authorities expressed doubt. A replica was, in due course, presented to Queen Elizabeth II, which is kept in Buckland Abbey, Drake's Devonshire property, now a museum. In 1977 a reported analysis of the composition of the brass by the Lawrence Berkeley Institute of the University of California and the Research Laboratory for Archaeology at Oxford found that it was of late 19th- or early 20th-century manufacture.

**False memory syndrome.** A term, often abbreviated FMS, that came into use in the 1990s following many cases in which individuals 'recall' child or adult sexual abuse or ritual satanic abuse that has not actually taken place. Such 'memories' have been coaxed out of children or those accused of abusing children by over-eager therapists or prosecutors, with the result that many lives have been blighted, not least those of parents, falsely implicated by their adult children. Cases of FMS first came to light in the USA in the late 1980s, when 22-year-old Ericka Ingram, of East Olympia, Washington, was obliged to 'admit' that she had been abused as a child by her father, an accusation supposedly supported by her 18-year-old sister, Julie, who 'evidenced' tales of satanic rituals involving their family and their father's friends. In 1993 Robert Kelly, of Edenton, North Carolina, was found guilty of some of the 183 charges of satanic paedophilia he was accused of committing at his day-care centre, despite the fact that some of the tales involved children being microwaved or thrown into tanks full of ravenous sharks. Most of the accusations came from stay-at-home mothers, and no one visiting the centre had ever noticed anything unusual. That same year 35-year-old Peter Ellis, of New Zealand, was accused of abusing over fifty young children at a similar centre. Much of the children's evidence was shown to be patently false, but Ellis was nevertheless found 'guilty' of sexual violation and indecent assault and jailed for ten years. The whole murky phenomenon subsequently surfaced in Britain, where in 1996 a man was acquitted of sexually abusing a woman thanks to psychological assessments concluding that the plaintiff was probably suffering from FMS and that her 'memories' had in fact been suggested by storylines in television dramas.

**Hitler diaries, The.** On 24 April 1983 the *Sunday Times* reported the discovery of 60 volumes of Hitler's diaries, which had been acquired by the Hamburg magazine *Stern* for £2,460,000 and delivered to them by their reporter Gerd Heidemann. They were said to have been salvaged from an aircraft wrecked in 1945 and found in a hayloft. Professor Hugh Trevor-Roper (Lord Dacre) had vouched for their authenticity and the *Sunday Times* (after paying *Stern* for publication rights) obtained two volumes (1932 and 1935) for testing. Dr Julius Grant, a chemical expert, proved that the paper in the diaries was not in use until after the Second World War. Two weeks after their alleged discovery the Bonn government also declared them to be forgeries. Heidemann revealed that he had obtained them from a Stuttgart dealer in military relics, Peter Fischer, real name Konrad Kujau, and the latter confessed to forgery. Both were imprisoned in May 1983, brought to trial in August 1984 and sentenced in July 1985. Kujau was jailed for 4 years 6 months for forgery and Heidemann for 4 years 8 months for fraud.

**Ireland forgeries, The.** One of the best known literary forgers was William Henry Ireland (1777–1835), the son of a bookseller and amateur antiquarian. When he was only 19 years old, Ireland produced a number of seemingly ancient leases and other documents purporting to be in Shakespeare's handwriting, including a love poem to 'Anna Hatherrawaye'. Emboldened by their acceptance, he next came out with two 'lost' Shakespeare plays: *Vortigern and Rowena* and *Henry II*. Ignoring the suspicions of Kemble, R.B. Sheridan produced *Vortigern* at DRURY LANE in 1796. During the rehearsals Mrs Siddons and Mrs Palmer resigned their roles, and Kemble helped to ensure the play was laughed off the stage. When he spoke the line 'When this solemn mockery is o'er', the house yelled and hissed until the curtain fell. Meanwhile Edmund Malone and George Steevens had studied the *Miscellaneous Papers*, said to be Shakespeare's, and had declared them forgeries. Ireland confessed later in the same year. His motive appears to have been a craving to secure the admiration of his father, whose antiquarian interests amounted to an obsession.

**Macaroni parson, The.** The Rev. Dr William Dodd (1729–77) was so nicknamed from his expensive habits, which resulted in a well-known forgery. He graduated in mathematics at Cambridge in 1750 and was soon ordained, becoming chaplain of the recently opened Magdalen hospital in London for unfortunate and fallen women, and his sermons soon attracted a fashionable following. He was editor of *The Christian Magazine* (1760–7) and published numerous books during his lifetime. He became a royal chaplain in 1763, but his attempt to secure the rich living of St George's Hanover Square by improperly offering money through the Lord Chancellor's wife cost him his chaplaincy. He held various other preferments during his career but became deeply in debt and signed a cheque for £4200 in the name of his former pupil, the 5th Lord Chesterfield. When the forgery was discovered he repaid much of the money but was confined in NEWGATE PRISON and sentenced to death. He received support from Dr Johnson and many others, but George III refused clemency to his one-time chaplain, who was hanged in July 1777. *See also* MACARONI.

**Pictures of Tom Keating, The.** Keating (1918–84), beginning as a picture restorer, produced about 2000 drawings and paintings and sold them as originals by Samuel Palmer (1805–81) and other English artists. He admitted his works were fakes in 1976, and in the last years of his life enjoyed brief fame on television as an expert on painting generally and IMPRESSIONISM in particular.

**Pigott forgeries, The.** In April 1887 *The Times* published in facsimile a letter attributed to Charles Stewart Parnell, the Irish leader, condoning the PHOENIX PARK MURDERS. Parnell denounced this as a forgery, but *The Times* continued to publish its damaging articles on 'Parnellism and Crime', which deeply influenced English opinion. In 1888 O'Donnell, one of those besmirched, sued *The Times* for libel. From the judicial inquiry which resulted, the letters were found to be forged by Richard Pigott, who had sold them to *The Times* for a large sum, money being his only motive. *The Times* had to pay £250,000 in costs. Pigott fled to Madrid and shot himself when arrest was impending.

**Piltdown skull** or **Piltdown man, The.** In 1908 and 1911 Charles Dawson (1864–1916) of Lewes 'found' two pieces of a highly mineralized human skull in a gravel bed near Piltdown Common, Sussex. By 1912 he and Sir Arthur Smith Woodward (1864–1944) had discovered the whole skull. This was thought to be that of a new genus of man and was called *Eoanthropus dawsoni*. It came to be accepted as such by prehistorians, archaeologists and others, although a few were sceptical. In 1953 J.S. Weiner, K.P. Oakley and W.E. Le Gros Clark issued a report (*Bulletin of the British Museum* (Natural History), Vol II, No. 3) announcing that the Piltdown mandible was a fake, in reality the jaw of a modern ape, the rest of the skull being that of *Homo sapiens*. The hoax, which duped most of the experts, was apparently planned by William Sollas, Professor of Geology at Oxford (1897–1937), through his dislike of Woodward.

**Poems of Ossian, The.** *See* OSSIAN.

**Protocols of the Elders of Zion, The.** Forged material published by Serge Nilus in Russia in 1905 and based on an earlier forgery of 1903, purporting to outline secret Jewish plans for achieving world power by undermining Gentile morality, family life and health, and by securing a monopoly in international finance, among other things. Their falsity was first exposed by Philip Graves, *The Times* correspondent in Constantinople, in 1921 and later judicially, at Berne (1934–5). Their influence in inciting anti-Semitism, notably among the Russians, and later providing Hitler and his associates with an excuse they knew to be a myth, provide tragic evidence of the power of the 'big lie'.

**Psalmanazar, George.** A classical example of the impostor. A Frenchman, whose real name is unknown to this day, he appeared in London in 1703 claiming to be a native of Formosa, at that time an almost unknown island. In 1704 he published an account of Formosa with a grammar of the language, which from beginning to end was a fabrication of his own. The literary and critical world of London was taken in, but his imposture was soon exposed by Roman Catholic missionaries who had laboured in Formosa, and after a time Psalmanazar publicly confessed his fraud. He turned over a new leaf and applied himself to the study of Hebrew and other genuine labours, ending his days in 1763 as a man of some repute and the friend of Dr Johnson. He apparently took his name from the biblical character Shalmaneser, king of Assyria (2 Kings 17:3), adding an initial P. *See also* OSSIAN; PROTOCOLS OF THE ELDERS OF ZION (*above*).

**Rowley poems, The.** Poems written by Thomas Chatterton (1752–70) were said by him to have been the work of a 15th-century priest of Bristol called Thomas Rowley (a fictitious character). Chatterton began to write them before he was 15 and, after having been refused by the playwright Robert Dodsley (1704–64), they were published in 1769. Many prominent connoisseurs and litterateurs, including Horace Walpole (until he consulted friends), were hoaxed.

**Turin Shroud, The.** The shroud of twill linen kept in Turin Cathedral and claimed to be the one in which the body of Christ was wrapped after the crucifixion. The pope agreed to RADIOCARBON DATING in 1987, and in 1988 the archbishop of Turin appointed the Oxford Research Laboratory for Archaeology, the Department of Physics of Arizona University and the Swiss Federal Institute of Technology at Zurich to date the shroud, pieces of which were given to these institutes in April 1988. The results were announced on 13 October and the cloth was dated between 1260 and 1390. There is no firm historical evidence that it was known before the 14th century. Although not accepted by all, the general conclusion is that the shroud is a medieval fake. *See also* SUDARIUM.

**Vermeer forgeries, The.** Hans (Henri) van Meegeren (1889–1947) began his series of brilliant fakes of Dutch masters in 1937 with *Christ at Emmaus*, which was sold as a 'Vermeer' for 550,000 gulden. Experts duly acclaimed it. His intention seems to have been to indulge his contempt and hatred of the art critics by a superlative hoax, but the financial success of his first fake led to others, mostly 'Vermeers'. Discovery came only in 1945 when Allied commissioners were seeking to restore to their former owners the art treasures that had found their way to Germany during the war. Among Goering's collection was an unknown Vermeer, *The Woman taken in Adultery*, and its original vendor was found to be van Meegeren. Sale of such a work of national importance involved a charge of collaboration with the enemy. To escape the heavy penalty, van Meegeren confessed to faking 14 Dutch masterpieces, 9 of which had been sold for a total of 7,167,000 gulden, and to prove his story agreed to paint another 'old masterpiece' in prison in the presence of the experts. He was sentenced to one year's imprisonment in October 1947 but died on 30 December.

**Vinland Map, The.** Norse exploration from the end of the 10th century led to the discovery of part of North America. According to the Norse Saga, *Flateyjarbók*: 'When spring came they made ready and left, and Leif named the land after its fruits, and called it Vinland.' In 1957 the discovery of a map of the northeast American coast was announced and said to be the most exciting cartographic find of the century. Supposedly drawn *c.*1440, it substantially preceded the voyages of Columbus (1492) and of John Cabot (1497), thus conclusively establishing the extent of the Viking explorations. It was presented to Yale University by an anonymous donor in 1965. In 1974 Yale announced that it was a fake. The pigment of the ink with which it was drawn was found to contain titanium dioxide, first used in the 1920s.

**Zinoviev Letter, The.** A letter purportedly signed by the Russian Communist leader Grigory Zinoviev (1883–1936), president of the Third International. It summoned the British Communist Party to intensify its revolutionary activities and to subvert the armed forces, and was published on 25 October 1924, four days before a general election. It helped to promote a 'red scare' and was instrumental in defeating Ramsay MacDonald's first Labour government. Many Labour leaders held it to be a forgery, and its authenticity was denied by the Russians. In December 1966 the *Sunday Times* published an article establishing that the letter was a forgery perpetrated by a group of WHITE RUSSIAN *émigrés*. At the same time it was suggested that certain leaders at the Conservative Central Office knew that it was a fake, although the Conservative party as a whole assumed it to be genuine. The 'informant' was paid for his services.

**Falange** (Spanish, 'phalanx'). At first the title of a right-wing party in Spain formed in 1933 by José Antonio Primo de Rivera (1903–36) to uphold his father's memory against republican criticism but later adopted by General Franco as the name of the one official party in the state. It basically represented a combination of European fascism and Spanish nationalism and was used to counterbalance royalist, army and church influence. In 1937 it forced the CARLISTS to join with it. The Falange lost its unique position after the CAUDILLO's death in 1975 and was formally disbanded in 1977.

**Falcon, Peregrine.** *See under* PEREGRINE.

**Falernian.** A choice Italian wine esteemed by the ancient Romans and celebrated by VIRGIL and HORACE. It was so called because it was made of grapes from Falernus.

**Fall.** (1) In music, a sinking of tone or cadence.

> That strain again; it had a dying fall.
> SHAKESPEARE: *Twelfth Night*, I, i (1599)

(2) Autumn, the time of the fall of the leaf. Though now commonly classed as an Americanism, the term is found in the works of Michael Drayton, Thomas Middleton, Sir Walter Ralegh and others.

> What Crowds of Patients the Town Doctor kills,
> Or how, last fall, he rais'd the Weekly Bills.
> JOHN DRYDEN: *Translations from Juvenal*, 'The Tenth Satyr' (1693)

**Fall, The.** The degeneracy of the human race in consequence of the disobedience of ADAM.

**Fall about, To.** To laugh uncontrollably. *See also* ROLLING IN THE AISLES *under* ROLL.

**Fall among, To.** To enter the company of a group of people by chance.

> A certain man went down from Jerusalem to Jericho, and fell among thieves.
> Luke 10:30

**Fall apart, To.** To disintegrate; to lose one's ability to cope.

**Fall away, To.** To lose flesh; to degenerate; to leave a group, as: 'His adherents fell away one by one.'

**Fall back on** or **upon, To.** To have recourse to.

**Fall behind, To.** To drop back, as in a race; to be in arrears, as with a series of payments.

**Fall between two stools, To.** To fail, through hesitation or indecision, between two choices. The French say, *être assis entre deux chaises* ('to sit between two chairs').

**Fall by the wayside, To.** To drop out; to be unable to finish a race or course. The reference is to the parable of the sower. *See also* FALL ON STONY GROUND.

> Behold, there went out a sower to sow: and it came to pass, as he sowed, some fell by the way side, and the fowls of the air came and devoured it up.
> Mark 4:3–4

**Fall down, To.** To collapse; to fail. To fall down on the job is to fail to fulfil one's obligations.

**Fallen angels.** Those cast out of heaven or, colloquially, women who have strayed from the paths of virtue.

**Fall flat, To.** To fall prostrate; to fail to interest, as: 'The last act fell flat.'

**Fall for, To.** To be captivated by; to become infatuated with; to be taken in by.

**Fall foul of, To.** To quarrel with; to make an assault on someone. The expression is of nautical origin. A rope is said to be foul when it is entangled, and one ship falls foul of another when they run against each other.

**Fall from, To.** To tumble or slip off; to abandon or depart from; to lapse into error or sin. In addition to the theological sense, 'to fall from grace' means to relapse from a moral position attained or to fall from favour.

**Fall guy, A.** An American term for a loser, dupe or victim. Towards the end of the 19th century professional wrestling became widely popular in America, but many of the bouts were rigged. One wrestler would promise to 'take a fall' if the other agreed to deal with him gently, but the winner often broke his word and handled his opponent roughly. In such circumstances the loser came to be known as a 'fall guy'.

**Fall in, To.** To take one's place in the ranks; to take one's place with others. *See also* FALL OUT.

**Falling sickness.** Epilepsy, in which the patient falls suddenly to the ground. Shakespeare plays on the term:

> *Brutus*: He hath the falling-sickness.
> *Cassius*: No, Caesar hath it not; but you, and I,
> And honest Casca, we have the falling-sickness.
> *Julius Caesar*, I, ii (1599)

**Falling star.** A meteor. A wish made as a star falls is supposed to come true. Muslims believe them to be firebrands, flung by good angels against evil spirits when they approach too near the gates of heaven.

**Fall in love, To.** To be sexually attracted to a person; to become very fond of a thing. 'Fall' here did not originally have the present sense of dropping from a higher state to a lower, but of passing suddenly from one state to another. 'To fall asleep' was originally similar, although the association is now with passing to a lower stage of consciousness.

> It's never too late to have a fling,
> For Autumn is just as nice as Spring,
> And it's never too late to fall in love.
> SANDY WILSON: 'It's Never Too Late to Fall in Love' (song) (1953)

**Fall into line with, To.** To agree with; to act in conformity with. The expression derives from the falling-in of soldiers into straight lines. *See also* FALL IN.

**Fall into place, To.** To begin to make sense.

**Fall in with, To.** To meet accidentally; to come across; to agree with, as: 'He fell in with my plans.'

**Fall line.** A natural junction that runs parallel to the east coast of the United States, between the hard rocks of the Appalachians and the softer coastal plain, where rivers form falls and rapids.

**Fall on, To.** To attack, as: 'To fall on the enemy.' To throw oneself on, as: 'He fell on his sword.' To occur, to take place, as: 'What date does Easter fall on next year?'

**Fall on deaf ears, To.** To go unheeded; to be deliberately ignored.

**Fall** or **land on one's feet, To.** To be unexpectedly lucky; to find oneself in a very favourable situation. The phrase seems to come from the old theory that the cat always falls on its feet unharmed.

**Fall on stony ground, To.** To meet with no response; to fail to be taken up. The expression is normally used of proposals, suggestions and the like, and it alludes to the parable of the sower. *See also* FALL BY THE WAYSIDE.

> And some [seed] fell on stony ground, where it had not much earth ... and because it had no root, it withered away.
> Mark 4:5–6

**Fallout.** The descent of radioactive dust from a nuclear explosion. Figuratively, fallout is used of the secondary consequences of some action.

**Fall out, To.** To quarrel; to happen. In military parlance, to fall out is to be dismissed or to disperse from the ranks. *See also* FALL IN.

**Fall over oneself, To.** To be keen or eager, as: 'He fell over himself to assist.'

**Fall short of, To.** To be deficient of a supply; not to come up to standard. To fall short of the mark is a figure taken from archery or some similar sport, where the missile falls to the ground before reaching the target.

**Fall sick, To.** To be unwell. *See also* FALLING SICKNESS.

**Fall through, To.** To come to nothing; to fail to materialize.

**Fall to, To.** To begin (eating, fighting and the like).

> Come, sir, fall to then; you see my little supper is always ready when I come home, and I'll make no stranger of you.
> IZAAK WALTON and CHARLES COTTON: *The Compleat Angler*, Pt II, ch ii (1653)

**Fall under, To.** To become subject to, as: 'He fell under the influence of bad companions.'

**Did she fall or was she pushed?** A RHETORICAL QUESTION asked about a girl who has lost her virginity. The phrase is said to have originated with reference to a murder case at the turn of the 20th century, when a young woman was found dead at the foot of a cliff near BEACHY HEAD.

**Free fall.** *See under* FREE.

**It fell off the back of a lorry.** Said of stolen goods or of something acquired fortuitously or by somewhat dubious means. The expression may have arisen among lorry drivers.

**Pride goes before a fall.** *See under* PRIDE.

**Ride for a fall, To.** *See under* RIDE.

**Fallacy, Pathetic.** *See under* PATHETIC.

**False. False alarm.** The term has two almost contrary meanings. It can either be a needless alarm, whether given in error or with the intention to deceive, or a justified alarm, given for a danger that does not in the event materialize.

**False dawn.** A transient light in the east before dawn; a promising sign which comes to nothing.

**False memory syndrome.** *See under* FAKES.

**False scent.** A scent laid to deceive or to put others off the track.

**False start.** A start disallowed in a race, often caused when one or more of the contestants JUMP THE GUN. Also generally an unsuccessful attempt to begin something.

**False step.** A slip; a mistake.

**Play false, To.** *See under* PLAY.

**Sail under false colours, To.** *See under* SAIL.

**Falstaff.** A fat, sensual, boastful and mendacious knight, full of wit and humour. He is the boon companion of Henry, Prince of Wales (the future Henry V) in Shakespeare's *Henry IV, Pts I and II* (1597) and *The Merry Wives of Windsor* (1600). His death is movingly described in *Henry V* (1598). Hence, 'Falstaffian', possessing the qualities and characteristics of Falstaff.

**Falutin.** *See* HIGH FALUTIN'.

**Fame, Temple of.** *See under* TEMPLE.

**Familiar** or **familiar spirit** (Latin *famulus*, 'servant'). A spirit slave, sometimes in human shape, sometimes appearing as a CAT, dog, RAVEN or the like, who attends or aids a witch, WIZARD or magician, and is said to be a demon in disguise.

> Away with him! he has a familiar under his tongue.
> SHAKESPEARE: *Henry VI, Pt II*, IV, vii (1590)

**Familiarity breeds contempt.** The proverb appears in English at least as early as the mid-16th century and was well known in Latin. The same idea is conveyed in the saying that a prophet is not appreciated in his own country.

**Familists.** Members of the Family of Love, an extremist sect founded by Hendrik Niclaes at Emden, about 1540. He derived his mysticism from David Joris, an ANABAPTIST of Delft, whose followers are sometimes called Davidists or Davists. He implanted his ideas in England in the reign of Edward VI, and the sect gained a hold in the eastern counties in spite of persecution. It revived under the COMMONWEALTH and lingered on until the 18th century, when many of its members joined the QUAKERS. As their name suggests, Familists maintained that all people were of one family and that religion consisted essentially of love.

**Family. Family Favourites.** A popular weekly record request show on the BBC's Light Programme linking London with the British Forces Network in Germany. It started in 1945 and went out for an hour at Sunday lunchtime, thereby becoming intimately associated with the aroma of roast and gravy wafting from the kitchen. It changed its title to *Two-Way Family Favourites* in 1960 and continued until 1984.

**Family newspaper.** Any regular newspaper regarded as an unsuitable medium for explicit sexual language. In some cases the phrase is introduced expressly to titillate the prurient reader.

> Hanging alongside ... are some superb examples of the erotic prints by Utamaro that inspired [Aubrey] Beardsley. I cannot describe them to you. This is a family newspaper.
> *Sunday Times* (11 October 1998)

**Family of Love.** *See* FAMILISTS.

**Addams Family, The.** *See under* ADDAMS.

**County family.** *See under* COUNTY.

**Happy families.** *See under* HAPPY.

**Happy family.** *See under* HAPPY.

**Holy Family, The.** *See under* HOLY.

**In the family way.** Pregnant.

**Larkin Family, The.** *See under* LARKIN.

**Run in the family, To.** *See under* RUN.

**Famous. Famous Five, The.** The four children and their dog who have unlikely adventures at various holiday locations around Britain in the novels of Enid Blyton. They are the two brothers Julian and Dick, their sister, Anne, and their tomboy cousin Georgina, known as 'George', together with the mongrel dog Timmy. They first appeared in *Five on a Treasure Island* (1942) and continued their exploits in a further 20 volumes, all with a title beginning *Five*. The tales were the inspiration for television farces in the *Comic Strip Presents* ... series of the 1980s, the first being *Five Go Mad in Dorset* (1982).

**Famous last words.** Many 'famous last words' are either apocryphal or have survived in inaccurate versions. The following, spoken or written at or shortly before the named person's death, are among the better known:

> John Adams (1735–1826; 2nd President of the USA): 'Independence for ever.'
>
> John Quincy Adams ( 1767–1848; 6th President of the USA): 'It is the last of earth. I am content.'
>
> Joseph Addison (1672–1719; English essayist): 'See in what peace a Christian can die.'
>
> St AGATHA (3rd century): 'Cruel tyrant, do you not blush to torture this part of my body, you that sucked the breasts of a woman yourself?'
>
> ALBERT, Prince Consort (1819–61): 'I have such sweet thoughts,' *or* 'I have had wealth, rank and power; but, if these were all I had, how wretched I should be!'
>
> Louisa M. Alcott (1832–88; US author): 'Is it not meningitis?'
>
> Alexander II 1818–81; tsar of Russia): 'I am sweeping through the gates, washed in the blood of the Lamb.'
>
> Vittorio Alfieri (1749–1803; Italian poet): 'Clasp my hand, dear friend, I am dying.'
>
> Anaxagoras (*c*.500–428 BC; Greek philosopher): he kept a school, and when asked if he wished for anything, replied: 'Give the boys a holiday.'
>
> ANTHONY OF PADUA (1195–1231): 'I see my God. He calls me to Him.'
>
> Archimedes (*c*.287–212 BC; Greek mathematician): when ordered by a Roman soldier to follow him replied: 'Wait till I have finished my problem.'

Sometimes rendered as: 'Stand away, fellow, from my diagram!'

Augustus (63 BC–AD 14; first Roman emperor): to his friends: 'Do you think I have played my part pretty well through the farce of life?'

Jane Austen (1775–1817; English author): when asked what she required: 'Nothing but death.'

Francis Bacon (1561–1626; English philosopher): 'My name and memory I leave to men's charitable speeches, to foreign nations and to the next age.'

Thomas à Becket (*c*.1118–70; English archbishop): before he was struck dead by Sir William de Tracy: 'I am prepared to die for Christ and His Church.'

VENERABLE BEDE (673–735): having dictated the last sentence of his translation of St John's Gospel and being told by the scribe that the sentence was now written: 'It is well; you have said the truth: it is indeed.'

Henry Ward Beecher (1813–87; US clergyman): 'Now comes the mystery.'

Ludwig van Beethoven (1770–1827; German composer, who was deaf): 'I shall hear in heaven.'

'Captain' Thomas Blood (*c*.1618–80; Irish adventurer): 'I do not fear death.'

Nicolas Boileau Despréaux (1636–1711; French poet): 'It is a great consolation to a poet on the point of death that he has never written a line injurious to good morals.'

Anne Boleyn (*c*.1504–36; wife of Henry VIII): 'The executioner is, I believe, very expert ... and my neck is very slender.'

Edmund Burke (1729–97; British statesman): 'God bless you.'

Robert Burns (1759–96; Scottish poet): 'Don't let the awkward squad fire over my grave.'

William S. Burroughs (1914–97; US writer): 'Love? What is it? Most natural painkiller. What there is ... love.'

George Gordon Byron, 6th Baron Byron (1788–1824; English poet): 'I must sleep now.'

Julius CAESAR (100–44 BC) to Brutus, his most intimate friend, when stabbed by him: *Et tu, Brute?* ('You, too, Brutus?')

Thomas Carlyle (1795–1881; Scottish essayist): 'So this is death, well ...'

Giacomo CASANOVA (1725–98): 'I have lived as a philosopher. I die as a Christian.'

Robert Stewart, Viscount Castlereagh (1769–1822; British politician): to his doctor: 'Bankhead, let me fall into your arms. It is all over.'

Robert Catesby (1673–1603; a conspirator in the GUNPOWDER PLOT): 'Stand by me, Tom, and we will die together.'

Marcus Porcius Cato, the Younger (95–46 BC; Roman politician): seeing that the sword's point was sharp, before thrusting it into his body: 'Now I am master of myself.'

Edith Cavell (1865–1915; English nurse): before facing the German firing party: 'Patriotism is not enough. I must have no hatred or bitterness towards anyone.'

Beatrice Cenci (1577–99; Roman beauty and murderer): before being executed: 'Jesus! Mary!' *See also* BEAUTIFUL PARRICIDE

CHARLEMAGNE (747–814): 'Lord, into Thy hands I commend my spirit.'

CHARLES I (1600–49; king of England): 'From a corruptible to an incorruptible crown where no disturbance can be, no disturbance in the world.' *See also* REMEMBER

Charles II (1630–85; king of England): 'I have been a most unconscionable time a-dying; but I hope you will excuse it,' *and* to his brother, James II: 'Do not ... do not let poor Nelly [Nell GWYN] starve.'

Charles VIII (1470–98; king of France): 'I hope never again to commit a mortal sin, nor even a venial one, if I can help it.'

Charles IX (1550–74; king of France, whose reign saw the St BARTHOLOMEW'S DAY MASSACRE): 'Nurse, nurse, what murder! what blood! O! I have done wrong: God pardon me.'

Philip Dormer Stanhope, 4th Earl of Chesterfield (1694–1773; English politician): 'Give Dayrolles a chair.'

Erskine Childers (1870–1922; British writer and politician): to the firing squad at his execution: 'Come closer, boys. It will be easier for you.'

CICERO (106–46 BC): to his assassins: 'Strike.'

Gaspard de Coligny (1519–72; French admiral): to the German who assassinated him in the St BARTHOLOMEW'S DAY MASSACRE): 'Honour these grey hairs, young man.'

Christopher Columbus (1451–1506; Spanish explorer): 'Lord, into Thy hands I commend my spirit.'

Nicolas Copernicus (1473–1543; Polish astronomer): 'Now, O Lord, set Thy servant free.'

Stephen Crane (1871–1900; US writer): 'When you come to the hedge that we must all go over, it isn't so bad. You feel sleepy, you don't care. Just a little dreamy anxiety, which world you're really in, that's all.'

Thomas Cranmer (1489–1556; English archbishop): as he held in the flames his right hand which had signed his apostasy: 'That unworthy hand! That unworthy hand!'

Oliver Cromwell (1599–1658; English soldier and statesman): 'My design [or 'desire'] is to make what haste I can to be gone.'

Georges Cuvier (1769–1832; French anatomist): to the nurse who was applying leeches: 'Nurse, it was I who discovered that leeches have red blood.'

Georges Danton (1759–94; French revolutionary leader): to the executioner: 'Be sure you show the mob my head. It will be a long time ere they see its like.'

Charles Darwin (1809–82; English naturalist): 'I am not in the least afraid to die.'

Demonax (d. *c*.176 BC; Greek philosopher): 'You may go home, the show is over.'

Denis Diderot (1713–84; French encyclopedist and philosopher): 'The first step towards philosophy is incredulity.'

DIOGENES (*c*.410–*c*.320 BC): 'One brother anticipates the other: Sleep before Death. Everything will shortly be turned upside down.'

Sir James Douglas (*c*.1286–1330; Scottish friend of Robert Bruce): 'Fight on, my merry men.'

Edward I (1239–1307; king of England): 'Carry my bones before you on your march, for the rebels will not be able to endure the sight of me, alive or dead.'

Jonathan Edwards (1703–58; American clergyman): 'Trust in God and you need not fear.'

John Scott, 1st Earl of Eldon (1751–1838; English jurist): 'It matters not where I am going whether the weather be cold or hot.'

Elizabeth I (1533–1603; queen of England): 'All my possessions for a moment of time.'

Ebenezer Elliott (1781–1849; English poet): 'A strange sight, sir, an old man unwilling to die.'

Louis-Antoine-Henri Condé, Duc d'Enghien (1772–1804; French soldier; shot by order of NAPOLEON BONAPARTE): 'I die for my king and for France.'

Epaminondas (*c*.418–362 BC; Theban general): on being told that the Thebans were victorious: 'Then I die happy.'

William Etty (1787–1849; English painter): 'Wonderful! Wonderful this death!'

Kathleen Ferrier (1912–53; English singer): 'Now I'll have eine kleine Pause.'

Gaston de Foix (1489–1512; French soldier): 'I am a dead man! Lord, have mercy upon me!'

Bernard Fontenelle (1657–1757; French man of letters): 'I suffer nothing, but I feel a sort of difficulty in living longer.'

Charles James Fox (1749–1806; English politician): to his wife: 'It don't signify, my dearest, dearest Liz.'

George Fox (1624–91; English founder of Society of Friends): 'Never heed! the Lord's power is over all weakness and death.'

Frederik V (1723–66; king of Denmark): 'There is not a drop of blood on my hands.'

Charles Frohman (1860–1915; US theatre manager): before drowning in the *Lusitania*: 'Why fear death? It is the most beautiful adventure in life.'

Thomas Gainsborough (1727–88; English painter): 'We are all going to heaven and Van Dyck is of the company.'

Sir Samuel Garth (1661–1719; English physician): to his physicians: 'Dear gentlemen, let me die a natural death.'

George IV (1762–1830, king of Britain): to his page, Sir Walthen Waller: 'Wally, what is this? It is death, my boy. They have deceived me.'

Johann Wolfgang von Goethe (1749–1832; German poet): 'Light, more light!'

General Ulysses Grant (1822–85; 18th President of the USA): 'I want nobody distressed on my account.'

Henry Grattan (1746–1820; Irish politician): 'I am perfectly resigned. I am surrounded by my family. I have served my country. I have reliance upon God and I am not afraid of the Devil.'

Horace Greeley (1811–72; US journalist): 'It is done.'

Gregory VII (*c*.1020–85; St HILDEBRAND): having retired to Salerno after his disputes with the emperor, Henry IV: 'I have loved justice and hated iniquity, therefore I die in exile.'

Lady Jane Grey (1537–54; queen of England for nine days): before being executed: 'Lord, into Thy hands I commend my spirit,' *or* 'I die in peace with all people. God save the Queen.'

Gustavus Adolphus (1594–1632; king of Sweden): 'I am sped, brother. Save thyself.'

Captain Nathan Hale (1755–76; American soldier in Revolutionary War, hanged by the British as a spy): 'I regret that I have but one life to give for my country.'

HAMLET (in Shakespeare's play, 1600): 'The rest is silence.'

Hannibal (247–182 BC): 'Let us now relieve the Romans of their fears by the death of a feeble old man.'

Sir Henry Havelock (1795–1857; British soldier): 'Come, my son, and see how a Christian can die.'

Joseph Haydn (1732–1809; Austrian composer): singing: 'God preserve the Emperor!'

William Hazlitt (1778–1830; English writer): 'Well, I've had a good life.'

Heinrich Heine (1797–1856; German poet): 'God will pardon me, it is His trade.'

Henry II (1133–89; king of England): when told that his favourite son John was one of those who were conspiring against him: 'Now let the world go as it will; I care for nothing more.'

Henry VIII (1491–1547; king of England): 'All is lost! Monks, Monks, Monks!'

O. Henry (1862–1910; US author; real name William Sydney Porter): 'Turn up the lights. I don't want to go home in the dark.'

George Herbert (1593–1633; English religious poet): 'Now, Lord, receive my soul.'

Thomas Hobbes (1588–1679; English philosopher): 'I am taking a fearful leap in the dark.'

Henry Richard Fox, 3rd Baron Holland (1773–1840; English politician): 'If Mr Selwyn calls, let him in. If I am alive I shall be very glad to see him, and if I am dead he will be very glad to see me.' (Selwyn was noted for his interest in viewing corpses and in attending executions.)

Thomas Hood (1799–1845; English poet): watching a mustard plaster being applied to his foot: 'There's very little meat for the mustard.'

Alexander von Humboldt (1769–1859; German naturalist): 'How grand these rays! They seem to beckon earth to heaven.'

Dr William Hunter (1718–83; Scottish anatomist): 'If I had strength to hold a pen, I would write down how easy and pleasant a thing it is to die.'

Jan Hus (1372–1415; Czech religious leader): to an old woman thrusting another faggot on the pile to burn him: 'Sancta simplicitas!'

Thomas Jonathan 'Stonewall' Jackson (1824–63; US Confederate general): 'Let us pass over the river, and rest under the shade of the trees.'

James V (1512–42; king of Scotland): when told that the queen had given birth to a daughter, the future Mary, Queen of Scots: 'It [the crown of Scotland] came [to the Stuarts] with a lass and it will go with a lass.'

Thomas Jefferson (1743–1826; 3rd President of the USA): 'I resign my spirit to God, my daughter to my country.'

Jerome of Prague (c.1365–1416; Czech religious leader and, like Hus, burned at the stake): 'Thou knowest, Lord, that I have loved the truth!'

JOAN OF ARC (*c*.1412–31): 'Jesus! Jesus! Jesus! Blessed be God.'

St JOHN CHRYSOSTOM (*c*.347–407): 'Glory to God for all things. Amen.'

Dr Samuel Johnson (1709–84; English lexicographer): to Miss Morris: 'God bless you, my dear.'

JULIAN THE APOSTATE (*c*.331–363): *Vicisti, O Galilaee*. ('Thou hast conquered, O Galilean.')

John Keats (1795–1821; English poet): 'Severn – I – lift me up – I am dying – I shall die easy; don't be frightened – be firm, and thank God it has come.'

Thomas Ken (1637–1711; English bishop): 'God's will be done.'

John Knox (*c*.1513–72; Scottish religious reformer): 'Now it is come.'

Charles Lamb (1775–1834; English essayist): 'My bed-fellows are cramp and cough – we three all in one bed.'

John Lambert, born Nicholson (d.1538; English martyr): as he was pitched into the flames: 'None but Christ! None but Christ!'

Hugh Latimer (*c*.1485–1555; English religious reformer): to Nicholas Ridley at the stake: 'Be of good comfort, Mr Ridley, and play the man. We shall this day light a candle by God's grace in England, as I trust never shall be put out.'

William Laud (1573–1645; English archbishop): 'No one can be more willing to send me out of life than I am desirous to go.'

Sir Henry Lawrence (1806–57; British general and defender of Lucknow): 'Let there be no fuss about me, let me be buried with the men.'

Robert Dudley, 1st Earl of Leicester (*c*.1532–88; English courtier): 'By the arm of St James, it is time to die.'

Leopold I (1640–1705; Holy Roman Emperor): 'Let me die to the sound of sweet music.'

John Locke (1632–1704; English philosopher): to Lady Masham, who was reading him some of the Psalms: 'Oh! the depth of the riches of the goodness and knowledge of God. Cease now.'

St LOUIS, Louis IX (1215–70; king of France): while on a crusade: 'Jerusalem, Jerusalem.'

Louis XIV (1638–1715; king of France): 'Why weep you! Did you think I should live for ever? I thought dying had been harder.'

Louis XVI (1754–95; king of France): on the scaffold: 'Frenchmen, I die guiltless of the crimes imputed to me. Pray God my blood fall not on France!'

Louis XVIII (1755–1824; king of France): 'A king should die standing.'

Thomas Babington Macaulay (1800–59; English writer): 'I shall retire early. I am very tired.'

Niccolò MACHIAVELLI (1469–1527): 'I love my country more than my soul.'

Chrétien Malesherbes (1721–94; French politician): to the priest: 'Hold your tongue! your wretched chatter disgusts me.'

Katherine Mansfield (1888–1923; British writer): 'I believe ... I'm going to die. I love the rain. I want the feeling of it on my face.'

Marie Antoinette (1755–93; queen of France): before being executed: 'Farewell, my children, for ever. I am going to your father.'

Harriet Martineau (1802–76; English writer): 'I see no reason why the existence of Harriet Martineau should be perpetuated.'

Mary I (1516–58; queen of England): 'You will find the word Calais written on my heart.'

Mary II (1662–94; queen of England): to Archbishop Tillotson, who had paused in reading a prayer: 'My Lord, why do you not go on? I am not afraid to die.'

Philipp MELANCHTHON (1497–1560): to the question, 'Do you want anything?' replied: 'Nothing but heaven.'

MICHELANGELO Buonarroti (1475–1564): 'My soul I resign to God, my body to the earth, my worldly goods to my next of kin.'

Honoré Riqueti, Comte de Mirabeau (1754–92; French politician): 'Let me fall asleep to the sound of delicious music.'

MOHAMMED: 'O Allah! Pardon my sins. Yes, I come.'

St Monica (332–387; mother of Augustine of Hippo and recorded in the *Confessions*): 'In peace I will sleep with Him and take my rest.'

James Scott, Duke of Monmouth (1649–85; claimant to the English throne ): to his executioner: 'There are six guineas for you and do not hack me as you did my Lord Russell.'

Lady Mary Wortley Montagu (1689–1762; English poet): 'It has all been very interesting.'

Dwight Lyman Moody (1837–99; US evangelist): 'I see earth receding: heaven is opening; God is calling me.'

Sir John Moore (1761–1809; British general): 'I hope my country will do me justice.'

Sir Thomas More (*c*.1477–1535; English statesman): 'See me safe up [to the scaffold]; for my coming down, let me shift for myself.'

Wolfgang Amadeus Mozart (1756–91; Austrian composer): 'You spoke of a refreshment, Emile; take my last notes, and let me hear once more my solace and delight.'

Joachim Murat (1767–1815; French cavalry commander and king of Naples): to the men detailed to shoot him: 'Soldiers, save my face; aim at my heart. Farewell.'

NAPOLEON BONAPARTE (1769–1821): *Mon Dieu! La Nation Française. Tête d'armée.* ('My God! The French nation. Head of the army.')

NAPOLEON III (1808–73): to Dr Conneau: 'Were you at Sedan?'

Admiral Horatio Nelson (1758–1805; British naval officer): 'I thank God I have done my duty. Kiss me, Hardy,' *or* 'Kismet [i.e. fate, destiny], Hardy.'

NERO (37–68; Roman emperor): *Qualis artifex pereo.* ('What an artist dies with me!')

Sir Isaac Newton (1642–1727; English physicist and mathematician): 'I don't know what I may seem to the world. But as to myself I seem to have been only like a boy playing on the seashore and diverting myself in now and then finding a smoother pebble or prettier shell than ordinary, whilst the great ocean of truth lay all undiscovered before me.'

John Palmer (1742–98; English actor): speaking, on stage, a line from the play *The Stranger*: 'There is another and a better world.'

Henry Temple, 3rd Viscount Palmerston (1784–1865; English politician): 'Die, my dear doctor? That's the last thing I shall do.'

Blaise Pascal (1623–62; French scientist and philosopher): 'My God, forsake me not.'

Pericles (*c*.490–429 BC; Athenian statesman): 'I have never caused any citizen to put on mourning on my account.'

Hugh Peters (1598–1660; English clergyman; tried as an accomplice in the execution of Charles I): to his executioner: 'Friend, you do not well to trample on a dying man.'

William Pitt, the Younger (1759–1806; English politician): 'My country! How I leave my country!' *or* 'How I love my country!'

PLATO (*c*.428–*c*.348 BC): 'I thank the guiding providence and fortune of my life, first, that I was born a man and a Greek, not a barbarian nor a brute; and next, that I happened to live in the age of Socrates.'

Edgar Allan Poe (1809–49; US poet and short story writer): 'Lord, help my soul!'

Jeanne-Antoinette Poisson, Madame de Pompadour (1721–64; French mistress of Louis XV):

'Stay a little longer, Monsieur le Curé, and we will go together.'
Alexander Pope (1688–1744; English poet): 'Friendship itself is but a part of virtue,' *or* 'I am dying, sir, of one hundred good symptoms.'
Dennis Potter (1935–94; English playwright): in the face of imminent death from cancer: 'The nowness of everything is absolutely wondrous.'
James Quin (1693–1766; English actor): 'I could wish this tragic scene were over, but I hope to go through it with becoming dignity.'
François Rabelais (*c*.1494–1553; French writer): 'Let down the curtain, the farce is over,' *or* 'I am going to seek the great perhaps.'
Sir Walter Ralegh (*c*.1554–1618; English courtier and navigator): speaking on the scaffold where he was beheaded: 'It matters little how the head lies, so the heart be right,' *or* (feeling the axe) "Tis a sharp remedy, but a sure one for all ills.'
Ernest Renan (1823–92; French philosopher): 'We perish, we disappear, but the march of time goes on for ever.'
Sir Joshua Reynolds (1723–92; English painter): 'I know that all things on earth must have an end, and now I am come to mine.'
Cecil John Rhodes (1853–1902; British colonial administrator): 'So little done, so much to do.'
Richard I (1157–99; king of England): to Bertrand de Gourdon, who shot him with an arrow at Chalus: 'Youth, I forgive thee!' Then, to his attendants: 'Take off his chains, give him 100 shillings, and let him go.'
Richard III (1452–85; king of England): at Bosworth, where his best men deserted him: 'Treason! treason!' *or* (according to Shakespeare): 'A horse, a horse, my kingdom for a horse!'
Marie Jeanne Philipon, Madame Roland (1754–93; French politician): on her way to the guillotine: 'O Liberty! What crimes are committed in thy name!'
Wentworth Dillon, 4th Earl of Roscommon (*c*.1633–85; British poet): quoting from his own translation of *Dies Irae*: 'My God, my Father, and my Friend,/Do not forsake me at my end.'
William, Lord Russell (1639–83; English politician and political martyr): 'The bitterness of death is now past.'
SALADIN (1137–93): 'When I am buried, carry my winding sheet on the point of a spear, and say these words: Behold the spoils which Saladin carries with him! Of all his victories, realms and riches, nothing remains to him but this.'
Ken Saro-Wiwa (1941–95; Nigerian writer): just before being hanged: 'Lord take my soul, but the struggle continues.'
Paul Scarron (1610–60; French comic poet and dramatist): 'Ah, my children, you cannot cry for me so much as I have made you laugh.'
Johann Schiller (1759–1805; German poet and playwright): 'Many things are growing plain and clear to my understanding.'
Sir Walter Scott (1771–1832; Scottish poet and novelist): to his family: 'God bless you all, I feel myself again.'
Michael Servetus (1511–53; Spanish theologian): at the stake: 'Christ, Son of the eternal God, Have mercy upon me.' (Calvin insisted on his saying 'the eternal Son of God' but he would not, and was burned to death.)
Lucius Septimius Severus (146–211; Roman emperor): 'I have been everything, and everything is nothing. A little urn will contain all that remains of one for whom the whole world was too little.'
Richard Brinsley Sheridan (1751–1816; Irish dramatist and politician): 'I am absolutely undone.'
Sir Philip Sidney (1554–86; English poet, politician and soldier): to his brother Robert: 'Govern your will and affections by the will and word of your creator, in me beholding the end of this world with all her vanities.'
Siward the Dane, Earl of Northumberland (d.1055; Danish warrior in England): 'Lift me up that I may die standing, not lying down like a cow.'
Socrates (469–399 BC; Greek philosopher: 'Crito, I owe a cock to AESCULAPIUS.'
Madame de Staël (1766–1817; French writer): 'I have loved God, my father, and liberty.'
Gertrude Stein (1874–1946; US writer): 'What *is* the answer?' And when no answer came: 'In that case what is the question?'
St STEPHEN (d.*c*.35; the first Christian martyr): 'Lord, lay not this sin to their charge.' (*See* Acts 7:60)
Lytton Strachey (1880–1932; English writer): 'If this is dying, then I don't think much of it.'
Thomas Wentworth, 1st Earl of Strafford (1593–1641; English politician): before his execution: 'Put not your trust in princes.'
Torquato TASSO (1544–95): 'Lord, into Thy hands I commend my spirit.'
General Zachary Taylor (1784–1850; 12th President of the USA): 'I have tried to do my duty, and am not afraid to die. I am ready.'
John Taylor (*c*.1578–1653; English pamphleteer; the 'Water Poet'): 'How sweet it is to rest!'
Alfred, Lord Tennyson (1809–92; English poet): 'I have opened it.'
Charles Abbott, 1st Baron Tenterden (1762–1832; English Lord Chief Justice): 'Gentlemen of the jury, you may retire.'
Theramenes (*fl*.411–403 BC; Athenian statesman): condemned by Critias to drink hemlock: 'To the health of the fair Critias.'
Arthur Thistlewood (1770–1820; English conspirator): 'I shall soon know the grand secret.' *See also* CATO STREET CONSPIRACY
Henry David Thoreau (1817–62; US writer): 'I leave this world without a regret.'
Edward Thurlow, 1st Baron Thurlow (1731–1806; English judge): 'I'll be shot if I don't believe I'm dying.'
William Tyndale (*c*.1494–1536; English Bible translator): 'Lord, open the eyes of the king of England [i.e. Henry VIII].'
Sir Henry Vane (1613–62; English politician): 'It is a bad cause which cannot bear the words of a dying man.'
Vespasian (9–79; Roman emperor): 'A king should die standing.' But his last words were: *Ut puto, deus fio* ('I suppose I am now becoming a god'), referring to the deification of the Caesars after death.
Queen Victoria (1819–1901; queen of Britain): referring to the war in South Africa then in progress: 'Oh, that peace may come.'
VOLTAIRE (1694–1778): 'Do let me die in peace.'
George Washington (1732–99; 1st President of the

USA): 'It is well, I die hard, but am not afraid to go.'

Daniel Webster (1782–1852; US lawyer and statesman): 'Life, life! Death, death! How curious it is!'

Charles Wesley (1707–88; English evangelist and hymn writer): 'I shall be satisfied with Thy likeness – satisfied.'

John Wesley (1703–91; English founder of Methodism): 'The best of all is, God is with us.'

WILLIAM THE SILENT (1533–84): 'O my God have mercy upon my soul! O my God, have mercy upon this poor people!'

Alexander Wilson (1766–1813; US ornithologist): 'Bury me where the birds will sing over my grave.'

George Wishart (*c.*1513–46; Scottish reformer and martyr): at the stake: 'I fear not this fire.'

Ludwig Wittgenstein (1889–1951; Austrian-born British philosopher): 'Tell them I've had a wonderful life.'

John Wolcot (1738–1819; Peter PINDAR): 'Give me back my youth!'

General James Wolfe (1727–59; British army officer): 'What! do they run already? Then I die happy.'

Thomas Wolsey (*c.*1475–1530; English cardinal and statesman): 'Had I but served God as diligently as I have served the king, He would not have given me over in my grey hairs.'

William Wordsworth (1770–1850; English poet): 'God bless you! Is that you, Dora?'

John Ziska (*c.*1370–1424; Bohemian general and Hussite leader): 'Make my skin into drumheads for the Bohemian cause.'

**Famous Sorites of Themistocles, The.** The premise was that his infant son commanded the whole world, proved thus:

My infant son rules his mother.
His mother rules me.
I rule the Athenians.
The Athenians rule the Greeks.
The Greeks rule Europe.
And Europe rules the world.

*See also* SORITES.

**Fan.** (1) A word used from the 19th century for an ardent admirer or devotee. It is an abbreviation of FANATIC. Admiring letters written to the object of such admiration are known as fan mail, and these are usually handled by the celebrity's agent or fan club.

(2) A device used to create a current of air, whether it is held in the hand or operated by electricity.

**Fanatic** (Latin *fanum*, 'temple'). Literally, a person who is possessed of the enthusiasm or madness of the temple engendered by over-indulgence in religious rites.

Earth's fanatics make
Too frequently heaven's saints.
ELIZABETH BARRETT BROWNING: *Aurora Leigh*, ii (1857)

**Fan dance.** A dance in which women manipulate large fans in front of their body, partly revealing (or suggesting) their nudity. Oriental fan dances do not normally involve nudity, however.

The dancer, a girl of about thirteen, is elaborately dressed as a page. Confined by the closely-folded robe, the feet and legs are not much used, the feet, indeed, never leaving the ground. Time is marked by undulations of the body, waving the arms, and deft manipulation of a fan. One movement succeeds another by transitions singularly graceful, the arms describing innumerable curves, and the fan so skilfully handled as to seem instinct with a life and liberty of its own.
H.A. GILES: *A Glossary of Reference on Subjects Connected with the Far East* (1900)

**Queen Anne's fan.** *See* COCK A SNOOK.

**Fancy.** Love, as the creation of the fantasy or imagination.

Tell me, where is fancy bred,
Or in the heart or in the head?
SHAKESPEARE: *The Merchant of Venice*, III, ii (1596)

**Fancy, The.** In early 19th-century slang parlance a collective name for prize fighters and devotees of the prize ring. It is now sometimes applied to supporters of other sports and pastimes, especially the breeding of birds and animals.

Du Loo was a heavy good-humoured stupid fellow in the Blues, who prided himself on ... his boxing, and who was going, at half-past twelve, to have a little play with Fighting Chatney, one of the Fancy.
OUIDA: *Held in Bondage*, ch vi (1863)

**Fancy dress.** A fanciful costume put on when masquerading as a different person or as an animal. Fancy dress plays a popular part in children's parties and adults readily don it to raise money for charity at fêtes and the like.

More than 40 volunteers marked the [sick] boy's birthday by abseiling down the City Hospital in fancy dress. The organisers hope the stunt will have raised money for a physiotherapy and exercise room for Jack.
*Ceefax, BBC East Midlands* (12 December 1998)

**Fancy-free.** Not in love, or more generally, carefree, having no commitments.

And the imperial votaress passed on,
In maiden meditation, fancy-free.
SHAKESPEARE: *A Midsummer Night's Dream*, II, i (1595)

**Fancy man, A.** Originally a *cavaliere servente* or CICISBEO, a man selected by a married woman to escort her, ride about with her and generally entertain her. The term is now more usually applied to a woman's lover or to a pimp.

**Fancy oneself, To.** To be conceited.

**Fancy that!** An exclamation of surprise or disbelief.

**Fancy woman.** A mistress.

**Footloose and fancy free.** *See under* FOOT.

**Tickle one's fancy, To.** *See under* TICKLE.

**Fanfaron** (Spanish *fanfaronada*, from *fanfarron*, 'to

boast'). A swaggering bully or cowardly boaster who blows his own trumpet. Sir Walter Scott uses the word for finery, especially for the gold lace worn by military men. Hence the now rare word fanfaronade for boastful or ostentatious behaviour.

**Fanny.** A slang word either for the buttocks or for the female genitals. The latter sense is traced back by some to the name of Fanny Hill, the libidinous heroine of John Cleland's *Memoirs of a Woman of Pleasure* (1748–9), her own name (often used as a short title of the book) apparently a pun on the anatomical term *mons veneris*. However, there is a long gap between the publication of this work and the emergence of fanny in this sense in the late 19th century. Fanny is also a colloquial acronymic name for a member of the First Aid Nursing Yeomanry.

**Fanny Adams.** *See* SWEET FANNY ADAMS.

**Lord Fanny.** A nickname given by Alexander Pope to Lord Hervey (1696–1743) for his effeminate and foppish manners.

> The lines are weak, another's pleased to say,
> Lord Fanny spins a thousand such a day.
> ALEXANDER POPE: *Imitations of Horace*, Satire i (1733)

**My Aunt Fanny.** *See under* AUNT.

**Sweet Fanny Adams.** *See under* SWEET.

**Fan tan.** A card game popular with children. Cards are dealt equally, with a seven starting the game. The next person must play either a six or an eight of the same suit, or start another suit with another seven. The next plays five or nine, and so on until the sequence is full. The winner is the first person to play all his or her cards. Adults can play the game for stakes. The game is a Western adaptation of a Chinese gambling game of the same name, *fan* meaning 'number of times' and *t'an* 'to apportion', alluding to the payment of stakes so many times the original amount.

**Fantom.** An old spelling of PHANTOM.

**Fantomas.** A French master criminal who turns over a new leaf and decides to use his skills for good causes instead of bad. He is a sort of French Sexton BLAKE, and first appears in the novel (1911) named after him by Pierre Souvestre and Marcel Allain. His fame became international when he was played by René Navarre in 1913 in a series of silent films, and there have been various comic books and strips starring him. His name is based on French *fantôme*, 'phantom', 'ghost'.

**Far. Far and away.** By a great amount, as, 'far and away the best', meaning easily the best.

**Far and near**. Everywhere.

**Far and wide.** To a good distance in every direction. 'To spread the news far and wide' is to make it known everywhere.

**Far be it from me.** I am reluctant to, as: 'Far be it from me to tell you what to do.'

**Far cry, A.** A long way, whether literally or metaphorically. The cry here is a loud shout, which would not be heard at a distance.

> One of the Campbells replied, 'It is a far cry to Lochow'; a proverbial expression of the tribe, meaning that their ancient hereditary domains lay beyond the reach of an invading enemy.
> SIR WALTER SCOTT: *A Legend of Montrose*, ch xii (1819)

**Far East, The.** The countries of eastern Asia, especially China, Japan, North and South Korea, Indonesia, Malaysia and the Philippines. The term is still sometimes extended to include all lands east of Afghanistan. *See also* MIDDLE EAST.

**Far-fetched.** Literally, 'brought from afar'; hence, improbable, unlikely, as, 'a far-fetched excuse'.

**Far-flung.** Extending far; widely distributed.

**Far from it.** Not in the least; by no means; on the contrary. If the answer to, 'Was he sober at the time?' is, 'Far from it,' the implication is that he was more than a little drunk.

**Far from the madding crowd.** In a peaceful place; away from turmoil. 'Madding' does not mean 'maddening' but acting madly. The phrase is familiar as the title of Thomas Hardy's novel (1874) and originated in Thomas Gray's *Elegy Written in a Country Churchyard* (1750), where it describes the 'rude forefathers' who are buried there:

> Far from the madding crowd's ignoble strife,
> Their sober wishes never learn'd to stray;
> Along the cool sequester'd vale of life
> They kept the noiseless tenor of their life.

**Far gone.** Advanced in time. Also, in an advanced state of illness, drunkenness or the like.

**Go too far, To.** *See under* GO.

**So far, so good.** *See under* SO.

**Farce, Bedroom.** *See under* BED.

**Fare** (Old English *faran*, 'to go', 'to travel', ultimately related to Latin *portare*, 'to carry'). The noun formerly denoted a journey for which a sum was paid, then the sum itself, and by extension, the person who pays it. In certain English dialects the verb 'fare' is used in its original sense, 'to go'. Hence farewell, meaning 'go well,' originally an expression of good wishes to a person setting out on a journey. The noun also means food and drink, the provisions of the table.

**Bachelor's fare.** *See under* BACHELOR.

**Bill of fare.** *See under* BILL.

**Farewell Address.** George Washington's famous retirement speech made on 17 September 1796 in the Fraunces Tavern, New York, at the conclusion of his second presidency. It was largely written by Alexander Hamilton (1757–1804) but expressed Washington's thoughts. Its main purpose was to offer carefully weighed words of wise advice to his country.

> The nation which indulges toward another an habitual hatred or an habitual fondness is in some degree a slave. It is a slave to its animosity or to its affection, either of which is sufficient to lead it astray from its duty and its interest.
>
> GEORGE WASHINGTON: *Farewell Address* (1796)

**Fargo, Wells.** *See* WELLS FARGO.

**Farm. Fat farm.** *See under* FAT.

**Funny farm.** *See under* FUNNY.

**Farmer. Farmer George.** George III (1738–1820). A keen and progressive farmer who transformed his agricultural holdings. Under the name of Ralph Robinson he contributed the Robinson Letters to Arthur Young's *Annals of Agriculture*. The nickname of farmer was used by his political critics to arouse ridicule, but it was appropriate. It was also etymologically tautologous, since the name George means 'farmer' in the original Greek (literally, 'earth worker'). *See also* UNCLE GEORGE.

**Gentleman farmer.** *See under* GENTLEMAN.

**Farnese.** A noted Italian family who ruled Parma and Piacenza from 1545 to 1731. As Pope Paul III (r.1534–49), Alessandro Farnese set up his son Pierluigi in the duchy and established the family politically.

**Farnese Bull, The.** A marble group executed by Apollonius of Tralles and his brother Tauriscus in the 2nd century BC. The group represents Zethus and AMPHION tying their stepmother Dirce to the horns of a wild bull as a punishment for tormenting their mother, Antiope. It was discovered in the Baths of Caracalla in 1546 and placed in the Farnese Palace at Rome. It is now in the Museo Nazionale at Naples.

**Farnese Hercules, The.** Glycon's copy of an original statue by Lysippus, the Greek sculptor of the time of Alexander the Great. It represents the hero leaning sideways on his club, with one hand on his back, as if he had just got possession of the apple of the HESPERIDES. It was moved from the Farnese Palace at Rome, with other well-known sculptures, to the Museo Nazionale at Naples.

**Farrago of nonsense, A.** A confused heap of nonsense. Latin *farrago* is properly a mixture of *far* ('meal') with other ingredients to make a mash for cattle.

**Farthing** (Old English *fēorthing*, 'fourthling', 'fourth part'). The early silver penny was divided into two or four parts on the reverse thus ⊕ on the lines of the cross. Each of these quarters was a farthing. Farthings ceased to be legal tender on 31 December 1960.

**Farthing Bundles.** Formerly held on the first Saturday of each month, the distribution of Farthing Bundles at the Fern Street Settlement, Tower Hamlets, London, is no longer a regular event. The bundles are of toys or trinkets given to children small enough to pass under an archway inscribed: 'Enter now ye children small, None can come who are too tall.' The recipients pay a penny each for their gift.

**Farthing dip, A.** A synonym for something almost valueless.

**Not worth a brass farthing.** *See under* WORTH.

**Penny farthing.** *See under* PENNY.

**Farthingale.** The hooped understructure of the large protruding skirt fashionable in the reigns of Elizabeth I and James I. The word is from French *verdugale*, from Old Spanish *verdugado*, 'green rods', which were used for the framework before whalebone (*see* MISNOMERS) took their place.

**Fasces** (Latin, 'bundles'). A bundle of rods tied round with a red thong from which an axe projected. In ancient Rome *fasces* were assigned to the higher magistrates as symbols of authority, representing power over life and limb. In modern times the fasces became the emblem of the Italian FASCISTS.

**Fascines.** Bundles of faggots used to build up military defences or to fill in ditches for impeding attack. They were much used in the First World War for road foundations and for horse standings and also used to impede attack in the Second World War. The name derives from the Roman FASCES.

**Fascism.** Originally an Italian political movement, taking its name from the old Roman FASCES. It was founded in 1919 by Benito Mussolini (1883–1945), who took advantage of the discontent in Italy after the First World War to form a totalitarian nationalist party against left-wing radicalism and socialism. In 1922 the Fascists marched on Rome and demanded power, and King Victor Emmanuel III made Mussolini Prime Minister. He styled himself DUCE (leader) and made himself dictator in 1925, suppressing all other political parties the following year. The Fascists controlled Italy until 1943.

The term Fascism soon came to be applied to similar totalitarian movements in other countries. Ruthlessness, inhumanity and dishonest and disreputable practices were notable characteristics of its adherents. *See also* HITLERISM; NAZI.

> Benito Mussolini provided Italy with a new theme of government which, while it claimed to save the Italian people from Communism, raised himself to

dictatorial power. As Fascism sprang from Communism, so Nazism developed from Fascism.
WINSTON CHURCHILL: *The Second World War*, Vol I, *The Gathering Storm*, ch i (1948)

**Fash. Dinna fash yersel'!** Don't get excited; don't get into a state about it. The word is not of Scottish origin, but comes from obsolete French *fascher* (modern *fâcher*), 'to anger'.

**Fashion. Fashion victim.** A slavish follower of fashion trends.

**In a fashion** or **after a fashion.** In a sort of way, as: 'He spoke French after a fashion.'

**In fashion.** Fashionable at the time in question. The converse is out of fashion, implying outmoded or even obsolete.

**Rank and fashion.** *See under* RANK.

**Fast** (noun). *See also* FASTING.

**Break one's fast.** *See under* BREAK.

**Cecil's fast.** *See under* CECIL.

**Fast** (adjective). The adjective is used figuratively of someone addicted to pleasure and dissipation or of a person who goes the pace.

**Fast and furious.** Eager(ly); uproarious(ly).

As Tammie glowr'd, amaz'd, and curious,
The mirth and fun grew fast and furious.
ROBERT BURNS: 'Tam O'Shanter' (1791)

**Fast colour.** A colour that does not run or wash out in water.

**Fast food.** Food that can be served up fast, since it requires little preparation.

**Fast lane, The.** The outer lane of a motorway, where traffic overtakes or travels at high speed. Metaphorically, to be in the fast lane is to have a busy or even hectic lifestyle.

**Fast talk.** Earnest but deceptive patter.

**Fast track.** Metaphorically, a route or method that provides rapid results or promotion in business, especially when up against keen competition.

**Fast worker, A.** A colloquialism for a person who achieves quick results, especially in a love affair.

**Hard and fast.** *See under* HARD.

**Play fast and loose, To.** *See under* PLAY.

**Pull a fast one, To.** *See under* PULL.

**Thick and fast.** *See under* THICK.

**Fasti.** In ancient Rome, working days when the law courts were open. Holy days (DIES NON) when the law courts and other establishments were not open were called *nefasti*.

The *fasti* were listed in calendars, and the list of events occurring during the year of office of a pair of consuls was called *fasti consulares*. Hence, any chronological list of events of office holders became known as *fasti*. The surviving six books of Ovid's *Fasti* (1st century BC) are a poetical account of the Roman festivals of the first six months of the year. *See also* CALENDS.

**Fasting.** Strictly, a complete abstention from food and drink, but the word is more usually applied to an extreme or fairly strict limitation of diet and is of proved value in treating certain complaints. It is ancient and widespread as a form of penance or purification, and was so used by the Jews. It was practised by Christ and adopted by the early church. As currently practised in the church, it is marked by abstinence from flesh meat and observance of a light diet. Throughout the ROMAN CATHOLIC CHURCH fasting is obligatory on ASH WEDNESDAY and GOOD FRIDAY. The main fast of the Muslims is during the month of RAMADAN.

Mahatma Gandhi (1869–1948) practised fasting, an ancient Hindu observance, as a form of asceticism and as a political protest. *See also* BREAK ONE'S FAST; HUNGER STRIKE; CAT AND MOUSE ACT.

Moreover when ye fast, be not, as the hypocrites, of a sad countenance: for they disfigure their faces, that they may appear unto men to fast.
Matthew 6:16

**Fat. Fat, The.** The byname of:

Alphonso II of Portugal (1185–1223)
Charles III of France, le Gros (839–888); also known as Charles II if CHARLEMAGNE is omitted from the list of French kings
Louis VI of France, le Gros (1081–1137)

**Fat cat, A.** A rich or influential person, especially a businessman, politician or civil servant. A fat cat is one that gets the 'cream'.

**Fat chance, A.** A slim chance. An ironical expression, as also, a fat lot of good, no good at all.

**Fat farm.** An American colloquialism for a health farm for overweight people.

**Fathead.** A silly fool; a stupid person.

**Fat is in the fire, The.** An action has been done that will probably have dire consequences. If, in cooking, the grease spills into the fire, it blazes up and smokes, so that the food is spoilt.

**Fat of the land, The.** The best available. To live off the fat of the land is to have the best of everything. The expression is biblical.

Ye shall eat the fat of the land.
Genesis 45:18

**Chew the fat, To.** *See under* CHEW.

**Laugh and grow fat.** *See under* LAUGH.

**When the fat lady sings.** *See under* WHEN.

**Fata** (Italian, 'fairy'). A female supernatural being, introduced in Italian medieval romance, usually under the sway of DEMOGORGON.

**Fata Morgana.** MORGAN LE FAY, the half-sister of King ARTHUR. The name is also used for a mirage often visible in the Straits of Messina, so named because Morgan le Fay was fabled by the Norman settlers in England to dwell in Calabria.

**Fatal. Fatal gifts.** *See* CADMUS; NIBELUNGENLIED; OPAL; SEIAN HORSE; SHIRT OF NESSUS.

**Fatal necklace, The.** The necklace that CADMUS gave to Harmonia, although some say that VULCAN, others Europa, gave it to him. It possessed the property of stirring up strife and bloodshed. It is said to have eventually become the property of Phaÿllus, who gave it to his mistress. Her youngest son set fire to the house and mother, son and the necklace were destroyed.

**Fatal raven, The.** The raven consecrated to ODIN, the Danish war god, and the emblem of the Danish standard, *Landeyda* ('desolation of the country'), which was said to have been woven and embroidered in one noontide by the daughters of Ragnar Lodbrok (Ragnar Leather-Trousers), son of SIGURD. If the Danish arms were destined to defeat, the raven hung its wings, but if victory was to attend them, it stood erect and soaring, as if inviting the warriors to follow.

> The Danish raven, lured by annual prey,
> Hung o'er the land incessant.
> JAMES THOMSON: *Liberty*, Pt IV (1735–6)

The two ravens that sit on the shoulders of Odin are called Huginn (Mind) and Muninn (Memory).

**Fatal Vespers, The.** On 26 October 1623 a congregation of some 300 had assembled in an upper room in the residence of the French ambassador, at Blackfriars, to hear Father Drury, a JESUIT, preach. The flooring gave way, and Drury with another priest and about 100 of the congregation were killed. This accident was attributed to God's judgement against the Jesuits.

**Fate. Fates, The.** The Greeks and Romans supposed there were three Parcae or Fates, who arbitrarily controlled the birth, life and death of everyone. They were CLOTHO, LACHESIS and ATROPOS. They are sometimes called the 'cruel Fates' because they paid no heed to anyone's wishes.

**Fate worse than death, A.** Formerly, a fearful ordeal that was regarded as worse than being killed, and that was implicitly understood as rape or the loss of one's virginity. The expression is now often used frivolously.

> [The ape] threw her roughly across his broad, hairy shoulders, and leaped back into the trees, bearing Jane Porter away toward a fate a thousand times worse than death.
> EDGAR RICE BURROUGHS: *Tarzan of the Apes*, ch xix (1914)

**Irony of fate, The.** *See under* IRONY.

**Father.** In the Holy TRINITY, God. The name is given as a title to Roman Catholic priests and sometimes to CHURCH OF ENGLAND clergy of a HIGH CHURCH tendency. It is also applied to the senior member of a body or profession, as the Father of the House of Commons, and to the originator or first leader of some movement or school, as the Father of Comedy, the Father of History. In ancient Rome the title was given to the senators and in ecclesiastical history to the early church writers and doctors. *See also* CONSCRIPT FATHERS; PATRICIAN.

**Father Brown.** *See under* BROWN.

**Father Christmas.** An English rather than American name for SANTA CLAUS, associating him specifically with CHRISTMAS. The name carries a somewhat socially superior cachet and is thus preferred by certain advertisers.

> Father Christmas is coming to town. Celebrations start at 8.00am this Saturday with a carnival outside Harrods. .... Shortly afterwards snow will fall as Father Christmas arrives in his sleigh drawn by reindeer, accompanied by a parade of elves, pipers and amongst others a giant snowman. At 9.00am, Father Christmas will make a tour of the store before arriving at his Grotto on the Fourth Floor at 9.30am, where he will remain until December 24th. So come along and meet Father Christmas.
> *The Times* (advertisement) (4 November 1998)

**Father-figure.** A person who is regarded or looked up to as a father in some sense.

**Father Ignatius.** *See under* IGNATIUS.

**Father Mathew.** *See under* MATHEW.

**Father of Angling, The.** Izaak Walton (1593–1683). *See also* GENTLE CRAFT.

**Father of Chemistry, The.** Robert Boyle (1627–91).

**Father of Christian Monasticism, The.** St ANTHONY OF EGYPT (*c*.250–356). *See also* FATHERS OF THE DESERT.

**Father of Comedy, The.** Aristophanes (*c*.450–385 BC), the Athenian dramatist.

**Father of Courtesy, The.** Richard de Beauchamp, Earl of Warwick (1382–1439).

**Father of Danish Drama, The.** Ludwig von Holberg (1684–1754).

**Father of Dithyrambic Poetry, The.** ARION of Lesbos.

**Father of Ecclesiastical History, The.** Eusebius of Caesarea (*c*.260–*c*.340).

**Father of English Botany, The.** William Turner (*c*.1520–68), dean of Wells, who wrote his *New Herball* (1551–62), which is held to begin the scientific study of botany in England.

**Father of English History, The.** The VENERABLE BEDE (673–735), author of the *Ecclesiastical History of the English People*, written in Latin and finished in 731.

**Father of English Poetry, The.** Geoffrey Chaucer (*c*.1340–1400).

**Father of English Song, The.** CAEDMON (*fl*.670).

**Father of Epic Poetry, The.** HOMER.

**Father of French Drama, The.** Étienne Jodelle (1532–73).

**Father of French History, The.** André Duchesne (1584–1640).
**Father of French Satire, The.** Mathurin Régnier (1573–1613).
**Father of Greek Drama, The.** Thespis (6th century BC).
**Father of Greek Music, The.** Terpander of Lesbos (*fl.*676 BC).
**Father of Greek Tragedy** or **Tragedy, The.** A title given to AESCHYLUS (*c.*525–456 BC), author of the Orestean trilogy and many other tragedies, and to the Greek poet Thespis (6th century BC). *See also* THESPIANS.
**Father of his Country, The.** CICERO (106–43 BC) was so entitled by the Roman senate. Julius CAESAR (100–44 BC) and AUGUSTUS (63 BC–AD 14) were among the several Caesars given the title. Others who were granted the sobriquet include:

Andronicus Palaeologus II (*c.*1260–1332)
Cosimo de Medici of Florence (1389–1464)
Andrea Doria (1466–1560) of Genoa
George Washington (1732–99), first President of the United States
Victor Emmanuel II (1820–78), first king of Italy, was popularly so designated in allusion to his sizeable progeny of bastard offspring.

**Father of Historic Painting, The.** Polygnotus of Thaos (*c.*500–*c.*440 BC).
**Father of History, The.** Herodotus (*c.*485–*c.*424 BC).
**Father of Iambic Verse, The.** Archilochos of Paros (*fl.c.*700 BC).
**Father of Landscape Gardening, The.** André Le Nôtre (1631–1700), who landscaped VERSAILLES.
**Father of letters, The.** Francis I (1494–1547), king of France. Also Lorenzo de Medici (1449–92), the Magnificent.
**Father of Lies, The.** SATAN.
**Father of Medicine, The.** Aretaeus of Cappadocia (2nd century AD) is sometimes so called, and especially HIPPOCRATES of Cos (469–399 BC).
**Father of Modern German Drama, The.** Andreas Gryphius (1616–64).
**Father of Modern Music, The.** Mozart (1756–91) has been so called.
**Father of Moral Philosophy, The.** St THOMAS AQUINAS (*c.*1225–74).
**Father of Musicians, The.** Jubal, 'the father of all such as handle the harp and organ' (Genesis 4:21).
**Father of Parody, The.** Hipponax of Ephesus (6th century BC).
**Father of Ridicule, The.** François Rabelais (*c.*1495–1553). *See also* RABELAISIAN.
**Father of Roman Poetry, The.** Ennius (239–169 BC), noted for his dramas and epic poetry.
**Father of Roman Satire, The.** Gaius Lucilius (*c.*180–*c.*102 BC).
**Father of Satire, The.** Archilochus of Paros (7th century BC).
**Father of Spanish Drama, The.** Lope de Vega (1562–1635).
**Father of the chapel.** *See* CHAPEL.
**Father of the English Novel, The.** Both Samuel Richardson (1689–1761) and Henry Fielding (1707–54) have been given the title.
**Father of the Faithful, The.** ABRAHAM (Romans 4:16, Galatians 3:6–9).
**Father of the people, The.** Louis XII, king of France (1462–1515); also Christian III, king of Denmark and Norway (1503–59). Henry IV, king of France (1553–1610) was termed the Father and Friend of the people.
**Father of the waters, The.** The Irrawaddy in Myanmar (Burma) and the Mississippi in North America. The Missouri is the latter's child. The Nile is so called by Dr Johnson in his *Rasselas* (1759). The epithet is not uncommonly applied to rivers, especially those on which cities are built.

Say, Father Thames, for thou hast seen
Full many a sprightly race
Disporting on thy margent green,
The paths of pleasure trace.
THOMAS GRAY: *Ode on a Distant Prospect of Eton College* (1747)

**Father's Day.** A day devoted to fathers in the annual calendar, falling on the third Sunday in June. Britain imported the occasion from the United States, where it was devised in 1910 in Spokane, Washington, as a counterpart to Mother's Day. It has never won the popularity of the older festival, however. *See also* MOTHERING SUNDAY.
**Fathers of the church.** All those church writers of the first 12 centuries whose works on Christian doctrine are considered of weight and worthy of respect. The term is, however, more strictly applied to those teachers of the first 12 centuries, and especially of the first six, who added holiness and orthodoxy to their learning. Representative among them are:

1st century: Clement of Rome
2nd century: Ignatius of Antioch, Justin, Irenaeus, Polycarp
3rd century: Cyprian, Dionysius, Origen, Tertullian, Clement of Alexandria, Gregory Thaumaturgus
4th century: Hilary, Cyril of Jerusalem, Gregory Nyssen, JOHN CHRYSOSTOM, Eusebius, JEROME, Epiphanius, Athanasius, Basil, AMBROSE
5th century: Rufinus, AUGUSTINE, Pope Leo the Great, Cyril of Alexandria, Vincent of Lerins
6th century: Caesarius of Arles
7th century: Isidore, Pope GREGORY THE GREAT
8th century: John of Damascus, VENERABLE BEDE

11th century: Peter Damian
12th century: Anselm, BERNARD

*See also* APOSTOLIC FATHERS.

**Fathers of the Constitution, The.** The framers of the constitution of the United States who took part in the Constitutional Convention at Philadelphia in 1787. In particular, James Madison (1751–1836) is known as the Father of the Constitution for the part he played in its formation.

**Fathers of the desert** or **desert fathers, The.** The monks and hermits of the Egyptian deserts in the 4th century from whom Christian monasticism derives. The best known were St ANTHONY THE GREAT, who founded his first monastery in 305, St Pachomius, the hermit and founder of monasteries, and St Hilarion. There is a good description of their mode of life in Charles Kingsley's *Hypatia* (1851).

**Father Time.** A personification of time, conventionally depicted as an old man with a beard and holding a scythe. In American New Year's Eve illustrations he represents the passing old year and is usually shown giving way to a cute little baby, the New Year.

**Apostolic Fathers.** *See under* APOSTOLIC.
**Conscript fathers.** *See under* CONSCRIPT.
**How's your father?** *See under* HOW.
**Land of My Fathers.** *See under* LAND.
**Last of the Fathers, The.** *See under* LAST.
**Lie with one's fathers, To.** *See under* LIE.
**Pilgrim Fathers.** *See under* PILGRIM.
**Seraphic Father.** *See under* SERAPHIC.
**White Fathers.** *See under* WHITE.
**Wish is father to the thought, The.** *See under* WISH.

**Fatima.** The last wife of BLUEBEARD. MOHAMMED's youngest daughter was also Fatima (*c*.605–633). She married his cousin, the fourth Muslim caliph ALI.

**Fatimids** or **Fatimites.** An Arab dynasty ruling in Egypt and North Africa (909–1171), descended from FATIMA and her husband ALI.

**Fatted calf.** *See* KILL THE FATTED CALF.

**Fatwa** (Arabic). A legal decision given by a MUSLIM religious leader. The word became familiar in the West in 1989 when Iran's Ayatollah Khomeini issued a *fatwa* sentencing the writer Salman Rushdie (b.1947) to death for writing *The Satanic Verses* (1988), a novel condemned as blasphemous and highly offensive. The Arabic word, which does not specifically mean a death sentence, is related to MUFTI. *See also* MAHOUND.

**Fault.** In geology, the break or displacement of a stratum of rock.

**At fault.** *See under* AT.
**Find fault, To.** *See under* FIND.
**To a fault.** *See under* TO.

**Fauna.** The animals of a country at any given period. The term was first used by Linnaeus in the title of his *Fauna Suecica* (1746), a companion volume to his *Flora Suecica* (1745), and it is the name of a rural goddess, with attributes similar to those of FAUNUS. *See also* PAN.

Nor less the place of curious plant he knows;
He both his Flora and his Fauna shows.
GEORGE CRABBE: *The Borough*, letter viii (1810)

**Fauni** or **Fauns.** Minor Roman deities of the countryside, merry and mischievous, small counterparts of FAUNUS. *See also* SATYR.

**Faunus.** A good spirit of forest and field, and a god of prophecy. He had the form of a SATYR and is identified with the Greek PAN. FAUNA is sometimes given as his wife, sometimes as his daughter. At his festivals, called *Faunalia*, peasants brought rustic offerings and made merry. He was also fabled to have been a king of Latium, subsequently deified for his devotion to agriculture.

**Fauntleroy, Little Lord.** *See under* LITTLE.

**Faust.** The hero of Christopher Marlowe's *Tragical History of Dr Faustus* (1604) and Goethe's *Faust* (1808, 1832) is founded on Dr Johann Faust, or Faustus (*c*.1480–*c*.1540), a magician and astrologer born in Württemberg, about whom many stories soon began to circulate crediting him with supernatural gifts and evil living. In 1587 *The History of Dr Faustus, the Notorious Magician and Master of the Black Art* was published by Johann Spies at Frankfurt. It immediately became popular and was soon translated into English, French and other languages. Many other accounts followed, and the Faust theme was developed by writers, artists and musicians over the years. It was Goethe who was responsible, however, for transforming the necromancer into a personification of the struggle between the higher and lower natures in man. Notable among musical compositions on the story are Spohr's opera *Faust* (1813), Wagner's overture *Faust* (1840), Berlioz's *Damnation de Faust* (1846), Gounod's opera *Faust* (1859), Boito's *Mefistofele* (1868) and Busoni's *Doktor Faust* (1925).

The idea of making a pact with the Devil for worldly reasons is of Jewish origin. The basis of the Faust story is that he sold his soul to the Devil in return for 24 years of further life during which he is to have every pleasure and all knowledge at his command. The climax comes when the Devil claims him for his own.

*O lente lente currite noctis equi.*
The stars move still, time runs, the clock will strike,
The devil will come, and Faustus must be damned.
O I'll leap up to my God: who pulls me down?
See, see, where Christ's blood streams in the firmament.

One drop would save my soul, half a drop, ah my Christ.
CHRISTOPHER MARLOWE: *Dr Faustus*, V, ii (1604)

**Faute de mieux** (French). For want of anything better.

'*Faute de* what?'
'*Mieux*, m'lord. A French expression. We should say "For want of anything better."'
'What asses these Frenchmen are. Why can't they talk English?'
P.G. WODEHOUSE: *Ring for Jeeves* (1953)

**Fauvism.** The name given to the work of a group of young French artists of the first decade of the 20th century, whose leader was Henri Matisse (1869–1954), and which included André Derain (1880–1954), Georges Braque (1882–1963), Maurice de Vlaminck (1876–1958), Raoul Dufy (1877–1953), Albert Marquet (1875–1947), Othon Friesz (1879–1949) and Georges Rouault (1871–1958). There was a corresponding German movement known as *Die Brücke* ('The Bridge'). The French school derives from the influence of Van Gogh, and their work was characterized by the imaginative use of brilliant colour, decorative simplicity, vitality and gaiety. The name Fauves ('wild beasts') arose from a remark of the French art critic Louis Vauxcelles, *Donatello au milieu des fauves*, occasioned by the sight of a quattrocento-like statue amid their spectacularly coloured paintings at an exhibition of their work in 1905. *See also* CUBISM; DADAISM; FUTURISM; IMPRESSIONISM; ORPHISM; SURREALISM; SYNCHROMISM; VORTICISM.

**Faux pas** (French, 'false step'). A breach of manners or good conduct.

The fact is, his Lordship, who hadn't, it seems,
Form'd the slightest idea, not ev'n in his dreams,
That the pair had been wedded according to law,
Conceived that his daughter had made a *faux pas*.
R.H. BARHAM: *Ingoldsby Legends*, 'Some Account of a New Play' (1840)

**Favonius.** The Latin name for the ZEPHYR or west wind. It means the wind favourable to vegetation.

If to the torrid zone her way she bend,
Her the cool breathing of Favonius lend,
Thither command the birds to sing their quires,
That zone is temp'rate.
WILLIAM HABINGTON: *Castara*: 'To the Spring' (1634)

**Favour.** Ribbons made into a bow are called favours from being bestowed by ladies on the successful champions of tournaments. *See also* TRUELOVE KNOT.

Here, Fluellen; wear thou this favour for me, and stick it in thy cap.
SHAKESPEARE: *Henry V*, IV, vii (1598)

**Curry favour, To.** *See under* CURRY.
**Family Favourites.** *See under* FAMILY.
**Worm oneself into another's favour, To.** *See under* WORM.

**Fawkes, Guy.** The Roman Catholic convert (1570–1606) who was one of the conspirators in the GUNPOWDER PLOT. His experience as a soldier and his reputation as a cool schemer won him the actual execution of the plan, but he was caught in the vault under the House of Lords on 4 November 1605, the plot having been betrayed to the government. Under fearful torture on the rack he disclosed the names of his fellow conspirators, but by then they had already been apprehended. He was executed before the old Palace of Westminster on 31 January 1606. *See also* GUY.

**Fay.** *See* FAIRY.
**Morgan le Fay.** *See* FATA MORGANA; MORGAN LE FAY.

**Feal and divot.** In Scotland the right to cut turf or peat, from which, by jocular derivation, comes the divot of golf, a piece of turf removed by a player's club. Both words mean 'turf'.

**Fear, No.** *See under* NO.

**Feast** or **festival.** A day or days specially set apart for religious observances, an ancient practice common to all religions. The number of feasts in the ROMAN CATHOLIC and GREEK CHURCHES is extensive, but after the REFORMATION the CHURCH OF ENGLAND retained only a limited number. The feasts in the Christian CALENDAR have been divided in various ways, one of which is to group them as movable or immovable. All Sundays are feast-days.

The chief immovable feasts are the four quarter days, i.e. the ANNUNCIATION OF LADY DAY (25 March), the Nativity of St JOHN THE BAPTIST (24 June), MICHAELMAS DAY (29 September) and CHRISTMAS Day (25 December). Others are the Naming of Jesus, formerly known as the Circumcision (1 January), EPIPHANY (6 January), ALL HALLOWS DAY (1 November), the various Apostles' days and the anniversaries of martyrs and saints.

The movable feasts are those that depend on EASTER Day. Also among them are the Sundays after the Epiphany, SEPTUAGESIMA SUNDAY, the Sundays of LENT, Rogation Sunday, ASCENSION DAY, Pentecost or WHITSUNDAY, TRINITY SUNDAY and the Sundays after Trinity.

**Feast of Fools, The.** A kind of clerical SATURNALIA, popular in the Middle Ages and not successfully suppressed until the REFORMATION, and even later in France. The feast usually centred on a cathedral and was most commonly held on the feasts of St STEPHEN (26 December), St JOHN THE EVANGELIST (27 December) and HOLY INNOCENTS (28 December). The mass was burlesqued, and braying often took the place of the customary responses. Obscene jests and dances were common as well as the singing of indecent songs. The ass was a central feature and the Feast of Asses was sometimes a separate festival. *See also* BOY BISHOP.

**Feast of Lanterns, The.** A popular Chinese festival, celebrated annually at the first full moon. Tradition says that one evening the daughter of a well-known mandarin fell into a lake. Her father and his neighbour took lanterns to look for her, and happily she was rescued. A festival was ordained to commemorate the rescue, which in time developed into the Feast of Lanterns.

**Feast of the Annunciation, The.** 25 March, also called LADY DAY, on which the angel GABRIEL announced to the Virgin MARY that she would be the mother of the MESSIAH (Luke 1:26–38).

**Feast of the Immaculate Conception, The.** 8 December, one of the FEASTS OF OBLIGATION.

**Feast of the Tabernacles, The.** One of the three main feasts of the Jewish year, lasting seven days followed by an eighth day of 'holy convocation' (*see* Leviticus 23:34–43, Numbers 29:12–34). It commemorates the way the Jews dwelt in booths or tents in the wilderness and also celebrates the final gathering-in of the harvest and the vintage. It begins on the 15th Tishri (mid-September to mid-October).

**Feast of Trumpets, The.** A Jewish festival held on the first two days of Tishri (about mid-September to mid-October), the beginning of the Jewish ecclesiastical year, at which the blowing of trumpets formed a prominent part of the ritual. *See* Numbers 29:1.

**Feasts of Obligation.** Days on which Roman Catholics are bound to hear MASS and to abstain from 'work or business that would inhibit the worship to be given to God, the joy proper to the Lord's Day, or the relaxation of mind and body'. The feasts vary slightly in different countries, but according to the *Codex Iuris Canonici* of 1983 are: all SUNDAYS, CHRISTMAS Day (25 December), the EPIPHANY (6 January), ASCENSION DAY, CORPUS CHRISTI, the Solemnity of the Blessed Virgin Mary (1 January), her ASSUMPTION (15 August) and IMMACULATE CONCEPTION (8 December), the feasts of St JOSEPH (1 May), Sts PETER and PAUL (29 June) and All Saints (*see* ALL HALLOWS DAY) (1 November).

**Egg feast.** *See under* EGG.

**Harvest festival.** *See under* HARVEST.

**Islamic festivals.** *See under* ISLAM.

**Movable Feasts.** *See under* MOVABLE.

**Ram Feast, The.** *See under* RAM.

**Skeleton at the feast, The.** *See under* SKELETON.

**Feather. Feather an oar, To.** To turn the blade parallel with the surface of the water and move it over it as the arms go forwards for the next stroke. The oar throws off the water in a feathery spray.

**Feather-bed, To.** To pamper or cushion, as in a feather bed. In the workplace, feather-bedding is the practice of limiting production, duplicating work and so forth in order to prevent redundancies.

**Feather in one's cap, A.** A personal achievement or honour to be proud of. The allusion is to the custom, general in Asia and among the Native Americans, of adding a feather to the headgear for every enemy slain. The ancient Lycians and many others had a similar custom, just as the sportsman who kills the first woodcock puts a feather in his cap. At one time in Hungary the only person who could wear a feather was the one who had killed a Turk. When CHINESE GORDON quelled the TAIPING rebellion he was honoured by the Chinese Government with the 'yellow jacket and peacock's feather'.

**Feather one's nest, To.** To provide for one's own interests, especially financially. The phrase is commonly used with an implication of disapproval. Many birds literally feather their nests to provide a warm and comfortable home for their chicks.

**Featherweight.** Something of extreme lightness in comparison with others of its kind. The term is applied to a professional boxer weighing 118–126 pounds (53.5–57kg) or to an amateur boxer weighing 119–126 pounds (54–57kg).

In the paper trade, the name is given to very light antique, laid, or wove book papers, which are loosely woven and made mainly from esparto.

**As light as a feather.** *See under* AS.

**Birds of a feather flock together.** *See under* BIRD.

**Fine feathers make fine birds.** *See under* FINE.

**Fur and feather.** *See under* FUR.

**In full feather.** *See under* FULL.

**Knocked down with a feather, To be.** *See under* KNOCK.

**Make the feathers** or **fur fly, To.** *See under* FUR.

**Peacock's feather.** *See under* PEACOCK.

**Prince of Wales's feathers.** *See* PRINCE OF WALES.

**Show the white feather, To.** *See under* SHOW.

**Smooth one's ruffled feathers, To.** *See under* SMOOTH.

**Tarred and feathered.** *See under* TAR.

**February.** The month of purification among the ancient Romans (Latin *februum*, 'purgation').

2 February, CANDLEMAS DAY, is the feast of the Purification of the Blessed Virgin MARY. It is said that if the weather is fine and frosty at the close of JANUARY and the beginning of February, there is more winter ahead than behind.

The Dutch used to call the month *Spokkelmaand* ('vegetation month'). The Anglo-Saxons knew it as *solmōnath* ('mud month'). In the FRENCH REVOLUTIONARY CALENDAR its equivalent, from 21 January to 19 February, was Pluviôse ('rain month'). *See also* FILL-DYKE.

**Fair maid of February.** *See under* FAIR.

**Fecit** (Latin, 'made it'). A word formerly appearing after the name of a painter or sculptor to indicate the particular artist who executed the work.

**Federalists.** Those Americans who supported the proposed new constitution of 1787, led by Alexander Hamilton, James Madison, John Adams, John Jay and others. Hamilton, Madison and Jay published 85 essays under the name Publius, in support of Federalism, known in their collected form as *The Federalist* (1788). The party controlled the government until 1801 and came to an end in 1816. *See also* CONFEDERATE STATES.

**Fedora.** A low soft felt hat with a crown creased lengthways. It takes its name from *Fédora* (1882), a preposterous play by the French dramatist Victorien Sardou, in which the heroine is a Russian princess named Fédora Romanoff.

**Fee.** A word from Old French *fie*, of Germanic origin, related to Old English *fēo*, 'cattle', 'goods', 'money', which itself gave modern fief. A similar relationship exists in Latin between *pecunia*, 'money', and *pecus*, 'cattle'. English 'capital' shares the development, since it derives from Latin *capita*, 'heads' (of cattle), and its own related word, through French, is chattels.

**Fee simple.** A property held by a person in his or her own right, free from condition or limitation. The converse is FEE TAIL.

**Fee tail.** An estate restricted to a person and his or her lawful heirs, otherwise an entailed estate. Fee tail as such was abolished by the Law of Property Act, 1925. *See also* ENTAIL.

**Hold in fee, To.** *See under* HOLD.

**Retaining fee.** *See under* RETAIN.

**Surplice fees.** *See under* SURPLICE.

**Feed. Feeding of the Five Thousand, The.** The occasion when Jesus fed a crowd of about 5000 people in the wilderness, using only five barley loaves and two fishes. The miracle is recounted in all four Gospels (Matthew 14:15–21, Mark 6:35–44, Luke 9:12–17, John 6:5–14), the loaves symbolizing Christ: 'I am the bread of life: he that cometh to me shall never hunger' (John 6:35).

**Feed the fishes, To.** To be seasick; to be drowned.

**Chicken feed.** *See under* CHICKEN.

**Feel. Feel bad about, To.** To be regretful or unhappy; to have a conscience about.

**Feel in one's bones, To.** To have an intuition about something.

**Feel** or **look like death warmed up, To.** To be utterly exhausted; to feel or look ghastly.

> I look like death warmed up and what I feel is nobody's business.
>
> NGAIO MARSH: *Death and the Dancing Footman*, ch ii (1942)

**Feel one's way, To.** To proceed cautiously.

**Feel small, To.** To feel humiliated; to be 'taken down a peg or two'.

**Feel the pinch, To.** To be affected by some kind of adversity; to suffer hardship or poverty. The allusion may be to shoes that have become tight and that one cannot afford to replace. Alternatively, the reference may be to the thinning of the body so that one has to TIGHTEN ONE'S BELT.

**Better feelings.** *See under* BETTER.

**Feet.** *See* FOOT.

**Feilding, Beau.** Robert Feilding (*c.*1651–1712), known generally as 'Beau Feilding' and called 'Handsome Feilding' by Charles II. He died at Scotland Yard, London, having been convicted of bigamously marrying (1705) the Duchess of Cleveland, a former mistress of Charles II and others. He figures as Orlando in Steele's *Tatler* (Nos. 50 and 51).

**Felix the Cat.** The feline hero of early animated film cartoons produced by Pat Sullivan in the 1920s. Throughout his many adventures, 'Felix kept on walking', and thus originated the formerly familiar catchphrase. Felix was actually created in 1919 by the animator Otto Messmer (1894–1985).

**Fell, Dr.**

> I do not love thee, Dr Fell,
> The reason why I cannot tell;
> But this I know, and know full well,
> I do not love thee, Dr Fell.

These well-known lines are by the satirist Thomas Brown (1663–1704), and the person referred to was Dr John Fell, dean of CHRIST CHURCH and bishop of Oxford (1625–86), who expelled him, but said he would remit the sentence if Brown translated the thirty-third Epigram of Martial:

> Non amo te, Sabidi, nec possum dicere quare;
> Hoc tantum possum dicere, non amo te.
> (I do not love you, Sabidius, and I cannot say why;
> All I can say is this, that I do not love you.)

Brown's translation, above, is said to have been given impromptu.

**Fellow.** At the colleges of Oxford and Cambridge, and at Trinity College, Dublin, a fellow is a member of the foundation, sharing in its government and drawing a stipend from the college revenues. There are also honorary fellowships. At University College and King's College, London, election as a fellow is a mark of honour to a distinguished member. At other universities there are research or postgraduate fellowships for further study.

**Fellow traveller.** A person in sympathy with a

political party but not a member of that party. The term, which came to be chiefly used of Communist sympathizers, is a translation of Russian *poputchik*, first used by Trotsky in this sense to refer to non-communist writers who sympathized with the Revolution. *See also* SPUTNIK.

**Jolly good fellow, A.** *See under* JOLLY.

**Phantom fellow.** *See under* PHANTOM.

**Felo de se** (Anglo-Latin, 'felon of himself'). A legal term for suicide and for the person who commits it. Murder is felony, and someone who murders himself commits this felony on himself.

**Female. Female Howard, The.** Elizabeth Fry (1780–1845), the QUAKER philanthropist and prison reformer, so called after John Howard (1726–90), her famous predecessor in this field.

**Female Marine, The.** Hannah Snell of Worcester (1723–92), who at the age of 22 disguised herself as a man under the name of James Gray and enlisted as a foot soldier, then a sailor, with the aim of finding her husband, whom she had married some two years before. Her lack of beard as a cabin boy earned her the nickname of 'Miss Molly Gray', but her skill and intrepidity in the carrying out of shipboard duties soon won her acceptance among the male crew members. She published the story of her experiences, *The Female Soldier; Or, The Surprising Life and Adventures of Hannah Snell* (1750).

**Feme. Feme covert.** A legal term for a married woman, from Anglo-French, literally 'covered woman', i.e. one protected by marriage.

**Feme sole.** A single woman, whether spinster, widow or divorcee.

**Feme sole merchant.** A woman, married or single, who carries on a trade on her own account.

**Feminine ending.** An extra unaccented syllable at the end of a line of verse, e.g. in lines 1 and 3 of the following:

> The candles burn their sockets,
> The blinds let through the day,
> The young man feels his pockets
> And wonders what's to pay.
> A.E. HOUSMAN: *Last Poems*, No. 21 (1922)

**Femme fatale** (French, 'fatal woman'). A dangerously seductive woman, who lures men to their downfall.

**Fen.** The Fens are a low-lying region of the East Midlands and East Anglia, mainly in Cambridgeshire, Norfolk and Lincolnshire. There are no specific boundaries, and the former marshy terrain of the area has changed since the 17th century, when much of the marshland was reclaimed and made suitable for farming. Even so, there are large parts below sea level, crossed by dykes that need constant pumping in order to avoid the ever-present threat of floods, as in Holland. The Fens are felt to be brooding and other-worldly, and they have inspired a number of literary and artistic works, such as Dorothy Sayers' crime story *The Nine Tailors* (1934) and Graham Swift's poetic novel *Waterland* (1983), filmed in 1992.

**Fence.** A slang term for a dealer in stolen goods. The name probably derives from 'defence', since the dealer is a trusted person and keeps the goods in a well protected or defended place.

**Sit on the fence, To.** *See under* SIT.

**Feng shui.** In Chinese thought a system of good and evil influences in the natural surroundings, now increasingly taken into account in the West when designing buildings or simply when deciding where to sit. The words represent Chinese *feng*, 'wind', and *shui*, 'water'. For the Chinese *feng shui* is both an art and a science, the former as a means of counteracting evil influences by good ones, the latter by determining the desirability of sites from the configuration of natural objects such as rivers, trees and hills. Many Chinese were at first concerned that the introduction of railways and telegraph lines would seriously damage the *feng shui* or prosperity of the districts through which they were laid.

**Fenians.** An anti-British secret society of Irishmen founded in New York in 1858 by John O'Mahony (1816–77) and in Ireland by James Stephens (1882–1950), with the object of making Ireland a republic and bringing English domination to an end. The word is properly from Irish *féne*, the name of an ancient Irish people, but this became confused with *fíann*, the legendary band of warriors led by FINN. *See also* CLAN-NA-GAEL; FIANNA FÁIL; FINE GAEL; PHOENIX PARK MURDERS; SINN FÉIN.

**Fenice, La** (Italian, 'The Phoenix'). The principal opera house of Venice, regarded as the most beautiful in the world. Many famous operas had their first performance here, including Rossini's *Tancredi* (1813) and Verdi's *Rigoletto* (1851) and *La Traviata* (1853). It was built in 1792 and is aptly named, since it has twice been destroyed by fire (1836, 1996) but each time has arisen from the ashes.

**Fennel.** This herb (*Foeniculum vulgare*) was at one time believed to be an aphrodisiac, thus 'to eat conger and fennel' was provocative of sexual licence. Hence Falstaff's remark to Poins:

> He plays at quoits well, and eats conger and fennel, and drinks off candles' ends for flap-dragons, and rides the wild mare with the boys.
> SHAKESPEARE: *Henry IV, Pt II*, II, iv (1597)

It was also emblematic of flattery and may have been included among the herbs distributed by Ophelia (*Hamlet*, IV, v (1600)) for this reason.

**Fenny Poppers.** St Martin's Day (11 November) is celebrated at Fenny Stratford, now a district of Bletchley, Buckinghamshire, by the firing of six mini-cannons known as the Fenny Poppers. They are taken from the belfry of St Martin's church, their normal resting place, to a local sports ground, and there loaded and fired at four-hour intervals from 8 am. The custom marks the founding of the church in 1730 by Dr Browne Willis.

**Fenrir.** In Scandinavian mythology the wolf of LOKI. He was the brother of HEL, and when he gaped one jaw touched earth and the other heaven. At the RAGNAROK he broke his fetters and swallowed ODIN, who was avenged by VIDAR thrusting his sword into the yawning gullet and piercing the beast's heart.

**Ferae Naturae** (Latin, 'of savage nature'). The legal term for animals living in a wild state, as distinguished from those that are domesticated.

> Women are not compris'd in our Laws of Friendship: they are *Feræ Naturæ*.
>
> JOHN DRYDEN: *An Evening's Love, or The Mock Astrologer*, iv (1668)

**Ferdia.** A hero of Irish legend who was persuaded to fight for Queen MAEVE against CUCHULAIN, his dearest friend. After a struggle lasting three days he was killed, to Cuchulain's bitter grief.

**Ferdinand the Bull.** The gentle, peace-loving bull in the children's tale *The Story of Ferdinand* (1936) by Munro Leaf. He is chosen for the bullring, but the matador is disappointed when all that Ferdinand wants to do is to sniff the scent of the flowers in the hats of the women spectators. An award-winning Disney cartoon, *Ferdinand the Bull* (1938), was based on the story, which has a simple moral: peace and gentleness are better than fighting and death.

**Fergus mac Roich.** The heroic tutor of CUCHULAIN, who left CONCHOBAR's court after the treacherous murder of the SONS OF USNECH.

**Ferrant d'Espagne** (French, 'shod one of Spain'). The horse of OLIVER.

**Ferrara.** *See* ANDREA FERRARA.

**Ferrara Bible, The.** *See under* BIBLE.

**Ferrex and Porrex.** Two sons of Gorboduc, a mythical British king, who divided his kingdom between them. Porrex drove his brother from Britain, and when Ferrex returned with an army he was slain, but Porrex was shortly after torn to pieces by his mother with the assistance of her women. The story is told in Geoffrey of Monmouth's *Historia Regum Britanniae*, ch xvi (*c*.1136), and it forms the basis of the first regular English tragedy, *Gorboduc, or Ferrex and Porrex*, written by Thomas Norton and Thomas Sackville, Lord Buckhurst, and acted in 1562.

**Ferris wheel.** A fairground attraction in the form of a gigantic revolving wheel with passenger cars suspended on its outer edge. It was originally designed by the American engineer George W.G. Ferris (1859–96) for the World's Columbian Exposition in Chicago in 1893.

**Ferry, Harpers.** *See under* HARPERS.

**FERT.** The ORDER OF THE ANNUNCIATION has these letters on its collar. *Fert* (Latin, 'he bears') is an ancient motto of the House of Savoy, but the letters have also been held to be the initials of *Fortitudo Ejus Rhodum Tenuit* ('His courage held Rhodes'), in allusion to the aid rendered to Rhodes by Savoy in 1310, *Foedere Et Religione Tenemur* ('We are bound by our word and oath'), which appears on the gold doubloon of Victor Amadeus I (1630–7), or *Fortitudo Ejus Rempublicam Tenet* ('His courage holds the state').

**Fesse.** *See* HERALDRY.

**Festina lente** (Latin, 'make haste slowly'). Words ascribed by Suetonius to Emperor Augustus. They form the punning motto of the Onslow family.

**Festival of the Popinjay, The.** The first Sunday in May, when a figure of a popinjay, decked with parti-coloured feathers and suspended from a pole, served as a target for shooting practice. The person whose ball or arrow brought down the bird, by cutting the string by which it was hung, received the title of Captain Popinjay for the rest of the day and was escorted home in triumph.

**Festschrift** (German, *Fest*, 'celebration', and *Schrift*, 'writing'). A term commonly used for the volume of essays, papers and so forth, prepared by colleagues and friends as a tribute to a scholar on some special occasion, usually the retirement or a particular anniversary.

> The 'Festschrift', the present *English Miscellany*, speaks for itself, and will remain a permanent record of the esteem in which [the philologist] Dr. Furnivall is held wherever English literature is read, or the English language studied.
>
> *An English Miscellany (Presented to Dr. Furnivall in Honour of his Seventy-fifth Birthday)* (1900)

**Fetch** (noun). A WRAITH or the disembodied ghost of a living person. Hence 'fetch light' or 'fetch candle', a light appearing at night that is supposed to foretell someone's death. Fetches most commonly appear to distant friends and relations at the very moment before the death of those they represent. The word is of uncertain origin.

> The very fetch and ghost of Mrs Gamp, bonnet and all, might be seen hanging up, any hour in the day, in at least a dozen secondhand clothes-shops about Holborn.
>
> DICKENS: *Martin Chuzzlewit*, ch xix (1843–4)

The word is also used in the sense of a stratagem, artifice or trick.

> Deny to speak with me! They are sick! they are
> weary,
> They have travelled hard to-night! Mere fetches,
> The images of revolt and flying off.
>
> SHAKESPEARE: *King Lear*, II, iv (1605

**Fetch** (verb). **Fetch and carry, To.** To run backwards and forwards with things, like a simple servant.

**Fetish** (Portuguese *feitiço*, 'sorcery', from Latin *facticius*, 'made by art'). The name given by early Portuguese voyagers to AMULETS and other objects supposed by the natives of the Guinea coast to possess magic powers. Hence an idol or an object of devotion. Fetishism is found in all primitive nations in which the services of a spirit may be appropriated by the possession of its material emblem. In psychology the word is used to denote a condition in which sexual gratification is obtained from handling some object or part of the body (other than the sexual organs).

**Fettle.** In some specialized and dialect senses, the verb means to repair, prepare or put in order. As a noun it means condition or state of health, as, 'in fine fettle'. It comes from Old English *fetel*, 'belt', alluding to the act of girding oneself up.

**Feudalism** (Medieval Latin *feudum*, 'fee'). The name given to an institutional growth in Europe from the time of the decay of the Roman Empire. It arose from the need of the individual and society to gain protection from attack, occasioned by internal disorder and external threat. In return for protection from some powerful individual, the dependant offered services or surrendered his land to an overlord, who then held it held subject to conditions. English feudalism is commonly held to begin with WILLIAM THE CONQUEROR, who acted on the principle that all land belonged to him. It was granted to the tenant-in-chief in return for homage and military service, and he in turn passed land on to subtenants in return for other services. Thus a pyramidal social structure developed in which every man was bound to an overlord and ultimately to the king.

**Feu de joie** (French, 'fire of joy'). A ceremonial discharge of musketry into the air by a line of soldiers on an occasion of rejoicing, with each man firing in turn down the line and back.

**Fever. Hay fever.** *See under* HAY.

**Milk fever.** *See under* MILK.

**Spring fever.** *See under* SPRING.

**Trench fever.** *See under* TRENCH.

**Yellow fever.** *See under* YELLOW.

**Feversham, Arden of.** *See under* ARDEN.

**Few. Few, The.** The RAF pilots of the BATTLE OF BRITAIN, so called from Winston Churchill's memorable tribute in the House of Commons on 20 August 1940: 'Never in the field of human conflict was so much owed by so many to so few.'

**Few and far between.** Scarce; at rare intervals.

**Have a few, To.** To be visibly drunk, as: 'He's had a few.'

**Not a few.** Several.

**FFI** (*Forces françaises de l'intérieur*, 'French Forces of the Interior'). The grouping together in February 1944 of the various forces fighting for liberation after the fall of France in 1940. It included partisans, FRANCS-TIREURS, MAQUIS and others and was subsequently merged with the army (November 1944).

**FFL** (*Forces françaises libres*, 'Free French Forces'). The forces organized by General de Gaulle (1890–1970) from June 1940, after the German occupation of France, to continue the struggle in cooperation with the Allies. They were later called the FIGHTING FRENCH.

**Fiacre.** A French cab or HACKNEY coach, so called from the hotel of ST FIACRE, Paris, where the first station of these coaches was established in about 1650.

**St Fiacre.** An Irish hermit, sometimes known as Fiachrach (*c*.610–670), who settled in France. His hermitage, near Meaux, became the monastery, and later the town, of Breuil (Saint-Fiacre-en-Brie). His day is 30 August, and he is the patron saint of gardeners and (punningly) coachmen.

**Fianna Fáil.** One of the two main political parties in Ireland, sometimes loosely called the Republican Party. It was constituted in 1926 under Éamon de Valera as a grouping of those opposed to the terms of the treaty with Great Britain that in 1921 brought the Irish Free State into existence. Its name derives from Irish *fianna*, 'band of warriors' and *Fáil*, the genitive form of *Fál*, an old name of Ireland, popularly understood to mean 'Destiny'. *See also* FENIANS; FINE GAEL.

**Fiasco** (Italian, 'flask'). A complete failure. In Italy an unpopular singer is sometimes greeted with the cry *Olà olà fiasco!* The word was used by the glassblowers of Venice to describe bad workmanship, and it may have some allusion to the bursting of a bottle. Various incidents in the Italian theatre have been put forward as the origin of this usage.

**Fiat** (Latin, 'let it be done'). A term for an official sanction or decree, or more generally for any act that brings something about.

**Fiat justitia ruat coelum** (Latin). 'Let justice be done though the heavens should fall.' *See also* PISO'S JUSTICE.

**Fico** (Italian, 'fig', from Latin *ficus*). A popular term in Shakespeare's England for an obscene gesture of contempt made by thrusting the thumb (representing the male sex organ) between the first and second fingers (forming the female) Figo is another form.

> 'Convey', the wise it call, 'Steal!' foh! a fico for the phrase.
>
> SHAKESPEARE: *The Merry Wives of Windsor*, I, iii (1600)

*See also* NOT TO CARE A FIG *under* CARE.

**Fiction, Science.** *See under* SCIENCE.

**Fiddle** (Old English *fithele*, probably from Medieval Latin *vitula*, from Latin *vitulari*, 'to celebrate'). The word *fithele* occurs in Layamon's *Brut* (12th century), and Chaucer refers to the *fidel* in the *Canterbury Tales* (*c*.1387). A stringed instrument of the violin type or a colloquial word, sometimes used disparagingly, for the violin generally.

**Fiddle, To.** To manipulate accounts or the like in a dishonest way in order to gain some advantage or to cover up a deficiency. To be 'on the fiddle' is to be involved in an illegal operation.

**Fiddle about** or **around, To.** To mess about; to waste time.

**Fiddle-de-dee!** An exclamation signifying that what has been said is nonsense.

**Fiddle-faddle.** To busy oneself with nothing; to trifle; to talk nonsense.

> Ye may as easily
> Outrun a cloud, driven by a northern blast,
> As fiddle-faddle so.
>
> JOHN FORD: *The Broken Heart*, I, iii (1633)

**Fiddler's Green.** The happy land imagined by sailors where there is perpetual mirth, a fiddle that never stops playing for dancers who never tire, plenty of GROG and unlimited tobacco.

**Fiddlesticks!** Much the same as FIDDLE-DE-DEE!, i.e. nonsense, rubbish.

**Fiddle while Rome burns, To.** To trifle during an emergency or crisis. An allusion to NERO's reputed behaviour during the burning of ROME in AD 64, when it is said that he sang to his lyre and enjoyed the spectacle from the top of a high tower.

**As fit as a fiddle.** *See under* AS.

**Cat and Fiddle.** *See under* CAT.

**Devil rides on a fiddlestick, The.** *See under* DEVIL.

**Face as long as a fiddle, A.** *See under* FACE.

**First fiddle.** *See under* FIRST.

**Play second fiddle, To.** *See under* PLAY.

**Second fiddle.** *See under* SECOND.

**Fidei Defensor.** *See* DEFENDER OF THE FAITH.

**Fidelity. High fidelity.** *See under* HIGH.

**Horn of fidelity.** *See under* HORN.

**Mantle of fidelity.** *See under* MANTLE.

**Fiduciary issue.** That part of a note issue that is not backed by gold, although it may be backed by government securities. If there is no such backing for the paper currency as a whole, the whole issue is fiduciary. Fiduciary means that which is held or given in trust (Latin *fiducia*).

**Fidus Achates.** A faithful companion; a bosom friend. Achates (in Virgil's *Aeneid* (1st century BC)) was the chosen comrade of AENEAS.

**Field.** In huntsman's language the field means all the riders. In horse-racing it means all the horses in any one race. In military parlance it is the place of battle, the battle itself or the place of campaign, and to take to the field means to make the opening moves in a military campaign. In HERALDRY it means the entire surface of the shield.

**Field day.** A military term for a day when troops have manoeuvres or exercises. Generally, a field day is a day or time of exciting activity and success. In the US Navy it is a day devoted to cleaning ship and preparing for inspection.

**Field events.** In athletics, sports other than races, such as shot-putting, jumping and discus-throwing.

**Field glasses.** Binoculars, as used when in the field.

**Field gun.** A gun specially designed to support front-line troops.

**Field marshal.** In the British army this title, the highest rank, is conferred on generals who have rendered conspicuous services. The title was first used in England in 1736. A field marshal remains on the active list (on half pay) for life, as does an admiral of the fleet and an air marshal, the equivalent ranks.

**Field notes.** Notes by a person engaged in FIELD WORK.

**Field of Aaru.** In ancient Egyptian religion this was the Paradise that Egyptians believed awaited them after death, so corresponding roughly with the Elysian Fields of Greek mythology. The Field of Aaru was a garden in the west and was near water, so that it was 'blessed with breezes'.

**Field of Blood, The.** ACELDAMA, the piece of ground purchased with the blood-money of Jesus. The battlefield of CANNAE, where Hannibal defeated the Romans, 216 BC, is also so called.

**Field officer.** In the British army, an officer above the rank of captain and below that of general.

**Field of fire.** The area that a weapon or group of weapons can cover, uninterrupted by contours, woods or other obstructions.

**Field of force.** A term used in physics to denote the range within which a force, such as magnetism, is effective.

**Field of honour.** The place where a battle or duel is fought.

**Field of the Cloth of Gold, The.** The plain in Picardy between Guines and Ardres where Henry VIII met Francis I of France in June 1520. Francis hoped for English support against the emperor, Charles V. A temporary palace was erected, lavish and spectacular arrangements were made for jousting, dancing and banqueting, and Henry was accompanied by a magnificent retinue. Henry, however, later met the emperor with whom he effected a treaty.

**Field of the Forty Footsteps** or **Brothers' Steps, The.** The land at the back of the British

Museum, once called Southampton Fields, near the extreme northeast of the present Montague Street. The tradition is that at the time of the Duke of MONMOUTH'S REBELLION (1685), two brothers fought each other here over a girl with whom they were both in love until both were killed, and for several years 40 of their footprints remained on the field. No grass would grow there nor upon the bank where the young woman sat to watch the fight. The site was built over in about 1800.

**Field of vision** or **view.** The space over which things can be seen, or the space or range within which objects are visible when looking through an instrument such as a telescope, microscope, viewfinder etc.

**Fieldpiece.** A former name for a FIELD GUN.

**Field studies.** Research carried out in the field. *See also* FIELD WORK.

**Field trip.** A visit by students or researchers to a site where they can carry out FIELD WORK.

**Field work.** Work such as archaeological research carried out on an actual site, as distinct from work done in a classroom or laboratory.

> Here we shall be in a field of research where the traditional methods of searching in archives are reinforced by the aerial survey and by field-work.
>
> MAURICE BERESFORD: *The Lost Villages of England*, Introduction (1954)

**Field works.** Defensive or protective works, or temporary fortifications, made by an army to strengthen its positions.

**Back the field, To.** *See under* BACK.

**Cold Bath Fields.** *See under* COLD.

**Hold** or **keep the field, To.** *See under* HOLD.

**Master of the field.** *See under* MASTER.

**Play the field, To.** *See under* PLAY.

**Potter's field.** *See under* POTTER.

**Three-field system.** *See under* THREE.

**Win the field, To.** *See under* WIN.

**Fierabras, Sir.** The son of BALAN, king of Spain. For height of stature, breadth of shoulder and hardness of muscle, he knew no equal, but his pride was laid low by OLIVER. He became a Christian, was accepted by CHARLEMAGNE as a PALADIN and ended his days in an odour of sanctity. His name, which means 'Iron-arm', is the same as the French *Bras-de-Fer*. He is also known in English as Sir Ferumbras. *See also* ISUMBRAS.

**Fieri facias** (Latin, 'cause it to be done'). A writ of execution to a sheriff to levy from the property of a debtor the sum according to the judgement given, together with the interest and any costs. The phrase is often abbreviated to 'fi fa'. The term was also punningly used in the 16th century in connection with red noses and 'fiery faces' through drink. The sheriff's return to the writ that the stated sum has been levied is known as *fieri feci*, 'I have caused it to be done.'

**Fiery cross, The.** An ancient signal in the Scottish Highlands when a chieftain wished to summon his clan in an emergency. It was symbolic of fire and the sword and consisted of a light wooden cross, the ends of which were dipped in the blood of a goat slain for the purpose. It was carried from settlement to settlement by swift runners. Disobedience to the summons implied infamy, hence the alternative name of Cross of Shame. Sir Walter Scott's *The Lady of the Lake* (iii (1810)), contains a graphic account of the custom.

When the KU KLUX KLAN arose after the American Civil War (1861–5) it adopted this symbol.

**Fifi.** A stock name for a cute and worldly Frenchwoman, so designated in various plays, stories and doubtful jokes. Guy de Maupassant's story *Mademoiselle Fifi* (1882) takes its title from the nickname of its main character, an effeminate Prussian officer who is killed by a woman for insulting the French flag.

**Fifteen, The.** The Jacobite rebellion of 1715, when James Edward Stewart, the OLD PRETENDER, (1688–1766) made an unsuccessful attempt to gain the throne. The Earl of Mar's Scottish forces were defeated at Sheriffmuir and the English JACOBITES under Squire Foster were beaten at Preston.

**Fifteen Os** or **Os of St Bridget, The.** Fifteen meditations on the Passion composed by St Bridget. Each begins with 'O Jesu' or a similar invocation.

**Fifteen points of a good horse, The.** *See under* HORSE.

**Fifth. Fifth-Amendment Communist.** In the United States anyone who refused to answer the charge of communist activities by invoking the Fifth Amendment to the Constitution (1791), which states that no person 'shall be compelled in any criminal case to be a witness against himself'.

**Fifth Avenue.** A New York street famed for its fashion, elegance and high society, and the legendary playground of the city's oldest and wealthiest families. It runs between Park Avenue and the AVENUE OF THE AMERICAS up the centre of Manhattan Island.

**Fifth column.** Traitors, those within a country who are working for the enemy, often by infiltrating into key positions and seeking to undermine the body politic from within. The origin of the phrase is attributed to General Mola, who, in the Spanish Civil War (1936–9), said that he had four columns encircling Madrid, and a fifth column working for him in the city.

**Fifth estate, The.** Jocularly applied to various

'authorities', such as the BBC, the trade unions, and so on, following on from the FOURTH ESTATE.

**Fifth-Monarchy Men.** Religious extremists of Cromwellian times, who maintained that the time had come for the rule of Christ and His Saints, the Fifth Monarchy, succeeding those of Assyria, Persia, Macedonia and Rome when the four monarchies described in the Book of Daniel give way to that set up by God. VENNER'S RISING of 1661 marked the end of their attempts to establish the Fifth Monarchy.

> And in the days of these kings shall the God of heaven set up a kingdom, which shall never be destroyed: and the kingdom shall not be left to other people, but it shall break in pieces and consume all these kingdoms, and it shall stand for ever.
> Daniel 2:44

**Fifth wheel.** Someone or something that is superfluous or unwanted. The reference is to the spare wheel carried on a four-wheel vehicle. In coaching days, the fifth wheel was a cumbersome object carried at the rear of the carriage, where it had to be unlashed and relashed whenever it was necessary to retrieve a piece of luggage from the storage space behind it.

**Fifty-four Forty or Fight.** The slogan of the Democratic party in the US presidential election campaign of 1844, which won the day for President Polk. It arose from the long-standing dispute between Britain and the USA over the northern boundary of Oregon. A convention of 1818 had provided for a ten-year joint occupation of the disputed area, and this was renewed in 1827 for an indefinite period. The question came to the forefront again in the 1840s with the growing popularity of the OREGON TRAIL, hence the appeal of the slogan. Nevertheless Polk and the Senate agreed to the British compromise proposal that the boundary between Canada and the USA be continued along the 49th parallel to the Pacific and not set at the more northerly latitude of 54° 40′.

**Fig.** Most phrases that include the word have reference to the fruit as being an object of trifling value, but in the phrase 'in full fig', meaning 'in full dress', the word is a variant of *feague*, itself from German *fegen*, 'to sweep'.

**Fig leaf.** The leaf of the fig tree was used by ADAM and EVE to cover their nakedness after the FALL. Hence its adoption in statues and paintings in times when 'modesty' was in fashion, notably in the Victorian period.

> And the eyes of them both were opened, and they knew that they were naked; and they sewed fig leaves together, and made themselves aprons.
> Genesis 3:7

**Fig Sunday.** An old local name for PALM SUNDAY. Figs were eaten on that day in commemoration of the blasting of the barren fig tree by Jesus (Mark 11:13–14). Many festivals still have their special dishes, such as the goose for MICHAELMAS DAY, pancakes for SHROVE TUESDAY, hot cross buns for GOOD FRIDAY etc.

**Fig tree.** It is said that JUDAS ISCARIOT hanged himself on a fig tree. *See also* ELDER TREE; JUDAS TREE.

**Not to care a fig.** *See under* CARE.

**Figaro.** A person of daring, cunning, roguery and intrigue. He is the central character in *Le Barbier de Séville* (1775) and *Le Mariage de Figaro* (1784) by Beaumarchais. There are several operas based on these dramas, such as Mozart's *Le Nozze di Figaro* (1786) and Paisiello's and Rossini's *Il Barbiere di Siviglia* (respectively 1782 and 1816). Figaro was invented by Beaumarchais, who may have based his name on *fils Caron*, 'son (of) Caron', this being his family name.

The character gave the name of the Parisian periodical, which appeared from 1826 to 1833, and of its successor which was first published in 1854. *Le Figaro* is one of the foremost French dailies to survive the Second World War.

**Fight. Fighting Fifth, The.** *See under* REGIMENTAL AND DIVISIONAL NICKNAMES.

**Fighting fit.** Fit enough to fit; at the peak of one's physical form.

**Fighting French, The** (French, *La France Combattante*). All those French people at home and abroad who combined with the Allied nations in their war against the AXIS powers after the fall of France (in June 1940). General de Gaulle and others escaped to England, and he formed them into the FFL (Free French) with the CROSS OF LORRAINE for their emblem. The name was later changed to the Fighting French (14 July 1942). One of their most noted feats was the march of General Leclerc's column across the Sahara, from Lake Chad, to join the British 8th Army in Libya. These men were honoured by being the first formation to enter Paris on 23 August 1944. The Fighting French supported the Allies in Africa, Italy and elsewhere and together with the FFI made a valuable contribution to the liberation of France.

**Fighting fund.** Money raised to support a campaign.

**Fighting Prelate, The.** Henry Spenser, or Despenser, bishop of Norwich (1370–1406), who put down the insurgents of Norfolk and Suffolk during the PEASANTS' REVOLT of 1381. At North Walsham he burned down the church in which they took refuge. He later fought in Flanders and in France for Pope Urban VI against the antipope's followers, and was denounced by Wyclif as a fighting bishop.

**Fighting words.** Belligerent words, as of one looking for a fight.

**Fight like Kilkenny cats, To.** To fight till both sides have lost or are destroyed. The story is that during the Irish rebellion of 1798 Kilkenny was garrisoned by a troop of Hessian soldiers, who amused themselves by tying two cats together by their tails and throwing them across a clothes-line to fight. When an officer approached to stop the 'sport', a trooper cut the two tails with a sword and the two cats fled. When asked to explain the two bloody tails, the trooper explained that two cats had been fighting and devoured each other all but the tails.

**Fight shy of, To.** To avoid; to resist being brought into conflict.

**Fight tooth and nail, To.** To fight with all one's might, as though biting and scratching.

**Fight with the gloves off, To.** To dispute mercilessly with NO HOLDS BARRED; not 'pulling one's punches'. *See also* WITH THE GLOVES OFF.

**Fight with the gloves on, To.** Figuratively, to spar or dispute without open animosity; to observe the courtesies and to show some consideration for one's opponent.

**Acre-fight.** *See under* ACRE.

**Bun fight.** *See under* BUN.

**Free fight.** *See under* FREE.

**Hero of the hundred fights.** *See under* HERO.

**He that fights and runs away may live to fight another day.** An old saying found in many languages. When Demosthenes was reproached for fleeing from Philip of Macedon at Chaeronea, he replied: 'A man that runs away may fight again.' The same sentiment is expressed in Samuel Butler's *Hudibras*, III, iii (1680):

> For those that fly may fight again
> Which he can never do that's slain.

**Spoiling for a fight, To be.** *See under* SPOIL.

**Three-cornered fight.** *See under* THREE.

**Figo.** *See* FICO.

**Figure** (Latin *figura*, 'shape', from *fingere*, 'to mould'). The word is not etymologically connected with the English 'finger', even though fingers are used for moulding and were used as a primitive method of calculating.

**Figurehead.** A carved figure on the head or bows of a sailing ship, which has ornamental value but is of no practical use. Hence, a nominal leader who plays no real part, but often one whose social or other position inspires confidence. *See also* CUTTY SARK.

**Figure of eight.** An outline of the figure 8, especially as traced in the ice by a skater or flown by an aircraft in the air. The figure can be repeated endlessly without a break. Hence the adoption of a horizontal figure of eight (∞) as the symbol for infinity in mathematics.

**Figure of fun, A.** A person of curious appearance or manner, whether through untidiness, eccentricity or some other quirk, and who is therefore laughed at or ridiculed.

**Figure of speech, A.** An established form of abnormal expression designed to produce a special effect, such as HYPERBOLE, METAPHOR, METATHESIS etc.

**Figure skating.** Skating in which the skater traces the outlines of particular figures or patterns on the ice.

**Cut a pretty or a sorry figure, To.** *See under* CUT.

**Father-figure.** *See under* FATHER.

**In round figures.** *See under* ROUND.

**Lay figures.** *See under* LAY.

**Roman figures.** *See under* NUMERALS.

**Filch.** To steal or purloin. A piece of 16th-century thieves' slang of uncertain origin.

> With cunning hast thou filched my daughter's heart.
> SHAKESPEARE: *A Midsummer Night's Dream*, I, i (1595)

**File** (French *file*, 'row').

**Indian file.** *See under* INDIAN.

**In single file.** *See under* SINGLE.

**Rank and file.** *See under* RANK.

**Viper and file.** *See under* VIPER.

**Filibuster** (Spanish *filibustero*, from French *flibustier*, itself probably from Dutch *vrijbuiter*, 'pirate', literally 'one plundering freely'). The earlier form of the word, flibuster, was applied to the pirates plundering in West Indian waters in the 17th century. Filibuster was later used of certain 19th-century bands organized from the United States, in defiance of international law, to invade and revolutionize certain Spanish-American territories. The most notable of these filibusters were those led by Narcisco Lopez against Cuba (1850–51) and William Walker against Sonora (1853–4). *See also* FREEBOOTER.

**Filibuster, To.** To obstruct legislation by means of delaying tactics. The word was first used in this sense in the USA in 1841. Such tactics were notably employed by the Irish Nationalists under Parnell. In July 1877 the House of Commons sat for 26 hours. *See also* CLOSURE.

**Filioque controversy.** An argument concerning the Procession of the Holy Spirit, which long disturbed the Eastern and Western Churches and which still forms one of the principal barriers between them. The point was: Did the HOLY GHOST proceed from the Father and the Son (Latin *Filio-que*), or from the Father only? The argument is basically this: If the Son is one with the Father, whatever proceeds from the Father must proceed from the Son also. The filioque was first introduced by the Western Church at the Council of Toledo in 589 and was added to the NICENE CREED in the 11th century.

**Fill. Fill-dyke.** The month of FEBRUARY, when rain and melting snow fill the ditches to overflowing.

February fill dyke, be it black or be it white;
But if it be white it's the better to like.
Old proverb

**Fill someone in, To.** To provide them with information. To fill someone in is also to beat them up. The expression probably derives from the earlier low sense of making a woman pregnant.

**Fill the bill, To.** To be suitable; to be right for the purpose. The reference is perhaps to the size of lettering used for the name of an actor on a theatrical poster or bill. If one actor was absent, the name of another would replace him and occupy the same space.

**Back and fill, To.** *See under* BACK.

**Fille de joie** (French, 'girl of pleasure'). A prostitute.

**Final, Cup.** *See under* CUP.

**Financial year.** In the United Kingdom the year ending 31 March. The taxation year, however, ends on 5 April as a consequence of the transition to the GREGORIAN CALENDAR. Until 1752, the year began on 25 March and the transition from the JULIAN CALENDAR was effected by omitting eleven days from the September of that year. Taxpayers objected to paying on a year thus shortened and so the taxation was correspondingly adjusted to end on 5 April.

**Find. Find a mare's nest, To.** To make what at first seems to be a great discovery but that proves to be nothing at all.

**Finders keepers.** A comment made when one has accidentally found something, implying that it is now the finder's property. This old saying is based on very dubious legal grounds. It is sometimes extended as 'losers weepers', meaning that the person who did not make the find has reason to be regretful.

**Find fault, To.** To blame; to express disapprobation.

**Find it in one's heart, To.** To be willing. The phrase is mostly found in the negative, as: 'I couldn't find it in my heart to punish him.'

**Find** or **get one's bearings, To.** To establish one's position with regard to surrounding objects.

**Find one's feet, To.** To become accustomed to one's situation, as in a new job.

**Find one's level, To.** To find one's appropriate or most suitable position socially or professionally.

**Find one's tongue, To.** To speak after recovery from initial shyness.

**Find one's way, To.** To manage to reach a place. Also to turn up, to be discovered, as: 'How did that find its way into your pocket?'

**Find the lady.** The THREE-CARD TRICK.

**Findabair.** In Irish legend the beautiful daughter of Queen MAEVE of Connacht. She was promised in marriage to the man who would challenge CUCHULAIN in the WAR OF THE BROWN BULL and died after her lover, Fraoch, was slain in battle by Cuchulain.

**Fin de siècle** (French, 'end of century'). A phrase implying decadence, with particular reference to the end of the 19th century.

**Fine. Fine arts, The.** Those arts that depend on creative imagination and the quest for the expression of beauty, as music, painting, poetry, sculpture and architecture, as opposed to the applied arts, which are those that are practised primarily for their utility, such as weaving, metalwork etc.

**Fine feathers make fine birds.** An expression said of an overdressed person who does not really match up to his or her clothes.

**Fine-tooth comb.** A comb with narrow, close-set teeth. To go over something with a fine-tooth comb is to search it thoroughly.

**Fine** or **fair words butter no parsnips.** Mere words are not enough to rectify the situation.

**Cut it fine, To.** *See under* CUT.

**Get something down to a fine art, To.** *See under* GET.

**In fine.** In short; briefly. This 'fine' comes from French *fin*, 'end', and is the equivalent of French *enfin*.

**Not to put too fine a point on it.** Not to be over delicate in stating it. The expression, often a prelude to a blunt though truthful remark, alludes to the sharp end of a tool or weapon.

**One of these fine days.** *See under* ONE.

**Their finest hour.** The famous phrase from Winston Churchill's speech (18 June 1940) given at the time when the collapse of France was imminent and the BATTLE OF BRITAIN about to begin.

Let us therefore brace ourselves to our duty, and so bear ourselves that, if the British Commonwealth and its Empire lasts for a thousand years, men will still say, 'This was their finest hour.'

**Fine Gael.** One of the two main political parties of Ireland, together with FIANNA FÁIL, its name being Irish for 'tribe of Gaels'. It arose in 1933 from William Thomas Cosgrave's Cumann na nGaedheal (Society of Gaels), whose members had supported the terms of the Anglo-Irish treaty of 1921 that brought the Irish Free State into existence. Little now separates it politically from Fianna Fáil, of which it is even so a distinctive rival.

**Fingal.** The great Gaelic legendary hero, father of OSSIAN and identified with FINN, who according to James Macpherson was the original author of the long epic poem *Fingal* (1762), which narrates the hero's adventures. His name represents Irish *Fhionghall*, 'white stranger', as an Irish name for a Norse settler in Ireland. 'White' here means 'fair-haired', as many Scandinavians are.

**Fingal's Cave.** The basaltic cavern on Staffa, said to have been a home of FINGAL. It is the name given to Mendelssohn's *Hebrides* Overture (1830).

**Finger.** The old names for the five fingers are:

(1) *Thūma* (Old English), the thumb.
(2) *Towcher* (Middle English, 'toucher'), foreman or pointer. This was called the *scite-finger* ('shooting finger') by the Anglo-Saxons. It is now usually known as the first finger or forefinger, or the index finger because it is used for pointing.
(3) Long-man or long-finger.
(4) Lec-man or ring-finger. The former means the 'medical finger' (literally 'leech finger') and the latter is the Roman *digitus annularis*, called by the Anglo-Saxons gold-finger. This finger was used as the ring finger (also annular finger) in the belief that a nerve ran through it to the heart. Hence the Greeks and Romans called it the medical finger, and used it for stirring mixtures under the notion that it would give instant warning to the heart if it came into contact with anything noxious. It is still a popular superstition that it is bad to rub ointment or scratch the skin with any other finger.
(5) Little man or little finger. The Anglo-Saxons called it the ear-finger, because it is the one used to poke inside the ear when it tickles or to worm out the wax. It is also known as the auricular finger.

The fingers each had their special significance in ALCHEMY, and Ben Jonson says:

The thumb, in chiromancy, we give to VENUS,
The fore-finger to JOVE; the midst to SATURN;
The ring to SOL; the least to MERCURY.
*The Alchemist*, I, ii (1610)

**Finger buffet.** A buffet meal at which food is served that can be picked up with the fingers, such as canapés or vol-au-vents. The food itself is known as finger food.

**Finger painting.** A method of painting using the fingers, hands or arms instead of a brush.

**Fingerprint.** An impression taken in ink of the whorls of lines on the finger. In no two persons are they alike, and they never change throughout life, hence their great value as a means of identifying criminals. From ancient times they were used for certifying documents by the Chinese and Japanese. Sir Francis Galton's *Finger Prints* (1892) and *Finger Print Directories* (1895) drew attention to their usefulness. Sir Edward Henry, Commissioner of the Metropolitan Police (1903–18), devised a widely adopted system for classifying impressions. The American Federal Bureau of Investigation uses his method. *See also* GENETIC FINGERPRINTING.

**Fingers crossed.** An allusion to the superstition that making the sign of the cross will avert bad luck.

**Finger someone or put the finger on someone, To.** To identify or inform on, especially to the police.

**Fingers were made before forks.** A saying used especially at mealtimes to imply that ceremony is unnecessary. Forks were not introduced into England until the early 17th century, before which fingers were used.

**Finger trouble.** A colloquial term for an error caused by operating a control wrongly or pressing a wrong key on an electronic instrument, such as a television or a computer.

**All fingers and thumbs.** *See under* ALL.

**At one's fingertips.** *See under* AT.

**Burn one's fingers, To.** *See under* BURN.

**Cross one's fingers, To.** *See under* CROSS.

**Dead men's fingers.** *See under* DEAD.

**Devil's fingers.** *See under* DEVIL.

**Five fingers.** *See under* FIVE.

**Genetic fingerprinting.** *See under* GENETIC.

**Get** or **pull one's finger out, To.** To get a move on or to make an effort, especially when one is slow or idle, or prevaricating. The allusion is to a male finger and a female anatomy. Perhaps because of the crude reference, the expression has undergone mock-pompous variants, such as 'to dedigitate'. The phrase startled some when it was used by Prince Philip, in a speech about British industry, on 17 October 1961: 'It is about time we pulled our fingers out!'

**Give someone the finger, To.** To make an obscene gesture at them with the middle finger as a sign of contempt. *See also* HARVEY SMITH.

**Green fingers.** *See under* GREEN.

**Have a finger in the pie, To.** To have a share in doing something, usually with the implication of officious interference or meddling.

**Have something at one's fingertips, To.** To be completely familiar with it and able to do it proficiently. The Latin proverb is, *Scire tanquam ungues digitosque suos*, 'to know [it] as well as one's fingers and nails'. The earlier equivalent was 'at one's fingers' ends'. The Latin tag is referred to by Shakespeare in *Love's Labour's Lost* (V, i (1594)):

*Costard*: Go to; thou has it *ad dunghill*, at the fingers' ends, as they say.
*Holofernes*: O! I smell false Latin; dunghill for *unguem*.

**Lay a finger on, To.** *See under* LAY.

**Lay** or **put one's finger on, To.** *See under* LAY.

**Let something slip through one's fingers, To.** *See under* LET.

**Light-fingered.** *See under* LIGHT.

**Medicinal finger.** *See under* MEDICINE.

**My little finger told me that.** *See under* LITTLE.

**Not to lift a finger.** *See under* LIFT.

**One's fingers itch to be at a person.** One longs to give someone a sound thrashing. *See also* ITCH.

**Physician finger.** *See under* PHYSICIAN.

**Put the finger on, To.** To inform against; to identify a potential victim.
**St Peter's fingers.** *See under* PETER.
**Snap one's fingers at, To.** *See under* SNAP.
**Stick to someone's fingers, To.** *See under* STICK.
**Twist** or **wrap someone round one's little finger, To.** *See under* TWIST.
**Wedding finger.** *See under* WED.
**Work one's fingers to the bone, To.** *See under* WORK.

**Finn.** A celebrated hero of Irish mythology, known also as Finn mac Cool (Fionn Mac Cumhail) or, in Scotland, as FINGAL. He may have originated as an aspect of the god Lugh, and folklore credits him with being a giant and building the GIANT'S CAUSEWAY. The Fenian or Ossianic Cycle tells the stories of his deeds, and his name has thus come to be associated in modern historic times with the FENIANS and with FIANNA FÁIL. *See also* OSSIAN.

**Finn, Huckleberry.** The likeable rogue of a boy who is the central character of Mark TWAIN's novels *The Adventures of Tom Sawyer* (1876) and *The Adventures of Huckleberry Finn* (1884). In the latter, Huck himself is the narrator, describing in a Mississippi dialect how he runs away from his guardian in the company of the escaped slave Nigger Jim and experiences a number of encounters and adventures as they travel down the river on a raft.

**Fionnuala.** In Irish legend, the daughter of King LIR, who was transformed into a swan and condemned to wander over the lakes and rivers until Christianity came to Ireland. *See also* BIRDS PROTECTED BY SUPERSTITIONS.

> Silent, O Moyle, be the roar of thy water,
> Break not, ye breezes, your chain of repose,
> While, murmuring mournfully, Lir's lonely daughter
> Tells to the night-star her tale of woes.
> THOMAS MOORE: *Irish Melodies*, 'The Song of Fionnuala' (1807)

**Firbolgs.** *See* MILESIANS.

**Fire** (Old English *fȳr*, related to Greek *pur*).
**Fire, To.** To discharge from employment suddenly and unexpectedly. An expression originating in the USA.
**Fire and brimstone.** Said of a fiery sermon that threatens transgressors with eternal damnation.

> Upon the wicked he shall rain snares, fire and brimstone, and an horrible tempest.
> Psalm 11:6

**Firearms.** Those weapons that originally required gunpowder, such as guns and pistols, as against swords, spears or bows, that did not.
**Fire away!** Go ahead, say what you have to say or ask what you want to ask. The allusion to the firing of a gun is obvious. You are loaded and cocked with something to say, so shoot.
**Fireball.** Literally, a meteor or a ball of flame, as from a nuclear explosion. Metaphorically, an energetic person.
**Firebrand.** An incendiary, a person who causes unrest or incites to rebellion, like a blazing brand that ignites everything it touches.
**Firebug.** An arsonist or person who deliberately sets fire to property; a FIRE RAISER.
**Firedog.** *See* ANDIRON.
**Firedrake** or **firedragon.** A fire-breathing dragon, superstitiously believed to be keeping guard over hidden treasures.
**Fire-eater.** A belligerent person. The allusion is to the conjuror who pretends to swallow fire.
**Fireman.** A word of opposite meanings. On the one hand, a member of a fire brigade, employed to put fires out. On the other, a person who keeps a fire going in a furnace or in a steam locomotive or steamship.
**Fire one's pistol in the air, To.** To desist deliberately from injuring an adversary. The phrase is often used of argument and refers to the old practice of duellists doing this when they wished to discharge a 'debt of honour' without incurring risks or wounding their opponent.

> A steady voice said 'Fire'; and the Duke raised his pistol. But Winchilsea's was still pointing at the ground. The Duke paused for an instant, fired, and hit his coat. Then Winchilsea fired in the air.
> PHILIP GUEDALLA: *The Duke*, ch viii (1931)

**Fire raiser.** An arsonist, especially a person who sets fire to property with the aim of collecting the insurance money.
**Fire ship.** A ship filled with combustibles sent against enemy vessels to set them on fire. English fire ships scattered the Spanish Armada in confusion when it was anchored off Calais in 1588.
**Fireside chats.** The name adopted by President F.D. Roosevelt for his broadcasts to the American people on topics of national interest and importance. They began in 1933 and became customary during his administration.
**Fire-walker.** A person who walks barefoot over hot stones or smouldering ashes, often as part of a ceremony. The act depends as much on strength of will as on the strategic placing of the feet, and wood ash in fact has a low 'specific heat' in any case. In modern times fire-walking has been adopted by some business companies as a test to foster leadership skills.

> After an intensive course of at least ten 12-hour days, participants are invited to a spectacular finale which involves fire-walking, breaking bricks with bare hands or group hypnosis.
> *The Times* (15 July 1998)

**Fire watcher.** The name given to those volunteers in Britain who watched for fires started by enemy air raids during the Second World War.

**Fireworks.** The devices that produce such spectacular effects are of ancient Chinese origin, and evolved in their present form from military rockets and explosive missiles. As such, they turned the 'thunder and lightning' of battle to a different end in order to mark a victory or a celebration of peace. The fireworks that form an essential part of BONFIRE Night more precisely represent the barrels of gunpowder prepared by Guy FAWKES and his fellows in the GUNPOWDER PLOT. The introduction of magnesium and aluminium in the 19th century added greatly to the brilliance of firework displays. The science of manufacturing fireworks and the art of displaying them is known as pyrotechnics.

**Fire worship.** A type of worship said to have been introduced into Persia by Phoedima, widow of Smerdis, and wife of Hystaspes. It is not the sun that is worshipped, but the god who is supposed to reside in it. However, the fire worshippers reverence the sun as the throne of the deity. *See also* PARSEES.

**Add fuel to the fire, To.** *See under* ADD.

**Baal fires.** *See under* BAAL.

**Baptism of fire.** *See under* BAPTISM.

**Breathe fire and brimstone, To.** *See under* BREATHE.

**Burned child dreads the fire, A.** *See under* BURN.

**Carry fire in one hand and water in the other, To.** *See under* CARRY.

**Dead fire.** *See under* DEAD.

**Draw someone's fire, To.** *See under* DRAW.

**Dropping fire.** *See under* DROP.

**Fat is in the fire, The.** *See under* FAT.

**Field of fire.** *See under* FIELD.

**Friendly fire.** *See under* FRIEND.

**Go through fire and water, To.** *See under* GO.

**Great Fire of London, The.** *See under* GREAT.

**Greek fire.** *See under* GREEK.

**Hang fire, To.** *See under* HANG.

**Heap coals of fire on, To.** *See under* HEAP.

**Helen's fire.** *See* CORPOSANT.

**Irons in the fire.** *See under* IRON.

**Kentish fire.** *See under* KENT.

**Line of fire.** *See under* LINE.

**No smoke without fire.** *See under* SMOKE.

**Ordeal of fire.** *See under* ORDEAL.

**Play with fire, To.** *See under* PLAY.

**Promethean fire.** *See under* PROMETHEUS.

**St Anthony's fire.** *See under* ANTHONY.

**St Elmo's fire** or **St Helen's fire.** *See* CORPOSANT.

**Set the Thames** or **world on fire, To.** *See under* SET.

**We do not fire first, gentlemen.** According to tradition, this very chivalrous reply was made to Lord Charles Hay (commanding the Guards) at the opening of the Battle of Fontenoy (1745) by the French Comte d'Auteroche after Hay had invited the French commander to order his men to fire. The story is told by the historian Espagnac and by VOLTAIRE, but it is not borne out by the description of the battle written shortly after the conflict by Lord Charles to his father, the Marquess of Tweeddale.

**Where's the fire?** *See under* WHERE.

**First. First aid.** Immediate medical attention, as in the case of an accident, before professional help arrives. The term originally translated German *Erste Hilfe*.

**First blood.** The first shedding of blood in a contest, especially boxing. Hence the first point or advantage scored in any challenge.

**First blow is half the battle, The.** Well begun is half done.

**First catch your hare.** This direction is generally attributed to Hannah GLASSE, dressmaker to the Prince of Wales, and author of *The Art of Cookery made Plain and Easy* (1747). Her actual directions are: 'Take your hare when it is cased.' To case is to skin, as in Shakespeare's *All's Well that Ends Well* (III, vi (1602)): 'We'll make you some sport with the fox ere we case him.' However, 'first catch your hare' already existed as a phrase and is recorded in the early 14th century.

> Et vulgariter dicitur quod primo oportet cervum capere, et postea, cum captus fuerit, illum excoriare. (And it is commonly said that you must first catch your deer, and afterwards, when it is caught, skin it.)
>
> HENRY DE BRACTON: *De legibus et consuetudinibus Angliae*, IV, xxi (*c*.1300)

**First cause.** A cause that does not depend on any other; the Creator of the universe.

**First come, first served.** Promptness reaps its own reward; the EARLY BIRD CATCHES THE WORM.

**First-day cover.** In philatelic parlance, an envelope ('cover') bearing stamps postmarked with the date on which they are first issued.

**First fiddle.** The leading or most distinguished of the company. The allusion is to the first violin, who leads the orchestra.

**First Fleet.** The first expedition of 11 convict ships under Captain Arthur Phillip, bringing convicts to Australia in 1788. The second fleet arrived in 1790. To have been a first fleeter became a matter of pride. *See also* FIRST FOUR SHIPS.

**First floor.** In England the first floor is that immediately above the ground floor; in America and certain European countries it is the ground floor.

**First foot** or **first footer.** The first visitor at a house after midnight on New Year's Eve. In Scotland and the north of England the custom of first footing is still popular.

**First Four Ships.** The earliest European settlers' ships that arrived in Canterbury Province,

New Zealand, in 1840. The founders of Canterbury are said to have come with the First Four Ships. *See also* FIRST FLEET.

**First fruits.** The first profitable results of labour. In husbandry the first corn that is cut at harvest, which by the ancient Hebrews was offered to JEHOVAH. Such offerings became customary in the early Christian church. ANNATES were also called first fruits. The word is used figuratively as well in such expressions as 'the first fruits of sin', 'the first fruits of repentance'.

**First Gentleman of Europe, The.** A nickname given to GEORGE IV, but W.M. Thackeray says in *The Four Georges* (1860): 'We can tell of better gentlemen.'

**First Grenadier of the Republic, The.** A title given by NAPOLEON BONAPARTE to La Tour d'Auvergne (1743–1800), a man of extraordinary courage and self-effacement. He refused all promotion beyond that of captain, as well as this title.

**First Lady.** In the United States the honorary title of the wife of the President or of a state governor.

> The nation's first professional first lady [Hillary Clinton] proved that she preferred to take the heat on Capitol Hill rather than in the kitchen.
>
> *Britannica Book of the Year* (1994)

**First light.** In the armed forces 'first light' denotes the earliest time (roughly dawn) at which light is sufficient for the movement of ships or for military operations to begin. Similarly last light is the latest time when such movements can take place. The expression was current in the Second World War.

**First movable, The.** *See* PRIMUM MOBILE.

**First name.** A forename or Christian name.

**First nighter.** One who makes a practice of attending opening performances of plays.

**First offender.** A person convicted of a criminal offence for the first time who is usually treated more leniently than a seasoned offender is likely to be.

**First past the post.** Said of a voting system in which a candidate is elected by means of a simple majority. The opposite is proportional representation, when voters number the candidates in order of preference, and a candidate wins when he or she has the minimum number of 'number one' votes needed to be elected. British parliamentary elections are run on the first-past-the-post system. The allusion is to horse-racing, in which the horse that reaches the winning post first is the one that wins. The expression is redolent of British FAIR PLAY.

**First post.** The first of two bugle calls giving the order to retire for the night. The second is the better known LAST POST.

**First refusal.** An agreement with a prospective buyer that the subject of the sale will not be sold to anyone else unless he or she refuses the offer.

**First school.** A school for young children from age five to age nine.

**First strike.** An aggressive atack on an enemy with nuclear weapons before the enemy has the chane to use them.

**First string.** The top player of a team in a one-to-one sport such as squash.

**First thing.** Before anything else; very early in the morning.

**First thing, The.** Anything at all. The phrase is normally used negatively, as: 'He doesn't know the first thing about gardening.'

**First things first.** Things must be done in an order of priority.

**At first blush.** *See under* AT.

**At first hand.** *See under* AT.

**At first sight.** *See under* AT.

**City of Firsts, The.** *See under* CITY.

**Diamond of the first water, A.** *See under* DIAMOND.

**Double first.** *See under* DOUBLE.

**From first to last.** Continuously, all the time, throughout.

**Fish.** The fish was used as a symbol of Christ by the early Christians on account of the fish mentioned in the FEEDING OF THE FIVE THOUSAND. Moreover, the letters of the Greek word for fish, *ikhthus* (ICHTHYS), formed an acronym of the initial letters of the words Jesus Christ, Son of God, Saviour.

**Fish day.** In France known as *jour maigre* ('lean day'), a day when Roman Catholics and others used to abstain from meat and customarily eat fish. In the ROMAN CATHOLIC CHURCH there was a general law of abstinence on all Fridays (unless any were feast-days), but the church now urges the faithful to practise this or some other form of self-denial voluntarily. *See also* EAT NO FISH.

**Fisher King.** In the legends of the HOLY GRAIL, the uncle of Sir PERCEVAL.

**Fisherman's ring.** A seal-ring with which the pope is invested at his election, bearing the device of St PETER fishing from a boat. It is used for sealing papal briefs, and is officially broken at the pope's death by the Chamberlain of the Roman Church.

**Fish for compliments, To.** To try to obtain praise, usually by putting leading questions.

**Fish in troubled waters, To.** To try to take advantage of confusion or disorder. Many anglers believe that fish bite better when the water is turbulent.

**Fish out of water, A.** A person who is in an unusual or unwelcome environment and who thus feels ill at ease or awkward. A fish out the water cannot swim.

**Fish royal.** Sturgeon and whales, dolphins and porpoises (although the latter are not fish). If any are caught within 3 miles (5km) of the coast of the United Kingdom, they are the property of the crown.

**Fishwife.** A woman who sells fish in a fish market or who hawks fish. Fishwives are renowned for their flow of invective, hence the term is sometimes applied to a vulgar, scolding female.

**Fishy.** Dubious; suspicious. The allusion may be to the concept 'slippery as a fish', or to food that tastes or smells of fish when it should not.

**Cold fish.** *See under* COLD.

**Cry stinking fish, To.** *See under* CRY.

**Drink like a fish, To.** *See under* DRINK.

**Eat no fish, To.** *See under* EAT.

**Feed the fishes, To.** *See under* FEED.

**Have other fish to fry, To.** *See under* OTHER.

**Hunting, shooting and fishing.** *See under* HUNT.

**Kettle of fish. A.** *See under* KETTLE.

**Neither fish, flesh nor fowl** or **neither fish, flesh nor good red herring.** *See under* NEITHER.

**Pilot fish.** *See under* PILOT.

**Queer fish, A.** *See under* QUEER.

**Ring of the Fisherman.** *See* FISHERMAN'S RING.

**St Peter's fish.** The JOHN DORY.

**Tin fish.** *See under* TIN.

**Fist. Hand over fist.** *See under* HAND.

**Iron fist in the velvet glove, The.** *See under* IRON.

**Mailed fist, The.** *See under* MAIL.

**Fit. As fit as a fiddle.** *See under* AS.

**Fighting fit.** *See under* FIGHT.

**See fit to, To.** *See under* SEE.

**Fitz.** The Norman form of modern French *fils*, 'son'. Hence names such as Fitzgerald, Fitzherbert, Fitzwilliam etc. It is sometimes assumed by the illegitimate or morganatic children of royalty, as Fitzclarence or Fitzroy, the latter meaning 'son of the king'. Henry Fitzroy, Duke of Grafton (1663–90), for example, was the illegitimate son of Charles II and Barbara Villiers, Duchess of Cleveland (1641–1704).

**Fitzrovia.** A region of London north of Oxford Street and west of Tottenham Court Road, so called after Fitzroy Square there. The name became associated in the 1930s with impecunious artists and writers and gained a somewhat dubious reputation.

> After leaving school he emigrated into what he calls Fitzrovia – a world of outsiders, down-and-outs, drunks, sensualists, homosexuals and eccentrics.
>
> *Times Literary Supplement* (10 January 1958)

**Fitzwilliam Museum.** A famous museum at Cambridge, so called from the 7th and last Viscount Fitzwilliam (1745–1816), who on his death left £100,000, with books, paintings and so on, to form the nucleus of a museum for the benefit of the university. The present building was begun in 1837 and has had several extensions since.

**Five.** The pentad, one of the mystic numbers, being the sum of 2 and 3, the first even and first odd compound. Unity is God alone, i.e. without creation. Two is diversity, and three (being 1 and 2) is the compound of unity and diversity, or the two principles in operation since creation, and representing all the powers of nature.

**Five Alls, The.** *See under* PUBLIC HOUSE SIGNS.

**Five Articles of Perth, The.** The Articles (1618) were imposed on the CHURCH OF SCOTLAND by James VI and I, enjoining kneeling at communion, the observance of CHRISTMAS, GOOD FRIDAY, EASTER and PENTECOST, confirmation, communion for the dying and early baptism of infants. They were ratified by the Scottish Parliament, 4 August 1621, a day called BLACK SATURDAY, and condemned by the General Assembly at Glasgow in 1638.

**Five Boroughs, The.** In English history the Danish confederation of Derby, Leicester, Lincoln, Nottingham and Stamford in the 9th and 10th centuries. The first four of these became county capitals, while Stamford retained a strategic position at the meeting point of three counties: Lincolnshire, Northamptonshire and Rutland. (In the county boundary changes of 1974, the northern part of Northamptonshire, the Soke of Peterborough, passed to Cambridgeshire, and Rutland passed to Leicestershire, so that Stamford stood at the crossroads of four counties, the only town in England to do so.)

**Five-finger exercise.** An exercise on the piano involving all five fingers. Hence generally an easy task, since such piano exercises are for beginners.

**Five fingers.** A fisherman's name for the starfish.

**Five joyful mysteries, The.** The first chaplet of the ROSARY, made up of the ANNUNCIATION, the Visitation, the Nativity of Christ, the Presentation of Christ in the Temple and the Finding of the Child Jesus in the Temple.

**Five Members, The.** Pym, Hampden, Haselrig, Holles and Strode, the five members of the LONG PARLIAMENT whom Charles I attempted to arrest in 1642.

**Five Mile Act, The.** An Act passed in 1665 (repealed in 1812), the last act of the CLARENDON CODE prohibiting Nonconformist clergy from coming within 5 miles (8km) of any corporate town or within that distance of the place where they had formerly ministered.

**Five Nations, The.** A description applied by Rudyard Kipling to the British Empire: the Old

Country, Canada, Australia, South Africa and India.

In American history the term refers to the five confederated Native American tribes inhabiting the present State of New York, i.e. the Mohawks, Oneidas, Onondagas, Cayugas and Senecas, also known as the IROQUOIS League. HIAWATHA is traditionally regarded as the Onondaga founder of this league, to which the Tuscarora were admitted in 1722, so that the league became known to the English as the Six Nations.

**Five o'clock shadow.** The beginnings of a new beard on a man's clean-shaven face, visible at about this time of day.

**Five Points of Calvinism, The.** *See* CALVINISM.

**Five Ps, The.** William Oxberry (1784–1824) was so called, because he was printer, poet, publisher, publican and player.

**Five sacraments, The.** These are Confirmation, Penance, Orders, Matrimony and EXTREME UNCTION. These are not counted 'Sacraments of the Gospel'. (*See* Book of Common Prayer, Articles of Religion, xxv.)

**Five senses, The.** Hearing, sight, smell, taste and touch. Hence sixth sense as a term for intuition or clairvoyance.

**Five-star.** Of the highest standard or class. The reference is to the system used to grade hotels. Sometimes crowns are substituted for stars, especially for hotels, but otherwise the system can be adopted for any type of rating. In some gradings the highest is four-star.

**Five Towns, The.** Towns in the Potteries that Arnold Bennett (1867–1931) used as the scene of the best known of his novels and stories. They are Tunstall, Burslem, Hanley, Stoke-on-Trent, Longton and Fenton. These actually number six, but for artistic purposes Bennett called them five, giving them the respective fictional names of Turnhill, Bursley, Hanbridge, Knype and Longshaw. All are now part of Stoke-on-Trent. *See also* ETRURIA.

**Five-year plan.** In the former USSR one of a series of plans for developing the whole of the nation's economy in a co-ordinated effort by a five-year programme. The first five-year plan was launched by Stalin in 1929 with the aim of making the Soviet Union self-supporting. Further five-year plans followed and the example was copied by some other countries.

**Big Five.** *See under* BIG.

**Bunch of fives.** *See under* BUNCH.

**Famous Five.** *See under* FAMOUS.

**Feeding of the Five Thousand, The.** *See under* FEED

**Fix, A.** In modern slang, and of American origin, a shot of heroin or other narcotic drug.

**Fixed assets.** Business assets that are not used in trade and that are relatively permanent, such as plant, fittings and goodwill.

**Fixed odds.** The odds when predetermined at the start of a horse race, by contrast with the STARTING PRICE (*see under* START).

**Fixed oil.** A true oil, as a natural animal or vegetable oil that is non-volatile. Fixed oils thus differ from essential oils. The glycerides, such as linseed and walnut oils, are examples. Such oils make a permanent greasy stain on paper.

**Fixed star.** A star whose relative position to other stars is always the same, as distinguished from a planet, which shifts its relative position. Fixed stars were originally thought to be attached to an outer crystal sphere, and this was believed to explain their apparent lack of movement.

**Fix up, To.** To mend or repair; to arrange.

**In a fix.** In an awkward predicament.

**Obtain a fix, To.** *See under* OBTAIN.

**Fizz, Buck's.** *See under* BUCK.

**Flaccus.** HORACE (65–8 BC), the Roman poet, whose full name was Quintus Horatius Flaccus.

**Flag.** A word of uncertain origin. National flags are flown as the symbols of a state and are particularly important as a means of recognition of ships at sea. Merchant ships usually fly their flag or ensign at the stern, whereas warships fly their flag or jack at the bows and their ensign at the stern. Flags are also used as personal banners or standards, especially by royalty and high-ranking naval and military officers, by regiments, as house flags by companies, for signalling purposes and the like. The part of a flag that is nearest the mast is called the hoist, and the disc-shaped block at the top of the flagstaff is the truck. The fly is the end of the flag furthest from the staff. *See also* TRICOLOUR.

**Flag captain.** The captain commanding the vessel in which the ADMIRAL is flying his flag.

**Flag Day.** In the USA 14 June, the anniversary of the adoption of the STARS AND STRIPES in 1777. In Britain a flag day is any day on which small stickers (originally little paper flags) for wearing on the lapel are sold for the support of charities, good causes and the like.

**Flag down, To.** To stop someone, nowadays usually a motorist or taxi driver, from the practice of stopping a train or other vehicle by waving or displaying a flag. Formerly, trains that did not usually stop at little-used stations or halts did so if the appropriate flag was displayed. Such stations were known as flag stations or flag stops.

**Flag lieutenant.** An ADMIRAL'S aide-de-camp, colloquially known as 'Flags'.

**Flag of convenience, A.** A foreign flag under which a vessel is registered, usually to lessen taxation and manning costs. Liberia, Honduras and Panama are the most widely used flags of convenience, and Liberia has the largest merchant fleet in the world.

**Flag of distress, The.** When a ship's ensign is flown upside down it is a signal of distress.

**Flag officer.** An ADMIRAL, vice admiral or rear admiral who flies the flag appropriate to his rank. An admiral of the fleet flies a UNION JACK; an admiral a St GEORGE'S CROSS on a white ground, a vice admiral the same, with one red ball in the upper canton next to the staff, and a rear admiral a second red ball in the canton immediately below.

**Flagship.** A ship carrying the FLAG OFFICER. Figuratively, a flagship is something that a company or organization regards as its 'showpiece', such as a particular car model.

**Flags on church flagstaffs.** In the CHURCH OF ENGLAND the proper flag to be flown is that of St GEORGE, with the diocesan arms on a shield in the first quarter. Where this cannot be obtained, however, it is acceptable to fly a plain St George's flag.

**Black flag.** *See under* BLACK.
**Blue Flag.** *See under* BLUE.
**Break a flag, To.** *See under* BREAK.
**City of Five Flags, The.** *See under* CITY.
**Dip a flag, To.** *See under* DIP.
**Fly the flag at half-mast, To.** *See under* FLY.
**Green flag.** *See under* GREEN.
**Red flag.** *See under* RED.
**Show the flag, To.** *See under* SHOW.
**Strike the flag, To.** *See under* STRIKE.
**Trade follows the flag.** *See under* TRADE.
**White flag.** *See under* WHITE.
**Yellow flag.** *See under* YELLOW.

**Flagellants** (Latin *flagellum*, 'scourge'). A name given to those extremists who scourged themselves in public processions in medieval times, and in more recent times, as penance for the sins of the world. There was a particular outbreak in Italy in 1260 and again in 1348–9, at the time of the BLACK DEATH, when the movement spread over Europe. The church has never encouraged such practices.

**Flagellum Dei** (Latin, 'the scourge of God'). *See* SCOURGE OF GOD.

**Flamberge** or **Floberge** ('flame cutter'). The name of one of CHARLEMAGNE's swords, and also of RINALDO and Maugis.

**Flamboyant architecture.** The last phase of French GOTHIC ARCHITECTURE, named from Old French *flambe*, 'flame'. Characterized by flame-like tracery and elaboration of detail, it flourished from about 1460 until the 16th century.

**Flame.** A lover or sweetheart. An old flame is a former sweetheart.

**Flamers, The.** *See under* REGIMENTAL AND DIVISIONAL NICKNAMES.

**Flaming sword.** A sword with a wavy or flamboyant edge, used now only for state ceremonies. The Dukes of Burgundy carried such swords, and they were worn in Britain until the time of William III (1689–1702).

**Flaminian Way.** The great northern road, the Via Flaminia, of ancient Italy, constructed by Gaius Flaminius in 220 BC. It led from the Flaminian gate of Rome to Ariminum (Rimini).

**Flanders Mare, The.** So Henry VIII ungallantly called Anne of Cleves (1515–57), on riding down to Rochester to meet her. He married her as his fourth wife in January 1540 and divorced her six months later.

> The King found her so different from her picture ... that ... he swore they had brought him a Flanders mare.
>
> TOBIAS SMOLLETT: *A Complete History of England*, Vol vi (1759)

**Flannel.** Evasive or flattering talk; 'soft soap'. Flannel may have acquired this kind of connotation in the same way as BOMBAST and FUSTIAN.

**Flannelled fools.** Cricketers. This term, used derisively or humorously, is taken from Rudyard Kipling:

> Then ye returned to your trinkets; then ye contented your souls
> With the flannelled fools at the wicket or the muddied oafs at the goals.
>
> 'The Islanders' (1903)

*See also* MUDDIED OAFS.

**Flap. Flapdoodle.** Foolish talk, nonsense.

**Flapjack.** A flat cake of batter baked on a griddle or in a shallow pan, so called from turning it by tossing it into the air.

> We'll have flesh for holidays, fish for fasting-days, and moreo'er puddings and flapjacks.
>
> SHAKESPEARE: *Pericles*, II, i (1608)

**In a flap.** In a state of anxious excitement, as birds flap and flutter when they are disturbed. A flap is thus the state itself. 'There's a flap on' is a military colloquialism meaning that there is an alert or state of special security.

**Flapper.** A term applied in the early years of the 20th century to a teenage girl, from her plaited pigtail tied at the end with a large bow. As she walked along, the pigtail flapped on her back. Subsequently her hair was 'put up' in a bun or other hairstyle. The term later became synonymous with the 'bright young things' of the 1920s and 1930s. It gained an added punning sense since it referred to a young woman who was 'flighty'.

**Flapper vote, The.** A contemptuous name for the vote granted to women of 21 by the Equal Franchise Act of 1928, sponsored by Baldwin's Conservative government.

**Flash.** Ostentatious or gaudy, as: a 'flash wedding', a 'flash hotel'.

**Flashback.** A scene in a film or novel set earlier

than the current action. It is a useful narrative device that allows a writer to be flexible in the temporal structure of the plot. Some films have a flashback within a flashback. In *The Barefoot Contessa* (1954) Humphrey Bogart, while attending Ava Gardner's funeral (in the present), reminisces about the night when she visited his hotel (flashback) to tell him about her wedding night (flashback within a flashback). *The Locket* (1946) famously has a fourfold flashback, i.e. a flashback within a flashback within a flashback within a flashback.

**Flash Gordon.** The spaceman hero created in imitation of Buck Rogers by the American strip cartoonist Alex Raymond in 1934. Together with his girlfriend, Dale Arden, he has a series of adventures on the planet Mongo and elsewhere, and subsequently moved to other media, notably the cinema but also in novel form.

**Flash in the pan, A.** A failure after a showy beginning; a NINE DAYS' WONDER. The allusion is to the attempt at firing an old flintlock gun that ends with a flash in the priming pan, the gun itself 'hanging fire'. *See also* HANG FIRE.

**As quick as a flash.** *See under* AS.

**Flashman.** The infamous school bully in Thomas Hughes's *Tom Brown's Schooldays* (1857), in which he notoriously 'roasts' young Tom in front of an open fire. He was revived as a type of cowardly scoundrel in a series of comic historical novels by George Macdonald Fraser, beginning with *Flashman: From the Flashman Papers 1839–1842* (1969).

**Flat. Flat-chested.** A purely relative term to describe a woman with a modest bust.

**Flatfoot.** A derogatory nickname for a policeman.

**Flat on one's back, To be.** To be laid up with ill health; to be incapacitated.

**Flat out.** At full speed; all out; fully extended.

**Flat race.** A horse race on a level course without jumps, as opposed to a STEEPLECHASE or a race over hurdles. The flat racing season is often known as simply 'the Flat'.

**Flat spin.** To be in a 'flat spin' is to be very flurried, to be in a panic. In flying, a flat spin is when the longitudinal axis of an aircraft inclines downwards at an angle of less than 45°. In the early days this inevitably involved loss of control. It later came to be an aerial manoeuvre performed at low level in air combat as an evasive action.

**Flat top.** A style of haircut in which the hair is cut short on the top of the head so that it stands up and appears flat.

**Flattop.** A colloquial American term for an aircraft carrier.

**As flat as a pancake.** *See under* AS.

**Caught flat-footed, To be.** *See under* CATCH.

**Cottage flat.** *See under* COTTAGE.

**Fall flat, To.** *See under* FALL.

**Granny flat.** *See under* GRANNY.

**That's flat.** Let there be no doubt about it. Said to reinforce a statement just made: 'You're not going out, and that's flat.'

**Flavour of the month.** A person, fad or craze that is temporarily fashionable or in favour. The term originated as a general advertising phrase aimed at US ice-cream consumers.

> When last she worked there she had been young, attractive, unattached. She had been 'flavour of the month'. But returning she was in a rather different situation: 'married, a mother, with outside commitments'.
>
> *The Times* (2 June 1998)

**Flea. Fleabag.** Originally a bed or sleeping-bag, but now more generally any shabby or unattractive person or thing.

**Flea market.** A street market selling second-hand goods and the like, so called because the clutter of bric-à-brac and old clothes is conducive to fleas. The French equivalent is the *marché aux puces*, or simply *les puces*, in Paris, the oldest and best known being that at St Ouen, on the northern edge of the city.

**Fleapit.** Any dingy or dirty place, and conventionally an old run-down cinema, where fleas may have been a real hazard.

**Flea's jump, A.** It has been estimated that if a man, in proportion to his weight, could jump as high as a flea, he could clear St Paul's Cathedral, 365ft (111.3m) high.

Aristophanes in the *Clouds* (423 BC) says that Socrates and Chaerephon tried to measure how many times its own length a flea jumped. They took the size of a flea's foot in wax, then calculated the length of its body. They then measured the distance of a flea's jump from the hand of Socrates to Chaerephon and resolved the problem by simple multiplication.

**Great fleas have lesser fleas.** *See under* GREAT.

**Mere flea-bite, A.** *See under* MERE.

**Sent off with a flea in one's ear, To be.** *See under* SEND.

**Fleece, The Golden.** *See under* GOLDEN.

**Fleet, The.** A London prison of medieval origin, which stood on the east side of Farringdon Street until its demolition (1846), on the site now partly occupied by the Memorial Hall. It took its name from the River Fleet, which (now piped) enters the THAMES at Blackfriars Bridge. As a royal prison it housed some distinguished prisoners in Tudor and Stuart times, including those committed by STAR CHAMBER, but it mainly owes its notoriety to its subsequent use as a debtors' prison. It was destroyed in the GREAT FIRE OF LONDON, rebuilt and again burned during the Gordon Riots. The Warden farmed out the prison to the highest bidder, which encouraged the shameful treatment of its occupants.

> Most of our readers will remember that, until within a very few years past, there was a kind of iron cage in the wall of the Fleet Prison, within which was posted some man of hungry looks, who, from time to time, rattled a money-box, and explained, in a mournful voice 'Pray, remember the poor debtors; pray, remember the poor debtors'.
> DICKENS: *Pickwick Papers*, ch xlii (1836–7)

**Fleet Street.** The famous thoroughfare that runs from Ludgate Circus to the Strand, taking its name from the River Fleet, which was once navigable for coal barges as far as Holborn. It was formerly noted for its bookshops, and was long synonymous with journalism and the newspaper world. All the newspaper offices have now gone, with many moving in the 1980s to new premises in the former DOCKLANDS region, although in the mid-1990s REUTERS and the Press Association still had offices in Fleet Street.

**Bishop of Fleet Street.** *See under* BISHOP.

**First Fleet.** *See under* FIRST.

**Flogging round** or **through the fleet.** *See under* FLOG.

**Liberties of the Fleet, The.** *See under* LIBERTY.

**Flemish school.** A school of painting founded by the van Eyck brothers, Jan and Hubert, in the 15th century. The chief early masters were Hans Memling (*c.*1433–94), Rogier van der Weyden (*c.*1400–64), Quinten Massys or Matsys (*c.*1465–1530) and Jan Mabuse (*c.*1470–*c.*1533), with a second period adding Peter Paul Rubens (1577–1640), Anthony Van Dyck (1599–1641), Frans Snyders (1579–1657) and David Teniers (1610–90). As well as for the invention of oil painting by Jan van Eyck the school was noted for its near-perfect representation of reality.

**Flesh. Flesh and blood.** One's own children, one's own brothers and sisters or other near kindred.

**Flesh-eating horses.** The horses of DIOMEDES, tyrant of Thrace, who fed his horses on the strangers who visited his kingdom. HERCULES vanquished the tyrant and gave the carcass to the horses to eat.

**Fleshly School, The.** In the *Contemporary Review* for October 1871 Robert Buchanan (1841–1901) published a violent attack on the poetry and literary methods of A.C. Swinburne, Dante Gabriel Rossetti, William Morris, Arthur O'Shaughnessy, John Payne and others under the heading *The Fleshly School of Poetry*, over the signature 'Thomas Maitland'. The incident created a literary sensation. Buchanan first denied the authorship but was soon obliged to admit it, and was reconciled to Rossetti, his chief victim, some years later. Swinburne's trenchant reply is to be found in his *Under the Microscope* (1872). Fleshly here means 'carnal', 'lascivious'.

**Fleshpots.** Literally, pots for cooking meat; metaphorically, luxurious living. The reference is biblical.

> And the children of Israel said unto them, Would to God we had died by the hand of the Lord in the land of Egypt, when we sat by the flesh pots, and when we did eat bread to the full.
> Exodus 16:3

**One flesh, To be.** *See under* ONE.

**Phantom flesh.** *See under* PHANTOM.

**Pound of flesh.** *See under* POUND.

**Thorn in the flesh, A.** *See under* THORN.

**Way of all flesh.** *See under* WAY.

**Fleur-de-lis, -lys** or **-luce** (French, 'lily flower'). The name of several varieties of iris or flags, and also of the heraldic lily, which was borne as a charge on the old French royal COAT OF ARMS. In the reign of Louis VII (1137–80) the national standard was thickly charged with lilies, but in 1376 the number was reduced to three by Charles V in honour of the Trinity. Guillim's *Display of Heraldrie* (1610) says the device is 'Three toads erect, saltant'; in allusion to which NOSTRADAMUS in the 16th century called Frenchmen *crapauds*. The fleur-de-lis was used to decorate the north point on the mariner's card before the end of the 15th century, and in the 20th century it was adopted as the badge of the BOY SCOUTS. *See also* FLORIN.

**Flibbertigibbet.** One of the five fiends that possessed 'poor Tom' in *King Lear* (IV, i (1605)). Shakespeare got the name from Samuel Harsnet's *Declaration of Egregious Popish Impostures* (1603), where one reads of 40 fiends, which the JESUITS cast out and among which was Fliberdigibbet, a name that had been previously used by Latimer and others for a mischievous gossip. Elsewhere the name is apparently a synonym for PUCK. Its origin is in a meaningless representation of chattering. The word is now used generally for a gossiping or restless person. Sir Walter Scott uses it as a nickname for Dickie Sludge, the 'queer, shambling, ill-made urchin' in *Kenilworth* (1821).

**Flicks, The.** The cinema, a film show, an expression deriving from the early days of such shows in the 1920s, when the pictures 'flickered' on the screen.

**Skin flick.** *See under* SKIN.

**Flight, Asmodeus.** *See under* ASMODEUS.

**Flimsy.** An old journalists' term for newspaper copy, arising from the thin paper (often used with a sheet of carbon paper to take a copy) on which reporters and others wrote up their matter for the press. The white £5 Bank of England note, which ceased to be legal tender in March 1961, was known as a flimsy. In the Royal Navy the name is also given to the brief certificate of conduct issued to an officer by his captain on the termination of his appointment to a ship or establishment. The derivation is again from the thin-quality paper.

**Fling. Have a fling at, To.** To have a go at; to try. The allusion is to throwing a stone at something with the aim of hitting it.

**Have one's fling, To.** To have full freedom of action; to indulge in pleasure to the fullest extent; to 'sow one's wild oats'.

**Flitch, Dunmow.** *See under* DUNMOW.

**Flog. Flog a dead horse, To.** To attempt to revive a question already settled or worn thin, thereby wasting time and energy.

**Flogging round** or **through the fleet.** In the Royal Navy, according to the ancient practice of the sea, this barbarous punishment consisted of a number of lashes from the CAT-O'-NINE-TAILS administered alongside each ship present, usually to the accompaniment of the ROGUE'S MARCH. Death frequently resulted. It ceased before the end of the 18th century, but flogging at the gangway was not finally 'suspended' until 1879. After the mutiny at the Nore in 1797 one seaman of the *Monmouth* was sentenced to 380 lashes.

**Flog to death, To.** To pursue and promote an idea or viewpoint so relentlessly and tediously that it loses its impact on those who hear it.

**Flood, The.** *See* DELUGE.

**Flook.** A bear-like beast with a trumpet-like snout, created for his strip cartoons in the *Daily Mail* by the artist Wally Fawkes under the pen name 'Trog'. He first appeared in 1949.

**Floor. Floor traders** or **room traders.** A name that is particularly used in New York for those members of a stock exchange who buy and sell stock on their own account, unlike commission brokers who act exclusively on behalf of clients.

**Cross the floor, To.** *See under* CROSS.

**First floor.** *See under* FIRST.

**Ground floor.** *See under* GROUND.

**Second floor.** *See under* SECOND.

**Shop floor.** *See under* SHOP.

**Take the floor, To.** To speak in a debate; to begin to dance.

**Wipe the floor with someone, To.** *See under* WIPE.

**Flora.** The Roman goddess of flowers especially associated with spring. Her festivals, the Floralia, were from 28 April to 3 May. The term 'flora' also denotes the native or indigenous plants of a country or region. *See also* FAUNA.

**Flora Macdonald.** *See under* MACDONALD.

**Florentine Diamond.** A large and famous diamond weighing 133 carats. It formed part of the Austrian crown jewels and previously belonged to Charles, Duke of Burgundy.

**Florida.** In 1512 Ponce de León sailed to the west in search of the FOUNTAIN OF YOUTH. He first saw land the following year shortly before EASTER, popularly called in Spain *Pascua florida*, 'flowery Easter', and on that account, prompted also by the lush spring vegetation, called the land Florida. It is also called the Peninsula State. Its city of St Augustine, founded in 1565, is the oldest European settlement in the original United States.

**Florin** (Italian *fiorino*, 'little flower'). A gold coin first minted in 13th-century Florence and named after the lily on the reverse. The FLEUR-DE-LIS was the badge of Florence. Edward III coined an English gold florin in 1344 valued at 6s. The English silver florin representing 2s was first issued in 1849 as a tentative introduction of a DECIMAL CURRENCY. It ceased to be LEGAL TENDER on 5 June 1993.

**Graceless** or **godless florin.** *See under* GRACE.

**Florizel.** GEORGE IV, when Prince of Wales, corresponded under this name with Mrs Robinson, the actress, generally known as PERDITA, in which character she first attracted his attention. The name comes from Shakespeare's *The Winter's Tale* (1610), in which Florizel, Prince of Bohemia, falls in love with Perdita. In Benjamin Disraeli's *Endymion* (1880), Prince Florizel represents NAPOLEON III.

**Flotsam and jetsam.** Properly, wreckage and other goods found in the sea. 'Flotsam' designates goods found floating on the sea (Old French *floter*, 'to float'), while 'jetsam' are the things thrown overboard to sink and remain under water (a shortening of jettison, from Old French *getaison*, related to modern French *jeter*, 'to throw'). The term is now also applied to wreckage found on the shore. Lagan, a word of uncertain origin, applies to goods thrown overboard but tied to a float for later recovery.

Flotsam and Jetsam were also the names adopted by two popular entertainers of variety stage and broadcasting fame. B.C. Hilliam (1890–1968), English composer and pianist, took the name Flotsam, and his partner, the Australian bass singer, Malcolm McEachern (1884–1945), that of Jetsam. The names were appropriate, since Flotsam had the high or 'floating' voice, and Jetsam the low or 'sinking' one. Flotsam and jetsam later became a composite phrase meaning odds and ends or vagrants.

**Flourish. Flourish like a green bay tree, To.** To prosper greatly. The bay throws out many fresh green branches every year from both base and trunk.

> I have seen the wicked in great power, and spreading himself like a green bay tree.
>
> Psalm 37:35.

**Flourish of trumpets, A.** An ostentatious introduction or arrival. The allusion is to the fanfare announcing the arrival of someone of high rank or distinction.

**Flowers and trees.**

Dedicated to heathen gods:

Cornel cherry-tree: APOLLO
CYPRESS: PLUTO
DITTANY: DIANA
LAUREL: APOLLO
LILY: JUNO
Maidenhair: PLUTO
MYRTLE: VENUS
NARCISSUS: CERES
OAK: JUPITER
OLIVE: MINERVA
Poppy: CERES
Vine: BACCHUS

Dedicated to saints:

Canterbury bells: St AUGUSTINE of Canterbury
Crocus: St VALENTINE
Crown imperial: EDWARD THE CONFESSOR
DAISY: St MARGARET
Herb Christopher: St CHRISTOPHER
LADY'S SMOCK: the Virgin MARY
ROSE: MARY MAGDALENE
St John's-wort: St JOHN
St Barnaby's thistle: St BARNABAS

National emblems:

LEEK, DAFFODIL: Wales
LILY (FLEUR-DE-LIS): BOURBON France
Lily (*Giglio bianco*): Florence
Lily (white): GHIBELLINES
Lily (red): GUELPHS
LINDEN: Prussia
Mignonette: Saxony
POMEGRANATE: Spain
Rose: England
Rose (red): LANCASTRIANS
Rose (white): YORKISTS
SHAMROCK: Ireland
Sugar maple: Canada
THISTLE: Scotland
VIOLET: Athens

In Christian symbolism:

Box: the Resurrection
Cedar: the faithful
Corn-ears: the Holy Communion
Dates: the faithful
Grapes: 'This is my Blood'
HOLLY: the Resurrection
IVY: the Resurrection
Lily: purity
OLIVE: peace
ORANGE BLOSSOM: virginity
PALM: victory
Rose: incorruption
Vine: 'Christ our Life'
YEW: death

The laurel, oak, olive, myrtle, rosemary, cypress and amaranth are all funereal plants.

**Flower de luce.** A corruption of FLEUR-DE-LIS.

**Flower of Chivalry, The.** A name given to several knights of spotless reputation, including:

Sir William Douglas, knight of Liddesdale (*c*.1300–53)
Chevalier de BAYARD
Sir Philip Sidney (1554–86)

**Flower of Kings, The** (Latin *Flos regum*). King ARTHUR was so called by John of Exeter, bishop of Winchester (d.1268).

**Flower people.** Supporters of a garishly clad youth cult of the mid-1960s who advocated peace and love, FLOWER POWER, as a substitute for materialism.

**Flower power.** The power of the FLOWER PEOPLE or Flower Children based on the slogan 'Make love, not war'. The Flower Children, also known as the Beautiful People, were a new form of HIPPIE movement, whose adherents were characterized by the wearing of bells and flowers. They appeared in Britain in 1967, taking their pattern from San Francisco.

**Flowers in Christian tradition.** Many plants and flowers play a part in Christian tradition. The ASPEN is said to tremble because the cross was made of its wood and there are other traditions connected with the ELDER TREE, FIG TREE, PASSION FLOWER, THISTLE etc. *See also* FIG LEAF; GLASTONBURY.

The following are said to owe their stained blossoms to the blood that trickled from the cross: the red anemone, the arum, the purple orchis, the crimson-spotted leaves of the vervain or 'herb of the cross', the spotted persicaria or snakeweed.

**Flowery Kingdom, The.** China, a rendering of the Chinese *huáguó*. A more precise translation would be Bright Land. The name does not necessarily imply the presence of flowers and is similar to *la belle France*.

**Cuckoo flowers.** *See under* CUCKOO.

**Language of flowers, The.** *See under* LANGUAGE.

**Passion flower.** *See under* PASSION.

**Fluff, A bit of.** *See under* BIT.

**Flush.** In cards, a whole hand of one suit.

**Flush game, To.** A gun dog is said to flush game when he disturbs them and they fly up from cover.

**Flush with money.** Very well supplied with money. Similarly a flush of water means a sudden and full flow of water.

**Royal flush.** *See under* ROYAL.

**Flute, The Magic.** *See under* MAGIC.

**Flutter.** A colloquial term for a small gamble. The allusion is to the excitement involved.

**Cause a flutter in the dovecote, To.** *See under* CAUSE.

**Fly** (noun) (1, plural flys). A one-horse HACKNEY-carriage. A contraction of fly-by-night, as SEDAN CHAIRS on wheels used to be called in the REGENCY. These 'fly-by-nights', much patronized by the Regent and his boon companions at

Brighton, were invented in 1809 by John Butcher, a carpenter.

(2, plural flies). An insect. It is said that no fly was ever seen in Solomon's temple, and according to Muslim legend, all flies shall perish except one, the bee fly.

**Flyblown.** Fouled by flyblows, i.e. the eggs or young larvae of a blowfly; hence tainted, spoiled. At one time naturalists thought that maggots were actually blown on to the meat by blowflies.

**Fly boy.** Another name for a PRINTER'S DEVIL.

**Fly in the ointment, A.** The trifling cause that spoils everything. A phrase of biblical origin.

> Dead flies cause the ointment of the apothecary to send forth a stinking savour: so doth a little folly him that is in reputation for wisdom and honour.
> Ecclesiastes 10:1

**Fly on the wall, A.** A hidden observer. A fly-on-the-wall technique, recording events as they happen without any overt artistic direction, is used by some makers of film and television documentaries.

**Crush a fly on a wheel, To.** *See under* CRUSH.

**God** or **Lord of Flies, The.** *See under* GOD.

**Rise to the fly, To.** *See under* RISE.

**Spanish fly.** *See under* SPAIN.

**There are no flies on him.** He is no fool; he won't be caught napping. The term derives from angling. A person was formerly said to be 'no fly' if they failed to rise to the bait.

**Venus' fly-trap.** *See under* VENUS.

**Fly** (verb). To move through the air by means of wings; to move swiftly; to depart rapidly.

**Fly a kite, To.** In commercial slang to raise money by means of accommodation bills. In practice this usually means the juggling of cheques between accounts so as to create a bogus balance of funds on which to draw. The increasing spiral of dishonesty is thus compared to the dizzying ascent of a kite. Today the phrase is more commonly used in the sense to test public opinion.

**Fly blind, To.** To pilot an aircraft solely by means of instruments, the opposite of visual navigation.

**Flyby.** A flight past a particular object, especially for purposes of observation, as a spacecraft past a planet or satellite.

**Fly-by-night.** A person who defrauds creditors by decamping in the night. *See also* FLY (a cab).

**Flying angel, A.** A ride given to a youngster seated astride someone's shoulders, holding hands with arms held high at full stretch.

**Flying bedstead.** A nickname of the experimental wingless and rotorless VTOL (vertical takeoff and landing) jet aircraft demonstrated in Britain in 1954. The name was inspired by its appearance.

**Flying circus.** An exhibition of aerobatics, as by aircraft at an air show.

**Flying dragon, A.** A meteor.

**Flying Duchess, The.** Mary du Caurroy Russell, Duchess of Bedford (1865–1937). After making record-breaking return flights to India (1929) and South Africa (1930) with Captain Barnard, she obtained an 'A' pilot's licence in 1933 and disappeared on a solo flight over the North Sea in March 1937.

**Flying Dutchman, The.** In maritime legend, a spectral ship that is supposed to haunt the seas around the Cape of Good Hope and to lure other vessels to their destruction or to cause other misfortune. According to Auguste Jal's *Scènes de la Vie Maritime*, he is said to be a Dutch captain, who persisted in trying to round the Cape, in spite of the violence of the storm and the protests of passengers and crew. Eventually a form, said to be the Almighty, appeared on the deck, but the Captain did not even touch his cap but fired upon the form and cursed and blasphemed. For punishment, the Dutchman was condemned to sail and to be a torment to sailors until the Day of Judgement. A skeleton ship appears in S.T. Coleridge's 'The Rime of the Ancient Mariner' (1798), and Washington Irving tells of 'the Flying Dutchman of the Tappan Sea' in his *Chronicles of Wolfert's Roost* (1839–40). Wagner has an opera *Der Fliegende Holländer* (1843), and Captain Marryat's novel *The Phantom Ship* (1839) tells of Philip Vanderdecken's successful but disastrous search for his father, the captain of the Flying Dutchman. Similar legends are found in many other countries.

> The Demon Frigate braves the gale;
> And well the doom'd spectators know
> The harbinger of wreck and woe.
> SIR WALTER SCOTT: *Rokeby*, II, xi (1813)

**Flying picket.** A picket that moves from one site to another in an industrial dispute. In the miners' strike of 1984 many flying pickets went to Nottinghamshire to support their colleagues in Britain's second largest coalfield. As a result of their activities, flying pickets were declared illegal under the 1980 Employment Act, and striking miners were confined to their own pits.

**Flying saucers.** Alleged mysterious objects resembling revolving, partially luminous discs that shoot across the sky at a high velocity and at a great height. They were largely brought to public attention by the American writer George Adamski, who in books such as *Flying Saucers Have Landed* (1953) told of travelling into space with extraterrestrials. The landing or sighting of flying saucers was reported on several occasions in the 1950s and 1960s, but their cult has now largely faded. *See also* UFO.

**Flying Scotsman.** A famous express train from London to Edinburgh. It has left King's Cross station at 10 am daily almost without interruption since 1862. When it first ran, it took 10½ hours over the journey, with a half-hour halt for passengers to take lunch at York. It later gradually speeded up, so that by the 1960s it was taking under six hours for the run, and by the 1970s less than five. In the late 1990s its journey was scheduled at only 4 hours 13 minutes. The up-train of the same name is timed to leave Glasgow at noon.

**Flying squad.** A police detachment able to proceed rapidly to the scene of a crime such as a robbery. In the Metropolitan Police, the Flying Squad became the best known department of SCOTLAND YARD, with the RHYMING SLANG nickname of Sweeney Todd, after the 'demon barber' of FLEET STREET in Victorian melodrama who cut his customers' throats. This name was popularly shortened to 'The Sweeney', itself used as the title of a fictional television series about the Squad first shown in 1974. The Flying Squad was reorganized in 1978 as the Central Robbery Squad, but its old name and nickname are still in use.

**Flying-the-garter.** Springing or jumping lightly over something. Flying-the-garter was a onetime children's game, in which the players jumped over the garter or line (usually of stones), and the back of another player. In circuses the tapes held up for performers to jump over were called garters.

> 'Who do you suppose will ever employ a professional man, when they see his boy playing at marbles, or flying the garter in the horse road?'
> DICKENS: *Pickwick Papers*, ch xxxviii (1836–7)

**Fly in the face of, To.** To defy; to oppose violently and unreasonably; to act in direct opposition to, as of authority. The allusion is to a dog that flies at the face of its enemy.

**Fly off the handle, To.** To burst out into angry and violent speech without control, as a hammer or axe loses its head when loose after a blow has been struck.

**Fly out at, To.** To burst or break into a rage.

**Flypast.** A ceremonial flight of aircraft over a particular building or area.

**Flyposting.** The posting of bills or advertisements on unauthorized places, such as the windows of empty shops. The expression presumably alludes to the fact that the posters fly as soon as they have stuck up their bills. *See also* FLY-TIPPING.

**Fly the flag at half-mast, To.** A sign of mourning. If the flag is already flying, it is lowered to half-mast. If it is not flying, it is raised to the top of the mast, broken, then lowered to half-mast. *See also* BREAK A FLAG.

**Fly-tipping.** The tipping of refuse in unauthorized sites. *See also* FLYPOSTING.

**As the crow flies.** *See under* AS.

**Bird has flown, The.** *See under* BIRD.

**Let fly, To.** *See under* LET.

**Make the feathers or fur fly, To.** *See under* FUR.

**Off to a flying start.** *See under* OFF.

**With flying colours, To.** *See under* WITH.

**Fob someone off, To.** To attempt to satisfy a person by means of trickery; to give a person something that is of inferior quality or quantity to that due. Fob is probably connected with German *foppen*, 'to hoax'.

**Fo'c's'le.** *See* FORECASTLE.

**Fodder, Cannon.** *See under* CANNON.

**Foggy Bottom.** A nickname for the US State Department, whose headquarters, to the southwest of the White House in Washington, are in a locality subject to fogs from the neighbouring Potomac River. The name has become punningly synonymous with political routine and government bureaucracy.

**Fogey. Old fogey** or **fogy.** *See under* OLD.

**Young fogey.** *See under* YOUNG.

**Foil.** A person or thing that sets off another to advantage. The allusion is to the metallic leaf used by jewellers to set off precious stones (French *feuille*, Latin *folium*, Greek *phullon*, 'leaf').

> I'll be your foil, Laertes; in mine ignorance
> Your skill shall, like a star i' the darkest night,
> Stick fiery off indeed.
> SHAKESPEARE: *Hamlet*, V, ii (1600)

**Folio.** The word come from the Latin phrase *in folio*, 'in a leaf'. In bibliography and printing it has distinct applications:

(1) A sheet of paper (for printing) in its standard size
(2) A book whose sheets have been folded once only, so that each sheet makes two leaves, hence a book of large size
(3) The leaf of a book of any size; until the mid-16th century, when printed pagination became common, books were foliated, i.e. numbered on the recto or front of the leaf only and not on the verso; printers call a page of manuscript or printed matter a folio regardless of size

In legal use, a folio is a unit of measurement used for a document, determined by the number of words. In Britain it is generally 72 words, or for parliamentary proceedings 90 words, while in the USA it is 100 words.

**Folk, Hill.** *See under* HILL.

**Folklore.** The traditional beliefs, customs, popular superstitions and legends of a people. The word was coined in 1846 by 'Ambrose Merton' (W.J. Thoms) (1803–85), editor of the *Athenaeum* and founder of *Notes and Queries*. He described the word as 'a good Saxon compound'. *See also* ATHENAEUM CLUB.

**Follow. Following bird.** A bird following a ship or boat at sea, believed by some to embody the restless spirit of one drowned.

> 'A follerin' bürrd', he said, again; and again I waited; questions were not grateful to him.
> 'There be a carpse there, sure enough, a carpse driftin' and shiftin' on the floor of the sea. There be those as can't rest, poor sawls, and her'll be mun, her'll be mun, and the speerit of her is with the bürrd.'
> 'MICHAEL FAIRLESS' (MARGARET FAIRLESS BARBER): *The Roadmender*, ch ii (1902)

**Follow in someone's footsteps, To.** To continue another person's job or tradition, as a son may do of his father.

> 'Mark my footsteps, good my page;
> Tread thou in them boldly:
> Thou shalt find the winter's rage
> Freeze thy blood less coldly.'
> J.M. NEALE: 'Good King Wenceslas' (1853)

**Follow-my-leader.** A game in which each player must exactly imitate the actions of the leader or pay a forfeit. Americans usually call it 'follow-the-leader'.

**Follow-on.** In CRICKET an innings forced on a team immediately after the first. This happens when the side scores a particular number of runs fewer than its opponents in the first innings.

**Follow one's nose, To.** To go straight ahead; to trust to instinct.

**Follow suit, To.** To follow the leader; to conform to another person's actions. The term is from card games.

**Follow through, To.** To continue an action to its conclusion. In sport, to follow through is to continue the movement of a stroke after the ball has been struck.

**Camp followers.** *See under* CAMP.

**Folly.** A fantastic or foolishly extravagant country seat or costly structure, built for amusement or idiosyncratic show. Fisher's Folly, a large and beautiful house in Bishopsgate, with pleasure gardens, bowling green and hothouses, built by Jasper Fisher, one of the six clerks of Chancery, is a historic example. Queen Elizabeth I slept there. In 1625 it was acquired by the Earl of Devonshire, and its site is now occupied by Devonshire Square.

A classic folly was that of Fonthill Abbey, Wiltshire, a huge and sumptuous house built by William Beckford (1759–1844), author of the oriental tale VATHEK (1786), at a cost of some £273,000. It took 18 years to complete and was sold in 1822 for £330,000. Hazlitt described it as a 'glittering waste of industrious idleness'. Three years later the octagonal tower, 260ft (79m) high, collapsed, destroying part of the house. The rest of the mansion was demolished soon after, and the present Fonthill Abbey is the one built in 1859 by the Marquess of Westminster on the same site.

With the growth of landscaping in the 18th century, follies multiplied rapidly, taking many forms. Towers, obelisks, mock ruins of castles and abbeys, chapels, temples, hermitages and grottoes became the pride of their owners. The style varied from 'gothick' to classical and Chinese pagodas were not uncommon.

**Palmerston's follies.** *See under* PALMERSTON.

**Font** or **fount.** A complete set of type of the same body and face with all the points, accents, figures, fractions, signs and so on that ordinarily occur in printed books and papers. A complete fount (which includes italics) consists of over 200 separate pieces of type, without the special characters needed in ALMANACS, astronomical and medical works and so forth. The word is Old French *fonte*, 'founding', ultimately from Latin *fundere*, 'to melt'. Like other printing terms, the word has now passed into computer jargon, in which it is used for the range of typefaces available. *See also* LETTER.

**Fontarabia.** A town properly called Fuenterrabia (Basque *Hondarrabia*, 'sandy river'), in northern Spain near the Gulf of Gascony. Here, according to legend, CHARLEMAGNE and all his chivalry fell by the swords of the SARACENS. French romancers say that when the rear of the king's army was cut to pieces, Charlemagne returned to life and avenged them by a complete victory.

**Food. Food for thought.** Something to ponder or mull over, especially something instructive.

**Food for worms** or **for the fishes, To become.** To be dead and buried; to be drowned. *See also* FEED THE FISHES.

> Your worm is your only emperor for diet: we fat all creatures else, to fat us; and we fat ourselves for maggots.
> SHAKESPEARE: *Hamlet*, IV, iii (1600)

**Food of the gods, The.** *See* AMBROSIA; NECTAR.

**Bolt one's food, To.** *See under* BOLT.

**Fast food.** *See under* FAST.

**Spagyric food.** *See under* SPAGYRIC.

**Fool.** There are many self-explanatory expressions or sayings regarding fool, such as: 'A fool and his money are soon parted,' 'Fortune favours fools' and 'There's no fool like an old fool.' Some others are given below.

**Fool about** or **around, To.** To play the fool; to play around, often in an aimless or annoying fashion.

**Fool Bible, The.** *See under* BIBLE.

**Fool for one's pains, To be a.** To have worked ineffectively; to have had no reward for one's labours.

**Fool's bolt is soon shot, A** (Shakespeare, *Henry V*, III, vii (1599)). Simpletons cannot wait for the fit and proper time, but waste their resources in random endeavours. The allusion is to bowmen, bolt being the arrow of a crossbow. The good soldier shot with a purpose, the foolish soldier at random.

> A fool uttereth all his mind: but a wise man keepeth it in till afterwards.
> Proverbs 29:11

**Fool's cap.** A conical cap with feather and bells, such as licensed fools used to wear.

**Foolscap.** Properly the jester's cap and bells or the conical paper hat of a DUNCE. The former standard size of printing paper measuring $13\frac{1}{2} \times 17$in (343 × 432mm) and of writing paper measuring $13\frac{1}{4} \times 16\frac{1}{2}$ in (337 × 419mm) took their name from an ancient watermark showing a fool's head and cap. *See also* FOOL'S CAP.

**Fool's errand, A.** A fruitless errand; one that is a waste of time.

**Fool's gold.** A name given to iron pyrites or pyrite, which, being of a brassy yellow colour, was sometimes mistaken for gold. It is often found in coal seams. Martin Frobisher (*c*.1535–94) returned with supposed 'gold minerall' from his voyage of 1576 in search of the NORTHWEST PASSAGE. Two further voyages were made in 1577 and 1578 for cargoes of the supposed ore, which proved to be nothing but 'fool's gold'.

**Fool's paradise, A.** A state of contentment or happiness founded on unreal, fanciful or insecure foundations.

**Fools rush in where angels fear to tread.** Those who are unintelligent and thoughtless become involved in matters where those with wisdom and understanding think twice.

> Nay, fly to altars; there they'll talk you dead;
> For fools rush in where angels fear to tread.
> Distrustful sense with modest caution speaks,
> It still looks home, and short excursions makes.
> ALEXANDER POPE: *Essay on Criticism* (1711)

**All Fools' Day.** 1 April. *See* APRIL FOOL.
**April Fool.** *See under* APRIL.
**As the fool thinks, so the bell clinks.** *See under* AS.
**Court fools.** *See under* COURT.
**Feast of Fools, The.** *See under* FEAST.
**Flannelled fools.** *See under* FLANNEL.
**Gooseberry fool.** *See under* GOOSEBERRY.
**Paradise of fools, The.** *See under* PARADISE.
**Play the fool, To.** *See under* PLAY.
**Ship of fools, The.** *See under* SHIP.
**Tomfool.** *See under* TOM.
**Wisest fool in Christendom, The.** *See under* WISE.

**Foot** or **feet.** The foot as a measure of length (12 inches, one-third of a yard, or 0.3048 of a metre) is common to most peoples and has never varied much more than does the length of men's feet, from which the name is taken.

In prosody, the term denotes a division in verse that consists of a certain number of syllables (or pauses), one of which is stressed. Here the term, which comes from Greece, refers to beating time with the foot.

**Foot-and-mouth disease.** A contagious viral disease of cattle, sheep, goats and pigs, among other cloven-footed animals. It is characterized by the formation of painful blisters on and in the mouth, between the two toes of the foot and around the top of the hoof. Vaccines can control epidemics but there is no effective cure for infected animals.

**Foothold.** A place where a foot can be securely placed when climbing. Figuratively, a secure initial position or advantage.

**Foot in the door, A.** An initial step in the right direction, especially in a difficult undertaking.

**Foot it, To.** To walk the distance instead of riding; also to dance.

> Foot it featly here and there;
> And, sweet sprites, the burden bear.
> SHAKESPEARE: *The Tempest*, I, ii (1611)

**Footloose and fancy free.** Unattached romantically; 'young, free and single'. Footloose is a term of nautical origin, referring to a sail on which the restraining ropes at the base (foot) have been slackened off (loosened) so that it flaps about capriciously.

**Footmen.** *See* RUNNING FOOTMEN.

**Foot the bill, To.** To pay it. The reference is to signing one's name at the foot of the bill as a guarantee that one will pay it. The modern equivalent is the signing of a cheque or credit card voucher.

**Best foot forward.** *See under* BEST.
**Bishop has put his foot in it, The.** *See under* BISHOP.
**Boot is on the other foot, The.** *See under* BOOT.
**Carried out feet foremost, To be.** *See under* CARRY.
**Change one's feet, To.** *See under* CHANGE.
**Cold feet.** *See under* COLD.
**Crow's feet.** *See under* CROW.
**Enter a house right foot foremost.** *See under* ENTER.
**Fall** or **land on one's feet, To.** *See under* FALL.
**Find one's feet, To.** *See under* FIND.
**First foot.** *See under* FIRST.
**Follow in someone's footsteps, To.** *See under* FOLLOW.
**Get one's feet wet, To.** To begin to participate.

**Have feet of clay, To.** Said of someone hitherto held in high regard or in an important position who shows disappointing weaknesses of character. The allusion is to Daniel 2:31–5, in which DANIEL describes 'the great image' in NEBUCHADNEZZAR's dream. It had a head of gold, breast and arms of silver, belly and thighs of brass, legs of iron and feet of iron and clay.

**Have itchy feet, To.** *See under* ITCH.

**Have the ball at one's feet, To.** *See under* BALL.

**Not to let the grass grow under one's feet.** *See under* LET.

**Not to put a foot wrong.** To do everything right; to make no mistakes.

**On a good** or **friendly footing with someone, To be.** *See under* GOOD.

**Play footsie, To.** *See under* PLAY.

**Put one's feet up, To.** To take a rest.

**Put one's foot down, To.** To take a firm stand; to refuse or insist upon something firmly and finally. In driving, to depress the accelerator and speed up.

**Put one's foot in it, To.** To blunder; to make a FAUX PAS; to get into trouble. There is a well-known Irish bull: 'Every time I open my mouth I put my foot in it.'

**Queen Anne's footstool.** *See under* ANNE.

**Right foot foremost.** *See under* RIGHT.

**Run** or **rushed off one's feet, To be.** *See under* RUN.

**Set off on the wrong foot, To.** *See under* SET.

**Shoot oneself in the foot, To.** *See under* SHOOT.

**Sit at someone's feet, To.** *See under* SIT.

**Stand on one's own two feet, To.** *See under* STAND.

**Tread** or **trample under foot, To.** *See under* TREAD.

**Under one's feet.** *See under* UNDER.

**Walk someone off their feet, To.** *See under* WALK.

**Washing the feet.** *See* MAUNDY THURSDAY.

**With one foot in the grave.** *See under* WITH.

**For. For all I care.** As far as I'm concerned. An expression denoting a lack of interest or concern. The person can vary, as: 'I could be at death's door, for all you care.'

**For a year and a day.** In law the period of time which in certain matters determines a right or liability. Thus the crown formerly had the right to hold the land of felons for a year and a day, and if a person wounded does not die within a year and a day, the assailant is not guilty of murder.

**For better, for worse.** Whatever the future may bring. The phrase is from the English marriage service, in which it expresses indissoluble union.

**For crying out loud.** A colloquial exclamation of astonishment or annoyance current since the 1920s, and probably a EUPHEMISM for 'For Christ's sake'.

**For dear life.** Urgently or desperately, as: 'She was running for dear life.'

**For good** or **for good and all.** Permanently; finally; conclusively.

> The good woman never died after this, till she came to die for good and all.
>
> SIR ROGER L'ESTRANGE: *Fables* (1692)

**For good measure.** As an extra precaution; as an addition beyond what is necessary.

**For life.** As long as life continues.

**For my part.** As far as I am concerned.

**For old sake's sake.** For the sake of old acquaintance, past times.

**For one's name's sake.** Out of regard for one's reputation or good name.

**For one's pains.** In return for one's trouble or well-meant efforts.

**For Pete's sake.** An exclamation of annoyance or impatience. The precise identification of Pete is problematical. The expression is perhaps a sort of oath in the name of St PETER. Alternatively, it may have evolved from 'for pity's sake'.

**For that matter.** As far as that is concerned.

**For the best.** With the best of motives; with a view to obtaining the best results.

**For the hell of it.** For the fun of it; for 'kicks'.

**For the life of me.** Even though I am trying desperately hard, as if my life depended on it.

> Nor could I for my life see how the creation of the world had anything to do with what I was talking about.
>
> OLIVER GOLDSMITH: *The Vicar of Wakefield*, ch xiv (1766)

**For the most part.** Generally; as a rule.

**For the record.** For the sake of complete accuracy.

**For want of a nail.** 'For want of a nail, the shoe is lost; for want of a shoe, the horse is lost; for want of a horse, the rider is lost.' (George Herbert: *Jacula Prudentum*, No. 499 (1651)).

**Forane, Vicar.** *See under* VICAR.

**Forbid. Forbidden City, The.** Lhasa, the ancient religious and political capital of Tibet, 11,830ft (3606m) above sea level. The palace of the Dalai Lama or Grand Lama stands on the neighbouring Potala Hill. This sacred city of Lamaist BUDDHISM containing 15 monasteries fell under Chinese control (*c.*1720) and when, in 1959, the Tibetans unsuccessfully tried to cast off the Chinese yoke, the Dalai Lama fled to India. Its first European mention was by Friar Odoric, the traveller (*c.*1330). It was closed to Westerners until the beginning of the 20th century. Hence the epithet. Its name means 'city of the gods'. Forbidden City is also the name of the walled section of Peking that contains the Imperial Palace and other buildings of the former Chinese Empire. *See also* LAMAISM.

**Forbidden fruit.** Forbidden or unlawful pleasure of any kind, especially illicit love. The reference is to Genesis 2:17: 'But of the tree of the knowledge of good and evil, thou shalt not eat of it.' According to Muslim tradition the forbidden fruit partaken of by ADAM and EVE was the banyan or Indian fig. According to popular Christian tradition it was an apple.

**Forbid the banns, To.** To object formally to the proposed marriage.

> And better fate did *Maria* deserve, than to have her Banns forbid, by the intrigues of the curate of the parish who published them——
>
> LAURENCE STERNE: *Tristram Shandy*, Bk IX, ch xxiv, 'The Invocation' (1759–67)

**Force. Force someone's hand, To.** To make a person reveal his or her plans earlier than intended, as in card playing.

**Force the issue, To.** To compel a decision to be made.

**Field of force.** *See under* FIELD.

**Fore!** A cry of warning used by golfers before driving. It is probably short for before.

**Fore and aft.** The whole length of a ship from stem to stern, i.e. lengthwise. Fore here is the forward (pronounced 'forrad') or bow part of the ship, and aft the after or stern part. Sailing vessels are classed as square-rigged or fore-and-aft rigged, the latter having their sails extending from the fore-and-aft line to the lee side. Such vessels carry no square sails and can sail closer to the wind. In the Royal Navy a seaman's uniform of cap, jumper and bell-bottomed trousers is termed square rig, while the peaked cap, jacket and trousers of petty officers and above is called fore-and-aft rig.

**Forecastle** or **fo'c's'le.** So called because at one time the fore part of a ship was raised and protected like a castle, so that it could command the enemy's deck. Similarly the after part (now termed the QUARTERDECK) was called the after castle. Soldiers were stationed in these castles to carry on the fighting. It has always been customary to place the crew's quarters in the fo'c's'le and the officers' quarters aft.

**Foregone conclusion, A.** An inevitable one.

**Come to the fore, To.** *See under* COME.

**To the fore.** *See under* TO.

**Foreign Legion.** A body of volunteer sympathizers fighting to aid a foreign cause. The name is now particularly associated with the French Foreign Legion or *Légion étrangère*, composed of volunteers of many nationalities. It was founded by law in 1831 and has been in almost continuous combat since then. After the Falklands War of 1981, British recruits to the Foreign Legion rose to some 10 per cent of the total.

**Forelock, Take time by the.** *See under* TIME.

**Forest. Forest City.** Cleveland, Ohio, from its many well-shaded, tree-lined streets.

**Forest courts.** The ancient courts established for the conduct of forest business and the administration of the forest laws, the main aim of which was to preserve the wild animals for the royal chase. Such laws existed in Saxon England and were reinforced by the Norman kings. William I (r.1066–87) created the New Forest in the sense that he placed the area under Forest Law, and the forests reached their greatest extent under Henry II (r.1154–89). The young Henry III was forced to concede a Forest Charter in 1217, modifying the laws and disafforesting lands afforested by Henry II. *See also* ROBIN HOOD.

**Forest Lawn.** One of the largest cemeteries in the world, outside Los Angeles, California. The fictional Whispering Glades Memorial Park in Evelyn Waugh's macabre comic novel *The Loved One* (1948) is loosely based on it.

**Forest of Arden.** In north Warwickshire, once part of a large Midland forest, famous as the probable setting of Shakespeare's *As You Like It* (1599). The name survives in the Warwickshire market town of Henley-in-Arden.

**Drunken forest.** *See under* DRUNK.

**Forgery. Ireland forgeries, The.** *See under* FAKES.

**Pigott forgeries, The.** *See under* FAKES.

**Vermeer forgeries, The.** *See under* FAKES.

**Forget. Forget-me-not.** According to German legend this flower takes its name from the last words of a knight, who was drowned while trying to pick some from the riverside for his lady. The generic name *Myosotis* ('mouse-ear') refers to the shape of the leaves. The native name translated Old French *ne m'oubliez mye* (modern French *ne-m'oubliez-pas*), and its equivalent is now found in other languages, such as German *Vergissmeinnicht*, Italian *nontiscordardime*, Spanish *nomeolvides* and Russian *nezabudka*. To wear the flower is to ensure against being forgotten by one's lover.

**Forgotten man, The.** This is a phrase derived from W.G. Summer (1840–1910), the American sociologist, to describe the decent, hardworking, ordinary citizen. It was later popularized by F.D. Roosevelt in 1932 during the presidential election campaign, although he actually used the expression before his nomination. He advocated a NEW DEAL and appealed to the 'forgotten man at the bottom of the economic pyramid'.

**Forgotten Sins Bible, The.** *See under* BIBLE.

**Gone but not forgotten.** Remembered although absent. A phrase formerly found on gravestones and memorials. The phrase may be used of a person whom one was glad to see go but whom one now reluctantly recalls.

**Fork. Forked cap.** A bishop's mitre.

**Forked lightning.** Zigzag lightning.

**Fork lunch** or **supper.** A light meal eaten with a fork, especially one to which guests are invited.

**Fork out, To.** Fork is old thieves' slang for a

finger, so 'to fork out' is to produce and hand over or to pay up.

**Forks, The** (Latin *furca*). Among the Romans crucifixion ranked as the most common method of execution, and a slave condemned to death by this method was made to wear the *furca*, a kind of V-shaped collar. It was fixed over the back of the neck, the ends resting on the shoulders. The criminal's hands were bound to his thighs. In this manner he was marched to the place of execution. All the way the executioners or *carnifices*, literally 'flesh-makers', walked behind him, beating him with cudgels or flogging him with whips.

**Caudine Forks, The.** *See under* CAUDINE.

**Fingers were made before forks.** *See under* FINGER.

**Morton's fork.** *See under* MORTON.

**White man speak with forked tongue.** *See under* WHITE.

**Forlorn hope.** The phrase has its origin in Dutch *verloren hoop*, 'lost troop'. The French equivalent is *enfants perdus*, 'lost children'. The forlorn hope was a picked body of men sent in front to begin an attack, particularly the body of volunteers who first entered a breach when storming a defensive fortification. The phrase is still sometimes applied to a body of men selected for some desperate enterprise, although it is mostly used of a faint or failing hope in general.

**Form** (Old French *forme*, Latin *forma*). Good form is behaviour in accordance with the established conventions of good manners. Bad form is the reverse.

**Form or make a ring, To.** To act together in order to control the price of a given article, usually to enhance the price and ensure greater profit. Dealers at auctions sometimes form such a ring and do not outbid each other, thus ensuring that articles are knocked down cheaply. After the auction, the dealers' ring then organizes a sale or distribution among its members.

**Bad form.** *See under* BAD.

**On form.** Playing or performing well.

**Fort, To hold the.** *See under* HOLD.

**Forth. Back and forth.** *See under* BACK.

**Hold forth, To.** *See under* HOLD.

**Fortnum & Mason.** The quality grocery store in Piccadilly was founded in 1707 by William Fortnum, a footman in the household of Queen Anne, together with his grocer friend, Hugh Mason. Mr Fortnum had already been selling candles at cut price to the household staff, and the two men's first commercial venture was little more than a stall in a Piccadilly doorway. A grocer's shop was then opened, and remained in the hands of both men's families until about 1800, since when neither a Fortnum nor a Mason has been connected with the business.

**Fortunatus.** A hero of medieval legend (derived from Eastern sources) who possessed an inexhaustible purse, a wishing cap and other attributes. He appears in a German *Volksbuch* of 1509. Hans Sachs dramatized the story in 1553, and Thomas Dekker's *Pleasant Comedy of Old Fortunatus* was first performed in December 1599.

**Fortune. Fortunate Islands.** An ancient name for the Canary Islands, as well as for any imaginary lands set in distant seas, like the 'Islands of the Blest'.

> Their place of birth alone is mute
> To sounds which echo further west
> Than your sires' 'Islands of the Blest'.
>
> LORD BYRON: *Don Juan*, III, lxxxvi (1819–24)

**Fortune cookie.** A small biscuit containing a motto or prediction on a slip of paper. The notion of putting such messages inside cakes dates back to the MING dynasty in China, when rebels planning secret meetings would distribute folded notes to their compatriots inside apparently innocent cakes. The Chinese introduced the idea to the Americans and the present-day cookie was first produced in San Francisco's CHINATOWN in the 19th century. Messages found in modern cookies are generally rather trite, and typically include such words of wisdom as: 'Flattery will go far tonight', 'Someone close to you will win a fortune' or, rather more inscrutably, 'Few things are as bad as enthusiastic ignorance'.

**Fortune favours the brave.** The expression is found in Terence: *Fortis fortuna adjuvat* (*Phormio*, I, ch iv (2nd century BC)); also in Virgil: *Audentis fortuna adjuvat* (*Aeneid*, x (1st century BC)), and other classical writers.

**Fortune hunter.** A person seeking wealth by marriage.

**Ball of fortune.** *See under* BALL.

**Gentleman of fortune.** *See under* GENTLEMAN.

**Soldiers of fortune.** *See under* SOLDIER.

**Wheel of fortune, The.** *See under* WHEEL.

**Forty.** A number of frequent occurrence in the scriptures and hence formerly treated as having special sanction. MOSES was 'in the mount 40 days and 40 nights'; ELIJAH was fed by ravens for 40 days; the rain of the Flood fell for 40 days and another 40 days expired before NOAH opened the window of the ark; 40 days was the period of embalming; Nineveh had 40 days to repent; Jesus fasted 40 days and was seen 40 days after His Resurrection, and so on.

St SWITHIN bestowed 40 days' rain or 40 days' dry weather; a QUARANTINE extended to 40 days; in Old English law 40 days was the limit for the payment of the fine for manslaughter; a stranger had 40 days within which to be enrolled in the TITHING; the privilege of the RIGHT OF SANCTUARY was for 40 days; a widow was allowed to remain in her husband's house for 40 days after his decease; a knight obliged his tenant to serve him for 40 days; a newly appointed burgess had to forfeit 40 pence unless he built a house within 40 days, and so on and so forth.

**Forty-Five, The.** The name given to the rebellion of 1745 led by Charles Edward Stuart, the YOUNG PRETENDER. He landed on Eriskay Island (23 July) and raised his standard at Glenfinnan (19 August). Joined by many Scottish clansmen, he proclaimed the OLD PRETENDER to be King James III, defeated Sir John Cope at Prestonpans (21 September) and marched south to Derby (4 December). His plan to proceed to London was frustrated by the advice of his supporters and lack of support from English JACOBITES. He retreated to Scotland and was decisively defeated by the Duke of Cumberland at CULLODEN Moor (16 April 1746). The Young Pretender escaped to France (20 September) with the help of Flora MACDONALD and others. Cumberland earned the nickname 'Butcher' for the subsequent reprisals taken against the Highlanders.

**Forty Immortals, The** or simply **The Forty.** The members of the French Academy, who number 40.

**Forty-niners.** Those who took part in the Californian gold rush, after the discovery of gold there in 1848. Most of the adventurers arrived in 1849, coming from many parts of the world, including Australia and China.

> In a cavern, in a canyon,
> Excavating for a mine,
> Dwelt a miner, Forty-niner,
> And his daughter Clementine.
> PERCY MONTROSE: 'Clementine' (1884)

**Forty stripes save one.** The Jews were forbidden by the LAW OF MOSES to inflict more than 40 stripes on an offender, and for fear of breaking the law, they stopped short of the number. If the scourge contained three lashes, 13 strokes would equal '40 save one'.

The THIRTY-NINE ARTICLES of the CHURCH OF ENGLAND used sometimes to be called 'the 40 stripes save one' by theological students.

**Forty-two Line Bible, The.** *See* MAZARIN BIBLE *under* BIBLE.

**Forty winks.** A colloquial term for a short nap or a doze.

**Forty Years On.** This oft-quoted phrase forms the opening of the Harrow Football Song, the first four lines of which are given below. It is also the school song. The words by Edward Bowen were set to music by his colleague John Farmer, who was director of music at Harrow from 1862 to 1885.

> Forty years on, when afar and asunder
> Parted are those who are singing today,
> When you look back and forgetfully wonder
> What you were like in your words and your play.
> 'Forty Years On' (published 1886)

**Field of the Forty Footsteps.** *See under* FIELD.

**Hungry Forties, The.** *See under* HUNGRY.

**Roaring Forties, The.** *See under* ROAR.

**Forwards, Marshal.** Field Marshal Blücher (1742–1819) was called Marschall Vorwärts, from his constant exhortation to his soldiers in the campaigns preceding the Battle of Waterloo (1815): *Vorwärts! immer Vorwärts!*

**Fosse** or **Foss Way.** One of the principal Roman roads in Britain. It runs on the route Axmouth – Ilchester – Bath – Cirencester – Leicester – Lincoln. Its name derives from the ditch (Latin *fossa*) on each side of the road. See also ERMINE STREET.

**Foul. Foul anchor.** A ship's cable that has taken a turn round the anchor. It was used as an official seal by Charles Howard, Earl of Nottingham (1536–1624), when Lord High Admiral, and later as a badge on naval uniform buttons, cap badges and the Admiralty crest.

**Foul-weather Jack.** Admiral John Byron (1723–86), grandfather of the poet, said to have been as notorious for foul weather as Queen Victoria was for fine. Admiral Sir John Norris (*c*.1660–1749) was also so called.

**Fall foul of, To.** *See under* FALL.

**Fountain. Fountain of Arethusa.** *See* ALPHEUS AND ARETHUSA.

**Fountain of Youth.** In popular legend, a fountain with the power of restoring youth. It was much sought after, and at one time was supposed to be in one of the Bahama Islands. Ponce de León, discoverer of FLORIDA, set out in search of BIMINI.

**Four. Four-ale.** Small ale or cheap ale, originally sold at fourpence per quart. Hence four-ale bar as a name in a public house or inn for the public bar, where prices are lowest.

> It is night in the chill, squat chapel ... night in the four-ale, quiet as a domino.
> DYLAN THOMAS: *Under Milk Wood* (1954)

**Four corners of the earth, The.** The uttermost ends of the earth; the remotest parts of the world. The expression appears to allude to the belief that the earth is flat. In 1965 members of the Johns Hopkins Applied Physics Laboratory named the four corners of the earth as being in Ireland, southeast of the Cape of Good Hope, west of the Peruvian coast, and between New Guinea and Japan. Each of these 'corners' (of several thousand square miles in area) is some 120ft (37m) above the geodetic mean and the gravitational pull is measurably greater at these locations.

**Four-eyes.** A derogatory nickname for a person who wears spectacles.

**Four Freedoms, The.** The human rights defined by F.D. Roosevelt in his message to Congress, 6 January 1941, as the freedom of speech, the freedom of expression, the freedom of worship and the freedom from fear and want. They were to be the aims of the USA and ultimately of the world.

**Four Horsemen of the Apocalypse, The.** The four agents of destruction described in Revelation 6, two being agents of war and two of famine and pestilence. The first appeared on a white horse, the second on a red horse, the third on a black horse and the fourth on a pale horse.

In 1916 the Spanish writer Vicente Blasco Ibáñez (1867–1928) published a novel of this title about the First World War, *Los cuatro jinetes del Apocalipsis*, which appeared in English in 1918.

**Four Hundred, The.** A late 19th-century term for New York's most exclusive social set, which came into general use as a designation of social exclusiveness. In 1892 Mrs William Astor, finding the need to limit her guests to the capacity of her ballroom, which was asserted to be suitable for 400 guests, asked Ward McAllister, the self-appointed organizer of New York society, to prune her invitations. McAllister is also reported to have claimed that there were only 400 people in New York City who could claim to be 'society'. *See also* UPPER TEN.

**Four Last Things, The.** Death, Judgement, Heaven and Hell. A theological encapsulation translating Latin *quattuor novissima*.

**Four-leaved clover.** A clover leaf with four leaflets, believed to bring good luck.

> I'm looking over a four leaf clover
> That I overlooked before.
> MORT DIXON: 'I'm Looking Over a Four Leaf Clover' (song) (1927)

**Four-letter man.** A EUPHEMISM for a person who is sufficiently unpleasant to be designated by a FOUR-LETTER WORD.

> Felix regarded Randall as a four-letter man of the first order.
> IRIS MURDOCH: *An Unofficial Rose*, ch xvii (1962)

**Four letters, The.** *See* TETRAGRAMMATON.

**Four-letter word.** One of various short English words relating to sex or excrement. The two words commonly regarded as the grossest are those that came to be widely known in the 1990s as the 'F-word' and the 'C-word'. The otherwise liberally minded *Oxford English Dictionary* did not even admit these two to its pages until it issued the first volume of its Supplement (A–G) in 1972. Although such words are still not used in polite society, they have gained an increasing degree of acceptance in the media and in literature. However, many newspapers still resort to dashes or asterisks when printing them, and their occurrence in literature, even of the 'serious' type, still offends many.

Four-letter words are sometimes referred to as 'Anglo-Saxon words', although some are not of Old English origin. Crap, for example, comes from Medieval Latin *crappa*, 'chaff', and piss from Old French *pisser*. The term itself is also sometimes punningly applied to everyday words with four letters. Henry Livings' play *Eh?* (1965) was turned into a film under the title *Work is a Four-Letter Word* (1968), while the novelist Nicholas Monsarrat entitled his two-volume autobiography *Life is a Four-Letter Word* (1966, 1970).

> Good authors too
> Who once used better words
> Now only use four-letter words.
> COLE PORTER: 'Anything Goes' (song) (1934)

**Four-minute men.** The name given in the USA during the First World War to the members of a volunteer organization some 75,000 strong who, in 1917–18, set out to promote the sale of Liberty Loan Bonds and stir up support for the war in Europe. They gave talks of four minutes' duration to church congregations, cinema audiences, lodges and the like.

**Four-minute mile.** The running of a mile in 4 minutes was for many years the eagerly sought goal of professional athletes. The rigorous training and timed pacing of P.J. Nurmi (Finland) achieved a time of 4 minutes 10.4 seconds in 1924, but Roger Bannister (b.1929) was the first man to achieve the ambition in 1954, when he breached the barrier at Oxford with a time of 3 minutes 59.4 seconds. In 1979 Sebastian Coe set a new world record of 3 minutes 49 seconds, only to be beaten almost immediately by Steve Ovett, who reduced this time by one-fifth of a second. The time has subsequently been gradually eroded. Coe beat his own record in 1981 with a running of 3 minutes 47.33 seconds, and in 1999 the Moroccan athlete Hicham El Guerrouj notched up a new world record with a mile in 3 minutes 43.14 seconds.

**Fourpenny one.** A hit or blow, especially one with the fist. The reference may be to the four knuckles. Some authorities derive the phrase from RHYMING SLANG, in which fourpenny bit means hit. *See also* BUNCH OF FIVES.

**Four PP** or **Ps, The.** A 'merry interlude' by John Heywood, written *c.*1540. The four principal characters are 'a Palmer, a Pardoner, a Potticary [apothecary] and a Pedlar'. *See also* GREATEST LIE.

**Four seas, The.** The seas surrounding Great Britain on the north, south, east and west.

**Four Sons of Aymon, The.** The *chanson de geste* of *Doon de Mayence* (13th century) describes the struggle of certain feudal VASSALS against

CHARLEMAGNE, including Doon of Mayence and Aymon of Dordogne. The exploits of the four sons of Aymon (Renauld or RINALDO, Alard, Guichard and Richard, with their horse BAYARD) is a central feature. They appear in many other poems and romances including Pulci's MORGANTE MAGGIORE (1485), Boiardo's ORLANDO INNAMORATO (1487), Ariosto's ORLANDO FURIOSO (1532), and Tasso's *Rinaldo* (1562) and JERUSALEM DELIVERED (1580–81).

**Four-square.** Solidly based; steady and resolute.

**All fours.** *See under* ALL.

**Annals of the Four Masters, The.** *See under* ANNALS.

**Devil's four-poster.** *See under* DEVIL.

**First Four Ships.** *See under* FIRST.

**Gang of four.** *See under* GANG.

**History of the Four Kings, The.** *See under* HISTORY.

**Plus fours.** *See under* PLUS.

**Fourierism.** A utopian socialist system advocated by François Marie Charles Fourier (1772–1837) of Besançon. Society was to be organized into 'phalanges' each consisting of about 1600 people sharing common buildings (the *phalanstère*) and working about 5000 acres (2023 hectares) of land, with suitable facilities for the development of handicrafts and sources of amusement and a harmonious social life. The most menial tasks were to be the best rewarded out of the common gain and pleasant labour the least well rewarded. The 'phalanges' were to be linked together in suitable groups and finally into one great federation with the capital Constantinople. A number of short-lived Fourierist phalanges were established in the USA in the middle years of the 19th century but all had disappeared by 1860.

**Fourteen.** The number has several curious coincidences in its connection with Henry IV and Louis XIV of France:

Henry IV:
- There are 14 letters in the name Henry of Bourbon
- He was the fourteenth king of France and Navarre on the extinction of the family of Navarre
- He was born on 14 December 1553, the sum of which year amounts to 14
- His first wife, Marguerite de Valois, was born on 14 May 1553
- On 14 March 1590 he won his decisive victory at Ivry
- On 14 May 1590 a great ecclesiastical and military demonstration was organized in Paris against him
- Gregory XIV placed Henry under the papal ban
- On 14 May 1610 Henry was assassinated by Ravaillac

Louis XIV:
- He was the fourteenth king of this name
- He ascended the throne in 1643, the sum of which figures equals 14
- He died in 1715, the sum of which figures equals 14
- He lived for 77 years, the sum of which figures equals 14
- He was born in 1638 and died in 1715, which added together equals 3353, the sum of which figures equals 14

**Fourteen hundred.** The cry raised on the Stock Exchange to give notice that a stranger has entered the 'House'. The term is said to have been in use in Defoe's time, and to have originated when, for a considerable period, the number of members had remained stationary at 1399.

**Fourteen Points.** The 14 conditions laid down by President Woodrow Wilson (1856–1924) as those on which the Allies were prepared to make peace with Germany on the conclusion of the First World War. He outlined them in a speech to Congress on 8 January 1918, and they were eventually accepted as the basis for the peace. They included the evacuation by Germany of all allied territory, the restoration of an independent Poland, freedom of the seas, reduction of armaments and OPEN DIPLOMACY.

**Fourth. Fourth dimension.** As a mathematical concept, a hypothetical dimension, whose relation to the recognized three of length, breadth and thickness is analogous to their relation with each other. Albert Einstein in 1921 introduced time as the fourth dimension in his Theory of Relativity. The expression is also occasionally used to describe something beyond the limits of normal experience.

**Fourth estate, The.** The press. Edmund Burke, referring to the Reporters' Gallery in the HOUSE OF COMMONS, is reputed to have said, 'Yonder sits the fourth estate, more important than them all,' but it does not appear in his published works. The phrase has also been applied to the working classes. It occurs in Hazlitt's *Table Talk* (vi, 115 (1821)) referring to the influence of William Cobbett.

> The gallery [in the Commons] where the reporters sit has become a fourth estate of the realm.
>
> LORD MACAULAY: *Hallam* (1828)

**Fourth of July.** *See* INDEPENDENCE DAY.

**Fourth of June, The.** King George III's birthday and speech day at Eton. The day is celebrated with a procession of boats, cricket matches and fireworks. George III was a particular patron of the school.

**Fourth Party.** The nickname of a group of four members of the CONSERVATIVE opposition who harassed W.E. Gladstone's second administration (1880–5). It consisted of Sir Henry Drummond Wolff, Sir John Gorst, A.J. Balfour and their leader, Lord Randolph Churchill. They seized their first opening during the disputes over Bradlaugh's admission to Parliament, when, as an atheist, Bradlaugh refused to take the parliamentary oath of allegiance. They made every use of their political opportunities against the government and strongly criticized their own FRONT BENCH under the somewhat ineffective leadership of Sir Stafford Northcote. The name Fourth Party arose when an MP referred to two parties (meaning LIBERAL and Conservative) and Charles Stewart Parnell, the leader of the Irish members, called out 'three'; Randolph Churchill then interjected to make it 'four'. *See also* PRIMROSE LEAGUE.

**Fourth Republic.** The French Republic established in 1946 to replace the provisional governments that followed the collapse of the VICHY regime after D-DAY. It was essentially a continuation of the THIRD REPUBLIC and gave way to the Fifth Republic in 1958.

**Fowl. Guinea fowl.** *See under* GUINEA.

**Neither fish, flesh nor fowl.** *See under* NEITHER.

**Fowler.** The short name of *A Dictionary of Modern English Usage*, by H.W. Fowler (1858–1933), first published in 1926 and soon established as a 'bible' for settling matters of dispute in the use of English. Fowler first made his name in 1906 with *The King's English*, a book about good and bad English written together with his brother, F.G. Fowler. A second edition of the *Dictionary*, revised by Sir Ernest Gowers, appeared in 1965, and a much more radical revision, edited by R.W. Burchfield, was issued in 1996 under the title *The New Fowler's Modern English Usage*. Fowler's name often occurs in the phrase 'according to Fowler'.

**Fowler, The.** Henry I (876–936), son of Otto, Duke of Saxony and king of Germany from 919 to 936. According to 11th-century tradition, when the deputies announced to him his election to the throne, they found him fowling (hunting birds) with a hawk on his fist.

**Fox. Fox, To.** To steal or cheat; to keep an eye on somebody without seeming to do so; to baffle. A dog, a fox and a weasel are said to sleep 'with one eye open'.

**Fox and Goose.** *See under* PUBLIC HOUSE NAMES.

**Fox and grapes.** Said of someone who wants a thing badly but cannot obtain it, and so tries to pretend that he or she does not really want it at all. *See also* SOUR GRAPES.

**Foxed.** A print or page of a book stained with reddish-brown marks is said to be 'foxed' because of its colour. Foxed is also used to imply baffled or bewildered, and fuddled or the worse for liquor.

**Foxfire.** The luminescent glow, without heat, that is emitted by some fungi on rotting wood. The word is said to derive from French *faux feu*, 'false fire'.

**Foxglove.** The flower *Digitalis purpurea* is named from the animal and the glove. It is not known how the fox came to be associated with it, but one suggestion is that it is a corruption of folk's glove, folk being the fairies or little people. In Welsh it is called *menig ellyllon* ('elves' gloves') or *menig y llwynog* ('the fox's gloves'), and in Ireland it is called fairy thimble.

**Foxhole.** A small slit trench or pit for one or more men.

**Fox terrier.** A short-haired breed of terrier originally used to unearth foxes.

**Foxtrot.** A short, quick walking pace, as of a fox. A foxtrot is also a ballroom dance originating in America, popular from the 1920s until the 1950s.

**Foxy.** As well as meaning 'crafty', as a fox is traditionally said to be, the word is also used in the sense sexually attractive.

> W/f [white female] ... 21 years old and foxy, would like to hear from a gorgeous man with a terrific body.
> *Easyriders* (February 1983)

**Br'er Fox and Br'er Rabbit.** *See under* BR'ER.

**Old Fox.** *See under* OLD.

**Reynard the Fox.** *See under* REYNARD.

**Foyle's.** A name synonymous with literature and luncheons. The bookstore of W. & G. Foyle Ltd in Charing Cross Road, London, arose from the textbook-selling business set up by the brothers William and Gilbert Foyle in 1903. Their initial stock was second-hand, but they added new books in 1912. In 1930 William's daughter, Christina Foyle (1911–99), inaugurated the literary luncheons, enabling book-lovers to see and hear well-known writers. William Foyle died in 1963, Gilbert in 1971.

**Fra. Fra Angelico.** *See under* ANGELICO.

**Fra Diavolo.** *See under* DIAVOLO.

**Fracasse, Captain.** A boisterous soldier of Italian comedy and a successor to the *Miles gloriosus* ('boastful soldier') of classical comedy. He was the inspiration for Théophile Gautier's picaresque novel *Le Capitaine Fracasse* (1863), in which his role is taken on by the impoverished Baron de Sigognac. His name comes from the legendary giant Fracassus, itself based on Italian *fracassare*, 'to smash', 'to shatter'.

**Frame. Frame-up.** A false or trumped-up criminal charge against an innocent victim. The term is of American origin, and it is said to derive from the framed photographs of criminals kept by law enforcement agencies.

**Oxford frame.** *See under* OXFORD.

**France.** *See* FRANKS.

**Lily of France, The.** *See under* LILY.

**Francesca da Rimini.** The daughter of Guido da Polenta, Lord of Ravenna. Her story is told in

Dante's *Inferno* (v (*c*.1309–20)). She was married to Gianciotto Malatesta for reasons of state, but on his discovery of her adultery with his younger brother, Paolo, he put both to death *c*.1283. Leigh Hunt wrote a poem on the subject, *The Story of Rimini* (1816), and there are tragedies by Silvio Pellico, *Francesca da Rimini* (1815); Stephen Phillips, *Paolo and Francesca* (1900); Gabriele d'Annunzio, *Francesca da Rimini* (1902); and F.M. Crawford, *Francesca da Rimini* (1902). This last play was written for Sarah Bernhardt. The story also inspired, among others, Tchaikovsky's symphonic fantasy (1876); the opera (based on d'Annunzio's play) by Riccardo Zandonai (1914); the opera by Sergei Rachmaninov (1906); and the symphonic poem by Henry Hadley (1905).

**Francis. Francis of Assisi, St.** The founder of the FRANCISCANS. Born in 1182, son of a wealthy merchant, he was rejected by his father for his generous gifts to the poor folk of Assisi, and his little chapel was soon thronged with disciples. His love of nature was a characteristic, together with his purity and gentleness of spirit, and his preaching to the birds became a favourite subject for artists. His begging friars lived in extreme poverty. He was canonized two years after his death (1226).

**Franciscans.** The Friars Minor, founded by St FRANCIS OF ASSISI in 1209 and now divided into three distinct and independent branches: the Friars Minor, the Friars Minor Conventual and the Friars Minor CAPUCHIN. These constitute the First Order. The Franciscans first appeared in England in 1224 and were called Grey Friars from the indeterminate colour of their habit, which is now brown. They had 65 religious houses in England at the time of the REFORMATION. The distinguishing feature of the order at the outset was insistence on poverty, which later produced dissension. Many of the stricter members, called Spirituals or Zealots, the less strict FRATICELLI, and in 1517 the Observantins, separated from the Conventuals, and in the 1520s the Capuchins became another order. Later groups were the Reformati, the Recollects and the Discalced (BAREFOOTED). The whole Order was reorganized into its present branches by Leo XIII in 1897. An ANGLICAN order of Franciscan friars was established in Dorset in 1931. *See also* CORDELIER; TERTIARIES.

Those nuns following a milder rule instituted by Urban IV in 1263 were called Urbanists, and a reformed order of Colettines founded by St Colette arose in the 15th century, other offshoots being the Grey Sisters, Capuchin Nuns, Sisters of the Annunciation and Conceptionists. For the Second Order (of Nuns) *see* ORDER OF ST CLARE.

**St Francis Xavier.** One of the earliest of the JESUITS and a Spanish missionary (1506–52), who was celebrated as the Apostle of the Indies and the Apostle of Japan. His day is 3 December.

**Franconi, King.** Joachim Murat (1767–1815), NAPOLEON BONAPARTE's great cavalry leader, who became king of Naples in 1808, was so named after the gold-laced circus-master.

**Francs-tireurs** (French, 'free-shooters'). Sharpshooters, skirmishers or irregular troops. They were originally unofficial military units or rifle clubs formed in France during the Luxembourg crisis of 1867, and they gave notable service in the Franco-German War of 1870–1. They wore no uniform until they were brought under proper French military control. They were shot if captured by the Germans.

**Frank, Anne.** A German Jewish girl (1929–45) who kept a lively and moving diary when in hiding from the Nazis with her family in Holland and who perished in a concentration camp. The only surviving member of her family was her father. Her diary was first published in abridged form in 1947 (in English in 1952). Many of the original entries relating to her repressed sexual feelings were issued separately in 1989 and a full 'definitive' edition appeared in 1997.

**Frankenstein.** The young student in Mary Wollstonecraft Shelley's romance of that name (1818), a classic horror story. Frankenstein made a soulless monster out of corpses from churchyards and dissecting rooms and endued it with life by galvanism. The tale shows that the creature longed for sympathy but was shunned by everyone and became the instrument of dreadful retribution on the student who usurped the prerogative of the Creator. The name is sometimes wrongly used as that of the monster itself, and hence for any monstrous creation. *See also* VAMPIRE.

> There are now growing indications that the Nationalists in South Africa have created a political Frankenstein which is pointing the way to a non-White political revival.
> *Daily Telegraph* (3 May 1971)

**Frankincense.** The literal meaning of the word is 'pure incense', from Old French *franc encens*. It is a fragrant gum exuded from several trees of the genus *Boswellia*, abundant on the Somali coast and in southern Arabia. It was ceremonially used by the Egyptians, Persians, Babylonians, Hebrews, Greeks and Romans and is an ingredient of the modern incense used in some churches.

> And when they had opened their treasures, they presented unto him gifts; gold, and frankincense, and myrrh.
> Matthew 2:11

**Frankpledge.** A system originating in Anglo-Saxon times by which all men were to be grouped in a TITHING or frankpledge with the responsibility for each other's actions. If one of their number committed an offence, the others would compel him to answer for it or see that reparation was made. Men of position were excused, as were freeholders, and the system came to apply only to the unfree over 12 years of age.

**Franks.** (1) Free letters for government officials and Members of Parliament. The privilege of franking a letter was held by numerous court officials in Tudor times. By writing their name and title on the corner of the letter they obtained free delivery. This concession was abused from the outset and after the RESTORATION was increasingly exploited by members of both Houses of Parliament signing the letters of friends and others. By an act of 1764 each member of either house of Parliament was permitted to send 10 free letters daily and to receive 15. The abuse continued and the right was abolished in 1840 on the introduction of the penny post. Today, however, MPs are entitled to free stationery, postage and inland telephone calls from within the House of Commons.

(2) The Germanic tribe, probably originating in Pomerania (on the southern shore of the Baltic Sea), which conquered GAUL after the fall of the Roman Empire, whence the name France.

**Frater.** The refectory or dining room of a monastery, where the brothers (Latin *fratres*) met together for meals. In old vagabond slang a frater was much the same as an ABRAM MAN, a usage derived from the friar's begging habits.

**Fraternity, The.** A term highwaymen used to apply to themselves as a body but the 'gentlemen of the road' were by no means always on friendly terms with one another.

**Fraticelli** (Italian, 'little brethren'). A name given to several groups of monks and friars in Italy in the 13th, 14th and 15th centuries, many of whom were originally FRANCISCANS. They were mostly fanatical ascetics and came to be branded as HERETICS.

**Frazzle, Worn to a.** *See under* WEAR.

**Frederick the Great.** While Frederick II (1712–86) was at SANS SOUCI, the palace he had built at Potsdam, he went into his anteroom to drink a cup of chocolate, but set his cup down to fetch a handkerchief. On his return he found a great spider had fallen from the ceiling into his cup. He called for fresh chocolate and the next moment heard the report of a pistol. The cook had been bribed to poison the chocolate and, supposing he had been found out, shot himself. On the ceiling of the room in Sans Souci a spider has been painted (according to tradition) in remembrance of this event.

**Fred Karno's army.** *See* KARNO.

**Free. Free and easy.** Casual and carefree. The expression has an implication of moral laxity.

> 'It's just that I don't believe in this – whatever you call it – this free-and-easy way of going on. It –' 'Anticipation of marriage is probably how they put it in your – in the advice columns.'
>
> KINGSLEY AMIS: *Take a Girl Like You*, ch iv (1960)

**Free association.** In psychology a method of investigating a person's unconscious by eliciting spontaneous associations with ideas or words proposed by the examiner. The word 'chair' might thus prompt a response 'table' in one subject, 'high' in another and 'electric' in a third. The second and third of these would alert the examiner more than the first would.

**Freebie.** A colloquialism for something provided free, especially as a bonus, PERK or inducement. The increasing prevalence of freebies by way of corporate hospitality in the business world has met with some criticism. *See also* FRINGE BENEFITS.

> The freebie-culture of certain professions – journalism, showbiz, PR – causes people to start believing, against all reason, that they shouldn't have to pay full price for *anything*.
>
> *The Times* (24 October 1994)

**Freebooter.** A pirate; an adventurer who makes his living by plundering; literally, one who obtains his booty free (Dutch *vrij*, 'free', and *buit*, 'booty'). *See also* FILIBUSTER.

**Free Churches.** The NONCONFORMIST churches, so called because they are free from any kind of official connection with the state.

**Free Church of Scotland.** The church formed by those who left the established CHURCH OF SCOTLAND after the disruption of 1843.

**Free companies.** A name given to groups of disbanded mercenaries who roamed France, plundering and pillaging during the HUNDRED YEAR'S WAR in the mid-14th century.

**Freedom Trail, The.** A famous tourist route through Boston, Massachusetts, starting at the Old South Meeting House, where in 1773 the decision was taken to dump English tea imports into the harbour (the BOSTON TEA PARTY). It passes many historic sites, especially those where heroes of the American Revolution (War of American Independence) are buried.

**Free fall.** A downward movement due solely to gravity, as of a parachutist before the parachute opens. The term is also generally used for any state of falling rapidly, as of a 'plunge' of share prices on the stock market.

**Free fight, A.** A fight in which all engage, rules being disregarded. A free-for-all is much the same, whether applied to a scuffle or an argument.

**Free-for-all.** A FREE FIGHT.

**Free French.** *See* FIGHTING FRENCH.

**Free, gratis and for nothing.** At no cost whatsoever to the recipient. The double tautology is sometimes used ironically, as: 'I'll tell you this free, gratis and for nothing'.

**Free hand, A.** Freedom of action, without the need of referring to others for approval.

**Freehold.** An estate held in FEE SIMPLE. *See also* COPYHOLD.

**Free house.** A public house or inn that is not tied to a particular brewery. Its landlord is thus free to sell any kind of beer he chooses.

**Freelance.** A self-employed person, especially a journalist, musician, writer or the like who is not employed continuously by a particular organization but is hired for individual assignments. The reference is to the FREE COMPANIES of the Middle Ages, which were free to sell themselves to any cause or master. The word was probably coined by Sir Walter Scott and first appears in his *Ivanhoe* (1820) as a term for a knight with no allegiance to any single cause.

**Freeloader.** A colloquial term for a person who eats and drinks at another's expense.

**Free love.** Sexual relations unrestricted by marriage.

**Free on board** or **FOB.** A term used of goods delivered on board ship or into a conveyance at the seller's expense.

**Free pardon.** A remission of the legal consequences of a crime or conviction.

**Free rein, A.** Unrestricted liberty or scope.

**Free speech.** The right to express one's opinions freely.

**Free spirit, A.** An individualistic or uninhibited person.

**Freethinker.** Someone who rejects dogma or authority, especially in matters of religion.

**Free trade.** The opposite of protection, when a government does not impose duties on imports to favour the home producer. Such a policy in Britain aroused increasing advocacy from the time of Adam Smith's *Wealth of Nations* (1776), when he attacked the existing protectionist policies which he called the Mercantile System. Largely as a result of Peel's Budgets of 1842 and 1845, the activities of the Anti-Corn Law League and the repeal of the CORN LAWS in 1846, and Gladstone's Budgets of 1853 and 1860, Britain became a free trade country. In spite of changed economic circumstances, free trade long remained a SACRED COW, but the country reverted to protection in 1932. Free trade is also an old slang term for smuggling.

**Free verse.** A breakaway from the regular classical metres, and the substitution of ordinary speech rhythms and loose or no rhyme patterns for regular stanza forms. John Milton experimented with irregular forms, and much of Robert Browning's poetry breaks away from the older tradition. From the early 20th century free verse came into its own through the influence of Ezra Pound, T.S. Eliot and others. There was a similar trend in France towards *vers libre*.

**Freewheeling.** The term first appeared in the late 19th century with the advent of the free wheel for bicycles, which allowed the rider to stop pedalling without impeding progress. In the metaphorical sense freewheeling is moving or acting without restaint.

**Free will.** The power of acting without any constraint; the ability to act as one wishes or thinks right.

**Apostle of Free Trade, The.** *See under* APOSTLE.

**As free as air.** *See under* AS.

**Bird of Freedom.** *See under* BIRD.

**It's a free country.** Said when a proposed action is not illegal, or is regarded as such by the speaker. An example might be: 'I'll park here if I want to – it's a free country.'

**Make free with, To.** To take liberties with; to use as one's own; to be too familiar with somebody.

**Wee Frees.** *See under* WEE.

**Freeman, Mrs.** The name assumed by Sarah Churchill, duchess of Marlborough (1660–1744), in her correspondence with Queen Anne. The queen called herself Mrs MORLEY.

**Freemasonry.** A secret society that has existed for many centuries and that professes to trace its origins to the building of the TEMPLE OF SOLOMON. In medieval times stonemasons banded together with their secret signs, passwords and tests. Freemasonry in its modern form, as a body with no trade connections, began to flourish in the 17th century and it is likely that Sir Christopher Wren was a member. The antiquarian Elias Ashmole (1617–92) was initiated in 1646. The first Grand Lodge of England was founded in London in 1717 and took under its aegis the many small lodges in the provinces. Even the ancient York Lodge, which has given its name to the rites of the Continent and the USA, acknowledged its authority. From this Grand Lodge of England derive all Masonic lodges throughout the world.

In Britain Masonry has three degrees: Entered Apprentice, Fellow of the Craft and Master Mason. Royal Arch Masonry is an adjunct to these and is peculiar to Britain. In the USA the first regular lodge was founded at Boston in 1733, although minutes exist of a lodge in Philadelphia in 1730. The ritual side of Freemasonry has appealed to American more than it has to British Masons, and many degrees are worked in the USA with elaborate ritual and mysteries. In addition to the three degrees of British Masonry, there are the Cryptic Degrees of Royal and Select Masters, the Chivalric Rite, with three degrees of Knights Red Cross, Temple and of Malta, and the 33 degrees of the Ancient and Accepted Scottish Rite. The various Grand Orients of the Continent (all disowned by the Grand Lodge of England because of their political activities) were founded at different times and work modifications of the Scottish Rite. Freemasonry has been condemned by the papacy, not only for being a secret society, but for its alleged subversive aims, which, if supported by continental Masons, were quite unknown to their British and American brethren. Freemasonry is not a Christian institution, but charity and 'brotherly love' are characteristics of the fraternity, and much is done to help members and their dependants with the provision of hospitals, schools and the like and to provide relief for widows and orphans.

**Lady Freemason, The.** Women were not admitted into FREEMASONRY, but the story goes that a lady was initiated in the early 18th century. She was the Hon Elizabeth St Leger, daughter of Lord Doneraile, who hid herself in an empty clockcase when the lodge was held in her father's house, and witnessed the proceedings. She was discovered and compelled to submit to initiation as a member. Today female relatives of Master Masons may join the Order of the Eastern Star. There are also separate orders for boys and girls.

**Freezing point.** The temperature at which liquid becomes solid. If mentioned without qualification, the freezing point of water is meant (32° Fahrenheit, 0° Centigrade). The zero of Fahrenheit's thermometer is 32° below freezing point, being the lowest temperature recorded by him in the winter of 1709.

**Freischütz** (German, 'freeshooter'). A legendary German marksman in league with the Devil, who gave him seven balls, six of which were to hit infallibly whatever the marksman aimed at, with the seventh to be directed as the Devil wished. Weber's opera, *Der Freischütz*, based on the legend (libretto by Friedrich Kind), was first produced in Berlin in 1821.

**French.** The national adjective has come to have sexual or at any rate 'naughty' connotations. Examples are French kiss, for a kiss with one's tongue in the other's mouth, French knickers, as a wide-legged kind worn by women, and French letter, as a euphemism for a condom. The French themselves call this last a *capote anglaise*, 'English cap'. *See also* DUTCH CAP.

**French bread.** A long, slender loaf of white bread with a crisp crust.

**French cricket.** A simplified form of cricket played by children, usually with the batsmen's legs serving as the wicket.

**French Devil, The.** Jean Bart (1651–1702), French admiral and a native of Dunkirk. He was a terror to English shipping during the wars between William III and Louis XIV.

**French dressing.** A salad dressing with an oil and vinegar base.

**French fries.** Potato chips.

**French leave.** Leave or absence without permission or without announcing one's departure. The reference is to the French custom of leaving without saying goodbye to one's host. The French associated the habit with the English, however. Hence their equivalent for 'to take French leave', which is *s'en aller* (or *filer*) *à l'anglaise*, 'to go away in the English way'.

**Frenchman.** *See* NATIONAL NICKNAMES.

**French mustard.** A mild mustard made with vinegar rather than water, and usually contrasted with the stronger English mustard.

**French Pléiade, The.** A 16th-century group, whose members wrote poetry in the metre and style of the ancient Greeks and Romans. Pierre de Ronsard (1524–85) was their leader, the others being Joachim du Bellay, Rémi Belleau, Jean Antoine de Baïf, Étienne Jodelle, Pontus de Tyard and Jacques Peletier. Scévole de Sainte-Marthe and Muretus are sometimes cited instead of Jodelle and Pontus de Tyard. *See also* CHARLEMAGNE'S PLEIAD.

**French Revolutionary Calendar.** Adopted by the NATIONAL CONVENTION on 5 October 1793, retrospectively as from 22 September 1792, and in force in France till 1 January 1806, when NAPOLEON BONAPARTE restored the GREGORIAN CALENDAR. It consisted of 12 months of 30 days each, with five intercalary days, called SANS CULOTTIDES. Every fourth or Olympic Year was to have six such days. It was devised by Gilbert Romme (1750–55), the months being named by the poet Fabre d'Eglantine (1755–94), as follows (beginning in autumn): VENDÉMIAIRE, BRUMAIRE, Frimaire, NIVÔSE, Pluviôse, VENTÔSE, Germinal, Floréal, Prairial, Messidor, THERMIDOR and Fructidor.

**French toast.** Bread that is buttered on one side and toasted on the other. Also a slice of bread soaked in milk, dipped in beaten egg and fried. The French know the latter as *pain perdu*, literally 'lost bread', since the bread virtually disappears under its smothering of milk, egg and fat.

**Fighting French.** *See under* FIGHT.

**Norman French.** *See under* NORMAN.

**Fresh. As fresh as a daisy.** *See under* AS.

**Breath of fresh air, A.** *See under* BREATH.

**Fresh blood.** *See* NEW BLOOD.

**Freyja.** In Norse mythology the sister of FREYR, goddess of love, marriage and of the dead. She was the wife of ODIN and always wore the shining necklace called Brisingamen and was consequently called 'ornament-loving'. Her husband is also given in some legends as Odhr, and she shed golden tears when he left her. She is the counterpart of VENUS, and is also commonly identified with Frigg, wife of Odin, who in Scandinavian myth ranked highest among the goddesses. Her name means 'lady', 'mistress', related to German *Frau*. *See also* FRIDAY.

**Freyr.** In Norse mythology, the brother of FREYJA and the god of fruitfulness and crops and of the sun and rain. He owned a miraculous boar called Gullinborsti ('Golden Bristle') and his ship was SKIDBLADNIR. His name means 'lord', 'master'.

**Friar** (Latin *frater*, 'brother'). A member of one of the mendicant orders, notably the AUGUSTINIANS, CARMELITES, DOMINICANS and FRANCISCANS. *See also* CRUTCHED FRIARS.

**Friar Bungay.** *See under* BUNGAY.

**Friar Rush.** A legendary house spirit who originated as a kind of mischievous ROBIN GOODFELLOW in German folklore. He later acquired more devilish attributes and appeared in the habit of a friar to lead astray those under religious vows. Thomas Dekker's play *If it be not Good, the Divel is in it* (printed 1612) was based on *The Pleasant History of Friar Rush* (1567).

**Friar's Lanthorn.** One of the many names given to the Will o' the Wisp. *See also* IGNIS FATUUS.

**Friars Major** (*Fratres majores*). Sometimes applied to the DOMINICANS in contrast to the FRIARS MINOR.

**Friars Minor** (*Fratres minores*). The FRANCISCANS.

**Friar Tuck.** *See under* TUCK.

**Augustinian** or **Austin Friars.** *See under* AUGUSTINE.

**Begging friars.** *See under* MENDICANT ORDERS.

**Black Friars.** *See under* BLACK.

**Crutched Friars.** *See under* CRUTCHED.

**Curtal Friar.** *See under* CURTAL.

**Grey Friars.** *See* FRANCISCANS.

**White Friars.** *See* CARMELITES.

**Friday.** The sixth day of the week (or fifth counting from Monday). In ancient ROME it was called *dies Veneris*, 'day of VENUS', hence French *vendredi*. The northern nations adopted the same nomenclature and the nearest equivalent to Venus was Frigg or FREYJA, hence Friday (Old English *frīgedæg*).

Friday was regarded by the Norsemen as the luckiest day of the week, when weddings took place, but among Christians it has been regarded as the unluckiest, because it was the day of the crucifixion. While no longer a day of compulsory abstinence for Roman Catholics, they are urged to set Friday apart for some voluntary act of self-denial.

Friday is the SABBATH for Muslims, who hold that ADAM was created on a Friday and that it was on Friday that Adam and EVE ate the FORBIDDEN FRUIT and on Friday that they died. It is also held unlucky among Buddhists and BRAHMANS.

In England it is not unlucky to be born on this day, since 'Friday's child is loving and giving'. It is held to be a bad day for ships to put to sea, but in 1492 Columbus set sail on a Friday and sighted land on a Friday. It was also sometimes called 'hanging day' because condemned criminals were often executed then.

**Friday the thirteenth.** A particularly unlucky Friday. One falling in February in a non-LEAP YEAR will also occur in March and November. *See also* THIRTEEN.

**Black Friday.** *See under* BLACK.

**Bloody Friday.** *See under* BLOODY.

**Good Friday**. *See under* GOOD.

**Man Friday.** *See under* MAN.

**Nine first Fridays, The.** *See under* NINE.

**Red Friday.** *See under* RED.

**Friend.** A QUAKER, i.e. a member of the Society of Friends. In the law courts counsel refer to each other as 'my learned friend', though they may be entire strangers, just as in the House of Commons one MP speaks of another member of his party as 'my honourable friend'. In the House of Lords the equivalent is 'my noble friend'.

**Friend at court, A.** A friend who is in a position to help by influencing those in power or authority.

**Friendly fire.** A military euphemism for fire coming from one's own side, especially when it results in accidental injury or death among one's own forces. The phrase was current in the Vietnam War (1955–75) but came into prominence during the Gulf War of 1991, when many fatal casualties among allied troops were attributed to it. 'Friendly bombing' is also found as a variant.

**Friend in need is a friend indeed, A.** The Latin saying (from Ennius) is, *Amicus certus in re incerta cernitur* ('A sure friend is made known when (one is) in difficulty').

**Friendly match.** In sport, a match played in friendly rivalry, not in competition for a cup or other trophy.

**Friendly society.** A voluntary self-help organization providing insurance against sickness, infirmity, death etc, payable from central funds. Friendly societies developed from the late 17th century and became widespread in the 19th and early 20th centuries. There are over 6000 registered societies in the UK, including the Odd Fellows, Foresters and Hearts of Oak.

**Friendly suit** or **action, A.** An action at law between parties by mutual arrangement with the object of obtaining a legal decision upon some point which concerns them both.

**Friend of Man, The.** The name given to the

Marquis de Mirabeau (1715–89), father of Honoré Gabriel Riqueti, Comte de Mirabeau (1749–91), of French revolutionary fame. His great work was *L'Ami des Hommes* (1756), hence the nickname.

**Friend of the court, A** (Latin *amicus curiae*). A legal term to denote anyone not concerned in a case who brings to the attention of the court some point or decision of law which seems to have been overlooked.

**Friendship.** The classical examples of lasting friendship between man and man are ACHILLES and PATROCLUS, PYLADES and ORESTES, NISUS and EURYALUS, DAMON and PYTHIAS. To these should be added DAVID and JONATHAN.

**Friends of the Earth.** An environmental pressure group, originating in the USA and existing in Britain since 1970. It now has branches in a number of countries. Protests and propaganda are furthered by public meetings, demonstrations and so on. Members are actively against all forms of pollution (especially nuclear power), developments that ruin the countryside and the destruction of wildlife. *See also* GREENPEACE.

**Best friend.** *See under* BEST.

**Bosom friend.** *See under* BOSOM.

**Fair-weather friends.** *See under* FAIR.

**King's Friends.** *See under* KING.

**Mutual friends.** *See under* MUTUAL.

**Next friend.** *See under* NEXT.

**Pen friend.** *See under* PEN.

**Prisoner's friend, The.** *See under* PRISONER.

**Society of Friends, The.** The QUAKERS.

**Soldier's friend, The.** *See under* SOLDIER.

**Frigate, Stone.** *See under* STONE.

**Frigg.** *See* FREYJA.

**Frills, To put on.** To give oneself airs, frill being an affectation of dress or manner. A similar concept is expressed by the phrase 'to put on airs and graces'.

**Fringe.** The fringe, or more correctly twisted cords or tassels worn on the four corners of the Jewish outer garment (*tzitzith*) in Old Testament times and later, was believed to have a special virtue. Hence the desire of the woman who had the issue of blood to touch the hem of Jesus' garment (Matthew 9:20–22). From the 13th century an undergarment with tassels attached, the *arba kanfoth* (four corners) worn at all times by orthodox Jews, replaced the *tzitzith*.

> Thou shalt make thee fringes upon the four quarters of thy vesture, wherewith thou coverest thyself.
> Deuteronomy 22:12

**Fringe benefits.** Concessions and benefits given to employees; PERKS that go with a job or appointment such as free fuel, use of a car, pensions, insurances, medical benefits and so forth. *See also* FREEBIE.

**Fringe party.** A British political or quasi-political party with a small or ephemeral membership, as distinct from the CONSERVATIVE Party, LABOUR PARTY or Liberal Democrats (*see* LIBERAL). Many such parties emerge only at the time of a GENERAL ELECTION, and are of narrow, local or frivolous appeal, with a policy that may be specific or deliberately nebulous. As such, they add a note of eccentricity to an otherwise serious and even portentous event. One of the best known fringe parties is the Monster Raving Loony Party, founded by the pop singer David 'Screaming Lord' Sutch (1940–99), its name aptly echoing its affinity with the LUNATIC FRINGE.

In the General Election of 1997, the following were among the 150 or so fringe parties that fielded one or more candidates:

All Night Party
British Democratic Party
Care in the Community
Christian Unity
Common Sense Sick of Politicians Party
Fancy Dress Party
Hemp Coalition
Independent No to Europe
Independent Royal Forest of Dean
Legalize Cannabis Party
Lord Byro versus the Scallywag Tories
Miss Moneypenny's Glamorous One Party
None of the Above Parties
Rainbow Dream Ticket Party
Ronnie the Rhino Party
Socialist Equality Party
Space Age Superhero from Planet Beanus
Top Choice Liberal Democrat
UK Pensioners Party
Universal Alliance
Wessex Regionalist
West Cheshire College in Crisis Party

**Celtic fringe.** *See under* CELTIC.

**Lunatic fringe, The.** *See under* LUNATIC.

**Frippery.** Rubbish of a tawdry character; worthless finery. A 'friperer' or 'fripperer' was one who dealt in old clothes. French *friperie*, means 'old clothes', 'cast-off furniture'.

**Frithiof.** A hero of Icelandic myth who married Ingeborg, daughter of a minor king of Norway and widow of Sigurd Ring, to whose dominions he succeeded. His name means 'peacemaker' and his adventures are recorded in the saga which bears his name. It was paraphrased by the Swedish poet Esaias Tegnér in his *Fritiofs saga* (1825). *See also* ANGURVADEL.

**Fritz.** FREDERICK THE GREAT of Prussia (1712–86) was known as Old Fritz. In the First World War the men in the trenches commonly called any German in the enemy lines Fritz. *See also* NATIONAL NICKNAMES.

**Frock.** A word and garment with something of a patchwork history. A frock was originally a long, gown-like garment worn by men, something like a monk's habit. Hence 'unfrocked' was applied to a priest deprived of his ecclesiastical status. The term then spread to denote any long outer garment worn by men and, subsequently, by women. In the 17th and 18th centuries it was mostly a type of gown worn only by children, and from the 19th century by girls only. In the early 20th century the frock made a comeback as a women's daytime dress, while for girls it continued as a lightish indoor garment, typically one for a special occasion. Hence 'party frock', 'simple little frock' and the like.

The origin of the word is equally tortuous. Its primary source is Old French *froc*, a word in modern use either for a monk's habit or as slang for trousers. Both words are also related in some way to French *frac*, the term for a frock coat or 'tails'. This in turn is probably from English frock. The word has thus gone full circle, even if the sense has not.

> This quiet Dust was Gentleman and Ladies
> And Lads and Girls—
> Was laughter and ability and Sighing
> And Frocks and Curls.
>
> EMILY DICKINSON: 'This quiet Dust was Gentlemen and Ladies' (*c*.1864)

**Frodo.** A HOBBIT in J.R.R. Tolkien's *The* LORD OF THE RINGS (1954–5) who went on a quest to destroy a ring that could make the wearer all-powerful, lest it fall into the hands of an evil lord. 'Frodo Lives' was a HIPPIE slogan of the 1960s.

**Froebel system.** The name given to a system of KINDERGARTEN teaching by which children's abilities are developed by means of clay modelling, mat-making and similar activities, developed by Friedrich Froebel (1782–1852), a German schoolmaster.

**Frog.** Frenchmen, or more properly Parisians, have been nicknamed Frogs or Froggies, from their ancient heraldic device, which was three frogs or toads. *Qu'en disent les grenouilles?* ('What do the frogs say?') was in 1791 a common court phrase at VERSAILLES. There was point in the pleasantry, as Paris was at one time a quagmire called LUTETIA ('mud-land'). Further point is given to the nickname by the fact that the back legs of the edible frog (*Rana esculenta*) form a delicacy in French cuisine that aroused much disparaging humour from the English. *See also* FLEUR-DE-LIS; NATIONAL NICKNAMES.

**Frog in the throat, A.** A temporary loss of voice; hoarseness. The expression is said to allude to the medieval fear of drinking water containing frogspawn, when it was believed frogs would grow inside the body. Hoarseness or 'gagging' was thus allegedly caused by a frog trying to escape from the stomach by way of the throat.

**Frog march.** A method of carrying an obstreperous prisoner face downwards by his four limbs, like a frog. The term is now more generally used, however, for a way of making a person walk somewhere by pinning his arms behind him and hustling him forwards.

**Frogmen.** In the Second World War strong swimmers dressed in rubber suits with paddles on their feet resembling the feet of frogs, who operated in enemy harbours by night attaching explosives to shipping etc. They are now used in salvage operations, searches for submerged bodies and the like.

**From. From China to Peru.** From one end of the world to the other; worldwide. The expression is the equivalent of the biblical FROM DAN TO BEERSHEBA. It comes from the opening of Johnson's *Vanity of Human Wishes* (1749):

> Let observation with extensive view
> Survey mankind from China to Peru.

Boileau (*Satire*, viii, 3 (1668)) had previously written:

> De Paris au Pérou, du Japon jusqu'à Rome.
> (From Paris to Peru, from Japan as far as Rome.)

**From cold.** Without advance notice; without any guidance or instruction.

**From cover to cover.** From beginning to end of a book.

**From Dan to Beersheba.** From one end of the kingdom to the other; everywhere. The phrase occurs several times in the Bible, Dan being the northernmost city and Beersheba the southernmost in the HOLY LAND. The equivalent English expression is FROM LAND'S END TO JOHN O'GROATS.

**From hand to hand.** From one person to another.

**From here to Timbuctoo.** Said of a very long range or distance. *See also* TIMBUCTOO.

**From hour to hour.** Hourly. So also 'from day to day', 'from week to week', 'from year to year', 'from age to age' etc.

> And so from hour to hour we ripe and ripe,
> And then from hour to hour we rot and rot,
> And thereby hangs a tale.
>
> SHAKESPEARE: *As You Like It*, II, vii (1599)

**From Land's End to John o'Groats.** From one end of Great Britain to the other; FROM DAN TO BEERSHEBA.

**From pillar to post.** Hither and thither; from one thing to another without definite purpose; badgered and bothered. The phrase was originally from post to pillar, and comes from the old covered tennis courts, in allusion to the banging about of the balls.

**From pole to pole.** Throughout the entire world. The allusion is to the north and south poles.

> Oh Sleep! it is a gentle thing,
> Beloved from pole to pole.
>
> S.T. COLERIDGE: 'The Rime of the Ancient Mariner', v (1798)

**From the bottom of one's heart.** Sincerely; without reservation.

**From the cradle to the grave.** From birth to death; throughout life.

**From the sublime to the ridiculous.** In his *Age of Reason* (1794), Pt II, Thomas Paine said, 'The sublime and the ridiculous are often so nearly related, that it is difficult to class them separately. One step above the sublime, makes the ridiculous; and one step above the ridiculous, makes the sublime again.' NAPOLEON BONAPARTE, who was a great admirer of Paine, used to say: *Du sublime au ridicule il n'y a qu'un pas*.

**From the word go.** From the very beginning. The allusion is to the start of a race. *See also* READY, STEADY, GO!

**From time immemorial.** For such a long time that one cannot recall the first occurrence. In English law 'time immemorial' is before 'legal memory', i.e. before the reign of Richard I (1189–99), because the Statute of Westminster of 1275 fixed his reign as the time limit for bringing certain types of action.

**From time to time.** Occasionally. The equivalent expression exists in several languages, such as French *de temps en temps*, German *von Zeit zu Zeit*, Russian *vremya ot vremeni*, and the like.

**From top to toe.** From head to foot.

**Fronde.** The name given to a civil contest in France (1648–53) during the minority of Louis XIV. It began as a struggle against the court party for the redress of grievances, but soon became a faction fight among the nobles to undo the work of Cardinal Richelieu and to overthrow Cardinal MAZARIN. *Fronde* means 'sling', and the name arose from the occasion when the Paris mob pelted Cardinal Mazarin's windows with stones.

**Spanish Fronde, The.** *See under* SPANISH.

**Front. Front bench, The.** In the HOUSE OF COMMONS, the leading members of the government occupy the front bench to the right of the SPEAKER. This is called the Treasury Bench. The OPPOSITION leaders occupy the opposite front bench, to the left of the Speaker. Hence, by extension, the leadership of either group. *See also* BACK-BENCHER.

**Eyes front!** *See under* EYE.

**Full frontal.** *See under* FULL.

**Popular Front.** *See under* POPULAR.

**Frontier, The Northwest.** *See under* NORTH.

**Frost. Frost saints.** *See* ICE SAINTS.

**Black frost.** *See under* BLACK.

**Ground frost.** *See under* GROUND.

**Jack Frost.** *See under* JACK.

**Frozen words.** An image used by the ancient Greeks. Antiphanes applies it to the discourses of PLATO: 'As the cold of certain cities is so intense that it freezes the very words we utter, which remain congealed till the heat of summer thaws them, so the mind of youth is so thoughtless that the wisdom of Plato lies there frozen, as it were, till it is thawed by the ripened judgement of mature age.' Baron MÜNCHAUSEN relates an incident of the 'frozen horn', and Rabelais tells how PANTAGRUEL and his friends, on the confines of the Frozen Sea, heard the uproar of a battle, which had been frozen the preceding winter, released by a thaw.

> Where truth in person doth appear.
> Like words congeal'd in northern air.
>
> SAMUEL BUTLER: *Hudibras*, I, i (1662)

**Fruit. Bear fruit, To.** *See under* BEAR.

**First fruits.** *See under* FIRST.

**Old fruit.** *See under* OLD.

**Forbidden fruit.** *See under* FORBID.

**Tree is known by its fruit, The.** *See under* TREE.

**Frusberta.** RINALDO'S sword.

**Fry. Devil's Frying Pan, The.** *See under* DEVIL.

**Lamb's fry.** *See under* LAMB.

**Out of the frying pan into the fire.** *See under* OUT.

**Small fry.** *See under* SMALL.

**Fuchsia.** A genus of highly ornamental flowering shrubs coming from Mexico and the Andes, although two species are found in New Zealand. They were so named in 1703 in honour of the German botanist Leonhard Fuchs (1501–66).

**Fudge.** A mild exclamation of annoyance or disagreement. Its derivation is uncertain. Today it is probably thought of as a euphemism for the 'F-word' (*see* FOUR-LETTER WORD), much as 'sugar' euphemises an exclamatory 'shit'. Fudge is also a kind of soft candy.

**Fuel to the fire** or **flames, To add.** *See under* ADD.

**Fugger.** A famous family of German merchant bankers, particularly influential in the 15th and 16th centuries, and proverbial for their great wealth, their newsletter and fine library. 'As rich as a Fugger' is common in Elizabethan dramatists. Charles V introduced some of the family into Spain, where they superintended the mines.

**Führer** (German, 'leader'). The title assumed by Adolf Hitler (1889–1945) when he acceded to supreme power in Germany on the death of Hindenburg in 1934.

**Full. Full-blown.** In full flower, hence fully developed or qualified. 'He is a full-blown doctor now' means he is no longer a student but fully qualified to practise.

**Full board.** The provision of a bed and all meals in a hotel or the like, as distinct from bed and breakfast only.

**Full dress.** Ceremonial dress, court dress, full uniform, academicals, evening dress or any similar complete and formal garb.

**Full frontal.** A painting or photograph of a nude

person with genitals exposed to full view or an actual person standing thus.

**Full house.** A term in the game of poker for a hand holding three of one kind and two of another, e.g. 3 tens and 2 sixes. More commonly the expression is used of a theatre, cinema or other auditorium that is filled to capacity. In BINGO, full house is the set of numbers needed to win.

**Full marks.** The maximum award in a school exercise or examination, 'ten out of ten'. Hence a term of approval, as: 'Full marks to her for being so enterprising.'

**Full monty, The.** Everything; the lot; 'the works'. Said of anything done to the utmost or fullest degree. The origin of the expression is uncertain. It may derive from 'the full amount' or the Spanish card game monte (literally 'mountain', i.e. heap of cards) or allude to a full three-piece SUNDAY BEST suit from the men's outfitters Montague Burton. One explanation traces the term to Field Marshal Bernard Montgomery, nicknamed 'Monty' (1887–1976), said to have begun every day with a full English breakfast when campaigning in the African desert in the Second World War. The British phrase became familiar generally in the English-speaking world from its use as the title of a film (1997) about a group of unemployed British factory workers who raise money by staging a strip act at a local club.

**Full of beans.** Full of energy and high spirits. Beans have long been popularly regarded as an aphrodisiac.

**Full of oneself.** Conceited, egotistic.

**Full speed ahead!** Go ahead as fast as possible; get cracking! An alternative is 'full steam ahead', showing the origin of the expression in nautical parlance.

**Full term.** The completion of a normal pregnancy, i.e. one that did not result in a premature birth or an abortion.

**At full tilt.** *See under* AT.

**In full cry.** Said of a pack of hounds that have caught the scent, and that give tongue simultaneously. Hence the use of the phrase to denote a person or group of people in hot pursuit of a quarry.

**In full feather.** In good spirits. Also, in fine feather, in good feather, in high feather etc.

**In full fig.** *See* FIG.

**In full swing.** Going well, and at the peak of activity.

**To the full.** *See under* TO.

**Fum** or **Fung-hwang.** The PHOENIX (*fèng*) of Chinese legend, one of the four symbolic creatures presiding over the destinies of China. It appears only at the golden epochs, feeds only upon the seeds of the bamboo, and drinks only from the sweetest springs. It has not been seen since the days of Confucius. It was this strange creature that was embroidered on the dress of certain MANDARINS.

**Fum.** GEORGE IV.

**Fu Manchu.** The Chinese master villain who is head of the dreaded 'Si-Fan' secret society. He was the creation of Sax Rohmer (Arthur Sarsfield Ward) in a series of stories that ran in the *Story-Teller Magazine* from 1912. These were soon collected to form best-selling novels such as *The Mystery of Dr Fu Manchu* (1913). Fu operates internationally, his ultimate aim apparently being to gain mastery of the world, but his evil plans are constantly foiled by the doughty Englishman Dennis Nayland Smith. Fu Manchu's adventures were later transferred to the screen, and he became established as the 'Yellow Peril incarnate', a familiar racial stereotype.

**Fuming.** In a bad temper, especially from impatience or frustration.

**Fun. Fun and games.** Enjoyable goings-on. The phrase is frequently used ironically, especially for amatory play.

**Fun run.** A long run undertaken by a large number of people for pleasure and exercise, and especially a sponsored run, as a marathon to raise money for charity.

**Barrel of fun.** *See under* BARREL.

**Figure of fun, A.** *See under* FIGURE.

**For fun.** Not for a serious reason.

**Have fun!** Enjoy yourself! Sometimes said when the coming action will hardly be fun.

**Like fun.** *See under* LIKE.

**Make fun of, To.** To make a butt of someone; to ridicule.

**Poke fun at someone, To.** *See under* POKE.

**What fun!** How amusing!

**Fund. Consolidated fund.** *See under* CONSOLIDATED.

**Fighting fund.** *See under* FIGHT.

**Public funds.** *See under* PUBLIC.

**Sinking fund.** *See under* SINK.

**Fundamental. Fundamental colour.** A fundamental colour is one of the seven colours of the spectrum, as seen in a RAINBOW: violet, indigo, blue, green, yellow, orange and red.

**Fundamentalism.** The maintenance of traditional Protestant Christian beliefs based upon a literal acceptance of the Scriptures as fundamentals. Fundamentalism as a religious movement arose in the USA about 1919 among various denominations. What was new was not so much its ideas and attitudes, but its widespread extent and the zeal of its supporters. It opposed all theories of evolution and anthropology, holding that God transcends all laws of nature and that He manifests Himself by exceptional and extraordinary activities, belief in the literal meaning of the Scriptures being an essential tenet. In 1925, John T. Scopes, a science teacher of Rhea High School, Dayton, Tennessee, was convicted of violating the state laws by teaching evolution, an incident arousing interest and controversy far beyond the religious circles of the USA. Their leader was William Jennings Bryan (1860–1925), the politician and orator. *See also* MODERNISM.

**Funeral** (Late Latin *funeralis*, from *funus*, 'funeral'). *Funus* is connected with *fumus*, 'smoke', and the word seems to refer to the ancient practice of disposing of the dead by cremation. Roman funerals were conducted by torchlight at night, lest magistrates and priests be made ceremonially unclean by seeing the corpse.

Most modern funeral customs derive from the Romans, such as dressing in black, walking in procession, carrying insignia on the bier, raising a mound on the grave (called *tumulus*, whence tomb) and the like. The Greeks crowned the dead body with flowers and also placed flowers on the tomb. The Romans had similar customs. In England the PASSING BELL or the Soul Bell used to be tolled from the church when a parishioner was dying, and the funeral bell would be tolled as many times as the dead person's years of age.

The custom of giving a feast at funerals also came to us from the Romans, who not only feasted the friends of the deceased but also distributed food to the persons employed. *See also* ISTHMIAN GAMES; NEMEAN GAMES.

**Funk. In a funk** or **blue funk, To be.** The word may derive from Old French *funkier*, 'to smoke', though the connection is uncertain. A funk is a state of apprehensive fear or abject fear. The word first appeared at Oxford in the first half of the 18th century.

> If I was going to be flogged next minute, I should be in a blue funk.
>
> THOMAS HUGHES: *Tom Brown's Schooldays*, Pt I, ch ii (1857)

**Funny. Funny bone.** A pun on the word *humerus*, the Latin name for the arm bone. It is the inner condyle or knob at the end of the bone where the ulnar nerve is close to the surface of the skin at the elbow. A knock on this part is naturally painful and produces a tingling sensation.

**Funny business.** Suspicious behaviour; craftiness.

**Funny-face.** A term of endearment.

**Funny farm.** A colloquial or facetious term for a psychiatric hospital.

**Funny money.** Inflated or counterfeit currency.

**Funny-peculiar or funny-ha-ha?** A question put to someone who uses the word 'funny' without making it clear which of the two senses is meant.

> *Chris*: That's funny.
> *Button*: What do you mean, funny? Funny-peculiar, or funny ha-ha?
>
> IAN HAY: *Housemaster*, III (1936)

**Too funny for words.** *See under* TOO.

**Fur. Fur and feather.** Game animals and birds.

**Make the fur** or **feathers fly, To.** To create a violent disturbance or to attack vigorously, either physically or by speech or writings, as when birds or animals are attacked or attack each other.

**Furies, The.** The Roman name (*Furiae*) for the Greek ERINYES, said by Hesiod to have been the daughters of GAIA (the Earth) and to have sprung from the blood of URANUS, and by other accounts to be daughters of Night or of Earth and Darkness. They were three in number: Tisiphone (the Avenger of Blood), ALECTO (the Implacable) and Megaera (the Jealous).

They were merciless goddesses of vengeance and punished all transgressors, especially those who neglected filial duty or claims of kinship. Their punishments continued after death. *See also* EUMENIDES.

**Furies of the guillotine, The.** *See* TRICOTEUSES.

**Furioso, Orlando.** *See under* ORLANDO.

**Furious, Fast and.** *See under* FAST.

**Furnace, The burning fiery.** *See under* BURN.

**Furry Dance.** Part of the spring festival held at Helston, Cornwall, on 8 May (or if this is a Sunday or Monday, on the preceding Saturday). 'Furry', which perhaps derives from Latin *feriae*, 'festivals', 'holidays', or is related in some way to English fair, was incorrectly changed to 'Flora' in the 18th century, and in the 19th century the dance was called the 'Floral Dance', as in the well-known song. It is derived from a pre-Christian festivity and is copied in some other towns. In its present form it begins at 7 am with the Early Morning Dance, led by the Mayor. The children then begin their dance at about 10 am, and the principal Furry Dance steps out from the Guildhall at noon. Hundreds of dancing couples try to weave in and out of all the houses, if possible entering and leaving though different doors, as this brings extra luck. At 5 pm a free-for-all ball begins. There is a similar spring festival at Padstow beginning at midnight on 30 April, when the revelry centres on the 'Obby 'Oss. *See also* HAL-AN-TOW; HOBBY.

**Fuss. As fussy as a hen with one chick.** *See under* AS.

**Kick up a fuss, To.** *See under* KICK.

**Fustian.** A coarse twilled cotton cloth with a velvety pile, probably so called from Fustat, a suburb of Cairo. It is chiefly used now in a figurative sense meaning inflated or pompous talk, CLAPTRAP, BOMBAST or pretentious words. *See also* FLANNEL.

**Futhorc** or **futhark.** The ancient runic alphabet of

the Anglo-Saxons and other Germanic peoples, so called (on the same principle as the ABC) from its first six letters: f, u, th, a, r, k.

**Futurism.** An art movement that originated at Turin in 1909 under the influence of Filippo Tommaso Marinetti (1876–1944). Its adherents sought to introduce into paintings a 'poetry of motion' whereby, for example, the painted gesture should become actually 'a dynamic condition'. The Futurists tried to indicate not only the state of mind of the painter but also that of the figures in the picture. It was another movement to shake off the influence of the past. The original Futurists included Marinetti, Umberto Boccioni (1882–1916), Carlo Carrà (1881–1966), Luigi Russolo (1885–1947) and Gino Severini (1883–1966), and they first exhibited at Paris in 1912. *See also* CUBISM; DADAISM; FAUVISM; IMPRESSIONISM; ORPHISM; SURREALISM; SYNCHROMISM; VORTICISM.

**Fylfot.** A mystic sign or emblem known also as the SWASTIKA and GAMMADION, and in HERALDRY as the cross cramponnée, used (especially in Byzantine architecture and among the North American Indians) as an ornament of religious import. It has been found at Hissarlik, on ancient Etruscan tombs, CELTIC monuments, Buddhist inscriptions, Greek coins and elsewhere. It was thought to have represented the power of the sun, of the four winds, of lightning and so on. It is used nowadays in jewellery as an emblem of luck and was also adopted as the NAZI badge. (*See* diagram on page 298.) The term fylfot was adopted by antiquaries from a 15th-century manuscript, and it possibly means fill foot, denoting a device to fill the foot of a stained glass or painted window.

# G

**G.** This letter is a modification of the Latin C, which was a rounding of the Greek *gamma*, Γ. Until the 3rd century BC the g and k sounds were both represented by the letter C. In the Hebrew and old Phoenician alphabets G is the outline of a camel's head and neck, and Hebrew *gimel* means 'camel'.

**Gab, The gift of the.** *See under* GIFT.

**Gabars.** Followers of the ancient Persian religion, reformed by Zoroaster. They are fire worshippers and PARSEES. The name, which was given them by their Muslim conquerors, is now applied to fire-worshippers generally. It is linguistically related to that of the KAFFIRS. *See also* ZOROASTRIANS.

**Gabbara.** The giant who, according to Rabelais, was 'the inventor of the drinking of HEALTHS'.

**Gabriel** (Hebrew *gavrī'el*, 'man of God'). One of the ARCHANGELS, sometimes regarded as the angel of death, the prince of fire and thunder but more frequently as one of God's chief messengers, and traditionally said to be the only angel who can speak Syriac and Chaldee. The Muslims call him the chief of the four favoured angels and the spirit of truth. Milton makes him chief of the angelic guards placed over Paradise (*Paradise Lost*, iv (1667)).

In the TALMUD Gabriel appears as the destroyer of the hosts of SENNACHERIB, as the man who showed Joseph the way, and as one of the angels who buried MOSES.

According to the KORAN it was Gabriel who took MOHAMMED to heaven on Al BORAK and revealed to him his 'prophetic love'. In the Old Testament Gabriel is said to have explained to DANIEL certain visions (Daniel 8:6–26), and in the New Testament he announced to Zacharias the future birth of JOHN THE BAPTIST (Luke 1:13 and elsewhere) and appeared to MARY the mother of Jesus (Luke 1:26 and elsewhere).

**Gabriel Bell.** In medieval England another name for the ANGELUS or Ave Bell, in remembrance of the archangel's salutation of the Virgin MARY.

**Gabriel's hounds.** Wild geese. The noise of geese in flight is like that of a pack of hounds in full cry. The legend is that they are the souls of unbaptized children, wandering through the air until the Day of Judgement.

**Gabrielle, La Belle.** Gabrielle d'Estrées (1573–99), daughter of Antoine d'Estrées, grandmaster of artillery, and governor of the Île de France. Towards the close of 1590, Henry IV happened to stay for a night at the Château de Coeuvres and was smitten with her. She married Nicolas d'Amerval but in 1592 went to live at court as Henry's mistress. She bore him three children, one of whom was César de Bourbon, Duc de Vendôme (1594–1665), leader of aristocratic revolts in the reign of Louis XIII (1610–43). She was made Duchess of Beaufort in 1597.

**Gad, By.** *See under* BY.

**Gadarene swine.** The herd of pigs into which Jesus drove demoniac spirits, so that they 'ran violently down a steep place into the sea' and were drowned. The story is told in three of the Gospels (Matthew 8:30, Mark 5:13, Luke 8:32) and symbolizes Jesus' power of exorcism as well as illustrating the general contempt in which pigs and their flesh were held. (The Prodigal Son was so hungry that he was tempted to eat their food.)

**Gaekwar** (Marathi, 'cowherd'). Formerly the title of the ruler of the Mahrattas, then that of the ruler of Baroda (his son being Gaekwad). The cow is a sacred animal to the Hindus. *See also* GURKHAS.

**Gaelic.** The language of the Gaelic branch of the CELTIC race. The name is now usually restricted to the Celtic language of the Scottish Highlands, but can also include that of Irish and Manx Celts. *See also* ERSE.

**Gaff.** A cheap public entertainment or a low-class MUSIC HALL, often called 'penny gaff' from the price of admission. Such theatres were common in Victorian times on the Surrey side of the Thames.

**Blow the gaff, To.** *See under* BLOW.

**Gaffer** (alteration of godfather). An old country fellow, or more specifically the boss, overseer or foreman. In the world of cinema and television, the gaffer is the senior electrician. *See also* GAMMER.

**Gag.** In theatrical parlance, an interpolation of lines not in the actor's stage part. When Shakespeare makes Hamlet direct the players to say no more 'than is set down' (III, ii) he cautions them against gagging. A gag is also a joke.

**Gaia** or **Ge** (Greek *gē*, 'earth'). The Greek goddess of the Earth, who gave birth to the sky, mountains and sea. By URANUS she brought forth the TITANS, the CYCLOPS and other giants and according to some legends she was the mother of the EUMENIDES.

**Gaiety Girl.** One of the beauty chorus for which the Old Gaiety Theatre in the Strand was famous in the 1890s and EDWARDIAN days. Several of them married into the peerage. *See also* GIBSON GIRL.

**Gain. Gain ground, To.** To make headway; to improve one's position.

**Gain time, To.** To improve one's chances by causing delay, or at any rate accepting it.

**Capital gain.** *See under* CAPITAL.

**Gaius Lusinus Fabricius.** *See* FABRICIUS.

**Gala** (Old French *gale*, 'pleasure'). In the general sense, a festivity or celebration, when people put on their best attire. The term is now usually used specifically for a particular sporting event, such as a swimming gala. The annual Durham miners' gala was for long a well-known demonstration of trade union pride and solidarity. First held in 1871, it was traditionally led by leading Labour politicians. From the early 1990s, however, the size and importance of the procession through the streets of Durham decreased, partly because there were fewer miners and partly because Labour politicians were less keen to align themselves publicly with the trade unions. Gala is usually pronounced to rhyme with 'parlour', but in the case of the Durham miners it traditionally rhymes with 'paler'.

**Galahad, Sir.** In the ARTHURIAN ROMANCES the purest and noblest knight of the ROUND TABLE. He is a late addition and first appears in the *Quest of the San Graal* attributed to Walter Map (*c*.1137–1209). He was the son of LANCELOT OF THE LAKE and ELAINE. At the institution of the Round Table one seat (the Siege Perilous) was left unoccupied for the knight who could succeed in the Quest. When Sir Galahad sat there it was discovered that it had been left for him. The story is found in Malory's *Morte d'Arthur* (1470) and the works of Tennyson. The knight's name may be based on a Celtic word meaning 'white', 'fair'. *See also* FINGAL.

**Galatea** (Greek *gala*, *galaktos*, 'milk'). A sea NYMPH, beloved by the monster POLYPHEMUS, but herself in love with the beautiful ACIS, who was killed by the jealous CYCLOPS. Galatea threw herself into the sea where she joined her sister nymphs. Handel has an opera entitled *Acis and Galatea* (1720). The Galatea beloved by PYGMALION was a different person.

**Galathe** (Greek, 'milk-coloured'). One of the horses of HECTOR.

**Galaxy, The** (Greek *gala*, *galaktos*, 'milk'). The Milky Way. A long, white, luminous track of stars, which seems to encompass the heavens like a girdle. It is composed of a vast collection of stars so distant that they are indistinguishable as separate stars but appear as a combined light. According to classic fable it is the path to the palace of ZEUS.

**Galen.** A Greek physician and philosopher of the 2nd century AD. For centuries he was the supreme authority in medicine. Hence 'Galenist', a follower of Galen's medical theories.

**Galère. Que diable allait-il faire dans cette galère?** ('What the Devil was he doing in that galley?'). This famous line is from MOLIÈRE's comedy *Les Fourberies de Scapin* (1671). Scapin wants to swindle Géronte out of his money and tells him that his master (Géronte's son) is detained prisoner on a Turkish galley, where he went out of curiosity. The above was Géronte's reply. The phrase is applied to someone who finds himself in difficulties through being where he ought not to be, or to express surprise that he should be found in such an unusual situation.

> 'One of the St Wilfrid's priests, I suppose,' Flaxman said to himself. 'What on earth is he doing *dans cette galère?* Are we to have a disputation? That would be dramatic.'
>
> MRS HUMPHRY WARD: *Robert Elsmere*, ch xl (1888)

**Vogue la galère.** *See under* VOGUE.

**Galilee.** A chapel or porch at the west end of some churches where penitents waited before admission to the body of the church and where clergy received women who had business with them. Examples remain at Durham, Ely and Lincoln cathedrals. The name probably has a biblical origin:

> The land of Zebulon, and the land of Nephthalim, by the way of the sea, beyond Jordan, Galilee of the Gentiles.
>
> Matthew 4:15

**Galilean.** An inhabitant of Galilee, and specifically Jesus Christ, who was called 'the Galilean'. The term was also applied to Christians as his followers. The dying words attributed to the Roman Emperor JULIAN THE APOSTATE were *Vicisti, Galilaee* ('Thou hast conquered, Galilean').

**Galimatias.** Nonsense; gibberish. The word first appeared in France in the 16th century, but its origin is unknown. It may be connected with GALLIMAUFRY. In his translation of Rabelais, Sir Thomas Urquart (1611–60) heads chapter ii of Book I a 'Galimatias of Extravagant Conceits found in an Ancient Monument'.

**Gall.** Bile, as the bitter fluid secreted by the liver.

Hence the figurative use of the word as a symbol for anything of extreme bitterness.

**Gall of bitterness, The.** The bitterest grief; extreme affliction. The ancients taught that grief and joy were subject to the gall, as affection was to the heart and knowledge was to the kidneys. The 'gall of bitterness' means the bitter centre of bitterness, as the 'heart of hearts' means the innermost recesses of the heart or affections. In Acts it is used to signify 'the sinfulness of sin', which leads to the bitterest grief.

> For I perceive that thou art in the gall of bitterness, and in the bond of iniquity.
> Acts 8:23

**Gall of pigeons.** The story goes that pigeons have no gall because the dove that was sent from the ark by NOAH burst its gall out of grief, and none of the pigeon family has had a gall ever since.

**Gallant.** The meaning of this word varies with its pronunciation. When stressed on the first syllable, it is an adjective meaning 'brave', 'honourable'. When stressed on the second, it means 'chivalrous', 'attentive to women', and exists as a noun in this sense. In origin it is related to GALA.

> These two gallants passed Peveril more than once, linked arm in arm ... staring broadly at Peveril and his female companions.
> SIR WALTER SCOTT: *Peveril of the Peak*, ch xxxii (1823)

**Gallery. Ladies' Gallery.** *See under* LADY.

**Play to the gallery, To.** *See under* PLAY.

**Rogues' gallery.** *See under* ROGUE.

**Whispering gallery.** *See under* WHISPER.

**Gallia.** Poetically, France, or more properly the Latin name for Gaul, as the region in Roman times that was more extensive than France and that was populated by CELTIC peoples.

**Gallia Bracata** or **Braccata** ('trousered Gaul'). Southwestern Gaul from the Pyrenees to the Alps, better known as *Gallia Narbonensis* ('Gaul of Narbona'), modern Narbonne, part of GALLIA TRANSALPINA. *See also* GENS BRACATA.

**Gallia Cisalpina** or **Citerior** ('Gaul this side of the Alps'). The part of Gaul corresponding to what is now northern Italy. It was also called *Gallia Togata* ('togaed Gaul') from the Roman form of dress worn.

**Gallia Comata** ('hairy Gaul'). That part of Gaul that belonged to the Roman emperor was so called from the long flowing locks of the inhabitants. It was also called *Tres Provinciae* ('three provinces'), since it included the provinces of Aquitania, Lugdunensis and Belgica, with a common capital at Lugdunum (Lyon).

**Gallia Togata.** *See* GALLIA CISALPINA; TOGA.

**Gallia Transalpina** or **Ulterior** ('Gaul beyond the Alps'). Often called simply GALLIA, it included modern France and Belgium and parts of Holland, Germany and Switzerland.

**Gallicism.** A phrase or sentence constructed in the French manner. In Matthew 15:32, 'They continue with me now three days' is a Gallicism, and sounds as if it has been translated not from the Greek but from the French (*Il y a déjà trois jours qu'ils ne me quittent point*). The term also applies to a single word used in a sense peculiar to the French language, as 'assist' in the sense of 'to be present': 'The dinner at which we have just assisted' (W.M. Thackeray, *The Newcomes* (1854)).

**Galligaskins** (obsolete French *gargesques*, perhaps influenced by 'galley' and 'Gascon'). A loose, wide kind of breeches worn by men in the 17th century.

> My galligaskins, that have long withstood
> The winter's fury and encroaching frosts.
> JOHN PHILIPS: *The Splendid Shilling* (1701)

**Gallimaufry.** A medley, a confused jumble, and properly a HOTCHPOTCH made of all the scraps of the larder, from French *galimafrée*, 'ragout', 'hash'. The origin of the word is unknown, although it may be related to GALIMATIAS.

> They have a dance which the wenches say is a gallimaufry of gambols, because they are not in't.
> SHAKESPEARE: *The Winter's Tale*, IV, iii (1610)

**Gallio.** A name applied to a person, particularly an official, whose chief characteristic is one of indifference, especially to things outside his province. The reference is to the biblical Gallio, L. Junius Gallio, Roman proconsul of Achaia in *c.*AD 52, who refused to be drawn into the dispute between St. Paul and his Jewish adversaries in Corinth.

> And Gallio cared for none of those things.
> Acts 18:17

**Galloglass** or **gallowglass** (Irish *gallóglach*, from *gall*, 'foreigner', and *óglach*, 'young warrior-servant'). An armed servitor or foot soldier in ancient Ireland. Shakespeare speaks of kerns and gallowglasses as coming from the Western Isles of Scotland. *See also* KERN.

**Gallows and gibbet.** *See* INVENTORS.

**Gallup Poll.** The best known of the public opinion surveys, instituted by Dr George Gallup (1901–84) of the American Institute of Public Opinion in 1935. Trained interviewers interrogate a carefully selected but small cross-section of the population. For the British parliamentary election of 1945, out of 25 million voters, 1809 were interviewed, but the Gallup Poll forecast was within 1 per cent. However, the forecast was wrong for the American presidential election of 1948. The LABOUR PARTY victory was forecast for the British parliamentary elections in 1964 and 1966. It is held that such polls in themselves influence the result. STRAW POLLS and market research surveys were the forerunners of the Gallup Poll. Most opinion polls in Britain are now conducted by MORI (Market and Opinion Research Institute), a joint Anglo-American organization, founded in 1969. *See also* MASS OBSERVATION.

**Galosh.** The word comes from Old French *galoche*, itself from Late Latin *gallicula*, 'Gallic shoe'.

It was originally applied to a kind of clog or patten worn as a protection against wet in the days when silk or cloth shoes were worn, and is used in this sense by Langland.

> As is the kynde of a knyght that cometh to be
> dubbed,
> To geten hem gylte spores or galoches ycouped.
> *Piers Plowman*, xxi (*c*.1367–70)

**Galvanized iron.** *See* MISNOMERS.

**Game** (Old English *gamen*, 'joy', 'sport'). This word is variously used to mean, among other things, play, sport, contest, trick and jest, and it is also applied collectively to certain wild animals and birds legally protected and pursued for sport. *See also* SPORTING SEASONS IN ENGLAND.

**Gamecock State, The.** An old nickname for South Carolina, from the supposedly warlike nature of its inhabitants. *See also* PALMETTO STATE; UNITED STATES OF AMERICA.

**Game is not worth the candle, The.** *See* NOT WORTH THE CANDLE *under* WORTH.

**Game is up, The.** The scheme, endeavour or plot has come to grief, and there is no longer a chance of success. In hunting the words have the same significance as the GAME'S AFOOT.

**Game laws.** A series of enactments akin to the old forest law, designed to protect game for the landowner and to prevent poaching, and formerly noted for their harshness. In 1671 a Game Law was passed that prevented all freeholders killing game except those with lands worth £100 a year. *The Extraordinary Black Book* of 1831 pointed out that 50 times more property was required to kill a partridge than to vote for a KNIGHT OF THE SHIRE. In the reign of George III (1760–1820) 32 Game Laws were passed. The modern game licence for the killing of game stems from the Game Act of 1831, which also demarcated the seasons during which certain game might be taken. From 1671 to 1831 the sale of game was totally prohibited, thus providing a lucrative market for poachers.

**Game leg.** A lame leg. Here, 'game' is probably from Irish *cam*, 'crooked'. It is of comparatively modern usage. 'Gammy' also has this sense.

**Game's afoot, The.** The hare has started; the enterprise has begun.

> I see you stand like greyhounds in the slips,
> Straining upon the start. The game's afoot:
> Follow your spirit.
> SHAKESPEARE: *Henry V*, III, i (1598)

**Actian games.** *See under* ACTIAN.

**As game as Ned Kelly.** *See under* AS.

**At one's little games again** or **at the same old game, To be.** *See under* AT.

**Big game.** *See under* BIG.

**Fair game.** *See under* FAIR.

**Flush game.** *See under* FLUSH.

**Fun and games.** *See under* FUN.

**Give the game away, To.** To reveal a secret or one's intentions.

**Have the game in one's hands, To.** To have such an advantage that success is assured; to hold the winning cards.

**Haxey Hood game.** *See under* HAXEY.

**Highland Games.** *See under* HIGHLANDS.

**Isthmian games.** *See under* ISTHMIAN.

**Name of the game, The.** *See under* NAME.

**Needle game** or **match.** *See under* NEEDLE.

**Nemean Games.** *See under* NEMEAN.

**Olympic Games.** *See under* OLYMPIA.

**On the game.** Involved in prostitution or robbery.

**Parlour game.** *See under* PARLOUR.

**Play a waiting game, To.** *See under* PLAY.

**Play the game, To.** *See under* PLAY.

**Pythian Games.** *See under* PYTHIA.

**Roaring game.** *See under* ROAR.

**Secular games.** *See under* SECULAR.

**Skin game.** *See under* SKIN.

**So that's your little game!** *See under* LITTLE.

**Wall game, The.** *See under* WALL.

**War game.** *See under* WAR.

**Gamelyn, The Tale of.** *See under* TALE.

**Gamesmanship.** A term popularized by Stephen Potter, whose book *The Theory and Practice of Gamesmanship* (1947) defines the meaning in its subtitle: 'The Art of Winning Games without actually Cheating.'

**Gammadion.** The FYLFOT OR SWASTIKA, so called because it resembles four Greek capital gammas, Γ, set at right angles.

**Gammer.** A former rustic term for an old woman, as a corruption of 'godmother' or 'grandmother', with an intermediate form of 'granmer'. *See also* GAFFER.

**Gammer Gurton's Needle.** The second earliest extant English comedy, which was probably written by William Stevenson of Christ's College, Cambridge, in the early 1550s but not published until 1575. The comedy is vigorous, and it closes with the painful discovery of Gammer Gurton's missing needle in the seat of her man Hodge's breeches.

**Gammon.** This word probably derives from the same original as 'game' and 'gamble', but in Victorian and later slang it meant to impose upon, delude, cheat, or play a game on. As an exclamation it meant: 'Nonsense, you're pulling my leg.' To gammon the flats is to dupe the fools, who are called 'flat' because they are not 'sharp'.

> A landsman said, 'I *twig* the chap — he's been upon the Mill —
> And 'cause he *gammons* so the *flats*, ve calls him Veeping Bill!'
>
> R.H. BARHAM: *Ingoldsby Legends*, 'Misadventures at Margate' (1840)

**Gammy leg.** *See* GAME LEG.

**Gamp.** Sarah Gamp is a disreputable monthly nurse in Dickens' *Martin Chuzzlewit* (1843–4), famous for her bulky umbrella and her perpetual reference to an imaginary Mrs Harris, whose opinions always confirmed her own. Hence a 'gamp' as a formerly common term for an umbrella.

**Gamut.** Originally, the first or lowest note in Guido d'Arezzo's scale, corresponding to G on the lowest line of the modern bass stave. The term was later extended to the whole series of notes recognized by musicians, and hence generally came to be used for the whole range or compass of anything. It comes from *gamma ut*, from *gamma*, the third letter of the Greek alphabet, used by Guido to mark the lowest note in the hexachord, and *ut*, the first of the notes of the scale. *See also* ARETINIAN SYLLABLES; TONIC SOL-FA.

**Run the gamut of, To.** *See under* RUN.

**Gandalf.** In J.R.R. Tolkien's novels *The* LORD OF THE RINGS (1954–5), the tall, good magician who sends FRODO on his quest and who helps him whenever possible.

**G and T.** Gin and tonic. *See also* B AND S.

**Ganelon.** The Count of Mayence, the villain and traitor in the CHARLEMAGNE romances, in which, through jealousy of ROLAND, he schemes for the defeat of the rearguard at Roncesvalles. He figures in Dante's *Inferno* (*c.*1309–20) and in Chaucer's 'Nun's Priest's Tale' (*c.*1387).

**Ganesa.** In Hindu mythology, the god of wisdom and good luck, lord of the Ganas, or lesser deities. He was the son of SIVA and is invoked at the beginning of a journey or when commencing important work, and on the first pages of books, especially ledgers. He is shown with a red or yellow human trunk, a big round stomach, four arms, and an elephant's head with a mouth from which a single tusk protrudes. *See also* HINDUISM.

**Gang. Gang day.** *See* ROGATION DAYS.

**Gang of four** (1). Leaders of a Chinese radical group who unsuccessfully attempted to seize control after the death of Mao Tse-tung in 1976. The gang, who were imprisoned in 1981, consisted of Jiang Qing (Mao's widow and third wife), Zhang Chunqiao, Wang Hongwen and Yao Wenyuan.

(2) In Great Britain the name was given to the four MPs who left the LABOUR PARTY in 1981 to form the Social Democratic Party (SDP), namely Roy Jenkins (leader until 1983), David Owen, Shirley Williams and Bill Rodgers. Owen became leader in 1983 and was succeeded by Robert Maclennan in 1987. *See also* LIBERAL.

**Gang saw.** A number of power-driven circular saws mounted together so that they can reduce a tree trunk to planks at one operation. Gang is similarly applied to various collections of tools, machines and the like working in combination. Other examples are a gang mower, used for mowing large areas of grass, and a gang plough, used for ploughing a field.

**Gang show.** A variety show performed periodically by BOY SCOUTS and GIRL GUIDES.

**Gang up, To.** To form a closely knit group, usually in a spirit of antagonism.

**Apple Tree Gang.** *See under* APPLE.

**Bloomsbury Gang.** *See under* BLOOMSBURY.

**Crazy Gang, The.** *See under* CRAZY.

**Press gang.** *See under* PRESS.

**Ganges, The.** So named from Sanskrit *gangā* 'river', as also in Kishenganga ('black river'), Neelganga ('blue river') and Naraingunga ('river of Naranyana' or VISHNU). This sacred river of the Hindus is said to flow from the toe of Vishnu.

**Gangway.** Originally the boarded way (sometimes called the gang-board) in the old galleys made for the rowers to pass from stem to stern, and where the mast was laid when it was unshipped (gang, 'alley'). The term is now used for the portable bridge or walkway by which passengers enter or leave a ship. When used as an exclamation, 'Gangway!' means 'Make way!'

**Below the gangway.** *See under* BELOW.

**Ganymede** or **Ganymedes** (Greek *ganumai*, 'to shine joyfully'). In Greek mythology the beautiful Trojan youth who was abducted by ZEUS and taken up to OLYMPUS, where he became cup-bearer to the gods. Hence a cup-bearer generally.

> Nature waits upon thee still,
> And thy verdant cup does fill;
> 'Tis fill'd wherever thou dost tread,
> Nature's self's thy Ganimede.
>
> ABRAHAM COWLEY: *Anacreontics*, 'The Grasshopper' (1656)

**Gaora.** According to Richard Hakluyt (*c.*1552–1616) this was a tract of land inhabited by people without heads, with eyes in their shoulders and their mouths in their breasts.

**Gap. Gap year.** A year between secondary and further or higher education, when some school-leavers go out 'into the world' to travel or find work before resuming their studies. Those who travel often go hitchhiking or back-packing abroad, especially to exotic or even dangerous places.

**Credibility gap.** *See under* CREDIBILITY.

**Gender gap.** *See under* GENDER.

**Generation gap.** *See under* GENERATION.

**Garden. Garden** or **Garden Sect, The.** The disciples of EPICURUS, who taught them in his own garden.

**Garden city.** A name given to both Norwich and Chicago, and also, as a general name, to model townships which have been specially planned to provide attractive layouts for housing and industry, and which have a surrounding rural belt and adequate open spaces. The term was first used by an American, A.T. Stewart, in 1869, and applied to an estate development on Long Island. The 'garden city' movement in England was due to the social ideas of Sir Ebenezer Howard (1850–1928), set out in his book *To-morrow* (1898). His first garden city was founded at Letchworth, Hertfordshire, in 1902 and his second at Welwyn (1920).

**Garden of . . . .** A term commonly applied to the more fertile areas as:

Garden of England: Kent and Worcestershire, both famous for their fruit
Garden of Europe: Italy
Garden of France: Amboise, in the department of Indre-et-Loire
Garden of India: Oudh
Garden of Ireland: Wicklow
Garden of Italy: the island of Sicily
Garden of Spain: Andalusia
Garden of Switzerland: Thurgau
Garden of the Gods: in the USA an area west of Colorado Springs at the foot of Pikes Peak, consisting of massive beds of red and pink sandstone rocks taking their colour from red oxide deposits; there are many fanciful shapes resembling cathedral spires, animals and carved faces
Garden of the Sun: the East Indian (or Malayan) Archipelago
Garden of the West: Illinois, also Kansas (the SUNFLOWER STATE)
Garden of the World: the region of the Mississippi

**Garden of Cymodoce, The.** Sark, one of the Channel Islands. It is the title of a poem by A.C. Swinburne in his *Songs of the Springtides* (1880). *See also* CYMODOCE.

**Garden of Eden, The.** *See* EDEN.

**Garden of the Hesperides.** *See* HESPERIDES.

**Garden party.** A social event held on a lawn or in a garden. The garden parties held at Buckingham Palace are among the most prestigious, with members of the royal family passing among the guests.

**Garden suburb.** A name applied to certain model suburbs with the characteristics of a GARDEN CITY. Hampstead Garden Suburb is a well-known example

**Bear garden.** *See under* BEAR.

**Common or garden.** *See under* COMMON.

**Cottage garden.** *See under* COTTAGE.

**Covent Garden.** *See under* COVENT.

**Cremorne Gardens.** *See under* CREMORNE.

**Cultivate one's garden, To.** *See under* CULTIVATE.

**Everything in the garden is lovely.** *See under* EVERY.

**Hanging Gardens of Babylon.** *See under* HANG.

**Lead someone up the garden path, To.** *See under* LEAD.

**Rosherville Gardens.** *See under* ROSHERVILLE.

**Vauxhall Gardens.** *See under* VAUXHALL.

**Gardy loo.** The cry of warning formerly given by Edinburgh housewives and servants when about to empty the contents of the slop pail out of the window into the street below. It is a corruption of false French *gare de l'eau*, 'beware of the water'. (Real French would be *gare l'eau*.)

> At ten o'clock at night the whole cargo of the chamber utensils is flung out of a back window that looks into some street or lane, and the maid calls 'Gardy loo' to the passengers.
>
> TOBIAS SMOLLETT: *Humphry Clinker*, II (1771)

**Gargamelle.** The mother of GARGANTUA. Her name existed before Rabelais' time, and comes from Old French *gargamelle*, 'throat'. She was inspired by a character of folklore called Galemelle. Gargantua's father, Grandgousier, has a similar name, meaning 'big gullet' (modern French *grand gosier*).

**Gargantua.** A giant of medieval or possibly CELTIC legend, famous for his enormous appetite. He was adopted by Rabelais in his great satire (1535), and made the father of PANTAGRUEL. One of his exploits was to swallow five pilgrims, complete with their staves, in a salad. He is the subject of a number of CHAPBOOKS, and became proverbial as a voracious and insatiable guzzler. His name is popularly derived from Occitan *garganta*, 'gullet', but there was a Celtic giant named Gargan whose name lies behind several French place-names, including that of Mont-Gargan, the historic name of Mont-Saint-Michel.

> You must borrow me Gargantua's mouth first: 'tis a word too great for any mouth of this age's size.
>
> SHAKESPEARE: *As You Like It*, III, ii (1599)

**Gargouille.** The great dragon that lived in the Seine, ravaged Rouen and was slain by St Romanus, archbishop of Rouen, in the 7th century. His name means 'throat' (English gargoyle).

**Garibaldi.** The name Garibaldi was given to a loose-fitting blouse for women, fashionable in the 1860s. It was copied from the red flannel shirts worn by the soldiers of the Italian patriot, Giuseppe Garibaldi (1807–82). *See also* GARIBALDI'S RED SHIRT.

**Garibaldi biscuit.** Currants are mixed in the pastry to make a form of food much favoured by Giuseppe Garibaldi on his farm in Caprera.

**Garibaldi's red shirt.** The famous red shirt

worn by Garibaldi and his followers during the liberation of Italy was of accidental origin. When Garibaldi was raising an Italian legion at Montevideo in 1843 a number of red woollen shirts came on the market owing to the difficulties in trade due to the war with Argentina. The government of Uruguay bought them up cheaply and gave them to Garibaldi for his men. When the Italian Legion came over to Italy in 1848 they brought their red shirts with them.

**Garland.** Primarily a wreath of flowers, either worn or else festooned round something. Its use has also been extended to apply to an anthology of prose or verse.

> What I now offer to your lordships is a collection of Poetry, a kind of Garland of Good Will.
>
> MATTHEW PRIOR: *Poems*, Dedication (1718)

**Garlic.** The old superstition that garlic can destroy the magnetic power of the LODESTONE has the sanction of Pliny, Solinus, PTOLEMY, Plutarch and others. Sir Thomas Browne includes it in his *Vulgar Errors* (Bk II, ch iii (1646)).

**Garlic Wall.** The satirical name applied by Gibraltarians to the Spanish barrier, which closed the frontier to La Linea in 1969 as a consequence of Spain's claim to the Rock. GIBRALTAR was ceded to Great Britain by the Treaty of Utrecht (1713). Spain reopened the frontier at La Linea in 1985. *See also* ROCK SCORPION.

**Garnet, All Sir.** *See under* ALL.

**Garnett, Alf.** The working-class Londoner played by Warren Mitchell in the television series *Till Death Us Do Part* (1964–74). He is an archetypal royalist and racist, and his forthright pronouncements had the unusual effect of simultaneously endearing him to the viewing public, who secretly agreed with his views, yet alienating him from them because of his bigoted attitude and his bad language. His appearance in a sequel, *In Sickness and in Health* (1985–6), seemed much less shocking.

**Garratt, The Mayor of.** *See under* MAYOR.

**Garrick.** The Garrick CLUB was founded in 1831 by the Duke of Sussex for actors, painters, writers and similarly creative and artistic individuals. It was named after the actor David Garrick (1717–79), whose portrait by Zoffany hangs here. Today its members are mainly lawyers, writers and publishers. It has consistently voted against the admission of women.

**Garter.** It was at one time a common custom for a man to wear the garters of a pretty girl either on the hat or knee. Brides usually wore on their legs a host of gay ribbons, to be distributed after the marriage ceremony among the bridegroom's friends, and the piper at the wedding dance never failed to tie a piece of the bride's garter round his pipe.

**Crewel garters.** *See under* CREWEL.

**Flying-the-garter.** *See under* FLY.

**Most Noble Order of the Garter, The.** *See under* MOST.

**Gas.** The word was coined from Greek *khaos*, 'chaos', by the Flemish physician and chemist Jan Baptista van Helmont (1579–1644) as a term for the occult principle supposedly present in all bodies. He was almost certainly influenced by PARACELSUS, who used the same Greek word to denote the proper element of spirits such as GNOMES. The present technical sense of the word for a fluid that can expand without limit, such as air, arose in the late 18th century. The colloquial expression 'a gas' applied to anything hilarious probably alludes to nitrous oxide, so-called LAUGHING GAS, used in anaesthetics since the 18th century.

**Laughing gas.** *See under* LAUGH.

**Gasconade.** Absurd boasting; BRAGGADOCIO. It is said that a Gascon, being asked what he thought of the Louvre in Paris, replied: 'Pretty well: it reminds me of the back part of my father's stables.' This was an especially boastful answer at a time when the Gascons were proverbial for their poverty. Another Gascon, in proof of his ancient nobility, asserted that they used no other fuel in his father's house than the batons of the family marshals.

**Gasp, Last.** *See under* LAST.

**Gat.** An American slang term for an automatic pistol. It is a contraction of Gatling, from the machine-gun invented (1861–2) by Richard Jordan Gatling (1818–1903) of North Carolina.

**Gate.** In street names the word gate often represents Old Norse *gata*, meaning 'street'. Examples are Briggate ('Bridge Street') in Leeds and Micklegate ('Great Street') in York. Most such names are in the north of England. But in some cases the meaning actually is 'gate', as Lincoln's Eastgate, Northgate and Westgate, named after the city's gates.

**-gate.** The second element of a noun denoting a scandal associated with the person, animal or place named in the first element. The analogy is with WATERGATE. Irangate was thus a scandal of 1986 in the USA following the revelation that members of the Reagan administration had sanctioned arms sales to Iran in exchange for the release of hostages in Lebanon, while in the UK Lawsongate was a scandal of 1988 caused by allegations that the Chancellor of the Exchequer, Nigel Lawson, had deliberately deceived the public about the economy. The format was still in active use in the late 1990s.

> The cumulative effect of Squidgygate, Fergiegate and Camillagate [in the royal family] has been to replace deference with popular disdain.
>
> GREG HADFIELD and MARK SKIPWORTH: *Class*, ch i (1994)

**Gate-crasher.** Someone who gains entrance to a social function without invitation or ticket of admission. The origin is obvious.

**Gate-leg table.** A table with one or two drop leaves that are supported by a hinged leg, which swings out like a gate from the centre.

**Gate money.** Money paid at the door or gate for admission to a sporting contest or entertainment of some kind.

**Gate of Italy, The.** A narrow gorge between two mountain ridges in the valley of the Adige, in the vicinity of Trent and Rovereto.

**Gate of Tears, The.** The passage into the Red Sea so called by the Arabs (*Bab-el-Mandeb*) from the number of shipwrecks that took place there.

**Gatepost.** The post on which a gate hangs is called the hanging post, and that against which it shuts is called the banging post.

**Gatepost bargain.** A 'cash down' deal. An old country custom of placing the purchase money on the gatepost before the stock being sold left the field.

**Gates of dreams, The.** There are two such gates in Greek legend, that of ivory and that of horn. Dreams that are false pass through the ivory gate; those that are true pass through the gate of horn. This fancy depends upon two puns: 'ivory' in Greek is *elephas*, and the verb *elephairomai* means 'to cheat with empty hopes'; the Greek for 'horn' is *keras*, and the verb *karanoō* means 'I accomplish'.

> Let it suffice me that my murmuring rhyme
> Beats with light wing against the ivory gate.
> WILLIAM MORRIS: *The Earthly Paradise*, i (1868–70)

**Between you and me and the gatepost.** *See under* BETWEEN.

**Bull and Gate.** *See under* BULL.

**Decuman gate.** *See under* DECUMAN.

**Golden Gate, The.** *See under* GOLDEN.

**Iron Gates, The.** *See under* IRON.

**Kiss gate.** *See under* KISS.

**Northern gate of the sun, The.** *See under* NORTH.

**Pearly Gates.** *See under* PEARL.

**Southern gate of the sun, The.** *See under* SOUTH.

**Tom Gate.** *See under* TOM.

**Traitors' Gate.** *See under* TRAITOR.

**Gateau, Black Forest.** *See under* BLACK.

**Gath, Tell it not in.** *See under* TELL.

**Gather. Gathering of the clans, A.** An assembly of like-minded persons, usually for convivial purposes. The allusion is to the gathering of Scottish clans at the Highland Games and elsewhere.

> Of the greater 'gatherings' the northern meeting at Inverness, the Braemar Gathering on Deeside, and the Oban Games are the outstanding examples.
> DUKE OF ATHOLL in H.W. Meikle, *Scotland*, ch xxxi (1947)

**Here we go gathering nuts in May.** This refrain of the old children's game is probably a corruption of 'Here we go gathering knots of may', referring to the old custom of gathering knots of flowers on MAY DAY. There are no nuts to be gathered in May.

**Gatling gun.** *See* GAT.

**Gatsby, Jay.** The central character of F. Scott Fitzgerald's novel *The Great Gatsby* (1925), a wealthy but mysterious man who gives lavish parties but whom nobody really knows. He epitomizes the type of man who has little or no self-esteem and no friends and who relies on wealth to enhance his social status.

**Gaudeamus igitur** (Latin). The opening words of the famous students' song of medieval origin. It has seven verses and was formerly often sung at student celebrations. Its traditional melody is the one that occurs as the fifth and final theme in Brahms' *Academic Festival Overture* (1881).

> Gaudeamus igitur,
> Juvenes dum sumus
> Post jucundam juventutem
> Post molestam senectutem,
> Nos habebit humus.
> (Let us then rejoice,
> While we are young,
> After the pleasures of youth
> And the burdens of old age
> Earth will hold us.)

**Gaudy** (Latin *gaudium*, 'joy'). A holiday, a feast-day, especially an annual celebration of some event, such as the foundation of a college. The word was in use at Oxford University by the 17th century to designate a generally commemorative feast at a college and many colleges there now regularly hold gaudies for the benefit of former members.

**Gauge, Standard.** *See under* STANDARD.

**Gaul.** The country inhabited by the Gauls. *See also* GALLIA.

**Amadis of Gaul.** *See under* AMADIS.

**Gauleiter** (German, 'district leader'). The ruler of a province under the NAZI regime (1933–45).

**Gaunt, John of.** *See under* JOHN.

**Gauntlet. Run the gauntlet, To.** *See under* RUN.

**Take up the gauntlet, To.** To accept a challenge. *See also* GLOVE.

**Throw down the gauntlet, To.** *See under* THROW.

**Gautama.** The family name of BUDDHA. His personal name was Siddhartha ('one whose aim is accomplished'), his father's name Suddhodana, and his mother's name Mahamaya. He assumed the title Buddha at about the age of 36, when, after seven years of seclusion and spiritual struggle, he believed himself to have attained perfect truth.

**Gavelkind.** A system of tenure, especially in Kent and Wales and also in other parts of England.

It was based on the freemen who gave rent or 'gafol' to their lord instead of services. Some of its principal features were that if a person died intestate, his property was divided equally among his sons or, in the absence of sons, his daughters. The dower was one-half instead of one-third of a husband's land, and a widower's courtesy one-half of the land while remaining unmarried. After the Norman Conquest (1066) it was replaced in England by the custom of primogeniture, except in Kent. It was abolished in Wales during the reign of Henry VIII and completely by Acts of Parliament of 1922 and 1925.

**Gawain.** One of the most famous of the knights of the ARTHURIAN ROMANCES, nephew of King ARTHUR and probably the original hero of the quest for the HOLY GRAIL. He appears in the Welsh TRIADS and in the MABINOGION as Gwalchmai, and in the Arthurian cycle he is the centre of many episodes and poems. The Middle English poem *Sir Gawain and the Green Knight* (*c*.1360) is a romance telling how Gawain beheads the Green Knight in single combat. Gwalchmai may derive from Welsh *gwalch*, 'falcon', and *Mai*, 'May'. His better known name gave the modern first name Gavin.

**Gay** (Old French *gai*). Light-hearted; merry; brightly coloured.

> Belinda smiled and all the world was gay.
> ALEXANDER POPE: *The Rape of the Lock*, ii (1714)

French *gai* became associated with effeminate roles in French burlesque theatre, and the English theatre similarly began to apply the word 'gay' to saucy or 'promiscuous' characters. These mock female roles were always played by men, because in Elizabethan times women were not allowed on the stage in either country. It was this use of the word that gave the general current one of 'homosexual', a use favoured by homosexuals themselves.

> Mr Huffington drew a fine distinction between 'homosexual' and 'gay', a word he felt carried too much 'baggage' and did not apply to him.
> *The Times* (7 December 1998)

**Gay deceiver, A.** A lothario or LIBERTINE. For a time the expression was also adopted as a slang term for a brassière lined with soft plastic padding, in other words 'falsies'.

**Gay dog, A.** A 'man about town', especially one who fancies himself with the ladies.

**Gay Gordons.** A lively old-time Scottish dance, taking its name from the Gordon Highlanders, the regiment whose members 'adopted' it and popularized it.

**Gay lothario, A.** A LIBERTINE, a seducer of women, a debauchee. The character is from Nicholas Rowe's tragedy *The Fair Penitent* (1703). He probably got the name from Sir William D'Avenant's *The Cruel Brother* (1630) in which there is a similar character with this name. *See also* LOVELACE.

> Is this that haughty, gallant, gay Lothario?
> NICHOLAS ROWE: *The Fair Penitent*, V, i

**Gayomart.** According to Persian mythology the first man. He was the creation of Ahura Mazda and lived as a spirit for 3000 years before assuming the corporeal form of a beautiful youth. He then lived 30 years, when he was poisoned by Ahriman. From his seed grew the father and mother of the human race, Mashye and Mashyane. His name represents Avestan *Gayo maretan*, 'mortal life'.

**Gazelle Boy, The.** In 1961 Jean-Claude Armen, travelling by camel through the Spanish Sahara in west Africa, was told by nomad tribesmen of the whereabouts of a young boy living with a herd of gazelles. In due time he sighted the boy and eventually attracted him to close quarters by playing a Berber flute. The boy fed on the same plants as the animals, sometimes eating worms and lizards. On a subsequent expedition in 1963, this time in a Jeep, the speed of the boy when galloping with the herd was established at over 30 mph. *See also* WILD CHILD.

**Gazette.** A newspaper. A word of Italian origin derived from the government newspaper issued in Venice from about 1536. It was named for its price, one gazet, a small copper coin whose own name may have come from *gazza*, 'magpie'.

**Gazetted.** Posted in the LONDON GAZETTE as having received some official appointment, service promotion or the like, or on being declared bankrupt.

**Gazetteer.** A geographical and topographical index or dictionary. It is so called because the name of one of the earliest such works in English was Laurence Echard's *The Gazetteer's or Newsman's Interpreter* (2nd edition, 1693), i.e. it was intended for the use of journalists, gazetteer being a word applied to writers of news.

**London Gazette.** *See under* LONDON.

**Gazing, Crystal.** *See under* CRYSTAL.

**Gazumping.** A colloquial term from the early 1970s relating to the property market. It denotes the dubious practice of raising the selling price of a house after agreement has been reached with an intending purchaser. After agreeing a price with the vendor, the purchaser finds that he is gazumped because the vendor has accepted a higher offer from another buyer before contracts have been signed and exchanged. The origin of the word is uncertain. It probably derives from a Yiddish verb meaning 'to swindle'.

**GCB.** *See* KNIGHTS OF THE BATH.

**Ge.** *See* GAIA.

**Gear.** Clothing, equipment and the like, as, for example, sports gear. The word also applies to the combination of toothed wheels and levers, which connect a motor with its work. 'High gear' is the arrangement whereby the driving part moves slowly in relation to the driven part, while 'low gear' is when the driving part moves relatively more quickly than the driven.

**Out of gear.** *See under* OUT.

**Gee.** A mild exclamation, originating as a EUPHEMISM for Jesus. It also occurs in the form 'Gee whiz!'

**Gee-up!** A call to a horse to encourage it to move off or go faster. The origin of the word is unknown. It gave 'gee-gee', the children's word for a horse, taken up by sporting men and others, as in 'a flutter on the gee-gees'.

**Geese.** *See* GOOSE.

**Gehenna** (Hebrew). The place of eternal torment. Strictly speaking, it means the 'Valley of Hinnom' (*Ge-Hinnom*), where sacrifices to BAAL and MOLOCH were offered (Jeremiah 19:6 and elsewhere). It came to be regarded as a place of unquenchable fire, possibly from the fires of Moloch.

**Geisha.** A member of a professional class of Japanese women trained to entertain men by dancing and singing. The word literally means 'art person', from *gei*, 'art', and *-sha*, 'person'. The geisha system probably evolved in the 17th century to provide a class of entertainers distinct from courtesans and prostitutes and was traditionally a form of indentured labour. In the 1920s there were as many as 80,000 geisha in Japan but by the end of the 20th century their numbers had dwindled to just a few thousand, mostly in Tokyo and Kyoto, where they were patronized by only the wealthiest businessmen and the richest politicians. *See also* BAYADERE.

**Gemara** (Aramaic, 'completion'). The second part of the TALMUD, consisting of annotations, discussions and amplifications of the MISHNA, which is the first part. The Mishna is the codification of the oral law; the Gemara is supplementary and a commentary on the Mishna.

**Gemini** (Latin, 'twins'). A constellation, also one of the signs of the ZODIAC (21 May to 21 June), representing CASTOR AND POLLUX, the great twin brethren of classical mythology.

**Gendarmes** (French *gens d'armes*, 'men-at-arms'). The armed police of France. The term was first applied to an armed knight or cavalier, then to the cavalry. In the time of Louis XIV (1638–1715) it was applied to a body of horse charged with the preservation of order, and after the Revolution to a military police chosen from old soldiers of good character. It is now the word for the ordinary police.

**Gender. Gender gap.** The difference in attitudes or viewpoints that can exist between men and women, especially in the political field.

> The gender gap – the marked difference between the political views of men voters and the increasingly sizeable body of women voters – rang out as the theme of the convention.
> *The Times* (25 July 1983)

**Gender words.** Words that, prefixed to the noun, indicate an animal's sex, for example:

Bull, cow: elephant, rhinoceros, seal and whale
Dog, bitch: ape, fox (the bitch is usually called a vixen), otter, wolf
Buck, doe: hare, rabbit
He, she: general gender words for quadrupeds, e.g. he-goat, she-wolf
Cock, hen: gender words for most birds, and in some cases forming part of their regular names, e.g. peacock, peahen; moorcock, moorhen (the red grouse, not the water bird)

In many cases a different word is used for each of the sexes: boar, sow; cockerel, pullet; colt, filly; drake, duck; gander, goose; hart, roe; ram, ewe; stag, hind; stallion, mare; steer (in the USA used of beef cattle of any age), heifer.

**General. General anaesthetic.** One that affects the whole body, leading to loss of consciousness. The opposite is a local anaesthetic, which numbs only a part of the body and does not lead to loss of consciousness.

**General election.** One in which representatives are chosen in all constituencies. The converse is a local election or, in political terms, a by-election.

**General John.** A nickname of John Churchill (1650–1722), 1st Duke of Marlborough.

**General Judgement, The.** *See* LAST JUDGEMENT.

**General Lud.** *See* LUDDITES.

**General practitioner.** The GP, or family doctor, who has a medical practice but who does not specialize. He or she is thus contrasted with a specialist, to whom patients requiring special treatment will be referred.

**General Strike, The.** The nationwide strike called by the Trades Union Congress on 3 May 1926 in support of the miners' union, which was resisting the mine-owners' demand for longer hours and lower wages. Stanley Baldwin's Conservative government used troops, volunteers and special constables to maintain food supplies and basic services, and it held a monopoly on the media, including BBC radio. The TUC ended the strike after nine days, leaving the miners, who felt betrayed by them, unsuccessfully continuing the strike until November 1926. The Trades Disputes Act of 1927 made general strikes illegal.

**General Synod, The.** The highest governing body in the Church of England. It comprises members of the upper houses of the convocations of Canterbury and York, a House of Clergy and a House of Laity, and is required to meet at least twice a year.

**General Wade.** *See under* WADE.

**General warrants.** Warrants issued for the arrest of unspecified persons, first by the Court of STAR CHAMBER and subsequently authorized by the Licensing Act of 1662, and continued after its lapse in 1695, when they were used against the authors and publishers of allegedly seditious or libellous writings. They were declared invalid as a result of actions brought against the crown (1763–5) by John Wilkes. A general warrant is now issued for the arrest of unnamed persons or for the search of unspecified premises or for unspecified property.

**Estates General.** *See under* ESTATE.

**States General.** *See under* STATE.

**Vicar general.** *See under* VICAR.

**Generalissimo.** The supreme commander, especially of a force drawn from two or more nations, or of a combined military and naval force. The title is said to have been coined by Cardinal Richelieu on taking supreme command of the French armies in Italy, in 1629.

In modern times the title has been applied to Marshal Foch (1851–1929), who commanded the Allied forces in France in 1918; to Joseph Stalin (1879–1953), who was made generalissimo of the Soviet forces in 1943; to General Franco (1892–1975) who proclaimed himself generalissimo of the Spanish army in 1939; and to Marshal Chiang Kai-shek (1888–1975), leader of the KUOMINTANG, who was in power in China from 1927 to 1949.

**Generation. Generation gap.** The years that separate an older generation from a younger, especially as discernible in a difference of outlook, values and attitudes. In some instances the disparity can lead to a lack of understanding or empathy between the two.

**Beat generation.** See under BEAT.

**Lost generation.** *See under* LOST.

**Generic names.** *See* BIDDY.

**Generous. As generous as Hatim.** *See under* AS.

**Genesis.** The first book of the Old Testamant and of the Bible as a whole tells the story of the creation of the world. Its name is thus the Greek for 'origin', 'creation', 'generation'.

**Genetic fingerprinting.** The pattern of DNA unique to each person that can be analysed in a sample of blood, saliva or tissue, and that is used as a means of identification as conventional FINGERPRINTS are.

**Genetrix, Venus.** *See under* VENUS.

**Geneva.** *See* GIN.

**Geneva bands.** The two white cloth strips attached to the collar of the clerical dress of some Protestants are so called. Like the Geneva gown, the black preaching gown worn by the early Reformed ministers, the name comes from Geneva in Switzerland, where they were originally worn by the Calvinists.

**Geneva Bible, The.** *See under* BIBLE.

**Geneva Convention.** In 1862 Jean Henri Dunant (1828–1910), a Swiss, published an account of the sufferings of the wounded at the Battle of Solferino in 1859. From this sprang the RED CROSS movement and an international conference at Geneva in 1864. The resulting Geneva Convention provided for the care of the wounded and the protection of the military medical services, under the international emblem of the Red Cross.

**Geneva Cross.** *See* RED CROSS.

**Geneva doctrines.** CALVINISM.

**Pope of Geneva, The.** *See under* POPE.

**Geneviève.** Patron saint (422–512) of PARIS. Her day is 3 January, and she is represented in art with the keys of Paris at her girdle, a Devil blowing out her candle and an angel relighting it, or as restoring sight to her blind mother, or as guarding her father's sheep. She was born at Nanterre and was influential in saving Paris from the FRANKS and the threatened attack of Attila the Hun. Her church has since become the PANTHEON. Her name is usually derived from the Germanic name Genowefa, in which *geno* means 'race' (Latin *genus*) and *wefa* means 'woman' (English 'wife'). She is thus 'generically female'.

**Genghis Khan.** The Mongol emperor (1167–1227), one of the most famous conquerors in history. His original name was Temujin, and he was born in Deligun Bulduk on the River Onon. He acquired a fighting force of some 20,000 tribesmen and through sheer brutality and relentless campaigning overcame all his rivals, both Mongolian and Tartar, until by 1206 he was acknowledged overlord of all Mongolian steppe people. It was at this stage that he was given the title Genghis Khan, meaning literally 'king of the ocean'. Resorting to rather more sophisticated military tactics, he went on to extend his realm from China in the east to the Adriatic Sea in the west.

**Genius** (plural genii). In Roman mythology the tutelary spirit that attended a man from cradle to grave, governed his fortunes and determined his character. The Genius wished a man to enjoy pleasure in life, and thus to indulge one's Genius was to enjoy pleasure. The Genius existed only for man; the woman had her JUNO. Another belief was that a man had two genii, one good and one evil, and bad luck was due to his evil genius. The Roman genii were somewhat similar to the guardian angels spoken of in Matthew 18:10. The word is from Latin *gignere*, 'to beget', from the notion that birth and life were due to these *dii genitales*. Hence genius is used for an innate talent.

The eastern genii were JINNS, who were not attendant spirits but fallen angels under the dominion of EBLIS.

**Genius loci** (Latin, 'genius of the place'). The tutelary deity of a place and so generally a place's special atmosphere.

> In the midst of this wreck of ancient books and utensils, with a gravity equal to Marius among the ruins of Carthage, sat a large black cat, which to a superstitious eye, might have presented the *genius loci*, the tutelar demon of the apartment.
>
> SIR WALTER SCOTT: *The Antiquary*, ch iii (1816)

**Genocide.** A word invented by the American jurist Raphael Lemkin, and used in the drafting of the official indictment of war criminals in 1945. It is a combination of Greek *genos*, 'race', and Latin *caedere*, 'to kill'. It is defined as acts intended to destroy, in whole or in part, national, ethnic, racial or religious groups, and in 1948 was declared by the General Assembly of the UNITED NATIONS to be a crime in international law.

**Genre painter** (French *genre*, 'mode', 'style'). A term applied to those who paint scenes of everyday life in the home, the village, the countryside and so on. The Dutch artists of Rembrandt's time were particularly characteristic of this style. The term is sometimes used of drama in the same sense.

**Gens** (Latin, plural *gentes*). A CLAN or SEPT in ancient Rome, as a group of aristocratic families having a common name and claiming descent from a common ancestor.

**Gens bracata** or **braccata** (Latin, 'trousered people'). Unlike the Gauls, Scythians and Persians, the Romans did not wear trousers or breeches, so had a designation for those races that did. *See also* GALLIA BRACATA.

**Gens togata.** *See* TOGA.

**Gentiles.** The word, applied generally to someone not Jewish, stems from the Hebrew term *goy*, meaning 'nation', and was originally used both for the Hebrews and for other races. The plural form, *goyim*, was used of all nations that were not Jewish and was translated in the Vulgate (Latin version of the Bible) as 'gentes' or 'gentiles', from Latin *gens*, 'race'. A singular form of this was adopted in English for a Gentile, an individual non-Jew, and in post-biblical Hebrew, *goy* acquired the same sense. As most non-Jews in the Western world were Christians, Gentile gained the narrower sense 'Christian', although strictly speaking it denotes any non-Jew, whether Christian or not.

**Gentle.** Belonging to a family of position, well-born, having the manners of genteel persons. The word is from Latin *gentilis*, 'belonging to the same family'. *See also* GENS.

> We must be gentle, now we are gentlemen.
>
> SHAKESPEARE: *The Winter's Tale*, V, ii (1610)

**Gentle breeze.** In meteorological terms, a light breeze of force 3 on the Beaufort Scale, blowing at 8–12 mph (13–19 kph/7–10 knots).

**Gentle craft, The.** Shoemaking. CRISPIN AND CRISPINIAN, the patron saints of shoemaking, were said to be brothers of noble birth.

> As I am a true shoemaker, and a gentleman of the Gentle Craft, buy spurs yourselfes, and I'll find ye bootes these seven yeeres.
>
> THOMAS DEKKER: *The Shoemaker's Holiday, or the Gentle Craft*, I, i (1600)

**Gentle giant.** A nickname for a tall and strong but kindly person.

**Gentle reader.** A formerly courteous address from the writer to the reader in the course of a novel or other work. In modern use it is mainly self-mocking or purely playful.

**Gentle sex, The.** Women.

**Gentle Shepherd, The.** A nickname given by the elder Pitt to George Grenville (1712–70). In the course of a speech on the cider tax (1763), Grenville addressed the House of Commons somewhat plaintively: 'Tell me where? Tell me where?' Pitt mimicked him with the words of the song 'Gentle shepherd, tell me where?' The House burst into laughter and the name stuck to Grenville. The line is from a song by Samuel Howard (1710–82).

**Gentleman** (from Old French *gentilz hom*). Historically a man entitled to bear arms but not of the nobility, hence one of gentle birth, of some position in society, and with manners, bearing and behaviour appropriate to one in such a position. The term then gradually came to mean any cultured man, and any man in general, as a polite form of reference ('I think this gentleman was here first').

**Gentleman farmer.** A term either for a person who engages in farming but who does not depend on it for a living or for someone who owns farmland but who does not farm it personally.

> My father was one of those whom they call gentlemen-farmers. He had a little estate of about 300l. a year.
>
> HENRY FIELDING: *Tom Jones*, Bk VIII, ch xi (1749)

**Gentleman in black velvet, The.** *See* LITTLE GENTLEMAN IN VELVET.

**Gentleman of fortune, A.** A pirate; an adventurer.

**Gentleman of the road.** A HIGHWAYMAN. In parts of North America a highwayman was called a road agent, and the term is still sometimes applied to bandits who hold up trains or road traffic. See also KNIGHT OF THE ROAD.

**Gentleman-ranker.** In the days of the small regular army before the First World War this term was applied to a well-born or educated man who enlisted as a private soldier, 'in the ranks'. This was considered a last resort of one who had made a mess of things.

We're poor little lambs who've lost our way,
Baa! Baa! Baa!
We're little black sheep who've gone astray,
Baa-aa-aa!
Gentleman-rankers out on the spree,
Damned from here to Eternity,
God ha' mercy on such as we,
Baa! Yah! Bah!

RUDYARD KIPLING: 'Gentlemen-Rankers' (1892)

**Gentleman's agreement, A.** An agreement or understanding as between gentlemen in which the only guarantee is the honour of the parties concerned.

**Gentleman's gentleman, A.** A manservant, especially a valet. A famous literary exemplar is JEEVES.

*Fag*: My master shall know this – and if he don't call him out I will.
*Lucy*: Ha! ha! ha! You gentlemen's gentlemen are so hasty!

R.B. SHERIDAN: *The Rivals*, II, ii (1775)

**Gentlemen Pensioners.** The old name for the members of the HONOURABLE CORPS OF GENTLEMEN AT ARMS.

**Gentlemen Ushers.** Court attendants in the Royal Household. They consist of Gentlemen Ushers, Extra Gentlemen Ushers, the Gentleman Usher to the Sword of State and the Gentleman Usher of the BLACK ROD.

**First Gentleman of Europe, The.** *See under* FIRST.

**Honourable Corps of Gentlemen at Arms, The.** *See under* HONOURABLE.

**Little gentleman in velvet.** *See under* LITTLE.

**Nation of gentlemen, A.** *See under* NATION.

**Old Gentleman, The.** *See under* OLD.

**Geomancy** (Greek *gē*, 'earth', and *manteia*, 'prophecy'). DIVINATION by means of the observation of points on the earth or by the patterns made by throwing some earth into the air and allowing it to fall on a flat surface.

**Geordie.** A Tynesider or the dialect spoken by the native inhabitants of this northeastern region of England. The name is a local form of George, used as a generic nickname for local miners, sailors and others. It is specifically associated with, if not actually derived from, the name of George Stephenson (1781–1848), the Newcastle engineer who built the first successful steam locomotive in 1814 and who became manager of the world's first public railway, the Stockton and Darlington, in 1821. Hence 'Geordieland' as a synonym for Tyneside or the northeast generally. Linguists trace the Geordie dialect back to Northumbrian, one of the three divisions of Old English.

**George.** The patron saint of England since his 'adoption' by Edward III (*see* MOST NOBLE ORDER OF THE GARTER). His day is 23 April. The popularity of St George in England stems from the time of the early CRUSADES, for he was said to have come to the assistance of the crusaders at Antioch in 1098. Many of the Normans under Robert CURTHOSE, son of WILLIAM THE CONQUEROR, took him as their patron.

Edward Gibbon and others argued that George of Cappadocia (d.361), the Arian bishop of Alexandria, became the English patron saint, but it is more generally accepted that he was a Roman officer martyred (*c*.300) near Lydda during the Diocletian persecution. He is also the patron saint of Aragon and Portugal.

The legend of St George and the DRAGON is simply an allegorical expression of the triumph of the Christian hero over evil, which St JOHN THE EVANGELIST envisioned through the image of a dragon. Similarly, St MICHAEL, St MARGARET, St Sylvester and St MARTHA are all depicted as slaying dragons. The legend forms the subject of the ballad 'St George for England' in PERCY'S RELIQUES (1765), and a gently humorous version of the tale, entitled 'The Reluctant Dragon', was included by Kenneth Grahame in *Dream Days* (1898), his evocation of orphan childhood.

**George-a-Green.** The mythical 'pinder' ('Pinner' or 'Pindar') or pound-keeper of Wakefield, who resisted ROBIN HOOD, Will Scarlet and LITTLE JOHN single-handed when they attempted to commit a trespass in Wakefield. Robert Greene wrote a comedy called *George-a-Green, or the Pinner of Wakefield* (1599).

**George Barnwell.** *See under* BARNWELL.

**George Cross** and **George Medal.** The George Cross is second only to the VICTORIA CROSS. It consists of a plain silver cross with a medallion showing St GEORGE and the DRAGON in the centre. The words 'For Gallantry' appear round the medallion, and in the angle of each limb of the cross is the royal cipher. It hangs from a dark blue ribbon. The George Cross was founded in 1940 for acts of conspicuous heroism, primarily by civilians. It has twice been awarded collectively: to Malta in 1942 (*see* GEORGE CROSS ISLAND) and to the Royal Ulster Constabulary in 1999. In 2000 there were 34 surviving recipients of the George Cross.

The George Medal (red ribbon with five narrow blue stripes) is awarded for similar but somewhat less outstanding acts of bravery.

**George Cross Island.** Malta is so called from the award of the George Cross to the island by George VI in April 1942, in recognition of the steadfastness and fortitude of its people while under siege in the Second World War. It had suffered constant aerial attacks from Italian and German bombers.

**George Eliot.** *See under* ELIOT.

**George III.** *See* FARMER GEORGE; UNCLE GEORGE.

**George IV.** The king (1762–1830) was given many nicknames. As Prince Regent he was known as 'Prinny', 'Prince FLORIZEL' (the name under which he corresponded with Mrs Robinson), 'The First Gentleman in Europe', 'The Adonis of Fifty' and 'The Prince of Whales', this last for his corpulence. As king (1820–30) he was called 'Fum the Fourth' by Byron. The FUM (phoenix) was a legendary bird of China that was symbolic of royal dignity.

> And where is 'Fum' the Fourth, our 'royal bird?'
> Gone down, it seems, to Scotland to be fiddled
> Unto by Sawney's violin, we have heard.
> LORD BYRON: *Don Juan*, xi (1819–24)

**George Orwell.** *See under* ORWELL.

**George Sand.** *See under* SAND.

**By George.** *See under* BY.

**Cavalier of St George.** *See under* CAVALIER.

**Farmer George.** *See under* FARMER.

**Let George do it.** *See under* LET.

**St George he was for England, St Denis was for France.** This refers to the battle cries of the two nations. That of England was 'St George!', that of France, 'MONTJOIE ST DENIS!'

> St George he was for England; St Denis was for France;
> Sing, Honi soit qui mal y pense.
> PERCY: *Reliques*, 'St George for England' (1765)

**St George's cross.** A red cross on a white background.

**Uncle George.** *See under* UNCLE.

**Geraint.** In ARTHURIAN ROMANCES, a tributary prince of Devon and one of the Knights of the ROUND TABLE. In the MABINOGION he is the son of Erbin, as he is in the French original *Erec et Enide*, from which Tennyson drew his 'Geraint and Enid' in the *Idylls of the King* (1842).

**Geranium.** The Turks say this was a common mallow, which was changed by the touch of MOHAMMED's garment. The name comes from Greek *geranos*, 'crane', and the wild plant is called 'crane's bill' from the resemblance of the fruit to the bill of a crane.

**Gerda** or **Gerd.** In Scandinavian mythology the giant daughter of the frost-giant Gymir and the wife of FREYR. She was so beautiful that the brightness of her naked arms illumined both air and sea. Her name may be connected with Old Norse *garthr*, 'enclosure', and her coupling with Freyr perhaps expresses the sacred marriage of the god of fertility to the cultivated land.

**Germain-en-Laye, St.** The favourite summer residence of the kings of France until Louis XIV moved the court to VERSAILLES. Situated some 13 miles (21km) southwest of Paris, the château was the childhood home of Mary, Queen of Scots and sheltered the exiled James II after the GLORIOUS REVOLUTION of 1688.

**German** or **germane.** Pertaining to or nearly related to, as: 'cousins-german' (first cousins), 'germane to the subject' (bearing on or pertinent to the subject). The word is Latin *germanus*, 'of the same race', and has no connection with the German nation.

**Germany.** The English name for *Deutschland* (French *Allemagne*) is the Latin *Germania*, the source of which is uncertain. It may be a Roman form of a Celtic name meaning 'neighbouring people', from words related to Old Irish *gair*, 'neighbour', and *maon*, 'people'.

In *The History of the Kings of Britain* Geoffrey of Monmouth says that Ebrancus, a mythological descendant of BRUTE, and founder of York (Eboracum), had 20 sons and 30 daughters by 20 wives. The 20 sons departed to Germany and obtained possession of it. Thus Edmund Spenser, speaking of Ebranck, writes:

> An happie man in his first dayes he was,
> And happie father of faire progeny:
> For all so many weekes as the yeare has,
> So many children he did multiply:
> Of which were twentie sonnes, which did apply
> Their minds to praise, and cheualrous desire:
> Those germans [brothers] did subdew all Germany,
> Of [after] whom it hight [was called].
> *The Faerie Queene*, II, x (1590)

**German measles.** The disease formerly known as rubella is so named as it is milder than 'proper' measles. 'German' here denotes inferiority, as DUTCH does in many expressions. It is similar in its application to GERMAN SILVER.

**German silver.** Another name for nickel silver, a cheap, silvery-looking alloy of copper, zinc and nickel. It was first made in Europe at Hildburghausen, Germany, in the early 19th century but had long been used by the Chinese.

**High German.** *See under* HIGH.

**Low German.** *See* HIGH GERMAN.

**Young Germany.** *See under* YOUNG.

**Gerrymander.** To redraw the boundaries of electoral districts in such a way as to give one political party undue advantage over others. The word is derived from Elbridge Gerry (1744–1814), governor of Massachusetts, who did this in 1812 in order to preserve control for his party. Gilbert Stuart (1755–1828), the artist, looking at a map of the new distribution, with a little imagination converted the outline of one district in Essex County to a salamander and showed it to Benjamin Russell, editor of the Boston *Sentinel*. 'Better say a gerrymander,' said Russell, and the name caught on. The practice was not new.

**Gert and Daisy.** The pair of Cockney gossips were created as a comic duo for BBC radio in the 1930s by the sisters Elsie and Doris Waters. They became national institutions in the Second World War to the extent that Lord HAW-HAW, in a broadcast from Germany, declared: 'the good folk of Grimsby should not expect Gert and Daisy to protect them from attacks by the Luftwaffe.' Doris Waters died in 1978, her sister in 1990.

**Gertrude of Nivelles, St.** The daughter of Pepin of Landen, aunt of Charles Martel's father, Pepin of Heristal. As abbess of Nivelles she was noted for her care of the poor and was reputed to have known most of the Bible by heart. In art she is usually represented as so rapt in contemplation that a mouse climbs her pastoral staff unnoticed. She died *c.*664 and her day is 17 March.

**Geryon.** In Greek mythology, a monster with three bodies and three heads, whose oxen ate human flesh and were guarded by Orthos (or Orthrus), a two-headed dog. HERCULES slew both Geryon and the dog.

**Gessler, Hermann.** The tyrannical Austrian governor of the three Forest Cantons of Switzerland who figures in the William TELL legend.

**Gesta. Gesta Danorum** or **Historia Danica.** *See* SAXO GRAMMATICUS.

**Gesta Romanorum.** A collection of popular tales in Latin, each with a moral attached, compiled at the end of the 13th or beginning of the 14th century. The name, meaning 'Deeds of the Romans', is merely fanciful since some of the episodes are of Oriental origin. It was first printed at Utrecht, and the earliest English edition is that of Wynkyn de Worde in about 1510. It is the source of many stories found in later literature. Chaucer, Shakespeare, D.G. Rossetti, H.W. Longfellow and many others use tales and plots that are found in it. It seems to have been compiled for the use of preachers.

**Gestapo.** A name shortened from German *Geheime Staatspolizei*, 'secret state police', which acquired sinister fame in NAZI Germany after 1933. It was formed by Hermann Goering (1893–1946) and later controlled by Heinrich Himmler (1900–45), and it was responsible for terrorizing both the Germans and the peoples of occupied territories. It was declared a criminal organization by the Nuremberg Tribunal in 1946.

**Gestas.** The traditional name of the impenitent thief. *See* DISMAS.

**Geste, Beau.** Michael Geste, a bold young Englishman who joins the French Foreign Legion and has a number of adventures in North Africa. He is the hero of P.C. Wren's *Beau Geste* (1924). His name puns on the French phrase *beau geste* (literally, 'fine gesture') used for a display of magnanimity. *See also* BEAU SABREUR.

> He gave in, but he gave in with a passionate reservation. He was not going to quarrel with a *beau geste*.
>
> WARWICK DEEPING: *Sorrell and Son*, ch xv (1925)

**Get.** With its past and past participle 'got', this is one of the hardest-worked words in the English language, as the following example from a mid-Victorian writer (Dr Withers) shows:

> I got on horseback within ten minutes after I got your letter. When I got to Canterbury I got a chaise for town; but I got wet through, and have got such a cold that I shall not get rid of it in a hurry. I got to the Treasury about noon, but first of all got shaved and dressed. I soon got into the secret of getting a memorial before the Board, but I could not get an answer then; however, I got intelligence from a messenger that I should get one next morning. As soon as I got back to my inn, I got my supper, and then got to bed. When I got up next morning, I got my breakfast, and, having got dressed, I got out in time to get an answer to my memorial. As soon as I got it, I got into a chaise, and got back to Canterbury by three, and got home for tea. I have got nothing for you, and so adieu.

For expressions containing the word 'get' that are not listed below, look under the first main word in the phrase.

**Get about, To.** To travel about; to attend many events. Of news or rumour, to spread.

**Get across, To.** To manage to communicate; to annoy or irritate.

**Get a life!** Find something worthwhile to do! A catchphrase of the 1990s. *See also* GET REAL!

**Get along, To.** To live harmoniously.

**Get around, To.** An expression of American origin, with the same meanings as to get about.

**Get at, To.** To reach; to mean or intend; to irritate or annoy.

**Get away, To.** To escape. 'Get away!' or 'Get away with you!' is an expression of disbelief.

**Get by, To.** To get along all right; to manage just satisfactorily; to pass muster.

**Get down to brass tacks** or **it, To.** To set about a task in earnest. To get down to business or to get down to brass tacks is to stop talking or idling and start concentrating on the matter in hand; to get down to the essentials or 'nitty gritty'. 'Brass tacks' is cockney rhyming slang for 'facts'.

**Get even with, To.** To retaliate.

**Get going, To.** To start; to set off.

**Get in, To.** To enter; to be elected.

**Get it?** Do you understand? Have I made myself clear? Sometimes written 'Geddit?' to reflect a colloquial pronunciation.

**Get off, To.** To escape, not to be punished. To 'tell someone where to get off' is to rebuke them.

**Get off someone's back, To.** To stop criticizing or harassing a person.

**Get off the ground, To.** To begin, to make a start, as of a successful project.

**Get off with, To.** To have a love affair with; to form a sexual relationship with.

**Get on someone's wick, To.** To annoy them. The final word is rhyming slang, 'wick' being short for 'Hampton Wick' (a locality in south-west London), representing 'prick'.

**Get one's own back, To.** To have one's revenge.

**Get out of, To.** To avoid or escape from; to abandon, as 'to get out of a habit'.

**Get out of bed on the wrong side, To.** To be in a bad temper from early morning. It was formerly held to be unlucky to set the left foot on the ground first when getting out of bed. The same superstition applies to putting on the left shoe first. AUGUSTUS Caesar was very superstitious in this respect.

**Get outside, To.** To eat or drink, as: 'He felt better once he'd got outside a pint.'

**Get over, To.** To recover from; to overcome.

**Get real!** Be realistic! An adjuration to face realities, usually with a specific reference. *See also* GET A LIFE!

**Get-rich-quick.** Designed to make money fast.

**Get round someone, To.** To persuade them by coaxing or cajoling.

**Get someone's back up, To.** To annoy a person. The allusion is to a cat, which arches its back when it is threatened by a dog or other animal.

**Get something down to a fine art, To.** To execute something to perfection; to be absolutely expert at it.

**Get something over with, To.** To complete it promptly; to have done with it.

**Get somewhere, To.** To make progress, as: 'Now we're getting somewhere.'

**Get there, To.** To succeed; to 'arrive'; to attain one's object, as: 'We got there in the end.'

**Get to the bottom of, To.** To investigate fully and explain.

**Get up, To.** To rise from one's bed; to devise or create, as: 'We will get up a show.'

**Get-up-and-go.** Energy; vim.

**Have got it bad or badly, To.** To be obsessed or affected emotionally.

**Gethsemane.** Aramaic *gat-semena*, 'oil press', gave the name of the Garden of Gethsemane, the scene of Jesus' agony, on the Mount of Olives (OLIVET), east of the ravine of the Kidron. There was presumably an oil press here.

**Gettysburg Address.** The speech delivered by President Lincoln at the dedication on 19 November 1863 of the National Cemetery at Gettysburg, Pennsylvania, the site of one of the most decisive battles of the American Civil War (1861–5). Although brief, the address came to be regarded as a masterpiece of prose poetry. It begins calmly and gradually works to a climax, so that the concluding words are the best known:

> We here highly resolve that these dead shall not have died in vain – that this nation, under God, shall have a new birth of freedom – and that government of the people, by the people, for the people, shall not perish from the earth.
>
> ABRAHAM LINCOLN: *Gettysburg Address* (19 November 1863)

**Ghibelline.** *See* GUELPHS.

**Ghost. Ghostbuster.** A person whose job it is to destroy apparitions or LAY A GHOST. The term was popularized by the American film *Ghostbusters* (1984).

**Ghost of a chance, The.** The least likelihood. 'He doesn't have the ghost of a chance' means that he has no chance at all.

**Ghost town.** A town that once prospered but that is now in decay with few inhabitants.

**Ghost train.** A train seen running at a time when none is scheduled, especially silently or after dark. Arnold Ridley's comedy thriller *The Ghost Train* (1925) was one of the most successful ever written, and formed the basis of many films, the best being *Oh Mr Porter* (1937). At a fun fair a ghost train is a miniature train that takes riders on a round trip of ghoulish sights, sounds and special effects. In railway slang a ghost train is a night-running de-icing train on electric railways equipped with conductor rails.

**Ghost walks, The.** Theatrical slang for 'we are going to be paid'. When there is no money available, actors say 'the ghost won't walk this time'. The allusion is to Shakespeare's *Hamlet* (I, i (1600)), where Horatio asks the ghost if it 'walks' because:

> Thou hast uphoarded in thy life
> Extorted treasure in the womb of earth.

**Ghost word.** A term invented by the lexicographer W.W. Skeat in 1886 to denote words that are not 'real' words because they have come into existence in error. ACRE-FIGHT and SLUGHORN are examples.

Intrusive letters that have no etymological justification in a word but have been inserted through false analogy with words similarly pronounced (like the gh in sprightly, the h in aghast or the h in ghost) are sometimes called ghost letters.

> We should jealously guard against all chances of giving any undeserved record of words which had never any real existence, being mere coinages due to the blunders of printers or scribes, or to the perfervid imaginations of ignorant or blundering editors.
>
> W.W. SKEAT: *Transactions of the Philological Society*, ii (1886)

**Ghost writer.** An anonymous author who writes speeches, articles or books (especially autobiographies) for which another, better known person gets the credit.

**Cock Lane Ghost.** *See under* COCK.

**Give up the ghost, To.** To die. The idea is that life is independent of the body and is due to the habitation of the ghost or spirit in the material body.

> Man dieth, and wasteth away: yea, man giveth up the ghost, and where is he?
> Job 14:10

**Holy Ghost, The.** *See under* HOLY.

**Lay a ghost, To.** *See under* LAY.

**Look like a ghost, To.** *See under* LOOK.

**Sampford ghost.** *See under* SAMPFORD.

**Stockwell ghost.** *See under* STOCKWELL.

**GI.** In the Second World War American enlisted men called themselves GIs, from an abbreviation of Government Issue. After becoming accustomed to GI shirts, GI blankets and other army issues, the soldiers began to apply the term to themselves.

**GI bride.** A woman who married an American serviceman (GI) after meeting him when he was stationed in England (or some other country) in the Second World War.

**Giants.** People well above normal height and size have existed as 'sports of nature' or 'freaks', but the widespread belief in pre-existing races of giants among primitive peoples is due partly to the ingrained idea that mankind has degenerated – 'There were giants in the earth in those days' (Genesis 6:4) – and partly to the existence from remote antiquity of cyclopean buildings, gigantic sarcophagi and the like, and to the discovery from time to time in pre-scientific days of the bones of extinct monsters, which were taken to be those of men. Among instances of the latter may be mentioned:

A 19ft (5.8m) skeleton was discovered at Lucerne in 1577. Dr Plater is the authority for this measurement.

'Teutobochus', whose remains were discovered near the Rhône in 1613. They occupied a tomb 30ft (9.1m) long. The bones of another gigantic skeleton were exposed by the action of the Rhône in 1456. If this was a human skeleton, the height of the living man must have been 30ft (9.1m).

Pliny records that an earthquake in Crete exposed the bones of a giant 46 cubits (roughly 75ft/22.9m) in height. He called this the skeleton of ORION, while others held it to be that of Otus (*see* EPHIALTES).

ANTAEUS is said by Plutarch to have been 60 cubits (about 90ft/27.4m) in height. Plutarch adds that the grave of the giant was opened by Serbonius.

The skeleton of the 'monster Polypheme' is said to have been discovered at Trapani, Sicily, in the 14th century. If this skeleton was that of a man, he would have been 300ft (91.4m) in height.

**Giant Despair.** In John Bunyan's PILGRIM'S PROGRESS (1678, 1684), the owner and occupant of DOUBTING CASTLE, where he imprisoned CHRISTIAN and Hopeful.

**Giants' cauldrons.** *See* GIANTS' KETTLES.

**Giant's Causeway.** A formation of some 40,000 basaltic columns, projecting into the sea about 8 miles (13km) east-northeast of Portrush, County Antrim, on the north coast of Ireland. It is fabled to be the beginning of a road to be constructed by the giants across the channel from Ireland to Scotland. Its Irish name is *Clochán na bhFomhoraigh* ('stepping stones of the Fomorians', the evil gods of Irish myth). Here are to be found the Giant's Loom, the Giant's Well and the Giant's Chair. Other formations in the locality are called the Giant's Organ, the Giant's Peephole and the Giant's Granny. There are also reefs called the Giant's Eye-glass. All these names are now traditionally treated as singular, although the original Irish was plural. This is the consequence of another legend, that the Causeway was built by a single giant, the folk hero Finn mac Cool, better known as FINGAL.

**Giants' Dance, The.** STONEHENGE, which Geoffrey of Monmouth says was brought from Killaurus, a mountain in Ireland, by Uther PENDRAGON and his men under the direction of MERLIN.

**Giants' kettles** or **cauldrons.** A name given to glacial pot-shaped cylindrical holes worn in rocks by the rotary currents of subglacial streams, often containing water-worn stones, boulders and the like. They are found in Norway, Germany, the USA and elsewhere.

**Giants' Leap, The.** A popular name in many mountainous districts for two prominent rocks, separated from each other by a wide chasm or stretch of open country across which some giant is fabled to have leapt and so baffled his pursuers.

**Giants of legend and literature.** The giants of Greek mythology were, for the most part, sons of URANUS and GAIA. When they attempted to storm heaven, they were hurled to earth by the aid of HERCULES, and buried under Mount ETNA. Those of Scandinavian mythology dwelt in JOTUNHEIM and these 'voracious ones' personified the unbridled forces of nature with superhuman powers against which man strove with the help of the gods. Giants feature prominently in nursery tales such as JACK THE GIANT-KILLER and Swift peopled BROBDINGNAG with giants. *See also* ALIFANFARON; ANTAEUS; ATLAS; BALAN; BELLERUS; BLUNDERBORE; BRIAREUS; BRONTES; CACUS; CORMORAN; COTTUS; CYCLOPS; ENCELADUS; EPHIALTES; FIERABRAS; GARGANTUA; GOG AND MAGOG; IRUS; MORGANTE MAGGIORE; ORGOGLIO; ORION; PANTAGRUEL; POLYPHEMUS; TITANS; TYPHOEUS; YMIR.

## Giants of other note.

Anak (*see* BRICE *below*)
Andronicus II, grandson of Alexius Comnenus, was 10ft (3m) tall; Nicetas asserts that he had seen him
Edward Bamford was 7ft 4in (2.2m); he died in 1768 and was buried in St Dunstan's churchyard, London
Captain Bates was 7ft 11½in (2.4m); a native of Kentucky, he was exhibited in London in 1871
Big Frank (*see* SHERIDAN *below*)
Big Sam (*see* Samuel McDONALD *below*)
Henry Blacker was 7ft 4in (2.2m) and most symmetrical; a native of Cuckfield, Sussex, he was called 'the British Giant'
William Bradley (1787–1820) was 7ft 9in (2.4m); he was born at Market Weighton, Yorkshire, and his right hand is preserved in the museum of the Royal College of Surgeons
M.J. Brice (b.1840), exhibited under the name of Anak, was 7ft 8in (2.3m) at the age of 26; he was born at Ramonchamp in the Vosges and visited England in 1862–5; his arms had a stretch of 7ft 11½in (2.4m)
Von Brusted of Norway was 8ft (2.4m); He was exhibited at London in 1880
Byrne (*see* O'BRIEN *below*)
Chang, the Chinese giant, was 8ft 2in (2.5m); he was exhibited in London in 1865–6 and in 1880
CHARLEMAGNE (747–814), according to tradition was nearly 8ft (2.4m) and was so strong that he could squeeze together three horseshoes with his hands
Patrick Cotter (1761–1806), an Irish bricklayer, who exhibited as O'Brien, was 8ft 1in (2.5m); he died at Clifton, Bristol; a cast of his hand is preserved in the museum of the Royal College of Surgeons
Daniel, the porter of Oliver Cromwell, was a man of 'gigantic stature'
Eleazer was 7 cubits (nearly 11ft/3.4m); Vitellius sent this giant to Rome, and he is mentioned by Josephus who also speaks of a Jew of 10ft 2in (3.1m)
Eleizegue (Joachim) was 7ft 10in (2.4m); a Spaniard, he was exhibited in the Cosmorama, Regent Street, London, in the mid-19th century
William Evans (d.1632) was 8ft (2.4m); he was a porter of CHARLES I
Gabara, the Arabian giant, was 9ft 9in (2.8m); Pliny says he was the tallest man seen in the days of Claudius
Gilly, the Swedish giant, was 8ft (2.4m); he was exhibited at London in the early part of the 19th century
Alice Gordon (d.1737 at the age of 19) was 7ft (2.1m); she was a native of Essex
Robert Hale (1802–62) was 7ft 6in (2.3m) and was born at West Somerton, Norfolk; he was called 'the Norfolk Giant'
Harald Hardrada (d.1066) was nearly 7ft (2.1m) and was called 'the Norway Giant'; he was slain at Stamford Bridge
Benjamin Holmes (d.1892) was 7ft 7in (2.3m); he was from Northumberland and became sword-bearer to the Corporation of Worcester
James McDonald (d.1760) of Cork, Ireland, was 7ft 6in (2.3m)
Samuel McDonald (d.1802), usually called 'Big Sam', was 6ft 10in (2.1m); a Scot, he was the Prince of Wales's footman
Cornelius Macgrath (1740–60) was 7ft 10in (2.4m) at the age of 16; he was an orphan and was reared by Bishop Berkeley
Maximus I, Roman emperor (r.235–238) was 8ft 6in (2.6m)
John Middleton was 9ft 3in (2.8m); according to Dr Plot's *Natural History of Staffordshire* (1686) he was born at Hale, Lancashire, in the reign of James I and his hand was 17in (43cm) long and 8in (22cm) broad; recent research suggests, however, that his actual stature may have been nearer 7ft 9in (2.4m)
Maximilian Christopher Miller (d.1734) was 8ft (2.4m); his hand measured 12in (30cm) and his forefinger 9in (23cm); he died at London at the age of 60
Murphy, an Irish giant of the late 18th century, was 8ft 10in (2.7m); he died at Marseilles
Charles O'Brien or Byrne (1761–83) was 8ft 4in (2.5m); he was Irish and died in Cockspur Street, London; his giant skeleton is preserved in the Royal College of Surgeons
O'Brien (*see* COTTER *above*)
Porus, an Indian king, was 5 cubits in height (about 7ft 6in/2.3m); according to Quintus Curtius, *De rebus gestis Alexandri Magni*, he fought against Alexander the Great near the Hydaspes
Francis Sheridan (d.1870), an Irishman who exhibited under the name Big Frank, was 7ft 8in (2.3m)
Anne Hannen Swan, a native of Nova Scotia, was the same height as Captain BATES (*above*) to whom she was married
James Toller (d.1819) was 8ft (2.4m) at the age of 24
Robert P. Wadlow (1918–40), of Illinois, USA, was 8ft 11in (2.7m); he is the tallest man of whose measurements there is complete certainty
Josef Winkelmaier (1865–87), an Austrian, was 8ft 9in (2.6m)
Zeng Jinlian (1964–82), of Hunan Province, China, was 8ft 1¾in (2.5m), and the tallest woman in medical history

### In addition to the above:

Del Rio says that he saw a Piedmontese in 1572 more than 9ft (2.7m) high
M. Thevet published (1575) an account of a South American giant, the skeleton of which he measured: it was 11ft 5in (3.5m)
Gaspard Bauhin (1560–1624), the anatomist and botanist, speaks of a Swiss 8ft (2.4m) high
C.F.S. Warren (in *Notes & Queries*, 14 August 1875) said that his father knew a woman 9ft (2.7m) in height, and adds: 'her head touched the ceiling of a good-sized room'
There is a human skeleton 8ft 6in (2.6m) in height in the museum of Trinity College, Dublin

There were over 100 applicants in response to an advertisement in *The Times* (25 July 1966) for 'giants' of minimum height 6ft 7in (2m) for the premiere of *Cast a Giant Shadow* at the London Pavilion. The tallest was 7ft 3in (2.2m). *See also* DWARF; HEAVIEST MEN.

## Giants of the Bible.

Anak: the eponymous progenitor of the Anakim (*see below*); Hebrew spies said they were mere grasshoppers compared with these giants (Joshua 15:14, Judges 1:20, Numbers 13:33)

GOLIATH of Gath (1 Samuel 17 and elsewhere): his height is given as 6 cubits and a span; the cubit varied and might be anything from about 18in to 22in (45–59cm); a span was about 9in (23cm); this would give Goliath a height of between 9ft 9in and 11ft 3in (2.9–3.4m)

OG, king of Bashan (Joshua 12:4, Deuteronomy 3:10, 4:47 and elsewhere): 'of the remnant of the giants'; according to tradition, he lived for 3000 years and walked beside the Ark during the Flood. One of his bones formed a bridge over a river, and his bed (Deuteronomy 3:11) was 9 cubits by 4 cubits

The Anakim and Rephaim were tribes of reputed giants inhabiting the territory on both sides of the Jordan before the coming of the Israelites. The Nephilim, the offspring of the sons of God and the daughters of men (Genesis 6:4), a mythological race of semi-divine heroes, were also giants.

**Giants' Ring.** A prehistoric circular mound south of Belfast, Northern Ireland. It is 580ft (177m) in diameter and has a CROMLECH in the centre.

**Giants' Staircase.** The staircase rising from the courtyard of the Doge's Palace, Venice, and so named from the figures of two giants at its head.

**Giants' War with Zeus.** The War of the Giants and the War of the TITANS should be kept distinct. The latter was before ZEUS became god of heaven and earth; the former was after that time. The Giants' War was a revolt by the giants against Zeus, which was readily put down by the help of the other gods and the aid of HERCULES.

**Battle of the Giants, The.** *See under* BATTLE.

**Gentle giant.** *See under* GENTLE.

**Jack the Giant-killer.** *See under* JACK.

**Giaour** (Turkish *giaur*, 'unbeliever'). A word used by the Turks for a person who was not a Muslim, especially a Christian. The word was popularized by Byron who wrote a poem called *The Giaour* (1813).

> The city won for Allah from the Giaour,
> The Giaour from Othman's race again may wrest.
> LORD BYRON: *Childe Harold's Pilgrimage*, ii (1812)

**Gib cat.** A tomcat. The male cat used to be called Gilbert. Tibert, or TYBALT, is the French form of Gilbert, and hence Chaucer, or whoever it was that translated that part of the *Romaunt of the Rose*, renders 'Thibert le cas' by 'Gibbe, our Cat' (line 6204). It is generally used of a castrated cat.

> I am as melancholy as a gib cat, or a lugged bear.
> SHAKESPEARE: *Henry IV*, *Pt I*, I, ii (1597)

**Gibeonite.** A slave's slave, a workman's labourer, a farmer's understrapper or Jack-of-all-work. The Gibeonites were made 'hewers of wood and drawers of water' to the Israelites (Joshua 9:27).

**Gibraltar.** The CALPE of the ancients and one of the PILLARS OF HERCULES. The name is a corruption of Arabic *Jabal-Tarik*, 'hill of Tarik', Tarik being the SARACEN leader who defeated RODERICK, the Gothic king of Spain in 711, and built a castle on the Rock. The Spanish finally took it from the Moors in 1462. It was captured by a combined English and Dutch force under Sir George Rooke in 1704 and unsuccessfully besieged by the Spanish and French in 1704, 1705 and subsequently from 1779 to 1783, when it was heroically defended by General Eliott. *See also* GARLIC WALL; ROCK SCORPION.

**Gibson Girl.** A representation of female beauty characteristic of its period depicted by Charles Dana Gibson (1867–1944) in several series of black-and-white drawings dating from 1896. His pictures of the American girl enjoyed an enormous vogue and the series, entitled *The Adventures of Mr Pipp*, which appeared in *Collier's Weekly* (1899), formed the basis of a successful play. The Gibson Girl was portrayed in various poses and occupations, her individuality accentuated by the sweeping skirts and large hats of the period. She was based on his wife Irene (née Langhorne) and her sisters, one of whom was Nancy, Viscountess Astor (1879–1964).

**Gideon.** The great warrior who delivered the Israelites from the Midianites. His deeds are chronicled in Judges 6–8, where two separate accounts are juxtaposed. The first tells how Gideon, having led his tribesmen to slay the Midianites, creates an idolatrous image from the booty, thus inducing ISRAEL to immorality. In the second version, he replaces the idol and altar of the pagan god BAAL with the worship of Yahweh, the God of Israel, who thus inspires him and his men to destroy the Midianites as a sign of Yahweh's supremacy.

**Gideons.** An international association of Christian business and professional men founded in 1899 and now functioning in many countries. They seek to lead others to Christianity, particularly by the distribution of Bibles and New Testaments on a large scale. Bibles are placed in hotel bedrooms and hospitals, and New Testaments are presented to pupils in schools. They are named after Gideon's men who overthrew the Midianites (Judges 7).

**Sword of Gideon.** *See under* SWORD.

**Gidget.** The nickname of Francine Lawrence, a sporty teenage 'California girl' who is the main character in several novels by Frederick Kohner, beginning with *Gidget* (1957). She appeared in a series of films based on the books from 1959, played in turn by Sandra Dee, Deborah Walley and Cindy Carol. In American slang, a 'gidget' is a lithe, pert young woman.

**Gift. Gift of the gab, The.** Fluency of speech, also the gift of boasting. The word 'gab' may be onomatopoeic or derive from the identical Gaelic word for mouth.

**Gift of tongues, The.** Command of foreign languages, also the power claimed by the early church and by some later mystics (as the IRVINGITES) of conversing in and understanding unknown tongues (from the miracle at PENTECOST, Acts 2:4, the implications of which are obscure).

**Cordelia's gift.** *See under* CORDELIA.

**Greek gift.** *See under* GREEK.

**Look a gift-horse in the mouth, To.** *See under* LOOK.

**New Year's gifts.** *See under* NEW.

**Seven gifts of the Holy Spirit, The.** *See under* SEVEN.

**Gigi.** The pet name of Gilberte, the young Parisian girl who is the heroine of Colette's novel titled after her (1944), in which she is trained by her aunt to become a courtesan. The story inspired a film of 1948, in which Gigi is played by Danièle Delorme, and a successful screen musical by Frederick Loewe and Alan Jay Lerner (1958), with Leslie Caron in the lead role. The later film has the popular numbers 'Thank heaven for little girls' and 'I remember it well'.

**Gig-lamps.** An old slang term for spectacles, especially large round ones. The allusion is to the lanterns attached to a 'gig' (a one-horse carriage).

**Gilbertian.** A term applied to anything whimsically topsy-turvy, any situation such as those W.S. Gilbert (1836–1911) depicted in the famous Gilbert and Sullivan operas. Of these perhaps *The Mikado* (1885) furnishes the best examples.

**Gilbertines.** The only medieval religious order of English origin, founded at Sempringham, near Bourne, Lincolnshire, in *c.*1135 by Gilbert of Sempringham (*c.*1083–1189). The monks observed the rule of the AUGUSTINIANS and the nuns that of the BENEDICTINES. There were some 25 houses at the Dissolution.

**Gild. Gilded cage.** A luxurious but restrictive environment.

> Her beauty was sold for an old man's gold,
> She's a bird in a gilded cage.
> ARTHUR J. LAMB: *A Bird in a Gilded Cage* (1900)

**Gilded Chamber, The.** A name for the HOUSE OF LORDS.

**Gilded youth.** Wealthy and fashionable young men, principally engaged in the pursuit of pleasure. A parallel expression to the French JEUNESSE DORÉE.

**Gild** or **paint the lily, To.** To try to improve a thing that is already excellent or beautiful. The phrase occurs in Shakespeare with regard to King John's second coronation:

> Therefore, to be possess'd with double pomp,
> To guard a title that was rich before,
> To gild refined gold, to paint the lily ...
> Is wasteful and ridiculous excess.
> *King John*, IV, ii (1596)

**Gild the pill, To.** It was the custom of old-time doctors, whether QUACKS or genuine, to make their nauseous pills more attractive, at least to the sight, by gilding them with a thin coating of sugar. Hence to make an unattractive thing at least appear desirable.

**Gildas.** The earliest British 'historian', also called Sapiens and Badonicus (*c.*516–*c.*570). Little is known about him, but he was most probably an ecclesiastic and much of his writing consists of a tirade against his countrymen. His works contain much scriptural matter, and the history covers the period from the Roman invasion to his own times. Although vague (with few dates) and inaccurate, his writing is important. His Latin sketch of the history of Britain, *De Excidio et Conquestu Britanniae* ('On the destruction and conquest of Britain'), was first published in modified form by the ecclesiastic Polydore Virgil in 1525.

**Gilderoy.** A noted robber and cattle-stealer of Perthshire who was hanged with five of his gang in July 1638 at Gallowlee near Edinburgh. He was noted for his handsome person, and his real name was said to be Patrick Macgregor. He is credited with having picked the pocket of Cardinal Richelieu, robbed Oliver Cromwell and hanged a judge. There are ballads on him in PERCY'S RELIQUES and elsewhere.

> Oh! sike twa charming een he had,
> A breath as sweet as rose,
> He never ware a Highland plaid,
> But costly silken clothes.
> PERCY: *Reliques*, 'Gilderoy' (1765)

**Hung higher than Gilderoy's kite, To be.** *See under* HANG.

**Gilead, Is there no balm in?** *See under* BALM.

**Giles.** A mildly humorous generic name for a farmer. The subject of Robert Bloomfield's poem *The Farmer's Boy* (1800) was so named. *See also* FARMER GEORGE.

**Giles of Antwerp.** Gilles Coignet, the Flemish painter (1538–99).

**St Giles.** The patron saint of cripples. The tradition is that Childeric, king of France, accidentally wounded the hermit in the knee when hunting, and he remained a cripple for life, refusing to be cured that he might the better mortify the flesh. His symbol is a hind, in allusion to the 'heaven-directed hind' that went daily to his cave near the mouth of the Rhône to give him milk. He is sometimes represented as an old man with an arrow in his hand and a hind by his side. Churches dedicated to St Giles were usually situated in the outskirts of a city, and originally outside the walls because cripples and beggars were not permitted to pass the gates.

**Gilgamesh epic.** A collection of ancient Babylonian stories and myths, older than HOMER, seemingly brought together around Gilgamesh, king of Erech, as the central hero. He was two-thirds a god, one-third a man, and his name probably means 'ancestral hero'. The epic appears to have covered 12 tablets (*c*.3000 lines), portions of which were found among the relics of the library of Assur-bani-pal, king of Assyria (668–626 BC). Some of the tablets date back to *c*.2000 BC. *See also* DELUGE.

**Gilles de Rais.** *See* BLUEBEARD.

**Gillie.** A Gaelic word (properly *gille*) for a boy or lad, manservant or attendant, especially one who attends a sportsman fishing or hunting.

**Gillies' Hill.** In the Battle of Bannockburn (1314), the king, Robert BRUCE, ordered all the gillies, drivers of carts and camp followers to go behind a hill. When the battle seemed to favour the Scots, those wishing to share in the plunder rushed from their concealment with such arms as they could lay hands on. The English, thinking them to be a new army, fled in panic. The height was ever after called the Gillies' Hill.

**Gillie-wet-foot.** A barefoot Highland lad; a running footman who had to carry his master over brooks and watery places when travelling.

**Gills.** Humorous slang for the mouth.

**White** or **pale about the gills.** *See under* WHITE.

**Gilpin, John.** The character in William Cowper's famous ballad *The Diverting History of John Gilpin* (1782) is said to represent William Beyer (1693–1791), a noted linen draper at the junction of Cheapside and Paternoster Row. It was Lady Austen, widow of Sir Robert Austen and Cowper's neighbour at Olney, Buckinghamshire, who told him the story to divert him from his melancholy. The marriage adventure of Commodore Trunnion in Tobias Smollett's *Peregrine Pickle* (1751) is very similar to that of Gilpin's wedding anniversary.

**Gilt. Gilt-edged investments.** A phrase introduced in the last quarter of the 19th century to denote securities of the most reliable character, such as CONSOLS and other government stock, first mortgages, debentures, shares in high-ranking companies and the like.

**Take the gilt off the gingerbread, To.** To spoil the illusion; to appropriate all the fun or profit and leave the dull base behind; to rob something of its attraction.

**Gimlet-eyed.** Keen-eyed; very sharpsighted; having eyes that 'bore through', like a gimlet.

**Gimmick.** The first use of this word in American slang was to describe some device by which a conjurer or fairground showman worked his trick. In later usage it applied to some distinctive quirk or trick associated with a film or radio star, then to any device. The origin of the word is uncertain. It may be an alteration of 'gimcrack' or even a form of 'magic'.

**Gin.** A contraction of Dutch *genever*, 'juniper', the berries of which are used to flavour the spirit. *See also* HOLLANDS.

> This calls the Church to deprecate our sin,
> And hurls the thunder of the laws on gin.
>
> ALEXANDER POPE: *Satires*, Epilogue, i (1738)

**Gin and It.** A mixture of gin and Italian vermouth.

**Gin palace.** A garishly ornate gin shop, especially in Victorian and Edwardian times.

**Gin sling.** A long drink composed mainly of gin and lemon. It has been attributed to JOHN COLLINS, famous bartender of Limmer's Hotel in London, but it dates from before his time and was found in the USA by 1800.

**Ginger.** A hot, spicy root used in cooking and in medicine, hence as a nickname applied to someone with red hair.

**Gingerbread.** A moist, dark brown cake mixed with treacle and flavoured with ginger. It is traditionally made up into toy shapes such as gingerbread men and decorated with DUTCH GOLD or gold leaf. It was commonly sold at fairs up to the middle of the 19th century.

**Ginger group.** A small group of people whose object is to stir the more passive majority into activity, especially in politics. The allusion is to the spice.

**Gingerly.** Cautiously, with hesitating, mincing or faltering steps. The word dates back to at least the 16th century and has nothing to do with ginger. It is perhaps from Old French *gensor*, 'dainty', from *gent*, 'of noble birth' (English 'gentle').

> They spend their goods ... upon their dansing minions, that minse it ful gingerlie, God wot, tripping like gotes, that an egge would not brek vnder their feet.
>
> JOHN STUBBES: *Anatomie of Abuses*, II, i (1583)

**Take the gilt off the gingerbread, To.** *See under* GILT.

**Ginnungagap.** In Scandinavian mythology the Great Void between NIFLHEIM, the region of fogs, and MUSPELHEIM, the region of intense heat. It was without beginning and without end, there was neither day or night, and it existed before either land or sea, heaven or earth.

**Ginseng** (Mandarin Chinese *rénshēn*, 'man image'). The plant *Panax schinseng*, whose root resembles a man's forked legs and when taken in medicinal form is a supposed source of strength and virility. Hence its name. According to popular Chinese superstition, the ginseng plant changes after 300 centuries into a man with white blood, and as such is the elixir of immortality, a few drops bringing a dead man back to life. The older the plant, the more it is valued, and experts are able to ascertain its age by examination of certain marks on the stem and peculiarities of its root structure.

**Gioconda smile.** An enigmatic smile, as that of the Mona Lisa. Leonardo da Vinci's famous painting (1503–6), also known as *La Gioconda* or *La Joconde*, is a portrait of the wife of Francesco del Giocondo. Aldous Huxley has a short story, 'The Gioconda Smile', in *Mortal Coils* (1922).

**Giotto's O.** The old story goes that the pope, wishing to employ artists from all over Italy, sent a messenger to collect specimens of their work. When the man visited Giotto (*c*.1267–1337), the artist paused for a moment from the picture he was working on and with his brush drew a perfect circle on a piece of paper. In some surprise the man returned to the pope, who, appreciating the perfection of Giotto's artistry and skill by his unerring circle, employed him forthwith.

> I saw ... that the practical teaching of the masters of Art was summed up by the O of Giotto.
> JOHN RUSKIN: *The Queen of the Air*, iii (1869)

*See also* AS ROUND AS GIOTTO'S O.

**Giovanni, Don.** *See* DON JUAN *under* JUAN.

**Gipsy.** *See* GYPSY.

**Giralda** (Spanish, 'weather vane'). The name given to the great square tower of the cathedral at Seville (formerly a Moorish minaret), which is surmounted by a statue of Faith, so pivoted as to turn with the wind.

**Gird, To.** The verb can mean 'to mock at' as well as 'to bind round'.

**Gird up one's loins, To.** To prepare for hard work or for a journey. The Jews wore loose garments, which they girded (belted) about their loins (waist) when travelling or working.

> Wherefore gird up the loins of your mind, be sober, and hope to the end for the grace that is to be brought unto you at the revelation of Jesus Christ.
> 1 Peter 1:13

**Girdle. Girdlecake.** A cake cooked over the fire on a girdle or griddle, a circular iron plate, also called a bakestone.

**Girdle of Venus, The.** The CESTUS.

**Aphrodite's girdle.** The CESTUS.

**Culross girdles.** *See under* CULROSS.

**Put a girdle round the earth, To.** To travel around it. PUCK says:

> I'll put a girdle round about the earth
> In forty minutes.
> SHAKESPEARE: *A Midsummer Night's Dream*, II, i (1595)

**Girl.** The word first appears in Middle English, and its etymology has given rise to many guesses. It may be related to Low German *göre*, 'child'. It was formerly applicable to a child of either sex, so that a boy was sometimes distinguished as a 'knave girl'. It is now applied solely to a female child or a young woman. The word appears nearly 70 times in Shakespeare, but only twice in the Authorized Version of the Bible (1611): 'sold a girl for wine' (Joel 3:3) and 'boys and girls playing in the streets' (Zechariah 8:5).

**Girl Guides.** The feminine counterpart to the BOY SCOUTS, organized in 1910 by General Baden-Powell (1857–1941) and his sister Agnes (1858–1945). Their training and organization is much the same as the Scouts and is based on similar promises and laws. The three sections of the movement, since 1992 officially named Guides rather than Girl Guides, were originally Brownies, Guides and Rangers, but the names and groupings have now been modified to: Rainbow Guides (aged 5–7), Brownie Guides (7 and over), Guides (10 and over), Ranger Guides (14 and over) and Young Leaders (15–18).

In the USA they are called Girl Scouts (formed 1912), with names and age groups as follows: Daisies (5–6), Brownies (6–8), Juniors (8–11), Cadettes (11–14) and Seniors (14–17).

**Girl meets boy.** The paradigm of a conventional love match, fictional or in fact. *See also* BOY MEETS GIRL.

**Girl next door, The.** A young woman, especially one known from childhood, regarded as a pleasant and decent but in the main conventional marriage partner.

**All girls together.** *See under* ALL.

**Bachelor girl.** *See under* BACHELOR.

**Best girl.** *See under* BEST.

**Bunny girl.** *See under* BUNNY.

**Call girl.** *See under* CALL.

**Cover girl.** *See under* COVER.

**Dancing girl.** *See under* DANCE.

**Essex girl.** *See under* ESSEX.

**Gaiety Girl.** *See under* GAIETY.

**Gibson Girl.** *See under* GIBSON.

**Good-time girl.** *See under* GOOD.

**Land girls.** *See under* LAND.

**Sweater girl.** *See under* SWEAT.

**Giro.** The word has come to have two main applications, one formal, the other informal. Formally, it is the name of the Girobank, a clearing bank set up as part of the Post Office in 1968. It operates like any other bank, but uses post offices as its outlets. Informally, as an abbreviation for girocheque, it is the name of the social security payment sent by post to those entitled, who then cash the cheque at a post office. The word ultimately goes back to Italian *giro*, 'circulation'.

'That my lager?' he inquired, feeling mean even as he uttered the question. 'Yeah, d'you mind?' said Raymond. 'I'll replace it when I get me next giro.'
DAVID LODGE: *Nice Work*, Pt III, ch ii (1988)

**Girondists** or **Gironde, The.** The moderate republicans in the French Revolution (1791–3), so called from the department of the Gironde, which elected for the Legislative Assembly men such as Vergniaud and Gensonné who championed its point of view. Condorcet, Madame Roland and Pétion were among them. Brissot became their chief spokesman, hence they were sometimes called Brissotins. They were the dominant party in 1792 but were overthrown in the Convention by the MOUNTAIN in 1793 and many of their leaders were guillotined.

**Gis.** A corruption of Jesus or J.H.S. Ophelia says 'By Gis and by St Charity' (*Hamlet*, IV, v (1601)).

**Giselle.** The central character of Adolphe Adam's ballet that bears her name (1841), with a libretto by Jules-Henri Vernoy de Saint-Georges, Théophile Gautier and Jean Coralli. The plot is based on a legend from Heinrich Heine's *Zur Geschichte der neueren schönen Literatur in Deutschland* ('On the History of Current Belles-Lettres in Germany') (1833), telling how the peasant girl Giselle loves Albrecht, unaware that he is a count and betrothed to another. On discovering his secret, she goes mad and kills herself. After her death she joins the Wilis, the embodied spirits of brides who died before their wedding day. When Albrecht comes to her grave the Wilis trap him as well, but Giselle recognizes him and manages to stave them off until dawn, when he will be safe.

**Give.** For phrases including the verb 'give' but not included below, see under the principal word.

**Give and take, To.** To be fair; to practise forbearance and consideration. In horse-racing a give and take plate is a prize for a race in which the runners that exceed a standard height carry more than the standard weight and those that fall short of it less.

**Give as good as one gets, To.** To retort with equal words or blows.

**Giveaway, A.** A revealing or betraying circumstance.

**Give away, To.** To hand the bride in marriage to the bridegroom; to act the part of the bride's father.

**Give in, To.** To confess oneself beaten; to yield.

**Give it someone, To.** To scold or thrash them, as: 'I'll give it you when I catch you.'

**Give me where to stand, and I will move the world.** (Greek *Dos moi pou stō kai kinō tēn gēn.*) So said ARCHIMEDES. The instrument he would have used is the lever.

**Given name, A.** A first name, forename or Christian name.

**Give oneself away, To.** To betray oneself by some thoughtless action or remark; to damage one's own cause by carelessly letting something out.

**Give one's word, To.** *See under* WORD.

**Give onto, To.** To look out over; to afford a view of, as: 'The hotel gave onto the sea.'

**Give out, To.** To make public. Also, to come to an end, as: 'The funds have given out.'

**Give someone to understand, To.** To inform them unambiguously.

**Give someone what for, To.** To punish or reprimand a person severely.

**Give up, To.** To renounce, resign or surrender; to admit defeat.

**Give way, To.** To break down; to yield.

**Not to give a damn.** *See under* DAMN.

**What gives?** What's happening? What's the latest?

**Gizzard.** The strong, muscular second stomach of birds, where the food is ground, attributed humorously to humans in some phrases.

**Stick in one's gizzard, To.** *See under* STICK.

**Glad. Glad rags.** A slang term for one's best clothes.

**Give someone the glad eye, To.** To look at someone lasciviously or provocatively.

**Gladiators** (Latin *gladius*, 'sword'). These combatants who fought to the death in Roman arenas were first drawn from condemned criminals and originally appeared at FUNERAL ceremonies in 164 BC. Slaves and prisoners of war came to be employed, when the taste for these grim spectacles grew, and their employment as hired bodyguards by wealthy patrons became a threat to law and order. They were trained in special schools (*ludi*), and gladiatorial games spread throughout the provinces. Such combats were suppressed in the Eastern Empire by Constantine in AD 325 and in the West by Theodoric in AD 500. *See also* THUMB.

**Gladstone bag.** A kind of leather portmanteau made in various sizes and named after the great Victorian statesman, W.E. Gladstone (1809–98).

**Glamorgan.** The historic southernmost county of Wales, in 1974 divided into West, Mid and South Glamorgan and since 1996 represented in name by the unitary authority of Vale of Glamorgan. Geoffrey of Monmouth says that Margan and Cunedagius, the sons of Gonorilla and Regan, divided the kingdom of Britain between them after the death of their aunt Cordeilla. Margan, resolving to take the whole, attacked Cunedagius but was put to flight and killed 'in a town of Kambria, which since his death has been by the country people called Margan to this day'.

The name actually means 'Morgan's shore', from Welsh *glan*, 'bank', 'shore', and Morgan, probably a 7th-century prince of Gwent. The Welsh name for Glamorgan is Morgannwg, the suffix -wg after the name indicating that it is his domain and so meaning 'territory'.

**Glasgow. Glasgow capon, A.** A salt herring.

**Glasgow magistrate.** A salt herring. The phrase is said to have originated when some wag placed a salt herring on the iron guard of the carriage of a well-known magistrate who made up part of a deputation to George IV.

**Arms of Glasgow.** *See* KENTIGERN.

**Glasnost** (Russian, 'openness'). Mikhail Gorbachev became General Secretary of the Soviet Communist party in 1985, and in 1986 he introduced a policy of *glasnost* (in conjunction with PERESTROIKA) relaxing repression on human rights but within the framework of socialism. The intention was to give more freedom in social and cultural affairs.

> Mr Gorbachev has said Moscow no longer claims a monopoly on the right path to Communism but he has been at pains to stress the international benefits of a bit of *glasnost*.
> *Sunday Telegraph* (17 July 1988)

**Glass. Glass ceiling.** An invisible barrier on the career ladder that some employees, in particular women, find they can see through but which they cannot surmount.

> If there are still glass ceilings in some offices, they are likely to shatter at the collective impact of the confident, well-qualified generation of girls now emerging from the nation's schools.
> *The Times* (7 September 1998)

**Glasshouse.** Army slang for a military prison. It was originally applied to the prison at North Camp, Aldershot, which had a glass roof.

**Glass of wine with the Borgias, A.** A great and sometimes fatal honour, since Caesar and Lucretia Borgia, son and daughter of Pope Alexander VI, were reputed to be adept in ridding themselves of foes or unwanted friends by inducing them to pledges in poisoned wine.

**Glass slipper.** *See* CINDERELLA.

**Cheval glass.** *See under* CHEVAL.

**Field glasses.** *See under* FIELD.

**Granny glasses.** *See under* GRANNY.

**Live in a glass house, To.** *See under* LIVE.

**Raise one's glass, To.** *See under* RAISE.

**Venice glass.** *See under* VENICE.

**Glasse, Mrs Hannah.** A name immortalized by the reputed saying in her cookery book, FIRST CATCH YOUR HARE.

**Glastonbury.** An ancient town in Somerset, almost 12 miles (19km) from Cadbury Castle, 'the many-towered CAMELOT'. It is fabled to be the place where JOSEPH OF ARIMATHEA brought the Christian faith to Britain, and the HOLY GRAIL in the year 63. According to legend, it was here that Joseph's staff took root and budded as the Glastonbury Thorn, *Crataegus monogyna*, a form of hawthorn, which flowers every Christmas in honour of Christ's birth. It is the isle of AVALON, reputed burial place of King ARTHUR. The Celtic revival of the late 20th century has made Glastonbury a place of pilgrimage for NEW AGE adherents, while its legendary Tor, topped by a 14th-century tower, is a draw for any WEST COUNTRY visitor.

**Glauber salts.** A strong laxative, so called from Johann Rudolph Glauber (1604–68), a German chemist who discovered it in 1658 in his search for the PHILOSOPHER'S STONE. It is the crystalline hydrated form of sodium sulphate.

**Glaucus.** The name of a number of heroes in classical legend, including:

(1) A fisherman of BOEOTIA, who became a sea-god endowed with the gift of prophecy by APOLLO. Milton alludes to him in *Comus* (1637), Spenser mentions him in *The Faerie Queene* (IV, xi (1596)), and John Keats gives his name to the old magician whom ENDYMION met in NEPTUNE's hall beneath the sea (*Endymion* (1818)). *See also* SCYLLA.

(2) A son of SISYPHUS who would not allow his horses to breed. VENUS so infuriated them that they tore him to pieces. Hence the name is given to one who is so overfond of horses that he is ruined by them.

(3) A commander of the Lycians in the TROJAN WAR (*Iliad*, vi (8th century BC)) who was connected by ties of ancient family friendship with his enemy, DIOMEDES. When they met in battle they not only refrained from fighting but exchanged arms in token of friendship. As the armour of the Lycian was of gold and that of the Greek of bronze, it was like bartering precious stones for paste.

**Gleipnir** (Old Norse, 'fetter'). In Scandinavian legend the fetter by which the dwarfs bound the wolf FENRIR. It was extremely light and made of the noise of the footfalls of a cat, the roots of a mountain, the sinews of a bear, the breath of a fish, the beard of a woman and the spittle of a bird.

**Glengarry bonnet.** A brimless Scottish wool cap with a crease down the crown, and sometimes with ribbons dangling at the back. It is named after the valley in Inverness.

**Glim.** *See* DOUSE THE GLIM.

**Globe. Globe Theatre.** The first theatre of this name on London's BANKSIDE was a round wooden edifice built in 1598 and named after its sign, which showed HERCULES with the world on his shoulders. Many of Shakespeare's plays were performed here, the first being *Henry V* (1598), with its reference to 'this wooden O'. In 1613, during a performance of *Henry VIII* (1612), two cannon set the thatch alight and the building was burned to the ground. It was speedily rebuilt and reopened in 1614, but was closed in 1642 by the PURITANS and demolished two years later. A replica was built near the original site in the 1990s, opening to its first full season in 1997.

Another London theatre of the name opened in Shaftesbury Avenue in 1906, originally as the Hicks Theatre. It became the Globe in 1909 and in 1994 was renamed the Gielgud Theatre in honour of the 90th birthday of the actor Sir John Gielgud (1904–2000).

**Reynard's globe of glass.** *See under* REYNARD.

**Gloria.** A silk, wool, cotton or nylon material for making umbrellas.

**Gloria in Excelsis.** The opening words of the ANGELIC HYMN, also called the Greater DOXOLOGY. The Latin *Gloria in Excelsis Deo* etc, is part of the ORDINARY OF THE MASS and the English translation 'Glory be to God on high' forms part of the CHURCH OF ENGLAND service for Holy Communion.

**Gloria Patri.** *See* DOXOLOGY.

**Gloria tibi.** The brief DOXOLOGY, *Gloria tibi Domine* ('Glory be to thee, O Lord'). In the Roman Catholic Mass, the Latin words are used after the announcement of the Gospel. In the CHURCH OF ENGLAND service for Holy Communion the English version is used similarly.

**Sic transit gloria mundi.** *See under* SIC.

**Gloriana.** Edmund Spenser's name in *The Faerie Queene* (1590, 1596) for the character who represents Queen Elizabeth I. Gloriana held an annual feast for 12 days, during which time adventurers appeared before her to undertake whatever task she chose to impose upon them. On one occasion 12 knights presented themselves before her, and their exploits form the scheme of Spenser's allegory.

**Glorious.** OLIVER's sword, which hacked to pieces the nine swords made by Ansias, Galasand and Munifican.

**Glorious First of June, The.** 1 June 1794, when the Channel Fleet under Lord Howe gained a decisive victory over the French under Admiral Villaret de Joyeuse. Off Ushant, six French ships were captured and one sunk, but the convoy of corn ships, which they were escorting, got through to Brest.

**Glorious Fourth, The.** *See* INDEPENDENCE DAY.

**Glorious Goodwood.** *See under* GOODWOOD.

**Glorious** or **Bloodless Revolution, The.** The revolution of 1688, which established parliamentary sovereignty, when James II, deserted by his followers, fled to France in December 1688 and William of Orange and his wife Mary (daughter of James II) were declared joint sovereigns.

**Glorious Twelfth, The.** 12 August, 'St Grouse's Day', the day grouse shooting begins, unless the day falls on a Sunday, when it is postponed to the Monday in accordance with the Game Act of 1831. Shooting ends on 10 December. *See also* PARTRIDGE; SPORTING SEASONS IN ENGLAND.

**Glorious uncertainty of the law, The.** The toast at a dinner given to the judges and counsel in Serjeant's Hall. The occasion was the elevation of Lord Mansfield to the peerage and to the office of Lord Chief Justice (1756).

**Glory. Glory hole.** A small room, cupboard or the like, where all sorts of odds and ends and junk are dumped.

**Hand of glory.** *See under* HAND.

**Knickerbocker glory.** *See under* KNICKERBOCKERS.

**Old Glory.** *See under* OLD.

**Queen of Glory, The.** *See under* QUEEN.

**Gloucestershire, As sure as God's in.** *See under* AS.

**Glove.** In the days of CHIVALRY it was customary for knights to wear a lady's glove in their helmets, and to defend it with their life.

On ceremonial occasions gloves are not worn in the presence of royalty, because a person is to stand unarmed, with helmet and gauntlets off to show there is no hostile intention.

In medieval times a folded glove was used as a pledge to fulfil a judgement of a court of law. A glove was also thrown down as a challenge. VASSALS were often enfeoffed by investing them with a glove, and fiefs were held by presenting a glove to the sovereign. Gloves used to be worn by the clergy to indicate that their hands were clean and not open for bribes. Bishops were sometimes given gloves as a symbol of accession to their see. At one time judges were not allowed to wear gloves on the Bench, so to give a judge a pair of gloves indicated that he need not take his seat. In a maiden assize the SHERIFF presented the judge with a pair of white gloves.

> Once a sign of a well-bred lady, gloves have become optional accessories, largely reverting to their original purpose of keeping the hands warm.
>
> *Debrett's Etiquette & Modern Manners* (1981)

**Glove money.** A bribe, a perquisite, so called from the ancient custom of a client presenting a pair of gloves to a counsel who undertook a cause. Mrs Croaker presented Sir Thomas More, the Lord Chancellor, with a pair of gloves lined with forty pounds in 'angels' as a 'token'. Sir Thomas kept the gloves but returned the 'lining'.

**Fight with the gloves off** or **on, To.** *See under* FIGHT.

**Hand in glove.** *See under* HAND.

**Handle with kid gloves, To.** *See under* HANDLE.

**Iron fist in the velvet glove, The.** *See under* IRON.

**With the gloves off.** *See under* WITH.

**Glubbdubdrib.** The land of sorcerers and magicians visited by GULLIVER in Jonathan Swift's *Gulliver's Travels* (1726). In an article in *Studies in Philology* (i, (1953)), the literary scholar P.O. Clark decoded the name as 'Dub-bul-lin', i.e. Dublin, Swift's birthplace. *See also* GLUMDALCLITCH.

**Gluckists.** C.W. von Gluck (1714–87), the German operatic composer and a notable innovator, came to Paris in 1773 and his controversial *Iphigénie en Aulide* was produced the following year with the support of the dauphiness, Marie Antoinette. The Italian composer Niccolò Piccinni (1728–1800) arrived in 1776 at the invitation of Madame du Barry as champion of the Italian school, and in Parisian musical circles a foolish rivalry developed between the adherents of Gluck (Gluckists) and the supporters of Piccinni (Piccinnists). Gluck remained in Paris until 1779 when his *Iphigénie en Tauride* marked the triumph of the Gluckists.

**Glumdalclitch.** A girl, nine years old and almost 40ft (12m) high, who in Swift's *Gulliver's Travels* (1726) took charge of GULLIVER in BROBDINGNAG, giving him the name of GRILDRIG. The 'little' girl's name has been decoded by P.O. Clark as 'grim doll clutch', although other authorities interpret it as 'grand *altrix*', i.e. 'big nurse', arriving at this by means of letter substitutions based on the code Swift used in his *Journal to Stella* (1710–13). (Swift makes GULLIVER call her his 'little Nurse'.) If so, Glumdalclitch may be based on 'Stella' (Esther Johnson) herself. *See also* GLUBBDUBDRIB.

> Soon as Glumdalclitch miss'd her pleasing care,
> She wept, she blubber'd, and she tore her hair.
> No British miss sincerer grief has known,
> Her squirrel missing, or her sparrow flown.
> ALEXANDER POPE: 'The Lamentation of Glumdalclitch for the Loss of Grildrig' (1727)

**Glyndebourne.** The country estate, near Lewes in Sussex, where John Christie (1882–1962) opened the Glyndebourne Festival Theatre in 1934 for operatic and musical performances, which became an annual summer event. A new opera house opened to general acclaim in 1994.

**G-man.** Short for Government man, an agent of the US Federal Bureau of Investigation (FBI).

**Gnat. To strain at a gnat and swallow a camel.** *See under* STRAIN.

**Gnome.** According to the ROSICRUCIAN system, a misshapen elemental spirit, dwelling in the bowels of the earth and guarding the mines and quarries. Gnomes of various sorts appear in many fairy tales and legends. The word seems to have been first used (and perhaps invented) by PARACELSUS and may have been based on Greek *gēnomos*, 'earth-dweller'. *See also* SALAMANDER.

**Gnomes of Zürich.** An uncomplimentary name given to those financiers of Zürich controlling international monetary funds. The phrase became popular after its use in 1964 by George Brown (then Labour Minister of Economic Affairs) at the time of a sterling crisis.

> What most infuriated George Brown, and Labour MPs such as John Mendelson and Ian Mikardo … was that the men they disparaged as the 'gnomes of Zürich' were really giants.
> T.R. FEHRENBACH: *The Gnomes of Zürich* (1966)

**Gnomic verse.** Verse characterized by pithy expression of sententious or weighty maxims. The Greek word *gnōmē*, 'thought', 'judgement', acquired specialized meanings such as EPIGRAM, 'proverb', 'maxim'. Hence gnomic verse. A group of gnomic poets existed in Greece in the 6th century BC. An English exemplar is Francis Quarles (1592–1644).

> Man is man's A.B.C. There is none that can
> Read God aright, unless he first spell Man.
> FRANCIS QUARLES: *Hieroglyphics of the Life of Man*, i (1638)

**Gnostics.** Various sects, mainly of Christian inspiration, which arose and flourished in the 2nd century with offshoots surviving into the 5th century. The name derives from the Greek word *gnōsis*, 'knowledge', but it was usually used by the Gnostics in the sense of 'revelation', which gave them certain mystic knowledge of salvation that others did not possess. It was essentially based on oriental DUALISM, the existence of two worlds, good and evil, the divine and the material. The body was regarded as the enemy of spiritual life. In most Gnostic systems there were seven world-creating powers, in a few their place was taken by one DEMIURGE. Christ was the final and perfect AEON. The Gnostic movement caused the Christian church to develop its organization and doctrinal discipline. In 1945, 52 Gnostic texts were found in Upper Egypt, which underline its intellectual challenge to the early church. *See also* MANICHEANS; MARCIONITES.

**Go** (Old English *gān*, 'start', 'move'). Both the verb and the noun are used in a wide range of expressions, some of which are given below. For others, see under the next or principal word.

**Go, A.** A fix, a scrape, as in 'here's a go' or 'here's a fine go', meaning 'here's a mess' or awkward state of affairs. Also an attempt, as to 'have a go'.

**Go ahead, To.** To make progress; to prosper; to start.

**Go all out, To.** To make every effort; to do one's utmost.

**Go along with, To.** To accept; to comply with, as: 'I'll go along with that.'

**Go as you please.** Not bound by any rules; not standing on ceremony.

**Go back on a person, To.** To betray a person.

**Go back on one's word, To.** To fail to keep one's promise; to withdraw from what one has promised or said.

**Go-between, A.** A person who acts as an intermediary; one who acts as an agent between two parties. The central character of L.P. Hartley's novel *The Go-Between* (1953) is a young boy who innocently carries messages between two doomed lovers, the daughter of an aristocratic family and a tenant farmer.

**Go-cart.** A device for training toddlers to walk, which at the same time combined some of the features of a playpen. They were in use from the later Middle Ages and were introduced into England in the early 17th century. They consisted of a small framework on wheels or rollers, splayed out at the base so that they could not be overturned. The top was usually in the form of a tray for containing toys with a circular opening in which the child could stand upright and be held secure at waist height.

The spelling 'go-kart' is used for a small, one-man racing vehicle propelled by a light engine.

**Go down, To.** In university parlance, to commence vacation or to leave the university finally.

**Go down with, To.** To succumb to (an illness).

**Goer, A.** A person of spirit and energy.

**Go for someone, To.** To attack them, whether physically or verbally.

**Go-getter.** An enterprising, ambitious person.

**Go-go dancer.** A scantily dressed female dancer who performs energetic and often erotic dances in a night-club or the like. The term has been influenced by English 'go', but it probably comes from French *à gogo*, 'aplenty', 'ad lib'. *See also* GO IT.

**Go in for, To.** To follow as a pursuit or occupation, as, 'to go in for DIY'.

**Going, going, gone!** An auctioneer's announcement that bidding is about to close ('going') and that it has closed ('gone').

**Go into a matter, To.** To explore or investigate a subject thoroughly.

**Go into the church, To.** To take HOLY ORDERS; to enter the ministry.

**Go into the wilderness, To.** A figurative description of being deprived of political office through a change of government.

**Go it!** An exclamation of encouragement, sometimes ironical.

**Go it, To.** To do something energetically or extravagantly.

> O blackbird, what a boy you are!
> How you do go it!
> T.E. BROWN: 'Vespers' (1900)

**Go it alone, To.** To play a lone hand; to carry on or do something without help; to assume sole responsibility.

> In battle or business, whatever the game,
> In law or in love, it is ever the same:
> In the struggle for power, or the scramble of pelf,
> Let this be your motto—Rely on yourself!
> For, whether the prize be a ribbon or throne,
> The victor is he who can go it alone!
> JOHN GODFREY SAXE: 'The Game of Life' (1861)

**Go-kart.** *See* GO-CART.

**Go off at half-cock, To.** To fail as a result of doing something prematurely or without proper preparation. The allusion is to a gun that goes off when the hammer is set at half-cock and supposedly secure.

**Go off the deep end, To.** To get unnecessarily angry.

**Go off the rails, To.** To behave abnormally: to go crazy.

**Go on!** An expression of encouragement or of disbelief.

**Go on all fours, To.** To crawl about on all four limbs like a quadruped or an infant. The phrase used to be 'all four', as in Leviticus 11:42: 'whatsoever goeth upon all four.'

**Go one better, To.** To improve on what someone else has done. The phrase is from card playing: at poker, if one wishes to continue betting, one has to 'go' at least 'one better', i.e. raise the stake.

**Go out with someone, To.** To have a romantic relationship with them.

**Go round the bend, To.** *See* ROUND THE BEND.

**Go somewhere, To.** To go to the lavatory. A euphemism.

**Go the pace, To.** *See* FAST.

**Go through fire and water, To.** To undergo trial or torment. The expression may derive from the ORDEAL OF FIRE.

**Go through the mill, To.** To undergo hardship; to be subjected to a severe course of probationary training.

**Go through the motions, To.** To make a pretence of doing something; to carry out an obligation or duty in a very half-hearted manner.

**Go to!** A former exclamation of impatience or reproof, or an exhortation like 'come'.

> *Cassius*: I am a soldier, I,
> Older in practice, abler than yourself
> To make conditions.
> *Brutus*: Go to; you are not, Cassius.
> SHAKESPEARE: *Julius Caesar*, IV, iii (1599)

**Go to it!** Begin work! Get on with it!

**Go too far, To.** To exceed reasonable limits; to overdo.

**Go under, To.** To become ruined; to fail utterly; to lose face. Also to pass as, to be known as, as: 'She goes under the name of "Miss Webb" but we all know she is really "Mrs Martin".'

**Go with a swing, To.** Said of a ceremony, function, entertainment or the like that runs well and is a great success.

**Go without a hitch, To.** To go entirely successfully or smoothly.

**Go with the tide** or **the flow, To.** To conform to the traditional or accepted norm; to do what everyone else does; to 'follow the herd'.

**All go.** *See under* ALL.

**All the go.** *See under* ALL.

**From the word go.** *See under* FROM.

**Give it a go, To.** To make an effort to succeed.

**Give someone the go-by, To.** To pass by and ignore a person; to snub or slight someone.

**Give the go-ahead, To.** To give permission to proceed in an undertaking.

**Have a go, To.** To make an attempt.

**Have gone and done it** or **been and gone and done it, To.** To have done exactly what one did not want to do; to have made a mess of something.

**It's no go.** It is not workable; it can't happen.

> It's no go my honey love, it's no go my poppet;
> Work your hands from day to day, the winds will blow the profit.
>
> LOUIS MACNEICE: *Earth Compels*, 'Bagpipe Music' (1938)

**On the go.** Busy and active with no time to rest, as: 'I've been on the go since nine this morning.'

**That goes without saying.** That is self-evident; that is well understood or indisputable. The French say *Cela va sans dire*.

**Touch and go.** *See under* TOUCH.

**Who goes there?** A sentry's traditional challenge. *See also* CEREMONY OF THE KEYS.

**Goal, Golden.** *See under* GOLDEN.

**Goat.** From early times the goat has been associated with the idea of sin and associated with Devil worship. The legend that the Devil created the goat may well be due to its destructiveness, and the Devil was frequently depicted as a goat. It is also a symbol of lust and lechery. *See also* SCAPEGOAT.

**Goat and Compasses.** The origin of this PUBLIC HOUSE SIGN is uncertain. A once popular suggestion was that it is a corruption of 'God encompasseth us'. Other suggestions are that it was derived from the arms of the Wine Coopers' Company of Cologne, or merely the addition of the masonic emblem of the compasses to an original sign of a goat.

**Goatsucker.** A name popularly given to the nightjar (*Caprimulgus europaeus*), from the ancient and widespread belief that this bird sucks the udders of goats. Its Latin generic name literally means 'goat-milker', as does its name in other languages, such as German *Ziegenmelker*, Italian *caprimulgo* and Russian *kozodoy*.

**Act** or **play the giddy goat, To.** *See under* ACT.

**Billy goat.** *See under* BILLY.

**Get someone's goat, To.** To annoy a person. The expression, an old Americanism, is said to relate to a practice among racehorse trainers of soothing a nervous horse by putting a goat in its stall. Someone wanting the horse to lose could sneak in and remove the goat. The horse would again succumb to an attack of nerves and would not run well. The explanation seems contrived, however.

**Separate the sheep from the goats, To.** *See under* SEPARATE.

**Gobbledygook.** A word invented by the Texan lawyer Maury Maverick, a descendant of the cattle-owner Samuel A. Maverick (*see* MAVERICK), to describe the convoluted, pretentious and often meaningless language of bureaucracy.

> People ask me where I got gobbledygook. I do not know. It must have come in a vision. Perhaps I was thinking of the old bearded turkey gobbler back in Texas, who was always gobbledy-gobbling and strutting with ludicrous pomposity. At the end of this gobble there was a sort of gook.
>
> *New York Times* (21 May 1944)

**Gobelin tapestry.** So called from a French family of dyers founded by Jehan Gobelin (d.1476). Their tapestry works in the Faubourg St Marcel, Paris, were taken over by Colbert as a royal establishment in 1662.

**Goblin.** A familiar demon, dwelling, according to popular legend, in private houses, chinks of trees and various other places. In many parts miners attributed to them the strange noises they heard in the mine. The word is French *gobelin*, from German *Kobold*. *See also* COBALT; GNOME.

**God.** A word common, in slightly varying forms, to all Germanic languages, and coming from a root word related to Old Irish *guth*, 'voice'. It is in no way connected with English 'good'.

It was VOLTAIRE who said: *Si Dieu n'existait pas, il faudrait l'inventer* ('If God did not exist, it would be necessary to invent him'). For the various gods listed in this Dictionary see under their individual names.

Greek and Roman gods were divided into *Dii Majores* and *Dii Minores*, the greater and the lesser. The *Dii Majores* were 12 in number:

| *Greek* | *Latin* |
|---|---|
| ZEUS | JUPITER (king) |
| Apollon | APOLLO (the sun) |
| ARES | MARS (war) |
| HERMES | MERCURY (messenger) |
| POSEIDON | NEPTUNE (ocean) |
| Hephaestus | VULCAN (smith) |
| HERA | JUNO (queen) |
| DEMETER | CERES (tillage) |
| ARTEMIS | DIANA (moon, hunting) |
| ATHENE | MINERVA (wisdom) |
| APHRODITE | VENUS (love and beauty) |
| Hestia | VESTA (home life) |

Their blood was ICHOR, their food was AMBROSIA, their drink NECTAR. Four other deities are often referred to:

| | |
|---|---|
| Dionysus | BACCHUS (wine) |
| EROS | CUPID (love) |
| Pluton | PLUTO (the underworld) |
| KRONOS | SATURN (time) |

Persephone (Greek) or PROSERPINA (Latin), was the wife of Pluto, CYBELE was the wife of Saturn, and RHEA of Kronos.

The Greeks observed a Feast of the Unknown Gods lest any be neglected.

**God bless the Duke of Argyle.** A phrase supposed to have been used by Scottish Highlanders when they scratched themselves. The story is that a Duke of Argyle (now Argyll) had posts erected on a treeless part of his estates so that his cattle might rub against them to ease themselves of the 'torment of flies'. The herdsmen saw the value of the practice, and as they rubbed their itching backs against the posts, gratefully uttered the above words.

**God bless** or **save the mark!** A kind of apology for introducing a disagreeable subject. Hotspur, apologizing to the king for not sending the prisoners according to command (Shakespeare, *Henry IV*, *Pt I*, I, iii (1597)), says the messenger was a 'popinjay', who made him mad.

> To see him shine so brisk and smell so sweet
> And talk so like a waiting-gentlewoman
> Of guns, and drums, and wounds, – God save the mark!

In *Othello* (I, i (1604)) Iago says he was 'God bless the mark! his Moorship's ancient', expressing derision and contempt.

Sometimes the phrase is used to avert ill fortune or an evil omen, as in *The Merchant of Venice* (II, ii (1596)):

> To be ruled by my conscience, I should stay with the Jew my master, who God bless the mark! is a kind of devil.

It is suggested that the 'mark' is possibly the sign of the cross and the phrase a kind of supplication.

**Goddam.** A name given by the French to the English at least as early as the 15th century on account of the favourite oath of the English soldiers. JOAN OF ARC is reported to have used the word on a number of occasions in contemptuous reference to her enemies.

> *Joan*: I came to know these three poor goddams quite well. They had not half my strength.
> *Robert*: Do you know why they are called goddams?
> *Joan*: No. Everyone calls them goddams.
> *Robert*: It is because they are always calling on their God to condemn their souls to perdition. That is what goddam means in their language.
> GEORGE BERNARD SHAW: *Saint Joan*, I (1924)

**God from the machine, A.** *See* DEUS EX MACHINA.

**God helps those who help themselves.** To this a wag has added 'but God help those who are caught helping themselves'. The French say AIDE-TOI, LE CIEL T'AIDERA.

**Godless florin.** *See* GRACELESS FLORIN.

**God** or **Lord of Flies, The.** Every year, in the temple of Actium, the Greeks used to sacrifice an ox to ZEUS, who in this capacity was surnamed Apomyios, 'averter of flies'. Pliny writes that at Rome sacrifice was offered to flies in the temple of HERCULES Victor, and the Syrians also offered sacrifice to these insects. *See also* ACHOR; BEELZEBUB.

**God of Love, The.** The title generally implies either EROS or CUPID. To the Scandinavians FREYJA was the goddess of sexual love, and among the Hindus KAMA is the approximate equivalent of Eros. Christians impute the title to God.

> Be perfect, be of good comfort, be of one mind, live in peace; and the God of love and peace shall be with you.
> 2 Corinthians 13:11

**Gods, The.** The gallery in a theatre or its occupants. Those 'up in the gods' were originally the most critical and vociferous section of the audience. The name alludes to the lofty location.

**God's acre.** A cemetery or churchyard. A translation of German *Gottesacker*, wrongly called by Longfellow an 'ancient Saxon phrase'.

**God save the King** or **Queen.** *See* NATIONAL ANTHEM.

**God sides with the strongest.** Fortune favours the strong. NAPOLEON BONAPARTE said: *Le bon Dieu est toujours du côté des gros bataillons* ('God is always on the side of the big battalions'). The phrase is of much earlier origin, however. Tacitus (*Histories* iv, 17 (2nd century AD)) has *Deos fortioribus adesse* ('The gods are on the side of the strongest'). The Comte de Bussy-Rabutin, in a letter to the Comte de Limoges of 18 October 1677, wrote: *Comme vous le savez, Dieu est d'ordinaire pour les gros escadrons contre les petits* ('As you know, God is usually on the side of the big squadrons against the small'). And VOLTAIRE in 'The Piccini Notebooks' (*c*.1735–50) remarked: *Dieu n'est pas pour les gros bataillons, mais pour ceux qui tirent le mieux* ('God is not on the side of the big battalions, but of those who are the best shots'). A more recent variation on the theme is found in Jean Anouilh's play *L'Alouette* ('The Lark') (1953): *Dieu est avec tout le monde. ... Et, en fin de compte, il est toujours avec ceux qui ont beaucoup d'argent et de grosses armées* ('God is on everyone's side. ... And, in the final analysis, he is always on the side of those with plenty of money and large armies').

**God tempers the wind to the shorn lamb.** The phrase comes from Laurence Sterne's *Sentimental Journey* (1768) but it was not original, for *Dieu mesure le froid à la brebis tondue* appears in Henri Estienne's *Les Prémices* (1594). The meaning is that God is specially tender in His protection of the weak. Correctly speaking, only sheep are shorn, not lambs.

> *God tempers the wind*, said Maria, to the shorn lamb. Shorn indeed! and to the quick, said I.
> *A Sentimental Journey*

**God ye good den!** An abbreviated form of the old salutation 'God give you good even(ing)', used at any time after noon.

> *Nurse*: God ye good morrow, gentlemen.
> *Mercutio*: God ye good den, fair gentlewoman.
> *Nurse*: Is it good den?
> *Mercutio*: 'Tis no less, I tell you; for the bawdy hand of the dial is now upon the prick of noon.
> SHAKESPEARE: *Romeo and Juliet*, II, iv (1594)

**Act of God.** *See under* ACT.
**Call God to witness, To.** *See under* CALL.
**Call of God, The.** *See under* CALL.
**Child of God.** *See under* CHILD.
**City of God, The.** *See under* CITY.
**Cleanliness is next to godliness.** *See under* CLEAN.
**Dog of God, The.** *See under* DOG.
**Good God!** *See under* GOD.
**Grace of God, The.** *See under* GRACE.
**Household gods.** *See under* HOUSEHOLD.
**House of God.** *See under* HOUSE.
**In the lap of the gods.** *See under* LAP.
**Lord God of Hosts.** *See under* LORD.
**Man proposes but God disposes.** *See under* MAN.
**St John of God.** *See under* JOHN.
**Scourge of God, The.** *See under* SCOURGE.
**Seven Gods of Luck, The.** *See under* SEVEN.
**Son of God.** *See under* SON.
**Sword of God, The.** *See under* SWORD.
**Take God's name in vain, To.** To use it profanely, thoughtlessly, or irreverently.

> Thou shalt not take the name of the Lord thy God in vain.
> Exodus 20:7

Among primitive peoples, as well as the ancient Hebrews, the name of a deity is regarded as his manifestation and is treated with the greatest respect and veneration. Among savage tribes there is a reluctance in disclosing one's name because this might enable an enemy by magic to work one some deadly injury. The Greeks were particularly careful to disguise uncomplimentary names. *See also* ADONAI; ERINYES; EUMENIDES; EUXINE SEA; TETRAGRAMMATON.

**Tin god.** *See under* TIN.
**Truce of God.** *See under* TRUCE.
**Twilight of the Gods, The.** *See* RAGNAROK.
**Whom God would destroy He first makes mad.** *See under* WHO.
**Whom the gods love die young.** *See under* WHO.

**Goddess of Reason, The.** The central figure in an attempt to supersede Christianity during the French Revolution. The first Feast of Reason (*fête de la Raison*) was held on 20 BRUMAIRE, Year II (10 November 1793), when the 'goddess', the actress and singer Julie Candeille (1767–1834), was enthroned in Notre-Dame Cathedral, which became the TEMPLE OF REASON. She was dressed in white, with a red Phrygian cap (LIBERTY CAP) and the pike of Jupiter-Peuple in her hand. Mme Momoro, wife of Antoine François Momoro (1756–94), a member of the CORDELIERS' CLUB who went to the guillotine for his stand against Robespierre, was later installed at St Sulpice. Goddesses of Liberty and Reason were soon set up throughout France, one allegedly wearing a fillet bearing the words 'Turn me not into Licence!' SATURNALIA of an uninhibited kind accompanied these installations.

**Godiva, Lady.** A famous patroness of Coventry. According to legend, in 1040 Leofric, Earl of Mercia (d.1057), imposed certain heavy taxes on his tenants, which his wife begged him to remove. He said he would do so if she would ride naked through the town. Lady Godiva did so, her modesty preserved by her long hair, and the earl kept his promise.

The legend is recorded by Roger of Wendover (d.1236), in his *Flores Historiarum*, and this was adapted by Paul de Rapin in his *History of England* (1723–7) into the story commonly known. An addition of the time of Charles II asserts that everyone stayed indoors at the time, but a certain tailor peeped through his window to see the lady pass and was struck blind as a consequence. He has ever since been called 'Peeping Tom'. Since 1768 the ride has been annually re-enacted at Coventry by a procession in which a modern 'Lady Godiva' in a body stocking is the cynosure.

**Godolphin Barb.** *See* DARLEY ARABIAN.

**Godzilla.** A fearsome dinosaur of the cinema that is awakened from its primordial slumbers by H-bomb tests and menaces Tokyo. It first appeared in the film that bears its name, in the original Japanese *Gojira* (1955). The name itself is a blend of Japanese *kujira*, 'whale', the nickname of a film production company employee at the time, and 'gorilla'. The monster reappeared in a number of sequels, some even more ridiculous than the original, including *King Kong vs. Godzilla* (1962), *Godzilla vs. the Thing* (1964) and *Destroy All Monsters* (1964). An all-new, all-American re-creation was *Godzilla* (1998).

**Goel** (Hebrew, 'claimant'). Among the ancient Hebrews the goel was the next of kin whose duty it was to redeem the property of a kinsman who had been forced to sell under stress of circumstances. He was also the AVENGER OF BLOOD.

**Goemagot** or **Goemot.** The names given in Geoffrey of Monmouth's *Historia Regum Britanniae* (I, xvi (*c*.1136)), and Spenser's *The Faerie Queene* (II, x (1590)), to the giant who dominated the western horn of England (Cornwall or Cornubia). He was slain by CORINEUS. *See also* GOG AND MAGOG.

**Gog and Magog.** In British legend the sole survivors of a monstrous brood, the offspring of demons and the 33 infamous daughters of the Emperor Diocletian, who murdered their husbands. Gog and Magog were taken as prisoners to London after their fellow giants had been killed by BRUTE and his companions, where they were made to do duty as porters at the royal palace, on the site of the Guildhall, where their effigies have stood at least from the reign of Henry V. The old giants were destroyed in the GREAT FIRE OF LONDON, and were replaced by figures 14ft (4.3m) high, carved in 1708 by Richard Saunders. These were subsequently demolished in an air raid in 1940 and new figures were set up in 1953. Wickerwork models of Gog and Magog were formerly carried in the LORD MAYOR'S SHOWS.

In the Bible Magog is spoken of as a son of Japhet (Genesis 10:2), in Revelation Gog and Magog symbolize all future enemies of the Kingdom of God, and in Ezekiel Gog is prince of Magog, a ruler of hordes to the north of Israel.

**Gogmagog Hill.** The higher of two hills some 4 miles (6km) southeast of Cambridge. The legend is that Gogmagog fell in love with the nymph Granta, but she would have nothing to say to the giant, and he was metamorphosed into the hill (Michael Drayton, *Polyolbion*, xxi (1598–1622)). The hills are popularly known to students and local people as the Gogs.

**Golconda.** An ancient kingdom and city in India, west of Hyderabad, which was conquered by Aurangzeb in 1687. The name is emblematic of great wealth and proverbially famous for its DIAMONDS, but the gems were only cut and polished there.

**Gold.** According to the ancient alchemists, gold represented the sun and silver represented the moon. In HERALDRY gold (called 'or') is depicted by dots. The gold CARAT is the unit used by goldsmiths, assayers and others to express the proportion of gold in any article in gold. Gold coins were struck in England as regular currency from the reign of Edward III until 1917.

**Gold and silver shield, The.** A medieval allegory tells how two knights, coming from opposite directions, stopped in sight of a shield suspended from a tree branch, one side of which was gold and the other silver, and disputed about its metal, proceeding from words to blows. Luckily a third knight came up. The point was referred to him, and the disputants were informed that the shield was silver on one side and gold on the other.

**Gold brick, A.** An American phrase descriptive of any form of swindling. It originated in the gold-rush days when a cheat would sell his dupe an alleged (or even a real) gold brick, in the latter case substituting a sham one before making his getaway. In the Second World War gold-bricking was synonymous with idling, shirking or getting a colleague to do one's job.

**Gold disc.** A record, usually of popular music, that has sold a specified high number of copies. In Britain the term applies to an album that has sold 100,000 copies or a single that has sold 400,000. In the USA the honour is awarded to either an album or a single that has sold 500,000 copies.

**Goldilocks.** A nickname for a fair-haired person, especially a young child. The popular reference is to the little girl in the story of Goldilocks and the Three Bears. In Robert Southey's version of the story (1837) she was originally 'Silver Hair'. Subsequent re-tellings had her as 'Silver-Locks' (1858) and 'Golden Hair' (1868) and she received her present name only in John Hassall's *Old Stories and Rhymes* (*c*.1904), which recounts how 'the little girl had long golden hair, so she was called Goldilocks'.

**Gold Key, The.** The office of GROOM OF THE STOLE, the holder of which had a golden key as his emblem.

**Gold of Nibelungen, The.** *See* NIBELUNGENLIED.

**Gold Standard, The.** A currency system based on keeping the monetary unit at the value of a fixed weight of gold. Britain adopted the Gold Standard from 1821 but suspended gold payments in 1914, returned to the Gold Standard in 1925 and abandoned it in 1931 during the slump. Most countries of the world were on the Gold Standard from 1894 to 1914. Gold became the monetary standard of the USA by the Coinage Act of 1873, but the Gold Standard was abandoned in 1933.

**Gold Stick.** The gilt rod carried before the sovereign on state occasions by the Colonel of the Life Guards or the Captain of the Gentlemen-at-arms. The term is also the designation of the bearer of the Stick.

**All he touches turns to gold.** *See under* ALL.

**All that glitters is not gold.** *See under* ALL.

**As good as gold.** *See under* AS.

**Bridge of Gold.** *See under* BRIDGE.

**Dutch gold.** *See under* DUTCH.
**Fool's gold.** *See under* FOOL.
**Go for gold, To.** To aim high; to set out to win or succeed. The allusion is to a gold medal as the highest sporting award.
**Heart of gold, A.** *See under* HEART.
**Pot of gold.** *See under* POT.
**Red gold.** *See under* RED.
**Worth its weight in gold.** *See under* WORTH.

**Golden. Golden Age.** An age when life was idyllic, or when a nation was at its peak of power, glory and reputation. The expression is sometimes qualified, as the golden age of innocence, the golden age of literature. *See also* AGE.

The 'Golden Ages' of a number of nations are often given as follows:

Assyria: from the reign of Esarhaddon, third son of Sennacherib, to the fall of Nineveh (*c*.700 to 600 BC)
Athens: during the supremacy of Pericles (443 to 429 BC)
Chaldaeo-Babylonian Empire: from the reign of Nabopolassar to that of Belshazzar (*c*.625–538 BC)
China: the era of the T'ang dynasty (618–906)
Egypt: the reign of Seti I and Rameses II (*c*.1312–1235 BC)
England: the reign of Elizabeth I (1558–1603)
France: the century 1640–1740, including the reign of Louis XIV
Germany: the reign of Charles V (1519–58)
Media: the reign of Cyaxares (*c*.634–594 BC)
Persia: from the reign of Khosru, or Chosroes I, to that of Khosru II (*c*.AD 531–628)
Portugal: from John I to the close of Sebastian's reign (1385–1578)
Prussia: the reign of Frederick the Great (1740–86)
Roman Empire: Edward Gibbon (*Decline and Fall*, ch iii (1776)) considered it to be from the death of Domitian (AD 96) to the accession of Commodus (180)
Russia: the reign of Peter the Great (1672–1725)
Spain: the reign of Ferdinand and Isabella when the crowns of Castile and Aragon were united (1474–1516)
Sweden: from Gustavus Vasa (r.1523–60) to the close of the reign of Gustavus Adolphus (r.1611–32)

**Golden apple.** A former name for the tomato, still found in some languages for this fruit, e.g. Italian *pomodoro*, Russian (from Italian) *pomidor*. *See also* APPLE OF DISCORD; ATALANTA; HESPERIDES.

**Golden Arrow.** A famous PULLMAN express train service from London to Paris, with a ferry crossing from Dover to Calais. On the French side of the English Channel the train had the equivalent name, *Flèche d'Or*. A train had been leaving Victoria Station at 11 am daily for many years on this route before the name was adopted in 1929. The service was withdrawn in 1972. The name itself comes from folklore, in which the Golden Arrow was the one sought by a pair of lovers in the land of their dreams. The legend is alluded to in the title and story of Mary Webb's early novel *The Golden Arrow* (1916). The name is fitting for a train that takes passengers to Paris, the 'City of Lovers'.

**Golden Ass, The.** Properly, *Metamorphoses*, a 2nd-century satirical romance by Apuleius, and apparently called the *Golden Ass* because of its excellency. It tells the adventures of Lucian, a young man who, being accidentally metamorphosed into an ass while sojourning in Thessaly, falls into the hands of robbers, eunuchs, magistrates and so on, and is ill-treated by them. Ultimately, however, he recovers his human form. The work includes the story of CUPID AND PSYCHE.

**Golden bowl is broken, The.** Death. A biblical allusion:

> Or ever the silver cord be loosed, or the golden bowl be broken, or the pitcher be broken at the fountain, or the wheel broken at the cistern. Then shall the dust return to the earth as it was: and the spirit shall return unto God who gave it.
>
> Ecclesiastes 12:6–7

**Golden boy** or **girl.** A popular or successful person, especially in sport or business. In Clifford Odets's play *Golden Boy* (1937) the hero, a violinist, becomes a successful boxer.

> Watching the golden boy [golfer] fail was a particular pleasure. It was a proper reward for his demeanour, and it corrected the ignorant.
>
> *Sunday Times* (19 July 1998)

**Golden Bull, The.** An edict issued by Emperor Charles IV at the Diet of Nuremberg in 1356 for the purpose of regularizing the election to the throne of the empire. It was sealed with a golden *bulla* or seal. *See also* ELECTOR; PAPAL BULL.

**Golden calf, The.** *See* WORSHIP THE GOLDEN CALF.

**Golden delicious.** A greenish-yellow (rather than golden-skinned) variety of dessert apple.

**Golden eagle, The.** This bird and the spread eagle are commemorative of the CRUSADES and they were the devices of the Eastern Roman Empire. France (under the Empires), Germany, Austria, Prussia and Russia also adopted the eagle as a royal or imperial emblem. The white-headed American eagle, *Haliaetus leucocephalus*, also known as the bald eagle, is specifically the emblem of the USA. It is depicted with outspread wings, as the 'eagle displayed' of HERALDRY. *See also* TWO-HEADED EAGLE.

**Golden Fleece, The.** The old Greek story is that Ino persuaded her husband Athamus that his son Phryxus was the cause of a famine that desolated the land. Phryxus was thereupon ordered to be sacrificed but, learning of this, he made his escape over the sea on the winged ram, Chrysomallus, which had a golden fleece. When he arrived at Colchis, he sacrificed the ram to ZEUS, and gave the fleece to King Aeëtes, who hung it on a sacred oak tree. JASON subsequently set out to recover it. *See also* HELLESPONT.

Australia has been called the Land of the Golden Fleece because of its abundant wool production.

**Golden Gate, The.** The strait forming the entrance to San Francisco Bay. San Francisco is hence called the City of the Golden Gate. The name was given by the American explorer John C. Frémont in 1846 in allusion to the GOLDEN HORN of the BOSPORUS, since he envisaged riches from the Orient pouring through the strait. He originally gave the name in the Greek form *Chrysopylae*, answering to that of the Golden Horn, *Chrysoceras*.

The state entrance to the city of Constantinople, built of three arches to commemorate the victory of Theodosius I over Maximus (388) and incorporated in the walls built by Theodosius II, was called the Golden Gate. The 11th-century fortifications of Kiev also incorporated a Golden Gate.

**Golden goal.** In football, the first goal scored in extra time following a draw. This wins the game under a SUDDEN DEATH system, as distinct from a penalty shoot-out. The modification to the rules was introduced in the first half of the 1990s and has now been extended to hockey.

> France became the first team in World Cup history to win a game under the new golden goal rule when they beat Paraguay 1–0 yesterday.
> *The Times* (29 June 1998)

**Golden goose.** A goose in folklore that laid a golden egg every day until its greedy owner killed it in an attempt to lay his hands on all the gold at once. The tale is traditionally incorporated into a PANTOMIME. *See also* KILL THE GOOSE THAT LAYS THE GOLDEN EGGS.

**Golden handcuffs.** Payments to an employee that are deliberately deferred over a number of years in an attempt to make him or her stay with a particular company. *See also* GOLDEN HANDSHAKE.

> Jeremy Paxman was named yesterday as the new presenter of Radio 4's *Start the Week* after signing a 'golden handcuffs' deal that will keep him at the BBC until 2002.
> *The Times* (28 July 1998)

**Golden handshake.** A phrase applied to the often considerable terminal payments made to individuals, especially business executives, whose services are prematurely dispensed with. It has also been applied to the final grants made to colonial dependencies on attaining their independence. The phrase was coined by Frederick Ellis (d.1979), City Editor of the *Daily Express*. *See also* BOWLER-HATTED.

> The average 'golden handshake' to departing directors has risen for the first time since 1994, from £328,000 for the year to October 1997 to £463,000 over the past 12 months.
> *The Times* (2 October 1998)

**Golden hello.** A special payment made by a company to a sought-after recruit when he or she signs a contract of employment with them. *See also* GOLDEN HANDSHAKE.

**Golden Hind, The.** The famous ship in which Sir Francis Drake made his voyage of circumnavigation (1577–80). Originally called the *Pelican*, it was renamed the *Golden Hind* at Port St Julian, near the entrance to the Straits of Magellan, in 1578. Drake was knighted on board the *Golden Hind* in the presence of Queen Elizabeth I on 4 April 1581. *See also* DRAKE BRASS PLATE *under* FORGERY. The *Golden Hind* was also the name of an express train service from London to Plymouth, the latter city being that from which Drake set sail.

**Golden Horde.** The Mongolian TARTARS who in the 13th century established an empire in south-eastern Russia under Batu, grandson of GENGHIS KHAN. They overran eastern Europe and parts of western Asia, being eventually defeated by TAMBERLANE in 1395. The name Golden derives from the magnificent trappings of Batu's field headquarters.

**Golden Horn, The.** The inlet of the BOSPORUS around which Istanbul (formerly Constantinople) is situated. Some 5 miles (8km) long, it may have derived its name both from its shape and from its abundance of fish, which made it a real cornucopia or HORN OF PLENTY. *See also* GOLDEN GATE.

**Golden Legend, The** (Latin *Legenda aurea*). A collection of so-called lives of the saints made in *c.*1260 by Jacobus de Voragine (*c.*1230–98), a Dominican friar of Genoa. It is valuable for the picture it gives of medieval manners, customs and thought. It was translated from the Latin into most of the languages of western Europe and an English edition was published by CAXTON in 1483. The first complete modern English edition was published only in 1993, in a translation by the American priest William Granger Ryan. The original title of the work was simply *Legenda Sanctorum* ('Readings on the Saints'), and its present title arose from its uplifting content and lasting popularity. The London printer Wynkyn de Worde, formerly Caxton's assistant, published an edition in 1498 with the following heading:

> Here begynneth the legende named in Latyn Legenda Aurea that is to saye in Englysshe the Golden Legende. For lyke as passeth golde in valewe all other metallys, so this legende excelleth all other bookes.

H.W. Longfellow's dramatic poem *The Golden Legend* (1851) is based on *Armer Heinrich* ('Poor Henry'), a story by Hartmann von Aue, a 12th-century German MINNESINGER. Longfellow so titled the work 'because the story upon which it is founded seems to me to surpass all other legends in beauty and significance' (Introduction).

**Golden mean.** The middle course between extremes; the principle of moderation. The phrase translates Latin *aurea mediocritas* in Horace's *Odes*, II, x (1st century BC).

**Golden-mouthed, The.** St JOHN CHRYSOSTOM (d.407), a father of the GREEK CHURCH, was so called for his great eloquence.

**Golden nose.** Tycho Brahe (1546–1601), the Danish astronomer. He lost his nose in a duel, so adopted a golden one, which he attached to his face by a cement that he carried about with him. The bloodthirsty Emperor Justinian II, nicknamed Rhinotmetus, had a golden nose in place of the nose that had been cut off by his general Leontius before he ascended the imperial throne. It used to be said that when Justinian cleansed this golden nose, those who were present knew that the death of someone had been decided upon.

**Golden number.** The number of the year in the METONIC CYCLE, which may therefore consist of any number from 1 to 19. In the ancient Roman and Alexandrian CALENDARS this number was marked in gold, hence the name. The rule for finding the golden number, which was used for determining the EPACT and the date of EASTER, is as follows:

> Add one to the year of our Lord, and then divide by 19; the remainder, if any, is the Golden Number; but if nothing remaineth, then 19 is the Golden Number.
>
> Book of Common Prayer (A Table to find Easter-Day)

**Golden ointment.** Eye ointment, in allusion to the ancient practice of rubbing a stye on the eye with a gold ring, which was supposed to cure it.

> 'I have a sty here, Chilax.'
> 'I have no gold to cure it.'
>
> FRANCIS BEAUMONT and JOHN FLETCHER: *The Mad Lover*, V, iv (*c*.1616)

Present-day 'golden eye ointment' is made from yellow mercuric oxide.

**Golden oldie.** Something that is an old favourite, such as a nostalgic song or piece of music. Also a person who is no longer young but still successful in a particular field.

**Golden parachute.** A clause in a senior executive's contract that grants him special benefits if he loses his post as the result of a takeover. There is a pun on 'bale out' and 'bail out' here. *See also* GOLDEN HANDSHAKE.

**Golden rivet.** A practice of leg-pulling among old hands in certain callings, especially in ships and shipyards, where an apprentice or GREENHORN is sent to look for the golden rivet, which is, of course, non-existent. *See also* SKYHOOK.

**Golden rose.** An ornament made of gold in imitation of a spray of roses, one of which contains a receptacle into which is poured balsam and musk. The rose is solemnly blessed by the pope on LAETARE SUNDAY and is conferred from time to time on sovereigns and others, as well as churches and cities distinguished for their services to the ROMAN CATHOLIC CHURCH. The last to receive it was Princess Charlotte of Nassau, Grand Duchess of Luxembourg, in 1956. The rose presented by Pius IX to the Empress Eugénie in 1856 is preserved in Farnborough Abbey.

**Golden rule, The.** 'Do as you would be done by.'

> All things whatsoever ye would that men should do to you, do ye even so to them: for this is the law and the prophets.
>
> Matthew 7:12

**Golden sands of the Pactolus, The.** The Pactolus is a small river in Lydia, Asia Minor, once famous for the particles of gold in its sands, which legendarily was due to MIDAS having bathed there. Its gold was exhausted by the time of AUGUSTUS.

**Golden section.** The division of a line into two parts such that the area of the rectangle contained by the smaller segment and the whole line equals that of the square on the larger segment (Euclid, *Elements*, ii (2nd century BC)).

**Golden share.** A share in a company that controls at least 51 per cent of the voting rights. Such shares are usually those held by the government on the occasion of a privatization. The figure of 51 per cent is a token one, indicating just over half of the total.

**Golden State, The.** California. So called from the gold discoveries of 1848. *See also* FORTY-NINERS; UNITED STATES OF AMERICA.

**Golden Stream, The.** St JOHN DAMASCENE (d.*c*.752), author of the first systematic treatise on dogmatic theology, was so called (*Chrysorrhoes*) for his flowing eloquence.

**Golden syrup.** A kind of pale treacle.

**Golden Temple.** The chief SIKH house of worship in India, in the city of Amritsar. It is known to Sikhs themselves as the Harimandir ('Temple of Hari', i.e. of VISHNU) or Darbar Sahib ('Divine Court'), and was built in 1604 by GURU Arjun, who sited it on a lower level so that even the humblest had to step down to enter it, and with entrances on four sides, so that it was open to all worshippers of all castes and creeds. It sustained some damage in 1984 when Indian troops fought their way in to crush Sikh extremists using it as a refuge.

**Golden-tongued, The** (Greek *Chrysologos*). St Peter, archbishop of Ravenna (d.*c*.450).

**Golden Triangle.** An opium-producing area of southeast Asia, consisting of parts of Myanmar (Burma), Laos and Thailand.

**Golden Vale** or **Valley.** The rich plain in the Irish counties of Limerick, Tipperary and Waterford, mainly in the valley of the Suir, is known as the Golden Vale, and the valley of the Dore in Herefordshire is similarly known as the Golden Valley. The latter name arose from mistaken etymology, however. The valley is not 'of gold' (French *d'or*) and the river name derives from a Celtic word meaning 'water' (Welsh *dwfr*).

**Golden verses.** Greek verses containing the moral rules of PYTHAGORAS, usually thought to have been composed by some of his scholars. He enjoins, among other things, obedience to God and one's rulers, deliberation before action, fortitude and temperance in exercise and diet. He also suggests making a critical review each night of the actions of the past day.

**Golden wedding.** The fiftieth anniversary of marriage, husband and wife being both alive.

**City of the Golden Gate, The.** *See under* CITY.

**Order of the Golden Fleece, The.** *See under* ORDER.

**Three golden balls, The.** *See under* THREE.

**Worship the golden calf, To.** *See under* WORSHIP.

**Golders Green.** The district of northwest London is synonymous with its crematorium, the resting place of the ashes of many famous people, including Sir Henry Irving, Rudyard Kipling, Neville Chamberlain, Stanley Baldwin, G.B. Shaw, Ralph Vaughan Williams and T.S. Eliot. It was opened in 1902.

**Goldfish Club.** *See* CATERPILLAR CLUB.

**Golf.** A basically straightforward yet at the same time esoteric sport, which has gained its own vocabulary. This chiefly relates to the names of clubs and strokes. Sources differ regarding the precise correspondence between the names of clubs and their numbers, but the most widely observed identifications are as follows:

Woods:
number 1: driver
number 2: brassie
number 3: spoon
number 4: baffy
number 5: (replaces number 3 or 4 iron)

Irons:
number 1: driving iron
number 2: midiron
number 3: mid-mashie
number 4: mashie iron
number 5: mashie
number 6: spade mashie
number 7: mashie-niblick
number 8: pitching niblick
number 9: niblick
number 10: wedge
no number: putter

In scoring, every course has its 'par', as the score an expert would be expected to make on it. (The word is interpreted by cynics as an acronym of 'pretty average really'.) Many courses also have a 'bogey', as the score that a moderate player would be expected to make. For the names of scores one or more strokes under par, *see also* ALBATROSS, BIRDIE, EAGLE.

**Clock golf.** *See under* CLOCK.

**Crazy golf.** *See under* CRAZY.

**Golgotha.** The place outside Jerusalem where Christ was crucified. The word is Aramaic and means 'skull'. It may have been a place of execution where bodies were picked clean by animals or was so named from the round, bare contour of the site. There is no biblical evidence for supposing that it was a hillock. The traditional site is that recovered by Constantine. Calvaria is the Greek and Latin equivalent of Golgotha. *See also* CALVARY.

In the University Church, Cambridge, Golgotha was the gallery in which the 'heads of the houses' sat. It was so called because it was the place of skulls or heads. It has been more wittily said that this Golgotha was the place of empty skulls.

**Goliards.** Educated jesters and buffoons who wrote ribald Latin verse, and who were noted for riotous behaviour. They flourished mainly in the 12th and 13th centuries. The word comes from the Old French *goliart* ('glutton'). The *Carmina Burana* is a collection of Goliardic poems, found in the German monastery of Benediktbeuern. Many were set to music (1937) by the German composer Carl Orff.

**Goliath.** The PHILISTINE giant, slain by the stripling DAVID with a small stone hurled from a sling (I Samuel 17:49–51). The name is sometimes used for any 'giant' object or organization. *See also* GIANTS OF THE BIBLE.

> Small companies can take on Goliaths.
> *The Times* (headline) (1 November 1994)

**Golightly, Holly.** The fascinating young heroine of Truman Capote's novella *Breakfast at Tiffany's* (1958). She has a calling card which states, 'Miss Holiday Golightly. Travelling', and it turns out that she is a farmer's child bride on the run. Her name symbolizes her role as a carefree travelling girl.

**Golliwog.** The black-faced doll with a shock of black hair began life as a character in a children's picture book by Bertha and Florence Upton, *The Adventures of Two Dutch Dolls and a 'Golliwogg'* (1895), Florence illustrating the text and Bertha, her mother, writing the verse text.

The character became immensely popular, and a 'golliwogg' (*sic*) craze soon developed. Debussy even included a 'Golliwog's Cake-Walk' in his *Children's Corner* suite (1905–6). The doll also caught on as a rather incongruous commercial symbol for Robertson's jam. However, a hundred years after his creation, the golliwog had become a serious victim of POLITICAL CORRECTNESS, and his centenary was only mutely marked, if at all. The origin of the name is uncertain. It may be a blend of 'golly' (what a sight!) and 'polliwog', an American term for a tadpole. It is perhaps itself the source of the also subsequently outlawed slang word 'wog'.

**GOM.** The initial letters of 'Grand Old Man', a nickname of honour given to W.E. Gladstone (1809–98), four times Prime Minister, in his later years. Lord Rosebery first used the expression in 1882.

**Gomorrah.** *See* SODOM.

**Gone.** *See* GO.

**Goneril.** One of LEAR's three daughters. Having received her share of Lear's kingdom, she first curtailed the old man's retinue, then gave him to understand that his company was troublesome. In Holinshed she appears as Gonerilla. *See also* CORDELIA; REGAN.

**Gong.** A service nickname for a medal.

**Gonged, To be.** To be signalled to stop by a police car for some traffic offence. The expression alludes to the loud electric bell formerly used to attract the offender's attention.

**Gonville and Caius.** *See* CAIUS.

**Good. Good, The.** Among the many who earned, or were given, this appellation are:

Alfonso VIII (or IX) of León, 'The Noble and Good' (1158–1214)
Haco I, king of Norway (*c*.920–961)
John II of France, le Bon (1319, 1350–64)
John III, Duke of Brittany (1286, 1312–41)
Philip the Good, Duke of Burgundy (1396, 1419–67)
René called the Good King René, Duke of Anjou, Count of Provence, Duke of Lorraine and king of Sicily (1409–80)
The Prince Consort, Albert the Good (1819–61), husband of Queen Victoria

**Good Book, The.** The BIBLE.

**Good clean fun.** Innocent amusement, free of vulgarity. The phrase is often used ironically.

**Good Duke Humphrey.** Humphrey, Duke of Gloucester (1391–1447), youngest son of Henry IV, said to have been murdered by Suffolk and Cardinal Beaufort. He was so called because of his devotion to the church. *See also* DINE WITH GOOD DUKE HUMPHREY.

**Good egg.** A good and helpful person. 'Good egg!' is also an exclamation of approval. *See also* BAD EGG.

**Goodfellow.** *See* ROBIN GOODFELLOW.

**Good-for-nothing.** A useless or irresponsible person.

**Good for** or **on you!** Well done! Well said! An expression of congratulation or approval.

**Good Friday.** The Friday before EASTER, held as the anniversary of the crucifixion. 'Good' here means 'holy'. Both CHRISTMAS and SHROVE TUESDAY used to be called 'the Good Tide'. *See also* ABSTINENCE.

**Good God!** One of a number of similar exclamations denoting surprise, horror or some similar emotion. Others are 'Good Lord!', 'Good heavens!', 'Good grief!', 'Good gracious!' The phrases 'Goodness!' and 'Goodness gracious!' also really belong here.

**Goodies.** *See* GOODY.

**Good job, A.** A fortunate state of affairs, as: 'It's a good job you missed the rain.'

**Goodman.** A husband or master. In Matthew 24:43: 'If the goodman of the house had known in what watch the thief would come, he would have watched.'

**Good News Bible, The.** *See under* BIBLE.

**Good Parliament, The.** Edward III's Parliament of 1376, so called because of the severity with which it pursued the unpopular party of the Duke of Lancaster.

**Good people, The.** A name for fairies.

**Good Queen Bess.** Elizabeth I (1533–1603).

**Good question, A.** One that cannot be easily answered. The phrase often occurs in the formula 'That's a good question'.

**Good Regent, The.** James Stewart, Earl of Moray (d.1570), an illegitimate son of James V and half-brother of Mary, Queen of Scots. He was appointed Regent of Scotland after the abdication of Queen Mary in 1567.

**Good round sum, A.** A large sum of money.

> Three thousand ducats; 'tis a good round sum.
> SHAKESPEARE: *The Merchant of Venice*, I, iii (1596)

**Good Samaritan, A.** A philanthropist, one who helps the poor and needy (Luke 10:30–7).

**Good Shepherd, The.** A title of Jesus Christ.

> I am the good shepherd: the good shepherd giveth his life for the sheep.
> John 10:11

**Good-time girl.** A young woman who seeks pleasure and 'plenty of action' to go with it.

**Good times.** A period of prosperity.

> Let the good times roll.
> SAM THEARD AND FLEECIE MOORE: 'Let the Good Times Roll' (song title) (1946)

**Good time was had by all, A.** Everyone enjoyed themselves. A stock expression formerly ending the account of a social event in a parish magazine or local newspaper, but now frequently used ironically following a disappointing or unwelcome experience.

**Good trencherman, A.** Usually said of a good eater. The trencher was the platter on which food was cut (Old French *trencier*, 'to cut') or served, and the term trencherman is sometimes applied to a convivial table companion, or a person who enjoys their food.

**Goodwife.** The feminine counterpart of GOODMAN.

**Goodwill.** Kindly feeling; cheerful consent. Also the established reputation of a business, regarded as enhancing its value.

**Good wine needs no bush.** If something has real worth, quality or merit it does not need to be advertised. An ivy bush, which in the ancient world was sacred to BACCHUS, was once the common sign of taverns and of ale and wine vendors.

**Good works.** Charitable acts.

> Let your light so shine before men, that they may see your good works, and glorify your Father which is in heaven.
> Matthew 5:16

**Goody Halliett.** *See under* HALLIETT.

**All to the good.** *See under* ALL.

**As good as.** *See under* AS.

**As good as gold.** *See under* AS.

**As good as one's word.** *See under* AS.

**Bad with the good.** *See under* BAD.

**Be good!** *See under* BE.

**Can there any good thing come out of Nazareth?** (John 1:46). A general insinuation against any family or place of ill repute. 'Can any great man come from such an insignificant village as Nazareth?'

**Cape of Good Hope, The.** *See* CAPE OF STORMS.

**Come good, To.** *See under* COME.

**For good** or **for good and all.** *See under* FOR.

**For good measure.** *See under* FOR.

**Give a good account of oneself, To.** To perform well, as in a sport or examination. One may conversely 'give a poor account of oneself' or fail to come up to expectations.

**Great and the good, The.** *See under* GREAT.

**Have a good mind to do something, To.** To feel strongly inclined to do it.

**Have good sea legs, To.** To be a good sailor; to be able to stand the ship's motion without getting seasick.

**Hold good, To.** *See under* HOLD.

**In good faith.** With complete sincerity, especially in a business negotiation.

**In good hands.** Safe, well cared for.

**In someone's good books, To be.** To be in favour with a person. Conversely, to be in someone's bad books is to be in disfavour with a person. *See also* BLACK BOOKS.

**In someone's good graces, To be.** To be in a person's favour.

**Keep a good house, To.** To supply a bountiful table.

**Keep a good table, To.** To provide a good and generous standard of fare at one's table.

**Keep good hours, To.** To go home early every night; to go to bed in good time; to be punctual at work.

**Make good, To.** To fulfil one's promises or to come up to expectations; to achieve success, often after an unpromising start. Also to replace, repair or compensate for as: 'You will have to make good the damage.'

**Never had it so good.** *See under* NEVER.

**On a good** or **friendly footing with someone, To be.** To be on amicable terms with a person.

**On good** or **bad terms, To be.** *See under* TERM.

**Only the good die young.** *See under* ONLY.

**On to a good thing, To be.** *See under* THING.

**Put in a good word for someone, To.** *See under* WORD.

**So far, so good.** *See under* SO.

**That's a good one.** A traditional rejoinder to an unbelievable statement, or more positively to an excellent joke.

**There's a good time coming.** A long-established familiar saying in Scotland. Charles Mackay (1814–89) wrote his once popular song of this title in 1846.

> 'I could have wished it had been ... when I could have better paid the compliments I owe your Grace; but there's a gude time coming.'
> SIR WALTER SCOTT: *Rob Roy*, ch xxxii (1817)

**Goodbye.** A contraction of 'God be with you', and so similar to the French *adieu*. 'God' became 'good' under the influence of similar expressions, such as good morning and good night.

**Kiss goodbye to, To.** *See under* KISS.

**Goods. Goods and chattels.** All kinds of person property. Chattels, a word related to 'cattle', is legally divided into chattels personal, as tangible goods, and chattels real, as leasehold interests.

**Capital goods.** *See under* CAPITAL.

**Deliver the goods, To.** *See under* DELIVER.

**Piece goods.** *See under* PIECE.

**Producer's goods.** *See under* PRODUCER.

**White goods.** *See under* WHITE.

**Goodwin Sands.** It is said that these dangerous sandbanks, stretching about 10 miles (16km) northeast and southwest some $5\frac{1}{2}$ miles (9km) off the east Kent coast, consisted at one time of about 4000 acres (1620 ha) of low land called Lomea (the *Infera Insula* of the Romans), fenced from the sea by a wall, and belonging to Earl Godwin. WILLIAM THE CONQUEROR gave them to the abbey of St Augustine, Canterbury, but the abbot allowed the sea wall to decay and in 1099 the sea inundated the site.

**Tenterden steeple was the cause of Goodwin Sands.** *See under* TENTERDEN.

**Goodwood.** The races so called are held on the estate of this name near Chichester, Sussex, the property of the Dukes of Richmond and Gordon. Racing dates from 1801 and the course was laid out under the direction of Lord George Bentinck (1802–48). The Gold Cup, 'Cup Day', was instituted in 1812, the Goodwood Stakes in 1823, and the Stewards' Cup in 1840. There are 18 days' racing there annually, but the best known are the five days of the Goodwood Festival, or 'Glorious Goodwood', which takes place at the end of July and traditionally marks the end of the London summer season. *See also* RACES.

**Goody.** A term for any nice small thing to eat, such as a sweet or cake. Children generally say 'Goody!' as a sign of approval. In a story or film, the 'Goody' is the hero or heroine, as contrasted with the 'Baddy'. The word is also a rustic variant of goodwife (*see* GOODMAN) and is sometimes used as a title, like GAMMER, as, 'Goody Blake', 'Goody Dobson'. *See also* HALLIETT. The word often occurs in the plural, so that goodies are pleasant titbits and the 'Goodies' are the good people in the story. *The Goodies* was the collective name adopted by three comedians in the television series so titled, first shown in 1970. They were Graeme Garden, Tim Brooke-Taylor and Bill Oddie. ('Goodies' actually represented letters from their surnames: *G*arden, Br*oo*ke and Od*die*.)

> Mr Benn never ceases to amaze. He is like those Christmas crackers packed with mystery surprises. You pull the taper, there is a flash, a bang, and out pops a selection of weird goodies.
> *The Times* (1 November 1994)

**Goody-goody.** A reduplication of GOODY, as a term for a smugly virtuous person.

**Goody Two-Shoes.** This nursery tale first appeared in 1765 under the full title *The History of Little Goody Two-Shoes; Otherwise Called Mrs Margery Two-Shoes, With the Means by Which She Acquired Her Learning and Wisdom, and in Consequence Thereof Her Estate*. It was written for John Newbery (1713–67), a notable publisher of children's books, probably by Oliver Goldsmith. Its heroine owned only one shoe and when given a pair she was so pleased that she showed them to everyone, saying 'Two shoes!'

**Googly.** In CRICKET, a deceptive delivery depending on hand action by the bowler in which an off-break is bowled to a right-handed batsman with what appears to be a leg-break action. It was invented and developed by B.J.T. Bosanquet from 1890, and he used it against the Australians in 1903. In Australia it is called a 'Bosey'. The origin of the term is uncertain. It may have evolved from 'goggle', since the bowl that you see is not the ball that you get. *See also* CHINAMAN.

**Goons, The.** A team of four comics who won a wide following for their absurd sense of humour in the weekly radio series *The Goon Show* (1951–60). The crazy quartet consisted of Spike Milligan (b.1918), Peter Sellers (1925–80), Harry Secombe (b.1921) and Michael Bentine (1921–96). The name Goon betrayed the wartime influence on Milligan and Secombe, who had first met in the North African desert. It was a word often used by prisoners-of-war for their German guards, as which it may have been a blend of 'gorilla' and 'baboon'. Milligan claimed, however, that he took the name from the creature called Alice the Goon in the POPEYE comic strip by the US cartoonist Elzie C. Segar (1894–1938). The former origin may have prompted one of the programme's catchphrases: 'Neddie Seagoon' (Secombe) would offer a cigarette with the words 'Have a gorilla', to which the reply was, 'No thanks, I only smoke baboons'.

**Goose** or **geese.** A foolish or ignorant person is called a goose because of the alleged stupidity of this bird. A tailor's pressing-iron is so called because its handle resembles the neck of a goose. The plural of the iron is 'gooses' not 'geese'. *See also* BOOBY.

> Come in, tailor; here you may roast your goose.
> SHAKESPEARE: *Macbeth*, II, iii (1605)

**Geese save the Capitol, The.** When the Gauls attacked Rome in 390 BC it is said that a detachment advanced up the Capitoline Hill so silently that the foremost man reached the top unchallenged. On climbing over the rampart, however, he disturbed some sacred geese, whose cackle awoke the garrison. Marcus Manlius rushed to the wall and hurled the fellow over the edge. To commemorate this event, the Romans carried a golden goose in procession to the Capitol every year. Manlius was given the name Capitolinus.

> Those consecrated geese in orders,
> That to the capitol were warders;
> And being then upon patrol,
> With noise alone beat off the Gaul.
> SAMUEL BUTLER: *Hudibras*, II, iii (1663)

**Goose and Gridiron.** A PUBLIC HOUSE SIGN, probably in ridicule of the Swan and Harp, a popular sign for the early music houses (*see* MUSIC HALL), but properly the coat of arms of the Company of Musicians, i.e. azure, a swan with wings expanded argent, within double tressure [the gridiron] flory counterflory.

In the United States the name is humorously applied to the national coat of arms, the American EAGLE with a gridiron-like shield on its breast.

**Goose Bible, The.** *See under* BIBLE.

**Goose egg.** *See* DUCK'S EGG.

**Goose fair.** A fair formerly held in many English towns about the time of MICHAELMAS, when geese were plentiful. The one still held in Nottingham was the most important. Tavistock Goosey Fair in Devon is still held in the second week in October, although geese no longer play a part, except at the cattle market on the Wednesday.

Tes jist a month cum Vriday nex'
Bill Champernown an' me
Us druv a-crost ole Dartymoor
Th' Goozey Vair to zee.
'Tavistock Goozey Vair' (traditional song)

**Gooseflesh.** A rough, pimply condition of the skin, especially on the arms and legs, like that of a plucked goose or fowl. It is usually occasioned by cold or shock.

**Goose step.** A military step in which the legs are swung forward rigidly to an exaggerated height. It was introduced as a form of recruit drill in the British army but never became popular, although it exists in a modified form in the slow march. As the *Stechschritt* it has been a full dress and processional march in the German army since the time of Frederick the Great (1712–86). When the AXIS flourished it was adopted by the Italian army but was soon ridiculed into disuse.

**All one's geese are swans.** *See under* ALL.
**As loose as a goose.** *See under* AS.
**Cook one's goose, To.** *See under* COOK.
**Ember goose.** *See under* EMBER.
**Fox and Goose.** *See under* PUBLIC HOUSE NAMES.
**Golden goose.** *See under* GOLDEN.
**Kill the goose that lays the golden eggs, To.** *See under* KILL.
**MacFarlane's geese.** *See under* MACFARLANE.
**Mother Carey's Goose.** *See under* MOTHER.
**Mother Goose.** *See under* MOTHER.
**Not to say boo to a goose.** *See under* SAY.
**St Martin's goose.** *See under* MARTIN.
**Wayzgoose.** *See under* WAYZGOOSE.
**What is sauce for the goose is sauce for the gander.** *See under* WHAT.

**Gooseberry. Gooseberry fool.** A dish essentially made of gooseberries, cream or custard, and sugar, the fruit being crushed through a sieve. Here the word 'fool' probably comes from its standard meaning, with a punning allusion to 'trifle'.
**Cape gooseberry.** *See under* CAPE.
**Play gooseberry, To.** *See under* PLAY.

**Gopher.** A native of Minnesota, USA. The word probably comes from the prairie rodent of that name.
**Gopher wood.** The wood of which NOAH made his ark (Genesis 6:14). It was probably some kind of cedar.

**Gorboduc.** *See* FERREX AND PORREX.

**Gordian knot.** A great difficulty. Gordius, a peasant, being chosen king of Phrygia, dedicated his wagon to JUPITER, and fastened the yoke to a beam with a rope of bark so ingeniously that no one could untie the knot. Alexander the Great was told that whoever undid it 'would reign over the whole East'. 'Well then,' said the conqueror, 'it is thus I perform the task,' and, so saying, he cut the knot in two with his sword. 'To cut the Gordian knot' is thus to get out of a difficult position by one decisive stroke, or to resolve a situation by force or by evasive action.

**Gordon. Chinese Gordon.** *See under* CHINESE.
**Flash Gordon.** *See under* FLASH.
**Gay Gordons.** *See under* GAY.

**Gordonstoun.** The Scottish public school, renowned for its emphasis on physical self-reliance, was founded in 1934 by the German educationalist Kurt Hahn after he was forced to flee from Nazi Germany. His aim was to counteract what he saw as the 'four social declines' of physical fitness, initiative, care and compassion. To combat the problems of puberty, he instigated a rigorous routine of morning runs and cold showers. He later devised the Duke of Edinburgh Award scheme. The school won royal approval, and no fewer than three royal princes, Charles, Andrew and Edward, were educated here, the former letting it be known subsequently that his time had not been a happy one. The school has now toned down its ruggedness and rigidity, but much of Hahn's legacy survives. It became coeducational in 1972.

**Gore.** A triangular or wedge-shaped piece of cloth in dressmaking, also a similarly shaped piece of land, as in the name Kensington Gore. The word is Old English *gara*, related to *gār*, 'spear'.

**Gorgon** (Greek *gorgos*, 'terrible'). A fierce or unpleasant-looking woman. In classical mythology there were three Gorgons, with serpents on their heads instead of hair. MEDUSA was their chief; the others, Stheno and Euryale, were immortal. They also had brazen claws and monstrous teeth. Their glance turned their victims to stone. *See also* PERSEUS.

**Gospel** (Old English *gōdspel*, 'good news', from Ecclesiastical Latin *bonus nuntius*, literally translating Latin *evangelium*, itself representing Greek *euaggelion*). The word is used to describe collectively the lives of Christ as told by the EVANGELISTS in the NEW TESTAMENT, to signify the message of redemption set forth in those books, to denote the entire Christian message and to apply to any doctrine or teaching set forth for some specific purpose.

The first four books of the New Testament, known as The Gospels, are ascribed to MATTHEW, MARK, LUKE and JOHN, although their exact authorship is uncertain. The first three of these are called the Synoptic Gospels because they follow the same lines and may be brought under one general view or synopsis. The fourth Gospel stands apart as the work of just one mind. There are many Apocryphal Gospels, examples of which are given below. *See also* APOCRYPHA.

**Gospel according to ...** The chief teaching of [so-and-so]. The Gospel according to MAMMON is the amassing of wealth or money.

**Gospel of Nicodemus, The.** Also known as the ACTS OF PILATE, this is an apocryphal book of uncertain date between the 2nd and 5th centuries. It gives an elaborate and fanciful description of the trial, death and resurrection of Jesus, names the two thieves (DISMAS and GESTAS), PILATE's wife (Procla), the centurion (LONGINUS) and others, and ends with an account of the *descensus ad inferos* ('descent into hell') of Jesus, by Charinus and Leucius, two men risen from the dead. The title first appears in the 13th century. The Gospel was much used by the writers of Miracle and MYSTERY PLAYS.

**Gospel of Peter, The.** An apocryphal book in fragmentary form, first mentioned by Serapion, bishop of Antioch, in the last decade of the 2nd century, and part of which was found in 1892.

**Gospel of Thomas, The.** A GNOSTIC work, probably of the 2nd century, containing much that is fanciful.

**Gospel of wealth, The.** The philosophy that holds that wealth is the great end and aim of man and that it is the one thing needful, i.e. the Gospel according to MAMMON.

**Gospel side of the altar, The.** To the left of the celebrant facing the altar, i.e. the north side. This is the side where the Gospel is still sometimes read in the Communion Service.

**Hot gospeller.** *See under* HOT.

**Hot Gospellers.** *See under* HOT.

**Synoptic Gospels.** *See under* SYNOPTIC.

**Gossamer.** According to legend, this delicate thread is the unravelling of the Virgin MARY's winding sheet, which fell to earth on her ascension to heaven. It is fancifully said to be God's seam, i.e. 'God's thread'. The word is actually from Middle English *gossomer*, 'goose summer', referring to St MARTIN'S SUMMER (early November), when goose was traditionally eaten. The filmy cobwebs are often seen at this time. Similarly, German *Gansemonat*, 'goose month', is used as a local name for November.

**Gossip.** Trivial or malicious talk, tittle-tattle. A gossip was formerly the sponsor of a child at its baptism, and the word is a corruption of Old English *godsibb*, 'godparent', with *sibb* appearing in modern English 'sibling'. From this specialized sense, the meaning expanded to denote a woman's female friends at the birth of a child, and hence to the casual chat that they indulged in. *See also* ALL STUARTS ARE NOT SIB.

> 'Tis not a maid, for she hath had gossips; yet 'tis a maid, for she is her master's maid, and serves for wages.
>
> SHAKESPEARE: *Two Gentlemen of Verona*, III, i (1594)

**Gotham. Gothamites.** Inhabitants of New York. The term was in use in 1800. The name of Gotham was given to New York by Washington Irving in his *Salmagundi* (1807).

**Wise men of Gotham.** *See under* WISE.

**Goths.** A barbarian Germanic tribe, which invaded and devastated Europe in the 3rd to 5th centuries, establishing kingdoms in Italy, France and Spain. Hence the use of the name to imply anyone who is uncultured, uncivilized or destructive. *See also* VANDALS.

**Gothic architecture.** The name for the style prevalent in western Europe from the 12th to the 16th centuries. The name was given contemptuously to imply 'barbaric' by the architects of the RENAISSANCE period who revived classical styles. A Gothic Revival was started by wealthy dilettanti such as Horace Walpole in the 18th century and was further popularized by Sir Walter Scott and John Ruskin. The works of A.W. Pugin (1812–52) and Sir Giles Gilbert Scott (1811–78) are notable examples of 19th-century Gothic.

**Last of the Goths, The.** *See* RODERICK.

**Götz von Berlichingen.** *See* IRON-HAND.

**Gourd, Jonah's.** *See under* JONAH.

**Gourmand** and **gourmet** (French). A gourmand is someone whose main pleasure is eating, while a gourmet is a connoisseur of food and wines. The gourmand rates quantity higher than quality, the gourmet adopts the opposite approach. *See also* APICIUS.

**Gout** (Old French *goute*, from Latin *gutta*, 'drop'). The disease is so called from the belief that it was due to 'drops of humours'.

**Govan. St Govan's Bell.** *See* INCHCAPE ROCK.

**Government. Coalition government.** *See under* COALITION.

**National governments.** *See under* NATIONAL.

**Petticoat government.** *See under* PETTICOAT.

**Gower, The Moral.** *See under* MORAL.

**Gowk** (Old Norse *gaukr*). The cuckoo, and hence a fool, a simpleton.

**Gowk storm, A.** One consisting of several days of windy weather, believed by country folk to take place periodically in early April, at the time that the gowk arrives in this country. It is also, curiously enough, a storm that is short and sharp.

**Hunting the gowk.** *See under* HUNT.

**Gown. Gown and town.** *See* TOWN AND GOWN.

**Cap and gown.** *See under* CAP.

**Stuff gown.** *See under* STUFF.

**GPU.** *See* OGPU.

**Graal.** *See* HOLY GRAIL.

**Gracchi.** Two Roman brothers, Gaius Sempronius Gracchus (*c*.159–121 BC) and Tiberius Sempronius Gracchus (168–133 BC), who became noted tribunes and social reformers. Accused of having violated the tribuneship by deposing his colleague Caecina, Tiberius was murdered, together with some 300 of his friends. Seneca relates that the brothers' mother, Cornelia, spoke of the boys as her jewels. Together with their sister, Sempronia, the two were the only survivors of their mother's 12 children.

**Cornelia, Mother of the Grachi.** *See under* CORNELIA.

**Grace.** A courtesy title used in addressing or speaking of dukes, duchesses and archbishops, e.g. 'His Grace the Duke of Devonshire', 'My Lord Archbishop, may it please Your Grace'.

**Grace and favour residence.** A residence belonging to the crown and granted to a notable person as free accommodation.

**Grace before** or **after meat.** A short prayer asking a blessing on, or giving thanks for, one's food, such as the old college grace *Benedictus benedicat* ('May the blessed one bless') before the meal, followed by *Benedicto benedicatur* ('It is blessed by the blessed one') at the end. The word is a relic of the old phrase 'to do graces' or 'to give graces', meaning to render thanks (French *rendre grâces*, Latin *gratias agere*).

**Grace cup** or **loving cup.** *See* LOVING CUP.

**Grace Darling.** *See under* DARLING.

**Graceless** or **godless florin.** The first English silver florin struck in 1849, called 'graceless' because the usual *Dei Gratia* ('by the grace of God') was omitted, and 'godless' because of the omission of FD (DEFENDER OF THE FAITH). Some attributed the cholera outbreak of that year to the new florin. The coins were called in and the Master of the MINT, Richard Lalor Sheil (1791–1851), a Roman Catholic, left the post the following year.

**Grace notes.** Musical embellishments not essential to the harmony or melody of a piece. They were more common in 16th-century music than in modern music.

**Grace of God, The.** The free and unmerited love and favour of God. 'There but for the grace of God go I' is a phrase used by the self-righteous or smug when others are faced with disaster, disgrace or the like as a result of their actions. It implies that they could well have been in the same position but have been fortunate enough to escape. The phrase is usually traced back to the PROTESTANT martyr John Bradford (*c*.1510–55), who on seeing a group of criminals being led to their execution, remarked, 'But for the grace of God there goes John Bradford.'

**Act of Grace.** *See under* ACT.

**Days of grace.** *See under* DAY.

**Herb of grace.** *See under* HERB.

**In someone's good graces, To be.** *See under* GOOD.

**Pilgrimage of Grace, The.** *See under* PILGRIMAGE.

**Three Graces, The.** *See under* THREE.

**Time of Grace.** *See* SPORTING SEASONS IN ENGLAND.

**With a good** or **bad grace.** *See under* WITH.

**Year of Grace.** *See under* YEAR.

**Grade.** This word is commonly used to denote a student's assessment or mark of attainment in schools and colleges, as the seven grades A to G in the GCSE (General Certificate of Secondary Education) examination. From 1994 there has been an additional 'starred' A grade (A*) to cater for the highest attainers.

**Grade crossing.** The American equivalent of the British level crossing.

**Make the grade, To.** To rise to the occasion; to reach the required standard or level; to overcome obstacles. The allusion is to climbing a hill or gradient.

**Gradual.** An antiphon sung between the Epistle and the Gospel as the deacon ascends the steps (Late Latin *graduales*) of the altar or pulpit. The word also refers to the book containing the musical portions of the service at mass: the graduals, introits, kyries, GLORIA IN EXCELSIS, credo and so on.

**Gradual Psalms, The.** Psalms 120–134 inclusive. They are probably so called because they were sung when the priests made the ascent to the inner court of the Temple at Jerusalem. In the Authorized Version of the Bible they are called Songs of Degrees, and in the Revised Version Songs of Ascents. *See also* HALLEL.

**Gradus ad Parnassum** (Latin, 'steps to Parnassus'). The fanciful title of a once popular dictionary of Latin prosody used in schools for the teaching of Latin verse. It was also the title of a well-known treatise on musical composition written in Latin by Johan Joseph Fux, published at Vienna in 1725, and of Muzio Clementi's collection of piano studies (1817). The first piece in Claude Debussy's suite *Children's Corner* (1906–8) is a parody of Clementi's studies and is entitled 'Dr Gradus ad Parnassum'. *See also* PARNASSUS.

**Graffiti** (Italian *graffito*, 'scratching'). A name applied originally to the 'wall scribblings' found at Pompeii and other Italian cities, as the work of schoolboys, idlers and the like, many of them obscene and accompanied by rough drawings. A collection of graffiti of Pompeii was published by Bishop Wordsworth in 1837, and it provides a useful insight into the life of the ancient Romans. Modern graffiti are found on walls, in lavatories, on posters and in other clearly visible places. They are sometimes crude and erotic, but some are genuinely witty. One seen in Manchester in 1978 read, 'If you hate graffiti, sign a partition'. Political graffiti were formerly common in the 1930s. *See also* ALEXANDER THE CORRECTOR; CHAD; KILROY.

**Graham's Dyke.** *See* GRIMSDYKE.

**Grail, The Holy.** *See under* HOLY.

**Grain. Against the grain.** *See under* AGAINST.

**With a grain of salt.** *See* WITH A PINCH OF SALT *under* WITH.

**Gram** ('grief'). One of the swords of SIEGFRIED.

**Grammar.** Suetonius writes (*De Grammaticis*, 22 (2nd century AD)) that Tiberius was rebuked by a grammarian for some verbal slip, and upon a courtier remarking that if the word was not good Latin it would be in future, now that it had received imperial recognition, he was rebuked with the words, *Tu enim Caesar civitatem dare potes hominibus, verbis non potes* ('Caesar, you can grant citizenship to men, but not to words'). Hence the saying, *Caesar non supra grammaticos* ('Caesar is not above the grammarians').

When the German Emperor Sigismund I stumbled into a wrong gender at the Council of Constance (1414), no such limitation would be admitted. He replied, *Ego sum Imperator Romanorum, et supra grammaticam* ('I am the Roman Emperor and am above grammar').

**Grammar schools.** The somewhat forbidding name has its origins in the medieval schools established by pious founders to provide free education for local children. The schools were largely dependent on the church, and as Latin was then the universal language of knowledge and communication, it figured largely in the timetable. Hence the grammar of the title. The schools gradually declined over the years, mainly because of a diminution in endowments, and by the 19th century they were in a poor state. The Grammar School Act of 1840 then authorized governing bodies to introduce a wider range of subjects. Both boarding and day schools developed, and it was from the former that PUBLIC SCHOOLS emerged. There are still several schools nominally designated grammar schools, but they are mostly comprehensive schools that have retained the name from the days when they were independent.

**Prince of Grammarians, The.** Apollonius the SOPHIST of Alexandria (1st century AD), so called by Priscian.

**Grammaticus, Saxo.** *See under* SAXO.

**Gramont.** The Comte de Gramont (1621–1707) became known for his short memory as the result of a story told of his marriage to Elizabeth Hamilton ('La Belle Hamilton') of the RESTORATION court. When leaving England in 1663, after a visit in which this young lady's name had been compromised by him, he was followed by her brothers with drawn swords, who asked him if he had not forgotten something. 'True, true,' said the Count pleasantly, 'I promised to marry your sister.' Upon which he returned to London and married Elizabeth.

**Granby, The Marquis of.** At one time this was a popular PUBLIC HOUSE SIGN, and such signs are still numerous. John Manners, Marquis of Granby (1721–70), commanded the Leicester Blues against the YOUNG PRETENDER in the FORTY-FIVE, was a Lieutenant General at Minden (1759), and commander-in-chief of the British army in 1766. He was a very bald man and this was exaggerated on most of the inn signs. *See also* GO FOR SOMEONE BALDHEADED *under* BALD.

**Gran Capitán, El** (Spanish, 'the Great Captain'). The name given to the famous Spanish general Gonsalvo de Cordova (1453–1515), through whose efforts Granada and Castile were united.

**Grand. Grand Alliance.** The coalition against France consisting of the Holy Roman Empire, Holland, Spain, Great Britain, Sweden and Savoy, which fought the War of the Grand Alliance or War of the League of Augsburg (1689–97) to check French aggression.

**Grand eagle.** Before metrication, paper 28¾ x 42in (730 x 1067mm), so called from a watermark first met with in 1314.

**Grand Guignol.** *See* GUIGNOL.

**Grand Lama, The.** *See* LAMAISM.

**Grand National.** The principal event in English steeplechasing, instituted at Liverpool in 1839, and now run at Aintree on a 4½-mile (7.2km) course of 30 jumps, including the famous Becher's Brook. *See also* RACES.

**Grand Old Duke of York, The.** The duke made famous in the nursery rhyme was Frederick Augustus, Duke of York and Albany (1763–1827), second son of George III, who commanded the English Army in Flanders (1794–5), cooperating with the Austrians against Revolutionary France. His part in the campaign of 1794 was derisively summarized in the rhyme:

> The grand old Duke of York
> He had ten thousand men,
> He marched 'em up to the top of the hill
> And he marched 'em down again.

In fact, there was no hill, he was young, and he commanded some 30,000 men. In variants of the rhyme he is the 'brave' or 'rare old Duke'. He was made commander-in-chief in 1798. *See also* DUKE OF YORK'S COLUMN.

**Grand opera.** Opera in which the entire libretto is set to music. *See also* LIGHT OPERA.

**Grand Seignior.** A term applied to the former Sultans of Turkey.

**Grand Tour, The.** In the 17th, 18th and early

19th centuries it was the custom of families of rank and substance to finish their sons' education by sending them under the guardianship of a tutor on a tour through France, Switzerland, Italy and home through western Germany. This was known as the Grand Tour, and sometimes a couple of years or more were devoted to it. The young men were supposed to study the history, language and so on of each country they visited and such travel was a distinguishing mark between the great landowners and the ordinary squires.

**Grand, Le** or **Grande, La** (French, 'the Great').

**Grand Bâtard, Le.** Antoine de Bourgogne (d.1504), a bastard son of Philip the Good, famous for his deeds and prowess.

**Grand Condé, Le.** Louis II of Bourbon, prince de Condé, one of France's greatest military commanders (1621–86). The funeral oration pronounced at his death was Jacques Bossuet's finest composition.

**Grand Dauphin, Le.** Louis (1661–1711), eldest son of Louis XIV, for whose use the Delphin Classics (a set of Latin classics published 1674–1730) were prepared. *See also* DAUPHIN.

**Grande Mademoiselle, La.** Anne, Duchesse de Montpensier (1627–93), daughter of Gaston, Duc d'Orléans, and cousin of Louis XIV, who was noted for her wealth, position and strength of character.

**Grand Monarque, Le.** Louis XIV, king of France (b.1638, r.1643–1715).

**Grand Pan, Le.** VOLTAIRE (1694–1778).

**Monsieur le Grand.** *See under* MONSIEUR.

**Grandfather clock.** The traditional name for the formerly common weight-and-pendulum eight-day clock in a tall wooden case. It derives from the popular song 'My Grandfather's Clock' by Henry Clay Work (1832–84) of Connecticut, author of the temperance song 'Come Home Father' (1864) and the patriotic 'Marching through Georgia' (1865). The clock that inspired the song now stands in the George Hotel, Piercebridge, County Durham.

> My grandfather's clock was too large for the shelf
> So it stood ninety years on the floor.
> H.C. WORK: 'My Grandfather's Clock' (1876)

**Grandison, Sir Charles.** The hero of Samuel Richardson's *History of Sir Charles Grandison*, published in 1753. Sir Charles is the perfect hero and English Christian gentleman, aptly described by Sir Walter Scott as 'a faultless monster that the world never saw'. Richardson's model for Sir Charles may have been the worthy Robert Nelson (1656–1715), a religious writer and eminent nonjuror, whose life was devoted to good works.

**Grandison Cromwell.** Mirabeau's nickname for Lafayette (1757–1834), implying that he had all the ambition of a Cromwell, but wanted to appear before men as a Sir Charles Grandison.

**Grandmontines.** An order of BENEDICTINE hermits, founded by St Stephen of Thiers in Auvergne in about 1100, with its mother house at Grandmont. They came to England soon after the foundation and established a few small houses in remote places, such as that at Craswall, near Hay-on-Wye, Herefordshire.

**Grandmother. Teach one's grandmother to suck eggs, To.** *See under* TEACH.

**Grange** (Anglo-French *graunge*, ultimately from Latin *granum*, 'grain'). Properly the granary or farm of a monastery, where the corn was stored. Houses attached to monasteries where rent was paid in grain were also called granges, and in Lincolnshire and the northern counties the name is given to any isolated farm, many now surviving as 'Grange Farm'. 'The Grange' also became a popular name for country houses built for the more prosperous Victorians.

In the USA the Grange of Patrons of Husbandry is a secret organization of farmers and their families. Founded at Washington, D.C., in 1867 by O.H. Kelley, a clerk in the Department of Agriculture, as a social fraternity, it stressed cultural and educational objectives and became politically involved in the agrarian discontent of the 1870s. The name derives from the local lodges called granges.

**Granger states.** Wisconsin, Illinois, Minnesota and Iowa. *See also* UNITED STATES OF AMERICA.

**Grangerize, To.** To supplement the illustrations of a book by inserting portraits, autograph letters, caricatures, prints, broadsheets, biographical sketches, anecdotes, scandals, press notices, parallel passages and any other matter directly or indirectly bearing on the subject. The name is that of James Granger (1723–76), vicar of Shiplake, Oxfordshire, who published his *Biographical History of England* (1769), which included blank pages for illustrations to be supplied by the reader. The book went through several editions with added material and it was continued by Mark Noble in 1806. Collectors made this book a core around which to assemble great collections of portraits, and in 1856 two copies were sold in London, one in 27 volumes with 1300 portraits, the other in 19 volumes with 3000 portraits. 'Grangerizing' books became a fashion with the result that many excellent editions of biographies and the like were ruined by having the plates removed for pasting in some amateur collection.

**Grani** (Old Norse, 'grey-coloured'). SIEGFRIED's horse, of marvellous swiftness.

**Granite. Granite City, The.** Aberdeen is so named, for its many granite buildings. Since 'granite' has connotations of greyness and coldness, the city has sought to attract visitors rather than repel them by devising a new title. 'Aberdeen, City of Opportunity' was thus the more neutral slogan chosen in 1997 as an equal lure to business people and tourists.

**Granite State, The.** New Hampshire, so called because the mountainous parts of the state are chiefly granite. *See also* UNITED STATES OF AMERICA.

**Granny. Granny flat.** A self-contained flat or annexe inside or built onto a house, designed as accommodation for an elderly relative.

**Granny glasses.** Spectacles with small circular lenses, in fashion in the 1960s during the heyday of the BEATLES and the FLOWER PEOPLE. Their popularity was largely due to John Lennon, who wore glasses of this type.

**Granny knot.** A reef knot with the ends crossing the wrong way, making it liable to slip.

**Granny Smith.** A green-skinned, crisp-fleshed dessert apple, named after its first cultivator, Maria Ann Smith (*c*.1801–70), known as Granny Smith, of Eastwood, New South Wales, Australia.

**Grantchester.** This historic village 2 miles (3km) south of Cambridge has a fine old church with many interesting features, but it owes its modern fame to its associations with Rupert Brooke (1887–1915). He lived at the Old Vicarage, and saw active service in the First World War, his reputation being much enhanced by his last poems.

> But Grantchester! ah, Grantchester,
> There's peace and holy quiet there.
>
> RUPERT BROOKE: 'The Old Vicarage, Grantchester' (1915)

**Grant quarter, To.** To spare the life of an enemy in one's power. The old suggestion that the expression derives from an agreement made between the Dutch and Spaniards, that the ransom of a soldier should be the quarter of his pay, is not borne out. It is possibly due to the fact that the victor would have to provide his captive with temporary QUARTERS.

**Grape. Grapeshot.** A form of ammunition for cannons consisting of cast-iron balls packed between iron plates, which were arranged in layers or tiers and held together by a central iron pin. When fired there was a wide spread of shot. The phrase 'a whiff of grapeshot' occurs in Carlyle's *History of the French Revolution* (I, v (1837)) and refers to the ease with which NAPOLEON BONAPARTE and his artillery dispersed the Paris insurrection of VENDÉMIAIRE, 1795.

**Grapevine, The.** Somewhat the same as the BUSH TELEGRAPH, the mysterious means and covert whisperings by which information, rumours, gossip and the like are spread around.

**Fox and Grapes.** *See under* FOX.

**Sour grapes.** *See under* SOUR.

**Grasp. Grasp the nettle, To.** To face up firmly to a difficulty, to tackle a situation boldly. A nettle is less likely to sting when grasped firmly, as the lines written by the English poet Aaron Hill (1685–1750) tell:

> Tender-handed stroke a nettle,
> And it stings you for your pains;
> Grasp it like a man of mettle,
> And it soft as silk remains.

**Within one's grasp.** *See under* WITHIN.

**Grass.** An old name for spring or early summer, the time when the grass grows.

> She is five years old this grass.
>
> MISS MITFORD: *Our Village*, 'The Copse' (1819)

It is also the name given to the dried leaves and flowers of the cannabis plant or hemp, also called marijuana. *See also* HASH.

In criminal slang 'to grass' is to inform, from RHYMING SLANG 'grasshopper' for COPPER. The particular reference was to a plain-clothes officer who 'hopped' from one criminal haunt to another with the aim of gathering intelligence. A supergrass is one who informs on a number of his associates.

**Grass roots.** An expression referring to that which is rooted in the earth, i.e. that which has its origins among the common folk. Hence 'at grass-roots level' alludes to the ordinary voters in an election or to rank-and-file party members.

**Grass widow.** Formerly, an unmarried woman who has had a child. The origin of the term is uncertain but 'grass' here may be the equivalent of 'bed', 'place of love-making'. *See also* BASTARD; ROLL IN THE HAY.

It now implies a wife temporarily parted from her husband, and in this sense it became current again in the days of British rule in India. The term was equally applicable, since in the heat of high summer the wives and children of colonial officials were sent to the hills where the climate was cooler and the grass still grew.

**Dog grass.** *See under* DOG.

**Not to let the grass grow under one's feet.** *See under* LET.

**Put out to grass.** Properly, turned into a pasture, as of a horse at the end of its working life. Hence, spoken of a retired person.

**Snake in the grass, A.** *See under* SNAKE.

**Grasshopper.** The grasshoppers on London signboards of goldsmiths, bankers and others commemorated the crest of Sir Thomas Gresham (1519–79), founder of the ROYAL EXCHANGE, the original building being decorated with stone grasshoppers.

**Gratis. Free, gratis and for nothing.** *See under* FREE.

**Grattan's Parliament.** The free Irish Parliament at Dublin between 1782 and 1800, so named after Henry Grattan (1746–1820), who obtained the repeal of Poynings' Law and the Declaratory Act of 1719, thereby theoretically abolishing English control. It came to an end with the ACT OF UNION (1800), which was a result of English bribery and influence.

**Grave.** Solemn, sedate and serious in look and manner. The word is Latin *gravis*, 'heavy', 'grave', but 'grave' as a burial place is from Old English *græf*, 'pit', 'trench'.

**Graveyard shift.** In the Second World War the name given by shift workers in munitions factories and other workplaces to the shift covering the midnight hours. The allusion is perhaps to the watchmen who at one time patrolled the graves of the wealthy in order to deter grave robbers.

**As silent as the grave.** *See under* AS.

**Early grave.** *See under* EARLY.

**Have one foot in the grave, To.** *See under* ONE.

**Someone is walking over my grave.** *See under* SOMEONE.

**Turn** or **spin in one's grave, To.** *See under* TURN.

**Gray. Gray's Inn.** One of the four INNS OF COURT, and formerly the residence of the de Greys, a family that, in the 13th century, had high-ranking legal associations. After the death of the 1st Lord Grey de Wilton (1308) the property was vacated, and at some time in the 14th century it was occupied by the Society of Gray's Inn. In 1594 Shakespeare's *Comedy of Errors* was first acted in the hall of Gray's Inn and the walks and gardens were laid out by Francis Bacon (1561–1626). The library, containing some 30,000 volumes and manuscripts, and the original hall were destroyed in the air raids of 1940–41.

**Bessie Bell and Mary Gray.** *See under* BESS.

**Grease. Grease monkey.** A motor or aircraft mechanic.

**Grease someone's palm, To.** To bribe them.

> Grease my fist with a tester or two, and ye shall find it in your pennyworth.
>
> FRANCIS QUARLES: *The Virgin Widow*, IV, i (1649)

**Axle grease.** *See under* AXLE.

**Elbow grease.** *See under* ELBOW.

**Like greased lightning.** *See under* LIKE.

**Great, The.** The term is usually applied to the following:

Abbas I, shah of Persia (1571–1629)
Albertus Magnus, the Schoolman (1206–80)
Alexander of Macedon (356–323 BC)
Alfonso III, king of Asturias and León (838–910)
Alfred of England (849–899)
St Basil, bishop of Caesarea (4th century)
CANUTE of England and Denmark (995–1035)
Casimir III of Poland (1310–70)
Catherine II, empress of Russia (1729–96)
Charles, king of the Franks and emperor of the Romans, called CHARLEMAGNE (742–814)
Charles III, Duke of Lorraine (1543–1608)
Charles Emmanuel I, Duke of Savoy (1562–1630)
Clovis, king of the Franks (465–511)
Condé, *see* Louis II
Constantine I, emperor of Rome (*c*.288–337)
Cyrus, founder of the Persian Empire (559–529 BC)
Darius, king of Persia (548–486 BC)
Douglas, Archibald, the great Earl of Angus, also called BELL-THE-CAT (*c*.1449–1514)
Ferdinand I of Castile and León (r.1028–65)
Frederick William, elector of Brandenburg, surnamed the Great Elector (1620–88)
Frederick II of Prussia (1712–86)
Gregory I, pope (540–604)
Gustavus Adolphus of Sweden (1594–1632)
Henri IV of France (1553–1610)
Herod, king of Judea (*c*.73–44 BC)
John I of Portugal (1357–1433)
Justinian I, emperor of the East (483–565)
Leo I, pope (440–461)
Leo I, emperor of the East (400–474)
Leopold I of Germany (1640–1705)
Lewis I of Hungary (1326–82)
Louis II, de Bourbon, Duc d'Enghien, prince of Condé (1621–86), always known as the Great Condé
Louis XIV, called Le GRAND MONARQUE (1638–1715)
Maximilian, Duke of Bavaria, victor of Prague (1573–1651)
Cosmo de Medici, 1st Grand Duke of Tuscany (1519–74)
Gonzales Pedro de Mendoza, great cardinal of Spain, statesman and scholar (1428–95)
Mohammed II, sultan of the Turks (1430–81)
NAPOLEON I, emperor of the French (1769–1815)
Nicholas I, pope (858–867)
Otho I, emperor of the Romans (912–973)
Peter I, tsar of Russia (1672–1725)
Pierre III of Aragon (1239–85)
Sancho III, king of Navarre (*c*.970–1035)
Shapur II, king of Persia from birth (310–379)
Sigismund II, king of Poland (1467–1548)
THEODORIC, king of the Ostrogoths (*c*.454–526)
Theodosius I, emperor (346–395)
Matteo Visconti, Lord of Milan (1255–1322)
Vladimir, Grand Duke of Russia (*c*.956–1015)
Waldemar I of Denmark (1131–82)

**Great and the good, The.** Those who are distinguished and worthy. The term is frequently used ironically.

> Great and good is the typical Don, and of evil and wrong the foe,
> Good, and great, I'm a Don myself, and therefore I ought to know.
>
> A.D. GODLEY: 'The Megalopsychiad' (1904)

**Great Bear and Little Bear, The.** These constellations were so named by the Greeks, and their word, *arktos*, 'bear', is preserved in the names Arcturus and ARCTIC. *See also* CHARLES'S WAIN; NORTHERN WAGONER.

**Great Bed of Ware, The.** A fourposter bed 11ft (3.3m) square and capable of holding 12 people. It dates from the late 16th century and was formerly at the Saracen's Head Inn, Ware, Hertfordshire, but in 1931 it passed to the Victoria & Albert Museum, London.

> Although the sheet were big enough for the bed of Ware in England.
>
> SHAKESPEARE: *Twelfth Night*, III, ii (1599)

**Great Bible, The.** *See under* BIBLE.
**Great Bullet-head, The.** Georges Cadoudal (1771–1804), a leader of the CHOUANS.
**Great Captain, The.** *See* GRAN CAPITÁN.
**Great Cham of Literature, The.** An epithet applied to Samuel Johnson (1709–84) by Tobias Smollett. 'Cham' is a French form of KHAN.
**Great Charter, The.** *See under* MAGNA CARTA.
**Great circle.** Any circle on the surface of a sphere which lies on a plane through its centre, or any circle which divides it into two equal parts. The great circle is of major importance in navigation by sea or in the air. The shortest distance between any two points on the earth's surface is on a great circle. The Equator and all lines of longitude are great circles.
**Great Commoner, The.** William Pitt the Elder (1708–78), 1st Earl of Chatham, so nicknamed for his great eloquence in the House of Commons.
**Great Council.** The *Magnum Concilium* of the Norman kings and their successors, the assembly of tenants-in-chief meeting at regular intervals with the king and his principal officers for consultation. It was the *curia regis* from which governmental, legal and political institutions derived.
**Great cry and little wool.** A proverbial equivalent expressive of contempt for someone who promises great things but never fulfils the promises, otherwise 'all talk and no do'. Originally the proverb ran: 'Great cry and little wool, as the Devil said when he sheared the hogs.' It appears in this form in the ancient MYSTERY PLAY of *David and Abigail*, in which Nabal is represented as shearing his sheep and the Devil imitates him by shearing a hog.
**Great Dauphin, The.** *See* GRAND DAUPHIN.
**Great Divide, The.** The boundary between life and death.
**Great Duke, The.** The Duke of Wellington (1769–1852), the victor at the Battle of Waterloo, who was also called the IRON DUKE.
**Great Elector, The.** Frederick William, elector of Brandenburg (1620–88), who left for his successors a position in Germany next in importance to that of Austria.
**Greatest lie, The.** In John Heywood's *The Four P's* (*c.*1540) a Palmer, a Pardoner, a Potticary [apothecary] and a Pedlar disputed as to which could tell the greatest lie. The Palmer said he had never seen a woman out of patience, whereupon the other three threw up the sponge, saying such falsehood could not possibly be outdone. *See also* FOUR PP.
**Greatest Show on Earth, The.** The name of the gigantic travelling combination of circus, menagerie and collection of human freaks in the USA, displayed by the American showman Phineas T. Barnum (1810–91) and his partners in 1871. In 1842 Barnum had exhibited General TOM THUMB and in 1850 had toured America with the SWEDISH NIGHTINGALE. He had a varied career of success and failure but the Greatest Show again made his fortune and that of his partner Bailey. In 1889 the show was presented at the London OLYMPIA.
**Great Exhibition, The.** The Exhibition of 1851, largely inspired by the Prince Consort and housed in the CRYSTAL PALACE, Hyde Park, London.

There were over 13,000 exhibitors in the four classes: raw materials, machinery, manufacturers and fine arts. It was a conspicuous success and the profits were mainly used for educational foundations at South Kensington. Its centenary was celebrated by another Exhibition on the South Bank in 1951.
**Great Fire of London, The.** The fire that broke out in the early hours of Sunday, 2 September 1666 at Master Farryner's bakehouse in Pudding Lane, Thames Street. Aided by high winds it spread from the TOWER OF LONDON to the TEMPLE BAR and from the THAMES to SMITHFIELD. St Paul's Cathedral and 87 other churches were destroyed and 13,200 houses. In five days the fire covered 387 acres within the city walls and 63 without. It was not the reason for the disappearance of the Plague, as is commonly held, since most of the slum quarters escaped. The fire was halted by blowing up houses at Pie Corner, Smithfield. A Frenchman, Robert Hubert, confessed to setting fire to the bakehouse and was hanged at TYBURN.
**Great fleas have lesser fleas.** No matter what our station in life, we all have some hangers-on.

> So, naturalists observe, a flea
> Hath smaller fleas that on him prey;
> And these have smaller fleas to bite 'em,
> And so proceed *ad infinitum*.
> JONATHAN SWIFT: 'On Poetry' (1733)

**Great gulf fixed, A.** An irreconcilable separation. The allusion is to the parable of DIVES and LAZARUS (Luke 16:26).
**Great Harry.** The name popularly given to the famous warship *Henry Grâce à Dieu* built at Erith and launched in 1514. With a displacement of about 1000 tons, the vessel had five masts and 21 guns as well as a multitude of small pieces.
**Great Head, The.** Malcolm III of Scotland (r.1057–93), also called Canmore (Gaelic *Ceannmor*, 'Great Head').
**Great** or **Long hundred.** Six score, 120.
**Great is Diana of the Ephesians.** A phrase sometimes used to signify that self-interest blinds the eyes, from the story of Demetrius, the Ephesian silversmith in Acts 19:24–28, who made shrines for the temple of DIANA. Demetrius

stirred the people to riot, claiming that: 'this Paul hath persuaded and turned away much people, saying that they be no gods, which are made with hands: so that not only this our craft is in danger to be set at nought; but also that the temple of the great goddess Diana should be despised, and her magnificence should be destroyed.' Hence their cry 'Great is Diana of the Ephesians'. *See also* DIANA OF EPHESUS.

**Great Lakes, The.** Lakes Erie, Huron, Michigan, Ontario and Superior, on the borders of Canada and the USA.

**Great Magician** or **Wizard of the North, The.** Professor John Wilson ('Christopher North') gave Sir Walter Scott the name because of the wonderful fascination of his writings.

**Great majority, The.** One of many euphemisms for the dead. The words usually occur in a phrase such as 'to join the majority', as which it renders Latin *abiit ad plures*, 'He passed to the majority'.

**Great Mogul.** *See* MOGUL.

**Great Peter.** A bell in York Minster, weighing $10\frac{3}{4}$ tons and hung in 1845.

**Great Piazza Coffee House.** A flourishing COFFEE house at the northeast angle of the COVENT GARDEN piazza opened in 1756, previously (1754–6) known as Macklin's. It was here that, in 1809, Sheridan watched the fire at the DRURY LANE Theatre saying: 'A man may surely be allowed to take a glass of wine at his own fireside.' It became a hotel in 1840 and was pulled down to make way for the Floral Hall in 1865.

**Great Plague, The.** The last occurrence (1665–6) of the bubonic plague, which had frequently erupted in various localities since the BLACK DEATH but less disastrously. Outbreaks were particularly bad in London in 1603, 1625 and 1636, doubtless due to growing congestion. The outbreak of 1625 was known as the Great Plague until it was overshadowed by that of 1665. Deaths in London are estimated at *c.*100,000, but the lord mayor remained at his post. *See also* GREAT FIRE OF LONDON.

**Great Plains, The.** The area east of the Rocky Mountains from the border of Canada to the mouth of the River Arkansas.

**Great primer.** A large-sized type, rather smaller than 18 point, $4\frac{1}{4}$ lines to the inch.

**Great** or **Major Prophets, The.** ISAIAH, JEREMIAH, EZEKIEL and DANIEL, so called because their writings are more extensive than the prophecies of the other twelve.

**Great Rebellion, The.** In English history the period of the Civil Wars (1642–51), the time of the rebellion against CHARLES I. *See also* RESTORATION; FORTY-FIVE.

**Greats.** The colloquial name of the final school of *Literae Humaniores* (Latin, 'the more humane studies'), the honours course at Oxford in classics, philosophy and ancient history. *See also* HUMANITIES; SMALLS.

**Great Schism, The.** The split in the CATHOLIC CHURCH when there were rival popes at Avignon and Rome. It began in 1378 and ended in 1417. After the death of Gregory XI, the last of the AVIGNON POPES proper, Urban VI (1378–89) alienated the French cardinals and their adherents, and they established an antipope, Clement VII, at Anagni. Clement soon retired to Avignon with his supporters, where the antipope remained until the schism ended.

**Great Scott!** An exclamation of surprise, wonder, admiration or the like. It seems to have originated in America in the late 1860s, and possibly evoked General Winfield Scott (1786–1866), a popular figure after his victorious Mexican campaign of 1847. More likely, it is simply a euphemism for 'Great God!'

**Great Seal, The.** The chief seal of the Sovereign used to authenticate important state documents. It is always round in shape and one side shows the sovereign crowned and enthroned (i.e. in majesty) and the other the sovereign mounted. The seal is kept by the LORD CHANCELLOR. *See also* E PLURIBUS UNUM.

**Great snakes!** An exclamation of surprise.

**Great Spirit, The.** *See* MANITOU.

**Great Synagogue, The.** According to Jewish tradition, a body of 120 men in the time of Ezra and NEHEMIAH (5th century BC) who were engaged in remodelling the religious life of the Jews after the return from exile and in establishing the text and canon of the Hebrew Scriptures.

**Great Tom of Lincoln.** A bell at Lincoln Cathedral weighing 5 tons 12 cwt.

**Great Tom of Oxford.** A bell in TOM GATE Tower, Oxford, tolled 101 times every night at 9.05 to signify the original number of scholars at Christ Church. It weighs 7.5 tonnes and is celebrated in the old round:

> Great Tom is cast
> And Christ Church bells ring one
> Two, three, four, five, six
> And Tom comes last.

**Great Trek, The.** The exodus of some fifth part of the Boers from Cape Colony from 1835 into the 1840s, leading to the establishment of Transvaal and the Orange Free State across the Vaal and Orange rivers and to the British control of Natal in 1843. The direct cause of the emigration was the Abolition of Slavery Act 1833, since it was on slave labour that the economy of the Boers largely depended.

**Great Unknown, The.** Sir Walter Scott, who published *Waverley* (1814) and the subsequent novels anonymously as 'by the author of Waverley'. He was first so called by his publisher,

James Ballantyne. It was not until 1827 that he admitted the authorship, although it was then well known.

**Great Unwashed, The.** Usually a derogatory reference to the lower classes of former days.

> There are individuals still alive who sneer at the people and speak of them with epithets of scorn. Gentlemen, there can be but little doubt that your ancestors were the Great Unwashed.
>
> W.M. THACKERAY: *Pendennis*, ch xxix (1848–50)

**Great Wall of China.** One of the greatest constructions ever realized, the Great Wall of China extends overall some 4000 miles (6400km) westwards from Po Hai, on the Yellow Sea. Parts of it date from the 4th century BC, and its prime aim was to serve as a defensive barrier against the incursions of the Hsiung-nu, the nomadic tribes of the Mongolian steppes. It was substantially rebuilt in the 15th and 16th centuries, and is generally about 30ft (9m) high with periodic towers at intervals of roughly 1000 yards (914m) that are about 40ft (12m) high. At its western end it is now little more than a huge bank of mud, although its main length is faced with brick. *See also* CHINESE WALL *under* CHINESE.

**Great War, The.** The war of 1914–18 was so called until that of 1939–45, when the term First World War largely replaced it, the latter becoming the Second World War.

**Great Wen, The.** *See* WEN.

**Great White Way, The.** A once popular name for BROADWAY, New York City, so called because of its abundance of electric signs used for advertising.

**Great Wizard of the North, The.** *See* GREAT MAGICIAN.

**Frederick the Great.** *See under* FREDERICK.

**Gregory the Great.** *See under* GREGORY.

**No great shakes.** Nothing extraordinary or particularly clever; not very good. The expression is said to derive from gambling with dice, but Admiral Smyth's *Sailor's Word-Book* (1867) says it comes from 'shaking a cask', which is to dismantle it and pick up the staves or shakes, a condition in which it has little value.

**St James the Great.** *See under* JAMES.

**Ten Great Persecutions, The.** *See under* TEN.

**Grecian.** A senior boy of Christ's Hospital, the BLUECOAT SCHOOL, so called because he is or was a Greek scholar.

**Grecian bend.** An affectation in walking with the body stooped slightly forward, assumed by some Englishwomen in the mid-19th century. The allusion is to the inclined figures on ancient Greek vases. *See also* ALEXANDRA LIMP.

**Grecian Coffee House.** The COFFEE house in Devereux Court, Essex Street, London, was possibly named after one Constantine, a Greek who opened one in Essex Buildings in 1681, but there is no written record of the Grecian until the reign of Anne (1709), and they were not necessarily connected. It is mentioned by Steele in the *Tatler* and by Addison in the *Spectator*. There was also a Grecian Coffee House in King Street, Covent Garden in 1673, and it was possibly older than that in Devereux Court, which closed in 1843.

**Grecian nose** or **profile, A.** One where the line of the nose continues that of the forehead without a dip, as represented on some ancient Greek statues.

**Greco, El** (Spanish, 'the Greek'). Domenikos Theotokopoulos (1541–1614), a Cretan, who studied under Titian and MICHELANGELO, and moved to Spain *c.*1570. He was the foremost 16th-century painter of the Castilian school.

**Greece. Amadis of Greece.** *See under* AMADIS.

**Wise men of Greece, The.** *See under* WISE.

**Wisest man of Greece, The.** *See under* WISE.

**Greek. Greek Anthology, The.** A 19th-century edition of Greek epigrammatic poetry, based on the 10th-century *Anthology* of Cephalas of Constantinople, which was rearranged by Maximus Planudes in 1301 and first published at Florence in 1494. The work of Cephalas incorporated the *Garland* of Meleager (1st century BC), the *Garland* of Philippus (1st century AD) and the *Circle* of Agathias (6th century). Planudes' text was superseded by the Palatine manuscript when the *Anthology* of Cephalas was discovered in the Count Palatine's Library at Heidelberg in 1606.

> The Greek Anthology is one of the great books of European literature, a garden containing the flowers and weeds of fifteen hundred years of Greek poetry, from the most humdrum doggerel to the purest poetry.
>
> PROFESSOR A.D.C. CAMERON in *The Oxford Classical Dictionary* (1996)

**Greek Calends.** Never. To defer something to the Greek CALENDS is to defer it indefinitely. There were no Calends in the Greek calendar. *See also* NEVER.

**Greek Church.** A name often given to the Eastern or ORTHODOX CHURCH, of which the Greek Church proper is an autocephalous unit, recognized as independent by the Patriarch of Constantinople in 1850.

**Greek cross.** *See under* CROSS.

**Greek fire.** A combination of nitre, sulphur and naphtha used for setting fire to ships, fortifications and the like. Blazing tow steeped in the mixture was hurled through tubes or fired tied to arrows. The invention is ascribed to Callinicus of Heliopolis, AD 668.

**Greek gift.** A treacherous gift. The reference is to the WOODEN HORSE OF TROY or to VIRGIL's *Timeo Danaos et dona ferentes* ('I fear the Greeks, even when they offer gifts' (*Aeneid*, ii (1st century BC)).

**Greeks had a word for it, The.** Said of something unmentionable. The phrase has its origin in the title of Zoë Akins' play produced on Broadway in 1929. This was based on the antics of the *hetairai* ('companions'), the women of Greece, whether slave, freed or foreign, who were paid for sexual favours.

**All Greek to me.** *See under* ALL.

**Father of Greek Drama, The.** *See under* FATHER.

**Father of Greek Music, The.** *See under* FATHER.

**Father of Greek Tragedy, The.** *See under* FATHER.

**Last of the Greeks, The.** *See under* LAST.

**When Greek meets Greek.** *See under* WHEN.

**Green.** Young, fresh; or a 'green old age', an old age in which the faculties are not impaired and the spirits are still youthful. Hence, immature in age or judgement, inexperienced; also simple, raw, easily imposed upon, as a characteristic GREENHORN. *See also* SALAD DAYS.

> 'He is so jolly green,' said Charley.
> DICKENS: *Oliver Twist*, ch ix (1837–8)

For its symbolism *see* COLOURS.

**Greenbacks.** Legal tender notes first issued in the United States in 1862, during the Civil War (1861–5), as a war-revenue expedient. They were so called because the back was printed in green. The name is now applied to paper currency issued by any national American bank.

**Green belt.** A stretch of country around a large urban area that has been scheduled for comparative preservation and where building development is restricted.

**Green Berets.** A nickname for British or US commandos.

**Green cheese.** Unripe cheese, or cheese that is eaten fresh, like cream cheese, and not kept to mature.

**Green Cross Code.** A code of road safety for children, first published in 1971 and now included in *The Highway Code* as a guide to crossing the road for all pedestrians.

**Green Dragoons, The.** *See under* REGIMENTAL AND DIVISIONAL NICKNAMES.

**Green eye.** A jealous or envious eye. Jealousy is figuratively described as a GREEN-EYED MONSTER.

**Green-eyed monster, The.** So Shakespeare called jealousy:

> *Iago*: O! beware, my lord, of jealousy;
> It is the green-ey'd monster which doth mock
> The meat it feeds on.
> *Othello*, III, iii (1604)

A greenish complexion was formerly held to be indicative of jealousy, and as all the green-eyed cat family 'mock the meat they feed on', so jealousy mocks its victim by loving and loathing it at the same time. *See also* GREEN WITH ENVY.

**Green fingers.** Said of a successful gardener.

**Green flag.** Used on railways, roads and so on for signalling 'Go ahead'.

**Greengage.** A variety of plum introduced into England in about 1725 from France by Sir William Gage (1657–1727) of Hengrave Hall, Bury St Edmunds, Suffolk, and named in his honour. The French know the fruit as *reine-claude* by way of compliment to the first wife of Francis I, daughter of Anne of Brittany and Louis XII. She became queen in 1515, on her husband's accession, and died in 1524, worn out by repeated child-bearing.

**Greenhorn.** A novice at anything. The allusion is to the 'green horns' of a young horned animal. *See also* GREEN.

**Greenhouse effect.** Literally, an effect occurring in greenhouses in which radiant heat from the sun passes through the glass and, trapped inside by the glass, warms the contents. The term came to apply to an analogous effect on the Earth's atmosphere in which carbon dioxide and other gases in the atmosphere absorb the infrared radiation emitted by the Earth's surface through being exposed to solar ultraviolet radiation. As a result, the Earth's mean temperature rises.

**Green Howards, The.** *See under* REGIMENTAL AND DIVISIONAL NICKNAMES.

**Green Isle, The.** Ireland. *See also* EMERALD ISLE.

**Green Linnets, The.** *See under* REGIMENTAL AND DIVISIONAL NICKNAMES.

**Greenmail.** The stock market practice in which a company buys enough shares in another company to threaten a takeover, so forcing the threatened company to buy them back at a higher price in order to retain control of the business. The term is a variant of BLACKMAIL, with 'green' here in the sense of money, as in GREENBACKS.

**Green Man.** This common PUBLIC HOUSE SIGN probably represents either a JACK-IN-THE-GREEN or a forester, who, like ROBIN HOOD, was once clad in green.

> But the 'Green Man' shall I pass by unsung,
> Which mine own James upon his sign-post hung?
> His sign, his image – for he once was seen
> A squire's attendant, clad in keeper's green.
> GEORGE CRABBE: *The Borough* (1810)

The public house sign the Green Man and Still is probably a modification of the arms of the Distillers' Company, the supporters of which were two Indians, for whom the sign painters usually substituted foresters or green men drinking out of a glass barrel.

Green Men are most tellingly to be found in the foliated stonework and ornamental wood carving of medieval churches throughout Europe. Their heads are wreathed in foliage, which is often shown growing from their mouths, eyes, ears and nostrils. This Green Man is believed to be a Celtic symbol of creative fertility in nature. In Christian terms, he is a symbol of EASTER and the Resurrection, and is usually depicted as a gentle and benevolent deity. Kathleen Basford, in her key work on the subject, *The Green Man* (1978), rejects this idea, and sees him as a demon or even the Devil himself. Kingsley Amis's novel *The Green Man* (1969) evokes a similarly sinister figure. Representations of Green Men exist in the parish churches of Crowcombe and Withycombe, both in Somerset.

To young children 'the green man' is the illuminated symbol of a human figure at a pedestrian crossing, indicating it is time to cross. *See also* GREEN CROSS CODE; LITTLE GREEN MEN.

**Green Mountain Boys.** Vermont (*Vert Mont*) is called the Green Mountain State from the evergreen forests on its mountains. The Green Mountain Boys were organized on a military basis under Ethan Allen (1738–89) when the settlers of the area found their titles to land in dispute between New York and New Hampshire. From 1775 they fought successfully in the American Revolution and Vermont declared itself an independent state in 1777.

**Green Paper.** In parliamentary parlance, a command paper containing policy proposals for discussion in the House. When the proposals have been discussed by all the parties concerned, they are published as a WHITE PAPER. This in turn usually leads to the introduction of a BILL, and finally to an ACT OF PARLIAMENT. An example is the Green Paper introduced by the Home Secretary after the Southall riots of 1979. This led in 1985 to a White Paper called 'The Review of Public Order', which in turn led to the introduction of the Public Order Bill and Act of 1986. The Green Paper is so called for the colour of its cover.

**Green Party.** In Britain a political party founded in 1973 after the publication of *Blueprint for Survival*, a work issued by the editors of the *Ecologist* magazine by way of offering radical solutions to environmental problems. The party was known as the Ecology Party until 1985. Despite the importance attached to environmental issues, the party has made only a minimal impact on the political scene. It fielded 95 candidates in the 1997 GENERAL ELECTION and polled 63,991 votes, just 0.2 per cent of the total.

**Greenpeace.** A movement originating in Canada in 1971, aiming to persuade governments to change industrial activities that threaten natural resources and the environment. It supports direct non-violent action and has gained wide attention by its efforts to protect whales and to prevent the killing of young seals. When acting against French nuclear tests in the South Pacific in 1985, its ship *Rainbow Warrior* was sunk by a French saboteur. *See also* FRIENDS OF THE EARTH.

**Green Ribbon Day.** In Ireland this is 17 March, St PATRICK's Day, when the SHAMROCK and green ribbon are worn as the national badge.

**Greenroom.** In a theatre the common waiting room for the performers near the stage. Originally such rooms were painted green to relieve the eyes from the glare of the stage.

**Greenshirt.** A supporter of the Social Credit Movement established in England by Major Douglas in the 1920s, and so named from the green uniform shirt adopted.

**Green sickness.** The old name for chlorosis, a form of anaemia once common in adolescent girls. It was characterized by a greenish pallor.

**Greensleeves.** A popular ballad in the time of Elizabeth I, published in 1581, given in Clement Robinson's *Handefull of Pleasant Delites* (1584) and mentioned by Shakespeare (*Merry Wives of Windsor*, II, i, and V, v (1600)). The air is of the same period and was used for many ballads. During the Civil Wars (1642–51) it was used by the CAVALIERS as a tune for political ballads, and Pepys (23 April 1660) mentions it under the title of *The Blacksmith*. It includes the following lines:

> Greensleeves was all my joy,
> Greensleeves was my delight,
> Greensleeves was my heart of gold,
> And who but Lady Greensleeves?

**Green wellies.** Green WELLINGTON boots, as typically worn by SLOANE RANGERS, or those members of the upper classes who practise the country sports of 'HUNTING, SHOOTING AND FISHING'.

**Green with envy, To be.** To be jealous or covetous of someone's achievements, attainments, wealth and so forth. Literally, to have one's face acquire a pale greenish hue as a result of envy. *See also* GREEN-EYED MONSTER.

**As green as grass.** *See under* AS.

**Board of Green Cloth, The.** *See under* BOARD.

**Fiddler's Green.** *See under* FIDDLE.

**Get the green light, To.** To get permission to proceed with an undertaking, green being the 'Go' sign on road and rail signals.

**Golders Green.** *See under* GOLDERS.

**Kendal green.** *See under* KENDAL.

**Lincoln green.** *See under* LINCOLN.

**Little green men.** *See under* LITTLE.

**Paris green.** *See under* PARIS.

**Rub of the green, The.** *See under* RUB.

**Verdant Green.** *See under* VERDANT.

**Wearing of the green, The.** *See under* WEAR.

**Wigs on the green.** *See under* WIG.

**Greenham Common.** A village near Newbury, Berkshire, that was the site of a United States cruise missile base and that from 1981 until its closure in 1991 was the focal point of a camp of 'peace women' protesting against nuclear weapons. The 'green' name was coincidentally fitting for the stance.

**Greenlander.** A native of Greenland, discovered by Eric the Red of Iceland in 982 and reputedly called Greenland 'for he said it would make men's minds long to go there if it had a fine name'. The name was actually not inappropriate for the point where he landed, a smooth grassy plain at the head of the Igaliku fjord, near the modern settlement of Julianehåb (Qaqortoq), at a latitude equal to that of the Shetland Islands. For the ice-clad country as a whole, however, it is a clear misnomer.

**Greenwich. Greenwich barbers.** Retailers of sand; so called because the inhabitants of Greenwich used to 'shave the pits' in the neighbourhood to supply London.

**Greenwich Time** or **Greenwich Mean Time.** The local time for the 0° meridian that passes through Greenwich. It is the standard time for Britain and a former basis for determining the time in most other countries of the world. In 1928 Greenwich Mean Time was officially redesignated Universal Time. *See also* MERIDEN; STANDARD TIME; SUMMER TIME.

**Greenwich Village.** The residential area of lower Manhattan, New York, gained a reputation from the early years of the 20th century for its bohemianism, and became established as a meeting-place of unconventional writers, artists and musicians, especially members of the BEAT GENERATION and of students generally. In more recent times it has lost much of its sense of creative originality, although its alternative lifestyle continues to be represented in that of its gay community. Many New Yorkers now wax lyrical about 'the Village', with its former feel of excitement and vitality.

**Gregorian. Gregorian calendar.** A modification of the JULIAN CALENDAR, also called the New Style, introduced in 1582 by Pope Gregory XIII. *See also* CALENDAR; GREGORIAN YEAR.

**Gregorian chant.** Another name for plainsong, as the traditional ritual melody of the Christian church of the West, so called because it was reformed and elaborated by GREGORY THE GREAT at the end of the 6th century.

**Gregorian epoch.** The epoch or day on which the GREGORIAN CALENDAR commenced in October 1582. *See also* GREGORIAN YEAR.

**Gregorian telescope.** The first form of the reflecting telescope, invented in 1663 by James Gregory (1638–75), professor of mathematics at St Andrews.

**Gregorian year.** The civil year according to the correction introduced by Pope Gregory XIII in 1582. The equinox, which occurred on 25 March in the time of Julius Caesar, fell on 11 March in the year 1582. This was because the Julian calculation of 365¼ days to a year was 11 minutes 14 seconds too long. Gregory suppressed 10 days by altering 5 October to 15 October, thus making the equinox fall on 21 March 1583. Further simple arrangements prevented the recurrence of a similar error in the future. The change was soon adopted by most Roman Catholic countries, but the Protestant countries did not accept it until much later. The New Style was not adopted by England and Scotland until 1752. At the same time the beginning of the civil or legal year was altered from LADY DAY (25 March) to 1 January, a change adopted in Scotland in 1600. Sweden adopted the New Style calendar in 1753, Japan in 1873, China in 1912, Russia in 1918 and Greece in 1923. The GREGORIAN CALENDAR differs from the JULIAN CALENDAR in that no century year is a leap year unless it is exactly divisible by 400, e.g. 1600 and 2000. *See also* GIVE US BACK OUR ELEVEN DAYS *under* ELEVEN.

**Gregory the Great** or **St Gregory.** The first pope of this name and DOCTOR OF THE CHURCH (540–604). The outstanding figure of his age, notable for church and monastic reform, for dealing with heresies, for wise administration and for kindness to the poor. He also refashioned the liturgy of the church and made a lasting contribution to church music. He sent St AUGUSTINE on his mission to the Anglo-Saxons, thus earning the title of Apostle of England. *See also* GREGORIAN CHANT.

**Gremlin.** One of a number of imaginary GNOMES OR GOBLINS humorously blamed by the RAF in the Second World War for everything that went wrong in an aircraft or an operation. The name was probably coined at the end of the First World War or in the 1920s and was apparently in use on RAF stations in India and the Middle East in the 1930s. The name is first traced in print in *The Aeroplane* (10 April 1929). One explanation claims that a gremlin was the goblin that came out of Fremlin's beer bottles (Fremlin being a brewer in Kent), although there are numerous other origins, some more plausible than the rest.

**Grenadier.** Originally a soldier, picked for his stature, whose duty in battle was to throw grenades. In time each regiment had a special company of them, and when, in the 18th century, the use of grenades was discontinued (not to be revived until the First World War) the name was retained for the company composed of the tallest and finest men. In the British Army it now survives only in the Grenadier Guards, the First Regiment of Foot Guards, noted for their height, physique, traditions and discipline.

**First Grenadier of the Republic.** *See under* FIRST.

**Grendel.** The mythical half-human monster killed by BEOWULF. Grendel nightly raided the king's hall and slew the sleepers.

**Gresham, Sir Thomas.** *See* CLEOPATRA AND HER PEARL; GRASSHOPPER.

**Gresham's law.** The law is usually summarized by the statement that 'bad money drives out good'. It may be explained by the following instance. If two coins have the same nominal value, but one is made of pure metal (worth more) and one of impure (worth less), the cheaper coin will tend to drive the dearer out of circulation. The law was promulgated by Gresham to Elizabeth I in 1558, although it had been explained earlier by Copernicus.

**Dine with Sir Thomas Gresham, To.** *See* DINE WITH DUKE HUMPHREY.

**Greta Hall, The Poet of.** *See under* POET.

**Gretchen.** In Goethe's *Faust* (1808, 1832), the pure young maiden whom FAUST eventually seduces. Her song at the spinning-wheel, *Meine Ruh' ist hin, / Mein Herz ist schwer* ('My peace is gone, / My heart is heavy') is one of the most famous passages in all literature and has been set to music by a number of composers, most memorably by Schubert in *Gretchen am Spinnrade* ('Gretchen at the Spinning-Wheel') (1814). Gretchen ('Maggie') is also a stock name for any German girl.

**Gretel.** *See* HÄNSEL.

**Gretna Green marriages.** Runaway marriages. Elopers from England reaching Gretna, near Springfield, Dumfriesshire, 10 miles (16km) northwest of Carlisle, could (until 1856) get legally married without licence, banns or priest. All that was required was a declaration before witnesses of the couple's willingness to marry. This declaration was generally made to a blacksmith, landlord, toll-keeper or other local official. By an Act of 1856, residence in Scotland for at least 21 days by one of the parties became essential before a marriage was possible. Gretna Green's prominence arose from the abolition of Fleet Marriages (the clandestine marriage of minors) in 1753. Although marriage by declaration ceased to be legal in July 1940, Gretna Green and other places in Scotland continued to attract young couples because minors could still marry there without parental consent. Following the Act of 1969 that fixed the legal age of consent at 18, however, this no longer applies. Even so, many couples seek to be married at Gretna Green for the romantic associations.

**Grève, Place de.** *See under* PLACE.

**Grey. Grey area.** Generally, an area or situation where distinctions cannot be clearly made or rules precisely determined. In a more specific sense, a grey area is a region of relatively high unemployment, first so called in Britain in 1966. The official term for such a region is a development area. The description 'grey' may have owed something to maps of Britain showing such areas shaded grey.

**Greybeard.** An old man, especially a wise one. The word is also used for an earthenware or stoneware pot for holding spirits. *See also* BELLARMINE.

**Grey economy.** Commercial activity that is unaccounted for in official statistics. The term was based on the GREY MARKET.

**Grey Eminence** (French *Éminence grise*). The name given to François Joseph Leclerc du Tremblay (1577–1638), or Père Joseph, as he was called, the CAPUCHIN agent and trusty counsellor of Cardinal Richelieu. It was inspired by his influence over Cardinal Richelieu's policies. He was, as it were, a 'shadow' cardinal in the background. ('Your Eminence' is the title used to address a cardinal.) Hence any close adviser who exercises power behind the scenes. The French form of the term is often used in English.

> Many Americans will no doubt find it strange that Mr Menon ... whom they have come to regard as a sinister *éminence grise* standing between two countries, should choose to act as their ambassador.
> *The Times* (2 May 1955)

**Grey Friars.** *See* FRANCISCANS.

**Greyfriars Bobby.** A terrier who watched over the grave of his master (John Gray) in Greyfriars Kirkyard, Edinburgh, from 1852 to 1872. A drinking fountain surmounted by a statue of Bobby stands in nearby Candlemaker Row.

**Grey hen, A.** A stone bottle for holding liquor. Large and small pewter pots mixed together are called hens and chickens.

**Grey mare is the better horse, The.** The woman is paramount, she 'wears the trousers'. The expression was formerly used of a 'bossy' wife.

**Grey market.** In the Second World War a transaction regarded as a lesser breach of the rationing regulations than the BLACK MARKET. In STOCK EXCHANGE parlance, a grey market is a market in the shares of a new issue by investors who have applied for the shares but not actually received them. *See also* GREY ECONOMY.

**Grey matter.** A pseudoscientific name for the brain, used generally to mean common sense. The active part of the brain is composed of a greyish tissue, which contains the nerve endings.

**Greys, The.** *See under* REGIMENTAL AND DIVISIONAL NICKNAMES.

**Grey Sisters.** *See* FRANCISCANS.

**Greysteel.** The sword of Koll the Thrall.

**Earl Grey.** *See under* EARL.

**Earl of Mar's Grey Breeks, The.** *See under* REGIMENTAL AND DIVISIONAL NICKNAMES.

**Lady Jane Grey.** The granddaughter of Henry VII and daughter of Henry Grey, Marquess of Dorset, Lady Jane Grey (1537–54) was at 15 married against her will to Lord Guildford Dudley during the final illness of Edward VI as part of Dudley's father's scheme to ensure a Protestant succession. She was declared queen in 1553 three days after Edward's death but was forced to abdicate nine days later in favour of his sister, BLOODY MARY, and imprisoned in the TOWER OF LONDON. Following a rebellion in her favour, she and her husband were executed. *See also* NINE DAYS' QUEEN.

**Old grey whistle test, The.** *See under* OLD.

**Gridiron.** The emblem of St LAWRENCE of Rome. One legend says that he was roasted on a gridiron, another that he was bound to an iron chair and roasted alive. He was martyred in 258, under Valerian. *See also* ESCORIAL.

It is also the American term for a football playing field, from the fact that the field was marked with squares or grids.

**Gridironer.** An Australian settler who bought land in strips like the bars of a gridiron, so that the land lying between was of little use and could be acquired later at a bargain price.

**Goose and Gridiron.** *See under* GOOSE.

**Grief, To come to.** *See under* COME.

**Griffin** (Old French *grifon*, from Latin *gryphus*, from Greek *grups*, from *grupos*, 'hooked'). A mythical monster, also called Griffon or Gryphon, fabled to be the offspring of the lion and the EAGLE. Its legs and all its body from the shoulders to the head are those of an eagle, while the rest of its body is that of a lion. This creature was sacred to the sun and kept guard over hidden treasures. *See also* ARIMASPIANS.

> [The Griffin is] an Emblem of valour and magnanimity, as being compounded of the Eagle and the Lion, the noblest Animals in their kinds; and so is it applicable unto Princes, Presidents, Generals, and all heroik Commanders; and so is it also born in the Coat-arms of many noble Families of Europe.
>
> SIR THOMAS BROWNE: *Pseudodoxia Epidemica*, III, xi (1646)

**Griffon.** A small, rough-haired terrier used in France for hunting. It is difficult to see why the dog was so named, since it has a monkey-like head. Possibly the namer of the breed had a fanciful idea of what a GRIFFIN looked like.

**Grig.** A grig is a young eel, a cricket (or grasshopper) or short-legged hen. The second sense presumably gave the phrase 'as merry as a grig' for a lively person, with 'grig' influenced by its similarity to 'cricket'. The word itself originally meant DWARF and is probably of Scandinavian origin.

**Grildrig.** The name given to GULLIVER by GLUMDALCLITCH on taking charge of him in BROBDINGNAG in Swift's *Gulliver's Travels* (1726). The name has been decoded by P.O. Clark as 'girl thing', i.e. doll, although derivations have also been proposed from Irish *grileag*, 'any small matter', 'a small potato' or Latin *gryllus*, 'grasshopper', this taking *-drig* as a diminutive suffix. Swift himself writes: 'The Word imports what the *Latins* call *Nanunculus*, the *Italians Homunceletino*, and the *English Mannikin*' (Pt II, ch ii).

**Grim. Grim Reaper, The.** Death, often depicted, like Time, with a scythe.

**Like grim death.** See under LIKE.

**Grimaldi, Joseph.** The most celebrated and irresistible clown of English PANTOMIME (1779–1837) was born at London, the son of an Italian actor. He appeared at Drury Lane theatre before he was two years old and at Sadler's Wells at the age of three. He was forced to retire in 1828, worn out by continuous overwork. He dressed in what became the traditional clown costume and the name 'Joey the clown' attests his popularity and importance.

**Grimalkin.** An old she-cat, especially a wicked or eerie-looking one, from grey and MALKIN. In Shakespeare's *Macbeth* (I, i (1605)) a Witch says 'I come, Graymalkin'. The cat was supposed to be a witch.

**Grimm's law.** The law of correspondence of consonants between the Germanic languages and other Indoeuropean languages. It was first comprehensively formulated by Jakob L. Grimm (1785–1863), the German philologist, in 1822. Thus what is p in Greek, Latin or Sanskrit, becomes f in Gothic and b or f in the Old High German, and what is t in Greek, Latin or Sanskrit, becomes th in Gothic and d in Old High German. Thus changing p into f, and t into th, Greek and Latin *pater* becomes German *Vater* and English 'father'. Certain exceptions to Grimm's Law have been noted by more recent philologists.

**Grimsdyke.** A name commonly found for an ancient earthwork or wall. Examples are Grim's Dyke (or DEVIL'S DYKE), near Wallingford, south Oxfordshire, and Grim's Ditch, between Salisbury and Blandford, south Wiltshire. The name is that of Grímr, literally 'masked person', as an Old Norse byname of ODIN, who had a habit of appearing in disguise. Old English *grīma* also meant 'mask', and the Anglo-Saxons would have used the name in the same way, equating it with that of WODEN (*see also* WANSDYKE). From the 16th century such earthworks were associated with the Devil, with whom Woden had long been popularly linked. In similar manner Scotland has Graham's Dyke, as a popular name for a section of the ANTONINE WALL between the Firth of Forth and Firth of Clyde. Sir Walter Scott, in his *Tales of a Grandfather* (1827–30), says that when the Picts and Scots attacked the wall, after the Romans left, Graham was the first person to climb over it!

The same name lies behind other important archaeological sites, such as Grimes Graves, the Neolithic flint mines north of Brandon, in East Anglia, and the Grimspound walled settlement near Manaton, Dartmoor, with the remains of over 20 stone hut circles. It was the latter name and location that inspired the Grimpen Mire of Sir Arthur Conan Doyle's story *The Hound of the Baskervilles* (1902).

**Grin. Grin and bear it, To.** To put up with things, to PUT A BOLD FACE ON THE MATTER (*see under* BOLD). A similar expedient was enjoined on BOY SCOUTS in the Scout Law: 'A Scout smiles and whistles under all difficulties' (Robert Baden-Powell, *Scouting for Boys* (1908)).

**Grin like a Cheshire cat, To.** An old simile popularized by Lewis Carroll:

> 'Please would you tell me,' said Alice a little timidly ... 'why your cat grins like that?' 'It's a Cheshire cat,' said the Duchess, 'and that's why.'
> *Alice in Wonderland*, ch vi (1865)

The phrase has never been satisfactorily explained. The two leading theories are: (1) Cheshire cheese was once sold moulded like a cat that appeared to be grinning; (2) a sign painter painted grinning lions on inn signs (such as the Red Lion) in an area of Cheshire.

**Grind. Grind someone down, To.** To oppress or tyrannize them.

**Grind to a halt, To.** To come laboriously to a standstill. The reference is to the clogging up of a piece of machinery until it can no longer function. In the days of the windmill, when the wind dropped, the grinding action of the millstones on the grain stopped the mill, and it literally ground to a halt.

**Bump and grind, To.** *See under* BUMP.

**Have an axe to grind, To.** *See under* AXE.

**Keep one's nose to the grindstone, To.** *See under* NOSE.

**Griselda.** The model of enduring patience and wifely obedience, also called Patient Griselda, Patient Grissel and the like. She was the heroine of the last tale in Boccaccio's *Decameron* (1353). This was translated into Latin by Petrarch under the title *De Obedientia ac Fide uxoria Mythologia* ('On mythological wifely obedience and fidelity') (1373) and thence used by Chaucer (*c*.1387) and by Dekker, Chettle and Haughton for their *Patient Grissil* (1603). The story is of the Marquis of Saluzzo, who marries a poor girl of great beauty. He subjects her to almost unendurable trials, including the pretence that he has married another woman. At last convinced of her patience and devotion, Chaucer concludes:

> 'This story does not mean it would be good
> For wives to ape Griseld's humility,
> It would be unendurable they should.
> But everybody in his own degree
> Should be as perfect in his constancy
> As was Griselda.' That is why Petrarch chose
> To tell her story in his noble prose.
> CHAUCER: *Canterbury Tales*, 'The Clerk's Tale' (*c*.1387) (modern translation by Nevill Coghill, 1951)

**Grist to the mill.** Anything useful or profitable, especially when added to what already exists. Grist is that quantity of grain which is to be ground at one time.

**Grizzle.** All skin and bone, the horse of Dr SYNTAX.

**Groaning chair.** An old rustic name for a chair in which a woman sat after her confinement to receive congratulations. Similarly 'groaning cake' and 'groaning cheese' (called in some dialects 'kenno') are the cake and cheese that were provided, and 'groaning malt' was a strong ale brewed for the occasion.

> For a nurse, the child to dandle,
> Sugar, soap, spiced pots and candle,
> A groaning chair and eke a cradle.
> *Poor Robin's Almanack* (1676)

**Groat.** The name given in medieval times to all thick silver coins, from Middle Dutch *groot*, 'thick'. In England the name was given specifically to the fourpenny piece first made in the reign of Edward I. Later it became a very small silver coin, the issue of which ceased in 1662 although they were still struck as MAUNDY MONEY. In 1836 the small fourpenny piece reappeared as the Britannia Groat. *See also* JOEY.

**Grockle.** *See* EMMETS.

**Grog.** Spirits; properly, rum diluted with water. In 1740 Admiral Vernon, when Commander-in-Chief West Indies, substituted watered-down rum for the neat spirit then issued to both officers and men. The admiral was nicknamed Old Grog from his GROGRAM coat and the name was transferred to the new beverage.

> A mighty bowl on deck he drew,
> And filled it to the brink;
> Such drank the Burford's gallant crew,
> And such the gods shall drink,
> The sacred robe which Vernon wore
> Was drenched within the same;
> And hence his virtues guard our shore,
> And Grog derives its name.
> THOMAS TROTTER: 'Written on board the Berwick' (printed in *Notes & Queries*, Series I, 1781)

Grog was originally issued twice daily, as a quarter of a pint of rum with a pint of water. The ration was cut to one issue in 1824 and reduced to a half-gill in 1850. The issue to officers was stopped in 1881 and to warrant officers in 1918. Grog ration to all ratings ended on 31 July 1970.

**Grogram** (French *gros grain*, 'coarse grain'). A coarse fabric made of silk and mohair or silk and wool, stiffened with gum.

**Grommet** (obsolete French *gourmette*, 'bit-chain', from *gourmer*, 'bridle'). A rubber or plastic ring designed to line a hole to prevent a cable or pipe from chafing as it passes through. The word is also used for a ring of rope hemp used to pack the gland of a pipe joint. The origin is in equestrian parlance, as a term for the chain that links the ends of a horse's bit.

**Groom of the Stole, The.** Formerly, the first lord of the bedchamber, a high officer of the Royal Household, ranking next after the vice-chamberlain. In the reign of Queen Anne the post was held by a woman, and on the accession of Queen Victoria the office was replaced by that of the Mistress of the Robes. 'Stole' here is not connected with Latin *stola*, but refers to the king's stool or privy. As late as the 16th century, when the king made a royal progress, his close stool formed part of the baggage and was in the charge of a groom.

**Groove. In a groove.** In a rut; confined to a narrow undeviating course of life or routine.

**In the groove.** In the right mood; doing something successfully, fashionable. Hence the dated (but revivable) slang word 'groovy' for something fashionable or exciting. The allusion is to the accurate reproduction of music by a needle in the groove of a gramophone record.

**Gross.** The French word *gros*, 'big', 'bulky', 'coarse', has developed many additional meanings in English. Thus a gross is twelve dozen (144), gross weight is the entire weight without deductions, and a gross payment similarly is one before tax or other deductions. A nation's gross national product (GNP) is the total value of all its goods and services produced annually. This is contrasted with its gross domestic product (GDP), which is the total value of its goods and services produced domestically over a year. This equals its GNP less net investment incomes from abroad.

**Grotesque.** The word derives from Old Italian *pittura grotesca*, 'cave painting'. The chambers of ancient buildings revealed in medieval times in Rome were called grottoes, and as their walls were frequently decorated with fanciful ornaments and designs, the word 'grotesque' came to be applied to similar ornamentations.

**Ground. Ground bass.** In music, a short melodic bass line that is repeated over and over again. One of the best known examples is Dido's lament 'When I am laid in earth' in Purcell's opera *Dido and Aeneas* (1690), in which the bass is heard once alone and is then repeated six times with varied harmonies above it.

**Ground control.** The personnel and equipment at an airbase or launch site that monitor and control the flight of aircraft or spacecraft.

**Ground floor.** The storey level with the ground, or, in a house with a basement, the floor above the basement. In the USA and certain European countries the ground floor is known as the FIRST FLOOR. To 'get in on the ground floor' is to secure an advantageous position in an enterprise through participation at the outset, especially in securing investments before they are available to the general public.

**Ground frost.** A state of frost that is indicated by a thermometer on the grass registering a temperature of 32°F (0°C) or less.

**Groundhog.** The woodchuck or North American marmot.

**Groundhog Day.** In the United States CANDLEMAS DAY (2 February), from the saying that the groundhog first appears from hibernation on that day. If he sees his shadow, he goes back to his burrow for another six weeks, indicating six more weeks of winter weather. The general idea is that a sunny day (when he sees his shadow) means a late spring, whereas a cloudy day (when he does not see it) means an early spring.

**Groundnut scheme.** Figuratively, an expensive failure or ill-considered enterprise. The reference is to a hastily organized and badly planned British government scheme (1947) to clear large areas of hitherto unprofitable land in Africa to grow groundnuts. The venture was abandoned three years later at considerable cost to the taxpayer.

**Ground rent.** Rent due on a long lease (traditionally 99 years) that enables the lessee to build on the land. The tenant usually pays an initial lump sum (called a fine or premium) followed by a regular rent at a lower rate.

**Ground rules.** The basic rules or principles.

**Ground swell.** A long, deep rolling or swell of the sea, caused by a recent or distant storm, or by an earthquake. The expression is also used figuratively of a strong public opinion that can be detected even though it is not expressed openly.

**Break new ground, To.** *See under* BREAK.

**Cut the ground from under someone's feet, To.** *See under* CUT.

**Ear to the ground.** *See under* EAR.

**Fall on stony ground.** *See under* FALL.

**Gain ground, To.** *See under* GAIN.

**Get in on the ground floor, To.** *See under* GROUND FLOOR.

**Get off the ground, To.** *See under* GET.

**Go to ground, To.** To make oneself inaccessible

for a long period. When a fox goes to ground it seeks refuge in its den. *See also* GONE TO EARTH *under* EARTH; RUN TO EARTH.

**Happy hunting ground.** *See under* HAPPY.

**Hit the ground running, To.** *See under* HIT.

**Hold one's ground, To.** *See under* HOLD.

**Lose ground, To.** *See under* LOSE.

**Meet someone on their own ground, To.** *See under* MEET.

**Run into the ground, To.** *See under* RUN.

**Shift one's ground, To.** *See under* SHIFT.

**Stand one's ground, To.** *See under* STAND.

**Suit one down to the ground, To.** *See under* SUIT.

**Thin on the ground.** *See under* THIN.

**Tom Tiddler's ground.** *See under* TOM.

**Groundlings.** Those who occupied the cheapest part of an Elizabethan theatre, i.e. the pit, which was the bare ground in front of the stage. The actor who today 'plays to the gallery', in Elizabethan times according to Shakespeare 'split the ears of groundlings' (*Hamlet*, III, ii (1600)).

**Group. Blood group.** *See under* BLOOD.

**Bloomsbury Group.** *See under* BLOOMSBURY.

**Ginger group.** *See under* GINGER.

**London Group.** *See under* LONDON.

**Oxford Group.** *See under* OXFORD.

**Grovely Wood.** In 1603 the villagers of Great Wishford, near Salisbury, Wiltshire, were granted the right to gather wood for all time from nearby Grovely Wood. Once a year on 29 May by way of confirming the privilege they march to the wood, cut branches and carry them back to the village. They then process through the streets bearing a banner with the words 'Grovely! Grovely! Grovely! and all Grovely! Unity is strength', chanting the words 'Grovely, Grovely and Grovely' as they go.

**Grow. Grow on trees, To.** To be plentiful. The expression is mostly found in the negative, as: 'Money doesn't grow on trees.'

**Let the grass grow under one's feet, Not to.** *See under* LET.

**May your shadow never grow less!** *See under* SHADOW.

**Growlers.** The old four-wheeled horse-drawn cabs were called growlers from the surly attitude of their drivers, and crawlers from their slow pace.

**Grub. Grub stake, To.** In the United States a miner's term for equipping a gold prospector with his requirements in exchange for a share of his finds.

**Grub Street.** The former name of a London street in the ward of CRIPPLEGATE Without, changed to Milton Street in 1830 after the carpenter and builder who was the ground landlord. It leads north out of Fore Street, Moorfields, to Chiswell Street, and the name came to refer generally to the world of literary hacks and impoverished authors. In his *Dictionary of the English Language* (1755), Samuel Johnson says it was

> Much inhabited by writers of small histories, dictionaries, and temporary poems; whence any mean production is called *grub street*.

**Hermit of Grub Street, The.** *See under* HERMIT.

**Gruel** (Old French, of Germanic origin). Properly, a type of thin porridge, made by boiling oatmeal in water or milk. The word is related to 'grout'.

**Gruelling.** Very demanding or tiring. The word is related to GRUEL in its verbal sense of 'to exhaust', 'to punish'.

**Grundy. What will Mrs Grundy say?** *See under* WHAT.

**Gryphon.** *See* GRIFFIN.

**G-string.** A minimal garment covering the genital area, as typically worn by striptease artistes. The source of the name has been the subject of much speculation. It is almost certainly of American Indian origin, and in its original spelling was gee-string.

> Around each boy's waist is the tight 'geestring', from which a single strip of cloth runs between the limbs from front to back.
>
> J.H. BEADLE: *The Western Wilds*, ch xvi (1878).

**Guard. Guards, The.** *See* HOUSEHOLD TROOPS.

**Coldstream Guards.** *See under* COLDSTREAM.

**Home Guard.** *See under* HOME.

**Horse Guards.** *See under* HORSE.

**Iron Guard, The.** *See under* IRON.

**Life Guards.** *See under* LIFE.

**National Guard.** *See under* NATIONAL.

**Off one's guard.** *See under* OFF.

**Old Guard.** *See under* OLD.

**Praetorian guard.** *See under* PRAETORIAN.

**Red Guard.** *See under* RED.

**Swiss Guard.** *See under* SWISS.

**Take guard, To.** In CRICKET of a batsman who selects a spot to receive the bowling in front of the wicket by requesting the umpire to indicate the bat's position relative to the stumps.

**'Up, Guards, and at them!'** *See under* UP.

**Guarneri** or **Guarnerius.** The name of one of the famous violin makers of CREMONA of the 17th and 18th centuries. Andreas (*c*.1626–98) was a pupil of Niccolò AMATI. Giuseppe (1687–1745), known as Giuseppe del Gesù, from his habit of inscribing the sacred initials IHS inside his violins, was held to be the greatest. *See also* STRAD.

**Gubbins.** An object of little or no value, or odds and ends generally; otherwise a stupid person. The name formerly applied to the wild and savage inhabitants of the region around Brent Tor, on the edge of Dartmoor. According to Fuller in his *Worthies* (1661), they lived in cots (rather holes than houses) ... having all in common, multiplying without marriage into many hundreds. ... Their language is the dross of the dregs of the vulgar Devonian.

He explains the name thus: 'We call the shavings of fish (which are of little worth) gubbins.' The word comes from obsolete gobbon, itself probably related to gobbet.

**Gudrun, Guthrun** or **Kudrun.** The heroine of the great 13th-century German epic poem of this name founded on a passage in the *Prose* EDDA. The third part describes how Gudrun, daughter of King Hettel, was carried off by Hochmut of Normandy and made to work like a menial in his mother's house, because she would not break her troth to Herwig, king of Zealand. She was eventually rescued by her brother. This poem is sometimes known as the German ODYSSEY.

**Gudule, Gudula** or **Gudila.** Patron saint (*c.*648–712) of Brussels, daughter of Count Witger. She is represented with a lantern or candle. The story goes that her lantern went out as she was making one of her regular early morning visits to the church at Moorsel but was relit by the Holy Virgin with her prayers. Her feast-day is 8 January.

**Guelphs and Ghibellines.** In medieval Italy two rival factions whose quarrels occupy much of the political history of the period. The Guelphs were the papal and popular party, the Ghibellines the imperial and aristocratic party. Both names are derived from two rival German factions of the 12th century. Ghibelline is an Italian form of Waiblingen, a small town in Württemberg and a possession of the Hohenstaufen Emperor Conrad III, the name of which is said to have been used as a war cry by his followers at the Battle of Weinsberg (1140). Their opponents similarly used the war cry Welf, the personal name of their leader, Welf VI of Bavaria. Guelph is the Italian form of Welf.

The Guelph dynasty ruled in Hanover until 1866 and the reigning dynasty of Great Britain is descended from it. Guelphs ruled in Brunswick from its raising into a duchy in 1235 until 1918.

**Guenevere.** *See* GUINEVERE.

**Guernsey lily.** *See* MISNOMERS.

**Guerrilla war.** Irregular warfare carried on by small groups acting independently, especially by patriots when their country is being invaded. From Spanish *guerrilla*, diminutive of *guerra*, 'war'. *See also* FFI.

**Guest, Be my.** *See under* BE.

**Gueux, Les** or **Beggars, The.** The name adopted by the confederates who rose against Spanish rule in the Netherlands in the 16th century. In 1556 Baron Berlaymont is said to have exclaimed to the Regent, Margaret of Parma: 'Is it possible that your highness can entertain fear of these beggars?' (Motley, *Rise of the Dutch Republic*, II, vi (1855)). The name then became an honoured title.

**Guides.** *See* GIRL GUIDES.

**King's** or **Queen's Guide**. See under KING.

**Guignol.** The principal character in a popular French puppet show, similar to PUNCH AND JUDY. As the performances came to involve macabre and gruesome incidents, the name was attached to short plays of this nature. Hence 'Grand Guignol', a series of such plays or the theatre in which they were performed. The character first appeared in a puppet theatre at Lyon in 1808, in which it was originally named Chignol, after Chignolo, the theatre owner's native village in northern Italy. The name seems to have been altered under the influence of French *guignon*, 'evil eye'.

**Guilds.** *See* LIVERY COMPANIES.

**Dean of Guild.** *See under* DEAN.

**Guillotine.** An instrument for inflicting capital punishment by decapitation, so named from Joseph-Ignace Guillotin (1738–1814), a French physician, who proposed its adoption to prevent unnecessary pain. It was first used in the Place de GRÈVE on 25 April 1792. For a time it was known as a Louisette after Antoine Louis (1723–92), the French surgeon who devised it. Similar instruments had been used in some countries from the 13th century. *See also* INVENTORS; MAIDEN.

In modern terms a guillotine is a paper-cutting machine and a surgical instrument.

In British parliamentary procedure, the guillotine or closure by compartments is an extension of the CLOSURE procedure, as a way of setting a time limit on the discussion of a bill. It arose as an emergency measure in 1887 to limit discussion on the Criminal Law Amendment (Ireland) Bill, which was debated for 35 days before the guillotine was introduced.

**Furies of the guillotine, The.** *See* TRICOTEUSES.

**Guinea.** A gold coin current in England from 1663 to 1817 (last struck 1813), originally made of gold from Guinea in West Africa. The early issues bore a small elephant below the head of the king. Its original LEGAL TENDER value was 20s, but from 1717 it was fixed at 21s. The actual value varied, and in 1694 it was as high as 30s. Before the advent of DECIMAL CURRENCY, it was still customary for professional fees, subscriptions, the price of race horses, pictures and other luxuries to be paid in guineas as money of account. *See also* SPADE GUINEA.

**Guinea fowl.** So called because it was introduced from Guinea, where it is common.

**Guinea pig.** Properly the cavy, a small South American rodent. The reason for its name is uncertain. The geographical name GUINEA was formerly used for any remote land, and this may have applied in the case of the cavy. Guinea pigs are often used in scientific and medical experiments, so that the name is now applied to anyone used in this way or to a person on whom something is tried out.

We're all of us guinea pigs in the laboratory of God.
Humanity is just a work in progress.
TENNESSEE WILLIAMS: *Camino Real*, Block xii (1953)

**Spade guinea.** *See under* SPADE.

**Guinevere, Guenevere** or **Guinever.** The wife of King ARTHUR and paramour of LANCELOT OF THE LAKE. The name represents the Old French form of Welsh Gwenhwyfar, itself made up of *gwen*, 'white', 'fair', and *hwyfar*, 'soft', 'smooth'. The name appears in various forms. In Geoffrey of Monmouth's *Historia Regum Britanniae* (*c*.1136), a principal source of ARTHURIAN ROMANCES, she is Guanhamara, and in Layamon's *Brut* (early 13th century) she is Wenhaver.

**Guinness.** As a commercial product, the name was initially that of Arthur Guinness (1725–1803), an Irish brewer in Leixlip, County Kildare. In 1759 he acquired a brewery in Dublin, at first producing standard ale and table beers, but in 1799 introducing the porter that became the Guinness of today. The business expanded under his three sons, Arthur, Benjamin and William, who inherited it after their father's death, and in 1886 it became a limited company.

The firm's products naturally found a home in British and Irish pubs, where convivial chatter often turns to a discussion or dispute regarding the facts of a particular claim. It was in order to resolve such disputes that the *Guinness Book of Records* was created. Its first edition appeared in 1955, and it now features in its own pages as the world's all-time bestselling book with the sole exception of the Bible.

**Gules.** The heraldic term for red. In engraving it is shown by perpendicular parallel lines. The word comes from Old French *gueules*, the term for a red fur worn round the neck, itself from *gole*, 'throat'. Like all heraldic colours (or tinctures, as they are properly called), the word occurs in poetical works.

Full on this casement shone the wintry moon,
And threw warm gules on Madeline's fair breast.
JOHN KEATS: *Eve of St Agnes*, xxv (1820)

**Gulf. Gulf Stream.** The great warm ocean current that flows northeastwards out of the Gulf of Mexico (hence its name). Off the eastern coast of the United States, near Newfoundland, it is deflected across the Atlantic to modify the climate of western Europe as far north as Spitsbergen and Novaya Zemlya. It also washes the shores of the British Isles.

**Great gulf fixed, A.** *See under* GREAT.

**Gulistan** (Persian, 'garden of roses'). The famous moral miscellany renowned for the quality of its prose and wit, written by Saadi (*c*.1184–1292), the name adopted by Sheikh Muslih Addin, the most celebrated Persian poet and writer after OMAR KHAYYÁM. It contains sections on kings, dervishes, contentment, love, youth and old age, among other subjects, and has numerous stories and philosophical sayings.

**Gull.** An Elizabethan synonym for one who is easily duped, especially a high-born gentleman (*see also* BEJAN). Thomas Dekker wrote his *Gull's Hornbook* (1609) as a kind of guide to the behaviour of contemporary GALLANTS.

The most notorious geck [fool] and gull
That e'er invention play'd on.
SHAKESPEARE: *Twelfth Night*, V, i (1599)

**Gulliver.** The hero of Jonathan Swift's *Gulliver's Travels* (1726), a sailor and doctor who goes on a number of travels to strange places, including LILLIPUT and BROBDINGNAG. His adventures and encounters serve as a satirical depiction of England and France. Gulliver's first name, Lemuel, means literally 'devoted to God' and was perhaps intended ironically. His surname may have been meant to suggest his gullibility.

**Gum. Gum up the works, To.** To clog up the proceedings; to make a mess of things. The expression relates to early methods of lubricating machinery, often an inexact science rather than a fine art.

**Up a gum tree.** *See under* UP.

**Gun.** This word was formerly used for a large stone-throwing military device of the catapult or mangonel type. It is probably a shortened form of the Scandinavian female name Gunnhildr, itself from Old Norse *gunnr*, 'war', and *hildr*, 'battle'. The bestowing of female names on arms is not uncommon: *see also* BIG BERTHA and MONS MEG.

**Gunboat diplomacy.** In the days of the Victorian colonial empire, gunboats and other naval vessels were often called upon to coerce local rulers in the interests of British traders, usually in response to local demand. Hence gunboat diplomacy, to imply the settling of issues with weaker powers by the use or threat of force. *See also* PACIFICO.

**Guncotton.** A highly explosive compound, prepared by saturating cotton or other cellulose material with nitric and sulphuric acids. *See also* GREEK FIRE.

**Gun dog.** A dog trained to work with sportsmen, especially in the task of retrieving, pointing at or flushing out game. As this description suggests, retrievers and pointers are well-known examples of gun dogs.

**Gun for someone, To.** To set out to get a person in order to reprimand, attack or even kill them. The expression alludes to the last of these.

**Gunman.** An armed criminal prepared to use his gun recklessly. A term of American origin.
**Gun money.** Money issued in Ireland by James II between 1689 and 1690 made from old brass cannon, bells, copper utensils and the like.
**Gun room.** In the Royal Navy, a room for the accommodation of junior officers, originally under the charge of the gunner. *See also* WARDROOM.

> The subordinate officers in a big ship mess together in the gun-room, and the King of the gun room is the Sub-Lieutenant.
>
> GIEVES LTD. *How to Become a Naval Officer*, ch iv (1933)

**Gunrunning.** The smuggling of guns and ammunition into a country for belligerent purposes.
**Barisal guns** or **Lake guns.** *See under* BARISAL.
**Blow great guns, To.** *See under* BLOW.
**Bren gun.** *See under* BREN.
**Evening gun.** *See under* EVENING.
**Field gun.** *See under* FIELD.
**Gatling gun.** *See* GAT.
**Go great guns, To.** To act or operate with great vigour or intensity.
**Jump the gun, To.** *See under* JUMP.
**Lay a gun, To.** *See under* LAY.
**Minute gun.** *See under* MINUTE.
**Son of a gun.** *See under* SON.
**Spike someone's guns, To.** *See under* SPIKE.
**Sten gun.** *See under* STEN.
**Stick to one's guns, To.** *See under* STICK.
**Sunset gun.** *See* EVENING GUN.
**Tommy gun.** *See under* TOM.

**Gunga Din.** An enduringly familiar fictional name from a single five-stanza poem. Gunga Din is the 'regimental bhisti' or loyal water-carrier in Kipling's poem named after him in *Barrack-Room Ballads* (1892). The Cockney verses tell how he is killed while tending a wounded English soldier.

> Though I've belted you an' flayed you,
> By the livin' Gawd that made you,
> You're a better man than I am, Gunga Din!
>
> RUDYARD KIPLING: 'Gunga Din' (1892)

**Gunnar.** The Norse form of GUNTHER.

**Gunner. Kiss the gunner's daughter, To.** *See under* KISS.

**Gunpowder Plot.** A plan to destroy James I and Parliament at the opening of the latter on 5 November 1605, as a prelude to a Roman Catholic rising. Barrels of powder were stored in a vault under the HOUSE OF LORDS and Guy Fawkes was to fire the train. Tresham, one of the plotters, warned his Catholic relative, Lord Monteagle, who revealed the plot to the authorities. The cellars were searched, and Guy FAWKES was captured. The ceremony of searching the vaults of Parliament prior to the annual opening is a result of this plot. *See also* GUY.

**Gunter. Gunter's chain.** A chain used in land surveying and so named from Edward Gunter (1581–1626), the great mathematician and professor of astronomy at Gresham College. It is 66ft (20m) long, and divided into 100 links. As 10 square chains make an acre, it follows that an acre contains 100,000 square links.
**According to Gunter.** *See under* ACCORDING.

**Gunther** or **Gunnar.** In the NIBELUNGENLIED saga, a Burgundian king, brother of KRIEMHILD, the wife of SIEGFRIED. He resolved to wed the martial BRUNHILD (or Brynhild), who had made a vow to marry only the man who could ride through the flames that encircled her castle. Gunther failed, but Siegfried did so in the shape of Gunther, and remained with her three nights, his sword between them all the time. Gunther then married Brunhild, but later Kriemhild told Brunhild that it was Siegfried who had ridden through the fire, thus arousing her jealousy. Siegfried was slain at Brunhild's instigation, and she then killed herself, her dying wish being to be burned at Siegfried's side. Gunther was slain by ATTILA THE HUN (Etzel) because he refused to reveal where he had hidden the hoard of the Nibelungs. The legends are said to be based on the historical character of Gundaharius, a Burgundian king, who with his men perished by the sword of the Huns in 436.

**Gurkhas.** A Nepalese people whose men have volunteered to serve in the British Army since the 19th century. They are respected for their martial spirit, and have built a reputation as some of the finest soldiers in the world. In the late 20th century they were stationed mainly in Hong Kong but in 1995 their headquarters moved to Britain. Their name is Sanskrit for 'cow protectors', the cow being a sacred animal to the Hindus. *See also* GAEKWAR.

**Guru.** A Sanskrit word meaning 'weighty'. It is now applied to a Hindu spiritual teacher and leader, or more generally, to any expert or adviser. As a title, the word is used for the founder of the SIKH religion, Nanak, and his nine successors. These are therefore known as Guru Nanak, Guru Angad, Guru Amar Das, and so on.

**Gutenberg Bible, The.** *See* MAZARIN BIBLE *under* BIBLE.

**Guthlac, St.** The saint, from Crowland, Lincolnshire, is represented in Christian art as a hermit punishing demons with a scourge, or consoled by angels while demons torment him. He was a Mercian prince who died as a hermit in 714.

**Guthrun.** *See* GUDRUN.

**Gutter. Gutter press.** A term applied contemptuously to the popular press, which indulges in sensationalism and scandalmongering.
**Guttersnipe.** A street urchin. The word was

originally a dialect nickname for the common snipe, *Gallinago gallinago*, a wading bird that uses its long bill to probe the rivulets ('gutters') of mud flats for worms.

**Born in the gutter, To be.** *See under* BORN.

**Guts. Blood and Guts.** *See under* BLOOD.

**Devil's guts.** *See under* DEVIL.

**Guy.** An effigy of a man stuffed with combustibles in mockery of Guy FAWKES, carried round and burned on a BONFIRE on 5 November, in memory of the GUNPOWDER PLOT. Hence, any dowdy or fantastic figure. Hence also, from American usage, the word applied to a person, as the equivalent of the British CHAP. The origin sometimes proposed in 'goy', a Jewish term for a non-Jew, is not tenable.

**Guy Fawkes.** *See under* FAWKES.

**Guy of Warwick.** An English hero of legend and romance, whose exploits were first written down by an Anglo-Norman poet of the 12th century and accepted as history by the 14th century.

Guy is the son of Siward, steward of Rohand, Earl of Warwick, and the story tells of the exploits he undertakes to win the hand of the Earl's daughter, Phelis (Felice). He first performs doughty deeds abroad, including rescuing the daughter of the emperor of Germany, fighting the SARACENS, and slaying the Soldan (sultan). Returning to England, he marries Phelis, but after 50 days sets off again on pilgrimage to the HOLY LAND to enact further deeds of prowess. Back in England he slays the Danish giant Colbrand and then the DUN COW. After these feats he becomes a hermit near Warwick, begging bread daily of his wife at his own castle gate. On his deathbed he sends her a ring, by which she recognizes him, and she goes to close his dying eyes. The story is told in the Legend of Sir Guy in PERCY'S RELIQUES (1765) and to some extent is paralleled by that of TIRANT LO BLANCH.

**Guy's Hospital.** A famous London hospital founded in 1721 by Thomas Guy (*c*.1645–1724), bookseller and philanthropist. He amassed an immense fortune in 1720 by speculations in South Sea Stock (*see* SOUTH SEA BUBBLE) and gave £238,295 to found and endow the hospital, which is situated in SOUTHWARK.

**Fall guy, A.** *See under* FALL.

**Gwyn, Nell.** A popular actress and mistress of Charles II, Nell (Eleanor) Gwyn (1651–87) first became known when selling oranges at the Theatre Royal, DRURY LANE. In 1665 she appeared as Cydaria in Dryden's *The Indian Emperour*. An illiterate child of the back streets, she was winsome, sprightly and good company. She had two sons by the king, the elder becoming Duke of St Albans, and the younger, James, Lord Beauclerk. She finally left the stage in 1682, and on his deathbed Charles said to his brother James, 'Let not poor Nelly starve.' James II fulfilled the request. She was buried in St Martin-in-the-Fields and the funeral sermon was given by Thomas Tenison, later archbishop of Canterbury.

> Nell Gwyn is said to have suggested to her royal lover the building of Chelsea Hospital, and to have made him a present of the ground for it.
>
> LEIGH HUNT: *The Town*, ch vii (1848)

**Gyges.** A king of Lydia of the 7th century BC, who founded a new dynasty, warred against Ashurbanipal of Assyria, and is memorable in legend for his ring and for his prodigious wealth.

According to PLATO, Gyges went down into a chasm in the earth, where he found a brazen horse. Opening the sides of the animal, he found the carcass of a man, from whose finger he drew a brazen ring, which rendered him invisible. It was by the aid of the ring that Gyges obtained possession of the wife of CANDAULES and through her, of his kingdom.

**Gymnosophists** (Greek *gumnos*, 'naked', and *sophistēs*, 'wise man'). A sect of ancient Hindu philosophers who went about barefoot and almost without clothing. They lived in woods, subsisted on roots and never married. They believed in the TRANSMIGRATION OF SOULS.

**Gyp.** At Cambridge (and at Durham) the name for a college servant, who acted as the valet to two or more undergraduates, the counterpart of the Oxford SCOUT. He ran errands, waited at table, woke men for morning chapel, brushed their clothes, and so on. The word is probably from gippo, a 17th-century term for a scullion.

**Give someone gyp, To.** To give them a rough time; to make them suffer; as: 'My tooth is giving me gyp.' The word may be a form of GEE-UP.

**Gypsy** or **gipsy.** A dark-skinned, nomadic people who first appeared in England in the 16th century, called Romanies by George Borrow from *romani*, the adjectival form of their native name, *rom* (*see* ROMANY). They were originally of low-caste Indian origin, but migrated to Persia and thence to Europe, reaching Germany and France in the 15th century. As they were first thought to have come from Egypt they were called Egyptians, which became corrupted to Gyptians, and so to the present form. This form of the name has its French and Spanish counterparts in *Gitan* and *Gitano* respectively. The largest group of European Gypsies is the Atzigan. This is an Old Bulgarian name that comes from Byzantine Greek *tsiganos*, a shortened form of *atsinganos*, itself a popular form of *athinganos*, 'not touching'. The name took various forms in different countries: Italian *zingaro* (*see* ZINGARI), Portuguese *cigano*, Romanian *ţigan*, German *Zigeuner*, Turkish *çingene*, Hungarian *cigány*, Russian *tsygan*, French *Tsigane* and English *Tzigane*.

Under the NAZIS they suffered the same fate as the Jews and large numbers were exterminated. Gypsies have an old reputation as tinkers, horse dealers, fortune-tellers and musicians. They practise a wide variety of crafts in many countries, and in England have gained a romantic veneer (partly thanks to Borrow) through their colourful horse-drawn caravans and their leisurely 'open road' lifestyle.

> Throughout my life the Gypsy race has always had a peculiar interest for me. Indeed I can remember no period when the mere mention of the name Gypsy did not awaken within me feelings hard to be described. I cannot account for this – I merely state a fact.
>
> GEORGE BORROW: *The Gypsies of Spain*, Introduction (1841)

**Gyromancy** (Greek *guros*, 'circle', and *manteia*, 'divination'). A kind of DIVINATION performed by walking round in a circle until one falls from dizziness, the direction of the fall being of significance.

**Gytrash.** A type of ghost or apparition, often taking the form of a huge black and shaggy animal, and chiefly found in northern English counties. It appeared after dark in certain spots and was thought to warn of the impending death of a close relative or friend. The origin of the word is unknown.

> I remembered certain of Bessie's tales, wherein figured a North-of-England spirit, called a 'Gytrash'; which, in the form of horse, mule, or large dog, haunted solitary ways, and sometimes came upon belated travellers.
>
> CHARLOTTE BRONTË: *Jane Eyre*, ch xii (1847)

# H

**H.** The form of the capital H is through the Roman and Greek from the Phoenician (Semitic) letter *Heth* or *Cheth*, which, having two crossbars instead of one, represented a fence. The corresponding Egyptian HIEROGLYPH was a sieve, and the Anglo-Saxon RUNE is called *hægl*, 'hail'.

**Habakkuk.** A prophet noted for preaching 'woe' to the wicked, this word beginning three verses in the brief Old Testament book that bears his name. His sayings are an expression of social indignation and an impassioned appeal to God to punish the oppressors who make the lives of the people so wretched.

**Habeas corpus** (Latin, 'you may have the body'). The name given to a prerogative writ (from the opening words) used to challenge the detention of a person either in official custody or in private hands and ordering the detainer to produce or 'have the body' of the accused before the court. Various forms of this writ developed from the 13th century, and by CHARLES I's reign such writs were the established means of testing illegal imprisonment. The freedom of the subject from wrongful imprisonment was formally established by the Habeas Corpus Act of 1679, and the Habeas Corpus Act of 1816 provided for the issue of such writs in vacation as well as in term.

The Habeas Corpus Act has been suspended in times of political and social disturbance. Its importance is that it prevents people being imprisoned on mere suspicion or left in prison an indefinite time without trial. Punning on the phrase, Dorothy M. Sayers wrote a detective novel titled *Have His Carcase* (1932).

**Haberdasher.** A dealer in small articles of dress. The word comes from Anglo-French *hapertas*, of uncertain etymology. The Haberdashers' Company was one of the '12 great' LIVERY COMPANIES and was noted for its benefactions, especially in the field of education.

**Habsburg** or **Hapsburg.** The name of the dynasty that ruled in Austria, Hungary, Bohemia, Spain and elsewhere, is a contraction of *Habichtsburg*, 'hawk's castle'. This was the name of the castle built in the 11th century near the junction of the Aar and the Rhine, in present-day Switzerland, by Werner, bishop of Strasbourg, whose nephew, Werner, was the first to assume the title of Count of Hapsburg. *See also* EMPEROR.

**Habsburg lip.** *See* AUSTRIAN LIP.

**Hack.** The word is short for HACKNEY, a horse let out for hire, and hence came to apply to a person whose services are for hire, especially a literary drudge or mediocre journalist. Oliver Goldsmith, who well knew from experience what such a life was, wrote this epitaph on Edward Purdon:

> Here lies poor Ned Purdon, from misery freed,
> Who long was a bookseller's hack:
> He led such a damnable life in this world,
> I don't think he'll wish to come back.
> 'Epitaph on Edward Purdon' (1774)

*See also* GRUB STREET.

**Hackney.** Originally (14th century) the name given to a class of medium-sized horses, distinguishing them from warhorses. They were used for riding, and later the name was applied to a horse let out for hire, whence hackney carriage. The name probably comes from the London borough of Hackney, where such horses were formerly raised. A hackney cab is an official term for a taxi. *See also* HACK.

**Hackneyed expression, A.** One that is well worn or over used. The allusion is to a weak hired horse, as originally raised at HACKNEY.

**Haddock.** Traditionally it was in a haddock's mouth in the fresh water of the Lake of Gennesaret that St PETER found the piece of money, the *stater* or *shekel* (Matthew 17:27), and the two marks on the fish's neck are said to be impressions of the finger and thumb of the apostle. Haddock, however, cannot live in fresh water. *See also* JOHN DORY.

**Hades.** In Homer the name of the god (PLUTO) who reigns over the dead, but in later classical mythology the abode of the departed spirits, a place of gloom but not necessarily a place of punishment and torture. As the abode of the dead, Hades corresponds to the Hebrew *Sheol*, a word that, in the Authorized Version of the Bible, has frequently been translated by the misleading 'Hell'. Hades is, therefore, often used as a EUPHEMISM for hell. In fact, Hades itself represents Greek *Aidēs*, traditionally derived from *a-*, 'not', and *eidō*, 'I see', so that the sense is 'invisible one'. But this is almost certainly a popular etymology.

**Hadith** (Arabic, 'saying', 'tradition'). A 10th-century compilation by the Muslim jurists Moshin and Bokhari of the traditional sayings and doings of MOHAMMED. It forms a supplement to the KORAN, as the TALMUD does to the Jewish scriptures. Originally the Hadith was not allowed to be committed to writing, but this became necessary later for its preservation.

**Hadrian's Wall.** The Roman wall that runs for 73½ miles (118km) between Wallsend in the east and Bowness on the Solway Firth in the west. It was built between AD 122 and 127, after the Emperor Hadrian had inspected the site, to keep back the PICTS. It was 16ft (4.9m) high with mile-castles and turrets between the castles. There were 17 forts on the south side and a parallel vallum or ditch, about 10ft (3m) deep and 30ft (9m) wide, on the north. It was attacked and overrun in the 2nd and 3rd centuries and ceased to be an effective barrier by the latter part of the 4th century. It has become a popular tourist attraction, and its fabric has to some extent suffered in recent years from the feet of those walking along it. *See also* ANTONINE WALL.

**Hafiz.** Mohammed Shams ad-Din Hafiz (*c.*1325–*c.*1389), a Persian poet, the Persian ANACREON. His *ghazels* (lyric poems) tell of love, wine, nightingales, flowers, the instability of all things human, of ALLAH and the Prophet and the like. He was a professed dervish, and his tomb at Shiraz is still the resort of pilgrims. *Hafiz* means 'one who has learned the KORAN by heart'.

**Hag.** A witch or sorceress; an ugly old woman.

> How now, you secret, black and midnight hags?
> SHAKESPEARE: *Macbeth*, IV, i (1605)

**Hag-ridden.** Disturbed by nightmares, as if by a witch. The term is also used facetiously of a man pestered by women.

**Hagstones.** Flints naturally perforated used in country places as charms against witches, the EVIL EYE and the like. They are hung on the key of an outer door, around the neck for luck, on the bedpost to prevent nightmare, on a horse's collar to ward off disease and so on.

**Haganah** (Hebrew, 'defence'). A clandestine Jewish militia organized in Palestine, when under British mandate, in preparation for the coming struggle for Zionist independence at the end of the Second World War. It formed the nucleus of the army of Israel, which was established as an independent state in 1948.

**Hagar.** The Egyptian servant of SARAH (Genesis 16 and 21). When Sarah continues to be barren, she encourages her husband ABRAHAM to sleep with Hagar. Sarah then treats Hagar badly so that she runs away. An angel comforts her and she returns, in due course giving birth to ISHMAEL. When Sarah later bears ISAAC, she fears that Ishmael may become a rival heir and persuades Abraham to send mother and son into the desert. There God sustains Hagar and Ishmael and remains with the boy until he grows up.

**Haggadah** (Hebrew, 'narration'). The variety of MIDRASH that contains rabbinical interpretations of the historical and legendary, ethical, parabolic and speculative parts of the Hebrew scriptures. The variety devoted to law, practice and doctrine is called *Halakhah* ('rule by which to walk').

**Haggai.** A prophet who helps prepare the Jewish people for the rebuilding of the Temple of Jerusalem after the Babylonian Exile. His message, powerful because single-minded, is expressed in the Old Testament book named after him.

**Haggis.** A traditional Scottish dish, popular on BURNS' NIGHT, made from the heart, lungs and liver of a sheep or calf, chopped up with suet, oatmeal, onions and seasonings, and boiled like a big sausage in a sheep's stomach bag. The derivation of the name is uncertain, but it may be related in some way to 'hack'.

The haggis was also an English dish until the 18th century. Gervase Markham says in his *English Housewife* (1615):

> ... and this small oatmeal mixed blood and the Liver of either Calfe, Sheep or Swine maketh that pudding which is called haggas, or haggus, of whose goodness it is in vain to boast because there is hardly to be found a man that does not affect them.

**Haha.** A type of ditch found in the grounds of country houses and perhaps so called from the exclamation of surprise when coming across it or of malicious pleasure when another is seen to fall into it. A haha serves as a barrier to keep out livestock and other interlopers and is constructed below ground level so as not to impede the view from the house. Often one side is steep and the other merely sloping, but occasionally both sides slope and there is an actual wall running along the bottom. Unlike a moat, however, a haha is never filled with water.

**Haiku** (Japanese, 'amusement verse'). A Japanese verse form consisting of 17 syllables in three lines of five, seven and five syllables respectively. The resulting poem normally encapsulates a single idea, image or 'mood'. A few Western poets have been influenced by it and attempted to imitate it, not always successfully. The following is an example by one of its classic practitioners, the poet Matsuo Basho (1644–94):

> *Shizukasa ya*
> *iwa ni shimiiru*
> *semi no koe.*
> ('How still it is!
> Stinging into the stones
> The locust's trill'.)

An example of an English haiku was quoted as a 'Lilliputian lyric' by the *Westminster Gazette* in its issue for 19 April 1904:

The west wind whispered
And touched the eyelids of Spring:
Her eyes, Primroses.

**Hail.** An exclamation of welcome like the Latin *salve*. It is from Old Norse *heill*, 'hale', 'whole', and represents the greeting *ves heill* (Old English *wes hāl*), 'be healthy'. *See also* WASSAIL.

*First Witch*: All hail, Macbeth! hail to thee, Thane of Glamis!
*Second Witch*: All hail, Macbeth! hail to thee, Thane of Cawdor!
*Third Witch*: All hail, Macbeth! that shalt be king hereafter.
SHAKESPEARE: *Macbeth*, I, iii (1605)

**Hail a taxi, To.** To attract the driver's attention in order to board the vehicle.

**Hail-fellow-well-met.** Friendly and familiar, often in an unwelcome fashion.

**Hail from, To.** To come from or belong to a place by birth or residence. The expression is of nautical origin and comes from the custom of hailing (attracting the attention of) passing ships to ascertain their port of departure.

**Hail Mary.** *See* AVE MARIA.

**Within hail.** *See under* WITHIN.

**Hair.** One single tuft is left on the shaven crown of a Muslim for MOHAMMED to grasp hold of when drawing the deceased to Paradise.

The scalp-lock on the otherwise bald head of Native Americans is for a conquering enemy to seize when he tears off the scalp.

The Ancient Greeks believed that until a lock of hair was devoted to PROSERPINA, she refused to release the soul from the dying body. When DIDO mounted the funeral pile, she lingered in suffering until JUNO sent IRIS to cut off a lock of her hair. THANATOS did the same for ALCESTIS when she gave her life for her husband, and in all sacrifices a forelock was first cut off from the head of the victim as an offering to the black queen.

Byron says in *The Prisoner of Chillon*, i (1816):

My hair is grey, but not with years,
Nor grew it white
In a single night,
As men's have grown from sudden fears.

It is well authenticated that this can happen and has happened. It is said that Ludovico Sforza (1451–1508) became grey in a single night, as did CHARLES I while undergoing trial, and Marie Antoinette grew grey from grief during her imprisonment. *See also* RED HAIR.

**Hair-brained.** *See* HARE-BRAINED.

**Hair of the dog that bit you, The.** The idea that the thing that causes the malady is the best cure or means of relief, as another drink in the morning is considered by some the best answer to a HANGOVER. The allusion is to the old notion that the burned hair of a dog is an antidote to its bite. The general principle that 'like cures like' is an ancient one, expressed in Latin as *Similia similibus curantur*.

**Hair's-breadth.** A very narrow margin.

Wherein I spake of most disastrous chances,
Of moving accidents by flood and field,
Of hair-breadth 'scapes i' the imminent deadly breach.
SHAKESPEARE: *Othello*, I, iii (1604)

**Hair shirt.** A garment of coarse haircloth (made from horsehair and wool or cotton) worn next to the skin as a penance by ascetics. *See also* WEAR SACKCLOTH AND ASHES.

**Hairspring.** The fine spiral spring in a clock or a watch for regulating the movement of the balance.

**Hair trigger.** A trigger that allows the firing mechanism of a rifle or pistol to be operated by a slight pressure. The device was invented in the 16th century.

**Hairy.** In addition to the regular sense, covered with hair, there is a colloquial meaning dangerous, frightening, scary. This has become associated with 'hair-raising' but probably does not derive from it. The word's original sense was 'difficult', then 'impressive'.

'Ave you 'eard o' the Widow at *Windsor*
With a hairy gold crown on 'er 'ead?
RUDYARD KIPLING: 'The Widow at Windsor' (1892)

**Adoption by hair.** *See under* ADOPTION.

**Bobbed hair.** *See under* BOB.

**Get in someone's hair, To.** To annoy them.

I'm Gonna Wash That Man Right out of My Hair.
OSCAR HAMMERSTEIN II: *South Pacific* (song title) (1949)

**Judas-coloured hair.** *See under* JUDAS.

**Keep your hair on!** Don't lose your temper; keep calm. 'Keep your wool on' is an alternative form.

**Let one's hair down, To.** *See under* LET.

**Make one's hair stand on end, To.** To terrify. Dr Andrews, once of Beresford Chapel, Walworth, who attended an execution, said: 'When the executioner put the cords on the criminal's wrists, his hair, though long and lanky, of a weak iron-grey, rose gradually and stood perfectly upright, and so remained for some time, and then fell gradually down again.'

**Not to turn a hair.** *See under* TURN.

**Red hair.** *See under* RED.

**Split hairs, To.** *See under* SPLIT.

**Tear one's hair, To.** *See under* TEAR.

**Venus' hair.** *See under* VENUS.

**Haizum.** According to the Koran the horse of the archangel GABRIEL.

**Hajj** (Arabic, 'pilgrimage'). The pilgrimage to the KAABA, which every Muslim is obliged to make at least once in a lifetime. Those who neglect to do so 'might as well die Jews or Christians'. The pilgrimage begins on the 7th day of the 12th month of the year, Dhu al-Hijjah, and ends on the 12th day. Until comparatively recent times none but a Muslim could make this pilgrimage except at risk of life, and the Hajj was performed only by Johann Burckhardt (1784–1817), Richard Burton (1821–90) and a few other travellers who disguised themselves as Muslims.

**Hajji.** A Muslim who has made the HAJJ and who is therefore entitled to wear a green turban.

**Halakhah.** *See* HAGGADAH.

**Hal-an-tow.** The play and procession at Helston, which precedes the FURRY DANCE on Furry Day as a crop-fertility ritual that is probably older than the dance itself. In its older form, men and maids went into the country in early morning and returned with green boughs and flowers, with twigs in their hats and caps. Led by an elderly person riding a donkey, they entered the decorated streets singing the 'Morning Song', the chorus of which is:

> Hal-an-Tow, jolly rum-be-low,
> And we were up as soon as any day-O,
> And for to fetch the summer home, the summer and the May-O,
> For summer is a-come-O and winter is a-gone-O.

The song also mentions many of the characters who take part in the play and the procession, such as St GEORGE and the DRAGON, ROBIN HOOD, LITTLE JOHN, FRIAR TUCK, and Aunt Mary Moses, the local version of MAID MARIAN. The name is possibly from Cornish *hal* and *tyow*, which, freely rendered, would mean 'in the moorland and in the town'.

**Halcyon days.** Times of happiness and prosperity. Halcyon represents Greek *alkuōn*, 'kingfisher', popularly derived from *hals*, 'sea', and *kuōn*, 'conceiving'. The ancient Sicilians believed that the kingfisher incubated its eggs for 14 days on the surface of the sea, during which period, before the winter SOLSTICE, the waters were always calm.

> Expect St Martin's summer, halcyon days.
> SHAKESPEARE: *Henry VI, Pt I*, I, ii (1590)

**Half. Half a loaf is better than none.** If you cannot get all you want, try to be content with part of it.

**Half-and-half.** A mixture of two liquors in equal quantities, such as porter and ale, old and mild, mild and bitter and the like, or more generally the mixture of any two things in more or less equal proportions.

**Half an eye.** A minimum of perceptiveness; an unobtrusive observing of someone or something.

**Half-baked.** Foolish, stupid, as: 'That's just one more of his half-baked ideas.' The implication is that the idea might have worked if it had been thought through, just as bread needs to be properly baked before it can be eaten. Half-baked bread is sold in shops as 'part-baked' to avoid the undesirable term.

**Half-blood.** The relationship between two people who have only one parent in common.

**Half-blue.** An OXBRIDGE award for a minor sport, such as squash, or a person who substitutes for a full BLUE in a major sport.

**Half board.** The provision by a hotel or the like of bed, breakfast and one main meal, as distinct from FULL BOARD.

**Half-hearted.** Unenthusiastic; lacking commitment. The converse is whole-hearted.

**Half holiday.** A holiday for half a day, usually the afternoon. In many boarding schools Wednesdays and Saturdays are usually half holidays. Sunday is a whole holiday.

**Half is more than the whole, The.** This is what Hesiod said to his brother Perseus, when he wished him to settle a dispute without going to law. He meant: 'Half of the estate without the expense of law will be better than the whole estate after the lawyers have had their pickings.' The remark, however, has a wide signification. Thus a large estate, to someone who cannot keep it up, is a financial burden.

> Unhappy they to whom God has not revealed,
> By a strong light which must their sense control,
> That half a great estate's more than the whole.
> ABRAHAM COWLEY: *Essays in Verse and Prose*, iv (1668)

**Half-life.** As a scientific term, the time taken for half the atoms of a given amount of radioactive substance to decay. This time may vary from a fraction of a second to millions of years according to the given substance. A knowledge of this process has enabled archaeologists and geologists to date materials with considerable accuracy.

**Half-mast.** *See* FLY THE FLAG AT HALF-MAST.

**Half-nelson.** A wrestling hold in which a wrestler puts his arm under one of his opponent's arms from the rear while simultaneously pressing with his hand on the other's neck. In a 'full nelson' he places both arms under his opponent's arms, though this is an illegal hold in professional wrestling. It is not certain who the Nelson was who gave his name to these holds.

**Half of it, The.** The rest of it; the most important part of it. The phrase is usually in a form such as: 'You don't know the half of it', meaning you don't know the full story.

**Half-seas over.** Drunk. The phrase originally meant 'halfway over the sea', hence halfway between one state and another. A drunk person is halfway between sobriety and oblivion.

> Our Friend the Alderman was half Seas over.
> *The Spectator*, No. 616 (5 November 1714)

**Half the battle.** *See* FIRST BLOW IS HALF THE BATTLE.

**Half the time.** Usually, as: 'Half the time he's in the pub.'

**Half-timer.** A person engaged in some occupation for only half the usual time. The term formerly applied to a child attending school for half the time and working the rest of the day. This practice was terminated by the Education Act of 1918. A more usual phrase today is part-timer.

**Halftone block.** A typographic printing block for illustrations, produced by photographing on to a prepared plate through a screen or grating, which breaks up the picture to be reproduced into small dots of varying intensity, thus giving the lights and shades, or tones.

**Halfway house.** A fairly common name for an inn situated midway between two towns or villages. The phrase is figuratively used for a compromise or moderate policy.

**Better half.** *See under* BETTER.

**By halves.** *See under* BY.

**Go halves, To.** To share something equally with another person.

**Go off at half-cock, To.** *See under* GO.

**Have half a mind, To.** To be disposed to; to have an inclination towards doing something.

**Not half.** Very much. If a thing is 'not half bad' it is very good.

**Wood's halfpence.** *See under* WOOD.

**Halifax. Go to Halifax.** A EUPHEMISM for 'Go to hell'. The coinage probably derives from association with the saying: 'From Hull, Hell and Halifax, Good Lord, deliver us.'

**Hull, Hell and Halifax.** *See under* HULL.

**Hall. Hall of Mirrors, The.** The *galeries des Glaces*, the state apartments of the Palace of VERSAILLES. It was here that King William I of Prussia was acclaimed German Emperor (18 January 1871) after the defeat of France under NAPOLEON III.

**Exeter Hall.** *See under* EXETER.

**Liberty hall.** *See under* LIBERTY.

**Tammany Hall.** *See under* TAMMANY.

**Hallel** (Hebrew, 'praise'). A Jewish hymn of praise recited at certain festivals, consisting of Psalms 113–18 inclusive, also called the 'Egyptian' or 'Common Hallel'. The name 'Great Hallel' is given to Psalm 126 and sometimes to Psalms 120–36, thus including the GRADUAL PSALMS.

**Hallelujah** (Hebrew *hallelūjāh*, 'praise the Lord', from *hellēl*, 'to praise', and *yāh*, 'the Lord'). Alleluia is one of the several variant spellings. *See also* JEHOVAH.

**Hallelujah lass.** In the early days of the SALVATION ARMY, a name given to female members. The phrase is defined somewhat disdainfully by Dr Brewer as: 'A young woman who wanders about with what is called "The Salvation Army".'

**Hallelujah victory.** A victory by the Britons *c*.429 over the combined Picts and Saxons, probably somewhere in the north Midlands. The Britons, many newly baptized, were led by Germanus, bishop of Auxerre, and when they raised the war cry 'Hallelujah', the Picts and Saxons, seeing themselves surrounded, fled without fighting.

**Hallé Orchestra.** Britain's oldest symphony orchestra, predating all current London ones by at least half a century. It was founded in 1858 in Manchester by the German-born pianist Charles Hallé (1819–95), who remained its conductor until his death. Later conductors have included Sir Thomas Beecham (1879–1961), Sir Malcolm Sargent (1895–1967) and Sir John Barbirolli (1899–1970).

**Halliett, Goody.** The witch of Cape Cod, Massachusetts, also known as the 'little old woman of Nauset Sea'. Tales dating from the 18th century tell how she danced the nights away in scarlet shoes, wailing like the wind as she heaped ill fortunes on wayfarers. She is said to have reigned over Eastham and the Cape's deadly shoals for almost a century, whipping up hurricanes and luring ships to their doom with a lantern hung from the tail of a whale. According to legend, she was eventually strangled by her consort, the Devil, and a pair of red shoes was found in the belly of a whale, confirming her death.

**Hallmark.** The official mark stamped on gold and silver articles after they have been assayed (tested), so called because the assaying was originally done at the Goldsmiths' Hall. Since 1999, hallmarks have officially consisted of three compulsory symbols: the standard (fineness) mark; the assay office mark, and the sponsor's mark. Traditional marks such as the date letter may be added voluntarily.

(1) The standard mark. For gold, a crown in England and a thistle in Scotland, followed by the number of CARATS in figures for 22 and 18 carat gold. In Ireland a crowned harp for 22 carat, three feathers for 20 carat and a unicorn's head for 18 carat. Lower standards of gold have the number of carats in figures, without the device.

For silver, a lion passant in England, a thistle in Edinburgh, a thistle and a lion rampant in Glasgow and a crowned harp in Dublin. In 1697 Britannia Standard was introduced, enforcing a higher proportion of silver to prevent the melting down of coins. Britannia and a lion's head erased replaced the lion passant. Britannia Standard or New Sterling was abolished in 1729 because the alloy was too soft for most uses.

In modern hallmarks the standard is expressed in millesimal figures as the minimum content of gold or silver by weight in parts per thousand. The figures are as follows:

| | | |
|---|---|---|
| Gold | 22 carat | 916.6 |
| | 18 carat | 750 |
| | 14 carat | 585 |
| | 9 carat | 375 |
| Silver | Britannia | 958.4 |
| | Sterling | 925 |

(2) The assay office or 'hall' mark.

London: a leopard's head
Sheffield: a York Rose for gold, a crown for silver
Birmingham: an anchor (on its side for gold, upright for silver)
Edinburgh: a castle

Marks of assay offices now closed:

Chester: three sheaves and a sword
Exeter: a castle
Glasgow: the city arms (a tree, a bird, a bell and a salmon with a ring in its mouth)
Newcastle: a castle over a lion
York: five lions on a cross

(3) The sponsor's or maker's mark, instituted in 1363 and originally a device such as a bird or a FLEUR-DE-LIS, but now the maker's or manufacturer's initials.

(4) The date letter, showing the year when an article was assayed and hallmarked. The London assay office used 20 letters of the alphabet, Glasgow 26 and most of the others 25. The letter is changed annually, and until 1975 a distinctive style of lettering was also adopted and the shape of the letter's shield changed. Given the date letter and the assay office mark, the date of manufacture may be easily discovered on referring to a table.

(5) Other marks. There are four other marks to commemorate special events: the Silver Jubilee of George V and Queen Mary in 1935, the Coronation of Queen Elizabeth II in 1953, the Silver Jubilee of Queen Elizabeth in 1977, and the Millennium in 2000. The first three have the heads of the appropriate sovereigns, while the fourth shows the number 2000 shaped into a cross.

**Halloo. Don't halloo till you are out of the wood.** *See under* CRY.

**Halloween, Hallowe'en** or **All Hallows Eve.** 31 October, which in the old Celtic calendar was the last day of the year, its night being the time when all the witches and warlocks were abroad. On the introduction of Christianity it was taken over as the eve (even or e'en) of ALL HALLOWS or All Saints, and in the late 20th century it was still a popular 'party' occasion. Adults don ghoulish garb and light candles in hollowed-out pumpkins to look like eerie grinning heads, and children, similarly attired, go round the houses to play TRICK OR TREAT.

> Like it or not, Hallowe'en as a fully fledged event, as a big night, as an excuse for off-licences and bars to try ever more feeble promotions to make more cash, is here to stay.
> *Sunday Times* (6 November 1994)

**Hallows. All Hallows Day.** *See under* ALL.

**All Hallow Eve.** *See* HALLOWEEN.

**All Hallows summer.** *See under* ALL.

**Hallstatt.** The name given to a culture marking the transition between the Bronze Age and IRON AGE in central and western Europe and the Balkans. It takes its name from Hallstatt, a village in Upper Austria where between 1846 and 1899 over 2000 graves were found, the earliest dating from *c.*900 BC. They contained many objects typical of the earliest Iron Age.

**Halo.** In Christian art the same as a NIMBUS. The luminous circle around the sun or moon caused by the refraction of light through a mist is called a halo. Figuratively, it implies the ideal or saintly glory surrounding a person and is often used derisively, as: 'You ought to be wearing a halo.' The word comes from Latin *halos*, in turn from Greek *halōs*, originally a circular threshing floor, then the sun or moon's disc. *See also* AUREOLE.

**Halt, To grind to a.** *See under* GRIND.

**Ham.** (1) The youngest son of NOAH (Genesis 5–9). He sees his father drunk and naked, and by way of punishment God curses his son Canaan, ordering him to live as a servant to the children of Ham's brothers, SHEM and Japheth. In the 19th century this was sometimes taken by apologists of slavery to be God's approval of servitude, so that Negroes were sometimes called 'children of Ham'.

(2) A ranting, inferior actor. The word is of uncertain origin, but apparently derives from 'hamfatter', a term of contempt for a low-grade actor, itself said to come from an old minstrel song called 'The Ham-fat Man'. Whatever the derivation, the word has undoubtedly become associated with amateur.

**Hamadryads.** *See* DRYAD.

**Hambletonian.** The name given to a superior strain of horse bred in the USA for trotting, and descended from the stallion Hambletonian (1849–76).

**Hamburger.** This popular American dish of fried minced beef, onion, egg and so forth, made into a flat cake, takes its name from Hamburg in Germany. It appears to have originated in the Baltic region some centuries ago, and it was introduced into America in the 19th century by immigrants from the port of Hamburg and subsequently 'naturalized'. The beefburger came to be so called by caterers to avoid confusion by association with ham. There are now various types of burgers with the first part of the name indicating the chief constituent. Examples are cheeseburger, chickenburger, steakburger, vegeburger.

**Hamelin, Pied Piper of.** *See under* PIED.

**Hamilton, Single-speech.** *See under* SINGLE.

**Hamlet.** The complex central figure of Shakespeare's play that bears his name (1600). He is one of the most widely known, quoted and analysed characters in English literature, his role on the stage presenting a challenge to even the most experienced or original of actors. His 'To be or not to be' speech, as his soliloquy on suicide, is subject to varying interpretation, some taking the opening words, 'that is the question', to have a subtext implying 'that is *not* the question'.

> I saw *Hamlet* Prince of Denmark played, but now the old play began to disgust this refined age.
>
> JOHN EVELYN: *Diary* (26 November 1661)

**Hamlet without the prince.** Said when the person who was to have taken the principal place at some function is absent. The play *Hamlet* would lose all its meaning if the part of the prince were omitted.

**Hammer.** In personal nicknames:

> Pierre d'Ailly (1350–1420): *Le Marteau* ('hammer') *des Hérétiques*, president of the council that condemned John Huss
>
> John Faber (1478–1541): the German controversialist, was surnamed *Malleus Hereticorum* ('Hammer of the Heretics'), from the title of one of his works
>
> St Hilary: bishop of Poitiers (d.368), was known as the Hammer of the ARIANS
>
> Charles the Hammer: *see* MARTEL
>
> Edward I (1239–1307): nicknamed Longshanks and called the Hammer of the Scots; the inscription on his tomb in Westminster Abbey reads *Edwardus Primus Malleus Scotorum hic est* ('Here lies Edward I Hammer of the Scots')
>
> Thomas Cromwell (*c*.1485–1540): called *Malleus Monachorum* ('Hammer of the Monks'); he carried out the dissolution of the monasteries (1536–9) as Henry VIII's right-hand man

The second name of Judas MACCABAEUS, the son of Mattathias the Hasmonean, is thought by some to denote that he was a 'Hammer' or 'Hammerer' and to be derived from Hebrew *makkabah*, 'hammer'.

**Hammer and sickle.** The emblem of the former USSR, symbolic of the union under Communism of workers in the factory and peasants on the land. The Russians themselves always referred to the emblem as 'Sickle and Hammer' (*Serp i molot*).

**Hammer and tongs.** With great energy, as: 'They were fighting hammer and tongs.' The allusion is to a blacksmith energetically at work, hammering the metal that he holds with the tongs.

**Hammered, To be.** A stock exchange term, used of a broking firm in the 'House' that cannot meet its commitments. This is done by the 'Head Waiter', who goes into the rostrum and attracts the attention of the members present by striking the desk with a hammer before making the announcement.

**Hammer out, To.** To arrive at the final form of a plan or scheme by effort, careful thought and discussion. A metaphor from the blacksmith's shop.

**Come under the hammer, To.** *See under* COME.

**Throwing the hammer.** *See under* THROW.

**Hammon.** *See* AMMON.

**Hampden clubs.** A series of clubs centred on the Hampden Club set up in London in 1811 by the veteran agitator Major Cartwright (1740–1824). The aim was to agitate for reform of Parliament and the extension of the franchise to all payers of direct taxes, although some years later the clubs became more democratic, extending membership to all willing to pay a subscription of a penny a week. Each club was technically a separate organization in order to evade the existing law that forbade societies with affiliated branches. The name is derived from the parliamentarian John Hampden (1594–1643), of SHIP MONEY fame.

**Hampshire hog.** An old established nickname for a native of Hampshire, from its famous breed of pigs.

**Hampstead.** This district of northwest London was a place of fashion and elegance even before John James Park, writing in 1814, called it 'a select, amicable, respectable and opulent neighbourhood'. Its residents have included the cream of culture and intellect in the persons of William Pitt, Byron, John Keats, John Constable, H.G. Wells, Kate Greenaway, Sigmund Freud, R.L. Stevenson, Anna Pavlova, Mary Webb, J.B. Priestley and Giles Gilbert Scott, among others. Despite its latter-day associations of left-wingism and 'radical chic', it remains one of London's most obviously gentrified communities. Its physical proximity to homely Hampstead Heath only points up its own image of somewhat self-conscious eclecticism.

**Hampton. Hampton Court.** The grand palace next to the Thames, about halfway between the City of London and Windsor, was built in 1520 by Cardinal Wolsey. Henry VIII confiscated it from him and then adapted and used it as a regular residence, as which it remained for Elizabeth I. It has rarely been a residence since but has become an extremely popular tourist attraction, two of its draws being its fine

Tudor interiors and its gardens, with the latter incorporating the famous Maze.

**Hampton Court Conference.** Discussions held at Hampton Court in 1604 between James I, the bishops and four PURITAN clergy in the presence of the Council. The bishops would make no concessions of importance and their most valuable decision was to effect a new translation of the Bible, which became the Authorized Version of 1611. *See also* AUTHORIZED VERSION *under* BIBLE.

**Bevis of Hampton.** *See under* BEVIS.

**Hanaper.** 'Hanap' was the medieval name for a goblet or wine cup, and the 'hanaper' (connected with 'hamper') was the wickerwork case that surrounded it. Hence the name was given to any round wicker basket and especially to one kept in the Court of CHANCERY containing documents that had passed the GREAT SEAL. The office was under the charge of the Clerk of the Hanaper until its abolition in 1842.

**Hancock.** *See* JOHN HANCOCK.

**Hand.** A symbol of fortitude in Egypt and of fidelity in Rome. Two hands symbolize concord. ZENO OF ELEA represented dialectics by a closed hand and eloquence by an open hand.

In early art, the Deity was frequently represented by a hand extended from the clouds, with rays issuing from the fingers, but generally it was in the act of benediction, i.e. two fingers raised.

In card games, 'hand' is used for the game itself, for an individual player (as 'a good hand at WHIST') or the cards held.

> A saint in heaven would grieve to see such hand
> Cut up by one who will not understand.
> GEORGE CRABBE: *The Borough* (1810)

Hand is also used for style of work, play, handwriting and the like, as: 'She is a good hand at bowls,' 'He writes a beautiful hand.' Workmen and sailors are also called 'hands'.

As a measure of length a hand is 4in (10cm). Horses are measured up the foreleg to the withers, and their height is expressed in hands.

**Hand down, To.** To leave for a later generation. When a judge 'hands down a sentence', it is to pass it; to announce the verdict.

**Handfasting.** A marriage 'on approval' was formerly in vogue in the Borders. A fair was at one time held in Dumfriesshire, at which a young man was allowed to pick a female companion to live with. If they both liked the arrangement after 12 months they became man and wife. This was called 'handfasting' or 'handfastening'.

This sort of contract was common among the Romans and Jews.

**Hand in glove.** In collusion; fitting each other intimately like hand and glove.

**Hand in hand.** In a friendly fashion; unitedly.

**Hand in one's checks** or **chips, To.** To die. A phrase of American origin derived from poker. Checks (counters) were handed in when one had finished or was 'cleaned out'. Variants are to pass in or to cash one's checks.

**Hand in the matter, A.** To have a hand in the matter is to be associated with it; to 'have a finger in the pie'.

**Hand it to someone, To.** To give credit to them; to recognize their success.

**Hand-me-down.** Something passed on to another person when one no longer has any use for it oneself, such as a child's outgrown garment.

**Hand of glory, The.** In folklore, a dead man's hand, preferably one cut from the body of a man who has been hanged, soaked in oil and used by witches for its special magical properties. Robert Graves points out that 'hand of glory' is a translation of the French *main de gloire*, itself a corruption of *mandragore*, the plant mandragora (mandrake), whose roots had a similar magic value. *See also* DEAD MAN'S HAND.

**Hand on the torch, To.** To maintain and transmit knowledge or learning to the succeeding generation. The allusion is to the runners at ancient Greek festivals passing on the torch in relays.

**Handout.** Primarily something handed out or given away, as sweets or cakes at a children's party or gifts of food or clothing to vagrants. It is now more commonly used to designate: (1) free advertising material given to potential customers; (2) a press release by a news service; (3) a prepared statement to the press by a government, official body, publicity agent or the like.

**Hand over fist.** Steadily and rapidly, as: 'He is making money hand over fist.' The allusion is to sailors climbing up or down the rigging. The notion is that one grasps a fistful of coins with one hand while reaching out for more with the other.

**Hand over hand.** With one hand above the other, as when climbing a rope or ladder. Sailors when hauling a rope put one hand before the other alternately and rapidly. The French say *main sur main*.

**Hand-picked.** Chosen specially; selected with great care.

**Hand round, To.** To pass from one person to another; to distribute.

**Hands off!** Don't touch! Keep clear!

**Hands-on.** Involving practical experience, especially of mechanical or electronic equipment.

**Hand's turn, A.** A small amount of work. The expression is usually with a negative, as: 'He hasn't done a hand's turn this week.'

**Hands up!** The order given by captors when taking prisoners. The hands are to be held high above the head so that the person cannot resist, use a weapon or otherwise impede his capture. 'Hands up' in the classroom is a request by a teacher to pupils to respond to a question by putting up their hand.

**Hand that rocks the cradle rules the world, The.** The mightiest world ruler was once a babe in a cradle rocked by his mother. The proverbial line is from 'What Rules the World' (1865) by the American poet William Ross Wallace:

> A mightier power and stronger
> Man from his throne has hurled,
> For the hand that rocks the cradle
> Is the hand that rules the world.

**Hand-to-mouth existence, A.** An economically precarious way of life; improvident living. The image is of someone eating food as soon as they get it instead of storing it.

**All hands.** *See under* ALL.

**All hands and the cook.** *See under* ALL.

**Ask the hand of someone, To.** *See under* ASK.

**At first hand.** *See under* AT.

**At hand.** *See under* AT.

**At someone's hands.** *See under* AT.

**Bear a hand, To.** *See under* BEAR.

**Bird in the hand is worth two in the bush, A.** *See under* BIRD.

**Bite the hand that feeds one, To.** *See under* BITE.

**Black Hand.** *See under* BLACK.

**Bloody hand.** *See under* BLOODY.

**By hand.** *See under* BY.

**Cap in hand.** *See under* CAP.

**Change hands, To.** *See under* CHANGE.

**Charge hand.** *See under* CHARGE.

**Clean hands.** *See under* CLEAN.

**Come to hand, To.** *See under* COME.

**Court hand.** *See under* COURT.

**Cross the hand, To.** *See under* CROSS.

**Dab hand, A.** *See* DAB.

**Dead hand.** *See under* DEAD.

**Dead man's hand.** *See under* DEAD.

**Eat out of someone's hand, To.** *See under* EAT.

**Force someone's hand, To.** *See under* FORCE.

**Free hand, A.** *See under* FREE.

**From hand to hand.** *See under* FROM.

**Get one's hand in, To.** To familiarize oneself with the task; to begin to take responsibility for a task or duty.

**Get** or **gain the upper hand, To.** *See under* UP.

**Give someone a big hand, To.** *See under* BIG.

**Have clean hands, To.** *See under* CLEAN.

**Have one's hands full, To.** To be fully occupied; to have as much work as one can manage.

**Have one's hands tied, To.** To be unable to act freely.

**High-handed.** *See under* HIGH.

**Hold someone's hand, To.** *See under* HOLD.

**Imposition of hands.** *See* LAYING ON OF HANDS.

**In good hands.** *See under* GOOD.

**In hand.** Under control; in possession; in progress.

**In one's own hands.** In one's sole control, ownership, management, responsibility or the like.

**Iron hand.** *See under* IRON.

**Keep one's hand in, To.** To maintain one's skill by practice.

**Kiss hands, To.** *See under* KISS.

**Lay hands on, To.** *See under* LAY.

**Laying on of hands, The.** *See under* LAY.

**Lend a hand, To.** *See under* LEND.

**Live from hand to mouth, To.** *See under* LIVE.

**Many hands make light work.** *See under* MANY.

**Note of hand, A.** *See under* NOTE.

**Offhand.** *See under* OFF.

**Off one's hands.** *See under* OFF.

**Oil someone's hand, To.** *See under* OIL.

**Old hand, An.** *See under* OLD.

**Out of hand.** *See under* OUT.

**Palm of the hand.** *See under* PALM.

**Play into someone's hands, To.** *See under* PLAY.

**Poor hand, A.** *See under* POOR.

**Put one's hand in one's pocket, To.** To give money (often to a charity).

**Put one's hand to the plough, To.** To undertake a task, to commence operations in earnest. Only by keeping one's eyes on an object ahead is it possible to plough straight.

> And Jesus said unto him, No man, having put his hand to the plough, and looking back, is fit for the kingdom of God.
> Luke 9:62

**Raise one's hand, To.** *See under* RAISE.

**Red Hand** or **Bloody Hand.** *See under* RED.

**Right-hand man.** *See under* RIGHT.

**Rub one's hands, To.** *See under* RUB.

**Set one's hand to, To.** *See under* SET.

**Shake hands, To.** *See under* SHAKE.

**Show of hands, A.** *See under* SHOW.

**Show one's hand, To.** *See under* SHOW.

**Sit on one's hands, To.** *See under* SIT.

**Slow handclap.** *See under* SLOW.

**Spencerian handwriting.** *See under* SPENCER.

**Stay one's hand, To.** *See under* STAY.

**Strike hands, To.** *See under* STRIKE.

**Take a hand, To.** To play a part, especially in a game of cards.

**Take someone in hand, To.** To take charge of a person; to control or discipline someone.

**Take something off a person's hands, To.** To relieve them of something troublesome.

**Take the law into one's own hands, To.** *See under* LAW.

**Throw in one's hand, To.** *See under* THROW.

**Throw up one's hands, To.** *See under* THROW.

**Try one's hand, To.** *See under* TRY.

**Turn one's hand to, To.** *See under* TURN.

**Under my hand and seal.** *See under* UNDER.
**Wait on someone hand and foot, To.** *See under* WAIT.
**Wash one's hands, To.** *See under* WASH.
**Wash one's hands of something, To.** *See under* WASH.
**Wax in someone's hands.** *See under* WAX.
**Win hands down, To.** *See under* WIN.
**With a heavy hand.** *See under* WITH.

**Handcuff. Handcuff king.** The nickname of Harry HOUDINI (1874–1926), American entertainer and expert escapist, especially from handcuffs. *See also* DAVENPORT TRICK.
**Golden handcuffs.** *See under* GOLDEN.

**Handicap, The Waterloo.** *See under* WATERLOO.

**Handiron.** *See* ANDIRON.

**Handle. Handle to one's name, A.** A title, such as 'Lord', 'Sir', 'Doctor' and so on.
**Handle with kid gloves, To.** To treat with great care and respect.
**Dead man's handle.** *See under* DEAD.
**Fly off the handle, To.** *See under* FLY.
**Get a handle on, To.** To understand the reason for something or the basis for it.
**Love handles.** *See under* LOVE.

**Handsel** (Old English *handselen*, 'delivery into the hand'). A gift for good luck at the beginning of the year. Hence Handsel Monday, the first Monday of the year, when small gifts were given, before Boxing Day and the associated CHRISTMAS BOX took its place.

**Handshake, Golden.** *See under* GOLDEN.

**Handsome is as handsome does.** It is one's actions that count, not merely one's appearances or promises. The proverb is in John Ray's *Collection of English Proverbs* (1670) and is also found in Oliver Goldsmith's *The Vicar of Wakefield* (ch i (1766)).

**Hang.** A mild substitute for damn, as in 'Hang it all!', 'I'll be hanged!' or 'I don't give a hang what you say.'
**Hang about** or **around, To.** To loiter; to loaf; to wait about. As an interjection, 'Hang about!' means 'Wait a minute!'
**Hang a jury, To.** To reduce them to disagreement so that they fail to bring in a verdict.
**Hang back, To.** To hesitate to proceed.
**Hang by a thread, To.** To be in a precarious situation. The allusion is to the SWORD OF DAMOCLES.
**Hangdog look.** A guilty or furtive look. The allusion is to someone who is about to hang a dog or who deserves to be hanged like a dog.
**Hanged, drawn and quartered.** Strictly, the phrase should read 'drawn, hanged and quartered', for the allusion is to the sentence usually passed on those guilty of high treason, which was that they should be drawn to the place of execution on a hurdle or at a horse's tail. Later, drawing, in the sense of disembowelling, was added to the punishment after the hanging and before the quartering. Thus the sentence (August 1305) on Sir William WALLACE was that he should be drawn (*detrahatur*) from the Palace of Westminster to the Tower of London, then hanged (*suspendatur*), then disembowelled or drawn (*devaletur*), then beheaded and quartered (*decapitetur et decolletur*). His quarters were gibbeted at Newcastle, BERWICK, Stirling and Perth.

According to official records, on October 19 1685, for the crime of high treason, John Fernley, William Ring and Henry Cornish were given the following sentence:

> 'You must, every one of you, be had back to the place from whence you came, from thence you must be drawn to the place of execution, and there you must severally be hanged by the necks, every one of you by the neck till you are almost dead; and then you must be cut down, your Entrails must be taken out and burnt before your faces, your several heads to be cut off, and your bodies divided into four parts, and these to be disposed of at the pleasure of the King; and the Lord have mercy on your souls.'
>
> GEORGE R. SCOTT: *A History of Torture*, ch xxi (1940)

**Hanger-on.** An unwelcome follower or dependant.
**Hang fire, To.** To delay; to be irresolute; to be slow in acting. The expression derives from gunnery. The gun could be slow in firing the charge if it had not been properly loaded and primed or if the powder was damp.
**Hanging Gardens of Babylon, The.** A square garden (according to Diodorus Siculus (*c*.40 BC)), 400ft (122m) each way, rising in a series of terraces and provided with earth to a sufficient depth to accommodate trees of a great size. Water was raised from the Euphrates by a screw, and the gardens were irrigated from a reservoir at the top.

These famous gardens, one of the SEVEN WONDERS OF THE WORLD, were said to have been built by Queen SEMIRAMIS and by NEBUCHADNEZZAR, to gratify his wife Amytis, who felt weary of the flat plains of Babylon and longed for something to remind her of her native Median hills. They may have been associated with the great ziggurat of Babylon.
**Hang in the balance, To.** To be in a state of doubt or suspense with regard to the outcome of a situation, not knowing on which side the scales of fate may descend.
**Hang in there, To.** To stick with it, even when the going is tough. The allusion is probably to the boxing ring, where a boxer getting the worst of it may seek relief by clinging on to his opponent or to the ropes. After such a brief respite, he is better able to continue.

> 'No, no,' said Simon. 'I'll hang in there now that I've waited this long.'
>
> JEFFREY ARCHER: *First among Equals*, ch xii (1984)

**Hang loose, To.** To have a relaxed attitude to everything. The expression probably originated in sport, where one often plays or performs better if one is not tense.

**Hangman.** A game for two in which the letters of a word are guessed. An incorrect guess results in a line drawn in the depiction of a gallows with a person hanging on it. When the drawing is complete, the guesser is 'dead'.

**Hangmen and executioners.** Some practitioners have achieved particular fame (or infamy):

- Gregory Brandon and his son Richard (d.1649), who executed Strafford, Laud and CHARLES I (1649), and were known as 'the two Gregories'; the gallows came to be known as the Gregorian tree
- Bull (*c*.1593), the earliest hangman whose name survives
- William Calcraft (1800–79) was appointed hangman in 1829 and was pensioned off in 1874
- Thomas Cheshire, nicknamed 'Old Cheese'
- Edward Dennis (*fl*.1780), introduced in Dickens' *Barnaby Rudge* (1841)
- DERRICK, who cut off the head of the 2nd Earl of Essex in 1601
- Squire Dun, mentioned in Samuel Butler's *Hudibras* (III, ii (1680))
- Jack KETCH (d.1686) executed Lord Russell (1683) and the Duke of Monmouth (1685); his name later became a generic word for a hangman
- William Marwood (1820–83), who invented the 'long drop'
- Albert Pierrepoint (1905–92), who succeeded his father in 1946 and who resigned in 1956; he executed 433 men and 17 women, including the murderer Ruth Ellis (1926–55), the last woman to receive the death penalty in Britain
- Rose, the butcher (1686)

Of French executioners, the most celebrated are Capeluche, headsman of Paris during the days of the Burgundians and Armagnacs, himself beheaded in 1418 on account of his atrocities, and father and son Charles Sanson (1740–1806) and Henri Sanson (1767–1840), who worked the GUILLOTINE during the French Revolution. The former executed Louis XVI (1754–93), the latter his queen, MARIE ANTOINETTE (1755–93), his sister, Madame Élisabeth (1764–94), and Philippe ÉGALITÉ, Duc d'Orléans (1747–93).

The fee given to the hangman at TYBURN used to be 13½d, with 1½d, for the rope. Noblemen who were to be beheaded were expected to give the executioner £7 to £10 for cutting off their head, and any peer who came to the scaffold could claim the privilege of being suspended by a silken rope.

**Hang on, To.** To cling to; to persist; to depend on. As a command, 'hang on' means 'wait', 'be reasonable', as: 'Hang on, you mustn't say that.'

**Hang on like grim death, To.** To cling tenaciously, literally or metaphorically; to refuse to be shaken off, as death persists once it has marked down its victim. *See also* LIKE GRIM DEATH.

**Hang out, To.** To live or stay, as: 'Where does he hang out these days?' The phrase may have arisen from the old custom of innkeepers, shopkeepers, tradesmen and so on hanging a sign outside their premises.

> 'I say, old boy, where do you hang out?' Mr Pickwick replied that he was at present suspended at the George and Vulture.
>
> DICKENS: *Pickwick Papers*, ch xxx (1838–9)

**Hang out one's shingle, To.** An American colloquialism meaning 'to begin one's professional career'. 'Shingle', properly a kind of wooden tile, refers to the small signboard displayed outside premises by professional men and others.

**Hangover.** Something remaining from a previous occasion, especially the headache and nausea experienced the 'morning after the night before', i.e. the morning after an evening of alcoholic overindulgence. A tradition remedy is A HAIR OF THE DOG THAT BIT YOU.

**Hang together, To.** To make sense; to remain in association.

**Hang up, To.** To end a telephone conversation by replacing the receiver, which in the older wall-mounted models hung down from the cradle-hook.

**Hang-up, A.** An emotional problem.

**Hang up one's hat, To.** To make oneself at home; to become one of the family.

> Wherever I lay my hat, that's my home.
>
> MARVIN GAYE: (song title) (1969)

**Hung higher than Gilderoy's kite, To be.** To be punished more severely than the very worst criminal. The greater the crime, the higher the gallows, was at one time a legal axiom. The gallows of Montrose were 30ft (9m) high, for example. The ballad in PERCY'S RELIQUES (1765) runs:

> Of Gilderoy sae fraid they were,
> They bound him mickle strong,
> Till Edenburrow they led him thair,
> And on a gallows hong;
> They hong him high abone the rest,
> He was so trim a boy.

*See also* GILDEROY.

**Hung Parliament, A.** One in which no party has an overall majority, so that the party that forms the government is dependent on the support of one or more of the smaller parties. Such a government, which is likely to prove unstable, is more probable when there are minority parties, especially under some forms of proportional representation.

**As well be hanged for a sheep as a lamb.** *See under* AS.

**Born to be hanged.** *See under* BORN.

**Get the hang of something, To.** To understand its general principles.

**Give a dog a bad name and hang him.** *See under* DOG.

**Let it all hang out, To.** *See under* LET.

**Hanky-panky.** Suspicious behaviour; covert sexual activity. The phrase is an altered form of HOCUS POCUS.

**Hannah. Mrs Hannah Glasse.** *See under* GLASSE.

**Hannah Snell.** *See* FEMALE MARINE.

**Hannibal.** The skill and daring of this Carthaginian general (247–182 BC) almost defeated Rome, but his most popular feat was a march through the Alps into Italy with an army that included elephants.

**Hansard.** The printed official report of the proceeding and debates in the British Houses of Parliament and its standing committees and also those of some of the COMMONWEALTH Parliaments.

The name is derived from T.C. Hansard (1776–1833), printer, then publisher, of the unofficial *Parliamentary Debates* begun by William Cobbett in 1803. After 1855 the firm was helped by government grants, until 1890, when the work was undertaken by several successive printers working at a loss. The name 'Hansard' was omitted from the title page in 1891 and restored in 1943. Luke Hansard, the father of T.C. Hansard, was the printer of the House of Commons Journals from 1774 until his death in 1828.

**Hanseatic League.** Originally an organization of German merchants trading in northern Europe in the 13th century. It became a loose federation of nearly 100 towns by the mid-14th century, headed by Lübeck. It acquired a monopoly of the Baltic trade and dominated the North Sea routes until challenged by English, Dutch and Scandinavian competitors in the 15th century. The last Diet of the League met in 1669, and only Lübeck, Bremen and Hamburg remained in it. Its London STEELYARD was sold in 1853 and its Antwerp premises in 1863.

**Hänsel and Gretel.** The inseparables of the fairy story found among the tales of the brothers Grimm. Hänsel was a woodcutter's son and Gretel a little girl found in the forest. When starvation threatened the household, the woodcutter, at his wife's behest, abandoned the children in the forest. Hänsel laid a trail by which they found their way home, but they were subsequently again cast adrift. After several escapes from the wiles of a wicked fairy, Hänsel was at last transformed into a fawn and taken with Gretel to the king's castle, where Hänsel was restored to human form and enabled to marry Gretel. The story forms the basis of Humperdinck's opera (1893) of this name.

**Hansom.** A light two-wheeled cab, popular in London before the introduction of taxicabs early in the 20th century. It was invented in 1834 by Joseph Aloysius Hansom (1803–83), the architect of Birmingham Town Hall. The original vehicle had two large wheels with sunk axle trees and a seat for the driver beside the passenger. The size of the wheels was subsequently reduced and the driver placed in a DICKY at the rear.

**Hanukkah** (Hebrew, 'consecration'). The Jewish Festival of Lights, commemorating the purification and rededication of the Temple at Jerusalem in 165 BC by JUDAS MACCABEUS after its pollution by the Syrians. It begins on the 25th day of Kislev (mid-December) and lasts eight days. Candles are lit on an eight-branched candlestick or menorah and oily potato pancakes (*latkes*) traditionally eaten. Because it falls shortly before CHRISTMAS, many Jews treat it as a surrogate festival. The menorah thus replaces the Christmas tree and children are given *gelt* (presents or gifts of money) instead of Christmas presents.

**Happy. Happy birthday!** A greeting to someone on their birthday. The birthday greeting song 'Happy birthday to you', with the person's name inserted in the third line after 'Dear', was originally 'Good Morning to All', written in 1893, with words by the American educator Patty Smith Hill and music by her sister, Mildred J. Hill. The present words by Clayton F. Summy were substituted in 1935.

**Happy clappy.** A term descriptive of a type of evangelical religious worship, with joyful hymn singing accompanied by rhythmic clapping. The phrase caught on in the early 1990s.

**Happy days!** A toast when drinking. *See also* HAPPY LANDINGS!

**Happy dispatch.** *See* HARA-KIRI.

**Happy ending.** The end of a story, play or the like in which, typically, the characters marry or come into money and 'live happily ever after'. A conclusion of this kind is common in many FAIRY TALES.

**Happy event, A.** The birth of a baby.

**Happy expression, A.** A well-turned phrase; an apt choice of words.

**Happy families.** A card game in which the cards represent the four members of a tradesman's family. The object is to make as many complete families as one can.

**Happy family.** A conventionally happy family or

a group of people living or working (or both) together, 'like one big happy family'.

**Happy-go-lucky.** Carefree; cheerfully casual. The phrase was originally used adverbially in the sense 'as luck will have it'.

**Happy hour.** A period in the early evening (not necessarily an hour) when some pubs or clubs sell drinks at reduced prices.

**Happy hunting ground.** The heaven of Native Americans. Figuratively, the place where one has a happy leisure occupation, as: 'Second-hand stalls are a happy hunting ground for many.'

**Happy landings!** A toast when drinking, especially among aircraft pilots.

**Happy medium.** A course or compromise that avoids extremes.

**Happy release.** Death, especially as a liberation from suffering.

**Happy ship.** One in which the crew work together harmoniously.

**Happy Valley.** A place where people live or work in peace and contentment. The term can be applied ironically. In the Second World War RAF pilots so named the Ruhr, as a much bombed area. The name belongs originally to Dr Johnson's prose romance *Rasselas* (1759), the story of a prince of Abyssinia who, weary of the joys of the 'happy valley' where the inhabitants know only 'the soft vicissitudes of pleasure and repose', travels far and wide in search of true happiness. *Happy Valley* (1939) is also the ironic title of the first novel of the Australian writer Patrick White. *See also* MERIDEN.

**As happy as a sandboy.** *See under* AS.

**As happy as Larry.** *See under* AS.

**Bomb-happy.** *See under* BOMB.

**Hapsburg.** *See* HABSBURG.

**Hara-kiri** (Japanese taboo slang *hara*, 'belly', and *kiri*, 'cut'). A method of suicide by disembowelment practised by Japanese military and governmental officials, among others, when in serious disgrace or when their honour was positively impugned. The act was performed with due ceremony. Hara-kiri or 'happy dispatch', as it was also known in English, was practised from medieval times but ceased to be obligatory in 1868. A law of 1870 granted the privilege of hara-kiri to the SAMURAI, in lieu of the death penalty. It was abolished as an official practice in 1873. The standard Japanese term for the act is *seppuku*, from *setsu*, 'to cut' and *fuku*, 'abdomen'. The word is liable to corruption in English as 'hari-kari' or 'hari-kiri'.

> She discloses her age – fifteen; her mother's poverty; that her father committed *hari kiri* [*sic*].
> *The New Kobbé's Opera Book* (1997)

**Hard. Hard and fast.** Strict; unalterable; fixed. A 'hard and fast rule' is one that must be rigidly kept. It was originally a nautical phrase, used of a ship run aground.

**Hard-bitten.** Tough; stubborn; worldly wise; realistic. The term was perhaps originally used of horses that were hard-mouthed and difficult to control. 'Bitten' here should be understood actively, i.e. as if biting. Compare 'soft-spoken', meaning 'speaking softly'.

**Hard-boiled.** One who is toughened by experience; a person with no illusions or sentimentalities.

**Hard by.** In close proximity to. 'Hard' here means close or pressed close together.

**Hard cash.** Money, especially actual currency, as opposed to cheques or IOUs. The expression originally applied to coin, which was 'hard', as distinct from banknotes.

**Hard cheese.** Bad luck.

**Hard copy.** Computer jargon for a paper printout of an output, as distinct from a machine-readable output on a disk.

**Hard core.** The members of a group or movement who remain at its centre and who are firmly against change. Hard-core pornography is 'explicit', describing or depicting sexual acts.

**Hard currency.** A country's currency that is hard to obtain by another country that has an adverse balance of payments with it. The term has also been used to mean metal money, or currency that is stable and unlikely to depreciate suddenly.

**Hard-done-by.** Unfairly treated.

**Hard hat.** A protective hat worn on building sites and the like.

**Hard-headed.** Shrewd; intelligent and businesslike; not readily duped.

**Hard-hearted.** Unfeeling; callous; pitiless.

**Hard hit.** Badly affected, especially by monetary losses.

**Hard-hitting.** Tough and uncompromising.

**Hard labour.** A punishment of enforced labour additional to that of imprisonment, introduced by statute in 1706. For a long time it consisted of working the treadmill, breaking stones, picking oakum and similar tedious toil. Hard labour was abolished by the Criminal Justice Act of 1948.

**Hard lines.** Bad luck. 'Lines' here means one's lot or portion marked off as if by a line, 'one's lot in life', as: 'The lines are fallen unto me in pleasant places: yea, I have a goodly heritage' (Psalm 16:6).

**Hard luck.** Luck worse than one deserves, and more than simply bad luck.

**Hard-nosed.** Shrewd and practical.

**Hard** or **tough nut to crack, A.** A difficult question to answer; a hard problem to solve.

**Hard of hearing.** Rather deaf.

**Hard on, To be.** To be difficult for; to be severe towards or critical of.

**Hard-pressed.** In difficulties; closely pursued.

**Hard put to it, To be.** To find it difficult.

**Hard and soft science.** NATURAL SCIENCE, physics and the 'traditional' sciences are sometimes called 'hard science' as opposed to 'soft science', meaning sociology, economics, psychology, political science and other social and behavioural sciences.

**Hard sell.** The aggressive promotion of a product or service.

**Hard shoulder.** The surfaced verge of a motorway, used for emergency stops.

> You MUST NOT use the hard shoulder for overtaking.
> *Highway Code*, Rule 167 (1996)

**Hard stuff, The.** Strong alcoholic drink, especially whisky.

**Hardtack.** Ship's biscuit; coarse bread. 'Tack' here has the sense foodstuff.

**Hard up.** Short of money. The phrase was originally nautical. When a vessel was forced by stress of weather to turn away from the wind, the helm was put hard up to windward to alter course. So, when someone is 'hard up' they must weather the storm as best they can.

**Hardware.** A traditional term for ironmongery (kettles, pots and pans, cutlery, tools and so on), which was sold in hardware stores. The word is now also used for the physical equipment in a computer system, such as the central processing unit and memory. *See also* SOFTWARE.

**As hard as nails.** *See under* AS.

**Go hard with one, To.** To fare ill with; to result in hardship; to be troublesome to, to make unhappy. 'It will go hard with me before I give up' means 'I won't give up until I have tried every means to success, no matter how difficult or painful it may prove.'

**Hold hard!** *See under* HOLD.

**No hard feelings?** Said to someone whom one may have upset or offended.

**Hardy.** Brave or daring, hence the phrase *Hardi comme un lion* (French, 'Brave as a lion'). Among those surnamed 'The Hardy' are:

> William Douglas, defender of Berwick (d.1298)
> Philip III of France (1245–85)
> Philip II, Duke of Burgundy (1342–1404)

**Kiss me, Hardy.** *See under* KISS.

**Hare.** *See* BURKE.

**Hare.** The hare is the subject of many superstitions. It is unlucky for a hare to cross your path, because witches were said to turn into hares. According to medieval 'science', the hare was a melancholy animal and ate wild succory (chicory) in the hope of curing itself. Its flesh was supposed to generate melancholy in those who ate it. Another belief was that hares are sexless, or that they change their sex annually. Among the Hindus the hare is sacred to the moon because, they say, it is distinctly visible in the full disc.

**Hare and hounds.** The name given to a form of cross-country running when one or two runners act as hares and set off in advance scattering a trail of paper. The remainder, the hounds, duly set off in pursuit. It is also a fairly common PUBLIC HOUSE SIGN.

> 'Well, my little fellows,' began the Doctor … 'what makes you so late?'
> 'Please, sir, we've been out big-side hare-and-hounds, and lost our way.'
> THOMAS HUGHES: *Tom Brown's Schooldays*, Pt I, ch vii (1857)

**Hare and the tortoise, The.** An allusion to the well-known fable of the race between them, which was won by the tortoise. The moral is, 'slow and steady wins the race'.

**Hare-brained.** Giddy or foolhardy. *See also* AS MAD AS A MARCH HARE; HARUM SCARUM.

**Harefoot.** The nickname given to Harold I (*c.*1016–40), younger son of CANUTE and Aelfgifu of Northampton, king of England (1037–40), in allusion to his fleetness of foot.

**Harelip.** A cleft lip, so called from its resemblance to the upper lip of a hare. It was fabled to be caused at birth by an ELF or malicious FAIRY.

**As mad as a March hare.** *See under* AS.

**First catch your hare.** *See under* FIRST.

**Jugged hare.** *See under* JUG.

**Run with the hare and hunt with the hounds, To.** *See under* RUN.

**Start a hare, To.** *See under* START.

**Hare Krishna.** A sect devoted to the worship of the Hindu deity KRISHNA. It arose in the USA in 1966 as the International Society for Krishna Consciousness and claims a lineage of spiritual masters dating back to Caitanya (1485–1533), whom it regards as an incarnation of Krishna. It has become familiar to the public from the shaven-headed, saffron-robed youths who chant and clash cymbals as they weave their way along the city streets. The chant, known as the Maha ('Great') Mantra, gave the present name, and in full runs: 'Hare Krishna, Hare Krishna, Krishna, Krishna, Hare Hare'. This is repeated, substituting RAMA, as the name of the second most popular Hindu deity, for Krishna every second verse. 'Hare' means 'O god'.

**Hari, Mata.** *See under* MATA.

**Harijan.** *See* UNTOUCHABLES.

**Harkaway, Jack.** The hero of PENNY-DREADFULS, or popular fiction for boys in Victorian times. He was the creation of S. Bracebridge Hemyng and first appeared in the story *Jack Harkaway's Schooldays*, published in 1871 in the magazine *Boys of England*. He is the quintessential

English schoolboy, both plucky and lucky, but a perpetrator of pranks and practical jokes and a punisher of sneaks and bullies. His very name evokes his subsequent adventures as a world rover, typically battling with pirates or prospecting for gold.

**Hark back, To.** To return to the subject. A call to hounds in foxhunting, when they have overrun the scent, 'Hark, hounds, hark back!' So also 'Hark forrard!', 'Hark away!' and so on.

**Harleian.** Robert Harley, Earl of Oxford (1661–1724), and his son Edward, the 2nd Earl (1689–1741), were great collectors of manuscripts, scarce tracts and the like. In 1742 the widow of the 2nd Earl sold his prints and printed books to Thomas Osborne, the Gray's Inn bookseller, for £13,000 (considerably less than the cost of their binding alone), and in 1753 the manuscript books, charters and rolls were purchased at the bargain price of £10,000 for the British Library (then part of the British Museum), where the Harleian Manuscripts are among its most valuable literary and historical possessions. The *Harleian Miscellany* (ten volumes, first published 1744–6 in eight volumes) contains reprints of nearly 700 tracts, mostly of the 16th and 17th centuries. Since 1870 the Harleian Society has published numerous volumes of Registers, Herald's Visitations and Pedigrees.

**Harlem.** The main black district of New York City, so named by the original Dutch settlers after the town of Haarlem in the Netherlands.

**Harlequin.** In British PANTOMIME, a mischievous fellow supposed to be invisible to all eyes but those of his faithful COLUMBINE. His function is to dance through the world and frustrate all the knavish tricks of the CLOWN, who is supposed to be in love with Columbine. He wears a tight-fitting spangled or parti-coloured costume and is usually masked. He derives his name from Arlecchino, a stock character of Italian comedy (like Pantaloon and SCARAMOUCH), whose name was in origin probably that of a sprite or HOBGOBLIN. It goes back to Old French *Hellequin* or *Herlequin*, which in turn could come from either Middle English *Herle king*, one of the names of WODEN, or German *Erlenkönig*, 'king of the alders'. One of the demons in Dante is named Alichino.

The Prince of Harlequins was John Rich (1682–1761).

The Emperor Charles V or Charles Quint (1550–58) was called 'Harlequin' by Francis I of France.

**Harley Street.** A street in Marylebone, London, generally regarded as the leading address for fashionable medical specialists. By extension the name includes the surrounding area, which houses many consultants and dental specialists. Its growth as a medical centre dates from late Victorian days.

**Harmonia's necklace.** An unlucky possession; something that brings evil to all who possess it. Harmonia was the daughter of MARS and VENUS and she received the FATAL NECKLACE on her marriage to King CADMUS. VULCAN, to avenge the infidelity of her mother, also gave the bride a present of a robe dyed in all kinds of crimes, which infused wickedness and impiety into all her offspring. Both Harmonia and Cadmus, having suffered many misfortunes, were changed into serpents. MEDEA, in a fit of jealousy, likewise sent Creusa (or Glauce) a wedding robe, which burned her to death. *See also* SHIRT OF NESSUS.

**Harmonious Blacksmith, The.** The name given, after his death, to the air and variations in Handel's fifth harpsichord suite (1720). An ingenious but baseless fabrication ascribed its origin to the hammering at his forge of a blacksmith, William Powell (*c.*1702–80), said to have inspired Handel to compose this air. Powell's grave at Little Stanmore, near Edgware, was originally surrounded by a wooden rail on one side of which was painted: 'Sacred to the memory of William Powell, the HARMONIOUS BLACKSMITH, died Feb. 27, 1780, aged about 78', and on the other: 'He was Parish Clerk at this Church many years, and during the Time the Immortal Handel resided much at Cannons with the Duke of Chandos'. In 1868 this was replaced by a stone bearing, in a sunk medallion, a hammer, anvil, laurel leaf and a bar of music, with a modified inscription to the effect that: 'He was parish clerk during the time the immortal Handel was organist of this church'.

**Harmony, Close.** *See under* CLOSE.

**Harness, To die in.** *See under* DIE.

**Harold. Harold Godwinsson.** Harold II (*c.*1022–66), son of Earl Godwin, succeeded to his father's earldom of Essex in 1053 and became the right-hand man of EDWARD THE CONFESSOR. Edward died in January 1066 and Harold was elected as his successor. He defeated the Norwegian king Harald Siggurdsson at Stamford Bridge in September that year, but four days later WILLIAM THE CONQUEROR landed at Pevensey in Kent. The men's armies met at Senlac, some 9 miles (14.5km) from Hastings. On 14 October, in the Battle of Hastings, Harold was killed, supposedly pierced through the eye by an arrow. The ill-starred outcome is recorded in the BAYEUX TAPESTRY.

**Childe Harold.** *See under* CHILD.

**Haroun al-Raschid.** CALIPH of Baghdad. *See also* ABBASSIDS.

**Harp.** The cognizance of Ireland. Traditionally,

one of the early Irish kings was named DAVID and this king took the harp of the Psalmist as his badge. King John (r.1199–1216), to distinguish his Irish coins from the English, had them marked with a triangle, either in allusion to St PATRICK's explanation of the Trinity or to signify that he was king of England, Ireland and France. The harp may have originated from this. Henry VIII was the first to adopt it as the Irish device, and James I placed it in the third quarter of the royal achievement of Great Britain.

**Harp on, To.** To reiterate; to return continually to one point of argument, like a harpist continually plucking the same string. The expression sometimes takes the form 'to carp on', but this is strictly a misuse. 'To carp', meaning to find fault, has even so been influenced by Latin *carpere*, 'to pluck', although this is not the origin of English 'harp'.

**Aeolian harp.** *See under* AEOLIAN.

**Jew's harp.** *See under* JEW.

**Welsh harp.** *See under* WELSH.

**Harpagus** (Latin, 'one that carried off rapidly'). One of the horses of CASTOR AND POLLUX.

**Harper, The Blind.** *See under* BLIND.

**Harpers Ferry.** The present quiet residential village in West Virginia was the scene of an assault by the Abolitionists under JOHN BROWN on 16 October 1859, their aim being to capture its arsenal and establish an independent stronghold of freed slaves. The armoury was captured, but Brown's forces were outnumbered and overwhelmed by state and federal troops. Seventeen men died in the two-day struggle, and Brown together with six surviving henchmen were hanged before the year was out.

**Harpocrates.** The Greek form of the Egyptian *Her-pa-khrad* ('HORUS the child'). The hieroglyph for 'child' represented him as a seated boy sucking his finger, and the Greeks, misunderstanding this, made him the god of silence and secrecy.

> I assured my mistress she might make herself perfectly easy on that score for I was the Harpocrates of trusty valets.
>
> ALAIN-RENÉ LESAGE: *Gil Blas*, IV, ii (1715–35)

**Harpy** (Greek *harpazein*, 'to seize'). In classical mythology a monster with the head and body of a woman and wings and claws of a bird. It was fierce, ravenous-looking and loathsome, and lived in an atmosphere of filth and stench, contaminating everything it came near. Homer mentions only one harpy, Hesiod gives two, and later writers three. Their names, Aello ('storm'), Celeno ('blackness') and Ocypete ('rapid'), indicate their early association with whirlwinds and storms.

In general terms, a harpy is a cruel, greedy woman.

> Was it my mother-in-law, the grasping, odious, abandoned, brazen harpy?
>
> W.M. THACKERAY: *The Virginians*, ch xviii (1857–9)

**Harrods.** The vast department store in Brompton Road, London, arose from the small grocer's shop opened there in 1849 by Henry Charles Harrod (1811–85), an Eastcheap tea merchant who had married a butcher's daughter. It had become one of London's leading stores by the turn of the century, and a hundred years on was still striving to live up to its old slogan: 'Everything, for everyone, everywhere.' (Its telegraphic address was 'Everything Harrods London'.) Its vast food halls are effectively a superior supermarket, stocking all one could conceivably wish to buy for the table. *See also* FATHER CHRISTMAS.

**Harry. Harry Houdini.** *See under* HOUDINI.

**Harry Tate's Navy.** A good-humoured sobriquet applied to the Royal Naval Volunteer Reserve from about the time of the First World War or a little earlier. The allusion is to the Scottish music hall artist Harry Tate, born Ronald MacDonald Hutchison (1873–1940), perhaps best known for his motoring sketch. The term 'Harry Tate' came to signify anything that was disorganized or chaotic. *See also* FRED KARNO'S ARMY *under* KARNO; WAVY NAVY.

**Bell Harry.** *See under* BELL.

**Copper-nose Harry.** *See under* COPPER.

**Great Harry.** *See under* GREAT.

**Light Horse Harry.** *See under* LIGHT.

**Old Harry.** *See under* OLD.

**Tom, Dick and Harry.** *See under* TOM.

**Hart.** The male deer. In Christian art, the emblem of solitude and purity of life. It was the attribute of St HUBERT, St JULIAN and St Eustace. It was also the symbol of piety and religious aspiration: 'As the hart panteth after the water brooks, so panteth my soul after thee, O God' (Psalm 42:1). *See also* HIND.

**Hart royal.** A male red deer, when the crown of the antler has made its appearance and the creature has been hunted by a king.

**White Hart, The.** *See under* WHITE.

**Harum scarum.** Giddy, HARE-BRAINED, or a person so constituted. The term perhaps comes from hare, 'to harass', and scare, a form of 'stare', with a possible additional allusion to the madness of a March hare. *See also* AS MAD AS A MARCH HARE.

**Haruspex** (Latin *hira*, 'gut', and *specere*, 'to look at'). A Roman official of Etruscan origins who interpreted the will of the gods by inspecting the entrails of animals offered in sacrifice. Cato said: 'I wonder how one haruspex can keep from laughing when he sees another.' *See also* AUSPICES; DIVINATION.

**Harvard University.** The senior university in the USA, at Cambridge, Massachusetts. A college was founded in 1636 by the general court of the colony and in 1639 was named after John Harvard (1607–38) who left to it his library and half his estate. In due course it developed into a complete university, especially after 1869, but the college remained its core. Harvard had himself been educated at Cambridge University, England.

**Harvest. Harvest festival.** On Sunday, 1 October 1843, the Rev. R.S. Hawker (1804–75), vicar of Morwenstow in Cornwall, set aside the day to thank God for the harvest. The popular CHURCH OF ENGLAND festival largely derives from this. The practice spread, and nowadays churches are decorated with corn, fruit, vegetables and produce of all kinds, especially in country parishes. Hawker also reverted to the offering of the LAMMAS DAY bread at the EUCHARIST. *See also* HARVEST HOME.

**Harvest home.** In former days the bringing in of the last load of the corn of the harvest with the harvesters singing the 'harvest home' song, or the supper provided by the farmer followed by a general jollification. It is also a PUBLIC HOUSE SIGN. *See also* CORN DOLLY; CRYING THE NECK; HARVEST FESTIVAL; MELL SUPPER.

> Come, ye thankful people, come,
> Raise the song of harvest-home:
> All is safely gathered in,
> Ere the winter storms begin.
> HENRY ALFORD: 'Harvest Hymn' (1844)

**Harvest moon.** The full moon nearest the autumnal equinox, which rises for several days at about the same time (nearly sunset), giving a longer run of moonlit evenings than usual.

**White harvest.** *See under* WHITE.

**Harvey. Harvey Smith.** A V-SIGN. At the Hickstead show-jumping finals, August 1971, it was alleged that the horseman Harvey Smith (b.1938), on completing his last, winning round, made the sign at Douglas Bunn, one of the judges. He was threatened with the loss of all prize money but claimed he had merely made a V FOR VICTORY sign to mark his triumph. The matter was subsequently dropped but his name became attached to the gesture. *See also* GIVE SOMEONE THE FINGER *under* FINGER.

**Harvey Wallbanger.** A cocktail of gin or vodka and orange juice. It emerged in the United States in the late 1960s and has a name that presumably compliments and commemorates its inventor and alludes to its disorientating effect on those who partake of it.

**Hash.** A mess or a muddle, as in 'to make a hash of it'. The allusion is to the dish of recooked, mixed-up meat and potatoes. It is also the name given to the compacted resin of the cannabis plant, often mixed with molasses, where it is an abbreviation of 'hashish'. *See also* GRASS.

**Settle someone's hash, To.** *See under* SETTLE.

**Hasideans** (Hebrew *Hasidim*, 'the pious'). The forerunners of the PHARISEES. A religious party in Palestine, which in the 2nd century BC sought to maintain strict adherence to the Hebrew law and Mosaism against Greek influences.

**Hassan ben Sabah** or **Hasan ibn-al-Sabbah.** The OLD MAN OF THE MOUNTAIN, founder of the sect of the ASSASSINS.

**Haste, Post.** *See under* POST.

**Hat.** According to the story, Lord Kingsale is supposed to have acquired the right of wearing his hat in the royal presence when King John and Philip II of France agreed to settle a dispute respecting the duchy of Normandy by single combat. John de Courcy, conqueror of Ulster and founder of the Kingsale family, was the English champion and no sooner appeared than the French champion put spurs to his horse and fled. The king asked the earl what reward he would like, and he replied: 'Titles and lands I want not, of these I have enough; but in remembrance of this day I beg the boon, for myself and successors, to remain covered in the presence of your highness and all future sovereigns of the realm.' The 18th Lord Kingsale wore his hat three times in the presence of William III.

The Spanish grandees are said to have had the privilege of being covered in the presence of the reigning monarch, and to this day in England, any peer of the realm has the right to sit in a court of justice with his hat on.

In the House of Commons, while a division is proceeding, a member may speak on a point of order arising out of or during a division, but if he does so he must speak sitting and with his head covered.

It was a point of principle with the early QUAKERS not to remove the hat, the usual mark of respect, even in the presence of royalty. The story goes that William Penn once entered the presence of Charles II and kept his hat on, whereupon Charles removed his own hat. 'Friend Charles,' said Penn, 'Why dost thou uncover thy head?' 'Friend Penn,' answered Charles with a smile, 'it is the custom here that only one person wears his hat in the king's presence.'

**Hat in hand.** *See* CAP IN HAND.

**Hats off to him.** Good for him; thanks to him. An expression of admiration or appreciation. The person is obviously variable.

**Hat trick.** In CRICKET, the taking of three wickets with three successive balls. A bowler who accomplished this formerly earned the right to take his hat round the ground for a collection. The phrase is now also applied to any success or achievement repeated three times in a row. Hat tricks are rare in a TEST MATCH. The following is a classic description of the feat in 1999 as the first by an English bowler against Australia for 100 years:

> Darren Gough earned himself a hat-trick. He removed Ian Healy, knocked out Stuart MacGill's middle stump with his next, an inswinging yorker, and then banged into the outside of Colin Miller's off stump with an away-swinger which was nearer a yorker than long half-volley.
> *Sunday Times* (3 January 1999)

**As black as your hat.** *See under* AS.
**At the drop of a hat.** *See under* AT.
**Bad hat, A.** *See under* BAD.
**Billycock hat.** *See under* BILLY.
**Bowler hat.** *See under* BOWLER.
**Brass hat.** *See under* BRASS.
**Cocked hat.** *See under* COCK.
**Cockle hat, A.** *See under* COCKLE.
**Dick's hatband.** *See under* DICK.
**Eat one's hat, To.** *See under* EAT.
**Hang up one's hat, To.** *See under* HANG.
**Hard hat.** *See under* HARD.
**High hat.** *See under* HIGH.
**Keep it under one's hat, To.** *See under* UNDER.
**Knock into a cocked hat, To.** *See under* KNOCK.
**My hat!** An exclamation of surprise or disbelief.
**Old hat.** *See under* OLD.
**Out of a hat.** *See under* OUT.
**Pass the hat round, To.** *See under* PASS.
**Picture hat.** *See under* PICTURE.
**Red hat.** *See under* RED.
**Runcible hat.** *See under* RUNCIBLE.
**Scarlet hat.** *See under* SCARLET.
**Shovel hat.** *See under* SHOVEL.
**Stovepipe hat.** *See under* STOVEPIPE.
**Take off one's hat to someone, To.** *See under* TAKE.
**Talk through one's hat, To.** *See under* TALK.
**Ten-gallon hat.** *See under* TEN.
**Throw one's hat into the ring, To.** *See under* THROW.
**Tin hat.** *See under* TIN.
**Tip one's hat, To.** *See under* TIP.

**Hatches. Hatches, matches and dispatches.** A long-established colloquialism for a newspaper's announcements of births, marriages and deaths.

**Batten down the hatches, To.** *See under* BATTEN.
**Booby hatch.** *See under* BOOBY.
**Under hatches.** *See under* UNDER.

**Hatchet. Hatchet-faced.** Grim-looking, like one wielding a hatchet.

**Hatchet job.** A malicious or highly critical attack on someone, especially in print.

**Hatchet man.** A hired killer, or a man employed to carry out a HATCHET JOB.

**Bury the hatchet, To.** *See under* BURY.

**Throw the helve after the hatchet, To.** *See under* THROW.

**Hathor.** A major Egyptian deity. She is both mother goddess and goddess of love, and she is invariably depicted as a cow. Her father is the sun god RA (Re), and she is often regarded as the mother of all the pharaohs. Her erotic aspects are expressed in her associations with music and dancing, and her priestesses carry rattles and necklaces as sexual symbols in their cultic rites. Many of the attributes of APHRODITE are modelled on her. She appears at an early period to have been regarded as the mother of HORUS. Hence her name, which means 'abode of Horus'.

**Hatim, As generous as.** *See under* AS.

**Hatto.** An archbishop of Mainz (*c.*850–913), a noted statesman and counsellor of Otto the Great, who, according to some, was noted for his oppression of the poor. In time of famine, in order to give more to the rich, he is said to have assembled the poor in a barn and burned them to death, saying: 'They are like mice, only good to devour the corn.' Presently an army of mice advanced on the archbishop, who moved to a tower on the Rhine to escape the plague, but the mice followed in their thousands and devoured him. The tower is still called the MOUSE TOWER. Robert Southey has a ballad on 'Bishop Hatto'.

**Haul over the coals, To.** *See* CALL OVER THE COALS.

**Hauteclaire** (French, 'very bright'). The swords of both OLIVER and Closamont were so called.

**Hautville's Quoit.** A huge stone said to weigh about 30 tons, near Stanton Drew, Somerset, so called from a tradition that it was a quoit or coit thrown by Sir John Hautville (13th century). In Oxfordshire three huge stones near Stanton Harcourt are called the Devil's Quoits, and there is a DOLMEN at St Breock, Cornwall, called the Giant's Quoit.

**Have.** For phrases beginning with 'have', look under the first main word of the expression.

**Have had it, To.** A colloquial expression widely popularized during the Second World War and possibly of Australian origin. It is applied to anyone or anything that is 'finished with' or 'done for'. Thus a man seriously wounded was said to 'have had it'. At Roman gladiatorial combats the spectators cried *hoc habet* or *habet* ('he has it', 'he is hit') when a gladiator was wounded or received his death wound. It is also applied to someone who has missed a chance or opportunity.

**Have what it takes, To.** To possess the necessary attributes for success; to CUT THE MUSTARD.

**Never had it so good.** *See under* NEVER.

**Havelock.** A white cloth covering for a soldier's cap with a flap hanging down, worn in hot climates to protect the back of the neck from the sun. It is so called after General Sir Henry Havelock (1795–1857), who effected the first relief of Lucknow (1857) during the INDIAN MUTINY.

**Havelock the Dane.** A hero of medieval romance, the orphan son of Birkabegn, king of Denmark. He was cast adrift on the sea through the treachery of his guardians and the raft bore him to the Lincolnshire coast. He was rescued by a fisherman called Grim and brought up as his son. He eventually became king of Denmark and of part of England. Grim was suitably rewarded and, so the story goes, with the money built Grim's town or Grimsby.

**Haversack** (German *Habersack*, 'oat bag'). The haversack was originally a bag to carry oats to feed a horse. The word was later used for any bag for rations or the like, either carried on the back or slung over the shoulder.

**Havoc** (Old French *havot*, 'pillage', apparently of Germanic origin). The word that now denotes destruction or chaos was originally a military command to massacre without quarter. This cry was forbidden in the ninth year of Richard II's reign (1377–1400) on pain of death. In a 14th-century tract entitled *The Office of the Constable and Mareschall in the Tyme of Werre* (contained in the *Black Book of the Admiralty*), one of the chapters is, 'The peyne of hym that crieth havock, and of them that followeth him' (*Item si quis inventus fuerit qui clamorem inceperit qui vocatur havok*).

> Cry 'Havoc!' and let slip the dogs of war.
> SHAKESPEARE: *Julius Caesar*, III, i (1599)

**Play, wreak** or **cause havoc, To.** *See under* PLAY.

**Hawcubites.** Street bullies in the reign of Queen Anne (1702–14) who molested and ill-treated the old watermen, women and children who chanced to be in the streets after sunset. The succession of these London pests after the RESTORATION was: the Muns, the TITYRE-TUS, the Hectors, the Nickers, then the Hawcubites (1711–14), and worst of all the MOHOCKS. The name is probably a combination of Mohawk and Jacobite.

**Haw-haw, Lord.** In the Second World War the name given by Jonah Barrington, a journalist with the *Daily Express*, in allusion to his upper-class accent, to William Joyce (1906–46) who broadcast anti-British propaganda in English from Germany. His broadcasts usually began 'Germany calling! Germany calling!' with 'Germany' pronounced more like 'Jairmany'. He was hanged for treason.

**Hawk.** Falconry, as a sport for kings and gentry, had a tremendous vogue and it retained its popularity until the advent of the shotgun. The various hawks used in England came mostly from Norway and the chief market was St Botolph's fair, Boston, Lincolnshire. Their maintenance was very expensive. In recent times there has been a serious revival of the sport.

The different parts of a hawk are known as:

Arms: the legs from the thigh to the foot
Beak: the upper and crooked part of the bill
Beams: the long feathers of the wings
Clap: the nether part of the bill
Feathers summed and unsummed: feathers full or not full grown
Flags: the feathers next to the principals
Glut: the slimy substance in the pannel
Gorge: the crow or crop
Haglurs: the spots on the feathers
Mails: the breast feathers
Nares: the two little holes on the top of the beak
Pannel: the pipe next to the fundament
Pendant feathers: those behind the toes
Petty singles: the toes
Pounces: the claws
Principal feathers: the two longest feathers
Sails: the wings
Sear or sere: the yellow part under the eyes
Train: the tail

The rankings of a hawk are:

Gerfalcon: for a king
Falcon or tercel gentle: for a prince
Falcon of the rock: for a duke
Falcon peregrine: for an earl
Bastard hawk: for a baron
Sacre and sacret: for a knight
Lanner and lanneret: for a squire
Merlin: for a lady
Hobby: for a young man
Goshawk: for a yeoman
Tercel: for a poor man
Sparrowhawk: for a priest
Musket: for a holy-water clerk
Kestrel: for a knave or servant

This somewhat fanciful list of hawks proper to the various individuals is taken from the *Boke of St Albans* (1486) by 'Dame Juliana Berners'. The writer Barry Hines took the title of his novel *A Kestrel for a Knave* (1968) from this book. It is the story of a north-country boy and the kestrel that he adopts, and was memorably filmed as *Kes* (1969). *See also* TASSEL-GENTLE.

The dress of a hawk is:

Bewits: the leathers with the hawk-bells, buttoned to the bird's legs
Creanse: a pack thread or thin twine fastened to the leash in disciplining a hawk
Hood: a cover for the head, to keep the hawk in the dark; a rufter hood is a wide one, open behind. To unstrike the hood is to draw the strings so that the hood may be in readiness to be pulled off
Jesses: the little straps by which the leash is fastened to the legs
Leash: the leather thong for holding the hawk

The terms used in falconry are:

Casting: something given to a hawk to cleanse their gorge
Cawking: treading
Cowering: when young hawks, in obedience to their elders, quiver and shake their wings
Crabbing: fighting with each other when they stand too near

Hack: the place where a hawk's meat is laid
Imping: repairing a hawk's wing by grafting on a new feather
Inke or ink: the breast and neck of a bird on which a hawk preys
Intermewing: the time of changing the coat
Lure: a figure of a fowl made of leather and feathers
Make: an old staunch hawk that sets an example to young ones
Mantling: stretching first one wing then the other over the legs
Mew: the place where hawks sit when moulting; *see also* MEWS
Muting: the dung of hawks
Pelf or pill: what a hawk leaves of the prey
Pelt: the dead body of a fowl killed by a hawk
Perch: the resting-place of a hawk when off the falconer's wrist
Plumage: small feathers given to a hawk to make her cast
Quarry: the fowl or game at which a hawk flies
Rangle: gravel given to a hawk to bring down its stomach
Sharp set: hungry
Tiring: giving a hawk the leg or the wing of a fowl to pull at

Further information about hawks and hawking and the *Boke of St Albans* may be found in Arnold Fleming's *Falconry and Falcons* (1934) and Major C.E. Hare's *The Language of Sport* (1939).

**Hawkeye.** An inhabitant of the state of Iowa. *See also* LEATHERSTOCKING NOVELS.

**Hawks and doves.** Politically, and generally, the hawks are those who favour war and resolute military action, the doves those who support peace or compromise and negotiation. In America the term Warhawk came into particular prominence for those agitating for war with Britain in 1811–12.

**Know a hawk from a handsaw, To.** *See under* KNOW.

**Hawthorn.** The symbol of 'good hope' in the LANGUAGE OF FLOWERS because it shows winter is over and spring is at hand. Athenian girls used to crown themselves with hawthorn flowers at weddings, and the marriage torch was made of hawthorn. The Romans considered it a charm against sorcery and placed leaves of it on the cradles of new-born infants.

The hawthorn was chosen by Henry VII as his device because Richard III's crown was recovered from a hawthorn bush at Bosworth. 'Haw' here is the Old English *haga*, 'hedge'. *See also* HAYWARD.

**Haxey Hood game.** A medieval game played annually on 6 January at Haxey, north Lincolnshire. It is overseen by 12 men known as 'Boggans', a 'King' and a 'Fool', all of whom wear colourful costumes. The game begins when a canvas 'hood' is thrown to the crowd. Whoever secures it, eludes the Boggans, and takes it to the nearest inn, receives one shilling. After 12 such hoods are thrown a leather one follows. In a general scrimmage, this also reaches a local inn. The game is then over, with free drinks all round. The origin is in the 13th century, when the hood of Lady de Mowbray blew away as she was riding home from church and was retrieved by 12 labourers. This so amused the lady that she gave a piece of land, still known as the Hoodlands, to the village, the rent being a leather hood to be contested for annually by 12 men dressed in scarlet.

**Hay. Hay fever.** An allergic reaction to pollen, dust or the like, with consequent itching eyes, running nose and sneezing. The name is a misnomer, since the condition, technically called pollinosis, is neither caused by hay nor results in a fever.

**Haymaker.** In boxing a vicious, swinging blow, like a man wielding a heavy pitchfork of hay.

**Hayseed.** An American term for a rustic or countryman.

**Hayward** (Old English *haga*, 'hedge', and *weard*, 'keeper'). A manorial and village officer whose duty it was to look after the hedges and boundaries and to impound straying livestock. He sometimes regulated the use of the common. *See also* HAWTHORN.

**Antic hay.** *See under* ANTIC.

**Cock of hay.** *See under* COCK.

**Go haywire, To.** To run riot; to behave in an uncontrolled manner. This American phrase probably arises from the difficulty of handling the coils of wire used for binding bundles of hay, which easily became entangled and unmanageable if handled unskilfully.

> No one who has ever opened a bale of hay with a hatchet, and had the leaping wire whirl about him and its sharp ends poniard him, will ever have any doubt how *to go haywire* originated.
>
> H.L.MENKEN: *The American Language*, Supplement I (1946)

**Hit the hay, To.** *See under* HIT.

**Look for a needle in a haystack, To.** *See under* LOOK.

**Make hay of something, To.** To cause confusion. Before the days of the hay baler, hay was tossed about with a pitchfork before being gathered in.

**Make hay while the sun shines, To.** To STRIKE WHILE THE IRON IS HOT.

**Roll in the hay, To.** *See under* ROLL.

**Haze.** To bully; to punish by hard work. A nautical expression.

> Every shifting of the studding-sails was only to 'haze' the crew.
>
> R.H. DANA: *Two Years Before the Mast*, ch viii (1840)

In the USA 'to haze' is to subject to horseplay or punishment in school or fraternity initiations.

**Head.** Cattle are counted by the head, manual workers by hands, soldiers formerly by their arms, diners by covers and so on. People are also counted by the head when being charged or catered for individually 'at so much a head'. *See also* POLL TAX.

**Head and shoulders.** 'Head and shoulders above the rest' means, literally, taller than everyone else; figuratively, it means greatly superior. A tall person may be a head higher than a short one.

**Head-hunting.** The practice among some peoples of cutting off the heads of slain enemies and keeping them as trophies. In the modern sense, head-hunting is the recruitment of executives by one company from another, often through an agency.

**Head off, To.** To intercept; to get ahead of and force to turn back.

**Head over heels.** Literally, turning a somersault, hence, completely, utterly, as 'head over heels in love', when one is quite 'bowled over'. The expression, originally 'heels over head', had a Latin equivalent in *per caputque pedesque*.

**Heads I win, tails you lose.** A catchphrase descriptive of a one-sided arrangement. *See also* HEADS OR TAILS.

**Heads or tails.** Said when guessing whether the coin spun will come down with headside uppermost or not. The word 'tail' includes all the various devices appearing on the reverse of a coin. The French say *pile ou face*, literally 'pillar or face', the 'pillar' being the die with which the reverse of the blank coin was stamped. The Russians say *orël ili reshka*, literally 'eagle or curlicue', from the former representation of an eagle on the obverse and an ornate letter (the tsar's initial, as 'A' for Alexander or 'N' for Nicholas) on the reverse.

**Head start.** An advantage in a competitive situation. The allusion is to a racehorse that has its head in front of others at the 'off'.

**Heads will roll.** People will be dismissed. The allusion is to the GUILLOTINE.

**Bang** or **run one's head against a brick wall, To.** *See under* BANG.

**Bang their heads together, To.** *See under* BANG.

**Beachy Head.** *See under* BEACHY.

**Bite off someone's head, To.** *See under* BITE.

**Boar's head.** *See under* BOAR.

**Boar's Head Tavern.** *See under* BOAR.

**Brazen head.** *See under* BRAZEN.

**Bury one's head in the sand, To.** *See under* BURY.

**Captain of the heads.** *See under* CAPTAIN.

**Cock one's head, To.** *See under* COCK.

**Come to a head, To.** *See under* COME.

**Death's head.** *See under* DEATH.

**Dip the headlights, To.** *See under* DIP.

**Do one's head in, To.** *See under* DO.

**Get** or **take it into one's head, To.** To come to believe something that may be untrue, as: 'She's got it into her head that dogs make better companions than cats.'

**Get one's head down, To.** To go to bed; to concentrate on one's work.

**Give someone their head, To.** To allow them complete freedom; to let them do what they like. The phrase is from horse management.

**Go to one's head, To.** To be unduly influenced; to become conceited as a result of success, praise or the like. The reference is to the 'heady' effect of alcoholic drinks.

**Great Head, The.** *See under* GREAT.

**Have a head, To.** To have a headache.

**Have one's head screwed on the right way, To.** To be clear-headed and right thinking; to know what one is doing.

**Hit the nail on the head, To.** *See under* HIT.

**Hold one's head high, To.** *See under* HOLD.

**Keep one's head, To.** To remain calm in an emergency; to keep one's wits about one.

**Keep one's head above water, To.** To avoid insolvency; to avoid being overwhelmed by one's tasks or commitments. The allusion is to a swimmer 'in deep water'.

**Keep one's head down, To.** To remain inconspicuous in difficult times.

> We have to stop keeping our heads down and learn how to explain why the Catholic faith truly is a glorious gift of God and not a contrivance of the devil.
>
> *Catholic Herald* (16 October 1998)

**King Charles's head.** *See under* KING.

**Laugh one's head off, To.** *See under* LAUGH.

**Lift up one's head, To.** *See under* LIFT.

**Lion's head.** *See under* LION.

**Lose one's head, To.** *See under* LOSE.

**Make head or tail of, To.** To understand; to puzzle out. The expression is usually negative, as: 'I can't make head or tail of this timetable.'

**Make headway, To.** To make progress; to succeed in one's efforts, as a ship makes headway against a tide or current.

**Off one's head.** *See under* OFF.

**Off the top of one's head.** *See under* OFF.

**Over someone's head.** *See under* OVER.

**Put one's head into the wolf's mouth, To.** To expose oneself to needless danger. The allusion is to AESOP's fable of the crane that put its head into a wolf's (or fox's) mouth in order to extract a bone.

**Put** or **get one's heads together, To.** To discuss or consult together.

**Roof over one's head, A.** *See under* ROOF.

**Shake of the head, A.** *See under* SHAKE.

**Snap off someone's head, To.** *See under* SNAP.

**Soft in the head.** *See under* SOFT.

**Speaking heads.** *See under* SPEAK.

**Swelled** or **swollen head.** *See under* SWELL.

**Turn someone's head, To.** *See under* TURN.
**Two heads are better than one.** *See under* TWO.
**Valois head-dress.** *See under* VALOIS.
**Win by a head, To.** *See under* WIN.
**With one's head in the clouds.** *See under* WITH.

**Headlines, To hit the.** *See under* HIT.

**Heal. Heal the breach, To.** To effect a reconciliation.

**Faith healing.** *See under* FAITH.

**Healths.** The old custom of drinking healths, according to WILLIAM OF MALMESBURY, arose from the death of young Edward the Martyr (*c.*963–978), who was ignobly stabbed in the back while drinking a horn of wine presented by his stepmother Aelfthryth. *See also* GABBARA.

The Greeks handed the cup to the person toasted and said, 'This to thee.' Our holding out the wine glass is a relic of this Greek custom. In drinking the health of a mistress, the Romans used to drink a bumper to each letter of her name. Samuel Butler (*Hudibras*, II, i (1663)) satirizes this custom in the line: 'And spell names over beer-glasses.' Plautus (*Stichus* V, iv (3rd century BC)) writes of a man drinking to his mistress with these words: *Bene vos, bene nos, bene te, bene me, bene nostram etiam Stephaniam* ('Here's to you, here's to us, here's to thee, here's to me, and here's to our Stephania'). Martial, Ovid, Horace and others refer to the same custom.

The Saxons were great health-drinkers, and Geoffrey of Monmouth (*Historia Regum Britanniae*, Bk VI, xii (*c.*1136)) says that Hengist invited King VORTIGERN to a banquet to see his new levies. After the banquet, ROWENA, Hengist's beautiful daughter, entered with a gold cup full of wine and curtseying said to him, *Lauerd king wacht heil!* ('Lord king, your health'). The king then drank and replied, *Drinc heil* ('Here's to you'). *See also* HERE'S TO YOU; WASSAIL.

**Bill of health.** *See under* BILL.

**Heap. Heap coals of fire on, To.** To cause a person remorse by repaying bad treatment with good.

> If thine enemy be hungry, give him bread to eat; and if he be thirsty, give him water to drink: For thou shalt heap coals of fire upon his head, and the Lord shall reward thee.
>
> Proverbs 25:21–22

**Struck all of a heap.** *See under* STRIKE.

**Hear, hear!** An exclamation approving what a speaker says. Originally disapproval was marked by humming. Those supporting the speaker protested by saying 'Hear him, hear him!', which eventually became 'Hear, hear!'

**Hearing, Hard of.** *See under* HARD.

**Heart.** In Christian art the heart is an attribute of St TERESA OF AVILA. The flaming heart is a symbol of charity and an attribute of St AUGUSTINE, denoting the fervency of his devotion. The heart of Jesus is sometimes so represented.

**Heartache.** Extreme anguish or mental torment. This is the only form of bodily ache that is mental, not physical. Compare headache, backache, toothache, earache and so on.

**Heartland.** A name for the central region of the United States, otherwise the Midwest. As the name of the chief continental part of the USA, rather than the coastal areas, it has connotations of the 'good old days' and of a country that has retained its original moral and spiritual values.

**Heart of gold, A.** A person with a kind and generous nature.

**Heart of Midlothian.** The old TOLBOOTH of Edinburgh. This old prison was demolished in 1817.

> 'Then the tolbooth of Edinburgh is called the Heart of Midlothian?' said I. 'So termed and reputed, I assure you.'
>
> SIR WALTER SCOTT: *The Heart of Midlothian*, ch i (1818)

**Heart of Oak.** This sea song and naval march is from David Garrick's pantomime, *Harlequin's Invasion*, with music by William Boyce. It was written in 1759, 'the year of victories' (Quiberon Bay, Quebec, Minden), hence the allusion to 'this wonderful year' in the opening lines. 'Heart of Oak' refers to the timber from which the ships were built.

> Heart of oak are our ships,
> Heart of oak are our men:
> We always are ready;
> Steady, boys, steady;
> We'll fight and we'll conquer again and again.

**Heart of stone, A.** A stubborn or unemotional nature.

**Heartsease.** The *Viola tricolor*. It has a host of popular names, including the butterfly flower, kiss-me-quick, a kiss behind the garden gate, LOVE-IN-IDLENESS, pansy, three faces under one hood, variegated violet and herb trinity or trinitatis.

**Heart-throb.** The object of one's love or infatuation, especially when a celebrity.

**Heart-to-heart, A.** A confidential talk in private, often one in which advice is offered or a warning or reprimand given.

**Absence makes the heart grow fonder.** *See under* ABSENT.
**After one's own heart.** *See under* AFTER.
**At heart.** *See under* AT.
**Break one's heart, To.** *See under* BREAK.
**Break someone's heart, To.** *See under* BREAK.
**Change of heart, A.** *See under* CHANGE.
**City of Kind Hearts, The.** *See under* CITY.
**Cross one's heart, To.** *See under* CROSS.
**Cry from the heart, To.** *See under* CRY.
**Dead Heart, The.** *See under* DEAD.

**Eat one's heart out, To.** *See under* EAT.
**Faint heart never won fair lady.** *See under* FAINT.
**Find it in one's heart, To.** *See under* FIND.
**From the bottom of one's heart.** *See under* FROM.
**Have one's heart in one's boots, To.** To be utterly despondent, depressed or drained of hope. When one's heart sinks into one's boots the image is of spirits sinking very low.
**Have one's heart in one's mouth, To.** One's heart is beating so fast that one's throat is taut with apprehension, fear or expectation.
**Have one's heart in the right place, To.** To be kind and sympathetic, although one's manner or appearance might suggest otherwise.
**Have something at heart, To.** To cherish something as a great hope or desire; to be set on something.
**Have the heart to, To.** An expression usually found in the negative, as: 'I didn't have the heart to tell him,' meaning 'I couldn't bring myself to tell him.' Said when one wants to spare a person's feelings.
**Hole in the heart.** *See under* HOLE.
**Immaculate Heart of Mary, The.** *See under* IMMACULATE.
**In one's heart of hearts.** In the depths of one's conscience or feelings.

> Give me that man
> That is not passion's slave and I will wear him
> In my heart's core, ay, in my heart of heart.
> SHAKESPEARE, *Hamlet*, III, ii (1600)

**Learn by heart, To.** *See under* LEARN.
**Lose one's heart to, To.** *See under* LOSE.
**My heart bleeds for you.** I feel very sorry for you. The phrase is often used ironically.
**My heart goes pit-a-pat.** *See under* PIT-A-PAT.
**Out of heart.** *See under* OUT.
**Purple Heart.** *See under* PURPLE.
**Queen of Hearts, The.** *See under* QUEEN.
**Sacred Heart, The.** *See under* SACRED.
**Set one's heart on something, To.** *See under* SET.
**Take heart, To.** To be encouraged. At one time moral courage was supposed to reside in the heart, physical courage in the stomach, wisdom in the head, affection in the REINS (kidneys), melancholy in the BILE and spirit in the BLOOD.
**Take something to heart, To.** To take it seriously; to be concerned about it.
**To one's heart's content.** As much as one likes.
**Warm the cockles of one's heart, To.** *See under* WARM.
**Wear one's heart on one's sleeve, To.** *See under* WEAR.
**With all one's heart.** *See under* WITH.

**Heat.** A single section of a sporting contest, such as a race, so called because of its intensity of will and action. If there are too many competitors to participate at once, it may be necessary for them to enter in heats.

> The same day in the morning will be run for, by Women, a Smock of 5*l.* value, 3 Heats, half a mile each Heat.
> *London Gazette*, No. 3315 (1697)

**Heat of the day, The.** The hottest part of the day; that part of the day when the heat is oppressive.

> And the Lord appeared unto him [Abraham] in the plains of Mamre: and he sat in the tent door in the heat of the day.
> Genesis 18:1

**Blood heat.** *See under* BLOOD.
**Dead heat, A.** *See under* DEAD.
**In the heat of the moment.** Impulsively; without pausing to think.
**On** or **in heat.** Sexually receptive, of certain female animals.
**Turn on the heat, To.** *See under* TURN.
**White heat.** *See under* WHITE.

**Heath Robinson.** A phrase sometimes applied to an absurdly complicated mechanical contraption, especially one performing a basically simple function. The name is that of William Heath Robinson (1872–1944), whose amusing drawings of such absurdities appeared in *Punch* and elsewhere.

**Heathrow.** London Airport, as it is officially known, takes its popular name from the small settlement that was formerly in that place, west of London, itself so called as it was simply a row of cottages at the western edge of Hounslow Heath. The site was acquired by the Ministry of Civil Aviation in 1946, and in 1955 Queen Elizabeth II opened the first of the airport's three permanent buildings.

**Heaven** (Old English *heofon*). The word properly denotes the abode of the Deity and the angels, but it is also used in the Bible and elsewhere for the air, meaning the upper heights, as 'the fowls of heaven', 'the dew of heaven', 'the clouds of heaven'.

In the PTOLEMAIC SYSTEM, the heavens were the successive spheres surrounding the central earth. *See also* EMPYREAN; PARADISE; SEVEN HEAVENS.

**Heaven cannot support two suns, nor earth two masters.** So said Alexander the Great before the Battle of Arbela when DARIUS sent to offer terms of peace. *See also* Shakespeare (*Henry IV*, *Pt I*, V, iv (1597)):

> Two stars keep not their motion in one sphere;
> Nor can one England brook a double reign,
> Of Harry Percy and the Prince of Wales.

**Heavenly body.** The sun, the moon, a star or other celestial object.

**Heavenly host, The.** The ANGELS and ARCHANGELS.

**Heavenly twins, The** A term sometimes used of a well-meaning couple, usually of the same sex, as two elderly sisters. Astrologically the heavenly twins are GEMINI.

**In seventh heaven, To be.** *See under* SEVEN.

**Lamp of heaven, The.** *See under* LAMP.

**Marriages are made in heaven.** *See under* MARRIAGE.

**Move heaven and earth, To.** *See under* MOVE.

**Pennies from heaven.** *See under* PENNY.

**Queen of Heaven, The.** *See under* QUEEN.

**Seven heavens, The.** *See under* SEVEN.

**Heavy. Heavies, The.** *See under* REGIMENTAL AND DIVISIONAL NICKNAMES.

**Heaviest men.** Among the heaviest men whose weights are recorded are:

Jon Brower Minnoch (1941–83): from Washington State, USA; the heaviest human in medical history, who weighed 69st 9lb (442kg) in 1976 and when admitted to hospital in 1978 had a weight calculated to be more than 100st (635kg), most of which was water accumulation

Robert Earl Hughes (1926–58): from Illinois, USA; he reached a weight of 74st 5lb (472kg)

Peter Yarnall (1950–84): from London; he was the heaviest man recorded in Britain, attaining 58st (368kg)

Daniel Lambert (1770–1809): the previous record-holder at 52st 11lb (335kg), was a keeper at Leicester gaol. He died at the Waggon and Horses Inn, Stamford, Lincolnshire, during a stay to attend the races; his clothes were displayed in the inn and were visited more than once by the American dwarf Charles Stratton (TOM THUMB), who left a set of his own miniature garments by way of comparison; both sets are now displayed in Stamford Museum

There are others said to have been heavier than these, but their weights are not verified. *See also* DWARF; GIANTS.

**Heaviest women.** The heaviest woman ever recorded is the American Rosalie Bradford (b.1943), who is said to have reached a peak of 85st (544kg) in 1987. She subsequently slimmed and in 1994 weighed 20st 3lb (128kg).

**Heavy breather.** An anonymous telephone caller, usually a man to a woman, who imitates heavy breathing to suggest sexual excitement.

**Make heavy weather of, To.** To make an undue labour of, from the labouring of a ship in rough seas.

**Hebe.** In Greek mythology the daughter of ZEUS and HERA, the goddess of youth and cup-bearer to the gods. She had the power of restoring youth and vigour to gods and men.

**He Bible, The.** *See under* BIBLE.

**Hecate.** In Greek mythology the daughter of the TITAN Perses and of Asteria and high in favour with ZEUS. Her powers extended over heaven and hell, the earth and the sea. She came to combine the attributes of SELENE, ARTEMIS and PROSERPINA and to be identified with them. She was represented as a triple goddess, sometimes with three heads, one of a horse, one of a dog and one of a boar, and sometimes with three bodies standing back to back. As goddess of the lower world she became the goddess of magic, ghosts and WITCHCRAFT. Her offerings consisted of dogs, honey and black lambs, which were sacrificed to her at crossroads.

**Hecatomb.** In ancient Greece, the sacrifice of 100 head of oxen, from Greek *hekaton*, 'hundred', and *bous*, 'ox'. Hence any large sacrifice or large number. It is said that PYTHAGORAS, who would never take life, offered up 100 oxen when he discovered that the square of the hypotenuse of a right-angled triangle equals the sum of the squares of the other two sides.

> Behold with sleepless eyes! regard this Earth
> Made multitudinous with thy slaves, whom thou
> Requitest for knee-worship, prayer, and praise,
> And toil, and hecatombs of broken hearts.
>
> P.B. SHELLEY: *Prometheus Unbound*, i (1821)

**Hector.** The eldest son of PRIAM, the noblest and most magnanimous of all the Trojan chieftains in Homer's ILIAD. After holding out for ten years, he was slain by ACHILLES, who lashed him to his chariot and dragged the dead body in triumph thrice round the walls of TROY. In 17th-century stage representations of him, he was played as a blustering bully. Hence 'to hector' means to browbeat or bluster.

**Hector of Germany, The.** Joachim II, Elector of Brandenburg (1505–71).

**Hecuba.** The second wife of PRIAM and mother of 19 children, including HECTOR. When TROY was taken she fell to the lot of ULYSSES. She was afterwards metamorphosed into a bitch and finding she could only bark, threw herself into the sea. Her sorrows and misfortunes are featured in numerous Greek tragedies.

**Hedge.** In betting, 'to hedge' is to protect oneself against loss by cross-bets. It is also to prevaricate.

> He [Godolphin] began to think ... that he had betted too deep on the Revolution and that it was time to hedge.
>
> LORD MACAULAY: *History of England*, ch xvii (1849–55)

The word is used attributively for people of lowly origin, vagabonds who plied their trade in the open, under or between the hedges. Hence hedge-priest, a poor or vagabond parson; hedge-writer, a GRUB STREET author; hedge-marriage, a clandestine union, performed by a hedge priest; and hedge-school, a school conducted in the open air, as in Ireland in former days. Brian Friel's play *Translations* (1981) is set in a hedge-school in County Donegal in 1833.

**Hedgehop, To.** An airman's term for flying low, as if skimming the hedgetops.

**Hedge one's bets, To.** *See* HEDGE.

**Hedonism** (Greek *hēdonē*, 'pleasure'). The doctrine of Aristippus (4th century BC), that pleasure or happiness is the chief good and end of man. *See also* EPICURUS.

**Heebie-jeebies.** An American slang term for a state of nervousness or jitters, coined by the cartoonist Billy De Beck in the *New York American* in 1923.

**Heel.** In American slang a heel is a CAD, a despicable fellow with no sense of decency or honour.

**Heel of Achilles.** *See* ACHILLES' TENDON.

**Heeltap.** A small amount of alcoholic drink left in a cup or glass after drinking. A heeltap was originally a layer of leather that went to make up the heel of a shoe. The word came to apply to the left-over liquor because the dregs were thought to resemble the leather heeltap in shape. *See also* DAYLIGHT.

**Cool one's heels, To.** *See under* COOL.

**Dig in one's heels, To.** *See under* DIG.

**Down at heel.** *See under* DOWN.

**Head over heels.** *See under* HEAD.

**High Heels and Low Heels.** *See under* HIGH.

**Kick up one's heels, To.** *See under* KICK.

**Lay by the heels, To.** *See under* LAY.

**Rock back on one's heels, To.** *See under* ROCK.

**Show a clean pair of heels, To.** *See under* SHOW.

**Take to one's heels, To.** To run off.

**Tar Heel.** *See under* TAR.

**Turn on one's heel, To.** *See under* TURN.

**Well-heeled.** *See under* WELL.

**Heep, Uriah.** An abject toady and a malignant hypocrite, making a great play of being ''umble', but in the end falling a victim to his own malice (Dickens, *David Copperfield* (1849–50)).

**Hegira** (Arabic *hijra*, 'departure'). The flight of MOHAMMED from MECCA to Yathrib, 16 July 622, which soon came to be called MEDINA, the City of the Prophet. The MUSLIM CALENDAR starts from this event. The word is pronounced almost as if 'hedgerow'.

**Heidelberg man.** A type of prehistoric man found near Heidelberg, Germany, in 1907, possibly of the genus *Pithecanthropus*. A single lower jaw was found along with other extinct mammal fossils of the Pleistocene period.

**Heidi.** The orphaned Swiss girl who is the central character of Johanna Spyri's children's novel named after her (1881). As a small child she lives in the mountains with her grandfather, a misanthrope and religious sceptic, spending her summer days idyllically playing with young Peter the goatherd. At the age of eight she is sent to Frankfurt to act as a companion to the crippled child of a rich family. She pines for the mountains, however, and at last returns there. She reads the biblical story of the Prodigal Son to her grandfather, and he recovers his faith. The novel is thus a tale of childhood grace and goodness, and of the triumph of Christian values. Even Heidi's name reflects the theme, since it is short for Adelheid, meaning 'noble sort'.

**Heil Hitler** (German, 'Hail Hitler'). The familiar salutation to the FÜHRER, often used derisively of one adopting dictatorial methods or attempting dictatorial policies. *See also* HITLERISM.

**Heimdall.** In Scandinavian mythology, a god of light who guards the rainbow bridge, BIFROST. He was the son of the nine daughters of AEGIR and in many attributes identical with TIU. His name is of uncertain meaning, but has been interpreted as 'world bow'.

**Heimskringla** (Old Norse, 'world orb'). An important collection of 16 sagas on the lives of the early kings of Norway to 1184, the work of Snorri Sturluson (1179–1241). *See also* EDDA.

**Heir. Heir apparent.** The actual heir who will succeed if he or she outlives the present holder of the crown or title, as distinct from the heir presumptive, whose succession may be broken by the birth of someone more closely related or of a son (who takes priority over daughters) to the holder. Thus Princess Victoria (1840–1901), the Princess Royal, was heir presumptive to Queen Victoria, as her eldest daughter, until the Prince of Wales, the future Edward VII, was born in 1841 as her eldest son and became heir apparent. Queen Elizabeth II (b.1926), when Princess Elizabeth, was heir presumptive from 1936 to 1952, as George VI could at any time have produced a son who would have been heir apparent. At the close of the 20th century the heir apparent to Elizabeth was Charles, Prince of Wales.

**Heir of Linne, The.** The hero of an old ballad given in PERCY'S RELIQUES (1765). It tells how he wasted his substance in riotous living and, having spent all, sold his estates to his steward, keeping only a poor lodge. When no one would lend him more money he tried to hang himself but fell to the ground instead. When he came to, he espied two chests full of beaten gold and a third full of white money, over which was written:

> Once more, my sonne, I sette thee clere;
> Amend thy life and follies past;
> For but thou amend thee of thy life,
> That rope must be thy end at last

He now returned to his old hall, where he was refused the loan of 40 pence by his former steward. One of the guests remarked to the steward that he ought to have lent it, as he had bought the estate cheap enough. 'Cheap, call you it?' said the steward. 'Why, he shall have it back for 100 marks less.' 'Done,' said the heir of Linne, and recovered his estates.

**Hel.** In early Scandinavian mythology, the name of the abode of the dead and of its goddess. Later, it was the home of those not slain in battle, whereas slain warriors entered VALHALLA. Hel and her realm eventually acquired more sinister attributes after the advent of Christianity.

**Heldenbuch** (German, 'book of heroes'). The name given to a collection of 13th-century German epic poetry. The stories are based upon national sagas, Dietrich of Bern (*see* THEODORIC) being a central figure.

**Helen.** The prototype and archetype of female beauty. In Greek legend she was the daughter of ZEUS and LEDA and the wife of MENELAUS, king of Sparta. She eloped with PARIS and thus brought about the siege and destruction of TROY. *See also* FACE THAT LAUNCHED A THOUSAND SHIPS.

**Helen's fire.** *See* CORPOSANT.

**Helena.** The saint (*c*.248–*c*.328) who was the mother of Constantine the Great. She is represented in royal robes, wearing an imperial crown as an empress, sometimes carrying a model of the HOLY SEPULCHRE, other times carrying a large cross. Sometimes she also bears the three nails by which the Saviour was affixed to the cross. Her day is 18 August. *See also* INVENTION OF THE CROSS.

The island of St Helena in the South Atlantic was discovered by the Portuguese on 21 May 1502, St Helena's Day as observed in the Eastern Church. It was the place of NAPOLEON BONAPARTE's exile from 1815 until his death in 1821.

**Helicon.** The home of the MUSES, a part of PARNASSUS. It contained the fountains of AGANIPPE and HIPPOCRENE, connected by 'Helicon's harmonious stream'. The name is used allusively of poetic inspiration.

> From Helicon's harmonious springs
> A thousand rills their mazy progress take.
> The laughing flowers, that round them blow,
> Drink life and fragrance as they flow.
> THOMAS GRAY: *The Progress of Poesy* (1757)

**Heliogabalus.** *See* ELAGABALUS.

**Heliopolis** (Greek, *hēlios*, 'sun', and *polis*, 'city'). The CITY OF THE SUN, a Greek form of (1) Baalbek, in Syria, and (2) On, in ancient Egypt (to the northeast of Cairo), where the sun was worshipped in the name of RA (Re) or ATEN.

**Helios** (Greek *hēlios*, 'sun'). The Greek sun god, who climbed the vault of heaven in a chariot drawn by snow-white horses to give light and in the evening descended into the ocean. He is called HYPERION by Homer and, in later times, APOLLO.

**Heliotrope** (Greek, *hēlios*, 'sun', and *tropos*, 'turn'). For the story of the flower, *see* CLYTIE.

The bloodstone, a greenish quartz with veins and spots of red, used to be called heliotrope, the story being that if thrown into water it turned the rays of the sun to blood colours. This stone also had the power of rendering its bearer invisible.

> Nor hope had they of crevice where to hide,
> Or heliotrope to charm them out of view.
> DANTE: *Vision, Hell*, xxiv (Cary's translation (1805))

**Hell.** The abode of the dead, then traditionally the place of torment or punishment after death (Old English *hell*, related to *helan*, 'to cover').

According to the KORAN, hell has seven portals leading into seven divisions (sura xv).

True BUDDHISM admits of no hell properly so called, but certain of the more superstitious Buddhists acknowledge as many as 136 places of punishment after death, where the dead are sent according to their deserts. *See also* NIRVANA.

According to classical authors, the Inferno is encompassed by five rivers: ACHERON, COCYTUS, STYX, PHLEGETHON and LETHE. *See also* AVERNUS; GEHENNA; HADES; HEAVEN; PURGATORY; TARTARUS.

**Hell-bent.** Grimly determined.

**Hell-cat.** A spiteful and fierce-tempered woman.

**Hellfire Club.** A notorious 18th-century coterie founded about 1755 by Sir Francis Dashwood, afterwards Baron Le Despencer (1708–81). Its 13 members conducted their profanities and revelries at Medmenham Abbey, Buckinghamshire, which formed part of the Dashwood property. Among the 'Monks of Medmenham' were John Wilkes, Paul Whitehead, the satirist, who was secretary and steward, Charles Churchill and the Earl of Sandwich. The motto of the fraternity was: *Fay ce que voudras* ('Do as thou shalt wish').

**Hell for leather.** As fast as possible; at top speed. The phrase originally applied to riding on horseback, the saddle being the 'leather'. Popular etymologists like to derive the expression from 'all of a lather' or 'L for leather', the latter as a letter of some phonetic alphabet.

**Hell hath no fury like a woman scorned.** A popular saying derived from William Congreve's *The Mourning Bride* (III, viii (1697)).

> Heav'n has no rage, like love to hatred turn'd,
> Nor Hell a fury, like a woman scorn'd.

Colley Cibber's *Love's Last Shift* (1696) has, 'we shall find no fiend in hell can match the fury of a disappointed woman, – scorned, slighted, dismissed without a parting pang.'

**Hell-hole.** A thoroughly unpleasant or disagreeable place.

**Hell-hound.** A hound from hell and especially CERBERUS. Also, any fiend.

**Hell, Hull and Halifax.** *See under* HULL.

**Hell of a** or **Helluva.** Great, very, as: 'A hell of a speed,' 'One helluva nice guy.'

**Hell-raiser.** A person who causes trouble or creates chaos.

**Hell's Angels.** Members of a group of unruly motorcyclists originating in California in the 1950s. They typically wear denim or leather jackets, and their symbol is a DEATH'S HEAD. In due course Hell's Angels appeared in Britain and Europe. They are often tattooed, flaunt Nazi symbols and badges and are infamous for their lawlessness and initiation rites.

**Hell's bells** or **Hell's teeth.** An exclamation of any strong emotion or reaction.

**Hell's Corner.** The triangle of Kent centring on Dover was so called in the Second World War from being both the recipient of German bombardment from across the English Channel and the scene of much of the fiercest air combat during the BATTLE OF BRITAIN (1940).

**Hell to pay.** Serious trouble or dire consequences.

**All hell broke loose.** *See under* ALL.

**Cat in hell's chance, A.** *See under* CAT.

**Come hell or high water.** *See under* COME.

**For the hell of it.** *See under* FOR.

**Give someone hell, To.** To make things very unpleasant for them.

**Lead apes in hell, To.** *See under* LEAD.

**Like a bat out of hell.** *See under* LIKE.

**Like hell.** *See under* LIKE.

**Not a hope in hell.** No hope at all.

**Play merry hell with, To.** *See under* PLAY.

**Raise hell, To.** *See under* RAISE.

**Road to hell is easy, The.** *See* AVERNUS.

**Road to hell is paved with good intentions, The.** *See under* ROAD.

**Vicar of Hell, The.** *See under* VICAR.

**What the hell?** *See under* WHAT.

**Hellenes.** According to J.E. Renan (*Life of Jesus*, xiv (1863)): 'This word had in Palestine three different meanings: sometimes it designated the pagans; sometimes the Jews, speaking Greek and dwelling among the pagans; and sometimes proselytes of the gate, that is, men of pagan origin converted to Judaism, but not circumcised.'

The Greeks were called Hellenes from Hellen, the son of DEUCALION AND PYRRHA, their legendary ancestors. The name has descended to the modern Greeks, and their sovereign was not 'king of Greece', but 'king of the Hellenes'. After the abolition of the monarchy in 1973 a 'Hellenic Republic' was instituted. The ancient Greeks called their country *Hellas*, and the republic has this as its modern Greek name. It was the Romans who called it *Graecia* which, among the inhabitants themselves, referred only to Epirus.

**Hellenic.** The common dialect of the Greek writers after the age of Alexander the Great. It was based on ATTIC.

**Hellenistic.** The dialect of the Greek language used by the Jews. It was full of Oriental idioms and metaphors. The term likewise particularly denotes Greek culture and art modified by foreign and oriental influences after the conquests of Alexander the Great.

**Hellenists.** Those Jews who used the Greek or Hellenic language. Hellenists are also Greek scholars.

**Hellespont.** The ancient name of the Dardanelles, meaning 'sea of Helle', and so called because Helle, the sister of Phryxus, was drowned there. She was fleeing with her brother through the air to Colchis on the golden ram to escape from Ino (LEUCOTHEA), her mother-in-law, who most cruelly oppressed her, but, turning giddy, she fell into the sea. It is celebrated in the legend of HERO AND LEANDER. *See also* GOLDEN FLEECE.

**Hello.** A common expression of greeting or of surprise, the latter sometimes in expanded form, as: 'Why, hello!' The word itself is a variant of 'hollo', in turn a form of 'holla', a call for attention, from French *holà*, 'ho, there'. Alternative spellings are 'hullo' and 'hallo'.

**Hello, sailor!** A camp greeting born of sailors' reputation for homosexuality induced by long spells at sea, but no doubt originally a prostitute's call to a sailor on shore leave. The phrase was made familiar by various radio and television programmes, such as *The Goon Show* (*see* GOONS) and *Monty Python's Flying Circus* (1969–74).

**Golden hello.** *See under* GOLDEN.

**Helm, Ease the.** *See under* EASE.

**Helmet.** The helmets of Saragossa were in most repute in the days of CHIVALRY.

Bever or drinking-piece: one of the movable parts, which was lifted up when the wearer ate or drank; the name derives from the old Italian verb *bevere*, 'to drink'

Close helmet: the complete headpiece, having in front two movable parts, which could be lifted up or down at pleasure

Morion: a low iron cap, worn only by infantry

Visor: one of the movable parts, an opening to look through

**Helmet in heraldry, The.** When it rests on the chief of the shield and bearing the crest, the helmet indicates rank.

Royalty: gold, with six bars, or with the visor raised (in full face)

Duke or marquess: silver, with five bars (in full face)

Earl, viscount or baron: silver, with four bars, with visor raised (in profile)

Knight or baron: steel, without bars, and with visor open (in full face)

Squire or gentleman: steel, with visor closed (in profile)

A helmet is never put over the arms of a woman, other than the sovereign.

**Helmet of Mohammed, The.** MOHAMMED wore a double helmet. It is known that the exterior one was called *al-mawashah* ('the wreathed garland').

**Helmet of Perseus, The.** This, the 'helmet of HADES', which rendered the wearer invisible, was taken with its winged sandals and magic wallet from certain NYMPHS, but after he had slain MEDUSA Perseus restored them again and presented the GORGON's head to ATHENE, who placed it in the middle of her AEGIS.

**Héloïse.** *See* ABELARD.

**Helot, A drunken.** *See under* DRUNK.

**Help. Help a lame dog over a stile, To.** To help someone in distress; to offer a helping hand.

> Do the work that's nearest,
> Though it's dull at whiles,
> Helping, when we meet them,
> Lame dogs over stiles.
> CHARLES KINGSLEY: 'The Invitation. To Tom Hughes' (1856)

**God helps those who help themselves.** *See under* GOD.

**Helve. Put the axe in the helve, To.** *See under* AXE.

**Send the axe after the helve, To.** *See under* SEND.

**Throw the helve after the hatchet, To.** *See under* THROW.

**Hemlock.** A poisonous biennial plant (*Conium maculatum*), with umbels of small white flowers, found in Britain, Europe and parts of Asia and western Africa, also naturalized in North and South America. The roots and fruit are specially dangerous. Poisoning by hemlock was used in ancient Greece to kill condemned criminals and evil-doers. *See also* SOCRATES.

**Hen. Hen and chickens.** In Christian art, this device is emblematic of God's providence. *See also* GREY HEN.

**Hen night.** An all-women party for a bride the night before her wedding. *See also* STAG NIGHT.

> I was the hen at a hen night. Consider it, your Honour, a case of high jinx [*sic*] and hilarity rather than debauchery. We ordered no stripagrams, we frequented no dive bars. I was simply the victim of a girls' night out.
> *The Times* (5 November 1994)

**Henpecked.** Of a husband, persistently nagged by his wife. *See also* CAUDLE LECTURE.

**As fussy as a hen with one chick.** *See under* AS.

**As scarce as hen's teeth.** *See under* AS.

**Grey hen, A.** *See under* GREY.

**Tappit-hen.** *See under* TAPPIT.

**Hendiadys** (Greek, 'one through two'). A figure of speech in which one idea is expressed by two words joined by 'and', as in 'gloom and despondency', 'nice and warm'.

**Hengist and Horsa.** The semi-legendary leaders who led the first Saxon band of warriors to settle in England. They are said to have arrived in Kent in 449 at the invitation of VORTIGERN, who offered them land on the understanding that they would help against the PICTS. Horsa is said to have been slain at the Battle of Aylesford (*c.*455), and Hengist to have ruled in Kent until his death in 488. The name Horsa derives from Old English *hors* and Hengist from Old English *hengest*, both meaning 'horse'. The traditional badge of Kent is a white horse.

**Henley, Orator.** *See under* ORATOR.

**Henry. Henry Grâce à Dieu.** *See* GREAT HARRY.

**Henry the Navigator.** The fourth son of King John I of Portugal, Henry (1394–1460) took part in 1415 in the capture of Ceuta from the Moors and then settled at Sagres, Cape St Vincent, where he built an observatory and training school for navigation. As a result the Madeiras were discovered in 1418, and the systematic exploration of the Guinea coast began in 1430. Cape Verde was rounded in 1446 and the Azores reached in 1448, by which time Prince Henry had aroused a national interest in further exploration.

**Hep** or **hip.** American slang meaning 'alive to', 'aware'. Despite much speculation, the exact origin of the word remains unknown. *See also* HIPPIE.

**Hepcat.** An obsolescent word for a person who is fond of jazz or swing. *See also* ZOOT SUIT.

**Hepatoscopy.** A very ancient form of DIVINATION based upon inspection of the liver from the animal sacrificed (Greek *hēpar, hēpatos*, 'liver'). It rested on the belief that the liver was the seat of vitality and of the soul.

> For the king of Babylon stood at the parting of the way, at the head of the two ways, to use divination: he made his arrows bright, he consulted with images, he looked in the liver.
> Ezekiel 21:21

**Hephaestus.** The Greek VULCAN.

**Heptameron, The.** A collection of Italian and other medieval stories written by, or ascribed to, Margaret of Angoulême, queen of Navarre (1492–1549), and published posthumously in 1558. They are said to have been related in seven days (Greek *hepta*, 'seven', and *hēmera*, 'day'). *See also* DECAMERON; HEXAMERON.

**Heptarchy** (Greek, 'seven governments', from *hepta*, 'seven', and *-arkhia*, 'rule'). The term is used of the seven English kingdoms of Kent, Sussex, Wessex, Essex, East Anglia, Mercia and Northumbria during the period of their co-existence, i.e. from the 6th to the 8th centuries. This is the period when overlordship was exercised by a BRETWALDA.

**Heptateuch** (Greek *hepta*, 'seven', and *teukhos*,

'book'). A name given to the first seven books of the Bible, the PENTATEUCH plus Joshua and Judges.

**Hera.** The Greek JUNO, the wife of ZEUS. Her name is of very uncertain origin. It has been related to Greek *hērōs*, 'hero', and the former word *era*, 'earth', as well as to the Indoeuropean root element that gave English year, German *Jahr* etc.

**Heracles.** *See* HERCULES.

**Herald** (Old French *herault*, of Germanic origin). The herald was an officer whose duty it was to proclaim war or peace or carry challenges to battle and messages between sovereigns. Heralds had their attendants called PURSUIVANTS. Nowadays war or peace is still proclaimed by the heralds, but their chief duty as court functionaries is to superintend state ceremonies such as coronations and installations of knights, and also to grant arms, trace genealogies, attend to matters of precedence, honours and the like.

Edward III appointed two heraldic kings at arms for south and north, called Surroy and Norroy. The English College of Heralds was incorporated by Richard III in 1483–4. It consists of three Kings of Arms, six Heralds and four Pursuivants, under the EARL MARSHAL, a hereditary office in the line of the Dukes of Norfolk.

The three Kings of Arms are

Garter King of Arms (blue): so called from his special duty to attend at the solemnities of election, investiture and installation of Knights of the Garter. He is Principal King of Arms for all England

CLARENCEUX KING OF ARMS: so called from the Duke of Clarence, brother of Edward IV. His jurisdiction extends over England south of the Trent

Norroy and Ulster King of Arms (purple): has jurisdiction over England on the north side of the Trent and over Northern Ireland

The six Heralds are styled Somerset, Richmond, Lancaster, Windsor, Chester and York. The four Pursuivants are Rouge Dragon, Blue Mantle, Portcullis and Rouge Croix. The Bath King of Arms is not a member of the Herald's College and is concerned only with the Order of the Bath.

In Scotland, heraldry is the function of the Lyon office and it consists of the LORD LYON KING OF ARMS, three Heralds (Albany, Marchmont and Rothesay), three ordinary Pursuivants (Unicorn, Carrick, Dingwell or Kintyre) and two Pursuivants Extraordinary (Linlithgow and Falkland).

**Windsor Herald.** *See under* WINDSOR.

**Heraldry.** Originally a term applied to the science and functions of a HERALD but now more usually restricted to the knowledge or science of armorial bearings, formerly known as ARMORY.

A COAT OF ARMS consists of the shield, the HELMET, crest, mantling and supporters. The motto is not strictly part of the coat of arms or armorial achievement.

The shield is the main part of the achievement and the colours used upon it are azure (blue), gules (red), purpure (purple), sable (black), vert (green). Argent (silver) and or (gold) are known as metals and the other tinctures are called furs (ermine, ermines, erminois, pean, potent and vair). The items put on the ground of the shield are called charges (e.g. bends, chevrons, piles, fesses, bars, crosses, animals, birds, reptiles and various inanimate objects).

'Differencing' is the alteration of a coat to distinguish between the various members and branches of a family.

'Marshalling' is the science of bringing together the arms of several families in one escutcheon.

In heraldry, punning on names and words is called 'canting'. *See also* CANTING ARMS.

The following are some of the principal terms used in heraldry:

Bars: horizontal bands (more than one) across the middle of the shield
Bend: a diagonal stripe
Bordure: an edge of a different colour round the whole shield
Chevron: a bent stripe, as worn by non-commissioned officers in the army, but with the point upwards
Chief: the upper one-third of the shield divided horizontally
Cinquefoil: a five-petalled formalized flower
Couchant: lying down
Counter-passant: moving in opposite directions
Couped: cut straight at the stem or neck
Coward: coué, with tail hanging between the legs
Displayed (of birds): with wings and talons outspread
Dormant: sleeping
Endorse: a very narrow vertical stripe; *see also* PALE
Erased: with nothing below the stem or neck, which ends roughly as opposed to the sharp edge of COUPED
Fesse: a broad horizontal stripe across the middle of the shield
File: a horizontal bar from which normally depend one or more smaller bars called labels
Gardant: full-faced
Hauriant: standing on its tail (of fishes)
Issuant: rising from the stop or bottom of an ORDINARY
Lodged: reposing (of stags and so forth )
Martlet: a swallow with no feet
Mullet: a star of a stated number of points
Naiant: swimming (of fishes)
Nascent: rising out of the middle of an ORDINARY
Ordinary: a primary charge (e.g. BEND, PALE, FESSE, CHEVRON, PILE, cross, roundel and so on)
Pale: a wide vertical stripe down the centre of the shield
Pallet: a narrow vertical stripe

**Heraldry: the basic ordinaries**

Passant: walking, the face in profile (emblematic of resolution)
Passant gardant: walking, with full face (emblematic of resolution and prudence)
Passant regardant: walking and looking behind
Pile: a narrow triangle
Rampant: rearing, with face in profile (emblematic of magnanimity)
Rampant gardant: erect on the hind legs, full face (emblematic of prudence)
Rampant regardant: erect on the hind legs, side face looking behind (emblematic of circumspection)
Regardant: looking back (emblematic of circumspection)
Salient: springing (emblematic of valour)
Sejant: seated (emblematic of counsel)
Statant: standing still
Trippant: running (of stags and so forth)
Volant: flying

**Beasts of heraldry.** *See under* BEAST.
**Cross in heraldry, The.** *See under* CROSS.
**Helmet in heraldry, The.** *See under* HELMET.
**Lion in heraldry, The.** *See under* LION.

**Herb. Herba sacra.** The 'divine weed', vervain, said by the Romans to cure the bites of all rabid animals, to arrest the progress of venom, to cure the plague, to avert sorcery and WITCHCRAFT, to reconcile enemies and so on. It was so highly esteemed that feasts called Verbenalia were annually held in its honour. HERALDS wore a wreath of vervain when they declared war, and the DRUIDS are said to have held it in veneration.

> Lift your boughs of vervain blue.
> Dipt in cold September dew;
> And dash the moisture, chaste and clear,
> O'er the ground and through the air.
> Now the place is purged and pure.
> W. MASON: *Caractacus* (1759)

**Herb of Grace.** Rue is probably so called because, owing to its extreme bitterness, it is the symbol of repentance.

> Here did she fall a tear; here in this place,
> I'll set a bank of rue, sour herb of grace;
> Rue, even for ruth, here shortly shall be seen,
> In the remembrance of a weeping queen.
> SHAKESPEARE: *Richard II*, III, iv (1595)

**Hercule Poirot.** *See under* POIROT.

**Hercules** (Greek *Hēra*, 'Hera', and *kleos*, 'glory'). In Greek mythology a hero of superhuman physical strength, the son of ZEUS and ALCMENA. He is represented as brawny, muscular and short-necked, often holding a club and a lion's skin. In a fit of madness inflicted on him by JUNO, he slew his wife and children, and as penance was ordered by APOLLO to serve the Argive king, Eurystheus, for 12 years. The latter imposed 12 tasks of great difficulty and danger on him:

(1) To slay the NEMEAN LION
(2) To kill the Lernaean HYDRA
(3) To catch and retain the Arcadian stag
(4) To destroy the Erymanthian boar
(5) To cleanse the AUGEAN STABLES
(6) To destroy the STYMPHALIAN BIRDS
(7) To take captive the Cretan bull
(8) To catch the horses of the Thracian Diomedes
(9) To get possession of the girdle of HIPPOLYTA, queen of the Amazons
(10) To capture the oxen of the monster GERYON
(11) To obtain the apples of the HESPERIDES
(12) To bring CERBERUS from the infernal regions

After these labours and many other adventures he was rewarded with immortality.

**Herculean knot.** A snaky device on the rod or CADUCEUS of MERCURY, adopted by Grecian brides as the fastening of their woollen girdles, which only the bridegroom was allowed to untie. As he did so, he invoked JUNO to render his marriage as those of HERCULES, whose numerous wives all had families, among them being the 50 daughters of Thestius, all of whom conceived in one night. *See also* TRUELOVER KNOT.

**Hercules and his load.** The sign of the Globe Theatre showing Hercules carrying the globe upon his shoulders. Shakespeare alludes to it in *Hamlet* (II, ii (1600)):

> *Hamlet*: Do the boys carry it away?
> *Rosencrantz*: Ay, that they do, my lord; Hercules and his load too.

**Hercules' choice.** Immortality, the reward of toil in preference to pleasure. Xenophon writes that when Hercules was a youth he was accosted by Virtue and Pleasure and asked to choose between them. Pleasure promised him all carnal delights, but Virtue promised immortality. Hercules gave his hand to the latter and, after a life of toil, was received among the gods.

**Hercules' horse.** *See* ARION.

**Hercules Secundus.** Commodus, the Roman emperor (AD 161–192), gave himself this title. Dissipated and inordinately cruel, he claimed divine honours and caused himself to be worshipped as Hercules. It is said that he killed 100 lions in the amphitheatre and that he slew over 1000 defenceless gladiators.

**Attic Hercules, The.** *See under* ATTIC.
**Columns** or **Pillars of Hercules.** *See under* PILLAR.
**Farnese Hercules, The.** *See under* FARNESE.

**Here. Here and now.** Immediately.
**Here and there.** In various places.
**Here goes!** Said at the start of some bold or even foolhardy act.
**Here's to you.** I drink your health. The person toasted will obviously vary. *See also* HEALTHS.

> Here's to the maiden of bashful fifteen,
> Here's to the widow of fifty;
> Here's to the flaunting extravagant queen,
> And here's to the housewife that's thrifty.
> R.B. SHERIDAN: *The School for Scandal*, III, iii (1777)

**Here, there and everywhere.** All over; said of something ubiquitous.

**Here today and gone tomorrow.** Said of someone or something transient or unreliable.

**Here we go again.** Said when the same events reoccur, especially when undesirable.

**Neither here nor there.** *See under* NEITHER.

**Heresy, Antonine.** *See under* ANTONINE.

**Heretic** (Greek *haeresis*, 'choosing'). A heretic is one who holds unorthodox opinions in matters of religion, i.e. he chooses his own creed.

The principal heretical sects of the first six centuries were:

1st century: Simonians (from SIMON MAGUS), Cerinthians (Cerinthus), Ebionites (Ebion) and Nicolaitans (Nicholas, deacon of Antioch)

2nd century: Basilidians (Basilides), Carpocratians (Carpocrates), Valentinians (Valentinus), GNOSTICS (Knowing Ones), NAZARENES, MILLENARIANS, CAINITES (Cain), Sethians (Seth), Quartodecimans (who kept EASTER on the 14th day of Nisan, our April), Cerdonians (Cerdon), MARCIONITES (Marcion), Montanists (Montanus), Alogians (who denied the 'Word'), Angelics (who worshipped angels), Tatianists (Tatian), QUINTILIANS

3rd century: The Patri-passians, Arabici, Aquarians, Novatians, Origenists (followers of Origen), Melchisedechians (who believed Melchisedec was the Messiah), SABELLIANS (from Sabellius) and MANICHEANS (followers of Mani)

4th century: ARIANS (from Arius), Colluthians (Colluthus), MACEDONIANS, AGNOITAE (they denied that God knew the past and the future), APOLLINARIANS (Apollinaris), Collyridians (who offered cakes to the Virgin Mary), Seleucians (Seleucus), Priscillians (Priscillian), Anthropomorphites (who ascribed a human form to God), Jovinianists (Jovinian), Messalians and Bonosians (Bonosus)

5th century: PELAGIANS (Pelagius), NESTORIANS (Nestorius), Eutychians (Eutychus), MONOPHYSITES (who held that Christ had but a single, and that a divine, nature), Predestinarians, Timotheans (Timothy, Monophysite Patriarch of Alexandria)

6th century: Theopaschites (Monophysites who held that God was crucified in Christ's Passion), the new Agnoitae (Monophysite followers of Themistus)

*See also* ALBIGENSES; BOGOMILS; WALDENSIANS.

**Hergest, The Red Book of.** *See under* RED.

**Heriot.** A feudal kind of death duty, as the lord of the manor's right to the best beast or chattel of a deceased villein. Freemen also owed heriots to their overlords of horses and armour. The word is from Old English *heregeatwa*, 'army trappings', which were originally on loan to the tenant.

**Hermann Gessler.** *See under* GESSLER.

**Hermaphrodite.** A person or animal with both male and female sexual characteristics, or in botany a flower with both male and female reproductive organs. The word is derived from Hermaphroditus, son of HERMES and APHRODITE. The nymph Salmacis became enamoured of him and prayed that she might be so closely united that 'the twain might become one flesh'. Her prayer was heard and the nymph and the boy became one body. According to fable, all persons who bathed in the fountain Salmacis, in Caria, became hermaphrodites.

**Hermas, The Shepherd of.** *See under* SHEPHERD.

**Hermes.** The Greek MERCURY, whose busts, known as Hermae, were affixed to pillars and set up as boundary marks at street corners. The Romans also used them for garden ornaments. The origin of the god's name is uncertain. It has been linked with Greek *hermeneus*, 'interpreter', meaning that Hermes was the interpreter of the gods. Hence hermeneutics as the science of interpretation, especially of the Scriptures.

**Hermes Trismegistus** ('Hermes Thrice Greatest'). A Greek name for the Egyptian god THOTH, identifying him with their own god HERMES. He was credited with 42 encyclopedic works on Egypt, many of them dealing with alchemy, mysticism and magic.

**Hermetically sealed.** Closed so as to be airtight. Disciples of HERMES TRISMEGISTUS would heat the neck of a vessel until it was soft and then twist it until the aperture closed up.

**Hermione.** In Greek mythology the wife of CADMUS, but better known as the daughter of HELEN and MENELAUS who was promised to ORESTES but given in marriage to Pyrrhus, himself passionately in love with ANDROMACHE. In Racine's tragedy *Andromaque* (1667) she plays Orestes against Pyrrhus and commits suicide when the latter is murdered at her own instigation. In Shakespeare's *The Winter's Tale* (1610), as the noble wife of Leontes, Hermione is wrongly accused of adultery.

**Hermit. Hermit of Grub Street, The.** Henry Welby (*c*.1552–1636) of Gedney, Lincolnshire, who became a recluse in GRUB STREET at the age of 40, having resolved to live alone after suffering a pistol attack from his younger brother. He was never seen outside his house and died at the age of 84. He lived abstemiously and was attended by an elderly servant maid, spending his means on the sick and the poor. He had been a student at St John's College, Cambridge, and seems to have spent his time reading.

**Hermit of Warkworth, The.** The subject of a poem of this name by Bishop Percy (of PERCY'S RELIQUES), former chaplain to the Duke of Northumberland. His ballad, which appeared in 1771, gives a realistic picture of the early hermitage on the north bank of the River Coquet about a quarter of a mile (400m) upstream of Warkworth Castle. It is hollowed out of the freestone cliff on the river bank and has an arched chapel with an altar and two other cells as well as steps cut in the rock leading to the hermit's small garden. The chapel is still used for occasional services.

> Then, scooped within the solid rock,
> Three sacred vaults he shows;
> The chief, a chapel, neatly arch'd,
> On branching columns rose.

**Hermit's Derby.** One of the best known races in the history of the TURF, when the race horse Hermit, belonging to Henry Chaplin (1840–1923), later Viscount Chaplin, won the DERBY STAKES of 1867 against all expectations and the notorious Marquess of Hastings lost £120,000 in bets.

**Peter the Hermit.** *See under* PETER.

**Queen's Square Hermit, The.** *See under* QUEEN.

**St Paul the Hermit.** *See under* PAUL.

**Herne the Hunter.** *See* WILD HUNTSMAN.

**Hero. Hero and Leander.** The old Greek tale is that Hero, a priestess of VENUS, fell in love with Leander, who swam across the HELLESPONT every night to visit her. One night he was drowned, and heartbroken Hero drowned herself in the same sea. The story is told in one of the poems of Musaeus and in Marlowe and Chapman's *Hero and Leander* (1598).

Lord Byron and Lieutenant Ekenhead repeated the ill-fated exploit of Leander in 1810 and accomplished it in 1 hour 10 minutes. The distance, allowing for drifting, would be about 4 miles (6km). In *Don Juan* (ii (1819–24)), Byron says of his hero:

> A better swimmer you could scarce see ever,
> He could, perhaps, have pass'd the Hellespont,
> As once (a feat on which ourselves we prided)
> Leander, Mr Ekenhead, and I did.

**Hero from zero.** A term sometimes used of a person who has 'made good' from humble beginnings, otherwise a SELF-MADE MAN.

**Hero of the hundred fights.** CONN, a semi-legendary Irish king of the 2nd century.

**Hero of the Nile, The.** Horatio, Lord Nelson (1758–1805), from his great victory at Aboukir Bay (1798), for which he was made Baron Nelson of the Nile.

**Herod, To out-herod.** *See under* OUT.

**Heroic. Heroic age.** The age of a nation that comes between the purely mythical period and the historic. This is the age when the sons of the gods were said to take unto themselves the daughters of men, and the offspring partake of the twofold character.

**Heroic size.** In sculpture, a stature that is larger than life without being colossal.

**Heroic verse.** Verse in which epic poetry is generally written. In Greek and Latin it is HEXAMETER verse, in English it is ten-syllable IAMBIC verse, whether rhyming or not, and in Italian it is the OTTAVA RIMA. It is so called because it is employed to celebrate heroic exploits.

**Heroin.** The so-called recreational drug was introduced in the 1890s by Friedrich Bayer & Co in Germany as a substitute for morphine. It gives an extraordinary sense of euphoria, suggesting that its name may derive from Greek *heros*, 'hero'. It can be 'snorted', injected into veins or smoked, when the user will probably CHASE THE DRAGON. It is produced from the opium poppy, grown extensively in the GOLDEN TRIANGLE. The hazards of heroin use are appalling and involve loss of appetite, convulsions, vomiting, loss of bowel control, sleeplessness, impotence in men, infertility in women and ultimately death. *See also* NICKNAMES OF DRUGS.

**Herrenvolk.** A German word meaning broadly 'master race'. In NAZI usage it implied the superiority of the German peoples.

**Herring. Herringbone.** In building, courses of stone or brick laid angularly, thus: <<<<<<. The term is also applied to strutting placed between thin joists to increase their strength.

In needlework, the name is that of an embroidery stitch, similar to cross-stitch, used as decoration or to fasten down heavy material.

**Herring Pond, The.** The ocean or dividing seas, especially the Atlantic, which separates America from the British Isles.

> I'le send an account of the wonders I meet on the Great Herring Pond.
>
> JOHN DUNTON: *Letters from New England* (1686)

**Battle of the Herrings, The.** *See under* BATTLE.

**Caller herrings.** *See under* CALLER.

**King of the Herrings, The.** *See under* KING.

**Neither fish, flesh, nor good red herring.** *See under* NEITHER.

**No herring, no wedding.** A bad fishing season discourages marriage among fisherfolk.

**Red herring.** *See under* RED.

**Hershey bar.** In the USA a well-known make of chocolate bar, which was available only to the troops in the Second World War. The name is that of Milton S. Hershey (1857–1945), who founded the Hershey Chocolate Corporation in 1903. General Lewis B. Hershey (1893–1977) was Director of the Selective Service System (1941–70), the agency that drafted millions of young American men into the armed forces. In US army slang the term Hershey bar was thus applied to the narrow gold bar worn by troops on the left sleeve to indicate that they had done six months' overseas service.

**Hertha.** *See* NERTHUS.

**Hesperia** (Greek, 'western'). Italy was so called by the Greeks, because it was to them the 'Western Land'. The Romans, for a similar reason, later transferred the name to Spain.

**Hesperides.** Three sisters who guarded the golden apples which HERA received as a marriage gift. They were assisted by the dragon LADON. HERCULES, as the eleventh of his labours, slew the dragon and carried some of the apples to Eurystheus.

Many poets call the place where these golden apples grew the 'Garden of the Hesperides'.

> But Beauty, like the fair Hesperian tree
> Laden with blooming gold, had need the guard
> Of dragon-watch with unenchanted eye,
> To save her blossoms, and defend her fruit,
> From the rash hand of bold Incontinence.
> MILTON: *Comus* (1637)

Shakespeare (*Love's Labour's Lost*, IV, iii (1595)) speaks of 'climbing trees in the Hesperides'.

**Hesperus.** The name given by the Greeks to the planet VENUS as an evening star. As a morning star it was called LUCIFER or Phosphorus. *See also* HESPERIA.

> Ere twice in murk and occidental damp
> Moist Hesperus hath quench'd his sleepy lamp.
> SHAKESPEARE: *All's Well that Ends Well*, II, i (1602)

**Wreck of the Hesperus, The.** *See under* WRECK.

**Hessian.** A coarse, strong cloth made from jute or hemp, originally made in Hesse in Germany.

Hessian boots were first worn by troops in Germany and became fashionable in England in the 19th century.

> While a lover's professions,
> When uttered in Hessians,
> Are eloquent everywhere!
> W.S. GILBERT: *Patience* (1881)

**Hesychasts** (Greek *hēsukhos*, 'quiet'). In the Eastern Church, supporters of the ascetic mysticism propagated by the monks of Mount Athos in the 14th century. They were also known as Palamists after Gregory Palamas (*c*.1296–1350), who became the chief exponent of Hesychasm. The object of their exercises was to attain a vision of the 'Divine Light', which they held to be God's 'energy'. Hesychasm lasted until the 17th century.

**Hexameron** (Greek *hex*, 'six', and *hēmera*, 'day'). A period of six days, especially the biblical six days of the Creation.

**Hexameter.** The metre in which Greek and Latin epics were written and which has been imitated in English in such poems as H.W. Longfellow's *Evangeline* (1847), Arthur Hugh Clough's *Bothie of Tober-na-Vuolich* (1848) and Charles Kingsley's 'Andromeda' (1858).

The line consists of six feet, dactyls or spondees for the first four, the fifth is almost always a dactyl (but sometimes a spondee), and the sixth a spondee or trochee.

Verse consisting of alternate hexameters and pentameters is known as ELEGIAC. S.T. Coleridge illustrates this:

> In the hexameter rises the fountain's silvery column;
> In the pentameter aye falling in melody back.
> 'The Ovidian Elegiac Metre' (1834)

**Hexateuch.** *See* ELOHISTIC AND YAHWISTIC SOURCES; HEPTATEUCH; PENTATEUCH.

**Hezekiah.** The twelfth king of JUDAH (2 Kings 18–20). His reign is saved by the intervention of the angel that killed SENNACHERIB's troops, and as he lies dying, God tells him that his life has been extended by 15 years. The repulse of Sennacherib, however, turns out to be only a reprieve.

**Hiawatha.** The Iroquois name of a hero of miraculous birth who came (under a variety of names) among the Native American tribes to bring peace and goodwill to man.

In H.W. Longfellow's poem (1855) he is an Ojibway, son of Mudjekeewis (otherwise Kabeyun, 'the west wind') and Wenonah ('first-born'), and married MINNEHAHA (interpreted as 'laughing water' but perhaps actually meaning 'he makes rivers'). He represents the progress of civilization among his people. When the white man landed and taught the Indians the faith of Jesus, Hiawatha exhorted them to receive the words of wisdom, to reverence the missionaries who had come far to see them.

**Hibernia.** The Latin name for Ireland, a variant of Celtic *Iveriu*. *See also* IRELAND.

**Hic jacets.** Tombstones, so called from the first two words of the Latin inscription: *Hic jacet* ('Here lies').

> And by the cold Hic Jacets of the dead.
> TENNYSON: *Idylls of the King*, 'Merlin and Vivien' (1859)

**Hickathrift, Tom.** A hero of nursery rhyme and mythical strong man, fabled to have been a labourer at the time of the Norman Conquest. Armed with an axletree and cartwheel, he killed a giant who dwelt in a marsh at Tilney All Saints, Norfolk. He was knighted and made a governor of Thanet.

**Hickok, Wild Bill.** James Butler Hickok (1837–76), American soldier and scout, was called Wild Bill. As a renowned pistol shot in his early days, he served as a stage driver and later in the Union army during the Civil War (1861–5) as a scout and sharpshooter. He became a deputy marshal in 1866 and served as a scout for General Custer and others. In 1869–71 he was marshal in Kansas. He was of great strength and courage and shot many thieves and outlaws, in 1872–3 touring in the east with BUFFALO BILL. He was killed from the rear at Deadwood, Dakota.

**Hickory. Hickory cloth.** Cloth dyed with hickory juice.

**Hickory Mormons.** MORMONS of half-hearted persuasion.

**Old Hickory.** *See under* OLD.

**Hide** (noun). In feudal England the term denoted the amount of land that was sufficient to support a family, usually varying between 60 and 120 acres (24–49 ha) according to the locality or quality of the land. A hide of good land was smaller than one of poorer quality. It was long used as the basis for assessing taxes. The name represents Old English *hīgid*, related to *hīw*, 'family', 'household', and ultimately to Latin *civis*, 'citizen'.

**Hide** (verb). **Hidden Imam.** *See* MAHDI.

**Hide one's light under a bushel, To.** To conceal one's talents; to be self-effacing and modest about one's abilities. A bushel here is a vessel that contained a bushel in measure.

> Neither do men light a candle, and put it under a bushel, but on a candlestick.
>
> Matthew 5:15

**Hieroglyphics** (Greek *hieros*, 'holy', and *gluphē*, 'carving'). The picture characters of ancient Egyptian writing. For many years these inscribed symbols of beasts and birds, men and women and the like, were indecipherable. Dr Thomas Young (1773–1829) was the first to decipher part of the demotic text of the ROSETTA STONE in 1819 and prove the alphabetic nature of the signs. This provided a basis for the construction of a complete alphabet (1821–2) by J.F. Champollion (1790–1832). Since then, knowledge of ancient Egypt and its customs has been transformed.

**High. High altar.** The main altar in a church, at the east end.

**High and dry.** Stranded; left out of the current of events. A nautical metaphor.

**High and low.** Everywhere; in all places, as: 'I've hunted high and low for that book but can't find it.'

**High and mighty.** Arrogant and overbearing. *See also* HOGEN MOGEN.

**Highball.** The American term for whisky, diluted with water, soda water or ginger ale and served in a tall glass with ice.

**Highbinder.** In the USA a gangster or corrupt politician. The term alludes to the High-Binders, a 19th-century New York City gang.

**Highbrow.** A learned person; an intellectual. The term originated in the USA in the early 20th century and is also used to denote cultural, artistic and intellectual matters above one's head. Derivatives are lowbrow and middlebrow.

**High camp.** A sophisticated or ostentatious form of camp as a style or manner. *See also* CAMP IT UP.

**High Church.** That section of the CHURCH OF ENGLAND distinguished by its 'high' conception of church authority, upholding sacerdotal claims and asserting the importance of the SACRAMENTS. It also stresses the historical links with Roman Catholic Christianity. It has its origins in the reign of Elizabeth I, although the name is of the late 17th century. Archbishop Laud was of this persuasion and High Church opinions were again strengthened and re-established by the OXFORD MOVEMENT. *See also* LOW CHURCH.

**High Court.** The High Court of Justice, which in England and Wales is one of the two divisions of the Supreme Court of Judiciary, the other being the COURT OF APPEAL.

**High days and holidays.** Special occasions, a high day being a festival or great occasion. *See also* HOLIDAYS.

**Higher criticism.** Critical inquiry into literary composition and sources, especially of the Bible, also called historical criticism. The term is used in contradistinction to textual or verbal criticism, which aims to establish the correctness of the text.

**Higher education.** Education at colleges and universities, usually from the age of 18 having taken A-levels. Further education is continuing education after leaving school at 16, after the GCSE.

**Higher mathematics.** Mathematics that is more abstract and advanced than standard arithmetic, algebra, geometry and trigonometry.

**High explosive.** Any very powerful type of explosive, such as TNT or gelignite.

**High falutin'.** Pompous or pretentious. 'Falutin'', may derive from 'fluting', denoting something strident and high-pitched.

**High fidelity** or **hi-fi.** Sound reproduction on electronic equipment that gives faithful reproduction with a minimum of distortion.

**High-five.** A form of greeting or mutual congratulation of American origin in which two people slap each other's raised right hand. 'Five' refers to the five fingers.

> 'And what are these girls after, O knowledgeable one?' McDermott asks, bowing slightly as he walks. Van Patten laughs and still in motion they give each other high-five.
>
> BRET EASTON ELLIS: *American Psycho* (1991)

**High-flier.** An ambitious person; a 'go-getter'; someone successful in a particular field.

**High-flown.** Extravagant or pretentious, as a high-flown style or manner.

**High German.** The standard German language, derived from the form of German spoken in High or southern Germany. Low German is the name applied to all other German dialects, or the language of Low or northern Germany. *See also* LANGUE D'OC.

**High-handed.** Overbearing and inconsiderate; arrogant and imperious.

**High hat.** A top hat; an affectedly superior person.
**High Heels and Low Heels.** The names of two factions in Swift's tale of LILLIPUT (*Gulliver's Travels* (1726)), satirizing the HIGH CHURCH and LOW CHURCH parties.
**High jinks.** Nowadays the phrase expresses the idea of pranks, fun and jollity.

> The frolicsome company had begun to practise the ancient and now forgotten pastime of *high jinks*. This game was played in several different ways. Most frequently the dice were thrown by the company, and those upon whom the lot fell were obliged to assume and maintain for a time, a certain fictitious character, or to repeat a certain number of fescennine verses in a particular order. If they departed from the characters assigned ... they incurred forfeits, which were ... compounded for by swallowing an additional bumper.
> SIR WALTER SCOTT: *Guy Mannering*, ch xxxvi (1815)

**High jump.** Someone who is for the high jump is about to receive a reprimand or punishment. The allusion is to the 'jump' made by a hanged person at the moment of execution.
**High life.** The life of HIGH SOCIETY. *See also* LOW LIFE.
**Highlight.** The most exciting or memorable part of something. To a hair stylist, highlights are more literally a bleached blond streak in the hair.
To highlight something is to give it prominence or draw attention to it.

> Two journalists arrested after gaining access to a room where the Prince of Wales was due to sleep in Hong Kong said they had wanted to highlight lax security.
> *The Times* (7 November 1994)

**High Mass.** A solemn sung MASS, especially a Roman Catholic one.
**High-muck-a-muck** or **Lord High-muck-a-muck.** An arrogant or conceited person. The expression has become associated with English 'high' and 'muck' but originated as Chinook Jargon *hiyu muckamuck*, 'plenty of food', from Nootka *hayo*, 'ten' (for which English 'high' was substituted) and *mahomaq*, 'choice whalemeat'.
**High opinion.** A favourable one.
**High places.** In the Authorized Version of the Bible this is a literal translation of the Hebrew word *bāmâ* and applied to the local places of sacrifice where JEHOVAH was worshipped. Such sites were often on a hilltop or mound, which may account for the origin of the name. Because of their association with forms of idolatry and sometimes immoral rites, they were denounced by HOSEA. HEZEKIAH removed the high places (2 Kings 18:4), so did Asa (2 Chronicles 14:3) and others. *See also* HILLS.
**High priest.** In Judaism, the priest of highest rank who was the only one permitted to enter the HOLY OF HOLIES in the Temple.
**High profile.** A prominent public position, especially when intentionally adopted. A converse position is adopted by one who prefers TO KEEP A LOW PROFILE (*see under* LOW).
**High school.** In the USA a secondary school from grade 7 to grade 12. In Britain the term is mostly found as the name of a former GRAMMAR SCHOOL for girls.
**High seas.** As defined in international law, all the area of sea not under the sovereignty of any state.
**High season.** The summer season at a seaside resort, or winter season at a skiing resort, when hotel and other accommodation is at its most expensive.
**High society.** The fashionable sector of the upper classes. *The Philadelphia Story* (1940), one of America's finest comedy films, was remade as *High Society* (1956) in a musical version that fell far short of the wit and glamour of the original.
**High spirits.** Exuberance; lively happiness.
**High spot, The.** The best or most exciting part of something; its peak or climax. *See also* HIT THE HIGH SPOTS.
**High Street.** The street of a town that has, or used to have, the principal shops or the most familiar chain stores. It is so called not because of its elevation but because it originated as the town's main thoroughfare. It thus corresponds to the Main Street of many American towns. Some Roman roads have sections called High Street, notably that between Penrith and Ambleside in Cumbria, but this runs through hill country and is certainly named for its height. The name is properly that of the highest mountain over which it passes.
**High table.** In a college dining hall, the table at the top end of the hall at which the dons sit.
**High tea.** A meal, at about the usual teatime, which includes a light cooked dish. It is common in Scotland and the north of England.
**High time.** A time that is overdue and almost too late.

> Now it is high time to awake out of sleep: for now is our salvation nearer than when we believed.
> Romans 13:11

**High treason.** An act of treachery against the SOVEREIGN of the state, a violation of one's allegiance. *See also* MISPRISION OF TREASON; PETTY TREASON.
**All-time high, An.** *See under* ALL.
**As high as a kite.** *See under* AS.
**Hit the high spots, To.** *See under* HIT.
**Lord High Constable of Scotland.** *See under* LORD.
**On one's high horse, To be.** To be overbearing and arrogant. Formerly people of rank rode on tall horses or chargers.

**Highgate, Sworn at.** *See under* SWEAR.

**Highlands, The.** Precise definitions vary, but generally the name can be taken to refer to the part of Scotland that lies northwest of the great fault that runs from Dumbarton to Stonehaven. Stirling is known as the Gateway to the Highlands. In the wars between England and Scotland, possession of this strong point gave great advantage. The Highlands are generally regarded as the 'real' Scotland, and it is to this region that Highland dress, the Highland Games and Highland cattle belong.

> The arbitrary line dividing the Highlands and Lowlands is really a myth (said to have been drawn by Queen Victoria's German tailor, from Aberdeen to Glasgow).
>
> WILLIAM KIRK: 'Prehistoric Scotland', in *Tartan Tapestry* (compiled by John Hay of Hayfield) (1960)

**Highland Clearances.** The forced removal of tenants from large estates in Scotland during the early 19th century. It occurred when landowners sought to improve their estates by converting from arable farming to sheep farming. Many families emigrated as a result, mostly to North America and Australia. Few issues in Scottish history arouse such deep feelings as this event, which was orchestrated with an uncanny combination of brutality and philanthropy.

**Highland Games.** The series of sporting events held at annual clan gatherings in the Scottish Highlands spring from earlier informal contests. These then gradually disappeared, partly through their suppression, but were subsequently revived in the new enthusiasm for things Scottish that stemmed from Sir Walter Scott's novels. They were also encouraged by Queen Victoria, who personally patronized those held at Braemar during her visits to Balmoral. Hence the present dominance of the Braemar gathering nearby. The sports cover a wide range of contests, in which tossing the caber is one of the toughest, Highland dancing one of the nimblest, and playing the bagpipes one of the most tuneful. There is also a gruelling race up and down Ben Nevis.

**Highland Mary.** A sweetheart of Robert Burns, to whom he addressed some of his finest poetry, including 'My Highland Lassie, O', 'Highland Mary', 'To Mary in Heaven' and perhaps 'Will ye go to the Indies, my Mary?' She is said to have been a daughter of Archibald Campbell, a Clyde sailor. Burns first made her acquaintance in the spring of 1786 and they pledged mutual fidelity. But he forgot his vows and she died young in the autumn of that same year, to be buried in Greenock.

> My Mary, dear departed shade!
> Where is thy blissful place of rest?
> Seest thou thy lover lowly laid?
> Hear'st thou the groans that rend his breast?
>
> 'To Mary in Heaven' (1788)

**Cameron Highlanders.** *See under* CAMERON.

**Highness, Royal.** *See under* ROYAL.

**Highway.** A public road, especially the main road for traffic that leads directly from one town to another.

**Highway Code, The.** The official booklet of rules and guidance for road users, pedestrians as well as drivers. It was first published in 1931.

**Highwayman.** A mounted robber of passengers and travellers on the HIGHWAY. The term has gained a romantic ring. The Highwayman was the name of a train that ran from London to Newcastle in the summers of 1970 and 1971, so called because by means of cheap fares it aimed to 'rob' passengers from road coaches. *See also* GENTLEMAN OF THE ROAD; KNIGHT OF THE ROAD; STAND AND DELIVER!

> The wind was a torrent of darkness among the gusty trees,
> The moon was a ghostly galleon tossed upon cloudy seas,
> The road was a ribbon of moonlight over the purple moor,
> And the highwayman came riding—
> Riding—riding—
> The highwayman came riding, up to the old inn-door.
>
> ALFRED NOYES: 'The Highwayman' (1907)

**King's** or **Queen's highway.** *See under* KING.

**Hijacker.** A term of American origin denoting a bandit who preys on BOOTLEGGERS and other criminals. It is now applied more generally to one who steals goods in transit, particularly lorries loaded with valuable merchandise. The name is popularly said to derive from the gunman's command to his victim, 'Stick 'em up high, Jack,' meaning that the arms were to be raised well above the head. *See also* SKYJACKER.

**Hilary Term.** The former legal term and the university term at Oxford and Trinity College Dublin corresponding to the LENT term elsewhere. It is named in honour of St Hilary whose day is 13 January (14 January in the Roman Catholic Church), near which day these terms begin.

The Hilary Law Sittings usually begin on 11 January and end on the Wednesday before EASTER.

**Hildebrand.** A celebrated character of German romance whose story is told in *Das Hildebrandslied*, an old German alliterative poem (written *c.*800). He also appears in the NIBELUNGENLIED and elsewhere. He is an old man, who returns home after many years among the Huns through following his master THEODORIC, only to be challenged to single combat by his own son Hadubrand.

The name is better known as that of the great reforming pope St Gregory VII (*c*.1020–85) whose attempts to prohibit lay investiture brought Henry IV to CANOSSA and made him many enemies. He did much to remove abuses and to regenerate the church.

**Hildegard.** St Hildegard of Bingen (1098–1179) appears in the Roman Martyrology although she was never officially canonized. The first 30 years of her life as a Benedictine nun were unremarkable, but she then began to have a number of visions, in one of which the Holy Spirit directed her to found a monastery on a hill near Bingen. The sacred music that she composed there has made her a modern cult figure among early music enthusiasts and she is now equally honoured by NEW AGE religious feminists. Her day is 17 September.

**Hildesheim.** Legend relates that a monk of Hildesheim, an old city of Hanover, doubting that with God 1000 years could be as one day, listened to the singing of a bird in a wood, as he thought for three minutes, but found the time had been 300 years. Longfellow makes use of the story in his *Golden Legend* (1851), calling the monk Felix.

**Hill. Hillbilly.** An American rustic or countryman of the hilly regions. The name is also applied to the characteristic traditional songs of the hill regions of the southeastern parts of the USA.

**Hill, Fanny.** *See* FANNY HILL.

**Hill folk.** Sir Walter Scott's name for the CAMERONIAN Scottish COVENANTERS, who met clandestinely among the hills after the Covenants were declared unlawful in 1662. Sometimes the Covenanters generally are so called.

In Scandinavian tradition they are a type of being between elves and human beings. The 'hill people' were supposed to dwell in caves and small hills.

**Hill of Tara, The.** The hill of this name in County Meath, some 20 miles (32km) north of Dublin, was the ancient seat of the high kings of Ireland until the 6th century AD. Only a series of earthworks now remains to mark the site of 'Tara's halls'. Here were held a national assembly, the Feis of Tara, and gatherings for music, games and literary contests. Here too was the LIA FAIL, which is supposed to have been JACOB's pillow taken from Tara to Scotland. *See also* TANIST STONE.

> The harp that once through Tara's halls
> The soul of music shed,
> Now hangs as mute on Tara's walls
> As if that soul were fled.
>
> THOMAS MOORE: *Irish Melodies*, 'The harp that once through Tara's halls' (1807)

**Hills.** Prayers were offered on the tops of high hills and temples built on HIGH PLACES, from the notion that the gods could better hear prayer on such places, as they were nearer heaven. Balak took BALAAM to the top of Peor and other high places when Balaam wished to consult God (Numbers 23, 24).

**As old as the hills.** *See under* AS.

**City of the Seven Hills, The.** *See under* CITY.

**Constitution Hill.** *See under* CONSTITUTION.

**Dragon Hill.** *See under* DRAGON.

**Gillies' Hill.** *See under* GILLIE.

**Gogmagog Hill.** *See under* GOG AND MAGOG.

**Marcle Hill.** *See under* MARCLE.

**Over the hill.** *See under* OVER.

**Salt Hill.** *See under* SALT.

**Savoy Hill.** *See under* SAVOY.

**Seven hills of Rome, The.** *See under* SEVEN.

**Vinegar Hill.** *See under* VINEGAR.

**Hind.** The animal that is the emblem of St GILES. *See also* HART.

**Hind of Sertorius, The.** Sertorius (*c*.122–72 BC), Marian governor of Hispania Citerior, was proscribed by Sulla and forced to flee. Later he was invited to return by the Lusitani and held Spain against the Senatorial party until his death through treachery. He had a tame white hind, which he taught to follow him and from which he feigned to receive the instructions of DIANA. By this artifice, says Plutarch, he imposed on the superstition of the people.

**Devil take the hindmost.** *See under* DEVIL.

**Golden Hind, The.** *See under* GOLDEN.

**Milk-white hind, The.** *See under* MILK.

**Talk the hind leg off a donkey, To.** *See under* TALK.

**Up hill and down dale.** *See under* UP.

**Hinduism.** According to Hinduism, the creative force of the universe is BRAHMA. Once he has brought the cosmos into being it is sustained by VISHNU and then annihilated by SIVA, only to be created once more by Brahma. These three chief gods, as creator, preserver and destroyer, thus form the triad of the TRIMURTI. Central beliefs of Hinduism are reincarnation and karma. The oldest scriptures are the Veda collection of hymns, followed by the philosophical UPANISHADS and the epics RAMAYANA and MAHABHARATA, all dating from before the Christian era. Some Hindu deities are particularly popular, such as KRISHNA, Hanuman, LAKSHMI and Durga, and some also manifest themselves in different incarnations or avatars. Examples are Rama and Krishna, both avatars of Vishnu. Hinduism does not regard women as the equals of men but teaches that they must be treated with kindness and respect. The caste system of India traditionally derives from early Hindu society, and it is within this system that Hinduism has its complex of rites and ceremonies. Temple worship is almost universally observed, and there are many festivals. *See also* HARE KRISHNA.

**Hindustan Regiment, The.** *See under* REGIMENTAL AND DIVISIONAL NICKNAMES.

**Hinny.** *See* MULE.

**Hip.** *See* HEP.

**Hip! Hip! Hurrah!** The old fanciful explanation of the origin of this cry is that 'hip' is a NOTARIKON, composed of the initials *Hierosolyma est perdita* and that when German knights headed a Jew-hunt in the Middle Ages, they ran shouting 'Hip! Hip!' as much as to say 'Jerusalem is destroyed.'

'Hurrah' was similarly fancifully derived from Slavonic *hu-raj* ('to Paradise'), so that Hip! Hip! Hurrah! would mean 'Jerusalem is lost to the infidel, and we are on the road to Paradise.'

Hip is actually of unknown origin, but hurrah or hurray (or hooray) are alterations of huzza, itself said by 17th-century writers to be a sailors' cheer.

> The sun has got his hat on,
> Hip, hip, hip, hooray,
> The sun has got his hat on
> And he's coming out to play.
> NOEL GAY and RALPH BUTLER: (song) (1932)

**Hippie.** Hippies originated in San Francisco in the late 1960s among young people who were anarchists but had a regard for the environment. The movement spread to Britain, where they adopted fantastic styles of dress, travelled around in ramshackle vehicles and were often given to drink and drugs. They lived to some extent by begging, scrounging and with the help of Social Security payments. By the 1990s they had largely been superseded by an amorphous group of young unemployed or homeless people, the most positively motivated of whom are the so-called NEW AGE travellers, who prefer a life in the natural environment of the countryside to one in the polluted prison of the cities. The word probably comes from 'hip' in the sense of fashionable. *See also* BEATNIK; DROPOUTS; HELL'S ANGELS.

**Hippocampus** (Greek, *hippos*, 'horse', and *kampos*, 'sea monster'). A sea horse, having the head and forequarters resembling those of a horse, with the tail and hindquarters of a fish or dolphin. The name was also that of the steed of NEPTUNE; it had only two legs, the hindquarters being the tail of a dragon or fish.

**Hippocrates.** A Greek physician (*c.*460–*c.*375 BC), known as the Father of Medicine. He was a member of the well-known family of priest-physicians, the Asclepidae, and was an acute and indefatigable observer, practising as both physician and surgeon. More than 70 treatises known as the *Hippocratic Collection* are extant, but their authorship is uncertain. Literally rendered, his name means 'horsepower', from Greek *hippos*, 'horse', and *kratos*, 'power'.

**Hippocratean school.** The 'Dogmatic' school of medicine, founded by HIPPOCRATES.

**Hippocrates' sleeve.** A woollen bag of a square piece of flannel, having the opposite corners joined, so as to make it triangular. It was used by apothecaries for straining syrups, decoctions and the like and formerly by vintners.

**Hippocratic oath.** An outstanding code of medical ethics contained in the *Hippocratic Collection*. The oath related particularly to the inviolability of secrecy concerning any communication made by a patient during consultation and demanded absolute integrity concerning the patient's welfare. It also enjoined members of the profession not to aid a woman to procure an abortion.

**Hippocrene** (Greek *hippos*, 'horse', and *krēnē*, 'spring'). The fountain of the MUSES on Mount HELICON, produced by a stamp of the hoof of PEGASUS. Hence, poetic inspiration.

> O for a beaker full of the warm South,
> Full of the true, the blushful Hippocrene.
> JOHN KEATS: 'Ode to a Nightingale' (1820)

**Hippodamia.** *See* BRISEIS.

**Hippogriff** (Italian *ippogrifo*, from *ippo-*, 'horse' (Greek *hippos*), and *grifo*, 'griffin'). The winged horse, whose father was a GRIFFIN and mother a filly. It was a symbol of love.

> So saying, he caught him up, and, without wing
> Of hippogrif, bore through the air sublime,
> Over the wilderness and o'er the plain.
> MILTON: *Paradise Regained*, iv (1671)

**Hippolyta.** Queen of the AMAZONS and daughter of MARS. Shakespeare introduced the character in *A Midsummer Night's Dream* (1595), in which he betroths her to THESEUS, Duke of Athens. In classic fable it is her sister Antiope who married Theseus, although some writers justify Shakespeare's account. Hippolyta was famous for a girdle given by her father, and it was one of the 12 labours of HERCULES to possess himself of this prize. Her name, like that of HIPPOLYTUS, means 'releaser of horses', from Greek *hippos*, 'horse', and *luō*, 'I release'.

**Hippolytus** (Greek *hippos*, 'horse', and *lūo*, 'I release'). Son of THESEUS, king of Athens. When he repulsed his stepmother PHAEDRA's advances she accused him of attempting her seduction. In anger his father sought NEPTUNE's aid, who sent a sea monster which so terrified Hippolytus' horses that they dragged him to death. He was restored to life by AESCULAPIUS.

**Hippomenes.** In Boeotian legend, the Greek prince who won the race with ATALANTA.

**Hipsters.** Trousers hanging from the hips instead of the waist. *See also* HIPPIE.

**Hiragana** (Japanese, 'plain kana'). A Japanese system of syllabic writing based on Chinese cursive ideograms. It is the more widely used of the two current systems, the other being KATAKANA, and is employed in newspapers and in literature generally. It has a set of 48 characters each representing a syllable, such as *fu*, *ju*, *mu* and the like. The hiragana characters were mainly used by women and were not originally mixed with other characters. *Kana* itself, as the name for the basic syllabary, literally means 'borrowed letters', as distinct from the *kanji*, literally 'Chinese characters', which are the 'real' letters.

**Hiram Abif.** A central figure in the legend and ritual of FREEMASONRY, the craftsman builder of the TEMPLE OF SOLOMON, who died rather than yield up the secrets of masonry. He appears as Huram, the alternative form of the name, in 2 Chronicles: 2 and 4. He must not be confused with Hiram or Huram, king of Tyre, who supplied much of the material.

**Hiring fair.** A STATUTE FAIR, virtually the same as a MOP FAIR, formerly an annual event in most market towns in England and Wales at MARTINMAS (11 November), when men and maids stood in rows to be inspected by those seeking servants, farm workers and the like.

**Hiroshima.** A Japanese city and military base, the target of the first atomic bomb dropped in warfare (6 August 1945). Over 160,000 people were killed or injured and far more rendered homeless. The flash of the explosion was seen 170 miles (275km) away and a column of black smoke rose over the city to a height of 40,000ft (12,190m). Hiroshima remains a solemn portent of the fate overshadowing mankind in the event of major world conflict.

**History. Historical materialism.** This is the application of DIALECTICAL MATERIALISM to the evolution of society. Broadly it comes down to a materialist or economic interpretation of history in which all historical developments are basically due to economic phenomena and all social, political and intellectual life, as well as religion, are basically determined by the material conditions of life. Furthermore, historical development is part of the dialectical process. *See also* MATERIALISM.

**History of the Four Kings, The (Livre des quatre rois, Le).** A pack of cards. In a French pack the four kings are CHARLEMAGNE, DAVID, Alexander the Great and CAESAR. *See also* COURT CARDS.

**Case history.** *See under* CASE.

**Father of Ecclesiastical History, The.** *See under* FATHER.

**Father of English History, The.** *See under* FATHER.

**Father of French History, The.** *See under* FATHER.

**Father of Historic Painting, The.** *See under* FATHER.

**Father of History, The.** *See under* FATHER.

**Life history.** *See under* LIFE.

**Make history, To.** To take part in events and actions that will shape the future or that will be of such significance as to become part of the historical record.

**Muse of History, The.** *See* CLIO.

**Hit. Hit-and-miss.** Aimed or done carelessly.

**Hit-and-run.** Descriptive of a road accident in which the driver of a motor vehicle has hit or knocked down a person, then driven on without stopping.

**Hit below the belt, To.** To hit someone unfairly; to ignore the rules of fair play. The allusion is to the boxing ring.

**Hit** or **knock for six, To.** *See under* KNOCK.

**Hit hard** or **hard hit.** Hurt or distressed by adversities of fortune.

**Hit it off, To.** To agree or get on well with each other.

**Hit list.** A list of people to be murdered or objects to be achieved.

**Hit man.** A hired assassin.

> A hitwoman broke down in tears at the Old Bailey yesterday as she described shooting a roofing contractor in the face in return for the money to buy a mobile home.
>
> *The Times* (8 November 1994)

**Hit on something, To.** To come across it unexpectedly; to guess it correctly.

**Hit-or-miss.** HIT-AND-MISS.

**Hit parade.** Formerly, a list of the most popular songs, as the forerunner of the Top 10.

**Hit something off, To.** To describe it tersely and epigrammatically; to mimic it truthfully and quickly.

**Hit the deck, To.** To fall to the ground or floor in order to escape injury.

**Hit the ground running, To.** To proceed with energy and enthusiasm. The imagery is military, of a person who has jumped from a landing craft or helicopter or even landed by parachute and who instantly springs into action.

**Hit the hay, To.** To go to bed. The image is of a weary wanderer in a barn of hay.

**Hit the headlines, To.** To receive prominent attention in the newspapers or the news media generally.

**Hit the high spots, To.** To excel or to go to excesses in 'living it up'. *See also* HIGH SPOT.

**Hit the jackpot, To.** *See* JACKPOT.

**Hit the nail on the head, To.** To surmise correctly; to arrive at the precise conclusion. The allusion is to an accurate hit with a hammer on the head of a nail. The French equivalent is *frapper au but* ('to hit the mark'), the Italian *dare in brocca* ('to hit the pitcher', alluding to a game where a pitcher took the place of AUNT SALLY).

**Hit the road, To.** To start one's journey; to be on one's way.

**Hit** or **go through the roof, To.** To be very angry; to be furious.

**Hit the sack, To.** To go to bed.

**Hit the white, To.** To be quite right; to make a good shot. The phrase is from the old days of archery, the white being the inner circle of the target, the BULL'S EYE.

**Hard hit.** *See under* HARD.

**Hard-hitting.** *See under* HARD.

**Make** or **score a hit, To.** To make a good impression; to meet with unexpected success.

**Not to know what has hit one.** *See under* KNOW.

**Hitch. Hitchhike, To.** To travel from place to place by getting lifts from passing vehicles. The action is essentially a form of hiking by 'hitching' oneself to a vehicle.

**Hitch your wagon to a star.** Aim high; do not be content with low aspirations. The phrase is from Ralph Waldo Emerson's essay 'Civilization' in *Society and Solitude* (1870).

**Get hitched, To.** To get married.

**Go without a hitch, To.** *See under* GO.

**Hitler. Hitler diaries, The.** *See under* FAKES.

**Hitlerism.** A generic term for the whole doctrine and practice of Fascism as exemplified by the NAZI regime of Adolf Hitler (1889–1945), who became German Chancellor in 1933 and ruled until his death. His regime was marked by tyranny, aggression and mass persecution of Communists and Jews. *See also* FASCIST.

**Heil Hitler.** *See under* HEIL.

**Hittites.** The ancient people who inhabited Anatolia and northern Syria from the 3rd to the 1st millennium BC. They had their capital at Hattusas, now Boghasköy in Turkey, and became a strong kingdom that overthrew the Babylonian Empire. They then went into eclipse, but re-emerged in a new empire *c.*1400 BC, successfully waging war with Egypt. The Hittites of the Old Testament, e.g. in Genesis 26:34, are not these people but probably members of a local Canaanite tribe.

**Uriah the Hittite.** *See under* URIAH.

**Hoarstone.** A stone marking out the boundary of an estate, properly an old, grey, lichen-covered one. They have been wrongly taken for druidical remains.

**Hob.** A short form of Robin.

**Hob and nob.** *See* HOBNOB.

**Hobbema.** Meindert Hobbema (1638–1709), the Dutch landscape painter.

**English Hobbema, The.** John Crome (1768–1821), 'Old Crome', of Norwich, whose last words are said to have been, 'O Hobbema, my dear Hobbema, how I have loved you!'

**Scottish Hobbema, The.** Patrick Nasmyth (1787–1831), the landscape painter.

**Hobbism.** The principles of Thomas Hobbes (1588–1679), author of *Leviathan* (1651). He was a sceptic noted for his MATERIALISM and ERASTIANISM. He emphasized the doctrine of state sovereignty based on the theory of a social contract, which he used as a support for absolutism. Man, according to Hobbes, is motivated by self-interest and the urge for self-preservation. Many regarded Hobbism as subversive freethinking.

**Hobbit.** One of an imaginary race of benevolent, half-size people, the creation of Professor J.R.R. Tolkien. They are featured in his two works, *The Hobbit* (1937) and *The* LORD OF THE RINGS (1954–5). The name was their own for themselves, and according to them meant 'hole-dweller'.

> In a hole in the ground there lived a hobbit.
> J.R.R. TOLKIEN: *The Hobbit* (1937)

*See also* BAGGINS; GANDALF.

**Hobble skirt.** A long skirt, in fashion between 1910 and 1914, that was so tight around the ankles that the wearer was impeded in walking, much as a horse is hobbled.

**Hobby.** A favourite pursuit; a pastime that interests or amuses. The origin is in 'hobby' as a small or medium-sized horse, itself probably from the name Robin. From this 'hobbyhorse' the name was transferred to a light wickerwork frame, appropriately draped, in which someone gambolled in the old MORRIS DANCES. Padstow in Cornwall has its ancient 'Obby 'Oss parade on MAY DAY. The horse is preceded by men clad in white known as 'teazers'. It also came to apply to a child's toy 'horse', consisting of a stick, across which he straddles, with a horse's head at one end. It was from this last, which was the child's pastime, that the name passed to the leisure-time pursuit. *See also* FURRY DANCE.

**Hobgoblin.** An impish, ugly and mischievous sprite, particularly PUCK or ROBIN GOODFELLOW. The word comes from 'hob', with the same meaning, as a variant of Rob and GOBLIN.

> Those that Hobgoblin call you, and sweet Puck,
> You do their work, and they shall have good luck.
> SHAKESPEARE: *A Midsummer Night's Dream*, II, i (1595)

**Hobnob, To.** To be on friendly terms; to socialize, especially when drinking together. The word comes from the old phrase 'hob or nob', 'to drink to one another by turns', from Old English *habban*, 'to have', and *nabban*, 'not to have'.

> 'Have another glass!' 'With you. Hob and nob,' returned the sergeant. 'The top of mine to the foot

of yours – the foot of yours to the top of mine – Ring once, ring twice – the best tune on the Musical Glasses! Your health.'

DICKENS: *Great Expectations*, ch v (1860–1)

**Hobo.** In American usage, a migratory worker who likes to travel. This is in contrast to a tramp, who travels without working, and a bum, who neither travels nor works. The origin of the word is uncertain.

**Hobson-jobson.** The expression is now applied to English words or phrases that have arisen by way of garbled adoption from a foreign language. It was originally used by British soldiers in India in the 19th century for the Muharram festival, and was their corruption of the Shi'ites' cry, *Ya Hasan! Ya Hosain!* ('O Hasan! O Husain!'). Hasan and Hosain, grandsons of MOHAMMED, were killed fighting for the faith. The phrase came about by association with the surnames Hobson and Jobson. Henry Yule and A.C. Burnell's dictionary *Hobson-Jobson* (1886) is a treasure trove of Anglo-Indian words and phrases that has never been superseded.

**Hobson's choice.** No choice at all. The saying derives from Thomas Hobson (*c.*1544–1631), a Cambridge carrier well known in his day, who refused to let out any horse except in its proper turn.

**Hock. Hock shop.** A pawnshop. In America 'to hock' is to pawn. It derives from the earlier English HOCKTIDE when small ransoms were demanded from those caught and bound.

**Hocktide** or **Hock Tuesday.** The second Tuesday after EASTER, long held as a festival in England and observed until the 16th century. According to custom, on Hock Monday, the women of the village seized and tied up men, demanding a small payment for their release. On the Tuesday the men similarly ensnared the women. The takings were paid to the churchwardens for parish work. The origin of 'hock' is unknown.

**Hockey.** A game having inevitable associations with girls' schools. The hockey stick became the militant symbol of the sporting schoolgirl, and 'jolly hockey sticks' was the slogan that epitomized her *joie de sport* as well as that of the games mistress who urged her to victory on the field. The expression itself was first heard in the late 1940s in the radio comedy series *Educating Archie*, in which it was uttered by Monica, Archie's schoolgirl friend. It should be mentioned that hockey to a North American implies ice hockey and that the game played on grass will need to be distinguished as field hockey.

**Hocus pocus.** Words traditionally uttered by conjurors when performing a trick. Hence the trick itself, also the juggler himself.

The phrase dates from the early 17th century and is the opening of an absurd string of mock Latin used by the performer: *Hocus pocus, tontus, talontus, vade celeriter, jubeo.* The first two words are probably a parody of the words of consecration in the Latin Mass, *Hoc est Corpus meum*, 'This is my Body'. As for the rest, *totus* means 'whole', *talontus* is perhaps based on *talentum*, 'talent', *vade celeriter* means 'go quickly' and *jubeo* means 'I bid'. Put together, the result is nonsense. It is equally possible that *hocus pocus* was suggested by HOTCHPOTCH (or HODGEPODGE). There is a juggler in the Chorus at the end of Act i of Ben Jonson's play *Magnetic Lady* (1632) called *Hokos-Pokos*.

Modern 'hoax' is probably a contraction of hocus pocus, which also supplied the now rare verb 'to hocus', meaning to cheat. *See also* HANKY-PANKY.

**Hodge.** A familiar and condescending name for a farm labourer or peasant, a country clown or rustic, in use in the 16th century. It is an abbreviated form of Roger.

**Hodgepodge.** A medley, a mixed dish of 'bits and pieces' all cooked together. The word is a corruption of HOTCHPOTCH.

**Hog.** A pig, properly a castrated male raised solely for slaughter and killed young. The origin of the word is uncertain, but it probably came into English from Celtic. The name is also applied to a sheep in its first year that has yet to be shorn. In general colloquial use, a hog is a gluttonous, greedy or unmannered person, hence 'road hog' as a term for a selfish driver.

**Hog it** or **pig it, To.** To live in a rough, uncouth fashion or to eat unceremoniously and greedily in a piggish fashion.

**Hogs Back.** The western end of the North Downs, the chalk ridge from Guildford to Farnham in Surrey, along which the A31 now runs. It is so called from its outline as seen from below.

**Hogs Norton.** A village in Oxfordshire, now long called Hook Norton, 5 miles (8km) north-east of Chipping Norton. The name owes its more recent fame to Gillie Potter, the English comedian and radio broadcaster, who in the 1930s described in mock erudite fashion a long series of unlikely events taking place in this village.

The humorous corruption to Hogs Norton, recently employed by Mr Gillie Potter, goes back to at least the 16th century, when the village had become proverbial for rusticity and boorishness. ... There was evidently a jingle about Hogs Norton, where pigs play on the organ.

MARGARET GELLING: *The Place-Names of Oxfordshire*, ii (1954)

**Go the whole hog, To.** To do something completely and thoroughly, without compromise or reservation: to go the whole way. William Cowper says (*The Love of the World; or Hypocrisy Detected* (1779)) that the Muslim divines sought to ascertain which part of the hog was proscribed as food by the Prophet.

> But for one piece they thought it hard
> From the whole hog to be debarred.

Unable to reach a decision, each thought that the portion of the meat he wanted was the one to be forbidden. As their tastes differed, they therefore decided to eat the whole hog. However, the origin of the expression may be simpler than this. Virginian butchers were said to sell a whole hog more cheaply, pound for pound, than for individual choice cuts, even though the customer had to pay more overall.

**Hampshire hog.** *See under* HAMPSHIRE.

**Like a hog on ice.** *See under* LIKE.

**Road hog.** *See under* ROAD.

**Hogen Mogen.** Holland or the Netherlands, so called from Dutch *Hooge en Mogende* ('HIGH AND MIGHTY'), the formula for addressing the STATES-GENERAL.

**Hogmanay.** In Scotland the last day of the year, the day when children demanded gifts or 'hogmanay' of oatcake or oaten bread.

In olden times it was a kind of annual SATURNALIA. The word is of uncertain origin and of the numerous suggestions made, the most likely is that it is from French *aguillaneuf*, 'a gift at the New Year'. Attempts to relate this word to French *gui*, 'mistletoe', have no historical backing.

**Hoi polloi** (Greek, 'the many'). The masses, usually used in a slighting sense. Since the first word of the expression means 'the' it is strictly speaking superfluous to prefix it with a second English 'the'.

> If by the people you understand the multitude, the *hoi polloi*, 'tis no matter what they think; They are sometimes in the right, sometimes in the wrong; their judgement is a mere lottery.
>
> JOHN DRYDEN: *Essay of Dramatic Poesy* (1668)

**Hoist with one's own petard, To be.** To be beaten with one's own weapons; caught in one's own trap; ensnared in the danger intended for others, as were some designers of instruments of torture. The 'petard' was a thick iron engine of war, filled with gunpowder and fastened to gates, barricades and the like to blow them up. The danger was that the engineer who fired the petard might be blown up by the explosion.

**Hoity-toity.** A reduplicated word on the pattern of HARUM SCARUM, mingle-mangle, hugger-mugger and so on, and probably formed from the obsolete verb *hoit*, 'to romp'. It is now mostly used as an adjective, meaning 'stuck-up', haughty or petulant, or as an interjection expressing disapproval or contempt of someone's airs or assumptions.

**Hokey-cokey.** A light-hearted Cockney dance, popular during the 1940s, with a song and tune of this name to go with it.

**Hokey-pokey.** An early form of cheap ice-cream, sold by street vendors until the 1920s with the cry 'Hokey-pokey penny a lump'. The name is derived from HOCUS POCUS, although mistakenly said by some to be from the Italian *Ecco un poco* ('Here is a little') or *O che poco* ('Oh how little'), Italian street vendors being associated with ice-cream. Hokey-pokey is also used to mean nonsense.

**Holborn.** A thoroughfare and district of London taking its name from the Holebourne ('stream in the hollow'), which was the name of the upper part of the Fleet River. The spanning of the valley by Holborn Viaduct (1867–9) did away with the old Holborn Hill along which criminals were taken to be hanged at TYBURN.

**Hold. Hold a candle to, To.** An expression more commonly heard in the negative to mean markedly inferior, as: 'He can't hold a candle to his brother.' The allusion is said to be to linkboys who held torches in streets or candles in theatres and other places of evening entertainment.

> Some say, that Signor Bononcini,
> Compared to Handel's a mere ninny;
> Others aver, that to him Handel
> Is scarcely fit to hold a candle.
>
> JOHN BYROM: 'On the Feuds between Handel and Bononcini' (1727)

**Hold a thing against someone, To.** To resent or regard it as unworthy that they have it. 'I won't hold it against you' means 'I won't let it adversely affect my opinion of you'.

**Hold court, To.** To preside over one's admirers like a sovereign.

**Hold down, To.** To manage or keep going, as: 'Can he hold down that sort of job?'

**Hold forth, To.** To speak in public; to harangue; to talk lengthily and tediously.

**Hold good, To.** To be valid or applicable, as: 'That holds good for both of us.'

**Hold hard!** Stop or go easy. The reference is to keeping a firm hold, seat or footing when travelling, to avoid the danger of being overthrown.

**Hold in, To.** To restrain. The allusion is to horses that are tightly reined in.

**Hold in fee, To.** To hold as one's lawful, absolute possession.

> Once did She hold the gorgeous east in fee;
> And was the safeguard of the west.
>
> WILLIAM WORDSWORTH: 'On the Extinction of the Venetian Republic' (1807)

**Hold it!** or **Hold on!** or **Hold everything!** Stop! Wait!

**Hold one's breath, To.** To deliberately stop breathing for a few moments, as when startled.

**Hold one's ground, To.** To maintain one's position or authority.

**Hold one's head high, To.** To be proud or confident.

**Hold one's horses, To.** To stop; to slow down. Often said when a person is impatient.

**Hold one's own, To.** To maintain one's position or advantage; to stand one's ground.

**Hold one's peace, To.** To remain silent.

**Hold one's tongue, To.** To keep silent when one might speak; to keep a secret. In COVERDALE'S BIBLE, where the Authorized Version has, 'But Jesus held his peace' (Matthew 26:63), the reading is: 'Jesus helde his tonge.'

**Hold out, To.** To endure or persist; not to succumb.

**Hold out for, To.** To wait patiently or determinedly for something.

**Hold out the olive branch, To.** To make overtures for peace. The allusion is to the olive being an ancient symbol of peace. In some of Numa's medals the king is represented holding an olive twig, indicative of a peaceful reign.

**Hold over, To.** To keep back; to retain in reserve; to defer or postpone.

**Hold someone's hand, To.** Metaphorically, to guide or counsel a person.

**Hold** or **keep the field, To.** To maintain one's position in the face of opposition.

**Hold the fort, To.** To maintain one's position; to be left to keep things running during the absence of others. 'Hold the fort!' was immortalized as a phrase by General Sherman during the American Civil War (1861–5), when in 1864 he signalled this message to General Corse from the top of Mount Kennesaw.

**Hold the purse strings, To.** To be the one who controls the money and its expenditure. *See also* CUTPURSE.

**Hold up, To.** To stop, as highwaymen did, with the intention of robbing. In this connection the order 'Hold 'em up!' means that the victim must hold his hands above his head to ensure that he or she is not reaching for a weapon. A hold-up is thus an outdoor robbery in which people or vehicles are held up. It is also a delay or obstacle. *See also* HIJACKER.

**Hold water, To.** To bear close inspection; to be thoroughly sound and consistent, as a vessel that holds water is sound. In this sense it is mostly used negatively, as, 'His statement will not hold water,' meaning that on examination it will be proved faulty. The expression also means to stay the progress of a boat by stemming the current with the oars.

**Hold with, To.** To approve of. The expression is mostly used negatively, as: 'I don't hold with such behaviour.'

**Hold your horses.** Be patient; wait a moment; do not be too hasty. Horses that show signs of nervousness must be held back.

**Get hold of the wrong end of the stick, To.** To misunderstand the story or the information. The wrong end of the stick is the dirty or muddy one.

**Left holding the baby.** *See under* LEFT.

**No holds barred.** *See under* NO.

**On hold.** Temporarily suspended or not operating, as of something mechanical.

**There's no holding him.** He is so keen or enthusiastic that it is impossible to stop from pursuing a course of action.

**Hole. Hole-and-corner business, A.** Something clandestine or furtive.

**Hole in one.** In golf a shot from the tee that finishes in the hole.

**Hole in the heart.** A common name for a septal defect, in which there is a hole in the septum (partition) between the left and right sides of the heart. Such defects develop before birth and in serious cases can usually be repaired surgically.

**Hole in the wall.** A dark and dingy place, especially one difficult to find. The name also exists for a number of restaurants, some of which are quite superior and anything but dingy. The source of the name in this sense is uncertain, but the hole may originally have been in the wall of a debtors' prison, used to pass gifts of food and drink to the inmates. A hole in the wall is also a term for an automatic cash dispenser in the outside wall of a bank.

**Hole out, To.** In golf to drive the ball into the appropriate hole of the course.

**Hole up, To.** To hide oneself.

**Better 'ole, A.** *See under* BETTER.

**Black hole.** *See under* BLACK.

**Black Hole of Calcutta.** *See under* BLACK.

**Burn a hole in one's pocket, To.** *See under* BURN.

**Devil's Hole, The.** *See under* DEVIL.

**Glory hole.** *See under* GLORY.

**Have an ace in the hole, To.** *See under* ACE.

**In a hole.** In an awkward predicament.

**Make a hole in something, To.** To consume a considerable portion of it.

**Nineteenth hole.** *See under* NINE.

**Pick holes in, To.** *See under* PICK.

**Square peg in a round hole, A.** *See under* SQUARE.

**Watering hole.** *See under* WATER.

**Wookey Hole.** *See under* WOOKEY.

**Holger Danske** (Danish, 'Danish Ogier'). The Danish name of OGIER THE DANE.

**Holiday. Holidays of Obligation.** *See* FEASTS OF OBLIGATION.

**Bank holidays.** *See under* BANK.

**Busman's holiday.** *See under* BUS.

**Give the boys a holiday.** *See under* BOY.
**Half holiday.** *See under* HALF.
**High days and holidays.** *See under* HIGH.
**Roman holiday.** *See under* ROMAN.
**St Crispin's holiday.** *See under* CRISPIN.

**Holland.** A coarse linen cloth, so called because it was originally made in Holland and originally known as 'holland cloth'.

**Hollands.** Dutch gin, traditionally sold in stone bottles. The word represents Dutch *Hollandsch genever*.

**Hollow. Beat someone hollow, To.** *See under* BEAT.
**Sleepy Hollow.** *See under* SLEEP.

**Holly.** The custom of decorating churches and houses with holly at CHRISTMAS is of great antiquity and may derive from its earlier use by the Romans in the festival of the SATURNALIA, which occurred at the same season, or from the old Germanic custom. It is held to be unlucky by some to bring it into the house before Christmas Eve. *See also* IVY; MISTLETOE.

**Holly Golightly.** *See under* GOLIGHTLY.

**Hollywood.** The internationally famous byname of the American film industry and of the glamorous actors and actresses who are its vital exponents. Geographically it is the suburb of Los Angeles where a number of independent producers set up their studios in 1912 and to the casual visitor looks far from glamorous. The location's actual name is said to have been given by its original developers in 1887.

**Holmes, Sherlock.** The most famous figure in detective fiction, the creation of Sir Arthur Conan Doyle (1859–1930). His solutions of crime and mysteries were related in a series of 60 stories that mainly appeared in the *Strand Magazine* between 1891 and 1927. The character was based on Dr Joseph Bell of the Edinburgh Infirmary, whose methods of deduction suggested a system that Holmes developed into a science: the observation of the minutest details and apparently insignificant circumstances scientifically interpreted. Dr Watson, Holmes' friend and assistant, was a skit on Doyle himself, and Baker Street acquired lasting fame through his writings.

> How often have I said to you that when you have eliminated the impossible, whatever remains, *however improbable*, must be the truth?
> SIR ARTHUR CONAN DOYLE: *The Sign of Four*, ch vi (1890)

**Holocaust.** The name given to the destruction of some 6 million Jews by Hitler in the Second World War. The terror began within a month of Hitler's becoming German chancellor in January 1933. The Nuremberg Laws of 1935 deprived Jews of German citizenship, and the night of 9–10 November 1938 saw the *Kristallnacht*, a night of violence against Jewish persons and property, so called ironically from the litter of broken glass left in the aftermath. Discussion of the *Endlösung* or Final Solution was held on 20 January 1942, when it was agreed that the Jews of central and western Europe would be deported and sent to camps in eastern Poland, where they would be exterminated or made to work as slave labourers until they perished.

The word holocaust literally means 'burned whole', from the Greek, and originally applied to a sacrifice wholly consumed by fire. This is the 'burned offering' of the Old Testament, when slaughtered sacrificial animals or birds were burned on the altar, the skin being given to the priest who performed the ritual. The current use of the word was introduced by historians in the 1950s as an equivalent of the Hebrew *Shoah* ('Catastrophe') or *Hurban* ('Destruction'). This particular word was probably suggested by the crematoria in which the bodies of the victims were burned.

**Holofernes.** In the APOCRYPHA, the Babylonian general who is beheaded by JUDITH after he becomes drunk when celebrating his delight that she has agreed to sleep with him (Judith 2–7, 10–15). The bloody subject was a favourite with Renaissance painters. There is an old-fashioned pedagogue of the same name in Rabelais' *Gargantua* (1534), as well as a ridiculous schoolmasterly character in Shakespeare's *Love's Labour's Lost* (1594).

**Holy. Holy Alliance.** A treaty signed originally by the rulers of Austria, Prussia and Russia in 1815 (after the fall of NAPOLEON BONAPARTE) and joined by all the rulers of Europe, except Great Britain and the president of the Swiss Republic. Sponsored by Tsar Alexander, the rulers undertook to base their relations 'upon the sublime truths which the Holy religion of our Saviour teaches'. In effect it became a reactionary influence, seeking to maintain autocratic rule.

**Holy Boys, The.** *See under* REGIMENTAL AND DIVISIONAL NICKNAMES.

**Holy City.** The city that adherents of a particular religion regard as being intimately connected with their faith:

Benares: Hindus
Cuzco: ancient Incas
Fez: western Arabs
Jerusalem: Jews and Christians
Mecca and Medina: Muslims

Figuratively, the Holy City is HEAVEN.

**Holy Coat.** Both the Cathedral at Trèves (Trier) and the parish church of Argenteuil claim the ownership of Christ's seamless coat, which the soldiers would not tear and therefore cast lots for (John 19:23, 25). The traditions date from about the 12th century, and the coat was supposed to have been found and preserved by St HELENA in the 4th century. Other places also claim this relic.

**Holy Cross** or **Holy Rood Day.** 14 September, the day of the Feast of the EXALTATION OF THE CROSS, called by the Anglo-Saxons 'Roodmass-day'. It was on this day that Jews in Rome used to be compelled to go to church to listen to a sermon, a custom abolished *c.*1840 by Pope Gregory XVI. It is the subject of Robert Browning's 'Holy-Cross Day' (1845).

**Holy Door.** The specially walled-up door of each of the four great basilicas of Rome: St Peter's, St John Lateran, St Paul's-Outside-the-Walls and St Mary's Major. That of St Peter's is ceremoniously opened by the pope on Christmas Eve to inaugurate the Holy Year, while the others are opened by Cardinals-Legate. They are similarly closed the following Christmas Eve. Many pilgrims pass through these doors during the year to perform their devotions and to receive INDULGENCES. *See also* JUBILEE.

**Holy Family, The.** Properly, the infant Jesus, MARY and JOSEPH. In art the Holy Family is usually depicted as the infant Jesus attended by Joseph, Mary, ELIZABETH, Anne the mother of Mary and JOHN THE BAPTIST.

**Holy Ghost, The.** The third person of the TRINITY, the Divine Spirit, also called the Holy Spirit and represented in art as a DOVE.

**Holy Grail, The.** The cup or chalice traditionally used by Christ at the LAST SUPPER, the subject of much medieval legend, romance and allegory. 'Grail' itself comes from Old French *graal*, in turn from Latin *gradalis*, 'bowl'.

According to one account, JOSEPH OF ARIMATHEA preserved the Grail and received into it some of Jesus' blood at the crucifixion. He brought it to England, but it disappeared. According to others it was brought by angels from heaven and entrusted to a body of knights who guarded it on top of a mountain. When approached by anyone not of perfect purity, it vanished, and its quest became the source of most of the adventures of the KNIGHTS OF THE ROUND TABLE. *See also* PERCEFOREST.

There is a whole mass of literature concerning the Grail Cycle, and it appears to be a fusion of Christian legend and pre-Christian ritual origins. Part of the subject matter appears in the MABINOGION in the story of Peredur, son of Efrawg. The first Christian Grail romance was that of the French TROUVÈRE Robert de Boron, who wrote *Joseph d'Arimathie* at the end of the 12th century, and it next became attached to the Arthurian legend. In Robert de Boron's work the Grail took the form of a dish on which the Last Supper was served. *See also* ARTHURIAN ROMANCES.

**Holy Innocents** or **Childermas.** This feast is celebrated on 28 December, to commemorate Herod's MASSACRE OF THE INNOCENTS. It used to be the custom on Childermas to whip the children (and even adults) 'that the memory of Herod's murder of the Innocents might stick the closer'. This practice forms the plot of several tales in the DECAMERON.

**Holy Island.** There are various islands of this name in the British Isles. The following are the best known, respectively in England, Wales and Scotland.

Lindisfarne ('domain of Lindis') in the North Sea, off the Northumberland coast some 5 miles (8km) north of Belford. It became the see of St Aidan in 635 and developed as a missionary centre. St CHAD, St Oswy, St Egbert and St WILFRID were among those educated there. It was the see of St CUTHBERT (685–687) and is now in the diocese of Newcastle. At low tide it can be reached across the sands by a causeway.

Ynys Gybi ('Cybi's island'), the island on which Holyhead is situated, off the west coast of Anglesey. It is one of the oldest sites of human habitation in Wales and has many ancient and medieval remains. It is connected with Anglesey by a road bridge and by a road and rail embankment.

A rocky and barely inhabited island off the east coast of the larger island of Arran, at the entrance to Lamash Bay. It has a cave with early Christian and Viking carvings on the walls.

Ireland has been called the Holy Island on account of its numerous saints, and Guernsey was so called in the 10th century as a result of the great number of monks residing there. *See also* SACRED ISLE.

**Holy Joe.** Nautical slang for a clergyman or chaplain. Also generally a nickname for a pious person.

**Holy Land, The.** Christians call Palestine the Holy Land because it was the scene of Christ's birth, ministry and death.

Muslims call MECCA the Holy Land because MOHAMMED was born there.

The Chinese Buddhists call India the Holy Land because it was the native land of Sakyamuni, the BUDDHA.

The Greeks considered Elis in the western Peloponnesus as the Holy Land, from the temple of Olympian ZEUS and the sacred festival held there. *See also* OLYMPIC GAMES.

**Holy League, The.** Several leagues are so called. The best known are:

1511 between Pope Julius II, Ferdinand of Aragon, Henry VIII and Venice to drive the French out of Italy; the Emperor Maximilian and the Swiss also joined

1526 the Holy League of Cognac between Clement VII and Francis I of France against the Emperor Charles V

1576 formed by Henry, Duke of Guise, and the JESUITS and joined by Henry III against the HUGUENOTS, for the defence of the Roman Catholic Church

**Holy Name of Jesus, The.** The name of JESUS as an object of formal devotion, both among Roman Catholics, who until 1969 celebrated it as a feast-day in the first week of January, and among Anglicans, for whom the BOOK OF COMMON PRAYER has assigned it the date of 7 August. Some modern Anglican liturgies use the Naming of Jesus as an alternative title for the feast of the Circumcision (1 January). The close relation between name and person is manifest in the many references to the name of Jesus in the NEW TESTAMENT. The disciples perform miracles and exorcisms 'in the name of Jesus' and regularly baptize in it.

At the name of Jesus every knee should bow, of things in heaven, and things in earth, and things under the earth.
Philippians 2:10

**Holy Office, The.** *See* INQUISITION.

**Holy of Holies.** The innermost apartment of the Jewish temple, in which the ARK OF THE COVENANT was kept and into which only the HIGH PRIEST was allowed to enter and even then only once a year on the DAY OF ATONEMENT. Hence a term for any private apartment or place of special privacy. *See also* ADYTUM.

**Holy Orders.** A clergyman is said to be in holy orders because he belongs to one of the orders or ranks of the church. In the CHURCH OF ENGLAND these are three: deacon, priest and bishop. In the ROMAN CATHOLIC CHURCH there is a fourth, that of subdeacon. In ecclesiastical use the term also denotes a fraternity of monks or friars (as the Franciscan Order), and also the Rule by which the fraternity is governed.

**Holy places.** A name particularly applied to those places in Palestine, and especially Jerusalem, that are associated with some of the chief events in the life of Christ, his death and resurrection. Christian pilgrimages to the holy places were a familiar feature of medieval life and the CRUSADES began when Muslims interfered with pilgrims visiting the HOLY SEPULCHRE. The Crimean War (1854–6) had its origins in a dispute between Orthodox and Roman Catholic rights over the holy places, which included the churches of the Holy Sepulchre and the Virgin in Jerusalem, GOLGOTHA and the Church of the Nativity at Bethlehem.

**Holy Roller.** A derogatory nickname for a member of any evangelical sect who expresses religious fervour in an extrovert or extravagantly physical way.

**Holy Roman Empire.** The unification of Europe, with papal blessing, under a Christian emperor (800–814, 962–1806), said to be neither holy, nor Roman, nor an empire. *See also* EMPEROR; THIRD REICH.

**Holy Rood Day.** *See* HOLY CROSS DAY.

**Holy Saturday.** *See* HOLY WEEK.

**Holy Scripture, The.** *See* SCRIPTURES.

**Holy See.** The see of Rome; as a term it is often used to denote the papacy and papal jurisdiction, authority and so on.

**Holy Sepulchre, The.** The cave outside the walls of old JERUSALEM in which the body of Christ is believed to have lain between his burial and the Resurrection. The tomb is said to have been discovered by St HELENA, and from at least the 4th century the spot has been covered by a Christian church, where today Greek, Catholic, Armenian, Syrian and Coptic Christians have their rights of occupation. *See also* INVENTION OF THE CROSS.

**Holy Spirit, The.** *See* HOLY GHOST.

**Holy Thursday.** In England a former name for ASCENSION DAY, the Thursday next but one before WHITSUNDAY. Roman Catholics and others also give the name to MAUNDY THURSDAY, i.e. the day before GOOD FRIDAY.

**Holy Trinity.** *See* TRINITY.

**Holy war.** A war in which religious motivation plays, or is purported to play, a prominent part. The CRUSADES, the THIRTY YEARS' WAR, the wars against the ALBIGENSES and so on were so called.

The Jehad, or Holy War of the Muslims, is a call to the whole Islamic world to take arms against infidels.

John Bunyan's *Holy War*, published in 1682, tells of the capture of Mansoul by SATAN and its recapture by the forces of Shaddai (EMMANUEL).

Although properly undertaken from religious motives, holy wars were fiercely and often bitterly contested, and the expression is often colloquially applied to relentless crusades of various kinds.

**Holy water.** Water blessed by a priest for religious purposes. It is particularly used in the ROMAN CATHOLIC CHURCH at the Asperges, the sprinkling of the altar and congregation before HIGH MASS and generally at blessings, dedications and the like, and it is kept in holy water stoups near church doors for the use of those entering.

**Holy Week.** The last week in LENT. It begins on PALM SUNDAY. The fourth day is called SPY WEDNESDAY, the fifth is MAUNDY THURSDAY, the sixth is GOOD FRIDAY, and the last is Holy Saturday or EASTER Eve.

**Holy Willie.** A nickname for an excessively pious person. The allusion is to Robert Burns' daring poem 'Holy Willie's Prayer' (1785), which he explained was about 'a rather oldish bachelor elder in the parish of Mauchline, and much and justly famed for that polemical chattering which ends in tippling orthodoxy'.

**Holy Writ.** The BIBLE.

**Holy Year.** *See* HOLY DOOR; JUBILEE.

**As the Devil loves holy water.** *See under* AS.

**Order of the Holy Ghost, The.** *See under* ORDER.

**Procession of the Holy Ghost, The.** *See* FILIOQUE CONTROVERSY.

**Seven gifts of the Holy Spirit, The.** *See under* SEVEN.

**Sin against the Holy Ghost, The.** *See under* SIN.

**Homburg.** A soft felt hat popularized by Edward VII (r.1901–10). It was originally made at Homburg in Prussia where the king 'took the waters'.

**Home. Home and dry.** Safe and successful, having satisfactorily completed some endeavour. The allusion is to a horse race home, when the winning rider has such a good lead that he can rub down his mount before the rest of the field arrive.

**Home Counties.** The counties surrounding London. These were originally Kent, Surrey, Essex, and Middlesex, but now Buckinghamshire, Berkshire, Hertfordshire and Sussex are often included in the term.

**Home economics.** A school subject usually studied by girls rather than boys and including diet management, budgeting, child care and other aspects of running a home. It was formerly familiar as domestic science.

**Home from home, A.** A place other than one's own home where it is possible to make oneself at home.

**Home Guard.** In Britain the force of volunteers raised early in the Second World War and trained for defence against the threat of invasion. It was originally known as the Local Defence Volunteers but was renamed the Home Guard at Winston Churchill's suggestion. It soon came to be affectionately known as DAD'S ARMY. The Home Guard was officially disbanded in 1957.

**Home, James, and don't spare the horses.** An expression from the days when the rich commanded their coachmen to drive them home as fast as possible. It is still used jocularly to mean 'let's get home as fast as we can', or to tell a driver to set off for home without delay. The expression itself is the title of a popular song of 1934 by Fred Hillebrand.

**Home Office.** The British government department that is responsible for the maintenance of law and order, immigration control and those domestic affairs that are not specifically assigned to another department. In many countries the equivalent department is known as the Ministry of the Interior. The head of the Home Office is the HOME SECRETARY.

**Home of lost causes, The.** Oxford. The university is referred to as such by the poet Matthew Arnold (1822–88) in his *Essays in Criticism* (1865):

> Whispering from her towers the last enchantments of the Middle Ages … Home of lost causes, and forsaken beliefs, and unpopular names, and impossible loyalties!

**Home Rule.** The name given by Isaac Butt (1813–79), its first leader, to the movement for securing governmental independence for Ireland under the British crown, after failures of earlier movements to secure the repeal of the Act of Union of 1800. The Home Government Association was founded in 1870 (renamed the Home Rule Association in 1873), and when Charles Stewart Parnell (1846–91) became leader in 1879 its policy of obstruction in Parliament became a growing thorn in the flesh of English governments. A Home Rule Bill was eventually passed in 1914, but its implementation was postponed by the outbreak of the First World War. The Easter Rising in 1916, the activities of SINN FÉIN and resistance in Ulster, led to the establishment of the Irish Free State in 1921, but Northern Ireland continues to be represented in the British Parliament.

**Home Secretary.** The title of the CABINET minister who is responsible for the HOME OFFICE. He is the equivalent of the Minister (or Secretary) of the Interior in many other countries, such as the United States, France and Germany.

**Home shopping.** Shopping carried out from home by means of mail order catalogues, satellite television channels and the like.

**Home straight, The.** The final stretch of a racecourse. Metaphorically, to be in the home straight is to be almost HOME AND DRY.

**Home, sweet home.** This popular English song first appeared in the opera *Clari, or, the Maid of Milan* (1823). The words were by the American actor and playwright John Howard Payne (1791–1852) and the music was by Sir Henry Bishop (1786–1855), who claimed to have based it on a Sicilian air. The sentiment expresses exactly that made by the Latin DULCE DOMUM.

> Mid pleasures and palaces though we may roam,
> Be it ever so humble, there's no place like home;
> A charm from the skies seems to hallow us there,
> Which, seek through the world, is ne'er met with elsewhere.
> Home, home, sweet, sweet home!
> There's no place like home! there's no place like home!

**Home truth.** An unpleasant or unwelcome truth delivered by another person about oneself, which 'goes home'.

**At home.** *See under* AT.
**Bring home the bacon, To.** *See under* BRING.
**Bring home to, To.** *See under* BRING.
**Bring something home to someone, To.** *See under* BRING.
**Charity begins at home.** *See under* CHARITY.
**Come home to roost, To.** *See under* COME.
**Do one's homework, To.** *See under* DO.
**Drive a point home, To.** *See under* DRIVE.
**England, home and beauty.** *See under* ENGLAND.
**Englishman's home is his castle, An.** *See under* ENGLISH.
**Harvest home.** *See under* HARVEST.
**House and home.** *See under* HOUSE.
**Not at home.** *See* AT HOME.
**Nothing to write home about.** *See under* NOTHING.
**Stately home.** *See under* STATELY.
**Strike home, To.** *See under* STRIKE.
**There's no place like home.** *See* HOME, SWEET HOME.
**Who goes home?** *See under* WHO.

**Homer.** The traditional author of the ILIAD and the ODYSSEY. Estimates of his birth date vary between 1159 BC and 685 BC. In antiquity, seven cities claimed the honour of being Homer's birthplace: Argos, Athens, Chios, Colphon, Rhodes, Salamis in Cyprus and Smyrna. *See also* MAEONIDES.

PLATO has been called the Homer of philosophers, MILTON the English Homer and OSSIAN the Gaelic Homer. BYRON called Henry Fielding the prose Homer of human nature, and John Dryden said: 'Shakespeare was the Homer, or father, of our dramatic poets.'

**Homer sometimes nods.** Even the best of us is liable to make mistakes. The line is from Horace's *Ars Poetica* (1st century BC):

> Indignor quandoque bonus dormitat Homerus,
> Verum operi longo fas est obrepere somnum.
> (I am aggrieved when sometimes even worthy
> Homer nods, but in so long a work it is allowable
> if drowsiness comes on.)

**Casket Homer, The.** *See under* CASKET.
**Scourge of Homer, The** *See under* SCOURGE.

**Honest. Honest Abe.** *See* OLD ABE.

**Honest Injun.** Settlers of the American West in the 19th century mistrusted the Indians they encountered and ironically or with tongue in cheek referred to themselves as 'honest Injuns' by comparison. The phrase was taken up in the stories of Mark Twain, and from them came to be adopted as a catchphrase meaning 'honour bright' or words to that effect.

**Honest to goodness.** Really; for sure.
**As honest as the day is long.** *See under* AS.

**Honey. Honeymoon.** A holiday spent together by a newly married couple. The word was originally used for the first month of marriage, although 'moon' does not mean 'month' here, as sometimes supposed. The reference is to the moon as sweetness and is ironic, for no sooner is it full than it begins to wane. Other languages have a like term, such as French *lune de miel*, Italian *luna di miele* and Russian *medovy mesyats*. A German honeymoon is *Flitterwochen*, literally 'fondling weeks'.

**Honeysuckle.** *See* MISNOMERS.

**Honey trap.** A scheme to lure a person into a compromising sexual situation in order to blackmail them. The scenario typically involves a seductive woman as the 'honey' and a senior civil servant as the victim.

> High-flyers in the Ministry of Defence no longer have to fear the 'honey traps' set by foreign spymasters. They can now confess their sexual peccadillos without their careers being ruined.
> *Sunday Times* (3 January 1999)

**Land of milk and honey.** *See under* LAND.
**Second honeymoon.** *See under* SECOND.

**Honi soit qui mal y pense.** The motto of the MOST NOBLE ORDER OF THE GARTER, usually rendered as 'evil be to him who evil thinks' although 'shame to him' would be more accurate. It has been the subject of several ribald variants, including 'honey sweet but smelly pants'.

**Honky-tonk.** A disreputable night-club or low roadhouse; a place of cheap entertainment. A honky-tonk piano is one from which the felts of the hammers have been removed, thus making the instrument more percussive and giving its notes a tinny quality. Such pianos are often used for playing ragtime and popular melodies in public houses.

**Honorificabilitudinitatibus.** A concocted word based on the Latin *honorificabilitudo*, 'honourableness', found in Shakespeare. Sir Edwin Durning-Lawrence, in support of the cryptographic theory that attributed Shakespeare's works to Francis Bacon, discovered this to be the all-revealing word, since its 27 letters were clearly an ANAGRAM of '*Hi ludi F Baconis nati tuiti orbi*', 'These plays, F. Bacon's offspring, are preserved for the whole world'. *See also* LONG WORDS; WILLIAM SHAKESPEARE.

> Thou are not so long by the head as honorificabilitudinitatibus.
> *Love's Labour's Lost*, V, i (1594)

**Honour. Affair of honour, An.** *See under* AFFAIR.
**Court of honour.** *See under* COURT.
**Debts of honour.** *See under* DEBT.
**Do the honours, To.** *See under* DO.
**Field of honour.** *See under* FIELD.
**Laws of honour.** *See under* LAW.
**Legion of Honour.** *See under* LEGION.
**Maid of honour.** *See under* MAID.
**Medal of Honor.** *See under* MEDAL.

**On one's word of honour.** *See under* WORD.
**Peace with honour.** *See under* PEACE.
**Point of honour.** *See under* POINT.
**Word of honour.** *See under* WORD.

**Honourable.** For the word's application to the nobility *see* COURTESY TITLES. This title of honour is also given to the children of life peers, to MAIDS OF HONOUR and to Justices of the HIGH COURT, except Lord Justices and Justices of Appeal. In the HOUSE OF COMMONS one member speaks of another, or addresses another, in the third person, as 'the honourable member for [name of constituency]'. When referring to an MP of the same party, a member calls him or her 'my honourable friend', and to an MP of another party, 'the honourable gentleman' or 'the honourable lady'. *See also* RIGHT HONOURABLE. In the USA 'honourable' is a courtesy title applied to persons of distinction in legal or civic life. The title was also borne by the East India Company. *See also* JOHN COMPANY.

**Honourable Artillery Company (HAC).** The oldest surviving British army unit, having been founded by Henry VIII, in 1537, as the Guild of St George. In Tudor and Stuart days the officers for the TRAINBANDS of London were supplied by the HAC, in whose ranks John Milton, Christopher Wren and Samuel Pepys served at one time or another. The HAC is not part of the Regular Army but is the senior regiment of the Territorial Army Volunteer Reserves. It maintains a headquarters in the City Road, London, and has four squadrons and a gun troop. It also provides the Company of Pikemen and Musketeers and has the right to march through the City of London with fixed bayonets.

In 1638 Robert Keayne, a member of the London company, founded the Ancient and Honourable Artillery Company of Boston, Massachusetts, which is the oldest military unit in the USA.

**Honourable Corps of Gentlemen at Arms, The.** The bodyguard of the sovereign (formerly called Gentlemen Pensioners), which acts in conjunction with the Yeomen of the Guard (BEEFEATERS). It has a Captain, Lieutenant, Standard Bearer, Clerk of the Cheque, Sub-officer and 39 Gentlemen at Arms, all of whom were chosen from retired officers of ranks from General to Major of the Regular Army and Royal Marines.

**Most Honourable.** *See under* MOST.
**Right Honourable.** *See under* RIGHT.

**Honours.** A general term for titles, distinctions, awards and the like. At bridge, the honours are the five highest trump cards: ace, king, queen, knave (jack) and ten.

**Honours of war.** The privilege, allowed to an enemy on capitulation, of being allowed to retain his weapons. This is the highest honour a victor can pay a vanquished foe. Sometimes the troops so treated are allowed to march with all their arms, drums beating and colours flying.

**Birthday honours.** *See under* BIRTHDAY.
**Do the honours, To.** *See under* DO.
**Last honours.** *See under* LAST.

**Hooch.** An American slang term for whisky or crude raw spirits, often made surreptitiously or obtained illegally. The word is a shortened form of Tlingit *Hoochinoo*, the name of an Alaskan tribe that distilled a particular type of liquor. *See also* MOONSHINE.

**Hood. Hood** or **cowl does not make the monk, The.** It is a person's way of life, not what he or she professes to be, that really matters. The expression is the equivalent of the Latin *Cucullus non facit monachum* and is probably derived from the lines in St Anselm's *Carmen de Contemptu Mundi* (11th century):

> Non tonsura facit monachum, non horrida vestis;
> Sed virtus animi, perpetuusque rigor.
> (It is not the tonsure that makes the monk, not the rough garments,
> But the virtue and constant discipline of the soul.)

**Robin Hood.** *See under* ROBIN.
**Robin Hood and Guy of Gisborne.** *See under* ROBIN.
**Robin Hood's Bay.** *See under* ROBIN.
**Robin Hood's bow and arrow.** *See under* ROBIN.
**Robin Hood's death.** *See under* ROBIN.
**Robin Hood's larder.** *See under* ROBIN.
**Robin Hood wind, A.** *See under* ROBIN.

**Hoodlum.** A street hooligan. The word originated in San Francisco in 1871 and rapidly spread throughout the USA. Its origin is uncertain, but it may be in German dialect *Huddellump*, 'ragamuffin'. A colloquial form is 'hood'.

**Hoof, Cloven.** *See under* CLOVEN.

**Hook. Hooked, To be.** To be caught, whether of a man 'hooked' by a woman (for marriage), of a person addicted to a drug, or generally of someone who has become interested in a thing or taken a liking to it.

**Hooker.** A prostitute. Originally a thief or pickpocket, who snatched his ill-gotten gains by means of a hook. A prostitute similarly 'hooks' her clients.

**Hook, line and sinker.** To swallow a tale hook, line and sinker is to be extremely gullible, like the hungry fish that swallows not only the baited hook, but the sinker (lead weight) and some of the line as well.

**By hook or by crook.** *See under* BY.

**Get one's hooks into** or **on, To.** To get hold of. The hooks are one's hands or fingers.

**Off the hook, to.** *See under* OFF.

**On one's own hook.** On one's own initiative or account. An angler's phrase.

**On the hook.** Kept waiting, or in a dangerous or difficult situation.

**Sling one's hook, To.** *See under* SLING.

**Hookey, To play.** *See under* PLAY.

**Hooligan.** A violent or lawless young person. The term dates from the late 19th century and is said to derive from the Irish surname Houlihan, alluding to a particular family.

> The original *Hooligans* were a spirited Irish family of that name whose proceedings enlivened the drab monotony of life in Southwark towards the end of the 19th century.
>
> ERNEST WEEKLEY: *The Romance of Words*, ch i (1922)

**Hooray.** *See* HIP! HIP! HURRAH!

**Hoosier.** An inhabitant of the state of Indiana, the Hoosier State. The origin of the name is unknown.

**Hoover.** The tradename of a firm of vacuum cleaner makers, which, to the company's displeasure, has come to be used as a noun and a verb relating to vacuum cleaners and vacuuming in general. The name was patented by the company in 1927, although this cannot legally stop people using it in a generic sense. The name is that of William H. Hoover (1849–1932), a saddler of North Canton, Ohio, who saw the potential of an 'electric suction cleaner' invented in 1907 by Murray Spangler, a department store guard.

**Hop. Hopalong Cassidy.** The black-garbed hero of the Old West was created by the American writer Clarence E. Mulford for his novel named after him (1910). Sequels followed, and he then reemerged on the cinema screen in the 1930s in a series of 60 cheaply made movies, in which he was played by William Boyd. Many Western fans regard his film persona as an improvement on the original.

**Hop in, To.** To get in quickly, as into a car.

Hop it. Be off with you; clear off; go away.

**Hop-o'-my-thumb.** A PYGMY OR DWARF. *See also* TOM THUMB.

**Hopping mad.** Very angry; literally so angry as to jump or hop about.

**Hopscotch.** A children's game involving hopping on one foot over lines or between boxes marked ('scotched') on the ground and retrieving a flat stone or similar object that lies in one of the boxes. The game may have given the HOP, SKIP AND JUMP of athletics.

**Hop, skip** or **step and jump.** In athletics, an informal name for the triple jump. The athlete runs up to the sandpit, hops by taking off and landing on the same foot, skips or steps by landing on the other foot, and jumps by landing in the pit in any manner, but usually with the feet together. The origins of the jump may lie in children's HOPSCOTCH.

**Hop the twig, To.** To depart suddenly; to decamp just before being caught. The phrase is from hunting jargon, referring to birds that take to the air just before, or just as, the hunter fires at them.

**Hope.** *See* PANDORA'S BOX.

**Hope Diamond.** A rare sapphire-blue Indian stone weighing $44\frac{1}{8}$ carats (now in America), which appeared on the market in 1830 and at one time was the property of Henry Thomas Hope. It is believed to be part of the large blue DIAMOND cut to 68 carats and sold to Louis XIV by Jean Baptiste Tavernier (1605–89). Like the SANCY DIAMOND, it disappeared (1792) during the French Revolution.

**Band of Hope.** *See under* BAND.

**Bard of Hope.** Thomas Campbell (1777–1844) was so called on account of his poem *The Pleasures of Hope* (1799).

**Forlorn hope.** *See under* FORLORN.

**Cape of Good Hope, The.** *See* CAPE OF STORMS.

**Land of Hope and Glory.** *See under* LAND.

**Young hopeful.** *See under* YOUNG.

**Horace.** Quintus Horatius Flaccus (65–8 BC), the Roman lyric poet.

**Horace of England, The.** George, Duke of Buckingham, preposterously declared Abraham Cowley (1618–67) to be the PINDAR, Horace and VIRGIL of England. Ben Jonson (1572–1637) was nicknamed Horace by Thomas Dekker in the so-called War of the Theatres.

**Horace of France, The.** Jean Macrinus or Salmon (1490–1557); also Pierre Jean de Béranger (1780–1857), alternatively called the French Burns.

**Horace of Spain, The.** The brothers Lupercio (1559–1613) and Bartolomé de Argensola (1562–1631).

**Horae** (Latin, 'hours', 'seasons'). In classical mythology, the three sisters Eunomia ('good order'), Dice ('justice') and Irene ('peace'), who presided respectively over spring, summer and winter. According to Hesiod they were the daughters of JUPITER and THEMIS.

**Horatius.** In Roman legend a great warrior who bravely and single-handedly held off an invading army at the bridge across the Tiber and who then swam the river in full armour when the bridge was finally broken. His story is familiar from Thomas Babington Macaulay's poem that bears his name.

> With weeping and with laughter
> Still is the story told,
> How well Horatius kept the bridge
> In the brave days of old.
>
> T.B. MACAULAY: *Lays of Ancient Rome*, 'Horatius' (1842)

**Horde, Golden.** *See under* GOLDEN.

**Horizon, The dip of the.** *See under* DIP.

**Horn.** The horn was a symbol of power and dominion and as such is found in classical writers and in the Old Testament. The original Hebrew SHOFAR or trumpet was made of a ram's horn.

**Hornbook.** A thin board about 9in (23cm) long and 5–6in (12.5–15cm) wide (with a handle) serving as backing to a leaf of vellum or sheet of paper on which were usually written (later printed) the alphabet, an exorcism, the Lord's Prayer and the Roman numerals. The whole was covered by a thin piece of transparent horn. The handle had a hole in it so that it could be tied to a schoolchild's girdle. Hornbooks continued to be used in England until well into the 18th century. *See also* CRISS-CROSS.

> He teaches boys the hornbook.
> SHAKESPEARE: *Love's Labour's Lost*, V, i (1594)

**Horn Dance.** *See* ABBOTS BROMLEY HORN DANCE.

**Horn in, To.** To interrupt or intrude.

**Horn of Africa.** The region of northeastern Africa occupied by present-day Somalia. It should not be confused with CAPE HORN.

**Horn of fidelity.** MORGAN LE FAY sent a horn to King ARTHUR, which had the following 'virtue': no lady could drink out of it who was not 'to her husband true'. All others who attempted to drink were sure to spill what it contained. This horn was carried to King MARK and 'his queene with a hundred ladies more' tried the experiment, but only four managed to 'drink cleane'.

**Horn of plenty** or **cornucopia.** AMALTHEA'S HORN, an emblem of plenty. CERES is drawn with a ram's horn in her left arm, filled with fruits and flowers. Sometimes these are being poured on the earth, and sometimes they are piled high in the horn as in a basket. 'Cornucopia' represents Latin *cornu copiae*, 'horn of plenty'.

**Hornpipe.** An obsolete wooden pipe with a reed mouthpiece at one end and horn at the other. The dance of this name, once associated with mariners, was originally accompanied by this instrument.

**Horns of a dilemma, The.** A difficult choice in which the alternatives appear equally distasteful or undesirable. Greek *lēmma* means 'assumption', 'proposition', from *lambanein*, 'to grasp'. A dilemma is a double lemma, or what the SCHOOLMEN called an *argumentum cornutum*, 'horned argument'. The allusion is to a bull that will toss you whichever horn you grasp.

**Horns of Moses' face, The.** MOSES is conventionally represented with horns, owing to a blunder in translation. In Exodus 34:29–30, where the text tells that when Moses came down from Mount Sinai 'the skin of his face shone', the Hebrew for this shining may be translated either as 'sent forth beams' or 'sent forth horns', and the VULGATE took the latter as correct, rendering the passage: *quod cornuta esset facies sua*. MICHELANGELO followed the earlier painters in depicting Moses with horns.

**Amalthea's horn.** *See under* AMALTHEA.

**Auld Hornie.** *See under* AULD.

**Blow one's horn, To.** *See under* BLOW.

**Cape Horn.** *See under* CAPE.

**Devil's horn.** *See* DEVIL'S CANDLESTICK.

**Draw** or **pull in one's horns, To.** *See under* DRAW.

**Golden Horn, The.** *See under* GOLDEN.

**King Horn.** The hero of a late 13th-century English metrical romance. His father, king of Sudenne, was killed by SARACEN pirates who set young Horn adrift in a boat with 12 other children. After many adventures he reconquered his father's kingdom and married Rymenhild, daughter of King Aylmer of Westernesse.

**Lock horns, To.** *See under* LOCK.

**Make horns at, To.** To show the fist with the first and fourth fingers extended, the others doubled in. This is an ancient gesture of insult to a person, implying that he is a CUCKOLD.

> Denmark was so disquised, as he would have lain with the Countess of Nottingham, making Horns in Derision at her Husband the High Admiral of England.
> SIR E. PEYTON: *The Divine Catastrophe of the Kingly Family of the House of Stuarts* (1652)

**Oldenburg Horn.** *See under* OLDENBURG.

**Swearing on the horns.** *See under* SWEAR.

**Take the bull by the horns, To.** *See under* BULL.

**Wear the horns, To.** *See under* WEAR.

**Horner, Little Jack.** *See under* JACK.

**Horoscope** (Greek *hōroskopos*, from *hōra*, 'hour', and *skopos*, 'observer'). The observation of the heavens at the hour of a person's birth, used by astrologers for predicting the future events of his life. The term is also used for a figure or diagram of the 12 houses of heaven, showing the positions of the planets at a given time, as used in ASTROLOGY. *See also* ASTROLOGICAL HOUSES.

**Hors** (French, 'out of', 'outside').

**Hors concours** ('out of competition'). In the narrow sense, a term applied to an artist or exhibitor who has been excluded from competing. In a general sense, the phrase is used for someone who is unrivalled or unequalled, who is in a class of his or her own.

**Hors de combat** ('out of battle'). Incapable of taking any further part in the fight; disabled.

**Hors d'oeuvre** ('outside the work'). An extra course served as an appetizer at the beginning of a dinner, such as anchovies, CAVIARE, continental sausage, soused herrings or the like. This part of the meal is now less pretentiously known in English as a STARTER. The word is usually found in the plural.

> Nor shall I, though your mood endure,
> Attempt a final Water-cure
> Except against my wishes;

For I respectfully decline
To dignify the Serpentine,
And make *hors-d'œuvres* for fishes.
AUSTIN DOBSON: 'To "Lydia Languish"' (1872)

**Horsa.** *See* HENGIST.

**Horse.** According to classical mythology POSEIDON created the horse, and according to VIRGIL the first person that drove a four-in-hand was ERICHTHONIUS. In Christian art the horse is held to represent courage and generosity. It is an attribute of St MARTIN, St Maurice, St GEORGE and St Victor, all of whom are represented on horseback.

It is a not uncommon emblem in the CATACOMBS and probably typifies the swiftness of life.

The use of horse attributively usually denotes something that is coarse, inferior or unrefined, as in horseradish, horse mushroom. *See also* COB; HAND.

**Horsebridge.** Another name for a pack-horse bridge, sometimes called a riding bridge or bridle bridge.

**Horse chestnut.** John Gerard mentions in his *Herball* (1597) that the tree is so called 'for that the people of the East countries do with the fruit thereof cure their horses of the cough'. Another, less likely, explanation is that when a leaf stalk is pulled off, it shows a miniature representation of a horse's hock and foot with shoe and nail marks. A third possibility is that the fruit is so called because of its coarseness, by comparison with the edible (sweet) chestnut. One thus has horse radish compared to the smaller, more delicate radish, and horse mackerel as a term for the larger kinds of mackerel.

**Horse Guards.** The British cavalry regiment, known as the 'Blues', which together with the Life Guards made up the cavalry section of the sovereign's Household Brigade until 1969, when they were amalgamated with the 1st Royal Dragoons to become the Blues and Royals. Their headquarters is in WHITEHALL. *See also* HOUSEHOLD TROOPS.

**Horse latitudes.** A region of calms about 30° north and south of the Equator, perhaps so named from the fact that sailing ships carrying horses to America and the West Indies were sometimes obliged to jettison their cargoes when becalmed in these latitudes through shortage of water for the animals. According to another theory, the name derives from 'dead horse', a nautical term for advance pay, which sailors expected to work off by the time they reached this region.

**Horse laugh.** A coarse, vulgar laugh, like a horse's whinny.

**Horseleech.** An old name for a veterinary surgeon, and formerly for a greedy person. The latter sense is at least partly from the biblical line: 'The horseleach hath two daughters, crying, Give, give' (Proverbs 30:15). John Marbeck, commentating in 1581, explains the 'two daughters':

> That is, two forks in her tongue, which he heere calleth her two daughters, whereby she sucketh the bloud and is never saciate.

**Horse Marines, The.** *See under* REGIMENTAL AND DIVISIONAL NICKNAMES.

**Horse of a different colour, A.** A different affair altogether. The allusion is to the identification of horses when selling or racing. A similar expression is 'a horse of the same colour'.

**Horse opera.** A Western film.

**Horseplay.** Boisterous play.

**Horsepower.** A common unit of power measurement as applied to machines, engines, motors and so on, equal to 550 foot-pounds per second (about 750 watts). It was first fixed by James Watt when seeking a suitable way of indicating the power exerted by his steam engine. He estimated that a strong dray horse working at a gin for eight hours a day averaged 22,000 foot-pounds per minute. He increased this by 50 per cent, and this became the recognized unit.

**Horse sense.** Plain common sense. The allusion is not to the animal but to the horse trader, noted for his shrewdness. *See also* HORSE TRADING.

**Horses for courses.** A course of action or policy that has been modified slightly from the original to allow for altered circumstances. A horse that runs well on a dry course will run less well on a damp course and vice versa.

**Horseshoes.** The belief that it is lucky to pick up a horseshoe is from the idea that it was a protection against witches and evil generally. According to John Aubrey, the reason is that 'MARS (iron) is the enemy of SATURN (God of the Witches)'. Consequently they were nailed to the house door with two ends uppermost, so that the luck did not 'run out'. Nelson had one nailed to the mast of the *Victory*.

One legend is that the Devil one day asked St DUNSTAN, who was noted for his skill as a farrier, to shoe his 'single hoof'. Dunstan, knowing who his customer was, tied him tightly to the wall and proceeded with the job, but purposely caused the Devil such pain that he roared for mercy. Dunstan at last agreed to release his captive on condition that he would never again enter a place where he saw a horseshoe displayed.

**Horse's neck.** A mixed long drink of flavoured ginger ale and brandy, served on ice. It seems to have been named after an earlier, less sophisticated drink of MOONSHINE and cider drunk in the American backwoods. 'Horse's neck' may be short for 'horse's necklace', in turn an alteration of 'horse's nightcap', meaning a strong final drink of the day.

**Horses of the Dioscuri, The.** Cyllaros, named from Cylla in Troas, and Harpagus, 'carrier-off', from Greek *harpazein*, 'to seize', 'to snatch'. *See also* HARPY.

**Horse trading.** Hard, shrewd bargaining, as when trading at a horse fair.

**Angels on horseback.** *See under* ANGEL.

**As strong as a horse.** *See under* AS.

**Back the wrong horse, To.** *See under* BACK.

**Banks's horse.** *See under* BANKS'S.

**Blood horse.** *See under* BLOOD.

**Brazen horse, The.** *See under* BRAZEN.

**Dark horse, A.** *See under* DARK.

**Devils on horseback.** *See under* DEVIL.

**Famous horses of myth and history.** In classical mythology the names given to the horses of HELIOS, the Sun, were:

Actaeon ('effulgence'), Aethon ('fiery red'), Amethes ('no loiterer'), Bronte ('thunderer'), Erythreos ('red producer'), Lampos ('shining like a lamp'), Phlegon ('burning one') and Purocis ('fiery hot')

AURORA's horses were:

Abraxa, Eoos ('dawn') and Phaethon ('shining one')

PLUTO's horses were:

Abaster ('away from the stars'), Abatos ('inaccessible'), Aeton ('swift as an eagle') and Nonios

The following list is arranged alphabetically:

AARVAK or Arvak ('early-waker'): in Norse mythology the horse that draws the sun's chariot driven by the maiden SOL

Al BORAK

Alfana ('mare'): Gradasso's horse in ORLANDO FURIOSO

Alsvid or Alswider (Old Norse, 'all-swift'): the horse that draws the chariot of the moon in Norse mythology

Aquiline ('like an eagle'): Raymond's steed, bred on the banks of the Tagus (Tasso, JERUSALEM DELIVERED).

ARION ('martial'): HERCULES' horse

Arundel: the horse of BEVIS OF HAMPTON; the word means 'swift as a swallow' (French *hirondelle*)

BALIOS: one of the horses given by NEPTUNE to PELEUS and afterwards belonging to ACHILLES

Barbary: the favourite horse of Richard II; *see also* BARBARY ROAN

BAVIECA: the CID's horse

BAYARD: the horse given by CHARLEMAGNE to the FOUR SONS OF AYMON

BAYARDO: the steed of RINALDO, which once belonged to AMADIS OF GAUL

Black Agnes: a palfrey of Mary, Queen of Scots, given by her brother Moray and named after Agnes of Dunbar

Black Bess: the mythical mare, created for Dick TURPIN by Harrison Ainsworth in his *Rookwood* (1834), which carried Dick from London to York

BLACK SALADIN: Warwick's coal-black horse

BRIGADORE or Brigliadore ('golden bridle'): Sir Guyon's horse in Spenser's *The Faerie Queene* (1590, 1596)

Brigliadoro: ORLANDO's charger, second only to BAYARDO in swiftness and wonderful powers

BUCEPHALUS ('ox-head'): the charger of Alexander the Great, who was the only person who could mount him, and he always knelt down to take up his master; he was 30 years old at death and Alexander built the city of Bucephala for a mausoleum

CARMAN: the Chevalier BAYARD's horse

CELER ('swift'): the horse of the Roman Emperor Lucius Versus

CERUS ('fit'): the horse of ADRASTUS

Clavileno: *see* WOODEN HORSE

COPENHAGEN: the horse ridden by the Duke of Wellington at Waterloo

CYLLAROS: a celebrated horse of CASTOR AND POLLUX

DAPPLE: the name given in Smollett's translation of *Don Quixote* to SANCHO PANZA's donkey

Dinos ('the marvel'): DIOMEDES' horse

Ethon ('fiery'): one of the horses of HECTOR

Fadda: MOHAMMED's white mule

Ferrant d'Espagne ('Spanish grey'): the horse of OLIVER

Galathe (Greek, 'milk-coloured'): one of the horses of HECTOR

Grani (Old Norse, 'grey-coloured'): SIEGFRIED's horse, of marvellous swiftness

Grizzle: all skin and bone, the horse of Dr SYNTAX

Haizum: the horse of the archangel GABRIEL

Harpagus ('one that carries off rapidly'): one of the horses of CASTOR AND POLLUX

HIPPOCAMPUS: one of NEPTUNE's horses

HRIMFAXI ('frost-mane'): in Scandinavian legend the horse of night

INCITATUS (Latin, 'spurred-on'): the horse of CALIGULA

Kantaka: the white horse of the BUDDHA

Lampon (Greek, 'bright one'): one of DIOMEDES' horses

Lamri (Celtic, perhaps 'curvetter'): King ARTHUR's mare.

Malech: *see* BLACK SALADIN

MARENGO: the white stallion of NAPOLEON BONAPARTE

Marocco: *see* BANKS' HORSE

PEGASUS

Phallus (Greek *phallos*, 'male sex organ', so 'stallion'): the horse of Heraclius

Phrenicos (Greek *phrēn*, 'mind', so 'intelligent'): the horse of Hiero of Syracuse, which won the prize for single horses in the 73rd OLYMPIAD

Podarge (Greek *podargos*, 'swift-footed' or 'white-footed'): one of the horses of HECTOR

Roan Barbary: *see* BARBARY ROAN

Rosabelle: the favourite palfrey of Mary, Queen of Scots; *see also* BLACK AGNES

Rosinante (Spanish *rocín*, 'hack', 'nag', and *antes*, 'before', so 'formerly a hack'): Don QUIXOTE's horse

SAVOY: the favourite black horse of Charles VIII of France

Shibdiz: the Persian BUCEPHALUS, fleeter than the wind, the charger of Chosroes II

Skinfaxi (Old Norse, 'shining mane'): the horse of day in Norse legend; *see also* HRIMFAXI

SLEIPNIR (Old Norse, 'sliding one'): ODIN's eight-legged grey horse

SORREL: the horse of William III
Strymon: the horse immolated by XERXES before he invaded Greece; it came from the vicinity of the River Strymon in Thrace
Tachebrune (French, 'brown patch'): the horse of OGIER THE DANE
TREBIZOND: the grey horse of Guarinos, one of the French Knights taken at Roncesvalles
Vegliantino (Italian, 'little vigilant one'): ORLANDO's steed, called Veillantif in French romance
WHITE SURREY: Richard III's favourite horse
Xanthos or Xanthus: ACHILLES' horse and brother to BALIOS

**Fifteen points of a good horse, The.**

A good horse sholde have three propyrtees of a man, three of a woman, three of a foxe, three of a hare, and three of an asse.
Of a man. Bolde, prowde and hardye.
Of a woman. Fayre-breasted, fair of haire and easy to move.
Of a foxe. A fair taylle, short eers, with a good trotte.
Of a hare. A grate eye, a dry head and well rennynge.
Of an asse. A bygge chynn, a flat legge and a good hoof.
WYNKYN DE WORDE (1496)

**Flesh-eating horses.** *See under* FLESH.
**Flog a dead horse, To.** *See under* FLOG.
**Four Horsemen of the Apocalypse, The.** *See under* FOUR.
**Grey mare is the better horse, The.** *See under* GREY.
**Hercules' horse.** *See* ARION.
**Hobby horse.** *See under* HOBBY.
**Hold one's horses, To.** *See under* HOLD.
**Hold your horses!** *See under* HOLD.
**Home, James, and don't spare the horses.** *See under* HOME.
**Liberty horses.** *See under* LIBERTY.
**Lock the stable door after the horse has bolted, To.** *See under* LOCK.
**Look a gift-horse in the mouth, To.** *See under* LOOK.
**Nod is as good as a wink to a blind horse, A.** *See under* NOD.
**One-horse town.** *See under* ONE.
**On one's high horse, To be.** *See under* HIGH.
**Pale Horse, The.** *See under* PALE.
**Put the cart before the horse, To.** *See under* CART.
**Put one's shirt on a horse, To.** *See under* SHIRT.
**Seian Horse, The.** *See under* SEIAN.
**Shire horse.** *See under* SHIRE.
**Straight from the horse's mouth.** *See under* STRAIGHT.
**Swap** or **change horses in midstream, To.** *See under* SWAP.
**Trojan horse. A.** *See under* TROJAN.
**White Horse, The.** *See under* WHITE.
**White horses.** *See under* WHITE.
**Winged horse.** *See* PEGASUS.
**Wild horse.** *See under* WILD.
**Wooden Horse, The.** *See under* WOOD.
**Wooden Horse of Troy, The.** *See under* WOOD.
**You can take a horse to the water but you cannot make him drink.** There is always some point at which it is impossible to get an obstinate or determined person to go any further in the desired direction. The proverb is found in John Heywood (1546).

**Horus.** One of the major gods of the ancient Egyptians, originally a great sky god and sun god, who became merged with Horus the son of OSIRIS and ISIS, and Horus the Child. He was also identified with the king himself, and the Horus name was the first of the five names of the Egyptian king. He was the best known of the falcon gods and was represented in hieroglyphics by the winged sun disc. *See also* HARPOCRATES.

**Hose, Trunk.** *See under* TRUNK.

**Hosea.** The Old Testament prophet who denounces idolatry, luxury and debauchery in ISRAEL, urging those in authority to concentrate on religious and moral reform. His strong but also compassionate views are expressed in the book that bears his name.

Hear the word of the Lord, ye children of Israel: for the Lord hath a controversy with the inhabitants of the land, because there is no truth, nor mercy, nor knowledge of God in the land.
Hosea 4:1

**Hospital** (Medieval Latin *hospitale*, from Latin *hospitalis*, an adjectival form of *hospes*, 'guest'). The word was originally applied to a hospice or hostel for the reception of pilgrims. It later denoted a charitable institution for the aged and infirm (as in Greenwich Hospital, Chelsea Hospital), then charitable institutions for the education of children (as in Christ's Hospital, Emmanuel Hospital, Greycoat Hospital) and finally the present institutions for treatment of the sick and injured. Hospital, hospice, hostel and hotel are all related words. *See also* MAGDALENE.

**Hospitallers.** The name first applied to those whose duty it was too provide *hospitium* ('lodging and entertainment') for pilgrims. The most noted institution of the kind was founded at Jerusalem (*c.*1048), which gave its name to an order called the Knights Hospitallers or the Knights of St John of Jerusalem. Later they were styled the Knights of Rhodes and subsequently the Knights of Malta, the islands of Rhodes (1310) and Malta (1529) being, in turn, their headquarters. The order became predominantly military in the 12th century, but in the late 18th century it reverted to its earlier purposes of tending the sick and poor, moving to Rome in 1834.

The order came to an end in England after the REFORMATION, but a branch was revived in 1831, which declared itself an independent order in 1858 and is now styled the Order of the Hospital of St John of Jerusalem. It founded the St John Ambulance Association in 1877.

**Hospital Sunday.** The Sunday nearest St LUKE's day (18 October), when churches have special collections for hospitals. The practice began in London in 1873.

**Cottage hospital.** *See under* COTTAGE.

**Guy's Hospital.** *See under* GUY.

**Hospodar** (Slavic, 'lord', 'master'). The title borne by the princes of Moldavia and Wallachia before their union with Romania.

**Host.** (1) From the Latin *hostia* ('sacrifice') meaning the consecrated bread of the EUCHARIST regarded as the sacrifice of the Body of Christ.

(2) An army or multitude, from the Latin *hostis*, 'enemy'. In Medieval Latin *hostem facere* came to mean 'to perform military service'. *Hostis* ('military service') then came to mean the army that went against the foe, whence our word 'host'.

(3) One who entertains guests, from the Latin *hospes*, 'a guest'.

**Elevation of the Host, The.** *See under* ELEVATION.

**Heavenly host, The.** *See under* HEAVEN.

**Lord God of Hosts** or **Lord of Hosts, The.** *See under* LORD.

**Hostler** or **ostler.** The name given to the man who looked after the horses of travellers at an inn was originally applied to the innkeeper (hosteller) himself. It has been jokingly said to be derived from 'oat-stealer'.

**Hot. Hot air.** Empty talk; BOMBAST. Hence hot-air merchant, one whose utterances are 'full of sound and fury, signifying nothing', otherwise a WINDBAG.

> A great warm wind ... has been blowing across the political landscape. And hot air, sirocco-like, is filling the sails of some unlikely navigators.
> *The Times* (8 November 1994)

**Hot and strong.** In good measure; fully.

**Hot cockles.** A CHRISTMAS game. One player kneels down with his eyes covered and lays his head in another's lap and on being struck has to guess who gave the blow.

> As at Hot cockles once I laid me down,
> And felt the weighty hand of many a clown,
> Buxoma gave a gentle tap and I
> Quick rose and read soft mischief in her eye.
> JOHN GAY: *The Shepherd's Week*, 'Monday' (1714)

**Hot cross buns.** *See* BUN.

**Hot dog.** A sausage, especially a frankfurter, served in a hot roll split lengthways. There may be a punning allusion to the 'sausage dog', or dachshund, although 'hot dog' is equally an American expression of approval.

**Hotfoot.** With speed; rapidly.

**Hot gospeller.** A revivalist preacher with an enthusiastic delivery of the Gospel message.

**Hot Gospellers.** An old nickname for PURITANS, in modern times applied to the more energetic and colourful EVANGELISTS and revivalists.

**Hot line.** A special direct telephone line, for use in emergencies. In commercial use, the term is applied to an ordinary line over which a customer can place an order.

**Hot on.** Strict on, as: 'The boss is very hot on punctuality.'

**Hot pants.** Very brief, skin-tight shorts, as worn by young women in the early 1970s. They are 'hot' because they are sexually arousing.

**Hotpot.** A dish of mutton or beef with sliced potatoes cooked in a sealed pot in an oven. It is traditionally a popular dish in the north of England. Hence its alternative name of 'Lancashire hotpot'.

**Hot potato.** A delicate or tricky situation, which, as the term suggests, has to be handled with great care.

> The maternity subject is such a hot potato that once you know you have a problem, legal advice from an employment specialist is a must.
> *The Times* (12 August 1998)

**Hot rod.** An old car stripped and tuned for speed and, by transference, the owner of such a vehicle.

**Hot seat.** A difficult or precarious position.

**Hot spot.** A region of potential violence or danger, as a war zone.

**Hot stuff.** A person, especially a girl or woman, who is sexually exciting. The phrase can also apply to an object of this nature, such as a pornographic film or book.

**Blow hot and cold, To.** *See under* BLOW.

**Get hot under the collar, To.** To become indignant, angry or irritated.

**Give it hot to someone, To.** To punish them.

**Go hot and cold, To.** To feel alternately hot and cold through fear or some other strong emotion.

**Go** or **sell like hot cakes.** *See under* CAKE.

**In hot pursuit.** Following closely or rapidly behind; in spirited chase.

**In hot water, To be.** To be in trouble.

**Long hot summer.** *See under* LONG.

**Make it hot for someone, To.** To make it unpleasant or dangerous for a person.

**Not so hot.** Not so good; not very satisfactory.

**Hotchpotch** (French *hochepot*, from *hocher*, 'to shake', and *pot*, 'pot'). A thick broth containing meat and vegetables and other mixed ingredients; a confused mixture or jumble. HODGEPODGE is another alternative form. 'Hotchpot', another variant, is a legal term. When a fund or estate has to be divided among certain beneficiaries and some of the number have already received their share, those shares must brought into hotchpot, i.e. collected up and redistributed. The situation typically arises when a parent has given property to children but dies intestate, so that other beneficiaries technically get nothing because there is no will. A 'hotchpot provision' is a clause in a settlement requiring the carrying out of this procedure.

**Hotel, Private.** *See under* PRIVATE.

**Hôtel de Rambouillet.** The house in Paris where, *c*.1615, the Marquise de Rambouillet (1588–1665), disgusted with the coarseness of the court and the immoral and puerile tone of the time, founded the salon out of which grew the Académie Française. Mme de Sévigné (1626–96), François de Malherbe (1555–1628), Pierre Corneille (1606–84), the Duchesse de Longueville (1619–79) and the Duc de la Rochefoucauld (1613–80) were among the members. They had a refinement of language of their own, but preciosity, pedantry and affectation eventually led to the disintegration of the coterie. The women were known as *Les* PRÉCIEUSES and the men as *Esprits doux* ('gentle spirits'). Rambouillet itself is a town just southwest of Versailles. Its château is the summer residence of the French president.

**Hotspur.** A fiery person of uncontrolled temper. Harry Percy (1364–1403), son of the 1st Earl of Northumberland (*see* Shakespeare's *Henry IV, Pt I* (1597)), was so called.

**Houdini, Harry.** The stage name of Ehrich Weiss (1874–1926), the most celebrated illusionist and escapologist to date. Born in Budapest to Jewish parents, who emigrated to New York, he began his career as a magician in 1890, but world fame began with his appearance at London in 1900. No lock could hold him, not even that of the condemned cell at Washington jail. He escaped from handcuffs, ropes, safes and similar restraints and was deservedly called 'the Great Houdini'. He took his professional name from the French illusionist Jean-Eugène Robert-Houdin (1805–71), with Erik anglicized as Harry. He died from a punch in the stomach, delivered before he had tensed his muscles. *See also* DAVENPORT TRICK; HANDCUFF KING. Houdini is sometimes used as a noun to refer to someone who is skilled at extricating themselves from difficult situations.

**Hound. Hound of Crete.** A bloodhound.

**Gabriel's hounds.** *See under* GABRIEL.

**Hare and hounds.** *See under* HARE.

**Wish hounds** or **yell hounds.** *See under* WISH.

**Hour. Hour is not yet come, The.** The time for action has not yet arrived, or properly, the hour of death has not yet come, from the idea that the hour of death is preordained.

> The hour is come, but not the man.
>
> SIR WALTER SCOTT: *Heart of Midlothian*, ch iv (title) (1818)

**At the eleventh hour.** *See under* AT.

**Bad quarter of an hour, A.** *See under* BAD.

**Book of Hours.** *See under* BOOK.

**Canonical hours.** *See under* CANON.

**Darkest hour is that before the dawn, The.** *See under* DARK.

**Devil's dancing-hour, The.** *See under* DEVIL.

**Early hours, The.** *See under* EARLY.

**From hour to hour.** *See under* FROM.

**Happy hour.** *See under* HAPPY.

**Keep good hours, To.** *See under* GOOD.

**Keep regular hours, To.** *See under* REGULAR.

**Small hours.** *See under* SMALL.

**Their finest hour.** *See under* FINE.

**Houri** (Arabic *hūr*, plural of *haurā'*, 'dark-eyed woman'). One of the black-eyed damsels of the Muslim Paradise, possessed of perpetual youth and beauty, whose virginity is renewable at pleasure and who are the reward of every believer. Hence, in English use, any dark-eyed, dusky beauty.

**Housain.** *See* HOUSSAIN.

**House. House, The.** A familiar name for CHRIST CHURCH, Oxford, the London STOCK EXCHANGE, the HOUSE OF COMMONS and HOUSE OF LORDS among the most familiar institutions.

**House and home.** Home, from the point of view of its domestic management.

**House builded upon rock, A.** A phrase descriptive of a person or a thing whose foundations are sure. The allusion is to Matthew 7:24.

**House husband.** A married man who, instead of going out to work, carries out the household duties traditionally undertaken by a housewife, including the care of children. The term first appeared in the United States in the early 1970s. *See also* NEW MAN.

> Nor was either of us keen on Bruce becoming – the dread phrase – a househusband. The answer for him was a part-time academic job. He would earn less but be able to do more around the house.
>
> *The Times* (11 December 1998)

**Housemaid's knee.** Bursitis, an acute inflammation of the bursa, which is between the patella and the skin. This complaint was so called because housemaids were particularly liable to it in the days when they spent much time kneeling to scrub and polish floors.

**House of call.** Some house, frequently a public house, that one visits or uses regularly; formerly, a house where journeymen and workmen assembled for hire when out of work.

**House of cards.** An unstable situation, which can collapse at any minute, like a house built of playing cards.

**House of Commons.** The elected house of the British PARLIAMENT. It is also the lower house in the Canadian Parliament. *See also* HOUSE OF LORDS.

**House of correction, A.** A jail. The term originally applied to a place where vagrants were made to work and offenders were kept in ward for the correction of small offences.

**House of God, A** or **The.** A church or place of worship, also any place sanctified by God's presence. Thus JACOB in the wilderness, where he saw the ladder leading from earth to heaven, said, 'This is none other but the House of God and this is the gate of heaven' (Genesis 28:17).

**House of ill repute** or **ill fame, A.** A brothel.

**House of issue.** An investment banking house which advertises, underwrites and sells stocks or bonds on behalf of a corporation.

**House of Keys.** *See* TYNWALD.

**House of Lords.** The upper house of the British PARLIAMENT, consisting of the LORDS SPIRITUAL and LORDS TEMPORAL, i.e. hereditary peers (some two-thirds of the total), life peers (Lords of Appeal and those created under the Life Peerages Act of 1958), Scottish Representative Peers, the archbishops and certain BISHOPS of the CHURCH OF ENGLAND. Increasingly from the 1980s there were calls by the LABOUR PARTY to abolish or at least reform the House of Lords as an anachronism, and a first move in this direction was made in 1998, when the Lords themselves debated a proposal to deprive hereditary peers of the right to vote.

> The House of Peers, throughout the war,
> Did nothing in particular,
> And did it very well.
>
> W.S. GILBERT: *Iolanthe*, II (1882)

**House of Loreto, The.** The *Santa Casa* or Holy House, the reputed house of the Virgin MARY at Nazareth. It was said to have been miraculously moved to Dalmatia in 1291, thence to Recanati in Italy in 1294 and finally to a site near Ancona in 1295. It was reputed to have been transported by angels to prevent its destruction by the Turks. The name is from Latin *lauretum*, 'laurel grove', in which it stood in Recanati. The Holy House itself is a small stone building, now surrounded by a marble screen.

**House of Representatives.** The lower legislative chamber in the USA and Australia and the sole such chamber (formerly the lower) in New Zealand.

**House of Windsor, The.** The style of the British Royal House adopted in 1917 in deference to anti-German sentiment to replace the then existing style of Saxe-Coburg-Gotha, derived from Albert the PRINCE CONSORT. It was changed in 1960 to Mountbatten-Windsor for the descendants of Queen Elizabeth II, other than those entitled to the style of ROYAL HIGHNESS or of prince and princess. After his abdication, 11 December 1936, Edward VIII was created Duke of Windsor.

**House party.** A weekend (or longer) party at a COUNTRY HOUSE to which several guests are invited. Such parties are traditionally associated with the wealthy 'country set' and are less common today than they were in their heyday, in the years before and after the First World War. They are by no means defunct, however.

**House that Jack built, The.** An intriguing cumulative nursery rhyme, whose final verse runs as follows:

> This is the farmer sowing his corn,
> That kept the cock that crowed in the morn,
> That waked the priest all shaven and shorn,
> That married the man all tattered and torn,
> That kissed the maiden all forlorn,
> That milked the cow with the crumpled horn,
> That tossed the dog,
> That worried the cat,
> That killed the rat,
> That ate the malt
> That lay in the house that Jack built.

Mention of 'the priest all shaven and shorn' suggests that the rhyme may be of medieval origin.

**House-to-house.** Calling at every house in turn, as a 'house-to-house canvass'.

**House-warming.** A party given to celebrate moving into a new or first home.

**Housey-housey.** A name for BINGO or lotto, from the cry of 'House!' shouted by a winner, who has a FULL HOUSE on his or her card.

**As safe as houses.** *See under* AS.
**Astrological houses.** *See under* ASTROLOGY.
**Big house.** *See under* BIG.
**Bring down the house, To.** *See under* BRING.
**Clearing house.** *See under* CLEAR.
**Clerk of the House.** *See under* CLERK.
**Committee of the Whole House.** *See under* COMMITTEE.
**Count out the House, To.** *See under* COUNT.
**Country house.** *See under* COUNTRY.
**Cry from the housetop, To.** *See under* CRY.
**Disorderly house, A.** *See under* DISORDERLY.
**Eat someone out of house and home, To.** *See under* EAT.
**Free house.** *See under* FREE.
**Full house.** *See under* FULL.
**Halfway house.** *See under* HALF.
**Have the run of the house, To.** *See under* RUN.
**Ice house.** *See under* ICE.
**Keep a good house, To.** *See under* GOOD.
**Like a house on fire.** *See under* LIKE.
**Lower House.** *See* HOUSE OF COMMONS.
**Mansion House.** *See under* MANSION.
**On the house.** Of drinks, paid for by the owner of the hotel or bar, or the landlord of the pub.
**Open house.** *See under* OPEN.
**Paper a house, To.** *See under* PAPER.
**Picts' houses.** *See under* PICTS.
**Rough house.** *See under* ROUGH.

**Rowton houses.** *See under* ROWTON.
**Safe house.** *See under* SAFE.
**Set** or **put one's house in order, To.** To reform one's affairs as necessary.
**Somerset House.** *See under* SOMERSET.
**Sponging house.** *See under* SPONGE.
**Tied house.** *See under* TIE.
**Tippling house.** *See under* TIPPLING.
**Upper House.** *See under* UPPER.
**White House, The.** *See under* WHITE.

**Household, The.** *See* ROYAL HOUSEHOLD.
**Household Brigade.** *See* HOUSEHOLD TROOPS.
**Household gods.** The LARES AND PENATES who presided over the dwellings and domestic concerns of the ancient Romans. Hence, in modern use, the valued possessions of one's home, all those things that endear it to one.
**Household name** or **word.** A person or thing that is well known or that everyone has heard of.
**Household Troops.** Those troops whose special duty it is to attend the sovereign. They consist of the Household Cavalry, comprising the two regiments of the LIFE GUARDS and the Blues and Royals (HORSE GUARDS), and the Guards Division (formerly Brigade of Guards), consisting of the five Foot Guards regiments of the GRENADIER, COLDSTREAM, Scots, Irish and Welsh Guards. The proper collective name for these seven regiments is the Household Division (until 1968 Household Brigade), and the title 'Household Troops' properly applies to the Household Division together with the King's Troop and Royal Horse Artillery.

**Houssain** or **Housain.** In the ARABIAN NIGHTS ENTERTAINMENTS the brother of Prince AHMED and owner of the MAGIC CARPET.

**Houyhnhnms.** In *Gulliver's Travels* (1726) a race of horses endowed with reason and all the finer qualities of man. Swift coined the word in imitation of 'whinny'.

**How. How are you getting on?** How are things going? What success have you had?
**How come?** How did it happen? What is the reason for that?
**How goes the enemy?** What is the time? Time is the enemy of man, especially of those who are behindhand.
**How long is a piece of string?** Who knows? How can one tell? Said to someone who asks a question to which there is no accurate or worthwhile answer.
**How many beans make five?** A retort to an unanswerable question similar to HOW LONG IS A PIECE OF STRING? One possible answer is: 'Two in each hand and one in the mouth'.
**How now, brown cow?** What's up? What next? 'Brown cow' is said to have originally referred to a barrel of beer. The expression may therefore suggest that a good solution to an unexpected development or arrival is to have a drink. The words are also a traditional elocution exercise.
**How's your father?** A purely rhetorical question that originated as a humorous catchphrase in the music halls before the First World War. It later came to be a synonym for 'nonsense' or meaningless ritual, so that the Northern Ireland MP Bernadette Devlin (later McAliskey) was reported in the *Daily Mail* of 23 April 1969, following her maiden speech, as saying: 'All this stand up, sit down, kneel down and how's-your-father was so funny.' Later still, the phrase acquired a sexual connotation on the lines of HANKY-PANKY, as 'a bit of the old how's-your-father'.
**How to ... .** The stock opening words of the title of a book offering practical help or advice. Two well-known titles of this type are Dale Carnegie's *How To Win Friends and Influence People* (1936) and Shepherd Mead's *How to Succeed in Business Without Really Trying* (1953), the latter turned into a musical by Frank Loesser in 1961. On the fictional front there is also Erica Jong's novel *How To Save Your Own Life* (1978), a tale of the personal pilgrimage of a pornographic writer.

**Howard, The Female.** *See under* FEMALE.

**Howler.** A glaring and unintentionally amusing mistake, as typically perpetrated by a school student in written work. The error may simply be the result of sloppy expression, such as the definition of a gynaecologist as 'a specialist in women and other diseases'. But it may equally come from a misuse of words, or by confusion between similar words, such as: 'The whole story was a virago of lies' (for 'farrago'). Translators and interpreters fear howlers like the plague, as do copywriters employed by companies marketing products overseas. One food company promoted its *burrito* (a type of tortilla) in Spanish-speaking countries as a *burrada*. This was something of a *faux pas*, because *burrada* is Spanish for 'big mistake'. Even the slip of a single letter can produce a howler, as that of the American motor company which advertised two new models with the words, 'Cars that break tradition, now your bank account' (instead of 'not'). Collections of genuine howlers like these make enjoyable but salutary reading.

**Hoyle, According to.** *See under* ACCORDING.

**HP Sauce.** A commercial brand of sauce first made in the 1870s. The initials that form its name are traditionally supposed to stand for 'Houses of Parliament', a picture of which appears on the label. However, the name was adopted by the Midland Vinegar Company, its original manufacturers, from that of another firm's product, 'Garton's H.P. Sauce', and it was thus ready-made, whatever the letters themselves might have actually meant.

**Hrimfaxi** (Old Norse, 'frost mane'). The horse of night in Scandinavian legend, from whose bit fell the 'rime-drops', which nightly bedew the earth.

**Hrothgar.** In the anonymous epic poem *Beowulf* the Danish king whose hall is attacked by GRENDEL but saved by BEOWULF.

**Hubbard, Old Mother.** *See under* OLD.

**Hubert.** The patron saint of huntsmen (656–727), reputedly the son of Bertrand, Duke of Guienne. He so neglected his religious duties for the chase that one day a stag bearing a crucifix menaced him with eternal perdition unless he reformed. Upon this he entered the cloister and duly became bishop of Liège and the apostle of Ardennes and Brabant. Those who were descended of his race were supposed to possess the power of curing the bite of a mad dog.

In art he is represented as a bishop with a miniature stag resting on the book in his hand, or as a huntsman kneeling to the miraculous crucifix borne by the stag. His day is 3 November.

**Huckleberry Finn.** *See under* FINN.

**Hudson, Jeffrey.** The famous DWARF (1619–82), who was served up in a pie at an entertainment given for CHARLES I by the Duke of Buckingham, who afterwards gave him to Queen Henrietta Maria for a page. He was 18in (46cm) high until the age of 30 but afterwards reached 3ft 6in (106cm) or so. He was a captain of horse in the English Civil War, but was captured by pirates and imprisoned for supposed complicity in the POPISH PLOT. His portrait was painted by Van Dyck, and he appears in Sir Walter Scott's *Peveril of the Peak* (1823). His armour is on show in the TOWER OF LONDON.

**Hue and cry.** An early system for apprehending suspected criminals. Neighbours were bound to join in a hue and cry and to pursue a suspect to the bounds of the manor. It became the old common law process of pursuing 'with horn and with voice'. 'Hue' is from Old French *hue*, 'outcry'.

**Hug. Hug the shore, To.** To keep as close to the shore as is compatible with a ship's safety.

**Hug the wind, To.** To keep a ship close-hauled.

**Bear hug.** *See under* BEAR.

**Bunny hug.** *See under* BUNNY.

**Cornish hug.** *See under* CORNISH.

**Hugh of Lincoln.** There are two saints so designated.

(1) St Hugh (*c.*1140–1200), a Burgundian by birth, also known as St Hugh of Avalon, and founder of the first CARTHUSIAN house in England. He became bishop of Lincoln in 1186. He was noted particularly for his charitable works and kindness to the Jews. His day is 17 November.

(2) St Hugh (d.1255), a boy of only nine years of age allegedly tortured and crucified in mockery of Christ. The story goes that the affair arose from his having driven a ball through a Jew's window while at play with his friends. The boy was finally thrown into a well from which he spoke miraculously. Eighteen Jews were purported to have been hanged. However, the discovery of the boy's body in the well may simply have been used as a basis for expressing anti-Semitic envy. The story is paralleled at a number of other places in England and on the European continent and forms the subject of Chaucer's 'The Prioress' Tale' (*c.*1387). *See also* WILLIAM OF NORWICH.

**Huguenots.** The French Calvinists of the 16th and 17th centuries. The name derives from Genevan dialect *eyguenot*, the term for an opponent of annexation by Savoy, itself ultimately from Swiss German *Eidgenoss*, 'confederate'. The dialect word was influenced by 'Hugues', the surname of a 16th-century burgomaster. Philippe de Mornay (1549–1623), called Duplessis-Mornay, their great supporter, was nicknamed 'the Huguenot pope'. *See also* BARTHOLOMEW'S DAY MASSACRE; CALVINISM.

**Hulda.** The old German goddess of marriage and fecundity. The name means 'benign'.

**Hulk, The Incredible.** *See under* INCREDIBLE.

**Hulks, The.** Old dismasted men-of-war anchored in the Thames and off Portsmouth and used as prison ships, first established as a 'temporary expedient' in 1778 and remaining until 1857. An impression of the Hulks is given by Dickens in the opening chapters of *Great Expectations* (1860–1).

**Hull, Hell and Halifax.** The first line of an old beggars' and vagrants' 'prayer' first recorded in Antony Copley's *Wits fittes and fancies* (1594) and traditionally quoted as

> From Hull, Hell and Halifax
> Good Lord, deliver us.

It is said that Hull was to be avoided because the beggars had little chance of getting anything there without doing hard labour for it, and Halifax because anyone caught stealing cloth there was beheaded without further ado. It has been suggested that 'Hell and' is a corruption of Elland, another cloth-making town only 3 miles (5km) from Halifax. Hull and Halifax are just over 60 miles (96km) apart on an almost parallel latitude in what were formerly and respectively the East Riding and West Riding of Yorkshire.

**Huma** (Persian *humā*, 'phoenix'). A fabulous oriental bird that never alights but is always on the wing. It is said that every head that it overshadows will wear a crown. The bird suspended over the throne of Tippoo Sahib at Seringapatam represented this poetical fancy.

**Human. Orator of the Human Race, The.** *See* CLOOTS, ANACHARSIS.

**Universal Declaration of Human Rights, The.** *See under* UNIVERSAL.

**Humanitarians.** A name given to certain ARIANS who held that Christ was only man. The name was also used of the UNITARIANS and of the followers of Saint-Simon (1760–1825), an early exponent of socialism. Nowadays the term is usually applied to philanthropists in general.

**Humanities, The.** The study of literature, philosophy and the arts, or more narrowly, of ancient Greek and Roman language and literature, otherwise, classics. The study of classics, philosophy and ancient history at Oxford is organized by the faculty of *Literae Humaniores*, literally, 'the more humane letters', as opposed to *Literae Divinae*, 'divine letters', or divinity. The first examination is Classical Honour Moderations ('Mods') and the final school is GREATS.

**Humanity Martin.** Richard Martin (1754–1834), one of the founders of the Royal Society for the Prevention of Cruelty to Animals. He secured the passage of several laws for the suppression of cruelty to animals.

**Humber.** The legendary king of the HUNS, fabled by Geoffrey of Monmouth to have invaded Britain about 1000 BC. He was defeated in a great battle by LOCRINUS near the river that bears his name. 'Humber made towards the river in his flight and was drowned in it, on account of which it has since borne his name.' The Humber actually has a name of Celtic origin, perhaps meaning 'good river'.

**Humble. Eat humble pie, To.** *See under* EAT.

**Humbug.** Deceptive or false talk or behaviour; a fraud or sham; an impostor. The word originally meant a trick or hoax. A humbug is also a striped boiled sweet flavoured with peppermint, perhaps so called because originally a confectionary ruse. The source of the word is uncertain. It may be connected in some way with 'hum' and 'bug' (the insect).

> 'Bah,' said Scrooge. 'Humbug!'
> CHARLES DICKENS: *A Christmas Carol*, Stave I (1843)

**Hume, Adversity.** *See under* ADVERSITY.

**Humour.** According to the ancient philosophers there were four principal humours in the body: phlegm, blood, choler (or yellow bile) and melancholy (or black bile). As any one of these predominated it determined the temper of the mind and body, hence the terms phlegmatic, sanguine, choleric and melancholic. A just balance made a good humour, and a preponderance of any one of the four an ill or bad humour.

**Cardinal humours.** *See under* CARDINAL.

**Humpback, The.** A nickname of the Italian burlesque poet Girolamo Amelunghi, *Il Gobbo di Pisa* (*fl.*1547–66), and also of Cristoforo Solario (or Solari), Italian sculptor and architect (1460–1527).

**Humphrey. Dine with Duke Humphrey, To.** *See under* DINE.

**Good Duke Humphrey.** *See under* GOOD.

**Humpty Dumpty.** Short and broad, like the egg-shaped figure in the nursery rhyme.

**Hun.** An uncivilized brute, from the barbarian tribe of Huns who invaded the East Roman Empire in the 4th and 5th centuries. In the First World War it became a colloquial name for the Germans. Ironically, it was a speech by Wilhelm II that promoted the latter sense. At Bremerhaven on 27 July 1900 the German emperor addressed troops about to set sail for China. As reported in the English press, the speech contained the following passage:

> No quarter will be given, no prisoners will be taken. Let all who fall into your hands be at your mercy. Just as the Huns a thousand years ago, under the leadership of Etzel [ATTILA THE HUN] gained a reputation in virtue of which they still live in historical tradition, so may the name of Germany become known in such a manner in China that no Chinaman will ever again even dare to look askance at a German.
> *The Times* (30 July 1900)

**Hundred.** From pre-CONQUEST times a division of the English shire, corresponding to the WAPENTAKE of Danish areas. Originally the hundred probably consisted of 100 HIDES, hence the name. The hundred court or MOOT, which survived until the late 19th century, met regularly in medieval times to deal with private pleas, criminals, matters of taxation and the like. The equivalent unit in Northumberland, Cumberland, Westmorland and Durham was a WARD. Yorkshire, Lincolnshire, Nottinghamshire, Derbyshire, Leicestershire and Rutland were divided into 'wapentakes'. Yorkshire had also three larger divisions called RIDINGS. Similarly Kent was divided into five LATHES and Sussex into six RAPES, each with subordinate hundreds.

**Hundred and one.** Very many, as: 'I have a hundred and one things to do today.' A hundred is many, but a hundred and one is even more than that. The phrase is common in titles of books and articles of the practical kind, such as *A Hundred and One Basic Recipes*. The notion of multiplicity is similar to that in *The Thousand and One Nights* (*see* ARABIAN NIGHTS ENTERTAINMENTS).

**Hundred Days, The.** The days between 20 March 1815, when NAPOLEON BONAPARTE reached the TUILERIES (after his escape from Elba) and 28 June, the date of the second restoration of Louis XVIII. Napoleon left Elba on 26 February, landed near Cannes on 1 March and finally abdicated on 22 June.

The address of Louis de Chabrol de Volvic, prefect of PARIS, to Louis XVIII on his second restoration in 1815 began: *Cent jours se sont écoulés depuis le moment fatal où votre majesté quitta sa capitale* ('A hundred days have elapsed since the fatal moment when Your Majesty quit his capital'). This is the origin of the phrase, which has since been applied to the first 100 days (or three and a half months) of a reign or tenure of office, as by a prime minister. 'The First Hundred Days' was the title of the first chapter of Harold Wilson's political study *Purpose in Power* (1966).

**Hundred-eyed, The.** ARGUS in Greek and Latin fable. JUNO appointed him guardian of IO (the cow), but JUPITER caused him to be put to death, whereupon Juno transplanted his eyes into the tail of her peacock.

**Hundred-handed, The.** Three of the sons of URANUS, namely BRIAREUS, COTTUS and Gyes. After the TITANS were overcome during the war with ZEUS and hurled into TARTARUS, the *Hecatoncheires* were set to keep watch and ward over them.

CERBERUS is sometimes so called because writhing snakes sprang from his three necks instead of hair.

**Hundreds and thousands.** A name given by confectioners to tiny, brightly coloured beads of sugar, used as cake decorations.

**Hundred Years' War.** The long series of wars between England and France, beginning in the reign of Edward III in 1337 and ending in that of Henry VI in 1453. The first battle was the naval victory of Sluys (1340) and the last a defeat at Castillon (1453). The war originated in English claims to the French crown and resulted in the English losing all their possessions except CALAIS, which was held until 1558.

**Chiltern Hundreds.** *See under* CHILTERN.

**Four Hundred.** *See under* FOUR.

**Fourteen hundred.** *See under* FOURTEEN.

**Great** or **Long hundred.** *See under* GREAT.

**Hero of the hundred fights.** *See under* HERO.

**Not a hundred miles away.** A way of saying 'in this very neighbourhood'. The phrase is used when it would be unwise to refer more directly to the person or place in question.

**Old Hundred** or **Old Hundredth.** *See under* OLD.

**Hung.** *See* HANG.

**Hungary, Elizabeth of.** *See* ELIZABETH.

**Hunger. Hunger march.** A march of the unemployed to call attention to their grievances, as that of 1932, the year in which Wal Hannington, the leader of the National Union of Unemployed Workers, led a march on London. The biggest of the marches organized by the union was that against the MEANS TEST in 1936. The march of the Blanketeers (1817) was in effect the first such march.

**Hunger strike.** The refusal of prisoners to take food in order to embarrass the authorities or to secure release, a common SUFFRAGETTE tactic. *See also* CAT AND MOUSE ACT.

**Hungry Forties, The.** The 1840s in Britain, so called from the widespread distress among the poor, especially before 1843. It was the period of CHARTISM, characterized by bad harvests, dear bread and unemployment. The years 1847 and 1848 were also bad, but the 1820s were probably worse than the 1840s. The situation was helped by the railway boom and by Peel's financial measures and repeal of the CORN LAWS.

**As hungry as a hunter.** *See under* AS.

**Hunky-dory.** An American expression of approval, dating from the mid-19th century. Its origin is uncertain, but it is perhaps an elaborated form of 'hunky', derived from Dutch *honk*, 'goal', 'station', 'home', as in TAG and other games. If one is 'home', one is thus in a good or satisfactory position.

**Hunt. Hunters and runners of classic renown.**

Acastus: who took part in the hunt for the CALYDONIAN BOAR
ACTAEON: the huntsman who was transformed by DIANA into a stag because he chanced to see her bathing
ADONIS: beloved by VENUS, slain by a wild boar while hunting
ADRASTUS: who was saved at the siege of Thebes by the speed of his horse ARION, given him by HERCULES
ATALANTA: who promised to marry the man who could outstrip her in running
CAMILLA: the swiftest-footed of all the companions of DIANA
Ladas: the swiftest-footed of all the runners of Alexander the Great
MELEAGER: who took part in the great hunt for the CALYDONIAN BOAR
ORION: the great and famous hunter, changed into the constellation conspicuous in November
Pheidippides: who ran 150 miles (240km) in two days

**Hunting, shooting and fishing.** The traditional sporting trinity of the British landed gentry, centring on the capturing, wounding and killing of animals. The phrase is sometimes written 'huntin', shootin' and fishin'' to convey the clipped accent of some of the more venerable practitioners. *See also* BLOOD SPORT.

> Hunting, shooting, fishing and sporting estates are all part of the job working for our Senior Director in a small friendly office.
>
> *The Times* (advertisement) (26 August 1998)

**Hunting the gowk.** Making someone an APRIL FOOL.

**Hunt's dog.** A Shropshire saying has it that 'Like

Hunt's dog, he would neither go to church nor stay at home'. The story is that one Hunt, a labouring man, kept a mastiff, which, on being shut up while his master went to church, howled and barked so as to disturb the whole congregation. Hunt thought he would take him to church next Sunday, but the dog refused to enter. The proverb is applied to a person who will be neither led nor driven.

**Hunt the slipper.** A party game in which one person, who is 'it', stands in the middle of a circle of players who pass a slipper or some other object behind their backs. The person aims to divine who has the slipper at a given moment and wrest it from them. Inevitably, this involves some degree of physical contact, even if decorous, which can add a certain spice to the proceedings.

**As hungry as a hunter.** *See under* AS.

**Fortune hunter.** *See under* FORTUNE.

**Mighty hunter, The.** *See under* MIGHTY.

**Orator Hunt.** *See under* ORATOR.

**Run with the hare and hunt with the hounds, To.** *See under* RUN.

**Wild Huntsman, The.** *See under* WILD.

**Huntingdonians.** Members of 'the Countess of Huntingdon's Connection', a sect of Calvinistic METHODISTS founded in 1748 by Selina, widow of the 9th Earl of Huntingdon, and George Whitefield, who had become her chaplain. The churches founded by the countess, numbering some 36, were mostly affiliated with the Congregational Union. *See also* UNITED REFORMED CHURCH.

**Hurdy-gurdy.** A stringed musical instrument, the music of which is produced by the friction of a rosined wheel on the strings, which are stopped by means of keys. It had nothing to do with the barrel organ or piano organ of the streets, which is sometimes so called, probably from its being played by a handle. The name itself is imitative of the jangling music produced. *See also* SQUEEZE-BOX.

**Hurlothrumbo.** A popular burlesque, which in 1729 had an extraordinary run at the Haymarket Theatre. So great was its popularity that a club called the Hurlo-Thrumbo Society was formed. The author was Samuel Johnson (1691–1773), an eccentric Manchester dancing master, who put this motto on the title page when the burlesque was printed:

> Ye sons of fire, read my *Hurlo-Thrumbo*,
> Turn it betwixt your finger and your thumbo,
> And being quite undone, be quite struck dumbo.

**Hurricane.** A destructive storm or cyclone, from a Taino (West Indian) word based on *hura*, 'wind', that was introduced through Spanish. In the 18th century the word was used for a large private party or ROUT. *See also* DRUM.

**Names of hurricanes.** The modern custom of assigning names to hurricanes originated with the Australian meteorologist Clement Wragge (1852–1922), who gave women's names to tropical storms and men's to non-tropical. The practice was officially adopted by US meteorologists in 1953, when an alphabet of women's names was created for the purpose: Alice, Barbara, Carol, Dolly, Edna, Florence, Gilda, Hazel, Irene, Jill, Katherine, Lucy, Mabel, Norma, Orpha, Patsy, Queen, Rachel, Susie, Tina, Una, Vickie and Wallis. These names were also used in 1954, when the severity of hurricanes Carol, Edna and Hazel prompted some to suggest that men's names would have been more suitable. Women's names remained, however, until the 1970s, when feminist pressure led to the adoption of alternate men's and women's names in 1977.

**Hurry-scurry.** A confused bustle through lack of time. A RICOCHET word.

**Husband.** The word is from Old English *hūsbonda*, from Old Norse *hūsbōndi*, from *hūs*, 'house', and *bōndi*, 'one who has a household'. Hence, literally, a husband is a man in his capacity as head of the household, and so the word came to be applied to a married man, who held this position.

**Husbandry.** The occupation of the HUSBAND (in the original sense), i.e. the management of the household. The word was later restricted to farm management, and the 'husband' became the 'husbandman'.

**House husband.** *See under* HOUSE.

**Hush. Hush-hush.** A term that came into use in the First World War to describe very secret operations, designs, or inventions, from the exclamation 'hush' demanding silence. *See also* TOP SECRET.

**Hush money.** Money given as a bribe for silence or hushing a matter up.

**Hush puppy.** An American aliment of deep-fried corn meal batter, often served with fried fish in the Southern states. Pieces thrown to hungry barking dogs with the injunction 'Hush, Puppy!' were said to effect an instant silence. 'Hush Puppies' were familiar in the 1960s as the trade name of a type of soft shoe. Here the suggestion was probably of homeliness rather than a specific reference to the food.

**Hussites.** Followers of John Huss, the Bohemian religious reformer (1369–1415), sometimes called WYCLIFFITES from the fact that many of the teachings of John Huss were derived from those of John Wyclif (*c.*1330–84).

**Hussy.** The word is now a contemptuous term for a shameless or promiscuous woman. In origin, however, it is simply the word 'housewife' in its colloquial pronunciation as 'hussif'. The small sewing outfit issued to sailors is called a housewife and is still pronounced 'hussif'.

**Hustings.** A word originating from Old Norse *hústhing*, from *hús*, 'house', and *thing*, 'assembly'. Hence the assembly of a king, earl or chief, and its subsequent application to open-air meetings connected with parliamentary elections. In many towns the hustings court transacted some legal business, particularly that of the City of London, which still exists and is presided over by the lord mayor and sheriffs, although shorn of most of its former powers. The use of the word for the platform on which nominations of parliamentary candidates were made (until the passing of the Ballot Act of 1872) derives from its first application to the platform in the Guildhall on which the London court was held. A realistic impression of the old hustings at a parliamentary election is given by Dickens in *Pickwick Papers* (ch xiii (1836–7)).

**Hut. Nissen hut.** *See under* NISSEN.

**Quonset hut.** *See under* QUONSET.

**Hutin, Louis le.** *See under* LOUIS.

**Hyacinth.** According to Greek fable, the son of Amyclas, a Spartan king. The boy was beloved by APOLLO and ZEPHYR and as he preferred the sun-god, Zephyr drove Apollo's quoit at his head and killed him. The blood became a flower, and the petals are inscribed with the signature AI, meaning woe (Virgil, *Eclogues*, iii (1st century BC)).

> The hyacinth bewrays the doleful 'AI',
> And culls the tribute of Apollo's sigh.
> Still on its bloom the mournful flower retains
> The lovely blue that dyed the stripling's veins.
> CAMOËNS: *Lusiads*, ix (1572)

**Hyades** (perhaps from Greek *huein*, 'to rain'). The collective name of seven NYMPHS, the daughters of ATLAS and Pleione, who were placed among the stars in the constellation TAURUS and who threaten rain when they rise with the sun. The fable is that they wept at the death of their brother Hyas so bitterly that ZEUS out of compassion took them to heaven. *See also* PLEIADES.

**Hyde. Hyde Park.** London's largest Royal Park, extending for over 340 acres (138 ha) and merging on its western edge with Kensington Gardens. Henry VIII had it as a deer park, but Charles II opened it to the public. It was at first rather dirty and disreputable, but by the 18th century had become much as it is now, the 'lungs of London' and a favourite place of relaxation for city workers. It has become associated with free speech and mass meetings, the former because of Speakers' Corner at its northeastern corner, the latter through its size and central location. Its name probably derives from 'hide' as a term for the area of land that belonged to the manor of Ebury on which it originally arose. *See also* HIDE.

**Dr Jekyll and Mr Hyde.** *See* JEKYLL.

**Hydra** (Greek *hudōr*, 'water'). A many-headed water snake of the Lernaean marshes in Argolis. It was the offspring of TYPHOEUS and ECHIDNA and was variously reputed to have 100 heads, or 50 or 9. It was one of the 12 labours of HERCULES to kill it, and, as soon as he struck off one of its heads, two shot up in its place. Hence the phrase 'hydra-headed' is applied to a difficulty that goes on increasing as it is combated. The monster was eventually destroyed by Hercules with the assistance of his charioteer, who applied burning brands to its wounds as soon as each head was severed by his master.

**Hydrophobia.** A once popular term for rabies. The literal meaning is 'fear of water', referring not to a morbid terror of water but to the inability of the sufferer to drink. Far from fearing water, the patient is often intensely thirsty, but attempts to drink induce violent spasms in the throat, making this impossible.

**Hyena.** An animal held in veneration by the ancient Egyptians, because it is fabled that a certain stone, called the 'hyaenia', is found in its eye of the creature. Pliny asserts that when the stone is placed under the tongue it imparts the gift of prophecy. The three species are the spotted or laughing hyena (*Crocuta crocuta*), the striped hyena (*Hyaena hyaena*) and the brown hyena (*Hyaena brunnea*). The generic name comes from Greek *huaina*, the feminine of *hus*, 'pig', the allusion apparently being to the animal's bristly back, which is rather like that of a pig.

**Hygeia** (Greek *hugieia*, 'good health'). The goddess of health in Greek mythology and the daughter of AESCULAPIUS. Her symbol was a serpent drinking from a cup in her hand.

**Hyksos.** The so-called 'shepherd kings' who ruled Egypt from the end of the 18th century BC to the beginning of the 16th, the period between the Middle and New Kingdoms. They were an Asiatic nomad people, and their name derives from a mistranslation of the Egyptian original, which more correctly means 'ruler of the lands of the nomads'.

**Hylas.** A boy beloved by HERCULES, carried off by the NYMPHS while drawing water from a fountain in Mysia.

**Hymen** (Greek *humēn*, 'membrane'). Properly, a marriage song of the ancient Greeks. The word was later adopted as a personification of the god of marriage, represented as a youth carrying a torch and veil, effectively a more mature EROS or CUPID.

**Hymn. Abecedarian Hymns.** *See under* ABECEDARIAN.

**Angelic Hymn, The.** *See under* ANGEL.

**Seraphic Hymn.** *See under* SERAPHIC.

**Hypallage** (Greek, 'exchange'). A figure of speech in which an adjective or participle is transferred from the appropriate noun to one associated with it. An example is 'the condemned cell', in which it is not the cell that is condemned but the prisoner. 'A sleepless night' is also a hypallage, as is 'a happy day'.

**Hype.** A slang abbreviation of 'hypodermic' meaning a hypodermic needle or an injection from it. 'To be hyped up' is to be self-injected with a drug or to be artificially excited or stimulated. Hype as used in the sense of a deception or racket, or for misleading, inflated or highly exaggerated advertising publicity, may be derived either from the prefix hyper- meaning 'more than normal', 'excessive' or possibly from hypodermic.

**Hyperbole** (Greek, 'overcasting'). A figure of speech which contains an exaggeration for special effect. Many everyday phrases contain a hyperbole, such as 'a flood of tears', 'tons of money', AS OLD AS THE HILLS.

**Hyperboreans.** In Greek legend, a happy people dwelling beyond BOREAS, the North Wind, from which their name was supposedly derived. They were said to live for 1000 years under a cloudless sky, knowing no strife or violence. The word is applied to those living in the extreme north.

**Hyperion** (Greek *huper*, 'over', and *eimi*, 'to go'). In Greek mythology one of the TITANS, son of URANUS and GAIA, and father of HELIOS, SELENE and EOS (the sun, moon and dawn). The name is sometimes given by poets to the sun itself, which 'goes over', but not by John Keats in his 'fragment' of this name (1820), where Hyperion is the fallen SATURN, conquered by JUPITER.

**Hypermnestra.** Wife of LYNCEUS and the only one of the 50 daughters of Danaus who did not murder her husband on their bridal night. *See* DANAIDES.

**Hypnotism.** The art or science of producing trance-sleep. Dr James Braid (*c.*1795–1860) of Manchester gave it this name (1843), after first calling it 'neuro-hypnotism', based on Greek *neuron*, 'nerve', and *hupnos*, 'sleep', or 'nervous sleep', as he called it. Hypnotism is today used by some psychoanalysts as a means of helping patients to recall and come to terms with disturbing events and also as a method of enabling patients to relax. Staged hypnotism is also offered for public entertainment, sometimes controversially, by such practitioners as Paul McKenna.

**Hypostatic union.** The union of three persons in the TRINITY; also the union of the divine and human in Christ, in which the two elements, although inseparably united, each retain their distinctness. The 'hypostasis' (Greek *hupo*, 'under', and *stasis*, 'standing', so 'foundation') is the personal existence as distinguished from both nature and substance.

**Hyssop.** King DAVID says (Psalm 51:7): 'Purge me with hyssop and I shall be clean.' The reference is to the custom of ceremonially sprinkling the unclean with a bunch of hyssop (marjoram or the thorny caper) dipped in water in which had been mixed the ashes of a red heifer. This was done as they left the Court of the Gentiles to enter the Court of the Women (Numbers 19:17–18).

**Hysteria.** Generally, a wild uncontrollable emotion or excitement, often accompanied by weeping or laughing. In a narrower medical sense, hysteria is a functional disturbance of the nervous system and of psychoneurotic origin. The word itself comes from Greek *hustera*, 'womb', since it was originally associated with a disturbance of the uterus and its functions. It was thus formerly believed to be a physical disorder confined to women.

**Hysteron proteron.** A term from the Greek meaning literally 'latter (placed as) former'. It is used in rhetoric to describe a figure of speech in which the word that should come last is placed first, or the second of two consecutive propositions is stated first, e.g. *Moriamur, et in media arma ruamus* ('Let us die and rush into the midst of the fray') (Virgil, *Aeneid*, ii (1st century BC)). *See also* PUT THE CART BEFORE THE HORSE *under* CART.

In logic, 'hysteron proteron' is a fallacious argument in which the proposition to be proved is taken as a premise. *See also* PETITIO PRINCIPII.

# I

**I.** The ninth letter of the alphabet, representing the Greek *iota* and Semitic *yod*. The written and printed i and j were for long interchangeable, and it was only in the 19th century that in dictionaries they were treated as separate letters. In Samuel Johnson's *Dictionary* of 1755, 'iambic' comes between 'jamb' and 'jangle'. Hence in many series, such as the signatures of sheets in a book or hallmarks on plate, either I or J is omitted. I is number one in Roman notation.

The dot on the small i was introduced about the 11th century as a diacritic in cases where two i's came together (e.g. *filii*), to distinguish between these and u. *See also* U.

**I Ching** (Chinese *yijing*, 'book of changes'). The Chinese manual of divination, one of the Five Classics of CONFUCIANISM, evolved from SCAPULIMANCY and dates from the 12th century BC. The first English edition appeared in 1882. It takes as its base the opposing forces of YIN AND YANG and for purposes of divination permutations of 64 hexagrams are consulted, each consisting of a pair of trigrams, themselves made up of three yin and/or yang lines. The eight basic trigrams have the following names and symbolic attributes:

Earth (receptive)
Mountain (immovable)
Water (dangerous)
Wind (gentle)
Thunder (arousing)
Fire (clinging)
Lake (joyful)
Heaven (active)

**Dot the i's and cross the t's, To.** *See under* DOT.

**Iambic.** An 'iamb', or 'iambus', is a metrical foot consisting of a short syllable followed by a long one, as 'away', 'deduce', or an unaccented followed by an accented, as 'be gone!' Iambic verse is verse based on iambs, as, for instance, the ALEXANDRINE measure, which consists of six iambuses:

> I think the thoughts you think; and if I have the knack
> Of fitting thoughts to words, you peradventure lack,
> Envy me not the chance, yourselves more fortunate!
>
> ROBERT BROWNING: *Fifine at the Fair*, lxxvi (1872)

**Father of Iambic Verse, The.** *See under* FATHER.

**I am his Highness' dog at Kew; Pray tell me sir, whose dog are you?** *See under* DOG.

**Ianthe** (Greek *ion*, 'violet', and *anthos*, 'flower'). A Cretan girl who, as told in Ovid's *Metamorphoses* (ix (1st century AD)) married Iphis, who had been transformed for the purpose from a girl into a young man. The Ianthe to whom Lord Byron dedicated Canto i of his *Childe Harold's Pilgrimage* (1812–18) was 12-year-old Lady Charlotte Harley. P.B. Shelley gave the name to his eldest daughter (1813–76).

**Iapetus.** The son of URANUS and GAIA, the father of ATLAS, PROMETHEUS, Epimetheus and Menoetius, and, for the Greeks, the father of the human race, which was hence called *genus Iapeti*, 'progeny of Iapetus'.

**Iberia.** Spain, the country of the Iberi or Hiberi, the ancient people who took their name from the River Iberus or Hiberus, the modern Ebro.

**Iberia's Pilot.** Christopher Columbus (*c.*1446–1506), a Genoese by birth but a servant of Spain from 1492.

**Ibis.** A sacred bird of the ancient Egyptians, with a white body and a black head and tail, which is still found in the Nile marshes of the upper Sudan. It was the incarnation of THOTH and was often mummified after death.

**Iblis.** *See* EBLIS.

**Ibn Sina.** *See* AVICENNA.

**Ibraham.** The ABRAHAM of the KORAN.

**Ibsenism.** A concern in drama with social problems, realistically rather than romantically treated, as in the works of the Norwegian dramatist Henrik Ibsen (1828–1906), whose plays, translated by William Archer and championed by George Bernard Shaw, infused new vigour into English drama.

**Icaria.** A communistic UTOPIA described by the French reformer and utopian Étienne Cabet in his 'philosophical and social romance' *Voyage en Icarie* (1840), a novel whose rather weak love-plot is based on Jean-Jacques Rousseau's *La Nouvelle Éloïse* (1761). In 1849 Cabet led a group to Texas to found the utopian settlement of Icaria on the Red River. His followers, known as Icarians, identified themselves with the Socialist Labor Party in the USA and with the First International (*see* INTERNATIONALS).

**Icarius.** In Greek legend an Athenian who was taught the cultivation of the vine by Dionysus (BACCHUS). He was slain by some peasants who had become intoxicated with wine he had given them and who thought they had been poisoned. They buried him under a tree. His daughter Erigone, searching for her father, was directed to the spot by the howling of his dog Moera, and when she discovered the body she hanged herself for grief. Icarius, according to this legend, became the constellation BOÖTES, Erigone the constellation VIRGO, and Moera the star PROCYON, which rises in July, a little before the DOG STAR.

**Icarus.** The son of DAEDALUS. He flew with his father from Crete, but the sun melted the wax with which his wings were attached, and he fell into the sea. Those waters of the Aegean were thenceforward called the Icarian Sea.

**Ice. Ice Age.** This term is usually applied to the earlier part of the Pleistocene, the existing geological period, when a considerable portion of the northern hemisphere was overwhelmed by ice caps. Palaeolithic man was contemporary with at least the latter periods of the Ice Age, his remains having been found, together with those of the mammoth and reindeer, in glacial deposits.

The Antarctic continent was also more completely ice-covered, and glaciers existed on the heights of Hawaii, New Guinea and Japan. The Ice Age is also called the glacial epoch.

**Ice dancing.** A form of decorative figure skating resembling ballroom dancing, performed by a couple dancing on a rink.

**Ice house.** In the days before the domestic refrigerator, large private houses often had their own stores of ice kept in a specially constructed chamber, usually below ground level, which was known as an ice house.

**Iceland.** The island state received its name from the Viking Floki, who landed here in 960. A century earlier, another Viking had named the island Snjoland, 'snowland'. The name was more appropriate then than now, when the climate was colder.

**Ice saints** or **frost saints.** Those saints whose days fall in what is called the BLACKTHORN WINTER, that is, the second week in May (between 11 and 14). Some authorities give only three days, but whether 11, 12 and 13 or 12, 13 and 14 is not agreed. 11 May is the day of St Mamertus, 12 May of St PANCRAS, 13 May of St Servatius and 14 May of St BONIFACE.

**Black ice.** *See under* BLACK.

**Break the ice, To.** *See under* BREAK.

**Cut little** or **no ice, To.** *See under* CUT.

**On ice.** Waiting or pending, as if kept refrigerated for use.

**Skate on thin ice, To.** *See under* SKATE.

**Tip of the iceberg, The.** *See under* TIP.

**Iceni.** *See* BOADICEA.

**Ichabod.** A son of Phinehas, born just after the death of his father and grandfather. The name, popularly understood to mean 'without glory', from the Hebrew, is rendered in the Bible as 'the glory has departed' (1 Samuel 4:21). Hence the use of Ichabod as an exclamation.

**Ich dien** (German, 'I serve'). The motto of the PRINCE OF WALES since the time of Edward, the BLACK PRINCE (1330–76). It is said, without foundation, to have been adopted, together with the three white ostrich feathers, from John, king of Bohemia, who fell at the Battle of Crécy in 1346.

According to Welsh tradition, Edward I promised to provide Wales with a prince 'who could speak no word of English', and when his second son Edward (later Edward II) was born at Caernarvon he presented him to the assembly, saying in Welsh *Eich dyn*, 'Your man'.

**Ichneumon.** A species of mongoose venerated by the ancient Egyptians and called 'pharaoh's rat' because it fed on vermin, crocodiles' eggs and the like. The word is Greek and literally means 'tracker', from *ikhneuein*, 'to track', itself from *ikhnos*, 'footprint'.

**Ichor** (Greek *ikhōr*). In classical mythology, the colourless blood of the gods.

> He patter'd with his keys at a great rate,
> And sweated through his apostolic skin:
> Of course his perspiration was but ichor,
> Or some such other spiritual liquor.
>
> LORD BYRON: *The Vision of Judgement* (1822)

**Ichthys** (Greek *ichthus*, 'fish'). From the 2nd century the fish was used as a symbol of Christ, and the word, in its Greek form ΙΧΘΥΣ, is also an acronym formed from the initial letters of Ἰησοῦς Χριστός Θεοῦ Υἱὸς Σωτήρ ('Jesus Christ, Son of God, Saviour'). It is found on many seals, rings, urns and tombstones of the early Christian period and was believed to be a charm of mystical power.

**Icknield Way.** An ancient trackway from the Wash to the source of the River Kennet in Wiltshire, running through Cambridgeshire, Letchworth, Tring and the Berkshire Downs (crossing the Thames near Goring). Part of it in East Anglia became a Roman road. The origin of the name is unknown, although it has been popularly linked with the Iceni, the ancient British people who lived in this part of England.

**Icon** or **ikon** (Greek *eikōn*, 'image', 'likeness'). A representation in the form of painting, low-relief sculpture or mosaic of Christ, the Virgin MARY or a saint and held as an object of veneration in the EASTERN CHURCH. Except for the face and hands, the whole is often covered with an embossed metal plaque (the *riza*), representing the figure and drapery.

By the early 1990s icon had acquired two new meanings: first, and generally, as a word for a well-known person regarded as a cult figure (as if worshipped, like the ecclesiastical icon); second, and more specifically, as a term for a small symbolic figure on a computer screen that represents a particular facility and that can be activated to provide that facility (by positioning the cursor or pointer on it and double-clicking the mouse).

> As the country [Russia] prepares to bury again the remains of its last emperor, Nicholas II is becoming an icon, as familiar as he is revered.
> *The Times* (16 July 1998)

**Icon Basilike.** *See* EIKON BASILIKE.

**Iconoclasts** (Late Greek *eikonoklastes*, 'image-breaker'). A term for the reformers of the 8th century, essentially in the EASTERN CHURCH, who were opposed to the use of sacred pictures, statues, emblems and the like. The movement against the use of images was begun by Emperor Leo III, the Isaurian (r.717–741), who was strongly opposed by the monks and also by Popes Gregory II (r.715–731) and Gregory III (r.731–741). The controversy continued under successive iconoclast emperors, notably Constantine V (r.741–775), called insultingly Copronymus, 'dung-named', by his opponents because he is said to have fouled the font at his baptism. It was finally ended by the Empress Theodora in 843 in favour of the image-lovers, and iconoclasm was proscribed.

**Id** (Latin, 'it'). In Freudian psychology the id is the whole reservoir of impulsive reactions that forms the unconscious mind, as modified by the EGO.

**Id est** (Latin, 'that is'). Normally abbreviated to i.e.

**Ida, Mount.** A mountain or ridge of mountains in the vicinity of TROY and the scene of the Judgement of PARIS. *See also* APPLE OF DISCORD.

**Idaean dactyls.** *See* DACTYLS.

**Idea, Big.** *See under* BIG.

**Idéal, Beau.** *See under* BEAU.

**Ideal commonwealths.** The best known ideal or imaginary commonwealths are those sketched by Plato in *The Republic* (4th century BC) (from which later examples derive), by Cicero in *De Republica* (1st century BC), by St Augustine in *De Civitate Dei* (413–427), by Dante in *De Monarchia* (1309–12), by Sir Thomas More in UTOPIA (1516), by Tommaso Campanella in *Civitas Solis* (1602), by Francis Bacon in *The* NEW ATLANTIS (1626), and by Samuel Butler in EREWHON (1872).

Others are Samuel Johnson's *Rasselas* (1759), Bulwer-Lytton's *The Coming Race* (1871), Edward Bellamy's *Looking Backward: 2000–1887* (1888), William Morris' *News from Nowhere* (1890) and H.G. Wells' *In the Days of the Comet* (1906) and *The World Set Free* (1914). *See also* ATLANTIS; CITY OF THE SUN.

**Idealism.** As a philosophical theory, idealism takes a variety of forms, but all agree that the mind is more fundamental than matter and that mind does not originate in matter; also that the material world is less real than that of the mind or spirit. Modern idealism has its roots in the philosophy of Bishop Berkeley (1685–1753), sometimes called theistic idealism. The more important theories of idealism are:

- Transcendental idealism: taught by Immanuel Kant (1724–1804)
- Subjective idealism: taught by J.G. Fichte (1762–1814)
- Absolute idealism: taught by G.W.F. Hegel (1770–1831)
- Objective idealism: taught by F.W.J. von Schelling (1775–1854)

Idealism in the general sense is applied to ethical and aesthetic concepts that adopt 'ideal' or perfectionist standards. *See also* MATERIALISM.

**Identikit.** A method of identifying criminals from composite photographs based on an assemblage of individual features selected by witnesses from a wide variety of drawings. The method was developed by Hugh C. McDonald and first used at Los Angeles in 1959.

**Ides.** In the ancient ROMAN CALENDAR the 15th day of March, May, July and October, and the 13th day of all the other months. The day always fell eight days after the NONES.

**Beware the Ides of March.** *See under* BEWARE.

**Idle. Idle Bible, The.** *See under* BIBLE.

**Bone idle.** *See under* BONE.

**Idomeneus.** King of Crete and ally of the Greeks at TROY. After the city was burned, he made a vow to sacrifice whatever he first encountered if the gods granted him a safe return to his kingdom. He met his own son and duly sacrificed him, but a plague followed, and the king was banished from Crete as a murderer. Mozart's opera *Idomeneo, Rè di Creta, ossia Ilia ed Idamante* was first performed in 1781. *See also* IPHIGENIA.

**Idris.** Traditionally a Welsh giant, prince and astronomer. His rock-hewn seat is on the summit (*Pen y Gadair*, 'head of the chair') of CADER IDRIS ('chair of Idris') in Gwynedd. According to legend, any person passing a night upon this will be either dead in the morning, in a state of frenzy or endowed with the highest poetical inspiration.

> The well-worn myth that one who sleeps there by night must wake mad, blind, or a poet need not detain us; it is a fancy embroidered by Mrs Hemans [in 'The Rock of Cader Idris'] in the last century.
> WYNFORD VAUGHAN-THOMAS and ALUN LLEWELLYN: *The Shell Guide to Wales* (1969)

**Iduna.** In Scandinavian mythology, daughter of the dwarf Svald and wife of BRAGI. She was guardian of the golden apples, which the gods tasted whenever they wished to renew their youth. Iduna was lured away from ASGARD by LOKI, but she was eventually brought back. The gods were thus once more able to grow youthful again, and spring came back to the earth.

**If.** 'If—', the title of a well-known moralistic poem by Rudyard Kipling, originally appeared in *Rewards and Fairies* (1910). It enumerates 12 conditions, the successful fulfilment of which will bring the doer 'the Earth and everything that's in it,/And—which is more—you'll be a Man, my son!' The poem gave the ironic title of the highly praised film *If...* (1968), an allegorical treatment of public school life as a metaphor for the established system that fewer and fewer people were willing to accept.

**If it comes to that.** In that case.

**Ifs and ans.**

If ifs and ans
Were pots and pans
Where would be the tinker?

An old-fashioned jingle to describe wishful thinking: 'If wishes were horses, beggars could ride.' The 'ans' are merely the old use of 'an' for 'if'.

**If the cap fits, wear it.** If the remark applies to you, apply it to yourself. Hats and caps vary only slightly in size but everyone knows their own when putting it on.

**If the mountain will not come to Mohammed.** When MOHAMMED was asked for miraculous proofs of his teaching he ordered Mount Safa to come to him, and as it did not move, he said: 'God is merciful. Had it obeyed my words, it would have fallen on us to our destruction. I will therefore go to the mountain and thank God that He has had mercy on a stiff-necked generation.' The phrase, sometimes in the form 'If the mountain will not come to Mohammed, Mohammed must go to the mountain', is now used of someone who is unable to get their own way and who is therefore obliged to bow to the inevitable.

**If the salt have lost his savour, wherewith shall it be salted?** A rhetorical question from Matthew 5:13. If people fall from grace, how shall they be restored? The reference is to rock salt, which loses its saltiness if exposed to the hot sun.

**If the worst comes to the worst.** Even if the very worst occurs.

**If youth knew; if age could.** An English rendering of the French apophthegm, *Si jeunesse savait; si vieillesse pouvait*, quoted by the printer and publisher Henri Estienne in *Les Prémices* (1594) and attributed to Louis VI of France (1081–1137), also called Louis the Fat. Abbot Suger, his friend and counsellor, said that it was the king's frequent regret never to be able to have knowledge and strength together: 'In my youth I had knowledge, and in my old age, had strength been mine, I might have conquered many kingdoms.'

**If you want peace, prepare for war.** A translation of the Latin proverb, *Si vis pacem, para bellum*.

**Igerna.** *See* IGRAINE.

**Ignatius. Father Ignatius.** The Rev. Joseph Leycester Lyne (1837–1908), a deacon of the CHURCH OF ENGLAND, who founded a pseudo-BENEDICTINE monastery at Capel-y-ffin, near Llanthony in South Wales in 1870. He was an eloquent preacher, but his ritualistic practices brought him into conflict with his ecclesiastical superiors who would not admit him to priest's orders. In 1898 he was ordained by Joseph Villatte, a wandering bishop, who had been consecrated by a schismatic JACOBITE prelate in Ceylon.

The Rev. and Hon George Spencer (1799–1864), a clergyman of the Church of England, who joined the ROMAN CATHOLIC CHURCH and became Superior of the English province of the Congregation of PASSIONISTS, was also known as Father Ignatius.

**St Ignatius.** According to tradition St Ignatius was the child whom Christ set in the midst of the disciples for their example. He was a convert of St JOHN THE EVANGELIST, was consecrated bishop of Antioch by St PETER, and is said to have been thrown to the beasts in the amphitheatre by TRAJAN *c*.107. His day is 17 October, and he is represented in art with lions or chained and exposed to them.

**St Ignatius Loyola.** The founder (1491–1556) of the Society of Jesus is depicted in art with the sacred monogram IHS on his breast or as contemplating it, surrounded by glory in the skies, in allusion to his claim that he had a miraculous knowledge of the mystery of the TRINITY vouchsafed to him. He was the son of the Spanish ducal house of Loyola and, after being severely wounded at the siege of Pamplona (1521), left the army and dedicated himself to the service of the Virgin. *See also* JESUIT.

**Ignis fatuus** (Medieval Latin, 'foolish fire'). The will o' the wisp or friar's lanthorn, a flame-like phosphorescence (caused by the spontaneous combustion of gases from decaying vegetable matter) that flits over marshy ground and deludes people who attempt to follow it. Hence any delusive aim or object, or some scheme that is utterly impracticable. It is also known by a number of other names, such as elf-fire, jack-o'-lantern, peg-a-lantern, kit o' the canstick, spunkie, walking fire, fair maid of Ireland and John in the wad.

> When thou rannest up Gadshill in the night to catch my horse, if I did not think thou hadst been an *ignis fatuus* or a ball of wildfire, there's no purchase in money.
>
> SHAKESPEARE: *Henry IV, Pt I*, III, iii (1597)

According to Russian folklore these wandering fires are the spirits of stillborn children, which flit between heaven and the Inferno.

**Ignoramus** (Legal Latin, 'we take no notice of it'). The grand jury used to write 'ignoramus' on the back of indictments 'not found' or not to be sent to court. This was often construed as an indication of the stupidity of the jury, hence its present meaning. The widespread use of the word is due to its adoption as the name of a character, an unlettered lawyer, in a farcical play by George Ruggle produced in 1615. The play was actually titled *Ignoramus*.

**Ignorantines.** A name given to the brothers of a Roman Catholic religious fraternity founded at Rheims by the Abbé de la Salle in 1680 with the aim of giving free education to the children of the poor. They now carry out teaching work in many countries. A clause in the order's constitution prohibited the admission of priests with theological training, hence the name, which was also given to a body of Augustinian mendicants, the Brothers of Charity, or Brethren of Saint Jean-de-Dieu, founded in Portugal in 1495.

**Igraine** or **Igerna.** In ARTHURIAN ROMANCES, the wife of Gerlois (Gorlois), Duke of Tintagel, in Cornwall, and mother of ARTHUR. His father, UTHER PENDRAGON, married Igraine the day after her husband was slain.

**Ihram.** The ceremonial garb of Muslim pilgrims to MECCA, and also the ceremony of assuming it.

> We prepared to perform the ceremony of *Al-Ihram* (assuming the pilgrim garb) ... we donned the attire, which is nothing but two new cotton cloths, each six feet long by three and a half broad, white with narrow red stripes and fringes ... One of these sheets, technically termed the *Rida*, is thrown over the back, and, exposing the arm and shoulder, is knotted at the right side in the style *Wishah*. The *Izar* is wrapped round the loins from waist to knee, and knotted or tucked in at the middle, supports itself.
>
> RICHARD BURTON: *Pilgrimage to El-Medinah and Meccah*, ch xxvi (1855–6)

**IHS.** The Greek ΙΗΣ, as the first two and last letters of Ιησους ('Jesus'), with the long η taken for a capital Roman H. St Bernadine of Sienna in 1424 applied them to *Iesus Hominum Salvator* ('Jesus, Saviour of men'). Other explanations were *In hac salus* ('in this [cross] salvation') and *In hoc signo* [*vinces*] ('in this sign [ye shall conquer]'). *See also* CONSTANTINE'S CROSS.

**Ikon.** *See* ICON.

**Iliad** (Greek *Iliados*, 'of Ilium', i.e. of Troy). The epic poem of 24 books attributed to HOMER (8th century BC) recounting the siege of TROY. PARIS, son of PRIAM, king of Troy, when a guest of MENELAUS, king of Sparta, ran away with his host's wife, HELEN. Menelaus induced the Greeks to lay siege to Troy to avenge the perfidy, and the siege lasted ten years. The poem begins in the tenth year with a quarrel between AGAMEMNON, king of Mycenae and commander-in-chief of the allied Greeks, and ACHILLES, the hero who had retired from the army in ill temper. The Trojans now prevail, and Achilles sends his friend PATROCLUS to oppose them, but Patroclus is slain. Enraged, Achilles rushes into the battle and slays HECTOR, the commander of the Trojan army. The poem ends with the funeral rites of Hector.

> He [the translator] will find one English book and one only, where, as in the *Iliad* itself, perfect plainness of speech is allied with perfect nobleness; and that book is the Bible.
>
> MATTHEW ARNOLD: *On Translating Homer*, Lecture iii (1861)

**Iliad in a nutshell, The.** Pliny writes that the ILIAD was copied in so small a hand that the whole work could lie in a walnut shell. His authority is Cicero (*Apud Gellium*, ix, 421 (1st century BC)).

Huet, bishop of Avranches (d.1721), proved by experiment that a parchment 10½ × 8¼in (267 × 210mm) could contain the entire *Iliad* and that such a parchment would go into a common-sized nut. He wrote 80 verses of the *Iliad* (which contains in all 501,930 letters) on a single line of a page similar to this dictionary. This would be 19,000 verses to the page or 2000 more than the *Iliad* contains.

In the Harleian Manuscripts is an account of Peter Bales, a clerk of the Court of Chancery *c*.1590, who wrote a Bible so small that he enclosed it in a walnut shell of English growth. Maxine Lalanne described, in his *Curiosités Bibliographiques*, an edition of La Rochefoucauld's *Maximes*, published by Didot in 1829, on pages 1in (25mm) square, each page containing 26 lines, and each line 44 letters. Charles Toppan, of New York, engraved on a plate ⅛in (3mm) square 12,000 letters. The *Iliad* would occupy 42 such plates engraved on both sides. George P. Marsh claimed to have seen the entire KORAN in a parchment roll 4in (10cm) wide and ½in (12mm) in diameter.

**Ilk, Of that** (Old English *ilca*, 'same family', 'same kind'). This phrase is often misused to mean 'of the same kind', but it is correctly used only when the surname of the person spoken of is the same as the name of his estate, thus 'Bethune of that ilk' means 'Bethune of Bethune'. Used adjectivally it means 'every', 'each', as in 'Ilka lassie has her laddie.' In origin the word is related to modern 'like'.

**Ill. Ill at ease.** Uneasy; anxious; uncomfortable.

> Seated one day at the organ,
> I was weary and ill at ease,
> And my fingers wandered idly
> Over the noisy keys.
>
> ADELAIDE ANN PROCTER: 'A Lost Chord' (1858)

**Ill-starred.** Unlucky; fated to be unfortunate. In Shakespeare's *Othello* (V, ii (1604)), Othello says of Desdemona, 'O ill-starr'd wench!' The allusion is to the astrological lore that the stars influence the fortunes of mankind.

**Bird of ill omen.** *See under* BIRD.

**House of ill repute** or **ill fame.** *See under* HOUSE.

**It's an ill wind that blows nobody any good.** Someone profits by every loss; someone usually benefits by every misfortune. The allusion is nautical, since a head wind for one ship will be a tail wind for another sailing in the opposite direction.

**Illuminati.** The baptized were at one time so called, because a lighted candle was given them to hold as a symbol that they were illuminated by the HOLY GHOST.

The name has been given to, or adopted by, several sects and secret societies professing to have superior enlightenment, especially to a republican society of deists founded by the German mystic Adam Weishaupt (1748–1830) at Ingolstadt in Bavaria in 1776, to establish a religion consistent with 'sound reasons'. They were also called Perfectibilists.

Among others to whom the name has been applied are the HESYCHASTS, the Alombrados of 16th-century Spain, the French Guernists, the ROSICRUCIANS, the French and Russian Martinists and in the USA the Jeffersonians.

**Illuminator, The.** The surname given to St Gregory of Armenia (*c.*240–322), the apostle of Christianity among the Armenians.

**Illustrious, The.** The following have been so called:

Albert V, Duke of Austria and Emperor Albert II (1397–1439)
Ptolemy V, Epiphanes (Illustrious), king of Egypt (*c.*210–180 BC)
JAMSHID (Jam the Illustrious), fourth king of the mythical Pishdadian dynasty of Persia
Ch'ien-lung, fourth emperor of the Manchu dynasty of China (1711–96)

**Il Milione.** *See* MILIONE.

**Image, Spitting.** *See under* SPIT.

**Imagism.** A school of poetry founded by Ezra Pound (1885–1972), derived from the ideas of the philosopher T.E. Hulme (1883–1917). The imagist poets were in revolt against excessive romanticism and proclaimed that poetry should use the language of common speech, create new rhythms, be uninhibited in choice of subject and present a precise image.

**Imam.** An Arabic word meaning 'leader', i.e. one whose example is to be followed. The title is given to the head of the Muslim community but is more familiar through its application to those leading the prayers in the mosques, the lesser Imams. The name is also given as an honorary title and formerly to the ruler of the Yemen.

**Hidden Imam.** *See* MAHDI.

**Imbroccata** or **imbrocata** (Italian). An old fencing term for a thrust over the arm.

> The special rules, as your punto, your reverso, your staccato, your imbroccato, your passado, your montanto.
>
> BEN JONSON: *Every Man in His Humour*, IV, vii (1598)

**Immaculate. Immaculate Conception.** The dogma that the Blessed Virgin MARY was 'preserved immaculate from all stain of original sin' from 'the first moment of her conception'. It was not declared by the ROMAN CATHOLIC CHURCH to be an article of faith until 1854, when Pius IX issued the Bull *Ineffabilis Deus*. It has a long history as a belief and was debated by the SCHOOLMEN. It was denied by St THOMAS AQUINAS but upheld by Duns Scotus. *See also* DUNCE; THOMISTS.

**Immaculate Heart of Mary, The.** In the ROMAN CATHOLIC CHURCH devotion to the heart of Mary is a special form of devotion, which developed from the 17th century. In 1944 Pius XII recognized 22 August as the Feast of the Immaculate Heart of Mary.

**Feast of the Immaculate Conception, The.** *See under* FEAST.

**Immanuel.** *See* EMMANUEL.

**Immolate.** To sacrifice, from the Latin *immolare*, 'to sprinkle with meal'. The reference is to the ancient Roman custom of sprinkling wine and fragments of the sacred cake (*mola salsa*) on the head of a victim to be offered in sacrifice.

**Immortal. Immortal, The.** Yung-Cheng, 3rd Manchu emperor of China (r.1723–33), assumed this title.

**Immortal Dreamer, The.** John Bunyan (1628–88), whose allegory, *The* PILGRIM'S PROGRESS (1678, 1684), is in the form of a dream.

**Immortals, The.** The bodyguard of the kings of ancient Persia. *See also* REGIMENTAL AND DIVISIONAL NICKNAMES.

**Immortal Tinker, The.** John Bunyan, a tinker by trade, is also known by this name.

**Forty Immortals, The.** *See under* FORTY.

**Immunity, Diplomatic.** *See under* DIPLOMAT.

**Imp, Lincoln.** *See under* LINCOLN.

**Impanation.** The dogma that the body and blood of Christ are locally present in the consecrated bread and wine of the EUCHARIST, just as God was present in the body and soul of Christ. The word means 'putting into the bread' and is found as early as the 11th century. *See also* TRANSUBSTANTIATION.

**Imperator.** *See* EMPEROR.

**Imperial.** From the Latin *imperialis* (from *imperium*), meaning pertaining to an emperor or empire. The following are some of the word's special and particular applications:

Before metrication, a standard size of printing and writing paper measuring 22 × 30in (559 × 762mm)
An 18th-century Russian gold coin, worth 10 roubles
A trunk for luggage adapted for the roof of a coach or diligence, also the carriage top itself; hence modern French *impériale* for the top deck of a bus, tram or railcar
A tuft of hair on the chin, the rest of the face being clean-shaven, a fashion so called from that set by the Emperor NAPOLEON III (1808–73)

**Imperial Conference.** The name given to the conferences held in London between the Prime Ministers of the various dominions of the British Empire between 1907 and 1946 inclusive. These conferences had their origin in the first Colonial Conference, which met in 1887 on the occasion of Queen Victoria's JUBILEE. Since 1948 the COMMONWEALTH Prime Ministers' Conference has replaced the Imperial Conference.

**Imperial Machiavelli, The.** Tiberius, the Roman emperor (42 BC–AD 37). His political axiom was: 'He who knows not how to dissemble knows not how to reign.' It was also the axiom of Louis XI of France (r.1461–83).

**Prince Imperial.** *See under* PRINCE.

**Imposition. Imposition of hands.** *See* LAYING ON OF HANDS.

**Impositions.** Duties levied on imports under royal prerogative were a point of dispute between James I and the Commons. CHARLES I continued to levy them until the fall of Strafford in 1642, when he consented to an Act of Parliament rendering them illegal. Extra written work, lines, detention and so on given to schoolchildren as punishments are also still sometimes called impositions, a word abbreviated by Victorian schoolboys to 'impot'.

**Impossibilities.** Examples of the many familiar expressions denoting the impossible are:

Catching wind in cabbage nets
Fetching water in a sieve
Flaying eels by the tail
Gathering grapes from thistles
Making a silk purse out of a sow's ear
Making cheese from chalk
Squaring the circle
Turning base metal into gold

**Impressionism.** The first of the modern art movements, taking its name from the painting of the harbour at Le Havre, *Impression: Sunrise* (1872), by Claude Monet (1840–1926). Édouard Manet (1832–83), Auguste Renoir (1841–1919), Camille Pissarro (1830–1903) and Edgar Degas (1834–1917) were the leading impressionist painters who upheld the new approach. As the name implies, they rejected the established conventions and sought to capture the impression of colour of transitory and volatile nature rather than its form. It broke down the distinction between a sketch and a finished painting. *See also* CUBISM; DADAISM; FAUVISM; FUTURISM; ORPHISM; POINTILLISM; POST-IMPRESSIONISM; SALON DES REFUSÉS; SURREALISM; SYNCHROMISM; VORTICISM.

**Imprimatur** (Latin, 'let it be printed'). An official licence to print a book. Such a licence or royal imprimatur was required under the Licensing Act of 1662 to secure ecclesiastical conformity. The act was initially for two years, was not renewed after 1695 and was in abeyance from 1679 to 1685.

In the ROMAN CATHOLIC CHURCH a book by a priest on theological and moral subjects has to receive an imprimatur and NIHIL OBSTAT. The former is granted by the bishop or his delegate. *See also* INDEX.

**Impropriation** (Latin *impropriare*, 'to take as one's own'). The profits of an ecclesiastical BENEFICE that are in the hands of a layman, who is called the impropriator. When the benefice is in the hands of a spiritual corporation it is called appropriation. At the REFORMATION many appropriated monastic benefices passed into the hands of lay rectors, who usually paid only a small part of the TITHE to incumbents, hence the need for Queen ANNE'S BOUNTY.

**In** (English). For phrases beginning with 'in' that are not included here, look under the next main word in the expression.

**In and Out, The.** The nickname of the Naval and Military Club, London, since the days of HANSOM cabs. To avoid confusion among the various service clubs of that time, the cabbies bestowed nicknames on them, and the 'In' and 'Out' directions on the posts of the respective gateways suggested the name 'In and Out'. In 1998 the Club moved from its longstanding base at 94 Piccadilly, the former home of Lord Palmerston, to new premises in St James's Square. *See also* CLUB.

**In at the death.** Present when the fox is caught and killed. Hence, present at the climax or final stage of an exciting event.

**In cahoots.** *See under* CAHOOTS.

**In for it, To be.** To be due for something unpleasant; to be due for a telling off or dressing down; to expect punishment.

**In it.** In trouble, as: 'One more word from you, and you're in it.'

**In one ear and out the other.** Forgotten as soon as heard.

**In on something, To be.** To be familiar or acquainted with it, as: 'I was in on his plan.'

**Ins and outs, The.** All the details of a thing.

**In with someone, To be.** To be friendly with them.

**In your face.** Right in front of someone; aggressively provocative. The phrase is also spelt 'in yer face'.

**Have it in for someone, To.** To wish them harm or evil.

**Have it in one, To.** To have the ability or power to do something.

**In** (Latin). **In banco** or **in banc.** A Late Latin legal phrase, meaning 'on the bench'. It is applied to sittings of a superior court of COMMON LAW in its own bench or court, and not on circuit or at NISI PRIUS. The work of the courts 'in banco' was transferred to Divisional Courts of the HIGH COURT of Justice by the Judicature Act of 1873.

**In camera** ('in the chamber'). In judicial proceedings, the hearing of a case either in the judge's private room or in a court from which the public has been excluded.

**In esse** ('in being'). In actual existence, as opposed to *in posse*, in potentiality. Thus a living child is 'in esse', but before birth is only 'in posse'.

**In extenso** ('in extension'). At full length; word for word; without abridgement.

**In extremis** ('in the furthest reaches'). In dire straits; at the point of death.

**In flagrante delicto** ('with the crime still blazing'). RED-HANDED; in the act.

**In gremio legis** ('in the bosom of the law'). Under the protection of the law.

**In loco parentis** ('in place of a parent'). Having temporary charge of children or young people in some capacity, as in a school, and therefore assuming parental functions.

**In medias res** ('into the midst of things'). In the middle of events or a story. The phrase is from Horace's *Ars Poetica* (1st century BC).

**In memoriam** ('in memory of'). Commemorating; as a memorial to. The phrase was popularized by the title of Alfred, Lord Tennyson's poem *In Memoriam A.H.H.* (1850) written in memory of his close friend Arthur Henry Hallam, who had died in 1833 aged only 22.

**In perpetuum** ('in perpetuity'). For ever.

**In personam** ('against the person'). Directed against a particular person (of a judicial act). Compare with IN REM.

**In petto** (Italian, 'in the breast'). In secrecy; in reserve. The pope creates cardinals *in petto*, i.e. in his own mind, and keeps the appointment to himself till he thinks proper to announce it. On the declaration of their names, their seniority dates from their appointment *in petto*. It is claimed that the English historian John Lingard (1771–1851) was made cardinal *in petto* by Leo XII (r.1823–9), who died before announcing the fact.

**In posse.** *See* IN ESSE.

**In propria persona** ('in one's own person'). Personally; not by a deputy or agents.

**In puris naturalibus** ('in pure naturals'). Naked.

> I thought it was a commonplace
> That a man or woman in a state of grace
> In puris naturalibus, don't you see,
> Had normal pudenda, like you and me.
>
> D.H. LAWRENCE: *Nettles* (1930)

**In re** ('in the matter'). Concerning or on the subject of, as, *In re* Jones *v* Robinson, referring to the case. This phrase gave the *re* sometimes used by letter writers when introducing a subject or simply referring to something, as: 'Any news yet re the sale of your house?'

**In rem** ('against the matter'). Against the property referred to (rather than a particular person). Compare with IN PERSONAM.

**In situ** ('in its place'). In its original or natural place; where it is; on the spot.

> I at first mistook it for a rock *in situ*, and took my compass to observe the direction of its cleavage.
>
> CHARLES DARWIN: *The Voyage of the 'Beagle'*, ch ix (1839)

**In statu pupillari** ('in an orphan state'). Under guardianship; as a pupil.

**In statu quo** or **In statu quo ante** ('in the state in which (before)'). In the same state as before. Hence STATUS QUO as a term for the existing state of affairs.

**In toto** ('in all'). Entirely; altogether.

**In vino veritas** ('in wine is truth'). When people have drunk more than usual they may mention things they would at other times keep to themselves.

**Inaugurate, To.** To install into an office with appropriate ceremony; to open formally. The word is from Latin *inaugurare*, which meant first to take OMENS by AUGURY, and then to consecrate or install after taking such omens.

**Inca** (Quechua *inka*, 'king'). A king or royal prince of the dynasty governing Peru before the Spanish conquest or a member of the tribe in Peru at that time. The capital of their extensive empire was at Cuzco, and the dynasty was mythologically descended from Manco Capac ('powerful band') who was high priest of the sun. His brothers were Cachi ('salt'), Uchu ('pepper') and Auca ('pleasure'). It was prophesied that Manco's golden rod would sink into the ground on reaching their destined home. This happened at Cuzco. The last of the Inca dynasty, Atahuallpa ('creator of chance in war or play') was murdered by the Spaniards in 1533. The Incas' own name for their empire was *Tawantinsuyu*, 'empire of the four regions'.

**Incarnation.** The Christian doctrine that the Son of God took human flesh and that Jesus Christ is truly God and truly man. From Late Latin *incarnare* ('to make flesh').

**Inch. Give him an inch and he'll taken an ell.** Give someone a little licence, and they will take great liberties.

**Within an inch.** *See under* WITHIN.

**Inchcape Rock.** A dangerous rocky reef (also called the Bell Rock) about 12 miles (19km) from Arbroath in the North Sea (Inch or Innis means 'island'). The abbot of Arbroath or 'Aberbrothok' fixed a bell to a timber float as a warning to mariners. Robert Southey's ballad 'The Inchcape Rock' (1796–8) tells how the pirate Ralph the Rover cut the bell adrift and was himself wrecked on the very rock as a consequence.

A similar tale is told of St Govan's bell at St Govan's Head in Pembrokeshire. In the chapel was a silver bell, which was stolen one summer evening by pirates, but no sooner had their boat put to sea than it was wrecked.

**Incitatus** (Latin, 'spurred-on'). The horse of CALIGULA, which the emperor made priest and consul. It had an ivory manger and drank wine from a golden pail.

**Incognito** (Italian, from Latin *incognitus*, 'unknown'). Under an assumed name or title. When a royal person, public figure or celebrity travels and does not wish to be treated ceremoniously or desires to avoid the public gaze they may adopt another name and travel incognito.

**Incorruptible, The.** Maximilien de Robespierre (1758–94), the French revolutionary leader. *See also* REIGN OF TERROR; SEA-GREEN INCORRUPTIBLE.

**Increase, Natural.** *See under* NATURAL.

**Incredible Hulk, The.** The huge green humanoid into which the humble scientist, Dr Bruce Banner, metamorphoses whenever he is possessed by anger. The creature was the brainchild of the American writer Stan Lee and first featured in Marvel Comics in 1962. It (he) later appeared in television versions, with Lou Ferrigno playing the part of the muscleman.

**Incubus** (Latin *incubare*, 'to lie on'). A nightmare, anything that weighs heavily on the mind. In medieval times the word denoted an evil demon who was supposed to have sexual intercourse with women during their sleep. *See also* SUCCUBUS.

> Women can now go safely up and down
> By every bush or under every tree;
> There is no other incubus but he,
> So there is really no one else to hurt you
> And he will do no more than take your virtue.
>
> CHAUCER: *Canterbury Tales*, 'The Wife of Bath's Tale' (*c*.1387) (modern translation by Nevill Coghill, 1951)

**Incunabula** (Latin, 'swaddling clothes', hence 'beginnings', from *cunae*, 'cradle'). The cradle, birthplace, origins or early stages of anything. The word is particularly and arbitrarily applied to the early days of printing and book production up to 1500, although this date does not mark any significant change in these crafts. The mid-16th century would be a more satisfactory termination of the early period of printing and book production.

**Incunabula Bible, The.** *See under* BIBLE.

**Indenture.** A document or agreement devised to prevent forgery, especially one between an apprentice and his master. It was so called because it was duplicated on a single sheet and separated or indented by a zigzag cut so that each party held identical halves. Their authenticity could be proved by matching the jagged edges. *See also* TALLY.

**Independence. Independence Day.** 4 July, which is kept as a national holiday in the USA because the Declaration of Independence, asserting the sovereign independence of the former British colonies, was adopted on 4 July 1776.

**Declaration of Independence, The.** *See under* DECLARE.

**Independent. Independent Labour Party.** A small socialist party formed by Keir Hardie (1856–1915) in 1893 to establish independent labour candidates in Parliament. It played a prominent part in the early days of the LABOUR PARTY and continued to advocate more radical policies. In 1923 it had 46 members in the House of Commons. When James Maxton (1885–1946), then its leader, died, it petered out as a parliamentary party.

**Independents.** A collective name for the various PROTESTANT separatist sects, especially prominent in 17th-century England, who rejected both Presbyterianism and EPISCOPACY, holding that each congregation should be autonomous or independent. The BAPTISTS and CONGREGATIONALISTS became the two main groups, but there were others more eccentric such as the FIFTH-MONARCHY MEN. They were notably strong in the Cromwellian army.

**Index, The.** The popular name for the 'Index Librorum Prohibitorum' ('list of prohibited books') of the ROMAN CATHOLIC CHURCH, which members were forbidden to read except in special circumstances. The first Index was made by the INQUISITION in 1557, although St Gelasius (pope 492–496) issued a list of prohibited writings in 494, and there had been earlier condemnations and prohibitions. In 1571 Pius V set up a Congregation of the Index to supervise the list, and in 1917 its duties were transferred to the Holy Office. In addition to the Index there was the 'Codex Expurgatorius' of writings from which offensive doctrinal or moral passages were removed. The Index and Codex were abolished in 1966.

All books likely to be contrary to faith and morals, including translations of the Bible not authorized by the church, were formerly placed on the Index. Among authors wholly or partly prohibited were: Joseph Addison, Francis Bacon, Geoffrey Chaucer, Benedetto Croce, Gabriele D'Annunzio, René Descartes, Edward Gibbon, Oliver Goldsmith, Victor Hugo, John Locke, John Milton, Michel Eyquem de Montaigne, Ernest Renan, Girolamo Savonarola, VOLTAIRE and, for a long time, Copernicus, Dante and Galen. *See also* IMPRIMATUR.

**Dow–Jones index, The.** *See under* DOW.

**Thumb index.** *See under* THUMB.

**India.** The country is so named from its main river, the Indus, itself from Sanskrit *sindhu*, 'river'. Related words are Hindu (the religion and its adherents) and Hindi (the language and its speakers). Hindustan is the *stan* or 'country' of the Hindus. *See also* HINDUISM.

**India paper.** A creamy coloured printing paper, originally made in China and Japan from vegetable fibre, and used for taking off the finest proofs of engraved plates. The India paper (or Oxford India paper) used for printing Bibles and high class 'thin paper' and 'pocket' editions is a very thin, tough and opaque imitation. The name 'India' given to these papers arises from their original importation through the 'India trade', which brought in the products of the Far East.

**Star of India, The.** *See under* STAR.

**Indian. Indian agent.** In North America an official who represents the American or Canadian authorities to a group of Indians, as Native Americans were formerly known. *See also* INDIAN TRIBES.

**Indian Bible, The.** *See under* BIBLE.

**Indian club.** A bottle-shaped club, one of a pair used by gymnasts or jugglers. The reference is perhaps to similarly shaped clubs used by American Indians in exercise.

**Indian file.** Singly; one after another. The allusion is to the North American Indian practice of progressing in single file, each member of the column stepping in the footprints of the person in front, and the last of the line obliterating them. Thus neither the track nor the number of people could be traced.

**Indian ink.** Despite its name, Indian ink is actually Chinese ink. It is a black pigment that was originally prepared from a lampblack produced by burning sesame oil together with varnish and pork fat. A paste was made from the lampblack, and a binding agent such as glue was added, as well as musk or camphor to scent it and some gold leaf to give a metallic sheen. The paste was beaten on wooden anvils with steel hammers and then placed in wooden moulds and ornamented with gold or coloured characters. It came to be called Indian ink because it was brought to Europe by East India merchants. *See also* MISNOMERS.

**Indian Mutiny.** The name given to the revolt in parts of British India (1857–9), which was primarily a mutiny of sepoys in the East India Company's Bengal army rather than a national revolt against British rule.

**Indian rope-trick.** The trick or illusion of climbing an apparently unsupported rope. Its traditional enactment is as follows. A boy climbs up a rope and disappears. A man climbs up after him, brandishes a dagger, and pieces of the boy's body fall to the ground. The man descends and places the pieces in a basket, which he then covers. A form slowly materialises in the basket. It is the boy. The ruse is first recorded in the 14th century.

**Indian summer.** A term of American origin now generally applied to a period of fine sunny weather in late autumn. In America it is applied to such a period of mild dry weather usually accompanied by a haze. The name arose from the fact that such weather was more pronounced in the lands formerly occupied by Native Americans than in the eastern regions inhabited by the white population. *See also* St MARTIN'S SUMMER.

**Indian tribes.** The Indian peoples of North and South America, so misnamed by Columbus, are the aboriginal inhabitants of the two continents. Their name derives from Columbus' belief that he had discovered a new route to India. They consequently came to be known as AMERICAN INDIANS (or Amerindians or Amerinds) or, more recently and accurately, Native Americans.

In the United States, the major Indian tribes and nations have reservations and trust lands in the following states:

Alabama: Poarch Creek
Alaska: Aleut, Eskimo, Athapascan, Haida, Tlingit, Tsimpshian
Arizona: Navajo, Apache, Papago, Hopi, Yavapai, Pima
California: Hoopa, Paiute, Yurok, Karok, Mission Bands
Colorado: Ute
Connecticut: Mashantucket Pequot
Florida: Seminole, Miccosukee
Idaho: Shoshone, Bannock, Nez Perce
Iowa: Sac and Fox
Kansas: Potawatomi, Kickapoo, Iowa
Louisiana: Chitimacha, Coushatta, Tunica-Biloxi
Maine: Passamaquoddy, Penobscot, Maliseet
Michigan: Chippewa, Potawatomi, Ottawa
Minnesota: Chippewa, Sioux
Mississippi: Choctaw
Montana: Blackfeet, Crow, Sioux, Assiniboine, Cheyenne
Nebraska: Omaha, Winnebago, Santee Sioux
Nevada: Paiute, Shoshone, Washoe
New Mexico: Zuni, Apache, Navajo

New York: Seneca, Mohawk, Onondaga, Oneida
North Carolina: Cherokee
North Dakota: Sioux, Chippewa, Mandan, Arikara, Hidatsa
Oklahoma: Cherokee, Creek, Choctaw, Chickasaw, Osage, Cheyenne, Arapahoe, Kiowa, Comanche
Oregon: Warm Springs, Wasco, Paiute, Umatilla, Siletz
Rhode Island: Narragansett
South Dakota: Sioux
Texas: Alabama-Coushatta, Tiwa, Kickapoo
Utah: Ute, Goshute, Southern Paiute
Washington: Yakima, Lummi, Quinault
Wisconsin: Chippewa, Oneida, Winnebago
Wyoming: Shoshone, Arapahoe.

In Canada the largest groups of Native Americans are the SIX NATIONS (Iroquois) and Inuit (Eskimo). In Central America there are the Maya and Aztecs, and in South America the Tupi, Guarani and Aruak, with the Araucanians, Patagonians and Puelche in the southern steppes, and the Fuegians, Chibcha and Quechua (including the Incas) in the upland regions. *See also* FIVE NATIONS.

Only in 1924 did a law in Congress grant all American Indians in the United States the status of citizenship.

Down the rivers, o'er the prairies,
Came the warriors of the nations,
Came the Delawares and Mohawks,
Came the Choctaws and Camanches,
Came the Shoshonies and Blackfeet,
Came the Pawnees and Omahas,
Came the Mandans and Dacotahs,
Came the Hurons and Ojibways,
All the warriors drawn together
By the signal of the Peace-Pipe.

H.W. LONGFELLOW, *The Song of Hiawatha*, i (1855)

*See also* PLAINS INDIANS; RED INDIANS.

**Honest Injun.** *See under* HONEST.

**Indirect taxation.** Tax, such as value added tax, which is levied on consumer commodities, as opposed to direct taxation on land, incomes and capital.

**Indoeuropean.** A term invented in 1814 by the Egyptologist Thomas Young (1773–1829) and later adopted by scientists, anthropologists and philologists to describe the racial and linguistic origins of the main Indian and European peoples. The Indoeuropean languages have been classified in groups such as Indo-Iranian, Greek, Italic, CELTIC, Germanic, Balto-Slavic and others.

**Indolence, Castle of.** *See under* CASTLE.

**Indra** (Sanskrit, 'best'). An ancient Hindu god of the sky, originally the greatest, who was the hurler of thunderbolts and giver of rain, a god of warriors and of nature. He is represented as having four arms, and his steed is an elephant. He is the son of Heaven and Earth and lives on the fabulous Mount MERU, the centre of the earth, north of the Himalayas.

**Induction** (Latin *inducere*, 'to lead in'). When a clergyman is inducted to a living he is led to the church door and his hand is laid on the key by the archdeacon or other person authorized to induct. The new incumbent then tolls the bell.

**Indulgence.** In the ROMAN CATHOLIC CHURCH the remission before God of the earthly punishment due for sins of which the guilt has been forgiven in the sacrament of penance. Such indulgences are granted out of the 'treasury of the church' (the store of merit of Christ). They are either plenary or partial. In the later Middle Ages the sale of indulgences by PARDONERS became a grave abuse, and it was the hawking of indulgences by the monk Johann Tetzel and the DOMINICANS in Germany that roused Martin Luther and precipitated the REFORMATION.

**Declarations of Indulgence.** *See under* DECLARE.

**Industry. Industrial action.** A term covering a variety of practices resorted to by dissatisfied employees collectively with the intent to disrupt industry or to embarrass the general public or government of the day. Such action includes bans on overtime, go-slow tactics, working to rule, strikes and picketing.

**Industrial Revolution.** A term popularized by Arnold Toynbee whose *Lectures on The Industrial Revolution of the 18th century in England* were published in 1884, although it had been used half a century earlier by French observers. It generally denotes the whole range of technological and economic changes that transformed Britain from an essentially rural society into an urban, industrialized state. The limiting dates usually assigned to this period of change vary somewhat, with years between 1750 and 1780 given for the beginning and between 1830 and 1850 for the end. The Industrial Revolution in Britain occurred earlier than elsewhere.

**Captain of industry.** *See under* CAPTAIN.

**Cottage industry.** *See under* COTTAGE.

**Indy 500, The.** The popular name of the Indianapolis 500 motor race, held annually with the exception of war years from 1911 at the Indianapolis Motor Speedway, near Indianapolis, Indiana. It was originally held on Memorial Day, 30 May, but later took place on the preceding Saturday or Sunday. It is 500 miles (805km) in length, which means that drivers of the 33 participating cars need to circuit the near-oblong 2½-mile (4km) track 200 times, starting three abreast from the initial line-up. The Indy 500 draws more spectators than any other American sporting event, and an attendance of 300,000 is not unusual.

**Inexactitude, A terminological.** *See under* TERMINOLOGICAL.

**Inexpressibles.** A 19th-century euphemism for trousers, also called ineffables, inexplicables and unmentionables. This absurdity is attributed to Peter PINDAR who used it in a biting lampoon on the dandy Prince Regent, later GEORGE IV.

I've heard, that breeches, petticoats, and smock,
Give to thy modest mind a grievous shock,
And that thy brain (so lucky its device)
Christ'neth them inexpressibles, so nice.
PETER PINDAR: 'A Rowland for an Oliver' (1790)

**Infallibility.** In the ROMAN CATHOLIC CHURCH the pope, when speaking EX CATHEDRA on a question of faith and morals, is held to be free from error. This dogma was adopted by the VATICAN COUNCIL of 1869–70 (many members dissenting or abstaining from voting) and was publicly announced by Pius IX (r.1846–78) at St Peter's.

**Infamy of Crete, The.** The MINOTAUR.

At the point of the disparted ridge lay stretch'd
The infamy of Crete, detested brood
Of the feigned heifer.
DANTE: *Inferno*, 'Hell', xii (*c*.1309–*c*.1320)
(translation by Henry Cary, 1805–14)

**Infant** (Latin *infans*, 'speechless', from *in-*, 'not', and *fari*, 'to speak'). Literally, one who is unable to speak, and hence a young child. The word was used as a synonym of CHILDE, as 'The Infant hearkned wisely to her tale' (Edmund Spenser, *The Faerie Queene*, VI, viii (1596)). Hence Infanta, any princess of the royal blood in Spain and Portugal except an heiress of the crown, and Infante, any son of the sovereigns of Spain and Portugal except the crown prince who, in Spain, is called the Prince of the Asturias. In 1999 there were two Infantas as daughters of King Juan Carlos I: Elena Maria Isabel Dominga (b.1963) and Cristina Federica Victoria Antonia (b.1965). The Prince of the Asturias was Felipe Juan Pablo Alfonso y Todos los Santos (b.1968).

**Infantry.** Foot soldiers. This is the same word as INFANT, from Italian *infanteria*, from *infante*, 'boy'. Hence a young and inexperienced male who acted as a page to a KNIGHT, and so in turn a foot soldier.

**Light infantry.** *See under* LIGHT.

**Inferiority complex.** A psychiatric term for a complex resulting from a sense of inferiority dating from childhood. Attempts to compensate for the sense of worthlessness may take an aggressive or violent form, or manifest themselves in an over-zealous involvement in activities.

**Infernal column.** The name given by the Spanish to the corps of La Tour d'Auvergne (1743–1800), the FIRST GRENADIER OF THE REPUBLIC, from its terrible charges with the bayonet.

The same name, *Colonnes infernales*, was given, because of their brutality, to the 12 bodies of republican troops which 'pacified' La Vendée in 1793 under General Turreau.

**Infinitive, To split an.** *See under* SPLIT.

**Influence, Backstairs.** *See under* BACK.

**Information. Worm out information, To.** *See under* WORM.

**Infra dig.** Not befitting one's position or public character. The expression is short for Latin *infra dignitatem*, 'beneath (one's) dignity'.

**Infralapsarian.** The same as SUBLAPSARIAN.

**Ingoldsby, Thomas.** The pseudonym of the Rev. Richard Harris Barham (1788–1845) as author of *The Ingoldsby Legends*, which appeared in Bentley's *Miscellany* and the *New Monthly Magazine*, and, in 1840, in book form.

**Ink.** The word is from Greek *enkaustos*, 'burned in'.

**Indian ink.** *See under* INDIAN.

**Ink-blot test.** *See* RORSCHACH TEST.

**Inkhorn term.** A 16th-century expression for a pedantic turn of phrase, which showed signs of having been laboured over. The inkhorn was the receptacle of horn, wood or metal, which pedants and pedagogues carried with them.

**Inkslinger.** A former contemptuous term for a writer, especially a newspaper journalist.

**Inn.** The word is Old English and originally meant a private dwelling-house or lodging. Hence Clifford's Inn, once the mansion of Baron Clifford, LINCOLN'S INN, the abode of the Earls of Lincoln, and GRAY'S INN. The word then came to be applied to a public house giving lodging and entertainment, or a tavern.

**Inns of Court.** The four voluntary societies in London that have the exclusive right of calling to the English BAR. They are the INNER TEMPLE, the MIDDLE TEMPLE, LINCOLN'S INN and GRAY'S INN. Each is governed by a board of BENCHERS.

**Barnard's Inn.** *See under* BARNARD.

**Gray's Inn.** *See under* GRAY.

**Lincoln's Inn.** *See under* LINCOLN.

**Tabard Inn, The.** *See under* TABARD.

**Innamorato, Orlando.** *See under* ORLANDO.

**Inner. Inner barristers.** *See* UTTER BARRISTERS.

**Inner city.** The parts of a city, not necessarily at its centre, that have become decayed or abandoned as a result of poverty, unemployment, poor housing conditions and racial tension. The term is American in origin.

**Inner light.** Inward or spiritual light, knowledge divinely imparted. As used by QUAKERS, the expression refers to the light of Christ in the soul.

**Inner man** or **woman, The.** The soul or mind of a person. Also, jocularly, the stomach.

**Inner Temple**. One of the four INNS OF COURT built on the site of the TEMPLE, the former headquarters of the Knights Templar (*see* TEMPLARS) in London. Like the MIDDLE TEMPLE, it is named for its proximity to the CITY and in relation to the Outer Temple. The latter was never more than a piece of land that belonged to the Templars and that later became the site of Essex House, the mansion of the Earl of Essex, favourite of Elizabeth I.

**Innings.** In CRICKET the time that the eleven or an individual has in, batting at the wicket. Hence the use of the word for the period of a person's activity, career or even life, as: 'He had a pretty good innings.'

**Inniskillings.** In 1689 one cavalry and one infantry regiment were raised in Enniskillen, County Fermanagh, to defend the town in the cause of William III. The former became the 6th (Inniskilling) Dragoons in 1751, and they later amalgamated with the 5th Dragoon Guards in 1922 to form the 5th/6th Dragoons and were renamed the 5th Inniskilling Dragoon Guards in 1927. The title 'Royal' was granted on the occasion of George V's JUBILEE (1935).

In 1751 the infantry regiment became the 27th (Inniskilling) Regiment of Foot. In 1881 they were renamed the Royal Inniskilling Fusiliers, with the 108th Foot as their 2nd battalion, becoming in 1968 the 1st Battalion Royal Irish Rangers.

**Innocent, An.** An idiot or born fool was formerly so called.

**As innocent as a lamb.** *See under* AS.

**Feast of the Holy Innocents, The.** *See* HOLY INNOCENTS.

**Holy Innocents.** *See under* HOLY.

**Massacre of the Innocents, The.** *See under* MASSACRE.

**Ring of Innocent, The.** *See under* RING.

**Ino.** *See* LEUCOTHEA.

**Inquisition, The** (Legal Latin *inquisitio*, 'enquiry'). The name given to the ecclesiastical jurisdiction in the ROMAN CATHOLIC CHURCH dealing with the prosecution of heresy. In the earlier days of the church EXCOMMUNICATION was the normal punishment, but in the later 12th and early 13th centuries, disturbed by the growth of the ALBIGENSES, the church began to favour seeking the aid of the state. The Inquisition as such was instituted by Pope Gregory IX in 1231, influenced by the activities of the Emperor Frederick II against HERETICS. Inquisitors were appointed, chiefly from the DOMINICAN and FRANCISCAN Orders, to uphold the authority of the church in these matters. They held court in the local monastery of their order. Proceedings were in secret, and torture, as a means of breaking the will of the accused, was authorized by Pope Innocent IV in 1252. Obstinate heretics were handed over to the secular authorities for punishment, which usually meant death at the stake (AUTO-DA-FÉ). In 1542 the Congregation of the Inquisition was set up as the final court of appeal in trials of heresy. Its title was changed to the Congregation of the Holy Office in 1908, and it was then renamed the Sacred Congregation for the Doctrine of the Faith in 1965. It is concerned with the maintenance of ecclesiastical discipline.

The Spanish Inquisition was established in 1479, closely bound up with the state and at first directed against 'converts' from Judaism and ISLAM. Its infamous first Grand Inquisitor was TORQUEMADA (1420–98), and during his term of office some 2000 heretics were burned. The Spanish Inquisition was abolished by Joseph Bonaparte in 1808, reintroduced in 1814 and terminated in 1834.

**INRI.** The initial letters of the inscription affixed to the cross of Christ by order of Pontius Pilate: *Iesus Nazarenus, Rex Iudaeorum* ('Jesus of Nazareth, King of the Jews' (John 19:19)). It was written in Greek, Latin and Hebrew (Luke 23:38). Alchemists interpreted the letters as *Igne Natura Renovatur Integra* ('All nature is renewed by fire'), and *Henri*, the nickname for a crucifix in French undertakers' jargon, is simply a perverted acronymic pronunciation of INRI.

**Insane root, The.** A plant, probably henbane or HEMLOCK, supposed to deprive of their senses anyone who took it. Banquo says of the witches:

> Were such things here as we do speak about?
> Or have we eaten of the insane root
> That takes the reason prisoner?
> SHAKESPEARE: *Macbeth*, I, iii (1605)

Similar properties were attributed to the BELLADONNA, MANDRAKE, poppy and so on. *See also* MOLY.

**Inscription** (on coins). *See* LEGEND.

**Installation.** The correct term for the induction of a CANON or prebendary to his stall in a cathedral or collegiate church. Members of certain orders of CHIVALRY are also installed.

**Insult** (Latin *insultare*, 'to jump on'). Originally, to leap on the prostrate body of a foe, hence, to treat with contempt. The priests of BAAL, to show their indignation against their gods, 'leaped upon the altar which was made' (1 Kings 18:26).

**Add insult to injury, To.** *See under* ADD.

**Pocket an insult, To.** *See under* POCKET.

**Stomach an insult, To.** *See under* STOMACH.

**Insurrection, Whiskey.** *See under* WHISKY.

**Intelligence quotient** or **IQ.** The ratio, expressed as a percentage, of a person's mental age to his or her actual age, the former being the level of test performance that is median for that age tested by the Binet type scale or some similar system. Thus if a ten-year-old has a mental age of nine years, the IQ is 90. 100 indicates average intelligence. The term was introduced by William Stern and popularized by L.M. Terman (1877–1956).

**Intent, Letter of.** *See under* LETTER.

**Inter alia** (Latin). Among other things or matters.

**Intercalary** (Latin *inter*, 'between', and *calare*, 'to proclaim'). An intercalary day is a day inserted between two others, as 29 February in a LEAP YEAR. It is so called because, among the Romans, this was a subject of solemn proclamation. *See also* CALENDS.

**Interdict.** In the ROMAN CATHOLIC CHURCH an ecclesiastical punishment placed on individuals, particular places or a district, restrictions being placed upon participation in, or performance of, certain SACRAMENTS, solemn services and public worship. Notable instances are:

1081: Poland was put under an interdict by Pope Gregory VII because Boleslaw II, the Bold, slew Stanislaus, bishop of Cracow, on the altar steps of his church

1180: Scotland was similarly treated by Pope Alexander III for the expulsion of the bishop of St Andrews

1200: France was interdicted by Pope Innocent III because Philip Augustus had his marriage with Ingelburge annulled

1208: England was put under an interdict lasting until 1213 by Innocent III for King John's refusal to admit Stephen Langton as archbishop of Canterbury

*See also* EXCOMMUNICATION.

**Interest** (Latin, 'it concerns'). The interest on money is the sum that a borrower agrees to pay a lender for its use. Simple interest is interest on the principal, or money lent, only, while compound interest is interest on the principal plus the interest as it accrues.

**Declare one's interest, To.** *See under* DECLARE.

**In an interesting condition.** Pregnant. The now dated phrase came into use in the 18th century.

**Interlard** (Old French *entrelarder*). Originally to 'lard' meat, i.e. to put strips of fat between layers of lean meat. Hence, metaphorically, to mix irrelevant matter with the solid part of a discourse.

> They interlard their native drinks with choice
> Of strongest brandy.
>
> JOHN PHILIPS: *Cyder*, ii (1708)

**Interlingua.** An international language consisting of the living Latin roots in all European languages. It dates from about 1908 and was the product of the former VOLAPÜK academy. *See also* ESPERANTO.

**International Date Line.** *See* DATE LINE.

**Internationale** (French *chanson internationale*, 'international song'). The official international socialist anthem, and the Soviet national anthem until 1944. The words were written in 1871 by Eugène Pottier, a Parisian transport worker, and set to music by Pierre Degeyter, a woodworker of Lille (1848–1932). It is not the same as the RED FLAG.

> C'est la lutte finale
> Groupons-nous, et, demain
> L'Internationale
> Sera le genre humain.
> (This is the final conflict,
> Let us form up, and, tomorrow
> The International
> Will be the human race.)

**Internationals.** The name usually applied to the international federations of Socialist and Communist parties, the first of which was set up under the auspices of Karl Marx in 1864 as the International Working Men's Association, lasting until 1876. The INTERNATIONALE was adopted as its anthem. The Second or Social-Democratic International was formed in 1889, and the Third or Communist International was set up by LENIN in 1919 and lasted until 1943. The abortive Trotskyite Fourth International dates from 1938, and in 1953 began a series of splits, each of the factions claiming that it was the 'real' one. There was also a '2½ International', as a nickname for the Vienna International of 1921–3. *See also* COMMUNISM.

**Interregnum, The.** In British history the term usually implies the period of the COMMONWEALTH and Protectorate from the execution of CHARLES I (30 January 1649) until the RESTORATION (18 May 1660). The period between the flight of James II (22 December 1688) and the accession of William and Mary (23 February 1689; 20 April 1689 in Scotland) was also an interregnum.

**Into. Into the bargain.** Besides what was bargained for.

**Into the blue.** Into the unknown; into the 'wide blue yonder'.

**Intolerable Acts, The.** The American name for a group of British measures directed against Massachusetts in 1774, after the BOSTON TEA PARTY. They consisted of the Boston Port Act, closing the port of Boston, the Massachusetts Government Act, increasing British control, the Transportation Act, permitting British officials accused of capital offences to be tried outside Massachusetts, and the Quartering Act, which stationed royal troops in the barracks of Boston.

**Introduction, Letter of.** *See under* LETTER.

**Invalides, Les** (*Hôtel des Invalides*). The great institution founded by Louis XIV at Paris in 1670 for infirm soldiers. It contains the Musée de l'Armée, a fine museum of military objects, and notably the parish church of Saint-Louis, containing the tomb of NAPOLEON BONAPARTE, whose body was brought here from St HELENA in 1840. Close by are the tombs of his son, NAPOLEON II (L'Aiglon), duc de Reichstadt (1811–32), who died at Schönbrunn, and whose ashes were returned to France in 1940 by Hitler, and Marshal Foch (1851–1929). Others buried here are Joseph Bonaparte (1768–1844), king of Naples and Spain; Jérôme Bonaparte (1784–1860), king of Westphalia; Marshal Turenne (1611–75); General Bertrand (1773–1844); Marshal Duroc (1772–1813); Marshal Grouchy (1766–1847); and General Kléber (1753–1800).

**Invention of the Cross, The.** Until its abolition by Pope John XXIII in 1960, this was a church festival held on 3 May in commemoration of the finding (Latin *invenire*, 'to find') of the 'true cross of Christ' by St HELENA. At her direction, after a long and difficult search in the neighbourhood of the HOLY SEPULCHRE (which had been over-built with heathen temples), the remains of the three buried crosses were found. These were applied to a sick woman, and the one which effected her cure was declared the 'true cross'. The Empress Helena had this enclosed in a silver shrine (after having taken a large piece to Rome) and placed in a church built on the spot for the purpose. *See also* IRON CROWN OF LOMBARDY.

**Inventors.** Certain inventors of instruments of death and punishment were to pay the price of their own ingenuity. The following are instances, although some probably belong to the realm of fable rather than of fact.

BASTILLE: Hugues Aubriot, provost of Paris, who built the Bastille (*c.*1369), was the first person confined therein; the charge against him was heresy.

Brazen bull: Perillus of Athens made a brazen bull for PHALARIS, Tyrant of Agrigentum, intended for the execution of criminals, who were shut up in the bull, fires being lighted under the belly; Phalaris admired the invention and tested it on Perillus, who was the first person baked to death in the fearful monster.

Eddystone lighthouse: Henry Winstanley erected the first Eddystone lighthouse, a wooden polygon, 100ft (30m) high, on a stone base; the architect perished in his own edifice when it was washed away by a storm in 1703.

Gallows and gibbet: the Book of Esther (7:9) tells how Haman devised a gallows 50 cubits high on which to hang MORDECAI, by way of commencing the extirpation of the Jews, but the favourite of AHASUERUS was himself hanged on it. Similarly, Enguerrand de Marigny, Minister of Finance to Philip the Fair (1284–1314), was hanged on the gibbet that he had caused to be erected at Montfaucon for the execution of certain felons. Four of his successors in office suffered the same fate.

GUILLOTINE: Dr J.B.V. Guillotin of Lyons was guillotined, but he was not the man after whom the guillotine was named. That honour falls to Joseph-Ignace Guillotin (1738–1814).

Iron cage: the bishop of Verdun, who invented the iron cage, too small to allow the person confined in it to stand upright or lie at full length, was the first to be shut up in one. Cardinal La Balue, who recommended them to Louis XI, was himself confined in one for ten years.

OSTRACISM: Cleisthenes of Athens introduced the practice of ostracism and was the first to be banished thereby.

Sanctuary: Eutropius (*fl.*4th century) induced the Emperor Arcadius to abolish the RIGHT OF SANCTUARY, but a few days afterwards he committed some offence and fled for safety to the nearest church. St JOHN CHRYSOSTOM told him that he had fallen into his own net, and he was put to death.

Turret-ship: Cowper Coles, inventor of the turret-ship, perished in the *Captain* off Finisterre on 7 September 1870.

WITCH-HUNTING: a story was long current that Matthew Hopkins, the witch-finder, was tried by his own tests and put to death as a WIZARD in 1647.

*See also* DEATH FROM UNUSUAL CAUSES.

**Investiture controversy.** The name given to disputes between the church and the emperor and other princes over the right to invest abbots and bishops with the ring and staff and to receive homage. The political and religious issues were strongly contested in the 11th and 12th centuries, especially between Pope Gregory VII (HILDEBRAND) and Emperor Henry IV (see CANOSSA). A compromise was reached in 1122 at the Concordat of Worms, when the emperor gave up his claim to invest with the ring and the staff but continued to grant the temporalities. In England the controversy between Anselm, archbishop of Canterbury, and Henry I over lay investiture was settled in a similar fashion in 1107.

**Investment, Gilt-edged.** *See under* GILT.

**Invincible. Invincible Doctor, The.** WILLIAM OF OCCAM or Ockham (a village in Surrey), FRANCISCAN friar and scholastic philosopher (1285–1349). He was also called Doctor Singularis and Princeps Nominalium, for he was the reviver of NOMINALISM. *See also* OCCAM'S RAZOR.

**Invincibles, The.** An Irish secret society of FENIANS founded in Dublin in 1881 with the object of doing away with the English 'tyranny' and killing the 'tyrants'. They were responsible for the PHOENIX PARK MURDERS.

**Invisibility.** According to fable, invisibility was obtainable in many ways. For example:

ALBERICH's cap, the TARNKAPPE: SIEGFRIED obtained this, which rendered him invisible; *see also* NIBELUNGENLIED

The HELMET OF PERSEUS: this, loaned by PLUTO and made by the CYCLOPS for the god of the underworld, rendered its wearer invisible

JACK THE GIANT-KILLER's cloak: this made him invisible; he also had a cap of knowledge

The ring of Otnit, king of Lombardy: according to the HELDENBUCH this rendered its wearer invisible

REYNARD'S WONDERFUL RING: according to REYNARD THE FOX, this ring had three colours, one of which (green) made the wearer invisible

*See also* DEAD MAN'S HAND; GYGES; HELIOTROPE.

**Invisible. Invisible Man, The.** There have been various fictional invisible men, but the best known is that of H.G. Wells' novel so titled (1897). He is the scientist Dr Griffin, who discovers the secret of making himself invisible and is driven mad from the consequences. There have been a number of filmed versions, some more light-hearted than others. For Wells' original, however, the science of invisibility was no laughing matter.

**Church Invisible.** *See under* CHURCH.

**Invulnerability.** There are many fabulous instances of this having been acquired:

ACHILLES: according to Greek legend he was rendered invulnerable by being dipped in the River STYX

JASON: MEDEA, who had fallen in love with him, rendered him proof against wounds and fire by anointing him with the Promethean unguent

SIEGFRIED: he was rendered invulnerable by anointing his body with dragon's blood

**Io.** The priestess of JUNO of whom ZEUS became enamoured. When Juno discovered his liaison, Jupiter transformed Io into a heifer and she wandered over the earth, finally settling in Egypt, when she was restored to human form.

**Ionic. Ionic order.** One of the Greek ORDERS OF ARCHITECTURE, so called from Ionia, where it originated. Its columns are fluted, and its capitals are decorated with volutes (scroll-like ornaments), which are its characteristic feature. *See also* CORINTHIAN ORDER; DORIC ORDER; TUSCAN ORDER.

**Ionic school.** A school of philosophy that arose in the 6th century BC in Ionia, notable as the nursery of Greek philosophy. It included Thales, Anaximander, Anaximenes, Heraclitus, Anaxagoras and Archelaus. They sought a primal substance from which the infinite diversity of phenomena has evolved. Thales said it was water, Anaximenes thought it was air, and Heraclitus claimed that it was fire. Anaxagoras developed a theory of fragments or particles from which all things emerged by process of aggregation and segregation.

**Iota.** *See* I; JOT.

**IOU.** 'I owe you.' The acknowledgement of a debt given by the borrower to the lender.

**Iphigenia.** In classical legend the daughter of AGAMEMNON and CLYTEMNESTRA. One account says that her father, having offended ARTEMIS by killing her favourite stag, vowed to sacrifice the most beautiful thing the year brought forth. This was his infant daughter. He deferred the sacrifice until the Greek fleet that was proceeding to TROY reached AULIS and Iphigenia had grown to womanhood. Then CALCHAS told him that the fleet would be held in harbour by a contrary wind until he had fulfilled his vow. Accordingly the king prepared to sacrifice his daughter, but Artemis at the last moment snatched her from the altar and carried her to heaven, substituting a hind in her place. Euripides wrote a tragedy *Iphigenia in Tauris* (5th century BC) and Christoph Gluck has an opera *Iphigénie en Tauride* (1779); the former's *Iphigenia in Aulis* was incomplete at his death. *See also* IDOMENEUS.

**Ipse dixit** (Latin, 'he himself said so'). A mere assertion, wholly unsupported. 'It is his *ipse dixit*' implies that there is no guarantee that what he says is so. The Latin phrase translates Greek *autos epha* used of PYTHAGORAS by his followers.

**Ipso facto** (Latin, 'by the very fact'). Irrespective of all external circumstances of right or wrong; absolutely. It sometimes means the act itself carries the consequences. Thus by burning the PAPAL BULL in 1520, Luther *ipso facto* denied the pope's supremacy.

**IRA.** The Irish Republican Army, a guerrilla force largely reorganized by Michael Collins (1890–1922) from the former Irish Volunteers, which confronted the Royal Irish Constabulary and the BLACK AND TANS from 1919 to 1921. After the Civil War that began at Easter 1922, extremists kept it in being as a secret organization, and although it was proscribed in 1936, the IRA continued to make occasional raids into Northern Ireland, its aim now being to establish a united Irish republic. After a period of quiescence, violence steadily increased from the mid-1950s. From 1969 to 1994, when it declared a cease-fire, its senseless acts of terrorism in Northern Ireland, England and elsewhere made a settlement of the Northern Ireland problem increasingly difficult. It subsequently resumed its activities on a sporadic basis, although an agreement reached between North and South on Good Friday 1998 appeared to bring a permanent peace settlement nearer. *See also* SINN FÉIN; SIX COUNTIES; ULSTER.

**IRB.** The Irish Republican Brotherhood, another name for the Irish branch of the FENIANS, which continued in use after the latter had ceased to operate.

**Ireland.** The name effectively means 'Eire land', with the first word being the country's Irish name. It may itself mean 'western land', from a word related to Gaelic *iar*, 'west', although some authorities derive it from Gaelic *i*, 'island', and *iarunn*, 'iron'. The Roman name of Ireland, Hibernia, evolved as a form of Iverna, itself representing Old Celtic *Iveriu*. This gave ERIN as the poetic name for the island.

**Church of Ireland.** *See under* CHURCH.

**Fair maid of Ireland, The.** The IGNIS FATUUS.

**Ireland forgeries, The.** *See under* FAKES.

**Irish rats.** It was once a common belief that rats in pastures could be destroyed by anathematizing them in rhyming verse or by metrical charms. Sir Philip Sidney says (*Defence of Poesie* (1595)): 'I will not wish unto you ... to be rimed to death, as is said to be done in Ireland'; and Shakespeare makes Rosalind say (*As You Like It*, III, ii (1599)): 'I was never so be-rhymed since Pythagoras' time, that I was an Irish rat.'

**Irish stew.** A stew of mutton, onions and potatoes, called 'Irish' from the predominance of potatoes, once regarded as the staple diet of the Irish.

**Toads unknown in Ireland.** *See under* TOAD.

**United Irishmen.** *See under* UNITED.

**Young Ireland.** *See under* YOUNG.

**Irene** (Greek *eirēnē*, 'peace'). The Greek goddess of peace and wealth. She is represented as a young woman carrying PLUTUS in her arms. Among her attributes are the OLIVE branch and a cornucopia (AMALTHEA'S HORN).

**Iris.** (1) The goddess of the rainbow or the rainbow itself. In classical mythology she was the messenger of the gods, and of JUNO in particular, and the RAINBOW is the bridge or road let down from heaven for her accommodation.

(2) Poetically applied to the rainbow, the name, in English, is also given to the coloured diaphragm surrounding the pupil of the eye.

(3) The Iridaceae is a large family of brightly coloured rhizomatous or cormous flowers, including the iris, crocus and gladiolus.

**Iron. Iron Age.** An archaeological term denoting the cultural phase conditioned by the introduction of the use of iron for edged tools, implements, weapons and so on. In the Near East the preceding Bronze Age ended about 1200 BC, and by 1000 BC the Iron Age was established. North of the Alps the first Iron Age, known as the HALLSTATT period, began about 750 BC, and in England *c*.500 BC. In Scotland the Bronze Age lasted until *c*.250 BC. *See also* TÈNE.

The era between the death of CHARLEMAGNE and the close of the Carolingian dynasty (814–987) is sometimes so called from its ceaseless wars. It is also called the leaden age for its worthlessness. *See also* AGE; DARK AGES.

**Iron-arm.** François de la Noue (1531–91), Bras de fer, the HUGUENOT soldier, was so called. FIERABRAS, another form of the name, was that of one of the PALADINS.

**Iron cage.** *See* INVENTORS.

**Iron Chancellor, The.** The name given to Prince Otto von Bismarck (1815–98), the creator of the German Empire. A century later, Gordon Brown (b.1951), CHANCELLOR OF THE EXCHEQUER in the Labour government elected in 1997, was also so dubbed for his proverbial frugality with the nation's resources.

**Ironclads.** The name originally applied to wooden warships when their hulls were first clad with iron armour plating. The idea originated with NAPOLEON III, and the French floating batteries used in the Crimean War (1854–6) were plated with iron. The first British warship of this type was the *Warrior* (1860), which was covered in plating to the waterline. The name persisted when warships were built of iron faced with steel.

**Iron Cross, The.** A Prussian military decoration in the form of an iron Maltese cross (✠) edged with silver, instituted by Frederick William III in 1813 during the struggle against NAPOLEON BONAPARTE. It was remodelled by William I in 1870 with three grades, in civil and military divisions, and some 3 million Iron Crosses were awarded in the First World War.

**Iron Crown of Lombardy, The.** The crown of the ancient Longobardic kings, said to have been bestowed by Pope GREGORY THE GREAT. CHARLEMAGNE was crowned (774) with it as king of Italy, as was Charles V in 1530. In 1805 NAPOLEON BONAPARTE put it on his head with his own hands. In 1866 it was restored to the king of Italy by Emperor Franz Joseph of Austria and replaced in the cathedral at Monza. It is so called from the inner fillet of iron, which is said to have been beaten out of a nail from the 'true cross', which was given to Constantine by his mother St HELENA. The outer circlet is of beaten gold and is set with precious stones. *See also* INVENTION OF THE CROSS.

**Iron Curtain, The.** The phrase denoting the barrier of secrecy created by the former USSR and its satellites along the Stettin-Trieste line, the Communist countries east of this line having cut themselves off from western Europe after the Second World War. The phrase was popularized by Winston Churchill in his Fulton Speech (5 March 1946), but it was used previously in Germany by Goebbels in *Das Reich* (25 February 1945) and by Churchill himself in a cable to President Truman (4 June 1945). It has earlier antecedents: Ethel Snowden used it in 1920 with reference to BOLSHEVIK Russia; Lord D'Abernon used it in 1925 with regard to the proposed Locarno Treaties; and in 1914 Elisabeth, the queen of the Belgians, spoke of a 'bloody iron curtain', between her and the Germans. The phrase occurs in the Earl of Munster's journal as far back as 1819.

> From Stettin, in the Baltic, to Trieste, in the Adriatic, an iron curtain has descended across the Continent.
>
> SIR WINSTON CHURCHILL: Fulton Speech

**Iron Duke, The.** The Duke of Wellington (1769–1852) was so called from his iron will. *See also* GREAT DUKE.

**Iron entered his soul, The.** This expression, used of one experiencing the pangs of anguish and embitterment, is found in the Prayer Book version of Psalm 105:18. It is a mistranslation of the Hebrew that appeared in the VULGATE. It was corrected in the Authorized Version of the Bible, which says 'whose feet they hurt with fetters: he was laid in iron', i.e. he was put in irons or fetters. Coverdale, following the Vulgate, says: 'They hurte his feet in the stocks, the yron pearsed his herte.'

**Iron fist** or **hand in the velvet glove, The.** Ruthlessness; severity or tyranny concealed by a polite and courteous manner. The expression is attributed to NAPOLEON BONAPARTE.

**Iron Gates, The.** The narrowing of the Danube below Orsova in southwest Romania is so called. It is about 2 miles (3km) long, with great rapids and an island in midstream. More popularly the term refers to the rocky bed of the river in this stretch, which was dangerous to navigation until a ship canal was opened in 1898.

**Iron Guard, The.** The title adopted by the Romanian FASCIST party of the 1930s.

**Iron hand.** Severe or harsh control, as: 'He imposed discipline with an iron hand.'

**Iron-hand.** Götz von Berlichingen (1480–1562), a German knight who lost his right hand at the siege of Landshut (1505) and contrived one of steel to replace it. He was brave and chivalrous but something of a brigand. His autobiography was used by Goethe for his drama *Götz von Berlichingen* (1773).

**Iron Lady, The.** The name bestowed upon Margaret Thatcher, when leader of the Conservative Opposition in the HOUSE OF COMMONS, by the Soviet Defence Ministry newspaper *Red Star* (24 January 1976). After she had warned the Commons of the increasing Russian threat to the West, the *Red Star* accused the 'Iron Lady' of trying to revive the Cold War, referring to her 'viciously anti-Soviet speech', and to 'the peace-loving policy of the Soviet Union'. Her speech (made on 19 January) had included the words: 'The Russians are bent on world dominance ... the Russians put guns before butter.'

**Iron lung.** An airtight metal cylinder that encloses a person's body and that provides artificial respiration in cases where the patient's respiratory muscles are paralysed, as in poliomyelitis.

**Iron maiden.** A medieval instrument of torture used for traitors, heretics, parricides and others. It was a box, large enough to admit a man, with folding doors, the inside of these being studded with sharp iron spikes. When the doors were closed on him the spikes were forced into the body of the victim. The name refers to the shape of the box, which bore some resemblance to a woman.

A noted example was the iron maiden of Nuremberg. This had a conical body constructed of sheet iron, topped with a female head wearing a bonnet and ruff. The front opened with two doors, through which the victim was backed into the Maiden's embrace. Protruding from the inside of one door were 13 square-sectioned spikes, and from the other eight more. These were so positioned that, as the doors were gradually closed, they pierced the victim's vital organs. Another two spikes were set at face level to enter the eyes. A full description appeared in the English journal *Archaeologia* (1838).

**Iron rations.** Emergency rations, especially as provided in the army, and traditionally consisting of tinned food, particularly BULLY BEEF and biscuit.

**Ironside.** Edmund II (*c*.998–1016), king of England from April to November 1016, was so called from his iron armour.

**Ironsides.** Cromwell's soldiers were so called after 1644. Their resolution at Marston Moor in July of that year caused Prince Rupert to nickname Cromwell 'Old Ironsides', and the name was thereafter applied to his men.

'Old Ironsides' was also the nickname of the US frigate *Constitution*, said to have been so called by American sailors when the British shot failed to penetrate her oaken sides during her victory over the *Guerrière* in 1812. She was saved from the breakers by Oliver Wendell Holmes' poem 'Old Ironsides' (1828).

**Irons in the fire.** Activities, projects and the like with which one is involved, as: 'I have several irons in the fire.' The allusion is to the smoothing iron, which was heated in the fire for pressing clothes. When one grew cool as it was being used, another was ready in the fire.

**In irons.** Handcuffed or chained.

**Man in the Iron Mask, The.** *See under* MAN.

**Pig iron.** *See under* PIG.

**Pump iron, To.** *See under* PUMP.

**Rule with a rod of iron, To.** *See under* RULE.

**Strike while the iron is hot, To.** *See under* STRIKE.

**Irony** (Greek *eirōneia*, 'simulated ignorance'). The use of words or expressions that have a meaning different from the usual one; otherwise a subtle form of sarcasm understood correctly by the initiated.

**Irony of fate, The.** The circumstance that brings about the opposite of what might have been expected. Thus by an irony of fate JOSEPH became the saviour of his brothers who had cast him into the pit.

**Socratic irony.** *See under* SOCRATES.

**Iroquois.** The French form of the Indian name of the FIVE NATIONS. *See also* INDIAN TRIBES.

**Irredentism.** The name given to national minority movements seeking to break away from alien rule and to join up with neighbours of their own nationality and language. It derives from *Italia irredenta* ('unredeemed Italy'), the name given by the Italians, between 1861 and 1920, to those Italian-speaking areas still under foreign rule. When the kingdom of Italy was formed in 1861, Venetia, Rome, Trieste, the Trentino, Nice and elsewhere were not included.

**Irrefragable Doctor, The.** Alexander of Hales (*c*.1186–1245), an English FRANCISCAN, author of *Summa Universae Theologiae*. Irrefragable means 'unable to be disproved'.

**Irresistible.** Before starting on his expedition against Persia, Alexander the Great went to consult the Delphic ORACLE on a day when no responses were made. Nothing daunted, he sought out PYTHIA, and when she refused to attend took her to the temple by force. 'Son,' said the priestess, 'thou art irresistible.' 'Enough,' cried Alexander, 'I accept your words as an answer.'

**Irus.** (1) The gigantic beggar who carried out the commissions of the suitors of PENELOPE. When he sought to hinder the returning ULYSSES, he was felled to the ground by a single blow. 'Poorer than Irus' was a classical proverb.

(2) The father of Eurytion and Eurydamas. When PELEUS accidentally killed Eurytion, Irus refused to accept the cattle offered by Peleus as blood money. Peleus left the animals at liberty, and the gods turned the wolf that attacked them to stone, the statue marking the boundary between Locris and Phocis.

**Irvingites.** Members of the CATHOLIC AND APOSTOLIC CHURCH. Edward Irving (1792–1834), a friend of Thomas and Jane Carlyle, claimed to revive the college of the APOSTLES, and established a complex hierarchy, with such symbolical titles as 'Angel', 'Prophet' and so on. In their early days they claimed to have manifested the GIFT OF TONGUES.

**Isaac.** The only son of ABRAHAM and SARAH, and the father of ESAU and JACOB. Although Sarah was past the age of childbearing, God promised Abraham that they would have a son, and Isaac was born. Later, to test Abraham's obedience, God ordered him to sacrifice the boy. He was prepared to do so, but God spared Isaac at the last moment, telling Abraham to sacrifice a ram in a nearby thicket instead. Abraham's acquiescence to God's command served the early Christians as a symbol of faith and obedience.

**Isabel.** *See* SHE-WOLF OF FRANCE.

**Isabel** or **Isabelle.** The colour so called is the yellow of soiled calico. A yellow dun horse is, in France, *un cheval isabelle*. According to Isaac D'Israeli (*Curiosities of Literature* (1791)), Isabel of Austria, daughter of Philip II, at the siege of Ostend vowed not to change her linen until the place was taken. The siege lasted three years (1601–04). Another story, equally unlikely, attaches to Isabella of Castile, who, it is said, made a vow to the Virgin not to change her linen until Granada fell into her hands. There is no reason for accepting these fanciful derivations, all the more as the word appears in a list of Queen Elizabeth's clothes dated July 1600, a year before the siege even began: 'one rounde gowne of Isabella-colour satten'.

**Isaiah.** One of the greatest of the Old Testament prophets, noted above all else for foretelling the coming of the MESSIAH. Much of the text of Handel's *Messiah* (1742) comes from his book.

> He shall feed his flock like a shepherd: he shall gather the lambs with his arm, and carry them in his bosom, and shall gently lead those that are with young.
>
> Isaiah 40:11

**I say.** The gentlemanly expostulation is found in writing much more often than it is heard in speech. It serves little more than a general attempt of the speaker to draw attention to himself, even when he has nothing to say. Indeed, it is complete in itself, and virtually meaningless. In fiction it is thus usually taken to symbolize the words and thoughts of the vacuous twit. In the reduplicated form, 'I say, I say, I say', it is the catchphrase of the music hall comedian, used as an introduction to a piece of repartee, however unoriginal. It has also been used in conjunction with other stock phrases in certain situations, as the schoolboys' 'I say, you fellows', or the young man's reaction to a pretty girl, 'I say, what a smasher!' These are all hopelessly dated, but their connotations are still well understood.

**Iscariot, Judas.** *See under* JUDAS.

**Isenbras.** *See* ISUMBRAS.

**Isengrym** or **Isegrin.** In REYNARD THE FOX the wolf who is forced to give his shoes to REYNARD after the fox tricks Isengrym's wife into dipping her tail into icy water to catch fish.

**Iseult.** *See* YSOLDE.

**Ish kabbible.** An exclamation of indifference, nonchalance or the like, the equivalent of 'I should worry'. It is presumably of Yiddish origin, although the precise sense is obscure. Possibly none was ever intended, although the 'ish' is certainly 'I'. It was apparently introduced, and perhaps even invented, by the American Jewish comedienne Fanny Brice (1891–1951) in the 1930s.

**Ishmael.** The son of ABRAHAM and his concubine HAGAR, handmaid of his wife SARAH. Hagar was driven into the wilderness by Sarah's harshness before her son was born. The Arabs regard Ishmael as their ancestor. His name has been used in general for an outcast. When the narrator of Herman Melville's novel *Moby-Dick* (1851) opens his story with the words, 'Call me Ishmael', he is recalling the biblical description of Ishmael: 'He will be a wild man; his hand will be against every man, and every man's hand against him' (Genesis 16:12).

**Ishtar.** The Babylonian goddess of love and war (Greek *Astarte*), corresponding to the Phoenician ASHTAROTH, except that, while the latter was identified with the moon, Ishtar was more frequently identified with the planet VENUS.

**Isis.** The principal goddess of ancient Egypt, sister and wife of OSIRIS and mother of HORUS, she typified the faithful wife and devoted mother. The cow was sacred to her, and she is represented as a queen, her head being surmounted by horns and the solar disc or by the double crown. Her chief shrines were at Abydos and Busiris. Later a splendid temple was built at Philae. Proclus mentions a statue of her which bore the inscription: 'I am that which is, has been, and shall be. My veil no one has lifted. The fruit I bore was the Sun.' Hence 'to lift the veil of Isis' is to pierce the heart of a great mystery.

She was worshipped as a nature goddess throughout the Roman world and was identified with JUNO, IO, APHRODITE, ASTARTE and others, in due course becoming an embodiment of the universal goddess. Milton, in *Paradise Lost* (i (1667)), places her among the fallen angels. Her name ultimately derives from Egyptian *set*, 'seat', 'throne', this being her symbol, as well as that of Osiris. *See also* CROWNS OF EGYPT.

**Isis.** *See* CAM AND ISIS.

**Isis, River.** *See* THAMES.

**Islam.** The Muslim religion; the whole body of Muslims. The word is Arabic and means 'resignation', 'submission', i.e. to the will of God. Islam involves five duties:

(1) Recital of the creed ('There is but one God and MOHAMMED is his Prophet')
(2) Recital of daily prayers
(3) Fasting in the month of RAMADAN
(4) Giving the appointed legal alms
(5) Making a pilgrimage to MECCA at least once in a lifetime; *see also* HAJJ

**Islamic festivals.** There are two major Islamic festivals: Id al-Fitr ('feast of breaking fast') celebrating the end of RAMADAN, the month of fasting, and observed on the day after the sighting of the new moon of the following month, and Id al-Adha ('feast of sacrifice'), celebrating the submission of the Prophet ABRAHAM to ALLAH, and occurring at the end of the HAJJ, or pilgrimage to MECCA. Because of the vast crowds, the prayers on these festivals are offered either in the larger mosques or on specially consecrated ground.

**Island** or **Isle. Island of Saints, The.** Ireland was so called in the Middle Ages.

**Island of the Moon, The.** Madagascar is so named by its indigenous inhabitants.

**Island of the Seven Cities, The.** A land of Spanish fable, where seven bishops, who left Spain during the dominion of the MOORS, founded seven cities. The legend says that many have visited the island, but no one has ever left it.

**Islands of the Blest.** *See* FORTUNATE ISLANDS.

**Isle of Apples.** *See* AVALON.

**Isle of Dogs, The.** A peninsula on the left bank of the THAMES between Limehouse and Blackwall reaches, opposite Greenwich. It is traditionally said to be named from the fact that Edward III (r.1327–77) kept hounds there for hunting in Waltham Forest. Another explanation is that it is a corruption of Isle of Ducks, from the number of wild fowl inhabiting the marshes. It has long been part of DOCKLANDS, and from the early 1980s has been the site of new commercial and residential development.

> The working men of the Isle of Dogs number some 15,000, engaged in the numerous factories and shipyards; for whose recreation has been formed a Free Library, to provide them with amusement for evenings too often spent in dissipation.
> JOHN TIMBS: *Curiosities of London* (1867)

**Isle of Man.** One explanation of the name is that given by Richard of Cirencester (d.*c.*1401): 'Midway between the two countries [Britain and Ireland] is the island called Monoeda, but now Monavia,' i.e. deriving the name from *menagh* or *meanagh* meaning middle. Another is that it is from Manannán Mac Lir, 'Manannán son of LIR', a Celtic sea god. It is almost certainly from a Celtic word meaning 'mountain', related to Welsh *mynydd*. The Manx name of the island is Ellan Vannan, 'island of Man'. Caesar recorded the name of the island as Mona in the 1st century BC. Supporters of the 'middle' origin point out that AS THE CROW FLIES a route running FROM LAND'S END TO JOHN O'GROATS has the Isle of Man as its exact halfway point. The island is also at the geographical centre of the British Isles, and a circle drawn with Man to LAND'S END OR JOHN O'GROAT'S as the radius will almost exactly encircle the British Isles. *See also* DEEMSTER; TRISKELION; TYNWALD.

**Isle of Portland.** *See* MISNOMERS.

**Apple Islanders, The.** *See under* APPLE.

**Devil's Island.** *See under* DEVIL.

**Emerald Isle, The.** *See under* EMERALD.

**Fair Isle.** *See under* FAIR.

**Fortunate Islands.** *See under* FORTUNATE.

**George Cross Island.** *See under* GEORGE.

**Holy Island.** *See under* HOLY.

**Lord of the Isles.** *See under* LORD.

**Magnetic Island.** *See under* MAGNET.

**Sacred Isle.** *See under* SACRED.
**Sea-girt isle, The.** *See under* SEA.
**Spice Islands.** *See under* SPICE.

**Islington, The Bailiff's Daughter of.** *See under* BAILIFF.

**Ismene.** In Greek legend the daughter of OEDIPUS and Jocasta. ANTIGONE was to be buried alive by order of King CREON for burying her brother Polynices (slain in combat with his brother Eteocles) against the tyrant's express command. Ismene declared that she had aided her sister and asked to share the same fate.

**Isms, The City of.** *See under* CITY.

**Isocrates.** One of the great orators of Athens, distinguished as a teacher of eloquence. He was born in 436 BC and died in 338 BC at the age of 98.

**Isolde.** *See* YSOLDE.

**Israel.** The name has gained different applications over the centuries. In the Old Testament it is the name given to JACOB when he was wrestling with God. Jacob's sons sired the TWELVE TRIBES OF ISRAEL (the Israelites or 'children of Israel' or Hebrews), who many years later conquered the PROMISED LAND and settled there. In due course their land became the kingdom of Israel, with SAUL, DAVID and SOLOMON as its rulers (*see* KINGS OF ISRAEL). On the death of Solomon, the kingdom divided into two unequal parts, the larger becoming Israel and the smaller, JUDAH. This Israel lasted for only 200 years, and its people became the LOST TRIBES OF ISRAEL. The name was resurrected in modern times for the republic established in 1948 in the former British mandate of Palestine. It is generally interpreted as representing the Hebrew words for 'man friend of God', although the Old Testament explanation differs slightly:

> Thy name shall be called no more Jacob, but Israel: for as a prince hast thou power with God and with all men, and hast prevailed.
> Genesis 32:28

**Kings of Israel.** *See under* KING.
**Lost Tribes of Israel, The.** *See under* LOST.
**Sweet singer of Israel, The.** *See under* SWEET.
**Twelve Tribes of Israel, The.** *See under* TWELVE.

**Israfel.** The angel of music for the Muslims. He possesses the most melodious voice of all God's creatures and is to sound the Resurrection Trump, which will ravish the ears of the saints in Paradise. Israfel, GABRIEL and MICHAEL were the three angels who, according to legend, warned ABRAHAM of Sodom's destruction.

**Issachar.** In John Dryden's *Absalom and Achitophel* (1681) the name is used for Thomas Thynne (1648–82), of Longleat, known as Tom of Ten Thousand. Issachar, the fifth son of JACOB by LEAH, was progenitor of one of the TWELVE TRIBES OF ISRAEL, and is described as 'a strong ass couching down between two burdens' (Genesis 49:14).

**Issue.** The point in debate or in question, especially in law.
**At issue.** *See under* AT.
**Fiduciary issue.** *See under* FIDUCIARY.
**Force the issue, To.** *See under* FORCE.
**House of issue.** *See under* HOUSE.
**Join** or **take issue, To.** *See under* JOIN.
**Side issue.** *See under* SIDE.

**Istar.** *See* ISHTAR.

**Isthmian games.** One of the four national festivals of the ancient Greeks, held every alternate spring, the second and fourth of each Olympiad. They took place on the isthmus of Corinth, hence the name. According to one legend they were instituted as funeral games in honour of MELICERTES. They included gymnastics, horse-racing and music contests. *See also* LEUCOTHEA; OLYMPIC GAMES.

**Isumbras** or **Isenbras, Sir.** A hero of medieval romance who made visits to the HOLY LAND and slaughtered thousands of SARACENS. He was at first proud and presumptuous and was visited by all sorts of punishments. He was afterwards penitent and humble when his afflictions were turned into blessings. It was in this latter stage that he one day carried a poor woodman's two children across a ford on his horse. This scene is depicted in J.E. Millais' painting *Sir Isumbras at the Ford* (1856–7). His name appears to be a part-Germanic equivalent of that of Sir Ferumbras, and so also mean 'Iron-arm'. *See* FIERABRAS.

**It.** A synonym for sex appeal, popularized by the novelist Elinor Glyn in *It* (1927) and promoted both visually and verbally by the film star Clara Bow, the 'It' Girl (1905–65), who appeared in a film version of this novel in 1928. 'It' was the word used in billings to describe her particular appeal. Kipling had used the word earlier, however, and it was used for sexual intercourse ('to do it') in the 19th century.

> 'Tisn't beauty, so to speak, nor good talk necessarily. It's just It. Some women'll stay in a man's memory if they once walk down a street.
> RUDYARD KIPLING: *Traffics and Discoveries*, 'Mrs Bathurst' (1904)

**Its.** One of the words by which Thomas Chatterton betrayed his forgeries (*see* ROWLEY POEMS *under* FAKES). In a poem purporting to be the work of a 15th-century priest, he wrote, 'Life and its goods I scorn,' but the word was not in use until more than two centuries later, 'it' ('hit') and 'his' being the possessive case.

'Its' does not occur in any play of Shakespeare published in his lifetime, but there is one instance in the First Folio of 1623 (*Measure for Measure*, I, ii), as well as nine instances of 'it's'. Nor does 'its' occur in the Authorized Version of the Bible (1611), the one instance of it in modern editions (Leviticus 25:5) having been substituted for 'it' in the Bible printed for Hills and Field in 1660.

'Its' in the sense 'belonging to it' was regularly written 'it's' by some down to the early 19th century, although this form is now regarded as illiterate. 'It's' is now properly used to represent 'it is' or 'it has'.

**You're it!** An expression used in children's games such as TAG to the one who has been touched or caught and who will now be chased by the others. 'It' is also used as the name of the game itself.

**That's it.** That's all there is; we've finished.

**This is it.** The big moment is about to arrive. The phrase is also used as a casual or ignorant response to a speaker, as: 'But why can't they get on together?' 'Well, this is it.'

**Where it's at.** *See under* WHERE.

**With it, To be.** *See under* WITH.

**Italia irredenta.** *See* IRREDENTISM.

**Italic.** Pertaining to Italy, especially ancient Italy and the parts other than Rome.

**Italic school of philosophy.** The Pythagorean, because PYTHAGORAS taught in Italy.

**Italic type** or **italics.** The type in which the letters, instead of being erect, as in roman, slope from the left to right, *thus*. It was first used in 1501 by Aldus Manutius (*c.*1450–1515), being the work of his type designer, Francesco Griffo of Bologna, and based on the *cancelleresca corsiva* of the papal chancery.

**Italic version.** An old Latin version of the Bible, prepared from the SEPTUAGINT. It preceded the VULGATE.

**Words italicized in the Bible.** *See under* WORD.

**Italy. Gate of Italy, The.** *See under* GATE.

**Young Italy.** *See under* YOUNG.

**Itch, To.** Properly, to have an irritation of the skin that gives one a desire to scratch the part affected. Hence, figuratively, to feel a constant teasing desire for something. In popular belief, itching of various parts foretold certain occurrences. For instance, if your right palm itched you were going to receive money, the itching of the left eye betokened grief, and of the right pleasure. Itching of the lips foretold kissing, of the nose, that strangers were at hand, and the thumb, that evil approaches. *See also* PRICKING OF ONE'S THUMB.

**Itching ears, To have.** To enjoy scandal-mongering, hearing news or current gossip.

> For the time will come when they will not endure the sound doctrine; but, having itching ears, will heap to themselves teachers after their own lusts.
> 2 Timothy 4:3

**Itching palm, An.** A hand ready to receive bribes; to have a grasping or greedy nature. The old superstition is that if your palm itches you are going to receive money.

> Let me tell you, Cassius, you yourself
> Are much condemned to have an itching palm.
> SHAKESPEARE: *Julius Caesar*, IV, iii (1599)

**Itching powder.** A powder used to make the skin itch, especially as a practical joke.

**Itchy feet, To have.** To be restless; to have a desire to travel.

**One's fingers itch to be at a person.** *See under* FINGER.

**Seven-year itch.** *See under* SEVEN.

**ITMA** (initials of *It's That Man Again*). A famous and popular British radio comedy series, and one that did much to brighten the dreariness of the BLACKOUT years of the Second World War. It was devised and maintained by the comedian Tommy Handley (1896–1949), the script being written by Ted Kavanagh, and ran from 1939 until Handley's death. Among the characters were the char Mrs Mopp, Funf the spy, Claude and Cecil the polite handymen, Ali Oop the saucy seaside postcard seller, Colonel Chinstrap, Signor Soso the 'funny foreigner' and the lugubrious laundress Mona Lott. Each character had his or her own catchphrase. Mrs Mopp's was 'Can I do yer now, sir?', Colonel Chinstrap's was 'I don't mind if I do', Mona Lott's was 'It's being so cheerful as keeps me going', Funf's was 'Ziss iss Funf speakink'. Mrs Mopp's farewell was 'Ta-ta for now', abbreviated as 'TTFN'. 'That man' was Handley. Kavanagh took the full title from a *Daily Express* headline referring to Hitler.

> It is sometimes forgotten that the full title of the opening broadcast, It's That Man Again, was merely the use of a catch-phrase already established. Hitler might not yet, on July 12, 1939, have made one territorial grab too many. But he had long exceeded what even the patient British thought was any reasonable speech ration.
> *The Times* (18 September 1958)

**Ivan. Ivan Ivanovitch.** Used of a Russian, as JOHNNY CRAPAUD was of a Frenchman.

**Ivan the Terrible.** Ivan IV of Russia (1530, 1533–84), infamous for his cruelties, but a man of great energy. He first adopted the title of Tsar (1547). The English nickname is something of a misnomer, since in the original Russian he is *Ivan Grozny*, 'Ivan the Awesome'.

**Ivanhoe.** Sir Walter Scott took the name of his novel (1819) and its hero from the village of Ivinghoe in Buckinghamshire. He recalled an old rhyme but changed the spelling of the name. (His spelling was not necessarily a mistake, and the name actually appears as Ivanhoe in a document dated 1665. Scott could not have seen this, however, since it was published only in 1905.)

> Tring, Wing and Ivinghoe
> For striking of a blow
> Hampden did forego
> And glad he could escape so.

The Hampden of this tradition, ancestor of the squire of SHIP MONEY fame, is said to have quarrelled with the BLACK PRINCE at tennis and struck him with his racket.

**Ivory. Ivories.** Teeth, dice, piano keys, billiard balls, dominoes and so on.

**Ivory shoulder of Pelops, The.** The distinguishing or distinctive mark of anyone. The tale is that DEMETER ate the shoulder of PELOPS when it was served by TANTALUS. When the gods put the body back into the cauldron to restore it to life, this portion was lacking, whereupon Demeter supplied one made of ivory.

**Ivory tower.** To live in an ivory tower is to live in seclusion, divorced from everyday life and wilfully or unwittingly excluding the harsh realities of the outside world. The phrase is first recorded in English in 1911 as a translation of French *tour d'ivoire*, a term used by the critic and poet Charles Sainte-Beuve to refer to his fellow poet Alfred de Vigny. The English phrase was then used by Henry James for the title of his novel *The Ivory Tower* (1916) and was popularized by the writings of Hart Crane, Ezra Pound, H.G. Wells, Aldous Huxley and others.

> Et Vigny plus secret,
> Comme en sa tour d'ivoire, avant midi, rentrait.
> (And Vigny more discreet, as if in his ivory tower, retired before noon.)
>
> CHARLES SAINTE-BEUVE: *Les Pensées d'Août, à M. Villemain* (1837)

**Ivy.** The plant was dedicated to BACCHUS from the notion that it prevents drunkenness. In Christian symbolism ivy typifies the everlasting life, from its remaining continually green.

**Ivy League.** The eight American universities that have a similar academic and social reputation to Oxford and Cambridge in England. They are all in the northeastern states and are, with year of foundation: Harvard (1636), Yale (1701), Pennsylvania (1740), Princeton (1746), Columbia (1754), Brown (1764), Dartmouth (1769) and Cornell (1853). The Ivy League is also the name of the athletic conference for intercollegiate (American) football and other sports to which they belong. Various explanations have been offered to account for the name, such as a derivation in the Roman numeral IV for an early sports league formed by four of them, but it seems likely that the allusion is simply to the ivy-clad walls that the buildings of some of them have or had.

> The fates which govern [football] play among the ivy colleges and academic boiler-factories alike seem to be going around the circuit.
>
> *New York Herald Tribune* (16 October 1933)

**Ixion.** In Greek legend a treacherous king of the LAPITHS who was bound to a revolving wheel of fire in the infernal regions for boasting of having won the favours of HERA. ZEUS had sent a cloud to him in the form of Hera, and by him the cloud became the mother of the CENTAURS.

# J

**J.** The tenth letter of the alphabet, a modern introduction, was differentiated from I only in the 17th century and not completely distinguished from it until the 19th. In Dr Johnson's *Dictionary of the English Language* (1755) 'joyous' is thus followed by 'ipecacuanha', and 'itself' is followed by 'jubilant'. It was a medieval practice to lengthen the I when it was the initial letter, usually with the consonantal function now assumed by J. In the Roman system of numeration it was used in place of i as the final figure in a series, e.g. iij for iii.

**Jabberwocky.** The eponymous central figure of a strange, almost nonsensical poem in Lewis Carroll's *Through the Looking-Glass* (1871). It contains many significant PORTMANTEAU WORDS, as subsequently explained to Alice by HUMPTY DUMPTY.

The creature's name appears to indicate a 'wock' that 'jabbers', but as the poem is a mock medieval ballad, with 'Anglo-Saxon' words invented by Carroll, one may look for a mock medieval derivation for the name itself. When a class in the Girls' Latin School, Boston, Massachusetts, wrote to Carroll to ask permission to name their magazine *The Jabberwock*, he replied in a letter dated 6 February 1888 as follows:

> Mr Lewis Carroll has much pleasure in giving to the editresses of the proposed magazine permission to use the title they wish for. He finds that the Anglo-Saxon word 'wocer' or 'wocor' signifies 'offspring' or 'fruit'. Taking 'jabber' in its ordinary acceptation of 'excited and voluble discussion', this would give the meaning of 'the result of much excited discussion'. Whether this phrase will have any application to the projected periodical, it will be for the future historian of American literature to determine. Mr Carroll wishes all success to the forthcoming magazine.
>
> MORTON N. COHEN (ed): *The Selected Letters of Lewis Carroll* (1982)

Carroll was not indulging in whimsy for once, for Old English *wōcer* or *wōcor* does mean 'offspring', as he says.

**Jachin and Boaz.** The two great bronze pillars set up at the entrance of the TEMPLE OF SOLOMON, Jachin being the right-hand (southern) pillar, with a Hebrew name literally meaning 'he [the Lord] makes firm', and Boaz being the left-hand (northern) pillar, with a name meaning 'in him [the Lord] is strength'. *See* 1 Kings 7:21, 2 Chronicles 3:17.

**Jack.** (1) A favourite name for JOHN, derived from Jan and Jankin, which developed from Johannes. It came to be a generic name for a boy, man, husband or similar male, and a familiar term of address among sailors, workmen and others.

(2) When the name is applied to animals it usually denotes the male sex or smallness of size: Jackass, Jack-baker (a kind of owl), Jack or dog fox, Jack hare, Jack rat, Jack shark, Jack snipe, Jack curlew (the whimbrel, a small species of curlew). A young pike is called a Jack, so also were the male birds used in falconry.

(3) The name is also found for certain common wild plants: Jack-at-the-hedge (cleavers), Jack-by-the-hedge (garlic mustard), Jack-go-to-bed-at-noon (goat's beard) and so on. Jack-in-the-pulpit is a North American woodland plant, *Arisaema triphyllum*, so called from its upright spadix, which is overarched by the spathe, resembling a parson in a pulpit.

(4) When applied to certain articles, the word usually implies smallness or inferiority of some kind. The jack is the flag smaller than the ensign, worn on the jackstaff in the bows of a warship, although the Union flag is usually called the UNION JACK. The small waxed leather vessel for liquor was called a jack. Jack was also the inferior kind of armour consisting of a leather surcoat worn by foot soldiers, formed by overlapping pieces of metal fastened between two layers of canvas, leather or quilted material. The jack at bowls is so called because it is small in comparison with the bowls themselves. A jack is an obsolete term for a FARTHING, and a jack and half-jack were names given to counters, used in gambling, resembling a SOVEREIGN and half-sovereign. *See also* BLACKJACK.

(5) Numerous appliances and contrivances that obviate the use of an assistant are called jacks. A jack is used for lifting heavy weights and is also applied to the rough stool or horse used for sawing timber on. A bottle-jack or roasting-jack was used for turning the meat when roasting before an open fire.

**Jack Adams.** A fool.

**Jack-a-dandy.** A smart, foppish, bright little fellow.

**Jack-a-Lent.** A kind of AUNT SALLY, which was thrown at in LENT, and hence a puppet or sheepish booby. Shakespeare says: 'You little Jack-a-Lent, have you been true to us?' (*The Merry Wives of Windsor*, III, iii (1600)).

**Jack among the maids.** A favourite with the ladies; a ladies' man.

**Jack-a-Napes.** The nickname of William de la Pole, Duke of Suffolk (1396–1450), who was beheaded at sea (off Dover), possibly at the instigation of the Duke of York. The name arose from his badge, the clog and chain of an ape, which also gave rise to his name 'Ape-clogge'. *See also* JACKANAPES.

**Jack and Jill.** In the familiar nursery rhyme Jack and Jill who went up the hill 'to fetch a pail of water' are probably generic names for lad and lass, and represent a typical courting couple. Norman Iles, in *Who Really Killed Cock Robin?* (1986), suggests that the rhyme has a specific sexual reference and that it was Jill, not Jack, who 'broke her crown', i.e. lost her virginity.

**Jack and the Beanstalk.** A nursery tale found among many peoples in varying forms. In the English version Jack exchanges his poor mother's cow for a handful of beans, which miraculously produce stalks reaching the sky. Jack climbs up them and steals treasures from the ogre's castle: a bag of gold, a wonderful lamp and the hen (or goose) that lays the golden eggs, thus redeeming their poverty. *See also* GOLDEN GOOSE; KILL THE GOOSE THAT LAYS THE GOLDEN EGGS.

**Jackboot.** A large boot extending over the knee, acting as protective armour for the leg, worn by troopers in the 17th and 18th centuries and later. It is still the type of boot worn by the Household Cavalry and was adopted by fishermen and others before the advent of gumboots. Figuratively, to be under the jackboot is to be controlled by a brutal military regime. *See also* MAILED FIST.

**Jack Cade legislation.** Pressure from without. An allusion to the Kentish insurrection of 1450 led by Jack Cade. He marched on LONDON, encamped on BLACKHEATH, and demanded redress of grievances from Henry VI (r.1422–61, 1470–1). He held London for two days, then his followers began to plunder and disperse. He attempted to reach the coast but was killed near Heathfield, East Sussex.

**Jack Dusty.** A stores rating in the Royal Navy, formerly called a Supply Assistant, is so named. Handling naval stores, especially flour, is sometimes a dusty job.

**Jack Frost.** The personification of frost or frosty weather.

**Jack Harkaway.** *See under* HARKAWAY.

**Jack Horner.** A fanciful explanation of the old nursery rhyme 'Little Jack Horner' is that Jack was steward to the abbot of Glastonbury at the time of the dissolution of the monasteries (1536–9), and that by a subterfuge he gained the deeds of the Manor of Mells. It is said that these deeds, with others, were sent to Henry VIII concealed, for safety, in a pasty. 'Jack Horner' was thus the bearer who, on the way, lifted the crust and extracted this 'plum'.

**Jack-in-a-bottle.** The long-tailed titmouse or bottle tit, so called from the shape of its nest.

**Jack-in-office.** A pompous overbearing official, who uses his powers unimaginatively.

**Jack-in-the-basket.** The basket or kindred device on the top of a pole, which serves as a leading mark to shipping.

> How comfortingly the cocoa boiled on an even keel at dawn with Jack-in-the-basket in sight!
> *Yachting Monthly* (March 1921)

**Jack-in-the-box.** A toy consisting of a box out of which 'Jack' springs when the lid is raised.

**Jack-in-the-green.** A youth or boy who moves about concealed in a wooden framework covered with leaves and boughs as part of the chimney-sweeps' revels on MAY DAY. This is now an obsolete English custom.

**Jack Ketch.** *See under* KETCH.

**Jack-knife.** A knife with a blade pivoted in such a way that it folds into the handle. A jack-knife is also a former name for a type of dive in which the diver bends at the waist in mid-air, then straightens out to enter the water head first. This is now known as a 'forward pike dive'. When an articulated lorry jack-knifes, usually through loss of control, the trailer swings round at an angle to the cab.

**Jack of all trades and master of none.** A term of contempt for someone who tries anything and everything but is not an expert in any one field.

**Jack of clubs.** The knave or servant of the king and queen of this suit. So also for the jack in the other three suits (diamonds, hearts and spades).

**Jack of Dover, A.** Some unidentified eatable mentioned by Chaucer in the Prologue to 'The Cook's Tale' (*c*.1387):

> Many's the Jack of Dover you have sold
> That has been twice warmed up and twice left cold.
> (Modern translation by Nevill Coghill, 1951)

In his edition of Chaucer W.W. Skeat says that it is 'probably a pie that has been cooked more than once'. Another suggestion is that it is some kind of fish. *See also* JOHN DORY.

**Jack of Newbury.** John Winchcombe alias Smallwood (d.1520), a wealthy clothier in the reign of Henry VIII (1509–47). He was the hero of many CHAPBOOKS and is said to have kept 100 looms in his own house at Newbury and to have equipped at his own expense 100–200 of his men to aid the king against the Scots at Flodden Field (1513).

**Jack-o'-lantern.** IGNIS FATUUS. In the USA the name is used for the hollowed-out pumpkin of HALLOWEEN games.

**Jack-o'-the-bowl.** The BROWNIE or house spirit of Switzerland, so called from the nightly custom of placing a bowl of fresh cream for him on the cowhouse roof. The contents are sure to disappear before morning.

**Jack-o'-the-clock.** The carved and painted human figure that, in some old public clocks, comes out to strike the hours on the bell. There is a good example at Wells Cathedral, where two quarter-jacks strike the quarter-hours, and Jack Blandifer strikes the hours.

**Jack out of office.** One no longer in office; one dismissed from his employment.

> I am left out; for me nothing remains,
> But long I will not be Jack-out-of-office.
> SHAKESPEARE: *Henry VI, Pt I*, I, i (1590)

**Jackpot.** In poker a pot that cannot be opened until a player has a pair of jacks or better. The word is generally applied to the 'pool' disgorged by a gaming machine or to the top prize in a contest, draw or lottery. To hit the jackpot is to win any great prize or unexpected 'bonanza'.

> Denis, the host for the evening, excitedly informed me that I had hit the jackpot: a large hen party and an all-female 21st birthday party had booked.
> *Sunday Times* (13 November 1994)

**Jack rabbit.** A large prairie hare of North America. The name is a shortened form of jackass rabbit, an appellation given it on account of its very long ears and legs.

**Jack rafter.** A rafter in a hipped roof, shorter than a full-sized one.

**Jack rib.** An inferior rib in an arch, shorter than the rest.

**Jackroll.** The cylinder around which the rope of a well coils; a windlass.

**Jack Russell.** A white-coloured sporting TERRIER first bred by the Devonshire cleric John Russell (1759–1883). Jack Russell, nicknamed 'The Sporting Parson', was much addicted to foxhunting and otter-hunting, and at one time kept his own pack of hounds. *See also* SQUARSON.

**Jack's as good as his master.** An old proverb indicating the equality of man. It was the wise Agur (Proverbs 30:22) who placed 'a servant when he reigneth' as the first of the four things that the earth cannot bear. *See also* WHEN ADAM DELVED.

**Jackscrew.** A large screw rotating in a threaded socket, used for lifting heavy weights.

**Jack Sheppard.** *See under* SHEPPARD.

**Jack Sprat.** A DWARF, as if sprats were dwarf herrings. Children, by a similar metaphor, are called SMALL FRY.

> Jack Sprat could eat no fat,
> His wife could eat no lean,
> And so, between them both, you see,
> They licked the platter clean.
> Nursery rhyme

**Jack Straw.** *See under* STRAW.

**Jack Tar.** A sailor. *See also* TARPAULIN.

**Jack the Giant-killer.** The hero of the old nursery tale owed much of his success to his four marvellous possessions. When he put on his coat no eye could see him, when he had his shoes on no one could overtake him, when he put on his cap he knew everything he required to know, and his sword cut through everything. The story is given by Walter Map (*c*.1140–*c*.1209), who obtained it from a French source.

**Jack the Lad.** A self-assured and carefree young man, especially when bold and brash. The nickname was that of the thief Jack SHEPPARD (1702–24), the subject of numerous ballads and popular plays. He was imprisoned four times and on each occasion effected a spectacular escape, even when manacled to the floor of his cell in solitary confinement. After his fifth arrest he was hanged, reputedly before a gathering of some 200,000 people. The popular hornpipe in Sir Henry Wood's *Fantasia on British Sea Songs* (1905), traditionally performed at the LAST NIGHT OF THE PROMS, is known as *Jack's the Lad*.

**Jack** or **John the Painter.** James Aitken, alias James Hill, alias James Hind, alias James Actzen was born at Edinburgh in 1752, the son of a whitesmith. He showed skill as an artist but abandoned his apprenticeship for the lure of London, where he lived by theft until capture seemed imminent. He joined the army but soon deserted. Early in the American war he apparently offered his services to the Americans, promising to burn British ships and dockyards. His first, unsuccessful, attempts were at Portsmouth Dock and Plymouth, and in January 1777 he set out for Bristol where he destroyed ships and warehouses and created panic. Rewards for his arrest were offered by the corporation, by Edmund Burke, MP for Bristol, and by George III. He was eventually arrested at Andover and in due course made his confession. On 10 March 1777, aged 24, he was hanged at the yardarm of the *Arethusa* at Portsmouth and then hung in chains on Blockhouse Point, at the mouth of the harbour.

**Jack the Ripper.** The name adopted by an unknown killer who murdered at least five prostitutes in Whitechapel in 1888 and mutilated ('ripped') their bodies. The victims included Mary Ann Nicholls, Annie Chapman, Elizabeth Stride, Catherine Eddowes and Mary Kelly.

Early theories that the killer was a 'gentleman' of some kind (an insane doctor and a cricket-playing lawyer have been proposed) are almost certainly wide of the mark. A recent suggestion is that the murders were planned by a group of high-ranking Freemasons (*see* FREEMASONRY), including Sir William Gull, the royal physician, their motive being to suppress scandals involving Prince Albert Victor, Duke of Clarence (1846–92), elder son of the then Prince of Wales (later Edward VII). Another theory is that the murderer was the Duke of Clarence himself, but a more likely candidate is J.K. Stephen, the duke's lover.

**Jack timbers.** Timbers in a building that are shorter than the rest.

**Before you can say Jack Robinson.** *See under* BEFORE.

**Bootjack.** *See under* BOOT.

**Cheap-jack.** *See under* CHEAP.

**Every Jack shall have his Jill.** *See under* EVERY.

**Every man jack of them.** *See under* EVERY.

**Foul-weather Jack.** *See under* FOUL.

**House that Jack built, The.** *See under* HOUSE.

**I'm all right, Jack.** *See* PULL UP THE LADDER, JACK, I'M INBOARD.

**Jumping jack.** *See under* JUMP.

**On one's jack.** On one's own. Short for 'on one's Jack Jones', RHYMING SLANG for 'alone'.

**Pull up the ladder, Jack, I'm inboard.** *See under* PULL.

**Radical Jack.** *See under* RADICAL.

**Sixteen-string Jack.** *See under* SIX.

**Strip Jack naked.** *See under* STRIP.

**Union Jack.** *See under* UNION.

**Yellow jack.** *See under* YELLOW.

**Jackal.** A toady; one who does the dirty work for another. It was once thought that the jackal hunted in troops to provide the lion with prey. *See also* LION'S PROVIDER.

**Jackanapes.** A conceited or impertinent person. It is uncertain whether the -napes is connected originally with the ape or with Naples, Jackanapes being a Jack (monkey) of (imported from) Naples, just as fustian-a-napes was fustian from Naples. By the 16th century, Jackanapes was in use as a proper name for a tame ape. It then came to be used as a term for a mischievous child. Mrs J.H. Ewing's *Jackanapes* (1883), originally serialised in *Aunt Judy's Magazine* in 1879, was a long popular Victorian tale for children. Jackanapes is a WILD CHILD whose father was killed at Waterloo. He is civilized when brought up by his maiden aunt, however, and grows up to lay down his life for a friend on the battlefield. *See also* JACK-A-NAPES.

**Jackass.** A stupid person; a fool.

**Laughing jackass.** *See under* LAUGH.

**Jackdaw.** A bird notorious for its thieving habits.

**Jackdaw of Rheims, The.** One of the best known of the INGOLDSBY *Legends* (1840), in which the cardinal's ring mysteriously vanishes. He solemnly curses the thief by BELL, BOOK AND CANDLE, and the jackdaw's bedraggled appearance, caused by the curse, reveals him as the culprit.

**Jackeroo.** A name used in Australia in the first half of the 19th century to describe a young Englishman newly arrived to learn farming, derived, according to some, from a combination of Jack and kangaroo. Later the name was applied simply to a station hand. Jilleroo, its feminine counterpart, was applied to the Australian LAND GIRLS of the Second World War.

**Jacket.** The word came into English from Old French *jaquet*. This was the term used for a short jacket worn by a typical peasant, who was nicknamed JACQUES. Baked potatoes when cooked unpeeled are called 'jacket potatoes'.

**Donkey jacket.** *See under* DONKEY.

**Shell jacket.** *See under* SHELL.

**Jackson, Stonewall.** Thomas J. Jackson (1824–63), one of the Confederate generals in the American Civil War (1861–5), so called from his firmness at the Battle of Bull Run (1861), when a fellow officer observed him with his brigade standing 'like a stone wall'.

**Jackstones.** A children's game played with a set of small stones and a small ball or marble. They are thrown up and caught on the back of the hand in various ways.

**Jackstraws.** In the USA a children's game similar to spillikins, but played with straws.

**Jacob.** A son of ISAAC and the father of the Jewish nation (Genesis 25:1). As a boy, he traded his brother ESAU for a 'mess of pottage' for the latter's birthright and then duped Isaac into giving him his blessing by disguising himself in hairy skins. In the land of LABAN, he fell in love with RACHEL and worked for seven years to win her hand but was tricked and given LEAH. After working for another seven years he won Rachel. On his return with his family, he wrestled with an angel and was given the name ISRAEL.

**Jacob's ladder.** The ladder seen by JACOB leading up to heaven (Genesis 28:12), hence its application to steep ladders and steps, especially the rope ladder with wooden rungs slung from a ship's boom to the water. The garden plant *Polemonium caeruleum* is also so called from the ladder-like arrangement of its leaflets.

**Jacob's staff.** A pilgrim's staff. The allusion is to St JAMES THE GREAT (Latin *Jacobus*), who is usually represented with a staff and SCALLOP SHELL. The term is also used for a surveyor's rod, used instead of a tripod, and for a former instrument for taking heights and distances.

**Jacob's stone.** The Coronation STONE OF SCONE is

sometimes so called, from the legend that JACOB's head had rested on this stone when he had the vision of angels ascending and descending the ladder (Genesis 28:11).

**Jacobins.** The DOMINICANS were so called in France from the Rue St Jacques, the location of their first house in Paris. The French Revolutionary Jacobin Club, founded at Versailles in 1789 as the Breton Club, moved to Paris and met in a former Jacobin convent. Hence its name. Among its famous members were Honoré Mirabeau (1749–91), Maximilien Robespierre (1758–94), Louis Saint-Just (1767–94), Jean Paul Marat (1743–93) and George Couthon (1756–94). It controlled the country at one stage through its hundreds of daughter societies in the provinces. The club was suppressed in 1794, after the fall of Robespierre. Their badge was the Phrygian or LIBERTY CAP.

**Jacobites.** (1) A sect of Syrian MONOPHYSITES, so called from Jacobus Baradaeus, bishop of Edessa in the 6th century. The present head of their church is called the PATRIARCH of Antioch. The term is also applied to the Monophysite Christians in Egypt.

(2) The name given to the supporters of James II (Latin *Jacobus*) and of his descendants who claimed the throne of Great Britain and Ireland. They came into existence after the flight of James II in 1688 and were strong in Scotland and the north of England. They were responsible for the risings of 1715 and 1745, the latter rising marking their virtual end as a political force. The last male representative of the Stuarts was Henry (IX), a cardinal and a pensioner of George III, who died in 1807.

**Jacobus.** The unofficial name of a hammered gold coin struck in the reign of James I (Latin *Jacobus*), originally worth 20s. It was properly called a UNITE.

**Jacquard loom.** So called from Joseph-Marie Jacquard (1752–1834) of Lyons, its inventor. Its particular importance was in facilitating the weaving of patterns, especially in silks.

**Jacques** (French, 'James'). A generic name for the French peasant, the equivalent of HODGE. Jacques Bonhomme is similarly used. *See also* JACKET.

**Jacquerie.** An insurrection of the French peasantry in 1358, provoked by the hardships caused by the HUNDRED YEARS' WAR, the oppressions of the privileged classes and Charles II, the Bad, of Navarre (r.1349–87). The Jacquerie committed many atrocities and savage reprisals followed. The name derives from JACQUES.

**Melancholy Jacques.** *See under* MELANCHOLY.

**Jactitation of marriage.** A false assertion by a person of being married to another. This was actionable until abolished by the Family Law Act of 1986. Jactitation derives from Latin *jactitare*, 'to utter publicly', itself from *jactare*, literally 'to toss about', from *jacare*, 'to throw'. The term comes from the old CANON LAW.

**Jacuzzi.** The 'whirlpool bath' takes its name from its Italian-born American inventor, Candido Jacuzzi (1903–86), who originally devised it for his young son, a victim of rheumatoid arthritis.

**Jade.** (1) The fact that in medieval times this ornamental stone was supposed, if applied to the side, to act as a cure for renal colic is enshrined in its name, for jade is from the obsolete Spanish *piedra de ijada*, 'stone of the side', and its other name, nephrite, is from Greek *nephros*, 'kidney'. Among the Native Americans it is still worn as an AMULET against the bite of venomous snakes, and to cure the gravel (small stones in the kidney or bladder), epilepsy and other conditions.

(2) The word jade, of unknown origin, is also applied to a worthless horse or, contemptuously, to a bad-tempered or disreputable woman.

**Jaeger.** The type of knitwear owes its name to the German hygienist and naturalist Gustav Jaeger (1832–1917), who was convinced that it was healthier for people to wear clothes made of wool, from animals, than of cotton and linen, from plants. The first shop to sell this type of clothing opened in London in the late 1870s, and George Bernard Shaw regularly wore a Jaeger suit.

**Jael.** The nomadic woman who offers shelter to Sisera after he loses the battle with DEBORAH, then kills him by hammering a nail through his head while he is resting. The story is told with poetic realism in Judges 4.

**Jagannath.** *See* JUGGERNAUT.

**Jahweh.** *See* JEHOVAH.

**Jains.** A sect of dissenters from HINDUISM, of as early an origin as BUDDHISM. Jains, being largely traders, are usually wealthy and therefore influential for their numbers.

**Jakes.** An old word for a privy, perhaps from French JACQUES. *See also* JOHN.

**Jam.** A word used colloquially for something agreeable or that comes easily, especially if unexpected. Hence a remark such as 'You want jam on it', meaning that it is not 'sweet' enough for you.

**Jam session.** A meeting of JAZZ musicians improvising spontaneously without rehearsal.

**Jam tomorrow.** A pleasant thing that is frequently promised but that never appears. The phrase is from Lewis Carroll's *Through the Looking-Glass* (1871), in which the White Queen wants Alice to be her maid and offers her twopence a week and jam every other day. However, she can never actually have it, for: 'The rule is, jam to-morrow and jam yesterday – but never jam *to-day*'. A similar concept is PIE IN THE SKY.

**In a jam, To be.** To be in a predicament, from the verb jam, to compress; to squeeze or press down, akin to champ.

**Money for jam.** *See under* MONEY.

**Jambres.** *See* JANNES.

**James.** *See* JACOBUS.

**James Bond.** *See under* BOND.

**Court of St James's, The.** *See under* COURT.

**Jesse James.** A notorious American bandit (1837–82). In 1867 he organized a band of bank and train robbers who perpetrated a number of infamous murders and daring crimes. A reward of $10,000 was put on his head. He retired to St Joseph, Missouri, under the name of Howard and was shot by a reward-seeker while hanging a picture in his house. He undeservedly passed into legend as another ROBIN HOOD.

**St James the Great.** The Apostle is the patron saint of Spain. One legend states that after his death in Palestine his body was placed in a boat with sails set, and that next day it reached the Spanish coast. At Padrón, near COMPOSTELA, they used to show a huge stone as the original boat. Another legend says that the relics of St James were miraculously conveyed from Jerusalem, where he was bishop, to Spain, in a marble ship. A knight saw the ship entering port and his horse took fright and plunged into the sea but the knight saved himself by boarding the vessel and found his clothes entirely covered with SCALLOP SHELLS.

The saint's body was discovered in 840 by Bishop Theudemirus of Iria through divine revelation, and a church was built at Compostela for its shrine.

St James is commemorated on 25 July and is represented in art sometimes with the sword by which he was beheaded and sometimes attired as a pilgrim, with his cloak covered with shells.

**St James the Less** or **James the Little.** He has been identified both with the Apostle James, the son of Alphaeus, and with James the brother of Christ. He is commemorated with St PHILIP on 1 May (on 3 May by Roman Catholics).

**Jameson Raid.** A foolhardy attempt by Dr L.S. Jameson (1853–1917) to overthrow the Transvaal government of Paul Kruger. On 29 December 1875 Jameson crossed the border with 470 men in the expectation of a simultaneous UITLANDER rising in the Transvaal. He was surrounded at Doornkop (2 January 1896) and subsequently handed over to the British authorities. Cecil Rhodes, the Cape Prime Minister, was involved, and Joseph Chamberlain, the Colonial Secretary, was almost certainly implicated. *See also* KRUGER TELEGRAM.

**Jamshid.** In Persian legend, the fourth king of the Pishdadian (earliest) dynasty who reigned for 700 years and had Devs (demons) as his slaves. He was credited with 300 years of beneficent rule, but when he forgot God he was driven out and remained hidden for 100 years. He was eventually sawn apart. Among his magical possessions was a cup containing the ELIXIR OF LIFE which is mentioned in Edward FitzGerald's *Omar Khayyám* (1859) and Thomas Moore's *Lalla Rookh* (1817).

**Jane.** (1) A small Genoese silver coin, so called from French *Gênes*, 'Genoa'.

(2) A jane is a (mainly American) slang term for a woman, derived from the name.

Jane is also the name of a strip cartoon heroine popular in the Second World War. She was created by the artist Norman Pett in 1932 for a strip (the operative word) in the *Daily Mirror*. She began as a reasonably recognizable 'bright young thing' (*see* FLAPPER) but in the war years progressed to more exotic roles, in many of which she managed to lose most of her clothes. The newspaper strip ran until 1959, but she was revived in 1982 for a semi-animated television series, in which she was played by Glynis Barber.

**Janeite.** A devotee of the works (and person) of Jane Austen (1775–1817).

**Calamity Jane.** *See under* CALAMITY.

**Lady Jane Grey.** *See under* GREY.

**Plain jane.** *See under* PLAIN.

**Janissaries** or **Janizaries** (Turkish *yeniçeri*, 'new troops'). Celebrated troops of the OTTOMAN EMPIRE, raised by Orchan in 1330; originally, and for some centuries, compulsorily recruited from Christian subjects of the Sultan. In 1826 the Janissaries, long a tyrannical military caste, rebelled when their privileges were threatened, and they were abolished by total massacre.

**Jannes and Jambres.** The names under which St PAUL (2 Timothy 3:8) referred to the two magicians of PHARAOH who imitated some of the miracles of MOSES (Exodus 7). The names are not mentioned in the Old Testament, but they appear in the TARGUMS and other rabbinical writings, where tradition has it that they were sons of BALAAM, and that they perished either in the crossing of the Red Sea or in the tumult after the WORSHIP OF THE GOLDEN CALF.

**Jansenists.** A sect of Christians, who held the doctrines of Cornelius Jansen (1585–1638), bishop of Ypres. Jansen professed to have formulated the teaching of AUGUSTINE, which resembled CALVINISM in many respects. He taught the doctrines of 'irresistible grace', ORIGINAL SIN and 'the utter helplessness of the natural man to turn to God'. Louis XIV opposed them and they were put down by Pope Clement XI, in 1713, in the Bull UNIGENITUS.

**Januarius.** The patron saint of Naples, a bishop of Benevento, who was martyred during the

Diocletian persecution *c.*304. He is commemorated on 19 September, and his head and two vials of his blood are preserved in the cathedral at Naples. This congealed blood is said to liquefy several times a year.

**January.** The month dedicated by the Romans to JANUS, who presided over the entrance to the year and, having two faces, could look back to the past year and forward to the new.

The Dutch used to call this month *Lauwmaand* ('frosty month'), while the Saxons knew it as *Wulfmōnath*, because wolves were very troublesome then from the great scarcity of food. After the introduction of Christianity, the name was changed to *æftera Gēola* ('after Yule'). It was also called *Formamōnath* ('first month'). In the FRENCH REVOLUTIONARY CALENDAR of the first French Republic the corresponding month was called NIVÔSE ('snow month'), from 22 December to 20 January.

**Janus.** The ancient Roman deity who kept the gate of heaven and is, therefore, the guardian of gates and doors. He was represented with two faces, one in front and one behind, and the doors of his temple in Rome were thrown open in times of war and closed in times of peace. The name is used allusively both with reference to the two-facedness and to war.

**Japanese vellum.** *See* MISNOMERS.

**Japhetic.** An adjective sometimes applied to the ARYANS, from their supposed descent from Japheth, one of the sons of NOAH. *See also* JAVAN.

**Jarndyce v. Jarndyce.** An interminable CHANCERY suit in *Bleak House* (1852–3). Dickens probably founded his story on the lengthy Chancery suit of *Jennens* v. *Jennens*, which related to property in Nacton, Suffolk, belonging to an intestate miser who died in 1798. The case was only finally concluded more than 80 years after its start.

**Jason.** The hero of Greek legend who led the ARGONAUTS in the quest of the GOLDEN FLEECE, the son of Aeson, king of Iolcus, brought up by the centaur CHIRON. When he demanded his kingdom from his uncle Pelias who had deprived him of it, and was told he could have it in return for the Golden Fleece, Jason gathered around him the chief heroes of Greece and set sail in the ARGO. After many tests and trials, including sowing the remaining dragon's teeth left unsown by CADMUS, he was successful through the help of MEDEA, whom he married. He later deserted her and subsequently killed himself through melancholy. Another account says he was crushed to death by the stern of his old ship *Argo*, while resting beneath it.

**Jaundiced eye, A.** A prejudiced eye that only sees faults. It was a popular belief that to the eye of a person who had jaundice (French *jaune*, 'yellow'), everything looked yellow.

> All seems infected that th' infected spy,
> As all looks yellow to the jaundiced eye.
>
> ALEXANDER POPE: *Essay on Criticism*, ii (1711)

**Jaunty.** In the Royal Navy the usual nickname for a chief petty officer of the regulating branch, officially called a MASTER-AT-ARMS. It is said to be a corruption of the French *gendarme*.

**Java man.** *See* PITHECANTHROPUS.

**Javan.** In the Bible the collective name of the Greeks (Isaiah 66:19 and elsewhere), who were said to be descended from Javan, the son of Japheth (Genesis 10:2).

**Jaw.** Impudent talk; idle conversation; moralizing talk.

> To jaw-jaw is always better than to war-war.
>
> WINSTON CHURCHILL: Speech at the White House (26 June 1954)

**Jaw-breaker** or **cracker.** A word that is hard to pronounce. Many foreign words are jaw-breakers to one unfamiliar with the language.

**Jaws.** Anything dangerous or threatening, that will bite and swallow one up, as the jaws of death.

**Lantern jaws.** *See under* LANTERN.

**Pi-jaw.** *See under* PI.

**Jay.** A foolish or gullible person.

**Jay Gatsby.** *See under* GATSBY.

**Jaywalker.** A person who crosses or walks in a street thoughtlessly, regardless of passing traffic. The word alludes both to the bird, which hops in an erratic fashion, and to the JAY that is a foolish person.

**Jazz** (of unknown origin). A type of dance music originating in the folk music of the American Negro of the cotton fields. It first developed in New Orleans and reached Chicago by 1914 where it gained its name. It was slightly influenced by RAGTIME and is characterized by syncopation and the noisy use of percussion instruments, together with the trombone, trumpet and saxophone. Its impact grew steadily and it has had many notable exponents. The name has been somewhat loosely appropriated by popular dance orchestras playing their own conception of the jazz idiom. *See also* BLUES; BOOGIE-WOOGIE; SWING.

**Jean Crapaud.** *See* JOHNNY CRAPAUD.

**Jeanne d'Arc.** *See* JOAN OF ARC.

**Jeep.** The registered name of a small all-purpose car first developed by the USA during the Second World War and known as GP, i.e. General Purpose, the US Army designation for this type of car. The name probably derives from this, although was influenced by 'Eugene the Jeep', a versatile cartoon character that had a cry of 'Jeep'. It was introduced in the comic strip 'Thimble Theater' (the forerunner of Popeye) by the cartoonist Elzie C. Segar in 1936 and used briefly for the name of a commercial vehicle the following year. According to another account, the name came from the exclamation, 'Jeepers creepers!', made by Major General George Lynch, US Army chief of infantry, when he first rode in a prototype of the vehicle at Fort Myer, Virginia, in 1939, and accordingly adopted then by the vehicle's designer, Charles H. Payne. The experimental models were also called Beeps, Peeps and Blitz Buggies, but the name Jeep came to stay in 1941.

**Jeeves.** Bertie WOOSTER's dignified and loyal butler in the books by P.G. Wodehouse. He is as intelligent as his master is vacuous, and as soberly resourceful as he is cheerfully inept. Wodehouse took his name from a Gloucestershire county cricketer, Percy Jeeves, killed in the First World War.

> At this point in the proceedings there was another ring at the front door. Jeeves shimmered out and came back with a telegram.
> P.G. WODEHOUSE: *Carry on, Jeeves!* (1925)

**Jeffrey Hudson.** *See under* HUDSON.

**Jehad.** *See* HOLY WAR.

**Jehennam, Bridge of.** Another name for AL-SIRAT.

**Jehoshaphat.** The fourth king of JUDAH, reigning in the 9th century BC. In the Old Testament his reign covers roughly the same period as that of AHAB in ISRAEL (1 Kings 22), and the two kings conduct a joint campaign against Syria. Jehoshaphat goes into battle wearing Ahab's clothes, while Ahab disguises himself as someone else. However, it is Ahab who is killed, while Jehoshaphat escapes. He subsequently defeats the Moabites and Ammonites.

**Jumping Jehoshaphat.** *See under* JUMP.

**Jehovah.** The name Jehovah is an instance of the extreme sanctity with which the name of God was invested, as it is a disguised form of JHVH, the TETRAGRAMMATON that was the 'ineffable name', too sacred to use. The scribes therefore added the vowels of ADONAI, thereby indicating that the reader was to say Adonai instead of JHVH. At the time of the RENAISSANCE these vowels and consonants were taken for the sacred name itself. Hence Jehovah or Yahweh. The name itself is believed to be based on the Hebrew verb *hāwāh*, 'to be', 'to exist'.

> And God said unto Moses, I AM THAT I AM: and he said, Thus shalt thou say unto the children of Israel, I AM hath sent me unto you.
> Exodus 3:14

**Jehovah's Witnesses.** A religious movement founded in 1872 by Charles Taze Russell (1852–1916) in Pittsburgh, Pennsylvania, and known as International Bible Students until 1931. It does not ascribe divinity to Jesus Christ, regarding him as the perfect man and agent of God. Recognition of JEHOVAH as their sole authority involves the Witnesses in refusal to salute a national flag or to do military service. *The Watch Tower* is their official organ.

**Jehu.** A coachman, especially one who drives at a rattling pace.

> The driving is like the driving of Jehu the son of Nimshi; for he driveth furiously.
> 2 Kings 9:20

**Companions of Jehu.** *See under* COMPANION.

**Jekyll. Dr Jekyll and Mr Hyde.** Two contrasting or opposed aspects of one person. Jekyll is the 'good man', Hyde is 'the evil that is present'. The phrase comes from R.L. Stevenson's *The Strange Case of Dr Jekyll and Mr Hyde* (1886). In this, Dr Jekyll is a physician who is conscious of the duality, the mixture of good and evil, in his own person, and he becomes fascinated by the possibility of what would happen if the two sides could be embodied in different personalities. He succeeds by means of a drug, and is taken over by the evil personality of Mr Hyde. The result for both is disaster.

**Jealousy, The Water of.** *See under* WATER.

**Jelly, Calf's-foot.** *See under* CALF.

**Jellyby, Mrs.** A character in Dickens's *Bleak House* (1852–3). She represents the eager, unthinking philanthropist whose own family and home are neglected in her enthusiasm for 'good works'.

**Jemima.** In the Old Testament (Job 42), the first daughter born to JOB after he was restored, noted for her beauty. In American 20th-century lore Jemima is a jolly plump Negress, a personification of the happy slave 'mammy'. The name was made familiar by labels on the 'Aunt Jemima' food products. Latterly the name in this sense has become unacceptable to blacks, implying that they are willing to be oppressed by whites.

**Jemmy. Jemmy Dawson.** *See under* DAWSON.

**Jemmy Twitcher.** *See under* TWITCHER.

**Je ne sais quoi** (French, 'I don't know what'). An indescribable something; an indefinable quality.

> Francesca da Rimini, miminy, piminy,
> *Je-ne-sais-quoi* young man!
> W.S. GILBERT: *Patience* (1881)

**Jenkins' Ear.** The name given to an incident that helped to provoke war between England and Spain in 1739, a conflict that became merged in the War of the Austrian Succession (1740–8), since Spain and Britain were on opposite sides. Captain Robert Jenkins, of the brig *Rebecca*, claimed to have been attacked by a Spanish coastguard off Havana in 1731, when homeward bound from the West Indies, and declared that his ship had been plundered and his ear severed. When he reached London, he carried his complaint to the king. The case was revived in 1738, and Walpole was forced to yield to the general clamour for war, which was backed by trading interests. The main incidents of this maritime war, basically caused by Spanish interference with British shipping, occasioned by large-scale illicit trading, were Edward Vernon's capture of Portobello (1739) and George Anson's voyage round the world (1740–4).

**Jephthah.** A great judge of ISRAEL (Judges 11, 12). In return for God's promise to defeat the Amorites, Jephthah rashly vows to sacrifice the first person to appear from his tent. When his beloved virgin daughter and only child comes to meet him, he hesitates, but with her encouragement eventually keeps his word. The story formed the basis of oratorios *Jephte* (1650) by Giacomo Carissimi and *Jephtha* (1751) by G.F. Handel.

**Jeremiah.** A doleful prophet, alluding to the 'Lamentations' of Jeremiah, the Old Testament prophet. He is particularly noted for his calls for moral reform and his prophecies of the fall of JERUSALEM TO BABYLON. His lamentations centred on the destruction of Jerusalem.

**Jeremiad.** A pitiful tale, a tale of woe to induce compassion, so called from the 'Lamentations' of JEREMIAH.

**Jerez.** Jerez de la Frontera, in southern Spain, at one time a frontier fortress between Moors and Christians, was the centre that produced the best SACK, which in the early 17th century came to be called sherry, from 'sherris', a word taken to be plural, but actually from Spanish *vino de Xeres*, 'wine of Xeres' (as Jerez was then called). Drake brought home some 3000 butts of Jerez wine when returning from the sack of Cadiz in 1587. *See also* SINGEING THE KING OF SPAIN'S BEARD.

**Jericho.** Used in various phrases to give verbal location to some altogether indefinite place, possibly in allusion to 2 Samuel 10:5 and 1 Chronicles 19:5 ('Tarry at Jericho until your beards be grown').

**Go to Jericho.** The equivalent of 'Go to hell.'

**Rose of Jericho, The.** *See under* ROSE.

**Jerk. Jerked beef.** 'Jerked' here is a corruption of Quechua *echarqui*, meat cut into strips and dried in the sun.

**Jerkwater.** An early American term for a small train on a branch railway, also a small township of little consequence, so generally anything of trifling importance. In such remote places a locomotive had to 'jerk' water from a stream or water tower into its tender. The township became known as a jerk town. Hence 'jerk' as a term for a stupid or dull person. *See also* ONE-HORSE TOWN.

**Jeroboam.** A very large wine bottle, so called in jocular allusion to the 'mighty man of valour' of this name who 'made Israel to sin' (1 Kings 11:28, and 14:16). Its capacity is not very definite but it usually contains the equivalent of four bottles. An English wine bottle contains approximately one-sixth of a gallon or 26⅔ fluid ounces (75 centilitres), also called a reputed quart. *See also* JORUM; MAGNUM; REHOBOAM; TAPPIT-HEN.

**Jerome.** A father of the Western Church, and compiler of the VULGATE (*c*.340–420). He died at Bethlehem and is usually represented as an aged man in a cardinal's dress, writing or studying, with a lion seated beside him. His day is 30 September.

**Jerry** (from 'German'). Since the First World War a nickname for a German or Germans collectively. Also an old colloquialism for a chamber pot, said to allude to the shape of an upturned German helmet.

**Jerry-built.** Cheaply and insubstantially built. The term has been linked with JERICHO (the walls of which came tumbling down) and with a JURY MAST (a temporary, makeshift one). However, it probably comes from the personal name Jerry, which is found in similar phrases denoting an inferior person or thing, such as jerrymumble, to tumble about, Jerry Sneak, a mean, sneaking fellow, and jerry-shop, a cheap beer house. These all existed before jerry-built was first recorded in 1869.

**Jerry can.** A 4½-gallon (20.5-litre) petrol or water container, which would stand rough handling and stack easily, developed by the Germans for the Afrika Korps in the Second World War. It was borrowed by the British in Libya and became the standard unit of fuel replenishment throughout the Allied armies. The name is an allusion to its origin.

**Tom and Jerry.** *See under* TOM.

**Jersey. Jersey Lily, The.** Emily Charlotte Langtry (1852–1929), known as Lillie (or Lily) Langtry, was already so known as a society beauty before she made her début on the professional stage in 1881. A one-time intimate of the Prince of Wales (later Edward VII), she was the wife of Edward Langtry and daughter of W.C. Le Breton, dean of Jersey. After Langtry's death she married Sir Hugo Gerald de Bathe in 1899. The Jersey Museum at St Helier, Jersey, has a three-quarter-length portrait of her by J.E. Millais, executed in 1878, in which she holds a lily in one hand.

**Yellow jersey.** *See under* YELLOW.

**Jerusalem.** ISRAEL's capital has a history more eventful than that of almost any other capital city. It became capital of the Hebrew kingdom after its capture by King DAVID *c*.1000 BC, was destroyed by NEBUCHADNEZZAR in 586 BC, taken by the Romans in 63 BC and devastated in 70 AD and 135 AD during the Jewish rebellions against Rome. After having fallen to the Arabs in 637 and to the Seljuk Turks in 1071, it was ruled by

Crusaders from 1099 to 1187 and by the Egyptians and Turks until conquered by the British in 1917. It was the centre of the British mandate of Palestine from 1920 to 1948, when the Arabs took the old city and the Jews held the new, and was unified under the Israelis after the Six Days' War in 1967. The United Nations does not recognize it as the rightful capital since East Jerusalem is part of the West Bank (Occupied Territories) captured that year.

Its name goes back to a Semitic root word *urushalim*. The meaning of this is uncertain, but it is likely that *uru* means 'house', 'town', and *shalim* means 'peace' (Hebrew *shalom*, from Arabic *salaam*). It is thus probably the 'town of peace', a name that belies its turbulent history.

**Jerusalem artichoke.** Jerusalem is here a corruption of Italian *girasole*, the sunflower, which this vegetable resembles in leaf and stem. *See also* HELIOTROPE; JORDAN ALMOND.

**Jerusalem Bible, The.** *See under* BIBLE.

**Jerusalem Chamber.** This chamber adjoins the south tower of the west front of Westminster Abbey and probably owes its name to the tapestries hung on its walls depicting scenes of Jerusalem. Henry IV died there on 20 March 1413. The WESTMINSTER ASSEMBLY (1643–9) which drew up the Calvinistic WESTMINSTER CONFESSION met in the Jerusalem Chamber, as did the compilers of the Revised Version of the Bible. It is now the chapter room.

**Jerusalem cross.** A CROSS POTENT.

**Jerusalem Delivered.** An Italian epic poem in 20 books by Torquato Tasso (1544–95). It was published in 1581 and translated into English by Edward Fairfax (*c*.1580–1635) in 1600. It tells the story of the First CRUSADE and the capture of Jerusalem by Godfrey of Bouillon in 1099.

**New Jerusalem, The.** *See under* NEW.

**Jesse** or **Jesse tree.** A genealogical tree, usually represented as a large vine or as a large brass candlestick with many branches, tracing the ancestry of Christ, called a 'rod out of the stem of Jesse' (Isaiah 11:1). Jesse is himself sometimes represented in a recumbent position with the vine rising out of his loins. A stained glass window representing him thus with a tree shooting from him containing the pedigree of Jesus is called a Jesse window. Two fine examples are those in the churches of St Mary the Virgin at Shrewsbury and St Laurence at Ludlow.

**Jesse James.** *See under* JAMES.

**Jesters.** *See* COURT FOOLS.

**Jesuits.** The name given to members of the Society of Jesus, begun by IGNATIUS LOYOLA in 1534, and formally approved by Pope Paul III in 1540. The Society was founded to combat the REFORMATION and to propagate the faith among the heathen. Through its discipline, organization and methods of secrecy it acquired such power that it came into conflict with both the civil and religious authorities. It was driven from France in 1594, from Portugal in 1759 and from Spain in 1767, was suppressed by Pope Clement XIV in 1773, but formally reconstituted by Pope Pius VII in 1814.

Because of the casuistical principles maintained by many of its leaders, the name Jesuit acquired an opprobrious sense, so that Jesuitical means 'dissembling', 'equivocating'.

**Jesus.** The founder of the Christian religion, surnamed Christ, 'anointed one'. His name is a Greek form of JOSHUA, so like that name it is of Hebrew origin and means 'JEHOVAH saves'. The meaning is referred to in the New Testament (Matthew 1:21) and is underscored in his title of 'Saviour', which occurs about 30 times in the New Testament. Other titles of Jesus, both prophetically, in the Old Testament, and at present, in the New Testament, are as follows:

Advocate: 1 John 2:1
Alpha and Omega: Revelation 1:8, 22:13
Amen: Revelation 3:14
Author and Finisher of our faith: Hebrews 12:2
Author of eternal salvation: Hebrews 5:9
Beginning of the creation of God: Revelation 3:14
Blessed and only Potentate: 1 Timothy 6:15
Branch: Zechariah 3:8, 6:12
Bread of God: John 6:33
Bread of Life: John 6:35
Bright and morning star: Revelation 22:16
Captain of Salvation: Hebrews 2:10
Corner-stone: Ephesians 2:20, 1 Peter 2:6
Counsellor: Isaiah 9:6
David: Jeremiah 30:9, Ezekiel 34:23, 37:24, Hosea 3:5
Day-spring: Luke 1:78
Day-star: 2 Peter 1:19
Deliverer: Romans 11:26
Desire of all nations: Haggai 2:7
Emmanuel: Isaiah 7:14, Matthew 1:23
Everlasting Father: Isaiah 9:6
Faithful witness: Revelation 1:5, 3:14
First and Last: Revelation 1:17
First begotten: Hebrews 1:6, Revelation 1:5
God: Isaiah 40:9, John 20:28, 1 John 5:20
God blessed for ever: Romans 9:5
Governor: Matthew 2:6
Great shepherd of the sheep: Hebrews 13:20
Head over all things: Ephesians 1:22
Heir of all things: Hebrews 1:2
High Priest: Hebrews 4:14, 5:10
Holy child: Acts 4:27
Holy One: Luke 4:34
Horn of Salvation: Luke 1:69
Image of God: 2 Corinthians 4:4
Just One: Acts 3:14, 7:52, 22:14
King of Israel: John 1:49
King of kings: 1 Timothy 6:15, Revelation 17:14, 19:16
King of the Jews: Matthew 2:2
Lamb of God: John 1:29, 36
Life, The: John 14:6

Light of the World: John 8:12, 9:5
Lion of the Tribe of Judah: Revelation 5:5
Living Stone: 1 Peter 2:4
Lord: Zechariah 14:3, Matthew 3:3, Mark 11:3
Lord God Almighty: Revelation 15:3
Lord of all: Acts 10:36
Lord of glory: 1 Corinthians 2:8
Lord of lords: 1 Timothy 6:15, Revelation 17:14, 19:16
Lord of the holy prophets: Revelation 22:6
Lord our righteousness: Jeremiah 23:6
Maker and Preserver of all things: John 1:3,10, 1 Corinthians 8:6, Colossians 1:16, Hebrews 1:2, 10, Revelation 4:11
Man, The: 1 Timothy 2:5
Mediator: 1 Timothy 2:5, Hebrews 12:24
Messiah: Daniel 9:25, John 1:41
Mighty God: Isaiah 9:6
Morning star: Revelation 22:16
Most holy: Daniel 9:24
My beloved Son: Matthew 3:17, 17:5, Luke 9:35
My fellow: Zechariah 13:7
My servant: Isaiah 52:13
Nazarene: Matthew 2:23
Only-begotten Son: John 1:18, 3:16, 18
Our passover: 1 Corinthians 5:7
Priest for ever: Hebrews 5:6
Prince: Acts 5:31
Prince of Life: Acts 3:15
Prince of Peace: Isaiah 9:6
Prince of the kings of the earth: Revelation 1:5
Prophet: Deuteronomy 18:15, Luke 24:19
Propitiation: Romans 3:25, 1 John 2:2
Redeemer: Job 19:25, Isaiah 59:20
Righteous, The: 1 John 2:1
Root and offspring of David: Revelation 5:5, 22:16
Ruler in Israel: Micah 5:2
Same yesterday, to-day and for ever: Hebrews 13:8
Second Adam, The: 1 Corinthian 15:45, 47
Second man: 1 Corinthians 1547
Shepherd and bishop of souls: 1 Peter 2:25
Shepherd in the land: Zechariah 11:16, 13:7
Shiloh: Genesis 49:10
Son, A: Hebrews 3:6
Son, The: Psalm 2:12
Son of David: Matthew 9:27, 21:9
Son of God: Matthew 8:29, Luke 1:35
Son of Man: Matthew 8:20, John 1:51, Acts 7:56
Son of the Highest: Luke 1:32
Star: Numbers 24:17
Sun of Righteousness: Malachi 4:2
True light: John 1:9, 12:35
Truth: John 14:6
Vine: John 15:1, 5
Way: John 14:6
Wonderful: Isaiah 9:6
Word: John 1:1
Word of God: Revelation 19:13

**Spouse of Jesus, The.** *See under* SPOUSE.

**Jetsam.** Goods cast into the sea to lighten a ship. *See also* FLOTSAM.

**Jeu. Jeu de mots** (French, 'play of words'). A pun, especially an erudite one.

**Jeu d'esprit** (French, 'play of spirit'). A witticism, especially in literature.

**Jeune Cupidon, Le** (French, 'young Cupid'). Count d'Orsay (1801–52), handsome dandy and wit, was so styled by Byron. He was also called Le beau D'ORSAY.

**Jeunesse dorée** (French, 'gilded youth'). Rich and fashionable young people. The expression was originally applied to the fashionable counter-revolutionaries who made their presence felt after the fall of Robespierre in 1794.

**Jew.** A Hebrew, or a person whose religion is Judaism.

**Jewish calendar.** This dates from the Creation, fixed at 3761 BC, and consists of 12 months of 29 and 30 days alternately, with an additional month of 30 days interposed in embolismic (intercalary) years to prevent any great divergence from the months of the solar year. The 3rd, 6th, 11th, 14th, 17th, and 19th years of the METONIC CYCLE are embolismic years. The names of the months are: Nisan, Iyyar, Sivan, Tammuz, Av, Elul, Tishri, Marcheshvan, Kislev, Tevet, Shevat and Adar.

**Jew's ear.** A fungus that grows on the JUDAS TREE. Its name is due to a mistranslation of its Latin name, *Auricula judae*, 'Judas' ear'.

**Jew's harp.** A simple musical instrument held between the teeth and twanged with the hand. The origin of the name is a matter of surmise. A corruption of jaw's harp is unlikely.

**Jew's myrtle.** Butcher's broom (*Ruscus aculeatus*) is so called, from the popular notion that it formed the crown of thorns placed by the Jews on the head of Christ.

**Ebrew Jew.** *See under* EBREW.

**Wandering Jew, The.** *See under* WANDERING.

**Jewels.** *See* PRECIOUS STONES.

**Crown Jewels.** *See under* CROWN.

**Setting of a jewel.** *See under* SET.

**Street jewellery.** *See under* STREET.

**Jezebel.** The infamous wife of AHAB, king of ISRAEL, who was denounced by ELIJAH for bringing in the worship of BAAL. Her name came to be used for a shameless or immoral woman. It is also used for such a woman who applies cosmetics liberally or gaudily, a 'painted Jezebel'.

> And when Jehu was come to Jezreel, Jezebel heard of it; and she painted her face, and tired her head [dressed her hair], and looked out at a window.
> 2 Kings 9:30

**Jezreelites.** A small sect founded in 1875 by James White (1849–85), a one-time army private, who took the name James Jershom Jezreel. Its members were also called the 'New and Latter House of Israel' and believed that Christ redeemed only souls and that the body is saved by belief in the Law. Their object was to be numbered among the 144,000 (Revelation 7:4) who, at the Last Judgement, will be endowed with immortal bodies. Their headquarters were at Gillingham, Kent, where their Tower of Jezreel was formerly a familiar landmark. Jezreel, in the Old

Testament, was the capital of Israel under AHAB. The first son of the prophet HOSEA was also named Jezreel, as a reminder of the bloodshed at Jezreel that brought King Jehu to power.

**Jib, The cut of someone's.** *See under* CUT.

**Jiffy, In a.** In a moment; in an instant. The origin of the word is unknown, but it gave the name to the handy 'Jiffy bag', a type of padded envelope in which books and other articles can be quickly packed for posting.

**Jig** (French *gigue*). A lively tune or dance in 6/8 time.

**Jiggered.** Dashed, damned, blowed, as: 'Well, I'm jiggered!' The word may be a euphemistic form of buggered.

**Jiggery-pokery.** Fraud; trickery. The phrase originated as Scottish dialect *joukery-pawkery*.

**Jill.** *See* JACK AND JILL.

**Jilleroo.** *See* JACKEROO.

**Jim. Jim Crow.** A popular 'NIGGER MINSTREL' song first introduced in Louisville by Thomas D. Rice (Daddy Rice) in 1828. It was brought to the Surrey Theatre, London, in 1836. A renegade or TURNCOAT was called 'Jim Crow', from the song's refrain:

> Wheel about and turn about
> And do jis so,
> Ebry time I wheel about
> I jump Jim Crow.

**Diamond Jim.** *See under* DIAMOND.

**Jimmy.** In the urban dialect of Central Scotland, Jimmy is used as an informal term of address to a stranger, usually (but not always exclusively) a male. James has long been a popular name in Scotland.

**Jimmy the One.** In naval jargon, the First Lieutenant.

**Ten-cent Jimmy.** *See under* TEN.

**Jingo.** A word from the patter and jargon of 17th-century conjurers, probably originating as a euphemistic form of Jesus. *See also* HOCUS POCUS; JINGOISM.

**Jingoism.** Aggressive British 'patriotism', the equivalent of French *chauvinisme*. The term derives from the popular music hall song by G.W. Hunt, which appeared at the time of the Russo-Turkish War (1877–8), when anti-Russian feeling ran high and Disraeli ordered the Mediterranean fleet to Constantinople.

> We don't want to fight, but by Jingo if we do,
> We've got the ships, we've got the men, and got the money too.
> We've fought the Bear before, and while we're Britons true,
> The Russians shall not have Constantinople.

The Russophobes became known as Jingoes, and any belligerent patriotism has been labelled jingoism ever since. *See also* CHAUVINISM.

**Jinks, High.** *See under* HIGH.

**Jinn.** Demons of Arabian mythology fabled to dwell in the mountains of Kâf, which encompass the earth. They were created 2000 years before ADAM and assume the forms of serpents, dogs, cats, monsters and even humans. The evil jinn are hideously ugly, but the good are singularly beautiful. The word is plural, and its singular is jinni or jinnee, with genii as a variant form, influenced by genius in the sense of 'spirit'. *See also* GENIUS.

**Jitter. Jitterbug.** Originally a swing music enthusiast in the late 1930s, with the name probably coming from Cab Calloway's song 'Jitter bug' (1934), in which a 'jitter bug' was a person who drank regularly and so 'has the jitters ev'ry morning'. The name passed to a person who danced the jitterbug, a fast, twirling, whirling American dance to a JAZZ accompaniment, popular in the 1940s. Hence also more generally, a nervous person, one who 'has the jitters'.

**Have the jitters, To.** A phrase of North American origin meaning to be nervously apprehensive, to be 'on edge'. Jittery is nervous or jumpy.

**Jive.** A type of fast, lively JAZZ, or the jerky dancing to it, popular in the 1920s and revived, to rock and roll, in the 1940s and 1950s. Hand jive, with synchronized movement of the hands and forearms, was a British development of it, as seen, for example, in the popular television series *Rock Follies* (1976–7). Jive talk is the specialized vocabulary of its adepts. In Black American English jive originally meant 'misleading talk'.

**Jix.** The nickname of Sir William Joynson-Hicks, 1st Viscount Brentford (1865–1932), noted puritan and tactless speaker. He was Home Secretary (1924–9), and was prominent in defeating the adoption of the Revised Prayer Book of 1928.

> We mean to tread the Primrose Path,
> In spite of Mr Joynson-Hicks.
> We're People of the Aftermath
> We're girls of 1926.
>
> JACQUES REVAL: *The Woman of 1926*, 'Mother's Advice on Father's Fears' (1926)

**Joab.** The nephew of King DAVID, and his most successful general and staunchest ally. His career was built on the cornerstone of his capture of JERUSALEM for David, so enabling his uncle to extend his power northwards and combat the PHILISTINES in the south. His story is told in 2 Samuel 2–3.

**Joachim.** The father of the Virgin MARY, generally represented as an old man carrying two turtle doves in a basket, an allusion to the offering made for the purification of his daughter. His wife was St Anne.

**Joan. Joan of Arc.** The Maid of Orleans (La Pucelle d'Orléans) (1412–31) was born at Domrémy in Lorraine, the daughter of a peasant. She was directed by heavenly voices to undertake her mission to deliver France, then undergoing the ravages of the HUNDRED YEARS' WAR. She convinced the DAUPHIN of her sincerity, donned male dress and inspired the French army in the relief of Orleans (1429) and then the advance to Rheims. She was captured by the Burgundians at Compiègne (May 1430) and sold to the English by the Count of Luxembourg for 10,000 livres. She was condemned to death by the bishop of Beauvais for WITCHCRAFT and heresy and burned at the stake at Rouen (30 May 1431). Her last words were the name of Jesus repeated thrice. She was canonized in 1920 as the second patron of France but is not recognized as such by the state. (There has been no official patron saint of France since the separation of church and state in 1905.) She has become a figure almost as popular in England as in her native France, and has been the subject of an impressive range of novels, plays, films and studies. *See also* ARMOISES.

> *Joan*: I could do without my warhorse; I could drag about in a skirt; I could let the banners and the trumpets and the knights and soldiers pass me and leave me behind as they leave the other women, if only I could still hear the wind in the trees, the larks in the sunshine, the young lambs crying through the healthy frost, and the blessed blessed church bells that send my angel voices floating to me on the wind. But without these things I cannot live; and by your wanting to take them away from me, or from any human creature, I know that your counsel is of the devil, and that mine is of God.
> GEORGE BERNARD SHAW: *Saint Joan*, VI (1924)

**Darby and Joan.** *See under* DARBY.

**Pope Joan.** A mythical female pope first recorded in the 13th century by the Dominican Stephen de Bourbon (d.*c.*1261) who is said to have derived the story from Jean de Mailly. It was widely and long accepted. She was said to have been born in Germany of English parents and eventually went to Rome after living with a monk at Athens. Passing under the name of Johannes Anglicus, her wide learning gained her election to the papacy in 855 as John VIII. After reigning more than two years, she is said to have died in childbirth during a solemn procession. The Calvinist scholar David Blondel exploded the myth in 1647 and it was again demolished in 1863, when the Bavarian Church historian Ignaz von Döllinger explained it as an ancient Roman folk-tale.

Pope Joan is also the name of a once popular card game played with an ordinary pack minus the eight of diamonds (the nine of diamonds is called the 'pope'). The term has also been used for a circular revolving tray with eight compartments.

**Joanna Southcott.** *See* SOUTHCOTTIANS.

**Job.** The personification of poverty and patience, in allusion to the PATRIARCH whose history is given in the Old Testament book named after him. He is a pious man who is sent terrible afflictions by God to test the strength of his piety. Although he loses his wealth, family and friends, and suffers a painful disease, he refuses to 'curse God and die'. Ultimately everything is restored to him.

> I am as poor as Job, my lord, but not so patient.
> SHAKESPEARE: *Henry IV*, *Pt II*, I, ii (1597)

*See also* AS POOR AS JOB.

**Job's comforter.** A person who means to sympathize with you in your grief but says that you brought it on yourself and so adds to your sorrow. The allusion is to the rebukes Job received from his friends.

> I have heard many such things: miserable comforters are ye all.
> Job 16:2

**As poor as Job.** *See under* AS.

**Job. Job lot, A.** A collection of miscellaneous goods, sold as one lot and usually bought at a low price.

**Job satisfaction.** The factor in one's work that brings fulfilment to one's hopes and desires.

**Jobs for the boys.** A form of favouritism giving jobs and appointments to friends and acquaintances or through the OLD BOY NETWORK, regardless of their qualifications or ability and not by fair and open competition. *See also* NEPOTISM.

**Jobsworth.** A minor official who insists on the letter of the law being applied in all cases, however unreasonable or unsympathetic this may seem. He dare not deviate or accommodate, because 'It's more than my job's worth'.

**Bad job.** *See under* BAD.

**Bob-a-Job Week.** *See under* BOB.

**Coggeshall job.** *See under* COGGESHALL.

**Good job.** *See under* GOOD.

**Hatchet job.** *See under* HATCHET.

**Just the job.** Exactly what is needed or required.

**Make a clean job of it, To.** *See under* CLEAN.

**Make the best of a bad job, To.** To do what one can with the materials, facilities or opportunities available.

**Nine-to-five job.** *See under* NINE.

**On the job.** Actively at work; engaged in sexual intercourse.

**Snow job.** *See under* SNOW.

**Jocasta.** *See* OEDIPUS.

**Jock.** A popular nickname for a Scotsman. It is a Scots form of the name Jack, here perhaps associated with JACQUES as the French equivalent of the common Scottish name James rather than with John, as more usually. Many Scots object to the name and do not call their children thus.

**Jockey.** Properly 'a little JOCK'.

**Jockey Club.** The select body which controls the English TURF. Its headquarters are at

Newmarket. It arose from a group of 'noblemen and gentlemen' who first met in 1750 at the Star and Garter COFFEE house in PALL MALL to remedy the abuses at Newmarket. It also controls the *General Stud Book* and, since 1902, the *Racing Calendar*. Its French counterpart was formed in 1833 and the American Jockey Club in 1880.

**Jockey for position, To.** To manoeuvre for position, literally or figuratively, as in a horse race.

**Jockey of Norfolk.** Sir John Howard (*c.*1430–85), the first Howard to be Duke of Norfolk, and a firm adherent of Richard III. On the night before the Battle of Bosworth, where he was slain, he found in his tent the warning couplet:

> Jockey of Norfolk, be not too bold,
> For Dickon thy master is bought and sold.

**Jodhpurs.** In the 1860s the maharajah of the Rajputana state of Jodhpur was an extreme devotee of polo which he played in breeches that were tight-fitting by the ankle and loose-fitting above. British army officers exported the game and the breeches to England.

**Joe.** American slang for the man in the street, and as a form of address for someone whose name is unknown. GI Joe was also applied to an American soldier. *See also* JACK.

**Joe Bloggs.** The average British man. His American equivalent is Joe Blow or Joe Six-Pack.

**Joe Muggins.** A simpleton or a dupe. *See also* MUG.

**Joe Public.** The general British public.

> Every journalist ought to be turned over by his rivals once in a while. ... It makes you understand just how Joe Public feels when he is monstered by us.
> *The Times* (15 January 1999)

**Joe Soap.** A person who is imposed on, as a stooge or innocent.

**Joey.** The small silver GROAT struck between 1836 and 1855 at the suggestion of Joseph Hume, MP (1777–1855), who advocated their usefulness for paying small cab fares and so on. The name was later sometimes applied to the silver threepenny piece.

In Australia a young kangaroo is called a joey.

**Holy Joe.** *See under* HOLY.

**Uncle Joe.** *See under* UNCLE.

**Vinegar Joe.** *See under* VINEGAR.

**Joel.** The prophet whose colourful warnings of disasters are set forth in the brief Old Testament book named after him.

**John.** The English form of Latin and Greek *Johannes*, from Hebrew *Yōhānān*, meaning God has forgiven'. The feminine form, Johanna or Joanna, is nearer the original. The French equivalent of the name is Jean (formerly Jehan), the Italian Giovanni, Russian Ivan, Gaelic Ian, Irish Sean or Shaun, Welsh Evan, German Johann or Johannes, which is contracted to Jan, Jahn and Hans.

For many centuries John has been one of the most popular of masculine names in England, probably because it is that of St JOHN THE EVANGELIST, St JOHN THE BAPTIST and other saints.

The name John has been used by popes more than any other, its last holder being John XXIII, elected in 1958. There have since been two popes John-Paul. Famous bearers of the name in English history are King John of England (*c.*1167–1216), John of Salisbury (1115 or 1120–80), supporter of Thomas à Becket against Henry II, and John of Gaunt (1340–99), fourth son of Edward III. John is also an American slang term for a lavatory, perhaps originating as a pun on JAKES.

**John Anderson, my Jo.** Burns' well-known poem (1790) is founded on an 18th-century version given in PERCY'S RELIQUES (1765) and is said to have been sung in derision of a Catholic Latin hymn. (Jo is an old Scottish word for a sweetheart.) The first verse is:

> John Anderson my jo, cum in as ze gae bye,
> And ze zall get a sheip's heid weel baken in a pye;
> Weel baken in a pye, and the haggis in a pat;
> John Anderson my jo, cum in, and ze's get that.

**John-a-Nokes** and **John-a-Stiles.** Names formerly given, instead of the impersonal 'A and B', to fictitious persons in an imaginary action at law. Hence either may stand for 'just anybody'. The names themselves mean 'John (who dwells) at the oak' and 'John (who dwells) at the stile'. *See also* STYLES, TOM.

> And doth the Lawyer lye then, when vnder the names of Iohn a stile and Iohn a noakes, hee puts his case?
> SIR PHILIP SIDNEY: *An Apologie for Poetry* (1595)

**John Barleycorn.** A personification of malt liquor. The term was popularized by Burns.

> Inspiring bold John Barleycorn,
> What dangers thou canst make us scorn!
> 'Tam o'Shanter' (1791)

**John Birch Society.** A reactionary American organization founded in 1958 to combat Communism. It was named after John Birch, a Baptist missionary and US Army Intelligence officer killed by Chinese Communists in 1945, and regarded by the Society as the first hero of the Cold War.

**John Brown.** An American ABOLITIONIST (1800–59) who on 16 October 1859 led a body of men to free Negro slaves at HARPERS FERRY, Virginia, and who was subsequently executed for treason. The Union song of the Civil War (1861–5), 'John Brown's Body', made him a legend. It arose among the soldiers at Fort Warren, Boston, in 1861, around Sergeant John Brown of their regiment, who was jokingly connected with the 'martyr' of Harpers Ferry.

**John Bull.** The nickname for an Englishman or Englishmen collectively. The name was used in Dr John Arbuthnot's satire, *Law is a Bottomless Pit* (1712), republished as *The History of John Bull*. Arbuthnot did not invent the name but established it.

**John Collins.** A long drink of gin, lemon or lime and soda water, sugar and a lump of ice. Curaçao is sometimes added. The name is perhaps that of the bartender who originally dispensed it. In the USA it is called a Tom Collins.

**John Company.** The old Honourable East India Company. It is said that John is a perversion of 'Hon', but it is possible that the name is allied to the familiar JOHN BULL. The Company was founded in 1600 and finally abolished in 1858.

**John Doe.** *See under* DOE.

**John Dory.** A golden yellow fish, *Zeus faber*, common in the Mediterranean and around the southwestern coasts of Britain. Its name was dory (French *doré*, 'golden') long before John was added. There is a tradition that it was from this fish that St PETER took the stater or shekel (Matthew 17:27). It has an oval black spot on each side, said to be his fingermarks when he held the fish to extract the coin. It is called in France the *saint-pierre*. *See also* HADDOCK.

**John Gilpin.** *See under* GILPIN.

**John Hancock.** American slang for one's own signature, derived from the fact that John Hancock (1737–93), the first of the signatories to the Declaration of Independence (1776), had an especially large and clear signature.

**John Knox cap.** An early form of the TRENCHER CAP, MORTARBOARD or COLLEGE CAP, worn at the Scottish universities.

**John of Gaunt.** The fourth son (1340–99) of Edward III, so called from his birthplace, Ghent in Flanders.

**John o'Groats.** The site of a legendary house 1¾ miles (2.8km) west of Duncansby Head, Caithness, northeastern Scotland. The story is that Malcolm, Gavin and John o' Groat (or Jan de Groot), three Dutch brothers, came to this part of Scotland in the time of James IV (r.1488–1513). There came to be eight families of the name, and they met annually to celebrate. On one occasion a question of precedence arose. Consequently John o'Groat built an eight-sided room with a door to each side and set an octagonal table in it so that all were 'head of the table'. This building went ever after with the name of John o'Groat's House. *See also* FROM LAND'S END TO JOHN O'GROATS.

**John Shorne.** *See under* SHORNE.

**Blue John.** *See under* BLUE.

**Dear John.** *See under* DEAR.

**From Land's End to John o'Groats.** *See under* FROM.

**General John.** *See under* GENERAL.

**Little John.** *See under* LITTLE.

**Long johns.** *See under* LONG.

**Long John Silver.** *See under* LONG.

**Prester John.** *See under* PRESTER.

**St John Chrysostom** (Greek *khrusostomos*, 'golden-tongued'). Bishop of Constantinople and one of the DOCTORS OF THE CHURCH (*c*.347–407). St John did much to purify the life of his see. He was banished by his enemies in 403 and died in exile. He was noted for his holiness and liturgical reforms. His day is 13 September (formerly 27 January).

**St John Damascene** ('of Damascus'). A DOCTOR OF THE CHURCH (*c*.675–*c*.749) and a defender of images during the ICONOCLAST controversy. His day is 4 December (formerly 27 March).

**St John Lateran.** This church, which is called the Mother and Head of all Churches, is the cathedral church of Rome. It occupies part of the site of the old Lateran palace.

**St John of Beverley.** Bishop of Hexham and subsequently archbishop of York (*c*.640–721). The VENERABLE BEDE was one of his pupils. His healing gifts are recorded by his biographers, and his shrine at Beverley Minster, which he founded, became a favourite resort of pilgrims. His day is 7 May.

**St John of God.** Patron (1495–1550) of hospitals, nurses and the sick, and a native of Portugal. In Ireland he is also held popularly to be the patron of alcoholics, through association with the Dublin clinic devoted to their cure and bearing his name. He founded the Order of Charity for the Service of the Sick or Brothers Hospitallers. His day is 8 March.

**St John of Nepomuk.** Patron saint (*c*.1340–93) of Bohemia, he was drowned by order of the dissolute King Wenceslas IV (r.1378–1400), allegedly because he refused to reveal to the king the confessions of the queen. His day is 16 May.

**St John of the Cross.** Founder (1542–91) of the Discalced CARMELITES under the influence of St TERESA OF AVILA. He is noted for his mystical writings, *The Ascent of Mount Carmel*, *The Dark Night of the Soul*, *The Spiritual Canticle* and so on. He was canonized in 1726, and his feast-day is 14 December.

**St John the Baptist.** The forerunner of Jesus, who was sent 'to prepare the way of the Lord'. His day is 24 June, and he is represented in a coat of sheepskin (in allusion to his life in the desert), either holding a rude wooden cross with a pennon bearing the words, *Ecce Agnus Dei* ('Behold the Lamb of God'), or with a book on which a lamb is seated, or holding in his right hand a lamb surrounded by a HALO, and bearing a cross on the right foot.

**St John the Evangelist** or **the Divine.** The 'beloved disciple'. Tradition says that he took the Virgin MARY to Ephesus after the crucifixion and that in the persecution of Domitian (AD 93–96) he was plunged into a cauldron of boiling oil but was delivered unharmed. Afterwards he was banished to the Isle of Patmos where he wrote the Book of Revelation. He died at Ephesus. His day is 27 December, and he is usually represented bearing a chalice with a snake coming out of it, in allusion to his removing the poison from a cup presented to him to drink.

**Sir John Mandeville.** *See under* MANDEVILLE.

**Johnnie Cope** or **Hey, Johnnie Cope.** This Scottish song celebrates the YOUNG PRETENDER'S victory at Prestonpans (20 September 1745). Sir John Cope (d.1760), who led the Government troops, was surprised by the Highlanders at daybreak and routed. He escaped and brought the news of his own defeat to BERWICK.

> Hey, Johnnie Cope, are ye wauking yet?
> Or are ye sleeping, I would wit?
> Oh, haste ye, get up, for the drums do beat!
> O fye, Cope, rise in the morning.

The Scots attacked before the English were awake.

**Johnny.** A general word used for a man or boy, a 'chap'.

**Johnny-cake.** An American name for a cake made of maize-meal, once much esteemed as a delicacy. It is said to be a corruption of journey-cake. In Australia, the cake of this name is made of wheatmeal.

**Johnny-come-lately.** A brash newcomer; a recent arrival.

**Johnny Crapaud** or **Crapaud.** A Frenchman, literally 'Johnny Toad'. *See also* FLEUR-DE-LIS.

**Johnny-Head-in-Air.** A dreamy fellow. 'The Story of Johnny-Head-in-Air' is one of the tales in the English version of STRUWWELPETER.

> Do not despair
> For Johnny-head-in-air;
> He sleeps as sound
> As Johnny Underground.
> JOHN PUDNEY: *Dispersal Point* (1942)

**Johnny Raw.** A raw recruit; a 'new chum'; a GREENHORN.

**Johnny Reb.** In the American Civil War (1861–5) a Federal name for a CONFEDERATE soldier, 'a rebel' from the Northern standpoint.

**Johnson, Pussyfoot.** W.E. Johnson (1862–1945), the temperance advocate, gained his nickname from his 'cat-like' policies in pursuing law breakers in gambling saloons and elsewhere in Indian territory when serving as Chief Special Officer of the US Indian Service (1908–11). After this he devoted his energies to the cause of prohibition and gave over 4000 lectures on temperance.

**Join** or **take issue, To.** To dispute or take opposite views of a question, or opposite sides in a suit.

**Joint.** In American slang, originally a sordid place where illicit spirits were drunk, and hence any cheap restaurant, place of low entertainment or the like.

**Joint committee.** A committee nominated by the HOUSE OF LORDS and the HOUSE OF COMMONS, in practice a SELECT COMMITTEE of the Commons, which meets a Select Committee of the Lords.

**Case a joint, To.** *See under* CASE.

**Clip joint.** *See under* CLIP.

**Out of joint.** *See under* OUT.

**Put someone's nose out of joint, To.** *See under* NOSE.

**Joke. Joker.** A playing card with a figure of a medieval court jester, used in many games as a WILD CARD. The standard pack of 52 cards usually contains two jokers.

> In the play ace may be high or low, as desired, and the jokers, of course, take any denomination the holder wishes.
> *Hoyle's Games Modernized* ('Coon-can') (1950)

**Dirty joke.** *See under* DIRTY.

**Sick joke.** *See under* SICK.

**Standing joke.** *See under* STAND.

**Jolly.** A sailor's nickname for a MARINE. A militiaman was a 'tame jolly'.

> But to stand and be still to the *Birken'ead* drill is a damn' tough bullet to chew,
> An' they done it, the Jollies, – 'Er Majesty's Jollies – soldier an' sailor too!
> RUDYARD KIPLING: 'Soldier an' Sailor Too' (1896)

**Jolly boat.** A small clinker-built ship's boat, or any small sailing boat used for pleasure. Jolly is probably the Danish *jolle*, English yawl.

**Jolly good fellow, A.** A sociable or generally popular person. A common chorus to a toast is the following, with each line except the last repeated three times:

> For he's a jolly good fellow,
> And so say all of us,
> For he's a jolly good fellow,
> And so say all of us!

**Jolly Roger, The.** The black flag with white SKULL AND CROSSBONES; the pirate flag. Roger was originally thieves' cant for a thief or beggar, perhaps based on 'rogue'. Other accounts of the name are not tenable, such as a source in French *joli rouge*, 'beautiful red' or in an Indian pirate named Ali Rajah, whom British sailors supposedly called 'Olly Roger'.

**Jonah.** A person whose presence brings misfortune upon his companions as did Jonah to his fellow mariners. God had sent him to preach at

Nineveh, but he took ship to Tarshish to 'flee from the presence of the Lord' (Jonah 1). A storm arises, and the other sailors attribute it to Jonah's presence. They throw him overboard to be rid of him, and he is swallowed by a great fish, traditionally thought of as a whale. When released, after three days and three nights, he preached so well that Nineveh repented and was spared. Jonas is an alternative name for him.

**Jonah's gourd.** This plant (*see* Jonah 4:6–10) was most probably the bottle gourd, *Lagenaria vulgaris*. It was often planted near such booths as the one in which JONAH sat. It is a very rapid grower and its broad leaves give plenty of shade. It is much more likely that it was a vine of this type than the castor-oil plant, as has been suggested by some.

**Jonathan.** In the Old Testament (1 Samuel), the son of SAUL. His close relationship with DAVID gave 'David and Jonathan' as a synonym for an intimate friendship. Jonathan was eventually killed in battle, as a result of which Saul committed suicide. *See also* BROTHER JONATHAN.

**Jonathan's.** A noted COFFEE house in Change Alley described in the *Tatler* as the general mart of stockjobbers. In 1773 those brokers who used Jonathan's moved to premises in Sweating's Alley, which came to be known as the STOCK EXCHANGE coffee house. In 1801 they raised capital to build the Stock Exchange in CAPEL COURT.

**Brother Jonathan.** *See under* BROTHER.

**David and Jonathan.** *See under* DAVID.

**Jones. Davy Jones.** *See under* DAVY.

**Keep up with the Joneses, To.** *See under* KEEP.

**Paul Jones.** *See under* PAUL.

**Potato Jones.** *See under* POTATO.

**Jongleur.** A medieval minstrel who recited verses to his own musical accompaniment. They wandered from castle to castle, performing the CHANSONS DE GESTE, and are linked with the TROUBADOURS. The word is related to English JUGGLER, and is from Old French *jogleour*, from Latin *joculator*, 'joker'.

**Jordan.** A name formerly given to the pot used by alchemists and doctors, then transferred to a chamber pot. It was perhaps originally Jordan-bottle, i.e. a bottle in which pilgrims and crusaders brought back water from the River Jordan.

> Why, they will allow us ne'er a jordan, and then we leak in the chimney; and your chamber-lie breeds fleas like a loach.
>
> SHAKESPEARE: *Henry IV, Pt I*, II, i (1597)

**Jordan almond.** Here Jordan has nothing to do with the river but is a corruption of French *jardin*, 'garden'. The Jordan almond is a fine variety that comes chiefly from Malaga. *See also* JERUSALEM ARTICHOKE.

**Jorum.** A large drinking bowl, intended especially for PUNCH. The name is thought to be connected with King Joram, who 'brought with him vessels of silver, and vessels of gold, and vessels of brass' (2 Samuel 8:10). *See also* JEROBOAM; MAGNUM; REHOBOAM; TAPPIT-HEN.

**Josaphat.** *See* BARLAAM AND JOSAPHAT.

**Joseph.** The son of JACOB and RACHEL (Genesis 30:24). His mother had long been barren, and spoiled him in childhood. This caused much jealousy from his brothers, especially when he was given a coat of many colours (Genesis 37:3). His brothers threw him in a well, telling Jacob he had been killed, and then sold him into slavery in Egypt. He served POTIPHAR there until Potiphar's wife accused him of attempted rape. In prison he interpreted Pharaoh's dream, as a consequence of which he was promoted to become Pharaoh's adviser and chief administrator. Long after, his brothers came to Egypt seeking aid, and he gave it to them, forgiving them and welcoming all their families.

A person who cannot be seduced from continence by the severest temptation is sometimes so called. The reference is to Joseph in Potiphar's house (Genesis 39). *See also* BELLEROPHON.

A woman's floor-length riding coat used to be known as a joseph, in allusion to the coat of many colours. The coat has provided inspiration for various artistic works, such as Andrew Lloyd Webber and Tim Rice's children's musical, *Joseph and the Amazing Technicolor Dreamcoat* (1968).

> Olivia would be drawn as an Amazon, dressed in a green joseph, richly laced with gold, and a whip in her hand.
>
> OLIVER GOLDSMITH: *The Vicar of Wakefield*, ch xvi (1766)

**Joseph Grimaldi.** *See under* GRIMALDI.

**St Joseph.** Husband of the Virgin MARY and the lawful father of Jesus. He is patron saint of carpenters, because he was of that craft. Joseph is represented in art as an aged man with a budding staff in his hand. His day is 19 March, and in 1955 Pope Pius XII instituted the feast of St Joseph the Workman on 1 May.

**St Joseph of Arimathea.** The rich Jew, probably a member of the SANHEDRIN, who believed in Christ, but feared to confess it, and, after the crucifixion, begged the body of Jesus and deposited it in his own tomb. His day is 17 March. Legend relates that he was imprisoned for 12 years and was kept alive miraculously by the HOLY GRAIL, and that on his release by Vespasian, *c*.63, he brought the Grail and the spear with which LONGINUS wounded the crucified Christ to Britain, founded the abbey of GLASTONBURY and commenced the conversion of Britain.

**Josephine.** Joséphine de Beauharnais, *née* Marie Josèphe Rose Tascher de la Pagerie (1763–1814), was born in Martinique and in 1779 married as her first husband the Vicomte de Beauharnais, who was executed in 1794. Two years later she married NAPOLEON BONAPARTE and accompanied him on his Italian campaign, but soon returned to Paris. He divorced her in 1809 in order to make a dynastic marriage with Austria, citing their childless marriage as a legitimate ground for the dissolution.

> Not tonight, Josephine.
> DAVID WORTON and LAWRENCE WRIGHT: song title (1915)

**Josephus.** Flavius Josephus (*c*.37–*c*.100), the celebrated Jewish historian and PHARISEE, took a prominent part in the last Jewish revolt against the Romans (66–70) and later wrote his *History of the Jewish War*. According to his own account, his prophecy that Vespasian, the captor of JERUSALEM, would become emperor of Rome, saved his life. The most important of his other writings was his *Jewish Antiquities*, dealing with the history of the Jews down to the end of Nero's reign.

**Joshua.** The leader of the Israelites after the death of MOSES. He brings them to the PROMISED LAND, defeats the city of Jericho, where the walls come tumbling down after his men blow their trumpets, and defeats the Amorites while the sun stands still. Exodus and Joshua recount his exploits.

**Josiah.** The king of JUDAH (2 Kings 22–23) who destroys the idols and re-establishes a strict observance of religious laws.

**Joss.** A Chinese god or idol. The word is probably a PIDGIN ENGLISH corruption of Portuguese *deos*, Latin *deus*, 'god'. A temple is called a joss house, and a joss stick is a stick made from clay mixed with the powder of various scented woods burned as incense.

**Jot.** A very little, the least possible bit, as: 'I don't care a jot.' The iota, (*see* I), is the smallest letter of the Greek alphabet.

**Jot or tittle.** A tiny amount. The jot is , or iota, and the tittle, from Medieval Latin *titulus*, 'label', is the mark or dot over the i.

> Till heaven and earth pass, one jot or one tittle shall in no wise pass from the law, till all be fulfilled.
> Matthew 5:18

**Jotunheim** (Old Norse *jötunnheimr*, 'giants' home'). The land of the Scandinavian GIANTS.

**Jourdain, Monsieur.** A bourgeois whose wealth has elevated him to the ranks of gentlemen and who makes himself ridiculous by his endeavours to acquire their accomplishments. The character is from MOLIÈRE'S *Le Bourgeois Gentilhomme* (1671). He is chiefly remembered for his delight in discovering that, whereas some write poetry, he himself had been speaking prose all his life.

**Journal** (Old French, from Latin *diurnalis*, 'daily', from *dies*, 'day'). As applied to newspapers, the word strictly means a daily paper, but it has come to be used of any periodical. *See also* JOURNEY.

**Journalism, Chequebook.** *See under* CHEQUE.

**Journey** (Old French *journee*, 'day'). The word originally applied to a day's travel, which in medieval times was usually reckoned as 20 miles (32km). It later came to apply to travel of any length of time from one place to another. *See also* BREAK A JOURNEY.

**Journeyman.** The name was originally used for a worker who was hired by the day (Old French *journee*), but later came to be used of any competent worker, especially a craftsman or artisan. *See also* JOURNEY.

**Break a journey, To.** *See under* BREAK.

**Sabbath day's journey.** *See under* SABBATH.

**Jousts, The Diamond.** *See under* DIAMOND.

**Jove.** Another name of JUPITER, from *Jovis pater*, 'father Jove'. Milton, in *Paradise Lost* (1667), makes Jove one of the fallen angels. *See also* EAGLE; OLYMPIAN JOVE; SUB JOVE.

**Jovial.** Merry and sociable, like those born under the planet JUPITER, which astrologers considered the happiest of the natal stars. *See also* SATURNINE.

**Jowl, Cheek by.** *See under* CHEEK.

**Joy. Joyride.** A pleasure ride in a car, especially a stolen one.

**Joystick.** The control column of an aircraft, which is linked to the elevators and ailerons. It is so nicknamed from the great pleasure and 'kicks' it gives to the pilot who operates it.

**Five joyful mysteries, The.** *See under* FIVE.

**Jump for joy, To.** *See under* JUMP.

**No joy.** *See under* NO.

**Seven joys of Mary, The.** *See under* SEVEN.

**Traveller's joy.** *See under* TRAVELLER.

**Juan. Juan Fernandez.** *See* CRUSOE, ROBINSON.

**Don Juan.** Don Juan Tenorio, the legendary hero of many plays, poems, stories and operas, was the son of a notable family in 14th-century Seville. The story is that he killed the commandant of Ulloa after seducing his daughter. He then invited the statue of the murdered man (erected in the FRANCISCAN convent) to a feast, at the end of which the sculptured figure delivered him to hell. He is represented as an archetypal philanderer.

He was introduced into literature by Tirso de Molina's play *El Burlador de Sevilla* ('The Seducer of Seville') (1635), and subsequently made notable appearances, with different aspects of his personality stressed, in Molière's play *Don Juan* (1665), Mozart's opera *Don Giovanni* (1787), and Byron's poem *Don Juan*

(1819). In the latter he is an innocent young man seduced by women who will not leave him alone and a man who would be honourable if only a depraved, 'civilized' society offered any honourable options.

**Jubilate** (Latin, 'make a joyful noise'). The name given to two psalms (65 and 99), which begin with this word in the VULGATE. In the English psalter they are Psalms 66 and 100.

**Jubilate Sunday.** The third Sunday after EASTER, when the introit at the MASS begins with two verses of the first of the JUBILATE psalms.

**Jubilee.** In Jewish history the year of jubilee was every 50th year, which was held sacred in commemoration of the deliverance from Egypt. In this year the fields were allowed to lie fallow, land that had passed out of the possession of those to whom it originally belonged was restored to them, and all who had been obliged to let themselves out for hire were released from bondage. The jubilee was proclaimed with trumpets made from ram's horn (*see* Leviticus 25:11–34, 39–54 and 27:17–24). The word actually comes from Hebrew *yōvhēl*, 'ram's horn', but was influenced by Latin *jubilare*, 'to shout for joy'. *See also* JUBILATE.

Jubilee subsequently came to apply to any 50th anniversary, especially one marked with great celebration, and was extended to a 25th anniversary or in some cases to one marking any number of years. George III's Jubilee was on 25 October 1809, the day before the commencement of the 50th year of his reign. Queen Victoria celebrated her Jubilee on 21 June 1887, and marked her Diamond Jubilee ten years later. George V celebrated the 25th year of his accession by a Silver Jubilee on 6 May 1935. Elizabeth II's Silver Jubilee was celebrated on 7 June 1977. If still reigning, she will mark her full Jubilee in 2002.

In the ROMAN CATHOLIC CHURCH Pope Boniface VIII instituted a jubilee in 1300 and INDULGENCES were granted to pilgrims visiting Rome. It was to be held at intervals of 100 years but in 1343 Clement VI altered it to 50 years and in 1389 Urban IV to 33. In 1470 Paul II reduced the interval to 25 years. The jubilee is the only occasion when the Porta Santa (HOLY DOOR) of St Peter's, Rome is opened. Pilgrimage to Rome ceased to be obligatory in 1500. A jubilee is also known as a Holy Year, and extends from Christmas to Christmas.

**Diamond Jubilee.** *See under* DIAMOND.

**Judah.** A son of JACOB and LEAH, and the father of one of the TWELVE TRIBES OF ISRAEL. When the Israelites divide into two kingdoms, this tribe dominates the southern one, which is named after him.

**Judas. Judas Bible, The.** *See under* BIBLE.

**Judas-coloured hair.** Fiery red. In the Middle Ages JUDAS ISCARIOT was represented with red hair and beard.

> *Rosalind*: His very hair is of the dissembling colour.
> *Celia*: Something browner than Judas's: marry, his kisses are Judas's own children.
> SHAKESPEARE: *As You Like It*, III, iv (1599)

**Judas' ear.** *See* JEW'S EAR.

**Judas Iscariot.** The apostle who betrays Jesus to the religious authorities for 30 pieces of silver (Matthew 26:15), covertly identifying Him by kissing Him in the Garden of GETHSEMANE. He bitterly repents his betrayal and returns the silver, but then hangs himself (or according to Acts 1:18 was disembowelled). His name is conventionally used for any traitor. The precise meaning of Iscariot is disputed. It may mean 'man of Keriot', this being a place identified with Kerioth (Joshua 15:25). Alternatively, it may simply mean 'false', from an Aramaic word.

**Judas kiss.** A deceitful act of courtesy or simulated affection. JUDAS betrayed Jesus with a kiss (Matthew 26:49).

**Judas Maccabeus.** The best known member of the family whose Jewish rebellions against the Syrians are recounted in 1 and 2 Maccabees in the Apocrypha. The recapture of JERUSALEM by Judas is celebrated in the festival of HANUKKAH. The Maccabees also led several unsuccessful revolts against the Romans.

**Judas tree.** A tree of southern Europe (*Cercis siliquastrum*), which flowers before the leaves appear, so called from a Greek tradition that Judas hanged himself on such a tree. The ELDER TREE is sometimes also so named. The American Judas tree is the *Cercis canadensis* or red-bud. *See also* JEW'S EAR *under* JEW.

**Judas window** or **hole.** A peephole in a prison door, which the warder uses to check on the prisoners.

**Jude.** One of the 12 apostles, the brother of James (i.e. Jesus' brother), also identified as brother of JAMES THE LESS. He is represented in art with a club or staff, and a carpenter's square in allusion to his trade. His day, 28 October, coincides with that of St SIMON, with whom he suffered martyrdom in Persia. He is the author of the Epistle of Jude and nowadays is regarded as the patron of hopeless causes. Hence personal advertisements thanking him when a wished-for matter has been happily resolved.

**Judge. Judge's black cap.** *See* BLACK CAP.

**Judge's robes.** In the English criminal courts, where the judges represent the sovereign, they appear in full court dress, and wear a scarlet robe, but in NISI PRIUS courts the judge sits merely to balance the law between citizens, and therefore appears in his judicial undress or violet gown.

**Judges' rules.** Rules concerning the questioning of suspects by the police and the taking of statements. They were first formulated in 1912, revised in 1918 and reformulated in 1964. They were superseded by the provisions regarding the detention, treatment and questioning of persons by the police contained in the Police and Criminal Evidence Act of 1984, Part V, and the Secretary of State's Code of Practice.

**As sober as a judge.** *See under* AS.

**Puisne judges.** *See under* PUISNE.

**Judgement. Judgement by default.** A verdict given when the defendant does not appear in court on the day appointed. The judge gives sentence in favour of the plaintiff, not because the plaintiff is right, but from the default of the defendant. The phrase is thus used of a judgement made in a person's absence.

**Judgement of Paris, The.** *See* PARIS.

**Judgement of the cross, The.** An ORDEAL instituted in the reign of CHARLEMAGNE. The plaintiff and defendant were required to cross their arms upon their breast, and he who held out the longer gained the suit. *See also* JUDICIUM CRUCIS.

**Daniel come to judgement, A.** *See under* DANIEL.

**Last** or **General Judgement, The.** *See under* LAST.

**Sit in judgement, To.** *See under* SIT.

**Judica Sunday.** The fifth Sunday in LENT (formerly also known as Passion Sunday) is so called from the first word of the introit at the MASS, *Judica me, Deus*, 'Give sentence with me, O God' (Psalm 43:1). *See also* CARE SUNDAY.

**Judicial. Judicial astrology.** *See* ASTROLOGY.

**Judicial circuit.** The journey through the counties formerly made by the judges twice a year to administer justice at the Assizes, a system changed by the Courts Act of 1971. Circuit judges are now appointed to have criminal jurisdiction in the Crown Courts and civil jurisdiction in the county courts. There are currently six circuits: the Midland and Oxford, the North-Eastern, the Northern, the South-Eastern, the Wales and Chester and the Western. Scottish High Court judges sit in Edinburgh and on circuit in other towns.

**Judicium crucis.** Trial of the cross. A form of ORDEAL, which consisted in stretching out the arms before a cross until one party could hold out no longer and lost his cause. *See also* JUDGEMENT OF THE CROSS.

**Judith.** In the book that bears her name in the APOCRYPHA Judith is a beautiful widow who, when her city was invaded by the Babylonian general HOLOFERNES, entered his camp and promised to lie with him. He duly anticipated the pleasant prospect with a feast. When drink took the better of him Judith beheaded him and saved her city. Her action is graphically depicted in a number of paintings, some of them gruesome.

**Judy.** *See* PUNCH AND JUDY.

**Jug.** The origin of the word may be in Jug, a pet form of the name Joan, Joanna or Jenny. As a slang word for a prison, the origin is in stone jug, an old nickname of NEWGATE PRISON.

**Jugged hare.** Hare stewed with wine and seasoning, properly in a jug or jar.

**Bottle and jug.** *See under* BOTTLE.

**Toby jug.** *See under* TOBY.

**Juggernaut.** A Hindu god, whose name is an alteration of Hindi *Jagannath*, from Sanskrit *Jagannātha*, 'lord of the world'. The name is a title of VISHNU, chief of the Hindu gods. The god is represented by an idol of KRISHNA (an avatar of Vishnu) in a temple at Puri in Orissa. The chief festival is the car festival when Jagganath is dragged in his car, 35ft (10.7m) square and 45ft (13.7m) high, over the sand to another temple. The car has 16 wheels, each 7ft (2.1m) in diameter. The belief that fanatical pilgrims threw themselves under the wheels of the car to go straight to Paradise on the last day of the festival is largely without foundation. However, it has led to the use of juggernaut to denote a regime or institution beneath which people are ruthlessly crushed. The word has also come to apply to a large lorry, especially one that travels throughout Europe. Such lorries or HGVs (heavy goods vehicles) have become increasingly common in Britain with the expansion of the European Union, and 'juggernaut' for this reason has become a dirty word with environmentalists. The word itself has become popularly associated with -naut in its application to long-distance voyagers such as the ARGONAUTS or an ASTRONAUT, while jugger- is in some cases misapprehended as a form of 'judder'.

**Juggler** (Latin *joculator*, 'jester', 'joker'). In the Middle Ages jugglers accompanied MINSTRELS and TROUBADOURS and added sleight of hand and feats of prowess to their musical talents in order to amuse their audience. In time the music was omitted and the tricks and antics became their prime offering. *See also* JONGLEUR.

**Juice, To stew in one's own.** *See under* STEW.

**Julian.** Pertaining to Julius CAESAR (100–44 BC).

**Julian calendar.** The calendar instituted by Julius CAESAR in 46 BC, which was in general use in western Europe until the introduction of the GREGORIAN CALENDAR in 1582 and was still used in England until 1752 and until 1918 in Russia. To allow for the odd quarter of a day, Caesar ordained that every fourth year should contain 366 days, the additional day being introduced after the 6th before the CALENDS of March, i.e. 24 February. Caesar also divided the months into the number of days they at present contain. It is now called OLD STYLE. *See also* CALENDAR; JULY.

**Julian of Norwich.** A religious recluse and mystic (*c.*1342–*c.*1413), who recorded her visions in *Sixteen Revelations of Divine Love*. Julian was formerly a woman's name as well as a man's.

**Julian the Apostate** (Greek *apostanai*, 'to stand apart'). Flavius Claudius Julianus (332–363), Roman emperor and nephew of Constantine the Great. He was so called from his attempts to restore paganism, having abandoned Christianity at about the age of 20. He set an example by the austerity of his life and his zeal for public welfare, and was notable for his literary and philosophical interests. Christians were not actively persecuted but there was discrimination against them. *See also* GALILEAN.

**Julian year.** The average year of 365¼ days, according to the JULIAN CALENDAR.

**St Julian.** A patron saint of travellers and of hospitality, looked on in the Middle Ages as the epicure of saints. He seems to be essentially a mythical saint. He is said to have unwittingly killed his parents and to have devoted his life to helping strangers by way of atonement.

**Juliet.** *See* ROMEO.

**Julius Caesar.** *See* CAESAR.

**July.** The seventh month, named by Mark Anthony in honour of Julius CAESAR. It was formerly called *Quintilis*, as it was the fifth month of the Roman year. The old Dutch name for it was *Hooy-maand* ('hay month'), while the Anglo-Saxons knew it as *Mǣdmōnath* ('meadow month'), because the cattle were turned into the meadows to feed then. In the FRENCH REVOLUTIONARY CALENDAR the equivalent was *Messidor* ('harvest gift'), corresponding to the period 20 June to 19 July.

Until the 18th century July was accented on the first syllable. Even as late as 1798 Wordsworth wrote:

> In March, December, and in July,
> 'Tis all the same with Harry Gill;
> The neighbours tell, and tell you truly,
> His teeth they chatter, chatter still.
> 'Goody Blake and Harry Gill'

**July Monarchy, The.** That of Louis Philippe, also called the Orleanist monarchy. *See also* JULY REVOLUTION.

**July Revolution, The.** The French revolution of 1830 (17–29 July) that overthrew Charles X and gave the throne to Louis Philippe, Duc d'Orléans, the CITIZEN KING.

**Column of July, The.** *See under* COLUMN.

**Jumbo.** The name of an exceptionally large African elephant, which, after giving rides to thousands of children in the London Zoo, was sold to Barnum's GREATEST SHOW ON EARTH in 1882. He weighed 6½ tons and was accidentally killed by a railway engine in 1885. His name is now synonymous with elephant in many minds, and has come to be applied to various large objects, such as a jumbo jet or a jumbo-size packet of commercial goods. The name may come from Swahili *jambe*, 'chief'.

**Jump. Jump at, To.** To accept something eagerly, such as an offer or an opportunity.

**Jump bail, To.** To forfeit bail by absconding before trial.

**Jump down someone's throat, To.** To reply or retort to a person unusually sharply.

**Jumped-up.** Suddenly elevated in importance, and arrogant with it.

**Jump for joy, To.** To express one's supreme pleasure. Young children sometimes literally jump for joy.

**Jumping bean.** The seed of a Mexican plant that 'jumps' with the movement of a moth larva inside it.

**Jumping jack.** A type of small firework that produces repeated explosions. Also a toy figure of a man with movable limbs.

**Jumping Jehoshaphat.** A mild expletive, first in American use in the mid-19th century. It is based on the name of the biblical JEHOSHAPHAT, and may have arisen as a variation on 'holy Moses'.

**Jumping-off place** or **point.** The edge of the earth; the end of civilization from which one leaped into nothingness. The phrase came to be used by settlers of any remote, desolate spot, and is now applied to a starting-point of some kind, as for an enterprise or operation.

**Jump leads.** A pair of cables fitted with crocodile clips that are used to start a motor vehicle when the battery is flat by connecting the battery to another battery.

**Jump-off.** An extra round in an equestrian contest, when two or more horses are equal winners.

**Jump on someone, To.** To reprimand or attack a person suddenly and forcefully.

**Jump out of one's skin, To.** To be very startled.

**Jump over the broomstick, To.** To live together without the proper ceremony of marriage. The derivation of the phrase is uncertain.

**Jump ship, To.** To desert the ship in which one is serving.

**Jump start.** A method of starting a car when the engine cannot be started by the ignition in the normal way. The car is pushed along or allowed to freewheel downhill and the gears are suddenly engaged. The term is also used for a similar start using JUMP LEADS.

**Jump suit.** A one-piece garment of combined trousers and jacket, as originally worn by paratroopers.

**Jump the besom, To.** To omit the marriage

service after the publication of the BANNS OF MARRIAGE, but to live together as man and wife. In Lowland Scots, 'besom' is a derogatory word for a woman.

**Jump the gun, To.** To anticipate; to start before the proper time, usually with a view to gaining an advantage. The reference is to a runner in a race who starts just before the gun is fired.

**Jump the queue, To.** To take a place in a queue ahead of those already in it.

**Jump to conclusions, To.** To draw inferences too hastily from insufficient evidence.

**Jump to it!** Get on with it!

**Flea's jump.** *See under* FLEA.

**High jump.** *See under* HIGH.

**Hop, step or skip and jump.** *See under* HOP.

**One jump ahead, To be.** To be one stage further on than a rival or opponent.

**Take a running jump at yourself.** Go away.

**Junction. Junction box.** *See under* BOX.

**Spaghetti Junction.** *See under* SPAGHETTI.

**June.** The sixth month, probably named from the Roman *gens* or clan name *Junius*, related to *juvenis*, 'young'. Some sources take the name from JUNO, however. Its old Dutch name was *Zomermaand* ('summer month'), while the Anglo-Saxons called it *Sēremōnath* ('dry month'). In the FRENCH REVOLUTIONARY CALENDAR the equivalent month was *Prairial* ('meadow month'), corresponding to the period 21 May to 19 June.

**Fourth of June, The.** *See under* FOURTH.

**Glorious First of June, The.** *See under* GLORIOUS.

**Jungle. Blackboard jungle, The.** *See under* BLACK.

**Law of the jungle, The.** *See under* LAW.

**Junior, Democritus.** *See under* DEMOCRITUS.

**Junius. Junius Brutus.** The son of Marcus Junius and Tarquinia and the nephew of TARQUIN. When his father and elder brother were murdered by Tarquin the Proud (Tarquinius Superbus), he feigned insanity, thereby saving his life, and was called Brutus for his apparent stupidity. He later inspired the Romans to get rid of the Tarquins and became one of the first consuls of Rome, fabled to have held office about 509 BC. He condemned to death his own two sons for joining a conspiracy to restore the banished Tarquin.

**Letters of Junius, The.** *See under* LETTER.

**Junk.** Nautically speaking, 'junk' was originally old or discarded rope. The word is now applied generally to a miscellany of cast-off or unwanted articles. It is also a slang term for narcotic drugs such as heroin and cocaine, an addict of which is called a 'junkie'.

> Junkies run on junk-time and junk metabolism. They are subject to junk-climate. They are warmed and chilled by junk.
> WILLIAM BURROUGHS: *Junkie* (1953)

**Junker.** A German land-owning aristocrat or squire, who formerly provided most of the officer class. Bismarck, the German Chancellor, came from the Prussian junker class. The word literally means 'young master', modern German *Jungherr*.

**Junket.** The present dish of flavoured milk set to a curd developed from a type of custard that was served in a rush basket. Hence the origin of the word in Old French *jonc*, 'rush' or 'reed'. The original cream dish was often eaten at feasts, and this gave junket as a word for a feast or merry-making occasion itself.

> You know there wants no junkets at the feast.
> SHAKESPEARE: *The Taming of the Shrew*, III, ii (1593)

**Juno.** In Roman mythology 'the venerable ox-eyed' wife and sister of JUPITER, and QUEEN OF HEAVEN. She is identified with the Greek HERA, was the special protectress of marriage and of women and was represented as a war-goddess. *See also* BIRD OF JUNO; GENIUS.

**Junoesque.** Said of a woman who has a regal and stately bearing, like that of Juno.

**Bird of Juno.** *See under* BIRD.

**Junta** (Spanish, 'council'). In Spain, a committee or council, especially a consultative or legislative assembly for the whole part of the country, the best known being the Junta of Regency set up under Murat's presidency after NAPOLEON BONAPARTE had secured King Ferdinand's abdication (1808) and the local juntas, backed by a central junta at Seville, formed to resist the French. The word is now usually applied to a group of military officers who have seized political power.

**Jupiter.** Also called JOVE, the supreme god of Roman mythology, corresponding to the Greek ZEUS, the son of SATURN or KRONUS, the Titan, whom he dethroned, and Ops or RHEA. He was the special protector of Rome, and as Jupiter Capitolinus (his temple being on the Capitoline Hill) presided over the Roman games. He determined the course of human affairs and made known the future through signs in the heavens, the flight of birds and other means. *See also* AUGURY.

As Jupiter was lord of heaven and bringer of light, white was the colour sacred to him. Among the alchemists Jupiter thus designated tin. In HERALDRY Jupiter stands for AZURE, the blue of the heavens. *See also* COLOURS.

Jupiter is also the name of the largest of the planets, given in honour of the greatest of the gods. The name itself comes from Greek *Zeus Patēr*, 'Father Zeus'. *See also* JOVE.

Jupiter's statue by Phidias at OLYMPIA was one of the SEVEN WONDERS OF THE WORLD. It was taken to Constantinople by Theodosius I and destroyed by fire in AD 475. *See also* THEMIS.

**Jupiter Ammon.** A name under which JUPITER was worshipped in Libya where his temple was famous for its ORACLE which was consulted by HERCULES. *See also* AMMON.

**Jury** (Latin *jurare*, 'to swear'). The jury arose in medieval times as a body of neighbours summoned by a public officer to give, on oath, a true answer to some question. There have long been 12 jurors in a court of law, and this figure is stipulated in the first clause of the Assize of Clarendon (1166). The Norman kings of England regarded the 12-man jury as an alternative to trial by combat or trial by ORDEAL, although juries of eight or nine had earlier been common in the Domesday Inquest (1086). The number 12 has always been a significant or mystical number, as that of the signs of the ZODIAC, APOSTLES and so on and was doubtless regarded as providing a sufficiently large number of people to give a reliable verdict in legal hearings.

**Jury is still out, The.** A decision has not yet been reached.

**Jury mast.** A temporary mast erected to replace one that has been carried away. Similarly, 'jury-rigged' means anything that has been set up in a makeshift manner. The origin of the word is uncertain. It may come ultimately from Old French *ajurie*, 'aid'.

**Challenge a jury, To.** *See under* CHALLENGE.

**Hang a jury, To.** *See under* HANG.

**Pack a jury, To.** *See under* PACK.

**Jus.** Latin for 'law', as in the following terms, in which it often includes a moral obligation as well as a legal:

**Jus canonicum.** CANON LAW.

**Jus civile.** Civil law, Roman law.

**Jus divinum.** Divine law.

**Jus gentium.** The law of nations or law common to all nations, otherwise international law.

**Jus mariti.** The right of the husband to the wife's property.

**Jus naturae** or **naturale.** Natural law, originally in essence the same as JUS GENTIUM.

**Jus primae noctis.** The 'right of the first night', an equivalent to the *droit du seigneur* ('lord's right'), meaning the right of the lord to share the bed of the bride of any one of his servants on the wedding night. The custom seems to have existed in early medieval Europe but was more often the excuse for levying dues in lieu.

**Jus sanguinis.** 'Right of blood', on the principle that a person's nationality at birth is the same as that of their parents.

**Just. Just, The.** Rulers and others who have been given this byname are, with regnal dates:

Aristides, the Athenian (d.*c.*468 BC)
Bahram II (r.276–293), fifth of the Sassanid kings of Persia
Casimir II, king of Poland (1177–94)
Ferdinand I, king of Aragon (1412–16)
Haroun al-Raschid ('Aaron the guided [by God]'), the most renowned of the ABBASSID caliphs (786–809); he appears in the ARABIAN NIGHTS ENTERTAINMENTS
James II, king of Aragon (1291–1327)
Khosrow or Chosroes I, king of Persia (531–579)
Peter I, king of Portugal (1356–67)

**Just my luck.** Typical of me. An ironic phrase said when one has lost out (as usual).

**Just the thing** or **very thing.** Just what is wanted; exactly what is needed.

**Just what the doctor ordered.** Precisely what is needed to rectify or improve the situation.

**Juste. Juste milieu** (French, 'the right mean'). The happy medium.

**Mot juste, Le.** *See under* MOT.

**Justice. Justices of the peace.** Local lords and gentry were initially given judicial authority as Conservators of the Peace in 1361. As unpaid Justices of the Peace they acted firstly through the courts or QUARTER SESSIONS. Summary jurisdiction developed in the 16th century and they also carried out much administrative work until the Local Government Acts of 1888 and 1894. Today, as lay magistrates appointed by the LORD CHANCELLOR, JPs largely deal with the lesser offences, the licensing of premises and the like.

**Clerk to the Justices.** *See under* CLERK.

**Piso's justice.** *See under* PISO.

**Poetic justice.** *See under* POET.

**Justify. End justifies the means, The.** *See under* END.

**Justinian, Pandects of.** *See under* PANDECTS.

**Juveniles.** In theatrical parlance, actors playing youthful roles. In publishing, juveniles are periodicals or books for the young.

**Juvenilia** (Latin, 'youthful things'). Creative work in art, music or literature produced by a young person before their mature style has developed.

# K

**K.** The eleventh letter of the alphabet, representing the Greek *kappa* and the Hebrew *kaph*. The Egyptian HIEROGLYPHIC for K was a bowl. The Romans, after the C was given the K sound, used the latter only for abbreviated forms of a few words from Greek. Thus, false accusers were branded on the forehead with a K for *kalumnia* (English 'calumny'), and the Carians, Cretans and Cilicians were known as the 'three bad K's'. K is the recognized abbreviation of KNIGHT in British Orders but the abbreviation of Knight as such is Kt.

**Kaaba** (Arabic *ka'bah*, 'cube'). The ancient stone building said to have been first built by ISHMAEL and ABRAHAM and incorporated in the centre of the Great Mosque at MECCA. It forms a rough square and is about 40ft (12m) high, containing the BLACK STONE in the east corner. The present Kaaba was built in 1626 and is covered with a cloth of black brocade that is replaced in an annual ceremony.

**Kaffir** (Arabic *kāfir*, 'infidel'). A now offensive name given to all Africans who were not Muslims or to Black Africans generally. The British and other Europeans restricted the term to the Bantu races.

**Kaffir King, The.** A nickname given to Barney Barnato (1852–97), the South African diamond magnate and speculator, who became an associate of Cecil Rhodes.

**Kaffirs.** The STOCK EXCHANGE term for South African mining shares and for the market dealing with them.

**Kai Lung.** The Chinese sage and teller of tales who is the hero of a series of short stories by the English writer Ernest Bramah (real name Ernest Bramah Smith). They are first collected in *The Wallet of Kai Lung* (1900), and abound with mock-Chinese aphorisms.

**Kailyard School.** A school of writers flourishing in the 1890s, who took their subjects from humble Scottish life. It included Ian Maclaren (pen-name of John Watson) (1850–1907), J.J. Bell (1871–1934), S.R. Crockett (1859–1914) and J.M. Barrie (1860–1937). The name is from the line 'There grows a bonnie brier bush in our Kailyard', used by Maclaren for his *Beside the Bonnie Brier Bush* (1894). Their sentimental assumptions about the realities of Scottish small town life were countered by George Douglas in his novel *The House with the Green Shutters* (1901), which 'let in the East wind', as J.B. Priestley put it, to 'this cosy chamber of fiction'.

**Kaiser.** The German form of CAESAR, as the title formerly used by the head of the HOLY ROMAN EMPIRE and by the emperors of Austria and Germany. It was Diocletian (*c*.284) who ordered that Caesar should be the title of the emperor of the West. Its particular Roman origin relates it directly to TSAR.

**Kalevala.** The national epic of the Finns, compiled from popular songs and oral tradition by the Finnish philologist Elias Lönnrot (1802–84), who published his first edition of 12,000 verses in 1835 and a second, of some 22,900 verses, in 1849. Its name is taken from the three sons of Kaleva ('of a hero') who inhabit Kalevala ('Kaleva's homeland', i.e. Finland) and who are the heroes of the poem: Väinämöinen, Ilmarinen and Lemminkäinen. Prominent in the action is the 'sampo', the magical mill that grants all one's wishes. The epic is influenced by Teutonic and Scandinavian mythology and to a lesser extent by Christianity. It is written in unrhymed, alliterative trochaic verse and is the prototype both in form and content of Longfellow's *Hiawatha* (1855). Jean Sibelius based several works on the myths, including *Kullervo* (1892), *Pohjola's Daughter* (1906), *The Swan of Tuonela* (1896) and *Lemminkäinen and the Maidens* and *Lemminkäinen's Homecoming* (1893–5).

**Kali.** The cult name, from Sanskrit *kāla*, 'black', of Durga, wife of SIVA, the Hindu goddess of death and destruction. Calcutta is said to have received its name from her, and it was to her that the THUGS sacrificed their victims. Her idol is black, besmeared with blood. She has red eyes, four arms, matted hair, huge, fang-like teeth and a protruding tongue that drips with blood. She wears earrings of corpses and a necklace of skulls, and her body is girdled with serpents. *See also* HINDUISM.

**Kalki.** *See* AVATAR.

**Kalyb.** The 'Lady of the Woods', who stole St GEORGE from his nurse and endowed him with gifts. St George enclosed her in a rock where she was torn to pieces by spirits. The story occurs in the first part of *Famous History of the Seven Champions of Christendom* (*c*.1597) by Richard Johnson (1573–*c*.1659). *See also* SEVEN CHAMPIONS.

**Kama.** The god of love in Indian mythology. His wife is Rati, and he is depicted as a handsome youth, surrounded by heavenly nymphs, shooting arrows of flowers that produce love. His name comes from Sanskrit *kāma*, 'love', a word that appears in the title of the KAMASUTRA.

**Kamasutra** (Sanskrit, literally 'thread of love', from *kāma*, 'love', and *sūtra*, 'thread'). An ancient Hindu text on erotic pleasure and related topics, attributed to the 1st-century AD Indian sage Vatsyayana.

**Ka me, ka thee.** The equivalent of 'You scratch my back and I'll scratch yours' or 'One good turn deserves another'. It is an old proverb and appears in John Heywood's collection of 1546. The origin of 'ka' is uncertain. It may have evolved from 'claw'.

**Kamerad** (German, 'comrade'). A word used by the Germans in the First World War as an appeal for mercy. For a while it was taken up in English to mean 'I surrender'.

> 'Kamerad, Bull! I'll come in,' said Loftie. Vaughan's hands had gone up first.
>
> RUDYARD KIPLING: *Limits and Renewals* (1930)

**Kami.** A god or divinity in SHINTOISM, the native religion of Japan, and also the title given to daimios (feudal nobles) and governors. The name represents Japanese *kami*, 'god', 'lord'. *See also* KAMIKAZE.

**Kamikaze.** A Japanese word meaning 'divine wind', referring to the providential typhoon that on a night in August 1281 balked a Mongol invasion. In the Second World War it was applied to the 'suicide' aircraft attacks organized under Vice-Admiral Onishi in the Philippines between October 1944 and January 1945. Some 5000 young pilots gave their lives when their bomb-loaded fighters crashed into their targets.

**Kamsa.** *See* KRISHNA.

**Kangaroo.** In British parliamentary procedure the process by which the SPEAKER, on the Report stage of a bill, selects the amendments to be debated, rather than having all the amendments discussed. The procedure was first used on the discussion of the Financial Bill of 1909. It is so named because the debate leaps from clause to clause. The word is also applied when the chairperson of a parliamentary committee selects some amendments for discussion but not others. *See also* CLOSURE; GUILLOTINE.

**Kangaroo court.** A term applied to an irregular court or tribunal which is conducted in disregard of proper legal procedure, as, for example, a mock court held among prisoners in a gaol. 'To kangaroo' means to convict a person on false evidence. The term, which probably arose from some resemblance of the 'jumps' of the kangaroo to the progress of 'justice' in such courts, was common in the USA during the 19th century. It obtained wide currency in Britain in 1966 when it was applied to the irregular punitive measures taken by certain TRADE UNIONS against their members who were regarded as strike-breakers.

**Kantaka.** The white horse of Prince GAUTAMA, the BUDDHA.

**Karaites.** *See* SCRIPTURISTS.

**Karenina, Anna.** The heroine of Tolstoy's novel *Anna Karenina* (1875–7) and one of the great tragic adulteresses of 19th-century fiction. She falls in love with Alexei Vronsky, an army officer, and leaves her husband and child to live with him. When his passion for her wanes, she commits suicide by throwing herself under a train at a station in Moscow. She is said to be based on a blend of Pushkin's daughter, Maria Alexandrovna Hartung (1832–1919), and Countess Alexandra Tolstoy (1817–1904), a cousin of Tolstoy's father. There have been filmed versions of her story, and she was memorably portrayed in the cinema by Greta Garbo in 1935 and in an acclaimed television adaptation by Nicola Pagett in 1978.

**Karma** (Sanskrit, 'action', 'effect'). In Buddhist philosophy the name given to the results of action, especially the cumulative results of a person's deeds in one stage of his existence as controlling his destiny in the next.

Among Theosophists the word has the rather wider meaning of an unbroken sequence of cause and effect, each effect being, in its turn, the cause of a subsequent effect.

**Karno. Fred Karno's army.** A humorous nickname applied to the new British army raised during the First World War, in allusion to Fred Karno, the comedian and producer of stage burlesques, whose real name was Frederick John Westcott (1866–1941). At the time Fred Karno's company was a household name through its high-spirited and eccentric performances. The well-known army chorus, sung to the tune of 'The Church's One Foundation', runs:

> We are Fred Karno's army,
> Fred Karno's infantry;
> We cannot fight, we cannot shoot,
> So what damn good are we?
> But when we get to Berlin
> The Kaiser he will say
> Hoch, hoch, mein Gott
> Vot a bloody fine lot,
> Fred Karno's infantry.

There are variants, of course, and in the Second World War 'Old Hitler' was substituted for 'The Kaiser'. The name is also applied derisively to other nondescript bodies. Karno himself adopted his stage name when he and two gymnast colleagues filled in at a music hall for an act called 'The Three Carnos'. His agent, Richard Warner, suggested they change the 'C' to a more distinctive 'K'. *See also* HARRY TATE'S NAVY.

**Karttikeya.** The Hindu god of war and the first-born son of SIVA. He is shown riding on a peacock, with a bow in one hand and an arrow in the other, and is also known as Skanda (Sanskrit, 'spurt of semen') and Kumara (Sanskrit, 'boy', 'adolescent'). According to one tradition, he was the son of the Krttikas, the six women who as stars make up the PLEIADES. Hence his name, meaning 'son of Krttikas'. (In Hindu mythology there are only six Pleiades, not the seven recognized by modern astronomers.) *See also* HINDUISM.

**Kaswa, Al.** MOHAMMED's favourite camel, which fell on its knees when the prophet delivered the last clause of the KORAN to the assembled multitude at MECCA.

**Katakana** (Japanese, 'side kana'). The Japanese system of writing syllabic characters that is complementary to the more common HIRAGANA. Its 48 characters are chiefly used for foreign or foreign-derived words. Its name of 'side kana' refers to its origin in mnemonic symbols that were placed alongside the Chinese characters as reading aids.

**Katerfelto.** A generic name for a QUACK or CHARLATAN. Gustavus Katerfelto (d.1799) was a celebrated quack who gained fame during the influenza epidemic of 1782, when he exhibited his solar microscope at London and created immense excitement by showing the infusoria of muddy water. He was a tall man, dressed in a long black gown and square cap, who was accompanied by a black cat.

> And Katerfelto, with his hair on end,
> At his own wonders, wondering for his bread.
>
> WILLIAM COWPER: *The Task*, 'The Winter Evening' (1785)

**Kathay.** *See* CATHAY.

**Katmir.** *See* KRATIM.

**Kay, Sir.** In ARTHURIAN ROMANCES the son of Sir Ector and foster-brother of King ARTHUR, who made him his seneschal.

**KB.** Knight Bachelor.

**Keating, Tom, The pictures of.** *See under* FAKES.

**Keblah.** *See* KIBLAH.

**Kedar's tents.** This world. Kedar was a son of ISHMAEL (Genesis 25:13) and was the ancestor of an important tribe of nomadic Arabs. The phrase comes from Psalm 120:5: 'Woe is me, that I sojourn in Mesech, that I dwell in the tents of Kedar!' Kedar's name means 'dark one'.

**Keel. Keelhauling.** An old naval punishment, which involved dragging the offender under the keel of the ship from one side to the other by means of ropes and tackles attached to the yards. The result was often fatal. Figuratively it is to haul or CALL OVER THE COALS; to castigate harshly.

**On an even keel.** Figuratively, well-balanced or steady.

**Keen. As keen as mustard.** *See under* AS.

**Keening.** A weird lamentation for the dead, once common in Ireland, practised at funerals. It is from the Irish word *caoine*, pronounced 'keen', from Old Irish *coīnim*, 'I wail'.

**Keep.** One's keep is the amount that it takes to maintain one, as: 'You're not worth your keep.' The keep of a medieval castle was the main tower or stronghold of the dungeon.

For expressions including 'keep' as a verb that are not included below, see under the first main word.

**Keep at it, To.** To continue hard at work; to persist.

**Keeper of the king's conscience, The.** *See* LORD CHANCELLOR.

**Keep one's head down, To.** *See under* HEAD.

**Keep one's word, To.** To do what one has promised.

**Keep on trucking, To.** To persevere. The reference is to long-distance haulage truckers, who keep going through the night.

**Keep up with the Joneses, To.** To endeavour to maintain one's social level, to keep up appearances with one's neighbours. The phrase was invented by Arthur R. Momand ('Pop'), the comic strip artist, for a series ('Keeping up with the Joneses – by Pop'), which began in the New York *Globe* on 1 April 1913 and ran 28 years. It was originally based on the artist's own attempts to keep up with his neighbours. *See also* STATUS SYMBOL.

**Finders keepers.** *See under* FIND.

**Kells, The Book of.** *See under* BOOK.

**Kelly, As game as Ned.** *See under* AS.

**Kelmscott Press.** A private printing press founded in 1890 by William Morris (1834–96) in a cottage adjoining his residence, Kelmscott House, at 26 Upper Mall, Hammersmith, which he had bought in 1878 from the novelist George MacDonald and renamed after his earlier home, Kelmscott Manor, near Faringdon, Berkshire (now Oxfordshire). Assisted by Emery Walker (1851–1933), who initially gave Morris the inspiration, and Sidney Cockerell, the aim was to revive good printing as an art. Their publications beneficially influenced printing and book production.

The delicately drawn frontispiece to the Kelmscott Press edition of Morris' *News from Nowhere* (1891) shows the gabled manor and its garden and has the following caption in capital lettering:

This is the picture of the old house by the Thames to which the people of this story went. Hereafter follows the book itself which is called *News from Nowhere or an Epoch of Rest* & is written by William Morris.

**Kelpie** or **kelpy.** In Scottish folklore a spirit of the waters in the form of a horse. It was supposed to delight in the drowning of travellers, but also occasionally helped millers by keeping the mill wheel going at night. The word is perhaps related to Scottish Gaelic *cailpeach*, 'heifer'.

**Kelter.** *See* KILTER.

**Kendal green.** Green cloth for foresters, so called from Kendal, Westmorland (now Cumbria), formerly famous for its manufacture. Lincoln was also renowned for its green cloth, hence LINCOLN GREEN.

**Kenelm.** An English saint, the son of Kenwulf, king of Mercia, in the early 9th century. He was only seven years old when, by his sister's order, he was murdered at Clent, near Stourbridge, Worcestershire. The murder, says Roger of Wendover, was miraculously reported in Rome by a white dove, which alighted on the altar at St Peter's, bearing in its beak a scroll with the verse:

In Clent cow pasture, under a thorn,
Of head bereft, lies Kenelm, king-born.

His day is 17 July.

**Kensal Green.** Churchyard burials in London had presented problems long before suburban cemeteries were established by joint-stock companies. Kensal Green, off the Harrow Road, was the first such cemetery, and it was opened in 1832. It contains the tombs of many notable 19th-century figures, including the Duke of Sussex (sixth son of George III) and his sister, the Princess Sophia, Thomas Hood, Sydney Smith, Isambard Kingdom Brunel, Leigh Hunt, W.M. Thackeray, Anthony Trollope, Wilkie Collins and BLONDIN.

For there is good news yet to hear and fine things to be seen,
Before we go to Paradise by way of Kensal Green.
G.K. CHESTERTON: 'The Rolling English Road' (1914)

**Kensington.** The London borough, now combined with Chelsea, has long had associations of royalty and prosperity. Kensington Gardens, at the western edge of HYDE PARK, was used by Queen Mary and Queen Anne as the gardens for Kensington Palace, which has been a London home of royalty since William III and Mary moved into it from Whitehall Palace in 1689. Kensington Park Gardens, formerly nicknamed 'Millionaires' Row' for its wealthy residents, is a private road to the west of the Palace where many embassies are located.

**Kent. Kentish fire.** Rapturous applause or 'three times three and one more'. The expression probably originated with the protracted cheers given to the No-popery orators in 1828–9 in Kent. Lord Winchelsea, proposing the health of the Earl of Roden on 15 August 1834, said: 'Let it be given with the Kentish fire.'

**Kentishman, A.** A native of West Kent, born west of the Medway. *See also* MAN OF KENT.

**Kentishman's tails.** *See* TAILED MEN.

**Kentish rag.** A dark-coloured, tough limestone used for building, found in parts of Kent.

**Kents Cavern.** A limestone cave at Torquay, Devon, a mile east of the harbour, once known as Kent's Hole. Apart from the fascination of its natural features, including the beauty of its stalagmite grotto, it is of major importance to archaeologists. Many relics, human and animal, have been found, including those of the mammoth and sabre-toothed tiger. Excavation was begun in the 1820s by a Roman Catholic priest, but he could not publish his results until much later because they clashed with contemporary religious belief. The origin of the cave's name is a matter for surmise.

**Fair Maid of Kent, The.** *See under* FAIR.

**Maid of Kent, The.** *See under* MAID.

**Man of Kent, A.** *See under* MAN.

**Kentigern.** The patron saint of Glasgow (*c.*510–*c.*600), the apostle of northwest England and southeast Scotland and the traditional founder of Glasgow Cathedral. He is represented with his episcopal cross in one hand and a salmon and ring in the other in allusion to the following legend:

Queen Langoureth had been false to her husband, King Roderich, and had given her lover a ring. The king, aware of the fact, stole upon the knight in sleep, abstracted the ring, threw it into the Clyde, and then asked the queen for it. The queen, in alarm, applied to St Kentigern, who after praying, went to the Clyde, caught a salmon with the ring in its mouth, handed it to the queen and was thus the means of restoring peace to the royal couple.

The Glasgow arms include the salmon with the ring in its mouth, an oak tree with a bell hanging on one of its branches and a bird at the top of the tree. The oak and the bell allude to the story that St Kentigern hung a bell on an oak to summon the wild natives to worship. His day is 13 January.

St Kentigern is also known as St Mungo, allegedly because Mungho ('dearest') was the name by which St Servan, his first preceptor, called him.

**Kentucky Derby.** One of the classic horse races in the USA. It is for three-year-olds, and has been run since 1875 at Churchill Downs, Louisville, Kentucky, over 1¼ miles (2km).

**Kepler's laws.** Astronomical laws of planetary motion first formulated by Johannes Kepler

(1571–1630). They formed the basis of Newton's work and are the starting point of modern astronomy. They are as follows:

(1) All planets move round the sun in elliptical orbits, with the sun as one of the foci
(2) A radius vector joining any planet to the sun sweeps out equal areas in equal lengths of time
(3) The squares of the sidereal periods (of revolution) of the planets are directly proportional to the cubes of their mean distances from the sun

**Kermis** or **Kirmess.** Originally the *Kirkmass* or church mass held in most towns of the Low Countries on the anniversary of the dedication of the parish church. It was accompanied by processions and by feasting, and sports and games often of a somewhat riotous nature. It still survives, essentially as a FAIR. A similar event of the name is held in North America with the aim of collecting money for charity. In France *kermesse* is used more generally to denote a fair or charity fête.

**Kermit.** The garrulous green-garbed puppet frog was the mainstay of the Muppets, created by Jim Henson. He first appeared on American television in 1957, but did not become generally familiar until 1969, when he featured in the children's educational programme *Sesame Street*. This in turn led to the *Muppet Show*, running from 1976 to 1981, in which Kermit pranced and parleyed with his equally esoteric friends, among them Miss Piggy and Fozzie Bear.

**Kern** (Middle Irish *cethern*, 'band of foot soldiers', from *cath*, 'battle'). In medieval Ireland a lightly armed foot soldier, one of the lowest grade. *See also* GALLOGLASS.

**Kern Baby.** *See* CORN DOLLY.

**Kersey.** A coarse cloth, usually ribbed and woven from long wool, said to be originally made at Kersey, a village near Hadleigh, Suffolk. It should not be confused with 'kerseymere', which is a fine soft woollen cloth of twill weave, taking its name as a blend of 'Kersey' and 'cassimere', itself a variant of 'cashmere'.

**Kestrel.** A common European falcon, or small HAWK, once regarded as of a mean or base variety. Hence the former use of the word for a worthless fellow.

> Ne thought of honour euer did assay
> His baser brest, but in his kestrell kind
> A pleasing vaine of glory vaine did find.
> EDMUND SPENSER: *The Faerie Queene*, II, iii (1590)

**Ketch, Jack.** A notorious hangman and executioner, who was appointed *c.*1663 and died in 1686. He was the executioner in 1683 of Lord William Russell, for his share in the RYE HOUSE PLOT and in 1685 of Monmouth (*see* MONMOUTH'S REBELLION). In 1686 he was removed from office for insulting a SHERIFF and succeeded by a butcher named Rose, who was himself hanged within four months, when Ketch was reinstated. As early as 1678 his name had appeared in a ballad, and by 1702 was associated with the PUNCH AND JUDY puppet play, which had recently been introduced from Italy. *See also* HANGMEN AND EXECUTIONERS.

**Kettle.** As well as meaning the vessel used for boiling water and cooking, the word is old thieves' slang for a watch. A tin kettle is a silver watch, a red kettle is a gold one.

**Kettledrum.** A drum made of a thin, hemispherical shell of brass or copper with a parchment top. In late Victorian times the word was also used for an afternoon tea party, in playful allusion to the presence of the tea kettle.

**Kettle of fish, A.** An old Border name for a kind of *fête champêtre* or riverside picnic where a newly caught salmon is boiled and eaten. The discomfort of this sort of party may have led to the phrase 'a pretty kettle of fish', meaning an awkward state of affairs, a mess or a muddle.

> As the whole company go to the water-side today to eat a kettle of fish, there will be no risk of interruption.
> SIR WALTER SCOTT: *St Ronan's Well*, ch xii (1823)

**Giants' kettles.** *See under* GIANT.

**Pot calling the kettle black, The.** *See under* POT.

**Kevin.** An Irish saint of the 6th century. Legend relates that he retired to a cave on the steep shore of a lake where he vowed no woman should ever land. A girl named Kathleen followed him, but the saint whipped her with a bunch of nettles or, according to a more romantic story, hurled her from a rock. Her ghost never left the place where he lived. A cave at Glendalough, County Wicklow, is said to be the bed of St Kevin. Moore has a poem on this tradition, its first stanza running:

> By that Lake whose gloomy shore
> Skylark never warbles o'er,
> Where the cliff hangs high and steep,
> Young Saint Kevin stole to sleep.
> 'Here, at least,' he calmly said,
> 'Woman ne'er shall find my bed.'
> Ah! the good Saint little knew
> What that wily sex can do.
> THOMAS MOORE: *Irish Melodies*, 'By that Lake whose Gloomy Shore' (1807)

In the 1990s Kevin came to be regarded as the name of a typical ESSEX MAN and thus to connote the attributes of such a person.

**Key.** Metaphorically, that which explains or solves some difficulty or problem, as the key to a problem, the means of solving it. *Keys to the Classics* was a well-known title for a series of CRIBS or literal translations. Key is also used for a place that commands a large area of land or sea, as Gibraltar is the Key to the Mediterranean, and in the Peninsular War Ciudad Rodrigo was known as the Key to Spain.

In music, the lowest note of a scale is the keynote and gives its name to the scale or key itself. Hence the phrases 'in key' or 'out of key', meaning in or out of harmony with.

**Key money.** The payment made by a new tenant before moving in.

**Key of the door, The.** A symbol of independence, popular on 18th birthday cards (and formerly on 21st).

I'm twenty-one today,
Twenty-one today,
I've got the key of the door,
Never been twenty-one before.

ALEC KENDAL: 'I'm Twenty-one Today' (song) (1912)

**Carriage return key.** *See under* CARRIAGE.

**Ceremony of the Keys, The.** *See under* CEREMONY.

**Cross Keys, The.** *See under* CROSS.

**Gold Key, The.** *See under* GOLD.

**House of Keys, The.** *See* TYNWALD.

**Power of the keys, The.** *See under* POWER.

**St Peter's Keys.** *See under* PETER.

**Keyne.** A Celtic saint of the 5th century, the daughter of Brychan, king of Brecknock. St Keyne's Well, near Liskeard, Cornwall, is reputed to give greater authority to the first of two marriage partners to drink from it.

**Keystone. Keystone Kops.** A troupe of SLAPSTICK film comedians led by Ford Sterling who from 1912 to 1920, under the inspiration of Mack Sennett (1880–1960), made a number of action-packed comedies at the Keystone Studios, Hollywood, complete with crazy chases and trick effects.

**Keystone State, The.** Pennsylvania, so called from its position and importance. *See also* UNITED STATES OF AMERICA.

**KGB.** *See* OGPU.

**Khaki.** An Urdu word, meaning 'dusty', from Persian *khak*, 'dust'. Khaki uniform was first used by an irregular corps of Guides raised by the British at Meerut during the INDIAN MUTINY. They were known as the *Khaki Risala* ('khaki squadron') and nicknamed 'the Mudlarks'. It was adopted as an active service uniform by several regiments and in the Omdurman campaign (1898) but was not generally introduced until the South African War of 1899–1902.

**Khaki Election.** The name given to the general election of 1900 (28 September to 24 October) by which the CONSERVATIVES sought to profit from the recent military victories in the South African War. It was promoted by Joseph Chamberlain (1836–1914), and the Conservatives won, although the gain in seats was very slight.

**Khalifa.** An Arabic word meaning 'successor' (English 'caliph'), and the title adopted by Abdullah el-Taashi, the successor of the MAHDI, in 1885. His power was broken by General Kitchener at the Battle of Omdurman in 1898.

**Khan** (Turkish, contraction of *khāqān*, 'ruler'). The chief rulers of Tartar, Mongol and Turkish tribes, as successors of GENGHIS KHAN (d.1227). The word means 'lord' or 'prince'. *See also* CHAM.

**Aga Khan.** *See under* AGA.

**Genghis Khan.** *See under* GENGHIS.

**Khayyám, Omar.** *See under* OMAR.

**Khedive.** The title, from Persian *khidīw*, 'prince', by which the ruler of Egypt as viceroy of the Turkish Sultan was known from 1867 to 1914. In 1914, when Turkey joined the Central Powers, Khedive Abbas II was deposed by the British and Hussein Kamil set up as SULTAN. The title of king was adopted by Fuad in 1922 when the British terminated their Protectorate.

**Kibbutz** (Modern Hebrew *qibbūs*, 'gathering'). A Jewish communal settlement in Israel organized on socialist lines by which land and property are shared. Work and meals are arranged collectively. Adults have private quarters but children are housed together. Kibbutzim were originally agricultural only, but various factories and industries later developed. The first kibbutz was set up in the Jordan Valley in 1909 by Jewish immigrants from Europe. They have played a considerable part in defending Jewish territory.

**Kiblah.** The point towards which Muslims turn when they worship, i.e. the KAABA at MECCA. The word is also used for the niche or slab (called the *mihrab*) on the interior wall of a mosque that indicates this direction. The word itself derives from Arabic *qiblah*, 'that which is placed opposite', related to *qabala*, 'to be opposite'.

**Kibosh. Put the kibosh on, To.** To put a stop to; to prevent from continuing. The word is of unknown origin.

**Kick.** Former slang for a sixpence, but only in compounds, as 'two-and-a-kick', otherwise two shillings and sixpence.

**Kick against the pricks, To.** To struggle against fate; to protest when the odds are against one. The expression occurs in Acts 9:5 and 26:14 ('It is hard for thee to kick against the pricks'), where the metaphorical reference is to an ox kicking when goaded, or a horse when pricked with the rowels of a spur. *See also* 1 Samuel 2:29: 'Wherefore kick ye at my sacrifice and at mine offering?'

**Kick ass, To.** To act forcefully or domineeringly. 'Ass' is 'arse'.

**Kickback.** Payment for collaboration in a matter involving illicit profit.

**Kicked upstairs.** Promoted to a position that is ostensibly higher but without the commensurate authority.

**Kick in, To.** To pay one's share; to make one's contribution.

**Kick in the pants** or **teeth.** A humiliating or hurtful rebuke or rebuff.

**Kick-off.** In football, the start or resumption of a game by kicking the ball from the centre of the field.

**Kick one's heels, To.** *See* COOL ONE'S HEELS.

**Kick over the traces, To.** To break away from control or to run riot, as a horse refusing to run in harness kicks over the traces (the two side straps that connect his harness to the swingletree).

**Kick-start.** A method of starting a motorcycle by kicking down (vigorously depressing) a pedal.

**Kick the bucket, To.** To die. The expression is of uncertain provenance. The following three possibilities have been proposed: (1) 'bucket' is from Old French *buquet*, 'balance', referring to the beam on which a pig was suspended by the heels for slaughter; (2) the bucket was the upturned one on which a suicide stood, kicking it away to hang himself; (3) the bucket is the one formerly put out to collect for the widow of a workmate, some of those passing simply kicking the bucket instead of throwing in a coin.

**Kick up a fuss** or **row, To.** To create a disturbance.

**Kick up a shindy, To.** To make a row or to create a disturbance. The word is probably connected with 'shinty', a primitive kind of hockey played in Scotland and the north of England.

**Kick up one's heels, To.** To enjoy oneself without inhibition. The allusion is to a horse set free, which often kicks up its heels when scampering off.

**Alive and kicking.** *See under* ALIVE.

**Get a kick out of something, To.** To derive pleasurable excitement from some event or action.

**Kickshaws** (French *quelque chose*, 'something'). Worthless trinkets and, formerly, small or elaborate delicacies.

> Some pigeons, Davy, a couple of short-legged hens, a joint of mutton, and any pretty little tiny kickshaws, tell William cook.
>
> SHAKESPEARE: *Henry IV, Pt II*, V, i (1597)

**Kid.** A child, from the kid that is the young of the goat, a very playful and frisky little animal. The related verb 'to kid' means to tease, as, 'Only kidding!'

**Kid brother** or **sister.** A younger brother or sister.

**Kiddies, The.** *See under* REGIMENTAL AND DIVISIONAL NICKNAMES.

**Kid-glove treatment.** Very gentle or tactful handling. Kid gloves, made from the skin of the young goat, were at one time a symbol of elegance and gentility.

**Kids' stuff.** Something very easy; CHILD'S PLAY.

**Billy the Kid.** *See under* BILLY.

**Dead end kids.** *See under* DEAD.

**Sundance Kid.** *See under* SUN.

**Whizz kid.** *See under* WHIZZ.

**Kidd, Captain.** William Kidd (1645–1701), privateer and pirate, about whom many stories and legends have arisen. He was commissioned with LETTERS OF MARQUE in 1696 to attack the French and seize pirates, but turned the expedition into one of piracy. He was eventually arrested at Boston and subsequently hanged at Execution Dock.

**Kidnapping.** A slang word of 17th-century origin. 'Nabbing' a KID was the popular term for the stealing of young black children and selling them to sea captains and others who transported them to the colonial plantations. Today people are usually kidnapped to be held to ransom, the kidnappers often being politically motivated. *See also* HIJACKER; NAB; SKYJACKER.

**Kidney.** Temperament, disposition or stamp, as 'of another kidney' or 'of the same kidney'. The REINS or kidneys were formerly supposed to be the seat of the affections.

**Kilkenny cats, To fight like.** *See under* FIGHT.

**Kill. Killing no murder.** A pamphlet published in Holland and sent over to England in 1657 advising the assassination of Oliver Cromwell. It purported to be by one William Allen, a JESUIT, and has frequently been attributed to Silas Titus (later made a colonel and Groom of the Bedchamber by Charles II), but it was actually by Colonel Edward Sexby, a LEVELLER, who had gone over to the Royalists and who, in 1657, narrowly failed in an attempt to murder Cromwell.

**Killing pace, A.** Too strong or too hot to last.

**Killjoy.** A person who spoils the pleasure of others.

**Kill off, To.** To destroy or annihilate a number of persons or things. When an author kills off a fictional character he arranges his death. Sir Arthur Conan Doyle tried to kill off SHERLOCK HOLMES in *The Final Problem* (1893) but was compelled to resurrect him in *The Adventure of the Empty House* (1903) after his 'posthumous' appearance in *The Hound of the Baskervilles* (1901). *See also* MORIARTY.

**Kill oneself, To.** To overexert oneself, as: 'Don't kill yourself, it's not worth it.'

**Kill or cure.** Said of a drastic remedy or extreme measure.

**Kill the fatted calf, To.** To celebrate; to welcome with the best of everything. The phrase is from the parable of the PRODIGAL SON (Luke 15:30).

**Kill the goose that lays the golden eggs, To.** To sacrifice future reward or benefit for the sake of present gain or satisfaction. *See also* GOLDEN GOOSE; JACK AND THE BEANSTALK.

**Kill time, To.** To while away spare time with amusements or occupations of various kinds in order to avoid or relieve boredom.

**Kill two birds with one stone, To.** To accomplish two things with a single action. The Italian equivalent is *Prendere due piccioni con una fava*, 'To catch two pigeons with one bean', for the Germans it is *Zwei Fliegen mit einer Klappe schlagen*, 'To swat two flies at once', and for the Russians *Ubit' dvukh zaytsev odnim udarom*, 'To kill two hares with a single blow'.

**Kill with kindness, To.** To overwhelm with benevolence. It is said that Draco, the Athenian legislator, was killed by his popularity, being smothered in the theatre of Aegina by the number of caps and cloaks showered on him by the spectators (590 BC). Thomas Heywood wrote a domestic tragedy called *A Woman Killed with Kindness* (1607).

**Dressed to kill.** *See under* DRESSED.

**In at the kill.** Present at the end or the climax. The allusion is to hunting.

**Make a killing, To.** To make a sudden financial profit, especially on the STOCK EXCHANGE.

**Kilroy.** During the Second World War the phrase 'Kilroy was here' was found written up wherever the Americans (particularly Air Transport Command) had been. Its origin is a matter of conjecture. One suggestion is that a certain shipyard inspector at Quincy, Massachusetts, chalked up the words on material he had inspected. *See also* CHAD; GRAFFITI.

**Kilt.** The Scotsman's tartan skirt was originally a long length of cloth wrapped round the waist, with one end thrown over the shoulder. It later became a nether garment, before which a sporran is worn, as a leather or fur pouch suspended from the belt. The word is of Scandinavian origin, related to Danish *kilte*, 'to tuck up'.

**Kilter** or **kelter.** Good condition, health, order or spirits. The word, of unknown origin, occurs in various local dialects in such expressions as 'out of kilter', 'in good kilter'.

**Kim.** The orphan boy, with full name Kimball O'Hara, who is the hero of the novel by Kipling that bears his name (1901), regarded by many as the writer's finest. He passes as a native Indian boy, takes up with a wise old Tibetan lama, and eventually becomes a secret agent on behalf of the British government.

**Kin. Count kin with someone.** *See under* COUNT.

**Kith and kin.** *See under* KITH.

**Next of kin.** *See under* NEXT.

**Kindergarten** (German, 'children's garden'). The name is applied to schools for training young children where the child is led rather than taught, using play materials, handwork, songs and the like. The system was initiated by Friedrich Froebel (1782–1852), when he opened his first kindergarten at Blankenburg in 1837. The word is now applied to any school for pre-primary-school-age children.

**Kindness. Kill with kindness, To.** *See under* KILL.

**Milk of human kindness, The.** *See under* MILK.

**King** (Old English *cyning*, probably from a Germanic word related to 'kin' plus the suffix *-ing*, as if meaning 'scion of the race'). In the game of chess a king is the chief piece, in draughts a crowned man is called a king, and in cards it is a card carrying a picture of a king.

**King and the Miller of Mansfield, The.** This old ballad, given in PERCY'S RELIQUES (1765), tells how Henry II, having lost his way, met a miller, who took him home to his cottage. Next morning the courtiers traced the king and the miller discovered the rank of his guest, who in merry mood knighted his host as 'Sir John Cockle'. On St GEORGE's Day, Henry II invited the miller, his wife and son to a royal banquet, and after being amused with their rustic ways, made Sir John overseer of Sherwood Forest with a salary of £300 a year.

**King Bomba.** *See under* BOMB.

**King** or **Queen can do no wrong, The.** The legal and constitutional principle that the crown acts on the advice and consent of ministers and therefore the sovereign cannot be held responsible. It is another way of expressing the principle of ministerial responsibility. Nor, according to Dicey (*Law of the Constitution*, 1885), 'can the king be made personally responsible at law for any act done by him'.

**King Charles's head.** A phrase applied to an obsession; a fixed fancy. It comes from Mr Dick, the harmless half-wit in Dickens's *David Copperfield* (1849–50) who, whatever he wrote or said, always got round to the subject of King Charles's head, about which he was composing a memorial.

**King Charles spaniel.** A small black and tan spaniel with a rounded head, short muzzle, silky coat and long soft drooping ears. The variety came into favour at the RESTORATION, but the colour of the dogs at that time was liver and white.

**King Cole.** *See* OLD KING COLE.

**King Cotton.** Cotton, the staple of the American South, called at one time the COTTON KINGDOM. The expression was first used by James H. Hammond in the United States Senate in 1858.

**King Dagobert and St Eloi.** There is a traditional French song in which the king's minister, St ELOI, tells Dagobert that his coat has a hole in it, and the king replies: *C'est vrai, le tien est bon: prête-le-moi* ('It is true, but yours is good: lend it me'). After many such complaints and answers St Eloi says: 'My lord, your death is at hand!' 'Why can't you die instead of me?' replies the king. Since the Revolution the song has been adapted to suit the political events of the day. In 1814, for example, it was banned by the authorities on account of verses against NAPOLEON BONAPARTE and the Russian campaign of 1812.

**King Demos** (Greek *dēmos*, 'people'). The electorate, the proletariat, those who choose the rulers of the nation and are therefore ultimately sovereign. A facetious or derisive term.

**King Dick.** *See under* DICK.

**Kingdom, United.** *See under* UNITED.

**King Franconi.** *See under* FRANCONI.

**King Horn.** *See under* HORN.

**King James's Bible.** *See* AUTHORIZED VERSION *under* BIBLE.

**King Kong.** The giant ape who is the fearsome yet curiously touching star of the horror film (1933) that bears his name. He is discovered on a Pacific island, and brought to America as a circus attraction. He breaks loose there, runs riot in New York, and climbs the Empire State Building. He is finally gunned down by fighter planes, but not before he has gently carried a young woman (played by Fay Wray) in his hairy hand to the top of the skyscraper. Both parts of his name suggests that he is a king (Danish *Kong*). The story was written by Edgar Wallace and the film was directed by Merian C. Cooper. Jessica Lange played Wray's part in the 1976 remake.

**King Lear.** *See under* LEAR.

**King Lir.** *See under* LIR.

**King Log, A.** *See under* LOG.

**Kingmaker, The.** Richard Neville, Earl of Warwick (1428–71), so called because when he supported Henry VI, Henry was king, but when he sided with Edward IV, Henry was deposed and Edward crowned. He was killed at the Battle of Barnet after seeking to re-establish Henry VI. He was apparently first called 'the kingmaker' by John Major in his *History of Greater Britain, both England and Scotland* (1521).

**King Mark.** *See under* MARK.

**King of Arms.** *See* HERALD.

**King of Bath.** *See under* BATH.

**King of beasts, The.** The lion.

**King of birds, The.** The eagle.

**King of Cockneys, The.** In former days, a master of the revels chosen by the students of LINCOLN'S INN on CHILDERMAS Day.

**King of kings.** The Deity. The title has also been assumed by various eastern rulers, especially the sovereigns of Ethiopia.

> The blessed and only Potentate, the King of kings, and Lord of lords.
> 1 Timothy 6:15

**King of metals, The.** GOLD.

**King of Misrule.** In medieval and Tudor times the director of the Christmastide horseplay and festivities, called also the Abbot or Lord of Misrule and in Scotland the Abbot of Unreason. A King of Misrule was appointed at the royal court, and at Oxford and Cambridge one of the Masters of Arts superintended the revelries. John Stow tells how the lord mayor of London, the sheriffs and the noblemen each had their Lord of Misrule. Philip Stubbs, in his *Anatomie of Abuses* (1595), says that these mock dignitaries had from 20 to 100 officers, furnished with HOBBY horses, dragons and musicians. They first paraded in church with such a babble of noise that no one could hear what was said. Polydore Vergil says that the Feast of Misrule was derived from the Roman SATURNALIA. According to Stow: 'this pageant potentate began his rule at All Hallows' Eve and continued the same till the morrow after the Feast of the Purification.'

**King of Rome, The.** A title conferred by NAPOLEON BONAPARTE on his son Francis Charles Joseph Napoleon, Duke of Reichstadt (1811–32), on the day of his birth. His mother was the Empress Marie Louise. He was called L'Aiglon ('the young eagle') by Edmond Rostand in his play so titled (1900). His ashes were transferred to the INVALIDES in 1940.

**King of shreds and patches, A.** In the old MYSTERY plays Vice used to be dressed in the motley of a clown or buffoon, as a mimic king in a multicoloured suit. Thus Shakespeare says (*Hamlet*, III, iv (1600)):

> *Hamlet*: A vice of kings;
> A cut-purse of the empire and the rule,
> That from a shelf the precious diadem stole,
> And put it in his pocket!
> *Queen*: No more!
> *Hamlet*: A king of shreds and patches.

Gilbert and Sullivan's *Mikado*, I (1885) has NANKI-POO sing:

> A wandering minstrel I –
> A thing of shreds and patches.

The phrase has also been applied to a HACK who compiles books for publishers but supplies no originality of thought or matter. *See also* GRUB STREET.

**King of the Beggars, The.** Bampfylde Moore Carew (1693–1770), a famous English vagrant who became king of the GYPSIES. He was transported to Maryland, where he escaped. He is said to have subsequently joined the YOUNG PRETENDER and followed him to Derby.

**King of the Border, The.** A nickname of Adam Scott of Tushielaw (executed 1529), a famous border outlaw and chief.

**King of the castle.** A children's game in which each child aims to stand alone on a sandcastle or mound of some kind by pushing the others off it. The successful child calls out, 'I'm the king of the castle!' *See also* WILLIE WASTLE *under* WILLIAM.

**King of the Dunces, The.** In his first version of the *Dunciad* (1712), Alexander Pope gave this place of honour to Lewis Theobald (1688–1744), but the edition of 1742 has Colley Cibber (1671–1757) in his stead.

**King of the forest, The.** The OAK.

**King of the Herrings, The.** The CHIMERA, or sea ape, a cartilaginous fish that accompanies a shoal of herrings in their migrations.

**King of the king.** Cardinal Richelieu (1585–1642) was so called because of his influence over Louis XIII of France.

**King of the Romans, The.** The title usually assumed by the sovereign of the HOLY ROMAN EMPIRE previous to his actual coronation at Rome. NAPOLEON BONAPARTE's son, afterwards the Duke of Reichstadt, was styled the KING OF ROME at his birth in 1811.

**King of the World, The.** The title (in Hindi *Shah Jehan*) assumed by Khorrum Shah, third son of Selim Jehangir and fifth of the Mogul emperors of Delhi (r.1627–58).

**King of waters, The.** The River Amazon, in South America. Although not as long as the Mississippi-Missouri (which is the longest river in the world), it discharges a greater volume of water.

**King of Yvetot, The.** *See under* YVETOT.

**King over the Water, The.** The name given by JACOBITES to James II after his flight to France, to his son the OLD PRETENDER (James III), and to his grandsons Charles Edward the YOUNG PRETENDER (Charles III) and Henry, cardinal of York (Henry IX).

**Kingpin.** In skittles, ninepins and other similar games, the pin in the centre when all the pins are in place, or the pin at the front, because if struck successfully it knocks down the others. Figuratively the word is applied to the principal person in a company, enterprise or other group.

**Kings and queens honoured as saints.** *See under* SAINT.

**King's** or **Queen's Bench.** The Supreme Court of COMMON LAW, so called because at one time the sovereign presided in this court, and the court followed the sovereign when he or she moved from one place to another. Originally called the *Aulia Regia*, it is now one of the three divisions of the HIGH COURT of Justice.

**King's Book, The.** The usual name given to Henry VIII's *Necessary Doctrine and Evolution for any Christian Man* (1543), issued after presentation to Convocation. It was based on the *Bishops' Book* of 1537 and the royal supremacy was more strongly emphasized. Its doctrinal tone was more Catholic than that of its predecessor. It was probably the work of Thomas Cranmer, although Henry VIII seems to have contributed the preface.

**King's Cave, The.** A cave on the west coast of the Isle of Arran, Scotland, so called because it was here that Robert BRUCE and his retinue are said to have lodged before they landed in Carrick (1307).

**King's Champion, The.** *See* CHAMPION OF ENGLAND.

**King's** or **Queen's Colour, The.** The UNION JACK, except in the case of Foot Guards, the first of the two colours borne by regiments. In the Guards it is a crimson flag bearing the royal cipher. The first colour was called 'King's' in 1751, 'Royal' in 1837, with the accession of Queen Victoria, and 'Queen's' in 1892. *See also* REGIMENTAL COLOURS.

**King's** or **Queen's Counsel.** In England a member of the BAR appointed by the crown or the nomination of the LORD CHANCELLOR, and in Scotland on the recommendation of the Lord Justice General. A KC or QC wears a silk gown and is thus often called a silk. He or she takes precedence over the junior Bar and in a case must be accompanied by a junior barrister.

**King's** or **Queen's County, The.** A former county in the province of Leinster in Ireland. It was so called in 1556 when planted by English settlers, but is now called Offaly, its former name. Similarly Queen's County is once more called Leix (Laois).

**King's** or **Queen's English, The.** English as it should be spoken. The term occurs in Shakespeare's *The Merry Wives of Windsor* (I, iv (1600)), but it is older and was evidently common. 'Queene's English' is found in Thomas Nashe's *Strange Newes of the Intercepting Certaine Letters* (1593), and 'thou clipst the Kinge's English' in Thomas Dekker's *Satiro-Mastix* (1602). *See also* FOWLER.

**King's** or **Queen's evil, The.** Scrofula, which was supposedly cured by the royal touch. Hence the name. The custom existed in France long before its introduction into England by EDWARD THE CONFESSOR (r.1042–66). Ceremonial touching was introduced by Henry VII (r.1485–1509) and the sufferers were presented with gold coins, although CHARLES I sometimes gave silver touch pieces instead of gold. The practice reached its height under Charles II, who is said to have touched nearly 100,000 people and in 1682 alone some 8500. Some of those who came to him for the touch were trampled to death. William III called it 'a silly superstition' and it was last practised by Queen Anne, who touched Dr Johnson without effecting a cure in 1712. Between the reign of Charles I (1625–49) and 1719 the Book of Common Prayer contained an office for the touching. The OLD and YOUNG PRETENDERS also claimed this power.

**King's Friends.** The name given in the early years of George III's reign (1760–1820) to those politicians, mainly Tories, who for various reasons supported the crown and its ministries. The term was used with derogatory implications by the WHIGS. Their subservience to the king has been overestimated, as well as their importance as a coherent political group.

**King's** or **Queen's Guide.** A GIRL GUIDE who has passed the highest proficiency tests.

**King's** or **Queen's highway.** Any public road or right of way.

**King's** or **Queen's messenger.** An official of the British Foreign Office whose duty it is to carry personally confidential messages from London to any embassy or legation abroad. He carries as his badge of office a silver greyhound, and although he receives courtesies and help in the countries across which he travels, he enjoys no diplomatic immunities or privileges except that of passing through the customs the 'diplomatic bag' he is carrying.

**King's Oak, The.** The OAK under which Henry VIII sat in Epping Forest, while Anne Boleyn was being executed (1536). Its name is preserved in the King's Oak Hotel, High Beech.

**Kings of Israel.** The kings of ISRAEL, and subsequently Israel and JUDAH separately, with dates when their reigns began, are as follows:

Kings of Judah-Israel:
- SAUL: *c*.1020 BC
- DAVID: *c*.1000
- SOLOMON: *c*.961

Kings of Israel:
- Jeroboam I: *c*.922 BC
- Nadab: *c*.901
- Baasha: *c*.900
- Elah: *c*.877
- Zimri: *c*.876
- Tibni: *c*.876
- Omri: *c*.876
- AHAB: *c*.869
- Ahaziah: *c*.850
- Jehoram: *c*.849
- Jehu: *c*.842
- Jehoahaz: *c*.815
- Joash: *c*.801
- Jeroboam II: *c*.786
- Zachariah: *c*.746
- Shallum: *c*.745
- Menahem: *c*.745
- Pekahiah: *c*.736
- Pekah: *c*.735
- Hoshea: *c*.732

Kings of Judah:
- Rehoboam: *c*.922 BC
- Abijah: *c*.915
- Asa: *c*.913
- JEHOSHAPHAT: *c*.873
- Jehoram: *c*.849
- Ahaziah: *c*.842
- Athaliah: *c*.842
- Joash: *c*.837
- Amaziah: *c*.800
- Uzziah: *c*.783
- Jotham: *c*.742
- Ahaz: *c*.735
- HEZEKIAH: *c*.715
- Manasseh: *c*.687
- Amon: *c*.642
- JOSIAH: *c*.640
- Jehoahaz: 609
- Jehoiaikim: 609
- Jehoiachin: 597
- Zedekiah: 597

**King's** or **Queen's peace, The.** The peace of law-abiding subjects; originally the protection secured by the sovereign to those employed on royal business.

**King's** or **Queen's proctor, The.** The Treasury solicitor who represents the crown in maritime and matrimonial cases. The proctor's main function is to intervene to show cause why a DECREE NISI should not be made absolute because material facts have not been disclosed.

**King's** or **Queen's ransom, A.** A very large sum of money.

**King's** or **Queen's Regulations.** Regulations governing the organization and discipline of the Royal Navy, the Army and the Royal Air Force.

**King's** or **Queen's Remembrancer, The.** Originally an EXCHEQUER clerk sharing the work of establishing and collecting fixed revenues and debts with the Lord Treasurer's Remembrancer. In 1323 the King's Remembrancer was assigned to casual crown revenues, proceedings against defaulters and the like, and other duties were added later. In 1877 the office was transferred to the Supreme Court and is now held by the Senior Master of the KING'S OR QUEEN'S BENCH division. His duties are concerned with the selection of sheriffs, the swearing-in of the lord mayor of London and with revenue cases.

**King's** or **Queen's scholar, A.** A student who holds a school or college scholarship in a royal foundation.

**King's** or **Queen's Scout, A.** A BOY SCOUT who has passed the highest tests of proficiency and endurance. His female equivalent is a KING'S OR QUEEN'S GUIDE.

**King's** or **Queen's shilling, The.** To take the king's or queen's shilling is to enlist. The allusion is to the former practice of giving each recruit a shilling when he was sworn in.

**King's** or **Queen's speech, The.** The speech from the throne in the HOUSE OF LORDS made at the opening of a parliamentary session outlining the government's programme for the session. It is always addressed to both Houses but the special clause relating to finance is addressed to the HOUSE OF COMMONS alone.

**King Stork.** *See under* STORK.

**Bean king.** *See under* BEAN.
**Bluff King Hall.** *See under* BLUFF.
**Cat may look at a king, A.** *See under* CAT.
**Citizen King, The.** *See under* CITIZEN.
**City of the Three Kings, The.** *See under* CITY.
**Cotton king.** *See under* COTTON.
**Dandy King, The.** *See under* DANDY.
**Days fatal to kings.** *See under* DAY.
**Factory King, The.** *See under* FACTORY.
**Fisher King.** *See under* FISH.
**Flower of Kings, The.** *See under* FLOWER.
**Handcuff king.** *See under* HANDCUFF.
**Kaffir King, The.** *See under* KAFFIR.
**Like a king.** *See under* LIKE.
**Lord Lyon King of Arms.** *See under* LORD.
**Maiden King, The.** *See under* MAIDEN.
**Master of the King's Music.** *See under* MASTER.
**Paper King, The.** *See under* PAPER.
**Pearly king.** *See under* PEARL.
**Railway King.** *See under* RAILROAD.
**Sailor King, The.** *See under* SAILOR.
**Snow King, The.** *See under* SNOW.
**Sun King, The.** *See under* SUN.
**Three Kings, The.** *See* MAGI.
**Three Kings' Day.** *See under* THREE.
**Three Kings of Cologne, The.** *See under* THREE.
**Valley of the Kings, The.** *See under* VALLEY.

**Kingdom. Kingdom come.** The next world; life after death.
**Cotton kingdom.** *See under* COTTON.
**Flowery Kingdom, The.** *See under* FLOWER.

**Kiplingcotes Derby.** The oldest FLAT RACE in Great Britain, run in March near Market Weighton, North Yorkshire. The 4-mile (6.4km) course of narrow roads and tracks dates from 1519. The second prize is often worth more than the first.

> Miss Cole-Walton's three-length lead cost her £24 (the first prize was £16, the second £40). 'But I don't really mind; it's much better to win.'
> *The Times* (17 March 1972)

**Kirk. Kirk of Skulls.** The long abandoned Kirk of St John at Gamrie, east of Banff, Scotland, so called because the skulls and other bones of the Norsemen who fell in the neighbouring field, the Bloody Pits, were built into its walls.
**Auld Kirk, The.** *See* CHURCH OF SCOTLAND.

**Kirke's Lambs.** *See under* REGIMENTAL AND DIVISIONAL NICKNAMES.

**Kismet.** Fate, destiny or the fulfilment of destiny. The word comes from Persian *qismet*, 'portion', 'lot'. *See also* KISS ME, HARDY.

**Kiss** (Old English *cyssan*). An ancient and widespread mode of salutation frequently mentioned in the Bible as an expression of reverence and adoration, and as a greeting or farewell among friends. ESAU ran to meet JACOB, 'and embraced him, and fell on his neck, and kissed him' (Genesis 33:4), the repentant woman continually kissed the feet of Christ (Luke 7:45), and the disciples of Ephesus 'fell on Paul's neck, and kissed him' (Acts 20:37). In the New Testament the kiss becomes a token of Christian brotherhood: 'Salute one another with an holy kiss' (Romans 16:16). Kissing between the sexes occurs in Proverbs 7:13, 14: 'So she caught him and kissed him, and with an impudent face said unto him, I have peace offerings with me.'

The old custom of 'kissing the bride' comes from the Salisbury rubric concerning the PAX.

In billiards (and bowls) a kiss is a very slight touch of one moving ball on another, especially a second touch. The term was also formerly used of a drop of sealing wax accidentally let fall beside the seal.

The sign 'X' to signify a kiss, as at the end of a letter, probably represents the meeting of two pairs of lips.

**Kissagram.** A greetings service for a party or celebration, in which a person is hired to come and kiss the celebrator. The word is a blend of 'kiss' and 'telegram'.

**Kiss and make up** or **be friends, To.** To be reconciled after a quarrel or disagreement.

**Kiss-and-tell.** A journalistic term for a practice favoured by the popular press, in which an 'ordinary' person tells of their sexual relationship, or supposed relationship, with a celebrity.

**Kiss-behind-the-garden-gate.** A rural name for a pansy.

**Kiss curl.** A circular curl of hair pressed flat against the forehead or cheek.

**Kisser.** A slang term for the mouth or face.

**Kiss goodbye to, To.** To accept the loss of something.

**Kiss hands, To.** To kiss the hand of the sovereign either on accepting or retiring from office.

Kissing the hand of, or one's own hand to, an idol was a usual form of adoration. God said he had in Israel 7000 persons who had not bowed unto BAAL, 'every mouth which hath not kissed him' (1 Kings 19:18).

**Kissing cousin.** A relative close enough to be kissed on formal occasions.

**Kissing gate.** A gate in a V-shaped or U-shaped enclosure, which allows only one person to pass through at a time. The person opens the gate, enters the enclosure, then closes the same gate behind him to leave. If there are two people, one has the chance to kiss the other while this is going on.

**Kissing the pope's toe.** Matthew of Westminster (15th century) says it was customary formerly to kiss the hand of his Holiness, but that a certain woman in the 8th century not only kissed the pope's hand but 'squeezed it'. Seeing the danger to which he was exposed, the pope cut off his hand and was compelled in future to offer his foot. In reality the pope's foot (i.e. the cross embroidered on his right shoe) may be kissed by the visitor. Bishops kiss the knee as well. This is an old sign of respect and does not imply servility. It is customary to bend the knee and kiss the ring of a cardinal, bishop or abbot.

**Kissing under the mistletoe.** An English CHRISTMAS custom, dating back at least to the early 17th century. The correct procedure, now seldom observed, is that a man should pick a berry when he kisses a girl under the MISTLETOE, and when the last berry is gone there should be no more kissing.

**Kiss-in-the-ring.** A game played by children or young people of both sexes. They all join hands in a ring except one, who runs round outside the ring and touches (or drops a handkerchief behind) a player of the opposite sex, who then leaves the ring and chases after the person, giving them a kiss when caught.

**Kiss it better.** A mother's kiss on a young child's hurt is said to be a relic of the custom of sucking poison from wounds. St MARTIN OF TOURS observed a leper covered with sores at the city gates of Paris. He went up to him and kissed the sores and the leper instantly became whole. There are many such stories.

**Kiss me, Hardy.** These famous words, often used facetiously, were uttered by the dying Lord Nelson when taking leave of his flag captain, Thomas Masterman Hardy (1769–1839), in the moment of victory at the Battle of Trafalgar (1805). Hardy knelt down and kissed his cheek. They were preceded by the request, 'Take care of poor Lady Hamilton.' According to some, the words actually spoken by Nelson were 'Kismet, Hardy,' i.e. 'Fate, Hardy'. *See also* KISMET.

**Kiss my arse** or **ass**. A crude challenge or rejection, inviting a person to perform the stated obsequious and degrading act.

**Kiss of death.** An action or relationship that has disastrous consequences. The allusion is to the kiss that JUDAS ISCARIOT gave Jesus in the garden of GETHSEMANE. *See also* JUDAS KISS.

**Kiss of life.** The name applied to the mouth-to-mouth method of artificial respiration. SLEEPING BEAUTY was awakened from her deathlike sleep by the Prince's kiss. The expression is also used metaphorically for anything that revives or re-invigorates.

**Kiss of peace.** A mutual greeting between members of the congregation in the EUCHARIST. It is not an actual kiss, but a shaking of hands. It is a revival of a custom in the primitive church, and is not welcomed by some of the faithful, who claim that it is artificial and disrupts the progression of the service. *See also* PAX.

**Kiss the book, To.** To kiss the Bible or the New Testament after taking an oath. The kiss is one of confirmation or promise to act in accordance with the words of the oath and a public acknowledgement of its sanctity.

In the English courts, the Houses of Parliament and certain other places, non-Christians are permitted to affirm without kissing the book, as a result of the struggle waged by the atheist Charles Bradlaugh (1833–91) to take his seat in the HOUSE OF COMMONS. He was first elected in 1880 and finally admitted to the House in 1886. Previously, in 1858, Baron Lionel de Rothschild (1808–79), the first Jew to be admitted to Parliament, as a Jew, had been allowed to swear on the Old Testament. He had been elected as WHIG MP for the City of London in 1847. The position was legalized by the Oaths Act of 1888.

In Roman Catholic and some HIGH CHURCH Anglican churches it is customary for the priest to kiss the Bible after reading the Gospel.

**Kiss the dust, To.** To submit abjectly; to be defeated.

**Kiss the gunner's daughter, To.** To be flogged on board ship. At one time sailors in the Royal Navy who were to be flogged were tied to the breech of a cannon.

**Kiss the mistress, To.** To make a good hit; to shoot right into the eye of the target. In bowls the expression means to graze another bowl with your own. The JACK (4) used to be called the 'mistress', and when one ball just touches another, it is said to kiss it.

**Kiss the rod, To.** To submit to punishment or misfortune meekly and without murmuring.

**Blow a kiss, To.** *See under* BLOW.

**Butterfly kiss.** *See under* BUTTERFLY.

**Judas kiss.** *See under* JUDAS.

**Kist of whistles.** A Scots term for a church organ. Kist is the same word as *cist* ('chest').

**Kit Carson.** *See under* CARSON.

**Kit-Cat Club.** A club formed about 1700 by the aristocratic WHIGS of the day who dined in the house of Christopher (Kit) Cat, a pastry cook of Shire Lane. His mutton pies, called 'kitkats', always formed part of their meals. Among the distinguished noblemen and gentlemen were Steele, Addison, Congreve, Sir Samuel Garth, Vanbrugh, Manwaring, Stepney, Sir Robert Walpole, Pulteney and the Duke of Somerset. Jacob Tonson (1656–1737), the publisher, was the secretary.

Sir Godfrey Kneller (*c.*1649–1723) painted 42 portraits (now in the National Portrait Gallery) of the club members for Tonson, in whose villa at Barn Elms the meetings were latterly held. The paintings were made three-quarter length (36 × 28in/91 × 71cm) in order to accommodate them to the size of the club's dining room. Hence a three-quarter length portrait came to be called a 'kitcat' (or 'kitkat'). The club closed *c.*1720.

**Kitchen. Kitchen cabinet.** An American term for an informal group of advisers used by a President and given more weight than the proper cabinet. The term was first used of such an unofficial group advising Andrew Jackson, known as OLD HICKORY, who was President 1829–37.

**Kitchen sink drama.** A type of drama popular in the 1950s, in which the plot centres on the more sordid aspects of working-class or lower-middle-class domestic life, much of which is spent at the kitchen sink.

**Devil's Kitchen.** *See under* DEVIL.

**Everything but the kitchen sink.** *See under* EVERY.

**Kite.** In lawyer's slang, a junior counsel who was allotted at an assize court to advocate the cause of a prisoner who was without other defence.

In RAF slang, the word denoted an aircraft, and in STOCK EXCHANGE jargon, it is used for an accommodation bill, i.e. a bill of exchange co-signed by a guarantor.

**Kitemark.** The label on a manufactured product that says it meets with the approval of the British Standards Institution. It consists of a kite-shaped monogram of the letters BSI, the Institution's initials. The BSI was founded in 1901 and the Kitemark was already in use in 1903 on tramway lines.

**As high as a kite.** *See under* AS.

**Fly a kite, To.** *See under* FLY.

**Kith and kin** (Old English *cȳthth*, 'relationship', and *cynn*, 'kind', 'family'). One's own people and kindred, one's friends and relations.

**Kit's Coty House.** A great CROMLECH 3½ miles (5.6km) north of Maidstone, Kent, on the Rochester road, consisting of a block of sandstone, 12ft (3.7m) long, resting on three standing stones. The name is said to derive from Celtic (British) *ket coed*, 'tomb (in a) wood'. It is near the ancient battlefield where Vortigern is said to have fought HENGIST AND HORSA.

**Kittens, Cat and.** *See under* CAT.

**Kiwanis.** An organization founded in the USA in 1915 aiming to improve business ethics and provide leadership for raising the level of business and professional ideals. There are many Kiwanis clubs in the USA and Canada, and also several in Britain. The name is said to come from a Native American language and to mean 'to make oneself known'.

**Kiwi.** A New Zealand bird of the genus *Apteryx*, which is incapable of flight. In flying circles the word is applied to a man of the ground staff of an airfield. It also denotes a New Zealander.

**Klondike.** A river and district of the Yukon, Canada. The rich gold-bearing gravel found at Bonanza Creek in 1896 resulted in a wild rush of prospectors. Gold production reached its peak in 1900.

**Knave** (Old English *cnafa*, related to modern German *Knabe*, 'boy'). The word originally meant a boy or male child, then a male servant, or a male of lowly estate, and subsequently a rascal.

In cards the knave (or jack), the lowest COURT CARD of each suit, is the common soldier or servant of the royalties.

**Knee. Knee-high to a grasshopper.** Very small; very young.

**Kneejerk reaction.** Literally, the reflex kick that a person's lower leg gives when it is tapped sharply just below the knee. Figuratively, the expression is used of any automatic or unthinking response or reaction.

**Knees-up.** A boisterous and energetic dance, in which the dancers raise alternate knees. Hence any lively party or celebration. The dance gets its name from the song to which it is traditionally performed, 'Knees up, Mother Brown!'

> Ooh! Knees up Mother Brown!
> Well! Knees up Mother Brown!
> ... knees up, knees up!
> Don't get the breeze up
> Knees up Mother Brown.
>
> HARRIS WESTON & BERT LEE: 'Knees up, Mother Brown!' (1939)

**Knee-trembler.** An act of sexual intercourse performed in a standing position.

**Knee tribute.** A former term for adoration or reverence by bending the knee, otherwise an act of homage. *See also* LIP SERVICE.

**Bring someone to their knees, To.** *See under* BRING.

**Housemaid's knee.** *See under* HOUSE.

**Weak-kneed.** *See under* WEAK.

**Wounded Knee.** *See under* WOUND.

**Knell, Death.** *See under* DEATH.

**Knickerbockers.** Loose-fitting breeches, gathered in below the knees, formerly worn by boys, cyclists, sportsmen and others, and by women as an undergarment. They were so named from George Cruikshank's illustrations for Washington Irving's *A History of New York from the Beginning of the World to the End of the Dutch Dynasty* (1809), written under the pseudonym Diedrich Knickerbocker, in which the Dutchmen wore such breeches. The name probably meant a baker of knickers, i.e. clay marbles. Hence modern knickers, as a short form of this. *See also* BLOOMERS.

**Knickerbocker glory.** A rich confection consisting of ice cream, jelly, cream and fruit served in a tall glass. It is not clear what relationship, if any, it has with KNICKERBOCKERS.

**Don't get your knickers in a twist.** Keep calm; don't lose your temper. The allusion is to a woman hurriedly dressing (or re-dressing).

**Knife.** The emblem of St AGATHA, St Albert and St

Christina. The flaying knife is the emblem of St BARTHOLOMEW, because he was flayed.

The custom of demanding a small coin when making a present of a knife or a pair of scissors is said to come from Sheffield, the home of the Cutlers' Company. The 'gift' having been 'bought' makes the purchaser responsible for any injury that may be sustained when using the knife or scissors. The custom is also found outside Britain.

**Knifeboard.** The long back-to-back seats that used to run longitudinally along the top of the old horse omnibuses. In the 1890s transverse 'garden seats' gradually took their place. The allusion is to the old board used for cleaning steel table knives.

**Before you can say knife.** Very quickly.

**Bowie knife.** *See under* BOWIE.

**Get one's knife into someone, To.** To treat a person maliciously; to victimize or harass someone.

**Live on a knife edge, To.** *See under* LIVE.

**Night of the Long Knives, The.** *See under* NIGHT.

**Under the knife.** *See under* UNDER.

**Knight** (Old English *cniht*, 'servant'). The word was originally used for a boy or servant; it then came to denote a man of gentle birth who, after serving at court or in the retinue of some lord as a page and ESQUIRE, was admitted with appropriate ceremonies to an honourable degree of military rank and given the right to bear arms. *See also* BACHELOR; BANNERET; BARONET.

Since the disappearance of KNIGHT SERVICE, knights, as men of standing in England, have continued to give service as KNIGHTS OF THE SHIRE or SHERIFFS and in similar positions of authority. Titles have long been bestowed on administrative officials, professional men, politicians, scholars, artists and the like, as well as those serving in the armed forces, trades union officials, sportsmen and others.

There are eight British Orders of Knighthood in regular use today, the oldest being that of the Garter (*see* MOST NOBLE ORDER OF THE GARTER), which takes precedence, and which was probably founded in 1348. The others are (in order of precedence):

MOST ANCIENT ORDER OF THE THISTLE (1687)
KNIGHTS OF THE BATH (1399, but revived in 1725 and subsequently reorganized)
ORDER OF MERIT (1902)
ORDER OF ST MICHAEL AND ST GEORGE (1818)
Royal Victorian Order (1896)
Order of the British Empire (1917)
Companions of Honour (1917)

No awards have been made for the Order of the STAR OF INDIA (1861) or Order of the Indian Empire (1868) since 1947, when that country gained its independence. Appointments to the Garter, Thistle, Order of Merit and Royal Victorian Order are in the personal gift of the sovereign. The others are on the recommendation of the Prime Minister.

The modern Knights Bachelor do not constitute an order and rank lowest in precedence. The wife of a knight is designated 'Dame' or, more usually, 'Lady'.

**Knight Bachelor.** *See* KNIGHT; BACHELOR.

**Knight Banneret.** *See* BANNERET.

**Knight Baronet.** The original title of a BARONET.

**Knight errant.** A medieval knight, especially a hero of those long romances satirized by Cervantes in *Don* QUIXOTE (1605), who wandered about the world in quest of adventure and in search of opportunities to rescue damsels in distress and to perform other chivalrous deeds.

**Knight in shining armour, A.** A chivalrous rescuer or helper, especially of a woman. *See also* DAMSEL IN DISTRESS.

**Knight Marshal.** *See* MARSHALSEA PRISON.

**Knight of Grace.** A member of the lower order of the Knights of Malta. *See also* HOSPITALLERS.

**Knight of La Mancha, The.** Don QUIXOTE de la Mancha, the hero of Cervantes' romance *Don Quixote* (1605). La Mancha, a former province of Spain, is now an arid plateau in the centre of the country and its most sparsely populated region. *La Mancha* derives from Arabic *mansha*, 'dry land'.

**Knight of the Rueful Countenance, The.** Don QUIXOTE.

**Knight of the road, A.** A HIGHWAYMAN; a commercial traveller; a tramp; a lorry or taxi driver. The name in each case is humorous or ironic. *See also* GENTLEMAN OF THE ROAD.

**Knight of the Shire.** The original name for the two men of the rank of knight who formerly represented a shire or county in Parliament. A 'knight of the shires' is now a term for a BACKBENCHER, usually a Conservative, who has been awarded a knighthood for long and dedicated service. He is typically a former landowner from MIDDLE ENGLAND.

**Knight of the Swan, The.** LOHENGRIN.

**Knight service.** The tenure of land in feudal times, on the condition of rendering military service to the crown for 40 days. By the time of Edward III (r.1327–77) knights were paid for their military service.

**Knights Hospitallers.** *See* HOSPITALLERS.

**Knights of Columbus.** A Roman Catholic fraternal and philanthropic society in the USA, founded in 1882 with the aim of uniting laymen of that church in corporate religious and civic usefulness.

**Knights of Malta.** *See* HOSPITALLERS.

**Knights of Pythias, The.** A benevolent fraternity in the USA and Canada, founded at Washington, D.C., in 1864. The Pythian Sisters, founded in 1888, are recruited from female relatives of the Knights.

**Knights of the Bath.** This order derives its name from the ceremony of bathing, which was formerly practised at the inauguration of a KNIGHT as a symbol of purity. The ceremony was established by Henry IV (r.1399–1413), and the last knights were created in the ancient manner at the coronation of Charles II in 1661. GCB stands for Grand Cross of the Bath (the first class), KCB, Knight Commander of the Bath (the second class), and CB, Companion of the Bath (the third class).

**Knights of the Holy Sepulchre.** An order of military knights founded by the French Crusader Godfrey of Bouillon (*c.*1060–1100) in 1099 to guard the Holy Sepulchre.

**Knights of the Round Table.** According to Sir Thomas Malory (*Le Morte d'Arthur*, iii (1485)) there were 150 knights who had 'sieges' at the round table. King Leodegraunce brought 100 when he gave the table to King ARTHUR, MERLIN filled up 28 of the vacant seats, and the king elected GAWAIN and Tor. The remaining 20 were left for those who might prove worthy.

A list of the knights (151) and a description of their armour is given in the *Theatre of Honour* (1622) by Andrew Fairne. These knights went forth in quest of adventures, but their chief exploits were concerned with the quest of the HOLY GRAIL.

Sir LANCELOT is a model of fidelity, bravery, frailty in love and repentance, Sir GALAHAD of chastity, Sir GAWAIN of courtesy, Sir KAY of a rude, boastful knight, and Sir MODRED of treachery. *See also* ARTHURIAN ROMANCES; ROUND TABLE.

**Knights of the White Camellia.** *See* KU KLUX KLAN.

**Knights of Windsor.** Originally a small order of knights founded by Edward III (r.1327–77) in 1348 after the wars in France to assist English knights who had been held prisoner in France and become impoverished through having to pay heavy ransoms. It was formed of 26 veterans, but under the will of Henry VIII (r.1509–47) their number was reduced to 13, with a Governor, a figure that has since remained. The members are meritorious military officers who are granted apartments in Windsor Castle with a small stipend in addition to their army pension. They take part in all ceremonies of the MOST NOBLE ORDER OF THE GARTER and attend Sunday morning service in St George's Chapel as representatives of the Knights of the Garter. Their present uniform of scarlet tailcoat with white cross sword-belt, crimson sash and cocked hat with plume was designed by William IV, who changed their title to Military Knights of Windsor.

**Knights Templar.** *See* TEMPLARS.

**Belted knight.** *See under* BELT.

**Carpet knight.** *See under* CARPET.

**City of Dreadful Knights, The.** *See under* CITY.

**Cross-legged knights.** *See under* CROSS.

**Distraint of knighthood.** *See under* DISTRAINT.

**Last of the Knights, The.** *See under* LAST.

**Teutonic Knights.** *See under* TEUTONS.

**White knight.** *See under* WHITE.

**Knillian, The.** A tradition enacted at John Knill's Monument on Worvas Hill near St Ives, Cornwall. Knill, a local bachelor benefactor, built the monument to himself and on his death in 1782 left provision for ten little girls clad in white to dance round it every fifth year on St James's Day (25 July) to the tune of the OLD HUNDRED played on a violin. It is now a civic ceremony, led by the mayor.

**Knob. With knobs** or **brass knobs on.** *See under* WITH.

**Knobkerrie.** A stick that can be used both as a walking sick and as a weapon. It is fashioned in such a way that it has a large knob on the top and is chiefly in use among South African tribesmen. Its name represents Afrikaans *knopkierie*, from *knop*, 'knob', and *kieri*, 'stick', a word of Hottentot (Khoikhoin) origin.

**Knobstick wedding, A.** The name given to an 18th-century practice whereby the churchwardens of a parish used their authority to encourage the marriage of a pregnant woman, which they attended officially. The term 'knobstick' was in allusion to the churchwarden's staff, his symbol of office. *See also* SHOTGUN WEDDING.

**Knock. Knock, To.** In slang of former days, to create a great impression; to be irresistible, as in Albert Chevalier's song 'Knocked 'em in the Old Kent Road' (1892), i.e. astonished the inhabitants or filled them with admiration. *See also* ALBERT THE GREAT.

In current colloquial usage the verb means to criticize adversely; to belittle; to disparage.

**Knock about** or **around, To.** To travel about, especially to distant or exotic places, as: 'He's knocked about a bit.'

**Knockabout turn, A.** A MUSIC HALL term for a noisy, boisterous act usually involving horseplay and SLAPSTICK.

**Knock down, To.** To dispose of an article to the highest bidder at an auction, when a sale is indicated by a knock of the auctioneer's gavel.

**Knocked down with a feather, To be.** To be overcome with surprise.

> I was so confounded at these words, you might have beat me down with a feather.
>
> SAMUEL RICHARDSON: *Pamela*, letter vii (1749)

**Knock for knock agreement.** An agreement between insurance companies by which each pays a policyholder regardless of liability.

**Knock** or **hit for six, To.** To demolish utterly an argument or to defeat completely an opponent, figuratively or literally. In CRICKET the ball is 'knocked for six' when the batsman, by hitting it over the boundary of the cricket field, scores six runs.

> 'It hit me for six. I am not proud of it', he told the jury. 'It was an extraordinarily passionate relationship that really did overwhelm me over the next few months'.
> *The Times* (27 January 1999)

**Knocking-shop.** A slang term for a brothel, from 'to knock', meaning to have sexual intercourse.

**Knock into a cocked hat, To.** To beat in a contest by a wide margin; to defeat easily. In the game of ninepins, three pins were set up in the form of a triangle, and when all the pins except these three were knocked down, the set was said to be 'knocked into a cocked hat'. The idea is that of a hat being knocked out of shape.

**Knock into shape, To.** To LICK INTO SHAPE.

**Knock into the middle of next week, To.** To beat someone thoroughly.

**Knock-kneed.** With the knees turned inwards so that they almost knock or rub together in walking.

**Knock, knock!** An invitation to respond to a riddle punning on a personal name. An old example is: 'Knock, knock!' 'Who's there?' 'Roland.' 'Roland who?' 'Roland mow the lawn.' More sophisticated examples may be allusive: 'Knock, knock!' 'Who's there?' 'Sam and Janet.' 'Sam and Janet who?' 'Sam and Janet evening.' A restriction to personal names is not essential: 'Knock, knock!' 'Who's there?' 'A little old lady.' 'A little old lady who?' 'I didn't know you could yodel.'

**Knock off, To.** To cease work; to steal; to kill.

**Knock** or **blow one's socks off, To.** To astound; to amaze.

**Knock-on effect.** An effect caused indirectly by some other event or circumstance.

**Knock on wood, To.** The American equivalent of to TOUCH WOOD. *See under* TOUCH.

**Knockout.** A disabling blow, especially in boxing, which renders the recipient unconscious, thus finishing the fight. Hence a complete surprise is 'a fair knockout'. A knockout contest is one in which competitors are gradually eliminated. If a person or thing is described generally as 'knockout' or 'a knockout', they are unusually impressive or attractive.

**Knockout drops.** A drug added to a drink to render the drinker unconscious.

**Knock out of the box, To.** In baseball, to score so highly against a pitcher that he is replaced by another in the box. Figuratively, to achieve an easy and decisive victory over an opponent.

**Knock spots off someone, To.** To beat them soundly; to get the better of them. The allusion is probably to pistol shooting at a playing card, when a good shot will knock out the pips or spots.

**Knock the bottom** or **the stuffing out of, To.** To invalidate an argument incontrovertibly.

**Postman's knock.** *See under* POSTMAN.

**Knot** (Old English *cnotta*, allied to modern *knit* and Latin *nodus*). As applied to the unit of speed for ships and aircraft, a knot is 1 NAUTICAL MILE (about 1.15 statute miles) per hour. It is so called from the knots tied on the log-line formerly used on a ship in conjunction with the sandglass, the speed being the number of knots run out during the time measured by the sandglass. *See also* LOG.

**Knotgrass.** This plant, *Polygonum aviculare*, if taken in an infusion, was at one time believed to check growth.

> Get you gone, you dwarf;
> You minimus, of hindering knot-grass made.
> SHAKESPEARE: *A Midsummer Night's Dream*, III, ii (1595)

**Knotty problem, A.** A difficult or intricate one.

**At a rate of knots.** *See under* AT.

**Cut the knot, To.** *See under* CUT.

**Get knotted!** An uncouth response expressing annoyance or rejection.

**Gordian knot.** *See under* GORDIAN.

**Granny knot.** *See under* GRANNY.

**Herculean knot.** *See under* HERCULES.

**Love knot.** *See under* LOVE.

**Marriage knot, The.** *See under* MARRIAGE.

**Tie in knots, To.** To baffle; to bewilder.

**Truelove** or **true-lovers' knot.** *See under* TRUE.

**Know. Know a hawk from a handsaw, To.** To be able to distinguish one thing from another. In *Hamlet*, II, ii (1600), Hamlet says: 'I am but mad north-north-west: when the wind is southerly I know a hawk from a handsaw'. 'Handsaw' is probably a corruption of *hernshaw* (a young heron), so the expression means 'I know a hawk from a heron', 'I know the bird of prey from the game flown at', and hence, 'I know one thing from another'. The expression is known only in Shakespeare.

**Know all men by these presents.** That is, know them by the writings or documents now present (Latin *per presentes*, 'by the [writings] present').

**Know all the answers, To.** To give the impression of being extremely well informed, resourceful and intelligent. But no one can know all the answers.

**Know a thing or two, To.** To be sharp; to be knowing; to be experienced.

**Know better than to, To.** To be not so stupid as to.

**Know-how.** Practical knowledge; expertise; natural skill. A term of American origin.

**Know-nothings.** An anti-Catholic, anti-immigrant movement that developed in the USA after 1852 but that faded out after 1856. It was properly known as the Native American party, and its members sought to keep out of public office anyone who was not native-born American. The nickname came from the members' stock reply to any question about the party's activities and programme: 'I know nothing.'

**Know one's onions, To.** To be knowledgeable in one's particular field. The expression is sometimes jokingly said to refer to the lexicographer C.T. Onions, co-editor of the *Oxford English Dictionary* and author of books on English, but it may actually derive from RHYMING SLANG, with onions short for 'onion rings' meaning 'things'.

**Know one's stuff, To.** To KNOW THE ROPES.

**Know the ropes, To.** To be thoroughly familiar with what is to be done; to be up to all the tricks and dodges. The expression derives from the days of sail when a sailor or apprentice had to become thoroughly familiar with the details of the rigging and how to handle the ropes.

> The captain, who ... 'knew the ropes', took the steering oar.
>
> R.H. DANA: *Two Years Before the Mast*, ch ix (1840)

**Know the score, To.** To appreciate the given situation; to understand the facts.

**Know the time of day, To.** To be smart and wide awake. The negative is more common, as, 'He doesn't know the time of day', meaning that he is 'dozy' and unaware of what is happening or what he should be doing.

**Know thyself.** The admonition inscribed on the temple of the oracle of APOLLO at DELPHI. The words have been attributed to Thales, SOLON the Athenian lawgiver, SOCRATES, PYTHAGORAS and others. Plato, in *Protagoras*, ascribes the saying to the Seven WISE MEN OF GREECE. The original Greek is *Gnothi sauton*.

**Know what one is talking about, To.** To be, or claim to be, expert or authoritative.

**Know what's what, To.** To be shrewd; to understand the true nature of things. One of the senseless questions of logic was *Quid est quid*?

> He knew what's what, and that's as high
> As metaphysic wit can fly.
>
> SAMUEL BUTLER: *Hudibras*, I, i (1662)

**Know which side one's bread is buttered, To.** To be mindful of one's own interest; to know what to do in order to gain any advantage.

> No man knows so well as Bittlebrains on which side his bread is buttered.
>
> SIR WALTER SCOTT: *The Bride of Lammermoor*, ch xviii (1819)

**Before you know where you are.** Unexpectedly soon or quickly; before you have time to realise what is happening.

**Don't I know it!** A phrase of rueful assent.

**I knew it!** I expected that! I was sure that would happen!

**I know what.** I've got an idea.

**In the know, To be.** To be aware, informed or party to what is happening.

**Lord knows.** *See under* LORD.

**Not to know B from a battledore** or **bull's foot.** To be quite illiterate; not to know even one's letters.

> He knew not a B from a battledore nor ever a letter of the book.
>
> JOHN FOXE: *Actes and Monuments* (1563)

**Not to know chalk from cheese.** To be unable to differentiate in essentials. *See also* AS DIFFERENT AS CHALK AND CHEESE *under* AS.

**Not to know someone from Adam.** To be quite unacquainted with someone; to have no knowledge of a person.

**Not to know what has hit one.** To be completely taken by surprise; to be the victim of something entirely unexpected.

**Not to know which way to turn.** To be at a complete loss; to be quite unsure what to do.

**You know something** or **what?** I am going to tell you something.

**You never know.** Nothing is certain; it could happen.

**Knowledge, Tree of.** *See under* TREE.

**Knox Version, The.** *See under* BIBLE.

**Knuckle. Knuckle down, To.** To work away; to be diligent.

**Knuckle-duster.** A loop of heavy metal, gripped in the hand and fitting over the knuckles, used as an offensive weapon. Its origin goes back to the days of Roman pugilism.

**Knuckle sandwich.** A punch in the mouth.

**Knuckle under, To.** To acknowledge defeat; to give in; to submit. An allusion to the old custom of striking the underside of a table with the knuckles when defeated in an argument.

**Near the knuckle.** *See under* NEAR.

**Rap over the knuckles, A.** *See under* RAP.

**Knurr and spell.** An old English game resembling trap ball. It is played with a knurr (or nurr) or wooden ball, which is released from a little brass cup at the end of a tongue of steel called a spell or spill. After the player has touched the spring, the ball flies into the air and is struck with the bat.

**Knut.** *See* NUT.

**Kobold.** A house spirit in German folklore, similar to the English ROBIN GOODFELLOW and the Scots BROWNIE. The word is also used for a GNOME who works in mines and forests. *See also* COBALT.

**Koh-i-Noor Diamond** (Persian, 'mountain of light'). A famous DIAMOND, so called by Nadir

Shah and now kept in the TOWER OF LONDON. Its early history is uncertain, but when Aurangzeb (d.1707), Mogul emperor of India, possessed the stone, it was used for the eye of a peacock in his peacock throne at Delhi. In 1739 it was acquired by Nadir Shah of Persia and later passed to Afghanistan, but when Shah Shuja was deposed he gave it to Ranjit Singh of the Punjab for promised assistance towards his recovery of the Afghan throne. Ten years after Ranjit's death (1839) the Punjab was annexed to the British crown, and in 1849, by stipulation, the diamond was presented to Queen Victoria. At this time it weighed $186\frac{1}{16}$ carats, but was subsequently cut down to $106\frac{1}{16}$ carats. It has been worn by all the queens of England since Victoria. There is a tradition that it brings good luck to women who wear it but bad luck to men.

**Kojak.** The tough New York cop played by Telly Savalas in the popular series named after him (1973–8). He was the creation of the writer Abby Man, and his 'trademarks' were his bald head and his habit of sucking lollipops.

**Kong, King.** *See under* KING.

**Kon-Tiki expedition.** The unique voyage made by the Norwegian Thor Heyerdahl (b.1914) with five companions in 1947, who sailed a balsa raft from Callao in Peru to Tuamotu Island in the South Pacific. Their object was to support the theory that the Polynesian race reached the Pacific islands in this fashion and were descendants of the Incas of Peru. Their raft was called *Kon-Tiki* after the INCA sun-god.

> The original name of the sun-god Virakocha, which seems to have been more used in Peru in old times, was Kon-Tiki or Illa-Tiki, which means Sun-Tiki or Illa-Tiki. Kon-Tiki was a high priest and sun-king of the Incas' legendary 'white men' who had left the enormous ruins on the shores of Lake Titicaca.
>
> THOR HEYERDAHL: *The Kon-Tiki Expedition* (1950)

**Koppa.** An ancient Greek letter, disused as a letter in classical Greek, but retained as the sign for the numeral 90. It was pronounced like K with the point of articulation further back in the throat. The Romans incorporated it into their alphabet as Q.

**Koran** or **Al Koran** (Arabic *qurān*, 'reading'). The sacred book of the Muslims, containing the religious teaching of the Prophet MOHAMMED with instructions on morality and Islamic institutions. The Koran (more correctly *Qur'an*), which contains 114 chapters or suras, is said to have been communicated to Mohammed at MECCA and MEDINA by an angel, to the sound of bells. It is written in Arabic and was compiled from the Prophet's own lips. The present text is of the 7th century, the chapters being arranged, except the first, in descending order of length.

**Kosher.** A YIDDISH word (from Hebrew) denoting that which is 'right', 'fit' or 'proper'. It is applied usually to food, especially meat that has been prepared in the prescribed manner. This implies four dietary laws: (1) the food must not be obtained from the animals, birds and fish prohibited in Leviticus 11 or Deuteronomy 14; (2) the animals or bird must have been ritually slaughtered by a special cut across the neck (a method called *shehitah*, 'slaughter'); (3) the meat must be salted to remove the blood (Deuteronomy 12:16, 23–5 and elsewhere) and the ischiatic nerve removed from the hindquarters (Genesis 32:32); (4) meat and milk must not be cooked together (Exodus 23:19). The term *terefah* ('that which has been torn by beasts') is applied to all food that violates the law.

**Kow-tow** (Chinese *ketou*, literally 'knock head'). A Chinese custom of kneeling down and knocking the head on the ground as a sign of reverence, homage or respect. Hence, in popular usage, to kow-tow is to behave obsequiously to someone, to fawn or to grovel.

**Kraken.** A fabulous sea monster supposedly seen off the coast of Norway and probably based on the sighting of a gigantic cuttlefish. It was first described by Pontoppidan in his *History of Norway* (1752). It was said to be capable of dragging down the largest ships and when submerging to suck down a vessel by the whirlpool it created. The creature was the inspiration for John Wyndham's science fiction novel, *The Kraken Wakes* (1953). *Kraken* itself is a Norwegian word of obscure origin. The final *-n* means 'the'. See *also* LOCH NESS MONSTER.

**Kralitz Bible, The.** *See under* BIBLE.

**Kratim.** The dog of the SEVEN SLEEPERS, more correctly called Katmir or Ketmir, which according to MOHAMMED sleeps with them and is one of the ten animals to be admitted into Paradise. He accompanied the seven noble youths to the cavern in which they were walled up and remained standing for the whole time, neither moving, eating, drinking nor sleeping.

**Kremlin** (Russian *kreml'*, 'citadel'). The Moscow Kremlin is on a scale of its own, comprising buildings of many architectural styles (Arabesque, Gothic, Greek, Italian, Chinese and so on) enclosed by battlemented and many-towered walls $1\frac{1}{2}$ miles (2.4km) in circuit. The Tsars and the PATRIARCH lived in the Kremlin until the time of Peter the Great (r.1682–1725) when the court moved to St Petersburg (former Leningrad). Much of it was damaged in the 1917 Revolution but all has now been fully restored. Before the Revolution its bells rang out 'Great is our Lord in Zion' at midday, and the Preobrazhensky March at midnight. After the Revolution these respectively became the INTERNATIONALE and

'You fell as a victim'. The Great Kremlin Palace was completed in 1849.

As the seat of Russian government the word is used symbolically of that government, just as VATICAN is of the papacy.

**Kreutzer.** An old German copper or silver coin stamped with a cross (German *Kreuz*, 'cross').

**Kreutzer Sonata.** Beethoven's violin sonata so named (1802–3) was dedicated to the French violinist Rodolphe Kreutzer (1766–1831), who even so is believed never to have played it. The work gave the name of Leo Tolstoy's story *The Kreutzer Sonata* (1891) in which the central character, Pozdnyshev, suspects his wife is having an affair with a neighbour with whom she plays the sonata.

**Kriegsspiel.** *See* WAR GAME.

**Kriemhild.** The legendary heroine of the NIBELUNGENLIED, a woman of unrivalled beauty, the daughter of King Dankrat and sister of GUNTHER, Gernot and Giselher. She first married SIEGFRIED and next ATTILA THE HUN (Etzel). Her name literally means 'battle helmet'.

**Krishna** (Sanskrit, 'black one', 'dark one'). A popular Hindu deity and an avatar of VISHNU. One myth says he was the son of Vasudeva and Devaki and was born at Mathura, between Delhi and Agra. His uncle, King Kamsa, who had been warned that one of his nephews would kill him, murdered Devaki's children on birth. Accordingly Krishna was smuggled away and brought up among cowherds and lived to kill his uncle. He was the APOLLO of India and the idol of women. He features in the MAHABHARATA, the BHAGAVAD-GITA and the *Bhagavata-Purana*. Another story is that Vishnu plucked out two of his own hairs, one white and one black, and the black one became Krishna. *See also* HINDUISM.

**Hare Krishna.** *See under* HARE.

**Kronus.** One of the TITANS of Greek mythology, son of URANUS and GAIA, father (by his sister RHEA) of Hestia, DEMETER, HERA, HADES, POSEIDON and ZEUS. He dethroned his father as ruler of the world and was in turn dethroned by his son Zeus. The Romans identified him with SATURN.

**Kruger telegram.** The congratulatory message sent on 3 January 1896 by Kaiser William II to President Kruger after the defeat of the JAMESON RAID. It embittered Ango-German relations and encouraged Kruger in his policies.

**Kublai Khan.** The grandson (1214–94) of GENGHIS KHAN. He extended the Mongol Empire to include China, where he founded a dynasty of Chinese emperors. His name is famously associated with Coleridge's poem:

> In Xanadu did Kubla Khan
> A stately pleasure-dome decree:
> Where Alph, the sacred river, ran
> Through caverns measureless to man
> Down to a sunless sea.
>
> S.T. COLERIDGE: 'Kubla Khan' (1816)

**Kudrun.** *See* GUDRUN.

**Kufic.** Ancient Arabic letters, so called from Kufa, on the Hindiya branch of the Euphrates, the capital of the CALIPHS before the building of Baghdad. It was noted for its skilled copyists. The KORAN was originally written in Kufic.

**Kufic coins.** Early Muslim coins inscribed in Kufic, which was superseded by Nashki characters in the 13th century AD. Their inscriptions carry much useful information for the historian.

**Ku Klux Klan.** An American secret society founded at Pulaski, Tennessee, in 1866 at the close of the Civil War (1861–5) as a social club with a fanciful ritual and hooded white robes. The name is an elaboration of Greek *kuklos*, 'circle'. It soon developed into a society to overawe the newly emancipated Negroes, and similar societies such as the Knights of the White Camellia, the White League, the Pale Faces and the Invisible Circle sprang up in 1867–8. Its terroristic activities led to laws against it in 1870 and 1871. Although it had been disbanded by the Grand Wizard in 1869, local activities continued for some time.

In 1915 a new organization, the Invisible Empire, Knights of the Ku Klux Klan, was founded by the Rev. William J. Simmons near Atlanta, Georgia. He adopted much of the ritual of the original, adding further puerile ceremonies and nomenclature of his own. Klansmen held Klanvocations and their local Klaverns were ruled by an Exalted Cyclops, a Klaliff etc. In addition to being anti-Negro, it was anti-Catholic, anti-Jewish and xenophobic. In advocating Protestant supremacy for the native-born whites, it grew rapidly from 1920 and gained considerable political control in the southern states by unsavoury methods. By 1930 it had shrunk again to small proportions but a revival began before the Second World War, and the Klan became noted for its FASCIST sympathies. In 1944 it was again disbanded but continued locally and was still active surreptitiously in the late 20th century, though on a much reduced scale.

**Kultur** (German, 'civilization'). When the word is used in English it implies civilization as conceived by the Germans. The English word 'culture' has its German equivalent as *Bildung*.

**Kulturkampf** (German *Kampf*, 'struggle'). The *Kulturkampf*, or so-called struggle for civilization, was the name used for Chancellor Bismarck's struggle with the Roman Catholic hierarchy in the 1870s to assert the supreme authority of the state over the individual and the church, at a time when the latter, under

Pope Pius IX, was asserting Catholic claims. The conflict began over the control of education and developed into a wider attack on the church, but Bismarck eventually (1879) effected a reconciliation with the Catholic Centre Party in order to avoid control by the National Liberal Party.

**Kuomintang** (Chinese, 'National People's Party'). A Chinese political party formed by Sun Yat-sen (1867–1925) in 1905, which, after his death, passed under the control of General Chiang Kai-shek (1887–1975). From 1927 to 1949 the Kuomintang was in power in China when it was driven out by the Communist Party under Mao Tse-tung (1893–1976). The Nationalists still maintain themselves in Formosa (Taiwan).

**Kwan. Kwan Ti.** The Chinese god of war, the equivalent of the Roman MARS. He was a real warrior who lived AD 162–220 and who began his life as an itinerant seller of bean curd. He was one of three heroes who entered a plot to support the Han dynasty against the rebel Yellow Turbans. He was finally taken prisoner and beheaded, after which he was canonized and subsequently (1594) raised to the rank of god. Images of Kwan Ti are kept by most households in China, facing the entrance of the building, to scare away evil influences.

**Kwan Yin.** The Chinese goddess of mercy, corresponding in some respects to the Roman Lucina. She is usually depicted seated upon a lotus and is worshipped by newly married couples who desire children. Her name means 'she who pays attention to sounds', i.e. she who hears prayers.

**Kyle.** A district of southwest Scotland, between the Irvine and the Doon.

> Kyle for a man, Carrick for a coo [cow],
> Cunningham for butter, Galloway for woo' [wool].

Kyle, between Ayr and Kilmarnock, has strong corn-growing soil; Carrick, south of Ayr, is a wild hilly portion, only fit for feeding cattle; Cunningham, north of Kilmarnock, has rich dairy land; Galloway, south of Carrick, has long been famous as pastoral country.

**Kyrie eleison** (Greek, 'Lord have mercy'). The short petition used in the liturgies of the Eastern and Western Churches, as a response at the beginning of the MASS and in the Anglican communion service. The name is also used for the musical setting for this.

# L

**L.** The twelfth letter of the alphabet. In Phoenician and Hebrew it represents an ox goad, *lamed*, and in the Egyptian HIEROGLYPHIC a lioness.

**£.** The pound sterling sign represents the initial of Latin *libra*, 'pound'. In the Roman notation L stands for 50 and, with a line drawn above the letter, 50,000.

**Laban.** The tight-fisted father of RACHEL and LEAH (Genesis 24–30). When JACOB works seven years to win Rachel, Laban substitutes Leah and then makes Jacob work another seven years for Rachel.

**Labarum.** The standard of the later Roman emperors. It consisted of a gilded spear with an eagle on the top, while from a cross-staff hung a splendid purple streamer, with a gold fringe, adorned with precious stones. *See also* CONSTANTINE'S CROSS.

**Labour. Labor Day.** A legal holiday in the USA and some provinces of Canada, held on the first Monday in September. Labour rallies in Britain and elsewhere are held on MAY DAY.

**Labour of love, A.** Work undertaken for the love of it, without regard to payment.

> Remembering without ceasing your work of faith, and labour of love, and patience of hope in our Lord Jesus Christ, in the sight of God and our Father.
> 1 Thessalonians 1:3

**Labour Party.** One of the major political parties of Britain, established with the aim of promoting socialism. It has been so called since 1906 but was originally formed as the Labour Representation Committee in 1900 from such elements as the INDEPENDENT LABOUR PARTY, the TRADE UNIONS and the FABIAN SOCIETY. The first Labour Government was that of Ramsay MacDonald in 1924; the second lasted from 1929 to 1931, when the party split over the cuts in unemployment benefit (*see* NATIONAL GOVERNMENT). It was not returned to power again until 1945 and was replaced by the CONSERVATIVES in October 1951. It was again in office from 1964 to 1970, 1974 to 1979, and from 1997 when, as 'New Labour', it was reborn in the image of its leader, Tony Blair, ridding itself of its commitment to public ownership and generally making itself more appealing to the electorate.

**Division of labour.** *See under* DIVISION.

**Hard labour.** *See under* HARD.

**Independent Labour Party.** *See under* INDEPENDENT.

**Statute of Labourers, The.** *See under* STATUTE.

**Labyrinth.** A Greek word of unknown origin denoting a structure with complicated passages through which it is baffling to find one's way. The maze at HAMPTON COURT, formed of high hedges, is a labyrinth on a small scale. The chief labyrinths of antiquity were:

- Egyptian: built 1800 BC by Petesuchis or Tithoes, near Lake Moeris; it had 3000 apartments, half of which were underground
- Cretan: built by DAEDALUS, in which the MINOTAUR was imprisoned; the only means of finding a way out was by following a skein of thread (*see* Virgil, *Aeneid*, v (1st century BC))
- Cretan conduit: had 1000 branches or turnings
- Lemnian: built by the architects Smilis, Rholus and Theodorus, it had 150 columns, so finely adjusted that a child could turn them; vestiges of this labyrinth were still in existence in the time of Pliny (1st century AD)
- Labyrinth of Clusium: made by Lars Porsena, king of Etruria, for his tomb
- Samian: built by Theodorus (540 BC); it is mentioned by Pliny, Herodotus, Strabo and others
- Labyrinth at Woodstock, Oxfordshire: built by Henry II to protect FAIR ROSAMOND

**Lace, Lavender and old.** *See under* LAVENDER.

**Lacedaemonians, The.** *See under* REGIMENTAL AND DIVISIONAL NICKNAMES.

**Lacedaemonian letter.** The Greek (*iota*), the smallest of the letters. *See also* JOT.

**Laches.** A legal term for negligence and delay in enforcing a right, from Old French *laschesse*, 'negligence', to which modern English 'lax' is related.

**Lachesis.** One of the three FATES, and the one who spins life's thread and determines its length. Her name represents Greek *lakhesis*, 'destiny'.

**Laconic.** Pertaining to Laconia or Sparta, hence very concise and pithy, for the SPARTANS were noted for their brusque and aphoristic speech. When Philip of Macedon wrote to the Spartan magistrates, 'If I enter Laconia, I will level Lacedaemon to the ground,' the EPHORS (magistrates) sent back the single word, 'If'. Julius CAESAR's words VENI, VIDI, VICI and Sir Charles

Napier's 'Peccavi' (*see* CRY PECCAVI) are well-known laconicisms.

**Lad, Jack the.** *See under* JACK.

**Ladder. Jacob's ladder.** *See under* JACOB.

**Pull up the ladder, Jack, I'm inboard.** *See under* PULL.

**Snakes and ladders.** *See under* SNAKE.

**La-di-da** or **Lah-di-dah.** Exaggeratedly refined. The phrase represents an affected drawl, and can be used as a noun for a la-di-da person.

**Lading, Bill of.** *See under* BILL.

**Ladon.** The name of the dragon that guarded the apples of the HESPERIDES; also one of the dogs of ACTAEON.

**Ladrones** (Spanish, 'thieves'). The name given to the Mariana Islands by Magellan's sailors in 1521 because of the thievish habits of the natives.

**Lady.** Literally 'bread kneader', from Old English *hlǣfdīge* (*hlāf*, 'bread', and *dīge*, 'kneader', related to modern 'dough'). The original meaning was simply the female head of the family, the mistress of the household, or what is now called 'the lady of the house'. *See also* COURTESY TITLES; COUSIN; LORD.

**Ladies' Gallery, The.** A public gallery in the HOUSE OF COMMONS that is reserved for women.

**Ladies' Mile, The.** A stretch of the road on the north side of the Serpentine, Hyde Park, much favoured in Victorian days by 'equestriennes'. The Coaching and Four-in-hand Clubs held their meets there in spring.

**Ladies' night.** An evening function at a men's club to which women are invited.

**Ladies' Rock, The.** A crag under the castle rock of Stirling, where ladies used to witness tournaments.

**Ladybird.** The small red insect with black spots, *Coccinella septempunctata*, called also ladybug, Bishop Barnabee and, in Yorkshire, the cushcow lady. The name means 'bird (beetle) of our Lady', apparently because of the service it performs by feeding exclusively on greenfly, one of the worst plant pests.

**Lady Bountiful.** A charitable but patronizing woman of a neighbourhood. The name is that of a character in George Farquhar's play *The Beaux' Stratagem* (1707).

**Lady Chapel.** A chapel dedicated to the Virgin MARY within a church or cathedral. It is usually situated to the east of the high altar.

**Lady Day.** 25 March, commemorating the ANNUNCIATION of our Lady, the Virgin MARY. It was formerly called St Mary's Day in Lent, to distinguish it from other festivals in honour of the Virgin, which were also, properly speaking, Lady Days. Until 1752 Lady Day was the legal beginning of the year, and dates between 1 January and that day are shown with two years, e.g. 29 January 1648/9, which by present reckoning is 29 January 1649. *See also* GREGORIAN YEAR.

**Lady Freemason, The.** *See under* FREEMASON.

**Lady Godiva.** *See under* GODIVA.

**Lady-in-waiting.** In a royal household a lady who attends a queen or princess. Ladies-in-waiting are officially styled Ladies of the Bedchamber, Women of the Bedchamber and MAIDS OF HONOUR. In the British royal household they deal with correspondence from the public, especially from children.

**Lady-killer.** A male flirt; a man who is a great favourite with the ladies or who thinks he is.

**Lady-love.** A sweetheart.

**Lady Luck.** A popular personification of Fortune.

> Lady luck could set you up for life, but don't bet on it.
>
> *Sunday Times* (20 November 1994)

**Lady Muck.** An ordinary woman who behaves as if she were an aristocrat.

**Lady of easy virtue, A.** A prostitute or promiscuous woman.

**Lady of England and Normandy, The.** The Empress Maud or Matilda (1102–67), daughter of Henry I of England and wife of the Emperor Henry V of Germany, who died in 1125. After his death she married Geoffrey of Anjou, and long contested Stephen's possession of the English crown on her father's death. She was acknowledged as Lady of England and Normandy by a council at Winchester in 1141, but finally withdrew to Normandy in 1145. Her son by Geoffrey of Anjou became king as Henry II in 1154. *See also* ALOE.

**Lady of Shalott, The.** A maiden in the ARTHURIAN ROMANCES, who fell in love with Sir LANCELOT OF THE LAKE, and died because her love was unrequited. Tennyson has a beautiful poem on the subject (1832) and the story of ELAINE is substantially the same.

> But Lancelot mused a little space;
> He said, 'She has a lovely face;
> God in his mercy lend her grace,
> The Lady of Shalott.'

Shalott is the ASTOLAT of Arthurian legend. Tennyson and other writers based the name on its French form, Ascolet or Escalot, and this was the spelling in Malory's *Le Morte d'Arthur*. When Caxton printed this work in 1485, however, he misread the c as a t. Hence Astolat.

**Lady of the Lake, The.** In ARTHURIAN ROMANCES Vivien, the mistress of MERLIN. She lived in the middle of a lake surrounded by knights and damsels. *See also* LANCELOT OF THE LAKE.

In Scott's poem of this name (1810), the lady is Ellen Douglas, who lived with her father near Loch Katrine.

**Lady of the Lamp, The.** A name given to Florence Nightingale (1820–1910), from her nightly rounds of the hospital wards at Scutari during the Crimean War (1854–6), carrying a lighted lamp.

**Lady of the night, A.** A prostitute.

**Lady's man, A.** One who is fond of the company of women and very attentive to them. The term lacks the more amorous implications of LADY-KILLER.

**Lady's mantle.** *See* ALCHEMILLA.

**Lady's slipper.** The largest of British wild orchids of the genus *Cypripedium*, now rare. The flower (*Cypripedium calceolus*) has yellow slipper-shaped petals, and is found in Yorkshire on limestone soil. It also occurs in Europe and the USA.

**Lady's smock.** A common name for the cuckoo flower or bittercress (*Cardamine pratensis*), so called because the flowers are supposed to resemble linen laid out to bleach on the grass. There are many other such names of plants, e.g. lady's bedstraw (*Galium verum*), lady's cushion (*Saxifraga hypnoides*), lady's delight (*Viola tricolor*), lady's finger (*Anthyllis vulneraria*), ladies' seal (*Bryonia dioica*), lady's thistle (*Silybum marianum*), lady's tresses (*Spiranthes spiralis*), and so on.

**Bag lady.** *See under* BAG.

**Dark Lady of the Sonnets, The.** *See under* DARK.

**Faint heart never won fair lady.** *See under* FAINT.

**Find the lady.** Another name for the THREE-CARD TRICK.

**First Lady.** *See under* FIRST.

**Iron Lady, The.** *See under* IRON.

**Leading lady.** *See under* LEAD.

**Lords and ladies.** *See under* LORD.

**Naked lady.** *See* NAKED BOY.

**Old lady, The.** *See under* OLD.

**Old Lady of the Bund, The.** *See under* OLD.

**Old Lady of Threadneedle Street, The.** *See under* OLD.

**Our Lady of Mercy.** *See under* OUR.

**Our Lady of the Snows.** *See under* OUR.

**When the fat lady sings.** *See under* WHEN.

**White Ladies.** *See under* WHITE.

**White lady.** *See under* WHITE.

**Young lady.** *See under* YOUNG.

**Laertes.** In Greek mythology the father of Odysseus (ULYSSES). The *Odyssey* (8th century BC) tells how he aids his son after the killing of the suitors.

**Laestrygones.** *See* LESTRIGONS.

**Laetare Sunday** (Latin, 'rejoice'). The fourth Sunday in LENT, so called from the first word of the introit, which is from Isaiah 66:10: 'Rejoice ye with Jerusalem, and be glad with her, all ye that love her.' It is also known as MOTHERING SUNDAY.

**La Fontaine, Jean de.** The fame of the French poet (1621–95) essentially depends on his *Contes* (1664–71) and his *Fables* (1668–93), the first six books of the latter being dedicated to the DAUPHIN. The complete collection consists of 12 books.

**Lag, Time.** *See under* TIME.

**Lagado.** In Jonathan Swift's *Gulliver's Travels* (1726) the capital of BALNIBARBI, celebrated for its grand academy of projectors, where the scholars spend their time in such projects as making pincushions from softened rocks, extracting sunbeams from cucumbers and converting ice into gunpowder. The name of the city has been decoded by P.O. Clark as Lonnod, an anagram of London.

**Lagan** or **ligan.** *See* FLOTSAM AND JETSAM.

**Lager louts.** A term in use from the late 1980s and applied to young hooligans who create disturbances, damage property and the like after drinking too much lager.

**Laid. Laid paper.** Paper having a ribbed appearance, due to manufacture on a mould or by a DANDY ROLLER on which the wires are laid side by side, instead of being woven transversely.

**Laid to rest.** Buried.

**Laid up.** Confined to bed or to one's house through illness or physical incapacity.

**Laide. Belle laide.** *See under* BELLE.

**Lais.** The name of three celebrated Greek courtesans. One flourished in Corinth in the 5th century BC and was visited by Aristippus the philosopher, but the best known was the daughter of Timandra, the mistress of Alcibiades. She was born *c.*420 BC and came to Corinth as a child. She was patronized by princes, philosophers and plebeians alike. Her charges were sufficiently exorbitant to deter Demosthenes. Her later success in Thessaly so enraged the women that they pricked her to death with their bodkins. There was a third Lais, contemporary with Alexander the Great, who sat for APELLES.

**Laissez faire** (French, 'let alone'). The principle of allowing things to look after themselves, especially the non-interference by government in economic affairs. The originator of the phrase may have been Legendre, a contemporary of Colbert, or possibly D'Argenson, a former minister of Louis XV. It became the accepted maxim of the French PHYSIOCRATS in the 18th century as a reaction against Colbertism and MERCANTILISM. Adam Smith was its advocate in Britain, as the prophet of FREE TRADE. The principle was extended to politics by Jeremy Bentham, the leader of the individualist school and philosopher of UTILITARIANISM. Since the

1870s the doctrine has steadily been eroded by collectivist policies, which increasingly limit the freedoms and activities of the individual in the name of public good. *Laissez passer, laissez aller* are similar phrases.

**Laius.** *See* OEDIPUS.

**Lake. Lake District.** The picturesque mountainous district of Cumbria that contains the principal English lakes, including Windermere, Grasmere, Derwentwater and Ullswater. It gave its name to the LAKE POETS and has other literary associations.

> Thousands who have never visited the Lakes have learnt something of their charm through the poetry of Wordsworth, who passed the greater part of his life at Grasmere, and knew every valley, stream, and pass in the district.
> *Cassell's Gazetteer of Great Britain and Ireland* (1896)

**Lake Poets.** The name applied derisively by the *Edinburgh Review* (1816), originally as 'the Lake School', to William Wordsworth (1770–1850), Samuel Taylor Coleridge (1772–1834) and Robert Southey (1774–1843), who lived in the LAKE DISTRICT and sought inspiration in nature, and to the writers who followed them. Charles Lamb, Charles Lloyd and Christopher North (John Wilson) are sometimes included in their number.

**Asphaltic Lake.** *See under* ASPHALTIC.

**Devil's Lake.** *See under* DEVIL.

**Great Lakes.** *See under* GREAT.

**Lady of the Lake, The.** *See under* LADY.

**Lancelot of the Lake.** *See under* LANCELOT.

**Lakshmi** (Sanskrit, 'prosperity', 'beauty'). One of the consorts of VISHNU and the mother of KAMA. She is the Hindu goddess of beauty, wealth and pleasure, and the RAMAYANA describes her as springing from the foam of the sea. *See also* APHRODITE.

**Lamaism** (Tibetan *blama*, 'spiritual teacher', 'lord'). A modified form of BUDDHISM, the religion of Tibet and Mongolia. The name is from the title given to monks in the higher ranks. The Grand Lama or Dalai Lama (the Sacred Lama) was the ruler of Tibet, although it came under Chinese control (1720) during the time of the 7th Dalai Lama. This control declined to nominal suzerainty, but the Chinese again invaded in 1950, and in 1959 the 14th Dalai Lama fled to India. There is another Grand Lama, the Tashi Lama or Panchen ('great jewel') Lama whose authority was confined to one province but who was supported by the Chinese as rival to the Dalai Lama. The priests live in lamaseries.

**La Mancha, The Knight of.** *See under* KNIGHT.

**Lamb.** In Christian art the emblem of the Redeemer, in allusion to John 1:29: 'Behold the Lamb of God, which taketh away the sin of the world.' It is also the attribute of St AGNES, St CATHERINE, St GENEVIÈVE and St Regina. JOHN THE BAPTIST either carries a lamb or is accompanied by one.

**Lamb-ale.** The 'ale' or merrymaking formerly held by the farmer when lambing was over. *See also* CHURCH-ALE.

**Lamb's fry.** Lamb's testicles or other offal as food.

**Lamb's tails.** A popular country name for catkins on the hazel tree.

**As innocent as a lamb.** *See under* AS.

**As well be hanged for a sheep as a lamb.** *See under* AS.

**Ewe lamb.** *See under* EWE.

**God tempers the wind to the shorn lamb.** *See under* GOD.

**In two shakes of a lamb's tail.** *See under* TWO.

**Larry the Lamb.** *See under* LARRY.

**Like a lamb to the slaughter.** *See under* LIKE.

**March comes in like a lion and goes out like a lamb.** *See under* MARCH.

**Mutton dressed as lamb.** *See under* MUTTON.

**Sheep dressed as lamb.** *See under* SHEEP.

**Paschal lamb.** *See under* PASCH.

**Lambert's Day, St.** 17 September. St Lambert (*c.*635–*c.*705) was bishop of Maastricht and patron of Liège. He supported the missionary work of St Willibrord and was energetic in suppressing vice. He met a violent death, probably the outcome of a blood feud, and hence is venerated as a martyr.

> Be ready, as your lives shall answer it,
> At Coventry, upon Saint Lambert's day.
> SHAKESPEARE: *Richard II*, I, i (1595)

**Lambeth.** A London borough on the south side of the River THAMES, formerly part of Surrey. The name derives from Old English *lamb*, 'lamb', and *hȳth*, 'landing place', as it was the place where lambs were landed. It includes the districts of VAUXHALL, Kennington and Brixton.

**Lambeth conferences.** Assemblies of the archbishops and bishops of the Anglican Church from around the world, held every ten years under the presidency of the archbishop of Canterbury. From 1867 to 1958 they were held at LAMBETH PALACE, in 1968 at Church House, Westminster, and in 1978, 1988 and 1998 at the University of Kent in Canterbury. An increasingly wide range of issues has been discussed, and the 1998 conference voted overwhelmingly in favour of a motion condemning homosexuality as incompatible with biblical teaching. The resolutions of Lambeth conferences, though not binding, are nevertheless regarded by member churches as significant.

**Lambeth degrees.** Degrees in divinity, arts, law, medicine, music and other subjects, conferred by the archbishop of Canterbury, who was empowered to do so by a statute of 1533.

**Lambeth Palace.** The London residence of the archbishops of Canterbury since the 12th century. The oldest part is the chapel built by Archbishop Boniface in 1245, and the buildings have been steadily added to and modified through the centuries. Originally called Lambeth House, it came to be called Lambeth Palace *c.*1658 owing to the decay of the palace at Canterbury. It is the archbishop's principal residence, but he now has another palace at Canterbury.

**Lambeth quadrilateral.** The four points suggested by the LAMBETH CONFERENCE of 1888 as a basis for Christian reunion: the Bible, the Apostolic and NICENE CREEDS, two Sacraments (BAPTISM and the EUCHARIST) and the historic Episcopate.

**Lambeth walk.** A thoroughfare in Lambeth leading from Black Prince Road to the Lambeth Road. It gave its name to the popular COCKNEY dance featured by Lupino Lane (from 1937) in the musical show *Me and My Gal* at the Victoria Palace.

> Any time you're Lambeth way,
> Any evening, any day,
> You'll find us all
> Doin' the Lambeth walk.
> DOUGLAS FURBER and ARTHUR ROSE: 'Doin' the Lambeth Walk' (1937)

**Lame duck, A.** A STOCKJOBBER or dealer who will not, or cannot, pay his losses, so that he has to 'waddle out the alley like a lame duck'. In business, the term is also used for a large and prestigious company that cannot meet foreign competition without government support. In general, the expression can be used of any person or thing that is disabled or ineffectual.

> 'I don't like the looks of Mr Sedley's affairs … He's been dabbling on his own account I fear … unless I see Amble's ten thousand down you don't marry. I'll have no lame duck's daughter in my family.'
> W.M. THACKERAY: *Vanity Fair*, ch xiii (1847–8)

**Lamia** (Greek *lamuros*, 'voracious', 'gluttonous'). Among the Greeks and Romans a female demon who devoured children and whose name was used to frighten them. She was a Libyan queen beloved by JUPITER, but, robbed of her offspring by the jealous JUNO, she became insane and vowed vengeance on all children, whom she delighted to entice and devour. The race of lamiae, in Africa, were said to have the head and breasts of a woman and the body of a serpent. They enticed strangers into their embraces to devour them.

In the Middle Ages witches were called lamiae, and Keats' poem *Lamia* (1820) recounts how a bride, when recognized by APOLLONIUS OF TYANA as a serpent or lamia, vanished in an instant. Keats took the substance of his poem from Robert Burton's *Anatomy of Melancholy* (1621), for which the source was Philostratus (*De Vita Apollonii*, Bk iv (3rd century AD)). *See also* LILITH.

**Lammas Day.** 1 August, one of the regular QUARTER DAYS in Scotland and a half-quarter or cross-quarter-day in England, the day on which, in Anglo-Saxon times, the FIRST FRUITS were offered. Formerly, bread for the Lammas Day EUCHARIST was made from the new corn of the harvest. The name derives from Old English *hlāfmæsse*, 'loaf mass'. It is also the feast of St PETER AD VINCULA. *See also* HARVEST FESTIVAL.

**Lamp. Lamp of heaven, The.** The moon. Milton calls the stars 'lamps':

> Why shouldst thou, but for some felonious end,
> In thy dark lantern thus close up the stars
> That Nature hung in heaven, and filled their lamps
> With everlasting oil, to give due light
> To the misled and lonely traveller?
> *Comus* (1637)

**Lamp of Phoebus, The.** The sun. PHOEBUS is the mythological personification of the sun.

**Lady of the Lamp, The.** *See under* LADY.

**Lampadion.** The received name of a lively, petulant courtesan in later Greek comedy.

**Lampon** (Greek, 'bright one'). One of DIOMEDES' horses.

**Lampoon.** A sarcastic or scurrilous personal satire, perhaps so called from French *lampons*, 'let us drink', part of the refrain of a 17th-century drinking song.

**Lampos** (Greek, 'bright'). One of the steeds of AURORA; also the name of one of the horses of HECTOR.

**Lamri** (Celtic, perhaps 'curvetter'). King ARTHUR's mare.

**Lancaster. Chancellor of the Duchy of Lancaster, The.** *See under* CHANCELLOR.

**Time-honoured Lancaster.** *See under* TIME.

**Lancasterian.** Of or pertaining to Joseph Lancaster (1778–1838), the QUAKER educational reformer, who claimed to have invented the MONITORIAL SYSTEM. His supporters founded the Royal Lancasterian Society in 1808, which later became the British and Foreign School Society. *See also* MADRAS SYSTEM; VOLUNTARY SCHOOLS.

**Lancastrian.** An adherent of the Lancastrian line of kings, or one of those kings (Henry IV, V, VI), who were descendants of Edward III. *See also* RED ROSE; WARS OF THE ROSES; YORKIST.

**Lance.** An attribute in Christian art of St MATTHEW and St THOMAS, the apostles; also of St LONGINUS, St GEORGE, St Adalbert, St BARBARA, St MICHAEL and others.

**Lance corporal.** The lowest grade of non-commissioned officer in the army.

**Lance-knight.** An old term for a foot soldier. The word is a corruption of *Landsknecht* or *Lansquenet*, literally 'land knight', a German mercenary foot soldier of the 16th century.

**Lance sergeant.** A corporal temporarily performing the duties of a sergeant. The rank derives its name ultimately from Italian *lancia spezzata*, 'broken lance', referring to an experienced soldier, one who has had his lance shattered in battle. *See also* LANCE CORPORAL.

**Lancers.** The dance so called, an amplified kind of QUADRILLE, was introduced by Laborde in Paris in 1836 and taken to England in 1850.

**Freelance.** *See under* FREE.

**St Crispin's lance.** *See under* CRISPIN.

**Lancelot of the Lake** or **Lancelot du Lac.** One of the KNIGHTS OF THE ROUND TABLE, the son of King BAN of Brittany, who was stolen in infancy by the LADY OF THE LAKE. She plunged with the baby into the lake (hence the name), and when her protégé was grown to manhood, she presented him to King ARTHUR. Sir Lancelot went in search of the HOLY GRAIL and twice caught sight of it. Though always represented in ARTHURIAN ROMANCES as the model of CHIVALRY, bravery and fidelity, Sir Lancelot was the adulterous lover of Queen GUINEVERE, and it was through this liaison that the war resulted that led to the disruption of the Round Table and the death of King Arthur.

**Land. Land girls.** Girls or women recruited for farmwork during the two world wars. In the Second World War they were organized as a Women's Land Army.

**Land League.** An Irish association formed in 1879 under the leadership of Michael Davitt (1846–1906), with Charles Stewart Parnell as president and two FENIANS as secretaries. It stimulated agrarian revolt and aimed to secure peasant proprietorship by forceful methods. It was declared illegal in 1881 but was renewed as the National League in 1882.

**Landlopers.** A Scottish term for vagabonds or vagrants. 'Loper' is from Dutch *loopen*, 'to run'.

**Landlubber.** An awkward or inept sailor is so called, or someone who has had no experience at sea. A 'lubber' is a heavy, clumsy person.

**Land of Beulah, The.** The name, meaning literally 'married woman', that is given to ISRAEL (Isaiah 62:4). In Bunyan's PILGRIM'S PROGRESS (1678, 1684) it is that land of heavenly joy where the pilgrims wait until they are summoned to enter the CELESTIAL CITY.

**Land of Cakes, The.** Scotland, famous for its oatmeal cakes.

**Land of Enchantment, The.** A name given to Mexico.

**Land office business.** Booming trade; thriving business. The US government land office of the 19th century was overburdened with work allotting land to a multitude of land-seekers. Hence the use of the phrase to mean a rush of business.

**Land of Hope and Glory.** Great Britain was so portrayed in the heyday of imperialism in Sir Edward Elgar's well-known melody with words by A.C. Benson. It was sung by Dame Clara Butt in 1902 and widely used at EMPIRE DAY celebrations and other occasions. It is now a traditional item at the LAST NIGHT OF THE PROMS. The tune was taken from Elgar's *Pomp and Circumstance* march, number 1 (1901). The words were originally written to be sung as the finale to Elgar's *Coronation Ode* of 1902.

> Land of Hope and Glory, Mother of the Free,
> How shall we extol thee who are born of thee?
> Wider still and wider shall thy bounds be set;
> God who made thee mighty, make thee mightier yet.

**Land of milk and honey.** Any fertile land or territory. The allusion is to the land of natural fertility, 'flowing with milk and honey', that was promised by God to the Israelites (Ezekiel 20:6).

**Land of My Fathers.** Wales, from the song *Hen Wlad fy Nhadau*, 'Land of My Fathers', which is the national anthem of Wales. The Welsh words are by Evan James and the music by his son, James James. It was first published in 1860.

**Land of Nod, The.** This was the land to which CAIN was exiled after he had slain ABEL (Genesis 4:16). Jonathan Swift, in *A Complete Collection of Genteel and Ingenious Conversation* (1738), said that he was 'going into the land of Nod', meaning that he was going to sleep, which meaning it has retained ever since.

> [It] had my lady into the land of Nod in half a minute.
> CHARLES READE: *Hard Cash*, ch xviii (1863)

**Land of Promise.** *See* PROMISED LAND.

**Land of the Midnight Sun, The.** Any land that lies north of the Arctic Circle and that has continuous daylight throughout the summer. In practice this means the northern regions of Norway, Sweden and Finland and almost the whole of Lapland.

**Land of the Rising Sun, The.** Japan. The title is a form of the country's indigenous name of Nippon, which literally means 'sun origin'. The allusion is to the geographical location of Japan with regard to China. The Japanese flag shows the sun's red disc on a white background.

**Land of the White Eagle, The.** Poland. The white eagle, with a crown on its head, formed part of the Polish COAT OF ARMS. An old legend tells how Prince Lech, when out hunting, came to a great oak tree, where he saw a pair of huge white eagles over their nest. The prince regarded this as a prophetic sign and decided to establish his capital there. He called it *Gniazdo*, 'nest', saying, 'Here shall be our nest'.

**Land on one's feet, To.** *See* FALL ON ONE'S FEET.

**Land o' the Leal, The.** The land of the faithful or blessed, a Scottish name for a 'Happy Land' or heaven.

**Land's End.** The westernmost tip of England, in CORNWALL, now commercialized for touristic purposes. Its Cornish name of identical meaning is Penwith, and the name has parallels in Pembroke, Wales (Welsh *Penbro*) and in Finistère, Brittany (from Latin *finis terrae*, 'end of the land') and Cape Finisterre, Spain. The unity of name suggests a westward drive of some kind in the past.

**Landslide.** The word is used metaphorically for a crushing election defeat, especially when it involves a reversal of fortune. A classic example was the overwhelming victory of the LABOUR PARTY in 1997 after 18 years of Conservatism.

**Bad Lands, The.** *See under* BAD.

**Belly landing.** *See under* BELLY.

**Clear the land, To.** *See under* CLEAR.

**Doric land.** *See under* DORIAN.

**Fat of the land, The.** *See under* FAT.

**From Land's End to John o'Groats.** *See under* FROM.

**Happy landings!** *See under* HAPPY.

**In the land of the living.** Still alive.

> Let us cut him off from the land of the living, that his name may be no more remembered.
>
> Jeremiah 11:19

**Holy Land, The.** *See under* HOLY.

**Promised Land, The.** *See under* PROMISE.

**See how the land lies, To.** *See under* SEE.

**Soft landing.** *See under* SOFT.

**Van Diemen's Land.** *See under* VAN DIEMEN.

**Landau.** A four-wheeled carriage with a divided top or hood, the two halves of which can be raised or lowered separately. It is said to have been first made in the 18th century at Landau in Bavaria.

**Landaulet.** A coupé with a LANDAU top; also an early type of car with a folding hood over the passengers' seats.

**Landscape.** A country scene or a picture representing this. The word was originally 'landskip', from Middle Dutch *lantscap*, 'region', with *-scap* related to English 'shape'. The English word has spawned a number of other 'scapes' as extensive views of particular regions, such as airscape, bodyscape (a 'map' of the body), cityscape, cloudscape, manscape (a sea of faces), moonscape, riverscape, seascape, skyscape, snowscape, townscape, waterscape and so on.

**Father of Landscape Gardening.** André Le Nôtre (1631–1700), who landscaped VERSAILLES.

**Landsknecht.** *See* LANCE-KNIGHT.

**Landsturm.** German forces of the militia type not used as first-line troops but usually employed on garrison duties or as labour forces. The forces were usually formed from those unfit for full military service or from the older age groups. The word literally means 'landstorm', referring to the storm-warning bells that originally summoned men to battle.

**Landtag** (German, 'land assembly'). The legislative assembly of a German state.

**Landwehr** (German, 'land defence'). In Germany the army reserve, used only in time of war.

**Lane. Drury Lane.** *See under* DRURY.

**Fast lane.** *See under* FAST.

**It's a long lane that has no turning.** *See under* LONG.

**Mincing Lane.** *See under* MINCE.

**Petticoat Lane.** *See under* PETTICOAT.

**Lang syne** (Scottish, 'long since'). In the olden time; in days gone by.

**Auld Lang Syne.** *See under* AULD.

**Langtry, Lillie.** *See* JERSEY LILY.

**Language. Language of flowers, The.** The traditional symbolic meanings attached to numerous flowers and plants. Some examples are:

> ASPHODEL: 'my regret follows you to the grave'
> BAY leaf: 'I change but in death'
> Bluebell: constancy
> FOXGLOVE: insincerity
> Honeysuckle: generous and devoted affection
> Jasmine: amiability
> Nasturtium: patriotism
> OAK leaves: bravery
> PEONY: shame, bashfulness
> Quince: temptation
> Snowdrop: hope
> Veronica: fidelity

Many herbs are associated with particular aspects of the character. Rosemary, for example, was believed to strengthen the memory and has come to be a symbol for memory.

> There's rosemary, that's for remembrance; pray, love, remember; and there is pansies, that's for thoughts.
>
> SHAKESPEARE: *Hamlet*, IV, v (1600)

**Body language.** *See under* BODY.

**Dead language.** *See under* DEAD.

**Parliamentary language.** *See under* PARLIAMENT.

**Romance languages.** *See under* ROMANCE.

**Semitic languages.** *See under* SEMITIC.

**Speak the same language, To.** *See under* SPEAK.

**Strong language.** *See under* STRONG.

**Three primitive languages, The.** *See under* THREE.

**Langue d'oc and langue d'oïl** (French *langue*, 'tongue'). The former is the old Provençal language, spoken south of the River Loire. The latter is Northern French, spoken in the Middle Ages to the north of that river, as the original of modern French. The languages are so called because 'yes' was in Provençal *oc*, from Latin *hoc*, 'this', and in the northern speech *oïl*, which later became *oui*, from Latin *hoc ille* (*fecit*), 'this he (did)'. *See also* HIGH GERMAN.

**Lansquenet.** *See* LANCE-KNIGHT.

**Lantern.** In Christian art, the attribute of St GUDULE and St Hugh.

**Lantern jaws.** Long jaws with cheeks so thin and hollow that it is almost possible to see daylight through them, as light shone through the horn of the lantern.

**City of Lanterns, The.** *See under* CITY.

**Dark lantern.** *See under* DARK.

**Feast of Lanterns, The.** *See under* FEAST.

**Lanthorn, Friar's.** *See under* FRIAR.

**Laocoön.** A son of PRIAM and priest of APOLLO, famous for the tragic fate of himself and his two sons, who were squeezed to death by serpents while he was sacrificing to POSEIDON. Their death was said to be in consequence of his having offended Apollo or for having sought to prevent the entry of the WOODEN HORSE into TROY. The group representing these three in their death agony, now in the VATICAN, was discovered in 1506 in a vineyard at Rome. It is a single block of marble and is attributed to the sculptors Hagesander, Polydorus and Athenodorus of Rhodes in the 1st century BC.

**Laodamia.** The wife of Protesilaus, king of Phylace, who was slain before TROY by HECTOR. According to one account, she begged to be allowed to converse with her dead husband for only three hours, and her request was granted. She afterwards voluntarily accompanied the dead hero to the underworld. William Wordsworth has a poem on the subject (1815).

**Laodicean.** Someone who is indifferent to religion, caring little or nothing about the matter, like the Christians of that church mentioned in the Revelation 3:14–18. Thomas Hardy's novel *A Laodicean* (1881) is on this theme and concerns a vacillating young woman, Paula Power, who cannot take the plunge when faced with the ordeal of total immersion as a Baptist.

**Lao's mirror.** It reflected the mind and its thoughts, as an ordinary mirror reflects the outward seeming (Oliver Goldsmith, *Citizen of the World*, xlv (1760–1)).

**Lao Zi.** *See* TAOISM.

**Lap. In the lap of the gods.** The unknown chances of the future; whatever may fall from the lap of the gods. The lap of fortune expresses the same idea.

**Live in the lap of luxury, To.** *See under* LIVE.

**Lapiths.** A people of Thessaly, noted in Greek legend for their defeat of the CENTAURS at the marriage feast of BRISEIS (Hippodamia), when the latter were driven out of Pelion. The contest was represented on the PARTHENON, the Theseum at Athens, the Temple of Apollo at Bassae and on various vases.

**Lapsus linguae** (Latin, 'slip of the tongue'). A mistake in uttering a word; an imprudent word inadvertently spoken. Similar adoptions from Latin are *lapsus calami*, 'a slip of the pen', and *lapsus memoriae*, 'a slip of the memory'. A SPOONERISM is usually a *lapsus linguae*.

**Laputa.** The flying island inhabited by scientific quacks in Jonathan Swift's *Gulliver's Travels* (1726). These dreamy philosophers were so absorbed in their speculations that they employed attendants called 'flappers', to flap them on the mouth and ears with a blown bladder when their attention was to be distracted from 'high things' to attend to vulgar mundane matters.

It has been suggested that the name could represent Spanish *la puta*, 'the whore', with reference to the proverb: 'Beware of the whore, who leaves the purse empty.' In the context of the novel this could be an allusion to England's impoverishment of Ireland.

**Lapwing.** Shakespeare refers to two peculiarities of this bird: (1) to lure people from its nest, it flies away and cries loudest when farthest from its nest; (2) the newly hatched birds fly with parts of shell still sticking to their heads.

> Far from her nest the lapwing cries away.
> *The Comedy of Errors*, IV, ii (1594)

> This lapwing runs away with the shell on his head.
> *Hamlet*, V, ii (1601)

The first peculiarity made the lapwing a symbol of insincerity; the second that of a forward person, one who is scarcely hatched. The name of the bird does not derive from 'lap' and 'wing' but from the equivalent of 'leap' and 'wink', the latter word in the sense to move from side to side. It is thus so called from the irregular, flapping manner of its flight.

**Lar.** *See* LARES AND PENATES.

**Larboard.** *See* STARBOARD AND LARBOARD.

**Larder.** A place for keeping bacon, from Old French *lardier*, from Latin *laridum*, 'bacon fat'. The origin of the word shows that pigs were the chief animals salted and preserved in olden times.

**Douglas larder, The.** *See under* DOUGLAS.

**Robin Hood's larder.** *See under* ROBIN HOOD.

**Wallace's larder.** *See under* WALLACE.

**Lares and penates.** A phrase used as a collective expression for home, and for those personal belongings that make it homely and individual. In ancient Rome the *lares* (singular *lar*) were the household gods, usually deified ancestors or heroes, and the *lar familiaris* was the spirit of the founder of the house, which never left it. The *penates* were the gods of the storeroom and guardian deities of the household and the state, whose duty was to protect and ward off dangers. Their images stood in a special shrine in each house, and offerings were made to them of wine, incense, cakes and honey on special family occasions. *See also* DII PENATES.

**Large. Large Family Bible, The.** *See under* BIBLE.

**Larger than life.** In exaggerated form.

**As large as life.** *See under* AS.

**At large.** *See under* AT.

**By and large.** *See under* BY.

**Loom large, To.** *See under* LOOM.

**Lark.** A spree or frolic. The word is perhaps a modern adaptation of dialect *lake*, 'sport', from Middle English *laik*, 'play', and Old English *lac*, 'contest'. Skylark, as in 'skylarking about', is a more recent extension.

**Dunstable larks.** *See under* DUNSTABLE.

**Larkin Family, The.** Pop and Ma Larkin are a happy-go-lucky farming couple who appear in a series of comically rustic novels by H.E. Bates (1905–74), beginning with *The Darling Buds of May* (1958). They have a large brood of children with names such as Zinnia, Petunia and Primrose. Surprisingly, the stories were not brought to the television screen until 1991, when they appeared to popular acclaim under the title of the first novel, with David Jason playing Pop Larkin, Pam Ferris as Ma and Catherine Zeta Jones as their eldest daughter, Marietta.

**Larrikin.** An Australian term dating from the 19th century denoting a young ruffian or rowdy given to acts of hooliganism. They flourished particularly in the 1880s and were known by their own style of dress, recognizable by its excessive neatness and severe colours. The word comes from the name Larry.

**Larry. Larry the Lamb.** The wooden toy lamb that first appeared in 1925 in a series of story books for young children by S.G. Hulme Beaman. From 1929, together with his friends, Dennis the Dachshund and Ernest the Policeman, Larry appeared regularly on BBC radio's 'Children's Hour', his voice bleatingly rendered by 'Uncle Mac' (Derek McCulloch).

**As happy as Larry.** *See under* AS.

**Larvae.** Among the ancient Romans, a name for malignant spirits and ghosts. The larva or ghost of Caligula was often seen (according to Suetonius) in his palace.

**Lass, Hallelujah.** *See under* HALLELUJAH.

**Lassie.** One of the most popular dogs in the cinema. The first film starring her (played by a male dog called Pal) was in 1943 and was itself based on Eric Knight's children's novel *Lassie Come Home* (1940). Lassie is an intelligent collie who is sold by her owners when they cannot afford to keep her, much to the distress of their young son. She promptly runs away from her new home in Scotland until, after travelling hundreds of miles, she 'comes home', and is reunited with the family she loves.

**Last. Last Day.** The final day of the present dispensation when Christ is to return to earth for the LAST JUDGEMENT, otherwise the day of judgement itself. *See also* BALANCE.

**Last-ditch attempt, A.** A final effort, like that made by a horse and rider over the final fence of a race. *See also* DIE IN THE LAST DITCH.

**Last gasp.** To be at one's last gasp is to be completely exhausted or even on the point of death. The phrase comes from the Apocrypha, in which it forms part of the story of the seven brothers and their mother who were tortured by King Antiochus when they refused to disobey the laws of their fathers:

> And when he was at the last gasp, he said, Thou like a fury takest us out of this present life, but the King of the world shall raise us up.
>
> 2 Maccabees 7:9

**Last honours.** Funeral rites, as the last tributes of respect to the dead.

**Last** or **General Judgement, The.** God's final sentence on mankind on the LAST DAY.

**Last light.** *See* FIRST LIGHT.

**Last Man, The.** CHARLES I was so called by the Parliamentarians, meaning that he would be the last king of Great Britain. His son, Charles II, was called the Son of the Last Man.

**Last Night of the Proms, The.** The final evening of the annual PROMENADE CONCERTS at the Royal Albert Hall, London, in September, popularly regarded as the apotheosis of the series. The audience is mainly made up of young promenaders who enthusiastically join in the traditional choruses of LAND OF HOPE AND GLORY and RULE, BRITANNIA while waving UNION JACKS, bursting balloons, throwing streamers and evincing other manifestations of patriotic fervour and good humour.

> Little, it seems, is ever going to change at the Last Night of the Proms. So there is no point in worrying about the hopefully good-natured jingoism of those who believe that, once a year at least, Britannia still Rules the Waves.
>
> *The Times* (14 September 1998)

**Last of the Barons, The.** Warwick the KING-MAKER. Lord Lytton has a novel of this title (1843).

**Last of the Dandies, The.** A title given to Count Alfred D'Orsay (1801–52).

**Last of the English, The.** Hereward the Wake (*fl.*1070), who led the rising of the English at Ely against William the Conqueror. Charles Kingsley's novel *Hereward the Wake* was published in 1866.

**Last of the Fathers, The.** St BERNARD (1090–1153), abbot of Clairvaux.

**Last of the Goths, The.** RODERICK (d.711), last king of the Visigoths in Spain.

**Last of the Greeks, The.** The general Philopoemen of Megalopolis (*c*.253–183 BC), whose great object was to infuse into the Achaeans a military spirit and to establish their independence.

**Last of the Knights, The.** The Holy Roman Emperor Maximilian I (1459–1519).

**Last of the Mohicans, The.** The Indian chief Uncas is so called by Fenimore Cooper in his novel of this title (1826).

**Last of the Romans, The.** A title given to a number of historical characters, including:

- Marcus Junius Brutus (*c*.85–42 BC), one of the murderers of Julius Caesar
- Caius Cassius Longinus (d.42 BC), so called by Brutus
- Stilicho (*c*.359–408), VANDAL, and Roman general under Theodosius
- Aetius, the general who defended the Gauls against the FRANKS and other barbarians and defeated Attila near Châlons-sur-Marne in 451; he is so called by Procopius
- Rienzi or Rienzo (1313–54), the Italian patriot and 'last of the Tribunes'
- François Joseph Terrasse Desbillons (1711–89), a French Jesuit, so called from the elegance and purity of his Latin

Alexander Pope called William Congreve *Ultimus Romanorum*, and the same title was conferred on Dr Johnson, Horace Walpole and C.J. Fox. *See also* ROMAN.

**Last of the Saxons, The.** King Harold (1022–66), who was defeated and slain at the Battle of Hastings. Lord Lytton has this as a subtitle for his novel *Harold* (1848).

**Last of the Tribunes, The.** Cola di Rienzi (*c*.1313–54), who led the Roman people against the barons.

**Last of the Troubadours, The.** Jacques Boé, called Jasmin (1798–1864), the Gascon poet who wrote in patois.

**Last post, The.** The bugle call that is the military order to retire for the night. It is traditionally sounded at military funerals.

**Last rites.** The religious rites in the Christian church that are prescribed for those close to death.

**Last straw, The.** The final annoyance or hurt that breaks one's patience or resilience. The expression comes from the proverb, 'It is the last straw that breaks the camel's back,' itself alluding to the final, minute addition to the burden that makes it literally unbearable.

**Last Supper, The.** The last meal Christ partook with his disciples on the night before the crucifixion and the institution of the EUCHARIST.

Leonardo da Vinci's picture of this was painted on a wall of the refectory of the Convent of Santa Maria delle Grazie, Milan, in about 1497. Although the refectory was reduced to ruins by Allied bombs in August 1943, the wall on which the Last Supper is painted was practically undamaged, and the picture left quite intact. It has worn badly with time and is now protected against further deterioration. Recent restoration has distorted the original.

**Last thing.** A final action, such as one carried out before retiring to bed.

**Last trump, The.** The final end of all things earthly; the Day of Judgement.

> We shall not all sleep, but we shall all be changed, in a moment, in the twinkling of an eye, at the last trump.
>
> 1 Corinthians 15:51–52

**Last word, The.** Anything that is conclusive or final. 'To have the last word' is to have the final say or decision; to make the last rejoinder in an argument. Like the French *le dernier cri*, the phrase 'last word' also has the meaning of the latest, most fashionable and up-to-date style in anything, as: 'the last word in elegance', 'the last word in boorishness'.

**Breathe one's last, To.** *See under* BREATHE.

**Cobbler should stick to his last, A.** *See under* COBBLER.

**Have the last laugh, To.** *See under* LAUGH.

**On its last legs.** *See under* LEG.

**Las Vegas.** The self-styled 'Gambling Capital of the World', in Nevada, USA. Its first settlers were MORMONS, attracted by the springs in the dry valley along the Old Spanish Trail. Hence its name, Spanish for 'the meadows'. The Mormons subsequently abandoned the site, and the present town grew up around a US Army fort, built in 1864. Its growth was stimulated when legal gambling was introduced in 1931, and this is the activity for which it is now chiefly renowned, with its luxury hotels and casinos grouped in a glamorous but garish area known as 'The Strip'.

**Late. Late Latin.** The period of LATIN that followed the AUGUSTAN AGE to about AD 600. It includes the works of the FATHERS OF THE CHURCH.

**Better late than never.** *See under* BETTER.

**Lateran.** The ancient palace of the Laterani family, which was appropriated by NERO (AD 66) and later given to Pope Sylvester I (r.314–335) by the Emperor Constantine. It remained the official residence of the popes until the departure to AVIGNON in 1309. The present palace is now a museum. Legend derives the name from Latin *latere*, 'to hide', and *rana*, 'frog', and accounts for it by saying that Nero once vomited a frog covered with blood, which he believed to be his own progeny and so hid in a vault. The palace built on its site was called the 'Lateran', or the palace of the hidden frog.

**Lateran Council.** The name given to the ECUMENICAL COUNCILS held in the church of St JOHN LATERAN at Rome. They are five:

1123: held under Calixtus II, confirming the Concordat of Worms, which ended the INVESTITURE CONTROVERSY
1139: Innocent II condemned Anacletus II and Arnold of Brescia
1179: convoked by Alexander III to regularize papal elections
1215: Innocent III condemned the ALBIGENSES and further defined Catholic doctrine
1512–17: Julius II and Leo X invalidated the work of the anti-papal Council of Pisa

**Lateran Treaty.** A treaty concluded between the HOLY SEE and the kingdom of Italy in 1929, establishing as sovereign the VATICAN CITY STATE, thus ending the 'Roman Question' begun in 1870 when the temporal power of the papacy was finally abrogated and Rome became the capital of the Italian kingdom. *See also* PRISONER OF THE VATICAN.

**St John Lateran.** *See under* JOHN.

**Lathe** (Old English *lǣth*, 'district'). An ancient unit of local government in Kent, which was ultimately divided into five lathes (Sutton-at-Hone, Sheppey, Scray, Aylesford, and St Augustine and Hedeling). The divisions for the former petty sessions (now magistrates' courts) were based on them. *See also* RAPE.

**Latin.** The language of the ancient inhabitants of Latium in Italy and spoken by the ancient Romans. According to one story, Latium is from *latere*, 'to lie hidden', and was so called because SATURN hid there, when he was driven out of heaven by the gods. According to Roman tradition the Latini were the aborigines. *See also* LATINUS.

The earliest specimen of the Latin language is an inscription on the Praeneste fibula, a gold brooch. It was found in 1886 and dates from the 6th century BC.

**Latin alphabet.** *See* ROMAN ALPHABET.

**Latin America.** The regions of America whose official languages are Spanish and Portuguese, spoken by LATIN RACES. This essentially means South America, Central America, Mexico and some of the Caribbean islands.

**Latin Church, The.** The Western or ROMAN CATHOLIC CHURCH, as distinct from the EASTERN OR GREEK CHURCH.

**Latin cross, The.** *See* CROSS AS A MYSTIC EMBLEM.

**Latin quarter.** *See* QUARTER.

**Latin races, The.** The peoples whose language is based on Latin, of whom the chief are the Italians, Spanish, Portuguese, French and Romanians. *See also* ROMANCE LANGUAGES.

**Classical Latin.** *See under* CLASSICAL.

**Dog Latin.** *See under* DOG.

**Late Latin.** *See under* LATE.

**Law Latin.** *See under* LAW.

**Low Latin.** *See under* LOW.

**Macaronic Latin.** *See under* MACARONI.

**Medieval Latin.** *See under* MEDIEVAL.

**New Latin.** *See under* NEW.

**Pig Latin.** *See under* PIG.

**Rogues' Latin.** *See* THIEVES' LATIN.

**Thieves' Latin.** *See under* THIEF.

**Vulgar Latin.** *See under* VULGAR.

**Latinus.** Legendary king of the Latini, the ancient inhabitants of Latium. According to Virgil, he opposed AENEAS on his first landing, but later formed an alliance with him, and gave him his daughter, Lavinia, in marriage. Turnus, king of the Rutuli, declared that Lavinia had been betrothed to him and the issue was decided by single combat. Aeneas, being the victor, became the husband of Lavinia and ancestor of ROMULUS and Remus (Virgil, *Aeneid*, vii (1st century BC)). *See also* LATIN.

**Latitudes, Horse.** *See under* HORSE.

**Latitudinarians.** In the CHURCH OF ENGLAND a name applied from the mid-17th century, at first opprobriously, to those clergy attaching little importance to dogma and practice in religion, which in the 18th century encouraged laxity and indifference. The Cambridge Platonists were prominent among them. Latitudinarianism was checked by the advent of the EVANGELICALS and the OXFORD MOVEMENT. The term is widely applied to those attaching little importance to dogma and orthodoxy in general.

**Latium.** *See* LATIN.

**Latona.** The Roman name of the Greek LETO, mother by JUPITER of APOLLO and DIANA. Milton refers to the legend that when she knelt with her infants in arms by a fountain at Delos to quench her thirst, some Lycian clowns insulted her and were turned into frogs.

> As when those hinds that were transformed to frogs
> Railed at Latona's twin-born progeny,
> Which after held the Sun and Moon in fee.
> *Sonnets*, xii, 'I did but prompt the age' (1673)

**Latrine lawyer.** *See* BARRACK-ROOM LAWYER.

**Latter-day Saints.** *See* MORMONS.

**Lauds.** In the Western Church the traditional morning prayer, so called from the repeated occurrence of the word *laudate* ('praise ye') in Psalms 147–50, which form part of the office. It is said in the early morning by religious orders who rise for the night office, but otherwise is now coupled with MATINS and said overnight. It forms part of the BREVIARY of the ROMAN CATHOLIC CHURCH, and the service of Morning Prayer, in the BOOK OF COMMON PRAYER, is essentially composed of parts of Lauds and Matins.

**Laugh. Laugh and grow fat.** An old saw, expressive of the wisdom of keeping a cheerful mind. Sir John Harington, in *The Metamorphosis of Ajax*

(1596), writes of 'many of the worshipful of the city, that make sweet gains of stinking wares; and will laugh and be fat'.

Laugh and be well. Monkeys have been
Extreme good doctors for the spleen.
MATTHEW GREEN: *The Spleen* (1737)

**Laughing Cavalier, The.** The name given to the portrait (1624) of an unknown gallant, by the Dutch painter Frans Hals, now in the Wallace Collection, London. The title is inaccurate, since the subject is smiling, not laughing.

**Laughing gas.** Nitrous oxide ($N_2O$), discovered by Joseph Priestley in 1772 and suggested as an anaesthetic by Sir Humphry Davy in 1802. It was formerly much used in dentistry and for minor operations. After inhalation it produces a feeling of exhilaration followed by unconsciousness. Hence the name.

**Laughing jackass.** Another name for the kookaburra (*Dacelo novaeguineae*), from its cackling cry.

**Laughing Philosopher, The.** Democritus of ABDERA (5th century BC), who viewed with supreme contempt the feeble powers of man. *See also* WEEPING PHILOSOPHER.

**Laughing stock.** A butt for jokes; an object of ridicule.

**Laugh in someone's face, To.** To show open contempt for them.

**Laugh like a drain, To.** To laugh noisily or coarsely, like water gurgling down a drain.

**Laugh off, To.** To dismiss a matter lightly; to shake off an insult or setback with a pleasantry.

**Laugh one's head off, To.** To laugh uproariously or excessively.

**Laugh on the other side of one's face, To.** To feel sudden annoyance after mirth or satisfaction; to be bitterly disappointed; to cry.

**Laugh out of court, To.** To cover with ridicule and so treat as not worth considering.

**Laugh to scorn, To.** To treat with contempt.

All they that see me laugh me to scorn: they shoot out the lip; they shake the head.
Psalm 22:7

**Laugh up one's sleeve, To.** To laugh inwardly; to hold in derision secretly. At one time it was quite possible to conceal amusement by hiding the face in the large loose sleeves formerly worn.

**Barrel of laughs.** *See* BARREL OF FUN.

**Belly laugh.** *See under* BELLY.

**Burst out laughing, To.** *See under* BURST.

**Canned laughter.** *See under* CANNED.

**Don't make me laugh.** I don't believe you; you must be joking.

**Have the last laugh, To.** To win in an argument or situation in which one had earlier been losing.

**Horse laugh.** *See under* HORSE.

**No laughing matter.** Something to be treated seriously. The expression is an example of LITOTES.

Starvation is no laughing matter.
W.M. THACKERAY: *The Adventures of Philip*, ch xvi (1861–2)

**Raise a laugh, To.** *See under* RAISE.

**Launcelot.** *See* LANCELOT.

**Launch. Launching pad.** Figuratively, the place that gives an impetus to, or sees the start of, an important enterprise. The expression derives from the technical term in aeronautics.

**Face that launched a thousand ships, The.** *See under* FACE.

**Launfal, Sir.** One of the KNIGHTS OF THE ROUND TABLE. His story is told in a metrical romance written by Thomas Chestre in the reign of Henry VI (1422–61, 1470–1). James Russell Lowell has a poem *The Vision of Sir Launfal* (1845).

**Laura.** The name given by Petrarch to the young woman who inspired his love poems. He first saw her in the church of St Clare, Avignon, on 6 April 1327. Her identity remains unknown.

Think you, if Laura had been Petrarch's wife,
He would have written sonnets all his life?
LORD BYRON: *Don Juan*, III, viii (1819)

**Laureate, Poet.** *See under* POET.

**Laurel.** The Greeks gave a wreath of laurels to the victor in the PYTHIAN GAMES, but the victor in the OLYMPIC GAMES had a wreath of wild olives, in the NEMEAN GAMES a wreath of green parsley, and in the ISTHMIAN GAMES a wreath of dry parsley or green pine leaves.

The ancients held that laurel communicated the spirit of prophecy and poetry, hence the custom of crowning the Pythoness (the PYTHIA) and poets, and of putting laurel leaves under one's pillow to acquire inspiration. Another superstition was that the BAY laurel could prevent a strike of lightning, but Sir Thomas Browne, in his *Vulgar Errors* (1646), recounts how Vicomereatus proved from personal knowledge that this is untrue.

The laurel in modern times is a symbol of victory and peace and of excellence in literature and the arts. In Christian art St GUDULE, patron saint of Brussels, carries a laurel crown. *See also* APOLLO; DAPHNE.

**Look to one's laurels, To.** *See under* LOOK.

**Rest on one's laurels, To.** *See under* REST.

**Laurence, St.** *See* LAWRENCE.

**Laurentian Library.** A LIBRARY opened by Cosimo de MEDICI (1519–74) in 1571, noted for its collection of Greek and Latin manuscripts, and named after Laurentius or Lorenzo de Medici. It was designed by MICHELANGELO and formed from the collections of Cosimo the Elder, Pietro de Medici and Lorenzo the Magnificent.

**Laurie, Annie.** The eldest of three daughters of Sir Robert Laurie of Maxwelton, born 16 December 1682. William Douglas of Fingland (Kirkcudbright) wrote the popular verses, which were altered by Lady Scott (1810–1900), who composed the air. In 1709 Annie married Alexander Fergusson of Craigdarroch. She was the grandmother of Alexander Fergusson, the hero of Burns' song called 'The Whistle'. She died in 1764.

**Laurin.** The dwarf king in the German folk legend *Laurin*, or *Der kleine Rosengarten*. He possesses a magic ring, girdle and cap, and is attacked by Dietrich of Bern (*see* THEODORIC) in his rose garden, which no one may enter on pain of death. The anonymous poem belongs to the late 13th century, and Laurin's name comes from *laur*, 'cunning'.

**Lavender.** The earliest form of the word is Medieval Latin *lavendula*, perhaps from Latin *lividus*, 'bluish'. However, since the plant was used by laundresses for scenting linen, it came to be associated with *lavare*, 'to wash'. The modern botanical name is *Lavandula*. The plant is a token of affection.

**Lavender and old lace.** Old-fashioned gentility. The phrase comes from the title of a novel by Myrtle Reed published in 1902. A dramatized version by Rose Warner appeared in 1938. This was given a new twist as a black comedy by Joseph Kesselring under the title *Arsenic and Old Lace* (1941), and an enjoyable film version was first screened in 1942.

**Lay up in lavender, To.** *See under* LAY.

**Lavengro.** The wandering hero of George Borrow's semi-autobiographical novel *Lavengro: the Scholar, the Gypsy, the Priest* (1851) and its sequel, *The Romany Rye* (1857). According to Borrow, *lavengro* is a gypsy (ROMANY) word meaning 'philologist' or, literally, 'word-master', and was a name allegedly given him in his youth by Ambrose Smith, who appears in the book as the gypsy Jasper Petulengro.

**Lavinia.** *See* LATINUS.

**Lavolta** (Italian, 'the turn'). A former lively dance, in which there was a good deal of jumping or capering. Hence its name. Troilus says: 'I cannot sing, nor heel the high lavolt' (Shakespeare, *Troilus and Cressida*, IV, iv (1601)). It originated in 16th-century Provence or Italy and is thus described:

> A lofty jumping or a leaping round,
> Where arm in arm two dancers are entwined,
> And whirl themselves with strict embracements
> bound,
> And still their feet an anapest do sound.
> SIR JOHN DAVIES: *The Orchestra* (1594)

**Law. Law is an ass, The.** The proverbial expression became popular from Dickens' *Oliver Twist* (1838), in which the words are spoken by Mr Bumble. But the phrase existed well before his time, and is found, for example, in Chapman's *Revenge for Honour* (1654).

**Law Latin.** The debased Latin used in legal documents. *See also* DOG LATIN.

**Lawless Parliament.** *See* PARLIAMENT OF DUNCES.

**Law Lords.** The Lords of Appeal in Ordinary; also, additionally, those members of the HOUSE OF LORDS who are qualified to deal with the judicial business of the House, i.e. the LORD CHANCELLOR, the Lord Chief Justice, the MASTER OF THE ROLLS and any peer who has held high judicial office. The Lords of Appeal in Ordinary were instituted in 1877 as life BARONS. Until 1873 the appellate jurisdiction of the Lords was open to the whole House. *See also* LIFE PEER.

**Law merchant.** Formerly, the practice of merchants as established by judicial decisions and administered in the courts of markets and fairs, such as a COURT OF PIEPOWDER. From the time of Lord Mansfield (Lord Chief Justice, 1756–88), law merchant became assimilated to the COMMON LAW.

**Law of averages.** The law that is popularly said to exist by which an event will reoccur with a frequency roughly the same as its probability. An example is that if a tossed coin lands heads up five times in a row, then 'according to the law of averages' it is best to bet on tails next time. Such reasoning is actually false, since the coin has an equal chance of falling either way each time it is tossed.

**Law of diminishing returns, The.** The principle that an increase in expenditure beyond a certain point will no longer produce a proportionate yield.

**Law of Moses, The.** The laws given in the PENTATEUCH including the TEN COMMANDMENTS.

**Law of supply and demand, The.** The economic statement that the competition of buyers and sellers tends to make such changes in price that the demand for any article in a given market will become equal to the supply. In other words, if the demand exceeds the supply the price rises, operating so as to reduce the demand and so enable the supply to meet it, and vice versa.

**Law of the jungle, The.** Ruthless competition, especially when motivated by self-interest. The phrase was popularized by Kipling's *Jungle Book* (1894):

> The Law of the Jungle, which never orders anything without a reason, forbids every beast to eat Man except when he is killing to show his children how to kill.
> 'Mowgli's Brothers'

**Law of the Medes and Persians, The.** That which is unalterable.

> Now, O King, establish the decree, and sign the writing, that it be not changed, according to the law of the Medes and Persians, which altereth not.
> Daniel 6:8

**Law's Bubble.** *See* MISSISSIPPI BUBBLE.

**Laws of honour.** Certain conventional rules that the fashionable world tacitly holds with regard to honourable conduct.

**Laws written in blood.** Demades said that the laws of Draco were written in blood, because every offence was punishable by death. *See also* DRACONIAN CODE.

**Law unto itself, A.** A thing that is outside established law. The phrase may equally be used of a person, as: 'He's a law unto himself.'

> For when the Gentiles, which have not the law, do by nature the things contained in the law, these, having not the law, are a law unto themselves.
> Romans 2:14

**Aemilian law.** *See under* AEMILIAN.
**Blue laws.** *See under* BLUE.
**Blue Sky Laws.** *See under* BLUE.
**Canon law.** *See under* CANON.
**Common law.** *See under* COMMON.
**Corn Laws.** *See under* CORN.
**Game laws.** *See under* GAME.
**Glorious uncertainty of the law, The.** *See under* GLORIOUS.
**Go to law, To.** To take legal proceedings.
**Gresham's law.** *See under* GRESHAM.
**Grimm's law.** *See under* GRIMM.

**In-laws.** A way of referring to one's relations by marriage: mother-in-law, brothers-in-law and so on. The law is that of CANON LAW, and it refers to the degrees of affinity within which marriage is allowed or prohibited.

**Jim Crow laws.** *See under* JIM CROW.
**Lay down the law, To.** *See under* LAY.
**Letter of the law.** *See under* LETTER.
**Lydford Law.** *See under* LYDFORD.
**Lynch Law.** *See under* LYNCH.
**Martian laws.** *See under* MARTIAN.
**Murphy's law.** *See under* MURPHY.
**Myrmidons of the law.** *See under* MYRMIDONS.
**Necessity knows no law.** *See under* NECESSITY.
**Nuremberg laws.** *See under* NUREMBERG.
**Parkinson's Law.** *See under* PARKINSON.
**Red laws, The.** *See under* RED.
**Rhodian law, The.** *See under* RHODIAN.
**Salic law.** *See under* SALIC.
**Sumptuary laws.** *See under* SUMPTUARY.

**Take the law into one's own hands, To.** To try to secure satisfaction by force or personal action; to reward or punish (usually the latter) on one's own responsibility.

**Unwritten law.** *See under* UNWRITTEN.

**Lawn.** Fine linen or cotton fabric, used for the rochets of Anglican bishops, ladies' handkerchiefs and the like. It is probably so called from Laon (Old French *Lan*), a town in the Aisne department of France, once noted for its linen manufacture.

**Lawrence** or **Laurence, St.** The patron saint of curriers, who was roasted on a GRIDIRON. He was archdeacon to Pope Sixtus II (d.258) and was charged with the care of the poor, the orphans and the widows. When summoned by the praetor to deliver up the treasures of the church, he produced the poor under his charge, and said: 'These are the church's treasures' (*see also* CORNELIA). His day is 10 August. Fragments of his relics were taken to the ESCORIAL.

**Lawyer. Lawyer's bags.** More properly 'barrister's bags', since they are not used by solicitors. Counsel traditionally use bags made of cotton damask to carry their robes from home or chambers to court. The ordinary bag of a junior counsel is blue, but it is customary for a KC or QC to present a junior who has given outstanding assistance in a particular case with a red bag, which that junior thereafter always uses, during the remainder of a career both as a junior and as a counsel. Bags are normally carried from chambers to court by counsel's clerk. The bag is closed by pulling the ends of a cord, which is threaded round the mouth. It is carried over the shoulder, the ends of the cord being held in one hand.

**Barrack-room lawyer.** *See under* BARRACK.
**Bush lawyer.** *See under* BUSH.
**Penang lawyer.** *See under* PENANG.
**Philadelphia lawyer.** *See under* PHILADELPHIA.

**Lay** (adjective). Pertaining to the people of laity (Latin *laicus*) as distinguished from the clergy. Thus, a lay brother is one who, though not in HOLY ORDERS, is received into a monastery and is bound by its vows.

**Lay figures.** Wooden figures with free joints, used by artists chiefly for the study of how drapery falls. The word was earlier layman, from Dutch *leeman*, a contraction of *ledenman*, literally 'joint man'. Horace Walpole uses layman (1762), but lay figure had taken its place by the end of the 18th century. Hence, figuratively, a character who is a mere foil or puppet.

**Layman, A.** Properly speaking, anyone not in HOLY ORDERS. The word is also used by professional men, especially doctors and lawyers, to denote one not of their particular calling or specialized learning.

**Lay reader.** In the CHURCH OF ENGLAND A LAYMAN licensed by a bishop to conduct church services, namely, Morning and Evening Prayer (except the absolution and the blessing) and the Litany. A lay reader may also publish BANNS OF MARRIAGE, preach, catechize children and perform certain other offices. The modern office dates from 1866.

**Lay vicar.** A cathedral officer, formerly called a clerk vicar, who sings those portions of the liturgy not reserved for the clergy.

**Lay** (verb). A verb inviting misusage, partly because 'lay' is both the present tense of the transitive verb 'lay' and the past tense of the intransitive verb 'lie'. The similarity of meaning between the verbs compounds the confusion. 'Lay' has 'laid' as both past tense and past participle; 'lie' has 'lay' as its past tense and 'lain' as its past participle. *See also* LIE.

> Joanne, victim of killer who laid low for a year?
> *Daily Mail* (headline) (25 August 1998)

**Lay about one, To.** To hit or lash out on all sides.

**Lay a charge at someone's door, To.** To accuse someone of some crime or misdeed.

**Lay a finger on, To.** To harm. The expression is often used negatively, as: 'Don't you dare lay a finger on her.'

**Lay a ghost, To.** To prevent it from 'walking'.

**Lay a gun, To.** To aim it; to direct it on the target. The term is not used of SMALL ARMS.

**Lay an egg, To.** In American usage, to relate a joke or give a performance that fails completely. The allusion is probably to the DUCK'S EGG that is a failure to score.

**Lay by the heels, To.** To render powerless. The allusion is to the stocks, in which vagrants and other petty offenders were confined by the ankles.

**Lay down arms, To.** To cease from armed hostilities; to surrender.

**Lay down the law, To.** To tell someone what to do; to speak with authority.

**Lay hands on, To.** To apprehend; to lay hold of. *See also* LAYING ON OF HANDS.

**Laying on of hands, The.** In church usage, the imposition of hands is the laying on or touch of a bishop's hands in confirmation and ordination.

Among the Romans, a hand laid on the head of a person indicated the right of property, as when someone laid claim to a slave in the presence of the praetor. *See also* LAY HANDS ON.

**Lay into, To.** To attack vigorously, either physically or verbally.

**Lay it on thick** or **with a trowel To.** To flatter extravagantly.

**Lay off, To.** To dismiss workmen, usually temporarily. Also, to cease to annoy or attack.

**Lay** or **put one's finger on, To.** To point out precisely; to detect with accuracy. The expression is often used in a negative sense, as: 'I can't quite put my finger on it.'

**Lay on the table, To.** The parliamentary phrase for postponing consideration of a motion, proposal, Bill or the like, indefinitely. Hence to table a matter is to defer it SINE DIE. It is also used to mean submitting something for discussion.

**Lay out, To.** To disburse; to display goods; to arrange. Also, to prepare a corpse for the coffin; to disable or render unconscious.

**Lay someone low, To.** To overthrow or kill them.

**Lay to one's charge, To.** To attribute an offence to a person. The expression is biblical.

> And he [Stephen] kneeled down, and cried with a loud voice, Lord, lay not this sin to their charge.
> Acts 7:60

**Lay up, To.** To store away; to reserve for future use. A person temporarily incapacitated through injury or illness is said to be 'laid up', especially if confined to bed.

**Lay up in lavender, To.** To put something aside carefully for future use. The expression is sometimes used facetiously of a criminal, who is laid up in lavender when locked up in prison.

> Lowestoffe is laid up in lavender only for having shown you the way into Alsatia.
> SIR WALTER SCOTT: *The Fortunes of Nigel*, ch xxiii (1822)

**Lazarus.** A poor person or beggar, so called from the Lazarus of the parable, who was laid daily at the rich man's gate. *See also* AS POOR AS LAZARUS; DIVES.

**Lazy. Lazy bed.** A type of potato patch formerly cultivated in parts of Scotland and Ireland. The potatoes were laid on the surface and grown by being covered with kelp and with soil from a trench either side of the bed.

**Lazybones.** An idle or indolent person.

**Lazy daisy stitch.** An embroidery stitch used in making flower patterns, and consisting of a long chain stitch.

**Lazy dog.** In American military jargon, a fragmentation bomb that detonates in mid-air and scatters steel pellets over a wide target area.

**Lazy eye.** An eye that has poor vision and so is little used, with the result that its sight deteriorates even further. It is most commonly the unused eye in a squint.

**Lazy susan.** A type of revolving stand or tray used for holding condiments and the like.

**Lazy tongs.** A set of tongs with extending arms that allows one to pick up objects at a distance.

**L-committee.** A short form of legislative committee. A committee formed annually from members of the CABINET to decide which legislation should be introduced in the following session (beginning in November). The workings and composition of this committee are secret, but it is known that it includes the leaders of both Houses and the Government WHIPS of both Houses.

**Lead** (noun). The ancient alchemists called the element SATURN.

The lead, or blacklead, of a lead pencil

contains no lead at all, but is composed of plumbago or graphite, an almost pure carbon with a touch of iron. It was so named in the 16th century when it was thought to be made of the metal or at least contain it.

**Leads, The.** The prison in Venice in which CASANOVA was incarcerated and from which he escaped.

**Swing the lead, To.** *See under* SWING.

**Lead** (verb).

**Lead a cat and dog life, To.** To be always snapping and quarrelling, like a cat and a dog.

**Lead a dog's life.** To be harried FROM PILLAR TO POST; to be nagged constantly, never to be left in peace.

**Lead apes in hell, To.** The depressing consequence of dying an old maid. Hence ape-leader, an old maid. Thus Beatrice says:

> I will even take sixpence in earnest of the bearward, and lead his apes into hell.
> SHAKESPEARE: *Much Ado About Nothing*, II, i (1598)

**Leader.** The first violin of an orchestra is called the leader.

**Leading article** or **leader.** A newspaper article by the editor or a special writer. It takes the lead or chief place as commentary on current issues and expresses the policy of the paper.

**Leading card.** The strongest point in one's argument or in one's favour. In card games a person leads from his or her strongest suit.

**Leading case.** A lawsuit that forms a precedent in deciding others of a similar kind.

**Leading counsel.** In a court case, the senior barrister of two or more.

**Leading lady** or **man.** The actress or actor who takes the chief role in a play or film.

**Leading light.** An important or prominent person, especially in a particular organization or company. The phrase is of nautical origin, a leading light being one that is illuminated at night to lead a ship past some local danger.

**Leading note.** In music the seventh note of the diatonic scale, which leads to the octave, only half a tone higher.

**Leading question.** A question so worded as to suggest an answer. 'Was he not dressed in a black coat?' leads to the answer 'Yes'. In cross-examining a witness, leading questions are permitted, because the chief object of a cross-examination is to obtain contradictions. As popularly understood, a leading question is simply an unfair question, as in the exchange: 'So why did you marry her?' 'Ah, that's a leading question.'

**Leading strings.** The straps or harness that are used to help a young child who is learning to walk. To be in leading strings is thus to be under the control of someone else.

**Lead one the Devil's own dance, To.** To give one endless trouble.

**Lead someone a dance, To.** To put someone to much trouble. The reference is to the complicated dances of former times, when all followed the leader.

**Lead someone astray, To.** To lead someone into error; to misguide them.

**Lead someone by the nose, To.** To make a person do what one wants; to dominate someone. Such a person has no will of his own but tamely follows where he is led, just as a horse is led by bit and bridle. Bulls, buffaloes, camels and bears are led by a ring through their nostrils.

> Because thy rage against me, and thy tumult, is come up into mine ears, therefore will I put my hook in thy nose, and my bridle in thy lips, and I will turn thee back by the way by which thou camest.
> Isaiah 37:29

**Lead someone up the garden path, To.** To deceive or trick someone; to entice a person with false promises of good prospects or the like. The expression may relate to the garden parties of the 19th century, when a male guest with his eye on a particular young lady would at first stroll in the garden with her in full view of her chaperones until an opportunity presented itself for him to lead her up a path screened by shrubs or bushes.

**Lead the way, To.** To go first; to set the example.

**Lead to the altar, To.** To marry. A bride is led up to the altar rail, where marriages are solemnized.

**Lead with one's chin, To.** To invite defeat. A boxer normally leads his attack with one fist while defending himself with the other. If he leads with his chin, he obviously renders himself vulnerable.

**Bear leader.** *See under* BEAR.

**Blind leading the blind, The.** *See under* BLIND.

**Jump leads.** *See under* JUMP.

**Leaf.** Before the invention of paper, leaves of certain plants were among the materials used for writing upon. The reverse and obverse pages are still called leaves, and the double page of a ledger is termed a FOLIO, from Latin *folium*, 'leaf'. The word paper itself derives from Greek *papurus* (English 'papyrus') and book is a related word to 'beech'.

**Fig leaf.** *See under* FIG.

**Strawberry leaves.** *See under* STRAWBERRY.

**Take a leaf out of someone's book, To.** To imitate someone; to do as someone else does. The allusion is to literary plagiarisms.

**Turn over a new leaf, To.** *See under* TURN.

**League. League of Nations, The.** A league, having at one time about 60 member nations with headquarters at Geneva, with the essential aim of preventing war as well as promoting other forms of international cooperation. It was formed on 10 January 1920, after the close of the First

World War, but was weakened from the outset by the refusal of the USA to participate (although President Woodrow Wilson had played a major part in its foundation) and the exclusion of Russia. Its achievements were considerable in many fields, but it failed in its primary purpose. It last met on 18 April 1946, being replaced by the UNITED NATIONS Organization, which had been established on 24 October 1945.

**League of the Three Emperors, The.** The Dreikaiserbund of 1872 whereby the emperors of Germany, Austria and Russia agreed to cooperate in maintaining the STATUS QUO in Europe. A formal treaty was signed at Berlin in 1881 on policy with regard to possible war between one of them and a fourth Great Power and also on matters in the Near East. The treaty was renewed in 1884 but terminated in 1888.

**Big league.** *See under* BIG.

**Catholic League.** *See under* CATHOLIC.

**Hanseatic League.** *See under* HANSEATIC.

**Holy League, The.** *See under* HOLY.

**Ivy League.** *See under* IVY.

**Land League.** *See under* LAND.

**Primrose League, The.** *See under* PRIMROSE.

**Solemn League and Covenant.** *See under* SOLEMN.

**White League.** *See under* WHITE.

**Leah.** In the Old Testament (Genesis 29–31), the first wife of JACOB following her substitution by her father, LABAN, for her sister, RACHEL. As Jacob loved Leah more, God made Rachel barren and Leah fertile, and she was the mother of REUBEN, Simeon, Levi, JUDAH, ISSACHAR and Zebulun.

**Leak. Leak out, To.** To come surreptitiously to public knowledge. As a liquid leaks out of an unsound vessel, so the secret filters through.

**Spring a leak, To.** *See under* SPRING.

**Leal** (Old French *leial*, related to English 'legal' and 'loyal'). Trusty, law-abiding; a word now practically confined to Scotland.

**Land o' the Leal.** *See under* LAND.

**Leander.** *See* HERO AND LEANDER.

**Leaning tower.** While there are a number of leaning campanili (bell towers) in Italy, the most celebrated is the eight-storey tower of the cathedral of Pisa, which stands apart from the main building. It is 179ft (54.5m) high, 57ft 6in (17.5m) in diameter at the base, and leans about 15ft (4.5m) from the perpendicular. It was begun in 1173 and the sinking commenced during construction, but it continued to stand because the centre of gravity was within its walls. Galileo used the overhanging tower to make his experiments in gravitation. The angle of incline has gradually increased, however, despite several efforts to rectify the situation. In 1934 ballast pumped into the foundations only increased the tilt, as did a later attempt in 1995, when engineers froze the sandy soil to solidify it. In 1998 giant steel cables were attached as braces to the second loggia in a bid to avert a final collapse.

Caerphilly Castle, south Wales, has a tower that leans 10° from the perpendicular, the result of attempts to dismantle the castle with gunpowder after the Civil Wars (1642–51). The church spires at Chesterfield, Derbyshire, and Ermington, Devonshire, also lean.

**Leap. Leap in the dark, A.** A step or action whose consequences cannot be foreseen. The phrase was used by Lord Derby, the Prime Minister, of his government's policy in promoting the Parliamentary Reform Act of 1867. He adopted the expression from Lord Cranborne who first 'taunted the government with taking a leap in the dark' (Justin McCarthy, *Short History of Our Own Times*, ch xxi (1879–80)). Thomas Hobbes possibly also said it as his FAMOUS LAST WORDS.

**Leap year.** A year of 366 days, a BISSEXTILE year, i.e. in the JULIAN and GREGORIAN CALENDARS any year whose date is exactly divisible by 4 except those that are divisible by 100 but not by 400. Thus 1900 (though divisible by 4) was not a leap year, but 2000 was.

In ordinary years, the day of the month that falls on Monday this year will fall on Tuesday next year, and Wednesday the year after, but the fourth year will 'leap over' Thursday to Friday. This is because a day is added to February, the reason being that the astronomical year (i.e. the time that it takes the earth to go around the sun) is approximately 365¼ days, or more precisely 365.2422, the difference between .25 and .2422 being righted by the loss of the three days in 400 years.

It is an old saying that during a leap year the ladies may propose, and, if not accepted, may claim a silk gown.

**Bayard's Leap.** *See under* BAYARD.

**Giants' Leap, The.** *See under* GIANT.

**Look before you leap.** *See under* LOOK.

**Lear, King.** A legendary king of Britain whose story is told by Shakespeare (1605). Shakespeare's immediate source was Holinshed, who in turn derived it from Geoffrey of Monmouth's *Historia Regum Britanniae* (*c*.1136). It is also given in the GESTA ROMANORUM and in PERCEFOREST. Spenser uses it in *The Faerie Queene* (II, x (1590)), and Camden tells a similar story of Ina, king of the West Saxons. According to Shakespeare's version, King Lear in his old age divided his kingdom between his daughters GONERIL and REGAN, who professed great love for him but then harassed him into madness. CORDELIA, left portionless, succoured him and came with an army to dethrone her sisters, but was captured and slain. King Lear died over her body. *See also* LIR.

**Learn. Learn by heart, To.** To LEARN BY ROTE; to memorize.

**Learn by rote, To.** To learn by means of repetition, i.e. by going over the same track again and again. Rote has been associated with route, but there is no good authority for this.

**Learned, The.** Kalman or Koloman, king of Hungary (1095–1116), was so called. *See also* BEAUCLERC.

**Learned Blacksmith, The.** Elihu Burritt (1810–79), the American pacifist, a one-time blacksmith, who by the age of 30 could read nearly 50 languages.

**Learned Painter, The.** Charles Lebrun (1619–90), so called from the great accuracy of his costumes.

**Learned Tailor, The.** Henry Wild of Norwich (1684–1734), who, while he worked at his trade, mastered Greek, Latin, Hebrew, Chaldaic, Syriac, Persian and Arabic.

**Learn someone to do something, To.** An expression that is now a provincialism or regarded as illiterate speech but was formerly quite good English. In the Prayer Book version of the Psalms there is 'Lead me forth in thy truth and learn me,' and 'Such as are gentle, them shall he learn his way' (25: 4, 8). Other examples of this use of learn as an active verb are found in Psalm 119:66 ('O learn me true understanding') and 132:13 ('If thy children will keep my covenant, and my testimonies that I shall learn them').

> The red plague rid you
> For learning me your language!
> SHAKESPEARE: *The Tempest*, I, ii (1611)

'I'll learn you' or 'I'll larn you' is still used as a threat, especially by exasperated mothers to troublesome children.

**New Learning.** *See under* NEW.

**Revival of learning.** *See under* REVIVAL.

**Leash, To strain at the.** *See under* STRAIN.

**Leather. Leather medal.** An American colloquial term for a BOOBY PRIZE.

**Leatherneck.** A soldier or a MARINE, so called from the leather stock formerly worn by them.

**Leatherstocking novels.** The novels by Fenimore Cooper (1789–1851) in which Natty Bumppo, nicknamed Leatherstocking and Hawkeye, is a leading character. They are *The Pioneers* (1823), *The* LAST OF THE MOHICANS (1826), *The Prairie* (1827), *The Pathfinder* (1840) and *The Deerslayer* (1841). 'Leatherstocking' was a hardy backwoodsman, a type of North American pioneer, ignorant of books but a philosopher of the woods.

**All leather or prunella.** *See under* ALL.

**Give someone a leathering, To.** To beat them with a leather strap; to give them a drubbing.

**Hell for leather.** *See under* HELL.

**Nothing like leather.** *See under* NOTHING.

**Leave. Leave a bad or nasty taste in the mouth, To.** To cause a strong sense of dislike or unease following a particular experience.

**Leave in the lurch, To.** To desert a person in a difficulty. In cribbage a player is left in the position called the lurch when his or her adversary has run out a score of 51 holes before the player has turned the corner or pegged out the 31st hole.

**Leave it at that, To.** To refrain from further action or comment.

**Leave no stone unturned, To.** To spare no trouble, time or expense in endeavouring to accomplish one's aim. After the defeat of Mardonius at Plataea (477 BC), a report was current that the Persian general had left great treasures in his tent. Polycrates the Theban sought long, but did not find them. The ORACLE of DELPHI, told him 'to leave no stone unturned', and the treasures were discovered.

**Leave one cold, To.** To have no effect on someone; to fail to move or interest them.

**Leave someone standing, To.** To make much more rapid progress than they.

**Leave well alone.** Do not try to alter a state of affairs that is reasonably satisfactory lest you make things worse. 'Why not let it alone' was a maxim of Lord Melbourne, the WHIG Prime Minister (1835–41), and the motto of his 18th-century predecessor, Sir Robert Walpole, was virtually the same: *Quieta non movere*, the equivalent of LET SLEEPING DOGS LIE.

**Left holding the baby, To be.** To carry the responsibility for faults committed by others; to CARRY THE CAN.

**Left holding the bag, To be.** To be deserted by one's comrades and left with the entire onus of what was originally a group responsibility. Similar expressions are to be LEFT HOLDING THE BABY and left to CARRY THE CAN.

**Left in the basket, To be.** To be neglected or uncared for. Formerly foundling hospitals used to place baskets at their doors where unwanted babies could be left. Basket is also a EUPHEMISM for BASTARD.

**French leave.** *See under* FRENCH.

**Take it or leave it.** *See under* TAKE.

**Take one's leave, To.** To bid farewell; to say goodbye; to depart.

**Ticket of leave.** *See under* TICKET.

**Lebensraum.** A German phrase ('room for living') applied to the territory required by a nation for overseas expansion, both for settlement and trade, to meet the population pressures in the MOTHER COUNTRY.

**Lecture. Bampton Lectures.** *See under* BAMPTON.

**Barnaby Lecturers.** *See under* BARNABAS.

**Caudle lecture.** *See under* CAUDLE.

**Curtain lecture.** *See under* CURTAIN.

**Romanes lecture.** *See under* ROMANES.

**Leda.** In Greek mythology the wife of Tyndarus. JUPITER came to her in the guise of a swan when she was bathing, and in due time she brought forth two eggs, from one of which came CASTOR and CLYTEMNESTRA, and from the other Pollux and HELEN. The two former are usually held to be the children of Tyndarus.

**Leda Bible, The.** *See under* BIBLE.

**Lee** (Old English *hlēow*, 'shelter'). Nautically, the side or quarter opposite to that against which the wind blows; in other words, the sheltered side.

**Leeboard.** A wooden board fixed on the side of a vessel and lowered on the lee side when on a wind, to prevent making too much leeway. The once familiar Thames sailing barge was equipped with leeboards.

**Lee shore.** The shore under the lee of a ship, or that towards which the wind blows. It is very dangerous for a vessel to come close to a lee shore.

**Lee side.** *See* LEEWARD.

**Lee tide.** A tide running in the same direction as the wind blows. If it runs in the opposite direction it is called a tide under the lee.

**Leeward.** Towards the LEE, or that part towards which the wind blows. The opposite is windward, the WEATHER side.

**Under the lee of a ship.** *See under* UNDER.

**Under the lee of the land.** *See under* UNDER.

**Leech.** Formerly, a doctor, literally a person skilled in 'leechcraft'. The word comes from Old English *lǣce*, from *lacnian*, 'to heal'. The blood-sucking worm, the leech, gets its name from the same source.

**Leek.** The national emblem of Wales. The story is that St DAVID, on one occasion, caused his countrymen under King Cadwaladr to distinguish themselves from their Saxon foes by wearing a leek in their caps. Shakespeare makes out that the Welsh wore leeks at the Battle of Poitiers, and Fluellen says:

> If your majesties is remembered of it, the Welshmen did good service in a garden where leeks did grow, wearing leeks in their Monmouth caps; which, your majesty know, to this hour is an honourable badge of the service; and I do believe, your majesty takes no scorn to wear the leek upon Saint Tavy's Day.
>
> *Henry V*, IV, vii (1598)

The reason the leek should have become the Welsh national plant is a matter for speculation. Shakespeare's allusion is to a garden of leeks where the Welsh are said to have won an important battle, each man plucking and wearing a leek so as to be distinguished from the enemy by their fellow-countrymen. *See also* DAFFODIL.

**Eat the leek, To.** *See under* EAT.

**Leet.** In East Anglia, a division of the HUNDRED, formed from a group of vills (feudal townships) for local government and taxation. The word occurs in the DOMESDAY BOOK and is of Anglo-French origin.

**Court leet.** *See under* COURT.

**Left** (adjective). The left side of anything is frequently considered to be unlucky, of bad omen; the right is considered the reverse. *See also* AUGURY; SINISTER.

In politics the left denotes the more RADICAL political group, and today is usually applied to Socialists. Within a particular party the left wing is made up of the 'progressives' or 'radicals'. Communists were often known as the 'extreme left'. In many legislatures the radicals sit on the left-hand side (as seen from the chair) and in most of the British Commonwealth assemblies the opposition sits on the left.

In the French National Assembly of 1789, the reactionaries sat on the right, moderates in the centre, and democrats and extremists on the left, and this established the custom.

**Left-handed compliment, A.** A compliment that implies a reproach.

**Left-handed marriage, A.** A MORGANATIC MARRIAGE.

**Left-handed oath, A.** One not intended to be binding.

**Left, right and centre.** In all directions; everywhere.

**Eyes left!** *See under* EYE.

**Have two left feet, To.** To be clumsy.

**Over the left.** *See under* OVER.

**Left** (verb). *See* LEAVE.

**Leg.** In many phrases, such as 'to find one's legs', 'to put one's best leg forward' and so on, leg is interchangeable with FOOT.

**Leg before wicket** or **lbw.** In CRICKET a method of dismissal. A batsman is declared out if his legs are struck by a bowled ball that would otherwise have struck the wicket.

**Leg break.** In CRICKET a ball that, after striking the ground from the batsman's leg side, turns towards the wicket. A fast leg break is known as a leg-cutter.

**Leg bye.** In CRICKET a run scored from a ball that has glanced off any part of the batsman's person except his hand.

**Leg it, To.** To run away.

**Legless.** Very drunk. An inebriated person finds it hard to stand.

**Legman.** In the United States a newsman who reports from the scene of the action or who obtains news from an original source. The word is also used for someone who runs errands.

**Legs eleven.** A call for the number 11 at bingo. The two figure 1s suggest a pair of legs.

**Leg show.** A variety performance in which dancing girls display their legs.

**Legwork.** Work that involves a lot of walking or travelling.

**Arm and a leg.** *See under* ARM.

**Break a leg!** *See under* BREAK.

**Game leg.** *See under* GAME.

**Give someone a leg up, To.** To help a person mount an obstacle; to help a person advance in some way. The original sense was to help a person up into the saddle by cupping one's hands for them to place one foot in as a 'step'.

**Have a bone in one's leg, To.** *See under* BONE.

**Have good sea legs, To.** *See under* GOOD.

**Have no legs, To.** Said of a golf ball that lacks the momentum to reach the desired point.

**On its last legs.** Moribund; obsolete; about to collapse or cease functioning.

**Peg leg.** *See under* PEG.

**Pull someone's leg, To.** *See under* PULL.

**Shake a leg!** *See under* SHAKE.

**Show a leg.** *See under* SHOW.

**Take to one's legs, To.** To run away.

**Stretch one's legs, To.** *See under* STRETCH.

**Without a leg to stand on.** *See under* WITHOUT.

**Legal. Legal bands.** A relic of the wide, falling collars, which formed a part of the ordinary dress in the reign of Henry VIII and which were especially conspicuous in Stuart times. In the showy days of Charles II the plain bands were changed for lace ends.

> The eighth Henry as I understand,
> Was the first prince that ever wore a band.
> JOHN TAYLOR (1580–1653)

**Legal tender.** Money that, by the law of a particular country, constitutes payment that a creditor is obliged to accept. In Britain gold dated 1838 onwards is legal tender for any amount. Various amounts of coins of different values are legal tender up to a stated amount at any one time. When notes or coins are about to be withdrawn from circulation they cease to be legal tender from a particular date. The farthing ceased to be legal tender on 31 December 1960, the halfpenny on 1 August 1969, the halfcrown on 1 January 1970, the threepence and pre-decimal penny on 31 August 1971, the sixpence on 30 June 1980, the decimal halfpenny on 31 December 1984, the old 5p on 31 December 1990, the old 10p on 30 June 1993, and the old 50p on 28 February 1998.

**Legend** (Latin *legenda*, 'things to be read'). The narratives of saints and martyrs were so termed from their having to being read, especially at MATINS and after dinner in monastic refectories. Exaggeration and a love for the wonderful so predominated in these readings that the word came to signify a traditional story, a fable or myth.

In numismatics the legend is the inscription impressed in letters on the edge or rim of a coin or medal and is often used synonymously with 'inscription', which is strictly the words in the field of a coin. (The field is the whole part of a coin not occupied by the device.) Legend is also applied to the title on a map or under a picture.

**Legenda aurea.** *See* GOLDEN LEGEND.

**Leger, St.** A horse race for three-year-olds run at Doncaster on a Saturday early in September. It was instituted in 1776 by Colonel Anthony St Leger, of Park Hill, near Doncaster, but was not called the St Leger until two years later. *See also* CLASSIC RACES; RACES.

**Legion.** Very large or numerous. The use of the word in this sense was popularized by the biblical line: 'My name is Legion: for we are many' (Mark 5:9).

**Legionnaires' disease.** A form of pneumonia first identified in 1976 as being caused by a previously unknown bacillus, *Legionella pneumophilia*, which thrives in contaminated air-conditioning units. The name comes from a convention held that year at a Philadelphia hotel by members of the American Legion, an organization of retired American servicemen. A total of 192 Legionnaires contracted the disease, 29 of them fatally.

**Legion of Honour.** An order of distinction and reward instituted by NAPOLEON BONAPARTE in 1802 for either military or civil merit. It was originally limited to 15 *cohortes*, each composed of 7 *grands officiers*, 20 *commandants*, 30 *officiers* and 350 *légionnaires*, making a total of 6105 members. It was reorganized by Louis XVIII in 1814, and again by NAPOLEON III in 1852, and now consists of 80 *grand-croix*, 200 *grands officiers*, 1000 *commandeurs*, 4000 *officiers* and an unlimited number of *chevaliers*.

The badge is a five-branched cross with a medallion bearing a symbolic figure of the republic and round it the legend, 'République Française'. This is crowned by a LAUREL wreath, and the ribbon is of red watered silk.

**British Legion.** *See under* BRITISH.

**City of Legions.** *See under* CITY.

**Foreign Legion.** *See under* FOREIGN.

**Thundering Legion, The.** *See under* THUNDER.

**Legislation, Jack Cade.** *See under* JACK.

**Legislator** or **Solon of Parnassus, The.** Nicolas Boileau (1636–1711) was so called by VOLTAIRE, because of his *Art of Poetry* (1674), a production widely regarded as unequalled in the whole art of didactic poetry.

**Leitmotiv.** A German word meaning the 'leading motive', applied in music to a theme associated with a character in an opera or similar work, and repeatedly recurring to emphasize the dramatic situation. The term first came into use in connection with Wagner (1813–83). It is also used for any word, phrase or theme that continually recurs in a literary work.

**Lemnos.** The Greek island onto which VULCAN fell when JUPITER flung him out of heaven. Lemnos was mythically celebrated for two massacres. The men were said to have killed all the children of their abducted Athenian consorts, and the Lemnian women to have murdered their husbands. Hence Lemnian or anything barbaric or inhuman.

**Lemon. Lemon sole.** The name of the flatfish has nothing to do with the fruit, lemon, but is from French *limande*, itself a word of uncertain origin.

**Answer's a lemon, The.** *See under* ANSWER.

**Salts of lemon.** *See under* MISNOMERS.

**Lemures.** The name given by the Romans to evil spirits of the dead, especially spectres that wandered about at night to terrify the living. *See also* LARVAE.

**Lemuria.** The lost land that is said to have connected Madagascar with India and Sumatra in prehistoric times. The German biologist E.H. Haeckel (1834–1919) thought that it was the original habitat of the lemur. *See also* ATLANTIS; LYONESSE.

**Lend. Lend a hand, To.** To help; to give assistance.

**Lend-Lease.** Reciprocal agreements made by the USA with Great Britain and the Allied Forces in the Second World War to foster the pooling of resources. The policy began with the destroyers sent to Britain in return for naval and air bases in parts of the British COMMONWEALTH, and was formalized by the Lend-Lease Act of March 1941. When Lend-Lease ended in 1945 the United States had received somewhat less than one-sixth, in monetary terms, of what they had expended in aid to their allies, over 60 per cent of which went to the British Commonwealth. *See also* RUM-RUNNERS.

**Lend me your ears.** Pay attention to what I am about to say.

> Friends, Romans, countrymen, lend me your ears;
> I come to bury Caesar, not to praise him.
> SHAKESPEARE: *Julius Caesar*, III, ii (1599)

**Lend one's name to, To.** To authorize the use of one's name in support of a cause or venture.

**Length, Cable's.** *See under* CABLE.

**Lenin.** The assumed name of Vladimir Ilyich Ulyanov (1870–1924), founder of the Soviet Union and propagator of its guiding doctrine of Marxist-Leninism. The origin of his pseudonym remains uncertain. It is popularly said to derive from the Siberian River Lena, but although he had been exiled to Siberia, it was not to this river. He first used the name in 1901. *See also* MARXISM.

**Leningrad.** The name given in 1924 on the death of LENIN to Petrograd which, until 1914, was known as St Petersburg, the former capital of Tsarist Russia founded by Peter the Great in 1703. In 1991 it reverted to its original name of St Petersburg.

**Lens** (Latin, 'lentil', 'bean'). Glasses used in optical instruments are so called because the double convex lens is shaped like a lentil.

**Stanhope lens.** *See under* STANHOPE.

**Lent** (Old English *lencten*, 'spring', literally 'lengthening'). The Saxons called MARCH *lenctenmōnath* because in this month the days noticeably lengthen. As the chief part of the great fast, from ASH WEDNESDAY TO EASTER, falls in March, it received the name *lenctenfæsten* or Lent. The fast of 36 days was introduced in the 4th century, but it did not become fixed at 40 days until the early 7th century, thus corresponding with Christ's fast in the wilderness.

**Lenten.** Frugal, stinted, as food in LENT. Shakespeare has 'lenten entertainment' (*Hamlet*, II, ii (1600)) 'a lenten answer' (*Twelfth Night*, I, v (1599)); 'a lenten pie' (*Romeo and Juliet*, II, iv (1594)).

**Lent lily.** The wild daffodil (*Narcissus pseudonarcissus*), which blooms in LENT. It is not a lily at all.

**Leo.** The Lion, a constellation and fifth sign of the ZODIAC. The stars in the constellation Leo depict a crouching lion, its head marked by a sickle-shaped cluster. At the figure's heart is its brightest star, Alpha Leonis.

**Leo Africanus.** The Arabian traveller, geographer and historian was born Al-Hasan ibn Muhammad al-Wazzan az-Zayatti al-Fasi *c.*1489, the son of a clerk in Granada. Soon after 1492 his family moved to Fez (Morocco), where he was educated and whence he began to travel widely on commercial and diplomatic missions to North Africa and the Middle East. In 1519 he was captured by Italian pirates and taken first to Naples, then to Rome, where he was presented as a gift to Pope Leo X. In 1520 the pope baptized him and named him after himself as Leo Giovanni, to which Africanus ('African') was soon added. Leo lived in Rome and Bologna, teaching Arabic. In 1528 he apparently left Italy for Tunis, but his subsequent fate is unknown. In *c.*1526 he completed his greatest work, *Descrittione dell'Africa* ('Description of Africa'), until the early 19th century the prime source of knowledge of Africa. It was originally written in Arabic but was translated by Leo himself into Italian, to be published in Venice in 1550. An English version followed in 1600.

**Leonard, St.** A Frank at the court of Clovis in the 6th century, the founder of the monastery of Noblac, now the town of Saint-Léonard, near

Limoges. He is the patron saint of prisoners, since Clovis gave him permission to release all whom he visited. He is usually represented as a deacon holding chains or broken fetters in his hand. His day is 6 November.

**Leonidas.** King of Sparta, who defended the pass of THERMOPYLAE against the Persians in 480 BC. Only one of the 300 SPARTANS survived.

**Leonine.** Lion-like or relating to one of the popes named Leo, especially Leo I (r.440–461). The Leonine City is the part of Rome surrounding the VATICAN, which was fortified by Leo IV (r.847–855).

**Leonine verses.** Latin HEXAMETERS or alternate hexameters and PENTAMETERS rhyming at the middle and end of each respective line. These were common in 12th-century literature and are said to have been popularized by Leoninus, a canon of the church of St Victor, Paris, but there are many such lines in the classic poets, particularly Ovid. In English verse any metre that rhymes at both the middle and the end may be called Leonine verse. The following is an example, from Tennyson's 'The Revenge' (1878):

> 'Spanish ships of war at sea! we have sighted fifty-three!'
> Then sware Lord Thomas Howard: "Fore God I am no coward;
> But I cannot meet them here, for my ships are out of gear,
> And the half my men are sick. I must fly, but follow quick.'

**Leopard.** The animal is so called because it was thought in medieval times to be a cross between the lion (*leo*) and the 'pard', the name given to a panther that had no white specks on it. In Christian art, the leopard represents that beast spoken of in Revelation 13:1–8, with seven heads and ten horns. Six of the heads bear a NIMBUS, but the seventh, being 'wounded to death', lost its power, and consequently is bare.

The leopard's head, or king's mark, on silver is really a lion's head. It is called a leopard because the Old French heraldic term leopard means a lion passant gardant. *See also* LION IN HERALDRY.

**Leopard cannot change its spots, A.** A person's character never changes fundamentally, and what is innate remains. The allusion is to Jeremiah 13:23: 'Can the Ethiopian change his skin, or the leopard his spots?'

**Leopolita Bible, The.** *See under* BIBLE.

**Leprechaun.** A mischievous ELF of Irish folklore, often said to have a treasure hoard. The word comes from Irish *leipreachán*, from Old Irish *lūchorpān*, itself based on *lū*, 'small', and *corp*, 'body'. He is also known as a CLURICAUNE.

**Lernaean Hydra.** *See* HYDRA.

**Lesbian.** Pertaining to Lesbos, one of the islands of the Greek Archipelago, or to SAPPHO, the poetess of Lesbos, to whom the term for a homosexual woman alludes.

**Lesbian poets, The.** Terpander, Alcaeus, Arion and SAPPHO, all of whom came from Lesbos.

**Lèse-majesté** (French, from Latin *laesa majestas*, 'wounded majesty'). A phrase commonly applied to presumptuous conduct by inferiors who do not show sufficient respect for their 'betters'. The legal phrase 'lese-majesty' denotes TREASON, a crime against the sovereign.

**Less, St James the.** *See under* JAMES.

**Lesser Prophets, The.** *See* MINOR PROPHETS.

**Lesson, To teach someone a.** *See under* TEACH.

**Lestrigons** or **Laestrygones.** A fabulous race of cannibal giants who lived in Sicily. Odysseus (ULYSSES) sent two sailors and a messenger to request that he might land, but the king of the place ate one for dinner and the other fled. The Lestrigons gathered on the coast and threw stones at Odysseus and his crew. They departed with all speed, but many men were lost. *See also* POLYPHEMUS.

**Let. Let down, To.** To disappoint; to fail to keep faith or trust; to fail in an obligation.

**Let fly, To.** To make a violent attack upon, either literally or with a torrent of abuse or the like.

**Let George do it.** Let someone else do it. The expression is said to derive from Louis XII of France (r.1498–1515) who, when an unpleasant task arose, was apt to say 'Let Georges do it', referring to his minister, Cardinal Georges.

**Let go, To.** To release.

**Let it all hang out, To.** To relax completely; to be quite uninhibited. The allusion is probably to a naked or 'unbuttoned' person, and the expression, which gained popularity in the counterculture of the 1960s, originated among American blacks.

> It's a fellow with hair curling over his neck shrieking: 'Up-tight–outasight! What you gonna doo–boogaloo! Let it all hang out!'
> RICHARD GILBERT in *Anatomy of Pop* (1970)

**Let me see.** Let me think for a moment.

> *Brutus*: Let me see, let me see; is not the leaf turn'd down
> Where I left reading? Here it is, I think.
> SHAKESPEARE: *Julius Caesar*, IV, iii (1599)

**Let off steam, To.** To give vent to pent-up feelings in words; to work off superabundant energy and high spirits in vigorous physical activity. The allusion is to the noisy escape of steam from the safety valve of a steam engine.

**Let on, To.** To reveal a secret; to pretend.

**Let oneself go, To.** To act in an uninhibited manner; to pay little attention to one's appearance.

**Let one's hair down, To.** To behave in a free and uninhibited manner, especially when among friends. The allusion is to the days when women wore their long hair pinned up in various ways over their head for all their public appearances, but occasionally 'let their hair down' and allowed it to flow free in the privacy of their homes.

**Let rip, To.** To speak or act without restraint, as: 'He really let rip when he saw the damage' or 'OK, lads, let her rip.'

**Let sleeping dogs lie, To.** To leave well alone; to preserve the status quo. The watchdog is the best to leave undisturbed.

**Let slip, To.** To tell unintentionally when off one's guard, as a hound might be let slip unintentionally in coursing.

**Let someone down gently, To.** To avoid reproaching or humiliating them abruptly.

**Let something slip through one's fingers, To.** To fail to seize a chance at the favourable moment, just as an unprepared fielder drops a catch in CRICKET.

**Let the cat out of the bag, To.** To disclose a secret. *See also* PIG IN A POKE.

> Letting the cat of selfishness out of the bag of secrecy.
> W.M. THACKERAY: *Vanity Fair*, ch xix (1847–8)

**Let the dead bury their dead.** Let bygones be bygones. Don't rake up old scores and dead grievances. The expression is biblical (Matthew 8:22).

**Let this cup pass from me.** Let this trouble or affliction be taken away, that I may not be compelled to undergo it. The reference is to Christ's agony in the Garden of GETHSEMANE (Matthew 26:39).

**Let up, To.** To relax; to cease to act vigorously; to ease up.

**Not to let the grass grow under one's feet.** To waste no time dealing with a matter.

**L'état, c'est moi.** *See under* ÉTAT.

**Lethe.** In Greek mythology, one of the rivers of HADES, which the souls of all the dead are obliged to taste that they may forget everything said and done when alive. The word means 'oblivion'.

**Leto.** In Greek mythology, the mother of APOLLO and Artemis (DIANA). She had an affair with ZEUS, for which HERA pursued her to the floating island of DELOS. She is also known by the Roman name of LATONA.

**Letter.** The name of a character used to represent a sound; also a missive or written message. The word came into English from Old French *lettre*, itself from Latin *littera*, 'letter of the alphabet'. The plural use of the word to refer to literature or learning (as in MAN OF LETTERS) dates from medieval times.

There are 26 letters in the English alphabet, but in a FONT or fount of type over 200 characters are required, these being made up of small letters (LOWER CASE), capitals (UPPER CASE) and small capitals. Also included are the diphthongs (Æ, æ etc), ligatures (ff, fi, fl, ffi, ffl), the ampersand (&), accented letters (é, è, ä, ñ, ô), numerals, fractions, points (, ; : ! ?), brackets, reference marks (*, †, ‡, ¶), and the various monetary, commercial and mathematical signs (£, $, @, ©, #, %, +, ÷, = ). *See also* PRINTERS' MARKS.

**Letter missive.** An official letter from the LORD CHANCELLOR to a peer requesting him to put in an appearance to a bill filed in CHANCERY and sent in lieu of a summons; also a letter from the sovereign to a dean and chapter nominating the person to be elected bishop.

**Letter of advice.** A commercial letter notifying the recipient about a consignment of goods.

**Letter of comfort.** An assurance about a debt, although not a legal guarantee, given to a bank by a third party.

**Letter of credence** or **letter credential.** The formal document with which a diplomatic agent is furnished, accrediting him on his appointment to a post at the seat of a foreign government. It is signed by the sovereign or head of the state, and he is not officially recognized until it has been presented.

**Letter of credit.** A letter from a banker to another, requesting him to credit the bearer with a sum of money up to a specified amount.

**Letter of intent.** A letter indicating that the writer has the intention of carrying out some action, such as signing a contract. It does not in itself constitute an undertaking or a contract.

**Letter of introduction.** A letter given by one person to another, introducing that person to a third party.

**Letter of licence.** An instrument in writing made by a creditor, allowing a debtor longer time for payment of his debt.

**Letter of marque.** A licence from the crown making a merchantman a PRIVATEER or legalized ship of war able to take reprisals on a hostile nation. Without such authorization the vessel would be a pirate.

**Letter of safe conduct.** A writ under the GREAT SEAL, guaranteeing safety of passage to the person named in the passport.

**Letter of the law.** To keep to the letter of the law is to observe it strictly; to follow out the regulations thoroughly and to avoid breaking them.

**Letter of Uriah.** A treacherous letter, implying friendship but in reality a death warrant.

> And it came to pass in the morning, that David wrote a letter to Joab, and sent it by the hand of Uriah. And he wrote in the letter, saying, Set ye Uriah in the forefront of the hottest battle, and retire ye from him, that he may be smitten, and die.
> 2 Samuel 11:14–15

**Letters of administration.** The legal instrument granted by the probate court to a person appointed administrator to someone who has died intestate.

**Letters of Junius, The.** A series of anonymous letters, the authorship of which has never been finally settled, which appeared in the London *Public Advertiser* from 21 November 1768 to 21 January 1772. They were directed against Sir William Draper, the Duke of Grafton and George III's ministers generally. The author said in his Dedication: 'I am the sole depository of my own secret, and it shall perish with me.' Among the many suggested authors are Edmund Burke, John Wilkes, George Grenville, Lord Temple, Henry Grattan, Edward Gibbon, Alexander Wedderburn, Lord George Sackville, Horne Tooke, Lord Shelburne and Philip Francis. This last finds most favour at present, and Alvar Ellegård's *Who Was Junius?* (1962) argues convincingly for Francis.

**Letters patent.** Documents from the sovereign or a crown office conferring a title, right, privilege or the like, such as a title of nobility, or the exclusive right to make or sell for a given number of years some new invention. They are so called because they are written on open sheets of parchment, with the seal of the sovereign or party by whom they were issued attached at the bottom.

**Begging letter.** *See under* BEG.
**Black letter.** *See under* BLACK.
**Cadmean letters.** *See under* CADMUS.
**Call letters.** *See under* CALL.
**Casket Letters, The.** *See under* CASKET.
**Chain letter.** *See under* CHAIN.
**Dead letter.** *See under* DEAD.
**Father of Letters, The.** *See under* FATHER.
**Lacedaemonian letter.** *See under* LACEDAEMONIANS.
**Man of letters, A.** *See under* MAN.
**Open letter.** *See under* OPEN.
**Poison-pen letter.** *See under* POISON.
**Proofs before lettering.** *See under* PROOF.
**Pythagoras' letter.** *See under* PYTHAGORAS.
**Red Letter, The.** *See* ZINOVIEV LETTER *under* FAKES.
**Republic of Letters, The.** *See under* REPUBLIC.
**Samian letter, The.** *See under* SAMIAN.
**Scarlet letter.** *See under* SCARLET.
**Snarling letter.** *See under* SNARLING.
**Sunday letters.** *See* DOMINICAL LETTERS.
**To the letter.** Adhering to every detail.
**Zinoviev Letter, The.** *See under* FAKES.

**Lettres de cachet** (French, 'letters with a seal'). Under the old regime in France, letters or orders which were issued by the king under the royal seal (*cachet*). The name is best known for those used to imprison or punish a subject without trial, there being no HABEAS CORPUS in France. In the 18th century they were often issued as blank warrants, leaving the name to be filled in subsequently by the authorities or parties concerned. They were used against lunatics and prostitutes, and also obtained by heads of families against their relatives. Mirabeau was consigned to prison by his father in this manner. During the administration of Cardinal Fleury (1726–34) 80,000 such cachets are said to have been issued, mostly against the JANSENISTS. They were abolished by the CONSTITUENT ASSEMBLY (January 1790).

**Leucothea** (Greek, 'goddess of the white foam', from *leukos*, 'white', and *thea*, 'goddess'). Ino, the mortal daughter of CADMUS and wife of Athamas, was so called when she became a sea-goddess. When Athamas in a fit of madness slew one of her sons, she threw herself into the sea with the other, imploring assistance of the gods, who deified both of them. Her son, then renamed PALAEMON, was called by the Romans Portunus or Portumnus, and became the protecting genius of harbours. *See also* ISTHMIAN GAMES; MELICERTES.

**Levant. Levant and couchant** (French, 'rising up' and 'lying down'). In legal parlance cattle that have strayed into another's field and have been there long enough to lie down and sleep. The owner of the field can demand compensation for such intrusion.

**Levant and ponent winds.** The east wind is the Levant, and the west wind the Ponent. The former is from Latin *levare*, 'to raise' (referring to the sunrise), and the latter from *ponere*, 'to set' (referring to the sunset).

> Forth rush the Levant and the Ponent winds.
> MILTON: *Paradise Lost*, x (1667)

The name Levant was formerly applied to the eastern shore of the Mediterranean, i.e. to the region now occupied by Lebanon, Syria and Israel. It also had a broader application, denoting the lands from Greece to Egypt. In the 16th and 17th centuries the FAR EAST was sometimes known as the High Levant. *See also* RIVIERA.

**Levanter.** A name for a person who lives in the Levant, or for an easterly wind that blows there, especially in late summer. A levanter is also a person who decamps without paying after losing a bet. This word has nothing to do with the Levant, but is from Spanish *levantar el campo*, 'to break up the camp'.

**Levee** (French *lever*, 'to rise'). A morning assembly or reception. In Britain the word is particularly associated with the royal levees formerly held at St James's Palace, official occasions when the sovereign received men only, most usually in the afternoon. Before the French Revolution it was customary for the French monarch to receive visitors (court physicians, nobles, messengers and the like) at the time of his *levée*, i.e. just after rising from bed.

**Level. Level-headed.** Shrewd; businesslike; full of common sense. The term is used to describe someone who has his or her head screwed on the right way.

**Level pegging.** Equality in a contest or rivalry with another person. The expression is from those games, such as cribbage, in which a pegboard is used for scoring.

**Level up** or **down, To.** To raise or lower to another level, status or condition.

**Do one's level best, To.** *See under* DO.

**Find one's level, To.** *See under* FIND.

**On the level.** Honest and sincere in whatever one is doing or saying. A term from FREEMASONRY.

**Levellers.** In Cromwellian times a group of RADICAL republicans who wanted the franchise for 'freeborn Englishmen' (not necessarily including servants and labourers) and who were prominent at London and in the ranks of the army until their power was broken by Cromwell, after the mutinies of 1647 and 1649. Their influence waned steadily, especially after the suppression in 1652–3 of their leader, John Lilburne (*c.*1614–57). In Irish history, the WHITEBOYS were also called Levellers.

**Lever. Lever de rideau** (French, 'curtain-raiser'). A short sketch or act performed on the stage before the main play begins.

**Lever le ban et l'arrière-ban** (French). 'To levy the ban' was to call the king's VASSALS to active service; to levy the *arrière-ban* was to levy the vassals of a suzerain or underlord. The French *arrière-ban* arose from words related to Germanic *heri*, 'army', and *ban*, 'summons'. The first part of the word was subsequently taken to be French *arrière*, 'behind', since it related to the summoning of the lesser vassals.

**Leviathan.** The name of a monster of the waters. In Job 41:1 and Psalm 74:14 it appears to refer to a crocodile, in Psalm 104:26 it is probably a whale and in Isaiah 27:1 it is a sea serpent.

> There go the ships: there is that leviathan, whom thou hast made to play therein.
>
> Psalm 104:26

The name came to apply to any huge sea creature or large ship. Hobbes took the name as the title for his treatise on 'the Matter, Forme, and Power of a Commonwealth Ecclesiastical and Civil' (1651) from the Bible as he also did for his BEHEMOTH. His *Leviathan* is the absolute state.

> I have set forth the nature of man (whose Pride and other Passions have compelled him to submit himselfe to Government;) together with the great power of his Governour, whom I compared to Leviathan, taking that comparison out of the two last verses of the one and fortieth of Job; where God having set forth the great power of Leviathan, called him King of the Proud.
>
> *Leviathan*, Pt II, ch xxviii

The name itself is probably from Hebrew *lawo*, 'to twist', 'to writhe', with *tan* (used only in the plural, *tannīm*, from Arabic *tinīn*, 'dragon') translated as 'whale', 'sea serpent', or whatever best suits the context. If this interpretation is correct, it could not refer to a crocodile, since that reptile does not writhe.

According to rabbinical tradition, it was Leviathan who seduced EVE in its male incarnation of Samael, and ADAM in its female incarnation of LILITH.

**Leviathan of Literature, The.** Dr Johnson (1709–84). *See also* GREAT CHAM OF LITERATURE.

**Levitation.** A term applied to the phenomenon of heavy bodies rising and floating in the air. It is frequently mentioned in Hindu and other writings, and it is a not uncommon attribute of Roman Catholic saints. Joseph of Cupertino (1603–63) was the subject of such frequent levitation that he was forbidden by his superiors to attend choir, and performed his devotions privately where he would not distract others. The Scottish spiritualist D.D. Home (1833–86) was alleged by Sir W. Crookes to have this power. Science has not yet found an explanation. As a magician's illusion, however, levitation has long been an art based on natural laws. It was the greatest creation of J.N. Maskelyne (1839–1917), whose displays were remarkable for the apparent absence of any apparatus.

**Levites.** The members of the tribe of Levi, third of the 12 sons of JACOB. They were given the special task of looking after the Tabernacle in the Temple, and they carried the ARK OF THE COVENANT as the bodyguard of God. They were not given a portion in the land of ISRAEL because God was their portion (Joshua 13:14). Today the Levites have only a residual role in Jewish religion. *See also* LEVITICUS.

**Leviticus.** The third book of the Old Testament, so named from the LEVITES who are its principal theme.

**Levy, Capital.** *See under* CAPITAL.

**Lewis, Monk.** *See under* MONK.

**Lex** (Latin, 'law').

**Lex domicilii** (Latin, 'law of the domicile'). The law of the country in which a person is domiciled.

**Lex fori** (Latin, 'law of the court'). The law of the country in which an action is brought.

**Lex loci** (Latin, 'law of the place'). The law of the country in which a transaction is performed, a tort committed or a property situated.

**Lex non scripta** (Latin, 'unwritten law'). The COMMON LAW, as distinct from STATUTE or written law, which is *lex scripta*. It does not derive its force from being recorded, such written compilations merely serving as reminders.

**Lex talionis** (Latin, 'law of retaliation'). The supposed law of revenge, whereby a punishment resembles the offence committed; TIT FOR TAT.

**Ley lines.** Imaginary mystic lines running across Britain, said to connect places of power such as churches and different types of ANCIENT MONUMENT and so to form 'power grids'. STONEHENGE is one of several monuments said to lie at the intersection of at least two ley lines. The idea of such lines was introduced to the public by Alfred Watkins in his *Early British Trackways* (1922). His original theory 'that mounds, moats, beacons and mark stones fall into straight lines throughout Britain' was firmly rejected by archaeologists and historians but in more recent times has generated a lively NEW AGE cult. 'Ley' is a variant of 'lea'.

**Lia Fail.** The Irish name for the Coronation Stone, or Stone of Destiny, of the ancient Irish kings, for whom it was used at the HILL OF TARA. Fergus mac Erca was said to have taken it to Scotland, where it became the STONE OF SCONE. However, there is a stone at Tara today which is known as the Lia Foil. Its name represents Irish *Lia Fáil*, 'stone of Ireland'. *See also* TANIST STONE.

**Libel.** Originally the word denoted a little book (Latin *libellus*), as in *The Libel of English Policy* (*c.*1436), the title of a poetic essay advocating a strong navy. A plaintiff's statement of his case, which often 'defames' the defendant, was also called a libel, for it made a 'little book'. Today it usually applies to a written or printed defamation and is actionable.

In 1637 the three PURITANS, William Prynne, Robert Burton and John Bastwick, among other punishments, were branded on the cheeks and forehead with the letters SL for 'seditious libeller'. Prynne later interpreted them as representing *Stigmata Laudis*, 'brandings of praise'.

**Liber** (Latin, 'book').

**Liber Albus** (Latin, 'white book'). A compilation of the laws and customs of the City of London, made in 1419 by John Carpenter, town clerk.

**Liber Niger.** *See* BLACK BOOK.

**Liberal.** As a political term, the word came to be applied to the more 'advanced' WHIGS in the early 19th century and acquired respectability after the Reform Act of 1832, when the name gradually supplanted that of Whig. The first administration generally called Liberal was that of Gladstone (1868–74), the last, that of Asquith (1908–15). In 1988 a majority of the Liberals merged with Social Democratic Party (SDP) to form the Social and Liberal Democrats, from 1989 being known as the Liberal Democrats ('Lib-Dems'). A minority continued separately as the Liberal Party.

**Liberal Nationals** or **National Liberals.** Those Liberals who supported the NATIONAL GOVERNMENTS formed after the financial crisis of 1931 and who continued to cooperate with the CONSERVATIVE party.

**Liberal Unionists.** Those Liberals who supported the maintenance of the parliamentary union with Ireland and who opposed Gladstone's HOME RULE measures. From 1886, under Lord Hartington and Joseph Chamberlain, they supported the CONSERVATIVES.

**Liberator, The.** Simón Bolívar (1783–1830), who established the independence of Bolivia, Colombia, Ecuador, Panama, Peru and Venezuela from Spain in 1825.

Daniel O'Connell (1755–1847), who secured emancipation for Roman Catholics in 1829, was also thus styled. The title derived from the 'Order of Liberators', which he founded in 1826 and which was open to anyone who had done an act of service to Ireland. He was also known as the Counsellor.

**Liberator of the World, The.** A name given to Benjamin Franklin (1706–90).

**Libertine.** A freethinker in religion and morals, hence (more commonly) a debauchee or a profligate; otherwise a person who puts no restraint on self-indulgence. The application of the word to 16th-century ANABAPTIST sects in the Low Countries and certain of Calvin's opponents at Geneva had derogatory implications. In the NEW TESTAMENT it is used to mean 'freedman' (Latin *libertinus*):

> Then there arose certain of the synagogue, which is called the synagogue of the Libertines.
> Acts 6:9

**Liberty.** Freedom from restraint or control (Latin *liber*, 'free').

**Liberties.** In medieval England the word applied to areas that were to varying extents free from royal jurisdictions in whole or in part, such as the Marcher lordships (*see* MARCHES) and Palatine earldoms (*see* PALATINATE). The areas belonging to the City of London immediately outside the City walls were called liberties, and in course of time these were attached to the nearest ward within the walls. *See also* TOWER LIBERTY.

**Liberties of the Fleet, The.** The district immediately surrounding the FLEET, in which prisoners were sometimes allowed to reside but beyond which they were not permitted to go. They included the north side of LUDGATE Hill and the OLD BAILEY to Fleet Lane, down the lane to the market, and on the east side along by the prison wall to the foot of Ludgate Hill.

**Liberty Bell.** The traditional symbol of American freedom. It is a large bell that was cast in London and hung in the State House in Philadelphia, Pennsylvania, in 1753. It cracked when its clapper was being initially tested, cracked again when tolling for the funeral of Chief Justice Marshall in 1835, and irreparably cracked in 1846 when being rung on George Washington's birthday. Around it run the words: 'Proclaim liberty throughout all the land unto all the inhabitants thereof' (Leviticus 25:10).

**Liberty boat.** The boat taking seamen from a ship for shore leave, such passengers being designated liberty-men.

**Liberty bodice.** A type of sleeveless vest formerly worn by young children. The name was a commercial one given to suggest a greater freedom of movement than that provided by the conventional bodice. It was first manufactured in the opening years of the 20th century by the firm of R. & W.H. Symington, of Market Harborough, Leicestershire, but ceased to be produced in the 1960s.

**Liberty cap.** When a slave was manumitted by the Romans, a small Phrygian cap, usually of red felt, called a *pileus*, was placed on his head and he was termed *libertinus* ('freedman'). When Saturninus took possession of the Capitol in 100 BC he hoisted a similar cap to the top of his spear to indicate that all slaves who joined his standard should be free. Marius employed the same symbol against Sulla, and when CAESAR was murdered, the conspirators marched forth with a cap elevated on a spear in token of liberty.

In the French Revolution the liberty cap (*bonnet rouge*) was adopted as an emblem of freedom from royal authority. *See also* CARMAGNOLE.

**Liberty Enlightening the World.** The formal title of the Statue of Liberty, the colossal statue standing on Bedloe's (now Liberty) Island at the entrance of New York Harbor, presented to the American people by the Republic of France in commemoration of the centenary of the American Declaration of Independence. It was unveiled in 1886 and is the work of the Alsatian sculptor Frédéric-Auguste Bartholdi (1834–1904). The bronze, 302ft (92m) high (including the pedestal), is of a draped woman holding a torch in her raised right hand and a tablet bearing the date 'July 4, 1776' in her left. A plaque at the entrance to the pedestal is inscribed with a sonnet, 'The New Colossus' (1883), by Emma Lazarus. This was written to help raise money for the pedestal, and begins:

> Not like the brazen giant of Greek fame,
> With conquering limbs astride from land to land;
> Here at our sea-washed, sunset gates shall stand
> A mighty woman with a torch, whose flame
> Is the imprisoned lightning, and her name
> Mother of Exiles.

The statue of Liberty over the entrance of the Palais Royal, Paris, was modelled on Mme Tallien, 'Notre-Dame de Thermidor', born Teresa de Cabarrùs (1773–1835), the daughter of a Spanish banker. Her name is that of her second husband, the politician Jean-Lambert Tallien, whose mistress she became when in prison in Bordeaux and whom she married in 1793. She divorced him in 1802 and in 1805 married the Comte de Caraman, the future Prince de Chimay.

**Liberty hall.** The numerous applications of this descriptive phrase may be gathered from Oliver Goldsmith's definition:

> This is Liberty-Hall, gentlemen. You may do just as you please here.
> *She Stoops to Conquer*, II, i (1773)

Charles Dibdin's opera, *Liberty Hall*, was first performed in 1785.

**Liberty horses.** Circus horses that perform revolutions without riders.

**Liberty of the press.** The right to publish without censorship or restraint, subject to the laws of LIBEL and proper judicial processes.

**Liberty ships.** Standardized prefabricated cargo ships of about 10,000 tons, much used by the USA during the Second World War.

**Civil liberty.** *See under* CIVIL.

**Natural liberty.** *See under* NATURAL.

**Political liberty.** *See under* POLITICAL.

**Religious liberty.** *See under* RELIGIOUS.

**Sons of Liberty.** *See under* SON.

**Take liberties, To.** To be unduly familiar or overpresumptuous.

**Take the liberty, To.** To venture or presume to do something, as in the polite preamble, 'May I take the liberty?'

> Excuse me,
> Your Majesty,
> For taking of
> The liberty,
> But marmalade is tasty if
> It's very Thickly Spread.
> A.A. MILNE: *When We Were Very Young*, 'The King's Breakfast' (1924)

**Tower Liberty.** *See under* TOWER.

**Tree of Liberty, The.** *See under* TREE.

**Libitina.** In ancient Italy the goddess who presided over funerals, her name often being a synonym for death itself. The Romans identified her with PROSERPINA.

**Libra** (Latin, 'balance'). The seventh sign of the ZODIAC and the name of one of the ancient constellations, which the sun enters about 22 September and leaves about 22 October. At this time the day and night, being 'weighed', would be found equal.

**Library.** Before the invention of paper the thin inner bark of certain trees was used for writing on. The Latin word for this was *liber*, which later also came to mean 'book'. Hence library, a place for books, and librarian, a keeper of books.

Strabo says that Aristotle (384–322 BC) was the first to own a private library. From an uncertain date, there were public libraries in Athens, and these were known to Demetrius of Phalerum (4th century BC) who suggested to Ptolemy I the founding of a library at Alexandria. This was begun but greatly increased by Ptolemy II, and Alexandria became the great library centre of the Greek world. It continued to flourish under the Romans but decline and destruction set in from the end of the 4th century AD.

Among the numerous great libraries of modern Europe, the Vatican Library is especially notable for its antiquity and manuscript wealth. The present building was erected by Sixtus V in 1588 and it contains some 905,000 volumes and 60,000 manuscripts. The Biblioteca Mediceo-Laurenziana, Florence (opened to the public in 1571), has a particularly fine collection of precious classical manuscripts. Others are the great national libraries, such as the Biblioteca Nazionale Centrale at Rome (founded in 1875), the Biblioteca Nacional, Madrid (founded 1716, formerly the Royal Library), the Bibliothèque Nationale, Paris (originating under Charles V and re-created under Louis XI), and the Russian State Library, Moscow (formerly the Lenin Library and originally the Rumyantsev Museum Collection, opened in 1862). The library of the Academy of Sciences in St Petersburg is a noteworthy example of the specialized library.

The BRITISH LIBRARY, founded as the British Museum library in 1753, is world famous. Its services are based on collections that include over 18 million volumes, 1 million disks and 55,000 hours of tape recordings. It is based at two sites: London (St Pancras and Colindale) and Boston Spa, West Yorkshire. The BODLEIAN LIBRARY, Oxford (1598), includes the original University Library based on the collection of Humphrey, Duke of Gloucester, and has about 6 million volumes and a large collection of manuscripts, as well as about 1 million maps. Cambridge University Library (early 15th century) has almost 5 million volumes. The John Rylands Library, Manchester, founded 1900, has a notable collection of manuscripts. It was amalgamated with Manchester University Library (founded 1851) in 1972. The oldest library in Scotland is that of St Andrews University, founded in 1456. The National Library of Scotland was founded as the ADVOCATES' LIBRARY in 1682 and has about 6 million books and pamphlets. The National Library of Wales, Llyfrgell Genedlaethol Cymru, was founded at Aberystwyth in 1907 and has about 4 million printed books and 40,000 manuscripts. Trinity College Library, Dublin, possesses many valuable manuscripts as well as the BOOK OF KELLS. All these institutions (except John Rylands and St Andrews) are COPYRIGHT LIBRARIES.

The oldest library in the USA is that of HARVARD UNIVERSITY (1638), which has almost 11 million volumes. The United States Library of Congress in Washington, DC, founded in 1800, has over 16 million books in the classified collections and over 88 million in non-classified, making it the largest library in the world. New York Public Library has almost 10 million volumes and nearly as many manuscript letters and documents. The Henry E. Huntington Library and Art Gallery, San Marino, California, is noted for rare books, and the Pierpont Morgan Library, New York, for INCUNABULA and manuscripts. The Folger Shakespeare Library, Washington, D.C., has the largest collection of Shakespeareana in the world. It should be emphasized that figures for holdings of larger libraries can be only approximate and comparison is difficult because of different methods of computation. *See also* TAUCHNITZ.

**Advocates' Library, The.** *See under* ADVOCATE.

**Ambrosian Library.** *See under* AMBROSE.

**Bodleian Library.** *See under* BODLEIAN.

**British Library.** *See under* BRITISH.

**Copyright Library.** *See under* COPY.

**Cottonian Library.** *See under* COTTONIAN.

**Laurentian Library.** *See under* LAURENTIAN.

**London Library.** *See under* LONDON.

**Mazarin Library.** *See under* MAZARIN.

**Radcliffe Library.** *See under* RADCLIFFE.

**Licence. Letter of licence.** *See under* LETTER.

**Poetic licence.** *See under* POET.

**Lich.** A corpse (Old English *līc*).

**Lich gate** or **lych gate.** The covered entrance to churchyards, intended to afford shelter to the coffin and mourners while awaiting the clergyman who is to conduct the cortège into church.

**Lich wake** or **lyke wake.** The funeral feast or the waking of a corpse, i.e. watching it all night.

In a pastoral written by Aelfric in 998 for Wilfsige, bishop of Sherborne, the attendance of the clergy at lyke wakes is forbidden. 'Lyke Wake' is also the name of an old Yorkshire funeral dirge. Its name was adopted in modern times for the long-distance trail known as the Lyke Wake Walk, which extends for some 40 miles (64km) from Osmotherly, northeast of

Northallerton, North Yorkshire, to Ravenscar on the coast in the same county.

**Lychway** or **lickway.** A trackway, especially in a remote upland area, along which corpses were borne for burial in a distant churchyard. Journeys of up to 15 miles (24km), lasting two days, were recorded along lychways in the Yorkshire Dales as recently as the 18th century. Lychways are also known as corpse roads or coffin paths.

**Lichfield, The Swan of.** *See under* SWAN.

**Lick. Lick and a promise, A.** A superficial wash or clean-up, as a cat might give to its face or fur.

**Lick into shape, To.** To make presentable; to mould into a satisfactory condition. The expression derives from the widespread medieval belief that bear cubs are born shapeless and have to be licked into shape by their mothers. The story gained currency apparently from the Arab physician AVICENNA (979–1037), who tells it in his encyclopedia.

> Enforced, as a Bear doth her Whelps, to bring forth this confused lump, I had not time to lick it into form.
>
> ROBERT BURTON: *The Anatomy of Melancholy* (1621)

**Lick one's lips** or **chops, To.** To give evident signs of pleasurable anticipation or recollection.

**Lick one's wounds, To.** To retire after a defeat in order to rally one's strength or muster one's resources.

**Lickpenny.** Something or someone that makes the money go, that 'licks up' the pennies. John Lydgate (*c*.1370–1449) wrote a humorous poem called 'London Lyckpenny' in which he shows that life in London makes the money fly.

**Lick someone's boots, To.** To CURRY FAVOUR; to be abjectly servile; to be a LICKSPITTLE or BOOTLICKER.

**Lickspittle.** A toady; a sycophant; a flatterer.

**Go at a great lick, To.** To go at a great speed.

**Salt lick.** *See under* SALT.

**Lictors.** Binders (Latin *ligare*, 'to bind'). These ancient Roman officials were so called because they bound the hands and feet of criminals before they executed the sentence of the law.

**Lido.** An outdoor bathing place, usually with sunbathing facilities and often providing entertainments. The name is taken from the sandy island called the Lido, facing the Adriatic outside Venice, long a fashionable bathing resort. Its own name comes from Latin *litus*, 'shore'.

**Lie** (noun or verb). A falsehood or untruth or to tell a falsehood or untruth.

**Lie detector.** An American invention that records the physiological changes of a person under questioning. It is based on the supposedly proven assumption that a human being cannot tell a lie without an increase in the heartbeat and an alteration in other physiological functions, and this can be recorded. In some States of the Union, the findings of this device are accepted as legal evidence.

**Lie in one's beard, teeth** or **throat, To.** To lie grossly, flagrantly or deliberately.

**As one makes one's bed, so one must lie on it.** *See under* AS.

**Big lie.** *See under* LIE.

**Father of Lies, The.** SATAN (John 8:44).

**Give someone the lie, To.** To accuse a person to his or her face of telling a falsehood.

**Give the lie to, To.** To show that a statement is false; to disprove.

**Greatest lie, The.** *See under* GREAT.

**Pack of lies, A.** *See under* PACK.

**White lie.** *See under* WHITE.

**Lie** (verb). A verb frequently confused with LAY.

**Lie at the catch, To.** In Bunyan's *Pilgrim's Progress* (I, xii (1678)), Talkative says to Faithful: 'You lie at the catch, I perceive.' To which Faithful replies: 'No, not I; I am only for setting things right.' To lie at or on the catch is to lie in wait or to lay a trap to catch someone.

**Lie doggo, To.** To get into hiding and remain there; to lie low.

**Lie in, To.** To be confined in childbirth; to stay in bed beyond one's usual time of rising.

**Lie in state, To.** Said of a corpse or coffin of a royal or distinguished person that is displayed to the general public.

**Lie low, To.** To conceal oneself or one's intentions; to avoid notice.

**Lie up, To.** To refrain from work through ill health; to rest or retire to one's room or bed.

**Lie with one's fathers, To.** To be buried in one's native place or with one's ancestors.

> But I will lie with my fathers, and thou shalt carry me out of Egypt, and bury me in their burying place.
>
> Genesis 47:30.

**Take it lying down, To.** *See under* TAKE.

**Lieutenant.** The military rank below a captain. The word derives from Old French and means literally 'place-holding', that is, standing in for an officer of higher rank. In combination with other ranks and offices it has the general implication of deputy or subordinate, as, LORD LIEUTENANT, Lieutenant Governor, Lieutenant General. The word is usually pronounced 'leftenant' in the British Army, 'letenant' in the Royal Navy and 'lootenant' in the United States.

**Flag lieutenant.** *See under* FLAG.

**Lord Lieutenant.** *See under* LORD.

**Life. Life and soul of the party, The.** The main source of fun and merriment in a company.

**Life Guards.** The regiment that with the Blues and Royals forms the Household Cavalry. *See also* HOUSEHOLD TROOPS.

**Life history.** The story of a person's life, especially when told at tedious length.

**Life is not all beer and skittles** or **cakes and ale.** Life is not all pleasure. *See also* CAKES AND ALE.

**Life peer.** A peer whose title lapses on death. Life peerages have been conferred since 1958 on distinguished men and women from all walks of life, granting them seats in the HOUSE OF LORDS in the degree of BARON or Baroness. In 1998 there were 479 life peers, including 39 LAW LORDS, against 625 hereditary peers who had succeeded to their titles and nine peers who had had their titles conferred on them, one such being the PRINCE OF WALES.

**Life preserver.** A club or bludgeon kept for self-defence; a life belt or life jacket.

**Life science.** A science that is concerned with living things, such as biology, botany or zoology.

**Life sentence.** A sentence of imprisonment for life, awarded in Britain as the mandatory sentence for murder and the maximum penalty for a number of serious offences such as robbery, rape, arson and manslaughter. Since 1997 courts in England and Wales have been required to impose life sentences also on those convicted for a second time on a serious violent or sexual offence. Unless 'life means life', people serving life sentences are normally detained for at least 20 years. They are then released but remain on licence for the rest of their lives and are subject to recall if their behaviour suggests that they could again be a danger to the public.

**Lifestyle.** A chosen way of living, especially when it is one to be admired or emulated.

**As large as life.** *See under* AS.

**Bear a charmed life, To.** *See under* BEAR.

**Book of life, The.** *See under* BOOK.

**Come to life, To.** *See under* COME.

**Drawn from life.** *See under* DRAW.

**Elixir of life, The.** *See under* ELIXIR.

**Facts of life, The.** *See under* FACT.

**For dear life.** *See under* FOR.

**For life.** *See under* FOR.

**For the life of me.** *See under* FOR.

**Get a life!** *See under* GET.

**High life.** *See under* HIGH.

**Kiss of life.** *See under* KISS.

**Larger than life.** *See under* LARGE.

**Light of one's life.** *See under* LIGHT.

**Line of life.** *See under* LIFE.

**Live the life of Reilly, To.** *See under* LIVE.

**Low life.** *See under* LOW.

**Matter of life and death, A.** *See under* MATTER.

**New lease of life.** *See under* NEW.

**Not on your life.** Certainly not.

**Save one's life, To.** *See under* SAVE.

**See life, To.** *See under* SEE.

**Simple life.** *See under* SIMPLE.

**Staff of life.** *See under* STAFF.

**Still life.** *See under* STILL.

**Time of one's life, The.** *See under* TIME.

**To the life.** *See under* TO.

**Web of life, The.** *See under* WEB.

**Lift. Lifter.** A thief; a person who lifts something with the aim of taking it. The word still exists in 'shoplifter'.

**Lift up one's head, To.** To hold one's head high with pride.

> Lift up your heads, O ye gates; and be ye lift up, ye everlasting doors; and the King of glory shall come in.
>
> Psalm 24:7

**Lift up one's voice, To.** To sing out.

**Airlift.** *See under* AIR.

**Not to lift a finger.** Not to make the slightest effort; not to give any assistance.

**Thumb a lift, To.** *See under* THUMB.

**Ligan.** *See* LAGAN.

**Light.** Old English *lēoht* is the same for both senses of this word, i.e. 'illumination' and 'not heavy', but in the former sense it is related to Old High German *lioht* and Latin *lux* and in the latter to Old High German *liht* (modern German *leicht*, 'easy').

**Light blue.** Related to Cambridge or Harrow.

**Light comedian.** One who takes humorous parts but not coarse parts.

**Light-fingered.** Having nimble or agile fingers, especially for thieving or picking pockets.

**Light-footed.** Nimble.

**Light-headed.** Giddy; frivolous; delirious.

**Light-hearted.** Cheerful; unduly casual.

**Light Horse Harry.** The nickname of Henry Lee (1756–1818), American cavalry officer and father of the Confederate Commander-in-Chief, Robert E. Lee. In 1779 he defeated the British at Paulus Hook in the War of Independence.

**Light Infantry.** In the British Army, infantry carrying less equipment than normal and trained to manoeuvre at high speed. They were introduced into the British Army by Sir John Moore (1761–1809).

**Light of Asia, The.** The BUDDHA. *The Light of Asia, or the Great Renunciation* (1879) was the name given by Sir Edwin Arnold (1832–1904) to his narrative poem dealing with the life and teachings of Buddha.

**Light of one's life, The.** A dearly loved one. The expression is often used semi-seriously, as: 'I must have a word with the light of my life'.

**Light of the Age, The.** Maimonides or Rabbi Moses ben Maimon of Cordova (1135–1204).

**Light of the World, The** (Latin *Lux Mundi*). Jesus Christ, who was allegorically portrayed by William Holman Hunt in his picture (1851–3) showing Christ, carrying a lantern, knocking at the door of the soul. The disused and overgrown door has no handle on the outside, since it can be opened only from within. Sir Arthur Sullivan has an oratorio of this title (1873), and Sir Edwin Arnold a poem (1891) in which Christ is the central figure as the founder of Christianity.

> Then spake Jesus again unto them, saying, I am the light of the world: he that followeth me shall not walk in darkness, but shall have the light of life.
> John 8:12

**Light o' love.** An inconstant, capricious or loose woman.

**Light opera.** An operetta, otherwise an opera on a light or humorous theme, as distinct from the 'heavy' themes of traditional opera. Classic examples are the works of Jacques Offenbach and Johann Strauss and the Savoy Operas of Gilbert and Sullivan. There is a similar distinction between light music, as 'easy listening', and the more demanding works of Bach, Beethoven, Brahms, Mozart, Schubert and other classical composers. *See also* GRAND OPERA.

**Lights out.** The time when those in an institution must retire to bed, such as soldiers in barracks or pupils in a boarding school.

**Light troops.** A term formerly applied to light cavalry, i.e. lancers and hussars, who were neither such large men as the 'Heavies' or DRAGOONS, nor so heavily equipped. It also applies to lightly equipped forces generally.

**Light upon, To.** To come across by chance; to discover by accident. Thus, Dr Johnson wrote to Mrs Thrale: 'How did you light upon your specifick for the tooth-ache?'

**Light year.** A scientific unit for measuring stellar distances. Light travels at the rate of 186,000 miles (299,274km) per second, so that a light year, or the distance travelled by light in a year, is just under 6 million million miles (9.46 × 1012km). In general terms a light year is a long distance or great amount, as: 'Japan is light years ahead of many Western countries in electronics'.

**Anchor light.** *See under* ANCHOR.

**Ancient lights.** *See under* ANCIENT.

**As light as a feather.** *See under* AS.

**Bright lights.** *See under* BRIGHT.

**Bring to light, To.** *See under* BRING.

**City of Light, The.** *See under* CITY.

**Come to light, To.** *See under* COME.

**Courtesy light.** *See under* COURTESY.

**Drummond light.** *See under* DRUMMOND.

**Fairy lights.** *See under* FAIRY.

**First light.** *See under* FIRST.

**Hide one's light under a bushel, To.** *See under* HIDE.

**Inner light.** *See under* INNER.

**Leading light.** *See under* LEAD.

**Make light of, To.** To treat as of no importance; to take little notice of.

> Tell them which are bidden, Behold, I have prepared my dinner: my oxen and my fatlings are killed, and all things are ready: come unto the marriage. But they made light of it, and went their ways, one to his farm, another to his merchandise.
> Matthew 22:4–5

**Make light work of, To.** To do something easily and quickly.

**Out like a light.** *See under* OUT.

**Owl light.** *See under* OWL.

**Pilot light.** *See under* PILOT.

**See the light, To.** *See under* SEE.

**Stand in someone's light, To.** *See under* STAND.

**Strike-a-light.** *See under* STRIKE.

**Sweetness and light.** *See under* SWEET.

**Throw** or **shed light on, To.** *See under* THROW.

**Tread the light fantastic, To.** *See under* TREAD.

**Lighthouse.** *See* PHAROS.

**Lighthouse of the Mediterranean.** The name given to the volcano Stromboli, one of the Lipari Islands in the Tyrrhenian Sea.

**Lightning.** Hamilcar (*c.*270–228 BC), the Carthaginian general, was called Barca, the Phoenician for 'lightning', 'thunderbolt' (Hebrew *baraq*), both on account of the rapidity of his march and for the severity of his attacks.

**Lightning conductor.** A copper rod raised above a building and in contact with the earth, to carry off the lightning and prevent its injuring the building. It was invented by Benjamin Franklin (1706–1790), who first used it in 1752.

**Lightning never strikes the same place twice.** The commonly held belief is a fallacy. Many tall buildings have been struck more than once. The statue of William Penn on City Hall, Philadelphia, is struck by lightning about five times a year, and the Empire State Building, New York, twice this number of times. Nor are humans immune. An American, Roy C. Sullivan, was struck on seven different occasions over a period of 35 years, although suffering relatively minor injuries.

**Lightning preservers.** The EAGLE, the sea calf and the LAUREL were the most approved classical preservers against lightning. JUPITER chose the first, Augustus CAESAR the second, and Tiberius the third.

**Lightning strike.** A strike by workers at short notice, especially when without official trade union backing.

**Ball lightning.** *See under* BALL.

**Chain lightning.** *See under* CHAIN.

**Forked lightning.** *See under* FORK.

**Like greased lightning.** *See under* LIKE.

**Sheet lightning.** *See under* SHEET.

**Liguria.** The ancient name of a part of Cisalpine GAUL, and now a modern territorial division of Italy including the provinces of Genoa, Imperia, Savona and La Spezia. NAPOLEON BONAPARTE founded a Ligurian Republic with Genoa as its capital and including also Venetia and a part of Sardinia. It was annexed by France in 1805.

**Ligurian Sage, The.** Aulus Persius Flaccus (AD 34–63), born at Volaterrae, in Etruria, and famous for his *Satires*.

**Like. Like a bat out of hell.** Very quickly. The implication seems to be that a bat would be keen to flee the light and heat of Hell.

**Like a bomb.** Very successfully. The phrase is often used ironically.

**Like a bull at a gate.** Hastily or rashly.

**Like a cat on a hot tin roof.** In an uneasy or apprehensive state.

**Like a dog with two tails.** Very pleased.

**Like a dream.** Very easily and effortlessly.

**Like a drowned rat.** Soaking wet; looking exceedingly dejected.

**Like a duck to water.** Readily or easily, as: 'He took to computing like a duck to water.' The expression would be particularly apt in: 'She took to swimming like a duck to water.'

**Like a dying duck in a thunderstorm.** Looking forlorn and sorry for oneself. Young ducks die speedily of chill if caught by a sudden downpour away from warmth and shelter.

**Like a hog on ice.** Supremely confident; cocky; self-assured. A phrase used in America, of unknown origin, although it may be Scottish, having connection with the hog used in curling. The phrase is discussed in detail by Charles Earle Funk in his book *A Hog on Ice* (1950).

**Like a house on fire.** Very rapidly. The old houses of timber and thatch burned very swiftly.

**Like a king.** When Porus, the Indian prince, was taken prisoner, Alexander the Great asked him how he expected to be treated. 'Like a king,' he replied, and Alexander made him his friend, restoring Porus to his kingdom.

**Like a lamb to the slaughter.** Meekly; innocently. The expression is biblical in origin:

> He is brought as a lamb to the slaughter
> Isaiah 53:7

**Like a shot.** With great rapidity; without hesitation; with alacrity.

**Like billy-o.** Very much; strongly. The word has been derived from the following: (1) Joseph Billio, rector of Wickham Bishops, Essex, ejected for nonconformity and the first Nonconformist minister of Maldon (1696), who was noted for his drive and energy; (2) Nino Biglio, one of Garibaldi's lieutenants, who would dash keenly into battle shouting, 'I am Biglio! Follow me, you rascals, and fight like Biglio!'; (3) Puffing Billy, George Stephenson's locomotive, so that 'puffing like Billy-o' and 'running like Billy-o' were common phrases.

**Like fun.** Quickly; energetically; with delight.

> Click, click, click, we heard in the old Madman's den. Then that stopped all of a sudden, and the bolts went to like fun.
> THOMAS HUGHES: *Tom Brown's Schooldays*, Pt II, ch iii (1857)

**Like greased lightning.** Very quickly indeed.

**Like grim death.** As if one's life depended on it. *See also* HANG ON LIKE GRIM DEATH.

**Like hell.** Very much; very hard, as: 'He wanted to win like hell.' The phrase is also used sarcastically, as: 'Like hell you did.'

**Like nobody's business.** In an unusual or extraordinary manner, as: 'He was knocking back the pints like nobody's business'.

**Like old boots.** Greatly; vigorously. 'I was working like old boots' means 'I was working as hard as I could'.

**Like something the cat brought in.** In a dishevelled or bedraggled state, like a small animal that a cat has caught and been sporting with before bringing it indoors.

**Like the blast of Roland's horn.** ROLAND had a wonderful ivory horn, named Olivant, which he won from the giant Jutmundus. When he was attacked by the Saracens at Roncesvalles (Roncesvaux) he sounded it to give CHARLEMAGNE notice of his danger. At the third blast it cracked in two, but it was so loud that birds fell dead and the whole SARACEN army was panic-struck. Charlemagne heard the sound at St-Jean-Pied-de-Port, and rushed to the rescue, but arrived too late.

> Oh, for a blast of that dread horn
> On Fontarabian echoes borne,
> That to King Charles did come.
> SIR WALTER SCOTT: *Marmion* (1808)

**Like water off a duck's back.** Having no influence or effect.

**Like** (verb). **Like it or lump it.** If you don't like it you must put up with it, i.e. take it in a lump.

> 'I'm a-going to call you Boffin, for short ... If you don't like it, it's open to you to lump it.'
> DICKENS: *Our Mutual Friend*, Bk IV, ch iii (1864–5)

**Like the look of, To.** To approve what one sees or discovers. The converse is 'not to like the look of', meaning to find a thing alarming or suspicious, as: 'I don't like the look of it.'

**Likeness, Speaking.** *See under* SPEAK.

**Li'l Abner.** The handsome hillbilly created by the American newspaper cartoonist Al Capp in 1934. He comes from the dead-end town of Dogpatch and has a 'dumb blonde' girlfriend, Daisy Mae. His adventures have been represented in stage and screen versions.

**Lil, Diamond.** *See under* DIAMOND.

**Lili Marlene.** A German song of the Second World War. It was based on a poem written in 1917 by a German soldier, Hans Leip (1894–1983), and was composed by Norbert Schultze in 1938. The German singer Lale Andersen initially made it known in 1939. It became increasingly popular, especially with the Afrika Korps, and the recorded version was played nightly by Radio Belgrade from the late summer of 1941 virtually until the end of hostilities. Other German stations relayed it, and it was picked up and adopted by the British 8th Army, the English version of the lyric being by Tommy Connor (who deleted an implication in the original that Lili Marlene was a prostitute). There were French, Italian and other renderings of what became the classic song of the war, and it was one of the theme songs of its namesake, the German-born actress Marlene Dietrich. A recording of the song by Ann Shelton in 1944 sold a million copies. Leip subsequently said he had based Lili Marlene on two girls, Lili and Marlene, whom he had known in Berlin when on leave.

> Bei der Kaserne
> Vor dem grossen Tor,
> Stand eine Lanterne
> Und steht sie noch davor ...
> Mit dir, Lili Marlene,
> Mit dir, Lili Marlen'.
> (Underneath the lantern
> By the barrack gate,
> Darling, I remember
> The way you used to wait ...
> My Lili of the lamplight,
> My own Lili Marlene.)

**Lilith.** A night monster and VAMPIRE, probably of Babylonian origin, said to haunt wildernesses in stormy weather and to be specially dangerous to children. The name is from a Semitic root meaning 'night', which was the special time of this demon's activities. In rabbinical writings, she is supposed to have been the first wife of ADAM. She is referred to in Isaiah 34:14 as the 'screech-owl' in the Authorized Version, as the 'night-monster' in the Revised Version and as LAMIA in the VULGATE. A superstitious cult of Lilith persisted among certain Jews until the 7th century. *See also* DEVIL AND HIS DAM; LEVIATHAN.

**Lilliburlero.** The refrain of a piece of political doggerel written by Lord Thomas Wharton (1648–1715), which influenced popular sentiment at the time of the GLORIOUS REVOLUTION of 1688. The orange lily was the symbol of the Irish supporters of William of Orange, and the words *Lilliburlero Bullenala* are said to be a corruption of Irish *An lile ba léir é ba linn an lá* ('the lily was triumphant and we won the day').

The song is referred to in Laurence Sterne's *Tristram Shandy* (1759–67) and is given in PERCY'S RELIQUES (1765). The air is attributed to Purcell but it has been traced back to a book of psalm tunes published at Antwerp in 1540.

> Ho, Brother Teague, dost hear de Decree?
> *Lilli Burlero Bullena-la.*
> Dat we shall have a new Debity [deputy],
> *Lilli Burlero Bullena-la.*
>
> THOMAS WHARTON: *Poems on Affairs of State*, 'A New Song' (1704)

**Lilliput.** The land of pygmies in Swift's *Gulliver's Travels* (1726). The name is apparently based on Danish *lille*, 'little', and Italian *putto*, 'child', although English 'little' and Latin *putus*, 'boy', would work almost as well. It is possible that Swift intended a pun on 'put', so that the land is one where little people have been put.

**Lily, The.** There is a tradition that the lily sprang from the repentant tears of EVE as she went forth from Paradise.

In Christian art the lily is an emblem of chastity, innocence and purity. In pictures of the Annunciation GABRIEL is sometimes represented as carrying a lily branch, while a vase containing a lily stands before MARY who is kneeling in prayer. St JOSEPH holds a lily branch in his hand, indicating that his wife Mary was a virgin.

The lily in the field in Matthew 6:29 ('even Solomon in all his glory was not arrayed like one of these') is the wild lily, probably a species of iris. The 'lily of the valley', with which this is sometimes confused, is a different plant, *Convallaria majalis*.

**Lily-livered.** *See* LIVER.

**Lily Maid of Astolat, The.** *See* ELAINE.

**Lily of France, The.** The device of CLOVIS was three black toads, but the story goes that an aged hermit of Joye-en-Valle saw a miraculous light stream into his cell one night and an angel appeared to him holding an azure shield of wonderful beauty, emblazoned with three gold lilies that shone like stars. This he was commanded to give to Queen Clothilde, who gave it to her husband, and his arms were everywhere victorious. The device thereupon became the emblem of France. *See also* FLEUR-DE-LIS.

**Lilywhites, The.** *See under* REGIMENTAL AND DIVISIONAL NICKNAMES.

**City of Lilies, The.** *See under* CITY.

**Gild** or **paint the lily, To.** *See under* GILD.

**Jersey Lily, The.** *See* JERSEY.

**Stone lilies.** St CUTHBERT'S BEADS.

**Limb.** A slang word for a mischievous rascal or a young imp. It is short for the older word 'limb of the Devil', where the word implies 'agent' or 'scion'. John Dryden called John Fletcher 'a limb of Shakespeare'.

**Out on a limb.** *See under* OUT.

**Phantom limb.** *See under* PHANTOM.

**Limbo** (Latin *in limbo*, 'on the edge', from limbus, 'border', 'fringe', 'edge'). The borders of hell, that portion assigned by the SCHOOLMEN to those departed spirits to whom the benefits of redemption did not apply through no fault of their own. There are distinguished: (1) the *limbus patrum*, 'limbo of the fathers', where the PATRIARCHS and prophets who died before Christ's crucifixion await the last day, when they will be received into heaven; and (2) the *limbus infantium*, 'limbo of infants', for children who die before baptism or before they are responsible for their actions.

**Limbus. Limbus of fools.** *See* PARADISE OF FOOLS.

**Limbus of the moon.** *See* MOON.

**Limelight.** A vivid light, giving off little heat, produced by the combustion of oxygen and hydrogen on a surface of lime. It was tried at the South Foreland lighthouse in 1861, but its main use developed in the theatre, where it was used to throw a powerful beam on one player on the stage to the exclusion of others. Hence the phrase 'to be in the limelight', to be in the full glare of public attention.

**Limerick.** A nonsense verse in the metre popularized by Edward Lear in his *Book of Nonsense* (1846), of which the following is an example:

> There was a young lady of Wilts,
> Who walked up to Scotland on stilts;
> When they said it was shocking
> To show so much stocking,
> She answered, 'Then what about kilts?'

The name has been said to come from the chorus 'Will you come up to Limerick', which at one time followed each verse as it was improvised by a member of a convivial party, but there is no firm evidence behind this. Nor is the derivation in 'Learic', from the name of Edward Lear, as sometimes stated. Many modern limericks are bawdy.

**Limey.** In American and Australian slang a British sailor or ship, or just a Briton. The nickname derives from the practice of issuing lime juice to a ship's crew to combat scurvy.

**Limit. Sky's the limit, The.** *See under* SKY.

**Three-mile limit.** *See under* THREE.

**Limp.** This word, formed from the initials Louis (XIV), James (II), his wife Mary (of Modena) and the Prince (of Wales), was used as a JACOBITE toast in the time of William III. *See also* NOTARIKON.

**Alexandra limp.** *See under* ALEXANDRA.

**Lincoln. Lincoln green.** Lincoln was noted formerly for its light green, as was Coventry for its blue, and Yorkshire for its grey cloth. *See also* KENDAL GREEN.

**Lincoln imp.** A grotesque carving with weird and prominent ears and nursing the right leg crossed over the left, in the Angel Choir of Lincoln Cathedral. He is said to have been turned to stone by the angels for misbehaving in the angel choir. He is now the county emblem.

**Lincoln's Inn.** One of the four INNS OF COURT in London. The inn takes its name from its landlord Thomas de Lincoln, king's serjeant, and is probably of late 14th-century origin. The Old Hall dates from the reign of Henry VII. The Chapel was completed by Inigo Jones in 1643.

**Devil looking over Lincoln, The.** *See under* DEVIL.

**Great Tom of Lincoln.** *See under* GREAT.

**Hugh of Lincoln.** *See under* HUGH.

**Linden.** The German name, also used in England, for a lime tree. *Unter den Linden* ('under the limes') is the name of a principal street in Berlin.

> An' there vor me the apple tree
> Do leän down low in Linden Lea.
>
> WILLIAM BARNES: *Hwomely Rhymes*, 'My Orcha'd in Linden Lea' (1859)

**Lindor.** One of the conventional names given by the classical poets to a rustic swain, or shepherd lover.

**Line. Line, The.** The equator. *See also* CROSSING THE LINE *under* CROSS.

In the British Army all regular infantry regiments except the Foot Guards and the Rifle Brigade are called 'line regiments'. The term sometimes includes cavalry regiments.

**Line engraving.** The incising of lines on a metal plate for subsequent printing. It differs from etching in that no chemicals are used. The process dates from the first half of the 15th century. *See also* LITTLE MASTER.

**Line of battle.** The formation of ships in line ahead or line abreast in a naval engagement. A 'line-of-battle' ship was a CAPITAL SHIP built and equipped to take part in a main attack. The expression can also apply to a line or lines of troops drawn up for battle.

**Line of beauty.** In art a line of undulating curvature, usually in the form of a slender, elongated letter S.

**Line of country.** One's business or specialization.

**Line of duty.** A necessary (and often undesired) part of what one is required to do.

**Line of fire.** The path taken by a bullet or other fired missile.

**Line of life.** In PALMISTRY the crease in the left hand beginning above the web of the thumb and running towards or up to the wrist. The nearer it approaches the wrist, the longer will be the life, according to palmists. If long and deeply marked, it indicates long life with very little trouble. If it is crossed or cut with other marks, it indicates sickness.

**Line one's pockets, To.** To make a good deal of money; to FEATHER ONE'S NEST. The phrase often implies that one is profiting at the expense of others.

**Line-up.** A row or grouping of people or things, such as an identity parade, an arrangement of players at the start of a game or the deployment of opposing forces before a battle.

**Line upon line.** Admonition or instruction repeated little by little, a line at a time.

> For precept must be upon precept, precept upon precept; line upon line, line upon line; here a little, and there a little.
>
> Isaiah 28:10

**All along the line.** *See under* ALL.
**Bring into line, To.** *See under* BRING.
**Crossing the line.** *See under* CROSS.
**Date Line.** *See under* DATE.
**Datum line.** *See under* DATUM.
**Draw the line at, To.** *See under* DRAW.
**Drop someone a line, To.** *See under* DROP.
**End of the line, The.** *See under* END.
**Fall into line with, To.** *See under* FALL.
**Fall line.** *See under* FALL.
**Hard lines.** *See under* HARD.
**Hook, line and sinker.** *See under* HOOK.
**Hot line.** *See under* HOT.
**Ley lines.** *See under* LEY.
**Maginot line.** *See under* MAGINOT.
**Mason–Dixon Line.** *See under* MASON.
**No day without a line.** *See under* NO.
**Party line.** *See under* PARTY.
**Plimsoll line.** *See under* PLIMSOLL.
**Punch line.** *See under* PUNCH.
**Read between the lines, To.** *See under* READ.
**Ship of the line, A.** *See under* SHIP.
**Shoot a line, To.** *See under* SHOOT.
**Siegfried Line.** *See under* SIEGFRIED.
**Sign on the dotted line, To.** *See under* SIGN.
**Silver lining.** *See under* SILVER.
**Snow line.** *See under* SNOW.
**Stag line.** *See under* STAG.
**Thin red line, The.** *See under* THIN.
**Toe the line, To.** *See under* TOE.
**Wallace's line.** *See under* WALLACE.

**Linen. Shoot one's linen, To.** *See under* SHOOT.

**Wash one's dirty linen in public, To.** *See under* WASH.

**Lingua Franca** (Italian, 'Frankish tongue'). A type of Italian mixed with French, Greek, Arabic and other languages spoken on the coasts of the Mediterranean, also (as lingua franca) any mixture of languages serving as a means of communication between different peoples. *See also* PIDGIN ENGLISH.

**Links**. The word links in its use as a field of play for golf derives from Old English *hlinc*, 'ledge'. This came to apply in Scotland to a narrow strip of coastal land with coarse grass and sand dunes. An example is Lundin Links on Largo Bay, Fife. Such areas of land provided the terrain for the first golf courses, with the coarse grass serving as the 'rough' and the sand dunes adapted to make bunkers.

**Linnaean system.** The system of classification adopted by the Swedish botanist Carolus Linnaeus (Carl von Linné) (1707–78), who arranged the three kingdoms of animals, vegetables and minerals into classes, orders, genera, species and varieties, according to certain characteristics.

**Linne, The Heir of.** *See under* HEIR.

**Lion.** An honourable nickname. Among its recipients are the following:

- Ali (*c*.597–661), son of Abu Taleb and son-in-law of MOHAMMED: called the Lion of God; his mother called him at birth Al Haidara, 'the Rugged Lion'
- Ali Pasha (1741–1822): called the Lion of Janina
- Daniel Romanovich of Galicia, who founded Lemburg, modern Lvov ('Lion City'), in 1259
- Gustavus Adolphus (1594–1632): called the Lion of the North
- Henry, Duke of Bavaria and Saxony (1129–95): called the Lion for his courage and daring
- John Nicholson (1821–57), Brigadier General of Indian Mutiny fame: called the Lion of the Punjab from his services in the Punjab and from his outstanding valour
- Louis VIII of France (1187–1226): called the Lion because he was born under the sign LEO
- Mohammed ibn Daud (*c*.1029–72), nephew of Toghril Beg, the Perso-Turkish monarch: surnamed Alp Arslan, the 'Valiant Lion'
- Richard I, Coeur de Lion (Lion's Heart) (1157–99): so called for his bravery
- William of Scotland, The Lion (1143–1214): so called because he chose a red lion rampant for his cognizance

St MARK the EVANGELIST is symbolized by a lion because he begins his gospel with the scenes of St JOHN THE BAPTIST and Christ in the wilderness.

A lion is the emblem of the tribe of JUDAH, and Christ is called 'the Lion of the tribe of Judah'.

Among the titles of the Emperor of Ethiopia were Conquering Lion of the Tribe of Judah, Elect of God and King of Kings of Ethiopia.

A lion is a symbol of Britain. (*see* BRITISH LION).

**Lion as an emblem of the Resurrection, The.** According to tradition, the lion's whelp is born dead, and remains so for three days, when the father breathes on it and it receives life.

**Lion at the feet of crusaders** or **martyrs, A.** In effigy the lion signifies that such persons died for their cause.

**Lion-Heart.** *See* COEUR DE LION.

**Lion in heraldry, The.** Ever since 1164, when it was adopted as a device by Philip I, Duke of Flanders, the lion has figured prominently as an emblem in HERALDRY and consequently in PUBLIC HOUSE SIGNS.

The earliest and most important attitude of the heraldic lion is RAMPANT (the device of

Scotland), but it is also shown as passant, passant gardant (as in the shield of England), salient, sejant and even dormant. A lion statant gardant is the device of the Dukes of Norfolk; a lion rampant, with the tail between the legs and turned over its back, is the badge of Edward IV as Earl of March; a sleeping lion is the device of Richard I; and a crowned lion the badge of Henry VIII.

In the arms of England there are three lions passant gardant, i.e. walking and showing full face. The first lion was that of Rollo, Duke of Normandy, and the second that of Maine, which was added to Normandy. These were the two lions borne by WILLIAM THE CONQUEROR and his descendants. Henry II added a third to represent the duchy of Aquitaine, which came to him through his wife Eleanor.

Any lion not rampant is called a 'lion leopardé', and the French call the lion passant a *léopard*. Hence NAPOLEON BONAPARTE said to his soldiers, 'Let us drive these leopards [the English] into the sea.'

Since 1603 the royal arms have been supported by (DEXTER) the English lion and (SINISTER) the Scottish UNICORN, but before the accession of James I the sinister supporter was a family badge. Edward III, with whom supporters began, had a lion and an EAGLE, Henry IV an antelope and a swan, Henry V a lion and an antelope, Edward IV a lion and a bull, Richard III a lion and a boar, Henry VII a lion and DRAGON, and Henry VIII, Mary I and Elizabeth I a lion and a greyhound.

The lion in the arms of Scotland is derived from the Earls of Northumberland and Huntingdon, from whom some of the Scottish monarchs were descended. *See also* LORD LYON KING OF ARMS.

**Lion in story and legend, The.** The story of ANDROCLES AND THE LION has many parallels, the best known of which are those related by St JEROME and St Gerasimus noted below. Similar tales are told by the Bollandists in the *Acta Sanctorum* ('Lives of Saints'), the Jesuit writers who, taking their name from the first editor, John Bolland, published the first volume in 1643.

CYBELE was represented as riding in a chariot drawn by two lions

HIPPOMENES and ATALANTA, the fond lovers, were metamorphosed into lions by Cybele

HERCULES is sometimes represented clad in the skin of the NEMEAN LION

St Jerome was lecturing one day when a lion entered the schoolroom and lifted up one of its paws. All his disciples fled, but Jerome, seeing the paw was wounded, drew a thorn out if it and dressed the wound. The lion, out of gratitude, showed a wish to stay with its benefactor, hence the saint is represented as accompanied by a lion

St Gerasimus, while on the banks of the Jordan, saw a lion coming to him limping on three feet. When it reached the saint it held up its right paw, from which St Gerasimus extracted a large thorn. The grateful beast attached itself to the saint and followed him about like a dog

Sir George Davis, an English consul at Florence at the beginning of the 19th century, was visiting the lions of the Duke of Tuscany and was shown one that the keepers could not tame. No sooner did Sir George appear than it showed every sign of joy. He entered its cage, and the lion licked his face and wagged its tail. Sir George told the duke that he had brought up the creature but had sold it when it became older and more dangerous

Sir Iwain de Galles, a hero of romance, was attended by a lion which he had delivered from the attacks of a serpent

Sir Geoffrey de Latour was aided by a lion against the SARACENS, but it was drowned when attempting to board the vessel that was carrying Sir Geoffrey away from the HOLY LAND

George Adamson (1906–89), a game warden of Kenya, together with his wife Joy (1910–85), brought up the lioness Elsa. After returning to the jungle and rearing cubs she frequently visited the Adamsons. She died in 1961. Both the Adamsons were murdered

**Lionize a person, To.** To treat someone as a celebrity. The notion is of treating the person as one of the LIONS.

**Lion of St Mark** or **of Venice, The.** A winged lion sejant, holding an open book with the inscription *Pax tibi, Marce, Evangelista Meus* ('Peace to thee, Mark, my Evangelist').

A sword-point rises above the book on the DEXTER side, and the whole is encircled by an AUREOLE.

**Lions.** The lions of a place are the sights worth seeing or the celebrities. The allusion is to the former custom of showing visitors the lions at the TOWER OF LONDON, as chief of the city's sights. The Tower menagerie was abolished in 1834.

**Lions Bible, The.** *See under* BIBLE.

**Lions Clubs.** Local clubs that form the International Association of Lions Clubs, founded in the USA in 1917 to encourage good relations and to provide service to the community.

**Lion Sermon, The.** A sermon preached annually on 16 October at St Katharine Cree Church, Leadenhall Street, London, to commemorate 'the wonderful escape' of Sir John Gayer from a lion that he met in the desert while he was travelling in Turkish dominions. Sir John was lord mayor of London in 1646.

**Lion's head.** In fountains the water is often made to issue from the mouth of a lion, an ancient custom. The Egyptians thus symbolized the inundation of the Nile, which happens when the sun is in LEO (23 July to 22 August), and the Greeks and Romans adopted the device for their fountains.

**Lions in public house signs.** *See under* PUBLIC HOUSE SIGNS.

**Lion's provider.** A JACKAL; a foil to another man's wit, a humble friend who plays into your hand to show you to the best advantage. The jackal feeds on the lion's leavings, and is said to yell to advise the lion that it has roused up his prey, serving the lion in much the same way as a dog serves a sportsman.

**Lion's share, The.** The larger part, all or nearly all. In AESOP's *Fables*, several beasts joined the lion in a hunt, but when the spoil was divided, the lion claimed one quarter as his own prerogative, another for his superior courage, a third for his dam and cubs, 'and as for the fourth, let who will dispute it with me'. Intimidated by his fierce frown, the other beasts silently withdrew.

**Androcles and the lion.** *See under* ANDROCLES.

**Ass in a lion's skin, An.** *See under* ASS.

**Beard the lion in his den, To.** *See under* BEARD.

**British Lion, The.** *See under* BRITISH.

**Nemean Lion, The.** *See under* NEMEAN.

**Paint the lion, To.** *See under* PAINT.

**Place** or **put oneself** or **one's head in the lion's mouth.** *See under* PLACE.

**Pride of lions, A.** *See under* PRIDE.

**Twist the lion's tail, To.** *See under* TWIST.

**Lip. Lip service.** Insincere respect, expressed with the lips but not acted upon.

> This people draweth nigh unto me with their mouth, and honoureth me with their lips; but their heart is far from me.
> Matthew 15:8

*See also* KNEE TRIBUTE.

**Austrian lip.** *See under* AUSTRIAN.

**Bite one's lip, To.** *See under* BITE.

**Button one's lip, To.** *See under* BUTTON.

**Curl one's lip, To.** *See under* CURL.

**Give someone lip, To.** To be cheeky or abusive to them.

**Habsburg lip.** *See* AUSTRIAN LIP.

**Keep a stiff upper lip, To.** *See under* STIFF

**Lick one's lips, To.** *See under* LICK.

**Lir, King.** The earliest known original of the king in Shakespeare's *King* LEAR (1605), an ocean-god of early Irish and British legend. He figures in the romance *The Fate of the Children of Lir* as the father of FIONNUALA. On the death of Fingula, the mother of his daughter, he married the wicked Aoife, who, through spite, transformed the children of Lir into swans.

Lir appears in the MABINOGION as Llyr and in Geoffrey of Monmouth's *Historia Regum Britanniae* (*c.*1136) as Leir, the supposed founder of Leicester, from which later source Shakespeare derived his plot.

**Lisbon.** Camoëns, in the LUSIADS, derives the name of the Portuguese capital from *Ulyssippo* ('Ulysses' city'), and says that it was founded by ULYSSES. In reality it probably comes from Phoenician *Alisubbo*, 'calm bay'.

**Lisieux, St Teresa of.** *See under* TERESA.

**List. Back list.** *See under* BACK.

**Civil List.** *See under* CIVIL.

**Hit list.** *See under* HIT.

**Short list.** *See under* SHORT.

**Listen to reason, To.** To be persuaded to do something by peaceful argument.

**Lists, To enter the.** *See under* ENTER.

**Literary place-names.** Many literary works are set in real places with fictional names, as Anthony Trollope's BARCHESTER and Arnold Bennett's FIVE TOWNS. Thomas Hardy created an entirely new WESSEX for the purposes of his novels, with Bournemouth recast as 'Sandbourne', Dorchester as 'Casterbridge', Exeter as 'Exonbury', Salisbury as 'Melchester' and Weymouth as 'Budmouth Regis', among others. The relationship beween the real and the created name, where one exists, is of peculiar interest to literary toponymists. Below is a selection of such renamings.

*Aberalva* Clovelly, Devon (Charles Kingsley)
*Babington* Abingdon, Oxon (Dorothy Richardson)
*Ballah* Sligo, Ireland (W.B. Yeats)
*Battersby* Langar, Notts (Samuel Butler)
*Belford Regis* Reading (Mary Russell Mitford)
*Bestwood* Eastwood, Notts (D.H. Lawrence)
*Birchester* Birmingham (W.H. Mallock)
*Blackstable* Whitstable, Kent (W. Somerset Maugham)
*Blunderstone* Blundeston, Suffolk (Charles Dickens)
*Bonnycliff* Sandgate, Kent (Dorothy Richardson)
*Bretton* Bridlington, East Yorks (Charlotte Brontë)
*Briarfield* Birstall, West Yorks (Charlotte Brontë)
*Brideshead* Castle Howard, North Yorks (Evelyn Waugh)
*Bridgepoint* Baltimore, MD (Gertrude Stein)
*Brocklebridge* Tunstall, Lancs (Charlotte Brontë)
*Brompton-on-Sea*, Kensington, London (Christina Rossetti)
*Bromstead* Bromley, London (H.G. Wells)
*Broxton* Roston, Derby (George Eliot)
*Chevron* Knole, Kent (Vita Sackville-West)
*Clavering St Mary* Ottery St Mary, Devon (W.M. Thackeray)
*Cloisterham* Rochester, Kent (Charles Dickens)
*Cockleton* Hartlepool (W.M. Thackeray)
*Coketown* Hanley, Staffs (Charles Dickens)
*Cossethay* Cossall, Notts (D.H. Lawrence)
*Crampsford* Langar, Notts (Samuel Butler)
*Cranford* Knutsford, Ches (Elizabeth Gaskell)
*Darling* Dartington, Devon (J.A. Froude)
*Deerbrook* Diss, Norfolk (Harriet Martineau)
*Delisleville* Knoxville, TN (Frances Hodgson Burnett)
*Dulditch* Shropham, Norfolk (Mary Mann)
*Dullborough* Rochester (Charles Dickens)
*Dunfield* Wakefield (George Gissing)
*Eagledale* Dovedale, Staffs (George Eliot)
*Eatanswill* Sudbury, Suffolk (Charles Dickens)
*Fairport* Arbroath, Tayside (Walter Scott)
*Fort Penn* Harrisburg, PA (John O'Hara)

*Gibbsville* Pottsville, PA (John O'Hara)
*Gudetown* Irvine, Strathclyde (John Galt)
*Hamnavoe* Stromness, Orkney (George Mackay Brown)
*Hillsborough* Sheffield (Charles Reade)
*Hillstone* Winchester (Florence Marryat)
*Hurstley* Bradenham, Bucks (Benjamin Disraeli)
*Jefferson* Oxford, MS (William Faulkner)
*Knarborough* Nottingham (D.H. Lawrence)
*Knebley* Astley, War (George Eliot)
*Lower Binfield* Henley, Oxon (George Orwell)
*Lowton* Kirkby Lonsdale, Cumbria (Charlotte Brontë)
*Lymport* Portsmouth, Hants (George Meredith)
*Marabar Caves* Barabar Caves, India (E.M. Forster)
*Middlemarch* Coventry (George Eliot)
*Milton* Manchester (Elizabeth Gaskell)
*Minton* Moorgreen, Notts (D.H. Lawrence)
*Monkshaven* Whitby, North Yorks (Elizabeth Gaskell)
*Moonfleet* Fleet, Dorset (J. Meade Falkner)
*Morton* Hathersage, Derby (Charlotte Brontë)
*Muggleton*, Maidstone, Kent (Charles Dickens)
*Nuttall* Underwood, Notts (D.H. Lawrence)
*Oakbourne* Ashbourne, Derby (George Eliot)
*Oniton* Clun, Shropshire (E.M. Forster)
*Polchester* Truro, Cornwall (Hugh Walpole)
*Rivermouth* Portsmouth, NH (T.B. Aldrich)
*San Spirito* Benicia, CA (Sinclair Lewis)
*Sawston* Tonbridge, Kent (E.M. Forster)
*Siddermorton* South Harting, West Sussex (H.G. Wells)
*Steepways* Clovelly, Devon (Charles Dickens)
*Stonyshire* Derbyshire (George Eliot)
*Stuffington* Darlington, Dur (W.M. Thackeray)
*Tercanbury* Canterbury (W. Somerset Maugham)
*Thrums* Kirriemuir, Scotland (J.M. Barrie)
*Thurchester* Winchester (Charles Palliser)
*Tilling* Rye, East Sussex (E.F. Benson)
*Troy Town* Fowey, Cornwall (Sir Arthur Quiller-Couch)
*Villette* Brussels (Charlotte Brontë)
*Whittlecombe* Stockingford, War (George Eliot)
*Wimblehurst* Midhurst, West Sussex (H.G. Wells)
*Yoknapatawpha Co* Lafayette Co, MS (William Faulkner)

**Litotes** (Greek *litos*, 'small'). Understatement, especially emphasizing an affirmative by a negative of its contrary, as, 'a citizen of no mean city', i.e. of a great or illustrious city.

**Litterbug.** A person who leaves litter all over the place. A more recent equivalent is a litter lout.

**Little. Little Bear.** *See* GREAT BEAR AND LITTLE BEAR.

**Little bird told me, A.** Someone whom I shan't name (but whose identity you can perhaps guess) told me.

> A bird of the air shall carry the voice, and that which hath wings shall tell the matter.
>
> Ecclesiastes 10:20.

**Little Britain.** The name given in the old romances to Armorica, now Brittany.

A street in the City of London, originally Bretton-Strete, eventually became Lyttell Bretton in late Elizabethan times. It is said to be named from a Duke of Brittany who had a residence there. It was once noted for its booksellers.

> Little Britain may truly be called the heart's core of the city, the stronghold of true John Bullism.
>
> WASHINGTON IRVING: *The Sketch Book*, 'Little Britain' (1819–20)

**Little by little.** Gradually; a little at a time.

**Little Corporal.** NAPOLEON BONAPARTE. He was so called after the Battle of Lodi in 1796, from his low stature, youthful age and great courage. He was barely 5ft 2in (1.57m) tall. See also CORPORAL VIOLET *under* VIOLET.

**Little Dauphin.** *See* SECOND DAUPHIN.

**Little-endians.** *See* BIG-ENDIANS.

**Little Englander.** An uncomplimentary term first applied in Victorian times to critics and opponents of imperialism and overseas expansion, mostly RADICAL and LIBERAL politicians and propagandists of Victorian England who, influenced by the doctrines of LAISSEZ FAIRE and the MANCHESTER SCHOOL, or from more positive and idealistic reasons, opposed imperialism and advocated retrenchment in the colonial field. W.E. Gladstone (1809–98), George Leveson-Gower, 2nd Earl Granville (1815–91), Richard Cobden (1804–65) and John Bright (1811–89) are examples.

**Little Entente.** The name given to the political alliance formed between Czechoslovakia, Yugoslavia and Romania (1920–2). It was originally designed to prevent the restoration of HABSBURG power but became broader in scope. It was brought to an end by the destruction of Czechoslovakia after the Munich Agreement (1938).

**Little gentleman in velvet** or **black velvet, The.** A favourite JACOBITE toast in the reign of Queen Anne. The reference was to the mole that raised the molehill against which William III's horse SORREL stumbled (21 February 1702). The king broke his collar bone and died at Kensington (8 March).

> He urged his horse to strike into a gallop just at a spot where a mole had been at work. Sorrel stumbled on the mole-hill, and went down on his knees. The king fell off and broke his collar bone.
>
> LORD MACAULAY: *History of England*, ch xxv (1849, 1855)

**Little go.** A nickname for the former Previous (Entrance) Examination for undergraduates at Cambridge, unless excused on account of successes at other examinations. It ceased to operate after 1961, owing to new regulations. *See also* SMALLS.

**Little green men.** Imaginary people of peculiar appearance, supposedly landed from outer space. The description derives from cartoons of such creatures emerging from FLYING SAUCERS.

**Little Jack Horner.** *See* JACK HORNER.

**Little John.** A character in the ROBIN HOOD cycle,

a big stalwart man whose surname was also said to be Nailor. On his first encounter with Robin Hood he 'tumbl'd him into the brook' and the outlaws changed the victor's name from John Little to 'Little John'.

> He was, I must tell you, but seven foot high,
> And, maybe, an ell in the waste;
> A sweet pretty lad; much feasting they had;
> Bold Robin the christ'ning grac'd.
>
> JOSEPH RITSON: *Robin Hood*, 'Robin Hood and Little John' (1795)

**Little local difficulty, A.** A euphemism for a major problem. The expression was popularized by Prime Minister Harold Macmillan's statement at London Airport on 7 January 1958 on leaving for a Commonwealth tour following the resignation of the Chancellor of the Exchequer, among others.

> I thought the best thing to do was to settle up these little local difficulties and then turn to the wider vision of the Commonwealth.
>
> HAROLD MACMILLAN: quoted in *The Times* (8 January 1958)

**Little Lord Fauntleroy.** The title of a popular children's story by Frances Hodgson Burnett, a household name in late Victorian and Edwardian days. It was first published in book form by Scribners in 1886 and was adapted as a play, *The Real Lord Fauntleroy*, in 1888. As a consequence many small boys, often to their embarrassment, were made to model themselves on the Fauntleroy image of polished manners, curly hair and black velvet suits with lace collars. The illustrations to the book by Reginald B. Birch were based on photographs of the author's costumed son Vivian (1876–1937), and the Fauntleroy suit was in vogue for at least a generation.

**Little man, A.** An insignificant man. The expression is also used of a local handyman who operates on a small scale.

**Little Mary.** A former euphemism for the stomach, from the play of that name by J.M. Barrie (1903). It is not the name of a character, but the colloquialism used by a children's doctor: 'How's little Mary today?'

**Little master.** A name applied to certain German designers who worked for engravers and others in the 16th century, because their designs were on a small scale, fit for copper or wood. They were Hans Sebald Beham (1500–50) and his brother Barthel Beham (1502–40), Georg Pencz (*c*.1500–50), Jacob Binck (b.*c*.1500), Heinrich Aldegraver (1502–55) and Albrecht Altdorfer (*c*.1480–1538). They continued in the tradition begun by Albrecht Dürer of Nuremberg (1471–1528). *See also* LINE ENGRAVING.

**Little old ladies in tennis shoes.** A nickname for conservative Republican women voters in American elections, said to be typified by an elderly resident in the western states who does not care about her appearance and who 'votes for values'.

The support of such voters did much to boost Barry Goldwater's position in the late 1950s and 1960s.

> 'Burt Reynolds has done more for little old ladies in tennis shoes than anyone else in the history of the world,' said Dinah Shore at the annual Friars Club roast, where Reynolds was the guest of honor.
>
> *Newsweek* (1 June 1981)

**Little Parliament.** *See* BAREBONES PARLIAMENT.

**Little people, The.** *See* FAIRY.

**Little pitchers have long ears.** Little children often hear and understand what adults are saying. The 'ear' of a pitcher is the handle, somewhat resembling a human ear.

**Little Red Riding Hood.** This nursery story is also common to Sweden, Germany and France. It comes from the French *Le Petit Chaperon Rouge*, in Charles Perrault's *Contes de ma mère l'Oye* ('Mother Goose Tales') (1697) and was probably derived from Italy. The finale, which tells how a huntsman slits open the wolf and restores Little Red Riding Hood and her grandmother to life, is a German addition.

**Little Rhody.** The state of Rhode Island, USA.

**Little stranger, A.** A new baby.

**Little Venice.** A London beauty spot centring on the western end of the Regent's Canal and famous for its artists. It is hardly like Venice, although it was romantically compared to that city in the 19th century by Lord Byron and Robert Browning. The present name appears not to have emerged until after the Second World War.

**Little woman, The.** A facetious term for a wife.

**My little finger told me that.** The same as a LITTLE BIRD TOLD ME, meaning: 'I know that, although you did not expect me to.' The popular belief was that an itching or tingling foretold that something was about to happen. *See also* ITCH; PRICKING OF ONE'S THUMB.

**So that's your little game!** So that's what you have been planning!

**Live** (verb).

**Live from hand to mouth, To.** To live with only just enough money or food. The phrase implies the ready consumption of whatever one can get hold of.

> Poor Frog ... is in hard circumstances, he has a numerous family and lives from hand to mouth.
>
> JOHN ARBUTHNOT: *History of John Bull* (1712)

**Live in a glass house, To.** To be in a vulnerable position morally; to be open to attack. An expression arising from the old proverb 'those who live in glass houses should not throw stones'. It is found in varying forms from the time of Chaucer.

**Live in the lap of luxury, To.** To have every material comfort and need supplied. The image is of luxury as a maternal figure in whose lap one can live with every want given before one asks.

**Live like a lord, To.** To fare luxuriously.

**Live on a knife edge, To.** To occupy such a precarious position that the slightest false move could result in disaster.

**Live on a shoestring, To.** To manage on very little money.

**Live on one's wits, To.** To live by temporary shifts and expedients rather than by honest work.

**Live the life of Reilly, To.** To live luxuriously. The allusion is said to be to a comic song by Pat Rooney, 'Is That Mr Reilly', popular in the USA in the 1880s, which described what the hero would do if he 'struck it rich'. The name is also spelt Riley.

**Living death.** A state of hopeless misery.

**Living will.** A written statement of a person's wish not to be kept alive by artificial means if terminally ill or seriously injured. It is not legally binding.

**Standard of living.** *See under* STANDARD.

**Their name liveth for evermore.** *See under* NAME.

**Live** (adjective).

**Live music.** Music performed in one's presence, i.e. not recorded.

**Livestock.** In colloquial usage, lice or other parasitic vermin.

**Live wire, A.** A wire charged with electricity. Hence also a lively person abounding with energy and enthusiasm.

**Liver.** In the AUSPICES taken by the Greeks and Romans before battle, if the liver of the animals sacrificed was healthy and blood-red, the OMENS were favourable, but if it were pale it augured defeat.

The liver was formerly believed to be the seat of love. Hence in Shakespeare's *Love's Labour's Lost* (IV, iii (1594)), when Longaville reads the verses, Biron says in an aside: 'This is the liver-vein, which makes flesh a deity.' In *The Merry Wives of Windsor* (II, i (1600)), Pistol speaks of Falstaff as loving Ford's wife 'with liver burning hot'.

Another superstition was that the liver of a coward contained no blood. Hence such expressions as WHITE-LIVERED, lily-livered, PIGEON-LIVERED, and Sir Toby's remark in Shakespeare's *Twelfth Night* (III, ii (1599)):

> For Andrew, if he were opened, and you find so much blood in his liver as will clog the foot of a flea, I'll eat the rest of the anatomy.

**Liverpool.** A native of Liverpool is called a SCOUSE or a Liverpudlian. The latter of these jokingly substitutes 'puddle' for 'pool' in the name.

**Livery.** That which is delivered, hence the clothes of a manservant delivered to him by his master, and the stables to which a horse is delivered for keep. Splendid uniforms were formerly given to members of royal households. Barons and knights gave them to their retainers, but in the reign of Edward IV a statute of 1468 forbade the latter practice and Henry VII prosecuted those giving or receiving liveries.

In modern terms the livery of a company or line is the distinctive colour scheme in which its vehicles are painted. Individual railway companies and airlines have distinctive liveries for their trains and aircraft.

> Another enjoyable exercise was embarked upon when, less than a month after nationalization, the Railway Executive held the first of several 'beauty contests' to decide upon the future livery for BR locomotives and coaching stock.
>
> MICHAEL R. BONAVIA: *British Rail: The First 25 Years* (1981)

**Livery companies.** The modern representatives in the City of London of the old craft guilds, which were originally associations for religious and social purposes and later trade organizations for fixing wages, standards of craftsmanship and the like. They also acted as friendly societies. Their members wore distinctive livery on special occasions, hence the name livery company.

The 12 'great' companies in order of civic precedence are:

(1) Mercers (1393)
(2) Grocers (1345)
(3) Drapers (1364)
(4) Fishmongers (1364)
(5) Goldsmiths (1327)
(6/7) Merchant Taylors (1326)
(6/7) Skinners (1327)
(8) Haberdashers (1448)
(9) Salters (1558)
(10) Ironmongers (1454)
(11) Vintners (1436)
(12) Clothworkers (1528)

The Pepperers and Spicers amalgamated in 1345 to become later known as the Grocers, and the Haberdashers were originally known as the Hurrers. Samuel Pepys was Master (1677) of the Clothworkers, which was a 16th-century incorporation of the Shearmen and the Fullers.

Among the 90-odd lesser livery companies are:

Apothecaries (1606)
Armourers and Brasiers (1453)
Blacksmiths (1571)
Butchers (1606)
Cordwainers (1438)
Dyers (1471)

Farmers (1952)
Furniture Makers (1963)
Glovers (1639)
Leathersellers (1444)
Plasterers (1501)
Stationers and Newspaper Makers (1556)

The Weavers (1184) claim to be the oldest company. Many still have their halls in the City and contribute largely from their funds to charities, especially to almshouses and education. Merchant Taylors' School, the Haberdashers' schools, St Paul's School, Goldsmiths' College and numerous such institutions, owe much to their benevolence. *See also* AT SIXES AND SEVENS.

**Liverymen.** The freemen of the London LIVERY COMPANIES are so called because they were entitled to wear the livery of their respective companies.

**Devil's livery.** *See under* DEVIL.

**Lizard.** The reptile was at one time believed to be venomous, hence a 'lizard's leg' was an ingredient of the witches' cauldron in Shakespeare's *Macbeth* (IV, i (1605)):

Eye of newt, and toe of frog,
Wool of bat, and tongue of dog,
Adder's fork, and blind-worm's sting,
Lizard's leg, and howlet's wing.

**Lounge lizard.** *See under* LOUNGE.

**Lizzie, A tin.** *See under* TIN.

**Llama.** The name of the South American beast of burden, famous for its soft woolly fleece, is probably of Quechua origin. It is popularly but falsely said to derive from the query of a Spanish explorer on first seeing the beast, *¿Cómo se llama?* ('What is it called?'). The tale runs that his native companion did not understand the question but merely repeated the final word, leading the Spaniard to take that as its name. A similar spurious etymology is still sometimes offered for the indigenous names of other animals, notably the KANGAROO.

**Llareggub.** The little town by the sea that is the fictional setting for Dylan Thomas' 'play for voices', *Under Milk Wood* (1954). The original title of the work was *Llareggub* (*A Piece for Radio Perhaps*), but the spelling of the town's palingrammatic name was altered after the author's death to the more delicate Llaregyb. The play was written in Thomas' home town of Laugharne, and its own name may have been the initial inspiration for the literary invention.

**LLD.** Doctor of Laws, i.e. both civil and canon. The double L is the plural, as in MSS (manuscripts), the plural of MS, pp (pages), the plural of p and so on.

**Lloyd's.** An international insurance market in the City of London and the world centre of shipping intelligence that began in the 17th-century COFFEE house of Edward Lloyd in LOMBARD Street. It was originally a market for marine insurance only but now deals with nearly all forms of insurance. Lloyd's was incorporated by Act of Parliament in 1871. Insurance is accepted at Lloyd's by individual underwriters, not by Lloyd's, which provides the premises, intelligence and other facilities. Lloyd's Agents throughout the world send shipping information, which is published in *Lloyd's List* and *Lloyd's Shipping Index*. *See also* BALTIC.

**Load. Load line.** Another name for the PLIMSOLL LINE.

**Hercules and his load.** *See under* HERCULES.

**Loadstone.** *See* LODESTONE.

**Loaf.** In sacred art, a loaf held in the hand is an attribute of St PHILIP the Apostle, St Osyth, St Joanna, St NICHOLAS, St Godfrey and other saints noted for their charity to the poor.

**Coburg loaf.** *See under* COBURG.

**Cottage loaf.** *See under* COTTAGE.

**Fairy loaves.** *See under* FAIRY.

**Half a loaf is better than none.** *See under* HALF.

**Use your loaf.** *See under* USE.

**Vantage loaf.** *See under* VANTAGE.

**Loamshire.** An imaginary county of southern England used as a setting by writers of fiction to avoid identification with actual towns and villages, loam being a kind of particularly fertile soil. Hence the Loamshires as an equally fictitious regiment of the LINE.

**Loan, A call.** *See under* CALL.

**Lo and behold.** Would you believe; just imagine. A phrase introducing a surprising or unexpected fact. 'Lo' is related to 'look'. The tautologous phrase is not as old as it seems, and apparently dates from the 19th century.

**Loathly lady.** A stock character of old romance who is so hideous that everyone is deterred from marrying her. When she at last finds a husband, however, her ugliness, which is the result of a spell, disappears, and she becomes a model of beauty. Her story is the feminine counterpart of BEAUTY AND THE BEAST.

**Lobby.** A vestibule or corridor, from Medieval Latin *lobia*, 'lodge', 'portico'. In the HOUSE OF COMMONS, the Lobby is the large hall to which the public are admitted, especially for interviews with members. Division lobbies are the corridors to which members retire to vote, and 'to lobby' is to solicit the vote of a member or to seek to influence members. A 'lobbyist' is someone who does this.

**Lobsters.** Soldiers were popularly so called because they were 'turned red' when they enlisted, i.e. they wore red coats. The name is also applied to Royal MARINES. The term was originally given to a troop of Parliamentary horse in the Civil Wars (1642–51).

**Died for want of lobster sauce.** *See under* DIE.

**Local, The.** In colloquial parlance, the local pub; also the local paper.

**Local Defence Volunteers.** *See* HOME GUARD.

**Local option.** The choice allowed to a local authority to decide what course it shall take on a given question, especially the sale of alcohol. In 1913 Scotland was given local option. Parishes, small towns and wards of large towns were allowed to vote on licensing: whether for no licence, for a reduction of licences or for no change. Very few places went 'dry'.

**Local rag, The.** A colloquial term for the local newspaper.

**Lochiel.** The title of the head of the Clan Cameron, so called from his domain.

The hero of Thomas Campbell's poem, *Lochiel's Warning* (1802), is Donald Cameron (*c*.1695–1748), known as The Gentle Lochiel. He was one of the YOUNG PRETENDER'S staunchest adherents, and escaped to France with him after CULLODEN (1746). He took service with the French army, but died in France two years later.

**Lochinvar.** The dashing knight of Sir Walter Scott's poem *Marmion* (1808) who comes to the bridal feast for the woman he loves and, after pleading one last dance, sweeps her out of the hall, up onto his horse, and away.

> O, young Lochinvar is come out of the west,
> Through all the wide Border his steed was the best;
> And save his good broadsword he weapons had
> none,
> He rode all unarm'd, and he rode all alone.
> So faithful in love, and so dauntless in war,
> There never was knight like the young Lochinvar.
> *Marmion*, V, xii

**Loch Ness Monster.** On 22 July 1933 a grey monster some 6ft (1.8m) long was spotted crossing a road near Loch Ness, and subsequent 'sightings' reported a strange object some distance out in the water. Descriptions of it varied, so that two years later its length was said to be nearer 20ft (6m) and its appearance a cross between a seal and a plesiosaur, with a snake-like head at the end of a long neck and two flippers near the middle of its body. From then on it became a continual object of media attention. Investigations showed no substantial evidence of the existence of the supposed monster but more recent observations have increased the belief in the presence of 'Nessie', and in 1987 a sonar scan of the loch revealed a moving object some 400lb (181kg) in weight which scientists could not identify. The ornithologist Sir Peter Scott dubbed the creature *Nessiteras rhombopteryx*, after its appearance on a photograph taken by some Americans. The name was taken to mean 'Ness monster with the diamond-shaped fin', but crossword fanatics pointed out a short while later that it was in fact an anagram of 'monster hoax by Sir Peter S.'

**Lock. Lock horns, To.** To become engaged in an argument. The allusion is to two stags, which often lock horns when battling head to head over a mate.

**Lock, stock and barrel.** The whole of anything; in entirety. The lock (firing mechanism), stock (butt) and barrel comprise a complete gun or rifle.

**Lock the stable door after the horse has bolted, To.** To take precautions or measures too late, when the damage has been done.

**Davy Jones' locker.** *See under* DAVY.

**Not a shot in one's locker.** *See under* SHOT.

**Rape of the Lock, The.** *See under* RAPE.

**Scalp lock.** *See under* SCALP.

**Lockhart.** Legend has it that Sir James Douglas (*c*.1286–1330), on his way to the HOLY LAND with the heart of Robert BRUCE, was killed in Spain fighting against the Moors. Sir Simon Locard of Lee was commissioned to carry the heart back to Scotland, and it was interred in Melrose Abbey. In consequence he altered his name to Lockheart, and adopted the device of a heart within a fetterlock, with the motto *Corda serrata pando* ('Locked hearts I open').

**Loco-foco.** An American name for a self-igniting cigar patented in New York in 1834 and soon applied to a friction OR LUCIFER MATCH. The name is seemingly based on locomotive, taken to mean 'self-moving', so that loco-foco was intended to mean 'self-lighting'. The name was then applied to the RADICAL wing of the Democratic Party and then to the Democratic Party generally. It arose from an incident that occurred at a party meeting in TAMMANY HALL (1835) when the gas lights were turned out by the opponents of the radicals to break up the assembly, but the radicals produced candles, which they lit with loco-focos.

> Here's full particulars of the patriotic loco-foco movement yesterday in which the Whigs was so chawed up.
> DICKENS: *Martin Chuzzlewit*, ch xvi (1843–4)

**Locrinus.** Father of SABRINA, and eldest son of the mythical BRUTUS, king of Britain. On the death of his father he became king of LOEGRIA (Geoffrey of Monmouth, *Historia Regum Britanniae*, ch i–v (*c*.1136)). *See also* HUMBER.

An anonymous tragedy called *Locrine*, based on Holinshed and Geoffrey of Monmouth, was published in 1595 bearing Shakespeare's initials (W.S.). This tragedy contains borrowings from Edmund Spenser, and Christopher Marlowe has also been suggested as its author. It is almost certainly not by Shakespeare.

**Locum tenens** or **locum** (Medieval Latin, 'holding the place'). One acting temporarily for another, especially a doctor or a clergyman.

**Locus** (Latin, 'place'). A word that begins a number of Latin expressions, many of them legal. The following is a selection.

**Locus classicus** ('classical place'). The most cited or most authoritative passage on a particular subject.

**Locus delicti** ('place of the crime'). The place where a crime was committed.

**Locus in quo** ('place in which'). The place in question; the spot mentioned.

**Locus poenitentiae** ('place of repentance'). The interval when it is possible to withdraw from a bargain or course before being committed to it. In the interview between ESAU and his father ISAAC, St PAUL says that the former 'found no place of repentance, though he sought it carefully with tears' (Hebrews 12:17), i.e. no means whereby Isaac could break his bargain with JACOB.

**Locus sigilli** ('place of the seal'). The place where the seal must be affixed on legal documents. The expression is usually abbreviated to LS or designated by a small circle.

**Locus standi** ('place of standing'). A recognized position; an acknowledged right or claim. In law, *locus standi* is the right to be heard in court.

**Locusta.** A woman who murders those she professes to nurse or those whom she is supposed to be looking after. Locusta lived in the early days of the Roman Empire, poisoned CLAUDIUS and Britannicus, and attempted to kill NERO. On being found out, she was put to death.

**Lode.** Originally a ditch that guides or leads water into a river or sewer, from Old English *lād*, 'way', 'course' (connected with lead and load). Hence in mines the vein that leads or guides to ore.

**Lodestar.** The North Star or Pole Star, the leading star by which mariners are guided. *See also* CYNOSURE.

**Lodestone** or **loadstone.** The MAGNET or 'guiding stone', a rock that consists of almost pure magnetite and that is thus naturally magnetic. In the Middle Ages pilots were called 'lodesmen'.

**Lodget, To tile a.** *See under* TILE.

**Lodona.** A personification of the Loddon, a river that enters the Thames at Shiplake, on the Oxfordshire-Berkshire border. Alexander Pope, in *Windsor Forest* (1713), says she was a NYMPH, fond of the chase, like DIANA. It chanced one day that PAN saw her and tried to catch her, but Lodona fled from him, imploring CYNTHIA to save her. No sooner had she spoken than she became 'a silver stream' which 'virgin coldness keeps'.

**Loegria.** England is so called by Geoffrey of Monmouth, from LOCRINUS, whose own name comes from *Lloegr*, the Welsh name for England, itself probably related to the Ligore or Legore, the Celtic people who gave the name of Leicester. *See also* BRUTUS.

**Log.** An instrument for measuring the speed of a ship. In its simplest form it is a flat piece of wood, some 6in (15cm) in radius, in the shape of a quadrant, and made so that it will float perpendicularly. To this is fastened the log-line, which is knotted at intervals. *See also* KNOT.

**Logbook.** In a ship the journal in which the LOGS are entered. It also contains the general record of proceedings on board, especially the navigational and meteorological records. The word later came to be used for the document that gave the ownership and other details of a motor vehicle.

**Log cabin.** In the United States a small house made of logs, as built in wooded localities by early settlers and hunters. To say of a person that he was 'born in a log cabin' is to mean that he was of humble origin. John N. Garner, twice Vice President under Franklin D. Roosevelt, said in a speech in 1959: 'That log cabin [in which he was born] did me more good in politics than anything I ever said.'

**Logged, To be.** To have one's name recorded in the ship's log for some misdemeanour or offence. The term can now be used of any record noted, such as a distance travelled.

**Logrolling.** A term applied in politics to the 'give and take' principle, by which one party will further certain interests of another in return for help given in passing its own measures.

In literary circles it means mutual admiration, the mutual admirers being called 'log-rollers'. The allusion, originally American, is to neighbours who assist a new settler to roll away the logs of his clearing.

> Reagan's objective is precisely to keep the coming battle out of the trenches, where the lobbyists and the log-rollers can coalesce and trade votes in a program-by-program defense of their interests.
> *Newsweek* (2 March 1981)

**As easy as falling off a log.** *See under* AS.

**King Log, A.** A king who rules in peace and quietness, but never makes his power felt. The allusion is to the FABLE of *The Frogs Desiring a King*. JUPITER first threw them down a log of wood, but they grumbled at so spiritless a king. He then sent them a stork, which devoured them eagerly. *See also* KING STORK *under* STORK.

**Sleep like a log, To.** *See under* SLEEP.

**Yule log.** *See under* YULE.

**Logan stones.** Rocking stones; large masses of stone so delicately poised that they will rock at a touch. There are many such stones in the British Isles, usually not far from the coast.

The Logan Rock at Land's End was toppled by Lieutenant Goldsmith, RN (nephew of the poet Oliver Goldsmith) and his boat's crew in

1824. It cost him over £2000 to have it replaced. There is a logan stone half a mile (800m) from St David's in southwest Wales which may be rocked with one finger. The word 'logan' itself comes from 'logging-stone', from the dialect word 'log' meaning 'to rock'.

**Loggerheads, To be at.** *See under* AT.

**Lohengrin.** A son of PERCEVAL in the German legend of the Knight of the Swan, and a character associated with the HOLY GRAIL cycle. He appears at the close of Wolfram von Eschenbach's *Parzival* (*c*.1210) and in other German romances, where he is the deliverer of Elsa, princess of Brabant, who has been dispossessed by Tetramund and Ortrud. He arrives at Antwerp in a skiff drawn by a swan, champions Elsa, and becomes her husband on the sole condition that she shall not ask him his name or lineage. She is persuaded to do so on the marriage night, and he, by his vows to the Grail, is obliged to disclose his identity but at the same time disappears. The swan returns for him, and he departs, but not before retransforming the swan into Elsa's brother Gottfried, who, by the wiles of the sorceress Ortrud, had been obliged to assume that form. Wagner's opera of this name was first performed in 1850.

His name has been derived from Old French, meaning 'Garin of Lorraine', but it has equally been traced back to Lohrangerin, a Persian god whose name means 'the red messenger'.

**Loins, To gird up one's.** *See under* GIRD.

**Loki.** The god of strife and spirit of evil in Norse mythology, the son of the giant Farbauti and Laufey, and father of the MIDGARD snake and of HEL and FENRIR. It was he who artfully contrived the death of BALDER. He was finally chained to a rock and, according to one legend, is to remain there until the Twilight of the Gods, when he will break his bonds, the heavens will disappear, the earth will be swallowed up by the sea, fire will consume the elements and even ODIN, with all his kindred deities, will perish. Another story has it that he was freed at RAGNAROK, and that he and HEIMDALL fought until both were slain. His name is said to come from Old Norse *lygi*, 'lie', 'untruth', or *logi*, 'flame', 'fire'.

**Lolita.** The 12-year-old 'nymphet' who is the beloved of Humbert Humbert in Vladimir Nabokov's brilliant but controversial novel that bears her name, a name subsequently used for any underage sexpot. Her full name is Dolores Haze. The book was filmed by Stanley Kubrick (1962) and Adrian Lyne (1997) but neither picture did proper justice to the original, partly because the actresses in the name part, respectively Sue Lyon and Dominique Swain, were necessarily some years older than the prototype.

> She was Lo, plain Lo, in the morning … She was Lola in slacks. She was Dolly at school. She was Dolores on the dotted line. But in my arms she was always Lolita.
>
> VLADIMIR NABOKOV: *Lolita*, ch i (1955)

**Lollards.** A name given to the followers of John Wyclif and, earlier, to a sect in the Netherlands. It is probably from the Middle Dutch *Lollaerd*, one who mumbles prayers or hymns. The word is recorded as having been used by William Courtenay, archbishop of Canterbury, when he spoke against their teachings in 1382.

The Lollards condemned TRANSUBSTANTIATION, INDULGENCES, clerical celibacy, the ecclesiastical hierarchy and the temporal possessions of the church.

**Lombard.** A banker or moneylender. In medieval London, Lombard Street became the home of Lombards and other Italian merchants who set up as goldsmiths, moneylenders and bankers. From the 13th century they flourished as pawnbrokers and the THREE GOLDEN BALLS of the pawnshop are said to be taken from the armorial bearings of the MEDICI of Florence.

> This merchant, who was wary and discreet,
> Soon managed to negotiate his loan;
> The bond that he had signed became his own
> For he paid down the money to a franc
> To certain Lombards at their Paris Bank.
>
> CHAUCER: 'The Shipman's Tale' (*c*.1387) (modern translation by Nevill Coghill, 1951)

**All Lombard Street to a China orange.** *See under* ALL.

**Iron Crown of Lombardy, The.** *See under* IRON.

**London.** The first surviving reference to London is to be found in Tacitus (*Annals*, xiv) written AD 115–117, and referring to events in AD 61. It is the Roman name *Londinium*, which is from a Celtic or even pre-Celtic name of uncertain meaning.

**London Bridge.** The present bridge of three spans over the Thames was built in 1967–72 and replaced the earlier five-arched one, completed in 1831. This was dismantled and in 1968 sold for $1.8 million to the McCulloch Oil Corporation, USA, who reerected it to span an inlet on the Colorado at Lake Havasu City, Arizona. (It was long rumoured that the Americans thought they were buying Tower Bridge, a canard hotly denied by the company chairman, George McCulloch.) The first London Bridge was probably made of wood and built during the Roman occupation some time between AD 100 and 400. The first stone bridge was erected in 1176. From the early 13th to the mid-18th century there were houses on London Bridge, and from the early 14th century to the RESTORATION the heads of executed traitors were displayed on it.

**London Gazette.** The official organ of the British government and the appointed medium for all official announcements of pensions, promotions, bankruptcies, dissolutions of partnerships and similar events. It appeared first as the *Oxford Gazette* in 1665, when the Court was at Oxford, and Henry Muddiman (b.1629) started it as a daily newsletter or newspaper. It was transferred to London in 1666 and is now published five times a week. A corresponding journal is published at Edinburgh, and the *Iris Oifigiúil* ('official journal'), formerly the *Dublin Gazette*, founded 1922, is the Irish equivalent. *See also* GAZETTE; NEWS; YELLOW PRESS.

**London Group.** A society of artists founded in 1913 by some painters associated with Walter Sickert (1860–1942). Its aim was to break away from academic tradition and to draw inspiration from French Post-Impressionism.

**London Library, The.** London's largest subscription library, in St James's Square, with a collection of over a million books. Its titles centre on the humanities, and it has no books on law, medicine, science or technology. It was founded by Thomas Carlyle (1795–1881) in 1841 and has had many distinguished writers among its members, who in 1998 were paying an annual subscription of £135.

**London pride.** The little red-and-white flowering plant *Saxifraga × urbium*, also called 'none-so-pretty' and 'St Patrick's cabbage'. The precise source of the name is uncertain. Bishop Walsham How (1823–97) once wrote a poem addressed to the flower, rebuking it for possessing the sinful attribute. A lady called his attention to the fact that the name did not mean that the plant was proud, but that London was proud of it, whereupon the bishop wrote a second poem apologizing to it.

> London Pride has been handed down to us.
> London Pride is a flower that's free.
> London Pride means our own dear town to us,
> And our pride it for ever will be.
> NOËL COWARD: 'London Pride' (song) (1941)

**London Regiment.** This regiment, now disbanded, consisted of two regular battalions of the City of London Regiment (Royal Fusiliers) and a number of territorial battalions, including the London Rifle Brigade, Kensingtons, Artists' Rifles and London Scottish.

**London season.** Formerly the part of the year when the Court and fashionable society were generally in town, i.e. May, June and July. This localized Victorian season has now broadened out into 'The Season', as the series of social events, cultural and sporting, at which it is the done thing 'to be seen'. They include, beginning in April, the GRAND NATIONAL, the GLYNDEBOURNE Festival, the Chelsea Flower Show, the DERBY, the ROYAL ACADEMY Summer Exhibition, the FOURTH OF JUNE, ROYAL ASCOT, WIMBLEDON, the Henley Royal Regatta, Polo Day at Cowdray Park, GLORIOUS GOODWOOD, Cowes Week, the GLORIOUS TWELFTH, the Edinburgh Festival, the Braemar Gathering and the LAST NIGHT OF THE PROMS.

**London Stone.** A stone set into the wall of No. 111 Cannon Street. It is an ancient relic of uncertain history. Camden thought it to be the point from which the Romans measured distances and another theory is that it is a Saxon ceremonial stone.

According to Holinshed's *Chronicles* (1577) Jack Cade struck it with his sword when proclaiming himself master of the city and the incident is mentioned in Shakespeare's *Henry VI, Pt II* (IV, vii (1590)). The stone was placed against the wall of St SWITHIN's Church in 1798 as a safeguard against its destruction, but in 1960 it was moved to its present position.

**Great Fire of London, The.** *See under* GREAT.

**Nine Worthies of London, The.** *See under* NINE.

**Tower of London, The.** *See under* TOWER.

**Londonderry.** The Northern Ireland county and city of this name took the prefix 'London' when in 1613 the confiscated lands of native chieftains were assigned to some of the London LIVERY COMPANIES and to the Corporation of London. Derry, now the more usual form of the name, represents Irish *doire*, 'oak wood'.

**Lone. Lone Ranger, The.** The masked adventurer of the American West, whose 'real' name was John Reid, was the creation of George W. Trendle and Fran Striker for an American radio series that began in 1933. The Lone Ranger is an ex-Texas Ranger who has become an enforcer of law. He is honest, upright and well-spoken, and shoots only to wound, using special silver bullets. He has an Indian friend, Tonto, and a horse, Silver, whom he urges off with a cry of 'Hi-ho, Silver, awaaaaay!' *See also* SLOANE RANGER.

**Lone Star State.** The state of Texas, USA. *See also* UNITED STATES OF AMERICA.

**Lone wolf, A.** A person who prefers his own company. A lone wolf is remarkable because wolves mostly hunt in packs.

**Lonely-heart.** A somewhat dated term for a single person seeking a relationship. Miss Lonelyhearts is an alternative name for an AGONY AUNT, and Nathanael West's novel *Miss Lonelyhearts* (1933) tells of a male reporter who takes on the job but is soon destroyed by his involvement with the pathetic problems of the people who write to him for advice.

**Long. Long and the short of it, The.** All that need be said; the essence or whole sum of the matter in brief. The allusion is probably to the telling of a tale. If recounted both at length and in brief, it has been fully and finally told.

**Long arm of the law, The.** The ability of the police to track down malefactors wherever they may hide.

**Longchamps.** The racecourse at the end of the Bois de Boulogne, Paris. An abbey formerly stood there, and it was long celebrated for the parade of smartly dressed Parisians that took place on the Wednesday, Thursday and Friday of HOLY WEEK.

The custom dates from the time when all who could do so went to the abbey to hear the TENEBRAE sung in Holy Week, and it survives as an excellent opportunity to display the latest spring fashions.

**Long dozen, A.** Thirteen. *See also* BAKER'S DOZEN.

**Long face, A.** A disappointed or miserable expression, with the mouth turned down at the corners so that the face seems elongated.

**Long hot summer.** A period of civil unrest, as that in the summer of 1967 in the USA, when riots erupted among underprivileged blacks in several cities. *The Long Hot Summer* was the title of a film of 1958 based on William Faulkner's story *The Hamlet* (1928) in which one of the chapters is headed 'The Long Summer'.

**Long hundred.** *See* GREAT HUNDRED.

**Long in the tooth.** Old. The reference is to horses, whose gums recede as they get older, making their teeth look longer. Something similar also occurs with humans.

**Long johns.** Long-legged underpants.

**Long John Silver.** The one-legged pirate who poses as a sea-cook aboard the *Hispaniola* in R.L. Stevenson's novel *Treasure Island* (1883). With his pet parrot, Captain Flint, and his sea-dog's turns of phrase, he is one of the most popular villains in 19th-century fiction.

**Long Knives.** *See* NIGHT OF THE LONG KNIVES.

**Long March, The.** The journey of about 6000 miles (9650km) made in 1934–5 by about 100,000 Chinese Communists when they were forced out of their base at Kiangsi in southeastern China. They made their way to Shensi in northwestern China, with only some 8000 surviving the ordeal.

**Long Meg and Her Daughters.** Six miles (9.7km) northeast of Penrith, Cumbria, is a large Bronze Age circle of 59 stones, some of them 10ft (3m) high. Some 17 paces off, on the south side, is a single outlier, about 18ft (5.5m) high, called Long Meg, the shorter ones being called Her Daughters. According to legend, these rocks are witches turned to stone.

**Long Meg of Westminster.** A noted virago in the reign of Henry VIII, around whose exploits a comedy (since lost) was performed in London in 1594.

> *Lord Proudly*: What d'ye this afternoon?
> *Lord Feesimple*: Faith, I have a great mind to see *Long Meg* and *The Ship* at the Fortune.
>
> NATHAN FIELD: *Amends for Ladies*, II, i (1610)

Her name has been given to several articles of unusual size. Thus, the large blue-black marble in the south cloister of Westminster Abbey, over the grave of Gervasius de Blois, is called 'Long Meg of Westminster'. Thomas Fuller says the term is applied to things 'of hop-pole height, wanting breadth proportionable thereunto', and refers to a great gun in the TOWER OF LONDON, so called, taken to Westminster in troublesome times. The *Edinburgh Antiquarian Magazine* (September 1769) tells of Peter Branan, aged 104, who was 6ft 6in (1.9m) high and commonly called Long Meg of Westminster.

**Long Melford.** A long stocking purse, such as was formerly carried by country folk. In boxing, according to George Borrow, it was a straight right-handed blow. The town of Long Melford in Suffolk owes the epithet to the length of its main street.

> 'Now, will you use Long Melford?' said Belle, picking me up.
> 'I don't know what you mean by Long Melford,' said I, gasping for breath.
> 'Why, this long right of yours,' said Belle, feeling my right arm.
>
> GEORGE BORROW: *Lavengro*, ch lxxxv (1851)

**Long Parliament, The.** The most familiar of this name is the Parliament summoned by CHARLES I (3 November 1640), the remnant of which was not dissolved until 16 March 1660 (*see* RUMP). It was especially notable for its resistance to the king and its part in the GREAT REBELLION. The name is also applied to Henry IV's Parliament of 1406 (1 March to 22 December), and to the CAVALIER PARLIAMENT (1661–79) in Charles II's reign.

**Long pull, The.** The extra quantity of beer supplied by a publican to his customer over and above the exact quantity ordered and paid for. In the USA the term is applied to long and diligent effort.

**Long pull, a strong pull and a pull all together, A.** A steady, energetic and systematic cooperation. The reference may be to the oarsmen in a boat, to a TUG OF WAR or to the act of hauling with a rope, for all of which a simultaneous strong pull is required.

**Long run, A.** Said of a theatrical or film show. 'It had a long run' means it was performed repeatedly over a long period because it was so popular. The allusion is to a long-distance run or race. A 'short run' means that the show did not take on with the public and therefore was soon withdrawn.

**Longshanks.** Edward I, king of England (r.1272–1307), nicknamed Longshanks and also called the Hammer of the Scots.

**Long shot, A.** A remote chance, such as hazarding a highly improbable guess.

**Long suit.** A thing at which one excels. The reference is to card-playing, in which a hand containing many cards of the same suit is a strong one, especially if the suit is trumps.

**Long time no see.** A mock traditional greeting to a person one has not seen for a long time. It is a form of PIDGIN ENGLISH based on Chinese *hǎo jiǔ méi jiàn*.

**Long Tom.** A familiar term for any gun of great length, especially the naval 4.7s used on land in the South African War (1899–1902). A brush for painting, on a long handle of the broomstick variety, is also called a long tom.

**Long words.** 'Honorificabilitudinitatibus' has often been called the longest word in the English language. 'Quadradimensionality' is almost as long, and 'antidisestablishmentarianism' beats it by one letter. The *Oxford English Dictionary* has 'pneumonoultramicroscopicsilicovolcano-coniosis' as its longest word, on which it comments: 'A factitious word alleged to mean "a lung disease caused by the inhalation of very fine silica dust" but occurring chiefly as an instance of a very long word.'

While there is some limit to the coining of polysyllabic words by the conglomeration of prefixes, combining forms, and suffixes, e.g. 'deanthropomorphization' and 'inanthropomorphizability', the chemists concoct such concatenations as 'nitrophenylenediamine' and 'tetraethyldiamidobenzhydrols'. They are far surpassed, however, by the nonsense words found in Urquhart and Motteux's translation of Rabelais (1693–4). The following comes from ch xv of Bk IV:

> He was grown quite esperruquanchurelebublouzerireliced down to his very heel.
> (J.M. Cohen in his Penguin Classics translation renders this as 'bruisedblueandcontused'.)

The film *Mary Poppins* (1963) provided 'supercalifragilisticexpialidocious', which is now in the *Oxford English Dictionary*.

The longest place-name in Britain is traditionally that of a village in Anglesey: Llanfairpwllgwyngyllgogerychwyrndrobwllllantysiliogogogoch (58 letters). It is usually popularly shortened to Llanfair PG. The meaning is: 'The church of St Mary in a hollow of white hazel, near to the rapid whirlpool and St Tysilio church, near to a red cave.' This was an artificial concoction, however, and has now been outdone by another such, created by the Fairbourne & Barmouth Steam Railway: Gorsafawddacha'idraigddanheddogleddollônpenrhynareurdraethceredigion (67 letters): 'The Mawddach station and its dragon teeth at the Northern Penrhyn Road on the golden beach of Cardigan Bay'. The longest English surname is said to be Featherstonehaugh, often pronounced 'Fanshaw'.

The German language lends itself to extensive agglomerations and the following would be hard to beat: *Lebensmittelzuschusseinstellungskommissionsvorsitzenderstellvertreter* ('Deputy-President of the Food-Rationing-Winding-up-Commission').

**As long as your arm.** *See under* AS.

**How long is a piece of string?** *See under* HOW.

**In the long run.** Eventually.

**It's a long lane that has no turning.** Every misfortune has an ending; things will eventually improve.

**Make a long arm, To.** To stretch for something, especially across the table.

**Not by a long chalk.** Not by any means; in no way. The allusion is probably to the chalk marks made on a floor to record the score of a player or team. A 'long chalk' would mean a high score. *See also* BY A LONG CHALK.

**Not long for this world.** Approaching death.

**So long.** *See under* SO.

**Longevity.** Among the traditional stock cases of longevity are Harry Jenkins, who is reputed to have lived 169 years; Thomas PARR, who died at the age of 152; Catherine, Countess of Desmond, who died at the age of 140; and Thomas Carn of Shoreditch, listed by Dr Brewer as living 207 years and in the reign of ten sovereigns. Carn's actual dates were 1471 to 1578 (107 years), a figure '2' having been superimposed over a '1' on his tombstone.

It must be noted that all these cases belong to the days before the Registration Act of 1836 ensured a really efficient system of recording births, marriages and deaths.

The longest authenticated life in the United Kingdom is that of Charlotte Hughes (née Milburn, 1877–1993), who lived to be 115. The American, Carrie White (née Joyner, 1874–1991), died at the age of 116. The Frenchwoman, Jeanne Calment (1875–1997), was 122 years old when she died, a world record officially recognized by the *Guinness Book of Records*.

**Longinus** or **Longius.** The traditional name of the Roman soldier who smote Jesus with his spear at the crucifixion. The only authority for this is the apocryphal ACTS OF PILATE, dating from the 6th century. According to ARTHURIAN ROMANCES this spear was brought by JOSEPH OF ARIMATHEA to Listenise, when he visited King Pellam, 'who was nigh of Joseph's kin'. Sir Balim the Savage seized the spear, with which he wounded King Pellam and destroyed three whole countries with that one stroke. William of Malmesbury says the spear was used by CHARLEMAGNE against the SARACENS.

**Longwood.** The residence on the island of St Helena where NAPOLEON BONAPARTE passed the last years of his life in exile, dying there on 5 May 1821.

**Longsword, William.** *See under* WILLIAM.

**Look. Look a gift-horse in the mouth, To.** Often used in a negative way, as: 'Don't look a gift-horse in the mouth.' When one is given a present one should not inquire too minutely into its intrinsic value. The normal way of assessing the age of a horse is to inspect its front teeth. The proverb has its counterpart in many languages, as French *A cheval donné on ne regarde pas aux dents*, German *Einem geschenkten Gaul sieht man nicht in's Maul*, and Russian *Darënomu konyu v zuby ne smotryat*. The Latin equivalent is *Donati non sunt ora inspicienda caballi*.

**Look alive!** Hurry up; be on the alert.

**Look as if butter would not melt in one's mouth, To.** To look innocent and harmless, when one is probably not.

**Look as if one came out of a bandbox, To.** To look very smart and neat. A 'bandbox' is a special lightweight box for holding hats, caps, collars and the like. In the 17th century it was a cardboard box used by parsons for keeping their BANDS in.

**Look askance, To.** To regard obliquely, with suspicion or disapproval. The word 'askance' is of uncertain origin, but may ultimately relate to Latin *quasi*, 'as if'.

**Look before you leap.** Consider well before you act; avoid doing anything hasty.

> And look before you ere you leap.
> For as you sow, you're like to reap.
> SAMUEL BUTLER: *Hudibras*, II, ii (1663)

**Look big, To.** To assume a consequential air.

**Look** or **feel blue, To.** To be depressed.

**Look daggers, To.** To glare with open hostility.

**Look down one's nose, To.** To treat disdainfully; to regard with disapproval. The allusion is to the gesture of disapproval made by half-closing one's eyelids and looking down one's nose.

**Look for a needle in a haystack, To.** To search for something very small in the midst of a great mass or large number of objects.

**Looking-glass.** As applied to words, a phrase implying that what is spoken or written is to be accepted in the reverse sense or turned upside down. Thus, as spoken by some, 'We are prepared to negotiate' really means 'We are ready for you to accept all our demands but will concede nothing in return'. Similarly, 'We believe in freedom of speech' really means 'We believe in freedom of speech only as long as you say what we want to hear'. A similar DOUBLESPEAK is sometimes cynically ascribed to estate agents, travel agents and other advertisers, who thus talk of a 'dream house' meaning one that is prohibitively expensive and a 'secluded location' meaning one far from any amenities. The allusion is to Lewis Carroll's *Through the Looking-Glass* (1871). *See also* MIRROR WRITING.

**Look like a ghost, To.** To look deathly pale, as pale as a ghost.

**Look on the bright side, To.** To be optimistic.

**Look out for squalls.** Be prepared for difficulties. A nautical term, a squall being a succession of sudden violent gusts of wind.

**Look-see, A.** A survey or inspection. The expression is imitative of PIDGIN ENGLISH.

**Look someone in the face, To.** To meet a person with a steady gaze, implying a lack of fear or shame.

**Look someone up and down, To.** To scrutinize someone closely or contemptuously.

**Look the other way, To.** To disregard what one should notice; to ignore a person one knows.

**Look to one's laurels, To.** To be on one's guard against rivals; to endeavour to maintain one's lead in a field in which one has already excelled.

**Look up, To.** To seek information in books; to visit an acquaintance, to pay a call. Things or persons are said to 'look up' when they are improving. If one 'looks up to' a person, one admires them.

**Black looks.** *See under* BLACK.

**Dirty look.** *See under* DIRTY.

**Hangdog look.** *See under* HANG.

**Like the look of, To.** *See under* LIKE.

**New Look.** *See under* NEW.

**Venus' looking-glass.** *See under* VENUS.

**Loom** (noun). **Jacquard loom.** *See under* JACQUARD.

**Loom** (verb). **Loom large, To.** To be very prominent or important.

**Loony left, The.** A term coined by the media in the 1980s to describe the more hard-line activists of the LABOUR PARTY. Notable among them were Tony Benn, Ken Livingstone and Bernie Grant. 'Loony' is 'lunatic'.

**Loop the loop, To.** The air pilot's term for the manoeuvre that consists of describing a perpendicular circle in the air. At the top of the circle, or loop, the pilot is upside down. The term is from a kind of switchback once popular at fairs in which a moving car or bicycle performed a similar revolution on a perpendicularly circular track.

**Loose.** Figuratively, lax, dissolute, promiscuous, as a 'loose woman'.

**As loose as a goose.** *See under* AS.
**At a loose end.** *See under* AT.
**Cut loose, To.** *See under* CUT.
**Hang loose, To.** *See under* HANG.
**Have a tile** or **slate loose, To.** *See under* TILE.
**On the loose.** Escaped from captivity; on a SPREE.

**Loosestrife.** This name of several species of plants of the genera *Lysimachia* and *Lythrum* is due to mistranslation. The Greek name was *lusimakhion*, from the personal name *Lusimakhos* (Lysimachus), who is said to have discovered it, and this was treated as if it were *lusimakhos* 'loosing (i.e. ending) strife'. Pliny says that the plant has a soothing effect upon oxen that will not draw in the same yoke and that it keeps off flies and gnats, thus relieving horses and oxen from their irritation.

> Yellow Lysimachus, to give sweet rest
> To the faint shepherd, killing, where it comes,
> All busy gnats, and every fly that hums.
> JOHN FLETCHER: *The Faithful Shepherdess*, II, ii (1610)

**Lord.** A nobleman, a peer of the realm, and formerly (and in some connections still) a ruler, a master, the holder of a manor. The word is Old English *hlāford*, 'bread keeper', i.e. the head of the household. *See also* LADY.

All members of the HOUSE OF LORDS are lords. The archbishops and bishops are LORDS SPIRITUAL, and the lay peers LORDS TEMPORAL. The word is used in COURTESY TITLES and as a title of honour to certain official personages, as the Lord Chief Justice and other judges, the Lord Mayor, Lord Advocate, Lord Rector and others. A BARON is called by his title of peerage (either a surname or territorial designation), prefixed by the title Lord, as 'Lord Dawson' or 'Lord Islington'. It may also be substituted in other than strictly ceremonial use for MARQUESS, EARL or VISCOUNT, the 'of' being dropped, 'Lord Salisbury' (for the Marquess of Salisbury), 'Lord Derby' (for the Earl of Derby) and so on. This cannot be done in the case of dukes.

**Lord Chancellor** or **Lord High Chancellor, The.** The highest judicial functionary of Great Britain, who ranks above all peers, except princes of the BLOOD and the archbishop of Canterbury. He is keeper of the GREAT SEAL, is called 'Keeper of His (or Her) Majesty's Conscience' and presides on the WOOLSACK in the HOUSE OF LORDS and in the CHANCERY Division of the Supreme Court of Judicature or HIGH COURT of Justice.

**Lord Fanny.** *See under* FANNY.

**Lord God of Hosts** or **Lord of Hosts, The.** In the Old Testament a frequently used title for JEHOVAH, no doubt arising from the belief that he led the hosts of the angels and celestial spheres.

**Lord Haw-haw.** *See* HAW-HAW.

**Lord High Constable.** *See* CONSTABLE OF ENGLAND.

**Lord High Constable of Scotland, The.** An office similar to those of England and France instituted by David I about 1147. It was conferred by Robert BRUCE in 1315 on Sir Gilbert Hay, created Earl of Erroll, in which family it was made hereditary and is still held.

**Lord High-muck-a-muck.** *See* HIGH-MUCK-A-MUCK.

**Lord it** or **lord it over, To.** To play the lord; to rule tyrannically; to domineer.

**Lord knows.** An expression used to denote one's ignorance of the matter, as: 'Lord knows why he left'.

**Lord Lieutenant.** In the mid-16th century lieutenants of the counties came into existence as crown representatives for control of the military with the power of raising the MILITIA. Lords Lieutenant appointed by the crown are now the chief executive authority in the counties, with the right of recommending the appointment of magistrates. Their extensive control over the militia ended in 1871. Until 1922 the Viceroy was the Lord Lieutenant of Ireland.

**Lord Lyon King of Arms.** The chief heraldic officer for Scotland, so called from the lion rampant in the Scottish royal arms. *See also* HERALDRY; LION IN HERALDRY.

**Lord Mayor's Day.** Originally the Lord Mayor of London was elected on the Feast of St SIMON and St JUDE (28 October), and although the election day was altered, admittance to office continued to take place on that day until 1751. From 1752, following the adoption of the GREGORIAN CALENDAR, Lord Mayor's Day became 9 November. Since 1959 the lord mayor has been sworn in at Guildhall on the second Friday in November, being presented to the Lord Chief Justice on the following Saturday. The change was made to avoid traffic congestion.

**Lord Mayor's Show, The.** The annual procession that accompanies the Lord Mayor through the City of London to the Royal Courts of Justice on the second Saturday in November. It has developed in scale over the years, and from 1453 until 1856 a river pageant was part of the proceedings. A few days later the Lord Mayor's banquet is held in the Guildhall, at which it is now customary for the Prime Minister to make a political speech. The bill for the procession and banquet is met by the Lord Mayor and the sheriffs.

**Lord of Creation, The.** Man.

> Replenish the earth, and subdue it: and have dominion over the fish of the sea, and over the fowl of the

air, and over every living thing that moveth upon the earth.
Genesis 1:28

**Lord of Flies.** *See* GOD OF FLIES.

**Lord of Hosts, The.** *See* LORD GOD OF HOSTS.

**Lord of Misrule.** *See* KING OF MISRULE.

**Lord of the Ascendant.** *See* ASCENDANT.

**Lord of the Isles, The.** A title once borne by descendants of Somerled, Lord of Argyll, who ruled the Western Isles of Scotland as VASSALS of the king of Scotland in the 14th and 15th centuries.

The Lordship of the Isles was taken over by the Scottish crown in 1540, and it subsequently became one of the titles of the PRINCE OF WALES. Scott has a poem *The Lord of the Isles* (1814).

**Lord of the manor.** The person or corporation in whom the rights of a manor are vested.

**Lord of the Rings, The.** The title of Sauron the Great, the Ruler of Middle-earth in J.R.R. Tolkien's sequel (1954–5) to *The* HOBBIT (1937). Sauron's power depended on the possession of certain rings, especially the One Ring, the Ruling Ring, the Master Ring, which he had lost many years ago and which he now sought to regain to give him strength to cover the land in a second darkness. This ring had eventually come into the hands of the HOBBIT Bilbo BAGGINS, who passed it on to FRODO Baggins, his adopted heir. If Sauron recovered it, the Hobbits would be doomed, and the only way to destroy the ring was to find the Cracks of Doom and cast it into the volcano Orodruin, the 'Fire-mountain'. The saga essentially concerns Frodo's struggles, trials and adventures to achieve this.

**Lord Peter Wimsey.** *See under* WIMSEY.

**Lord Protector of the Commonwealth, The.** Oliver Cromwell (1599–1658) was declared such in 1653. His son Richard succeeded to the title in 1658, but resigned in May 1659.

**Lord's.** The Headquarters of the Marylebone Cricket Club (MCC) and of CRICKET generally is at St John's Wood, London. The ground was opened by Thomas Lord (1757–1832) who was groundsman at the White Conduit Club, London, in 1780. In 1797 he started a cricket ground of his own on the site of what is now Dorset Square, moving the turf in 1811 to a new site near Regent's Canal, whence in 1814 he transferred to the present ground.

> I doubt if there be any scene in the world more animating or delightful than a cricket-match – I do not mean a set match at Lord's ground for money, hard money, between a certain number of gentlemen and players, as they are called.
>
> MISS MITFORD: *Our Village*, 'A Country Cricket-Match' (1832)

**Lords and ladies.** The popular name of the wild arum, *Arum maculatum*. *See also* CUCKOO FLOWERS.

**Lord's Day, The.** SUNDAY.

**Lords in Waiting, Gentlemen in Waiting** and **Grooms in Waiting.** Functionaries in the Royal Household for personal attendance upon the sovereign.

**Lord's Prayer, The.** The words in which Jesus taught his disciples to pray, beginning 'Our Father' (Matthew 6:9–13). *See also* PATERNOSTER.

**Lords Spiritual.** The bishops who have seats in the HOUSE OF LORDS.

**Lord's Supper, The.** The name given to the Holy Communion that commemorates the LAST SUPPER of Jesus with his disciples.

**Lord's Table, The.** The communion table or ALTAR.

**Lords Temporal.** The lay members of the HOUSE OF LORDS.

**As drunk as a lord.** *See under* AS.

**In the year of our Lord.** *See* ANNO DOMINI.

**House of Lords.** *See under* HOUSE.

**Law Lords.** *See under* LAW.

**Live like a lord, To.** *See under* LIVE.

**My Lord.** The correct form to use in addressing judges of the Supreme Court (usually slurred to 'M'Lud'); also the respectful form of address to bishops, noblemen under the rank of duke, lord mayors, lord provosts and the lord advocate.

**Shepherd Lord, The.** *See under* SHEPHERD.

**Lorelei.** The name of a steep rock, some 430ft (130m) high, on the right bank of the River Rhine south of Koblenz, noted for its remarkable echo. It is the traditional haunt of a SIREN who lures boatman to their death. Heinrich Heine and others have poems on it, and Max Bruch made it the subject of an opera, *Die Lorelei*, produced in 1864. Mendelssohn has an incomplete opera of the same title (1847). The name, properly Loreley and formerly Lurley, is that of the rock itself, and perhaps means 'peeping cliff'. Heine and others gave the name a romantic ring by associating it with the female forename *Lore*, English Laura.

**Loreto, The House of.** *See under* HOUSE.

**Lorrain** or **Lorraine.** *See* CLAUDE.

**Lorraine, Cross of.** *See under* CROSS.

**Lorry, It fell off the back of a.** *See under* FALL.

**Lose. Lose count, To.** To fail to take note how many there have been; to lose the running total in counting.

**Lose face, To.** To be humiliated. The expression translates Chinese *diulian*, the literal covering of the face with a fan as a sign of disgrace or humiliation.

**Lose ground, To.** To become less successful or popular; to drift away from the object aimed at.

**Lose one's bearings, To.** To be off course; to be lost; to be bewildered or perplexed.

**Lose one's bottle, To.** To LOSE ONE'S NERVE.

**Lose one's cool, To.** To LOSE ONE'S TEMPER.

**Lose one's head, To.** To become so excited or confused that one behaves irrationally.

**Lose one's heart to, To.** To fall in love with.

**Lose one's nerve, To.** To become timid or irresolute.

**Lose one's temper, To.** To become angry.

**Lose one's tongue, To.** To become tongue-tied or speechless through shyness, fear or the like.

**Lose out, To.** To be unsuccessful; to fail to gain the advantage.

**Lose sleep over, To.** To be worried about. The expression is usually found in the negative, as: 'I shan't lose any sleep over it.' Anxieties sometimes assume exaggerated importance at night and may mar one's sleep.

**Lose the day, To.** To lose the battle; to be defeated.

**Lose the thread, To.** To lose a train of thought or of an argument because of a digression, interruption, mental aberration or the like.

**What you lose on the swings you gain on the roundabouts.** *See under* WHAT.

**Loss. At a loss, To be.** *See under* AT.

**At a loss for words, To be.** *See under* AT.

**Dead loss.** *See under* DEAD.

**Lost. Lost Generation.** A name sometimes applied to the young men, especially of the cultivated upper and middle classes, who lost their lives in the First World War. Rupert Brooke (1887–1915) became their symbol. He was 27 when he died (not in battle, but of blood-poisoning).

**Lost property office.** Many languages name this more logically as the 'found property office', as French *bureau des objets trouvés*, German *Fundbüro*, Russian *byuro nakhodok*. The term makes sense, since 'found' implies a positive quality, which can be recorded and evaluated, but 'lost' a negative one, which nullifies the object's very existence.

**Lost Sunday.** Another name for SEPTUAGESIMA SUNDAY, from its having no special name.

**Lost Tribes of Israel, The.** The term applied to the ten tribes of ISRAEL who were carried away from north Palestine (721 BC) into Assyria about 140 years before the BABYLONIAN CAPTIVITY (586 BC) exiled the tribes of JUDAH. After breaking with Judah under Jeroboam to form the northern kingdom of Israel, the tribes of Reuben, Simeon, Issachar, Zebulun, Dan, Naphtali, Gad, Asher, Ephraim and Manasseh were carried away (2 Kings 17:6, 18:11), and are still believed to be in the land of their exile. Their disappearance has caused much speculation, especially among those who look forward to a restoration of the Hebrews as foretold in the OLD TESTAMENT. In 1649, John Sadler suggested that the English were of Israelitish origin. This theory was expanded by Richard Brothers, the half-crazy enthusiast who declared himself Prince of the Hebrews and Ruler of the World (1792), and has since been developed by others. The British Israelite theory is still held by some without any serious supporting evidence. *See also* TWELVE TRIBES OF ISRAEL.

**Home of lost causes, The.** *See under* HOME.

**It got lost in the wash.** *See under* WASH.

**Lot. Bad lot.** *See under* LOT.

**Have a lot on one's plate, To.** To have much to do or worry about.

**Job lot.** *See under* JOB.

**Scot and lot.** *See under* SCOT.

**Throw in one's lot with someone, To.** *See under* THROW.

**Whale of a lot, A.** *See under* WHALE.

**Lot and his wife.** Lot journeys out of Egypt with ABRAHAM and settles near SODOM AND GOMORRAH. When God decides to destroy these 'cities of the plain' for their wickedness, he warns Lot to leave and not look back. Lot's wife does so, however, and is turned into a pillar of salt. The story, in Genesis 13 and 19, gives neither the name of Lot's wife nor those of his two daughters, who later seduce him when he is drunk.

**Lothario, A gay.** *See under* GAY.

**Lothian.** A region of Scotland, which traditionally takes its name from King Lot, or Lothus Llew, the brother-in-law of King ARTHUR and father of MODRED. It is now divided administratively into East Lothian, Midlothian and West Lothian. *See also* HEART OF MIDLOTHIAN.

**Lotophagi.** *See* LOTUS-EATERS.

**Lots, To cast.** *See under* CAST.

**Lotus.** A name given to many plants. For example, by the Egyptians to various species of water lily, by the Hindus and Chinese to the Nelumbo (a water bean), their 'sacred lotus', and by the Greeks to *Zizyphus lotus*, probably the jujube tree, a North African shrub of the order *Rhamnaceae*, the fruit of which was used for food.

According to MOHAMMED a lotus tree stands in the seventh heaven, on the right hand of the throne of God, and the Egyptians pictured the creator springing from the heart of a lotus flower. Iamblichus says the leaves and fruit of the lotus tree, being round, represent 'the motion of intellect', while its towering up through mud symbolizes the eminency of divine intellect over matter. The deity sitting on it implies his intellectual sovereignty.

The classic myth is that Lotis, a daughter of NEPTUNE fleeing from PRIAPUS, was changed into a tree, called Lotus after her. Another story is that Dryope of Oechalia and her infant son

Amphisus were each changed into a lotus.

**Lotus-eaters** or **Lotophagi.** In Homeric legend a people who ate of the lotus tree, the effect of which was to make them forget their friends and homes and lose all desire of returning to their native country, their only wish being to live in idleness in Lotus-land (*Odyssey*, xi). Hence a lotus-eater is one living in ease and luxury. One of Tennyson's greatest poems is 'The Lotos-Eaters' (1833).

**Lotus position.** In yoga a seated cross-legged position, so named for the leaf of the lotus tree, which, as long as it rests on the surface of the water, represents detachment.

**Louis. Louis le Hutin.** Louis X of France (1289–1316) was so called. His nickname means 'the stubborn', an epithet that he gained after his quarrel with the archbishop of Lyon, who was arrested. His father's treasurer, Enguerrand de Marigny (*c.*1260–1315), was hanged and his first wife, Margaret of Burgundy (*c.*1290–1315), was executed for alleged adultery.

**St Louis.** Louis IX of France (1214–70) is usually represented as holding Christ's crown of thorns and the cross, but sometimes he is pictured with a pilgrim's staff and sometimes with the standard of the cross, the allusion in all cases being to the CRUSADES. He was canonized in 1297, his feast-day being 25 August. He is considered a saint offering special protection to France.

**Louisette.** *See* GUILLOTINE.

**Louisiana.** The American state was so named in 1682 as a compliment to Louis XIV of France. The name was originally applied to the French possessions in the Mississippi valley.

**Louisiana Purchase, The.** The acquisition by the US government in 1803 of the French territory of Louisiana for the sum of about $15 million. Some 828,000 square miles (2,144,500 sq km), between the Mississippi and the Rocky Mountains, were thus obtained.

**Lounge lizard.** A popular phrase in the 1920s to describe a young man, a gigolo, who spent his time, or often made his living, by dancing and waiting upon rich women, typically in the lounge of a grand hotel. A lizard is colourful, reptilian, and 'suns' itself as if lazily lounging.

**Lourdes.** A centre of pilgrimage in the southwest of France. In 1858 Bernadette Soubirous (1844–79), a simple peasant girl, claimed that the Virgin Mary had appeared to her on 18 occasions. Investigations failed to shake her story, and a spring with miraculous healing properties that appeared at the same time began to draw invalids from all over the world. The pilgrimage received ecclesiastical recognition in 1862 and Bernadette was canonized in 1933. There is little doubt that some visitors benefit by bathing in the mineral springs at Lourdes, and by drinking the spring water there, but such treatment has become popularly confused with the healing stories.

**Louts, Lager.** *See under* LAGER.

**Louvre.** The former royal palace of the French kings in Paris. Dagobert (605–639) is said to have built a hunting seat there, but the present buildings were begun by Francis I (r.1515–47) in 1541. Since the French Revolution, the greater part of the Louvre has been used for the national museum and art gallery.

**Love.** The word is from Old English *lufu*, connected with Sanskrit *lubh*, 'to desire', and Latin *lubere*, 'to please'.

In the sense 'nil score in tennis', as 'forty-love' (40–0), 'love-all' (0–0), love probably comes from the phrase 'to play for love', meaning to play for the love of the game, i.e. without stakes. It is not likely to be a corruption of French *l'œuf*, 'the egg', as sometimes stated, on the grounds that a figure 0 resembles an egg. In CRICKET, however, 'out for a duck', said of a batsman dismissed without having scored any runs, derives from DUCK'S EGG, from the similarity between the egg and a large figure 0 on the scoreboard.

**Love apple.** The tomato, which the Spaniards introduced to Europe from South America. It was said to have aphrodisiac properties, but this may have in part resulted from its name, which in its English form translates French *pomme d'amour*, literally 'apple of love'. The red skin of the tomato became associated with red as the colour of passion, while the apple itself has long played a traditional role in love rituals. An old German name for the tomato, *Liebesapfel*, is similar.

**Lovebird.** A small African parrot of the genus *Agapornis*, so named for its remarkable display of affection for its mate. An affectionate human couple are also sometimes called lovebirds.

**Lovebite.** A red mark on the skin caused by biting or sucking during sexual play.

**Love child.** An illegitimate child.

**Love feast.** *See* AGAPE.

**Love handles.** Bulges of fat either side of the waist, so called because they afford a 'hold' to a lover during an embrace.

**Love in a cottage.** A marriage for love without sufficient means to maintain one's social status. *See also* WHEN POVERTY COMES IN AT THE DOOR, LOVE FLIES OUT AT THE WINDOW.

> Love in a hut, with water and a crust,
> Is – Love, forgive us! – cinders, ashes, dust;
> Love in a palace is perhaps at last
> More grievous torment than a hermit's fast.
> JOHN KEATS: *Lamia*, Pt II, i (1819)

**Love-in-a-mist.** The flower *Nigella damascena*, also called devil-in-a-bush and love-in-a-puzzle.

**Love-in-idleness.** The HEARTSEASE or wild pansy, *Viola tricolor*. Fable has it that it was originally white, but was changed to purple by CUPID.

> Yet mark'd I where the bolt of Cupid fell:
> It fell upon a little western flower.
> Before milk-white, now purple with love's wound,
> And maidens call it, Love-in-idleness.
> SHAKESPEARE: *A Midsummer Night's Dream*, II, i (1595)

**Love is blind.** Lovers cannot see each other's weaknesses and shortcomings. *See also* CUPID.

**Love knot.** A bow, usually fashioned of ribbon, that symbolizes the love between two lovers.

**Love-lies-bleeding.** The red AMARANTH, *Amaranthus caudatus*, also known as the tassel flower, from its hanging panicles of small crimson flowers.

**Lovelock.** A small curl worn by women, fastened to the temples, also called a bow-catcher. At the end of the 16th century the lovelock was a long lock of hair hanging in front of the shoulders, curled and decorated with bows and ribbons.

**Lovelorn.** Pining from unrequited love.

**Love match.** An engagement or marriage made for love alone and no other considerations.

**Love me, love my dog.** If you love someone, you must love all that belongs to them. St BERNARD quotes this proverb in Latin, *Qui me amat, amat et canem meum.*

**Love's girdle.** CESTUS.

**Love spoons.** The giving of elaborately carved love spoons by a lover to his lady as a token during courtship was common in 18th-century Wales and later.

**Loving** or **grace cup.** A large cup, tankard or goblet passed round from guest to guest at formal banquets. Agnes Strickland (1786–1874) says that Margaret Atheling, wife of Malcolm Canmore, in order to induce the Scots to remain for grace, devised the grace cup, which was filled with the choicest wine and of which each guest was allowed to drink *ad libitum*, after grace had been said.

The monks took over the WASSAIL bowl of their heathen predecessors and called it *poculum caritatis*, or the loving cup. At the Lord Mayor's or City livery companies' banquets the loving cup is a silver bowl with two handles, a napkin being tied to one of them. Two people stand up, one to drink and the other to defend the drinker. Having taken his draught, the first wipes the cup with the napkin and passes it to his 'defender', when the next person rises up to defend the new drinker and so on.

At the universities of Oxford and Cambridge, the term 'grace cup' is more general. The name is also applied to a strong brew of beer flavoured with lemon peel, nutmeg and sugar, and very brown toast.

**Abode of Love, The.** *See* AGAPEMONE.

**Calf love.** *See under* CALF.

**Court of love.** *See under* COURT.

**Cupboard love.** *See under* CUPBOARD.

**Fall in love.** *See under* FALL.

**Family of Love, The.** *See* FAMILISTS.

**Free love.** *See under* FREE.

**God of Love, The.** *See under* GOD.

**Labour of love, A.** *See under* LABOUR.

**Light o'love.** *See under* LIGHT.

**Make love, To.** Originally, to court. Now, to engage in sexual intercourse.

> Then I solemnly declare, said the lady, blushing—you have been making love to me all this while.
> LAURENCE STERNE: *A Sentimental Journey* (1768)

**Not for love or money.** Not under any circumstances.

**Platonic love.** *See under* PLATO.

**Queen of love, The.** *See under* QUEEN.

**There is no love lost between us.** We dislike each other. Formerly the phrase was used in exactly the opposite sense: it was all love between us, and none of it went elsewhere.

**Tug of love.** *See under* TUG.

**When poverty comes in at the door, love flies out at the window.** *See under* WHEN.

**Lovelace.** A LIBERTINE; a lothario. The name is taken from the principal male character in Samuel Richardson's *Clarissa, or the History of a Young Lady* (1748). He is a selfish voluptuary, a man of fashion, whose sole ambition is to seduce young women.

**Lovell, the Dog.** *See* RAT, CAT AND DOG.

**Lovers' acronyms.** Love letters between couples or spouses have long carried coded messages of passion, in particular when the man is away from home on military service. The following are some of the better-known examples, mostly based on place-names:

> BOLTOP: Better on lips than on paper (of a kiss)
> BURMA: Be undressed ready, my angel
> EGYPT: Eager to grab your pretty tits
> HOLLAND: Hope our love lasts and never dies
> ITALY: I trust and love you
> NORWICH: (K)nickers off ready when I come home
> SWALK: Sealed with a loving kiss

**Low. Low Church.** The essentially Protestant section of the CHURCH OF ENGLAND, which gives a relatively low place to the value of the priesthood and the sacraments; it has more in common with NONCONFORMIST than Roman Catholic teaching. The name contrasts with HIGH CHURCH.

**Low comedy.** Comedy close to farce.

**Low Countries, The.** The Netherlands, Belgium and Luxembourg, the first of which has a precisely equivalent name.

**Low-down, The.** Inside information. The phrase implies that it was once thought mean or 'low down' to give such information.

**Lower case.** The printer's name for the small letters of a FONT or fount of type, as opposed to the capitals. In a typesetter's 'case' these were originally on a lower level than the others. *See also* UPPER CASE.

**Lower deck.** In the Royal Navy the rank and file of the ship's company as distinct from the officers. In the ships of former days the lower deck, above the orlop, was the lowest of the continuous gun decks, where the crew had their messes and slung their hammocks.

**Lower Empire.** The later Roman, especially the Western Empire, from about the time of the foundation of the Eastern Empire in 330 to the fall of Constantinople in 1453.

**Lower House, The.** The HOUSE OF COMMONS, a term in use in the 15th century; in the USA, the HOUSE OF REPRESENTATIVES.

**Low German.** *See* HIGH GERMAN.

**Low Latin.** Any form of Latin that differs from CLASSICAL LATIN, such as VULGAR LATIN or MEDIEVAL LATIN.

**Low life.** The life of the lower levels of society. *See also* HIGH LIFE.

**Lowlight.** A humorous term for the opposite of a HIGHLIGHT, i.e. a boring or dull period. To a hair stylist, lowlights are dark tints in the hair produced by dyeing.

**Low Mass.** In the Western Church, MASS said by the celebrant without the assistance of other clergy. No part of the service is sung.

**Low Sunday.** The Sunday next after EASTER. It is probably so called by contrast with the 'high' feast of Easter Day. *See also* QUASIMODO SUNDAY.

**High and low.** *See under* HIGH.

**Keep a low profile, To.** To avoid publicity deliberately; to choose to LIE LOW.

**Lay someone low, To.** *See under* LAY.

**Lie low, To.** *See under* LIE.

**Loyal.** The Loyal North Lancashire Regiment was so called in 1793, the only British regiment given this designation.

**Loyal Toast, The.** This time-honoured toast to the monarch is normally drunk while standing, but it is the Royal Navy's privilege to drink it sitting. The story is that this custom arose when George IV (or William IV), when acknowledging the toast in a ship, bumped his head on a beam as he stood up. However apocryphal such stories may be, it is probably due to the difficulty of standing upright between decks in the old wooden warships.

**Empire Loyalist.** *See* UNITED EMPIRE LOYALISTS.

**Loyola, St Ignatius.** *See under* IGNATIUS.

**LS.** *See* LOCUS SIGILLI.

**LSD.** The pre-decimal abbreviation for British money, from Latin *libra*, 'pound', *solidus*, 'shilling' and *denarius*, 'penny'.

LSD also stands for lysergic acid diethylamide 25, a powerful drug, colloquially known as acid, that induces hallucinations.

**Luce, Flower de.** A corruption of FLEUR-DE-LIS.

**Lucian.** The personification of the follies and vices of the age. Such was Lucian, the chief character in the GOLDEN ASS of Apuleius (2nd century AD).

**Lucifer** (Latin, 'light-bearer'). The name was first applied logically to Jesus (as 'day star', 2 Peter 1:19) as well as to VENUS, the MORNING STAR. When Venus follows the sun and is an evening star, she is called HESPERUS.

ISAIAH applied the epithet 'day star' to the king of Babylon who proudly boasted he would ascend to the heavens and make himself equal to God, but who was fated to be cast down to the uttermost recesses of the pit. This epithet was translated into 'Lucifer':

> How art thou fallen from heaven, O Lucifer, son of the morning!
> Isaiah 14:12

St JEROME and other Fathers applied the name to Satan. Hence poets write that Satan, before he was driven out of heaven for his pride, was called Lucifer.

**Luciferians.** A 4th-century sect, so called from their leader, Lucifer, bishop of Cagliari in Sardinia. They resisted all conciliation with repentant ARIANS.

**Lucifer match** or **Lucifer.** A match. The friction match was invented by John Walker (*c*.1781–1859) in 1826 and at first called a 'friction light'. The invention was copied by Samuel Jones of the Strand and sold as the 'Lucifer' (*c*.1829). The term 'match' was taken over from the name given to the spill used as secondary tinder in the days of the tinderbox. *See also* CONGREVES; LOCO-FOCO; PROMETHEAN; SAFETY MATCHES.

**Lucius.** One of the mythical kings of Britain, the son of Coillus, and fabled as the first Christian British king, according to Geoffrey of Monmouth.

**Luck** (Middle Dutch *luc*, related to modern German *Glück*). Accidental good fortune.

**Luck in odd numbers.** It was an ancient fancy that odd numbers were lucky. According to the PYTHAGOREAN SYSTEM nine represents the deity. A major chord consists of a fundamental or tonic, its major third and its fifth. Because the odd numbers are the fundamental notes of nature, the last being the deity, it is understandable how they came to be considered the great or lucky numbers.

The odd numbers 1, 3, 5, 7, 9 seem to play a far more important part than the even numbers. VIRGIL (*Eclogues*, viii (1st century BC)) says

*Numero deus impare gaudet* ('the god delights in odd numbers'). THREE indicates the 'beginning, middle and the end'. The Godhead has three persons, while in classical mythology HECATE had threefold power, JOVE's symbol was a triple thunderbolt, NEPTUNE's a sea trident, PLUTO's a three-headed dog, and there were three Horae. There are SEVEN notes, seven days a week, NINE planets, nine orders of ANGELS, thirteen lunar months, or 365 days a year and so on, as well as FIVE senses, five fingers, five toes, five continents and the like. *See also* DIAPASON; NUMBERS.

**Luck of Eden Hall, The.** An enamelled drinking glass (probably made in Venice in the 10th century) in the possession of the Musgrave family at Eden Hall near Penrith, Cumbria, and said to have fortune-bringing properties. The story is that it was taken from St Cuthbert's well in the garden where it was left by the fairies while they danced. The superstition is:

If that glass should break or fall,
Farewell the luck of Eden Hall.

The estate was broken up in 1920, and the glass is now in the Victoria and Albert Museum, London.

**Luck of the draw, The.** The situation that one finds oneself in, like it or not. The allusion is to a card drawn 'blind' from a pack.

**Lucky break.** A sudden favourable opportunity. The allusion is to the game of snooker, in which each player's turn is called a break, because it breaks the game up into stages.

**Lucky dip.** A tub or other container in which are placed various articles covered with sawdust or something similar, popular at fêtes and children's parties. The visitors 'dip' and draw out a prize or present at random.

**Lucky stone, A.** A stone with a natural hole through it. John Aubrey (1697) writes that flints with holes in them were hung on a horse or in its stall as a preservative against being hag-ridden.

**Lucky you.** I envy you.

**As luck would have it.** *See under* AS.

**Beginner's luck.** *See under* BEGIN.

**Best of British luck, The.** *See under* BEST.

**Born under a lucky** or **unlucky planet, To be.** *See under* BORN.

**Chance one's luck, To.** *See under* CHANCE.

**Devil's luck.** *See under* DEVIL.

**Down on one's luck.** *See under* DOWN.

**Just my luck.** *See under* JUST.

**Lady Luck.** *See under* LADY.

**No such luck.** *See under* NO.

**Pot luck.** *See under* POT.

**Push one's luck, To.** *See under* PUSH.

**Seven Gods of Luck, The.** *See under* SEVEN.

**Spitting for luck.** *See under* SPIT.

**Strike lucky, To.** *See* STRIKE IT RICH.

**Try one's luck, To.** *See under* TRY.

**Wish me luck.** *See under* WISH.

**With luck.** If all goes well.

**Worse luck.** *See under* WORSE.

**Lucretia.** In Roman legend the beautiful and virtuous wife of the nobleman Lucius Tarquinius Collatinus. She is raped by Sextus Tarquinius, son of Lucius Tarquinius Superbus, tyrant of Rome, and stabs herself after exacting an oath of vengeance against the Tarquins from her father and husband. The event, traditionally dated 509 BC, marks the end of the Roman monarchy and the foundation of the Republic. Shakespeare's *The Rape of Lucrece* was published in 1594.

**Lucullus sups with Lucullus.** Said of a glutton who gourmandizes alone. Lucius Lucullus (*c*.117–56 BC) was a successful Roman military leader and administrator whose latter years were given over to rich and elegant living. On one occasion a superb supper was prepared, and when asked who were to be his guests, he replied: 'Lucullus will sup tonight with Lucullus.' He was essentially a man of cultural tastes and more of a gourmet than a GOURMAND.

**Lucus a non lucendo.** An etymological contradiction. The Latin phrase was formerly used by philologists who explained words by deriving them from their opposites. It means literally 'a grove (so called) from not producing light', from *lucus*, 'grove' and *lucere*, 'to shine', 'to be light'. It was the Roman grammarian Honoratus Maurus (*fl.* late 4th century AD) who provided this famous etymology. In the same way *ludus*, 'school', where pupils work, may be said to come from *ludere*, 'to play', and English 'linen' from 'lining', because it is not used for linings.

**Lucy. Lucy Stoner.** An American colloquialism for a married woman who keeps her maiden name, after Lucy Stone (1818–93), a US SUFFRAGETTE. Her married name was Blackwell.

**St Lucy.** Patron saint for those afflicted in the eyes. She is said to have lived in Syracuse and to have suffered martyrdom there *c*.304. One legend relates that a nobleman wanted to marry her for the beauty of her eyes, so she tore them out and gave them to him, saying: 'Now let me live to God.' She is accordingly represented in art carrying a palm branch and a dish with two eyes on it.

**Lud.** A mythical king of Britain. According to Geoffrey of Monmouth, he was the beautifier of London who was buried by LUDGATE, named after him. It is also suggested that the name is that of a Celtic river-god.

**Ludgate.** One of the former western gates of the City of London, first mentioned in the 12th century. It stood halfway up Ludgate Hill, was rebuilt after extensive damage in 1586 and demolished 1760–62. It was used as a prison for several centuries. The statues of LUD and his two sons that once adorned the gate are now in the entrance of St Dunstan's School. The name probably derives from Old English *ludgeat*, 'postern', 'back gate'.

**General Lud.** *See* LUDDITES.

**Luddites.** The name given to the machine-breaking rioters in the manufacturing districts of Nottinghamshire, Lancashire, Cheshire and Yorkshire in 1811–16. The textile workers blamed the new machinery for their unemployment and suffering. They were called Luddites after their legendary leader, Ned Ludd, and the leadership of such rioters was often attributed to 'General Ludd'. *See also* SWING, CAPTAIN.

**Ludo** (Latin, 'I play'). A simple and popular board game, resembling a horse race. Each player has four counters of the same colour and on throwing the dice moves the given number of spaces along the squares of a 'course' until the centre is reached. If a counter lands on a square occupied by another player, that player's counter goes back to the start. If it lands on a square occupied by the player's own counter, it simply stays there until the next move. As in many games of this type, a throw of six on the dice brings another throw.

**Lughnasa.** In Irish mythology the feast of the pagan sun-god Lugh, who is said to have introduced it to commemorate his foster mother Tailtu. It was one of the major pre-Christian festivals and was essentially an agrarian feast celebrating the harvest. Christianity took it over as LAMMAS DAY. The name survives in modern Irish for the name of the month of August, Lúnasa. Brian Friel's highly acclaimed play *Dancing at Lughnasa* (1990) is a tender evocation of his childhood in rural Ireland in the 1930s.

**Luke. St Luke.** The patron saint of artists and physicians. Tradition says he painted a portrait of the Virgin Mary, and Colossians 4:14 states that he was a physician. His day is 18 October.

**St Luke's summer.** The latter end of autumn. *See also* SUMMER.

**Lumber.** Formerly a pawnbroker's shop, from LOMBARD. Thus Lady Murray (*Lives of the Baillies* (1749)) writes: 'They put all the little plate they had in the lumber, which is pawning it, till the ships come home.'

From its use as applied to old broken boards and bits of wood, the word was extended to mean timber sawn and split, especially when the trees have been felled and sawn on the spot.

**Lumberjack.** A person whose work is felling trees.

**Lumber-jacket.** A bright checked jacket such as a LUMBERJACK wears. Hence any similar jacket.

**Lumber-room.** A room in a house where unused or useless household articles are stored away.

> Often and often Nicholas had pictured to himself what the lumber-room might be like, that region that was so carefully sealed from youthful eyes and concerning which no questions were ever answered. It came up to his expectations.
>
> SAKI (H.H. MUNRO): *Beasts and Super-Beasts*, 'The Lumber-Room' (1914)

**Luminary of the English Church, The.** Bishop Bartholomew of Exeter (1161–84), a Breton, was so called by Pope Alexander III (r.1159–81). He was one of the five bishops sent to Sens with Henry II's appeal to the pope, after Archbishop Becket's flight to France in 1164. He conscientiously used his learning and abilities for the good of the church.

**Lump. Like it or lump it.** *See under* LIKE.

**Lunar. Lunar month.** From new moon to new moon, i.e. the time taken by the moon to revolve round the earth, about 29½ days. Popularly, the lunar month is 28 days. In the JEWISH and MUSLIM CALENDARS the lunar month commences at sunset on the day when the new moon is first seen after sunset and varies in length from 29 to 30 days.

**Lunar year.** Twelve lunar months, i.e. about 354⅓ days.

**Lunatics.** Literally, moon-struck persons. The Romans believed that the mind was affected by the moon and that lunatics grew more and more frenzied as the moon increased to its full (Latin *luna*, 'moon').

**Lunatic fringe, The.** The small section of the community who follow and originate extremist ideas, and whose behaviour is sometimes eccentric by conventional standards, but whose influence on the majority is mostly minimal. *See also* LOONY LEFT *under* LOONY.

**Lundi, St.** *See* ST MONDAY *under* MONDAY.

**Lung, Iron.** *See under* IRON.

**Lunn, Sally.** *See under* SALLY.

**Lupercal, The.** In ancient Rome the spot where ROMULUS and Remus were suckled by the wolf (Latin *lupus*). An annual festival, the Lupercalia, was held there on 15 February, in honour of Lupercus the Lycaean PAN (so called because he protected the flocks from wolves). The name Lupercal is sometimes, inaccurately, used for the Lupercalia. It was on one of these occasions that Antony thrice offered Julius CAESAR the crown, but he refused, saying: 'JUPITER alone is king of Rome.'

> You all did see that on the Lupercal,
> I thrice presented him a kingly crown,
> Which he did thrice refuse.
>
> SHAKESPEARE: *Julius Caesar*, III, ii (1599)

**Lurch, To leave in the.** *See under* LEAVE.

**Lush.** Beer and other intoxicating drinks. A word of uncertain origin, said by some to be derived from the name of a London brewer called Lushington. Up to about 1895, there was a convivial society of actors called the 'City of Lushington', which met in the Harp Tavern, Russell Street, and claimed to be 150 years old. 'Lush' is also American slang for an alcoholic.

**Lusiads, The.** The Portuguese national epic, written by Luis de Camoëns (1524–80) and published in 1572. It relates the stories of illustrious actions of the Lusians or Portuguese, and primarily the exploits of Vasco da Gama and his comrades in their 'discovery of India' (1497–9). The intervention of VENUS and BACCHUS and other classical deities makes it far more than the narrative of a voyage. It has been said that Camoëns did for the Portuguese language what Dante did for Italian and Chaucer for English. *See also* LUSUS.

**Lustral.** Properly, pertaining to the LUSTRUM, hence purificatory, as lustral water, the water used in Christian as well as many pagan rites for asperging worshippers. In Rome the priest used a small OLIVE or LAUREL branch for sprinkling infants and the people.

**Lustrum** (Latin *lustrare*, 'to purify'). In ancient Rome the purificatory sacrifice made by the censors for the people once in five years, after the census had been taken. Hence the word for a period of five years.

**Lusus.** Pliny writes that Lusus was the companion of BACCHUS in his travels and settled a colony in Portugal. As a result, the country was called Lusitania and the inhabitants Lusians, 'sons of Lusus'. The origin of the name is uncertain. It has been associated by some with the Celtic god Lug.

**Lute, A rift in the.** *See* RIFT.

**Lutetia** (Latin *lutum*, 'mud'). The ancient name of PARIS, which, in Roman times, was a collection of mud hovels. CAESAR called it *Lutetia Parisiorum* ('mud town of the Parisii'), which gives the present name Paris.

**Lutine bell.** HMS *Lutine*, a captured French warship, recommissioned by the British, left Yarmouth for Holland on 9 October 1799 with bullion and specie to the value of some £500,000. The same night she was wrecked on a sandbank off the Zuyder Zee with the loss of every soul on board save one, who died as soon as rescued. It was a black day for LLOYD'S underwriters. In 1858 some £50,000 was salvaged, as well as the *Lutine*'s bell and rudder, among other things. The latter was made into the official chair for Lloyd's chairman and a secretary's desk. The bell was hung at Lloyd's and for many years was rung once whenever a total wreck was reported, and twice for an overdue ship. It is now rung on ceremonious occasions and when important announcements are to be made to the market, with two strokes for good news and one for bad. It was rung in 1963 to signal the death of President Kennedy and in 1965 for that of Sir Winston Churchill, who was an honorary member of Lloyd's.

**Luxury. Live in the lap of luxury.** *See under* LIVE.

**LXX.** A common abbreviation for the SEPTUAGINT, from the Roman numeral 70.

**Lycanthropy.** The insanity afflicting those who imagine themselves to be some kind of animal and exhibit the tastes, voice and so on of that animal. In ancient times the name was given to those who imagined themselves to be wolves (Greek *lukos*, 'wolf', and *anthropos*, 'man').

The WEREWOLF has sometimes been called a lycanthrope, and the word lycanthropy was sometimes applied to the form of WITCHCRAFT by which witches transformed themselves into wolves.

**Lycaon.** In classical mythology a king of ARCADIA, who, desirous of testing the divine knowledge of JOVE, served up human flesh on his table, for which the god changed him into a wolf. His daughter, CALLISTO, was changed into the constellation the Bear, which is sometimes called Lycaonis Arctos.

**Lych gate.** *See* LICH GATE.

**Lycopodium.** A genus of perennial plants consisting of the club mosses, so called from their fanciful resemblance to a wolf's foot (Greek *lukos*, 'wolf', and *pous, podos*, 'foot'). The powder from the spore cases of some of these is used in surgery as an absorbent and also (as it is highly inflammable) for stage lighting. *See also* LIMELIGHT.

**Lycurgus.** The impious king of Thrace in Greek legend who drove away the worshippers of Dionysus (BACCHUS) and was then driven mad by this god. He thought his son was a tree and killed him with an axe, then lopped off his own legs, thinking they were branches.

**Lyddite.** A high explosive composed of picric acid and GUNCOTTON. It is so called from Lydd in Kent, where it was first tested on the artillery ranges in 1888.

**Lydford law.** Punish first and try afterwards. Lydford was one of the four Saxon boroughs of Devon, and its Norman castle became the prison of the STANNARIES. Offenders were imprisoned in a dungeon so loathsome and dreary that they frequently died before they could be brought for trial. *See also* LYNCH LAW.

**Lydia.** In the New Testament, a 'seller of purple' (Acts 16:14) who is converted when she hears PAUL preach. She is traditionally regarded as the first Christian convert in Europe.

**Lyke-wake.** *See* LICH-WAKE.

**Lynceus.** One of the ARGONAUTS. His sight was so

keen that he could see through the earth and distinguish objects that were miles off. It was also the name of the husband of HYPERMNESTRA. *See also* DANAIDES.

**Lynch law.** Mob law. Law administered by private individuals and followed by summary execution. The origin of the term is uncertain. None of the suggested derivations, from James Lynch, a 15th-century mayor of Galway in Ireland, or Charles Lynch (1736–96) of Virginia, has been substantiated. From the 18th century the practice was particularly associated with the more lawless districts of the USA. *See also* LYDFORD LAW.

**Lynx.** The animal proverbial for its piercing eyesight is a fabulous beast, half-dog and half-panther, but not like either in character. The cat-like animal now called a lynx is not remarkable for its sharp sight. *See also* LYNCEUS.

**Lyon. Lyon King of Arms, Lord.** *See under* LORD.

**William the Lyon.** *See under* WILLIAM.

**Lyonesse.** A rich tract of land fabled to stretch between Land's End and the Scilly Isles on which stood the City of Lions and some 140 churches. King ARTHUR came from this mythical country. 'That sweet land of Lyonesse' was, according to Edmund Spenser (*The Faerie Queene* (1590, 1596)), the birthplace of TRISTRAM, and, according to Tennyson, the scene of Arthur's death. Its name has been associated with the Breton town of St-Pol-de-Léon, known to the Romans as Castellum Leonense, 'Leo's castle'.

**Lyons, The Butcher of.** *See under* BUTCHER.

**Lyre.** The most ancient of all stringed instruments. That of Terpander and Olympus had only three strings, the Scythian lyre had five, that of Simonides had eight, and that of Timotheus had twelve. It was played either with the fingers or with a plectrum. The lyre is called by poets a 'shell', because the cords of the lyre used by ORPHEUS, AMPHION and APOLLO were stretched on the shell of a tortoise. HERCULES used boxwood. In addition to these:

Amphion built Thebes with the music of his lyre

Arion charmed the dolphins by the music of his lyre, and when the bard threw himself into the sea, one of them carried him safely to Taenarus

Hercules was taught music by Linus; one day, being reproved, the strong man broke the head of his master with his own lyre

Orpheus charmed savage beasts, and even the infernal gods, with the music of his lyre; mountains moved to hear his song and rivers ceased to flow

**Lysenkoism.** *See* MICHURINISM.

**Lysistrata.** In Aristophanes' play of this name (4th century BC) an Athenian woman who, exasperated at the futility of the war with Sparta, organizes the women of both cities to refuse to have sexual relations with any of the men until the war is ended.

# M

**M.** The thirteenth letter of the English alphabet, the twelfth of the ancient Roman, and the twentieth of the FUTHORC. M in the Phoenician character represented the wavy appearance of water, and in Hebrew it is called *mem* ('water'). The Egyptian HIEROGLYPHIC represented the owl. In English M is always sounded, except in words from Greek in which it is followed by n, as MNEMONIC and MNEMOSYNE (the Greek goddess of memory).

In Roman numerals M stands for 1000 (Latin *mille*), so that MCMXCVIII = 1998 (one thousand, nine hundred and ninety-eight).

Persons convicted of manslaughter and admitted to BENEFIT OF CLERGY used to be branded with an M on the ball of the left thumb.

**M to represent the human face.** Add two dots for the eyes, thus, •M•. If these dots are taken as Os, the result is OMO, which can be understood as Latin *homo*, 'man'.

**What is your name? N or M.** *See* N OR M.

**M'.** The first letter of certain Celtic surnames, such as M'Cabe, M'Ian, M'Mahon, represents Mac ('son') and should be pronounced as such.

**Mab** (perhaps Welsh *maban*, 'baby'). The 'fairies' midwife', employed by the fairies as midwife to deliver man's brain of dreams. Thus when Romeo says, 'I dreamed a dream tonight,' Mercutio replies: 'Oh, then, I see Queen Mab hath been with you.' When Mab is called 'queen' it does not mean sovereign, for TITANIA as wife of King OBERON was queen of the fairies, but simply 'female' (Old English *cwēn*, modern *quean*).

Imaginative descriptions of Mab are given by Shakespeare (*Romeo and Juliet*, I, iv (1594)), by Ben Jonson, by Robert Herrick and by Michael Drayton in *Nymphidia* (1627).

**Mabinogion.** A collection of eleven medieval Celtic stories of which the Four Branches of the Mabinogi are the most outstanding. Originally they were probably essentially concerned with the life and death of Pryderi, but a considerable amount of additional material has complicated the structure. The tales are basically Welsh mythology and folklore together with ARTHURIAN ROMANCE. The title 'Mabinogion' was given by Lady Charlotte Guest to her translations of these stories (1838–49), but this only properly applies to the Four Branches (*Pwyll*, *Branwen*, *Manawydan* and *Math*) and not the remainder. The last three stories, 'The Lady of the Fountain', 'Peredur' and 'Geraint, son of Erbin', show marked Norman-French influence, often attributed to Chrétien de Troyes, but it is now thought that his material may have derived from Welsh sources.

*Mabinogi* is derived from *mab*, 'youth', and was applied to a 'tale of youth', then to any 'tale'. Lady Guest's translation long held the field, but a better and more complete English version is that of Gwyn Jones and Thomas Jones (1948).

**Macabre, Danse.** *See* DANCE OF DEATH.

**Macadamization.** A method of road-making introduced after 1810 by John L. McAdam (1756–1836), consisting of layers of broken stones of nearly uniform size, each being separately crushed into position by traffic or (later) by a heavy roller.

**Macaire.** A French CHANSON DE GESTE of the 12th century. Macaire was the name of the murderer of Aubry de Montdidier, and he was brought to justice by the sagacity of AUBRY'S DOG. The story was transferred to the 14th century in another version and a 15th-century mural painting of the legend in the chateau of Montargis gave rise to Aubry's dog being called the 'dog of Montargis'.

**Macaroni.** A dandy who affects foreign manners and style. The word is derived from the Macaroni CLUB, instituted in London about 1760 by a set of flashy men who had travelled in Italy and who introduced at ALMACK's subscription table the new-fangled Italian food, macaroni. The Macaronis were exquisite fops, vicious, insolent, fond of gambling, drinking and duelling, and they became the curse of VAUXHALL GARDENS. *See also* MOHOCKS.

An American regiment raised in Maryland during the War of Independence was called The Macaronies from its showy uniform. *See also* YANKEE DOODLE.

**Macaronic Latin.** DOG LATIN. From Italian dialect *maccarone*, 'macaroni', a mixture of coarse meal, eggs and cheese.

**Macaronic verse.** Verses in which foreign words are ludicrously distorted and jumbled together, as in Richard Porson's lines on the threatened invasion of England by NAPOLEON BONAPARTE or J.A. Morgan's 'translation' of Canning's *The Elderly Gentleman*, the first two verses of which are:

Prope ripam fluvii solus
A senex silently sat
Super capitum ecce his wig
Et wig super, ecce his hat.
Blew Zephyrus alte, acerbus,
Dum elderly gentleman sat;
Et a capite took up quite torve
Et in rivum projecit his hat.

Macaronic verse seems to have been originated by Odaxius of Padua, but it was popularized by his pupil, Teofilo Folengo or Merlinus Coccaius (1491–1544), a Mantuan monk of noble family whose *Liber Macaronicorum* (1520), a poetical rhapsody made up of words of different languages, treated of 'pleasant matters' in a comical style.

John Skelton's *Phyllyp Sparowe* (1512) contained somewhat similar verse. It begins:

Pla ce bo,
Who is there, who?
Di le xi,
Dame Margery.

In 1801 Allan Cunningham published *Delectus Macaronicorum Carminum*, a history of macaronic poetry, and the issue of *Notes & Queries* for 27 March 1852 contained the following fine example of macaronic verse, in which the Latin words represent English:

O pateo tulis aras cale fel O,
Hebetis vivis id, an sed, 'Aio puer vello!'
Vittis nox certias in erebo de nota olim, –
A mite grate sinimus tonitis ovem.
(O Paddy O'Toole is a rascally fellow,
He beat his wife's head, and said, 'I hope you are well, O!'
With his knocks, sir, she has in her body not a whole limb, –
A mighty great sin I must own it is of him.)

Some macaronic verse mixes more languages than two, as the following, from a poem called 'The Suitor with Nine Tongues':

Ti soi legō, meirakion,
Now that this fickle heart is won?
Me semper amaturam te
And never, never, never stray?
Herzschätzchen, Du verlangst zu viel
When you demand so strict a seal.
N'est-ce pas assez que je t'aime
Without remaining still the same?
Gij daarom geeft u liefde niet
If others may not have a treat.
Muy largo es mi corazón,
And fifty holds as well as one.
Non far nell' acqua buco che
I am resolved to have my way;
Im lo boteach atta bi,
I'm willing quite to set you free:
Be you content with half my time,
As half in English is my rhyme.

**Macaroni parson, The.** *See under* FAKES.

**Macbeth.** The central character of Shakespeare's play of the same name (1605) is based on the historical Macbeth who was king of the Scots from 1040 until his death in 1057. He established himself on the Scottish throne after killing his uncle, Duncan, in battle, a death that Shakespeare alters to his murder in bed. The real Macbeth is buried on the island of Iona.

**Maccabeus.** The surname given to JUDAS, the central figure in the Jewish struggle (*c*.170–160 BC) against the SELEUCIDAE, and hence to his family or clan. He was the third son of Mattathias the Hasmonaean. The most probable derivation of the name is from Aramaic *maqqavā*, Hebrew *maqqav*, 'hammer', just as Edward I was called *Scotorum malleus* ('Hammer of the Scots').

**Maccabees, The.** The family of Jewish heroes descended from Mattathias the Hasmonaean and his five sons, John, Simon, Judas, Eleazar and Jonathan, which delivered its race from the persecutions of the Syrian king, Antiochus Epiphanes (r.175–163 BC). It established a line of priest-kings, which lasted until it was supplanted by Herod in 37 BC. Their exploits are told in the four Books of the Maccabees, of which two are in the APOCRYPHA.

**Judas Maccabeus.** *See under* JUDAS.

**McCarthyism.** Political WITCH-HUNTING, as the hounding of Communist suspects to secure their removal from office and public affairs. It is so called after US Senator Joseph McCarthy (1908–57) who specialized in these activities somewhat unscrupulously.

**McCoy, The Real.** *See under* REAL.

**Macdonald, Flora.** The Scottish heroine (1722–90) who aided the escape of Prince Charles Edward after the failure of the FORTY-FIVE Rebellion. She conducted the YOUNG PRETENDER, disguised as Betty Burke, an Irishwoman, from Benbecula to Monkstadt in Skye and thence via Kingsburgh to Portree, often in imminent danger from the military search parties. She was subsequently imprisoned in the TOWER OF LONDON but released in 1747 under the Act of Indemnity. She married Allan Macdonald in 1750, emigrated to North Carolina in 1774, but returned to Scotland in 1779.

After dinner, Flora Macdonald on horseback, and her supposed maid and Kingsburgh, with a servant carrying some linen, all on foot, proceeded towards that gentleman's house. Upon the road was a small rivulet which they were obliged to cross. The Wanderer [the Prince], forgetting his assumed sex,

that his clothes might not be wet, held them up a great deal too high. Kingsburgh mentioned this to him, observing, it might make a discovery.
JAMES BOSWELL: *Journal of a Tour to the Hebrides* (13 September 1773)

**Mace.** Originally a club armed with iron and used in war, and now a staff of office pertaining to certain dignitaries, as the SPEAKER of the HOUSE OF COMMONS, lord mayors, mayors and so on. Both sword and mace are symbols of dignity, suited to the times when men went about in armour, and sovereigns needed champions to vindicate their rights.

**Macedonians.** A religious sect named after Macedonius (d.*c*.362), bishop of Constantinople, an upholder of semi-Arianism. He was deposed by the ARIAN Council of Constantinople in 360.

**Macedonia's madman.** Alexander III, the Great, of Macedon (356–323 BC).

**MacFarlane's geese.** According to the proverb: 'MacFarlane's geese like their play better than their meat.' The wild geese of Inchtavoe (Loch Lomond) used to be called MacFarlane's geese because the MacFarlanes had a house on the island, and it is said that the geese never returned after the destruction of the house. One day James VI visited the chieftain and was highly amused by the gambols of the geese, but one served at table was so tough that the king exclaimed: 'MacFarlane's geese like their play better than their meat.'

**MacGregor.** The motto of the MacGregors is, 'E'en do and spair nocht,' said to have been given them in the 12th century by a king of Scotland. While the king was hunting, he was attacked by a wild boar, and Sir Malcolm asked permission to encounter the creature. 'E'en do,' said the king, 'and spair nocht.' Whereupon the baronet tore up an oak sapling and dispatched the enraged animal. For this the king gave Sir Malcolm permission to use the said motto, and, in place of a Scots fir, to adopt for crest an oak tree eradicate, proper.

Another motto of the MacGregors is *'S rioghal mo dhream* ('My race is royal').

The MacGregors furnish the only instance of a clan being deprived of its family name. In 1603, as a result of their ruthless ferocity at the Battle of Glenfruin against the Colquhouns of Luss, it was proscribed by James VI, so that the clan assumed the names of neighbouring families such as the Campbells, Buchanans, Grahams and Murrays. The laws against them were annulled by Charles II in 1661, but in 1693, under William and Mary, similar measures were enacted against them. These penalties were finally abolished by the British Parliament and John Murray of Lanrick resumed the name MacGregor as chief of the clan in 1822. *See also* ROB ROY.

**Robert (Rob Roy) MacGregor.** *See* ROB ROY.

**Machiavelli, Niccolò.** The celebrated Florentine statesman (1469–1527) and author of *Il Principe* ('The Prince'), a treatise on the art of government addressed to Lorenzo de MEDICI, putting forward the view that only a strong and ruthless prince could free Italy from devastation by foreigners. In view of the distracted state of the country, he held that terrorism and deceit were justifiable means of achieving a peaceful and prosperous Italy. Hence the use of his name as an epithet or synonym for an unscrupulous politician, and Machiavellianism or Machiavellism to denote political deceit and intrigue and the use of unscrupulous methods generally.

Am I politic? am I subtle? am I a Machiavel?
SHAKESPEARE: *The Merry Wives of Windsor,* III, i (1600)

**Imperial Machiavelli, The.** *See under* IMPERIAL.

**Machismo** (Spanish *macho*, 'male'). A US usage denoting assertive masculinity that emphasizes such features as bravery, virility and the domination of the opposite sex.

**Mach number.** An expression of the ratio of flight speed to the speed of sound, devised by the Austrian physicist and psychologist Ernst Mach (1838–1916). An aircraft flying at Mach 2 is travelling at twice the speed of sound.

**Macintosh.** *See* MACKINTOSH.

**Mackerel. Mackerel sky.** A sky dappled with detached rounded masses of white cloud, something like the markings on the back of a mackerel.

Yorkshire farmers ... call a sky which is flecked with many small clouds a 'mackerel sky': A mackerel sky / Is never long dry.
SIDNEY O. ADDY: *Household Tales* (1895)

**Throw a sprat to catch a mackerel, To.** *See under* THROW.

**Mackintosh** or **macintosh.** Cloth waterproofed with rubber by a process patented in 1823 by Charles Macintosh (1766–1843); also a coat made of this or, loosely, any raincoat.

**Macmillanites.** A religious sect in Scotland that seceded from the CAMERONIANS in 1743 because they wished for stricter adherence to the principles of the REFORMATION in Scotland. They were so named from John Macmillan (1670–1753), their leader. They called themselves the Reformed Presbytery.

**McNaughten Rules.** The guidelines used in criminal cases to determine insanity. The rules, also known as M'Naghten Rules, are based on the questions first used in the case of Daniel McNaughten, tried in 1843 for murdering the Prime Minister's secretary, whom he took for the

Prime Minister himself. He was suffering from delusions of persecution, and was acquitted with a verdict of 'not guilty by reason of insanity'. The original statute defining the rule said that such a person must be detained in a hospital 'during Her Majesty's pleasure', effectively imposing a life sentence for murder.

**MacPherson.** Fable has it that during the reign of David I of Scotland (1124–53), a younger brother of the chief of the powerful clan Chattan became abbot of Kingussie. His elder brother died childless, and the chieftainship devolved on the abbot. He is supposed to have obtained a papal dispensation (a most unlikely story) to marry the daughter of the thane of Calder. A swarm of little 'Kingussies' was the result. The people of Inverness-shire called them the Macphersons, i.e. 'sons of the parson'.

**Macrocosm** (Greek, 'great world'). The ancients looked on the universe as a living creature, and the followers of PARACELSUS considered man a miniature representation of the universe. The universe was termed the Macrocosm, and man the MICROCOSM.

**Macy's.** The New York department store, long physically the largest in the United States, took its name from Rowland Hussey Macy (1822–77), who founded a partnership in Manhattan in 1858. His store attracted custom by its competitive prices, boosted by its slogan, 'It's smart to be thrifty.' There are many branches, often operating under different names. Macy's was purchased in a buy-out in 1986, but a combination of shady dealing and economic recession forced it into liquidation in 1992. The branch stores continued to operate, however.

**Mad. Mad Cavalier, The.** Prince Rupert (1619–82), noted for his impetuous courage and impatience of control as the Royalist cavalry leader during the English Civil Wars (1642–51). He was the son of James I's daughter, Elizabeth, and Frederick V, elector Palatine.

**Mad Mullah, The.** A nickname given to Mohammed bin Abdullah, a mullah who caused great problems for the British in Somaliland at various times between 1899 and 1920. He claimed to be the MAHDI and made extensive raids on tribes friendly to the British. The dervish power was not finally broken until 1920 when the Mad Mullah escaped to Ethiopia, where he died in 1921.

**Mad Parliament, The.** The Parliament that met at Oxford in 1258 and that produced the Provisions of Oxford to limit the power of Henry III. The epithet 'Mad' seems to have arisen through error, probably a substitution of *insane* for *insigne* ('famous') in a contemporary description.

**Mad Poet, The.** Nathaniel Lee (*c*.1653–92) who lost his reason towards the end of his life through intemperance and was confined for five years in BEDLAM.

**As mad as a hatter.** *See under* AS.

**As mad as a March hare.** *See under* AS.

**Brilliant Madman** or **Madman of the North, The.** Charles XII of Sweden (1682–1718).

**Hopping mad.** *See under* HOP.

**Madame.** The wife of Philippe, Duc d'Orléans (1640–1701), brother of Louis XIV, was so styled. The title was usually reserved for the eldest daughter of the king or the DAUPHIN. *See also* MONSIEUR.

**Madam Cresswell.** *See under* CRESSWELL.

**Madame Butterfly.** *See under* BUTTERFLY.

**Madame Déficit.** *See under* DÉFICIT.

**Madame Sans-Gêne.** *See under* SANS.

**Madame Tussaud's.** The widely known London exhibition of wax models of prominent as well as notorious people established by Marie Tussaud (née Grosholtz) in 1802. She was born at Berne in 1760 and was taught the art of modelling in wax in Paris and in due course gave lessons to Louis XVI's sister, Madame Élisabeth. After a short imprisonment during the French Revolution she came to London where she died in 1850. The Chamber of Horrors is filled with figures of notorious murderers and instruments of torture and punishment, including the GUILLOTINE blade that beheaded Marie-Antoinette in 1793. *See also* HANGMEN AND EXECUTIONERS.

**Made.** *See* MAKE.

**Mademoiselle. Mademoiselle from Armenteers.** In the First World War Armentières in northern France was held by the British until the great German offensive of 1918. The army song 'Mademoiselle from Armenteers', which became widely known, originated in 1916. It was a modification of the much earlier song and tune 'Three Prussian Officers Crossed the Rhine'. As before it readily lent itself to improvisation, especially of a scurrilous nature. One version ran:

> O Madam, have you any good wine?
> Parlez-vous;
> O Madam, have you any good wine?
> Parlez-vous.
> O Madam, have you any good wine?
> Fit for a soldier of the line?
> Inky-pinky, parlez-vous.

**Mademoiselle Rachel.** *See* RACHEL.

**Grande Mademoiselle, La.** *See under* GRAND.

**Madge.** A MAGPIE, with the name an abbreviated form of Margaret.

**Madoc** or **Madog.** A Welsh prince, son of Owain Gwynedd and legendary discoverer of America in 1170. He is supposed to have sailed from Aber-Cerrig-Gwynion near Rhos-on-Sea with two ships and to have reached Mobile Bay, Alabama. The Mandan Indians (extinct since the mid-19th century) have been held as the descendants of Madoc's voyagers, and there are fortifications north of Mobile Bay resembling Welsh pre-Norman castles. Madoc is also supposed to have made a second voyage to establish a colony, supposedly setting out from Lundy.

Robert Southey has a poem *Madoc* (1805), which also embodies the foundation of the Mexican Empire by the Aztecs from Aztlan. The story is first found in a 15th-century Welsh poem.

**Madonna** (Italian, 'my lady'). A title especially applied to the Virgin MARY.

**Sistine Madonna.** *See under* SISTINE.

**Madras system.** The MONITORIAL SYSTEM devised by Andrew Bell (1753–1832), when superintendent of the Madras Orphanage for sons of soldiers (1789–97). The so-called LANCASTERIAN system was derived from it. Bell subsequently became Superintendent for the NATIONAL SOCIETY.

**Maeander.** *See* MEANDER.

**Maecenas.** A patron of letters, so called from the Roman statesman Gaius Maecenas (d.8 BC), who kept an open house for men of letters in the reign of AUGUSTUS. He was the special friend and patron of HORACE and VIRGIL. Nicholas Rowe so dubbed the Earl of Halifax on his installation to the MOST NOBLE ORDER OF THE GARTER (1714).

**Last English Maecenas, The.** Samuel Rogers (1763–1855), poet and banker.

**Maelduin** or **Maeldune, The Voyage of.** *See under* VOYAGE.

**Maenads** (Greek *mainas*, 'madwoman'). The Bacchae or Bacchantes, female attendants of BACCHUS. The name arises from their extravagant gestures and frenzied rites.

**Maeonides** or **Maeonian Poet, The.** HOMER, either because he was the son of Maeon or because he was born in Maeonia (Asia Minor).

**Maeve** or **Medb.** In Irish legend a mythical queen of Connaught, wife of Ailill and mother of FINDABAIR who sought the downfall of CUCHULAIN and trained sorcerers to help bring this about. She instigated the 'cattle raid of Cooley' or 'Cuailnge', thus initiating the WAR OF THE BROWN BULL.

**Maeviad.** *See* BAVIAD.

**Mae West.** The name given by aircraft personnel in the Second World War to the inflatable life jacket or vest worn when there was danger of being forced into the sea. It was an allusion to the buxom figure of the American film star of this name (1892–1980).

**Mafficking.** Extravagant and boisterous celebration of an event, especially on an occasion of national rejoicing. The term arose from the uproarious scenes and unrestrained exultation that took place in the centre of London on the night of 18 May 1900, when the news of the relief of Mafeking (besieged by the Boers for 217 days) became known. The 'heroic' character of Baden-Powell's defence has been questioned, but the impact made at the time is not in dispute.

**Mafia.** A network of Sicilian criminal organizations, which became increasingly powerful during the 19th century. 'Protection' by blackmail, boycotting, terrorization and the vendetta are characteristic, and Sicilian politics came to be dominated by the *mafiosi*. Its power was largely broken under Mussolini in the 1920s, but it has not been exterminated. Sicilian immigrants introduced it into the United States, where it became a growing nuisance from the 1890s, and Mussolini's firm measures caused a fresh influx to join the BOOTLEGGERS and gangsters of Al CAPONE's era. These groups eventually adopted the name *Cosa Nostra* (Italian 'our thing'), controlling much of the drugs, gambling and prostitution in the big cities, although its use is mainly confined to the eastern seaboard.

*Mafia* is a word in the Sicilian dialect of Italian meaning literally 'boldness', itself perhaps from Arabic *mahyah*, 'bragging'. This would have been a result of the Arab conquest of Sicily in the 9th century. Many Sicilian families became peasant bandits in the hills, and patriotism and family loyalties took hold and developed. Their resistance continued after the Norman conquest of the 11th century and later control by Spain. After the liberation and unification of Italy the Mafia made crime a full-time pursuit.

Nowadays the word 'mafia' is frequently misused, becoming a vogue word loosely applied to any clique, exclusive circle or influential group. *See also* CAMORRA.

**Maga.** A once familiar name for *Blackwood's Magazine* (1817–1980), said to derive from the affectionate reference to it by its Scottish founder, William Blackwood (1776–1834), as 'ma magazine'.

**Magazine.** Originally a place for stores, with the word ultimately from Arabic *makhzan*, 'storehouse'. This sense is still retained in military usage. The word now more commonly denotes a periodical publication containing contributions by various authors. How this came about is seen from the Introduction to *The Gentleman's Magazine* (1731), the first to use the word in this way:

> This Consideration has induced several Gentlemen to promote a Monthly Collection to treasure up, as in a Magazine, the most remarkable Pieces on the Subjects above mention'd.

**All Souls' Parish Magazine.** *See under* ALL.

**Parish magazine.** *See under* PARISH.

**Magdalene.** A former term for an asylum for reclaiming prostitutes, so called from St MARY MAGDALENE or Mary of Magdala, 'out of whom he had cast seven devils' (Mark 16: 9). It is probably a misnomer, because the identification of Mary Magdalene with the sinner in Luke 7:37–50 is highly problematical. *See also* MAUDLIN.

**Magdalen College, Oxford.** The college was founded in 1458 by William Waynflete.

**Magdalene College, Cambridge.** The college was founded in 1542 by Lord Audley.

**Magdalenian.** The name given to the late (upper) Palaeolithic period from the village of La Madeleine, in Dordogne, France, where representative relics have been found. These people used wood and bone as well as flint, including bone needles and barbed harpoons. The cave paintings of Altamira in Spain belong to this period. In England the Creswellian culture is akin to the Magdalenian.

**Magdeburg Centuries.** The first great PROTESTANT history of the Christian church, compiled in Magdeburg under the direction of Matthias Flacius Illyricus (1520–75). It was written in Latin and first published at Basle (1559–74) as the *Historia Ecclesiae Christi*, and takes the story to 1400.

**Magellan, Strait of.** *See under* STRAIT.

**Magenta.** A brilliant red aniline dye derived from coal tar, named in commemoration of the bloody Battle of Magenta (1859), when the Austrians were defeated by the French and Sardinians. This was just before the dye was discovered.

**Maggot.** There was an old idea that whimsical or crotchety persons had maggots in their brains:

> Are you not mad, my friend? What time o' th' moon is't?
> Have not you maggots in your brain?
> JOHN FLETCHER: *Women Pleased*, III, iv (1620)

Hence 'maggoty' is used to mean 'whimsical' or 'full of fancies'. Fanciful dance tunes used to be called 'maggots', as in *The Dancing Master* (1716), where there are such titles as 'Barker's maggots', 'Cary's maggots', 'Draper's maggots' and so on, and in 1685 Samuel Wesley, father of John and Charles Wesley, published a volume called *Maggots; or Poems on Several Subjects*. The word appears in the same sense in the titles of such modern novels as *Mr Fortune's Maggot* (1927) by Sylvia Townsend Warner and *A Maggot* (1985) by John Fowles.

**Magi** (Latin, plural of *magus*). Literally 'wise men', and specifically the Three Wise Men of the East who brought gifts to the infant Jesus. Tradition calls them Melchior, Gaspar and Balthazar, three kings of the East. The first offered gold as the emblem of royalty, the second, FRANKINCENSE, in token of divinity, and the third, myrrh, in prophetic allusion to the persecution unto death that awaited the MAN OF SORROWS. Melchior means 'my king of light', from Hebrew *malkī-ōr*; Gaspar or Caspar, which is the same name as Jasper, has been derived from Old Persian *Kansbar*, 'treasurer'; and Balthazar is a corrupt form of the Aramaic name Belshazzar, itself from Babylonian *Belu-sharu-usur*, 'Bel protect the king'.

Medieval legend calls them the THREE KINGS OF COLOGNE, and the cathedral there claimed their relics. They are commemorated on 2, 3 and 4 January, and particularly at the Feast of the EPIPHANY.

Among the ancient Medes and Persians the Magi were members of a priestly caste credited with great occult powers, and in Camoëns' LUSIAD (1572) the term denotes Indian BRAHMANS. Ammianus Marcellinus says the Persian magi derived their knowledge from the Brahmans of India, and Arianus expressly calls the Brahmans 'magi'.

**Magic. Magic carpet, The.** The apparently worthless carpet, which transported whoever sat upon it wherever they wished, is one of the stock properties of Eastern storytelling. It is sometimes Prince Hussain's carpet, because of the popularity of the story of Prince AHMED in the ARABIAN NIGHTS ENTERTAINMENTS, when it supplies one of the main incidents. The main magic carpet, however, is that of King SOLOMON, which was of green silk. His throne was placed on it when he travelled, and it was large enough for all his forces to stand on, men and women on his right hand, and spirits on his left. When ready, Solomon told the wind where he wished to go, and the carpet rose in the air and landed at the place required. The birds of the air, with wings outspread, protected the party from the sun.

**Magic Flute, The.** In Mozart's opera of this name (*Die Zauberflöte* (1791)) the magic flute was bestowed by the powers of darkness and had the power of inspiring love. By it Tamino and Pamina are guided through all worldly dangers to knowledge of divine truth.

**Magician of the North, The.** The title assumed by Johann Georg Hamann (1730–88), a German philosopher and theologian.

**Magic lantern.** The old name for an optical instrument for the projection of slides and pictures. It is said to have been invented in 1636 by Athanasius Kircher.

**Black magic.** *See under* BLACK.

**Great Magician of the North.** *See under* GREAT.

**White magic.** *See under* WHITE.

**Maginot line.** A zone of fortifications built along the eastern frontier of France between 1929 and 1934 and named after André Maginot (1877–1932), Minister of War, who sponsored its construction. The line, essentially to cover the returned territories of Alsace-Lorraine, extended from the Swiss border to that of Belgium and lulled the French into a belief that they were secure from any German threat of invasion. In the event, Hitler's troops entered France through Belgium in 1940. *See also* SIEGFRIED LINE.

**Magistrate. Blind Magistrate, The.** *See under* BLIND.

**Glasgow magistrate.** *See under* GLASGOW.

**Mirror for Magistrates, A.** *See under* MIRROR.

**Magna Carta** or **Magna Charta** (Medieval Latin, 'great charter'). The charter of liberties extorted from King John in 1215. Its main effect was to secure the liberties of the English church and the rights of the baronial classes, and to restrict abuses of royal power. It gained a new, but historically inaccurate, importance in the constitutional quarrels of the 17th century as a charter of 'English liberty'.

**Magnanimous, The.** Alfonso V of Aragon (*c.*1394–1458) was so called.

**Magnet.** The LODESTONE or loadstone so called from Magnesia in Lydia, where the magnetic iron ore was said to abound.

**Magnetic Island.** An island in Halifax Bay, Queensland, Australia, so named by Captain Cook because he thought his compass was affected by metallic ore in the rocks, although later navigators found no confirmation of this.

**Magnetic Mountain.** A mountain of medieval legend which drew out the nails of any ship that approached within its influence. It is referred to in Sir John MANDEVILLE's *Travels* (1356–7) and in other stories.

**Magnificat.** The hymn of the Virgin (Luke 1:46–55) beginning 'My soul doth magnify the Lord' (*Magnificat anima mea Dominum*), used as part of the daily service of the church since the beginning of the 6th century and at evening prayer in England for over 800 years.

**Magnificent, The.** The following were so named:

Lorenzo de MEDICI (1449–92), 'Il Magnifico', Duke of Florence
Robert, Duke of Normandy (d.1035), also called Le Diable
Soliman or Suleiman I (*c.*1494–1566), greatest of the Turkish sultans

**C'est magnifique, mais ce n'est pas la guerre.** *See under* C'EST.

**Magnolia.** A genus of North American flowering trees, so called from Pierre Magnol (1638–1715), professor of botany at Montpellier.

**Magnum.** A wine bottle, twice the size of an ordinary bottle, or two 'reputed quarts'. A double magnum holds the contents of four ordinary bottles. *See also* JEROBOAM; JORUM; REHOBOAM; TAPPIT-HEN.

**Magnum bonum** (Latin, 'great and good'). A name given to certain choice potatoes and also plums.

**Magnum opus** (Latin, 'great work'). The chief or most important of one's learned or literary works.

> My magnum opus, the 'Life of Dr Johnson' ... is to be published on Monday, 16th May.
>
> JAMES BOSWELL: Letter to Rev. W. Temple (1791)

**Magog.** *See* GOG.

**Magoo, Mr.** The incompetent, myopic cartoon character was the creation of animators John Hubley and Robert Cannon. He first appeared in the late 1940s, and 'played' various fictional characters, such as Dr Jekyll and Long John Silver, in a television series of the 1960s.

**Magpie.** The bird was formerly known as a 'maggot pie', 'maggot' representing Margaret (compare Robin redbreast, Tomtit, and the old Phyllyp-sparrow), and 'pie' being 'pied', in allusion to its white and black plumage.

The magpie has generally been regarded as an uncanny bird, and in Sweden is connected with WITCHCRAFT. In Devon it was a custom to spit three times to avert ill luck when the bird was sighted, and in Scotland magpies flying near the windows of a house foretold death. One old rhyme about the number of magpies seen says:

> One for sorrow, two for joy
> Three for a girl, four for a boy,
> Five for silver, six for gold,
> Seven for a secret never to be told,
> Eight for a wish, nine for a kiss,
> Ten for a marriage never to be old.

An old Lancashire version runs:

> One for anger, two for mirth,
> Three for a wedding, four for a birth,
> Five for rich, six for poor,
> Seven for a bitch, eight for a whore,
> Nine for a burying, ten for a dance,
> Eleven for England, twelve for France.

In target shooting the score made by a shot striking the outermost division but one is called a magpie because it was customarily signalled by a black and white flag, and formerly bishops were humorously or derisively called magpies because of their black and white vestments.

**Magus.** *See* MAGI; SIMON MAGUS.

**Mahabharata.** One of the two great epic poems of ancient India, the other being the RAMAYANA. It is about seven times the combined length of the ILIAD and ODYSSEY. Its main story is the war between the Kauravas (descendants of Dhrtarstra) and the Pandavas (descendants of Pandu), but there are innumerable episodes. Dhrtarstra and Pandu were sons of Kuru, a descendant of Bharata from whom the poem gets its name, meaning 'great epic of the Bharata dynasty'. It contains the BHAGAVAD-GITA.

**Maharajah** (Hindi, 'great king'). The title of many of the native rulers of Indian states.

**Mahatma** (Sanskrit, 'great soul'). The title given by Buddhists to adepts of the highest order, a community of whom is supposed to exist in Tibet, and by Theosophists to a person who has reached perfection spiritually, intellectually and physically. As his knowledge is perfect he can produce effects that, to the ordinary man, appear miraculous. The title is particularly associated with Mohandas Karamchand Gandhi (1869–1948), the Hindu nationalist leader who identified himself with the poor, practised prayer and fasting, and sought to achieve his political ends by non-violence. *See also* BUDDHISM; THEOSOPHY.

**Mahayana** (Sanskrit, 'great vehicle'). A development from the earlier form of BUDDHISM, which occurred about 2000 years ago. It enjoined, besides the pursuit of NIRVANA, that each individual should strive to become a BUDDHA, thereby becoming able to preach and serve the welfare of others.

**Mahdi** (Arabic, 'guided one'). The expected MESSIAH of the Muslims. There have been numerous bearers of this title since early on in the Muslim era and the Hidden IMAM (head of the true faith) of the Ismaelis was another such. The most popularly known to the British was Mohammed Ahmed, who led the revolt in the Sudan and who died in 1885. His tomb was destroyed after the Battle of Omdurman in 1898. The best known was Ubaid Allah al-Mahdi, first CALIPH of the Fatimite dynasty, who reigned from 909 to 933.

**Mah-jongg.** A Chinese game played with 'tiles' like dominoes, made of ivory and bamboo, with usually four players. The tiles, 136 or 144 in all, are made up of numbered bamboo, circle and character suits, honours (red, green and white dragons), winds (north, east, south and west) and, additionally, numbered flowers and seasons.

It appears to be of 19th-century origin. The game was introduced to the USA by Joseph P. Babcock about 1919 under the trade name Mah-jongg, which he coined. It is Chinese for 'sparrows', referring to the mythical 'bird of 100 intelligences' that appears on one of the tiles.

**Mahogany.** An old Cornish drink used by the fishermen on account of its warming quality, so called from its colour. The name has also been given to a strong concoction of brandy and water. Boswell at a dinner party at Sir Joshua Reynolds' says:

> Mr Eliot mentioned a curious liquor peculiar to his country, which the Cornish fishermen drink. They call it Mahogany; and it is made of two parts gin, and one part treacle, well beaten together. … I thought it very good liquor and said it was a counterpart of what is called Athol Porridge in the Highlands of Scotland, which is a mixture of whisky and honey. Johnson … observed, 'Mahogany must be a modern name; for it is not long since the wood called mahogany was known in this country'.
>
> JAMES BOSWELL: *The Life of Dr Johnson* (30 March 1781)

**Mahomet.** *See* MOHAMMED.

**Mahound.** A name of contempt for MOHAMMED, a MUSLIM or a Moor, particularly in the romances of the CRUSADES. The name is sometimes used as a synonym for the Devil. The FATWA imposed on the novelist Salman Rushdie in 1989 was partly brought about by his use of the word in *The Satanic Verses* (1988), condemned as blasphemous by the Iranian authorities. The name itself, which has several variant forms such as Mahoun and Mahun, is simply a shortened form of 'Mohammed'. It is found in English literature dating from at least the 13th century.

> The presence seems, with things so richly odd,
> The mosque of Mahound, or some queer pagod.
>
> ALEXANDER POPE: *The Satires of Dr John Donne*, iv (1735)

**Maia.** The eldest and most lovely of the PLEIADES and mother, by JUPITER, of MERCURY. *See also* MAY.

**Maid. Maid Marian.** A female character in the old May games and MORRIS DANCES, usually as queen of the May. The original Marian was associated with quite a different Robin, first appearing in the 13th-century French play *Robin et Marion*. In the later ROBIN HOOD ballads she became attached to the cycle as the outlaw's sweetheart, probably through the performance of Robin Hood plays at MAY DAY festivities. The part of Maid Marian, both in the games and the dance, was frequently played by a man in female costume.

**Maid of all work.** A female servant doing work of all kinds.

**Maid of Athens.** The girl immortalized in Lord Byron's poem of this name is said to have been 12-year-old Theresa Macri, daughter of a widow whose husband had been vice-consul in Athens.

> Maid of Athens, ere we part,
> Give, oh give me back my heart!
> Or, since that has left my breast,
> Keep it now, and take the rest!
> Hear my vow before I go,
> Ζωη μου, σας αγαπω, ('My life, I love you').
>
> LORD BYRON: 'Maid of Athens' (1810)

**Maid of Buttermere, The.** Mary Robinson, the beautiful and innocent daughter of the landlord of the Fish Inn, beside Lake Buttermere, Cumbria, who in 1802 was deceived into marrying John Hatfield, an unscrupulous impostor posing as the Hon Alexander Augustus Hope, younger brother of the Earl of Hopetoun. He proved to be a much-married confidence trickster who had served numerous prison sentences.

Exposed by S.T. Coleridge, Hatfield was eventually hanged for forgery in 1803. The story was the subject of numerous songs, ballads and poems at the time.

I mean, O distant Friend! a story drawn
From our own ground, – the Maid of Buttermere, –
And how, unfaithful to a virtuous wife
Deserted and deceived, the Spoiler came
And wooed the artless daughter of the hills,
And wedded her, in cruel mockery
Of love and marriage bonds.

WILLIAM WORDSWORTH: *The Prelude*, vii (1805)

**Maid of honour.** An unmarried woman in attendance on a queen or princess, or in the USA, the principal unmarried attendant of the bride. Also the name of a small almond-flavoured tartlet.

**Maid of Kent, The.** Elizabeth Barton (*c*.1506–34), a servant girl who incited Roman Catholics to resist the REFORMATION and who believed that she acted under inspiration from God. Having denounced Henry VIII for his intention to divorce Anne Boleyn, she was hanged at TYBURN.

**Maid of Norway, The.** *See* FAIR MAID OF NORWAY.

**Maid of Orleans, The.** JOAN OF ARC.

**Maid of Saragossa, The.** Agustina Zaragoza Doménech (1790–1858), known as Agustina of Aragon, distinguished for her heroism when Saragossa was besieged by the French in 1808 and 1809 during the Peninsular War.

Is it for this the Spanish maid, aroused,
Hangs on the willow her unstrung guitar,
And, all unsex'd, the anlace [dagger] hath espoused,
Sung the loud song, and dared the deed of war?

LORD BYRON: *Childe Harold's Pilgrimage*, I, liv (1812–18).

**Maid of the Hairy Arms, The.** *See* MAY MOLLOCH.

**Jack among the maids.** *See under* JACK.

**Nut-brown Maid, The.** *See under* NUT.

**Old maid.** *See under* OLD.

**Maida.** Sir Walter Scott's favourite deerhound. He was a gift from Scott's friend Glengarry, who named him 'out of respect for that action in which my brother had the honour to lead the 78th Highlanders to victory', i.e. the Battle of Maida (1806), in which the English defeated the French in the Napoleonic Wars.

**Maida Vale.** The region of west London, noted for its handsome Victorian mansions, developed in the early 19th century round the Hero of Maida inn. This was itself named after the Battle of Maida in southern Italy, where British forces under General Sir John Stuart defeated the French in 1806. The section of road by the inn was at first called Maida Hill, but subsequently (and conversely) Maida Vale, presumably as this was more mellifluous, suggesting a secluded location. There is hardly a vale or valley here in the accepted sense.

**Maiden.** (1) A form of GUILLOTINE used in Scotland in the 16th and 17th centuries for beheading criminals, and also called 'the widow'. It was introduced by Regent Morton, James Douglas, 4th Earl of Morton (1516–81), for the purpose of beheading the laird of Pennycuik. Morton is erroneously said to have been the first to suffer by it, but Thomas Scott, one of the murderers of Rizzio, was beheaded by it in 1566. Morton did not suffer that fate until 1581.

(2) In many expressions 'maiden' is used figuratively for something that is untouched or 'virginal', or that involves a first attempt or event. Thus, a 'maiden castle' or 'maiden fortress' is one that has never been taken, a 'maiden over' in CRICKET is one from which no runs are made, a 'maiden speech' is a first public speech, a 'maiden tree' is one that has never been lopped, and a 'maiden voyage' is the initial voyage of a ship. A 'maiden assize' was an assize when there was nobody to be brought to trial. In such an assize, the sheriff of the county presented the judge with a pair of white gloves.

**Maiden Castle.** The site in Dorset is the best surviving IRON AGE fortification in Britain, occupying 120 acres (48.5 ha), and the site of earlier Neolithic settlement. Although a maiden castle is properly one that has never been captured, the reference here may be to a castle that is so strong it is capable of being defended by maidens.

**Maiden King, The.** Malcolm IV of Scotland (r.1153–65).

Malcolm ... son of the brave and generous Prince Henry ... was so kind and generous in his disposition, that he was usually called Malcolm the Maiden.

SIR WALTER SCOTT: *The Tales of a Grandfather*, iv (1827–30)

**Maiden name.** A woman's name before she is married.

**Maiden or Virgin Queen.** Elizabeth I, queen of England (r.1558–1603), who never married.

**Maiden town.** A town never taken by the enemy, but specifically Edinburgh, from the tradition that the maiden daughters of a Pictish king were sent there for protection during a local war.

**Answer to a maiden's prayer, The.** *See under* ANSWER.

**Swan maidens.** *See under* SWAN.

**Mail. Mailed fist, The.** Aggressive military might, from a phrase (*gepanzerte Faust*) used by William II of Germany (1859–1941) when bidding adieu to Prince Henry of Prussia as he was starting on his tour of the Far East (16 December 1897): 'Should anyone essay to detract from our just rights or to injure us, then up and at him with your mailed fist.' *See also* JACKBOOT.

**Coat of mail.** *See under* COAT.

**Maillotins.** Parisians who in 1382 rose up against the taxes imposed by the regents early in the reign of Charles VI (1368–1422). They seized iron mallets (*maillets*) from the arsenal and killed the tax collectors. The insurrection was harshly suppressed.

**Main. Main chance, The.** Profit or money, probably from the game called hazard, in which the first throw of the dice is called the main, which must be any number from 5 to 9 inclusive, the player then throwing his chance, which determines the main. *See also* HAVE AN EYE TO THE MAIN CHANCE *under* EYE.

**Main Plot.** Lord Cobham's plot (1603) to replace James I by his English-born cousin Arabella Stuart. Sir Walter Ralegh was one of the conspirators, and there were contacts with Spanish agents. They were tried with the contrivers of WATSON'S PLOT, which was also known as the Bye Plot, the names Main Plot and Bye Plot arising from their supposed connection.

**Main squeeze.** A man's principal girl-friend. The allusion is to the squeeze of an embrace.

**Main Street.** The principal thoroughfare in many of the smaller towns and cities of the USA. Sinclair Lewis' novel of this name (1920) epitomized the social and cultural life of these towns and gave the phrase a significance of its own.

**Spanish Main.** *See under* SPAIN.

**Welsh main.** *See under* WELSH.

**Mainbrace, To splice the.** *See under* SPLICE.

**Maintenance** (ultimately Latin *manu tenere*, 'to hold in the hand'). Means of support or sustenance. In law, maintenance was formerly a term for interference in a legal action by a person having no interest in it. The offence was abolished by the Criminal Law Act 1967.

**Cap of maintenace.** *See under* CAP.

**Maitland club.** A club of literary antiquaries, instituted at Glasgow in 1828. It published or reprinted works of Scottish historical and literary interest. *See also* BANNATYNE CLUB; ROXBURGHE CLUB.

**Maize.** American superstition had it that if a damsel found a blood-red ear of maize, she would have a suitor before the year was out.

> Then in the golden weather the maize was husked, and the maidens
> Blushed at each blood-red ear, for that betokened a lover.
>
> H.W. LONGFELLOW: *Evangeline*, II, iv (1849)

**Majesty.** In medieval England it was usual to refer to the king as 'the lord king'. Henry VIII (r.1509–47) was the first English king styled 'His Majesty', although it was not until the time of the Stuarts that this form of address became stereotyped, and in the dedication to James I prefixed to the Authorized Version of the Bible (1611) the king is addressed also as 'Your Highness'.

> The Lord of Heaven and earth blesse your Majestie with many and happy dayes, that as his Heavenly hand has enriched your Highnesse etc.

Henry IV (r.1399–1413) was 'His Grace'; Henry VI (r.1422–61, 1470–1) 'His Excellent Grace'; Edward IV (r.1461–83) 'High and Mighty Prince'; Henry VII (r.1485–1509) 'His Grace' and 'His Highness'; and Henry VIII in the earlier years of his reign 'His Highness'. 'His Sacred Majesty' was a title assumed by subsequent sovereigns, but was afterwards changed to 'Most Excellent Majesty'. The king of Spain was 'His Catholic Majesty', and the king of France 'His Most Christian Majesty'.

In HERALDRY, an eagle crowned and holding a sceptre is said to be 'an eagle in his majesty'.

**Apostolic Majesty.** *See under* APOSTOLIC.

**His Catholic Majesty.** *See under* CATHOLIC.

**Major. Major Prophets, The.** *See* GREAT PROPHETS.

**Drum major.** *See under* DRUM.

**Ursa Major.** *See under* URSA.

**Majority. Great majority.** *See under* GREAT.

**Moral majority.** *See under* MORAL.

**Majorette, Drum.** *See under* DRUM.

**Make.** In America this word is more frequently used with the meaning 'put ready for use' than in Britain, as in 'Have you made my room?' (i.e. put it tidy). In Britain the verb is more often used in such constructions as 'to make the bed', but compare Shakespeare's use of the expression 'make the door'. 'To make good', 'to make one's pile', 'to make a place' (i.e. to arrive there) are Americanisms.

For expressions beginning with make and not listed below, look under the first main word of the expression.

**Made to measure.** Of clothes, tailored or made to fit a particular person's measurements. So generally, appropriate or suitable for an occasion, as: 'The Cup Final is made to measure for television.'

**Make and break.** A device that alternately closes (makes) and opens (breaks) an electric circuit.

**Make and mend.** In the Royal Navy an afternoon free from work, originally, and still often, used for mending clothes.

**Make away with, To.** To take away or run off with; to squander. Also, to murder, so that 'to make away with oneself' is to commit suicide.

**Make do, To.** To manage.

**Make for, To.** To help bring about as: 'His actions make for peace.' Also, to move towards, hence, in slang, to attack.

**Make it, To.** To succeed in catching a train, in

keeping an appointment and so forth on time. Also, to be successful generally, or specifically, to score a sexual conquest.

**Make it up, To.** To become reconciled.

**Make off, To.** To run away, to abscond.

**Make or break.** 'This will make or break you' means this will bring you either success or failure.

**Make out, To.** To obtain an understanding of, as: 'I can barely make out the meaning.' To assert, to establish by evidence or argument, as: 'to make out one's case.' To draw up or prepare, as: 'I am tired of making out receipts.' In the USA it is to achieve one's purposes, particularly amorous, as: 'Mark is making out with Joanne.'

**Make over, To.** To transfer ownership; to re-fashion or renovate a garment.

**Makeshift.** A temporary improvisation during an emergency.

**Make-up.** As a verb and a noun denoting face cosmetics and their application, the term is of theatrical origin, and an actor is said to be 'made up for the stage' after the necessary application of greasepaint and the like. Hence, colloquially, the sum of one's characteristics and idiosyncrasies.

**Make up to, To.** To approach or to try to make friends with, usually for personal ends; to court.

**Makeweight.** A small addition in compensation or an 'extra', as a piece of meat, cheese or other food, put into the scale to make the weight correct.

**Make with, To.** Colloquially, to proceed with, as: 'Let's make with the music.'

**On the make.** Looking after one's own personal advantage or gain, intent on the MAIN CHANCE.

**Makyne, Robin and.** *See under* ROBIN.

**Malachi.** A prophet whose main prophecy is devoted to a coming day of judgement. The book named after him is the last in the Old Testament. His name is not really a personal name but a title, from the Hebrew meaning 'my messenger', and is drawn from the text of the book itself.

> Behold, I will send my messenger, and he shall prepare the way before me.
> Malachi 3:1

**Malachi Malagrowther.** The signature of Sir Walter Scott to a series of letters contributed to the *Edinburgh Weekly Journal* in 1826 on the lowest limitation of paper money to £5. They caused a great sensation at the time. He had previously called a querulous old courtier in *The Fortunes of Nigel* (1822) Sir Mungo Malagrowther. *See also* DRAPIER'S LETTERS.

**Malakoff.** This fortification, which was captured by the French (8 September 1855) during the Crimean War (1854–6), was named from a Russian, Alexander Ivanovich Malakhov, who kept a liquor shop outside Sebastopol. Other houses sprang up round it, and 'Malakoff', as the settlement came to be called, was ultimately fortified. It is now also the name of a southern suburb of Paris.

**Malaprop, Mrs** (French *mal à propos*, 'not to the purpose'). The character in Sheridan's *The Rivals* (1775), noted for her misuse of words. 'As headstrong as an allegory [alligator] on the banks of the Nile' (III, iii), is one of her grotesque misapplications. Hence the words 'malaprop' and 'malapropism' to denote such mistakes.

Malapropisms frequently flourish where the uninitiated attempt technical or professional language. Philip Norman, writing in *The Times* (4 May 1985), reported a miners' leader who denounced his bosses as 'totally incontinent', a parishioner who compained to her vicar about the church's poor 'agnostics', a motorcyclist's girlfriend who rode on the 'pavilion', and a housewife who was not 'enamelled' of her kitchen's colour scheme. Medical terms are particularly prone to malapropism, genuine examples including 'teutonic' ulcers, 'malingering' tumours, 'hysterical rectums' and 'Cistercian' deliveries. *See also* MISPRONOUNCED WORDS.

**Malbrouk** or **Marlborough.** The old French song *Marlbrouk s'en va-t-en guerre* is said to date from 1709, when the Duke of Marlborough was winning his battles in Flanders, but it did not become popular until it was applied to Charles Spencer, 3rd Duke of Marlborough, at the time of his failure against Cherbourg (1758). It was popularized after becoming a favourite of Marie-Antoinette about 1780, and by its being introduced by Beaumarchais into *Le Mariage de Figaro* (1784). In Britain it is sung to the tune of 'We won't Go Home till the Morning' or 'For He's a Jolly Good Fellow'. According to a tradition recorded by Chateaubriand, the air came from the Arabs, and the tale is a legend of Mambron, a crusader.

> Malbrouk s'en va-t-en guerre,
> Mironton, mironton, mirontaine;
> Malbrouk s'en va-t-en guerre,
> Ne sait quand reviendra.
> (Marlborough is off to war,
> Fol-de-rol, fol-de-rol, fol-de-la;
> Marlborough is off to war,
> He doesn't know when he'll return.)

**Malebolge.** The eighth circle of Dante's *Inferno* (xviii (*c*.1309–*c*.1320)), containing ten *bolge* or pits. The name is used figuratively of any cesspool of filth or iniquity.

**Maleficia.** The evil deeds formerly attributed to witches. In 1435 the theologian Johannes Nider categorized the offences into seven groups: (1) inspiring love, (2) stirring up hatred, (3) causing impotence, (4) introducing disease, (5) taking life, (6) inducing madness, or (7) injuring property or animals. Many witches were tried and executed on charges of *maleficia*, one such being the 34-year-old Frenchwoman Jehenne de Brigue, who in 1390 was alleged to have used sorcery to heal the seriously ill Jehan de Ruilly. She admitted to being a witch and gave a full confession on being threatened with torture. She was burned in Paris on 19 August 1391.

**Maleval, St William of.** *See under* WILLIAM.

**Malice.** In addition to its common meaning, 'malice' is a term in English law to designate a wrongful act carried out against another intentionally, without just cause or excuse. This is commonly known as 'malice aforethought'. 'Malicious damage' was a legal term meaning damage done to property wilfully and purposely (since 1971 it has been known as criminal damage), and 'malicious prosecution' means the instituting of a criminal prosecution, or the presentation of a bankruptcy petition, maliciously and without reasonable cause.

**Malice prepense.** Malice aforethought, malice designed or deliberate, from Latin *prae*, 'before', and *pensare*, 'to think'.

> Mr Pryce, to commence his 'ingenious defence',
> Made a 'powerful appeal' to the jury's 'good sense':
> 'The world he must defy ever to justify
> Any presumption of "Malice Prepense"'.
>
> R.H. BARHAM: *Ingoldsby Legends*, 'Patty Morgan the Milkmaid's Story' (1840)

**Malignants.** A term applied by the Parliamentarians to the Royalists who fought for CHARLES I and Charles II in the Civil Wars (1642–51). They were also called DELINQUENTS.

**Malkin.** An old diminutive of Matilda, formerly used as a generic term for a kitchen wench or untidy slut, also for a cat (*see* GRIMALKIN), and for a scarecrow or grotesque puppet, from which latter meaning derives the mop called a malkin, used especially for cleaning a baker's oven.

The name was also sometimes given to the queen of the MAY. *See also* MAID MARIAN.

> Put on the shape of order and humanity,
> Or you must marry Malkin, the May lady.
>
> FRANCIS BEAUMONT and JOHN FLETCHER: *Monsieur Thomas*, II, ii (1619)

**Mall, The.** A broad thoroughfare in St James's Park, London, so called because the game of PALL MALL used to be played there by Charles II and his courtiers. The 'mall' was the mallet with which the ball was struck.

**Malmesbury, William of.** *See under* WILLIAM.

**Malmsey.** A sweet Madeira wine. It derives its name from Medieval Latin *Malmasia*, a corruption of Greek Monembasia, the port in Greece from which it was originally shipped. George, Duke of Clarence (1449–78), son of Richard, Duke of York, is said to have been put to death in the TOWER OF LONDON by being drowned in a butt of malmsey by order of his brother, Edward IV. It is more likely that he was drowned in a bath.

**Malta.** *See* GEORGE CROSS ISLAND.

**Maltese cross.** The cross made thus: ✠. It was originally the badge of the Knights of Malta, formed of four barbed arrowheads with their points meeting in the centre. In various forms it is the badge of many well-known orders, including the British VICTORIA CROSS and ORDER OF MERIT, and the German IRON CROSS. *See also* CROSS.

**Knights of Malta** or **Hospitallers of St John of Jerusalem.** *See* HOSPITALLERS.

**Malthusian doctrine.** The theory that population tends to outrun the means of subsistence, put forward by the Rev. T.R. Malthus (1766–1834) in his *Essay on Population* (1798). It was not novel, but his systematic exposition drew attention to the population problem.

**Malum.** Latin *malum* means 'apple', *malus* means 'apple tree', and *malus, mala, malum* mean 'bad'. In his *Commonplace Book*, Robert Southey (1774–1843) quotes a witty derivation given by Nicolson and Burn, making the noun come from the adjective, possibly in allusion to the apple eaten by EVE. There is also the schoolboy quatrain, which adds *malo*, 'I wish', to the others:

> *Malo*, I would rather be
> *Malo*, up an apple tree
> *Malo*, than a bad boy be
> *Malo*, in adversity.

**Malvolio.** The pompous and puritanical steward in Shakespeare's *Twelfth Night* (1599) who dreams of marrying the lady Olivia. He is ridiculed by means of a ruse that persuades him to wear ridiculous 'cross-garters' and to smile, for which he is deemed insane. His name means 'ill-will'.

**Mambrino.** A pagan king of old romance, introduced by Ariosto into ORLANDO FURIOSO. He had a helmet of pure gold that made the wearer invulnerable and that was taken possession of by RINALDO. This is frequently referred to in *Don* QUIXOTE, and when the barber was caught in a shower, and clapped his brazen basin on his head, Don Quixote insisted that this was the enchanted helmet of the Moorish king.

**Mamelukes** (Arabic *mamlūk*, 'slave'). The slaves brought from the Caucasus and Asia Minor to Egypt who formed a bodyguard for the SULTAN, a descendant of SALADIN. In 1250 they set up one of their number as Sultan, and the Mamelukes reigned until they were overthrown by the Turkish Sultan Selim I in 1517. The country was subsequently governed by 24 Mameluke beys under the PASHA, but they retained virtual control. In 1811 they were exterminated by Mohammed Ali.

**Mammon.** The god of this world. The origin of the word is unknown. According to St AUGUSTINE, it is Punic for 'greed'. It occurs in the Bible (Matthew 6:24, Luke 16:13): 'Ye cannot serve God and mammon.' Both Edmund Spenser (*The Faerie Queene*, II, vii (1590)) and Milton, who identifies him with VULCAN or MULCIBER (*Paradise Lost*, i (1667)), make Mammon the personification of the evils of wealth and miserliness.

Mammon led them on –
Mammon, the least erected spirit that fell
From Heaven; for even in Heaven his looks and thoughts
Were always downward bent; admiring more
The riches of Heaven's pavement, trodden gold,
Than aught divine or holy else enjoyed
In beatific vision.

MILTON: *Paradise Lost*, i (1667)

**Mammon of unrighteousness, The.** Money.

Make to yourselves friends of the mammon of unrighteousness; that, when ye fail, they may receive you into everlasting habitations.

Luke 16:9

**Mammoth Cave.** The largest known cave system in the world is that under the Mammoth Cave National Park, Kentucky. It consists of many chambers with connecting passages said to total 300 miles (483km). Rivers, streams and lakes add to the majesty and scenic variety of this vast limestone cave. In 1972 a passage was discovered linking the Mammoth Cave with the Flint Ridge Cave System.

**Man** or **men. Man about town.** A fashionable idler.

**Man and boy.** From childhood, as: 'He'd worked on the farm man and boy.'

**Man Friday.** The young savage found by Robinson CRUSOE on a Friday and kept as his servant and companion on the desert island. Hence a faithful and willing attendant, ready to turn his hand to anything. Hence, in turn, 'girl Friday' as a female employee with a wide range of duties, in many cases the equivalent of a personal assistant (PA). (The name is appropriate for someone whose working week ends, and weekend begins, on this day.) The term fell from favour in the 1980s as being sexist.

Person Friday required for this busy Interior Design and Architectural Practice.

*The Times* (advertisement) (26 October 1994)

**Man in the Iron Mask, The.** In the reign of Louis XIV, a mysterious state prisoner held for over 40 years in various gaols until he finally died in the BASTILLE on 19 November 1703. When travelling from prison to prison he always wore a mask of black velvet, not iron. His name was never revealed, but he was buried under the name of 'M. de Marchiel'. Many conjectures have been made about his identity, one of them being that he was the Duc de Vermandois, an illegitimate son of Louis XIV. Dumas *père*, in his romantic novel on the subject, adopted VOLTAIRE's suggestion that he was an illegitimate elder brother of Louis XIV with Cardinal Mazarin for his father. The most plausible suggestion is that of the historians Lord Acton and Funck-Brentano, who suggested a minister of the Duke of Mantua (Count Mattiolo, b.1640), who, in his negotiations with Louis XIV, was found to be treacherous and imprisoned at Pignerol.

**Man in the Moon, The.** Some say it is a man leaning on a fork, on which he is carrying a bundle of sticks picked up on a Sunday. The origin of this fable is from Numbers 15: 32–36. Some add a dog. Another tradition says that the man is CAIN, with his dog and thorn bush, the bush being emblematic of the thorns and briars of the fall, and the dog being the 'foul fiend'. Some poets make out the 'man' to be ENDYMION, taken to the moon by DIANA.

**Man in the street, The.** The ordinary citizen, who in the aggregate makes public opinion.

**Man of Brass, The.** In Greek mythology, the byname of Talus, the work of Hephaestus (VULCAN). He was the guardian of Crete and threw rocks at the ARGONAUTS to prevent them from landing. He used to make himself red hot and then hug intruders to death.

**Man of December, The.** NAPOLEON III (1808–73). He was elected president of the Second French Republic on 10 December 1848, made his coup d'état on 2 December 1851, and became emperor on 2 December 1852.

**Man of Destiny, The.** NAPOLEON BONAPARTE (1769–1821). He regarded himself as an instrument in the hands of destiny. G.B. Shaw used the epithet as the title of a play about Napoleon.

**Man of Kent, A.** One born east of the Medway. These men went out with green boughs to meet WILLIAM THE CONQUEROR and obtained in consequence a confirmation of their ancient privileges from the new king. *See also* HENGIST AND HORSA; KENTISHMAN.

**Man of letters, A.** An author; a literary scholar.

**Man of mark, A.** A notable or well-known person; one who has 'made his mark' in some walk of life.

**Man of parts, A.** An accomplished person; one who is clever, talented or of high intellectual ability.

**Man of Ross, The.** John Kyrle (1637–1724) who spent most of his life at Ross, Herefordshire. He was noted for his benevolence and for supplying needy parishes with churches.

Who taught that heaven-directed spire to rise?
'The Man of Ross', each lisping babe replies.
Behold the market-place with poor o'erspread!

He feeds yon almshouse, neat, but void of state,
Where Age and Want sit smiling at the gate;
Him portion'd maids, apprenticed orphans bless'd,
The young who labour, and the old who rest.
ALEXANDER POPE: *Moral Essays*, Epistle iii (1731–5)

**Man of Sedan, The.** NAPOLEON III was so called because he surrendered his sword to William I, king of Prussia, after the Battle of Sedan (2 September 1870).

**Man of Silence, The.** NAPOLEON III.

**Man of Sin, The.** The biblical phrase (2 Thessalonians 2:3) is generally held to signify ANTICHRIST, and is applied by the PURITANS to the pope, by the FIFTH-MONARCHY MEN to Oliver Cromwell, and similarly by others elsewhere.

**Man of Sorrows.** Jesus Christ, from the prophecy in Isaiah 53:3 that the MESSIAH would be 'a man of sorrows, and acquainted with grief'.

**Man of straw, A.** A person without means, with no more substance than a straw doll; also, an imaginary or fictitious person put forward for some reason.

**Man of the moment, The.** The person best able to deal with a current situation.

**Man of the world, A.** Someone who is acquainted with the 'ways of the world', a socially experienced, practical person. Henry Mackenzie brought out a novel (1773) with this title and Charles Macklin a comedy (1871). A worldly man or woman, however, is one who cares only for the material things of this world.

In Shakespeare's time a woman of the world signified a married woman.

*Touchstone*: To-morrow will we be married.
*Audrey*: I do desire it with all my heart; and I hope it is no dishonest desire to be a woman of the world.
*As You Like It*, V, iii (1599)

**Man-of-war.** (1) A warship. Like other ships, a man-of-war is traditionally referred to as 'she'. Formerly the term denoted a fighting man ('the Lord is a man of war', Exodus 15:3).

(2) The popular name of the marine hydrozoan, *Physalia physalis*, is the Portuguese man-of-war, or simply, man-of-war.

**Man-of-war bird.** The frigate bird; any member of the family Fregatidae.

**Man of wax, A.** A model person, like one fashioned in wax. Horace speaks of the 'waxen arms of Telephus', meaning model arms, or of perfect shape and colour; and in Shakespeare's *Romeo and Juliet* (I, iii (1594)), the nurse says of Paris, 'Why, he's a man of wax,' which she explains by saying, 'Nay, he's a flower; in faith, a very flower.'

**Man on the Clapham omnibus, The.** In legal parlance, 'the reasonable person'. Possibly the phrase was first used by Sir Charles Bowen, QC (later Lord Bowen), who was junior council against the claimant in the TICHBORNE CASE (1871–4).

**Man proposes but God disposes.** An old proverb found in Hebrew, Greek and Latin, among other languages. The germ of the maxim lies in Proverbs 16:9: 'A man's heart deviseth his way: but the Lord directeth his steps.' *De Imitatione Christi* (*c*.1418) by Thomas à Kempis has the Latin origin of the English: *Homo proponit, sed Deus disponit* (I, xix, 2). Many writers, in English, French and other languages have repeated the words since.

**Man to man.** Frankly; as one man to another; in a manly fashion, as when two individuals talk 'man to man'.

**Man who broke the bank at Monte Carlo, The.** Joseph Hobson Jagger, who, in 1886, won over 2 million francs in eight days. An expert on spindles, he suspected one of the roulette wheels of a faulty spindle and had it watched for a week. Thereafter he staked on the numbers that were turning up with much more than mathematical probability and won a fortune. He died in 1892, probably mainly from boredom. His exploit became the subject of the Victorian MUSIC HALL ballad in the repertoire of the inimitable Charles Coborn, written and composed in 1891 by Fred Gilbert.

As I walk along the Bois Boolong, with an independent air,
You can hear the girls declare – 'He must be a millionaire';
You can hear them sigh and wish to die,
You can see them wink the other eye
At the man who broke the bank at Monte Carlo.

**Man without sandals, A.** A prodigal, so called by the ancient Jews, because the seller gave his sandals to the buyer as a ratification of his bargain (Ruth 4:7).

**Men stand with their backs to the fire.** An old explanation for this habit, now less common since the ubiquity of central heating, is that when the dog's nose proved too small to stop a leak in the Ark, NOAH sat on the hole to keep the water out. Ever since, men have felt the need to warm their backs, and dogs have had cold noses.

**As one man.** *See under* AS.
**Best man.** *See under* BEST.
**Cro-Magnon man.** *See under* CRO-MAGNON.
**Dead men.** *See under* DEAD.
**Elephant Man, The.** *See under* ELEPHANT.
**Essex man.** *See under* ESSEX.
**Fancy man.** *See under* FANCY.
**Forgotten Man.** *See under* FORGET.
**Four-letter man.** *See under* FOUR.
**Four-minute men.** *See under* FOUR.
**Friend of Man, The.** *See under* FRIEND.
**Green Man.** *See under* GREEN.

**Heidelberg man.** *See under* HEIDELBERG.
**Hit man.** *See under* HIT.
**I'm your man.** I'm the person you need.
**Inner man.** *See under* INNER.
**Invisible Man, The.** *See under* INVISIBLE.
**Isle of Man.** *See under* ISLE.
**Lady's man.** *See under* LADY.
**Last Man.** *See under* LAST.
**Leading man.** *See under* LEAD.
**Many men, many minds.** *See under* MANY.
**More I see of men the more I love dogs, The.** *See under* MORE.
**Neanderthal man.** *See under* NEANDERTHAL.
**New man, The.** *See under* NEW.
**No man's land.** *See under* NO.
**Old Man of the Mountains, The.** *See under* OLD.
**Old Man of the Sea, The.** *See under* OLD.
**One's own man again, To be.** To fully recover good health after an illness or other setback.
**Peking man.** *See under* PEKING.
**Poor man's (something), A.** *See under* POOR.
**Rag-and-bone man.** *See under* RAG.
**Red man.** *See under* RED.
**Rights of Man, The.** *See under* RIGHT.
**Sandwich man.** *See under* SANDWICH.
**See a man about a dog, To.** *See under* SEE.
**Self-made man, A.** *See under* SELF.
**Separate** or **sort out the men from the boys, To.** *See under* SEPARATE.
**Son of Man.** *See under* SON.
**Style is the man.** *See under* STYLE.
**Tailed men.** *See under* TAIL.
**Third man.** *See under* THIRD.
**Threefold man, The.** *See under* THREE.
**To a man.** *See under* TO.
**Twelfth man.** *See under* TWELVE.
**White man.** *See under* WHITE.
**White man's burden.** *See under* WHITE.
**White man's grave.** *See under* WHITE.
**White man speak with forked tongue.** *See under* WHITE.
**Wild man of the woods.** *See under* WILD.
**Wisest man of Greece, The.** *See under* WISE.

**Mañana** (Spanish, 'tomorrow'). A word frequently used to imply some vague unspecified future date.

> 'Mañana – is soon enough for me'
> PEGGY LEE and DAVE BARBOUR: song title (1948)

**Manasseh.** The elder of the two sons of JOSEPH, the other being Ephraim (Genesis 41, 48, 50). When presenting his sons to his father, JACOB, Joseph took Manasseh by his left hand and Ephraim by his right, but Jacob laid his right hand on the head of Ephraim and his left on that of Manasseh, saying that the younger son would be the greater. Both sons were progenitors of separate tribes among the TWELVE TRIBES OF ISRAEL. Manasseh is also the name of a king of Judah noted for his long reign and his idolatry (2 Kings 21).

**Mancha, The Knight of La.** *See under* KNIGHT.

**Manchester.** The name of the city was recorded in the 4th century AD as Mamucio, from a Celtic root word *mamm*, meaning 'breast', referring to the rounded hill on which Manchester arose. To this was added *ceaster*, the Old English form of Latin *castra*, 'camp', referring to its former status as a Roman walled town. A native of Manchester is a Mancunian, from Mancunium, the Medieval Latin name of the city. This seems to have come from a miscopying of the Roman name, Mamucium. *See also* COTTONOPOLIS.

**Manchester Martyrs, The.** The name given to the three Irishmen who were hanged for attempting to rescue two FENIAN prisoners in Manchester (November 1867). In the course of the struggle a policeman was killed.

**Manchester Massacre, The.** *See* PETERLOO MASSACRE.

**Manchester Poet, The.** Charles Swain (1801–74).

**Manchester school, The.** A term applied to a group of RADICALS and supporters of FREE TRADE originating from businessmen of the Manchester Chamber of Commerce and sponsors of the Anti-Corn Law League. They were supporters of LAISSEZ FAIRE and against the growth of the colonial empire. Led by Richard Cobden (1806–65) and John Bright (1811–89), they were derisively so called by Benjamin Disraeli in 1848, and the name came to be applied to Victorian advocates of free trade and a pacific foreign policy generally.

**Manchu, Fu.** *See under* FU.

**Mancus.** An Anglo-Saxon coin in both gold and silver. In the reign of Ethelbert of Kent (d.616) money accounts were kept in pounds, mancuses, shillings and pence. Five pence = one shilling, and 30 pence = one mancus.

**Mandaeans.** A GNOSTIC sect, also called Nasoreans and Christians of St John, which arose in the 1st or 2nd century and is still found near Baghdad. Their teachings were akin to those of the MANICHEANS, and St JOHN THE BAPTIST featured prominently in their writings. They favoured frequent baptism.

**Mandamus** (Latin, 'we command'). A former writ (now an order) of KING'S OR QUEEN'S BENCH commanding the person or body named to do what the writ directs. It is so called from the opening word.

**Mandarin.** A name given by the Portuguese to the official called by the Chinese *kuan*. Its ultimate origin is in Sanskrit *mantrin*, 'counsellor'. The word is sometimes used derisively for over-pompous officials, as: 'The mandarins of our Foreign Office.'

The nine ranks of mandarins were distinguished by the button in the cap: (1) ruby, (2) coral, (3) sapphire, (4) an opaque blue stone, (5) crystal, (6) an opaque white shell, (7) wrought gold, (8) plain gold and (9) silver.

**Mandate** (Latin *mandatum*, from *mandare*, 'to command'). An authoritative charge or command. Also, the authority conferred upon certain 'advanced nations' by the LEAGUE OF NATIONS after the First World War to administer the former German colonies and Turkish dependencies outside Europe. In practice 'advanced nations' meant the victorious powers. After the Second World War, under the UNITED NATIONS, Mandates became Trusteeships.

**Mandeville, Sir John** or **Jehan de.** The name assumed by the compiler of a well-known and influential 14th-century book of travels, originally written in French. The author claimed to have been born at St Albans and from 1322 to have travelled through Turkey, Armenia, Tartary, Persia, Syria, Arabia, Egypt, Libya, Ethiopia, Amazonia and India, and to have visited PRESTER JOHN and served under the emperor of China. The work contains many stories of fabulous monsters and legends, but was essentially derived from the writings of others, especially such noted medieval travellers as Friar Odoric and John de Plano Carpini. The book was probably the work of a Liège physician, Jean de Bourgogne or Jehan à la Barbe. An English version had appeared by the beginning of the 15th century. *See also* MÜNCHAUSEN.

**Mandrake.** The root of the mandrake or mandragora (*Mandragora officinarum*) often divides in two, presenting an approximate appearance of a man. In ancient times human figures were cut out of the root and wonderful virtues ascribed to them, such as the production of fecundity in women (Genesis 30:14–16). They could not be uprooted without supposedly producing fatal effects, so a cord used to be fixed to the root and around a dog's neck, and the dog, when chased, drew out the mandrake and died. A small dose of the drug was held to produce vanity in one's appearance, and a large dose, idiocy. The mandrake screamed when uprooted. Of this latter property Thomas Newton, in *An Herbal for the Bible* (1587), says: 'It is supposed to be a creature having life, engendered under the earth of the seed of some dead person put to death for murder.' Nicholas Culpeper, in *The Complete Herbal* (1653), says that the mandrake is 'a root dangerous for its coldness, being cold in the fourth degree'. The original name, mandragora, probably became mandrake by association with 'man' (for its forked root) and 'drake' (dragon), the latter associated with its magical powers.

> *Cleopatra*: Give me to drink mandragora.
> *Charmian*: Why, madam?
> *Cleopatra*: That I might sleep out this great gap of time
> My Antony is away.
> SHAKESPEARE: *Antony and Cleopatra*, I, v (1606)

**Manes.** *See under* MANI.

**Manger, A dog in the.** *See under* DOG.

**Mangi.** The name used by Marco Polo for southern China. *See also* CATHAY.

**Manhattan.** A COCKTAIL made from whisky and vermouth, with a dash of Angostura bitters and Curaçao or Maraschino. It is named from Manhattan Island, New York.

**Mani.** The MOON. In Scandinavian mythology the beautiful boy driver of the moon car, the son of Mundilfoeri. He is followed by a wolf, which, when time shall cease to exist, will devour both Mani and his sister SOL.

**Mani, Manes** or **Manicheus.** The founder of Manicheism, who was born in Persia (*c.*215) and was prominent in the reign of Shapur or Sapor I (*c.*241–272). Mani began his teaching *c.*240 and was put to death *c.*275. His name is of uncertain origin. The many enemies of Manicheism derived it from Greek *mania*, 'folly', 'madness', while his followers took it from Sanskrit *mani*, 'pearl', 'jewel'. According to one school of thought, the true origin is probably in Syriac *mono hayo*, 'living mud'.

**Manicheans** or **Manichees.** Followers of Mani, who taught that the universe is controlled by two antagonistic powers, light or goodness (identified with God), and darkness, chaos or evil. The system was based on the old Babylonian religion modified by Christian and Persian influences. St AUGUSTINE was for nine years a Manichean, and Manicheism influenced many Christian heretical sects and was itself denounced as a heresy. One of Mani's claims was that, although Christ had been sent into the world to restore it to light and banish darkness, the APOSTLES had perverted his doctrine, and he, Mani, was sent as the PARACLETE to restore it. Manicheism survived in Turkestan until the 13th century.

Manichean is now used in a general sense to mean 'pessimistic', 'basic', 'primitive'.

> But the more credible guess is that Reagan's philosophy is the creation of his own scissor research and his own increasingly Manichean vision of American liberty under siege by the forces of darkness in Moscow – and in Washington.
> *Newsweek* (21 July 1980)

**Mania, Tulip.** *See under* TULIP.

**Manitou.** The Great Spirit of certain Native Americans, either the Great Good Spirit or the Great Evil Spirit. The word is Algonquian, meaning 'spirit'. According to Native American beliefs, each hunter and warrior must 'win' Manitou by means of special tests and visions.

Christian missionaries used the concept of Manitou as an analogue of God, and this parallelism is implicit in H.W. Longfellow's *The Song of Hiawatha* (1855):

Gitche Manito, the mighty,
The creator of the nations,
Looked upon them with compassion,
With paternal love and pity.
I, 'The Peace-Pipe'

**Manna.** The miraculous food provided for the children of Israel on their journey from Egypt to the HOLY LAND.

And when the children of Israel saw it, they said to one another, It is manna: for they wist not what it was. And Moses said unto them, This is the bread which the Lord hath given you to eat.
Exodus 16:15

The word is popularly said to be a corrupt form of Aramaic *man-hu* ('what is this?') but it is probably Hebrew *mān*, the term for the honey-like secretion of a plant louse that congeals in the evening but melts in the sun.

And the house of Israel called the name thereof Manna: and it was like coriander seed, white; and the taste of it was like wafers made with honey.
Exodus 16:31

**Manna of St Nicholas of Bari.** AQUA TOFANA.

**Manner. Bedside manner.** *See under* BED.

**To the manner born.** *See under* TO.

**Manoa.** The fabulous capital of EL DORADO, the houses of which city were said to be roofed with gold. Sir Thomas Roe, Sir Walter Ralegh and others made numerous attempts to locate it during the reigns of Elizabeth I and James I.

**Manon.** The young heroine of Abbé Prévost's novel *Manon Lescaut* (1731). She runs away from a convent to be with her lover, Des Grieux, who remains faithful to her despite her own many infidelities. She is transported to Louisiana, where he joins her, and they finally die together in the wilderness. Her story inspired Massenet's opera *Manon* (1884) and Puccini's better known *Manon Lescaut* (1893).

**Manor** (Old French *manoir*, from Latin *manere*, 'to remain'). A word introduced after the Norman Conquest and used of a dwelling of a man of substance but not necessarily a large holding. It ultimately came to denote the self-contained estate in which the demesne (domain) land was worked for the lord's private benefit, the remainder being worked by free and unfree tenants, VILLEINS, who were subject to the COURT BARON. *See also* COMMON; OPEN-FIELD SYSTEM; WEEKWORK.

**Lord of the manor.** *See under* LORD.

**Mansard roof.** Also called a curb roof, this was named after the French architect François Mansart (1598–1666), although the style was used by Pierre Lescot (*c.*1510–78) at the Louvre in about 1550. Instead of forming a Λ-shape, the lower slope is almost perpendicular, while the upper is at a gentler angle. It was in use in America in the old colonial days, and there the term denotes a double-pitched roof, sloping up from the four sides of a building. Where it ends in two gables it is called a gambrel roof.

**Mansfield, The King and the Miller of.** *See under* KING.

**Mansion** (Latin *mansio*, from *manere*, 'to remain', 'to dwell'). The Latin word means a stay or continuance, a halting-place or night quarters, hence an inn or residence. *See also* MANOR.

**Mansion House, The.** The official residence of the lord mayor of London, built on the site of the old Stocks Market. It was first used in 1752, when Sir Crisp Gascoyne took up residence.

**Manticore** (perhaps Persian *mardkhora*, 'man-eater'). A fabulous beast usually given as having the head of a man, the body of a lion, a porcupine's quills and the tail of a scorpion. It is mentioned by Ctesias, a Greek living in the late 5th and early 4th centuries BC, who wrote a history of Persia. It features in medieval BESTIARIES and also in HERALDRY where it generally has horns and the tail and feet of a DRAGON.

**Mantle. Mantle of Elijah, The.** A symbol of authority or leadership. When someone succeeds to the established authority of a predecessor, he is said to assume 'the mantle of Elijah'. ELIJAH the prophet cast his mantle upon ELISHA to show he was his chosen successor (1 Kings 19:19).

**Mantle of fidelity.** The old ballad 'The Boy and the Mantle' in PERCY'S RELIQUES (1765) tells how a little boy showed King ARTHUR a curious mantle, which would suit no wife 'that hath once done amisse'. Queen GUINEVERE tried it, but it changed from green to red, and red to black, and seemed rent into shreds. Sir KAY's lady tried it, but fared no better. Others followed, but only Sir Cradock's wife could wear it. The theme, which is a very common one in old tales, was used by Edmund Spenser in the incident of Florimell's girdle (*The Faerie Queene*, III, IV (1590, 1596)).

**Mantuan Swan** or **Bard.** VIRGIL.

**Manu.** In Hindu philosophy one of a class of DEMIURGES, of whom the first is identified with BRAHMA. Brahma divided himself into male and female, these producing Viraj, from whom sprang the first Manu, a kind of secondary creator. He gave rise to ten Prajapatis ('lords of all living'). From these came seven Manus, each presiding over a certain period. The seventh was Manu Vaivasvata ('the sun-born') who is now reigning and who is looked upon as the creator of the living races of beings. To him are ascribed the Laws of Manu, now called Manavadharmashastra, a section of the VEDAS containing a code of civil and religious law compiled by the Manavans. *See also* DELUGE.

**Manual. Manual seal.** A signet.

**Royal Sign Manual.** *See under* ROYAL.

**Manumit.** To set free; properly 'to send from one's hand' (Latin *e manu mittere*). One of the Roman ways of freeing a slave was to take him before the chief magistrate and say, 'I wish this man to be free.' The LICTOR or master then turned the slave round in a circle, struck him with a rod across the cheek and let him go. The ancient ceremony has a relic in the Roman Catholic rite of Confirmation when the bishop strikes the candidate lightly on the cheek, saying: 'Peace be with you.'

**Manure** (Medieval Latin *manuopera*, 'manual work'). The original sense of 'handwork', which also lies behind English 'manoeuvre', became narrowed to 'tillage by manual labour' and hence 'dressing applied to land'. Milton uses the word in its original sense in *Paradise Lost* (iv (1667)):

> And at our pleasant labour, to reform
> Yon flowery arbours, yonder alleys green,
> Our walk at noon, with branches overgrown
> That mock our scant manuring.

**Manx cat.** A tailless species of cat found in the ISLE OF MAN where it is popularly known as a 'rumpee'. It was a practice to dock other cats in order to sell them to visitors as Manx cats. *See also* MODDEY DHOO.

**Many. Many a mickle makes a muckle.** The original Scottish proverb is 'A wheen o'mickles mak's a muckle', where *mickle* means 'little' and *muckle* 'much'. However, Old English *micel* or *mycel* means 'much', so that if the Scots proverb is accepted, a converse meaning must be given to *mickle*.

**Many hands make light work.** An old proverb (given in Ray's *Collection* (1670)) enshrining the wisdom of the division of labour. The Romans had a similar saying, *Multorum manibus magnum levatur onus* ('By the hands of many a great load is lightened').

**Many men, many minds.** There are as many opinions as there are men, as Terence says, *Quot homines tot sententiae* (*Phormio*, II, iv, 14 (2nd century BC)).

**Many talk of Robin Hood who never shot with his bow.** Many brag of deeds in which they took no part.

**Map, The Vinland.** *See under* FAKES.

**Maple leaf.** The emblem of Canada, appearing in the centre of the national flag.

**Maquis.** The thick scrubland in Corsica and Mediterranean coastal lands, to which bandits retreat to avoid capture.

In the Second World War French patriots, who formed guerrilla groups in the countryside during the German occupation (1940–5), attacking their patrols, depots and so on, were known as the Maquis. *See also* FFI.

**Marabou.** A large stork or heron of western Africa, from Arabic *murābit*, MARABOUT, 'hermit', because among the Arabs these birds were held sacred.

**Marabouts.** A priestly order of Morocco (Arabic *murābit*, 'hermit'), which founded a dynasty in 1075 and ruled over Morocco and part of Spain until it was abolished by the Almohads in the 12th century.

**Marais, Le.** *See* PLAIN.

**Maranatha.** An Aramaic word that occurs in 1 Corinthians 16:22: 'If any man love not the Lord Jesus Christ, let him be Anathema Maranatha.' Because it follows Anathema, it is usually taken to represent some kind of curse. Its precise meaning is uncertain, and it has been variously translated as 'Our Lord has come', 'Our Lord will come', or 'Our Lord, come!' The last seems the most likely, as a prayer for the imminent coming of the Lord, i.e. the SECOND COMING. The two words together were probably a stock liturgical expression forming a threat to 'those who do not love the Lord'.

**Marathon.** A long-distance race, named after the Battle of Marathon (490 BC), the result of which was announced at Athens by an unnamed courier who fell dead on his arrival, having run nearly 23 miles (37 km). This runner is sometimes cited as Pheidippides (or Philippides), who actually ran from Athens to Sparta to seek help against the Persians before the battle.

In the modern OLYMPIC GAMES the Marathon race was instituted in 1896, the distance being standardized at 26 miles 385 yards (42.195km) in 1924.

**Maravedi** (Spanish, ultimately from Arabic *Murābitīn*, plural of *murābit*, MARABOUT, the name of a Moorish dynasty of Spain from 1087 to 1147). Originally (11th century) a gold coin, later (16th to 19th centuries) a very small Spanish copper coin, worth less than a farthing. *See also* NOT WORTH A MARAVEDI *under* WORTH.

**Marble. Marble Arch.** The London landmark was originally erected in front of Buckingham Palace and moved to its present position at Cumberland Gate (formerly TYBURN Gate) in 1851. It is now on an 'island'. It was designed by John Nash (1752–1835), and it is said to be modelled on Constantine's Arch at Rome. The central entrance gates cost 3000 guineas and the statue of George IV by Sir Francis Leggatt Chantrey (9000 guineas), now in Trafalgar Square, was originally to have been placed upon it.

**Andaman marble.** *See under* ANDAMAN.

**Arundel Marbles.** *See under* ARUNDEL.

**Elgin Marbles.** *See under* ELGIN.

**Phigalian marbles.** *See under* PHIGALIAN.

**March** (month). The month is so called from MARS. The old Dutch name for it was *Lentmaand* (*see* LENT). The old Saxon name was *hrēthmōnath*, perhaps meaning 'rough-month', from its boisterous winds. This subsequently became *lenctenmōnath* ('lengthening month'). In the FRENCH REVOLUTIONARY CALENDAR the corresponding month was called VENTÔSE ('windy'), extending from 20 February to 21 March.

**March borrowed three days from April.** *See* BORROWED DAYS.

**March comes in like a lion and goes out like a lamb.** March begins with rough, boisterous weather and ends calmly.

**As mad as a March hare.** *See under* AS.

**March. March table.** A British military term for the instruction setting out the order in which parts of a convoy should proceed, the exact time each should pass a given starting point and the average speed at which each should proceed.

**Marching watch.** The guard of civilians enrolled in medieval London to keep order in the streets on the Vigils of St Peter (29 June) and St John the Baptist (24 June) during the festivities. The phrase was used also of the festivities themselves.

**Dead march.** *See under* DEAD.

**Frog march.** *See under* FROG.

**Hunger march.** *See under* HUNGER.

**Long March, The.** *See under* LONG.

**Rogue's march.** *See under* ROGUE.

**Steal a march on someone, To.** *See under* STEAL.

**Marches** (Old English *mearc*, 'mark', 'border', Old French *marche*, 'frontier'). The boundaries between England and Wales, and England and Scotland, were called marches. Hence 'marcher lords', the powerful vassals with special rights who guarded the Welsh Marches at Hereford, Shrewsbury and Chester. The title Earl of March held by certain great feudal families is similarly derived. *See also* MARQUESS.

A territorial and historic division of Italy is called the Marches, which includes Pesaro and Urbino, Ancona, Macerata and Ascoli Piceno.

**Ride the marches, To.** *See under* RIDE.

**Marchpane.** The old name for the confection of almonds, sugar and other ingredients that is now better known as marzipan, this being the German form of the original Italian *marzapane*, which was adopted in the 19th century in preference to the earlier word because this confection was largely imported from Germany.

**Marcionite.** A heretical sect founded by Marcion of Sinope in the 2nd century, and largely absorbed by the MANICHEANS in the late 3rd century. They rejected the God of DEMIURGE of the Old Testament as a God of Law, and worshipped only Jesus Christ as the God of Love, whose mission was to overthrow the Demiurge. Much of the New Testament was regarded by them as uncanonical and they had a certain kinship with the GNOSTICS.

**Marcle Hill.** Legend states that this hill in Herefordshire, at 6 pm on 17 February 1575, 'roused itself with a roar, and by seven next morning had moved 40 paces'. It kept on the move for three days, carrying all with it. It overthrew Kinnaston chapel and diverted two roads at least 200 yards (182m) from their former course. Altogether, 26 acres (10.5 ha) of land are said to have been moved 400 yards (366m). The site is known locally as 'The Wonder' and is marked as such on modern Ordnance Survey maps ('The Wonder. Landslip AD 1575').

> Marcle Hill ... the scene of a remarkable landslip in 1575, which continued for three days (Feb. 17 to 19), resulting in the complete displacement of the hill, which in its progress carried with it and overturned trees, hedges, and sheepcotes, and destroyed a chapel; the movement was accompanied by loud subterranean noises, and was at the time supposed to be caused by an earthquake; it has, however, been shown by Sir R. Murchison and others that the phenomenon was due to a landslip, depending on the geological structure of the district, and similar to that which occurs not infrequently in the Alps.
>
> *Cassell's Gazetteer of Great Britain and Ireland* (1896)

**Marco. Marco Milione.** *See under* MILIONE.

**Marco Polo.** *See under* POLO.

**Marcus. Marcus Brutus.** Caesar's friend (85–42 BC), who joined the conspiracy to murder him.

**Marcus Valeris Corvus.** *See* CORVUS.

**Mardi gras** (French, 'fat Tuesday'). SHROVE TUESDAY, the last day of the LENT Carnival in France. At Paris, a fat ox, crowned with a fillet, used to be paraded through the streets. It was accompanied by mock priests and a band of tin instruments in imitation of a Roman sacrificial procession.

**Marduk.** The Babylonian god of heaven and earth, light and life, and god of battle. He was identified with numerous other Babylonian deities. His name is said to come from Sumerian *Amar-utu*, 'young calf of the Sun'. *See also* BEL.

**Mare.** The Latin word for 'sea'. *Mare clausum* is a closed sea or one that is closed by a certain power or powers to the unrestricted passage of foreign shipping. *Mare liberum* is the free and open sea. In 1635 John Selden (1584–1654) published a treatise called *Mare Clausum*. FASCIST Italy called the Mediterranean *Mare Nostrum*, 'our sea', in their expansionist heyday. This was originally the Roman name for it.

**Mare. Mare's-tail sky.** A sky with wisps of trailing clouds, indicating winds at high altitudes.

**Cry the mare, To.** *See* CRYING THE NECK.

**Find a mare's nest, To.** *See under* FIND.

**Flanders Mare, The.** *See under* FLANDERS.

**Grey mare is the better horse, The.** *See under* GREY.

**Ride shanks's mare or pony, To.** *See under* RIDE.

**Serve a mare, To.** *See under* SERVE.

**Two-legged mare, The.** *See under* TWO.

**Win the mare or lose the halter, To.** *See under* WIN.

**Marengo.** The white stallion which NAPOLEON BONAPARTE rode at Waterloo, named commemoratively for the Battle of Marengo (1800), Italy, in which Napoleon won a narrow victory in the War of the Second Coalition. Marengo ended his days in England, dying in 1829.

**Marforio.** *See* PASQUINADE.

**Margaret.** A country name for the MAGPIE and also for the daisy or marguerite (Old French, 'pearl'), so called from its pearly whiteness.

**Margaret Catchpole.** *See under* CATCH.

**St Margaret.** A virgin martyr of the 3rd century, known as St Marina among the Greeks. It is said that Olybrius, governor of Antioch, captivated by her beauty, sought her in marriage but, being rejected, threw her into a dungeon, where the Devil came to her in the form of a DRAGON. She held up the cross and the dragon fled. Sometimes she is described as coming from the dragon's mouth, for one legend says that the monster swallowed her, but on her making the sign of the cross he suffered her to quit his maw.

She is the archetype of female innocence and meekness, represented as a young woman of great beauty, bearing the martyr's palm and crown, or with the dragon as an attribute, sometimes standing on it. She is the patron saint of the borough of King's Lynn, where the handsome St Margaret's church in the Saturday Market Place is dedicated to her.

**St Margaret of Scotland.** The wife of Malcolm III of Scotland (r.1057–93) and granddaughter of Edmund Ironside, king of England, St Margaret (*c.*1045–93) was noted for her services to the church in Scotland and for her learning, piety and religious benefactions. She was canonized in 1250 and died on 16 November, now her feast-day.

**Margin.** In many old books a commentary was printed in the margin, as notably in the Bible. Hence the word was often used for a commentary itself, as in Shakespeare's:

> His face's own margent did quote such amazes,
> That all eyes saw his eyes enchanted with gazes.
> *Love's Labour's Lost*, II, i (1594)

**Marguerite des Marguerites** (French, 'pearl of pearls'). So Francis I called his sister, Marguerite d'Angoulême (1492–1549), author of the HEPTAMERON (published posthumously in 1558) and a collection of poems entitled *Les Marguerites de la marguerite des princesses* (1547). She married twice, first the Duc d'Alençon (d.1525), and then Henri d'Albret, king of Navarre. She was known for her PROTESTANT leanings.

**Maria. Maria Marten.** *See* MURDER IN THE RED BARN.

**Ave Maria.** *See under* AVE.

**Black Maria.** *See under* BLACK.

**Mariage de convenance** (French, 'marriage of expediency'). A marriage for money and position. *See also* KNOBSTICK WEDDING; SHOTGUN WEDDING.

**Marian. Marian year.** The method of reckoning 25 March, the FEAST OF THE ANNUNCIATION, as the first day of the year. This was used until the reform of the calendar in 1752. The beginning of the FINANCIAL YEAR follows this reckoning, and the eleven days added in 1752 make it 5 April.

**Maid Marian.** *See under* MAID.

**Marianne.** *See* MARY ANNE.

**Marie Antoinette.** Josèphe Jeanne Marie Antoinette (1755–93), queen of Louis XVI, was one of the French Revolution's saddest victims, despite her reputation for frivolity and her spendthrift ways. She ended her days as a symbol of the decadence and selfishness that characterized the period and has gone down in history for allegedly saying 'Let them eat cake' when told that the poor had no bread.

**Marie Celeste.** Properly MARY CELESTE.

**Marigold.** The plant *Calendula officinalis* with its bright yellow or orange flowers is so called in honour of the Virgin MARY.

**Mari Lwyd.** 'Singing with Mari Lwyd' ('Grey Mare') is an old Welsh Christmastide custom surviving at Llangynwyd near Bridgend, south Wales, and may have derived from the old MYSTERY or miracle plays. The chief character wears a white cowl and a horse's skull bedecked with ribbons and is accompanied by two or three fantastically dressed followers. They used to sing outside houses, demanding entrance, when they were made welcome and suitably refreshed or recompensed. Today Mari Lwyd still performs her songs in and around *Yr Hen Dy* (The Old House) inn at midnight on New Year's Eve. The ritual is part of the mumming and WASSAIL tradition found elsewhere at this season.

**Marine.** A 'sea soldier'. In the Royal Navy the Marines have been an established force since 1755, although they had earlier origins in the Duke of York and Albany's Maritime Regiment of Foot (1664). A marine is familiarly known as a JOLLY, 'bootneck' and 'leatherneck', among other things. This last name arose from the leather lining of the stand-up collar of the old scarlet tunic (now only full dress).

Empty bottles were at one time called 'marines' (because the seamen regarded them as useless) but now, more usually, DEAD MARINES, or, in the USA, 'dead soldiers'.

According to one story, the Duke of York, when dining in the mess, said to the servant: 'Here, take away these marines.' A marine officer present asked for an explanation, and the duke replied: 'They have done their duty, and are prepared to do it again.'

A GREENHORN OR LANDLUBBER afloat is sometimes contemptuously called 'a marine' by seamen.

**Dead marines.** *See under* DEAD.

**Female Marine, The.** *See under* FEMALE.

**Tell that to the Marines!** *See under* TELL.

**Mariner. Mariner's compass.** China traditionally claims the invention of the compass in 2634 BC, but the earliest authentic reference to the LODESTONE is in AD 121, and not until the 12th century is there mention of a compass in a ship. Claims for its discovery have also been made for the Arabs, Greeks, Italians and others, but it may have arrived independently in both Europe and China. The belief that Marco Polo introduced it from China in 1260 is unfounded, as it was in use in Europe a century before this. *See also* FLEUR-DE-LIS.

**Ancient Mariner.** *See under* ANCIENT.

**Maritimes.** The Maritime Provinces of Canada: Nova Scotia, New Brunswick and Prince Edward Island.

**Marivaudage.** An imitation of the style of the French writer Pierre Marivaux (1688–1763), author of several comedies and novels, many of them written in a refined style with a content of exaggerated sentiment.

**Mark.** Government equipment of various kinds issued to the armed services in the original form is labelled Mark I. Subsequent modifications are labelled Mark II, Mark III and so on.

**Marked with a B, To be.** In the Middle Ages and as late as the 17th century (especially in America), this letter was branded on the forehead of convicted blasphemers. In France *être marqué au b* meant to be one-eyed, humpbacked or lame (*borgne*, *bossu* or *boiteux*). Hence the letter became associated with an ill-favoured person.

**Marked with a T, To be.** To be notified as a felon. Persons convicted of felony and admitted to the BENEFIT OF CLERGY, were branded on the thumb with the letter T (thief). The law authorizing this was abolished in 1827.

**Marked with BC, To be.** When a soldier disgraced himself by insubordination he was formerly marked with BC (bad character) before he was finally drummed out of the regiment.

**Mark of the beast, The.** To set the 'mark of the beast' on an object of pursuit (such as dancing, gambling, drinking and so forth) is to denounce it as an evil. The biblical 'mark of the beast' symbolizes the Satanic Roman Empire and the priests of its imperial cult.

> And there fell a noisome and grievous sore upon the men which had the mark of the beast, and upon them which worshipped his image.
>
> Revelation 16:2

**Marks of gold and silver.** *See* HALLMARK.

**Mark time, To.** To raise the feet alternately as in marching but without advancing or retreating. Also, to keep things going while waiting for something to happen or for an opportunity to arise. *See also* RUNNING ON THE SPOT.

**Beside the mark.** *See under* BESIDE.

**Full marks.** *See under* FULL.

**God bless** or **save the mark!** *See under* GOD.

**Make one's mark, To.** To distinguish oneself; to achieve note. It is an ancient practice for persons who cannot write to 'make their mark'. In old documents, the mark was the sign of the cross, which was followed by the name of the person concerned.

**Man of mark.** *See under* MAN.

**Near the mark.** *See under* NEAR.

**Printers' marks.** *See under* PRINT.

**Strawberry mark.** *See under* STRAWBERRY.

**Up to the mark.** *See under* UP.

**Wide of the mark.** *See under* WIDE.

**Mark** (name).

**Mark Tapley.** *See under* TAPLEY.

**Mark Twain.** *See under* TWAIN.

**King Mark.** In ARTHURIAN ROMANCES a king of Cornwall, Sir TRISTRAM'S uncle. He lived at TINTAGEL and is principally remembered for his treachery and cowardice and as the husband of YSOLDE the Fair, who was passionately enamoured of Tristram.

**Lion of St Mark, The.** *See under* LION.

**St Mark.** The Gospel writer who died in prison *c.*68 is represented in art as in the prime of life, sometimes dressed as a bishop and with a lion at his feet and scroll on which is written: 'Peace be to thee, O Mark, My Evangelist.' He is also represented with a pen in his right hand and the Gospel in his left. His day is 25 April.

**St Mark's Eve.** An old custom in north country villages was for people to sit in the church porch on this day (24 April) from 11 pm until 1 am for three years running, in order to see pass into the church in the third year the ghosts of those who were to die that year. In other parts this custom was observed on MIDSUMMER Eve (23 June). POOR ROBIN'S ALMANACK for 1770 refers to another superstition:

> On St Mark's Eve, at twelve o'clock,
> The fair maid will watch her smock,
> To find her husband in the dark,
> By praying unto good St Mark.

Keats has an unfinished poem on the subject.

**Market. Market cross.** A prominent feature in the centre of many towns and villages, the market cross had and in some cases still has a variety of functions, but it especially served as a focal point from which market traders and local townspeople could be addressed. Many crosses are of medieval origin and are of architectural interest, such as that formerly in Bristol, removed to the gardens of Stourhead, Wiltshire, in 1753. Some bear an inscription recording a significant local event, as the following, at Devizes, Wiltshire:

> The MAYOR and CORPORATION of Devizes avail themselves of the Stability of this Building, to transmit to future time, the Record of an awful Event which occured in this Market Place, in the year 1753, hoping that such a Record may serve as a salutary Warning against the Danger of impiously invoking Divine Vengeance, or of calling on the Holy Name of GOD to conceal the Devices of Falsehood and Fraud.
>
> On Thursday the 25th of January 1753, Ruth Pierce, of Pottern, in this County agreed with three other Women to buy a Sack of Wheat in the Market, each paying her due Proportion towards the same. One of these Women, in collecting the several Quotas of Money discovered a Deficiency, and demanded of Ruth Pierce the Sum which was wanting to make up the Amount; Ruth Pierce protested that She had paid her Share, and said, "*She wished She might drop down dead, if She had not.*" She rashly repeated this awful Wish, when, to the Consternation and Terror of the surrounding Multitude, She instantly fell down and expired, having the Money concealed in her Hand.

**Marketese.** The abbreviated names of fruit, flowers and vegetables, used not only on the price labels of market stalls and in the shops of fruiterers, florists, greengrocers etc, but also on domestic shopping lists. Examples are 'strawbs' for strawberries, 'toms' for tomatoes and 'mums' or 'xanths' for chrysanthemums. This last is a linguistic curiosity, since although 'xanth' represents an abbreviated pronunciation, the name itself means 'golden flower', from the Greek, yet Greek *xanthos* means 'yellow', which is equally appropriate.

**Black market.** *See under* BLACK.

**Caledonian Market.** *See under* CALEDONIA.

**Common Market.** *See under* COMMON.

**Drug on the market, A.** *See under* DRUG.

**Flea market.** *See under* FLEA.

**Grey market.** *See under* GREY.

**Marks and Sparks.** A colloquial jingling name for the Marks & Spencer clothes and food stores, current from about the 1940s.

> In their Marks and Sparks' woollies and living in what looks like a remarkable nice housing estate, Topsy and Tim clearly stand in for classless society.
>
> *Sunday Times* (5 April 1964)

**Marlborough.** *See* MALBROUK.

**Marlene, Lili.** *See under* LILI.

**Marlowe, Philip.** The honest but cynical Californian detective created by Raymond Chandler (1888–1959). He first appeared in *The Big Sleep* (1939).

**Marmalade, Oxford.** *See under* OXFORD.

**Maro.** VIRGIL.

**Marocco** or **Morocco.** The name of BANKS'S HORSE.

**Maronites.** A UNIAT body, mainly in the Lebanon, in communion with Rome and having their own liturgy. Although probably of 7th-century origin, they are traditionally said to have arisen in the early 5th century as followers of Maro, an anchorite living near Antioch. They became MONOTHELITES, but recognized Rome's authority in the 12th century.

**Marple, Miss.** The elderly spinster detective, full name Jane Marple, who is the heroine of a number of crime novels by Agatha Christie (1890–1976), beginning with *Murder at the Vicarage* (1930), in which she is 74 years old. She bases her methods on the belief that 'human nature is much the same everywhere', and regards her village, St Mary Mead, as a microcosm of the world. She has been played by various well-known actresses in film and television versions of the stories, including Margaret Rutherford in the former medium and Joan Hickson in the latter.

**Marplot.** An officious person who defeats some design by gratuitous meddling. The name is given to a silly, cowardly, inquisitive Paul PRY in *The Busie Body* (1709) by Susannah Centlivre. There are also Shakespeare's 'Sir Oliver Martext', the clergyman in *As You Like It* (1599) and 'Sir Martin Mar-All', the hero of Dryden and the Duke of Newcastle's comedy (1667) of that name, which was based on MOLIÈRE'S *L'Etourdi* (1655).

**Marprelate controversy.** The name given to the vituperative pamphlet war between the PURITAN writer 'Martin Marprelate' and the supporters of the established church. The Marprelate Tracts (1587–9) were scurrilous attacks on the bishops, secretly printed and distributed. They threatened to establish a 'young Martin' in every parish 'to mar a prelate'. The church commissioned John Lyly (*c*.1554–1606), Thomas Nashe (1567–1601) and Robert Greene (1558–92) to launch a counterattack. The tracts led to a Conventicle Act and another against seditious writings, and the presumed chief author, John Penry, was caught and hanged in 1593.

**Marque, Letter of.** *See under* LETTER.

**Marquess** or **marquis** (Old French *marchis*, 'count of the marches'). A title of nobility in England below that of DUKE. It was first conferred on Richard II's favourite, Robert de Vere, Earl of

Oxford, who was created Marquess of Dublin in 1385. A marquess is addressed as 'The Most Honourable the Marquess of ...'. *See also* COURTESY TITLE; COUSIN; MARCHES; PEERS OF THE REALM.

**Marquis of Granby, The.** *See under* GRANBY.

**Marriage. Marriage knot, The.** The bond of marriage effected by the legal marriage ceremony. The Latin phrase is *nodus Herculeus*, and part of the marriage service was for the bridegroom to loosen (*solvere*) the bride's girdle, not to tie it. In the Hindu marriage ceremony the bridegroom knots a ribbon round the bride's neck. Before the knot is tied, the bride's father may refuse consent, but immediately it is tied the marriage is indissoluble. The PARSEES bind the hands of the bridegroom with a sevenfold cord, seven being a sacred number. The ancient Carthaginians tied the thumbs of the betrothed with a leather lace. *See also* RICE.

**Marriages are made in heaven.** This implies that partners joined in marriage were foreordained to be so united. Edward Hall (*c*.1499–1547) says: 'Consider the old proverbe to be true that saieth: Marriage is destinie.'

> They say marriages are made in heaven; but I doubt, when she was married, she had no friend there.
>
> JONATHAN SWIFT: *A Complete Collection ... in Three Dialogues* (1738)

**Banns of marriage.** *See under* BANNS.

**Close seasons for marriage.** *See under* CLOSE.

**Gretna Green marriages.** *See under* GRETNA.

**Jactitation of marriage.** *See under* JACTITATION.

**Left-handed marriage, A.** A MORGANATIC MARRIAGE.

**Morganatic marriage, A.** *See under* MORGANATIC.

**Marry!** An old oath, meaning 'by Mary', the Virgin.

**Marry come up!** An exclamation of surprise, disapproval, incredulity or the like. The meaning is: 'May Mary come up to my assistance, or to your discomfort!'

**Mars.** The Roman god of war, identified in certain aspects with the Greek ARES. He was also the patron of husbandmen. The planet of this name was so called because of its reddish tinge.

Among the alchemists Mars designated iron, and in Camoëns' LUSIADS (1572) typified divine fortitude. *See also* MARTIANS.

**Mars of Portugal, The.** Alfonso de Albuquerque (1453–1515), viceroy of India.

**Marseillaise.** The hymn of the French Revolution and the national anthem of France. The words and music were written by Claude Rouget de Lisle (1760–1835), an artillery officer in the garrison at Strasbourg in 1792, and its original title was *Chant de guerre pour l'armée du Rhin* ('War song for the Rhine army'). It was first made known in Paris by troops from Marseilles, hence the name. *See also* CHANT DU DÉPART.

**Marshal** (Old French *mareschal*, related to Old High German *marahscalc*, 'groom', from *marah*, 'horse', and *scalc*, 'servant'). The word was originally used for a groom or farrier, but is now the title of high officials about the Court, in the armed forces and elsewhere. In the army field marshal is the highest rank, while in the RAF it is marshal of the Royal Air Force. Air chief marshal, air marshal and air vice marshal thus correspond to general, lieutenant-general and major-general respectively.

The military rank of Marshal of France was revived by NAPOLEON BONAPARTE, who gave the baton to some of his most able generals. No Marshals were created after 1870 until 1916 when the title was given to General Joffre (1852–1931). Generals Foch (1851–1929), Lyautey (1854–1934) and Pétain (1856–1951) were also Marshals of France. *See also* EARL MARSHAL.

**Marshal of the Army of God and of Holy Church, The.** The Baron Robert Fitzwalter, appointed by his brother barons to lead their forces in 1215, to obtain redress of grievances from King John. MAGNA CARTA was the result.

**Marshal Vorwärts.** *See* FORWARDS, MARSHAL.

**Earl Marshal.** *See under* EARL.

**Field marshal.** *See under* FIELD.

**Marshall Plan.** The popular name for the European Recovery Programme sponsored by US Secretary of State George C. Marshall (1880–1959), to bring economic aid to stricken Europe after the Second World War. It was inaugurated in June 1947. Most states, apart from the Soviet Union and her satellites, participated. Britain ceased to receive Marshall Aid in 1950. *See also* LEND-LEASE.

**Marshalsea Prison.** An old prison in High Street, SOUTHWARK, the prison of the Marshalsea Court, which was originally a court of the royal household, presided over by the EARL MARSHAL. The court, with the Knight Marshal for judge, existed until December 1849. From the 1430s, the prison also received admiralty prisoners and debtors. It moved to newer premises in 1799 and was closed in 1842. In 1381 its marshal was beheaded by the rebels under Wat Tyler. Charles Dickens' father was imprisoned there in 1824.

> Necessarily, he was going out again directly, because the Marshalsea lock never turned upon a debtor who was not.
>
> DICKENS: *Little Dorrit*, ch vi (1855–7)

**Marshland, The Bailiff of the.** *See under* BAILIFF.

**Marsyas.** The Phrygian flute player who challenged APOLLO to a contest of skill, and, being beaten by the god, was flayed alive for his presumption. From his blood arose the River

Marsyas. The flute on which Marsyas played had been discarded by MINERVA, and, being filled with the breath of the goddess, discoursed most beautiful music. The interpretation of this fable is as follows. The DORIAN MODE, employed in the worship of Apollo, was performed on lutes, and the Phrygian mode, employed in the rites of CYBELE, was executed by flutes, the reeds of which grew on the River Marsyas. As the Dorian mode was preferred by the Greeks, they said that Apollo beat the flute player.

**Martel.** The byname given to Charles (*c*.688–741), son of Pepin II, MAYOR OF THE PALACE, probably because of his victory over the SARACENS, who had invaded France under Abd-el-Rahman in 732. It is said that Charles 'knocked down the foe, and crushed them beneath his axe, as a martel or hammer crushes what it strikes'.

**Martello towers.** Round towers about 40ft (12m) high and of great strength. Many of them were built on the southeastern coasts of England about 1803 against the threat of French invasion. They took their name from Cape Mortella, Corsica, where a tower, from which these were designed, had proved extremely difficult to capture in 1794. Forty-three Martello towers have survived, and that at Dymchurch, Kent, has been restored to its original condition. *See also* PALMERSTON'S FOLLIES.

**Marten, Maria.** *See* MURDER IN THE RED BARN.

**Mar-text.** *See* MARPLOT.

**Martha. Martha's Vineyard.** An island some 100 square miles (260 sq km) in area off the southeast coast of Massachusetts. It was first recorded in 1602 by the navigator Bartholomew Gosnold and named by his fellow explorer Gabriel Archer. It is not known who the Martha of the name was.

**St Martha.** Sister of St LAZARUS and St MARY MAGDALENE, and the patron saint of good housewives. She is represented in art in homely costume, bearing at her girdle a bunch of keys, and holding a ladle or pot of water in her hand. Like St MARGARET she is accompanied by a bound DRAGON, for she is said to have destroyed one that ravaged the neighbourhood of Marseilles. She is commemorated on 29 July and is patron of Tarascon.

**Martial, Court.** *See under* COURT.

**Martian laws.** Laws said to have been compiled by Martia, wife of King Guithelin of Britain. According to Geoffrey of Monmouth (*Historia Regum Britanniae* (*c*.1136)) Martia was 'a noble lady ... accomplished in all kinds of learning', and her work was translated into Saxon by King Alfred.

**Martians.** The hypothetical inhabitants of the planet MARS, which has a much less dense atmosphere than the earth. In 1898 H.G. Wells wrote *The War of the Worlds*, in which he recounted the adventures and horrors of a war between the men of Mars and the dwellers on earth.

**Martin.** A bird of the swallow family, probably so called from the Christian name Martin (*see* St MARTIN'S BIRD), but possibly because it appears in Britain about March (the Martian month) and migrates about MARTINMAS.

**Martinmas.** The feast of St MARTIN OF TOURS, 11 November.

**Humanity Martin.** *See under* HUMANITY.

**St Martin of Bullions.** The St SWITHIN of Scotland. His feast-day is 4 July, and the saying is that if it rains then, rain may be expected for 40 days.

**St Martin of Tours.** The patron saint of innkeepers and reformed drunkards, usually shown in art as a young mounted soldier dividing his cloak with a beggar, in allusion to the legend that in midwinter, when a military tribune at Amiens, he divided his cloak with a near-naked beggar who sought alms and that at night Christ appeared to him arrayed in this very garment. This effected his conversion.

He was born *c*.316 of heathen parents in Pannonia (now in Hungary) but was converted at Rome and became bishop of Tours in 371, dying at Candes in 397. His day is 11 November, the day of the Feast of BACCHUS. Hence his purely accidental patronage.

**St Martin's beads.** Cheap counterfeit beads, jewellery, lace, rings and so on are so called. When the old collegiate church of St Martin's-le-Grand in London was demolished at the dissolution of the monasteries (1536), hucksters established themselves on the site and carried on a considerable trade in artificial jewellery and cheap wares generally. Hence the use of the saint's name in this connection. *See also* TAWDRY.

**St Martin's bird.** The hen harrier, called *l'oiseau de Saint Martin* in France, because it makes its passage through the country about 11 November (St Martin's Day).

**St Martin's goose.** St Martin's Day (11 November) was at one time the great goose feast in France. The legend is that the saint was annoyed by a goose, which he ordered to be killed and served up for dinner. Hence, the goose was 'sacrificed' to him on each anniversary. *See also* GOOSE FAIR; MICHAELMAS DAY.

**St Martin's summer.** A late spell of fine weather. St Martin's day is 11 November. *See also* INDIAN SUMMER.

**Martinet.** A strict disciplinarian, so called from Jean, Marquis de Martinet, colonel commanding Louis XIV's own regiment of infantry. The king required all young noblemen to command a platoon in this regiment before purchasing command of an infantry regiment. Martinet's system for training these wild young men in the principles of military discipline gained him lasting fame. He perished at the siege of Duisburg in 1672.

**Martini.** A COCKTAIL essentially consisting of Martini vermouth and gin, taking its name from the firm of Martini & Rossi, makers of vermouth. There are three forms of this cocktail, dry, medium and sweet, each containing two parts gin to one of vermouth, the latter two cocktails having additional ingredients. In the USA the proportion of gin in a dry Martini is considerably higher.

**Martinus Scriblerus.** A merciless satire on the false taste in literature current in the time of Alexander Pope (1688–1744), for the most part written by John Arbuthnot (1667–1735) and published in 1741. Cornelius Scriblerus, the father of Martin, was a pedant, who entertained all sorts of absurdities about the education of his son. Martin grew up a man of capacity, but although he had read everything, his judgement was poor and taste atrocious. Pope, Jonathan Swift and Arbuthnot founded a Scriblerus club with the object of pillorying all literary incompetence.

**Martyr** (Greek, 'witness'). Originally, someone who bears testimony, and hence someone who bears witness to their faith with their blood.

**Martyr King, The.** CHARLES I of England, beheaded 30 January 1649.

**Manchester Martyrs.** *See under* MANCHESTER.

**Tolpuddle Martyrs.** *See under* TOLPUDDLE.

**Marvel, Captain.** The red-suited, tough-muscled superhero of American comics, nicknamed 'the Big Red Cheese'. He first appeared in Fawcett's *Whiz* comics in 1940. His real name is Billy Batson, implying he is a son of BATMAN, who made his début the previous year. He begins as a weedy youth but is transformed when he meets a wizard who gives him a magic word to say. This is Shazam, an acronym of the names of six traditional heroes: SOLOMON, HERCULES, ATLAS, ZEUS, ACHILLES and MERCURY.

**Marxism.** The philosophical and political and economic theories or system propounded by Karl Marx (1818–83) and Friedrich Engels (1820–95), which formed the basis of Communist dogma. It involved a materialist conception of history, a theory of class war, a belief in the ultimate destruction of capitalism and the formation of a classless society. *See also* COMMUNISM; LENIN; MATERIALISM.

**Mary.** There are three women of this name in the New Testament: Mary, the mother of Jesus, MARY MAGDALENE, and Mary of Bethany, sister of MARTHA. All four Gospels agree that the first two of these were at the foot of the cross at the time of the crucifixion. John says that there were three Marys, the third being the sister of Mary, mother of Jesus, and the wife of Cleopas.

Mary, the Mother of Christ is represented in art as follows:

- Virgin: with flowing hair, emblematic of her virginity
- Mater Dolorosa: somewhat elderly, clad in mourning, head draped, and weeping over the dead body of Christ
- Our Lady of Dolours: seated, her breast pierced with seven swords, emblematic of her seven sorrows
- Our Lady of Mercy: with arms extended, spreading out her mantle and gathering sinners beneath it
- Glorified Madonna: bearing a crown and sceptre, or an orb and cross, in rich robes and surrounded by angels

The seven joys of Mary are: the ANNUNCIATION, the VISITATION, the NATIVITY, the EPIPHANY, the Finding in the Temple, the Resurrection and the Ascension. Her seven sorrows are: Simeon's prophecy, the Flight into Egypt, the loss of the Holy Child, meeting Christ on the way to CALVARY, the crucifixion, the taking down from the cross and the entombment. Her festival is 8 September.

**Mary Ambree.** *See under* AMBREE.

**Mary Anne** or **Marianne.** A slang name for the GUILLOTINE. *See also* MARY ANNE ASSOCIATIONS.

**Mary Anne associations.** Secret republican societies in France. The name was adopted by the Republican party because François Ravaillac was moved to assassinate Henry IV in 1610 by his reading *De Rege et Regis Institutione* by Juan de Mariana (1536–1624), the LIVY OF SPAIN.

**Marybuds.** The flower of the MARIGOLD. Like many other flowers, they open at daybreak and close at sunset.

> And winking Mary-buds begin
> To ope their golden eyes.
> SHAKESPEARE: *Cymbeline*, II, iii (1609)

**Mary Celeste.** An American brigantine found abandoned, with sails set, between the Azores and Portugal on 5 December 1872. The ship's one boat, sextant, chronometer, register and crew were missing, and no trace of them was ever found. It remains one of the unsolved mysteries of the sea. Hence the use of the ship's name for any deserted place, especially one that has signs of normally being occupied. The name is properly as given here, not 'Marie Celeste'.

**Maryland.** The US state was so named in compliment to Henrietta Maria, queen of CHARLES I. In the Latin charter it is called *Terra Mariae*.

**Marylebone.** This London district was originally called TYBURN, being situated on that little river. The name derives from St Mary-at-Bourne, a village near the River Tyburn, also called Marybourne, Maryborne, Marybone or Mary-le-bone. The -le- was probably inserted by association with St Mary-le-Bow, a similar name.

**Mary of Arnhem.** The name used by Helen Sensburg in her NAZI propaganda broadcasts to British troops in northwest Europe, 1944–5. Her melting voice made her programmes very popular with the British, but without the results for which she hoped.

**Mary Poppins.** *See under* POPPINS.

**Mary, Queen of Scots.** The daughter of James V of Scotland, Mary Stuart (1542–87) became queen when only a week old. She was promised in marriage to Prince Edward of England, son of Henry VIII, but the promise was annulled and she was sent to France to be betrothed to the DAUPHIN, later Francis II, and married him in 1558. Following his death a year later, she married her cousin, Lord Darnley. He was mysteriously killed in 1567, when she married the Earl of Bothwell, regarded by many as Darnley's murderer. She then abdicated in favour of her son, later James I of England, and threw herself on the mercy of Elizabeth I only to find herself a prisoner in a series of strongholds. She was eventually beheaded at Fotheringhay. Her Catholic allegiance has sometimes resulted in her being popularly confused with BLOODY MARY.

**Mary Stuart.** *See* MARY, QUEEN OF SCOTS.

**Bloody Mary.** *See under* BLOODY.

**Highland Mary.** *See under* HIGHLAND.

**Immaculate Heart of Mary, The.** *See under* IMMACULATE.

**Little Mary.** *See under* LITTLE.

**Seven joys of Mary, The.** *See under* SEVEN.

**Seven sorrows of Mary, The.** *See under* SEVEN.

**St Mary Magdalene.** The patron saint of penitents, and herself the model penitent of Gospel story. She is the prototype of the reformed prostitute and the chief witness of the Resurrection. After the crucifixion, on 'the first day of the week', she goes while it is still dark to Jesus' tomb and finds the stone rolled away and the tomb empty. She tells PETER and JOHN, who come running to see for themselves. When they have gone, she is left there weeping. Seeing a man whom she takes to be the gardener, she asks him if he has taken away the body and, if so, where to. He is no gardener, however, but Christ himself, who tells her not to touch him, but to go and tell the others (John 20:1–18). Her feast is 22 July.

In art Mary Magdalene is represented either as young and beautiful, with a profusion of hair and holding a box of ointment, or as a penitent, in a sequestered place, reading before a cross or skull. *See also* MAGDALENE; MAUDLIN.

**Typhoid Mary.** *See under* TYPHOID.

**Masada.** The great rock on the edge of the Judaean desert, the site of Herod the Great's palace, where the ZEALOTS made their last heroic stand against the Romans. When defeat was certain, their leader Eleazar ben Ya'ir persuaded them to draw lots to select ten men to kill the remaining 960 defenders. One of these finally slew his nine fellows and then pushed his sword through his own body. The story is told by JOSEPHUS. Among the relics revealed by Professor Yigael Yadin's excavation exhibited at London in 1966 were eleven small potsherds inscribed with names, on one of which was the name 'ben Ya'ir'. They are probably the lots in question.

**Masaniello.** A corruption of Tommaso Aniello (1623–47), a fisherman's son who led the Neapolitan revolt of July 1647 and ruled Naples for nine days. He was finally betrayed and shot. His body was flung into a ditch but was reclaimed and interred with great pomp and ceremony. The discontent was caused by excessive taxation, and Masaniello's immediate grievance was the seizure of his property because his wife had smuggled flour. Daniel Auber's opera *La Muette de Portici* (1828) is based on these events.

**Mascot.** A person or thing that is supposed to bring good luck. The word is French slang (perhaps connected with Provençal *masco*, 'sorcerer'), and was popularized in England by Edmond Audran's opera, *La Mascotte* (1880).

**Masculine ending.** The stress or accent falling on the final syllable of a line of verse. *See also* FEMININE ENDING.

> I must go down to the seas again, to the lonely sea and the sky,
> And all I ask is a tall ship and a star to steer her by.
> JOHN MASEFIELD: 'Sea Fever' (1902)

**Mask, The Man in the Iron.** *See under* MAN.

**Masochism.** The name for the condition in which sexual gratification is derived from humiliation and pain inflicted by another person, so called after Leopold von Sacher-Masoch (1836–95), the Austrian novelist who described this. *See also* SADISM.

**Mason–Dixon Line.** The southern boundary line that separated Pennsylvania from MARYLAND, fixed at 39° 43′ 26 north, marked out (1763–7) by two British surveyors, Charles Mason (1730–87) and Jeremiah Dixon (d.1777). From about 1820 it was popularly used to signify the boundary between North and South, 'free' and 'slave' states.

**Mass** (Latin *missa*, 'a dismissal'). The EUCHARIST. In the early church the unbaptized were dismissed before the Eucharist proper began and the remaining congregation were solemnly dismissed at the end. By the 8th century the name *missa* had become transferred to the service as a whole, and the original meaning of the word faded out. The name Mass is used by the ROMAN CATHOLIC CHURCH and by the HIGH CHURCH of the CHURCH OF ENGLAND.

HIGH MASS, or *Missa solemnis*, in which the celebrant is assisted by a deacon and subdeacon, requires the presence of choir and acolytes. Sung Mass, or *Missa cantata*, is a simplification in which the celebrant and congregation sing the musical parts of the service, but without the deacon and subdeacon. The plain form of Mass is called LOW MASS. A Pontifical High Mass is one celebrated by a bishop or higher prelate with very full ritual. A Nuptial Mass follows the marriage service and a Requiem Mass is one offered for the dead. There are also other special forms of Mass.

**Black Mass.** *See under* BLACK.

**Canons of the Mass.** *See under* CANON.

**Devil's Mass.** *See under* DEVIL.

**High Mass.** *See under* HIGH.

**Low Mass.** *See under* LOW.

**Ordinary of the Mass, The.** *See under* ORDINARY.

**Massacre. Massacre of the Innocents, The.** The slaughter of the male children of Behlehem 'from two years old and under' when Jesus was born (Matthew 2:16). This was done at the command of Herod the Great in order to destroy 'the babe' who was destined to become 'King of the Jews'.

In parliamentary parlance, the phrase denotes the withdrawal at the close of the session of those bills that there has been no time to consider or pass.

**Manchester Massacre.** *See* PETERLOO MASSACRE.

**Peterloo Massacre.** *See under* PETERLOO.

**St Bartholomew's Day Massacre.** *See under* BARTHOLOMEW.

**September Massacres, The.** *See under* SEPTEMBER.

**Mass Observation.** A British trade name for a system of obtaining information as to popular opinion, similar to the GALLUP POLL. It grew out of a voluntary organization started by Charles Madge and Tom Harrison in 1937.

**Mast, Jury.** *See under* JURY.

**Master.** The word is derived partly from Old English *magister* and partly from Old French *maistre*, both ultimately from Latin *magister*, related to Latin *magis*, 'more'.

**Master-at-arms.** In the Royal Navy, a chief petty officer of the Regulating Branch concerned with police and disciplinary duties. He takes precedence over other CPOs.

**Master mason.** A FREEMASON who has been raised to the third degree.

**Master of Arts.** One who holds a Master's degree of a university in arts. In the English universities it is the degree above that of Bachelor. At the modern universities it is awarded for further examination or research, but at Oxford and Cambridge no further tests are required. In the Scottish universities it is a first degree. At most universities there are corresponding Master's degrees in other faculties.

**Master of ceremonies.** A court official, first appointed by James I to superintend the reception of ambassadors and strangers of rank and to prescribe the formalities to be observed in LEVEES and other public functions. The title is now given to a person who presides over a public ceremony, such as a formal dinner or entertainment. His main role is to introduce items planned for the evening, as well as speakers and performers. It is often abbreviated to MC.

**Master of the field.** The winner; the victor in battle.

**Master of the King's** or **Queen's Music.** A musician appointed by the sovereign to compose music for state occasions. The post, the equivalent of the POET LAUREATE, is for life, and carries an annual honorarium (in the late 1990s it was £100). The title was that originally given (as Master of the King's Musick) to the official who presided over the Court band in the reign of Charles I. Composers holding the post since 1626 with appointment year following the life dates are:

Nicholas Lanier (1588–1666; 1626)
Louis Grabu (*fl.*1665–94; 1666)
Nicholas Staggins (1650–1700; 1674)
John Eccles (1668–1735; 1700)
Maurice Greene (1695–1755; 1735)
William Boyce (1710–79; 1755)
John Stanley (1713–86; 1779)
William Parsons (1746–1817; 1786)
William Shield (1748–1829; 1817)
Christian Kramer (d.1834; 1829)
Franz Cramer (1772–1848; 1834)
George Frederick Anderson (d.1870; 1848)
Sir William Cusins (1833–93; 1870)
Sir Walter Parratt (1841–1924; 1893)
Sir Edward Elgar (1857–1934; 1924)
Sir Walford Davies (1869–1941; 1934)
Sir Arnold Bax (1883–1953; 1941)
Sir Arthur Bliss (1891–1975; 1953)
Sir Malcolm Williamson (b.1931; 1975)

**Master of the Rolls.** The judge who presides over civil cases in the COURT OF APPEAL, and as such the most important civil judge outside the House of Lords. His title goes back to the 16th century, when he was the keeper of CHANCERY records or rolls and legal assistant to the CHANCELLOR. In 1838 he was given control of the newly created Public Record Office, a post that in 1958 was transferred to the LORD CHANCELLOR.

**Master of the Sentences.** The SCHOOLMAN, Peter Lombard (*c.*1100–60), and Italian theologian and bishop of Paris, author of *The Four Books of Sentences* (*Sententiarum libri IV*), a compilation from the Fathers of the leading arguments PRO AND CON, bearing on the hair-splitting theological questions of the Middle Ages.

The medieval graduates in theology, of the second order, whose duty it was to lecture on the *Sentences*, were called Sententiatory Bachelors.

**Bearded Master.** *See under* BEARD.

**Jack of all trades and master of none.** *See under* JACK.

**Jack's as good as his master.** *See under* JACK.

**Little Master.** *See under* LITTLE.

**Old Masters.** *See under* OLD.

**Past master.** *See under* PAST.

**Servant of two masters, A.** *See under* SERVANT.

**Seven Wise Masters, The.** *See under* SEVEN.

**Matador.** In bull fights, the final actor in the drama, his part being to play the bull alone and kill it.

In the game of OMBRE Spadille (the ace of spades), Manille (the seven of trumps) and Basto (the ace of clubs) are called 'Matadors'.

In the game of dominoes of this name, the double blank and all the 'stones' that of themselves make seven (6–1, 5–2 and 4–3) are 'matadors' and can be played at any time.

**Mata Hari.** The assumed name of the Dutch dancer and courtesan Margaretha Gertruida MacLeod, née Zelle (1876–1917), from a Malay expression for the sun, meaning 'eye of the day'. She was shot by the French on charges of spying for the Germans in the First World War, although precise details of her espionage activities remain rather obscure. Her own story was that she had agreed to act as a French spy in occupied Belgium without telling the French intelligence authorities of her agreement with the Germans. Her physical allure and glamorous role meant that her stage name was afterwards used for any seductive female spy.

**Match. Friendly match.** *See under* FRIEND.

**Hatches, matches and dispatches.** *See under* HATCHES.

**Love match.** *See under* LOVE.

**Lucifer match.** *See under* LUCIFER.

**Safety matches.** *See under* SAFE.

**Slanging match.** *See under* SLANG.

**Test Match.** *See under* TEST.

**Matchless Orinda, The.** Katherine Philips, *née* Fowler (1631–64), poet and letter-writer. She first adopted the signature 'Orinda' in her correspondence with Sir Charles Cotterell, and afterwards used it for general purposes. Her praises were sung by Abraham Cowley, John Dryden and others.

**Mate, Running.** *See under* RUN.

**Maté.** Paraguay tea made from the leaves of Brazilian holly (*Ilex paraguarienis*). Its full name is *Yerba de maté* (*yerba*, 'herb', and *mate*, 'vessel') from the hollow gourd in which it was infused. It is also called Brazil tea, Jesuit's tea and yerba. The tea was drunk from the gourd through a *bombilla* or tube (South American Spanish *bomba*, 'pump'), and customarily the Paraguayan Indian host, after taking the first suck to signify that no treachery was possible, would pass the bombilla and gourd to his guests. *See also* CALUMET.

**Mater. Mater familias** (Latin). The mother of a family.

**Alma mater.** *See under* ALMA.

**Stabat Mater.** *See under* STABAT.

**Materialism.** In philosophy, the doctrines of a materialist, who maintains that there is nothing in the universe but matter, that mind is a phenomenon of matter and that there is no ground for assuming a spiritual first cause. In general, Materialism is opposed to IDEALISM, free will and belief in God. In the ancient world its chief exponents were EPICURUS and Lucretius, while in modern times the French philosophers Julien Offray de la Mettrie (1709–51) and Paul Heinrich Holbach (1723–89) espoused the philosophy. In the 19th century Materialism was much influenced by the theory of evolution and became involved with problems of interpretation in science, while later Marx put forward DIALECTICAL MATERIALISM.

In everyday parlance 'materialism' implies devotion to material things and interests.

**Dialectical materialism.** *See under* DIALECTIC.

**Historical materialism.** *See under* HISTORY.

**Materialize, To.** In psychical research, to assume the bodily form of psychical phenomena. The principles governing materialization are as yet unknown.

**Materia medica** (Medieval Latin, 'medical matter'). The branch of medicine that deals with the remedial substances employed for the cure and alleviation of disease, including their uses, properties and physiological effects. Dioscorides wrote his *Materia medica* (1st century AD), giving the properties of some 600 medicinal plants and also animal products of medical and dietetic use, which served to enlighten the herbalists of the 15th and 16th centuries.

**Mathematics, Higher.** *See under* HIGH.

**Mathew, Father.** Theobald Mathew (1796–1856), an Irish priest called the Apostle of Temperance. His work on behalf of total abstinence was truly remarkable. When the centenary of his death was celebrated in Cork in 1956, 60,000 people gathered to honour his memory.

**Matilda, Waltzing.** *See under* WALTZING.

**Matins** or **mattins.** The BREVIARY office for the night called Vigiliae until the 11th century, and originally held at midnight, but in the BENEDICTINE rule at 2 am. It is now anticipated and said the previous afternoon or evening. The name was retained in the BOOK OF COMMON PRAYER

(1549) for the service of morning prayer, which was derived from the ancient office. The name was discarded in the book of 1552.

**Matriculate** (Latin *matricula*, 'roll', 'register'). Students at universities matriculate when they enrol after fulfilling certain entrance requirements. To matriculate used to mean to pass the entrance examination qualifying one to enter as a student at a university, although many sat for such examinations simply to obtain a qualification. This examination no longer exists.

In Scottish HERALDRY when persons register their arms with the LORD LYON KING OF ARMS they are said to matriculate.

**Matron** (Latin *matrona*, 'married woman', 'wife'). The word has acquired specific associations in English. In its most general sense it is still sometimes used of a middle-aged married woman with a large family, especially one who is staid or dignified. In a specialized sense it is the term for a woman professionally involved in medicine, from a senior member of the nursing staff in a hospital to the woman in charge of the domestic and medical arrangements in a boarding school. The latter are not necessarily married, however.

**Matter. Matter-of-fact.** Ordinary; prosaic; unimaginative; as a 'matter-of-fact account'.

**Matter of life and death, A.** A crucial or urgent matter.

**As a matter of course.** *See under* AS.

**For that matter.** *See under* FOR.

**Grey matter.** *See under* GREY.

**Hand in the matter, A.** *See under* HAND.

**No matter.** Regardless of, as in, 'no matter what happens'.

**Root of the matter, The.** *See under* ROOT.

**What's the matter?** *See under* WHAT.

**Matterhorn.** The German name of the mountain in the Pennine Alps known to the French as Mont Cervin and to the Italians as Monte Cervino, both meaning 'deer-like mountain', from the peak's similarity to a deer's curved antlers. The German name also refers to its curved peak (*Horn*) but the first part of the name refers to the meadows or pastures (*Matter*) that lie at its base. It was first scaled in 1865 by Edward Whymper (1840–1911), when four of his party lost their lives.

Figuratively used, the name is sometimes applied to any danger or desperate situation, as the 'matrimonial Matterhorn'.

**Matthew. Matthew Parker's Bible.** *See* BISHOPS' BIBLE *under* BIBLE.

**Matthew's Bible.** *See under* BIBLE.

**St Matthew.** One of the 12 apostles, also known as Levi, son of Alphaeus. He was a tax collector in the service of the tetrarch of Galilee, but is not generally regarded as being the writer of the Gospel of St Matthew. It must nevertheless be called by his name since its true author is uncertain. He is represented in art either as an EVANGELIST, old and with a long beard, with an angel generally standing near by dictating his Gospel, or as an APOSTLE, bearing a purse in reference to his being a publican. He sometimes carries a spear, and sometimes a carpenter's rule or square. His symbol is an angel or a man's face, and his day is 21 September.

One legend says that St Matthew preached for 15 years in Judaea after the Ascension, and that he carried the Gospel to Ethiopia, where he was murdered.

**Matthias, St.** The APOSTLE chosen by lot to take the place left by the traitor JUDAS ISCARIOT (Acts 1:21–26). The name is a shortened form of Mattathias. His day is 14 May (formerly 24 February).

**Mattins.** *See* MATINS.

**Maudlin.** Mawkishly sentimental. 'Maudlin drunk' is sentimentally drunk and inclined to tears. The word is derived from the repentant tears of MARY MAGDALENE, who was often portrayed with eyes swollen after weeping. *See also* MAGDALENE.

**Maul of Monks, The.** Thomas Cromwell (*c*.1485–1540), VICAR GENERAL (1535), who arranged for the visitation of the English monasteries and their subsequent dissolution.

**Maundy. Maundy Money.** Gifts in money given by the sovereign on MAUNDY THURSDAY to the number of aged poor men and women that corresponds with his or her age. Broadcloth, fish, bread and wine were given in the reign of Elizabeth I, later clothing and provisions. The clothing was replaced by money in 1725 and the provisions in 1837. In due course the ceremony was transferred from the chapel at WHITEHALL to Westminster Abbey. Personal distribution of the doles ceased in 1688 until George V restarted it in 1932, as did Edward VIII in 1936. Queen Elizabeth II has made a personal distribution in most years since 1953, and the ceremony is no longer held at Westminster every year. The 1979 service, for example, attended by the Queen and Prince Philip, was held in Winchester cathedral. The money is specially struck in silver pennies, twopennies, threepences and fourpences and is unaffected by decimalization. Each recipient receives one complete set of coins for every 10 years of the sovereign's age, with the odd years made up by coins to the appropriate value. Thus in 1990, when Elizabeth II was in her 64th year, 64 men and 64 women each received six complete sets and one fourpenny coin. The coins bear the young head of the sovereign, as when first struck, throughout his or her reign.

**Maundy Thursday.** The day before GOOD FRIDAY is so called from the first words of the antiphon for that day: *Mandatum novum do vobis* ('A new commandment I give unto you,' John 13:34), with which the ceremony of the washing of the feet begins. This is still carried out in Roman Catholic cathedrals and monasteries. It became the custom of popes, Catholic sovereigns, prelates and priests to wash the feet of poor people. In England the sovereign did the same as late as the time of James II (r.1685–8). The word has been incorrectly derived from *maund* ('a basket'), because on the day before the great fast it was an ancient church custom to bring out food in 'maunds' to distribute to the poor. (The 'new commandment' given by Christ was 'that ye love one another'.)

**Mauretania.** Parts of Morocco and Algiers, the land of the Mauri or MOORS. The kingdom of Mauretania was annexed to the Roman Empire in AD 42 and finally disintegrated when overrun by the VANDALS in 429.

**Mauritania.** The modern Islamic Republic of Mauritania is situated in the southwest Sahara.

**Mauritius.** Despite the similarity of name, this island state, east of Madagascar, has nothing in common with MAURITANIA. Already known to Arab voyagers of the 8th century, its first European discoverers were the Portuguese, who visited it in 1505 but did not settle it. The Dutch occupied it in 1598 and named it after Maurice of Nassau (1567–1625), Stadtholder of the Dutch Republic, later Prince of Orange. In 1715 it passed to the French, who renamed it *Île de France*. The British captured it in 1810, and in 1814 it formally passed to them, at the same time reverting to the Dutch name. It gained its independence in 1968.

**Mausoleum.** The name was originally that of the tomb of Mausolus, king of Caria, to whom his wife Artemisia erected a splendid monument at Halicarnassus (353 BC). Parts of the sepulchre, one of the SEVEN WONDERS OF THE WORLD, are now in the British Museum. The name is now applied to any magnificent tomb, usually with a sepulchral chamber.

Notable examples are those of:

AUGUSTUS
Hadrian in the castle of St Angelo at Rome
St Peter the Martyr in the church of St Eustatius at Milan
Frederick William III and Queen Louisa at Charlottenburg near Berlin
Albert, the Prince Consort at Frogmore in Windsor Park

Moscow's Red Square has long contained the modern Mausoleum of Lenin (and formerly also of Stalin), originally a wooden structure erected in 1924, the year of Lenin's death, but replaced by a stone building in 1930.

**Mauthe dog.** *See* MODDEY DHOO.

**Mauvais** or **mauvaise** (French, 'bad').

**Mauvaise honte.** Bad or silly shame; false modesty; bashfulness; sheepishness.

**Mauvaise plaisanterie.** A rude or ill-mannered jest; a joke in bad taste.

**Mauvais pas.** In mountaineering a 'bad step'; a place that represents a particularly difficult passage or climb.

**Mauvais quart d'heure.** A 'bad quarter of an hour'; a briefly unpleasant experience.

**Mauvais ton.** Bad manners; ill breeding; vulgar ways.

**Maverick.** An unbranded animal; a stray; a masterless person or rover. Samuel A. Maverick (1803–70), a Texan cattle raiser, did not bother to brand his cattle, hence the practice arose of calling unbranded calves mavericks, and the usage extended to other animals. In the USA it acquired a political connotation from the 1880s, applying to politicians who did not acknowledge any party leadership. Rudyard Kipling called an imaginary regiment 'The Mavericks'. 'To maverick' is to seize or brand mavericks, hence to appropriate anything without legal claim.

**Mavourneen.** Irish (*mo mhuirnín*) for 'my darling'.

> Kathleen Mavourneen! the grey dawn is breaking,
> The horn of the hunter is heard on the hill;
> The lark from her light wing the bright dew is shaking;
> Kathleen Mavourneen! what, slumbering still?
> JULIA CRAWFORD: 'Kathleen Mavourneen' (1835)

**Maxim's.** The well-known and elegant French restaurant, a symbol of gastronomic perfection and gaiety. It is in the rue Royale, Paris, where it was opened by Maxime Gaillard in 1893. His rich and famous clientele grew steadily, aided by the patronage of fashionable courtesans. Its characteristically opulent ART NOUVEAU décor is still maintained but it is now more noted for food than frolics. It has featured in various productions including *The Merry Widow* and *Gigi*.

**Maxims, Copybook.** *See under* COPY.

**May.** The Anglo-Saxons called this month *thrimilce*, because then cows can be milked three times a day. The present name is the Latin *Maius*, probably from MAIA, the goddess of growth and increase, connected with *major*. It was the fifth month in the JULIAN and GREGORIAN CALENDARS. The old Dutch name was *Bloumaand* ('blossoming month'). The corresponding month in the FRENCH REVOLUTIONARY CALENDAR was *Floréal* ('floral'), with a period from modern 21 April to 20 May.

**May and January.** A young woman and an old man as husband and wife. The allusion is to 'The Merchant's Tale' in Chaucer's *Canterbury Tales* (*c*.1387), in which May, a girl under 20, marries January, a Lombard baron over 60.

They made a careful marriage-treaty. She,
The girl agreed upon, whose name was May,
(And with the smallest possible delay)
Was to be married to this January.
(Modern translation by Nevill Coghill, 1951)

**May Day.** Polydore Virgil says that the Roman youths used to go into the fields and spend the CALENDS of May in dancing and singing in honour of FLORA, goddess of fruits and flowers. The English celebrated May Day with games and sports, particularly archery and MORRIS DANCES and the setting up of the MAYPOLE. In due time ROBIN HOOD and MAID MARIAN came to preside as Lord and Lady of the May, and by the 16th century May Day was Robin Hood's day and Robin Hood plays became an integral part of the festivities.

May Day was also formerly the day of the London chimney-sweepers' festival. *See also* LABOR DAY.

**Mayfair.** A fashionable district in the West End of London, north of PICCADILLY, to Oxford Street and between Park Lane and Berkeley Square. It was originally Brookfield, but takes its present name from the May fair, which occupied the site of the present Hertford Street, Curzon Street and Shepherd Market. There was an annual fair in the area from the reign of Edward I, called St James's Fair, which began on the eve of St JAMES THE LESS and was suppressed in 1664. It was renewed by James II to commence on 1 May, hence the name. From the beginning of the 18th century it became a centre for drinking and gaming, was temporarily suppressed in 1708, and finally abolished at the end of the 18th century.

**May meetings.** The yearly gatherings of religious and charitable societies, usually held in London in May or June to hear the annual reports and appeals for further support. *See also* EXETER HALL.

**May Molloch** or **Maid of the Hairy Arms, The.** An ELF of folklore who mingles in ordinary sports, and will even direct the master of the house how to play dominoes or draughts. Like the White Lady of Avenel in Sir Walter Scott's *The Monastery* (1820), May Molloch is a sort of BANSHEE.

**Maypole** and **May queen.** Dancing around the Maypole on MAY DAY, 'going-a-Maying', electing a May queen and lighting bonfires are all ancient relics of nature worship. In Cornhill, London, a great shaft or maypole was set up before the church of St Andrew. The annual dancing of people under the pole gave the church's present name of St Andrew Undershaft. In the first May morning people went 'a-maying' to fetch fresh flowers and branches of hawthorn (hence its name 'may') to decorate their houses, and the fairest maid of the locality was crowned 'queen of the May'.

**Maypole in the Strand, The.** This once famous London landmark was erected probably in the time of Elizabeth I, on a spot now occupied by the church of St Mary-le-Strand. It was destroyed by the PURITANS in 1644, but another, 134ft (41m) high, was set up in 1661, reputedly by the farrier John Clarges to celebrate the marriage of his daughter to General Monck. By 1713 this was decayed, and another erected, which was removed in 1718. It was bought by Sir Isaac Newton, who sent it to a friend in Wanstead, where it was erected in the park to support the then largest telescope in Europe.

**May unlucky for weddings.** This is a Roman superstition, and is referred to by Ovid. In this month were held the festivals of BONA DEA (the goddess of chastity) and the feasts of the dead called Lemuria.

**Cast not a clout till May is out.** *See under* CAST.

**Here we go gathering nuts in May.** *See under* GATHER.

**January and May.** *See under* JANUARY.

**Maya.** The mother of GAUTAMA who saw in a dream the future BUDDHA enter her womb in the shape of a little white elephant. Seven days after his birth she died from joy.

**Mayflower.** The 180-ton ship in which the PILGRIM FATHERS finally sailed from Plymouth, Devon, on 6 September 1620. They arrived off Cape Cod on 11 November and established their colony, although the original intention was to land on the shore of Delaware Bay. At Jordans, Buckinghamshire, the burial place of William Penn, there is a barn traditionally held to be built from the timber of this ship.

In 1957 a replica of the ship under the command of A.J. Villiers, and built of Devonshire oak and elm, sailed from Plymouth to Massachusetts following the route of its predecessor.

**Mayflower compact, The.** An agreement signed by 41 adults in the cabin of the *Mayflower* acknowledging their allegiance to the king of England and setting up a body politic 'to frame just and equal laws' (21 November 1620).

**Mayhem.** An early form of 'maim' and an archaic legal term for the crime of depriving a person of the use of an arm, leg, eye and so on, thus rendering him less able to defend himself in a violent struggle or to trouble his opponent. The word is now back in popular use for violent and injurious action.

**Mayonnaise.** A sauce made with pepper, salt, oil, vinegar, the yolk of egg and so on, beaten up together. When the Duc de Richelieu captured Port Mahon, Minorca, in 1756, he demanded food on landing. In the absence of a prepared meal, his chef took whatever he could find and beat it up together. Hence the original form 'mahonnaise'.

**Mayor.** The chief magistrate of a city, elected by the council, of which he becomes chairman. He holds office for 12 months.

The chief magistrate of London is the Lord Mayor, a Privy Councillor. York has had a lord mayor since 1389 and in more recent times the honour has been bestowed on Birmingham, Bradford, Bristol, Cardiff, Hull, Leeds, Leicester, Liverpool, Manchester, Newcastle upon Tyne, Norwich, Nottingham, Plymouth, Portsmouth, Sheffield and Stoke-on-Trent. The Norman *maire* (mayor) was introduced by Henry II (r.1154–89) and it supplanted the old name of PORTREEVE. *See also* LORD MAYOR'S DAY; LORD MAYOR'S SHOW.

**Mayor of Garratt, The.** The 'mayor' of Garratt, Wandsworth, was really the chairman of an association of villagers formed to resist encroachments on the common in the latter part of the 18th century. It became the practice to choose a new 'mayor' at the same time as the occurrence of a general election. These events became popular public occasions and at one such there were more than 80,000 people present, the candidates usually being lively characters. During one election a dead cat was thrown at the hustings and a bystander remarked that it stank 'worse than a fox.' 'That's no wonder', replied Sir John Harper (one of the mayors), 'for you see, it's a poll-cat.'

Samuel Foote has a farce called *The Mayor of Garratt* (1764), and the place-name still survives in Garratt Lane, Wandsworth.

**Mayor of the Bullring.** In the Dublin of former times, this official and his sheriffs were elected on MAY DAY and St Peter's Eve 'to be captaine and guardian of the batchelers, and the unwedded youth of the civitie'. For the year the 'mayor' had authority to punish those who frequented houses of ill-fame. He was termed 'Mayor of the Bullring' because he conducted any bachelor who married during his term of office to an iron ring in the market place to which bulls were tied for baiting and made him kiss it.

**Mayor of the Palace** (*Maire du Palais*). Originally the *major domus* or steward of the Frankish kings whose functions expanded into the affairs of state. By the 7th century, they were chief ministers until, in 751, Pepin III, son of Charles MARTEL, and mayor of the palace of Neustria and Burgundy, became king of the Franks and suppressed the office. He was the founder of the Carolingian dynasty and father of CHARLEMAGNE.

**Lord Mayor's Day.** *See under* LORD.

**Lord Mayor's Show, The.** *See under* LORD.

**Maypole, Dancing around the.** *See under* MAY.

**Mazarin. Mazarinades.** Pamphlets in prose or verse published against Cardinal Mazarin by supporters of the FRONDE.

**Mazarin Bible, The.** *See under* BIBLE.

**Mazarin Library.** The first public library (1642) at Paris. The great Cardinal Mazarin left his collection of 40,000 books to the city on his death in 1661, and himself drew up the rules for its conduct.

**Cardinal Jules Mazarin.** The Italian-born successor (1602–61) to Cardinal Richelieu and minister to the queen-regent during the minority of Louis XIV.

**Mazeppa.** The hero of Lord Byron's poem *Mazeppa* (1819), a Polish nobleman who is tied naked to a wild horse that runs until it falls dead, almost killing its rider. The story inspired many plays, in which Mazeppa was almost always played by a woman.

**Mazikeen** or **Shedeem.** A species of being in Jewish mythology resembling the Arabian JINN and said to be agents of magic and enchantment. When ADAM fell, says the TALMUD, he was excommunicated for 130 years, during which time he begat demons and spectres.

**Swell out like the Mazikeen ass, To.** *See under* SWELL.

**MCC.** The Marylebone Cricket Club, founded in 1787, which moved to LORD's in 1814. It is the accepted authority on cricket and is responsible for its laws. It is famous for its pavilion and its Long Room, and in 1998 admitted women members for the first time in its 211-year history.

**Meal. Meal Tub Plot.** In 1679 during the POPISH PLOT scare, Thomas Dangerfield (1650–85) pretended to have discovered a WHIG plot to prevent the Duke of York's succession to the throne. The evidence was claimed to be concealed under the meal tub of his associate Mrs Cellier. The falsity of this was discovered and he next accused prominent Roman Catholics of promoting the conspiracy as cover for a popish plot. Dangerfield was convicted of perjury and Mrs Cellier finally pilloried for libel in connection with her trial.

**Mealy-mouthed.** From 'mealy' in the sense of 'soft-spoken', as if having meal in one's mouth. The word is now used to mean velvet-tongued, afraid of giving offence, hypocritical or 'smarmy'.

**Square meal.** *See under* SQUARE.

**Mean, Golden.** *See under* GOLDEN.

**Meander.** To wind, to saunter about at random, so called from the Maeander, now the Menderes, a winding river of Phrygia. It is said to have given DAEDALUS his idea for a LABYRINTH. The term is also applied to an ornamental pattern of winding lines, used as a border on pottery, wall decorations and the like.

**Swan of Meander, The.** *See under* SWAN.

**Means. Means test.** The principle of supplying evidence of need before qualifying for relief from public funds, i.e. a test of one's means. Such a test was introduced by the NATIONAL GOVERNMENT in 1931 when a person's unemployment benefit was exhausted, and the resulting inquisition was much resented by those concerned. It took note of any earnings by members of the household and all monetary assets, and penalized the provident. The regulations governing public assistance were modified after the Second World War.

**Committee of Ways and Means.** *See under* COMMITTEE.

**Ways and means.** *See under* WAY.

**Measles, German.** *See under* GERMAN.

**Measure** (Old French *mesure*, from Latin *mensura*).

**Measure one's length, To.** To fall flat on the ground; to be knocked down.

**Measure up, To.** To meet the standard or requirement; to fulfil expectations.

**Beyond measure** or **out of all measure.** *See under* BEYOND.

**For good measure.** *See under* FOR.

**Get the measure of someone, To.** To assess them in some way, often with a view to outdoing them.

**Made to measure.** *See under* MAKE.

**Poulter's measure.** *See under* POULT.

**Tread a measure, To.** *See under* TREAD.

**Meat** and **bread.** Both words can connote food in general. For Italians and Asiatics bread stands for food, an indication of their lower consumption of animal food. The English, being greater consumers of meat, which simply means food, use the word almost exclusively for animal food. In the banquet given to his brethren, JOSEPH commanded the servants 'to set on bread' (Genesis 43:31). In Psalm 104:27, it is said of fishes, creeping things and crocodiles that God gives them 'meat in due season'. In parts of Devon potatoes for the table are still called meat potatoes, as opposed to seed potatoes or feed potatoes for livestock.

**Meat and drink.** Something very agreeable, a source of pleasure. Literally, something a person has an appetite for, or can 'feed' on. Meat here is food in general.

> It is meat and drink to me to see a clown.
> SHAKESPEARE: *As You Like It*, V, i (1599)

**After meat, mustard.** *See under* AFTER.

**Baked meats.** *See under* BAKE.

**Grace before** or **after meat.** *See under* GRACE.

**One man's meat is another man's poison.** *See under* ONE.

**Plates of meat.** *See under* PLATE.

**Strong meat.** *See under* STRONG.

**White meat.** *See under* WHITE.

**Meaux, The Eagle of.** *See under* EAGLE.

**Mebyon Kernow** (Cornish, 'Sons of Cornwall'). The society of Cornish nationalists, established in 1951. Their flag is the emblem of St PIRAN: a white cross, which symbolizes tin, on a black field, which represents the ground rock from which it is extracted.

**Mecca.** The birthplace of MOHAMMED in Saudi Arabia. It is one of the two holy cities (the other is MEDINA) and the most sacred pilgrimage for Muslims. Hence, a place one ardently longs to visit, a place outstandingly frequented by the followers of a particular cult or pursuit. Thus Stratford-upon-Avon could be called a Mecca for the devotees of Shakespeare while Wimbledon is the same for tennis players.

**Mecklenburg Declaration.** The first declaration of independence in the USA, made at Mecklenburg, North Carolina, on 20 May 1775.

**Medal. Medal of Honor.** In the USA, a medal instituted in 1862 for conspicuous acts of gallantry in the Civil War (1861–5). It is the premier decoration of the United States, the equivalent of the VICTORIA CROSS.

**George Medal.** *See* GEORGE CROSS.

**Leather medal.** *See under* LEATHER.

**Putty medal.** *See under* PUTTY.

**Victory Medal.** *See under* VICTORY.

**Médard, St.** The French St SWITHIN, whose day is 8 June.

> Quand il pleut à la Saint-Médard
> Il pleut quarante jours plus tard.
> (When it rains on St Médard
> It rains for the next forty days.)

Médard (*c*.470–*c*.560) was bishop of Noyon and Tournai and founded the Festival of the Rose at Salency, in which the most virtuous girl in the parish receives a crown of roses and a purse of money. Legend says that a sudden shower once fell, which soaked everyone except St Médard, who remained dry as a bone, for an EAGLE had spread its wings over him, and ever after he was termed *maître de la pluie*, 'rainmaster'.

**Medb.** *See* MAEVE.

**Medea.** In Greek legend a sorceress, daughter of Aeëtes, king of Colchis. She married JASON, the leader of the ARGONAUTS, whom she aided to obtain the GOLDEN FLEECE, and was the mother of Medus, regarded by the Greeks as the ancestor of the Medes.

**Medea's kettle** or **cauldron.** A means of restoring lost youth. MEDEA cut an old ram into pieces, threw the bits into her cauldron and a young lamb came forth. The daughters of Pelias accordingly killed and cut up their father, thinking to restore him to youth in the same way, but Medea would not save the situation.

**Medes and Persians.** *See* LAW OF THE MEDES AND PERSIANS.

**Medici.** A great and powerful family that ruled in Florence from the 15th to the 18th centuries, founded by Giovanni de Medici, a banker, whose son Cosimo (1389–1464) was famous as a patron of art and learning. His grandson Lorenzo the Magnificent (1449–92) was one of the outstanding figures of the RENAISSANCE.

From Lorenzo, brother of Cosimo the Elder, came the line of Grand Dukes of Tuscany, the first being his great-grandson Cosimo (1519–1574), who was regarded by many as the original of MACHIAVELLI's *Prince*. The Medici family gave three popes to the church: Leo X (1475–1521, r.1513–21), in whose pontificate the REFORMATION began; Clement VII (1478–1534, r.1523–34), who refused Henry VIII's divorce from Catherine of Aragon; and Leo XI, who was pope for only a few months in 1605.

**Venus de Medici.** *See under* VENUS.

**Medicine** (Latin *medicina ars*, 'art of healing', from *medicus*, 'doctor'). The alchemists applied the word to the PHILOSOPHER'S STONE and the ELIXIR OF LIFE, hence Shakespeare's

> How much unlike art thou Mark Antony!
> Yet, coming from him, that great medicine hath
> With his tinct gilded thee.
> *Antony and Cleopatra*, I, v (1606)

The word was, and is, frequently used in a figurative sense, as

> The miserable have no other medicine
> But only hope.
> SHAKESPEARE: *Measure for Measure*, III, i (1604)

Among the Native Americans, medicine is a spell, charm or FETISH, and sometimes even MANITOU himself, hence medicine man, a witch doctor or magician.

**Medical number.** In the PYTHAGOREAN SYSTEM, the number 7.

**Medicinal days.** In ancient practice the 6th, 8th, 10th, 12th, 16th, 18th and so on of a disease, so called because according to HIPPOCRATES no crisis occurs on these days and medicine may be safely administered.

**Medicinal finger.** Also the leech finger or leechman. The finger next to the little finger, the RING finger, so called in medieval times because of the notion that it contained a vein that led direct to the heart. *See also* FINGER.

**Medicine ball.** A large heavy ball tossed from one person to another as a form of exercise.

**Medicine lodge.** A tent or other form of structure used by Native Americans for ceremonial purposes.

**Medicine man.** A healer or shaman (*see* SHAMANISM) among the North American Indians. He is supposed to have special healing skills and to derive his power from another world. He is essentially the spiritual leader of a tribe. The expression is also sometimes used colloquially for a doctor, as: 'I think you ought to see the medicine man.'

**Father of Medicine, The.** *See under* FATHER.

**Take a dose of one's own medicine, To.** *See under* DOSE.

**Medieval. Medieval Latin.** Latin from the 6th to the 16th century inclusive. In this Latin, prepositions frequently supply the cases of nouns.

**Medieval times.** *See* MIDDLE AGES.

**Medina.** The second holy city of the Muslims, called Yathrib before the Prophet fled there from MECCA but afterwards Madinat-al-Nabiy ('city of the prophet'). *See also* HEGIRA.

**Meditation, Transcendental.** *See under* TRANSCENDENTAL.

**Mediterranean.** The midland sea, the sea in the middle of the (Roman) earth, from Latin *medius*, 'middle', and *terra*, 'land'.

**Key of the Mediterranean, The.** The Rock of GIBRALTAR.

**Lighthouse of the Mediterranean, The.** *See under* LIGHTHOUSE.

**Medium, Happy.** *See under* HAPPY.

**Medmenham, Monks of.** *See* HELLFIRE CLUB.

**Medusa** (Greek *medousa*, 'ruler', 'queen'). In classical mythology the chief of the GORGONS. Her face was so terrible that all who looked on it were turned to stone. Her head was struck off by PERSEUS. Medusa was the mother, by POSEIDON, of Chrysaor and PEGASUS.

**Meerschaum** (German, 'sea foam'). This mineral (used for making tobacco pipes), from having been found on the seashore in rounded white lumps, was popularly believed to be petrified sea foam. It is a compound of silica, magnesia, lime, water and carbonic acid. It is also known as sepiolite, and its chemical formula is $Mg_2Si_3O_6(OH)_4$. When first dug it lathers like soap, and it is used as soap by the Tartars.

**Meet. Meet behind closed doors, To.** To meet in secret, without the press or public present.

**Meeting for Sufferings, The.** The standing representative committee of the Yearly Meeting of the Society of Friends, so called because originally its chief function was to relieve the sufferings imposed upon QUAKERS by distraint of TITHES and other petty persecutions.

**Meet one's Waterloo, To.** To suffer a crushing defeat. The allusion is to the final defeat of NAPOLEON BONAPARTE by the Duke of WELLINGTON and Blücher (*see* FORWARDS, MARSHAL) at Waterloo (1815).

**Meet someone halfway, To.** To make a compromise; to respond agreeably to the advances of another.

**Meet someone on their own ground, To.** To meet them on their own terms.

**Meet the case, To.** To be adequate.

**Meet the eye, To.** To attract attention.
**Make ends meet, To.** *See under* END.
**There's more to this than meets the eye.** There are hidden qualities or complications.

**Meg. Long Meg and Her Daughters.** *See under* LONG.
**Long Meg of Westminster.** *See under* LONG.
**Meg Merrilies.** *See under* MERRILIES.
**Mons Meg.** *See under* MONS.
**Roaring Meg.** *See under* ROAR.

**Megrims.** A corruption of Greek *hēmikrania*, 'half the skull', through French *migraine*. A neuralgic affection generally confined to one brow or to one side of the forehead, hence a term for whims or fancies.

**Meinie** or **meiny.** An obsolete word for a company of attendants or household, from Old French *mesnie*, from Latin *mansio*, 'house'. Modern English 'menial' has much the same derivation and significance.

**Mein Kampf** (German, 'My Struggle'). The name adopted by Adolf Hitler (1889–1945) for the book embodying his political and racial theories and misreadings of history, which in due course became the Nazi 'bible'. The first part was written when he was in prison after the abortive 'Beer Hall Putsch' of 1923. It was published in two parts (1925 and 1927). *See also* HITLERISM; NAZI.

**Meiosis** (Greek, 'lessening'). A figure of speech by which an impression is deliberately given that a thing is of less size or importance than it actually is. An example is the typical English understatement 'rather good', said of something that is excellent, or 'rather a setback', said of a major disaster. A famous modern meiosis was Harold Macmillan's LITTLE LOCAL DIFFICULTY.

**Meistersinger.** Bürger poets of Germany, who, in the 14th to 16th centuries, attempted to revive the national minstrelsy of the MINNESINGER, which had fallen into decay. Hans Sachs, the cobbler (1494–1576), was the most celebrated. Wagner has an opera *Die Meistersinger von Nürnberg* (1868) in which he protested at his critics.

**Mekon, The.** The deadly foe of DAN DARE in the comic strip by Frank Hampson in the *Eagle*. The Mekon is a 'Treen' from the planet Venus. He is green-skinned and slitty-eyed, with a small body and a huge head, and generally resembles, perhaps intentionally, a monstrous human foetus.

**Melampode.** Black hellebore (*Helleborus niger*), so called from Melampus, a soothsayer and physician of Greek legend, who used it to cure the daughters of Proetus of their madness (Virgil, *Georgics*, iii (1st century BC)).

**Melancholy.** Lowness of spirits, supposed at one time to arise from a superfluity of black BILE (Greek *melas kholē*).

**Melancholy Jacques.** Jean-Jacques Rousseau (1712–78) was so called for his morbid sensibilities and unhappy spirit. The expression is from Shakespeare's *As You Like It* (1599).

**Melanchthon.** The Greek name by which Philipp Schwartzerd ('black earth'), the German reformer (1497–1560), was called. Similarly the German scholar Oecolampadius (1482–1531) took a name that is the Greek version of the name Hauschein or Huszgen ('house lamp'). *See also* AUGSBURG CONFESSION.

**Melba.** Melba toast is narrow slices of thin toast. Peach or Pêche Melba is a confection of peach on vanilla ice cream, covered with raspberry purée.

These take their name from Dame Nellie Melba (1861–1931), the Australian coloratura soprano. Her original name was Helen Porter Mitchell, with Nellie from Helen and Melba from Melbourne, her birthplace. The peach dish was created and named for her in London in 1894 by the French chef Auguste Escoffier following his receipt from the singer of two stalls for *Lohengrin*. The peach and ice cream represents the purity and sweetness of her voice, as well as her own 'peaches and cream' complexion, while the raspberry stands for her 'colour'.

**Meleager.** A hero of Greek legend, the son of Oeneus of Calydon and ALTHAEA, distinguished for throwing the javelin, for slaying the CALYDONIAN BOAR, and as one of the ARGONAUTS.

**Melford, Long.** *See under* LONG.

**Melicertes.** The son of Ino, a sea deity of Greek legend. Athamas imagined his wife Ino to be a lioness, and her two sons to be lion's cubs. In his frenzy he slew one of the boys and drove Melicertes and his mother into the sea. *See also* ISTHMIAN GAMES; LEUCOTHEA.

**Mélisande.** *See* MELUSINA.

**Melissa.** In Greek mythology the sister of AMALTHEA. She was a Cretan princess who helped nurse the infant ZEUS. Her name means 'bee', and she is the discoverer of honey (Greek *meli*).

**Mell supper.** In the northern counties a harvest supper, usually called kern or churn supper in Scotland. *See also* CRYING THE NECK; CORN DOLLY; HARVEST HOME.

> Mell is plainly derived from the French word *mesler*, to mingle together, the master and servant promiscuously at the same table. At the mell-supper, Bourne tells us, 'the servant and his master are alike, and everything is done with equal freedom; they sit at the same table, converse freely together, and spend the remaining part of the night in dancing and singing, without any difference or distinction'.
>
> JOSEPH STRUTT: *Sports and Pastimes*, Bk IV, ch iii (1801)

**Melodrama** (Greek *melos*, 'a song'). Properly (and in the early 19th century) a drama in which song and music were introduced, an OPERA. These pieces were usually of a sensational character and the musical parts were gradually dropped. The word now denotes a lurid, sensational and highly emotional play with a happy ending in which the villain gets what he richly deserves. *See also* MURDER IN THE RED BARN.

**Melon.** The Muslims say that the eating of a melon produces a thousand good works.

**Melpomene** (Greek, 'singer'). The MUSE of tragedy.

**Melting pot.** A pot in which metals or other substances are melted; hence, figuratively, a state of flux or transition.

**Melusine** or **Mélisande.** The most famous of all the *fées* of French romance, looked upon by the houses of Lusignan, Rohan, Luxembourg and Sassenaye as their ancestor and founder. Having enclosed her father in a high mountain for offending her mother, she was condemned to become every Saturday a serpent from her waist downward. She married Raymond, Count of Lusignan, and made her husband vow never to visit her on a Saturday, but the count hid himself on one of the forbidden days, and saw his wife's transformation. Melusine was now obliged to leave her husband, and was destined to wander about as a spectre till the day of doom, though some say that the count immured her in the dungeon of his castle.

The French call a sudden scream *un cri de Mélusine*, in allusion to the scream of despair uttered by Melusine when she was discovered by her husband, and in Poitou certain gingerbread cakes bearing the impression of a beautiful woman with a serpent's tail, made by confectioners for the MAY fair in the neighbourhood of Lusignan, are still called Mélusines, since her name is popularly interpreted as Mère Lusigne, 'mother of the Lusignes', alluding to the Lusignan family (from Lusignan) who reigned over Cyprus from 1192 to 1489.

**Members, The Five.** *See under* FIVE.

**Memento mori** (Latin, 'remember you must die'). An emblem of mortality, such as a skull, that reminds people of the inevitability of death. Muriel Spark has a black comedy of this title (1959), in which elderly people one by one receive an anonymous telephone call with an identical message, 'Remember you must die'.

**Memnon.** The Oriental or Ethiopian prince who, in the TROJAN WAR, went to the assistance of his uncle PRIAM and was slain by ACHILLES. His mother EOS (the Dawn) was inconsolable for his death, and wept for him every morning. The Greeks called the statue of Amenophis III at Thebes that of Memnon. When first struck by the rays of the rising sun it is said to have produced a sound like the snapping of a cord. Poetically, when Eos kissed her son at daybreak, the hero acknowledged the salutation with a musical murmur.

**Memory. Memorial Day.** 30 May, also known as Decoration Day, observed in most states of the USA as a holiday to honour those killed in war and originally held to commemorate those who fell in the CIVIL WAR (1861–5). In VIRGINIA it is observed as Confederate Memorial Day. In Louisiana and Tennessee Confederate Memorial Day is 3 June, the birthday of Jefferson Davis, President of the Confederate States; in Alabama, Florida, Georgia and Mississippi it is 26 April; and in the Carolinas it is 10 May.

**Memory man.** A person who uses MNEMONIC devices to recall and recite a lengthy text or an enumeration of objects. A popular practitioner so nicknamed was the broadcaster Leslie Welch (1908–80), who specialized in the recall of sporting facts and feats. Modern memory men include Dominic O'Brien, who memorized a random sequence of 40 packs of cards on 26 November 1993, although admitting one error, and Hiroyuki Goto of Japan, who on 18 February 1995 recited π to 42,195 places.

**Memory Woodfall.** *See under* WOODFALL.

**Down memory lane.** A nostalgic reminiscence or sentimental journey into the past. Some local newspapers run a regular feature so titled.

**False memory syndrome.** *See under* FAKES.

**Men.** *See* MAN.

**Menace, Dennis the.** *See under* DENNIS.

**Menalcas.** Any shepherd or rustic. The name figures in Virgil's *Eclogues* (1st century BC) and the *Idylls* (3rd century BC) of Theocritus.

**Mencius** or **Meng-tzu.** The Chinese philosopher who ranks next to Confucius. After his death (290 BC) his teachings were gathered by his disciples to form the *Mencius*, the fourth of the sacred books of China. Confucius, or Kung-futse, wrote the other three, namely *Ta-heo* ('School of Adults'), *Chong-yong* ('Golden Mean') and *Lunyu* ('Book of Maxims').

**Mend. Mend one's fences, To.** To make peace with a person.

**Mend one's manners, To.** To improve one's behaviour.

**Mend one's pace, To.** To go faster; to adjust one's pace to that of another.

**Mend one's ways, To.** To improve one's hitherto unsatisfactory habits and behaviour; to TURN OVER A NEW LEAF.

**Make and mend.** *See under* MAKE.

**On the mend.** Improving in health.

**Mendelism.** The theory of heredity propounded by Gregor Johann Mendel (1822–84), the Austrian botanist and abbot of Brünn, showing that the characteristics of the parents of crossbred offspring reappear in certain proportions in successive generations according to definite laws.

**Mendicant orders** or **Begging friars.** The orders of the FRANCISCANS (Grey Friars), DOMINICANS (Black Friars), AUGUSTINIANS (Austin Friars), CARMELITES (White Friars), Servites and other lesser orders.

**Menechmians.** Persons exactly like each other, so called from the *Menaechmi* of Plautus, the basis of Shakespeare's *Comedy of Errors* (1592), in which not only are the two Dromios exactly alike but Antipholus of Ephesus is the image of his brother, Antipholus of Syracuse.

**Menelaus.** The son of ATREUS, brother of AGAMEMNON, and husband of HELEN whose desertion of him brought about the TROJAN WAR. He was the king of Sparta or Lacadaemon.

**Mene, mene, tekel, upharsin.** *See* WRITING ON THE WALL.

**Menevia.** A form of the old name, Mynyw ('grove'), of St DAVID's, Pembrokeshire. Its present name is from Dewi or David. The saint is said to have been educated at a place called *Henfynyw* ('old grove').

> The sons of Liethali obtained the country of the Dimetae where is a city called Menavia.
>
> NENNIUS: *Historia Britonum* (9th century)

**Meng-tzu.** *See* MENCIUS.

**Menippus.** The CYNIC was born at Gadara, Syria, in the 3rd century BC. He was called by Lucian the greatest snarler and snapper of all the dogs (cynics).

Varro wrote the *Satyrae Menippeae* (1st century BC) and, in imitation, a French political *Satyre Menippée* was published in 1593. It was the work of Leroy, Gillot, Passerat, Rapin, Chrestien, Pithou and Durant, and was directed against the CATHOLIC LEAGUE.

**Mennonites.** Followers of Menno Simons (1496–1561), a parish priest of Dutch Friesland, who joined the ANABAPTISTS in 1536. They still exist in Holland, Germany, America and some other places. They reject church organization, infant baptism and, usually, military service and the holding of public office. They attach high importance to preaching, and both men and women may preach.

**Mensheviks.** A Russian word for a minority party (Russian *men'she*, 'less'). The name was applied to the moderate Russian social democrats who opposed the BOLSHEVIKS in the Russian Revolution of 1917.

**Mens sana in corpore sano.** A Latin tag meaning 'a healthy mind in a healthy body'. It is found in the *Satires* of Juvenal (2nd century AD).

**Mention in dispatches.** A reference by name to an officer in British naval, army and air force dispatches commending his conduct in action. An officer so mentioned is entitled to wear a small bronze oak leaf on the left breast or upon the medal ribbon for that particular campaign.

**Mentor.** A guide, a wise and faithful counsellor, so called from Mentor, a friend of ULYSSES, whose form ATHENE (MINERVA) assumed when she accompanied TELEMACHUS in his search for his father.

**Menu.** *See* MANU.

**Mephistopheles.** An evil spirit of German legend to whom FAUST sold his soul. He became well known from Christopher Marlowe's drama *The Tragical History of Dr Faustus* (*c.*1592) and as the sneering, jeering, leering tempter in Goethe's masterpiece based on this work, *Faust* (1808, 1832). His name is popularly understood to mean 'not loving the light', i.e. 'loving the dark', from Greek *me*, 'not', *phos, photos*, 'light' and *philos*, 'loving', although some take its origin from Hebrew *mephir*, 'destroyer' and *tophel*, 'liar'.

**Mercantilism.** A term embracing a wide range of policies at different times in various countries and first popularized by Adam Smith's attack on Britain's 'Mercantile System' in his *The Wealth of Nations* (1776). Mercantilism held sway in Britain between the mid-16th and the mid-18th centuries and was bound up with ideas of state power and security. National self-sufficiency, a favourable balance of trade, which would bring an influx of the precious metals, and protection, were all basic to it, and colonial trade was primarily regulated in the interest of the mother country. Adam Smith taught that labour, not trade, was the real source of wealth and aimed to replace mercantilism by FREE TRADE and LAISSEZ FAIRE.

**Mercator's projection.** A chart or map used for nautical purposes. The meridian lines are at right angles to the parallels of latitude. It is so called after its inventor Gerhard Kremer (1512–94), whose surname latinized is Mercator, meaning 'merchant'.

**Merchant. Merchant adventurers.** Local guilds of merchant adventurers were formed in the 14th century to develop English export of cloth to Europe, and in 1407 a regulated company of Merchants Adventurers was formed at London. It became a national organization with headquarters at Bruges, but political difficulties led to its removal at different times to other centres in the Low Countries and Germany. In the 16th century the company successfully rivalled the HANSEATIC LEAGUE and it was not finally dissolved until 1808.

**Law merchant.** *See under* LAW.

**Royal merchants.** See under ROYAL.

**Merchant-Ivory film.** A so called 'heritage film' that is typically a rich visual dramatisation of an Edwardian novel but that replaces its original irony with a lovingly nostalgic re-creation of the past. The name is that of the Indian producer Ismail Merchant (b.1936) and the American director James Ivory (b.1928), who became Indian on marriage to the novelist and screenwriter Ruth Prawer Jhabvala (b.1927). The first Merchant-Ivory film was *Shakespeare Wallah* (1965) (*see* WALLAH). Adaptations of novels include Henry James's *The Bostonians* (1984), E.M. Forster's *Howards End* (1991) and Kazuo Ishiguro's *The Remains of the Day* (1993).

**Mercia.** One of the ancient Anglian kingdoms of England, which first rose in importance under Penda (*c*.577–655) in the first half of the 7th century. In the 8th century, under Ethelbald and Offa, it became the dominant kingdom of the HEPTARCHY, and Mercian kings were supreme south of the Humber, but in 829 it was temporarily incorporated with WESSEX under Egbert.

It was subjected to Danish attacks from 855. The Danes settled the eastern part and the remainder came under the control of Wessex by the early 10th century. The earldom of Wessex, created by CANUTE, came to an end in 1070. The name is from Old English *mearc*, 'border', 'march', referring to the MARCHES or frontier against the Britons (Welsh). Mercia occupied territory between the Humber to the north, the Thames to the south, Wales to the west and East Anglia to the east.

**Mercury.** The Roman counterpart of the Greek HERMES, son of MAIA and JUPITER, to whom he acted as messenger. He was the god of science and commerce, the patron of travellers and also of rogues, vagabonds and thieves. Hence, the name of the god is used to denote both a messenger and a thief. Mercury is represented as a young man with winged hat and winged sandals (*talaria*), bearing the CADUCEUS, and sometimes a purse. Posts with a marble head of Mercury were erected where two or more roads met to point out the way (Juvenal, *Satires*, viii (2nd century AD)).

In astrology, Mercury 'signifieth subtill men, ingenious, inconstant: rymers, poets, advocates, orators, phylosophers, arithmeticians, and busie fellowes'. The alchemists credited mercury with great powers and used it for many purposes, for which see Ben Jonson's masque, *Mercury Vindicated from the Alchemists at Court* (1616). *See also* QUICKSILVER.

**Mercurial.** Light-hearted, gay or volatile. Those of such temperament were said by the astrologers to be born under the planet MERCURY.

**Mercurial finger.** The little finger, which, if pointed, denotes eloquence, but if square, sound judgement.

> The thumb in Chiromancy, we give Venus,
> The forefinger to Jove, the midst to Saturn,
> The ring to Sol, the least to Mercury.
> BEN JONSON: *The Alchemist*, I, i (1610)

**Mercy. Merciless** or **Unmerciful Parliament, The.** The PARLIAMENT (3 February to 3 June 1388) in which the Lords Appellant secured the condemnation of Richard II's friends. Four knights of the king's chamber were executed and some of his supporters were exiled to Ireland. *See also* WONDERFUL PARLIAMENT.

**Bowels of mercy.** *See under* BOWELS.

**Seven corporal works of mercy, The.** *See under* SEVEN.

**Seven spiritual works of mercy, The.** *See under* SEVEN.

**Mere. Mere flea-bite, A.** A thing of no consequence; a very small portion or contribution.

**Mere nothings.** Trifles; unimportant things or events.

**Meriden.** The village of Meriden, between Birmingham and Coventry, lies roughly 80 miles (130km) from the Wash, the Irish Sea and the Bristol Channel and is one of a dozen or so places claiming to be the exact centre of England, the precise spot supposedly marked by an old cross on a little green. Support for the uniqueness is mistakenly drawn by some from the name of the village, as if it came from 'meridian', but it actually means HAPPY VALLEY.

The situation even so links curiously with that of GREENWICH, which lies on the unique 0° meridian. Its name means 'green harbour' and it in turn links with Valverde, 'green valley', in the Canary Islands, on a line of longitude that in 1637 Louis XIII of France ordered geographers to take as the 0° meridian. Louis XIV later overturned his father's decree when in 1667 he constructed the Paris Observatory on a new 0° meridian at a site south of (now part of) the city called Vauvert, a name also meaning 'green valley'. A 'green valley' is more than likely to be a happy valley. *See also* NASEBY.

**Merit, Order of.** *See under* ORDER.

**Merlin.** The supposedly historical Merlin was a Welsh or British BARD, born towards the close of the 5th century, to whom a number of poems have been very doubtfully attributed. He is said to have become a bard of King ARTHUR and to have perished after a terrible battle about 570 between the Britons and their Romanized compatriots.

His story has been mingled with that of the enchanter Merlin of the ARTHURIAN ROMANCES. This Prince of Enchanters was the son of a damsel seduced by a friend, but was baptized by Blaise, and so rescued from the power of Satan. He became an adept in NECROMANCY, but was beguiled by the enchantress Nimue who shut him up in a rock. Later Vivien, the LADY OF THE LAKE, entangled him in a thornbush by means of spells, and there he still sleeps, though his voice may be sometimes heard.

He first appears in Nennius as the boy Ambrosius and in Geoffrey of Monmouth's *Historia Regum Britanniae* (*c*.1136), Part V of which is the *Vita Merlini* ('Life of Merlin'). These were developed by Robert Wace and Robert de Borron and later writers.

Geoffrey tells how Merlin was born in Carmarthen, and his name is said to derive from the Welsh name of this town, *Caerfyrddin*, 'Merlin's castle'. *Myrddin* was then latinized as *Merlinus*, with the dd becoming l in order to avoid a possible name *Merdinus*, which would suggest an origin in Latin *merda*, 'dung' (modern French *merde*).

**Merlin's magic mirror.** Given by MERLIN to King Ryence, it informed the king of treason, secret plots and projected invasions (Spenser, *The Faerie Queene*, III, ii (1590)).

**English Merlin, The.** William Lilly (1602–81), the astrologer, who published two tracts under the name of 'Merlinus Anglicus' and was the most famous CHARLATAN of his day.

**Mermaid.** The popular stories of this fabulous marine creature, half-woman and half-fish, allied to the SIREN of classical mythology, probably arose from sailors' accounts of the dugong, a cetacean whose head has a rough resemblance to the human outline. The mother while suckling her young holds it to her breast with one flipper, as a woman holds her baby in her arm. If disturbed, she suddenly dives under water, and tosses up her fishlike tail. *See also* MERROW.

In later 16th-century plays the term is often used for a courtesan.

**Mermaid's glove.** The largest of the British sponges (*Halichondria palmata*), so called because its branches resemble fingers.

**Mermaid's purse.** The horny egg case of the ray, skate or shark, frequently washed up by the waves on the beach.

**Mermaid Tavern.** The meeting-place in Bread Street, Cheapside, of the wits, literary men and men about town in the early 17th century. Among those who met there at a sort of early CLUB were Ben Jonson, Sir Walter Ralegh, Francis Beaumont, John Fletcher, John Selden and, in all probability, Shakespeare. *See also* MERMAID THEATRE.

**Mermaid Theatre.** The theatre at Puddle Dock by the Thames developed from that created in 1951 by Sir Bernard Miles and his wife in the garden of their house in St John's Wood. They named it for the historic MERMAID TAVERN, famous for its literary connections.

**Merope.** One of the PLEIADES. She is dimmer than the rest, because, according to Greek legend, she married SISYPHUS, a mortal. She was the mother of GLAUCUS.

**Merovingian dynasty.** The dynasty of Merovius, Merovech or Merwig ('great warrior'), grandfather of CLOVIS (d.511), who ruled over the FRANKS in the 5th century. The dynasty rose to power under Clovis and gradually gave way before the MAYORS OF THE PALACE, until, in 751, the dynasty was brought to an end by PEPIN THE SHORT's usurpation.

**Merrie England.** *See* MERRY.

**Merrilies, Meg.** The tall and awesome gypsy prophetess in Scott's novel *Guy Mannering* (1815), described by one of the characters, Dominie Sampson, as 'harlot, thief, witch and gypsy'. She is much more formidable than the Meg Merrilies of Keats' poem:

> Old Meg she was a Gipsy,
> And liv'd upon the Moors:
> Her bed it was the brown heath turf,
> And her house was out of doors.
>
> JOHN KEATS: 'Meg Merrilies' (1818)

**Merrow** (Irish *murbhach*). A MERMAID, believed by Irish fishermen to forebode a coming storm.

> It was rather annoying to Jack that, though living in a place where the merrows were as plenty as lobsters, he never could get a right view of one.
>
> W.B. YEATS: *Fairy and Folk Tales of the Irish Peasantry* (1888)

**Merry.** The original meaning is pleasing, delightful, hence giving pleasure, hence mirthful, joyous.

The old phrase 'Merrie England' merely signified that it was pleasant and delightful, not necessarily full of merriment, and so it is with 'the merry month of May'.

**Merry Andrew.** A buffoon, jester or attendant on a QUACK doctor at fairs. It is claimed by Thomas Hearne (1678–1735), with no supporting evidence, to derive from Andrew Boorde (*c*.1490–1549), physician to Henry VIII, who to his vast learning added great eccentricity. Matthew Prior has a poem on 'Merry Andrew'. *See also* ANDREW.

**Merry dancers.** The Northern lights or AURORA BOREALIS, so called from their undulatory motion. The French call them *chèvres dansantes* ('dancing goats').

**Merry-go-round.** A revolving machine with wooden horses or cars for riding on at a fair. Hence also any whirl of bustling activity.

**Merry Maidens.** A superb circle of 19 stones southeast of St Buryan, near Penzance, Cornwall. Two pillar stones nearby, 120ft (36.5m) apart, are called the Pipers. The whole group is said to have been petrified for making sport on the SABBATH.

**Merry Men of May.** An expanse of broken water, which boils like a cauldron in the southern side of the Stroma Channel, Pentland Firth.

**Merry Monarch, The.** Charles II. *See also* OLD ROWLEY.

**Merrythought.** The furcula or WISHBONE in the breast of a fowl. The word is sometimes used jocularly of the human breastbone.

> A lively din of splashing betokened that Comus had at least begun his toilet.
>
> 'You wicked boy, what have you done?' she cried reproachfully.
>
> 'Me washee,' came a cheerful shout; 'me washee from the neck all the way down to the merrythought, and now washee down from the merrythought to –'
>
> SAKI (H.H. MUNRO): *The Unbearable Bassington*, ch iii (1912)

**Merry widow, A.** An amorous or designing widow. The phrase comes from the English title of Franz Lehár's operetta *Die Lustige Witwe* (1905), in which the widow is Hanna Glawari.

**As merry as a cricket** or **grig.** *See* GRIG.

**Make merry, To.** To celebrate; to be festive; to make merry over; to treat with amusement; to ridicule; to make fun of.

**Mersey.** A river synonymous with Liverpool, and giving its name not only in 1974 to the new county of Merseyside but ten years earlier to the Mersey beat and Mersey sound, the English type of rhythm 'n' blues music associated with the BEATLES and with such groups as Gerry and the Pacemakers, the Searchers, and the Swinging Blue Jeans. The geographical name itself derives from the Old English words for 'boundary river'. The Mersey formed the boundary between the counties of Cheshire and Lancashire, and before that, between the Anglo-Saxon kingdoms of MERCIA and NORTHUMBRIA. This long historic link was broken overnight when the new county was created.

**Merton. Merton College.** The oldest Oxford college, founded in 1264 by Walter de Merton, bishop of Rochester and LORD HIGH CHANCELLOR. He was, through this foundation, the originator of the collegiate system developed at Oxford and Cambridge. The college was originally intended for training SECULAR CLERGY.

**Sandford and Merton.** *See under* SANDFORD.

**Meru, Mount.** The OLYMPUS of the Hindus, a fabulous mountain in the centre of the world, 80,000 leagues high, the abode of VISHNU, and a perfect Paradise. *See also* HINDUISM; INDRA.

**Merveilleuse** (French, 'marvellous'). The sword of Doon of Mayence. It was so sharp that when placed edge downwards it would cut through a slab of wood without the use of force.

The term is also applied to the dress worn by the fops and ladies of the DIRECTORY period in France, who were noted for their extravagance and for their aping of classical Greek modes.

**Mesmerism.** So called from Franz Anton Mesmer (1734–1815), an Austrian physician who introduced his theory of 'animal magnetism' at Paris in 1778. It was the forerunner of HYPNOTISM, which is increasingly studied for therapeutic purposes by the medical and psychiatric professions. Mesmerism was formerly used as a synonym for hypnotism.

**Mesolithic Age** (Greek *mesos*, 'middle', and *lithos*, 'stone'). The Middle STONE AGE in Europe, between the PALAEOLITHIC and NEOLITHIC AGES.

**Mesopotamia** (Greek, 'land between the rivers', i.e. Euphrates and Tigris). One of the cradles of civilization. Iraq now occupies the territory. The actor David Garrick (1717–79) said of the power of George Whitfield's voice that 'he could make men laugh or cry by pronouncing the word Mesopotamia' and Sir Paul Harvey, in his *Companion to English Literature* (1932), relates the story of an old woman who told her pastor that she found great support in 'that comfortable word Mesopotamia'.

**Mess.** The usual meaning today is a dirty, untidy state of things, a muddle, a difficulty (to make a mess), but the word originally signified a portion of food (Latin *missum*, from *mittere*, 'to send'; compare with French *mets*, 'viands', Italian *messa*, 'a course of a meal'). Hence it came to mean mixed food, especially for an animal, and so a confusion, medley or jumble.

Another meaning was a small group of persons (usually four) who sat together at banquets and were served from the same dishes. This gave rise to the army and navy mess, the place where meals are served and eaten, and to the Elizabethans using it in place of 'four' or 'a group of four'. Thus, Shakespeare has Berowne say in *Love's Labour's Lost* (IV, iii (1594)), 'You three fools lack'd me fool to make up the mess.' In the INNS OF COURT, London, the members still dine in groups of four.

**Mess of pottage.** For such ESAU sold his birthright to JACOB (Genesis 25: 29–34). Hence, figuratively, some material comfort or advantage obtained at the expense of something of much greater value or lasting worth.

**Benjamin's mess.** *See under* BENJAMIN.

**Messalina.** Wife of the Emperor CLAUDIUS of Rome, executed, aged 22, by order of her husband in AD 48. Her name has become a byword for lasciviousness and incontinence. Catherine the Great of Russia (1729–96) has been called the Modern Messalina.

**Messenger, King's** or **Queen's.** *See under* KING.

**Messiah** (Hebrew *māshīach*, 'anointed one'). It is the title of the expected leader of the Jews who shall deliver the nation from its enemies and reign in permanent triumph and peace. Equivalent to the Greek word Christ, it is applied by Christians to Jesus. *Messiah* (incorrectly *The Messiah*) is the title of an oratorio by Handel, first produced in Dublin in 1742. *See also* ISAIAH.

**Nunawading Messiah.** *See under* NUNAWADING.

**Mestizo.** A Spanish-American term of 16th-century origin for a half-breed, ultimately from Latin *mixtus*, 'mixed'. At first it denoted the offspring of a Spaniard and a Native American Indian, but later also of a NEGRO.

**Metals.** Metals used to be divided into two classes, noble and base. The noble or perfect metals were gold, silver and platinum, because they were not acted on by air (or oxygen) at any temperature. The base or imperfect metals are subject to oxidation in air and change their character. The only metals used in HERALDRY are 'or' (gold) and 'argent' (silver).

**Bath metal.** *See under* BATH.

**King of metals, The.** *See under* KING.

**Seven metals in alchemy.** *See under* SEVEN.

**Metaphor** (Greek, 'transference'). A figure of speech in which a name or descriptive term is applied to an object or action to which it is not literally applicable, as: 'The yacht spread her wings to the breeze.'

**Mixed metaphor, A.** *See under* MIXED.

**Metaphysics** (Greek, 'after-physics'). The branch of philosophy that deals with first principles, so called because the name was posthumously given to ARISTOTLE'S 'First Philosophy' which he wrote after his *Physics* (4th century BC). At various times the whole range of philosophical inquiry has been classed as metaphysics and the contrast between philosophy and science is comparatively modern.

**Metaphysical poets.** A term used to describe certain poets of the 17th century, notably John Donne (1572–1631), George Herbert (1593–1633), Richard Crashaw (*c*.1612–49), Henry Vaughan (1621–95) and Andrew Marvell (1621–78). They are characterized by subtlety of thought, expressed frequently in compressed though sometimes far-fetched images, and the use of complex versification. They mostly show strong religious feeling. The word 'metaphysical' in relation to poetry was first used by William Drummond of Hawthornden about 1630, then applied to this particular group of poets by John Dryden in 1693, and used derogatively of them by Dr Johnson in 1781.

**Metathesis** (Greek, 'transposition'). A change in the relative order between sounds or letters in a word, as Old English *bridd* becoming bird and *thrid* becoming third. *See also* SPOONERISM.

**Method, The Socratic.** *See under* SOCRATES.

**Methodists.** A name given in 1729 to the members of Charles Wesley's 'Holy Club' at Oxford, from the methodical way in which they observed their principles. They were originally members of the CHURCH OF ENGLAND, and the separatist Methodist Church was not established until after John Wesley's death (1791). The movement was itself soon faced with secessions, the first being the Methodist New Connection (1797), followed by the Independent Methodists (1805), Primitive Methodists (1810), the Bible Christians (1815), the Wesleyan Methodist Association (1835) and the Wesleyan Reformers (1849). Reunion began in 1857 with the formation of the United Methodist Free Church and was completed with the formation of the Methodist Church of Great Britain in 1932. Methodism was introduced into the USA in the 1760s and grew steadily in importance. *See also* WESLEYAN.

The name was at one time applied to the JESUITS, because they were the first to give systematic representations of the method of polemics.

**Methuselah. As old as Methuselah.** *See under* AS.

**Metonic cycle, The.** A cycle of 19 years at the end of which period the new moons fall on the same days of the year. It is so called because discovered by the Greek astronomer, Meton, 433 BC. *See also* CALLIPPIC PERIOD.

**Metonymy.** The use of one thing for another related to it, as 'the bench' for the magistrates or judges sitting in court, 'a silk' for a KING'S or QUEEN'S COUNSEL, 'the bottle' for alcoholic liquor. The word is Greek, meaning 'change of name'.

**Metroland.** An early 20th-century term for the region around a metropolis. As a proper name, Metroland is the region northwest of London served by the Metropolitan Railway, lovingly evoked in Sir John Betjeman's poem 'The Metropolitan Railway' (1954). The name was adopted by the railway in 1915 as a term for the districts through which it ran, and *Metro-Land* was the title of its guidebook, issued annually from that year to 1932, the last full year of its existence as an independent company. Lady Metroland, née Margot Beste-Chetwynde, is the wife of Lord Metroland, né Sir Humphrey Maltravers, Minister of Transportation, in Evelyn Waugh's *Decline and Fall* (1928) and later novels.

> Metro-Land is a country with elastic borders which every visitor can draw for himself, as Stevenson drew his map of Treasure Island.
>
> *Metro-Land* (1932)

**Metropolitan.** A bishop who controls a province and its SUFFRAGANS. The two metropolitans of England are the archbishops of Canterbury and York, and in Ireland the archbishops of Armagh and Dublin. The archbishop of Canterbury is *metropolitanus et primus totius Angliae* ('metropolitan and primate of all England') and the archbishop of York *metropolitanus et primus Angliae* ('metropolitan and primate of England'). In the early church the bishop of the civil metropolis (mother city) was usually given rights over the other bishops (suffragans) of the province. In the GREEK CHURCH a metropolitan ranks next below a PATRIARCH and next above an archbishop.

**Meum and tuum** (Latin, 'mine and thine'). That which belongs to me and that which is another's, a legal phrase expressing rights to property. If someone is said not to know the difference between *meum* and *tuum*, it is another way of saying he is a thief.

**Mews.** Stables, but properly a cage for HAWKS when moulting (Old French *mue*, from Latin *mutare*, 'to change'). The word acquired its new meaning because the royal stables built in the 17th century occupied the site of the King's Mews where formerly the king's hawks were kept. It is now the site of the National Gallery in Trafalgar Square. With the development of fashionable London in the 19th century, rows of stabling, with accommodation above for the coachman, were built and called mews. Since the 1920s these have been steadily converted into garages with flats or into fashionable maisonettes.

**Mexican wave.** A stunt indulged in periodically by spectators at a sporting event such as an athletics contest or football match. Successive sections of the crowd stand up with their arms raised then sit down with them lowered, causing a rising-and-falling 'wave' effect. The procedure was repeatedly carried out at the World Cup football competition at Mexico City in 1986 but was practised before this by American football crowds.

**Mezzotint** (Italian *mezzotinto*, 'half tint'). A process of engraving in which a copper plate is uniformly roughened so as to print a deep black, lights and half lights being then produced by scraping away the burr. Also a print from this, which is usually a good imitation of an Indian ink drawing.

**Micah.** A prophet who was particularly disturbed by the poverty of the agricultural workers. He championed the poor against the rich and the countryside against the town, and urged repentance before it was too late. The passion of his feelings is expressed in the Old Testament book that bears his name.

**Micah Rood's apples.** Apples with a spot of red in the heart. The story is that Micah Rood was a prosperous farmer at Franklin, Pennsylvania. In 1693 a pedlar with jewellery called at his house, and next day was found murdered under an apple tree in Rood's orchard. The crime was never brought home to the farmer, but next autumn all the apples of the fatal tree bore inside a red blood spot, called 'Micah Rood's Curse', and the farmer died soon afterwards.

**Micawber.** An incurable optimist, from Dickens' Mr Wilkins Micawber in *David Copperfield* (1849–50), a great speechifier and letter writer and projector of BUBBLE schemes sure to lead to fortune, but always ending in grief. Notwithstanding his ill success, he never despaired but felt certain that something would 'turn up' to make his fortune. Having failed in every adventure in the old country, he emigrated to Australia, where he became a magistrate.

**Mice.** *See* MOUSE.

**Michael. Michaelmas Day.** 29 September, the Festival of St MICHAEL and all Angels, one of the QUARTER DAYS when rents are due and the day when magistrates are chosen.

The custom of eating goose at Michaelmas is very old and is probably due to geese being plentiful and in good condition at this season. Tenants formerly presented their landlords with a bird to keep in their good graces. The popular story is that Queen Elizabeth I, on her way to Tilbury Fort on 29 September 1588, dined with Sir Neville Umfreyville, and partook of geese, afterwards calling for a bumper of Burgundy, and giving as a toast 'Death to the Spanish Armada!' Scarcely had she spoken when a messenger announced the destruction of the fleet by a storm. The queen demanded a second bumper, and said, 'Henceforth shall a goose commemorate this great victory.' The tale is unfortunately invalidated by the fact that the Armada was dispersed by winds in July and the thanksgiving sermon for victory was preached at St Paul's on 20 August. *See also* St MARTIN'S GOOSE.

**City of St Michael, The.** *See under* CITY.

**Order of St Michael and St George, The.** *See under* ORDER.

**St Michael.** The ARCHANGEL. The great prince of all the angels and leader of the celestial armies.

> Go, Michael, of celestial armies prince,
> And thou, in military prowess next,
> Gabriel; lead forth to battle these my sons
> Invincible; lead forth my armed saints
> By thousands and by millions ranged for fight.
> MILTON: *Paradise Lost*, vi (1667)

His day, St Michael and All Angels, is 29 September, MICHAELMAS DAY. He appears in the Bible in Daniel 10:13 and 12:1, Jude 9 and Revelation 12:7–9, where he and his angels fight the DRAGON. His cult was popular in the Middle Ages, and he was also looked on as the presiding spirit of the planet MERCURY and bringer to man of the gift of prudence.

In art St Michael is depicted as a handsome young man with severe countenance, winged, and clad in either white or armour, bearing a lance and shield, with which he combats a dragon. In the final judgement he is represented with scales, in which he weighs the souls of the risen dead.

**St Michael's Mount.** An island off the Cornish coast east of Penzance where according to an old legend St Michael appeared before some fishermen in *c.* AD 500. Historically it is known that monks from Mont St Michel in Normandy founded a monastery here in 1044. By 1425 it had become a royal fortress. Control of the mount then passed from noble to noble until the St Aubyn family bought it in 1657. They still live in the castle today although the island is now owned by the National Trust. The physical resemblance between the mount and its French namesake is remarkable.

**Michelangelo.** The supreme Italian sculptor, celebrated painter, architect and poet (1475–1564). His full name was Michelangelo di Lodovico Buonarroti Simoni.

**Michelangelo of battle scenes, The.** Michelangelo Cerquozzi (1602–60), a native of Rome, famous for his battle scenes and shipwrecks.

**Michelangelo of Music, The.** Christoph Willibald von Gluck (1714–87), the German composer.

**Michelangelo of Sculptors, The.** Pierre Puget (1620–94), the French sculptor. Also René Slodtz (1705–64).

**Miching** or **mitching** (Middle English *michynge*). Skulking; dodging; sneaking. It is probably derived from Old French *muchier* or *mucier*, 'to hide'. It is still a common term in the West Country and Wales for 'truanting'. Hence 'to mich' is to truant, and a truant is a 'micher'.

> *Third Neighbour*: Saw him in the bushes.
> *Fourth Neighbour*: Playing mwchins.
> *Third Neighbour*: Send him to bed without any supper.
>
> DYLAN THOMAS: *Under Milk Wood* (1954)

**Michurinism.** A genetic theory, named after the Soviet horticulturist I.V. Michurin (1855–1935), repudiating the laws of Mendel and essentially claiming that acquired characteristics can be inherited. It is alternatively called Lysenkoism, after T.D. Lysenko (1898–1976), the Soviet agriculturist, whose pamphlet *Heredity and its Variability* attempted to discredit orthodox genetics. Its revolutionary character was more due to Marxist wishful thinking than scientific proof, and the acceptability of such teaching to the Soviet government. Lysenkoism replaced orthodox genetics in the USSR in 1948 but after 1952 lost ground. Lysenko was dismissed from his key position in 1965. *See also* MENDELISM.

**Mickey. Mickey Finn.** A draught or powder slipped into liquor to render the drinker unconscious. The term is said to come from a notorious figure in 19th-century Chicago.

**Mickey Mouse.** One of the best known cartoon characters of all time. He is the hero of Walt Disney films and first appeared in the short silent movie *Plane Crazy* (1928), followed soon after the same year by a sound cartoon, *Steamboat Willie*. His main friends are Minnie Mouse and the clumsy dog Pluto. They were joined later in the 1930s by another dog, Goofy, and by Mickey's closest rival in popularity, DONALD DUCK. He is represented 'live' by a costumed human at Disneyland and elsewhere and has a whole host of toys, games and artefacts bearing his eternally cheery image.

**Take the mickey out of someone, To.** To tease them. 'Mickey' probably represents 'Mickey Bliss', RHYMING SLANG for 'piss', so that the expression is a euphemism for 'to take the piss'. This in turn alludes to the deflating of a person, as a bladder deflates when emptying.

**Mickle. Many a mickle makes a muckle.** *See under* MANY.

**Microcosm** (Greek *mikros kosmos*, 'little world'). So man is called by PARACELSUS. The ancients considered the world as a living being, the sun and moon being its two eyes, the earth its body, the ether its intellect and the sky its wings. When man was seen as the world in miniature, it was thought that the movements of the world and of man corresponded, and if one could be ascertained, the other could be easily inferred. Hence arose the system of ASTROLOGY, which professed to interpret the events of a person's life by the corresponding movements of the stars. The word is now used of any unit, group or place that is regarded as a miniature version of a larger one. *See also* MACROCOSM.

**Micromegas.** The central character of VOLTAIRE's tale named after him (1752). He is 24 miles (39km) high and an inhabitant of the star SIRIUS. Together with an inhabitant of Saturn only a mile high, he visits Earth. The two meet up with a party of philosophers just back from the Pole, and learn with horror of the massacres that have taken place among the humans, who are mere insects to them. His name represents a combination of Greek *mikros*, 'small', and *megas*, 'big'.

**Midas.** A legendary king of Phrygia who requested of the gods that everything that he touched might be turned to gold. His request was granted, but as his food became gold the moment he touched it, he prayed the gods to take their favour back. He was then ordered to bathe in the Pactolus, and the river ever after rolled over golden sands.

Another story told of Midas is that when appointed to judge a musical contest between APOLLO and PAN, he gave judgement in favour of the SATYR, whereupon Apollo in contempt gave the king a pair of ass's ears. Midas hid them under his Phrygian cap, but his barber discovered them, and, not daring to mention the matter, dug a hole and relieved his mind by whispering in it 'Midas has ass's ears', then covering it up again. Budaeus gives a different version. He says that Midas kept spies to tell him everything that transpired throughout his kingdom, and the proverb 'kings have long arms' was changed to 'Midas has long ears'.

A parallel of this tale is told of Portzmach, king of a part of Brittany. He had all the barbers of his kingdom put to death, lest they should announce to the public that he had the ears of a horse. A friend was found willing to shave him, after swearing profound secrecy, but unable to contain himself, he confided his secret to a river bank. The reeds of this river were used for pan pipes and hautbois, which repeated the words, 'Portzmach, King Portzmach has horse's ears.'

**Middle. Middle Ages.** A term used by historians to denote the period of European history between the downfall of the ancient classical civilization of Greece and Rome consequent upon the barbarian invasions and the Europe of the RENAISSANCE and REFORMATION, roughly a period of 1000 years. It has no obvious beginning or end and is usually taken to begin about the 5th century and to extend to the late 15th. It is a term of convenience, but has resulted in popular misconceptions, giving the medieval period a spurious unity and distinctness that it did not really possess. *See also* DARK AGES.

**Middle America.** The central and western states of the USA, regarded as typifying the 'model' American citizen, with his conservative political views and an unadventurous way of life. *See also* MIDDLE ENGLAND.

> Laid out like a sheet of rolled steel on the Great Miami River, a major industrial center plopped down on the placid, undulating farmland of southwestern Ohio, Dayton is about as Middle America as you can get.
> *The Atlantic* (September 1971)

**Middle East, The.** The area surrounding the Mediterranean, especially Israel and the Arab countries from Turkey to North Africa, and extending eastwards to Iran. This region was formerly often known as the Near East, by contrast with the FAR EAST.

**Middle England.** The lower middle classes in England outside London, regarded as representing a conservative political viewpoint. They are self-reliant in their outlook, hold national values higher than international, dislike change, and aspire to self-improvement. It was essentially Middle England that brought a fresh-faced LABOUR PARTY into power in the 1997 GENERAL ELECTION. The concept is thus not a geographical one, despite the analogy with MIDDLE AMERICA.

> While Middle England is in vogue with politicians, research suggests that the traditional values it is seen as espousing may be under threat.
> *Sunday Times* (4 October 1998)

**Middle Kingdom.** A term denoting the period of ancient Egyptian history covered by the 12th–14th Dynasties from about 2130 to 1600 BC, and essentially the period of the 13th Dynasty.

In the feudal period of Chinese history, the appellation *Chung Kwo*, 'The Middle Kingdom', denoted the royal domain or the civilized states of China proper, and was not used to express the idea that China was in the middle of the world.

**Middle name.** A personal name following the first name and preceding the surname, as typically found for Americans, where it is often represented by an initial. The middle name of Dwight D. Eisenhower (1890–1956) was thus David. The expression is also used to denote a person's most characteristic quality, as: 'Caution is my middle name'. The quality or attribute may actually serve as a sobriquet in the manner of a middle name, as typically with gangsters. George 'Machine Gun' Kelly (1895–1954) is an example.

**Middle-of-the-road.** Moderate; not extreme; especially in political views.

> Much could depend on the men Reagan chooses to help form the policies, and on whether he moves closer to the middle of the road once he assumes office.
> *Newsweek* (17 November 1980)

**Middle Passage.** The region of the middle Atlantic that lies between West Africa and the West Indies, the usual route for the slave-traders of former days.

**Middle Temple.** One of the four INNS OF COURT, so called from its location with regard to the INNER TEMPLE and the former Outer Temple.

**Middle West.** In the USA, properly, the states of Ohio, Indiana, Illinois, Michigan and Wisconsin. It is the industrial centre of the United States and in many ways the political pivot of the country.

**Fair to middling.** *See under* FAIR.

**Middlesex.** The original territory of the Middle Saxons, which seems to have included the area of the later counties of Middlesex and Hertford, between Essex and WESSEX. It became a SHIRE in the 10th century, was much reduced in area by the Local Government Act of 1888, and was finally absorbed by the Greater London Council, Surrey and Hertfordshire in 1965. Its name continues to serve for postal address purposes, however.

**Midgard** (Old Norse *mithgarthr*, 'middle garden'). In Scandinavian mythology the abode of the first pair, from whom sprang the human race. It was midway between NIFLHEIM and MUSPELHEIM, formed from the flesh and blood of YMIR and joined to ASGARD by the rainbow bridge BIFROST. *See also* UTGARD.

**Midinettes.** Young French female shop assistants, especially in the Paris fashion or millinery business, are so known, from their thronging of the parks and cafés at midday. The word is a blend of *midi*, 'midday' and *dînette*, 'snack'.

> The midinettes are working girls who appear (for their lunch hour) at noon. The place to see them in crowds is in the Jardin de la Trinité, about half-past twelve.
>
> E.I. ROBSON: *A Guide to French Fêtes*, ch iv (1930)

**Mid-Lent Sunday.** The fourth Sunday in LENT. It is called *dominica refectionis* (Refreshment Sunday) because the first lesson is the banquet given by JOSEPH to his brethren, and the Gospel of the day is the miraculous FEEDING OF THE FIVE THOUSAND. It is the day on which SIMNEL CAKES are eaten and is also called MOTHERING SUNDAY.

**Midlothian, Heart of.** *See under* HEART.

**Midnight. Burn the midnight oil, To.** *See under* BURN.

**Land of the Midnight Sun, The.** *See under* LAND.

**Midrash.** Rabbinical commentary on, or exposition of, the Old Testament writings, from the Hebrew root meaning 'to teach', 'to investigate'. Midrashim of the 2nd century are the *Sifra* on Leviticus, the *Sifra* on Numbers and Deuteronomy, and the *Mekilta* on Exodus. *See also* HAGGADAH; MISHNA.

**Midshipman.** A probationary rank of young naval officer, when under training, the successful completion of which meant promotion to sub-lieutenant. They were originally boys rather than young men, and in many cases were simply the sons of gentry. They were thus on board ship for the purposes of serving an apprenticeship, and were so called because they were stationed amidships when on duty. A colloquial name for a midshipman is 'middy', while a small or young one could be dubbed a 'midshipmite'. Less flatteringly, he could equally be a SNOTTY.

**Midsummer.** The week or so round about the summer SOLSTICE (21 June). Midsummer Day is 24 June, St JOHN THE BAPTIST'S day and one of the QUARTER DAYS.

**Midsummer ale.** Festivities which used to take place in rural districts at this season. Here ale has the same extended meaning as in CHURCH-ALE.

**Midsummer madness.** The height of madness. Olivia says to Malvolio in Shakespeare's *Twelfth Night* (III, iv (1599)): 'Why, this is very midsummer madness.' The reference is to the heat of the sun or the wild celebrations on midsummer eve or possibly the midsummer moon when lunacy was held to be widespread.

**Midsummer-men.** A name for the mountain plant *Sedum rosea*, so called because it used to be set in pots or shells on midsummer eve, and hung up in the house to tell maids whether their lovers were true or not. If the leaves bent to the right, it was a sign of fidelity, and if to the left, the 'true-love's heart was cold and faithless'.

**Midwife** (Old English *mid*, 'with', and *wīf*, 'woman'). The nurse who is with the mother in her labour.

**Midwife of men's thoughts.** So SOCRATES termed himself, and, as George Grote observed, 'No man ever struck out of others so many sparks to set light to original thought.' Out of his intellectual school sprang PLATO and the DIALECTIC school, EUCLID and the Megarian, Aristippus and the Cyrenaic, ANTISTHENES and the CYNIC.

**Mighty. Mighty hunter, The.** NIMROD was so called (Genesis 10:9). The allusion seems to be to a conqueror.

> Proud Nimrod first the bloody chase began,
> A mighty hunter, and his prey was man.
>
> ALEXANDER POPE: *Windsor Forest* (1713)

**High and mighty.** *See under* HIGH.

**Mignon.** The central character of Ambroise Thomas' opera named after her (1866). She has been abducted as a child by a band of gypsies who mistreat her. Wilhelm Meister buys her from them to rescue her, and she serves him as his page. She grows to love him, and is jealous of his love for the actress Philine. Meanwhile, she has befriended an elderly and deranged minstrel, Lothario, who is in fact her father, out searching for her. He overhears her saying that she wishes the castle in which Philine is acting would catch fire. He sets light to it, unaware that Mignon is inside. Wilhelm rescues her from the fire and realizes that he loves her. The story is based on Goethe's *Wilhelm Meisters Lehrjahre* ('Wilhelm Meister's Apprenticeship') (1795). Mignon's name means 'dainty', 'sweet', from the French.

**Mihrab.** *See* KIBLAH.

**Mikado** (Japanese *mi-*, 'honourable', and *kado*, 'door', 'gate'). The title used by foreigners for the Emperor of Japan. The Japanese title is *Tenno*. *See also* SHOGUN; TYCOON.

One of Gilbert and Sullivan's most popular comic operas is *The Mikado* (1885).

**Mike.** A common abbreviation for a microphone.

**For the love of Mike.** An exclamation of frustration or dismay. The expression may have evolved among Irish Roman Catholics as a euphemism for 'For the love of Christ'.

**Milan.** The English form of Milano, the capital city of Lombardy, in Latin *Mediolanum*, from Gaulish words meaning 'in the middle of the plain' (of Lombardy). In the Middle Ages it was famous for its steel, used for making swords, chain armour and the like. *See also* MILLINER.

**Milan Decrees, The.** Decrees issued by NAPOLEON BONAPARTE at Milan, 23 November and 17 December 1807. The second decree declared that all neutral shipping obeying the British

Orders in Council (aimed to prevent neutrals from trading with Napoleonic Europe) were lawful prizes if taken by France or its allies.

**Edict of Milan, The.** *See under* EDICT.

**Milanion.** *See* ATALANTA.

**Mile.** A measure of length, in the British Commonwealth and the United States, 1760 yards (1609m). It is so called from Latin *mille*, 'thousand', the Roman lineal measure being 1000 paces, or about 1680 yards (1536m) The old Irish and Scottish miles were longer than the standard English, that in Ireland (still in use in country parts) being 2240 yards (2048m), and the Scottish 1980 yards (1810m).

**Five Mile Act, The.** *See under* FIVE.

**Four-minute mile.** *See under* FOUR.

**Ladies' Mile.** *See under* LADY.

**Nautical** or **geographical mile.** *See under* NAUTICAL.

**Not a hundred miles away.** *See under* HUNDRED.

**Square Mile, The.** *See under* SQUARE.

**Stick out a mile, To.** *See under* STICK.

**Miles Gloriosus** (Latin, 'braggart soldier'). The hero of Plautus's comedy so titled (2nd century BC) and the type of all absurdly pompous soldiers since, down to Larry Gelbart and Burt Shevelove's musical play *A Funny Thing Happened on the Way to the Forum* (1962), with its famous 'I am a parade'.

**Milesians.** Properly, the inhabitants of Miletus, but the name has been given to the ancient Irish because of the legend that two sons of Milesius, a fabled king of Spain, conquered the country, and re-peopled it after exterminating the Firbolgs (the aborigines).

**Milesian fables.** A Greek collection of witty but obscene short stories by Antonius Diogenes, no longer extant, and compiled by Aristides of Miletus (2nd century BC), whence the name. They were translated into Latin by Sisenna about the time of the civil wars of Marius and Sulla, and were greedily read by luxurious SYBARITES. Similar stories are still sometimes called Milesian Tales.

**Milione, Il** or **Marco Milione** (Italian, 'the million'). The name given by the Venetians to Marco POLO and his writings. It may have been a reference to his stories of CATHAY and its millions of wonders, or the millions of riches that he gained. Eugene O'Neill has a play on the subject, *Marco Millions* (1927).

**Militant, Church.** *See under* CHURCH.

**Militia.** A development of the fyrd (the Anglo-Saxon division of the peasantry into those who fought and those who worked the land) into the form of a national levy for defence, organized by the lords lieutenant on a county basis and so called in the 17th century. The obligation to provide men and arms was placed on property owners and those called upon to serve were allowed to call on substitutes. It was never properly trained and became essentially a volunteer force after 1852. It came to an end with the passing of the Territorial and Reserve Forces Act of 1907, but the name was applied to the Special Reserve in 1921 and was revived by the Military Training Act of 1939.

**Milk. Milk, To.** Slang for to extract money out of somebody in an underhand way, also to plunder one's creditors, and (in mining) to exhaust the veins of ore after selling the mine.

**Milk and water.** Insipid; without energy or character; baby pap; feeble stuff.

**Milk fever.** A fever in women caused by infection after childbirth. It is so called as it was formerly believed to be caused by the swelling of the breasts with milk.

**Milk in the coconut, The.** A puzzling fact; a mystery. The contents of the coconut are not known until it is cracked open. The expression is of American origin.

> 'Nobody can really be christened Waveney: it's a river …'
>
> 'In East Anglia. Hence, as they say, the milk in the coconut. Rolffe's father … called his eleven children after East Anglian rivers.'
>
> LAURENCE MEYNELL: *Death by Arrangement*, ch i (1972)

**Milk of human kindness, The.** Sympathy; compassion.

> *Lady Macbeth*: Yet do I fear thy nature;
> It is too full o' the milk of human kindness
> To catch the nearest way.
>
> SHAKESPEARE: *Macbeth*, I, v (1605)

**Milk run.** An RAF expression of the Second World War for any sortie flown regularly day after day, or a sortie against an easy target on which inexperienced pilots could be used with impunity. It was as safe and simple as a milkman's early morning round.

**Milksop.** An effeminate or babyish person; someone without any backbone. The allusion is to young, helpless children, who are fed on pap (soft food).

**Milk** or **baby teeth.** A child's first set of teeth.

**Milk-white hind, The.** In John Dryden's *The Hind and the Panther* (1687) the phrase means the ROMAN CATHOLIC CHURCH, milk-white because 'infallible'. The panther, full of the spots of error, is the CHURCH OF ENGLAND.

**Milky Way, The.** The GALAXY.

**Bristol milk.** *See under* BRISTOL.

**Cry over spilt milk, To.** *See under* CRY.

**Devil's milk.** *See under* DEVIL.

**Land of milk and honey.** *See under* LAND.

**Pigeon's milk.** *See under* PIGEON.

**Mill. Mill, To.** To fight, or a fight. It is the same word as the mill that grinds flour (Latin *molere*, 'to grind'). Grinding was originally performed by pulverizing with a stone or pounding with the hand. 'To mill' is to beat with the fist, as persons used to beat corn with a stone.

**Mill about** or **around, To.** To move aimlessly in a circle, like a herd of cattle.

**Mills of God grind slowly, The.** Retribution may be delayed, but it is sure to overtake the wicked. The sentiment is to be found in many authors, ancient and modern.

> Gottes Mühlen mahlen langsam, mahlen aber trefflich klein;
> Ob aus Langmut Er sich säumet, bringt mit Schärf' Er alles ein.
> (Though the mills of God grind slowly, yet they grind exceeding small;
> Though with patience He stands waiting, with exactness grinds He all.)
>
> FRIEDRICH VON LOGAU: *Sinngedichte* (1624) (translated by Longfellow)

**Millstone around one's neck, A.** A burden or imposition, especially a constant one.

> Whoso shall offend one of these little ones which believe in me, it were better for him that a millstone were hanged about his neck, and that he were drowned in the depth of the sea.
>
> Matthew 18:5

**Go through the mill, To.** *See under* GO.

**Grist to the mill, To.** *See under* GRIST.

**Run of the mill.** *See under* RUN.

**Millenary Petition, The.** An appeal to James I in 1603 from some 1000 PURITAN clergy asking for certain changes in liturgy and worship, and for the prevention of pluralities and non-residence of clergy and the like. Their requests included the discontinuance of the sign of the cross in baptism, of the ring in marriage and of confirmation, also optional use of the cap and surplice, more scope for preaching, simplification of music and so on. As a result James summoned the conference at HAMPTON COURT in 1604, at which, to the dismay of the Puritans, the king declared his intention of maintaining and even enhancing the episcopacy: 'A Scottish presbytery agreeth as well with monarchy as God and the devil.'

**Millennium.** A thousand years (Latin *mille*, 'thousand', and *annus*, 'year'). In Revelation 20:2 it is said that an angel bound Satan for a thousand years, and verse 4 tells of certain martyrs who will come to life again who 'lived and reigned with Christ a thousand years'. 'This,' says St JOHN, 'is the first resurrection.' This is what is meant by the millennium: the period of a thousand years during which Christ will return to earth and live with his saints, and finally take them to heaven.

The arrival of the year 2000 fired the imagination of many countries and special ceremonies were devised to mark the event. In Britain a vast Millennium Dome was erected by the Thames in London at a site called the Millennium Experience, millennial postage stamps were issued, and grants were made through the National Lottery to a whole host of organizations and enterprises. *See also* MILLENNIUM BUG.

**Millennium bug.** The name given to the nightmare that threatened the correct operation of computer systems in the first second after midnight on 31 December 1999, the opening moment of the year 2000 and of the new MILLENNIUM. The problem arose because most computers manufactured before 1993 used only two digits instead of four to represent the year portion of the date. The danger was thus that as the new era dawned, the untreated computer chips would register the year as 1900, not 2000. In consequence the closing years of the 20th century saw several companies racing against the clock to debug their 'non-compliant' systems in order to avert widespread chaos.

**Millenarians** (Latin *mille*, Greek *khilioi*, 'thousand'). The name applied to early Christian sects who believed in a future MILLENNIUM. Such views were held by some post-REFORMATION sects and by some of the 17th-century Independents in England, and more recently by MORMONS, IRVINGITES and ADVENTISTS. *See also* CHILIASTS.

**Miller. Dusty Miller.** *See under* DUST.

**King and the Miller of Mansfield, The.** *See under* KING.

**Milliner.** A corruption of Milaner, so called from Milan in Italy, which at one time gave the law in Europe on all matters of taste, dress, and elegance. The straw work in hats manufactured there was already in vogue in the 15th century.

**Mills, Bertram.** A name synonymous with circuses. Bertram Mills (1873–1938) was the son of a coach proprietor, and originally helped his father with coaches. After the First World War, when there was little call for coaches, he entered the circus world, setting up his own first circus at Olympia, London, in 1920. The circus continued after his death but closed in 1967.

**Mills & Boon.** The byname for accessible, affordable romantic fiction had its origin in the publishing partnership of Gerald Mills (d.1927) and Charles Boon (1877–1943), who in the early 20th century began with editions of standard popular authors such as P.G. Wodehouse, Jack London and Hugh Walpole. Later, during the depressed interwar years, when people took to reading as a form of escapism, they decided that the genre to cultivate was romantic fiction. Their combined name is now generic for a GIRL MEETS BOY love story or even a real-life 'love match'.

> Girl meets boy, momentous events force separation, girl meets second boy, what happens next? If you

have read much Mills & Boon — and it's surprising the people who have — you may also recognise the style.

*Sunday Times* (23 August 1998)

**Milo.** A celebrated Greek athlete of Crotona in the late 6th century BC. It is said that he carried through the stadium at OLYMPIA a heifer four years old, and ate the whole of it afterwards. When he was old, he attempted to tear in two an oak tree, but the parts closed upon his hands, and while he was thus held fast he was devoured by wolves.

**Venus of Milo.** *See under* VENUS.

**Milton, John.** The English poet (1608–74) and author of, *inter alia*, *Comus* (1633), *Paradise Lost* (1667), *Paradise Regained* (1671) and *Samson Agonistes* (1671).

> Milton is the deity of prescience; he stands *ab extra*, and drives a fiery chariot and four, making the horses feel the iron curb which holds them in.
>
> SAMUEL TAYLOR COLERIDGE: *Table Talk* (1835)

**Milton of Germany.** Friedrich G. Klopstock (1724–1803), author of *The Messiah* (1773).

**Mimir.** In Norse mythology, the wisest of the gods of the tribe AESIR. He lives in the land of the Frost Giants and guards the well of knowledge, filled by a spring which flows from YGGDRASIL, the world tree. Some stories make him out to be more of a giant than a god, while others relate that he was a sage, from whose severed head, preserved in herbs, ODIN drew knowledge. Another story tells how Odin received wisdom by throwing one of his eyes into Mimir's well.

**Mimosa.** The plant is so called from the notion that it mimics the sensitivity of animals. The leaves fold upward at the slightest touch, hence the name 'sensitive plant' for the most commonly cultivated variety, *Mimosa pudica*.

> And one whose name I may not say, –
> For not Mimosa's tender tree
> Shrinks sooner from the touch than he.
>
> SIR WALTER SCOTT: *Marmion*, Introduction, iv (1808)

**Mimung.** The sword that Wittich lent SIEGFRIED. *See also* NIBELUNGENLIED.

**Mince. Mince matters, To.** To avoid giving offence by speaking or censuring in mild terms. The expression is more commonly used in the negative, so that 'I shan't mince matters' means that I shall speak bluntly. The allusion is to the mincing of meat to make it more digestible or palatable.

> A candid ferocity, if the case call for it, is in him; he does not mince matters.
>
> THOMAS CARLYLE: *Heroes and Hero-Worship*, ch ii (1841)

**Mince pies.** Traditional CHRISTMAS fare, said to symbolize the manger in which Christ was laid. The paste over the 'offering' was made in the form of a hay rack.

'Mince pies' is also RHYMING SLANG for 'eyes'.

**Mincing Lane.** The London lane was called in the 13th century Menechinelane, Monechenlane, and the like, and in the time of Henry VIII (r.1509–47) Mynchyn Lane. The name is from Old English *mynecen*, 'nun' (feminine of *munuc*, 'monk'), and the street is probably so called from the tenements held there by a house of nuns. Mincing Lane is the centre of the tea trade, for which it was formerly often used as a generic term.

**Make mincemeat of, To.** To completely defeat an opponent, literally or figuratively. Minced meat is meat cut up very fine.

**Mind. Mind one's own business, To.** To concern oneself with one's own affairs and not to meddle in those of others. The injunction 'Mind your own business' is sometimes abbreviated 'MYOB', letters that schoolboys liked to read as 'Mess your own breeches'.

**Mind one's Ps and Qs, To.** To be careful; to be circumspect in one's behaviour. The expression probably derives from an admonition to children learning to write to be careful to distinguish between the forms of p and q (although no such admonition was apparently necessary for the equally confusible b and d), or to printers' apprentices when handling and sorting type. More fancifully it is suggested that in public houses accounts were scored up for beer, with P for pints and Q for quarts, and a customer needed 'to mind his Ps and Qs' when the reckoning came. Another is that in the France of Louis XIV (r.1643–1715), when huge wigs were fashionable, dancing masters would warn their pupils to 'mind your Ps [*pieds*, 'feet'] and Qs [*queues*, 'wigs']' lest the latter fall off when bending low to make a formal bow.

**Mind's eye.** The visual perception of one's memory.

**Mind the shop, To.** To be in temporary charge.

**Mind you.** A phrase qualifying what one has just said, as: 'I just love the countryside. Mind you, I wouldn't like to live in the country.'

**Mind your backs!** An appeal to make way by a person who wishes to get past, especially when transporting something.

**At the back of one's mind.** *See under* AT.

**Bear in mind, To.** *See under* BEAR.

**Blow one's mind, To.** *See under* BLOW.

**Bring to mind, To.** *See under* BRING.

**Call to mind, To.** *See under* CALL.

**Change one's mind, To.** *See under* CHANGE.

**Cross one's mind, To.** *See under* CROSS.

**Give someone a piece of one's mind, To.** *See under* PIECE.

**Have a good mind to do something, To.** *See under* GOOD.

**Have a mind like a cesspool, To.** To have a dirty mind that harbours unclean thoughts. A similar expression is 'to have a mind like a sewer'. The origin of the word is in French *souspirail*, 'vent', from *soupirer*, 'to sigh'. The second half of this was altered by association with English 'pool'.

**In one's right mind.** *See under* RIGHT.

**In two minds, To be.** *See under* TWO.

**Make up one's mind, To.** To decide what one intends to do.

**Never mind.** It doesn't matter; don't worry about it; it's all right.

**Never you mind.** It is none of your business.

**One-track mind.** *See under* ONE.

**Out of one's mind.** *See under* OUT.

**Piece of one's mind, A.** *See under* PIECE.

**Read someone's mind, To.** *See under* READ.

**Set one's mind on, To.** *See under* SET.

**Set someone's mind at rest, To.** *See under* SET.

**Speak one's mind, To.** *See under* SPEAK.

**Spring to mind, To.** To suggest itself suddenly.

**Time out of mind.** *See under* TIME.

**Minden Boys, The.** *See* MINDEN REGIMENTS *under* REGIMENTAL AND DIVISIONAL NICKNAMES.

**Mine. Fairy of the mine.** *See under* FAIRY.

**Salt a mine, To.** *See under* SALT.

**Minerva.** The Roman goddess, possibly of Etruscan origin, of wisdom and the patroness of the arts and trades. She was fabled to have sprung, with a tremendous battle cry, fully armed from the brain of JUPITER. With JUNO and Jupiter she became part of the Capitoline triad. She was subsequently identified by the Romans with the Greek ATHENE (Athena), and she is represented as being grave and majestic, clad in a helmet and with drapery over a coat of mail, and bearing the AEGIS on her breast. Phidias made a statue of her of ivory and gold 39ft (12m) high, which was placed in the PARTHENON.

**Minerva Press, The.** A printing establishment in Leadenhall Street, London, which was famous in the late 18th century for its trashy and sentimental novels, characterized by complicated plots.

**Ming** (Chinese, 'bright'). The imperial dynasty of China from 1368 to 1644, noted for the severity of its laws. The name is also applied to porcelain produced during this period, which if genuine is characterized by brilliant colours and a fine quality of body.

**Miniature.** Originally, a rubrication or a small painting in an illuminated manuscript, which was done with 'minium' or red lead. Hence the word came to express any small portrait or picture on vellum or ivory. It is in no way connected with Latin *minor* or *minimus*.

**Minims** (Latin *Fratres Minimi*, 'least of the brethren'). A term of self-abasement assumed by a mendicant order founded by St Francis of Paula or Paola (1416–1507) in 1453. They went barefoot and wore a coarse black woollen robe, which they never took off, day or night. The FRANCISCANS had already adopted the title of Fratres Minores ('inferior brothers'). The superior of the Minims is called 'corrector'.

**Minister.** Literally, an inferior person, in opposition to 'magister', a superior. One is connected with the Latin *minus*, and the other with *magis*. Christ says, 'Whosoever will be great among you, let him be your minister' (Matthew 20:26), where the antithesis is well preserved.

The minister of a church is the person who serves the parish or congregation, and a minister of the crown is the sovereign's or state's servant.

Florimond de Remond, speaking of Albert Babinot, one of the disciples of John Calvin, says: 'He was student of the *Institutes*, read at the hall of the Equity school in Poitiers, and was called *la Ministerie.*' Calvin, speaking of the same, used to call him 'Mr Minister', whence not only Babinot but all the other clergy of the Calvinistic Church were called ministers.

**Prime minister.** *See under* PRIME.

**Ministry of all the Talents, The.** *See* ALL THE TALENTS.

**Minnehaha.** The beautiful Indian maiden who marries HIAWATHA in H.W. Longfellow's *The Song of Hiawatha* (1855). Her name perhaps means 'waterfall', although Longfellow renders it rather more romantically, repeating a popular etymology:

> From the waterfall he named her,
> Minnehaha, Laughing Water.

The waterfall in question is the one in the river of the same name near Minneapolis, Minnesota, in which names *Minne-* represents the Sioux word for 'water'.

**Minnesinger.** The poet musicians of 12th- to 14th-century Germany were so called, because the subject of their lyrics was the *Minnesang* ('song of courtly love'). The chief *Minnesinger* were Heinrich von Veldeke, Heinrich von Ofterdingen, Wolfram von Eschenbach and Walther von der Vogelweide. In addition to several *Love Songs* and a short epic, Wolfram von Eschenbach, who appears as a character in Wagner's *Tannhäuser* (1845), wrote the epic *Parzival* and two fragments known as *Titurel*. *Parzival* took as its subject the story of PERCEVAL and the HOLY GRAIL and became the basis for Wagner's *Parsifal* (1882), while *Titurel* was about the guardianship of the Grail. All the *Minnesinger* were men of noble birth, and they were succeeded by the MEISTERSINGER.

**Minnows, A Triton among the.** *See under* TRITON.
**Minoan.** *See* MINOS.
**Minor. Minoresses.** *See* ORDER OF ST CLARE.
**Minories.** The London street is so called from the abbey of the Minoresses of the ORDER OF ST CLARE, which stood on the site until the dissolution of the monasteries (1536).
**Minorites** or **Minors.** *See* FRANCISCANS.
**Minor** or **Lesser Prophets, The.** HOSEA, JOEL, AMOS, Obadiah, JONAH, MICAH, NAHUM, HABAKKUK, ZEPHANIAH, HAGGAI, ZECHARIAH and MALACHI, whose writings are less extensive than those of the four GREAT PROPHETS.
**Ursa Minor.** *See under* URSA.

**Minos.** The title of a legendary king and law-giver of Crete. At death, Minos was made supreme judge of the lower world, before whom all the dead appeared to give an account of their stewardship and to receive the reward of their deeds. He was the husband of PASIPHAE and the owner of the LABYRINTH constructed by DAEDALUS. From the name comes the adjective Minoan, pertaining to Crete. The Minoan period is the Cretan bronze age, roughly about 2500–1200 BC.

**Minotaur** (Greek *Minōtauros*, 'bull of Minos'). A mythical monster with the head of a bull and the body of a man, fabled to have been the offspring of PASIPHAE and a bull that was sent to her by POSEIDON. MINOS kept it in his LABYRINTH and fed it on human flesh, seven youths and seven maidens being sent as tribute from Athens every year for the purpose. THESEUS slew this monster and escaped from the Labyrinth with the aid of ARIADNE.

**Minstrel.** Originally, a person who had some official duty to perform (Latin *ministerialis*), but quite early in the Middle Ages the word was restricted to a wandering musician who entertained his master with juggling and with songs sung or poetry recited to his own musical accompaniment.
**Border Minstrel.** *See under* MINSTREL.
**Christy Minstrels.** *See under* CHRISTY.
**Nigger minstrels.** *See under* NIGGER.

**Mint.** The name of the herb is from Latin *mentha* (Greek *minthē*), said to be so called from Minthe, a NYMPH of the COCYTUS, and beloved by PLUTO. This nymph was metamorphosed by PROSERPINA (Pluto's wife), out of jealousy, into the herb called after her.
**Mint, The.** A place where MONEY is coined gets its name from Old English *mynet*, in turn from Latin *moneta*, 'money', itself from the temple of JUNO Moneta, used as a mint in ancient Rome.

The chief seat of the Mint was at London and was situated in the TOWER OF LONDON from its erection until 1810, when it moved to new premises upon Tower Hill and was one of the earliest public buildings lighted with gas. In Saxon times and in Henry VIII's reign (1509–47), there was also a Mint at Southwark which later became a refuge or asylum for debtors and vagabonds and a place for illicit marriages. The Mint was removed to Llantrisant, west of Cardiff, in 1968. *See also* TRIAL OF THE PYX.

**Minute.** (1) A minute of time (one-sixtieth part of an hour) is so called from Medieval Latin *pars minuta prima*, 'first small part', which, in the old system of sexagesimal fractions denoted one-sixtieth part of the unit. In the same way, the mathematical minute is one-sixtieth part of a degree. *See also* SECOND OF TIME.

(2) From the same Latin word as above, 'minute' also denotes something very small. Hence the minutes of a speech, meeting or the like are brief notes taken down during the proceedings to be subsequently written up in as a summarized record of what was said and of any decisions taken.
**Minute gun, A.** A signal of distress at sea or a gun fired at the death of some distinguished person, so called because a minute elapses between the discharges.
**Minutemen.** American militiamen who, at the onset of the Revolutionary War (1775–83) promised to take arms at a minute's notice. Hence someone who is similarly vigilant and ready to take prompt action. The name was adopted by a small, secret, ultra-right-wing American organization armed to conduct guerrilla warfare in the event of a Communist invasion. Minuteman is also the name of the intercontinental ballistic missile (ICBM) that constituted most of the land-based nuclear arsenal of the USA from the 1960s.

**Miocene** (Greek *meiōn*, 'less', and *kainos*, 'new'). The geological period immediately preceding the Pliocene, when the mastodon, *Dinotherium*, *Protohippus* and other creatures flourished.

**Miracle. Miracle plays.** *See* MYSTERY.
**Miracles of Mohammed.** *See under* MOHAMMED.

**Miranda.** In Shakespeare's *The Tempest* (1611), Prospero's innocent daughter, who falls in love with Ferdinand. Shakespeare apparently invented her name, basing it on Latin *mirandum*, 'fit to be admired'.

> *Ferdinand*: I do beseech you–
> Chiefly that I might set it in my prayers–
> What is your name?
> *Miranda*: Miranda ...
> *Ferdinand*: Admir'd Miranda!
> Indeed, the top of admiration.
>
> SHAKESPEARE: *The Tempest*, III, i (1611)

**Mirror. Mirror for Magistrates, A.** A large collection of poems (published 1555–9) by William

Baldwin, George Ferrers and many others, with an 'Induction' by Thomas Sackville (1536–1608). It contains in metrical form biographical accounts of British historical figures. The 'mirror' reflects the falls of the great. It was much extended in four later editions up to 1587.

**Mirror of Diana, The.** A lake in the Alban hills in the territory of ancient Aricia, in Italy, on the shores of which stood the earliest known temple of DIANA. The priest of this temple, called *Rex Nemorensis* ('King of the Wood'), was either a gladiator or runaway slave who retained office until slain by a successor. The cult is described in the first chapter of Sir James Frazer's *Golden Bough* (1890). The lake, Nemorensis Lacus (modern Nemi), is 110ft (33.5m) deep and some 3½ miles (5.6km) in diameter.

**Mirror of Human Salvation, The.** *See* SPECULUM HUMANAE SALVATIONIS.

**Mirror writing.** Writing that is reversed and that can be read only when held before a mirror. It sometimes occurs in left-handed people and those with certain derangements. The manuscripts of Leonardo da Vinci were written from right to left. The opening stanza of the poem *Jabberwocky* is printed as mirror writing in Lewis Carroll's *Through the Looking-Glass* (1872). *See also* LOOKING-GLASS.

**Cambuscan's mirror.** *See under* CAMBUSCAN.

**Hall of Mirrors, The.** *See under* HALL.

**Lao's mirror.** *See under* LAO.

**Merlin's magic mirror.** *See under* MERLIN.

**Reynard's wonderful mirror.** *See under* REYNARD.

**It is unlucky to break a mirror.** *See under* UNLUCKY.

**Vulcan's mirror.** *See under* VULCAN.

**Mirza** (Persian, 'son of a lord'). When prefixed to a surname it is a title of honour, but when annexed to the surname it means a prince of the blood royal.

**Miscreant** (Old French *mescreant*, 'unbelieving'). A term first applied to the Muslims who, in return, call Christians infidels and who associate with this word all that Christians imply by 'miscreants'.

**Mise** (Old French, 'putting', from *mettre*, 'to put'). A word used to denote a payment or disbursement, and in particular the payment made by the COUNTY PALATINE of Chester to a new EARL, or by the Welsh to a new lord of the MARCHES and subsequently to a new PRINCE OF WALES, who is also Earl of Chester.

The word is also applied to the settlement of a dispute by agreement or arbitration, as in the Mise of Amiens (1264), when Louis IX of France arbitrated between Henry III and the supporters of Simon de Montfort, and the subsequent Mise of Lewes 'for re-establishment of peace in the realm of England and the reconciliation of the discords which have arisen'.

**Mise en scène** (French, 'setting on stage'). The stage setting of a play, including the scenery, properties and so on, and the general arrangement of the piece. The expression is also used metaphorically.

**Misère** (French, 'misery'). In solo WHIST and some other games, the declaration made when the caller undertakes to lose every trick.

**Miserere.** The 51st psalm is so called because its opening words are *Miserere mei, Deus* ('Have mercy upon me, O God'). *See also* NECK VERSE.

One of the evening services of LENT is called miserere, because this penitential psalm is sung, after which a sermon is given. The underside of a folding seat in choir stalls is called a miserere, or more properly, a misericord. When turned up it forms a ledge-seat sufficient to rest the aged in a standing position. A shorter dagger used by knights to end the agony of a wounded man was also known as a misericord (Latin *misereri*, 'to have pity'; *cor, cordis*, 'heart').

**Misers.** Among the most renowned are:

Baron Aguilar or Ephraim Lopes Pereira d'Aguilar (1740–1802): born at Vienna and died at Islington, London, worth £200,000

Daniel Dancer (1716–94): his sister lived with him and was similar in character, but she died before him, and he left his wealth to the widow of Sir Henry Tempest, who nursed him in his last illness

Sir Hervey Elwes (d.1763): worth £250,000 but never spent more than £110 a year; his sister-in-law inherited £100,000, but actually starved herself to death, and her son John (1714–89), an MP and eminent brewer in Southwark, London, never bought any clothes, never allowed his shoes to be cleaned, and grudged every penny spent on food

Thomas Guy (*c*.1645–1724): founder of Guy's Hospital

William Jennings (1701–97): a neighbour and friend of Elwes, died worth £200,000

Henrietta (Hetty) Howland Green (née Robinson) (1835–1916): her estate proved to be worth $95 million and she kept a balance of over $31,400,000 in one bank alone, but she ate cold porridge because she begrudged the fuel to heat it and her son was obliged to have his leg amputated because of her delay in finding a free medical clinic for him

**Mishnah** (Hebrew, 'learning', 'instruction', from *shānāh* 'to repeat'). The collection of moral precepts and traditions that form the basis of the TALMUD. It is divided into six parts: (1) agriculture, (2) Sabbaths, fasts and festivals, (3) marriage and divorce, (4) civil and penal laws, (5) sacrifices, and (6) holy persons and things. *See also* GEMARA.

**Misnomers.** There are many misnomers in English, which have arisen through ignorance or confusion of ideas or from the changes that time brings about. CATGUT for instance, was in all probability once made from the intestines of a cat but now never is, although the name remains.

Misnomers entered in the present book include: CLEOPATRA'S NEEDLE; EAT HUMBLE PIE; FORLORN HOPE; GERMAN SILVER; GUINEA PIG; HAY FEVER; INDIAN INK; INDIAN TRIBES (American); JERUSALEM ARTICHOKE; JORDAN ALMOND; MEERSCHAUM; MOTHER-OF-PEARL; POMPEY'S PILLAR; SAND-BLIND; SLUGHORN; TURKISH BATHS; VENTRILOQUISM; WORMWOOD.

Some others are:

Blacklead: is plumbago or graphite, a form of carbon, and has no LEAD in its composition

Blindworms: are legless lizards (*Anguis fragilis*); they are neither blind nor worms; *see* SLOW-WORM *below*

China: as a name for porcelain the word gives rise to the contradictory expressions Sèvres china, Dresden china and so on; similar are iron milestones, brass shoehorns and silver for current cupro-nickel coins

Dutch clocks: are of German (*Deutsch*), not Dutch, manufacture

ELEMENTS: fire, earth, air and water, still often called 'the four elements', are not elements at all

Galvanized iron: is not usually galvanized, but is simply iron dipped into molten zinc

Guernsey lily (*Nerine sarniensis*): not a native of Guernsey, but of South Africa, transported from there, it is said, when a ship bringing specimens to Europe was wrecked on the coast of Guernsey; some of the bulbs were washed ashore and took root

Honeysuckle: so named from the old idea that bees extracted honey from it, but it is quite useless to the bee

Isle of Portland in Dorset: is a peninsula

Japanese vellum: not vellum but a costly, hand-beaten Japanese paper made from the inner bark of the mulberry tree

Rice paper: is not made from rice, but from the pith of a plant of Taiwan, *Tetrapanax papyriferum*

Salts of lemon: in reality potassium acid oxalate or potassium quadroxalate

Slow-worm (or blindworm): neither slow nor a worm; *see* BLINDWORM *above*

Titmouse: the word 'tit' implies 'small' and the second syllable represents Old English *mase*, used of several small birds; it has no connection with 'mouse'

Turkeys: do not come from Turkey, but from North America, and were brought to Spain from Mexico

Whalebone: not bone at all but a horny substance (baleen) attached to the upper jaw of the whale, which serves to strain the algae and plankton that it consumes, from the water it takes into its mouth

**Misprision** (Old French *mesprision*, 'error', from *mesprendre*, 'to mistake'). Concealment, a serious offence in law.

**Misprision of felony.** Neglecting to reveal a felony when known. The offence lapsed following the abolition in 1967 of the distinction between felony and misdemeanour.

**Misprision of treason.** Neglecting to disclose or purposely concealing a treasonable design.

**Mispronounced words.** Many words in English are regularly mispronounced. In some cases the cause is confusion with a similar-sounding word of quite different meaning, in others it is ignorance of the word's composition. The following, based on Professor J.C. Wells's *Longman Pronunciation Dictionary* (1990), is a selection of 50 common corruptions, the words so garbled being annexed in brackets. Incorrect or disputed syllable stresses, as *con*troversy/con*tro*versy, are not included.

anenome (anemone)
anythink (anything)
artheritis (arthritis)
athelete (athlete)
Bolzac (Balzac)
bought (brought)
cerstificate (certificate)
dash-hound (dachshund)
deterorate (deteriorate)
dimunution (diminution)
ecsetera (etcetera)
everythink (everything)
Febury (February)
fith (fifth)
funery (funerary)
geneologist (genealogist)
grievious (grievous)
haitch (aitch, the letter H)
hari-kari (hara-kiri)
height-th (height)
hyperbowl (hyperbole)
intregal (integral)
itinary (itinerary)
libary (library)
loathe (loath or loth)
macco (macho)
maintainance (maintenance)
meterologist (meteorologist)
mischievious (mischievous)
nucular (nuclear)
obsequous (obsequious)
pacifically (specifically)
particly (particularly)
perculate (percolate)
portentious (portentous)
pronounciation (pronunciation)
protruberance (protuberance)
reconise (recognize)
revelant (relevant)
reverent (reverend)
sacrosant (sacrosanct)
secetry (secretary)
sikth (sixth)
somethink (something)
stipendary (stipendiary)
suffrajan (suffragan)
supernumary (supernumerary)
tempory (temporary)
tenderhooks (tenterhooks)
Westminister (Westminster)

**Misrule, King of.** *See under* KING.

**Miss, Mistress, Mrs.** Miss used to be written 'Mis' and is the first syllable of Mistress. Mrs is the contraction of 'mistress' and is pronounced 'Missis'. As late as the time of George II (r.1727–60), single women used to be styled Mrs, as Mrs Lepel, Mrs Bellenden and Mrs Blount, all unmarried women mentioned by Alexander Pope (1688–1744).

Mistress was originally an honourable term for sweetheart or lover ('Mistress mine, where are you roaming'), and in the 17th century Miss was often used for a paramour, e.g. Charles II's 'misses'. Mistress has since come to mean a woman who has an extramarital sexual relationship with a man.

A further development is Ms, pronounced 'Miz', as an abbreviation of either Mrs or Miss, designed to avoid distinguishing between married and unmarried women. This title first arose in the USA in the 1940s.

> As an old-fashioned man, the President [Richard Nixon] prefers the old conventions, such as addressing a woman as 'Miss' or 'Mrs' rather than the new, liberated, statusless 'Ms' – not pronounced 'Muss' or 'Mess' as certain fastidious male chauvinists have suggested. No, for reasons that elude me, 'Ms' is pronounced 'Miz'.
> *New York Post* (3 January 1972)

**Miss Marple.** *See under* MARPLE.

**Miss Right.** A woman regarded as making a perfect marriage partner. Mr. Right is the male equivalent.

> While those who wait, as age advances,
> Aloof for Ms. or Mr. Right
> Weep to themselves in the still night.
> VIKRAM SETH: *The Golden Gate*, I (1986)

**Miss World.** The annual beauty contest was inaugurated by Eric Morley in 1951 as a British equivalent of the American Miss Universe. It was regularly televised until 1988, when mounting feminist protests resulted in its withdrawal for ten years, during which period it was held in Asia and Latin America. A Mr World competition was introduced in 1996.

**Mistress of the Night, The.** The tuberose (*Polianthes tuberosa*) is so called because it emits its strongest fragrance after sunset. In the 'language of flowers' the tuberose signifies 'the pleasures of love'.

**Mistress of the Robes.** The senior lady of the royal household, usually a duchess, who is responsible for arranging the rota for the attendance of LADIES-IN-WAITING on the sovereign. The position had its origin in the reign of Elizabeth I (1558–1603).

**Mistress of the World, The.** Ancient Rome was so called because it controlled all the known world.

**Mrs Beeton.** *See under* BEETON.

**Mrs Candour.** *See under* CANDOUR.

**Mrs Freeman.** *See under* FREEMAN.

**Mrs Hannah Glasse.** *See under* GLASSE.

**Mrs Jellaby.** *See under* JELLABY.

**Mrs Malaprop.** *See under* MALAPROP.

**Mrs Morley.** *See under* MORLEY.

**Kiss the mistress, To.** *See under* KISS.

**What will Mrs Grundy say?** *See under* WHAT.

**Miss. Miss, To.** To fail to hit; to lack; to feel the want of. The English say 'I miss you', but some other languages say 'You are missing to me', as French *Vous me manquez*, German *Sie fehlen mir.*

**Missing link, The.** A popular term for that stage in the evolution of man when he was developing characteristics that differentiated him from the other primates with whom he shared a common ancestry. The 'missing link' is thus that between man and the ape. The expression is sometimes applied disparagingly or jocularly.

**Miss is as good as a mile, A.** A failure is a failure by however small an amount; a narrow escape is an escape. An old form of the phrase was 'an inch in a miss is as good as an ell'.

> He was very near being a poet – but a miss is as good as a mile, and he always fell short of the mark.
> SIR WALTER SCOTT: *Journal*, iii (1825)

**Miss the boat** or **bus, To.** To miss a chance or an opportunity; to be too late to participate in something.

**Give something a miss, To.** To avoid it, as: 'I think I'll give the meeting a miss.'

**Missal** (Latin *liber missalis*, 'book of the mass'). The book containing the liturgy of the MASS with ceremonial instructions as used in the ROMAN CATHOLIC CHURCH. *See also* BREVIARY.

**Missionary, The Devil's.** *See under* DEVIL.

**Mississippi Bubble.** The French counterpart of the SOUTH SEA BUBBLE and equally disastrous. In 1716 John Law (1671–1729), a Scottish financier, obtained permission to establish a *Banque générale* in France. He set up the *Compagnie de la Louisiane ou d'Occident* in 1717 and was granted control of the mint and the farming of the revenue. For these concessions he undertook the payment of the NATIONAL DEBT and at one time shares were selling at nearly 40 times their nominal value. The crash came in 1720 and many people were ruined.

**Missive, Letter.** *See under* LETTER.

**Missouri Compromise.** An arrangement whereby Missouri was in 1820 admitted to the Union as a slave state, but with the proviso that there should be no slavery in the state north of 36° 30′.

**Mist, Scotch.** *See under* SCOTCH.

**Mister** or **Mr. Mr Chad.** *See* CHAD.

**Mr Chips.** *See under* CHIP.

**Mr Dowlas.** *See under* DOWLAS.

**Mr Magoo.** *See under* MAGOO.

**Mr Patel.** *See under* PATEL.

**Mr Spock.** *See under* SPOCK.

**Mr W.H..** *See under* W.H..

**Dr Jekyll and Mr Hyde.** *See under* JEKYLL.

**Mistletoe** (Old English *misteltān*, from *mistel*, 'mistletoe', and *tān*, 'twig'). The plant grows on various trees as a parasite, especially the apple tree, and was held in great veneration by the DRUIDS when found on the OAK. Shakespeare calls it 'the baleful mistletoe' (*Titus Andronicus*, II, iii (1593)), perhaps in allusion to the Scandinavian legend that it was with an arrow made of mistletoe and wielded by the blind god Hoder that BALDER was slain, or to the tradition that it was once a tree from which the wood of Christ's cross was formed, or possibly with reference to the popular belief that mistletoe berries are poisonous, or to the connection of the plant with the human sacrifices of the Druids. It is probably for this latter reason that it is excluded from church decorations.

**Kissing under the mistletoe.** *See under* KISS.

**Mistpoeffers.** *See* BARISAL GUNS.

**Mistress.** *See* MISS.

**Mite, Widow's.** *See under* WIDOW.

**Mithra** or **Mithras.** The god of light of the ancient Persians, one of their chief deities, and the ruler of the universe, sometimes used as a synonym for the sun. The Avestan word means 'friend', and this deity is so called because he befriends man in this life and protects him against evil spirits after death. He is represented as a young man wearing a Phrygian cap and plunging daggers into the neck of a bull that lies upon the ground. As for ABRAXAS, the letters of his name, if written in the Greek form Μειθρασ (*Meithras*), add up to 365, the solar figure, i.e. $\mu = 40$, $\epsilon = 5$, $\iota = 10$, $\theta = 9$, $\rho = 100$, $\alpha = 1$, $\sigma = 200$.

Sir Thomas More called the Supreme Being of his UTOPIA (1516) 'Mithra', and the cult of Mithraism had certain affinities with Christianity. (Mithra was born in a cave, and shepherds came to worship him and offer him presents.)

**Mithridate.** A former concoction named from Mithridates VI, king of Pontus and Bithynia (d.*c*.63 BC), who is said to have made himself immune from poisons by the constant use of antidotes. It was believed to be an antidote against poisons and contained 46 or more ingredients.

**Mitre** (Greek and Latin *mitra*, 'turban'). The episcopal mitre is said to symbolize the cloven tongues of fire that descended on the apostles on the day of PENTECOST (Acts 2:1–12).

**Mitre Tavern, The.** A tavern in FLEET STREET, London, first mentioned in 1603, but probably a good deal older. It was a frequent resort of Samuel Johnson and James Boswell and ceased to be a tavern in 1788. Another Mitre, mentioned by Ben Jonson and Samuel Pepys, existed in Wood Street.

**Mitten, The Pardoner's.** *See under* PARDON.

**Mittimus** (Latin, 'we send'). A command in writing to a jailer, to keep the person named in safe custody. Also a writ for removing a record from one court to another. It is so called from the first word of the writ.

**Mitty, Walter.** *See* WALTER MITTY.

**Mitzvah, Bar.** *See* BAR MITZVAH.

**Mix. Mixed metaphor, A.** A figure of speech in which two or more inconsistent metaphors are combined, as: 'The government was accused of burying its head in the sand and driving a coach and four through the educational system.' *See also* METAPHOR.

**Mixed race offspring.** The terms are: white father and black mother = MULATTO; white father and mulatto mother = quadroon; white father and quadroon mother = quintero; white father and quintero mother = white; white parent and quadroon parent = octoroon.

**Dolly mixture.** *See under* DOLLY.

**Pick and mix.** *See under* PICK.

**Mnemonic.** A mental device to help one remember a sequence, formula or other verbal or numerical grouping. A common example is a rhyme, such as that beginning 'Thirty days hath September' to give the number of days in each month (*see* MONTH). Another recourse is a sentence whose initial letters act as prompts, as 'Go Down And Enter By Force' to give the keynotes for the 'sharp' signatures in music, G with one sharp, D with two etc. The statement 'Dick is a duck with fur on his back, and that's a fact' gives the irregular Latin imperatives *dic*, *duc*, *fer*, *fac*, while the plea 'Oh Be A Fine Girl Kiss Me Right Now Sweetie' provides the sequence of letters in the Morgan-Keenan classification of stellar spectra: O, B, A, F, G, K, M, R, N, S. The first 15 numbers of pi ($\pi$), beginning 3.14159, may be remembered with the aid of the following: 'How I want a drink, alcoholic of course, after the heavy lectures involving quantum mechanics'. French has a quatrain to remember 31 digits, beginning: '*Que j'aime à faire apprendre un nombre utile aux sages!*' ('How I love to teach the wise a useful number!') The number of letters in each word corresponds to the relevant figure.

**Mnemosyne.** The goddess of memory (Greek *mnēmē*) and mother by ZEUS of the nine MUSES of Greek mythology. She was the daughter of heaven and earth (URANUS and GAIA).

**Moab.** The son of Lot and of Lot's eldest daughter (Genesis 19:37). He was the ancestor of the Moabites, the best known of whom was RUTH.

**Moabite Stone, The.** An ancient stele, bearing the oldest extant Semitic inscription, now in the Louvre, Paris. The inscription, of 34 lines in Hebrew-Phoenician characters, gives an account of the war of Mesha, king of Moab, who reigned about 830 BC, against Omri, AHAB and other kings of Israel (*see* 2 Kings 3:4, 5). Mesha sacrificed his eldest son on the city wall in view of the invading Israelites. The stone, which was found in 1868 by F.A. Klein at Dhiban (biblical Dibon), east of the Dead Sea, is 3ft 6in (106cm) high, 2ft (61cm) wide and 14½in (37cm) thick. The Arabs resented its removal and splintered it into fragments, but it has been restored.

**Moaning Minnie.** A Second World War term for a six-barrelled German mortar. The first word alludes to the rising shriek when it was fired; the second was based on the German word for 'mortar', *Minenwerfer* (literally 'mine thrower'). The name was also given to the air-raid warning siren from its repetitive wail, and it is colloquially applied to any constant moaner or habitual grumbler.

**Mob.** A contraction of Latin *mobile vulgus*, 'the fickle crowd'. The term was first applied to the people by the members of the Green Ribbon Club, a short-lived political club (*c*.1675–88), whose members included such WHIG supporters as the 1st Earl of Shaftesbury, 2nd Duke of Buckingham, Mulgrave, Thomas Shadwell, Thomas Dangerfield and Titus Oates. The RYE HOUSE PLOT made membership dangerous. In subsequent years the word was applied to an organized criminal gang.

**Mobcap.** A bag-shaped cap worn indoors in the 18th century by women and useful for concealing hair that was not yet 'done'. It was so called from 'mob', a term for a loose-living woman.

**Moby Dick.** The great white whale who is the 'hero' of Herman Melville's novel named after him (1851). He is pursued by Captain Ahab, whose one aim is to kill him. In the end both whale and man are destroyed. Moby Dick is regarded as representing the elusive reality of life, which in the end brings only death. The whale and his name were apparently based on a real whale, Mocha Dick, which caused loss of life to whalers and damage to whaling ships in the 1830s and 1840s.

**Mock. Mock-beggar hall** or **manor.** A grand, ostentatious house, where no hospitality is afforded, neither is any charity given.

> No times observed, nor charitable lawes,
> The poor receive their answer from the dawes
> Who, in their cawing language, call it plaine
> Mock-beggar Manour, for they come in vaine.
> JOHN TAYLOR: 'The Water Cormorant' (1622)

**Mock turtle soup.** A soup made from a calf's head or the like so as to resemble green turtle soup. The Mock Turtle is a character in Lewis Carroll's *Alice's Adventures in Wonderland* (1865) and tells his story in ch ix. Sir John Tenniel's illustrations for the book depict him with the head, hind hoofs and tail of a calf to show his culinary origin.

**Mock-up.** A phrase originating in the Second World War for a trial model or full-size working model. In the American Air Force, a panel mounted with models of aircraft parts and used for instructional purposes was so called.

**Mockney.** An affected imitation of COCKNEY speech or vocabulary, or a person who adopts such a turn of speech, often with the aim of winning STREET CRED. The name is a felicitous blend of 'mock' and 'Cockney'.

> With her large, inquisitive eyes, tousled Brit-girl hair, well-behaved Mockney accent and the twentysomething uniform of black sporty clothes, she [fashion designer Stella McCartney] looks like someone who can't wait to get back to her own quarters.
> *The Times* (26 October 1998)

**Moddey Dhoo** (pronounced 'Mawther Doo', Manx, 'black dog'). A ghostly black spaniel that for many years haunted Peel Castle in the ISLE OF MAN. It used to enter the guard room as soon as candles were lighted and leave it at daybreak. While this spectral dog was present, the soldiers forbore all oaths and profane talk, but they always carried out their nightly duties of locking up and conveying the keys to the captain accompanied by one of their fellows. One night a drunken trooper, from bravado, performed the rounds alone but lost his speech and died in three days. The dog never appeared again.

During excavations in 1871 the bones of Simon, bishop of Sodor and Man (died 1247) were uncovered, with the bones of a dog at his feet.

**Mode. Aeolian mode.** *See under* AEOLIAN.

**Dorian mode.** *See under* DORIAN.

**Phrygian mode.** *See under* PHYGIAN.

**Model Parliament, The.** Summoned by Edward I (r.1272–1307) in 1295, it consisted of representatives of the clergy, nobility and commonalty. It included 20 bishops, 67 abbots, 7 earls and 41 barons. In addition there were two knights from every SHIRE and two burgesses from each city or BOROUGH within a shire. It thus set the pattern for subsequent Parliaments.

**Modernism.** A movement in the ROMAN CATHOLIC CHURCH that sought to interpret the ancient teachings of the church with due regard to the current teachings of science, modern philosophy and history. It arose in the late 19th century and was formally condemned by Pope Pius X in 1907 in the encyclical *Pascendi*, which stigmatized it as the 'synthesis of all heresies'.

The term 'modernist' is also applied to liberal and radical critics of traditional theology in other churches. The Modern Churchmen's Union was founded in 1898 and was strongly critical of Anglo-Catholic and Roman Catholic ideals. Dean Inge (1860–1954) and Bishop Barnes (1874–1953) were prominent among its members.

**Modesty. Modesty Blaise.** *See under* BLAISE.

**Modesty panel.** A panel at the front of an office desk that prevents the immodest exposure of the legs and lap of a woman seated at it.

**Modred.** In ARTHURIAN ROMANCES one of the KNIGHTS OF THE ROUND TABLE, nephew and betrayer of King ARTHUR. He is represented as the treacherous knight. He revolted against the king, whose wife he seduced, was mortally wounded in the BATTLE OF CAMLAN and was buried in AVALON. The story is told, with a variation, in Alfred, Lord Tennyson's 'Guinevere' (1859).

**Mods.** A contraction of Moderations, the first public examination taken by candidates in certain subjects for the BACHELOR OF ARTS degree at Oxford. It is conducted by 'Moderators'. Honour Moderations are now taken in Classics, Engineering Science, English, Mathematics, Modern History, Music and Physics. There are also Law Moderations. The first public examination in other subjects is the Preliminary Examination. *See also* LITTLE GO; MATRICULATE; SMALLS.

**Mods and Rockers.** The Mods developed as a teenage cult in London in the early 1960s, initially putting their emphasis on fastidiousness and extravagance in dress and fashion. The rise of CARNABY STREET as their dress centre was a consequence. Mainly devoid of social conscience, they had some association with homosexuality and drugs, and their mode of life reflected the less desirable results of the AFFLUENT SOCIETY. With the rise of the rival gangs of leather-jacketed Rockers, akin to Teddy Boys (*see* EDWARDIAN) of the 1950s, trouble began. Bank holiday clashes between Mods and Rockers, who arrived in their hordes on scooters and motorcycles, made some seaside resorts hazardous places. Rowdyism reigned until the authorities took firm measures against them.

**Modus. Modus operandi** (Latin, 'way of operating'). The method of procedure; the way in which a thing is done or should be done.

**Modus vivendi** (Latin, 'way of living'). A working arrangement whereby persons, not on friendly terms at the time, can be induced to live peacefully. The term may be applied to individuals, societies and peoples.

**Moera** or **Maera.** The dog of ICARIUS.

**Moffatt's Translation.** *See under* BIBLE.

**Mogul** (Persian *mughul*, 'Mongol'). The title of the emperors of Delhi from the 16th to the 19th century. Noteworthy among them were AKBAR, his son, Jahangir (1569–1627), Shah Jahan (1592–1666), builder of the TAJ MAHAL, and the latter's son, Aurangzeb (1618–1707). An alternative form of the title was Grand Mogul, translating Portuguese *o grão Mogor*. The first to be so called was Babur (1483–1530), a descendant of TAMBERLANE (or Timur), whose reign began in 1526. The last of the Moguls was Bahudar Shah II, whose reign ended in 1857. The term later came to apply to any important, wealthy or influential person. A particularly prominent type was the 'movie mogul' of HOLLYWOOD.

**Mohammed, Mahomet** (Arabic, 'praised one'). There are various spellings of the name, the most correct being Muhammad. It is the titular name of the founder of ISLAM, adopted by him at the time of the HEGIRA. He was born at MECCA *c.*570 and died at MEDINA in 632. His full name was Abu al-Qasim Muhammad ibn Abdallah ibn Abd-al-Muttalib al-Hashimiyy, 'father of Al-Qasim Muhammad son of Abdallah son of Abd-al-Muttalib the Hashemite'. His first wife, Kadija, was a rich widow of the tribe of Koreish, who had been twice married already, and was 40 years old. For 25 years she was his only wife, but he subsequently married a number of others, nine of whom survived him, his favourite being AYESHA. He also had concubines. *See also* MAHOUND.

Angel of: when Mohammed was transported to heaven, he said: 'I saw there an angel, the most gigantic of all created beings. It had 70,000 heads, each head had 70,000 faces, each face had 70,000 mouths, each mouth had 70,000 tongues, and each tongue spoke 70,000 languages. All were employed in singing God's praises'

Banner of: Sanjaksherif (Turkish, 'noble banner'), which is kept in the Eyab mosque at Istanbul

Bible of: the KORAN

Camel (swiftest) of: Adha

Cave of: the cave in which GABRIEL appeared to Mohammed (610) was in the mountain of Hira, near Mecca

Coffin of: legend held that Mohammed's coffin was suspended in mid-air at Medina without any support

Daughter (favourite) of: Fatima

Dove of: Mohammed had a dove, which he fed with wheat out of his ear

Father of: ABDULLAH of the tribe of Koreish, who died just before the Prophet's birth

Father-in-law of: ABU-BEKR (father of AYESHA) and the first CALIPH

Flight from Mecca: the Hegira

Helmet of: *see under* HELMET

Horse of: Al BORAK

Miracles of: several are traditionally mentioned. The best known is that of the Moon. The story is that Habib the Wise asked Mohammed to prove his mission by cleaving the Moon in two. Mohammed raised his hands towards heaven and commanded the moon to do Habib's bidding. Accordingly it descended to the top of the KAABA, made seven circuits and, coming to the prophet, entered his right sleeve and came out of the left. It then entered the collar of his robe, descended to the skirt, and clove itself into two plaits, one of which appeared in the east of the skies and the other in the west. The two parts ultimately reunited

Mother of: Amina, of the tribe of Koreish, who died when Mohammed was six years old

Paradise of: *see* PARADISE

Tribe of: on both sides, the Koreish

Uncle of: Abu Tâlib, who took charge of Mohammed on the death of his grandfather

Year of Deputations: AD 630, the 8th of the Hegira

**Mohammed and the spider.** When MOHAMMED fled from MECCA he hid in a certain cave, with the Koreishites close upon him. Suddenly an acacia in full leaf sprang up at the mouth of the cave, a wood pigeon had its nest in the branches, and a spider had woven its web between the tree and the cave. When the Koreishites saw this, they felt sure that no one could have entered recently, and went on their way.

**Mohammed and the stepping-stone.** The stone on which he placed his foot when he mounted Al BORAK on his ascent to heaven rose as the beast rose. Mohammed, putting his hand upon it, forbade it to follow him, whereupon it remained suspended in mid-air, where the True Believer, if he has faith enough, may still behold it.

**Dine with Mohammed, To.** *See under* DINE.

**Helmet of Mohammed, The.** *See under* HELMET.

**If the mountain will not come to Mohammed.** *See under* IF.

**Mohawks.** One of the best known Native American tribes, who occupied villages west of what is now Schenectady, New York. They frequently warred against Algonquian tribes, but according to tradition, their leader, HIAWATHA, was the first to accept the principles of peace preached by the prophet of peace, Dekanawida.

**Mohicans, The Last of the.** *See under* LAST.

**Mohocks.** A class of ruffians who in the 18th century infested the streets of London. They were so called from the MOHAWK Indians. One of their 'new inventions' was to roll people down Snow Hill in a tub. Another was to overturn coaches on rubbish heaps.

A vivid picture of the misdoings of these and other brawlers is given in the *Spectator*, No. 324. *See also* MODS AND ROCKERS; TITYRE-TUS.

**Moira.** Fate or necessity, supreme even over the gods of OLYMPUS. The Moirai were the FATES, ATROPOS, CLOTHO and LACHESIS, who embodied laws that even the gods could not break.

**Moke.** A donkey. *See also* DICKEY.

**Mole.** A small animal, *Talpa europaea*, that burrows underground throwing up small heaps of soil called molehills. The name is currently also applied to spies and traitors obtaining positions of trust in organizations, especially government departments, intelligence and secret service. The most notorious of these moles was Kim Philby (1912–88), who worked for the USSR, as did his fellow Cantabrigians Anthony Blunt (1907–83), Guy Burgess (1911–63) and Donald Maclean (1913–83).

**As blind as a mole.** *See under* AS.

**Little gentleman in velvet** or **black velvet, The.** *See under* LITTLE.

**Molech.** *See* MOLOCH.

**Molière.** The name adopted by the great French comic dramatist and actor Jean Baptiste Poquelin (1622–73). He was taken ill when acting in his latest comedy *Le Malade Imaginaire* (1673) and died the same night.

**Moll.** An American term for a gunman's girlfriend or, more generally, for a prostitute. It is a pet form of the name Mary.

**Moll Cutpurse.** *See under* CUTPURSE.

**Molloch, May.** *See under* MAY.

**Molly. Mollycoddle.** A pampered person; a NAMBY-PAMBY. To mollycoddle is to fuss over or pamper. Molly is probably from the woman's name, perhaps influenced by French *molle*, 'soft'. 'Coddle' exists independently in the sense 'to indulge'. It may be related to 'caudle'.

**Molly Maguires.** An Irish secret society organized in 1843. Stout, active young Irishmen dressed up in women's clothes and otherwise disguised themselves to surprise rent collectors. Their victims were ducked in bog holes or more ruthlessly handled.

A similar Irish-American secret society of the same name flourished in the mining districts of Pennsylvania between 1854 and 1877, intimidating the German, Welsh and English miners. *See also* PINKERTON.

**Molly Mog.** This celebrated beauty was an innkeeper's daughter at Wokingham, Berkshire. She was the toast of the gay sparks of her day and died unmarried in 1766, at the age of 67. Gay has a ballad on this 'Fair Maid of the Inn', in which the 'swain' alluded to is Mr Standen, of Arborfield, who died in 1730. It is said that Molly's sister Sally was the greater beauty. A portrait of Gay long stood in the inn, the Rose, now demolished.

**Moloch** or **Molech** (Hebrew, 'king'). A term now used for anything that demands the sacrifice of what one holds most dear. Thus, war is a Moloch, and the GUILLOTINE was the Moloch of the French Revolution. The allusion is to the god of the AMMONITES, to whom parents sacrificed their children (2 Kings 23:10). Milton says he was worshipped in 'Rabba, in Argob, and Basan, to the stream of utmost Arnon' (*Paradise Lost*, i (1667)). His victims were slain and burnt.

**Molotov.** The alias (meaning 'hammer') of the

Russian diplomat Vyacheslav Mikhailovich Skryabin (1890–1986) was given in the Second World War to two weapons:

**Molotov breadbasket.** A canister of incendiary bombs which, on being launched from a plane, opened and showered the bombs over a wide area.

**Molotov cocktail.** A home-made anti-tank bomb, invented and first used by the Finns against the Russians in 1940 and developed in Britain as one of the weapons of the HOME GUARD. It consisted of a bottle filled with inflammable and glutinous liquid, with a slow match protruding from the top. When thrown at a tank, the bottle burst, the liquid ignited and spread over the plating of the tank.

**Moly.** According to Homer, the mythical herb given by HERMES to ULYSSES as an antidote against the sorceries of CIRCE.

The name is given to a number of plants, especially of the *Allium* (onion) family, the Indian moly, the moly of Hungary, serpent's moly, the yellow moly, Spanish purple moly, Spanish silver-capped moly and Dioscorides' moly. They all flower in late spring except 'the sweet moly of Montpelier', which blossoms in early autumn.

**Moment. At this moment in time.** *See under* AT.

**In a weak moment.** *See under* WEAK.

**Man of the moment, The.** *See under* MAN.

**Psychological moment.** *See under* PSYCHOLOGICAL.

**Momus.** Someone who carps at everything. Momus was the god of ridicule and the son of Nox (Night), who was driven out of heaven for his criticisms of the gods. VENUS herself was censured for the noise made by her feet, although he could find no fault with her naked body, while ZEUS was blamed for placing the bull's horns not on its shoulders, the strongest part, but on its head.

According to Hesiod, Momus was female, the sister of the HESPERIDES, and it was at her suggestion that Zeus, to reduce the burden on Earth of too many humans, married THETIS to a mortal. The daughter born of the union, HELEN, eventually led to the TROJAN WAR.

**Mona Lisa.** Leonardo da Vinci's famous portrait (1506) is of an otherwise obscure Florent-ine lady named Lisa Gerhardini, wife of the merchant Francesco di Zanobi del Giocondo. Her husband's name gave the painting's alternative Italian title, *La Gioconda*, i.e., wife of (Francesco del) Giocondo. *Mona* means 'Lady'. *La Gioconda* happens to translate as 'the merry one', but this is hardly appropriate for the enigmatically smiling lady.

**Monarch** or **Monarchy. Dual Monarchy.** *See under* DUAL.

**Fifth-Monarchy Men.** *See under* FIFTH.

**July Monarchy.** *See under* JULY.

**Merry Monarch, The.** Charles II.

**Monday.** The second day of the week, called by the Anglo-Saxons *Mōnandæg*, 'day of the Moon'. It is now commonly regarded as the first day, and usually appears as such in calendars, diaries and the like. *See also* SUNDAY.

**Monday Club.** A club of right-wing Conservatives founded in 1961, so named because they originally met regularly for lunch on a Monday.

**Monday morning blues** or **feeling.** Disinclination to start work after the weekend break.

> Tell me why I don't like Mondays.
>
> BOB GELDOF: 'I Don't Like Mondays' (song title) (1979)

**Monday's child.** The traditional rhyme says:

> Monday's child is fair of face,
> Tuesday's child is full of grace,
> Wednesday's child is full of woe,
> Thursday's child has far to go;
> Friday's child is loving and giving,
> Saturday's child works hard for a living;
> But the child that is born on the Sabbath-day
> Is bonny and blithe and good and gay.

Another rhyme says:

> If you sneeze on Monday, you sneeze for danger;
> Sneeze on Tuesday, kiss a stranger;
> Sneeze on Wednesday, sneeze for a letter;
> Sneeze on Thursday, something better;
> Sneeze on Friday, sneeze for sorrow;
> Sneeze on Saturday, see your sweetheart tomorrow.

**St Monday** or **St Lundi.** A facetious name given to Monday (also called Cobblers' Monday) because it was observed by shoemakers and others as a holiday ('holey' day).

There is a story that, while Oliver Cromwell lay encamped at Perth, one of his zealous partisans, named Monday, died and Cromwell offered a reward for the best lines on his death. A shoemaker of Perth brought the following:

> Blessed be the Sabbath Day,
> And cursed be worldly pelf,
> Tuesday will begin the week,
> Since Monday's hanged himself.

This so pleased Cromwell that he not only gave the promised reward but decreed that shoemakers should be allowed to make Monday a standing holiday.

**Black Monday.** *See under* BLACK.

**Oatmeal Monday.** *See under* OATMEAL.

**Plough Monday.** *See under* PLOUGH.

**Monde, Beau.** *See under* BEAU.

**Money.** Following after the Gallic invasion of Rome in 344 BC, Lucius Furius (or according to other accounts, Camillus) built a temple to JUNO Moneta (the Monitress) on the spot where the house of Manlius Capitolinus stood, and to this temple was attached the first Roman MINT, as the public treasury (*aerarium*) was attached to the temple of SATURN. Hence the 'ases' there coined were called *moneta*, and hence English 'money'. Juno is represented on medals with instruments of coinage, as the hammer, anvil, pincers and die. The oldest coin of Greece bore the impress of an ox. Hence a bribe for silence was said to be an 'ox on the tongue'. Subsequently each state had its own impress:

Athens: an owl (the bird of wisdom)
Boeotia: BACCHUS (the vineyard of Greece)
Delphos: a dolphin
Macedonia: a buckler (from its love of war)
Rhodes: the disc of the sun (the COLOSSUS was an image of the sun)

Rome had a different impress for each coin:

As: the head of JANUS on one side, and the prow of a ship on the reverse
Semi-as: the head of JUPITER and the letter S
Sextans: the head of MERCURY and two points to denote two ounces
Triens: the head of a woman (perhaps MINERVA) and three points to denote three ounces
Quadrans: the head of HERCULES and four points to denote four ounces

In every country there are popular nicknames for common coins and sums of money. Thus a 'BAWBEE' in Scotland means a halfpenny and also is applied to money generally. In England money is called 'brass', current colloquialisms being 'bread' and 'lolly', and there are or were (before decimalization):

COPPER: 1d
JOEY: 4d and 3d
TANNER or TIZZY: 6d
BOB: 1s
half a DOLLAR or two and a KICK: 2s 6d
dollar or cartwheel: 5s
QUID: 20s/£1
jimmy o'goblin: SOVEREIGN
fiver: £5
TENNER: £10
PONY: £25
MONKEY: £500

Similarly, in North America:

penny or a Red Indian: 1¢
NICKEL: 5¢
DIME: 10¢
quarter or two bits: 25¢
four bits: 50¢
BUCK: $1 (in silver, a cartwheel or a smacker)
SAWBUCK: $10
century: $100
MONKEY: $500
grand or a G: $1000

**Money for jam.** An easy job, yielding a profitable reward for little effort; an unexpected bit of luck. An expression conveying the same idea as MONEY FOR OLD ROPE.

**Money for old rope.** Easy money; money for nothing or very little; something that can be effected easily. In former sailing days, crew members would unpick the odd lengths of rope lying about the ship and sell the strands and strips to shipyards in the next port of call. There they would be hammered into the gaps in the deck planking before being covered in pitch.

**Money is the root of all evil.** Many people will do anything, however unscrupulous it may be, if there is money to be gained. According to 1 Timothy 6:10: 'Love of money is the root of all evil.'

**Money of account.** A monetary denomination used in reckoning and often not employed as actual coin. For example, a GUINEA as British money of account, when no coin of this value was in circulation. The US 'mill', being one-thousandth of a dollar or one-tenth of a cent, is money of account.

**Money talks.** The moneyed have considerable influence in many ways.

**Money to burn.** Money that can be spent without causing any hardship or sense of deprivation.

**Beer money.** *See under* BEER.
**Blood money.** *See under* BLOOD.
**Caution money.** *See under* CAUTION.
**Colour of one's money, The.** *See under* COLOUR.
**Conscience money.** *See under* CONSCIENCE.
**Dirty money.** *See under* DIRTY.
**Easy money.** *See under* EASE.
**Even money.** *See under* EVEN.
**Fairy money.** *See under* FAIRY.
**Flush with money.** *See under* FLUSH.
**For my money.** In my opinion; for my preference.
**Funny money.** *See under* FUNNY.
**Gate money.** *See under* GATE.
**Give someone a run for their money, To.** *See under* RUN.
**Glove money.** *See under* GLOVE.
**Gun money.** *See under* GUN.
**Have a run for one's money, To.** *See under* RUN.
**Hush money.** *See under* HUSH.
**Maundy Money.** *See under* MAUNDY.
**Not for love or money.** *See under* LOVE.
**Paper money.** *See under* PAPER.
**Pin money.** *See under* PIN.
**Pinched for money, To be.** *See under* PINCH.
**Pocket money.** *See under* POCKET.
**Prize money.** *See under* PRIZE.
**Put one's money where one's mouth is, To.** To be true to one's word; to support what one has said.
**Ready money.** *See under* READY.
**Run for one's money, A.** *See under* RUN.
**Ship money.** *See under* SHIP.
**Smart money.** *See under* SMART.
**Spur money.** *See under* SPUR.
**Table money.** *See under* TABLE.
**Throw away one's money, To.** *See under* THROW.
**Throw good money after bad, To.** *See under* THROW.
**Whisky money.** *See under* WHISKY.

**Mongol.** A member of the Asian people who live not only in Mongolia but also in China and parts of the former Soviet Union. They were united as an 'empire' in the 13th century under GENGHIS KHAN, but after his death fragmented into a number of separate chiefdoms. The name is sometimes loosely used for all the so called 'yellow' races, such as the Chinese, East Siberian Eskimos, Japanese, and even the American Indians. *See also* GOLDEN HORDE; MOGUL; TAMBERLANE.

**Mongrel Parliament.** The Parliament that Charles II summoned at Oxford in 1681 to deprive the WHIGS of the support of the City of London in their struggle to alter the succession, i.e. to exclude the Duke of York, a Roman Catholic.

**Monica.** St Monica (332–387), the mother of AUGUSTINE, is seen as the model of all Christian mothers, especially in her patient treatment of her wayward son in the years before his conversion.

**Monism.** The doctrine of the oneness of mind and matter that explains everything in terms of a single reality, ignoring all that is supernatural; otherwise any one of the philosophical theories that denies the dualism of mind and matter and seeks to deduce all the varied spiritual and physical phenomena from a single principle.

**Monitor** (Latin, from *monere*, 'to advise').

(1) The Romans called the nursery teacher the *monitor*. The 'military monitor' was an officer to tell young soldiers of the faults committed against the service. The 'house monitor' was a slave to rouse the family in the morning, among other duties. The term has long been applied to school pupils chosen to assist the staff in a variety of duties.

(2) The name was that of a shallow-draught IRONCLAD with a flat deck, low freeboard and one or two revolving turrets of heavy guns, especially designed for coastal bombardment. The first such craft was designed by Captain John Ericsson in 1861 and used by the Federals in the American Civil War (1861–5) and was so called, as the designer said, because it was intended to 'admonish the leaders of the Southern Rebellion' and to 'prove a severe monitor' to them. The battle between the *Monitor* and the Confederate former frigate *Merrimac* (properly the *Virginia* as renamed after being rebuilt as an ironclad) in 1862 is notable as the first conflict between ironclads.

(3) The word is also used to designate a broadcasting official employed to listen in to foreign (especially enemy) radio transmissions in order to analyse the news announced and to study propaganda. In normal circumstances the duties of a monitor include checking the quality of transmissions.

**Monitorial system.** The name given to the system of instruction, originally called the MADRAS SYSTEM, devised by Andrew Bell (1753–1832) when a superintendent of the Madras Orphanage (1789–96). Because of the dearth of suitably qualified masters, he used senior scholars or monitors to instruct their juniors. These monitors were taught to pass on factual information learned by rote, usually in the form of simple questions and answers. The system was adopted in England by the early LANCASTERIAN and National Schools for the same reasons that caused Bell to devise it in the first place. *See also* NATIONAL SOCIETY.

**Monk** (Old English *munuc*, from Late Latin *monachus*, 'solitary'). In the Western Church, properly a member of those religious orders living a community life under vows of poverty, chastity and obedience. *See also* BENEDICTINES; CARTHUSIANS; CISTERCIANS; FRIAR; MENDICANT ORDERS.

**Monk Lewis.** Matthew Gregory Lewis (1775–1818), so called from his highly coloured 'Gothic' novel *Ambrosio, or the Monk* (1796).

**Monks of Medmenham.** *See* HELLFIRE CLUB.

**Black Monks, The.** The BENEDICTINES.

**Devil sick would be a monk, The.** *See under* DEVIL.

**Hood or cowl does not make the monk, The.** *See under* HOOD.

**Maul of Monks, The.** *See under* MAUL.

**White Monks.** *See under* WHITE.

**Monkey.** Slang for £500 or (in America) $500; also for a mortgage (sometimes extended to 'a monkey with a long tail'), and among sailors the vessel that contained the full allowance of GROG for a MESS. A child, especially an active, meddlesome one, is often called 'a little monkey', for obvious reasons. In army parlance a monkey is a military policeman.

**Monkey business.** Mischievous or meddlesome behaviour, like that of monkeys. There is an excellent Marx Brothers film of this title (1931).

**Monkey jacket.** A short jacket formerly worn by seamen, possibly so called from its likeness to the jacket of the organ grinder's monkey of bygone days, or because it has no more tail than a monkey (or more strictly speaking, an ape). *See also* BUMFREEZER.

**Monkey nuts.** Another name for peanuts.

**Monkey on one's back, A.** An addict's dependence on a drug.

**Monkey puzzle.** The Chilean pine, *Araucaria araucana*, whose twisted and prickly branches puzzle even a monkey to climb.

**Monkey spoons.** Spoons having on the handle a heart surmounted by a monkey, at one time given in the Netherlands at marriages to some immediate relative of the bride, and at christenings and funerals to the officiating clergyman. *See also* SUCK THE MONKEY.

**Monkey suit.** In the USA services the term applied to full dress uniform; also to an aviator's overalls and sometimes to men's formal dress on important occasions.

**Monkey tricks.** Mischievous, ill-natured or deceitful actions.

**Monkey with** or **about, To.** To tamper with or play mischievous tricks. To monkey with the cards is to try to arrange them so that the deal will not be fair.

**Monkey wrench.** A wrench with adjustable jaws.

**Bonnet money.** *See under* BONNET.

**Brass monkey.** *See under* BRASS.

**Get one's monkey up, To.** To be riled or enraged. Monkeys are often irritable and easily provoked. *See also* GET SOMEONE'S GOAT.

**Grease monkey.** *See under* GREASE.

**Suck the monkey, To.** *See under* SUCK.

**Three Wise Monkeys.** *See under* THREE.

**Monmouth.** The town in Monmouthshire at the mouth of the Monnow, and also the surname of Henry V of England (r.1413–22), who was born there.

**Monmouth's Rebellion.** The disastrous final attempt of James, Duke of Monmouth (1649–85), the son of Charles II's mistress Lucy Walter (1630–58), to overthrow James II as champion of the Protestant religion. He landed at Lyme in 1685 and was hailed as king at Taunton and Bridgwater in Somerset but was routed by James II's army at Sedgemoor (6 July). Monmouth was executed and his rustic followers were dealt with at the BLOODY ASSIZES.

**Monmouth Street.** This London street in SOHO was once noted for its second-hand clothes shops. Hence the old expression 'Monmouth Street finery' for TAWDRY, pretentious clothes. *See also* CARNABY STREET.

**Monophysites** (Greek *monos*, 'one', and *phusis*, 'nature'). A religious sect in the Levant that maintained that Jesus Christ had only one nature, and that divine and human were combined in much the same way as body and soul were combined in man. It arose upon the condemnation at the Council of Chalcedon in 451 of the Eutychian heresy (which held that after incarnation Christ had only one nature, the divine), and it is still represented by the Coptic (*see* COPTS), Armenian, Abyssinian, Syrian and Malabar JACOBITE churches.

**Monopoly.** The popular board game, based on the acquisition of real estate, originated in the United States in about 1930 as the brainchild of Charles B. Darrow, a heating equipment engineer. The game sells in different languages around the world, and the properties on the board are named after the streets of a city in the appropriate country. This is usually the capital, so that the British version has London streets, the French those of Paris and so on. However, the original North American game has streets in Atlantic City, New Jersey, as this was where the Darrows spent their holidays.

**Monothelites** (Greek *monos*, 'one', and *thelein*, 'to will'). A 7th-century heretical sect holding that Christ had only one will, namely the divine. Monothelitism, which was akin to the teaching of the MONOPHYSITES, was an attempt to reconcile the latter to their fellow-Christians in the Eastern Empire against Persian and Muslim invaders. Monothelitism was finally condemned by the Council of Constantinople (680). *See also* MARONITES.

**Monroe Doctrine.** The doctrine first promulgated in 1823 by James Monroe (5th US president, 1817–25) to the effect that the American states would not entangle themselves in the broils of the Old World nor suffer European powers to interfere in the affairs of the New. There was to be no future colonization by any European powers. The Monroe Doctrine was invoked by the UNITED STATES during the Anglo-Venezuelan boundary dispute over the limits of British Guiana (1894–6). The capture of Manila, however, and the cession of the Philippines to the United States in 1898, and still more the part the Americans took in the First and Second World Wars, have abrogated a large part of this Doctrine.

**Mons. Mons Meg.** A great 15th-century piece of ordnance in Edinburgh Castle, made at Mons in Flanders and much esteemed by the Scots. It was taken to London in 1754 but at the request of Sir Walter Scott was restored to Edinburgh in 1829. A local story tells how the cannon was made by a smith named Mouncey of Carlingwark (now Castle Douglas) for the purposes of battering the neighbouring castle of Thrave, then in the possession of the Douglas family. It was thus nicknamed 'Mouncey's Meg' in jocular allusion to the maker's noisy wife. Meg is a pet form of Margaret, a popular Scottish name and one familiar from the country's history.

**Mons Star.** The British war medal ('The 1914 Star') given for service in France or Belgium in 1914 is popularly so called. The Battle of Mons was fought on 23 August 1914.

**Angels of Mons, The.** *See under* ANGEL.

**Monseigneur.** The title given to the DAUPHIN from the time of Louis XIV.

**Monsieur.** The eldest brother of the king of France was so called from the time of Louis XIV (r.1643–1715). Philippe, Duc d'Orléans (1640–1701) was the first to be so known.

**Monsieur de Paris.** The public executioner or Jack KETCH of France.

**Monsieur Jourdain.** *See under* JOURDAIN.

**Monsieur le Grand.** The Grand Equerry of France. The ill-fated Marquis de Cinq-Mars (1620–42) held this office in the reign of Louis XIII.

**Peace of Monsieur, The.** *See under* PEACE.

**Monsignor** (plural Monsignori). A title pertaining to all prelates in the ROMAN CATHOLIC CHURCH, which includes all prelates of the Roman court, active or honorary. Used with the surname, as 'Monsignor Newman', it does away with the solecism of speaking of Bishop so-and-so, which is like calling the Duke of Marlborough 'Duke Churchill'.

**Monster. Bug-eyed monster.** *See under* BUG.

**Green-eyed monster.** *See under* GREEN.

**Loch Ness Monster.** *See under* LOCH.

**Mont** (French, 'hill'). The technical term in PALMISTRY for the eminences at the roots of the fingers.

Mont de Mars at the root of the thumb
Mont de Jupiter at the root of the index finger
Mont de Saturne at the root of the middle finger
Mont du Soleil at the root of the ring finger
Mont de Vénus at the root of the little finger

That between the thumb and the index finger is called the Mont de Mercure, and that opposite it the Mont de la Lune.

**Mont-de-piété.** A pawnshop in France, first instituted as *monti di pietà*, literally 'banks of pity', at Rome under Pope Leo X (r.1513–21), by charitable persons who wished to rescue the poor from usurers. They advanced small sums of money on the security of pledges, at a rate of interest barely sufficient to cover the working expenses of the institution. Both the name and the system were introduced into France and Spain. Public granaries for the sale of corn were called in Italian *monti frumentarii*.

**Montagnard.** *See* MOUNTAIN.

**Monte Carlo, The man who broke the bank at.** *See under* MAN.

**Monteer cap.** *See* MONTERO.

**Monteith.** A scalloped basin in which the stems of glasses can be held so that the bowls of the glasses may be cooled and washed, a sort of punch bowl, made of silver or pewter, occasionally porcelain, sometimes with a movable rim scalloped at the top. According to the historian and antiquary, Anthony Wood (1632–95), it is so called from 'a fantastical Scot called "monsieur Monteigh" who about that time wore the bottome of his coate so notched'.

**Montem.** A custom observed triennially until 1847 by the boys of Eton College, who proceeded on Whit Tuesday *ad montem* ('to a mound' (called Salt Hill)), near Slough, and exacted a gratuity called salt money from all who passed by. Sometimes as much as £1000 was thus collected, and it was used to defray the expenses of the senior scholar at King's College, Cambridge.

**Montero** or **monteer cap.** So called from the headgear worn by the *monteros* ('mountaineers') *de Espinosa*, who once formed the interior guard of the palace of the Spanish king. It had a spherical crown and flaps that could be drawn over the ears, rather like a Victorian shooting-cap.

**Montessori method.** A system of training and educating young children evolved by the Italian educationalist, Dr Maria Montessori (1870–1952). Based on 'free discipline' and the use of specially devised 'educational apparatus' and 'didactic material', it has exercised considerable influence on work with young children. *See also* FROEBEL SYSTEM.

**Montevergine, St William of.** *See under* WILLIAM.

**Montezuma.** The Aztec emperor (d.1520) who was overthrown in Mexico by the invading Spaniards. His wealth was legendary, and his name is a byword for cruel human sacrifice. His uncle, of the same name, preceded him as emperor (d.1464), in a reign that was much more constructive than destructive. He rebuilt Tenochtitlán, the chief Aztec city, on the site of modern Mexico City.

**Montezuma's revenge.** One of several colourful euphemisms for diarrhoea suffered by visitors to Mexico or abroad in general, in allusion to the emperor's supposed reprisal after his defeat. Others of similar local reference are Aztec two-step, Cairo crud, Delhi belly, gippy (i.e. Egyptian) tummy, Hong Kong dog and Rangoon runs. *See also* RUNS.

**Month.** One of the 12 divisions of a year. At one time, a new month started on the day of the new moon or the day after. Hence the name (Old English *mōnath*), which is connected with 'moon'. For the individual months see their names. *See also* LUNAR MONTH.

The MNEMONIC for remembering the number of days in each month runs, in one popular version:

Thirty days hath September,
April, June, and November;
All the rest have thirty-one
Excepting February alone,
And that has twenty-eight days clear
And twenty-nine in each leap year.

This, with slight variations, dates from at least the 16th century. Thomas Hood (1799–1845) has a parody, reflecting the fickleness of English weather:

Dirty days hath September,
April, June, and November,
From January up to May

The rain it raineth every day.
February hath twenty-eight alone,
And all the rest have thirty-one.
If any of them had two and thirty
They'd be just as wet and dirty.

**Month of Sundays, A.** An indefinite but long time. The expression is usually combined with a negative to mean 'never', as: 'I wouldn't go there in a month of Sundays.'

**Month's mind, A.** Properly the Requiem MASS said for the deceased on the 30th day after death or burial. The term often occurs in old wills in connection with charities to be disbursed on that day.

**Flavour of the month.** *See under* FLAVOUR.

**Lunar month.** *See under* LUNAR.

**Pinch and a punch for the first of the month, A.** *See under* PINCH.

**Montjoie** or **Montjoie St Denis.** The war cry of medieval France. The Burgundians had for their war cry, 'Montjoie St André', the Dukes of Bourbon, 'Montjoie Notre Dame', and the kings of England used to have 'Montjoie St George'. 'Montjoie' was also the cry of the French HERALDS in the TOURNAMENTS, and the title of the French herald or king of arms.

Much has been conjectured about the origin of Montjoie, or its English equivalent, Mountjoy. According to popular tradition, it is a corruption of *Mons Jovis* ('mount of Jupiter'), as the little mounds were called that served as direction posts in ancient times. Hence it was applied to whatever showed or indicated the way, as the banner of St DENYS, called the ORIFLAMME. However, according to Jacqueline Picoche, in her *Dictionnaire étymologique du français* (1979), the mounds derive their name from Frankish *mund-gawi*, 'protector of the country', and the two elements of this were corrupted by association with *mont*, 'mound', and *joie*, 'joy'.

Where is Mountjoy the herald? speed him hence:
Let him greet England with our sharp defiance.
SHAKESPEARE: *Henry V*, III, v (1598)

**Montpelier.** The name is frequently found in English streets and squares because the town of Montpellier, in the south of France, was a fashionable resort in the 19th century. Montpelier, the capital of Vermont, USA, is named after the same town. The British pronunciation of the name approximates to the French, but the American is closer to 'Montpeelier'.

**Montserrat** (Latin *mons serratus*, 'serrated mountain'). The Catalonians aver that this mountain, in northeastern Spain, was riven and shattered at the crucifixion. Every rift is filled with evergreens. The monastery of Montserrat is famous for its printing press and for its Black Virgin.

**Monty, The full.** *See under* FULL.

**Monument. Monument, The.** The fluted Roman-Doric column of Portland stone, 202ft (61.5m) high, designed by Sir Christopher Wren to commemorate the GREAT FIRE OF LONDON in 1666. It stands near the north end of LONDON BRIDGE, near the spot where the fire started. It was erected between 1671 and 1677. In 1681 the following inscription was made on the base (erased 1831):

This Pillar was set up in perpetual remembrance of that most dreadful burning of this Protestant city, begun and carried out by ye treachery and malice of ye popish faction, in ye beginning of Septem in ye year of Our Lord 1666, in order to ye carrying on their horrid plott, for extirpating the Protestant religion and old English liberty, and the introducing Popery and slavery.

It was this that made Alexander Pope write:

Where London's column, pointing at the skies
Like a tall bully, lifts the head and lies.
*Moral Essays in Four Epistles to Several Persons*, 'To Lord Bathurst' (1733)

**Monumental City.** Baltimore, MARYLAND, is so called because of its many monuments and churches.

**Monuments and effigies in churches.** The following points usually apply:

Founders of chapels and so on: lie with their monument built into the wall
Priests: represented by figures with their hands on their breasts and chalices
Knights: represented by figures with armour
Crusaders or married men: represented by figures with legs crossed; a SCALLOP SHELL certainly indicates a crusader
Nuns: female figures with a mantle and large ring

In the age of CHIVALRY the woman was placed on the man's right hand, but when chivalry declined she was placed on his left hand.

It may be generally taken that inscriptions in Latin, cut in capitals, are of the 12th century or earlier, that those in Lombardic script and Norman French are of the 13th century, that those in Old English text are of the 14th century, and that those in English and Roman characters date from the 15th century or later.

Tablets against the wall came in with the REFORMATION, and brasses are mostly post-13th century.

**Ancient monument.** *See under* ANCIENT.

**Moody & Sankey.** Dwight Lyman Moody (1837–99) was the son of a Massachusetts bricklayer who began his evangelical work in 1860. He was joined by Ira David Sankey (1840–1908) in 1870, who backed up Moody's preaching with singing and organ music. The 'Sankey & Moody Hymn Book', first published in 1873, properly called *Sacred Songs and Solos*, was 'compiled and sung' by Sankey. Their type of 'Gospel Hymn' was partly popularized in Britain during their visits to this country and particularly by the SALVATION ARMY.

**Moon.** The word is probably connected with the Sanskrit root *men-*, 'to measure', because time has long been measured by the phases of the moon. Hence also MONTH. It is common to all Germanic languages (Gothic *mena*, Old Frisian *mona*, Old Norman *mane*, Old English *mōna*, German *Mond*, Dutch *maan*, Swedish *mån*, and so on) and is almost invariably masculine (although not in Dutch). In the EDDA the son of Mundilfoeri is MANI ('moon'), and daughter SOL ('sun').

The moon is represented in five different phases: (1) new, (2) full, (3) crescent or decrescent, (4) half and (5) gibbous or more than half. In pictures of the Assumption it is shown as a crescent under MARY's feet; in the crucifixion it is eclipsed, and placed on one side of the cross, the sun being on the other; and in the Creation and Last Judgement it is also depicted.

In classical mythology the moon was known as HECATE before she had risen and after she had set; as ASTARTE when crescent; as DIANA or CYNTHIA (she who 'hunts the clouds') when in the open vault of heaven; as PHOEBE when looked upon as the sister of the sun (i.e. PHOEBUS); and was personified as SELENE or Luna, the lover of the sleeping ENDYMION, i.e. moonlight on the fields.

The moon is called triform, because it presents itself either round or waxing (with horns towards the east) or waning (with horns towards the west).

One legend connected with the moon was that there was treasured everything wasted on earth, such as misspent time and wealth, broken vows, unanswered prayers, fruitless tears, unfulfilled desires and intentions and the like. In Ariosto's ORLANDO FURIOSO (1532), Astolpho found on his visit to the moon (Bk XXXIV) that bribes were hung on gold and silver hooks, princes' favours were kept in bellows, and wasted talent was kept in vases, each marked with the proper name, while in *The* RAPE OF THE LOCK (v (1712)), Pope writes that when the Lock disappeared:

> Some thought it mounted to the lunar sphere,
> Since all things lost on earth are treasured there.
> There heroes' wits are kept in pond'rous vases,
> And beaux' in snuff-boxes and tweezer-cases.
> There broken vows, and death-bed alms are found,
> And lovers' hearts with ends of riband bound,
> The courtier's promises, and sick man's prayers,
> The smiles of harlots, and the tears of heirs,
> Cages for gnats, and chains to yoke a flea,
> Dried butterflies, and tomes of casuistry.

Hence the phrase, the 'limbus of the moon'. *See also* LIMBO.

**Mooncalf.** An inanimate, shapeless abortion, formerly supposed to be produced prematurely owing to the malign influence of the moon; also a dolt or dunderhead.

**Moondrop.** In Latin, *virus lunare*, a vaporous foam supposed anciently to be shed by the moon on certain herbs and objects, when influenced by incantations.

> Upon the corner of the moon
> There hangs a vaporous drop profound;
> I'll catch it ere it come to ground.
> SHAKESPEARE: *Macbeth*, III, v (1605)

**Moonies.** A religious sect, properly called the Unification Church, founded by Sun Myung Moon (b.1920) in South Korea in 1954. It spread to the USA in the 1960s and subsequently to Great Britain, Australia and elsewhere. Moon claims to be the Second MESSIAH, and his devotees will save mankind from Satan. Funds built up by his followers by selling artificial flowers and other items were used by Moon to create a large property and business organization in America where he has lived since 1973. Tax avoidance led to his prosecution and imprisonment (1984–5).

**Moon is made of green cheese, The.** Said of an absurdity, as: 'He wants me to believe the moon is made of green cheese.'

> Writing a great book ... in which he proved that the moon was made of green cheese.
> CHARLES KINGSLEY: *The Water Babies*, ch iv (1863)

**Moonlight flit. A.** A clandestine removal of one's furniture during the night, to avoid paying one's rent or having the furniture seized in payment for it.

**Moonlighting.** In the Ireland of former days the name given to acts of agrarian violence at night. In Australia riding after cattle by night and, in the USA, holding a night job in addition to one's regular employment are also thus known. In Britain the term is now somewhat loosely applied to the additional employment outside regular working hours predominantly undertaken by building workers, craftsmen, electricians and the like also to undeclared employment by the registered unemployed. The employer usually pays in cash and tax evasion is thus possible.

**Moonrakers.** A nickname of Wiltshire folk and also of simpletons. The name alludes to the story that Wiltshire yokels, with typical country guile, when raking a pond for kegs of smuggled brandy, feigned stupidity when surprised by the excise men, and said that they were trying to rake out the moon, which was reflected in the water. Local lore links the tale with Bishop's Cannings, near Devizes, and with the pond known as the Crammer at Devizes itself.

**Moonrakers, The.** *See* SPRINGERS *under* REGIMENTAL AND DIVISIONAL NICKNAMES.

**Moonshine.** In the USA, especially Florida, a colloquial term for illicitly distilled liquor, the keeper of an illicit still being called a moonshiner. The liquor, called 'corn', 'shine', or 'white lightning', is made from maize, sugar and water. *See also* BOOTLEGGER.

In general colloquial usage the word means 'nonsense', as: 'It's all moonshine.' Here the allusion is to the supposed effects of moonlight on mental stability. *See also* LUNATIC.

**Moons of Mars.** In *Gulliver's Travels* (1726) Jonathan Swift tells how astronomers had 'discovered two lesser Stars, or *Satellites*, which revolve around Mars' (Pt III, ch iii). And although this is now true, it was unknown and unknowable at the time. Swift's prediction may not have been a fluke. He probably based the statement on the theory, advanced by the German astronomer Johannes Kepler (1571–1630), that each planet should have twice as many moons as the one preceding it in order of distance from the Sun. The Earth had one moon, Jupiter had four (known) moons, so Mars, between the two, must have two moons. They were actually discovered in 1877 by the American astronomer Asaph Hall.

**Moonstone.** A variety of feldspar, so called on account of the play of light which it exhibits. It contains bluish-white spots, which, when held to the light, present a silvery play of colour not unlike that of the moon.

**Bark or bay at the moon.** *See under* BARK.

**Bottled moonshine.** *See under* BOTTLE.

**Captain Moonlight.** In Ireland a mythical person to whom was attributed the performance of atrocities by night especially in the latter part of the 19th century. Arson, murder and the maiming of cattle were his specialities.

**Cry for the moon, To.** *See under* CRY.

**Cycle of the moon, The.** *See under* CYCLE.

**Drawing down the moon.** *See under* DRAW.

**Harvest moon.** *See under* HARVEST.

**Island of the Moon, The.** *See under* ISLAND.

**Man in the Moon, The.** *See under* MAN.

**Mohammed and the moon.** *See under* MOHAMMED.

**Mountains of the Moon, The.** *See under* MOUNTAIN.

**Once in a blue moon.** *See under* ONCE.

**Over the moon, To be.** *See under* OVER.

**Shoot the moon, To.** *See under* SHOOT.

**Moor.** The word is from Greek and Latin *Maurus*, an inhabitant of MAURETANIA. In the Middle Ages, Europeans called all Muslims Moors; similarly the eastern nations called all Europeans Franks. Camoëns, in the LUSIADS (Bk VIII (1572)), gives the name to the Indians.

**Moore, Anacreon.** Thomas Moore (1779–1852), who not only translated ANACREON into English (1800) but also wrote original poems in the same style.

**Moot** (Old English *gemōt*, 'meeting'). In Anglo-Saxon times, the assembly of freemen. The main moots were those of the SHIRE and HUNDRED, which served as units of local government. In a few towns, such as Aldeburgh in Suffolk, the town hall is still called the Moot Hall. *See also* WITENAGEMOT.

In legal circles the name is given to the students' debates on supposed cases, which formerly took place in the halls of the INNS OF COURT. The BENCHERS and BARRISTERS took part, as well as the students.

**Moot case** or **moot point.** A doubtful or unsettled question, one that is open to debate. In 'moot point' the word is often popularly confused with 'mute'.

**Mop. Mop** or **mop fair.** A statute or HIRING FAIR, probably taking its name from the tufts or badges worn by those seeking employment. Carters fastened a piece of whipcord to their hats; shepherds, a lock of wool; grooms, a piece of sponge. Others carried a pail, a broom, a mop or some similar implement.

**Mopping-up operations.** In military parlance the final reduction of isolated pockets of enemy resistance, involving the capturing and killing of enemy soldiers left there.

**Mops and mows.** Grimaces. Here 'mop' is connected with Dutch *moppen*, 'to pout'.

**Dame Partington and her mop.** *See under* DAME.

**Moral. Moral Gower, The.** John Gower (*c*.1325–1408), the poet, is so called by Chaucer (*Troilus and Criseyde*, V (*c*.1385)).

**Moral Majority, The.** In the USA an association of fundamentalist Christians founded in 1979 by the television evangelist Jerry Falwell (b.1933) with the aim of promoting 'traditional values' and reversing what he saw as the godless advance of liberal political and social attitudes.

> The Moral Majority, an organization that once struck fear into the hearts of liberals and inspired bumper stickers like 'The Moral Majority is Neither', has been laid to rest. In March, it came in like a lion in 1979 and went out like a lamb. Jerry Falwell, who proclaimed its creation, announced its demise in Las Vegas, Nevada, a city that shows off many sins he tried to fight. The Moral Majority never lived up to its supporters' highest expectations or its detractors' worst fears.
>
> *International Herald Tribune* (15 June 1989)

**Moral Rearmament.** A movement, known as MRA, founded in 1938 by the American evangelist Frank Buchman (1878–1961), who had earlier founded the OXFORD GROUP. Its purpose is to counter the MATERIALISM of present-day society by persuading people to live according to the highest standards of morality and love, to obey God, and to unite in a worldwide association according to these principles.

**Moral virtue.** An ethical virtue as opposed to the theological virtues.

**Father of Moral Philosophy, The.** *See under* FATHER.

**Morality. Morality play.** An allegorical dramatic form in vogue from the 15th to the 16th centuries in which the vices (SEVEN DEADLY SINS) and SEVEN VIRTUES were personified and the victory of the latter established. It was developed from the earlier MYSTERY plays. EVERYMAN, a 15th-century play translated from the Dutch *Elkerlijk*, is the best known. *See also* PASSION PLAY.

**New morality.** *See under* NEW.

**Moran's collar.** In Irish folklore the collar of Moran, the wise councillor of King Feredach the Just, which strangled the wearer if he deviated from the strict rules of equity.

**Moravians.** A PROTESTANT church that is a direct continuation of the BOHEMIAN BRETHREN. Theirs is a simple and unworldly form of religion, and John Wesley was influenced by them. They are now to be found in Denmark, Holland, Germany, Switzerland, Great Britain and America.

**Mordecai.** A cousin of ESTHER, in the Old Testament book of that name. He interprets the king's dreams, but incenses Haman, who had planned to massacre all the Jews. When Mordecai tells Esther what Haman is aiming to do, she saves the Jews, and Mordecai is promoted to high office and favour. *See also* INVENTORS.

**More. More I see of men the more I love dogs, The.** A misanthropic saying of obvious meaning, attributed to Madame de Sévigné (1626–96) as well as to Madame Roland (1754–93) and FREDERICK THE GREAT of Prussia (1712–86).

**More of More Hall.** *See* DRAGON OF WANTLEY.

**More one has, the more one wants, The.** In French: *Plus il en a, plus il en veut*. In Latin: *Quo plus habent, eo plus cupiunt*.

**More or less.** Approximately or in round numbers, as: 'It takes more or less three hours to get there,' i.e. 'it takes about three hours'.

**More power to your elbow.** A jocular toast of encouragement and support implying that a stronger elbow will lift more glasses to the mouth.

**More Sea Bible, The.** *See under* BIBLE.

**More (to that) than meets the eye.** More to something than appears at first sight or on the surface.

**More the merrier, The.** The proverb is found in Heywood's *Collection* (1546) and elsewhere. The full version is: 'The more the merrier; the fewer the better cheer [or fare].'

**No more, To be.** To exist no longer; to be dead.

> This parrot is no more. It's ceased to be. It's expired. It's gone to meet its maker. This is a late parrot.
>
> MONTY PYTHON'S FLYING CIRCUS (television comedy series): (14 December 1969)

**That's more like it.** That's better; that is an improvement. 'It' here is the desired perfection.

**Morganatic marriage.** One between a man of high (usually royal) rank and a woman of lower station, as a result of which she does not acquire the husband's rank and neither she nor any children of the marriage are entitled to inherit the title or possessions. It is often called a left-handed marriage because the custom is for the man to pledge his troth with his left hand instead of his right. George William, Duke of Zell, married Eleanora d'Esmiers in this way, and she took the name and title of Lady Harburg. Her daughter was Sophia Dorothea, the wife of George I. George, Duke of Cambridge (1819–1904), cousin of Queen Victoria, contracted a morganatic marriage in 1840. His children took the surname Fitz-George. The word comes from the Medieval Latin phrase *matrimonium ad morganaticam*, 'marriage based on the morning-gift', the latter being a token present given by a husband to his wife after consummation and representing his only liability. *Morganatica* is related ultimately to German *Morgen*, 'morning'.

**Morgan le Fay.** The fairy sister of King ARTHUR, a principal figure in Celtic legend and ARTHURIAN ROMANCES, also known as Morgane, Morgaine, Morgue la Faye and (especially in ORLANDO FURIOSO) as Morgana. *See also* FATA MORGANA.

It was Morgan le Fay who revealed to King Arthur the intrigues of LANCELOT and GUINEVERE. She gave him a cup containing a magic draught and he had no sooner drunk it than his eyes were opened to the perfidy of his wife and friend.

In *Orlando Furioso* she is represented as living at the bottom of a lake, and dispensing her treasures to whom she likes. In ORLANDO INNAMORATO she first appears as 'Lady Fortune' but subsequently assumes her witch-like attributes. TASSO introduces her three daughters, Morganetta, Nivetta and Carvilia.

In the romance of OGIER THE DANE she receives Ogier in the Isle of AVALON when he is over 100 years old, restores him to youth and becomes his bride.

Her name is of very uncertain origin, as are many names of Celtic mythology. It may come from Breton *Morigena*, 'born of the sea', or else Gaulish *mawr*, 'great', and *can*, 'shining'. Some say it means 'dawn', and so relate it to English 'morning'. Finally, there is the oriental school that traces it back to Arabic *marjan*, 'coral', from Greek *margaris*, 'pearl' (*see* MARGARET). Some

Celtic scholars relate Morgan to the ancient mother goddess Modron, herself apparently a form of the Roman goddess Matrona. *See also* MATRON.

**Morgante Maggiore.** A serio-comic romance in verse (1482) by Luigi Pulci of Florence (1432–84). The characters had appeared previously in many old romances. Morgante is a ferocious giant, converted by ORLANDO (the real hero) to Christianity. After performing the most wonderful feats he finally dies from the bite of a crab.

Pulci was practically the inventor of this burlesque form of poetry, called by the French BERNESQUE, from the Italian, Francesco Berni (1497–1535), who excelled in it.

**Morgiana.** In the ARABIAN NIGHTS ENTERTAINMENTS 'Ali Baba and the Forty Thieves' Morgiana is the clever, faithful slave of ALI BABA, who peers into the 40 jars and discovers that every jar but one conceals a man. She takes the oil from the only jar containing it, and having made it boiling hot, pours enough into each jar to kill the thief inside. She finally kills the captain of the gang and marries her master's son.

**Morglay** ('big glaive'). The sword of BEVIS OF HAMPTON.

**Moriarty.** The arch-enemy of Sherlock HOLMES. His full name is Professor James Moriarty, and he is a brilliant mathematician who has turned his genius to the cause of crime. He was devised by Conan Doyle as a character who could effectively KILL OFF Holmes. The two men finally meet in a 'clash of the titans' above the Reichenbach Falls in Switzerland. After a hand-to-hand struggle, they apparently fall to their deaths in the cataracts below. However, Conan Doyle subsequently resurrected Holmes, although the evil Moriarty remained dead.

**Morley, Mrs.** The name under which Queen Anne corresponded with 'Mrs FREEMAN' (Sarah Churchill, Duchess of Marlborough).

**Mormons.** Properly the Church of Jesus Christ of Latter-Day Saints, regarding itself as a restoration of the one and only Gospel of Christ.

Joseph Smith (1805–44), a farmer's son of Western New York, claimed (in 1820) that God the Father and his Son Jesus Christ had appeared to him, (in 1823) that an account of the early inhabitants of America and of the everlasting Gospel inscribed on gold plates had been revealed to him and (in 1827) that these plates were delivered to him. The result was the *Book of Mormon* produced at Palmyra, New York, in 1830, the book taking its name from the prophet Mormon, who had condensed earlier plates. In the same year Smith and his associates founded the church. Smith was later murdered by a mob when imprisoned by his enemies in Carthage, Illinois, and his place was taken by Brigham Young (1801–77), a carpenter. He led the persecuted 'Saints' to the valley of the Salt Lake, 1500 miles (2414km) distant, generally called Utah, but by the Mormons, DESERET ('bee country'), the NEW JERUSALEM where they have been settled since 1847, despite many disputes with the US government.

The Mormons accept the Bible as well as the *Book of Mormon* as authoritative, they hold doctrines of repentance and faith, that ZION will be built on the American continent, and believe in baptism, the EUCHARIST, the physical resurrection of the dead, and in the Second ADVENT when Christ will have the seat of his power in Utah. Marriage may be for 'time and eternity'. They were long popularly associated with polygamy and practised it until 1890 when the US Supreme Court finally declared against it. This was accepted by the church.

After Smith's death, those who refused to recognize Brigham Young's presidency subsequently established the Reorganized Church of Jesus Christ of Latter-Day Saints at Wisconsin in 1852. Notably it rejected polygamy, claiming that it was introduced by Brigham Young, and also that it is the true successor of the original church. Its headquarters are now at Independence, Missouri.

Mormon missionaries first arrived in Britain in 1837 and there are now some 350 congregations in the United Kingdom following a strict code of behaviour and self-sufficiency.

Smith explained the prophet's name as deriving from English 'more' and Egyptian *mon*, 'good', but this was almost certainly an invention designed to appease questioners. *See also* HICKORY MORMONS.

**Morning. Morning after** or **morning after the night before, The.** A hangover, after overindulgence the previous evening.

**Morning sickness.** Nausea soon after rising, as an early symptom of pregnancy.

**Morning Star.** The planet VENUS, seen just before sunrise when it is west of the sun. It was also Lord Byron's name for his cousin Mary Anne Chaworth, later Mrs Musters, with whom he was in love early in his life and whom he described in his poem 'The Dream' (1816).

**Morning Star of the Reformation.** John Wyclif (*c.*1324–84).

**Morning watch.** In nautical parlance, the watch between 4 am and 8 am. *See also* WATCH.

**Monday morning blues** or **feeling.** *See under* MONDAY.

**Coffee morning.** *See under* COFFEE.

**Pride of the morning, The.** *See under* PRIDE.

**Morocco.** Strong ale made from burnt malt, used in the annual feast at Levens Hall, Westmorland (now Cumbria), on the opening of Milnthorpe

Fair. It was put into a large glass of unique form, and the person whose turn it was to drink (called the 'colt') had to 'drink the constable', i.e. stand on one leg and say 'Luck to Levens as long as Kent flows', then drain the glass or pay a forfeit. The custom ended in the late 1870s.

**Morocco men.** Men who, about the end of the 18th century, used to visit London public houses touting for illegal lottery insurances. Their rendezvous was a tavern in Oxford Market, at the Oxford Street end of Great Portland Street

**Moros.** The name of the Muslim inhabitants of the island of Mindanao and the Sulu Archipelago in the Philippine Islands, and applied to them by the Spanish conquerors because of their supposed resemblance to MOORS.

**Morpheus.** Ovid's name for the son of Sleep, and god of dreams, from Greek *morphē*, 'form', because he gives these airy nothings their form and fashion. Hence the name of the narcotic, 'morphine' or 'morphia'.

**Morrice, Gil** or **Childe.** The hero of an old Scottish ballad, a natural son of an earl and the wife of Lord Barnard, and brought up 'in gude grene wode'. Lord Barnard, thinking the Childe to be his wife's lover, slew him with a broadsword, and setting his head on a spear gave it to 'the meanest man in a' his train' to carry to the lady. When she saw it she said to the baron, 'Wi' that saim speir, O pierce my heart, and put me out o' pain,' but the baron replied, 'Enouch of blood by me's bin spilt ... sair, sair I rew the deid,' adding:

> I'll ay lament for Gill Morice,
> As gin he were mine ain;
> I'll neir forget the dreiry day
> On which the youth was slain.
>
> PERCY: *Reliques* (*Gil Morrice*), xxvi (1765)

Percy says this pathetic tale suggested to John Home the plot of his tragedy, *Douglas* (1756).

**Morris dance.** A dance, popular in England in the 15th century and later, in which the dancers often represented characters from the stories of ROBIN HOOD and MAID MARIAN. Other stock characters were Bavian the fool, MALKIN the clown, the HOBBY horse or a DRAGON, and foreigners, probably MOORS or Moriscos. It was commonly part of the MAY games and other pageants and festivals, and the dancers were adorned with bells. It was brought from Spain in the reign of Edward III (1327–77) and was originally a military dance of the Moors or Moriscos, hence its name.

**Nine men's morris.** *See under* NINE.

**Morrison shelter.** Whereas the Second World War ANDERSON SHELTER was erected outdoors and was more or less permanent, the Morrison shelter was a transportable indoor refuge against bombs and falling masonry. It was made of steel and table-shaped, so that it could actually be used as a table when people were not sheltering under it. It took its name from Herbert S. Morrison (1888–1965), Home Secretary during the war.

**Mortal sin, A.** A 'deadly' sin, one that deserves everlasting punishment, as opposed to a VENIAL SIN.

> Sky loured, and muttering thunder, some sad drops
> Wept at completing of the mortal sin
> Original; while Adam took no thought,
> Eating his fill.
>
> MILTON: *Paradise Lost*, ix (1667)

**Mortarboard.** A COLLEGE CAP surmounted by a square 'board' usually covered with black cloth. The word is possibly connected with French *mortier*, the cap worn by the ancient kings of France, and still used officially by the chief justice or president of the court of justice. It is perhaps more likely an allusion to the small square board or hawk on which a bricklayer or plasterer carries his mortar. *See also* PHARISEES.

**Morte d'Arthur, Le.** *See* ARTHURIAN ROMANCES.

**Mortgage, Welsh.** *See under* WELSH.

**Mortmain** (Old French *mortemain*, from Medieval Latin *mortua manus*, 'dead hand'). A term applied to land that was held inalienably by ecclesiastical or other corporations. In the 13th century, it was common for persons to make over their land to the church and then receive it back as tenants, thus escaping their feudal obligations to the king or other lay lords. In 1279 the Statute of Mortmain was passed prohibiting the practice without the king's licence. The law of mortmain was abolished by the Charities Act 1960.

**Morton's fork.** John Morton (*c*.1420–1500), cardinal and archbishop of Canterbury and minister of Henry VII, when levying forced loans or BENEVOLENCES from rich men, so arranged it that none should escape. Those who were ostentatiously rich were forced to contribute on the grounds that they could well afford it; those who lived without display were made to contribute on the grounds that their economies must mean they had savings. The argument was dubbed 'Morton's fork', which was two-pronged.

> These two arguments alone provide a Morton's Fork on which to impale a womanising President: if he owns up, he's bringing his office into disrepute. If he covers up, he's bringing his integrity into question.
>
> *The Times* (9 January 1999)

**Mortstone.** A rock off Morte Point, Devon.

**He may remove Mortstone.** A Devonshire proverb, said incredulously of husbands who pretend to be masters of their wives. It also means: 'If you have done what you say, you can accomplish anything.'

**Mortuary.** Formerly a gift of the second-best beast of the deceased to the incumbent of the parish church, and later of the best or second-best possession. In due course mortuaries became fees, and in 1529 Parliament limited them to moderate amounts. The custom lingered on in some parishes into the 18th century.

**Mosaic law.** *See* LAW OF MOSES.

**Moses.** The great leader who guides the Jews out of Egypt to the PROMISED LAND. He was left in a basket of reeds at the edge of the Nile as a baby and adopted by Pharaoh's daughter. When he had grown, God appeared to him in a burning bush and appointed him leader of the Jews. He asked Pharaoh to release the Jews, and when Pharaoh refused, God sent ten plagues. Moses then led the Jews to the Red Sea and miraculously parted the waters for them. They continued, with Moses as their leader, to the desert, where he found water by striking a rock. Moses' brother AARON encouraged the Jews to worship a golden calf while Moses himself was on Mount Sinai, where God gave him the TEN COMMANDMENTS. God punished the Jews for their idolatry by condemning them to wander in the desert for 40 years. Moses continued to lead them throughout this time, until at last they came to the Promised Land. God forbade Moses from entering the Promised Land, however, and he died after seeing it from afar. According to tradition, Moses is the author of the PENTATEUCH.

The name of Moses is almost certainly Egyptian in origin. According to the Bible, however, when Pharaoh's daughter adopted the child, 'She called his name Moses: and she said, Because I drew him out of the water' (Exodus 2:10). But this is simply a pun on Hebrew *Moshe*, 'Moses', and *masho*, 'to pull', 'to draw out'. The -*ses* of his name thus really means 'son of', as for Rameses, 'son of RA' (the sun god), so that the initial *Mo*- must equally have been the name of a god. According to Manetho, a priest of HELIOPOLIS in the 3rd century BC, Moses was an Egyptian priest named Hosarsiph, a statement also made by JOSEPHUS in the 1st century AD.

**Moses basket.** A portable cot for babies in the form of a basket with handles. The name alludes to the 'ark of bulrushes' in which the baby MOSES was left by the Nile (Exodus 2:3).

**Moses boat.** A type of boat made at Salisbury, Massachusetts, by a famous boatbuilder, Moses Lowell, in the 18th century. Further south (in the West Indies), it is said to have been a boat of sufficient capacity to take a hogshead of sugar from shore to ship in one trip.

**Moses' rod.** The DIVINING ROD is sometimes so called, after the rod with which Moses worked wonders before pharaoh (Exodus 7:9), or the rod with which he smote the rock to bring forth water (Exodus 17:6).

**Horns of Moses' face, The.** *See under* HORN.

**Law of Moses, The.** *See under* LAW.

**Moshoeshoe.** The founder and first chief of the African Sotho (Basuto) nation, more accurately known as Mshweshwe (*c*.1786–1870). He was born Lepoqo, and after his circumcision became Letlama, 'Binder', a name given for the daring cattle raids he conducted as a young man. In 1809 he took the name Mshweshwe, an imitation of the sound a knife makes when shaving. His cattle raids and conquests brought him increased power, and his many wives added to his general prestige. He finally united the different groups under a single nation, called by the English Basutoland. His stronghold was at Thaba Bosiu ('Mountain of the Night'), where he pursued his policy of peace and prosperity almost until his death, when the arrival of the British, and their annexation of Sotho lands in 1868, diminished his influence.

**Moslem.** *See* MUSLIM.

**Mosque, The Pearl.** *See under* PEARL.

**Moss Bros.** The well-known firm of tailors and outfitters ultimately takes its name from Moses Moses, a Jewish bespoke tailor who set up shop in Covent Garden, London, in 1860. The 'Bros' were two of his five sons, George and Alfred, who inherited the business on their father's death in 1894, anglicizing their surname to Moss. The firm's shops are best known for hiring out dress suits.

**Most. Most Ancient Order of the Thistle, The.** This Scottish order of knighthood (ranking second to the MOST NOBLE ORDER OF THE GARTER) is not very ancient, being instituted by James II (James VII of Scotland) in 1687. It is inaccurately said to have been 'refounded' then. Legend has it that it was founded by Achaius, king of the Scots in 787. It fell into abeyance after 1688 but was revived again by Queen ANNE in 1703 and now consists of 16 knights (besides members of the royal family). Its officers are the dean, the secretary, the LORD LYON KING OF ARMS and the Gentleman USHER OF THE GREEN ROD. Its insignia consist of the Badge (an elongated eight-pointed star with a figure of St ANDREW and his cross), Star, Collar of golden thistles and sprigs of RUE, Mantle and dark green ribbon. It is sometimes called the Order of St Andrew. Its motto is NEMO ME IMPUNE LACESSIT.

**Most Christian King, The.** The style of the king of France since 1429, when it was conferred on Louis XI by Pope Paul II (r.1458–64). Previously the title had been given in the 8th century to Pepin le Bref (the Short, r.751–768) by Pope Stephen III (r.768–772), and again in the 9th century to Charles le Chauve (the Bald, r.843–877).

**Most Honourable.** The form of address for a MARQUESS, for members of the PRIVY COUNCIL and for the KNIGHTS OF THE BATH.

**Most Noble Order of the Garter, The.** The highest order of knighthood in Great Britain, traditionally instituted by Edward III about 1348, and reconstituted in 1805 and 1831. The popular legend is that the Countess of Salisbury accidentally dropped her garter at a court ball. It was picked up by the king who, noticing the significant looks of the spectators, rebuked them by binding the blue band round his own knee, saying as he did so, HONI SOIT QUI MAL Y PENSE. The lady has also been named as Joan, the FAIR MAID OF KENT, her cousin, Alice Montague and Queen Philippa. The order is limited to the sovereign and other members of the royal family, with 24 Knights Companions and such foreign royalties as may be admitted by statute. The only Ladies of the Garter are the sovereign's queen and his eldest daughter when she is heir presumptive. In the late 1990s the Ladies of the Garter were Queen Elizabeth, the Queen Mother, and Princess Anne, the Princess Royal. Until Viscount Grey (then Sir Edward Grey) was admitted to the order in 1912, no commoner for centuries had been able to put KG after his name. Sir Winston Churchill received the Order of the Garter from Queen Elizabeth II in 1953.

**Most unkindest cut of all.** Treachery from a friend, the proverbial 'last straw'. The phrase, with its tautological superlative, comes from Shakespeare's *Julius Caesar* (III, ii (1599)). When Mark Antony was showing the dagger cuts in Caesar's mantle he thus referred to the thrust made by MARCUS BRUTUS, whom he described as 'Caesar's angel'.

**His Most Religious Majesty.** The title by which the kings of England were formerly addressed by the pope. It still survives in the BOOK OF COMMON PRAYER in the Prayer 'for the High Court of Parliament under our most religious and gracious Queen at this time assembled' (which was written, probably by hand, in 1625), and in James I's *Act for Thanksgiving on the Fifth of November* occurs the expression 'most great, learned, and religious king'.

Similarly the pope addressed the king of France as 'Most Christian', the emperor of Austria as 'Most Apostolic', the king of Portugal as 'Most Faithful', and so on. *See also* MAJESTY.

**Moth, Death's-head.** *See under* DEATH.

**Mother.** Properly a female parent; hence, figuratively, the origin of anything, the head or headquarters of a religious or other community, the source of something. The word is similar in many languages, such as Sanskrit *mātr*, Greek *mētēr*, Latin *mater*, Old English *mōdor*, German *Mutter*, French *mère*, Russian *mat'* etc.

Mother is also the name given to a stringy gummy substance, sometimes called 'mother of vinegar', which forms on the surface of a liquor undergoing acetous fermentation, consisting of the bacteria that are causing that fermentation.

**Mother, To be.** To pour the tea, as: 'Shall I be mother?'

**Mother Ann.** Ann Lee (1736–84), the founder and 'spiritual mother' of the American sect of SHAKERS.

**Mother Carey's chickens.** Sailor's name for STORMY PETRELS, perhaps derived from *mater cara* or *madre cara* ('mother dear', with reference to the Virgin Mary). Sailors also call falling snow Mother Carey's chickens. Captain Marryat's *Poor Jack* (1840) has an account of sailors' superstitions on such matters.

**Mother Carey's goose.** The great black petrel or fulmar of the Pacific.

**Mother Church.** The church considered as the central fact, the head, the last court of appeal in all matters pertaining to conscience or religion. St JOHN LATERAN, at Rome, is known as the Mother and Head of all churches. Also, the principal or oldest church in a country or district, or the cathedral of a diocese.

**Mother country.** One's native country, or the country whence one's ancestors came to settle. England is the mother country of Australia, New Zealand and Canada, for example. The equivalent German term is *Vaterland* ('fatherland').

**Mother Earth.** When JUNIUS BRUTUS (after the death of LUCRETIA) formed one of the deputation to DELPHI to ask the ORACLE which of the three would succeed TARQUIN, the response was, 'He who should first kiss his mother.' Junius instantly threw himself on the ground, exclaiming, 'Thus, then, I kiss thee, Mother Earth,' and he was elected consul.

In modern terms Mother Earth is essentially a personification of the EARTH MOTHER and readily identified as such by NEW AGE adherents.

> Before the Romans foisted their Straight Lines upon us, these [British] isles undulated with all that was the wonder of our Mother Earth.
>
> JULIAN COPE: *The Modern Antiquarian*, Introduction (1998)

**Mother Goose.** The character famous from *Mother Goose's Nursery Rhymes*, which first seems to have been used in *Songs for the Nursery or, Mother Goose's Melodies for Children*, published by Thomas Fleet in Boston, Massachusetts, in 1719. The rhymes were free adaptations of Perrault's *Contes de ma mère l'oye* ('Tales of My Mother Goose'), which appeared in 1697. The term *conte de la mère l'oye* was then already in existence for a tale and its teller and is mentioned, for example, in the issue of 12 June 1650 of Jean Loret's weekly gazette *La Mvze historique*

**Mother Hubbard.** *See* OLD MOTHER HUBBARD.

**Mothering Sunday.** MID-LENT SUNDAY or LAETARE SUNDAY, when the pope blesses the GOLDEN ROSE, and children feast on mothering cakes and SIMNEL CAKES. A bunch of violets is emblematic of this day, and it is customary for children to give small presents to their mothers. It is said that it is derived from the pre-Reformation custom of visiting the MOTHER CHURCH on that day. Children away from home, especially daughters in service, normally returned to their family. The modern and secular equivalent is Mother's Day, introduced to Britain from the USA, where it is observed on the second Sunday in May.

**Mother-in-law.** The mother of a person's husband or wife and long the butt of popular humour, which aims to mock and thus belittle her autocratic authority and meddling manner.

**Mother of Believers, The.** Among Muslims, AYESHA, the second and favourite wife of MOHAMMED, who was called the Father of Believers. Mohammed's widows are also sometimes called 'mothers of believers'.

**Mother of God.** A title of the Virgin MARY, used of her by the Greek Fathers from Origen onwards. The term is common among Roman Catholics and in the ORTHODOX CHURCH. Its equivalent in the languages of these churches means literally 'God-bearer': Latin *Deipara*, Greek *Theotokos*, Russian *Bogoroditsa*.

**Mother of Parliaments.** The British Parliament, as the model for many other parliaments. The expression was originally used of England itself, not Parliament, by John Bright in 1865.

**Mother-of-pearl.** The inner iridescent layers of the shells of many bivalve molluscs, especially that of the pearl oyster. The name translates obsolete French *mère perle*, corresponding to Italian *madreperla* and German *Perlmutter*.

**Mother of Presidents.** The state of VIRGINIA. George Washington, first President of the USA (1789–97), was a Virginian.

**Mother's Day.** *See* MOTHERING SUNDAY.

**Mother Shipton.** *See under* SHIPTON.

**Mothers' meeting.** A meeting of mothers held periodically in connection with some church or denomination, at which the women can get advice or religious instruction, drink tea, gossip and sometimes do needlework. Hence, facetiously, a group of gossiping people, whether women or men.

**Mother's ruin.** A nickname for GIN.

**Mothers' Union.** A CHURCH OF ENGLAND women's society to safeguard and strengthen Christian family life, to uphold the lifelong vows of marriage and generally to play a proper part in the life of the church. It was incorporated by Royal Charter in 1926 and generally operates as a parish institution.

**Mother tongue.** Native language.

**Mother wit.** Native wit; a ready reply; the wit that 'our mother gave us'.

**Does your mother know you're out?** A jeering remark addressed to a presumptuous youth or to a simpleton. It is the title of a comic poem published in the *Mirror* of 28 April 1838 and rapidly became a catchphrase in both England and America.

> I went and told the constable my property to track;
> He ask'd me if 'I did not wish that I might get it back?'
> I answer'd, 'To be sure I do!—it's what I'm come about'.
> He smiled and said, 'Sir, does your mother know that you are out?'
>
> R.H. BARHAM: *Ingoldsby Legends*, 'Misadventures at Margate' (1840)

**Old Mother Hubbard.** *See under* OLD.

**Old Mother Riley.** *See under* OLD.

**Queen mother.** *See under* QUEEN.

**Tied to one's mother's apron strings.** *See under* TIE.

**Motion.** The laws of motion, according to Galileo and Newton, are:

(1) If no force acts on a body in motion, it will continue to move uniformly in a straight line
(2) If force acts on a body, it will produce a change of motion proportionate to the force, and in the same direction (as that in which the force acts)
(3) When one body exerts force on another, that other body reacts on it with equal and opposite force

**Go through the motions, To.** *See under* GO.

**Perpetual motion.** *See under* PERPETUAL.

**Mot juste, Le** (French, 'the right word'). The word or phrase that exactly conveys the meaning desired.

**Motley.** Varied, mixed, of things or people, as a motley collection or motley crew. The word originally applied to a clown's particoloured costume, or to a clown or jester himself, and it is found in this sense in Shakespeare.

**On with the motley.** On with the show. A phrase used when one determines to keep going, despite difficulties or interruptions. It arose as an English translation of Italian *Vesti la giubba*, which properly means 'Put on the jacket'. These are the words spoken by the clown Canio in Leoncavallo's opera *I Pagliacci* (1892) when he bewails his duty to keep amusing people although his heart is broken. *See also* MOTLEY.

**Mould, To break the.** *See under* BREAK.

**Moulin Rouge.** The Paris dance hall, with its cancan dancers, opened in Montmartre in 1889 and took its name from another hall nearby that had closed. Over its entrance it had a model of a red windmill (French *moulin rouge*), with working sails and the figures of a miller and his wife at different windows. When the sails turned, the couple waved to each other. The model itself typified the many windmills that at one time stood on the heights of Montmartre. The English equivalent is or was the coincidentally named WINDMILL THEATRE.

**Mount** or **Mountain. Mountain, The** (French *La Montagne*). The JACOBINS and extremists in the National Assembly at the time of the French Revolution, so called because they occupied the topmost benches on the left. Among its leaders were Robespierre, Danton, Marat, Collot d'Herbois, Camille Desmoulins, Carnot and St Just. They gained ascendancy in the Convention, supporting the execution of the king and the REIGN OF TERROR. The terms Montagnard and Jacobin were synonymous. Extreme RADICALS in France are still sometimes called Montagnards. *See also* GIRONDISTS; PLAIN.

**Mountain ash.** *See* ROWAN.

**Mountain dew.** Scotch whisky, formerly that from illicit stills hidden away in the mountains. *See also* MOONSHINE.

**Mountain in labour, The.** A mighty effort made for a small result. The allusion is to the celebrated line, *Parturiunt montes, nascetur ridiculus mus* ('Mountains will go into labour and a silly little mouse will be born') by Horace (*Ars Poetica* (1st century BC)). A similar quotation occurs in AESOP.

There is a story that the Egyptian king, Tachos, sustained a long war against Artaxerxes Ochus, and sent to the Lacedaemonians for aid. King Agesilaus went with a contingent, but when Tachos saw a little lame, ill-dressed man, he said: *Parturiebat mons; formidabat Jupiter; ille vero murem peperit*. ('The mountain laboured, Jupiter stood aghast, and a mouse ran out.') Agesilaus replied, 'You call me a mouse, but I will soon show you I am a lion.'

**Mountains of the Moon, The.** The name refers to mountains that are pale or white because of a covering of snow and ice. Ptolemy used the name of the Ruwenzori Range in central Africa, although it has also been applied to the Virunga Mountains, further to the east.

**Mount Carmel.** *See under* CARMEL.

**Mount Etna.** *See under* ETNA.

**Mount Ida.** *See under* IDA.

**Mount Meru.** *See under* MERU.

**Mount of Olives.** *See* OLIVET.

**Mount Pilatus.** *See under* PILATUS.

**Delectable Mountains.** *See under* DELECTABLE.

**If the mountain will not come to Mohammed.** *See under* IF.

**Magnetic Mountain.** *See under* MAGNET.

**Make a mountain out of a molehill, To.** To make a difficulty of trifles. Latin has *Arcem e cloaca facere* ('to make a stronghold out of a sewer'), and the French have *Faire d'une mouche un éléphant* ('to make an elephant out of a fly').

**Old Man of the Mountains, The.** *See under* OLD.

**Sermon on the Mount, The.** *See under* SERMON.

**Shivering Mountain.** *See under* SHIVER.

**Table Mountain.** *See under* TABLE.

**Mountebank** (Italian *montambanco*, 'climber on a bench'). A vendor of quack medicines at fairs or elsewhere, who attracts the crowd by his tricks and antics. Hence any CHARLATAN or self-advertising pretender. The 'bank' or bench was the counter on which traders displayed their goods, and street vendors used to climb on their bench to patter to the public.

**Mourning.** The colours of mourning dress vary from one part of the world to another, depending on the symbolic value of the particular shade. The following are some of the chief.

Black: expressing the privation of light and joy, the midnight gloom of sorrow for the loss sustained, is the colour of mourning in Europe and also formerly in ancient Greece and the Roman Empire

Black and white striped: expressing sorrow and hope, it is the mourning of the South Sea Islanders

Greyish-brown: the colour of the earth to which the dead return

Pale brown: the colour of withered leaves is the mourning of Persia

Sky blue: expressing the assured hope that the deceased has gone to heaven, is the mourning used in Syria, Armenia and some other Asian countries

Deep blue: the colour of mourning in Bokhara and also that of the Romans of the Republic

Purple and violet: expressing royalty, 'kings and priests to God', is the colour of mourning for cardinals and the kings of France; in Turkey the colour is violet

White: the emblem of 'white-handed hope', was used by the ladies of ancient Rome and Sparta; also in Spain till the end of the 15th century; Henry VIII wore white for Anne Boleyn; also the colour of mourning in China

Yellow: expressing the sere and yellow leaf, is the colour of mourning in Egypt and in Burma (Myanmar), where it is also the colour of the monastic order; in Brittany, widows' caps among the *paysannes* are yellow; Anne Boleyn wore yellow for Catherine of Aragon (some say yellow is in token of exaltation)

*See also* BLACK CAP.

**Mouse** or **mice.** The soul was at one time supposed to pass at death through the mouth of man in some animal form, sometimes a mouse or rat. A red mouse indicated a pure soul; a black mouse, a polluted soul; a pigeon or dove, a saintly soul.

'Mouse' is also a term of endearment, like 'duckie' and 'lamb'.

> 'God blesse thee Mouse' the Bridegroome sayd,
> And smakt her on the lips.
>
> WILLIAM WARNER: *Albion's England*, II, x (1592)

**Mouse Tower, The.** A medieval watchtower on

the Rhine, near Bingen, so called from the tradition that Archbishop HATTO was there devoured by mice. Actually it was built by Bishop Siegfried 200 years after Hatto's death, as a toll house. German *Maut* means 'toll' ('mouse' is *Maus*), and the similarity of these words together with the unpopularity of the toll on corn gave rise to the legend.

Many similar legends are told of the medieval Rhineland, among them the following:

(1) Count Graaf raised a tower in the centre of the Rhine, and if any boat attempted to avoid payment of a toll, the warders shot the crew with crossbows. In a famine year the count profiteered greatly by cornering wheat, but the tower was invaded by hungry rats who worried the old baron to death and then devoured him.

(2) Widerolf, bishop of Strasbourg (in 997), was devoured by mice because he suppressed the convent of Seltzen, on the Rhine.

(3) Bishop Adolf of Cologne was devoured by mice or rats in 1112.

(4) Freiherr von Güttingen collected the poor in a great barn and burnt them to death. He was pursued to his castle of Güttingen by rats and mice who gnawed him clean to the bone. His castle then sank to the bottom of the lake 'where it may still be seen'. *See also* PIED PIPER OF HAMELIN.

**As poor as a church mouse.** *See under* AS.

**As quiet as a mouse.** *See under* AS.

**Cat and Mouse Act, The.** *See under* CAT.

**Mickey Mouse.** *See under* MICKEY.

**When the cat's away the mice will play.** *See under* WHEN.

**Mousterian.** A name given to the epoch of NEANDERTHAL MAN, from the cave of Le Moustier near Les Eyzies, in the Dordogne in France, where Palaeolithic remains were found.

**Mouth. Mouth-watering.** Appetizing, whether literally of food or figuratively of anything tempting or attractive.

**By word of mouth.** *See under* BY.

**Down in the mouth.** *See under* DOWN.

**Keep one's mouth shut, To.** To keep a secret.

**Live from hand to mouth, To.** *See under* LIVE.

**Look a gift-horse in the mouth, To.** *See under* LOOK.

**Look as if butter would not melt in one's mouth, To.** *See under* LOOK.

**Make one's mouth water, To.** To cause one's keen anticipation. The sight, smell or thought of a tasty dish causes one's saliva to flow and stimulates one's appetite.

**Open one's big mouth, To.** *See under* OPEN.

**Put words into someone's mouth, To.** *See under* WORD.

**Shoot off one's mouth, To.** *See under* SHOOT.

**Take the bread out of someone's mouth, To.** *See under* BREAD.

**Take the words out of someone's mouth, To.** *See under* WORD.

**Word of mouth.** *See under* WORD.

**Moutons, Revenons à nos.** *See under* REVENONS.

**Movable. Movable Feasts.** Annual church feasts that do not fall on a fixed date but are determined by certain established rules. EASTER Day, which can fall on any date from 22 March to 25 April, is a notable example.

**First movable, The.** *See* PRIMUM MOBILE.

**Move. Move heaven and earth, To.** To make extradordinary efforts.

**Move mountains, To.** To achieve remarkable results. Also to make a supreme effort.

**Ecumenical movement.** *See under* ECUMENICAL.

**Get a move on, To.** To hurry.

**Oxford Movement.** *See under* OXFORD.

**Romantic movement.** *See under* ROMANTIC.

**Movie. Blue movie.** *See under* BLUE.

**Snuff movie.** *See under* SNUFF.

**Mow.** The three 'mows' in English are wholly distinct words.

(1) Mow, a heap of hay ('barley mow'), is Old English *mūwa*, connected with Old Norse *mūgr*, 'heap'.

(2) Mow, to cut down grass, is Old English *māwan*, connected with Latin *metere*, 'to reap'.

(3) Mow, to grimace (in 'mops and mows'), is Old French *moe*, 'pout' (modern French *moue*).

**Mowgli.** The boy raised by wolves in the forests of India, in Rudyard Kipling's *Jungle Book* (1894) and *Second Jungle Book* (1895). According to the story, his name means 'Frog', from his appearance as a naked 'man cub', but Kipling subsequently admitted that he had invented the name. Much of the lore and language of the WOLF CUBS was based on the Mowgli stories.

**Mpret** (Albanian, from Latin *imperator*). The old title of the Albanian rulers, revived in 1913 in favour of the German prince Wilhelm zu Wied whose mpretship lasted only a few months.

**MS** (plural **MSS**). Manuscript, as an abbreviation applied to literary works in handwriting, and also popularly to typescript (Latin *manuscriptus*, 'written by hand').

**Much.** The miller's son in the ROBIN HOOD stories. In the MORRIS DANCE he played the part of the Fool, and his great feat was to bang the head of the gawping spectators with a bladder of peas.

**Muck. As common as muck.** *See under* AS.

**Lady Muck.** *See under* LADY.

**Where there's muck, there's brass.** *See under* WHERE.

**Muckle, Many a mickle makes a.** *See under* MANY.

**Muckraking.** The searching out and revealing of

scandal. The term was coined by President Theodore Roosevelt in 1906 to describe journalism that exposed corruption and exploitation. He likened its practitioners to the anonymous 'man with the muck-rake' in Part II of John Bunyan's *Pilgrim's Progress* (1684) who 'could look no way but downwards' and so missed the sky above.

> The men with the muck-rakes are often indispensable to the well-being of society; but only if they know when to stop raking the muck.
>
> THEODORE ROOSEVELT: Speech in Washington (14 April 1906)

**Muddied oafs.** Footballers. *See also* FLANNELLED FOOLS.

**Muff.** One who is awkward at games and sports, or who is effeminate, dull or stupid. The word may be a sneering allusion to the use of muffs to keep one's hands warm. The term does not seem to be older than the early 19th century, but there is a Sir Harry Muff in Dudley's interlude, *The Rival Candidates* (1774), as a stupid, blundering dolt.

> 'I didn't think, Madman, that you'd have been such a muff as to let him be getting wet through at this time of day.'
>
> THOMAS HUGHES: *Tom Brown's Schooldays*, Pt II, ch iv (1857)

**Muffins and crumpets.** Muffin is perhaps Low German *muffen*, 'cakes'. The French scholar Charles Du Fresne, Sieur Du Cange, describes the *panis mofletus* as bread of a more delicate nature than ordinary, and says it was made fresh every day. Crumpet, the unsweetened soft cake, is a word of uncertain origin.

**Mufti.** An Arabic word meaning an official, an expounder of the KORAN and Muslim law. Thus the Mufti of JERUSALEM is the chief religious official of the Muslims of Jerusalem. The word passed into English to denote civil, as distinct from military or official costume. The modern meaning dates from the early 19th century, and probably arose from the resemblance that the flowered dressing gown and tasselled smoking cap worn by off-duty officers bore to the costume of an Eastern Mufti. The word itself comes from Arabic *muftī*, from *aftā*, 'to give a (legal) decision'. *See also* FATWA.

**Mug.** The word is used as slang for 'face' and also for one who is easily taken in, possibly coming from the gypsy meaning, a simpleton or MUFF.

**Mugging.** Now the common term for assault followed by robbery. From the old slang use of 'mug' meaning to rob or swindle.

**Muggins.** Slang for a fool or simpleton, often with reference to the speaker, as: 'Nobody had any money, so muggins had to pay'. The word may allude to MUG. *See also* JOE MUGGINS.

**Mug's game, A.** A foolish activity.

**Mugshot.** A photograph of someone's face, especially for an official purpose, such as a news item or in support of an application form.

**Mug up, To.** To study hard for a specific purpose, e.g. to pass an examination. This old university phrase may come from the theatre, where an actor, while making up his face or 'mug', would hurriedly scan his lines.

**Muggletonian.** A follower of Lodovic Muggleton (1609–98), a journeyman tailor, who in about 1651 made himself out to be a prophet. He was sentenced for blasphemous writings to stand in the pillory, and was fined £500. The members of the sect, which maintained some existence until *c.*1865, believed that their two founders, Muggleton and John Reeve, were the 'two witnesses' spoken of in Revelation 11:3.

**Mugwump.** An Algonquian word meaning literally 'great chief'. In Eliot's INDIAN BIBLE (*see under* BIBLE) the word 'centurion' in Acts is rendered 'mugwump'. It is now applied in the USA to independent members of the Republican Party, those who refuse to follow the dictates of a CAUCUS and all politicians whose party vote cannot be relied on. It is also used in the sense of 'big shot' or 'boss'. In 1936 Congressman Albert J. Engel is said to have explained a mugwump as 'a bird who sits with its mug on one side of the fence and its wump on the other'.

**Mulatto** (Spanish, from *mulo*, 'a mule'). A term for a person of mixed black and white parentage, or generally for any half-breed. A mule is the offspring of a female horse and a male donkey. *See also* CREOLE.

**Mulberry.** Fable has it that the fruit was originally white and became blood-red from the blood of PYRAMUS and Thisbe. In the 'language of flowers' black mulberry (*Morus nigra*) means 'I shall not survive you', while white mulberry (*Morus alba*) signifies 'wisdom'. The astrologer Nicholas Culpeper says that the tree is ruled by MERCURY and it is noted as a vermifuge. An old Gloucestershire proverb runs: 'After the mulberry tree has shown green leaf, there will be no more frost.' Silkworms are fed on the leaves of the mulberry, especially the white mulberry. The paper mulberry (*Broussonetia papyrifera*) is so called from its former use in Japan and the Far East for making paper from its inner bark.

In the Second World War Mulberry was the code name given to the prefabricated ports towed across to the Normandy coast to make possible the supply of the Allied armies in France in 1944 consequent upon the D-DAY landings. Submersible sections of concrete formed a breakwater and quay alongside which the transports were unloaded. The name was chosen at the time because it was the next in rotation on the British Admiralty's list of names available for warships. Two such Mulberries were set up, but the one serving the US beaches was wrecked by a storm (19 June). That serving the British beaches was kept in service until Antwerp was available.

**Here we go round the mulberry bush.** An old game in which children take hands and dance round in a ring, singing the song of which this is the refrain.

**Mulciber.** Among the Romans, a name of VULCAN. It means the softener, because he softened metals.

And round about him lay on euery side
Great heapes of gold, that neuer could be spent;
Of which some were rude owre, not purifide
Of *Mulcibers* deuouring element.
EDMUND SPENSER: *The Faerie Queene*, II, vii (1590)

**Mule.** The offspring of a female horse and a male donkey, hence a hybrid between other animals (or plants), as a mule canary, a cross between a canary and a goldfinch. The offspring of a stallion and a she-ass is not, properly speaking, a mule, but a hinny.

Very stubborn or obstinate people are sometimes called mules, in allusion to the reputed characteristic of the beast.

**Crompton's mule** or **spinning mule.** *See under* CROMPTON.

**Mulla. Bard of Mulla's silver stream, The.** *See under* BARD.

**Mullah** (Arabic *mawlā*, 'master'). A title of respect given by Muslims to religious dignitaries versed in the sacred law.

**Mad Mullah, The.** *See under* MAD.

**Mulled ale.** Ale spiced and warmed, similarly mulled wine. The derivation of the word is uncertain, but it may come from Middle English *mold-ale*, 'funeral feast', from *mold*, 'earth', 'grave'.

**Mulligan.** The word has several colloquial uses in the USA: (1) a stew; (2) a nickname for an Irishman; (3) an underworld term for a policeman; (4) a second drive in golf, allowed by an opponent on the first tee of a round if the first drive is missed. The origin of some or all of these appears to be in the surname Mulligan.

**Mulready envelope.** An envelope resembling a half-sheet of letter-paper when folded, having on the front an ornamental design by William Mulready (1786–1863), the artist. These were the stamped penny postage envelopes introduced in 1840, but the Mulreadies remained in circulation for one year only owing to ridicule of their ludicrous design. They are prized by stamp collectors.

The manager rings, and the Prompter springs
To his side in a jiffy, and with him brings
A set of those odd-looking envelope things,
Where Britannia (who seems to be crucified) flings
To her right and left funny people with wings
Amongst Elephants, Quakers, and Catabaw Kings;
And a taper and wax
And small Queen's heads in packs,
Which, when notes are too big, you're to stick on their backs.
R.H. BARHAM: *Ingoldsby Legends*, 'A Row in an Omnibus (Box)' (1840)

**Multitude, Nouns of.** *See under* NOUNS.

**Multum in parvo** (Latin, 'much in little'). Much information condensed into few words or into a small compass. The motto is that of Rutland, England's smallest county.

**Mum.** A strong beer made in Brunswick, said to be so called from Christian Mumme, by whom it was first brewed in the late 15th century.

**Mumchance.** Silence. Mumchance was a game of chance with dice, in which silence was indispensable. 'Mum' is connected with 'mumble' (German *mummeln*, Danish *mumle*, 'to mumble').

**Mum's the word.** An admonition to keep what is told you a profound secret. The phrase 'to keep mum' means to keep silent or not to speak to or tell anyone something. The word 'mum' represents a sound made with closed lips. *See also* MUMCHANCE.

Seal up your lips, and give no words but – mum.
SHAKESPEARE: *Henry, VI, Pt II*, I, ii (1590)

**Mumbo jumbo.** The name given by Europeans to a BOGY or grotesque idol venerated by certain African tribes, hence any object of blind unreasoning worship.

Mungo Park, in his *Travels in the Interior of Africa* (1795–7), says (ch iii) that Mumbo Jumbo 'is a strange bugbear, common to all Mandingo towns, and much employed by the Pagan natives in keeping their women in subjection'. When the ladies of the household become too quarrelsome, Mumbo Jumbo is called in. He may be the husband or his agent suitably disguised, who comes at nightfall making hideous noises. When the women have been assembled and songs and dances performed, 'Mumbo fixes on the offender'. She is 'stripped naked, tied to a post, and severely scourged with Mumbo's rod, amidst the shouts and derision of the whole assembly'. The original Mandingo form of the name is probably *Mama Dyumbo*, said to mean 'venerable ancestor with pompon'.

The term is now used for any meaningless or confusing language or action. *See also* JUMBO.

**Mummer.** A contemptuous name for an actor, from the parties that formerly went from house to house at CHRISTMAS mumming, i.e. giving a performance of St GEORGE and the DRAGON, and the like, in dumb show.

Peel'd, patch'd and piebald, linsey-woolsey brothers,
Grave mummers! sleeveless some, and shirtless others.
ALEXANDER POPE: *The Dunciad*, iii (1728)

**Mummy.** The word for an embalmed body comes from Persian *mum*, 'wax', alluding to the custom of anointing the body with wax and preparing it for burial.

**Mummy wheat.** Wheat (*Triticum compositum*) commonly grown on the southern shores of the Mediterranean, the seed of which is traditionally said to have been taken from ancient Egyptian tombs.

**Mumping day.** St THOMAS' Day, 21 December, is so called in some parts of the country, because on this day the poor used to go about 'mumping' or begging,.or, as it was called, 'a-gooding', that is, getting gifts to procure good things for CHRISTMAS, or begging corn. In Lincolnshire the name used to be applied to Boxing Day. In Warwickshire the term used was 'going a-corning'.

**Mumpsimus.** This word is an example of the practice of making new words by declaration. With the meaning, 'an erroneous doctrinal view obstinately adhered to', 'mumpsimus' was put into currency by Henry VIII in a speech from the throne in 1545. He remarked: 'Some be too stiff in their old mumpsimus, others be too busy and curious in their sumpsimus.' He referred to a familiar story in the jest books of a priest who always read in the MASS *quod in ore mumpsimus* instead of *sumpsimus*, as his MISSAL was incorrectly copied. When his mistake was pointed out, he said that he had read it with an m for forty years, 'and I will not change my old mumpsimus for your new sumpsimus'. The word is now used to mean 'an established reading that, though obviously incorrect, is retained blindly by old-fashioned scholars'.

**Münchhausen, Baron.** Karl Friedrich Hieronymus, Freiherr von Münchausen (1720–97) served in the Russian army against the Turks, and after his retirement told extraordinary stories of his war adventures. Rudolf Erich Raspe (1737–94), a German scientist, antiquarian and writer, collected these tales, and when living in England as a mining engineer, published them in English in 1785 as *Baron Münchausen's Narrative of his Marvellous Travels and Campaigns in Russia*. The text of *Münchausen* as reprinted latterly contains *Sea Adventures*, an account of Baron de Tott (a character founded on a real French hussar) partly written by Raspe, with much additional matter from various sources by other hands. *See also* MANDEVILLE.

**Mundane egg, The.** The Phoenicians, Egyptians, Hindus, Japanese and others maintained that the world was egg-shaped and was hatched from an egg made by the Creator. In some mythologies a bird is represented as laying the mundane egg on the primordial waters. Anciently this idea was attributed to ORPHEUS, hence the 'mundane egg' is also called the Orphic egg.

The opinion of the oval figure of the earth is ascrib'd to Orpheus and his disciples; and the doctrine of the mundane egg is so peculiarly his that 'tis called by Proclus the Orphick egg.
THOMAS BURNET: *The Sacred Theory of the Earth* (1684)

**Mundungus.** Bad tobacco, originally offal or refuse, from Spanish *mondongo*, 'black pudding'.

In Laurence Sterne's *Sentimental Journey* (1768), the word is used as a name for Samuel Sharp, a surgeon, who published *Letters from Italy*, and Tobias Smollett, who published *Travels through France and Italy* (1766), 'one continual snarl', is called 'Smelfungus'.

**Mungo, St.** An alternative name for St KENTIGERN.

Cheap felted fabric, made from second-hand woollens, is also known as 'mungo'.

**Muratorian fragment.** A fragment of a late 2nd-century document found embodied in an 8th-century codex. Written in Latin, it reveals the New Testament canon of the period as consisting of the four Gospels, thirteen Epistles of Paul, two Epistles of John, the Epistle of Jude, the Apocalypse of John, and the Apocalypse of Peter. It was discovered by Lodovico Antonio Muratori (1672–1750), librarian of the Ambrosian Library at Milan.

**Murder. Murderers' Bible, The.** *See under* BIBLE.

**Murder in the Red Barn, The.** A sensational murder at Polstead, near Hadleigh, Suffolk, that won lasting notoriety in melodrama and story. The anonymous *Maria Marten; or, the Murder in the The Red Barn* was a roaring success on the Victorian stage in the 1830s. The theme was essentially that of an innocent village maiden, seduced and murdered by a local man of property. The named melodrama and other titles were all founded on the murder of Maria Marten, a mole-catcher's daughter of loose morals who first bore a child to Thomas Corder, the son of a prosperous farmer. Later William Corder, his younger brother, became enamoured of her with inevitable consequences, but avoided marriage. In May 1827 an arrangement was apparently made for Maria to meet him at the Red Barn on his farm with the intention of going to Ipswich to be married. Maria was not seen alive again, but Corder went to London and married one Mary Moore, who kept a school. Eventually Maria's body was discovered in the Red Barn and William Corder was hanged for her murder at Bury St Edmunds on 11 August 1828 at the age of 24.

> The Red Barn, the scene of the tragic death of Maria Martin [*sic*], still exists, but the Corders have entirely left the place.
>
> *The National Gazetteer of Great Britain and Ireland* (1868)

**Murder will out.** The secret is bound to be revealed; 'be sure your sins will find you out'.

> 'O blessed God, that art so just and true,
> Thus thou revealest murder! As we say,
> "Murder will out." We see it day by day.'
>
> CHAUCER: 'Nun's Priest's Tale' (*c.*1387) (modern translation by Nevill Coghill, 1951)

**Phoenix Park murders.** *See under* PHOENIX.

**Scream blue murder.** *See under* SCREAM.

**Murphy.** A potato, from its long established prominence as a staple crop in Ireland.

**Murphy's law.** Of uncertain origin but with an Irish implication, Murphy's Law can be summed up by the saying 'If anything can go wrong, it will'. It has something in common with CATCH-22.

**Muscular Christianity.** Hearty or strong-minded Christianity, which braces a believer to fight the battle of life bravely and manfully. The term was applied to the teachings of Charles Kingsley (1819–75), somewhat to his annoyance.

**Muse. Muses.** In Greek mythology the nine daughters of ZEUS and MNEMOSYNE. They were originally goddesses of memory only, but later identified with individual arts and sciences. The paintings of Herculaneum show all nine with their respective attributes. Their names are: CALLIOPE, CLIO, EUTERPE, THALIA, MELPOMENE, TERPSICHORE, ERATO, POLYHYMNIA, URANIA. Three earlier Muses are sometimes given: Melete (Meditation), Mneme (Remembrance) and Aoede (Song). *See also* TENTH MUSE.

**Attic muse, The.** *See under* ATTIC.

**Museum.** Literally, a home or seat of the MUSES. The first building to have this name was the university erected at Alexandria by Ptolemy Soter about 300 BC.

**Museum piece, A.** An object of historic or antiquarian interest and value. The phrase is used in a derogatory or facetious sense for any article that is antiquated or out of fashion, or sometimes for an old-fashioned person.

**Ashmolean Museum.** *See under* ASHMOLEAN.

**British Museum.** *See under* BRITISH.

**Fitzwilliam Museum.** *See under* FITZWILLIAM.

**Mushroom.** A word applied figuratively to anything that springs up 'overnight', as a rapidly built housing estate. In 1787 Jeremy Bentham said, somewhat unjustly: 'Sheffield is an oak, Birmingham is a mushroom.'

**Mushroom, To.** To grow rapidly; to expand into a mushroom shape. Said especially of certain soft-nosed rifle bullets used in big game shooting, or of a dense cloud of smoke that spreads out high in the sky, especially after an atomic explosion.

**Sacred mushroom.** *See under* SACRED.

**Music** (Greek *mousikē tekhnē*, 'art of the muses').

**Music hall.** This essentially popular form of variety entertainment had its origins in the 'free and easy' of the public houses and in the song and supper rooms of early Victorian London. Food, drink and the singsong were its first ingredients, and its patrons came from the working classes. The first music hall proper, the Canterbury, was opened in 1852 by Charles Morton (1819–1905), 'the Father of the Halls', and a native of Hackney. It was specially built for the purpose, consequent upon the success of his musical evenings at the Canterbury Arms, Lambeth, of which he became the landlord in 1849. Music halls eventually became more numerous in London and the provinces than the regular theatres, and such names as Palladium, Palace, Alhambra, Coliseum, Empire, Hippodrome and so on proclaim their former glories. Their best days were before 1914, after which revue, the cinema, radio and, later, television, helped to bring about their eclipse. They have left a legacy of popular ballad and song, and memories of a host of great entertainers whose fame depended upon the intrinsic qualities of their individual acts. *See also* EVANS MUSIC-AND-SUPPER ROOMS.

**Music hath charms.** The opening words of Congreve's *The Mourning Bride* (1697):

> Music hath charms to soothe the savage breast,
> To soften rocks or bend a knotted oak.

The allusion is to ORPHEUS:

> Orpheus with his lute made trees,
> And the mountain-tops that freeze,
> Bow themselves when he did sing.
>
> SHAKESPEARE: *Henry VIII*, III, i (1612)

**Music of the spheres, The.** PYTHAGORAS, having ascertained that the pitch of notes depends on the rapidity of vibrations and also that the planets move at different rates of motion, concluded that the planets must make sounds in their motion according to their different rates, and that, as all things in nature are harmoniously made, the different sounds must harmonize, whence the old theory of the 'harmony of the spheres'. *See also* SPHERES.

**Canned music.** *See under* CANNED.

**Early music.** *See under* EARLY.

**Evans Music-and-Supper Rooms.** *See under* EVANS.

**Face the music, To.** *See under* FACE.

**Father of Greek Music, The.** *See under* FATHER.

**Father of Modern Music, The.** *See under* FATHER.

**Father of Musicians, The.** *See under* FATHER.

**Live music.** *See under* LIVE.

**Master of the King's Music.** *See under* MASTER.
**Prince of Music, The.** *See under* PRINCE.
**Programme music.** *See under* PROGRAMME.
**Rough music.** *See under* ROUGH.

**Musketeers, The Three.** *See under* THREE.

**Muslim** or **Moslem.** An adherent of ISLAM, with both words coming from Arabic *aslama*, 'he surrendered himself', i.e. to God.

**Muslim calendar.** A calendar used in Islamic countries, which dates from 16 July 622, the day of the HEGIRA. It consists of 12 lunar months of 29 days 12 hours 44 minutes each. As a result the Muslim year consists of only 354 or 355 days. A cycle is 30 years. The names of the months are: Muharram, Safar, Rabi' I, Rabi' II, Jumada I, Jumada II, Rajab, Shaaban, RAMADAN, Shawwal, Dhu'l-Qa'da, Dhu'l-Hijjah.

**Black Muslims.** *See under* BLACK.

**Muspelheim.** In Scandinavian mythology, the 'Home of Brightness' to the south of NIFLHEIM, where Surt (black smoke) ruled with his flaming sword and where dwelt the sons of Muspel the fire giant. The origin of 'Muspel' is uncertain.

**Mussulman.** An old word for a MUSLIM. The plural is properly Mussulmans, not Mussulmen.

**Mustard.** The condiment is so called because originally 'must', new wine (Latin *mustus*, 'fresh', 'new'), was used in mixing the paste.

**After meat, mustard.** *See under* AFTER.
**As keen as mustard.** *See under* AS.
**Cut the mustard, To.** *See under* CUT.
**French mustard.** *See under* FRENCH.

**Muster, To pass.** *See under* PASS.

**Mutantur.** *See* TEMPORA MUTANTUR.

**Mutatis mutandis** (Latin, 'things being changed that have to be changed'). After making the necessary changes. The phrase is used when those things have been changed that had to be changed.

**Mute, To stand.** *See under* STAND.

**Mutiny. Mutiny on the Bounty.** This celebrated mutiny broke out on 28 April 1789, and was as much due to the mutineers' attachment to the nubile maidens of Tahiti as to the exacting discipline of Captain William Bligh (1754–*c*.1817). The *Bounty* had been engaged in a breadfruit-collecting voyage in the South Seas, and Bligh was unaware of the impending mutiny. The mutineers reached Tahiti and some of them, accompanied by native men and women, sailed to Pitcairn Island, where they were not discovered until 1808, John Adams being the only surviving mutineer. Bligh, with 18 loyal companions, was set adrift in an open boat and made the remarkable voyage of 3618 nautical miles to Timor near Java.

**Indian Mutiny.** *See under* INDIAN.

**Mutton** (French *mouton*, 'sheep').

**Muttonchops.** Side whiskers trimmed to the shape of mutton chops.

**Mutton dressed as lamb.** A middle-aged or elderly woman dressed up to look younger. The allusion may not simply be to a butcher's tempting display of meat, but to 'mutton' in its slang sense of 'prostitute' and to 'lamb' in its colloquial sense of 'young innocent', 'virgin'.

**Mutton fist.** A large, coarse, red fist.
**Muttonhead.** A stupid or ignorant person.
**Mutton Lancers.** *See* KIRKE'S LAMBS *under* REGIMENTAL AND DIVISIONAL NICKNAMES.
**As dead as mutton.** *See under* AS.
**Return to our muttons, To.** *See* REVENONS À NOS MOUTONS.
**Saddle of mutton, A.** *See under* SADDLE.

**Mutual friends.** Can people have mutual friends? Strictly speaking not, but since Dickens adopted the solecism in the title of his novel *Our Mutual Friend* (1864–5), many people have objected to the correct term 'common friends'. 'Mutual' implies reciprocity from one to another (Latin *mutare*, 'to change'). The friendship between two friends should be mutual, but this mutuality cannot be extended to a third party.

**My. My hat!** *See under* HAT.
**My Lord.** *See under* LORD.
**My old Dutch.** *See under* DUTCH.

**Myrmidons** (literally 'ant people', from Greek *murmēx*). The name comes from the legend that when Aegina was depopulated by a plague, its king, Aeacus, prayed to JUPITER that the ants running out of an oak tree should be turned to men. According to one account they emigrated with PELEUS to Thessaly, whence they followed ACHILLES to the siege of TROY. They were noted for their fierceness, diligence and devotion to their leader, hence their name is applied to a servant who carries out his orders remorselessly.

**Myrmidons of the law.** Bailiffs, sheriffs' officers, policemen and other servants of the law. Any rough fellow employed to annoy another is the employer's myrmidon.

**Myron.** A Greek sculptor of the 5th century BC, noted for his realistic statues of gods, heroes, athletes and animals. Among his best known works is *Discobolos* ('The Discus Thrower'). It is said that he made a cow so lifelike that even bulls were deceived and made their approaches. He was an older contemporary of Phidias.

**Myrrha.** The mother of ADONIS, in Greek legend. She is fabled to have had an incestuous love for her own father, and to have been changed into a MYRTLE. The resinous juice called myrrh is obtained from the Arabian myrtle (*Balsamodendron myrrha*).

**Myrrophores** (Greek, 'myrrh-bearers'). The Marys who went to see the sepulchre, bearing sweet spices (Mark 16:1), are represented in Christian art as carrying vases of myrrh.

**Myrtle.** A leaf of myrtle, viewed in a strong light, is seen to be pierced with innumerable little punctures. According to fable, PHAEDRA, wife of THESEUS, fell in love with HIPPOLYTUS, her stepson. When Hippolytus went to the arena to exercise his horses, Phaedra repaired to a myrtle tree in Troezen to await his return, and beguiled the time by piercing the leaves with a hairpin.

In ORLANDO FURIOSO (1532) Astolpho is changed into a myrtle tree by Acrisia. *See also* MYRRHA.

The ancient Jews believed that the eating of myrtle leaves conferred the power of detecting witches, and it was a superstition that if the leaves crackled in the hands the person beloved would prove faithful.

**Myrtle which dropped blood, The.** AENEAS (Virgil, *Aeneid*, iii (1st century BC)) tells how he tore up a myrtle to decorate a sacrificial altar, but was terrified to find it dripped blood, while a voice came from the ground saying: 'Spare me, now that I am in my grave.' It was that of Polydorus, the youngest son of PRIAM and HECUBA, who had been murdered with darts and arrows for the gold he possessed. The deed was perpetrated by Polymnestor, king of Thrace, to whose care Polydorus had been entrusted.

**Jew's myrtle.** *See under* JEW.

**Mysterium.** The letters of this word, which, until the time of the REFORMATION, was engraved on the pope's tiara, are said to make up the number 666. *See also* NUMBER OF THE BEAST.

> And upon her forehead was a name written, MYSTERY, BABYLON THE GREAT, THE MOTHER OF HARLOTS AND ABOMINATIONS OF THE EARTH.
>
> Revelation 17:5

**Mystery.** In English two distinct words are represented: mystery, the archaic term for a handicraft, as in the art and mystery of printing, is the same as the French *métier* ('trade', 'craft', 'profession'), and is Middle English *mistere*, from Medieval Latin *misterium*, from Latin *ministerium*, 'ministry'. Mystery, meaning something hidden, inexplicable or beyond human comprehension, is from Latin *mysterium* (through French) and Greek *mustērion*, 'secret rites', from *mustēs*, 'mystery initiate', from *muein*, 'to close the eyes'. This last alludes to the fact that only those already initiated were permitted to witness secret rites.

It is from this second sense that the old miracle plays, medieval dramas in which the characters and story were drawn from sacred history, came to be called mysteries or mystery plays, although they were frequently presented by members of a guild or mystery. Miracle plays (as they were called at the time) developed from liturgical pageantry, especially in the CORPUS CHRISTI processions, and were taken over by the laity. They were performed in the streets on a wheeled stage or on stages erected along a processional route, and non-biblical subjects were also introduced. They flourished in England from the 13th to the 15th century but MORALITY PLAYS continued into the 16th century. *See also* PASSION PLAY.

**Mysteries of the rosary.** The 15 subjects of meditation from the life of Christ and the Virgin MARY, connected with the 15 decades of the ROSARY. They are divided into three groups of five, corresponding to the three chaplets of which the devotion is composed, and known as the FIVE JOYFUL MYSTERIES, the Five Sorrowful Mysteries, and the Five Glorious Mysteries. The Sorrowful Mysteries are the Agony in GETHSEMANE, the Scourging, the Crowning with Thorns, the Carrying of the Cross and the Crucifixion. The Glorious Mysteries are the Resurrection, the Ascension (*see* ASCENSION DAY), the Descent of the Holy Spirit at PENTECOST and the Coronation of the Blessed Virgin Mary.

**Mysteries of Udolpho, The.** A romance by Mrs Radcliffe (1764–1823), which was published in 1794 and founded the so-called 'terror school' of English Romanticism, although Walpole's *Castle of Otranto* (1764) had broken the ground. *See also* FRANKENSTEIN.

**Mystery tour.** An excursion, usually by coach, to an unspecified location.

**Bags of mystery.** *See under* BAG.

**Coventry Mysteries.** *See under* COVENTRY.

**Eleusinian mysteries.** *See under* ELEUSINIAN.

**Five joyful mysteries, The.** *See under* FIVE.

**Three greater mysteries, The.** *See under* THREE.

**Mystic. Cross as a mystic emblem.** *See under* CROSS.

**Myton, The Chapter of.** *See under* CHAPTER.

# N

**N.** The fourteenth letter of the English alphabet, represented in Egyptian HIEROGLYPHIC by a waterline ~~. It was called *nun* ('fish') in Phoenician, whence the Greek letter $\nu$ (*nu*). As a numeral, Greek $\nu$ = 50, but ͵$\nu$ = 50,000. N (Medieval Latin) = 90 or 900, but N̄ = 90,000 or 900,000.

**n.** The sign ~ (*tilde*) over an 'n' indicates that the letter is to be pronounced as though followed by a 'y', as *cañon* ('canyon'). It is used thus almost solely in words from Spanish. In Portuguese the accent (called *til*) is placed over vowels to indicate that they have a nasal value, as *divisão* ('division').

**nth** or **nth plus one.** The expression is taken from the index of a mathematical formula, where *n* stands for any number, and *n* + 1, one more than any number. Hence, n-dimensional, having an indefinite number of dimensions, and n-tuple (on the analogy of quadruple, quintuple and so forth), having an indefinite number of duplications. To the nth degree generally expresses something that is very great or even extreme, as: 'She was elated to the nth degree.'

**NAAFI.** The popular acronym for the Navy, Army, and Air Force Institutes, set up in 1921 to provide canteens for servicemen and developing to run shops and recreational facilities for service personnel wherever they are posted.

> The NAAFI is a sort of caafi
> Where soldiers are rude
> About the food.
> *Spectator* (23 January 1959)

**Nab.** Colloquial for to seize suddenly or without warning. Hence 'nabman' as a former term for a sheriff's officer or police constable. *See also* KIDNAPPING.

**Nabob.** Corruption of the Hindi *nawwāb*, English NAWAB, 'deputy governor', used of the governor or ruler of a province under the MOGUL Empire. Such men acquired great wealth and lived in splendour, eventually becoming independent princes. The name was sarcastically applied in the late 18th century to servants of the English East India Company who retired to England, having made their fortunes, bought estates, won seats in Parliament and so on.

**Nabonassar, The Era of.** *See under* ERA.

**Naboth's vineyard.** The possession of another person that is coveted by someone who will use any means, however unscrupulous, to acquire it. The reference is to the story told in 1 Kings 21.

**Nabu.** *See* NEBO.

**Nadir.** A word from the Arabic phrase *nazīr as-samt*, 'opposite the ZENITH', i.e. the point in the heavens that is directly below an observer's feet. Hence, figuratively, the lowest point in one's fortunes, the depth of degradation and so on.

**Naevius.** *See* ACCIUS NAEVIUS.

**Nagelring** (German, 'nail ring'). The sword of Dietrich of Bern, king of the Ostrogoths. *See also* THEODORIC.

**Nag's head consecration.** An early 17th-century story designed to deride the validity of the APOSTOLIC SUCCESSION in the CHURCH OF ENGLAND and in particular the validity of Archbishop Parker's consecration. The story is that on the passing of the Act of Uniformity of 1559 in Queen Elizabeth's reign, 14 bishops vacated their sees, and all the other sees were vacant except that of Llandaff, whose bishop refused to officiate at Parker's consecration. He was, therefore, irregularly consecrated at the Nag's Head tavern in Cheapside, by John Scory who had been deprived of the see of Chichester under Mary. In fact, the consecration took place at LAMBETH PALACE on 17 December 1559 by four bishops (Barlow, Scory, Coverdale and Hodgkin) who had held sees under Edward VI. Those who took part in the consecration apparently dined at the Nag's Head afterwards. The story was first put into circulation by the JESUIT Christopher Holywood in *De Investigenda Vera ac Visibili Christi Ecclesia Libellus*, published in Antwerp in 1604.

**Nahum.** An Old Testament prophet who writes gleefully, in the book that bears his name, about the coming destruction of Nineveh, which took place in 612 BC, soon after his prophecy.

> Woe to the bloody city! it is all full of lies and robbery.
> Nahum 3:1

**Naiad** (Greek *nāias*, related to *naein*, 'to flow'). In classical mythology a NYMPH of lake, fountain, river or stream.

> You nymphs, call'd Naiades, of the windring brooks,
> With your sedg'd crowns, and ever-harmless looks,
> Leave your crisp channels, and on this green land
> Answer your summons: Juno does command.
> SHAKESPEARE: *The Tempest*, IV, i (1611)

**Nail.** A nail was formerly a measure of weight of 8lb (3.6kg). It was used for wool, hemp, beef, cheese and other provisions. It was also a measure of length of 2¼in (6cm).

In ancient Rome a nail was driven into the wall of the temple of JUPITER every 13 September. This was originally done to tally the year, but subsequently it became a religious ceremony for warding off calamities and plagues from the city. Originally the nail was driven by the *praetor maximus*, subsequently by one of the consuls, and lastly by the dictator.

In the First World War patriotic Germans drove nails into a large wooden statue of Field Marshal Hindenburg (1847–1934), buying each nail in support of a national fund.

In the Middle Ages the nails with which Christ was fastened to the cross were objects of great reverence. Sir John MANDEVILLE says: 'He had two in his hondes, and two in his feet; and of on of theise the emperour of Constantynoble made a brydille to his hors, to bere him in bataylle; and throghe vertue thereof he overcam his enemyes.' Several places have 'true nails' displayed and venerated as relics. *See also* IRON CROWN OF LOMBARDY.

**Nail, To.** To convict and expose as false or spurious, as: 'I nailed that lie at once.' The allusion is said to be to the custom of shopkeepers nailing counterfeit coins to the counter as a warning to others.

**Nail in someone's coffin, A.** A thing or state that seems to increase the risk of death. The expression is often used in connection with smoking or drinking. *See also* COFFIN NAIL.

**Nail one's colours to the mast, To.** To refuse to admit defeat. Colours nailed to a ship's mast in battle cannot be lowered as a sign of defeat or capitulation.

**Nail-paring.** Superstitious people are particular as to the day on which they cut their nails. The old rhyme is:

> Cut them on Monday, you cut them for health,
> Cut them on Tuesday, you cut them for wealth,
> Cut them on Wednesday, you cut them for news,
> Cut them on Thursday, a new pair of shoes,
> Cut them on Friday, you cut them for sorrow,
> Cut them on Saturday, you see your true love tomorrow,
> Cut them on Sunday, your safety seek,
> The devil will have you the rest of the week.

A Herefordshire rhyme conveys an even stronger warning on the danger of nail-cutting on a Sunday:

> He that on the Sabbath Morn
> Cutteth either hair or horn
> Will rue the day that he was born.

**As hard as nails.** *See under* AS.

**Bed of nails.** *See under* BED.

**Fight tooth and nail, To.** *See under* FIGHT.

**For want of a nail.** *See under* FOR.

**Hit the nail on the head, To.** *See under* HIT.

**On the nail.** Immediately or on the spot, as: 'to pay on the nail.' One meaning of nail (possibly from medieval times) was a shallow vessel mounted on a stand, and business was concluded by payment into the vessel. It may have been so named from the rough resemblance of the stand to a nail's shape.

Outside the Corn Exchange at Bristol such 'nails' can still be seen in the form of four bronze pillars, and it is said that if a buyer was satisfied with the sample of grain shown 'on the nail' he paid on the spot. *See also* SUPERNACULUM.

**Tenpenny nails.** *See under* TEN.

**Nain rouge** (French, 'red dwarf'). A *lutin* or house spirit of Normandy, who is kind to fishermen. There is another called *Le petit homme rouge* ('the little red man').

**Naked** (Old English *nacod*, related to Latin *nudus* and so to English 'nude'). Destitute of covering, hence, figuratively, defenceless, exposed, without extraneous assistance, as 'with the naked eye', i.e. without the aid of an optical instrument such as a telescope or binoculars. A 'naked light' or 'naked flame' is one that is unprotected or unenclosed.

**Naked ape.** A human being. The term was introduced by the ethologist Desmond Morris:

> There are one hundred and ninety-three living species of monkeys and apes. One hundred and ninety-two of them are covered with hair. The exception is a naked ape self-named *Homo sapiens*.
> DESMOND MORRIS: *The Naked Ape*, Introduction (1967)

**Naked boy** or **lady.** The autumn crocus (*Colchicum autumnale*), so called because, like the almond or peach, the flowers come out before the leaves. It is poetically called 'the leafless orphan of the year', the flowers being orphaned or destitute of foliage.

**Naked Boy courts** and **alleys.** There are several in the City of London, all of which are named from the PUBLIC HOUSE SIGN of CUPID.

**Naked truth, The.** The plain, unvarnished truth; truth without trimmings. The fable says that Truth and Falsehood went bathing. Falsehood came first out of the water, and dressed herself in Truth's garments. Truth, unwilling to take those of Falsehood, went naked.

**Namby-pamby.** Wishy-washy, insipid or weakly sentimental, said especially of novelists and poets. It was the nickname of Ambrose Philips (1674–1749), bestowed on him by the dramatist Henry Carey (*c*.1687–1743) for his verses addressed to babies, and was adopted by Alexander Pope. It is also applied to a MOLLYCODDLE. The following is a typical example of Philips's artless art:

> Timely blossom, infant fair,
> Fondling of a happy pair,
> Every morn, and every night,
> Their solicitous delight,
> Sleeping, waking, still at ease,
> Pleasing without skill to please,
> Little gossip, blithe and hale,
> Tattling many a broken tale.
> 'Ode to Mistress Charlotte Pulteney' (1727)

**Name.**

> What's in a name? That which we call a rose
> By any other name would smell as sweet.
> SHAKESPEARE: *Romeo and Juliet*, II, ii (1594)

**Name, To.** In parliamentary parlance, to ban an MP from the House of Commons by mentioning their actual name, instead of referring to the Member by the name of the constituency, as is the usual custom. This happens if a member disobeys the Speaker's request for order. The Speaker rises and says: 'I must name the Honourable Member for [name of constituency, title and member's surname], for disregarding the authority of the Chair.' The MP must then leave the chamber, if necessary under escort. The first time a member is 'named' thus, the suspension lasts for five days. The next time it lasts for 20 days. If a member is 'named' a third time, the MP is suspended until the House allows him or her to return.

**Name-child.** A child named after a particular person.

**Name-day.** The feast-day of a saint after whom a person is named. In many countries with a strong Christian tradition it is still the custom to name a child after the saint on whose day it is born. On the stock exchange a name-day is the day before settling day, when the names of actual purchasers are handed to stockbrokers. It is also known as ticket-day.

**Name-dropper.** A person who seeks to impress by casual reference to well-known or prominent people, implying that they are personally known to the speaker.

**Name names, To.** To single out people by name, especially for purposes of accusation or blame.

**Name of the game, The.** The purpose or essence of anything. The expression is of American origin and may come from sports journalism.

> Call my bluff was the name of the game at last week's meeting of the International Whaling Commission.
> *Nature* (6 July 1973)

**Namesake.** A person having the same name as one's own. The word probably has its origin in the earlier phrase 'for the name's sake'.

**Name the day, To.** To fix the day of the wedding, a privilege of the bride-to-be.

**Name to conjure with, A.** A famous name or one of great influence. To conjure a name was to evoke a spirit. Thus Shakespeare says (*Julius Caesar*, I, ii (1599)):

> Why should that name be sounded more than yours?
> Write them together, yours is as fair a name;
> Sound them, it doth become the mouth as well;
> Weigh them, it is as heavy; conjure with 'em,
> 'Brutus' will start a spirit as soon as 'Caesar'.

**Call a person names, To.** *See under* CALL.

**First name.** *See under* FIRST.

**For one's name's sake.** *See under* FOR.

**Give it a name.** Tell me what it is you want, said when offering a reward, a drink or the like.

**Given name.** *See under* GIVE.

**Handle to one's name, A.** *See under* HANDLE.

**Holy Name of Jesus.** *See under* HOLY.

**Household name.** *See under* HOUSEHOLD.

**In the name of.** By the authority of, as: 'In the name of justice.'

**Lend one's name to, To.** *See under* LEND.

**Maiden name.** *See under* MAIDEN.

**Make a name for oneself, To.** To become well known or famous.

**No names, no pack drill.** *See under* NO.

**Pet names.** *See under* PET.

**Rose by any other name would smell as sweet, A.** *See under* ROSE.

**Take God's name in vain, To.** *See under* GOD.

**Take someone's name in vain, To.** To use it lightly or profanely.

**Their name liveth for evermore.** These consolatory words, frequently used on war memorials, are from the APOCRYPHA:

> Their bodies are buried in peace; but their name liveth for evermore.
> Ecclesiasticus 44:14

**Use someone's name, To.** *See under* USE.

**You name it.** Whatever you say or can think of, as: 'Our local antiques market has an amazing collection of Victoriana: you name it, they'll have it.'

**Nan, Brandy.** *See under* BRANDY.

**Nana.** In the story of PETER PAN, the gentle and faithful old dog who always looked after the children of the Darling family. (Hence her name, as 'nana' is a children's word for 'nurse'.) When Mr Darling played a trick on Nana by giving her unpleasant medicine, which he himself had promised to drink, the family did not appreciate his humour. This put him out of temper, and Nana was chained up in the yard before he went out for the evening. As a consequence Peter Pan effected an entry into the children's bedroom. *See also* DOGHOUSE.

**Nancy. Nancy boy.** A derogatory term for an effeminate or homosexual man.

**Miss Nancy.** An effeminate, foppish youth. The celebrated actress 'Mrs' Anne Oldfield was nicknamed 'Miss Nancy'. *See also* NARCISSA.

**Nankeen.** The buff-coloured cotton fabric is so called from Nanking in China, as is its pale greyish-yellow colour. 'Nankeens' are trousers made from this fabric.

**Nanki-Poo.** In Gilbert and Sullivan's operetta *The Mikado* (1885) the son of the Mikado. Disguised as a strolling musician, he courts Yum-Yum, who is one of the three wards of Ko-Ko, the Lord High Executioner. Like the other characters in the operetta, he has a mildly amusing mock-Chinese name.

**Nanny-Goats, The.** *See under* REGIMENTAL AND DIVISIONAL NICKNAMES.

**Nantes, Edict of.** *See under* EDICT.

**Naomi.** In the Old Testament the mother-in-law of RUTH. When her husband dies, she decides to return to her homeland and Ruth forsakes all her relations to go with her and care for her.

**Nap.** There are three distinct words.

(1) The doze or short sleep is so called from Old English *hnappian*, 'to sleep lightly'.

(2) The surface of cloth gets its name from Middle Dutch *noppe*.

(3) The card game, similar to whist, is so called in honour of NAPOLEON III.

**Caught napping, To be.** *See under* CATCH.

**Go nap, To.** To set oneself to make five tricks (all one can) in the game of NAP. Hence, to risk all one has on a venture; to back it through thick and thin.

**Naphtha.** The Greek name for an inflammable, bituminous substance coming from the ground in certain districts. In the MEDEA legend it is the name of the drug used by the witch for anointing the wedding robe of Glauce (Creusa), daughter of King CREON, whereby she was burnt to death on the morning of her marriage with JASON.

**Napier's bones.** The calculating square rods of bone, ivory or boxwood with numerical tables on each of their sides, invented by the Scottish mathematician John Napier (1550–1617), laird of Merchiston, in 1615. This ingenious arrangement was used for shortening the labour of multiplications and divisions. The previous year he had invented logarithms. *See also* ABACUS.

**Naples. See Naples and die.** *See under* SEE.

**Napoleon. Napoleon Bonaparte.** Emperor of the French (1769–1821). His reign (1804–15) is known in French history as the First Empire and his name is sometimes used to denote supremacy in a particular sphere, as a 'Napoleon of finance'. *See also* BONEY.

**Napoleon II.** Francis Joseph Charles (1811–32), the son of Napoleon and Marie Louise of Austria, created king of Rome, although he never reigned, was known to the Bonapartists as Napoleon II. He was given the compensatory title of Duke of Reichstadt in 1818.

**Napoleon III.** Napoleon (1808–73) was the third son of Louis Bonaparte, king of Holland (brother of NAPOLEON BONAPARTE), and Napoleon I's step-daughter Hortense de Beauharnais. In 1853 he married Eugénie (1826–1920), who fled with him to England after the Battle of Sedan (1870). His reign (1852–70) is called the Second Empire. Few men have had so many nicknames:

Man of December, so called because his *coup d'état* was on 2 December 1851, and he was made emperor on 2 December 1852
Man of Sedan, and, by a pun, 'M. Sedantaire'; it was at Sedan he surrendered his sword to William I, king of Prussia (1870)
Man of Silence, from his great taciturnity
Comte d'Arenenberg, the name and title he assumed when he escaped from the fortress of Ham
Badinguet, the name of the mason who changed clothes with him when he escaped from Ham; the emperor's partisans were called Badingueux, those of the empress were Montijoyeaux
Boustrapa, as a compound of Boulogne, Strasbourg, and Paris, the places of his noted escapades
Rantipole, harum-scarum, half fool and half madman

There are some curious numerical coincidences connected with Napoleon III and Eugénie. The last complete year of their reign was 1869. (In 1870 Napoleon was dethroned and exiled.) If to the year of coronation (1852) that of the birth of Napoleon or the birth of Eugénie is added, or the date of marriage, or the capitulation of Paris, the sum will always be 1869. For example:

| | |
|---|---|
| 1852 + 1 + 8 + 0 + 8 = 1869 | (1808 = birthday of Napoleon) |
| 1852 + 1 + 8 + 2 + 6 = 1869 | (1826 = birthday of Eugénie) |
| 1852 + 1 + 8 + 5 + 3 = 1869 | (1853 = date of marriage) |
| 1852 + 1 + 8 + 7 + 1 = 1869 | (1871 = capitulation of Paris) |

And if to the year of marriage (1853) these dates are added, they will give 1870, the fatal year.

**Napoleon of the ring.** James Belcher, the pugilist (1781–1811), who was remarkably like Napoleon in looks.

**Code Napoléon.** *See under* CODE.

**Napoo.** Soldier slang of the First World War for something that is of no use or does not exist. It represents the French phrase *il n'y en a plus* ('there is no more of it'). It occurs in a popular song in which the returning British soldier bids a fond farewell to his French mam'zelle:

Good-bye-ee! good-bye-ee!
Wipe the tear, baby dear, from your eye-ee.
Tho' it's hard to part, I know,
I'll be tickled to death to go.
Don't cry-ee! – don't sigh-ee! –
There's a silver lining in the sky-ee! –
Bonsoir, old thing! cheerio! chin-chin!
Nahpoo! Toodle-oo! Good-bye-ee!

R.P WESTON and BERT LEE: 'Good-Bye-Ee' (1918)

**Naraka.** In Hindu mythology and BUDDHISM the place of torture for departed evil-doers. It consists of many kinds of hells, hot and cold.

**Narcissa.** In Pope's *Moral Essays* (1731–5) 'Narcissa' represents the actress Anne Oldfield (1683–1730). When she died, her remains lay in state attended by two noblemen. She was buried in Westminster Abbey in a fine Brussels lace head-dress, a holland shift, with a tucker and double ruffles of the same lace, and new kid gloves. *See also* NANCY, MISS.

'Odious! In woollen! 'twould a saint provoke'
(Were the last words that poor Narcissa spoke).

ALEXANDER POPE: *Moral Essays*, i (1731–5)

'In woollen' is an allusion to the old law enacted for the benefit of the wool trade, that all shrouds were to be made of wool. *See also* BURIAL IN WOOLLEN *under* BURY.

**Narcissus.** In Greek mythology, the son of Cephisus, a beautiful youth who saw his reflection in a fountain and thought it the presiding NYMPH of the place. He repeatedly strained to reach it, but all his attempts resulted in failure, so that he pined away. The nymphs came to take up the body to pay it funeral honours but found only a flower, which they called by his name. The story is told by Ovid and others.

Plutarch says the plant is called Narcissus from the Greek *narkē*, 'numbness', and that it is properly *narcosis*, meaning the plant that produces numbness or palsy. ECHO fell in love with Narcissus.

**Narcissism.** The psychoanalytical term for excessive love and admiration of oneself.

**Nark** or **copper's nark.** A police spy or informer, from a ROMANY word, *nāk*, 'nose', on the analogy of NOSEY Parker. The term is also applied to a policeman. In colloquial parlance, 'to be narked' is to be angry or annoyed, and 'nark it' means stop it, 'give over'.

**Narnia.** The fictional land in which are set the seven children's books by C.S. Lewis, beginning with *The Lion, the Witch and the Wardrobe* (1950). It is visited only by select children, and peopled by talking beasts, giants, witches and other characters of myth and legend. To the north lie Ettinsmoor and the Wild Lands of the North; to the south, Archenland and Calormen.

**Narrow. Narrow Seas, The.** The Irish Sea and the English Channel, especially the area around the Straits of Dover.

**Narrow squeak, A.** A narrow escape; a goal barely attained. A squeak is a thin sound.

**Straight and narrow.** *See under* STRAIGHT.

**Nasbys.** A generic nickname in the USA for postal officials, particularly postmasters. The American humorist David Ross Locke (1833–88) wrote a series of satirical articles in the form of letters, which first appeared in 1861 in the *Jeffersonian*, published in Findlay, Ohio, and later in the *Blade*, published in Toledo, Ohio. These *Nasby Letters* purported to be those of a conservative, ignorant and whisky-drinking politician, one Petroleum Vesuvius Nasby, who hated Negroes and who was determined to be the postmaster of his little town. Comically spelled, and full of sly humour, the *Nasby Letters* were very popular, and soon gave rise to the generic title.

**Naseby.** Fable has it that this Northamptonshire village is so called because it was considered the navel (Old English *nafela*) or centre of England, just as DELPHI was considered 'the navel of the earth'. In fact the name appears in DOMESDAY BOOK as Navesberie, showing that it was a 'burh' or stronghold of a man called Hnæf. *See also* MERIDEN.

**Nash, Beau.** Richard Nash (1674–1762). A noted Welsh-born and Oxford-educated gambler, who nevertheless achieved distinction as Master of Ceremonies at Bath, which he made the leading English spa.

**Nasier, Alcofribas.** *See under* ALCOFRIBAS.

**Naso.** Ovid (Publius Ovidius Naso, 43 BC–AD 18), the Roman poet, author of *Metamorphoses*. Naso means 'nose', hence Holofernes' pun: 'And why, indeed, Naso, but for smelling out the odoriferous flowers of fancy' (Shakespeare, *Love's Labour's Lost*, IV, ii (1594)).

**Nasty bit** or **piece of work, A.** An unpleasant person.

**Nathan.** The Old Testament prophet who advises DAVID to build the Temple (2 Samuel 7) and who, with ZADOK the Priest, anoints SOLOMON king (1 Kings 1, 1 Chronicles 17).

**Nation. Nation of gentlemen, A.** So George IV called the Scots when, in 1822, he visited their country and was received with great expressions of loyalty.

**Nation of shopkeepers, A.** This phrase, applied to Englishmen by NAPOLEON BONAPARTE in contempt, comes from Adam Smith's *The Wealth of Nations* (iv, 7 (1776)). This book, well known to the emperor, says:

To found a great empire for the sole purpose of raising up a people of customers, may at first sight appear a project fit only for a nation of shopkeepers.

**Battle of the Nations, The.** *See under* BATTLE.

**Five Nations, The.** *See under* FIVE.
**League of Nations, The.** *See under* LEAGUE.
**Six Nations, The.** *See under* SIX.
**United Nations.** *See under* UNITED.

**National. National anthem.** The composition of 'God Save the Queen', the British National Anthem, has been attributed to Dr John Bull (*c*.1562–1628), organist at Antwerp Cathedral (1617–28), and quite erroneously to Henry Carey (*c*.1690–1743), but the following, by Mme de Brinon, was sung before Louis XIV in 1686:

Grand Dieu sauvez le roi,
Grand Dieu vengez le roi,
Vive le roi!
Qu'à jamais glorieux,
Louis victorieux,
Voie ses ennemis toujours soumis,
Vive le roi!
(Great God, save the king
Great God, avenge the king,
Long live the king!
May ever glorious
Louis victorious
See his foes always beaten,
Long live the king!)

The Authorized Version of the BIBLE has:

And all the people shouted, and said, God save the king.
1 Samuel 10:24

It became popular at the time of the FORTY-FIVE Rebellion as a demonstration of loyalty to George II and opposition to the JACOBITES, to whom the phrase 'confound their politics' may well refer.

The following are examples of the national anthems or principal patriotic songs of other nations:

Argentina: *Oíd, mortales, el grito sagrado Libertad* ('Hear, O Mortals, the Sacred Cry, Liberty')
Australia: 'Advance, Australia Fair'
Austria: *Land der Berge, Land am Strome* ('Land of Mountains, Land on the River')
Belgium: *La* BRABANÇONNE
Brazil: *Ouviram do Ipiranga às margens plácidas* ('A Cry Rang Out from Peaceful Ipiranga's Banks')
Canada: *O Canada! terre de nos aïeux* ('O Canada, Land of our Ancestors')
Colombia: *Oh gloria inmarcesible* ('Oh Unfading Glory')
Croatia: *Lijepa naša domovina* ('Our Beautiful Homeland')
Czech Republic: *Kde domov můj?* ('Where is my Home?')
Denmark: *Det er et yndigt land* ('There is a Lovely Land'); *Kong Kristian stod ved højen Mast* ('King Christian Stood Beside the Lofty Mast')
Finland: *Oi maamme, Suomi, synnyinmaa!* ('O Our Land, Finland, Native Land!')
France: *La* MARSEILLAISE
Germany: *Einigkeit und Recht und Freiheit* ('Unity and Right and Freedom')
Greece: *Imnos eis tin eleftherian* ('Hymn to Freedom')
Hungary: *Isten áldd meg a magyart* ('God Bless the Hungarians')
Iceland: *Ó Guð vors lands* ('Our Country's God')
Ireland: *Amhrán na bhFiann* ('Song of the Soldiers')
Israel: *Hatikvah* ('The Hope')
Italy: *Inno di Mameli* ('Mameli's Hymn'; words by Goffredo Mameli (1827–49))
Japan: *Kimigayowa* ('May Thy Reign Last Long')
Luxembourg: *Ons Hémécht* ('Our Homeland')
Mexico: *Mexicanos, al grito de guerra* ('Mexicans, to the War Cry')
Netherlands: *Wilhelmus van Nassouwe* ('William of Nassau')
New Zealand: God Save the Queen; God Defend New Zealand
Norway: *Ja, vi elsker dette landet, som det stiger frem* ('Yes, We Love This Country, Just As It Is').
Peru: *Somos libres, seámoslo siempre* ('We are Free, Let us Always be So')
Poland: *Jeszcze Polska nie zginęła* ('Poland has not Yet been Destroyed')
Portugal: *Herois do mar* ('Heroes of the Sea')
Romania: *Desteapta-te, romane* ('Awake, Romanian')
Russia: Patriotic Song (melody only) from Act I of Glinka's *A Life for the Tsar* (1836); former USSR: *Soyuz nerushimy respublik svobodnykh* ('Unbreakable Union of Free Republics')
Scotland: Scots wha hae wi' Wallace bled ('Scots who have with Wallace Bled')
Slovenia: *Zdravljica* ('A Toast')
South Africa: *Die Stem van Suid-Afrika* ('The Voice of South Africa'); *Nkosi Sikelel' iAfrika* ('God Bless Africa')
Spain: *Marcha Real Española* ('Royal Spanish March')
Sweden: *Du gamla, du fria* ('Thou Ancient, Thou Free')
Switzerland: *Trittst im Morgenrot daher* ('Thou Stridest Forth in Morning Glow')
Turkey: *Istiklal marşi* ('Independence March')
USA: The Star-Spangled Banner; *see also* STARS AND STRIPES
Wales: *Mae hen wlad fy nhadau* ('Land of my Fathers'); 'Men of Harlech'
Yugoslavia: *Hej, Slaveni, jošte zivi duh naših dedova* ('Oh, Slavs, The Spirit of our Ancestors Still Lives')

**National convention.** For the French assembly of this name *see* CONVENTION PARLIAMENTS.

In the USA the National Convention is the meeting of state delegates called by the national committees of the political parties which nominates candidates for President and Vice President. The party platform is also drawn up.

**National dances.** When Handel was asked to point out the peculiar taste of the different nations of Europe in dancing, he ascribed the minuet to the French, the saraband to the Spaniard, the arietta to the Italian, and the HORNPIPE and the MORRIS DANCE to the English. To these might be added the reel to the Scots, and the JIG to the Irish.

**National debt.** The public debt of the central

government of a state and secured on the national revenue. The 'funded debt' is the portion of the national debt that is converted into bonds and annuities etc. The remainder, essentially short-term debt, is called the 'floating debt'.

The British national debt assumed a permanent form in the reign of William III (1689–1702) and it has been managed by the Bank of England since 1750. The rapid increase of the national debt has been mainly due to wars. *See also* MISSISSIPPI BUBBLE; SINKING FUND; SOUTH SEA BUBBLE.

**National governments.** As a result of the financial crises and the collapse of the LABOUR government in 1931 an all-party coalition was formed under James Ramsay MacDonald (1931–5), the first of a series of governments called 'National' that held office in succession until 1940, under MacDonald, then Stanley Baldwin (1935–7) and lastly Neville Chamberlain (1937–40). Those LIBERAL and Labour MPs who supported these governments called themselves National Liberal candidates and National Labour candidates. The administrations became increasingly CONSERVATIVE in character.

**National Guard.** In France, the revolutionary leaders formed a National Guard at Paris in July 1789, and similar citizen armies were formed in the provinces. It supported Robespierre, but turned against the Convention and was defeated by NAPOLEON BONAPARTE with regular troops. Under Napoleon, a National Guard or militia was re-established and continued in existence until the Paris commune of 1871.

In the USA the National Guard is an organization of volunteer military units similar to the British Territorial Army. When called upon in a national emergency, they become an integral part of the US armed forces. The oldest unit is the 182nd infantry of Massachusetts, which traces its origins back to 1636. *See also* MINUTEMEN.

**National Liberals.** *See* LIBERAL NATIONALS.

**National nicknames.** *See under* NICKNAME.

**National Society.** The shortened form of the name of the association formed in 1811 as the 'National Society for the Education of the Poor in the Principles of the Established Church'. It played a great part in the development of English education, especially before direct state participation and control. Principally known for the establishment of church schools, or 'National Schools', and teacher training colleges, it still promotes religious education. *See also* MONITORIAL SYSTEM; VOLUNTARY SCHOOLS.

**Grand National.** *See under* GRAND.

**Native, To go.** To abandon civilized ways and to share the life and habits of a more primitive society.

**Nativity, The.** CHRISTMAS Day; the day set apart in honour of the Nativity or Birth of Christ.

**Cave of the Nativity, The.** *See under* CAVE.

**Natural. Natural, A.** A born idiot, i.e. someone who is born half-witted. The word is now commonly used to denote someone who is naturally adept at some particular skill, especially at games.

In music, a natural is a white key on a keyboard, as distinguished from a black key. In musical notation the sign is employed to counteract the following note from a sharp or flat in the signature or from a preceding sharp or flat in the same bar.

**Natural child, A.** A BASTARD. The Romans called the children of concubines *naturales*, i.e. children according to nature and not according to law.

**Natural increase.** In population statistics, the excess of births over deaths in a given period, usually a year. *See also* MALTHUSIAN DOCTRINE.

**Natural liberty.** Unrestricted liberty limited only by the laws of nature.

**Natural science.** The sciences used in the study of the physical world, such as physics, chemistry, geology, biology and botany, as distinct from mathematics, logic, and mental and moral science. The general principles of natural science are commonly called 'the laws of nature'.

**Natural wastage.** A gradual decrease in a workforce achieved by not appointing new employees to replace those who leave or retire.

**Nature. Nature abhors a vacuum.** This maxim is used by Spinoza in his *Ethics* (1677) and by Rabelais in its Latin form, *natura abhorret vacuum*, in his GARGANTUA (Bk I, ch v (1534)). *See also* TORRICELLI.

**Back to nature.** *See under* BACK.

**Balance of nature.** *See under* BALANCE.

**Call of nature, A.** *See under* CALL.

**Child of nature.** *See under* CHILD.

**Debt of nature, The.** *See under* DEBT.

**In a state of nature.** *See under* STATE.

**In the nature of things.** As is to be expected; as is typical or inevitable.

**Second nature.** *See under* SECOND.

**Naught, nought.** These are merely variants of the same word, 'naught' representing Old English *nāwhiht*, and 'nought', *nōwiht*, both meaning literally 'no thing'. In most senses they are interchangeable, but 'naught' now mainly occurs in set phrases, such as 'to set at naught', while 'nought' is used for the figure '0'.

'Naught' was formerly applied to things that were bad or worthless, and 'naughty' has this sense in older texts:

> One basket had very good figs, even like the figs that are first ripe: and the other basket had very naughty figs, which could not be eaten, they were so bad.
> Jeremiah 24:2

**Naughty Nineties, The.** The 1890s in England, when the puritanical Victorian code of behaviour and conduct gave way in certain wealthy and fashionable circles to growing laxity in sexual morals, a cult of hedonism, and a more light-hearted approach to life generally. MUSIC HALLS were at the height of their popularity, and the EMPIRE PROMENADE was in its heyday.

**Nausicaa.** The Greek heroine whose story is told in the ODYSSEY. She was the daughter of Alcinous, king of the Phaeacians, and the shipwrecked Odysseus (ULYSSES) found her playing ball with her maidens on the shore. Pitying his plight, she conducted him to her father, by whom he was entertained.

**Nautical** or **geographical mile.** A unit supposed to be one minute of a GREAT CIRCLE of the earth, but as the earth is not a true sphere the minute is variable, so a mean length of 6080ft (2026yd 2ft/1853m) was adopted by the British Admiralty. The geographical mile varies slightly with different nations, so there is a further International Nautical Mile of 1852m (6076ft). *See also* KNOT; MILE.

**Navigator, Henry the.** *See under* HENRY.

**Navvy.** A former name for a labourer employed on heavy work such as digging or excavating. It is a contraction of navigator, and derives from the days of canal construction, because the canals were called navigations.

**Navy. Harry Tate's Navy.** *See under* HARRY.

**Wavy Navy.** *See under* WAVE.

**Nawab** (Hindi, from Arabic, plural of *na'īb*, 'viceroy'). The title of a distinguished Muslim in Pakistan, and formerly also of a governor or nobleman in India.

**Nazarene.** A native of Nazareth. Christ is so called (John 8:5, 7). He was brought up in Nazareth, but was born in Bethlehem (Matthew 2:23). Hence the early Christians were called Nazarenes (Acts 24:5). The Nazarenes were also an early sect of Jewish Christians, who believed Christ to be the MESSIAH, but who nevertheless conformed to much of the Jewish law.

**Can there any good thing come out of Nazareth?** *See under* GOOD.

**Nazarites** (Hebrew *nāzār*, 'to consecrate'). A body of Israelites set apart by the vows they had taken. They refrained from strong drink and allowed their hair to grow long (Numbers 6:1–21).

**Nazi.** The shortened form of *Nationalsozialist* ('National Socialist'), the name given to Adolf Hitler's party. *See also* FÜHRER; HITLERISM; MEIN KAMPF; NIGHT OF THE LONG KNIVES; SWASTIKA.

**NB** (Latin *nota bene*). Note well.

**Neaera.** Any sweetheart or lady love. She is mentioned by Horace, Virgil and Tibullus.

> To sport with Amaryllis in the shade,
> Or with the tangles of Neaera's hair?
> MILTON: *Lycidas* (1637)

**Neanderthal man.** A species of Palaeolithic man inhabiting Europe during the MOUSTERIAN period. It was named from the bones discovered in 1856 in a grotto of the Neanderthal ravine near Düsseldorf. Similar remains have been found in many parts of Europe.

**Neap tides.** Those tides that attain the least rise and fall at or near the first and last quarters of the moon. The high water rises little more than half as high above the mean level as it does at SPRING TIDES, and the low water sinks about half as little below it.

**Near.** In its sense of 'mean', the word is rather a curious pun on 'close', meaning 'close-fisted'. What is 'close by' is near.

**Nearside** and **offside.** In Britain left side and right side when facing forward. 'Near wheel' means that to the driver's left hand, and 'near horse' (in a pair) means that to the left hand of the driver. In a four-in-hand, the two horses on the left side of the coachman are the 'near wheeler' and the 'near leader'. Those on the right-hand side are 'off' horses. This apparent anomaly arose when the driver walked beside his team. The teamster always walks with his right arm nearest the horse, and thus in a pair of horses the horse on the left side is nearer than the one on his right. *See also* OFFSIDE.

**Near the knuckle.** Bordering on the improper or indecent.

**Near the mark.** Nearly correct; fairly close to the truth. The phrase is derived from archery.

**Near** or **close to the bone.** Risqué or indecent.

**Nearest and dearest.** One's closest friends and relatives.

**As near as damn it.** *See under* AS.

**Neat. As neat a new pin.** *See under* AS.

**Nebo.** A god of the Babylonians (properly, Nabu) mentioned in Isaiah 46:1. He was the patron of Borsippa, near Babylon, and was regarded as the inventor of writing, as well as the god of wisdom. The name occurs in many Babylonian royal names, as, Nebuchadrezzar (Jeremiah 39:11), Nebushasban (Jeremiah 39:13), Nebuzaradan (2 Kings 25:8) etc. *See also* NEBUCHADNEZZAR.

**Nebuchadnezzar.** An incorrect form of Nebuchadrezzar (as it appears in Jeremiah 21:2 and elsewhere). The name represents Babylonian *Nabu-kudurru-usur*, meaning 'NEBO protect the boundary stone'.

Nebuchadnezzar, the greatest king of Babylon, reigned from 604 to 561 BC. He restored his country to its former prosperity and importance, practically rebuilt Babylon, restored the temple of BEL, erected a new palace, embanked the Euphrates, and probably built the HANGING GARDENS OF BABYLON. His name became the focus of many legends.

**Necessary.** The 17th- and 18th-century term for a privy. In large houses the emptying and cleaning of this was carried out by a servant known as the 'necessary woman'. 'The necessary' is now a colloquial term for money or for anything that is needed for a particular purpose, as: 'If the garden is too much for you, let me know and I'll do the necessary'.

**Necessity. Necessity knows no law.** These were the words used by the German Chancellor Theobald von Bethmann-Hollweg (1856–1921) in the Reichstag on 4 August 1914, as a justification for the infringement of Belgian neutrality.

> Gentlemen, we are now in a state of necessity, and necessity knows no law. Our troops have occupied Luxembourg and perhaps have already entered Belgian territory.

The phrase is common to most languages. Publilius Syrus has *Necessitas dat legem, non ipsa accipit* ('Necessity gives the law, but does not herself accept it'), and the Latin proverb *Necessitas non habet legem* appears in *Piers Plowman* (14th century) as, 'Neede hath no law.'

**Make a virtue of necessity, To.** *See under* VIRTUE.

**Neck.** Slang for cheek or impudence. The Americanism 'get it in the neck' means to be severely reprimanded.

**Neck and crop.** Entirely. The crop is the gorge of a bird. A former variant of the phrase was 'neck and heels'. There was once a punishment that consisted of bringing the chin and knees of the culprit forcibly together, and then thrusting him into a cage.

**Neck and neck.** Very close competitors; very near in merit. A phrase from the TURF, when two or more horses run each other very closely.

**Necking.** A common expression for 'petting'. In the western states of the USA, necking is to tie a restless animal by the neck to a tame one in order to render it more tractable. Necking is also part of a column between the shaft and capital, as the annulets of a DORIC capital.

**Neck of the woods.** In original American use, a settlement in the forest, but now a term for any neighbourhood or area, whether there are woods or not, as: 'We don't have any trouble in our neck of the woods.'

**Neck or nothing.** Whatever the risk; at any cost. The term comes from racing: if you can't win by a neck you are nowhere.

**Neck verse.** The first verse of Psalm 51: 'Have mercy upon me, O God, according to thy lovingkindness: according unto the multitude of thy tender mercies blot out my transgressions.' This verse was so called because it was the trial verse of those who claimed BENEFIT OF CLERGY, and if they could read it, the prison chaplain said, '*Legit ut clericus*' ('He reads like a clerk'), and the prisoner saved his neck. By an Act of Henry VII convicted clerks were branded on the hand before release. *See also* MISERERE.

**Break one's neck, To.** *See under* BREAK.

**Breathe down someone's neck, To.** *See under* BREATHE.

**Crew neck.** *See under* CREW.

**Crying the neck.** *See under* CRY.

**Dead from the neck up.** *See under* DEAD.

**Horse's neck.** *See under* HORSE.

**Pain in the neck, A.** *See under* PAIN.

**Risk one's neck, To.** *See under* RISK.

**Save one's neck, To.** *See under* SAVE.

**Stick one's neck out, To.** *See under* STICK.

**Stiff-necked.** *See under* STIFF.

**Swan with Two Necks, The.** *See under* SWAN.

**Talk through the back of one's neck, To.** *See under* TALK.

**Tread on someone's neck, To.** *See under* TREAD.

**Up to one's neck.** *See under* UP.

**Necklace.** A necklace of coral or white bryony beads used to be worn by children to aid their teething. Necklaces of hyoscyamus or henbane root have been recommended for the same purpose, although the alkaloid hyoscyamine that occurs in henbane is poisonous.

**Affair of the Diamond Necklace, The.** *See under* AFFAIR.

**Anodyne necklace, An.** *See under* ANODYNE.

**Fatal necklace.** *See under* FATAL.

**Harmonia's necklace.** *See under* HARMONIA.

**Necromancy** (Greek *nekros*, 'corpse', and *manteia*, 'prophecy'). Prophesying by calling up the dead, as the WITCH OF ENDOR called up Samuel (1 Samuel 28:7–14). Also the art of magic generally, the BLACK ART. *See also* DIVINATION.

**Nectar** (Greek). In classical mythology the drink of the gods. Like their food AMBROSIA, it conferred immortality, hence the name of the nectarine, so called because it is as 'sweet as nectar'. The word itself probably derives from the Greek root *ne-*, 'death' (as in *nekros*, 'corpse') and an element *-tar* related to Sanskrit *tarati*, 'he overcomes', itself related to Latin *trans*, 'across'.

**Neddy.** Little Edward, an old familiar name for a DONKEY. *See also* CUDDY; DICKEY; DOBBIN.

'Neddy' was also the popular name for the National Economic Development Council set up by the Government in 1962 (discontinued in 1992). The numerous Economic Development Committees for particular industries that subsequently appeared were called 'Little Neddies'.

**Need. Needful, The.** Ready money; cash.

**Needless to say.** Of course; it goes without saying.

**Needs must.** Necessity compels. A shortening of the old saying: 'Needs must when the Devil drives.'

> He must needs go that the Devil drives.
> SHAKESPEARE: *All's Well that Ends Well*, I, iii (1602)

**Friend in need is a friend indeed, A.** *See under* FRIEND.

**Needle. Needle, To.** To provoke, goad or tease, as if pricking with a needle.

**Needle game** or **match.** A game or match that is very close or that arouses a personal grudge.

**Needle time.** The time allocated to the broadcasting of recorded music and entertainment. The reference is to the old gramophone records, played with needles.

**Adam's needle.** *See under* ADAM.

**Cleopatra's Needle.** *See under* CLEOPATRA.

**Devil's darning needle.** *See under* DEVIL.

**Gammer Gurton's Needle.** *See under* GAMMER.

**Get the needle, To.** To be annoyed or nervous.

**Look for a needle in a haystack, To.** *See under* LOOK.

**On pins and needles.** *See under* PIN.

**Pins and needles.** *See under* PIN.

**St Wilfrid's needle.** *See under* WILFRID.

**Nefertiti.** The queen of Egypt and wife of King AKHENATEN who supported her husband's religious revolution and who adhered to the new cult of the sun god ATEN. She lived in the 14th century BC and is famous from the elegant painted bust of her in the Berlin Museum. Her name means 'The beautiful one is come'.

**Negative. Answer is in the negative, The.** *See under* ANSWER.

**Double negative.** *See under* DOUBLE.

**Negus.** (1) The drink of this name, consisting of hot port and lemon juice with sugar and spices, is so called from a Colonel Francis Negus (d.1732), who first concocted it.

(2) The ruler of Ethiopia was entitled the Negus, from Amharic *n'gus*, meaning 'king'.

**Nehemiah.** The governor of Jerusalem who managed to create a NEW JERUSALEM and to build what came to be called the Second Temple following the return of the Jewish exiles from their Captivity in Babylon.

**Neiges d'antan, Les** (French). A thing of the past. Literally 'last year's snows', from the refrain of François Villon's familiar 'Ballade des dames du temps jadis' in *Le Grand Testament* (1461):

> Mais ou sont les neiges d'antan?
> (But where are the snows of yesteryear?)

**Neighbourhood Watch.** As a result of increasing crime, especially burglary, residents in particular areas began organizing Neighbourhood Watch groups from the early 1980s with police cooperation. Suspicious activities and circumstances are reported to the police, and some worthwhile effect on burglary has resulted. The idea was copied from similar schemes in the USA.

**Neither. Neither fish, flesh, nor fowl** or **Neither fish, flesh nor good red herring.** Neither one thing nor the other. Not fish (food for the monk), nor flesh (food for the people generally), nor yet red herring (food for the poor).

> Damn'd Neuters, in their middle way of steering,
> Are neither Fish nor Flesh nor good Red-Herring.
> JOHN DRYDEN: *The Duke of Guise*, Epilogue (1679)

**Neither here nor there.** Irrelevant to the subject under discussion; a matter of no moment.

**Neither one thing nor the other.** Indefinite; undetermined.

**Neither rhyme nor reason.** Fit neither for amusement nor instruction. An author took his book to Sir Thomas More, Chancellor of Henry VIII, and asked his opinion. Sir Thomas told the author to turn it into rhyme. He did so and submitted it again to the Lord Chancellor. 'Ay! ay!' said the witty satirist, 'that will do, that will do. 'Tis rhyme now, but before it was neither rhyme nor reason.' *See also* WHAT! ALL THIS FOR A SONG?

**Nell. Black Nell.** *See under* BLACK.

**Nell Gwyn.** *See under* GWYN.

**Sweet Nell of Old Drury.** *See* Nell GWYN.

**Nelly. Not on your Nellie or Nelly.** Not likely; not on any account; not on your life. Probably from RHYMING SLANG, 'Not on your Nellie Duff', 'Duff' rhyming with 'puff', which is old slang for 'breath' and thus life itself.

**Nelson. Nelson's blood.** The Royal Navy's nickname for rum, issued to ratings between 1731 and 1970.

**Nelson's Column.** A CORINTHIAN column of Devonshire granite on a square base in Trafalgar Square, London, completed in 1843. The four lions, by Edwin Landseer (1802–73), were added in 1867. It stands 185ft (56.4m) high overall. The column is a copy of one in the temple of MARS Ultor (the Avenger) at Rome. The statue, by Edward Hodges Baily (1788–1867), is 17ft (5.2m) high. The following bronze reliefs are on the sides of the pedestal: (north) the Battle of the Nile (1798), (south) Nelson's death at Trafalgar (1805), (east) the Battle of Copenhagen (1801), (west) the Battle of Cape St Vincent (1797).

**Nelson's Pillar.** Formerly Dublin's most controversial monument, erected in honour of the great sailor by a committee of bankers and merchants in 1808–9, who raised the funds by public subscription. It was sited in Sackville Street (now O'Connell Street), and the statue of Nelson on the top was the work of Thomas Kirk. The column contained a spiral staircase leading to the top of the Doric abacus and somewhat fresher air. The whole monument was 134ft

(41m) high. It was blown up by young Republican extremists on 8 March 1966, and the 50ft (15m) of masonry left standing was demolished by army engineers. Nelson's head was moved to a Corporation depot whence it was taken by a group of art students and flown to London for subsequent sale to an antique dealer.

**Nemean. Nemean Games.** One of the four great festivals of ancient Greece, held in the valley of Nemea in Argolis every alternate year, the first and third of each OLYMPIAD. Legend states that they were instituted in memory of Archemorus who died from the bite of a serpent as the expedition of the SEVEN AGAINST THEBES was passing through the valley. It was customary for the games to open with a funeral oration in his honour. After HERCULES had slain the NEMEAN LION, the games were held in honour of ZEUS. Athletic contests were added after the model of the OLYMPIC GAMES. The victor's reward was at first a crown of OLIVES, later of green parsley. Pindar has eleven odes in honour of victors.

**Nemean Lion, The.** A terrible lion which kept the people of the valley of Nemea in constant alarm. The first of the 12 labours of HERCULES was to slay it. He could make no impression on the beast with his club, so he caught it in his arms and squeezed it to death. Hercules ever after wore the skin as a mantle.

**Nemesis** (Greek, 'righteous indignation', from *nemein*, 'to give what is due'). The Greek goddess of retribution or vengeance, the daughter of Nox. She rewarded virtue and punished the wicked and all kinds of impiety. As such, she was the personification of divine retribution. Hence the use of her name for retributive justice generally.

**Nemine. Nemine contradicente** (Latin). No one opposing; unanimously. Usually contracted to nem. con.

**Nemine dissentiente** (Latin). Without a dissentient voice; usually contracted to nem. diss.

**Nemo** (Latin, 'Nobody'). In the ODYSSEY the alias used by Odysseus (ULYSSES) when captured by POLYPHEMUS. In consequence Polyphemus cannot obtain help against Odysseus, for 'Nobody' harmed him. In Jules Verne's novel *Twenty Thousand Leagues under the Sea* (1870) Captain Nemo is the mysterious genius who builds a submarine and tours the world destroying ships.

**Nemo me impune lacessit.** No one provokes me with impunity. The motto of the MOST ANCIENT ORDER OF THE THISTLE and of the kings of Scotland. Its authorship is unknown. *See also* SLOGAN.

**Neolithic Age** (Greek *neos*, 'new', and *lithos*, 'stone'). The later STONE AGE of Europe. Neolithic stone implements are polished, more highly finished and more various than those of the PALAEOLITHIC AGE. Mankind knew something of agriculture, kept domestic animals, used boats, slings, and bows and arrows. It was superseded by the Bronze age.

**Nepenthe** or **Nepenthes** (Greek *nē*, 'not', and *penthos*, 'grief'). An Egyptian drug mentioned in the ODYSSEY (iv, 228) that was fabled to drive away care and make people forget their woes. Polydamna, wife of Thonis, king of Egypt, gave it to HELEN.

**Nephew** (French *neveu*, Latin *nepos*). Both in Latin and archaic English the word means grand-child or descendant. Hence NEPOTISM. In the Authorized Version of the Bible, 1 Timothy 5:4 reads, 'But if any widow have children or nephews', but in the Revised Version 'grandchildren'.

'Niece' (Latin *neptis*) similarly means granddaughter or female descendant.

**Ne plus ultra** (Latin, 'not more beyond'). The most perfect state to which a thing can be brought. *See* PLUS ULTRA.

**Nepman.** A term applied in the former USSR to the man allowed to engage in private enterprise business under the New Economic Policy (NEP) begun in 1921.

**Nepomuk, St John of.** *See under* JOHN.

**Nepotism** (Italian *nepote*, 'nephew'). The practice of specially favouring relatives in matters of employment, promotion and the like. The usage derives from the days when popes and high ecclesiastics gave preferment and advancement to their nephews, as their illegitimate sons were euphemistically labelled.

**Neptune.** The Roman god of the sea corresponding to the Greek POSEIDON, hence, allusively, the sea itself. Neptune is represented as an elderly man of stately mien, bearded, carrying a trident and sometimes astride a dolphin or horse. *See* HIPPOCAMPUS; PLANETS.

**Nereus.** The OLD MAN OF THE SEA, a sea-god of Greek mythology represented as a very old man. He was the father of the NEREIDS and his special dominion was the Aegean Sea.

**Nereids.** The sea nymphs of Greek mythology, the 50 daughters of NEREUS and 'grey-eyed' Doris. The best known are AMPHITRITE, THETIS and GALATEA. Milton refers to another, Panope, in *Lycidas* (1637):

> The air was calm and on the level brine
> Sleek Panope with all her sisters played.

The names of all 50 are found in Edmund Spenser's *The Faerie Queene*, IV, xi, verses 48–51 (1596), almost all with an appropriate descriptive word or phrase:

> Swift *Proto*, milde *Eucrate*, *Thetis* faire,
> Soft *Spio*, sweete *Eudore*, *Sao* sad,
> Light *Doto*, wanton *Glauce*, and *Galene* glad.

White hand *Eunica*, proud *Dynamene*,
Ioyous *Thalia*, goodly *Amphitrite*,
Louely *Pasithee*, kinde *Eulimene*,
Light foote *Cymothoe*, and sweete *Melite*,
Fairest *Pherusa*, *Phao* lilly white,
Wondred [wonderful] *Agaue*, *Poris*, and *Nesæa*,
With *Erato* that doth in loue delite,
And *Panopæ*, and wise *Protomedæa*,
And snowy neckd *Doris*, and milkewhite *Galathæa*.
Speedy *Hippothoe*, and chaste *Actea*,
Large *Lisianassa*, and *Pronæa* sage,
*Euagore*, and light *Pontoporea*,
And she, that with her least word can asswage
The surging seas, when they do sorest rage,
*Cymodoce*, and stout *Autonoe*,
And *Neso*, and *Eione* well in age,
And seeming still to smile, *Glauconome*,
And she that hight [was called] of many heastes [names] *Polynome*.
Fresh *Alimeda*, deckt with girlond greene;
*Hyponeo*, with salt bedewed wrests [wrists]
*Laomedia*, like the christall sheene;
*Liagore*, much praisd for wise behests;
And *Psamathe*, for her brode snowy brests;
*Cymo*, *Eupompe*, and *Themiste* iust;
And she that vertue loues and vice detests
*Euarna*, and *Menippe* true in trust,
And *Nemertea* learned well to rule her lust.

**Nergal.** The Babylonian god of the underworld, usually appearing as a god of war and sudden death. He is depicted as a bearded figure emerging from the ground, carrying a double-edged sword topped with lion heads. He is mentioned in the Bible as being created by 'the men of Cuth' (2 Kings 17:20). His name represents Sumerian *Ne-unu-gal*, 'lordship of the great city' (i.e. the underworld). In later mythology he was sometimes identified with MARS.

**Neri.** *See* BIANCHI.

**Nero. Nero, A.** Any bloody-minded man, relentless tyrant or evil-doer of extraordinary cruelty, from the depraved and infamous Roman emperor, Nero Claudius Caesar (AD 37–68), whom contemporaries believed to be the instigator of the great fire that destroyed most of Rome in AD 64, and to have recited his own poetry and played his lyre while enjoying the spectacle. Nero blamed the Christians.

**Nero of the North, The.** Christian II of Denmark (1481–1559), also called 'The Cruel'. He conquered Sweden in 1520 and massacred over 80 nobles and others in 'the blood bath' at Stockholm. Several hundred prominent people were put to death subsequently. The Danish oppressors were driven out by Gustavus Vasa in 1523.

**Neroli.** The essential oil of orange blossoms, used in EAU DE COLOGNE and other perfumes, is said to have been named after Anne Marie de la Trémoïlle (1635–1722), wife of Flavino Orsini, prince of Nerola, the French-born Italian princess who is believed to have discovered it.

**Nerthus** or **Hertha.** The name given by Tacitus to a German or Scandinavian goddess of fertility or 'Mother Earth', who was worshipped on the island of Rügen. She roughly corresponds to the classical CYBELE, and is probably confused with the Scandinavian god NIORD or Njorthr, the protector of sailors and fishermen. Nerthus and Niord both probably mean 'mother earth'.

**Nerve. Bundle of nerves.** *See under* BUNDLE.

**Lose one's nerve, To.** *See under* LOSE.

**War of nerves.** *See under* WAR.

**Nessus, The shirt of.** *See under* SHIRT.

**Nest. Nest egg.** Money laid by. The allusion is to the custom of placing a china egg in a hen's nest to induce her to lay her eggs there. If a person has saved a little money, it serves as an inducement to increase the store.

**Crow's nest.** *See under* CROW.

**Feather one's nest, To.** *See under* FEATHER.

**Nestor.** King of Pylos, in Greece, the oldest and most experienced of the chieftains who went to the siege of TROY. Hence the name is frequently applied as an epithet to the oldest and wisest man of a class or company. Samuel Rogers (1763–1855), for instance, who lived to be 92, was called 'the Nestor of English poets'.

**Nestorians.** Followers of Nestorius, Patriarch of Constantinople, 428–431 (d.*c*.451). He is traditionally said to have asserted that Christ had two distinct natures and that MARY was the mother of his human nature. His teaching was condemned by Pope Celestine I in 430. A separate Nestorian Church was established which spread to Asia where most of their churches were destroyed by TAMBERLANE (Timur) in about 1400. A small group called Assyrian Christians survived in parts of Asia Minor and Persia.

**Nettle, To grasp the.** *See under* GRASP.

**Network, Old boy.** *See under* OLD.

**Neustria.** The western portion of the ancient Frankish kingdom, originally corresponding to northwestern France between the Loire and the mouth of the Scheldt. In the 8th century the name was applied to western Lombardy.

**Never.** There are numerous locutions to express this idea, including:

At the GREEK CALENDS
At the latter LAMMAS
In the reign of QUEEN DICK
Not in a MONTH OF SUNDAYS
Not in a million years
Not in DONKEY'S YEARS
Once in a blue moon
On St TIB'S EVE
Over my dead body
When Dover and Calais meet
When hell freezes over
When pigs fly
When the world grows honest
When the yellow river runs clear
When two Fridays *or* three Sundays come together

**Never eat an oyster unless there's an R in the month.** Good advice that limits the eating of native oysters to the months from September to April, the normal marketing time. The legal close time for oysters in England and Scotland, however, extends only from 15 June to 4 August. The advice does not necessarily apply to imported oysters.

**Never had it so good.** Earlier current in the USA, the phrase became popular in Britain after its use by Harold Macmillan, Conservative Prime Minister (1957–63), in a speech at Bedford (20 July 1957). Referring to the overall prosperity and general improvement of living standards, he said: 'Most of our people have never had it so good.'

**Never Never Land.** The land (originally 'the Never Land') where the Lost Boys and Red Indians lived, and where Pirates sailed up the lake in J.M. Barrie's PETER PAN (1904). The phrase was applied to the whole of the Australian outback, but since the publication of *We of the Never-Never* (1908) by Jeannie Gunn it has been restricted to the Northern Territory.

**Never say die.** Never despair; never give up; never give in. Die here is 'to cease to live'.

**On the never-never.** To get or buy something on the never-never is to obtain it on hire purchase, a system of deferred payment.

**New. New Age.** A philosophy of the late 1980s centring on alternative medicine, astrology, spiritualism, animism and the like. Two notable phenomena of the period were New Age music, as a type of gentle melodic music combining elements of jazz, folk and classical music, played largely on electronic instruments, and New Age travellers, as groups of latter-day hippies, who lead a nomadic existence, travelling the country with their children and animals in ancient vehicles to set up camp at such spiritually significant sites as STONEHENGE and GLASTONBURY.

**New Albion.** The name under which Sir Francis Drake annexed territory in what is now California in 1579, during his voyage of circumnavigation. He recorded this act by setting up a brass plate. Such a plate was found near San Francisco in 1937. *See also* ALBION; DRAKE BRASS PLATE *under* FORGERY.

**New Atlantis, The.** An allegorical romance by Francis Bacon (1561–1626), published in unfinished form in 1626, in which he describes a visit to an imaginary island of Bensalem in the Pacific and the social conditions prevailing there. *See also* ATLANTIS; CITY OF THE SUN; UTOPIA.

In 1709 Mary de la Rivière Manley (*c.*1672–1724) published a similarly titled work, *The New Atlantis*, a scandalous chronicle of crimes purportedly committed by people of high rank, with the names of contemporaries so thinly disguised as to be readily recognized.

**New, fresh** or **young blood.** New young members or workers, regarded as bringing an invigorating force into a business or organization.

**New brooms sweep clean.** Those new in office are generally very zealous at first, and often keen to make changes, sometimes ruthlessly.

**New Deal.** The name given to President Roosevelt's policy of economic reconstruction announced in his first presidential campaign (1932). 'I pledge you, I pledge myself, to a new deal for the American people.' A relief and recovery programme known as the 'First New Deal' was inaugurated in March 1933, and a 'Second New Deal', which was concerned with social reform, in January 1935. The 'Third New Deal' of 1938 sought to preserve such gains made by its predecessors.

**New England.** The collective name of the northeastern states of the USA: Connecticut, Massachusetts, Rhode Island, Vermont, New Hampshire and Maine. In colonial days Plymouth and New Haven formed part of the group before they lost their separate identities as part of Massachusetts and Connecticut respectively. The name was given to the area by Captain John Smith in 1614, and colonization was begun by the PILGRIM FATHERS after the Plymouth Company of Virginia had been revived as the Council for New England. During the English Civil Wars (1642–51) a New England Confederation was set up consisting of Massachusetts, Plymouth, Connecticut and New Haven to maintain a common front. James II formed a short-lived Dominion of New England (1687–9), consisting of Massachusetts, Rhode Island, Connecticut, Plymouth, Maine and New Hampshire, to which NEW YORK and New Jersey were added.

**New English Bible, The.** *See under* BIBLE.

**New International Version, The.** *See under* BIBLE.

**New Jersey tea.** The popular name for *Ceanothus americanus*, a white-flowered plant found in the northeastern areas of the USA. The name derives from the fact that Native Americans and colonists made a kind of tea from the plant, the former regarding the drink as possessing medicinal properties. Some colonists are said to have used this tea to avoid the British tax on imported tea.

**New Jerusalem, The.** Heaven or the Paradise of Christians.

> And I saw a new heaven and a new earth: for the first heaven and the first earth were passed away; and there was no more sea. And I John saw the holy city,

new Jerusalem, coming down from God out of heaven, prepared as a bride adorned for her husband.
Revelation 21:1

Hence, figuratively, the perfect society.

**New Latin.** Latin written since *c*.1500, especially that used in scientific classifications and in theological and philosophical works.

**New Learning.** The name given to the revival of Greek and Latin classical learning during the period of the 15th- and 16th-century RENAISSANCE.

**New lease of life.** Renewed health and vigour, especially applied to someone who appears to gain a 'second wind' after a serious illness or change of circumstances.

**New Look.** The name given to the long-skirted women's dress of 1947. The style was reminiscent of Edwardian days and was short-lived. The phrase is also used generally for a redesigned periodical or restructured radio or television programme. An annual 'makeover' of this kind usually takes place in the autumn.

Next week, your New Statesman will have a new look. Alongside a brighter, easier-to-read design, we shall bring you an extended arts, culture and books section.
*New Statesman* (11 September 1998)

**New man, The.** The regenerated man. In scriptural phrase the unregenerated state is called the old man. The expression is also used to describe a type of modern man who actively expresses his latent caring nature by helping with domestic work and young children in the home. *See also* BREADWINNER; HOUSE HUSBAND; NEW WOMAN.

**New Model Army, The.** In the English Civil Wars (1642–51) the Parliamentary army organized in 1645 under Sir Thomas Fairfax in place of a variety of local forces. Most of the officers were INDEPENDENTS and the troopers of the Eastern Association (raised in Norfolk, Suffolk, Essex, Cambridge and Hertfordshire) became its backbone. Initially more than half of the infantry were pressed men. Regular pay (not available to the CAVALIERS) resulted in better discipline. Oliver Cromwell took command in 1650.

**New morality.** A popular term of the 1960s implying that the hitherto publicly accepted canons of morality are no longer relevant to present-day society, owing to the rapid spread of social and technical change, the advent of the PILL, and more 'enlightened' attitudes generally. Such thinking was induced by the growth of the AFFLUENT SOCIETY, the diminishing of individual responsibility occasioned by the WELFARE STATE, the declining influence of Christian standards and 'middle-class morality', and the championship of hedonism and self-indulgence by AVANT-GARDE writers and scientific theorists, who seem to lack the balance of historical perspective. In the sphere of sexual behaviour it was defined by Lord Shawcross as 'the old immorality', although it subsequently took a noticeable turn for the moral. *See also* NEW WOMAN.

**New Revised Standard Version, The.** *See under* BIBLE.

**New Style.** *See* GREGORIAN YEAR; STILO NOVO.

**New Testament, The.** The name given to the second group of sacred writings in the Bible, consisting of 27 books in all (the 4 Gospels, The Acts of the Apostles, 21 Epistles and the Revelation of St John the Divine), but which more correctly could be called 'The New Covenant' or 'The New Dispensation'.

The religion of Israel was regarded as a covenant between Jehovah and his chosen people and in due time a new covenant was promised by the prophets:

Behold, the days come, saith the Lord, that I will make a new covenant with the house of Israel, and with the house of Judah.
Jeremiah 31:31

This new covenant, for the Christians, was established by the life and death of Christ, and towards the end of the 2nd century a generally accepted collection of new scriptures, worthy of complementing the OLD TESTAMENT, was evolving. The present canon is that established by the Council of Carthage in 397. The name Testament is from the Latin *testamentum*, which is an inaccurate rendering of the Greek *diathēkē*, 'disposition', 'covenant'. Thus, in the Authorized Version, 'This cup is the new testament in my blood, which is shed for you.' (Luke 22:20), in the Revised Version reads, 'This cup is the new covenant in my blood, even that which is poured out for you.' *See also* APOCRYPHA.

**New Testament in Modern English, The.** *See under* BIBLE.

**New Testament in Modern Speech, The.** *See under* BIBLE.

**New Thought.** A general term for a system of therapeutics based on the theory that the mental and physical problems of life should be met, regulated and controlled by the suggestion of right thoughts. This system has nothing in common with CHRISTIAN SCIENCE, autosuggestion or psychotherapy.

**New town.** A town established as an entirely new settlement with the aim of relocating populations away from large cities. The first new towns in Britain were inspired by the garden city concept formulated at the end of the 19th century. They were proposed in the New Towns Act of 1946, and twelve were designated in England and Wales over the next four years, with a further two in Scotland. Each had its own development corporation financed by the government.

Further new towns were set up in the 1960s. Their tally is:

ENGLAND: Basildon (Essex), Bracknell, Crawley, Harlow, Hatfield, Hemel Hempstead, Stevenage, Welwyn Garden City, Newton Aycliffe, Corby, Milton Keynes, Northampton, Peterborough, Peterlee, Redditch, Runcorn, Skelmersdale, Telford, Warrington, Washington

WALES: Cwmbran, Mid-Wales (Newtown)

SCOTLAND: Cumbernauld, East Kilbride, Glenrothes, Irvine, Livingston

**New Wave** (French *Nouvelle Vague*). A movement in the French cinema of the 1960s characterized by a free or fluid use of the camera and an abandonment of traditional editing techniques. New Wave is also used for a type of rock music of the late 1970s that was related to PUNK but was more complex.

**New wine in old bottles.** To put new wine in old bottles is to add or impose something new to an old or established order, with disastrous results. New wine expands as it matures. If it is put in a new skin (bottle), the skin expands with it. If it is put in an old skin, the skin will burst when the wine expands.

> Neither do men put new wine into old bottles: else the bottles break, and the wine runneth out, and the bottles perish: but they put new wine into new bottles, and both are preserved.
>
> Matthew 9:17

**New woman, The.** A type of 'liberated', independently minded and self-motivated woman who emerged in the late 19th century as a successor to the feminist crusaders of the 1860s. Her own successors in the 20th century include the 'career girl' or 'career woman' of the 1950s and, in the backlash to the open promiscuity and AIDS scares of the 1980s, the NEW MORALITY 'virgin' or sexual abstainer of the 1990s. The term has largely been a creation of the media, however. *See also* NEW MAN.

**New World.** The Americas, North and South. The eastern hemisphere is called the Old World.

**New Year's Day.** 1 January. The Romans began their year in March, hence September, October, November, December for the 7th, 8th, 9th and 10th months. Since the introduction of the Christian era, CHRISTMAS Day, LADY DAY, EASTER Day, 1 March and 25 March have in turns been considered as New Year's Day. With the introduction of the GREGORIAN YEAR, 1 January was accepted as New Year's Day by most Christian countries, but not until 1600 in Scotland and 1752 in England.

**New Year's gifts.** The giving of presents at this time was a custom among both the Greeks and the Romans, the latter calling them *strenae*, whence the French term *étrenne* ('New Year's gift'). Nonius Marcellus says that Tatius, king of the SABINES, was presented with some branches of trees cut from the forest sacred to the goddess STRENIA ('strength') on New Year's Day, and from this incident the custom arose.

Magistrates were formerly bribed with gifts on New Year's Day, a custom abolished by law in 1290. Even down to the reign of James II, however, the monarchs received their 'tokens'.

**New York.** Formerly New Amsterdam, so named in honour of James, Duke of York (1633–1701), the future James II of England, Scotland and Ireland, to whom it was granted in 1664 after its capture from the Dutch by the British.

**New Zealand.** The name of this former British colony is derived from the Dutch province of Zeeland as a result of its discovery in 1642 by Abel Tasman (*c*.1603–59), the great Dutch navigator. *See also* WAITANGI DAY.

**That's a new one on me.** That's something I didn't know; I hadn't heard that. A phrase often used of a joke or anecdote one had not previously heard, or of a new and surprising variation on a traditional theme.

> He said there was blood pouring through his ceiling. That was a new one on the station sergeant.
>
> MICHAEL INNES (J.I.M. STEWART): *Private View*, ch iii (1952)

**Newbury, Jack of.** *See under* JACK.

**Newcastle, To carry coals to.** *See under* CARRY.

**Newgate.** According to John Stow, this was first built in the city wall of London in the time of Henry I, but excavations have shown that there was a Roman gate here about 31ft (9.5m) wide. It may have fallen into disuse, and have been repaired by Henry I (r.1100–35), the present name being given at the time.

**Newgate Calendar, The.** A biographical record of the more notorious criminals confined at Newgate. It was begun in 1773 and continued at intervals for many years. In 1824–8 Andrew Knapp and William Baldwin published, in 4 volumes, *The Newgate Calendar, comprising Memoirs of Notorious Characters*, partly compiled by George Borrow, and in 1886, C. Pelham published his *Chronicles of Crime or the New Newgate Calendar* (2 volumes). Another such calendar was published in 1969. The term is often used as a comprehensive expression embracing crime of every sort.

**Newgate prison.** The first prison (over the gate) existed in the reign of King John. The last prison on the site (designed in 1770) was closed in 1880 and demolished in 1902, and it was for long the prison for the City of London and County of Middlesex. Many notorious criminals and state prisoners were confined there, as well as debtors. Condemned criminals were executed in the street outside, 'condemned sermons' being preached the preceding Sunday, to which the public were formerly admitted.

From its prominence, Newgate came to be applied as a general name for gaols, and Thomas Nashe, in *Pierce Pennilesse, his Supplication to the Divell* (1592), says it is 'a common name for all prisons, as homo is a common name for a man or woman'.

The name came to be associated with various styles and fashions. A Newgate fringe was thus hair worn under the chin, so called because it occupied the position of the rope around the neck of a man about to be hanged. A Newgate knocker was a lock of hair twisted into a curl, once worn by COSTERMONGERS and persons of similar status. It was so called because it resembled a knocker, and the wearers were often Newgate inmates.

**Newgrange.** A chambered burial mound in the valley of the Boyne, Ireland. It is one of the finest STONE AGE monuments in Europe, and its entrance and chambers are aligned with the rays of the rising sun on 21 December, the winter SOLSTICE. The purposes of the alignment are uncertain. The tomb may have been built by sun worshippers who hoped that the rays would reawaken the spirits of the dead whose ashes were placed within. It received its name in medieval times, when the land on which it stands became one of the outlying farms, or 'new granges', of Mellifont Abbey. It was discovered in 1699 by the Welsh antiquary Edward Llwyd.

**News.** The letters E$\frac{N}{S}$W used to be prefixed to newspapers to show that they obtained information from the four quarters of the world, and the supposition that the word 'news' is thence derived is an ingenious conceit but spoilt by the old spelling 'newes'. The word is actually from French *nouvelles*.

The word is now nearly always treated as singular ('the news is very good'), but it was formerly taken as a plural, and in the *Letters of Queen Victoria* the queen and most of her correspondents so used it:

> The news from Austria are very sad, and make one very anxious.
>
> To the king of the Belgians (20 August 1861)

*See also* BREAK THE NEWS.

**Bad news.** *See under* BAD.

**Newspaper, Family.** *See under* FAMILY.

**Newspeak.** Language in which the words change their meaning to accord with the official party-political views of the state. The term was coined by George Orwell in his *1984* (1949). *See also* LOOKING-GLASS.

**Newt.** *See* APRON.

**Newton. Newton and the apple.** The well-known story of Isaac Newton (1642–1727) and the apple originated with VOLTAIRE, who says that he was told it by Mrs Conduit, Newton's niece. In 1666 Newton was visiting his mother at his birthplace, Woolsthorpe in Lincolnshire. On seeing an apple fall from a tree in the garden, he was led to the train of thought that resulted in his contribution to the laws of gravitation.

**Newtonian philosophy.** The astronomical system that in the late 17th century displaced COPERNICANISM, and also the theory of universal gravitation. It is so called after Sir Isaac Newton, who established the former and discovered the latter.

> Nature, and Nature's laws lay hid in night;
> God said, *Let Newton be!* and all was light.
>
> ALEXANDER POPE: 'Epitaph: Intended for Sir Isaac Newton' (1730)

**Next. Next friend.** In law an adult (usually a relation) who brings an action in a court of law on behalf of a minor or a person of unsound mind.

**Next of kin.** The legal term for a person's nearest relative, more especially where an estate is left by an intestate. In English law the next of kin in priority is: (1) husband or wife, (2) children, (3) father or mother (equally if both alive), (4) brothers and sisters, (5) half-brothers and half-sisters, (6) grandparents, (7) uncles and aunts, (8) half-uncles and half-aunts, (9) the crown.

**Next to nothing.** Very little, as: 'It will cost next to nothing,' 'She eats next to nothing.'

**Girl next door, The.** *See under* GIRL.

**Nibelungenlied, The.** A great medieval German epic poem founded on old Scandinavian legends contained in the VOLSUNGS and the EDDA.

Nibelung was a mythical king of a race of Scandinavian dwarfs dwelling in Nibelheim ('home of mist'). These Nibelungs or Nibelungen were the possessors of the wonderful 'hoard' of gold and precious stones, guarded by the dwarf ALBERICH, and their name passed to later holders of the hoard, SIEGFRIED's following and the Burgundians being in turn called 'the Nibelungs'.

Siegfried, the hero of the first part of the poem, became possessed of the hoard and married KRIEMHILD, sister of GUNTHER, king of Worms, whom he helped to secure the hand of BRUNHILD of Iceland. After Siegfried's murder by Hagen at Brunhild's instigation, Kriemhild carried the treasure to Worms, where it was seized by Gunther and his retainer Hagen. They buried it in the Rhine, intending later to enjoy it, but they were both slain for refusing to reveal its whereabouts, and the hoard remains for ever in the keeping of the Rhine Maidens.

The second part of the Nibelungenlied tells of the marriage of the widow Kriemhild to King Etzel (ATTILA THE HUN), her invitation of the Burgundians to the court of the Hunnish king and the slaughter of all the principal characters, including Gunther, Hagen and Kriemhild. *See also* RING OF THE NIBELUNG; WOTAN.

**Nicaea, The Council of.** *See under* COUNCIL.

**Niccolò Machiavelli.** *See under* MACHIAVELLI.

**Nicene Creed.** The creed properly so called was a comparatively short statement of beliefs issued in 325 by the COUNCIL OF NICAEA to combat the ARIAN heresy. The 'Nicene Creed' commonly referred to is that properly called the Niceno-Constantinopolitan Creed, referred to in Article VIII of the THIRTY-NINE ARTICLES given in the BOOK OF COMMON PRAYER, which ultimately derives from the Baptismal Creed of Jerusalem. It is used in the EUCHARIST of the ROMAN CATHOLIC CHURCH, the CHURCH OF ENGLAND and the EASTERN CHURCH, where it still forms part of the service of baptism. It was first used at Antioch in the late 5th century and gradually gained acceptance in both East and West. *See also* APOSTLES' CREED; ATHANASIAN CREED; FILIOQUE CONTROVERSY.

**Nicholas. Manna of St Nicholas of Bari.** *See* AQUA TOFANA.

**St Nicholas.** One of the most popular saints in Christendom, especially in the East. He is the patron saint of Russia, of Aberdeen, of parish clerks, of scholars (who used to be called clerks), of pawnbrokers (because of the three bags of gold, transformed to the THREE GOLDEN BALLS, that he gave to the daughters of a poor man to save them from earning their dowers in a disreputable way), of young boys (because he once restored to life three little boys who had been cut up and pickled in a tub to serve for bacon), and is invoked by sailors (because he allayed a storm during a voyage to the HOLY LAND) and against fire. Finally, he is the original of SANTA CLAUS.

Little is known of his life but he is said to have been bishop of Myra (Lycia) in the early 4th century, and one story relates that he was present at the COUNCIL OF NICAEA (325) and buffeted Arius on the jaw. His day is 6 December, and he is represented in episcopal robes with either three purses of gold, three golden balls or three little boys, in allusion to one or other of the above legends. *See also* LOMBARD.

**St Nicholas' bishop.** *See* BOY BISHOP.

**St Nicholas' clerks.** Old slang for thieves and highwaymen. It has been suggested that it may be an allusion to the liberties taken by choristers on St Nicholas' day when they chose their BOY BISHOP.

**Nick, Old.** *See under* OLD.

**Nick.** To nick is slang for to steal or to arrest.

**Nick the nick, To.** To hit the exact moment. Tallies used to be called 'nick-sticks'. Hence, to make a record of anything is 'to nick it down', as publicans used to nick a score on a TALLY.

**In good nick.** In good condition.

**In the nick.** In prison; in custody.

**In the nick of time.** Just in time; at the right moment. The allusion is to tallies marked with nicks or notches. *See also* NICK THE NICK; TALLY.

**Nickanan Night.** The night preceding SHROVE TUESDAY was so called in the West Country, especially in Cornwall, because boys played tricks and practical jokes on that night. The following night they went from house to house singing:

> Nicky, nicky nan,
> Give me a pancake and then I'll be gone;
> But if you give me none
> I'll throw a great stone
> And down your door shall come.

**Nickel.** The metal is so called from the German *Kupfernickel*, the name given to the ore (niccolite) from which it was first obtained (1751) by Axel F. von Cronstedt (1722–65). *Kupfer* means 'copper', and *Nickel* is the name of a mischievous GOBLIN fabled to inhabit mines in Germany. The name was given to it because, although it was copper-coloured, no copper could be got from it, and so the *Nickel* was blamed.

In the USA a nickel is a coin of five cents, so called from being made of an alloy of nickel and copper.

**Nickelodeon.** The first cinema theatre called a 'Nickelodeon' (i.e. 'Nickel Odeon', because the admission price was only five cents), was that opened by John P. Harris and Harry Davis at McKeesport, near Pittsburgh, Pennsylvania, in 1905. The picture shown was *The Great Train Robbery*. It was the first real motion-picture theatre and thousands more nickelodeons soon sprang up throughout the USA. Hence, a cheap entertainment, and also its application to a jukebox.

> Put another nickel in,
> In the nickelodeon,
> All I want is loving you
> And music, music, music.
>
> STEPHEN WEISS and BERNIE BAUM: 'Music, music, music' (1950)

**Wooden nickels.** *See under* WOOD.

**Nicker** or **nix** (from a root related to Greek *nisein*, 'to wash'). In Scandinavian folklore a water wraith, or KELPIE, inhabiting sea, lake, river and waterfall. They are sometimes represented as half-child, half-horse, the hoofs being reversed, and sometimes as old men sitting on rocks wringing the water from their hair. The female equivalent of a 'nicker' is a 'nixie'.

**Nickname.** Originally 'an eke-name', eke being an adverb meaning 'also' (modern German *auch*). A newt was formed in the same way (an ewt). The 'eke' of a beehive is a piece added to the bottom to enlarge the hive. *See also* APRON; NONCE.

Surnames as such were not common in

England before the 13th century, so that identification was helped by nicknames such as 'Long', 'Brown', 'Bull', 'Russell' ('red-haired'), 'Sour milk', 'Barefoot' and so on.

**Nicknamed doctors.** Many learned and pious figures have earned the nickname Doctor, this honorary appellation accompanied by a particularizing adjective. They include the following:

Admirable Doctor (Doctor Admirabilis): Roger Bacon (*c*.1220–92)
Angelic Doctor: St THOMAS AQUINAS (*c*.1225–74)
Divine Doctor or Ecstatic Doctor: Jan van Ruysbroeck (1293–1381)
Eloquent Doctor: Peter Aureolus (14th century)
Evangelic Doctor: John Wyclif (*c*.1320–84)
Illuminated Doctor: Raymond Lully (1235–1315) and Johann Tauler (*c*.1300–61)
Illustrious Doctor: Adam de Marisco (d.1257)
Invincible Doctor: WILLIAM OF OCCAM (*c*.1280–1349)
Irrefragable Doctor: Alexander of Hales (*c*.1175–1245)
Mellifluous Doctor: St BERNARD of Clairvaux (1090–1153)
Perspicuous Doctor: Walter Burley (1275–1345)
Profound Doctor: Thomas Bradwardine (*c*.1290–1349)
Resolute Doctor: John Baconthorpe (*c*.1290–1346)
Seraphic Doctor: St Bonaventura (Giovanni di Fidanza) (1221–74)
Singular Doctor: William of Occam (*c*.1280–1349)
Solid (i.e. sound) Doctor: Richard Middleton (*fl*.1280)
Subtle Doctor: Duns Scotus (*c*.1265–1308)
Universal Doctor: Albert of Cologne or Albertus Magnus (*c*.1206–80) and Alain de Lille (*c*.1128–1202)
Wonderful Doctor: Roger Bacon (*c*.1220–92)

**Nicknames of drugs.** Drug users and dealers have evolved a jargon of their own, and most drugs, whether legal or not, have evolved their individual nicknames. They include the following:

Amphetamine: bennies, dexies, goof balls, ice, speed
Cannabis (marijuana): baby, black, boo, bush, doobie, draw, ganja, grass, green, hash, hemp, Mary Jane, pot, reefer, shit, tea, weed
Cocaine: bernies, C, Charlie, coke, crack, dust, flake, freebase, leaf, nose, rock, snow
HEROIN: beast, black tar, H, horse, poison, scag, scat, schmeck, smack, stuff, sugar
LSD: A, acid, chief, purple
MDMA: Adam, E, ECSTASY, XTC
Phencyclidine: angel dust, corn flakes, goon, hog, loopy dust, rocket fuel

**National nicknames.** Among the best known, although some are dated and others are now derogatory, are:

American: BROTHER JONATHAN, YANK or Yankee; for the USA personified: UNCLE SAM
Argentinian: Argie
Australian: AUSSIE, DIGGER, Ozzie
Briton: Brit
Canadian: CANUCK
Chinese: Chink, Pong
Costa Rican: Tico
Dutchman: Dutchy, Mynheer
Englishman: JOHN BULL, LIMEY, POMMY or Pommie
French Canadian: Jean Baptiste
Frenchman: Frenchy, FROG or Froggie, JOHNNY CRAPAUD, Mossoo
German: Boche, FRITZ, Heinie, HUN, JERRY, Kraut
Irishman: Mick, MULLIGAN, PADDY, Pat,
Italian: Eyetie, Guinea, Tony
Japanese: Jap, Nip
Mexican: Mex
New Zealander: Kiwi
Pakistani: Paki
Pole: POLACK
Russian: Russky
Scot: JOCK, Mac, Sandy
Spaniard or Portuguese: Dago (Diego), Spic
Welshman: Taff or TAFFY

Other languages have similar names. French shares *Boche* and *Jap* with English, but also has *Angliche* or *Rosbif* ('roast beef') for a Briton, *Amerloque* or *Rican* for an American, *Chinetoc* for a Chinese, *Espingouin* for a Spaniard, *Fridolin* or *Frisé* for a German, *Portos* or *Tos* for a Portuguese, *Rital* for an Italian and *Ruskoff* for a Russian. *See also* GODDAM.

**Regimental and divisional nicknames.** *See under* REGIMENTAL.

**Traditional nicknames.** *See under* TRADITIONAL.

**Nicodemus.** In the New Testament (John 3), a PHARISEE to whom Jesus explains the meaning of being 'born again'. He later tries to defend Jesus to other Pharisees and assists in Christ's burial.

**Gospel of Nicodemus, The.** *See under* GOSPEL.

**Nicotine.** So named from *Nicotiana*, the Latin name of the tobacco plant, given to it in honour of Jean Nicot (*c*.1530–1600), French ambassador to Portugal, who introduced tobacco into France about 1560.

**Niece.** *See* NEPHEW.

**Niflheim** (Old Norse, 'mist home'). In Scandinavian mythology, the region of endless cold and everlasting night, ruled over by the goddess HEL. It consisted of nine worlds, to which were consigned those who died of disease or old age. It existed in the north, and out of its spring Hvergelmir flowed 12 ice-cold streams. *See also* MUSPELHEIM.

**Nigger** (Latin *niger*, 'black'). A Negro or anyone of very dark skin. It is now generally an offensive term although some Blacks adopted it in in the 1980s as a designation of pride.

**Nigger in the woodpile, A.** The phrase, of American origin, was originally a way of accounting for the disappearance of fuel. It then came to be used for any hidden snag or problem.

**Nigger minstrels.** The common name for the once popular 'coon' shows of the MUSIC HALL and seaside concert party who drew their inspiration from the CHRISTY MINSTREL shows. The Kentucky Minstrels and Black and White Minstrels are more recent revivals of this type of performance. Their songs were characterized by humour and pathos. Plantation life was romanticized but it was essentially good humoured and without any offensive intent. *See also* UNCLE TOM'S CABIN.

**Nigh, The end is.** *See under* END.

**Night. Night of the Long Knives, The.** A descriptive phrase applied to the night of 30 June 1934, when Hitler, assisted by Himmler's SS, secured the murder of the leaders of the SA. The shootings (mainly at Munich and Berlin) actually began on the Friday night of the 29th and continued through the Sunday. The estimates of those killed vary between 60 and 400, and Ernst Röhm and Kurt von Schleicher were among them. Hitler had decided to rely on the *Reichswehr* rather than risk dependence on Röhm and the SA. Himmler presented the assassins with 'daggers of honour' inscribed with his name.

The term, now applied allusively to any treacherous massacre or betrayal, has its antecedents. George Borrow, referring to a treacherous murder of South British chieftains by Hengist in 472, writes:

> This infernal carnage the Welsh have appropriately denominated the treachery of the long knives. It will be as well to observe that the Saxons derived their name from the saxes, or long knives, which they wore at their sides, and at the use of which they were terribly proficient.
>
> *Wild Wales*, ch lii (1862)

**Night on the tiles, A.** An evening or night of merrymaking or debauchery. The allusion is to the nocturnal activities of cats, especially in the mating season.

**Ambrosian Nights.** *See under* AMBROSE.

**Arabian Nights Entertainments, The.** *See under* ARABIAN.

**Burns' Night.** *See under* BURNS.

**Colcannon night.** *See under* COLCANNON.

**Dog in the night-time, The.** *See under* DOG.

**Early night, An.** *See under* EARLY.

**First nighter.** *See under* FIRST.

**Hen night.** *See under* HEN.

**Ladies' night.** *See under* LADY.

**Lady of the night.** *See under* LADY.

**Last Night of the Proms.** *See under* LAST.

**Nickanan Night.** *See under* NICKANAN.

**Ships that pass in the night.** *See under* SHIP.

**Stag night.** *See under* STAG.

**Twelfth Night.** *See under* TWELVE.

**Walpurgis Night.** *See under* WALPURGIS.

**Watch Night.** *See under* WATCH.

**White night.** *See under* WHITE.

**Nightingale.** The Greek legend is that Tereus, king of Thrace, fetched Philomela to visit his wife, Procne, who was her sister, but when he reached the 'solitudes of Heleas' he raped her, cutting out her tongue to prevent her from revealing what he had done. Tereus told his wife that Philomela was dead, but Philomela made her story known by weaving it into a robe, which she sent to Procne. Procne, in revenge, cut up her own son and served him to Tereus, and as soon as the king discovered it he pursued his wife, who fled to Philomela, whereupon the gods changed all three into birds: Tereus became the hawk, his wife the swallow, and Philomela the nightingale, which is still called Philomel ('lover of song') by the poets.

**Swedish Nightingale, The.** *See under* SWEDISH.

**Nightmare.** A sensation in sleep as if something heavy were sitting on one's chest, formerly supposed to be caused by a monster who actually did this. It was not infrequently called the 'night hag' or the 'riding of the witch'. The second part of the word is Old English *mare* (Old Norse *mara*), an INCUBUS, and it appears in the French *cauchemar*, 'the fiend that tramples'. The word now usually denotes a frightening dream, a night terror.

**Nightmare of Europe, The.** NAPOLEON BONAPARTE was so called.

**Nihil** (Latin, 'nothing').

**Nihilism.** The name given to an essentially philosophical and literary movement in Russia that questioned and protested against conventional and established values. The term was popularized by Ivan Turgenev's novel *Fathers and Sons* (1862) and was subsequently confused with a kind of revolutionary anarchism. Although nihilism proper was basically non-political, it strengthened revolutionary trends. The term was not new, and had long been applied to negative systems of philosophy.

**Nihil obstat.** The words by which a Roman Catholic censor of books (*Censor Librorum*) declares that he has found nothing contrary to faith or good morals in the book in question. The full Latin phrase is *nihil obstat quominus imprimatur*, 'nothing hinders it from being printed'.

The IMPRIMATUR is granted by the bishop or his delegate. *See also* INDEX.

**Nike** (Greek, 'victory'). The Greek winged goddess of victory, according to Hesiod, the daughter of Pallas and STYX. A US Army ground-to-air missile for use against high-flying attacking aircraft was also named from this goddess.

**Nil desperandum** (Latin). Never say die or never give up in despair; a tag from Horace (*Odes*, Bk I, vii (1st century BC)):

> Nil desperandum Teucro duce et auspice Teucro.
> (No need to despair with Teucer as your leader and Teucer to protect you.)

A modern jocular adaptation of this is *Nil carborundum illegitimi* or simply *Nil carborundum*, mock Latin for 'Don't let the bastards grind you down'.

**Nile.** The Egyptians used to say that the rising of the Nile was caused by the tears of ISIS. The feast of Isis was celebrated at the anniversary of the death of OSIRIS, when Isis was supposed to mourn for her husband.

**Hero of the Nile, The.** *See under* HERO.

**Nimbus** (Latin, 'cloud'). In Christian art a HALO of light placed round the head of an eminent personage. There are three forms:

(1) VESICA PISCIS, or fish form, used in representations of Christ and occasionally of the Virgin MARY, extending round the whole figure; *see also* ICHTHYS

(2) a circular halo

(3) radiated like a star or sun

The enrichments are:

(1) Christ: a cross
(2) Mary: a circlet of stars
(3) angels: a circlet of small rays, and an outer circle of quatrefoils
(4) saints and martyrs: the same as for angels but with the name often inscribed round the circumference
(5) God: the rays diverge in a triangular direction

Nimbi of a square form signify that the persons so represented were living when they were painted.

The nimbus was used by heathen nations long before painters introduced it into sacred pictures of saints, the TRINITY and the Virgin Mary. PROSERPINA was represented with a nimbus, and the Roman emperors were also decorated in the same manner because they were *divi* (gods). *See also* AUREOLE.

**Niminy-piminy.** Affectedly refined. Lady Emily, in General Burgoyne's *The Heiress* (III, ii (1786)), tells Miss Alscrip to stand before a glass and keep pronouncing *nimini-pimini*: 'The lips cannot fail to take the right plie.' A similar concept is used by Dickens in *Little Dorrit* (Bk II, ii (1855–7)), where Mrs General tells Amy Dorrit:

> Father is rather vulgar, my dear. The word Papa, besides, gives a pretty form to the lips. Papa, potatoes, poultry, prunes, and prism, are all very good words for the lips: especially prunes and prism.

**Nimrod.** Any daring or outstanding hunter, from the 'mighty hunter before the Lord' (Genesis 10:9), which the TARGUM says means a 'sinful hunting of the sons of men'. Alexander Pope says of him, he was 'a mighty hunter, and his prey was man' (*Windsor Forest* (1713)), and Milton also interprets the phrase thus (*Paradise Lost*, xii (1667)).

The legend is that the tomb of Nimrod still exists in Damascus, and that no dew ever falls upon it, even though all its surroundings are saturated.

Nimrod was the pseudonym of Major Charles Apperley (1779–1843), a devotee of hunting and contributor to the *Sporting Magazine*. His best known works are *The Life of John Mytton Esq*, *The Chase, the Turf, and the Road* and the *Life of a Sportsman*.

**Nine.** Nine, FIVE and THREE are mystical numbers: the DIAPASON, *diapente* and *diatrion* of the Greeks. Nine consists of a trinity of trinities. According to PYTHAGORAS, man is a full chord, or eight notes, and deity comes next. Three, being the TRINITY, represents a perfect unity. Twice three is the perfect dual, and three times three is the perfect plural. This explains why nine is a mystical number.

From ancient times the number nine has been held of particular significance. There are nine orders of ANGELS. DEUCALION's ark was tossed about for nine days when it stranded on the top of Mount PARNASSUS. There were nine MUSES, nine Gallicenae or virgin priestesses of the ancient Gallic ORACLE, and Lars Porsena swore by nine gods. NIOBE'S children lay in their blood for nine days before they were buried, and the HYDRA had nine heads. At the Lemuria, held by the Romans on 9, 11 and 13 May, people who were haunted threw black beans over their heads, pronouncing nine the words 'Avaunt, ye spectres, from this house!' nine times, and the EXORCISM was complete.

There were nine rivers of hell, or, according to some accounts, the STYX encompassed the infernal regions in nine circles, and Milton makes the gates of hell 'thrice three-fold', 'three folds were brass, three iron, three of adamantine rock'. They had nine folds, nine plates and nine linings (*Paradise Lost*, ii (1667)). *See also* DANTE AND BEATRICE.

When he was kicked from OLYMPUS, VULCAN was nine days falling to the island of LEMNOS, and when the fallen angels were cast out of heaven, Milton says 'Nine days they fell' (*Paradise Lost*, vi (1667)).

In the early PTOLEMAIC SYSTEM of astronomy, before the PRIMUM MOBILE was added, there were nine SPHERES. Hence Milton, in the 'Arcades' (*c*.1630–3), speaks of

> The celestial sirens' harmony,
> That sit upon the nine enfolded spheres.

In Scandinavian mythology there were nine earths, HEL being the goddess of the ninth. There were nine worlds in NIFLHEIM, and ODIN's ring dropped eight other rings every ninth night.

In folklore nine appears frequently. The ABRACADABRA was worn for nine days, and then flung into a river. In order to see fairies, one is directed to put 'nine grains of wheat on a four-leaved clover'. Nine knots are made in black wool as a charm for a sprained ankle. It used to be said that if a servant found nine green peas in a peascod, she should lay them on the lintel of the kitchen door, and the first man to enter would be her cavalier. To see nine MAGPIES is most unlucky, a cat has nine lives, and the nine of diamonds in a pack of cards is known as the CURSE OF SCOTLAND.

The weird sisters in Shakespeare's *Macbeth* (I, iii (1605)) sang as they danced around the cauldron: 'Thrice to thine, and thrice to mine, and thrice again to make up nine', and then declared 'the charm wound up'. A toast of 'Three-times-three' is drunk to those most highly honoured.

Leases are sometimes granted for 999 years, i.e. three times three-three-three. Many run for 99 years, the dual of a trinity of trinities. In HERALDRY there are nine marks of cadency and nine different crowns recognized. *See also* CAT-O'-NINE-TAILS; POSSESSION IS NINE POINTS OF THE LAW; NINE WORTHIES.

**Nine days' queen.** Lady Jane GREY (1537–54). She was proclaimed queen at the age of 15 in London on 10 July 1553 and succeeded by BLOODY MARY nine days later.

**Nine days' wonder.** Something that causes a great sensation for a few days, and then passes into the LIMBO of things forgotten. An old proverb is, 'A wonder lasts nine days, and then the puppy's eyes are open,' alluding to dogs, which like cats, are born blind. As much as to say, the eyes of the public are blind in astonishment for the space of nine days, but then their eyes become fully open, and they see too much to wonder any longer.

> *King Edward*: You'd think it strange if I should marry her ...
> *Gloucester*: That would be ten days' wonder, at the least.
> *Clarence*: That's a day longer than a wonder lasts.
> SHAKESPEARE: *Henry VI, Pt III*, III, ii (1590)

**Nine first Fridays, The.** In the ROMAN CATHOLIC CHURCH, the special observance of the first Friday in each of nine consecutive months, marked by receiving the EUCHARIST. The practice derives from St Margaret Mary Alacoque (1647–90), who held that Christ told her that special grace would be granted to those fulfilling this observance. *See also* SACRED HEART.

**Nine men's morris.** An ancient game (similar to draughts) once popular with shepherds and still found in East Anglia. It is played either on a board or on flat greensward. Two players have each nine pieces or 'men' which they place down alternately on the spots (*see* diagram), and the aim of either player is to secure a row of three men on any line on the board, and to prevent his opponent achieving this by putting one of his own men on a line that looks like being completed.

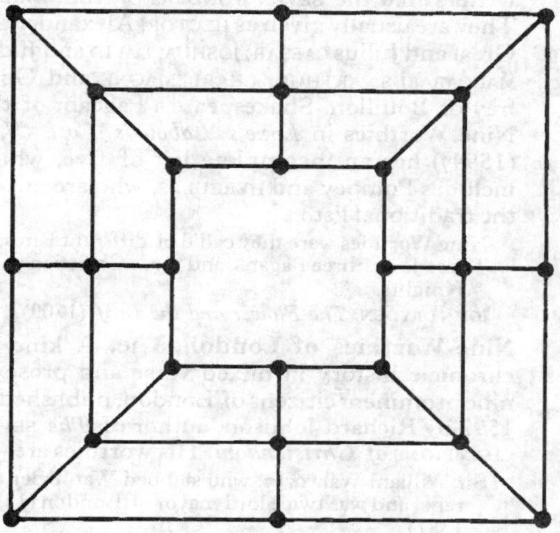

Joseph Strutt, in his *Sports and Pastimes of the People of England* (1801), writes: 'The rustics, when they have not materials at hand to make a table, cut the lines in the same form upon the ground, and make a small hole for every dot.'

> The fold stands empty in the drowned field,
> And crows are fatted with the murrion flock;
> The nine men's morris is fill'd up with mud.
> SHAKESPEARE: *A Midsummer Night's Dream*, II, i (1595)

*See also* MORRIS DANCE.

**Nine tailors make a man.** An old expression of contempt at the expense of tailors, implying such physical feebleness that it would take nine of them to make a man of good physique, the occupation not being conducive to sound physical development. It has been suggested that 'tailor' is a facetious adaptation of 'teller', a teller being a stroke on the funeral bell, three being given for a child, six for a woman and nine for a man.

The number mentioned is sometimes only three:

> Some foolish knave, I thinke, at first began
> The slander that three taylors are one man.
> JOHN TAYLOR: *Workes*, iii, 73 (1630)

**Nineteenth hole, The.** The bar at a golf club, reached after completing a standard round of 18 holes. One can here 'sink' a drink as one sinks the ball in each hole of the course.

**Nine times out of ten.** Far more often than not.

**Nine-to-five job.** A standard working day of eight hours, from 9 am to 5 pm.

**Nine Worthies, The.** Nine heroes: three from the Bible, three from the classics and three from romance, or three pagans, three Jews and three Christians, who were bracketed together by writers like the SEVEN WONDERS OF THE WORLD. They are usually given as HECTOR, Alexander the Great and Julius CAESAR; JOSHUA, DAVID and Judas MACCABAEUS; ARTHUR, CHARLEMAGNE and Godfrey of Bouillon. Shakespeare's Pageant of the Nine Worthies in *Love's Labour's Lost* (V, ii (1594)) has an incomplete list of five, which includes Pompey and HERCULES, who are not on the traditional list.

> Nine Worthies were they call'd of diff'rent Rites,
> Three Jews, three Pagans, and three Christian Knights.
>
> JOHN DRYDEN: *The Flower and the Leaf* (1700)

**Nine Worthies of London, The.** A kind of chronicle history in mixed verse and prose of nine prominent citizens of London, published in 1592 by Richard Johnson, author of *The* SEVEN CHAMPIONS *of Christendom*. His worthies are:

- Sir William Walworth, who stabbed Wat Tyler the rebel and was twice lord mayor of London (1374, 1381)
- Sir Henry Pritchard, who, in 1357, feasted Edward III and 5000 followers, Edward, the Black Prince, John, king of France, the king of Cyprus and David, king of Scotland
- Sir William Sevenoke, who fought with the Dauphin of France, was lord mayor in 1418 and who endowed a grammar school
- Sir Thomas White, a merchant taylor, who was lord mayor in 1553, founder of St John's College, Oxford, and a founder of Merchant Taylors' School
- Sir John Bonham, entrusted with a valuable cargo for the Danish market and made commander of an army raised to stop the progress of the army of Suleiman the Magnificent
- Christopher Croker, famous at the siege of Bordeaux and companion of the Black Prince, when he helped Don Pedro to the throne of Castile
- Sir John Hawkwood (d.1394), famous soldier and commander of the WHITE COMPANY in Italy, who is known in Italian history as Giovanni Acuto, the latter a corruption of his surname
- Sir Hugh Calveley (d.1393), soldier and commander of free companies; he fought under the Black Prince against the French and became governor of the Channel Islands and famous for ridding Poland of a monstrous bear
- Sir Henry Maleverer, generally called Henry of Cornhill, who lived in the reign of Henry IV; he was a crusader and became the guardian of 'Jacob's Well'

The above are essentially noted for their military rather than their civic achievements.

**As right as ninepence.** *See under* AS.

**Cat has nine lives, A.** *See under* CAT.

**Dressed up to the nines.** *See under* DRESSED.

**Naughty Nineties, The.** *See under* NAUGHTY.

**Possession is nine points of the law.** *See under* POSSESSION.

**Talk nineteen to the dozen, To.** *See under* TALK.

**Ninus.** The son of Belus and husband of SEMIRAMIS, and the reputed builder of Nineveh. It is at his tomb that the lovers meet in the PYRAMUS and Thisbe travesty:

> *Pyramus*: Wilt thou at Ninny's tomb meet me straightway?
> *Thisbe*: 'Tide life, 'tide death, I come without delay.
>
> SHAKESPEARE: *A Midsummer Night's Dream*, V, i (1595)

**Niobe.** The personification of maternal sorrow. According to Greek legend, Niobe, the daughter of TANTALUS and wife of AMPHION, king of Thebes, was the mother of 14 children, and taunted LATONA because she had only two, APOLLO and DIANA. Latona commanded her children to avenge the insult, and in consequence they destroyed Niobe's sons and daughters. Niobe, inconsolable, wept herself to death, and was changed into a stone, from which ran water, 'Like Niobe, all tears' (Shakespeare, *Hamlet*, I, ii (1600)).

**Niord, Niordhr** or **Njorthr.** A Scandinavian god, the protector of wealth and ships, who dwelt at Noatun by the seashore. His wife, Skadi, lived in the mountains, for the gulls disturbed her sleep. *See also* CUP OF VOWS; NERTHUS.

**Nip. Nip and tuck.** A NECK AND NECK race; a close fight. The phrase may have come from fencing, in which a nip is a light touch, and a tuck (from Italian *tocco*, 'blow'), a heavier contact.

**Nip in the bud, To.** To destroy something before it has had time to develop; to stop something in its early stages, as a bud is nipped by frost or pests, thus preventing further growth.

**Nip of whisky, A.** Short for nipperkin. This was a small measure for wine and beer, containing about half a pint (about 285ml), or a little under.

The traditional Devon and Cornish song 'The Barley Mow' starts with drinking the health out of the 'jolly brown bowl', and at each chorus increases the size of the receptacle until in the sixteenth there is a cumulative listing:

> We'll drink it out of the ocean, my boys,
> Here's a health to the barley mow!
> The ocean, the river, the well, the pipe, the hogshead, the half-hogshead, the anker, the halfanker, the gallon, the half-gallon, the pottle, the quart, the pint, the half pint, the quarter pint, the nipperkin and the jolly brown bowl!

**Nipper.** Slang for a small boy, so called because he is 'nippy', or swift and agile.

**Nippon.** The Japanese name for Japan, from *nichi*, 'sun', and *hon*, 'origin'. Hence the LAND OF THE RISING SUN.

**Nirvana** (Sanskrit, 'blowing out', 'extinction'). In BUDDHISM the cessation of individual existence, the attainment of a calm, sinless state of mind, which is achieved by the extinction of passion, a state that can be attained during life.

**Nisi** (Latin, 'unless'). In law, a 'rule nisi' is a rule, unless cause be shown to the contrary.

**Nisi prius** (Latin, 'unless previously'). Originally a writ commanding a SHERIFF to empanel a jury that should be at the Court of Westminster on a certain day, unless the justices of assize have previously come to his county. The second Statute of Westminster (1285) instituted judges of *nisi prius*, who were appointed to travel through the shires three times a year to hear civil causes. A trial at *nisi prius* was later a trial by jury in a civil cause before a single judge.

**Decree nisi.** *See under* DECREE.

**Rule nisi.** *See under* RULE.

**Nisroch.** The Assyrian god in whose temple SENNACHERIB was worshipping when he was slain (2 Kings 19:37). Nothing is known of this god, but the name is probably a corruption of Asur or a by-form of Asuraku. *See also* ASSHUR.

**Nissen hut.** A type of semi-cylindrical corrugated-iron hut, named after its inventor, Colonel P.N. Nissen (1831–1930). *See also* QUONSET HUT.

**Nisus and Euryalus.** An example of proverbial friendship, comparable to that of PYLADES AND ORESTES. Nisus with a Trojan friend raided the camp of the Rutulians and slaughtered many of the enemy in their drunken sleep, but the youthful Euryalus was killed by Volscens. Nisus rushed to avenge his death and in slaying Volscens was himself killed (Virgil, *Aeneid*, ix (1st century BC)).

**Nivelles, St Gertrude of.** *See under* GERTRUDE.

**Nivôse** (Latin *nivosus*, 'snowy'). The fourth month of the FRENCH REVOLUTIONARY CALENDAR, corresponding to the period from 22 December to 20 January.

**Nix.** *See* NICKER. The word is also slang for 'nothing' (German *nichts*, 'nothing'). 'He won't work for nix' means he won't work without payment.

**Nizam** (Arabic, 'order'). The title of sovereignty of the ruler of the state of Hyderabad, India, from 1724 to 1948. The word is a contraction of Arabic *Nizam-al-mulk*, literally 'governor of the empire'.

**Njorthr.** *See* NIORD.

**NKVD.** *See* OGPU.

**No** (Japanese, 'talent'). A type of Japanese lyrical play, dating from the 14th century. They are characterized by music, dancing, chanting, elaborate costumes and religious themes, and arose as a form of propitiation to Shinto gods. *See also* SHINTOISM.

**No. No better than one should be, To be.** A phrase of disparagement, implying an immoral or amoral character.

> ... and exprest some wonder at his having strayed so far out of his way, and at meeting him, as she said, 'in the company of that wench, who she feared was no better than she should be'.
>
> HENRY FIELDING: *Joseph Andrews*, Bk II, ch xiii (1742)

**No can do.** I cannot do it.

**No day without a line.** A saying attributed to the Greek artist APELLES (*nulla dies sine linea*), who said he never passed a day without doing at least one line and to this steady industry owed his great success. The words were adopted by Anthony Trollope as his motto.

**No dice.** NOTHING DOING. An American expression.

**No fear.** Certainly not. The implication is that you need not fear an affirmative response.

**No holds barred.** Anything goes. An allusion to a wrestling match in which normal rules are set aside.

**No joy.** No luck; no success.

**No love lost between us, There is.** *See* THERE IS NO LOVE LOST BETWEEN US *under* LOVE.

**No man's land.** The name given to the area between hostile lines of entrenchments or to any space contested by both sides and belonging to neither. In the OPEN-FIELD SYSTEM, the name was used for odd scraps of land, also called 'Jack's land' or 'anyone's land'.

**No names, no pack drill.** The information will not be revealed. The allusion is to military punishment. Offenders may be sent on a forced march in full kit. But if the drill sergeant does not have the names of the miscreants, he is unable to impose this ordeal on them.

**No problem.** It's all right; That is easily done. A catchphrase of the late 20th century, often used as a stock response to 'Thank you'. There is usually no question of a problem existing in the first place.

**No skin off my nose.** Said of something that has no adverse effect on oneself. The allusion may be to a fight, in which one has scratched one's adversary while remaining unscathed oneself. An American variant is: 'No skin off my tail.'

**No such luck.** Unfortunately not, as: 'Did you manage to get a ticket?' 'No such luck.'

**No way.** It is impossible; I will not agree to it.

**No wonder.** It is not surprising; one might have guessed. An expression used when an explanation is suddenly apparent, as: 'No wonder he looked so pleased with himself.'

**Not to take no for an answer.** *See under* ANSWER.

**Noah.** The man chosen by God to build an ark when he planned the Flood. *See also* DELUGE; NOAH'S ARK.

**Noah's ark.** The ark, or ship, built by NOAH, in which he took not only his own family but a male and female pair of every animal at the time of the Flood sent by God (Genesis 5–10). After 40 days and 40 nights, the rain stopped, and the inhabitants of the ark were the only surviving living things. The ark came to rest on Mount Ararat, and Noah sent out birds to search for dry land. The dove eventually returned with an olive leaf, and Noah knew that the waters had subsided. He then released the animals and his children, who bred and repopulated the earth. Searches for remains of the ark on Mount Ararat or any neighbouring mountain have so far proved inconclusive, despite claimed sightings by Russian airmen and others.

Noah's Ark is also the name given by sailors to a white band of cloud spanning the sky like a rainbow and shaped something like the hull of a ship. If it appears to run from east to west, expect dry weather, if from north to south, expect wet. Noah's Ark is also used as a PUBLIC HOUSE SIGN.

**Noah's wife.** According to legend, she was unwilling to go into the ark, and the quarrel between the patriarch and his wife forms a prominent feature of 'Noah's Flood' in the Chester and Townley MYSTERY play.

**Nobby.** Smart, elegant or neat. The word is from 'nob', a slang term for one of the upper classes, a contraction of 'noble' or 'nobility'. Hence the nickname Nobby for someone called CLARK, a clerk being originally a learned or literate person, as the nobility (mostly) were.

**Noble.** A former English gold coin, from the superior quality of its gold. It was first minted by Edward III (1344), possibly in commemoration of the Battle of Sluys (1340). It was originally valued at 6s 8d and replaced by the royal or ROSE NOBLE in 1465.

**Noble, The.** Charles III of Navarre (1361–1425).

**Noble Duke of York, The.** The duke of nursery rhyme fame was George III's second son, Frederick Augustus (1763–1827).

> The noble Duke of York,
> He had ten thousand men;
> He marched 'em up to the top of the hill,
> And he marched 'em down again.

The rhyme was a derisive commentary on the duke's abortive operations against the French in Flanders (1794). He was young at the time, although some versions of the rhyme refer to 'the rare old duke' or 'the grand old duke'. Moreover, the land was flat, so the rhyme is hardly accurate. He was made Commander-in-Chief in 1798. *See also* DUKE OF YORK'S COLUMN.

**Noble Savage, The.** The idealized human prototype, inherently good in a state of nature before being corrupted by 'civilization'. The concept was developed by Jean-Jacques Rousseau in his novel *Émile* (1762), a simple romance about a child reared apart from other children as an experiment. Other examples in life and literature include Huckleberry FINN and the WILD CHILD in his various manifestations. The Tahitian natives encountered by the crew of the *Bounty* were also of this type (*see* MUTINY ON THE BOUNTY).

**Noble science, The.** An old epithet for fencing or boxing, sometimes called 'The Noble Art of Self-Defence'.

**Noble Yachtsman, The.** A nickname given to the 7th Earl of CARDIGAN, during the Crimean War (1854–6), who for some weeks lived aboard his yacht in Balaclava harbour, thus escaping the hardships ashore.

**Rose noble.** *See under* ROSE.

**Noblesse oblige** (French, 'nobility obliges'). Noble birth imposes the obligation of high-minded principles and noble actions. *Noblesse Oblige* (1956), edited by Nancy Mitford, and subtitled 'An enquiry into the identifiable characteristics of the English aristocracy', gives an entertaining and revealing insight into the distinctive usage of English by the upper classes of the day.

**Noctes ambrosianae.** *See* AMBROSIAN NIGHTS.

**Nod. Nodding acquaintance, A.** A slight acquaintance; a person with whom one exchanges a nod for recognition when passing without seeking to become more closely acquainted. When used of one's acquaintance with literary works or the like, it means a superficial or slight knowledge.

**Nod is as good as a wink to a blind horse, A.** However obvious a hint or suggestion may be, it is useless if the other person cannot see it or will not take the hint.

> But you're a dutiful son, so I'll say no more about it – a nod's as good as a wink to a blind horse.
> CAPTAIN MARRYAT: *Peter Simple*, ch li (1834)

**Homer sometimes nods.** *See under* HOMER.

**Land of Nod, The.** *See under* LAND.

**On the nod.** On credit. To get a thing on the nod is to get it without paying for it at the time. The phrase is from the auction room where one signifies a bid by a mere nod of the head, the formalities of paying being attended to later. *See also* ON THE NEVER-NEVER *under* NEVER.

**Tom Noddy, A.** A very foolish or half-witted person, 'a noodle'. The marine birds called noddies are so silly that anyone can go up to them and knock them down with a stick. It seems more than likely that the word is connected with 'to nod', but it has been suggested that it was originally a pet form of NICODEMUS.

**Noddy.** The little pixie who lives in Toyland and drives a bright red motor car was the creation of Enid Blyton (1897–1968). His friends include Big Ears, a bearded gnome, and Mr Plod, a policeman. Noddy first appeared in *Little Noddy Goes to Toyland* (1949). He and his pals have subsequently been criticized by teachers, librarians and others as infantile stereotypes, and the stories in which they appear as undesirable and patronizing. They remain popular with their young readers, however.

**Noel.** In English (also written Nowell), a Christmas CAROL, or the shout of joy in a carol, and also, as in French, an alternative name for Christmas (as 'The first Nowell'). Noël (or Noel) is a traditional name given to a person born at Christmastime. Noël Coward (1899–1973) was born on 16 December and the writer Noel Streatfeild (1895–1986), famous for her children's books, on 24 December. The word ultimately comes from Latin *dies natalis*, 'birthday'.

**Nolens volens.** Whether willing or not. The phrase consists of two Latin participles meaning 'being unwilling (or) willing'. *See also* WILLY-NILLY.

**Noli me tangere** (Latin, 'touch me not'). The words Christ used to MARY MAGDALENE after his resurrection (John 20:17) and given as a name to a plant of the genus *Impatiens*. The seed vessels consist of one cell in five divisions, and when the seed is ripe, each of these, on being touched, suddenly folds itself into a spiral form and leaps from the stalk.

**Noll, Old.** *See under* OLD.

**Nolle prosequi** (Latin, 'to be unwilling to prosecute'). A petition from a plaintiff to stay a suit. *See also* NON PROS.

**Nolo. Nolo contendere** (Latin, 'I am unwilling to contend'). A plea in law by which the defendant, while not admitting guilt, declares he will not offer any defence. The plea is tantamount to that of 'guilty'.

**Nolo episcopari** (Latin, 'I am unwilling to be made a bishop'). The formal reply formerly returned to the royal offer of bishopric. Edward Chamberlayne says (*Present State of England* (1669)) that the person about to be elected modestly refused the office twice, but if he did so a third time his refusal was accepted.

> The landlord agreed with this view, and after taking the sense of the company, and duly rehearsing a small ceremony known in high ecclesiastical life as *nolo episcopari*, he consented to take on himself the chill dignity of going to Kench's.
>
> GEORGE ELIOT: *Silas Marner*, Pt I, ch vii (1861)

**Nom. Nom de guerre** (French, 'war name'). An assumed name. It was once customary for every entrant into the French army to assume a name, especially in the times of CHIVALRY, when knights were known by the device on their shields.

**Nom de plume.** Pseudo-French for 'pen name' or pseudonym, the name assumed by a writer or artist who does not choose to use his own name. Examples are Currer Bell (Charlotte Brontë) and Stendhal (Henri Beyle). *See also* CARAN D'ACHE; ELIOT, GEORGE; PHIZ; SAND, GEORGE; VOLTAIRE.

**Nominalism.** The SCHOOLMEN'S name for the theory of knowledge that denies the objective existence of abstract ideas. A form of Nominalism was proposed by Roscelin (Johannes Roscellinus) in the 11th century, but in its more pronounced form by WILLIAM OF OCCAM in the 14th century. Those who held the opposite view were called Realists. *See also* REALISM.

**Nominated Parliament.** *See* BAREBONES PARLIAMENT.

**Non.** The Latin negative, 'not', adopted in English and very widely employed as a prefix of negation, e.g. non-alcoholic, nonconformist, non-existent, non-residence, nonsense and so on.

**Non amo te, Sabidi.** *See* FELL, DOCTOR.

**Non Angli sed angeli.** *See under* ANGLES.

**Non assumpsit** (Latin, 'he has not undertaken'). The legal term for a plea denying a promise or undertaking.

**Non-com.** A non-commissioned officer in the army. The term is more usual in the USA.

**Non compos mentis** (Latin, 'not in control of one's mind'). Said of a mentally disturbed person or someone who has lost their memory and understanding because of accident or disease.

**Non-ego.** *See* EGO.

**Non est.** A contraction of Latin *non est inventus* ('not to be found'). These are the words that the sheriff writes on a writ when the defendant is not to be found in his bailiwick.

**Non mi ricordo** (Italian, 'I do not remember'). A roundabout way of saying: 'I don't choose to answer that question.' It was the usual answer of the Italian witnesses when under examination at the trial of Caroline of Brunswick, wife of George IV, in 1820.

**Non placet** (Latin, 'it is unpleasing'). The formula used, especially by the governing body of a university, for expressing a negative vote.

**Non pros.** A shortening of Latin *non prosequitur* ('he does not follow up'). Judgement *non pros* for a defendant was pronounced in an action when the plaintiff failed to take the necessary steps within the prescribed time.

**Non sequitur** (Latin, 'it does not follow'). A conclusion that does not follow from the premises stated; an inconsequent statement.

**Nonce.** The word derives from the phrase 'for the nonce', in origin a mistaken division of Middle English *for then anes*, 'for the once'. *See also* NICKNAME.

**Nonce word.** A word coined for a particular occasion, such as LIMEHOUSE or PUSEYITE.

**Nonconformists.** In England members of PROTESTANT bodies who do not conform to the doctrines of the CHURCH OF ENGLAND. They had their origins in the BROWNISTS and BAPTISTS of Elizabeth I's reign and among the 17th-century PURITANS and sectaries. After the RESTORATION and the subsequent Act of Uniformity of 1662, which enforced strict observance of the BOOK OF

COMMON PRAYER, some 2000 clergy were ejected and a lasting division resulted. The DISSENTERS or Nonconformists were subjected to the CLARENDON CODE until relief came with the Toleration Act of 1689 and later measures. Nonconformity received further recruits particularly with the advent of the METHODISTS.

**Nones.** In the ancient ROMAN CALENDAR the ninth (Latin *nonus*) day before IDES, and in the ROMAN CATHOLIC CHURCH, the office for the ninth hour after sunrise, i.e. between 12 noon and 3 pm.

**Nonjurors.** Those HIGH CHURCH clergy who refused to take the oath of allegiance to William and Mary after the Revolution of 1688 and who were deprived of their livings in 1690. Their numbers included Archbishop Sancroft and five other bishops. They maintained their own episcopal succession until the death of their last bishop in 1805. *See also* SEVEN BISHOPS.

**Nonresistance.** In the CHURCH OF ENGLAND passive obedience to royal commands was a natural corollary of the DIVINE RIGHT OF KINGS, but it acquired a particular importance after the RESTORATION, when TORY-minded clergy advocated nonresistance to combat NONCONFORMIST doctrines and WHIG policies. When James II (r.1685–8) tried to promote Roman Catholicism, many advocates of nonresistance abandoned their support of the monarchy and others became NONJURORS after the accession of William of Orange.

**Nonsense, Farrago of.** *See under* FARRAGO.

**Norfolk. Norfolk Broads.** *See* BROADS.

**Norfolk capon, A.** A RED HERRING.

**Jockey of Norfolk.** *See under* JOCKEY.

**N or M.** The answer given to the first question in the CHURCH OF ENGLAND Catechism. It means that here the person being catechized gives his or her name or names, Latin *nomen vel nomina*. The abbreviation for the plural *nomina* was the doubled initial (*see* LLD, for example), and when this was printed (as it was in old prayer books) in BLACK LETTER and close together, NN came to be taken for M.

In the same way the M and N in the marriage service ('I M take thee N to my wedded wife') merely indicate that the name is to be spoken in each case. However, the M and N in the publication of banns ('I publish the BANNS OF MARRIAGE between M of — and N of —') stand for *maritus*, 'bridegroom', and *nupta*, 'bride'.

**Norma.** In Bellini's opera of this name (1831), a druid priestess seduced by a Roman soldier. When he seeks to marry another priestess she considers murdering her children, then the other woman, but finally sacrifices herself. Her most memorable aria is 'Casta diva' ('Chaste goddess'), in which she prays to the moon for peace between Gaul and Rome.

**Norman French.** The dialect of Old French spoken in Normandy at the time of the CONQUEST and by the dominant class in England for some two centuries subsequently. Vestiges remain, particularly in legal terminology, and in other connections, such as 'Fitz' (*fils*, 'son') that precedes certain family surnames. The royal assent to bills passed by Parliament is still given in Norman French in the form *Le Roy* or *La Reine remercie ses bons sujets, accepte leur benevolence, et ainsi le veult* ('The king or queen thanks his or her subjects, accepts their benevolence, and also their wishes') and so on.

**Norns, The.** The FATES, dispensers of destiny in Norse mythology. They lived at the foot of the ash tree YGGDRASIL, which they watered daily from the fountain called Urd. The sisters eventually became three in number in imitation of the three Fates of classical legend.

**Norroy** (i.e. north *roy* or king). The third King of Arms (*see* HERALD) is so called, because his jurisdiction is on the north side of the River Trent. That to the south is exercised by CLARENCEUX KING OF ARMS. In 1943 the office of ULSTER KING OF ARMS was united with that of Norroy.

**North.** There was an old belief that only evil-doers should be buried on the north side of a churchyard, which probably arose from the lack of sun on this side. The east was God's side, where his throne is set, the west was man's side, the GALILEE of the Gentiles, the south was the side of the 'spirits made just', where the sun shines in his strength, and the north was the Devil's side. *See also* DEVIL'S DOOR.

**North Briton.** A periodical founded by John Wilkes in 1762 to air his animosity against Lord Bute and the Scottish nation. 'Number 45' is the edition (23 April 1763) in which the King's Speech referring to the Treaty of Paris of that year as 'honourable to my Crown and beneficial to my people' was held to be a lie. Wilkes escaped a charge of libel by pleading parliamentary privilege.

**Northeast Passage, The.** A hoped-for route to the east round the north extremity of Asia. It was first attempted by Sir Hugh Willoughby (d.*c*.1554) and Richard Chancellor (d.1556) in 1553–4, and its only practical result was the establishment of the Muscovy Company (1555). The passage was traversed by the Swedish explorer Nils Nordenskjöld in 1879.

**Northern Bear, The.** An old nickname for Russia. In political cartoons the former USSR was often depicted as a bear.

**Northern gate of the sun, The.** The sign of CANCER, or summer SOLSTICE, so called because it marks the northern tropic.

**Northern lights, The.** The AURORA BOREALIS.

**Northern Wagoner, The.** The genius presiding over the GREAT BEAR OR CHARLES'S WAIN, which contains seven large stars.

> By this the Northerne wagoner had set
> His seuenfold teme behind the stedfast starre [the pole star].
>
> EDMUND SPENSER: *The Faerie Queene*, I, ii (1590)

John Dryden calls the Great Bear the Northern Car, and similarly the crown in Ariadne has been called the Northern Crown. *See also* CYNOSURE.

**North Pole, The.** The pole was first reached on 6 April 1909 by the American explorer Robert Edwin Peary (1856–1920). In May 1933 it was claimed by the Russians, and four years later they established a polar station there under Professor Otto Schmidt.

**Northwest Frontier, The.** In particular, the northwest frontier of British India and the province of that name, now part of PAKISTAN. Because of the warlike nature of the local tribesmen and the Russian advance into central Asia, it gained a special importance from the later 19th century, and was a constant drain in men and money.

**Northwest Passage, The.** The name given to the long-sought route to the east round the north of the American continent, the search for which began with Sebastian Cabot's voyage of 1509. The search continued through the centuries by men such as Frobisher, Davis, Hudson, Baffin and Bylot, Cook and Vancouver. It was first navigated in 1903–6 by the Norwegian Roald Amundsen (1872–1928).

**Church of North America.** *See under* CHURCH.

**Christopher North.** A pseudonym of John Wilson. *See also* AMBROSIAN NIGHTS.

**Cock of the North.** *See under* COCK.

**Nero of the North.** *See under* NERO.

**Semiramis of the North, The.** *See under* SEMIRAMIS.

**Northamptonshire Poet, The.** *See* PEASANT POET.

**Northumbria.** The Anglo-Saxon kingdom formed in the early 7th century, which included all England north of the Humber, and southwest and east Scotland to the Firth of Forth. For most of the 7th century it was the most powerful English kingdom, and its kings Edwin, Oswald and Oswy held the office of BRETWALDA. Its dominance was replaced by that of MERCIA. It was long noted as a centre of learning.

**Norton, Hogs.** *See under* HOG.

**Norway, The Fair Maid of.** *See under* FAIR.

**Norwich. Julian of Norwich.** *See under* JULIAN.

**St William of Norwich.** *See under* WILLIAM.

**Nose. Nose tax.** It is said that in the 9th century the Danes imposed a poll tax in Ireland and that this was called the 'Nose Tax', because those who neglected to pay were punished by having their noses slit.

**Nose trick.** If one splutters a drink through the nose when choking or laughing one is said to 'do the nose trick'.

**Nosey.** Very inquisitive; overfond of poking one's nose into the business of others. One who does this is a Nosey Parker, a name popularly said to allude to Matthew Parker, archbishop of Canterbury (1504–75), who was noted for the detailed articles of inquiry concerning ecclesiastical affairs generally and the conduct of the clergy, which he issued for the visitations of his province and diocese. However, the nickname is first recorded only in the early 20th century, so such a reference seems unlikely. The phrase may instead be an embroidery on 'nose-poker' as a term for a prier. The Duke of Wellington was called 'Old Nosey' by his troops from his strongly accentuated aquiline nose. The nickname was also given to Oliver Cromwell. *See also* COPPER NOSE.

**As plain as the nose on your face.** *See under* AS.

**Bite** or **snap off someone's nose, To.** *See under* BITE.

**Bleeding of the nose.** *See under* BLEED.

**Cleopatra's nose.** *See under* CLEOPATRA.

**Conqueror's nose.** *See under* CONQUEROR.

**Copper nose.** *See under* COPPER.

**Copper-nose Harry.** *See under* COPPER.

**Count noses, To.** *See under* COUNT.

**Cut off one's nose to spite one's face, To.** *See under* CUT.

**Dog's nose.** *See under* DOG.

**Follow one's nose, To.** *See under* FOLLOW.

**Get up someone's nose, To.** To annoy or irritate a person.

**Golden nose.** *See under* GOLDEN.

**Grecian nose.** *See under* GRECIAN.

**Keep one's nose clean, To.** To ensure that one does not get involved in dealings or practices of a dubious or shady character; to avoid any suspicion of malpractice.

**Keep one's nose to the grindstone, To.** To keep hard at work. Tools such as scythes and chisels were formerly constantly sharpened on a stone or with a grindstone.

**Lead someone by the nose, To.** *See under* LEAD.

**Look down one's nose, To.** *See under* LOOK.

**No skin off my nose.** *See under* NO.

**Old Nosey.** *See under* OLD.

**One on the nose.** *See under* ONE.

**On the nose.** An American expression meaning exactly on time. It originated in the broadcasting studio, where the producer, when signalling to the performers, puts his finger on his nose when the programme is running to the scheduled time.

**Parson's nose.** *See under* PARSON.

**Pay through the nose, To.** *See under* PAY.

**Poke one's nose in, To.** *See under* POKE.

**Pope's nose, The.** *See under* POPE.

**Powder one's nose, To.** *See under* POWDER.

**Put someone's nose out of joint, To.** To supplant a person in another's good grace; to upset their plans; to humiliate or thwart someone.

**Roman nose.** *See under* ROMAN.

**Rub noses.** *See under* RUB.

**Rub someone's nose in it, To.** *See under* RUB.

**See no further than the end of one's nose, To.** *See under* SEE.

**Turn up one's nose, To.** *See under* TURN.

**Under one's very nose.** *See under* UNDER.

**With one's nose in the air.** *See under* WITH.

**Nostradamus.** The name assumed by Michel de Nostre-Dame, French physician and astrologer (1503–66) who published an annual 'Almanack' as well as the famous *Les Centuries* (1555), which were condemned by the pope in 1781. His controversial prophecies were couched in very ambiguous language.

**Nostrils, The Devil's.** *See under* DEVIL.

**Notables, The Assembly of.** *See under* ASSEMBLY.

**Notarikon** (Greek, from Latin *notarius*, 'shorthand writer'). A cabalistic word denoting the old Jewish art of using each letter in a word to form another word, or the initials of the words in a sentence similarly, as the word CABAL itself was fabled to have been from Clifford, Ashley, Buckingham, Arlington and Lauderdale, and as the term ICHTHYS was applied to the Saviour. *See also* AEIOU; CLIO; HIP! HIP! HURRAH!; LIMP; SMECTYMNUUS.

**Notation, Binary.** *See under* BINARY.

**Note. Note of hand, A.** A promise to pay made in writing and duly signed.

**Notes and Queries.** A periodical, known to its regular readers as 'N and Q', founded in 1849 as a medium in which academics of all kinds could exchange information with one another. Until 1923 its motto was 'When found, make a note of', Captain Cuttle's dictum in Dickens's *Dombey and Son* (1847).

> Letters and Folk-lore, Art, the Play;
> Whate'er, in short, men think or say,
> We make our theme—we make our own,
> In 'N and Q'.
>
> AUSTIN DOBSON: 'On "Notes and Queries"' (1882)

**Notes of the church.** The four characteristic marks of the church, i.e. one, holy, catholic and apostolic, as set forth in the NICENE CREED. These 'notes' were used by Roman Catholic theologians and others, and by the Tractarians (*see* OXFORD MOVEMENT) to demonstrate their claims.

**Compare notes, To.** *See under* COMPARE.

**Cover note.** *See under* COVER.

**Grace notes.** *See under* GRACE.

**Leading note.** *See under* LEAD.

**Strike the right note, To.** *See under* STRIKE.

**Treasury notes.** *See under* TREASURY.

**Nothing. Nothing doing.** What is requested or hoped for will not happen; I am not interested in your offer.

**Nothing if not.** At the very least, as: 'He's nothing if not enterprising.'

**Nothing like leather.** The story is that a town in danger of a siege called together a council of the chief inhabitants to know what defence they recommended. A mason suggested a strong wall, a shipbuilder advised WOODEN WALLS, and when others had spoken, a currier arose and said: 'There's nothing like leather.' Another version is: 'Nothing like leather to administer a thrashing.'

**Nothing loath.** Quite willing.

**Nothing short of.** Real or true, as: 'The picnic was nothing short of disaster.'

**Nothing to write home about.** A matter of no great interest.

**Nothing venture, nothing win.** An old proverb: if you don't take a chance, you can't expect to gain anything.

**Come to nothing, To.** *See under* COME.

**Free, gratis and for nothing.** *See under* FREE.

**Have nothing on, To.** To be naked; to have no engagements.

**Have nothing to do with, To.** To avoid; to have no connection with.

**Make nothing of, To.** To fail to understand; to make light of.

**Mere nothings.** *See under* MERE.

**Neck or nothing.** *See under* NECK.

**Next to nothing.** *See under* NEXT.

**Say nothing of, To.** *See under* SAY.

**Stop at nothing, To.** *See under* STOP.

**That's nothing to do with you.** It's none of your business; it is not your concern.

**There's nothing for it but to...** There's no alternative; there is only one thing that can be done.

**There's nothing** or **very little in it.** There is no or very little difference or interval.

**There's nothing to it.** It's easy.

**Think nothing of, To.** *See under* THINK.

**Notice, To sit up and take.** *See under* SIT.

**Nought.** *See under* NAUGHT.

**Nouns. Nouns of assemblage.** Long custom and technical usage have ascribed certain words to assemblages of animals, persons or things. Some of the most common are:

Animals:

antelopes: a herd
apes: a shrewdness
asses: a pace, a herd
badgers: a cete
bears: a sloth
bees: a swarm, a grist
birds: a flock, a flight, a congregation, a volery

bitterns: a sedge, a siege
boars: a sounder
bucks: a brace, a leash
buffaloes: a herd
cattle: a drove, a herd
cats: a clowder
chickens: a brood
choughs: a chattering
colts: a rag
coots: a covert
cranes: a herd, a sedge, a siege
crows: a murder
cubs: a litter
curlews: a herd
deer: a herd
dolphins: a school
doves: a flight
ducks: (in flight) a team, (on water) a paddling
elk: a gang
ferrets: a business
finches: a charm
fishes: a shoal, a draught, a haul, a run, a catch
flies: a swarm
foxes: a skulk
geese: (in flight) a skein; (on the ground) a gaggle
gnats: a swarm, a cloud
goats: a herd, a tribe
goldfinches: a charm
grouse: (a single brood) a covey; (several broods) a pack
gulls: a colony
hares: a down, a husk
hawks: a cast
hens: a brood
herons: a sedge, a siege
hounds: a pack, a mute
kangaroos: a troop
kittens: a kindle
larks: an exaltation
leopards: a leap
lions: a pride
mares: a stud
martens: a richesse
moles: a labour
monkeys: a troop
mules: a barren
nightingales: a watch
oxen: a yoke, a drove, a team, a herd
partridges: a covey
peacocks: a muster (in medieval times, a pride)
pheasants: a nye, a nide
plovers: a wing, a congregation
porpoises: a school
pups: a litter
quails: a bevy
rabbits: a nest
racehorses: a field, a string
rooks: a building, a clamour
seals: a herd, a pod
sheep: a flock
snipe: a walk, a wisp
starlings: a murmuration
swallows: a flight
swans: a herd, a bevy
swifts: a flock
swine: a sounder, a drift
teal: a spring
whales: a school, a gam, a pod
wolves: a pack, a rout, a herd
woodcock: a fall

People:
actors: a company, a cast, a troupe
angels: a host
baseball: a team, a nine
beaters: a squad
bishops: a bench
cricketers: an eleven
dancers: a troupe
footballers: (Association) an eleven or a squad; (Rugby) a fifteen or a squad
girls: a bevy
labourers: a gang
magistrates: a bench
minstrels: a troupe
musicians: a band, an orchestra, a group
police: a posse
rowers: an eight, a four, a pair
runners: a field
sailors: a crew
savages: a horde
servants: a staff
soldiers: a squadron, a troop, a battalion, a company, a platoon, a section, a squad, a detail, a party
worshippers: a congregation

Things:
aircraft: a squadron, a flight, a group, a wing
arrows: a sheaf
bells: a peal
bowls: a set
bread: a batch
cards: a pack, a deck
cars: a fleet
eggs: a clutch
flowers: a bunch, a bouquet, a nosegay
golf-clubs: a set
grapes: a cluster, a bunch
onions: a rope
pearls: a rope, a string
rags: a bundle
sails: a suit
ships: a fleet, a squadron, a flotilla
stars: a cluster, a constellation
steps: a flight
trees: a clump

**Nouns of multitude.** Dame Juliana Berners, in her *Booke of St Albans* (1486), says that the names of multitudes must not be used promiscuously in designating companies, and examples her remark thus:

> We say a congregacyon of people, a hoost of men, a felyshyppynge of yeomen, and a bevy of ladyes; we must speak of a herde of deer, swannys, cranys, or wrenys, a sege of herons or bytourys [bitterns], a muster of pecockes, a watche of nyghtyngales, a flyghte of doves, a claterynge of choughes, a pryde of lyons, a slewthe of beeres, a gagle of geys, a skulke of foxes, a sculle of frerys, a pontificalitye of prestys, and a superfluyte of nonnes.

She adds that a strict regard to these niceties better distinguishes 'gentylmen from ungentylmen', than regard to the rules of grammar, or even to the moral law. *See also* NOUNS OF ASSEMBLAGE.

**Nous** (Greek, 'mind', 'intellect'). A word adopted in English to denote 'intelligence', 'horse sense', 'understanding'.

'Nous' was the Platonic term for mind, or the first cause, and the system of divinity referred to above is that which springs from blind nature.

**Nous avons changé tout cela** (French, 'We have changed all that'). A facetious reproof to someone who lays down the law on everything and talks contemptuously of old customs, old authors, old artists and the like. The phrase is taken from MOLIÈRE's *Le Médecin malgré lui* (II, iv (1666)).

**Nouveaux riches** (French, 'the new rich'). A phrase with derogatory implications applied to those who have newly acquired considerable affluence and who often seek to use their money for social climbing. William Cobbett wrote of the 'damned aristocracy of money' in this connection and in his *Rural Rides* (30 October 1821) he describes 'a park' belonging to a Mr Montague with Dutch gardens and pseudo-Gothic dwelling and says: 'I do not know who this gentleman is. I suppose he is some honest person from the 'Change or its neighbourhood; and that these gothic arches are to denote the antiquity of his origin!'

**Nova Scotia.** *See* ACADIA.

**Novel. Novelist of Wessex** or **Dorset Novelist, The.** Thomas Hardy (1840–1928), the scenes of whose novels are set in this area. Hardy deliberately revived the historic name in his writings.

> It was in the chapters of *Far From the Madding Crowd*, as they appeared month by month in a popular magazine, that I first ventured to adopt the word 'Wessex' from the pages of early history, and give it a fictitious significance as the existing name of the district once included in that extinct kingdom ... Finding that the area of a single county did not afford a canvas large enough for this purpose, and that there were objections to an invented name, I disinterred the old one.
>
> THOMAS HARDY: *Far From the Madding Crowd*, Preface (1874)

**Dime novel.** *See under* DIME.
**Leatherstocking novels.** *See under* LEATHER.
**Waverley Novels.** *See under* WAVERLEY.

**Novella.** A diminutive from Latin *novus*, 'new'. A short story of the kind contained in Boccaccio's DECAMERON (1349–51) and immensely popular in the 16th and 17th centuries. Such stories were the forerunners of the long novel and also of the short story of more recent times.

**November** (Latin *novem*, 'nine'). The ninth month in the ancient ROMAN CALENDAR, when the year began in March, but now the eleventh. The old Dutch name was *Slaghtmaand*, 'slaughter month', the time when the beasts were slain and salted down for winter use. The Anglo-Saxon name was similar, as *Blōtmōnath*, literally 'blood month'. Another Saxon name was *Windmōnath*, 'wind month', when fishermen beached their boats and stopped fishing until the next spring. The equivalent in the FRENCH REVOLUTIONARY CALENDAR was BRUMAIRE ('mist month'), corresponding to the period from 23 October to 21 November.

> No sun – no moon!
> No morn – no noon –
> No dawn – no dusk – no proper time of day.
> No warmth, no cheerfulness, no healthful ease,
> No comfortable feel in any member –
> No shade, no shine, no butterflies, no bees,
> No fruits, no flowers, no leaves, no birds –
> November!
>
> THOMAS HOOD: 'No!' (1844)

**Novena** (Latin *novenus*, 'nine each'). In Roman Catholic devotions, a prayer for some special object or occasion extended over a period of nine days.

**Nowell.** *See* NOEL.

**Now you're talking.** What you are saying now is much more acceptable than what was said earlier.

**Noyades** (French, 'drownings'). During the REIGN OF TERROR in France (1793–4), the Revolutionary agent Jean-Baptiste Carrier (1756–94) drowned many of his prisoners in the Loire at Nantes by stowing them, bound, in boats and opening the cocks. NERO, at the suggestion of Anicetus, attempted to drown his mother in the same manner.

**Nugget, Welcome.** *See under* WELCOME.

**Nulla linea.** *See* NO DAY WITHOUT A LINE.

**Null and void.** No longer of binding force; having no further validity.

**Nullarbor Plain** (Latin *nulla arbor*, 'no tree'). The vast bare plain north of the Great Australian Bight, so named from its treeless character.

**Nulli secundus** (Latin, 'second to none'). The motto of the COLDSTREAM GUARDS, which regiment is hence sometimes spoken of as the Nulli Secundus Club.

**Numbers, numerals.** PYTHAGORAS looked on numbers as influential principles. In his system:

1 was Unity, and represented Deity, which has no parts
2 was Diversity, and therefore disorder, the principle of strife and all evil
3 was Perfect Harmony, or the union of unity and diversity
4 was Perfection, as the first square ($2 \times 2 = 4$)
5 was the prevailing number in Nature and Art
6 was Justice
7 was the CLIMACTERIC number in all diseases

With the ancient Romans, 2 was the most fatal of all the numbers. They dedicated the second month to PLUTO, and the second day of the month to the Manes.

In old ecclesiastical symbolism the numbers from 1 to 13 were held to denote the following:

1 The Unity of God
2 The HYPOSTATIC UNION of Christ, both God and man

3 The TRINITY
4 The number of the EVANGELISTS
5 The wounds of the Redeemer: two in the hands, two in the feet, one in the side
6 The creative week
7 The gifts of the HOLY GHOST and the seven times Christ spoke on the cross
8 The number of BEATITUDES (Matthew 5:3–11)
9 The nine orders of ANGELS
10 The number of the Commandments
11 The number of the APOSTLES who remained faithful
12 The original college
13 The final number after the conversion of PAUL

With one exception, the names of the English numerals, both cardinal and ordinal, up to a million are Anglo-Saxon. The one exception is second, which is French. The Anglo-Saxon word was 'other', as first, other, third and so on, but as this was ambiguous, the French *seconde* was early adopted. (*See* OTHER DAY *under* OTHER.) Million itself is from Latin *mille*, a thousand.

The primitive method of counting was by the fingers (*see also* DIGITS). Thus, in the Roman system of numeration, the first four were simply i, ii, iii, iiii. Five was the outline of the hand simplified into a v. The next four figures were the four combined, thus, vi, vii, viii, viiii, and ten was a double v, thus x. At a later period, iiii and viiii were expressed by one less than five (i – v) and one less than ten (i – x), while 19 was ten-plus-nine (x + ix) etc. *See also* ABSTRACT; ABUNDANT; AMICABLE; APOCALYPTIC; ARABIC NUMERALS; CYCLIC; DEFICIENT; PERFECT; PRIME.

**Number of the Beast, The.** 666, a mystical number of unknown meaning but referring to some man mentioned by St JOHN.

> Let him that hath understanding count the number of the beast: for it is the number of a man: and his number is Six hundred threescore and six.
> Revelation 13:18

One of the most plausible suggestions is that the number refers to Neron Caesar, which, when written in Hebrew characters with numerical values, gives 666, whereas NERO, without the final n, as in Latin, gives 616 (n = 50), the number given in many early manuscripts, according to Irenaeus.

Among the CABBALISTS every letter represented a number, and one's number was the sum of these equivalents to the letters in one's name. If, as is probable, Revelation was written in Hebrew, the number would suit Nero, Hadrian or Trajan, all persecutors. If in Greek, it would fit Caligula or Lateinos, i.e. the Roman Empire. But almost any name in any language can be twisted into this number, and it has been applied to many persons assumed to have been ANTICHRIST or Apostates, Diocletian, Evanthas, JULIAN THE APOSTATE, Luther, MOHAMMED, Paul V, Sylvester II, NAPOLEON BONAPARTE, Charles Bradlaugh, William II of Germany and several others, as well as to certain phrases supposed to be descriptive of 'the Man of Sin', as Vicar-General of God. The following are just two of the many examples in cabbalistic texts:

| | | | | | | | | | |
|---|---|---|---|---|---|---|---|---|---|
| M | a | o | m | e | t | i | s | | |
| 40 | 1 | 70 | 40 | 5 | 300 | 10 | 200 | = | 666 |
| L | a | t | e | i | n | o | s | | |
| 30 | 1 | 300 | 5 | 10 | 50 | 70 | 200 | = | 666 |

One suggestion is that St John chose the number 666 because it just fell short of the holy number 7 in every particular. It was straining at every point to get there, but never could. *See also* MYSTERIUM.

**Number one, two etc.** *See under* NUMBERS.

**Number phrases.** Below are some expressions with 'number' and a numeral.

*Number one*: (1) oneself; 'to look after number one' is to be selfish or to seek one's own interest; (2) in the Royal Navy, the first lieutenant of a ship, also known as 'Jimmy the One'; (3) a thing or person that is top-class or first-rate; (4) a bestselling record, CD, video etc when 'top of the pops'; (5) in young children's talk, urine, as: 'I want to do number one'; (6) (number ones) in the Royal Navy, No. 1 dress, a best dress uniform

*Number two*: (1) a person second in importance; a second in command; (2) a provincial town, especially one lacking a theatre; (3) in young children's talk, faeces, as: 'To do a number two' (*see also* NUMBER ONE)

*Number six*: (1) an American colloquialism for a household medicine, so called from its position on the pharmaceutical list of its inventor, Samuel Thomson; (2) a curl on the forehead in the shape of a figure 6; similar is a 'number six nose', also supposedly of this shape

*Number eight*: (1) in rugby football, the forward whose position is at the back of the scrum, which normally has three men in the front row, four in the second, and one man at the rear; (2) (number eights) in the Royal Navy, working dress

*Number nine*: in British army slang, a purgative pill, especially when prescribed as a panacea for minor ailments or dubious symptoms, so called from its listed position in the field hospital case

*Number ten*: No. 10, DOWNING STREET, London, the official residence of the prime minister

*Number eleven*: No. 11, DOWNING STREET, London, the official residence of the chancellor of the exchequer, next door to NUMBER TEN

**Abstract number.** *See under* ABSTRACT.

**Abundant numbers.** *See under* ABUNDANT.

**Amicable numbers.** *See under* AMICABLE.

**Apocalyptic number.** *See under* APOCALYPSE.

**Arabic numerals.** *See under* ARABIA.

**Back number, To be a.** *See under* BACK.

**Book of Numbers.** *See under* BOOK.

**Box number.** *See under* BOX.

**By numbers.** *See under* BY.

**Cardinal numbers.** *See under* CARDINAL.

**Concrete number.** *See* ABSTRACT NUMBER.

**Golden number.** *See under* GOLDEN.

**Have someone's number, To.** To understand them closely; to have an insight into their thoughts, actions and character.

**Have someone's number on it, To.** An expression used by members of the armed forces to refer to a bullet or other missile destined to hit a particular person, since it is supposedly marked by fate for their extinction.

**Luck in odd numbers.** *See under* LUCK.

**Mach number.** *See under* MACH.

**Medical number.** *See under* MEDICINE.

**My number's up.** I have been caught or am about to die. A soldier's phrase. In the American army a soldier who has just been killed or has died is said to have 'lost his mess number'. An older phrase in the Royal Navy was 'to lose the number of his mess'.

**Prime number.** *See under* PRIME.

**Nunawading Messiah.** James Cowley Morgan Fisher (*c.*1832–1915) of Nunawading, Victoria, Australia, was so called. The son of Gloucestershire immigrants, he ran away to sea at the age of 14 and settled at Nunawading in the mid-1850s. In the 1860s he succeeded his mother-in-law as head of the New Church of the Firstborn. In a law suit of 1871 he was accused of claiming to be the Messiah or the Christ and of practising polygamy, with three sisters as his wives. His following was small, estimated at about 100 in 1871, but was probably less. *See also* SOUTHCOTTIANS.

**Nunc dimittis.** The Song of SIMEON (Luke 2:29), 'Lord, now lettest thou thy servant depart in peace', so called from the opening words of the Latin version, *Nunc dimittis servum tuum, Domine*.

The Canticle is sung at evening prayer in the CHURCH OF ENGLAND, and has been anciently used at COMPLINE OR VESPERS throughout the church.

**Nuncheon.** Properly, 'the noontide draught', from Middle English *noneschench* (*none*, 'noon', and *schench*, 'cup', 'draught'). Hence, formerly, light refreshments between meals, otherwise lunch. The word luncheon has been affected by the older nuncheon. *See also* TIFFIN.

> So munch on, crunch on, take your nuncheon,
> Breakfast, supper, dinner, luncheon!
> ROBERT BROWNING: 'The Pied Piper of Hamelin' (1842)

**Nuremberg. Nuremberg laws.** The infamous NAZI laws promulgated in September 1935. Jews, and all those of Jewish extraction, were deprived of all rights of German citizenship, and regulations were made against those of partial Jewish ancestry. Marriage between Jew and 'German' was forbidden. Nuremberg (Nürnberg) was the centre of the annual Nazi Party convention.

**Nuremberg trials.** The trial of 23 NAZI leaders conducted by an Inter-Allied tribunal at Nuremberg after the Second World War (September 1945 to May 1946). Three were acquitted; Göring, Ribbentrop and nine others were condemned to death; and the remainder sentenced to various terms of imprisonment. Hitler, Himmler and Goebbels avoided retribution by committing suicide, as did Göring.

**Nurr and spell.** *See* KNURR.

**Nurse. Charge nurse.** *See under* CHARGE.

**Dry nurse.** *See under* DRY.

**Nursery nurse.** *See under* NURSERY.

**Wet nurse.** *See under* WET.

**Nursery.** A room set apart for the use of young children (Latin *nutrire*, 'to nourish'). Hence, a garden for rearing plants (tended by a nurseryman).

In horse-racing, nursery stakes are races for two-year-olds. Figuratively the word is used of any place of training or practising, as the nursery slopes for amateur skiers.

**Nursery cannons.** In billiards, a series of cannons played so that the balls move as little as possible.

**Nursery nurse.** A person, usually a woman, who has been trained to look after babies and young children.

**Nursery rhymes.** The traditional metrical jingles learned by children 'in the nursery' and frequently used in their games. They contain survivals of folklore, ancient superstitions, festival games, local customs and various references to history. Most of them are very old, but some are more recent, such as OLD MOTHER HUBBARD and the NOBLE DUKE OF YORK.

**Nut.** Slang for the head, perhaps from its shape. Also slang for a 'dude', a swell young man about town. In this sense it is sometimes spelled 'knut', and this form of the word was popularized by Arthur Wimperis' song 'I'm Gilbert, the Filbert, the Colonel of the Knuts', sung in the revue *The Passing Show* (1914) by Basil Hallam (1889–1916).

**Nut-brown Maid, The.** An English ballad probably dating from the late 15th century, first printed (*c.*1520) in Arnold's *Chronicle* at Antwerp. It tells how the 'Not-browne Mayd' was wooed and won by a knight who gave out that he was a banished man. After describing the hardships she would have to undergo if she married him, and finding her love true to the test, he revealed himself to be an earl's son, with large estates in Westmorland.

The ballad is given in PERCY'S RELIQUES (1765) and forms the basis of Matthew Prior's 'Henry and Emma' (1709).

> For in my mind, of all mankind
> I love but you alone.
> *The Nut-Brown Maid*, refrain

**Nutcase, A.** A crazy or foolish person.

**Nutcrackers, The.** *See under* REGIMENTAL AND DIVISIONAL NICKNAMES.

**Nuthouse, A.** A psychiatric institution.

**Nuts!** An expression of defiance or contempt; a statement of refusal or negation. A story of the Second World War tells how General McAuliffe, acting commander of the American 101st Airborne Division in the Ardennes at the time of the BATTLE OF THE BULGE (December 1944), when surrounded by enemy forces, was informed by the Germans that they would accept a surrender. His terse, one-word response to this proposal was 'Nuts!', a message that the Germans initially interpreted as meaning 'crazy'. Agence France Presse subsequently reported the incident, translating the General's retort more expansively but not altogether accurately as, *Vous n'êtes que de vieilles noix* ('You're just old fogeys').

**Nuts and bolts, The.** The practical details of a plan, operation, procedure or the like.

**Nuts on** or **dead nuts on, To be.** To be very keen on or fond of.

> My aunt is awful nuts on Marcus Aurelius; I beg your pardon, you don't know the phrase; my aunt makes Marcus Aurelius her Bible.
>
> WILLIAM BLACK: *A Princess of Thule*, ch xi (1873)

**Nutters' dance.** A dance still performed at Bacup, Lancashire, on Easter Saturday. The 'nutters', formally known as the Britannia Coconut Dancers, are eight men with blackened faces, clad in short white skirts, white plumed hats, black breeches and clogs, and with wooden 'nuts' like castanets fastened to their hands, waist and knees. The dance is performed to music and time is kept by clapping the nuts. The dance is led by a 'Whipper-In', who symbolically whips away the winter as they go.

**Do one's nut, To.** *See under* DO.

**Hard** or **tough nut to crack, A.** *See under* HARD.

**Here we go gathering nuts in May.** *See under* GATHER.

**Iliad in a nutshell, The.** *See under* ILIAD.

**Off one's nut.** *See under* OFF.

**Use a sledgehammer to crack a nut. To.** *See under* USE.

**Nutmeg State.** The nickname of CONNECTICUT, where WOODEN NUTMEGS were allegedly manufactured for export. *See also* UNITED STATES OF AMERICA.

**Nymphs** (Greek, 'young maidens'). In classical mythology, minor female divinities of nature, of woods, groves, springs, streams, rivers and other haunts. They were young and beautiful and kindly to mortals. They themselves were not immortal, but their life span was several thousand years. Particular kinds of nymphs were associated with the various provinces of nature. *See also* DRYADS; NAIADS; NEREIDS; OCEANIDS; OREADS. More generally a nymph is a poetic term for a beautiful young woman. Hamlet addresses Ophelia as 'nymph' at the end of his 'To be or not to be' speech (*Hamlet*, III, i (1601)).

# O

**O.** The fifteenth letter of our alphabet, the fourteenth of the ancient Roman and the sixteenth of the Phoenician and Semitic (in which it was called *ain*, 'eye').

**O'.** An Irish patronymic (Irish *ó*, 'grandson', 'descendant').

In phrases such as TAM-O'-SHANTER, five o'clock and CAT-O'-NINE-TAILS it stands for 'of', but in such phrases as 'He comes home late o' night', 'They go to church o' Sundays', it represents Middle English *on*.

**O tempora! O mores!** (Latin, 'O the times! O the manners!'). Alas, how the times have changed for the worse! Alas, how the morals of the people have degenerated! The tag is from Cicero's *In Catilinam* (i, 1 (1st century BC)).

**O Yes! O Yes! O Yes!** *See* OYEZ.

**As round as Giotto's O.** *See under* AS.

**Fifteen Os** or **Os of St Bridget, The.** *See under* FIFTEEN.

**Giotto's O.** *See under* GIOTTO.

**Seven Os** or **Great Os of Advent, The.** *See under* SEVEN.

**Oaf.** A variant of Old English *ælf* ('elf'). A foolish lout or dolt is so called from the notion that an idiot is a CHANGELING, a child left by the fairies in place of a stolen one.

**Oak.** In ancient times the oak was sacred to the god of thunder because these trees are said to be more likely to be struck by lightning than any other. The DRUIDS held the oak in great veneration, and the WOODEN WALLS of England depended upon it. About 3500 full-grown oaks or 900 acres of oak forest were used in selecting the timber for a large THREE-DECKER line-of-battle ship. The strength, hardness and durability of the timber, as well as the longevity of the tree, have given the oak a special significance to Englishmen, hence its name the Monarch of the Forest.

> As when, upon a trancèd summer-night,
> Those green-robed senators of mighty woods,
> Tall oaks, branch-charmèd by the earnest stars,
> Dream, and so dream all night without a stir.
>
> JOHN KEATS: 'Hyperion: A Fragment' (1820)

*See also* HEART OF OAK.

Among the famous oaks of Britain are:

Abbot's Oak, near Woburn Abbey: so called because the abbot of Woburn was hanged on one of its branches in 1537, by order of Henry VIII (r.1509–47)

Boscobel Oak: *see* OAK-APPLE DAY

Bull Oak, Wedgnock Park, near Warwick: growing at the time of the CONQUEST

Cowthorpe Oak, near Wetherby, Yorkshire: will hold 70 persons in its hollow and is said to be over 1600 years old

Ellerslie Oak, near Paisley, Renfrew: Sir William WALLACE and 300 of his men are said to have sheltered there

Fairlop Oak, Hainault Forest, Essex: before it was blown down in 1820 it was the site of an annual fair, held each July under its spreading branches; *see also* ROMANY NAMES OF TOWNS AND COUNTRIES *under* ROMANY

Hanging Tree, in Fort William, Inverness-shire: an oak believed to have been a 'joug tree' on which the local chief hanged wrong-doers; it was cut down in 1985 to make way for a new public library

Herne's Oak, Windsor Great Park: reputed to be haunted by the ghost of Herne the Hunter (*see* WILD HUNTSMAN), it is mentioned by Shakespeare in *The Merry Wives of Windsor* (1600) but was cut down in 1796; the present oak was planted in 1906 on its site

Honour Oak: a boundary oak at Whitchurch, Tavistock, Devon, marking the Tavistock limit for French prisoners on parole from Princetown prison in 1803–14, when England was at war with France, and also the place where money was left in exchange for food during the cholera epidemic of 1832

King Oak: *see* WILLIAM THE CONQUEROR'S OAK *below*

Major Oak, Edwinstowe, near Mansfield in Sherwood Forest: said to have been full-grown in the time of King John (r.1199–1216), the hollow of the trunk will hold 15 people (although new bark has diminished the opening); its girth is 37–38ft (11.3–11.6m), and the head covers a circumference of 240ft (73m); ROBIN HOOD is said to have hidden in it. Originally called the Queen Oak, its present name is said to honour Major Hayman Rooke, an 18th-century local antiquarian, who was particularly fond of it. In 1990 the tree was being drenched daily with thousands of gallons of water because of fears that in hot, dry weather it could be destroyed by fire or drought. In 1992 it was cloned in a test tube so that exact copies will be growing when it dies

Meavy Oak: standing in front of the lich gate of Meavy Church, near Yelverton, Devon, it is some 25ft (7.6m) in circumference, and in the hollow nine people are once reputed to have dined; according to tradition it dates back to Saxon times

Owen Glendower's Oak, Shelton, just west of Shrewsbury: in full growth in 1403, for in this tree

Owen Glendower witnessed the battle between Henry IV and Henry Percy; six or eight persons can stand in the hollow of its trunk, and its girth is 40ft 3in (12.3m)

Parliament Oak, Clipston, in Sherwood Forest: the tree under which Edward I held a Parliament in 1282. The king was hunting when a messenger announced the Welsh were in revolt under Llewelyn ap Gruffydd. He hastily convened his nobles under the oak, and it was resolved to march against the Welsh at once. The tree no longer exists

Queen's Oak, Huntingfield, Suffolk: so named because near this tree Queen Elizabeth I shot a buck

Reformation Oak, on Mousehold Heath, northeast of Norwich: the rebel Robert Kett (d.1549) held his court in 1549, and when the rebellion was stamped out nine of the ringleaders were hanged on this tree

ROBIN HOOD'S LARDER

Royal Oak: *see* OAK-APPLE DAY

Sir Philip Sidney's Oak, near Penshurst, Kent: planted at his birth in 1554 and commemorated by Ben Jonson and Edmund Waller

Swilcar Oak, in Needwood Forest, Staffordshire: between 600 and 700 years old

Watch Oak, Windsor Great Park: said to be 800 years old and so called because the Duke of Cumberland (third son of George II, who defeated the Jacobites at Culloden in 1745) was said to have stationed a lookout in its branches during target practices to signal the accuracy of the cannon shots

William the Conqueror's Oak or the King Oak, Windsor Great Park: said to have afforded the king shelter; it has a girth of 38ft (11.5m)

**Oak-apple Day** or **Royal Oak Day.** This falls on 29 May, the birthday of Charles II (1630–85) and the day on which he entered London at the RESTORATION. It was commanded by Act of Parliament in 1664 to be observed as a day of thanksgiving. A special service (expunged in 1859) was inserted in the BOOK OF COMMON-PRAYER, and people wore sprigs of oak with gilded oak-apples on that day. It commemorates Charles II's concealment with Major Careless in the 'Royal Oak' at Boscobel, near Shifnal, Shropshire, after his defeat at Worcester (3 September 1651). *See also* CHARLES AND THE OAK.

**Oak before the ash.** The old proverbial forecast, referring to whichever is in leaf first, says:

If the oak's before the ash
Then you'll only get a splash;
If the ash precedes the oak,
Then you may expect a soak.

**Oak boys.** Bands of PROTESTANT agrarian rioters in Ulster in the 1760s, so called from the oak sprays they wore in their hats. The main grievance was against the system of TITHES. *See also* STEELBOYS.

**Charles and the oak.** *See under* CHARLES.

**Heart of Oak.** *See under* HEART.

**King's Oak, The.** *See under* KING.

**Sport one's oak, To.** *See under* SPORT.

**Oakley, Annie.** An expert American markswoman (1860–1926), who in BUFFALO BILL's Wild West Show, using a playing card as a target, centred a shot in each of the pips. From this performance, and the resemblance of the card to a punched ticket, springs the American use of the name 'Annie Oakley' to mean a complimentary ticket to a show, a meal ticket or a pass on a railway.

**Oaks, The.** The 'Ladies' Race', one of the CLASSIC RACES of the TURF. It is for three-year-old fillies, and is run at Epsom the day before the DERBY. It was instituted in 1779 and so called from an estate of the Earl of Derby near Epsom named The Oaks.

**Oakum, Picking.** *See under* PICK.

**Oannes.** A Babylonian god having a fish's body and a human head and feet. In the daytime he lived with men to instruct them in the arts and sciences, but at night he returned to the depths of the Persian Gulf. His name is probably a Greek form of Akkadian *ummamu*, 'master'.

**Oar. Feather an oar, To.** *See under* FEATHER.

**Put** or **stick one's oar in, To.** To interfere; to interrupt.

**Rest on one's oars, To.** *See under* REST.

**Toss the oars, To.** *See under* TOSS.

**Oasis.** A fertile spot in the middle of desert country where water and vegetation are to be found. A delightful spot, or a charming and sheltered retreat from a stressful or noisy environment, is sometimes called 'an oasis'. The word itself is probably of Egyptian origin, with a literal meaning of 'dwelling-place'.

O me, my pleasant rambles by the lake,
My sweet, wild, fresh three quarters of a year,
My one Oasis in the dust and drouth
Of City life!

TENNYSON: 'Edwin Morris; or The Lake' (1842)

**Oat. Oatmeal Monday.** The mid-term Monday at the Scottish Universities, when the father of a poor student would bring him a sack of oatmeal, which would provide his staple diet for the rest of the term.

**Oatmeals.** A 17th-century nickname given to profligate bands in the streets of London. *See also* MOHOCKS; TITYRE-TUS.

**Sow one's wild oats, To.** *See under* SOW.

**Oath. Hippocratic oath.** *See under* HIPPOCRATES.

**Left-handed oath, A.** *See under* LEFT.

**Saucer oath.** *See under* SAUCER.

**Tennis-court Oath, The.** *See under* TENNIS.

**Obadiah.** The shortest book in the Old Testament, bearing the name of the prophet who foresaw the destruction of Edom. Obadiah is also (1 Kings 18) the governor of the house of AHAB who tried to protect the Hebrew prophets from persecution by JEZEBEL.

**Obeah** or **obi.** The belief in, and practice of, obeah, i.e. a kind of sorcery or witchcraft prevalent in West Africa and formerly in the West Indies. 'Obeah' is a native word and signifies something put into the ground to bring about sickness, death or other disaster. *See also* VOODOO.

**Obedience, Canonical.** *See under* CANON.

**Obelisk.** A tapering pillar of stone, originally erected by the Egyptians, who placed them in pairs before the portals of temples. The base was usually one-tenth of the height, and the apex was copper-sheathed. Each of the four faces bore incised HIEROGLYPHICS. The best known in Britain is CLEOPATRA'S NEEDLE.

The tallest obelisk, nearly 110ft (33.5m) high, is at Rome. It was taken there from HELIOPOLIS by the Emperor CALIGULA (37–41 AD) and later (1586) re-erected in the piazza of St Peter's by order of Pope Sixtus V. It weighs some 320 tons and was moved bodily on rollers. Spectators were forbidden on pain of death to utter a sound during the operation, but when the ropes were straining to breaking point, one of the workmen, a sailor from San Remo, is said to have shouted *Acqua alle funi* ('Water on the ropes'), so saving the situation at risk of the death penalty.

The Obelisk of Luxor, in the Place de la Concorde, Paris, came from Thebes, and it was presented to Louis Philippe in 1831, by the then KHEDIVE of Egypt. Its hieroglyphics record the deeds of Rameses II (12th century BC). *See also* COLUMN.

**Oberammergau.** *See* PASSION PLAY.

**Oberon.** King of the Fairies and the husband of TITANIA. Shakespeare introduced both of them in *A Midsummer Night's Dream* (1595). The name is perhaps connected with ALBERICH, the king of the elves.

Oberon first appeared in the 13th-century French romance, *Huon de Bordeaux*, in which he is the son of Julius CAESAR and MORGAN LE FAY. He was only 3ft (90cm) high, but had an angelic face, and was the lord and king of Mommur. At his birth, the fairies bestowed their gifts: one was insight into men's thoughts, and another was the power of transporting himself to any place instantaneously. In the fullness of time, legions of angels conveyed his soul to Paradise.

**Obi.** *See* OBEAH.

**Obiter dictum** (Latin, 'something said in passing'). An incidental remark. In law the term is used for a judge's expression of opinion backed by his knowledge and experience, but not forming part of a judgement and therefore not legally binding.

**Objector, Conscientious.** *See under* CONSCIENCE.

**Obligation, Feasts of.** *See under* FEAST.

**Obolus.** An ancient Greek bronze or silver coin of small value; also a medieval silver coin of small value. *See also* BELISARIUS.

**Observantins.** *See* FRANCISCANS.

**Obtain a fix, To.** In navigation to fix one's exact position by the intersection at a suitable angle of two or more position lines obtained at the same time.

**Obverse.** The side of a coin or medal that contains the principal device. Thus, the obverse of British coins is the side that bears the sovereign's head, while the other side is the reverse.

**Occam** or **Ockham. Occam's razor.** *Entia non sunt multiplicanda praeter necessitatem* (Latin, 'No more things should be presumed to exist than are absolutely necessary'), a maxim that means that all unnecessary facts or constituents in the subject being analysed should be eliminated. These exact words do not appear in Occam's works but the principle expressed occurs in several other forms.

WILLIAM OF OCCAM (1285–1349), the great FRANCISCAN scholastic philosopher, was born at Ockham, Surrey, Occam being the latinized form of the name. *See also* SCHOLASTICISM.

**William of Occam.** *See under* WILLIAM.

**Occasion. Rise to the occasion, To.** *See under* RISE.

**Occult sciences** (Latin *occultus*, related to *celare*, 'to hide'). Magic, ALCHEMY, ASTROLOGY, PALMISTRY, DIVINATION and so on, so called because they are, or were, hidden mysteries.

**Ocean. Atlantic Ocean.** *See under* ATLANTIC.

**Drop in the ocean, A.** *See under* DROP.

**Pacific Ocean.** *See under* PACIFIC.

**Shepherd of the Ocean, The.** *See under* SHEPHERD.

**Oceanids** or **Oceanides.** In Greek mythology sea NYMPHS, the daughters of OCEANUS and TETHYS, among whom were Doris, Electra and AMPHITRITE. Offerings were made to them by mariners.

**Oceanus.** A Greek sea-god, also the river of the world, which circles the earth and as such is represented as a snake with its tail in its mouth. As a sea-god, Oceanus is an old man with a long beard and bull's horns.

**Ockham.** *See* OCCAM.

**Octahedron, A regular.** *See under* REGULAR.

**Octavo.** A size of paper made by folding the sheet three times, giving eight leaves or 16 pages, hence, a book composed of sheets folded thus. The word is often written '8vo'. *See also* FOLIO; QUARTO.

**October.** The eighth month of the ancient ROMAN CALENDAR (Latin *octo*, 'eight') when the year began in March, but now the tenth month. The old Dutch name was *Wynmaand*, the Old English *Winmōnath*, 'wine month', or the time of vintage. Another Old English name was *Winterfylleth*, perhaps meaning 'winter full moon', but possibly from *fyllan*, 'to fell', as a time of tree-felling. In the FRENCH REVOLUTIONARY CALENDAR the equivalent month was VENDÉMIAIRE, 'time of vintage', corresponding to the period from 23 September to 22 October.

**October Club.** In the reign of Queen Anne, a group of High TORY MPs who met at a tavern near the Houses of Parliament to drink October ale and to abuse the WHIGS. It became politically prominent about 1710 although it had probably existed from the end of William III's reign.

**October Revolution.** In Russian history the BOLSHEVIK revolution of October 1917 (November in the western calendar), which led to the overthrow of Kerensky and the MENSHEVIKS and the triumph of LENIN.

**Octobrists.** A 'constitutionalist' centre party in Russia, supported by the landlords and wealthy mercantile interests, which was prominent in the *dumas* between 1907 and 1914, after the Tsar's liberal manifesto published in October 1905.

**Od.** *See* ODYLE.

**Odd. Oddfellows.** A FRIENDLY SOCIETY of 18th-century origins, first formed at London. During the period of the French Revolutionary Wars many lodges were prosecuted for alleged 'seditious' activities, as were many harmless organizations. In 1813 the Independent Order of Odd Fellows was formed at Manchester and it became the most influential in England. The movement spread to the United States and Canada and allied bodies now exist in various European countries. 'Odd' here means 'different from the rest'.

**Odd man out.** The one of a group who fails to get selected or included when numbers are made up; more generally a person who does not fit into a group or gathering for some reason.

**Odds and ends.** Fragments; remnants; bits and pieces of small value. A colloquial variant applicable to people is 'odds and sods'.

**Odds-on.** A state when success is more likely than failure. The reference is to betting odds.

**At odds.** *See under* AT.

**Fixed odds.** *See under* FIX.

**It makes no odds.** It makes no difference; it is no excuse. An application of the betting phrase.

**Luck in odd numbers.** *See under* LUCK.

**Over the odds.** *See under* OVER.

**Shout the odds, To.** *See under* SHOUT.

**What's the odds?** What does it matter?

**Odette.** In Tchaikovsky's ballet *Swan Lake* (1877) the beautiful swan queen who each night assumes the form of a young girl in search of a man who will faithfully love her, for whom in return she will preserve her human guise. She meets and loves the noble young prince Siegfried, but he is lured away by Odile, an evil enchantress disguised as a black swan, and Odette kills herself.

**Odin.** The Scandinavian name of the god called WODEN by the Anglo-Saxons. He was god of wisdom, poetry, war and agriculture. As god of the dead, he presided over banquets of those slain in battle. He became the all-wise either by receiving MIMIR's severed head or by drinking from Mimir's fountain, but had to purchase the distinction at the pledge of one eye, and he is thus often represented as a one-eyed man wearing a hat and carrying a staff. His remaining eye is the sun, and his horse is SLEIPNIR. He was master of magic and discovered the RUNES. *See also* VALHALLA.

**Promise of Odin, The.** *See under* PROMISE.

**Vow of Odin, The.** *See under* VOW.

**Odium theologicum** (Latin). The bitter hatred of rival theologians. There are no wars so sanguinary as holy wars, no persecutions so relentless as religious persecutions, no hatred so bitter as theological hatred.

**Odor lucri** (Latin). The sweets of gain; the delights of money-making.

**Odour.** To be in good (or bad) odour is to be in or out of favour.

**Odour of sanctity, The.** In the Middle Ages it was held that a sweet and delightful odour was given off by the bodies of saintly persons at their death, and also when their bodies, if 'translated', were disinterred. Hence the phrase, 'he died in the odour of sanctity', i.e. he died a saint. The SWEDENBORGIANS say that when the celestial angels are present at a deathbed, what is then cadaverous excites a sensation of what is aromatic.

There is an 'odour of iniquity' as well, and Shakespeare has a strong passage on the 'odour of impiety'. Antiochus and his wicked daughter were killed by lightning, and:

> A fire from heaven came and shrivell'd up
> Their bodies, even to loathing; for they so stunk,
> That all those eyes ador'd them ere their fall
> Scorn now their hand should give them burial.
> *Pericles, Prince of Tyre*, II, iv (1608)

**Comparisons are odorous.** *See under* COMPARE.

**Ods.** An expression used in such former oaths as: Od's bodikins! ('God's body'); Od's pittikins! ('God's pity'); Od-zounds! ('God's wounds'); Od rot'em! (DRAT).

**Odyle.** The name formerly given to the hypothetical force that emanates from a medium to produce the phenomena connected with MESMERISM, such as spirit-rapping, table-turning and so on. Baron von Reichenbach (1788–1869) called it 'Od', and taught that it pervaded all nature, especially heat, light, crystals, magnets and the like. He held that it was developed in chemical action and that it streamed from the fingers of specially sensitive persons. He proposed the word, a monosyllable beginning with a vowel, 'for the sake of convenient conjunction in the manifold compound words'.

> If that od-force of German Reichenbach,
> Which still from female finger-tips burns blue,

Could strike out as our masculine white heats
To quicken a man.
ELIZABETH BARRETT BROWNING: *Aurora Leigh*, vii (1857)

**Odysseus.** *See* ULYSSES.

**Odyssey.** The epic poem of HOMER which records the adventures of Odysseus (ULYSSES) on his homeward voyage from TROY. The word implies the things or adventures of Ulysses, and is now used generally for any great journey or undertaking, especially one that is pioneering.

**Oedipus.** The son of King Laius of Thebes and his queen, Jocasta. To avert the fulfilment of the prophecy that he would murder his father and marry his mother, Oedipus was exposed (abandoned) on the mountains as an infant, but he was taken in and reared by the shepherds. When grown to manhood, he unwittingly slew his father, then, having solved the riddle of the SPHINX, he became king of Thebes, thereby gaining the hand in marriage of Jocasta, his mother, both being unaware of their mutual relationship. When the facts came to light, Jocasta hanged herself and Oedipus tore out his own eyes.

**Oedipus complex.** The psychoanalytical term for the sexual desire (usually unrecognized by himself) of a son for his mother and conversely an equally unrecognized jealous hatred of his father.

**Oeil-de-boeuf** (French, 'bull's-eye'). A large reception room (*salle*) in the Palace of VERSAILLES was so named from its round 'bull's-eye' window. The ceiling, which was decorated by Adam Franz van der Meulen (1632–90), contains likenesses of Louis XIV's children. The courtiers waited and gossiped in the anteroom, hence the name became associated with backstairs intrigues.

**Oenone.** A NYMPH of Mount IDA, the wife of PARIS before he abducted HELEN. She prophesied the disastrous consequences of his voyage to Greece and, on the death of Paris, killed herself.

**Of. Of course.** Naturally; as would be expected.

**Of the first water.** Of the highest type; superlative. *See also* DIAMOND OF THE FIRST WATER.

**Off** (Latin *ab*, 'from', 'away'). If the house is 'a mile off', it is a mile away. The word preceding 'off' defines its scope. To be 'well off' is to be away or on the way towards prosperity or well-being, and to be 'badly off' is the reverse.

**Off-Broadway.** In the American theatre, a term relating to productions that are experimental, low budget or not commercially viable, as against the mainstream productions of BROADWAY. They are, in turn, contrasted with off-off-Broadway productions, which are highly experimental and often staged in small halls, cafés, churches and the like.

For proof that the theme of sexual diversion can be honestly and yet dramatically treated, one has to go, not to off-Broadway but to what is called off-off-Broadway. Actually the distinction between the two is quite real.
*Manchester Guardian Weekly* (17 October 1968)

**Off colour.** In poorish health; seedy. Of a remark, joke or the like, risqué.

**Off day.** A day when one is not at one's best.

**Offhand.** Casual; slighting; discourteous.

**Off one's guard.** Unprepared; caught unawares.

**Off one's hands.** No longer one's responsibility.

**Off one's head.** Deranged; delirious; extremely excited.

**Off one's nut** or **nuts.** Crazy; demented.

**Off one's own bat.** By one's own exertions; of one's own accord. In CRICKET the expression refers to runs made by a single player.

**Offside, The.** The side of a motor vehicle that is to the right hand of the driver. *See also* NEARSIDE.

In Association Football the referee signals offside and awards a free kick when the ball is played and a player of the attacking side is nearer to his opponent's goal-line and there are not two of his opponents between himself and the goal.

If an action or type of behaviour is 'a bit off', it is not quite up to proper standards. *See also* OFF COLOUR.

**Off the cuff.** Without previous preparation. The phrase may refer to the habit of some after-dinner speakers of making jottings on their stiff shirt cuffs as ideas occurred to them during the meal.

**Off the hook.** Out of a danger; freed from an obligation. When a telephone is off the hook the receiver is not on the rest and no incoming calls can be received. This expedient is resorted to by those who do not wish to be disturbed or to hear from a particular caller. In the early days of telephony, when it was not in use, the receiver hung from a hook next to the mouthpiece.

**Off the peg.** Of clothes, ready-made, and hanging on the peg for sale. The opposite is MADE TO MEASURE (*see under* MAKE).

**Off the point.** Irrelevant.

**Off the record.** Originally a legal term whereby a judge directs that improper or irrelevant evidence should be struck off the record. This later became commonly synonymous with 'in confidence' or an unofficial expression of views.

**Off the top of one's head.** Extempore; without any preparation or advance notice.

**Off the wall.** Unorthodox; unconventional. The allusion may be to a shot in squash or handball that comes off the wall at an unexpected or erratic angle.

**Off to a flying start.** Making a good beginning; having an initial advantage. The reference is to a runner who springs from the starting block at the very moment when the starter's pistol fires.

**Offa's Dyke.** An earthwork running from the River Wye, near Monmouth, to near Prestatyn, in Clwyd, probably built by Offa of MERCIA (r.757–796) as a boundary between him and the Welsh. *See also* GRIMSDYKE; WANSDYKE.

**Offender, First.** *See under* FIRST.

**Offensive, Charm.** *See under* CHARM.

**Office. Box office,** *See under* BOX.

**Circumlocution Office.** *See under* CICUMLOCUTION.

**Divine Office, The.** *See under* DIVINE.

**Holy Office, The.** *See* INQUISITION.

**Home Office.** *See under* HOME.

**Jack out of office.** *See under* JACK.

**Oval Office, The.** *See under* OVAL.

**Officer. Field officer.** *See under* FIELD.

**Flag officer.** *See under* FLAG.

**Second an officer.** *See under* SECOND.

**Offing, In the.** Said of a ship visible at sea off the land. Such a ship is often approaching port, hence the phrase is used figuratively to mean 'about to happen', 'likely to occur', 'likely to take place', as: 'It looks as if there is a storm in the offing.'

**Og.** The king of Bashan, according to Rabbinical legend, was an antediluvian giant, saved from the Flood (*see* DELUGE) by climbing on the roof of the ark. After the crossing of the Red Sea, MOSES first conquered Sihon, and then advanced against the giant Og whose bedstead, made of iron, was 9 cubits long and 4 cubits broad (Deuteronomy 3:11). The legend says that Og plucked up a mountain to hurl at the Israelites, but he got so entangled with his burden that Moses was able to kill him without much difficulty.

In John Dryden's *Absalom and Achitophel* (1681), Og represents Thomas Shadwell, who was fat.

**Ogam** or **Ogham.** The alphabet in use among the ancient Irish and British peoples. There were 20 characters, each of which was composed of a number (from one to five) of thin strokes arranged and grouped above, below or across a horizontal line

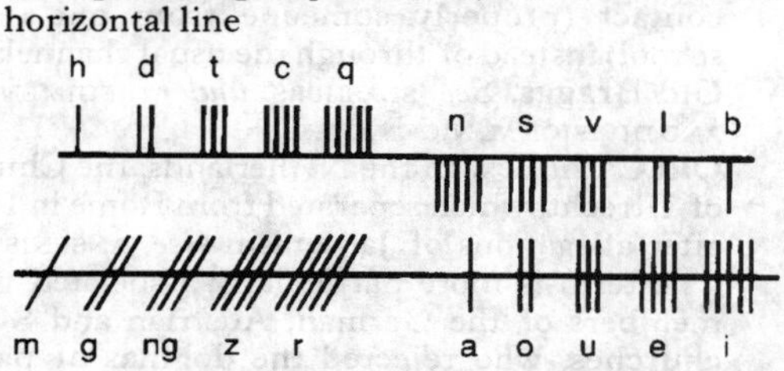


The word is connected with Ogma, the name of a Gaulish god, likened to HERCULES by Lucian, who performed his feats through eloquence and the gift of languages. *See also* RUNE.

**Ogier the Dane.** One of the great heroes of medieval romance whose exploits are chronicled in the CHANSONS DE GESTE. He was the son of Geoffrey, king of Denmark, of which country he is still the national hero. In one account, his son was slain by CHARLEMAGNE's son Charlot and in revenge Ogier killed the king's nephew and was only just prevented from slaying Charlemagne himself. He eventually returned from exile to defend France against the Saracen chief Brehus. In another romance, it is said that his birth was attended by fairies, among them MORGAN LE FAY, who eventually took him to AVALON where he dwelt for 200 years. She then sent him to defend France against invasion, after which she took him back to Avalon. William Morris gives a rendering of this romance in his *Earthly Paradise* ('August') (1868–70).

**Ogpu.** The secret political police of the former USSR. It was set up in 1917 as the Cheka, *Chrezvychaynaya komissiya* ('Extraordinary Commission' i.e. to combat counter-revolution). In 1922 this became the GPU, *Gosudarstvennoye politicheskoye upravleniye* ('State Political Administration'), and the following year Ogpu, adding *Obyedinyonnoye* ('United') to the previous title. In 1934 it was renamed the NKVD, *Narodnyy komissariat vnutrennykh del* ('People's Commissariat for Internal Affairs'). In 1946 this was superseded by the MGB, *Ministerstvo gosudarstvennoy bezopasnosti* ('Ministry of State Security'), which in 1953 was renamed the MVD, *Ministerstvo vnutrennykh del* ('Ministry of Internal Affairs'). Its major successor in 1954 was the KGB, *Komitet gosudarstvennoy bezopasnosti* ('Committee for State Security'). The KGB ceased to exist in 1991 on the demise of the Soviet Union, and it was succeeded by the FSK, *Federal'naya sluzhba kontrrazvedki* ('Federal Counter-Intelligence Service'). In 1995 this was renamed the FSB, *Federal'naya sluzhba bezopasnosti* ('Federal Security Service').

**Ogres.** In nursery stories ogres are giants of very malignant disposition, who live on human flesh. The word was first used (and probably invented) by Perrault in his *Histoires ou Contes du temps passé* (1697), and it is thought to based on Orcus, a name of PLUTO.

**Ogygia.** *See* CALYPSO.

**Ogygian deluge.** In Greek legend a flood said to have occurred when Ogyges was king of Boeotia, some 200 years before DEUCALION's flood. Varro says that the planet VENUS underwent a great change in the reign of Ogyges. It changed its diameter, its colour, its form and its course.

**Oh dear!** A very common exclamation, more likely to be a EUPHEMISM for 'Oh damn' than a form of French *O Dieu* ('O God'), as some claim.

**Oil. Oil someone's hand** or **palm, To.** To bribe someone.

**Oil the wheels, To.** To help make things run smoothly.

**Burn the midnight oil, To.** *See under* BURN.

**Fixed oil.** *See under* FIX.

**He's no oil painting.** He is not good-looking. Many painted portraits aim to enhance the appearance of the sitter, although there have been exceptions. *See also* WARTS AND ALL.

**Pour oil on troubled waters, To.** *See under* POUR.

**Strike oil, To.** *See under* STRIKE.

**Walpurgis oil.** *See under* WALPURGIS.

**Well-oiled.** *See under* WELL.

**Ointment. Fly in the ointment, A.** *See under* FLY.

**Golden ointment.** *See under* GOLDEN.

**Oisin.** *See* OSSIAN.

**OK.** All correct; all right. The expression is a reassuring affirmative that, coming from the USA to Britain, has spread colloquially throughout several European languages. Its first recorded use occurs in 1839. It is generally regarded as standing for 'Orl Korrect' ('all correct'), but has also been said to derive from the political society called 'Democratic OK', the 'OK' signifying 'Old Kinderhook', a nickname of the Democratic leader, Martin Van Buren (1782–1862).

**Old.** A word used colloquially as a term of endearment or friendship, as in 'my dear old fellow', 'my old man' (my husband); as a general disparagement, as in 'old cat', 'OLD FOGEY', 'old rascal', 'old stick-in-the-mud'; and as a common intensive, as in Shakespeare's 'Here will be an old abusing of God's patience and the King's English' (*Merry Wives of Windsor*, I, iv (1600)). It is also an intensive in such phrases as 'any old thing' (stronger than anything), 'good old sleep' (stronger than good sleep).

**Old Abe** or **Honest Abe.** Abraham Lincoln, President of the United States from 1861 until his death in 1865, when he was shot by a fanatical Southern sympathizer while at the theatre.

**Old Adam, The.** The evil that is supposedly inherent in all humans.

> Consideration, like an angel, came
> And whipped the offending Adam out of him.
> SHAKESPEARE: *Henry V*, I, i (1598)

*See also* ADAM.

**Old bag, An.** An elderly and unattractive or slovenly woman; a 'lady of easy virtue'.

> Ah reckon you must have fired that old bag you had in the kitchen and got yourself a hundred per cent American cook.
> PAUL GALLICO: *Mrs Harris goes to New York*, ch xvi (1960)

**Old Bailey.** The Central Criminal Court of the City of London and of (approximately) the Greater London area, situated in the thoroughfare of this name. 'Bailey' comes from Old French *baille* ('enclosed court'), referring to the enclosure of the City wall between LUDGATE and NEWGATE. The area has historic associations with crime owing to the proximity of NEWGATE PRISON and its being the site of public executions, the last victim being a FENIAN executed by William Calcraft in 1868. It was also the site of a pillory.

**Old bean.** A colloquial expression of good-natured familiarity. Compare with 'old boy', 'old chap', 'old man' and the like, popular in the interwar years. *See also* OLD FRUIT.

**Old Believers.** Those members of the Russian ORTHODOX CHURCH who rejected the liturgical reforms of the Patriarch Nikon and who were excommunicated in 1667. They were subjected to violent persecution and eventually resolved into two groups, the Popovtsy ('priestly') and the Bespopovtsy ('priestless'), the latter rejecting the priesthood altogether. The former attained state recognition in 1881.

**Old biddy.** A colloquial term for an old woman, especially one who gossips or interferes. 'Biddy' is a pet form of the name Bridget.

**Old Bill.** *See* BETTER 'OLE.

**Old Blood and Guts.** *See* BLOOD AND GUTS.

**Old Bold Fifth.** *See* FIGHTING FIFTH *under* REGIMENTAL AND DIVISIONAL NICKNAMES.

**Old Bona Fide.** Louis XIV (1638–1715). *See also* BONA FIDE.

**Old bones.** To make old bones is to live to a ripe old age.

**Old boy.** A friendly colloquial form of address between men of any age. The term also denotes a former pupil of a particular school, hence 'old boys' clubs', 'old boys' dinners' etc. 'Old girl' is similarly used to denote old scholars, and by some men as an affectionate term of address to a woman. It is also applied to certain female animals, especially horses. Both terms are applied in the obvious sense to elderly men and women. *See also* OLD SCHOOL TIE.

**Old boy network.** To arrange something on the old boy network is to fix it through a social contact (properly someone from one's old school) instead of through the usual channels.

**Old Braggs.** *See* SLASHERS *under* REGIMENTAL AND DIVISIONAL NICKNAMES.

**Old Catholics.** In the Netherlands, the Church of Utrecht, which separated from Rome in 1724 after allegations of Jansenism (*see* JANSENISTS). The term is more particularly associated with members of the German, Austrian and Swiss churches, who rejected the dogmas of papal INFALLIBILITY after the VATICAN COUNCIL of 1870 and who were joined by others as a result of the KULTURKAMPF. Their episcopal succession is derived from the Church of Utrecht, and they are in communion with the CHURCH OF ENGLAND. There are also others in the USA and small groups of Poles and Croats.

**Old Chapel, The.** An unusual public house at the corner of Duke Street, Devonport, which still has some of its original features. It was opened as a Unitarian church in what was then Plymouth Dock, in 1791. This was the time of the French Revolution, and UNITARIANS were regarded with suspicion, as is evidenced by the burning down of Joseph Priestley's Unitarian church in Birmingham. Commissioner Fanshawe, Controller of the Dockyard, suspecting the Unitarians, many of whom were government employees, of revolutionary intrigues, closed their chapel and it was converted to an inn in 1801.

**Old codger.** An old or eccentric person who is, even so, regarded with affection and even respected for his worldly wisdom. From 1936 to 1990 the *Daily Mirror* ran a 'Live Letters' column in which a couple of supposed 'Old Codgers' answered readers' questions on a variety of subjects in an entertaining and anecdotal way. For the origin of codger *see* COD.

> If we Old Pair had to nominate one single word as the most interesting in the English language, we'd plump for 'salt'.
> *The Daily Mirror Old Codgers Little Black Book No. 3* (1977)

**Old Conky.** The Duke of Wellington (1769–1852) was thus nicknamed from the shape of his nose or 'conk'. *See also* OLD NOSEY.

**Old Contemptibles, The.** Members of the British Expeditionary Force of 160,000 men that left Britain in 1914 to join the French and Belgians against Germany. The soldiers are said to have given themselves this name from an army order (almost certainly apocryphal) issued by the Kaiser at Aix on 19 August and published in an annexe to BEF Routine Orders of 24 September 1914:

> It is my royal and imperial command that you exterminate the treacherous English, and walk over General French's contemptible little army.

He may have actually called the BEF 'a contemptibly little army', which is not nearly so disparaging.

The surviving veterans held their last parade at the garrison church of All Saints, Aldershot, on Sunday, 4 August 1974 in the presence of Queen Elizabeth II, who took tea with them before their final dispersal.

**Old country, The.** In the days of the British Empire, Great Britain, the mother country.

**Old Cracow Bible, The.** *See* LEOPOLITA BIBLE *under* BIBLE.

**Old dear.** An elderly woman.

**Old Dominion, The.** The state of VIRGINIA, formerly an English colony.

**Old Dozen, The.** *See under* REGIMENTAL AND DIVISIONAL NICKNAMES.

**Old Dun Cow, The.** A derisive nickname given by the troops to the steamer *River Clyde* beached at Gallipoli in 1915 during the First World War. It was probably a reference to the popular song containing the words 'The Old Dun Cow she's done for now', the Old Dun Cow in question being a public house that had run dry.

**Olde worlde.** Quaint; in a mock old style. The words imitate Shakespearean spelling. 'Olde' is similarly found in the names of some shops with the aim of attracting custom, as 'Ye Olde Tea Shoppe'. London's Olde Mitre Tavern in Ely Place is a genuine 16th-century building.

**Old Fogs, The.** *See under* REGIMENTAL AND DIVISIONAL NICKNAMES.

**Old fogey** or **fogy.** An old-fashioned person or a person with old-fashioned ideas. The origin of 'fogey' is uncertain. *See also* YOUNG FOGEY.

**Old Fox.** A nickname of George Washington. Marshal Soult (1769–1851) was also so nicknamed from his strategic talents and fertility of resource. The term 'fox', as applied to a crafty person, has biblical precedent:

> Go ye, and tell that fox [Herod], Behold I cast out devils, and I do cures to day and to morrow.
> Luke 13:32

**Old fruit.** A now dated familiar form of address to a man.

**Old Gentleman, The.** The DEVIL, OLD NICK. Also a special card in a prepared pack, used for tricks or cheating.

**Old Glory.** The flag of the United States. *See also* STARS AND STRIPES.

**Old grey whistle test, The.** In TIN PAN ALLEY songwriters used to play their compositions to the 'old greys', the elderly doorkeepers and other employees in the offices of the music publishers. If the 'old greys' were still whistling the tunes after a week or so, then they were likely to be worth publishing. The phrase was adopted for the title of a weekly television pop music programme first shown in 1971 on BBC2 as a 'serious' partner to *Top of the Pops* on BBC1.

**Old Grog.** *See* GROG.

**Old Guard.** The veteran regiments of NAPOLEON BONAPARTE's Imperial Guard, the flower of the French army. Devoted to the emperor, the Old Guard could be relied upon in any desperate strait, and it was they who made the last charge of the French at Waterloo. Figuratively, the phrase Old Guard is used for the stalwarts of any party or movement.

**Old hand.** A person who has gained knowledge of some skill through long experience; a veteran.

**Old Harry.** A familiar name for the DEVIL, probably from the personal name but perhaps with some allusion to the word 'harry', meaning to plunder, harass, lay waste, from which comes the old 'harrow', as in the title of the 13th-century MYSTERY play, *The Harrowing of Hell*. *See also* OLD NICK.

**Old hat.** Outworn or obsolete. The expression probably arises from the fact that hats tend to date long before they are worn out.

**Old Hickory.** The nickname of General Andrew Jackson (1767–1845), 7th President of the United States (1829–37). He was first called 'Tough', from his great powers of endurance, then 'Tough as hickory' and finally 'Old Hickory'. *See also* KITCHEN CABINET; JACKSON, STONEWALL.

**Old Hundred** or **Old Hundredth.** A well-known and dignified psalm tune that owes its name to its being so designated in the Tate and Brady Psalter of 1696. Its name there indicated the retention of the setting of W. Kethe's version of the 100th psalm in the Psalter of 1563 by Sternhold and Hopkins. The tune is of older origin and is found as a setting to the 134th psalm in Marot and Béza's Genevan Psalter of 1551, and an even earlier version of it appears in the Antwerp collection *Souter Liederkens* of 1540.

**Old Ironsides.** *See* IRONSIDES.

**Old King Cole.** A legendary British king, described in the nursery rhyme as 'a merry old soul', who was fond of his pipe, his glass and his fiddlers three. Robert of Gloucester says he was father of St HELENA (and consequently grandfather of the Emperor Constantine). Colchester is popularly but erroneously said to have been named after him.

**Old lady, The.** A person's mother or wife.

**Old Lady of the Bund, The.** The nickname given by British residents in China to *The North China Daily News*, published at Shanghai (1855–1950).

**Old Lady of Threadneedle Street, The.** A synonym for the Bank of England, which stands in this street. The term dates from the late 18th century, and there is a caricature by James Gillray, dated 22 May 1797, depicting the Bank as an old lady with a dress made of paper money, seated firmly on the Bank's gold and ignoring the advances of the then Prime Minister, William Pitt the Younger. It was entitled *Political Ravishment: or the Old Lady of Threadneedle Street in Danger*, and it referred to Pitt's instruction that the Bank should not redeem its notes in gold and that it should issue £1 notes instead.

**Old maid.** A woman who is unlikely to marry, or any prim or fastidious woman in general. The name is also that of a card game. One card is removed from the pack, and players pair cards until one is left at the end of the game as the 'old maid' with an unpaired card. The LAPWING is also so called, from the fancy that old maids are changed into lapwings after death.

**Old Man of the Mountain, The** (*Sheikh-al-Jebal*). Rashid ad-Din (d.1192), leader of the Syrian branch of the ASSASSINS, who made his stronghold at a fortress in Masyaf, in northwest Syria. He made several attempts on the life of SALADIN, who opposed the Assassins.

**Old Man of the Sea, The.** In the story of SINBAD THE SAILOR in the ARABIAN NIGHTS ENTERTAINMENTS, the Old Man of the Sea hoisted himself on Sinbad's shoulders and clung there for many days and nights, much to the discomfort of Sinbad, who finally got rid of the Old Man by making him drunk. Hence, any burden, real or figurative, of which it is impossible to free oneself without the greatest exertions is called an 'old man of the sea'. *See also* NEREUS.

**Old man's beard.** *Clematis vitalba* is so called from its heads of long-bearded fruits. It is also known as traveller's joy.

**Old Masters.** The great painters (especially of Italy and the Low Countries) who worked from the 13th century to about the early 17th. The term is also used for their paintings.

> About suffering they were never wrong,
> The Old Masters: how well they understood
> Its human position; how it takes place
> While someone else is eating or opening a window
> or just walking dully along.
>
> W.H AUDEN: 'Musée des Beaux Arts' (1940)

**Old Mother Hubbard.** This lastingly popular nursery rhyme is one of definitely known origin. It was first published in 1805 and was written by Sarah Catherine Martin (1768–1826) while she was staying with her future brother-in-law, John Pollexfen Bastard, of Kitley, near Yealmpton, east of Plymouth in Devon. It is traditionally said that Mother Hubbard was the housekeeper at Kitley, and there is a cottage at Yealmpton purporting to be her former residence.

> Old Mother Hubbard
> Went to the cupboard
> To fetch her poor dog a bone;
> But when she came there
> The cupboard was bare
> And so the poor dog had none.

**Old Mother Riley.** The garrulous old washerwoman was the creation and persona of the MUSIC HALL comedian Arthur Lucan, whose wife stood in as her daughter, Kitty. Her heyday was the interwar years, when she appeared solely on stage. She then transferred to the cinema and a number of radio series.

**Old Nick.** The DEVIL. The term was in use in the

17th century, and it is perhaps connected with the German NICKEL, a GOBLIN, or in some forgotten way with St NICHOLAS. Samuel Butler's derivation from Niccolò MACHIAVELLI is, of course, poetic licence:

Nick Machiavel had ne'er a trick
(Though he gave name to our old Nick).
*Hudibras*, III, i (1680)

**Old Noll.** Oliver Cromwell (1599–1658) was so called, Noll being a familiar form of Oliver.

**Old Nosey.** Arthur Wellesley, 1st Duke of Wellington (1769–1852), so called by his troops from his strongly accentuated aquiline nose. *See also* OLD CONKY.

**Old pals act.** A colloquial term for the idea that friends should always help one another.

**Old Pretender, The.** James Francis Edward Stewart or Stuart (1688–1766), son of James II, the WARMING-PAN BABY, and known as the Old Chevalier. He was called James III by the JACOBITES on the death of his father in 1701. The word 'Pretender' here denotes one who makes a claim or pretension to a title.

**Old retainer.** A light-hearted term for an old and faithful friend or servant. A retainer is properly the dependant or follower of a person of rank, who retains him, if only nominally, in service.

**Old Reekie.** *See* AULD REEKIE.

**Old Rough and Ready.** General Zachary Taylor (1784–1850), 12th President of the USA (1849–50), so nicknamed for his readiness to accept rough-and-ready, common-sense arrangements, such as his agreement to an armistice in the Mexican War (1846–8).

**Old Rowley.** Charles II (1630–85) was so called after his favourite stallion. A portion of the Newmarket racecourse is still called Rowley Mile, and the Rowley Stakes are also held there.

'Old Rowley himself, madam,' said the King, entering the apartment with his usual air of easy composure.
SIR WALTER SCOTT: *Peveril of the Peak*, ch xxxi (1823)

**Old salt, An.** A long-experienced sailor, who has been well salted by the sea.

**Old school tie.** Literally, a distinguishing neck-tie worn by OLD BOYS of a particular school. Such ties being essentially associated with the public schools and the older grammar schools led to 'old school tie' being given a pejorative use as a symbol of class distinction, e.g. 'the old school tie brigade', meaning the members of a privileged class. *See also* OLD BOY NETWORK.

If you are entitled to wear what is generically known as an Old School Tie, whether it represents your public school, university, regiment, golf club, rowing club, or any other sporting or social associations, wear it sparingly.
GUY EGMONT: *The Art of Egmontese*, ch i (1961)

**Old Scratch.** OLD NICK, the DEVIL. From *skratta*, an old Scandinavian word for GOBLIN or monster (modern Icelandic *skratti*, 'a devil').

**Old Serpent, The.** SATAN.

And he laid hold on the dragon, that old serpent, which is the Devil, and Satan, and bound him a thousand years.
Revelation 20:2

**Old soldier, An.** A person who has had long experience of something, such as making do in basic conditions; an empty bottle. *See also* DEAD MARINES.

**Old Spanish custom, An.** *See* SPANISH PRACTICES.

**Old stager.** One of long experience; an old hand at the game. The expression originally referred to an experienced stage player.

All the girls declare
That I'm a gay old stager,
Hey! Hey! clear the way
Here comes the galloping major!
F.W. LEIGH and GEORGE BASTOW: *The Galloping Major* (1907)

**Old Style** and **New Style.** Terms used in chronology. 'Old Style' refers to dating by the JULIAN CALENDAR and 'New Style' by the GREGORIAN CALENDAR. *See also* STILO NOVO.

**Old sweat, An.** An experienced soldier of long service; any old soldier.

**Old Testament, The.** The collective name of the first 39 books in the BIBLE inherited as sacred scripture from the Jewish church, and referred to by Christ and his disciples as 'the Scriptures'.

Jesus saith unto them, Did ye never read in the scriptures ... ?
Matthew 21:42

The Hebrew canon, which is that of the Reformed churches and consists of the 39 books printed in most Bibles, is substantially that adopted by a Jewish council at Jamnia (*c*.AD 90). The Roman Catholic canon includes the APOCRYPHA. *See also* NEW TESTAMENT.

**Old thing.** A formerly familiar mode of address between friends. *See also* NAPOO.

**Old-time dance.** A formal or formation dance, of the kind danced in olden times.

**Old-timer.** A person with long experience; one who has lived long and seen life.

**Old Tom.** A specially potent gin. The story goes that a Thomas Norris, employed in Messrs Hodges' distillery, opened a GIN PALACE in Great Russell Street, Covent Garden, London, in the late 18th century, and called the gin concocted by Thomas Chamberlain, one of the firm of Hodges, 'Old Tom', in compliment to his former master.

**Old Uncle Tom Cobbleigh.** The last named of the seven village worthies who borrowed Tom Pearce's grey mare on which to ride to WIDECOMBE FAIR and whose names form the refrain of the ballad of that name, which has become as much the county song of Devon as 'D'ye ken John Peel' is of Cumberland.

When the wind whistles cold on the moor of a
night,
All along, down along, out along lee,
Tom Pearce's old mare doth appear gashly white,
Wi' Bill Brewer, Jan Stewer, Peter Gurney,
Peter Davy, Dan'l Whidden, Harry Hawk,
Old Uncle Tom Cobbleigh and all,
Old Uncle Tom Cobbleigh and all.

**Old Vic.** The theatre in Waterloo Road, London, which became famous for its Shakespearean productions under the management of Lilian Baylis (1874–1937), who took over from her aunt, Emma Cons, in 1912. It was opened in 1818 as the Coburg and was renamed the Royal Victoria Hall in 1833. It was the temporary home of the National Theatre from 1963 to 1976. In 1977 the Prospect Theatre moved in but they failed in 1981. In 1982 the Old Vic was bought by a Canadian businessman, Edwin Mirvich, and after extensive renovations reopened in 1983. *See also* SADLER'S WELLS.

**Old wives' tale, An.** Legendary lore or a story usually involving the marvellous and only accepted by the credulous. George Peele has a play *The Old Wives' Tale* (1595) and Arnold Bennett a novel (1908) of the same title.

**Old woman.** Colloquially, a fusspot, an old ditherer, as: 'He's a proper old woman.'

**Old World.** Europe, Asia and Africa are so called when contrasted with the NEW WORLD.

**As old as Adam, Methuselah or the hills.** *See under* AS.

**At the same old game, To be.** *See under* AT.

**Cathdrals of the Old Foundation.** *See under* CATHEDRAL.

**Dirty old man.** *See under* DIRTY.

**For old sake's sake.** *See under* FOR.

**Golden oldie.** *See under* GOLDEN.

Like old boots. *See under* LIKE.

**My old Dutch.** *See under* DUTCH.

**Oldenburg Horn.** A horn long in the possession of the reigning princes of the House of Oldenburg, but now in the collection of the king of Denmark. According to tradition, Count Otto of Oldenburg, in 967, was offered drink in this silver-gilt horn by a 'wild woman', at the Osenborg. Because he did not like the look of the liquor, he threw it away and rode off with the horn.

**Olio** (Spanish *olla*, 'stew', 'stewpot', from Latin *olla*, 'pot'). In Spain a mixture of meat, vegetables, spices and so on, boiled together and highly seasoned. Hence any HOTCHPOTCH of various ingredients, such as a miscellaneous collection of verses, drawings or pieces of music. *See also* OLLA PODRIDA.

**Olive.** In ancient Greece the olive was sacred to ATHENE, in allusion to the story that at the naming of Athens she presented it with an olive branch. It was the symbol of peace and fecundity, and brides wore or carried an olive garland, as British brides often do a wreath of ORANGE BLOSSOM. A CROWN OF WILD OLIVE was the highest distinction of a citizen who deserved well of his country, and was the highest prize in the OLYMPIC GAMES.

In the Old Testament, the subsiding of the Flood was demonstrated to NOAH by the return of a DOVE bearing an olive leaf in its beak (Genesis 8:11).

**Olive Branch Petition.** A peace move adopted by Congress (5 July 1775) after the Battle of Bunker Hill in that year, in which the British had defeated the Americans, to secure reconciliation with Britain and drawn up by John Dickinson. Lord North's conciliation proposals were rejected by the Americans, and George III refused to receive the Petition.

**Crown of Wild Olive.** *See under* CROWN.

**Hold out the olive branch, To.** *See under* HOLD.

**Oliver.** CHARLEMAGNE's favourite PALADIN who, with ROLAND, rode by his side. He was the son of Regnier, Duke of Genoa (another of the paladins), and brother of the beautiful Aude. His sword was HAUTECLAIRE and his horse was FERRANT D'ESPAGNE.

**Bath Oliver.** *See under* BATH.

**Oliver Twist.** *See under* TWIST.

**Roland for an Oliver, A.** *See under* ROLAND.

**Olivet** or **the Mount of Olives.** The range of hills to the east of Jerusalem, closely connected with ancient Jewish ceremonies and intimately associated with the events of the New Testament. Here Jesus retired for prayer and meditation and to talk to his disciples, and here he came on the night of his betrayal.

**Olivetan.** Pierre Robert (*c.*1506–38), a cousin of John Calvin and a Protestant reformer and translator of the Old Testament was called Olivetanus in allusion to his 'burning the midnight oil'.

**Olivetans.** Brethren of Our Lady of Mount Olivet, an offshoot of the BENEDICTINES. The order was founded in 1319 by St Bernard Ptolomei. For a time they were total abstainers.

**Olla podrida** (Spanish, 'putrid pot'). Odds and ends, a mixture of scraps or *pot-au-feu*, into which every sort of eatable is thrown and stewed. Figuratively, the term means an incongruous mixture; a miscellaneous collection of any kind; a medley. *See also* OLIO.

This volume is something of an olla podrida.
ERNEST WEEKLEY: *Adjectives and Other Words*, Preface (1930)

**Olympia.** The ancient name of a valley in Elis, Peloponnesus, so called from the games held there in honour of the OLYMPIAN ZEUS. The ALTIS, an enclosure about 500 × 600ft (153 × 183m), was built in the valley, containing the temple of Zeus, the Heroeum, the Metroum and other buildings, as well as the STADIUM, with gymnasia, baths and the like. Hence the name is applied to large buildings for sporting events, exhibitions and so on, such as the Olympia at Kensington, London. The valley Olympia should not be confused with the mountain OLYMPUS. Édouard Manet's painting *Olympia* (1865), a portrait of a striking female nude, signalled a radical departure from the conventional depiction of the nude.

**Olympiad.** Among the ancient Greeks, a period of four years, being the interval between the celebrations of the OLYMPIC GAMES. The first Olympiad began in 776 BC, and the last (the 293rd) in AD 392.

**Olympian Zeus** or **Jove.** A statue by Phidias, one of the SEVEN WONDERS OF THE WORLD. Pausanias (2nd century BC) says that when the sculptor placed it in the temple at OLYMPIA (433 BC), he prayed to the god to indicate whether he was satisfied with it, and immediately a thunderbolt fell on the floor of the temple without doing the slightest harm.

It was a chryselephantine statue (i.e. made of ivory and gold), and, although seated on a throne, was 60ft (18m) high. The left hand rested on a sceptre, and the right palm held a statue of Victory in solid gold. The robes were of gold, and so were the four lions that supported the footstool. The throne was of cedar, embellished with ebony, ivory, gold and precious stones. It was removed to Constantinople in the 5th century AD, and perished in the great fire of 475.

**Olympic Games.** The greatest of the four sacred festivals of the ancient Greeks, held every fourth year at OLYMPIA in July. After suitable sacrifices, racing, wrestling and other contests followed, ending on the fifth day with processions, sacrifices and banquets, and the presentation of OLIVE garlands to the victors.

The games were revived in 1896 as international sporting contests, the first Summer Olympics being held at Athens, and subsequently at Paris (1900), St Louis (1904), London (1908), Stockholm (1912), Antwerp (1920), Paris (1924), Amsterdam (1928), Los Angeles (1932), Berlin (1936), London (1948), Helsinki (1952), Melbourne (1956), Rome (1960), Tokyo (1964), Mexico City (1968), Munich (1972), Montreal (1976), Moscow (1980), Los Angeles (1984), Seoul (1988), Barcelona (1992), Atlanta (1996), Sydney (2000) and Athens (2004).

Winter Olympic Games were inaugurated in 1924 at Chamonix, with subsequent sites at St Moritz (1928), Lake Placid (1932), Garmisch-Partenkirchen (1936), St Moritz (1948), Oslo (1952), Cortina d'Ampezzo (1956), Squaw Valley (1960), Innsbruck (1964), Grenoble (1968), Sapporo (1972), Innsbruck (1976), Lake Placid (1980), Sarajevo (1984), Calgary (1988), Albertville (1992), Lillehammer (1994), Nagano (1998) and Salt Lake City (2002).

**Olympus.** The home of the gods of ancient Greece, where ZEUS held his court. It is a mountain 9550ft (2895m) high on the border between Macedonia and Thessaly. The name is used for any PANTHEON, as: 'Odin, Hort, Balder and the rest of the Northern Olympus.'

**Om.** Among the BRAHMANS the mystic equivalent for the name of the deity. It has been adopted by modern occultists to denote absolute goodness and truth or the spiritual essence.

**Om mani padme hum** (Sanskrit, 'Hail! Jewel in the lotus! Amen'). The mystic formula of the Tibetans and northern Buddhists used as a charm and for many religious purposes. They are the first words taught to a child and the last uttered on the deathbed of the pious. The LOTUS symbolizes universal being, and the jewel the individuality of the utterer.

Ah! Lover! Brother! Guide! Lamp of the Law!
I take my refuge in thy name and thee!
I take my refuge in thy Law of Good!
I take my refuge in thy Order! – OM!
The Dew is on the Lotus! – Rise, Great Sun!
And lift my leaf and mix me with the wave.
Om mani padme hum, the Sunrise comes!
The Dewdrop slips into the shining Sea!
SIR EDWIN ARNOLD: 'The Light of Asia' (1879)

**Omar Khayyám.** The Persian poet, astronomer and mathematician lived at Nishapur, where he died at about the age of 50 in about AD 1123. He was known chiefly for his work on algebra until Edward FitzGerald (1809–83) published a poetical translation of his poems in 1859. Little notice of this was taken, however, until the early 1890s, when the RUBÁIYÁT took Britain and America by storm. It is frankly hedonistic in tone, but touched with a melancholy that attunes with eastern and western pessimism alike. FitzGerald never pretended that his work was other than a free version of the original. He made several revisions, but did not improve on his first text.

**Ombre** (Spanish *hombre*, 'man'). A card game, introduced into Britain from Spain in the 17th century. It was very popular until it was supplanted by QUADRILLE *c.*1730. It was usually played by three persons, and the eights, nines and tens of each suit were left out. Matthew Prior has an epigram on the game. He was playing with two ladies, and Fortune gave him 'success in every suit but hearts'. Alexander Pope immortalized the game in *The Rape of the Lock* (1712).

**Ombudsman** (Swedish, 'commissioner'). In Scandinavian countries an official appointed by the legislature whose duty it is to protect the rights of the citizen against infringement by the government. Sweden has had one since 1809, Denmark since 1955, and Norway since 1962. New Zealand was the first COMMONWEALTH country to appoint such a commissioner (1962) and Britain appointed a Parliamentary Commissioner for Administration in 1967, commonly known as the 'Ombudsman'. Local Commissioners, or local government ombudsmen, were later appointed to investigate complaints from the public against local authorities, and independent ombudsmen schemes were similarly set up for banks, building societies, insurance companies, financial institutions and independent financial advisers.

**Omega.** *See* ALPHA.

**Omelette. You can't make omelettes without breaking eggs.** Said by way of warning to someone who is trying to 'get something for nothing', that is, to accomplish some desired object without being willing to take the necessary trouble or to make the necessary sacrifice. The phrase is a translation of the French: *On ne saurait faire une omelette sans casser des œufs.*

**Spanish omelette.** *See under* SPAIN.

**Omens.** Phenomena or unusual events taken as a prognostication of either good or evil; otherwise prophetic signs or auguries. *Omen* is a Latin word adopted into English in the 16th century. Some traditional examples of accepting what appeared to be evil omens as being of good AUGURY are:

Leotychides II of Sparta was told by his augurs that his projected expedition would fail because a viper had got entangled in the handle of the city key. 'Not so,' he replied, 'the key caught the viper.'

Julius Caesar, on landing at Adrumetum, tripped and fell on his face. This would have been considered a fatal omen by his army, but, with admirable presence of mind, he explained, 'Thus I take possession of thee, O Africa!' A similar story is told of Scipio.

William the Conqueror leaped upon the English shore and fell on his face. A great cry went forth that it was an ill omen, but the duke exclaimed: 'I have taken seisin of this land with both my hands.'

*See also* LIVER.

**Omnibus** (Latin, 'for all', dative plural of *omnis*, 'all'). The name was first applied to the public vehicle in France in 1828. In the following year it was adopted by George Shillibeer (1797–1866) for the vehicles that he started to run on the Paddington (now Marylebone) Road, London. The plural is 'omnibuses', and the word is now normally abbreviated to 'bus'. Other vehicles gained similarly abbreviated names, such as 'cab' from cabriolet, 'van' from caravan, and 'truck' from truckle.

**Omnibus bill.** The parliamentary term for a bill embracing clauses that deal with a number of different subjects, as a Revenue Bill dealing with Customs, Taxes, Stamps, Excise and so on.

**Omnibus box.** A box at a theatre for which the subscription is paid by several different parties, each of which has the right of using it.

**Omnibus train.** An old name for a train that stops at all stations, i.e. a train 'for all', as distinct from the specials and the expresses that ran between only a few stations. *See also* JERKWATER.

**Omnibus volume.** A collection in one volume of an author's works, of short stories, essays and so forth.

**Omnium** (Latin, 'of all', genitive plural of *omnis*, 'all'). The particulars of all the items, or the assignment of all the securities, of a government loan.

**Omnium gatherum.** DOG LATIN for a gathering or collection of all sorts of persons and things; a miscellaneous gathering together without regard to suitability or order.

**Omphale.** In Greek legend the queen of Lydia of masculine inclinations to whom HERCULES was bound as a slave for three years. He fell in love with her and led a submissive life spinning wool. Omphale wore the lion's skin while Hercules wore a female garment.

**On.** For expressions containing the word 'on' and not listed below, look under the first main word in the phrase.

**On end.** In succession, without a break, as: 'He goes away for days on end.'

**On its last legs.** *See under* LEG.

**On the beach.** Retired from naval service. In the Merchant Service to be 'on the beach' is to be without a ship, i.e. unemployed.

**On the loose.** *See under* LOOSE.

**On the nail.** *See under* NAIL.

**On the shelf, To put.** *See under* SHELF.

**On the spree.** *See under* SPREE.

**On the table.** *See under* TABLE.

**Have something on a person, To.** To possess damaging evidence or information about them, as: 'You've got nothing on me,' meaning, 'You know nothing that can incriminate me.'

**It's not on.** It cannot be done. A phrase from snooker that is used when the object ball is obscured.

**Onan.** A son of JUDAH who was ordered to marry his late brother's wife, TAMAR. In order to avoid fathering children on his brother's behalf, he resorted to coitus interruptus ('spilled it on the ground') when lying with Tamar, for which sin

God killed him (Genesis 38:6–10). Hence 'onanism' as a synonym for this technique, as well as more generally for masturbation.

**Once. Once and for all.** Finally; emphatically; decisively, as: 'Let's settle this once and for all.'

**Once bitten, twice shy.** Having been caught once, one is wary or cautious the next time; one learns from previous experience.

**Once in a blue moon.** Very rarely. On rare occasions the moon does appear to be blue. The cause is minute dust particles in the upper atmosphere. These block the light from the red end of the spectrum and scatter light from the blue end, with the result that the reflected sunlight from the moon shines through as blue to observers on earth.

**Once in a while.** Only occasionally.

**Once upon a time.** The traditional opening phrase in fairy stories or stories for children; at some indefinite time long ago.

> Once upon a time and a very good time it was there was a moocow coming down along the road and this moocow that was coming down along the road met a nicens little boy named baby tuckoo.
>
> JAMES JOYCE: *A Portrait of the Artist as a Young Man*, ch i (1916)

**Give someone or something the once-over, To.** To make a quick examination or assessment of something.

**On dit** (French, 'they say'). A rumour, a report or a piece of gossip, as: 'There is an *on dit* that the prince is to marry soon.'

**One. One above, The.** God.

**One and all.** Everybody, individually and jointly. The phrase is the motto of Cornishmen.

**One-armed bandit.** A gaming or 'fruit' machine operated by the insertion of coins and the pulling of an arm or lever. It is so called because it frequently 'robs' one of loose change. It has now mostly been superseded by electronic machines.

**One bell in the last dogwatch.** It is a common story in the Royal Navy that one bell has been struck at 6.30 pm instead of five since the mutinies of 1797, because in one port five bells in the dog watches was to be the signal for mutiny. This was prevented by the foreknowledge of officers, who ordered one bell to be struck instead.

**One-eyed.** An expression of contempt, as: 'I've never seen such a one-eyed town,' i.e. such a dull and lifeless place.

**One-eyed peoples.** *See* ARIMASPIANS; CYCLOPS.

**One flesh, To be.** To be closely united, as in marriage.

> Therefore shall a man leave his father and his mother, and shall cleave unto his wife: and they shall be one flesh.
>
> Genesis 2:24

**One for the road.** One last drink before departing, a popular call at the end of a night on the SPREE.

**One good turn deserves another.** A benefit received ought to be repaid.

**One-horse race.** A competition in which one competitor is clearly superior to all the others.

**One-horse town.** A very small town with few amenities. An expression of American origin when a small community might boast only one horse. It is now used figuratively of anything small or amateurish, as 'a one-horse set-up'. *See also* JERKWATER; ONE-EYED.

**One in a thousand** or **million.** Said of someone who is distinguished by excellent qualities, as 'a wife in a thousand', meaning a perfect wife or one who exactly suits the speaker's ideas of what a wife should be.

**One in the eye** or **on the nose.** A blow on the named part of the body. 'One in the eye' is also used figuratively for a telling blow.

**One-liner.** A short joke or witty remark.

> [President] Reagan's substitute for strong emotions seems to be humor, both memorized and spontaneous. He is a walking repertory theater of show-biz anecdotes, one-liners, elaborate routines.
>
> *Time* (20 October 1980)

**One man's meat is another man's poison.** What is palatable or beneficial for one person is distasteful or harmful for another.

**One-night stand.** A single evening performance by a touring theatrical company or the like at a town likely to provide an audience only for one night. Also, a sexual liaison lasting only one night.

**One-off.** Done or made only once, as: 'a one-off payment'.

**One of the boys.** One of a group of male friends or associates.

**One of these days.** Some day; at some unspecified time in the future; when the opportunity occurs.

**One over the eight.** Slightly drunk. In this expression, the 'eight' is a reference to eight pints of beer, which were traditionally regarded as a reasonable amount for an average person to drink.

**One-stop shop.** A shop providing a wide range of goods, so that a customer can make various purchases in a single visit.

**One swallow does not make a summer.** You are not to suppose summer has come to stay just because you have seen a swallow, nor that the troubles of life are over because you have surmounted one difficulty. The Greek proverb, 'One swallow does not make a spring', is found in Aristotle's *Nicomachean Ethics* (I, vii, 16 (4th century BC)).

**One-track mind.** A mind with one dominant

preoccupation, which constantly reverts to the one subject, as a single-track railway allows traffic in only one direction at a time.

**One-upmanship.** The art or knack of being 'one up', or gaining an advantage over other people. The term was popularized by Stephen Potter in his book of this title (1952). *See also* GAMESMANSHIP.

**Go one better, To.** *See under* GO.

**Have one foot in the grave, To.** To be near death.

**Keep oneself to oneself, To.** To avoid the society of others; to keep apart.

**Jimmy the One.** *See under* JIMMY.

**Neither one thing nor the other.** *See under* NEITHER.

**Oneida Community, The.** *See* PERFECTIONISTS.

**Oneiromancy** (Greek *oneiros*, 'dream', and *manteia*, 'prophecy'). DIVINATION based on the interpretation of dreams.

**Onions, To know one's.** *See under* KNOW.

**Only. Only the good die young.** A popular saying derived ultimately from one of the Greek Gnomic poets and echoed by several writers. *See also* GNOMIC VERSE; WHOM THE GODS LOVE DIE YOUNG.

**Only two Alexanders.** Alexander the Great said: 'There are but two Alexanders: the invincible son of Philip, and the inimitable painting of the hero by APELLES.'

**Onomatopeia** (Greek *onomatopoiia*, 'word-making'). The forming of a word that has a sound imitating that associated with the object designated, or a word that appears to suggest its nature or qualities. Examples are cuckoo, murmur and tingle.

**Onus** (Latin). The burden, the responsibility, as: 'The whole onus is on you.'

**Onus probandi** (Latin, 'the burden of proving'). The obligation of proving some proposition, accusation or the like, as: 'The *onus probandi* rests with the accuser.'

**Onyx** (Greek, 'fingernail'). The gemstone, a variety of chalcedony, is so called because its veined appearance resembles that of a fingernail.

**Oom Paul.** 'Uncle' Paul, the name familiarly applied to Paul Kruger (1825–1904), President of the Transvaal Republic and leader of Boer resistance to British rule in South Africa.

**Oops-a-daisy.** The expression of sympathy as one picks up a child who has fallen over arose as an elaboration of 'oops', a spontaneous exclamation after a mistake or slight accident, itself perhaps based on 'up'. The second part of the phrase may have been influenced by 'lackadaisy', a form of 'lackaday', another expression of misfortune.

**Oozlum bird.** This fanciful bird is reputed to fly backwards. It thus does not know where it is going, but it does like to know where it has been.

It's a curious bird, the Oozlum,
And a bird that's mighty wise,
For it always flies tail-first to
Keep the dust out of its eyes!

W.T. GOODGE: *Hits, Skits, and Jingles* (1899)

**Opal** (Greek *opallios*, probably from Sanskrit *upala*, 'gem'). This semi-precious stone, well known for its play of iridescent colours, a vitreous form of hydrous silica, has long been deemed to bring bad luck. Alphonso XII of Spain (1857–85) presented an opal ring to his wife on his wedding day, and her death occurred soon afterwards. Before the funeral he gave the ring to his sister, who died a few days later. The king then presented it to his sister-in-law, and she died within three months. Alphonso, astounded at these fatalities, resolved to wear the ring himself, and within a very short time he, too, was dead. The queen regent then suspended it from the neck of the Virgin of Almudena of Madrid.

**Op. cit.** (Latin *opere citato*). In the work quoted.

**Open. Open-and-shut case, An.** One that is straightforward and conclusive. No sooner do you open it that you can close it.

**Open book, An.** A person or thing that is transparently clear. For example, 'I know you like an open book' means 'I know you through and through' or 'I can always tell what is in your mind.'

**Open diplomacy.** The opposite of secret diplomacy, as defined in the first of Woodrow Wilson's FOURTEEN POINTS, 'open covenants of peace openly arrived at, after which there shall be no private international understandings of any kind'. It is perhaps significant that the Treaty of VERSAILLES was an 'open treaty' negotiated in secret, ultimately by President Wilson, Georges Clemenceau and David Lloyd George.

**Open door.** In political parlance, the principle of admitting all nations to a share in a country's trade. The term is also used for any loophole left for the possibility of negotiation between contending parties or nations.

**Open-field system.** The old manorial common-field system of agriculture in which the villages cultivated their individual 'strips' in the unfenced (open) arable fields. It was essentially a THREE-FIELD SYSTEM based on a triennial crop rotation. From the 15th century, and especially in the 18th and 19th centuries, the system gave way to enclosures. *See also* COMMON; MANOR; NO MAN'S LAND.

**Open house.** To keep open house is to dispense hospitality freely and generously at all times.

**Open letter.** A letter, usually of a critical nature or protesting about a particular issue, addressed to a particular person but published in a newspaper or periodical so that its contents may be publicly known.

**Open one's big mouth, To.** To speak indiscreetly. The expression is sometimes punningly elaborated as 'To open one's big mouth and put one's foot in it'.

**Open question, An.** A statement, proposal, doctrine or supposed fact about which differences of opinion are permissible. In the HOUSE OF COMMONS every member may vote as he likes, regardless of party considerations, on an open question.

**Open season.** The season when restrictions on the killing of game are lifted. *See* SPORTING SEASONS IN ENGLAND

**Open secret, An.** A piece of information generally known, but not formally announced.

**Open sesame!** The password at which the door of the robbers' cave flew open in the tale of ALI BABA in the ARABIAN NIGHTS ENTERTAINMENTS. Hence a key to a mystery or anything that acts like magic in obtaining favour, admission, recognition or the like.

Sesame (*Sesamum indicum*) is an East Indian annual herb, with an oily seed which is used as food or laxative. In Egypt they eat sesame cakes, and the seeds are a traditional flavouring in bread, rolls and so forth.

**Open shop, An.** The reverse of a CLOSED SHOP.

**Open someone's eyes, To.** To enlighten someone; to make a person realize what is happening.

**Open the ball, To.** To lead off the first dance at a ball; hence to begin the matter by taking the lead.

**Open the door to, To.** To create an opportunity for.

**Open verdict.** A verdict affirming that a crime has been committed but specifying neither the criminal nor, in the case of violent death, the cause.

**With open arms.** *See under* WITH.

**Opera** (Italian, from Latin, 'work'). Drama set to music, this being an integral part of the composition. Dialogue is mostly verse and sung to orchestral accompaniment. Lyrics are an important element, and in older operas a ballet was often included. The rise of opera dates from the end of the 16th century, and it became popular after the first opera house was opened at Venice in 1637. Alessandro Scarlatti (1659–1725) established the aria as a legitimate form of soliloquy, and introduced the *recitativo* (recitative). Henry Purcell (*c.*1658–95) was the father of English opera, writing some 42 musical works for the stage, including some semi-operas and one full opera, *Dido and Aeneas* (1689). *See also* LIGHT OPERA *under* LIGHT.

**Opéra bouffe** (French *bouffe*, 'buffoon'). A form of comic opera or operetta. *See also* OPERA BUFFA.

**Opera buffa.** A form of light opera, with musical numbers and dialogue in recitative. The plot may even be farcical. Mozart's *Le nozze di Figaro* (1786) and Donizetti's *Don Pasquale* (1843) are examples of the form. It is the opposite of OPERA SERIA.

**Opéra comique.** A type of opera that contains spoken dialogue. It does not necessarily imply 'comic opera', and is not the same as OPERA BUFFA. Beethoven's *Fidelio* (1805) could strictly be classified as *opéra comique*, although it would not be called such.

**Opera seria** (Italian, 'serious opera'). A formal opera, especially popular in the 17th and 18th centuries and often based on classical or mythological themes, characterized by the extensive use of arias. Mozart's *Idomeneo, Rè di Creta* (1780) is an *opera seria*.

**Operetta.** A short or light opera, usually with spoken dialogue. The works of Gilbert and Sullivan may be included in this category.

**Beggar's Opera, The.** *See under* BEG.

**Grand opera.** *See under* GRAND.

**Horse opera.** *See under* HORSE.

**Light opera.** *See under* LIGHT.

**Savoy Operas.** *See under* SAVOY.

**Soap opera.** *See under* SOAP.

**Ophelia.** In Shakespeare's *Hamlet* (1600) the naïve daughter of POLONIUS who falls in love with HAMLET. She is manipulated into spying for him, but is humiliated by him. When Hamlet kills Polonius she loses her reason and soon after drowns. Her deranged words are some of the most poignant in all literature.

> *Ophelia*: There's rosemary, that's for
> remembrance; pray, love, remember: and there is
> pansies, that's for thoughts.
> IV, vi

**Ophir.** An unidentified territory, famed in the Old Testament for its fine gold, possibly in southeast Arabia (1 Kings 9:26–28).

**Opinicus.** A fabulous monster in HERALDRY, compounded from DRAGON, CAMEL and LION. It forms the crest of the Barber-Surgeons of London. The name seems to be a corruption of Ophiucus, the classical name of the constellation the Serpent-Holder (Greek *ophis*, 'snake').

**Opium. Opium-eater, The.** Thomas de Quincey (1785–1859), author of *The Confessions of an English Opium-Eater* (1821).

**Opium of the People, The.** A CATCHPHRASE applied to religion. It comes from the Introduction to Karl Marx's *Contribution to the Critique of Hegel's Philosophy of Right* (1843–4):

> Religion is the sigh of the hard-pressed creature, the heart of a heartless world, as it is the soul of soulless circumstances. It is the opium of the people.

**Opium War.** The name given to the war between Britain and China, the First Chinese War (1839–42). The British government did not contest the Chinese right to prohibit trade in opium but opposed their demand that foreign merchants should agree that, if opium were found on a British ship, the culprits would be handed over for execution and the ship or cargo confiscated. Hostilities began when the British refused to surrender an innocent British subject for execution after the death of a Chinese man in a brawl.

**Oppidan** (Latin *oppidum*, 'town'). At Eton College, all those who are not collegers (King's Scholars). Originally those not on the foundation boarded in the town.

**Opposition.** The constitutional term for whichever of the major political parties is out of power. The leader of the Opposition receives a salary as such. In the HOUSE OF COMMONS, the Opposition sits on the benches to the SPEAKER's left, its leader occupying the FRONT BENCH. 'The opposition' is also used generally in business to denote a commercial rival.

> BT [British Telecommunications] was 'concerned' about telephone boxes being used as targets. 'It's a new one on us; perhaps they were working for the opposition.'
> *The Times* (6 December 1994)

**Ops.** The old SABINE fertility goddess and wife of SATURN. She was later identified with RHEA.

**Optime.** In the phraseology of Cambridge University a graduate in the second or third division of the Mathematical TRIPOS, the former being Senior Optime and the latter Junior Optime. The term comes from the Latin phrase formerly used: *Optime disputasti* ('You have disputed very well'). The class above the Optimes is composed of WRANGLERS.

**Optimism.** The doctrine that 'whatever is, is right', that everything that happens is for the best. It was originally set forth by Gottfried Wilhelm von Leibniz (1646–1716) from the postulate of the omnipotence of God, and is cleverly travestied by VOLTAIRE in CANDIDE (1759). *See also* PANGLOSS.

**Option. Local option.** *See under* LOCAL.

**Soft option.** *See under* SOFT.

**Opus** (Latin, 'work'). *See* MAGNUM OPUS.

**Opus Anglicanum** (Latin, 'English work'). Rich medieval embroidery dominated by work in silver and gold thread, so called because England's reputation was unrivalled in this art, which showed the skill of English goldsmiths and silversmiths in making wire. It was mostly employed on ecclesiastical vestments and frontals, but also on banners, palls, robes and hangings.

**Opus Dei** (Latin, 'God's work'). An international Roman Catholic organization of lay people and priests founded in Spain in 1928 by José Maria Escriva de Balaguer with the aim of spreading Christian principles.

**Or.** The heraldic term for the metal gold. *See also* HERALDRY.

**Oracle** (Latin *oraculum*, from *orare*, 'to speak', 'to pray'). The answer of a god or inspired priest to an inquiry respecting the future, or the deity giving responses to such an inquiry. Hence the place where the deity could be consulted, and thus generally a person whose utterances are regarded as profoundly wise and authoritative.

The best known of the numerous oracles of ancient Greece were those of:

AESCULAPIUS at Epidaurus and at Rome
APOLLO at DELPHI, the priestess of which was called the Pythoness, at DELOS and at Claros
DIANA at Colchis
HERCULES at Athens and Gades
JUPITER at DODONA (the most noted), AMMON in Libya and in Crete
MARS in Thrace
MINERVA at Mycenae
PAN in ARCADIA
TROPHONIUS in BOEOTIA, where only men made the responses
VENUS at Paphos and elsewhere

In most of the temples, women, sitting on a tripod, made the responses, many of which were ambiguous and so obscure as to be misleading. To this day, our word 'oracular' is still used of obscure as well as of authoritative pronouncements. Examples are:

When Croesus consulted the Delphic oracle respecting a projected war, he received for answer, *Croesus Halyn penetrans magnum pervertet opum vim* ('When Croesus crosses over the River Halys, he will overthrow the strength of an empire'). Croesus believed the oracle meant that he would overthrow the enemy's empire, but it was his own that he destroyed when defeated by CYRUS.

Pyrrhus, being about to make war against Rome, was told by the oracle: *Credo te, Aeacide, Romanos vincere posse*, which can mean either 'I believe that you, Pyrrhus, can conquer the Romans' or else 'I believe, Pyrrhus, that the Romans can conquer you.' The accusative and infinitive construction results in an ambiguity of object.

Another prince, consulting the oracle on a similar occasion, received for answer, *Ibis redibis nunquam per bella peribis* ('You shall go you shall return never you shall perish by the war'), the interpretation of which depends on the position of the comma. It may be, 'You shall return, you shall never perish in the war' or 'You shall return never, you shall perish in the war', which latter was the fact.

Philip of Macedon sent to ask the oracle of Delphi if his Persian expedition would prove successful, and received for answer:

The ready victim crowned for death
Before the altar stands.

Philip took it for granted that the 'ready victim' was the king of Persia, but it was Philip himself.

When the Greeks sent to Delphi to know if they would succeed against the Persians, they were told:

Seed-time and harvest, weeping sires shall tell
How thousands fought at Salamis and fell.

But whether the Greeks or the Persians were to be the 'weeping sires', no indication was given, nor whether the thousands 'about to fall' were to be Greeks or Persians. *See also* WOODEN WALLS.

When Maxentius was about to encounter Constantine, he consulted the guardians of the SIBYLLINE BOOKS as to the fate of the battle, and the prophetess told him: *Illo die hostem Romanorum esse periturum* ('That day the enemy of the Romans shall be destroyed'). Whether Maxentius or Constantine was the 'enemy of the Romans' the oracle left undecided.

The Bible tells (1 Kings 22:15, 35) that when AHAB, king of Israel, was about to wage war on the king of Syria, and asked Micaiah if Ramoth-Gilead would fall into his hands, the prophet replied, 'Go, for the Lord will deliver the city into the hand of the king.' In the event, the city fell into the hands of the king of Syria.

**Oracle of the Holy Bottle, The.** The oracle to which Rabelais (Bks IV and V) sent PANURGE and a large party to obtain an answer to a question that had been put to SIBYL and poet, monk and fool, philosopher and witch, judge and fortune-teller. This was whether Panurge should marry or not. The oracle was situated at BACBUC 'near Catay in Upper India', and the story has been interpreted as a satire on the church. The celibacy of the clergy was for long a moot point, and the 'Holy Bottle' or cup to the laity was one of the moving causes of the schisms from the church. The crew setting sail for the Bottle refers to Anthony, Duke of Vendôme, afterwards king of Navarre, setting out in search of religious truth.

**Sibylline oracles.** *See under* SIBYL.

**Work the oracle, To.** *See under* WORK.

**Orange. Orange blossom.** The conventional decoration for the bride at a wedding, introduced as a custom into Britain from France about 1820. The orange is said to indicate the hope of fruitfulness, few trees being more prolific, while the white blossoms symbolise innocence.

**Orange Lilies, The.** *See under* REGIMENTAL AND DIVISIONAL NICKNAMES.

**Orange lodges.** *See* ORANGEMEN.

**Orangemen** or **Orange Order.** A society founded in 1795 in ULSTER to maintain 'the Protestant Constitution, and to defend the King and his heirs as long as they maintain the Protestant ascendancy'. It was formed after an armed clash between Roman Catholics and Protestants in Armagh, known as the Battle of the Diamond. The name commemorated WILLIAM OF ORANGE (William III), who defeated James II and his Catholic supporters at the Battle of the Boyne in 1690. Orange lodges or clubs of militant Protestants spread throughout the province, their members being known as Orangemen, an earlier association of this name having been formed in the time of William III (r.1689–1702). Gladstone's championship of HOME RULE after 1886 led to a revival of the movement. The Orange Order still flourishes, imposing ethical obligations on its members. Orangeman's Day, 12 July, is the day when Protestants in Northern Ireland annually commemorate the anniversary of the Battle of the Boyne, with Orangemen to the fore in the parades and processions through the streets.

**Orange Peel.** A nickname given to Sir Robert Peel when Chief Secretary for Ireland (1812–18), on account of his PROTESTANT bias and opposition to Roman Catholic emancipation.

**Agent orange.** *See under* AGENT.

**Blood orange.** *See under* BLOOD.

**William of Orange.** *See under* WILLIAM.

**Oration, Creweian.** *See under* CREWEIAN.

**Orator. Orator Henley.** John Henley (1692–1756), who for about 30 years delivered lectures on theological, political and literary subjects.

**Orator Hunt.** Henry Hunt (1773–1835), a RADICAL politician. He presided at the meeting that led to the PETERLOO MASSACRE and as MP for Preston (1830–3) presented the first petition to Parliament in favour of women's rights.

**Orator of the Human Race, The.** *See* CLOOTS, ANACHARSIS.

**Stump orator.** *See* STUMP SPEAKER.

**Oratorians** (Medieval Latin *oratorium*, 'place of prayer'). A congregation founded at Rome by St Philip Neri (1515–95), but with origins in the late 1550s. Now called the Institute of the Oratory of St Philip Neri, membership consists of secular priests and lay brothers, who take no vows but live communally and are free to leave if and when they wish. Each oratory is autonomous, and its members work under the ORDINARY of their diocese. John Henry (later Cardinal) Newman (1801–90) was so impressed with the Oratory at Rome that he obtained papal permission to found the Birmingham Oratory in 1847, and in 1849 he sent Frederick William Faber (1814–63) to found the London Oratory, which moved to Brompton in 1854. *See also* ORATORIO.

**Oratorio.** A sacred story or drama set to music,

in which solo voices, chorus and instrumental music are employed. St Philip Neri introduced the acting and singing of sacred dramas in his Oratory at Rome in the late 16th century, and it is from this that the term comes. The first oratorio is generally accepted to be Emilio de' Cavalieri's *La rappresentazione di anima e di corpo* (1600).

**Oratory, Soapbox.** *See under* SOAP.

**Orc.** A sea monster fabled by ARIOSTO, Michael Drayton, Joshua Sylvester and others to devour men and women. The name was sometimes used for a whale.

> An island salt and bare,
> The haunt of seals, and orcs, and sea-mews' clang.
> MILTON: *Paradise Lost*, xi (1667)

**Orcades.** The Roman name for the Orkneys, probably connected with the old ORC, a whale.

**Orchestra, Hallé.** *See under* HALLÉ..

**Orcus.** A Latin name for HADES. Edmund Spenser speaks of a DRAGON whose mouth was:

> All set with yron teeth in raunges twaine,
> That terrifide his foes, and armed him,
> Appearing like the mouth of *Orcus* griesly grim.
> *The Faerie Queene*, VI, xii (1596)

**Ordeal** (Old English *ordēl*, 'judgement'). The ancient Anglo-Saxon and Germanic practice of referring disputed questions of criminality to supernatural decision by subjecting the accused to physical trials in the belief that God would defend the right, even by miracle if needful. Hence, figuratively, an experience testing endurance, patience, courage and the like. All ordeals, except that by battle and cold water for witches, were abolished in England in the early 13th century, when trial by jury took their place. Similar methods of trial are found among other races. *See also* ACT OF TRUTH.

**Ordeal by cold water.** The accused was bound and tossed into water. If the person floated, guilt was presumed. If the accused sank, they were hauled out. This became a common test for WITCHCRAFT.

**Ordeal** or **wager of battle.** The accused was obliged to fight his accuser. Lords often chose vassals to represent them and priests and women were allowed champions. It was legally abolished in 1818 when the right was claimed by a person charged with murder.

**Ordeal of boiling water.** Usual for the common people, the ordeal involved plunging the hand into hot water either up to the wrist or elbow. Guilt was presumed if the skin was injured.

**Ordeal of fire.** For persons of high rank. Carrying a red-hot iron or walking barefoot and blindfolded over red-hot ploughshares were the usual forms. If the accused showed no wound after three days he was adjudged innocent.

**Ordeal of the bier.** A suspected murderer was required to touch the corpse and was deemed guilty if blood flowed from the body.

**Ordeal of the Corsned.** *See* CORSNED.

**Ordeal of the cross.** The accuser and accused stood upright before a cross and he who moved first was adjudged guilty. *See also* JUDICIUM CRUCIS.

**Ordeal of the Eucharist.** For priests. It was believed that if the guilty partook of the SACRAMENT, divine punishment would follow for the sacrilege committed.

**Cold-water ordeal.** *See under* COLD.

**Damiens' ordeal.** *See under* DAMIEN.

**Order!** When members of the HOUSE OF COMMONS and other debaters call out 'Order!' they mean that the person speaking is in some way breaking the rule of order of the assembly and should be called to order. The command is most frequently heard from the mouth of the Speaker. *See also* NAME.

> Roars and bellows from all sides ('*Order! All* of you!' – Madam Speaker) and, wings flapping, our two principal chickens were pulled back into their boxes.
> *The Times* (7 December 1994)

**Order of battle.** The arrangement and disposition of an army or fleet according to the situation prior to engagement. *See also* LINE OF BATTLE.

**Order of Danebrog, The.** The second of the Danish orders of knighthood, which was traditionally instituted in 1219 by Waldemar II, although the present order derives from that founded by Christian V in 1671. *See also* ORDER OF THE ELEPHANT.

**Order of Merit.** A British order for distinguished achievement in all callings founded by Edward VII in 1902, with two classes, civil and military. The Order is limited to 24 men and women and confers no precedence. It is designated by the letters OM, following the first class of the Order of the KNIGHTS OF THE BATH, and precedes all letters designating membership of other Orders. The badge is a red and blue cross patté, with a blue medallion in the centre surrounded by a LAUREL wreath, and it bears the words 'For Merit'. The ribbon is blue and crimson. Crossed swords are added to the badge for military members.

**Order of St Catherine, The.** (1) An extinct military order established in 1063 to guard the remains of St CATHERINE and to protect pilgrims. It followed the rule of St Basil.

(2) A Russian order founded by Peter the Great (r.1682–1725), confined to female members, and so named as a compliment to his second wife, who succeeded him as Catherine I.

**Order of St Clare.** A religious order of women founded in 1212, the second that St Francis instituted. The name derives from their first abbess, Clare of Assisi. The nuns are also called Clarisses, Poor Clares, Minoresses or Nuns of the Order of St Francis. *See also* FRANCISCANS.

**Order of St Michael and St George, The.** A British order of knighthood instituted in 1818 to honour natives of the Ionian Isles and Malta. In 1864 the Ionian Islands were restored to Greece and the order was remodelled. It was extended in 1868, 1879 and subsequently to British subjects serving abroad or in British overseas possessions, but it is now largely awarded to members of the diplomatic and foreign service and for administrative service in the COMMONWEALTH.

It is now limited to 125 Knights and Dames Grand Cross, 375 Knights and Dames Commander and 1750 Companions.

**Order of St Patrick, The.** A British order of knighthood instituted by George III in 1783, originally consisting of the sovereign, the lord lieutenant, and 15 knights (increased to 22 in 1833). Its motto is *Quis separabit* ('Who shall separate [us]'). In 1968 the Order consisted of the sovereign and two knights: the Duke of Windsor and Duke of Gloucester. There have been no elections since 1922, when the Irish Free State was formed. The Order ceased with the death of the Duke of Gloucester in 1974.

**Order of the Annunciation, The.** An Italian order of military knights was thus named from 1518, but it was founded by Amadeus VI, Count of Savoy, in 1362 as the Order of the Collar, from its badge, a silver collar bearing devices in honour of the Virgin. *See also* FERT.

**Order of the boot, The.** The sack; a notice of dismissal from one's employment or office.

**Order of the day, The.** The prevailing state of things.

**Order of the Elephant, The.** A Danish order of knighthood said to have been instituted by Christian I in 1462, but reputedly of earlier origin. It was reconstituted by Christian V in 1693 and, besides the sovereign and his sons, consists of 30 knights. The collar is of gold elephants and towers. *See also* ORDER OF DANEBROG.

**Order of the Golden Fleece, The** (French *L'ordre de la toison d'or*). A historic order of knighthood once common to Spain and Austria, instituted in 1429 for the protection of the church by Philip the Good, Duke of Burgundy, on his marriage with the Infanta Isabella of Portugal. It became two separate orders in 1713. Its badge is a golden sheepskin with head and feet attached, adopted in allusion to Greek legend. It has been suggested that it may also have been influenced by the fact that the manufacture of woollens had long been the staple industry of the Netherlands. *See also* GOLDEN FLEECE.

**Order of the Holy Ghost, The.** A French order of knighthood (*Ordre du Saint-Esprit*), instituted by Henry III in 1578 to replace the Order of St Michael. It was limited to 100 knights and was not revived after the revolution of 1830. *See also* CORDON BLEU.

**Order of the Swan, The.** An order of knighthood founded by Frederick II of Brandenburg in 1440 (and shortly after in Cleves) in honour of the LOHENGRIN legend. It died out in the 16th century but was revived by Frederick William IV of Prussia in 1843. After the arrival of Anne of Cleves in England to marry Henry VIII the White Swan was adopted as a PUBLIC HOUSE SIGN. The badge of the Order was a silver swan surmounted by an image of the Virgin.

**Order of the Visitation** or **Visitandines, The.** A contemplative order for women founded by St Francis de Sales and St Jane Frances de Chantal in 1610. They adopted a modification of the AUGUSTINIAN rule, and their chief work is now concerned with education.

**Orders in Council.** Orders issued by the PRIVY COUNCIL with the sanction of the sovereign under the royal prerogative. In practice they are drawn up on the advice of ministers who are answerable to Parliament, usually to deal with matters demanding immediate attention. Orders in Council are also issued on matters of administrative detail under certain Acts of Parliament.

**Orders of architecture.** In classical architecture: CORINTHIAN, DORIC, IONIC, TUSCAN and Composite, which is a compound of Ionic and Corinthian. *See also illustration on page 858*

**Orders of Knighthood.** *See* KNIGHT.

**Orders of the day, The.** In the HOUSE OF COMMONS the items of business set down for a particular day on the Order Papers; the main business of the day.

**Order to view.** An estate agent's request for a prospective customer to be allowed to inspect premises.

**Apple-pie order.** *See under* APPLE.

**Call to order, To.** *See under* CALL.

**Corinthian order.** *See under* CORINTH.

**Court order.** *See under* COURT.

**Doric order.** *See under* DORIAN.

**Holy Orders.** *See under* HOLY.

**Ionic order.** *See under* IONIC.

**Most Ancient Order of the Thistle, The.** *See under* MOST.

**Most Noble Order of the Garter, The.** *See under* MOST.

**Orange Order.** *See* ORANGEMEN.

**Point of order.** *See under* POINT.

**Provincial of an order, The.** *See under* PROVINCIAL.

**Sealed orders.** *See under* SEAL.

**Standing orders.** *See under* STAND.

**Orders of architecture**

**Take orders, To.** To enter HOLY ORDERS by ordination.

**Tall order.** *See under* TALL.

**Tuscan order.** *See under* TUSCAN.

**Ordinal numbers.** *See* CARDINAL NUMBERS.

**Ordinance, The Self-denying.** *See under* SELF.

**Ordinary.** In the CHURCH OF ENGLAND an ecclesiastic who has ordinary or regular jurisdiction in his own right and not by depute, usually the bishop of a diocese and the archbishops. The chaplain of NEWGATE PRISON was called the Ordinary. In the ROMAN CATHOLIC CHURCH the pope, diocesan bishops, abbots, apostolic vicars and others are classed as ordinaries. In Scotland certain judges of the Court of Sessions are called Lords Ordinary, and those legal experts appointed to aid the HOUSE OF LORDS in the determination of appeals are called Lords of Appeal in Ordinary.

In HERALDRY the ordinary is a simple charge, such as the chief, pale, fesse, bend, bar, chevron, cross or saltire.

**Ordinary of the Mass, The.** That part of the MASS that varies in accordance with the church calendar as opposed to the CANONS OF THE MASS, which do not change.

**Ordnance Survey.** The government body responsible for mapping Britain was founded in 1791 to carry out a survey for the Board of Ordnance, the body of partly military and partly civilian composition that provided stores and equipment for the army. This was at a time when an invasion of Britain by Napoleon was expected. For this reason the first map was of Kent, the part of England nearest to France.

**Oreads** or **Oreades.** NYMPHS of the mountains (Greek *oros*, 'mountain').

> The Ocean nymphs and Hamadryades,
> Oreads and Naiads with long weedy locks,
> Offered to do her bidding through the seas,
> Under the earth, and in the hollow rocks.
>
> PERCY BYSSHE SHELLEY: 'The Witch of Atlas', xxii (1820)

**Oregon Trail.** A pioneer route some 2000 miles (3220km) long from Independence, Missouri, across the plains, thence up the North Platte, through South Pass, Wyoming, along the Snake River, across southern Idaho and the Blue Mountains to the Columbia River and finally by raft to the mouth of the Willamette. It was first followed by Nathaniel Wyeth of Massachusetts in 1833, and in the 1840s it became a regular emigrant route. It was also used as the overland route to the Californian goldfields.

The modern highway called the Oregon Trail follows a slightly different route.

**Orellana.** A former name of the River Amazon, after Francisco do Orellana (*c.*1500–49), lieutenant of Pizarro, who first explored it in 1541.

**Orestes.** In Greek legend the son of AGAMEMNON and CLYTEMNESTRA, who killed his mother and her lover AEGISTHUS in revenge for their murder of his father. He appears in various classical works, but most importantly in Aeschylus' trilogy *Oresteia* (5th century BC), in which he hesitates to kill Clytemnestra but is pressurized into doing so by APOLLO, his sister ELECTRA and the chorus. He is then driven mad by the FURIES, who demand that he be tried for his crime. He is finally acquitted by ATHENE.

**Plyades and Orestes.** *See under* PYLADES.

**Organ stops.** Many of the names of the stops found on church organs are music in themselves and include the following, with the tones they produce:

*Bourdon* (French, 'humming tone'), low and booming
*Clarabella* (Latin *clarus*, 'clear' and *bellus*, 'beautiful'), bright and fluting
*Cor de nuit* (French, 'night horn', i.e. watchman's horn), lowish and metallic
Dulciana (Latin *dulcis*, 'sweet'), soft and string-like
*Flûte d'amour* (French, 'love flute'), bright and fluting
*Lieblich gedact* (German, 'lovingly covered'), soft and fluting
*Salicional* (Latin *salix*, 'willow'), quiet and reedy
*Unda maris* (Latin, 'wave of the sea'), soft and tremulous
*Voix céleste* (French, 'angelic voice'), soft and tremulous
*Vox angelica* (Latin, 'angelic voice'), the same as *Voix céleste*
*Vox humana* (Latin, 'human voice'), reedy.
*Zauberflöte* (German, 'magic flute'), pleasant and fluting

**Orgies.** Drunken revels; riotous feasts; wild or licentious extravagance. They are so called from the Greek *orgia*, the secret nocturnal festivals in honour of BACCHUS.

**Orgoglio** (Italian, 'Arrogant Pride' or 'Man of Sin'). In Edmund Spenser's *The Faerie Queene* (I, vii and viii (1590)), Orgoglio is a hideous giant as tall as three men, son of Earth and Wind, who typifies the tyrannical power of the Church of Rome.

**Oriana.** The beloved of AMADIS OF GAUL, who called himself Beltenebros when he retired to the Poor Rock (*Amadis de Gaula*, ii, 6).

Queen Elizabeth I is sometimes called the 'peerless Oriana', especially in the group of madrigals entitled the *Triumphs of Oriana* (1601).

**Orientation** (Latin *oriens*, 'east'). The placing of the east window of a church due east, so that the rising sun, representing Christ, the Sun of Righteousness, may shine on the altar. Originally, churches were built with their axes pointing to the rising sun on the saint's day, so that a church dedicated to St John was not parallel to one dedicated to St Peter. In the building of modern churches, however, the saint's day is not normally taken into account. It has recently been suggested that because many churches were built on pagan sites, the eastern orientation reflects the pagan practice of praying towards the sunrise.

**Oriflamme** (French, 'flame of gold'). The ancient banner of the kings of France, first used in battle in 1124, which replaced the blue hood of St MARTIN OF TOURS. It was the standard of the abbey of St DENYS and was a crimson flag on a gilded staff, said by some writers to have had three points or tongues with tassels of green silk. It was last used in the field at Agincourt (1415) and was replaced by a blue standard powdered with FLEUR-DE-LIS.

It is reputed that infidels were blinded by merely looking at it. In the *Roman de Garin* the Saracens cry, 'If we only set eyes on it we are all dead men', and Jean Froissart records that it was no sooner unfurled at Rosbecq than the fog cleared away from the French, leaving their enemies in misty darkness.

**Original sin.** That corruption that is born with humankind and is the inheritance of all the offspring of ADAM. Theology teaches that as Adam was founder of his race, when Adam fell, the taint and penalty of his disobedience passed to all posterity.

**Orinda, The Matchless.** *See under* MATCHLESS.

**Orion.** A giant hunter of Greek mythology, noted for his good looks. He was blinded by Oenopion, ruler of Chios, who did not want Orion to marry his daughter Merope, but VULCAN sent the child Cedalion to be his guide, and his sight was restored by exposing his eyeballs to the sun. Being slain by DIANA (either because he tried to rape Diana or her attendant Opis, or because he challenged the goddess to a discus contest), he was made one of the constellations and is supposed to be attended by stormy weather. His wife was named Side, and his dogs were Arctophonos ('bear killer') and Ptoöphagos ('glutton of Ptoüs'). His own name may be related to Greek *oros*, 'mountain'.

The constellation Orion is pictured as a giant hunter with a belt and sword and surrounded by his dogs and animals. Betelgeuse and Bellatrix are the 'shoulder' stars, and three bright stars in a line form the belt, below which is the sword handle containing a remarkable nebula.

**Orkneys.** *See* ORCADES.

**Orlando.** The Italian form of ROLAND, one of the great heroes of medieval romance, and the most celebrated of CHARLEMAGNE'S PALADINS.

**Orlando Furioso** ('Orlando mad'). An epic poem in 45 cantos, by Ludovico ARIOSTO (1474–1535), published in its complete form in 1532. Orlando's madness is caused by the faithlessness of ANGELICA, but the main subject of the work is the siege of Paris by Agramant the Moor, when the Saracens were overthrown.

The epic is full of ANACHRONISMS. For example, in Book VI, CHARLEMAGNE (d.814) and his PALADINS are joined by Edward IV of England (r.1461–83), Richard, Earl of Warwick (1428–71) and other later historical characters. In Book IV, cannon are employed by Cymosco, king of Friza. In Book XVII, the late medieval PRESTER JOHN appears, as in the last three books does Constantine the Great, who died in 337.

Among English translations are those of Sir John Harington, by the command of Queen Elizabeth I (1591), John Hoole (1783), W.S. Rose (1823–31), G. Wadman (1974) and B. Reynolds (1975).

About 1589 a play (printed 1594) by Robert Greene entitled *The Historie of Orlando Furioso* was produced. In this version Orlando marries Angelica. *See also* MOON.

**Orlando Innamorato** ('Orlando in love'). An unfinished romance by Matteo Maria Boiardo (*c.*1441–94), published in 1487 and featuring the love of ROLAND and ANGELICA. ARIOSTO wrote ORLANDO FURIOSO as a sequel, and in 1541 the Tuscan poet Francesco Berni (*c.*1496–1535) turned Boiardo's work into a burlesque.

**Orleans, The Maid of.** *See* JOAN OF ARC.

**Ormulum, The.** A long poem in Middle English, of which only a 'fragment' of some 20,000 lines is extant. It is so called from its author Orm or Ormin, an Augustinian canon who wrote in the late 13th century. It consists of a simple narrative of the gospels appointed to be read in church, each with a homily upon it and expositions out of Aelfric, the VENERABLE BEDE and St AUGUSTINE. It is preserved in the Bodleian Library, Oxford, and its orthography makes it particularly valuable evidence of the vowel-length at the time (the writer always doubles a consonant after a short vowel).

Thiss boc iss nemmnedd Orrmulum
Forr thi thatt Orrm itt wrohhte.
(This book is named Ormulum,
For the (reason) that Orm wrought it.)

**Ormuzd** or **Ahura Mazda.** ZOROASTRIANS regard Ormuzd as the principle or angel of light and good, and as the creator of all things and judge of the world. He is in perpetual conflict with AHRIMAN but in the end will triumph. Ormuzd is an abbreviated form of the Old Persian name Ahura Mazda, which means 'Lord Wisdom', from Avestan *ahura*, 'lord', and *Mazda*, 'enlightenment', 'wisdom', the name that Zarathustra added to the supreme god Ahura, itself from Indo-European *mendh*, 'to give to', and *dhe*, 'to put'.

And Oromaze, Joshua, and Mahomet,
Moses, and Buddh, Zerdusht, and Brahm, and Foh,
A tumult of strange names, which never met
Before, as watchwords of a single woe,
Arose.

PERCY BYSSHE SHELLEY: *The Revolt of Islam*, x (1817)

**Orosius.** An early 5th-century Spanish presbyter and historian whose *Historia Adversus Paganos*, from the Creation to AD 417, was translated into Anglo-Saxon from the Latin by ALFRED THE GREAT. It was a popular textbook of general history in the Middle Ages, and Orosius presented some of his works to St AUGUSTINE when he visited him in 415.

**Orpheus.** In Greek legend a Thracian poet, the son of Oeagrus and CALLIOPE (held by some to be a son of APOLLO), who could move even inanimate things by his music, a power that was also claimed for the Scandinavian ODIN. When his wife, EURYDICE, a DRYAD, died, he went into the infernal regions and so charmed PLUTO that she was released on the condition that he would not look back until they reached the earth. Just as he was about to place his foot on the earth, he turned round and Eurydice vanished instantly. The prolonged grief of Orpheus at his second loss so enraged the Thracian MAENADS, with whom he had often celebrated the rites of BACCHUS, that they tore him to pieces. The fragments of his body were collected by the MUSES and buried at the foot of Mount OLYMPUS, but his head, thrown into the River Hebrus, was carried into the sea, and so borne to Lesbos, where it was buried.

The name of Orpheus has been linked with both Greek *orphnē*, 'darkness', for his descent to the infernal regions, and *orphanos*, 'orphan', alluding to his state after the death of Eurydice, but it is almost certainly pre-Greek in origin.

What could the Muse herself that Orpheus bore,
The Muse herself, for her enchanting son,
Whom universal nature did lament,
When, by the rout that made the hideous roar,
His gory visage down the stream was sent,
Down the swift Hebrus to the Lesbian shore?

MILTON: *Lycidas* (1638)

The legend has formed the basis of operas by Gluck, *Orfeo ed Euridice* (1762), Telemann, *Orpheus* (1726), Haydn, *Orfeo ed Euridice* (1806) and Offenbach, *Orphée aux Enfers* ('Orpheus in the Underworld' (1858)), a symphonic poem (1854) by Liszt and a ballet (1948) by Stravinsky.

**Orphic egg, The.** *See* MUNDANE EGG.

**Orphism.** A movement in painting started by Robert Delaunay (1885–1941), characterized by patches and swirls of intense and contrasting colours. The name, given by the poet Guillaume Apollinaire in 1912, alludes to the poetry of ORPHEUS. *See also* CUBISM; DADAISM; FAUVISM; FUTURISM; IMPRESSIONISM; SURREALISM; SYNCHROMISM; VORTICISM.

**Orrery.** A complicated piece of mechanism showing by means of clockwork the movements of celestial bodies within the solar system. It was invented about 1700 by George Graham, who sent his model to Rowley, an instrument maker, to make one for Prince Eugene. Rowley made a copy of it for Charles Boyle (1676–1731), 3rd Earl of Orrery, in whose honour it was named. One of the best is Fulton's, in the Kelvingrove Museum, Glasgow.

**Orson** (French *ourson*, 'little bear'). The twin brother of Valentine in the old romance of VALENTINE AND ORSON.

**Orthodox. Orthodox Church, The.** The Eastern Church, properly, the Holy Orthodox Catholic Apostolic Eastern Church. Its separation from the Western Church was partly due to the historic division of the empire by Constantine, but also to the differences arising between 'Greek' and 'Latin' Christianity which culminated in complete separation in 1054 over the FILIOQUE CONTROVERSY. The Eastern Church now consists of seven patriarchates and is oligarchical in structure. *See also* CATHOLIC CHURCH; GREEK CHURCH; PATRIARCH.

**Orthodox Sunday** or **Feast of Orthodoxy.** In the Eastern Church, the First Sunday in LENT, to commemorate the restoration of the icons in 842. *See also* ICONOCLASTS.

**Orthos** or **Orthrus.** The two-headed dog of GERYON, which was destroyed by HERCULES. *See also* ECHIDNA.

**Orwell, George.** The pseudonym adopted by Eric Arthur Blair (1903–50), Old Etonian and socialist, author of *The Road to Wigan Pier* (1937), ANIMAL FARM (1945) and *Nineteen Eighty-four* (1949), among other works. His derived his pen name from St George, patron saint of England, and the River Orwell in Suffolk, on whose banks he had once lived. *See also* DOUBLETHINK; NEWSPEAK.

**Oscar.** A gold-plated figurine awarded annually by the American Academy of Motion Picture Arts and Sciences for the best film acting, writing, production and so on of the year. There are two claims for the origin of this name. One is that in 1931 the future executive secretary of the Academy, Mrs Margaret Herrick, joined as librarian, and on seeing the then nameless gold statue for the first time, exclaimed, 'It reminds me of my Uncle Oscar.' The other claim is that it derives indirectly from Oscar Wilde (1854–1900). When on a lecture tour of the USA he was asked if he had won the Newdigate Prize for Poetry, and he replied, 'Yes, but while many people have won the Newdigate, it is seldom that the Newdigate gets an Oscar.' When Helen

Hayes was presented with the award, her husband Charles MacArthur, a noted wit and playwright, said, 'Ah, I see you've got an Oscar,' and the name stuck.

**Osiris.** One of the chief gods of ancient Egypt, the son of Nut and brother of SET, his jealous and constant foe, and the husband of ISIS. Set arranged his death, but Osiris underwent resurrection with the aid of THOTH. His son HORUS became his avenger. He was the god of the dead and of the afterlife and resurrection. His name derives from Egyptian *ūsir*, perhaps from *ūser*, 'powerful one'.

**Osmand.** A necromancer in *The Seven Champions of Christendom* (I, xix (*c*.1597)) by Richard Johnson. By magic means, Osmand raised an army to resist the Christians, and six of the Champions fell, whereupon St GEORGE restored them. Osmand tore out his own hair, in which lay his magic power, bit his tongue in two, disembowelled himself, cut off his arms and then, not surprisingly, died. *See also* SEVEN CHAMPIONS.

**Os sacrum** (Latin, 'sacred bone'). A triangular bone which lies at the lower part of the vertebral column. It may have been so called from the bone known in Rabbinical legend as the 'luz', and it was regarded as the nucleus of the resurrection body.

> Os sacrum ... so called from being offered in sacrifice by the ancients.
> *Encyclopædia Britannica* (1771)

**Ossian** or **Oisin.** The legendary Gaelic bard and warrior hero of the 3rd century, the son of Fionn Mac Cumhail (FINGAL). He is best known from the publications (1760–3) of the Scottish writer James Macpherson, purporting to be translations of poems by Ossian, the son of Fingal, from original manuscripts. Macpherson became famous, and his works were widely translated, but their authenticity was challenged by Dr Johnson in his *Journey to the Western Islands of Scotland* (1775) and others. They seem to have been essentially made up by Macpherson himself with some use of ancient sources. Ossian's name represents Irish *oisín*, 'fawn'.

> 'I [Johnson] look upon M'Pherson's Fingal to be as gross an imposition as ever the world was troubled with.'
> BOSWELL: *The Journal of a Tour to the Hebrides* (Wednesday, 22 September)

**Ostler.** *See* HOSTLER.

**Ostracism** (Greek *ostrakon*, 'potsherd'). Blackballing or boycotting; otherwise, the exclusion of a person from society. The word arose from the ancient Greek custom of banishing, by a popular vote, anyone whose power was a danger to the state, the citizens writing on a sherd the name of the one whose banishment was deemed desirable. *See also* BLACKBALL; BOYCOTT; INVENTORS.

**Ostrich.** At one time the ostrich was fabled, when hunted, to run a certain distance and then thrust its head into the sand, thinking that, because it cannot see, it cannot be seen. Hence the application of 'ostrich-like' and similar terms to various forms of self-delusion. What it actually does is to lie flat on the ground and extend its neck to look for danger. Standing up, it would present an easy target. On a further factual basis it is remarkable for its size and speed. It is the largest living bird, with a weight of 175–265lb (80–120kg), and although unable to fly can run when alarmed at 43mph (70kmh) and maintain a pace of 30mph (50kmh) for 20 to 30 minutes at a time.

The attractive sheen of ostrich feathers made them popular among Africans for the adornment of hairstyles, hats and weapons and the fashion caused a severe reduction in the ostrich population. When a vogue for the finery spread to the West, it was thus necessary to set up ostrich farms to cope with the huge demand for the ornamentation.

The ostrich eats indigestible things such as stones and pebbles to assist the functions of its gizzard. This has given rise to such phrases as 'to have the stomach of an ostrich', i.e. to be able to digest anything.

**Ostrich eggs.** These are often suspended in Eastern churches as symbols of God's watchful care. It used to be thought that the ostrich hatches her eggs by gazing on them and that if she looks away for even a minute, the eggs will be addled. Furthermore, the story goes, if an egg is bad the ostrich will break it. Thus also will God deal with evil men.

> Oh! even with such a look as fables say
> The mother ostrich fixes on her egg,
> Till that intense affection
> Kindle its light of life.
> ROBERT SOUTHEY: *Thalaba the Destroyer*, iii (1801)

**Ostrog Bible, The.** *See under* BIBLE.

**Othello.** In Shakespeare's play that bears his name (1604), a Moor and a general of Venice whose noble character and status are destroyed by his jealousy of his wife DESDEMONA. His murder of her after his discovery of her supposed affair with Cassio is in turn followed by his own suicide.

**Other. Other Club, The.** A dining CLUB founded in 1911 by Sir Winston Churchill and F.E. Smith (Lord Birkenhead) and said to be so called because they were not wanted at an existing fraternity known as The Club. It still meets at the Savoy, and membership is not confined to Tories or politicians.

**Other day, The.** Originally this meant 'the second day', either forwards or backwards, 'other' being the Old English equivalent for second, as in Latin *unus*, *alter*, *tertius* or *proximus*, *alter*, *tertius*. Starting from today, and going backwards, yesterday was the *proximus ab illo*, the day before yesterday was the *alterus ab illo*, or the other day, and the day preceding that was *tertius ab illo*, or three days ago. Now the phrase is used to express 'a few days ago', 'not so long since'.

**Other things being equal.** If conditions are alike in all but the point in question.

**Have other fish to fry, To.** To have other things to do that are more important.

**Ottava rima** (Italian, 'eighth rhyme'). A stanza of eight ten-syllable lines, rhyming a b a b a b c c, as used by John Keats in *Isabella* (1820), Lord Byron in *Don Juan* (1819–24) and others. It originated in Italy and was used by Torquato TASSO, Ludovico ARIOSTO and many others, the lines being eleven-syllable. The following is an example, as the last stanza of W.B. Yeats' 'Among School Children' (1928):

> Labour is blossoming or dancing where
> The body is not bruised to pleasure soul,
> Nor beauty born out of its own despair,
> Nor blear-eyed wisdom out of midnight oil.
> O chestnut tree, great-rooted blossomer,
> Are you the leaf, the blossom or the bole?
> O body swayed to music, O brightening glance,
> How can we know the dancer from the dance?

**Ottoman Empire.** The Turkish Empire founded by Othman or Osman I (1258–1324), which lasted until 1919.

**Otus.** *See* EPHIALTES.

**Ouida.** The pseudonym of Maria Louise de la Ramée (1839–1908), originally Maria Louise Ramée, a prolific writer of romantic novels of high society, the best known being *Under Two Flags* (1867). She was an unconventional, and later eccentric, character, herself unlucky in pursuit of romance. She was the daughter of a French father and an English mother, the name Ouida being her early childhood attempt to pronounce 'Louise'.

**Ouija.** A device employed by spiritualists for receiving spirit messages. It consists of a small piece of wood on wheels, placed on a board marked with the letters of the alphabet and certain commonly used words. When the fingers of the communicators are placed on the Ouija board, it moves from letter to letter and thus spells out sentences. The word is a combination of French *oui* and German *ja*, both meaning 'yes'. Ouija is a registered trade mark in the USA. *See also* TABLE-RAPPING.

**Our. Our Lady of Mercy.** A Spanish order of knighthood instituted in 1218 by James I of Aragon for the deliverance of Christian captives among the Moors.

**Our Lady of the Snows.** A fanciful name given by Rudyard Kipling in *The Five Nations* (1903) to Canada. William Wordsworth has a poem 'Our Lady of the Snow' (1820), inspired by Mount Righi in Switzerland.

**Out. Out and about.** Engaged in one's normal activities, as when recovered after an illness.

**Out and away.** By far or incomparably, as: 'He is out and away the best batsman.'

**Out and out.** Thoroughly; absolutely; without qualification. Thus 'an out and out liar' is a complete and utter fabricator of untruths.

**Out at elbow.** Shabbily dressed, like one who wears a coat worn out at the elbows. DOWN AT HEEL has a similar meaning.

**Outback.** The more remote and sparsely populated areas in the Australian interior; the bush. The word should be understood as an ellipsis for 'out in the back country', the back country being territory behind the settled regions.

**Outdoors** or **out of doors.** Outside the house; in the open air. The adjectival form is 'outdoor', as for an outdoor seat.

**Out for, To be.** To have one's mind set on achieving some particular end.

**Out-herod Herod, To.** To outdo in wickedness or violence; to rant and roar louder and fiercer than any other. Herod, who slew the babes of Bethlehem (Matthew 2:16), was portrayed as a ranting, roaring tyrant in medieval MYSTERY plays.

> I would have such a fellow whipped for o'er-doing Termagant; it out-herods Herod: pray you, avoid it.
> SHAKESPEARE: *Hamlet*, III, ii (1600)

**Outing.** The word has a general and a more specific meaning. In a general sense, an outing is a trip or excursion, usually one for pleasure. In a more specific and recent sense, it denotes the act of making it publicly known that a particular person, especially when prominent, is homosexual, i.e. when he or she has not voluntarily 'come out'. The verb for this action is thus 'to out'. *See also* COME OUT OF THE CLOSET.

> Chris Smith, Labour's national heritage spokesman who is homosexual, said: 'I don't believe that outing is either just or sensible. More is gained by gay people coming out voluntarily.'
> *Sunday Times* (4 December 1994)

**Out in the cold.** Ignored or neglected.

**Out like a light.** Quickly asleep, like a candle that has had its flame extinguished.

**Out of a hat.** As if by magic. A traditional conjuror's trick is to pull a rabbit (or some other live creature) out of an apparently empty hat.

**Out of breath.** Panting from exertion; temporarily short of breath.

**Out of character.** Not typical of a person. *See also* IN CHARACTER *under* CHARACTER.

**Out of countenance.** Ashamed; disconcerted; discomfited.

**Out of court.** Not admissible evidence within the terms of reference of the trial being conducted. Generally, too trivial to merit attention. To laugh someone or something out of court is to ridicule them.

**Out of date.** No longer valid or current; outmoded.

**Out of gear.** Not working properly.

**Out of God's blessing into the warm sun.** One of John Ray's proverbs, meaning from good to less good. In Shakespeare's *Hamlet* (I, ii (1600)), when the king says to Hamlet, 'How is it that the clouds still hang on you?', the prince answers, 'Not so, my lord; I am too much i' the sun,' meaning, 'I have lost God's blessing, for too much of the sun,' i.e. this far inferior state.

**Out of hand.** Out of control, as: 'The children often got out of hand.'

**Out of heart.** Despondent; without real hope.

**Out of it.** Left on one side; not included.

**Out of joint.** Figuratively, a disrupted or confused state of affairs, as a broken joint is out of order.

**Out of one's mind.** Insane; foolish.

**Out of sight.** Extreme; unusual; excellent; WAY OUT.

**Out of sight, out of mind.** Said of someone or something that is forgotten if not actually seen. The proverb appears as the title of one of Barnabe Googe's *Eglogs* in 1563. Fulke Greville, Lord Brooke (1554–1628), in his 56th sonnet gives it as: 'Out of mind as soon as out of sight'. A tale legendary in the business world tells how the saying was mistranslated by a firm in Thailand as 'Invisible things are insane'.

**Out of sorts.** Not in good health and spirits. The French *être dérangé* explains the metaphor. If cards are out of sorts they are deranged, and if a person is out of sorts the health or spirits are out of order.

In printer's language 'sorts' is applied to particular pieces of type considered as part of the FONT or fount, and a printer is out of sorts when he has run short of some particular letters or characters.

**Out of spirits.** Depressed and despondent.

**Out of the blue.** Unexpectedly, as if falling from the sky.

**Out of the frying pan into the fire.** From a bad situation to an even worse one. The Greeks said: 'Out of the smoke into the flame.'

**Out of the question.** Not worth discussing; not to be thought of or considered.

**Out of the running.** Out of the competition or not worthy of consideration, like a horse that has been scratched (*see* SCRATCH) from a race and is thus not 'in the running'.

**Out of the woods.** Clear of danger; free of problems.

**Out of this world.** Something quite exceptional; quite out of the ordinary; indescribably luxurious; very beautiful. A modern phrase.

**Out of touch.** Not up with current developments; behind the times.

**Out on a limb.** Isolated, stranded or cut off, as an animal on the end of a branch of a tree.

**Out on one's ear.** Peremptorily dismissed; 'sent packing'.

**Out with it.** Say what you are thinking.

**Have it out, To.** To contest either physically or verbally with another to the utmost of one's ability, as: 'I had it out with him,' i.e. 'I spoke my mind freely and without reserve.' The idea is that of releasing and expressing pent-up disapprobation.

**Outsider, An.** A person who is not a member of a particular circle or group, or one who is not considered a socially desirable companion; also a horse or person not thought to be in the running. The usage comes from coaching days when the humbler passengers travelled outside (other than on the box next to the coachman). In more recent times the word has been specifically applied to a person who in some way is alienated from society, and *The Outsider* in this sense is the title of a novel (1953) by the black American writer Richard Wright, of a study (1956) by Colin Wilson of the alienation of a man of genius, and as the English rendering (1946) of the title of Albert Camus' novel *L'Étranger* (1942), about a rebel or misfit who is out of tune with the times.

**Oval, The.** The cricket ground at Kennington, London, the headquarters of the Surrey Cricket Club, a former market garden, was opened in 1846. It was after Australia's victory at the Oval in 1882 that the ASHES came into being. *See also* LORD'S.

**Oval Office, The.** The official office of the President of the United States, in the WHITE HOUSE, so named for its shape. It is the place where key meetings are held, interviews granted, and important policy decisions made.

> With the convention still in progress, an aide to the President's media man, Gerald Rafshoon, plastered a hotel-room wall with ideas for negative T.V. spots – 'Empty Oval Office', 'Places He Would Attack' and 'He Is Not Active, He Means It'.
>
> *Newsweek* (25 August 1980)

**Ovation.** An enthusiastic display of popular favour, so called from the ancient Roman *ovatio*, a minor form of TRIUMPH in which the conqueror entered the city on horseback or on foot wearing a crown of MYRTLE instead of gold.

**Oven, A bun in the.** *See under* BUN.

**Over. Over a barrel.** In a helpless position; at someone's mercy. The allusion is said to be to the practice of draping over a barrel someone who has been rescued from the water when close to drowning, so encouraging the ejection of water from the lungs. A more likely reference may be to a form of punishment in which the victim is bent over a barrel and beaten.

**Over and above.** In addition to; besides.

**Over and over again.** Very frequently; repeatedly.

**Over Edom will I cast out my shoe.** I shall march and triumph. A reference to Psalms 60:6, 108:9.

**Overlander.** An Australian term for the stockmen employed in driving cattle or sheep from one station to another. Tramps and settlers who arrived 'overland' were called 'overland men'. As the 19th-century ballad says:

> We're not fenced in with walls or gates,
> No monarch's realms are grander.
> Our sheep and cattle eat their fill,
> And wander blithely at their will
> O'er forest, valley, plain or hill,
> Free as an Overlander.
> 'The Overlander'

**Overlord.** The code name given to the Allied operation for the invasion of German-occupied Normandy, which began on D-DAY 1944. It was so named because it was regarded as the over-riding operation of the day.

**Over my dead body.** Not if I have any say in the matter.

**Over someone's head.** Without considering or consulting the appropriate person, as: 'She was promoted over the head of her colleague' or 'He complained to the manager over the head of his boss.'

**Over the hill.** Past one's prime, as a woman is popularly supposed to be at 40 and a man at 50. Life after these ages is seen as coasting downhill.

**Over the left.** In early Victorian days, a way of expressing disbelief, incredulity or a negative.

> Each gentleman pointed with his right thumb over his left shoulder. This action, imperfectly described in words by the very feeble term 'over the left', when performed by any number of ladies or gentleman who are accustomed to act in unison, has a very graceful and airy effect; its expression is one of light and playful sarcasm.
> DICKENS: *Pickwick Papers*, ch xlii (1836–7)

**Over the moon, To be.** To be highly excited; extremely delighted; in raptures about something. An elated person may well feel so 'high' that they could jump over the moon. The expression is routine among sportsmen.

**Over the odds.** More than expected.

**Over the sticks.** Over the hurdles; hence a hurdle race or a STEEPLECHASE.

**Over the top.** Excessive; gross. The expression is often abbreviated as OTT, popularized by a television series of this title (1982). The allusion is perhaps to troops going 'over the top' of the trenches in battle.

**Overture** (Old French, ultimately from Latin *apertura*, 'opening'). An opening; a preliminary proposal; a piece of music for the opening of an OPERA. Independent pieces of instrumental music in overture style are called concert overtures.

**Make overtures, To.** To be the first to make an advance, as with a view to acquaintanceship, some business deal or a reconciliation.

**Overy** or **Overie.** The priory church of St Mary Overy, renamed St Saviour's in 1540 and which became SOUTHWARK Cathedral in 1905. It is said in legend to have been founded by a ferryman's daughter called Mary Overs. Her miserly father, Awdrey, feigned death in the hope that sorrow would restrain his household's consumption of victuals. Instead they rejoiced and made merry, whereupon Awdrey rose up in anger, only to be slain as a ghost. Mary, now possessed of his fortune, sent for her lover, but he was thrown from his horse and was killed. In sorrow she founded the nunnery, which she entered. Overy is probably a corruption of 'over the river'.

**Owain.** The hero of a 12th-century legend, *The Descent of Owain*, written by Henry of Saltrey, an English CISTERCIAN. Owain was an Irish knight of Stephen's court who, by way of penance for a wicked life, entered and passed through St PATRICK'S PURGATORY.

**Owl.** The emblem of Athens, where owls abounded. Hence MINERVA (ATHENE) was given the owl for her symbol. The Greeks had a proverb, 'to send owls to Athens', which meant the same as English CARRY COALS TO NEWCASTLE.

**Owlglass.** *See* EULENSPIEGEL.

**Owl light.** Dusk; the gloaming.

**Owl was a baker's daughter, The.** According to a Gloucestershire legend Christ went into a baker's shop for something to eat. The mistress put a cake into the oven for him, but her daughter said it was too large and reduced it by half. The dough, however, swelled to an enormous size, and the daughter cried out, 'Hoo! hoo! hoo!' and was transformed into an owl. Ophelia alludes to the tradition:

> Well, God 'ild you! They say the owl was a baker's daughter.
> SHAKESPEARE: *Hamlet*, IV, v (1600)

**As blind as an owl.** *See under* AS.

**Ox.** One of the four figures that made up the cherubim in Ezekiel 1:10. It is the emblem of the priesthood, and was assigned to St LUKE as his symbol because he begins his Gospel with the Jewish priest sacrificing in the Temple. It is also an emblem of St Frideswide, St LEONARD, St Sylvester, St MÉDARD, St Julietta and St Blandina.

Oxen is one of the few words in modern English that has retained the old Anglo-Saxon plural ending *-en*. Others are brethren and children.

**Oxbow.** A horseshoe bend in a river. An oxbow cut-off is a lake that has formed at a point where the original bend has been flooded.

**Oxgang.** An Anglo-Saxon measure of no very definite quantity, essentially denoting as much as an ox could 'gang over' or cultivate. It was also called a bovate. Eight oxgangs made a carucate. An oxgang became a conventional unit varying from about 10 to 25 acres (4–10 ha) in different places.

**Dumb Ox, The.** *See under* DUMB.

**Put the plough before the oxen, To.** *See under* PLOUGH.

**Oxbridge.** A word widely used as an abbreviation for Oxford and Cambridge collectively, and for the type of historic English university. For some it is a convenient term, for others it has tendentious and snobbish implications. *See also* CAMFORD; REDBRICK.

> Repeated differences with the university authorities caused Mr Foker to quit Oxbridge in an untimely manner.
>
> W.M. THACKERAY: *Pendennis*, ch xviii (1848–50)

**Oxford. Oxford accent.** The accent associated with spoken OXFORD ENGLISH.

**Oxford bags.** Very wide-bottomed flannel trousers, first fashionable among Oxford undergraduates in the 1920s.

**Oxford blue.** A dark blue colour; also a person who has been awarded a BLUE from Oxford University.

**Oxford Blues, The.** *See under* REGIMENTAL AND DIVISIONAL NICKNAMES.

**Oxford English.** The form of spoken English supposed to be typical of members of Oxford University and thus regarded as affected or pretentious. In recent years the term has come to be used by Oxford University Press as a virtual trade name for books designed to help people learning English as a foreign language.

**Oxford frame.** A picture frame the sides of which cross each other at the corners forming a cross-like projection. This was once much used for photographs of college groups.

**Oxford Group.** The name first adopted in South Africa by the followers of Frank Buchman (1878–1961), also called Buchmanism, which developed into the MORAL REARMAMENT movement. He had a considerable following at Cambridge in the 1920s, but later wider support at Oxford. The movement was EVANGELICAL in character and also became concerned with many social, industrial and international questions.

**Oxford marmalade.** A type of coarse-cut marmalade originally manufactured in Oxford. Oxford Marmalade is now a registered trade name for the marmalade produced by Frank Cooper.

**Oxford Movement.** A HIGH CHURCH revival movement in the CHURCH OF ENGLAND 'started and guided' by Oxford clerics, especially John Keble (1792–1866), John Henry Newman (1801–90), Richard Hurrell Froude (1803–36) and Edward Bouverie Pusey (1800–82), after whom the movement is sometimes known as Puseyism. They were dissatisfied with the decline of church standards and with the increase of liberal theology, and they feared that the Catholic Emancipation Act of 1829 endangered the English Church. The movement began in 1833 with Keble's sermon against the suppression of ten Irish bishoprics. It was published under the title of *National Apostasy*. Three tracts setting forth their views were published in 1833, and many *Tracts for the Times* followed, hence the name Tractarianism. They stressed the historical continuity of the Church of England and the importance of the priesthood and the sacraments. The hostility of both mainstream PROTESTANTS and the EVANGELICAL churches was aroused, especially after Newman's reception into the ROMAN CATHOLIC CHURCH in 1845, but in spite of much official opposition the movement had a lasting influence on the standards and ceremonial of the church.

**Great Tom of Oxford.** *See under* GREAT.

**Provisions of Oxford.** *See* MAD PARLIAMENT.

**Oxymoron.** A rhetorical figure in which effect is produced by the juxtaposition of contradictory terms, such as: 'Make haste slowly,' 'Faith unfaithful kept him falsely true.' The word is the Greek for 'pointedly foolish'.

**Oyer and terminer.** An Anglo-French legal phrase meaning 'to hear and determine'. Commissions or writs of oyer and terminer were issued to judges on circuit twice a year in every county, directing them to hold courts for the trial of offences.

**Oyez! Oyez! Oyez!** (Old French, 'Hear ye!'). The call made by the town crier, court officer or some similar official to attract attention when a proclamation is about to be read out. The cry is sometimes written 'O yes!'

**Oyster. Bush oyster.** *See under* BUSH.

**Never eat an oyster unless there's an R in the month.** *See under* NEVER.

**Prairie oyster.** *See under* PRAIRIE.

**World is his oyster, The.** *See under* WORLD.

**Oz.** A colloquialism for Australia, as a phonetic rendering of Aus, an abbreviation frequently used for that country. It is also the name of the magical country in the popular children's novel, *The Wonderful Wizard of Oz* (1900), by L. Frank Baum (1856–1919).

More sinisterly, it was the title of a hippie-style 'underground' magazine of the 1960s, so named as it was founded by an Australian, Richard Neville. The publication became widely known through a court case in 1971, when it was accused of 'corrupting morals'.

**Ozark country.** A popular tourist region in the south central United States, in Missouri, Arkansas and Oklahoma, taking its name from the Ozark Mountains there. It also has its local folklore, expressed in sayings such as: 'An Ozarkian's wealth is mostly dogs.' The tourist trade was boosted by Harold Bell Wright's novel *The Shepherd of the Hills* (1907), which romanticized the Missouri mountains. The name itself is said to be a corruption of 'Aux Arcs', a French trading post set up in the region in the early 18th century.

# P

**P.** The sixteenth letter in the English alphabet, called *pe*, 'mouth', by the Phoenicians and ancient Hebrews, and represented in Egyptian HIEROGLYPHICS by a shutter.

In the 16th century Placentius, a Dominican friar, wrote a poem of 253 HEXAMETER verses, called *Pugna Porcorum*, every word of which begins with the letter P. It opens thus:

> Plaudite, Porcelli, porcorum pigra propago

which may be translated:

> Piglets, praise pigs' prolonged progeny.

As a medieval numeral P stands for 400, $\overline{P}$ stands for 400,000. P is also the abbreviation for 'penny' in the British DECIMAL CURRENCY. Unlike d, its pre-decimal equivalent, it is used in everyday speech, so that '50p' is more commonly said '50 pee' than '50 pence'.

**p, pp, ppp.** Musical directions, with p = *piano* (Italian, 'soft'). P is thus 'soft', pp is 'very soft' and ppp or *pianissimo*, is 'very very soft'.

**Five Ps, The.** *See under* FIVE.

**Four PP** or **Ps, The.** *See under* FOUR.

**Mind one's Ps and Qs, To.** *See under* MIND.

**Pace.** From Latin *pax*, meaning peace or pardon. The word, pronounced 'pacy' or 'paachay', is used to mean 'with due deference to', when preceding the mention of some person with whom the speaker or writer disagrees, as: '*Pace* Mr Jones, I think the answer is to increase funding, not decrease it.'

**Pace eggs.** *See under* PASCH.

**Pace. At a round pace.** *See under* AT.

**Cracking pace, A.** *See under* CRACK.

**Put someone through their paces, To.** To test a person's capabilities, as the intending purchaser of a horse might try out the animal.

**Set the pace, To.** *See under* SET.

**Pacific, The.** The following were so named:

> Amadeus VIII, Duke of Savoy (1383–1451); as Felix V (1440–9) he was an antipope
> Frederick III, emperor of Germany (1415–93)
> Olaf III of Norway (1030–93)

**Pacific Ocean.** So named by the Portuguese navigator Fernão de Magelhães (Ferdinand Magellan (*c*.1480–1521)) in 1520, because there he enjoyed calm weather, and a placid sea after the stormy and tempestuous passage of the STRAIT OF MAGELLAN. It was first sighted by the Spanish explorer Vasco Núñez de Balboa (1475–1519) in 1513.

**Crossroads of the Pacific.** *See under* CROSS.

**Pacifico, Don.** David Pacifico, a Portuguese Jew born at Gibraltar, claimed exorbitant damages of £26,618 from the Greek government when his house at Athens was burned down by rioters. They refused payment, whereupon he asserted his British citizenship, and in January 1850 Lord Palmerston, who was Foreign Secretary, sent the Mediterranean fleet to the Piraeus where it seized Greek shipping. Eventually compensation was agreed at some £5000 after it was discovered that Pacifico claimed as much as £150 for a bedstead and £10 for a pillowcase. The handling of the affair aroused a vigorous criticism in Parliament. *See also* PAM.

**Pack. Package deal.** A settlement including a number of conditions that must be accepted in its entirety by the parties concerned. The allusion is to a parcel or package containing in one wrapping a number of different items. Similarly, a package tour or holiday includes provision for meals, entertainment, gratuities, lodging and the like for a single payment.

**Pack a jury, To.** To select for a jury persons whose verdict is likely to be partial. This form of 'pack' may have originated as 'pact', alluding to an implicit agreement.

**Pack it in!** Stop it!

**Pack of lies, A.** An entirely false story or account.

**Pack one's bags, To.** To get ready to leave.

**Pack up, To.** To put things away; to cease from a task; to stop working (of something mechanical).

**Pack up your troubles in your old kit-bag.** The opening line of one of the most memorable choruses of the First World War. It was written by George Asaf and composed by Felix Powell in 1915.

> Pack up your troubles in your old kit-bag,
> And smile, smile, smile.
> While you've a lucifer to light your fag,
> Smile, boys, that's the style.
> What's the use of worrying?
> It never was worth while,
> So, pack up your troubles in your old kit-bag,
> And smile, smile, smile.

**Send someone packing, To.** *See under* SEND.
**Wolf pack.** *See under* WOLF.

**Packet. Packet of Woodbines, The.** The nickname given to the Russian cruiser *Askold* from its five long, thin funnels, Woodbine cigarettes being thin and sold in packets of five. She was taken from the BOLSHEVIKS after the OCTOBER REVOLUTION of 1917 and used by the Royal Navy against the revolutionaries in the White Sea.
**Catch, get** or **cop a packet, To.** *See under* CATCH.
**Red packet.** *See under* RED.

**Packstaff.** *See* AS PLAIN AS A PIKESTAFF.

**Pact, The Anzac.** *See under* ANZAC.

**Pactolus, The golden sands of the.** *See under* GOLDEN.

**Pad, Launching.** *See under* LAUNCH.

**Paddington fair.** A public execution. TYBURN was in the parish of Paddington. Public executions were abolished in 1868.

**Paddle. Paddle one's own canoe, To.** To be self-reliant. The expression, offered as words of advice, was popularized by Sarah Bolton's poem in *Harper's Magazine* for May 1854:

> Voyage upon life's sea,
> To yourself be true,
> And, whatever your lot may be,
> Paddle your own canoe.

**Dog paddle.** *See under* DOG.

**Paddock, As cold as a.** *See under* AS.

**Paddy** or **Paddywhack.** An Irishman, from PATRICK (Irish *Padraig*). In slang both terms are used for a loss of temper, a childish temper-tantrum.

**Padishah.** The Turkish form of the Persian *Padshah*, a king or reigning sovereign, from *pādi*, 'lord', and *shah*. It was formerly applied exclusively to the SULTAN of Turkey.

**Padmasambhava.** The legendary Buddhist monk who introduced Tantric BUDDHISM to Tibet is credited with establishing the first Buddhist monastery there some time in the 8th century. His name represents Sanskrit *padma sambhava*, 'lotus-born'. He was also known as *Guru Rimpoche*, the latter word a Tibetan honorary title approximating to 'His Excellency'.

**Padre.** A chaplain is so called by personnel of the armed forces. The word, which is Spanish, Italian and Portuguese for 'father', was adopted by the British Army in India, where it was introduced by the Portuguese.

**Padua.** The Italian town was long supposed in Scotland to be the chief school of NECROMANCY, hence Sir Walter Scott says of the Earl of Gowrie:

> He learned the art that none may name
> In Padua, far beyond the sea.
> *The Lay of the Last Minstrel* (1805)

**Anthony of Padua.** *See under* ANTHONY.

**Paean.** According to Homer the name of the physician of the gods. It was used in the phrase *Io Paean* as the invocation in the hymn to APOLLO and later in hymns of thanksgiving to other deities. Hence paean has come to mean any song of praise or thanksgiving, any shout of triumph or exultation. It should not be confused with a paeon, a metrical foot of one long syllable and three short, although the origin is identical.

**Pagan** (Latin *paganus*, 'countryman', 'villager'). The word's present meaning of a heathen or non-Christian has usually been held to be derived from the fact that heathen practices lingered in the villages long after the Christian church was established in the towns. It was also a Roman contemptuous name for a civilian, and it is likely that when the early Christians called themselves *milites Christi* ('soldiers of Christ'), they adopted the military usage, *paganus*, for those who were not 'soldiers of Christ'.

**Page. Page Three.** A 'page three girl', as a euphemistic term for a nude female model, is so called from the daily photos of bare-breasted young women that first appeared on page 3 of the *Sun* newspaper on 17 November 1970. The feature was so popular that other tabloids copied it.

> Lovely Jackie Brocklehurst makes her bow today as a super Sun Page Three Girl.
> *Sun* (12 June 1975)

**Yellow Pages.** *See under* YELLOW.

**Paget's Irregular Horse.** *See under* REGIMENTAL AND DIVISIONAL NICKNAMES.

**Pagoda.** A Buddhist temple or sacred tower in India and the Far East, and also the name of gold and silver coins formerly current in southern India, from the representation of a pagoda on the reverse. The word came into English from Portuguese, and ultimately goes back to Sanskrit *bhagavatī*, 'divine'.

**Paid.** *See* PAY.

**Pain.** To be on or under pain of something is to be under the threat of punishment or penalty for non-compliance.
**Pain in the neck, A.** An annoying person or thing.
**At pains, To be.** *See under* AT.
**Fool for one's pains, To be a.** *See under* FOOL.
**For one's pains.** *See under* FOR.

**Paint. Paint the lily, To.** *See* GILD THE LILY.
**Paint the lion, To.** In old nautical parlance, to strip a man naked and then smear his body all over with tar.
**Paint the town red, To.** To celebrate without inhibition; to cause some disturbance in town by having a noisy and disorderly spree. A phrase of American origin, perhaps originally alluding to a town's RED LIGHT DISTRICT, which raunchy cowboys and their molls would extend to the whole town.
**As smart as paint.** *See under* AS.

**Devil's paintbrush.** *See under* DEVIL.
**Finger painting.** *See under* FINGER.
**Not as black as one is painted.** *See under* BLACK.
**War paint.** *See under* WAR.

**Painter.** It is said that APELLES, being at a loss to delineate the foam on BUCEPHALUS, dashed his brush at the picture in despair and achieved by accident what he could not accomplish by art. Similar stories are told of many other artists and also of the living quality of their paintings. It is reputed that Apelles painted Alexander the Great's horse so realistically that a living horse mistook it and began to neigh. Diego Velázquez (1599–1660) painted a Spanish admiral that was so true to life that Philip IV mistook the painting for the man and reproved the portrait for not being with the fleet. Birds flew at grapes painted by the Greek painter Zeuxis (*fl.* late 5th century BC), and the artist Jan Mandyn tried to brush off a fly from a man's leg, both having been painted by Quinten Massys or Matsys (*c.*1465–1530). Parrhasios of Ephesus (*fl.* 400 BC) painted a curtain so well that Zeuxis told him to draw it aside to reveal the picture behind it, and the Greek sculptor MYRON (5th century BC) is said to have fashioned a cow so well that a bull mistook it for a living creature. *See also* TROMPE L'OEIL.

**Cut the painter, To.** *See under* CUT.
**Genre painter.** *See under* GENRE.
**Jack the Painter.** *See under* JACK.
**Sunday painter.** *See under* SUNDAY.

**Pair. Pair off.** When two Members of Parliament of opposite parties agree to absent themselves, so that, when a vote is taken, the absence of one neutralizes the missing vote of the other, they are said to pair off. In the HOUSE OF COMMONS this is usually arranged by the WHIPS. If there are more Government than Opposition backbenchers, as with the large Government majority after the 1983 election, pairing can be physically difficult. In such cases, the MPs concerned are allowed to be absent on certain night, according to a rota known as a bisque (a sports term of obscure origin).

**Pigeon pair.** *See under* PIGEON.
**Second pair back.** *See under* SECOND.

**Paix** (French, 'peace').

**Paix des Dames, La** ('The Ladies' Peace'). The treaty, by which France lost Italy, concluded at Cambrai in 1529, between Francis I and Charles V, the Holy Roman Emperor, so called because it was effected by Louise of Savoy, mother of the French king, and Margaret, the emperor's aunt.

**Pakistan.** The name of this state formed in 1947 was coined in 1933 by a Cambridge student, Chaudarie Rahmat Ali, to represent the units that should be included when the time came: P for Punjab, A for the Afghan border states, K for Kashmir, S for Sind and 'stan' for Baluchistan. At the same time the name can be understood to mean 'land of the pure', from Iranian or Afghani *pāk*, 'pure', and Old Persian *stān*, 'land' (as in Afghanistan itself).

**Pal.** A ROMANY word meaning brother or mate.

**Old pals act.** *See under* OLD.

**Palace.** Originally a dwelling on the Palatine Hill of Rome, where AUGUSTUS, and later Tiberius and NERO, built their mansions. The word was then transferred to other royal and imperial residences and subsequently to similar buildings, such as BLENHEIM PALACE, Dalkeith Palace and to the official residence of a bishop, and finally to a place of amusement as the CRYSTAL PALACE, the People's Palace and, ironically, a GIN PALACE. *See also* ALLY PALLY; PALATINATE.

**Palace of Westminster, The.** Until 1512 a royal residence and the place to which Parliament was summoned, but now the seat of Parliament. In 1547 St STEPHEN's Chapel within the Palace became the home of the HOUSE OF COMMONS until the fire of 1834, when new buildings were erected. The House of Commons Chamber was again destroyed by enemy bombing in 1940. The HOUSE OF LORDS occupied other parts of the Palace, which ceased to be a royal residence after a serious fire in 1512. STAR CHAMBER stood in these precincts, but the only ancient building now remaining is Westminster Hall, parts of which date from 1097.

**City of Palaces, The.** *See under* CITY.
**Crystal Palace.** *See under* CRYSTAL.
**Gin palace.** *See under* GIN.
**Lambeth Palace.** *See under* LAMBETH.

**Paladin.** Properly, an officer of, or one connected with, the PALACE, but usually confined in romance to the 'Twelve Peers' (*les Douze Pairs*) of CHARLEMAGNE's court. Hence the use of the word for any renowned hero or KNIGHT ERRANT.

The most noted of Charlemagne's paladins were:

Allory de l'Estoc
Astolfo
Basin de Genevois
FIERABRAS or Ferumbras
Florismart
GANELON the traitor
Geoffroy, Seigneur de Bordelois
Geoffroy de Frises
Guérin or Gérin, Duc de Lorraine
Guillaume de l'Estoc, brother of Allory
Guy de Bourgogne
Hoël, Comte de Nantes
Lambert, Prince de Bruxelles
Malagigi
Nami or Nayme de Bavière
OGIER THE DANE
OLIVER
Otuël

Richard, Duc de Normandie
RINALDO
Riol du Mans
ROLAND (ORLANDO)
Samson, Duc de Bourgogne
Thiry or Thiery d'Ardaine

Of these, 12 at a time seem to have formed a special bodyguard to the king. Traditionally, however, the 12 are regarded as those listed in the *Chanson de Roland*: Roland, Oliver, Gérin, Gérier, Bérengier, Otton, Samson, Engelier, Ivon, Ivoire, Anséis and Girard.

**Palaemon.** In Roman legend a son of Ino (*see* LEUCOTHEA), and originally called MELICERTES. Palaemon is the name given to him after he was made a sea-god, and as Portumnus he was the protecting god of harbours. He is mentioned in Edmund Spenser's *The Faerie Queene* (IV, xi (1596)), and in the same poet's *Colin Clout's Come Home Againe* (1595), his name is used for the poet Thomas Churchyard (*c*.1520–1604).

**Palaeolithic Age** (Greek *palaios*, 'old', and *lithos*, 'stone'). The first of the STONE AGES, when man was essentially a hunter using somewhat primitive stone or flint implements and weapons. *See also* NEOLITHIC AGE.

**Palamedes.** In Greek legend one of the heroes who fought against TROY. He was the son of Nauplius and Clymene, and was the reputed inventor of lighthouses, scales and measures, the discus, dice and the like, and was said to have added four letters to the original alphabet of CADMUS. It was he who detected the assumed madness of ULYSSES, in revenge for which the latter brought about his death.

In ARTHURIAN ROMANCES Sir Palamedes is a SARACEN knight who was overcome in single combat by TRISTRAM. Both loved YSOLDE, the wife of King MARK, and after the lady was given up by the Saracen, Tristram converted him to the Christian faith, and stood as his godfather at the font.

**Palamon and Arcite.** *See* ARCITE.

**Palatinate.** The province of a palatine, who was originally an officer of the imperial palace at Rome. This was on the Palatine Hill.

In Germany the Palatinate was the name of a former state on the Rhine, and later that of a detached portion of Bavaria to the west of the Rhine, which in 1946 became part of the newly formed Land Rhineland-Palatinate. *See also* COUNTY PALATINE; PALACE.

**Pale. Pale about the gills.** *See* WHITE ABOUT THE GILLS.

**Paleface.** A name for a white man, attributed to the Native American Indians, as if a translation of an Indian phrase, but largely owing its popularity to the novels of James Fenimore Cooper (1789–1851).

> 'The pale faces make themselves dogs to their women,' muttered the Indian, in his native language.
>
> J. FENIMORE COOPER: *The Last of the Mohicans*, ch iv (1826)

**Pale Horse, The.** Death. 'I looked, and behold a pale horse: and his name that sat on him was Death' (Revelation 6:8). *See also* FOUR HORSEMEN OF THE APOCALYPSE.

**English Pale, The.** *See under* ENGLISH.

**Pales.** The Roman god (later a goddess) of shepherds and their flocks whose festivals, the Palilia or Parilia, were celebrated on 21 April, the 'birthday of Rome', to commemorate the day when ROMULUS, the wolf boy, drew the first furrow at the foot of the hill, and thus laid the foundations of the 'Roma Quadrata', the most ancient part of the city.

**Palgrave.** The short title of *Palgrave's Golden Treasury*, an anthology of poems first published in 1861 and compiled by the poet Francis Turner Palgrave (1824–97). The poems typify contemporary Victorian taste and were selected with the help and advice of Palgrave's friend Alfred, Lord Tennyson. A second series appeared in 1896, after which the standard anthology was *The Oxford Book of English Verse* (1900), edited by Sir Arthur Quiller-Couch (*see* Q), although Palgrave continued to be published in various editions. The Everyman enlarged edition of 1955, for example, had an 88-page supplement of poems 'chosen to conform to the Palgrave tradition'.

**Palimpsest** (Greek *palin*, 'again', and *psēstos*, 'rubbed smooth'). A parchment or other writing surface on which the original writing has been effaced and something else has been written, a practice that used to be common owing to the shortage of materials. Because the writing was not always entirely effaced, many works, otherwise lost, have been recovered. Thus Cicero's *De Republica* (1st century BC) was restored, even though it had been partially erased to make way for a commentary of St AUGUSTINE on the PSALMS.

**Palindrome** (Greek *palindromos*, 'running back again'). A word or line that reads backwards and forwards alike, as 'Madam' or 'Was it a cat I saw?' They have also been called Sotadics, from their reputed inventor, Sotades, a scurrilous Greek poet of the 3rd century BC.

One of the longer palindromes in English is:

> Dog as a devil deified
> Deified lived as a god.

There is also NAPOLEON BONAPARTE's reputed saying:

> Able was I ere I saw Elba.

ADAM'S reputed self-introduction to EVE:

> Madam, I'm Adam.

Also

Lewd did I live, evil I did dwel[l].

The following Latin lines are said to have been addressed to St MARTIN by the Devil:

Signa te signa; temere me tangis et angis;
Roma tibi subito motibus ibit amor.
(Cross, cross yourself; you annoy and vex me without cause;
Through my exertions, Rome, the object of your longing, will soon be near.)

A celebrated Greek palindrome appears as the legend around many fonts, notably that in the Basilica of St SOPHIA, Istanbul, those at St Stephen d'Egres, Paris, and St Menin's Abbey, Orleans, and, in England, around the fonts of St Martin's on Ludgate Hill, St Mary's in Nottingham, and Dulwich College Chapel, and in churches at Worlingworth (Suffolk), Harlow (Essex), Knapton (Norfolk) and Hadleigh (Suffolk):

NION ANOMHMATA MH MONAN OIN
(Wash my transgressions, not only my face.)

One of the best long palindromes in English was that devised by Joyce Johnson for a *New Statesman* competition in 1967. It has 126 words and 467 letters and represents a headmaster's notes on his memo pad. It begins 'Test on Erasmus' and ends, predictably, as 'Sums are not set'.

27.9.1972 is an example of a palindromic date. There are also numerical palindromes: add 132 to 231 for the total 363. Musical palindromes equally exist. The prelude and postlude to Paul Hindemith's *Ludus tonalis* ('The Play of Notes') (1942) are palindromic, as more extensively is the same composer's opera *Hin und zurück* ('There and Back') (1927). Haydn's symphony no. 42 in G (1772) is called the Palindromic. The allusion is to the minuet in the third movement, marked *al rovescio*, 'in reverse', since its second half is obtained by playing the first half backwards. The prelude to Constant Lambert's ballet *Horoscope* (1937) is yet another example.

**Palinode** (Greek, 'singing again'). A song or discourse recanting a previous one, such as that of Stesichorus to HELEN after he had been struck blind for singing evil of her, saying that she had caused the TROJAN WAR. Ovid is said to have written his *Remedia Amoris* (1st century AD) in order to retract his *Ars Amatoria* (1st century BC).

An early palinode in English is Chaucer's *Legend of Good Women* (*c*.1372–86), which he wrote to atone for the story of the false Criseyde in *Troilus and Criseyde* (*c*.1385). It was a favourite form of versification among Jacobean poets, and the best known is that of Francis Quarles (1592–1644), in which man's life is likened to all the delights of nature, all of which fade, and man too dies.

Isaac Watts (1674–1748) had a palinode in which he retracted the praise bestowed upon Queen Anne in a laudatory poem on the earlier years of her reign, saying that the latter part deluded his hopes.

**Palinurus** or **Palinure.** Any pilot, especially a careless one, from the steersman in Virgil's *Aeneid* (1st century BC), who went to sleep at the helm, fell overboard and was swept ashore three days later, only to be murdered on landing.

Lost was the nation's sense, nor could be found,
While the long solemn unison went round;
Wide and more wide, it spread o'er all the realm;
Even Palinurus nodded at the helm.
ALEXANDER POPE: *The Dunciad*, iv (1728)

**Palissy ware.** Dishes and similar articles of pottery, covered with models of fish, reptiles, shells, flowers, leaves and the like, carefully coloured and enamelled in high relief. It is so called after Bernard Palissy (1510–89), the French potter and enameller.

**Pall.** The small linen cloth, stiffened by cardboard, that covers the chalice at the EUCHARIST; also the covering thrown over a coffin. The word comes from Latin *pallium*, 'robe', 'mantle'. There is also the long sweeping robe or pall worn by sovereigns at their coronation, as well as by the pope and archbishops. *See also* PALLIUM.

Sometime let gorgeous Tragedy
In sceptred pall come sweeping by.
MILTON: 'Il Penseroso' (1645)

**Pallbearers.** The custom of appointing men of mark for pallbearers came down from the Romans. Julius CAESAR had magistrates for his pallbearers, AUGUSTUS Caesar had senators, Germanicus had tribunes and centurions, and Lucius Aemilius Paulus had the chief men of Macedonia, who happened to be at Rome at that time. The poor, however, were carried on a plain bier by ordinary citizens.

**Palladian.** An architectural style drawing on the ancient classical principles, introduced by the Italian architect Andrea Palladio (1518–80), who based his work largely on the *Ten Books of Architecture* by Vitruvius, who had been architect to Augustus. Palladio's own *I quattro libri dell' architettura* (1570) influenced his successors. The style was first used in England by Inigo Jones (1573–1652), and the Banqueting Hall, WHITEHALL (1637) and LINCOLN'S INN Chapel (1643) are examples of his work.

**Palladium.** In classical legend the colossal wooden statue of ATHENE in the citadel of TROY, which was said to have fallen from heaven and on the preservation of which the safety of the city was held to depend. It was reputed to have been taken by the Greeks and the city burned down, and was later said to have been removed to Rome by AENEAS. Hence the word is now figuratively applied to any type of safeguard.

> The liberty of the press is the palladium of all the civil, political, and religious rights of an English man.
> *Letters of Junius*: Dedication (1769–72)

*See also* ANCILE; LUCK OF EDEN HALL.

The rare metallic element, found associated with platinum and gold, was named palladium in 1803 by its discoverer, William Hyde Wollaston (1766–1828), from the newly discovered asteroid, Pallas. The London theatre called the Palladium (from 1934, London Palladium) appears to derive its name from the misapprehension that the ancient Palladium, like the COLOSSEUM, was something like a circus.

**Pallas** or **Pallas Athene.** *See* ATHENE.

**Pallium.** The Roman name for a square woollen cloak worn by men in ancient Greece, especially by philosophers and courtesans, corresponding to the Roman TOGA. Hence the Greeks were called *gens palliata*, and the Romans were known as *gens togata*. *See also* GALLIA BRACATA; GENS BRACATA.

At the present time, the scarf-like vestment of white wool with red crosses, worn by the pope and archbishops, is called the pallium. It is made from the wool of lambs blessed in the church of St Agnese, Rome, and until he has received his pallium, no Roman Catholic archbishop can exercise his functions. Its use in the Church of England ended with the REFORMATION, although it is still displayed heraldically in the arms of the archbishop of Canterbury in the shape of a letter Y. It is also called a PALL.

**Pall Mall.** This dignified WEST END thoroughfare, the centre of London's CLUBLAND, takes its name from the old 'alley' where pall mall was played long before Charles II introduced it in St James's Park. When the street was first built it was named Catherine Street, after Catherine of Braganza, Charles II's queen. 'Pale-maille,' says Randle Cotgrave, 'is a game wherein a round box ball is struck with a mallet through a high arch of iron, which he that can do at the fewest blows, or at the number agreed upon, wins.' The name comes from Italian *palla*, 'ball', and *maglio*, 'mallet'. *See also* CROQUET; MALL.

**Pally, Ally.** *See under* ALLY.

**Palm.** The well-known tropical and subtropical tree gets its name from Latin *palma*, 'palm of the hand', from the spread-hand appearance of its fronds. It is a symbol of resolution overcoming calamity. It is said by Orientals to have sprung from the residue of the clay of which ADAM was formed.

**Palma Christi** (Latin, 'palm of Christ'). The castor oil plant (*Ricinus communis*).

**Palm court.** In the interwar years many fashionable hotels had a lounge or tea room decorated with potted palms, where a string ensemble played to provide light background music for guests. Such players gave the name to the various palm court orchestras that evolved, one of them broadcasting regularly even in the years after the Second World War.

> David Galliver sings with the Palm Court Orchestra in Grand Hotel at 9.0 tonight.
> *Radio Times* (22 April 1955)

**Palmer** (Latin *palmifer*, 'palm-bearer'). A pilgrim to the HOLY LAND who was given a consecrated palm branch to carry back, which was usually laid on the altar of his parish church on his return.

> His sandals were with travel tore,
> Staff, budget, bottle, scrip he wore;
> The faded palm-branch in his hand
> Showed pilgrim from the Holy Land.
> SIR WALTER SCOTT: *Marmion*, i (1808)

**Palmistry** or **chiromancy** (Greek *kheir*, 'hand', and *manteia*, 'divination'). The art of reading the palm (of the hand) and deducing the character, temperament, fortune and so on of the owner from the lines on it. The art is ancient and was practised by the Greeks, Chaldean astrologers, Gypsies and others. *See also* DIVINATION.

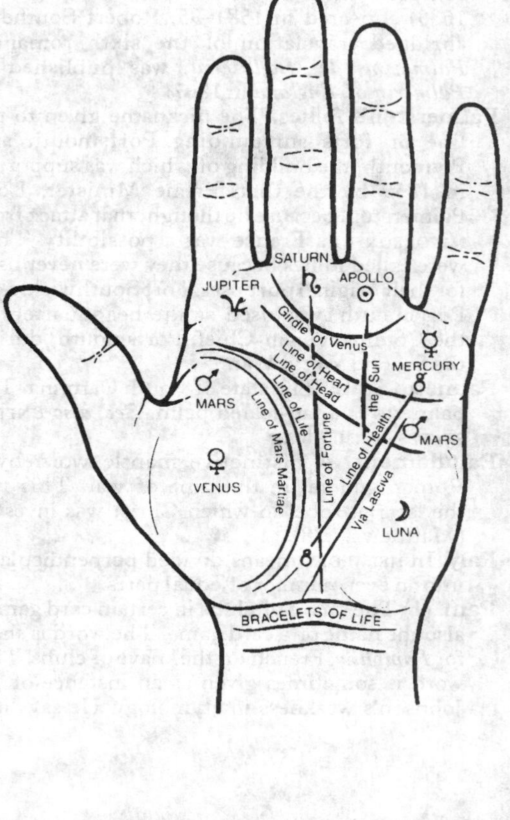

**Palm off, To.** To pass off fraudulently. The allusion is to a juggler, who conceals in the palm of a hand what he pretends to dispose of in some other way.

**Palm of the hand.** The inner area of the hand, between the wrist and the fingers. To have someone in the palm of one's hand is to have them at one's mercy or command.

**Palm Sunday.** The Sunday preceding EASTER, so called in memory of Christ's triumphant entry into JERUSALEM, when the multitude strewed the way (John 12:12–19). In medieval England 'palms' were often made from willow, box and yew.

**Palmy days.** Prosperous or happy days, as those were to a victorious gladiator when he went to receive the palm branch as the reward of his prowess.

**Bear the palm, To.** *See under* BEAR.

**Cross the palm, To.** *See under* CROSS.

**Grease someone's palm.** *See under* GREASE.

**Itching palm, An.** *See under* ITCH.

**Oil someone's hand** or **palm, To.** *See under* OIL.

**Yield the palm, To.** *See under* YIELD.

**Palmerin d'Oliva.** The hero of a cycle of eight 16th-century Spanish romances of CHIVALRY, on the lines of AMADIS OF GAUL. They are thought to be by the Portuguese writer Francisco de Moraes, and an English translation of the complete work by Anthony Munday (1560–1633) appeared in 1581–95. Robert Southey's abridged translation of the sixth romance, *Palmerim de Inglaterra*, was published as *Palmerin of England* in 1807.

**Palmerston's follies.** The nickname given to the line of forts surrounding Portsmouth and Plymouth, the building of which was supported in 1859 by the then Prime Minister, Lord Palmerston, because he thought that attack from NAPOLEON III's France was a possibility. They were called follies because they were never used for their original purposes. Fort Southwick, near Portsmouth, was used as the headquarters of the Commander-in-Chief, Portsmouth, during the Second World War.

**Palmetto State.** The state of South Carolina. The palmetto is a fan-leafed palm. *See also* UNITED STATES OF AMERICA.

**Paludament.** A distinctive mantle worn by a Roman general in the time of war. This was the 'scarlet robe' in which Christ was invested (Matthew 27:28).

**Paly.** In HERALDRY means divided perpendicularly into an even number of equal parts.

**Pam.** (1) The knave of clubs in certain card games, also the name of a card game. The word is short for *Pamphile*, French for the knave of clubs. This word is sometimes given as an instance of Dr Johnson's weakness in etymology. He says it is 'probably from palm, victory; as trump from triumph'.

(2) Pam was the usual nickname of the Victorian statesman Henry John Temple, 3rd Viscount Palmerston (1784–1865), who was Foreign Secretary in 1830–41 and 1846–51, Home Secretary in 1853–5 and Prime Minister in 1855–8 and 1859–65. *See also* PACIFICO, DON; PALMERSTON'S FOLLIES.

**Pamphlet.** A small written work of comparatively few sheets, often controversial and of only temporary interest. The word comes from the name of a 12th-century amatory Latin poem, *Pamphilus seu de Amore* ('Pamphilus ('All-Loving'), or On Love').

**Pan** (Greek, 'all', 'everything'). In Greek mythology, the god of pastures, forests, flocks and herds, and also the universal deity. Some sources derive the name from the same root as that of Latin *pascere*, 'to graze'. His parentage is variously given as born of JUPITER and Calisto, HERMES and Penelope, among others, and he is represented with the upper part of a man and the body and legs of a goat, and with little goat horns on his head. The medieval image of the Devil was based on him. Because his mother deserted him at birth, he was reared by nymphs. His lustful nature was a characteristic and he was the symbol of fecundity. The Romans identified him with their woodland god Silvanus and with FAUNUS.

> Universal Pan,
> Knit with the Graces and the Hours in dance,
> Led on th' eternal Spring.
>
> MILTON: *Paradise Lost*, iv (1667)

Legend has it that at the time of the crucifixion, just when the veil of the Temple was rent in twain, a cry swept across the ocean in the hearing of a pilot, 'Great Pan is Dead', and at the same time the responses of the ORACLES ceased for ever. Early Christians believed that this marked the beginning of the end of the pagan era. It has been suggested that what the mariner heard was a ritual lamentation in honour of ADONIS or for the Babylonian god THAMMUZ. *See also* PANIC.

**Panpipes.** A wind instrument of great antiquity, consisting of a series of pipes, from four to twelve or more, of graduated length, across the upper ends of which the player blows, obtaining a scale of thin, reedy notes. The story is that it was first formed by PAN from the reeds into which the nymph SYRINX was transformed when fleeing from his amorous advances. It is the instrument played by Papageno in *The* MAGIC FLUTE.

**Grand Pan, Le.** *See under* GRAND.

**Peter Pan.** *See under* PETER.

**Pan** (noun). **Flash in the pan, A.** *See under* FLASH.

**Sop in the pan, A.** *See under* SOP.

**Pan** (verb). To criticize harshly.

**Pan out, To.** To turn out or to happen, as, 'it has panned out satisfactorily'. The allusion is to the pan used by a prospector to wash out gold from the gravel of streams and riverbeds.

**Panacea** (Greek, 'all-healing'). A universal remedy. Panacea was the daughter of AESCULAPIUS (Asclepius) and Epione, and the medicine that cures is the daughter or child of the healing art.

In the Middle Ages the search for the panacea was one of the self-imposed tasks of the alchemists. Fable tells of many panaceas, such as the PROMETHEAN UNGUENT, which rendered the body invulnerable, ALADDIN'S ring, the balsam of FIERABRAS and PRINCE AHMED'S APPLE. *See also* ACHILLEA; MEDEA'S KETTLE.

**Panache.** The literal meaning of this French word is a plume of feathers flying in the wind as from the crest of a helmet. Figuratively, it is applied to courage or spirit; to keeping one's end up.

**Pancake.** A thin, flat cake of batter fried in fat, traditionally cooked and eaten on Pancake Day (SHROVE TUESDAY) before the long period of Lenten fasting began on ASH WEDNESDAY. The ingredients are eggs, symbols of creation, flour for the staff of life, salt for wholesomeness and milk for purity. Shrove Tuesday became a day of revelry, sounded off by the ringing of the Pancake Bell, which was the signal for the villagers to cease work and go home to make pancakes or join in the games and merrymaking. A Pancake Day race is still held at Olney, Buckinghamshire, and at Westminster School the Pancake Greaze or Scrimmage persists. In the latter contest, the school cook tosses the pancake over a bar separating the Upper and Lower School, and the boy who secures the largest piece of pancake is rewarded with a guinea. (He cannot eat the pancake, for in modern times it is made from Polyfilla and horsehair.)

**As flat as a pancake.** *See under* AS.

**Panchaea.** A fabulous land, possibly belonging to Arabia Felix (*see* ARABIA), renowned among the ancients for the quality of its perfumes, such as myrrh and incense.

**Pancras, St.** One of the patron saints of children, Pancras was martyred in the Diocletian persecution (304) at Rome at the age of 14. His feast-day is 12 May, and he is usually represented as a boy with a sword in one hand and a palm branch in the other.

The first church to be consecrated in England by St AUGUSTINE, at Canterbury, was dedicated to St Pancras.

**Pandarus.** In Greek legend a Lycian leader and ally of the Trojans. His later connection with the story of TROILUS and CRESSIDA, derived from Boccaccio's *Filostrato* (*c.*1350), led to his being depicted by the romance writers of the Middle Ages as a procurer. He occurs as such in both Chaucer's and Shakespeare's versions of the story. *See also* PANDER.

**Pandects of Justinian** (Greek *pandektēs*, 'all-receiving', 'all-containing'). The great compendium or DIGEST of Roman law made in the 6th century by order of Justinian (*c.*482–565), consisting of 50 books. These superseded all previous law books and decisions in his empire. *See also* CODE NAPOLÉON.

**Pandemonium** (Greek, 'all the demons'). A wild, unrestrained uproar, a tumultuous assembly. The word, formed on the analogy of PANTHEON, was first used by Milton as the name of the principal city in hell.

> The rest were all
> Far to the inland retired, about the walls
> Of Pandemonium, city and proud seat
> Of Lucifer.
>
> *Paradise Lost*, x (1667)

*See also* CORDELIERS' CLUB.

**Pander.** To pander to one's vices is to act as an agent to them, and such an agent is termed a pander, from PANDARUS, who procures for TROILUS the love of CRESSIDA. In Shakespeare's *Much Ado About Nothing* (1598) it is said that Troilus was 'the first employer of pandars' (V, ii).

**Pandora.** In Greek legend and according to Hesiod, she was the first mortal female. To punish PROMETHEUS (who had stolen fire to give to man), ZEUS ordered Hephaestus (VULCAN) to fashion a beautiful woman who was named Pandora ('All-Gifted'), because each of the gods gave her some power or attribute, such as beauty, grace and intelligence, which were to bring about the ruin of man, for Hephaestus gave her the power to lie and deceive.

**Pandora's box.** A present that seems valuable but that in reality is a curse, like that of MIDAS, who found his very food was turned to gold and was thus uneatable. PANDORA was sent by ZEUS as a gift to Epimetheus who married her, against the advice of his brother, PROMETHEUS.

She brought with her a large jar or vase (Pandora's box) which she opened and all the evils flew forth, and they have ever since continued to afflict the world. Hope alone remained in the box.

> The favours of Government are like the box of Pandora, with this important difference, that they rarely leave hope at the bottom.
>
> J.E.T. ROGERS: *Economic Interpretations of History* (1888)

**Pandy, Andy.** *See under* ANDY.

**Pangloss, Dr** (Greek, 'all tongues'). The pedantic old tutor to the hero in VOLTAIRE'S CANDIDE, *ou l'Optimisme* (1759). His greatest characteristic was his incurable and misleading OPTIMISM. It did him no good and brought him all sorts of misfortune, but to the end he reiterated 'all is for the best in this best of all possible worlds'. This was an attack upon the current theories of Gottfried Leibniz.

**Panhandle.** In the USA a narrow strip of territory belonging to one state that runs between two others, such as the Texas Panhandle and the Panhandle of Idaho. West Virginia is known as the Panhandle State.

**Panhandler, A.** Not an inhabitant of such territory, but American slang for a street beggar, perhaps from carrying a pan or tin for the reception of any oddments he may be given.

**Panic.** The word comes from the god PAN, because the sounds heard by night in the mountains and valleys, which give rise to sudden and unwarranted fear, were attributed to him. There are various legends accounting for the name. One is that BACCHUS, in his eastern expeditions, was opposed by an army far superior to his own, and Pan advised him to command all his men at dead of night to raise a simultaneous shout. The innumerable echoes made the enemy think that they were surrounded on all sides, and they took to sudden flight. (*See* Judges 7:18–21.) Another belief is that he could make men, cattle and other creatures bolt in 'Panic' terror.

**Panjandrum.** A pretentious or pompous official, a local 'potentate'. The word occurs in the farrago of nonsense composed in 1755 by Samuel Foote (1720–77) to test Charles Macklin (*c.*1697–1797), the Irish actor, who said he had brought his memory to such perfection that he could remember anything after reading it over once. There is more than one version of the following test passage:

> So she went into the garden to cut a cabbage-leaf to make an apple-pie, and at the same time a great she-bear came running up the street and popped its head into the shop. 'What! no soap?' So he died, and she – very imprudently – married the barber. And there were present the Picninnies, and the Joblillies, and the Garyulies, and the Grand Panjandrum himself, with the little round button at top, and they all fell to playing the game of catch-as-catch-can till the gunpowder ran out at the heels of their boots.

It is said that Macklin was so outraged at this nonsense that he refused to repeat a word of it.

**Panope.** *See* NEREIDS.

**Panopticon** (Greek *pan*, 'all', and *optikos*, 'of sight'). The name given by Jeremy Bentham (1748–1832) to his proposed circular prison with a warder's well in the centre from which convicts could be inspected. The Royal Panopticon of Science and Art, in Leicester Square, was opened in 1854 as a place of popular instruction and a home for the sciences and music. It was built in the Moorish style but failed in its original intention. It was renamed the ALHAMBRA in 1858 and became a theatre in 1871. It was burned down in 1882 and finally demolished in 1936. The Odeon cinema stands on the site. *See also* UTILITARIANISM.

**Pantagruel.** The principal character in Rabelais' great satire *The History of Gargantua and Pantagruel* (the first part published in 1532, the last posthumously in 1564). He was king of Dipsodes and son of GARGANTUA and by some identified with Henri II of France. He was the last of the giants, and Rabelais says he got his name from the Greek *panta*, 'all', and Arabic *gruel*, 'thirsty', because he was born during the drought which lasted thirty and six months, three weeks, four days, thirteen hours, and a little more, in that year of grace noted for having 'three Thursdays in one week'. Although he was chained in his cradle with four great iron chains, like those used in ships, he stamped out the bottom, which was made of weavers' beams. When he grew to manhood he knew all languages, all sciences, and all knowledge of every sort, out-Solomoning SOLOMON in wisdom. His immortal achievement was his voyage to UTOPIA in quest of the ORACLE OF THE HOLY BOTTLE.

He was based on a character who already existed. This was Panthagruel, in the 15th-century work, *Le Mystère des Actes des Apôtres*, in which he is a mischievous imp whose main role in life is to throw salt down the throat of drunkards. His name comes from Greek *panta*, 'all', and *gruel*, a corruption of Arabic *jiryāl*, 'wine'. *See also* PANURGE.

**Pantaloons.** Breeches, trousers, underdrawers or pants get their name from Pantaloon, a lean and foolish old Venetian of 16th-century Italian comedy, who was dressed in loose trousers and slippers. His name is said to come from San Pantaleone (a patron saint of physicians and very popular in Venice), and he was adopted in later harlequinades and PANTOMIMES as the butt of the clown's jokes. *See also* HARLEQUIN.

**Pantechnicon** (Greek, 'belonging to all the arts'). The name was originally coined for a bazaar for the sale of artistic work built *c.*1830 in Motcomb Street, Belgrave Square. As this was unsuccessful, the building was converted into a warehouse for storing furniture, and the name retained. It is now still sometimes used in place of pantechnicon van, a furniture removal van.

**Pantheism.** The doctrine that God is everything and everything is God, a monistic theory elaborated by Baruch Spinoza (1632–77), who by his doctrine of the Infinite Substance sought to overcome the opposition between mind and matter, body and soul. It also denotes PAGAN worship of all the gods. *See also* DUALISM.

**Pantheon** (Greek *pan*, 'all', and *theos*, 'god'). A temple dedicated to all the gods, especially that at Rome built by Hadrian (*c*.120 AD), its predecessor (begun by Agrippa in 27 BC) having been largely destroyed by fire. It is circular and over 140ft (42.6m) in diameter and of similar height. Since the early 7th century, as Santa Maria Rotunda, it has been used as a Christian church. Among the national heroes buried there are the painter Raphael (1483–1520), the first king of Italy, Victor Emmanuel II (1820–78), and Umberto I (1844–1900). Hadrian also built the Pantheon at Athens.

The Panthéon at Paris was originally the church of St GENEVIÈVE, started by Louis XV in 1764 and completed in 1812. In 1791 the CONSTITUENT ASSEMBLY renamed it the Panthéon and decreed that men who had deserved well of their country should be buried there. Among them are Jean Jacques Rousseau (1712–78), VOLTAIRE (1694–1778) and Victor Hugo (1802–85). Hence the term is used for a building to commemorate national heroes, or a MAUSOLEUM for such people. Thus Westminster Abbey has been called the British Pantheon.

The Pantheon opened in Oxford Street in 1772 was designed in the neoclassical style by James Wyatt (1746–1813) for musical promenades, and it was much patronized by those of rank and fashion. It was converted into a theatre for Italian opera in 1791 and the orchestra included Johann Baptist Cramer, La Motte and Cervetto. It was burned down in 1792, rebuilt as a theatre in 1795 and eventually became a bazaar in 1835. It was subsequently used for business premises. The original building was ornamented with Grecian reliefs, and statues of classical deities, and of Britannia, George III and Queen Charlotte.

**Panther** (earlier **Panthera**). In medieval times this animal was supposed to be friendly to all beasts, except the DRAGON, and to attract them by the peculiarly sweet odour that it exhaled. A.C. Swinburne, in 'Laus Veneris' (1866), gives this characteristic a more sinister significance:

> As one who hidden in deep sedge and reeds
> Smells the rare scent made when the panther feeds,
> And tracking ever slotwise the warm smell
> Is snapped upon by the warm mouth and bleeds,
> His head far down the hot sweet throat of her –
> So one tracks love, whose breath is deadlier.

In the old Greek bestiary *Physiologus*, the panther was the type of Christ, but later, when the savage nature of the beast became more widely known, it became symbolical of evil and hypocritical flattery. Hence John Lyly's comparison (in *Euphues, The Anatomy of Wit* (1578)) of the beauty of women to 'a delicate bait with a deadly hook, a sweet panther with a devouring paunch, a sour poison in a silver pot'.

The medieval idea perhaps arose from the name, which was popularly taken from Greek *panthēr*, 'all beasts'. *See also* REYNARD'S WONDERFUL COMB.

**Black Panthers.** *See under* BLACK.

**Pantile.** A roofing tile curved transversely to an ogee shape. In the 18th century, because the chapels (and also often the cottages) of NONCONFORMISTS were frequently roofed with these, such meeting-houses were sometimes called pantile shops, and the word was used in the sense of dissenting. Susannah Centlivre, in *A Gotham Election* (1715), contrasts the 'pantile crew' with a good churchman.

The Parade at TUNBRIDGE WELLS, known as the Pantiles, was so called because the name was erroneously applied to the flat Dutch tiles with which it is paved.

**Pantisocracy** (Greek, 'all of equal power'). The name given by S.T. Coleridge to the communistic, Utopian society, based on a joint-stock farm, that he, with Robert Southey, George Burnett and others, intended (*c*.1794) to form on the banks of the Susquehannah River in New England. The scheme came to nothing, chiefly because of the absence of funds.

> I other climes
> Where dawns, with hope serene, a brighter day
> Than e'er saw Albion in her happiest times,
> With mental eye exulting now explore,
> And soon with kindred minds shall haste to enjoy
> (Free from the ills which here our peace destroy)
> Content and Bliss on Transatlantic shore.
>
> S.T. COLERIDGE: 'On the Prospect of Establishing a Pantisocracy in America' (1794)

**Pantomime.** According to etymology this should be 'all dumb show' (Greek *panta*, 'all', and *mimos*, 'imitator', 'mime'), but the word was commonly applied to an adaptation of the old Commedia dell'Arte that lasted down to the 19th century. The principal characters are HARLEQUIN and COLUMBINE, who never speak, and the CLOWN and Pantaloon, who keep up a constant fire of joke and repartee. Harlequin, Columbine and the clown are the parts taken by the characters, 'the strolling players', in Ruggiero Leoncavallo's opera *I Pagliacci* (1892).

The old Christmas pantomime or harlequinade as an essentially British entertainment was first introduced by John Weaver (1673–1760), a dancing-master of Shrewsbury, in 1702. It is now usually based on a nursery tale such as CINDERELLA, JACK AND THE BEANSTALK, MOTHER GOOSE and PUSS IN BOOTS, enlivened by catchy, topical songs, pretty chorus girls and considerable buffoonery.

**Pants. Ants in one's pants.** *See under* ANT.

**Hot pants.** *See under* HOT.

**Panurge** (Greek *pan*, 'all', and *ergos*, 'worker'). The 'all-doer', i.e. the rogue who will 'do anything or anyone'. It is the name of the rascally companion of PANTAGRUEL and one of the principal characters in Rabelais' satire. A desperate rake, always in debt, he had a dodge for every scheme, knew everything and something more, and was a boon companion of the mirthfullest temper and most licentious bias, while also being timid of danger and a desperate coward. He consulted lots, dreams and so on and, finally, the ORACLE OF THE HOLY BOTTLE, and found insuperable objections to every one of its obscure answers.

Some commentators on Rabelais have identified Panurge with John Calvin, others with Charles of Guise, the cardinal of Lorraine, and this part of the satire seems to be an echo of the great REFORMATION controversy on the celibacy of the clergy.

**Panza, Sancho.** *See under* SANCHO.

**Papal. Papal bull.** An edict issued by the pope, named from the seal (Latin *bulla*) appended to the document. *See also* GOLDEN BULL.

**Papal dispensation, A.** Permission from the pope to dispense with something enjoined, otherwise a licence to do what is forbidden, or to omit what is commanded by the law of the ROMAN CATHOLIC CHURCH.

> A papal dispensation enabled Catherine to wed the brother of her late husband, the younger sovereign himself.
>
> J.R. GREEN: *History of the English People*, ch vi (1874)

**Paparazzi.** The Italian term for press photographers who pester celebrities is not related to any form of the word 'paper'. It comes from the name of such a photographer in Federico Fellini's film *La Dolce Vita* (1960), a cynical evocation of modern Roman high life. The name was supplied by Fellini's scenarist, Ennio Flaiano, who himself took it from George Gissing's travel narrative *By the Ionian Sea* (1901). In this book, Gissing devotes two paragraphs to the worthy proprietor of the Albergo Centrale, Catanzaro, where he spent a few days in 1897. He noted that the owner, Coriolano Paparazzo, had put up a notice on the door of each room expressing his regret that some of his clients chose to dine in other establishments. Flaiano found this 'prestigious' name, as he called it, in *Sulle rive dello Ionio* (1957), Margherita Guidacci's translation of Gissing's work.

**Paper.** So called from papyrus, the giant water reed from which the Egyptians manufactured a material for writing on.

**Paper a house, To.** In theatrical phraseology, to fill the theatre with 'deadheads', or non-paying spectators, admitted by paper orders.

**Paper credit.** Credit allowed against bills, promissory notes and the like that show that money is due to the borrower.

**Paper King, The.** John Law (1671–1729), the Scottish financier. *See also* MISSISSIPPI BUBBLE.

**Paper money** or **currency.** Bank notes as opposed to coin, or bills used as currency.

**Paper over the cracks, To.** To prevent an open breach, by a temporary expedient or settlement unlikely to last, and to ignore the fundamental points at issue that require more radical treatment. Bismarck alluded thus to the convention of Gastein of August 1865, after the defeat of Denmark, by which Austria was to administer Holstein, and Prussia, Denmark. 'We have papered over the cracks,' he said. The Austro-Prussian War broke out in June 1866. The allusion is to the decorator who papers over the cracks in a wall without bothering to repair them, thus only effecting a makeshift job.

**Paper profits.** Hypothetical profits shown in a company's report.

**Paper sizes.** Since metrication paper has been standardized into three series: A (which is used for writing-paper, books and magazines), B (which is used for posters) and C (which is used for envelopes). Each size within each series is identified by a numeral, which increases as the size diminishes. Thus A0 is $33\frac{1}{4} \times 46\frac{3}{4}$in/841 × 1189mm and A10 is $1 \times 1\frac{1}{2}$in/26 × 37mm; C0 is $36 \times 51\frac{1}{4}$in/917 × 1297mm and C6 is $4\frac{1}{2} \times 6\frac{1}{4}$in/114 × 162mm. In all the series, the sides of the paper decrease in the proportion of $1:\sqrt{2}$.

**Paper tiger.** A person or thing that seems strong, forceful or powerful, but that is, in fact, feeble or ineffective; a balloon when pricked. The expression arose from a Chinese saying applied by Chairman Mao in the 1950s to the USA (in the original, *zhǐ lǎohǔ*).

**Elephant paper.** *See under* ELEPHANT.

**Green Paper.** *See under* GREEN.

**India paper.** *See under* INDIA.

**Laid paper.** *See under* LAID.

**Not worth the paper it is written on.** *See under* WORTH.

**Post paper.** *See under* POST.

**Scrap of Paper, The.** *See under* SCRAP.

**Soul papers.** *See under* SOUL.

**Sound all right on paper, To.** *See under* SOUND.

**Walking papers.** *See under* WALK.

**White Paper.** *See under* WHITE.

**Papier mâché** (French, 'chewed paper'). Pulped paper mixed with adhesive and, while pliable, moulded to form various articles, or layers of paper glued together and shaped over a form of some kind. Papier mâché articles, lacquered and often inlaid with mother of pearl, were greatly in vogue in the 18th and 19th centuries.

In 1772 Henry Clay of Birmingham used it to make coaches, applying layers of japan and lacquer to strengthen the finished articles. Clay also used papier mâché to make trays, screens and even pieces of furniture. It was also widely employed for architectural mouldings, and in 1833 ten cottages and a villa were prefabricated in papier mâché and shipped to Australia. Papier mâché is probably of ancient Chinese origin, but the name is probably due to the popularity of French articles in 18th-century England. *See also* POTICHOMANIA; PYROGRAPHY.

**Papyrus.** The written scrolls of the ancient Egyptians are called papyri because they were written on papyrus. *See also* PAPER.

**Par** (Latin, 'equal'). Stock at par means that it is to be bought at the price it represents. Thus £100 stock if quoted at £105 would be £5 above par, while if at £95 it would be £5 below par. A person in low spirits or ill health is said to be 'below par'.

**Paracelsus.** The name coined for himself by the Swiss physician Theophrastus Bombastus von Hohenheim (1493–1541), implying that he was superior to (Greek *para*, 'beyond') Celsus, the 1st-century writer and physician. He studied chemistry and ALCHEMY and, after learning about metals and minerals by working in the mines of the Tyrol, became a medical practitioner. He made many enemies because of his disputatious temperament and flouting of academic traditions, and he wrote numerous treatises propounding his theories, which showed a keen concern for the development of medicine. He was essentially a neo-Platonist and held that, as man contained all elements, a knowledge of alchemy and the physical sciences was neces-sary for the treatment of disease. He did much to encourage innovation, but his work was marred by a streak of charlatanism and superstition.

**Parachute, Golden.** *See under* GOLDEN.

**Paraclete.** Literally, 'the advocate', as someone called to aid or support another, from Greek *parakalein*, 'to summon as a helper'. The word is used as a title of the HOLY GHOST, the Comforter.

> O source of uncreated light,
> The Father's promised Paraclete!
>
> JOHN DRYDEN: *Veni, Creator Spiritus* (1700)

*See also* ABELARD AND HÉLOÏSE.

**Paradise.** The Greeks borrowed this word from the Persians, among whom it denoted the enclosed and extensive parks and pleasure grounds of the Persian kings. The SEPTUAGINT translators adopted it for the Garden of EDEN, and in the New Testament and by early Christian writers it was applied to heaven, the abode of the blessed dead.

The ten animals admitted to MOHAMMED's Paradise are:

(1) the dog KRATIM, which accompanied the SEVEN SLEEPERS
(2) BALAAM's ass, which spoke with the voice of a man to reprove the disobedient prophet
(3) SOLOMON's ant, of which he said; 'Go to the ant, thou sluggard, consider her ways, and be wise'
(4) JONAH's whale
(5) The ram caught in the thicket, and offered in sacrifice in lieu of ISAAC
(6) The calf of ABRAHAM
(7) The camel of Saleb
(8) The cuckoo of Bilkis
(9) The ox of MOSES
(10) Mohammed's steed, Al BORAK

**Paradise and the Peri.** The second tale in Thomas Moore's *Lalla Rookh* (1817). The Peri laments her expulsion from heaven, and is told she will be readmitted if she brings to the gate of heaven the 'gift most dear to the Almighty'. After a number of unavailing offerings, she brought a guilty old man, who wept with repentance and knelt to pray. The Peri offered the 'Repentant Tear', and the gates flew open.

> One morn a Peri at the gate
> Of Eden stood, disconsolate;
> And as she listened to the Springs
> Of Life within, like music flowing,
> And caught the light upon her wings
> Through the half-open portal glowing,
> She wept to think her recreant race
> Should e'er have lost that glorious place!
>
> THOMAS MOORE: *Lalla Rookh*, 'Paradise and the Peri' (1817)

**Paradise Lost.** John MILTON's epic poem was first published in 1667. It tells the story:

> Of Man's first disobedience, and the fruit
> Of that forbidden tree, whose mortal taste
> Brought death into the World, and all our woe,
> With loss of Eden.

SATAN rouses the panic-stricken host of fallen angels with tidings of a rumour current in heaven of a new world about to be created. He calls a council to discuss what should be done, and they agree to send him to search for this new world. Seating himself on the TREE OF KNOWLEDGE, Satan overhears ADAM and EVE talking about the prohibition made by God, and he at once resolves upon the nature of his attack. He takes the form of a mist, and, entering the serpent, induces Eve to eat of the FORBIDDEN FRUIT. Adam eats 'that he may perish with the woman whom he loved'. Satan returns to hell to tell of his triumph, and MICHAEL is sent to lead the guilty pair out of the Garden.

Milton borrowed largely from the epic of Guillaume de Salluste du Bartas (1544–90), entitled *La Semaine* ('The First Week of Creation' (1578)), which was translated into almost every European language, and he was indebted to St

Avitus (d.523), who wrote in Latin hexameters *The Creation*, *The Fall* and *The Expulsion from Paradise*, for his description of Paradise (Bk i), of Satan (Bk ii), and other parts.

In 1671 *Paradise Regained* (in four books) was published. The subject is the Temptation. Eve, being tempted, fell and lost Paradise. Christ, being tempted, resisted and regained Paradise.

**Paradise of fools, The.** Also known as the limbus of fools or *Limbus fatuorum*. Because fools or idiots are not responsible for their actions, the SCHOOLMEN held that they were not punished in PURGATORY and could not be received into heaven, so they were destined to go to a special Paradise. *See also* FOOL'S PARADISE.

**Apples of Paradise.** *See under* APPLE.

**Earthly Paradise, The.** *See under* EARTH.

**Fool's paradise, A.** *See under* FOOL.

**Paraphernalia** (Greek *para*, 'beside', and *pherne*, 'dowry'). Literally, all that a married woman could legally claim as her own, i.e. personal articles, wearing apparel, jewellery and so on. Hence, personal attire, articles in general, anything for show or decoration.

**Parasite** (Greek *parasitos*, 'one who lives at the expense of another'). A plant or animal that lives on another, hence, a hanger-on, someone who fawns and flatters for the sake of what he can get out of it, otherwise a SPONGER.

**Parcae.** *See* FATES.

**Parcel, Part and.** *See under* PART.

**Parchment.** Material for manuscripts or bookbinding made from the skins of animals, so called from Pergamum, in Mysia, Asia Minor, where it was used for writing material when Ptolemy prohibited the export of PAPYRUS from Egypt.

**Pardon. Pardon bell.** The ANGELUS bell. So called because of the INDULGENCE once given for reciting certain prayers forming the Angelus.

**Pardoner.** A medieval cleric licensed to preach and collect money for a definite object such as a CRUSADE or the building of a church, for contributing to which letters of INDULGENCE were exchanged. By many they were regarded as licences to sin, and they were denounced by Chaucer, Langland and Wycliff and the other Protestant reformers.

**Pardoner's mitten, The.** Whoever put this mitten on would be sure to thrive in all things.

> 'Whoever wears this mitten on his hand
> Will multiply his grain. He sows his land
> And up will come abundant wheat or oats,
> Providing that he offers pence or groats.'
>
> CHAUCER: Prologue to 'The Pardoner's Tale' (*c*.1387) (modern translation by Nevill Coghill, 1951)

**Free pardon.** *See under* FREE.

**Pari. Pari mutuel** (French, 'mutual stake'). The name first given to the totalizator, which ensures that the winners of a race share the money staked on the horses after the cost of management, taxes and so on have been deducted.

**Pari passu** (Latin, 'at the same pace'). At the same time, in equal degrees. Two or more schemes carried on at once and driven forward with equal energy are said to be carried on *pari passu*.

**Pariah.** A low-caste Hindu of southern India, from a Tamil word meaning 'drummer', because such Hindus beat the drums at certain festivals. Europeans extended the term to those of no caste at all, hence its application to outcasts generally. *See also* UNTOUCHABLES.

**Parian.** Pertaining to the island of Paros, one of the Cyclades, renowned for its white marble. Hence a fine white porcelain used for making statuettes, vases and other objects.

**Parian chronicle.** One of the ARUNDELIAN MARBLES, found on the island of Paros, and bearing an inscription that contains a chronological register of the chief events of the mythology and history of ancient Greece from the reign of Cecrops (*c*.1580 BC) to the archonship of Diognetus (264 BC), of which approximately the last 100 years is missing.

**Paris.** (1) In Greek legend, the son of PRIAM, king of TROY, and HECUBA, and through his abduction of HELEN, the cause of the siege of Troy. Hecuba dreamed that she was to bring forth a firebrand, and as this was interpreted to mean that the unborn child would bring destruction to his house, the infant Paris was exposed (abandoned) on Mount IDA. He was, however, brought up by a shepherd and grew to perfection of beautiful manhood. At the judgement on the APPLE OF DISCORD, HERA, APHRODITE and ATHENE had each offered him a bribe: the first power, the second the most beautiful of women, and the third martial glory. In return for her victory, Aphrodite assisted him in the abduction of Helen, for whom he deserted his wife OENONE, daughter of the river-god, Cebren. At Troy, having killed ACHILLES, Paris was fatally wounded with a poisoned arrow by PHILOCTETES at the taking of the city.

(2) The capital of France (*see* LUTETIA). Rabelais gives a whimsical derivation of the name. He tells how GARGANTUA played a disgusting practical joke on the Parisians who came to stare at him, and the men said that it was a sport *par ris* ('to be laughed at'), wherefore the city was called Par'is.

The heraldic device of the city of Paris is a ship. As Henri Sauval says: *L'île de la cité est faite comme un grand navire enfoncé dans la vase, échoué au fil de l'eau vers le milieu de la Seine* ('The island of the city is formed like a great ship stuck in the mud, grounded downstream almost in the middle of the Seine'). This form of a ship struck the authorities, who, in the later Middle Ages, emblazoned it on the shield of the city.

**Paris-garden.** A bear garden; a noisy, disorderly place. The allusion is to the Tudor bull-baiting and bear-baiting gardens of that name at BANKSIDE, on the site of a house owned by Robert de Paris, who held the manor in the time of Richard II (r.1377–99). About 1595 the Swan Theatre was erected here and, in 1613, this gave way to the Hope.

**Paris green.** A vivid, light green pigment composed of aceto-arsenite of copper, also used as an insecticide. It is named from the French capital, where it was manufactured.

**Parisian Wedding, The.** The St BARTHOLOMEW'S DAY MASSACRE, which took place on 24 August 1572 during the festivities at the marriage of Henry of Navarre and Margaret of France.

**Monsieur de Paris.** *See under* MONSIEUR.

**Plaster of Paris.** *See under* PLASTER.

**Parish.** The term is used for both an ecclesiastical unit, as the subdivision of a diocese, with its own church and a clergyman, and a civil unit of local government. The latter was at one time territorially within the former, but with the growth of towns and increasing industrialization, the civil parish boundaries no longer matched those of the church parishes. Moreover, town councils took away much of their earlier authority, so that parish councils are now concerned with administering allotments, encouraging local arts and crafts, running community halls and community centres, such as swimming pools, and managing cemeteries and crematoria, as well as being responsible for a number of minor functions. They are funded by the district councils.

**Parish magazine.** The weekly magazine put out by a parish church. At one time they were proper magazines, with articles, serial stories and the like, provided for a whole diocese by the bishop's office, but having locally printed sections of news for particular parishes. Today they are often little more than home-produced photocopied pages of interest to churchgoers of a single village or group of villages, with announcements of church services, flower-arranging rosters, local advertisements and the like.

**Parish pump.** At one time a centre for local gossip in a parish among those who had come to draw water. Today the expression is used of an outlook or attitude that is parochial or restricted, as at times among politicians.

**Parish school.** Formerly, a school run by the local parish, usually in return for a small termly payment. They provided a basic education for the bulk of the population until board schools were set up in the 1870s. When free compulsory education was introduced in 1891, most parish schools became primary schools, then known as elementary schools. *See also* SCHOOLBOARDS.

**Peel parish, A.** *See under* PEEL.

**Park. Central Park.** *See under* CENTRAL.

**Champ de Mars.** *See under* CHAMP.

**Hyde Park.** *See under* HYDE.

**Regent's Park.** *See under* REGENT.

**Richmond Park.** *See under* RICHMOND.

**Safari park.** *See under* SAFARI.

**Parker. Archbishop Parker's table.** *See under* ARCHBISHOP.

**Parkhurst.** One of the better known prisons in Britain, on the Isle of Wight. It opened in 1838, and although traditionally regarded as one of the most secure, experienced embarrassing escapes in the late 20th century.

**Parkinson's Law.** As satirically promulgated by C. Northcote Parkinson (1909–93) in his book with this title (1958), the law states that 'work expands so as to fill the time available for its completion'. The 'law' is directed mainly at public administration, but it is aimed also at inefficient business administration.

**Parlement.** Under the old regime in France, the sovereign court of justice at Paris, where councillors were allowed to plead, and where justice was administered in the king's name. It was a development of the *curia regis*. In due course, 12 provincial parlements were created. They did not have the function of a court of peers as the parlement of Paris did, but they had certain administrative powers. The Paris parlement received appeals from all inferior tribunals, but its own judgements were final. It took cognizance of all offences against the crown, the peers, the bishops, the corporations and all high officers of state. It had no legislative power, however, but had to register the royal edicts before they could become law. The parlements were abolished by the CONSTITUENT ASSEMBLY in 1790.

**Parliament** (Anglo-Latin *parliamentum*, from Old French *parlement*, from *parler*, 'to speak'). The application of the word to assemblies of the king and his magnates became common in 13th-century England, and a representative element was introduced at these meetings. It became an established institution during the 14th century.

A number of Parliaments have been given characteristic names for various reasons, including the PARLIAMENT OF DUNCES. *See also* ADDLED; BAREBONES; BLACK; CAVALIER; CLUB; CONVENTION; DEVIL'S; DRUNKEN; GOOD; GRATTAN'S; LONG; MAD; MERCILESS; MODEL; MONGREL; PENSIONER; RUMP; SHORT; USELESS; WONDERFUL.

**Parliamentary borough.** A borough that sent at least one 'burgess' or member to PARLIAMENT.

**Parliamentary language.** Restrained and seemly language, such as is properly required of any Member speaking in Parliament.

**Parliamentary train.** By the Regulation of Railways Act of 1855 every railway in Great Britain was obliged to run at least one train a day over its system, at a minimum speed of 12 mph (19 kph), calling at every station, at a fare not greater than 1d a mile. This was repealed in 1915. *See also* JERKWATER.

**Parliament of Dunces, The.** Henry IV's second Parliament, convened at Coventry in 1404, also called the Lawless Parliament or the Unlearned Parliament, because the king hoped for a more tractable assembly by directing the sheriffs not to return any lawyers.

**Act of Parliament.** *See under* ACT.

**Contempt of Parliament.** *See under* CONTEMPT.

**Hung Parliament, A.** *See under* HANG.

**Parlour.** Originally the reception room in a monastery where the inmates could see and speak (French *parler*) to their friends.

**Parlour game.** An informal indoor game, typically a word game.

**Parlour tricks.** Accomplishments that are useful in company or at parties. 'Don't try any of your parlour tricks here' is used in the sense of 'Don't try any of your games with me'.

**Parmenio. You think of Parmenio and I of Alexander.** *See under* THINK.

**Parnassus.** A mountain near DELPHI, Greece, with two summits, one of which was consecrated to APOLLO and the MUSES, the other to BACCHUS. It is supposedly named from Parnassus, a son of NEPTUNE, and DEUCALION's ark came to rest there after the flood. Because of its connection with the Muses, it came to be regarded as the seat of poetry and music; hence 'to climb Parnassus' is to write poetry.

**Parnassian school.** The name given to a group of French poets flourishing from about 1850 to 1890, from a collection of their poems entitled *Le Parnasse contemporain* (1866). They included Théophile Gautier, Leconte de Lisle, Charles Baudelaire, François Coppée, Sully Prudhomme and Paul Verlaine. They were nicknamed *les impassibles* for their supposed devotion to 'art for art's sake' and represented a reaction against the romanticism of Victor Hugo and Alphonse Lamartine.

In England, the group of poets following D.G. Rossetti and William Morris have sometimes been referred to as 'the Parnassians'. *See also* PRE-RAPHAELITE BROTHERHOOD.

**Gradus ad Parnassum.** *See under* GRADUS.

**Legislator** or **Solon of Parnassus, The.** *See under* LEGISLATOR.

**Parody.** Parody means an ode that perverts the meaning of another ode (Greek *paroidia*). Parodies were frequent in ancient times. Aristophanes parodies the style of Aeschylus and Euripides in his *Frogs* (5th century BC), and parody was so common among Roman writers that Cicero lists its varieties. In English literature, Henry Fielding's *Shamela* (1741) was a complete parody of Samuel Richardson's *Pamela* (1740), while Richard Brinsley Sheridan's *The Critic* (1779) parodies the sentimental drama of his day. In modern times a classic parody of the 'primitive' novels of Mary Webb and others was Stella Gibbons' *Cold Comfort Farm* (1930). More recently, complete books of parodies have been compiled, such as Dwight MacDonald's *Parodies: An Anthology from Chaucer to Beerbohm and After* (1960) and E.O. Parrott's *Imitations of Immortality* (1986).

**Father of Parody, The.** *See under* FATHER.

**Parquet.** The word is a diminutive of Old French *parc*, 'enclosure' (in Modern French it has the meanings of both BAR and BENCH). In Britain it is commonly used of a form of wooden flooring made up of blocks laid in a pattern. In the USA it denotes the ground floor of a theatre (more commonly called the 'orchestra' nowadays) corresponding to the English 'pit', the latter deriving from the bear-baiting pit of the 16th century.

**Parr, Thomas.** The 'old, old, very old man', who was said to have lived in the reigns of ten sovereigns, to have done penance for sexual excesses at the age of 105, to have married a second wife when he was 122 years old and to have had a child by her. He was a husbandman, reputedly born at Alberbury, near Shrewsbury, in 1483, and he died in 1635. He was taken to the court of CHARLES I by the Earl of Arundel in 1635, and the change of his mode of life killed him. He was buried in the south transept of Westminster Abbey. There is no real evidence supporting his alleged age of 152, but he was doubtless a very old man. *See also* LONGEVITY.

**Parricide, The Beautiful.** *See under* BEAUTY.

**Parsees.** Guebres (or Ghebers) or fire worshippers. The descendants of Persians who fled to India during the Muslim persecution of the 7th and 8th centuries and who are still ZOROASTRIANS. The word means 'People of Pars', i.e. Persia. *See also* TOWERS OF SILENCE.

**Parsifal, Parsival.** *See* PERCEVAL.

**Parsnips, Fine** or **fair words butter no.** *See under* FINE.

**Parson.** *See under* CLERICAL TITLES.

**Parson Adams.** *See under* ADAM.

**Parson and clerk.** An old children's game played with burned paper, the sparks representing parsons.

So when a child (as playful children use)
Has burnt to tinder a stale last-year's news,
The flame extinct, he views the roving fire –
There goes my lady, and there goes the squire,
There goes the parson, oh illustrious spark!
And there, scarce less illustrious, goes the clerk!

WILLIAM COWPER: 'On Observing Some Names of Little Note Recorded in the Biographia Britannica' (1782)

Two red sandstone rocks at Dawlish in Devon are known as the Parson and Clerk. The story is that an inland parson used to visit a certain bishop of Exeter who was in ill health in the hope that he might gain the see on the bishop's death. One winter's night, when on his now customary errand guided by the parish clerk, they lost their way, but with the aid of a country fellow eventually found shelter at Dawlish. They passed the night in carousal among rough company, and in the morning heard that the bishop was dead. In haste the parson pushed his clerk into the saddle, but the horses refused to budge. 'I believe the Devil is in the horses,' said the parson. 'I believe he is,' answered the clerk, only to be greeted with laughter from the company who had now turned into jeering demons. The house disappeared and they found themselves on the seashore. The horses still ignored the whip and they both lost consciousness. Neither parson nor clerk returned to his parish, but two strange rocks now stood on the shore.

**Parson's nose.** The rump of a fowl, also called the POPE'S NOSE. The latter name, which probably gave the former, may have originated in the anti-Catholic period that followed the reign of the pro-Catholic king James II (1685–8).

**Parson's Pleasure.** The well-known bathing enclosure on the bank of the Cherwell at Oxford, known as Patten's Pleasure in the 17th century. It was acquired by the university in 1865, eventually coming to be called Parson's Pleasure, either from its use by local clergy or, more possibly, as a corruption of its original name. As a 'men only' enclosure, bathing in the nude became the common practice there. Its equivalent, not far away, was Dames' Delight, originally known as the Ladies' Pool. It opened in 1934 for family bathing but closed in 1970 following damage from floods.

**Macaroni parson, The.** *See under* FAKES.

**Part.** A portion; a piece; a fragment. To take the part of someone is to side with them.

**Part and parcel.** An essential part, portion or element.

**Part company, To.** To cease to associate.

**Parting of the ways, The.** Said of a critical moment when one has to choose between two different courses of action. The allusion is to a place at which a road branches off in different directions.

**Parts of speech.** A grammatical class of words of a particular character. The old rhyme by which children used to be taught the parts of speech is:

Three little words you often see
Are articles, *a*, *an*, and *the*.
A noun's the name of anything;
As *school* or *garden*, *hoop* or *swing*.
Adjectives tell the kind of noun;
As *great*, *small*, *pretty*, *white*, or *brown*.
Instead of nouns the pronouns stand;
*Her* head, *his* face, *our* arms, *your* hand.
Verbs tell of something being done;
To *read*, *count*, *sing*, *laugh*, *jump*, or *run*.
How things are done the adverbs tell;
As *slowly*, *quickly*, *ill*, or *well*.
Conjunctions join the words together;
As, men *and* women, wind *or* weather.
The preposition stands before
A noun, as *in* or *through* a door.
The interjection shows surprise;
As, *oh!* how pretty! *ah!* how wise!
The whole are called nine parts of speech,
Which reading, writing, speaking teach.

Lines 7 and 8 are now completely misleading because the so-called 'pronouns' here function as possessive adjectives, but it must be remembered that 'her', 'his', 'our', 'your' etc, were formerly regarded as personal pronouns of the possessive or genitive case. *See also* NOUNS.

**Best part of, The.** *See under* BEST.

**Better part of, The.** *See under* BETTER.

**Double a part, To.** *See under* DOUBLE.

**For my part.** *See under* FOR.

**For the most part.** *See under* FOR.

**Man of parts, A.** *See under* MAN.

**Play a part, To.** *See under* PLAY.

**Private parts.** *See under* PRIVATE.

**Till death us do part.** *See* DEPART.

**Walk-on part.** *See under* WALK.

**Walk through one's part, To.** *See under* WALK.

**Partant pour la Syrie** (French, 'Departing for Syria'). The official march of the French troops in the Second Empire. The words were by Count Alexandre de Laborde (1774–1842), and the music, attributed to Queen Hortense, mother of NAPOLEON III, was probably by the flautist Louis François-Philippe Drouet (1792–1873). The ballad tells how young Dunois followed his lord to Syria, and prayed to the Virgin 'that he might prove the bravest warrior, and love the fairest maiden'. Afterwards the count said to Dunois, 'To thee we owe the victory, and my daughter I give to thee'. The refrain was: *Amour à la plus belle; honneur au plus vaillant* ('Love to the fairest; honour to the bravest').

**Parthenon** (Greek, 'maiden's temple'). The great temple of ATHENE at Athens, many of the sculptured friezes and fragments of pediments of which are now in the British Museum among the ELGIN MARBLES. The temple was begun by the architect Ictinus *c*.445 BC and was mainly embellished by Phidias, whose colossal chryselephantine statue of Athene was its chief treasure. The Parthenon was destroyed during the siege of Athens in 1687 by the Venetians, when the powder stored in it by the Turks exploded.

**Parthenope.** Naples, so called from Parthenope ('Maiden-Face'), the SIREN, who threw herself into the sea out of love for ULYSSES, and was washed ashore in the Bay of Naples. Parthenope was an early Greek settlement, later called Palaeopolis ('old city'), after subsequent settlers had established Neapolis ('new city'), from which Naples derives its name.

**Parthian shot** or **shaft.** A parting shot; a telling or wounding remark made on departure, giving one's adversary no time to reply. The allusion is to the ancient practice of Parthian horsemen turning in flight, to discharge arrows and missiles at their pursuers.

**Partington. Dame Partington and her mop.** *See under* DAME.

**Parti pris** (French, 'side taken'). A preconceived opinion; a bias.

**Partlet** (Old French *Pertelote*, a female name). A neckerchief or ruff worn in the 16th century by women, named after the hen with reference to the frill-like feathers round the neck of some hens. The hen in Chaucer's 'The Nun's Priest's Tale' is called Partlet. The origin of the name is uncertain.

> This gentle cock was master in some measure
> Of seven hens, all there to do his pleasure.
> They were his sisters and his paramours,
> Coloured like him in all particulars;
> She with the loveliest dyes upon her throat
> Was known as gracious Lady Pertelote.
> CHAUCER: 'The Nun's Priest's Tale' (*c*.1387)
> (modern translation by Nevill Coghill, 1951)

**Partner, Sleeping.** *See under* SLEEP.

**Partridge. St Partridge's Day.** A whimsical name for 1 September, when partridge shooting begins. *See also* GLORIOUS TWELFTH; SPORTING SEASONS IN ENGLAND.

> 'Well, this *is* friendship! What on earth brings you here, old fellow? Why aren't you in the stubbles celebrating St Partridge?'
> MRS HUMPHRY WARD: *Robert Elsmere*, ch xlviii (1888)

**Parturiunt montes.** *See* MOUNTAIN IN LABOUR.

**Party.** Person, as in the legendary *Punch* cartoon caption ending 'Collapse of stout party'.

**Party line.** The official 'line' or policy of a political party; a telephone line shared by two or more subscribers.

**Party politics.** Politics conducted only through the machinery of the party, as against people's interests generally.

**Party pooper.** A person whose behaviour or attitude spoils other people's enjoyment; a 'wet blanket'. An antidote to a party pooper might be a PARTY POPPER.

**Party popper.** A device that throws forth a paper streamer, used at parties as a diversion and as a corrective to a PARTY POOPER.

**Party wall.** In law, a wall separating two people's property or land to which each of them has certain defined rights.

**Boston Tea Party.** *See under* BOSTON.

**Bottle party.** *See under* BOTTLE.

**Centre party.** *See under* CENTRE.

**Fourth Party.** *See under* FOURTH.

**Fringe party.** *See under* FRINGE.

**Garden party.** *See under* GARDEN.

**Green Party.** *See under* GREEN.

**House party.** *See under* HOUSE.

**Labour Party.** *See under* LABOUR.

**Third party.** *See under* THIRD.

**Toe the party line, To.** *See under* TOE.

**Ultramontane party.** *See under* ULTRAMONTANE.

**Parvenu** (French, 'arrived'). An upstart, a person who has risen from the ranks. The word was made popular in France by Pierre Marivaux's *Paysan Parvenu* (1735).

> The insolence of the successful *parvenu* is only the necessary continuance of the career of the needy struggler.
> W.M. THACKERAY: *Pendennis*, II, xxi (1848–50)

**Parvis** (Old French corruption of Late Latin *paradisus*, 'church close'). The term was originally applied to the court in front of St Peter's at Rome in the Middle Ages, and hence came to denote the court before the main entrance of a cathedral. In the parvis of St Paul's Cathedral, lawyers used to meet for consultation as brokers do on the Exchange. The word is now applied to the room above a church porch. There is a noted example at Cirencester, where the three-storeyed south porch of the church of St John the Baptist, dating from the late 15th century, was adopted for use as a town hall in the 17th century.

**Pasch.** EASTER, from the Greek form of the Hebrew *Pesach*, PASSOVER.

**Paschal lamb.** The lamb sacrificed and eaten at the Jewish PASSOVER. For Christians, Jesus Christ is called the Paschal Lamb because he was called the 'Lamb of God' (John 1:29) and in allusion to 1 Corinthians 5:7: 'For even Christ our passover is sacrificed for us.'

In HERALDRY a Paschal lamb is a white lamb passant carrying a banner of St GEORGE.

**Pasch, pasque** or **pace eggs.** EASTER EGGS, given as an emblem of the Resurrection.

**Pasha.** A Turkish title borne by governors of provinces and certain military and civil officers of high rank. There were three grades of pashas, which were distinguished by the number of horsetails carried before them and planted in front of their tents. The highest rank were those of three tails. The grand VIZIER was always such a pasha, as also were commanding generals and admirals. Generals of divisions were pashas of two tails, and generals of brigades, rear admirals and petty provincial governors, were pashas of one tail.

**Pasiphaë.** In Greek legend, a daughter of the sun and wife of MINOS, the king of Crete. She was the mother of ARIADNE and PHAEDRA and also, through intercourse with a white bull (given by POSEIDON to Minos), of the MINOTAUR.

**Pasque eggs.** *See* PASCH EGGS.

**Pasquinade.** A LAMPOON or political squib, having ridicule as its object. It is so called from Pasquino, an Italian tailor or barber of the 15th century, noted for his caustic wit. After his death, a mutilated statue was dug up and placed near the Piazza Navona. Because it was not clear whom the statue represented, and because it stood opposite Pasquin's house, it came to be called 'Pasquin'. The people of Rome affixed their political, religious and personal satires to it, and thus created the name. At the other end of the city was an ancient statue of MARS, called Marforio, to which were affixed replies to the Pasquinades.

**Pass. Pass away, on** or **over, To.** To die.

**Pass degree.** At the universities an ordinary degree; one without honours.

**Passing bell.** The bell that used to be rung when a person was on the point of death, to scare away any evil spirits that might be lurking ready to snatch the soul while passing from the body. A secondary object was to announce to the neighbourhood that all good Christians might pray for the safe passage of the soul into Paradise. The bell rung at a funeral is sometimes called the 'passing bell'.

Athenians used to beat on brazen kettles at the moment of death to scare away the FURIES.

**Pass muster, To.** To pass inspection; to 'get by'; to be allowed to pass.

**Pass off, To.** To be carried out in a particular way; to misrepresent as something else; to evade or lightly dismiss a remark or the like. In legal terms passing off is the pretence by one person that his goods or business are those of another, for example by using the same name, trade mark or description.

**Pass on, To.** To proceed on one's way. *See also* TO PASS AWAY.

**Pass over, To.** To omit; to ignore the claims of a person to promotion. *See also* PASS AWAY.

**Pass the buck, To.** To evade blame or responsibility and to shift it on to someone else. An American phrase, coming from the game of poker, the term is said to refer to the buckhorn knife that was placed in front of a player to indicate that he was the next dealer. When he had dealt, he 'passed the buck' to another player. The knife itself was so called because its handle was made from the horn of a buck. An alternative explanation is that the 'buck' was a piece of buckshot or a 'bucktail'. The earliest recorded use of the phrase is by Mark Twain in 1872.

**Pass the hat round, To.** To collect contributions of money, originally in a hat or cap.

**Pass the time of day, To.** To exchange a greeting by some remark appropriate to the time of day or the weather, as 'Good morning', 'Bit better today' and so forth.

**Pass under the spear, To.** To be sold by auction; to be sold 'under the hammer'. Writing to Samuel Pepys (12 August 1689), John Evelyn speaks of 'the noblest library that ever passed under the speare'. The phrase is from the Latin *sub hasta vendere*.

**Pass under the yoke, To.** To make a humiliating submission; to suffer the disgrace of a vanquished army. The Romans made a yoke of three spears, two upright and one across on top. When an army was vanquished, the soldiers had to lay down their arms and pass under this archway.

**Pass water, To.** To urinate.

**Bring to pass, To.** *See under* BRING.

**Come to pass, To.** *See under* COME.

**Let this cup pass from me.** *See under* LET.

**Make a pass at someone, To.** To make amorous or sexual advances to them.

> Men seldom make passes
> At girls who wear glasses.
>
> DOROTHY PARKER: *Not So Deep as a Well*, 'News Item' (1937)

**Pretty pass, A.** *See under* PRETTY.

**St Bernard Passes.** *See under* BERNARD.

**Selling the pass.** *See under* SELL.

**Passage. Back passage.** *See under* BACK.

**Bird of passage.** *See under* BIRD.

**Northeast Passage.** *See under* NORTH.

**Northwest Passage.** *See under* NORTH.

**Passepartout** (French, 'pass everywhere'). A master key; also a simple method of picture framing in which the picture is placed between a sheet of cardboard and a piece of glass, the whole being held together by strips of fabric pasted round the edges. As a name, Passepartout is the name of Phileas Fogg's French valet in Jules Verne's novel *Around the World in Eighty Days* (1873).

**Passim** (Latin, 'here and there', 'in many places'). A direction often found in the index of an annotated book that tells the reader that reference to the matter in hand will be found in many passages in the book, section or pages mentioned. The term is sometimes preceded by *et* ('and').

Human sacrifices in Africa, 112 *et passim*; in Caucasus, 27–31, 188; in Brazil, 150, 193; in the Himalayas, 198; in India, 65 *et passim*, 194; in Mexico, 165.

GUY CADOGAN ROTHERY: *The Amazons*, Index (1910)

**Passion, The.** The sufferings of Jesus Christ, which had their culmination in his death on the cross.

**Passion flower.** A plant of the genus *Passiflora*, whose flowers bear a fancied resemblance to the instruments of the PASSION. It seems to have been given the name by 16th-century Spanish missionaries to South America.

The leaf symbolizes the spear
The five petals and five sepals, the ten apostles (PETER, who denied, and JUDAS ISCARIOT, who betrayed, being omitted)
The five anthers, the five wounds
The tendrils, the scourges
The column of the ovary, the pillar of the cross
The stamens, the hammers
The three stigmas, the three nails
The filaments within the flower, the crown of thorns
The calyx, the glory or nimbus
The white tint, purity
The blue tint, heaven

It keeps open three days, symbolizing the three years' ministry, or the three days from the crucifixion (Good Friday) to the resurrection (Easter Day). *See also* PIKE.

**Passionists.** Members of the Congregation of Discalced Clerks of the Most Holy Cross and Passion of Our Lord Jesus Christ, founded by St Paul of the Cross in 1720. The first house, at Monte Argentario, an island off the coast of Tuscany, was opened in 1737. Their chief work is in the holding of retreats and missions. The fathers wear on the breast of their black habit a white heart with the inscription *Jesu XPI Passio*, surmounted by a cross, the *XPI* being the first three letters of the Greek name of Christ (XPICTOC).

**Passion play.** A development of the medieval MYSTERY play with especial reference to the story of Christ's passion and death. The best known survival of such plays, which were common in 14th-century France, is the Oberammergau Passion Play, which takes place every ten years. In 1633 the BLACK DEATH swept over the village of Oberammergau, in southern Germany, and when it abated the inhabitants vowed to enact the PASSION every ten years, starting in 1634. This has been done, although there have been some exceptions, as in 1870, when it was omitted because of the Franco-Prussian War, 1920, when the world situation led it to be postponed to 1922, and 1940, when the Second World War prevented production. An extra performance took place in 1934 to commemorate the tercentenary of the first performance. It is now a highly commercial undertaking, although the cast is still of villagers. It takes over five hours to enact, with as many as 850 people on the stage, together with 100 musicians and some animals.

**Passion Sunday.** *See* JUDICA SUNDAY.

**Passover.** A Jewish festival to commemorate the deliverance of the Israelites, when the angel of death, which slew the first-born of the Egyptians, passed over their houses and spared all who did as MOSES commanded them. The festival began on 14th of Nisan (about 12 April) when the PASCHAL LAMB was eaten, and the Festival of Unleavened Bread lasted seven days.

**Paste, Scissors and.** *See under* SCISSORS.

**Past master.** One who has held the office of dignity of master, hence an adept, one who is long experienced in a skill or matter.

**Pasty face, A.** Pale-faced and unhealthy-looking, like paste.

**Patch.** A fool, so called from the nickname of Cardinal Wolsey's jester, Sexton, who got his name either from Italian *pazzo*, 'fool', or from the motley or patched dress worn by licensed fools.

**Patch up a quarrel, To.** To arrange the matter in a not very satisfactory way; a coat that has been torn and then 'patched up' is pretty sure to break out again; so is a quarrel. *See also* PAPER OVER THE CRACKS.

**Bad patch, A.** *See under* BAD.

**Crosspatch.** *See under* CROSS.

**Face patches.** *See under* FACE.

**King of shreds and patches.** *See under* KING.

**Not a patch on.** Greatly inferior to, as, 'His garden isn't a patch on mine.' The phrase is probably a reduced form of 'not fit to be a patch on', alluding to a piece of inferior cloth deemed unsuitable to mend a garment of superior quality.

**Purple patches.** *See under* PURPLE.

**Patel, Mr.** A stock derogatory nickname for an immigrant Indian or Pakistani, often implying the owner of a corner shop. The name is as common as Smith is in England, and it is found in large numbers in cities where Indians and Pakistanis have settled. The name itself is the Hindi word for the headman of a village.

**Patent** (through French, from Latin *patens*, genitive *patentis*, 'lying open'). Open to the perusal of anybody. A thing that is patented is protected by LETTERS PATENT.

**Patent Rolls.** CHANCERY enrolment of LETTERS PATENT under the GREAT SEAL collected on parchment rolls and first dating from 1201. Each roll contains a year, although in some cases the roll is subdivided into two or more parts. Each sheet of parchment is numbered and called a membrane, so that the 8th sheet, say, of the 10th year of Henry III is cited thus: 'Pat. 10 Hen. III, m.8'.

If the document is on the back of the roll it is called dorso, and 'd' is added to the citation. Patents of invention were last enrolled in 1853 and they are now registered at the Patent Office.

**Letters patent.** *See under* LETTER.

**Paternoster** (Latin, 'Our Father'). The LORD'S PRAYER, from the first two words in the Latin version. Every eleventh bead of a ROSARY is so called, because at that bead the Lord's Prayer is repeated. The name is also given to a certain kind of fishing tackle, in which hooks and weights to suit them are fixed alternately on the line somewhat in rosary fashion.

**Paternoster Row.** The London street of this name was probably so named from the ROSARY or paternoster makers. There is mention as early as 1374 of a Richard Russell, a 'paternosterer', who dwelt there, and archives tell of 'one Robert Nikke, a paternoster maker and citizen', in the reign of Henry IV. Another suggestion is that it was so called because funeral processions on their way to St Paul's Cathedral began their *Pater noster* at the beginning of the Row.

For three centuries Paternoster Row was the home of publishers and booksellers. It was devastated in an air raid in December 1940, when thousands of books were destroyed. *See also* AMEN CORNER.

**Path. Bridle path.** *See under* BRIDLE.

**Cross someone's path, To.** *See under* CROSS.

**Primrose path.** *See under* PRIMROSE.

**Pathetic fallacy.** A term coined by John Ruskin (1819–1900) in the third volume (1856) of his *Modern Painters* to describe the figure of speech that attributes human feelings to nature. Ruskin claimed that a writer was pathetically fallacious when he ascribed such feelings to the inanimate. By way of example, he quoted the following lines from S.T. Coleridge's *Christabel* (1816):

> The one red leaf, the last of its clan,
> That dances as often as dance it can.

**Pathfinder.** One of the names of Natty Bumppo in James Fenimore Cooper's LEATHERSTOCKING NOVELS. It was given to the American Major-General John Charles Fremont (1813–90), who conducted four expeditions across the Rocky Mountains. In the Second World War RAF pilots who identified targets and dropped flares to guide the attacking force were called Pathfinders.

**Patience. Sit like patience on a monument.** *See under* SIT.

**Patient Grisel.** *See* GRISELDA.

**Patmos.** The island of the Sporades in the Aegean Sea to which St JOHN THE EVANGELIST was exiled (Revelation 1:9) and where he wrote Revelation. Hence the name is sometimes used allusively for a place of banishment or solitude.

**Patres conscripti.** *See* CONSCRIPT FATHERS.

**Patriarch** (Greek *patria*, 'family', and *arkhein*, 'to rule'). The head of a tribe or family who rules by paternal right, applied specially in the Bible (after Acts 7:8) to the 12 sons of JACOB, and to ABRAHAM, ISAAC, and Jacob and their forefathers. In one passage (Acts 2:29) DAVID is spoken of as a patriarch.

In the early church, Patriarch, which was first mentioned in the Council of Chalcedon but virtually existing from about the time of the COUNCIL OF NICAEA (325), was the title of the highest church officer. A Patriarch ordained METROPOLITANS, convened councils, received appeals and was the chief bishop over several countries or provinces, as an archbishop is over several dioceses. It was also the title given by the popes to the archbishops of Lisbon and Venice, in order to make the patriarchal dignity appear lower and distinct from the papal. It is also the title of the chief bishop of various Eastern churches, as the JACOBITES, Armenians and MARONITES.

In the Eastern or ORTHODOX CHURCH the bishops of Constantinople, Alexandria, Antioch and JERUSALEM are patriarchs, the Patriarch of Constantinople bearing the style of Ecumenical Patriarch. Within a religious order the title is given to the founder, as St Benedict, St FRANCIS and St DOMINIC.

**Patrician.** Properly one of the *patres* ('fathers') or senators of Rome and their descendants. As they long held all the honours of the state, the word came to signify the magnates or nobility of a nation, the aristocrats or 'patrician class'. *See also* CONSCRIPT FATHERS; PLEBEIAN; PROLETARIAT.

**Patrick.** The apostle and patron saint of Ireland, who is commemorated on 17 March, was not an Irishman but was born (*c.*389) at a place in western Britain usually named as Bannavem Taberniae. The location of this is uncertain. Its original name was probably Bannaventa Berniae, and a tentative identification has been made with Banwen Pyrddin, near Neath in South Wales. Patrick's father, Calpurnius, was a Roman official and deacon. As a boy Patrick was captured in a Pictish raid and sold as a slave in Ireland. He escaped to Gaul, where he probably studied in the monastery of Lérins before returning to Britain. After receiving a supernatural call to preach to the heathen of Ireland, he returned to Gaul and was ordained deacon. He landed in Wicklow (432) and travelling north, converted the people of Ulster and later those of other parts of Ireland. He established many communities and churches, including the cathedral church of Armagh. He is said to have died in 461 and to have been buried at Down in Ulster.

St Patrick left his name in many places, and numerous legends are told of his miraculous powers. One such is that he cleared Ireland of its vermin. The story goes that one old SERPENT resisted him, so he made a box and invited the serpent to enter it. The serpent objected, saying it was too small, but St Patrick insisted it was quite large enough to be comfortable. Eventually the serpent got in to prove it was too small, whereupon St Patrick slammed down the lid and cast the box into the sea. In commemoration of this he is usually represented banishing the serpents, and with a SHAMROCK leaf.

**Order of St Patrick, The.** *See under* ORDER.

**St Patrick's cross.** The same shape as St ANDREW's cross (X), only different in colour, i.e. red on a white ground.

**St Patrick's purgatory.** A cave on Station Island in Lough Derg, County Donegal, a resort of pilgrims from the 13th century. (The island is so named because the pilgrims there perform the 'stations' or traditional exercises of penitence.) The legend is that Christ revealed it to St PATRICK and told him that all who visited it in penitence and faith would gain a full INDULGENCE of their sins and they would gain sight of the torments of hell and the joys of heaven. Henry of Saltrey tells how Sir OWAIN visited it, and FORTUNATUS was one of the adventurers. Excesses caused the pilgrimage to be banned, and the cave blocked up by order of the pope on St Patrick's Day, 1497. Calderón (1600–81) has a play on the subject, *El Purgatorio de San Patricio*.

> Why then should all your chimney-sweepers be Irishmen? ...
>
> Faith, that's soon answered, for St Patrick, you know, keeps purgatory; he makes the fire, and his countrymen could do nothing if they cannot sweep chimneys.
>
> THOMAS DEKKER: *The Honest Whore*, Pt II, I, i (*c*.1604)

**Patriots' Day.** In the USA the anniversary of the Battle of Lexington, 19 April 1775, the first battle in the War of Independence. It is a public holiday in Massachusetts and Maine.

**Patroclus.** The gentle and amiable friend of ACHILLES. When the latter refused to fight in order to annoy AGAMEMNON, Patroclus appeared in the armour of Achilles at the head of the MYRMIDONS and was slain by HECTOR.

**Patron saints.** *See under* SAINT.

**Patter.** The running talk of CHEAPJACKS, conjurers, entertainers, comedians and the like. The word is from PATERNOSTER. When saying MASS, the priest often recited in a low, rapid, mechanical way until he came to the words 'and lead us not into temptation', which he spoke clearly and deliberately.

In music, a 'patter song' is one in which there is a rapid iteration of words, the accompaniment being only lightly supportive. There are several examples in LIGHT OPERA, as in Gilbert and Sullivan's *The Sorcerer* (1877):

> My name is John Wellington Wells.
> I'm a dealer in magic and spells,
> In blessings and curses
> And ever-filled purses,
> In prophecies, witches, and knells.

The 'patter' of feet or rain is not connected with the above. It is a frequentative of 'pat', to strike gently.

**Pattern.** From the same root as 'patron' (Latin *pater*, 'father'). As the patron ought to be an example, so pattern has come to signify a model.

**Willow pattern.** *See under* WILLOW.

**Paul. Paul Bunyan.** *See* BUNYAN, PAUL.

**Paul Jones.** A dance popular in Britain in the 1920s, in which the ladies formed an outward-facing circle moving in the opposite direction to the men, who faced inwards. The couples facing each other when the music stopped became partners for the next part of the dance, this pattern being repeated several times. It was earlier one of the 'sets' in American barn-dancing, and is perhaps named after the naval adventurer John Paul Jones (1747–92).

**Paul Pry.** *See under* PRY.

**Paul's cross.** A pulpit in the open air situated on the north side of Old St Paul's Cathedral, London, in which, from 1259 to 1643, eminent divines preached in the presence of the lord mayor and aldermen every Sunday. It was demolished in 1643 by order of Parliament. A new pulpit and cross were erected on the site in 1910.

**Oom Paul.** *See under* OOM.

**Rob Peter to pay Paul, To.** *See under* ROB.

**St Paul.** The patron saint of preachers and tentmakers (Acts 18:3). He was originally called SAUL, but changed his name, according to tradition, in honour of Sergius Paulus, whom he converted (Acts 13:6–12).

His symbols are a sword and an open book, the former the instrument of his martyrdom, the latter indicative of the new law propagated by him as the apostle of the Gentiles. He is represented as of short stature, with a bald head and a grey, bushy beard, and legend relates that when he was beheaded at Rome (*c*.AD 66), after converting one of NERO's favourite concubines, milk instead of blood flowed from his veins. He is commemorated on 25 January.

**St Paul the Hermit.** The first of the Egyptian hermits. When 113 years old, he was visited by St ANTHONY OF EGYPT, himself over 90, and when he died in 341, St Anthony wrapped his body in the cloak given to him by St Athanasius, and his grave was dug by two lions. He lived in a cave, and he is represented as an old man, clothed with palm leaves, and seated under a palm tree, near which are a river and loaf of bread.

**Pavan** or **pavane.** A stately Spanish dance of the 16th and 17th centuries, said to be so called because in it the dancers stalked like peacocks (Latin *pavones*), the gentlemen with their long robes of office, and the ladies with trains like peacock's tails. This etymology is uncertain, and it is more probable that the name is from Padova (Padua). The pavan, like the minuet, ended with a quick movement called the galliard, a sort of gavotte.

**Paving, Crazy.** *See under* CRAZY.

**Pavlovian response.** Ivan Petrovich Pavlov (1849–1936) pioneered the study of the conditioned reflex in animals. In his classic experiment, he first rang a bell when feeding a hungry dog, then trained the dog to salivate on hearing the bell even when there was no sight of food. A Pavlovian response is now generally regarded as any reaction made unthinkingly or under the influence of others.

> The report does not hesitate to name names, a procedure that will inevitably touch off a Pavlovian response from Leftist circles to deride it as a 'Reds under the Beds' scare.
> *Daily Telegraph* (8 February 1974)

**Paw. Bear sucking his paws, A.** *See under* BEAR.

**Cat's paw.** *See under* CAT.

**Pawnbroker's sign, The.** *See* THREE GOLDEN BALLS.

**Pawnee.** Anglo-Indian for water (Hindi *pani*, 'water'). It is also the name of a Native American people.

**Pax** (Latin, 'peace'). The KISS OF PEACE, which is given at MASS. It is omitted on MAUNDY THURSDAY.

Also a sacred utensil used when mass is celebrated by a high dignitary. It is sometimes a crucifix, sometimes a tablet and sometimes a reliquary, and it is handed round to be kissed as a symbolic substitute for the 'kiss of peace'. The old custom of 'kissing the bride', whic took place immediately before the Communion of the newly married couple and still obtains in some churches, is derived from the 'kiss of peace'.

**Pax!** The schoolboy's cry of truce.

**Pax Britannica.** The peace formerly imposed by Britain in her colonial empire. The phrase is modelled on the Latin *Pax Romana*, the peace existing between the different parts of the ROMAN EMPIRE. Since the USA increasingly took over Britain's former role, the term *Pax Americana* came into vogue.

> Never in the history of the world had any single nation dominated the international system as fully as the United States did for almost a quarter of a century after the Second World War. But the logic of Pax Americana led to the war in Vietnam, and the American people have learned their lesson.
> *Newsweek* (28 November 1983)

**Pax vobis** (Latin, 'Peace be unto you'). The formula used by a bishop instead of 'The Lord be with you', wherever this versicle occurs in Divine service. They are the words used by Christ to His APOSTLES on the first EASTER morning (Luke 24:26).

**Pay.** The English word comes from Old French *payer*, ultimately from Latin *pax*, 'peace', the allusion being to the appeasing of a creditor. The nautical 'pay', meaning to cover with hot tar when caulking, represents Old French *peier*, from Latin *picare*, 'to cover with pitch' (Latin *pix*).

**Pay court to, To.** To pay attention to someone because one wants their interest, favours or love.

**Pay dirt.** A mining term for ground that pays for working. Hence 'to hit pay dirt', meaning to attain one's objective.

**Pay for something, To.** To hand over the price of it; to be punished for it. 'You'll pay for it' means 'You will suffer the unpleasant consequences of your action'.

**Payload.** The goods or passengers carried in a ship, aircraft and the like that pay for their carriage, as opposed to the crew and equipment.

**Payoff, The.** The climax of a series of events or of a story, especially when it is unexpected or unlikely. The allusion is to the payment made by way of a bribe to a criminal after the execution of some trick or 'operation'.

**Payola.** A bribe given to gain a special favour, e.g. a payment made to a disc jockey to 'plug' certain records or tapes, or to promote a particular commercial product. The word is a blend of 'pay' and either 'Pianola' or 'Victrola', the latter being an American make of gramophone.

**Pay one's last respects, To.** To show respect for someone who has died, particularly by being present at the funeral.

**Pay one's respects, To.** To show polite regard for someone, usually by making a call.

**Pay one's way, To.** To contribute to the expenses of an undertaking.

**Pay on the nail, To.** *See* ON THE NAIL *under* NAIL.

**Pay out a rope, To.** To let it out gradually.

**Pay someone (back) in their own coin, To.** To treat them as they have treated you: to give them TIT FOR TAT.

**Pay through the nose, To.** To pay too much. Of many conjectured origins, the most likely is that this phrase derives from the NOSE TAX.

> She knows nothing of business, and is made to pay for everything through the nose.
> FANNY BURNEY: *Cecilia*, Pt X, ch vi (1782)

**Balance of payments, The.** *See under* BALANCE.

**Dance and pay the piper, To.** *See under* DANCE.

**Devil to pay, The.** *See under* DEVIL.

**Devil to pay and no pitch hot.** *See under* DEVIL.

**He who pays the piper calls the tune.** The one who foots the bill has the control.

**Pitch and pay.** *See under* PITCH.

**Put paid to, To.** To finish with, to destroy. The expression comes from the old counting-house, and even now when 'paid' is put to an account, it is settled.

**Take-home pay.** *See under* TAKE.

**Token payment.** *See under* TOKEN.

**Paynim.** The word formerly used for a heathen or pagan, from Old French *paienisme*, itself from Late Latin *paganismus*, was also the chivalric term for a Muslim.

**PC.** The Roman *patres conscripti*. *See also* CONSCRIPT FATHERS.

**PC49.** A rather dated nickname for a policeman, especially a 'bobby on the beat'. It derives from the central character of the radio series *The Adventures of P.C. 49* broadcast from 1949 to 1953, in which the improbably upper-class constable so numbered was actually named Archibald Berkeley Willoughby. 'P.C. 49' was earlier the title of a popular song by W.F. Hargreaves (1846–1919), author of 'Burlington Bertie from Bow'. *See* BURLINGTON BERTIE.

**Peace. Peace at any price.** Lord Palmerston (1784–1865) sneered at the QUAKER statesman John Bright (1811–89) as a 'peace-at-any-price man'. *See also* CONSCIENTIOUS OBJECTOR.

> Though not a 'peace-at-any-price' man, I am not ashamed to say I am a peace-at-almost-any-price man.
>
> LORD AVEBURY: *The Use of Life*, xi (1894)

**Peace Corps.** The US government agency of volunteers so named was set up in 1961 by President John F. Kennedy to assist other countries in their development efforts by providing skilled workers in a wide range of fields. Once abroad, the volunteer is expected to remain as a good neighbour in the host country for at least two years, speaking its language and living on a level comparable to that of his or her counterparts in the USA. The initial intake of 900 volunteers served in 16 countries, but the latter number was nearer 90 by the 1990s.

**Peace in our time.** The unfortunate phrase used by Prime Minister Neville Chamberlain (1869–1940), on his return from the Munich Conference with Adolf Hitler on 30 September 1938. It comes from the versicle in Morning Prayer: 'Give peace in our time, O Lord.'

**Peace of Monsieur, The.** The peace that the HUGUENOTS, the POLITIQUES and the Duke of Alençon ('Monsieur') obliged Henry III of France to sign in 1576. The Huguenots and the duke gained great concessions by it.

**Peace-pipe.** *See* CALUMET.

**Peace Pledge Union.** A body pledged to renounce war, organized by Canon Dick Sheppard (1880–1937) of St Martin-in-the-Fields in 1936.

**Peace with honour.** A phrase popularized by the then Prime Minister, Benjamin Disraeli, 1st Earl of Beaconsfield (1804–81), on his return from the Congress of Berlin (1878), when he said:

> Lord Salisbury and myself have brought you back peace – but a peace I hope with honour, which may satisfy our Sovereign and tend to the welfare of the country.

**Bill of Peace, A.** *See under* BILL.

**Breach of the peace.** *See under* BREACH.

**Clerk of the Peace.** *See under* CLERK.

**Conservator of the Peace.** *See under* CONSERVATOR.

**Disastrous Peace.** *See under* DISASTROUS.

**Hold one's peace, To.** *See under* HOLD.

**If you want peace, prepare for war.** *See under* IF.

**Justices of the Peace.** *See under* JUSTICE.

**Keep the peace, To.** To refrain from disturbing the public peace. Wrongdoers are sometimes bound over to keep the peace for a certain time by a magistrate, subject to entering into a recognizance, i.e. by officially acknowledging the obligation.

**King's** or **Queen's Peace, The.** *See under* KING.

**Kiss of peace.** *See under* KISS; *see also* PAX.

**Make one's peace with someone, To.** To be reconciled with a person.

**Perpetual Peace.** *See under* PERPETUAL.

**Prince of Peace.** *See under* PRINCE.

**Peacock. Peacock in his pride, A.** A peacock with his tail fully displayed.

**Peacock's feather, The.** An emblem of vainglory, and in some eastern countries a mark of rank. As a literary term the expression is used of a borrowed ornament of style spatchcocked into the composition, the allusion being to the fable of the jay who decked herself out in a peacock's feathers, making herself an object of ridicule. The peacock's tail is an emblem of an EVIL EYE, or an ever-vigilant traitor, hence the feathers are considered unlucky. *See also* ARGUS; PAVAN.

**Peak. Peak District.** Britain's first national park, over half of which lies in northern Derbyshire. It opened in 1951 and includes a highly popular tourist area, with the moors of the so-called 'dark peak' and vales of the 'white peak'. Together with the Lake District, it is the only national park to be financially independent, unlike the other parks, which are funded by the local county council.

**Adam's Peak.** *See under* ADAM.

**Widow's peak.** *See under* WIDOW.

**Peal, To ring a.** *See under* RING.

**Pear. Alligator pear.** *See under* ALLIGATOR.

**Warden pear.** *See under* WARDEN.

**William pear.** *See under* WILLIAM.

**Pearl.** Dioscorides and Pliny mention the belief that pearls are formed by drops of rain falling into oyster shells while they are open, with the raindrops thus received being hardened into pearls by some secretions of the animal. They are actually a secretion forming a coating and repeated so often that they attain considerable thickness, caused by the attempts of marine and freshwater molluscs to get rid of a foreign object, such as a grain of sand or a tiny parasitic worm.

According to Horace (*Satires* II, iii (1st century BC)), Clodius, son of Aesop the tragedian, drew a pearl of great value from his ear, melted it in vinegar, and drank to the health of Cecilia Metella. This story is referred to by Valerius Maximus, Macrobius and Pliny. *See also* CLEOPATRA AND HER PEARL.

**Pearl Coast, The.** The name given by early Spanish explorers to the Venezuelan coast from Cumaná to Trinidad, with the islands off this coast called the Pearl Islands. This area was the site of large pearl fisheries.

**Pearl Mosque, The.** A mosque at Agra, India, built of white marble at the orders of Shah Jahan (1592–1666), who also ordered the more famous TAJ MAHAL in the same city. There is another Pearl Mosque at Delhi, which was the private place of prayer of Aurangzeb (1618–1707), the third son of Shah Jahan who became emperor after ousting his brothers.

**Pearl of great price, A.** Something highly treasured or of especial value. One of the doctrinal works of the MORMONS is called *The Pearl of Great Price*. The expression is of biblical origin.

> The kingdom of heaven is like unto a merchant man, seeking goodly pearls: who when he had found a pearl of great price, went and sold all he had, and bought it.
> Matthew 13: 45–6

**Pearly Gates.** In popular allusion, the entrance to heaven, and also a nickname for the teeth. Pearly Gates, the black American popular singer (b.1946), was born Viola Billups, and was so renamed by her manager, Bruce Welch.

> The god-men say when die go sky
> Through Pearly Gates where river flow,
> The god-men say when die we fly
> Just like eagle-hawk and crow –
> Might be; but I don't know.
> ANONYMOUS: North Australian Aborigine version of Christianity

**Pearly king.** The coster 'kings' and 'queens', 'princes' and 'princesses' of the London boroughs are so named from their glittering attire studded with innumerable pearl buttons. There has been a pearly king of London since the Festival of Britain (1951). They were originally elected by the street traders of London to safeguard their rights from interlopers and bullies, but they now devote their efforts to collecting and working for charities. Their tradition is an old one, and they are a reminder of the more colourful London when barrow boys were more common than supermarkets. *See also* COSTERMONGER.

**Cast pearls before swine, To.** *See under* CAST.

**Cleopatra and her pearl.** *See under* CLEOPATRA.

**Peas, As like as two.** *See under* AS.

**Peasant. Peasant Poet, The.** John Clare (1793–1864), the son of a labourer, who began work as a shepherd boy at the age of seven, was so called. His first publication, *Poems Descriptive of Rural Life and Scenery* (1820), attracted attention and *The Village Minstrel* followed in 1821. *The Shepherd's Calendar* appeared in 1827 and *The Rural Muse* in 1835. He drifted through various occupations and was dogged by poverty. Mental disturbances began in 1836, and he eventually died in Northampton Asylum. He was born at Helpston, Northamptonshire (now Peterborough), and is buried there. 'Peasant Poet' is inscribed on his tombstone.

> I long for scenes where man has never trod;
> A place where woman never smil'd or wept;
> There to abide with my Creator, GOD,
> And sleep as I in childhood sweetly slept:
> Untroubling and untroubled where I lie;
> The grass below – above the vaulted sky.
> JOHN CLARE: 'I Am!' (1848)

**Peasants' Revolt, The.** The name given to the English peasant risings of 1381, which were immediately occasioned by an unpopular POLL TAX at a time when there was a growing spirit of social revolt. Its chief centre was southeastern England, especially Kent and Essex. Wat Tyler's men beheaded the archbishop of Canterbury (Sudbury) and temporarily held London, and John Ball (d.1381), an excommunicated priest, joined the Kentish rebels. Richard II (b.1367, r.1377–99) promised free pardon and redress of grievances (including the abolition of villeinage). In 1381 Wat Tyler was slain by Walworth, the mayor of London, severe retribution followed, and the boy king's promises were not kept.

In Germany the Peasants' Revolt or Peasant War of 1524–5 was caused by tyranny and oppression by the nobility and further stimulated by the seeming encouragement of religious reformers. Martin Luther disowned the peasants and threw in his lot with the princes, and the risings were put down with great severity.

**Peasant's or shepherd's weatherglass, The.** Another name for the SHEPHERD'S SUNDIAL.

**Peascod. Winter for shoeing, peascod for wooing.** *See under* WINTER.

**Peccavi, To cry.** *See under* CRY.

**Pecker. Keep your pecker up.** As the mouth is in the head, pecker (the mouth) means the head, and so 'keep your pecker up' means 'keep your head up'; in other words 'keep your chin up', 'never say die'.

**Peckish.** Hungry; desirous of something to eat. The allusion is to hens and other birds, which peck their food.

**Pecksniff.** A canting hypocrite, who speaks homilies of morality but does the most heartless things 'as a duty to society' and forgives wrongdoing in nobody but himself. The allusion is to the arch-hypocrite of this name in Dickens' *Martin Chuzzlewit* (1843–4). *See also* PODSNAP.

**Pecos Bill.** A cowboy of American folklore who performed superhuman feats on the frontier in early days. He was said to have been born in 1832 and raised by coyotes after his parents lost him near the Pecos River, Texas. As a man he rode a mountain lion and used a rattlesnake as a lasso, out-performing the best of cowboys. According to one account, he died after washing down a meal of barbed wire with nitroglycerine. He was the creation of journalists, primarily Edward O'Reilly in *Century* magazine.

**Pectoral cross.** *See* CRUX PECTORALIS.

**Peculiar.** A parish or group of parishes exempt from the jurisdiction of the ORDINARY of the diocese. There were many such in medieval England, e.g. monastic peculiars, royal peculiars, archiepiscopal and diocesan peculiars, peculiars belonging to Orders and cathedral peculiars. In 1832 there were still over 300 peculiars, which were abolished between 1838 and 1850, the exceptions being cathedral peculiars, Westminster Abbey and those of the royal residences including the Chapel Royal of the Savoy. *See also* DEAN OF THE ARCHES; DEANS OF PECULIARS.

**Peculiar People, The.** Properly, the Jews, the 'Chosen People'. The title was also assumed by a London sect, the Plumstead Peculiars, founded in 1838. They refuse medical aid, but not surgical, and rely on the efficacy of prayer and on anointing with oil by the elders. The name is based on Titus 2:14: 'Who gave himself for us, that he might ... purify unto himself a peculiar people'.

**Court of Peculiars.** *See under* COURT.

**Dean of Peculiars.** *See under* DEAN.

**Pecuniary** (Latin *pecuniarius*, from *pecunia*, 'money'). The word is ultimately from Latin *pecus*, cattle, sheep and so on. Varro says that sheep were the ancient medium of barter and standard of value. Ancient coins were commonly marked with the image of an ox or sheep.

**Pedagogue** (Greek *pais*, 'boy', and *agōgos*, 'leader'). A 'boy leader', hence a schoolmaster, now usually one who is pompous and pedantic. In ancient Greece the *paidagōgos* was a slave whose duty it was to take his master's son to school and back again.

**Pedestal, To set on a.** *See under* SET.

**Pedlar.** This word for an itinerant vendor of small wares is not from Latin *pedes*, 'feet', but is probably from *ped*, 'basket', in which his goods were carried. In Norwich, the ped market was where women used to display eggs, butter, cheese and other farm produce in open hampers. Peddars Way, i.e. pedlar's road, is an old route running from Ixworth, near Bury St Edmunds, Suffolk, to Holme next the Sea, near Hunstanton, Norfolk.

**Pedlar's Acre.** A portion of Lambeth Marsh bequeathed to the parish church of St Mary, and possibly originally a 'squatting place' of pedlars. In the church is a window containing a representation of a pedlar and his dog, and the story is that a pedlar bequeathed 'his acre' to the church on the condition that he and his dog were commemorated in a window. It has been suggested that it is a REBUS on Chapman, the name of a benefactor.

There is a similar representation in Swaffham Church, Norfolk, of one John Chapman, and a like tradition persists there.

**Peel.** A fortified keep or tower, particularly one built in the 16th century along the border areas of England and Scotland as a defence against raids. The word derives from Latin *palus*, 'stake'. Perhaps the best known is the Peel on St Patrick's Isle, off the ISLE OF MAN, connected to the main island by a causeway. *See also* MODDEY DHOO.

**Peeler.** Old slang for a policeman, first applied to the Irish constabulary founded by Sir Robert Peel when he was Chief Secretary for Ireland (1812–18), and later to the Metropolitan Police which he established in 1829 when he was Home Secretary. *See also* BOBBY; ORANGE PEEL.

In the 16th century the word was applied to robbers, from 'peel' (later 'pill'), to plunder, strip of possessions or rob. Holinshed, in his *Scottish Chronicle* (1570), refers to Patrick Dunbar, who 'delivered the countrie of these peelers'.

**Peelites.** Those CONSERVATIVES who supported and remained loyal to Sir Robert Peel (1788–1850) at the time of the repeal of the Corn Laws in 1846. Among them were the 4th Earl of Aberdeen (1784–1860), W.E. Gladstone (1809–98), Henry Goulburn (1784–1856), Sir James Graham (1792–1861) and Sidney Herbert (1810–61), and they did not return to the Conservative party after the rift in 1846.

**Peel parish, A.** In the Church of England a district taken out of an existing parish that may, with due formalities, be constituted a new parish. It is so called from the fact that Sir Robert Peel was Prime Minister in 1843 when the Act of Parliament authorizing such changes was passed.

**Emma Peel.** The neat and nimble black-dressed heroine of the television series *The Avengers* (1961–8) who is the assistant of the secret agent John Steed. She was played by Diana Rigg. Her name is meant to suggest 'M appeal', i.e. 'man appeal', in which role she undoubtedly succeeded.

**Orange Peel.** *See under* ORANGE.

**Peep. Peeping Tom.** *See* GODIVA, LADY.

**Peep-o'-Day Boys.** The Irish Protestant faction in ULSTER of the 1780s and 1790s, so called because they used to visit the houses of the DEFENDERS at 'peep of day' searching for arms or plunder etc. *See also* ORANGEMEN.

**Peer. Peers of the realm.** The five orders of DUKE, MARQUESS, EARL, VISCOUNT and BARON. The word 'peer' comes from Latin *par*, 'equal', and in feudal times all great vassals were held as equals. *See also* COURTESY TITLES.

**Life peer.** *See under* LIFE.

**Twelve Peers of Charlemagne, The.** *See* PALADINS.

**Peg.** To take someone down a peg is to take the conceit out of a braggart or pretentious person; to lower their self-esteem. The allusion is to a ship's colours, which used to be raised and lowered by pegs. The higher the colours are raised, the greater the honour, and to take them down a peg would be to diminish the honour. An earlier explanation refers to the ancient practice of sharing drink from a pegged container down to one's allotted peg.

**Peg a price, To.** To fix or maintain a market price, as by buying, selling or subsidy.

**Peg away at something, To.** To stick at it persistently, often in spite of difficulties and discouragement. The expression may allude to the peg tankard, a communal container, especially popular in Scandinavian countries and in the northeast of England as late as the early 19th century, with an internal row of pegs marking off each person's share.

**Peg leg.** A person with a wooden leg, from the days when wooden legs were rods strapped at the knee.

**Peg out, To.** To die. The allusion is to the game of cribbage, in which the game is ended by a player pegging out the last holes.

**Level pegging.** *See under* LEVEL.

**Off the peg.** *See under* OFF.

**Square peg in a round hole, A.** *See under* SQUARE.

**Pegasus.** The winged horse that arose from the blood that fell when PERSEUS struck off the head of MEDUSA. BELLEROPHON mounted on Pegasus when he rode against the CHIMERA. When the MUSES contended with the daughters of Pieros, HELICON rose heavenward with delight, but Pegasus gave it a kick, stopped its ascent and brought out of the mountain the soul-inspiring waters of HIPPOCRENE. Hence the use of its name for the inspiration of poetry. After Bellerophon's death, Pegasus returned to the gods.

In the Second World War the horse, with Bellerophon on his back, in pale blue on a maroon ground, was adopted as the insignia of all British airborne troops.

**Peine forte et dure** (French, 'severe and hard punishment'). A species of torture applied to contumacious felons who refused to plead. It usually took the form of pressing the accused between boards until the person accepted a trial by jury or died. Juliana Quick (1442), Anthony Arrowsmith (1598), Walter Calverly (1605) and Major Strangeways (1657) suffered death in this way. Even in 1741 this torture was invoked at the Cambridge assizes. It was abolished in 1772. The 1720 edition of John Stow's *Survey of London* (1598) offers a more detailed account:

> The criminal is sent back to the prison whence he came, and there laid in some low dark room, upon the bare ground on his back, all naked, except his privy parts, his arms and legs drawn with cords fastened to several parts of the room; and then there is laid on his body, iron, stone, or lead, so much as he can bear; the next day he shall have three morsels of barley bread, without drink; and the third day shall have to drink some of the kennel water with bread. And this method is in strictness to be observed until he is dead.

**Peking.** The Chinese capital city has long been familiar under this name, although in recent times the media have more frequently resorted to the more 'correct' designation of Beijing. Either way, the name itself means 'northern capital', the implicit contrast being with Nanking, the 'southern capital'. The city has borne its present name only since 1403. Previous to this it was known as Khanbalik, 'town of the khan', a name transcribed by Marco POLO as *Cambaluc*. The 'khan' in question was the Mongol conqueror KUBLAI KHAN, who himself called the new capital Ta-tu, 'great capital'. Peking's great public place is T'ien-an Men Square, the name meaning 'Gate of Heavenly Peace'. *See also* FORBIDDEN CITY.

**Peking man** (*Sinanthropus pekinensis*). The name given to remains of a skull found near Peking in 1929 that, in many respects, resembled that of PITHECANTHROPUS *erectus*, and it was held as being intermediate between Java and NEANDERTHAL MAN.

**Pelagians.** Heretical followers of the British monk Pelagius (*c.*360–*c.*420), whose name is a Latinized form of his Welsh name Morgan, 'sea'. They denied the doctrine of ORIGINAL SIN or the taint of ADAM, and maintained that we have power of ourselves to receive or reject the Gospel. They were opposed by St AUGUSTINE, and condemned by Pope Innocent I (r.402–417) in 417 and again by Pope Zosimus (r.417–418) in 418.

**Peleus.** In Greek legend the husband of THETIS, the father of ACHILLES, and the king of the MYRMIDONS. It was at his marriage that Eris introduced the golden APPLE OF DISCORD which initiated the Judgement of PARIS.

**Pelf.** Money, usually with a contemptuous implication. The word is from Old French *pelfre*, 'booty', related to English 'pilfer', and was originally used of stolen or pilfered goods, otherwise ill-gotten gains.

**Pelican.** In Christian art the bird is a symbol of charity and also an emblem of Jesus Christ, by 'whose blood we are healed'. St JEROME gives the story of the pelican restoring its young ones destroyed by serpents, and his own salvation by the blood of Christ. The popular fallacy that pelicans feed their young with their blood arose from the fact that the parent bird transfers macerated food from the large bag under its bill to its young. The correct term for the heraldic representation of the bird in this act is 'a pelican in her piety', piety having the classical meaning of filial devotion.

Medieval BESTIARIES recount that the pelican is very fond of its brood but that, when they grow, they often rebel against the male bird and provoke his anger, so that he kills them. The mother returns to the nest in three days, sits on the dead birds, pours her blood over them and revives them, and they feed on her blood.

**Pelican crossing.** A type of road crossing that can be controlled by pedestrians. Hence its name, from 'pedestrian light controlled crossing', with the acronym assimilated to 'pelican'.

> It is safer to cross at subways, footbridges, islands, Zebra, Pelican and Puffin crossings, traffic lights or where there is a police officer, school crossing patrol or traffic warden.
>
> *The Highway Code*, The Green Cross Code, 7a (1996)

**Pelican State, The.** Louisiana, USA, which has a pelican in its device. Pelicans are plentiful on its coasts. *See also* UNITED STATES OF AMERICA.

**Pelleas, Sir.** One of the KNIGHTS OF THE ROUND TABLE, famed for his great strength. He is introduced in Edmund Spenser's *The Faerie Queene* (VI, xii (1596)) as going after the BLATANT BEAST. Tennyson's also has him in *Pelleas and Ettare* (1870).

**Pelmanism.** A system of mind and memory training. It takes its name from Christopher Louis Pelman, who in 1899 founded the Pelman Institute for the Scientific Development of Mind, Memory and Personality in London. Because of the extensive advertising, the verb 'to pelmanize', meaning to obtain good results by training the memory, was coined. It also gave its name to a card game, popular with children, which largely depends on mental concentration and memory.

**Pelops.** The son of TANTALUS, and father of ATREUS and THYESTES. He was king of Pisa in Elis, and was cut to pieces and served as food to the gods. The Morea was called Peloponnesus, 'the island of Pelops', from this mythical king.

**Ivory shoulder of Pelops, The.** *See under* IVORY.

**Pen.** The word comes from Latin *penna*, 'a feather', with both words ultimately derived from the Indoeuropean root *pet-* 'to fly'. This also gave Sanskrit *patram*, 'wing', Greek *pteron*, 'wing', German *Feder*, 'pen', 'feather', and English 'feather' itself. In Old French *penne* meant both 'feather' and 'pen', but in Modern French it is restricted to the long wing and tail feathers and to heraldic plumes on crests, while 'pen' is *plume* (or now more usually *stylo*). Thus the French and English usages have evolved counter to each other.

**Pen friend** or **pen pal.** A person with whom one keeps in friendly contact by correspondence, in some cases never actually meeting, but in others, even marrying.

**Pen name.** A pseudonym. *See also* NOM DE PLUME.

**Penalty envelopes.** In the USA envelopes franked for official use by government departments like those printed 'On Her Majesty's Service' in Britain. 'Penalty' refers to the penalty for their misuse.

**Penang lawyer.** A type of heavy walking stick with a big knob, formerly sold in Penang and Singapore generally. It is popularly said to be so called either because the power and wisdom of lawyers lies in their nobs (heads) or because there was formerly no law in Penang and people were obliged to use a heavy stick in order literally to 'take the law into their own hands'. The name may actually be a corruption of Malay *pinang liyar*, 'wild areca', or *pinang láyor*, 'fire-dried areca', referring to the species of palm from which it was made.

**Penates.** *See* DII PENATES; LARES AND PENATES.

**Pence. Take care of the pence and the pounds will look after themselves.** *See under* CARE.

**Pencil.** The word was originally used for a painter's brush and is still in use for very fine paintbrushes. It comes from Latin *penicillum*, 'paintbrush', a diminutive of *peniculus*, 'a brush', itself a diminutive of *penis*, 'tail'. Hence also the word penicillin, from the tufted appearance of the sporangia of the *Penicillium* fungus from which the antibiotic is obtained. When the modern pencil came into use in the early 17th century, it was known as a dry pencil or a pencil with black lead.

**Pencil of rays.** All the rays of light that issue from one point or that can be found at one point are so called since a representation of them has the appearance of a pointed pencil.

**Blue pencil.** *See under* BLUE.

**Pendant, pennant** or **pennon.** A pennon (Latin *penna*, 'feather') was originally the small pointed or swallow-tailed flag borne on the lance of a knight. It was later adopted by Lancer regiments, and led to the custom of noblemen flying their banners or pennons from the masthead when afloat. In the Royal Navy it came to be called a pendant (Latin *pendere*, 'to hang'), and the word is particularly used of the broad pendant of a commodore and the long narrow flag flown at the masthead of a warship. There are also special pendants used in naval signalling. It is pronounced 'pennan', and this latter and more general spelling arose from a blending of 'pennon' and 'pendant'. A pennant, sometimes called a streamer, is taken as the 'whip' with which the English Admiral Blake (1599–1657) nullified Van Tromp's boast to sweep the English from the seas, when he hoisted a BROOM at the masthead during the Dutch War of 1652–3. The story is almost certainly legendary.

**Pendragon.** A title conferred on several British chiefs in times of great danger when they were invested with supreme power, especially, in ARTHURIAN ROMANCES, on UTHER Pendragon, father of King ARTHUR. The word is Welsh *pen*, 'head', and 'dragon', referring to the war chief's dragon standard. It corresponded to the Roman *dux bellorum*.

Geoffrey of Monmouth relates that when Aurelius, the British king, was poisoned by Ambron during the invasion of Pascentius, son of Vortigern, 'there appeared a star of wonderful magnitude and brightness, darting forth a ray, at the end of which was a globe of fire in the form of a dragon, out of whose mouth issued forth two rays, one of which seemed to stretch itself beyond the extent of Gaul, the other towards the Irish Sea, and ended in seven lesser rays' (*Historia Regum Britanniae*, Bk VIII, ch xiv (*c*.1136)). Uther, brother of Aurelius and his predestined successor, ordered two golden dragons to be made, one of which he presented to Winchester Cathedral and the other 'to be carried along with him to his wars', whence he was called Uther Pendragon.

**Penelope.** The wife of ULYSSES and mother of TELEMACHUS in Homeric legend. She was a model of all the domestic virtues.

**Web of Penelope, The.** *See under* WEB.

**Penetralia** (Latin, 'innermost parts'). The private rooms of a house; the secrets of a family. Properly, the part of a Roman temple to which the priest alone had access, where the sacred images were housed, the responses of the ORACLES made and the sacred mysteries performed. The HOLY OF HOLIES was the *penetralia* of the Jewish Temple.

**Peneus, The daughter of.** *See under* DAUGHTER.

**Penguin.** The name of this flightless bird is applied to a training aircraft used on the ground, also, formerly, to a member of the Women's Royal Air Force, a FLAPPER who does not fly. *See also* KIWI.

**Penguin Books.** The paperbacks so called take their name from the publishing firm founded in 1935 by Allen Lane, the name itself being one suggested by his secretary. According to Sir Allen, the logo appealed because it 'had an air of dignified flippancy and was easy to draw in black and white'.

**Penitential psalms.** The seven psalms expressive of contrition (6, 32, 38, 51, 102, 130, 143). FROM TIME IMMEMORIAL they have all been used at the ASH WEDNESDAY services, the first three at MATINS, the 51st at the Commination, and the last three at Evensong.

**Pennant** or **pennon.** *See* PENDANT.

**Pennsylvania Dutch** (German *Deutscher*, 'German'). The name given to the German settlers in Pennsylvania who first began to arrive in 1683 and whose immigration was actively promoted by William Penn (1644–1718). A steady influx continued through much of the 18th century, and in some parts a German patois is still spoken. The influence of their culture and industry has been notable. *See also* MENNONITES; TUNKERS.

**Penny** (Old English *pening*). The English coin, before decimalization (*see* DECIMAL CURRENCY) worth one-twelfth of a SHILLING, was originally made of silver and was used by the Anglo-Saxons. A few silver pennies are still coined as MAUNDY MONEY, but they were last struck for general circulation in the reign of Charles II. A few gold pennies (worth 20 silver pennies) were struck in the reign of Henry III. The first English COPPER penny was made in 1797 by Matthew Boulton (1728–1809) at the Soho Mint, Birmingham, hence a 'copper' as a common synonym for a penny. In 1860 bronze coins were substituted for copper.

The plural 'pennies' is used of the number of coins and 'pence' of the value. A penny is sometimes used to denote low-value coins of other nations, as in Luke 20:24, where it stands for the Roman *denarius* from which the symbol d for a penny is derived. *See also* P.

**Pennies from heaven.** Unexpected benefits.

> Every time it rains, it rains
> Pennies from heaven.
> Don't you know each cloud contains
> Pennies from heaven?
> You'll find your fortune falling
> All over town
> Be sure that your umbrella
> Is upside down.
>
> JOHNNY BURKE: 'Pennies from Heaven' (song) (1936)

**Penny-a-liner.** The old name for a contributor to a newspaper who was not on the staff and was paid a penny a line. As it was in his interest to 'pad' as much as possible, the word is still used in a contemptuous way for a second-rate writer or newspaper HACK.

**Penny Black.** The first adhesive postage stamp, issued in Britain in May 1840. It was imperforate and bore the profile of Queen Victoria on a dark background.

**Penny-dreadful.** Originally, a cheap boy's paper full of crude situations and highly coloured excitement. The term was later extended to trashy periodicals in general, although costing more than a penny. A 'shilling shocker' was a similar but more expensive publication.

**Penny dropped, The.** The meaning or significance became clear. The allusion is to the old penny-in-the-slot machine or device, such as a chocolate machine or doorlock, which could not operate until the penny was inserted and dropped. *See also* SPEND A PENNY.

**Penny farthing.** The nickname of what was also called the 'ordinary' bicycle that came into vogue in 1872. The front wheel was sometimes as much as 5ft (1.5m) in diameter, while the rear was only 12in (30cm), hence the name. The drive was on the front wheel, the seat being directly above it and slightly back from the perpendicular of the axle. The 'Safety' bicycle, much on the lines of the usual cycle of today, was introduced in 1885.

**Penny for your thoughts, A.** Tell me what you are thinking about. A phrase addressed humorously to one in a BROWN STUDY. The phrase occurs in John Heywood's *Proverbs* (1546).

**Penny plain, twopence coloured.** A phrase originating in the shop of a maker of toy theatres in East London. The scenery and characters for the plays to be 'acted' were printed on sheets of thick paper ready to be cut out, these being sold at 1d if plain, 2d if coloured.

> I own I like a definite form in what my eyes are to rest upon; and if landscapes were sold, like the sheets of characters of my boyhood, one penny plain and twopence coloured, I should go to the length of twopence every day of my life.
>
> R.L. STEVENSON: *Travels with a Donkey*, 'Father Apollinaris' (1879)

**Penny readings.** Parochial entertainments consisting of readings, music and the like, for which one penny (1d) admission was charged.

**Pennyroyal.** A species of mint (*Mentha pulegium*). The name is a corruption of Anglo-Norman *puliol real*, from Latin *pulegium*, 'pennyroyal', as if from *pulex*, 'flea' (according to Pliny the plant was harmful to fleas), and Anglo-Norman *real*, 'royal'. The plant's other common names include run-by-the-ground, lurk-in-the-ditch, pudding grass and piliolereial. *The Boke of Secretes of Albertus Magnus of the vertues of Herbes, Stones and certaine Beastes* states that if drowning flies and bees are placed in the warm ashes of pennyroyal 'they shall recover their lyfe after as little tyme as by ye space of one houre'.

**Penny saved is a penny gained** or **earned, A.** An old adage to encourage thrift in the young.

**Penny weddings.** Weddings formerly in vogue among the poor in Scotland and Wales at which each guest paid a small sum of money not exceeding a shilling. After defraying expenses, the residue went to the newly-weds to aid in furnishing their home.

**Pennyweight.** 24 grains, i.e. one hundred and fortieth of a pound Troy, so called because it was formerly the same proportion of the old TOWER POUND (i.e. 22½grains), which was the exact weight of a new silver penny. The abbreviation is dwt, from denarius weight. *See also* PENNY; TROY WEIGHT.

**Penny whistle.** A cheap type of metal flageolet with six finger holes.

**Penny wise and pound foolish.** A phrase said of someone who is in danger of 'spoiling the ship for a ha'porth of tar'. Someone who is thrifty in small matters and careless over large ones is said to be penny wise.

**Pennywort.** A rock plant, *Umbilicus rupestris* (or *Cotyledon umbilicus*), so named for its rounded leaves, which are the shape of pennies. 'Wort' in plant names represents Old English *wyrt*, 'root', related to the second half of 'mangel-wurzel'.

**Bun penny.** *See under* BUN.

**In for a penny, in for a pound.** Once undertaken, the matter must be carried through, whatever obstacles or difficulties may arise, and there can be no drawing back.

**Not to have a penny to bless oneself with.** To be very poor; to be almost bankrupt.

**Peter's Pence.** *See under* PETER.

**Pretty penny, A.** *See under* PRETTY.

**Spend a penny, To.** *See under* SPEND.

**Take care of the pence and the pounds will take care of themselves.** *See under* CARE.

**Two a penny.** Worth next to nothing although easily obtained.

**Turn an honest penny, To.** *See under* TURN.

**Turn up like a bad penny To.** *See under* TURN.

**Pension.** (1) Etymologically, that which is weighed out (Latin *pensio*, 'payment', from *pendere*, 'to weigh'), but also related to 'pay', because payment was originally weighed out. *See also* POUND.

(2) A relatively cheap boarding-house, in which one lives *en pension*, i.e. as a boarder. The word is now pronounced in the French manner ('*pon*sion'), but was formerly the same as the English retirement pension. This use arose because pension was the term for any regular payment made for services rendered, such as for board and lodging.

**Pensioner.** The counterpart at Cambridge of the Oxford COMMONER, i.e. a student who pays for his own commons.

At the INNS OF COURT the pensioner is the officer who collects the periodical payments made by the members for the upkeep of the Inn.

**Pensioner** or **Pensionary Parliament.** The LONG PARLIAMENT or CAVALIER PARLIAMENT of Charles II (1661–79), so called from the bribes or pensions accepted by many of its members and noted for the growth of party faction.

**Chelsea Pensioner.** *See under* CHELSEA.

**Gentlemen Pensioners.** *See under* GENTLEMAN.

**Pentacle.** A five-pointed star or five-sided figure, also called the Wizard's Foot, used in sorcery as a TALISMAN against WITCHCRAFT and other evil influences, and sometimes worn as a folded head-dress of fine linen, as a defence against demons in the act of conjuration. It is said to typify the five senses, although, because it resolves itself into three triangles, its efficacy may spring from its being a triple symbol of the TRINITY. It is also a candlestick with five branches. *See also* SOLOMON'S SEAL.

The Holy Pentacles numbered forty-four, of which seven were consecrated to each of the planets SATURN, JUPITER, MARS and the sun, five to both VENUS and MERCURY, and six to the moon. The various figures were enclosed in a double circle, containing the name of God in Hebrew, and other mystical words.

**Pentagon.** A vast five-sided building erected in Washington, D.C., to house government officials. It now houses the US Department of Defense, and Pentagon is a synonym for the official American line in military matters.

**Pentameron** (Greek *pente*, 'five', and *hēmera*, 'day'). A collection of 50 folk-tales modelled on the DECAMERON and written in the Neapolitan dialect by Giambattista Basile (*c.*1575–1632) and first published at Naples in 1637. The stories were supposed to have been told by ten old women during five days to a Moorish slave who had taken the place of the true princess. *The Pentameron* (1837) of Walter Savage Landor is a collection of five long imaginary conversations between Boccaccio and Petrarch, who discuss Dante's works.

**Pentameter.** In prosody, a line of five feet, DACTYLS or spondees divided by a caesura into two parts of two-and-a-half feet each, the line used in alternation with the HEXAMETER in Latin elegiac verse. The name is sometimes wrongly applied to the English five-foot IAMBIC line. This came about because the line of verse was misanalysed as two dactyls (or spondees), a spondee and two anapaests.

> In the hexameter rises the fountain's silvery column,
> In the pentameter aye falling in melody back.
>
> S.T. COLERIDGE: 'Example of Elegiac Metre' (1799)

**Pentateuch** (Greek *pente*, 'five', and *teukhos*, 'tool', later 'scroll'). The first five books of the OLD TESTAMENT, anciently attributed to MOSES.

**Samaritan Pentateuch, The.** *See under* SAMARITAN.

**Pentathlon.** An athletic contest of five events, usually the jump, javelin throw, 200-metre race, discus throw and 1500-metre flat race. In the OLYMPIC GAMES the modern pentathlon is a team event consisting of a 600-metre equestrian steeplechase, a series of fencing matches, pistol shooting, a 300-metre swim and a 4000-metre cross-country run. Women do not compete in this, although from 1964 to 1980 in the Olympics there was a pentathlon for individual women athletes consisting of shot put, high jump, 80-metre hurdles, 200-metre race and long jump. In the ancient Olympic Games the contest consisted of running (the length of the stadium, about 180 or 200 yards/162–182m), long jump, throwing the discus and javelin and wrestling.

**Pentecost** (Greek *pentēkostē*, 'fiftieth'). The festival held by the Jews on the fiftieth day after the second day of the PASSOVER, the equivalent of the Christian WHITSUNDAY.

**Pentecostal churches.** PROTESTANT sects associated with manifestations of the GIFT OF TONGUES such as had occurred at PENTECOST (Acts 2:1–4), and evangelical and healing campaigns.

**Pentecostals.** In medieval England offerings made to the parish priest at WHITSUNTIDE were called Pentecostals or Whitsun farthings. The term is also used of offerings paid by the parish church to the cathedral of the diocese. *See also* PETER'S PENCE.

**Penthesilea.** The queen of the AMAZONS who, in the post-Homeric legends, fought for TROY. She was slain by ACHILLES. Hence a general name for any strong, commanding woman. Sir Toby Belch in Shakespeare's *Twelfth Night* (II, iii (1599)) calls Maria by this name.

**Peony.** According to fable, the flower (*Paeonia* species) is so called from Paeon, the physician who cured the wounds received by the gods in the TROJAN WAR. At one time, the seeds were worn round the neck as a charm against the powers of darkness.

> About an Infants neck hang Peonie,
> It cures Alcydes cruell Maladie.
>
> JOSHUA SYLVESTER: *Du Bartas*, I, iii (1605)

**People. Flower people.** *See under* FLOWER.

**Opium of the People, The.** *See under* OPIUM.

**Peculiar People, The.** *See under* PECULIAR.

**Tribune of the people, A.** *See under* TRIBUNE.

**Pepin** or **Pippin the Short** (French *Pépin le Bref*). Pepin III (*c*.715–768), illegitimate son of Charles MARTEL, MAYOR OF THE PALACE, father of CHARLEMAGNE and founder of the CAROLINGIAN dynasty of French kings. He deposed the last of the MEROVINGIANS, Childeric III, in 751 and reigned as king of the FRANKS. Most of his reign was spent in war against the Saxons and the Saracens.

**Donation of Pepin, The.** *See under* DONATION.

**Pepper. Pepper-and-salt.** A cloth mixture of light and dark wools making a pattern of light and dark dots. The phrase is also used of hair that is dark but streaked with grey.

**Peppercorn rent.** A nominal rent. A peppercorn is of very slight value and is a token rental of virtually free possession without the ownership of the freehold.

**Pepperpot.** A stew of tripe, dumplings and vegetables originating in Philadelphia; also a celebrated West Indian dish of cassareep (the juice of the cassava root), fish, vegetables (chiefly the unripe pods of the okra) and chillies.

**Pioneers, The Rochdale.** *See under* ROCHDALE.

**Pippin, Ribston.** *See under* RIBSTON.

**Per. Per contra** (Latin, 'on the contrary'). A commercial term for 'on the opposite side of the account'. Used also of arguments, disagreements and the like.

**Per saltum** (Latin, 'by a leap'). A promotion or degree given without going through the usual stages, as the ordination to the priesthood of a man who is not yet a deacon. Such ordinations, now prohibited, were common in earlier times.

**Perambulator.** A wooden wheel that, when pushed along by a man on foot, records exactly the distance traversed. Such apparatuses were used by the employees of John Cary (*c*.1754–1835) in the production of the first accurate *Itinerary of the Great Roads of England and Wales* (1798). The word gave modern 'pram' for the vehicle in which babies are taken for walks.

**Perceforest.** An early 14th-century French prose romance (said to be the longest in existence), belonging to the ARTHURIAN ROMANCES, but mingling with it the life of Alexander the Great. After Alexander's war in India, he comes to England, of which he makes Perceforest, one of his knights, king. The romance tells how Perceforest establishes the Knights of the Franc Palais, how his grandson brings the HOLY GRAIL to England, and includes many popular tales, such as that of the SLEEPING BEAUTY. Perceforest is said to be so called because he had killed a magician in an impenetrable forest.

**Perception, The Doors of.** *See under* DOOR.

**Perceval, Sir.** The Knight of the ROUND TABLE who, according to Sir Thomas Malory's *Le Morte d'Arthur* (1485) and Alfred, Lord Tennyson's *Idylls of the King* (1842), finally won a sight of the HOLY GRAIL. He was the son of Sir Pellinore and brother of Sir Lamerocke. In the earlier French romances (based probably on the MABINOGION and other Celtic originals) he has no connection with the Grail, but here (as in the English also) he sees the lance dripping with blood and the severed head surrounded with blood in a dish. The French version of the romance is by Chrétien de Troyes (12th century), which formed the basis of Sebastian Evans' *The High History of the Holy Graal* (1893). The German version, *Parsifal* or *Parzival*, was written some 50 years later by the MINNESINGER Wolfram von Eschenbach, and it is principally on this version that Wagner drew for his opera, *Parsifal* (1882).

**Percy.** When Malcolm III of Scotland (r.1058–93) invaded England and attacked the castle of Alnwick, Robert de Mowbray brought to him the keys of the castle suspended on his lance, and handing them from the wall, thrust his lance into the king's eye, from which circumstance, the tradition says, he received the name of 'Pierce-eye', which has ever since been borne by the Dukes of Northumberland. Scott gives the true origin:

> This is all a fable. The Percies are descended from a great Norman baron, who came over with William, and who took his name from his castle and estate in Normandy.
>
> SIR WALTER SCOTT: *The Tales of a Grandfather*, iv (1827–30)

**Percy's Reliques.** The collection of old ballads and poems published as *Reliques of Ancient English Poetry* by Thomas Percy (1729–1811) in 1765. He became bishop of Dromore in 1782 and was encouraged in his project by William Shenstone, Samuel Johnson, David Garrick and others. Sir Walter Scott acknowledged his debt to Percy's work: 'To read and to remember was in this instance the same thing, and henceforth I overwhelmed my schoolfellows, and all who would hearken to me, with tragical recitations from the ballads of Percy.'

**Perdita.** In Shakespeare's *The Winter's Tale* (1610) the daughter of Leontes and Hermione of Sicily. She was abandoned by order of her father (hence her name, meaning 'lost'), and put in a vessel which drifted to 'the sea-coast of Bohemia' where the infant was discovered by a shepherd, who brought her up as his own daughter. In time, FLORIZEL, the son and heir of the Bohemian King Polixenes, fell in love with the supposed shepherdess. The match was forbidden by Polixenes and the young lovers fled to Sicily. Here the story is cleared up, and all ends happily in the restoration of Perdita to her parents, and her marriage with Florizel.

Mrs Robinson, the actress and mistress of George IV when Prince of Wales, was especially successful in the part of Perdita, by which name she came to be known, the prince being known as Florizel.

**Peregrine falcon.** A falcon (*Falco peregrinus*) of wide distribution, formerly held in great esteem for hawking, and so called (13th century) because taken when on passage or 'peregrination', from the breeding place, instead of straight off the nest, as was the case with most others (Latin *peregrinus*, 'foreigner'). The hen is the falcon of falconers, and the cock the tercel. *See also* HAWK.

The word 'peregrine' was formerly used as synonymous with 'pilgrim', to which it is etymologically related, and (adjectivally) for someone travelling about.

**Père Lachaise.** This great Parisian cemetery is on the site of a religious settlement that was founded by the JESUITS in 1626 and later enlarged by Louis XIV's confessor, Père François d'Aix La Chaise (1624–1709). After the Revolution, the grounds were laid out as a cemetery and were first used in 1804. Many well-known writers, musicians and artists are buried here, among them Lafontaine, Molière, Alphonse Daudet, Charles Nodier, Alfred de Musset, Honoré de Balzac, Frédéric Chopin, Gioacchino Rossini, Eugène Delacroix and Dominique Ingres, as well as military and political leaders such as Marshal Ney and André Masséna, Duc de Rivoli. It was here, too, that the COMMUNARDS made their last stand in May 1871.

**Perestroika** (Russian, 'restructuring'). A policy, linked with GLASNOST, much publicized since 1986 when it became the intention of Mikhail Gorbachev (b.1931) to introduce economic and political reform and to allow greater freedom of expression, which included the publication of formerly banned books. Gorbachev became President and Communist Party leader in the autumn of 1988, but his policies led to the collapse of Communism and the break-up of the Soviet Union in 1991, when he relinquished this post.

**Perfect. Perfectibilist.** *See* ILLUMINATI.

**Perfectionists.** Members of a communistic sect formed by J.H. Noyes (1811–86) in Vermont about 1834, and transferred by him to Oneida, New York, in 1847. Its chief features were that the community was held to be one family, mutual criticism and public opinion took the place of government, and wives were (theoretically, at least) held in common, until 1879, when, owing to opposition, this was abandoned. In 1881 the sect, which had prospered exceedingly through its thrift and industry, voluntarily dissolved and was organized as a joint-stock company.

**Perfect number.** A number that is equal to the sum of its divisors. The smallest perfect number is thus 6, the divisors of which are 1, 2 and 3, which added together make 6. Perfect numbers are very rare, and between 1 and 40 million there are only five: 6, 28, 496, 8128 and 33,550,336.

**Perfect rhyme.** A rhyme of two words spelled or pronounced alike but with different meanings, as 'rain' and 'reign', 'thyme' and 'time'.

**Perfect ruby, The.** An alchemist's term for the ELIXIR OF LIFE or PHILOSOPHER'S STONE.

> He that has once the flower of the sun,
> The perfect ruby which we call elixir …
> Can confer honour, love, respect, long life,
> Give safety, valour, yea, and victory,
> To whom he will.
>
> BEN JONSON: *The Alchemist*, II, i (1610)

*See also* RUBY.

**Counsel of perfection.** *See under* COUNSEL.

**Perfidious Albion.** An English rendering of French *la perfide Albion*, referring to England's alleged treacherous policy towards foreigners. The phrase is said to have been first used by the Marquis de Ximenès (1726–1817). It attracted no particular attention and next appears in 1809 in both a poem by Henri Simon and a song. Its later currency stems from its wide use in the Napoleonic recruiting drive of 1813, and it was well established by the end of the war in 1815. *See also* ALBION.

**Perfume.** The word means simply 'through smoke' (Latin *per fumum*), the first perfumes having been obtained by the combustion of aromatic woods and gums. Their original use was in sacrifices to counteract the offensive odours of burning flesh.

**Peri** (Persian, 'fairy', from Avestan *pairikā*, 'witch'). Originally, a beautiful but malevolent sprite of Persian myth, one of a class that was responsible for comets, eclipses, failure of crops and the like. In later times the word was applied to delicate, gentle, fairy-like beings, begotten by fallen spirits who direct with a wand the pure in mind on the way to heaven. These lovely creatures, according to the KORAN, are under the sovereignty of EBLIS, and MOHAMMED was sent for their conversion, as well as for that of man. The name used sometimes to be applied to any beautiful girl.

**Paradise and the Peri.** *See under* PARADISE.

**Pericles.** An Athenian statesman (*c*.490–429 BC) noted for his political skill, his promotion of democratic processes and his patronage of the arts. His 'funeral oration', reported by Thucydides, is one of the most famous in history. The Pericles of Shakespeare's play that bears his name (1608) is a prince of Tyre who is shipwrecked, meets and marries Thaisa, imagines his wife dead, leaves his daughter Marina with his unreliable friend Cleon, and is finally and miraculously reunited with both wife and daughter.

**Peril, Yellow.** *See under* YELLOW.

**Perillus and the brazen bull.** *See under* INVENTORS.

**Perilous Castle.** The castle of 'the good' Lord DOUGLAS was so called in the time of Edward I (r.1272–1307), because Douglas destroyed several English garrisons stationed there, and vowed to be revenged on anyone who should dare to take possession of it. Sir Walter Scott calls it 'Castle Dangerous' (*see* Introduction of *Castle Dangerous* (1831)).

**Siege Perilous.** *See under* SIEGE.

**Peripatetic school** (Greek *peri*, 'about', and *patein*, 'to walk'). The school or system of philosophy founded by ARISTOTLE, who used to walk about as he taught his disciples in the covered walk of the Lyceum. This colonnade was called the *peripatos*.

**Periphrasis** (Greek *peri*, 'around', 'about', and *phrasis*, 'speech'). A roundabout or long-winded form of expression, a circumlocution. A fair example is, 'Persons prejudicial to the public peace may be assigned by administrative process to definite places of residence', i.e. breakers of the law may be sent to prison.

**Perish the thought!** Do not entertain such an idea for a moment! A quotation from Colley Cibber's version of Shakespeare's *Richard III*, V, v (1592).

**Periwinkle.** The plant's generic name, *Vinca*, is from Latin *vincire*, 'to bind around'. It is a trailing plant. In Italy it used to be wreathed round dead infants and was thus called *fiore di morto*, 'flower of death'. The gastropod of this name was called in Old English 'pinewinkle', the first syllable perhaps being related to Latin *pina*, 'mussel', and 'winkle' from Old English *wincel*, 'corner', with reference to its much convoluted shell.

**Perk.** The word is possibly allied to 'perch'. Perks, in the plural, is a contraction of 'perquisites'.

**Perk up, To.** To get more lively; to feel better.

**Permissive society.** A term widely used in Britain in the 1960s to denote the increasingly tolerant and liberal attitudes in society that tend to blur the distinctions between right and wrong. Gambling clubs, strip clubs, the legalizing of homosexual practices between 'consenting adults', and the growing use of 'bad language' and obscenities in publications, in the theatre and on television, are all evidences. The borderline between permissiveness and decadence is not always apparent. *See also* AVANT-GARDE; NEW MORALITY.

**Perpetual. Perpetual motion.** The term applied to some theoretical force that will move a machine for ever of itself, a magnet that holds attractions for some minds much as did the search for the PHILOSOPHER'S STONE, the ELIXIR OF LIFE, and the FOUNTAIN OF (perpetual) YOUTH. According to the laws of thermodynamics, perpetual motion is impossible.

**Perpetual Peace.** The peace concluded 24 June 1502 between England and Scotland, whereby Margaret, daughter of Henry VII, was betrothed to James IV of Scotland. However, the Scots invaded England in 1513. The name has been given to other treaties, as that between Austria and Switzerland in 1474, and between France and Switzerland in 1516.

**Persecute. Science persecuted.** *See under* SCIENCE.

**Ten Great Persecutions, The.** *See under* TEN.

**Persephone.** *See* PROSERPINA.

**Persepolis.** The capital of the ancient Persian Empire. It was situated some 35 miles (56km) northeast of Shiraz. The palaces and other public buildings were some miles from the city and were approached by magnificent flights of steps.

**Perseus.** In Greek legend, the son of ZEUS and DANAË. He and his mother were set adrift in a chest but rescued by the intervention of Zeus. He was brought up by King Polydectes, who, wishing to secure DANAË, got rid of him by encouraging him in the almost hopeless task of obtaining the head of the MEDUSA. With the help of the gods, he was successful, and with the head (which turned all who looked on it into stone) he rescued ANDROMEDA, and later metamorphosed Polydectes and his guests to stone.

Before his birth, an ORACLE had foretold that Acrisius, father of Danaë, would be slain by Danaë's son (hence Perseus being originally cast adrift to perish). This came to pass, for while taking part in the games at Larissa, Perseus accidentally slew his grandfather with a discus.

**Helmet of Perseus, The.** *See under* HELMET.

**Person.** From Latin *persona*, which meant originally a mask worn by actors (perhaps from Etruscan *phersu*), and later transferred to the character or personage represented by the actor, and so to any definite character, at which stage the word was adopted in English through Old French *persone*. *See also* DRAMATIS PERSONAE.

**Persona grata** (Latin). An acceptable person; someone who is approved of or liked. When a diplomatic representative becomes no longer acceptable to the government to which he is accredited he is no longer *persona grata*, which virtually requests his recall. *Persona non grata* is the reverse of *persona grata*.

**Displaced persons.** *See under* DISPLACED.

**Personality. Dual personality.** *See under* DUAL.

**Split personality.** *See under* SPLIT.

**Perth. Fair Maid of Perth, The.** *See under* FAIR.

**Five Articles of Perth, The.** *See under* FIVE.

**Peru. Peruvian bark.** CINCHONA bark, called also Jesuit's bark, because it was introduced into Spain by the JESUITS. 'Quinine', from the same tree, is called by the Indians *quinquina*.

**From China to Peru.** *See under* FROM.

**Petard, To be hoist with one's own.** *See under* HOIST.

**Peter. Peterhouse** or **St Peter's College.** The oldest of the Cambridge colleges, having been founded in 1284 by Hugo de Basham, bishop of Ely.

**Peterman.** A burglar skilled in the art of breaking into safes. The word comes from 'peter' as a term for a safe or box itself, from the proper name Peter. It is uncertain why this particular name should have been chosen.

**Peter out, To.** To come gradually to an end; to give out. A phrase from the American mining camps of the 1840s of unknown origin.

**Peter Pan.** The little boy who never grew up, the central character of J.M. Barrie's play of this name (1904). One night Peter entered the nursery window of the house of the Darling family to recover his shadow. He flew back to NEVER NEVER LAND accompanied by the Darling children, to rejoin the Lost Boys. Eventually all were captured by the pirates, except Peter, who secured their release and the defeat of the pirates. The children, by now homesick, flew back to the nursery with their new friends, but Peter refused to stay as he did not wish to grow up. In their absence Mr Darling lived in the dog kennel as penance for having taken NANA away, thus making possible the children's disappearance in the first place.

The statue of Peter Pan by Sir George James Frampton (1860–1928) was placed in Kensington Gardens by Barrie in 1912.

**Peter Pindar.** *See under* PINDAR.

**Peter Principle, The.** The theory, usually taken not too seriously, that all members of a hierarchy rise to their own levels of incompetence. It is named after the Canadian-born American educationalist Dr Laurence J. Peter (1919–90), who, with Raymond Hull, first propounded it in *The Peter Principle* (1969).

**Peter Rabbit.** The most familiar of the animal characters created by Beatrix Potter (1866–1943) for her nursery tales. He is small and harmless, and first appears in *The Tale of Peter Rabbit* (1901).

**Peter Schlemihl.** *See under* SCHLEMIHL.

**Peter-see-me.** A favourite Spanish wine so called in the 17th century. The name is a corruption of Pedro Ximenes, the name of a grower who introduced a special grape.

> Peter-see-me shall wash thy noul [head]
> And malaga glasses fox thee;
> If, poet, thou toss not bowl for bowl
> Thou shalt not kiss a doxy.
>
> THOMAS MIDDLETON: *The Spanish Gipsy*, III (1625)

**Peter's Pence.** An annual tribute of one penny, paid at the feast of St Peter to the see of Rome, collected at first from every family, but afterwards restricted to those 'who had the value of thirty pence in quick or live-stock'. This tax was collected in England from the late 8th century until its abolition by Henry VIII in 1534. It was also called Rome-scot, Rome fardynges or Peter's farthings. Much of it never got as far as Rome. *See also* PENTECOSTALS.

Peter's Pence now consists of voluntary offerings made to the HOLY SEE by Roman Catholics.

**Peter the Hermit.** A French monk (*c*.1050–1115) and preacher of the first CRUSADE. He took part in the siege of Antioch (1098) and entered JERUSALEM with the victorious crusaders. He afterwards became prior of Huy.

**Peter the Wild Boy.** In 1724 a boy was found walking on his hands and feet and climbing trees like a squirrel in a wood near Hameln, Hanover. He was taken to George I, who brought him to England and put him under the care of Dr John Arbuthnot (1667–1735), who had him christened 'Peter'. He never became articulate and eventually lived with a farmer who equipped him with a brass collar inscribed 'Peter the Wild Boy, Broadway Farm, Berkhamsted'. On the farmer's death (1785), Peter refused food and soon died. *See also* WILD CHILD.

**Blue Peter.** *See under* BLUE.

**Chair of St Peter.** *See under* CHAIR.

**Gospel of Peter, The.** *See under* GOSPEL.

**Great Peter.** *See under* GREAT.

**Rob Peter to pay Paul, To.** *See under* ROB.

**St Peter.** The patron saint of fishermen, being himself a fisherman, the 'Prince of the Apostles'. His feast is kept universally on 29 June, and he is usually represented as an old man, bald, but with a flowing beard, dressed in a white mantle and a blue tunic, and holding in his hand a book or scroll. His peculiar symbols are the keys, and a sword (Matthew 16:19, John 18:10).

Tradition tells that he confuted SIMON MAGUS, who was at NERO's court as a magician, and that in AD 65 he was crucified with his head downwards at his own request, as he said he was not worthy to suffer the same death as Christ. The location of his bones under the high altar of St Peter's, Rome, was announced in 1950, and the pope confirmed their authenticity in 1968.

**St Peter ad Vincula.** The church dedication, wherever it is found, means 'St Peter in Chains', and refers to the miraculous release of St PETER from his prison chains by an angel (Acts 12:7). The best known church so dedicated is that of San Pietro in Vincoli in Rome, built in the 5th century with money from the Empress Eudoxia for the veneration of Peter's chains from his imprisonment in Jerusalem. Later, his Roman chains were added. In England, the best known church is that of St Peter ad Vincula, Tower Green, London, founded in the 12th century for the use of prisoners in the TOWER OF LONDON. There are about a dozen other churches elsewhere in England so dedicated, one being at Ashwater in Devon.

**St Peter's fingers.** The fingers of a thief. The allusion is to the fish caught by St PETER with a piece of money in its mouth. It is said that a thief has a fish-hook on every finger.

**St Peter's fish.** The JOHN DORY; also the HADDOCK.

**St Peter's Keys.** The CROSS KEYS, the insignia of the papacy borne, saltire-wise, one of gold and the other of silver, symbolizing the POWER OF THE KEYS.

**Peterloo Massacre.** On 16 August 1819 a large crowd (between 50,000 and 60,000) gathered at St Peter's Fields, Manchester, to hear Henry Hunt (ORATOR HUNT) address them on parliamentary reform, and fearing a riot, the magistrates ordered the yeomanry to disperse the assembly. Eleven people were killed, including two women, and some 500 injured. Hunt was arrested and given three years' imprisonment. The 'massacre' caused great indignation throughout England.

The name was founded on WATERLOO, then fresh in the public mind.

**Petition. Petitioners and Abhorrers.** Names given to political groupings in the reign of Charles II, eventually superseded by WHIGS and TORIES. When Charles II prorogued a newly elected Parliament in October 1679, Shaftesbury and the Country party petitioned the king to summon Parliament. The Court party abhorred this attempt to encroach on the royal prerogative. Hence the names as party labels.

**Petition of Right, The.** A document presented by Parliament to CHARLES I that eventually gained his assent (1628). It forbade the raising of gifts, loans, BENEVOLENCES and taxes without parliamentary consent and forbade also arbitrary imprisonment, compulsory billeting of soldiers and sailors and the issue of commissions of martial law.

**Olive Branch Petition.** *See under* OLIVE.

**Petitio principii** (Latin). A form of fallacious reasoning in logic, in which the conclusion is assumed in the premises, so to BEG THE QUESTION. In medieval logic, a ***principium*** was an essential, self-evident principle from which particular truths were deducible. The assumption of this principle was the *petitio*, i.e. begging of it. It is the same as 'arguing in a circle'.

**Pet names.** The change of m into p in pet names is by no means rare, e.g. as diminutives for Margaret, Maggie becomes Peggy, and Meg becomes Peg. For Martha, Matty becomes Patty.

For Mary, there is a single change for Molly, with r to ll, and a double change for Polly, with m to p as well. Similarly, Sarah becomes Sally, Dora becomes Dolly, and Henry becomes Hal.

**Petrel, storm.** *See under* STORM.

**Petrushka.** The puppet, the Russian equivalent of HARLEQUIN, who is the central character of Stravinsky's ballet named after him (1911). The story is simple but tragic. Petrushka falls in love with the Ballerina. She, however, prefers the Moor, who kills him. Although Russian *petrushka* happens to be the standard word for 'parsley', it is here a diminutive of *Pyotr*, 'Peter'. Perhaps 'Peterkin' would be the nearest English equivalent.

**Petticoat. Petticoat government.** Control by women, i.e. when women 'wear the trousers'.

**Petticoat Lane.** The Sunday street market, since the 1840s officially called Middlesex Street, and originally known as Hogham Lane, situated between Aldgate and Bishopsgate. It was settled by HUGUENOT silk weavers, later by Jews, and became a noted centre for second-hand clothes and general goods. It continues as a market for clothes, fruit, toys, cheap jewellery and the like, and is still a popular East End feature. The name derives from the original trade in women's petticoats.

**Petty treason.** An act of treachery against a subject (as distinct from the sovereign), as the murder of a master by his servant. *See also* HIGH TREASON; MISPRISION OF TREASON.

**Pfister's Bible, The.** *See* THIRTY-SIX-LINE BIBLE *under* BIBLE.

**Phaedra.** The daughter of MINOS and PASIPHAË, who fell in love with her stepson HIPPOLYTUS. On her rejection by him, she brought about his death by slandering him to her husband THESEUS. She subsequently killed herself in remorse. *See also* MYRTLE.

**Phaedrus.** A freedman of AUGUSTUS, who, in the reign of Tiberius, translated AESOP's Fables into Latin verse, interspersing them with anecdotes of his own. A prose version of his work, written about the 10th century, served as a model for the medieval fabulists.

**Phaeton.** In classical myth the son of PHOEBUS (the Sun). He undertook to drive his father's chariot and overturned it. He thereby caused Libya to be parched into barren sands and all Africa to be more or less injured, the inhabitants blackened and the vegetation nearly destroyed. He would have set the world on fire had not ZEUS transfixed him with a thunderbolt.

> Gallop apace, you fiery-footed steeds,
> Towards Phoebus' lodging; such a waggoner
> As Phaeton would whip you to the west,
> And bring in cloudy night immediately.
> SHAKESPEARE: *Romeo and Juliet*, III, ii (1594)

The name was given to a light, four-wheeled open carriage usually drawn by two horses.

**Phaeton's bird.** The swan. Cygnus, a son of NEPTUNE, was the friend of PHAETON and lamented his fate so grievously that APOLLO changed him into a swan, and placed him among the constellations.

**Phalanx.** The battle order of the heavy infantry (hoplites) of ancient Greece, first used by the Spartans and made famous by Philip of Macedon and Alexander the Great. The hoplites with lances 16ft (4.8m) or more long and with shields joined, were drawn up in from 12 to 16 close parallel lines. Alexander used a 16-rank formation, the first 5 ranks carrying their spears horizontally and the remainder carrying theirs across the shoulder. Although resistant to hostile onset, the phalanx lacked mobility. Hence the word has come to be used of any number of people presenting an unyielding front or distinguished for firmness and solidity of union.

**Phalaris. Brazen bull of Phalaris, The.** *See under* INVENTORS.

**Epistles of Phalaris, The.** *See under* EPISTLE.

**Phallus** (Greek *phallos*, 'male sex organ', so 'stallion'). The horse of Heraclius.

**Phantom.** A spirit or apparition, an illusory appearance. The word comes from Old French *fantosme*, from Greek *phantasma* (from *phainein*, 'to show').

**Phantom corn.** The mere ghost of corn; corn that has as little body as a spectre.

**Phantom fellow.** Someone who is under the ban of some HOBGOBLIN; a half-witted person.

**Phantom flesh.** Flesh that hangs loose and flabby, formerly supposed to be bewitched.

**Phantom limb.** The illusion that a limb is still present when it has actually been amputated.

**Phantom pregnancy.** The occurrence of the signs of pregnancy when no foetus is present. The cause is hormonal imbalance.

**Phantom Ship, The.** The FLYING DUTCHMAN.

**Pharamond.** In the ARTHURIAN ROMANCES, a KNIGHT OF THE ROUND TABLE, said to have been the first king of France and to have reigned in the early 5th century. He was the son of Marcomir and father of Clodion.

Gautier de Costes de la Calprenède's novel *Pharamond, ou l'Histoire de France* was published in 1661.

**Pharaoh.** A word from the Egyptian meaning 'great house', applied to the kings of ancient Egypt in much the same way as the HOLY SEE came to be used for the pope, or the Sublime PORTE for the government of the Sultan of Turkey. Its popular use stems from the Bible, but its use as a term for the king of Egypt begins during the 18th Dynasty with AKHENATEN. In HIEROGLYPHICS the old usage of four or five titles persisted.

The pharaohs of the Bible are mostly not identifiable because of the vagueness of the references and absence of reliable chronological data, but the pharaoh of the Oppression is usually taken to be RAMSES II and his son Merenptah, the pharaoh of the Exodus.

According to the TALMUD, the name of the pharaoh's daughter who brought up MOSES was BATHIA.

In John Dryden's *Absalom and Achitophel* (finished by Tate in 1682), 'Pharaoh' stands for Louis XIV of France.

**Pharaoh's chicken** or **hen.** The Egyptian vulture, so called from its frequent representation in Egyptian HIEROGLYPHICS.

**Pharaoh's corn.** The grains of wheat sometimes found in mummy cases. *See also* MUMMY WHEAT.

**Pharaoh's rat.** *See* ICHNEUMON.

**Pharaoh's serpent.** An indoor firework consisting of sulphocyanide of mercury, which fuses into a serpentine shape when lighted. It is so called in allusion to the magic serpents of Exodus 7: 9–12.

**Pharisees** (Old English *Farīsēus*, ultimately from Aramaic *perīsh*, 'separated'). 'Those who have been set apart.' The Jewish party of this name first appeared in Judea in the reign of John Hyrcanus I (135–104 BC) and strove to ensure that the state was governed in strict accordance with the TORAH. Their influence in the development of orthodox Judaism was profound. The condemnations of Jesus were essentially against the more extremist followers of the Pharisee Shammai, who were open to charges of narrow literalism and hypocrisy. The TALMUD mentions the following groups:

Dashers or Bandy-legged (Nikfi), who scarcely lifted their feet from the ground in walking but 'dashed them against the stones', that people might think them absorbed in holy thought (Matthew 21:44)
Mortars, who wore a 'mortier' or cap, which would not allow them to see the passers-by, that their meditations might not be disturbed; 'Having eyes they saw not' (Mark 8:18)
'Bleeders', who inserted thorns in the borders of their gaberdines to prick their legs in walking
Cryers or Inquirers who went about crying: 'Let me know my duty, and I will do it' (Matthew 19:16–22)
Almsgivers, who had a trumpet sounded before them to summon the poor together (Matthew 6:2)
Stumblers or Bloody-browed (Kizai), who shut their eyes when they went abroad that they might see no women, being 'blind leaders of the blind' (Matthew 15:14). Christ calls them 'blind Pharisees', 'fools and blind'
Immovables, who stood like statues for hours together, 'Praying in the market places' (Matthew 6:5)
Pestle Pharisees (Medinkia), who kept themselves bent double like the handle of a pestle
Strong-shouldered (Shikmi), who walked with bent back as if bearing the whole burden of the law
Dyed Pharisees, called by Christ 'Whited Sepulchres', whose externals of devotion cloaked hypocrisy and moral uncleanliness

**Pharos.** A lighthouse, so called from the lighthouse built by Ptolemy Philadelphus on the island of Pharos, off Alexandria, Egypt. It was 450ft (137m) high, and according to JOSEPHUS could be seen at a distance of 42 miles (68km). Part was blown down in 793, and it was totally destroyed by an earthquake in 1375. *See also* SEVEN WONDERS OF THE WORLD.

**Pharsalia.** An epic in Latin hexameters by Lucan. It tells of the civil war between Pompey and CAESAR, and of the Battle of Pharsalus (48 BC) in which Pompey, with 45,000 legionaries, 7000 cavalry, and a large number of auxiliaries, was decisively defeated by Caesar, who had only 22,000 legionaries and 1000 cavalry. Pompey's battle cry was *Hercules invictus* ('Hercules invincible'), that of Caesar, *Venus victrix* ('Venus conqueror').

**Phasian bird.** The pheasant (*Phasianus colchicus*), so called from Phasis, a river of Colchis, from where the bird is said to have been introduced elsewhere in Europe by the ARGONAUTS.

**Pheidippides.** *See* MARATHON.

**Phigalian marbles.** A series of 23 sculptures in ALTO RELIEVO, forming part of the ELGIN MARBLES. They were removed from the temple of APOLLO at Bassae, near Phigalia, in 1812, and represent the combat of the CENTAURS and the LAPITHS, and that of the Greeks and AMAZONS.

**Philadelphia.** The first city of the state of Pennsylvania, founded in 1682 by William Penn (1644–1718) and others of the Society of Friends (*see* QUAKER) and so named from the Greek *philadelphia*, 'brotherly love'. It was also the Greek name of two ancient cities: Rabbath-Ammon (now Amman) in southeastern Palestine, and Philadelphia in Asia Minor, named after Attalus II, king of Pergamum (159–138 BC), called Philadelphus for his devotion to his brother and predecessor, Eumenes II. This city was the seat of one of the SEVEN CHURCHES OF ASIA (Revelation 1:11).

**Philadelphia lawyer.** A lawyer of outstanding ability, with a keen scent for the weaknesses in an adversary's case, and a thorough knowledge of the intricacies of the law. 'You will have to get a Philadelphia lawyer to solve that' is a familiar American phrase. It is said that in 1735, in a case of criminal libel, the only counsel who would undertake the defence was Andrew Hamilton, the Philadelphia barrister, who obtained his client's acquittal in face of apparently irrefutable evidence, and charged no fee. In NEW ENGLAND there was a saying that three Philadelphia lawyers were a match for the Devil.

**Philandering.** Flirting with a woman, and leading her to think you love her, but never declaring your preference. 'Philander' literally means 'lover of men' (Greek *philos*, 'loving', and *anēr*, *andros*, 'man'), but as the word was made into a proper noun and used for a lover by Ariosto in ORLANDO FURIOSO (followed by Beaumont and Fletcher in *The Laws of Candy* (1647)), it obtained its present significance. In Thomas Norton and Thomas Sackville's *Gorboduc* (1561), Philander is the name of a staid old counsellor.

**Philanthropists, Spencean.** *See under* SPENCEAN.

**Philemon and Baucis.** Poor cottagers of Phrygia (husband and wife), who, in Ovid's story (*Metamorphoses*, viii (1st century AD)), entertained JUPITER and MERCURY, disguised as travellers, so hospitably that Jupiter transformed their cottage into a temple, making them its priest and priestess. They asked that they might die together, and it was so. Philemon became an oak, Baucis a linden tree, and their branches intertwined at the top.

**Philip. Philip Marlowe.** *See under* MARLOWE.

**Philip sober.** When a woman, who asked Philip of Macedon to do her justice, was snubbed by the petulant monarch, she exclaimed, 'Philip, I shall appeal against this judgement.' 'Appeal!' thundered the enraged king, 'and to whom will you appeal?' 'To Philip sober,' was her reply.

**Cooing and billing, like Philip and Mary on a shilling.** *See under* COOING.

**St Philip.** The saint is usually represented bearing a large cross, or a basket containing loaves in allusion to John 6:5–7. He is commemorated with St JAMES THE LESS on 1 May (since 1985, 11 May by Roman Catholics).

The name Philip is also applied to a sparrow, probably from its chirp.

**Philippan.** The sword of Antony, one of the triumvirs.

**Philippe Égalité.** *See under* ÉGALITÉ.

**Philippic.** A severe scolding, a speech full of acrimonious invective. It is so called from the orations of Demosthenes against Philip of Macedon, to rouse the Athenians to resist his encroachments. The orations of CICERO against Antony are called 'Philippics'.

**Philistines.** Properly, a warlike immigrant people of ancient Palestine or Philistia who contested its possession with the Israelites, hence a heathen foe. Its application to the ill-behaved and ignorant, those lacking culture and sensibility, or of materialistic outlook, stems from the term *Philister* as used by German university students to denote the townspeople, the 'outsiders'. This is said to have arisen at Jena, because of a TOWN AND GOWN row in 1693, which resulted in a number of deaths, when the university preacher took for his text, 'The Philistines be upon thee' (Judges 16:9). Its use was much popularized in England by Matthew Arnold's frequent employment of the term in his *Culture and Anarchy* (1869).

**Philoctetes.** The most famous archer in the TROJAN WAR, to whom HERCULES, at death, gave his arrows. In the tenth year of the siege, Odysseus (ULYSSES) commanded that he should be sent for, as an ORACLE had declared that TROY could not be taken without the arrows of Hercules. Philoctetes accordingly went to Troy, slew PARIS and Troy fell.

Sophocles' *Philoctetes* (5th century BC) is one of the most famous Greek tragedies.

**Philomela.** *See* NIGHTINGALE.

**Philosopher.** The sages of Greece used to be called *sophoi* ('wise men'), but PYTHAGORAS thought the word too arrogant, and adopted the compound *philosophos* ('lover of wisdom'), whence 'philosopher', one who courts or loves wisdom.

Marcus Aurelius (121–180) was surnamed the Philosopher by Justin Martyr, and the name was also conferred on Leo VI, emperor of the East (d.911), and Porphyry, the neo-Platonic opponent of Christianity (d.*c*.305).

The leading philosophers and schools of philosophy in Ancient Greece were:

Academic sect: PLATO, Speusippos, Xenocrates (*see* XENOCRATIC), Polemo, Crates of Athens, Crantor, Arcesilaos, Carneades, Clitomachos, Philo and Antiochos
Cynic sect: ANTISTHENES, DIOGENES of Sinope, Monimos, Onesicritos, Crates of Thebes, Metrocles, Hipparchia, MENIPPUS and Menedemos of Lampsacos
Cyrenaic sect: Aristippos, Hegesias, Anniceris, Theodoros and Bion
Eleac and Eretriac sects: Phaedo, Plisthenes and Menedemos of Eretria
Eleatic sect: Xenophanes, Parmenides, Melissos, ZENO OF ELEA, Leucippos, DEMOCRITUS, Protagoras and Anaxarchos
Epicurean sect: EPICURUS and a host of disciples
Heraclitan sect: Heraclitos; the names of his disciples are unknown
Ionic sect: Anaximander, Anaximenes, Anaxagoras and Archelaos
Italic sect: PYTHAGORAS, EMPEDOCLES, Epicharmos, Archytas, Alcmaeon, Hippasos, Philolaos and Eudoxos
Megaric sect: Euclid, Eubulides, Alexinos, Euphantos, Apollonius Chronosis, Diodorus, Ichthyas, Clinomachos and Stilpo
Peripatetic sect: ARISTOTLE, Theophrastos, Strato, Lyco, Aristoxenus, Critolaos and Diodoros
Sceptic sect: Pyrrho (*see* PYRRHONISM) and Timon
Socratic sect: SOCRATES, Xenophon, Aeschines, Crito, Simon, Glauco, Simmias and Cebes
Stoic sect: ZENO OF TARSUS, Cleanthes, Chrysippus, Zeno the Less, Diogenes of Babylon, Antipater, Panaetios, Epictetus, Marcus Aurelius, Posidonios and Seneca

**Philosopher of Sans Souci, The.** FREDERICK THE GREAT (r.1740–86).

**Philosopher's egg.** A medieval preservative against poison and a cure for the plague. The shell of a new egg was pricked, the white blown out and the space filled with saffron or a yolk of an egg mixed with saffron.

**Philosopher's stone.** The hypothetical substance that, according to the alchemists, would convert all baser metals into gold. Many believed it to be compounded of the purest sulphur and mercury. Medieval experimenters toiled endlessly in the search, thus laying the foundations of the science of chemistry, among other developments. It was in this quest that Johann Friedrich Böttger (1682–1719) stumbled on the manufacture of Dresden porcelain, Roger Bacon (*c*.1220–92) on the composition of gunpowder, Geber (14th century) on the properties of acids, Jan Baptista van Helmont (1579–1644) on the nature of gas, and Johann Rudolph Glauber (1604–68) on the 'salts' that bear his name.

In Ripley's treatise, *The Compound of Alchemie* (*c*.1471), the 12 stages or 'gates' in the transmutation of metals are given as follows: (1) Calcination, (2) Dissolution, (3) Separation, (4) Conjunction, (5) Putrefaction, (6) Congelation, (7) Cibation, (8) Sublimation, (9) Fermentation, (10) Exaltation, (11) Multiplication and (12) Projection. Of these, the last two were much the most important, the former consisting of the elixir, the latter in the penetration and transfiguration of metals in fusion by casting the powder of the philosopher's stone upon them, which is then called the POWDER OF PROJECTION. According to one legend, NOAH was commanded to hang up the true philosopher's stone in the ark, to give light to every living creature in it. Another tale related that DEUCALION had it in a bag over his shoulder, but threw it away and lost it. *See also* ALKAHEST; GLAUBER SALTS; PARACELSUS.

**Philosopher's tree** or **Diana's tree.** An amalgam of crystallized silver, obtained from mercury in a solution of silver. It was so called by the alchemists, with whom DIANA stood for silver.

**Philosophical Pleiad, The.** The seven WISE MEN OF GREECE are sometimes so called.

**Laughing Philosopher, The.** *See under* LAUGH.

**Weeping Philosopher, The.** *See under* WEEP.

**Philosophy. Alexandrine philosophy.** *See under* ALEXANDRINE.

**Aristotelian philosophy.** *See under* ARISTOTLE.

**Cartesian philosophy.** *See under* CARTESIAN.

**Corpuscular philosophy.** *See under* CORPUSCULAR.

**Cracker-barrel philosophy.** *See under* CRACKER.

**Newtonian philosophy.** *See under* NEWTON.

**Philtre** (Greek *philtron*, from *philos*, 'loving'). A draught or charm to incite in another the passion of love. The Thessalian philtres were the most renowned, but both Greeks and Romans used these dangerous potions, which sometimes produced insanity. Lucretius is said to have been driven mad by one, and CALIGULA's death is attributed to some philtres administered by his wife, Caesonia.

**Phineus.** In Greek mythology, a suitor who lacked the courage to rescue ANDROMEDA from the sea monster but who tried to claim her after she was rescued by PERSEUS, whereupon the latter turned him to stone. Another Phineus is a blind prophet tormented by the HARPIES.

**Phiz.** The face, a contraction of 'physiognomy'.

Phiz was the pseudonym assumed by the artist Hablot Knight Browne (1815–82), who became well known for his amusing and clever book illustrations. He adopted the name when he began illustrating the works of Charles Dickens (to match up with BOZ).

**Phlegethon** (Greek, 'blazing'). A river of liquid fire in HADES, flowing into the ACHERON.

> Fierce Phlegethon,
> Whose waves of torrent fire inflame with rage.
>
> MILTON: *Paradise Lost*, ii (1667)

**Phlogiston** (Greek, 'combustible'). The inflammable substance that was believed to be a constituent of all combustible material. The theory regarding it was originated by the German chemist Johann Becher (1635–82) and developed in 1702 by George Stahl (1660–1734). It held sway until overthrown in the 1770s by Antoine Lavoisier with the theory of oxygenation.

**Phoebe.** A female TITAN of classical myth, the daughter of URANUS and GAIA. It was also a name of DIANA, as goddess of the moon.

**Phoebus** (Greek, 'shining one'). An epithet of APOLLO, god of the sun. In poetry the name is sometimes used of the sun itself, sometimes of Apollo as leader of the MUSES.

> Wake, now my loue, awake; for it is time,
> The Rosy Morne long since left Tithones bed,
> All ready to her siluer coche to clyme;
> And Phœbus gins to shew his glorious hed.
>
> EDMUND SPENSER: *Epithalamion* (1595)

*See also* LAMP OF PHOEBUS.

**Phoenicians.** The inhabitants of Phoenicia, an ancient land corresponding to modern Lebanon with parts of neighbouring Syria and Israel. They were noted merchants and sea traders, and colonized the Mediterranean area in the 1st millennium BC. Their chief cities were Tyre, Sidon and Berot (modern Beirut). It is not known what the Phoenicians' own name for themselves was. It may have been *Kinahna*, 'Canaanites', from a word related to Hebrew *kena'ani*, which has the secondary meaning 'merchant'.

**Phoenix** (Greek *phoinix*, 'Phoenician', 'purple'). A fabulous Arabian bird, the only one of its kind, which according to Greek legend lives a certain number of years, at the end of which it makes a nest of spices, sings a melodious dirge, flaps its wings to set fire to the pile, burns itself to ashes and comes forth with new life. The phoenix was adopted as a sign over chemists' shops through the association of this fabulous bird with ALCHEMY. PARACELSUS wrote about it, and several of the alchemists employed it to symbolize their vocation. The phoenix is also a symbol of the Resurrection.

*The Phoenix and the Turtle* (1601), attributed to Shakespeare, is based on the legendary love and death of this bird and the turtledove.

Phoenix, the son of Amyntor, king of Argos, was tutor to ACHILLES.

**Phoenix dactylifera.** The date palm, so called from the ancient idea that this tree, if burned down or if it falls through old age, will rejuvenate itself and spring up fairer than ever.

**Phoenix Park.** The Dublin park has a name that is a corruption of Irish *fionn uisge*, 'clear water', so called from a spring at one time resorted to as a chalybeate spa. Despite this origin, the handsome Phoenix Column, erected by Lord Chesterfield in 1747, is surmounted by a figure of a phoenix, serving to perpetuate the misconception.

**Phoenix Park murders, The.** The assassination, on 6 May 1882, of Lord Frederick Cavendish, Chief Secretary for Ireland, and T.H. Burke, Under-Secretary, by Irish INVINCIBLES, when walking in Phoenix Park near the viceregal lodge. They were hacked to death by surgical knives on the day of Lord Spencer's arrival in Dublin as viceroy. James Carey, a Dublin councillor, one of the Invincibles, turned Queen's Evidence, and five of the gang were hanged, others being given life sentences. Carey was shot later by an avenger. The affair aroused great horror and proved a great embarrassment to the Irish leader, Charles Stewart Parnell, and to the cause of Anglo-Irish relations generally. *See also* FENIANS.

**Phoenix period** or **cycle.** Generally said to be 500 years. Tacitus writes that it was 500 years, R. Stuart Poole that it was 1460 Julian years, like the SOTHIC PERIOD, and Lipsius that it was 1500 years. Opinions vary between 250 and 7000 years.

**Phoney** or **phony.** Fraudulent, bogus or insincere. The word is an American colloquialism and slang term that became anglicized about 1920. It is said to derive from 'fawney', an obsolete underworld CANT word meaning the imitation gold ring used by confidence tricksters, itself from Irish *fáinne*, 'ring'. The period of comparative inactivity at the beginning of the Second World War, from the outbreak to the invasion of Norway and Denmark, was characterized by American journalists as the Phoney War. The French knew this period as *La drôle de guerre*.

**Phonograph.** In Britain the name of the old sound-reproducing machine with cylindrical records, which gave way to the gramophone, which in turn was supplanted by the electrical record player. In America the flat-disc gramophone was called a phonograph.

**Phony.** *See* PHONEY.

**Phrase, To coin a.** *See under* COIN.

**Phrenicos** (Greek *phrēn*, 'mind', so 'intelligent'). The horse of Hiero, king of Syracuse, which won the prize for single horses in the 73rd OLYMPIAD.

**Phrygians.** An early Christian sect of the late 2nd century, so called from Phrygia, where they abounded. They are also called Montanists, from Montanus, a Phrygian who asserted that he had received from the HOLY GHOST knowledge that had not been vouchsafed to the Apostles. They were extreme ascetics and believed in the imminence of the SECOND COMING. *See also* QUINTILIANS.

**Phrygian cap.** The LIBERTY CAP.

**Phrygian mode.** In music the second of the 'authentic' ecclesiastical modes. It had its 'final' on E and its 'dominant' on C, and was derived from the ancient Greek mode of this name, which was warlike.

**Phryne.** An Athenian courtesan of the 4th century BC, who acquired so much wealth by her beauty that she offered to rebuild the walls of Thebes if she might put on them the inscription: *Alexander diruit, sed meretrix Phryne refecit* ('Alexander destroyed them, but Phryne the prostitute rebuilt them'). This was refused. It is recorded of her that, when she was being tried on a capital charge, her defender, who failed to move the judges by his eloquence, asked her to unveil her bosom. She did so, and the judges, struck by her natural beauty, acquitted her on the spot. She is said to have been the model for Praxiteles' VENUS OF CNIDUS, and also for APELLES' picture APHRODITE ANADYOMENE.

**Phylactery** (Greek *phulaktērion*, 'outpost', from *phulax*, 'guard'). A charm or amulet worn by conforming Jews on the forehead and arm during morning prayer. It consisted of four slips of parchment, each bearing a text of Scripture, enclosed in two black leather cases. One case contained Exodus 13:1–10 and 11–16, and the other case Deuteronomy 6:4–9 and 11:13–21. The practice arose from the command of MOSES:

> Therefore shall ye lay up these my words in your heart and in your soul, and bind them for a sign upon your hand, that they may be as frontlets between your eyes.
>
> Deuteronomy 11:18

**Phyllis.** In Greek legend a Thracian princess who loved Demophon, son of THESEUS, and who hanged (or drowned) herself when he absented himself for a month. In Virgil's ECLOGUES Phyllis is a simple country girl, and her name and type are a regular feature in English poetry of the 16th and 17th centuries. Her Greek name means 'foliage'.

> Phyllis is my only joy,
> Faithless as the winds or seas,
> Sometimes coming, sometimes coy
> Yet she never fails to please.
>
> SIR CHARLES SEDLEY: 'Song' (1702)

**Physician** (Greek *phusis*, 'nature').

**Physician finger, The.** The third. *See also* MEDICINAL FINGER.

**Beloved Physician, The.** St LUKE, so called by St PAUL in Colossians 4:14.

**Prince of Physicians, The.** AVICENNA.

**Physiocrats.** A school of French political economists in the second half of the 18th century, founded by François Quesnay (1694–1774), a court physician. They attacked the economic regulations of MERCANTILISM, and held that wealth consisted in the products of the soil, not in coin or bullion. They advocated a predominantly agricultural society, FREE TRADE and LAISSEZ FAIRE. All revenue was to be raised by a land tax. The word is from Greek, meaning 'government according to nature'.

**Piazza.** An Italian word meaning square or market place, such as the piazza of COVENT GARDEN. In America it is applied to the veranda of a dwelling house.

**Great Piazza Coffee House.** *See under* GREAT.

**Pica.** *See* PIE.

**Picards.** An extremist early 15th-century sect prevalent in Bohemia and the VAUDOIS, said to be so called from Picard of Flanders, their founder, who called himself the New ADAM and tried to introduce the custom of living in the nude, like Adam in Paradise. They were suppressed by the Bohemian Hussite leader John Ziska (*c.*1370–1424) in 1421. *See also* ADAMITES.

**Picaresque** (Spanish *picaresco*, 'roguish', 'knavish'). The term applied to the class of literature that deals sympathetically with the adventures of clever and amusing rogues. The anonymous Spanish novel *Lazarillo de Tormes* (1554) is the earliest example of its kind, and Alain-René Lesage's *Gil Blas* (1715) is perhaps the best known. Nash's *Jack Wilton* (1594) is the earliest English example, and others are Daniel Defoe's *Moll Flanders* (1722) and *Colonel Jack* (1722). Mark Twain's *Huckleberry Finn* (1884) and Rudyard Kipling's *Kim* (1901) have also been described as picaresque, the 'rogue' in each being a travelling boy.

**Picayune.** Formerly, in FLORIDA and LOUISIANA, the Spanish half-real, from French *picaillon*, an old small coin of Piedmont. Hence the use of the word for anything of trifling value or contemptible character. The ultimate source of the word is unknown.

**Piccadilly.** The London street takes its name from Piccadilly Hall, which existed in the vicinity in the early 17th century, the home of Robert Baker, a tailor. The name is derived from 'pickadills' or 'peccadilloes', which, according to Blount's *Glossographia* (1656), were the round hems about the edge of a skirt or garment, also a kind of stiff collar or band for the neck and shoulders. The name may be in allusion to the tailor's source of wealth or that it was the 'skirt house' or outermost house in the district.

**Piccadilly weepers.** *See* WEEPER.

**Piccinnists.** *See* GLUCKISTS.

**Pick. Pickaback.** Carried on the back or shoulders, as a pack is carried. The term dates at least from the early 16th century, but its precise origin, and the force of the 'pick-', are unknown. Another form of it is 'piggyback'.

**Pick and choose, To.** To select fastidiously.

**Pick and mix** or **pick 'n' mix.** A commercial term for choosing mixed small objects for purchase, such as sweets.

**Pick holes in, To.** To find fault with. The older phrase was 'to pick a hole in one's coat', thus a hole in one's coat is a blot on one's reputation.

**Picking oakum.** Employment formerly given to prisoners, the picking and unravelling of old rope, which was used for caulking the seams of wooden ships. The word comes from Old English *ācumba*, 'off-combings'.

**Pick-me-up, A.** A tonic, especially a stimulating drink.

**Pickpocket.** A thief who steals from one's pocket or handbag in a public place.

**Pick someone's brains, To.** To obtain ideas or information from someone.

**Pick-up, A.** A casual acquaintance, whom one has 'picked up', often with sexual intentions. A pick-up truck is one that makes light deliveries, having an open body in which goods that are picked up can easily be placed.

**Pick up the tab, To.** To accept the responsibility of paying a bill. The 'tab' is the bill, perhaps as a shortening of 'tabulation'.

**Pick up the threads, To.** To resume one's line of argument; to get back into the way of things after absence, illness or the like.

**Have a bone to pick, To.** *See under* BONE.

**Picket. Flying picket.** *See under* FLY.

**Secondary picketing.** *See under* SECOND.

**Pickle. Pickled, To be.** To be drunk.

**In a pickle.** In a sorry plight or state of disorder.

**Rod in pickle, A.** *See under* ROD.

**Pickwickian. In a Pickwickian sense.** Said of words or epithets, usually of a derogatory or insulting kind, that, in the circumstances in which they are employed, are not to be taken as having quite the same force or implication as they naturally would have. The allusion is to the scene in the opening chapter of *Pickwick Papers* (1836–7) when Mr Pickwick accused Mr Blotton of acting in 'a vile and calumnious mode', whereupon Mr Blotton retorted by calling Mr Pickwick 'a humbug'. It finally was made to appear that both had used the offensive words only in a Pickwickian sense, and that both actually had the highest regard and esteem for each other.

**Picts.** The ancient inhabitants of Scotland before the coming of the Scots (Goidelic-speaking Celts) from Northern Ireland, in the 5th century. The Scots settled in Dalriada (Argyll) and the Pictish kingdom survived until the mid-9th century when it was conquered by Kenneth Mac Alpine, king of Dalriada. The name is popularly said to derive from Latin *picti*, 'painted', i.e. 'tattooed men', but some scholars dispute this, preferring instead to relate it to the 'Pit-' with which several Scottish place-names begin, as Pitlochry, Perth and Kinross, and Pittenweem, Fife, this representing Pictish *pett*, 'piece of land'.

The pseudo-learned etymology which derives the name of the Picts from their supposed habit of tattooing or painting themselves is not acceptable from a linguistic point of view.

W.F.H. NICOLAISEN: *Scottish Place-Names*, ch viii (1976)

**Picts' houses.** Underground prehistoric dwellings found in the Orkneys and on the east coast of Scotland and attributed to the Picts.

**Picture** (Latin *pictura*, 'painting', from *pingere*, 'to paint'). A person who closely resembles another, as: 'He is the picture of his father.' Also, a beautiful person, as: 'The children were a picture in their new hats'.

**Picture Bible.** A name given to the BIBLIA PAUPERUM.

**Picture hat.** A decorated hat with a very wide brim, as seen in some portraits, notably those of women by 18th-century painters such as Thomas Gainsborough and Joshua Reynolds.

**Pictures, The.** A colloquial term for the cinema or 'picture house'.

**Pictures of Tom Keating, The.** *See under* FAKES.

**Picture window.** A large window with a single pane of glass, with the view beyond seen as a 'picture'.

**As pretty as a picture.** *See under* AS.

**Get the picture, To.** To understand the essence of a situation.

**Put someone in the picture, To.** To inform someone of the proceedings or developments to date.

**Pidgin English.** Originally a form of Anglo-Chinese jargon which developed on the China coast from the 17th century as a consequence of contact with English traders and businessmen. It is essentially a form of basic English with some Chinese and additions from other tongues, but with certain Chinese constructions and a characteristic Chinese pronunciation, e.g. *ploper* for 'proper', *solly* for 'sorry', *makee* for 'make', *tinkee* for 'think' and so on. 'Pidgin' is a corruption of 'business', hence, 'That's not my pidgin', that is not my business, the responsibility for that is not mine. The word in this sense is often taken as 'pigeon', perhaps from an association with the bird as a carrier of messages, giving: 'That's not my pigeon.'

The following is a specimen of Pidgin English, purportedly as a letter from a *naima* or Chinese wet nurse, disappointed that the colours were not trooped as usual on the Queen's birthday:

Sir, Long time my have stop Hongkong side, any year Queen's bursday have got that soldier man play-pidgin City Hall overside. My chin-chin you tluly talkee my what for this year no got – no have got largee lain! How fashion? Some flen talkee my that soldier man b'long alla same olo man – two time one day he no can – some man talkee that soldier man taipan he more likee walkee that horse go topside sleep! Spose b'long tlue talkee my so fashion no likee. Too spensee my have catchee that seelick jacket, that bangle, that diamond ling, allo that thing. Tluly too muchee trub – long time stop that side waitee, no man talkee my no got. Spose soldier man b'long so fashion no can take care people that smallo pidgin, more better my chop-chop go Macao – that side have got plenty number one soldier man – no got fear. My too muchee no likee that foolo pidgin just now Hongkong any tim have got.

Chin-chin. Naai Ma. Hongkong, 27th May, 1878.

**Pie.** A printer's term to describe the mix-up of types (as when dropped), or a jumble of letters when a word or sentence is badly printed. It may be an allusion to the mixed ingredients in a pie, or it may come from the assortment of types used in the old pie or pre-REFORMATION books of rules for finding the prayers proper for the day. The ordinal was called the pica or pie from the colour and confused appearance of the rules which were printed in old black-letter type on white paper, thus giving a pied appearance (Latin *pica*, 'magpie').

**Pie in the sky.** The good time or good things promised that will never come; that which will never be realized.

You will eat, bye and bye,
In the glorious land above the sky;
Work and pray, live on hay,
You'll get pie in the sky when you die.

JOE HILL: *Songs of the Workers*, 'The Preacher and the Slave' (1911)

**As easy as pie.** *See under* AS.

**Cock and Pie.** *See under* COCK.

**Cottage pie.** *See under* COTTAGE.

**Eat humble pie, To.** *See under* EAT.

**Have a finger in the pie, To.** *See under* FINGER.

**Squab pie.** *See under* SQUAB.

**Stargazy pie.** *See under* STAR.

**Piece. Pièce de résistance** (French, 'piece of resistance'). The 'substantial piece' i.e. the main dish of a meal, the joint or meat dish. Figuratively, the most important feature; the main event; the best part of the show; the outstanding item.

**Piece goods.** Fabrics, especially Lancashire cottons, woven in recognized lengths for certain purposes for sale by the piece.

**Piece of cake.** Something easy, or easily obtained. The allusion is to the ease with which a slice of cake is taken and eaten. The RAF appropriated the expression in the Second World War, and a cartoon at the time of the Berlin airlift in 1948 depicted a pilot saying, 'Piece of Gatow, old boy'. (Gatow was a strategic Berlin airfield used for this operation.)

**Pieces of eight.** The old Spanish silver *peso* (piastre) or DOLLAR of 8 reals of the 17th and 18th centuries. It was marked with an 8.

**Piecework.** A term used when an industrial

worker is paid by the piece or job, instead of by the hour. The opposite is 'timework'.

**Bonnet piece.** *See under* BONNET.

**Give someone a piece of one's mind, To.** To say what one thinks about them.

**Go to pieces, To.** To lose control over oneself; to have a nervous or mental breakdown.

**Nasty bit of work, A.** *See under* NASTY.

**Set piece.** *See under* SET.

**Pied. Pied-à-terre** (French, 'foot on the ground'). A temporary lodging or a country residence; a footing.

> Mr Harding, however, did not allow himself to be talked over into giving up his own and only little *pied-à-terre* in the High Street.
>
> ANTHONY TROLLOPE: *Barchester Towers*, ch xliv (1857)

**Au pied de la lettre** (French, 'to the foot of the letter'). Quite literally, close to the letter.

> A wild enthusiastic young fellow, whose opinions one must not take *au pied de la lettre*.
>
> W.M. THACKERAY: *Pendennis*, I, xi (1848–50)

**Pied Piper of Hamelin.** The story is that the town of Hamelin (Hameln), in Westphalia, was infested with rats in 1284, and that a mysterious piper in a parti-coloured suit appeared in the town and offered to rid it of vermin for a certain sum, which offer was accepted by the townspeople. The Pied Piper fulfilled his contract, but payment was not forthcoming. On the following St John's Day he reappeared and again played his pipe. This time all the children followed him and he led them to a mountain cave, where all disappeared save two: one blind, the other dumb or lame. Another version is that they were led to Transylvania where they formed a German colony. The story, familiar in England from Robert Browning's poem (1842), appeared earlier in James Howell's *Familiar Letters* (1645–55). The legend has its roots in the story of the CHILDREN'S CRUSADE.

**Piepowder, Court of.** *See under* COURT.

**Piercing, Body.** *See under* BODY.

**Pierrot.** A traditional character in French PANTOMIME, a kind of idealized clown. He is generally tall and thin, has his face covered with white powder or flour, and wears a white costume with very long sleeves and a row of big buttons down the front. His name is a per form of *Pierre*, 'Peter'. *See also* HARLEQUIN.

**Piers Plowman.** *See* VISION OF PIERS PLOWMAN.

**Pietà** (Italian, 'pity'). A representation of the Virgin MARY embracing the body of the dead Christ. Filial or parental love was called *pietas* by the Romans.

**Pietists.** A 17th-century Lutheran movement seeking to revive the life of the Lutheran Church in Germany. It was started by P.J. Spener (1635–1705), and the name was applied derisively by the orthodox in the same way as the term METHODIST was used in England.

**Pig.** The pig was held sacred by the ancient Cretans because JUPITER was suckled by a sow. It was immolated in the ELEUSINIAN MYSTERIES, and was sacrificed to HERCULES, to VENUS, and to the LARES by all who sought relief from bodily ailments. The sow was sacrificed to CERES 'because it taught men to turn up the earth'. The pig is unclean to Jews and Muslims.

The five dark marks on the inner side of each of a pig's forelegs are supposed to be the marks of the Devil's claws when they entered the swine (Mark 5:11–15). *See also* HOG; PORK.

**Pig and the Tinderbox, The.** An old colloquial name for the ELEPHANT AND CASTLE public house in allusion to its sign of a pig-like elephant surmounted by the representation of a castle, which might pass as a tinderbox.

**Pig and Whistle.** *See under* PUBLIC HOUSE SIGNS.

**Piggyback.** *See* PICKABACK.

**Piggybank.** The traditional pig-shaped money box, still manufactured, nowadays often in plastic but formerly of earthenware or glass. Such money boxes, with a coin or coins inside, were given to apprentices in Tudor times as CHRISTMAS BOXES.

**Pig-headed.** Obstinate; blindly stubborn.

**Pig in a poke, A.** A blind bargain. The reference is to a former common trick of trying to palm off a cat as a sucking pig on a GREENHORN. Opening the poke or sack LET THE CAT OUT OF THE BAG, and the trick was disclosed. The use is referred to in Thomas Tusser's *Five Hundreth Good Pointes of Husbandrie* (1580). The French *chat en poche* refers to the fact, while the English proverb refers to the trick. 'Pocket' is a diminutive of 'poke'.

**Pig iron.** Iron cast in oblong ingots now called pigs but formerly sows. Sow is now applied to the main channel in which the molten liquid runs, the smaller branches that diverge from it being called pigs, and it is the iron from these that is called pig iron.

**Pig it, To.** To eat in a greedy fashion; to bolt one's food; to live in a slovenly piggish fashion. To make a pig of oneself is to overindulge.

**Pig Latin.** A secret language used by children, in which any consonants at the beginning of a word are placed at the end followed by '-ay'. Thus 'market' becomes 'arketmay'. *See also* VERLAN.

**Pig's ear.** In RHYMING SLANG, beer. To make a pig's ear of something, however, is to botch it. The ear of a slaughtered pig is its most worthless part, no good for anything. *See also* MAKE A SILK PURSE OUT OF A SOW'S EAR *under* SILK.

**Pigs in clover.** People who have money but don't know how to behave decently. Also, a game consisting of a box divided into recesses into which one has to roll marbles by tilting the box.

**Pigskin.** A saddle, the best being made of pigskin. 'To throw a leg across a pigskin' is to mount a horse.

**Pigtail.** In Britain the word first appeared (17th century) as the name of a tobacco that was twisted into a thin rope. It was used of the plait of twisted hair worn by sailors until the early 19th century, as it was a century later of that worn by schoolgirls. *See also* FLAPPER.

When the Manchu invaded and conquered China in the 17th century, the Chinese were required to wear queues or pigtails as a sign of servitude until the advent of the republic in 1912.

**Pig together, To.** To huddle together like pigs in a sty. To share and share alike, especially in lodgings. The phrase carries with it implications of disorderliness. It formerly meant to sleep two (or more) in the same bed.

**Bartholomew pig.** *See under* BARTHOLOMEW.

**Guinea pig.** *See under* GUINEA.

**St Anthony's pig.** *See under* ANTHONY.

**Sucking pig.** *See under* SUCK.

**When pigs fly.** NEVER. The particular animal may have been suggested by the pigeon, a bird that flies all too readily.

**Pigeon.** Slang for a dupe, an easily gullible person, a GULL. Pigeons are very easily caught by snares, and in the sporting world rogues and their dupes are called 'rooks and pigeons'.

**Pigeon breast.** A narrow or pinched chest as a deformity caused by rickets or obstructed breathing in infancy.

**Pigeonhole.** A small compartment for filing papers; hence, a matter that has been put on one side is often said to have been pigeonholed. In dovecots a small hole is left for the pigeons to walk in and out.

**Pigeon-livered.** Timid, easily frightened, like a pigeon. *See also* LIVER.

**Pigeon pair.** Boy and girl twins. It was once supposed that pigeons always sit on two eggs, which produce a male and a female, and these twin birds live together in love the rest of their lives.

**Pigeon's milk.** Partly digested food, regurgitated by pigeons for their young, also a non-existent liquid that gullible children and APRIL FOOLS are sometimes sent to fetch. *See also* ELBOW-GREASE.

**Pigeon-toed.** Having the toes turning inwards, like a pigeon's feet.

**Black pigeons of Dodona, The.** *See under* BLACK.

**Cat among the pigeons, The.** *See under* CAT.

**Gall of pigeons.** *See under* GALL.

**Stool pigeon.** *See under* STOOL.

**That's not my pigeon.** That is not my responsibility. *See also* PIDGIN ENGLISH.

**Pigmy.** *See* PYGMY.

**Pigott forgeries, The.** *See under* FAKES.

**Pi-jaw.** A contemptuous term for a moralizing 'lecture', as formerly by parents to their offspring or by masters to schoolboys. The first part of the word is 'pious'.

**Pike.** The Germans have a tradition that when Christ was crucified, all fishes dived under the water in terror, except the pike, which, out of curiosity, lifted up its head and beheld the whole scene. Hence the fancy that in a pike's head all the parts of the crucifixion are represented, the cross, three nails and a sword being clearly delineated. *See also* PASSION FLOWER.

**Pikestaff,** As plain as a. *See under* AS.

**Pilate.** In the New Testament the Roman governor of Judea who tries Jesus. Although he finds Christ not guilty, he 'washes his hands' of the matter, succumbing to the pressure of Jewish religious leaders, and sentences Jesus to be crucified.

One tradition has it that Pontius Pilate's later life was so full of misfortune that in CALIGULA's time he committed suicide at Rome. His body was thrown into the River Tiber, but evil spirits so disturbed the water that it was retrieved and taken to Vienne, where it was cast into the Rhône, eventually coming to rest in the recesses of a lake on Mount PILATUS. Another legend is that he committed suicide to avoid the sentence of death passed on him by Tiberius because of his having ordered the crucifixion of Christ. His wife is given as Claudia Procula, or Procla, and by some she has been identified with the Claudia of 2 Timothy 4:21. There is a story that they both became penitent and died peaceably in the faith.

In the Coptic Church, Pilate is regarded as a martyr, and his feast-day is 25 June. Procla has been canonized in the GREEK CHURCH. *See also* GOSPEL OF NICODEMUS.

**Acts of Pilate, The.** *See under* ACT.

**Pilatus, Mount.** A mountain in Switzerland, between the canton of Lucerne and Unterwalden. It is probably so called because during westerly winds it is covered with a white 'cap' of cloud (Latin *pileatus*, 'covered with the *pileus*, or felt cap'). The similarity of the name gave rise to a fabled connection with PILATE. One tradition is that Pilate was banished to GAUL by Tiberius and threw himself into the lake near the summit of this mountain, where he appears annually. Whoever sees the ghost will die before the year is out. In the 16th century a law was passed forbidding anyone to throw stones into the lake for fear of bringing a tempest on the country.

**Pile, Cross and.** *See under* CROSS.

**Pilgrim. Pilgrim Fathers.** The term (first used in 1799) applied to the emigrants who founded the colony of Plymouth, NEW ENGLAND, in 1620. In 1608 a PURITAN congregation from Scrooby, Nottinghamshire, settled at Leiden and eventually decided to migrate to America. They finally left Plymouth in the MAYFLOWER. Of the 102 settlers, 24 were women and only 35 of the party were Puritans. Their tradition is part of American folklore.

**Pilgrims, The.** A club founded in honour of the PILGRIM FATHERS in 1902, with one branch in London and the other in New York.

**Pilgrim's Progress, The.** The allegorical masterpiece of John Bunyan, the first part of which appeared in 1678 and the second in 1684. It tells of Christian's pilgrimage, beset with trials and temptations, but with incidental encouragement, until he reached the CELESTIAL CITY, where he was later joined by his wife and children. The rustic simplicity and directness of its story gave it lasting appeal and many expressions have become part of the language. They include 'The SLOUGH OF DESPOND', 'VANITY FAIR', 'The Valley of the Shadow of Death', 'DOUBTING CASTLE', 'The Celestial City', 'Mr Worldly Wiseman' and 'Mr Facing-Both-Ways'.

**Pilgrims' Way.** The road from Winchester in Hampshire to Canterbury in Kent, used by pilgrims from Europe and the south and west of England when visiting the shrine of Archbishop Becket. The route used by medieval pilgrims follows a much more ancient trackway. The name particularly applies to that part of the road in Kent and Surrey that forms part of the prehistoric Harrow Way, which crosses the south of England from Kent to Wiltshire.

**Pilgrimage.** A journey to a sacred place undertaken as an act of religious devotion, either as an act of veneration or penance, or to ask for the fulfilment of some prayer. In the MIDDLE AGES the chief venues in the West were Walsingham and Canterbury (England), Fourvière, Le Puy and St DENYS (France), Rome, Loreto and Assisi (Italy), COMPOSTELA, Guadalupe and MONTSERRAT (Spain), Mariazell (Austria), Cologne and Trier (Germany) and Einsiedeln (Switzerland). The pre-eminent pilgrimage was, of course, to the HOLY LAND. LOURDES became a noted place of pilgrimage for Roman Catholics after 1858.

Miraculous cures were sometimes effected upon those who worshipped at these shrines, and spiritual and bodily welfare were the main concerns of most pilgrims. For others, a pilgrimage was an occasion for a holiday and an opportunity to visit distant parts or foreign lands. *See also* CANTERBURY TALES; COCKLE HAT; CRUSADES; PALMER.

**Pilgrimage of Grace, The.** A rising in Yorkshire (1536–7) caused by political unrest among the gentry occasioned by enclosures and other restrictions and by the religious changes culminating in the dissolution of the monasteries. Under Robert Aske (d.1537), the 'pilgrims' took the five wounds of Christ as their banner and captured York and Hull. Among the insurgents were the archbishop of York, Lords Darcy, Latimer, Lumley and Scrope, and Sir Thomas Percy. The Duke of Norfolk effected a truce based on promises of redress, which were not kept. A full pardon was offered but further outbreaks in 1537 gave Henry VIII the excuse to execute some 220 rebels, including Aske.

**Pill, The.** Since the introduction of the oral contraceptive in the early 1960s, its impact has caused it to be known as 'the' pill, to the exclusion of all others. In Victorian England pills were popular 'universal remedies' for many maladies, but especially associated with liver complaints and constipation. Thomas Holloway (1800–83) and Joseph Beecham (1848–1916) were the two richest pill magnates of the day, the former entering the market in 1837. Aloes, ginger and soap formed the basis of their products, and both became millionaires.

**Beecham's Pills.** *See under* BEECHAM.

**Bitter pill to swallow, A.** *See under* BITTER.

**Gild the pill, To.** *See under* GILD.

**Poison pill.** *See under* POISON.

**Pillar. Pillar of Salt, The.** Lot's wife, when escaping from Sodom with her husband and daughters, looked back on the cities of SODOM AND GOMORRAH against God's command and 'She became a pillar of salt' (Genesis 19:26). Christ, when teaching indifference to worldly affairs and material possessions, refers to the episode saying, 'Remember Lot's wife' (Luke 17:32).

**Pillar saints.** *See* STYLITES.

**Pillars of Hercules, The.** The opposite rocks at the entrance to the Mediterranean, one in Spain and the other in Africa, at one time called CALPE and Abyla, now GIBRALTAR and Jebel Musa. The tale is that they were bound together till HERCULES tore them asunder in order to get to Gades (Cadiz). Macrobius ascribes the feat of making the division to Sesostris (the Egyptian Hercules), Lucan follows the same tradition, and the Phoenicians are said to have set on the opposing rocks two large pyramidal columns to serve as seamarks, one dedicated to Hercules and the other to ASTARTE.

**From pillar to post.** *See under* FROM.

**Nelson's Pillar.** *See under* NELSON.

**Pompey's Pillar.** *See under* POMPEY.

**Pillory.** A wooden framework into which wrongdoers were locked by the neck and wrists, and so exposed to the taunts and abuse of the public.

Punishment by the pillory was not finally abolished in England till 1837, but since 1815 it had been used only for cases of perjury. In Delaware, USA, it was a legal punishment until 1905. It was abolished in France in 1832. It was a popular punishment for libel, and among those pilloried for this offence were the pamphleteer William Prynne (1600–69) and Daniel Defoe (1660–1731) and, in 1797, Thomas Evans, the preacher, for singing a seditious Welsh song.

**Pilot.** The word came into English through French from Italian *pilota*, formerly *pedota*, which is probably connected with Greek *pēdon*, 'rudder'.

**Pilot balloon.** A small balloon sent up to find the direction of the wind. Hence, figuratively, a feeler or a hint thrown out to ascertain public opinion on some point. *See also* FLY A KITE.

**Pilot engine.** The leading engine when two are needed to draw a railway train; also, in the years before the First World War, a light engine running ahead of a royal train or other train carrying important people to make sure that the line was clear.

**Pilot fish.** The small fish *Naucrates ductor*, so called because it is said to pilot the shark to its prey.

**Pilot light.** A small flame in a gas appliance that lights the main burner when the control valve is opened.

**Pilot scheme** or **project.** An experimental try-out.

**Drop the pilot, To.** *See under* DROP.

**Iberia's pilot.** *See under* IBERIA.

**Sky pilot.** *See under* SKY.

**Piltdown Skull** or **Piltdown Man, The.** *See under* FAKES.

**Pimlico.** Formerly the pleasure gardens of Hoxton, but the better known Pimlico is the district of Westminster in London, between Knightsbridge and the Thames and St James's Park and Chelsea. It was once noted for its pleasure gardens, such as the Mulberry Garden (now the site of Buckingham Palace), RANELAGH, and Jenny's Whim. The name in Hoxton is said to derive from Ben Pimlico, a local brewer and tavern keeper, famous for his ales. A tract of 1598, *Newes from Hogsdon*, has: 'Have at thee, then, my merrie boys, and hey for old Ben Pimlico's nut-browne.' He apparently eventually settled just south of the site occupied by the present Victoria Station, which may account for the name of this district of Westminster.

Professor Richard Coates, in the American onomastic journal *Names*, Vol 43, No. 3 (September 1995), plausibly shows the name Pimlico to have been copied from a place in America called Pamlico and to be linked with Sir Walter Raleigh's abortive Roanoke settlements of the 1580s. As such, it may thus have been the first American place-name to be exported to England.

**Pimm's.** The proprietary cocktail takes its name from James Pimm, the London barman who invented it in 1840. The best known is Pimm's No. 1, which is gin-based. For many years there were five other varieties based on other spirits. Pimm's No. 2 had a base of whisky, Pimm's No. 3 of brandy, Pimm's No. 4 of rum, Pimm's No. 5 of rye, and Pimm's No. 6 of vodka.

**Pimpernel, Scarlet.** *See under* SCARLET.

**Pin. Pin money.** A woman's allowance of money for her own personal expenditure. Pins were once very expensive, and in 14th- and 15th-century wills there were often special bequests for the express purpose of buying pins. When they became cheap, women spent their allowances on other fancies, but the term 'pin money' remained in vogue.

> *Miss Hoyden*: Now, nurse, if he gives me two hundred a year to buy pins, what do you think he'll give me to buy fine petticoats?
>
> *Nurse*: Ah, my dearest, he deceives thee foully, and he's no better than a rogue for his pains! These Londoners have got a gibberage with 'em would confound a gipsy. That which they call pin-money is to buy their wives everything in the versal world, down to their very shoe-ties.
>
> THOMAS VANBRUGH: *The Relapse*, V, v (1696)

**Pinprick, A.** A minor irritation or annoyance.

**Pins.** Legs, as: 'He's not too steady on his pins.'

**Pins and needles.** The tingling that is felt in a limb when it has been numbed or has 'gone to sleep'. It is caused by the return of normal blood circulation after this has been temporarily impaired.

**Pin someone down, To.** To 'nail' someone; to compel a person to reveal their intentions or to state their views.

**Pin something on a person, To.** To fasten the blame, guilt or responsibility on a person.

**Pin something to someone's sleeve, To.** 'I shan't pin my faith to your sleeve' means 'I shall not slavishly believe or follow you'. The allusion is to the practice of knights, in the days of CHIVALRY, pinning to their sleeve some token given them by their lady love. This token was a pledge that they would do or die.

**Pin-up.** In the Second World War servicemen used to pin up in their quarters pictures of film stars and actresses (often scantily clad) or their own particular girlfriends. These were called 'pin-up girls'.

**Not worth a pin.** *See under* WORTH.

**On pins and needles.** On TENTERHOOKS; in a state of fearful expectation or great uneasiness.

**Tirl at the pin, To.** *See under* TIRL.

**You could have heard a pin drop.** Said of a state

of compete silence, especially when it occurs suddenly in the midst of din. Leigh Hunt speaks of 'a pin-drop silence' (*The Story of Rimini*, i (1816)).

**Pinch. Pinch, To.** Slang for 'to steal'.

**Pinch and a punch for the first of the month, A.** An old-established children's trick, usually carried out fairly gently on their fellows on the first of a month. Sometimes 'And no returns' is added as a safeguard against retaliation. *See also* APRIL FOOL.

**Pinched for money, To be.** To be in financial straits; to be hard up. Hence 'to pinch and scrape' or 'to pinch it' means to economize.

**Pinch-hitter.** A person who substitutes for another in a crisis. The term is from baseball where the pinch-hitter, who always hits the ball hard, is put in to bat when the team is in desperate straits.

**At a pinch.** *See under* AT.

**Feel the pinch, To.** *See under* FEEL.

**With a pinch of salt.** *See under* WITH.

**Pinchbeck.** An alloy of 5 parts copper and 1 part zinc, closely resembling gold and so called from Christopher Pinchbeck (1670–1732), a manufacturer of trinkets, watches and jewellery in Fleet Street, London. The term is used figuratively of anything spurious, of deceptive appearance or of low quality.

**Pindar.** A renowned lyric poet (*c.*522–443 BC) of Thebes who achieved great respect and public honour for his verse from his contemporaries.

**Pindaric verse.** Irregular verse, in various metres and lofty in style. The fashion for imitating in English the Greek versification of Pindar was started in the early 17th century by Ben Jonson (*c.*1572–1637), and his 'Ode to Sir Lucius Cary and Sir H. Morison' (1629) contains the following lines:

It is not growing like a tree
In bulk, doth make a man better be;
Or standing long an Oak, three hundred year,
To fall a log at last, dry, bald, and sear.
A Lily of a day
Is fairer far in May
Although it fall and die that night;
It was the plant and flower of light.
In small proportions, we just beauties see;
And in short measure, life may perfect be.

The fashion was taken up by Abraham Cowley (1618–67) in his 15 *Pindarique Odes* (1656), and the flexibility of his style was copied by many, including John Dryden and Alexander Pope.

**Peter Pindar.** The pseudonym of Dr John Wolcot (1738–1819), one-time physician-general in Jamaica and incumbent of Vere, Jamaica. He obtained an MD at Aberdeen in 1767 and was ordained in London in 1769. He returned to Britain to practise medicine at Truro, Cornwall, but moved to London in 1780 to devote his time to the writing of satirical verse and caricatures on the WHIG side. He had few scruples or convictions and George III was a victim of his pen. His verses include *The Lousiad* (1785–95), *Bozzy and Piozzi* (1786), and *Instructions to a Celebrated Laureate* (1787), in which he claimed to teach Thomas Warton (1728–90), then POET LAUREATE, how he should celebrate the visit of George III to Whitbread's brewery. *See also* INEXPRESSIBLES.

**Pink.** The flower is so called because the edges of the petals are pinked or notched. The verb 'to pink' means to pierce or perforate, also to ornament dress material by punching holes in it so that the lining can be seen, scalloping or zigzagging the edges and so on. In the 17th century it was commonly used of stabbing an adversary, especially in a duel.

> 'There went another eyelet-hole to his broidered jerkin!' – 'Fairly pinked, by G–d!' In fact, the last exclamation was uttered amid a general roar of applause, accompanying a successful and conclusive lunge, by which Peveril ran his gigantic antagonist through the body.
>
> SIR WALTER SCOTT: *Peveril of the Peak*, ch xxxii (1823)

**Pink elephants.** Hallucinations supposedly experienced by those who have drunk to excess.

**In pink.** In the scarlet coat of a foxhunter. The colour is not pink, but no hunter would call it anything else. *See also* REDCOATS.

**In the pink.** In excellent health. The phrase is an abbreviation of the expression 'in the pink of health' or 'in the pink of condition', meaning in the 'flower' or best state.

**Tickled pink.** *See under* TICKLE.

**Pinkerton.** Pinkerton's National Detective Agency was founded at Chicago (1852) by Allan Pinkerton (1819–84), Glasgow-born deputy sheriff of Kane County, Illinois, who had proved himself a detective of some resource. It came to the forefront during the Civil War (1861–5), when, in 1861, Pinkerton's men uncovered a plot to assassinate Lincoln, the President elect. Pinkerton also found the means of obtaining military and political information from the southern states during the war and eventually organized the Federal Secret Service. His most sensational coups were the discovery of the thieves of $700,000 stolen from the Adams Express in 1866 and the breaking-up of the MOLLY MAGUIRES (1877), an Irish-American secret society with many subversive and lawless deeds to their discredit.

**Pinocchio.** The mischievous hero of the puppet story *Le Avventure di Pinocchio* (1883) by Carlo Lorenzini, who wrote under the name of Collodi, that of his mother's home-town.

The story tells how a carpenter found a piece

of wood that laughed and cried like a child and gave it to his friend Geppetto, who fashioned from it the puppet Pinocchio. His creation proved unusually mischievous and had many bizarre adventures including having his feet burned off, his nose elongated and being transformed into a donkey. Eventually he learned to show sympathy and goodness, and 'the fairy' changed him to a real boy back at home with Geppetto. Pinocchio's name means 'pine seed', since he 'grew' from a piece of pine wood.

**Pious.** The Romans called a man who revered his father *pius*, hence Antoninus was called *pius*, because he requested that his adoptive father (Hadrian) might be ranked among the gods. AENEAS was called *Pius* because he rescued his father from the burning city of TROY. The Italian word PIETÀ has a similar meaning.

**Pious, The.** The following were so called:

Ernest I, founder of the House of Gotha (1601–74)
Robert II, son of Hugh Capet (*c*.970–1031)
Louis I of France (778–840); he was also called the DEBONAIR
Eric IX of Sweden (r.1150–60)
Frederick III, elector Palatine (1515–76)

**Pip.** The pips on cards and dice were named from the seeds of fruit (earlier *peep*, origin obscure). This is merely an abbreviated form of 'pippin', which denoted the seed long before it denoted apples raised from seed.

**Pip emma.** Military usage in the First World War for pm. It was originally telephonese, since 'ten pip emma' avoids any possibility of misunderstanding. In the same way 'ack emma' stood for am. *See also* ACK ACK; TOC H.

**Pipped, To be.** To be BLACKBALLED or defeated, the black ball being the pip.

**Pipped at the post, To be.** To be just beaten or defeated, when success seemed certain. To 'pip' in this sense was originally to BLACKBALL. See also BEATEN AT THE POST.

**Get one's second pip, To.** *See under* SECOND.

**Have** or **get the pip, To.** To be thoroughly 'fed up', downhearted and miserable. The word is probably connected with 'pip', the poultry disease that causes birds to pine away.

**Till the pips squeak.** *See under* TILL.

**Pipe. Pipe down.** Stop being aggressive or noisy; stop talking. A naval colloquialism derived from the boatswain's call of this name meaning 'hands turn in', i.e. 'lights out'.

**Pipe dream.** An impossible, imaginary and fanciful hope or plan indulged in at one's ease when smoking a pipe. The expression originated with opium smoking.

**Pipe rolls** or **great rolls of the pipe.** The name given to a class of EXCHEQUER records on account of their being kept in rolls in the form of a pipe. They begin in 1131 and continue till 1831, and contain the annual accounts of SHERIFFS with the Exchequer, county by county. They are now in the Public Record Office.

**Pipes of Pan.** *See* PANPIPES.

**Piping hot.** Hot as water that 'pipes' or sings, hence, new, only just out.

**As you pipe, I must dance.** *See under* AS.

**He who pays the piper calls the tune.** *See under* PAY.

**Pied Piper.** *See under* PIED.

**Put that in your pipe and smoke it.** Accept that if you can; 'swallow that one'. An expression used by someone who has given an opponent a rebuke or 'something to think about'.

**Tom Piper.** *See under* TOM.

**Pipeline, In the.** Already under way; in the process of being made or organized. The allusion is the transportation of oil by pipeline.

**Pippa.** The pure young girl in Robert Browning's poem *Pippa Passes* (1841) who wanders singing through the town on her holiday, her songs affecting all who hear her. One of her songs is sweeter than sweet:

The year's at the spring
And day's at the morn;
Morning's at seven;
The hill-side's dew-pearled;
The lark's on the wing;
The snail's on the thorn:
God's in his heaven –
All's right with the world!
*Pippa Passes*, I

**Pippin.** *See* PIP.

**Pippin the Short.** *See under* PEPIN.

**Piran, St.** The 5th- or 6th-century patron saint of Cornish miners, said to have been sent to Cornwall by St PATRICK. According to another legend he was cast into the sea by his fellow Irishmen bound to a millstone and landed at Perranzabuloe (St Piran in the Sands) near Perranporth. He set up a hermitage and discovered tin when he saw it streaming from the stone of his fireplace. Two churches of St Piran were buried in the sand dunes and the remains of one have been uncovered, hence legends of bells ringing in the sand. His day is 5 March. *See also* MEBYON KERNOW.

**Pis aller** (French, 'worst going'). A makeshift; something for want of a better; a last resort.

**Pisces** (Latin, 'the fishes'). A constellation and the twelfth sign of the ZODIAC.

**Piso's justice.** Verbally right, but morally wrong. Seneca says that Piso condemned a man on circumstantial evidence for murder, but when the execution was about to take place, the man believed to have been murdered appeared. The centurion sent the prisoner to Piso, and explained the situation to him, whereupon Piso condemned all three to death, saying, *Fiat* *justitia* (Latin, 'let justice be done'). The condemned man was executed because he had been sentenced, the centurion because he had disobeyed orders and the man believed to have been murdered because he had been the cause of death of two innocent men.

**Pistol.** The word has been popularly associated with Pistoia, the Italian city famed for its manufacture of weapons. The true origin is in Czech *píšťala*, 'pipe', 'pistol'.

**Fire one's pistol in the air, To.** *See under* FIRE.

**Pocket pistol.** *See under* POCKET.

**Queen Elizabeth's pocket pistol.** *See under* QUEEN.

**Pit, The Bottomless.** *See under* BOTTOM.

**Pit-a-pat, My heart goes.** It palpitates or races. A REDUPLICATED or an echoic word, as 'fiddle-faddle', 'harum-scarum', 'ding-dong' and so forth.

> 'Anything like the sound of a rat
> Makes my heart go pit-a-pat!'.
>
> ROBERT BROWNING: 'The Pied Piper of Hamelin' (1842)

**Pitch.** The black resinous substance gets its name from Latin *pix*, but the verb (to fling, settle and so on) is Middle English *picchen*, probably related to 'pick'.

**Pitch and pay.** Pay up at once. There is a pun in the phrase: 'to pay a ship' was to cover the oakum in the seams with pitch.

**Pitch and toss.** A game in which coins are pitched at a mark, the player getting nearest having the right to toss all the other's coins into the air and take those that come down with heads up. Hence, to play pitch and toss with one's money, prospects and so on is to gamble recklessly.

**Pitched battle.** A battle that has been planned, with the place and time chosen beforehand.

**Pitch into someone, To.** To assail them vigorously, to castigate them.

**Concert pitch.** *See under* CONCERT.

**Queer someone's pitch, To.** *See under* QUEER.

**Pitcher.** From Medieval Latin *picarium*, a variant of *bicarium*, related to English 'beaker'.

**Asses as well as pitchers have ears.** *See under* ASS.

**Little pitchers have long ears.** *See under* LITTLE.

**Pithecanthropus** or **Java Man.** The name given by Ernst Haeckel in 1868 to the hypothetical MISSING LINK, from Greek *pithēkos*, 'ape', and *anthrōpos*, 'man'. Later, *pithecanthropus* was the generic name given to the remains of the extinct man-like ape discovered near Trinil, Java, in 1891. *See also* PEKING MAN.

**Pitt Diamond.** A diamond of just under 137 CARATS found at the Parteal mines, India, and bought by Thomas Pitt (*see* DIAMOND PITT) in 1702 from a thief for a sum (said to have been £20,400) far below its real value. Hence Pope's reference:

> Asleep and naked as an Indian lay,
> An honest factor stole a gem away:
> He pledged it to the knight, the knight had wit,
> So kept the diamond, and the rogue was bit.
>
> ALEXANDER POPE: *Moral Essays*, Epistle iii (1731–5)

Pitt sold the diamond in 1717 to the Regent Orleans (hence its alternative name the 'Regent Diamond') for £135,000. It later adorned the sword hilt of NAPOLEON BONAPARTE, and it is still in the possession of France. Its original weight before cutting was 410 carats.

**Pius** (Latin, 'pious'). A name adopted by 12 popes, the most notorious being Pius V (r.1566–72), a relentless opponent of Protestantism and particularly reliant on the remedial rigours of the INQUISITION. A later controversial bearer of the name was Pius XII (r.1939–58), admired on the one hand for his moral authority but criticized on the other for his lack of action regarding the extermination of European Jews in the HOLOCAUST.

**Pixie** or **pixy.** A sprite or FAIRY of folklore, especially in Cornwall and Devon, where some held pixies to be the spirits of infants who died before baptism. In Cornwall and west Devon figures of 'piskeys' or pixies are still very much in evidence as souvenirs and lucky charms for tourists. The name is of obscure origin.

**Place. Place aux dames** (French). Make way for the ladies; ladies first.

**Place de Grève.** The TYBURN of old Paris, where for centuries public executions took place, now called the Place de l'Hôtel-de-Ville. It is on the bank of the Seine, the word *grève* here meaning 'shore', 'bank'. The same word also means 'strike' (of the industrial kind). This came about because the Place de Grève was a rallying point for unemployed workers.

**Place in the sun, A.** A favourable position; a share in something to which one has a natural right. The phrase achieved a particular significance when Kaiser Wilhelm II of Germany spoke of his nation taking steps to ensure that 'no one can dispute with us the place in the sun that is our due'.

**Placemakers' Bible, The.** *See under* BIBLE.

**Place** or **put oneself** or **one's head in the lion's mouth.** To expose oneself to danger needlessly and recklessly.

**Fall into place.** *See under* FALL.

**High places.** *See under* HIGH.

**Holy places.** *See under* HOLY.

**Watering place.** *See under* WATER.

**Placebo** (Latin, 'I shall please', 'I shall be acceptable').

(1) VESPERS for the dead, because the first antiphon at vespers of the office of the dead

began with the words *Placebo Domino in regione vivorum*, 'I will walk before the Lord in the land of the living' (Psalm 116:9). As sycophants and those who hoped to get something out of the relatives of the departed used to make a point of attending this service and singing the *Placebo*, the phrase 'to sing placebo' came to mean to play the flatterer or sycophant. Chaucer gives the name to such a parasite in 'The Merchant's Tale' (*c.*1387).

(2) An innocuous medicine designed to humour a patient, and which may have a beneficial psychological and physical effect, is called a placebo.

**Placemen.** A name given to those members of the HOUSE OF COMMONS who held 'places' or offices of profit under the crown. Their numbers grew steadily after the RESTORATION with the corrupt use of crown patronage by the Treasury to gain support for the government of the day. Placemen included ministers, civil servants, court officials, contractors, and army and navy officers. Attempts to limit their influence by Place Bills excluding them from the Commons were frequent, particularly from the 1690s until the 1740s, but few were passed. The objective was mainly secured by administrative reforms (1782–1870) which abolished places. The problem of patronage, however, still exists. *See also* PLACEMAKERS' BIBLE *under* BIBLE.

**Plagiarist.** The word for someone who appropriates another's ideas or material in literature, music and so on, means strictly a kidnapper or manstealer, from Latin *plagiarus*, 'plunderer', from *plagium*, 'kidnapping'. Martial applies it to a literary thief.

**Plagues. Plagues of Egypt.** The Old Testament book of Exodus tells how God imposed ten plagues on the Egyptians to persuade pharaoh to release his chosen people from captivity. They were:

(1) The waters of the Nile were turned to blood
(2) Hordes of frogs covered the land
(3) The dust was turned into swarms of gnats
(4) Swarms of flies infested the land
(5) Cattle were struck dead
(6) The people were covered with boils
(7) Lightning and hail destroyed crops and cattle
(8) The land was darkened with locusts
(9) A darkness covered the land for three days
(10) The first-born throughout the land were smitten

The tenth and final plague was the basis for the PASSOVER, after which the great Exodus of the Israelites began.

Scientists have sought to explain the plagues in terms of a cosmic disruption, but there is also an ecological theory. According to this, the Nile flooded catastrophically, filling with blood-red soil and red-coloured micro-organisms from the surrounding plateaux. As a result the fish were poisoned and the frogs forced onto dry land. The insects that then fed on the dead fish transmitted anthrax, so killing both humans and animals.

**Great Plague, The.** *See under* GREAT.

**Plaid Cymru** (Welsh, 'Party of Wales'). The Welsh nationalist party was set up in 1925 with the object of achieving Welsh home rule. Support grew from the 1960s and the party gained three seats in the HOUSE OF COMMONS in 1974, two in 1979 and 1983, three in 1987 and four in 1992 and 1997.

**Plain, The.** The GIRONDISTS were so called in the French Revolutionary National Convention because they sat on the level floor or plain of the hall. After their overthrow this part of the House was called the *marais* or swamp, and included such members as were under the control of the MOUNTAIN.

**Plains Indians.** The name given to the Native American tribes of the central prairie areas of North America from Alberta to Texas, once the land of the American bison or buffalo. They are the 'redskins' of popular fame, with their feather head-dresses, teepees and peace pipes. Among the numerous tribes are the APACHE, BLACKFOOT, Cheyenne, Comanche, Dakota and PAWNEE.

**Plains of Abraham.** A plateau of southern Quebec province, Canada, the scene of the decisive battle (13 September 1759) between the British under James Wolfe (1727–59) and the French under Louis Joseph Montcalm (1712–59), as a result of which the conquest of Canada was effected. Both leaders were killed. The plateau is named after Martin Abraham (1589–1664), a ship's pilot who earlier owned part of the land.

**Cities of the Plain, The.** SODOM AND GOMORRAH.

**Great Plains.** *See under* GREAT.

**Nullarbor Plain.** *See under* NULLARBOR.

**Salisbury Plain.** *See under* SALISBURY.

**Sermon on the Plain, The.** *See under* SERMON.

**Plain** (adjective). **Plain English.** Plain, unmistakable speech or writing. To tell someone in plain English what you think of them is to give your very candid opinion.

**Plain jane.** An unattractive woman or girl. *See also* JANE.

**Plain sailing.** Something is perfectly straightforward; there need be no hesitation about the course of action. A nautical phrase which has been influenced by 'plane sailing', the art of determining a ship's position on the assumption that the earth is flat. She is sailing, therefore, on a plane, instead of a spherical surface, which is a simple and easy method of determining the course and distance over short passages.

**As plain as a pikestaff.** *See under* AS.

**As plain as the nose on your face.** *See under* AS.

**Plan, Five-year.** *See under* FIVE.

**Planets.** The celestial bodies that revolve round the sun in approximately circular orbits, so called from Greek *planētēs*, 'wanderer', because to the ancients they appeared to wander about among the stars instead of having fixed places.

The primary planets are MERCURY, VENUS, the Earth, MARS, JUPITER, SATURN, URANUS, NEPTUNE and PLUTO (discovered in 1930). These are known as the major planets, the asteroids between the orbits of Mars and Jupiter being the minor planets.

The secondary planets are the satellites, or moons revolving round a primary.

Mercury and Venus are called inferior planets since their orbits are nearer to the Sun than the Earth's. The remaining planets are superior planets. Only five of the planets were known to the ancients (the Earth not being reckoned), i.e. Mercury, Venus, Mars, Jupiter and Saturn, but to these were added the sun and moon, making seven in all.

For the relation of metals and precious stones to the planets *see* PRECIOUS STONES.

**Born under a lucky** or **unlucky planet, To be.** *See under* BORN.

**Plank.** Any one portion or principle of a political PLATFORM.

**As thick as two short planks.** *See under* AS.

**Walk the plank, To.** *See under* WALK.

**Plant, Divine.** *See under* DIVINE.

**Plantagenet.** A name commonly given since the mid-17th century to the royal line now more properly called ANGEVIN and to the LANCASTRIAN and YORKIST kings from Henry II to Richard III. These were the descendants of Geoffrey, Count of Anjou, and Matilda, daughter of Henry I. It may have arisen from Geoffrey of Anjou's habit of wearing a sprig of BROOM (*plante genêt*) in his cap, or from the fact that he planted broom to improve his hunting covers. Henry II was Geoffrey's son. The House of Plantagenet therefore includes the following kings: Henry II (r.1154–89), Richard I (r.1189–99), John (r.1199–1216), Henry III (r.1216–72), Edward I (r.1272–1307), Edward II (1307–27), Edward III (r.1327–77), Richard II (r.1377–99), Henry IV (r.1399–1413), Henry V (r.1413–22), Henry VI (r.1422–61, 1470–71), Edward IV (r.1461–70, 1471–83), Edward V (r.1483) and Richard III (r.1483–5). It was historically only a nickname, first used as a surname by Richard, Duke of York, father of Edward IV.

**Plaque, Blue.** *See under* BLUE.

**Plaster. Plaster of Paris.** Gypsum, especially calcined gypsum used for making statuary casts, keeping broken limbs rigid for setting and so on. The name derives from the gypsum quarries of Montmartre, Paris.

**Court plaster.** *See under* COURT.

**Plate.** In horse racing, the gold or silver cup forming the prize, and hence the race for such a prize.

**Plates of meat.** RHYMING SLANG for 'feet', often abbreviated to 'plates'.

**Drake brass plate, The.** *See under* FAKES.

**Have a lot on one's plate, To.** *See under* LOT.

**Sheffield plate.** *See under* SHEFFIELD.

**Platform.** The policy or declaration of a political party; that on which the party stands. In this sense it is an Americanism dating from before the mid-19th century. It was, however, used in the late 16th century of a plan or scheme of church government. *See also* PLANK.

**Plato.** The great Athenian philosopher (*c*.428–348 BC), the pupil of SOCRATES and founder of the ACADEMY. Of his numerous writings, *The* REPUBLIC has perhaps been the most influential. He was originally called Aristocles, but the name Plato is said to have been bestowed by his gymnastic teacher, from his broad shoulders (Greek *platus*, 'flat'). Some say it arose from the breadth of his forehead.

**Platonic cycle** or **great year, The.** That space of time that, according to ancient astronomers, elapses before all the stars and constellations return to their former positions in respect to the equinoxes. Tycho Brahe calculated this period at 25,816 years, and Riccioli at 25,920 years.

> Cut out more work than can be done
> In Plato's year, but finish none.
>
> SAMUEL BUTLER: *Hudibras*, III, ii (1680)

**Platonic love.** Spiritual love between persons of opposite sexes; the friendship of man and woman, without any sexual implications. The phrase is founded on a passage towards the end of *The* SYMPOSIUM (4th century BC) in which PLATO was extolling not the non-sexual love of a man for a woman but the loving interest that SOCRATES took in young men. This was pure and therefore noteworthy in the Greece of the period.

> I am convinced, and always was, that Platonic Love is Platonic nonsense.
>
> SAMUEL RICHARDSON: *Pamela*, III, lxxviii (1740–1)

**Platonic year.** *See* PLATONIC CYCLE.

**Platonism.** A philosophy characterized by the doctrine of pre-existing eternal ideas, which teaches the immortality and pre-existence of the soul, the dependence of virtue upon discipline, and the trustworthiness of cognition.

**Plattdeutsch.** Low German, which, until 1500, was the business language of northern Europe. *See also* HIGH GERMAN.

**Play. Play along, To.** To cooperate temporarily.

**Play a part, To.** To perform some duty or pursue some course of action, also, to act deceitfully. The phrase is from the stage, where an actor's part is the words or the character assigned to him.

**Play a waiting game, To.** To bide one's time, knowing that that is the best way of winning, to adopt FABIAN TACTICS.

**Play ball, To.** A colloquial phrase on both sides of the Atlantic, meaning to agree to a suggestion or to cooperate in some plan or action. It takes two or more to play ball.

**Play chicken, To.** To play a physically dangerous 'game' or dare, such as children's 'last across': the first to cross a railway line before an oncoming train is 'chicken', the last to cross is the winner.

**Play down, To.** To minimize the importance of an action or event; to make light of something.

**Played out.** Exhausted; out of date; no longer in VOGUE.

**Play false, to.** To act treacherously; to be faithless.

**Play fast and loose, To.** To RUN WITH THE HARE AND HUNT WITH THE HOUND; to blow both hot and cold, to say one thing and do another. The allusion is probably to an old cheating game once practised at fairs. A belt or strap was doubled and rolled up with the loop in the centre and placed on edge on a table. The player then had to catch the loop with a skewer while the belt was unrolled, but this was done in such a way by the trickster as to make the feat impossible.

> To sell a bargain well is as cunning as fast and loose.
> SHAKESPEARE: *Love's Labour's Lost*, III, i (1594)

**Play footsie, To.** To touch the foot or leg of another person with one's own foot flirtatiously, especially under a table where others cannot see.

**Play for time, To.** To prolong or delay negotiations, or the arriving at a decision, in the hope of staving off defeat, failure or the like. In CRICKET, when victory for the batting team is no longer possible in the remaining time, cautious play may lead to a drawn game instead of defeat.

**Play gooseberry, To.** To be an unwanted third person when two lovers are together. The origin of the phrase is obscure, but it may derive from the tact of the person occupying the time in picking gooseberries while the others were more romantically occupied.

**Play, wreak** or **cause havoc, To.** To cause destruction, damage, distress, disruption or the like.

> The noise and clatter of high-revving engines can play havoc with a driver's nerves.
> *The Times* (25 March 1969)

**Play hookey, To.** To play truant, from the idea that 'to hook' something is to make off with it.

**Play into someone's hands, To.** To act unwittingly or carelessly, thus giving the advantage to the other person.

**Play it by ear, To.** To proceed instinctively or by dealing with each circumstance as it arises and as it merits. The metaphor is from music, when to play by ear is to perform without having seen the score.

**Play merry hell with, To.** To disrupt; to throw into disarray.

**Play one's cards close to one's chest, To.** To be cautious or secretive about what one plans to do. The allusion is to a card player who holds his cards close to his body so that others cannot see his hand.

**Play one's cards right, To.** To carry out one's plans, as a card player plans which cards to play.

**Play one's trump card, To.** To outdo or surpass, especially at a chosen moment. The phrase is from card playing. *See also* TRUMP CARD.

**Play on words.** A pun.

**Play possum, To.** To lie low; to feign quiescence; to dissemble. The phrase comes from the opossum's habitual attempt to avoid capture by feigning death. *See also* UP A GUM TREE.

**Play second fiddle, To.** To take a subordinate part, but next after the leader.

> 'I've played a second fiddle all through life,' he said with a bitter laugh.
> W.M. THACKERAY: *Pendennis*, ch xvii (1848–50)

**Play someone up, To.** To be a nuisance to someone; to harass and annoy a person; to behave in a troublesome fashion, as schoolchildren 'play up' some teachers.

**Play the ape, To.** To play practical jokes or silly tricks; to pull faces like an ape.

**Play the field, To.** To disperse one's interests or involvements widely.

**Play the fool, To.** To act foolishly; to behave in a frivolous manner.

**Play the game, To.** To act in a straightforward, honourable manner; to keep to the rules of fair play.

> There's a breathless hush in the Close to-night –
> Ten to make and the match to win –
> A bumping pitch and a blinding light,
> An hour to play and the last man in.
> And it's not for the sake of a ribboned coat,
> Or the selfish hope of a season's fame,
> But his Captain's hand on his shoulder smote –
> 'Play up! play up! and play the game!'
> SIR HENRY NEWBOLT: 'Vitaï Lampada' (1897)

**Play the sedulous ape to, To.** To study the style of another person and model one's own on theirs as faithfully and meticulously as possible. The phrase is said, usually with more or less contempt, of literary people. It is taken from R.L. Stevenson, who, in his essay, 'A College Magazine' (*Memories and Portraits* (1887)), said that he had:

> Played the sedulous ape to Hazlitt, to Lamb, to Wordsworth, to Sir Thomas Browne, to Defoe, to Hawthorne; to Montaigne, to Baudelaire, and to Obermann … That, like it or not, is the way to learn to write.

**Play the very Devil with something, To.** To thoroughly mar or spoil.

**Play to the gallery, To.** To court popularity in the same way as an actor seeking applause from the patrons of the cheapest seats in the theatre, those in the gallery.

> The instant we begin to think about success and the effect of our work – to play with one eye on the gallery – we lose power and touch and everything else.
>
> RUDYARD KIPLING: *The Light that Failed*, ch vii (1890)

*See also* GODS.

**Play up to someone, To.** To flatter a person with the aim of gaining favour.

**Play with fire, To.** To meddle with something that is potentially dangerous or harmful.

**Bring into play, To.** *See under* BRING.

**Child's play.** *See under* CHILD.

**Fair play.** *See under* FAIR.

**Passion play.** *See under* PASSION.

**Seeded players.** *See under* SEED.

**Two can play at that game.** *See under* TWO.

**Pleading, Special.** *See under* SPECIAL.

**Please. As pleased as a dog with two tails.** *See under* AS.

**As pleased as Punch.** *See under* AS.

**Pretty please.** *See under* PRETTY.

**Pleasure, Parson's.** *See under* PARSON

**Plebeian.** A member of the common people, properly a free citizen of Rome, neither PATRICIAN nor client. From Latin *plebs*, 'the common people'.

**Plebiscite.** In Roman history a law enacted by the *comitia* or assembly of tribes. The modern meaning is the direct vote of the whole body of citizens of a state on some definite question. Thus Louis Napoleon's COUP D'ÉTAT (2 December 1851) was confirmed by a carefully 'rigged' plebiscite, and in November 1852 another plebiscite approved the re-establishment of the empire.

**Pledge.** To guarantee; to assign as security. Hence, in drinking a toast, to give assurance of friendship by the act of drinking.

> Drink to me only with thine eyes,
> And I will pledge with mine.
>
> BEN JONSON: 'To Celia' (1616)

**Sign** or **take the pledge, To.** *See under* SIGN.

**Pleiades.** In classical myth, the seven daughters of ATLAS and Pleione, sisters of the HYADES. They were transformed into stars, one of which, MEROPE, is invisible, out of shame, because she married a mortal, SISYPHUS, while others say it is ELECTRA who hides herself from grief for the destruction of TROY and its royal race. Electra is known as 'the lost Pleiad'.

The great cluster of stars in the constellation TAURUS, especially the seven larger ones, were called the Pleiades by the Greeks from the word *plein*, 'to sail', because they considered navigation safe at the rising of the constellation, and their setting marked the close of the sailing season.

**Pleiad, The.** A name frequently given to groups of seven particularly illustrious persons.

**Pleiad of Alexandria, The.** A group of seven contemporary poets in the 3rd century BC: Apollonius of Rhodes, Aratus, Callimachus, Lycophron, Nicander, Philiscus (called Homer the Younger) and THEOCRITUS.

**Charlemagne's Pleiad.** *See under* CHARLEMAGNE.

**French Pléiade, The.** *See under* FRENCH.

**Philosophical Pleiad, The.** The WISE MEN OF GREECE..

**Plenty, Horn of.** *See under* HORN.

**Plight one's troth, To.** To pledge one's word, especially in marriage or betrothal. One may equally pledge one's troth, although 'plight' and 'pledge' are unrelated words. 'Troth' is a form of 'truth', as in 'betrothal' itself.

> I *M.* take thee *N.* to my wedded wife, to have and to hold from this day forward, for better for worse, for richer for poorer, in sickness and in health, to love and to cherish, till death us do part, according to God's holy ordinance; and thereto I plight thee my troth.
>
> *Book of Common Prayer* (Solemnization of Matrimony) (1662)

**Plimsoll line** or **mark.** The mark fixing the maximum load line of a merchant vessel in salt water. It takes its name from Samuel Plimsoll (1824–98), MP for Derby, who from 1870 led a campaign of protest against the overloading and overinsuring of unsafe shipping. His sensational outburst when Disraeli's government decided to drop the Shipping Bill in 1875 led to the Merchant Shipping (Plimsoll) Act of 1876.

**Plonk.** An Australian term for cheap red wine fortified by methylated spirit. It is also popularly applied to any cheap red wine. Despite this, the origin of the word may be in French *vin blanc*, 'white wine'.

**Plon-plon.** The sobriquet of Prince Napoleon Joseph Charles Paul Bonaparte (1822–91), son of Jérôme Bonaparte, an adaptation of *Craint-plon* ('Fear-bullet'), the nickname he earned in the Crimean War (1854–6).

**Plot. Bandbox Plot.** *See under* BANDBOX.

**Cobham's Plot.** *See* MAIN PLOT.

**Gunpowder Plot.** *See under* GUNPOWDER.

**Main Plot.** *See under* MAIN.

**Meal Tub Plot.** *See under* MEAL.

**Popish Plot.** *See under* POPE.

**Property plot.** *See under* PROPERTY.

**Rye House Plot.** *See under* RYE.

**Scotch Plot.** *See under* SCOTCH.

**Screw Plot.** *See under* SCREW.

**Watson's Plot.** *See under* WATSON.

**Plough.** Another name for the GREAT BEAR.

**Plough alms.** In medieval England a payment of one penny for each plough team in the parish, paid to the priest a fortnight after EASTER.

**Plough back profits, To.** To reinvest them.

**Ploughed, To be.** To fail to pass an examination. *See also* PLUCK.

**Plough Monday.** The first Monday after TWELFTH NIGHT is so called because it was the end of the CHRISTMAS holidays when men returned to their plough or daily work. It was customary for farm labourers to draw a plough from door to door and to solicit 'plough money' to spend in a frolic. The queen of the banquet was called Bessy. The plough itself was called the white, fond or fool plough; 'white', because the MUMMERS were dressed in white, gaudily trimmed with flowers and ribbons, 'fond' or 'fool', because the procession is fond or foolish, i.e. not serious or of a business character. *See also* St DISTAFF'S DAY.

**Plough** or **number the sands, To.** To undertake an endless or impossible task.

> Alas! poor duke, the task he undertakes
> Is numbering sands and drinking oceans dry.
>
> SHAKESPEARE: *Richard II*, II, ii (1595)

**Put one's hand to the plough, To.** *See under* HAND.

**Put the plough before the oxen, To.** Another way of saying to PUT THE CART BEFORE THE HORSE (*see under* CART).

**Speed the plough** or **God speed the plough.** *See under* SPEED.

**Plowden. 'The case is altered,' quoth Plowden.** There is more than one story accounting for the origin of this old phrase, used by Ben Jonson as the title of one of his comedies (*c.*1597). One is that Edmund Plowden (1518–85), the great lawyer, was defending a gentleman who was accused of hearing MASS and elicited the fact that the service was performed by a layman masquerading in priestly vestments for the purpose of informing against the worshippers. Thereupon the brilliant lawyer observed, 'The case is altered, no priest, no mass', thus securing the acquittal of his client. Another version is that Plowden was asked what legal remedy there was against some pigs that trespassed on a complainant's ground. 'There is a very good remedy,' began the lawyer, but when informed that they were the complainant's own pigs, said, 'Nay, then, the case is altered.' *See also* CASE IS ALTERED; PUBLIC HOUSE SIGNS.

**Pluck.** In its meaning of courage, determination, the word was originally pugilistic slang of the late 18th century and was used in the same way as 'heart'. A 'pug' who was lacking in pluck was a coward. The pluck of an animal is the heart, liver and lungs, that can be removed by one pull or pluck. Compare the expressions 'bold heart', 'lily-livered' (*see under* LIVER), 'a man of another KIDNEY', 'BOWELS OF MERCY', 'to vent one's SPLEEN', 'it raised his BILE' etc.

A rejected candidate at an examination is said to be plucked, because formerly at the ancient universities, when degrees were conferred and the names were read out before presentation to the vice chancellor, the PROCTOR walked once up and down the room, and anyone who objected might signify his dissent by plucking the proctor's gown. This was occasionally done by tradesmen to whom the candidate was in debt.

> 'No, it isn't that, sir. I'm not afraid of being shot; I wish to God anybody would shoot me. I have not got my degree. I – I'm plucked, sir.'
>
> W.M. THACKERAY: *Pendennis*, ch xx (1848–50)

**Plug. Plug a song, To.** To give a song copious and frequent publicity, as on the radio.

**Plug ugly.** A rowdy, unpleasant character, a term said to have originated at Baltimore, and applied to ruffians who attempted to exert political pressure. The origin of the term is uncertain.

**Pull the plug, To.** *See under* PULL.

**Plum.** Old slang for a very large sum of money (properly £100,000), or for its possession. Nowadays the figurative use of the word means the very best part of anything, the prize, the 'pick of the basket' or a WINDFALL.

**Plunger.** A reckless gambler, who goes on when he cannot afford it in the hope that his luck will turn. The 4th and last Marquess of Hastings was the first person so called by the TURF. He may have been the original of CHAMPAGNE CHARLIE and was certainly the most notorious spendthrift and wastrel of the mid-19th century. One night he lost three games of draughts for £1000 a game. He then cut a pack of cards for £500 a cut, and lost £5000 in an hour and a half. He paid both debts before he left the room.

**Plus. Plus fours.** Loose KNICKERBOCKERS overlapping the knee and thereby giving added freedom for active outdoor sports. They were particularly popular with golfers in the 1920s. The name derives from the four extra inches (about 10cm) of cloth required below the knee in tailoring.

**Plus ultra.** The motto in the Spanish royal arms. It was once *Ne plus ultra* ('thus far and no farther') in allusion to the PILLARS OF HERCULES, the *ne plus ultra* of the world, but after the discovery of America, and when Charles V (Holy Roman Emperor 1519–56) inherited the crown of Aragon and Castile, with all the vast American possessions, he struck out *ne*, and assumed the words *plus ultra* for the national motto, the implication being that Spain could go farther.

**Pluto.** In Roman mythology, the ruler of the infernal regions, the son of SATURN, brother of JUPITER and NEPTUNE, and husband of PROSERPINA. Hence, the grave, the place where the dead go before they are admitted into ELYSIUM or sent to TARTARUS.

In the Second World War Pluto was the code name (from the initials of Pipe Line Under The Ocean) given to the pipelines to carry oil fuel laid across the bed of the English Channel, from Sandown to Cherbourg and from Dungeness to Boulogne.

**Plutonian** or **Plutonist.** *See* VULCANIST.

**Plutonic rocks.** Granites, certain porphyries and other igneous unstratified crystalline rocks, believed to have been formed at a great depth and pressure, as distinguished from the volcanic rocks, which were formed near the surface. They are so called from PLUTO, as the lord of elemental fire. The Irish chemist Richard Kirwan used the term in his *Elements of Mineralogy* (1796).

**Plutus.** In Greek mythology the god of riches. Hence, 'as rich as Plutus', and 'plutocrat', one who exercises influence or possesses power through his wealth. The legend is that Plutus was blinded by ZEUS so that his gifts should be equally distributed and not go only to those who merited them.

**Plymouth Brethren.** A sect of Evangelical Christians founded in Ireland *c.*1828 by J.N. Darby (1800–82), one-time Anglican priest (hence they are sometimes called DARBYITES), and deriving their name from Plymouth, the first centre set up in England (1830). In 1849 they split up into Open Brethren and Exclusive Brethren. They have no organized ministry and lay emphasis on the BREAKING OF BREAD each Sunday.

**Pneumonia, Double.** *See under* DOUBLE.

**Pocahontas.** The daughter of Powhatan, an Indian chief of Virginia. She is said to have rescued Captain John Smith (1580–1631) when her father was on the point of killing him. She subsequently married John Rolfe, the first Englishman to plant and cure tobacco. In 1616 she came to England with her husband and infant son and was presented to James I and the queen. She died off Gravesend on 21 March 1617, aged about 22, when about to return to Virginia, and was buried in St George's Church. She actually passed her stay at the Bell-Savage. *See also* BELLE SAUVAGE.

**Pocket** (Anglo-Norman *poket*, 'small bag', from Middle Dutch *poke*, 'bag'). From the word's attributive use for small articles designed to be carried in the pockets of a garment, as pocket handkerchief, pocket watch and so on, it is figuratively used of things and people of less than normal or average size. Thus, Germany, forbidden to build warships of over 10,000 tons by the Treaty of VERSAILLES (1919), constructed several formidable battleships purporting to be within this limit which were known as pocket battleships (in German, *Westentaschenkreuzer*, literally 'waistcoat pocket cruiser').

**Pocket an insult, To.** To submit to an insult without showing annoyance.

**Pocket borough.** *See* ROTTEN BOROUGH.

**Pocket money.** A small (or not so small) sum of money given weekly to children by their parents as an allowance or for 'expenses'.

**Pocket pistol.** Colloquial for a flask carried in 'self-defence', because one may not be able to get a dram on the road.

**Pocket veto.** When the President of the USA refuses to sign a Bill that has passed both Houses, he is said to pocket it. It thus dies.

**In or out of pocket, To be.** To be a gainer or loser by some financial transaction.

**In someone's pocket, To be.** To be under their control; to be close to them.

**Line one's pockets, To.** *See under* LINE.

**Put one's hand in one's pocket, To.** *See under* HAND.

**Pococurante** (Italian *poco curante*, 'caring little'). Insouciant, DEVIL-MAY-CARE or easy-go-lucky. Hence, pococurantism, indifference to matters of importance but concern about trifles. The term is also used for someone who in arguments leaves the main thrust and veers off on some minor and indifferent point.

**Podarge** (Greek *podargos*, 'swift-footed' or 'white-footed'). One of the horses of HECTOR.

**Podsnap.** A pompous, self-satisfied man in Dickens' *Our Mutual Friend* (1864–5), the archetype of someone who is overburdened with stiff-starched etiquette and self-importance. Hence, 'Podsnappery'. *See also* PECKSNIFF.

> He always knew exactly what providence meant. Inferior and less respectable men might fall short of that mark, but Mr Podsnap was always up to it. And it was very remarkable (and must have been very comfortable) that what Providence meant was invariably what Mr Podsnap meant.
>
> *Our Mutual Friend*, Bk I, ch xi (1864–5)

**Podunk.** A term for a little American ONE-HORSE TOWN, from the place near Hartford, Connecticut, of this name, which is of Native American origin.

**Poem. Poems of Ossian, The.** *See* OSSIAN.

**Emblematical poems.** *See under* EMBLEM.

**Rowley poems, The.** *See under* FAKES.

**Poet. Poeta nascitur, non fit.** POETS ARE BORN, NOT MADE.

**Poetic justice.** The ideal justice, which poets exercise in making the good happy and the bad unsuccessful. The phrase is now used to mean little more than 'just deserts', 'comeuppance'.

Poetic Justice, with her lifted scale,
Where, in nice balance, truth with gold she weighs,
And solid pudding against empty praise.
ALEXANDER POPE: *The Dunciad*, Bk I (1742)

**Poet laureate.** A court official, now appointed by the Prime Minister, who has no specific duties but who traditionally composes odes in celebration of royal birthdays and national occasions. The appointment essentially dates from the time of James I, but there had earlier been an occasional *Versificator Regis* and the universities gave the LAUREL wreath to graduates in rhetoric and Latin versification and to meritorious poets, among whom John Skelton (*c*.1460–1529) was styled *Laureatus*. The laurel crown was anciently a mark of distinction and honour. The following is the list of poets laureate, the year after the life dates being that of the appointment to the post:

Ben Jonson (1572–1637; 1619)
Sir William D'Avenant (1606–68; 1638)
John Dryden (1631–1700; 1668)
Thomas Shadwell (*c*.1642–92; 1689)
Nahum Tate (1652–1715; 1692)
Nicholas Rowe (1674–1718; 1715)
Laurence Eusden (1688–1730; 1718)
Colley Cibber (1671–1757; 1730)
William Whitehead (1715–85; 1757)
Thomas Warton (1728–90; 1785)
Henry James Pye (1745–1813; 1790)
Robert Southey (1774–1843; 1813)
William Wordsworth (1770–1850; 1843)
Alfred, Lord Tennyson (1809–92; 1850)
Alfred Austin (1835–1913; 1896)
Robert Bridges (1844–1930; 1913)
John Masefield (1878–1967; 1930)
Cecil Day-Lewis (1904–72; 1968)
Sir John Betjeman (1906–84; 1972)
Ted Hughes (1930–98; 1984)
Andrew Motion (b.1952; 1999)

**Poetic licence.** A poet's transgression of accepted rules for special effect, defined by Dryden as 'the liberty which poets have assumed to themselves in all ages, of speaking things in verse, which are beyond the severity of prose'. A poet who takes liberties in the use of figurative speech, rhyme, archaism or syntax will be seen to display such licence. The term has been extended to artists who take an equivalent artistic licence.

**Poet of Greta Hall, The.** Robert Southey (1774–1843), who lived at Greta Hall, Keswick, Cumberland (now Cumbria).

**Poets are born, not made.** One can never be a poet by mere training if one has been born without the necessary creative power and inspiration. A translation of the Latin tag *Poeta nascitur non fit*, of which an extension is *Nascimur poetae fimus oratores* ('We are born poets, we are made orators'). The application has been extended to other callings.

**Poet's Corner.** The southern end of the south transept of Westminster Abbey, first so called by Oliver Goldsmith because it contained the tomb of Chaucer. Joseph Addison had previously (*The Spectator*, No. 26 (1711)) alluded to it as the 'poetical quarter', in which he says:

I found there were Poets who had no Monuments, and Monuments which had no poets.

Among writers buried here are Edmund Spenser, John Dryden, Samuel Johnson, Richard Brinsley Sheridan, Charles Dickens, Robert Browning, Alfred, Lord Tennyson, Lord Macaulay, Thomas Hardy and Rudyard Kipling. There are also many monuments to writers not buried here. Ben Jonson was buried in the north aisle of the Abbey, and Joseph Addison in Henry VII's Chapel.

**Barber Poet.** *See under* BARBER.
**Battle of the Poets, The.** *See under* BATTLE.
**Cean Poet, The.** *See under* CEAN.
**Cobbler Poet, The.** *See under* COBBLER.
**Cumberland Poets.** *See under* CUMBERLAND.
**Cyclic poets.** *See under* CYCLE.
**Devonshire Poet, The.** *See under* DEVONSHIRE.
**Dorsetshire Poet, The.** *See under* DORSET.
**Lake Poets.** *See under* LAKE.
**Mad Poet, The.** *See under* MAD.
**Maeonian Poet, The.** *See under* MAEONIDES.
**Manchester Poet, The.** *See under* MANCHESTER.
**Metaphysical poets.** *See under* METAPHYSICS.
**Peasant Poet.** *See under* PEASANT.
**Postman Poet.** *See* DEVONSHIRE POET.
**Samian Poet.** *See under* SAMIAN.
**Water Poet.** *See under* WATER.

**Poetry. Acrostic poetry.** *See under* ACROSTIC.
**Bernesque poetry.** *See under* BERNESQUE.
**Epic poetry.** *See under* EPIC.

**Point.** Defined by EUCLID as 'that which hath no parts'. John Playfair (1748–1819) defined it as 'that which has position but not magnitude', and Adrien-Marie Legendre (1752–1833) says it 'is a limit terminating a line', which suggests that a point could not exist without a line, and presupposes knowledge of what a line is.

**Point-blank.** Direct. A term from gunnery. When a cannon is so placed that the line of sight is parallel to the axis and horizontal, the discharge is point-blank, and was supposed to go direct, without curve, to an object within a certain distance. In French *point blanc* is the white mark or BULL'S EYE of a target, to hit which the ball or arrow must not deviate by the least amount.

**Point d'appui** (French, 'point of support'). A standpoint; a fulcrum; a base for action; a pretext to conceal the real intention.

**Point-device.** An archaic expression meaning punctilious; minutely exact. It represents the French *à point devis*, 'to the point arranged'.

Men's behaviour should be like their apparel, not too strait or point device, but free for exercise or motion.
FRANCIS BACON: *Essayes* (1597–1625)

**Point duty.** The positioning of a police officer or traffic warden at a road junction to direct traffic.
**Point of honour.** An obligation that is binding because its violation would offend some scruple or notion of self-respect.
**Point of no return.** The point in an aircraft's flight at which it has not enough fuel to return to its point of departure and must continue. Hence the figurative application of the expression to a point or situation from which there is no going back.
**Point of order, A.** In a formal deliberative assembly, a question raised as to whether a particular proceeding is in accordance with the rules of the body itself.
**Point of sale.** In commercial terms, the place at which a sale is made. This is usually either the counter or the supermarket check-out, the latter now operating an EFTPOS (electronic funds transfer at point of sale) system for customers paying by credit or debit card.
**Point of view.** Literally, the position from which one can observe. Figuratively, one's opinion or mental standpoint.
**Points.** A term from the Second World War relating to the system of rationing food, clothing and other commodities. Apart from direct rationing of meat, bacon, sugar, fats and tea, miscellaneous groceries were given 'points' values and each ration book holder was given a certain number of points to spend in an allotted period. Hence 'it's on points' was a common reference to many commodities.
**Points system.** A system used by a local authority for granting a council house to a tenant. Points are awarded according to the person's status, depending on such factors as length of residence in the area, number of children in the family and so on.
**Point-to-point race, A.** A race, especially a STEEPLECHASE, direct from one point to another, otherwise a cross-country race.
**Beside the point.** *See under* BESIDE.
**Boiling point, To be at.** *See under* BOIL.
**Break point.** *See under* BREAK.
**Brownie points.** *See under* BROWN.
**Cardinal points.** *See under* CARDINAL.
**Carry one's point, To.** *See under* CARRY.
**Case in point, A.** A relevant instance.
**Come to the point, To.** *See under* COME.
**Cuckold's Point.** *See under* CUCKOLD.
**Devil's Point.** *See under* DEVIL.
**Drive a point home, To.** *See under* DRIVE.
**Fourteen Points.** *See under* FOURTEEN.
**Freezing point.** *See under* FREEZING.
**In point of fact.** A stronger way of saying 'As a fact' or 'As a matter of fact'.
**Make a point of doing something, To.** To treat something as a matter of duty or to make it a special object. The phrase is a translation of the older French *faire un point de*.
**Make** or **prove one's point, To.** To make clear what one thinks or wishes; to prove one's contention.
**Not to put too fine a point on it.** *See under* FINE.
**Off the point.** *See under* OFF.
**Score points off someone, To.** *See under* SCORE.
**Selling point.** *See under* SELL.
**Sticking point.** *See under* STICK.
**Stretch a point, To.** *See under* STRETCH.
**Strong point.** *See under* STRONG.
**Take someone's point, To.** To concede that they have made a valid contention. A discussion or argument frequently contains a rejoinder such as: 'I take your point, but ... .'
**Up to a point.** *See under* UP.
**Win on points, To.** *See under* WIN.

**Pointillism** (French *pointiller*, 'to dot', 'to stipple'). A neo-Impressionist technique of painting with dots of pure colour, popularized by the French painter Georges Seurat (1859–91). *See also* IMPRESSIONISM.

**Poirot, Hercule.** The small and unassuming Belgian detective, with his waxed moustache and slightly comical manner, was the creation of Agatha Christie (1890–1976) and appeared in her first detective novel, *The Mysterious Affair at Styles* (1920). He went on to play a key role in some 40 further novels, including *Murder on the Orient Express* (1934). He has since starred on the cinema and television screen in a number of popular adaptations of the stories, being played by such disparate actors as Austin Trevor, Albert Finney, Peter Ustinov, Ian Holm and David Suchet.

'This affair must all be unravelled from within.' He tapped his forehead. 'These little grey cells. It is "up to them" – as you say over here.'
AGATHA CHRISTIE: *The Mysterious Affair at Styles*, ch x (1920)

**Poison.** *See* MITHRIDATE.
**Poison-pen letter.** A malicious letter, usually written anonymously with the aim of frightening, disturbing or warning someone.
**Poisoned chalice.** An award or honour which will probably prove a disadvantage to its recipient. There are many stories involving a cup or chalice that contains a deadly drink. In Shakespeare's *Hamlet* (1600) such a cup, prepared for Hamlet, actually kills Gertrude.
**Poison pill.** A pill containing a fast-acting poison such as cyanide, a traditional resort by captives in some countries as a means of suicide when defeat in combat is inevitable. In the world

of commerce a poison pill is a ploy used by a company to deter a bidder when faced with an unwelcome takeover bid.

**One man's meat is another man's poison.** *See under* ONE.

**What's your poison?** *See under* WHAT.

**Poisson d'Avril** (French, 'April fish'). The French equivalent of the British APRIL FOOL.

**Poke.** A bag, pouch or sack. The word gave POCKET, as a 'little poke'. It is now virtually obsolete except in the phrase 'to buy a PIG IN A POKE'.

**Poke bonnet.** A long, straight, projecting bonnet, commonly worn by women in the 18th and early 19th centuries and later by women members of the SALVATION ARMY and old-fashioned QUAKER women. It was perhaps so called because it projects or pokes out in front.

**Poke fun at someone, To.** To ridicule them.

**Poke one's nose in, To.** To meddle in other people's affairs, to intrude where one is not wanted.

**Pig in a poke, A.** *See under* PIG.

**Poker. Poker face, A.** An expressionless face characteristic of the good poker player, who assumes it to conceal from his adversaries any idea of what cards he may be holding.

**As stiff as a poker.** *See under* AS.

**Strip poker.** *See under* STRIP.

**Poky.** Cramped, narrow or confined, as a 'poky little room'. Also poor and shabby.

> The ladies were in their pokiest old headgear.
> W.M. THACKERAY: *The Newcomes*, ch lvii (1853–5)

As a noun 'poky' is American slang for a prison.

**Polack.** An inhabitant of Poland, a term now superseded by 'Pole', although humorously used in the USA.

**Poland.** There are many legends of early Poland. One is that Prince Popiel invited all his family to a banquet and when they were drunk killed them off with poisoned wine. He was duly punished when millions of mice entered his castle and devoured him. The chiefs then elected one Piast, a wheelmaker, to be their ruler, on the grounds of a report that when he had been sitting in the garden with his wife, two young men with white wings on their shoulders were with them, and this was deemed a favourable omen. The two angels were Cyril and Methodius, the apostles of central Europe. The Piast dynasty ruled from *c.*960 until 1370. *See also* LAND OF THE WHITE EAGLE.

**Polish Corridor, The.** The territory given to Poland by the Treaty of VERSAILLES (1919) to give access to the Baltic Sea west of Danzig. The Corridor cut off East Prussia from the rest of Germany and proved to be a bone of contention from the outset. It followed roughly the line of the River Vistula.

**Pole.** The word for the stake, mast and measure ($5\frac{1}{2}$ yards/5m) derives from Latin *palus*, 'stake', but 'pole' as in North Pole, magnetic pole and the like, is from Greek *polos*, 'axis', 'pivot'.

**Pole position.** In motor racing the starting position in the front row and on the inside of the first bend, usually regarded as the best and most advantageous. The reference is to the pole as the term for the inside fence on a racecourse.

**Poles apart** or **asunder.** Having widely different views or tastes. The reference is to the north and south poles.

**Barber's pole.** *See under* BARBER.

**From pole to pole.** *See under* FROM.

**North Pole.** *See under* NORTH.

**Totem pole.** *See under* TOTEM.

**Touch with a bargepole, To.** *See under* TOUCH.

**Up the pole.** *See under* UP.

**Policeman, Sleeping.** *See under* SLEEP.

**Polish. Polish off, To.** To finish rapidly; to conclude speedily; to dispatch summarily. An allusion to the action of cleaning an object by giving it a final polish. To polish off a meal is to eat it up quickly. To polish someone off is to dispose of or kill them.

**Polish up, To.** Figuratively, to improve one's knowledge of something by studying, practising or revising it; to 'brush it up'.

**Spit and polish.** *See under* SPIT.

**Politburo.** Formerly, the chief policy-making body of the Communist Party in the USSR, first formed in 1917. It examined matters before they were submitted to the government and consisted of five members. It was superseded by the PRESIDIUM of the Central Committee of the Communist Party in 1952. The word is a typical Soviet abbreviation, here for *Politicheskoye byuro* ('political bureau').

**Politics** or **political. Political correctness.** A philosophy of the 1990s, of American origin, that promoted the avoidance of expressions or actions that could be understood to denigrate groups or minorities traditionally regarded as disadvantaged in some way, as by race, gender, class, disability, religious or political leanings, or sexual orientation. Propagandists of this new morality recommended particular expressions that can and should be substituted for the traditional ones, such as 'the common citizen' for 'the common man' and 'childcare worker' for 'nursemaid'.

Dictionaries of such terms have been published, such as Henry Beard and Christopher Cerf's *The Official Politically Correct Dictionary and Handbook* (1992). Such revisionism extended even to the rewriting of established religious texts, such as the Bible, one version of which, published in 1994, not only avoided most 'gender-specific' words but substituted 'God's mighty hand' for 'God's right hand' for fear of offending the left-handed.

> Political Correctness (or P.C. for short) ... is now ascendant on American campuses large and small. ... Affirmative action, busing, gay rights, bilingualism, the self-segregation of blacks on campus and censorship in the pursuit of tolerance are all politically correct. The following are non-P.C.: The SAT [Scholastic Aptitude Test], doubts about abortion, Catholics, wearing fur, any emphasis on standards of excellence, and any suggestion that gender and ethnicity might not be the most overwhelmingly important issues of the modern era.
>
> *U.S. News & World Report* (December 1990)

**Political economy.** The former name of economics, as the social science that deals with the production and consumption of goods and services.

**Political liberty.** The freedom of a nation from any unjust abridgement of its rights and independence, also the right of the citizen to participate in political government and public office.

**Body politic.** *See under* BODY.

**Party politics.** *See under* PARTY.

**Politiques.** In French history, a party of 'moderates', formed after the St BARTHOLOMEW DAY'S MASSACRE around the Duke of Montmorency and the Marshal de Cossé-Brissac, who reacted against the fanaticism of CATHOLIC LEAGUE and HUGUENOT alike, and sought to bring the wars of religion to an end. The *Satyre Ménippée* (*see* MENIPPUS) was its work, and it championed the cause of Henry of Navarre as the future king of France.

**Polka** (Czech *půlka*, 'half-step'). A round dance said to have been invented about 1830 by a Bohemian servant girl, which soon took Europe by storm. It is danced by couples in 2/4 time, the characteristic feature being the rest on the second beat.

> You should see me dance the Polka,
> You should see me cover the ground,
> You should see my coat-tails flying,
> As I jump my partner round;
> When the band commences playing,
> My feet begin to go,
> For a rollicking romping Polka,
> Is the jolliest fun I know.
>
> GEORGE GROSSMITH: 'See Me Dance the Polka' (song) (*c.*1887)

**Poll.** A word of Germanic origin meaning the head, hence, the number of persons in a crowd ascertained by counting heads, hence the counting of voters at an election, and such phrases as 'to go to the polls', to stand for election and POLL TAX, a tax levied on everybody.

The Cambridge term, 'the poll', meaning students who obtain a PASS DEGREE, is probably from Greek *hoi polloi*, the common herd.

**Poll tax.** A graduated tax levied per head in England in 1377 led to the PEASANTS' REVOLT in 1381. Another was imposed in 1513 and on subsequent occasions, but it was abolished in 1689. In most of the southern states of the USA it was used as a condition of suffrage from 1889 and was still imposed by a few well into the 20th century. A poll tax replaced domestic rates in Scotland in 1989 and in England and Wales in 1990. Its official name was community charge, and in 1993 it was replaced by the council tax, a system closer to the original domestic rates.

**Deed poll.** *See under* DEED.

**Gallop Poll.** *See under* GALLOP.

**Straw poll.** *See under* STRAW.

**Pollux.** In classical mythology, the twin brother of CASTOR.

**Pollyanna.** The cheerfully optimistic young heroine of the novel named after her (1913) by Eleanor H. Porter (1868–1920). Her full name is Pollyanna Whittier, and she is known as the 'glad girl' for her determination to remain cheerful whatever happens. She is orphaned at the age of 11 and sent to live with a grim spinster aunt, but melts the hearts of everyone she meets, no matter how sour and dour they may be. Her name has entered the language to describe anyone who is unduly optimistic or who is able to remain happy through self-delusion.

> You're not fooling anyone, Babe, but yourself with this Pollyanna stuff. I want another drink, you want another drink, so we both have another little drink.
>
> TERENCE RATTIGAN: *While the Sun Shines*, I (1944)

**Polo, Marco.** The Venetian merchant (1254–1324) famous for his account of his travels in Asia. He visited China in 1274 bearing letters from Pope Gregory X to KUBLAI KHAN and spent 24 years in the East. He gained the nickname of *Marco Millione*, 'Marco Millions', from his frequent use of this word to describe the wealth of China and the Great Khan. His surname, Polo, is a form of *Paolo*, 'Paul'.

**Polonius.** A garrulous old courtier in Shakespeare's *Hamlet*, typical of a pompous, sententious old man. He is the father of OPHELIA and lord chamberlain to the king of Denmark.

**Poltergeist.** A household spirit well known to spiritualists, notorious for throwing things about, making noises and so on. It is a German word literally meaning 'noisy ghost'. *See also* SAMPFORD GHOST.

**Poltroon.** A coward. The word represents Old Italian *poltrone*, 'lazy good-for-nothing', ultimately from *poltro*, 'bed'. Cowards are sluggards and feign themselves sick abed in times of war.

In falconry the name was given to a bird of prey, with the talons of the hind toes cut off to prevent it flying at game. The origin here is perhaps from the old idea that the word was the Latin *pollice truncus*, 'maimed in the thumb'.

**Polycarp.** One of the most noted martyrs of the 2nd century, whose life was linked with the Apostolic age. Born *c.*69, he was probably converted to Christianity by St JOHN THE EVANGELIST and was bishop of Smyrna for over 40 years, during which time he became a staunch and vigorous leader. Persecution of Christians arose in Smyrna in 155 and the mob soon demanded Polycarp, 'the father of the Christians', as their next victim. The proconsul, Statius Quadratus, had him arrested, and he was burned alive after refusing to deny his faith. His faithfulness to the Apostolic tradition is recorded by Irenaeus, his disciple. Polycarp's only surviving writing is his *Epistle to the Philippians*. His day is 23 February (formerly 26 January).

**Polycrates.** *See* RING OF AMASIS.

**Polyhymnia** or **Polymnia.** The MUSE of lyric poetry and the inventor of the lyre. She invented harmony and presided over singing. Her Greek name means literally '(singing) many songs'.

**Polynices.** In Greek mythology the son of OEDIPUS, who agreed to alternate on the throne with his brother Eteocles after Oedipus went into exile. When Eteocles refused to leave at the end of his year, Polynices raised an army that included the SEVEN AGAINST THEBES and he and Eteocles killed each other.

**Polyphemus.** One of the CYCLOPS, who ruled over Sicily. When Odysseus (ULYSSES) landed on the island the monster made him and 12 of his crew captives. He ate six of them, and then Odysseus managed to blind him and escape with the rest of the crew. *See also* ACIS; GALATEA; LESTRIGONS.

**Pomander** (Old French *pome d'ambre*, 'apple of AMBER'). A ball made of perfume, such as ambergris, which was worn or carried in a perforated case in order to ward off infection or counteract bad smells. The cases, usually of gold or silver, were also called 'pomanders'.

**Pomegranate.** The fruit is a Christian symbol of the Resurrection through its association in classical mythology with PROSERPINA, who returned every spring to regenerate the earth. Its many seeds in a single case also make it a symbol of the unity of many under one authority, as well as of chastity. As a Resurrection symbol, the pomegranate is held by the infant Christ in some paintings.

**Pomfret cakes.** *See under* PONTEFRACT.

**Pommard.** A red Burgundy wine, so called from a village of that name in the Côte d'Or. The word is sometimes colloquially used for cider, the pun being on French *pomme*, 'apple'.

**Pommel.** The pommel of a sword is the rounded knob terminating the hilt, so called from its apple-like shape (French *pomme*, 'apple'), and to 'pummel' someone, meaning to pound them with one's fists, was originally to beat them with the pommel of one's sword.

**Pommy** or **Pommie.** An Australian and New Zealand term for an Englishman, used both affectionately and disparagingly. The name is of uncertain origin. Evidence suggests that it arose as a blend of 'pomegranate' and 'immigrant', the former word referring to the ruddy complexions of the English. A less convincing explanation is that it was formed from the initials POME, 'Prisoner of Mother England', alluding to the transportation of English convicts to Australia. Expansions of the name are 'Pommy Bastard' and 'Whingeing Pom', the latter with reference to the British national pastime of 'grousing'.

**Pomona.** The Roman goddess of fruits and fruit trees (Latin *pomum*, 'apple').

**Pompadour.** When used as a colour, the word means claret purple, so called from Louis XV's mistress, the Marquise de Pompadour (1721–64).

There is an old song said to be an elegy on John Broadwood, a QUAKER, which introduces the word:

> Sometimes he wore an old brown coat,
> Sometimes a pompadore,
> Sometimes 'twas buttoned up behind,
> And sometimes down before.

The word is also applied to a fashion of hairdressing in which the hair is raised (often on a pad) in a wave above the forehead.

The original name of the Marquise was Jeanne Antoinette Poisson. Her title comes from the small town of Pompadour in south central France, southeast of Limoges, which was raised to the status of a marquisate.

**Pompadours, The.** *See under* REGIMENTAL AND DIVISIONAL NICKNAMES.

**Pompey.** In British naval slang, Portsmouth. The precise origin of the name is uncertain. It is probably an arbitrary alteration of the city's name influenced by that of the Roman general Pompey (106–48 BC), defeated by Caesar at the Battle of Pharsalus (48 BC). Pompey is also the nickname of Portsmouth Football Club.

**Pompey's Pillar.** A Corinthian column of red granite, nearly 100ft (30m) high, erected at Alexandria by Publius, Prefect of Egypt, in honour of Diocletian and to record the conquest of Alexandria in 296. It was probably miscalled by travellers through ignorance. *See also* CLEOPATRA'S NEEDLE.

**Pond. Dew ponds.** *See under* DEW.

**Herring Pond.** *See under* HERRING.

**Ponent.** *See* LEVANT AND PONENT WINDS.

**Pongo.** In the old romance of *The* SEVEN CHAMPIONS *of Christendom*, Pongo was an amphibious monster of Sicily who preyed on the inhabitants of the island for many years. He was slain by the three sons of St GEORGE.

Pongo was also a nickname for a monkey, an Australian Aboriginal name for a flying squirrel and military slang for a marine or a soldier.

**Pons asinorum** (Latin, 'the asses' bridge'). The fifth proposition in Book I of Euclid, the first difficult theorem, which dunces rarely got over for the first time without stumbling. It is really more a stumbling block than a bridge. The geometric proposition itself is actually quite straightforward: that the angles opposite the two equal sides of an isosceles triangle are equal.

**Pontefract** or **Pomfret cakes.** Liquorice lozenges impressed with a castle and made at Pontefract, West Yorkshire, since the 16th century. The name of the town is still sometimes pronounced 'pumfret', representing the Anglo-Norman and Middle English 'Pontfret'. The name was recorded as Fractus Pons in 1097 and as Pontefractus *c*.1165. This represents Latin *pontus fractus* ('broken bridge') and is traditionally said to refer to the old Roman bridge over the River Aire, broken down by William I in 1069. It is now thought the original 'broken bridge' was one over the small stream known as the Wash Dike, at the point where Bubwith Bridge is today, near the A645 road. The stream is small, but the bridge over it would have been important, giving access to the main route to the north. It is not known when or how it was broken.

**Pontiff.** The term formerly applied to any bishop but now only to the pope, the Supreme Pontiff. The word has come to be associated with Latin *pontifex*, 'bridge-maker', referring to the *Pontifex Maximus*, the pagan title of the chief priest of Rome. But it may actually be of Etruscan origin.

**Pontius Pilate's Bodyguard.** *See under* REGIMENTAL AND DIVISIONAL NICKNAMES.

**Pony.** Slang for £25, perhaps because in betting circles the amount was seen as a small sum. The word is also used (especially in the USA) for a translation CRIB, and for a small beer glass. In card games, the person on the right hand of the dealer is called the pony, from Latin *pone*, 'behind', being behind the dealer.

**Pony Express.** This was the US government mail system across the continent just before the days of railways and telegraphs. It ran from St Joseph, Missouri, to the Pacific Coast and was inaugurated in 1860. Less than two years later it was superseded by the electric telegraph. The scheduled time for the whole distance was ten days, but Lincoln's inaugural address was taken across the continent in 7 days 17 hours. Fleet horses were used, not ponies, ridden for stages of 10–15 miles (16–24km), the rider doing three stages before handing over the wallet. The service was operated by the firm of Russell, Majors and Waddell. *See also* WELLS FARGO.

**Poodle-faker.** A man who cultivates female society for the purposes of promotion or social advancement, otherwise a 'ladies' man' or socialite generally. The term is also used for a young, newly commissioned army officer. It implies that the person so designated is a 'fake poodle', impersonating the actions of a fawning lapdog.

**Pooh-Bah.** A nickname for a pompous official who holds numerous offices simultaneously, usually from motives of self-interest. Pooh-Bah, The Lord-High-Everything-Else, is a character in Gilbert and Sullivan's *The Mikado* (1885), who was First Lord of the Treasury, Lord Chief Justice, Commander-in-Chief, Lord High Admiral, Master of the Buckhounds, Groom of the Back Stairs, Archbishop of Titipu and Lord Mayor, 'all rolled into one'. The name happens to represent exclamations of contempt ('pooh' and 'bah'), suggesting that it was intended ironically or even satirically.

**Pooper, Party.** *See under* PARTY.

**Poor. Poor Clares.** *See* ORDER OF ST CLARE.

**Poor hand, A.** An unskilful person; ill-formed handwriting; unsatisfactory cards, dealt to a player in a game of cards.

**Poor man's (something), A.** A thing that is a cheaper substitute for something else, as: 'My old Mini is a poor man's Mercedes.'

**Poor relation, A.** Something that is a cheaper or inferior substitute for 'the real thing', as: 'Plastic is a poor relation of leather.'

**Poor Richard.** The assumed name of Benjamin Franklin (1706–90) in a series of ALMANACS from 1732 to 1757. They contained maxims and precepts on temperance, economy, cleanliness, chastity and other virtues, and several ended with the words 'as poor Richard says'.

**Poor Robin's Almanack.** A humorous ALMANAC, parodying those who seriously indulged in prophecy, published at intervals from 1662 to as late as 1828. The early issues were almost certainly the work of William Winstanley (*c*.1628–98). As a specimen of the 'predictions', the following, for January 1664, may be cited:

> Strong Beer and good Fires are fit for this Season as a Halter for a Thiefe; and, when every Man is pleas'd, then 'twill be a Merry World indeed. ... This month we may expect to hear of the Death of some Man, Woman, or Child, either in Kent or Christendom.

**Poor thing, A.** A person (or sometimes an inanimate object) that is regarded with pity or disparagement. Touchstone's remark about Audrey, 'An ill-favoured thing, sir, but mine own' (Shakespeare, *As You Like It*, V, iv (1599)), is frequently misquoted, 'A poor thing, but mine own', when employed in half-ironical disparagement of one's own work.

**Poor white.** A derogatory nickname for an impoverished or underprivileged white person in the southern states of the USA or in South Africa.

**As poor as a church mouse, Job** or **Lazarus.** *See under* AS.

**Take a poor view of, To.** To regard with disfavour or regret.

**Pop. Pop goes the weasel.** Now regarded as a children's song, the original was obviously intended for their parents:

Up and down the City Road,
In and out the Eagle.
That's the way the money goes,
Pop goes the weasel.

The Eagle was a tavern and old-time MUSIC HALL in the City Road, London, and a popular rendezvous for singing and Saturday night drinking, which explains the need to 'pop' or pawn the 'weasel'. What the 'weasel' was is not clear, but it may have been slang for a tailor's iron.

**Pop the question, To.** To propose marriage. As this request is supposedly unexpected, the question is said to be 'popped'.

**Pope.** The word represents Old English *papa*, from ecclesiastical Latin, and Greek *pappas*, the infants' word for father.

In the early church the title was given to many bishops. Leo I, the Great (440–461) was the first to use it officially, and in the time of Gregory VII (1073–85) it was, by decree, specially reserved for the bishop of Rome. *See also* PONTIFF.

According to the Italian historian Platina, Sergius II (844–847) was the first pope who changed his name on assuming office. Some accounts have it that his name was Hogsmouth, others that it was 'Peter de Porca' and he changed it out of deference to St PETER, thinking it arrogant to style himself Peter II. However, the first clear case of changed name was when, on election, Peter, bishop of Pavia, changed his name to that of John XIV (r.983–984).

GREGORY THE GREAT (r.590–604) was the first pope to adopt the title *Servus Servorum Dei* ('Servant of the Servants of God'). It is founded on Mark 10:44. The title Vicar of Christ or Vicar of God was adopted by Innocent III (r.1198–1216) in 1198.

Including John Paul II, there are commonly 263 popes enumerated. The nationality of two of them is unknown. Of the remainder, 209 have been Italian, 15 French, 12 Greek, 6 German, 6 Syrian, 3 African, 3 Spanish, 2 Dalmatian, and 1 each Dutch, English, Polish, Portuguese and Jewish (St Peter).

For the drink called a 'pope' *see* BISHOP.

**Pope Joan.** *See under* JOAN.

**Popemobile.** The special bulletproof vehicle, with a raised viewing area, used by the pope on official visits. It was introduced by Pope John Paul II following his election in 1978.

**Pope of Geneva, The.** A name given to John Calvin (1509–64).

**Pope's eye, The.** The tender piece of meat (the lymphatic gland) surrounded by fat in the middle of a leg of an ox or a sheep. The French call it 'Judas' eye', and the Germans 'the priest's titbit'.

**Pope's nose, The.** The rump of a fowl, which is also called the PARSON'S NOSE. The phrase is said to have originated during the years following James II's reign (1685–8), when anti-Catholic feeling was high.

**Popes numbered among the saints.** *See under* SAINT.

**Popish Plot.** A fictitious JESUIT plot (1678) to murder Charles II and others, enthrone the Duke of York and set fire to the City of London, after which, with the aid of French and Irish troops, a massacre of Protestants was to ensue. The plot was invented by the scoundrelly Titus Oates (1649–1705). Before the anti-Catholic panic abated in 1681, some 35 Catholics were judicially murdered, including the Roman Catholic Primate of Ireland. Oates was eventually pilloried, whipped and imprisoned when James II became king.

**Avignon popes.** *See under* AVIGNON.

**Black Pope, The.** *See under* BLACK.

**Kissing the pope's toe.** *See under* KISS.

**Protestant Pope, The.** *See under* PROTESTANT.

**Red Pope, The.** *See under* RED.

**Popeye.** The muscle-bound sailor man came into the cartoon world in 1929 when the comic strip artist Elzie Segar created him for his classic strip, *Thimble Theatre*. He was at first known as Ham Gravy, but soon acquired his familiar sobriquet. He gains his muscular might from the can of spinach that he carries with him. His girlfriend is the stick-like Olive Oyl. Popeye's first appearance in a film was in the Betty BOOP cartoon, *Popeye the Sailor* (1933). He has a unique, strangulated delivery, and catch lines such as, 'Blow me down, I eats my spinach'. When not actually talking or eating, he has his jaws clamped jauntily on his pipe.

**Popinjay** (Spanish *papagayo*, from Arabic *babaghā*). An old word for a parrot, and hence a conceited or empty-headed fop.

I then all smarting with my wounds being cold,
To be so pester'd with a popinjay,
Out of my grief and my impatience,
Answer'd neglectingly, I know not what,
He should, or he should not.
SHAKESPEARE: *Henry IV, Pt I*, I, iii (1597)

**Festival of the Popinjay, The.** *See under* FESTIVAL.

**Poplar.** The poplar was consecrated to HERCULES, because he destroyed Kakos in a cavern of Mount Aventine, which was covered with poplars. In the moment of triumph, the hero plucked a branch from one of the trees and bound it round his head. When he descended to the infernal regions, the heat caused a profuse perspiration, which blanched the undersurface of the leaves, while the smoke of the eternal flames blackened the upper surface. Hence the leaves of the poplar are dark on one side and white on the other.

**White poplar, The.** *See under* WHITE.

**Popper, Party.** *See under* PARTY.

**Poppers, Fenny.** *See under* FENNY.

**Poppins, Mary.** The children's nanny who possesses magical powers in the stories by P.L. Travers, beginning with the one named after her (1934). She can not only slide *up* the banisters but walk into a picture, understand what dogs are saying and travel round the world in seconds. She was played by Julie Andrews in the film of 1964, also named after her.

**Poppy.** In medieval art the poppy sometimes represents Christ's blood, from its red colour. After the First World War the Allies adopted the poppy as a symbol of sacrifice, both from its blood-red colour and from its prominence on the fields of Flanders where many soldiers lost their lives. Poppy Day for this reason became an alternative name for REMEMBRANCE DAY.

In Flanders fields the poppies blow
Between the crosses, row on row
That mark our place: and in the sky
The larks still bravely singing, fly
Scarce heard amid the guns below.
JOHN McCRAE in *Punch* (8 December 1915)

**Popski's Private Army.** A British raiding and reconnaissance force of about 120 men formed in October 1942 under Lieutenant Colonel Vladimir Peniakoff (1897–1951), who had previously worked with the Libyan Arab Force. He was familiarly known as 'Popski', and his men wore the initials PPA on their shoulders. He was born in Belgium of Russian parents, educated at Cambridge and resident in Egypt from 1924. Popski and a few of his force, together with the Long Range Desert Group, reconnoitred the route by which Montgomery conducted his surprise attack around the Mareth Line, and subsequently operated in Italy and Austria.

**Popular Front.** A political alliance of left-wing parties (communists, socialists, liberals, radicals and so on) against reactionary government, especially dictatorship. The idea of an anti-FASCIST Popular Front was proposed by the Communist International in 1935. Such a government was set up in Spain in 1936, but the Civil War (1936–9) soon followed. The French Popular Front government, set up by Léon Blum in 1936, ended in 1938.

**Populist.** A term applied in the USA to a member of the People's Party, an agrarian protest movement formed at St Louis in 1891. They demanded free and unlimited silver currency, the prohibition of alien land ownership, state control of transport and similar measures.

**Porcelain.** The word comes from Italian *porcellana*, 'cowrie shell', referring to the ceramic material's pale and glossy shell-like finish. This word itself is the adjective of *porcella*, 'little sow', the allusion apparently being to the curve in a pig's back and to its similar colour.

**Porch, The.** A philosophic sect, generally called STOICS (Greek *stoa*, 'porch'), because ZENO, the founder, gave his lectures in the public ambulatory, *stoa poikile* ('painted colonnade'), in the *agora* or market place of Athens.

**Bachelor's porch.** *See under* BACHELOR.

**Pork, pig.** The former word is Norman (French), the latter Saxon (English). As in the case of most edible domestic animals, the Norman word is used for the meat and the Saxon for the live animal. *See also* PIG.

**Pork barrel.** An American term applied to legislation, normally achieved by LOGROLLING, which makes available Federal funds for local improvements or developments in the district of the congressman who promotes the measure to maintain popularity with the electorate. It is an allusion to old plantation days, when slaves assembled at the pork barrel for the allowance of pork reserved for them. Similarly, 'pork barrel' for the congressman is a reward for party service.

**Porphyrogenitus.** A surname of the Byzantine emperor, Constantine VII (905–959). It means 'born in the purple' (Greek *porphuros*, 'purple', and *genētos*, 'born'), and a son born to a sovereign after his accession is so designated. It was specifically an epithet of the Byzantine emperors born while their father was reigning. The term refers specifically to the purple room used by the empress for her lying-in.

**Porrex, Ferrex and.** *See* FERREX AND PORREX.

**Porridge. Do porridge, To.** *See under* DO.

**Save** or **keep one's breath to cool one's porridge.** *See under* SAVE.

**Port.** The left-hand side of a vessel when facing forward, with the word perhaps from 'port', 'harbour'. It replaced the earlier 'larboard', which was easily confused with STARBOARD, so called from the days when the steerboard or rudder was carried over the right-hand side. It was therefore necessary to come alongside on the larboard side. It is presumed that 'port' derives from the fact that the larboard was towards the side of the port.

A vessel's portholes are so called from Latin *porta*, 'door'. The harbour is called a 'port' from Latin *portus*, 'haven'. The dark red wine gets its name from Oporto, Portugal (which is again Latin *portus*), and 'port', the way of bearing oneself, is from Latin *portare*, 'to carry'.

**Any port in a storm.** *See under* ANY.

**Cinque Ports.** *See under* CINQUE.

**College port.** *See under* COLLEGE.

**Crusted port.** *See under* CRUST.

**On the port** or **starboard bow.** Within 45 degrees to the port or starboard of straight ahead.

**Porte** or **Sublime Porte.** Originally the official name of the Ottoman Court at Constantinople, and later used as a synonym for the Turkish government. The word is the French translation of the Turkish (Arabic) title Bab Ali, 'High Gate', the gate in question being the Imperial Gate of the SERAGLIO at Constantinople.

**Divan of the Sublime Porte, The.** *See under* DIVAN.

**Porteous Riots.** At Edinburgh, in September 1736, a smuggler awaiting death for robbing an excise collector escaped with the aid of Andrew Wilson, a fellow culprit. At the latter's execution, Lieutenant Porteous ordered the town guard to fire on the mob, which had become tumultuous. About six people were killed and eleven injured. Porteous was condemned to death but temporarily reprieved, whereupon some citizens burst into the jail and, dragging him to the Grassmarket, hanged him by torchlight on a barber's pole. The Lord Provost was dismissed as a consequence and the city fined £2000. The episode appears in Sir Walter Scott's *The Heart of Midlothian* (1818).

**Porter.** *See* STOUT.

**Portia.** A rich heiress and 'lady barrister' in Shakespeare's *The Merchant of Venice* (1596), in love with Bassanio. Her name is sometimes used for a female advocate.

**Portland vase.** A cinerary urn of the 1st century AD made of dark blue glass decorated with white figures, the finest surviving Roman example of cameo glass. It was found in a tomb near Rome in the 17th century and in 1770 was purchased from the Barberini Palace by Sir William Hamilton for 1000 guineas. In 1787 it came into the possession of the Duke of Portland, one of the trustees of the British Museum, who placed it in that institution for exhibition. In 1845 a deranged person named Lloyd dashed it to pieces, but it was so skilfully repaired that the damage is barely visible. It is 10in (25cm) high and 6in (15cm) in diameter at the broadest part.

**Portmanteau word.** A portmanteau is a type of leather travelling bag for clothes which opens out flat into two parts. A portmanteau word is thus a word made up of two others, and expressive of a combination denoted by those parts, such as SQUARSON, a cross between a squire and parson. Lewis Carroll invented the term in *Through the Looking-Glass* when Humpty Dumpty explains the meanings of words in the poem 'Jabberwocky':

> 'That's enough to begin with,' Humpty Dumpty interrupted: 'there are plenty of hard words there. "Brillig" means four o'clock in the afternoon – the time when you begin broiling things for dinner.'
>
> 'That'll do very well,' said Alice: 'and "slithy"?'
>
> 'Well, "slithy" means "lithe and slimy" ... You see it's like a portmanteau – there are two meanings packed up into one word.'
>
> LEWIS CARROLL: *Through the Looking-Glass*, ch vi (1872)

**Portobello.** There is a single source for the various places of this name in Britain, among them a district of Edinburgh, a service area on the A1(M) south of Gateshead, a district of Wolverhampton and a location in Wakefield south of the city centre. The source is the small port of Portobello ('beautiful harbour') in Panama, founded in 1597 by the Spanish and called after the bay here, itself named by Columbus in 1502. Its location made it a place of strategic and commercial importance, and it was attacked many times by the British. The Edinburgh Portobello took its name directly from a house called Portobello Hut that is said to have been so called by a sailor present at Admiral Vernon's capture of the Panamanian port in 1739. London's Portobello Road was so named similarly, after a Portobello Farm nearby.

**Portreeve.** In Saxon times and later, the chief magistrate of a town or BOROUGH, 'port' here meaning 'town'. There was a portreeve in Tavistock, Devon, as late as 1886. *See also* REEVE.

> It [Tavistock] was never chartered, but is governed by a portreeve, who is elected annually by the freeholders, and sworn in at the court leet, and who is also returning-officer, and may qualify to act as a magistrate for the borough.
>
> *The National Gazetteer of Great Britain and Ireland* (1868)

**Port-Royal.** A convent of CISTERCIAN nuns about 8 miles (13km) southwest of VERSAILLES, which in the 17th century became a centre of the JANSENIST influence. In 1626 the community had moved to Paris and Port-Royal des Champs was occupied mostly by laymen living a semi-monastic existence, among them many distinguished scholars. In 1648 some of the nuns returned and the hermits moved elsewhere in the neighbourhood.

From 1653 it came under papal condemnation for its adherence to Jansenism, and Louis XIV began active persecution from 1661. By 1669 the conformist nuns were all at the Paris house, and the supporters of Jansen remained at Port-Royal des Champs until forcibly removed in 1709. The buildings were duly destroyed but Port-Royal-de-Paris remained in being until the French Revolution.

**Portsoken ward.** The most easterly ward of the City of London, with the name coming from 'port' ('town') and 'soke' ('franchise'). It was the soke of the old Knightenguild outside the wall in the parish of St Botolph, Aldgate.

**Portumnus.** *See* PALAEMON.

**Poseidon.** In Greek mythology the god of the sea, the counterpart of the Roman NEPTUNE. He was the son of KRONUS and RHEA, brother of ZEUS and HADES, and husband of AMPHITRITE. It was he who, with APOLLO, built the walls of TROY, and as the Trojans refused to give him his reward he hated them and took part against them in the TROJAN WAR. Earthquakes were attributed to him, and he was said to have created the first horse.

**Poser.** Formerly used of an examiner, one who poses (i.e. 'opposes') questions, especially a bishop's examining chaplain. Also the name given to each of the two representatives of the fellows of King's College, Cambridge, among the examiners for scholarships to the Foundation of Eton and King's in the days when scholarships at King's were closed to all except scholars of Eton.

> The examination [for an Eton scholarship] was conducted by the Provosts of Eton and King's, the Fellows of Eton and two representatives of the Fellows of King's called Posers, so called either because they posed you with questions you could not answer, or because they placed you on the list.
>
> OSCAR BROWNING: *Memoirs of Sixty Years* (1910)

Nowadays the word usually denotes a puzzling question or proposition.

**Posh.** This colloquialism for 'grand', SWELL or 'first rate' is said to have originated in the old days of constant steamship travel between England and India. Passengers travelling by the P & O (Peninsular and Oriental) would, at some cost, book their return passage with the arrangement 'Port Outward Starboard Homeward', thus ensuring cabins on the cooler side of the ship, as it was usually unbearably hot when crossing the Indian Ocean. Passages were booked 'POSH' accordingly, and 'posh' soon came to be applied to a first-class passenger who could afford this luxury. This traditional explanation is almost certainly fictitious, however, and the word may have evolved its sense from the slang 'posh', meaning a dandy.

**Position. Jockey for position.** *See under* JOCKEY.

**Pole position.** *See under* POLE.

**Positivism.** A term originally applied to the system of Auguste Comte (1798–1857), which recognized only observable ('positive') facts scientifically established and disregarded metaphysical and theological considerations. Its chief English exponent was Frederic Harrison (1831–1923), who actively promoted it as a religious system centred on the worship of humanity.

In the wider sense, Positivism applies to any philosophical approach that rejects metaphysics and confines itself to the facts of experience.

**Posse** (Latin, 'to be able'). A body of men, especially CONSTABLES, who are armed with legal authority.

**Posse comitatus** (Medieval Latin, 'strength of the county'). The whole power of a county, i.e. all male members of the county over 15 years of age with the exception of clergymen and peers, summoned by a SHERIFF to assist in preventing a riot, or enforcing process. In modern times assistance is provided by constables and special constables.

**Possession is nine points of the law.** It is every advantage a person can have short of actual right. The 'nine points of the law' have been given as: (1) a good deal of money, (2) a good deal of patience, (3) a good cause, (4) a good lawyer, (5) a good counsel, (6) good witnesses, (7) a good jury, (8) a good judge and (9) good luck.

**Possum, To play.** *See under* PLAY.

**Post. Posted, To be.** In a club, to have one's name put upon the notice board as no longer a member, for non-payment of dues or other irregularity. In the Army and RAF it means to be assigned to a specific post or appointment. The equivalent naval term is to be drafted.

**Post haste.** With great speed or expedition. The phrase is said to derive from an old direction on letters, 'Haste, post, haste', meaning 'Hurry, post, hurry', as a forerunner of the special delivery of today's Post Office. The term was current by the 16th century.

**Post paper.** Before metrication, a standard size of paper measuring 15 × 19¼in (381 × 489mm) in writing papers and 15½ × 19¼in (394 × 489mm) in printing papers, so called from an ancient watermark, which has been supposed to represent a posthorn. This horn or bugle mark was, however, in use as early as 1314, long before anything in the nature of a postman or his horn existed. It is probably the famous horn of ROLAND.

**As deaf as a post.** *See under* AS.
**Beaten at the post.** *See under* BEAT.
**First past the post.** *See under* FIRST.
**First post.** *See under* FIRST.
**Keep someone posted, To.** To keep a person informed and up to date. The expression is of American origin, and probably originated from the counting-house, where ledgers are posted.
**Last post, The.** *See under* LAST.
**Pipped at the post, To be.** *See under* PIP.
**Whipping post.** *See under* WHIP.

**Post** (Latin, 'after').
**Post factum** (Latin). After the act has been committed.
**Post hoc, ergo propter hoc** (Latin). After this, therefore because of this. The phrase is expressive of the fallacy that because one thing follows another, the former is the cause of the latter. Because a man drinks a glass of beer and then falls over it does not follow that the beer was the cause of his fall. He may have tripped or slipped.
**Post-Impressionism.** The name applied to the phase of painting that followed IMPRESSIONISM. The chief exponents were Paul Cézanne (1839–1906), Paul Gauguin (1848–1903), Vincent van Gogh (1853–90) and Georges Seurat (1859–91). It aimed at synthesis and the expression of the material and spiritual significance of the subject free from restraint. *See also* POINTILLISM.
**Post meridiem** (Latin). After noon, usually contracted to pm. *See also* PIP EMMA.
**Post mortem** (Latin). After death. A post-mortem examination is for the purpose of ascertaining the cause of death.
**Post nati** (Latin, 'those born after'). Historically, a term referring to a judicial decision of 1607 that declared that all those born in Scotland after James VI's accession as James I of England in 1603 were natural born subjects of the king of England. James unsuccessfully tried to bring about the union of England and Scotland and to get the English Parliament to agree to the naturalization of his Scottish subjects.
**Post obit** (Latin *post obitum*, 'after decease', i.e. of the person named in the bond). An agreement to pay for a loan by a larger sum to be paid on the death of the person specified from whom the borrower has expectations.
**Post term** (Latin *post terminum*, 'after the term'). The legal expression for the return of a writ after the term, and for the fee that is then payable for its being filed.

**Poste restante** (French, 'post remaining'). A department at a post office to which letters may be addressed for callers, and where they will remain (within certain limits) until called for.

**Posteriori.** *See* A POSTERIORI.

**Postman. Postman Poet.** *See* DEVONSHIRE POET.
**Postman's knock.** An old PARLOUR GAME. The girls are each given a number. The 'postman' knocks on the door a certain number of times and the girl whose number answers to the number of knocks has to kiss the postman.

**Posy.** The word properly means a verse or sentence inscribed on a ring or other object and is a contraction of 'poesy'. The meaning of a bunch of flowers, a nosegay, probably comes from the custom of sending verses with gifts of flowers. *See also* GARLAND; RING POSIES.

> About a hoop of gold, a paltry ring
> That she did give me; whose poesy was,
> For all the world, like cutlers' poetry
> Upon a knife, 'Love me, and leave me not'.
> SHAKESPEARE: *Merchant of Venice*, V, i (1596)

**Ring posies.** *See under* RING.

**Pot.** Apart from designating a variety of vessels and containers, the word 'pot' is one of the many slang terms for the drug marijuana. As such, it is perhaps a shortened form of Mexican Spanish *potiguaya*.
**Pot belly.** A protruding stomach, which is not only suggestive of the roundness of a pot but implies an over-fondness for tasty edibles from the cooking pot.
**Potboiler.** Anything done merely for the sake of the money it will bring in, because it will 'keep the pot boiling', i.e. help to provide the means of livelihood. The word is applied especially to work of small merit by artists and writers, and is sometimes misused to apply to a fictional domestic narrative.

To keep the pot boiling, on the other hand, is to keep things going briskly; to see that interest does not flag.
**Pot calling the kettle black, The.** Said of someone accusing another of faults similar to those committed by the accuser. The allusion is to the old household in which the copper kettle would be kept polished, while the iron pot would remain black. The kettle's bright side would reflect the pot. The pot, seeing its reflection, would thus see black, which would appear to be on the side of the kettle. The pot could then accuse the kettle of a fault it did not have.
**Pothook.** The hook over an open fire on which the pot hung. The term was applied to a 'hooked' stroke used in writing, especially to the stroke terminating in a curve formerly practised by children in learning to write, as in the second element of n.
**Pothunter.** A person whose main aim is the collecting of prizes rather than enjoying a sport or activity for its own sake, the 'pot' being the cup commonly awarded for sporting events.
**Pot luck.** To take pot luck is to share a meal of

whatever food is available, one that has not been specially prepared for visitors; to take a chance. The expression comes from the days when the family cooking pot, containing a variety of edibles, was kept boiling over the fire. When it was ladled out at mealtimes, what anyone received was 'pot luck'.

**Pot of gold.** An imaginary reward; a longed-for treasure. An old legend tells of a pot or crock of gold that lies 'where the rainbow ends'. *See also* RAINBOW.

**Pot shot.** A random shot, or one aimed at an animal within easy reach. The reference is to a shot that lacks any niceties but that is simply to 'bag' an animal for the pot.

**Pot-wallopers.** Before the Reform Act of 1832, those who possessed a vote as householders because they had boiled their own pot at their own fireplace in the constituency for at least six months. The earlier form was 'pot-waller', from Old English *weallan*, 'to boil'.

**Big pot, A.** *See under* BIG.

**Death in the pot.** *See under* DEATH.

**Go to pot, To.** To go to ruin, to deteriorate. The allusion is to the pot in which leftovers of cooked meat are put ready for their last appearance as a hash.

**Six-hooped pot, A.** *See under* SIX.

**Watched pot never boils, A.** *See under* WATCH.

**Potato.** This useful and common vegetable (*Solanum tuberosum*) was brought from South America into Europe by the Spanish in the latter part of the 16th century. Sir Walter Ralegh (1552–1618) is said to have introduced it on his Irish lands from Virginia about 1585, but it did not arrive in Virginia until more than a century later. Potatoes were introduced to North America from Ireland in 1719. Sir John Hawkins (1532–95) brought back the sweet potato from the Caribbean in 1565. This latter plant, *Ipomoea batatas*, from which the word potato is derived, is supposed to have aphrodisiac qualities, and Falstaff refers to this when he says, 'Let the sky rain potatoes' (Shakespeare, *The Merry Wives of Windsor*, V, v (1600)).

Both 'spud' and 'murphy' are slang terms for a potato, and anyone with the name Murphy is often nicknamed 'Spud'.

**Potato Jones.** Captain D.J. Jones, who died in 1962 aged 92. In 1937, with his steamer *Marie Llewellyn* loaded with potatoes, he tried to run General Franco's blockade off Spain, but was prevented by a British warship. Two other blockade-running captains were called 'Ham-and-Egg' Jones and 'Corncob' Jones.

**Potato War.** The Prussian name for the War of the Bavarian Succession (1778–9), because the operations largely revolved around the acquisition or denial of suplies to the enemy.

**Couch potato.** *See under* COUCH.

**Hot potato, A.** *See under* HOT.

**Small potatoes.** *See under* SMALL.

**Poteen** (Irish *poitín*, 'little pot'). Illicitly distilled Irish whiskey, usually in small amounts. The practice arose in the late 18th century when the government refused to license small stills.

> An' that I tould yer Honour whativer I hard an' seen,
> Yer Honour 'ill give me a thrifle to dhrink yer health in potheen.
>
> TENNYSON: 'Tomorrow', xvi (1885)

**Potent, Cross.** *See under* CROSS.

**Potichomania.** The word is a combination of French *potiche*, 'glass vase', and *manie*, 'craze', 'fad'. It denotes the art of decorating plain glass vases and the like on the inside with designs of patterned paper to imitate decorated porcelain of various kinds. Glass panels, cheval screens, chiffoniers and other furniture were similarly dealt with. The art spread from France to England in the early 19th century and is fully described in Cassell's *Household Guide* of 1875. A debased form of potichomania consisted in sticking figures on the outside of pottery jars and varnishing over the whole. Such jars were called 'DOLLY VARDEN' jars.

**Potiphar.** An Egyptian captain of the guard who is the master of JOSEPH (Genesis 39). His wife, who is unnamed in the Bible, once tried to seduce Joseph and even tore off his clothes, after which she claimed that Joseph had tried to rape her, offering his clothes as proof. As a result of this, Joseph was imprisoned.

Some Arabian commentators have named Potiphar's wife as Rahil, others ZULEIKA, and it is this latter name that the 15th-century Persian poet Jami gives her in his *Yusuf and Zulaikha*. In C.J. Wells' poetic drama *Joseph and His Brethren* (1824), of which she is the heroine, she is named Phraxanor.

**Potlatch.** Among certain Native Americans of the northwest coast, a feast at which gifts are distributed lavishly to the guests while the hosts sometimes destroy some of their own valuable possessions. It is a social barbarity to refuse an invitation to a potlatch, or not to give one in return. The word comes from Nootka *patshatl*, 'giving', 'present'.

**Potomac.** The American river, rising in the Appalachians and flowing into Chesapeake Bay through the District of Columbia, has many historical associations, and Mount Vernon, George Washington's home, lies on its banks below Washington, D.C. The words 'All quiet along the Potomac' relate to the American Civil War (1861–5), and are attributed to the soldier and partisan George B. McClellan, although also appearing in a poem by Ethel Lynn Beers:

All quiet along the Potomac to-night.
No sound save the rush of the river,
While soft falls the dew on the face of the dead—
The picket's off duty for ever.
ETHEL L. BEERS: 'The Picket Guard' (1861)

**Potpourri** (French). A mixture of dried sweet-smelling flower petals and herbs preserved in a vase. *Pourri* means 'rotten' and *potpourri* is literally the vase containing the 'rotten' flowers. It is also a HOTCHPOTCH OR OLLA PODRIDA, and in music, a medley of favourite tunes.

**Potter's field.** A name applied to a burial ground formerly reserved for strangers and the friendless poor. It is an allusion to the field bought by the chief priests with the THIRTY PIECES OF SILVER returned to them by the repentant JUDAS ISCARIOT.

And they took counsel, and bought with them the potter's field, to bury strangers in.
Matthew 27:7

**Poult.** A chicken, or the young of the turkey, guinea fowl or other gallinaceous bird. The word is a contraction of 'pullet', from Late Latin *pulla*, 'hen', whence 'poultry', 'poulterer' and so on.

**Poulter's measure.** In prosody, a metre consisting of alternate ALEXANDRINES and fourteeners, i.e. 12-syllable and 14-syllable lines. The name was given to it by George Gascoigne (1576) because, it is said, poulterers, then called 'poulters', used to give 14 eggs to the second dozen. The following is from the Earl of Surrey's 'Complaint of the Absence of her Lover, being upon the Sea' (1547):

Good ladies, ye that have your pleasure in exile.
Step in your foot, come take a place, and mourn with me awhile,
And such as by their lords do set but little price
Let them sit still, it skills them not what chance come on the dice.

**Pound.** The unit of weight (Latin *pondus*, 'weight'), also, before the decimalization of the British currency, cash to the value of 20 SHILLINGS sterling, because in the CAROLINGIAN period the Roman pound (12 ounces) of pure silver was coined into 240 silver pennies. The symbol £ and letters lb are for *libra*, the Latin for a pound. *See also* DECIMAL CURRENCY.

**Pound of flesh.** The whole of the bargain, to the last letter of the agreement. The allusion is to Shakespeare's *The Merchant of Venice* (IV, i (1596)), where SHYLOCK bargained with Antonio for a 'pound of flesh' but was foiled in his suit by PORTIA, who said the bond was expressly a pound of flesh, and therefore first, the Jew must cut the exact quantity, neither more nor less than a just pound, and second, in so doing he must not shed a drop of blood.

**Pound Scots, A.** English and Scottish coins were of equal value until 1355, after which the Scottish coinage steadily depreciated, and when James VI of Scotland became James I of England (1603) the pound Scots was worth 1s 8d, one-twelfth the value of an English pound. A pound Scots was divided into 20 Scots shillings each worth an English PENNY. The Scottish MINT closed in 1709.

**In for a penny, in for a pound.** *See under* PENNY.

**Penny wise and pound foolish.** *See under* PENNY.

**Take care of the pence and the pounds will look after themselves.** *See under* CARE.

**Tonnage and poundage.** *See under* TONNAGE.

**Tower pound.** *See under* TOWER.

**Pour. Pour down the drain, To.** Figuratively, to waste one's resources, especially money, on useless, totally unproductive or unprofitable projects.

**Pour oil on troubled waters, To.** To soothe by gentle words, to use tact and diplomacy to restore calm after excited anger and quarrelsome argument.

The allusion is to the fact that the violence of waves is much decreased when oil is poured upon them. In Bede's *History of the English Church and People* (731) it is said that St AIDAN gave a young priest, who was to escort a maiden destined for the bride of King Oswy, a cruse of oil to pour on the sea if the waves became stormy. The priest did so when a storm arose and thereby calmed the waters.

**It never rains but it pours.** *See under* RAIN.

**Poverty. When poverty comes in at the door, love flies out at the window.** *See under* WHEN.

**Powder. Powder of projection.** A form of the PHILOSOPHER'S STONE, which was supposed to have the virtue of changing baser metals into gold. A little of this powder, being cast into the molten metal, would project from it pure gold.

**Powder one's nose, To.** To visit the lavatory. A euphemism applicable to women, who may well use the visit for the ostensible purpose.

**Itching powder.** *See under* ITCH.

**Keep one's powder dry, To.** To be prepared for action; to be on the *qui vive*. The phrase comes from a story told of Oliver Cromwell. During his campaign in Ireland, he is said to have concluded an address to his troops, who were about to cross a river before attacking, with the words: 'Put your trust in God, my boys, and keep your powder dry.' However, these words were put into his mouth by the Anglo-Indian soldier Valentine Blacker (1738–1823). They are quoted in 'Oliver's Advice' in E. Hayes' *Ballads of Ireland* (1856).

**Power. Power of attorney.** A deed by which one person empowers another to represent him or to act for him, either generally or in some specific matter. The giver of the power is called the principal; the person given the power is called the ATTORNEY.

**Power of the keys, The.** The supreme ecclesiastical authority claimed by the pope as the successor of St PETER. The phrase is derived from Matthew 16:19:

> And I will give unto thee the keys of the kingdom of heaven: and whatsoever thou shalt bind on earth shall be bound in heaven: and whatsoever thou shalt loose on earth shall be loosed in heaven.

**Powers that be, The.** A common expression applied to those in authority, especially those who exercise control of society as a whole. The phrase is taken from Romans 13:1: 'The powers that be are ordained of God.'

**Balance of power, The.** *See under* BALANCE.

**Black Power.** *See under* BLACK.

**Corridors of power.** *See under* CORRIDOR.

**Flower power.** *See under* FLOWER.

**More power to your elbow.** *See under* MORE.

**Thrones, Principalities and Powers.** *See under* THRONE.

**Pow-wow.** A consultation. The word is from the Native American Indians, and is related to the Algonquian word *powwaw* ('magician', literally 'he dreams').

**PPC.** *See* CONGÉ.

**Practitioner, General.** *See under* GENERAL.

**Praemunire.** The title of numerous statutes passed from 1353, and especially that of 1393 designed to assert the rights of the crown against encroachments from the papacy, particularly rights of patronage, the removal of cases from the king's courts and EXCOMMUNICATION. The name also denotes the offence, the writs and the punishment under these statutes. The writ begins with the words *praemunire facias* ('that you cause (someone) to be forewarned'). The best known case of praemunire was when Henry VIII invoked the statute against Cardinal Wolsey in 1529 because of his activities as papal legate. A peer so charged cannot be tried by his peers, but must accept a jury. The last statute involving praemunire was the Royal Marriage Act of 1772.

**Praetorian guard** or **praetorians.** Praetor was the title given to a provincial consul who had military powers and the general's bodyguard was the *cohors praetoria*. From the time of AUGUSTUS to that of Constantine, the praetorians were the household guard of the Roman emperors. In due course they acquired a dangerous power of making and unmaking emperors in times of national crisis and they were eventually (312) dispersed among the legions.

**Pragmatic. Pragmatic sanction** (Greek *pragmatikos*, 'businesslike', 'official'). A term originating in the BYZANTINE EMPIRE to denote a public decree and later used by European sovereigns for important declarations defining their powers, settling the succession and the like. Prominent among such was the Pragmatic Sanction of St Louis, 1269, and that of Charles VII in 1438, asserting the rights of the Gallican Church against the papacy, that which settled the empire of Germany in the House of Austria in 1439, the instrument by which Charles VI of Austria settled the succession of his daughter, Maria Theresa, in 1713, and that of Naples, 1759, whereby Charles III of Spain ceded the succession to the kingdom of Naples to his third son and his heirs in perpetuity. The Pragmatic Sanction of 1713 is the one usually referred to unless some qualification is added.

**Pragmatism** (Greek *pragma*, 'deed'). The philosophical doctrine that the only test of the truth of human cognitions or philosophical principles is their practical results, i.e. their workableness. It does not admit absolute truth, as all truths change their trueness as their practical utility increases or decreases. The word was introduced in this connection about 1875 by the American logician C.S. Peirce (1839–1914) and was popularized by William James (1842–1910), whose *Pragmatism* was published in 1907. Peirce later renamed his pragmatism as 'pragmaticism' to distinguish it from James's work.

> So then, the writer, finding his bantling 'pragmatism' so promoted, feels that it is time to kiss his child good-by and relinquish it to its higher destiny; while to serve the precise purpose of expressing the original definition, he begs to announce the birth of the word 'pragmaticism', which is ugly enough to be safe from kidnappers.
>
> C.S.PEIRCE: *Monist*, XV (1905)

**Prague, Defenestration of.** *See under* DEFENESTRATION.

**Prairie. Prairie oyster.** A seasoned raw egg, often served in spirits, and swallowed whole as a supposed cure for a hangover. The name presumably refers to the glistening molluscous appearance of the egg in its glass. Prairie oysters are also calves' testicles cooked and eaten as a delicacy.

**Prairie schooner.** A large covered wagon, drawn by oxen or mules, used to transport settlers across the North American continent during the mid-19th century, and usually built watertight for crossing rivers.

**Praise. Praise the Lord and pass the ammunition.** A phrase from the Second World War, said to have been used by an American naval chaplain during the Japanese attack on Pearl Harbor, although the actual identity of the chaplain has since been in dispute. One candidate is

Lieutenant Howell M. Forgy; another is Captain William H. Maguire. It was made the subject of a popular song by Frank Loesser in 1942. It is actually said to date from the American Civil War (1861–5).

**Damn with faint praise, To.** *See under* DAMN.

**Prajapatis.** *See* MANU.

**Prang.** RAF slang in the Second World War meaning to bomb a target with evident success, to shoot down another or to crash one's own aircraft, and generally to collide with, or bump into, any vehicle. Hence, also, 'wizard prang', for an accurate hit or other successful strike. According to Eric Partridge, *A Dictionary of RAF Slang* (1945), the word may be a blend of 'paste' and 'bang' but it is more likely to be simply imitative.

**Pratique.** The licence given to an incoming vessel when she can show a clean BILL OF HEALTH or has fulfilled the necessary QUARANTINE regulations. *See also* YELLOW JACK.

**Pray. Pray a tales, To.** To pray that the number of jurymen may be completed. In the celebrated action Bardell *v* Pickwick:

> It was discovered that only ten special jurymen were present. Upon this, Mr Serjeant Buzfuz prayed a *tales*; the gentlemen in black then proceeded to press into the special jury, two of the common jurymen; and a greengrocer and a chemist were caught directly.
>
> DICKENS: *Pickwick Papers*, ch xxxiv (1836–7)

*See also* TALES.

**Prayer wheel.** A device used by the Tibetan Buddhists as an aid to, or substitute for, prayer, supposedly founded on a misconception of the BUDDHA's instructions to his followers that they should 'turn the wheel of the law', i.e. preach BUDDHISM incessantly. It varies from a small pasteboard cylinder inscribed with prayers to a larger water wheel. Among the many prayers is the mystic formula OM MANI PADME HUM, and each revolution represents one repetition of the prayers. In Europe the term is used for a wheel with bells, sometimes called a WHEEL OF FORTUNE, used as a means of DIVINATION, a favourable or unfavourable response being indicated by the position at which it comes to rest.

**Bidding prayer.** *See under* BID.

**Lord's Prayer, The.** *See under* LORD.

**On a wing and a prayer.** *See under* WING.

**Wicked Prayer Book, The.** *See under* WICKED.

**Pre-adamites.** The name given by Isaac de la Peyrère (1655) to a race of men whom he supposed to have existed before the days of ADAM. He held that only the Jews are descended from Adam, and that the Gentiles derive from these 'Pre-adamites'.

**Prebend** (Medieval Latin *praebenda*, 'pension'). A cathedral BENEFICE, its holder being a prebendary. In the 19th century nearly all prebends became honorary offices only, and members of CHAPTERS came to be designated CANONS.

**Precarious** (Latin *precarius*, 'obtained by begging'). A word applied to what depends on prayers or requests. A precarious tenure is one that depends solely on the will of the owner to concede to a request, hence the general use of the word to mean uncertain or not to be depended on.

**Preceptor.** Among the Knights TEMPLAR, a preceptory was a subordinate house or community (the larger being a commandery) under a Preceptor or Knight Preceptor. The Grand Preceptor was the head of all the preceptories in a province, those of Jerusalem, Tripolis and Antioch being the highest ranking.

**Précieuses, Les** (French). The ladies of the intellectual circle that centred about the HÔTEL DE RAMBOUILLET in 17th-century Paris. It may be interpreted as 'persons of distinguished merit'. Their affected airs were the subject of MOLIÈRE's comedy *Les Précieuses Ridicules* (1659), and they were further satirized in *Les Femmes Savantes* (1672).

**Precious stones.** The ancients divided precious stones into male and female, the darker being the males and the light ones the females. Male sapphires approach indigo in colour, but the females are sky blue. Theophrastus mentions the distinction.

> And the tent shook, for mighty Saul shuddered: and sparkles 'gan dart
> From the jewels that woke in his turban, at once with a start,
> All its lordly male-sapphires, and rubies courageous at heart.
>
> ROBERT BROWNING: 'Saul', viii (1855)

According to the Poles, each month is under the influence of a precious stone:

| | | |
|---|---|---|
| January | Garnet | Constancy |
| February | AMETHYST | Sincerity |
| March | Bloodstone | Courage |
| April | DIAMOND | Innocence |
| May | EMERALD | Success in love |
| June | AGATE | Health and long life |
| July | Cornelian | Content |
| August | SARDONYX | Conjugal felicity |
| September | Chrysolite | Antidote to madness |
| October | OPAL | Hope |
| November | Topaz | Fidelity |
| December | Turquoise | Prosperity |

In relation to the signs of the ZODIAC:

| | | | |
|---|---|---|---|
| Aries | Ruby | Libra | Jacinth |
| Taurus | Topaz | Scorpio | Agate |
| Gemini | Carbuncle | Sagittarius | Amethyst |
| Cancer | Emerald | Capricorn | Beryl |
| Leo | Sapphire | Aquarius | ONYX |
| Virgo | Diamond | Pisces | Jasper |

In relation to the planets:

| | | |
|---|---|---|
| Saturn | Turquoise | Lead |
| Jupiter | Cornelian | Tin |
| Mars | Emerald | Iron |
| Sun | Diamond | GOLD |
| Venus | Amethyst | Copper |
| Moon | Crystal | SILVER |
| Mercury | Loadstone | Quicksilver |

In HERALDRY:

Topaz represents 'or' (gold), or Sol, the sun
Pearl or crystal represents 'argent' (silver), or Luna, the moon
Ruby represents 'gules' (red), or the planet Mars
Sapphire represents 'azure' (blue), or the planet Jupiter
Diamond represents 'sable' (black), or the planet Saturn
Emerald represents 'vert' (green), or the planet Venus
Amethyst represents 'purpure' (purple), or the planet Mercury

Many precious stones were held to have curative and magical properties, e.g. loadstone prevented quarrels between brothers, jasper worn by the ploughman ensured the fertility of a field, turquoise protected the wearer from injury if he fell, and, for the Chinese, jade was the most pure and divine of natural materials and had many properties, including stimulating the flow of milk in nursing mothers when powdered and mixed with milk and honey.

**Precocious.** The word literally means early ripened, from Latin *prae*, 'before', and *coquere*, 'to ripen'. Hence the general sense of 'premature', relating to development of mind or body before the normal age.

> Many precocious trees, and such as have their spring in the winter, may be found in most parts of Europe.
> SIR THOMAS BROWNE: *Vulgar Errors*, ii (1646)

**Pregnancy, Phantom.** *See under* PHANTOM.

**Prelate, The Fighting.** *See under* FIGHT.

**Preliminary canter, A.** Something which precedes the real business in hand; a trial run. The reference is to the trial trip of horses before racing.

**Premier** (French, from Latin *primus*, 'first'). First, chief, hence Prime Minister (French *premier ministre*), the first minister of the crown.

**Première.** The feminine form of the French *premier*, commonly denoting the first performance of a play, film or the like.

**Première danseuse.** The leading female dancer in a ballet. The principal male is the *premier danseur*.

**Ce n'est que le premier pas qui coûte.** *See under* CE.

**Premillenarians.** *See* SECOND ADVENTISTS.

**Premonstratensian.** An order, also known as the Norbertine Order, founded by St Norbert in 1120 in the diocese of Laon, France, which adopted the rule of St AUGUSTINE. A spot was pointed out to him in a vision, hence the name, from Medieval Latin (*locus*) *praemonstratus*, '(place) foreshown' (rather than *pratum monstratum*, 'meadow pointed out', as sometimes explained). The order's earliest house in England was established at Newhouse in Lincoln in *c.*1143. Its members generally in England were known as White Canons, from the colour of their habit.

**Prepared, Be prepared.** *See under* BE.

**Prepense, Malice.** *See under* MALICE.

**Pre-Raphaelite Brotherhood, The.** A group of artists formed in London in 1848 consisting of William Holman Hunt, John Everett Millais, Dante Gabriel Rossetti and the sculptor Thomas Woolner. It was later joined by James Collinson, Walter Howell Deverell, Frederick Stephens and William Michael Rossetti. Ford Madox Brown and John Ruskin supported their movement, which espoused a closer study of nature than was practised by those tied to academical rules, and the study of the method and spirit of the artists before ('pre') Raphael (1483–1520). Hence the name. Nevertheless, their works contained much artificiality of literary origins. The group was attacked by many artists and critics, especially by Charles Dickens in *Household Words* (1850). From this date D.G. Rossetti ceased to exhibit publicly. Their works are characterized by exaggerated attention to detail and a high degree of finish, and their earlier lives, at least, by BOHEMIAN activities.

**Presbyterians.** Members of a church governed by elders or presbyters (Greek *presbuteros*, 'elder'), and ministers in a hierarchy of representative courts. Their doctrine is fundamentally Calvinistic. The CHURCH OF SCOTLAND became presbyterian after the REFORMATION, but the growth of Presbyterianism in 17th-century England was checked by the rise of the INDEPENDENTS and the Act of Uniformity of 1662. The Presbyterian Church of Wales is of 18th-century origin.

**Cumberland Presbyterians.** *See under* CUMBERLAND.

**Presence.** *See* REAL PRESENCE.

**Presents, Know all men by these.** *See under* KNOW.

**Preserver. Life preserver.** *See under* LIFE.

**Lightning preservers.** *See under* LIGHTNING.

**Presidium.** In the former USSR the Presidium of the Supreme Soviet was a body elected by the Supreme Soviet to fulfil the role of constitutional head of the state. Its chairman was its representative in ceremonial affairs and it issued ordinances when the Supreme Soviet was not in session. Apart from its chairman, it consisted of 15 deputies (one for each of the republics), a secretary and 20 members. *See also* POLITBURO.

**Press. Clarendon Press.** *See under* CLARENDON.

**Gutter press.** *See under* GUTTER.

**Kelmscott Press.** *See under* KELMSCOTT.

**Liberty of the Press.** *See under* LIBERTY.

**Stanhope press.** *See under* STANHOPE.

**Yellow press, The.** *See under* YELLOW.

**Press gang.** The name formerly given to those naval parties that carried out the task of impressment, an ancient and arbitrary method of obtaining men for military service dating back to the early 13th century. Individual captains of ships provided their own parties until the demands of the 18th-century Navy led to the establishment of an Impress Service with depots where seafarers abounded. Apart from seizing men from taverns, they seized merchant sailors from ships at sea and other places, and pressed men formed about half of a ship's crew. The Royal Navy relied on this method until the 1830s, when improvements in pay and conditions encouraged adequate voluntary enlistment, although impressment has, strictly speaking, never been abolished. The word has nothing to do with 'pressing' in the sense of 'forcing' but derives from the 'prest' or 'imprest' money (French *prêter*, 'to lend') advanced on enlistment, rather like the army's KING'S SHILLING.

> But woe is me! the press-gang came,
> And forc'd my love away
> Just when we named next morning fair
> To be our wedding day.
> 'The Banks of the Shannon', Irish ballad (1785)

**Press-ganged into something, To be.** To be forced to do a thing or join it; or to take part against one's will or inclination.

**Prester John.** In medieval legend a fabulous Christian emperor of Asia who occurs in documents from the 12th century onwards. In Marco Polo's *Travels* he is lord of the TARTARS. From the 14th century he becomes the emperor of Ethiopia or Abyssinia, where he was apparently still reigning in the time of Vasco da Gama (*c*.1469–1525). In John Buchan's novel *Prester John* (1910) he is a Negro preacher who returns to South Africa to lead a native uprising. Prester means 'priest'.

**Prestige.** A word with a curiously metamorphosed meaning. Latin *praestigiae*, from which it is derived, means juggling tricks, hence the extension to illusion, fascination, charm and so to the present meaning of standing, influence, reputation, based on past achievements and associations.

**Presto.** The name frequently applied to himself by Swift in his *Journal to Stella*. According to his own account (*Journal*, 1 August 1711) it was given him by the notorious Duchess of Shrewsbury, an Italian:

> The Duchess of Shrewsbury asked him, was not that Dr –, Dr –, and she could not say my name in English, but said Dr Presto, which is Italian for Swift.

**Pretender. Old Pretender, The.** *See under* OLD.

**Young Pretender, The.** *See under* YOUNG.

**Pretext.** A pretence or excuse. The word is from Latin *praetexta*, a dress embroidered in the front, worn by Roman magistrates, priests, and children of the aristocracy between the age of 13 and 17. The *praetextatae* were dramas in which actors personated those who wore the *praetexta*. Hence persons who pretended to be what they were not.

**Pretty. Pretty fair.** Fairly well; reasonably satisfactory; 'not bad'.

**Pretty kettle of fish, A.** *See* KETTLE OF FISH.

**Pretty pass, A.** A difficult or deplorable state of affairs.

**Pretty penny, A.** A considerable sum of money; an unpleasantly large sum.

**Pretty please.** An earnest request for a thing, implying a sort of gift-wrapped 'please'.

**Pretty-pretty.** Too pretty; over-ornamented.

**As pretty as a picture.** *See under* AS.

**Sitting pretty.** *See under* SIT.

**Prevarication.** The Latin word *varico* means 'I straddle', and *praevaricor*, 'I go crooked'. The verb, says Pliny, was first applied to men who ploughed crooked ridges, and afterwards to men who gave crooked answers in the law courts or deviated from the straight line of truth. *See also* DELIRIUM.

**Previous question.** The question whether the matter under debate shall be put to the vote. In the HOUSE OF COMMONS to 'move the previous question' is to move 'that the question be not now put'. If the motion is carried, the question that was previously before the house is abandoned. If not carried, the question concerned must be put forthwith. The motion is now rarely used. The previous question may not be moved on an amendment or business motion or in committee.

**Priam.** King of TROY when that city was sacked by the Greeks, husband of HECUBA, and father of 50 children, the eldest of whom was HECTOR. When the gates of Troy were thrown open by the Greeks who had been concealed in the WOODEN HORSE, Pyrrhus, the son of ACHILLES, slew the aged Priam.

**Priapus.** In Greek mythology, the son of Dionysus (BACCHUS) and APHRODITE, the god of reproductive power and fertility (hence of gardens), the protector of shepherds, fishermen and farmers. He was later regarded as the chief deity of lasciviousness and obscenity and the phallus was his attribute.

**Price. Peace at any price.** *See under* PEACE.

**Pearl of great price, A.** *See under* PEARL.

**Peg a price, To.** *See under* PEG.

**Spot price.** *See under* SPOT.

**Starting price.** *See under* START.

**Upset price.** *See under* UPSET.

**Prick. Prick-eared.** Said of a dog with upstanding ears. The PURITANS or ROUNDHEADS were so called because they had their hair cut short and covered their heads with a black skull-cap drawn down tight, leaving the ears exposed.

**Pricking for sheriffs.** The annual choosing of SHERIFFS used to be done by the king, who marked the names on a list by pricking them with a bodkin at random. Sheriffs are still 'pricked' by the sovereign, but the names are chosen beforehand.

**Pricking of one's thumb, The.** In popular superstition, a portent of evil. The Second Witch in Shakespeare's *Macbeth* (IV, i (1605)) says:

> By the pricking of my thumbs
> Something wicked this way comes.

Macbeth then enters. *See also* ITCH.

**Prick of conscience, The.** Remorse, tormenting reflection on one's misdeeds. Richard Rolle de Hampole (*c*.1290–1349) wrote a devotional treatise with this title.

**Prick up one's ears, To.** To listen attentively to something not expected, as horses or dogs prick up their ears at a sudden sound.

> Like unbacked colts, they pricked their ears.
> SHAKESPEARE: *The Tempest*, IV, i (1611)

**Kick against the pricks, To.** *See under* KICK.

**Pride.** The word has both a bad and a good sense. The bad is conceit; the good is a sense of personal worth. It has further the meaning of ostentation, finery, magnificence or anything that one can be proud of. Thus Edmund Spenser (*The Faerie Queene*, I, i (1590)) talks of 'loftie trees yclad with sommer's pride' (their verdure), and Alexander Pope (*Odyssey*, viii (1725–6)), of a 'sword whose ivory sheath [was] inwrought with curious pride' (its ornamentation).

**Pride goes before a fall.** An adaptation of Proverbs 16:18: 'Pride goeth before destruction, and an haughty spirit before a fall.'

**Pride of lions, A.** A company or group of lions. The term dates from at least the 15th century. *See also* NOUNS OF ASSEMBLAGE.

**Pride of the morning, The.** A country term for the early mist or shower that promises a fine day. The morning is too proud to come out in her glory all at once, or is a proud beauty who, being thwarted, frets and pouts awhile.

**London pride.** *See under* LONDON.

**Peacock in his pride, A.** *See under* PEACOCK.

**Swallow one's pride, To.** To repress it.

**Pride's Purge.** When CHARLES I was a captive, after his defeat in the field, the LONG PARLIAMENT declared for a reconciliation (5 December 1648), but on the following day, 6 December, a body of soldiers under Colonel Thomas Pride expelled from the House of Commons those MPs who favoured further negotiations with the king. The remainder formed the RUMP.

**Priest. Priest or son of Bacchus, A.** A sot or toper. *See also* BACCHUS.

**High priest.** *See under* HIGH.

**Prig.** An old CANT word for to filch or steal, also for a thief. In Shakespeare's *The Winter's Tale* (IV, ii (1610)) the clown calls AUTOLYCUS a 'prig' who 'haunts wakes, fairs, and bear-baitings'. Thomas Shadwell (*The Squire of Alsatia*, I, i (1688)) uses the term of a pert COXCOMB, 'and thou shalt shine, and be as gay as any spruce prig that ever walked the street'.

Today 'prig' denotes a conceited, formal or didactic person; one who tries to teach others how to behave; one who is narrow-minded and self-righteous. The word is of unknown origin.

**Prima. Prima donna** (Italian, 'first lady'). The principal female singer in an opera. The phrase is also generally applied to a self-important person, a 'real prima donna'.

**Prima facie** (Latin, 'at first sight'). A *prima facie* case is a case or statement that, without minute examination into its merits, seems plausible and correct.

**Primary colour.** Any of the colours red, green and blue or, for pigments, red, blue and yellow, from which all other colours can be obtained by mixing.

**Primate.** The title of the bishop of the 'first' or chief see of a state (Latin *prima sedes*), originally the METROPOLITAN of a province. The archbishop of York is the Primate of England and the archbishop of Canterbury the Primate of All England.

**Prime** (Latin *primus*, 'first'). In the Western Church, the office appointed for the first hour (6 am), the first of the CANONICAL HOURS. Milton terms sunrise 'that sweet hour of prime' (*Paradise Lost*, v (1667)), and the word is used in a general way of the first beginnings of anything, especially of the world itself.

**Prime Minister.** The first minister of the crown, the PREMIER.

**Prime number.** The GOLDEN NUMBER, also called simply the 'prime'. In mathematics a prime number is any positive number that cannot be expressed as the product of two others, e.g. 1, 3, 5, 7 and 11.

**Prime the pump, To.** To give financial aid to an enterprise in the hope that it will become self-supporting. The allusion is to starting a pump working by pouring in water to establish suction.

**In one's prime.** In one's youth; at the flowering period of one's life.

One's prime is elusive. You little girls, when you grow up, must be on the alert to recognize your prime at whatever time of your life it may occur.
MURIEL SPARK: *The Prime of Miss Jean Brodie*, ch i (1961)

**Unknown Prime Minister, The.** *See under* UNKNOWN.

**Primer.** Originally the name of a book of devotions used by the laity in pre-REFORMATION England. This was used as a first reading book. The name was then applied to a small book by which children were taught to read and pray and hence to a first school book on any subject.

**Great primer.** *See under* GREAT.

**Primero.** A very popular card game for about a hundred years after 1530, in which the cards had three times their usual value. Four were dealt to each player, the principal groups being flush, prime and point. 'Flush' was the same as in poker, 'prime' was one card of each suit, and 'point' was reckoned as in piquet.

**Primrose.** The name of the flower is from Medieval Latin *prima rosa*, 'first rose'. The flower is one of the first to appear in the spring, with 'rose' here used generally to mean 'flower'.

**Primrose Day.** 19 April, the anniversary of the death of Benjamin Disraeli, 1st Earl of Beaconsfield, the season when primroses are at their best. *See also* PRIMROSE LEAGUE.

**Primrose League, The.** A Conservative party organization founded by members of the FOURTH PARTY in 1883, having as its objects 'the maintenance of religion, of the estates of the realm, and of the imperial ascendancy'. The name was taken in the mistaken belief that the primrose was Lord Beaconsfield's favourite flower, from the wreath of primroses sent to his funeral with the words: 'His favourite flowers from Osborne, a tribute of affection from Queen Victoria.' The league had its greatest influence and popularity in the days before the First World War when imperial sentiment was at its height.

**Primrose path.** The easy way, the path of pleasure and self-indulgence. Shakespeare refers to the 'primrose path of dalliance' (*Hamlet*, I, iii (1600)), and to 'the primrose way to the everlasting bonfire' (*Macbeth*, II, i (1605)).

**Primum mobile** (Latin, 'first moving [thing]'). In the PTOLEMAIC SYSTEM of astronomy, the ninth (later the tenth) sphere. It was believed to revolve round the earth from east to west in 24 hours, carrying with it all the other spheres. Milton refers to it as 'that first mov'd' (*Paradise Lost*, iii (1667)) and Sir Thomas Browne (*Religio Medici* (1642)) used the phrase, 'Beyond the first movable', meaning outside the material creation. According to Ptolemy, the *primum mobile* was the boundary of creation, above which came the EMPYREAN or seat of God.

The term is figuratively applied to any machine that communicates motion to others, and also to any great sources of motion or in the development of ideas. Thus, SOCRATES may be called the *primum mobile* of the DIALECTIC, Megarian, Cyrenaic and CYNIC systems of philosophy.

**Primus** (Latin, 'first'). The presiding bishop of the Episcopal Church of Scotland. He is elected by the other six bishops, and presides in Convocation, and at meetings relative to church matters.

**Primus inter pares** (Latin). The first among equals.

**Prince** (Latin *princeps*, 'chief', 'leader'). A title that was formerly in common use as the title of a reigning sovereign. It is still used in a few cases, e.g. the Prince of Monaco, the Prince of Liechtenstein. In England it is now limited to the sons of the sovereign and their sons. 'Princess' is limited to the sovereign's daughters and sons' (but not daughters') daughters.

**Prince Ahmed's apple.** A PANACEA or cure for every disorder. In the ARABIAN NIGHTS ENTERTAINMENTS the story is told of Prince AHMED, who purchased his apple at SAMARKAND.

**Prince Charming.** The fairy-tale prince who awakens SLEEPING BEAUTY, and in some versions of the story the prince who awakens SNOW WHITE. The name originally arose in English as a partial translation of French *Roi Charmant*, 'King Charming', the hero of the Contesse d'Aulnoy's *L'Oiseau bleu* (1697). The term is also loosely used of any paragon sought by a young woman as her lover.

Way back in the days of Dr Kildare, Richard Chamberlain must have been every girl's idea of Prince Charming.
*Daily Mail* (25 March 1976)

**Prince consort.** A prince who is the husband of the reigning queen.

**Prince Imperial.** The title of the heir apparent in the French Empire of NAPOLEON III (1852–70).

**Prince of Artists, The.** Albrecht Dürer (1471–1528) of Nuremberg was so called by his countrymen.

**Prince of Critics.** Aristarchus of Byzantium (2nd century BC), who compiled a critical edition of the Homeric poems and commentaries.

**Prince of Darkness.** The DEVIL; SATAN.

**Prince of Demons.** ASMODEUS, also called 'the Demon of Matrimonial Unhappiness'.

**Prince of Destruction, The.** TAMBERLANE, or Timur, the Tartar (1336–1405), the famous oriental conqueror of Persia and a great part of India. He was threatening China when he died.

**Prince of Grammarians, The.** Apollonius the SOPHIST of Alexandria (1st century AD), so called by Priscian.

**Prince of Harlequins, The.** John Rich (1682–1761).

**Prince of Hypocrites, The.** Tiberius Caesar (42 BC–AD 37) was so called because he affected a great regard for decency, but indulged in the most detestable lust and cruelty.

**Prince of Music, The.** Giovanni Pierluigi da Palestrina (*c*.1525–94).

**Prince of Peace, The.** MESSIAH; Jesus Christ.

> For unto us a child is born, unto us a son is given ... and his name shall be called Wonderful, Counsellor, The mighty God, The everlasting Father, The Prince of Peace.
>
> Isaiah 9:6

The Spanish statesman Manuel de Godoy (1767–1851) was called Prince of the Peace for his negotiations with France in the Treaty of Basle, 1795.

**Prince of Physicians, The.** A title given to AVICENNA.

**Prince of Piedmont.** The heir apparent to the House of Savoy, former kings of Italy.

**Prince of the Apostles.** St PETER (Matthew 16:18, 19).

**Prince of the Asturias.** The traditional title of the heir apparent to the Spanish throne.

**Prince of the church.** A CARDINAL.

**Prince of the Sonnet, The.** Joachim du Bellay, Apollo of the FRENCH PLÉIADES (1522–60), French sonneteer, was so called.

**Prince of Wales, The.** When Edward I extinguished Welsh independence (1282–3), he is popularly said to have presented Wales with a new prince in the form of his son Edward, who was born at Caernarvon (1284). In fact Edward was created Prince of Wales in 1301. The last native prince, Llywelyn ap Gruffydd, was killed at Builth in 1282. Since 1337 the king's or queen's eldest son has been born Duke of Cornwall, and the title Prince of Wales has been conferred upon him subsequently.

**Prince of Wales's feathers, The.** *See* ICH DIEN.

**Prince Regent.** A prince ruling on behalf of the legal sovereign. In British history George, PRINCE OF WALES, who acted as regent for his father, George III. *See also* REGENCY.

**Prince Rupert's drops.** Bubbles made by dropping molten glass into water. Their form is that of a tadpole, and if the smallest portion of the 'tail' is nipped off, the whole flies into fine dust with explosive violence. They were introduced into England by Prince Rupert (1619–1682), grandson of James I and Royalist cavalry leader during the Civil Wars (1642–51). Prince's metal, seemingly an alloy of brass or copper, was also his invention.

**Princes in the Tower, The.** The boy king Edward V and his younger brother Richard, Duke of York, who were lodged in the TOWER OF LONDON (May and June 1483), after which their uncle Richard, Duke of Gloucester, assumed the crown as Richard III. The princes disappeared at this time and are generally presumed to have been murdered by their uncle, but there is no conclusive evidence. Bones found during excavations near the WHITE TOWER in 1674 were transferred to Westminster Abbey. In 1933, experts proclaimed them to be bones of children of 12 or 13, the very ages of the princes.

**Prince's metal.** *See* PRINCE RUPERT'S DROPS.

**Black Prince, The.** *See under* BLACK.

**Crown prince.** *See under* CROWN.

**Hamlet without the prince.** *See under* HAMLET.

**Scourge of Princes, The.** *See under* SCOURGE.

**Princess Royal.** The title customarily conferred by a British sovereign on his or her eldest daughter. It was introduced by Charles I for his eldest daughter, Princess Mary. It then fell from use until the reign of George II, whose daughter Princess Anne was called Princess Royal. George III's eldest daughter, Princess Charlotte, was then Princess Royal until her death in 1828. As neither George IV nor William IV had daughters, the title was in abeyance until 1840 when Queen Victoria's daughter, Princess Victoria, succeeded to it. She remained Princess Royal until her death in 1901. In 1905 Edward VII's eldest daughter, Princess Louise, succeeded to the title. On her death in 1931 the title passed to Princess Mary, daughter of George V. She died in 1965, and the title was conferred on Princess Anne by Elizabeth II in 1987.

**Principal boy.** The chief character in the seasonal Christmas and New Year pantomime, such as Dick WHITTINGTON, ALADDIN, Robinson CRUSOE, Idle Jack in JACK AND THE BEANSTALK, or Prince Charming in CINDERELLA. Although male, the part has long been traditionally played by a young woman, perhaps as a modern equivalent of the Roman feast of SATURNALIA, one feature of which was the exchange of costume between sexes. It was also probably influenced by the custom in Shakespeare's day for boys to take female roles. In the pantomime it effectively balances the other main gender displacement: the acting of the Ugly Sisters by men. In the latter half of the 20th century the part of the principal boy was increasingly played by young men, notably pop stars.

**Principalities.** Members of one of the nine orders of angels in medieval angelology. *See also* ANGEL.

**Thrones, Principalities and Powers.** *See under* THRONE.

**Principle. Archimedes' principle.** *See under* ARCHIMEDES.

**Peter principle.** *See under* PETER.

**Print. Printers' Bible, The.** *See under* BIBLE.

**Printer's devil.** A printer's errand boy, and formerly the boy who took the printed sheets from the press.

> The Press-man sometimes has a Week-Boy to Take Sheets, as they are Printed off the Tympan: These Boys do in a Printing-House, commonly black and Dawb themselves: Whence the Workmen do jocosely call them Devils; and sometimes Spirits, and sometimes Flies.
>
> JOSEPH MOXON: *Mechanick Exercises*, ii (1683)

**Printers' marks.**

? is $\overset{q}{o}$, that is, the first and last letters of *quaestio* ('question')
! is $\overset{I}{o}$. Io in Latin is the interjection of joy
¶ is the initial letter of 'paragraph' (reversed)
§ the S-mark or section mark
* is used by Greek grammarians to arrest the attention to something striking (asterisk or star)
† is used by Greek grammarians to indicate something objectionable (obelisk or dagger)
# is the hash or 'number sign'; 'hash' is probably a corruption of 'hatch', the figure representing a crosshatching in which the digits 1 to 9 can be entered
& is the AMPERSAND

Both the asterisk (*) and obelisk (†) are now used to indicate footnotes, in this order. If a third footnote is needed, the next symbol conventionally used is a double dagger (‡). In linguistic works, the asterisk is used before a word to denote a reconstructed form, as Vulgar Latin **panna* for the origin of English 'pan'. The dagger is used for an obsolete word, as Middle English †*gnacche* for modern English 'gnash'. *See also* LETTER.

**Printing House Square.** Often used as synonymous with *The Times* newspaper, which was produced there from its inception until 1974. It began in 1785 as *The Daily Universal Register*, which became *The Times* in 1788. Printing House Square is at Blackfriars in the City of London and was earlier the site of the King's Printing House.

**Proof prints.** *See under* PROOF.

**Small print, The.** *See under* SMALL.

**Priori.** *See* A PRIORI.

**Priory, Alien.** *See under* ALIEN.

**Prisca, St.** A Roman Christian lady, tortured and beheaded (*c.*270) under the Emperor Claudius II. There is a church of St Prisca at Rome. She is represented between two lions who, it is said, refused to attack her. St Priscilla, a Christian convert of the 1st century, and mentioned several times in the New Testament (Acts 18, Romans 16:3, 1 Corinthians 16:19, 2 Timothy 4:19), is also known as St Prisca. *See also* EAGLE.

**Priscilla.** In the New Testament (Acts 18), a particularly devout woman. She and Aquila act as PAUL's hosts in Corinth and accompany him when he leaves to return to Syria.

**Prisoner. Prisoner at the bar, The.** The prisoner in the dock before the judge.

**Prisoner of Chillon.** François de Bonnivard (1493–1570), a Genevan prelate and politician. In his poem (1816), Lord Byron makes him one of six brothers, all of whom suffered for their opinions. The father and two sons died in battle, one was burned at the stake, and three were imprisoned in the dungeon of Chillon, on the edge of Lake Geneva. Of these, two died, and François, who had been gaoled for republican principles by the Duke-Bishop of Savoy, was released, after four years, by the BÉARNAIS.

**Prisoner of the Vatican, The.** The pope was so called after 1870, when Pius IX (r.1846–78) retired into the VATICAN after the occupation of Rome. He proclaimed himself a prisoner for conscience's sake and his successors remained in the precincts of the Vatican until the LATERAN TREATY of 1929.

**Prisoner's friend, The.** At a naval court martial, the person (usually an officer) who acts on behalf of, or assists, the accused, unless the person charged conducts his own case.

**Marshalsea Prison.** *See under* MARSHALSEA.

**Private. Private Bill.** The draft of an Act of Parliament affecting private persons, groups or corporations. *See also* ACT; PUBLIC BILL.

**Private eye.** One of the various nicknames for a private detective. The phrase was adopted for its title by the satirical magazine *Private Eye*, founded in 1961.

**Private hotel.** A hotel that is not obliged to take all comers.

**Private Member's Bill.** A public bill introduced by a private member as distinct from a member of the government. Few reach the STATUTE Book. *See also* ACT.

**Private parts.** The genitals, as the only parts of the body not normally seen in public.

**Private ship.** In the Royal Navy a ship other than a FLAGSHIP. A term in use by the early 17th century.

**Privateer.** A privately owned vessel commissioned under a LETTER OF MARQUE by a belligerent state to wage war on the enemy's commerce. The practice of issuing such commissions ceased as a result of the Declaration of Paris, 1856, but it did not finally become obsolete until the Hague Convention of 1907.

**Privilege.** In the parliamentary sense, the word applies to Parliament's right to regulate its own proceedings and in the case of the House of Commons the right to regulate membership. It also denotes the right to punish for breach of privilege or contempt, the right to freedom of speech and freedom from civil arrest. In addition, there is still the freedom of access as a body to the sovereign to present an address and the request for a favourable construction on its proceedings.

**Privy. Privy Council.** The council chosen by the sovereign originally to administer public affairs, but now never summoned to assemble as a whole except to proclaim the successor to the crown on the death of the sovereign, or to listen to the sovereign's announcement of intention to marry. It usually includes Princes of the Blood, the two PRIMATES, the bishop of London, the great officers of state and of the royal household, the LORD CHANCELLOR and Judges of the Courts of Equity, the Chief Justices of the Courts of COMMON LAW, the Judge Advocate, some of the PUISNE JUDGES, the SPEAKER of the HOUSE OF COMMONS, the lord mayor of London, the High Commissioners and many politicians. Today the business of the Privy Council is to give formal effect to proclamations and ORDERS IN COUNCIL. For this a quorum of three suffices. The CABINET and the Judicial Committee are, in theory, merely committees of the Privy Council. Privy Councillors are entitled to the prefix 'the Right Honourable', and to the use of the initials PC after their names. They rank next after those Knights of the Garter who may be commoners. The Lord President of the Council is the fourth great officer of state.

**Privy Seal.** The seal that the sovereign uses in proof of assent to a document, kept in the charge of a high officer of state known as the Lord Privy Seal. In matters of minor importance it is sufficient to pass the Privy Seal, but instruments of greater moment must have the GREAT SEAL also.

**Prize. Prize court.** A court of law set up in time of war to examine the validity of capture of ships and goods made at sea by the navy.

**Prize money.** The name given to the net proceeds of the sale of enemy shipping and property captured at sea. Before 1914 the distribution was confined to the ships of the Royal Navy actually making the capture. Since that date all prize money has been pooled and shared out among the navy as a whole. Prize money was paid at the end of the Second World War for the last time.

**Prize ring, The.** The boxing ring in which a prize fight takes place, a prize fight being a boxing match for a money prize or trophy.

**Booby prize.** *See under* BOOBY.

**Booker Prize.** *See under* BOOKER.

**Pulitzer prizes.** *See under* PULITZER.

**Pro** (Latin, 'for', 'on behalf of'). 'Pro' is also a common shortening of 'professional' as: 'He is a golf pro.'

**Pro and con** (Latin). For and against. 'Con' is a contraction of *contra*. The pros and cons of a matter are all that can be said for or against it.

**Pro bono publico** (Latin). For the public good or benefit.

**Pro rata** (Latin). Proportional or proportionally.

**Pro tempore** (Latin). Temporarily, for the time being; until something is permanently settled. The expression is often colloquially contracted into *pro tem*.

**Problem, No.** *See under* NO.

**Synoptic problem.** *See under* SYNOPTIC.

**Procès-verbal** (French). A detailed and official statement of some fact, especially a written and authenticated statement of facts in support of a criminal charge.

**Procne.** *See* NIGHTINGALE.

**Proconsul.** A magistrate of ancient Rome who was invested with the power of a consul and charged with the command of an army or the administration of a province. The name has often been applied to some of the great colonial administrators of the former British Empire.

**Procris.** *See* CEPHALUS.

**Procrustes' bed.** In Greek legend Procrustes was a robber of Attica, who placed all who fell into his hands upon an iron bed. If they were longer than the bed he cut off the overhanging parts, if shorter he stretched them until they fitted it. He was slain by THESEUS. Hence, any attempt to reduce men to one standard, one way of thinking, or one way of acting, is called 'placing them on Procrustes' bed'.

> Tyrants more cruel than Procrustes old,
> Who to his iron-bed by torture fits
> Their nobler parts, the souls of suffering wits.
>
> DAVID MALLET: *Verbal Criticism* (1733)

**Proctor.** Literally this is one who manages the affairs of another, the word being a contraction of 'procurator'. At the universities of Oxford and Cambridge the proctors are two officials whose duties include the maintaining of discipline. Representatives of ecclesiastical bodies in Convocation are called proctors.

**King's** or **Queen's Proctor, The.** *See under* KING.

**Procyon.** The Lesser DOG STAR, *alpha* in *Canis Minor*, so called because it rises before the Dog Star (Greek *pro*, 'before' and *kuōn*, 'dog'). It is the eighth brightest star in the heavens. *See also* ICARIUS.

**Prodigal.** Festus the Latin lexicographer (2nd century AD) says that the Romans called victims wholly consumed by fire *prodigae hostiae* ('wasted victims'), and adds that those who waste their substance are therefore called prodigals. The word ultimately goes back to Latin *prodigere*, 'to squander', literally 'to drive forth', from *pro*, 'forth', and *agere*, 'to drive'. The notion was that persons who had spent all their patrimony were 'driven forth' to be sold as slaves to their creditors.

**Prodigal son, The.** The younger of two sons who wastes his share of his father's inheritance on riotous living. On his return in poverty, his father KILLS THE FATTED CALF in celebration. When the elder son, who had stayed at home and worked faithfully, protests, the father replies that we should always celebrate when one that was dead returns to life. The parable is told in Luke 15.

**Prodigy** (Latin *prodigium*, 'portent', 'prophetic sign'). One endowed with surprising qualities.

**Prodigy of France, The.** Guillaume Budé (1467–1540), the French humanist, was so called by Erasmus.

**Prodigy of Learning, The.** Samuel Hahnemann (1755–1843), the German physician and scholar, was so named by J. Paul Richter.

**Producer's goods.** An economist's term for goods such as tools and raw material, which satisfy needs only indirectly, through making other goods. They are more commonly known as capital goods.

**Profane.** Literally before or outside the temple (Latin *pro fano*). Hence *profanus* was applied to those persons who came to the temple and, remaining outside and unattached, were not initiated. Hence the idea of irreverence, disregard of sacred things, blasphemy, secularism and the like.

**Profession, Adam's.** *See under* ADAM.

**Professor, Regius.** *See under* REGIUS.

**Profile.** Literally, shown by a thread, from Latin *pro*, 'forth', and *filum*, 'thread'. A profile is an outline, but especially a view or drawing or some other representation of the human face outlined by the median line. The term 'profile' for a biographical sketch came into journalistic use in the 1920s.

**High profile.** *See under* HIGH.

**Keep a low profile, To.** *See under* LOW.

**Profit. Paper profits.** *See under* PAPER.

**Plough back profits, To.** *See under* PLOUGH.

**Programme music.** Instrumental music based on a literary, historical or pictorial subject and intended to describe or illustrate the theme musically. Examples are Beethoven's 6th ('Pastoral') Symphony, Berlioz's *Symphonie fantastique* (1830) and Richard Strauss's tone poem *Don Quixote* (1896–7).

**Progress, The Pilgrim's.** *See under* PILGRIM.

**Projection, Powder of.** *See under* POWDER.

**Prolepsis** (Greek, 'a taking beforehand'). A literary device whereby a future event is presumed to have already happened. In the following example, the 'murder'd man' has not yet been murdered, but he will be by the 'two brothers' who are taking him into a forest:

> So the two brothers and their murder'd man
> Rode past fair Florence, to where Arno's stream
> Gurgles through straiten'd banks.
>
> JOHN KEATS: *Isabella*, xxvii (1820)

**Proletariat.** The labouring classes, the unpropertied wage-earning classes. In ancient Rome the *proletarii* could hold no office, and were ineligible for the army and served the state only with their offspring (*proles*).

> The proletariat, the lowest stratum of our present society, cannot stir, cannot raise itself up, without the whole superincumbent strata of official society being sprung into the air.
>
> MARX and ENGELS: *Communist Manifesto* (1848)

**Promenade. Promenade concert.** A concert in which some of the audience stand in an open area of the concert room floor. Promenade concerts, familiarly called 'Proms', date back to the days of the London pleasure gardens such as VAUXHALL and RANELAGH. Mansard had conducted similar concerts at Paris in the 1830s and from 1838 his example was followed at London. In 1895 Sir Henry Wood (1869–1944) began the concerts at the Queen's Hall, which he conducted for over half a century and which became a regular feature of London life. In 1927 the BBC took over their management from Chappell's. The destruction of the hall by enemy action in 1941 caused a break in the concerts but they were renewed at the Royal Albert Hall. The popular high point of the annual series is the LAST NIGHT OF THE PROMS.

In the USA a 'prom' is a dance or ball given by members of a class at school or college, a usage that has now been taken up in Britain.

**Empire Promenade, The.** *See under* EMPIRE.

**Prometheus** (Greek, 'Forethought'). One of the TITANS of Greek myth, the son of IAPETUS and the ocean nymph Clymene (or Themis), and famous as a benefactor to man. It is said that ZEUS, having been tricked by Prometheus over his share of a sacrificial ox, denied mankind the use of fire. Prometheus then stole fire from Hephaestus (VULCAN) to save the human race. For this he was chained by Zeus to Mount Caucasus, where an eagle preyed on his liver all day, the liver being renewed at night. He was eventually released by HERCULES, who slew the eagle. It was to counterbalance the gift of fire to mankind that Zeus sent PANDORA to earth with her box of evils.

**Promethean.** Capable of producing fire, pertaining to PROMETHEUS.

A somewhat dangerous match invented in 1828 was known as a 'Promethean'. It consisted of a small glass bulb containing sulphuric acid, the outside being coated with potassium chlorate, sugar, and gum surrounded by a paper wrapping in the form of a spill. When the glass was bitten with the teeth the chlorate fired the paper. *See also* CONGREVES; LUCIFER MATCH.

> I carried with me some promethean matches, which I ignited by biting; it was thought so wonderful that a man should strike fire with his teeth, that it was usual to collect the whole family to see it.
>
> CHARLES DARWIN: *The Voyage of the 'Beagle'*, ch iii (1839)

**Promethean fire.** The vital principle, the fire with which PROMETHEUS quickened into life his clay figures from which he created the first humans.

**Promethean unguent.** Unguent made from a herb on which some of the blood of PROMETHEUS had fallen. MEDEA gave JASON some of it, thus rendering his body proof against fire and weapons. *See also* PANACEA.

**Promise. Promised Land** or **Land of Promise.** Canaan, so called because God promised ABRAHAM, ISAAC and JACOB that their offspring should possess it. The promise is mentioned in Exodus 12:25, Deuteronomy 9:28 and elsewhere. Figuratively, it is a name for heaven or any place of expected happiness or fulfilment.

> Through the night of doubt and sorrow
> Onward goes the pilgrim band,
> Singing songs of expectation,
> Marching to the Promised Land.
>
> SABINE BARING-GOULD: 'Through the night of doubt and sorrow' (hymn) (1867)

**Promise of Odin, The.** The most binding of all oaths to a Norseman. In making it, the hand was passed through a massive silver ring, which was kept for the purpose, or through a sacrificial stone, like that called the Circle of Stennis. *See also* STANDING STONES OF STENNESS.

**Breach of promise.** *See under* BREACH.

**Break a promise, To.** *See under* BREAK.

**Lick and a promise, A.** *See under* LICK.

**Proms, Last Night of the.** *See under* LAST.

**Proof.** A printed sheet to be examined and approved before it is finally printed. The first, or foul, proof is that which contains all the compositor's errors. When these are corrected the impression next taken is called a clean proof and is submitted to the author. The final impression, which is corrected by the reader, is termed the press proof. With the advent of computerization, the foul proof became a thing of the past.

**Proof Bible, The.** *See under* BIBLE.

**Proof of the pudding is in the eating, The.** An old proverb meaning that performance is the true test, not appearances or promises, just as the best test of a pudding is to eat it, not just to look at it.

**Proof prints.** The first impressions of an engraving. India proofs are those taken off on INDIA PAPER.

**Proofs before lettering.** Those proofs taken off before any inscription is engraved on the plate. After the proofs, the connoisseur's order of value is: (1) prints that have the letters only in outline, (2) those in which the letters are shaded with a black line, (3) those in which some slight ornament is introduced into the letters, (4) those in which the letters are filled up quite black.

**Proof spirit.** A term formerly applied (until 1980) to a standard mixture of alcohol and water used as a basis for customs and excise purposes. It was legally defined as having 49.2 per cent of alcohol by weight, 57.1 per cent by volume, at 51°F (10.5°C). When the mixture had more alcohol it was said to be 'over proof', and when less, 'under proof'. In earlier days proof spirit was held to be that which if poured over gunpowder and ignited would eventually ignite the powder. If the spirit was under proof the water remaining would prevent the firing of the powder.

**Burden of proof.** *See under* BURDEN.

**Prooshan blue.** A former term of endearment, when after the Battle of Waterloo (1815) the Prussians were immensely popular in England. Sam Weller in *Pickwick Papers* (ch xxxiii (1836–7)) addresses his father as 'Vell, my Prooshan Blue'. *See also* PRUSSIAN BLUE.

**Propaganda.** The Sacred Congregation for Propagating the Faith (New Latin *Sacra Congregatio de Propaganda Fide*) is a committee of cardinals established at Rome by Gregory XV (r.1621–3) in 1622 for propagating the faith throughout the world. Hence the term is applied to any scheme, association, publication or the like for making PROSELYTES or influencing public opinion in political, social and religious matters.

**Properly speaking.** *See* STRICTLY SPEAKING.

**Property. Property plot.** In theatrical language, the phrase means a list of all the 'properties' or articles that are needed for the production of a particular play. Everything used on the stage is termed a 'prop'. 'Actor's props' are articles of personal use, the remainder are termed 'manager's props'.

**Lost property office.** *See under* LOST.

**Prophet, The.** The special title of MOHAMMED. According to the KORAN there have been 200,000 prophets, but only six of them brought new laws or dispensations, i.e. ADAM, NOAH, ABRAHAM, MOSES, Jesus and Mohammed.

**Banner of the Prophet, The.** *See under* BANNER.

**City of the Prophet, The.** *See under* CITY.

**Great** or **Major Prophets, The.** *See under* GREAT.

**Is Saul also among the prophets?** *See under* SAUL.

**Minor** or **Lesser Prophets, The.** *See under* MINOR.

**Props.** *See* PROPERTY PLOT.

**Proscription.** Outlawry or the denunciation of citizens as public enemies, so called from the Roman practice of writing the names of those proscribed on tablets, which were posted up in the forum, sometimes with the offer of a reward for those who should aid in bringing them to court. If the proscribed did not answer the summons, their goods were confiscated and their persons outlawed. In this case the name was engraved on brass or marble, the offence stated and the tablet placed conspicuously in the market place.

**Prose.** Straightforward speaking or writing (Latin *oratio prosa*), in opposition to foot-bound speaking or writing, *oratio vincta* ('fettered speech'), i.e. poetry.

It was Monsieur Jourdain, in MOLIÈRE's comedy *Le Bourgeois Gentilhomme* (1660), who suddenly discovered that he had been talking prose for 40 years without knowing it.

**Proselyte.** From Greek *proselutos*, one who has come to a place, hence, a convert, especially (in its original application) to Judaism. Among the Jews, proselytes were of two kinds: 'The proselyte of righteousness' and the 'stranger that is within thy gates' (Hellenes). The former submitted to circumcision and conformed to the laws of MOSES. The latter went no further than to refrain from offering sacrifice to heathen gods and from working on the SABBATH.

**Proserpina** or **Proserpine.** The Roman counterpart of the Greek goddess Persephone, queen of the infernal regions and wife of PLUTO, and sometimes identified with HECATE. *See also* DAFFODIL.

**Prosit** (Latin, 'May it benefit [you]'). Good luck to you! A salutation used in drinking a person's health. It is particularly associated with German university students.

**Prosperity Robinson.** *See under* ROBINSON.

**Prospero.** In Shakespeare's last play *The Tempest* (1611), the Duke of Milan who is marooned on an island, where he becomes a magician. He uses his magic to control the monster CALIBAN and the spirit ARIEL, and brings the ship of his usurping brother Antonio to the island for a reconciliation and the marriage of his daughter MIRANDA to Prince Ferdinand. His farewell speech is sometimes interpreted as Shakespeare's own farewell to the stage.

**Protean.** *See* PROTEUS.

**Protectionist.** One who advocates the imposition of import duties, to 'protect' home produce and manufactures. *See also* MERCANTILISM.

**Protector, The.** A title sometimes given in England to the regent during the sovereign's minority.

John of Lancaster, Duke of Bedford, was made Regent of France and Protector of England during the minority (1422–42) of his nephew, Henry VI, and Humphrey, Duke of Gloucester, was Protector during Bedford's absence in France, which was, in fact, for most of the time.

Richard, Duke of Gloucester, was Protector from 1483 until his assumption of the crown as Richard III. He took Edward V into his custody on the death of Edward IV. *See also* PRINCES IN THE TOWER.

Edward Seymour, Duke of Somerset, was Protector (1547–50) and Lord Treasurer in the reign of his nephew, Edward VI (1547–53).

**Protectorate, The.** *See* COMMONWEALTH.

**Lord Protector of the Commonwealth, The.** *See under* LORD.

**Protest, Dirty.** *See under* DIRTY.

**Protestant.** A member of a Christian church upholding the principles of the REFORMATION or (loosely) of any church not in communion with Rome. In the time of Martin Luther (1483–1546) his followers called themselves 'evangelicals'. The name arose from the Lutheran protest against the recess of the Diet of Spires (1529), which declared that the religious *status quo* must be maintained.

**Protestant Pope, The.** Clement XIV (r.1769–74), who ordered the suppression of the JESUITS in 1773. He was a patron of art and a liberal-minded statesman but was under pressure from the BOURBON kings.

**Proteus.** In Greek legend NEPTUNE's herdsman, an old man and a prophet, famous for his power of assuming different shapes at will. Hence the phrase, 'as many shapes as Proteus', i.e. full of shifts, aliases, disguises and so on, and the adjective 'protean', readily taking on different aspects, ever-changing, versatile.

Proteus lived in a vast cave, and his custom was to count up his herds of sea calves at noon, and then to sleep. There was no way of catching him but by stealing upon him at this time and binding him, otherwise he would elude anyone by a rapid change of shape.

**Protevangelium.** The first (Greek *protos*) GOSPEL, a term applied to an apocryphal gospel, which has been attributed to St JAMES THE LESS. It was supposed by some critics that all the gospels were based on this, but it appears to be the compilation of a Jewish Christian from a variety of sources and dates from the 2nd century. The name is also given to the curse upon the SERPENT in Genesis 3:15, which has been regarded as the earliest utterance of the gospel:

> And I will put enmity between thee and the woman, and between thy seed and her seed; it shall bruise thy head, and thou shalt bruise his heel.

*See also* APOCRYPHA.

**Prothalamion.** The term coined by Edmund Spenser (from Greek *thalamos*, 'bridal chamber') as a title for his 'Spousall Verse' (1596) in honour of the double marriage of Lady Elizabeth and Lady Katharine Somerset, daughters of the Earl of Worcester, to Henry Gilford and William Peter, Esquires. Hence a song sung in honour of the bride and bridegroom before the wedding. *See also* EPITHALAMIUM.

**Protocol.** In diplomacy the original draft of a diplomatic document such as a dispatch or treaty. The word comes from Greek *protos*, 'first', and *kolla*, 'glue', this being a sheet glued to the front of a manuscript, or the case containing it, giving certain descriptive particulars. The word also denotes the code of correct procedure, etiquette and ceremonial to be observed in official international exchanges.

**Protocols of the Elders of Zion, The.** *See under* FAKES.

**Protomartyr.** The first martyr (Greek *protos*, 'first'). STEPHEN the deacon is so called (Acts 6, 7), and St ALBAN is known as the protomartyr of Britain.

**Proud. Proud, The.** The following rulers were so called:

Otto IV, Emperor of Germany (*c*.1182–1218)
Tarquin II of Rome, Superbus (r.535–510 BC, d.496)

**Proud Duke, The.** Charles Seymour, 6th Duke of Somerset (1662–1748). He would never permit his children to sit in his presence, and would never communicate with his servants except by signs.

**Do oneself proud, To.** *See under* DO.

**Do someone proud, To.** *See under* DO.

**Stand proud, To.** *See under* STAND.

**Prove one's point, To.** *See* MAKE ONE'S POINT *under* POINT.

**Provider, Lion's.** *See under* LION.

**Provinces, United.** *See under* UNITED.

**Provincial.** Someone who lives in the provinces, at a distance from the metropolis, hence the meaning of narrow and unpolished.

**Provincial of an order, The.** In a religious order, one who has authority over all the houses of that order in a province or given area. He is usually elected by the provincial chapter.

**Provocateur, Agent.** *See under* AGENT.

**Proxime accessit** (Latin *proxime*, 'next', and *accessit*, 'he approached'). An expression used in prize lists and the like for the runner-up, the one who came very near the winner.

**Prud'homme.** In Old French, the word meant a man endowed with all the knightly virtues (*preux homme*), but it later implied a man of proven honesty, experience and knowledge in his craft or trade, whence its specialized meaning in modern French for a member of an Industrial Arbitration Board.

**Prudhommerie.** The loud and pompous enunciation of the obvious, derived from the character Joseph Prud'homme, created by the French writer Henri Monnier (1830).

**Prunella.** A dark, smooth, woollen stuff of which clergymen's and barristers' gowns used to be made, also gaiters and the uppers of boots. It is probably so named from its plum colour (French *prunelle*, 'sloe').

**All leather or prunella.** *See under* ALL.

**Prunes and prisms.** *See* NIMINY-PIMINY.

**Prussian blue.** So called because it was discovered by a Prussian, Diesbach, a colourman of Berlin, in 1704. It was sometimes called Berlin blue. It is made by adding a ferrous sulphate solution to one of potassium ferrocyanide to which ferric chloride is subsequently introduced. Prussic acid (hydrocyanic acid) can be made by distilling Prussian blue. *See also* PROOSHAN BLUE.

**Pry, Paul.** A meddlesome fellow, who has no occupation of his own, and is always interfering with other folk's business. The term comes from the hero of John Poole's comedy, *Paul Pry* (1825).

**PS** (Latin *post scriptum*). Literally, written afterwards, i.e. after the letter or book was finished. Anything added after a PS is a PPS, anything after that, a PPPS and so on.

**Psalmanazar, George.** *See under* FAKES.

**Psalms.** Of the 150 songs in the Book of Psalms, 73 are inscribed with DAVID's name, 12 with that of ASAPH the singer, 11 are attributed to the sons of Korah, a family of singers, and one (Psalm 90) to MOSES. The whole compilation is divided into five books: Book I from 1 to 41, Book II from 42 to 72, Book III from 73 to 89, Book IV from 90 to 106, and Book V from 107 to 150.

Much of the Book of Psalms was for centuries attributed to David (hence called 'the sweet psalmist of Israel') but it is doubtful if he wrote any of them. The tradition comes from the author of Chronicles, and 2 Samuel 22 is a psalm attributed to David that is identical with Psalm 18. Also, the last verse of Psalm 72 ('The prayers of David the son of Jesse are ended') seems to suggest that he was the author up to that point.

In explanation of the confusion between the Roman Catholic and Protestant psalters, it should be noted that Psalms 9 and 10 in the BOOK OF COMMON PRAYER version (also in the Authorized and Revised Versions of the Bible) are combined in the Roman Catholic Psalter to form Psalm 9, and Psalms 114 and 115 in the Book of Common Prayer are combined in the Roman Catholic Psalter to form Psalm 113. Again, Psalm 116 in the Book of Common Prayer is split to form Psalms 114 and 115 in the Roman Catholic Psalter, and Psalm 147 in the Book of Common Prayer is split to form Psalms 146 and 147 in the Roman Catholic Psalter. Thus only the first eight and the last three Psalms coincide numerically in both psalters.

**Bay Psalm Book, The.** *See under* BAY.
**Gradual Psalms.** *See under* GRADUAL.
**Penitential psalms.** *See under* PENITENTIAL.
**Seven penitential psalms.** *See under* SEVEN.

**Pseudepigrapha** (Greek, 'falsely ascribed'). In biblical scholarship, a term applied to certain pseudonymous Jewish writings such as the 'Book of Enoch', the 'Assumption of MOSES', the 'Psalms of SOLOMON', the 'Fourth Book of the MACCABEES' and others, which were excluded from the CANON of the OLD TESTAMENT and from the APOCRYPHA.

**Pseudonym.** *See* NOM DE PLUME.

**Psmith.** The eccentric young snob created by P.G. Wodehouse (1881–1975) for a series of stories, and first appearing in a boys' paper, the *Captain*, in 1908. His full name is Ronald Eustace Rupert Smith, and the initial P is an affectation, as is the monocle that he sports. Although educated at Eton, he claims to be a socialist and calls everyone 'Comrade'.

**Psyche** (Greek, 'breath', hence, 'life', 'soul'). In 'the latest-born of the myths', *Cupid and Psyche*, an episode in the GOLDEN ASS, Psyche is a beautiful maiden beloved by CUPID, who visited her every night but departed at sunrise. Cupid bade her never seek to know who he was, but one night curiosity got the better of her. She lit the lamp to look at him, a drop of hot oil fell on his shoulder, and he awoke and fled. The abandoned Psyche then wandered far and wide in search of her lover. She became the slave of VENUS, who imposed on her heartless tasks and treated her most cruelly. Ultimately she was united to Cupid and became immortal. The tale appears in Walter Pater's *Marius the Epicurean* (1885).

**Psychological moment, The.** The moment when the mind is readiest to receive suggestions from another. It is an inaccurate translation of the German *das psychologische Moment*, which means 'momentum', not 'moment'. It is incorrectly applied when the idea of mental receptivity is absent, but it is popularly used to mean 'the opportune moment', 'the most effective time'.

**Ptah.** The builder of the world in Egyptian mythology. He was originally the local deity of Memphis, but his cult then spread to cover the whole of Egypt. The Greeks identified Ptah with Hephaestus (VULCAN). His name means 'to ask' or 'to open'.

**Ptolemy.** The name of a dynasty of 15 Macedonian kings of Egypt. They reigned longer than any other house in the Alexandrian Empire, and succumbed to the Romans only in 30 BC. Chronologically, with their Greek bynames, they run as follows:

Ptolemy I, Soter ('saviour') (367–283 BC), general of Alexander the Great
Ptolemy II, Philadelphus ('brother-loving') (308–246 BC)
Ptolemy III, Euergetes ('benefactor') (*fl.*246–221 BC)
Ptolemy IV, Philopator ('father-loving') (*c.*238–205 BC)
Ptolemy V, Epiphanes ('illustrious') (*c.*210–180 BC)
Ptolemy VI, Philometor ('mother-loving') (*fl.c.*180–145 BC)
Ptolemy VII, Neos Philopator ('new Philopator') (d.144 BC)
Ptolemy VIII, Euergetes II ('benefactor') (d.116 BC)
Ptolemy IX, Soter II ('saviour') (*fl.* 2nd–1st century BC)
Ptolemy X, Alexander (d.88 BC)
Ptolemy XI, Alexander II (*c.*115–80 BC)
Ptolemy XII, Auletes ('flute player') (*c.*112–51 BC)
Ptolemy XIII, Theos Philopator ('god and father-lover') (63–47 BC), co-ruler with his sister, CLEOPATRA
Ptolemy XIV, Theos Philopator II (*c.*59–44 BC), co-ruler with his elder sister, Cleopatra
Ptolemy XV, Caesar (47–30 BC), son of Julius CAESAR and Cleopatra

Distinct from them is Ptolemy (*fl.* AD 127–145), the ancient astronomer, geographer and mathematician, who considered the earth to be the centre of the universe.

The name Ptolemy represents Greek *Ptolemaios*, from *ptolemos*, a poetic form of *polemos*, 'battle'.

**Ptolemaic system.** The system to account for the apparent motion of the heavenly bodies expounded in the 2nd century by PTOLEMY, the astronomer of Alexandria. He taught that the earth is fixed in the centre of the universe and that the heavens revolve around it from east to west, carrying with them the SUN, the PLANETS and the fixed stars, in their respective spheres, which he imagined as solid coverings (like so many skins of an onion) each revolving at a

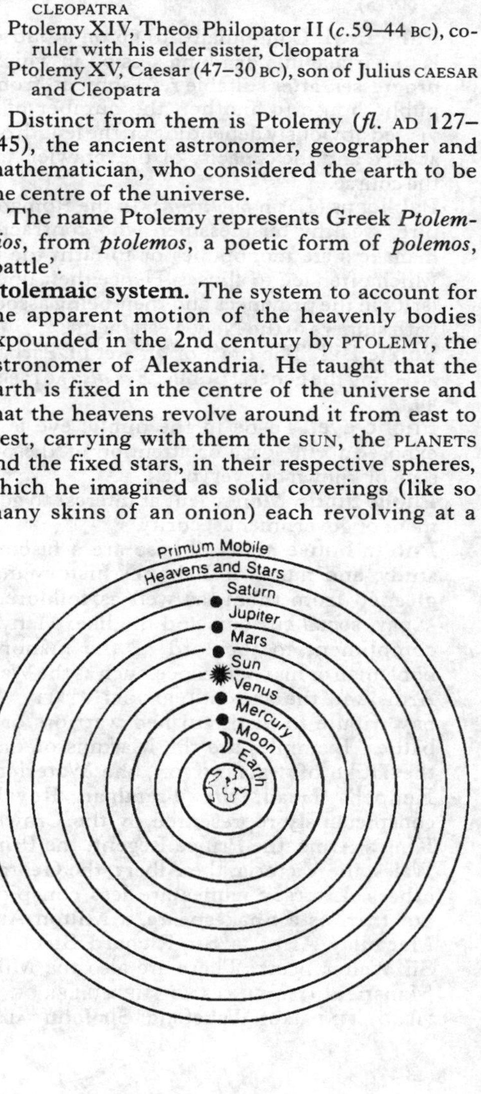

different velocity. The tenth or outer sphere was the PRIMUM MOBILE. This theory was an attempt to systematize theories long held by PLATO, ARISTOTLE, Hipparchus and others, and it substantially held sway until replaced by the COPERNICAN SYSTEM.

**Puberty, Age of.** *See under* AGE.

**Public** (Latin *publicus*, from *populus*, 'the people'). The people, generally and collectively, of a state, nation or community. Also a former contraction of 'public house', now more usually contracted to 'pub'.

> The simple life I can't afford,
> Besides, I do not like the grub –
> I want a mash and sausage, 'scored' –
> Will someone take me to a pub?
>
> G.K. CHESTERTON: 'Ballad of an Anti-Puritan' (1915)

**Pub-crawl.** Colloquially, to go on a pub-crawl is to partake in a drinking session in which one progresses, after suitable refreshment, from one public house to another, the number of such visited obviously depending on the length of stay at each and the capacity of the 'crawler' to stay the course.

**Publicans** (Latin *publicani*). In the Roman Empire, wealthy businessmen who contracted to manage state monopolies or to farm the taxes, which often led to abuses. Hence their unpopularity in the provinces and their being associated with sinners in the New Testament.

**Public Bill.** The draft of an Act of Parliament affecting the general public. *See also* ACT; PRIVATE BILL.

**Public eye.** To be in the public eye is to be exposed to the gaze or attention of the public, seen or known by everyone.

**Public funds.** Money lent at interest to government or government security.

**Public house signs.** These are a fascinating study, and much of Britain's history may be gleaned from them, as well as folklore, HERALDRY, social customs and the like. Many are a compliment to the lord of the manor or a nobleman or his cognizance, such as the Warwick Arms and the BEAR AND RAGGED STAFF. Others pay tribute to distinguished warriors or their battles. Examples are the Marquis of GRANBY, the Duke of WELLINGTON, the Waterloo, the Keppel's Head, the Trafalgar. Royalty is conspicuously represented by the Crown, the King's Arms, the Prince Regent, the Prince of Wales, the Victoria, the Albert, the George and others. Literary names are less conspicuous, but there is a Shakespeare, a Milton Arms, a Macaulay Arms, a Sir Richard Steele and a Sir Walter Scott. There are also the Miller of Mansfield (*see* KING AND THE MILLER OF MANSFIELD), PINDAR of Wakefield, Sir John FALSTAFF, Robinson CRUSOE and VALENTINE AND ORSON. Simon the Tanner, the GOOD SAMARITAN, NOAH'S ARK, the Gospel Oak and the Angel have a biblical flavour, while myth and legend are represented by the APOLLO, the HERCULES, the PHOENIX, King LUD, MERLIN's Cave, the MAN IN THE MOON, Punch, the ROBIN HOOD, the MOONRAKERS, Cat and the Fiddle and many others.

Some signs indicate sporting associations, such as the Cricketers, the Bat and Ball, the Bowling Green, the Angler's Rest and the Huntsman, or else trades associations, such as Coopers', Bricklayers', Plumbers', Carpenters', Masons' Arms and the like. Others show a whimsical turn as the Who'd a Thought It, the Five Alls, the WORLD TURNED UPSIDE DOWN and the Good Woman. More recently a fashion for homely names has shown itself, as the Slug and Lettuce, the Crab and Winkle, the Flower Pot, the Hungry Horse and the Spotted Cow.

Among the most common signs are the Bell, the Black Bull, the Blue Bell, the Crown, the Five Bells, the George, the King's Head, the Nag's Head, the New Inn, the Plough, the Red Lion, the Rose and Crown, the Royal Oak, the Ship, the Three Horseshoes, the Three Tuns, the Wheatsheaf, the White Hart and the White Horse.

The following list will exemplify the subject:

Bag o'Nails: from a tradesman's sign, that of an ironmonger; said unconvincingly by some 19th-century writers to be a corruption of 'Bacchanals'
Bear: from the popular sport of bear-baiting
Bell: mostly derived from the national addiction to bell-ringing
Bell Savage: *see* BELLE SAUVAGE
BLUE BOAR
Blue Lion: the sign of Denmark, possibly a compliment to James I's queen, Anne of Denmark (1574–1619), but also the badge of the Earl of Mortimer
BOLT IN TUN: the punning heraldic badge of Prior Bolton, last of the clerical rulers of St Bartholomew's before the REFORMATION
BULL AND GATE
CASE IS ALTERED
CAT AND FIDDLE
CAT AND KITTENS
Cat and Wheel: a corruption of St CATHERINE's wheel
CHEQUERS
Coach and Horses: a favourite sign of a posting house or stage coach inn
COCK AND BOTTLE
CROSS KEYS
Devil: *see* GO TO THE DEVIL
DIRTY DICK'S
Dog and Duck : an indication that the 'sport' so called could be seen there; a duck with pinioned wings was put in the water and a dog set to hunt it; the fun was to see the duck dive as its sole means of escape and the dog follow it under water
Five Alls: consists of a king (I rule all), a priest

(I pray for all), a soldier (I fight for all), a JOHN BULL or a farmer (I pay for all) and a lawyer (I plead for all)

Four Alls: the first four of the FIVE ALLS

Fox and Goose: sometimes signifying that there were arrangements within for playing the game of fox and goose

GOAT AND COMPASSES

Golden Cross: a reference to the emblems carried by the crusaders

GOLDEN FLEECE: an allusion to the Greek fable and to the woollen trade

Golden Lion: the badge of Henry I and the PERCY family of Northumberland

GOOSE AND GRIDIRON

GREEN MAN and the Green Man and Still

HEARTS OF OAK: a compliment to the British naval tradition

HOLE IN THE WALL: perhaps an allusion to the hole in the wall of a prison through which the inmates received donations, or a reference to the narrow alley or passage by which the tavern was approached

Horse and Jockey: an obvious allusion to the TURF

Man with a Load of Mischief: a sign in Oxford Street, London, nearly opposite Hanway Yard, said to have been painted by Hogarth, showing a man carrying a woman with a glass of gin in her hand, a magpie and a monkey

Marquis of GRANBY: in compliment to John Manners (1721–70), eldest son of John, 3rd Duke of Rutland, a bluff, brave soldier, generous and greatly beloved by his men

Nag's Head: probably indicating that this small riding horse was available for hire at the inn

New Inn: replacing an earlier inn on the site; inns of this name are often very old

PIG AND TINDERBOX

Pig and Whistle: said by some to be a corruption of pig and wassail, pig being an abbreviation of piggin, an earthen vessel; or a facetious form of the BEAR AND RAGGED STAFF; or simply a sign-painter's whimsy

Plough: the agricultural implement rather than the group of seven stars, although often represented as the latter

Plume of Feathers: the Prince of Wales's Feathers, the plume of three ostrich feathers first adopted as a crest by the Black Prince.

QUEEN OF BOHEMIA: in honour of James I's daughter Elizabeth, who married Frederick, Elector of the Palatinate, who was chosen king of Bohemia in 1619

Red Cow: possibly because at one time red cows were more esteemed in England than the more common 'black'

Red Lion: the Scottish lion rampant; also the badge of JOHN OF GAUNT, Duke of Lancaster, the most common pub name and sign in Britain

Rising Sun: a badge of Edward III

ROSE: a symbol of England

Rose and Crown: a sign of loyalty to the monarch and to England

Royal Oak: a reference to Charles II, who hid in an oak tree after his defeat at the Battle of Worcester in 1651; *see also* OAK-APPLE DAY

RUNNING FOOTMAN: from the liveried servant who used to run before the nobleman's carriage to clear people from its path.

Salutation: refers to the Annunciation, the greeting and proclamation of the angel Gabriel to the Virgin MARY

Saracen's Head: reminiscent of the CRUSADES

SEVEN STARS: an astrological sign

Ship: a general allusion to Britain's maritime heritage

Ship and Shovel: refers to the labourers who shovelled grain or coal from ships and barges

Star and Garter: the insignia of the MOST NOBLE ORDER OF THE GARTER

St GEORGE and the Dragon: in compliment to the patron saint of England

Swan and Harp: *see* GOOSE AND GRIDIRON

SWAN WITH TWO NECKS

TABARD

Talbot (a hound): the arms of the Talbot family

Three Horseshoes: the arms of the Worshipful Company of Farriers and of the Ferrers family, the earls of Derby

Three Kings: an allusion to the THREE KINGS OF COLOGNE, the MAGI

Three Tuns: a reference to the arms of both the Worshipful Company of Vintners and the Worshipful Company of Brewers

Turk's Head: like the Saracen's Head, an allusion to the CRUSADES

Two Chairmen: found in the neighbourhood of fashionable quarters when sedan chairs were in vogue

UNICORN: the Scottish supporter in the royal arms of Great Britain

Wheatsheaf: found in many coats of arms, including that of the Brewers' Company

WHITE HART: the cognizance of Richard II

White Horse: a widespread heraldic symbol, occurring in many coats of arms, including those of many London Guilds; it was also the symbol of the kings of Wessex

White Lion: the cognizance of Edward IV as Earl of March; also the device of the Dukes of Norfolk, the Earls of Surrey etc

Stephen Glover's *History and Directory of the Borough of Derby* (1843) includes the following names of taverns and public houses:

Bishop Blaze, Black Boy, Brick and Tile, Brown Bear, Buck-in-the-Park, Bunch of Grapes, Castle and Falcon, Dog and Duck, Dog and Partridge, Druids' Arms, Dusty Miller, Earl Grey, Fox and Goose, Green Man, Hawk and Buckle, Hen and Chickens, Horse and Trumpet, Jolly Toper, Lion and Tigress, Noah's Ark, Old Flower Pot, Old Neptune, Old Spot, Old Tiger, Punch Bowl, Seven Stars, Stag and Pheasant, Swan with Two Necks, Three Jolly Butchers, Woodman's Stroke.

*See also* COCK AND BULL STORY; MERMAID TAVERN; OLD CHAPEL.

**Public school.** The schools so designated are in fact private (fee-paying) and independent. They came to be so called in the 18th century when the reputation of GRAMMAR SCHOOLS spread beyond their immediate neighbourhood and they began taking resident students from elsewhere. They were thus public, or open to all, and not simply local.

The nine best known public schools, with their location and years of foundation, are:

Winchester College, Hampshire (1382)
Eton College, Berkshire (1440)
St Paul's School, London (1509)
Shrewsbury School, Shropshire (1552)
Westminster School, London (1560)
Merchant Taylors' School, London (1560)
Rugby School, Warwickshire (1567)
Harrow School, Greater London (1571)
Charterhouse School, Godalming, Surrey (1611)

Most public schools, although originally founded as boys' schools, are now coeducational, or at least take girls in the sixth form. Of those above, however, in the late 1990s, only Rugby was fully coeducational, with Westminster and Charterhouse having simply a sixth form intake.

The 12 oldest girls' public schools are:

Red Maids' School, Bristol (1634)
New Hall School, Chelmsford (1642)
Queen Anne's School, Reading (1698)
Dame Allan's Girls' School, Newcastle (1705)
Lady Eleanor Holles School, Hampton (1711)
St David's School, Ashford, Middlesex (1716)
Sir William Perkins's School, Chertsey (1725)
Godolphin School, Salisbury (1726)
James Allen's Girls' School, London (1741)
St Margaret's School, Bushey (1749)
Royal Masonic School, Hertfordshire (1788)
Ockbrook School, Derby (1799)

In American usage, a public school is just the opposite, as its name rightly implies, and is thus a school that is not under private ownership and control.

**Joe Public.** *See under* JOE.

**Pucelle, La** (French, 'The Maid'). The Maid of Orleans, JOAN OF ARC. Both Jean Chapelain and VOLTAIRE wrote poems with this title, respectively in 1656 and 1755.

**Puck.** A mischievous sprite of popular folklore, also called ROBIN GOODFELLOW. In Edmund Spenser's *Epithalamion* (1595) he is an evil goblin, but Shakespeare's *A Midsummer Night's Dream* (II, i (1595)) shows him as:

> that shrewd and knavish sprite
> Call'd Robin Goodfellow: are you not he
> That frights the maidens of the villagery;
> Skim milk, and sometimes labour in the quern,
> And bootless make the breathless housewife churn;
> And sometime make the drink to bear no barm;
> Mislead night-wanderers, laughing at their harm?
> Those that Hobgoblin call you and sweet Puck,
> You do their work, and they shall have good luck.

**Pudding. College pudding.** *See under* COLLEGE.

**Proof of the pudding is in the eating, The.** *See under* PROOF.

**Summer pudding.** *See under* SUMMER.

**Pueblo.** The Spanish word meaning 'people' (Latin *populus*), hence a town or village. It has been applied particularly to the peace-loving Indians of New Mexico and Arizona, and to their communal villages.

**Puff.** An onomatopoeic word, suggestive of the sound made by puffing wind from the mouth. Since at least the early 17th century it has been applied to extravagantly worded advertisements, reviews and the like with the implication that they have as much lasting value as a 'puff of wind'.

In R.B. Sheridan's *The Critic*, I, ii (1779), Puff, who, he himself says, is 'a practitioner in panegyric, or, to speak more plainly, a professor of the art of puffing', gives a catalogue of puffs:

> Yes, sir – puffing is of various sorts, the principal are, the puff direct, the puff preliminary, the puff collateral, the puff collusive and the puff oblique, or puff by implication. These all assume, as circumstances require, the various forms of letter to the editor, occasional anecdote, impartial critique, observation from correspondent, or advertisement from the party.

**Puffball.** A fungus of the genus *Lycoperdon*, so called because it is ball-shaped and when it is ripe it bursts and the spores come out in a 'puff' of fine powder.

**Puffed up.** Conceited; elated with conceit or praise; filled with wind. A puff is a tartlet with a very light or puffy crust.

**Puisne judges.** Formerly justices and barons of the COMMON LAW courts at Westminster other than the Chief Justices, and by the Judicature Act of 1877, Judges of the High Court other than the LORD CHANCELLOR, the Lord Chief Justice, the MASTER OF THE ROLLS, the Lord Chief Justice of the Common Pleas and the Lord Chief Baron (the last two offices becoming defunct). Since the Judicature Act of 1925 the term has applied to Judges of the High Court other than the Lord Chancellor, the Lord Chief Justice, or the President of the Probate Division (now the Family Division), but is not usually attached to the Master of the Rolls. *Puisne* is etymologically the same as 'puny'. It comes from Old French *puisne*, 'born later' (Latin *post natus*) and signifies 'junior' or 'inferior in rank'.

**Pukka sahib.** A now dated term for a 'real gentleman'. It arose as a military slang term in India in the 19th century, with *pukka* a Hindi word meaning 'cooked', 'substantial' and *sahib* an Urdu word from Arabic, meaning literally 'friend'.

**Pulitzer prizes.** Prizes for literary work, journalism, drama and music, which are awarded annually from funds left for the purpose by Joseph Pulitzer (1847–1911), a prominent and wealthy Hungarian-born American editor and newspaper proprietor.

**Pull.** The act of drawing or tugging to oneself, hence, figuratively, 'influence', especially with those in control. *See also* PULL STRINGS.

**Pull a face, To.** To grimace, especially intentionally in order to insult or amuse.

**Pull a fast one, To.** To obtain an advantage by a trick or by somewhat questionable means. The phrase is said to have its origin in cricket matches of the 1930s, when the English captain, Douglas Jardine, instructed his fast bowlers, Larwood and Voce, to abandon gentlemanly deliveries and simply hurl the ball at the far wicket. Such 'bodyline' bowling produced the desired results, and the intimidated batsmen were speedily dismissed.

**Pull a rabbit out of the hat, To.** To come up with a solution to a problem when success seemed impossible; to bring off a coup. An allusion to the conjuror's art.

**Pull Devil, pull baker.** Said in encouragement of a contest, usually over the possession of something.

**Pull oneself together, To.** To rouse oneself to renewed activity; to shake off depression or inertia.

**Pull one's punches, To.** Not to be as blunt as one could be, to soften the blow and to avoid offence by holding back a little. In boxing, blows delivered intentionally ineffectively are said to be 'pulled'.

**Pull one's socks up, To.** To PULL ONESELF TOGETHER and endeavour to do better.

**Pull one's weight, To.** To do the very best one can, to play one's proper part. A phrase from rowing: an oarsman who does not put all his weight into the stroke is a drag on the rest of the crew and something of a passenger.

**Pull out all the stops, To.** To make a supreme effort to achieve one's objective. The allusion is to a church organist, who produces maximum volume by pulling out all the stops.

**Pull rank, To.** To obtain an advantage or concession by virtue of one's superior position.

**Pull someone's leg, To.** To tease a person; to chaff someone; to make fun of them. The reference is to tripping someone up by kicking their legs from under them or by hooking their legs with a stick or with one's own leg.

**Pull strings, To.** To use private influence 'behind the scenes'. The allusion is to the puppeteer who controls the movements of the puppets by the strings attached to them. A person who essentially controls the actions of another is similarly said to pull the strings.

**Pull the chestnuts out of the fire, To.** To retrieve a difficult situation for someone, to get someone out of an embarrassment. The allusion is to the fable of the monkey and the cat. *See also* CAT'S PAW.

**Pull the other one!** Said as an expression of disbelief to a person regarded as teasing one. A person inclined to PULL SOMEONE'S LEG might well wish to pull the other one as well.

**Pull the plug, To.** To put an end to an enterprise; to cut off supplies or the like. The allusion is to letting the water run out of a bath or basin.

**Pull the wool over someone's eyes, To.** To deceive or hoodwink them; to blind them temporarily to what is going on.

**Pull through, To.** To get oneself well out of difficulty or serious illness.

**Pull together, To.** To cooperate harmoniously.

**Pull up the ladder, Jack, I'm inboard.** The nautical equivalent of 'I'm all right, Jack' denoting the pursuit of self-interest and the complete disregard of the interest of others. The allusion is obvious. *I'm All Right Jack* (1959), starring Peter Sellers as a shop steward, was a shrewd satirical farce on the industrial and political attitudes of the day and one of his finest films.

> It's 'Damn you, Jack – I'm all right!' with you chaps.
>
> SIR DAVID BONE, *Brassbounder*, ch iii (1910)

**Pull wires, To.** The same as to PULL STRINGS.

**Have a pull over someone, To.** To have an advantage over them; to be able to dictate terms or make them do what one wants.

**Long pull, The.** *See under* LONG.

**Long pull, a strong pull, and a pull all together, A.** *See under* LONG.

**Pullman.** Properly a well-fitted railway saloon or sleeping car built at the Pullman Carriage Works, Illinois. It is so called from the designer, George M. Pullman (1831–97) of Chicago. The word is now applied to other well-appointed railway coaches and motor transport.

**Pummel.** *See* POMMEL.

**Pump. Pump iron, To.** To do body-building exercises, the idea being that one 'pumps' one's body so that it is firm and 'hard as iron'.

**Pump someone, To.** To extract information from them by artful questions, as one draws water from a well by gradual pumping.

**Parish pump.** *See under* PARISH.

**Prime the pump, To.** *See under* PRIME.

**Pumpernickel.** The name of a slightly sour black bread, made of coarse rye flour, eaten in Germany, especially in Westphalia. W.M. Thackeray applied the term as a satirical nickname to petty German princelings ('His Transparency, the Duke of Pumpernickel') who made a great show with the court officials and etiquette, but whose revenue was almost nil. The word is of uncertain origin, although a derivation in German *pumpern*, 'to break wind', and NICKEL, 'goblin', has been proposed. Such a term of abuse (roughly meaning 'Farty Nick') would then have been transferred to the bread for the latter's own gas-creating potential in the human digestive system.

**Punch.** The name of this beverage, which was introduced into England in the early 17th century, is usually held to derive from Hindi *pānch*, 'five', because it has five principal ingredients (spirit, water, spice, sugar and fruit juice). It may equally derive from 'puncheon', the large wine cask.

**Punch and Judy.** The name of Mr Punch, the hero of the puppet play, probably comes from Italian *pulcinello*, a diminutive of *pulcino*, a young chicken. His identification with Pontius Pilate and of Judy with JUDAS ISCARIOT is imaginary. The story roughly in its present form is attributed to an Italian comedian, Silvio Fiorillo (*fl.*1600), and it appeared in England about the time of the RESTORATION. Punch, in a fit of jealousy, strangles his infant child, whereupon his wife Judy belabours him with a bludgeon until he retaliates and beats her to death. He flings both bodies into the street, but is arrested and shut in prison whence he escapes by means of a golden key. The rest is an allegory showing how the light-hearted Punch triumphs over (1) Ennui, in the shape of a dog, (2) Disease, in the disguise of a doctor, (3) Death, who is beaten to death, and (4) the Devil himself, who is outwitted. In subsequent English versions JACK KETCH, instead of hanging Punch, gets hanged himself.

The satirical humorous weekly paper, *Punch, or The London Charivari*, was named after Mr Punch, who naturally featured prominently on the cover design for very many issues. It first appeared in July 1841 under the editorship of Mark Lemon (1809–70) and Henry Mayhew (1812–87). Its falling circulation led to its closure in 1992 but it was relaunched in 1996.

**Punch drunk, To be.** To experience a form of concussion to which boxers are liable, causing unsteadiness of gait resembling drunkenness, used figuratively of someone 'reeling from heavy punishment'.

**Punch line.** A vivid, often surprising climax to an anecdote, joke, story or the like, which gives point to all that has gone before. The figurative 'punch' suggests that the listener is struck by this line.

**As pleased as Punch.** *See under* AS.

**Devil's Punch Bowl.** *See under* DEVIL.

**Pinch and a punch for the first of the month, A.** *See under* PINCH.

**Pull one's punches, To.** *See under* PULL.

**Suffolk punch.** *See under* SUFFOLK.

**Sunday punch.** *See under* SUNDAY.

**Punctual.** No bigger than a point, exact to a point or moment (Latin *ad punctum*). Hence the angel, describing this earth to ADAM calls it, 'This spacious earth, this punctual spot', i.e. a spot not bigger than a point (Milton, *Paradise Lost*, viii (1667)).

**Punctuality is the politeness of kings** (French *L'exactitude est la politesse des rois*). A favourite maxim of Louis XVIII, but erroneously attributed by Samuel Smiles to Louis XIV.

**Pundit** (Hindi *pandit*). In India, a learned man, one versed in Sanskrit, law, religion and the like. The word came to be used generally for a learned man, an expert, an authority.

**Punic. Punic apple.** A POMEGRANATE or apple belonging to the genus *Punica*.

**Punic faith** (Latin *punica fides*). Treachery; violation of faith; the faith of the Carthaginians. The Phoenicians (Latin *Punicus*, 'Phoenician') founded Carthage, and the long-drawn-out Punic Wars between Rome and Carthage ended in the latter's destruction. The Roman accusations of breach of faith were classic instances of the POT CALLING THE KETTLE BLACK. *See also* ATTIC FAITH.

**Punishment, Capital.** *See under* CAPITAL.

**Punk.** An old word for a harlot, a worthless person or thing. In recent times it came to be applied to certain young people wearing bizarre clothes and hairstyles, and to the music they favoured. *See also* HELL'S ANGELS; MODS AND ROCKERS; SKINHEADS.

**Punk rock.** A form of pop music of a coarse and cacophonous character, as typified by the Sex Pistols. The heyday of British punk was the 1970s, and when this group disbanded in 1978, the punk revolution was to all intents and purposes over. Punk rock itself was then succeeded by a rather more melodious 'post-punk' idiom.

**Pup.** As applied to the young of dogs, the word is an abbreviation of 'puppy', which represents French *poupée*, a dressed doll, a plaything. An empty-headed, impertinent young fellow is frequently called a young puppy

**Hush puppy.** *See under* HUSH.

**Sold a pup, To be.** *See under* SELL.

**Purchase, Louisiana, The.** *See under* LOUISIANA.

**Pure. As pure as the driven snow.** *See under* AS.

**Simon Pure.** *See under* SIMON.

**Purgatory.** The doctrine of Purgatory, according to which the souls of the departed suffer for a time until they are purged of their sins, is of ancient standing, and in certain phases of Jewish belief GEHENNA seems to have been regarded partly as a place of purgatory.

The early church Fathers developed the concept of purgatory and support for the doctrine was adduced from 2 Maccabees 39–45, Matthew 12:32, 1 Corinthians 3:11–13, and elsewhere. The first decree on the subject was promulgated by the Council of Florence in 1439. It was rejected by the CHURCH OF ENGLAND in 1562 by Article XXII of the Articles of Religion.

**St Patrick's Purgatory.** *See under* PATRICK.

**Purge, Pride's.** *See under* PRIDE'S.

**Purification, Feast of.** *See* CANDLEMAS DAY.

**Puritans.** The more extreme PROTESTANTS inside and outside the CHURCH OF ENGLAND who found the Elizabethan religious settlement unacceptable and wished a further 'purification' of religion. They looked more and more to the Bible as the sole authority, rejecting all tradition in matters of public worship, and were mainly Calvinist in outlook and theology. They feature in the 16th and 17th centuries as BAPTISTS, BARROWISTS, PRESBYTERIANS, SEPARATISTS and INDEPENDENTS, and were sometimes called Precisionists from their punctiliousness over religious rules and observances. After the RESTORATION and the Act of Uniformity (1662), they became collectively known as DISSENTERS or NONCONFORMISTS.

**Purlieu.** The outlying parts of a place, the environs and originally the borders or outskirts of a forest, especially that which was formerly part of the forest. The word is a corruption of Old French *pouralee* ('a going round'), the *lieu*, as though for 'place', being an erroneous addition due to English pronunciation and spelling of the French. Thus Henry III (r.1216–72) allowed certain portions around the forests, acquired by his predecessors by unlawful encroachment, to be freed from the forest laws and restored to former owners. The boundaries were then settled by a perambulation or 'purale'. *See also* FOREST COURTS.

**Purple.** A synonym for the rank of Roman emperor, derived from the colour of the emperor's dyed woollen robe, hence phrases such as 'raised to the purple'. Purple robes were a mark of dignity among the ancient Greeks and Romans and were worn by kings, magistrates and military commanders, hence purple became a symbol of luxury and power. It was obtained from shellfish (*Buccinum*, *Murex*) and the deep colour was termed *purpura* (from the name of one of these molluscs). Tyrian purple, which was made from a mixture of these shellfish, was very costly to produce. Differing shades were obtained by various combinations and methods. Since Roman times, purple has been used in the insignia of emperors, kings and prelates, and a priest is said to be raised to the purple when he is created CARDINAL, although his insignia are actually red. Purpure is one of the tinctures used in HERALDRY, and in engravings it is shown by lines running diagonally from sinister to dexter (i.e. from right to left as one looks at it). *See also* COLOURS.

**Purple emperor.** One of the largest and most richly coloured British butterflies, *Apatura iris*. Only the male has the purple sheen.

**Purple Heart.** A US army medal awarded for wounds received by enemy action while on active service. It consists of a silver heart bearing the effigy of George Washington, suspended from a purple ribbon with white edges.

The heartwood of *Copaifera pubiflora* and *C. bracteata* is called purple heart or purple wood. It is native to Guyana and a rich plum colour, and was used in making ramrods for guns. 'Purple heart' is also the popular name of a stimulant pill (Drinamyl), once favoured by drug-takers and so called from its shape and colour.

**Purple patches.** Highly coloured or florid patches in a literary work that is generally undistinguished. The allusion is to Horace's *De Arte Poetica*, xiv (1st century BC):

> Inceptis gravibus plerumque et magna professis
> Purpureus, late qui splendeat, unus et alter
> Adsuitur pannus.
> (Often to weighty enterprises and such as profess great objects, one or two purple patches are sewn on to make a fine display in the distance.)

**Born in the purple, To be.** *See* PORPHYROGENITUS.

**Purposes, At cross.** *See under* AT.

**Purse. Hold the purse strings, To.** *See under* HOLD.

**Make a silk purse out of a sow's ear, To.** *See under* SILK.

**Pursuivant.** The lowest grade of the officers of arms consisting of the Heralds' College, the others, under the EARL MARSHAL, being (1) the Kings of Arms, and (2) the HERALDS. England has four Pursuivants, i.e. ROUGE CROIX, BLUEMANTLE, ROUGE DRAGON and Portcullis; Scotland has three, i.e. Carrick, Kintyre and Unicorn.

**Purveyance.** A doublet of providence, from Latin *providentia*, 'foresight'. Historically, it is the crown prerogative of purchasing provisions and the like for the royal household at an appraised price and of impressing horses and vehicles. With an itinerant court such compulsory purchases caused much local hardship, especially as ready payment was rare, and from the late 13th century protests led to statutes against its abuse. It was largely abolished in 1660 but the purveyance of horses by the army was practised in the First World War, and this and the right of impressment of vehicles still exist for the armed services. The current use of compulsory purchase orders on properties has much in common with practices denounced under the early Stuart kings.

**Puseyite.** A HIGH CHURCH follower of Edward Bouverie Pusey (1800–82), who was Professor of Hebrew at Oxford, one of the leaders of the OXFORD MOVEMENT, and a contributor to *Tracts for the Times*. Hence Puseyism as an unfriendly name for Tractarianism.

**Push. Push-button civilization.** A phrase descriptive of the highly industrialized nations of the world where household chores are performed and entertainment provided by electrical appliances operated by 'push-button' controls.

**Pushed, To be.** To be pushed for time. The idea is that one is under pressure to complete something in a limited time.

**Push off, To.** To depart, to commence the operations. A phrase from boating: one starts by pushing the boat off from the bank. Used imperatively, 'Push off' means 'Go away', 'Get out of here'.

**Push one's luck, To.** To exceed what one can reasonably hope to gain from a favourable situation; to go too far in one's greed or ambition.

**Push the boat out, To.** A popular expression meaning to celebrate by treating one's acquaintances to a drinking session. The expression is of nautical origin, probably from the idea of a final celebration before sailing, to give impetus to one's departure.

**Push up the daisies, To.** To be dead and buried.

**Did she fall or was she pushed?** *See under* FALL.

**Get the push, To.** To be dismissed; to be sacked.

**When push comes to shove.** *See under* WHEN.

**Puss.** A conventional call-name for a cat, possibly imitative of a cat-like sound. The word was also applied in the 17th century to hares. The derivation from Latin *lepus*, 'a hare', Frenchified into *le pus*, is, of course, only facetious.

**Puss in Boots.** This nursery tale, *Le Chat Botté*, is from Straparola's *Nights* (1530), No. xi, in which Constantine's cat procures his master a fine castle and the king's heiress. It was translated from the Italian into French, in 1585, and appeared in Charles Perrault's *Les contes de ma Mère l'Oye* (1697), through which medium it reached England. In the story the clever cat secures a fortune and a royal partner for his master, who passes off as the Marquis of Carabas but is, in reality, a young miller without a penny in the world.

**Puss in the corner.** An old game in which a boy or a girl stands in each corner of a room and a fifth player in the middle. Those in the corners change positions in a succession and the centre player tries to occupy a vacated corner before another can reach it. If achieved, the loser occupies the centre.

**Pussyfoot.** A person with a soft, cat-like, sneaking tread, and from Pussyfoot JOHNSON, the word is now applied as a noun to advocates of, and as an adjective to opinions or legislation promoting, total abstinence.

**Pussyfoot Johnson.** *See under* JOHNSON.

**Put.** For expressions containing the verb 'put' see under the first main word of the phrase or expression.

**Putsch.** A German word, the same as English 'push', applied to a COUP DE MAIN or political uprising.

**Putty medal.** Used in expressions such as 'that's worth a putty medal' and at first as a sarcastic comment implying that a putty medal was a suitable reward for an incompetent performance or attempt. Subsequently it became a jocular recognition of a praiseworthy effort and was intended to encourage.

**Pygmalion.** In Greek legend, a sculptor and king of Cyprus. According to Ovid's *Metamorphoses* (1st century AD) he fell in love with his own ivory statue of his own ideal woman. At his earnest prayer the goddess APHRODITE gave life to the statue and he married it. The story is found in John Marston's *Metamorphosis of Pygmalion's Image* (1598). William Morris retold it in *The Earthly Paradise* (*August*) (1868–70), and W.S. Gilbert adapted it in his comedy of *Pygmalion and Galatea* (1871), in which the sculptor is a married man. His wife, Cynisca, was jealous of the animated statue (Galatea), which, after considerable trouble, voluntarily returned to its original state. The name was used figuratively by George Bernard Shaw for a play produced in 1912 from which the popular musical *My Fair Lady* (1957) was derived.

**Pygmy.** The name used by Homer and other classical writers for a supposed race of DWARFS said to dwell in Ethiopia, Africa or India. The name comes from Greek *pugme*, the length of the arm from elbow to the knuckles. They cut down corn with hatchets and made war against cranes which came annually to plunder them. When HERCULES visited their country they climbed up his goblet by ladders to drink from it, and while he was asleep two whole armies of pygmies fell upon his right hand and two on his left, but they were rolled up by Hercules in the skin of the NEMEAN LION and taken to Eurystheus. Jonathan Swift's debt to this legend is apparent in *Gulliver's Travels* (1726).

The term is now applied to certain dwarfish races of central Africa. Full-grown males are scarcely more than 4ft 9in (145cm) tall, and the existence of pygmies in general came to light only in the 19th century. Their culture is archaic, and stone implements are unknown. Their weapon is the bow and arrow, the latter often poisoned and tipped with iron obtained by bartering with neighbouring tribes. Snares and traps are also frequently employed. The word is also used used for the small members of a genus, as the pygmy hippopotamus.

**Pyjamas.** The word (in its American spelling, pajamas) and the form of dress have their origins in India, where it originally applied to loose trousers worn by men or women. This was then adopted in the late 19th century as sleepwear, and gradually superseded the nightshirt. The word itself is of Urdu origin and literally means 'leg clothing'.

**Cat's pyjamas.** *See under* CAT.

**Pylades and Orestes.** Two friends in Homeric legend, whose names have become proverbial for friendship, like those of DAMON AND PYTHIAS and DAVID AND JONATHAN. Orestes was the son, and Pylades the nephew, of AGAMEMNON, after whose murder Orestes was put in the care of Pylades' father (Strophius), and the two became fast friends. Pylades assisted Orestes in obtaining vengeance on AEGISTHUS and CLYTEMNESTRA, and afterwards married ELECTRA, his friend's sister.

**Pylon.** Properly a monumental gateway (Greek *pulon*, 'gateway'), especially of an Egyptian temple, consisting of two massive towers joined by a bridge over the doorway. The word is now usually applied to the obelisks that mark out the course on an airfield or to the standards for electric cables or the like.

**Pyramid** (Greek *puramis*, 'wheat cake'). The Greek name of these massive royal tombs of ancient Egypt was probably of humorous application. Zoser's step-pyramid at Saqqara (3rd Dynasty) was the forerunner of the true pyramid. The next stage was when the step-pyramid at Meidum was covered with a uniform slope from base to top by filling in the steps (*c.*2670 BC). The Great Pyramid at Giza, covering some 13 acres (5.3 ha) and originally rising to a height of 481ft (147m) , was built by Cheops or Khufu (*c.*2650 BC). That of Chephren or Khafra (*c.*2620 BC), his son, is slightly smaller, and the third, the tomb of Mycerinus or Menkaura (*c.*2600 BC), is 204ft (62m) high. Each contains entrances with passages leading to an antechamber and the burial chamber. Other pyramids are to be found at Abusir, Saqqara, Dahshur, Lisht and in the Faiyum.

The kings of the 11th Dynasty built small brick pyramids at Thebes.

**Pyramus.** A Babylonian youth in classic story (*see* Ovid's *Metamorphoses*, iv (1st century AD)), the lover of Thisbe. Thisbe was to meet him at the white MULBERRY tree near the tomb of NINUS, but she, scared by a lion, fled and left her veil, which the lion besmeared with blood. Pyramus, thinking his lady love had been devoured, killed himself, and Thisbe, coming up soon afterwards, stabbed herself also. The blood of the lovers stained the white fruit of the mulberry tree into its present colour. The 'tedious brief scene' and 'very tragical mirth' presented by the rustic characters in Shakespeare's *A Midsummer Night's Dream* (1595) is a travesty of this legend.

**Pyrography.** The art of decorating woodwork, furniture, panelling and the like by designs and pictures burned in with hot steel points. Some of the best work was as fine in detail as a good etching. Pyrography dates from the 17th century and reached its highest standard in the 19th century. In its crude form it is pokerwork.

**Pyromancy** (Greek *pur*, 'fire', and *manteia*, 'divination'). DIVINATION by fire or the shapes observed in fire.

**Pyrrha.** The wife of DEUCALION.

**Pyrrhic. Pyrrhic dance.** The war-dance of the Greeks, so called from its inventor, Pyrrichos, a Dorian. It was a quick dance, performed in full armour to the flute, and its name is still used for a metrical foot of two short 'dancing' syllables. The *Romaika*, still danced in Greece, is a relic of the ancient Pyrrhic dance.

**Pyrrhic victory.** A victory won at too heavy a price, like the costly victory won by Pyrrhus, king of Epirus, at Asculum in 279 BC ('One more such victory and we are lost.'). Pyrrhus lost all his best officers and many men.

**Pyrrhonism.** Scepticism, or philosophic doubt, so named from Pyrrho (4th century BC), the founder of the first Greek school of sceptical philosophy. Pyrrho maintained that nothing was capable of proof and admitted the reality of nothing but sensations.

**Pythagoras.** The Greek philosopher and mathematician of the 6th century BC (born at Samos), to whom was attributed the enunciation of the doctrines of the TRANSMIGRATION OF SOULS and of the harmony of the spheres, and also the proof of the 47th proposition in the 1st book of Euclid, which is hence called the Pythagorean proposition. He taught that the sun, moon and planets have a motion independent of their daily rotation but seems to have held that the universe was earth-centred. *See also* PYTHAGOREAN SYSTEM.

Pythagoras was noted for his manly beauty and long hair. Many stories are related of him, such as that he distinctly recollected previous existences of his own, having been (1) Aethelides, son of MERCURY, (2) Euphorbus the Phrygian, son of Panthous, in which form he ran PATROCLUS through with a lance, leaving HECTOR to kill him, (3) Hermotimus, the prophet of Clazomenae, and (4) a fisherman. To prove his Phrygian existence he was taken to the temple of HERA, in Argos, and asked to point out the shield of the son of Panthous, which he did without hesitation.

Other legends assert that one of his thighs was of gold, and that he showed it to ABARIS, and exhibited it in the OLYMPIC GAMES.

It was also said that Pythagoras used to write on a mirror in blood and place it opposite the moon, when the inscription would appear reflected on the moon's disc, and that he tamed a savage Daunian bear by 'stroking it gently with his hand', subdued an eagle by the same means and held absolute dominion over beasts and birds by 'the power of his voice' or 'influence of his touch'.

At Croton he became the centre of the Pythagorean brotherhood, which sought the moral reformation of society, practising temperance and abstinence from fleshly food.

**Pythagoras' letter.** The Greek letter upsilon, Y, so called because it was used by him as a symbol of the divergent paths of virtue and vice.

**Pythagoras' table.** The common multiplication table, carried up to ten. The table is divided into a hundred little squares. The name is taken from a corrupt text of Boethius, who was really referring to the ABACUS.

**Pythagoras' theorem.** That the square on the hypotenuse of a right-angled triangle is equal to the sum of the squares on the other two sides.

**Pythagorean system, The.** The astronomical system so called that held the universe to be spherical in shape with fire at its centre, around which revolved the counter-earth, the earth, then the moon, the sun, the five planets and lastly the sphere of fixed stars. It is a forerunner of the COPERNICAN SYSTEM and seems to be a later hypothesis of the Pythagoreans and not to have been originated by PYTHAGORAS himself.

**Pythia.** The priestess of APOLLO at DELPHI who delivered ORACLES. Inspiration was obtained by inhaling sulphurous vapours, which issued from the ground from a hole over which she sat on a three-legged stool or tripod. Oracles were only available in the spring and were originally spoken in HEXAMETER verses.

**Pythian Games.** The Greek games held in honour of APOLLO at Pytho in Phocis, subsequently called DELPHI. They took place every fourth year, in the third year of each OLYMPIAD, and were next in importance to the OLYMPIC GAMES.

**Pythias.** *See* DAMON.

**Knights of Pythias, The.** *See under* KNIGHT.

**Python.** The monster serpent hatched from the mud of DEUCALION's deluge, and slain by APOLLO at DELPHI (Pytho).

**Pyx** (Greek *puxis*, 'boxwood vessel'). A small metal receptacle or box in which the reserved HOST is taken to sick people. It is also the vessel in which the Host is reserved in the TABERNACLE in Roman Catholic (and some Anglican) churches.

**Trial of the Pyx.** *See under* TRIAL.

# Q

**Q.** The seventeenth letter of the English alphabet, and nineteenth of the Phoenician and Hebrew alphabets. In English q is invariably followed by u except in transliterations of some Arabic words, as in 'Qatar'. Qu in English normally represents the sound kw as in 'quinquennial' but occasionally k as in 'grotesque' and 'quay'. Without the u it is pronounced k as in 'Iraq'. Formerly, in Scotland, qu replaced hw as in 'quhat', or 'hwat' ('what'). Q as a medieval Latin numeral represents 500.

**Q.** The *nom de plume* of Sir Arthur Quiller-Couch (1863–1944), Cornish author and novelist, professor of English literature at Cambridge (1912–44) and editor of the first *Oxford Book of English Verse* (1900).

**'Q'.** In biblical criticism the symbol used for the theoretical document used by MATTHEW OR LUKE or both. In the SYNOPTIC GOSPELS there is much material common to both Matthew and Luke, which is designated 'Q' (usually held to be German *Quelle*, 'source'). These passages mainly consist of the sayings of Jesus.

**QC.** Queen's Counsel.

**QED** (Latin *quod erat demonstrandum*, 'which was to be demonstrated'). A tag originally appended to the theorems of EUCLID: Thus have we proved the proposition stated above, as we were required to do. In schoolboy parlance: 'Quite easily done.'

> Hence, contranominally, if *each* of the original sets consists of 2 *different* squares, their product gives the sum of 2 squares in 2 *different* ways. Q.E.D.
>
> CHARLES L. DODGSON (LEWIS CARROLL): *Pillow-Problems*, ch iii, 29 (1895)

**QEF** (Latin *quod erat faciendum*, 'which was to be done'). A tag originally appended to the problems of EUCLID: Thus have we done the operation required.

> Hence, on July 31, when clock indicates this time, it is *true* noon. Q.E.F.
>
> CHARLES L. DODGSON (LEWIS CARROLL): *Pillow-Problems*, ch iii, 31 (1895)

**QP** (Latin *quantum placet*, 'as much as it pleases'). Used in prescriptions to signify that the quantity may be as little or as much as you like. Thus, in a cup of tea one might say, 'Milk and sugar qp'.

**QS** (Latin *quantum sufficit*, 'as much as suffices'). Thus, after giving the drugs in minute proportions, the pharmacist may be told to 'mix in liquorice, qs'.

**Q ships.** In the First World War the name given to warships camouflaged as tramp steamers. These 'mystery ships' were used to lure U-BOATS to their destruction. 'Q' represents 'query'.

**Q.T., On the.** Secretly; unofficially. 'Q.T.' stands for 'quiet'.

**Quack** or **quack doctor.** Once called a quacksalver, an itinerant drug vendor at fairs who 'quacked' (hawked) his wares to the credulous rustics. Hence, a CHARLATAN. The word is today sometimes used in mock disparagement of the doctor one is obliged to consult, as: 'Better see the quack, I suppose'.

**Quad.** The university contraction for quadrangle, the rectangular courtyard of a college, often with a lawn in the middle. The quads at Oxford correspond to the courts at Cambridge. The word 'quad' is also applied to one of a family of quadruplets. *See also* QUOD.

**Tom Quad.** *See under* TOM.

**Quadragesima.** The 40 days of LENT.

**Quadragesima Sunday.** The first Sunday in LENT, so called because it is, in round numbers, the fortieth day before EASTER. *See also* QUINQUAGESIMA SUNDAY.

**Quadrant, The.** The name given to the curved southern end of Regent Street, London, which describes a quarter-circle. It was designed by John Nash (1752–1835) in 1813, and when built had two DORIC colonnades, the cast iron columns being made at the Carron ironworks. These were removed in 1848. The original buildings were demolished in 1928.

**Quadriga.** A contraction of *quadrijugae* (Latin *quadri-*, 'four', and *jugum*, 'yoke'). In classical antiquity a two-wheeled chariot drawn by four horses harnessed abreast. The Wellington Arch at Hyde Park Corner, London, is surmounted by a fine bronze group, the *Quadriga*, executed by Adrian Jones in 1912. The cost of the sculpture was met by Lord Michelham, a Jewish financier, whose 11-year-old son served as a model for the boy who pulls at the reins of the four horses harnessed to the quadriga as a huge figure of Peace descends upon them from heaven.

**Quadrilateral.** The combination of four fortresses mutually supporting one another during the Austrian rule of northern Italy. They were Peschiera and Mantua on the Mincio and Verona and Legnago on the Adige. They are now demolished.

**Lambeth quadrilateral.** *See under* LAMBETH.

**Quadrille.** (1) An old card game played by four people with an ordinary pack of cards from which the eights, nines and tens have been withdrawn. It displaced OMBRE in popular favour in about 1730 and was followed by WHIST.

(2) The square dance of this name was of French origin and was introduced into England in 1813 by the Duke of Devonshire. It was one of the most difficult ballroom dances in fashion at the time when Lewis Carroll wrote *Alice's Adventures in Wonderland* (1865) and features in ch x of his tale, 'The Lobster Quadrille'.

**Quadrivium.** The collective name given by the SCHOOLMEN of the Middle Ages to the four 'liberal arts' (Latin *quadri-*, 'four', and *via*, 'way'), i.e. arithmetic, music, geometry and astronomy. The quadrivium was the 'fourfold way' to knowledge, while the TRIVIUM was the 'threefold way' to eloquence. Together they were regarded as the seven liberal arts.

**Quadroon.** *See* MIXED RACE OFFSPRING.

**Quai d'Orsay.** The quay in Paris running along the left bank of the River Seine where are situated the departments of Foreign Affairs and other government offices. The name is applied to the French Foreign Office and sometimes to the French government as a whole.

**Quail.** This bird was formerly believed to be of an inordinately amorous disposition, hence its name was given to a courtesan.

> Here's Agamemnon, an honest fellow enough, and one that loves quails.
>
> SHAKESPEARE: *Troilus and Cressida*, V, i (1601)

**Quaker.** A familiar name for a member of the Society of Friends, a religious body having no definite creed and no regular ministry, founded by George Fox (1624–91), who began his preaching in 1647. His followers created an organized society during the 1650s and 1660s. It appears from the founder's *Journal* that they first obtained the appellation (1650) from the following circumstances: 'Justice Bennet, of Derby,' says Fox, 'was the first to call us Quakers, because I bid them Tremble at the Word of the Lord.'

> Quakers (that, like to lanterns, bear
> Their light within them) will not swear.
>
> SAMUEL BUTLER: *Hudibras*, II, ii (1663)

The name was previously applied to a sect whose adherents shook and trembled with religious emotion, and it was generally applied in the COMMONWEALTH period as an abusive term to religious and political radicals. *See also* SHAKERS.

**Quaker City.** PHILADELPHIA, which was founded by a group of Quakers led by William Penn (1644–1718) and intended as a haven of religious freedom.

**Quaker poet, The.** Bernard Barton (1784–1849); also John Greenleaf Whittier (1807–92).

**Quality of mercy is not strained, The.** 'Strained' in this famous line from Shakespeare (*The Merchant of Venice*, IV, i (1596)) means constrained or forced, so that mercy comes down freely as the rain, which is God's gift.

**Quarantine** (Italian *quaranta*, 'forty'). The period, originally 40 days, that a ship suspected of being infected with some contagious disorder is obliged to lie off port. The term is now applied to any period of segregation to prevent infection. In law the term was applied to the 40 days during which a widow who was entitled to a dower was entitled to remain in the chief house of her deceased husband. *See also* YELLOW JACK.

**Quare impedit** (Latin, 'wherefore he hinders'). A form of legal action by which the right of presentation to a Church of England benefice is tried (from the opening words of the writ). When a bishop has failed to institute a clergyman presented by the patron of the benefice, the latter may apply for a writ of *Quare impedit* against the bishop. It is now used only when the bishop's objections relate to matters of doctrine and ritual.

**Quarrel** (Old French *quarel*, 'pane', from Medieval Latin *quadrellus*, diminutive of Latin *quadrus*, 'square'). A square or lozenge; a small square or diamond-shaped tile, or a similarly shaped pane of glass as used in lattice-windows. Also a short stout square-headed bolt or arrow used in the crossbow.

**Quarrel, To** (Old French *querele*, from Latin *querella*, 'complaint'). To engage in contention; to fall out; to argue.

**Patch up a quarrel, To.** *See under* PATCH.

**Quarry.** (1) An object of chase, especially the bird flown at in hawking or the animal pursued by hounds or hunters. Originally the word (Old French *cuirée*, 'skinned') denoted the entrails of the deer, which were placed on the animal's skin after it had been flayed and given to the hounds as a reward.

> Your castle is surpris'd; your wife and babes
> Savagely slaughtered; to relate the manner,
> Were, on the quarry of these murder'd deer,
> To add the death of you.
>
> SHAKESPEARE: *Macbeth*, IV, iii (1605)

(2) The place where slate, stone and the like is dug out is called a quarry from Old French *quarrière*, from Latin *quadrare*, 'to make square',

because the stones were cut in square blocks on the spot. *See also* QUARREL.

**Quarter.** The fourth part of anything, as of a year or an hour or any material thing. In weights a quarter is 28lb (12.7kg), i.e. a fourth of a hundredweight. As a measure of capacity for grain it is 8 bushels, which used to be one-fourth, but is now one-fifth of a load. In the meat trade a quarter of a beast is a fourth part, which includes one of the legs. A quarter in the US coinage is the fourth part of a DOLLAR. In a heraldic shield or on a flag the quarters are the divisions made by central lines drawn at right angles across them. When looking at a shield, the first and fourth quarters are in the dexter chief and sinister base (left-hand top and right-hand bottom), and the second and third in the sinister chief and dexter base.

**Quarter.** Exemption from death upon surrender.

**Quarter** or **quarters.** Residence or place of abode. A district of a town or city is sometimes known as a quarter, as the poor quarter, the native quarter. The *Quartier Latin* ('Latin quarter') of Paris is the university area. Although popularly renowned as the cosmopolitan and BOHEMIAN quarter, it derives its name from its ancient fame as a centre of learning when Latin was the common language for the students, who came from all over Europe. Winter quarters is the place where an army lodges during the winter months, and married quarters is the accommodation for married servicemen and their families.

**Quarter days.** The days on which certain payments are traditionally due and tenancies begin and end, so called as they fall at quarter-yearly intervals.

New Style:
LADY DAY: 25 March
MIDSUMMER Day: 24 June
MICHAELMAS DAY: 29 September
CHRISTMAS Day: 25 December

Old Style:
Lady Day: 6 April
Old Midsummer Day: 6 July
Old Michaelmas Day: 11 October
Old Christmas Day: 6 January

In Scotland the quarter days are CANDLEMAS DAY (2 February), WHITSUNDAY (15 May), LAMMAS DAY (1 August) and MARTINMAS Day (11 November).

**Quarterdeck.** The upper deck of a ship from the mainmast to the stern. In the Royal Navy it is the promenade reserved for officers. The naval custom of saluting the quarterdeck is of uncertain origin, one suggestion being that at one time a shrine was kept in this part of the ship. *See also* FORECASTLE.

**Quartered.** *See* HANGED, DRAWN AND QUARTERED.

**Quarter Sessions.** From the mid-14th century JUSTICES OF THE PEACE sat four times a year in Quarter Sessions to deal with appeals from Petty Sessions, criminal charges and some civil cases as well as administrative work. Generally trial was by jury before two or more justices, but in 1882 a qualified barrister known as a recorder replaced them in the boroughs, and from 1962 the chairman in other courts of Quarter Sessions had to be a qualified lawyer. In 1842 the more serious criminal cases were transferred to the assizes and most of their administrative work was lost to the County Councils by the Local Government Act of 1888. Quarter Sessions were abolished by the Courts Act of 1971.

**At close quarters.** *See under* AT.

**Bad quarter of an hour.** *See under* BAD.

**Cry quarter, To.** *See under* CRY.

**Grant quarter, To.** *See under* GRANT.

**Hanged, drawn and quartered.** *See under* HANG.

**Quarterly, The.** A common name for the *Quarterly Review*, a literary and political review first published by John Murray at Edinburgh in 1809. It was a TORY rival of the EDINBURGH REVIEW. Its first editor was William Gifford (1756–1826), and Sir Walter Scott and Robert Southey were principal contributors. John Gibson Lockhart (1794–1854) took over the editorship from John Taylor Coleridge, nephew of Samuel Taylor Coleridge, in 1824 and continued in office until 1853. It ceased publication in 1967.

**Quartermaster.** In the army the officer whose duty it is to attend to the QUARTERS of the soldiers. He superintends the issue of all stores and equipment.

In the navy the rating or petty officer who supervises the steering of the ship at sea and in harbour keeps watch under the Officer of the WATCH.

**Quarto.** A size of paper made by folding the sheet twice, giving four leaves or eight pages, hence, a book composed of sheets folded thus. The word is often written '4to'. *See also* FOLIO; OCTAVO.

**Quashee.** A generic name for an unsophisticated West Indian black, from Akan *Kwasi*, a name often given to a boy born on a Sunday. *See also* QUASSIA.

**Quasi** (Latin, 'as if'). An element prefixed to a word to indicate 'seeming', 'as it were', denoting that what it qualifies is not the real thing but has some of its qualities. Thus a quasi-historical account is seemingly historical but not really or fully so.

**Quasi-contract.** In law an obligation similar to that created by a formal contract.

**Quasimodo Sunday.** The first Sunday after EASTER or LOW SUNDAY, so called from the Introit at MASS on this day, which begins *Quasimodo* *geniti infantes*, 'as new-born babes' (1 Peter 2:2). *See also* CANTATE SUNDAY.

Quasimodo is also the name of the hunchback in Victor Hugo's *Notre-Dame de Paris* (1831).

> He [Archdeacon Frollo] christened the adopted child by the name of Quasimodo, either because he chose thus to commemorate the day when he had found him, or because he meant to mark by that name how incomplete and imperfectly moulded the poor little creature was. Indeed, Quasimodo, one-eyed, hump-backed, bow-legged, could hardly be considered as anything more than an *as if*.
> Bk IV, ch ii

**Quassia.** An American plant, or rather genus of plants, named after Graman ('Grand Man') Quassi, a Surinamese slave, who, in 1730, was the first to make known its medicinal properties as a tonic. *See also* QUASHEE

> Linnaeus applied this name to a tree of Surinam in honour of a negro, Quassi ... who employed its bark as a remedy for fever; and enjoyed such a reputation among the natives as to be almost worshipped by some.
> JOHN LINDLEY and THOMAS MOORE: *The Treasury of Botany*, Pt ii (1866)

**Quattrocento** (Italian, from Latin *quattuor*, 'four', and *centum*, 'hundred'). An abbreviation of *mille quattrocento*, 1400. The name given to the 15th century as a period of art and literature, especially with reference to Italy. *See also* CINQUECENTO.

**Queen.** A female sovereign or a king's wife (also nowadays, an effeminate male homosexual). The word comes from Old English *cwēn*, 'woman', 'wife' (which also gives *quean*, formerly used of an impudent woman or prostitute), from an Indo-European base element that gave Greek *gunē* (English *gyno-*), Russian *zhena*, Irish *bean* and so on, all meaning 'woman'. *See also* KING; MAB.

**Queen Anne.** *See under* ANNE.

**Queen bee.** In a metaphorical sense, a woman who is in a position of power or authority in a group.

**Queen can do no wrong, The.** *See under* KING.

**Queen City**. Cincinnati. The city is called 'Queen of the West' in a poem of 1854 by Longfellow, but the present appellation to some extent puns on the city's name.

**Queen consort.** The wife of a reigning king.

**Queen Dick.** *See under* DICK.

**Queen dowager.** The widow of a deceased king.

**Queen Elizabeth's pocket pistol.** An ancient bronze cannon given to Elizabeth I by the Netherlands in recognition of her help against Philip II of Spain. It used to overlook the Channel from the Dover Cliffs and is now in Dover Castle.

**Queen Mab.** *See* MAB.

**Queen mother.** The consort of a king is so called after her husband's death and when her son or daughter has succeeded to the throne.

**Queen of Bohemia, The.** This old PUBLIC HOUSE SIGN was in honour of Elizabeth (1596–1662), daughter of James I, and wife of Frederick V, elector Palatine, whose election to the throne of Bohemia in 1619 touched off the THIRTY YEARS' WAR. George I, king of England, was their descendant. *See also* QUEEN OF HEARTS.

**Queen of Crime, The.** A promotional nickname given to the crime novelist Agatha Christie (1891–1976), and subsequently to her successor in this role, P.D. James (b.1920).

**Queen of Glory, The.** An epithet of the Virgin MARY.

**Queen of Hearts, The.** Elizabeth (1596–1662), daughter of James I, wife of Frederick V, elector Palatine, and ill-starred QUEEN OF BOHEMIA. She was so called in the Low Countries from her amiable character and engaging manners, even in her adversity. In Lewis Carroll's *Alice's Adventures in Wonderland* (1865) the Queen of Hearts is the tyrannical queen who plays croquet with flamingos and later orders 'Off with her head!' (Alice is saved when she points out that the queen and her court are all simply cards.) Diana, Princess of Wales (1961–97), was dubbed 'Queen of Hearts' by the media for her charity work and caring concern for the victims of misfortune.

> The BBC last night defended its decision to cut footage of the Princess Royal reacting angrily to a comparison with the late Diana, Princess of Wales. The film apparently showed the Princess's clear resentment of her former sister-in-law's popular image as a 'Queen of Hearts'.
> *The Times* (3 October 1998)

**Queen of Heaven, The.** The Virgin MARY. In ancient times the title was also applied by the Phoenicians to ASTARTE, by the Greeks to HERA, by the Romans to JUNO and HECATE, and by the Egyptians to ISIS. As a general title it applied to DIANA, or the moon, also called Queen of the Night and Queen of the Tides. Jeremiah 7:18 has: 'The children gather wood, and the fathers kindle the fire, and the women knead their dough, to make cakes to the queen of heaven', i.e. the moon.

**Queen of love, The.** APHRODITE OR VENUS.

> Poor queen of love, in thine own law forlorn
> To love a cheek that smiles at thee in scorn!
> SHAKESPEARE: *Venus and Adonis* (1593)

**Queen of Scots' Pillar, The.** A column in Poole's Cavern, Buxton, Derbyshire, as clear as alabaster. It is said to be so called because on one occasion, when going to throw herself on the mercy of Elizabeth I, Mary, Queen of Scots proceeded thus far and then turned back.

**Queen of Sheba, The.** *See under* SHEBA.
**Queen of the Blues, The.** A nickname given by Dr Johnson to Mrs Elizabeth Montagu (1720–1800), a noted BLUESTOCKING.
**Queen of the May, The.** *See* MAY QUEEN.
**Queen of the suburbs, The.** Ealing, on the western outskirts of Edwardian London, was at one time so called from the social status or genteel lifestyle of its residents. *See also* GARDEN SUBURB.
**Queen regnant.** A queen who holds the crown in her own right, as distinct from a QUEEN CONSORT.
**Queen's Bays, The.** *See under* REGIMENTAL AND DIVISIONAL NICKNAMES.
**Queen's Bench.** *See under* KING.
**Queen's College** (Oxford) and **Queens' College** (Cambridge). Note the position of the apostrophe in each case. The Oxford college was founded (1340) by Robert Eglesfeld in honour of Queen Philippa, consort of Edward III, to whom he was chaplain. The Cambridge college numbers two queens as its founders: Margaret of Anjou (1430–82), consort of Henry VI in 1448, and Elizabeth Woodville (1437–92), Edward IV's consort, who refounded the college in 1465.
**Queen's Colour, The.** *See under* KING.
**Queen's Counsel.** *See under* KING.
**Queen's County, The.** *See under* KING.
**Queen's Day.** 17 November, the day of the accession of Queen Elizabeth I in 1558, first publicly celebrated in 1570. Until the 19th century, Queen's Day was observed as a holiday in government offices and at Westminster School. Queen's Day was also occasionally known as Queen Elizabeth's Day to avoid association with any other queen.
**Queen's English, The.** *See under* KING.
**Queen's evil, The.** *See under* KING.
**Queen's Guide.** *See under* KING.
**Queen's highway.** *See under* KING.
**Queen's messenger.** *See under* KING.
**Queen's peace, The.** *See under* KING.
**Queen's proctor, The.** *See under* KING.
**Queen's ransom, A.** *See under* KING.
**Queen's Regulations.** *See under* KING.
**Queen's Remembrancer, The.** *See under* KING.
**Queen's scholar, A.** *See under* KING.
**Queen's Scout.** *See under* KING.
**Queen's shilling.** *See under* KING.
**Queen's speech, The.** *See under* KING.
**Queen Square Hermit, The.** Jeremy Bentham (1748–1832), the philosopher and father of UTILITARIANISM, who lived at No. 1 Queen Square, London. His embalmed figure, seated and fully dressed, is preserved at University College, London.
**Queen's ware.** Glazed Wedgwood earthenware of a creamy colour.
**Beauty queen.** *See under* BEAUTY.
**Faerie Queene, The.** *See under* FAERIE.
**Maiden Queen.** *See under* MAIDEN.
**Master of the Queen's Music.** *See under* MASTER.
**Nine days' queen.** *See under* NINE.
**Republican Queen, The.** *See under* REPUBLIC.
**Valley of the Queens, The.** *See under* VALLEY.
**Virgin Queen, The.** *See under* VIRGIN.
**White Queen, The.** *See under* WHITE.

**Queenhithe.** The hithe, or landing place, off Upper Thames Street, London, on the north bank of the Thames upstream of Southwark Bridge. It is mentioned in a charter of ALFRED THE GREAT as *Æðeredes hyd* ('Ethelred's wharf'), probably from Ethelred II of Wessex, and eventually became the property of Queen Matilda, first wife of Henry I, and subsequently it came to be called 'queen's hithe' or Queenhithe. In early times it was a flourishing port, mainly handling corn and fish.

**Queensberry Rules.** The regulations governing boxing matches in which gloves were worn, formulated by John Sholto Douglas, 8th Marquess of Queensberry (1844–1900) and John G. Chambers (1843–83) in 1867. They were first fully used at a London tournament in 1872. The present rules governing glove contests are those issued by the British Boxing Board of Control in 1929. *See also* BELOW THE BELT.

**Queer.** Colloquial for 'out of sorts', 'not up to the mark'; also thieves' CANT for anything base and worthless and a modern, usually pejorative term for a homosexual (although in recent years the term has been reclaimed by homosexuals, in an attempt, by using the word positively, to defy its negative use and connotations).
**Queer** or **rum customer, A.** A strange person who is to be treated cautiously.
**Queer fish, A.** An eccentric person.
**Queer someone's pitch, To.** To forestall or thwart someone; to render a person's efforts useless by underhand means, as a street or market vendor might find his trade spoilt by an interloper.
**Come over all queer, To.** *See under* COME.
**In Queer Street, To be.** To be in financial difficulties. The punning suggestion has been made that the origin of the phrase is to be found in a query (?) with which a tradesman might mark the name of a dubious customer on his ledger. More likely, it is a 'crooked' or 'cross' street, as compared with a 'straight' one (with possibly an implied pun on the biblical 'street which is called Straight' of Acts 9:11). German *Querstraße*, meaning 'cross-street', 'street running off at right angles', is the exact equivalent.

**Quern-biter** (Germanic, 'foot breadth'). Both Haco I and Thoralf Skolinson had a sword of this name.

**Querno.** Camillo Querno of Apulia, hearing that

Pope Leo X (b.1475, 1513–22) was a great patron of poets, went to Rome with a harp in his hand and sang a poem called *Alexias*, which had 20,000 verses. He was introduced to the pope as a buffoon, but was made poet laureate and became a constant frequenter of the pope's table.

Rome in her Capitol saw Querno sit,
Thron'd on seven hills the Antichrist of wit.
ALEXANDER POPE: *The Dunciad*, ii (1728)

**Query. Notes and Queries.** *See under* NOTE.

**Que sçais-je?** (French, 'What do I know?'). The motto adopted by Michel Eyquem de Montaigne (1533–92), the great French essayist, as expressing the sceptical and inquiring nature of his writings. The phrase (in the modern form, *Que sais-je?*) was adopted as a general title for the excellent series of informative paperbacks founded as a *Collection encyclopédique* by Paul Angoulvent in 1941 and published by Presses Universitaires de France. Over 2000 volumes had been published by the early 1980s.

**Question.** When members of the HOUSE OF COMMONS or other debaters call out 'Question', they mean that the speaker is wandering away from the subject under consideration.

**Questionists.** In examinations for degrees at Cambridge it was customary, at the beginning of the January term, to hold 'Acts', and candidates for the Bachelor's degree were called 'Questionists'. They were examined by a moderator, and afterwards the fathers of other colleges 'questioned' them for three hours in Latin, and the dismissal uttered by the REGIUS PROFESSOR indicated in which class each would be placed, or if a respondent were to be plucked (*see* PLUCK), in which case the words were simply *Descendus domine*.

**Question time.** In parliamentary parlance, a period of time set aside each day for members to question government ministers. There are three kinds of question that can be asked in the House of Commons: (1) oral questions, actually answered in the Chamber, for 55 minutes every Monday to Thursday; (2) written questions, which receive written answers; and (3) priority written questions, which the department concerned must have at least two days to answer. MPs submit oral questions a fortnight before they are due to be answered. The Prime Minister answers oral questions for half an hour every Wednesday when the House is sitting.

**Beg the question, To.** *See under* BEG.

**Beyond question.** *See under* BEYOND.

**Burning question.** *See under* BURN.

**Call in** or **into question, To.** *See under* CALL.

**Cross questions and crooked answers.** *See under* CROSS.

**Eastern Question, The.** *See under* EAST.

**Good question, A.** *See under* GOOD.

**Leading question, A.** *See under* LEAD.

**Open question, An.** *See under* OPEN.

**Out of the question.** *See under* OUT.

**Pop the question, To.** *See under* POP.

**Previous question, The.** *See under* PREVIOUS.

**Rhetorical question.** *See under* RHETORICAL.

**Sixty-four** or **sixty-four thousand dollar question.** *See under* SIX.

**Quetzalcoatl.** An Aztec deity whose name means 'feathered serpent', a god of the air or a sun-god and a benefactor of their race who instructed them in the use of agriculture, metals and the like. According to one account, he was driven from the country by a superior god and on reaching the shores of the Mexican Gulf promised his followers that he would return. He then embarked on his magic skiff for the land of Tlapallan. W.H. Prescott (*The History of the Conquest of Mexico*, ch iii (1843)) writes that: 'He was said to have been tall in stature, with a white skin, long, dark hair and a flowing beard. The Mexicans looked confidently to the return of the benevolent deity; and this remarkable tradition, deeply cherished in their hearts, prepared ... for the future success of the Spaniards.'

**Queue. Queue de Renard, Une** (French, 'a fox's tail'). A mockery. At one time it was a common practical joke to fasten a fox's tail behind a person whom it was intended to mock. PANURGE never lost a chance of attaching a fox's tail, or the ears of a leveret, behind a Master of Arts or Doctor of Divinity (Rabelais, *Gargantua*, II, xvi (1534)). *See also* REYNARD.

**Jump the queue, To.** *See under* JUMP.

**Qui** (French, 'who').

**Qui s'excuse, s'accuse** (French). He who excuses himself, accuses himself.

**Qui vive** (French, '(long) live who?'). The French sentry's equivalent of 'Who goes there?', which in French would be *Qui va là?* The sentry's words were originally designed to ascertain the loyalty of the person he challenged, and a correct response would have been '*Vive la France*' or '*Vive le roi*'.

**On the qui vive, To be.** To be on the alert; to be quick and sharp; to be on the lookout like a sentinel.

**Quick.** Living, and hence animated or lively. Also, fast, active or brisk.

**Quick and the dead, The.** The living and the dead.

**Quickie.** Anything done or made rapidly. In everyday speech a 'quickie' usually means a quick drink as: 'Can I get you a quickie?'

**Quicksand.** Sand that shifts its place as if it were alive. *See also* QUICK.

**Quickset.** Living hawthorn set in a hedge, instead of dead wood, hurdles and palings. *See also* QUICK.

**Quicksilver.** *Argentum vivum* ('living silver'), silver that moves about like a living thing, i.e. mercury.

**As quick as a flash.** *See under* AS.

**Cut to the quick.** *See under* CUT.

**Quid.** Slang for a sovereign (or a pound). It occurs in Thomas Shadwell's *Squire of Alsatia* (1688), but its origin is uncertain. It may ultimately come from Latin *quid*, 'what'.

In a 'quid' of tobacco, meaning a piece for chewing, quid is another form of 'cud'.

**Quiddists** or **Quids.** In the USA sectionalists of the Democratic-Republican party under John Randolph (1773–1833) who sought to maintain the ascendancy of Virginia and its planter aristocracy against the more democratic elements. They were active between 1805 and 1811, and opposed Madison's succession to Jefferson as party leader. The name was from *tertium quid*, 'a third something or other' opposed to the Federalists and administration Republicans.

**Quiddity.** The essence of a thing, or that which differentiates it from other things: 'the blackness of black', 'the freeness of the free'. Hence used of subtle, trifling distinctions, quibbles or captious argumentation. SCHOOLMEN say *Quid est?* ('what is it?') and the reply is, the *Quid* is so and so, the 'What' or the nature of the thing is as follows. The latter *quid* being formed into a barbarous Latin noun becomes *Quidditas*. Hence *Quid est?* ('what is it?'). Answer: *Talis est quidditas* ('Its essence is as follows').

**Quidlibet.** *See* QUODLIBET.

**Quidnunc** (Latin, 'What now?'). One who is curious to know everything that's going on, or pretends to know it; a self-important newsmonger and gossip. It is the name of the leading character in Arthur Murphy's farce *The Upholsterer, or What News?* (1757) and a gossip column in *The Sunday Times* in the 1990s bore the name.

**Quid pro quo** (Latin, 'something for something'). A return made for something; an equivalent; a TIT FOR TAT; or in legal parlance, a consideration.

**Quids.** *See* QUIDDISTS.

**Quids in.** Extremely lucky; very profitable; in a favourable situation. *See* QUID.

**Quién sabe?** (Spanish, 'Who knows?'). Sometimes used as a response in the sense of 'How should I know?'

**Quiet. As quiet as a mouse.** *See under* AS.

**Quietism.** A form of religious mysticism based on the doctrine that the essence of religion consists in the withdrawal of the soul from external objects and in fixing it on the contemplation of God. It is especially used for the doctrine of Miguel Molinos (1640–96), who taught the direct relationship between the soul and God. His followers were called Molinists or Quietists. Outward acts of mortification were held to be superfluous, and when a person has attained the mystic state by mental prayer, even if he transgresses in the accepted sense, he does not sin, since his will has been extinguished. Molinos was accused of heresy and condemned by the Inquisition.

**Quietus** (Latin *quietus est*, 'he is quit'). The writ of discharge formerly granted to those barons and knights who personally attended the king on a foreign expedition, exempting them also from the claim of SCUTAGE or knight's fee. Subsequently the term was applied to the acquittance that a SHERIFF receives on settling his account at the EXCHEQUER, and, later still, to any discharge, as of an account, or even of life itself.

> For who would bear the whips and scorns of time,
> Th'oppressor's wrong …
> When he himself might his quietus make
> With a bare bodkin?
> SHAKESPEARE: *Hamlet*, III, i (1601)

**Quinapalus.** A high-sounding, pedantic name invented by Feste, the Clown in Shakespeare's *Twelfth Night*, when he wished to give some saying the weight of authority. Hence someone 'dragged in' when one wishes to clinch an argument by some supposed quotation.

> For what says Quinapalus? 'Better a witty fool than a foolish wit.'
> *Twelfth Night*, I, v (1599)

**Quinine.** *See* CINCHONA.

**Quinquagesima Sunday** (Latin, 'fiftieth'). Shrove Sunday, or the first day of the week that contains ASH WEDNESDAY. It is so called because in round numbers it is the fiftieth day before EASTER. *See also* QUADRAGESIMA SUNDAY.

**Quins** or **Quints, The.** The popular name for the Dionne quintuplets, Marie, Émilie, Yvonne, Cécile and Annette, daughters born (1934) to a farmer's wife near Callander, Ontario. They became wards of the government in 1935 but their father regained control in 1941. Émilie died in 1954 and Marie in 1970. Quints is more usual North American usage.

**Quinsy.** The word is from Medieval Latin *quinancia*, derived from Greek *kunankhē*, 'dog-throttling', because those suffering from quinsy throw open the mouth like dogs, especially mad dogs. It appeared in English (14th century) as *qwinaci*, and later forms were *quynnancy* and *squinancy*. Squinancy-wort and quinsy-wort are still names given to the small woodruff (*Asperula cynanchica*) which was used as a cure for quinsy by the herbalists.

**Quintain, Tilting at the.** *See under* TILT.

**Quintessence.** The fifth essence. The ancient Greeks said that there are four ELEMENTS or forms in which matter can exist: fire, air, water and earth. The Pythagoreans (*see* PYTHAGOREAN SYSTEM) added a fifth, the fifth essence, ether, more subtle and pure than fire and possessed of an orbicular motion, which flew upwards at creation and formed the basis of the stars. Hence the word stands for the essential principle or the most subtle extract of a body that can be procured. Horace speaks of 'kisses that Venus has imbued with the quintessence of her own nectar'.

> Swift to their several quarters hasted then
> The cumbrous elements, Earth, Flood, Air, Fire;
> And this ethereal quintessence of Heaven
> Flew upward , spirited with various forms,
> That rolled orbicular, and turned to stars
> Numberless, as thou seest.
> MILTON: *Paradise Lost*, iii (1667)

**Quintilians.** Members of a 2nd-century heretical sect, said to have been founded by one Quintilia, a prophetess. They made the EUCHARIST of bread and cheese and allowed women to become priests and bishops. *See also* HERETIC; PHRYGIANS.

**Quip modest, The.** 'Sir, it was done to please myself,' in Shakespeare's *As You Like It* (V, iv (1599)). Touchstone's reasoning is as follows: If I sent a person word that his beard was not well cut and he replied he cut it to please himself, he would answer with a Quip Modest, which is six removes from the lie direct. Shakespeare is satirizing the formalities and code of honour of the Italianate style of duelling, then in vogue, in which the 'lie direct' involved a settlement by fighting. The other degrees of lie provided an opportunity for disputants to wax valiant but to retreat from the risk of bloodshed. *See also* REPLY CHURLISH; REPROOF VALIANT; RETORT COURTEOUS.

**Quipu.** A device of the INCAS of Peru used for keeping accounts, recording information and the like. The word means a knot, and the quipu was a length of cord, about 2ft (60cm) long, made of different coloured threads and tied with knots. The various threads and knots represented simple objects and numerical combinations. The word is Quechua *quipu*, 'knot'.

> The Quipus, thus used, might be regarded as the Peruvian system of mnemonics.
> W.H. PRESCOTT: *The Conquest of Peru*, Pt I, ch iv (1847)

**Quirinal.** One of the seven hills of ancient Rome, named after Quirinus, the SABINE name of MARS, and given to ROMULUS after deification. It is now called Monte Cavallo. Also the name of the palace originally built on its slopes as a papal summer residence and subsequently used by the kings of Italy and now by the president. The term was applied emblematically to the Italian kingdom and government as opposed to the VATICAN, the seat of papal authority and ecclesiastical government.

**Quis** (Latin, 'who?'). Formerly commonly used, especially among preparatory schoolboys, when offering to give away something. When only one thing was being offered, the first to call *Ego* ('I [do]') after the cry *Quis?* ('Who [wants]?') gained the reward.

**Quis custodiet ipsos custodes?** (Latin, 'Who will guard the guards themselves?'). The shepherds keep watch over the sheep, but who is there to keep watch over the shepherds? Said when one is uncertain of the person whom one has placed in a position of trust. The phrase is from Juvenal (*Satires*, VI (2nd century AD)) and is used to question the wisdom of setting guards over wives to prevent infidelities.

**Quis separabit?** (Latin, 'Who shall separate [us]?'). The motto adopted by the Most Illustrious ORDER OF ST PATRICK when it was founded.

**Quisling.** A traitor or fifth columnist, from Vidkun Quisling (1887–1945), the Norwegian admirer of Mussolini and Hitler, who acted as advance agent for the German invasion of Norway in 1940. He duly became puppet minister-president. He surrendered (9 May 1945) after the German defeat and was tried and shot (24 October).

**Quit** (French *quitter*, 'to leave', 'to depart'). In general this word is more commonly used in the sense of to leave a job or place.

**Quit of, To be.** To be free from; to be rid of.

**Quit rent.** A rent formerly paid to the lord of a MANOR by freeholders and copyholders which was an acquittal of all other services. It is nowadays a token or nominal rent. The ancient ceremony of rendering the quit rent service due to the crown by the Corporation of the City of London is still held before the KING'S OR QUEEN'S REMEMBRANCER.

**Call it quits.** *See under* CALL.

**Double or quits.** *See under* DOUBLE.

**Quite.** A word of almost opposite application. 'The box is quite full' can mean that it is completely full or that it is fairly full.

**Quite something.** A remarkable thing, as: 'My first parachute jump was quite something.'

**Quixote, Don.** The hero of the romance of this name by Miguel de Cervantes Saavedra (1547–1616). It was published at Madrid in 1605 with the continuation or second part in 1615. It ridicules the more tedious chivalric romances. Don Quixote is a gaunt country gentleman of La Mancha, gentle and dignified, affectionate and simple-minded, but so crazed by reading books of knight-errantry that he believes himself called upon to redress the wrongs of the whole world. Hence a quixotic person is a romantic idealist, one with impractical ideas of honour or schemes for the general good. *See also* KNIGHT OF LA MANCHA; SANCHO PANZA.

**Quixote of the North, The.** Charles XII of Sweden (b.1682, 1697–1718), also called the Madman.

**Quiz.** Originally, someone who banters or chaffs another. The origin of the word, which appeared *c.*1780, is unknown, but fable accounts for it by saying that a Mr Daly, manager of a Dublin theatre, laid a wager that he would introduce into the language within 24 hours a new word of no meaning. Accordingly, on every wall, or all places accessible, were chalked up the four mystic letters, and all Dublin was inquiring what they meant. The wager was won and the word became part of the language. A monocular eye-glass with, or without, a handle was called a quizzing glass, and any odd or ridiculous person or thing a quiz.

Quiz is also applied to a test, usually competitive, of knowledge, general or otherwise.

**Quo. Quo vadis?** *See* DOMINE, QUO VADIS?

**Quo warranto** (Latin, 'by what authority'). A writ issued by the crown against a person who has claimed or usurped any office or liberty to enquire by what authority he supports his claim.

**Quod.** Slang for prison. It is probably the same word as QUAD, which is a contraction of quadrangle, the enclosure in which prisoners are allowed to walk and where whippings used to be inflicted. The word was in use in the 17th century.

**Quodlibet** (Latin, 'what you please'). Originally a philosophical or theological question proposed for purposes of scholastic debate, hence a nice and knotty point, a subtlety. In music a quodlibet is a light-hearted composition consisting of various popular tunes or fragments of tunes. A classic example is the finale of Bach's *Goldberg Variations* (1742) which incorporates two popular melodies of the day, *Ich bin so lang nicht bei dir g'west* ('I've been away from you so long') and *Kraut und Rüben* ('Cabbages and Turnips').

**Quoit, Hautville's.** *See under* HAUTVILLE.

**Quondam** (Latin, 'formerly'). A word used in such expressions as a quondam schoolfellow (a former schoolfellow), my quondam friend, the quondam chancellor and so on.

**Quonset hut.** The American equivalent of a NISSEN HUT as a type of military shelter. It takes its name from Quonset Point, Rhode Island, where such huts were first erected at a US Air Force base in the Second World War.

**Quorum** (Latin, 'of whom'). The lowest number of members of a committee, board or the like whose presence is necessary before business may be transacted. The word comes from the stock formula used when forming Latin commissions: *quorum vos* […] *duos* (etc) *esse volumus*, 'of whom we wish you […] to be two (etc)', the ellipsis standing for the persons' names and the number variable.

**Quos ego.** A threat of punishment for disobedience. The words, from Virgil's *Aeneid* (i (1st century BC)), were uttered by NEPTUNE to the disobedient and rebellious winds and are sometimes given as an example of aposiopesis, i.e. a stopping short for rhetorical effort. 'Whom I –,' said Neptune, the 'will punish' being left to the imagination. A modern equivalent might be, 'Just let me –'.

**Quot. Quot homines, tot sententiae** (Latin). As many minds as men, i.e. there are as many opinions as there are people to hold them. The phrase is from Terence's *Phormio* (II, iv (2nd century BC)).

**Quot linguas calles, tot homines vales** (Latin). As many languages as you know, so many men are you are worth. A saying attributed to Charles V.

**Quotient, Intelligence.** *See under* INTELLIGENCE.

**Qur'an.** *See* KORAN.

**QV** (Latin *quantum vis*, 'as much as you wish'). In prescriptions, as much as you like, or *quantum valeat*, as much as is proper.

**qv** (Latin *quod vide*). Which see.

# R

**R.** The eighteenth letter of the English alphabet (seventeenth of the Roman) representing the twentieth of the Phoenician and Hebrew. As a medieval Roman numeral, R stood for 80 and $\bar{R}$ for 80,000. In England it was formerly used as a branding mark for rogues.

It has been called the 'snarling letter' or 'dog letter', because a dog in snarling utters a sound resembling r-r-r-r or gr-r-r-r.

In his *English Grammar Made for the Benefit of All Strangers* (1636) Ben Jonson says:

> R is the dog's letter and hurreth in the sound; the tongue striking the inner palate, with a trembling about the teeth.

The letter appears as ℞ in prescriptions. The ornamental part of this letter is the symbol of JUPITER (♃), under whose special protection all medicines were placed. The letter itself (Latin *recipe*, 'take') and its flourish may thus be paraphrased: 'Under the good auspices of Jove, the patron of medicines, take the following drugs in the proportions set down.' *See also* RECIPE.

**R months, The.** *See* NEVER EAT AN OYSTER UNLESS THERE'S AN R IN THE MONTH.

**Three Rs, The.** *See under* THREE.

**Ra** or **Re** (Egyptian, 'sun'). The sun god of ancient Egypt, and from the time of Chephren (6th Dynasty) the supposed ancestor of all the PHARAOHS. His chief centre was at HELIOPOLIS where he was also known as Atum. His great enemy was the serpent Apep, with whom he fought continually, but always eventually defeated. According to one legend, Ra was born as a child every morning and died at night as an old man. His name and cult was assimilated with that of Amen (AMEN-RA) and many others, and he was commonly represented with the head of a falcon surmounted by a solar disc surrounded with the Uraeus, the sacred flame-spitting asp that destroyed his enemies.

**Rabbit.** The nickname for a novice or poor performer at a sport such as cricket alludes to the legendary timidity of the animal in question.

**Br'er Fox and Br'er Rabbit.** *See under* BR'ER.

**Jack rabbit.** *See under* JACK.

**Peter Rabbit.** *See under* PETER.

**Pull a rabbit out of the hat, To.** *See under* PULL.

**Welsh rabbit.** *See under* WELSH.

**Rabelaisian.** Coarsely and boisterously satirical, extravagant and licentious in language, in a literary style reminiscent of the great French satirist François Rabelais (1495–1553). When Rabelaisian is used it implies coarseness and complete frankness and ignores Rabelais' humanism. *See also* PANTAGRUEL.

**English Rabelais, The.** A title somewhat unsuitably given to Jonathan Swift (1667–1745), Thomas Amory (*c*.1691–1788), author of *The Life and Opinions of John Buncle, Esq* (1756, 1766), and Laurence Sterne (1713–68).

**Raboin.** *See* TAILED MEN.

**Race** or **Races.** The principal horse races in England are chiefly run at Newmarket, Doncaster, Epsom, Goodwood and ROYAL ASCOT. The GRAND NATIONAL is the greatest of the STEEPLECHASES. The following is a selection of the main races, with distance and venue:

Ascot Gold Cup (Ascot) $2\frac{1}{2}$ miles (4km)
Benson & Hedges Gold Cup (York) $1\frac{1}{2}$ miles (2.4km)
Cambridgeshire Handicap (Newmarket) 1 mile (1.6km)
Cesarewitch (Newmarket) $2\frac{1}{4}$ miles (3.6km)
Champion Hurdle (Cheltenham) 2 miles (3.2km)
Champion Stakes (Newmarket) $1\frac{1}{4}$ miles (2km)
Cheltenham Gold Cup (Cheltenham) $3\frac{1}{4}$ miles (5.2km)
Cheveley Park Stakes (Newmarket) $\frac{3}{4}$ mile (1.2km)
Coronation Cup (Epsom) $1\frac{1}{2}$ miles (2.4km)
Derby (Epsom) $1\frac{1}{2}$ miles (2.4km)
Dewhurst Stakes (Newmarket) 7 furlongs (1.4km)
Eclipse Stakes (Sandown) $1\frac{1}{4}$ miles (2km)
Futurity Stakes (Doncaster) 1 mile (1.6km)
Goodwood Cup (Goodwood) 2 miles (3.2km)
Grand National (Liverpool) $4\frac{1}{2}$ miles (7.2km)
Hennessy Gold Cup (Newbury) $3\frac{1}{4}$ miles (5.2km)
Jockey Club Stakes (Newmarket) $1\frac{1}{2}$ miles (2.4km)
July Cup (Newmarket) $\frac{3}{4}$ mile (1.2km)
King George VI and Queen Elizabeth Diamond Stakes (Ascot) $1\frac{1}{2}$ miles (2.4km)
King George VI Chase (Kempton) 3 miles (4.8km)
Lincoln Handicap (Doncaster) 1 mile (1.6km)
Middle Park Stakes (Newmarket) $\frac{3}{4}$ mile (1.2km)
The Oaks (Epsom) $1\frac{1}{2}$ miles (2.4km)
One Thousand Guineas (Newmarket) 1 mile (1.6km)
Queen Mother Champion Chase (Cheltenham) 2 miles (3.2km)
St Leger (Doncaster) $1\frac{3}{4}$ miles (2.8km)
Sussex Stakes (Goodwood) 1 mile (1.6km)
Two Thousand Guineas (Newmarket) 1 mile (1.6km)

Whitbread Gold Cup (Sandown) $3\frac{1}{2}$ miles (5.6km)
Yorkshire Oaks (York) $1\frac{1}{2}$ miles (2.4km)

*See also* CLASSIC RACES.

**Alpine race.** *See under* ALPINE.

**Bumping races.** *See under* BUMP.

**Dirt-track racing.** *See under* DIRT.

**Epsom races.** *See under* EPSOM.

**Flat race.** *See under* FLAT.

**One-horse race.** *See under* ONE.

**Point-to-point race.** *See under* POINT.

**Rat race.** *See under* RAT.

**Sack race.** *See under* SACK.

**Selling race.** *See under* SELL.

**Three-legged race.** *See under* THREE.

**Weight-for-age race, A.** *See under* WEIGH.

**Rache.** In medieval England, a hound that hunts by scent. They were later called 'running hounds' (*canes currentes*). *See also* ALANS.

> At first I will begin with raches and their nature, and then greyhounds and their nature, and then alaunts and their nature ... and then I shall devise and tell the sickness of hounds and their diseases.
>
> EDWARD, 2ND DUKE OF YORK: *The Master of Game*, Prologue (*c.*1410)

**Rachel.** The younger and prettier daughter of LABAN and the wife of JACOB. Jacob loves her and works seven years for Laban to get her, but he is tricked into taking her elder sister, LEAH. He serves another seven years and marries Rachel as well. Rachel is barren, however, and persuades Jacob to sleep both with Leah and with her servant Bilhah. Her prayers are finally answered and she gives birth to JOSEPH. Later she bears BENJAMIN, but dies in childbirth. Her story is told in Genesis 29–33, 35.

**Rachel** or **Mademoiselle Rachel.** A French actress whose real name was Élisabeth Rachel Félix (1821–58). She was the daughter of poor Jewish pedlars, but going on the stage as a girl, she won a great triumph in 1843 in the name part of Racine's *Phèdre* (1677). As Adrienne Lecouvreur, in Augustin Eugène Scribe's play of that name (1849), she confirmed her position as one of the greatest tragic actresses in Europe.

**Rachmanism.** RACK-RENTING, extortion and the general exploitation of tenants and purchasers of house property. The name comes from that of Peter Rachman (1920–62), a Polish immigrant whose undesirable activities of this kind in the Paddington area of London were brought to light in 1962–3.

**Rack.** The instrument of torture so called (connected with German *recken*, 'to strain') was a frame in which a man was fastened and his arms and legs stretched by windlass arrangements. Not infrequently the limbs were wrenched from their sockets. Its use in England was abolished in 1640. *See also* DUKE OF EXETER'S DAUGHTER.

**Rack and ruin.** Utter decay or destitution. Here 'rack' is a variant of wrack and wreck.

**Rack one's brains, To.** To strain them to discover or recollect something; to puzzle about something.

**Rack-rent.** Legally regarded as the annual rent that can be reasonably charged for a property, being that which equals, or nearly equals, its value in the open market. The term is used generally for any excessive rent, one which is 'racked' or stretched. *See also* RACHMANISM.

**Rack up, To.** To achieve a score.

**Racket.** Noise or confusion. The word is probably imitative, like crack, bang, splash, rattle and so on. Also, colloquially, a revelry; one's line of business; BLACKMAIL or extortion.

**Racketeer.** A person engaged in an illegal enterprise for profit, from the practice (of American origin) of creating a noise, commotion or racket to enable a theft or crime to be carried out without attracting attention. The term was next applied to blackmailers and extortioners, and their activities became rackets.

**Radar.** A term formed from *ra*dio *d*etection *a*nd *r*anging, as a means of detecting the direction and range of aircraft, ships and the like by the reflection of radio waves. It is particularly valuable at night or in fog when the eye is of no avail. It was first developed effectively for the purposes by Sir Robert Watson-Watt in 1934–5 (and independently in the USA, France and Germany) and was of great importance during the Second World War, especially during the BATTLE OF BRITAIN.

**Radcliffe Library.** A library at Oxford, founded with a bequest of £40,000 left for the purpose by Dr John Radcliffe (1650–1714) and originally intended for a medical library. Dr Radcliffe was a prominent London physician, known for his candour. When summoned to Queen ANNE he told her that there was nothing the matter with her but 'vapours', and he refused to attend her on her death bed.

**Radegund, St.** A Thuringian princess (518–587) who was captured by the Franks when she was 12, educated by King Clotaire, and made his wife at the age of 18. Disgusted with the crimes of the royal family, she became a nun and founded the monastery of St Croix at Poitiers. Her feast-day is 13 August.

**St Radegund's lifted stone.** A stone 60ft (18m) in circumference, placed on five supporting stones, said by the historians of Poitou to have been so arranged in 1478, to commemorate a great fair held on the spot in October of that year. Country folk claimed that Queen Radegonde brought the impost stone on her head and the five uprights in her apron, and arranged them all as they appear today.

**Radical.** A political label denoting an ultra-liberal, which came into use about 1816 and is applicable to ORATOR HUNT, Major Cartwright, William Cobbett and many others of that period. The early radicals drew their inspiration mainly from the French Revolution, but John Wilkes (1727–97) may be considered representative of a somewhat earlier tradition.

> If the Whigs most inclined to popular courses adhere steadily to their determination of having no communication with the Radicals of any description, I trust the session may pass over without any schism among Opposition.
>
> Letter from Mr Allen to Mr Creevey (20 November 1816)

**Radical Jack.** John George Lambton (1792–1840), 1st Earl of Durham. He was prominent in the Whig party, and acquired the nickname for his persistent advocacy of radical reforms. He took a major part in the struggle for the Reform Act of 1832.

**Radiocarbon dating.** A scientific method of estimating the age of organic materials. Carbon dioxide from the atmosphere, which contains the radioactive isotope Carbon-14, is taken up by all living matter. After the organism has died, the amount of Carbon-14 diminishes at a known rate, thus permitting the age of the material to be dated approximately.

**Raffles.** The gentleman crook, with full name A.J. Raffles, invented by E.W. Hornung (1866–1921) for a series of short stories published in the 1890s in the *Strand* and other popular magazines. He is an 'upper crust' sportsman and patriot, and his adventures are told by his former public school fag and admirer, Bunny Manders. The stories inspired similar tales by other writers and there were various films starring him, in which he was played by such actors as John Barrymore and David Niven.

**Rafter, Jack.** *See under* JACK.

**Rag.** A tatter, hence a remnant (as 'not a rag of decency', 'not a rag of evidence'), hence a vagabond or RAGAMUFFIN.

In university slang, a rag is a boisterous escapade or jollification, usually involving horseplay and practical jokes. Many universities have a rag day or even a rag week, in which the students organize colourful events to raise money for charity. A traditional ingredient is the parading of gaudy floats through the town streets.

**Rag, The.** The nickname of the Army and Navy CLUB, PALL MALL. It is said to have originated in the remark of a dissatisfied member who described the entertainment there as 'rag and famish'. Another suggestion is that the 'rag' is the flag.

**Rag, To.** To tease and torment a person; to badger them.

**Ragamuffin.** A ragged and unkempt person, especially a child. The word comes from the name of Ragamoffyn, a demon in the great poem *Piers Plowman* (*c*.1367–70), itself probably based on rag.

**Rag-and-bone man.** A man who buys and sells (or used to buy and sell) old clothes, furniture and the like, making his way around the streets of a town or city. The 'rags' are the clothes, and the 'bones', left over from meals, were used for boiling down to make glue (for the furniture).

**Ragged robin.** A wild flower (*Lychnis floscuculi*), so named from the ragged appearance of its fringed petals. The word is used by Tennyson for a pretty damsel in ragged clothes.

> And should some great court-lady say, the Prince
> Hath pick'd a ragged-robin from the hedge,
> And like a madman brought her to the court,
> Then were you shamed, and, worse, might shame the Prince.
>
> TENNYSON: *Idylls of the King*, 'The Marriage of Geraint' (1859)

**Ragged schools.** VOLUNTARY SCHOOLS for the education of destitute children, originated by John Pounds (1766–1839), a Portsmouth shoemaker, about 1818. Ragged SUNDAY SCHOOLS, day schools and evening schools made an important contribution to the welfare of the homeless young of 19th-century London and elsewhere. The philanthropic 7th Earl of Shaftesbury was a notable benefactor.

**Ragtag and bobtail.** The RIFF-RAFF, rabble or GREAT UNWASHED. The common expression in the 16th and 17th centuries was 'the rag and tag'.

**Ragtime.** Medium-tempo syncopated music of American Negro origin, properly solo piano music, although also played by bands. Scott Joplin's *Maple Leaf Rag* (1899) was the first of its kind. *See also* BLUES; BOOGIE-WOOGIE; JAZZ; SWING.

**Rag trade, The.** The clothing and fashion industries.

**Rag water.** In thieves' jargon, whisky.

**Bear and ragged staff, The.** *See under* BEAR.

**Chew the rag, To.** *See under* CHEW.

**Glad rags.** *See under* GLAD.

**Local rag, The.** *See under* LOCAL.

**Red rag.** *See under* RED.

**Raglan.** An overcoat that has no shoulder seams, the sleeves extending up to the neck. Such a coat was first worn by Lord Raglan (1788–1855), the British commander in the Crimean War (1854–6).

**Ragman rolls.** The returns of each HUNDRED to Edward I's inquest of 1274–5, also called Hundred rolls. Their colloquial name is apparently from their ragged appearance, which is the result of their numerous pendant seals, from a game called 'ragman' involving a roll with strings attached. The roll of Homage and Fealty made by the Scottish clergy and barons to Edward I at Berwick in 1297 is likewise so called. *See also* RIGMAROLE.

**Ragnarok.** The *Götterdämmerung* or Twilight of the Gods in Scandinavian mythology (from Old Norse *ragnarökkr*, from *regin*, 'the gods', and *rökkr*, 'twilight'). The day of doom, when the old world and all its inhabitants were annihilated. Out of the destruction a new world was born, a world at peace. Of the old gods, BALDER returned, as well as ODIN's two sons VIDAR and Vail, Vili and Ve (Odin's brother's sons), Magni and Modi, sons of THOR, and Hoenir (Odin's companion).

**Rahu** (Sanskrit, 'eclipse'). The demon that, according to Hindu legend, causes eclipses. One day he quaffed some of the NECTAR of immortality, but was discovered by the sun and moon, who informed against him, and VISHNU cut off his head. As he had already taken some of the nectar into his mouth, the head was immortal, and he ever afterwards hunted the sun and moon, which he sometimes caught, thus causing eclipses.

**Raid. Baedeker raids.** *See under* BAEDEKER.

**Jameson Raid.** *See under* JAMESON.

**Tip and run raid.** *See under* TIP.

**Railroad** or **railway.** Both terms were originally used in England, but railway has long been the normal English usage, while railroad is the accepted American form.

> Alas! even the giddiness attendant on a journey on this Manchester rail-road is not so perilous to the nerves, as that too frequent exercise in the merry-go-round of the ideal world.
>
> SIR WALTER SCOTT: *Count Robert of Paris*: Introductory Address (1831)

**Railroad, To.** An American term, meaning to hustle someone through (as of school) or out (as of an assembly) with unseemly haste and without reference to the proper formalities. The term dates from the 19th century, when American railroad companies were fiercely competitive in the race to open up the West and link the coastlines.

**Railway King, The.** George Hudson (1800–71), MP and chairman of the York and North Midland Railway Company, Midland Railway Company and others, whose ventures in railway amalgamations and speculations at first proved so profitable that he dominated the market. The railway mania of 1847–8 brought his ruin, however. He was accused of 'cooking the books', and legal proceedings stripped him of his fortune. He remained an MP until 1859.

**Underground railroad.** *See under* UNDER.

**What a way to run a railway!** *See under* WHAT.

**Rain. Rain cats and dogs, To.** To rain very heavily. In northern mythology the cat is supposed to have great influence on the weather, and 'The cat has a gale of wind in her tail' is a seafarer's expression for when a cat is unusually frisky. Witches that rode on storms were said to assume the form of cats. The dog is a signal of wind, like the wolf, both of which were attendants of ODIN, the storm god. Thus cat may be taken as a symbol of the pouring rain, and dog of the strong gusts of wind accompanying a rainstorm.

**Rain check.** In the USA a receipt or the counterfoil of a ticket entitling one to see another baseball game if the original match for which the ticket was purchased is rained off. The phrase is now in general use of a promise to accept an invitation at a later date, so that if one is invited and cannot accept, one says, 'I'll take a rain check'.

**Rain tree.** Old travellers to the Canary Islands told of a linden tree from which sufficient water to supply all the men and beasts of the island of Hierro was said to fall. In certain weather conditions moisture condenses and collects on the broad leaves of many trees. The genisaro or guango, *Pithecolobium saman*, or ornamental tropical tree, one of the Leguminosae, is known as the rain tree. In this case ejections of juice by the cicadas are responsible for the 'rain' under its branches. Another is the *Andira inermis*, found in tropical Africa and America.

**As right as rain.** *See under* AS.

**Come rain or shine.** *See under* COME.

**It never rains but it pours.** One occurrence is frequently the harbinger of many more; strokes of good or ill fortune are often accompanied by additional benefits or misfortunes. An 18th-century proverb. 'But' here means 'without', i.e. 'It never rains without pouring', 'Every time it rains, it is a real downpour'.

**Put something by for a rainy day, To.** To save something against bad times.

**Rainbow.** The old legend is that if one reaches the spot where a rainbow touches the earth and digs there, one will be sure to find a pot of gold. Hence visionaries, wool-gatherers, day-dreamers and the like are sometimes called rainbow chasers, because of their habit of hoping for impossible things.

> Somewhere over the rainbow
> Way up high,
> There's a land that I heard of
> Once in a lullaby.
>
> E.Y. HARBURG: 'Over the Rainbow' (song in the film *The Wizard of Oz*) (1939)

**Rainbow Corner.** In the Second World War Messrs Lyons' Corner House in Shaftesbury Avenue, London, was taken over and turned into a large café and lounge for American servicemen under this name, and it became a general meeting place for Americans in London. The name was in reference to the 42ND: RAINBOW Division (*see* UNITED STATES ARMY *under* REGIMENTAL AND DIVISIONAL NICKNAMES), and the rainbow in the insignia of SHAEF (Supreme Headquarters Allied Expeditionary Forces).

**Raise. Raise a laugh, To.** To cause others to laugh.

**Raise an eyebrow, To.** To give a look of surprise or uncertainty.

**Raise Cain, To.** To cause a commotion or make a noisy disturbance. CAIN here is either used as an alternative to 'the Devil', or is a direct allusion to Cain's violent anger, which drove him to kill his brother (Genesis 4:5).

> Seven men from all the world back to Docks again,
> Rolling down the Ratcliffe Road drunk and raising
> Cain.
>
> RUDYARD KIPLING: Ballad of the 'Bolivar' (1890)

**Raised to the bench, To be.** To be made a judge.

**Raised to the episcopal bench, To be.** To be made a BISHOP.

**Raise** or **kick up dust, To.** To make a commotion or fuss.

**Raise hell, To.** To create a disturbance; to protest vigorously.

**Raise one's glass, To.** To drink someone's health.

**Raise one's hand, To.** To make as if to strike a person.

**Raise someone's spirits, To.** To cheer or reinvigorate them; to give them optimism.

**Raise the Devil, To.** To cause a commotion.

**Raise the roof, To.** To be very noisy; to make a real hullabaloo.

**Raise the wind, To.** To obtain necessary money or funds.

**Fire raiser.** *See under* FIRE.

**Raison. Raison d'état** (French, 'reason of state'). The doctrine that the interests of the state take precedence even at the expense of moral considerations.

**Raison d'être** (French). The reason for a thing's existence, its justification, as: 'If crime were abolished there would be no *raison d'être* for the police.'

**Rajah.** Hindi for 'king', from Sanskrit, and cognate with Latin *rex*. The title of an Indian king or prince, given later to tribal chiefs and comparatively minor rulers of various states. Maharajah means 'great rajah'.

**Raleigh, Sir Walter.** Raleigh or Ralegh (1552–1618), a courtier of Elizabeth I, has gone down in history as privateer and poet, saint and sinner. He led an expedition in search of EL DORADO but lost his fleet and broke the terms of the mission by razing a Spanish town. He is popularly remembered for laying his cloak over a puddle so that Elizabeth could cross without wetting her feet, but the story was probably invented by Sir Walter Scott for his novel *Kenilworth* (1821). Raleigh's secret affairs and machinations earned him a suspended death sentence, which was finally carried out at WHITEHALL.

**Ralph. Ralph Robinson.** *See* FARMER GEORGE.

**Ralph Roister Doister.** The name of the earliest English comedy on classical lines, so called from its chief character. It probably appeared in 1552 or 1553 and was written by Nicholas Udall, headmaster of Eton (1534–41) and headmaster of Westminster (1555–6).

**Ram** (noun). At one time, the ram was the usual prize at wrestling matches.

**Ram and Teazle, The.** A PUBLIC HOUSE SIGN, in compliment to the Clothworkers' Company. The ram symbolizes wool, and the teazle is used for raising the nap of woollen cloth.

**Ram Feast, The.** Formerly held on May morning at Holne, Dartmoor, Devon, when a ram was run down in the 'Ploy Field' and roasted, complete with fleece, close by a granite pillar. At midday, a scramble took place for a slice, which was supposed to bring luck to those who got it. At Kingsteignton, Devon, a decorated carcass is still escorted through the town on Whit Monday (now Spring Bank Holiday Monday) and afterwards roasted in the open.

**Ram of the Zodiac, The.** This is the famous Chrysomallus, whose GOLDEN FLEECE was stolen by JASON. *See also* ARIES.

**Ram** (verb). **Ram** or **force something down someone's throat, To.** To force an opinion on a person that they may be unwilling to 'swallow'; to assert insistently without allowing an opportunity for reply or being prepared to listen.

**Rama.** The seventh incarnation of VISHNU (*see also* AVATAR). His beautiful wife, Sita, was abducted by Ravana, the demon king of Ceylon. With the aid of a nation of monkeys who collected trees and rocks, a bridge, Adam's bridge, was built across the straits. Rama and his invading army gradually overcame the enemy, and Rama's arrow slew the demon monster. The story is told in the RAMAYANA.

**Ramayana** (Sanskrit, 'deeds of Rama'). The history of Rama, the great epic poem of ancient India, ranking with the MAHABHARATA and almost with the ILIAD. It is ascribed to the poet Valmiki and contains 24,000 verses in 7 books.

**Ramadan.** The ninth month of the Muslim year and the Muslim equivalent of Lent or Holy Month. It is the month in which the KORAN was revealed. Because the MUSLIM CALENDAR is lunar, it sometimes means that Ramadan falls in midsummer when the fast causes much discomfort, since it involves abstinence from drinking between sunrise and sunset.

**Rambo.** The tough Vietnam War veteran first appeared in David Morrell's violent thriller, *First Blood* (1971), in which he runs into trouble with a local sheriff, takes to the hills and finally massacres an entire unit of the National Guard single-handed. He was brought before a wide public by the film of the same title (1982), in which he is played by Sylvester Stallone, and by its unashamedly melodramatic sequels, *Rambo First Blood Part II* (1985) and *Rambo III* (1988). His name became a household word when President Reagan praised the second film in one of his speeches, as a result of which 'Rambo' became a nickname for Reagan himself, especially with regard to his policy of foreign military intervention.

> Given the bomb-'em-kill-'em suggestions pulsing from the typewriters of 100 literate Rambos, a boycott of the airport was the most reasonable act suggested.
> *Washington Post* (6 July 1985)

**Rambouillet, Hôtel de.** *See under* HÔTEL.

**Rameses.** *See* RAMSES.

**Ramilie** or **Ramillies.** A name given to certain articles of dress in commemoration of the Duke of Marlborough's victory over the French at Ramillies (near Namur in modern Belgium) in 1706. The Ramillies hat was the cocked hat, worn between 1714 and 1740, on which the brim was turned up in three equal-sized cocks. The Ramillies wig, which lasted until after 1760, had a long, gradually diminishing plait, called the Ramillies plait, with a large bow at the top and a smaller one at the bottom.

**Raminagrobis.** The name of an old poet in Rabelais' *Gargantua and Pantagruel* (1534) who gives advice as to whether or not PANURGE should get married. There is also an old cat of the name in the fables of La Fontaine. It represents the words *Domine grobis*, from Latin *Domine*, 'O Lord', and *grobis*, an Old French word for a fat cat.

**Rampage, On the.** Acting in a violently excited or angry manner. The word was originally Scottish and is probably connected with 'ramp', to storm and rage.

**Rampant.** The heraldic term for an animal, especially a lion, shown rearing up with the forepaws in the air. Strictly speaking, a lion rampant should stand on the SINISTER hind leg, with both forelegs elevated, and the head in profile.

**Ramses** or **Rameses.** The name of several PHARAOHS. The most notable were Ramses II (1304–1237 BC), who built the temple of Luxor, and Ramses III (1198–67 BC), traditionally thought to be the pharaoh from whom MOSES secured the release of the Jews. The name Ramses is of Egyptian origin and means 'RA bore him'.

**Ran.** *See* AEGIR.

**Ranch, Dude.** *See under* DUDE.

**Randan, On the.** On a spree, having a high old time in town. Randan is perhaps a variant of 'random'. Formerly, at Coal Aston, Derbyshire, when a man was 'rantanned', a straw likeness was made and carried around the village on three successive nights, accompanied by people banging tin cans and making a general din. The image was burned after the last parade. Matrimonial upsets usually provided the occasion for such performances. *See also* RIDING; SHALLAL; SKIMMINGTON.

**Ranee** or **Rani.** A Hindu queen, the feminine of RAJAH.

**Ranelagh.** An old London place of amusement on the site that now forms part of the grounds of Chelsea Hospital. It was named after Richard Jones, 1st Earl of Ranelagh, who built a house and laid out gardens there in 1690. From 1742 to 1803 Ranelagh rivalled VAUXHALL GARDENS for concerts, masquerades and the like. A notable feature was the Rotunda, which was built in 1742 and was not unlike the Albert Hall in design. It was 185ft (56m) across with numerous boxes in which refreshments were served, while the brightly lit floor formed a thronged promenade. There was also a Venetian pavilion in the centre of a lake.

The Ranelagh Club was established in 1894 in Barn Elms Park, in southwest London, to provide facilities for polo, tennis, golf and other sports.

**Ranger. Rangers.** Picked men in the US Army who worked with British COMMANDOS. They were named after ROGERS' RANGERS, an intrepid body of frontiersmen organized by Major Robert Rogers (1731–95). Rangers first appeared at the Dieppe Raid in 1942 on which a small party went as armed observers.

**Lone Ranger.** *See under* LONE.

**Rogers' Rangers.** *See under* ROGERS.

**Sloane Ranger.** *See under* SLOANE.

**Texas Rangers.** *See under* TEXAS.

**Rani.** *See* RANEE.

**Rank.** A row, a line (especially of soldiers); also high station, dignity, eminence, as:

> The rank is but the guinea's stamp,
> The man's the gowd for a' that!
> ROBERT BURNS: 'For a' that and a' that' (1790)

**Rank and fashion.** People of high social standing; the UPPER TEN.

**Rank and file.** Soldiers and non-commissioned officers as distinct from commissioned officers, hence the followers in a movement as distinct from its leaders. 'Rank' refers to men in line abreast or side by side, 'file' to men standing one behind the other.

**Close ranks, To.** *See under* CLOSE.

**Pull rank, To.** *See under* PULL.

**Rise from the ranks, To.** *See under* RISE.

**Ransom.** In origin the same word as redemption, from Latin *redemptio*, through Old French *rançon*, earlier *redempçon*.

**King's** or **queen's ransom, A.** *See under* KING.

**Rantan.** *See* RANDAN.

**Ranz des vaches.** Literally procession of the cows. Simple melodies sung by the Swiss cowherds or played on the alpenhorn when they drive their cows to pasture or call them home from the mountain-side.

**Rap. Rap over the knuckles, A.** Figuratively, a rebuke. The allusion is to the once common practice in schools, when children were punished for a misdemeanour in class by a sharp rap on the knuckles from the teacher's ruler.

**Not worth a rap.** *See under* WORTH.

**Rape.** One of the six divisions into which Sussex is divided, intermediate between HUNDRED and SHIRE. It is said that each had its own river, forest and castle. The word is identical with Old English *rāp*, 'rope', and alludes to the fact that the land so delimited was fenced off with a rope. *See also* LATHE.

**Rape of the Lock, The.** Lord Petre, in a thoughtless moment of frolic and gallantry, cut off a lock of Miss Arabella Fermor's hair, and this liberty gave rise to the bitter feud between the two families, which Alexander Pope worked up into the best heroic-comic poem of the language. The first sketch was published in 1712 in two cantos, and the complete work, including the most happily conceived machinery of SYLPHS and GNOMES, in five cantos in 1714. Pope, under the name of Esdras Barnevelt, apothecary, later pretended that the poem was a covert satire on Queen ANNE and the Barrier Treaty.

> Say what strange motive, goddess! could compel
> A well-bred lord to assault a gentle belle?
> O say what stranger cause, yet unexplored,
> Could make a gentle belle reject a lord?
> *The Rape of the Lock*, i (1712)

*See also* MOON.

**Rape of the Sabine Women, The.** The legend, connected with the foundation of Rome, is that, as ROMULUS had difficulty in providing his followers with wives, he invited the men of the neighbouring tribes to a festival. In the absence of the menfolk, the Roman youths raided the Sabine territory and carried off all the women they could find. The incident has frequently been depicted in art. Rubens' canvas in the National Gallery, London, painted *c*.1635–40, is one of the best known examples. Rape here thus means 'carrying off'.

**Raphael.** One of the principal ANGELS of Jewish angelology. The Book of TOBIT tells how he travelled with Tobias into Media and back again, instructing him on the way how to marry Sara and to drive away the wicked spirit. Milton calls him the 'sociable spirit' and the 'affable archangel' (*Paradise Lost*, vii (1667)), and it was he who was sent by God to warn ADAM of his danger.

> Raphael, the sociable Spirit, that deigned
> To travel with Tobias, and secured
> His marriage with the seven-times-wedded maid.
> *Paradise Lost*, v

Raphael is usually distinguished in art by a pilgrim's staff or carrying a fish, in allusion to his aiding Tobias to capture the fish that performed the miraculous cure of his father's eyesight.

**Raphaelesque.** In the style of the great Italian painter Raffaello Sanzio (1483–1520), known as Raphael, who was specially notable for his supreme excellence in the development of all the essential qualities of art: composition, expression, design and colouring.

**Rapparee.** A wild Irish plunderer. He was so called from his being armed with a rapaire, or half-pike, this word itself related to Irish *rapaire*, 'rapier', 'treacherous person' or 'robber'.

**Rappee.** A coarse kind of snuff manufactured from dried tobacco by an instrument called in French a *râpe* or rasp. It is so called because it is *râpé*, rasped or scraped.

**Rara avis** (Latin, 'rare bird'). A phenomenon; a prodigy; something quite out of the ordinary. The term was first applied by Juvenal to the black swan, which until its discovery in Australia was unknown.

> Rara avis in terris nigroque simillima cycno
> (A bird rarely seen on the earth, like nothing so much as a black swan).
> JUVENAL: *Satires*, i (2nd century AD)

**Rare.** Underdone, as of a steak, or less commonly, lightly cooked, as of an egg. The word is a variant of the obsolete *rear*, from Old English *hrēr*, perhaps related to *hrēran*, 'to stir', 'to move'.

**Rare Ben.** The inscription on the tomb of Ben Jonson (1573–1637), the dramatist, in the north nave aisle of Westminster Abbey. 'O rare Ben Jonson', was, says John Aubrey, 'done at the charge of Jack Young (afterwards knighted), who, walking there when the grave was covering, gave the fellow eighteen pence to cut it.' 'Rare' here is Latin *rarus*, 'uncommon', 'remarkable'.

**Raree show.** A peepshow, a show carried about in a box. In the 17th century most of the travelling showmen were Savoyards, and perhaps this represents their attempt at pronunciation of 'rare'.

> Bowed to the earth with bitter woe,
> Or laughing at some raree-show,
> We flutter idly to and fro.
> LEWIS CARROLL: *Sylvie and Bruno*, Dedication (1889)

**Rascal.** This word, originally a collective term for the rabble of an army, the commonalty, the mob, was early (14th century) adopted as a term of the chase, and for a long time almost exclusively denoted the lean, worthless deer of a herd. In the late 16th century it was retransferred to people, and so to its present meaning, a mean rogue, a scamp, a base fellow. Shakespeare says, 'Horns? the noblest deer has them as huge as the rascal' (*As You Like It*, III, iii (1599)), and 'Come, you thin thing; come, you rascal' (*Henry IV*, *Pt II*, V, iv (1597)). The word itself ultimately goes back to Latin *radere*, *rasus*, 'to scrape'.

**Raspberry, To blow a.** *See under* BLOW.

**Rasputin.** Grigoriy Yefimovich Novykh (*c*.1871–1916), the Siberian monk notorious for his baneful influence over the Russian monarchy in its last years, was apparently so called by his fellow villagers. Rasputin means 'dissolute' and he lived up to his nickname until the end. His easy conquests over women were helped by his assertion that physical contact with him was itself a purification. His gross indecencies and disgusting coarseness did not prevent his excessive familiarity with the Empress Alexandra and Tsar Nicholas II, which arose from his undoubted success in healing and sustaining the Tsarevich Alexis, a victim of haemophilia. Rasputin was first called to the palace in 1905 and his power increased steadily, until his murder by Prince YUSUPOV and his associates.

**Rastafarians.** Members of the Ras Tafari, a black political and religious group originating in the 1920s in Jamaica. They recognized Haile Selassie (1892–1975), emperor of Ethiopia, as a god. They consider that blacks are superior to whites, that Ethiopia is heaven and that Haile Selassie would arrange that all of African origin will find a homeland in Ethiopia. *Ras* means 'duke' and *Tafari* was a family name of Haile Selassie ('Might of the Trinity'). There are now Rastafarians in the West Indies, the USA, Canada and Europe, conspicuous by their long matted curls (dreadlocks).

**Rat.** The Egyptians and Phrygians deified rats. Egyptians believed that the rat symbolized utter destruction and also wise judgement; Phrygians believed that rats always chose the best bread.

Pliny writes (*Naturalis Historia*, VIII, lvii (1st century AD)) that the Romans drew presages from rats and that to see a white rat was an omen of good fortune. Clothing or equipment gnawed by rats presaged ill fortune.

It was an old superstition among sailors that rats deserted a ship before she set out on a voyage that was to end in her loss. Similarly rats were said to leave a falling house.

> In few, they hurried us aboard a bark,
> Bore us some leagues to sea; where they prepar'd
> A rotten carcass of a boat, not rigg'd,
> Nor tackle, sail, nor mast; the very rats
> Instinctively have quit it.
> SHAKESPEARE: *The Tempest*, I, ii (1611)

**Rat, To.** To forsake a losing side for the stronger party, as rats are said to forsake unseaworthy ships; to become a renegade; to 'squeal' or to inform.

**Rat, cat and dog.**

> The Cat, the Rat, and Lovell our dog,
> Rule all England under a hog.

These lines were affixed to the door of St Paul's and other places in the City of London in 1484 at the instigation of William Collingbourne (or Colyngbourne), a Wiltshire gentleman of Edward IV's household, who may have been an agent for Henry Tudor (later Henry VII). For this deed, according to the *Great Chronicle of London*, 'he was drawn unto the Tower Hill and there full cruelly put to death, at first hanged and straight cut down and ripped, and his bowels cast into the fire'. The rhyme implied that the kingdom was ruled by Francis, Viscount Lovell, whose crest was a dog, Sir Richard Ratcliffe, the Rat, and Sir William Catesby, Speaker of the HOUSE OF COMMONS, the Cat. The Hog was the white boar or cognizance of Richard III. *See also* BLUE BOAR.

**Rat-killer, The.** APOLLO received this derogatory title from the following incident: Apollo sent a swarm of rats against Crinis, one of his priests, for neglect of his office, but the priest, seeing the invaders coming, repented and obtained pardon. The god annihilated the rats with his far-darting arrows.

**Rat race.** The relentless struggle to get ahead of one's rivals, particularly in professional and commercial occupations.

**Rat run.** A residential street used by drivers as a short cut or to avoid a congested main road, especially during the rush hour.

> The rat-run has become the front line in the war between people and cars. As the number of vehicles rises and traffic calming measures proliferate, more roads are being used as short cuts.
> *Sunday Times* (6 December 1998)

**Rats!** Nonsense, or an exclamation of annoyance. It is of 19th-century American origin and may have arisen as a form of drat. It seems to have a pre-echo in Browning's popular poem for children, 'The Pied Piper of Hamelin', ii (1842), where it has an exclamatory line to itself:

> Rats!
> They fought the dogs and killed the cats,
> And bit the babies in the cradles.

**Irish rats.** *See under* IRISH.

**Like a drowned rat.** *See under* LIKE.

**Smell a rat, To.** *See under* SMELL.

**Ratatouille.** A type of vegetable casserole or stew, typically containing tomatoes, aubergines, courgettes and the like, and often called *ratatouille* *provençale*. The word itself is apparently based on French *touiller*, 'to stir'.

**Rate of knots, At a.** *See under* AT.

**Ration. Draw rations.** *See under* DRAW.

**Iron rations.** *See under* IRON.

**Raven.** A bird of ill omen, fabled to forebode death, and to bring disease and ill luck.

> The raven himself is hoarse
> That croaks the fatal entrance of Duncan
> Under my battlements.
> SHAKESPEARE: *Macbeth*, I, v (1605)

CICERO was forewarned of his death by the fluttering of ravens, and Lord Macaulay relates the legend that a raven entered the chamber of the great orator on the very day of his murder and pulled the clothes off his bed. Like many other birds, ravens indicate the approach of foul weather. When ravens forsake their normal abode, one may look for famine and mortality, because ravens bear the characters of SATURN, the author of these calamities, and have a very early knowledge of the bad disposition of that planet.

According to Roman legend ravens were once as white as swans and not inferior in size, but one day a raven told APOLLO that CORONIS, a Thessalian NYMPH whom he passionately loved, was faithless. The god shot the nymph with his dart, while hating the telltale bird.

In Christian art, the raven is an emblem of God's Providence, in allusion to the ravens that fed ELIJAH. St Oswald holds in his hand a raven with a ring in its mouth, St BENEDICT has a raven at his feet, and St PAUL THE HERMIT is drawn with a raven bringing him a loaf of bread.

**Ravenstone** (German *Rabenstein*). The old stone gibbet of Germany, so called from the ravens that were wont to perch on it.

> Do not think
> I'll honour you so much as save your throat
> From the Ravenstone, by choking you myself.
> LORD BYRON: *Werner*, ii (1822)

**Fatal raven, The.** *See under* FATAL.

**Raw. Raw deal, A.** A transaction that is harsh or unfair to a person, perhaps from the idea that it leaves them feeling 'raw' or hurt.

**In the raw.** In an undressed or naked state; in a natural or unmodified state.

**Johnny Raw.** *See under* JOHNNY.

**Touch someone on the raw, To.** *See under* TOUCH.

**Rays, Pencil of.** *See under* PENCIL.

**Razor. Occam's razor.** *See under* OCCAM.

**On a razor's edge.** In a hazardous position or an acutely critical situation.

**Razzia.** An incursion made by the military into enemy territory for the purpose of carrying off cattle or slaves, or for enforcing tribute. It is the French form of Arabic *ghaziya*, 'raid', usually employed in connection with Algerian and North African affairs.

**Razzle-dazzle.** A boisterous spree; a jollification.

**On the razzle** or **razzle-dazzle.** On a spree; on a wildly drunken frolic.

**Re** (Latin). Respecting, in reference to, as 're Brown', in reference to the case of Brown. *See also* IN RE.

**Reach.** The stretch of a river that lies between two points or bends, so called because it reaches from point to point.

> The reach of the Thames off Runnimede is picturesque and pleasant, fringed with willows, varied by eyots, and brightened with abundant water-lilies.
> JAMES THORNE: *Handbook to the Environs of London* (1876)

**Reach-me-down.** Ready-made; second-hand. Used of clothes that one reaches up to take down from the shelf, hook etc.

**Read. Read between the lines, To.** To discern the hidden meaning; to draw certain conclusions that are not apparent on the surface. One method of cryptography is to write so that the hidden message is revealed only when alternate lines are read.

**Read oneself in, To.** Said of an Anglican clergyman on entering upon a new incumbency, because one of his first duties was formerly to give a public reading of the THIRTY-NINE ARTICLES in the church to which he has been appointed, and to make the Declaration of Assent.

**Read someone like a book, To.** To understand a person clearly, even from their slightest word or action.

> That lady, who read him like a book, preserved an appearance of complete unconsciousness.
> GEORGE JOHN WHYTE-MELVILLE: *Uncle John*, ch v (1874)

**Read someone's mind, To.** To discern their thoughts; to know what they are thinking.

**Read the riot act, To.** The original Riot Act was that of 1715, which stated that when 12 or more people were committing a riot it was the duty of the magistrates to command them to disperse, and that anyone who continued to riot for one hour afterwards was guilty of a felony. (The Public Order Act of 1986 superseded it.) Figuratively to read the riot act is to check noise, commotion and misbehaviour of children and others by vigorous and forceful protests, to threaten them with the consequences of disobedience.

**He that runs may read.** *See under* RUN.

**Penny readings.** *See under* PENNY.

**Third reading.** *See under* THIRD.

**Reader.** The designation of certain senior lecturers at many of the universities, and at the INNS OF COURT one who reads lectures in law. In printing, a reader is someone who reads and corrects proofs before publication. In a publisher's office, a reader is a person who reads and reports on manuscripts submitted for publication.

**Gentle reader.** *See under* GENTLE.

**Lay reader.** *See under* LAY.

**Readies.** An elliptical expression for READY MONEY.

**Ready. Ready money.** Cash down; money available for immediate payment. *See also* MONEY.

> *Algernon* (*picking up empty plate in horror*): Good heavens! Lane! Why are there no cucumber sandwiches? I ordered them specially.
>
> *Lane*: There were no cucumbers in the market this morning, sir. I went down twice.
>
> *Algernon*: No cucumbers!
>
> *Lane* (*gravely*): No, sir. Not even for ready money.
>
> OSCAR WILDE: *The Importance of Being Earnest*, I (1895)

**Ready, steady, go!** A traditional formula for starting a race, especially among children. At the word 'ready' the runner prepares himself, at 'steady' he braces himself, at 'go!' he starts to run. In professional athletics, when contestants are UNDER STARTER'S ORDERS, the formula is usually 'On your marks, get set, go!', or simply 'Marks, set', with 'go!' replaced by the firing of the starter's pistol.

**Rough and ready.** *See under* ROUGH.

**Real. Real McCoy, The.** An expression used in the USA, but formerly in Britain it was the Real MacKay. Various stories about an American boxer have been suggested as the origin of the phrase, but Eric Partridge, in *From Sanskrit to Brazil* (1952), says with more probable truth that it dates from the 1880s and originated in Scotland, where it was applied to whisky, men and things of the highest quality. The whisky was exported to both the USA and Canada, where people of Scottish origin drank the whisky and kept the phrase alive. In the 1890s, however, there is no doubt that it was applied to a famous boxer, Kid 'the Real' McCoy (1873–1940).

**Real presence.** The doctrine that Christ himself is present in the bread and wine of the EUCHARIST after consecration, as contrasted with doctrines that maintain that the Body and Blood are only symbolically present.

**Real thing, The.** True love, not infatuation.

**Realism.** In medieval scholastic philosophy the opposite of NOMINALISM, and the belief that abstract concepts or universals are real things existing independently of our conceptions and their expression. It was a development from PLATO's metaphysic and was held in varying forms by Johannes Scotus Erigena (*c*.815–*c*.877), REMIGIUS, St Anselm (1033–1109), Peter ABELARD, ALBERT THE GREAT, St THOMAS AQUINAS, Duns Scotus and others. *See also* DUNCE; SCHOLASTICISM.

In literature and art it denotes the attempt to present life as it is, however unpleasant, ugly or distasteful. Émile Zola (1840–1902) and Guy de Maupassant (1850–93) were leaders of this school in France at the end of the 19th century. The brutality and outspokenness of their writings led to an outcry, thus Anatole France described Zola's novel *La Terre* (1877), about farming and peasant life, as 'a heap of ordure'. Realism often tends to emphasize the crude, the perverted and the immoral somewhat disproportionately, at the expense of the more balanced, admirable or beautiful.

**Realm. Estates of the Realm.** *See under* ESTATE.

**Peers of the Realm.** *See under* PEER.

**Realpolitik** (German). Practical politics; political realism; otherwise politics based on national 'interests' or material considerations as distinct from moral objectives.

**Reaper, The Grim.** *See under* GRIM.

**Rearmouse** or **reremouse.** The bat. The word comes from Old English *hrēremūs*, probably from *hrēran*, 'to move', and *mūs*, 'mouse', as if the bat were a flying mouse.

**Reason. Age of reason, The.** *See under* AGE.

**Goddess of reason, The.** *See under* GODDESS.

**Listen to reason, To.** *See under* LISTEN.

**Stand to reason, To.** *See under* STAND.

**Temple of reason, The.** *See under* TEMPLE.

**Within reason.** *See under* WITHIN.

**Reb, Johnny.** *See under* JOHNNY.

**Rebecca.** The wife of ISAAC. When she conceived ESAU and JACOB as twins, they fought in her womb, and when they were born, she favoured Jacob, the younger, and helped him disguise himself so that he received his father's blessing. Her name appears in the Bible (Genesis 24, 26–8) in the form Rebekah.

**Rebeccaites.** Bands of Welsh tenant-farmers dressed as women were responsible for the Rebecca Riots of 1839 and 1842–3, which were suppressed with military aid. They demolished turnpike gates and were largely a reaction against tolls, rates, TITHES, rents and an unfair system of landholding. These riots occurred in Carmarthenshire, Pembroke and Brecon. The rioters took their name from Genesis 24:60: when REBECCA left her father's house, LABAN and his family 'blessed her', and said: 'Let thy seed possess the gate of those which hate them.'

**Rebellion, The Great.** *See under* GREAT.

**Rebus** (Latin, 'with things'). A pictorial riddle. The origin of the word has, somewhat doubtfully, been traced to the lawyers of Paris, who, during the carnival, used to satirize the follies of the day in SQUIBS called *De rebus quae geruntur* ('on the things that are happening'), and, to avoid libel actions, employed pictures either wholly or in part.

In HERALDRY the name is given to punning

devices on a coat of arms suggesting the name of the family to whom it belongs, such as the broken spear on the shield of Nicholas Breakspear (Pope Adrian IV).

**Reception room.** Estate agents' jargon for a living room, drawing room (lounge) or dining room, as one of the rooms in a house in which guests are received.

> A well proportioned detached 1920's residence conveniently located close to the heart of the village and transport. Five bedrooms, two bathrooms, large loft, three reception rooms, kitchen/breakfast room, cloakroom, boiler room, two garages, off road car parking for several cars.
> *The Times* (advertisement) (20 January 1999)

**Recessional.** The music or words, or both, accompanying the procession of clergy and choir when they retire after a service. Rudyard Kipling's 'Recessional' (1897) written for Queen Victoria's Diamond JUBILEE begins:

> God of our fathers, known of old,
> Lord of our far-flung battle-line,
> Beneath whose awful Hand we hold
> Dominion over palm and pine –
> Lord God of Hosts, be with us yet,
> Lest we forget – lest we forget!

**Rechabites.** Members of a teetotal benefit society (the Independent Order of Rechabites), founded in 1835, and so named from Rechab, who enjoined his family to abstain from wine and to dwell in tents (Jeremiah 35:6, 7).

**Recipe** or **receipt.** *Recipe* is Latin for 'take', and contracted into ℞ is used in doctors' prescriptions. A recipe is now more usually a list of ingredients and instructions for making a food dish. *See also* R.

**Reck one's own rede, To.** To be governed by one's own better judgement.

> Do not, as some ungracious pastors do,
> Show me the steep and thorny way to heaven,
> Whilst, like a puffed and reckless libertine,
> Himself the primrose path of dalliance treads,
> And recks not his own rede.
> SHAKESPEARE: *Hamlet*, I, iii (1600)

**Reckon. Reckon, To.** In the sense of 'to guess' (to suppose), the verb was in use in England by the early 17th century and later became widely used in the USA.

**Reckon up, To.** To count up; to settle accounts.

**Day of reckoning.** *See under* DAY.

**Dead reckoning.** *See under* DEAD.

**Someone to be reckoned with.** *See under* SOMEONE.

**Recollects.** The name given to (1) a reformed branch of the FRANCISCAN Observants first formed in France, and (2) a reformed group of AUGUSTINIAN Hermits founded in Spain. Both orders were first formed in the late 16th century.

**Record.** That which is recorded, originally 'got by heart', from Latin *cor*, *cordis*, 'heart'. Hence the best performance or most striking event of its kind known, especially in such phrases as 'to beat or break the record'; 'to win in record time'.

In a legal context a record is a list of crimes of which a person has previously been convicted, and to have a record is to be known as a criminal.

**Court of record.** *See under* COURT.

**For the record.** *See under* FOR.

**Off the record.** *See under* OFF.

**Set** or **put the record straight, To.** *See under* SET.

**Recorder.** Originally, the title of the official who was responsible for maintaining the legal customs of a local court. By the mid-19th century, the recorder had become the judge of a city or borough court who presided at the QUARTER SESSIONS. The Courts Act of 1971, however, permitted a barrister or solicitor of ten years' standing to be appointed a recorder, acting as a part-time judge of the CROWN COURT.

**Recreant.** One who yields (from Old French *recroire*, 'to yield in trial by combat'), alluding to the judicial combats, when the person who wished to give in cried for mercy, and was held a coward.

**Rector.** *See* CLERICAL TITLES.

**Recusants.** The name given from the time of Elizabeth I (r.1558–1603) to those who refused to attend the services of the CHURCH OF ENGLAND (from Latin *recusare*, 'to refuse'). The term commonly denoted 'popish recusants' although properly it included Protestant dissenters. Fines were first exacted under statute in 1552 and 1559 at the rate of 1s per Sunday, but they were raised to the exorbitant sum of £20 per month in 1587. Fortunately they were intermittently imposed, and the last fines for recusancy were those in 1782 on two Yorkshire labourers and their wives.

**Red.** One of the PRIMARY COLOURS. In HERALDRY it is said to signify magnanimity and fortitude; in liturgical use it is worn at certain seasons; and in popular folklore it is the colour of magic.

> Red is the colour of magic in every country, and has been so from the very earliest times. The caps of fairies and musicians are well-nigh always red.
> W.B. YEATS: *Fairy and Folk Tales of the Irish Peasantry*, 'The Trooping Fairies – The Merrow' (1888)

Today it is more often symbolical of anarchy and revolution: 'Red ruin, and the breaking up of laws' (Tennyson, *Idylls of the King*, 'Guinevere' (1859)). In the French Revolution the Red Republicans were those extremists who never hesitated to dye their hands in blood. In Russia, red (Russian *krasny*) is etymologically beautiful (*krasivy*), but in the former Soviet Union red was mostly regarded as the colour of radicalism, socialism (*see* RED FLAG) and revolution.

Red is the colour of the royal livery, and it is said that this colour was adopted by huntsmen because fox hunting was declared a royal sport by Henry II. *See also* IN PINK *under* PINK.

In the old ballads red was frequently applied to gold ('the gude red gowd'), and in thieves' CANT a gold watch is a 'red kettle', and the chain a 'red tackle'. One of the names given by the alchemists to the PHILOSOPHER'S STONE was the 'red tincture', because with its help they hoped to transmute the base metals into gold.

**Red admiral.** The butterfly *Vanessa atalanta*, which has black wings with distinctive red and white markings. Its name may have originally been the Admirable.

**Red Army.** The combined Soviet army and air force were officially so named from 1918 to 1946, when the forces were renamed the Soviet Army. The original name was long preferred by the Western media, however.

**Red biddy.** A highly intoxicating concoction of red wine and methylated spirit, such as an impoverished OLD BIDDY might drink.

**Red Book.** A directory relating to the court, the nobility and the UPPER TEN generally. *The Royal Kalendar*, published from 1767 to 1893, was known by this name, as also was Webster's *Royal Red Book*, a similar work first issued in 1847.

The name is also given to certain special works covered in red, such as the official parliamentary records of the old Austro-Hungarian Empire, similar to the English BLUEBOOKS.

**Red Book of Hergest, The** (*Llyfr Coch Hergest*). A Welsh manuscript of the late 14th or early 15th century containing the MABINOGION, poems by TALIESIN and Llywarch Hen, and a history of the world from ADAM to 1318. It is now in the library of Jesus College, Oxford.

**Red Book of the Exchequer** (*Liber ruber Scaccarii*). A collection of EXCHEQUER documents in the Public Record Office compiled by Alexander of Swerford in the earlier part of the 13th century, with subsequent additions. It contains material from the 12th to the 16th centuries and includes such important documents as the Laws of Henry I, the *Dialogue of the Exchequer* and the *Carte Baronum* (the returns of tenants in chief in 1166 certifying how many knights' fees they held and the services due to the king).

**Redbreasts.** The old BOW STREET RUNNERS. Dickens says:

> The Bow Street Runners ceased out of the land soon after the introduction of the new police. I remember them very well as standing about the door of the office in Bow Street. They had no other uniform than a blue dress-coat, brass buttons ... and a bright red cloth waistcoat ... The slang name for them was 'Redbreasts' in consequence.
>
> *Letters* (18 April 1862)

**Redbrick.** A term that came to be loosely applied to all English universities of a late 19th or early 20th century foundation. The name was introduced by 'Bruce Truscot' (Professor E. Allison Peers) in his book *Redbrick University* (1943). He was primarily dealing with the universities of Birmingham, Bristol, Leeds, Liverpool, Manchester, Reading and Sheffield, and expressly excluded London. In his Introduction he says: 'Though red brick, rather than dingy stone, has been chosen as the symbol of the new foundations, it must be categorically stated that no one university alone has been in the author's mind.' *See also* CAMFORD; OXBRIDGE.

**Red Brigades** (Italian, *Brigate rosse*). The group of urban guerrillas who emerged in Italy in 1969 and who in 1978 kidnapped and murdered the Christian Democrat statesman Aldo Moro.

**Red Button.** In the former Chinese Empire a MANDARIN of the first class wore in his cap a button or knob of red coral or ruby as a badge of honour.

**Redcap.** A colloquial term for the British military police, who wear red covers on their caps. In the USA, a redcap is a porter at a railway or bus station.

**Red card.** In football a red-coloured card displayed to a player by the referee to indicate that he has repeated an offence or disregarded a caution and is thus sent off the field.

**Red carpet.** A ceremonial carpet unrolled for the arrival or departure of an important visitor.

**Redcoats.** British soldiers, from the colour of their uniforms in line regiments before the introduction of KHAKI. Oliver Cromwell's NEW MODEL ARMY was the first to wear red coats as a uniform. Regiments were distinguished by the colour of their facings: Blue, Green, Buff etc. *See also* REGIMENTAL AND DIVISIONAL NICKNAMES.

**Red Comyn.** Sir John Comyn the younger of Badenoch, nephew of John Balliol, king of Scotland, was so called from his ruddy complexion and RED HAIR. He was the son of Black Comyn, John Comyn the elder, who was swarthy and black-haired. He was stabbed by Robert BRUCE in 1306 in the church of the Minorites at Dumfries, and afterwards dispatched by Lindsay and Kirkpatrick.

**Red Crescent.** The equivalent in Muslim countries of the RED CROSS.

**Red Cross, The.** A red cross on a white ground, sometimes called the Cross of Geneva, is the Swiss flag reversed, and indicates the neutrality of hospitals and ambulances. Hence its adoption by the Red Cross, the international humanitarian organization established by the GENEVA CONVENTION of 1864. *See also* RED CRESCENT.

The Red Cross is also the cross of St GEORGE.

**Red Cross Knight, The.** In Edmund Spenser's *The Faerie Queene* (I (1590)), the Red Cross Knight is a personification of St GEORGE, the patron saint of England. He typifies Christian holiness and his adventures are an allegory of the CHURCH OF ENGLAND. The knight is sent by the queen to destroy a DRAGON, which is ravaging the kingdom of Una's father. After many adventures and trials Una and the knight are united in marriage.

**Red dragon.** Anciently the badge of the Parthians, it was introduced in Britain by the Romans. In the 7th century it became the standard of King Cadwaladr and later was one of the supporters of the Tudor arms. The present Welsh flag consists of a red dragon *passant* on a ground of two horizontal strips (white over green). *See also* DRAGON; UNICORN.

**Red Dragons, The.** *See under* REGIMENTAL AND DIVISIONAL NICKNAMES; ROUGE DRAGON.

**Red duster.** The Red Ensign, the flag of British merchant ships since 1674, but also, until 1864, the senior ensign of the Royal Navy where it was used as squadronal colour. Its use was solely reserved for the Merchant Navy in 1864. It is a red flag with a union device in the upper canton, but before 1707 it bore a St GEORGE'S CROSS.

**Red-faced.** Embarrassed; ashamed. An abashed person frequently flushes up. Hence the mock self-reproach of someone who has 'put his foot in it': 'Was my face red!'

**Red Feathers, The.** *See under* REGIMENTAL AND DIVISIONAL NICKNAMES.

**Red flag.** Generally used to indicate danger or as a stop signal. It is also the symbol of international socialism and *The Red Flag* is a socialist anthem still used, somewhat incongruously, by the British LABOUR PARTY. It is not the same as the INTERNATIONALE.

> Then raise the scarlet standard high!
> Within its shade we'll live or die.
> Tho' cowards flinch and traitors sneer,
> We'll keep the red flag flying here.
> JAMES CONNELL: 'The Red Flag' (1889)

**Red Friday.** Friday 31 July 1925, when a stoppage in the coal industry, planned to meet the threat of wage cuts, was averted by promise of government subsidies to support wages and so on. It was so called by the Labour press to distinguish it from Black Friday of 15 April 1921, when union leaders called off an impending strike of railwaymen and transport workers designed to help the miners who were locked out.

**Red gold.** Payment made by the KGB in former Soviet Russia to Western spies and informants.

> In his resignation letter ... [he] admitted taking 'red gold' in the form of expenses for foreign trips paid for by the KGB, but not cash for information.
> *Sunday Times* (11 December 1994)

**Red Guard.** A movement of armed workers in Russia prior to the October Revolution of 1917. A militant youth movement of the name also existed in China from 1966 to 1976.

**Red hair.** For centuries the red-haired have been popularly held to be unreliable and quick-tempered. The fat of a dead red-haired person used to be in demand as an ingredient for poisons, and George Chapman says that flattery, like the plague:

> Strikes into the brain of man,
> And rageth in his entrails when he can,
> Worse than the poison of a red-hair'd man.
> *Bussy d'Ambois*, III, i (*c*.1604)

It was a former notion that a person with red hair could not be trusted, from the tradition that JUDAS ISCARIOT had red hair. Shakespeare says:

> *Rosalind*: His very hair is of the dissembling colour.
> *Celia*: Something browner than Judas's.
> *As You Like It*, III, iv (1599)

A man with black hair and a red beard was the worst of all. The old rhyme says:

> A red beard and a black head,
> Catch him with a good trick and take him dead.

Many Scots are red-haired, and Sandy is one of their NATIONAL NICKNAMES. Hence also the names of RED COMYN and ROB ROY. *See also* HAIR.

**Red Hand** or **Bloody Hand.** In coat armour, the device of ULSTER, a SINISTER hand, erect, open and couped at the wrist, gules. Carried as the Red Hand of the O'Neills as a charge on the coats-of-arms of English and Irish BARONETS (not on those of Scotland or Nova Scotia). The 'bloody hand' is also borne privately by a few families when its presence is generally connected with some traditional tale of blood. *See also* BLOODY HAND.

**Red-handed.** To be caught red-handed is to be caught in the act; IN FLAGRANTE DELICTO; as if with blood on the hands.

**Red hat, The.** The flat broad-brimmed hat formerly bestowed upon CARDINALS, hence the office of cardinal itself.

**Red herring.** A deliberate or sometimes unintentional diversion, which distracts from a line of enquiry or a topic under discussion. A red herring (i.e. one dried, smoked and salted) drawn across a fox's path destroys the scent and faults the hounds. It is also known as a Norfolk or a Yarmouth capon.

**Red Indians** or **Redskins.** The Native Americans of North America, so called because of their copper-coloured skin. The name is now regarded as derogatory. *See also* INDIAN TRIBES.

**Red laws, The.** The civil code of ancient Rome. The civil laws, being written in vermilion, were called *rubrica*. The praetor's laws were inscribed in white letters and imperial rescripts were written in purple. *See also* RUBRIC.

**Red Letter, The.** *See* ZINOVIEV LETTER *under* FAKES.

**Red-letter day.** A lucky day; a day to be recalled with delight. In ALMANACS, and more commonly in ecclesiastical calendars, important feast-days and saints' days were printed in red, with other days in black. *See also* BLACK-LETTER DAY.

**Red-light district.** The brothel quarter of a large town, from the red light frequently displayed outside a prostitute's premises.

**Red man.** A term in ALCHEMY, used in conjunction with 'white woman', to express the affinity and interaction of chemicals. In the long list of terms that Surly scoffingly gives (Ben Jonson's *The Alchemist*, II, iii (1610)) 'your red man and your white woman' are mentioned. The French say that a red man commands the elements and that he wrecks off the coasts of Brittany those whom he dooms to death. The legend affirms that he appeared to NAPOLEON BONAPARTE and foretold his downfall.

**Redneck.** In the USA a disparaging term for one of the 'uneducated' masses, or for a racist Southerner who supports the segregation of blacks. *See also* ROOINEK.

**Red packet.** In Hong Kong and Malaysia a gift of money folded inside red paper and given at the Chinese New Year to unmarried younger relatives.

**Red Pope, The.** The Prefect of the PROPAGANDA, the Sacred Congregation for Propagating the Faith.

**Red rag.** In the phrase 'like a red rag to a bull', the reference is to anything that is calculated to excite rage. Toreadors' capes are lined with red. There is no evidence that the colour itself incenses bulls, however.

**Red Rose, The.** One of several badges of the House of Lancaster, but not necessarily the most prominent. It was used by Edmund, Earl of Lancaster (1245–96), called Crouchback, second son of Henry III, and it was one of the badges of Henry IV and Henry V, but it does not appear to have been used by Henry VI. The rose-plucking scene in Shakespeare's *Henry VI, Pt I*, II, iv (1590) is essentially a fiction.

**Red Sea.** So called by the Romans (*Mare rubrum*) and by the Greeks, as a translation of the Semitic name, the reason for which is uncertain. One explanation is that it is the colour of the algae in its waters and along its shores. Another is that it refers to the Himarites, a people who lived by its shores and whose own name means 'red'. A recent theory is that 'red' here means 'south', just as 'black' means 'north'. (This may explain the name of the BLACK SEA.)

**Red Shirt.** *See* GARIBALDI'S RED SHIRT.

**Redskins.** *See* INDIAN TRIBES; RED INDIANS.

**Red snow.** Snow reddened by the presence of a minute alga, *Protococcus nivalis*, not uncommon in arctic and alpine regions, where its sanguine colour formerly caused it to be regarded as a portent of evil.

**Red Square.** Moscow's central square has a name that existed long before the advent of Communism. It means 'beautiful square'.

**Red tape.** Official formality, or rigid adherence to rules and regulations, carried to excess; so called because lawyers and government officials tie their papers together with red tape. Charles Dickens is said to have introduced the expression, but the scorn poured on this evil of officialdom by Carlyle brought the term into popular use.

**Better red than dead.** *See under* BETTER.

**In the red.** Overdrawn; in debt; running at a loss. The allusion is to the former banking practice of showing overdrawn accounts in red (as opposed to black for in credit).

**Little Red Riding Hood.** *See under* LITTLE.

**Murder in the Red Barn, The.** *See under* MURDER.

**Not a red cent.** No money at all; 'stony broke'. The American cent used to be copper, but is now an alloy of copper, tin and zinc. Hence, 'not worth a red cent' means 'worth nothing at all'.

**Paint the town red, To.** *See under* PAINT.

**Robin Redbreast.** *See under* ROBIN.

**Saturn red.** *See under* SATURN.

**See red, To.** *See under* SEE.

**See the red light, To.** *See under* SEE.

**Rede** (Old English *rǣdan*, 'to rule'). As a noun, an archaic word meaning counsel, advice. Ethelred II, king of England (r.978–1016), was nicknamed the 'Redeless' or UNREADY, i.e. destitute of counsel.

**Reck one's own rede, To.** *See under* RECK.

**Redemptioner.** An immigrant who was obliged to pay back his passage money out of his earnings after landing in the new country, or who paid the master of the ship by his services.

**Redemptionists.** Members of a religious order whose object was to redeem Christian captives and slaves from the Muslims. They are also known as TRINITARIANS.

**Redemptorists.** Members of the Congregation of the Most Holy Redeemer, a religious order founded at Scala, Italy, in 1732 by St Alfonsus Maria di Liguori (1696–1787), who was canonized in 1839. Also known as Liguorians, they are largely concerned with mission work among the poor and foreign missions.

**Reductio ad absurdum** (Latin, 'reduction to the absurd'). Proof of the falsity of a principle by demonstrating that its logical consequence involves an absurdity. It is used loosely of taking an argument or principle to impractical lengths, as: 'The more sleep one has the longer one lives.

Thus to sleep all the time ensures the longest possible life.'

**Reduplicated** or **ricochet words.** There are probably hundreds of these words in English, which usually have an intensifying force, such as: chit-chat, click-clack, clitter-clatter, DILLY-DALLY, DING-DONG, drip-drop, fal-lal, FIDDLE-FADDLE, flim-flam, flip-flap, flip-flop, HANKY-PANKY, HARUM SCARUM, helter-skelter, higgledy-piggledy, HOBNOB, HODGEPODGE, HOITY-TOITY, hubble-bubble, hugger-mugger, hurly-burly, mingle-mangle, mish-mash, NAMBY-PAMBY, NIMINY-PIMINY, nosy-posy, PELL-MELL, ping-pong, PIT-A-PAT, pitter-patter, RANDEM-TANDEM, randy-dandy, RAZZLE-DAZZLE, RIFF-RAFF, ROLY-POLY, SHILLY-SHALLY, slip-slop, slish-slosh, tick-tack, TIP-TOP, tittle-tattle, wibble-wobble, wig-wag, wiggle-waggle, wish-wash, wishy-washy.

**Reed. Reed shaken by the wind, A.** A person blown about by every wind of doctrine. JOHN THE BAPTIST, said Christ, was not a 'reed shaken by the wind' (Matthew 11:7), but from the very first had a firm belief that the Son of MARY was, in fact, the Messiah, and this conviction was not shaken by fear or favour.

**Broken** or **bruised reed, A.** *See under* BREAK.

**Reefer.** An old name for a MIDSHIPMAN because they attended to reefing in the tops. A reefer is also a closely fitting double-breasted jacket or short coat as worn by seamen. As a slang term for a marijuana cigarette, reefer refers to the resemblance of the cigarette to the rolled reef of a sail.

**Reekie, Auld.** *See under* AULD.

**Reeve** (Old English *gerēfa*). The local officer and representative of his lord. The manorial reeve was generally a VILLAIN elected by his fellows. He was responsible for organizing the daily work of the MANOR and it was his duty to see that people were at their tasks. The shire-reeve or SHERIFF was an official of the SHIRE and the PORTREEVE of a town.

**Reformation, The.** Specifically, the religious revolution of the 16th century, which destroyed the religious unity of western Europe and resulted in the establishment of 'Reformed' or PROTESTANT churches. It aimed at reforming the abuses in the ROMAN CATHOLIC CHURCH and ended in schism, its chief leaders being Martin Luther, Huldrych Zwingli and John Calvin. *See also* CALVINISM.

**Counter-Reformation, The.** *See under* COUNTER.

**Refresher.** An extra fee paid to a BARRISTER during long cases in addition to his RETAINING FEE, originally to remind him of the case entrusted to his charge.

**Refreshment Sunday.** *See* MID-LENT SUNDAY.

**Refuge, Cities of.** *See under* CITY.

**Refusal, First.** *See under* FIRST.

**Regan.** The second of King LEAR's unfilial daughters, in Shakespeare's *King Lear* (IV, ii (1605)) called 'most barbarous, most degenerate'. She was married to the Duke of Cornwall, and in Geoffrey of Monmouth's *Historia Regum Britanniae*, (*c*.1136) from where the story originally comes, she is called Regau. *See also* CORDELIA; GONERIL.

**Regatta.** A boat race, or organized series of boat races. The name was originally given to the races held between Venetian gondoliers, from obsolete Italian (Venetian dialect) *rigatta*, meaning 'strife', 'contention'. The Henley Royal Regatta, one of the high points of the LONDON SEASON, was first held in 1839 and had Prince Albert as its first royal patron.

**Regency.** In British history, architecture, clothing and furniture the term is usually applied to the period 1811–20 when George, PRINCE OF WALES (afterwards George IV), acted as regent during the illness of his father, George III. The style is characterized by its imitation of classical architecture, especially that of ancient Greece, and a restrained simplicity. John Nash's rigidly geometric design for REGENT'S PARK in London exemplifies the neoclassicism of Regency architectural style. In French history it refers to the years from 1715 to 1723 when the Duke of Orleans was regent for the minor Louis XV.

> I pulled aside the thick magenta curtains
> – So Regency, so Regency, my dear –
> JOHN BETJEMAN: *A Few Late Chrysanthemums*, 'Sun and Fun' (1954)

**Regent. Regent's Park.** This London park, formerly called Marylebone Park Fields, covering 410 acres (166ha) of crown property, was laid out from 1812 by John Nash (1752–1835) for the PRINCE REGENT, who had the ultimate intention of building a palace there. Regent Street was the connecting link with Carlton House.

**Good Regent, The.** *See under* GOOD.

**Prince Regent.** *See under* PRINCE.

**Regicides.** The name given to those men who sat in judgement on CHARLES I in 1649 and especially the 59 who signed his death warrant. Of the 41 regicides still alive at the RESTORATION, 9 were executed. The bodies of Oliver Cromwell (1599–1658), Henry Ireton (1611–51) and John Bradshaw (1602–59) were disinterred, and after a solemn trial for treason were dismembered and exhibited at TYBURN and elsewhere.

**Regiment. Regimental colours.** The flags peculiar to regiments, carried into battle until 1881, on which they are entitled to embroider their battle honours, by permission of the sovereign. The Royal Regiment of Artillery has no colours, regarding the capture of its guns as the same disgrace as having one's colours captured. The regimental colours of NAPOLEON BONAPARTE'S army were the famous eagle standards, copied from the eagles of the Roman legions. The capture of a Napoleonic eagle was such an unusual feat that regiments that did so (such as the Scots Greys) incorporated the eagle into their regimental device. *See also* KING'S COLOUR.

**Regimental and divisional nicknames.** The following is a fairly select list of the nicknames of British Army regiments and United States Army divisions. As a result of amalgamations, especially in the last quarter of the 20th century, some of the regiments have ceased to have an independent existence, while others have been disbanded altogether. But their nicknames live on in many cases and are part and parcel of British military history.

BRITISH ARMY

**Assaye Regiment, The.** The 74th Foot, later the 2nd Battalion Highland Light Infantry, subsequently part of the Royal Highland Fusiliers (Princess Margaret's Own Glasgow and Ayrshire Regiment). The regiment distinguished itself at the Battle of Assaye (1803) when 2000 British and 2500 sepoy troops under Wellesley (later the Duke of Wellington) defeated 50,000 Mahrattas.

**Barrell's Blues.** The 4th Foot or King's Own Royal Regiment, so called from their blue facings and blue breeches and from William Barrell, colonel of the regiment (1734–9).

**Belfast Regiment, The.** The old 35th Foot, later the 1st Battalion Royal Sussex Regiment, subsequently the 3rd Battalion the Queen's Regiment, was raised in Belfast in 1701.

**Bengal Tigers.** The 17th Foot, later the Royal Leicestershire Regiment, subsequently the 4th Battalion Royal Anglian Regiment, was granted a badge of a royal tiger to honour their services in India (1804–23).

**Bingham's Dandies.** The 17th Lancers, later 17th/21st Lancers. When the regiment was commanded by Lord Bingham (later the Earl of Lucan) from 1826 to 1837, it was noted for its smart appearance.

**Bird Catchers, The.** This name is used for three regiments, each of which captured a French eagle standard. (1) 1st Dragoons, later Royal Dragoons (1st Dragoons), captured an Eagle at Waterloo in 1815. The regiment merged with the Royal Horse Guards (the Blues) in 1969 to form the Blues and Royals. (2) The 2nd Dragoons, the GREYS, also captured an eagle at Waterloo. (3) The 87th Foot, later the Royal Irish Fusiliers, captured an eagle at Barossa (1811). Disbanded 1968.

**Black Horse, The.** The 7th Dragoon Guards, later the 4th/7th Royal Dragoon Guards, from their black facings.

**Black Watch, The.** In 1725 six companies of clansmen loyal to the king were raised and were stationed in small detachments to keep watch on the Highlands and the clans of Scotland. Their tartan was dark, and their name, which was coined from a combination of this and their function, was used to distinguish them from the English troops performing the same duty. These companies later became the 42nd Foot and subsequently the Black Watch (Royal Highland Regiment). Black Watch has been a part of the official regimental title for over one hundred years.

**Blayney's Bloodhounds.** The 87th Foot, the Royal Irish Fusiliers (Princess Victoria's). The regiment received this name for its success in capturing Irish rebels in 1798 when commanded by Lord Blayney. Disbanded 1968.

**Blind Half-hundred, The.** Many of the men of the 50th Foot suffered from ophthalmia (a common cause of blindness) during the Egyptian campaign of 1801. The regiment later became the 1st Battalion Queen's Own Royal West Kent Regiment and, after that, part of the 2nd Battalion the Queen's Regiment.

**Bloody Eleventh, The.** The 11th Foot, later the Devonshire Regiment, subsequently part of the Devonshire and Dorset Regiment. After its stubborn fight in the Battle of Salamanca (1812), the regiment had 71 out of over 400 men left fit for duty, and many of these survivors were wounded.

**Blues, The.** *See* OXFORD BLUES.

**Bob's Own.** The Irish Guards. Field-Marshal Earl Roberts (known to the Army as 'Bobs') was the first colonel of the regiment.

**Brickdusts, The.** The name is derived from the brick-red facings of the 53rd Foot King's Shropshire Light Infantry. The regiment became the 3rd Battalion the Light Infantry in 1958, and was also known as the 'Five and Threepennies', a play on their old number and the old rate of an ensign's pay.

**Buckmaster's Light Infantry.** The 3rd West India Regiment (disbanded 1870) was so called after Buckmaster, a tailor who sold unauthorized Light Infantry uniforms to the officers of the regiment.

**Buffs, The.** The 3rd Foot was descended from a regiment raised for Dutch service in 1572 and the London TRAINBANDS, all of which had buff uniforms or facings. The regiment had become popularly known as the Buffs by 1702, and this became part of the official name in 1751. In 1935 it became the Buffs (Royal East Kent Regiment) and subsequently part of the 2nd Battalion the Queen's Regiment. *See also* STEADY THE BUFFS!

**Cheesemongers, The.** The 1st Life Guards. From 1788, when the regiment was remodelled, some commissions were refused because certain officers were the sons of merchants and were not 'gentlemen'. The 1st and 2nd Life Guards were amalgamated in 1922 to form a new regiment.

**Cherry-pickers, The.** This name was given to the 11th Hussars when a detachment was surprised by French cavalry while picking cherries in a Spanish orchard in 1811 and had to fight a dismounted action. This regiment amalgamated with the 10th Royal Hussars to form the Royal Hussars (Prince of Wales's Own) in 1969.

**Cherubims, The.** The 11th Hussars, also called Cherry-breeches and Cherrybums from the very tight pink trousers enforced upon their officers in 1840 by their regimental commander, the 7th Earl of Cardigan. *See also* CHERRY-PICKERS.

**Crossbelts, The.** The 8th Hussars, later part of the Queen's Royal Irish Hussars. During the Battle of Almenara (1710), the regiment almost destroyed a Spanish cavalry regiment. The 8th Hussars removed the Spaniards' crossbelts and wore them over the right shoulder.

**Death or Glory Boys, The.** The 17th Lancers, later 17th/21st Lancers. The regimental badge, chosen by the first colonel in memory of General Wolfe, is a Death's Head with the motto 'Or Glory'.

**Delhi Spearmen, The.** The 9th (Queen's) Royal Lancers, amalgamated in 1960 with the 12th Lancers to form the 9th/12th Royal Lancers. The name was acquired at the time of the Indian Mutiny (1857–8) when the regiment was surprised in bivouac by the mutineers who were dispersed so effectively that they fled shouting 'Delhi Bhala Wallah' (Delhi Spearman).

**Desert Rats, The.** The name associated with the 7th Armoured Division, whose divisional sign was the desert rat (jerboa), which was adopted during its 'scurrying and biting' tactics in Libya. The final design of the badge was a red rat outlined on a black background. The division served throughout the North Africa campaign of 1941–2 and in northwestern Europe from Normandy to Berlin. The name was subsequently associated with the 7th Armoured Brigade, and was again to the fore when this force was in action in the Middle East during the Gulf War of 1991.

**Devil's Own, The.** The name has been given to two regiments. (1) Tradition has it that it was given to the INNS OF COURT and Bloomsbury Volunteers, later renamed the Inns of Court Rifles (afterwards a Territorial unit) by George III (r.1760–1820) when he found that the regiment consisted mainly of lawyers. (2) It was also applied to the 88th Foot, later the 1st Battalion Connaught Rangers (disbanded in 1922), by General Picton (1758–1815) in honour of their bravery in the Peninsular War.

**Diehards, The.** At the Battle of Albuera (1811), the 57th Foot, later the 1st Battalion Middlesex Regiment, and afterwards the 4th Battalion the Queen's Regiment, had three-quarters of the officers and men either killed or wounded. Colonel Inglis was badly wounded, but refused to be moved, instead he lay where he had fallen crying: 'Die hard, my men, die hard.'

**Dirty Half-hundred, The.** The 50th Foot, later the 1st Battalion Royal West Kent Regiment, and subsequently part of the 2nd Battalion the Queen's Regiment. At Vimiera in 1808, the men wiped their sweating faces on their cuffs, transferring the black dye from their facings.

**Dirty Shirts, The.** The 101st Foot, later the 1st Battalion Royal Munster Fusiliers (disbanded 1922), fought in their shirtsleeves at Delhi during the Indian Mutiny (1857–8).

**Duke of Wellington's Bodyguard, The.** The 5th Foot, Royal Northumberland Fusiliers. The name dates from the Peninsular War, when the regiment was attached to Army Headquarters for a long period. The regiment became the 1st Battalion Royal Regiment of Fusiliers in 1968.

**Earl of Mar's Grey-breeks, The.** The 21st Foot, later Royal Scots Fusiliers, and later again part of the Royal Highland Fusiliers (Princess Margaret's Own Glasgow and Ayrshire Regiment), from the colour of their breeches when the regiment was raised by the Earl of Mar in 1678.

**Elegant Extracts, The.** The 105th Foot, the King's Shropshire Light Infantry, was remodelled in 1813 when the officers were removed after a number of courts martial. New officers were selected from other regiments to take their places. This regiment became the 3rd Battalion the Light Infantry in 1958.

**Eliott's Tailors.** The 15th (King's) Hussars, subsequently part of the 15th/19th King's Royal Hussars. In 1759 Lieutenant-Colonel Eliott (later Lord Heathfield) enlisted a large number of London tailors into a new cavalry regiment modelled on the Prussian Hussars. In 1768 the regiment was granted the title of King's Light Dragoons. The later title was adopted in 1806.

**Emperor's Chambermaids, The.** The 14th King's Hussars, later the 14th/20th King's Hussars, who captured Joseph Bonaparte's carriage and retained a silver chamber pot as a trophy after the Battle of Vitoria (1813).

**Ever-sworded 29th, The.** The 29th Foot, the Worcestershire Regiment. When the regiment was serving in North America in 1746, the officers were attacked in their mess by Native American Indians who had been thought to be loyal. The Indians were beaten off, but to guard against any similar attack in the future, the unique custom of officers wearing swords at dinner in the mess was instituted. The custom was subsequently observed by the Captain of the Week and the Orderly Officer at dinner and on certain other occasions. This regiment amalgamated with the Sherwood Foresters to form the Worcestershire and Sherwood Foresters' Regiment in 1970.

**Fighting Fifth, The.** The 5th Foot, the Royal Northumberland Fusiliers. The name came from a saying attributed to the Duke of Wellington: 'The ever-fighting, never-failing Fifth.' The regiment became the 1st Battalion Royal Regiment of Fusiliers in 1968. It was also called the Old Bold Fifth.

**Flamers, The.** The 54th Foot, later the 2nd Battalion Dorset Regiment, and subsequently part of the Devonshire and Dorset Regiment. In September 1781 the 54th Foot was part of a force that captured the privateer base of New London, Connecticut, after a fierce fight. The force burned the town and a number of ships in the harbour.

**Green Dragoons, The.** The name given to the 13th Dragoons in the period 1715–84 when they wore green facings. They were later the 13th Hussars and subsequently part of the 13th/18th Royal Hussars (Queen Mary's Own). The facings later changed to buff and subsequently white. *See also* LILYWHITES.

**Green Howards, The.** The 19th Foot, from their facings and Sir Charles Howard, Colonel of the Regiment 1738–48. The name became part of the official title of the regiment in 1920, and the title subsequently became the Green Howards (Alexandra, Princess of Wales's Own Yorkshire Regiment). Green is the colour of the regimental facings. The name was originally given to distinguish them from the 3rd BUFFS, which were also commanded by a Colonel Howard.

**Green Linnets, The.** The 39th Foot, later the 1st Battalion Dorset Regiment, and subsequently part of the Devonshire and Dorset Regiment. The name refers to the green facings of the regiment and dates from about 1741.

**Greys, The.** The Royal Scots Greys (2nd Dragoons) were raised in 1678. It is now uncertain whether the name comes from their grey horses or uniform, but within 30 years of formation the regiment was known as the Grey Dragoons. Scots Greys became part of the official title in 1866, with Royal added in 1877. In 1971 they were amalgamated with the 3rd Carabiniers (Princess of Wales's Dragoon Guards) to form the Royal Scots Dragoon Guards (Carabiniers and Greys).

**Heavies, The.** The heavy cavalry, especially the Dragoon Guards, which consisted of men of greater build and height than Lancers and Hussars. This term has been applied to the larger guns manned by the Royal Artillery and one of its predecessors, the Royal Garrison Artillery.

**Hindustan Regiment, The.** The 76th Foot, later the Duke of Wellington's Regiment (West Riding), was so called because the Regiment distinguished itself in the Hindustan campaign of 1803–5.

**Holy Boys, The.** The 9th Foot, later the Royal Norfolk Regiment, and subsequently part of the 1st Battalion Royal Anglian Regiment. During the Peninsular War, the Spanish thought that the regimental badge of BRITANNIA represented the Virgin MARY.

**Horse Marines, The.** The 17th Lancers, subsequently the 17th/21st Lancers. In 1795, two troops of the regiment served on board the frigate HMS *Hermione* on the West Indies station.

**Immortals, The.** The 76th Foot, later the Duke of Wellington's Regiment (West Riding). During the Mahratta War (1803–5), almost every man had one or more wounds.

**Kiddies, The.** A name given to the Scots Guards, when in 1686 James II formed a large camp on Hounslow Heath as a precaution against unrest in London. The (then) three existing Guards regiments were present, and the Scots, being the junior of the three, were given this name.

**Kirke's Lambs.** The 2nd Foot, later the Queen's Royal Regiment (West Surrey), subsequently the 1st Battalion the Queen's Regiment. Raised in 1661 for service in Tangier, which had become a British possession as part of the dowry of Charles II's queen, Catherine of Braganza, and ranged against Muslim forces, the badge adopted was the Christian emblem of the PASCHAL LAMB. After MONMOUTH'S REBELLION (1685), the regiment under Colonel Percy Kirke (hence Kirke's Lambs) was noted for its ruthlessness against the defeated rebels in Somerset and adjacent areas. Kirke's Lambs were also nicknamed the Tangerines in allusion to their origin, and Mutton Lancers from their badge.

**Lacedaemonians, The.** A nickname of the 46th Foot, later the 2nd Battalion Duke of Cornwall's Light Infantry, then part of the Somerset and Cornwall Light Infantry. In 1777, during the American War of Independence, their colonel is supposed to have made a long speech under heavy fire on Spartan discipline and the military system of the Lacedaemonians. In 1968 this regiment became the 1st Battalion the Light Infantry.

**Lilywhites, The.** The 13th Hussars, later 13th/18th Hussars. When the regiment was converted from Light Dragoons to Hussars in 1861, buff facings were adopted, but for some reason they were pipeclayed white. When the 13th Hussars and the 18th Hussars were amalgamated in 1922, the nickname was adopted by the new regiment. *See also* GREEN DRAGOONS.

**Minden Regiments.** (1) The 12th Foot, later the Suffolk Regiment, later the 1st Battalion Royal Anglian Regiment. (2) The 20th Foot, the Lancashire Fusiliers, known as 'the Minden Boys', later the (disbanded) 4th Battalion Royal Regiment of Fusiliers. (3) The 23rd Foot, the Royal Welch Fusiliers. (4) The 25th Foot, the King's Own Scottish Borderers. (5) The 37th Foot, later the Royal Hampshire Regiment. (6) The 51st Foot, the King's Own Yorkshire Light Infantry, which became the 2nd Battalion the Light Infantry in 1968.

On 1 August 1759 these six regiments won the most spectacular victory of the SEVEN YEARS' WAR by attacking and defeating a superior force of French cavalry. As the regiments advanced to the attack across Minden Heath, the men picked wild roses and stuck them in their caps. To commemorate this victory, the regiments (with the exception of the Royal Welch Fusiliers) took to wearing roses in their caps on Minden Day.

**Moonrakers, The.** *See* SPRINGERS.

**Mutton Lancers, The.** *See* KIRKE'S LAMBS.

**Nanny-Goats** or **Royal Goats, The.** The 23rd Foot, later the Royal Welch Fusiliers, which has a regimental mascot, a goat, supplied from the royal herd. *See also* RED DRAGONS.

**Nutcrackers, The.** The 3rd Foot, later the BUFFS (Royal East Kent Regiment), and subsequently the 2nd Battalion the Queen's Regiment, from their exploits against the French during the Peninsular War.

**Old Bold Fifth.** *See* FIGHTING FIFTH.

**Old Braggs.** *See* SLASHERS.

**Old Dozen, The.** The 12th Foot, later the Suffolk Regiment, and subsequently part of the 1st Battalion Royal Anglian Regiment.

**Old Fogs, The.** The 87th Foot, the Royal Irish Fusiliers (Princess Victoria's). The name comes from their war cry at Barossa (1811): 'Faugh-a-Ballagh' ('Clear the Way'). Disbanded 1968.

**Orange Lilies, The.** 35th Foot, later 1st Battalion Royal Sussex Regiment, and subsequently the 3rd Battalion the Queen's Regiment. The regiment was raised in Belfast in 1701 by the Earl of Donegal, who chose orange facings in honour of William III. The lilies come from the white plumes that the regiment took from the French Regiment of Royal Roussillon, which they defeated at Quebec (1759).

**Oxford Blues, The.** The Royal Horse Guards were so called in 1690, from the Earl of Oxford, their commander, and the blue uniform, which dates from 1661. The nickname was later shortened to the Blues and was incorporated in the regiment's title as the Royal Horse Guards (The Blues). In 1969 the regiment amalgamated with the Royal Dragoons (1st Dragoons) to form the Blues and Royals (Royal Horse Guards and 1st Dragoons).

**Paget's Irregular Horse.** The 4th Hussars, later part of the Queen's Royal Irish Hussars. When the regiment returned to England in 1842 under Colonel Paget, it had lost almost 900 officers and men in its 20 years in India. As the replacements were not as highly trained as the original men, the general standard of drill fell, and the name was coined.

**Pompadours, The.** The 56th Foot, later the 2nd Battalion Essex Regiment, later part of the 3rd Battalion Royal Anglian Regiment. When the regiment was raised in 1755, the facings chosen were purple, the favourite colour of the Marquise de POMPADOUR, the mistress of Louis XV.

**Pontius Pilate's Bodyguard.** The 1st Foot, later the Royal Scots (the Royal Regiment). Tradition states that when in French service as *Le Régiment de Douglas*, a dispute arose with the *Régiment de Picardie* as to seniority, and an officer of the latter claimed that his regiment was on duty on the night of the crucifixion, to which an officer of Douglas' replied: 'Had we been on duty, we would not have slept at our post.'

**Queen's Bays, The.** The 2nd Dragoon Guards. From 1767 the regiment was mounted on bay-coloured horses, while other cavalry regiments had black horses. In 1870 the name became official, the regiment being titled the 2nd Dragoon Guards (Queen's Bays). It subsequently became part of the 1st (Queen's) Dragoon Guards.

**Red Dragons, The.** The Royal Welch Fusiliers, the 23rd Foot, so named from the Welsh national emblem, the Red Dragon, which forms part of their badge. In 1958 it was included in the Welsh Brigade. *See also* NANNY-GOATS.

**Red Feathers, The.** The 46th Foot, later the 2nd Battalion Duke of Cornwall's Light Infantry, then part of the Somerset and Cornwall Light Infantry. During the American War of Independence, the 46th Foot defeated an American force at Brandywine (1777). The Americans promised to have their revenge, so the regiment dyed their cap feathers red to aid identification by the enemy. The regiment became the 1st Battalion the Light Infantry in 1968.

**Ross-shire Buffs, The.** The 78th Foot, later the 2nd Battalion Seaforth Highlanders (Ross-shire Buffs, the Duke of Albany's), and subsequently part of the Queen's Own Highlanders (Seaforth and Camerons). This name became part of the official title soon after the formation of the regiment, and commemorates the colour of their facings and the recruiting area.

**Sankey's Horse.** The 39th Foot, later the 1st Battalion Dorset Regiment, subsequently part of the Devonshire and Dorset Regiment. Sankey was colonel of the regiment when in Spain (1708–11), and tradition has it that he mounted the men on mules to enable them to reach the scene of a battle in time to take part.

**Saucy Seventh, The.** The 7th Queen's Own Hussars, later part of the Queen's Own Hussars. A regimental recruiting poster of *c.*1809 uses this name, an allusion to the regiment's smart appearance.

**Saucy Sixth, The.** The 6th Foot, the Royal Warwickshire Regiment. In 1795 the Regiment returned from the West Indies and recruited in Warwickshire, but the required standard was so high that few recruits were found, and the name was coined. In 1968 this regiment became the 2nd Battalion Royal Regiment of Fusiliers.

**Scarlet Lancers, The.** The 16th Lancers, whose tunic was red. It later became the 16th/5th the Queen's Royal Lancers. They were the only Lancer regiment to retain the DRAGOON's scarlet tunic in the latter half of the 19th century.

**Slashers, The.** The 28th Foot, later Gloucestershire Regiment. When the regiment was stationed in Canada in 1764, a magistrate harassed the soldiers and their families. A party of heavily disguised soldiers broke into the magistrate's house one night, and during a scuffle the man's ear was cut off. Officially, the identity of the culprits was never discovered, but the 28th acquired the nickname of the Slashers. Two other names attached to the regiment are the Braggs and the Old Braggs, from Lieutenant-General Philip Bragg, colonel of the regiment (1734–59).

**Snappers, The.** The 15th Foot, later East Yorkshire Regiment, and subsequently part of the Prince of Wales's Own Regiment of Yorkshire. During the Battle of Brandywine (1777), with ammunition exhausted, the men 'snapped' their muskets to give the impression that they were firing. This misled the Americans, and they retired.

**Springers, The.** The 62nd Foot, later the 1st Battalion Wiltshire Regiment, and subsequently part of the Duke of Edinburgh's Royal Regiment (Berkshire and Wiltshire). In 1775–6, during the American War of Independence, the 62nd were used as Light Infantry and the nickname commemorates their alertness and speed in their temporary role. They are probably better known, however, as the Moonrakers.

**Tangerines, The.** *See* KIRKE'S LAMBS.

**Vein-openers, The.** The 29th Foot, later the Worcestershire Regiment, and subsequently part of the Worcestershire and Sherwood Foresters' Regiment. In 1770, when American colonial discontent with England was increasing, the 29th was in Boston, and while a detachment was guarding the Customs House it was pelted by a mob. During a scuffle, a soldier mistook a shout from the crowd for an order and he fired. Other shots followed and four rioters were killed and several wounded. The name was given to the regiment by the Americans for their part in what was called the Boston Massacre.

**Virgin Mary's Bodyguard, The.** The 7th Dragoon Guards, later part of the 4th/7th Royal Dragoon Guards. During the reign of George II, the regiment was sent to assist the Archduchess Maria Theresa of Austria.

**Wolfe's Own.** The 47th Foot, later the Loyal Regiment (North Lancashire), so called for their distinguished service under General Wolfe at Quebec (1759). In 1970 they merged with the Lancashire Regiment (Prince of Wales's Volunteers) to form the Queen's Lancashire Regiment.

UNITED STATES ARMY

In the following representative selection all are Infantry Divisions unless otherwise stated. Unofficial nicknames are marked thus *.

**1st: The Big Red One.** A name given it by the Germans, who saw the red 1 on their shoulder patch. According to legend, the original red 1 was improvised from the cap of an enemy soldier killed by a 1st Division DOUGHBOY in the First World War when the division earned the right to proclaim itself the first American division (1918) in France, the first to fire on the enemy, the first to suffer casualties, the first to take prisoners, the first to stage a major offensive and the first to enter Germany.

**2nd: Indianhead.** A long-forgotten truck driver of the division in the First World War adorned the side of his vehicle with a handsome shield framing an Indian head, which was adopted by the division as its shoulder insignia. Hence the name Indian Division.

**3rd: The Marne Division.** So named because of its impregnable stand against the Germans' last counter-offensive in the First World War. The three diagonal stripes in its insignia symbolize its participation in three major battles in 1918.

**4th: The Ivy Division.** From its insignia. The selection of that design is one of the few known instances of authorized military frivolity. 'Ivy' represents a spelling out of the Roman numeral 'IV' (4).

**5th: The Red Diamond.** From its insignia. The Red Diamond was selected at the suggestion of Major Charles A. Meals that their insignia be the 'Ace of Diamonds, less the Ace'. Originally there was a white '5' in the centre. This was removed when they reached France.

**8th: Pathfinder.** From their insignia, which is a golden arrow through a figure 8 pointing the way. They are also called the Golden Arrow Division.

**9th: Hitler's Nemesis***. A newspaper at home dubbed them this. Also called Old Reliable* and Varsity*.
**10th: The Mountaineers** (formerly 10th Mountain division). This division was given the task of dislodging crack German mountain troops from the heights of Mount Belvedere. It was composed of famous American skiers, climbers, forest rangers and Wild Life Service men.
**13th: (Airborne) Blackcats***. So named from its flaunting of superstition. Its number is 13, and it was reactivated on Friday the 13th.
**17th: (Airborne) Golden Talon***. Named from its shoulder patch, stretching golden talons on a black field, representing ability to seize. Black suggests darkness, under which many operations are effected. Also called Thunderbolt*.
**23rd: The America Division.** Although without a nickname, it was the only Division in US Army history with a name and not a number, until the war in Vietnam. It was formed from Task Force 6814 in New Caledonia and joined in the invasion of Guadalcanal in 1942, subsequently fighting in Leyte and other Philippine Islands. It won an arrowhead for the invasion of Cebu.
**24th: Victory.** The Filipinos on Leyte greeted them with the V sign.
**25th: Tropic Lightning.** Activated from elements of the Hawaiian Division, Regular Army troops.
**26th: Yankee.** Originally composed of National Guard troops from the New England (YANKEE) states.
**28th: Keystone.** Troops from Pennsylvania, which is known as the Keystone State.
**29th: Blue and Gray.** Organized in the First World War from National Guardsmen of New Jersey, Delaware, Virginia, Maryland and the District of Columbia. Its shoulder patch of blue and grey, the colours of the rival armies in the Civil War (1861–5), symbolizes the unity of former embattled states. They are combined in a monad, the Korean symbol for eternal life.
**30th: Old Hickory.** Composed after the First World War from National Guardsmen of the Carolinas, Georgia and Tennessee, Andrew Jackson's old stamping grounds. He was known as OLD HICKORY.
**31st: Dixie.** Originally composed of men of the DEEP SOUTH or Dixie.
**32nd: Red Arrow.** On tactical maps the enemies' lines are indicated in red. Their patch is a reminder to those who wear it that the enemy has never stopped them. Another name, 'Les Terribles', was given them by an admiring French general during the First World War, when they earned four battle streamers and were first to crack the Hindenburg line.
**34th: Red Bull.** Its patch is a red bull's skull on an *olla*, a Mexican water bottle. It was inspired by the desert country of the southwest where it trained in the First World War.
**35th: Santa Fe.** So called because the ancestors of its personnel blazed the old SANTA FE TRAIL. Its insignia is the original marker used on the trail.
**36th: Texas.** Its personnel was from Oklahoma and Texas. The arrowhead of its insignia represented Oklahoma and the T was for Texas.
**37th: Buckeye.** Composed of Ohio troops. Ohio is known as the Buckeye State. Insignia is that of the state flag.
**38th: Cyclone.** So named in 1917 at Shelby, Mississippi, when the tent city in which it was bivouacked was levelled by winds. The division struck like a cyclone when it landed in Luzon.
**42nd: Rainbow.** The nickname originated from the fact that the division was composed of military groups from the District of Columbia, and 25 states, representing several sections, nationalities, religions and viewpoints. They blended themselves into one harmonious unit. A major in the First World War, noting its various origins, said: 'This division will stretch over the land like a rainbow.'
**43rd: Winged Victory.** Received its name on Luzon. It is formed from the name of its commanding general, Major-General Leonard F. Wing, and the ultimate goal of the division.
**63rd: Blood and Fire.** When the division was activated in June 1943 following the Casablanca Conference, they adopted the Conference's resolution, to make their enemies 'bleed and burn in expiation of their crimes against humanity', as their symbol.
**65th: Battleaxe***. Its patch is a white halbert on a white shield. The halbert, a sharp-pointed battleaxe, was a potent weapon of the 15th-century foot soldier, being suitable either for a powerful cutting smash or for a quick thrust. It is an emblem that signifies both the shock action and the speed of the modern infantry division.
**66th: Black Panther***. The black panther on its shoulder patch symbolizes the attributes of a good infantryman: the ability to kill and to be aggressive, alert, stealthy, cunning, agile and strong.
**70th: Trailblazer.** Their insignia combines an axe, a snowy mountain and a green fir tree, symbols of the pioneers who blazed the trail to Oregon and the Willamette Valley, where most of their training was accomplished.
**76th: Onaway.** The alert call of the Chippewa Indians in whose hunting grounds they trained. Also unofficially called Liberty Bell* from the shoulder patch of a Liberty Bell worn in the First World War. The 76th was the first draft division

from civilian ranks, and in 1919 the device became a shield with a white label, indicating the eldest son.

**77th: Statue of Liberty.** The insignia bears the picture of the Statue of Liberty, because most of the personnel in the First World War were from New York City.

**78th: Lightning.** The shoulder patch originated in the First World War because the battles of that division were likened by the French to a bolt of lightning, leaving the field blood red.

**79th: Cross of Lorraine.** Having distinguished itself at Montfaucon in Lorraine, the division selected the Cross of Lorraine, a symbol of triumph, as its insignia.

**80th: Blue Ridge.** Its insignia symbolizes the three Blue Ridge states, Pennsylvania, Virginia and West Virginia, from which most of its First World War personnel were drawn.

**81st: Wildcat.** Its name comes from Wildcat Creek, which flows through Fort Jackson, South Carolina. It is generally credited as the first to wear the shoulder patch.

**82nd: (Airborne) All American.** In the First World War the division was composed of men from every state in the union. Originally an infantry division, when it was reactivated as an airborne division it retained its insignia, adding the word 'Airborne' above.

**84th: Railsplitters.** Primarily made up of National Guard units from Illinois, Kentucky and Indiana, the Lincoln states. They called themselves the Lincoln Division. Their insignia is a red disc with a white axe, which splits a rail. In the Second World War they called themselves the Railsplitters. The Germans called them the Hatchetmen.

**85th: Custer.** The initials CD on its insignia stand for Custer Division, because it was activated at Camp Custer, Michigan, in the First World War.

**86th: Blackhawk*.** Its insignia is a black hawk with wings outspread superimposed on a red shield. On the breast of the hawk is a small red shield with black letters BH for its nickname. In the First World War its personnel were drawn from Illinois, Wisconsin and Minnesota, the territory inhabited by Chief Blackhawk and his tribe. The bird symbolizes keenness, cunning and tenacity.

**87th: Golden Acorn.** Their patch is a green field with a golden acorn, which symbolizes strength.

**88th: Blue Devil.** Their patch is a blue four-leaf clover formed from two crossed Arabic numerals, 88.

**89th: Rolling W*.** The W on its insignia within a circle forms an M when it is inverted, the two letters standing for Middle West, the section of the country from which its personnel were drawn. The circle indicates speed and stability. Also called Middle West*.

**90th: Tough 'Ombres.** The letter T of its insignia, standing for Texas, bisects the letter O for Oklahoma. The men of the division say it stands for Tough 'Ombres.

**92nd: Buffalo*.** The insignia is a black buffalo on an olive drab background with black border. In the days of war against the Native Americans, the Indians called Negro soldiers Black Buffaloes from their hair, which the Native Americans thought was similar to that found on a buffalo's neck. The men of this Negro division in the First World War were trained at Fort Huachuca in the same locality.

**96th: Deadeye*.** The name came from their perfect marksmanship while in training.

**97th: Trident*.** The insignia is a white trident on a blue field. NEPTUNE's trident represents the coastal states of Maine, Vermont and New Hampshire, from which they came. There is a prong for each state. The blue represents their freshwater lakes, and the white their snowy mountains.

**98th: Iroquois.** Its patch consists of a shield in the shape of the great seal of the state of New York. The head of the Iroquois chief is in orange. These are the colours of the Dutch House of Nassau, which was responsible for the settlement of New Amsterdam, later New York. The five feathers worn by the Iroquois chief represent the FIVE NATIONS which formed the Iroquois Confederacy. The personnel were from New York.

**99th: Checkerboard*.** The blue and white squares, resembling a checkerboard, formed part of the coat of arms of William Pitt (sable, a fess chequé or and AZURE between three BEZANTS). The home station of the division was Pittsburgh.

**101st: (Airborne) Screaming Eagle.** Its white eagle's head with gold beak on a black shield is based on tradition from Civil War (1861–5). The black shield recalls the Iron Brigade, one regiment of which possessed the famous eagle Old Abe, which went into battle with them as their screaming mascot.

**102nd: Ozark.** A large golden O on a field of blue. Within the O is the letter Z, from which is suspended an arc. This represents the word 'Ozark'. The personnel came from the Ozark Mountain region.

**103rd: Cactus.** A green saguaro cactus in a blue base superimposed on a yellow disc was adopted by this Reserve division, which had its headquarters in Denver, Colorado. The yellow disc represents the golden sky, while the green cactus growing in the blue sage-covered earth is characteristic of the southwest.

**106th: Golden Lion*.** Their patch represents a golden lion's face on a blue background encircled by white and red borders. The blue represents the infantry, red the supporting artillery and the lion's face strength and power.

**Cameron Highlanders.** *See under* CAMERON.

**Cameronian Regiment.** *See under* CAMERONIAN.

**London Regiment.** *See under* LONDON.

**Royal American Regiment.** *See under* ROYAL.

**Regius professor** (Latin *regius*, 'royal'). At the Universities of Oxford and Cambridge, an academic who holds a professorship founded by Henry VIII and certain others of subsequent foundation. At Oxford the first Regius Professor of Hebrew was appointed in 1535, and there have been Regius Professors of Civil Law, Divinity, Greek and Medicine since 1546, of Modern History since 1724, and of Moral and Pastoral Theology and Ecclesiastical History since 1842. At the Scottish universities, the title is used for any professorship instituted by the crown.

**Regnal year.** The year beginning with a monarch's accession. In Great Britain Acts of Parliament are still referred to by the regnal year in which they were passed. Thus the Local Government Act 1929, is also dated 19 Geo 5, the 19th year of the reign of George V. Edward VIII's Declaration of Abdication Act, which took effect on 11 December 1936, was dated 1 Edw 8. *See also* CALENDAR.

**Regnant, Queen.** *See under* QUEEN.

**Regular.** In the early 19th century this word, in its American sense, meant thorough, absolute. In the 20th century it has more often applied to people as, a regular guy, i.e. a straightforward, dependable person. The term is also applied to literary characters, such as a regular Becky Sharp for an unprincipled, scheming young woman, from W.M. Thackeray's *Vanity Fair* (1847–8), a regular Romeo for a young man who fancies himself as a LADY-KILLER, and a regular Scrooge for a skinflint or miser, in allusion to Ebenezer Scrooge in Dickens' *A Christmas Carol* (1843). A person who fancies himself as an amateur detective might likewise be derisively dubbed a regular SHERLOCK.

**Regular octahedron.** A solid figure whose eight faces are each an equilateral triangle. It is one of the five types of regular polyhedra, others being the tetrahedron, with four equilateral triangular faces, the cube, with six square faces, the dodecahedron, with twelve regular pentagons, and the icosahedron, with twenty equilateral triangles.

**Regulars.** A term for personnel of the British (and US) armed forces who adopt their respective service as a career, as opposed to members of reserve forces or conscripts.

**Keep regular hours, To.** To do the same thing each day at more or less the same hour, in particular in one's rising and going to bed.

**Regulations, King's or Queen's.** *See under* KING.

**Regulus, St.** *See* St RULE.

**Rehearsal, Dress.** *See under* DRESS.

**Rehoboam.** (1) In the Old Testament (1 Kings 12), the son of SOLOMON. Ten tribes revolted during his reign and set up a new kingdom of ISRAEL, separate from his own kingdom, which was called JUDAH. *See also* KINGS OF ISRAEL.

(2) As a wine measure, the equivalent of six bottles (2 Chronicles 13:7). *See also* BOTTLE; JEROBOAM; JORUM; MAGNUM; TAPPIT-HEN.

(3) In her description of the Rev. Matthewson Helstone, Charlotte Brontë applied the name to a clerical SHOVEL HAT.

> A personage short of stature, but straight of port, and bearing on broad shoulders a hawk's head, beak and eye, the whole surmounted by a Rehoboam, or shovel-hat, which he did not seem to think it necessary to lift or remove before the presence in which he then stood.
>
> *Shirley*, ch i (1849)

**Reich, Third.** *See under* THIRD.

**Reign of Terror.** The period in the French Revolution from April 1793 to July 1794, when supreme power was in the hands of the Committee of Public Safety, and the JACOBINS, dominated by Robespierre, St Just and Couthon. During this period, the historian Hippolyte Taine estimated that 17,000 people were put to death, although this is perhaps an exaggeration, but some 2600 were sentenced at Paris alone. The excuse was the external threat from the European coalition, 'royalist plots' and the like. Robespierre formulated the doctrine that 'in times of peace the springs of popular government are in virtue, but in times of revolution, they are both in virtue and terror'.

**Reilly, To live the life of.** *See under* LIVE.

**Rein** (ultimately from Latin *retinere*, 'to hold back'). The strap attached to the bit, used in guiding a horse.

**Draw rein, To.** *See under* DRAW.

**Free rein, A.** *See under* FREE.

**Keep a tight rein on, To.** *See under* TIGHT.

**Take the reins, To.** To assume the guidance of direction; to assume control.

**Reine s'avisera, La.** *See under* ROY.

**Reins** (Latin *renes*). The kidneys, believed by the Hebrews and others to be the seat of knowledge, pleasure and pain, as is evidenced at various points in the Old Testament: 'I will bless the Lord, who hath given me counsel: my reins also instruct me in the night seasons' (Psalms 16:7); 'Yea, my reins shall rejoice, when thy lips speak right things' (Proverbs 23:16); 'He hath caused the arrows of his quiver to enter into my reins'

(Lamentations 3:13). This last means that God sent pain into Jeremiah's kidneys.

**Relation. Blood relation.** *See under* BLOOD.

**Poor relation.** *See under* POOR.

**Release, Happy.** *See under* HAPPY.

**Relic.** In the Christian sense, the corpse of a saint, any part of the body, any part of the clothing or anything ultimately connected with him or her. The veneration of Christian relics goes back to the 2nd century and led to many spurious relics being brought back from the HOLY LAND. Miracle-working relics brought wealth to many monasteries and churches, and the remains of saints were often dismembered, with trickery and violence used to obtain them. Relics such as the tip of LUCIFER's tail, the blood of Christ and the candle lit by the Angel of the Lord in Christ's tomb were among the many accepted by the credulous.

**Religion, South Bank.** *See under* SOUTH.

**Religious. Religious liberty.** The freedom to adopt whatever religious beliefs or opinions one chooses and to practise them, provided such freedom in no way interferes with the equal liberty of others.

**His Most Religious Majesty.** *See under* MOST.

**Reliquary.** A receptacle of various kinds for RELICS. The smaller relics were preserved in monstrances, pyxes, pectoral reliquaries (usually in the form of a cross), shapes of arms and legs and so on. The entire remains of a saint were kept in shrines. *See also* ARM SHRINES.

**Reliques of Ancient English Poetry.** *See* PERCY'S RELIQUES.

**Remember!** The mysterious injunction of CHARLES I, on the scaffold, to Bishop Juxon (1582–1663), but not his actual last words. *See also* FAMOUS LAST WORDS.

**Remembrance Day** or **Remembrance Sunday.** After the First World War ARMISTICE DAY, or Remembrance Day, commemorating the fallen, was observed on 11 November. It was also called Poppy Day from the artificial poppies (recalling the poppies of Flanders fields) sold by the BRITISH LEGION in aid of ex-servicemen. From 1945 to 1956 Remembrance Sunday was observed on the first or second Sunday of November, commemorating the fallen of the First and Second World Wars. In 1956 it was fixed on the second Sunday of November. *See also* POPPY.

**Remembrancer, King's** or **Queen's, The.** *See under* KING.

**Remigius** or **Remy, St.** Bishop and confessor, and apostle of the FRANKS, St Remigius (438–533) is represented as carrying a vessel of holy oil, or in the act of anointing CLOVIS, who kneels before him. Remigius is said to have given Clovis the power of touching for the KING'S EVIL. His day is 1 October.

**Remonstrants.** Another name for the ARMINIANS. In Scottish history the name is also given to those who presented a remonstrance to the Committee of Estates in 1650 refusing to acknowledge Charles II as king until he had established his good faith and devotion to the Covenant. *See also* COVENANTERS.

**Remus.** *See* ROMULUS.

**Uncle Remus.** *See under* UNCLE.

**Remy.** *See* REMIGIUS.

**Renaissance, The** (French, 'rebirth'). The term applied to the intellectual movement characteristic of the period of European history that marks the transition between the medieval and modern. Chronologically it is usually taken to fall in the 15th and 16th centuries, occurring earliest in Italy and later in England. In a more limited sense, it implies what was formerly called the REVIVAL OF LEARNING.

The period was marked by a rediscovery of the classics, questioning of religious dogmas, the growth of a more scientific outlook, major developments in art and literature, new inventions and overseas discoveries, and a general assertion and emancipation of the human intellect.

The name is now also given to certain earlier periods, such as the 'Twelfth-century Renaissance'. *See also* CINQUECENTO; QUATTROCENTO.

**Renard, Une queue de.** *See under* QUEUE.

**Rent. Ground rent.** *See under* GROUND.

**Peppercorn rent.** *See under* PEPPER.

**Rack-rent.** *See under* RACK.

**Sin rent.** *See under* SIN.

**Repairs, Running.** *See under* RUN.

**Repentance, Stool of.** *See under* STOOL.

**Repenter curls.** The long ringlets of a lady's hair. *Repentir* is the French for 'penitence', and *les repenties* are the girls doing penance for their misdemeanours. MARY MAGDALENE had such long hair that she wiped off her tears from the feet of Jesus with it. Hence the association of long curls and reformed (*repenties*) prostitutes.

**Reply churlish.** 'Sir, you are no judge; your opinion has no weight with me.' Or, to paraphrase Touchstone's illustration (Shakespeare, *As You Like It*, V, iv (1599)): 'If I tell a courtier his beard is not well cut, and he disables my judgement, he gives me the reply churlish, which is the fifth remove from the lie direct, or rather, the lie direct in the fifth degree.' *See also* QUIP MODEST; REPROOF VALIANT; RETORT COURTEOUS.

**Representatives, House of.** *See under* HOUSE.

**Reproof valiant.** 'Sir, allow me to tell you that is not the truth.' This is Touchstone's fourth remove from the lie direct, or, rather, the lie direct in the fourth degree. *See also* QUIP MODEST; REPLY CHURLISH; RETORT COURTEOUS.

**Republic. Republic, The.** The English name for PLATO'S best known work, the *Politeia* ('Society'), written in the 4th century BC. It is his IDEAL COMMONWEALTH. *The Republic* is especially regarded for its philosophical and ethical teachings, and it gave Sir Thomas More the inspiration for his UTOPIA.

**Republican Queen, The.** Sophia Charlotte (1668–1705), wife of Frederick I of Prussia, was so nicknamed on account of her advanced political views. She was the sister of George I of Britain, the friend of Leibniz and a woman of remarkable culture. Charlottenburg, now part of Berlin, was named after her.

**Republic of Letters, The.** The world of literature, authors generally and their influence. Oliver Goldsmith, in *The Citizen of the World*, No. 20 (1760), says 'it is a very common expression among Europeans'. It is found in MOLIÈRE'S *Le Mariage Forcé*, vi (1664).

**Fourth Republic.** *See under* FOURTH.

**Third Republic.** *See under* THIRD.

**Parthenopean Republic.** *See under* PARTHENOPE.

**Roman Republic.** *See under* ROMAN.

**Weimar Republic.** *See under* WEIMAR.

**Requests, Court of.** *See under* COURT.

**Requiem.** The first word of the prayer *Requiem aeternam dona eis, Domine, et lux perpetua luceat eis* ('Eternal rest give them, O Lord, and let everlasting light shine upon them') used as the introit of a MASS for the Dead. Hence a word for a Requiem Mass.

**Reremouse.** *See* REARMOUSE.

**Residence, Grace and favour.** *See under* GRACE.

**Resolute Doctor, The.** John Baconthorpe (*c*.1290–1346), grand-nephew of Roger Bacon, head of the CARMELITES in England (1329–33) and commentator on Aristotle, the Bible and other works.

**Respects. Pay one's last respects, To.** *See under* PAY.

**Pay one's respects, To.** *See under* PAY.

**Response, Pavlovian.** *See under* PAVLOVIAN.

**Responsibility, To saddle with.** *See under* SADDLE.

**Responsions.** *See* SMALLS.

**Rest. Rest is silence, The.** The last words of the dying Hamlet (Shakespeare, *Hamlet*, V, ii (1600)).

**Rest one's case, To.** To conclude one's argument; to make one's final and definitive point. The expression is of American origin, representing the voluntary conclusion of evidence in a legal case.

> Let's put it this way – in 20 years' time, will everyone have DVD [digital versatile disc]? Possibly. And will everyone have digital TV? Most definitely. We rest our case.
>
> *Toys For The Boys* (Awards 1998)

**Rest on one's laurels, To.** To be satisfied with the degree of success one has already achieved and to refrain from further effort.

**Rest on one's oars, To.** To take a rest or breathing space after hard work or strenuous effort. A boating phrase.

**Chapel of rest.** *See under* CHAPEL.

**Day of rest.** *See under* DAY.

**Laid to rest.** *See under* LAID.

**Restaurant, Chinese.** *See under* CHINESE.

**Restoration, The.** In British history the recall of the Stuarts to the throne in 1660 in the person of Charles II (r.1660–85), thus bringing the Puritan COMMONWEALTH to an end. The Restoration period was marked by a relaxation in standards of conduct, but scholarship, science, literature and the arts blossomed and flourished with the cessation of Puritan restraints.

In France, the royal house of Bourbon was restored after the fall of NAPOLEON BONAPARTE in 1815 in the person of Louis XVIII, brother of the late king, Louis XVI, whose son, dynastically known as Louis XVII, did not survive to rule.

**Resurrectionists** or **Resurrection men.** BODYSNATCHERS, those who broke open the coffins of the newly buried to supply the demands of the surgical and medical schools. The first recorded instance of the practice was in 1742, and it flourished particularly until the passing of the Anatomy Act of 1832. The resurrectionist took the corpse naked, this being in law a misdemeanour, as opposed to a felony if garments were taken as well. Murders were sometimes committed for the same market. *See also* BURKE.

**Retaining fee** or **retainer.** A fee paid to secure the right to call on the services of someone, especially a lawyer. *See also* REFRESHER.

**Old retainer.** *See under* OLD.

**Retiarius** (Latin). A gladiator who made use of a net (*rete*), which he threw over his adversary. *See also* TRIDENT.

> As in the thronged amphitheatre of old
> The wary Retiarius trapped his foe.
>
> JAMES THOMSON: *Castle of Indolence*, ii (1748)

**Retirement, Early.** *See under* EARLY.

**Retort courteous, The.** 'Sir, I am not of your opinion; I beg to differ from you' or, to use Touchstone's illustration (Shakespeare, *As You Like It*, V, iv (1599)), 'If I said his beard was not cut well, he was in the mind it was.' The lie seven times removed, or rather, the lie direct in the seventh degree. *See also* QUIP MODEST; REPLY CHURLISH; REPROOF VALIANT.

**Retreat, To beat.** *See under* BEAT.

**Return. Return to the charge, To.** To renew the attack.

**By return of post.** *See under* BY.

**Law of diminishing returns, The.** *See under* LAW.

**Point of no return.** *See under* POINT.

**Reuben.** The first son of JACOB and the progenitor of one of the TWELVE TRIBES OF ISRAEL. He sleeps with his father's concubine, and when his brothers are about to kill JOSEPH, he persuades them to throw him into the pit instead. His story is told from Genesis 29 onwards.

**Reuters.** The premier international news agency, reputed for its integrity and impartiality, founded by Paul Julius Reuter (1816–99), a native of Kassel, Germany. He was of Jewish parentage and originally named Israel Beer Josaphat, but became a Christian in 1844 and adopted the name of Reuter. The agency was established at London in 1851, taking full advantage of the developing telegraph service, although links had to be completed by railway and pigeon post. Reuter developed a worldwide service in the ensuing years, and in 1871 he was made Baron de Reuter. It became a private trust in 1916 and was later (1926–41) taken over by the British Press Association, the Newspaper Publishers Association, the Australian Associated Press and the New Zealand Press Association, becoming a public company in 1984.

**Reveille** (French *réveiller*, 'to awaken'). The bugle call used in the armed forces announcing that it is time to rise.

**Revenant** (French, 'returning one'). Someone who returns after long exile, or more usually, an apparition, a ghost, a person who returns from the dead.

**Revenons à nos moutons** (French, 'Let us return to our sheep'). A phrase used to mean 'Let us return to the subject'. It is taken from the French comedy *La Farce de Maistre Pathelin*, or *l'Avocat Pathelin* (*c*.1460), in which a woollen draper charges a shepherd, Aignelet, with ill-treating his sheep. In telling his story, he continually digresses from the subject, and to throw discredit on the defendant's attorney (Pathelin), accuses him of stealing a piece of cloth. The judge has to pull him up every moment, with *Mais, mon ami, revenons à nos moutons*. The phrase is frequently quoted by Rabelais and has a jocular equivalent among some English speakers: 'Let's return to our muttons.'

**Reverend.** An archbishop is addressed as 'The Most Reverend (Father in God)', a bishop as 'The Right Reverend', a DEAN as 'The Very Reverend', an archdeacon as 'The Venerable', and all other clergy as 'The Reverend'. A person in orders should always be referred to as 'The Reverend Mr Jones' or 'The Reverend John Jones', not 'Reverend' or 'The Reverend Jones'.

**Review, The Edinburgh.** *See under* EDINBURGH.

**Revise. Revised Standard Version, The.** *See under* BIBLE.

**Revised Standard Version Common Bible, The.** *See under* BIBLE.

**Revised Version, The.** *See under* BIBLE.

**Revising barrister.** A BARRISTER appointed to revise the list of electors for Members of PARLIAMENT.

**Revival of learning** or **letters.** A term applied to that aspect of the RENAISSANCE that involved the revival of classical learning, especially of Greek literature, freed from the cramping influences of medieval SCHOLASTICISM and ecclesiastical restraint. Its keynote was humanism, which demanded that human reason should be free to pursue its intellectual and aesthetic purposes. It was marked by the enthusiastic pursuit of scholarship, the investigation of manuscript sources and the establishment of libraries and museums, and received added impetus from the invention of printing (*c*.1440). Italy was the centre of this European revival, where it was in evidence by the late 14th century, reaching its full development in the early 16th century.

**Revolt, The Peasants'.** *See under* PEASANT.

**Revolution. Diplomatic Revolution.** *See under* DIPLOMAT.

**Glorious Revolution.** *See under* GLORIOUS.

**Industrial Revolution.** *See under* INDUSTRIAL.

**July Revolution.** *See under* JULY.

**October Revolution.** *See under* OCTOBER.

**Rex.** The Latin equivalent of 'king', connected with *regere*, 'to rule', and with Sanskrit *rājan* (whence RAJAH), 'king'.

**Reynard.** A fox, and Caxton's form of the name in his translation (from the Dutch) of the *Roman de Renart* (REYNARD THE FOX). *Renart* was the Old French form, from German *Reginhart*, a personal name. The name gave *renard* as the present standard French word for the fox, which was earlier known as *goupil*.

**Reynard's globe of glass.** Reynard, in REYNARD THE FOX, said he had sent this invaluable treasure to her majesty the queen as a present, but it never came to light as it had no existence except in the imagination of the fox. It was supposed to reveal what was being done, no matter how far off, and also to afford information on any subject that the person consulting it wished to know.

**Reynard's wonderful comb.** Like the globe, the mirror and the ring this existed only in Reynard's head. He said that it was made of the Panthera's bone, the perfume of which was so fragrant that no one could resist following it, and that the wearer of the comb was always cheerful and merry. *See also* PANTHER.

**Reynard's wonderful mirror.** This mirror existed only in the brain of Master Fox. He told the queen lion that whoever looked in it could see what was done a mile off. The wood of the frame was not subject to decay, being made of the same block as King Crampart's magic horse.

**Reynard's wonderful ring.** This ring, which existed only in the brain of the fox, had a stone of three colours, red, white and green. The red made the night as clear as day, the white cured all manner of diseases, and the green rendered the wearer invisible.

**Reynard the Fox.** A medieval beast epic (*c.*1175–1250) satirizing contemporary life and events, found in French, Dutch and German literature. Episodes include a globe, comb, mirror and ring (*see above*). Chaucer's 'Nun's Priest's Tale' (*c.*1387) is part of the Reynard tradition. Most of the names in the Reynard cycle are German but it found its greatest vogue in France as the *Roman de Renart*. Caxton's *Hystorie of Reynart the Foxe* (1481) was based on a Dutch version published at Gouda in 1479. The oldest version (12th century) is in Latin. *See also* RUSSEL.

**Reyne le veult, La.** *See under* ROY.

**Rhabdomancy.** A form of DIVINATION by means of a rod or wand, dowsing, from Greek *rhabdos*, 'rod', and *manteia*, 'prophecy'. If carried out in the strictly approved manner, it involves throwing sticks, rods or arrows on the ground rather than holding them above it. It thus has a parallel in the 'throwing the wands' of I CHING fortune-telling. *See also* DOWSE.

**Rhadamanthus.** In Greek mythology, one of the three judges of hell, MINOS and Aeacus being the other two.

**Rhapsody.** Originally the word meant 'songs strung together', from Greek *rhaptein*, 'to sew together', and *ōidē*, 'song'. The term was applied to portions of the ILIAD and ODYSSEY, which bards recited.

**Rhea.** In Greek mythology, the mother of the gods, daughter of URANUS and GAIA, and sister of KRONUS, the Titan, by whom she bore ZEUS, HADES, POSEIDON, HERA, Hestia and DEMETER. She is identified with CYBELE and also known as AGDISTIS.

**Rhea Sylvia** or **Rea Silvia.** (1) The mother of ROMULUS and Remus. According to some legends, her name was Ilia, and she was the daughter of AENEAS and Livia. Other sources say that she was the daughter of Numitor, the king of Alba Longa. After deposing Numitor, the new king, her uncle, Amulius, forced her, for his own protection, to become a Vestal Virgin. MARS saw her and made her the mother of the twins Romulus and Remus. Amulius imprisoned Ilia (or threw her into the Tiber) and exposed (abandoned) the children, who later rescued her.

(2) HERCULES fell in love with a priestess of this name after slaying GERYON. Their son's name was Aventinus, after whom the Aventine Hill in Rome was named.

**Rheims. Rheims-Douai Version, The.** *See* DOUAI BIBLE *under* BIBLE.

**Jackdaw of Rheims.** *See under* JACKDAW.

**Rhetorical question.** A question asked for the sake of effect rather than demanding an answer as, 'Who cares?' i.e. nobody does. A rhetor was an ancient Greek or Roman teacher or professor of rhetoric.

**Rhiannon.** The Celtic horse goddess, featuring in the MABINOGION. She is the daughter of Hefaidd Hen and the wife of Pwyll, and she rides on a white mare. She is associated with the underworld and with fertility, and has been identified with the Romano-Celtic goddess Rigantona, whose name means 'great queen'.

**Rhine. Confederation of the Rhine.** *See under* CONFEDERATION.

**Watch on the Rhine, The.** *See under* WATCH.

**Rhino.** Slang for money, and a term in use in the 17th century. Its origin is uncertain but one possible suggestion is that it derives from an Eastern belief that the powdered horn of the rhinoceros increased sexual potency and therefore commanded a high price.

**Rhoda.** In the New Testament (Acts 12), a housemaid who recognized PETER by his voice after his release from prison and who was so excited by his arrival that she 'opened not the gate for gladness'.

**Rhodesia.** The former country of Southern Africa was named after Cecil Rhodes (1853–1902). It consisted of the historic territories of Matabeleland and Mashonaland, which became part of the British Empire by 1894 through the enterprise of Rhodes and his British South Africa Company. In 1964 Northern Rhodesia was renamed Zambia, and Southern Rhodesia became Zimbabwe in 1980. Both are independent republics within the COMMONWEALTH. *See also* JAMESON RAID.

**Rhodes scholars.** Students holding a scholarship at Oxford under the will of Cecil Rhodes, whose wealth largely accumulated from his mining activities in South Africa. These scholars are selected from candidates in the British COMMONWEALTH, the USA and Germany.

> [President] Clinton enrolled at Georgetown University largely to be near the U.S. Congress he hoped one day to enter. Then came Oxford, on a Rhodes scholarship, and Yale Law School, where he met the brightest woman in the class, Hillary Rodham.
> *Time* (27 January 1992)

**Rhodian. Rhodian bully, The.** The COLOSSUS of Rhodes.

> Yet fain wouldst thou the crouching world bestride,
> Just like the Rhodian bully o'er the tide.
> JOHN WOLCOT: *The Lousiad*, ii (1785–95)

**Rhodian law, The.** The earliest system of maritime law known to history, compiled by the Rhodians about 900 BC.

**Rhopalic verse** (Greek *rhopalon*, 'club that is thicker at one end'). Verse consisting of lines in which each successive word has more syllables than the one preceding it or each line is a foot longer. The following is an English example:

Whoe'er she be,
That not impossible she
That shall command my heart and me.
RICHARD CRASHAW: 'Wishes to His (Supposed) Mistress' (1646)

**Rhyme. Rhyming slang.** Slang, much used by the COCKNEY, in which the word intended is replaced by one that rhymes with it, as 'plates of meat' for feet, 'Rory O'More' for door, 'dicky dirt' for shirt, 'dicky-bird' for word. When the rhyme is a compound word, the rhyming part is often dropped, leaving the uninitiated somewhat puzzled. Thus Chivy (Chevy) Chase rhymes with 'face', but by dropping 'chase', Chivy remains. Similarly daisies are boots, from 'daisy roots', the 'roots' being dropped. Numerous colloquial expressions derive from it. *See also* BLOW A RASPBERRY *under* BLOW; USE YOUR LOAF *under* USE.

**Corn-law Rhymer, The.** *See under* CORN.

**Eye rhyme.** *See under* EYE.

**Neither rhyme nor reason.** *See under* NEITHER.

**Nursery rhymes.** *See under* NURSERY.

**Perfect rhyme.** *See under* PERFECT.

**Thomas the Rhymer.** *See under* THOMAS.

**Rib. Adam's rib.** *See under* ADAM.

**Jack rib.** *See under* JACK.

**Riband, Blue.** *See under* BLUE.

**Ribbon. Ribbon development.** Single-depth building, chiefly houses, along main roads extending out of built-up areas. Such development was banned by the Town and Country Planning Act of 1947.

**Ribbonism.** The activities and aims of the Ribbon or Riband societies, secret Irish Catholic associations flourishing from *c.*1820 to 1870 and at their peak in 1835–55. Ribbonism began in ULSTER to defend Catholics against ORANGEMEN, but spread south and by the 1830s was essentially agrarian. Its character and methods varied somewhat from district to district. It was basically a movement of the lower classes concerned with sporadic acts of outrage and took the place of the Whitefeet, MOLLY MAGUIRES, TERRY ALTS and other groups. The name arose from the green ribbon worn as a badge.

**Blue Ribbon.** *See under* BLUE.

**Blue Ribbon Army.** *See under* BLUE.

**Blue Ribbon of the Turf, The.** *See under* BLUE.

**Ribston pippin.** The apple is so called from Ribston, North Yorkshire, where the first pippins, introduced from Normandy about 1707, were planted. It is said that Sir Henry Goodriche planted three pips. Two died, and from the third came all the Ribston apple trees in England.

**Rice.** The custom of throwing rice after a bride comes from India, rice being, with the Hindus, an emblem of fecundity. The bridegroom throws three handfuls over the bride, and the bride does the same over the bridegroom. *See also* MARRIAGE KNOT.

**Rice Christians.** Converts to Christianity for worldly benefits, such as a supply of rice to Indians. The expression relates to Christianity born of gain, not faith.

**Rice paper.** *See* MISNOMERS.

**Rich. As rich as Croesus.** *See under* AS.

**Richard. Richard Roe.** *See under* DOE.

**Poor Richard.** *See under* POOR.

**Richmond. Richmond Park.** The largest park in Greater London, so extensive that it still contains wildlife, was originally the private chase or hunting ground of Henry VII, who built Richmond Palace here in the early 16th century, naming it after his former title of Duke of Richmond, from the Yorkshire town of this name.

**Another Richmond in the field.** *See under* ANOTHER.

**Rickshaw.** The two-wheeled passenger vehicle drawn by one or two men in Asian countries has a name that is a shortened form of jinrickshaw, literally 'man power carriage', from Japanese *jin*, 'man', *riki*, 'power', and *sha*, 'carriage'. The man who draws the carriage was formerly familiar as a coolie, from a Hindi word ultimately meaning 'hireling'. A similar vehicle with three wheels is known as a trishaw, and is propelled by a man pedalling as on a tricycle.

**Ricochet.** The bound of a bullet or other projectile after striking; the skipping of a flung stone over water (DUCKS AND DRAKES). The term is hence applied to anything repeated again and again. Marshal Vauban introduced ricochet firing at Philipsburg in 1688. The word is of unknown French origin.

**Ricochet words.** *See* REDUPLICATED WORDS.

**Riddle.** JOSEPHUS relates how Hiram, king of Tyre, and SOLOMON once had a contest in riddles, when Solomon won a large sum of money, but subsequently lost it to Abdemon, one of Hiram's subjects. Plutarch says that HOMER died of chagrin because he could not solve a certain riddle. *See also* SPHINX.

**Riddle me** or **riddle me ree.** Expound my riddle rightly.

**Riddle of claret, A.** Thirteen bottles, a MAGNUM and twelve quarts, said to be so called because in certain old golf clubs, magistrates invited to the celebration dinner presented the club with this amount, sending it in a riddle or sieve.

**Ride** (Old English *rīdan*). To go on horseback; to be carried in a vehicle and so on. In the USA; 'to ride' is also used to mean to oppress, to pick on and irritate a person.

**Ride a cockhorse, To.** A cockhorse is really a hobbyhorse, but when a child 'rides a cockhorse' he or she sits astride a person's foot or knee while they jig it up and down.

A cockhorse was also a horse kept ready at the bottom of a steep hill to help a coach and its team to the top. It was hitched to the front of the team.

**Ride again. To.** To reappear unexpectedly, usually in altered circumstances. The metaphor is from the American West.

> *Destry Rides Again* (film title) (1939)

**Ride and tie, To.** Said of a couple of travellers with only one horse between them. One rides on ahead and then ties the horse up and walks on. The other takes his turn on the horse when he has reached it.

**Ride for a fall, To.** To proceed with one's business recklessly, usually regardless of the consequences; almost to invite trouble by thoughtless or reckless actions.

**Rider of the Shires, The.** William Cobbett (1762–1835), the warm-hearted countryman and radical journalist, has been so called. His journeys on horseback through many of the southern counties of England are described in his *Rural Rides*, which were written after days in the saddle.

> This morning I set off, in a rather drizzling rain, from Kensington, on horse-back, accompanied by my son James, with an intention of going to Uphusband, near Andover, which is situated in the North West corner of Hampshire.
>
> *Rural Rides*, Chilworth, near Guildford, Surrey; Wednesday, 25th Sept. 1822 (1830)

**Ride roughshod over someone, To.** To treat them without any consideration; to disregard their feelings and interests completely. The shoes of a horse that is roughshod for slippery weather have projecting nail-heads.

**Ride shanks's mare** or **pony, To.** To walk or go on foot, the shanks being the legs.

**Ride the marches, To.** In Scotland to BEAT THE BOUNDS of the parish.

**Ride the Spanish mare, To.** An old nautical punishment. The victim was put astride a boom with the stay slackened off when the ship was at sea. This was a hazardous position and one of considerable discomfort.

**Riding.** (1) In Cornwall a 'riding' was a practice similar to the SKIMMINGTON, designed to shame and publicize those guilty of marital infidelity. Two people, representing the offenders, were driven through the streets in a cart pulled by a donkey with a suitable accompanying din. *See also* RANDAN; SHALLAL.

(2) The three historic divisions of Yorkshire East, North and West Riding, were so called because each formed a third part of the county. They arose during the Danish occupation. The word was originally 'thriding', from Old Norse *thrithjung*, 'a third part', but the initial *th-* of this was lost by assimilation to the final *t* or *th* in east, north or west. The divisions of the district of Lindsey, in north Lincolnshire, were also called ridings. The Yorkshire ridings were abolished in 1974 in the reorganisation of local government, but the East Riding of Yorkshire (so called in full to avoid confusion with the Lincolnshire one) was restored in 1996 as one of the four unitary authorities in the former county of Humberside. Winifred Holtby's novel *South Riding* (1936) drew on her own background in the East Riding of Yorkshire to portray a wide social panorama of the region. See *also* LATHE; RAPE.

**Go along for the ride, To.** To be present without contributing; to join an activity without particular motive. The expression dates from the age of the motor car, when originally journeys were made for a purpose.

**Rough Riders.** *See under* ROUGH.

**Taken for a ride, To be.** To have one's leg pulled; to be made the butt of a joke. More sinisterly, the expression is also a gangster EUPHEMISM for murder. The victim is induced or forced into a vehicle and murdered in the course of the ride. Such methods were used by the NAZI regime in Germany.

**White-knuckle ride.** *See under* WHITE.

**Ridiculous, From the sublime to the.** *See under* FROM.

**Ridotto** (Italian). An entertainment with music and dancing, popular in 18th-century England. The Italian word means literally 'retreat', ultimately from Latin *reducere*, 'to lead back'. The reference is to music 'reduced' from the full score, i.e. arranged for a smaller group of performers.

**Riff-raff.** Sweepings; refuse; the rabble. The Old French term was *rif et raf*, whence the phrase *Il n'a laissé ni rif ni raf* ('He has left nothing behind him'). Rif is related to *rifler*, 'to plunder', and raf to *rafle*, 'sweeping up'.

**Rift in the lute, A.** A rift is a split or crack, hence a defect betokening the beginning of disharmony or incipient dissension.

> It is the little rift within the lute,
> That by and by will make the music mute,
> And ever widening slowly silence all.
>
> TENNYSON: *Idylls of the King*, 'Vivien' (1859)

**Rig.** There is more than one word rig but their etymology and division are not clear-cut. In the sense of dressing, it was originally applied to a ship, which is said to be well-rigged, fully-rigged and so on. The ropes, stays, shrouds, braces, halyards and the like used to stay its masts and work the sails are its rigging, as also are the cordage, masts and sails as a whole. Hence rig-out as a person's clothing or costume.

In the USA, before the days of the motor car, a rig was a carriage or private conveyance.

The word was also formerly used of a whore, and a lewd woman was said to be riggish.

The word also meant a hoax or dodge, hence a swindle, and 'to rig the market' means to cause an artificial rise or fall in prices in order to make a profit.

**Bermuda rig.** *See under* BERMUDA.

**Rigadoon.** A lively dance of French origin for two people, in French *rigaudon*. Jean-Jacques Rousseau, in his *Dictionnaire de musique* (1767), says it was invented towards the close of the 17th century by a dancing master of Marseilles named Rigaud.

> Dance she would, not in such court-like measures as she had learned abroad, but some high-placed jig, or hopskip rigadoon, befitting the brisk lasses at a rustic merrymaking.
>
> NATHANIEL HAWTHORNE: *The House of the Seven Gables*, xiii (1851)

**Right.** In politics the right is the CONSERVATIVE side. *See also* LEFT.

**Right foot foremost.** It is considered unlucky to enter a house, or even a room, on the left foot, and in ancient Rome a boy was stationed at the door of a wealthy man's home to caution visitors not to cross the threshold with the left foot.

**Right-hand man.** An invaluable or chief assistant, as indispensable as one's right hand. The expression is an old one. Similarly, a person's 'right hand' is their principal assistant, their most trusted and loyal helper.

**Right Honourable.** A prefix to the title of EARLS, VISCOUNTS, BARONS and the younger sons of DUKES and MARQUESSES, Lord Justices and Justices of Appeal, all privy councillors, some lord mayors and lord provosts and certain other civic dignitaries, and some COMMONWEALTH ministers.

**Right now.** At this very moment; immediately.

**Righto!** or **righty-ho!** All right, a colloquial form of cheerful assent. 'Right you are' is a similar exclamation.

**Right of Sanctuary.** In Anglo-Saxon England all churches and churchyards generally provided refuge for fugitives for 40 days, while permanent refuge was available at the great LIBERTIES of Beverley, Durham, and Ripon. Sanctuary for treason was disallowed in 1486 and most of the remaining rights were severely restricted by Henry VIII. Eight cities of refuge were finally provided on the biblical model: Chester, Derby, Launceston, Northampton, Norwich, Wells, Westminster and York. Sanctuary for criminals was abolished in 1623 and for civil offenders by acts of 1697 and 1723. These latter measures were aimed at such rookeries as ALSATIA, the SAVOY, the CLINK and the MINT.

In Scotland the best known sanctuaries were those of the church of Wedale (Stow), near Galashiels, and that of Lesmahagow (Abbey Green), Lanark. These were abolished at the REFORMATION. The abbey of Holyrood House remained a sanctuary for debtors until the late 19th century. *See also* INVENTORS.

**Right of Tabouret.** In the old French court certain ladies of the highest rank had the *droit de tabouret*, the right of sitting on a tabouret or low stool in the presence of the queen. Gentlemen similarly privileged had the *droit de fauteuil*, the right of sitting in an armchair.

**Right of way.** The right of passing through the land of another. A highway is a public right of way. A private right of way is either customary or an easement (a legal right for the benefit of an adjoining owner). Rights of way may be for special purposes as an agricultural way, a way to church, a footway, a carriageway and so on.

**Right on!** A colloquial expression of agreement or approval.

**Right one, A.** A silly or foolish person, as: 'You're a right one, aren't you?'

**Rights of common.** The four principal rights that one person may have over the land of another are for: pasture (the right of feeding stock), piscary (the right of fishing), estovers (the right of cutting wood, furze and so on) and turbary (the right of cutting turves).

**Rights of Man, The.** According to political philosophers of the 17th and 18th centuries, there are certain unalienable human rights, which, as stated by John Locke, are the right to life, liberty and property. The social contract theorists also included the right to resistance from tyranny. Such rights were formally embodied in the French DECLARATION OF THE RIGHTS OF MAN, and a DECLARATION OF RIGHTS was drawn up by the First American Continental Congress in 1774. The American DECLARATION OF INDEPENDENCE (1776) says:

> We hold these truths to be self-evident, that all men are created equal, that they are endowed by their Creator with certain inalienable Rights, that among these are Life, Liberty, and the pursuit of Happiness.

**Right to bear arms, The.** This is based on proven descent, through the male line, from an ancestor entitled to bear certain arms, or by a grant from the College of Arms (Heralds' College) in England and Wales, the NORROY and ULSTER KING OF ARMS in Ulster, and the LORD LYON KING OF ARMS in Scotland. A person having such right is said to be armigerous. There is in fact little to prevent individuals from adopting arms without the consent of these authorities. *See also* HERALDRY.

In the USA the right to bear arms means the right of a citizen to have a gun, a right still zealously championed by many. It derives from Article II in the BILL OF RIGHTS which reads: 'A well-regulated militia being necessary to the security of a free State, the right of the people to keep and bear arms shall not be infringed.'

**As right as a trivet, ninepence** or **rain.** *See under* AS.

**Bill of Rights.** *See under* BILL.

**Bit of all right, A.** *See under* BIT.

**Dead right.** *See under* DEAD.

**Declaration of Rights.** *See under* DECLARE.

**Declaration of the Rights of.** *See under* DECLARE.

**Divine Right of Kings, The.** *See under* DIVINE.

**Eyes right!** *See under* EYE.

**In one's right mind.** Sane; in a normal state after mental excitement. The phrase is of biblical origin:

> And they come to Jesus, and see him that was possessed with the devil, and had the legion, sitting, and clothed, and in his right mind.
> Mark 5:15

**Left, right and centre.** *See under* LEFT.

**On the right side of forty.** Younger than forty. The age can of course vary.

**On the right side of someone.** In favour with them.

**On the right** or **wrong tracks.** *See under* TRACK.

**Petition of Right, The.** *See under* PETITION.

**Put things to rights, To.** To tidy up; to put everything in its proper place; to correct matters.

**See someone right, To.** *See under* SEE.

**Rigmarie.** An old Scottish coin of low value. The word originated from one of the 'billon' coins struck in the reign of Queen Mary, which bore the words *Reg. Maria* as part of the legend.

Billon is mixed metal for coinage, especially silver largely alloyed with copper.

**Rigmarole.** A rambling disconnected account, an unending yarn. The word is said to be a popular corruption of RAGMAN ROLL, and is recorded from the early 18th century.

> You never heard such a rigmarole ... He said he thought he was certain he had seen somebody by the rick and it was Tom Bakewell who was the only man he knew who had a grudge against Farmer Blaize and if the object had been a little bigger he would not mind swearing to Tom and would swear to him for he was dead certain it was Tom only what he saw looked smaller and it was pitch dark at the time [etc].
> GEORGE MEREDITH: *Richard Feverel*, ch ix (1859)

**Rigoletto.** The hunchbacked court jester who is the central character of the opera by Verdi that bears his name (1851). He laughs at the grief of the elderly Count Monterone, whose daughter has been seduced by the Duke of Mantua, and Monterone lays a curse on him. The courtiers discover that Rigoletto has a young girl hidden away. Unaware that she is actually his beloved daughter Gilda, they assume she is his mistress and abduct her for the duke's pleasure, tricking Rigoletto into helping them. The duke visits Gilda and she falls in love with him. The courtiers do not spare Rigoletto even when they discover who Gilda is, and he vows vengeance on the duke for having his way with her, hiring an assassin to kill him. Gilda still loves the duke, despite being dishonoured by him, and when she learns about the planned assassination, she takes his place, so that she is fatally stabbed. Rigoletto gloats over the sack delivered to him, believing it to contain the duke's body. He finds it is the dying Gilda, and collapses in anguish. Rigoletto's name is a diminutive of Arrigo, a vernacular form of Enrico, 'Henry'. Verdi's opera was based on the novel *Le Roi s'amuse* (1832) by Victor Hugo, and Verdi originally intended the title to be *La maledizione* ('The Curse').

**Rig-Veda.** *See* VEDAS.

**Rile.** A dialect word, common in Norfolk and other parts, for stirring up water to make it muddy. Hence to excite or disturb, and hence the colloquial meaning, to vex, annoy or make angry. The word is a variant form of 'roil', itself perhaps from Old French *ruiler*, 'to mix mortar', from Late Latin *regulare*, 'to regulate'.

**Riley.** *See* LIVE THE LIFE OF REILLY.

**Old Mother Riley.** *See under* OLD.

**Rimini, Francesca da.** *See under* FRANCESCA.

**Rimmon.** The Babylonian god who presided over storms. Milton identifies him with one of the fallen angels:

> Him followed Rimmon, whose delightful seat
> Was fair Damascus, on the fertile banks
> Of Abbana and Pharphar, lucid streams.
> *Paradise Lost*, i (1667)

**Bow down in the house of Rimmon, To.** *See under* BOW.

**Rinaldo.** One of the great heroes of medieval romance (also called Renault of Montauban), a PALADIN of CHARLEMAGNE, cousin of ORLANDO, and one of the FOUR SONS OF AYMON. He was the owner of the horse BAYARDO, and is always described with the characteristics of a borderer: valiant, ingenious, rapacious and unscrupulous.

Tasso's romantic epic *Rinaldo* appeared in 1562, and his masterpiece JERUSALEM DELIVERED, in which Rinaldo was the ACHILLES of the Christian army, despising gold and power but craving renown, was published (without permission) in 1581.

In Ariosto's ORLANDO FURIOSO (1516), Rinaldo appears as the son of the 4th Marquis d'Este, Lord of Mount Auban or Albano, eldest son of

Amon or Aymon, nephew of Charlemagne. He was the rival of his cousin Orlando.

**Ring.** In the sense 'circle', the word represents Old English *hring*. In the sense 'to sound a bell', it comes from Old English *hringan*, 'to clash', 'to ring', related to Latin *clangere*, 'to clang'.

A ring worn on the forefinger is supposed to indicate a haughty, bold and overbearing spirit. Worn on the middle finger a ring denotes prudence, dignity and discretion; if on the marriage finger, love and affection; and if on the little finger, a masterful spirit.

The wearing of a wedding ring by married women is now universal in Christian countries, but the custom varies greatly in detail. It appears to have originated in the betrothal rings given as secular pledges by the Romans. Until the end of the 16th century it was the custom in England to wear the wedding ring on the third finger of the right hand, not the left, as now. *See also* WEDDING FINGER.

As the forefinger was held to be symbolical of the HOLY GHOST, priests used to wear a ring on this in token of their spiritual office. Episcopal rings, worn by cardinals, bishops and abbots, are of gold with a stone (cardinals a sapphire, bishops and abbots an amethyst), and are worn on the third finger of the right hand. The pope wears a similar ring, usually with a cameo, emerald or ruby. A plain gold ring is placed on the third finger of the right hand of a nun on her profession.

In ancient Rome, the free Roman had the right to wear an iron ring, only senators, chief magistrates and, in later times, knights (*equites*), enjoyed the *jus annuli aurei*, the right to wear a ring of gold. The emperors conferred this upon whom they pleased and Justinian extended the privilege to all Roman citizens. *See also* CRAMP RINGS.

**Ring, The.** Bookmakers or pugilists collectively, and the sports they represent, because the spectators at a prize fight or race form a ring around the competitors. Specifically, 'The Ring' was the hall for prize fights in the Blackfriars Road, London.

The word is also applied to unscrupulous dealers, as a group, who form or make a ring.

**Ring a bell, To.** To strike a chord; to sound familiar; to remind someone of something. The expression may have derived from the fairground, where a bell on top of a tall column could be struck by a contestant hammering a pivot at the base and sending a projectile upwards.

**Ring a peal, To.** Correctly speaking, a set of bells is called a ring of bells and the sound made is a peal. Specifically, to ring a peal is to ring a series of changes on a set of bells, although the expression is commonly used more loosely.

**Ring a ring o'roses.** *See* BLACK DEATH.

**Ring down the curtain, To.** To bring a matter to an end. A theatrical term. *See also* RABELAIS *under* FAMOUS LAST WORDS.

**Ringer.** A one-ringer and so on. In the Royal Navy and Royal Air Force the rank of an officer is designated by the braided rings worn around the lower part of the sleeve. One ring denotes a sub-lieutenant and a flying officer, two rings, a lieutenant and a flight lieutenant, and these are called colloquially a one-ringer or two-ringer respectively. Warrant officers and pilot officers wear a thin ring, hence the term half-ringer. Lieutenant commanders and squadron leaders wear two rings with a narrow one between them and are thus called two-and-a-half-ringers. In the Navy a four-ringed captain denotes an officer of captain's rank as opposed to the 'captain' of a ship, who may be of much lower rank.

The term ringer is also applied on the racecourse, running track and the like to a runner who is entered for a race by means of a false return with regard to the detailed conditions of entry.

It is also used of a person or thing which closely resembles another. Hence, 'dead ringer' for someone who bears an exact resemblance to another.

**Ring in, To.** To welcome the New Year by ringing church bells, while simultaneously ringing out the old year.

> Ring out the old, ring in the new,
> Ring, happy bells, across the snow:
> The year is going, let him go;
> Ring out the false, ring in the true.
>
> ALFRED, LORD TENNYSON: *In Memoriam A.H.H.*, cvi (1850)

**Ringleader.** The moving spirit; the chief in some enterprise, especially of a mutinous character. The term comes from the old phrase 'to lead the ring', the ring being a group of associated persons.

**Ring of Agramant, The.** The tale of this enchanted ring is recounted in ORLANDO FURIOSO. It was given by Agramant, the emperor of Africa, to the dwarf Brunello from whom it was stolen by BRADAMANTE, the sister of RINALDO, and given to Melissa. It passed successively into the hands of ROGERO and ANGELICA, who carried it in her mouth

**Ring of Amasis, The.** Herodotus narrates (*Histories*, III, iv (5th century BC)) that Polycrates, tyrant of Samos, was so fortunate in everything that Amasis, king of Egypt, fearing such unprecedented luck boded ill, advised him to part with something that he highly prized. Polycrates accordingly threw an extremely valuable ring into the sea. A few days afterwards, a fish was presented to him, in which the ring was found. Amasis now renounced friendship with Polycrates, as a man doomed by the gods. Not long after, Polycrates was crucified by his host, the satrap Oroetes.

**Ring of bells, A.** A set of bells from 5 to 12 in number for change ringing.

**Ring off. To.** A phrase meaning to end a telephone conversation or connection by hanging up or replacing the receiver, as, 'I must ring off now'.

**Ring of Innocent, The.** On 29 May 1205 Innocent III sent John, king of England, four gold rings set with precious stones, and explained that the rotundity signifies eternity ('Remember we are passing through time into eternity'), the number signifies the four virtues, which make up constancy of mind (justice, fortitude, prudence and temperance), the material signifies 'the wisdom from on high', which is as gold purified in the fire, the green emerald is an emblem of 'faith', the blue sapphire of 'hope', the red garnet of 'charity' and the bright topaz of 'good works'.

**Ring of the Fisherman.** *See* FISHERMAN'S RING.

**Ring of the Nibelung** or **Ring Cycle.** The festival cycle by Richard Wagner, first performed at Bayreuth in 1876. Its constituent parts are *Das Rheingold* (1869), *Die Walküre* (1870), *Siegfried* (1876) and *Götterdämmerung* ('The Twilight of the Gods') (1876). *See also* NIBELUNGENLIED.

**Ring posies** or **mottoes.** These were commonly inscribed on the inside of rings in the 16th, 17th and 18th centuries. The inscriptions included:

AEI (Greek for 'Always')
For ever and for aye
In thee my choice,/ I do rejoice
Let love increase
May God above/ Increase our love
Not two but one/ Till life is gone
My heart and I,/ Until I die
When this you see,/ Then think of me
Love is heaven, and heaven is love
Wedlock, 'tis said/ In heaven is made

**Rings noted in fable and legend.**

RING OF AGRAMANT
RING OF AMASIS
CAMBALO'S RING
Doge's Ring: *see* BRIDE OF THE SEA
Ring of Edward the Confessor: the king was once asked for alms by an old man, and gave him his ring; later, when some English pilgrims to the HOLY LAND happened to meet the same old man, he told them he was JOHN THE EVANGELIST and gave them the identical ring to take to 'Saint' Edward. It was preserved in Westminster Abbey
Ring of Gyges: *see under* GYGES
RING OF INNOCENT
Luned's Ring: this, which rendered the wearer invisible, was given by Luned to Owain, one of King ARTHUR's knights
Ring of Ogier: given him by MORGAN LE FAY, the ring removed all infirmities and restored the aged to youth again
Otnit's Ring of Invisibility: according to the HELDENBUCH this belonged to Otnit, king of Lombardy, and was given to him by the queen mother when he went to gain the soldan's daughter in marriage; the stone had the virtue of directing the wearer to the right road to take in travelling
Polycrates' Ring: *see* RING OF AMASIS
Reynard's Wonderful Ring: *see under* REYNARD
Solomon's ring: *see under* SOLOMON
Talking ring: *see under* TALK

**Ring someone up, To.** To telephone them. The expression is now rather dated, and the usual term is now 'to call' or simply 'to phone'.

**Ring the bells backwards, To.** To ring a muffled peal. When serving as a tocsin or warning of danger, or to express grief or sorrow, bells were formerly rung backwards, that is, the peal began with the bass bell, not the treble. The expression was later applied to a muffled peal, especially one at a funeral.

**Ring the changes, To.** To repeat the same thing in a different way. The allusion is to bell-ringing. To know how many changes can be rung on a peal, multiply the number of bells in the peal by the number of changes that can be rung on a peal consisting of one fewer bells, thus: 1 bell, no change; 2 bells, 1 by 2 = 2 changes; 3 bells, 2 by 3 = 6 changes; 4 bells, 6 by 4 = 24 changes; 5 bells, 24 by 5 = 120 changes; 6 bells, 120 by 6 = 720 changes and so on.

**Ring true, To.** To appear authentic; to seem likely. The allusion is to the former method of testing coins by dropping them on a hard, cold surface. Those of pure silver or gold had a distinctive ring, i.e. they 'rang true', while those of base metal had a duller sound.

**Ring up the curtain, To.** In the theatre, to order the curtain to be raised or opened, the signal originally being the ringing of a bell. Metaphorically the phrase means to initiate or inaugurate something. Similarly to ring down the curtain is to terminate a thing or bring it to an end.

**Cambalo's ring.** *See under* CAMBALO.
**Cramp rings.** *See under* CRAMP.
**Fairy ring.** *See under* RING.
**Fisherman's ring.** *See under* FISH.
**Form** or **make a ring, To.** *See under* FORM.
**Giants' Ring.** *See under* GIANT.
**Lord of the Rings, The.** *See under* LORD.
**Napoleon of the ring.** *See under* NAPOLEON.
**Prize ring, The.** *See under* PRIZE.
**Reynard's wonderful ring.** *See under* REYNARD.
**Run rings around someone, To.** *See under* RUN.
**Solomon's ring.** *See under* SOLOMON.

**Talking ring.** *See under* TALK.
**Toplady ring.** *See under* TOPLADY.
**Tweed ring, The.** *See under* TWEED.

**Rio Grande.** The North American river, forming the frontier between the United States and Mexico, has a Spanish name meaning simply 'big river'. In Mexico itself it is known as the Río Bravo, 'wild river'. Its name is found elsewhere for other rivers, including two in Brazil.

**Riot. Porteous Riots.** *See under* PORTEOUS.
**Read the riot act, To.** *See under* READ.
**Run riot, To.** *See under* RUN.

**RIP** (Latin *Requiescat in pace*, 'Rest in peace'). An abbreviation used on mourning cards, tombstones and similar places. The initial letters of the Latin phrase happen to correspond to those of the English.

**Rip. Rip Van Winkle.** *See under* WINKLE.
**Let rip, To.** *See under* LET.

**Ripper, Jack the.** *See under* JACK.

**Rise. Rise and shine.** An order to get out of one's bed on the instant and become active. The words evoke the rising of the sun.

**Rise from the ranks, To.** A commissioned officer of the army who has worked his way up from a private soldier is said to have risen from the ranks; he is often called a ranker. Hence, the expression is applied to a SELF-MADE MAN in any walk of life.

**Rise in the world, To.** To attain a superior social position.

**Rise to the fly, To.** To rise to the bait or to fall for a hoax or trap, as a fish rises to the angler's fly and is caught.

**Rise to the occasion, To.** To show oneself equal to a demanding situation or task; to speak or act as the emergency requires.

**Rising in the air.** *See* LEVITATION.
**Easter Rising, The.** *See under* EASTER.

**Get a rise, To.** To be given an increase in salary or wages.

**Land of the Rising Sun, The.** *See under* LAND.

**Take a rise out of someone, To.** To raise a laugh at their expense; to make them angry. The metaphor may be from fly-fishing, since the fish rise to the fly and are caught. In the USA a pay increase is called a raise, and to get a raise out of someone is to call forth the desired reaction or response.

**Venner's rising.** *See under* VENNER.

**Risk. Risk one's neck, To.** To take a great risk.
**Security risk.** *See under* SECURITY.

**Risorgimento** (Italian, 'resurrection'). The name given to the 19th-century movement for Italian liberation. It can be said to have had its roots in the enlightened despotism of the 18th century and the influence of the French Revolution and French occupation. The CARBONARI in Naples and Sicily, the Federati in Sardinia, and Mazzini's YOUNG ITALY all played a part, and the Risorgimento was strengthened by the revolutionary events of 1848–9. Its political aims were largely achieved by Cavour (1810–61) in the events of 1859–60, and Garibaldi's radicalism made a further contribution, but the idealism of the Risorgimento was submerged by Cavour's realistic policies.

**Rites, Last.** *See under* LAST.

**Ritualism, The six points of.** *See under* SIX.

**Ritzy.** In colloquial usage, fashionable and luxurious; ostentatiously smart. The allusion is to one or other of the Ritz-Carlton Hotel, New York, the Ritz Hotel, Paris, or the Ritz Hotel, London, which became identified with wealth. The last of these was established in 1906 by the Swiss hotelier César Ritz (1850–1918).

**Rivals.** The word originally meant 'persons dwelling on opposite sides of a river', from Latin *rivalis*, 'one who shares the same river'. Caelius says there was no more fruitful source of contention than river-right, both with beasts and men, not only for the benefit of its waters, but also because rivers are natural boundaries.

**River. Sell down the river, To.** *See under* SELL.
**Sent up the river, To be.** *See under* SEND.
**Yellow River, The.** *See under* YELLOW.

**Rivet, Golden.** *See under* GOLDEN.

**Riviera** (Italian, 'shore', 'coast'). The name has come to be used for any fashionable or popular stretch of sea coast. It originally applied to the coastline around Genoa, Italy, where it has been traditionally divided into the Riviera di Ponente (western coast), taking in San Remo and Imperia, and the Riviera di Levante (eastern coast), with Rapallo. From there it passed to the French Riviera, which extends eastwards from Marseilles to La Spezia, across the Italian border. The French themselves do not use the term, but know the region as the Côte d'Azur ('azure coast'). England followed suit in due course with the Cornish Riviera, a name familiar from the express train so called (originally the 'Riviera Express'), running from London to Penzance, first in 1904. This Riviera is generally reckoned to be the coast of Mounts Bay, from Penzance in the west to the Lizard in the east. The Devon and Dorset coast, further east, has also been known as the English Riviera.

**Riwle, Ancren.** *See under* ANCREN.

**Rizieri of Risa.** *See* ROGERO OF RISA.

**Road. Road, The.** The name by which CHARING CROSS Road, in its heyday as the centre of the second-hand book trade in London, was known to booksellers and bibliophiles.

**Road hog.** A selfish motorist. The term dates back to the early days of motoring.

**Roadhouse.** An inn, hotel or the like by the roadside, usually at some distance outside a town, where parties can go for meals, dancing and so on.

**Roads** or **roadstead.** A place where ships can safely ride at anchor, as Yarmouth Roads. Road and ride are related words.

**Road sense.** The ability to behave safely on the road, especially in traffic.

**Road show.** A radio show broadcast live from different towns or venues, which are visited by a disc jockey or other radio presenter.

**Road to hell is paved with good intentions, The.** As 'Hell is paved with good intentions', this occurs as a saying of Dr Johnson (Boswell's *Life*, entry for 16 April 1775), but it is a good deal older. It is given by George Herbert (*Jacula Prudentum* (1633)) as: 'Hell is full of good meanings and wishings.'

**All roads lead to Rome.** *See under* ALL.

**Any road.** A north of England equivalent of anyway.

**Burma Road.** *See under* BURMA.

**Corduroy road.** *See under* CORDUROY.

**End of the road, The.** *See under* END.

**Gentleman of the road.** *See under* GENTLEMAN.

**Hit the road, To.** *See under* HIT.

**Knight of the road.** *See under* KNIGHT.

**One for the road.** *See under* ONE.

**On the road.** Progressing towards, as, 'on the road to recovery'. The expression is also used of a travelling salesman.

**Rule of the road, The.** *See under* RULE.

**Silk Road, The.** *See under* SILK.

**Take to the road, To.** To become a highwayman or a tramp.

**Trunk road.** *See under* TRUNK.

**Roan barbary.** *See* BARBARY ROAN.

**Roar. Roarer.** A broken-winded horse is so called from the noise it makes in breathing.

**Roaring boys.** The riotous blades of Ben Jonson's time, whose delight it was to annoy quiet folk. At one time their pranks in London were carried on to an alarming extent. Thomas Dekker and Thomas Middleton wrote a play about Moll CUTPURSE called *The Roaring Girl* (1621). *See also* MODS AND ROCKERS; MOHOCKS; SCOWERERS.

**Roaring drunk.** Noisily drunk.

**Roaring Forties, The.** A sailor's term for the stormy regions between 40° and 50° south latitude, where heavy westerly winds prevail. In the days of sail these winds often led mariners to return to Europe via CAPE HORN instead of the Cape of Good Hope. The term has also been applied to the North Atlantic crossing between Europe and America between 40° and 50° north latitude.

> Twice I have entered the Roaring Forties and been driven out by gales and squalls. The last one was on Tuesday when I handled the boat badly and it was damaged.
>
> SIR FRANCIS CHICHESTER in *The Sunday Times* (30 October 1966)

**Roaring game, The.** Curling, so called because the Scots when playing or watching support their side with noisy cheering, and because the stones, which are made of granite or whinstone and are shaped like a round flat cheese, roar as they cross the ice.

**Roaring Meg.** Formerly any large gun that made a great noise when fired was so called, as MONS MEG herself. Robert Burton says: 'Music is a roaring Meg against melancholy.'

**Roaring trade, A.** Brisk and profitable trading.

**Roaring twenties, The.** The 1920s, noted for their optimism and buoyancy after the First World War.

**Roar like a bull of Bashan, To.** To roar loudly and excessively. In Old Testament times Bashan was a territory in northern Palestine noted for its breed of cattle.

**Roast. Roast someone, To.** To give a person a severe dressing-down.

**Rule the roast, To.** *See under* RULE.

**Sunday roast.** *See under* SUNDAY.

**Rob** (verb). **Rob Peter to pay Paul, To.** To take away from one person in order to give to another; to pay off one debt only to incur another. The expression is said to allude to the fact that on 17 December 1540 the abbey church of St Peter, Westminster, was advanced to the dignity of a cathedral by LETTERS PATENT, but ten years later was joined to the diocese of London, and many of its estates appropriated to the repairs of St Paul's Cathedral. But it was a common saying long before this and was used by Wyclif about 1380:

> How should God approve that you rob Peter, and give this robbery to Paul in the name of Christ.
>
> *Select Works*, III

**Alexander and the robber.** *See under* ALEXANDER.

**Daylight robbery.** *See under* DAY.

**Rob Roy** (Robert the Red). The nickname of Robert M'Gregor (1671–1734), Scottish outlaw and FREEBOOTER, on account of his red hair. He assumed the name of Campbell about 1716, and was protected by the Duke of Argyll. He is the central character of Sir Walter Scott's novel named after him (1818), in which he is the embodiment of romance, loyalty and honour, and may generally be termed the ROBIN HOOD of Scotland. *See also* RED HAIR.

**Robe. Judge's robes.** *See under* JUDGE.

**Robert.** A name sometimes formerly applied to a policeman, 'the man in blue', in allusion to Sir

Robert Peel (1788–1850), who founded the London police force in 1829. *See also* BOBBY; PEELER.

**Robert the Bruce.** *See* BRUCE, ROBERT.

**Robert the Devil** or **le Diable.** Robert, 6th Duke of Normandy (1028–35), father of WILLIAM THE CONQUEROR. He supported the English ATHELINGS against Canute, and made the pilgrimage to JERUSALEM. He got his name for his daring and cruelty. He is also called Robert the Magnificent. A Norman tradition is that his wandering ghost will not be allowed to rest until the LAST JUDGEMENT, and he became a subject of legend and romance. One story tells that his mother, anxious for a child, prayed to the Devil for a son. In 1496 Wynken de Worde published *The Life of Robert the Devil*, an English translation of a French verse account of his life, and Thomas Lodge's play *Robin the Divell* dates from 1596. Giacomo Meyerbeer's opera *Roberto il Diavolo* (1831) portrays the struggle between the virtue inherited from his mother and the vice imparted by his father.

Robert François Damiens (1715–57), who attempted to assassinate Louis XV, was also called Robert le Diable. *See also* DAMIENS' ORDEAL.

**Robespierre.** Maximilien Marie Isidore de Robespierre (1758–94), a prime mover behind the REIGN OF TERROR, was himself executed following a brief career of growing autocracy. He was apprehended by the National Guard after being shot in the face on 27 July 1794 and the following day guillotined without trial, the executioners first callously tearing the bandage from his badly injured jaw.

**Robin.** A diminutive of Robert.

**Robin and Makyne.** An ancient Scottish pastoral by Robert Henryson or Henderson (*c*.1430–*c*.1506) given in PERCY'S RELIQUES (1765). Robin is a shepherd for whom Makyne sighs. She goes to him and tells her love, but Robin turns a deaf ear, and the damsel goes home to weep. After a time the tables are turned, and Robin goes to Makyne to plead for her heart and hand, but the damsel replies:

> The man that will not when he may,
> Sall have nocht when he wald [Shall have nothing when he would].

**Robin Goodfellow.** Another name for PUCK. His character and activities are given fully in the ballad of this name in PERCY'S RELIQUES (1765) as exemplified in the following verse:

> When house or harth doth sluttish lye,
> I pinch the maidens black and blue;
> The bed-clothes from the bedd pull I,
> And lay them naked all to view.
> 'Twixt sleepe and wake,
> I do them take,
> And on the key-cold floor them throw.
> If out they cry
> Then forth I fly,
> And loudly laugh out, ho, ho, ho!

**Robin Hood.** This traditional outlaw and hero of English ballads is mentioned by Langland in *The* VISION OF PIERS PLOWMAN, Bk V (1377), and there are several mid-15th-century poems about him. He also appears in Andrew Wyntoun's chronicle of Scotland, *The Orygynale Cronykil* (*c*.1420). The first published collection of ballads about him, *A Lytell Geste of Robyn Hode* was printed by Wynkyn de Worde (*c*.1489). The earliest tales were set in Barnsdale, near Doncaster, South Yorkshire, or in Sherwood Forest, Nottinghamshire, and his adventures have been variously assigned from the reign of Richard I (1189–99) to that of Edward II (1307–27). One popular legend was that he was the outlawed Earl of Huntingdon, Robert Fitzooth, in disguise. The name may have been that of an actual outlaw around whose name the legends accumulated. He suffered no woman to be harassed and he is credited with robbing the rich and helping the poor.

Robin's earlier companions included LITTLE JOHN, Will Scarlet, MUCH, the miller's son, Allen-a-dale, GEORGE-A-GREEN, and later Friar TUCK and MAID MARIAN.

The stories formed the basis of early dramatic representations, including Ben Jonson's last (and unfinished) play, *The Sad Shepherd, or, A Tale of Robin Hood* (*c*.1635), and were later amalgamated with the MORRIS DANCE and other MAY DAY revels. *See also* TWM SHON CATTI.

> Robyn was a proude outlawe,
> Whyles he walked on grounde,
> So curteyse an outlawe as he was one
> Was never none yfounde.
> *A Lytell Geste of Robyn Hode*, i

**Robin Hood and Guy of Gisborne.** A ballad given in PERCY'S RELIQUES (1765). Robin Hood and LITTLE JOHN, having had a tiff, part company, when Little John falls into the hands of the Sheriff of Nottingham, who ties him to a tree. Meanwhile Robin Hood meets with Guy of Gisborne, who has sworn to slay the 'bold forrester'. The two bowmen struggle together, but Guy is slain and Robin Hood rides on until he comes to the tree where Little John is bound. The sheriff mistakes him for Guy of Gisborne, and gives him charge of the prisoner. Robin cuts the cord, hands Guy's bow to Little John, and the two soon put the sheriff and his men to flight.

**Robin Hood's Bay.** The bay of this name between Whitby and Scarborough, North Yorkshire, is first recorded in 1532. According to local legend, Robin Hood kept fishing boats there to put to sea when pursued by the soldiery. He also went fishing in them in the summer.

**Robin Hood's bow and arrow.** The traditional bow and arrow of Robin Hood are religiously preserved at Kirklees Hall, Yorkshire, the seat of the Armytage family, and the site of his grave is marked in the park.

**Robin Hood's death.** The outlaw was reputedly bled to death treacherously by a nun, instigated to the foul deed by his kinswoman, the prioress of Kirklees, near Halifax (1247).

**Robin Hood's larder.** An oak in Sherwood Forest. The tradition is that ROBIN HOOD used its hollow trunk as a hiding place for the deer he had slain. Late in the 19th century a group of schoolgirls boiled a kettle in it and burned down a large part of the tree, which was reputed to be a thousand years old. It was blown down in 1966, and the Duke of Portland gave a suitably inscribed remnant to the mayor of Toronto.

**Robin Hood wind, A.** A thaw wind, which is particularly raw and piercing as it is saturated with moisture scarcely above freezing point. Tradition runs that ROBIN HOOD used to say he could bear any cold except that which a thaw wind brought with it.

> Every Yorkshireman is familiar with the observation that Robin Hood could brave all weathers but a thaw wind.
>
> *Life & Ballads of Robin Hood*, ii (*c*.1855)

**Robin Redbreast.** The popular name for the small songbird *Erithacus rubecula*. The tradition is that when Christ was on his way to CALVARY, a robin picked a thorn out of his crown, and the blood that issued from the wound fell on the bird and dyed its breast red.

Another fable is that the robin covers the dead with leaves. This is referred to in John Webster's *White Devil* (V, i (1612)):

> Call for the robin-red-breast and the wren,
> Since o'er shady groves they hover,
> And with leaves and flowers do cover
> The friendless bodies of unburied men.

When so covering Christ's body, their white breasts touched his blood and they have ever since been red. *See also* RUDDOCK.

**Auld Robin Gray.** *See under* AULD.

**Christopher Robin.** *See under* CHRISTOPHER.

**Cock Robin.** *See under* COCK.

**Many talk of Robin Hood who never shot with his bow.** *See under* MANY.

**Poor Robin's Almanack.** *See under* POOR.

**Ragged robin.** *See under* RAG.

**Round robin, A.** *See under* ROUND.

**Robinson. Robinson Crusoe.** *See under* CRUSOE.

**Before you can say Jack Robinson.** *See under* BEFORE.

**Heath Robinson.** *See under* HEATH.

**Prosperity Robinson.** Frederick John Robinson (1782–1859), Viscount Goderich, afterwards 1st Earl of Ripon, Chancellor of the Exchequer (1823–7), so called by William Cobbett, who also dubbed him 'Goody Goderich'. In 1825 he boasted in the House of the prosperity of the nation, but unfortunately the autumn and winter were marked by bank failures, bankruptcies and a STOCK EXCHANGE collapse. However, his economic policies were generally progressive.

**Ralph Robinson.** *See* FARMER GEORGE.

**Robot** (Czech *robota*, 'forced labour'). An automaton with semi-human powers and intelligence. From this the term is often extended to mean a person who works automatically without employing initiative. The name comes from the mechanical creatures in Karel Čapek's play *R.U.R.* (*Rossum's Universal Robots*), which was successfully produced in London in 1923. The word was also applied to various forms of 'flying bombs' sent against England by the Germans in the Second World War.

**Roc.** In Arabian legend a fabulous white bird of enormous size and such strength that it can 'truss elephants in its talons' and carry them to its mountain nest, where it devours them. It is described in the story of SINBAD THE SAILOR in the ARABIAN NIGHTS ENTERTAINMENTS, in which it carries Sinbad from the valley of the diamonds.

**Roch** or **Roque, St.** The patron saint of those afflicted with the plague, because 'he worked miracles on the plague-stricken, while he was himself smitten with the same judgement'. He is depicted in a pilgrim's habit, lifting his robe to display a plague spot on his thigh, which an angel is touching in order to cure it. Sometimes he is accompanied by a dog bringing bread in its mouth, an allusion to the legend that a hound brought him bread daily while he was perishing of pestilence in a forest. His feast-day, 16 August, was formerly celebrated in England as a general HARVEST HOME, and styled 'the great August festival'.

**St Roch et son chien** (French, 'St Roch and his dog'). Inseparables; DARBY AND JOAN.

**Rochdale Pioneers, The.** The name given to the sponsors of the first financially successful cooperative store. In December 1844, a group of 28 weavers, calling themselves the Equitable Pioneers, opened their store in Toad Lane, Rochdale, Lancashire, with a capital of £28. They sold their wares at market prices and gave a dividend to purchasers in proportion to their expenditure. It was on this basis that the cooperative movement grew.

**Rochelle salt.** Seidlitz powder, an effervescent powder, a mixture of sodium hydrogen carbonate with tartaric acid, acid sodium tartrate or another similar acid or salt, so called because it was discovered by an apothecary of La Rochelle, named Seignette, in 1672. In France it is called *sel de Seignette* or *sel des tombeaux*.

**Rocinante.** *See* ROSINANTE.

**Rock.** A symbol of solidity and strength.

> Thou art Peter, and upon this rock I will build my church; and the gates of hell shall not prevail against it.
> Matthew 16:18

It is Greek *petros* 'rock', from which the name Peter is derived. *See also* ROCK OF AGES.

GIBRALTAR is commonly known as 'The Rock'. *See also* ROCK ENGLISH.

ALCATRAZ Island in San Francisco Bay, the site of the former American prison for the most dangerous criminals, consists of 12 acres (4.8 ha) of solid rock and became known as 'The Rock'. It is now part of a recreation area.

In US thieves' slang a rock is a diamond or other precious stone.

**Rock back on one's heels, To.** To be surprised or astonished.

**Rock bottom.** The lowest one can get, literally or metaphorically. The expression is of mining origin, and alludes to the layers of bedrock that are reached when the mine is exhausted.

**Rock dove.** The domestic and feral pigeon is a semi-domesticated descendant of the rock dove (*Columba livia*). The wild rock dove is native to Mediterranean countries and is confined to mountainous areas and cliffs, hence the name. It can be distinguished from the STOCK DOVE and wood pigeon by its black wingbars and white lower back.

**Rock English.** The mixed patois of Spanish and English spoken by the native inhabitants of GIBRALTAR, who are colloquially referred to as Rock Lizards or ROCK SCORPIONS. Similarly, Malta or Mediterranean fever, which is common in Gibraltar, is also called rock fever.

**Rocking stones.** *See* LOGAN STONES.

**Rock 'n' roll.** Rock and roll, or just rock, was the pop music of the latter half of the 1950s, characterized by its swing or rhythm and the style of dancing that went with it. Its fans were called rockers and they belonged to the days of the teddy boy (*see* EDWARDIAN), before the advent of the Mods. *See also* MODS AND ROCKERS.

**Rock of Ages.** Christ, as the unshakeable and eternal foundation. In a marginal note to Isaiah 26:4, the words 'everlasting strength' are stated to be in Hebrew 'rock of ages'. In one of his hymns Wesley wrote (1788):

> Hell in vain against us rages;
> Can it shock
> Christ the Rock
> Of eternal Ages?
> 'Praise by all to Christ is given'

The well-known hymn 'Rock of Ages' was written by Augustus Montague Toplady (1740–78) and first published in *The Gospel Magazine* (1775). One account says that he wrote it while seated by a great cleft of rock near Cheddar, Somerset. A more unlikely story is that the first verse was written on the ten of diamonds in the interval between two rubbers of WHIST at Bath. *See also* TOPLADY RING.

**Rock Scorpion.** A colloquial name for a Gibraltarian. GIBRALTAR is commonly known as 'the Rock'. *See also* GARLIC WALL.

**Rock the boat, To.** To unsettle the stability of a situation; to create difficulties for one's associates, companions or partners.

**Aeolian rocks.** *See under* AEOLIAN.

**As steady as a rock.** *See under* AS.

**Between a rock and a hard place.** *See under* BETWEEN.

**Cyanean rocks.** *See under* CYANEAN.

**House builded upon rock, A.** *See under* HOUSE.

**Inchcape Rock.** *See under* INCHCAPE.

**Ladies' Rock.** *See under* LADY.

**Mods and Rockers.** *See under* MODS.

**On the rocks.** A sailor's phrase meaning 'stony broke', i.e. having no money. A ship that is on the rocks will soon disintegrate unless she can be floated off. A marriage that is 'on the rocks' is similarly one in danger of breaking up. A glass of whisky or other alcoholic drink 'on the rocks', however, is one served with ice cubes.

**Plutonic rocks.** *See under* PLUTO.

**Punk rock.** *See under* PUNK.

**Silurian rocks.** *See under* SILURIAN.

**Tarpeian rock.** *See under* TARPEIAN.

**Rockefeller.** A name synonymous with wealth and influence. The American family came into prominence in the 19th century through their oil holdings. John D. Rockefeller (1839–1937) established the Rockefeller Foundation in 1913, avowedly 'to promote the well-being of mankind', and his grandson, Nelson A. Rockefeller (1908–79), was first governor of New York then from 1974 US vice-president.

**Rocket. Congreve rocket.** *See under* CONGREVE.

**Give someone a rocket, To.** To reprimand them severely; 'to blow them up'.

**Rococo.** A style in the fine and decorative arts, particularly characterized by motifs taken from shells, which developed in 18th-century France and spread to Germany, Austria and Spain. The name is from French *rocaille*, rockwork, grotto work, as exemplified in the extravagances at VERSAILLES. At its best it was a lighter and more graceful development from Baroque, as is seen in the furniture and architecture of France during the reign of Louis XV (1715–74). At its worst, it was florid and ornate, hence the use of the word rococo to denote anything in art and literature that is pretentious and tasteless.

**Rod. Rod in pickle, A.** A rod ready to use to chastise with at any moment; one 'preserved' for use.

**Aaron's rod.** *See under* AARON.

**Black Rod.** *See under* BLACK.

**Divining rod.** *See under* DIVINATION.

**Hot rod.** *See under* HOT.

**Kiss the rod, To.** *See under* KISS.

**Make a rod for one's own back, To.** To do something that will lead to trouble, difficulties or hardship for oneself in the future.

**Rule with a rod of iron, To.** *See under* RULE.

**Spare the rod and spoil the child.** *See under* SPARE.

**Usher of the Green Rod.** *See under* USHER.

**Rodeo** (Spanish *rodear*, 'to go around'). A contest or exhibition of skill among COWBOYS, a feature of the ROUND-UP. As a travelling show it was first introduced by BUFFALO BILL, and it depends for its popularity on professional skill with the lasso, the riding of broncos and steers and the like.

**Roderick, Roderic** or **Rodrigo.** A Spanish hero around whom many legends have collected. He was the last of the Visigoth kings. He came to the throne in 710, and was routed, and probably slain, by the Moors under Tarik in 711. According to legend he raped Florinda, daughter of Count Julian of Ceuta, who summoned the SARACENS by way of revenge. It is related that he survived to spend the rest of his life in penance and was eventually devoured by snakes until his sin was atoned for. It was also held that he would return in triumph to save his country. Robert Southey took him as the hero of his narrative poem *Roderick, the Last of the Goths* (1814), in which he appears as the son of Theodofred, and W.S. Landor told the same story in *Count Julian* (1812), while in Sir Walter Scott's poem, *The Vision of Don Roderigo* (1811), Roderick sees in a vision the history of Spain, culminating in the Napoleonic Wars.

**Rodomontade.** Bluster, brag or a blustering and bragging speech. The word comes from Rodomont, the brave but braggart leader of the SARACENS in Boiardo's ORLANDO INNAMORATO and Ariosto's ORLANDO FURIOSO.

**Rodrigo.** *See* RODERICK.

**Roe, Richard.** *See under* DOE.

**Rogation Days.** Rogation Sunday is the Sunday before ASCENSION DAY, and the Rogation Days are the Monday, Tuesday and Wednesday following that Sunday. Rogation is the Latin equivalent of the Greek *litaneia*, supplication or litany (Latin *rogatio*), and in the ROMAN CATHOLIC CHURCH on the three Rogation days 'the Litany of the Saints' is appointed to be sung by the clergy and people in public procession.

The Rogation Days used to be called gang days, from the custom of ganging (going) around the country parishes to BEAT THE BOUNDS at this time. Similarly, the weed milkwort (*Polygala vulgaris*) is called rogation or gang flower from the custom of decorating the pole carried on such occasions with its flowers.

**Roger.** In radio communications, a term meaning 'message received and understood'. It represents a former telephonic name for the letter R, the initial of 'received'. The complete alphabet was:

> A = Able, B = Baker, C = Charlie, D = Dog, E = Easy, F = Fox, G = George, H = How, I = Item J = Jig, K = King, L = Love, M = Mike, N = Nan, O = Oboe, P = Peter, Q = Queen, R = Roger, S = Sugar, T = Tare, U = Uncle, V = Victor, W = William, X = X-ray, Y = Yoke, Z = Zebra

After 1956, the NATO alphabet was generally adopted (although Roger was kept for 'received'):

> A = Alpha, B = Bravo, C = Charlie, D = Delta, E = Echo, F = Foxtrot, G = Golf, H = Hotel, I = India, J = Juliet, K = Kilo, L = Lima, M = Mike, N = November, O = Oscar, P = Papa, Q = Quebec, R = Romeo, S = Sierra, T = Tango, U = Uniform, V = Victor, W = Whiskey, X = X-ray, Y = Yankee, Z = Zulu

**Jolly Roger, The.** *See under* JOLLY.

**Sir Roger de Coverley.** *See under* COVERLEY.

**Rogero, Ruggiero** or **Rizieri of Risa.** In legend the ancestor of the house of d'Este and in Ariosto's ORLANDO FURIOSO, the brother of Marphisa, and son of Rogero and Galacella. His mother was slain by Agolant and his sons, and he was nursed by a lioness. He deserted from the Moorish army to CHARLEMAGNE, and was baptized. His marriage with BRADAMANTE, Charlemagne's niece, and election to the crown of Bulgaria conclude the poem.

**Rogers' Rangers.** A body of daring American frontiersmen raised by Major Robert Rogers (1731–95) to fight with the British troops during the French and Indian war of 1756–63. They took possession of Detroit and other posts. During the War of Independence, the uncertainty of Rogers' allegiance led to his rejection by both sides, and his undoubted abilities were wasted. He died in London in drunken obscurity.

**Roget's Thesaurus.** A reference work, first published by Longman, Brown, Green and Longmans in 1852, which lists synonyms classified in groups not only by meaning but also by spirit and idea. The compiler was Dr Peter Mark Roget (1779–1869), the son of a Genevan pastor. A new enlarged edition appeared in 1879 compiled by his son, John Lewis Roget, and a further edition by John's son, Samuel Romilly Roget, was published in 1933. Subsequent revised and modernized editions were those of Robert A.

Dutch (1962), Susan A. Lloyd (1982), and Betty Kirkpatrick (1987 and 1998).

**Rogue.** One of the CANT words first used in the 16th century to describe sturdy beggars and vagrants, and perhaps related to Latin *rogare*, 'to beg'. The expression 'rogues and vagabonds' has been used in the various Vagrancy Acts for all sorts of wandering or idle fellows, such as fortune tellers, sellers of obscene prints and the like. The term 'incorrigible rogues' is similarly used of persons twice convicted of being rogues and vagabonds, or of persons who escape from imprisonment as rogues and vagabonds.

**Rogue elephant, A.** A vicious dangerous elephant that lives apart from the herd.

**Rogue's badge.** A racehorse or a hunter that becomes obstinate and refuses to do its work is known as a rogue, and the blinkers that it is made to wear are the rogue's badge.

**Rogues' gallery.** A collection of photographs of known criminals, used for the identification of suspects.

**Rogues' Latin.** The same as THIEVES' LATIN.

**Rogue's march.** The tune played when an undesirable soldier was drummed out of his regiment. Hence an ignominious dismissal.

**Rogue's yarn.** The name given to the coloured strand forming part of a government rope inserted to deter thieves. In the former main dockyard roperies yellow denoted Chatham cordage, blue Portsmouth, and red Devonport. *See also* BROAD ARROW.

**Rois Fainéants, Les** (French, 'the do-nothing kings'). An epithet particularly applied to the later kings of the MEROVINGIAN DYNASTY of France, whose powers were increasingly wielded by the MAYOR OF THE PALACE. The first of these largely nominal monarchs was Thierry III (d.690), followed by Clovis III, Childebert III, Dagobert III, Chilpéric II, Thierry IV and lastly Childéric III, who was deposed by PEPIN THE SHORT, Mayor of the Palace, who assumed the title of king in 751. Louis V (d.987), last of the CAROLINGIANS, was also so called.

> 'My signet you shall command with all my heart, madam,' said Earl Philip. ... 'I am, you know, a most complete Roi Fainéant, and never once interfered with my Maire de palais in her proceedings.'
>
> SIR WALTER SCOTT: *Peveril of the Peak*, ch xv (1823)

**Roland** or **Orlando.** The best known of the PALADINS of CHARLEMAGNE, Roland was called the Christian Theseus and the Achilles of the West. He was Count of Mans and Knight of Blaives, and son of Duke Milo of Aiglant, his mother being Bertha, the sister of Charlemagne. Fable has it that he was 8ft (2.4m) tall and that he had an open countenance, which invited confidence but at the same time inspired respect. When Charlemagne was returning from his expedition against Pamplona and Saragossa, the army fell into a natural trap at Roncesvalles (Roncevaux), in the Basque territory of the Pyrenees, and Roland, who commanded the rearguard, was slain with all the flower of the Frankish CHIVALRY (778).

In later renderings of the tale, the Basques become SARACENS, and the disaster of Roncesvalles is ascribed to a plot between Marsile, the Saracen king, and the treacherous GANELON. Roland's achievements are recorded in the Chronicle attributed to Turpin (d.794), archbishop of Rheims, which was not written until the 11th or 12th century, and in the coeval *Carmen de Proditione Guenois*. He is the hero of the 12th-century SONG OF ROLAND, and, as Orlando, of Boiardo's ORLANDO INNAMORATO and Ariosto's ORLANDO FURIOSO. He is also a principal character in Pulci's MORGANTE MAGGIORE, in which he converts the giant Morgante to Christianity. Roland's sword was Durandal and the horn, which, through pride, he failed to sound until it was too late, was Olivant. *See also* LIKE THE BLAST OF ROLAND'S HORN; OLIVER.

**Roland for an Oliver, A.** A blow for a blow; TIT FOR TAT. The exploits of these two PALADINS are so similar that it is difficult to keep them distinct. What Roland did Oliver did, and what Oliver did Roland did. At length the two met in single combat, and fought for five consecutive days, but neither gained the least advantage. Shakespeare alludes to the phrase: 'England all Olivers and Rolands bred' (*Henry VI*, *Pt I*, I, ii (1590)). Almost a century before Shakespeare, the historian Edward Hall (*c*.1499–1547) wrote:

> But to haue a Roland to resist an Oliuer, he sent solempne ambassadors to the Kyng of Englande, offeryng hym his doughter in mariage.
>
> *The Union of the Two Noble and Illustre Families of Lancastre and York* (*c*.1547)

**Rolandseck Tower.** A tower opposite the DRACHENFELS on the Rhine, 22 miles (35km) above Cologne. The legend is that when ROLAND went to the wars, a false report of his death was brought to his betrothed, who retired to a convent in the isle of Nonnenwerth. When he returned flushed with glory and found she had taken the veil, he built the castle to overlook the nunnery, that he might gain a glimpse of his lost love.

**Roland's sword.** Durandal, Durindana or Duranda, which was fabled to have once belonged to HECTOR, and which, like the horn, Olivant, ROLAND won from the giant Jutmundus. It had in its hilt a thread from the Virgin Mary's cloak, a tooth of St Peter, one of St DENYS' hairs and a drop of St Basil's blood. Legend relates that Roland, after he had received his death wound, strove to break Durandal on a rock to prevent it falling to the Saracens, but it was unbreakable so he hurled it into a poisoned stream, where it remains for ever. The name of the sword is probably related to Latin *durare*, 'to last', and therefore to English 'endure'.

**Childe Roland.** *See under* CHILD.

**Die like Roland, To.** *See under* DIE.

**Like the blast of Roland's horn.** *See under* LIKE.

**Song of Roland, The.** *See under* SONG.

**Role, Title.** *See under* TITLE.

**Roll. Rolling drunk.** Swaying or staggering from drunkenness.

> Before the Roman came to Rye or out to Severn strode,
> The rolling English drunkard made the rolling English road.
>
> G.K. CHESTERTON: 'The Rolling English Road' (1914)

**Rolling in it.** Rich; having plenty of money.

**Rolling in the aisles.** Said of a theatre or cinema audience laughing uncontrollably, so that their bodies rock and roll about. The aisles are the passages between the seats. *See also* AISLE; FALL ABOUT.

**Rolling stock.** All the wheeled vehicles of a railway that run on rails, i.e. the engines (locomotives), carriages (passenger coaches), goods trucks (freight wagons), guards' vans and the like.

**Rolling stone gathers no moss, A.** Someone who is always on the move and does not settle down will never become prosperous or wealthy. The proverb is an old one, and the anonymous *The Good Wife would a Pilgrimage* (*c*.1450–1500) has:

> Syldon [seldom] mossyth the ston that oftyn ys tornnyd and wende [turned]

**Roll in the hay, To.** To indulge in heavy petting or sexual intercourse.

**Roll of honour.** A list of those honoured, especially those who lost their lives in war.

**Roll up, To.** To arrive; to put in a appearance.

**Roll up one's sleeves, To.** To prepare oneself for work or a fight. By rolling up one's sleeves one frees one's hands and arms for action.

**Roll-your-own.** A hand-rolled cigarette.

**Barrel roll.** *See under* BARREL.

**Bridge roll.** *See under* BRIDGE.

**Catholic roll.** *See under* CATHOLIC.

**Dandy roller.** *See under* DANDY.

**Heads will roll.** *See under* HEAD.

**Holy Roller.** *See under* HOLY.

**Rollo.** A Norman pirate (*c*.860–932) who attacked Paris and Chartres and eventually secured from Charles III of France a large district on condition that he be baptized and become Charles' vassal. His descendants included WILLIAM THE CONQUEROR.

**Rollright Stones.** An ancient stone circle between the villages of Great and Little Rollright north of Chipping Norton, Oxfordshire, near the Warwickshire border. The structure consists of the King Stone, a circle of about 70 stones called the King's Men, and a few others called the Whispering Knights. 'The King' at this point could look over Oxfordshire and said:

> When Long Compton I shall see,
> King of England I shall be.

But he and his men were petrified by a witch. (Long Compton is a village just over the Warwickshire border.)

**Rolls. Chapel of the Rolls.** *See under* CHAPEL.

**Master of the Rolls.** *See under* MASTER.

**Patent Rolls.** *See under* PATENT.

**Pipe rolls.** *See under* PIPE.

**Ragman rolls.** *See under* RAGMAN.

**Struck off the rolls, To be.** *See under* STRIKE.

**Roly-poly.** A suet crust with jam rolled up into a pudding, or a plump or buxom person. Roly is a thing rolled, with poly a sort of diminutive. In some parts of Scotland the game of ninepins is called rouly-pouly.

**Romaic.** Modern or romanized Greek.

**Roman.** Pertaining to Rome, especially ancient Rome, or to the ROMAN CATHOLIC CHURCH. As a surname or distinctive title the adjective has been applied to:

- Jean Dumont (1700–81), the French painter, called le Romain
- Stephen Picart (1631–1721), the French engraver, called le Romain
- Giulio Pippi (*c*.1492–1546), the Italian Mannerist painter, known as Giulio Romano
- Rienzi or Rienzo (1313–54), the Italian patriot and 'last of the Tribunes', otherwise Ultimus Romanorum, the LAST OF THE ROMANS
- Adrian von Roomen (1581–1615), the mathematician, known as Adrianus Romanus
- Marcus Terentius Varro (116–27 BC), called the Most Learned of the Romans

**Roman alphabet.** The alphabet used by the Romans and for most European languages (except some Slavic) today.

**Roman architecture.** A style of architecture distinguished by its massive character and abundance of ornament, largely derived from the Greek and Etruscan. The Greek orders were adapted and the IONIC and CORINTHIAN were combined to form what came to be called the Roman or Composite order. Their greatest works were baths, amphitheatres, basilicas, aqueducts, bridges, triumphal arches and gateways.

**Roman birds.** EAGLES, so called because the ensign of the Roman legion was an eagle.

**Roman calendar.** The calendar of ancient Rome. It originally consisted of 10 months and had a special 'extra' month intercalated between 23 and 24 February. It was superseded by the JULIAN CALENDAR in 45 BC. *See also* CALENDAR; IDES; NONES.

**Roman candle.** A firework that produces a continuous shower of sparks interspersed with coloured balls of fire. It is so called because it originated in Italy.

**Roman Catholic Church, The.** A name introduced by non-Catholics for members of the Catholic or Western Church under the jurisdiction of the papacy. The term is a consequence of the REFORMATION and came into use in the early 17th century. It was a translation of Latin (*Ecclesia*) *Romana Catholica* (*et Apostolica*), 'Catholic (and Apostolic) (Church) of Rome', and appears to have arisen as a conciliatory term in place of the earlier Roman, Romanist or Romish, which had gained derogatory overtones. *See also* POPE.

**Roman Empire, The.** Properly, the empire established by AUGUSTUS in 27 BC, on the ruins of the Republic. It was finally divided into the Western or Latin Empire and the Eastern or Greek in AD 395. The Western Empire was eventually extinguished in 476, the last nominal emperor being Romulus Augustulus (r.475–476). The term 'Roman empire' is also applied to the territories and dominions of the ROMAN REPUBLIC. *See also* BYZANTINE EMPIRE.

**Roman figures.** *See* NUMBERS.

**Roman holiday.** An allusion to Byron's *Childe Harold's Pilgrimage*, IV, cxli (1818), in which he describes the death of a gladiator in the arena: 'Butcher'd to make a Roman holiday.' The expression is now current to describe enjoyment derived from the discomfiture of others.

**Roman nose.** A nose with a high bridge, as many aristocratic Romans had.

**Roman Republic, The.** The republic established in 509 BC after the overthrow of the last of the seven kings, Tarquinius Superbus (534–510 BC). It was superseded by the empire (27 BC).

For a few months in 1849, after the flight of Pius IX (r.1846–78), the people of Rome declared themselves a republic under the triumvirate of Mazzini, Saffi and Armellini. *See also* PRISONER OF THE VATICAN; YOUNG ITALY.

**Roman roads.** *See* ERMINE STREET; FOSSE WAY; ICKNIELD WAY; WATLING STREET.

**Roman snail.** A type of large edible snail, *Helix pomatia*, the *escargot* of the French. It is so called because it was (wrongly) believed to have been introduced to northern Europe by the Romans.

**Roman type.** The first printing types were based upon the national or local handwriting. Roman type, the character in which this book is printed, developed from the *littera antiqua*, the conscious revival of the old Roman capital and the CAROLINGIAN minuscule, which the Humanist scholars of the Italian RENAISSANCE considered more appropriate for the transcription of recently discovered classical manuscripts than the everyday forms of Gothic handwriting. First used in print *c*.1465, Roman type had virtually superseded Gothic letter in less than 100 years in all parts of Europe except Germany, the British Isles and Scandinavia. Roman type steadily took over in Britain from the late 16th century.

**Roman Wall, The.** *See* ANTONINE WALL; GRIMSDYKE; HADRIAN'S WALL; WALL OF SEVERUS.

**Holy Roman Empire, The.** *See under* HOLY.

**King of the Romans.** *See under* KING.

**Last of the Romans.** *See under* LAST.

**Romana, Rota.** *See under* ROTA.

**Romance.** A term applied in linguistics to the languages, especially Old French, that evolved from the Latin spoken in the European provinces of the ROMAN EMPIRE. The dialect spoken in parts of Switzerland is Romansh. Hence, as a noun, the word came to mean a medieval tale in Old French or Provençal describing (usually in mixed prose and verse) the marvellous adventures of a hero of CHIVALRY. The modern application to a work of fiction containing incidents more or less removed from ordinary life, or to a love story or love affair, followed from this.

The medieval romances fall into three main groups or cycles: the cycle related to the life of King ARTHUR and the KNIGHTS OF THE ROUND TABLE, the CHARLEMAGNE cycle and the cycle of Alexander the Great. In modern terms, to romance is to tell extravagant lies.

**Romance languages.** Those languages that are the immediate offspring of Latin, as Italian, Spanish, Portuguese, French and Romanian.

**Romance of the Rose, The** (French *Roman de la Rose*). An early French poem of some 22,000 lines, an elaborate allegory on the Art of Love, beneath which can be seen a faithful picture of contemporary life. It was begun by Guillaume de Lorris in the latter half of the 13th century, and continued by Jean de Meung in the early part of the 14th. The poet is accosted by Dame Idleness, who conducts him to the Palace of Pleasure, where he meets Love, accompanied by Sweet-looks, Riches, Jollity, Courtesy, Liberality and Youth, who spend their time in dancing, singing and other amusements. By this retinue the poet is conducted to a bed of roses, where he singles out one and attempts to pluck it, when an arrow from CUPID's bow stretches him fainting on the ground, and he is carried far from the flower of his choice. As soon as he recovers, he finds himself alone, and resolves to return to his rose. Welcome goes with him, but Danger, Shame-face, Fear and Slander obstruct him at every turn. Reason advises him to abandon the pursuit, but this he will not do, whereupon Pity and Liberality aid him in reaching the rose of his choice, and VENUS permits him to touch it with his lips. Meanwhile Slander rouses up Jealousy, who seizes Welcome, and casts him into a strong castle, giving the key of the castle door to an old hag. Here the poet is left to mourn over his fate, and the original poem ends.

In the second part, which is much the longer, the same characters appear, but the spirit of the poem is altogether different, the author being interested in life as a whole instead of solely love, and directing his satire against women especially.

An English version, *The Romaunt of the Rose*, was translated by Chaucer, but in the extant version (first printed in 1532) it is generally held that only the first 1700 lines or so are his.

**Arthurian Romances.** *See under* ARTHURIAN.

**Roman de la Rose.** *See* ROMANCE OF THE ROSE.

**Romanes lecture.** An annual lecture at Oxford University, given by an eminent authority, on a subject relating to science, art or literature. It was founded in 1891 by George John Romanes (1848–94) of Christ Church. Among the speakers and their subjects have been Lord Curzon on 'Frontiers' (1907), Gilbert Murray on 'Then and Now: or the Changes of the Last Fifty Years' (1935) and Lord Butler on 'The Difficult Art of Autobiography' (1967).

**Romanesque architecture.** This term embraces the style of architecture in western Europe from the virtual collapse of Roman rule in the 6th century until the emergence of GOTHIC ARCHITECTURE in the late 12th century. Although a style with considerable regional variations, such as SAXON and Norman in England, CAROLINGIAN and Rhenish in Germany, it is generally characterized by the round arch, great thickness of walls, shallow (if any) buttressing and, in the later phases, by profuse decoration, arcading and other features.

**Romantic movement, The.** The literary movement that began in Germany in the last quarter of the 18th century, having for its object a return from the Augustan or classical formalism of the time, to the freer fancies and methods of ROMANCE. It was led by J.C.F. von Schiller (1759–1805), Johann Goethe (1749–1832), Novalis (Friedrich von Hardenberg, 1772–1801) and Johann Ludwig Tieck (1773–1853), and thence spread to Britain, where it influenced the work of William Collins (1721–59) and Thomas Gray (1716–71) and received an impetus from the publication of PERCY'S RELIQUES and Macpherson's OSSIAN. It was immensely stimulated by the French Revolution and effected a transformation of English literature through the writings of John Keats (1795–1821), Lord Byron (1788–1824), William Wordsworth (1770–1850), Percy Bysshe Shelley (1792–1822), S.T. Coleridge (1772–1834), Sir Walter Scott (1771–1832) and others. In France its chief exponents were Jean Jacques Rousseau (1712–78), François René, Vicomte de Chateaubriand (1768–1848), Mme de Staël (1766–1817), Alphonse Lamartine (1790–1869), Alfred de Musset (1810–57), Alfred Victor, Comte de Vigny (1797–1863) and Victor Hugo (1802–85).

**Romany.** A GYPSY, or the Gypsy language, the speech of the Roma or Zincali. The word is from Romany *rom*, 'man', 'husband'.

> 'Aukko tu pios adrey Rommanis. Here is your health in Romany, brother,' said Mr Petulengro; who, having refilled the cup, now emptied it at a draught.
> GEORGE BORROW: *Lavengro*, ch liv (1851)

**Romany names of towns and countries.** The following GYPSY names of places are listed by George Borrow in his *Romano Lavo-Lil*, or 'Word-Book of the Romany' (1874):

Baulo-mengreskey tem (Swineherds' country): Hampshire
Bitcheno padlengreskey tem (Transported fellow's country): Botany Bay
Bokra-mengreskey tem (Shepherds' country): Sussex
Bori-congriken gav (Great church town): York
Boro-rukeneskey gav (Great tree town): Fairlop
Boro-gueroneskey tem (Big fellows' country): Northumberland
Chohawniskey tem (Witches' country): Lancashire
Choko-mengreskey gav (Shoemakers' town): Northampton
Churi-mengreskey gav (Cutlers' town): Sheffield
Coro-mengreskey tem (Potters' country): Staffordshire
Cosht-killimengreskey tem (Cudgel players' country): Cornwall
Curo-mengreskey gav (Boxers' town): Nottingham
Dinelo tem (Fools' country): Suffolk
Giv-engreskey tem (Farmers' country): Buckinghamshire
Gry-engreskey gav (Horsedealers' town): Horncastle
Guyo-mengreskey tem (Pudding-eaters' country): Yorkshire
Hindity-mengreskey tem (Dirty fellows' country): Ireland
Jinney-mengreskey gav (Sharpers' town): Manchester
Juggal-engreskey gav (Dog-fanciers' town): Dudley
Juvlo-mengreskey tem (Lousy fellows' country): Scotland
Kaulo gav (The black town): Birmingham
Levin-engreskey tem (Hop country): Kent
Lil-engreskey gav (Book fellows' town): Oxford
Match-engreskey gav (Fishy town): Yarmouth
Mi-develeskey gav (My God's town): Canterbury
Mi-krauliskey gav (My King's town): London
Nashi-mescro gav (Racers' town): Newmarket
Pappin-eskey tem (Duck country): Lincolnshire
Paub-pawnugo tem (Apple-water country): Herefordshire
Porrum-engreskey tem (Leek-eaters' country): Wales
Pov-engreskey tem (Potato country): Norfolk

Rashayeskey gav (Clergyman's town): Ely
Rokrengreskey gav (Talking fellows' town): Norwich
Shammin-engreskey gav (Chairmakers' town): Windsor
Tudlo tem (Milk country): Cheshire
Weshen-eskey gav (Forest town): Epping
Weshen-juggal-slommo-mengreskey tem (Fox-hunting fellows' country): Leicestershire
Wongareskey gav (Coal town): Newcastle
Wusto-mengreskey tem (Wrestlers' country): Devonshire

'Gav' means town, 'tem' is country, 'engro' denotes a male, and 'eskey' is for the sake of. 'Weshen-juggal', in Leicestershire's name, is literally dog of the wood. For Fairlop, *see under* OAK. *See also* BOTANY BAY; HAMPSHIRE HOG; LAVENGRO; LEEK; SILLY SUFFOLK.

**Romany rye.** One who enters into the GYPSY spirit, learns their language and lives with them as one of themselves. 'Rye', a Gypsy word for 'gentleman', is from Romany *rai*, related to RAJAH. George Borrow's book with this title, a sequel to LAVENGRO, was published in 1857.

> 'I'll bet a crown,' said the jockey, 'that you be the young chap what certain folks call "the Romany Rye."'
>
> *The Romany Rye*, ch xl

**Rome.** The greatest city of the ancient world, according to legend founded in 753 BC by ROMULUS and named after him, but possibly in reality either from Ruma, a former name of the River Tiber, of Etruscan origin, or from Greek *rhein*, 'to flow' or *rhōmē*, 'strength'. This last suggestion is supported by its other name, Valentia (Latin *valens*, 'strong'). It acquired a new significance as the seat of the papacy.

**Rome–Berlin Axis.** *See* AXIS.

**Rome penny** or **Rome scot.** The same as PETER'S PENCE.

**Rome was not built in a day.** Achievements of great moment, worthwhile tasks and the like, are not accomplished without patient perseverance and a considerable interval of time. The saying is an old one.

> Rome was not bylt on a daie (quoth he) and yet stood Tyll it was fynysht.
>
> JOHN HEYWOOD: *A dialogue conteinyng the nomber in effect of all the prouerbes in the englishe tongue*, I, xi (1546)

**All roads lead to Rome.** *See under* ALL.

**Fiddle while Rome burns, To.** *See under* FIDDLE.

**King of Rome, The.** *See under* KING.

**Seven hills of Rome, The.** *See under* SEVEN.

**Sword of Rome, The.** *See under* SWORD.

**When in Rome, do as the Romans do.** *See under* WHEN.

**Romeo and Juliet.** A typification of romantic love, as exemplified in Shakespeare's play of this title (1594). Romeo, of the house of Montague, falls in love with Juliet, one of the Capulet family, long-standing enemies of the Montagues. Romeo and Juliet are secretly married, but Romeo is banished from Verona before their wedding day is over as punishment for the unfortunate slaughter of a Capulet in an affray. Old Capulet now orders Juliet to prepare for marriage with Count Paris forthwith, and to avoid this, she drugs herself into a death-like trance. Romeo, hearing of her 'death', returns, enters the tomb where Juliet lies, and kills himself. Juliet awakens, sees her lover dead, and dispatches herself with Romeo's dagger. Shakespeare closely based his play on Arthur Brooke's long narrative poem, *The Tragicall History of Romeo and Juliet* (1562), which was derived ultimately from an earlier Italian story (1535) by Luigi da Porto, through a French version (1559) by Pierre Boisteau.

**Romulus.** The legendary and eponymous founder of ROME, together with his twin brother Remus. They were sons of MARS and RHEA SYLVIA (Ilia), who, because she was a VESTAL virgin, was condemned to death, while the sons were exposed (abandoned). They were, however, suckled by a she-wolf, and eventually set about founding a city, but quarrelled over the plans, so that Remus was slain by his brother in anger. Romulus was later taken to the heavens by his father, MARS, in a fiery chariot, and was worshipped by the Romans under the name of Quirinus.

**Second Romulus, The.** *See under* SECOND.

**Third Romulus, The.** *See under* THIRD.

**Roncesvalles.** *See* ROLAND; SONG OF ROLAND.

**Rood.** The cross of the crucifixion, or a crucifix, especially the large one that was formerly set on the stone or timber rood-screen that divides the nave from the choir in many churches. This is usually richly decorated with statues, carvings of saints, emblems and the like, and frequently surmounted by a gallery called the rood-loft. The word is related to rod.

**Rood Day.** HOLY CROSS DAY, 14 September, the EXALTATION OF THE CROSS, or 3 May, the INVENTION OF THE CROSS.

**By the rood.** *See under* BY.

**Roof. Roof of the world.** A name given to the Pamirs, the great region of mountains covering 30,000 square miles (77,700 sq km), devoid of trees and shrubs, and most of it in Tajikistan. The name is a translation of Wakhani *bam-i-dunya*, a native appellation. The name also applies to Tibet.

**Roof over one's head, A.** Somewhere to live.

**Hit** or **go through the roof, To.** *See under* HIT.

**Mansard roof.** *See under* MANSARD.

**Raise the roof, To.** *See under* RAISE.

**Under one roof.** In the same building.

**Rooinek** (Afrikaans, 'redneck'). A name given by the Boers to the British in the South African Wars (1881, 1899–1902), and used later to mean any British or European immigrant to South Africa.

**Rook.** A cheat. 'To rook' is to cheat, and 'to rook a pigeon' is to fleece a GREENHORN.

**Rook.** The castle in CHESS derives its name, through French and Spanish, from Persian *rukh*, said to have meant a warrior.

**Rookery.** Any low, densely populated neighbourhood, especially one frequented by thieves and vagabonds. The allusion is to the way in which rooks build their nests closely together. Colonies of seals, and places where seals or seabirds collect in their breeding season, are also known as rookeries.

**Rookie.** In army slang, a recruit, a novice or GREENHORN. In the USA the name is given to a raw beginner in professional sport. It is an altered form of 'recruit'.

**Room. Clear the room, To.** *See under* CLEAR.

**Drawing room.** See under DRAWING.

**Elbow room.** See under ELBOW.

**Gun room.** See under GUN.

**Have no room to swing a cat, To.** To be in a restricted or cramped area. There are various suggested origins of the phrase. Swinging cats by their tails as a mark for sportsmen was once a popular amusement. Cat was an abbreviation for CAT-O'-NINE-TAILS and in view of the restricted space in the old sailing ships where the cat was often administered, the expression is more likely to refer to this kind of cat. However, cat is also an old Scottish word for rogue, and if the derivation is from this, the 'swing' is that of the condemned rogue hanging from the gallows. *See also* FIGHT LIKE KILKENNY CATS.

> At London, I am pent up in frouzy lodgings, where there is not room to swing a cat.
>
> TOBIAS SMOLLETT: *The Expedition of Humphry Clinker*, ii (1771)

**Reception room.** *See under* RECEPTION.

**Smoke-filled room, A.** *See under* SMOKE.

**Roosevelt.** Two of the most prominent members of this wealthy American family were Theodore Roosevelt (1858–1919), 26th president of the USA and a Nobel prize winner, and his cousin, Franklin D. Roosevelt (1882–1945), Democratic statesman and 32nd president. The former's love of hunting gave the name of the TEDDY BEAR.

**Roost, To rule the.** *See* RULE THE ROAST.

**Root. Root and branch.** The whole of something, without any exceptions or omissions; otherwise LOCK, STOCK AND BARREL. The Puritans who supported the Root and Branch Bill of 1641 to abolish the EPISCOPACY were known as 'Root-and-branch men', or 'Rooters', and the term has since been applied to other political factions who are anxious for radical reform.

**Root for, To.** An American term meaning to support a sporting team. The origin here is in Old English *wrōt*, 'snout'.

**Root of the matter, The.** Its heart or essence; its actual base and foundation. The phrase comes from Job 19:28:

> But ye should say, Why persecute we him, seeing the root of the matter is found in me?

**Daisy roots.** *See under* DAISY.

**Grass roots.** *See under* GRASS.

**Insane root.** *See under* INSANE.

**Strike at the roots of, To.** *See under* STRIKE.

**Take root, To.** To become permanently or firmly established.

**Rope. Rope of sand, A.** A proverbially weak link or tie; a union which is easily broken; that which is virtually worthless and untrustworthy.

**Rope someone in, To.** To persuade them to take part in something. An expression from the cattle lands of America, where animals are roped in with a lasso.

**Ropewalk, The.** Former barristers' slang for an OLD BAILEY practice. Thus 'Gone into the ropewalk' means that the barrister concerned has taken up practice in the Old Bailey. The allusion is to the murder trials there, and to the convicted murderer 'getting the rope'.

**Ropy.** A slang expression meaning inferior or of poor quality, as a 'ropy outfit'. The word can also mean slightly unwell, 'one degree under', as: 'I'm feeling rather ropy.'

**Dead ropes.** *See under* DEAD.

**Give someone enough rope, To.** To allow them to continue on a particular course of action (usually bad) until they reap the consequences. 'Give him enough rope and he will hang himself' is the common saying.

**Indian rope-trick.** *See under* INDIAN.

**Know the ropes, To.** *See under* KNOW.

**Money for old rope.** *See under* MONEY.

**On the ropes.** On the verge of ruin or collapse. The allusion is to the boxing ring, where a fighter who is driven back against the ropes is often close to defeat.

**Pay out a rope, To.** *See under* PAY.

**Serve a rope, To.** *See under* SERVE.

**Taste of the rope's end, A.** *See under* TASTE.

**Roque, St.** *See* ROCH.

**Roquelaure.** A type of man's hooded cloak reaching to the knees. It was worn in the 18th century, and is so named from Antoine-Gaston, Duc de Roquelaure (1656–1738), a Marshal of France.

> Your honour's roquelaure, replied the corporal, has not once been had on, since the night before your honour received your wound.
>
> LAURENCE STERNE: *Tristram Shandy*, Bk VI, ch vi, 'The Story of Le Fever' (1759–67)

**Rorschach test.** A type of psychological personality test in which the subject looks at a series of ink-blots and describes what they suggest or resemble. The test was devised by the Swiss psychologist Hermann Rorschach (1884–1922), who introduced it in 1921. The ink-blots in the test are usually symmetrical, which to some extent restricts the degree of subjectivity of their interpretation.

**Rory O'More.** *See* RHYMING SLANG.

**Rosabelle.** The favourite palfrey of Mary, Queen of Scots.

**Rosalia** or **Rosalie, St.** The patron saint of Palermo, Sicily, depicted in art in a cave with a cross and skull, or else in the act of receiving a ROSARY or chaplet of roses from MARY. She lived in the 13th century, and is said to have been carried by angels to an inaccessible mountain, where she dwelt for many years in the cleft of a rock, a part of which she wore away with her knees in her devotions. A chapel has been built there, with a marble statue, to commemorate the event.

**Rosalind.** In Shakespeare's *As You Like It* (1599) the beautiful, witty woman who runs away to the FOREST OF ARDEN disguised as a boy and there gives her beloved Orlando lessons in courtship. She is one of the playwright's most attractive characters.

> From the east to western Ind,
> No jewel is like Rosalind.
> III, ii

**Rosamond, The Fair.** *See under* FAIR.

**Rosary** (Latin *rosarium*, 'rose garden', 'garland'). The bead-roll used by Roman Catholics for keeping count of the recitation of certain prayers, also the prayers themselves. The usual modern rosary consists of five decades of ten recitations, or one-third of the complete rosary known as a corona or chaplet. The full rosary consists of 15 decades of Aves (Hail Marys, small beads), each preceded by a Pater (Our Father, a large bead), and followed by a Gloria (Glory be to the Father, a large bead). While the first, second and third chaplets are being recited, the MYSTERIES OF THE ROSARY are contemplated, beginning with the FIVE JOYFUL MYSTERIES. Only one group of mysteries is usually contemplated at a time. Traditionally the devotion of the rosary is said to have begun with St DOMINIC early in the 13th century but this is not established. Sometimes the VENERABLE BEDE is credited with its introduction but quite erroneously; the idea is based upon the fanciful derivation of bead from his name Beda. *See also* GAUDY; PATERNOSTER.

**Mysteries of the rosary.** *See under* MYSTERY.

**Rosciad, The.** A satire by Charles Churchill (1732–64), published in 1761, on well-known metropolitan actors. It describes the attempt to find a worthy successor to ROSCIUS. Churchill was a member of the HELLFIRE CLUB.

**Roscius.** A first-rate actor, after Quintus Roscius (d.*c*.62 BC), the Roman actor unrivalled for his grace of action, melody of voice, conception of character and delivery.

> What scene of death has Roscius now to act?
> SHAKESPEARE: *Henry VI, Pt III*, V, vi (1590)

**Roscius of France, The.** Michel Boyron (1635–1729), generally called Baron.

**Another Roscius.** William Camden's name for Richard Burbage (d.1619).

**British Roscius, The.** Thomas Betterton (1635–1710), of whom Colley Cibber says: 'He alone was born to speak what only Shakespeare knew to write.' Garrick was also given the title.

**Young Roscius, The.** The boy actor William Henry West Betty, 'Master Betty' (1791–1874). He made his debut at the age of 11 in Belfast as Osman in *Zara*, an English version of Voltaire's *Zaïre* (1732). After achieving astonishing success, he left the stage in 1824.

**Rose.** Medieval legend asserts that the first roses appeared miraculously at Bethlehem as the result of the prayers of a 'fayre Mayden' who had been falsely accused and sentenced to death by burning. In Christian symbolism the rose, as being emblematic of a paragon or one without peer, is peculiarly appropriated to the Virgin MARY, one of whose titles is the Mystical Rose. It is also the attribute of St DOROTHEA, who carries roses in a basket; of St Casilda, St Elizabeth of Portugal and St Rose of Viterbo, who carry roses in either their hands or their caps; of St Thérèse of Lisieux, who scatters red roses; and of St Rosalia, St Angelus, St Rose of Lima and St Victoria, all of whom wear crowns of roses.

The rose is an emblem of England and in HERALDRY is used as the mark of cadency for a seventh son. *See also* RED ROSE; TUDOR ROSE; WHITE ROSE.

In the language of flowers different roses signify different characteristics or attributes, among them the following:

> Burgundy rose: simplicity and beauty
> China rose: grace or beauty ever fresh
> Daily rose: a smile
> DOG ROSE: pleasure mixed with pain
> Faded rose: beauty is fleeting
> Japan rose: beauty is your sole attraction
> Moss rose: voluptuous love
> Musk rose: capricious beauty
> Provence rose: my heart is in flames
> White rosebud: too young to love
> White rose full of buds: secrecy
> Wreath of roses: beauty and virtue rewarded
> Yellow rose: infidelity

**Rose Alley Ambuscade, The.** The attack on John Dryden in London by masked ruffians, probably in the employ of John Wilmot, 2nd Earl of Rochester (1647–80) and the Duchess of Portsmouth (1649–1734), the mistress of Charles II, on 18 December 1679, in revenge for an anonymous *Essay on Satire* attacking Charles II, Rochester, and the Duchesses of Cleveland and Portsmouth, which was erroneously attributed to Dryden but actually written by John Sheffield, 3rd Earl of Mulgrave and, later, 1st Duke of Buckingham and Normanby (1648–1721). The attack took place in Rose Alley, now Rose Street, near Leicester Square, where Dryden had been on his way home from WILL'S COFFEE HOUSE.

**Rose between two thorns, A.** A woman between two men; a good-looking, virtuous or gentle person between two plain, evil or ill-tempered ones.

**Rose by any other name would smell as sweet, A.** The name is of little consequence, it does not affect the inherent qualities of the person or thing under consideration. Thus Shakespeare's Juliet says:

> What's in a name? that which we call a rose
> By any other name would smell as sweet;
> So Romeo would, were he not Romeo call'd.
> *Romeo and Juliet*, II, ii (1594)

The expression is now commonly used sarcastically.

**Rose Coffee House, The.** The tavern standing at the corner of Russell Street and Bridge Street, Covent Garden, London, from about 1651. *See also* WILL'S COFFEE HOUSE.

**Rose-coloured spectacles.** *See* SEE THROUGH ROSE-COLOURED SPECTACLES.

**Rose noble.** A gold coin, also called a ryal, or royal, so named because it bore a rose in a sun on the reverse. It was first minted in 1465 and was valued at 10s, but the issue ceased by 1470. It was revived by Henry VII and again by Mary and Elizabeth I. A rose-ryal was issued by James I (r.1603–25).

**Rose of Jericho, The.** The popular name of *Anastatica hierochuntica*, a small branching plant, native to the sandy deserts of Arabia, Egypt and Syria. When it is dry, if it is exposed to moisture, the branches uncurl. It is also called the Resurrection plant.

**Rose of Sharon.** *Hypericum calycinum*, a small, shrub-like plant with yellow flowers, which is also known as Aaron's beard. The rose of Sharon in the Song of Solomon (2:1) was probably a bulbous plant. *See also* SHARON.

**Rose-red City.** Petra, the ancient capital of the Nabataean kings, from which Arabia Petraea took its name. It was occupied by the Romans in 105 AD and is noted for its ancient tomb and temple ruins as well as Roman remains. The epithet derives from the line in J.W. Burgon's Newdigate Prize poem of 1845:

> Match me such marvel, save in Eastern clime, –
> A rose-red city – 'half as old as Time!'

The local rocks are essentially red and much enhanced by red sunsets.

**Rose Sunday.** The fourth Sunday in LENT, when the pope blesses the GOLDEN ROSE.

**Alexandra Rose Day.** *See under* ALEXANDRA.

**Bed of roses, A.** *See under* BED.

**Dog rose.** *See under* DOG.

**Golden rose.** *See under* GOLDEN.

**Red Rose, The.** *See under* RED.

**Romance of the Rose, The.** *See under* ROMANCE.

**See through rose-coloured spectacles, To.** *See under* SEE.

**Sub rosa.** *See under* SUB.

**Tokyo Rose.** *See under* TOKYO.

**Tudor Rose, The.** *See under* TUDOR.

**Under the rose.** *See* SUB ROSA.

**Union rose, The.** *See* TUDOR ROSE.

**Wars of the Roses, The.** *See under* WAR.

**White Rose, The.** *See under* WHITE.

**Rosemary** (Latin *ros marinus*, 'sea dew'). The shrub (*Rosmarinus officinalis*) is said to aid the amatory art. As VENUS, the love goddess, was sprung from the foam of the sea, rosemary or sea dew would have amatory qualities.

> The sea his mother Venus came on;
> And hence some rev'rend men approve
> Of rosemary in making love.
> SAMUEL BUTLER: *Hudibras*, II, i (1663)

In Shakespeare's *Hamlet* (IV, v (1600)) Ophelia says, 'There's rosemary, that's for remembrance.' The herb was once extensively taken to quieten the nerves, and it was used to flavour wine and ale. It was highly popular at weddings, and to wear rosemary in ancient times was as significant of a wedding as to wear a white favour. When the Nurse in Shakespeare's *Romeo and Juliet* (II, iv (1594)) asks, 'Doth not rosemary and Romeo begin both with a [the same] letter?' she refers to the emblematic characteristics of the herb. In the language of flowers rosemary means 'fidelity in love'.

**Rosetta Stone, The.** A stone found in 1799 by a French officer of engineers named Bouchard or Boussard in an excavation made near Rosetta (Rashid), in the Nile delta northeast of Alexandria. It has an inscription in two languages, Egyptian and Greek, and in three writing systems: HIEROGLYPHICS, demotic script, and the Greek alphabet. It was erected (195 BC) in commemoration of the accession to the throne of Ptolemy Epiphanes. The great value of the stone is that it provided a key to the translation of Egyptian hieroglyphic writing. It is now in the British Museum.

**Rosherville Gardens.** In Victorian times, 'the place to spend a happy day' (as it was advertised at every railway station). These gardens were established by Jeremiah Rosher in disused chalk quarries near Gravesend, Kent. A theatre, zoological collections and music formed part of their attraction, and the gardens were particularly favoured by river excursionists. The site has long been given over to industry. *See also* CREMORNE GARDENS; RANELAGH; VAUXHALL GARDENS.

> Rosherville Gardens are exceedingly pretty, and will repay a visit. But it should be in the morning: in the afternoon and evening, theatrical and acrobatic performances, ballets and outdoor dancing, fireworks, the company, and the accompaniments, are a trying drawback on the beauty of the gardens.
>
> JAMES THORNE: *Handbook to the Environs of London* (1876)

**Rosicrucians.** A secret society of CABBALISTS, occultists and alchemists that is first heard of in 1614 when the anonymous *Fama fraternitatis des löblichen Ordens des Rosenkreuzes* ('Account of the Brotherhood of the Commendable Order of Rosicrucians') was published at Cassel, duly followed by the *Confessio* and *The Chemical Wedding of Christian Rosenkreutz*. The Rosicrucian Order was reputedly founded by the mythical Rosenkreutz ('cross of roses') in 1459. In FREEMASONRY there is still a degree known as the Rose Croix. Rosicrucian philosophy played a part in the early struggle for intellectual progress by clothing its progressive ideas in mystical guise. It seems to have influenced Dr John DEE (1527–1608) and Sir Francis Bacon (1561–1626) among others, and to have some links with the work of PARACELSUS. Rosicrucian societies still exist.

**Rosinante, Rozinante** or **Rocinante.** The wretched jade of a riding horse belonging to Don QUIXOTE. Although it was nothing but skin and bone, and worn out at that, he regarded it as a priceless charger surpassing 'the Bucephalus of Alexander and the Babieca of the Cid'. The name, which is applied to similar hacks, is from Spanish *rocín*, a jade, the *ante* ('before') implying that once upon a time, perhaps, it had been a proper horse.

> Al fin le vino á llamar Rocinante, nombre, á su parecer, alto, sonoro y significativo de lo que había sido cuando fué rocín, antes de lo que ahora era, que era antes y primero de todos los rocines del mundo. (He ended by calling him Rocinante, a name, it seemed to him, that was lofty, sonorous, and indicative of what he had been when he was a hack, before what he was now, and of how he was the first and foremost of all hacks in the world.)
>
> CERVANTES: *Don Quixote*, Pt I, Bk 1, ch i (1608)

*See also* GRIZZLE.

**Rosin Bible, The.** *See under* BIBLE.

**Ross. Ross-shire Buffs, The.** *See under* REGIMENTAL AND DIVISIONAL NICKNAMES.

**Betsy Ross.** Betsy Ross (1752–1836) is said to have made the first STARS AND STRIPES in 1776. The story is that George Washington, with Robert Morris and General George Ross, visited Betsy's upholstery shop in Philadelphia and asked her to make a flag from their design. The stars had six points, but Betsy said they would look better with five. This was agreed and she eventually produced the flag.

**Fair Maid of Ross, The.** *See under* FAIR.

**Man of Ross, The.** *See under* MAN.

**Rosse.** A famous sword, which the dwarf ALBERICH gave to Otwit, king of Lombardy. It struck so fine a cut that it left no 'gap', shone like glass and was adorned with gold.

**Rostrum.** A pulpit or stand for public speakers. Latin *rostrum* is the bill or beak of a bird, also the beak or curved prow of a ship. In the Forum at Rome, the platform from which orators addressed the public was ornamented with *rostra*, or ship-prows taken from the Antiates in 338 BC, hence this use of the word.

**Rota Romana.** A Roman Catholic ecclesiastical court of medieval origin composed of auditors under the presidency of a DEAN. It was reconstituted by Pius X in 1908 and has been reorganized a number of times since then. It appears to take its name from the circular table originally used by the judges at Avignon. It is the normal appeal tribunal for judging cases brought before the Holy See and is perhaps best known as the court to which certain nullity of marriage cases are referred.

**Rotary Club.** A movement among business men, which takes for its motto 'Service above Self'. The idea originated with Paul Harris, a Chicago lawyer, in 1905. In 1911 it took root in Britain and there are now clubs in most towns, membership being limited to one member each of any trade, calling or profession. Lectures are delivered at weekly meetings by guest speakers. The name derives from the early practice of holding meetings in rotation at the offices or business premises of its members. The Rotary Clubs are now members of one association called Rotary International.

**Rote, To learn by.** *See under* LEARN.

**Rothschild.** The name is associated with the great wealth of the international banking family of Rothschild, whose name derives from the red shield by which their parent house at Frankfurt was known. The family banking business really stems from the activities of Mayer Amschel Rothschild (1744–1812), who made a fortune during the Napoleonic Wars. His five sons separated, extending the business throughout Europe. Nathan Mayer Rothschild (1777–1836) established a branch at London in 1798 and made a financial scoop by his advance knowledge of the defeat of NAPOLEON BONAPARTE at Waterloo in 1815. His son Lionel Nathan (1808–79) was best known for his work for Jewish emancipation in Great Britain. Lionel's son Nathan Mayer (1840–1915) was made a baron in 1885 and was the first Jew to be admitted to the House of Lords. Nathan's son Lionel Walter (1868–1937), the 2nd Baron Rothschild, was a noted collector and taxonomist. The 3rd baron, Nathan's grandson, was Nathaniel Mayer Victor Rothschild (1910–90), a zoologist and administrator. His own son, Nathaniel Charles Jacob (b.1936), 4th Baron Rothschild, largely assumed his father's administrative mantle. Jacob's heir is Nathaniel Philip Victor James Rothschild (b.1971).

**Rotten. Rotten** or **pocket borough.** A borough of much diminished population with the parliamentary seat at the disposal of a patron (frequently the crown). Fifty-six such boroughs were disenfranchised by the Reform Act of 1832.

**Rotten Row.** The equestrian track in HYDE PARK, London, is said to be so called from Old French *route le roi* or *route du roi*, because it formed part of the old royal route from the palace of the PLANTAGENET kings at WESTMINSTER to the royal forests. However, it is unlikely that this road should have been given a French name, and 'rotten' probably means what it says, referring to the soft state of the ground here.

**Roué.** The profligate Duke of Orleans, Regent of France (1674–1723), first used this word in its modern sense *c.*1720. It was his ambition to collect around him companions as worthless as himself, and he used facetiously to boast that there was not one of them who did not deserve to be broken on the wheel (French *roue*), hence these profligates went by the name of Orleans' *roués*. The most notorious *roués* were the Dukes of Richelieu, Broglie, Biron and Brancas.

**Rouge** (French, 'red').

**Rouge Croix.** One of the PURSUIVANTS of the Heralds' College, so called from the red cross of St GEORGE, the patron saint of England. Rouge Croix was instituted by Henry V (r.1413–22).

**Rouge Dragon.** The PURSUIVANT established by Henry VII (r.1485–1509). The RED DRAGON was the ensign of the Welsh princes from whom Henry VII traced his ancestry.

**Rouge et noir** (French, 'red and black'). A game of chance, so called because of the red and black diamond-shaped compartments on the board. After the stakes have been placed on the table the cards are dealt in the prescribed manner and the player whose 'pips' amount nearest to 31 is the winner. The game is also called *Trente-et-un* (31) or *Trente-et-quarante* (30 and 40).

**Rough. Rough and ready.** Rough in manner but prompt in action; not elaborate; roughly adequate. General Zachary Taylor (1784–1860), 12th President of the United States, was called Old Rough and Ready, a name he won in the Seminole Wars.

**Rough diamond, A.** A person of worth or good moral character who lacks refinement or social polish. Literally, a diamond in its natural state, before it is cut and polished.

> She is very honest,
> And will be hard to cut as a rough diamond.
> JOHN FLETCHER: *A Wife for a Month*, IV, ii (1624)

**Rough-hewn.** Shaped in the rough; not finished; uncouth; unrefined.

> There's a divinity that shapes our ends,
> Rough-hew them how we will.
> SHAKESPEARE: *Hamlet*, V, ii (1600)

**Rough house, A.** A disorderly scrimmage or brawl.

**Rough music.** A din or noisy uproar made by clanging together pots and pans and other noise-producing instruments usually as a protest outside the house of a person who has outraged propriety. In Somerset it was called 'skimmity-riding', by the Basques *toberac*, and in France CHARIVARI. *See also* SKIMMINGTON.

**Roughneck.** A tough or violent person; a thug. The term is of American origin, and it arose in the early 19th century to refer to carnival workers, whose manual labour and outdoor life in all weathers gave them rough and red skin at the back of their necks.

**Rough Riders.** The 1st Regiment of US Cavalry Volunteers under Colonel Leonard Wood and Lieutenant-Colonel Theodore Roosevelt were so designated in the Spanish-American War (1898), noted for their successful charge up San Juan Hill. The force was made up from COWBOYS, Native Americans, rangers and college students.

In the British cavalry, rough riders were non-commissioned officers and highly skilled horsemen who acted as assistants to the regimental riding master. They owed their position to their abilities in riding unbroken (rough) horses.

**Bit of rough, A.** *See under* BIT.

**Cut up rough, To.** *See under* CUT.

**Old Rough and Ready.** *See under* OLD.

**Ride roughshod over someone, To.** *See under* RIDE.

**Rouncival** or **rounceval.** Very large or strong; of gigantic size. Certain large bones said to have been dug up at Roncesvalles were believed to have belonged to the heroes who fell with ROLAND, hence the usage. 'Rouncival peas' are the large marrowfat peas, and a very big woman is (or was) called a rouncival.

**Round. Round dealing.** Honest, straightforward dealing, without branching off into underhand tricks. The same as square dealing.

**Round on someone, To.** To turn on a person; to retort angrily to someone.

**Round peg in a square hole, A.** The same as a SQUARE PEG IN A ROUND HOLE.

**Round robin, A.** A petition or protest signed in a circular form, so that no name heads the list. The device is French, and according to some authorities the term is a corruption of *rond* ('round') and *ruban* ('ribbon'), and was originally used by sailors. It is also used for a sporting contest in which all participants compete against all others. In its written form, a round robin is now often simply a circular letter sent by one person to many, rather than by many to one.

> Today I returned home with a great sense of satisfaction, having posted our Christmas cards which, because my wife and I have just spent our first year abroad, for the first time contain a round-robin letter.
>
> *The Times* (Letter to the Editor) (14 December 1994)

**Round Table, The.** The Table fabled to have been made by MERLIN at Carduel for Uther PENDRAGON. Uther gave it to Leodegraunce of Cameliard, who gave it to King ARTHUR when the latter married GUINEVERE, his daughter. It was circular to prevent any jealousy on the score of precedency. It seated 150 knights, and a place was left in it for the SANGRAIL. The first reference to it is in Wace's *Roman de Brut* (1155). These legendary details are from Malory's *Morte d'Arthur*, III, i and ii (1485).

The table called King Arthur's Round Table in the Castle Hall at Winchester was recognized as ancient in the time of Henry III (r.1216–72), but its earlier history is unknown. It is of wedge-shaped oak planks and is 17ft (5.2m) in diameter and 2¾ in (7cm) thick. At the back are 12 mortise holes in which 12 legs probably used to fit. It was for the accommodation of 12 favourite knights. Henry VIII showed it to Francis I, telling him that it was the one used by the British king.

In the eighth year of Edward I (i.e. 1280), Roger de Mortimer established a Round Table at Kenilworth for 'the encouragement of military pastimes'. At this foundation, 100 knights and as many ladies were entertained at the founder's expense. About 70 years later, Edward III erected a splendid table at Windsor. It was 200ft (61m) in diameter, and the expense of entertaining the knights amounted to £100 a week. *See also* JOHN O'GROATS.

**Round table conference.** A conference in which no participant has precedence and at which it is agreed that the question in dispute shall be settled amicably with the maximum amount of 'give and take' on each side.

The expression came into prominence in connection with a private conference in the house of Sir William Harcourt on 14 January 1887, with the view of trying to reunite the Liberal Party after the split occasioned by Gladstone's advocacy of Irish Home Rule. Other politically notable Round Table Conferences were those on Indian government held in London (1931–2).

**Round the bend.** Mad; crazy. The sense is of being 'out of the true'.

**Round the twist.** Crazy; eccentric; ROUND THE BEND.

**Round-up.** The gathering up of cattle in the western USA by riding around them and driving them in. Hence, a gathering-in of scattered objects or persons such as criminals. *See also* RODEO.

**As round as Giotto's O.** *See under* AS.

**At a round pace.** *See under* AT.

**Get round someone, To.** To take advantage of a person by wheedling or flattery; to get one's own way through deception.

**In round figures** or **numbers.** Disregarding fractions or (in higher figures) units, so that the amount is expressed in a whole number or a conveniently approximate figure. Thus an annual income of £19,975 would in round figures be £20,000. An amount may be either rounded up (increased) in this way, or else rounded down (decreased).

> Round down your income and gains, to the nearest pound, and round up your tax credits and tax deductions.
>
> *Tax Return Guide* (1998)

**In the round.** In the theatre, the production of plays on a central stage surrounded by the audience as in an arena, without proscenium arch or curtains.

**Sellinger's round.** *See under* SELLINGER.

**Roundabout.** A large revolving platform at fairs, circuses and the like, with horses or similar mounts, which go round and round and are ridden by passengers to the strains of music, known in the USA as a carousel. From this arises the device at crossroads, whereby traffic circulates in one direction only.

**What you lose on the swings you gain on the roundabouts.** *See under* WHAT.

**Roundel** or **roundle.** In HERALDRY a charge of a circular form. There are a number of varieties, distinguished by their colours or tinctures, as:

BEZANT: or
Golpe: purpure
Guze: SANGUINE
Hurt: azure
Ogress or pellet: SABLE
Orange: tenney
Plate: argent
Pomey (because said to resemble an apple, French *pomme*): VERT
Torteau: GULES

**Roundheads.** PURITANS of the time of the Civil Wars (1642–51), especially Cromwell's soldiers.

They were so called from their close-cropped hair, as contrasted with the long hair fashionable among the Royalists or CAVALIERS. The name appears in 1641 in the affrays at Westminster when apprentices were demonstrating against the EPISCOPACY. *See also* NEW MODEL ARMY.

**Roup.** A name given to an auction in Scotland. It is of Scandinavian origin and is connected with Middle Swedish *ropa*, 'to shout'.

**Rout.** A common term in the 18th century for a large evening party or fashionable assemblage. *See also* DRUM; HURRICANE.

**Rove.** The original meaning was to shoot with arrows at marks that were selected at haphazard, the distance being unknown, with the object of practising judging distance. Hence 'to rove' in the sense 'to wander'.

**Roving eye, A.** An amorous interest in the opposite sex, especially of a man for women.

**Row. Paternoster Row.** *See under* PATERNOSTER.

**Death row.** *See under* DEATH.

**Rotten Row.** *See under* ROTTEN.

**Savile Row.** *See under* SAVILE.

**Skid row.** *See under* SKID.

**Rowan** or **mountain ash.** Called in Westmorland (now Cumbria) the Wiggentree. The tree, *Sorbus aucuparia*, was greatly venerated by the DRUIDS and was formerly known as the Witchen because it was believed to ward off witches.

Rowan tree or reed
Put the witches to speed.

Many mountain ash berries are said to denote a deficient harvest. In Aberdeenshire it was customary to make crosses of rowan twigs on the eve of the INVENTION OF THE CROSS and to put them over doors and windows to ward off witches and evil spirits.

**Rowena.** In semi-legendary British history the daughter of HENGIST who married VORTIGERN. Better known is 'the fair Rowena' of literature, the Saxon maiden whom IVANHOE comes to marry. She is a type of the quintessential 19th-century heroine, beautiful but bland.

**Rowley. Rowley poems, The.** *See under* FAKES.

**Old Rowley.** *See under* OLD.

**Rowton houses.** The hotel-type housing of this name was first provided in 1892 for poor working men who had previously been able to find only dormitory-type lodgings. The name is that of their provider, Montague William Lowry-Corry, 1st Lord Rowton (1838–1903).

**Roxana.** The captive Persian princess who became the wife (327 BC) of Alexander the Great. She murdered his second wife Stateira (323) and so became identified with the type of the jealous wife. She was murdered (310), together with her 12-year-old son, Alexander IV, by order of Cassander.

**Roxburghe Club, The.** An association of bibliophiles founded in 1812 for the purpose of printing rare works or manuscripts. It was named after John Ker, 3rd Duke of Roxburghe (1740–1804), a celebrated collector of ancient literature, and it remains the most distinguished gathering of bibliophiles in the world. It was the forerunner of a number of similar printing societies, as the Camden, Chetham, Percy, Shakespeare, Surtees and Wharton in England, the Abbotsford, BANNATYNE CLUB, MAITLAND CLUB and Spalding in Scotland, and the Celtic Society of Ireland.

**Roy. Roy s'avisera, Le** (Norman French, 'The king will consider it'). This is the royal veto on a parliamentary Bill, last put into force 11 March 1707, when Queen Anne refused her assent to a Scottish Militia Bill. The equivalent when the sovereign is a queen is *La reine s'avisera*. *See also* ROYAL ASSENT.

**Roy le veult, Le** (Norman French, 'The king wishes it'). The form of royal assent to parliamentary Bills. Dissent is expressed by *Le* ROY S'AVISERA. The formula for money Bills is *Le roy remercie ses bons sujets, accepte leur benevolence, et ainsi le veult* ('The king thanks his subjects, accepts their kindness, and so wishes it'), and for personal bills, *Soit fait comme il est désiré* ('Be it done as it is desired'). In the reign of a queen, *Le roy* becomes *La reine*.

**Rob Roy.** *See under* ROB.

**Royal. Royal Academy, The.** Founded in 1768, with Sir Joshua Reynolds (1723–92) as the first president, 'for the purpose of cultivating and improving the arts of painting, sculpture and architecture'.

**Royal American Regiment.** The original name of the King's Royal Rifle Corps, which was first raised under that title in Maryland and Pennsylvania, 1755. It subsequently became the 2nd Battalion the Royal Green Jackets.

**Royal and Ancient.** The name by which the game of golf has been known since early days when the Scottish kings practised it. James IV of Scotland (r.1488–1513) is the first recorded royal patron and Mary, Queen of Scots, was playing golf when news was brought to her of Lord Darnley's death in 1567. The Royal and Ancient Golf Club of St Andrews, Scotland, widely known as the 'R and A', is the ruling body of the game, and the links at St Andrews are the Mecca of all golfers.

**Royal Arms of England, The.** The systematic use of Royal Arms begins with Richard I (r.1189–99), who introduced the three lions passant gardant. In 1340 Edward III (r.1327–77) styled himself 'of Great Britain, France and Ireland, King', and quartered the arms of France with those of England. This title and practice was abandoned in 1801 when the Arms were remarshalled following the Union with Ireland. During Mary Tudor's reign the arms of Philip II of Spain were impaled on the existing Arms. James I of England and VI of Scotland introduced the lion rampant of Scotland and the harp of Ireland (derived from the badge assigned to Ireland in the reign of Henry VIII). During the reign of William III and Mary II, the arms of Nassau were added, and on the accession of George I in 1714 the White Horse of Hanover was superimposed until the Hanoverian connection ended with the accession of Victoria in 1837. The lion supporter for England and the UNICORN for Scotland were introduced by James I (r.1603–25). The lion statant gardant on the crest was first used by Edward III.

The correct emblazoning of the arms of the United Kingdom of Great Britain and Northern Ireland is:

> Quarterly, first and fourth gules, three lions passant gardant in pale, or, for England; second or, a lion rampant within a double tressure flory counterflory gules, for Scotland; third azure, a harp or, stringed argent, for Ireland; all surrounded by the Garter. Crest. Upon the royal helm, the imperial crown proper, thereon a lion statant gardant or, imperial crown proper. Supporters. A lion rampant gardant, or, crowned as the crest. Sinister, a unicorn argent, armed, crined, and unguled proper, gorged with a coronet composed of crosses patées and fleurs de lis, a chain affixed thereto, passing between the forelegs, and reflexed over the back, also or. Motto. 'Dieu et mon Droit' in the compartment below the shield, with the Union rose, shamrock, and thistle engrafted on the same stem.

*See also* LION IN HERALDRY.

**Royal Ascot.** A fashionable four-day race meeting held in June at Ascot Heath, Berkshire, and traditionally attended by the royal family. The meeting was instituted by Queen ANNE in 1711. *See also* CLASSIC RACES; RACES.

**Royal Assent.** Assent to parliamentary Bills is still given in Norman French. The form of assent to public and private Bills is *Le* ROY LE VEULT (or *La Reine le veult*), to personal Bills, *Soit fait comme il est désiré*, and to taxation and supply, *Le Roy* or *La Reine remercie ses bons sujets, accepte leur bénévolence, et ainsi le veult*. *See also* ROY S'AVISERA.

**Royal bounty.** A part of the CIVIL LIST out of which the British sovereign makes gifts to charities and pays for official subscriptions.

**Royal Exchange, The.** The original exchange at Cornhill, London, was founded by Sir Thomas Gresham, whose crest was a GRASSHOPPER, was opened by Queen Elizabeth I in 1568 and was modelled on the Bourse at Antwerp as a place for London merchants to transact their business. It was burned down during the GREAT FIRE OF LONDON and a new exchange was opened in 1670, but this was again destroyed by fire in 1838. It is said that before the bells fell they had chimed: 'There's nae luck aboot the hoose.' The third building was opened by Queen Victoria in 1844. In 1939 the Exchange ceased its origin function and the building was taken over by the Royal Exchange Assurance Corporation (now Guardian Royal Exchange Assurance Company), which had occupied offices there since 1720.

**Royal flush.** In poker a hand consisting of the ace, king, queen, jack and ten of one suit.

**Royal Goats, The.** *See* NANNY-GOATS *under* REGIMENTAL AND DIVISIONAL NICKNAMES.

**Royal Highness.** In 1917 George V restricted this title in Britain to the children of the sovereign, to the children of the sons of the sovereign, and to the eldest son of the eldest son of the Prince of Wales. Their wives would also receive the title. The husbands and children of the daughters of the sovereign do not receive the title, but in 1947 Prince Philip was created His Royal Highness The Duke of Edinburgh just before his marriage to Princess Elizabeth, the heir presumptive (*see* HEIR APPARENT), and in 1948 LETTERS PATENT decreed that their children would also be His or Her Royal Highness. *See also* HOUSE OF WINDSOR.

**Royalist Butcher, The.** Blaise de Montluc (1502–77), Marshal of France, notorious for his cruelty to the Huguenots in the time of Charles IX (r.1560–74).

**Royalists.** *See* CAVALIERS.

**Royal merchants.** The wealthy medieval families such as the MEDICI of Florence and the Grimaldi of Genoa.

Sir Thomas Gresham, founder of the ROYAL EXCHANGE, was called a 'royal merchant' from his wealth and influence; and in 1767 John Fletcher's comedy, *The Beggar's Bush* (1622), was produced as an opera with the title *The Royal Merchant*. *See also* GRASSHOPPER.

**Royal Oak.** *See* OAK-APPLE DAY; PUBLIC HOUSE SIGNS.

**Royal Sign Manual.** The signature of the monarch used on orders, commissions and warrants. The earliest known royal signature is that of Edward III (r.1327–77), before which marks or seals were used. Under certain restrictions a stamp is used for minor documents.

**Royal Society, The.** The premier scientific society in Britain. It was established in 1660 and incorporated as the Royal Society in 1662, but its origins can be traced to the meetings of philosophers and scientists held at Gresham College in 1645. It met at the college until 1710 and then moved to Crane Court, Fleet Street. In 1780 it transferred to Somerset House and thence to Burlington House in 1857. Fellowship of the

Royal Society is the most coveted honour among scientists.

**Royal stag.** One with a head of 12 or more points.

**Royal titles.** *See* RULERS.

**Royal 'we', The.** The use of 'we' instead of 'I' by a single person, as by a sovereign. *See* WE.

> Mrs Margaret Thatcher informed the world with regal panache yesterday that her daughter-in-law had given birth to a son. 'We have become a grandmother,' the Prime Minister said.
>
> *The Times* (4 March 1989)

**Battle royal.** *See under* BATTLE.

**Café Royal.** *See under* CAFÉ.

**Chapel Royal.** *See under* CHAPEL.

**Fish royal.** *See under* FISH.

**Hart royal.** *See under* HART.

**Princess Royal.** *See under* PRINCESS.

**Rozinante.** *See* ROSINANTE.

**Rub. Rub along, To.** To cope or manage without too much difficulty.

**Rub noses, To.** A traditional form of greeting among Eskimos.

**Rub of the green, The.** An expression used in golf that has spread into ordinary life. It means a piece of good or ill fortune that is outside the competence of the player (or individual). The situation can be illustrated as follows. Player A hits a shot to the green, which glances off a stone into the trees. Player B hits the same stone at a different angle, and his ball runs on to the green and into the hole. Since neither was aiming at the stone, or even aware of it, the resulting disparity of fortune is 'the rub of the green'.

**Rub one's hands, To.** An action of satisfaction, glee, keen anticipation or the like.

**Rub salt into someone's wounds, To.** To make a person's pain or shame even worse. The allusion is to the old sailing days, when errant sailors were flogged on the bare back and afterwards had salt rubbed in their wounds. This was to help heal the lacerations, but it also made them much more painful.

**Rub shoulders with someone, To.** To mix in their company.

**Rub someone's nose in it, To.** To remind someone forcefully or graphically of what they have done wrong. The allusion is to the house training of a puppy, whose nose is rubbed in its 'doings'. *See also* DON'T RUB IT IN!

**Rub someone up the wrong way, To.** To annoy someone; to irritate a person by lack of tact, as a cat is irked when its fur is rubbed the wrong way.

**Rub up, To.** To refresh the memory; to revive one's knowledge of a subject.

**Brass rubbing.** *See under* BRASS.

**Don't rub it in!** I know I've made a mistake, but you needn't go on emphasizing the fact. *See also* RUB SOMEONE'S NOSE IN IT.

**There's the rub.** That's the difficulty; that's the snag. The phrase comes from Hamlet's 'To be or not to be' speech, with the rub itself alluding to anything that checks or hinders the smooth passage of the ball in a game of bowls.

> To sleep: perchance to dream: ay, there's the rub;
> For in that sleep of death what dreams may come
> When we have shuffled off this mortal coil.
>
> SHAKESPEARE: *Hamlet*, III, i (1600)

**Rubáiyát** (plural of Arabic *rubā'īy*, 'comprising four elements'). A word meaning 'quatrains', much used by Arabic poets, and familiar to English readers through FitzGerald's *Rubáiyát* of OMAR KHAYYÁM (1859).

**Rubber.** In WHIST, bridge and some other games, a set of three games, the best two of three, or the third game of the set. The origin of the term is uncertain, but it may be a transference from bowls, in which the collision of two woods is a rubber, because they rub against each other.

**Rubberneck.** A person who stares or gapes inquisitively; a tourist who gawps at everything there is to see.

**Rubber-stamp, To.** To authorize as a matter of routine; to approve automatically, without any personal examination or check. The allusion is to the use of rubber stamps on routine documents in place of a written authorization.

**Rübezahl.** A mountain spirit of German folklore, the ruler of the weather, also called Herr Johannes, whose home is in the Riesengebirge (Giant Mountains), the mountain range that separates Prussian Silesia (now in Poland) and Bohemia (Czech Republic).

**Rubicon, To cross the.** *See under* CROSS.

**Rubik's Cube.** A teasing puzzle invented by the Hungarian Ernö Rubik (b.1944) in 1974. A cube, apparently composed of 27 cubelets, initially has each of its six faces made up of nine cubelets of the same colour. An interior system of pivots allows any layer of nine cubelets to be rotated with respect to the rest, so that repeated rotations cause the cubelet faces to become scrambled. The challenge is to restore a scrambled cube to its initial configuration. With millions of combinations, there is only one possible way of achieving the desired solution.

**Rubric** (Latin *rubrica terra*, 'red earth'). The Romans called an ordinance or law a rubric, because it was written with vermilion.

The liturgical directions and titles in a Prayer Book are known as the Rubrics because these were (and sometimes still are) printed in red. *See also* RED-LETTER DAY.

> No date prefix'd
> Directs me in the starry rubric set.
>
> MILTON: *Paradise Regained*, iv (1671)

The directions given on formal examination

papers concerning the selection of questions to be answered are also sometimes called the rubrics.

**Ruby.** The ancients considered the ruby to be an antidote to poison and to have the power of preserving people from plague, banishing grief, repressing the ill effects of luxuries and diverting the mind from evil thoughts. It has always been a valuable stone, and even today a fine Burma ruby will cost more than a diamond of the same size.

Marco Polo said that the king of Ceylon had the finest ruby he had ever seen: 'It is a span long, as thick as a man's arm, and without a flaw.' KUBLAI KHAN offered the value of a city for it, but the king would not part with it, even though all the treasures of the world were to be laid at his feet.

**Perfect ruby, The.** *See under* PERFECT.

**Ruddock.** The redbreast 'sacred to the household gods'. The word is related to Old English *rudu*, 'redness', whence 'ruddy'. *See also* ROBIN REDBREAST.

**Rudge, Barnaby.** *See under* BARNABAS.

**Rue.** The HERB OF GRACE, because it was employed for sprinkling holy water. Ophelia says:

> There's rue for you, and here's some for me! we may call it 'herb of grace' o' Sundays.
> SHAKESPEARE: *Hamlet*, IV, v (1600)

*See also* DIFFERENCE.

**Ruff.** An early forerunner of WHIST, very popular in the late 16th and early 17th centuries, later called 'slamm'. The act of trumping at whist and other card games is still called 'the ruff'.

**Rufus** (Latin, 'red'). The following were so called:

William II of England (b.*c*.1056, 1087–1100)
Otto II of Germany (b.955, 973–983), son of the Emperor Otto the Great
Gilbert de Clare, Earl of Gloucester (1243–95)

William Rufus, the son of WILLIAM THE CONQUEROR, was so nicknamed for his ruddy countenance rather than his red hair.

**William Rufus.** *See under* WILLIAM.

**Rug, As snug as a bug in a.** *See under* AS.

**Rugby.** The sport of rugby football, or rugger, as it is sometimes called, takes its name from Rugby School (see PUBLIC SCHOOL), where one afternoon in 1823 a pupil of the school, William Webb Ellis (1805–72), participating in an interclass football match, suddenly picked up the ball and ran with it. A plaque at the school commemorates the event. The sport subsequently adopted two forms: Rugby Union, played only by teams of amateurs, with teams of 15 players, and Rugby League, played between teams of 13 players, with professionalism allowed. The former takes its name from the Rugby Football Union, set up in 1871 to draw up the rules for the game originally played at Rugby. The latter has rules formed in the north of England in 1895 by the Rugby Football League, a breakaway branch of the Rugby Football Union.

**Arnold of Rugby.** *See under* ARNOLD.

**Ruggiero of Risa.** *See* ROGERO OF RISA.

**Ruin, Rack and.** *See under* RACK.

**Rule. Rule, Britannia.** The words of this well-known song are by James Thomson (1700–48), author of *The Seasons* (1726–30). The music is by Dr Thomas Arne (1710–78). It first appeared in a masque entitled *Alfred* produced in August 1740 at Cliveden House, near Maidenhead, Berkshire. It was written at the command of the PRINCE OF WALES and performed before him. The original opening was:

> When Britain first, at Heaven's command,
> Arose from out the azure main,
> This was the charter of the land,
> And guardian angels sung this strain:
> 'Rule, Britannia, rule the waves;
> Britons never will be slaves.'

In the rising of 1745 'Rule, Britannia' was sung by the JACOBITES with modifications appropriate to their cause.

**Rule 43.** A prison regulation whereby prisoners, especially sex offenders, can be isolated for their own protection.

**Rule nisi.** A 'rule' is an order from one of the superior courts, and a 'rule nisi' is such an order 'to show cause'. That is, the rule is to be held absolute unless the party to whom it applies can 'show cause' why it should not be so. *See also* NISI.

**Rule of the road, The.**

> The rule of the road is a paradox quite,
> In riding or driving along;
> If you go to the left you are sure to go right,
> If you go to the right you go wrong.

This is still the rule in Britain and Ireland. In most other European countries and in the USA, traffic keeps to the right.

**Rule of three, The.** The method of finding the fourth term of a proportion where three are given, the numbers being such that the first is to the second as the third is to the fourth. By multiplying the second and third terms together and dividing the result by the first, the fourth term is arrived at.

> Multiplication is vexation,
> Division is as bad;
> The Rule of three doth puzzle me,
> And Practice drives me mad.
> Elizabethan MS (1570)

**Rule of thumb.** A rough, guesswork measure, practice or experience, as distinct from theory, in allusion to the use of the thumb for rough measurements. The first joint of the adult thumb measures almost exactly 1in (2.5cm).

**Rule the roast, To.** To have the main control;

to be paramount. The phrase was common in the 16th century, apparently deriving from the master of the household, as head of the table, carving the joint. It has been suggested that the expression is really 'to rule the roost' (now the common form), from the cock deciding which hen is to roost near him, but roost is more likely a corruption of roast, the old spelling for which was rost or roste.

**Rule the roost, To.** *See* RULE THE ROAST.

**Rule with a rod of iron, To.** To rule tyrannically.

**Bend the rules, To.** See under BEND.

**Divide and rule.** *See under* DIVIDE.

**Exception proves the rule, The.** *See under* EXCEPTION.

**Golden rule, The.** *See under* GOLDEN.

**Ground rules.** *See under* GROUND.

**Home Rule.** *See under* HOME.

**Judge's rules.** *See under* JUDGE.

**McNaughten Rules.** *See under* MCNAUGHTEN.

**Queensberry Rules.** *See under* QUEENSBERRY.

**Scammozzi's rule.** *See under* SCAMMOZZI.

**Thirty-year rule.** *See under* THIRTY.

**Twelve good rules.** *See under* TWELVE.

**Work to rule, To.** *See under* WORK.

**Rule** or **Regulus, St.** A priest of Patrae in Achaia, who is said to have come to Scotland in the 4th century, bringing with him relics of St ANDREW, and to have founded the town and bishopric of St Andrews. The old Scots name of the town, Kilrule (*Cella Reguli*), perpetuates his memory.

**Rulers.** The following titles of rulers are (1) designations that approximately correspond to English king or emperor (e.g. Bey, Mikado, Sultan), and (2) appellatives that were originally the proper name of some individual ruler (e.g. Caesar). Some, of course, are now obsolete. It should also be noted that many of these titles refer to former rulers (e.g. those of Indian States and Persia).

Abgarus: a title of the kings of Edessa (99 BC – AD 217)

Abimelech (Hebrew, 'father of the king'): a title of the king of the ancient Philistines

Akhoond or Akond: king and high priest of the Swat (northwestern provinces of India)

Ameer or Amir (Arabic, 'commander', English EMIR): ruler of Afghanistan, Sind, and the title of certain other Muslim princes

Archon (Greek, 'ruler'): chief of the nine magistrates of ancient Athens

AUGUSTUS: the title of the Roman emperor when the heir presumptive was styled Caesar

Basileus: next in rank below ARCHON

Beglerbeg: *see* BEY

Begum (Urdu, from Eastern Turkish *begim*, 'my lady', related to BEY): a queen, princess or lady of high rank in India

Bey (Turkish, 'lord'): in the Turkish Empire, a superior military officer, or the governor of a minor province or sanjak

Brenn or brenhin: a war chief of the ancient Gauls; a dictator appointed by the DRUIDS in times of danger

BRETWALDA

Cacique: *see* CAZIQUE

Caesar: originally a surname of the Julian family, then assumed by successive Roman emperors and later by their heir presumptive

CALIPH or Calif (Arabic *khalīfa*, 'successor'): successors of MOHAMMED in temporal and spiritual affairs

Candace: a title of the queens of Meroe in Upper Nubia

CAUDILLO

Cazique or cacique (Arawak, 'chief'): a native prince of the ancient Peruvians, Cubans, Mexicans and others, also applied to chiefs of Indian tribes in South America and the West Indies

Chagan: the chief of the Avars

Cham: *see* KHAN

Czar: *see* TSAR

Dey (Turkish *dayi*, literally 'maternal uncle'): governor of Algiers before it was annexed to France in 1830; also the title of 16th-century rulers of Tunis and Tripoli

Diwan or Dewan (Hindi, from Persian *dēvan*, 'register'): the native chief of Palanpur, India

Doge (Venetian dialect, from Latin *dux*, 'leader'): the ruler of the old Venetian Republic (*c*.700–1797); also that of Genoa (1339–1797)

DUCE

Duke (Latin *dux*, 'leader'): the ruler of a duchy formerly in many European countries of sovereign rank

Elector: a prince of the HOLY ROMAN EMPIRE of sovereign rank entitled to take part in the election of the emperor

Emir: the independent chieftain of certain Arabian provinces as Bokhara, Nejd and elsewhere; also given to Arab chiefs who claim descent from Mohammed

Emperor (Latin *imperator*, 'commander'): the ruler of an empire, especially of the Holy Roman Empire

Exarch (Greek *exarkhos*, 'leader'): the title of a viceroy of the BYZANTINE EMPIRE, especially the Exarch of Ravenna, who was *de facto* governor of Italy

FÜHRER

Gaekwar (Marathi, 'cowherd'): formerly the title of the ruler of the Mahrattas, then that of the ruler of Baroda (his son being Gaekwad); the cow is a sacred animal to the Hindus

Gauleiter (German, 'district leader'): the ruler of a province under the NAZI regime in Germany (1933–45)

Holkar: the title of the Maharajah of Indore

Hospodar (Slavic, 'lord', 'master'): the title borne by the princes of Moldavia and Wallachia before their union with Romania

Imperator: *see* EMPEROR

INCA (Quechua, 'king'): the title of the sovereigns of Peru up to the conquest by Pizarro (1532)

Kabaka: the native ruler in the Buganda province of Uganda

Kaiser: the German form of Caesar and the old title of the Holy Roman Emperor and of the later Austrian and German emperors

Khan (Turkish, contraction of *khāqān*, 'ruler'): the chief rulers of Tartar, Mongol and Turkish tribes, as successors of Genghis Khan (d.1227); the word means 'lord' or 'prince'

Khedive (Persian *khidīw*, 'prince'): the title conferred in 1867 by the SULTAN of Turkey on the viceroy or governor of Egypt but abandoned in favour of 'Sultan' in 1914; *see also* VALI

KING

Lama: *see* LAMAISM

Maharajah (Hindi, 'great king'): the title of many of the native rulers of Indian states

Maharao: the title of the rulers of Cutch, Kotah and Sirohi, India

Maharao Rajah: the ruler of Bundi, India

Maharawal: the rulers of Banswana, Dungarpur, Jaisalmer and Partabgarh, India

MIKADO: *see also* SHOGUN; TYCOON

Mir: the ruler of Khairpur, India

MOGUL

Mpret (Albanian, from Latin *imperator*): the old title of the Albanian rulers, revived in 1913 in favour of Prince William of Wied, whose mpretship lasted only a few months

Nawab (Hindi, from Arabic, plural of *na'īb*, 'viceroy'): the native rulers of Bhopal, Tonk, Jaora and elsewhere, and formerly of Bengal

Negus (Amharic, 'king'): the native name of the emperor of Ethiopia

Nizam (Arabic, 'order'): the title of the ruler of Hyderabad

Padishah (Persian, 'protecting lord'): a title of the former SULTAN of Turkey, the SHAH of Persia, and of the former GREAT MOGULS

PENDRAGON

PHARAOH

Prince: formerly in common use as the title of a reigning sovereign, and still used in a few cases, e.g. the Prince of Monaco, the Prince of Liechtenstein

Rajah (Hindi, from Sanskrit *rājan*, 'king'): the title of the rulers of Cochin, Ratlam, Tippera, Chamba, Faridkot, Mandi, Pudukota, Rajgarh, Rajpipla, Sailana, and Tehri (Garhwal); *see also* MAHARAJAH; REX

Rex: the Latin equivalent of 'king', connected with *regere*, 'to rule', and with Sanskrit *rājan* (whence RAJAH)

Sachem or Sagamore (Abnaki *sāgimau*, literally 'he overcomes'): chieftains of certain tribes of Native Americans

Satrap (Old Persian *khshathrapāvan*, 'protector of the land'): the governor of a province in ancient Persia

Shah (Persian, 'king'): the supreme ruler of Persia and some other Eastern countries; *see also* PADISHAH

Shaikh or Sheikh (Arabic *shaykh*, 'old man'): an Arab chief, or head man of a tribe

SHOGUN

Sindhia: the special title of the Maharajah of Gwalior

Sirdar (Persian *sardār*, literally 'head possession'): the commander-in-chief of the Egyptian army and military governor of Egypt (a British officer during the occupation, 1882–1922); also applied to certain nobles in India

Stadtholder (Dutch, 'city holder'): originally a provincial viceroy in the Netherlands, later the chief executive officer of the United Provinces

Sultan (Arabic, 'rule'): the title of the rulers of certain Muslim states

Tetrarch (Greek *tetrarkhēs*, 'one of four rulers'): the governor of the fourth part of a province in the ancient Roman Empire

Thakur Sahib (Hindi, 'lord', and Urdu 'sir', from Arabic, literally 'friend'): the title of the native ruler of Gondal, India

Tsar or Czar (from Latin *Caesar*): the common title of the former emperors of Russia, first assumed by Ivan the Terrible in 1547

TYCOON

Vali (Turkish, 'governor'): the title of the governors of Egypt prior to their holding of the style KHEDIVE

Voivode or Vaivode (Slavic, 'leader of an army', Russian *voyevoda*): a title once used by the princes of Moldavia and Wallachia, later called HOSPODARS

Wali (same as VALI): a title of the ruler or Khan of Kalat, India

**Rum, Bay.** *See under* BAY.

**Ruminate.** To think; to meditate upon some subject; literally, 'to chew the cud' (Latin *ruminare*, from *rumen*, 'throat').

**Rump, The.** The end of the backbone, with the buttocks. The term was applied contemptuously to the remnant of the LONG PARLIAMENT that was left after PRIDE'S PURGE in 1648. It first numbered fewer than 60 MPs and, when augmented, not more than 125. It abolished the HOUSE OF LORDS and the monarchy and declared England a COMMONWEALTH. It was dismissed by Oliver Cromwell on 20 April 1653, but resumed its sitting in 1659. On 21 February 1660 General Monck secured the readmittance of its purged members, so ending its independent existence.

**Rump and dozen.** A rump of beef and a dozen of CLARET; or a rump steak and a dozen oysters. A not uncommon wager among sportsmen of the late 18th and early 19th centuries.

**Rumpelstiltskin.** A passionate little deformed DWARF of German folklore. A miller's daughter was enjoined by a king to spin straw into gold, and the dwarf did it for her, on condition that she would give him her first child. The maiden married the king, and grieved so bitterly when the child was born that the dwarf promised to relent if within three days she could find out his name. Two days were spent in vain guesses, but on the third day one of the queen's servants heard a strange voice singing:

> Little dreams my dainty dame
> Rumpelstiltskin is my name.

The child was saved, and the dwarf killed himself with rage. The name literally means 'wrinkled foreskin'.

**Rum-runners.** During the prohibition era in the USA, those engaged in smuggling illicit liquor by speedboats across the lakes from Canada or from ships outside the THREE-MILE LIMIT. The limit was subsequently increased to 12 miles (19km) by agreement with other powers and enforced by USN destroyers. These, when superannuated, were passed to Great Britain in 1940 under the LEND-LEASE arrangements. *See also* BOOTLEGGER; MOONSHINER.

**Run. Run across, To.** To chance to meet.

**Run along, To.** To depart; to be on one's way. An injunction to a lingering child is: 'Run along now'.

**Run amok** or **amuck, To.** To indulge in physical violence while in a state of frenzy. Amuck or amok is the Malay word *amoq*, 'furious assault'.

**Run away with, To.** To elope with; to steal; to win a prize easily; to bolt (of a horse) with its rider; to lose one's self-control or common sense, as: 'He lets his imagination run away with him.'

**Run down, To.** To cease to go or act from lack of motive force, as a clock when the spring is fully unwound. *See also* RUN SOMEONE DOWN.

**Run down, To be.** To be in poor health, and in need of a tonic or thorough rest. The allusion is to a clock that has run down and needs rewinding.

**Run for it!** Said to someone making their escape: now is your chance, get away quickly!

**Run for one's money, A.** A return or reward for one's efforts, often involving a sense of enjoyment and achievement.

**Run in, To be.** To be arrested and taken into custody.

**Run in the family, To.** To be inherited or characteristic of the family or its members.

**Run into the ground, To.** To take too far; to overwork; to destroy by overuse.

**Run** or **take its course, To.** To continue until it has finished, as of an illness.

**Run** or **go like clockwork, To.** To work smoothly and precisely; the phrase is generally applied to a routine, mode of working, journey or the like.

**Runners.** *See* REDBREASTS.

**Runner-up.** The competitor or team that finishes in second place, next after the winner.

**Running footmen.** Men servants in the early part of the 18th century whose duty it was to run beside the slow-moving coach horses and advise the innkeeper of his approaching guests, bear torches, pay turnpikes and so on. The pole that they carried was to help the cumbrous coach out of the numerous sloughs. William Douglas, 3rd Earl of March and 4th Duke of Queensberry (1724–1810), was said to be the last to employ them. The Running Footman used as a PUBLIC HOUSE SIGN derives from the old Tudor foot postmen.

**Running mate.** In American elections, a candidate for the subordinate of two linked positions, and especially the candidate for the Vice Presidency.

**Running on the spot.** The act of raising the feet alternately, as in running, but without moving forwards or backwards. The feat is familiar from military training. To perform the same action as if marching is to MARK TIME.

**Running repairs.** Repairs to a machine or vehicle that can be carried out in such a way that its running or operation can continue with little or no interruption.

**Run** or **rushed off one's feet, To be.** To be very busy; to be kept running around.

**Run of the mill.** The expected or usual type or sequence of events. If a steady flow of water issues from the millpond, the mill will run smoothly and normally.

**Run out, To.** In cricket to stump the wicket of a batsman as he is running so that he is out.

**Run out of steam, To.** To lose one's impetus or energy, like a steam engine low on water.

**Run rings round someone, To.** To defeat a person completely in some sport or competition; to outclass a person easily.

**Run riot, To.** To act without restraint or control; to act in a very disorderly way. The phrase was originally used of hounds that had lost the scent.

**Runs, The.** Diarrhoea. A descriptive word that also implies the sufferer's fleetness of foot to the lavatory. 'The trots' is a similar expression. *See also* MONTEZUMA'S REVENGE.

**Run someone down, To.** To denigrate or discredit someone to a third party.

**Run the gamut of, To.** To experience or perform the full range of. *See also* GAMUT.

**Run the gauntlet, To.** To be attacked on all sides, to be severely criticized. The word came into English at the time of the THIRTY YEARS' WAR (1618–48) as 'gantlope', meaning the passage between two files of soldiers. It is from Swedish *gatlopp*, literally 'passageway', from *gata*, 'way', and *lop*, 'course'. The reference is to a former punishment among soldiers and sailors. The company or crew, provided with rope ends, were drawn up in two rows facing each other, and the delinquent had to run between them, while every man dealt him as severe a blow as he could. The spelling 'gauntlet' is due to confusion with *gauntlet*, 'glove' (Old French *gantelet*, a diminutive of *gant*, 'glove').

**Run the show, To.** To take charge of an event; to be dominant in an activity.

**Run through, To.** 'To run through one's inheritance' is to squander it at a rapid rate; 'to run through one's part in a play' is to read or rehearse it; 'to run through the accounts' is to make a quick general survey of them; 'to run someone through' is to pass one's sword or rapier through their body.

**Run to earth, To.** To discover someone or something in a hiding place; to get to the bottom of a matter. A metaphor from fox hunting, when the quarry is run to its earth. *See also* GONE TO EARTH *under* EARTH.

**Run up against, To.** To encounter a difficulty.

**Run wild, To.** To grow or stray unchecked, as of an unkempt garden or an unruly child.

**Run with the hare and hunt with the hounds, To.** To play a double game; to try to keep in with both sides.

**Also ran, An.** *See under* ALSO.

**Bow Street Runners.** *See under* BOW.

**Bull run.** *See under* BULL.

**Cresta Run.** *See under* CRESTA.

**Cut and run.** *See under* CUT.

**Do a runner, To.** To leave hastily; to abscond.

**Dry run.** *See under* DRY.

**Fun run.** *See under* FUN.

**Give someone a run for their money, To.** To make them expend considerable effort; to lead them a pretty dance.

**Have a run for one's money, To.** To obtain satisfaction or pleasure from one's expenditure or efforts, even if the outcome is not entirely successful. A bet on a horse may give the backer some excitement whether the horse wins or not.

**Have the run of the house, To.** To have free access and liberty to make full use of what it offers.

**He that runs may read.** The Bible quotation in Habakkuk 2:2 is, 'Write the vision, and make it plain upon tables, that he may run that readeth it.'

> There is a book, who runs may read,
> Which heavenly truth imparts,
> And all the lore its scholars need,
> Pure eyes and Christian hearts.
> JOHN KEBLE: *The Christian Year*, 'Septuagesima' (1827)

**Hunters and runners of classic renown.** *See under* HUNT.

**Long run, A.** *See under* LONG.

**Make the running, To.** To set the pace or standard.

**Milk run, A.** *See under* MILK.

**My cup runs over.** *See under* CUP.

**On the run.** Moving from place to place and hiding from the authorities, said especially of criminals, escaped prisoners and the like.

**Out of the running.** *See under* OUT.

**Rat run.** *See under* RAT.

**Rum-runners.** *See under* RUM.

**Sands are running out, The.** *See under* SAND.

**Take a running jump at yourself.** Go away.

**Up and running.** *See under* UP.

**What a way to run a railway.** *See under* WHAT.

**Runcible hat** and **spoon.** In the preface to Edward Lear's *Nonsense Songs* (1871) there is mention of a runcible hat, and in 'The Owl and the Pussy-Cat', in the same collection, a runcible spoon. What runcible denotes is not apparent. Some who profess to know describe the spoon as a kind of fork having three broad prongs, one of which has a sharp cutting edge. However, the illustrations that Lear himself provided for his books do not support this definition. The word may actually be based on ROUNCIVAL.

> They dined on mince and slices of quince
> Which they ate with a runcible spoon.
> 'The Owl and the Pussycat' (1871)

**Rune.** A letter or character of the earliest alphabet in use among the Gothic tribes of northern Europe. Runic inscriptions most commonly occur in Scandinavia and parts of the British Isles. Runes were employed for purposes of secrecy, charms or DIVINATION, and the word is also applied to ancient lore or poetry expressed in runes. Rune is related to Old Norse *rūn*, 'secret'. The deeds of warriors were recorded on runic staves, and knowledge of rune writing was supposed to have been introduced by ODIN. *See also* FUTHORC; OGAM.

**Runic staff** or **wand.** *See* CLOG ALMANAC.

**Rupert. Rupert Bear.** The distinctive strip cartoon bear, with his check trousers, red jersey and scarf, was the creation of the illustrator Mary Tourtel, who introduced him in the pages of the *Daily Express* in 1920. The picture books with his adventures in rhyme began to appear in the mid-1920s, and the Rupert Annuals in 1936, the latter illustrated by Alfred Bestall. Rupert's world centres on his village of Nutwood, but he travels far and wide and has companions in the form of Bill the Badger, Algy Pug, Edward Trunk and others.

**Rupert of Debate, The.** Edward Stanley, 14th Earl of Derby (1799–1869). It was when he was Mr Stanley, and the opponent of Daniel O'Connell, that Lord Lytton so described him, in allusion to the brilliant Royalist cavalry leader, Prince Rupert.

**Prince Rupert's drops.** *See under* PRINCE.

**Rural dean.** An incumbent who assists in administering part of an archdeaconry. The office is an ancient one effectively revived from the mid-19th century.

**Ruritania.** An imaginary kingdom in pre-First

World War Europe where Anthony Hope placed the adventures of his hero in the novels *The Prisoner of Zenda* (1894) and *Rupert of Hentzau* (1898). The name is frequently applied to any small state where politics and intrigues of a melodramatic and romantic interest are the natural order of the day. The name is based on Latin *rus, ruris*, 'country', and the name of a Roman province such as Lusitania.

**Rush. Rush-bearing Sunday.** A Sunday, generally close to the festival of the saint to whom the church is dedicated, when at one time it was customary to renew the rushes with which the church floor was strewn. The custom is still observed at St Mary Redcliffe, Bristol, on WHITSUNDAY and at Ambleside, Grasmere, and elsewhere in Cumbria. At Ambleside a rush-bearing procession is held on the Saturday nearest St Anne's Day (26 July), the church being dedicated to St Anne.

**Friar Rush.** *See under* FRIAR.

**Not worth a rush.** *See under* WORTH.

**Russel.** A name given to a fox, from its russet colour.

> Sir Russel Fox then leapt to the attack,
> Grabbing his [Chanticleer's] gorge he flung him o'er his back
> And off he bore him to the woods, the brute,
> And for the moment there was no pursuit.
>
> CHAUCER: *Canterbury Tales*, 'The Nun's Priest's Tale' (*c*.1387) (modern translation by Nevill Coghill, 1951)

**Russell, Jack.** *See under* JACK.

**Russia. Black Russia.** *See under* BLACK.

**White Russian.** *See under* WHITE.

**Young Russia.** *See under* YOUNG.

**Rustam** or **Rustum.** The Persian HERCULES, the son of Zal, prince of Sedjistan, famous for his victory over the white dragon Asdeev. His combat for two days with Prince Isfendiar is a favourite subject with the Persian poets. Matthew Arnold's poem 'Sohrab and Rustum' (1853) gives an account of Rustam fighting with and killing his son Sohrab.

**Ruth.** In the Old Testament a woman who leaves her homeland when her husband dies to return to the home of her mother-in-law, Naomi. She there makes a sparse living by gleaning corn in the fields of Boaz, who notices her and marries her. Her story is told in the book that bears her name.

**Rutland.** England's smallest county, which although still a historic entity was removed from the political map when it was absorbed by Leicestershire in the local government county boundary changes of 1974, much to the annoyance of the local people. The name itself means 'Rota's land', referring to an Anglo-Saxon landowner. The county motto is *Multum in parvo*, 'Much in little'. The county was reinstated as a unitary authority in 1997.

**Rye. Rye House Plot.** A conspiracy in 1683 to murder Charles II and his brother James on their return to London from Newmarket as they passed near the Rye House, Hoddesdon, Hertfordshire, the home of Rumbold, a Cromwellian, where the plot was hatched. It was the work of WHIG extremists and former Cromwellians, but miscarried because the royal party left sooner than planned owing to a fire. Lord William Russell (1639–83) and Algernon Sidney (*c*.1622–83), the grand-nephew of Sir Philip Sidney, although not active participants, were executed for complicity.

**Romany Rye.** *See under* ROMANY.

**Rymenhild.** *See* HORN, KING.

# S

**S.** The nineteenth letter of the English alphabet (eighteenth of the ancient Roman), representing the Greek *sigma* from the Phoenician and Hebrew *shin*. As a medieval Roman numeral S stood for 7, also 70, and S̄ for 70,000.

**'S.** A euphemistic abbreviation of 'God's', formerly common in oaths and expletives, as ''Sdeath' (God's death), ''Sblood' (God's blood), ''Sdeins' (God's dignes, i.e. dignity), ''Sfoot' and so on.

> 'Sdeins, I know not what I should say to him, in the whole world! He values me at a crack'd three farthings, for aught I see.
>
> BEN JONSON: *Every Man in His Humour*, II, i (1598)

**$.** The typographical sign for the DOLLAR is thought to be a variation of the figure 8 with which pieces of eight were stamped, and it was in use in the United States before the adoption of the Federal currency in 1785. Another, perhaps fanciful, derivation is from the letters US.

**SA** (German *Sturmabteilung*, 'assault division'). Hitler's NAZI paramilitary organization, founded in 1921 and drawing its early members chiefly from the *Freikorps* ('Free Corps'), armed freebooter groups consisting mainly of former soldiers. It was kitted out in brown uniforms after the fashion of Mussolini's BLACKSHIRTS and accordingly became known as the Brownshirts. It was notorious for its methods of violent intimidation, both before and after its reorganization in 1925. Its leadership was purged in the NIGHT OF THE LONG KNIVES. *See also* SS.

**Sabaeans** or **Sabeans.** The ancient people of Yemen in southwestern Arabia, from Arabic *Saba'* or SHEBA (Job 6:19).

**Sabaism.** The worship of the stars, or the 'host of heaven' (from Hebrew *çābā*, 'host'). The term is also sometimes applied to the religion of the SABIANS.

**Sabaoth.** The biblical phrase Lord God of Sabaoth means 'Lord God of Hosts' not 'of the Sabbath', 'Sabaoth' being from Hebrew *ç'bāōth*, 'hosts', plural of *çābā*. The epithet has been frequently misunderstood, as in the last stanza of Edmund Spenser's *The Faerie Queene* (VII, viii (1596)):

> For, all that moueth, doth in *Change* delight:
> But thence-forth all shall rest eternally
> With Him that is God of Sabbaoth hight [called]:
> O that great Sabbaoth God, graunt me that
> Sabaoths sight.

**Sabbataeans.** The disciples of Sabbatai Sebi or Shabbetai Tzevi (1626–76) of Smyrna, a Jew of Spanish descent who proclaimed himself MESSIAH in 1648. He was imprisoned in Constantinople in 1666 and accepted the Muslim faith. His learning and personal appeal were extraordinary, and in his heyday he had thousands of followers.

**Sabbath** (Hebrew *shābath*, 'to rest'). Properly, the seventh day of the week, enjoined on the ancient Hebrews by the fourth Commandment (Exodus 20:8–11) as a day of rest and worship. The Christian SUNDAY, 'the Lord's Day', the first day of the week, is often inaccurately referred to as 'the Sabbath'. For Muslims, FRIDAY is the weekly day of rest.

**Sabbatarians.** Those who observe the day of rest with excessive strictness, a peculiar feature of English and Scottish Puritanism enforced during the period of the COMMONWEALTH when sport and recreation were forbidden. Some relaxation occurred after the RESTORATION, but the Lord's Day Observance Act of 1782 closed on a Sunday all places of entertainment where an admission fee was charged. A Sunday Entertainments Act, 1932, empowered local authorities to license the Sunday opening of cinemas and musical entertainments, and the opening of museums and the like was permitted. The Bill was opposed by the Lord's Day Observance Society. More recently, the same Society has opposed Sunday trading and the increased opening of shops and stores on Sunday.

**Sabbath day's journey, A.** The journey so mentioned from the Mount of Olives to Jerusalem (Acts 1:12) was not, with the Jews, to exceed the distance between the ark and the extreme end of the camp. This was 2000 cubits (about 1.2km). It arose from the injunction (Exodus 16:29) against journeying on the Sabbath with that (Joshua 3:4) providing for a distance of 2000 cubits between the ark and the people when they travelled in the wilderness. As their tents were this distance from the ark, it was held that they might properly travel this distance, since the injunction could not have been intended to prevent their attendance at worship.

**Witches' Sabbath.** *See under* WITCH.

**Sabbatical year.** One year in seven, when the land, according to Mosaic law, was to lie fallow (Exodus 23:10, Leviticus 25: 2–7, Deuteronomy 15: 1–11). The term is used in universities and the academic world generally for a specified period of freedom from duties, during which time a professor or lecturer is released to study or travel.

**Sabean.** *See* SABAEANS.

**Sabians.** A semi-Christian sect of Babylonia, akin to the MANDAEANS or Christians of St John, a GNOSTIC sect that arose in the 2nd and 3rd centuries and still survives south of Baghdad.

**Sabines, The.** An ancient people of central Italy, living in the Apennines, to the north and northeast of Rome, and subjugated by the Romans *c.*290 BC.

**Rape of the Sabine Women, The.** *See under* RAPE.

**Sable.** The heraldic term for black, shown in engraving by horizontal lines crossing perpendicular ones. The fur of the animal of this name is brown, but it is probable that in the 15th century, when the heraldic term was first used, the fur was dyed black, as seal fur has been in modern times. Sable fur was always much sought after and was very expensive.

**Sabotage.** Wilful and malicious destruction of machinery or plant by strikers, rebels, fifth columnists and the like. The term came into use after the great French railway strike in 1912. The word is traditionally said to to have referred to the action of the strikers, who threw sabots into the machinery to damage it. This explanation cannot be sustained, however, and the allusion is probably to the noise made by the wooden shoes in walking, evoking a clumsy or bungling action.

**Sabres.** *See* BAYONETS.

**Sabreur, Le Beau.** *See under* BEAU.

**Sabrina.** The Roman name of the River Severn, but according to Geoffrey of Monmouth (*Historia Regum Britanniae* (*c.*1136)) it is from Sabre, daughter of LOCRINUS and his concubine Estrildis, whom he married after divorcing Guendoloena. The ex-queen gathered an army and Locrinus was slain. Estrildis and Sabre were consigned to the waters of the Severn. NEREUS took pity on Sabre, or Sabrina, and made her the river-goddess.

> There is a gentle Nymph not far from hence,
> That with moist curb sways the smooth Severn
> stream,
> Sabrina is her name, a virgin pure.
>
> MILTON: *Comus* (1637)

**Sac and soc.** Sac is Old English *sacu*, 'strife', 'contention', 'litigation', and soc is Old English *soc*, 'inquiry', 'investigation', 'jurisdiction'. The expression was common both before and after the Norman Conquest in 1066 and was used in grants of land to denote the conveyance of rights in private jurisdiction to the grantee.

**Saccharissa.** The name bestowed by Edmund Waller (1606–87) on Lady Dorothy Sidney (1617–84), eldest daughter of the Earl of Leicester, who in 1639 married Lord Spencer of Wormleighton, afterwards Earl of Sunderland. John Aubrey says that Waller was passionately in love with the lady, but the poems themselves give the impression that the affair was merely a poetical pose. The name can be understood to mean 'sweetest'.

**Sacco benedetto** or **saco bendito** (Italian, Spanish, 'blessed cloak'). The yellow linen robe with two crosses on it, and painted over with flames and Devils, worn by those going to the stake after condemnation by the Spanish INQUISITION. Penitents who had been taken before the Inquisition had to wear this habit for a stated period. Those worn by Jews, sorcerers and renegades bore a St Andrew's cross in red on the back and front. *See also* AUTO-DA-FÉ.

**Sachem** (Narraganset *sachim*, 'chief') or **Sagamore** (Abnaki *sākimau* or *sāgimau*, literally 'he overcomes'). A chief among some of the Native American tribes. Sachem was also applied to certain high officials of the Tammany Society of New York. *See also* TAMMANY HALL.

**Sacheverell Affair, The.** On 5 November 1709, the anniversary of William III's landing at Torbay, Dr Henry Sacheverell (*c.*1674–1724) preached a sermon in St Paul's before the lord mayor of London reasserting the doctrine of NON-RESISTANCE and by implication attacking the principles of the GLORIOUS REVOLUTION and the DISSENTERS. The sermon, *The Perils of False Brethren*, was subsequently printed, and the WHIG ministry ill-advisedly impeached him (1710). The affair aroused great excitement. Queen ANNE attended Westminster Hall daily, and the London mob burned Dissenters' chapels. Sacheverell was declared guilty by 69 votes to 52 and sentenced to abstain from preaching for three years and to have his sermon burned by the common hangman. It was substantially a moral victory for Sacheverell and his TORY adherents.

**Sack.** (1) According to tradition, this was the last word uttered before the tongues were confounded at BABEL. In modern times it has come to be applied to certain loose garments and ladies' gowns hanging from the shoulders. It derives from Latin *saccus* ('bag').

(2) The old word for dry wines of the sherry type such as Madeira sack or Canary sack. It is

now found only in commercial names. It derives from French *vin sec*, 'dry wine'.

**Sack race, A.** A contest in which each runner is put up to the armpits in a sack to jump or run as well as the size of the sack permits.

**Get the sack or be sacked, To.** To be dismissed from employment. The phrase was current in 17th-century France (*On luy a donné son sac*), and the probable explanation of the term is that workmen carried their implements in a bag or sack, and when they were discharged they took up their bags of tools and departed to seek a job elsewhere. The SULTAN used to put in a sack and throw into the BOSPORUS any member of his harem he wished to dispose of, but this has no connection with the phrase.

**Hit the sack, To.** *See under* HIT.

**Sad sack.** *See under* SAD.

**Wear sackcloth and ashes, To.** *See under* WEAR.

**Sackerson.** The bear kept at PARIS-GARDEN in Shakespeare's time.

**Saco bendito.** *See* SACCO BENEDETTO.

**Sacrament** (Latin *sacramentum*). Originally 'a military oath' taken by the Roman soldiers not to desert their standard, turn their back on the enemy or abandon their general. Traces of this meaning survive in early Christian usage, but its present meaning comes from its employment in the Latin New Testament to mean 'sacred mystery'. Hence its application to baptism, confirmation, the EUCHARIST and so on. *See also* FIVE SACRAMENTS; SEVEN SACRAMENTS.

**Sacramentarians.** The name given by Martin Luther to those who maintained that no change took place in the eucharistic elements after consecration and that the bread and wine are the body and blood of Christ in a metaphorical sense only. The name was thus applied in the 16th century to those who did not accept the REAL PRESENCE.

**Five sacraments, The.** *See under* FIVE.

**Seven sacraments, The.** *See under* SEVEN.

**Two sacraments, The.** *See under* TWO.

**Sacra Via** (Latin, 'Holy Street'). The street in ancient Rome where ROMULUS and Tatius (the second king of Rome and the SABINE king) swore mutual alliance.

**Sacred** (Latin *sacrare*, 'to consecrate'). That which is consecrated or dedicated to religious use.

**Sacred Banner of France, The.** The ORIFLAMME.

**Sacred City, The.** *See* HOLY CITY.

**Sacred College, The.** The COLLEGE OF CARDINALS.

**Sacred cow, A.** Any institution, long-cherished practice or custom that is treated as immune from criticism, modification or abolition. The allusion is to the fact that the cow is held sacred by the Hindus.

**Sacred Heart, The.** In the ROMAN CATHOLIC CHURCH devotion to the Sacred Heart of Jesus, essentially directed at the Saviour himself. It originated from visions experienced in 1673–5 by a French nun, Marguerite Marie Alacoque (1647–90). This devotion in France was approved by Clement XIII in 1758 and extended to the whole church in 1856 by Pius IX. The festival is celebrated on the Friday in the week after CORPUS CHRISTI. There are various Congregations of the Sacred Heart.

The church of Sacré-Cœur in Paris is dedicated to the Sacred Heart, and its full name is Basilique du Vœu de la Nation au Sacré-Cœur ('Basilica of the National Vow to the Sacred Heart'). It was planned in 1873 with the aim of expiating the spiritual and moral collapse of France, which was felt to have led to the defeat of the French by the Prussians in 1870. Its siting on Montmartre ('martyrs' mount') was deliberate. It was completed only in 1919.

**Sacred Isle, The or Holy Island.** Ireland has been so called from its many saints, and Guernsey has been so called from its many monks. The island referred to by Thomas Moore in his *Irish Melodies* (1801–34) is Scattery, to which St Senanus retired, vowing that no woman should ever set foot there.

> 'Oh! haste and leave this sacred isle,
> Unholy bark, ere morning smile;
> For on thy deck, though dark it be,
> A female form I see;
> And I have sworn this sainted sod
> Shall ne'er by woman's foot be trod.'
> 'St Senanus and the Lady'

Enhallow (Norse *Eyinhalga*, 'holy isle') is a small island in the Orkney group where cells of the Irish anchorite fathers long existed. *See also* HOLY ISLAND.

**Sacred majesty.** *See* MAJESTY.

**Sacred mushroom.** A name given to various hallucinogenic mushrooms, especially species of *Psilocybe* and *Amanita*, which have been ritually eaten in different parts of the world. John Allegro (1923–88), author of books on the DEAD SEA SCROLLS, aimed to prove in *The Sacred Mushroom and the Cross* (1970) that an intrinsic interrelationship exists between the mushroom as cause and catalyst of heightened spiritual awareness and the essentially mystic mainspring of Christianity.

**Sacred war, The.** In Greek history, one of the wars waged by the Amphictyonic League in defence of the temple and ORACLE OF DELPHI.

> Against the Cirrhaeans (594–587 BC)
> For the restoration of Delphi to the Phocians, from whom it had been taken (448–447 BC)
> Against Philip of Macedon (346 BC)

*See also* AMPHICTYONIC COUNCIL.

**Sacred Way, The.** *See* SACRA VIA.

**Sacred weed, The.** VERVAIN or, humorously, tobacco, also called 'divine'. *See also* HERBA SACRA.

**Dean of the Sacred College.** *See under* DEAN.

**Sacring bell.** From the obsolete verb 'to sacre', 'to consecrate', used especially of sovereigns and bishops, this is the bell rung in churches to draw attention to the most solemn parts of the MASS. In medieval times it served to announce to those outside that the Mass was in progress, and for this purpose a handbell was often rung out of a side window. It is more usually called the Sanctus bell because it was rung at the saying of the Sanctus at the beginning of the CANONS OF THE MASS, and also at the Consecration and Elevation and other moments. It is still used in the ROMAN CATHOLIC CHURCH and certain other churches.

**Sacy's Bible.** *See under* BIBLE.

**Sad. Sad bread** (Latin *panis gravis*). Heavy bread; bread that has not risen properly. Shakespeare calls it 'distressful bread', meaning not the bread of distress, but the *panis gravis* or ill-made bread eaten by those who cannot get any better. In America, unleavened cakes are known as sad cakes.

**Sad sack.** A colloquial phrase for an incompetent person who is well-intentioned but cannot help making mistakes. The name was originally that of an American cartoon character, a lugubrious little GI, created by the artist George Baker in the Second World War for an army magazine.

**Saddle. Saddle of mutton, A.** The two loins with the connecting vertebrae.

**Saddle with responsibility, To.** To put the responsibility on someone; to make a person responsible for something.

**Boot and saddle.** *See under* BOOT.

**In the saddle, To be.** Literally, to be mounted. Figuratively, to be in office; to be in a position of authority.

**Sadducees.** A Jewish party opposed to the PHARISEES. They did not accept oral tradition, but only the written Law, denied the existence of angels and spirits and rejected the idea of future punishments in an afterlife, as well as the resurrection of the body. They were major opponents of Christ and the disciples and were involved in the events leading to the crucifixion. Substantially, they represented the interests and attitudes of the privileged and wealthy, and nothing more is heard of them after the destruction of Jerusalem (AD 70).

The name probably means descendants of Zadok (2 Samuel 8:17), high priest at the time of SOLOMON.

**Sadism.** The obtaining of sexual satisfaction through the infliction of pain or humiliation on another person or even an animal, also the morbid pleasure those in certain psychological states experience in being cruel or in watching certain acts of cruelty. The name derives from the Marquis de Sade (1740–1814), a French soldier and writer of plays and novels with sexual perversion as their theme, notably *Justine* (1791), *Philosophie dans le boudoir* (1793) and *Les Crimes de l'amour* (1800). *See also* MASOCHISM.

**Sadler's Wells.** There was once a holy well at this place belonging to St John's Priory, CLERKENWELL. It was blocked up at the REFORMATION but rediscovered by Thomas Sadler in 1683 when workmen were digging for gravel. The waters were pronounced to contain salts of iron, and the discovery was turned to immediate profit. However, when attendance at the well declined, MUSIC HALL entertainment was provided, and from the 1690s this became the chief attraction under James Miles. In 1765 a builder named Rosoman erected a proper theatre, which became famous for burlettas, musical interludes and PANTOMIMES. Edmund Kean, Charles Dibdin and Joseph GRIMALDI all appeared there. In 1844 Samuel Phelps took over and produced Shakespeare, but after his retirement the boom in West End theatres cast the Wells into the shade and it eventually became a cinema, which closed in 1916. A new theatre, built with the help of the Carnegie United Kingdom Trust, opened in 1931 under Lilian Baylis of the OLD VIC and it became one of the leading houses in London for the production of ballet and opera. In 1946 the ballet company transferred to the Royal Opera House, COVENT GARDEN, leaving the Sadler's Wells theatre vacant. (A new company formed there became the Birmingham Royal Ballet in 1990 when it transferred to that city.) A royal charter in 1956 transformed the Sadler's Wells Ballet into the Royal Ballet. Sadler's Wells features in Tobias Smollett's *Humphry Clinker* (1771).

**Safari** (Swahili, from Arabic *safarīya*, 'journey'). To be on safari is to be on a hunting expedition in Africa. The phrase is often used in the sense of 'on trek' in the wilds with a company of followers.

**Safari park.** As an imitation of an African game park, where lions and other large wild animals are kept in open spaces for public viewing, the safari park in Britain was the brainchild of the circus owner Jimmy Chipperfield (1912–90). The first such park opened at Longleat in 1966 and was soon copied elsewhere.

**Safari suit.** A lightweight suit, typically with short sleeves and four pleated pockets in the jacket, as originally worn by quasi-colonials or military men on safari.

**Safe. Safe and sound.** Secure and uninjured.

**Safe conduct.** A privilege of immunity from arrest or attack on a particular occasion. In wartime it is more concretely a pass issued to an enemy subject by a belligerent state. *See also* LETTER OF SAFE CONDUCT.

**Safe house.** A place of refuge or rendezvous for spies or criminals.

**Safe seat.** A seat in parliament that is usually won with a large majority. Rural constituencies were long seen as providing safe seats for Conservative candidates.

**Safe sex.** Sexual activity in which precautions are taken to avoid against the risk of spreading sexually transmitted diseases.

**Safety bicycle.** *See* PENNY FARTHING.

**Safety matches.** Matches that light only when struck on the specially prepared surface on the side of the box, since the match head only contains part of the ingredients of combustion. They derive from the discovery of red phosphorus by Anton von Schrötter in 1845. J.E. Lundström of Sweden is credited with their introduction in 1855. *See also* CONGREVES; LOCO-FOCO; LUCIFER MATCH; PROMETHEAN.

**As safe as houses.** *See under* AS.

**Better safe than sorry.** *See under* BETTER.

**In safe keeping.** Preserved in a secure place.

**Letter of safe conduct.** *See under* LETTER.

**On the safe side.** With a margin of caution, as: 'I'll take a mac to be on the safe side'.

**Saga** (Old Norse, 'narrative', related to English 'say'). In Icelandic the word is applied to any kind of narrative, but in English it particularly denotes heroic biographies written in Iceland and Norway mainly during the 12th, 13th and 14th centuries. From this comes its English application to a story of heroic adventure.

The sagas are a compound of history and myth in varying proportions, the *King's Sagas* being the oldest, the *First Saga of King Olaf* dating from 1180. Other notable examples are the *Saga of Hallfred*, the *Saga of Björn*, the *Grettis Saga*, the *Saga of Burnt Njáll*, the *Egils Saga*, the *Islendinga Saga*, the *Ynglinga Saga*, the *Volsunga Saga*, *Tristram's Saga* and the *Karlamagnus Saga*. Snorri Sturluson's *Heimskringla* ('Orb of the World') is a collection of biographies of Norwegian kings from the 9th to the 12th century. *See also* EDDA; VOLSUNGS.

**Sagamore.** *See* SACHEM.

**Sage. Sage of Chelsea, The.** Thomas Carlyle (1795–1881), essayist and historian, was so called. He and his wife Jane moved from Dumfriesshire to No. 5 (now 24) Cheyne Row, Chelsea, London, in 1834, where they lived for the remainder of their lives.

**Bactrian Sage.** *See under* BACTRIAN.

**Crotona's Sage.** *See under* CROTONA.

**Ligurian Sage, The.** *See under* LIGURIA.

**Samian Sage, The.** *See under* SAMIAN.

**Seven Sages, The.** *See* WISE MEN OF GREECE.

**Sagittarius** (Latin, 'archer'). One of the old constellations, the ninth sign of the ZODIAC, which the sun enters about 22 November. *See also* CHIRON.

**Sagittary.** The name given in medieval romances to the CENTAUR, whose eyes sparkled like fire and struck dead like lightning, fabled to have been introduced into the armies of TROY.

**Sahib** (Urdu, 'friend'). A form of address used by Hindus to Europeans in India corresponding to English 'Sir' in 'Thank you, sir.' Also a term for an Englishman or European, a woman being Memsahib, i.e. 'Ma'am Sahib'. The word is also used colloquially to describe a cultured, refined man. *See also* PUKKA SAHIB.

**Sail. Sail against the wind, To.** To swim against the tide; to oppose popular or current trends, opinions and the like.

**Sail before the wind, To.** To prosper; to go on swimmingly; to meet with great success, as a ship sails smoothly and rapidly with a following wind.

**Sail close to the wind, To.** To keep the vessel's head as near as possible to the quarter from which the wind is blowing yet keeping the sails filled. Figuratively, to go to the verge of what decency or propriety allows; to act so as just to escape the letter or infringement of the law; to take a risk.

**Sail into, To.** To 'sail into' someone is to attack or reprimand them forcefully, and to 'sail into' a task or the like is to set about it vigorously, as attackers 'sail into' an enemy to commence a naval engagement.

**Sail under false colours, To.** To pretend to be what one is not with the object of personal advantage. The allusion is to pirate ships, which approached the object of their prey with false colours at the mast.

**Plain sailing.** *See under* PLAIN.

**Set sail, To.** *See under* SET.

**Strike sail, To.** *See under* STRIKE.

**Take the wind out of someone's sails, To.** *See under* WIND.

**Trim one's sails, To.** *See under* TRIM.

**Sailor. Sailor King, The.** William IV of England (b.1765, r.1830–7), also called Silly Billy, who entered the navy as a midshipman in 1779 and was made Lord High Admiral in 1827.

**Sinbad the Sailor.** *See under* SINBAD.

**Saint.** Individual saints are entered under their respective names.

From early Christian times the title of saint was applied to APOSTLES, EVANGELISTS, MARTYRS and Confessors of remarkable virtue, especially martyrs. In due course the need arose for bishops to intervene against local recognition of the undeserving, and eventually Pope Alexander III (r.1159–81) asserted the exclusive right of the papacy to add to the roll of saints. Today canonization is dependent on a lengthy legal process during which the case for the canonization of a particular person is thoroughly explored and contested. JOAN OF ARC was canonized in 1920, Sir Thomas More (1478–1535) and John Fisher (1459–1535), bishop of Rochester, in 1935.

In the Roman Catholic Church canonization is regarded as conferring a sevenfold honour: (1) the name is inscribed in the catalogue of saints; (2) the new saint is invoked in the prayers of the Church; (3) churches may be dedicated to the saint; (4) the Mass and Office are publicly offered to God in the saint's honour; (5) festival days are celebrated in the saint's honour; (6) pictorial representations are made of the saint, who is shown surrounded by an AUREOLE or glory; (7) the saint's relics are enclosed in a precious vessel and publicly honoured.

*See also* SYMBOLS OF SAINTS *below*.

**Saint, The.** The 'ROBIN HOOD of modern crime' created by Leslie Charteris. 'The Saint' is his crime name, and his real name is Simon Templar. He lives beyond the law, but he is otherwise a perfect English gentleman, a rescuer of damsels in distress and a jolly joker. He first appeared in the novel *Meet the Tiger* (1928), and went on to star in a long series of stories and novels in both magazines and book form, as well as in film and television versions.

**Battle of the Saints, The.** *See under* BATTLE.

**City of Saints, The.** *See under* CITY.

**Ice** or **frost saints.** *See under* ICE.

**Island of Saints, The.** *See under* ISLAND.

**Kings and queens honoured as saints.** Among them are, with regnal dates:

EDWARD THE CONFESSOR (1042–66)
Edward the Martyr (975–978)
Eric VIII of Sweden (1150–60)
Ethelred I, king of Wessex (866–871)
Ferdinand III of Castile and Leon (1217–52)
Louis IX of France (1226–70)
Margaret, queen of Scotland (d.1093), wife of Malcolm III
Olaf II of Norway (1015–30)
Stephen I of Hungary (997–1038)

**Latter-day Saints.** *See* MORMONS.

**Patron saints.**

(1) A selected list of trades and professions with their patron saints:

Accountants, bankers and book-keepers: St Matthew
Actors: St Genesius
Advertising: St Bernadine of Sienna
Airmen and air travellers: Our Lady of Loreto, St Thérèse of Lisieux, St Joseph Cupertino
Architects: St Thomas, St Barbara
Artists: St Luke
Astronauts: St Joseph Cupertino
Astronomers: St Dominic
Athletes and archers: St Sebastian
Authors and journalists: St Francis de Sales
Bakers: St Elizabeth of Hungary, St Nicholas
Bankers: St Matthew
Barbers: Sts Cosmas and Damian, St Louis
Bee-keepers: St Ambrose, St Bernard, St Modomnoc
Blacksmiths: St Dunstan
Bookkeepers: St Matthew
Booksellers: St John of God
Boys: St Nicholas, St Aloysius
Brewers: St Augustine of Hippo, St Luke, St Nicholas of Myra
Bricklayers: St Stephen
Broadcasters: St Gabriel
Builders: St Vincent Ferrer
Cab drivers: St Fiacre
Carpenters: St Joseph
Children: St Nicholas, St Lambert
Cobblers: Sts Crispin and Crispinian
Comedians: St Vitus
Conservationists: St Francis of Assisi
Cooks: St Lawrence, St Martha
Dancers: St Vitus
Dentists: St Apollonia
Dieticians (medical): St Martha
Doctors: St Luke, Sts Cosmas and Damian
Domestic servants: St Zita
Editors: St John Bosco
Engineers: St Ferdinand III
Farmers: St George, St Isidore
Fathers: St Joseph
Firefighters: St Florian
Florists: St Dorothea, St Thérèse of Lisieux
Funeral directors: St Joseph of Arimathea, St Dismas
Gardeners: St Dorothea, St Adelard, St Tryphon, St Fiacre, St Phocas
Girls: St Agnes, St Catherine, St Nicholas, St Ursula
Goldsmiths and metalworkers: St Dunstan, St Anastasius
Gravediggers: St Anthony
Grocers: St Michael
Gunners: St Barbara
Hairdressers (ladies'): St Mary Magdalen
Hairdressers (men's): St Martin de Porres, Sts Cosmas and Damian
Hoteliers and innkeepers: St Amand, St Julian, St Martha
Housewives: St Anne, St Martha, St Zita
Huntsmen: St Hubert
Infantrymen: St Maurice
Jewellers: St Eloi
Lawyers: St Ivo, St Genesius, St Thomas More
Librarians: St Jerome
Lighthouse keepers: St Venerius
Lovers: St Valentine
Merchants: St Nicholas, St Homobonus
Miners: St Barbara
Mothers: Blessed Virgin Mary, St Giles, St Monica
Motorcyclists: Our Lady of Grace
Motorists: St Frances of Rome, St Christopher
Musicians and singers: St Gregory the Great, St Cecilia, St Dunstan
Nurses: St Camillus of Lellis, St John of God, St Agatha, St Alexius, St Raphael
Painters: St Luke
Paratroopers: St Michael

Pawnbrokers: St Nicholas
Philosophers: St Justin
Pin-makers: St Sebastian
Poets: St David, St Cecilia, St Columba, St John of the Cross
Policemen: St Michael
Postal workers: St Gabriel
Printers: St John of God, St Augustine of Hippo
Prisoners: St Dismas, St Leonard, St Roch
Publishers: St John the Apostle
Sailors: St Cuthbert, St Brendan, St Eulalia, St Christopher, St Peter Gonzales, St Erasmus
Scholars: St Bede, St Jerome, St Bridget
Schoolboys: St Nicholas, St John Bosco
Schoolgirls: St Catherine, St Ursula
Scientists: St Albert
Scouts: St George
Sculptors: St Claude
Secretaries: St Genesius, St Cassian
Shepherds: St Cuthbert, St Bernadette
Singers: St Cecilia, St Gregory
Soldiers: St Adrian, St George, St Ignatius, St Sebastian, St Martin, St Joan of Arc
Speleologists: St Benedict
Students: St Thomas Aquinas, St Catherine
Surgeons: Sts Cosmas and Damian, St Luke
Tailors: St Homobonus
Tax collectors: St Matthew
Teachers: St Gregory the Great, St Catherine, St John Baptist de la Salle
Television: St Clare
Travellers: St Anthony of Padua, St Nicholas, St Christopher, St Raphael
Virgins: Blessed Virgin Mary
Weavers: St Maurice, St Bernardino of Sienna
Widows: St Monica, St Paula
Wine-growers: St Vincent
Workers: St Joseph
Writers: St John the Evangelist, St Francis de Sales
Yachtsmen: St Adjutor

(2) Some European and Commonwealth countries with their patron saints:

Australia: Our Lady Help of Christians
Belgium: St Joseph
Canada: St Joseph, St Anne
Czech Republic: St Wenceslas, St John of Nepomuk, St Procopius
Denmark: St Asgar, St Canute
England: St George
France: Our Lady of the Assumption, St Joan of Arc, St Denys, St Louis, St Thérèse (there is no official patron saint of France, those listed are recognized as patron saints by the church)
Germany: St Boniface, St Michael
Greece: St Nicholas, St Andrew
Holland: St Willibrord
Hungary: Our Lady, St Stephen
India: Our Lady of the Assumption
Ireland: St Patrick
Italy: St Francis of Assisi, St Catherine of Sienna
New Zealand: Our Lady Help of Christians
Norway: St Olaf
Poland: Our Lady of Czestochowa, St Casimir, St Stanislaus
Portugal: Immaculate Conception, St Francis Borgia, St Anthony of Padua, St George, St Vincent
Russia: St Andrew, St Nicholas, St Thérèse of Lisieux
Scotland: St Andrew, St Columba
South Africa: Our Lady of the Assumption
Spain: St James, St Teresa
Sweden: St Bridget, St Eric
Wales: St David
West Indies: St Gertrude

**Popes numbered among the saints.** From the time of St PETER to the end of the 4th century all the popes (with a few minor and doubtful exceptions) are popularly entitled 'Saint'. Since then the following are the chief of those given the honour, with papal dates:

Celestine V (1294)
Deusdedit I (615–618)
Gregory the Great (590–604)
Gregory VII (Hildebrand) (1073–85)
Innocent I (401–417)
John I (523–526)
Leo the Great (440–461)
Leo II (682–683)
Leo III (795–816)
Leo IX (1049–54)
Martin I (649–653)
Nicholas the Great (858–867)
Paschal I (817–824)
Paul I (757–767)
Pius V (1566–72)
Pius X (1903–14)
Sergius I (687–701)
Zacharias (741–752)

**Sunday saint.** *See under* SUNDAY.

**Symbols of saints.** The symbol common to all saints is the NIMBUS, which encircles the head. Martyrs alone have the common symbols of the crown of eternal life won by their heroism and the palm of triumph. With these is generally associated some symbol peculiar to the individual saint, often the instrument of his or her martyrdom, such as the GRIDIRON of St LAWRENCE or the windlass on which the bowels were drawn from St Erasmus' body. Angels, singly or in a host, have constantly appeared to aid and protect the saints and are depicted as their companions in sacred iconography.

Saints that are not martyrs will be depicted with an object symbolizing their particular virtue (St AMBROSE has the beehive emblematic of eloquence) or relating to some incident in their lives (as St DUNSTAN pinching the Devil's nose). All saints are depicted in their proper dress, as soldiers in armour, bishops or priests in appropriate vestments, kings robed and crowned, religious in the habits of their order.

Below is a selection of some of the many symbols of saints with some of the saints to which they are applied. *See also* APOSTLES, MARY and entries for individual saints.

Almsbox around his neck: St John of God
Anchor: St Clement, St Felix, St Nicholas
Angel or angels: St Bernard (angel holding a crosier), St Bertold (angel with fish on a plate), St Boniface (angel bearing a fish), St Cecilia (angel playing an organ), St Congal (angel bearing a

fish), St Dorothea (angel holding a basket of flowers), St Francis of Assisi (angel playing violin), St Hugh of Lincoln (angel defending from lightning), St Isidore of Madrid (angel holding plough), St Leontius (angel holding a bottle), St Pachomius (angel bringing monastic rule), St Paphnutius (angel bringing monastic rule)

Anvil: St Adrian, St Eloi

Apple: St Malachy, St Nicholas (three golden apples)

Arrow or arrows (as instruments of martyrdom): St Anastasius, St Canute, St Christina, St Edmund, St Faustus, St Sebastian, St Ursula

Arrow(s): St Augustine (two piercing the heart), St Mackesoge (arrow and bent bow), St Otto (holding bunch of arrows)

Ass: St Anthony of Padua (ass kneeling to Blessed Sacrament), St Gerlach, St Germanus, St Philibert

Axe (as instrument of martyrdom): St Anastasius, St Josaphat, St Malchus, St Martian, St Matthew, St Matthias, St Proculus, St Rufus

Barge: St Bertulphus

Barn: St Ansovinus, St Bridget of Kildare

Barrel: St Antonia, St Bercher, St Willibrord (cross in barrel)

Basket: St Ann (basket of fruit), St Dorothea (basket of flowers or of fruit), St Elizabeth of Hungary (basket of roses), St Frances, St Joanna, St John Damascene, St Philip (basket of bread), St Romanus (basket of bread), St Sitha (basket of fruit)

Bear: St Columba, St Corbinian (bear laden with baggage), St Edmund, St Florentius (bear keeping sheep), St Gallus, St Humbert, St James (bear ploughing), St Maximinus (bear is sometimes laden with baggage)

Beard (obtained by the prayers of): St Galla, St Paula Barbata, St Wilgefortis (*see also* St UNCUMBER)

Bed of iron: St Faith

Beehive: St Ambrose, St Bernard, St John Chrysostom

Bell: St Anthony of Egypt, St Gildas, St Kenan, St Paul de Leon (bell in fish's mouth), St Winwaloc (bell and fishes)

Bellows (held by Devil): St Genevieve

Boar: St Emilion

Boat: St Bertin, St Jude, St Mary Magdalene

Boathook: St Jude

Bodkin: St Leger, St Simon of Trent

Book (a common attribute of apostles, abbots, abbesses, bishops etc, but specifically with the following): St Anthony of Padua (the child Jesus standing on it), St Antoninus, St Hubert (with hunting horn or stag with crucifix between horns), St Sitha (book in bag), St Urban (with wine vessel on it)

Broom: St Gisella, St Martin of Siguenza, St Petronilla

Bull: St Adolphus, St Blandina (tossed or gored by bull), St Marciana (tossed or gored by bull), St Regnier, St Saturninus (tossed or gored by bull), St Sylvester

Calves: St Walstan (two at feet)

Camel: St Aphrodicius, St Hormisdas, St Julian of Cilicia (bound to camel)

Candle: St Beatrix

Cauldron (as an instrument of martyrdom by boiling in lead, oil, pitch, water and so on): St Boniface, St Cecilia, St Emilian, St Erasmus, St Felicity, St John the Evangelist, St Lucy, St Vitus

Chafing dish: St Agatha

Church: a common symbol of abbots, abbesses, bishops and so on as builders of churches and monasteries

City: the attribute of a saint as protector of a particular city

Club or clubs (as instrument of martyrdom): St Boniface, St Ewald the White, St Eusebius, St Fabian, St Lambert, St Magnus, St Nicomedes, St Pantaleon, St Valentine, St Vitalis

Colt: St Medard

Cow: St Berlinda, St Bridget, St Modwena, St Perpetua

Crocodile: St Helenus, St Theodore

Crow: St Vincent

Cup and serpent (symbolizing poison detected by): St Benedict, St James of Marchia, St John a Facundo, St John the Evangelist

Dagger (as instrument of martyrdom): St Agnes, St Canute, St Edward, St Irene, St Kilian, St Olave, St Solange

Deer: St Henry

Devil or Devils: in Christian art the Devil is shown both tormenting the saints (e.g. throwing St Euphrasia down a well, disturbing the prayers of St Cuthbert or St Madalberte) and being worsted by their virtue (holding a candle for St Dominic or seized by the nose in St Dunstan's pincers); the incidents are too various for separate mention

Distaff: St Genevieve, St Rosalie

Doe: St Fructuosus, St Mammas, St Maximus of Turin

Dog: St Benignus, St Bernard, St Dominic (dog with torch), St Roch (dog with a loaf)

Dolphin: St Adrian (dolphin bearing corpse), St Calistratus (dolphin supporting), St Martianus

Dove (on or over): St Ambrose, St Basil, St Bridget of Sweden, St Catherine, St Catherine of Sienna, St Cunibert, St David, St Dunstan, St Gregory the Great, St Hilary of Arles, St John Columbini, St Lo, St Louis, St Medard, St Oswald, St Peter Celestin, St Peter of Alcantara, St Sampson, St Thomas Aquinas

Eagle: St Augustine, St Gregory the Great, St John the Evangelist, St Prisca

Ear or ears of corn: St Bridget, St Fara, St Walburge

Falcon or hawk: St Bavo, St Edward, St Julian Hospitator, St Otto (hawk on cottage)

Feather: St Barbara

Firebrand: St Anthony of Egypt

Fish or fishes: St Andrew, St Eanswide, St Gregory of Tours, St John of Burlington, St Raphael, St Simon; *see also* Angel, Bell *above and* Key *below*

Fish hooks: St Zeno

Flail: St Varus

Flower or flowers: St Dorothea, St Hugh of Lincoln, St Louis of Toulouse, St Zita (flowers in apron)

Fountain (obtained by prayer): St Alton, St Antoninus of Toulouse, St Apollinaris, St Augustine of Canterbury, St Clement, St Egwin, St Guntilda, St Humbert, St Isidore of Madrid, St Julian of Mans, St Leonard, St Nicholas of Tolentino, St Omer, St Philip Beniti, St Riquier, St Servatius, St Trond, St Venantius, St Wolfgang

Fountain (springing from their blood): St Boniface, St Eric
Frog or frogs: St Huvas, St Rieul, St Sinorina, St Ulphia
Goose: St Martin
Gosling: St Pharaildis
Gridiron (as instrument of martyrdom): St Cyprian, St Donatilla, St Erasmus, St Faith, St Lawrence, St Vincent
Hammer: St Adrian, St Bernward (hammer and chalice), St Eloi (hammer and chalice), St Reinoldus
Hare: St Albert of Sienna
Harp: St Cecilia, St Dunstan
Hatchet: St Adjutus, St Matthew, St Matthias
Heart: St Augustine, St Catherine of Sienna, St Francis de Sales, St Jane Frances, St Ignatius (heart with sacred monogram), St Teresa (heart with sacred monogram)
Hen: St Pharaildis
Hind: St Bassian (hind with two fawns), St Catherine of Sweden, St Genevieve of Brabant, St Lupus of Sens
Hoe: St Isidore of Madrid
Hook (as instrument of martyrdom): St Agatha, St Eulalia, St Felician, St Vincent
Hops: St Arnold of Soissons
Horse: St Barochus, St Irene, St Severus of Avranches
Hourglass: St Hilarion, St Theodosius
Ink-bottle: St Jerome
Jug or pitcher: St Agatha, St Bede, St Benedict, St Elizabeth of Portugal, St Vincent
Key: St Egwin (key in fish's mouth), St Ferdinand, St Germanus of Paris, St Hubert, St Peter, St Petronilla (key and book), St Raymond of Peñafort, St Sitha (key and rosary)
Keys (two): St Hippolytus, St Maurilius, St Riquier
Keys (bunch of): St Genevieve, St James the Great, St Martha, Blessed Virgin Mary, St Nothburge
Knife: St Agatha, St Bartholomew, St Christina, St Ebba, St Peter Martyr
Ladder: St Emmeran, St John Climacus
Ladle: St Martha
Lamp: St Francis, St Hiltrudis (lamp and book), St Lucy
Lance or spear (as instrument of martyrdom): St Barbara, St Canute, St Emmeran, St Gerhard, St Germanus, St Hippolytus, St John of Goto, St Lambert, St Longinus, St Matthias, St Oswin, St Thomas
Lantern: St Gudule, St Hugh, St Mary of Cabeza
Leopard and ox or lions: St Marciana
Lily: St Anthony of Padua, St Cajetan, St Casimir, St Catherine of Sweden, St Clare, St Dominic, St Joseph, St Kenelm, St Philip Neri, St Sebastian, St Vincent Ferrer
Lion or lions: St Adrian, St Dorothea, St Euphemia, St Germanus, St Ignatius, St Jerome, St Mark, St Prisca
Loom: St Anastasia, St Gudule
Mason's tools: St Marinus
Nail or nails (as instrument of martyrdom, held or piercing the body): St Alexander, St Denys, St Fausta, St Gemellus, St Julian of Emesa, St Pantaleon, St Quintin, St Severus of Rome, St William of Norwich
Oar: St Jude
Organ: St Cecilia
Ox or oxen: St Blandina, St Frideswide, St Fursey, St Julitta, St Leonard, St Lucy, St Luke, St Medard, St Otto
Padlock on lips: St John of Nepomuk
Pickaxe: St Leger
Pig: St Anthony of Egypt
Pilgrim's staff: St Dominic, St Louis
Pincers: St Agatha, St Apollonia, St Lucy
Plough: St Exuperius, St Richard
Purse: St Brieuc (three purses), St Cyril of Jerusalem, St Nicholas (three purses)
Rats: St Gertrude of Nivelles
Raven: St Benedict, St Erasmus (raven bringing food), St Ida (raven with ring in beak), St Oswald (raven with ring in beak), St Paul the Hermit (raven bringing food)
Razor: St Pamphilius
Ring: St Barbara, St Damascus, St Edward
Saw: St James the Less, St Simon
Scales: St Manous, St Michael (scales weighing souls)
Scourge: St Ambrose, St Boniface, St Dorotheus, St Gervase, St Gutlac, St Peter Damian
Scythe: St Guntilda, St Nothburge, St Sidwell (scythe and well), St Walstan
Serpent: St Cecilia, St Euphemia, the Virgin Mary, St Patrick
Shears: St Agatha, Sts Cosmas and Damian (shears and bottle), St Fortunatus, St Marca
Shovel (baker's): St Aubert, St Honorius
Sieve: St Benedict, St Hippolytus
Spade: St Fiacre
Sparrow: St Dominic
Spit (roasting): St Gengulph, St Quentin
Stag or stags: St Aidan, St Eustace, St Felix of Valois, St Hubert, St Julian Hospitator (Hospitaller), St Kenan (ploughing with stag), St Kentigern (ploughing with stag), St Osyth, St Rieul
Star (on or over): St Anastasia, St Bernadin, St Bruno, St Dominic, St Humbert, St Nicholas of Tolentino, St Peter of Alcantara, St Thomas Aquinas
Swans (two): St Cuthbert, St Hugh of Grenoble, St Kentigern
Sword (as instrument of martyrdom, piercing head or body): St Boniface, St Euphemia, St Lucy, St Thomas of Canterbury
Sword (held): St Adrian (sword and hammer), St Agnes, St Aquila, St Arcadius (sword and club), St Beztert (sword and stone or stones), St Catherine (sword and wheel or book), St Ewald the Black (sword and chalice), St Irene, St James the Great, St Kilian (sword and crosier or dagger), St Pancras (sword and stone or stones), St Paul, St Prisca, St Pantaleon (sword and vase)
Taper: St Gudule
Thistle: St Caroline, St Narcissus
Tongs: St Christina, St Felician, St Martina
Torch: St Aidan, St Barbara, St Dorothea, St Eutropia, St Irenaeus, St Medard
Tower: St Barbara, St Praxedes
Trowel: St William of Montevergine, St Winibald
Trumpet: St Vincent Ferrer
Vine: St Elpidius, St Urban, St Urban of Langres
Weaver's loom: St Severus of Ravenna
Wheel: St Catherine, St Euphemia, St Quentin (broken wheel)
Wolf: St Blaise (wolf stealing pig), St Simpertus (wolf bringing child), St Vedast (wolf bringing goose), St William of Montevergine

Wolfdog: St Donatus
Woolcomb: St Blaise

**Weeping Saint, The.** *See under* WEEP.

**Sainte ampoule, La** (French, 'the holy phial'). The sacred vessel containing oil used in anointing the kings of France, said to have been brought from heaven by a dove for the coronation service of St LOUIS. It was preserved at Rheims until the French Revolution, when it was destroyed.

**Saint-Simonism.** The social and political theories derived from the teachings of Claude Henri, Comte de Saint-Simon (1760–1825), the French utopian socialist. He advocated a social order based on large-scale industrial production controlled by benevolent industrial leaders. The aim of his society was to improve the lot of the poorest. His disciples advocated that the state should become the sole proprietor and supported a form of socialism in which social groups were to manage the state properties. Everyone was to be placed and rewarded in the social hierarchy according to their capacities.

**Sake.** A form of the obsolete word sac. *See also* SAC AND SOC.

In the common phrases 'for God's sake', 'for goodness' sake', 'for heaven's sake' etc, it means 'out of consideration for' God, goodness, heaven and so on.

**Sakes! or sakes alive!** An expression of surprise, admiration or the like, more common in the USA than in England.

**For old sake's sake.** *See under* FOR.

**For one's name's sake.** *See under* FOR.

**For Pete's sake.** *See under* FOR.

**Saker.** A piece of light artillery, used especially on board ship, in the 16th and 17th centuries. The word is borrowed from the saker hawk (falcon).

> The cannon, blunderbuss, and saker,
> He was the inventor of and maker.
> SAMUEL BUTLER: *Hudibras*, I, ii (1662)

**Saki.** The pseudonym of Hector Hugh Munro (1870–1916), the author of many short stories, such as the collections *Reginald* (1904), *The Chronicles of Clovis* (1911), *Beasts and Super-Beasts* (1914) and *The Toys of Peace* (1919), and three novels, of which the best is *The Unbearable Bassington* (1912). He took his pen name either from a line in FitzGerald's *The Rubáiyát of Omar Khayyám* (1859) ('And when like her, O Saki, you shall pass') or as a contraction of SAKYA MUNI, one of the names of the BUDDHA. He was killed in the First World War in France, shot in the head while resting in a crater. His style is often wickedly but wittily satirical. His stories frequently involve animals who take their revenge on humans and children who display their superiority of spirit over feckless adults.

**Sakuntala** or **Shakuntala** (Sanskrit *sakunta*, 'bird'). The heroine of Kalidasa's great Sanskrit drama *Abhijnanasakuntala* ('Recognition of Sakuntala'). She was the daughter of Viswamita, a sage, and Menaka, a water nymph, and was brought up by a hermit. One day King Dushyanta came to the hermitage during a hunt, and persuaded her to marry him, and later, giving her a ring, returned to his throne. A son was born and Sakuntala set out with him to find his father. On the way, while bathing, she lost the ring, and the king did not recognize her because of enchantment. Subsequently the ring was found by a fisherman in a fish he had caught. The king recognized his wife, she was publicly proclaimed his queen, and Bharata, his son and heir, became the founder of the glorious race of the Bharatus. Sir William Jones (1746–94) translated the work into English. *See also* KENTIGERN.

**Sakya Muni** (Sanskrit, 'Sage of the Sakyas'). One of the names of Gautama Siddartha, the BUDDHA.

**Salad days.** Days of youthful inexperience, when people are very green. The expression has come down from Shakespeare.

> My salad days,
> When I was green in judgement, cold in blood,
> To say as I said then!
> *Antony and Cleopatra*, I, v (1606)

**Saladin** (Arabic *Salah ad-Din*, 'Honour of the Faith'). Saladin (1138–93) was SULTAN of Egypt and Syria and founder of the Ayubite dynasty, and his capture of JERUSALEM in 1187 led to the Third CRUSADE. He appears in Walter Scott's *The Talisman* (1825) as a chivalrous warrior.

**Saladin tithe.** The tax levied by Henry II in 1188 for the recovery of JERUSALEM after its capture by SALADIN.

**Black Saladin.** *See under* BLACK.

**Salamander** (Greek *salamandra*, a kind of lizard). The name is now given to tailed amphibians of the Salamandridae family of the order Caudata, but formerly to a mythical lizard-like monster that was supposed to be able to live in fire, which, however, it quenched by the chill of its body. Pliny refers to this belief (*Naturalis Historia* x, 86; xxix, 23 (1st century BC)). It was adopted by PARACELSUS as the name of the elemental being inhabiting fire (GNOMES being those of the earth, SYLPHS those of the air, and UNDINES those of the water), and was hence taken over by the ROSICRUCIAN system, from which source Alexander Pope introduced salamanders into *The Rape of the Lock* (1712).

Francis I of France (r.1515–47) adopted as his badge a lizard in the midst of flames, with the legend *Nutrisco et extinguo* ('I nourish and extinguish'). The Italian motto from which it derived was *Nutrisco il buono e spengo il reo* ('I nourish the good and extinguish the bad'). Fire purifies good metal, but consumes rubbish.

Shakespeare's Falstaff calls Bardolph's nose 'a burning lamp', 'a salamander', and the drink that made such 'a fiery meteor' he calls 'fire'.

I have maintained that salamander of yours with fire any time this two-and-thirty years.
*Henry IV, Pt I*, III, iii (1597)

**Salary.** Originally 'salt money' (Latin *salarium*, from *sal*, 'salt'). The ancient Romans gave sums of money to their soldiers and civil servants to buy rations of salt, and the word subsequently passed to the pay itself.

**Salariat, The.** Salaried employees collectively, such as civil servants.

**Sale. Bring-and-by sale.** *See under* BRING.

**Point of sale.** *See under* POINT.

**Salem.** The city in Massachusetts is notorious for the WITCHCRAFT trials of 1692 that earned it the nickname of 'Witch City'. More memorably, it is the birthplace of Nathaniel Hawthorne (1804–64) and the setting for many of his stories. The 17th-century house that gave the title and subject of *The House of the Seven Gables* (1851) is preserved here. *See also* WITCHES OF SALEM.

**Salic.** Pertaining to the Salian FRANKS, a tribe of Franks who in the 4th century established themselves on the banks of the Sala (now known as the Yssel), and from whom the kings of MEROVINGIAN DYNASTY of France were descended.

Which Salique, as I said, 'twixt Elbe and Sala,
Is at this day in Germany called Meisen.
SHAKESPEARE: *Henry V*, I, ii (1598)

**Salic law, The.** The compilation of laws of the Salian Franks, supposedly begun in the 5th century and with later additions. Several Latin texts of what was essentially a penal code still exist. Lex Salica lix stated that a wife could not inherit the land of her husband, but this proviso regarding Salic lands in no way applied to the succession to the French crown. The so-called 'Salic Law' invoked in 1316 to exclude the daughters of Louis X (r.1314–16) and, later, Philip V (r.1316–22) from the throne of France never existed. Subsequent exclusions of females from European thrones rested on precedent rather than Salic Law. The so-called 'Spanish Salic Law', an Act of Philip V of Spain (r.1700–46) published in 1713 and giving preference to male succession, was to satisfy European pressure, and it aimed at preventing the future union of the French and Spanish thrones. This law was abrogated by Charles IV (r.1788–1808) in 1789, although the fact was not made public until 1830.

**Salii** or **Saliens.** In ancient Rome a college of 12 priests of MARS traditionally instituted as guardians of the ANCILE. Every year these young patricians paraded the city, singing and dancing, and finishing the day with a banquet, so that the expression *saliaris coena* became proverbial for a sumptuous feast. The word *saliens* means 'dancing', from Latin *salire*, 'to leap'.

**Salisbury. Salisbury Crags.** The range of cliffs on the flank of ARTHUR'S SEAT, Edinburgh, are said to be so called from William de Montacute, 1st Earl of Salisbury (1301–44) who in 1327 accompanied Edward III in an expedition against the Scots. However, the name is not recorded until the 15th century, and the commemoration itself seems unlikely.

**Salisbury Plain.** An extensive and largely uninhabited and uncultivated tract of chalk upland in Wiltshire north of Salisbury. It abounds in ancient earthworks and is specifically famed for STONEHENGE. In modern times it has been given over to military training, and much of it is closed to the public.

Oh, Salisbury Plain is bleak and bare, –
At least so I've heard many people declare
For I fairly confess I never was there; –
Not a shrub, nor a tree, nor a bush can you see,
No hedges, no ditches, no gates, no stiles,
Much less a house or a cottage for miles; –
– It's a very sad thing to be caught in the rain
When night's coming on upon Salisbury Plain.
R.H. BARHAM: *Ingoldsby Legends*, 'The Dead Drummer' (1840)

**Shepherd of Salisbury Plain, The.** *See under* SHEPHERD.

**Sallee-man** or **Sallee rover.** A pirate ship, so called from Sallee (now more usually Salé), a seaport near Rabat on the west coast of Morocco, formerly a notorious haunt of pirates.

**Sally. Sally Army.** A nickname of the SALVATION ARMY. *See also* POKE BONNET.

**Sally Lunn.** A type of teacake, said to be so called from a woman pastrycook of that name who used to sell them in the streets of Bath at the close of the 18th century. Dalmer, a baker and musician, bought her business and made a song about the buns. Sally Lunn's house still exists in Lilliput Alley. The original cakes were made like plain teacakes without any fruit but with a yeasted mix.

**Aunt Sally.** *See under* AUNT.

**Salmacis.** *See* HERMAPHRODITE.

**Salmagundi.** A mixture of minced veal, chicken or turkey, anchovies or pickled herrings, and onions, all chopped together and served with lemon juice and oil. The word appeared in the 17th century. Its origin is uncertain (it may be from Italian *salami conditi*, 'pickled salami'), but fable has it that it was the name of one of the ladies attached to the suite of Marie de Medici (1573–1642), wife of Henry IV of France, who invented or popularized the dish.

In 1807 Washington Irving published a humorous periodical with this as the title.

**Salome.** Although not identified by name in the Bible (Matthew 14), Salome is the daughter of Herodias who so delights Herod with her dancing that he offers her anything she wishes. She asks for the head of JOHN THE BAPTIST, and this is brought to her on a dish. Her name comes from Josephus' account of the incident, and tradition has subsequently associated her with the 'dance of the seven veils' as a form of seductive striptease. Oscar Wilde's play *Salomé* (1896) is now perhaps best known from Richard Strauss's opera (1906), but it was also the basis for Antoine Mariotte's opera (1908). *La tragédie de Salomé* (1907) by Florent Schmitt is a mimodrama, and the story was the basis of a ballet (1978) to the music of Sir Peter Maxwell Davies.

**Salon des Refusés.** The exhibition of paintings opened at Paris in 1863 at the instigation of NAPOLEON III, of works from artists (especially Claude Monet) rejected by the French Salon. Monet's 1872 picture *Impression: Soleil levant* ('Impression: Sunrise') gave rise to the term IMPRESSIONISM, which was coined in derision by a journalist.

**Salop.** *See* SHROPSHIRE.

**Salt.** Flavour; smack. The 'salt of youth' is that vigour and strong passion that predominates in that early stage of life.

> Though we are justices and doctors and churchmen, Master Page, we have some salt of our youth in us.
> SHAKESPEARE: *The Merry Wives of Windsor*, II, iii (1600)

Shakespeare uses the term on several occasions for sexual passion. Thus Iago refers to it as 'hot as monkeys, salt as wolves in pride' (*Othello*, III, iii (1604)). The Duke calls Angelo's base passion his 'salt imagination', because he supposes his victim to be Isabella, and not his betrothed wife whom the Duke forced him to marry (*Measure for Measure*, V, i (1604)).

**Salt a mine, To.** To introduce pieces of ore and the like into the workings so as to delude prospective purchasers or shareholders into thinking that a worthless mine is profitable.

**Salt an account, To.** To put an extreme value on each article, and even something more, to give it piquancy and raise its market value.

**Salt away** or **down, To.** To store or preserve for future use, especially money.

**Salt Hill.** The mound where boys at Eton used to collect money for the Captain at the MONTEM. All the money collected was called salt. *See also* SALARY.

**Salt lick.** A place where salt is found naturally and where animals that go there may lick it from the rocks or other surface.

**Salt of the earth.** The perfect; the elect; the worthiest and most honest of the human race. Christ told his disciples they were 'the salt of the earth' (Matthew 5:13).

**Salt on the tail.** To put salt on someone's tail is to catch or apprehend them. The phrase is from the advice given to young children to lay salt on a bird's tail if they want to catch it.

**Salts of lemon.** *See* MISNOMERS.

**Attic salt.** *See under* ATTIC.

**Bread and salt.** *See under* BREAD.

**Covenant of salt, A.** *See under* COVENANT.

**Eat salt with someone, To.** *See under* EAT.

**Epsom salts.** *See under* EPSOM.

**Glauber salts.** *See under* GLAUBER.

**If the salt have lost its savour, wherewith shall it be salted?** *See under* IF.

**Old salt, An.** *See under* OLD.

**Pillar of Salt, The.** *See under* PILLAR.

**Rochelle salt.** *See under* ROCHELLE.

**Rub salt into someone's wounds, To.** *See under* RUB.

**Sit above the salt, To.** *See under* SIT.

**Spilling salt.** *See under* SPILL.

**True to one's salt.** *See under* TRUE.

**With a pinch** or **grain of salt.** *See under* WITH.

**Worth one's salt.** *See under* WORTH.

**Salutation** or **salute** (Latin *salutare*, 'to keep safe', 'to greet'). Military salutes take various forms according to the occasion, and include touching the cap, presenting arms, the lowering of sword-points, lowering the flag and the firing of guns. The number of guns fired for a Royal Salute in the Royal Navy is 21, in the Army 101. The lowering of swords indicates a willingness to put oneself in the power of the person saluted, as does the presenting of arms.

Other common forms of salutation are the kiss, the handshake, the bow, the curtsey, the raising of the hat and so on.

**Salvation Army.** A religious organization founded by William Booth (1829–1912), originally a METHODIST minister. Its origins are to be found in 1865 in his Christian Mission, WHITECHAPEL, London, and the movement took its present name in 1878. Booth himself became the 'General' and the 'Army' was planned on semi-military lines. The motto adopted was 'Through Blood and Fire', and the activities were directed towards the poor, outcast and destitute. The movement grew worldwide, and its brass bands and open-air meetings became a familiar feature of the street scene, as did the bonnets of the Salvation Army 'lasses'. Much good has been done by the selfless devotion of its members.

**Salve** (Latin, 'hail', 'welcome'). The word is sometimes woven on doormats.

**Salve, Regina.** An ancient antiphonal hymn recited at the end of some of the canonical hours and still widely used in Roman Catholic churches. So called from the opening words,

*Salve, regina, mater misericordiae* ('Hail, O queen, Mother of Mercy').

**Weapon salve.** *See under* WEAPON.

**Sam. Sam Browne belt.** The leather belt with a strap over the shoulder and originally with a sword-frog, compulsory for officers and warrant officers in the British Army until 1939, when it was declared optional. This belt was invented by General Sir Sam Browne, VC (1824–1901), a veteran of the INDIAN MUTINY. Its pattern has been adopted by almost every military power in the world.

**Sam Spade.** *See under* SPADE.

**Soapy Sam.** *See under* SOAP.

**Uncle Sam.** *See under* UNCLE.

**Samanids.** A Persian dynasty founded by Ismail at Samani. They ruled from 892 to 1005 and were notable patrons of Persian literature.

**Samaritan. Samaritan Pentateuch, The.** The Hebrew text of the Pentateuch as preserved by the Samaritans, said to date from the 4th century BC.

**Samaritans, The.** An organization founded by the Rev. Chad Varah of St Stephen Walbrook, London, in 1953, to help the despairing and suicidal. By the early 1990s there were more than 180 centres in the British Isles as well as some overseas. Trained volunteers give their help at any hour to those who make their needs known, mostly by telephone, but also by letter or a personal visit.

**Good Samaritan, A.** *See under* GOOD.

**Samarkand.** An ancient city of Central Asia, now in Uzbekistan. From the 4th century BC to the 6th century AD the Sogdian capital of Marakanda stood on the site. In AD 329 it was captured by the forces of Alexander the Great. In the early 8th century the city fell to the Arabs and then passed through various hands before it was laid waste by MONGOL Tartars in 1220. It was the capital of TAMBERLANE from the late 14th to the early 15th century and soon after gained renown as one of Central Asia's greatest cultural centres. Its name, meaning 'stone fort', has become a byword for oriental riches and exotic romance.

> For lust of knowing what should not be known,
> We take the Golden Road to Samarkand.
> JAMES ELROY FLECKER: *Hassan*, V, ii (1922)

**Same breath, In the.** *See under* BREATH.

**Samian. Samian letter, The.** The letter Y, PYTHAGORAS' LETTER.

> When reason doubtful like the Samian letter,
> Points him two ways, the narrower the better.
> ALEXANDER POPE: *The Dunciad*, iv (1728)

**Samian Poet, The.** Simonides of Amorgos, Greek iambic poet and native of Samos, who flourished in the mid-7th century BC.

**Samian Sage** or **Samian, The.** PYTHAGORAS, who was born at Samos.

> Not so the Samian sage; to him belongs
> The brightest witness of recording Fame.
> JAMES THOMSON: *Liberty*, Pt III (1726–30)

**Samite.** A rich silk fabric with a warp of six threads, generally interwoven with gold, held in high esteem in the Middle Ages. It is so called after the Greek *hexamiton*, 'having six threads', from *hex*, 'six', and *mitos*, 'thread'. *See also* DIMITY.

**Sampford ghost.** An uncommonly persistent POLTERGEIST which haunted a thatched house (destroyed by fire *c.*1942) at Sampford Peverell, near Tiverton, Devon, for about three years until 1810. In addition to the usual knockings, the inmates were beaten, curtains agitated and damaged, levitations occurred, and in one instance an 'unattached arm' flung a folio Greek Testament from a bed into the middle of the room. The Rev. Charles Caleb Colton, rector of the Prior's Portion, Tiverton (credited as author of these freaks), offered £100 to anyone who could explain the matter except on supernatural grounds. No one claimed the reward.

**Sampo.** *See* KALEVALA.

**Samson.** Any man of unusual strength, so called from the ancient Hebrew hero (Judges 13–16) who once killed 1000 men with the jawbone of an ass. His strength comes from his vow never to cut his hair, but DELILAH, learning his secret, cuts it and delivers him back to his enemies, the PHILISTINES, who blind him. As his hair grows back, his strength returns, and when he is paraded for public display, he pushes down the pillars of the temple, so destroying the Philistines as well as himself.

The name has been specially applied to Thomas Topham, the 'British Samson', son of a London carpenter. He lifted three hogsheads of water, weighing 1836lb (833kg) in the presence of thousands of spectators at COLD BATH FIELDS on 28 May 1741. He stabbed his wife and committed suicide in 1749. The name has also been given to Richard Joy, the Kentish Samson, who died in 1742 at the age of 67. His tombstone is in St Peter's churchyard, Isle of Thanet.

**Samuel.** The last of the judges of ISRAEL, and a prophet second only to MOSES. He anoints both King SAUL and DAVID, and the events concerning him are related in 1 Samuel.

**Samurai.** The military class of old Japan. In early feudal times the term (which means 'guard') was applied to all who bore arms, but eventually the Samurai became warrior knights and administrators as retainers of the *daimyo* or nobles. From 1869 the rigid feudal stratification of society came to an end, and in 1876 they were forbidden to wear two swords, the symbol of a warrior. With the creation of a new nobility in

1884 they became *shizoku* ('gentry') and many took posts in administration and industry. The formal reorganization of society into *kazoku* ('nobility'), *shizoku* ('gentry') and *heimin* ('common people') set up in 1869, and subsequently modified, was abolished in 1947. *See also* HARA-KIRI; SEVEN SAMURAI (*under* SEVEN).

**San benito.** *See* SACCO BENEDETTO.

**Sancho Panza.** The squire of Don QUIXOTE in Cervantes' romance. A short pot-bellied rustic, full of common sense, but without a grain of 'spirituality', he became governor of BARATARIA. He rode upon an ass, DAPPLE, and was famous for his proverbs. His name effectively means 'St Paunch', from the Spanish name Sancho, from Latin *sanctus*, 'saint', and *panza*, 'paunch'. Hence a Sancho Panza as a rough-and-ready, sharp and humorous justice of the peace, an allusion to Sancho, as judge in the isle of Barataria.

**Sanchuniathon.** The *Fragments of Sanchuniathon* are the literary remains of a Phoenician philosopher said to have lived before the TROJAN WAR. They are incorporated in the *Phoenician History* by Philo of Byblos (1st and 2nd centuries AD), which was drawn upon by Eusebius (*c.*260–*c.*340), the Father of Church History. The name is Greek and may mean 'the whole law of Chon' or it may be a proper name. It is unlikely that the name was invented by Philo to give ancient authority to his writings.

**Sanction, Pragmatic.** *See under* PRAGMATIC.

**Sanctity, The odour of.** *See under* ODOUR.

**Sanctuary, Right of.** *See under* RIGHT.

**Sanctum sanctorum.** Latin for HOLY OF HOLIES. *See also* ADYTUM.

**Sanctus bell.** *See* SACRING BELL.

**Sancy Diamond, The.** A DIAMOND (55 carats), said to have once belonged to Charles the Bold of Burgundy, and named after the French ambassador in Constantinople, Nicholas de Harlay, Sieur de Sancy, who, *c.*1575, bought it for 70,000 francs. Later it was owned by Henry III and Henry IV of France, then by Queen Elizabeth I. James II took it with him in his flight to France in 1688 and sold it to Louis XIV for £25,000. Louis XV wore it at his coronation, but during the French Revolution it was stolen and, in 1828, sold to Prince Pavel Demidov for £80,000. It remained in his family until 1900, and was subsequently acquired by Lady Nancy Astor.

**Sand. Sand-blind.** Dim-sighted, not exactly blind, but with eyes of very little use. 'Sand' here is a corruption of the obsolete prefix 'sam-' meaning 'half' (modern 'semi-'), as in the old sam-dead, sam-ripe and sam-sodden, which still survives in some dialects. In Shakespeare's *The Merchant of Venice* (II, ii (1596)) Launcelot Gobbo connects it with 'sand', the gritty earth:

> This is my true-begotten father, who, being more than sand-blind, high gravel blind, knows me not.

**Sandcastle.** A castle, or apology for one, built by a child on a sandy beach, and serving as a symbol of the transience of things when it is invaded and razed by the rising tide.

**Sandgropers.** Nickname for the inhabitants of Western Australia, originally applied to the gold rush pioneers.

**Sandman is here, The.** A playful remark addressed to children who are tired and 'sleepy-eyed'.

**Sands are running out, The.** Time is getting short; there will be little opportunity to do what you have to do unless you take the chance now. The phrase is often used with reference to one who has not much longer to live. The allusion is to the hourglass. A fuller version is: 'The sands of time are running out'.

**As happy as a sandboy.** *See under* AS.

**Golden sands of the Pactolus, The.** *See under* GOLDEN.

**Goodwin Sands.** *See under* GOODWIN.

**Plough** or **number the sands, To.** *See under* PLOUGH.

**Rope of sand, A.** *See under* ROPE.

**Sand, George.** The pen name of the French novelist Amandine-Aurore Lucille Dupin, baronne Dudevant (1804–76). It was adopted during her liaison with Jules Sandeau.

**Sandabar** or **Sindibad.** Names given to a medieval collection of tales much the same as those in the Greek *Syntipas the Philosopher* and the Arabic *Romance of the Seven Viziers* known in western Europe as *The Seven Sages* (SEVEN WISE MASTERS), and derived from the Indian animal fables known in Europe as the *Fables of Bidpay*. These names probably result from Hebrew mistransliterations of the Arabic equivalent of Bidpay or Pilpay, itself the name of the Indian narrator.

**Sandal. Man without sandals, A.** *See under* MAN.

**Wear the sandals of Theramenes, To.** *See under* WEAR.

**Sandford and Merton.** The schoolboy heroes of Thomas Day's old-fashioned children's tale of this name (published in three parts, 1783–9). 'Master' Tommy Merton is rich, selfish, untruthful and generally objectionable, while Harry Sandford, the farmer's son, is depicted as being the reverse in every aspect. Tommy was duly reformed under the guidance of Mr Barlow the local clergyman, and by association with Harry. In the last paragraph of the book Tommy says to Harry:

> To your example I owe most of the little good that I can boast; you have taught me how much better it is to be useful than rich or fine; how much more amiable to be good than great.

Desmond Coke, author of books for boys, wrote an amusing burlesque of *Sandford and Merton* entitled *Sandford of Merton* (1903) under the pen name Belinda Blinders. *See also* STROKE.

**Sandwich.** Meat or other filling between two slices of bread, so called from the 4th Earl of Sandwich (1718–92), the notorious 'Jemmy TWITCHER'. He passed whole days in gambling, bidding the waiter to bring him for refreshment a slice of cold beef between two pieces of bread, which he ate without stopping play. The word has passed into many languages including Russian *sandvich*, Chinese *sanmíngzhi* and Japanese *sandoitchi*. *See also* CLUB SANDWICH.

**Sandwich man.** A perambulating advertisement displayer, 'sandwiched' between a pair of advertisement boards carried before him and behind.

**Beer and sandwiches.** *See under* BEER.

**Club sandwich.** *See under* CLUB.

**Sang. Sang-de-boeuf** (French, 'ox blood'). The deep red with which ancient Chinese porcelain is often coloured.

**Sang-froid** (French, 'cold blood'). Freedom from excitement or agitation. One does a thing 'with perfect *sang-froid*' when one does it coolly and collectedly.

**Sanger's Circus.** One of the most spectacular entertainments of Victorian England. In 1845 the brothers John (1816–89) and George (1825–1911) Sanger began a conjuring exhibition at Birmingham and from this they ventured into a travelling circus business. Their success was such that they were eventually able to lease the Agricultural Hall, Islington, and in 1871 purchased ASTLEY'S. Their mammoth shows were a distinctive feature of the entertainment world, but they subsequently dissolved the partnership and after John's death only 'Lord' George's circus continued on the road.

**Sanglamore** ('big bloody blade'). Braggadochio's sword in Edmund Spenser's *The Faerie Queene* (1590, 1596).

**Sangrado, Dr.** A name applied to an ignorant or 'fossilized' medical practitioner, from the humbug in Alain René Le Sage's *Gil Blas* (1715), a tall, meagre, pale man, of very solemn appearance, who weighed every word he uttered and gave an emphasis to his sage 'dicta'. 'His reasoning was geometrical, and his opinions angular.' He prescribed warm water and bleeding for every ailment, for his great theory was that: 'It is a gross error to suppose that blood is necessary for life.'

**Sangrail** or **Sangreal.** The HOLY GRAIL. Popular etymology used to explain the word as deriving from Old French *sang real*, real blood or royal blood, meaning the real or royal blood of Christ or the wine used in the LAST SUPPER, and a tradition arose that some of this wine-blood was preserved by JOSEPH OF ARIMATHEA in the Saint or Holy Grail. The true origin is in Old French *saint graal*.

**Sanguine** (Latin *sanguis*, *sanguinis*, 'blood'). The term used in HERALDRY for the deep red or purplish colour usually known as murrey (from the mulberry). In engravings it is indicated by lines of vert and purpure crossed, that is, diagonals from left to right. This is a word with a curious history. Its actual meaning is bloody, or of the colour of blood, hence it came to be applied to someone who was ruddy, whose cheeks were red with good health and well-being. From this it was easy to extend the meaning to a person who was full of vitality, vivacious, confident and hopeful. An artist's drawing in red chalk or crayon is called a sanguine, as also is the chalk itself.

**Sanhedrin** or **Sanhedrim** (Greek *sun*, 'together', and *hedra*, 'seat', i.e. 'a sitting together'). The supreme council and highest court of justice of the ancient Jews held at Jerusalem. It consisted of 70 priests and elders and a president, dealt with religious questions, and acted as a civil court for Jerusalem. It was the Sanhedrin that condemned Christ to death. The Sanhedrin proper came to an end with the fall of the Jewish state (AD 70). Some authorities, taking their evidence from the MISHNA, hold that there was a Great Sanhedrin of 71 members possessing civil authority and a little Sanhedrin of 23 with religious authority under the high priest. The English has preserved the Hebrew form of the word, and a nearer Greek equivalent would be 'synedrion'.

In John Dryden's *Absalom and Achitophel* (1681) the Sanhedrin stands for the English Parliament.

**Sankey's Horse.** *See under* REGIMENTAL AND DIVISIONAL NICKNAMES.

**Sans** (French, 'without'). In *As You Like It*, II, vii (1599), Shakespeare describes SECOND CHILDHOOD as 'sans teeth, sans eyes, sans taste, sans everything'.

**Sans culottes** (French, 'without knee-breeches'). A name given during the French Revolution to the extremists of the working classes, so called because they wore the *pantalon* or long trousers instead of the *culotte* (from *cul*, bottom, backside) or knee-breeches of the upper classes. Hence Sansculottism, the principles of 'red republicans'.

**Sans culottides.** The five complementary days added to the 12 months of the FRENCH REVOLUTIONARY CALENDAR, each month being made to consist of 30 days. The days were named in honour of the SANS CULOTTES, and served as the respective republican festivals of Virtue, Genius, Labour, Opinion and Reward.

**Sans peur et sans reproche** (French, 'without fear and without reproach'). The CHEVALIER DE BAYARD was known as *Le chevalier sans peur et sans reproche*.

**Sans Souci** (French). Free and easy; void of care. It is the name given by FREDERICK THE GREAT to the little palace he built in imitation of VERSAILLES near Potsdam (1745), and has been adopted as a typical suburban house name in England.

**Enfants Sans Souci.** *See under* ENFANT.

**Madame Sans-Gêne.** The nickname of Catherine Hubscher, a washerwoman and VIVANDIÈRE who in 1783 became the wife of François Joseph Lefebvre, Duke of Danzig (1755–1820), one of NAPOLEON BONAPARTE's marshals. She was kind and pleasant, but her rough-and-ready ways and ignorance of etiquette soon made her the butt of the court. She was the heroine of Victorien Sardou's comedy so titled (1893). The name itself means 'without constraint', 'free and easy'.

**Philosopher of Sans Souci, The.** *See under* PHILOSOPHER.

**Sansei.** An American citizen whose grandparents were immigrants to the USA, from a Japanese word meaning 'third generation'.

**Santa. Santa Casa.** *See* HOUSE OF LORETO.

**Santa Claus.** An American modification of Dutch dialect *Sante Klaas* (St NICHOLAS), the patron saint of Dutch and German children. His feast-day is 6 December, and the vigil is still held in some places, but for the most part his name is now associated with Christmas. The custom used to be for someone, on 5 December, to assume the costume of a bishop and to distribute small gifts to 'good children'. The present custom, introduced into England from Germany about 1840, is to put toys and other small presents into a stocking late on Christmas Eve, when the children are asleep, and when they wake on Christmas Day they find at the bedside the gifts brought by Santa Claus, who supposedly travels round in a sleigh pulled by reindeer, which he 'parks' by a house's chimney, descending it to leave his presents. *See also* FATHER CHRISTMAS.

**Santa Fe Trail, The.** The wagon trail between Independence, Missouri, and Santa Fe, New Mexico, used by Missouri traders. The first wagon train traversed the trail in 1821–2 and a steady trade in mules, furs, silver and the like developed. For several years detachments of troops were used to protect the caravans against Indian attacks. The railway reached Santa Fe in 1880.

**Santa Sophia.** *See under* SOPHIA.

**Sapho.** Mlle de Scudéry (1607–1701), the French novelist and poet, went by this name among her own circle.

**Sappho.** The Greek poetess of Lesbos, known as the TENTH MUSE. She lived *c.*600 BC, and is fabled to have thrown herself into the sea from the Leucadian promontory in consequence of her advances having been rejected by the beautiful youth Phaon.

Alexander Pope used the name in his *Moral Essays* (II) for Lady Mary Wortley Montagu (1689–1762). *See also* ATOSSA; SAPHO.

**Sapphics.** A four-lined stanza-form of classical lyric poetry, named after SAPPHO of Lesbos, who employed it, the fourth line being an Adonic. There must be a caesura after the fifth syllable of each of the first three lines which run thus:

– ∪|– –|–||∪ ∪|– ∪|– ∪

The Adonic is:

– ∪ ∪|– ∪ or – –

The first and third stanzas of the *Ode* of Horace, *Integer vitae*, i (1st century BC), may be translated thus, preserving the metre:

He of sound life, who ne'er with singers wendeth,
Needs no Moorish bow, such as malice bendeth,
Nor with poisoned darts life from harm defendeth.
Fuscus, believe me.
Once I, unarmed, was in a forest roaming,
Singing love lays, when i' the secret gloaming
Rushed a huge wolf, which though in fury foaming
Did not aggrieve me.

Probably the best example of Sapphics in English is George Canning's 'Needy Knife-grinder' (1797), which begins:

Needy Knife-grinder! whither are you going?
Rough is the road, your wheel is out of order –
Bleak blows the blast; – your hat has got a hole in't.
So have your breeches.

**Sapphism.** Another name for lesbianism. *See also* LESBIAN.

**Sappho of Toulouse, The.** Clémence Isaure (*c.*1450–*c.*1500), a lady of Toulouse who composed an *Ode to Spring* and who is legendarily supposed to have founded and endowed the Jeux Floraux, the Toulouse Academy, which gives an annual prize of poetry. In fact the Academy was founded by the TROUBADOURS in 1323 and originally known as the Consistoire du Gai Savoir ('Consistory of the Gay Science').

**Saracen** (Late Greek *Sarakēnos*, possibly from Arabic *sharq*, 'sunrise'). A name applied to Arabs generally by medieval writers, especially to those of Syria and Palestine, and also to all infidel nations who opposed the CRUSADERS. The name was given by the Greeks and Romans to the nomadic tribes of the Syro-Arabian desert.

**Saragossa, The Maid of.** *See under* MAID.

**Sarah.** In the Old Testament (Genesis 17–21), the wife of ABRAHAM and mother of ISAAC, whom she bears at the age of 90, so demonstrating the power of faith while helping to found the tribe of ISRAEL.

**Divine Sarah, The.** *See under* DIVINE.

**Saratoga trunk, A.** A huge trunk, such as used to be taken by fashionable ladies to the watering place of that name in New York State.

**Sarcenet.** *See* SARSENET.

**Sarcophagus** (Greek *sarx*, 'flesh', and *phagein*, 'to eat'). A stone coffin, so called because it was made of stone that, according to Pliny, consumed the flesh in a few weeks. The stone was sometimes called *lapis Assius*, because it was found at Assos in Lycia.

**Sardanapalus.** A name applied to any luxurious, extravagant and self-willed tyrant. It is the Greek name of Assurbanipal (mentioned in Ezra 4:10 as Asnappar), king of Assyria in the 7th century BC. Byron, in his poetic drama of the same name (1821), makes him a voluptuous tyrant whose effeminacy led Arbaces, the Mede, to conspire against him. Myrra, his favourite concubine, roused him to appear at the head of his armies. He won three successive battles, but was then defeated, and was induced by Myrra to place himself on a funeral pyre. She set fire to it, and jumping into the flames, perished with him. The painting *Sardanapalus* (1827) by Eugène Delacroix was inspired by Byron's drama. The name Assurbanipal is Assyrian in origin and means '(the god) Assur creates the son'.

**Sardines.** A party game played mainly by children. One person hides and is looked for by everyone else. When someone finds the hider, they join him, so that ultimately all except the final searcher are packed like sardines into a single hiding place. The game is also played by adults, since it provides a legitimate excuse for close physical contact.

**Sardonic smile** or **laughter.** A smile of contempt or bitter, mocking laughter, so used by Homer.

The *Herba Sardonia* (so called from Sardis, in Asia Minor) is so acrid that it produces a convulsive movement of the nerves of the face, resembling a painful grin, but the word probably represents Greek *sardanios*, a 'bitter laugh'.

**Sardonyx.** A precious stone composed of white chalcedony alternating with layers of sard, which is an orange-brown variety of cornelian. Pliny says it is called *sard* from Sardis, in Asia Minor, where it is found, and *onyx*, the nail, because its colour resembles that of the skin under the nail (*Naturalis Historia*, xxxvii, 31 (1st century AD)).

**Sark, Cutty.** *See under* CUTTY.

**Sarong** (Malay, 'sheath'). The Western garment so called is an adaptation of the draped skirt-like dress originally worn by men and women in the East, notably in the Malay Archipelago, Sri Lanka and the islands of the Pacific. It consists of an oblong length of cloth from 2 to 4ft (61 to 122cm) in width and about 6ft (183cm) in length. The ends are sewn together, and the garment is then worn as a kind of kilt, tightened about the waist by a series of special twists. It is frequently of a check pattern and usually bright in colour. It can be made of silk or cotton, or a blend of both.

> Paramount concocted its own South Sea island on which only a sarong separated Dorothy Lamour from the imaginings of any G.I.
>
> DAVID THOMSON: *A Biographical Dictionary of the Cinema* (1975)

**Sarsenet.** A very fine soft silk material, so called from its Saracenic or Oriental origin. The word is sometimes used adjectivally of soft and gentle speech.

**Sarsen stones.** The sandstone boulders of Wiltshire and Berkshire are so called. The early Christian Saxons used the word Saresyn (i.e. SARACEN) as a synonym of pagan or heathen, and as these stones were popularly associated with DRUID worship, they were called Saresyn (or heathen) stones. In the tin mining areas of Cornwall old attle or rock waste was called 'Sarsen' or 'Jews' leavings' on the assumption that Saracens, Jews and Phoenicians had once worked there. *See also* STONEHENGE.

> Scattered over the [Marlborough] Downs are upright stones, 'sarsens' (locally known as 'Grey Wethers', from their resemblance to sheep). Many of these stones have, however, been used for building purposes, or broken up for road-making.
>
> *Cassell's Gazetteer of Great Britain and Ireland* (1896)

**Sash, Black.** *See under* BLACK.

**Sassanides.** A powerful Persian dynasty, ruling from about AD 225 to 641, so named because Ardeshir, the founder, was son of Sassan, a lineal descendant of XERXES.

**Sassenach.** A Scots name for an Englishman, from Gaelic *Sasunnach*, itself from Late Latin *Saxones*, 'Saxons'. The word is related to Welsh *Saesneg*, 'English'.

> The name of 'Saxon' has always adhered to our nation, though we have seemed almost as if we had been willing to divest ourselves of it. We have called our country *England*, and our language *English*: yet our neighbours west and north, the Welsh and the Gael, have still called us Saxons, and our language Saxonish.
>
> JOHN EARLE: *The Philology of the English Tongue* (1887)

**Satan.** The name, in the original Aramaic, means adversary or enemy, and is traditionally applied to the DEVIL, the personification of evil.

> To whom the Arch-enemy
> (And thence in heaven called Satan).
>
> MILTON: *Paradise Lost*, i (1667)

He appears as the SERPENT, tempter of mankind in Genesis 3:1, and the existence of Satan as the centre of evil is part of the teaching of both the Old and New Testament.

> But when they have heard, Satan cometh immediately, and taketh away the word that was sown in their hearts.
> Mark 4:15

The name is often used of a tempter or of a person of whom one is expressing abhorrence. Thus the Clown says to Malvolio:

> Fie, thou dishonest Satan! I call thee by the most modest terms; for I am one of those gentle ones that will use the devil himself with courtesy.
> SHAKESPEARE: *Twelfth Night*, IV, ii (1599)

**Satanic school, The.** So Robert Southey, in the Preface to his *Vision of Judgement* (1821), called Lord Byron, Percy Bysshe Shelley and those of their followers who set at defiance the generally received notions of religion.

**Satan rebuking sin.** The POT CALLING THE KETTLE BLACK.

**Satin, White.** *See under* WHITE.

**Satire.** A derivation of this word from SATYR is quite untenable. It is from Latin *satura*, 'medley', originally *lanx satura*, a dish of varied fruits. The term was applied to a medley or hotchpotch in verse, and later to compositions in verse or prose in which folly, vice or individuals are held up to ridicule.

**Father of French Satire, The.** *See under* FATHER.

**Father of Roman Satire, The.** *See under* FATHER.

**Father of Satire, The.** *See under* FATHER.

**Satisfaction, Job.** *See under* JOB.

**Satrap** (Old Persian *khshathrapāvan*, 'protector of the land'). The governor of a province in ancient Persia.

**Saturday.** The seventh day of the week, or popularly the sixth (*see* SUNDAY). It was called by the Anglo-Saxons *Sæternes dæg*, after the Latin *Saturni dies*, the day of SATURN.

**Black Saturday.** *See under* BLACK.

**Bloody Saturday.** *See under* BLOODY.

**Holy Saturday.** *See* HOLY WEEK.

**Saturn.** A Roman deity, identified with the Greek Kronos (time). He devoured all his children except JUPITER (air), NEPTUNE (water) and PLUTO (the grave). These time cannot consume. The reign of Saturn was celebrated by the poets as a GOLDEN AGE. According to the old alchemists and astrologers, Saturn typified LEAD, and was a very evil planet to be born under. He was the god of seedtime and harvest and his symbol was a scythe, and he was finally banished from his throne by his son Jupiter.

**Saturnalia.** The ancient Roman festival of SATURN, celebrated on 19 December and eventually prolonged for seven days, was a time of freedom from restraint, merrymaking and often riot and debauchery. During its continuance public business was suspended, the law courts and schools were closed and no criminals were punished.

**Saturnian.** Pertaining to SATURN, with reference to the GOLDEN AGE, to the god's sluggishness or to the baleful influence attributed to him by the astrologers.

> Then rose the seed of Chaos, and of Night,
> To blot out order, and extinguish light,
> Of dull and venal a new world to mould,
> And bring Saturnian days of lead and gold.
> ALEXANDER POPE: *The Dunciad*, iv (1728)

**Saturnian verses.** A rude metre in use among the Romans before the introduction of Greek metres. Also a peculiar metre consisting of three iambics and a syllable over, joined to three trochees, as in the lines, 'The queen was in the parlour', 'The maid was in the garden'.

> The Fescennine and Saturnian were the same, for as they were called Saturnian from their ancientness, when Saturn reigned in Italy, they were called Fescennine, from Fescennia [*sic*] where they were first practised.
> JOHN DRYDEN: *A Discourse concerning the original and progress of Satire* (1693)

**Saturnine.** Grave, phlegmatic, gloomy, dull and glowering. Astrologers affirm that such is the disposition of those who are born under the influence of the leaden planet SATURN. *See also* JOVIAL.

**Saturn red.** Red lead.

**Saturn's tree.** An alchemist's name for Diana's Tree or PHILOSOPHER'S TREE.

**Satyr.** One of a body of forest gods or demons who, in classical mythology, were the attendants of BACCHUS. Like the FAUNI, they are represented as having the legs and hindquarters of a goat, budding horns and goat-like ears, and they were very lascivious.

Hence, the term is applied to a brutish or lustful man, and the neurotic condition in men characterized by the desire to have sexual intercourse with as many women as possible is known as satyriasis.

**Sauce** (Latin *salsus*, 'salted food'). Used to give a relish to meat, as pickled roots, herbs or the like.

In familiar usage it means 'cheek' or impertinence, of the sort one expects from an impudent youngster or 'saucebox'.

**Saucy Seventh, The.** *See under* REGIMENTAL AND DIVISIONAL NICKNAMES.

**Saucy Sixth, The.** *See under* REGIMENTAL AND DIVISIONAL NICKNAMES.

**HP Sauce.** *See under* HP.

**What is sauce for the goose is sauce for the gander.** *See under* WHAT.

**Saucer.** Originally a dish for holding sauce, the Roman *salsarium*.

**Saucer eyes.** Big, round, glaring eyes.

> Yet when a child (good Lord!) I thought
> That thou a pair of horns had'st got
> With eyes like saucers staring.
> PETER PINDAR: 'Ode to the Devil' (1782–5)

**Saucer oath.** When a Chinese is put in the witness box, he says: 'If I do not speak the truth may my soul be cracked and broken like this saucer.' So saying, he dashes the saucer on the ground. The Jewish marriage custom of breaking a wineglass has a similar basis.

**Flying saucers.** *See under* FLY.

**Saudi Arabia.** The kingdom in southwestern Asia was founded in 1932 by the Muslim leader Ibn Saud (1880–1953), and named after him. His name derives from the Arabic word meaning 'good fortune', 'happiness', but it is purely a coincidence that the main part of the Arabian peninsula was known to the Romans as Arabia Felix, 'Arabia the fortunate'.

**Saul.** There are two noteworthy biblical personages of the name. In the Old Testament (1 Samuel 9–31), Saul is the first king of ISRAEL. He was subsequently deserted by God in favour of DAVID, whom Saul persecuted for many years until he himself committed suicide when all his sons were killed in battle. In the New Testament (Acts), Saul is the name of the Pharisee who is converted to Christianity while on the road to Damascus, where he was intending to persecute the Christians. He thereupon changes his name to PAUL.

**Is Saul also among the prophets?** (1 Samuel 10:11). Said of one who unexpectedly bears tribute to a party or doctrine that he has hitherto vigorously assailed. At the conversion of Saul, afterwards called PAUL, the Jews asked, in effect, 'Is it possible that Saul can be a convert?' (Acts 9:21).

**Sausage, Not a.** Nothing at all. The expression originally denoted a lack of money, and is said to derive from RHYMING SLANG, in which 'bangers and mash' (i.e. sausages and mash) represents 'cash'.

**Sauvage, Belle.** *See under* BELLE.

**Sauvagine.** *See* COURTAIN.

**Sauve qui peut** (French, 'save himself who can'). One of the first uses of the phrase is by Nicolas Boileau (1636–1711). The phrase thus came to mean a rout.

> What a fine satirical picture we might have had of that general *sauve qui peut* amongst the Tory party!
> W.M. THACKERAY: *The Four Georges*, ch i (1855–6)

**Savage, The noble.** *See under* NOBLE.

**Save. Save appearances, To.** To do something to obviate or prevent embarrassment or exposure.

**Save face, To.** To avoid disgrace or discomfiture. The allusion is to the aspect that one figuratively presents to the world. 'Saving face' is very important to the Chinese and Japanese. *See also* LOSE FACE *under* LOSE.

**Save one's bacon, To.** To save oneself from injury; to escape loss. The allusion may be to the care formerly needed to save from the dogs of a household the bacon that was stored for winter use.

> But here I say the Turks were much mistaken,
> Who hating hogs, yet wish'd to save their bacon.
> BYRON: *Don Juan* vii (1819–24)

**Save** or **keep one's breath to cool one's porridge, To.** A blunt remark to someone who is giving unwanted or unsought advice.

> *Charles*: If you are going to say 'Son of St Louis: gird on the sword of your ancestors, and lead us to victory' you may spare your breath to cool your porridge; for I cannot do it.
> GEORGE BERNARD SHAW: *Saint Joan*, II (1924)

**Save one's life, To.** However hard one tries, as: 'He couldn't drive a car to save his life'.

**Save one's neck, To.** To escape from a dangerous or difficult situation.

**Save one's skin, To.** To get off with one's life.

**Save the mark!** *See* GOD BLESS THE MARK!

**Save the situation** or **day, To.** To produce a solution to a difficulty or disaster.

**Savile Row.** The Mayfair street has been synonymous with high-class men's tailoring since the late 19th century, when tailors here introduced stylish new suits. The name of the street is also 'quality' although not male. It is that of Lady Dorothy Savile, wife of Richard Boyle, 3rd Earl of Burlington (1695–1753), who developed the estate here in the early 18th century.

**Savoir. Savoir-faire** (French, literally 'a knowing how to do'). Readiness in doing the right thing; tact; skill.

**Savoir-vivre** (French, literally 'a knowing how to live'). Good breeding; being at ease in society and knowing what to do.

**Savoy.** The favourite black horse of Charles VIII of France (r.1483–98), so called from its donor, the Duke of Savoy. It had only one eye and 'was mean in stature'.

**Savoy, The.** A precinct off the STRAND, London, between the present ADELPHI and the TEMPLE. It is so called after Peter of Savoy, the uncle of Henry III's queen, Eleanor of Provence. Henry granted it to Peter in 1245 and, after his departure in 1263, it became the residence of Eleanor of Castile, wife of Prince Edward (afterwards Edward I). It was later given to Queen Eleanor's second son, Edmund of Lancaster. On the accession of Henry IV in 1399, it was annexed to the crown as part of the estates of the Duchy of Lancaster. Most of the original buildings were destroyed by Wat Tyler's followers in 1381, but Henry VII bequeathed funds for reconstruction of the palace as a hospital for the poor under the name of St John's Hospital. It became a military hospital, then a barracks under Charles II, but this was demolished with the construction of John Rennie's Waterloo Bridge, which was completed in 1831.

In the late 17th century, the Savoy precinct became a notorious ROOKERY for evil-doers claiming RIGHTS OF SANCTUARY. The Savoy Hotel and Savoy Theatre now occupy part of the area. The Savoy Chapel was first built in 1505 and, after the destruction of St Mary le Strand by Protector Somerset, became known as St Mary le Savoy. It was repaired and restored several times in the 18th century and again by Queen Victoria in 1843 and 1864. *See also* ALSATIA.

**Savoy Conference, The.** After the RESTORATION the conference at the Savoy (1661) between the bishops and PRESBYTERIAN clergy to review the BOOK OF COMMON PRAYER. It resulted in only minor changes, which were included in the revised book of 1662. Most of the Presbyterian demands were rejected.

**Savoy Hill.** The site of the first studios of the British Broadcasting Company (1922) and until 1932 the headquarters of the British Broadcasting Corporation, the original BBC call sign being 2LO (i.e. No. 2, London).

**Savoy Operas.** The comic operas with words by W.S. Gilbert (1836–1911) and music by Arthur Sullivan (1842–1900), produced by Richard D'Oyly Carte. Most of the operettas, from *Iolanthe* (1882), were first produced at the SAVOY Theatre, which D'Oyly Carte built specially for his productions. The players performing in these operas were known as the 'Savoyards'.

**Saw.** In Christian art an attribute of St SIMON and St JAMES THE LESS, in allusion to the tradition of their being sawn to death.

**Gang saw.** *See under* GANG.

**Sawbuck.** In American usage a $10 bill. A sawbuck is a sawing-horse used for cutting up firewood, the legs at each end of which are crossed and bolted in an X-shape. Before note issue became a monopoly of the Federal Reserve Bank, many had an X instead of a 10 to show the denomination. A double sawbuck is a $20 bill.

**Saxifrage.** A member of a genus (*Saxifraga*) of small plants probably so called because they grow in the clefts of rocks (Latin *saxum*, 'a rock', and *frangere*, 'to break'). Pliny, and later writers following him, held that the name was due to the fact that the plant had a medicinal value in the breaking up and dispersal of stones in the kidney or bladder.

**Saxo Grammaticus** ('Saxo the Grammarian'). A Danish chronicler living in the latter part of the 12th century (d.*c.*1208). His *Gesta Danorum*, a chronicle of the early Danish kings to 1185, is a valuable source for the times nearer his own. The earlier parts, derived from old songs, traditions and Runic inscriptions, are less reliable.

In 1930 the philologist Ernest Weekley produced a short volume of guidance for the aspiring English writer under the title *Saxo Grammaticus, or First Aid for the Best-Seller*. It was one of a series on the theme 'To-day and Tomorrow' published by Kegan Paul Trench Trubner in which many of the titles began with a classical name appropriate for the subject. Bertrand Russell was thus the author of *Hypatia, or Woman and Knowledge*, Oliver Stewart of *Aeolus, or the Future of the Flying Machine*, Vera Brittain of *Halcyon, or the Future of Monogamy* and Gerald Heard of *Narcissus, an Anatomy of Clothes*.

**Saxons.** A Germanic people who invaded Britain in the late 5th and early 6th centuries; also the general name given by the Romans to the Teutonic raiders who from the 2nd century ravaged the coasts of Roman Britain. Essex, Sussex, Middlesex and Wessex are names that commemorate their settlements.

**Saxon Shore.** The coast of Norfolk, Suffolk, Essex, Kent, Sussex and Hampshire, fortified by the Romans against the attacks of Saxon and Frisian pirates, under the charge of the COUNT OF THE SAXON SHORE (*Comes Litoris Saxonici per Britanniam*). His garrisons were at Brancaster (Branodunum) in Norfolk; Burgh Castle (Gariannonum) and Walton Castle in Suffolk; Bradwell-on-Sea (Othona) in Essex; Reculver (Regulbium), Richborough (Rutupiae), Dover (Dubris) and Lympne (Portus Lemanis) on the Kent coast; Pevensey (Anderitum) on the Sussex coast; and perhaps Portchester (Portus Ardaoni) near Portsmouth.

**Last of the Saxons.** *See under* LAST.

**Say. Say cheese!** A traditional injunction from a photographer to a group of people about to be photographed, in order to make them smile (by saying the word 'cheese').

**Say ditto, To.** To endorse or agree with somebody else's expressed opinion.

> Two people who are going to be married ought to say ditto to each other in everything.
> MRS HUMPHRY WARD: *Marcella*, ii (1894)

**Say nothing of, To.** As well as, or in addition, as: 'He shouldn't be tired, he slept nine hours last night, to say nothing of a nap this after-noon.'

**Says you!** You may say that, but I disagree. *See also* SEZ YOU!

**Say the word, To.** To give the order; to indicate that one agrees or gives permission.

**Say when.** Stop me when I have given you enough (food or drink).

**I say.** *See* I SAY.

**Needless to say.** *See under* NEED.

**Not to say boo to a goose.** To be very mild or timid.

> There is a story related of the celebrated Ben Jonson, who always dressed very plain; that being introduced to the presence of a nobleman, the peer, struck by his homely appearance and awkward manner, exclaimed, as if in doubt, 'you Ben Jonson! why you look as if you could not say Boh to a goose!' 'Boh!' replied the wit.
>
> FRANCIS GROSE: *Dictionary of the Vulgar Tongue* (1811)

**Take the say, To.** To taste meat or wine before it is presented, in order to prove that it is not poisoned. 'Say' is short for 'assay', a test. The phrase was common in the time of Elizabeth I (r.1558–1603).

**You can say that again!** I quite agree. The suggestion is that I approve of what you say and would be pleased to hear it again.

**'Sblood, 'Sdeath etc.** *See under* 'S.

**Scaevola** (Latin, 'left-handed'). So Gaius Mucius (6th century BC) and his house were called because he had burned off his right hand.

Intending to kill Lars Porsena, who was besieging Rome (509 BC), he entered the king's camp but slew Porsena's secretary by mistake. He was captured and taken before the king and sentenced to the flames. He deliberately held his right hand over the sacrificial fire until it was destroyed to show the Etruscan he would not shrink from torture. This fortitude was so remarkable that Porsena at once ordered his release and made peace with the Romans.

**Scales.** FROM TIME IMMEMORIAL the scales have been one of the principal attributes of justice, it being impossible to outweigh even a little right with any quantity of wrong.

According to the KORAN, at the Judgement Day everyone will be weighed in the scales of the archangel GABRIEL. The good deeds will be put in the scale called 'Light', and the evil ones in the scale called 'Darkness', after which all men have to cross the bridge AL-SIRAT, not wider than the edge of a scimitar. The faithful will pass over in safety, but the rest will fall into the dreary realms of GEHENNA.

**Scales fell from his eyes, The.** The cause of his inability to recognize the truth having been removed, he now saw the facts clearly. 'Scale' here is the shell or thin covering, a scab. It is related to the scale or dish of a balance.

After Ananias put his hands on Saul (St PAUL) the Bible tells:

> And immediately there fell from his eyes as it had been scales; and he received sight forthwith.
>
> Acts 9:18

**Sliding scale.** *See under* SLIDING.

**Turn** or **tip the scales, To.** *See under* TURN.

**Scallop shell.** The emblem of St JAMES THE GREAT of Compostela, adopted, says Erasmus, because the shore of the adjacent sea abounds in them. It was also the emblem of the pilgrims to his shrine and of medieval pilgrims generally. *See also* COCKLE HAT.

> Give me my scallop-shell of quiet,
> My staff of faith to walk upon,
> My scrip of joy, immortal diet,
> My bottle of salvation,
> My gown of glory, hope's true gage,
> And thus I'll take my pilgrimage.
>
> SIR WALTER RALEIGH: 'The Passionate Man's Pilgrimage' (1604)

**Scalp lock.** A long lock of hair allowed to grow on the scalp by men of certain Native American tribes as a challenge to their scalp-hunting enemies.

**Scammozzi's rule.** The jointed 2ft (60cm) rule used by builders, said to have been invented by Vincenzo Scammozzi (1552–1616), the Italian architect.

**Scandal** (Greek *skandalon*, 'trap'). The word means properly a pitfall or snare laid out for an enemy, hence a stumbling-block, and morally an aspersion.

**Scandalmonger.** A person who spreads (and enjoys) scandal.

**Scandalum magnatum** (Latin, 'scandal of magnates'). Words in derogation of the crown, peers, judges and other great officers of the realm, made a legal offence in the time of Richard II (r.1377–1400).

**Scanderbeg.** A name given by the Turks to George Castriota (1403–68), the Albanian patriot. The name is a corruption of Iskander (Alexander) Beg or BEY.

**Scapegoat.** Part of the ancient ritual among the Hebrews for the DAY OF ATONEMENT laid down by the LAW OF MOSES (*see* Leviticus 16) was as follows: two goats were brought to the altar of the TABERNACLE and the high priest cast lots, one for the Lord, and the other for AZAZEL. The Lord's goat was sacrificed, the other was the scapegoat, and the high priest having, by confession, transferred his own sins and the sins of the people to it, it was taken to the wilderness and allowed to escape. *See also* GOAT.

**Scaphism** (Greek *skaphē*, 'anything scooped out', 'boat'). A mode of torture formerly practised in Persia. The victim was enclosed in the hollow trunk of a tree, with head, hands and legs projecting. These were smeared with honey to attract wasps. The sufferer had to linger in this state in the burning sun for several days.

**Scapulimancy** (Latin *scapula*, 'shoulder-blade' and Greek *manteia*, 'prophecy'). An ancient form of DIVINATION, involving examination of the cracks that appeared in an animal's shoulder-blade when it was burned in a slow fire. The Chinese I CHING evolved from it.

**Scarab.** A trinket in the form of a dungbeetle, especially *Scarabaeus sacer*. It originated in ancient Egypt as an AMULET, and was made of polished or glazed stone, metal or glazed faience and then perforated lengthways for suspension. By the 13th Dynasty, scarabs became used as seals, worn as pendants or mounted on signet rings. The insect was believed to conceal in itself the secret of eternal life, since the scarab was believed to be only of the male sex. Hence their use as amulets. They are still the most popular of Egyptian souvenirs.

**Scaramouch.** The English form of Italian *Scaramuccia* (through French *Scaramouche*), a stock character in old Italian farce, introduced into England soon after 1670. He was a braggart and fool, very valiant in words, but a POLTROON, and was usually dressed in a black Spanish costume caricaturing the dons. The Neapolitan actor Tiberio Fiorilli (*c*.1608–94) was named Scaramuccia Fiorilli. He came to England in 1673, and astonished audiences with his feats of agility. The name probably derives from Italian *schermire*, 'to fence', 'to fight with the sword', related to English 'skirmish'. *See also* COLUMBINE; HARLEQUIN.

**Scarborough warning.** No warning at all; otherwise blow first, warning after. In Scarborough robbers were said to be dealt with in a very summary manner by a sort of Halifax gibbet-law or LYNCH LAW.

Thomas Fuller says that the expression arose from Thomas Stafford's unexpected seizure of Scarborough Castle in 1557, but the phrase occurs earlier than this. *See also* LYDFORD LAW.

> The true man for giving Scarborough warning – first knock you down, then bid you stand.
>
> SIR WALTER SCOTT: *Redgauntlet*, ch xix (1824)

**Scarce. As scarce as hen's teeth.** *See under* AS.

**Scare the living daylights out of, To.** To frighten badly or startle suddenly. The daylights were originally the eyes, but the term was extended to any vital organ.

**Scarlet.** The colour of certain official costumes as those of judges, cardinals, holders of certain academic qualifications and the like. Hence the word is sometimes applied to these dignitaries themselves. *See also* PURPLE.

**Scarlet hat.** A CARDINAL, from his once traditional RED HAT.

**Scarlet Lancers, The.** *See under* REGIMENTAL AND DIVISIONAL NICKNAMES.

**Scarlet letter.** In the early days in Puritan New England a scarlet A for 'adulteress' was branded or sewn on a guilty woman's dress.

> She turned her eyes downwards at the scarlet letter, and even touched it with her finger, to assure herself that the infant and the shame was real.
>
> NATHANIEL HAWTHORNE: *The Scarlet Letter*, ch ii (1850)

**Scarlet pimpernel.** A plant of the primrose family, *Anagallis arvensis*. Sir Percy Blakeney, the hero of Baroness Orczy's novel, *The Scarlet Pimpernel* (1905), and of several others in the series, took his nickname from the use of the pimpernel as his emblem. *See also* SHEPHERD'S SUNDIAL.

**Scarlet woman** or **scarlet whore.** The woman seen by St JOHN THE EVANGELIST in his vision 'arrayed in purple and scarlet colour', sitting 'upon a scarlet coloured beast, full of names of blasphemy, having seven heads and ten horns', 'drunken with the blood of the saints, and with the blood of the martyrs', upon whose forehead was written 'Mystery, Babylon the Great, The Mother of Harlots and Abominations of the Earth' (Revelation 17:1–6).

St John was probably referring to Rome, which, at the time he was writing, was 'drunken with the blood of the saints'. Some controversial Protestants have applied the words to the Church of Rome, and some Roman Catholics have applied it to the Protestant churches generally. *See also* MYSTERIUM.

**Will Scarlet.** One of the companions of ROBIN HOOD. In some accounts he is named as William Scarlocke.

**Scat singing.** In JAZZ a form of singing without words, using the voice as a musical instrument. It is said to have been started by Louis Armstrong in the 1920s when he forgot the words or dropped the paper on which they were written while singing a number. Jelly Roll Morton, on the other hand, claimed to have sung scat as early as 1906. The word itself is presumably imitative.

**Scavenger's daughter.** An instrument of torture whose invention has been attributed to Sir Leonard Skevington or Skeffington, Lieutenant of the TOWER OF LONDON in the reign of Henry VIII (1509–47). It was also known as Skeffington's gyves, and consisted of a large iron hoop hinged in two halves. Victims were made to kneel on the lower half. The upper half was then closed on them with a screw. As this was tightened, the body was pressed ever closer together, chest against knees, belly against thighs, and thighs against legs. The spine was thus gradually dislocated and the breastbone and ribs fractured.

**Scene.** Many expressions with this word allude to the theatre and to the action of the players on or off the stage.

**Behind the scenes.** *See under* BEHIND.

**Change of scene, A.** *See under* CHANGE.

**Come on the scene, To.** To arrive; to appear.

**Quit the scene, To.** To die.

**Set scene, A.** *See under* SET.

**Set the scene, To.** *See under* SET.

**Scent, False.** *See under* FALSE.

**Sceptic.** A word with the literal meaning of one who thinks for himself and does not rely on another's testimony, from Greek *skeptesthai*, 'to consider'. Pyrrho (*c*.365–270 BC) founded the philosophic sect called Sceptics, and Epictetus (1st century) combated their dogmas. In theology the word is applied to those who do not accept revelation. *See also* PYRRHONISM.

**Sceptre** (Greek *skeptron*, 'staff'). The jewelled gold wand carried by a sovereign as an emblem of royalty, hence, royal authority and dignity.

> This hand was made to handle nought but gold:
> I cannot give due action to my words,
> Except a sword, or sceptre, balance it.
> A sceptre shall it have, have I a soul,
> On which I'll toss the flower-de-luce of France.
> SHAKESPEARE: *Henry VI, Pt II*, V, i (1590)

The sceptre of the kings and emperors of Rome was of ivory, bound with gold and surmounted by a golden eagle. The British sceptre is of richly jewelled gold, and bears immediately beneath the cross and ball the great CULLINAN DIAMOND.

Homer says that AGAMEMNON's sceptre was made by VULCAN, who gave it to the son of SATURN. It passed successively to JUPITER, MERCURY, PELOPS, ATREUS and THYESTES until it came to Agamemnon. It was looked on with great reverence, and several miracles were attributed to it.

**Schadenfreude** (German *Schade*, 'harm', and *Freude*, 'joy'). A malicious delight in the bad luck of others.

**Scheherazade.** The mouthpiece of the tales related in the ARABIAN NIGHTS ENTERTAINMENTS, daughter of the grand vizier of the Indies. The Sultan Schahriah, having discovered the infidelity of his sultana, resolved to have a fresh wife every night and have her strangled at daybreak. Scheherazade entreated to become his wife, and so amused him with tales for a thousand and one nights that he revoked his cruel decree, bestowed his affection on her and called her 'the liberator of the sex'. Her name is of Persian origin and means 'daughter of the town', from *shahr*, 'town', and *zāde*, 'son', 'daughter' (Persian does not distinguish gender). The sense is that she was the most beautiful girl in the town.

> I had noticed that the Young Girl – the story-writer, our Scheherazade, as I called her – looked as if she had been crying or lying awake half the night.
> OLIVER WENDELL HOLMES: *The Poet at the Breakfast-Table*, ch iii (1872)

**Schelhorn's Bible.** *See* THIRTY-SIX-LINE BIBLE *under* BIBLE.

**Scheme. Groundnut scheme.** *See under* GROUND.

**Pilot scheme.** *See under* PILOT.

**Schism, The Great.** *See under* GREAT.

**Schlemihl, Peter.** The man who sold his shadow to the Devil in the story *Peter Schlemihls wundersame Geschichte* ('Peter Schlemihl's Strange Story' (1814)) by Adelbert von Chamisso (1781–1838). The name is a synonym for any person who makes a desperate and silly bargain. *Schlemihl* is Yiddish for a clumsy person, the word being adopted from his name.

**Scholar. King's** or **Queen's scholar, A.** *See under* KING.

**Rhodes scholars.** *See under* RHODES.

**Scholasticism.** The term usually denotes the philosophy and doctrines of the medieval SCHOOLMEN from the 9th to the early 15th century. It was largely concerned with applying Aristotelian logic to Christian theology. On the whole, reason took second place to faith, and the apparent reconciliation and harmony between the two established by St THOMAS AQUINAS in his 13th-century *Summa Theologiae* was undermined by Duns Scotus and WILLIAM OF OCCAM. It taught men to discipline their thought and to classify their knowledge. Scholasticism owed much of its decline to its own internal quibblings, verbal subtleties and intellectual exhaustion, but it never completely lost its vitality and still attracts theologians, especially in the ROMAN CATHOLIC CHURCH. *See also* DIALECTIC; DUNCE; NOMINALISM; REALISM.

**School. Schoolboards.** The name given to the special local committees elected under Forster's Education Act of 1870 to administer the undenominational elementary schools set up under the Act, hence the term 'board schools'. Schoolboards were abolished by the Balfour Act of 1902, and their work was taken over by education committees of the various local government authorities. These schools then became known as council schools, then provided schools, then county schools (as a type of maintained school). *See also* PARISH SCHOOL.

**Schoolmaster is abroad, The.** Education is spreading and it will bear fruit. Lord Brougham, a champion of popular education, said in a speech to the HOUSE OF COMMONS (1828) on the general diffusion of education, and of the intelligence arising therefrom: 'Let the soldier be abroad, if he will; he can do nothing in this age. There is another personage abroad ... the schoolmaster is abroad, and I trust to him, armed with his primer, against the soldier in full military array.' The phrase lends itself to ironical usage to explain a state of ignorance.

**Schoolmen.** The name given to the teachers of philosophy and theology who lectured in the ecclesiastical schools attached to certain abbeys and cathedrals as instituted by CHARLEMAGNE, and in the medieval universities. Among the best known are:

Flaccus Alcuin or Albinus (735–804)
Johannes Scotus Erigena or John the Scot (*c*.815–*c*.877)
Gerbert of Aurillac (*c*.950–1003),
Pope Sylvester II (r.999–1003)
Berengar of Tours (*c*.998–1088)
Lanfranc (*c*.1005–89), archbishop of Canterbury (1070–89)
Anselm (*c*.1033–1109), archbishop of Canterbury (1093–1109)
Roscellinus of Compiègne (*c*.1050–*c*.1122)
Peter ABELARD (1079–1142)
Peter Lombard (*c*.1100–*c*.1160)
John of Salisbury (*c*.1115–80)
Alain de Lille (*c*.1128–1202)
Alexander of Hales (*c*.1175–1245)
ALBERT THE GREAT, Albertus Magnus (*c*.1206–80)
St Bonaventura or John of Fidanza (1221–74)
St THOMAS AQUINAS (*c*.1225–74)
Raymond Lully (*c*.1235–1315)
Duns Scotus (*c*.1265–1308)
WILLIAM OF OCCAM (*c*.1280–1349)
Thomas Bradwardine (*c*.1290–1349)
Robert Holcot (d.1349)
Jean Buridan (*c*.1300–*c*.1368)

*See also* DUNCE; MASTER OF THE SENTENCES; OCCAM'S RAZOR; SCHOLASTICISM.

**Alexandrian school.** *See under* ALEXANDRIAN.
**As every schoolboy knows.** *See under* AS.
**Bluecoat School.** *See under* BLUE.
**Boarding school.** *See under* BOARD.
**Bolognese school.** *See under* BOLOGNESE.
**Cockney School.** *See under* COCKNEY.
**Della Cruscan school.** *See* DELLA CRUSCANS.
**First school.** *See under* FIRST.
**Flemish school.** *See under* FLEMISH.
**Fleshly school.** *See under* FLESH.
**Grammar schools.** *See under* GRAMMAR.
**High school.** *See under* HIGH.
**Hippocratean school.** *See under* HIPPOCRATEAN.
**Ionic school.** *See under* IONIC.
**Manchester school.** *See under* MANCHESTER.
**Old school tie.** *See under* OLD.
**Parish school.** *See under* PARISH.
**Parnassian school.** *See under* PARNASSUS.
**Peripatetic school.** *See under* PERIPATETIC.
**Public school.** *See under* PUBLIC.
**Ragged schools.** *See under* RAG.
**Satanic school, The.** *See under* SATAN.
**Silver-fork school, The.** *See under* SILVER.
**Spasmodic school.** *See under* SPASMODIC.
**Sunday school.** *See under* SUNDAY.
**Tell tales out of school, To.** *See under* TELL.
**That schoolgirl complexion.** A popular phrase, used in compliment or in jest, which owes it familiarity to its long use (from the early 1920s) in advertisements for Palmolive Soap.
**Voluntary schools.** *See under* VOLUNTARY.

**Schooner.** In the USA a tall glass for beer. The word is also applied to a standard pint-size beer glass in Australia and to a large glass for sherry in England.

**Prairie schooner.** *See under* PRAIRIE.

**Science.** The word literally means 'knowledge', from Latin *scientia*, from *scire*, 'to know'. Shakespeare uses it in this old, wide meaning:

> Plutus himself,
> That knows the tinct and multiplying medicine,
> Hath not in nature's mystery more science
> Than I have in this ring.
>
> *All's Well That Ends Well*, V, iii (1602)

**Science, The.** Pugilism.
**Science fiction.** A fiction based on imagined future developments in science, especially with regard to space or time travel, life on other planets, visits to Earth from aliens and the like. Much science fiction is sophisticated and fires the imagination, but the worst types of the genre are mostly risible and fit only for crude comic strips or picture stories. The term first gained general currency in the 1920s.
**Science persecuted.** Anaxagoras of Clazomenae (d.*c*.428 BC) held opinions in NATURAL SCIENCE so far in advance of his age that he was accused of impiety and condemned to death. Pericles, with great difficulty, got his sentence commuted to fine and banishment.

Galileo (1564–1642) was imprisoned by the INQUISITION for maintaining that the earth moved, but recanted to gain his liberty. *See also* EPPUR SI MUOVE.

Roger Bacon (*c*.1220–92) was excommunicated and imprisoned for diabolical knowledge, chiefly on account of his chemical researches. Dr John DEE was imprisoned under Queen Mary for using enchantments to compass the queen's death. Averroes, the Arabian philosopher, who flourished in the 12th century, was denounced as a madman and degraded solely on account of his great eminence in natural philosophy and medicine.

**Blind with science, To.** *See under* BLIND.
**Christian Science.** *See under* CHRISTIAN.
**Dismal science, The.** *See under* DISMAL.
**Hard** and **soft science.** *See under* HARD.
**Life science.** *See under* LIFE.
**Natural science.** *See under* NATURAL.
**Noble science, The.** *See under* NOBLE.
**Occult sciences.** *See under* OCCULT.
**Seven sciences** or **seven liberal sciences, The.** *See under* SEVEN.

**Scipio, Continence of a.** *See under* CONTINENCE.

**Sciron.** A robber of Greek legend, the son of either POSEIDON or PELOPS, who was slain by THESEUS. He infested the region about Megara, forcing travellers on the road to Eleusis over the rocks into the sea, where they were devoured by a sea monster or, in some accounts, a giant turtle.

**Scissors.** *See* KNIFE.

**Scissors and paste.** Compilation, as distinct from original literary work. The allusion is to the materials needed for this operation, which is also known as cut and paste.

**Scold's bridle, A.** A metal bridle with a tongue plate put upon shrewish women as a punishment. They were used from medieval times until the 18th century. There was a ring over the nose aperture for a rope or chain by which the wearer was led through the streets. *See also* SKIMMINGTON.

**Sconce.** A word with several meanings: a lantern; a candlestick; a wall bracket for one or more candles (from Old French *esconse*, 'lantern'); a small fortified earthwork or fort (from Dutch *schans*, 'fort'); the head or skull; and a verb meaning to mulct or fine (derivation uncertain).

**Sconced, To be.** At Oxford University to pay a forfeit of ale to the company for a breach of table etiquette. Formerly, university officials imposed sconces or fines for breaches of discipline.

**Scone. Drop scone.** *See under* DROP.

**Stone of Scone, The.** *See under* STONE.

**Scorched earth policy.** A policy of burning and destroying crops and anything that may be of use to an invading force. The term probably translates Chinese *shaotu zhèngcè*, from *shao*, to burn, *tu*, earth and *zhèngcè*, policy.

**Score** (Old English *scora*, related to Old Norse *skor*, 'notch'). A word originally applied to a notch on a TALLY, hence a reckoning or account. As the word for the quantity 20, the allusion is probably to the special score or mark made on a tally to indicate that figure. Drovers passing their animals through a tollgate always based their counting on twenties or scores.

**Score off** or **score points off someone, To.** To gain an advantage over a person; to be 'one up'.

**Know the score, To.** *See under* KNOW.

**Score a hit, To.** *See* MAKE A HIT *under* HIT.

**Settle a score, To.** *See under* SETTLE.

**Three score years and ten.** *See under* THREE.

**Scorn, To laugh to.** *See under* LAUGH.

**Scorpio** or **Scorpion.** Scorpio is the eighth sign of the ZODIAC, which the sun enters about 24 October. ORION had boasted that he could kill any animal the earth produced. A scorpion was sent to punish his vanity and it stung Orion to death. JUPITER later raised the scorpion to heaven.

Fable has it that scorpions carry with them an oil which is a remedy against their stings.

> 'Tis true, a scorpion's oil is said
> To cure the wounds the venom made,
> And weapons dress'd with salves restore
> And heal the hurts they gave before.
> SAMUEL BUTLER: *Hudibras*, III, ii (1680)

The oil was extracted from the flesh and given to the sufferer as a medicine. It was also said to be very useful for bringing out the descending stone of the kidneys. Another belief was that if a scorpion was surrounded by a circle of fire it would sting itself to death with its own tail. Byron, in *The Giaour* (1813), extracts a simile from the legend:

> The Mind, that broods o'er guilty woes,
> Is like the Scorpion girt by fire;
> In circle narrowing as it glows,
> The flames around their captive close,
> Till inly search'd by thousand throes,
> And maddening in her ire,
> One sad and sole relief she knows,
> The sting she nourish'd for her foes,
> Whose venom never yet was vain,
> Gives but one pang, and cures all pain,
> And darts into her desperate brain.

**Scorpion, Rock.** *See under* ROCK.

**Scot.** Payment or reckoning. The same word as shot.

**Scot and lot.** The rough equivalent of the modern domestic rates or council tax, i.e. payments by householders for local and national purposes. They became in due course a qualification for the franchise. 'Scot' is the tax and 'lot' the allotment or portion allotted. Scot came from the Old Norse *skot*, 'a contribution', corresponding to Old English *sceot*.

**Go scot-free, To.** To be let off payment; to escape payment or punishment.

**Scotch, Scots** or **Scottish.** These three adjectives all mean belonging to, native of or characteristic of Scotland, but their application varies, and the Scots themselves usually prefer Scottish rather than Scotch, which is applied to whisky and certain standard foods or dishes, such as Scotch broth (a thick kind of soup), Scotch egg (a hard-boiled egg in sausage meat), Scotch pancake (a drop scone) and Scotch woodcock (scrambled egg and anchovies on toast). *See also* WELSH RABBIT *under* WELSH.

**Scotch, To.** To cut with shallow incisions; to slash. Shakespeare's *Macbeth* (III, ii (1605)) has, 'We have scotch'd the snake, not killed it', but in the First Folio the word appears as 'scorch'd'. Izaac Walton's *Compleat Angler* (1653) tells the reader that to dress a chub: 'Give him three or four scotches or cuts on the back with your knife, and broil him on charcoal.' The derivation of the word is uncertain.

**Scotch cap.** A cloth cap worn in Scotland as part of the national dress.

**Scotch-Irish.** The American name for the PRESBYTERIAN immigrants from Ulster who mainly settled in Pennsylvania and the Carolinas during the 18th century. The name derives from the Scottish ancestry of the Ulstermen.

**Scotch mist.** Fine, misty rain.

**Scotch Plot.** An alleged conspiracy, called the Queensberry Plot in Scotland, for a JACOBITE rising and invasion of Scotland in 1703. Simon

Fraser, Lord Lovat (*c*.1667–1747), after intriguing at the courts of St GERMAIN-EN-LAYE and VERSAILLES, returned to Scotland with a letter from Mary of Modena (James II's widow) to be delivered to an unnamed nobleman. He addressed it to John Murray, Duke of Atholl, his personal enemy, and then took it to the Duke of Queensberry, Atholl's rival in the Scottish Ministry. This broke up the ministry and drove Atholl over to the Jacobites. It led to disputes between the English and Scottish Parliaments, but no punitive action was taken.

**Scotch woodcock.** A savoury dish of scrambled eggs on toast, livened up with anchovies or anchovy paste. The name is a blatant misnomer and was actually inspired by WELSH RABBIT.

**Scots Greys, The.** *See* GREYS *under* REGIMENTAL AND DIVISIONAL NICKNAMES.

**Broad Scotch (Braid Scots).** *See under* BROAD.

**Mary, Queen of Scots.** *See under* MARY.

**Pound Scots, A.** *See under* POUND.

**Queen of Scots' Pillar, The.** *See under* QUEEN.

**Scotists.** Followers of Duns Scotus, who maintained the doctrine of the IMMACULATE CONCEPTION in opposition to THOMAS AQUINAS. *See also* DUNCE.

**Scotland.** St ANDREW is the patron saint of Scotland, and tradition says that his remains were brought by St RULE (Regulus) to the coast of Fife in 368.

The old royal arms of Scotland were:

Or: a lion rampant gules, armed and langued azure, within a double tressure flory counter-flory of fleur-de-lis of the second.

Crest: an imperial crown proper, surmounted by a lion sejant affronté gules crowned or, holding in his dexter paw a naked sword and in the sinister a sceptre both proper.

Supporters: two UNICORNS argent, armed, crined, and unguled or, imperially crowned, gorged with open crowns with chains reflexed over the back of the last, the dexter supporting a banner charged with the arms of Scotland, the sinister supporting a similar banner azure, thereupon a saltire argent.

Mottoes: NEMO ME IMPUNE LACESSIT and, over the crest, *In Defens*.

In Scotland today the royal arms of Great Britain are used with certain alterations: the collar of the MOST ANCIENT ORDER OF THE THISTLE encircles that of the MOST NOBLE ORDER OF THE GARTER, the Scottish crest takes the place of the English, and the unicorn supporter crowned and gorged takes precedence over the lion. *See also* HERALDRY.

The last Scottish coronation was that of Charles II at Scone on 1 January 1651.

**Scotland Yard.** As commonly used the name denotes the Criminal Investigation Department of the Metropolitan Police. The name arose from the fact that Great Scotland Yard, Whitehall, was the headquarters of the Metropolitan Police from *c*.1842 to 1890 and thereafter New Scotland Yard, Parliament Street, until 1967 when 'Scotland Yard' was transferred to Broadway, Westminster. The name of the original Scotland Yard comes from the fact that it was the residence of the kings of Scotland when they came to London. Scotland Yard, or its detective force, is often simply referred to as 'the Yard', especially in crime fiction.

**Church of Scotland.** *See under* CHURCH.

**Curse of Scotland, The.** *See under* CURSE.

**Lord High Constable of Scotland.** *See under* LORD.

**St Margaret of Scotland.** *See under* MARGARET.

**Scotsman, Flying.** *See under* FLY.

**Scott, Great.** *See under* GREAT.

**Scotus, Duns.** *See* DUNCE; SCOTISTS.

**Scourge.** A whip or lash, and a word also applied to epidemics that carry off great numbers as well as to persons who seem to be the instruments of divine punishment, as Edward I, 'The Scourge of Scotland'.

**Scourge of God, The** (Latin *flagellum Dei*). Attila (d.453), king of the Huns, so called by medieval writers because of the widespread havoc and destruction caused by his armies.

**Scourge of Homer, The.** The carping critic ZOILUS.

**Scourge of Princes, The.** Pietro Aretino (1492–1556), the Italian satirist.

**Scouse.** A name applied to a native of the port of Liverpool, also to Liverpudlian speech and mannerisms. The word is a shortened form of 'lobscouse', a sailor's name for a stew, particularly of meat, vegetables and ship's biscuit. Hence 'lobscouser' as a former name for a sailor.

**Scout.** This word comes from the Old French *escoute*, 'a spy', 'eavesdropper', akin to the modern French *écouter*, 'to listen'. It is applied to an individual, an aeroplane, warship or the like sent to observe enemy movements or to obtain information. In the early days of CRICKET the fielders were called scouts. College servants at Oxford are still called scouts, even though they are now mostly women, and the word is now officially used for a member of the former BOY SCOUTS.

**King's** or **Queen's Scout, A.** *See under* KING.

**Scrambled egg.** *See* BRASS HAT.

**Scrap.** A colloquial term for a fight or argument.

**Scrap of Paper, The.** The treaty of 1839 maintaining the independence of Belgium, signed by Lord Palmerston for Great Britain, Count Sebastiani for France, Baron von Bülow for Prussia, Count Pozzi di Borgo for Russia, Count Senfft for Austria and M. Van de Weyer for Belgium. It was this treaty that the Germans violated when they invaded Belgium in August 1914.

This brought Great Britain into the struggle and the German Chancellor Bethmann Hollweg declared that Great Britain had entered the war 'just for a scrap of paper'.

**Scrape. Scrape acquaintance with, To.** To contrive to get to know a person by currying favour and by insinuation. According to the *Gentleman's Magazine* (NS xxxix), Hadrian went one day to the public baths and saw an old soldier, well known to him, scraping himself with a potsherd for want of a strigil. The emperor sent him a sum of money. Next day Hadrian found the bath crowded with soldiers scraping themselves with potsherds, and said: 'Scrape on, gentlemen, but you'll not scrape acquaintance with me.'

**Scrape the barrel, To.** To be reduced to one's last resources; to make the best of what is left. The term is said to allude to the barrels of meat lined and sealed with fat which formed a ship's provisions. When the meat was used up, the crew would gain such sustenance as they could from the layers of fat in the discarded barrels.

**Scrape through, To.** To pass a test or examination BY THE SKIN OF ONE'S TEETH, just escaping failure.

**Bread and scrape.** *See under* BREAD.

**Scrimp and scrape, To.** *See under* SCRIMP.

**Scratch.** There are two colloquial sporting uses of this word: (1) a horse or other entrant in a race or sporting event when withdrawn is said to be scratched; (2) a person starting from scratch in a sporting event is one starting from the usual starting point (i.e. the line marked, originally scratched out), whereas his fellow competitors would be starting ahead of him with handicaps awarded to their respective merits. In golf the term par is used instead of scratch. To start from scratch in general usage means to start from nothing or without particular advantages.

**Scratch crew, side** or **team, A.** One scraped together, not a regular team.

**Scratch the surface, To.** To deal with something superficially.

**Come up to scratch, To.** *See under* COME.

**Old Scratch.** *See under* OLD.

**You scratch my back and I'll scratch yours.** If you help me, I'll help you.

**Scream, shout** or **yell blue murder, To.** To scream or shout loudly; to yell at the top of one's voice, especially from terror. The expression seems to pun on the French exclamation *morbleu*, which is actually a form of *mort Dieu*, 'God's death' (or in archaic English, ''sdeath').

**Screen, The small.** *See under* SMALL.

**Screw.** Slang for wages or pay, possibly because in some employments it was handed out 'screwed up in paper' or because it was 'screwed out' of one's employer. The word is also slang for a prison warder, from the days when the locks were operated with a screw-like movement.

**Screwball.** A colloquial term for an erratic, eccentric or unconventional person. It is also a baseball term for a ball pitched to break with a particular kind of slant away from the apparent curve of flight.

**Screwed.** Intoxicated. A playful synonym of 'tight'.

**Screwed up.** Confused, anxious or nervous, as: 'He was all screwed up about his exams.'

**Screw Plot, The.** The story is that before Queen Anne went to St Paul's in 1708 to offer thanksgiving for the victory of Oudenaarde, conspirators removed certain screw-bolts from the roof beams of the cathedral so that the fabric might fall on the queen and her entourage and kill them. In fact, it appears that certain iron fastenings were omitted by one of the workmen because he thought the timbers were already sufficiently secured.

**Screw up one's courage, To.** To summon up one's courage; to 'take the plunge'.

**Archimedes' screw.** *See under* ARCHIMEDES.

**Have a screw loose, To.** To be 'not quite all there'; to be 'a little touched' or mad. The mind of such a person, like a piece of machinery, is in need of adjustment.

**Put on the screw, To.** To press for payment, as a screw presses by gradually increasing pressure. A phrase surviving from the days when the THUMBSCREW was used as a form of torture to extract confessions or money. Hence also 'to put the screws on', to increase the pressure in order to enforce one's demands.

**Scribe.** In the New Testament the word means a Jewish doctor of the law, and Scribes were generally coupled with the PHARISEES as upholders of the ancient ceremonial tradition. In the Old Testament the word has a wider application, and generally means a scholar and teacher of the Jewish law.

**Scriblerus, Martinus.** *See* MARTINUS SCRIBLERUS.

**Scrimp and scrape, To.** To be very economical or sparing; to restrict one's expenses to the minimum.

**Scrimshaw.** A word from sailing-ship days applied to carved or scratched engraving on shells, bone, ivory and the like done to while away the time at sea. 'To scrimshaw' is to make any ingenious useful article on shipboard. The origin of the word is uncertain. It may be from a personal name.

**Scriptores Decem.** A collection of ten ancient chronicles on English history edited by Sir Roger Twysden (1597–1672) and published in 1652 as *Historiae Anglicanae Scriptores Decem* with the 'Glossary' of William Somner, the first Anglo-Saxon word-list. The chroniclers are

Simeon of Durham, John of Hexham, Richard of Hexham, Ailred of Rievaulx, Ralph de Diceto (Archdeacon of London), John Brompton of Jorval, Gervase of Canterbury, Thomas Stubbs, William Thorn of Canterbury and Henry Knighton of Leicester.

Thomas Gale (*c*.1635–1702) published a similar collection of five chronicles, *Historiae Anglicanae Scriptores Quinque* in 1687, and in 1691 *Historiae Britannicae, Saxonicae, Danicae Scriptores Quindecim*.

**Scriptorium** (Medieval Latin, from *scribere*, 'to write'). A writing-room, especially the chamber set apart in the medieval monasteries for the copying of manuscripts. Sir James Murray (1837–1915) gave the name to the corrugated-iron outhouse in his garden at Mill Hill in which he started the great *New English Dictionary* (now the *Oxford English Dictionary*).

**Scriptures, The** or **Holy Scripture** (Latin *scriptura*, 'a writing'). The Bible, hence the application of the term to the sacred writings of other creeds, as the KORAN, the Scripture of the Muslims, or the VEDAS and ZEND-AVESTA, the Scripture of the Hindus and Persians.

**Scripturists.** A name given to the Karaites ('Readers of the Scripture'), those Jewish literalists who kept biblical injunctions to the letter. For them 'an eye for an eye' meant just this, and 'Ye shall kindle no fire throughout your habitations upon the sabbath day' (Exodus 35:3) left them shivering in the winter. The movement began in the 8th century under Anan ben David, and spread from Babylonia to Persia and Egypt. Its decline set in from the 10th century, although it has lingered on in isolated pockets.

**Scrolls, The Dead Sea.** *See under* DEAD.

**Scrubs, Wormwood.** *See under* WORM.

**Scruple.** The name of the weight (20 grains or $\frac{1}{24}$oz) and the term for doubt or hesitation (as in 'a scruple of conscience'). Both come from Latin *scrupulus*, meaning a sharp little pebble, such as will cause great uneasiness if it gets into one's shoe. The second is the figurative use, with the name of the little weight contrasted with that of the big one, stone (i.e. 224oz).

**Scullabogue, The Barn of.** *See under* BARN.

**Sculls, The Diamond.** *See under* DIAMOND.

**Sculptures, Aeginetan.** *See under* AEGINETAN.

**Scunner.** A Scottish term for a feeling of distaste amounting almost to loathing. To 'take a scunner' to something is to take a violent dislike to it.

**Scunthorpe.** A place-name for some reason regarded as amusing, and thus in the same category as BASINGSTOKE. The humour may partly lie in the fact that most places with 'thorpe' in the name have remained small villages, as Scunthorpe itself was until the 19th century. It then grew rapidly following the discovery of iron ore here in North Lincolnshire. Its name means simply 'Skuma's farmstead', from a Scandinavian landowner.

**Scurry.** In horse racing, a scratch race for inferior mounts, or a short, quick race.

**Scutage** or **escuage.** In feudal times, a payment in commutation of KNIGHT SERVICE (i.e. military service). It developed after the Norman Conquest of 1066, but the term, from Latin *scutum*, a shield, did not come into use until the beginning of the 12th century. The method of assessment was regularized in the time of Henry II (r.1154–89), and TENANTS-IN-CHIEF passed on the levy to their tenants. Scutage came to an end in 1327.

**Scuttle.** The scuttle for coal is Old English *scutel*, 'a dish', from Latin *scutella*, 'a dish', 'a platter'. The scuttle or opening in the side or deck of a ship is Spanish *escotilla*, 'a hatchway'.

**Scuttle a ship, To.** To hole it in order to make it sink. This is from SCUTTLE in the sense of a hatch-opening or hole.

**Scuttle off, To.** To make off hurriedly. This was originally 'to scuddle off', 'scuddle' being a frequentative of 'scud', to run or skim along, perhaps also influenced by 'shuttle'.

**Scylla.** (1) In Greek legend the name of a daughter of King Nisus of Megara. She promised to deliver Megara into the hands of her lover, MINOS, and, to effect this, cut off a golden (or purple) hair on her father's head while he was asleep thus causing his death. Minos despised her for this treachery, and Scylla threw herself from a rock into the sea. Other accounts say she was changed into a lark (or an egret) by the gods and her father into a hawk.

(2) Scylla, the sea monster, was a beautiful NYMPH beloved by GLAUCUS, who applied to CIRCE for a love potion, but Circe became enamoured of him and metamorphosed her rival into a hideous creature with twelve feet and six heads, each with three rows of teeth. Below the waist her body was made up of hideous monsters, like dogs, which barked continuously and ate all those who came within reach. She dwelt on the rock of Scylla, opposite CHARYBDIS, on the Italian side of the Straits of Messina, and was a terror to ships and sailors. Whenever a ship passed, each of her heads would seize one of the crew.

**Between Scylla and Charybdis.** *See* CHARYBDIS.

**Scythian.** Pertaining to the peoples or region of Scythia, the ancient name of a great part of European and Asiatic Russia.

**Scythian defiance.** When DARIUS approached Scythia, an ambassador was sent to his tent with a bird, a frog, a mouse and five arrows, then left without a word. Darius, wondering what was meant, was told by Gobrias it meant this: either fly away like a bird, hide your head in a hole like a mouse or swim across the river like a frog, or in five days you will be laid prostrate by the Scythian arrows.

**Sea.** Any large expanse of water, more or less enclosed, hence the expression 'molten sea' meaning the great brazen vessel that stood in the TEMPLE OF SOLOMON (2 Chronicles 4:2, 1 Kings 7:23). Even the NILE, the Euphrates and the Tigris are sometimes called sea by the prophets. The world of water is the Ocean.

**Seabees, The.** A nickname for members of the US Navy's Construction Battalions, who build airstrips. They are thus to do with the air, but not necessarily with that other great element, the sea.

**Sea-born city, The.** Venice.

**Sea-born goddess, The.** APHRODITE.

**Sea change, A.** An apparently magical change, as though brought about by the sea. The phrase comes from Ariel's song in *The Tempest* (I, ii (1611)):

> Full fathom five thy father lies;
> Of his bones are coral made:
> Those are pearls that were his eyes:
> Nothing of him that doth fade,
> But doth suffer a sea-change
> Into something rich and strange.

**Sea deities.** In classical myth, besides the 50 NEREIDS, the OCEANIDS, the SIRENS and others, there were numerous deities connected with the sea. Chief among them are: AMPHITRITE; GLAUCUS; Ino (*see* LEUCOTHEA); NEPTUNE; NEREUS and his wife TETHYS; Portumnus (*see* PALAEMON); POSEIDON (the Greek Neptune); PROTEUS; THETIS; TRITON.

**Sea dog.** An old and seasoned sailor; an OLD SALT.

**Sea-girt isle, The.** England. So called because, as Shakespeare has it, it is 'hedged in with the main, that water-walled bulwark' (*King John*, II, i (1596)).

> This precious stone set in the silver sea,
> Which serves it in the office of a wall,
> Or as a moat defensive to a house,
> Against the envy of less happier lands.
> *Richard II*, II, i (1595)

**Sea-green Incorruptible, The.** So Thomas Carlyle called Robespierre in *The French Revolution* (1837). He was of a sallow, unhealthy complexion. *See also* INCORRUPTIBLE.

**Sea-island cotton.** A fine, long-stapled cotton, *Gossypium barbadense*, so called from being grown on the islands off the coast of Florida, South Carolina and Georgia.

**Sea serpent.** A serpentine monster said to inhabit the depths of the ocean. Many reports of such a creature have been made by mariners over the centuries but its existence has never been established. *See also* LEVIATHAN; LOCH NESS MONSTER.

**At sea** or **all at sea.** *See under* AT.

**Black Sea, The.** *See under* BLACK.

**Bride of the Sea, The.** *See under* BRIDE.

**Celtic Sea.** *See under* CELTIC.

**Dead Sea.** *See under* DEAD.

**Euxine Sea.** *See under* EUXINE.

**Four seas, The.** *See under* FOUR.

**Half-seas over.** *See under* HALF.

**Have good sea legs, To.** *See under* GOOD.

**High seas, The.** *See under* HIGH.

**Narrow Seas, The.** *See under* NARROW.

**Old Man of the Sea, The.** *See under* OLD.

**Red Sea.** *See under* RED.

**Seven seas, The.** *See under* SEVEN.

**Seal.** (1) The sire is called a bull, his females are cows, the offspring are called pups, the breeding place is called a rookery, a group of young seals is a pod, and a colony of seals is a herd. The immature male is called a bachelor. A sealer is a seal hunter, and seal hunting is called sealing.

(2) A seal (Old French *seel*, from Latin *sigillum*) is also an impressed device, in wax, lead or something similar.

**Sealed orders.** Orders delivered in a sealed package to naval and military commanders that they must not open before a certain time or before reaching a certain locality.

**Seal of confession.** In the ROMAN CATHOLIC CHURCH the obligation that binds a priest never to divulge outside the confessional anything he may hear inside it. He cannot be forced to reveal in the witness box of a court of law any information he may have thus obtained.

**Seal women.** Sea-fairies of Celtic folklore who turn into seals and come ashore to seek a human mate. Seal women originated in Norse mythology, and in the Faroes it is a local belief that seals cast off their skins every ninth night, assume human form, and sing and dance like men and women until daybreak, when they resume their sealskins.

**Bachelor seal.** *See under* BACHELOR.

**Great Seal, The.** *See under* GREAT.

**Hermetically sealed.** *See under* HERMES.

**My lips are sealed.** I am not allowed to say; I shall keep it secret.

> I shall be but a short time tonight. I have seldom spoken with greater regret, for my lips are not yet unsealed.
> STANLEY BALDWIN: *Hansard* (10 December 1935)

**Privy Seal.** *See under* PRIVY.

**Set one's seal on something, To.** *See under* SET.

**Solomon's seal.** *See under* SOLOMON.

**Under my hand and seal.** *See under* UNDER.

**Seamy side.** The 'wrong' or worse side, as the 'seamy side of London', the 'seamy side of life'. In joined fabrics, Brussels carpets, tapestry and the like, the 'wrong' side shows the seams or threads of the pattern exhibited on the right side.

**Search. Searchlight tattoo.** A military entertainment, carried out at night in the open air with illuminations, military exercises and martial music. The best known is that at Edinburgh Castle, staged during the Edinburgh Festival on the Castle Esplanade, with the floodlit castle as a dramatic backdrop.

**Body search.** *See under* BODY.

**Strip search.** *See under* STRIP.

**Seasons.** The four seasons are spring, summer, autumn and winter. Spring starts (officially) on 21 March, the spring EQUINOX, when the sun enters ARIES; summer on 22 June, the summer SOLSTICE, when the sun enters CANCER; autumn on 23 September, the autumn EQUINOX, the sun entering LIBRA; and winter on 22 December, when the sun enters CAPRICORN. *See also* ZODIAC.

The ancient Greeks characterized spring by MERCURY, summer by APOLLO, autumn by BACCHUS and winter by HERCULES.

James Thomson's poetic series *The Seasons* was not published as a collection until 1730. 'Winter' first appeared in 1726 and fetched three guineas from the publisher, but gave Thomson a reputation. 'Summer', dedicated to George Bubb Dodington, was published in 1727, 'Spring' in 1728, and 'Autumn' in 1730.

**Season ticket.** A ticket entitling the holder to any number of journeys, admittances to an exhibition or the like, in a stated period.

**High season.** *See under* HIGH.

**In and out of season.** Always or all the time; constantly.

**London season.** *See under* LONDON.

**Open season.** *See under* OPEN.

**Silly season, The.** *See under* SILLY.

**Sporting seasons in England.** *See under* SPORT.

**Seat. Arthur's Seat.** *See under* ARTHUR.

**Back seat, A.** *See under* BACK.

**Hot seat.** *See under* HOT.

**Safe seat, A.** *See under* SAFE.

**Sebastian, St.** The patron saint of archers, who was martyred in 288. He was bound to a tree and shot at with arrows before being beaten to death. Because the arrows stuck in his body as pins in a pincushion, he was also made the patron saint of pinmakers. As he was a captain of the guard, he is the patron saint of soldiers. His feast-day, coupled with that of St Fabian, is kept on 20 January.

**English St Sebastian, The.** St Edmund, the martyr king of East Anglia (855–870), who is said to have been tied to a tree by the Danes and shot dead with arrows at Hoxne, Suffolk, because he refused to rule as a Danish vassal. His body was taken to the royal manor of Bedricsworth, which came to be called St Edmund's Burgh, and his remains, miraculously incorrupt, became the chief relic of the abbey of Bury St Edmunds.

**Second.** The next after the first (Latin *secundus*).

In duelling, the second is the representative of the principal. He carries the challenge, selects the ground, sees that the weapons are in order and is responsible for all the arrangements.

**Second Adam, The.** Jesus Christ.

> A second Adam to the fight
> And to the rescue came.
>
> J.H. NEWMAN: *The Dream of Gerontius* (1865)

Milton calls MARY a 'second Eve' (*Paradise Lost*, v and x (1667, 1674)).

**Second Adventists.** Those who believe that the SECOND COMING of Christ (*see* 1 Thessalonians 4:15) will precede the MILLENNIUM. Hence they are sometimes also called Premillenarians.

**Second an officer, To.** With the accent on the last syllable, the word means, in military parlance, to remove an officer temporarily from his or her present duties to take up another extraregimental or staff appointment.

**Secondary colour.** A colour that results from the mixture of two PRIMARY COLOURS, such as orange (from red and yellow), green (from blue and yellow) and purple (from red and blue).

**Secondary picketing.** The picketing of the premises of a firm that is not otherwise involved in the original strike or dispute.

**Second Augustine, The.** St THOMAS AQUINAS, the ANGELIC DOCTOR.

**Second banana.** In American theatrical parlance, a vaudeville performer who plays a secondary role to another. Also anyone generally who occupies such a position. *See also* TOP BANANA.

**Second chamber.** In a legislature of two houses the nonelected or indirectly elected house is so called. In Great Britain the HOUSE OF LORDS is the second chamber, and in the USA it is the Senate.

**Second childhood.** Old age; dotage; the time when some folk 'regress' to the simple tastes and pleasures of their youth. *See also* SANS; SEVEN AGES OF MAN (*under* SEVEN).

**Second Coming, The.** The prophesied return of Jesus Christ at the Last Judgement. The event is alluded to directly or indirectly at several points in the New Testament, and is summarized in the Apostles' Creed: 'From thence he shall come to judge the quick and the dead' (Order for Morning Prayer, Book of Common Prayer). *See also* ADVENT.

**Second** or **Little Dauphin.** Louis (1682–1712), son of the GRAND DAUPHIN.

**Second Empire.** *See* NAPOLEON III.

**Second fiddle.** In musical terms, the second violin in a string quartet or one of the second violins in an orchestra. Figuratively, to play second fiddle is to adopt a subordinate status to someone else.

**Second floor.** Two flights above the ground floor. In the USA the second floor is the English first floor.

**Second-guess, To.** The term has two almost contradictory senses. On the one hand, to second-guess is to appraise or criticize someone or something with hindsight, after the event, but on the other it is simply to attempt to anticipate or predict what someone will do or what may happen.

**Second-hand.** Not new or original; that which has already been the property of another, as second-hand books, clothes, opinions and the like.

**Second honeymoon.** A holiday, something like a HONEYMOON, that a couple take after they have already been married for some years. The aim, both nostalgically and romantically, is to 're-capture that first fine careless rapture'.

**Second nature.** Said of a habit or way of doing things that has become so ingrained that it is instinctive.

**Second of time, A.** So called because the division of the minute into sixtieths is the second of the sexagesimal operations, the first being the division of the hour into minutes.

**Second pair back.** The back room on the floor two flights of stairs above the ground floor. Similarly the front room is called the second pair front.

**Second Romulus, The.** CAMILLUS was so called because he saved Rome from the Gauls in 365 BC.

**Second self.** One's ALTER EGO; a person whose tastes, opinions, habits and so on correspond so entirely with one's own that there is practically no distinction.

**Second sight.** The power of seeing things invisible to others; the power of foreseeing future events.

**Second string.** An alternative course of action, which one has in reserve or 'up one's sleeve' if the first action fails. The full expression is 'to have a second string to one's bow'.

**Second to none.** Surpassed by no other, i.e. first.

**Second wind.** A recovery of one's normal breathing after exertion or breathlessness. The sense may also figuratively denote a renewal of energy during a sustained effort.

**Get one's second pip, To.** In the army, to be promoted from second to first lieutenant, these ranks and that of captain being marked by 'pips', a nickname for the stars on the shoulder straps.

**Get one's second wind, To.** To recover and go about one's pursuits with renewed vigour, as a runner, after initial breathlessness, warms up and regains more regular respiration, known as the second wind.

**On second thoughts.** Said when one has revised one's opinion or changed one's mind, as: 'I was going to give her a ring but on second thoughts I think I'll write.'

**Split second.** *See under* SPLIT.

**Secret. Secret Service, The.** The popular name for governmental intelligence, espionage and counterespionage organizations. The US Secret Service, under the Treasury Department, is mainly concerned with Federal crime.

**Open secret, An.** *See under* OPEN.

**Top secret.** *See under* TOP.

**Trade secret.** *See under* TRADE.

**Secretary, Home.** *See under* HOME.

**Sect, Clapham.** *See under* CLAPHAM.

**Section. Caesarian section.** *See under* CAESAR.

**Golden section.** *See under* GOLDEN.

**Secular.** From Latin *saecularis*, pertaining to a *saeculum* or age or generation; also a period of 100 years (the longest duration of a person's life); any long period of indefinite length. The meaning 'lay', 'temporal', 'of this world', is from Late Latin, when *saecularis* had acquired the meaning 'belonging to the world', 'worldly'.

**Secular arm.** Civil as opposed to ecclesiastical jurisdiction.

**Secular clergy.** Clergy living 'in the world' as opposed to the regular clergy of the cloister, who live under a rule. In the ROMAN CATHOLIC CHURCH secular clergy take precedence over the regular clergy.

**Secular games** (Latin *Ludi saeculares*). In ancient Rome the public games, lasting three days and three nights, that took place once in an age (*saeculum*) or every 100 years (sometimes every 110 years). They were instituted in obedience to the Sibylline verses with the promise that 'the empire should remain in safety so long as this admonition was observed'. They derived from the Tarentine Games instituted in 249 BC to propitiate PLUTO and PROSERPINA.

**Secularism.** The name given in 1846 by George Jacob Holyoake (1817–1906) to an ethical system founded on 'natural morality' and opposed to the tenets of revealed religion and ecclesiasticism.

**Secundus, Hercules.** *See under* HERCULES.

**Security risk.** Governmental security is concerned with the prevention of leakages of confidential information, and a security risk denotes a person of questionable loyalty, whose background and associations make employment in state service inadvisable, especially in posts that involve access to confidential information likely to be of use to a potentially hostile government.

**Sedan chair.** The covered seat, so called, carried by two bearers back and front, originated in Italy in the late 16th century, and was introduced into England by Sir Sanders Duncombe in 1634.

The name is probably derived from Latin *sedere*, 'to sit', but Dr Johnson's suggestion that it is connected with the town of Sedan in north-east France remains a possibility.

**Man of Sedan, The.** *See under* MAN.

**Sedgwick, Doomsday.** *See under* DOOM.

**Sedulous. Play the sedulous ape to, To.** *See under* PLAY.

**See** (noun). The seat or throne of a BISHOP, hence the town or place where the bishop's cathedral is located and from which he takes his title. A see, strictly speaking, thus has to be distinguished from a diocese, the territory over which he has jurisdiction. It is derived from the Latin *sedes*.

**Holy See.** *See under* HOLY.

**See** (verb). To perceive by the eye.

**See a man about a dog, To.** To excuse oneself; to leave a meeting, party and so forth, often specifically in order to go to the lavatory. The suggestion is that one is about to place a bet on a dog in a race.

**See eye to eye, To.** To be precisely of the same opinion; to agree completely.

> For they shall see eye to eye, when the Lord shall bring again Zion.
> Isaiah 52:8

**See fit to, To.** To consider it appropriate or proper to.

**See how** or **which way the cat jumps, To.** To see what develops before taking action or committing oneself. The allusion is either to the game of tipcat, in which a player must see which way the 'cat' (a short piece of wood) goes before 'tipping' (hitting) it, or to the cruel sport mentioned under NO ROOM TO SWING A CAT.

**See how the land lies, To.** To see whether things are propitious or not; to examine the immediate prospects. According to an old army dictum, time spent on reconnaissance is never wasted.

**Seeing Eye, The.** An American organization that provides guide dogs for blind people, corresponding to the Guide Dogs for the Blind Association in Britain. It was founded in 1929 by Mrs Dorothy Harrison Eustis. The first Seeing Eye dog was a German shepherd bitch named Buddy, assigned to guide Morris Frank, a young blind man in Tennessee.

> The hearing ear, and the seeing eye, the Lord hath made even both of them.
> Proverbs 20:12

**See into something, To.** To investigate something.

**See life, To.** To 'knock about' town, where life may be seen to the full; to move in smart or fashionable society.

**See Naples and die.** An old Italian saying, implying that nothing more beautiful remains to be seen on earth. There is also a pun involved since Naples was once a centre of typhoid and cholera. *See also* PARTHENOPE.

**See no further than the end of one's nose, To.** To be lacking in foresight, perception and discernment. The expression is also literally used of a very short-sighted person.

**See one's way, To.** To find it possible, as, 'Can you see your way to settling this bill?'

**See red, To.** To give way to excessive passion or anger; to be violently moved; to RUN AMOK. The reference is to an angry bull.

**See snakes, To.** To suffer from delirium tremens. This is one of the delusions common to those so afflicted.

**See someone off, To.** To accompany a person to the point of departure on a journey. Also, colloquially, to outwit or get the better of them. This can be done physically, as a dog 'sees off' unwanted prowlers.

**See someone right, To.** Colloquially, to make sure that a person is treated fairly.

**See someone through, To.** To help a person through a difficulty; to 'tide someone over'.

**See stars, To.** To receive a blow on the head so that one experiences the optical illusion of seeing brilliant streaks, radiating and darting in all directions.

**See the back of, To.** To get rid of.

**See the elephant, To.** An American expression meaning to see life or to gain experience.

**See the light, To.** To be converted; to come to a full understanding or realization of something.

**See the light of day, To.** To come into existence; to be born.

**See the red light, To.** To be aware of approaching disaster; to realize it is time to desist; to take warning. The allusion is to the railway signal, where the red light signifies danger.

**See the sights, To.** *See under* SIGHT.

**See the world, To.** To travel widely; to gain experience.

> We joined the Navy to see the world,
> And what did we see? We saw the sea.
> IRVING BERLIN: 'We Saw the Sea' (song) (1936)

**See things, To.** To have hallucinations; to imagine one sees what is not there, as: 'When he waved at me I thought I was seeing things.'

**See things in their true colours, To.** To see things as they really are.

**See through rose-coloured spectacles, To.** To regard circumstances with unjustified optimism. Spectacles of such a hue would show the world as uniquely but misleadingly rosy, bright and hopeful. The French equivalent is *voir la vie en rose*, 'to see life in pink'.

**See through someone, To.** To perceive a person's true character and motives; not to be taken in by someone.

**See to, To.** To attend to.

**See which way the wind blows, To.** To discover the true state of affairs.

**See you** or **see you later.** Goodbye for now.

**As seen on TV.** *See under* AS.

**I'll be seeing you.** An expression on parting. *See also* SEE YOU.

**I'll see you damned first.** I absolutely refuse to do what you ask.

**Let me see.** *See under* LET.

**Not to be seen dead in** or **with.** Said of a thing or person that one dislikes or detests.

> I have to hang on to one [a car] that my daughters say they wouldn't be seen dead in.
>
> A.G. MACDONELL: *England, Their England*, ch xiii (1933)

**Not to see the wood for the trees.** To fail to pick out the essentials from the surrounding mass of detail; not to recognize the main issues or facts of the matter.

**Wait and see.** *See under* WAIT.

**We shall see.** Let us await the outcome; we may not do what has been planned or asked.

**You see.** You understand; you will appreciate the situation. The phrase is sometimes used apologetically or to preface an excuse.

> At the hotel we had separate rooms, but in the middle of the night she came sobbing into mine, and we made it up very gently. You see, she had absolutely nowhere else to go.
>
> VLADIMIR NABOKOV: *Lolita*, Pt I, ch xxxiii (1955)

**Seed. Seeded players.** Those players regarded by the organizers of a tournament (e.g. lawn tennis at the All England Club, Wimbledon) as likely to reach the final stages, and who are so placed in the order of play that they do not meet each other until the closing rounds. These players are numbered in the order of likelihood. The allusion is to sowing seeds in such a way that those of the best plants are not 'weeded out' before their time.

**Go to seed, To.** To lose one's vigour or usefulness. The allusion is to a plant that has produced its seeds and shed them.

**Seekers.** A 17th-century PURITAN sect akin to the QUAKERS in their outlook who rejected the existing church and claimed to seek the true church that God would reveal in his own time. Roger Williams (*c.*1603–83) founded Providence, NEW ENGLAND, as a refuge for the sect.

**Seian Horse, The.** A possession that invariably brings bad luck with it, hence the Latin proverb *Ille homo habet equum Seianum* ('That man has the Seian horse'). Cneius Seius had a beautiful bay horse from Argos and bred from Diomedes' horses, but it was fatal to its possessor. Seius was put to death by Mark Antony. The next owner, Cornelius Dolabella, who bought it for 100,000 sesterces, was killed in Syria during the civil wars. Caius Cassius, who next took possession of it, perished after the Battle of Philippi by the very sword that had stabbed Julius Caesar. Antony himself had the horse next and, after the Battle of Actium, killed himself. *See also* FATAL NECKLACE; HARMONIA'S NECKLACE; OPAL; SHIRT OF NESSUS.

**Seignior, Grand.** *See under* GRAND.

**Selah.** A Hebrew word occurring often in the Psalms (and three times in Habakkuk 3), indicating some musical or liturgical direction, such as a pause, a repetition or the end of a section. Its precise sense is uncertain, but it could mean 'lift up', indicating either the raising of the voice or the 'raising up' of instrumental music in an interlude to the singing.

> The Lord of hosts is with us; the God of Jacob is our refuge. Selah.
>
> Psalm 46:11

**Select. Select committee.** A fact-finding body of members selected from the whole House, such as the Select Committee on European Legislation, set up in 1974.

**Select-men.** Town officers in NEW ENGLAND deputed to be responsible for certain local concerns. They are elected annually at town meetings, and their office derives from the select vestrymen of former days. *See also* VESTRY.

**Selene.** The moon goddess of Greek mythology, corresponding approximately to the Roman DIANA. According to Hesiod she was the daughter of HYPERION and Theia; other sources say she was the daughter of Pallas (the TITAN) and Euryphaessa. Selene had 50 daughters by ENDYMION and three by ZEUS, including Herse, the dew, and Pandia. Selene is represented with a diadem and wings on her shoulders, riding in a chariot drawn by two white horses, while Diana is represented with a bow and arrow running after a stag.

**Seleucidae.** The dynasty of Seleucus Nicator (*c.*358–281 BC), one of Alexander the Great's generals who in 312 conquered Babylon and succeeded to part of Alexander's vast empire. The monarchy consisted of Syria, a large part of Asia Minor, and all the eastern provinces (Persia, Bactria and others). The last of the line was dispossessed by the Romans in 64 BC.

**Self. Self-denying Ordinance, The.** The measure passed by the LONG PARLIAMENT (April 1645) providing that Members of either House should give up their military commands and civil offices within 40 days. Nothing was said to prevent their reappointment. The indecisive second Battle of Newbury in 1644 led to this measure, which was directed against incompetent commanders, particularly in the HOUSE OF LORDS.

**Self-determination.** In politics, the concept that every nation, no matter how small or weak, has the right to decide on its own form of government and to manage its own affairs. The phrase acquired this significance during the attempts to resettle Europe after the First World War.

**Self-made man, A.** One who has risen from poverty and obscurity to comparative opulence or a position of importance by his own efforts.

**Second self.** *See under* SECOND.

**Seljuks.** The name of several Turkish dynasties descended from Seljuk, a Ghuzz (or Oghuz) chieftain, which ruled in Persia, Syria and Asia Minor between the 11th and 13th centuries. In 1055 Togril Beg (*c.*990–1063), grandson of Seljuk, was made Commander of the Faithful (*see* CALIPH) for coming to the assistance of the ABBASSID caliph of Baghdad. His successor, Alp Arslan (*c.*1030–72), great-grandson of Seljuk, took Syria and Palestine and a large part of Anatolia from the Byzantine emperor. The territories were eventually partitioned among branches of the family, but were subject to Mongol onslaughts from 1243. Their power steadily declined and their place was eventually taken by the Ottomans.

**Sell.** A swindle or hoax, so that the person swindled or hoaxed is said to be 'sold'.

**Sell-by date.** The date by which a perishable item, such as a food product, must be sold if it is to be consumed in a fresh or fit state. It is not the same as a use-by or best-before date, which is usually a day or two later. The expression has gained a facetious general sense to refer to a person who is 'getting on', so that if one is past one's sell-by date, one is past one's prime.

**Sell by the candle, To.** A form of sale by auction. A pin is thrust through a candle a short distance from the top, and bidding goes on until the candle is burned down to the pin. When the pin drops into the candlestick, the last bidder is declared the purchaser. Such an auction was held at Aldermaston and reported in the *Reading Mercury* of 16 December 1893.

**Sell down the river, To.** To deceive; to betray. The allusion is to the days when American owners sold domestic slaves to plantation owners lower down the Mississippi, where harsher conditions often prevailed.

**Selling out.** In stockbroking to sell in open exchange those shares that a purchaser failed to take up at the specified time, the original purchaser having to make good the difference between the original contract price and the price at which they are actually sold. The term also applied to an officer's retirement from the army in the days when commissions were bought and sold.

**Selling point.** An advantageous feature of a thing, which might persuade a potential purchaser to buy it.

**Selling race.** A horse race in which owners of runners must agree beforehand that the winner shall be sold at an agreed price.

**Selling the pass.** Betraying one's own side. The phrase was originally Irish and applied to those who turned King's or Queen's evidence or who impeached their comrades for money. The tradition is that a regiment was sent by Crotha, 'lord of Atha', to hold a pass against the invading army of Trathal, 'king of Cael'. The pass was betrayed for money, the Firbolgs (*see* MILESIANS) were subdued, and Trathal assumed the title of 'king of Ireland'.

**Sell like hot cakes, To.** *See* GO LIKE HOT CAKES.

**Sell off the family silver, To.** To dispose of valuable assets that, once gone, cannot be retrieved. The allusion was made memorable from its use in a speech by Sir Harold Macmillan to the Tory Reform Group on 8 November 1985 in which he criticized the Thatcher government's privatization of nationalized industries.

**Sell oneself, To.** To convince a person of one's true worth or competence.

**Sell-out, A.** A betrayal. The expression originated in the USA for a corrupt agreement by a public body that involves a sacrifice of the public interest to the private.

**Sell short, To.** A STOCK EXCHANGE phrase meaning to sell stock that one does not at the moment possess, on the chance that it may be acquired at a lower rate before the date of delivery. It is the same as selling for a fall or selling a BEAR.

**Sell the** or **a dummy, To.** In rugby to deceive an opponent by pretending to pass the ball to a team-mate but then continuing to run with it.

**Sell the skin before one has caught the bear, To.** To COUNT ONE'S CHICKENS BEFORE THEY ARE HATCHED. Shakespeare alludes to a similar practice:

> The man that once did sell the lion's skin
> While the beast lived, was killed with hunting him.
> *Henry V*, IV, iii (1598)

**Sold a pup, To be.** To be swindled. The allusion is to selling something that is worth far less than one expects. A pup is only a small young dog, who will have to be trained.

**Bestseller.** *See under* BEST.

**Bill of sale.** *See under* BILL.

**Hard sell.** *See under* HARD.

**Soft sell.** *See under* SOFT.

**Sellinger's round.** An old country dance, very popular in Elizabethan times, in which:

the dancers take hands, go round twice and back again; then all set, turn, and repeat; then lead all forward, and back, and repeat; two singles and back, set and turn single and repeat; arms all and repeat.
JOHN PLAYFORD: *The English Dancing Master* (1651)

It is said to be so called either from Sir Thomas Sellynger, buried in St George's Chapel, Windsor, *c.*1470, or from Sir Anthony Saint-Leger, Lord Deputy of Ireland (*c.*1496–1559).

**Semele.** In Greek mythology the daughter of CADMUS and Harmonia. By ZEUS she was the mother of Dionysus (BACCHUS) and was slain by lightning when he granted her request to visit her in his glory. Dionysus went to the Underworld to search for her, and she was taken up into heaven and given the name Thyone. For his oratorio *Semele* (1744), which tells the story of Semele's love for Zeus and which contains the well-known aria 'Where'er you walk', Handel adapted the libretto William Congreve had written for the opera, also called *Semele*, by John Eccles (*c.*1650–1735).

**Semiramis.** In ancient legend the daughter of the goddess Derceto and a young Assyrian. She married Menones, but he hanged himself when NINUS, king of Assyria and founder of Nineveh, demanded Semiramis from him. She forthwith married Ninus, who was so smitten that he resigned the crown to her. After this she put him to death, but was herself ultimately slain by her son Ninyas. She is sometimes identified with ISHTAR and her doves. These and other legends accumulated around an Assyrian princess of this name who lived *c.*800 BC. The name itself derives from Akkadian *Shammuramat*, 'friend of doves'. *See also* HANGING GARDENS OF BABYLON.

**Semiramis of the North, The.** Margaret of Denmark, Sweden and Norway (1353–1412) and Catherine the Great of Russia (1729–96) have both been so called.

**Semitic.** Pertaining to the descendants of SHEM (*see* Genesis 10), i.e. the Hebrews, Arabs, Assyrians, Aramaeans and others. The name is nowadays applied to the Jews.

**Semitic languages.** The ancient Afro-Asiatic branch of languages that includes Akkadian, Aramaic, Amharic, Syriac, Arabic, Hebrew, Samaritan and Phoenician.

**Semper aliquid novi Africam adferre** (Latin, 'Africa always brings something new'). A Greek proverb quoted by Pliny (1st century AD) in allusion to the belief that Africa abounded in strange monsters. It is often quoted as *Ex Africa semper aliquid novi* ('Always something new out of Africa'), in which form it provided the title of Karen Blixen's classic account *Out of Africa* (1937) and of the film (1985) based on it.

**Send. Send a shot across someone's bows, To.** To give them a warning. The allusion is to an encounter with an enemy or potential enemy at sea.

**Send someone about their business, To.** To dismiss them; to send them away.

**Send someone packing, To.** To dismiss them summarily.

'Rouse up, sirs! Give your brains a racking
To find the remedy we're lacking,
Or, sure as fate, we'll send you packing!'
ROBERT BROWNING: 'The Pied Piper of Hamelin' (1842)

**Send the axe after the helve, To.** To THROW THE HELVE AFTER THE HATCHET.

**Send the cap round, To.** To make a collection. From the custom of street musicians, singers and the like, sending a cap round to collect pennies among the onlookers.

**Send to Coventry, To.** To ostracize a person or to ignore them. It is said that the citizens of Coventry once had so great a dislike of soldiers that a woman seen speaking to one was instantly outlawed. Hence when a soldier was sent to Coventry he was cut off from all social intercourse. Edward Hyde, Earl of Clarendon, in his *History of the Great Rebellion* (1702–4), says that Royalist prisoners captured in Birmingham were sent to Coventry, which was a Parliamentary stronghold. *See also* BOYCOTT.

**Sent down, To be.** To be sent from a university as a punishment.

**Sent off with a flea in one's ear, To be.** To be sent away discomfited by a reproof or repulse. A dog that has a flea in its ear is restless and runs around in distress. The expression dates from at least the 15th century in English, and earlier in French.

And manye oothere grete wundres [ye haue seyd] whiche ben fleen in myne eres.
*Pilgrimage of the Lyf of the Manhode* (from the French of Guillaume de Guilleville) (*c.*1430)

**Sent up the river, To be.** In American colloquial usage, to be sent to prison, from the fact that Sing Sing, one of the most widely known prisons, is at Ossining, up the Hudson River from New York.

**That sends me.** A now dated phrase used of certain lively or emotional music, which sends its hearers into ecstasies.

**Sennacherib.** In the Old Testament (2 Kings 18, 19), the Assyrian king who besieged JUDAH only to have 5000 of his men killed by an angel while they were asleep. He thereupon returned to Nineveh, where he was murdered by his two sons, Adrammelech and Sharezer, who 'escaped into the land of Armenia'.

**Se'nnight.** A week, literally seven nights, on the same lines as 'fortnight' for fourteen nights.

These words are relics of the ancient Celtic custom of beginning the day at sunset, a custom observed by the ancient Greeks, Babylonians, Persians, Syrians and Jews, and by the modern heirs of these peoples. Genesis 1:5 tells how the evening precedes the morning, as: 'The evening and the morning were the first day.' The word for a week in some languages still contains the notion of seven days or nights, as French *semaine*, from ecclesiastical Latin *septimana*.

> He shall live a man forbid.
> Weary se'nnights nine times nine
> Shall he dwindle, peak and pine.
> SHAKESPEARE: *Macbeth*, I, iii (1605)

**Sense.** Sense has the general meaning of 'mental perception', so, for example, to take leave of one's senses is to behave in an irrational or crazy way.

**Bring someone to their senses, To.** *See under* BRING.

**Come to one's senses, To.** *See under* COME.

**Common sense.** *See under* COMMON.

**Five senses.** *See under* FIVE.

**Horse sense.** *See under* HORSE.

**Road sense.** *See under* ROAD.

**Seven senses, The.** *See under* SEVEN.

**Sixth sense.** *See under* SIX.

**Take leave of one's senses, To.** To go mad; to act irrationally.

**Sensitive plant.** *See* MIMOSA.

**Sentence. Life sentence.** *See under* LIFE.

**Master of the Sentences.** *See under* MASTER.

**Serve a sentence, To.** *See under* SERVE.

**Separate. Separate** or **sort out the men from the boys, To.** To separate the experienced from the inexperienced; to distinguish those who can from those who can't.

**Separate the sheep from the goats, To.** To divide the worthy from the unworthy, the good from the evil, the favoured from the disfavoured. The allusion is biblical. *See also* SEPARATE THE WHEAT FROM THE CHAFF.

> And before him shall be gathered all nations; and he shall separate them one from another, as a shepherd divideth his sheep from the goats.
> Matthew 25:32

**Separate the wheat from the chaff, To.** To distinguish the good from the bad. The comparison is implicit in certain biblical texts.

> What is the chaff to the wheat? saith the Lord.
> Jeremiah 23:28

**Separatists.** A name given to the INDEPENDENTS of the 17th century who separated from the Established Church.

**Sephardim.** The Jews of Spain and Portugal, as distinct from those of Poland and Germany, called Ashkenazim (from the location given in Genesis 10:3). The name is from Sepharad (Obadiah 20) where Jews were in captivity. The TARGUM of Jonathan wrongly identified it with Spain, possibly from some similarity with Hesperis, hence the application of the name to Spanish Jews.

**Sept.** From Old French *septe*, possibly a variant of *secte* or sect, a term especially applied to an Irish CLAN, which was a division of the tribe. The freemen of the sept bore the clan name with the prefix Ua, grandson, written in English as O.

**September.** The seventh month from MARCH, when the year formerly commenced. The old Dutch name was *Herstmaand*, 'autumn month', and the Anglo-Saxon *Hærfestmōnath*, 'harvest month', or after the introduction of Christianity *Hāligmōnath*, 'holy month', the nativity of the Virgin MARY being on the 8th, the EXALTATION OF THE CROSS or HOLY CROSS DAY on the 14th and St MICHAEL's Day on the 29th. In the FRENCH REVOLUTIONARY CALENDAR the equivalent month was *Fructidor*, 'fruit month', corresponding to the period from 19 August to 22 September.

**September Bible, The.** *See under* BIBLE.

**September Massacres, The.** An indiscriminate slaughter during the French Revolution, directed at the royalists confined in the Abbaye and other prisons, lasting from 2 to 7 September 1792. Over 1500 were massacred with revolting brutalities. It was occasioned by the dismay at the fall of Verdun to the Prussians. Those taking part in the atrocities were called Septembrists.

**Black September.** *See under* BLACK.

**Septentrional signs.** The first six signs of the ZODIAC, because they belong to the northern celestial hemisphere. The north was called the septentrion from the SEVEN STARS of the GREAT BEAR (Latin *septem*, 'seven', and *triones*, 'ploughing oxen'). *See also* URSA MAJOR.

**Septuagesima Sunday.** The third Sunday before LENT, which in round numbers is 70 (in fact 64) days (Latin *septuagesima dies*) before EASTER.

**Septuagint** (Latin *septuaginta*, 'seventy'). The most important Greek version of the OLD TESTAMENT and APOCRYPHA, so called because it was traditionally said to have been translated from the Hebrew SCRIPTURES by 72 learned Jews in the 3rd century BC, at the command of Ptolemy II, known as Philadelphus (308–246 BC), for the Alexandrian Library. They worked on the island of Pharos and completed the task in 72 days.

The name Septuagint is commonly abbreviated as LXX. The translation was probably the work of Jewish scholars at Alexandria working over a long period of time.

**Sepulchre. Holy Sepulchre, The.** *See under* HOLY.

**Knights of the Holy Sepulchre.** *See under* KNIGHT.

**Whited sepulchre.** *See under* WHITE.

**Seraglio.** The word is Italian, from Persian *saray*, 'palace', and especially denotes the former palace of the SULTANS at Constantinople, situated on the GOLDEN HORN and enclosed by walls containing many buildings. The chief entrance was the Sublime Gate (*see* PORTE), and the chief edifice the harem or 'forbidden spot', which contained numerous dwellings, both for the sultan's wives and for his concubines. The seraglio was able to be visited by strangers, but not the harem. Mozart's opera *Die Entführung aus dem Serail* ('The Abduction from the Seraglio') was first performed in Vienna in 1782.

**Seraphic. Seraphic Blessing.** The blessing written by St FRANCIS OF ASSISI at the request of Brother Leo on Mount Alvernia in 1224. It is based on Numbers 6:24: 'May the Lord bless thee and keep thee. May he show His face to thee and have mercy on thee. May he turn his countenance on thee and give thee peace. May the Lord bless thee, Brother Leo.'

**Seraphic Doctor, The.** The Scholastic philosopher, St Bonaventura (1221–74).

**Seraphic Father** or **Saint, The.** St FRANCIS OF ASSISI (1182–1226), whence the FRANCISCANS are sometimes called the Seraphic Order.

**Seraphic Hymn, The.** The Sanctus, 'Holy, holy, holy' (Isaiah 6:3), which was sung by the SERAPHIM.

**Seraphim.** The highest of the nine choirs of ANGELS, so named from the seraphim of Isaiah 6:2. The word is perhaps the same as *saraf*, 'a serpent', from *saraf*, 'it burned', possibly alluding to the 'fiery serpents' that 'bit the people' in Numbers 21:6. The connection with burning suggested to early Christian interpreters that the seraphim were specially distinguished by their zeal and love.

Seraphim is a plural form. The singular, seraph, was first used in English by Milton. ABDIEL was

> The flaming Seraph, fearless, though alone,
> Encompassed round with foes.
> *Paradise Lost*, v (1667)

**Serapis.** The Ptolemaic form of APIS, an Egyptian deity who, when dead, was honoured under the attributes of OSIRIS. He was lord of the underworld, and was identified by the Greeks with HADES. His name represents Egyptian *Usar-Hep*, 'dead Apis'.

**Serat, Al.** *See* AL-SIRAT.

**Serbonian Bog, The.** A great morass, now covered with shifting sand, between the isthmus of Suez, the Mediterranean and the Nile delta. In Strabo's time it was a lake, stated by him to be 200 stadia long and 50 broad, and by Pliny to be 150 miles (240km) long. TYPHOEUS was said to dwell at the bottom of it, hence its other name, Typhoeus' Breathing Hole.

> A gulf profound as that Serbonian bog,
> Betwixt Damiata and Mount Casius old,
> Where armies whole have sunk.
> MILTON: *Paradise Lost*, ii (1667)

The term is used figuratively of a mess from which there is no way of extricating oneself.

**Serendipity.** A happy coinage by Horace Walpole to denote the faculty of making lucky and unexpected 'finds' by accident. In a letter to Sir Horace Mann (28 January 1754) he says that he formed it on the title of a fairy story, *The Three Princes of Serendip*, because the princes

> were always making discoveries, by accidents and sagacity, of things they were not in quest of.

Serendip is an ancient name of Ceylon (modern Sri Lanka), and is a corruption of Sanskrit *Sinhaladvipa*, 'Sinhalese island'.

**Serene** (Latin *serenus*, 'clear', 'calm'). A title mainly given formerly to certain German princes. Those who used to hold it under the empire were entitled Serene or Most Serene Highnesses.

**All serene.** *See under* ALL.

**Sergeanty** or **serjeanty.** Various forms of land tenure akin to KNIGHT SERVICE involving military service or some form of household service for the king or lord, such as looking after his wine. Serjeanty comes from Norman French *serjantie* (Latin *serviens*, 'servant'). They eventually came to be classed as Grand Serjeanties and Petit or Petty Serjeanties, the latter involving some obligation such as the rendering of a bow or a sword. These services were retained when military tenures were abolished in 1661.

The old royal manor of Woodstock, the site of BLENHEIM PALACE, was granted to the Duke of Marlborough 'in grand serjeanty', as a mark of the nation's gratitude for his victory over the French and Bavarians at Blenheim in 1704. The incidents were preserved by the Law of Property Acts, 1922 and 1925.

**Serjeants-at-Arms.** Officials of the royal household with certain ceremonial functions. In addition, there is the SPEAKER's Serjeant-at-Arms in the HOUSE OF COMMONS, who carries the MACE and acts as the disciplinary officer, and another who carries the mace of the LORD CHANCELLOR in the HOUSE OF LORDS.

**Serjeants-at-law.** A superior order of barristers superseded by KING'S COUNSEL in 1877. Their title comes from Low Latin *servientes ad legem*, those who serve the king in matters of law. They formed an Inn called Serjeants' Inn which was in Fleet Street and later in Chancery Lane.

**Colour sergeant.** *See under* COLOUR.

**Lance sergeant.** *See under* LANCE.

**Sergius.** Patron of Moscow and later of all Russia, St Sergius of Radonezh (1315–92) is the most loved and honoured of all Russian saints. He was the founder of many monasteries and a teacher of simple communal life in accord with nature. He was buried in his monastery church at Sergiyev near Moscow, a place of unceasing pilgrimage even in Soviet times (when the town was renamed Zagorsk).

**Sermon. Sermon on the Mount, The.** The long discourse delivered by Christ to a crowd assembled on a mountainside, noted especially for the eight BEATITUDES contained within it. *See also* SERMON ON THE PLAIN.

**Sermon on the Plain, The.** A discourse delivered by Christ to a crowd gathered on the plain. It is similar to the SERMON ON THE MOUNT but is briefer, with only four BEATITUDES. As cited by Luke 6:20–22, blessed are: (1) ye poor: for yours is the kingdom of God; (2) ye that hunger now: for ye shall be filled; (3) ye that weep now: for ye shall laugh; (4) ye, when men shall hate you, and when they shall separate you from their company, and shall reproach you, and cast out your name as evil, for the Son of man's sake.

**Action sermon.** *See under* ACTION.

**Lion Sermon.** *See under* LION.

**Spital sermons.** *See under* SPITAL.

**Serpent.** The serpent is symbolical of:

(1) Deity: according to Plutarch 'it feeds upon its own body, even so all things spring from God and will be resolved into deity again'
(2) Eternity (as a corollary of the former): it is represented as forming a circle, holding its tail in its mouth
(3) Renovation and the healing art: it is said that when old, it has the power of growing young again 'like the eagle', by sloughing its skin, which it does by squeezing itself between two rocks. It was sacred to AESCULAPIUS and was supposed to have the power of discovering healing herbs. *See also* CADUCEUS
(4) A guardian spirit: it was thus employed by the ancient Greeks and Romans and not infrequently the figure of a serpent was depicted on their altars. In the temple of ATHENE at Athens a serpent, believed to be animated by the soul of ERICHTHONIUS, was kept in a cage and called the Guardian Spirit of the Temple
(5) Wisdom: 'Be ye therefore wise as serpents and harmless as doves' (Matthew 10:16)
(6) Subtlety: 'Now the serpent was more subtil than any beast of the field' (Genesis 3:1)
(7) The DEVIL: as the Tempter (Genesis 3:1–6); in early pictures the serpent is sometimes placed under the feet of the Virgin MARY, in allusion to the promise made to EVE after the Fall (Genesis 3:15)

In Christian art the serpent is an attribute of St CECILIA, St Euphemia, St PATRICK and many other saints, either because they trampled on SATAN, or because they miraculously cleared some country of snakes.

Fable has it that the cerastes (horned viper) hides in sand that it may bite the horse's foot and get the rider thrown. In allusion to this belief, Jacob says: 'Dan shall be a serpent by the way, an adder in the path, that biteth the horse heels, so that his rider shall fall backward' (Genesis 49:17). The Bible also tells that the serpent stops up its ears lest it be charmed by the charmers, 'charming never so wisely' (Psalm 58:4, 5).

Another old idea about snakes was that when attacked they would swallow their young and not eject them until reaching a place of safety.

It was in the form of a serpent, runs the legend, that JUPITER AMMON appeared to Olympia and became by her the father of Alexander the Great. *See also* SNAKE.

**Serpentine.** The long curved lake in Hyde Park and Kensington Gardens was created when the small River Westbourne was dammed in 1730, the idea originating with Caroline of Anspach (1683–1737), consort of George II. It has long been popular for swimming and boating in summer and for skating in winter, and has a less fortunate claim to fame as a chosen spot for suicides. Its name refers to its winding shape.

**Serpentine verses.** Verses that begin and end with the same word. The following are examples:

> Crescit amor nummi, quantum ipsa pecunia crescit.
> (Greater grows the love of money, as money itself grows greater).
>
> Ambo florentes aetatibus, Arcades ambo.
> (Both in the spring of life, Arcadians both).

The allusion is to the old representations of snakes with their tails in their mouths, having no beginning and no end.

**Cherish a serpent in one's bosom, To.** *See under* CHERISH.

**Old Serpent, The.** *See under* OLD.

**Pharaoh's serpent.** *See under* PHARAOH.

**Sea serpent.** *See under* SEA.

**Sertorius, The hind of.** *See under* HIND.

**Servant. Servant of two masters, A.** A parable told by Christ in Luke 16, the import being that no man can serve two masters and that therefore each person must choose between 'God and MAMMON'. Carlo Goldoni has a comedy *The Servant of Two Masters* (1745).

**Is thy servant a dog?** Said in contempt when asked to do something derogatory or beneath one. The phrase is from 2 Kings 8:13. When Sir Edwin Landseer, the celebrated painter of dogs and animals, asked John Gibson Lockhart if he would like to sit for his portrait, Lockhart's answer was: 'Is thy servant a dog that he should do this thing?' The phrase was adopted and much used by Sydney Smith.

**What did your last servant die of?** *See under* WHAT.

**Serve. Serve a mare, To.** To place a stallion to her for breeding.

**Serve a rope, To.** To wind a rope around with spun yarn or other suitable cord or twine, to protect it from wet or chafing. Serving is always put on against the lay of the rope.

**Serve a sentence, To.** To undergo the punishment awarded.

**Serve a writ on someone, To.** To deliver a legal writ into the hands of the person concerned.

**Serve its turn, To.** To answer the purpose; to be sufficient for the occasion, sometimes with the implication of being a makeshift or of barely meeting requirements.

**Serve one's time, To.** To hold an office or appointment for the full period allowed; to go through one's apprenticeship; to go through one's length of service in the armed forces; to serve one's sentence in a prison.

**Serve you right!** You got what you deserved.

**First come, first served.** *See under* FIRST.

**Service. Break service, To.** *See under* BREAK.

**Civil service.** *See under* CIVIL.

**Diplomatic service.** *See under* DIPLOMAT.

**Eye service.** *See under* EYE.

**Lip service.** *See under* LIP.

**Secret Service.** *See under* SECRET.

**Yeoman service.** *See under* YEOMAN.

**Servus servorum** (Latin). The slave of slaves; the drudge of a servant. *Servus servorum Dei* ('the servant of the servants of God') is one of the honorific epithets of the pope. It was first adopted by GREGORY THE GREAT (r.590–604).

**Sesame!, Open.** *See under* OPEN.

**Sesquipedalian.** A word sometimes applied in heavy irony to cumbersome and pedantic words. It comes from Horace's *sesquipedalia verba*, words a foot-and-a-half long.

> 'Sesquippledan,' he would say. 'Sesquippledan verboojuice'.
>
> H.G. WELLS: *The History of Mr Polly*, ch i (1909)

**Session. Bull session.** *See under* BULL.

**Court of Session.** *See under* COURT.

**Jam session.** *See under* JAM.

**Sestina.** A set form of poem, usually rhymed, with six stanzas of six lines each and a final triplet. The terminal words of stanzas 2–6 are the same as those of stanza 1 but arranged differently. Sestinas were invented by the Provençal TROUBADOUR Arnaut Daniel (13th century). Dante, Petrarch and others employed them in Italy, Cervantes and Camoëns in Spain and Portugal, and an early use in English was by William Drummond of Hawthornden (1585–1649). A.C. Swinburne's sestinas are probably the best in English.

**Set** or **Seth.** The Egyptian original of the Greek TYPHOEUS. He was the jealous brother of OSIRIS whom he murdered by tricking him into a coffer, nailing the lid and having it sealed with molten lead. He was later castrated by HORUS and came to be regarded as the incarnation of evil. He is represented as having the body of a man with a thin, curved snout and square-shaped ears, and sometimes with a tail and the body of an animal, which has not been identified with any certainty, although some say his body resembles that of a massive dog.

**Set.** The word set has a multitude of meanings, and the *Oxford English Dictionary* records 58 noun uses, 126 verbal uses and 10 uses as a participial adjective. Some of the more common and colourful phrases with the word are given below.

**Set about someone, To.** To attack them physically or verbally.

**Set eyes on, To.** To see; to catch sight of. The phrase is often used negatively, as: 'I'd never set eyes on her before.'

**Set off on the wrong foot, To.** To make an inauspicious start. The opposite is 'to set off on the right foot'.

**Set off something to advantage, To.** To display something in its best light.

**Set on a pedestal, To.** To idolize or to idealize. From the custom of showing reverence to figures of saints and others set on pedestals.

**Set one's cap at, To.** Of a woman, to try to win a man as one's lover or husband. In the days when ladies habitually wore caps they would naturally put on the most becoming to attract the attention of the favoured gentleman.

**Set one's face against something, To.** To oppose something firmly; to resist its being done.

**Set one's hand to, To.** To sign; to begin a task.

**Set one's heart on something, To.** To earnestly desire something.

**Set one's mind on, To.** To be firmly resolved on; to aim to achieve or obtain.

**Set one's seal on** or **to something, To.** To give it one's authority; to authenticate it. From the affixing of seals to documents as an official sign of their authenticity.

**Set one's sights on, To.** To aim for; to strive to achieve, as: 'He's set his sights on winning.'

**Set one's teeth, To.** To clench them, usually as a sign of determination.

**Set one's teeth on edge, To.** Literally, to cause a tingling or grating sensation in one's teeth, as from a harsh noise. Figuratively, to jar one's nerves or irritate one.

> In those days they shall say no more, The fathers have eaten a sour grape, and the children's teeth are set on edge.
>
> Jeremiah 31:29

**Set piece.** In the theatre a piece of scenery designed to stand independently on a stage set. Also, a fireworks display.

**Set sail, To.** To start a voyage.

**Set scene, A.** In theatrical parlance a scene built up by the stage carpenters, or a furnished interior, as a drawing room, as distinct from an ordinary or shifting scene.

**Set someone's mind at rest, To.** To reassure them.

**Set store by, To.** To value highly.

**Set the ball rolling.** *See* START THE BALL ROLLING.

**Set the pace, To.** To set the standard for others to emulate or keep up with, as in a race.

**Set** or **put the record straight, To.** To correct a mis-statement or a misunderstanding.

**Set the scene, To.** To indicate to an audience where the action of a play is taking place and what has prompted it. *See also* SET THE STAGE.

**Set the stage, To.** To prepare the way for something. *See also* SET THE SCENE.

**Set the Thames on fire, To.** Usually used in such expressions as 'he'll never set the Thames on fire', meaning 'he'll never make a name for himself', 'he'll never do anything memorable'. The popular explanation is that the word Thames is a pun on the word 'temse', a corn sieve, and that the parallel French locution 'he will never set the Seine on fire' is a pun on 'seine', a dragnet. But these solutions are not tenable. There is a Latin saw, *Tiberum accendere nequaquam potest* ('He can in no wise set the Tiber on fire'), which is probably the source of other parallel sayings. The Germans had *den Rhein anzünden* ('to set the Rhine on fire') as early as 1630.

> His second novel was successful, but not so successful as to arouse the umbrageous susceptibilities of his competitors. In fact it confirmed them in their suspicions that he would never set the Thames on fire.
>
> W. SOMERSET MAUGHAM: *Cakes and Ale*, ch i (1930)

**Setting of a jewel.** The frame or mount of gold or silver surrounding a jewel in a ring, brooch or the like.

> This precious stone set in the silver sea.
>
> SHAKESPEARE: *Richard II*, II, i (1595)

**Setting of the current, The.** The direction or point of the compass towards which the current flows.

**Set-to, A.** A fight or a tussle, literally or verbally. In pugilism the combatants were by their seconds 'set to the scratch' or line marked on the ground. *See also* COME UP TO SCRATCH.

**Set-up, A.** An event, such as a sporting contest, whose result or outcome has been prearranged.

**All set.** *See under* ALL.

**Cliveden set, The.** *See under* CLIVEDEN.

**Dead set against.** *See under* DEAD.

**Setebos.** A god or demon worshipped by the Patagonians, and introduced by Shakespeare into *The Tempest* as the god of Sycorax, CALIBAN's mother.

> His art is of such power,
> It would control my dam's god, Setebos,
> And make a vassal of him.
>
> *The Tempest*, I, ii (1611)

The cult of Setebos was first known in Europe through Magellan's voyage around the world, 1519–21.

**Settle. Settle a score, To.** To settle accounts, a phrase used sometimes of money debts, but usually in the sense of revenging an injury, of 'getting even' with someone.

**Settle one's affairs, To.** To make the necessary arrangements when death is near, especially by making a will.

**Settle out of court, To.** To agree on the sum to be paid in a case, through the two sides' solicitors, without it going to court.

**Settle someone's hash, To.** To subdue or silence someone; to 'fix' them. The 'hash' here is a jumble or mess.

**Seven.** A mystic or sacred number. It is composed of four and three, which among the Pythagoreans were, and FROM TIME IMMEMORIAL have been, accounted lucky numbers. Among the Babylonians, Egyptians and other ancient peoples there were seven sacred planets, and the Hebrew verb 'to swear' means literally 'to come under the influence of seven things'. Thus seven ewe lambs figure in the oath between ABRAHAM and ABIMELECH at Beersheba (Genesis 21:28), and Herodotus (*Histories*, III, viii (5th century BC)) describes an Arabian oath in which seven stones are smeared with blood.

There are seven days in creation, seven days in the week, SEVEN VIRTUES, seven divisions in the Lord's Prayer, seven ages in the life of man, climacteric years are seven and nine with their multiples by odd numbers, and the seventh son of a seventh son was always held notable.

Among the Hebrews every seventh year was SABBATICAL, and seven times seven years was the JUBILEE. The three great Jewish feasts lasted seven days, and between the first and second were seven weeks. Levitical purifications lasted seven days. The number is associated with a variety of occurrences in the Old Testament.

The Book of Revelation tells of SEVEN CHURCHES OF ASIA, seven candlesticks, seven stars, seven trumpets, seven spirits before the throne of God, seven horns, seven vials, seven plagues, a seven-headed monster and the Lamb with seven eyes.

The old astrologers and alchemists recognized seven planets, each having its own 'heaven'. *See also* SEVEN BODIES.

**Seven, The.** Used of groups of seven people, especially:

(1) the 'men of honest report' chosen by the APOSTLES to be the first Deacons (Acts 6:5), i.e. Stephen, Philip, Prochorus, Nicanor, Timon, Parmenas and Nicolas
(2) the SEVEN BISHOPS
(3) the Seven Sages of Greece (WISE MEN OF GREECE)

The original members of the European Free Trade Association (EFTA) formed in 1959 and comprising Denmark, Norway, Sweden, Austria, Portugal, Switzerland and the United Kingdom, were known as 'The Seven' as distinct from the SIX.

**Seven against Thebes, The.** An expedition in Greek legend, fabled to have taken place against Thebes of Boeotia before the TROJAN WAR. The Seven were the Argive chiefs POLYNICES, Eteocles, Tydeus, Amphiaraus, Hippomedon, Capaneus and Parthenopaeus. (In some versions of the legend ADRASTUS is substituted for Polynices or Eteocles.) When OEDIPUS abdicated, his two sons agreed to reign alternate years, but at the end of the first year, the elder, Eteocles, refused to give up the throne, whereupon Polynices, the younger brother, induced the chiefs to espouse his cause. The allied army laid siege to Thebes, but without success, and all the heroes perished except Adrastus. Subsequently, seven sons of the chiefs, resolved to avenge their fathers' deaths, marched against the city, took it and placed Terpander, one of their number on the throne. These are known as the *Epigoni* (Greek, 'descendants'). The poets Aeschylus and Euripides dramatized the legend. *See also* NEMEAN GAMES.

**Seven ages of man, The.** According to Jaques in Shakespeare's *As You Like It,* II, vii (1599) the seven ages of man are: (1) the infant, (2) the schoolboy, (3) the lover, (4) the soldier, (5) the justice, (6) the pantaloon and (7) SECOND CHILDHOOD.

**Seven Bishops, The.** Archbishop Sancroft of Canterbury, and Bishops Lloyd of St Asaph, Turner of Ely, Ken of Bath and Wells, White of Peterborough, Lake of Chichester and Trelawny of Bristol, who petitioned James II against the order to have his second Declaration of Indulgence read in every church on two successive Sundays (20 and 27 May 1688). James foolishly sent them to the TOWER OF LONDON and had them duly tried on a charge of seditious libel. They were acquitted amid universal rejoicing. *See also* NONJURORS.

> And have they fix'd the where and when?
> And shall Trelawny die?
> Here's twenty thousand Cornish men
> Will know the reason why!
>
> R.S. HAWKER: 'Song of the Western Men' (19th century)

**Seven bodies, The.** According to alchemists, the seven metals believed to correspond with the seven PLANETS.

> As for the seven bodies I mention
> Here they all are, if they are worth attention:
> Gold for the sun and silver for the moon,
> Iron for Mars and quicksilver in tune
> With Mercury, lead which prefigures Saturn
> And tin for Jupiter. Copper takes the pattern
> Of Venus if you please!
>
> CHAUCER: 'The Canon's Yeoman's Tale' (*c.*1387) (modern translation by Nevill Coghill, 1951)

**Seven Champions, The.** The medieval designation of the national patron saints of England, Scotland, Wales, Ireland, France, Spain and Italy. In about 1597 Richard Johnson (1573–*c.*1659) published a chapbook *The Famous History of the Seven Champions of Christendom*. In this he relates that St GEORGE of England was for seven years imprisoned by the Almidor, the black king of Morocco; St DENYS of France lived in the form of a hart for seven years; St JAMES THE GREAT of Spain was dumb for seven years through love of a fair Jewess; St Anthony of Italy, with the other champions, was enchanted into a deep sleep in the Black Castle, and was released by St George's three sons, who quenched the seven lamps by water from the enchanted fountain; St ANDREW of Scotland liberated six ladies who had lived seven years under the form of white swans; St PATRICK of Ireland was immured in a cell where he scratched his grave with his own nails; and St DAVID of Wales slept for seven years in the enchanted garden of Ormandine before being redeemed by St George. *See also* KALYB.

**Seven churches of Asia, The.** Those churches mentioned in Revelation 1:11, that is:

- Ephesus: founded by St PAUL in 57, but in a ruinous state in the time of Justinian
- Smyrna: POLYCARP was its first bishop
- Pergamum: renowned for its library
- Thyatira: now called Ak-Hissar ('White Castle')
- Sardis: now Sart, a small village
- Philadelphia: now called Allah Shehr ('City of God')
- Laodicea: now a deserted place called Eski-Hissar ('Old Castle')

**Seven corporal works of mercy, The.** According to Matthew 25:35–45 the seven corporal works of mercy are: (1) to tend the sick, (2) to feed the hungry, (3) to give drink to the thirsty, (4) to clothe the naked, (5) to harbour the stranger, (6) to minister to prisoners, and (7) to bury the dead. *See also* SEVEN SPIRITUAL WORKS OF MERCY.

**Seven Deacons, The.** In Acts 6:1–6, the 'seven men of honest report, full of the Holy Ghost and wisdom'. These are held to be the first deacons of the church. Their names were Stephen, Philip, Prochorus, Nicanor, Timon, Parmenas and Nicolas.

**Seven deadly** or **capital sins, The.** Pride, covetousness, lust, envy, gluttony, anger and sloth ('accidie').

**Seven Dials.** St Giles in the Fields, HOLBORN. When first developed in the reign of Charles II a DORIC pillar with (actually) six sundials stood facing the seven streets radiating from it, two of the streets opening on one face of the dial-stone. The column and dials were removed in 1773 and in 1882 set up on Weybridge Green. The district came to be notorious for squalor, vice, crime and degradation generally and was long the headquarters of the ballad printers and balladmongers. In 1989 a new pillar with dials was erected on the original site and ceremoniously unveiled by Queen Beatrix of the Netherlands.

Hearts just as pure and fair
May beat in Belgrave Square
As in the lowly air
Of Seven Dials!

W.S. GILBERT: *Iolanthe*, I (1882)

**Seven Dwarfs, The.** The dwarfs who try to protect SNOW WHITE in the film *Snow White and the Seven Dwarfs* (1937). They whistle while they work and individually are Happy, Sleepy, Doc, Bashful, Sneezy, Grumpy and Dopey.

**Seveners.** The Isma'ilis, a SHI'ITE following of Isma'il, whom they hold to be the seventh IMAM. They include the ASSASSINS, Carmathians, DRUSES and FATIMIDS. *See also* TWELVERS.

**Seven gifts of the Holy Spirit, The.** (1) Wisdom, (2) understanding, (3) counsel, (4) fortitude, (5) knowledge, (6) piety and (7) fear of the Lord. The list is taken from the VULGATE text of Isaiah 11:2, which adds *pietas* (piety) to the six in the AUTHORIZED VERSION (*see under* BIBLE).

**Seven Gods of Luck, The** (Japanese *Shichi-fuku-jin*). In Japanese folklore they are: (1) Benten, goddess of music, (2) Bishamon, god of war, (3) Daikoku, god of wealth, (4) Ebisu, god of commerce, (5 and 6) Fukurokuju and Jurojin, gods of longevity, and (7) Hotei, god of joviality.

**Seven heavens, The.** Among Muslims the seven heavens are:

(1) Pure silver: here the stars, each with its ANGEL warder, are hung out like lamps on golden chains. It is the abode of ADAM and EVE.
(2) Pure gold: it is the domain of JOHN THE BAPTIST and Jesus.
(3) Pearl: it is allotted to JOSEPH. Here AZRAEL is stationed and is forever writing in a large book (the names of the new-born) or blotting names out (those of the newly dead).
(4) White gold: it is Enoch's. Here dwells the angel of Tears, whose height is '500 days' journey' and who sheds ceaseless tears for the sins of man.
(5) Silver: it is AARON's. Here dwells the Avenging Angel, who presides over elemental fire.
(6) Ruby and garnet: presided over by MOSES. Here dwells the Guardian Angel of heaven and earth, half snow and half fire.
(7) Formed of divine light beyond the power of tongue to describe: it is ruled by ABRAHAM. Each inhabitant is bigger than the whole earth and has 70,000 heads, each head 70,000 faces and each face 70,000 mouths, each mouth 70,000 tongues and each tongue speaks 70,000 languages, all for ever employed in chanting the praises of the Most High.

**Seven hills of Rome, The.** The Palatine, Capitoline, Aventine, Caelian, Esquiline, Viminal and QUIRINAL or Colline. The walls of ancient Rome were built about them.

**Seven joys of Mary, The.** The seven joys of the Virgin Mary are: the ANNUNCIATION, the VISITATION, the NATIVITY, the EPIPHANY, the Finding in the Temple, the Resurrection and the Ascension. *See also* SEVEN SORROWS OF MARY.

**Seven-leagued boots.** The boots worn by the giant in the fairy tale called *The Seven-leagued Boots*. A pace taken in them measured seven leagues.

**Seven liberal arts, The.** *See* QUADRIVIUM.

**Seven metals in alchemy.** *See* SEVEN BODIES.

**Seven Os** or **Great Os of Advent, The.** The seven antiphons to the MAGNIFICAT sung during the week preceding CHRISTMAS. They commence respectively with *O Sapientia*, *O Adonai*, *O Radix Jesse*, *O Clavis David*, *O Oriens Splendor*, *O Rex gentium* and *O Emmanuel*. They are sometimes called the Christmas Os.

**Seven penitential psalms, The.** Psalms 6, 32, 38, 51, 102, 130 and 143, in use from early Christian times and in the MIDDLE AGES ordered to be recited after LAUDS on Fridays in LENT.

**Seven planets, The.** *See* PLANETS.

**Seven sacraments, The.** These are BAPTISM, Confirmation, the EUCHARIST, Penance, Orders, Matrimony and EXTREME UNCTION.

**Seven sages of Greece, The.** *See* WISE MEN OF GREECE.

**Seven Samurai, The.** In the film of this name (1954), the seven SAMURAI who defend a Japanese peasant village from bandits, in the process learning about the true values of life.

**Seven sciences** or **seven liberal sciences, The.** The same as the seven liberal arts. *See* QUADRIVIUM.

**Seven seas, The.** The Arctic and Antarctic, North and South PACIFIC, North and South ATLANTIC, and Indian Oceans.

**Seven senses, The.** According to ancient teaching the SOUL of man or his 'inward holy body' is compounded of seven properties, which are under the influence of the seven PLANETS. The properties are fire, which animates; earth, which gives the sense of feeling, water, which gives speech; air, which gives taste; mist, which gives sight; flowers, which give hearing; and the south wind, which gives smelling. Hence the seven senses are animation, feeling, speech, taste, sight, hearing and smelling (*see* Ecclesiasticus 17:5).

**Seven Sisters, The.** An old name of the PLEIADES. The name has also been given to a set of seven cannon, cast by one Robert Borthwick and used at Flodden (1513), and to the chalk cliffs between Cuckmere Haven and Beachy Head on the Sussex coast. The latter individual heights are Went Hill Brow, Baily's Brow, Flagstaff Point, Brass Point, Rough Brow, Short Brow and Haven Brow.

**Seven sleepers, The.** Seven Christian youths of Ephesus, according to the legend, who fled during the Diocletian persecution (303) to a cave in Mount Celion. The cave was walled up by their pursuers, and they fell asleep. In the reign of Theodosius II, some 200 years later, they awoke and one of them went into the city for provisions. They then fell asleep again, this time until the Resurrection. Their names are given as Constantius, Dionysius, Joannes, Maximianus, Malchus, Martinianus and Serapion. The legend was current in the 6th century and is referred to by Gregory of Tours. *See also* KRATIM.

**Seven sorrows of Mary, The.** The seven sorrows of the Virgin Mary are: SIMEON'S prophecy, the flight into Egypt, the loss of the Holy Child, meeting Christ on the way to CALVARY, the crucifixion, the taking down from the cross and the entombment. *See also* SEVEN JOYS OF MARY.

**Seven spiritual works of mercy, The.** The seven spiritual works of mercy are: (1) to convert the sinner, (2) to instruct the ignorant, (3) to counsel those in doubt, (4) to comfort those in sorrow, (5) to bear wrongs patiently, (6) to forgive injuries, (7) to pray for the living and the dead. *See also* SEVEN CORPORAL WORKS OF MERCY.

**Seven stars, The.** A name used formerly of the PLANETS, also of the PLEIADES and the GREAT BEAR.

> *Fool*: The reason why the seven stars are no more than seven is a pretty reason.
> *Lear*: Because they are not eight?
> *Fool*: Yes, indeed; thou wouldst make a good fool.
> SHAKESPEARE: *King Lear*, I, v (1605)

**Seventh-day Adventists.** A sect of ADVENTISTS, which grew out of a movement begun by William Miller (1781–1849) in the United States in 1831. He preached that the present world would end in about 1843. The Seventh-day Adventists adopted their name in 1860 and were formally organized from 1863. They observe Saturday as their SABBATH and insist on temperance and abstinence from alcohol and tobacco and a strict adherence to the SCRIPTURES.

**Seventh-day Baptists.** In the USA, a group of German Baptist brethren who keep Saturday, the seventh day of the week, as their SABBATH.

**Seven virtues.** Faith, hope, charity, justice, fortitude, prudence and temperance. The first three are called the supernatural, theological or Christian virtues, while the remaining four are Plato's cardinal or natural virtues. *See also* SEVEN DEADLY SINS.

**Seven Weeks' War, The.** The war between Austria and Prussia, engineered by the German Chancellor Prince Otto von Bismarck (1815–98), which lasted from 14 June to 26 July 1866. Austria and her allies were decisively defeated at Sadowa or Königgrätz (3 July) and the war ended with the Treaty of Prague (23 August). Austria withdrew from the German Confederation, and Prussia was left to assume the leadership of Germany.

**Seven Wise Masters, The.** A collection of oriental tales (*see* SANDABAR) said to be told to the king by his advisers. The king's son returned to court after being educated in the seven liberal arts (*see* QUADRIVIUM) by the Seven Wise Masters. By consulting the stars, he learned that his life was in danger if he spoke before the elapse of seven days. One of the royal consorts then endeavoured to seduce him without success, whereupon she denounced him to the sovereign and the prince was condemned to death. The Wise Masters, by their tales against women, secured a suspension of the sentence for one day. The woman then told a contrary tale to secure the confirmation of Prince Lucien's punishment. The Wise Masters counteracted this with further tales and so on, until the seventh day, when the prince revealed the truth and his accuser was sentenced to death instead. There are numerous versions of these stories, which date from 10th century. *See also* SCHEHERAZADE.

**Seven wonders of the world, The.** In the ancient world:

- COLOSSUS of Rhodes
- HANGING GARDENS OF BABYLON
- PHAROS of Alexandria
- PYRAMIDS of Egypt.
- Statue of OLYMPIAN ZEUS by Phidias
- Temple of DIANA OF EPHESUS
- Tomb of Mausolus (*see* MAUSOLEUM)

A later list gives:

- Catacombs of Alexandria
- COLOSSEUM of Rome
- GREAT WALL OF CHINA
- LEANING TOWER of Pisa
- Mosque of Santa SOPHIA at Constantinople (Istanbul)
- Porcelain Tower of Nanking
- STONEHENGE

**Seven words from the cross, The.** The final utterances of Christ in his mortal life: (1) 'Father, forgive them; for they know not what they do' (Luke 23:34); (2) 'Today shalt thou be with me in paradise' (Luke 23:43); (3) 'Woman, behold thy son! ... Behold thy mother!' (John

19:26–7); (4) 'Eli, Eli, lama sabachthani? [that is to say] My God, my God, why hast thou forsaken me?' (Matthew 27:46); (5) 'I thirst' (John 19:28); (6) 'It is finished' (John 19:30); (7) 'Father, into thy hands I commend my spirit' (Luke 23:46).

**Seven works of mercy, The.** *See* SEVEN CORPORAL WORKS OF MERCY; SEVEN SPIRITUAL WORKS OF MERCY.

**Seven-year itch.** A tendency towards infidelity, said to set in after about seven years of marriage. The expression was popularized by George Axelrod's comedy of the name (1952), made into a film (1955), in which a married man has a fling with the girl upstairs.

**Seven Years' War, The.** A war fought (1756–63) over European and colonial and commercial rivalries by France, Austria, Saxony, Russia and Sweden against Prussia, Great Britain and Hanover. Spain joined in 1761 and attacked Portugal. It began with FREDERICK THE GREAT's invasion of Saxony and was ended by the Treaty of Paris between Great Britain, France, Portugal and Spain, which gave Canada and other colonial territories to Great Britain, New Orleans to Spain, among other grants. By the Peace of Hubertusburg between Austria and Prussia, the latter retained Silesia.

**At sixes and sevens.** *See under* AT.

**In seventh heaven, To be.** To be supremely happy. The CABBALISTS maintained that there are seven heavens, each rising above the other, the seventh being the abode of God and the highest class of ANGELS.

**Island of the Seven Cities, The.** *See under* ISLAND.

**Severn.** *See* SABRINA.

**Severus, The Wall of.** *See under* WALL.

**Seville, The Barber of.** *See under* BARBER.

**Sèvres ware.** Fine porcelain made at the French state factory at Sèvres near Paris. It was first opened at Vincennes in 1745 and moved to Sèvres in 1756. Louis XV became the proprietor in 1760. The king took a personal interest in the manufactory, and expositions were held at VERSAILLES for the sale of the products to the nobility at court. There is a story that Louis XV one day noticed a nobleman quietly pocketing a pretty cup. The next day a servant approached him and presented him with a saucer together with an invoice.

**Sewer, To have a mind like a.** *See* HAVE A MIND LIKE A CESSPOOL *under* MIND.

**Sex. Fair sex, The.** *See under* FAIR.

**Gentle sex, The.** *See under* GENTLE.

**Safe sex.** *See under* SAFE.

**Sexagesima Sunday.** The second Sunday before LENT, so called because in round numbers it is 60 days (Latin *sexagesima dies*) before EASTER.

**Sextile.** The aspect of two PLANETS when distant from each other sixty degrees or two signs. This position is marked by astrologers thus ★.

> In sextile, square, and trine, and opposite,
> Of noxious efficacy.
> MILTON: *Paradise Lost*, x (1667)

**Sexton Blake.** *See under* BLAKE.

**Sez you!** A contemptuous exclamation expressing disbelief in what someone has said, holding it up to ridicule. It is an expression of American origin that became popular in England in the 1930s. Its anglicized equivalent, milder in import, is SAYS YOU!

**Sganarelle.** A comic character who appears in several plays by Molière and who was often played by the dramatist himself. In *Le Médecin malgré lui* (1666) he is an earthy peasant who is forced to become a doctor and who succeeds far better than the real doctors, while in *L'École des maris* (1661) he is the jealous but strict guardian of a young girl. His name ultimately comes from Italian *sgannare*, 'to disabuse'.

**Shades.** The abode of the departed or HADES, also the spirits or ghosts of the departed. Hence 'shades of ...' to refer to something reminiscent of another person, as: 'I prefer my coffee black: shades of my father.'

Wine vaults with a bar attached are often known as shades. The term originated at Brighton, when the Old Bank in 1819 was turned into a smoking-room and bar. There was an entrance by the Pavilion Shades, or Arcade, and the name was soon transferred to the bar.

**Put someone in the shade, To.** To outdo a person; to attract to oneself all the applause and plaudits another had been enjoying.

**Shadow.** A word with numerous figurative and applied meanings. One is a ghost, so that Macbeth says to the ghost of Banquo:

> Hence, horrible shadow! unreal mockery, hence!
> SHAKESPEARE: *Macbeth*, III, iv (1605)

Another is an imperfect representation, as: 'I haven't the shadow of a doubt.' A third is a constant attendant, as in Milton's 'Sin and her shadow Death' (*Paradise Lost*, ix (1667)). Yet another is moral darkness or gloom, as: 'He has outsoar'd the shadow of our night' (Percy Bysshe Shelley, *Adonaïs*, xl, 1 (1821)). And a further is a protecting influence:

> Hither, like yon ancient Tower,
> Watching o'er the River's bed,
> Fling the shadow of thy power,
> Else we sleep among the dead.
> WORDSWORTH: 'Jesu! bless our slender Boat' (hymn) (1820)

**Shadow, To.** To follow someone about like a shadow, especially as a detective, with the object of spying out all his or her doings. In a more positive sense, a trainee or employee who accompanies a person at work to see what they do and learn how they do it is said to shadow them.

**Shadow cabinet.** A potential CABINET formed from leaders of the OPPOSITION party in PARLIAMENT, who also take the lead as critics of particular features of government policy.

**Shady character, A.** A person of very doubtful reputation; one whose character would scarcely bear investigation in the light of day.

**Five o'clock shadow.** *See under* FIVE.

**May your shadow never grow less!** May your prosperity always continue and increase. A phrase of Eastern origin. Fable has it that when those studying the black arts had made certain progress, they were chased through a subterranean hall by the Devil. If he caught only their shadow, or part of it, they lost all or part of it, but became first-rate magicians. This would make the expression mean, 'May you escape wholly and entirely from the clutches of the Devil', but a more simple explanation is: 'May you never waste away, but always remain healthy and robust.' *See also* SCHLEMIHL.

**Wrangle for an ass's shadow, To.** *See under* WRANGLE.

**Shaggy dog story, A.** A supposedly funny story told laboriously and at great length with an unexpected twist at the end. It is usually more amusing to the teller than the hearer and is so called from the shaggy dog that featured in many stories of this genre in the 1940s. The following classic shaggy dog story is recounted by Eric Partridge:

> Travelling by train to London from one of its outer dormitories, a businessman got into a compartment and was amazed to see a middle-aged passenger playing chess with a handsome Newfoundland. The players moved the pieces swiftly and surely. Just before the train pulled in at the London terminus, the game ended, with the dog victorious. 'That's an extraordinary dog, beating you like that – and obviously you're pretty good yourself.' – 'Oh, I don't think he's so hot; I beat him in the two games before that.'
>
> ERIC PARTRIDGE: *A Charm of Words*, 'The Shaggy Dog' (1960)

**Shah** (Persian, 'king'). The supreme ruler of Persia and some other Eastern countries. *See also* PADISHAH.

**Shaikh.** *See* SHEIKH.

**Shaka.** The African chief (*c*.1787–1828) who founded the Zulu Empire. He took over the Zulus on the death of his father, Senzangakona, in 1816, and made his first act the reform of their army, equipping them with long-bladed assegais instead of the feeble throwing spears they had previously used. He divided the regiments, known as the impi, into four groups: the 'chest', as the strongest group, designed to pin down the enemy, two 'horns', which ran out to encircle the foe and attack him from behind, and the 'loins', as the reserve. He was murdered by two of his half-brothers when he pushed his impi too hard, allowing them no respite in battle.

His name, also spelt Chaka, is Zulu for 'intestinal beetle', in allusion to the fact that his mother Nandi, an orphaned princess, had been pregnant without being officially married. According to popular Zulu belief, the 'intestinal beetle' had the power to suppress a woman's menstruation.

**Shake.** To agitate; to move violently or quickly.

**Shake a leg!** Hurry up! Get a move on! Also, 'to shake a leg' is to dance.

**Shake hands, To.** To take another person's hand in one's own and shake or momentarily clasp it, as typically on meeting or departing.

> Fortune and Antony part here; even here
> Do we shake hands,
>
> SHAKESPEARE: *Antony and Cleopatra*, IV, xx (1606)

It is customary to shake hands after settling a quarrel, also on confirming an agreement or a business deal and before embarking on a contest of some kind. While shaking hands one could not get at one's sword to strike a treacherous blow. When Jehu asked Jehonadab if his 'heart was right' with him, he said, 'If it be, give me thine hand', and Jehonadab gave him his hand (2 Kings 10:15). Similarly NESTOR shook hands with ULYSSES on his return to the Grecian camp with the stolen horses of Rhesus.

> Then Judas, thinking indeed that they would be profitable in many things, granted them peace; whereupon they shook hands, and so they departed to their tents.
>
> 2 Maccabees 12:12

**Shake in one's shoes, To.** To be in a state of fear or nervous terror.

**Shake of the head, A.** An indication of refusal, disapproval, annoyance, frustration or the like.

**Shake one's sides, To.** To be convulsed with laughter.

**Shake on it, To.** To SHAKE HANDS to seal an agreement.

**Shake-out.** On the Stock Exchange a crisis that drives the weaker speculators out of the market. The term is also applied to the reduction of the labour force in a trade or industry in order to reduce costs.

**Shakers.** A sect of ADVENTISTS started by James and Jane Wardley at Manchester in 1747 who seceded from the QUAKERS and who, from their excited behaviour, were derisively dubbed 'Shakers' or 'Shaking Quakers'. Ann Lee, known as MOTHER ANN, the 'bride of the Lamb' and the 'Female Christ', soon became their acknowledged leader and the sect left for

America in 1774. They practised celibacy, temperance and communal living, and a few small communities still survive.

Another sect of English Shakers was founded at Battersea by Mary Anne Girling (1827–86), a farmer's daughter. The 'Children of God' settled in the New Forest but the sect petered out after Mrs Girling's death.

**Shakes, The.** A state of uncontrollable trembling, either from fear or from some physical cause, such as a fever or alcoholism.

**Shake the dust from one's feet, To.** To show extreme dislike of a place and to leave it with the intention of never returning. The allusion is to the Eastern custom.

> And whosoever shall not receive you, nor hear your words, when ye depart out of that house or city, shake off the dust of your feet.
>
> Matthew 10:14

**Shake-up.** A drastic upheaval or radical reorganization. *See also* SHAKE-OUT.

**Give me a shake.** Wake me up (at the requested time).

**In a couple of shakes.** *See under* COUPLE.

**In two shakes of a lamb's tail.** *See under* TWO.

**No great shakes.** *See under* GREAT.

**Shakespeare, William.** The greatest English poetic dramatist. The Shakespearian canon comprises the 36 plays of the First Folio (1623), which include collaborative contributions that cannot be determined with certainty, the *Sonnets* (1609), *The Rape of Lucrece* (1594), *Venus and Adonis* (1593), a few lyrics and the 16 lines contributed to the play of *Sir Thomas More* (*c*.1593).

The theory that William Shakespeare (1564–1616) was not the writer of the works attributed to him, based on the assumption that he did not possess the knowledge and culture revealed in those works, was first put forward by Herbert Lawrence in 1769. In 1857 William Henry Smith suggested that the only writer of that age competent to produce such writings was Francis Bacon. Thus the Baconian theory began its lengthy career. In 1887 Ignatius Donnelly, a former senator of Minnesota, published *The Great Cryptogram*, which professed to show that cryptograms in the plays revealed Bacon as the undoubted author. The cryptographic method was further advanced by Sir Edwin Durning-Lawrence in *Bacon is Shakespeare* (1910), where he claimed that the all-revealing cryptic word was HONORIFICABILITUDINITATIBUS. The Baconians still persist and others have put forward many additional candidates, including a school of thought which assigns Shakespeare's work to a group of seven writers. *See also* DARK LADY OF THE SONNETS.

**German Shakespeare, The.** August von Kotzebue (1761–1819) has been so styled.

**Spanish Shakespeare, The.** Pedro Calderón de la Barca (1600–81).

**Shakuntala.** *See* SAKUNTALA.

**Shallal.** In former days in Cornwall, a band of ROUGH MUSIC, which visited newly married couples and those suspected of immorality. *See also* RIDING; SKIMMINGTON.

**Shalott, The Lady of.** *See under* LADY.

**Sham Abraham, To.** To pretend to be mentally or physically sick, like an ABRAHAM MAN. The phrase was formerly current among sailors.

> 'Look out,' he cried in some alarm; 'he's shamming Abraham.'
>
> CHARLES READE: *Hard Cash*, II, xix (1863)

**Shamanism.** A primitive form of religion, in which it is believed that the world is governed by good and evil spirits who can be propitiated through the intervention of a Shaman, a priest or sorcerer. The word is immediately Slavic, the cult being practised by the Samoyeds and other Siberian peoples. Its ultimate source, however, is Sanskrit *srama*, 'religious exercise'.

**Shambles.** The ultimate source of the word is in Old English *sceamul*, 'stool', 'table', from a word related to Latin *scamnum*, 'bench'. This was adopted for the stall on which meat was sold in a market, and from there it passed, in the plural form, to the term for a slaughter-house, where the meat was actually prepared. Hence 'shambles' in its colloquial use for any scene of disorder or confusion, as formerly applied to slaughter-houses. The 'meat stall' sense of the word remains in the streets or markets called Shambles in some older towns, as in York.

**Shame. Shamefaced.** With a sheepish or guilty expression. The word was originally 'shamefast' (like steadfast), meaning 'bashful', 'modest'.

**Tell the truth and shame the Devil.** *See under* TELL.

**Shamrock.** The symbol of Ireland, because it was selected by St PATRICK to illustrate to the Irish the doctrine of the TRINITY. According to the elder Pliny, no serpent will touch this plant.

**Shamus.** US slang for a policeman or private detective. It may derive from Shammash, the sexton of a SYNAGOGUE, or be an anglicization of the Irish Séamas (James), or a mixture of both.

**Shandean.** Characteristic of Tristram Shandy or the Shandy family in Laurence Sterne's novel, *Tristram Shandy* (9 volumes, 1759–67). Tristram's father, Walter Shandy, is a type of metaphysical Don QUIXOTE, full of superstitious and idle conceits. He believes in long noses and propitious names, but his son's nose is crushed, and his name becomes Tristram instead of Trismegistus. Tristram's Uncle Toby was wounded at the siege of Namur, and is benevolent and generous, simple as a child, brave as a lion, and gallant as a courtier. His modesty with Widow Wadman and his military tastes are admirable. He is said to be based on Sterne's father. The mother was the epitome of nonentity, and of Tristram himself one reads almost more before he was born than after. *See also* YORICK.

**Shandon, The Bells of.** *See under* BELL.

**Shanghai, To.** An old nautical phrase, meaning to make a man drunk or to drug him insensible and to get him on board an outward-bound vessel in need of crew. It originated on the west coast of the USA where Shanghai was a likely destination for an impressed sailor.

**Shango.** In the pantheon of the Yoruba people of Nigeria the god of thunder and lightning. He lives in the clouds in a vast palace of shining copper, whence he rains down red-hot rocks on any who displease him. Those struck by lightning are left unburied, since Shango has need of them. Houses struck by lightning are ransacked by priests and worshippers and their owners fined, for Shango has punished them with his lightning for lying and oath-breaking. Figures of Shango usually show him with bow and sword surrounded by his three wives, goddesses of the rivers Niger, Osun and Oba, who stand with palms pressed together before their breasts.

**Shangri La.** The hidden Buddhist lama PARADISE described in James Hilton's *Lost Horizon* (1933). The name was also applied to CAMP DAVID and to the secret 'base' used for the great American air raid on Tokyo in 1942. The name is now applied to any imagined earthly 'Paradise' or idyllic utopia.

**Shanks' mare** or **pony, To ride.** *See under* RIDE.

**Shannon, To be dipped in the.** *See under* DIP.

**Shanties.** Songs of the days of sail sung by a 'shanty man' to help rhythmical action among sailors hauling on ropes, working the capstan and so on. The workers joined in the choruses. The word is probably from French *chanter*, 'to sing'. The chorus of one of the most popular runs thus:

> Then away, love, away,
> Away down Rio.
> O fare ye well my pretty young gel,
> For we're bound for the Rio Grande.

A shanty is also a small wooden house or hut, from Canadian-French *chantier*, 'log hut', 'workshop' (French, 'timber-yard').

**Shan Van Voght.** This fine song, composed in 1798, has been called the Irish MARSEILLAISE. The title is a corruption of *An t-sean bhean bhocht*, 'the poor old woman', i.e. Ireland. The last verse is:

> Will Ireland then be free?
> Said the Shan Van Voght. [repeat]
> Yes, Ireland shall be free
> From the centre to the sea,
> Hurrah for liberty!
> Said the Shan Van Voght.

**Shape, To lick into.** *See under* LICK.

**Share. Golden share.** *See under* GOLDEN.

**Lion's share, The.** *See under* LION.

**Sharecropper.** After the American Civil War (1861–5) Southern plantations were divided into one-man holdings worked by a freedman and his family, or by a white, usually planting cotton or tobacco. They were called sharecroppers because the planter or storekeeper, from whom they obtained their supplies, usually took from one-quarter to one-half of the crop, according to the service rendered. From the 1940s, with the growth of mechanization in agriculture and the spread of industry in the South, many blacks moved to the cities of the North. Sharecropping, however, is still a common form of rent payment in many parts of the USA.

**Sharif.** *See* SHERIF.

**Shark.** A swindler; a pilferer; an extortionate dealer, landlord or the like. The allusion is to a shark, which snaps up its food alive or dead regardless.

**Sharon.** A female forename of biblical origin: 'I am the rose of Sharon, and the lily of the valley' (Song of Solomon 2:1). The name was adopted by attraction of the rose that here accompanies it, although Sharon itself is not a person but a plain in the north of Palestine. The forename had became very popular by the 1970s but subsequently came to gain a pejorative patina, especially when coupled with the name TRACY. To say, for example, that a club was full of Sharons and Tracys is to say that it was full of ESSEX GIRL types. John Steinbeck has a character named Rosasharn (a shortening of Rose of Sharon) in his novel *The Grapes of Wrath* (1939).

**Rose of Sharon.** *See under* ROSE.

**Sharp. Sharp practice.** Smart, underhand or dishonourable dealing; low-down trickery intended to advantage oneself.

**Sharp's the word!** Look alive! Brace yourself!

**At the sharp end.** *See under* AT.

**Shave, A.** A grazing touch. A near or close shave is a narrow escape.

**Shaveling.** Used in contempt of a young man and, especially after the REFORMATION, of a priest. At a time when the laity wore beards and moustaches the clergy were not only usually clean-shaven but they also wore large shaven TONSURES.

**Shaver.** A young lad, especially one who has just begun to shave.

> Who would imagine now, that this young shaver
> could dream of a woman so soon.
>
> GEORGE FARQUHAR: *Love and a Bottle*, III, i (1698)

**Close shave.** *See under* CLOSE.

**Dry shave.** *See under* DRY.

**Shavian.** After the manner of George Bernard Shaw (1856–1950), or descriptive of his philosophy and style of humour.

**She. She Bible, The.** *See* HE BIBLE *under* BIBLE.

**She-wolf of France, The.** Isabella of France (1292–1358), daughter of Philip the Fair and adulterous wife of Edward II. She executed the Despensers and procured her husband's death (1327) at Berkeley Castle. His murderers thrust a hot iron into his bowels.

She-wolf of France, with unrelenting fangs,
That tear'st the bowels of thy mangled Mate.
THOMAS GRAY: *The Bard*, II, i (1757)

**Shears, Sieve and.** *See under* SIEVE.

**Sheathe the sword, To.** To cease hostilities; to make peace. Figuratively, to put aside enmity.

**Sheba.** In the Old Testament (2 Samuel 20), an Israelite who raises a revolt against DAVID. He is trapped in the city of Abel by JOAB and is beheaded there by the inhabitants.

**Queen of Sheba, The.** The queen who visited SOLOMON (1 Kings 10) is known to the Arabs as BALKIS, queen of Sheba (Koran, ch 27). Sheba was thought by the Romans to have been the capital of what is now Yemen, and the people over whom the queen reigned were the SABAEANS.

**Shebang.** American slang for a hut or one's quarters, also for a cart, and in a humorous deprecatory way, for any matter or thing. The word is of uncertain origin, but it could be a mischievous inversion of bang shoot, as in 'the WHOLE BANG SHOOT'.

**Shebeen.** A place (originally only in Ireland) where liquor is sold without a licence, and hence applied to any low-class public house. The word represents Irish *síbín*, 'weak beer'.

**Shechina.** *See* SHEKHINAH.

**Shed light on, To.** *See* THROW LIGHT ON.

**Shedeem.** *See* MAZIKEEN.

**Sheena.** Essentially the female counterpart of TARZAN, the jungle girl of American comic books has the real name Janet Ames. She is a white foundling raised by an African tribe who teach her martial arts and shamanistic skills. She was the creation of Will Eisner and S.M. Iger for Jumbo Comics, and made her debut in 1938. She subsequently appeared in a television series and in a film of 1984, named after her, in which she is played by Tanya Roberts.

**Sheep.** The ram or tup is the sire, the ewe is the dam, the lamb is the young until weaned, when it is called a tup hogget or ewe hogget, as the case may be, or, if the tup is castrated, a wether hogget. After the removal of the first fleece, the tup hogget becomes a shearling, the ewe hogget a gimmer, and the wether hogget a dinmont. After the removal of the second fleece, the shearling becomes a two-shear tup, the gimmer a ewe, and the dinmont a wether. After the removal of the third fleece, the ewe is a twinter-ewe, and when it ceases to breed, a draft-ewe.

**Sheep dressed as lamb.** Said of a woman of some maturity who 'dolls herself up' to give the appearance of being much younger. *See also* MUTTON DRESSED AS LAMB.

**Sheepish.** Awkward and shy; bashful through not knowing how to deport oneself in the circumstances; embarrassed through shame.

**Sheep's eyes.** A now rather dated term for an amorous or 'come-hither' look. *See also* MAKE EYES AT *under* EYE.

**As well be hanged for a sheep as a lamb.** *See under* AS.

**Black sheep of the family, The.** *See under* BLACK.

**Separate the sheep from the goats, To.** *See under* SEPARATE.

**Wolf in sheep's clothing, A.** *See under* WOLF.

**Sheer** or **Shere Thursday.** An old name for MAUNDY THURSDAY. It is generally supposed to be from Middle English *schere*, 'clean', i.e. free from guilt, from the custom of receiving absolution, or of cleansing the altars on this day.

**Sheet. Sheet lightning.** A diffuse discharge, caused by a flash of lightning in a cloud, or cloud-to-cloud discharge.

**As white as a sheet.** *See under* AS.

**Charge sheet.** *See under* CHARGE.

**Clean sheet.** *See under* CLEAN.

**Three sheets in the wind.** *See under* THREE.

**Sheffield plate.** A process of fusing a copper sheet between two sheets of silver foil, discovered by Thomas Bolsover (or Boulsover), a Sheffield cutler, about 1742 and developed by Bolsover's apprentice Joseph Hancock. Domestic articles such as candlesticks, coffee pots, trays and dishes of quality were produced by Sheffield craftsmen until the industry gave way to electroplated products and came to an end in about 1865.

**Sheikh** or **Shaikh** (Arabic *shaykh*, 'old man'). A title of respect among the Arabs, but properly the head of a BEDOUIN clan, family or tribe, or the headman of an Arab village.

**Sheikh-al-Islam.** The Grand MUFTI or supreme head of the Muslim hierarchy in Turkey.

**Sheila.** The female forename derives from Irish *Síle*, a form of English Cecily. In Australia the name came to be used for any girl or woman, while in South Africa a sheila is (or was) a white teddy girl (*see* EDWARDIAN).

**Sheila-na-gig.** A fertility symbol in the form of a stone nude female figure with legs wide apart and hands placed so as to draw attention to the genitals. They are found on churches in

Britain and Ireland, and the term itself derives from Irish *Síle na gcíoch*, 'Sheila of the breasts'. The figures may have been introduced by the Normans. An example may be found on the south side of the apse of the fine Norman church at Kilpeck near Hereford.

**Shekels.** A colloquial word for money. It was anciently part of the Babylonian weight and monetary systems, and in general use among the peoples of Mesopotamia and Syria. The Hebrew heavy gold shekel weighed about 252 grains TROY and the light gold shekel about 126 grains, while the heavy silver shekel weighed about 224 grains troy and the light silver shekel about 112 grains. The standard English gold SOVEREIGN was about 123 grains troy. Phoenician shekels of about 224 and about 112 grains were also commonly found throughout the Near East.

**Shekhinah** or **Shechina** (Hebrew *shekhīnāh*, 'that which dwells'). A word used frequently in the TARGUMS as an equivalent for the divine presence of God. It does not occur in the Bible. The Shekhinah is God's omnipresence and is everywhere. God is not identical with the world, He is of the world and yet afar off. Thus when JACOB says (Genesis 28:16), 'The Lord is in this place', the Targum says, 'The glory of the Shekhinah of J is in this place'.

**Sheldonian Theatre.** The Senate House of Oxford University, so called from Gilbert Sheldon (1598–1677), archbishop of Canterbury, who provided the money for the building designed by Sir Christopher Wren and opened in 1699. Formerly the senate's meetings were held in St Mary's Church. *See also* ENCAENIA.

**Shelf, To put on the.** To put aside as of no further use, superannuated. Said of officials and others no longer actively employed, or of a project begun and set aside. An object pawned at the brokers is also put on the shelf. A single woman beyond the average age of marriage is said to be on the shelf.

**Shell.** The hard outside covering of nuts, eggs, molluscs and so on, and hence applied to other hollow coverings, as the hollow projectile filled with explosives.

It is also applied to a form or class in some public schools, usually an intermediate form of some kind between those distinguished by numbers. This latter usage derives from Westminster School, where the intermediate form between the fifth and sixth occupied a schoolroom of which one end was shell-shaped or apsidal.

**Shellback.** Nautical slang for a hardened and seasoned sailor, an 'old salt'. In the US Navy the term is reserved for one who has crossed the line and been duly initiated. *See also* CROSSING THE LINE.

**Shell jacket.** An army officer's waist-length mess jacket.

**Shell out, To.** To pay or 'stump up' or to FORK OUT, as peas are shelled out of a pod.

**Shell shock.** An acute neurasthenic condition due to the explosion of a shell or bomb at close quarters. The term originated in the First World War.

**Shell suit.** A lightweight tracksuit, which has an inner cotton layer covered by a waterproof nylon outer layer or 'shell'.

**Cockleshell.** *See under* COCKLE.

**Come out of one's shell, To.** *See under* COME.

**Eggshells.** *See under* EGG.

**Scallop shell.** *See under* SCALLOP.

**Venus on the Half Shell.** *See under* VENUS.

**Shelter. Anderson shelter.** *See under* ANDERSON.

**Morrison shelter.** *See under* MORRISON.

**Shem.** The traditional ancestor of the Hebrews and other kindred peoples. Semite and SEMITIC derive from Shem, the eldest of the three sons of NOAH (Genesis 9:18).

**Shemozzle.** A fuss, a rumpus or a rough and tumble. The word represents Yiddish *shlimazl*, 'misfortune'.

**Shenandoah.** Although hardly one of America's greatest rivers, the Shenandoah, in Virginia, is memorable for the role it played in the American Civil War (1861–5). In 1865 there was a strategic campaign for control of its valley, running between the Blue Ridge and Allegheny Mountains, and the South exploited its transportational advantages so effectively that it frequently became a 'valley of humiliation' for the North.

> Oh, Shenandoah, I long to hear you,
> Way-hay, you rolling river!
>
> Anonymous shanty, 'Shenandoah'

**Sheol.** *See* HADES.

**Shepherd. Shepherd Lord, The.** Henry, 14th Baron Clifford (*c.*1455–1523), sent by his mother to be brought up as a shepherd, in order to save him from the fury of the YORKISTS. At the accession of Henry VII he was restored to all his rights and seigniories. He is celebrated in Wordsworth's 'The Song for the Feast of Brougham Castle' (1807) and *The White Doe of Rylstone* (1815).

**Shepherd of Banbury, The.** The ostensible author of a weather guide (published 1744), written by John Claridge, which attained considerable popularity at the time.

**Shepherd of Hermas, The.** An allegorical work of the mid-2nd century, essentially a collection of instructions and revelations from an angelic guide for the benefit of good Christians. It has been called the PILGRIM'S PROGRESS of the early church. The identity of Hermas is largely a matter of conjecture.

**Shepherd of Salisbury Plain, The.** A religious tract by the BLUE STOCKING Hannah More, first published in *The Cheap Repository Tracts* (1795), a series of moral 'tales for the people'. It had enormous popularity. The story was founded on the life of one David Saunders, who with his father had kept sheep upon SALISBURY PLAIN for 100 years and who lived in a lonely cottage on Cheverell Down. He was noted for his homely wisdom and practical piety, and was turned by Miss More into a sort of idealized Christian peasant.

**Shepherd of the Ocean, The.** So Sir Walter Raleigh (1552–1618) was called by Edmund Spenser.

> Whom when I asked from what place he came,
> And how he hight, himselfe he did ycleepe [call],
> The shepheard of the Ocean by name,
> And said he came far from the main-sea deepe.
> *Colin Clout's Come Home Againe* (1595)

**Shepherd's sundial, The.** The SCARLET PIMPERNEL, which opens at a little past seven in the morning and closes at a little past two. When rain is at hand or the weather is unfavourable, it does not open at all. It is also called the shepherd's calendar, clock and watch, and the shepherd's (or poor man's) weatherglass. In Norfolk it is known as change-of-the-weather.

**Shepherd's warning, The.**

> Red sky at night, shepherd's delight,
> Red sky in the morning, shepherd's warning.

The Italian equivalent is *Sera rossa e bianco mattino, allegro il pellegrino* ('a red evening and a white morning rejoice the pilgrim').

**Ettrick Shepherd, The.** *See under* ETTRICK.

**Gentle Shepherd, The.** *See under* GENTLE.

**Good Shepherd, The.** *See under* GOOD.

**Sheppard, Jack.** A notorious thief, the son of a carpenter in Smithfield, London, and brought up in Bishopsgate workhouse. Sheppard (1702–24) was known for his prison escapes, especially when he broke out of 'the Castle' of NEWGATE via the chimney. He was soon afterwards taken and hanged at TYBURN, allegedly in sight of 200,000 spectators.

> 'I say, master, did you ever hear tell of Mr Wood's famous 'prentice?'
> 'What apprentice?' asked the stranger, in surprise.
> 'Why, Jack Sheppard, the notorious housebreaker – him as has robbed half Lunnon to be sure.'
> W.H. AINSWORTH: *Jack Sheppard*, III, i (1839)

**Shere Thursday.** *See* SHEER THURSDAY.

**Sherif** or **Sharif** (Arabic, 'noble'). A descendant of the Prophet MOHAMMED through his daughter FATIMA. The title was formerly applied to the chief magistrate of MECCA, and it was also adopted by the rulers of Morocco, who claimed descent from the Prophet through his grandson Hasan.

**Sheriff** (Old English *scīrgerēfa*, literally 'shire-reeve'). In medieval and later times the sheriff was an official who looked after the royal demesne in the SHIRE and, by the 11th century, the chief official for local administration. After the 13th century, the sheriffs declined in importance with the rise of new courts and officials, and today they are largely of ceremonial and minor judicial importance. The high sheriff is still the chief officer of the crown in a county. The City of London has two sheriffs, and certain ancient cities, among them Norwich, Bristol, York and Oxford, still have one. In Scotland the sheriff is a judge. In the USA the sheriff, usually elected, has administrative and limited judicial functions. *See also* PRICKING FOR SHERIFFS; REEVE.

**Sheriff of Nottingham, The.** In the stories about ROBIN HOOD, the evil sheriff who is Robin's persistent enemy.

**Sherlock, A.** A person who shows an unusual ability in observation and deduction and in solving mysteries, like Sherlock HOLMES. The nickname is sometimes used derisively.

**Sherlock Holmes.** *See under* HOLMES.

**Sherry.** *See* JEREZ; SACK.

**Shewbread.** The word was adopted by William Tyndale, modelled on Martin Luther's *Schaubrot*. It is more correctly 'presence-bread'. Tyndale explains it as 'always in the presence and sight of the Lorde'. Shewbread denotes the 12 loaves for the 12 tribes, arranged in two piles on the table of shittim wood set beside the altar each week. When they were removed, only the priest was allowed to partake of them. This ancient oblation is referred to in Exodus 25:30, Leviticus 24:5–9 and elsewhere.

**Shibboleth.** A test word, a catchword or principle to which members of a group adhere long after its original significance has ceased, hence a term for a worn-out or discredited doctrine. Shibboleth (meaning 'flood', 'stream') was the word the Ephraimites could not pronounce when they were challenged at the ford on the Jordan by their pursuers, Jephthah and the Gileadites. The Ephraimites could only say Sibboleth, thus revealing themselves to the enemy.

> Then said they unto him, Say now Shibboleth: and he said Sibboleth: for he could not frame to pronounce it right. Then they took him, and slew him at the passages of Jordan.
> Judges 12:6

**Shibdiz.** The Persian BUCEPHALUS, fleeter than the wind, the charger of Chosroes II (591–628), who conquered Syria and Egypt.

**Shield.** The most famous shields in story are those of ACHILLES, described by Homer, of HERCULES, described by Hesiod, of AENEAS, described by Virgil, and the AEGIS.

Other shields, with their devices, are those of:

Amycos (son of POSEIDON): a crayfish, symbol of prudence
ATHENE: a Gorgon
CADMUS and his descendants: a dragon to indicate their descent from the dragon's teeth
Eteocles: a man scaling a wall
HECTOR: a lion
IDOMENEUS: a cock
MENELAUS: a serpent at his heart, alluding to the elopement of his wife with Paris
Odysseus (ULYSSES): a dolphin, whence he is sometimes called Delphinosemos
Parthenopaeus (one of the SEVEN AGAINST THEBES): a Sphinx holding a man in its claws

Servius says that in the siege of TROY the Greeks had, as a rule, NEPTUNE on their bucklers, and the Trojans MINERVA.

It was a common custom, after a great victory, for the victorious general to hang his shield on the wall of some temple.

**Shield of David, The.** *See* STAR OF DAVID.

**Shield of expectation, The.** The perfectly plain shield given to a young warrior on his maiden campaign. As he achieved glory, his deeds were recorded or symbolized on it.

**Clang of shields, The.** *See under* CLANG.

**Gold and silver shield, The.** *See under* GOLD.

**Shift. Shift one's ground, To.** To try a different plan of attack; to alter one's argument or viewpoint.

**Graveyard shift.** *See under* GRAVE.

**Shi'ites** (Arabic *shī ʿah*, 'sect'). Those Muslims who regard ALI, MOHAMMED's son-in-law, as the first rightful IMAM and CALIPH. They reject the first three SUNNI caliphs and all Sunnite tradition.

**Shillelagh.** The conventional cudgel of the Irish, made from oak or blackthorn. It is popularly believed to be so called from the village of this name in County Wicklow, which is said to have supplied the roof timbers for Westminster Hall from its once extensive oak forest. The more likely origin, however, is in Irish *sail*, 'cudgel', and *éille*, 'thong'.

**Shilling** (Old English *scilling*, perhaps related to Germanic *skel-*, 'to resound', 'to ring', or *skil-*, 'to divide'). The shilling, as such, dated from 1504, and was originally made with a deeply indented cross, and could be easily divided into halves and quarters. Before decimalization, a shilling (1s) was worth 12 pence (12 × 1d), and there were 20 shillings in a pound (£1). After decimalization, the shilling coin was replaced by the 5p piece.

**Shilling shocker.** *See* PENNY-DREADFUL.

**Cooing and billing, like Philip and Mary on a shilling.** *See under* COOING.

**Cut off with a shilling.** *See under* CUT.

**King's or Queen's shilling, The.** *See under* KING.

**Shilly-shally, To.** To hesitate or act in an undecided, irresolute way, The word is a corruption of 'shill I shall I', a reduplication of 'shall I'. *See also* DILLY-DALLY; REDUPLICATED WORDS.

> 'You're a shilly-shally fellow: you take after your poor mother. She never had a will of her own.'
> GEORGE ELIOT: *Silas Marner*, Pt I, ch ix (1861)

**Shindig.** A slang term for a dance, a noisy celebration party or the like. The word is a form of SHINDY.

**Shindy, To kick up a.** *See under* KICK.

**Shine. Come rain or shine.** *See under* COME.

**Rise and shine.** *See under* RISE.

**Take a shine to someone, To.** To be attracted to someone; to 'fancy' a person, as if seeing them in a special light.

**Shingle, To hang out one's.** *See under* HANG.

**Shintoism** (Japanese, 'the way of the gods', from Chinese *shén*, 'gods', and *dào*, 'way'). The ancient national religion of Japan, now partly supplanted by BUDDHISM. The chief of innumerable deities is Amateraru Ōmikami ('the great holy goddess shining in the sky'), the sun-goddess, from whom the imperial dynasty supposedly descended. In 1946 the emperor divested himself of any divine attributes.

**Ship. Ship money.** An old-established levy exacted from maritime towns and countries to strengthen the navy in time of need. CHARLES I extended the demand to inland areas in 1635, which resulted in John Hampden's refusal (1637) to pay his due of 20s. The judges decided against Hampden, contrary to the PETITION OF RIGHT. Ship money was made illegal by the LONG PARLIAMENT in 1641.

**Ship of Fools, The.** The adaptation by Alexander Barclay (*c*.1475–1552) of Sebastian Brant's *Narrenschiff* (1494), published as *The Shyp of Folys of the Worlde* (1509). The ship was manned by fools of various types, and the device was used for a satire on the vices and follies of the times. It had a considerable vogue and was imitated by W.H. Ireland in his *Modern Ship of Fools* (1807).

**Ship of the desert, The.** The camel.

**Ship of the line, A.** Formerly, a man-of-war with sufficient gunpower to take a place in 'line of battle'. Fighting ships were not grouped specifically for this purpose before the mid-18th century when line battleships were divided into First Rates (THREE-DECKERS with at least 100 guns), Second Rates (three-deckers with 90 guns), Third Rates (two-deckers with 64 or 74 guns).

**Shipshape.** In proper order; as methodically arranged as things in a ship. When a sailing vessel was properly rigged and equipped she was said to be 'shipshape'. *See also* ALL SHIPSHAPE AND BRISTOL FASHION.

**Ships that pass in the night.** Chance acquaintances, encountered only once. The phrase is from Longfellow:

> Ships that pass in the night, and speak each other in passing,
> Only a signal shown and a distant voice in the darkness;
> So on the ocean of life we pass and speak one another,
> Only a look and a voice; then darkness again and a silence.
>
> *Tales of a Wayside Inn*, III, 'The Theologian's Tale: Elizabeth', iv (1874)

**All shipshape and Bristol fashion.** *See under* ALL.
**Break ship, To.** *See under* BREAK.
**Capital ship.** *See under* CAPITAL.
**Drive a ship, To.** *See under* DRIVE.
**Fire ship.** *See under* FIRE.
**Happy ship.** *See under* HAPPY.
**Jump ship, To.** *See under* JUMP.
**Liberty ships.** *See under* LIBERTY.
**Private ship.** *See under* PRIVATE.
**Scuttle a ship, To.** *See under* SCUTTLE.
**Spoil the ship for a ha'porth o' tar, To.** *See under* SPOIL.
**Swing a ship, To.** *See under* SWING.
**When one's ship comes in** or **home.** *See under* WHEN.
**White Ship, The.** *See under* WHITE.

**Shipton, Mother.** A prophetess and witch of legendary fame, first recorded in a pamphlet of 1641, who is said to have foretold the death of Wolsey, Lord Percy and others, and to have predicted the steam engine and telegraph, among other technological advances. However, these latter prophecies have now been shown to be forgeries. She was born Ursula Southeil in 1488 as the daughter of a 16-year-old orphan pauper of Knaresborough, Yorkshire, and married Toby Shipton, a carpenter, when she was 24. In 1677 Richard Head brought out a *Life and Death of Mother Shipton*, which relates how she was carried off by the Devil, by whom she bore an imp. She died in *c.*1560. There is a fake 'Mother Shipton's tomb' at Williton, Somerset. A small moth with wing markings resembling a witch's face, *Callistega mi*, is also named after her.

**Shire** (Old English *sīr*, 'office'). The main unit of local government in Anglo-Saxon England, presided over by an ealdorman (alderman) but from the 10th century by a SHERIFF. Shires were divided into HUNDREDS or WAPENTAKES, and after the Norman Conquest in 1066 the name county was applied to shire.
**Shire horse.** A large heavy breed of carthorse, originally bred in the SHIRES.
**Shire moot.** *See* MOOT.
**Shires, The.** The English counties whose names terminate in -shire, but in a narrower sense, the Midland counties noted for fox-hunting, especially Leicestershire, Northamptonshire and Rutland. The inhabitants of East Anglia, Kent, Sussex, Essex and Surrey apply this term to the rest of England.
**Knight of the Shire.** *See under* KNIGHT.
**Rider of the Shires, The.** *See under* RIDER.

**Shirt. Shirt of Nessus, The.** A source of misfortune from which there is no escape. Nessus was a CENTAUR, a son of IXION and Nephele. He was the ferryman on the River Evenus and while carrying DEIANEIRA, the second wife of HERCULES, across the river, he tried to rape her. Hercules killed him, but before he died, Nessus persuaded Deianeira to collect his blood to make a potion or to smear it on Hercules' tunic, which would be sure to make Hercules love her. Years later, when Deianeira feared that Hercules loved Iole, she sent him a tunic smeared with the blood, which, containing poison from the HYDRA, caused Hercules to die in agony, and so Nessus was revenged. *See also* HARMONIA'S NECKLACE.
**Shirts as party emblems.** *See* BLACKSHIRTS; BLUE SHIRTS; GARIBALDI'S RED SHIRT; GREENSHIRT.
**Shirty.** Bad tempered; very cross and offended, i.e. in the state you are in when someone has 'got your shirt out' or annoyed you.
**Boiled shirt, A.** *See under* BOIL.
**Give the shirt off one's back, To.** To give all one has.
**Hair shirt.** *See under* HAIR.
**Keep your shirt on!** There is no need to lose your temper. One who removes his shirt may be spoiling for a fight.
**Put one's shirt on a horse, To.** To back a horse with all the money one possesses.
**Stuffed shirt, A.** *See under* STUFF.
**Take the shirt off someone's back, To.** To strip someone of all they have.

**Shiva.** *See* SIVA.

**Shivaree.** The word is a corruption of CHARIVARI and in the USA means the mocking serenade accorded to newly married people.

**Shiver. Shivering Mountain.** Mam Tor, a hill about 1700ft (518m) above sea level, one of the Seven Wonders of the PEAK DISTRICT, so called from the crumbling of its southern face by 'shivering', that is, breaking away in 'shivers' or small pieces. This has been going on for ages, as the hill consists of alternate layers of shale and gritstone. The former, being soft, is easily reduced to powder, and as it crumbles small 'shivers' of the gritstone break away for want of support.
**Shiver my timbers.** An imprecation used by 'stage sailors' and popular with children's story writers. It is presumably of nautical origin, with

'shiver' here used in the sense of 'to shatter' or 'splinter into pieces', the 'timbers' being those of the ship.

> I won't thrash you Tom. Shiver my timbers if I do.
>
> CAPTAIN MARRYAT: *Jacob Faithful*, ch ix (1834)

**Shock, Shell.** *See under* SHELL.

**Shoe.** It was once thought unlucky to put on the left shoe before the right, or to put either shoe on the wrong foot.

It has long been a custom to throw an old shoe at the bride and bridegroom when they depart from the wedding breakfast or when they go to church to get married. Now it is more usual to tie an old shoe to their carriage or car. To throw a shoe after someone is an ancient way of bringing good luck. The custom has been variously interpreted.

In Anglo-Saxon marriages, the father delivered the bride's shoe to the bridegroom, who touched her on the head with it to show his authority.

Loosing the shoe (Joshua 5:15) is a mark of respect in the East. The Muslim leaves his slippers outside the mosque. Deuteronomy 25: 5–10 tells how the widow, refused by her husband's surviving brother, asserted her independence by 'loosing his shoe', and Ruth 4:7 explains that 'a man plucked off his shoe, and gave it to his neighbour' by way of confirming an agreement. 'A MAN WITHOUT SANDALS' was a proverbial expression among the Jews for a prodigal, from the custom of giving one's sandals in confirmation of a bargain.

Reginald Scot, in *The Discoverie of Witchcraft* (1584), tells how 'many will go to bed again if they sneeze before their shoes be on their feet'.

**Shoemakers.** Shoemaking is called the GENTLE CRAFT and its patron saints are CRISPIN AND CRISPINIAN.

**Shoe the wild colt, To.** To exact a fine called 'footing' from a newcomer, who is called the 'colt'. Colt is a common synonym for a GREENHORN or a youth not broken in.

**Another man's shoes.** *See under* ANOTHER.

**Court shoes.** *See under* COURT.

**Devil's shoestrings, The.** *See under* DEVIL.

**Die in one's shoes, To.** *See under* DIE.

**I wouldn't like to be in his shoes.** I am glad I am not in his position; I don't envy him.

**Live on a shoestring, To.** *See under* LIVE.

**Shake in one's shoes, To.** *See under* SHAKE.

**Where the shoe pinches.** *See under* WHERE.

**Shofar** (Hebrew *shōphār*, 'ram's horn'). A trumpet still used in the modern SYNAGOGUE. It is made of the horn of a ram or any ceremonially clean animal, and produces only the natural series of harmonics from its fundamental note. It is sounded daily during the month of Elul and repeatedly in Rosh Hashanah.

**Shogun** (Japanese, from Chinese *chān*, 'to lead', and *qún*, 'army'). The Shoguns were hereditary commanders-in-chief who seized political power in Japan at the end of the 12th century. The MIKADO did not fully regain power until 1868. *See also* TYCOON.

**Shoot.** *See also* SHOT.

**Shoot!** Go ahead; say what you have to say. In filming it is the command for the cameras to begin turning.

**Shoot a line, To.** To exaggerate; to tell a tall story; to boast. The expression may come from the theatre, alluding to an actor's line declaimed with too much emphasis or emotion.

**Shoot down in flames, To.** To refute the arguments of an opponent devastatingly and completely. A metaphor from aerial warfare.

**Shooting stars.** Incandescent meteors shooting across the sky, formerly, like comets, fabled to presage disaster:

> A little ere the mightiest Julius fell,
> The graves stood tenantless and the sheeted dead
> Did squeak and gibber in the Roman streets;
> As stars with trains of fire and dews of blood,
> Disasters in the sun.
>
> SHAKESPEARE: *Hamlet*, I, i (1600)

They were called in ancient legends the 'fiery tears of St LAWRENCE', because one of the periodic swarms of these meteors is between 9 and 14 August, about the time of St Lawrence's festival, which is on the 10th. Other periods are from 12 to 14 November, and from 6 to 12 December.

Shooting stars are said by the Arabs to be firebrands hurled by the angels against the inquisitive genii, who are forever clambering up on the constellations to peep into heaven.

**Shooting war.** A 'real' war, as distinct from a COLD WAR.

**Shoot off one's mouth, To.** To talk indiscreetly.

**Shoot one's bolt, To.** To exhaust one's efforts; to do all that one can. The bolt here is that of the archer.

**Shoot oneself in the foot, To.** To damage one's own cause inadvertently; to spoil one's chances.

**Shoot one's linen, To.** To display an unnecessary amount of shirt cuff; to show off.

**Shoot the moon, To.** To remove one's household goods by night to avoid distraint, to 'do a moonlight flit'.

> I told him who were responsible tenants; I warned him when shootings of moons seemed likely.
>
> SIR WALTER BESANT: *All Sorts and Conditions of Men*, ch iv (1882)

**Shoot the sun, To.** A nautical colloquialism meaning to take the sun's altitude with a sextant.

**Hunting, shooting and fishing.** *See under* HUNT.

**Whole bang shoot** or **whole shooting match, The.** *See under* WHOLE.

**Shop. Shop, The.** In military slang, the former Royal Military Academy at Woolwich, which moved to Sandhurst in 1946. On the Stock Exchange it is the South African gold market.

**Shop around, To.** To look for the 'best buy'; to visit a variety of shops comparing prices and quality before making one's choice.

**Shop floor.** The part of a factory where the production processes are undertaken. The term can also mean 'workers'.

**Shop someone, To.** To betray them or inform on them.

**Shop steward.** The elected trade union representative of a factory or workshop who acts as the link with the local union branch, monitors union membership and the like, and has certain negotiating functions with the management.

**All over the shop.** *See under* ALL.

**Bucket shop.** *See under* BUCKET.

**Bull in a china shop, A.** *See under* BULL.

**Closed shop.** *See under* CLOSE.

**Hock shop.** *See under* HOCK.

**Home shopping.** *See under* HOME.

**Nation of shopkeepers, A.** *See under* NATION.

**One-stop shop.** *See under* ONE.

**Open shop.** *See under* OPEN.

**Shut up shop, To.** *See under* SHUT.

**Talk shop, To.** *See under* TALK.

**Window shopping.** *See under* WINDOW.

**You've come to the wrong shop.** *See under* COME.

**Shore. Cornubian shore.** *See under* CORNUBIAN.

**Hug the shore, To.** *See under* HUG.

**Lee shore.** *See under* LEE.

**Saxon Shore.** *See under* SAXON.

**Shoreditch.** The legend that this district of London takes its name from Edward IV's mistress, Jane Shore (d.*c*.1527), derives from a ballad in the Pepys collection, a version of which is given in PERCY'S RELIQUES (1765):

> Thus, weary of my life, at lengthe
> I yielded up my vital strength
> Within a ditch of loathsome scent,
> Where carrion dogs did much frequent:
> The which now since my dying daye,
> Is Shoreditch called, as writers saye.

It is also suggested that the name comes from Soerdich, or Shorditch, the family who once held the manor, and Bishop Percy says it is 'from its being a common sewer (vulgarly "shore") or drain'. In fact, it is probably 'the ditch draining the slope'. The shore would not be that of the Thames, as Shoreditch is separated from the river by the City of London.

**Duke of Shoreditch, The.** An archer of this parish is said to have been so called by Henry VIII for his success in an archery contest at Windsor. The title was long playfully applied to the Captain of the Company of Archers of London.

**Shorne** or **Schorne, John.** Rector of North Marston, Buckinghamshire (*c*.1290–1314), in the church of which was once a shrine in his honour. He was renowned for his piety and miraculous powers. He blessed a local well giving it legendary healing properties and also 'conjured the Devil into a boot'. His shrine became so frequented by pilgrims that, in 1481, the DEAN and CHAPTER of Windsor, owners of the ADVOWSON, with papal permission, removed his shrine and relics to Windsor.

**Short. Short and sweet.** Briefer than one was expecting, as: 'Her stay was short and sweet'. The implication is that one is glad it was not longer.

**Short-change someone, To.** To cheat or swindle them, as if not giving enough change.

**Short-circuit, To.** Metaphorically to take a short cut, especially when dealing with officialdom. The metaphor is from electrical engineering, in which a short circuit is a deviation of current along a path of lower resistance.

**Short commons.** Insufficient rations; scant fare. 'Commons' here originally referred to the food provided for a community, especially a college, where meals were eaten at a common table.

**Short cut is often the longest way round, The.** It does not always pay to avoid taking a little trouble; short cuts do not always pay. Francis Bacon says:

> It is in life as it is in ways, the shortest way is commonly the foulest, and surely the fairer way is not much about.
>
> *Advancement of Learning*, Bk II, ch iii, sect 45 (1605)

**Shorter Catechism.** One of the two Catechisms (the Larger and Shorter) drawn up by the WESTMINSTER ASSEMBLY in 1647 and adopted by the English Parliament and the Scottish General Assembly. The Shorter Catechism proved its instructional worth and came into regular use among PRESBYTERIANS, BAPTISTS and, later, WESLEYANS.

**Short list.** A final list of candidates for a post or the like. The original list was much longer, and many have been weeded out.

**Short Parliament.** The abortive PARLIAMENT (13 April to 5 May 1640) summoned by CHARLES I after his ELEVEN YEARS' TYRANNY to procure supplies to fight the Scots. The Commons insisted on redress of grievances and Charles dissolved Parliament.

**Bermuda shorts.** *See under* BERMUDA.
**Caught short.** *See under* CATCH.
**Cut it short!** *See under* CUT.
**Cut short, To.** *See under* CUT.
**Fall short, To.** *See under* FALL.
**Get someone by the short and curlies, To.** To have someone completely in one's power. The allusion is to pubic hair, or more precisely to the short hairs that sprout on the scrotum.
**Give someone short shrift, To.** To treat them peremptorily and unsympathetically. Short shrift was the few minutes in which a criminal about to be executed was allowed to make his confession.
**In short supply.** Scarce.
**Long and short of it, The.** *See under* LONG.
**Make short work of it, To.** To dispose of it quickly; to deal summarily with it.
**Nothing short of.** *See under* NOTHING.
**Sell short, To.** *See under* SELL.
**Win by a short head, To.** *See under* WIN.

**Shot.** A missile weapon.
**Shotgun wedding.** One forced upon the couple, usually by the bride's parents, when the bride is pregnant. The image is of a threat with a firearm.
**Shot in the arm, A.** A drink of whisky or the like; something that puts new life into one. The allusion is to a hypodermic injection of cocaine or some other stimulant drug.
**Shot in the dark, A.** A wild guess; a random conjecture. A shot in the dark at a target may well miss.
**Bad shot, A.** *See under* BAD.
**Big shot, A.** *See under* BIG.
**Call the shots, To.** *See under* CALL.
**Dead shot.** *See under* DEAD.
**Have a shot at, To.** To have a try; to make an attempt at something in which one makes no particular claim to expertise.
**Like a shot.** *See under* LIKE.
**Long shot, A.** *See under* LONG.
**Not a shot in one's locker.** With no money or resources left. The phrase comes from the days of the sailing warship. The ammunition was kept in lockers and when these were empty the ship could no longer fight or fulful its main function.
**Parthian shot** or **shaft.** *See under* PARTHIAN.
**Pot shot.** *See under* POT.
**Send a shot across someone's bows, To.** *See under* SEND.

**Shoulder. Shoulder to cry on, A.** A person one can turn to for sympathy.
**Shoulder to shoulder.** In solidarity; in a corporate effort.
**Atlantean shoulders.** *See under* ATLANTEAN.
**Cold shoulder, The.** *See under* COLD.
**Hard shoulder.** *See under* HARD.
**Have a chip on one's shoulder, To.** *See under* CHIP.
**Head and shoulders.** *See under* HEAD.
**Ivory shoulder of Pelops, The.** *See under* IVORY.
**Put one's shoulder to the wheel, To.** To make a determined effort, as a carter would put his shoulder to the wheel to assist his horses hauling his wagon out of a rut.

> Putting your shoulder to the wheel when the coach gets into the mud. That's what I've been doing all my life.
>
> ANTHONY TROLLOPE: *The Small House at Allington*, ch xlvi (1864)

**Rub shoulders with someone, To.** *See under* RUB.
**Straight from the shoulder.** *See under* STRAIGHT.

**Shout. Shout the odds, To.** To make a noisy protest or fuss, as a bookmaker noisily proclaims the odds.
**All over bar the shouting.** *See under* ALL.
**It's my shout.** It's my turn to buy the next round of drinks. The allusion is to shouting in order to catch the landlord's attention or calling one's order.

**Shove, When push comes to.** *See under* WHEN.

**Shovel hat.** A broad-brimmed black hat curved up at the sides producing a shovel-like projection at back and front, and formerly favoured by clergy. Hence 'shovel hat' as a former colloquialism for an ecclesiastic.

**Show. Show a clean pair of heels, To.** To run away; to make one's escape by superior speed. Here 'clean' means free from obstruction.
**Show a leg.** Jump out of bed and be quick about it. A naval phrase, from the traditional formula used to call the hands from their hammocks, 'Wakey, wakey, rise and shine, the morning's fine … show a leg, show a leg, show a leg.' It comes from the days when women were allowed to sleep on board. They were allowed to 'lie in' and had to 'show a leg' to ensure that no rating was still turned in.
**Show of hands, A.** A vote at a meeting, taken by those present raising their hands for or against a motion.
**Show one's face, To.** To put in an appearance, often only briefly.
**Show one's hand, To.** To reveal one's intentions or resources, as when exposing a hand of cards to an opponent.
**Show one's teeth, To.** To adopt a menacing or aggressive tone, as a dog bares its teeth when it snarls.
**Show one's true colours, To.** To reveal one's true nature or proper character.
**Show someone the door, To.** To ask a person to leave; to get rid of someone whose presence is unwelcome.

**Show stopper.** A stage act, song or the like that receives so much applause that it interrupts the show.

**Show the flag, To.** To assert one's claim to a territory, or more generally, to put in an appearance, so that one is seen to be present.

**Show the white feather, To.** To show cowardice, a phrase from COCKFIGHTING, a white feather in a gamecock's tail being taken as a sign of degenerate stock, not a true gamebird.

**Gang show.** *See under* GANG.

**Good show!** Well done! I approve of that!

**Greatest Show on Earth.** *See under* GREAT.

**Have a showdown, To.** To reveal the strength of one's position; to have a final confrontation in a dispute to settle the matter or to clear the air. In poker, a showdown is the act of placing one's cards face upwards on the table at the end of the game.

**Leg show.** *See under* LEG.

**Raree show.** *See under* RAREE.

**Road show.** *See under* ROAD.

**Run the show, To.** *See under* RUN.

**Steal the show, To.** *See under* STEAL.

**Shred. King of shreds and patches.** *See under* KING.

**Shrewmouse.** This small insectivorous animal was fabled to have the power of harming cattle and other beasts by running over their backs and of laming any foot over which it ran. Gilbert White tells of a shrew ash whose twigs give relief if applied to the limbs of beasts harmed by the shrewmouse. This tree was one in which a deep hole had been bored and a shrewmouse thrust in alive. The hole was then plugged (*Natural History of Selbourne*, Letter xxviii (1788)). It was also ill luck to encounter a shrewmouse when beginning a journey.

**Shrift** or **shrive** (ultimately from Latin *scribere*, 'to write'). To shrive a person was to prescribe penance after confession and to absolve. *See also* SHROVETIDE.

**Give someone short shrift, To.** *See under* SHORT.

**Shropshire.** The Old English name for the county was *Scrobbesbyrigscir*, literally 'Shrewsbury-shire'. The Norman name was *Salopescira*, hence Salop as a synonym for the county (and its official name from 1974 to 1980) and Salopian for a native.

**Shroud, The Turin.** *See under* FAKES.

**Shrovetide.** The three days just before the beginning of LENT, when people went to confession and afterwards indulged in all sorts of sports and merrymaking.

**Shrove Tuesday.** The day before ASH WEDNESDAY, otherwise PANCAKE Day. It used to be the great time for COCKFIGHTING in England.

**Shut. Shut** or **close one's eyes to, To.** To pretend not to see or notice; to ignore.

**Shut the door in someone's face, To.** To shut the door deliberately and to refuse to have any dealings with the caller. Figuratively, to end negotiations with someone.

**Shut up!** Stop talking! Stop interrupting! The allusion is to shutting one's mouth.

**Shut up shop, To.** To retire or withdraw from participation in an undertaking.

**Shut your face!** An abrupt command to someone to stop talking. An even abrupter one is 'Shut it!'

**Door must be either shut or open.** *See under* DOOR.

**Shy. Fight shy of.** *See under* FIGHT.

**Shylock, A.** A grasping, stony-hearted money-lender. The allusion is to the Jew in Shakespeare's *The Merchant of Venice* (1596).

**Si.** *See* ARETINIAN SYLLABLES; TONIC SOL-FA.

**Si quis** (Latin, 'if anyone'). A notice to all whom it may concern, given in the parish church before ordination, that a resident means to offer himself as a candidate for HOLY ORDERS and that if anyone knows any just cause or impediment to this, they are to declare the same to the bishop.

**Siamese twins.** Identical twins physically joined together when born and often inseparable. The name originated with two children, Eng and Chang Bunker (1811–74), born in Siam (now Thailand) of Chinese parents. Joined in the area of the waist, they were duly sold by their mother and exhibited in America, England and Europe. They enjoyed good health, married two sisters, fathered normal healthy children and lived to the age of 63.

The medical term for waist-joined twins is xiphopagi, from Greek *xiphos*, 'sword', referring to the xiphoid (sword-shaped) cartilage at the site of conjoining, and *pagos*, 'firmly fixed'. Twins joined at the buttocks are known as pygopagi, the first half of the word meaning 'rump'. Most pygopagi are female or HERMAPHRODITE. The Czech twin sisters Rosa and Josefa Blazek (1878–1920) were a noted example. They also enjoyed good health and lived to be 42. They were exhibited in Paris as the 'Bohemian Twins' and were brought to London in 1891. At the age of 32 they entered hospital and Rosa give birth to a boy.

A sign on a green at Biddenden, Kent, depicts two young women joined together. They are the Siamese twins Mary and Eliza Chulkhurst, said to have been born here in 1100. The date is unlikely, however, and probably arose as a misreading of 1500. At their death aged 34 the sisters left the income from their property to provide bread and cheese for the poor. This dole is still distributed on Easter Monday morning.

**Sibyl.** A prophetess of classical legend, who was supposed to prophesy under the inspiration of a deity. The name is now applied to any prophetess or woman fortune-teller. There were a number of sibyls, and they had their seats in widely separate parts of the world, Greece, Italy, Babylonia and Egypt among them. Plato mentions only one, i.e. the Erythraean, identified with AMALTHEA, the Cumaean sibyl, who was consulted by AENEAS and accompanied him into HADES and who sold the SIBYLLINE BOOKS to TARQUIN. Martin Capella speaks of two, the Erythraean and the Phrygian. Aelian tells of four, the Erythraean, Samian, Egyptian and Sardian. Varro writes that there were ten: the Cumaean, the Delphic, Egyptian, Erythraean, Hellespontine, Libyan, Persian, Phrygian, Samian and Tiburtine.

The medieval monks 'adopted' the sibyls, as they did so much of pagan myth. They made them 12, and gave to each a separate prophecy and distinct emblem:

(1) Libyan (emblem, a lighted taper): 'The day shall come when men shall see the king of all living things.'
(2) Samian (emblem, a rose): 'The Rich One shall be born of a pure virgin.'
(3) Cuman (emblem, a crown): 'Jesus Christ shall come from heaven, and live and reign in poverty on earth.'
(4) Cumaean (emblem, a cradle): 'God shall be born of a pure virgin, and hold converse with sinners.'
(5) Erythraean (emblem, a horn): 'Jesus Christ, Son of God, the Saviour.'
(6) Persian (emblem, a dragon under the sibyl's feet and a lantern): 'Satan shall be overcome by a true prophet.'
(7) Tiburtine (emblem, a dove): 'The Highest shall descend from heaven and a virgin be shown in the valleys of the deserts.'
(8) Delphic (emblem, a crown of thorns): 'The Prophet born of the virgin shall be crowned with thorns.'
(9) Phrygian (emblem, a banner and a cross): 'Our Lord shall rise again.'
(10) European (emblem, a sword): 'A virgin and her Son shall flee into Egypt.'
(11) Agrippine (emblem, a whip): 'Jesus Christ shall be outraged and scourged.'
(12) Hellespontic (emblem, a T-cross): 'Jesus Christ shall suffer shame upon the cross'.

**Sibylline books, The.** A collection of oracular utterances preserved in ancient Rome and consulted by the Senate in times of emergency or disaster. According to Livy, there were originally nine books offered to TARQUIN by the SIBYL of Cumae but the offer was rejected, and she burned three of them. She offered the remaining six at the same price. Again, being refused, she burned three more. The remaining three were then bought by the king for the original sum.

The three books were preserved in a vault of the temple of JUPITER Capitolinus, and committed to the charge of custodians, ultimately 15 in number. They were destroyed by fire in 83 BC. A new collection of verses was made from those preserved in the cities of Greece, Italy and Asia Minor, and deposited in the rebuilt temple. They were transferred to the temple of APOLLO by AUGUSTUS in 12 BC and were said to have been destroyed by Stilicho (*c*.405).

**Sibylline oracles.** A collection of 15 books, 12 of which are extant, of 2nd- and 3rd-century authorship, and written by Jews and Christians in imitation of the SIBYLLINE BOOKS. Their aim was to gain converts to their respective faiths.

**Sic** (Latin, 'thus', 'so'). A word used in quoting after a doubtful or unusual word or phrase, or a misspelling, to indicate that it is here printed exactly as in the original and to call attention to the fact that it is wrong in some way or different from what is to be expected.

**Sic transit gloria mundi** (Latin, 'So passes away the glory of the world'). A quotation from *De Imitatione Christi* by Thomas à Kempis (1380–1471), a classic statement on the transitory nature of human vanities. At the coronation ceremony of the pope, a reed surmounted with flax is burned, and as it flickers and dies the chaplain intones *Pater sancte, sic transit gloria mundi* ('Holy Father, thus doth the glory of the world depart').

> Tell me, where are now those learned Doctors and Professors, who, while the honours of literature were blooming around them, you so well knew and so highly reverenced? … While living, they seemed to be something: but dead, the tongue is utterly silent about them. O how suddenly passeth away the glory of this world!
>
> *Of the Imitation of Christ*, Bk I, ch iii (anonymous English translation)

**Sicily. Sicilian Vespers.** The massacre of the French in Sicily on Easter Monday (30 March) 1282, which began on the stroke of the vesper bell. It was occasioned by the brutality and tyranny of the rule of Charles of Anjou (1227–85).

**Two Sicilies, The.** *See under* TWO.

**Sick. Sick and tired.** Disgusted, weary or fed up, as: 'I'm sick and tired of his behaviour.'

**Sick joke.** An insensitive, morbid or sadistic joke, not amusing in the normal way but the product of warped wit. An example is the following:

> What's a thousand metres long and eats vegetables? A Moscow meat queue.
>
> 'NORMA P. LAMONT': *The Official Ministry of Fun Joke Book* (1992)

**Sick Man of Europe, The.** So Nicholas I of Russia (in 1844 and subsequently) called the Turkish Empire, which had long been in decline. His hints to Britain in 1853 of a partition were ignored.

**As sick as a cat** or **a dog.** *See under* AS.
**Falling sickness.** *See under* FALL.
**Fall sick, To.** *See under* FALL.
**Green sickness.** *See under* GREEN.
**Sleeping sickness.** *See under* SLEEPING.
**Sweating sickness.** *See under* SWEAT.

**Sickle, Hammer and.** *See under* HAMMER.

**Side. Sideburns.** Short side whiskers, originally called burnsides after the American Federal General Ambrose Everett Burnside (1824–81) who wore such whiskers.

**Side issue.** A subsidiary issue, of secondary importance to the main issue.

**Sidetrack, To.** Originally an American RAILROAD term, hence to divert; to distract.

**Bit on the side, A.** *See under* BIT.
**Distaff side.** *See under* DISTAFF.
**East Side.** *See under* EAST.
**God sides with the strongest.** *See under* GOD.

**Let the side down, To.** To fail one's colleagues, especially by embarrassing them.

**On the side.** As a sideline; in addition to one's regular work; secretly or illegally.

**On the side of the angels.** The phrase with which Disraeli thought he had settled the problems raised by Darwin's theory of the origin of species. It occurred in his speech at the Oxford Diocesan Conference, 25 November 1864:

> The question is this: Is man an ape or an angel? Now I am on the side of the angels.

It was the same statesman who said in the HOUSE OF COMMONS (14 May 1866): 'Ignorance never settles a question.'

**Put on side, To.** To give oneself airs; to be arrogant or pretentious. 'To put on side' in billiards is to give one's ball a twist or spin with the cue when striking it.

**Seamy side.** *See under* SEAMY.
**Shake one's sides, To.** *See under* SHAKE.
**Spear side.** *See under* SPEAR.
**Spindle side.** *See under* SPINDLE.
**Split one's sides, To.** *See under* SPLIT.
**Sunny side.** *See under* SUN.
**West Side.** *See under* WEST.

**Siege. Siege of Troy, The.** *See* ACHILLES; HELEN; ILIAD; TROJAN WAR; ULYSSES; WOODEN HORSE OF TROY.

**Siege Perilous.** In the cycle of ARTHURIAN ROMANCES, a seat at the ROUND TABLE, which was kept vacant for whoever should accomplish the quest of the HOLY GRAIL. For any lesser person to sit in it was fatal. At the crown of his achievement, Sir GALAHAD took his seat in the Siege Perilous. *See also* KNIGHTS OF THE ROUND TABLE.

**Siegfried** or **Sigurd.** The hero of the first part of the NIBELUNGENLIED. He was the youngest son of Siegmund and Sieglind, king and queen of the Netherlands. Wagner's opera *Siegfried* (1876) is the third part of *Der Ring des Nibelungen*. *See also* TARNKAPPE.

**Siegfried Line.** The defences built by the Germans on their western frontier before and after 1939 as a reply to France's MAGINOT LINE. The British song, popular in 1939, 'We're gonna hang out the washing on the Siegfried Line' was somewhat premature. When Canadian troops penetrated the Line in 1945 they hung up a number of sheets with a large notice on which was written 'The Washing'.

**Siegfried's cloak of invisibility.** *See* TARNKAPPE.

**Siena, Catherine of.** *See under* CATHERINE.

**Sierra.** The word is Spanish for 'saw' and is used for the name of a chain of mountains with jagged peaks, especially in America or Spain itself. Some of the best known such chains are the Sierra Madre, 'mother chain', in Mexico, and the Sierra Nevada, 'snowy chain', in both California and southeastern Spain. The word also gave the name of the West African state of Sierra Leone, 'lion chain'.

**Sieve and shears.** An ancient form of DIVINATION mentioned by Theocritus (*c*.310–250 BC). The points of the shears were stuck in the wooden rim of the sieve and two persons supported it upright with the tips of their two fingers. Then a verse of the Bible was read aloud, and St PETER and St PAUL were asked if the guilty person was A, B or C (naming those suspected). When the guilty person was named the sieve would suddenly turn round. This method was also used to tell if a couple would marry.

> Searching for things lost with a sieve and shears.
> BEN JONSON: *The Alchemist*, I, i (1610)

**Sighs, Bridge of.** *See under* BRIDGE.

**Sight.** In colloquial usage, the word can denote a great quantity or degree, as: 'It's a sight more peaceful here than it is in the city'.

**Sight for sore eyes, A.** A person or thing that it is a pleasure or a relief to see, especially when long awaited, such as a visitor.

**Sight unseen.** Without having actually seen the thing mentioned, as when one buys something by telephone or mail order.

**At first sight.** *See under* AT.

**Lower one's sights, To.** To become less ambitious.

**Out of my sight!** Go away at once! Don't let me see you again!

**Out of sight.** *See under* OUT.
**Out of sight, out of mind.** *See under* OUT.
**Second sight.** *See under* SECOND.

**See the sights, To.** To visit the interesting or historic features of a town or region, or those promoted as such by touristic literature. 'Sights' here means the things worth seeing, as more precisely indicated by the equivalent word in other languages, such as German *Sehenswürdigkeiten* or the equally lengthy Russian *dostoprimechatel'nosti*. The Chinese is *míngshèng*, literally 'name successes'.

**Set one's sights on, To.** *See under* SET.

**Sigismonda.** In Boccaccio's DECAMERON, a princess of Salerno whose true love is murdered by her father, TANCRED.

**Sign. Sign off, To.** In the 19th century this expression denoted finally leaving one religious organization for another. It is generally used to mean terminating attendances, registering when leaving work, finishing a broadcast or the like.

**Sign on the dotted line, To.** To accept fully the terms offered, from the space indicated by dots reserved for a person's signature on printed forms.

**Signs of the Zodiac, The.** *See* ZODIAC.

**Sign or take the pledge, To.** To bind oneself by one's pledged word to abstain from intoxicating liquors. Such a pledge was taken by members of the BAND OF HOPE.

**Call sign.** *See under* CALL.

**Cardinal signs.** *See under* CARDINAL.

**Royal Sign Manual.** *See under* ROYAL.

**Septentrional signs.** *See under* SEPTENTRIONAL.

**Signature. Signature tune.** A musical theme played regularly as a means of identification to introduce a particular artist or regularly broadcast programme. One of the best known signature tunes in the days of 'steam radio' was 'Here's To the Next Time', played in the 1930s at the close of every broadcast by Henry Hall and the BBC Dance Orchestra.

> If one wished to be facetious, one could say that the *leitmotiv* of characters in Wagner's *Ring* are their 'signature-tunes'.
>
> MICHAEL KENNEDY: *The Oxford Dictionary of Music* (1994)

**Episcopal signatures.** *See under* EPISCOPACY.

**Signet, A writer to the.** *See under* WRITE.

**Sigurd.** The SIEGFRIED of the VOLSUNGS Saga, the Scandinavian version of the NIBELUNGENLIED. He falls in love with BRUNHILD but under the influence of a love potion marries Gudrun, a union that has fateful consequences.

**Sikes, Bill.** A name at one time used for a ruffianly housebreaker, from the character in Dickens' *Oliver Twist* (1837–8).

**Sikh** (Hindi, 'disciple'). All Sikhs are ultimately disciples of GURU Nanak (1469–1539) and his nine successors, who lived in the Punjab region of India. The son of a local tax official, Nanak at the age of about 30 underwent an experience that changed his life. He bathed in the river as usual one morning but returned only three days later claiming that he had been chosen to preach the oneness of God and the potential for anyone, regardless of caste or sex, to receive God's grace and receive spiritual liberation without waiting for death. This was to be accomplished by undertaking socially acceptable work and by caring for the needy by deed or gift. There are 20 million Sikhs worldwide, their chief house of worship in India being the GOLDEN TEMPLE.

**Silence. Silence gives consent.** A saying, common to many languages, founded on the old Latin legal maxim: *Qui tacet consentire videtur* ('whoever is silent is held to consent').

**Silence is golden.** *See* SPEECH IS SILVER, SILENCE IS GOLDEN.

**Amyclaean silence.** *See under* AMYCLAEAN.

**Argument of silence, The.** *See under* ARGUE.

**Man of Silence.** *See* NAPOLEON III.

**Rest is silence, The.** *See under* REST.

**Towers of Silence.** *See under* TOWER.

**Two-minute silence.** *See under* TWO.

**Silent. As silent as the grave.** *See under* AS.

**William the Silent.** *See under* WILLIAM.

**Silenus.** The drunken attendant and nurse of BACCHUS, represented as a fat, jovial old man, always full of liquor, riding a donkey. Silenus was the son of PAN or of HERMES, and he is often associated with his counterpart, Bacchus (or Dionysus), the god of wine:

> Within his car, aloft, young Bacchus stood,
> Trifling his ivy-dart, in dancing mood,
> With sidelong laughing;
> And little rills of crimson wine imbrued
> His plump white arms, and shoulders, enough white
> For Venus' pearly bite:
> And near him rode Silenus on his ass,
> Pelted with flowers as he on did pass
> Tipsily quaffing.
>
> JOHN KEATS: *Endymion*, iv (1818)

**Silhouette.** A profile drawing of a person giving the outline only, with the whole area within the outline in black; hence a shadow and, figuratively, a slight literary sketch of a person or other subject. The word is derived from the name of the French minister of finance, Étienne de Silhouette (1709–67), noted for his parsimony in public expenditure. His name was applied to things made cheaply, and the first silhouettes were cut out from scraps of paper, rather than being drawn.

**Silk. Silk Road, The.** The ancient caravan route along which silk was carried from China, through central Asia, thence to Antioch and the eastern Mediterranean and eventually to other parts of Europe. It was in use for about 1500 years, particularly in the days of the Roman Empire. Parts of it were traversed by the Venetian Marco POLO (1254–1324) on his visits to China in the late 13th century.

**Make a silk purse out of a sow's ear, To.** To attempt to make something good from what is by nature bad or inferior in quality. *See also* PIG'S EAR.

**Take silk, To.** Said of a BARRISTER who has been appointed a KING'S OR QUEEN'S COUNSEL (KC or QC) because he or she then exchanges a stuff gown for a silk one.

**Wild silk.** *See under* WILD.

**Silly.** The word comes from Old English *sǣlig*, 'happy', related to modern German *selig*, 'blessed', so that the original sense was 'happy through being innocent'. Hence medieval carols term the infant Jesus 'a harmless silly babe', and sheep were called 'silly'. As the innocent are easily taken in by worldly cunning, the word came to signify 'gullible', 'foolish'.

**Silly Billy.** A nickname applied to William IV (1765–1837), also to William Frederick, Duke of Gloucester (1776–1834).

**Silly season, The.** An old journalistic expression for the part of the year when Parliament and the Law Courts are not sitting (usually August and September), when, through lack of news, the papers had to fill their columns with trivial items, such as news of giant gooseberries and sea serpents, and long correspondence on subjects of ephemeral or little interest.

> The silly season for newspapers is usually thought of as August. This year there is a second silly season, in December, and it is built around the national lottery ... The nation is gripped by some ridiculous argument about whether a lottery winner should be named.
>
> *Sunday Times* (18 December 1994)

**Silly Suffolk.** The county has possibly come to be so nicknamed from its many churches and religious houses.

**Silurian.** Of or pertaining to the ancient British tribe, the Silures, or the district they inhabited, i.e. southeastern Wales. The 'sparkling wines of the Silurian vats' are cider and perry.

**Silurian rocks.** A name given by Sir Roderick Murchison (1835) to what miners call graywacke and Werner termed transition rocks, because it was in the SILURIAN district (English-Welsh border) that he first investigated their structure.

**Silurist, The.** A surname adopted by the mystical poet Henry Vaughan (1621–95), who was born and died in Brecknockshire.

**Silver.** In England standard silver (i.e. that used for coinage) formerly consisted of $\frac{37}{40}$ of fine silver and $\frac{3}{40}$ of alloy (fineness, 925). In 1925 the proportions were changed to one-half silver, one-half alloy (fineness, 500). In 1946 cupronickel coins were introduced to replace silver. *See also* HALLMARK; LEGAL TENDER.

Among the ancient alchemists silver represented the MOON OR DIANA. In HERALDRY it is known by its French name argent, and it is indicated on engravings by the silver (argent) portion being left blank.

**Silver Age, The.** According to Hesiod and the Greek and Roman poets, the second of the Ages of the World, fabled as a period that was voluptuous and godless, and much inferior in simplicity and true happiness to the GOLDEN AGE.

**Silver-fork school, The.** A name given *c.*1830 in amused contempt to the novelists who were sticklers for the etiquette and graces of the UPPER TEN and showed great respect for the affectations of gentility. Theodore Hook (1788–1841), Marguerite, Countess of Blessington (1789–1849) and Lord Lytton (1803–73) may be taken as representatives of it.

**Silver lining.** A comforting or optimistic aspect of an otherwise bleak or black situation. *See also* EVERY CLOUD HAS A SILVER LINING.

**Silver Star.** A United States military decoration for gallantry in action. It consists of a bronze star bearing a small silver star in its centre.

**Silver Streak, The.** The English Channel.

**Silver-tongued.** An epithet bestowed on many persons famed for eloquence, such as William Bates, the PURITAN divine (1625–99), Anthony Hammond, the poet (1688–1738), Henry Smith, preacher (*c.*1550–91), and Joshua Sylvester (1563–1618), translator of Du Bartas.

**Silver wedding.** The twenty-fifth anniversary, when presents of silver plate (in Germany a silver wreath) are given to the happy pair.

**Born with a silver spoon in one's mouth, To be.** *See under* BORN.

**Every cloud has a silver lining.** *See under* EVERY.

**German silver.** *See under* GERMANY.

**Long John Silver.** *See under* LONG.

**Sell off the family silver, To.** *See under* SELL.

**Speech is silver, silence is golden.** *See under* SPEECH.

**Thirty pieces of silver.** *See under* THIRTY.

**Silvia.** In Roman mythology the mother of ROMULUS and Remus. In Shakespeare's *The Two Gentlemen of Verona* (1594) Silvia is a paragon of beauty. The song about her in the play has been set to music by several composers, but most memorably by Schubert.

> Who is Silvia? what is she,
> That all our swains commend her?
> IV, ii

**Simeon.** In the Old Testament (Genesis) the second of the 12 sons of JACOB. In the New Testament (Luke 2) Simeon is a devout aged Jew who is the first to recognise the child Jesus as the MESSIAH and who then dies in peace. His song of praise and thanks to God, the 'Song of Simeon', is more usually known as the NUNC DIMITTIS.

**St Simeon Stylites.** *See* STYLITES.

**Similia similibus curantur** (Latin). Like cures like, or take a HAIR OF THE DOG THAT BIT YOU.

**Simnel cakes.** Rich cakes formerly eaten on MID-LENT SUNDAY (MOTHERING SUNDAY) and at EASTER. The recipes varied from county to county, but the Lancashire recipe was especially rich. The ingredients were enriched with almonds and eggs, and the cakes were traditionally decorated with marzipan formed into small balls. The cakes were eaten at Mid-Lent in commemoration of the banquet given by JOSEPH to his brethren, which forms the first lesson of Mid-Lent Sunday, and the feeding of the five thousand, which forms the GOSPEL of the day.

The word simnel comes through Old French from Latin *simila*, 'fine flour'.

**Simon. Simon Magus.** Isidore of Seville writes that Simon Magus died in the reign of NERO, and adds that he had proposed a dispute with St PETER and St PAUL, and had promised to fly up to heaven. He succeeded in rising high into the air, but at the prayers of the two apostles he was cast down to earth by the evil spirits who had enabled him to rise.

Henry Milman, dean of St Paul's, in his *History of Latin Christianity*, ii (1854–5) tells another story. He says that Simon offered to be buried alive, and declared that he would reappear on the third day. He was actually buried in a deep trench, 'but to this day,' says Hippolytus, 'his disciples have failed to witness his resurrection'.

His followers were known as Simonians, and the sin of which he was guilty, i.e. the trafficking in sacred things and the buying and selling of ecclesiastical offices, is still called simony.

> And when Simon saw that through laying on of the apostles' hands the Holy Ghost was given, he offered them money.
> Acts 8:18

**Simon Pure.** The real man, the authentic article. In Susannah Centlivre's *A Bold Stroke for a Wife* (1718) a Colonel Feignwell passes himself off for Simon Pure, a QUAKER, and wins the heart of Miss Lovely. No sooner does he get the assent of her guardian than the Quaker turns up, and proves beyond a doubt he is the 'real Simon Pure'. In modern usage, the expression is used of a hypocrite, one who makes a great parade of virtue.

**St Simon (Zelotes).** The saint and martyr is represented with a falchion in his hand, in allusion to the instrument with which the heathen priests hewed him to death. He sometimes bears fish in his other hand, in allusion to his occupation as a fisherman. His feast-day is 28 October.

**Simple Simon.** *See under* SIMPLE.

**Simonism.** *See* SAINT-SIMONISM.

**Simple. Simple, The.** Charles III of France (879–929), the son of Louis the Stammerer, was so called. Having ceded Normandy to the Vikings under Rollo, he was dethroned in 923.

**Simple life, The.** A mode of living in which the object is to eliminate as far as possible all luxuries and extraneous aids to happiness, while returning to the simplicity of life as imagined by the pastoral poets. One who essayed the simple life with singular success was the American writer Henry D. Thoreau (1817–62), who in his book *Walden; or, Life in the Woods* (1854) describes his experiment in basic living on the shores of Walden Pond near Concord, his Massachusetts birthplace.

**Simple Simon.** A simpleton, a gullible booby, from the character in the well-known nursery tale, who met a pieman but had no money to buy any pies, who went fishing for a whale in a bucket of water, and who pricked his finger when looking to see if plums grew on thistles.

**Fee simple.** *See under* FEE.

**Sin.** According to Milton, Sin is twin keeper with Death of the gates of hell. She sprang full-grown from the head of SATAN.

> The one seemed woman to the waist, and fair,
> But ended foul in many a scaly fold
> Voluminous and vast, a serpent armed
> With mortal sting.
> *Paradise Lost*, ii (1667)

**Sin against the Holy Ghost, The.** Much has been written about this sin, the definition of which has been based upon several passages in the Gospels, such as Matthew 12: 31, 32 and Mark 3:29, and it has been interpreted as the wilful denunciation of that which is manifestly good, thus revealing a state of soul beyond the divine influence.

> Whosoever speaketh against the Holy Ghost, it shall not be forgiven him, neither in this world, neither in the world to come.
> Matthew 12:32

**Sin-eaters.** Poor people hired at funerals in olden days to eat beside the corpse and so take upon themselves the sins of the deceased, that the soul might be delivered from PURGATORY. In Carmarthenshire the sin-eater used to rest a plate of salt on the breast of the deceased and place a piece of bread on the salt. After saying an incantation over the bread, the sin-eater consumed it and with it the sins of the dead.

**'Sin on' Bible, The.** *See under* BIBLE.

**Sin rent.** In medieval England a fine imposed upon the laity by the church for living in sin, i.e. for concubinage. *See also* CRADLE CROWN.

**As ugly as sin.** *See under* AS.

**Earn the wages of sin, To.** *See under* EARN.

**Man of Sin, The.** *See under* MAN.

**Mortal sins.** The same as the SEVEN DEADLY SINS.

**Original sin.** *See under* ORIGINAL.

**Seven deadly sins, The.** *See under* SEVEN.

**Venial sin.** *See under* VENIAL.

**Sinbad the Sailor.** The hero of the story of this name in the ARABIAN NIGHTS ENTERTAINMENTS. He was a wealthy citizen of Baghdad, called 'The Sailor' because of his seven voyages in which, among many adventures, he discovered the ROC's egg and the Valley of Diamonds, and killed the OLD MAN OF THE SEA.

**Sindhia.** The family name of the princely rulers of Gwalior from 1726 to 1947.

**Sindibad.** *See* SANDABAR.

**Sine** (Latin). Without.

**Sine die** (Latin, 'without a day'). With no time fixed; indefinitely with regard to time. When a proposal is deferred *sine die*, it is deferred without fixing a day for its reconsideration, which is virtually 'for ever'.

**Sine qua non** (Latin). An indispensable condition. The fuller expression in Latin is *sine qua non potest esse* or *fieri* ('that without which (the thing) cannot be or be done').

**Sinecure** (Latin *(beneficium) sine cura*, '(benefice) without cure'). An enjoyment of the emoluments attached to a benefice without having the trouble of the pastoral or spiritual 'cure' or care of the parishioners. The word is applied to any office to which a salary is attached without any duties to perform. Government sinecures were a particular feature of 18th-century political life and were not entirely unknown in the 20th. *See also* PLACEMEN.

**Sing. Singing bread** (French *pain à chanter*). An old term for the larger altar bread used in celebration of the MASS, because singing or chanting was in progress during its manufacture. It was also called singing cake and singing loaf.

**Sing out, To.** To cry or squeal from chastisement; to shout or call out.

**Make someone sing another tune, To.** To make them change their behaviour; to make them submit or be humble.

**Scat singing.** *See under* SCAT.

**When the fat lady sings.** *See under* WHEN.

**Singeing the king of Spain's beard.** Sir Francis Drake's daring attack on the Spanish ships and stores at Cadiz (1587), which delayed the sailing of the Armada until 1588. He referred to it as his 'singeing of the Spanish king's beard'. The king of Spain then was Philip II (r.1556–98). *See also* JEREZ.

**Single. Single currency.** A unified currency proposed for all member states of the European Union, the currency itself being the EURO. More generally the term symbolizes the relationship between national sovereignty and economic and monetary union. *See also* WAIT AND SEE *under* WAIT.

**Single-speech Hamilton.** William Gerard Hamilton (1729–96), Chancellor of the Exchequer in Ireland (1763–84), was so called from his maiden speech in Parliament (1755), a masterly torrent of eloquence, which astounded everyone.

**Single ticket.** A ticket for a single journey on public transport to a destination, with no return. The equivalent in the USA is, more logically, a 'one-way' ticket.

**In single file.** One behind another. *See also* INDIAN FILE.

**Sinis.** A Corinthian robber of Greek legend, according to some a giant and the son of POSEIDON. He was known as the Pinebender, because he used to fasten his victims to two pine trees bent towards the ground, and then leave them to be torn asunder when the trees were released. He was captured by THESEUS and put to death in the same way. Theseus is said to have founded the Isthmian games in honour of Sinis.

**Sinister** (Latin, 'on the left hand'). Foreboding ill; ill-omened. According to AUGURY, birds appearing on the left-hand side forebode ill luck, but on the right-hand side, good luck. Plutarch, following Plato and Aristotle, gives as the reason that the west (or left side of the augur) was towards the setting or departing sun.

In HERALDRY the word denotes the left side of the shield viewed from the position of its bearer, i.e. in illustrations it is the right-hand side.

**Bar sinister.** *See under* BAR.

**Bend sinister.** *See under* BEND.

**Sink. Sinking fund.** The name given to the government fund established in 1717, the interest from which was to 'sink' or pay off the NATIONAL DEBT. The fund was re-established by Pitt the Younger in 1786, and, as a result of the French Revolutionary Wars, created a loss and was abandoned in 1828. A new fund was set up in 1875, which was remodelled in 1923 and 1928. According to Sir William Blackstone, it was intended 'to sink and lower the National Debt'.

> The Sinking Fund's unfathomable sea,
> That most unliquidating liquid, leaves
> The debt unsunk, yet sinks all it receives.
>
> LORD BYRON: *Don Juan* (1819–24)

**Sink or swim.** No matter what happens. Convicted witches were thrown into the water to 'sink or swim'. If they sank, they were drowned, but if they swam it was clear proof they were in league with the Evil One. They were thus in a CATCH-22 situation. *See also* ORDEAL.

**Hook, line and sinker.** *See under* HOOK.

**Kitchen sink drama.** *See under* KITCHEN.

**Sinn Féin** (Irish, 'we ourselves'). The Irish nationalist movement formed in 1905, which set up the Irish Republic (1919) under De Valera and carried on guerrilla warfare with the English until the treaty of 1922. Disagreements over this settlement disrupted the party, which still aims to bring Northern Ireland into the Republic. *See also* FENIANS; IRA; SIX COUNTIES; ULSTER.

**Sir.** The word evolved as a shortening of 'sire', itself through Old French from Latin *senior*, 'elder', and ultimately from Latin *senex*, 'old man'. Spanish *señor*, Italian *signor* and French *sieur* are related.

As a title of honour prefixed to the Christian name of BARONETS and KNIGHTS, Sir is of great antiquity, and the clergy at one time had Sir prefixed to their name. This is merely a translation of the university word *dominus* given to graduates, as 'Dominus Hugh Evans'.

The word is traditionally used as a form of address to a superior in general and in particular by a schoolboy to a master.

> 'Sir, please sir, I think he's to do with the church, sir', said Cole Slaw. 'I saw him, talking to Wells Fargo, sir, after the service'.
>
> JOHN LE CARRÉ: *Tinker, Tailor, Soldier, Spy*, ch xiv (1974)

**Sirat, Al.** *See* AL-SIRAT.

**Sirdar** (Persian *sardār*, literally 'head possession'). The commander-in-chief of the Egyptian army and military governor of Egypt (a British officer during the occupation, 1882–1922). Also applied to certain nobles in India.

**Siren** (perhaps from Greek *seira*, 'rope', so 'entangler'). One of the mythical monsters, half-woman and half-bird, said by Greek poets to entice seamen by the sweetness of their song to such a degree that the listeners forgot all and died of hunger. The word thus came to be applied to any dangerous, alluring woman.

In Homeric mythology there were two sirens, but later writers name three: PARTHENOPE, Ligea and Leucosia. The number was still further augmented by others. The sirens were the daughters of Achelous and either MELPOMENE, Sterope or TERPSICHORE.

ULYSSES escaped their blandishments by filling his companions' ears with wax and lashing himself to the mast of his ship. While the ARGONAUTS sailed past their island, ORPHEUS sang and played on his harp so that he and his companions would not be lured towards them.

Plato says there were three kinds of sirens: the celestial, the generative and the cathartic. The first were under the government of JUPITER, the second under that of NEPTUNE and the third of PLUTO. When the soul is in heaven, the sirens seek, by harmonic motion, to unite it to the divine life of the celestial host, and when it is in HADES, to conform it to the infernal regimen, but on earth they spawn generation, of which the sea is emblematic (Proclus, *On the Theology of Plato*, Bk vi (5th century AD)).

In 1819 the word was adopted by the French physicist Charles Cagniard de la Tour (1777–1859) as the name of an acoustical instrument used to produce musical tones and to measure the number of vibrations in a note. It was this that gave the term for the modern mechanical whistle sounded at a factory to indicate that work is to be started or finished for the day. Sirens with two or more notes were employed in the Second World War to give warning of an air raid, sounding the 'alarm' beforehand and the 'all clear' after.

> What song the Syrens sang, or what name Achilles assumed when he hid himself among women, though puzzling questions, are not beyond all conjecture.
>
> SIR THOMAS BROWNE: *Hydriotaphia*, ch v (1658)

**Siren suit.** A one-piece lined and warm garment on the lines of a boiler suit, sometimes worn in London during the air raids of the Second World War. It was much favoured by Sir Winston Churchill and was so named from its being slipped on over night clothes at the first wail of the SIREN.

**Sirius.** The DOG STAR, so called by the Greeks from the adjective *seirios*, 'hot and scorching'. The Romans called it *canicula*, whence CANICULAR DAYS, and the Egyptians *sept*, which gave the Greek alternative *Sothis*. *See also* SOTHIC PERIOD.

**Sirloin.** Properly surloin, from Old French *surlonge*, 'above the loin'. The mistaken spelling 'sir-' has given rise to a number of stories of the joint having been 'knighted' because of its estimable qualities. Thomas Fuller (1608–61) tells how Henry VIII did so:

> Dining with the Abbot of Reading, he [Henry VIII] ate so heartily of a loin of beef that the abbot said he would give 1,000 marks for such a stomach. 'Done!' said the king, and kept the abbot a prisoner in the Tower, won his 1,000 marks, and knighted the beef.
>
> *Church History*, VI, ii (1655)

Another tradition turns the joke on James I:

> 'I vow, 'tis a noble sirloin!'
> 'Ay, here's cut and come again.'
> 'But pray, why is it called a sirloin?'
> 'Why you must know that our King James I, who loved good eating, being invited to dinner by one of his nobles, and seeing a large loin of beef at his table, he drew out his sword, and in a frolic knighted it. Few people know the secret of this.'
>
> JONATHAN SWIFT: *Polite Conversation*, ii (1738)

He is said to have performed this act in 1617 when passing the night at Hoghton Tower, near Blackburn, Lancashire, as the guest of Sir Richard Hoghton.

**Sirocco.** *See* AUSTER.

**Sister. African Sisters, The.** The HESPERIDES.

**Brontë sisters, The.** *See under* BRONTË.

**Seven Sisters, The.** *See under* SEVEN.

**Sob sister.** *See under* SOB.

**White Sisters.** *See under* WHITE.

**Sistine. Sistine Chapel, The.** The principal chapel in the VATICAN, reserved for ceremonies at which the pope is present, so called because it was built by Sixtus IV (1471–84). It is decorated with frescoes by MICHELANGELO and others.

**Sistine Madonna, The** (Italian *Madonna di San Sisto*). The Madonna painted by Raphael (*c.*1513) for the church of St Sixtus (San Sisto) at Piacenza. St Sixtus is shown kneeling at the right of the Virgin. The picture is now in the Gemäldegalerie, Dresden.

**Sisyphus.** In Greek legend the son of AEOLUS and husband of MEROPE, and in post-Homeric legend, the father of Odysseus (ULYSSES). His punishment in the world of the SHADES was to roll a huge stone up a hill to the top. As it constantly rolled down again just as it reached the summit, his task was everlasting. Hence 'a labour of Sisyphus' or 'Sisyphean toil' is an endless, heart-breaking job.

The reasons given for this punishment vary. Some sources say that ZEUS decided to punish Sisyphus because he revealed to Aegina's father, the river-god Asopus, that she had been abducted by Zeus. Another reason suggested was that Zeus sent THANATOS to kill Sisyphus, who took Thanatos by surprise and imprisoned him so that no mortals could die. Zeus forced Sisyphus to release Thanatos, whose first victim was Sisyphus, but he had asked his wife, MEROPE, to make sure that no funerary honours were paid so that when he reached the Underworld he persuaded the gods to permit him to return to earth to punish his wife. He was allowed to leave the Underworld, and then lived to a great age. When he eventually died, the gods of the Underworld, determined that he should not escape again, set him the unending task. His name has been popularly derived from Greek *sophos*, 'wise', but it is almost certainly the case that it is of pre-Greek origin. *See also* ANTICLEA; AUTOLYCUS.

**Sit. Sit above the salt, To.** To sit in a place of distinction. Formerly the family 'saler' (salt cellar) was of massive silver, and placed in the middle of the table. Persons of distinction sat above the 'saler', i.e. between it and the head of the table, while dependants and inferior guests sat below.

**Sit at someone's feet, To.** To be their pupil or disciple.

**Sit-down strike.** A form of mass protest in which the strikers remain at their workplace but refuse to work themselves or allow others to do so. The tactic first came to the fore in the 1930s.

**Sit-in, A.** A form of mass protest similar to a SIT-DOWN STRIKE, in which students occupy college premises but BOYCOTT lectures. The aim is to redress grievances or dictate policy.

**Sit in judgement, To.** To take upon oneself the right to pass judgement on others; to be censorious.

**Sit like patience on a monument, To.** To be exceptionally patient and long suffering. From the apparent patience of a statue.

> She sat like patience on a monument,
> Smiling at grief.
> SHAKESPEARE: *Twelfth Night*, II, iv (1599)

**Sit on one's hands, To.** To take no action; to refuse to applaud.

**Sit on someone, To.** To 'squash' someone; to put them in their place.

**Sit on the fence, To.** To take care not to commit oneself; to hedge. A fence traditionally separates different territories or properties, so to sit on it is to adopt a neutral position.

> Sitting on the fence is a much maligned practice. For one thing, you get a better view. You also keep your feet dry and your options open. Of course, it may not look very elegant, but there are times when refusing to decide shows a firmer purpose than sheepishly climbing down off the railing, muttering: 'Oh, all right then, if you insist'.
> *Sunday Times* (6 September 1998)

**Sit tight, To.** Not to give up one's seat; to bide one's time; to remain in, or as if in, hiding. The phrase is from poker, where, if a player does not want to continue betting and at the same time does not wish to throw in his cards, he 'sits tight'.

**Sitting Bull.** A Sioux chief (*c.*1831–90) who resisted the governmental policy of reservations for his tribe. He defeated Custer in 1876 and later appeared in BUFFALO BILL's show. He was killed while his warriors were trying to rescue him during the Sioux rebellion of 1890. His Indian name was Tatanka Iyotake. *See also* CUSTER'S LAST STAND.

**Sitting pretty.** Well placed; 'on to a good thing'. Pretty here means prettily.

**Sit up and take notice, To.** To become interested suddenly. The image is of one rapidly recovering after an illness.

**Make someone sit up, To.** To astonish or considerably disconcert someone.

**Sitzkrieg** (German). The 'sitting war', the descriptive term applied (in contrast to BLITZKRIEG) to the period of comparative quiet and seeming military inactivity at the outset of the Second World War (September 1939 to April 1940), the period of the PHONEY war.

**Siva** or **Shiva.** The third member of the Hindu TRIMURTI, representing the destructive principle in life and also the reproductive or renovating power. He has other contrasting qualities, being a god of ascetics as well as of music, dancing and learning, and in all is a god of many attributes and functions. Siva, representing the Sanskrit word meaning 'benevolent', is only one of his many names. He is generally represented with three eyes and four arms and his symbol is the lingam.

**Six. Six, The.** The six countries Belgium, France, Germany, Italy, the Netherlands and Luxembourg, as the original participants in three economic communities: the European Coal and Steel Community (1951); the European Economic Community (now European Community) or Common Market, set up by the Treaty of Rome (1957); and the European Atomic Energy Community or Euratom (1957). *See also* The SEVEN.

**Six, Les.** A group of French composers formed at Paris in 1918 under the aegis of Jean Cocteau and Erik Satie to further their interests and those of modern music generally. The group lost its cohesion in the 1920s. Its members were Arthur Honegger (1892–1955), Darius Milhaud (1892–1974), Francis Poulenc (1899–1963), Louis Durey (1888–1979), Georges Auric (1899–1983) and Germaine Tailleferre (1892–1983).

**Six Acts, The.** The name given to the six measures sponsored by the Liverpool Ministry in 1819 to curb RADICAL agitation and popular disorder after the PETERLOO MASSACRE. These measures were designed to:

(1) restrict public meetings
(2) shorten procedures in bringing cases to trial so that political agitators could be dealt with more speedily
(3) forbid the drilling of private persons
(4) empower magistrates to seize blasphemous and seditious literature
(5) authorize the seizure of arms
(6) extend the stamp duties on newspapers and periodicals

**Six Articles, The.** The so-called 'six-stringed whip', otherwise known as the 'Bloody Bill', the Statute of Six Articles passed in 1539 to secure uniformity in matters of religion. It was repealed in 1547 under Edward VI. The articles maintained

(1) TRANSUBSTANTIATION
(2) the sufficiency of Communion in one kind
(3) clerical celibacy
(4) the obligation of monastic vows
(5) the propriety of private masses
(6) the necessity of auricular confession

Penalties were imposed for nonobservance, including death at the stake for those who spoke against transubstantiation.

**Six Counties, The.** Another name for Northern Ireland, as the six former ULSTER counties of Antrim, Armagh, Down, LONDONDERRY or Derry, Fermanagh and Tyrone. *See also* IRA; ORANGEMEN; SINN FÉIN.

**Six-foot way, The.** The strip of ground between two adjacent railway lines, measured between the outsides of the adjacent rails. It is usually in fact about 6ft 6in (1.98m).

**Six-hooped pot, A.** A two-quart pot. Quart pots were bound with three hoops, and when three men joined in drinking, each man drank his hoop. Mine host of the Black Bear (Sir Walter Scott, *Kenilworth*, ch iii (1821)), calls Tressilian 'a six-hooped pot of a traveller', meaning a first-class guest, because he paid freely and made no complaints.

**Six Nations, The.** The FIVE NATIONS together with the Tuscaroras. *See also* INDIAN TRIBES.

**Six of one and half a dozen of the other.** There is nothing to choose between two people or two propositions, for they are equally good or equally bad.

**Six of the best.** In the earlier decades of the present century, when corporal chastisement was still the normal and usually effective way of punishing schoolboys for wrongdoing and bad behaviour, it meant six strokes of the cane across the delinquent's posterior given by the headmaster or one of his assistants.

**Sixpence.** *See* TANNER.

**Six points of ritualism, The.** Altar lights, eucharistic vestments, the mixed chalice, incense, unleavened bread and the eastward position. So called when English Ritualists and upholders of the OXFORD MOVEMENT sought to reintroduce them in the 1870s.

**Six-stringed whip, The.** The SIX ARTICLES.

**Sixteen-string Jack.** John Rann, a highwayman (hanged 1774), noted for his foppery. He wore 16 tags, eight at each knee.

**Sixth sense.** Intuition, or a supposed extrasensory knowledge. It is so called as additional to the five physical senses: sight, hearing, smell, taste, touch.

**Sixty-four** or **sixty-four thousand dollar question.** The last and most difficult question; the crux of the problem. From the stake money awarded in an American radio quiz for answering the final question.

> Did that mean the whole area had extractable tin underneath it? 'That's the 64,000 dollar question.'
>
> *Sunday Telegraph* (5 August 1979)

**At sixes and sevens.** *See under* AT.

**Knock or hit someone for six, To.** *See under* KNOCK.

**Sizar.** An undergraduate of Cambridge, or of Trinity College, Dublin, who receives a grant from his college to assist in paying his expenses. Formerly sizars were expected to undertake certain menial duties now performed by college servants, and the name is taken to show that one so assisted received his sizes or SIZINGS free.

**Size. About the size of it.** *See under* ABOUT.

**Cut down to size, To.** *See under* CUT.

**Heroic size.** *See under* HEROIC.

**Paper sizes.** *See under* PAPER.

**Sizings.** The allowance of food provided by the college for undergraduates at a meal. A pound loaf, two inches of butter and a pot of milk used to be the 'sizings' for breakfast, meat was provided for dinner, but any extras had to be 'sized' for. The word is a contraction of 'assize', a statute to regulate the size or weight of articles sold.

**SJ** (Latin *Societas Jesu*). The Society of Jesus, denoting that the priest after whose name those letters are placed is a JESUIT.

**Skanda.** *See* KARTTIKEYA.

**Skate. Skate on thin ice, To.** To behave rashly or take risks, especially by broaching a subject that properly requires tactful handling.

**Figure skating.** *See under* FIGURE.

**Get one's skates on, To.** To make haste.

**Skeleton. Skeleton at the feast, The.** The thing or person that acts as a reminder that there are troubles as well as pleasures in life. Plutarch says in his *Moralia* (2nd century AD) that the Egyptians always had a skeleton in a prominent position at their banquets.

**Skeleton in the cupboard** or **closet, A.** A domestic source of worry or shame that a family conspires to keep to itself. Every family is said to have at least one.

A story goes that someone without a single care or trouble in the world had to be found. After long and unsuccessful search a lady was discovered who all thought would 'fill the bill', but to the great surprise of the inquirers, after she had satisfied them on all points and the quest seemed to be achieved, she took them upstairs and there opened a closet which contained a human skeleton. 'I try to keep my trouble to myself', said she, 'but every night my husband makes me kiss that skeleton.' She then explained that the skeleton was that of her husband's rival, killed in a duel. The expression was given literary use by Thackeray:

> And it is from these that we shall arrive at some particulars regarding the Newcome family, which will show us that they have a skeleton or two in their closets as well as their neighbours.
>
> *The Newcomes*, ch lv (1853–5)

**Skevington's daughter.** *See* SCAVENGER'S DAUGHTER.

**Skidbladnir.** In Scandinavian mythology the magic ship made by the DWARFS for FREYR. It was big enough to take all the AESIR with their weapons and equipment, yet when not in use could be folded up and carried by Freyr in his pouch. It sailed through both air and water, and went straight to its destination as soon as the sails were hoisted. Its name means 'Thin-Planked'. *See also* MAGIC CARPET.

**Skid row.** An American expression applied to a district abounding in vicious characters and down-and-outs. In the lumber industry a skid row was a row of logs down which other felled timber was slid or skidded. Early on, Tacoma, near Seattle, flourished on its lumber production and in due course liquor and women became available for loggers descending the skid row. The usage may well derive from this situation. *See also* BOWERY.

**Skiffle.** A name given to a style of JAZZ of the 1920s, and subsequently to a type of jazz folk music current in Britain in the late 1950s played by a skiffle group, consisting of guitar, drums, kazoo, washboard and other improvised instruments. The word is perhaps of imitative origin.

**Skimmington.** It was an old custom in rural England and Scotland to make an example of nagging wives by forming a ludicrous procession through the village accompanied by ROUGH MUSIC to ridicule the offender. A man, mounted on a horse with a distaff in his hand, rode behind the woman with his face to the horse's tail, while the woman beat him about the chops with a ladle. As the procession passed a house where the woman was paramount, the participants gave the threshold a sweep. The event was called 'riding the Skimmington'. The origin of the name is uncertain, but in an illustration of 1639 the woman is shown belabouring her husband with a skimming-ladle. Unfaithful husbands were similarly ridiculed. The procession is fully described in Butler's *Hudibras*, II, ii (1663):

> Near whom the Amazon triumphant
> Bestrid her beast, and, on the rump on't,
> Sat face to tail and bum to bum,
> The warrior whilom overcome,
> Arm'd with a spindle and a distaff,
> Which, as he rode, she made him twist off:
> And when he loiter'd, o'er her shoulder
> Chastis'd the reformado soldier.

For another example *see* Hardy's *The Mayor of Casterbridge*, ch xxxix (1886), where the skimmity ride causes the death of Lucetta Farfrae. *See also* RIDING; SHALLAL.

**Skin. Skin and bones, To be.** To be very thin.

**Skin flick.** A pornographic film containing nudity and explicit sex.

**Skinflint.** A miserly person. To skin a flint was to be very exacting in making a bargain. Latin *lana caprina*, literally 'goat's wool', similarly meant something as worthless as the skin of a flint (which has no skin) or the fleece of an eggshell (which has no fleece).

**Skin game.** A rigged gambling game; a swindle. The allusion is presumably to 'skin' meaning to fleece or strip someone of their money by sharp practice or fraud. John Galsworthy has a play of this title (1920).

**Skinhead.** A young person, usually the member of a gang, with hair very closely cropped or shaved, making an appearance from the late 1960s. *See also* MODS AND ROCKERS; PUNK.

It is at these shows that Rosko the brash, shrieking voice, becomes flesh and blood to his different fans – reggae-loving skin-heads, draped and winkle-pickered rockers, tumescent girls.
RICHARD GILBERT in *Anatomy of Pop* (1970)

**Skinners.** A predatory band in the American Revolutionary War, which roamed over Westchester County, New York, robbing and fleecing those who refused to take the oath of fidelity to the Republic.

**Skinny dipping.** Swimming in the nude.

**Skin-popping.** The subcutaneous injection of drugs, in which the skin is 'popped' or broken.

**Beauty is only skin deep.** *See under* BEAUTY.

**By the skin of one's teeth.** *See under* BY.

**Change one's skin, To.** *See under* CHANGE.

**Dane's skin.** *See under* DANE.

**Get under someone's skin, To.** *See under* UNDER.

**Jump out of one's skin, To.** *See under* JUMP.

**No skin off my nose.** *See under* NO.

**Save one's skin, To.** *See under* SAVE.

**Sell the skin before one has caught the bear, To.** *See under* SELL.

**Thick-skinned.** *See under* THICK.

**Skinfaxi** (Old Norse, 'shining-mane'). The horse of day in Norse legend. *See also* HRIMFAXI.

**Skirt, A bit of.** *See under* BIT.

**Skittles, Life is not all beer and.** *See under* LIFE.

**Skull. Skull and crossbones.** An emblem of mortality and specifically the pirate's flag or JOLLY ROGER. The 'crossbones' are two human thigh bones laid across each other. This particular flag was used only by British and British-American pirates in the first quarter of the 18th century. Other pirates attacked either under the flag of their own ruler or else that of the prince issuing their commandeering commissions.

**Kirk of Skulls.** *See under* KIRK.

**Sky. Skyhook.** Where an overhead hook could be useful or necessary in certain work operations, a GREENHORN is despatched by his more experienced workmates to fetch a 'skyhook'. *See also* GOLDEN RIVET.

**Skyjacker.** A criminal who secures passage on an airliner with the intent to terrorize the crew into furthering his particular ends. Skyjackers are mostly anarchists or terrorists but robbers and crazed folk are also among them. *See also* HIJACKER.

**Skylark, To.** To amuse oneself in a frolicsome way; to jump around and be merry; to indulge in mild horseplay. The phrase was originally nautical and referred to the sports of the boys among the rigging after their work was done. Hence perhaps the popular boat name, as in: 'All aboard the Skylark'.

**Sky pilot.** A clergyman or padre. Originally this was a sailor's expression which was in use from the late Victorian period. The allusion is obvious.

**Skysail.** In a square-rigged ship, a sail next above the fore-royal, the main-royal or the mizzen royal.

**Skyscraper.** A very tall building, especially one in New York or some other American city. Some of them run to a hundred storeys or more. The word was also formerly applied by sailors to a SKYSAIL. The word for the building is translated literally in most languages, as French *gratte-ciel*, German *Wolkenkratzer* ('cloud-scraper'), Russian *neboskrëb* and Chinese *mótianlóu* ('touch-sky-building').

**Sky's the limit, The.** There is no limit.

**Skywriting.** The forming of words in the sky by an aircraft's release of smoke or vapour.

**Columbus of the Skies, The.** *See under* COLUMBUS.

**Mackerel sky.** *See under* MACKEREL.

**Mare's-tail sky.** *See under* MARE.

**Pie in the sky.** *See under* PIE.

**Water sky.** *See under* WATER.

**Slam.** A term in card-playing denoting winning all the tricks in a deal. In bridge this is called a grand slam, and winning all but one, a little or small slam. The word itself was originally the name of a card game, and is perhaps from obsolete *slampant*, 'trickery'. *See also* RUFF.

**Slang.** As denoting language or jargon of a low or colloquial type, the word first appeared in the 18th century. It is perhaps connected with 'sling' (compare 'mud-slinging', for hurling abuse). Slang is of various kinds, as business, racing, schoolboy, army, nautical, thieves' and so on, and usually has some element of humour about it. Certain lexicographers have made the study of slang their speciality, one of the most notable being Eric Partridge (1894–1979), author of *Slang Today and Yesterday* (1933), *A Dictionary of Slang and Unconventional English* (1937), *A Dictionary of RAF Slang* (1945), *A Dictionary of the Underworld* (1949) and related works. More recently, Jonathon Green published the fruits of five years' research into the subject in *The Cassell Dictionary of Slang* (1998). *See also* BACK SLANG; CANT; RHYMING SLANG.

**Slanging match.** A lengthy exchange of abuse and insults.

**Back slang.** *See under* BACK.

**Rhyming slang.** *See under* RHYME.

**Slap. Slap and tickle.** Amorous play or sexual foreplay.

I was, to put it politely, jolly annoyed with my husband, who I discovered had taken to popping round to a young journalist's flat for a bit of slap and tickle.
*The Times* (15 January 1999)

**Slap-bang.** At once; without hesitation; done with a slap and a bang. The term was formerly applied to a cheap eating house, where one 'slapped' one's money down as the food was 'banged' on the table.

> They lived in the same street, walked to town every morning at the same hour, dined at the same slap-bang every day.
>
> DICKENS: *Sketches by Boz*, iii (1836–7)

**Slapdash.** In an off-hand manner; done hurriedly as with a slap and a dash. Rooms used to be decorated by slapping and dashing the walls to imitate paper, and at one time slapdash walls were common.

**Slap-happy.** Foolish and irresponsible, as one who is dazed; akin to being PUNCH DRUNK.

**Slaphead.** A bald or balding man, whose head is readily slapped.

**Slap in the face, A.** An insult; a rebuff.

**Slap on the back, A.** Congratulations.

**Slap on the wrist, A.** A reprimand, as administered to a naughty child. An adult who has made some slip may make the gesture to his or her own wrist by way of self-rebuke.

**Slapper.** A promiscuous woman, who has slapped make-up on her face as a rough and ready allure.

**Slapstick.** Literally the two or more laths bound together at one end with which HARLEQUINS, CLOWNS and other performers strike one another with a resounding slap or crack. The word is now more often applied to any broad comedy with knockabout action and horseplay. *See also* KEYSTONE KOPS.

**Slap-up.** First-rate, grand or lavish.

> The more slap-up still have the two shields painted on the panels with the coronet over.
>
> W.M. THACKERAY: *The Newcomes*, ch xxxi (1853–5)

**Slashers, The.** *See under* REGIMENTAL AND DIVISIONAL NICKNAMES.

**Slate. Slate club.** A sick benefit club for working men. Originally the names of the members and the money paid in were entered on a folding slate.

**Slate someone, To.** To reprove or criticize them savagely. It is not known how the term arose, but perhaps it is because at school the names of bad boys were chalked up on the slate as an example.

**Clean slate.** *See under* SLATE.

**Have a slate** or **tile loose, To.** *See* HAVE A TILE LOOSE *under* TILE.

**On the slate.** On the account; to be paid for later. From the custom of chalking up debts on a slate in shops and public houses.

**Start with a clean slate, To.** *See under* START.

**Wipe the slate clean, To.** *See under* WIPE.

**Slave.** An example of the way words acquire changed meanings. The Slavs were a tribe that once dwelt on the banks of the Dnieper, but as, in later days of the Roman Empire, many of them were spread over Europe as captives, the word acquired its present meaning.

**Slave Coast, The.** The west coast of Africa around the Bight of Benin, between the River Volta and Mount Cameroon, from the 16th to the 19th century the chief source of African slaves.

**Slave States, The.** A phrase current in the period before the American Civil War (1861–5) and applied to the states where domestic slavery was practised, i.e. Delaware, Maryland, Virginia, North Carolina, South Carolina, Georgia, Florida, Alabama, Mississippi, Louisiana, Texas, Arkansas, Missouri, Kentucky and Tennessee. *See also* UNITED STATES OF AMERICA.

**Chinese slavery.** *See under* CHINESE.

**White slave.** *See under* WHITE.

**Sledgehammer. Sledgehammer argument, A.** A clincher; an argument that annihilates opposition at a blow. The sledgehammer (Old English *slecg*) is the largest hammer used manually, and is wielded in both hands.

**Sledging.** In cricket, the heaping of insults on an opposing player so as to break his concentration. The analogy is with giving him a battering with a sledgehammer.

**Use a sledgehammer to crack a nut, To.** *See under* USE.

**Sleep. Sleep around, To.** To be sexually promiscuous.

**Sleep away, To.** To pass away in sleep; to consume in sleeping, as: 'To sleep one's life away.'

**Sleeper, The.** EPIMENIDES, the Greek poet, is said to have fallen asleep in a cave when a boy and not to have waked for 57 years, when he found himself possessed of all wisdom.

In medieval legend, stories of those who have gone to sleep and have been, or are to be, awakened after many years are very numerous. Such legends are associated with King ARTHUR, CHARLEMAGNE and BARBAROSSA. *See also* OGIER THE DANE; SEVEN SLEEPERS; TANNHÄUSER; WINKLE, RIP VAN.

**Sleeper Awakened, The.** *See* SLY, CHRISTOPHER.

**Sleepers.** In Britain the supports for the chairs (usually of timber) that carry railway lines. In the USA these supports are called ties. A sleeper is also a railway sleeping car.

**Sleep in, To.** To remain asleep longer than usual in the morning. It is not necessarily the same as to oversleep, which is to sleep longer than one intended.

**Sleeping Beauty, The.** This charming nursery tale comes from the French *La Belle au Bois Dormant*, by Charles Perrault (1628–1703) (*Contes de ma mère l'Oye*, 1697). The Princess is shut up by enchantment in a castle, where she sleeps for a hundred years, during which time an impenetrable wood springs up around. She is finally released by the kiss of a young prince, who marries her.

**Sleeping partner.** A partner in a business who takes no active share in running it beyond supplying capital. Such a partner is also called a silent partner in the USA.

**Sleeping policeman.** A slight bump built across a road in order to slow the speed of traffic. The image is of a recumbent police officer, and for this reason other names are now mostly used, such as (unofficially) speed bump or (officially) traffic calming measure.

**Sleeping sickness.** A West African disease caused by a parasite, *Trypanosoma brucei*, characterized by fever and great lethargy, and often terminating fatally. The disease known in England with similar symptoms, as a form of encephalitis or inflammation of the brain, is sometimes called sleepy sickness for distinction. Its medical name is encephalitis lethargica.

**Sleep like a log or top, To.** To sleep very soundly or excellently; to go the night through without waking or discomfort. When peg tops are at the ACME of their gyration, they become so steady and quiet that they do not seem to move. In this state they are said to 'sleep'. William Congreve plays on the two meanings:

> Hang him, no, he a dragon! If he be, 'tis a very peaceful one. I can ensure his anger dormant, or should he seem to rouse, 'tis but well lashing him and he will sleep like a top.
> *The Old Bachelor*, I, v (1693)

**Sleep off, To.** To get rid of by sleep, especially the aftereffects of alcohol.

**Sleep on it, To.** To postpone a decision on a matter until the following day.

**Sleepover.** A night spent away from home, especially by a young person in a friend's house.

> Stepchildren and siblings often coexist happily in a loose arrangement of weekend sleepovers.
> *The Times* (30 December 1998)

**Sleepy.** Said of pears and other fruits when they are beginning to rot.

**Sleepy Hollow.** Any village far removed from the active concerns of the outside world. From Washington Irving's story 'The Legend of Sleepy Hollow' (*Sketch Book* (1820)), which deals with a quiet old-world village on the Hudson.

**Sleepy sickness.** *See* SLEEPING SICKNESS.

**Beauty sleep.** *See under* BEAUTY.

**Dog sleep.** *See under* DOG.

**Let sleeping dogs lie, To.** *See under* LET.

**Lose sleep over, To.** *See under* LOSE.

**Put to sleep, To.** Commonly used as a euphemism for painlessly killing pet animals.

**Seven sleepers, The.** *See under* SEVEN.

**Twilight sleep.** *See under* TWILIGHT.

**Sleeve. Sleeveless.** In the 16th and 17th centuries 'sleeveless' was commonly used to signify fruitless or unprofitable, as 'a sleeveless message', 'a sleeveless errand' and so on. The reason for this usage is uncertain.

**Have a card up one's sleeve, To.** *See under* CARD.

**Have an ace up one's sleeve, To.** *See under* ACE.

**Have something up one's sleeve, To.** To hold a thing in reserve; to have it ready to produce in case of need. The allusion is to conjurers, who frequently conceal up their sleeve the means by which they do the trick.

**Hippocrates' sleeve.** *See under* HIPPOCRATES.

**Laugh up one's sleeve, To.** *See under* LAUGH.

**Pin something to someone's sleeve, To.** *See under* PIN.

**Roll up one's sleeves, To.** *See under* ROLL.

**Wear one's heart on one's sleeve, To.** *See under* WEAR.

**Sleipnir** (Old Norse, 'sliding one'). ODIN's eight-legged grey horse, which could traverse both land and sea. The horse typifies the wind, which blows from the eight principal points.

**Sleuthhound.** A bloodhound that follows the sleuth (Old Norse *sloth*, modern English *slot*) or track of an animal. Hence used, especially in America, of a detective.

**Sliding scale.** A scale of duties, prices, payments and the like, which 'slides' upwards and downwards in relation to the fluctuations in the cost to which it relates. Thus in the Sliding-scale CORN LAW of 1828, the duty varied inversely to the home price of corn, i.e. as the price of corn went up the duty went down.

**Sling. Sling one's hook, To.** To go away; to depart. The expression may be of nautical origin and allude to the anchor (hook), which must be secured in its sling at the bow before the ship can get under way.

**Gin sling.** *See under* GIN.

**Slip. Slip of a boy or girl, A.** One who is small and slim. Slip here is related to 'sliver'.

**Slippery slope, The.** The broad and easy way 'that leadeth to destruction'. *See also* AVERNUS.

**Slip something over on, To.** To outwit; to PULL A FAST ONE.

**Slip the cable, To.** To release the cable from the inboard end and let it run out through the hawse, so releasing the anchor.

> To preserve their close order the Armada's vessels were riding to two anchors each, and there was no time to weigh. The majority did not even slip, but cut their cables and drifted off in the darkness.
> J.A. WILLIAMSON: *The Age of Drake*, ch xvi (1938)

Figuratively, to slip one's cable is to die.

**Slip up, To.** Metaphorically, to make a mistake, usually through an oversight.

**As slippery as an eel.** *See under* AS.

**Give someone the slip, To.** To steal away from someone unnoticed; to elude pursuit. The expression probably arose from the idea of a hound slipping its collar or from the slipping of an anchor when it is necessary to get away quickly from an uncomfortable berth. The normal practice in such cases is to buoy the cable before letting it slip through the hawsepipe, so that anchor and cable can be recovered afterwards. *See also* SLIP THE CABLE.

What's become of Waring
Since he gave us all the slip?
ROBERT BROWNING: 'Waring' (1842)

**Let slip, To.** *See under* LET.

**Let something slip through one's fingers, To.** *See under* LET.

**There's many a slip 'twixt cup and lip.** Everything is uncertain until you possess it; things can go wrong at the last moment. The saying was known to the ancient Greeks. *See also* ANCAEUS.

**Slipper. Carpet slippers.** *See under* CARPET.

**Hunt the slipper.** *See under* HUNT.

**Lady's slipper.** *See under* LADY.

**Sloane Ranger.** A young upper class or upper-middle class person who is disciplined, well mannered and speaks educated English. Sloanes are conservative in dress, the women having no freakish hair styles and the men being clean shaven. The women wear expensive but informal country clothes and the men the attire of a city gentleman or country squire, those in town living around Sloane Square, Holland Park and Kensington. The term first emerged in the 1970s and was originated by Peter York, writer on fashion. (The name puns on LONE RANGER, the cowboy hero of western stories and films.) The *Official Sloane Ranger Handbook* (1982) by Ann Barr and Peter York elaborated the theme.

**Slogan.** Originally, the war cry of the old Highland clans, from Gaelic *sluagh*, 'army', and *gairm*, 'cry'. Hence, any war cry, and in later use, a political party cry or advertising catchphrase. *See also* SLUGHORN.

**Slope, Slippery.** *See under* SLIP.

**Sloper, Ally.** *See under* ALLY.

**Slops.** An old name for ready-made or cheap clothing, and in the Royal Navy the term long applied to the clothing, towels, blankets and the like sold from the ship's store, which is known as the slop shop.

**Slough of Despond.** A period of, or fit of, great depression. In Bunyan's PILGRIM'S PROGRESS, Pt I (1678), it is a deep bog which Christian has to cross in order to get to the Wicket Gate. Help comes to his aid, but Neighbour Pliable turns back.

**Slow. Slow but sure.** Taking one's time in order to be certain of eventually achieving one's objective. An expanded form of the phrase is: 'Slow but sure wins the race'.

**Slowcoach.** A person who acts, thinks or moves slowly.

**Slow handclap.** A slow, usually unison clapping by an audience to express their displeasure or boredom.

**Slow-worm.** *See* MISNOMERS.

**Go slow.** The deliberate slowing down of work or production by employees engaged in an industrial dispute. In Canada and the USA the term is 'slowdown'.

**Slubberdegullion.** A base fellow; a nasty oaf. 'To slubber' is to do things carelessly, in a slovenly way, and 'degullion' is a fanciful addition, 'gullion' perhaps being a variant of 'cullion', a base fellow.

Quoth she, Although thou hast deserved,
Base-slubber degullion, to be served
As thou didst vow to deal with me.
SAMUEL BUTLER: *Hudibras*, I, iii (1662)

**Slugabed.** A late riser. 'To slug' used to be quite good English for 'to be thoroughly lazy'.

The Soldier, slugging long at home in Peace,
His wonted courage quickly doth decrease.
GUILLAUME DU BARTAS: *Collected Works*, I, vii (1592)

**Slughorn.** A battle trumpet. The word was the result of an erroneous reading by Thomas Chatterton of the Gaelic SLOGAN. He thought the word sounded rather well and as he did not know what it meant, gave it a meaning that suited him:

Some caught a slughorne and an onsett wounde.
*The Battle of Hastings*, ii (1770)

Browning adopted it in the last two lines of 'Childe Roland to the Dark Tower Came' (1855), and thus this GHOST WORD got a footing in the language.

Dauntless the slug-horn to my lips I set,
And blew.

**Sly. Sly-boots.** A cunning one; a WAG. A similar compound to lazy-boots, clumsy-boots and the like.

**Christopher Sly.** A keeper of bears and a tinker, son of a pedlar, and a sad drunken sot in the Induction of *The Taming of the Shrew* (1593). Shakespeare mentions him as a well-known character of Wincot, a hamlet near Stratford-on-Avon, and it is likely that he is an actual portrait of a contemporary.

Sly is found dead drunk by a lord, who commands his servants to put him to bed and on his waking to attend upon him like a lord and trick him into the belief that he is a great man. The play is performed for his delectation. The same trick was played by the Caliph HAROUN AL-RASCHID ON ABU HASSAN, the rich merchant, in the story 'The Sleeper Awakened' in the ARABIAN NIGHTS ENTERTAINMENTS.

**On the sly.** In a secretive manner; covertly.

**You're a sly dog.** You're a cunning one.

**Smack.** A slang term for heroin, from the 'smack' that is a smell or flavour.

**Smack one's lips, To.** *See* LICK ONE'S LIPS.

**Small. Small arms** (Latin *arma*, 'arms', 'fittings'). Weapons fired from the hand or shoulder, such as revolvers and rifles, also light portable machine guns and the like, which originally did not require carriages, as distinct from artillery, which did.

**Small beer.** Properly, beer of only slight alcoholic strength, hence, trivialities, persons or things of small consequence.

**Small change.** Money in the form of coins rather than notes. Small change is also a collective expression for trivial remarks.

**Small claims court.** A local court in which claims for small amounts can be heard and decided quickly and cheaply.

**Smallclothes.** Once a term for men's close-fitting breeches, now for underclothes or 'smalls'.

**Small deer.** Any small animal. The expression came to be used metaphorically for trifling matters or any collection of trifles. *See also* SMALL BEER.

> But mice and rats, and such small deer
> Have been Tom's food for seven long year.
> SHAKESPEARE: *King Lear*, III, iv (1605)

**Small-endians.** *See* BIG-ENDIANS.

**Small fry.** A way of referring to young children, from the numerous fry or young of fish and other creatures. *See also* JACK SPRAT.

**Smallholding.** A small plot of agricultural land bigger than an allotment, but not big enough to be called a farm. The term received legal significance under the Small Holdings Act of 1892, which permitted county councils to provide them for letting. The Small Holdings and Allotments Act of 1926 defined them as of not less than an acre (0.4 ha) and not more than 50 acres (20 ha), and of not more than £100 in annual value.

**Small hours, The.** The hours from midnight to dawn, or from 1 am to 4 or 5 am, when the numbered hours are 'small' or low.

**Small is beautiful.** A phrase and concept popularized by the German-born British economist E.F. Schumacher in the title of his book subtitled 'A Study of Economics as if People Mattered' (1973). It does not, of course, follow that small is generally beautiful.

**Small of the back, The.** The slenderer, narrower part, just above the buttocks.

**Small potatoes.** Someone or something of little importance. The allusion is probably to potatoes that are so small they are hardly worth cleaning or peeling.

**Small print, The.** The detailed clauses or conditions pertaining to an agreement or contract. These are usually printed in small type and are often skipped by the unwary, who suffer in consequence.

**Smalls.** The undergraduate name at Oxford for Responsions, which at one time were the first of the three examinations for the BA degree, similar to the Cambridge LITTLE GO, the final examination being called GREATS. It later became the official university entrance examination until the growing use of the School Certificate (later General Certificate of Education) examinations led to its discontinuance. Smalls were last held in 1960. *See also* SMALLCLOTHES.

**Small screen, The.** Television, as distinct from 'the big screen', or cinema.

**Small talk.** Trifling conversation; social chit-chat.

**Feel small, To.** *See under* FEEL.

**Smart. Smart Alec** or **Aleck.** An American term for a bumptious, conceited know-all. The name goes back to at least the 1860s, but the identity of Alec is uncertain. The allusion may be to Aleck Hoag, a notorious pimp, thief and confidence man in New York in the 1840s.

**Smart money.** Money paid by a person to obtain exemption from some disagreeable office or duty. It was applied to money paid by an army recruit to obtain release before being sworn in, and also to money paid to soldiers and sailors for wounds. In law it denotes heavy damages. It is something that makes the person 'smart' (i.e. suffer) or that is received in payment for 'smarting'.

**Smarty-pants** or **boots.** A would-be clever or smart person. 'Pants' here are trousers.

**As smart as paint.** *See under* AS.

**Smear campaign, A.** A planned or organized attempt to tarnish someone's character or reputation.

**Smectymnuus.** The name under which was published (1641) an anti-episcopal tract in answer to Bishop Hall's *Humble Remonstrance* (1640). The name was composed of the initials of its authors: Stephen Marshall, Edward Calamy, Thomas Young, Matthew Newcomen and William Spurstow. Young was Milton's former tutor, and Milton seems to have had a part in it and wrote pamphlets in defence of the Smectymnuans.

> The handkerchief about the neck,
> Canonical cravat of Smec.
> SAMUEL BUTLER: *Hudibras*, I, iii (1662)

**Smell, To.** Often used figuratively for to suspect or to discern intuitively, as in to SMELL A RAT.

Shakespeare has, 'Do you smell a fault?' (*King Lear*, I, i (1605)), and Iago says to Othello, 'One may smell in such a will most rank' (*Othello*, III, iii (1604)). St JEROME says that St Hilarion had the gift of knowing what sins and vices anyone was inclined to by smelling either the person or their garments, and by the same faculty could discern good feelings and virtuous propensities.

**Smell a rat, To.** To perceive some underhand work or treachery afoot; to detect something suspicious. The allusion is to a cat that smells a rat but cannot see it.

**Bells and smells.** *See under* BELL.

**Rose by any other name would smell as sweet, A.** *See under* ROSE.

**Smile. Come up smiling, To.** *See under* COME.

**Giaconda smile.** *See under* GIACONDA.

**Sardonic smile.** *See under* SARDONIC.

**Smith. Smithfield.** The London district has a name meaning smooth field (Old English *smēthe*, 'smooth'). It was called in Latin *Campus Planus* and was described by Fitz-Stephen in the 12th century as a 'plain field where every Friday there is a celebrated rendezvous of fine horses brought thither to be sold'. It was originally outside the city wall and was used for races, quintain matches, TOURNAMENTS and the like, as well as for a market. BARTHOLOMEW FAIR was held here until 1855, at which time the cattle market was transferred to the CALEDONIAN MARKET. Its less pleasant associations were the gibbet and the stake, and most of the martyrs of Mary's reign suffered death at Smithfield. It is now London's largest meat market.

**Smith of Smiths, The.** The Rev. Sydney Smith (1771–1845), a Whig clergyman and canon of St Paul's, was so called by Macaulay. He was renowned as a conversationalist for his drollery and brilliance of wit as well as for the incisive quality of his writings. *See also* PARTINGTON.

**Smith Square.** The London square has long had contrasting political associations, and at one time held the headquarters of the Conservative, Labour and Liberal Parties. The Conservative Party remains here at No. 32, and until 1980 the Labour Party was at Transport House, the former headquarters of the Transport and General Workers' Union.

**Granny Smith.** *See under* GRANNY.

**Harvey Smith.** *See under* HARVEY.

**Wayland Smith.** *See under* WAYLAND.

**Smithereens.** If something is smashed to smithereens it ends up in very small pieces. This is the literal meaning of the word, which represents Irish *smidirín*, 'fragment', with an English plural s.

**Smock, Lady's.** *See under* LADY.

**Smoke. Smoke** or **Big Smoke, The.** London. An old slang name of obvious origins. *See also* AULD REEKIE.

> Till that last awful winter! ... when the farmers had been mostly ruined, and half the able-bodied men of Mellor had tramped 'up into the smoke', as the village put it, in search of London work.
>
> MRS HUMPHRY WARD: *Marcella*, Bk I, ch ix (1894)

**Smoke-filled room, A.** A room filled with tobacco smoke from which political leaders emerge with a decision after long hours of discussion or bargaining. The original smoke-filled room was a suite in the Blackstone Hotel, Chicago, in which Warren Harding was selected as the Republican presidential candidate in June 1920. The phrase itself appears to have come from a comment by Harding's chief supporter, Harry Daugherty, that the meeting would not be able to decide between the two obvious candidates and that a group of bleary-eyed senators would 'sit down about two o'clock in the morning around a table in a smoke-filled room in some hotel and decide the nomination'. That was what actually happened, and Harding was duly selected as the candidate. The smoke in this instance was probably emitted by cigars.

**Smokescreen.** In military operations, a cloud of smoke dispersed to conceal manoeuvres. Figuratively a smokescreen is a device or ruse employed to disguise one's activities.

**Smoke someone out, To.** To drive them out of hiding, literally or metaphorically.

**Smoke the pipe of peace, To.** *See* CALUMET.

**Chain smoker.** *See under* CHAIN.

**End in** or **up in smoke, To.** *See under* END.

**No smoke without fire.** Every report or rumour has some foundation. The reverse proverb, 'no fire without smoke', means no good without some drawback.

**Valley of Ten Thousand Smokes, The.** *See under* VALLEY.

**Smooth. Smooth one's ruffled feathers, To.** To recover one's poise after an insult or the like.

**Smooth** or **still waters run deep.** Deep thinkers are persons of few words; silent conspirators are the most dangerous. A calm exterior is far more to be feared than a loud-mouthed braggart.

> Smooth runs the water where the brook is deep,
> And in his simple show he harbours treason.
> The fox barks not when he would steal the lamb:
> No, no, my sov'reign; Gloucester is a man
> Unsounded yet, and full of deep deceit.
>
> SHAKESPEARE: *Henry VI, Pt II*, III, i (1590)

**Snack, To take a.** To have a little to eat; to 'snatch a bite of something'. The word is probably from Middle Dutch *snacken*, a variant of *snappen*, 'to snap'.

**Snail, Roman.** *See under* ROMAN.

**Snake.** It was an old idea that snakes in annually sloughing their skins gained new vigour and fresh strength, hence Shakespeare's allusion:

When the mind is quicken'd out of doubt,
The organs, though defunct and dead before,
Break up their drowsy grave, and newly move
With casted slough and fresh legerity.
*Henry V*, IV, i (1598)

**Snake charmer.** A person who seems to make snakes rise up by playing music. The feat is chiefly associated with India, where charmers have been seen to bring up cobras with the music of their gourd pipe. It is a fallacy, however, that the snakes respond to the music. The cobra that sits up and sways to and fro does so in its attraction to the rhythmic movements of the player, who himself sways in time with his melody.

**Snake-eyes** (USA). In throwing dice, a double one.

**Snake in the grass, A.** A hidden or hypocritical enemy; a disguised danger. The phrase is from Virgil (*Eclogues*, iii (1st century BC)), *Latet anguis in herba* ('a snake is lurking in the grass').

**Snakes and ladders.** A favourite board game among children. The board is divided into 100 numbered squares and decorated with snakes and ladders running respectively from a higher number to a lower and vice versa. A counter landing at the foot of a ladder thus takes the player nearer to the finish, while one landing on the head of snake is a setback or reversal. The symbolism is vaguely biblical, the ladder going up to heaven and the snake representing a 'fall'.

**Snake stones.** AMMONITES, from the old belief that these were coiled snakes petrified.

**Great snakes!** *See under* GREAT.

**See snakes, To.** *See under* SEE.

**Snap. Snapdragon.** The same as 'flap-dragon', an old name for raisins soaked in spirit and set alight; also a plant of the genus *Antirrhinum* with a flower opening like a mouth when a bee alights on the lower part.

**Snap off someone's head, To.** Virtually the same as 'to snap off someone's nose' or to BITE OFF SOMEONE'S NOSE.

**Snap one's fingers at, To.** To brush aside contemptuously; to disregard authority.

**Snap out of it, To.** To shake off a fit of depression; to regain one's good humour; to pull oneself together.

**Snappers, The.** *See under* REGIMENTAL AND DIVISIONAL NICKNAMES.

**Snapshot** or **snap.** A snapshot was originally a shot fired without taking aim, but the term is now applied almost exclusively to a photograph, especially one taken with a simple, unsophisticated camera. Hence 'to snap a person' is to take a photograph of them.

**Snap vote, A.** A vote taken unexpectedly, especially in Parliament. The result of a 'snap vote' has, before now, been the overthrow of a ministry.

**Make it snappy.** Be quick about it.

**Snare and a delusion, A.** Something that raises hopes only to dash them. Lord Denman's judgement in O'Connell *v* the Crown (September 1844) has: 'Trial by jury itself, instead of being a security to persons who are not accused, will be a delusion, a mockery and a snare.'

**Snark.** The imaginary animal invented by Lewis Carroll as the subject of his mock-heroic poem *The Hunting of the Snark* (1876). It was most elusive and gave endless trouble, and when eventually the hunters thought they had tracked it down, their quarry proved to be a Boojum. The name (a PORTMANTEAU WORD of snake and shark) has sometimes been given to the quests of dreamers and visionaries.

It was one of Dante Gabriel Rossetti's delusions that in *The Hunting of the Snark* Lewis Carroll was caricaturing him.

**Snarling letter** (Latin *litera canina*). The letter r. *See also* R.

**Snatch. Body snatcher.** *See under* BODY.

**Cradle** or **baby snatcher.** *See under* CRADLE.

**Sneeze.** St GREGORY has been credited with originating the custom of saying 'God bless you' after sneezing, the story being that he enjoined its use during a pestilence in which sneezing was a mortal symptom. Aristotle, however, mentions a similar custom among the Greeks, and Thucydides writes that sneezing was a crisis symptom of the great Athenian plague.

The Romans followed the same custom, their usual exclamation being *Absit omen!* The PARSEES hold that sneezing indicates that evil spirits are abroad, and there are similar beliefs in India, Africa, ancient and modern Persia, among the Native American tribes and elsewhere. The English response BLESS YOU! is on similar lines. The nursery rhyme goes:

If you sneeze on Monday you sneeze for danger,
Sneeze on Tuesday, kiss a stranger,
Sneeze on Wednesday, sneeze for a letter,
Sneeze on Thursday, something better,
Sneeze on Friday, sneeze for sorrow,
Sneeze on Saturday, see your sweetheart tomorrow.

**It is not to be sneezed at.** It is not to be underrated; it is worthy of consideration.

**Snell, Hannah.** *See* FEMALE MARINE.

**Snobs, Cotton.** *See under* COTTON.

**Snood.** The snood was originally a ribbon with which a Scots lass braided her hair and was the emblem of her maiden character. When she married, she changed the snood for the curch or coif, but if she lost the rank of virgin before she obtained that of wife, she 'lost her silken snood' and was not privileged to assume the curch.

In more recent times the word has been applied to the net in which women confine their hair. The origin of the word itself is unknown.

> No hunter's hand her snood untied,
> Yet ne'er again to braid her hair
> The virgin snood did Alice wear.
> SIR WALTER SCOTT: *The Lady of the Lake* (1810)

**Snooks.** An old exclamation of incredulity or derision.

**Cock a snook, To.** *See under* COCK.

**Snoopy.** The day-dreaming beagle first appeared in Charles M. Schulz's comic strip *Peanuts* in 1950. He is Charlie Brown's dog, and although he never speaks, he makes up for it by his endless dreams of glory, enacting in his imagination roles that will make him world famous.

**Snotty.** Naval slang for a MIDSHIPMAN, allegedly from their habit of wiping their noses on their sleeves. It is said that the three buttons on the cuffs of their jackets were to prevent their doing this. New entries were called 'warts' and the lieutenant who overlooked the gunroom was known as the 'snotty nurse'. But perhaps the 'middies' were so called simply because they were young and as yet untrained, like small boys with runny noses.

**Snow.** A slang term for cocaine, heroin or morphine.

**Snowed under, To be.** To be overwhelmed with paperwork.

**Snow job, A.** In the USA the act of deceiving someone or overwhelming them with elaborate talk or persistent persuasion.

**Snow King, The.** So the Austrians called Gustavus Adolphus of Sweden (1594–1632), because, they said, he 'was kept together by the cold, but would melt and disappear as he approached a warmer soil'.

**Snow line.** The line above which a mountain is continually under snow.

**Snow White.** The beautiful princess of the fairy stories has her origins in German folklore, and in the tales collected by the Brothers Grimm. She was brought before a wide English-speaking audience in the feature-length Disney cartoon film *Snow White and the Seven Dwarfs* (1937). In this version, she eats a poisoned apple given her by the queen, who is jealous of her beauty, but is brought back to life when kissed by a prince. Her name alludes to her milk-white skin.

**Abominable Snowman.** *See under* ABOMINABLE.

**As pure as the driven snow.** *See under* AS.

**Red snow.** *See under* RED.

**Snudge.** *See* BOOTSIE AND SNUDGE.

**Snuff. Snuffed out, To be.** To be put down or killed. Hence snuff movie for a pornographic film depicting an actual murder.

**Snuff it, To.** To die, the allusion being to the snuffing out of a candle.

> 'Tis strange the mind, that very fiery particle,
> Should let itself be snuffed out by an article.
> LORD BYRON: *Don Juan*, xi (1819–24)

**Snuff movie.** A pornographic film depicting an actual killing, usually with preliminary harrowing torture.

**Devil's snuffbox.** *See under* DEVIL.

**Dip snuff, To.** *See under* DIP.

**Up to snuff.** *See under* UP.

**Snug. As snug as a bug in a rug.** *See under* AS.

**So. So far so good.** Progress has been satisfactory up to this point.

**So long.** Goodbye; until we meet again.

**So much for.** That is all that needs to be said about, as: 'So much for his promises'.

**So what?** What of it? A colloquialism of American origin, often shortened to 'So?'

**Soap. Soap** or **soft soap.** Flattery, especially of an oily, unctuous kind.

**Soapbox oratory.** Tub-thumping or demagogic utterance. From the use of a 'soapbox' as a stand or platform. Soap was formerly packed in strong wooden boxes.

**Soap bubble.** Figuratively, anything attractive that is ephemeral.

**Soap opera** or **soap.** A term for a sentimental type of play, usually in serial form, as originally used by commercial radio and television in advertising soap and other commodities. Such programmes were sponsored by soap manufacturers, perhaps because they were obviously 'clean'. Radio producers then nicknamed the plays 'soaps', and when they were taken up by television, 'opera' was added as a humorous allusion to their increasingly 'heavy' content.

**Soapy Sam.** Samuel Wilberforce (1805–73), bishop of Oxford, and afterwards of Winchester, founder of Cuddesdon Theological College (1854), so called because of his persuasive and unctuous way of speaking. It is somewhat remarkable that the floral decorations above the stall of the bishop and of the principal of Cuddesdon were S.O.A.P., the initials of Sam[uel] Oxon[iensis] and Alfred Port[smouth].

Someone asking the bishop why he was so called received the answer: 'Because I am often in hot water and always come out with clean hands.'

**Joe Soap.** *See under* JOE.

**Sob. Sob sister.** A now dated nickname for a female journalist who writes the answers to readers' personal problems, so called because of the tear-provoking sentimentality involved.

**Sob story.** A story or explanation, especially an excuse, that plays on the emotions.

**Sob stuff.** A phrase describing newspaper, film or other stories of a highly sentimental kind, otherwise cheap or tear-jerking pathos.

**Sober. As sober as a judge.** *See under* AS.

**Philip sober.** *See under* PHILIP.

**Soc.** *See* SAC AND SOC.

**Socage.** A free feudal nonmilitary tenure, held in FEE SIMPLE, service being in the form of rent or some form of agricultural duty. The word is from Old English *soc*, 'jurisdiction', 'franchise', modern 'soke'.

**Socialism. Social and Liberal Democrats.** *See* GANG OF FOUR (2); LIBERAL.

**Social Democratic Party.** *See* GANG OF FOUR (2); LIBERAL.

**Champagne socialism.** *See under* CHAMPAGNE.

**Society.** In the restricted sense, the world of fashion, high society or the UPPER TEN.

**Society of Friends.** *See* QUAKERS.

**Society of Jesus.** *See* JESUITS.

**Society of the Temple, The.** *See under* TEMPLE.

**Society verse.** *See* VERS DE SOCIÉTÉ.

**Affluent society, The.** *See under* AFFLUENT.

**Camden Society.** *See under* CAMDEN.

**Dorcas Society.** *See under* DORCAS.

**Fabian Society.** *See under* FABIUS.

**Friendly society.** *See under* FRIEND.

**High society.** *See under* HIGH.

**John Birch Society.** *See under* JOHN.

**National Society.** *See under* NATIONAL.

**Permissive society.** *See under* SOCIETY.

**Royal Society.** *See under* ROYAL.

**Sock.** The light shoe worn by the comic actors of Greece and Rome (Latin *soccus*), hence applied to comedy itself.

> Then to the well-trod stage anon,
> If Jonson's learned sock be on.
> MILTON: 'L'Allegro' (1645)

The difference between the sock of comedy and the buskin of tragedy was that the sock reached only to the ankle, but the buskin extended to the knee.

**Sock it to them.** Let them have it; impress them. 'Sock' here is the verb meaning 'to hit'.

**Blow one's socks off, To.** *See under* BLOW.

**Bobby socks.** *See under* BOBBY.

**Knock** or **blow one's socks off, To.** *See under* KNOCK.

**Pull one's socks up, To.** *See under* PULL.

**Put a sock in it.** Be quiet; shut up; make less noise. In the late 19th century and earlier years of the 20th, when gramophones or phonographs amplified the sound through large horns, woollen socks were often stuffed in them to deaden the volume.

**Socrates.** The great Greek philosopher of Athens (*c*.470–399 BC). He used to call himself 'the midwife of men's thoughts' and out of his intellectual school sprang those of PLATO and the Dialectic system, EUCLID and the Megarian, Aristippus and the Cyrenaic, ANTISTHENES and the CYNIC, and the Elean and Eretrian schools. Phaedo and Xenophon were also among his disciples. Cicero said of him, 'he brought down philosophy from the heavens to earth', and he was the first to teach that 'the proper study of mankind is man'. He was condemned to death for the corruption of youth by introducing new gods (thus being guilty of impiety) and drank hemlock in the presence of his followers.

**Socratic irony.** The assumption of ignorance as a means of leading on and eventually disproving an opponent. This was a form of procedure used with great effect by SOCRATES.

**Socratic method, The.** The method of conducting an argument, imparting information and the like by means of question and answer.

**Sodom and Gomorrah.** Figuratively, any town or towns regarded as exceptional centres of vice and immorality. An allusion to the cities that God destroyed for their wickedness (*see* Genesis 18–19). Sodom, in particular, was the city whose inhabitants wanted to 'know' the two angels staying with Lot (Genesis 19:5), but Lot offered them his two daughters instead. Hence sodomy as an alternative term for buggery. Hence also sodomite as the word for a person who practises this, 'sod' as a slang term for an unpleasant person or any person in general ('lucky sod'), and 'sod off' as one of several fairly crude expressions meaning 'go away'. *See also* LOT AND HIS WIFE.

> Gary told the economics teacher, who managed the first XI, to 'sod off' and so was expelled from the first XI after one match.
> *The Times* (Letter to the Editor) (4 January 1999)

**Apples of Sodom.** *See under* APPLE.

**Soft. Soft answer.** A gentle or good-tempered answer to abuse or accusation. The phrase is of biblical origin.

> A soft answer turneth away wrath.
> Proverbs 15:1

**Softening of the brain.** A morbid degeneration of the brain, especially in the elderly. *See also* SOFT IN THE HEAD.

**Soft focus.** A slight deliberate blurring of the focus in a photograph, often for advertising effect or to tone down an otherwise pornographic image. In a film it may be used to photograph an actress who may not stand up to sharper definition or to enhance an exotic shot in a musical number.

**Soft in the head.** Feeble-minded.

**Soft landing.** Figuratively, a painless resolution of an economic or other problem.

**Softly-softly.** Said of any action that is gradual and cautious. The term comes from the quasi-proverb, 'Softly, softly, catchee monkey'. The present phrase was popularized by the television series *Softly, Softly* (1966–70), based on the work of the Lancashire police.

**Soft option.** The easiest of a number of choices, involving the least difficulty or effort.

**Soft science.** *See* HARD SCIENCE.

**Soft sell.** A method of selling based on persuasion or inducement, rather than direct appeal (HARD SELL).

**Soft soap.** *See* SOAP.

**Soft touch, A.** Someone who is soft-hearted and easily imposed on, especially someone easy to 'touch' for money.

**Software.** Computer programs, also video cassettes and disks. *See also* HARDWARE.

**As soft as butter.** *See under* AS.

**Have a soft spot for, To.** To have a special affection or sympathy for.

**Soho!** An exclamation used by huntsmen, especially in hare coursing when a hare has been started. It is a very old call dating from at least the 13th century, and corresponds to the TALLY-HO! of fox hunters when the fox breaks cover. It was the password used by the duke's forces in the ill-starred night attack at Sedgemoor in 1685 during MONMOUTH'S REBELLION.

**Soho.** This cosmopolitan area of London apparently derives its name from the old hunting cry, when fields here were used for hunting. Its first use as a place-name is found (as So Ho) in 1632. Its first foreign influx was that of the HUGUENOTS after the revocation of the EDICT OF NANTES in 1685, and in the 1860s and 1870s Germans and Italians came to settle, followed by Swiss, Russians, Poles, Greeks and others. It has long been a noted centre for foreign restaurants and delicatessen shops and a haunt of gastronomes, and in the 1950s and 60s they were joined by a proliferation of STRIPTEASE shows, near-beer clubs and CLIP JOINTS. New legislation in the 1970s, however, reduced the number of such premises.

**Soi-disant** (French, literally 'calling oneself'). Self-styled; would-be.

**Soil, A son of the.** *See under* SON.

**Sol** (Latin, 'sun'). The Roman sun god, and the sun itself. In Scandinavian mythology Sol was the maiden who drove the chariot of the sun.

The name was given by the alchemists to gold, and in HERALDRY it represents or (gold). It is also the monetary unit of Peru. In music sol is the fifth note of the diatonic scale.

**Sold.** *See* SELL.

**Soldier.** Originally a hireling, one paid a wage, especially for military service, from Late Latin *solidus*, 'gold coin', hence 'pay'.

**Soldier on, To.** To perservere doggedly; to plod on steadily like a good soldier.

**Soldier's friend, The.** An official appointed to assist soldiers in making out and presenting their claims to the various pension boards.

**Soldiers of fortune.** Men who live by their wits; *chevaliers d'industrie*. The allusion is to those men in medieval times who let themselves for hire to any army.

**Come the old soldier over, To.** *See under* COME.

**Old soldier, An.** *See under* OLD.

**Tin soldier.** *See under* TIN.

**Solecism.** A deviation from correct idiom or grammar, from the Greek *soloikismos*, 'speaking incorrectly', so named from Soloi, a town in Cilicia, the ATTIC colonists of which spoke a debased form of Greek. The word is also applied to any impropriety or breach of good manners. *See also* SPLIT AN INFINITIVE.

**Solemn League and Covenant, The.** An agreement between the English Parliament and the Scots in 1643 to strengthen their position in the struggle against CHARLES I. Presbyterianism was to be established in England and Ireland, and the Scots undertook to provide an army in return for payment. Charles II swore to abide by the Covenant when he was crowned at Scone in 1651, but after the RESTORATION it became a dead letter. *See also* COVENANTERS.

**Sol-fa.** *See* TONIC SOL-FA.

**Solicitor.** *See* ATTORNEY.

**Solicitor-General.** The second law officer of the crown and deputy of the ATTORNEY-GENERAL. He is a member of the House of Commons, and his period of office terminates with the fall of the ministry. It is customary to confer a knighthood on the holder of this office.

**Solid** (Latin *solidus*, 'firm', 'dense', 'compact'). As applied to individuals, the word commonly denoted soundness, as in a 'man of solid worth', or gravity and depth, also a man of substance.

**Solid South, The.** The white electorate of the Southern states of the USA, regarded as giving unified support to the Democratic Party.

> It is possible for the GOP [Grand Old Party, i.e. Republican Party] to revitalize itself by becoming the necessary counterweight to the newly reconstituted Solid South.
>
> *Chicago Tribune* (2 October 1977)

**Solipsism** (Latin *solus*, 'alone', and *ipse*, 'self'). Absolute egoism; the metaphysical theory that the only knowledge possible is that of oneself.

**Solomon.** King of Israel (d.*c*.930 BC). He is the son of DAVID and BATHSHEBA, the builder of the TEMPLE, and a ruler specially noted for his wisdom and justice. This is evidenced in the case where two women claim the same baby. Solomon offers to cut it in half, thereby prompting the true mother to renounce her claim in order to preserve the child. Solomon is also said to have had 1000 wives and concubines and to have written the sensual Song of Solomon. His life and times are described in 1 Kings and 1 and 2 Chronicles.

**Solomon of France, The.** Charles V (1338–80), le Sage ('the Wise').

**Solomon's carpet.** *See* MAGIC CARPET.

**Solomon's ring.** This enabled the monarch to overcome all opponents and to transport himself to the celestial spheres where he learned the secrets of the universe. The ring also sealed up the refractory JINN in jars and cast them into the Red Sea, and conferred upon the wearer the ability to understand and converse with the animal world.

**Solomon's seal.** A plant, *Polygonatum multiflorum*, with drooping white flowers. As the stems decay, the rootstock becomes marked with scars that have some resemblance to seals. This is one explanation of the name. Another is that the root has medicinal value in sealing up and closing green wounds. Yet another claims that the seal is one of the flowers, which hangs like a seal from a document. Solomon's seal is also another name for the STAR OF DAVID.

**English Solomon, The.** James I (r.1603–25), who was a Scot, also called by Sully 'the wisest fool in Christendom'.

**Temple of Solomon, The.** *See under* TEMPLE.

**Wisdom of Solomon, The.** *See under* WISDOM.

**Solomonids.** A dynasty of Ethiopian emperors and NEGUSes reigning from *c.*1270 to 1974. Its first historically reliable member was Yekuno Amlak (r.*c.*1270–85), originally a ruler of a small Christian kingdom in central Ethiopia. He and his seven successors were 'holy' rulers, living in seclusion and making no royal visits. The real founder of the medieval Ethiopian empire was 'Amda Seyon I (r.1314–44), who extended the territory as far as the Red Sea and Gulf of Aden. He and his successors were 'warrior' rulers. They had several wives, who, with the entire court and royal army, accompanied them on their visits to various parts of the country. During such sorties they received gifts, fed and feasted their entourage and troops, repelled enemy attacks or invaded their territory and fortified the frontiers of their kingdom. It was probably in the reign of 'Amda Seyon that the legend arose attributing the origin of Yekuno Amlak's line to King SOLOMON. The story is told in the *Kebra Negast* ('Glory of the Kings'), used as a mythological 'royal charter' from the 14th century to the fall of Haile Selassie in 1974.

**Solon.** Athenian statesman and sage (*c.*638–*c.*558 BC), a great lawgiver and one of the Seven Sages or WISE MEN OF GREECE.

**Solon of Parnassus, The.** So VOLTAIRE called Nicolas Boileau (1636–1711). *See also* LEGISLATOR OF PARNASSUS.

**Solstice.** The summer solstice is 21 June and the winter solstice is 22 December. They are so called because on or about these dates the sun reaches its extreme northern and southern points in the ECLIPTIC and appears to stand still (Latin *sol*, 'sun', and *sistere*, 'to stand still') before it turns back on its apparent course. The term is often popularly confused with EQUINOX.

> Sir, What on Earth (literally) is the 'summer equinox' (letters headline June 27)? Is it something visible from the east pole?
>
> *The Times* (Letter to the Editor) (1 July 1998)

**Soma.** An intoxicating drink anciently made, with mystic rites and incantations, from the juice of some Indian plant by the priests, and drunk by the BRAHMANS as well as offered as libations to their gods. It was fabled to have been brought from heaven by a falcon, or by the daughters of the sun. It was itself personified as a god, and represented the moon. The plant was probably a species of *Asclepias*.

**Someone. Someone is walking over my grave.** An exclamation when one is seized with an involuntary, convulsive shuddering.

**Someone to be reckoned with.** A person of power or influence, to whom one must pay due heed.

**Someone** or **somebody up there likes me.** An expression that is commonly used in the event of a narrow escape or a piece of good fortune. 'Someone up there' is God.

**Somerset House.** The present building off the Strand, London, housing the Board of Inland Revenue, the Registrar-General (to 1973), and the Principal Probate Registry, was built (1776–86) by Sir William Chambers. It occupies the site of the former princely mansion of Lord Protector Somerset, brother of Jane Seymour and uncle of Edward VI. The building became crown property after Somerset's execution (1552) and was later renamed Denmark House by James I, in honour of his queen, Anne of Denmark. It was occupied in turn by three queens, Anne of Denmark, Henrietta Maria of France and Catherine of Braganza. From 1990 it has housed the Courtauld Gallery.

**Something is rotten in the state of Denmark.** There is something wrong, although it is hard to say precisely what. The quotation, from Shakespeare's *Hamlet*, I, iv (1600), is often used facetiously.

**Son. Son of a bitch.** A general term of abuse, dating from at least the time of Shakespeare.

> Nothing but the composition of a knave, beggar, coward, pandar, and the son and heir of a mongrel bitch.
>
> *King Lear*, II, ii (1605)

**Son of a gun.** This familiar designation, originally implying contempt but now used with friendly familiarity, derives from the days when women were allowed to live in naval ships. The 'son of a gun' was one born in the ship, often near the midship gun, behind a canvas screen. If paternity was uncertain the child was entered in the log as 'Son of a gun'.

**Son of Ammon, The.** Alexander the Great was thus greeted by the priests of the Libyan temple of JUPITER AMMON.

> Ammon's great son one shoulder had too high.
> ALEXANDER POPE: *Epistle to Dr Arbuthnot* (1735)

*See also* AMEN-RA.

**Son of Bacchus, A.** *See* PRIEST OF BACCHUS.

**Son of God.** An angel or Christian believer.

> As many as are led by the Spirit of God, they are the sons of God.
> Romans 8:14

**Son of Man.** In the Gospels, a title of Christ.

**Son of the Devil.** Ezzelino da Romano (1194–1259), the noted GHIBELLINE leader and Governor of Vicenza, so called for his infamous cruelty.

**Son of the soil, A.** The native of a district whose family has well-established local roots; also a worker on the land.

**Sons of Belial.** Lawless, worthless, or rebellious people.

> Now the sons of Eli were sons of Belial; they knew not the Lord.
> 1 Samuel 2:12.

**Sons of Liberty.** American secret radical associations formed after the passing of the Stamp Act (1765) to resist British attempts at taxation. They had considerable influence in arousing revolutionary feeling.

**Sons of Thunder.** *See* BOANERGES.

**Sons of Usnech or Uisnech, The.** Naoise, Ainle and Ardan. DEIRDRE was told by her foster father that she would fall in love with a man who had hair as black as a raven, cheeks as red as blood, and a body white as snow. Naoise was such a man and Deirdre eloped with him.

**Four Sons of Aymon.** *See under* FOUR.

**Prodigal son, The.** *See under* PRODIGAL.

**Son et lumière** (French, 'sound and light'). Pageantry and dramatic spectacles presented after dark in an appropriate natural or historic setting, in vogue in Britain during the 1960s and adopted from enactments of this type at French châteaux such as Chambord. They are accompanied by, and dependent on, lighting effects, suitable music and narrative.

**Song. Song and dance, A.** A fuss, especially an unnecessary one, as: 'There's no need to make such a song and dance about it.'

**Song of Roland, The.** The 11th-century CHANSON DE GESTE ascribed to the Norman TROUVÈRE Théroulde or Turoldus, which tells the story of the death of ROLAND and all the PALADINS at Roncesvalles, and of CHARLEMAGNE's vengeance. When Charlemagne had been six years in Spain he sent GANELON on an embassy to Marsillus, the pagan king of Saragossa. Ganelon, out of jealousy, betrayed to Marsillus the route that the Christian army planned to take on its way home, and the pagan king arrived at Roncesvalles just as Roland was conducting through the pass a rear-guard of 20,000 men. He fought until 100,000 SARACENS lay slain, and only 50 of his own men survived, when another army of 50,000 men poured from the mountains. Roland now blew his enchanted horn. Charlemagne heard the blast but Ganelon persuaded him that Roland was merely hunting deer. Thus Roland was left to his fate.

The *Chanson* runs to 4000 lines, the oldest manuscript being preserved in the Bodleian Library, Oxford and Wace (*Roman de Rou*) tells that the Norman minstrel sang parts of this to encourage William's soldiers at the Battle of Hastings.

> Taillefer, the minstrel-knight, bestrode
> A gallant steed, and swiftly rode
> Before the Duke, and sang the song
> Of Charlemagne, of Roland strong,
> Of Oliver, and those beside
> Brave knights at Roncesvaux that died.
> A.S. Way's rendering (1913)

**Song of Songs, The.** The Song of Solomon in the OLD TESTAMENT, also known as Canticles.

**Song of the Three Holy Children, The.** An APOCRYPHAL book in the SEPTUAGINT and the VULGATE included as part of the Book of Daniel. It contains the prayer of Azarias and a narrative of the three Hebrews in the fiery furnace ending with the thanksgiving for their deliverance. The canticle known as the Benedicite is taken from this.

**Going for a song.** For sale very cheaply. The allusion is probably to the trifling cost of the old ballad sheets or to the small change given to itinerant songsters outside inns and public houses.

**On song.** Performing very well.

**Plug a song, To.** *See under* PLUG.

**Swan song.** *See under* SWAN.

**Theme song.** *See under* THEME.

**Sonnet. Dark Lady of the Sonnets, The.** *See under* DARK.

**Prince of the Sonnet.** Joachim du Bellay, Apollo of the Pleiad (1522–60), French sonneteer, was so called. *See also* FRENCH PLÉIADE.

**Sooner.** A native of Oklahoma. The name alludes to those who reached their claims sooner than was legal in the great Oklahoma land rush of 1889.

**Sooterkin.** A kind of false birth fabled to be produced by Dutch women through sitting over their stoves, hence an abortive proposal or scheme, and, as applied to literature, an imperfect or a supplementary work.

For knaves and fools being near of kin
As Dutch boors are t'a sooterkin,
Both parties join'd to do their best
To damn the public interest.
SAMUEL BUTLER: *Hudibras*, III, ii (1680)

**Sop. Sop in the pan, A.** A titbit; a dainty morsel. Literally it is a piece of bread soaked in the dripping of meat caught in the dripping pan. The phrase is also used for a bribe.

**Sop to Cerberus, A.** A bribe. To give a sop to CERBERUS is to quiet a troublesome customer. Cerberus is PLUTO's three-headed dog, stationed at the gates of the infernal regions. When people died, the Greeks and Romans used to put a cake in their hands as a sop to Cerberus to allow them to pass without molestation.

**Soph.** A contraction of sophister. At Cambridge, a second-year student was formerly called a Junior Soph and in his third year a Senior Soph. These students had to maintain a given question in the schools by opposing the orthodox view of it. The word is from Greek and Latin *sophister*, a SOPHIST.

In American universities soph is an abbreviation of sophomore, a term applied to second-year students.

**Sophia, Santa.** The great metropolitan cathedral of the ORTHODOX CHURCH at Istanbul. It was built by Justinian (532–537), but since the capture of the city by the Turks (1453) has been used as a mosque and is now a museum. It was not dedicated to a saint named Sophia, but to the 'Logos', or Second Person of the TRINITY, called Hagia Sophia ('Sacred Wisdom').

**Sophist, sophistry, sophism, sophisticated etc.** These words have quite departed from their original meaning. The Seven Sages or WISE MEN OF GREECE were called sophists ('wise men') and in the 5th and 4th centuries BC the term denoted those who made a profession of teaching the various branches of learning. PYTHAGORAS (*fl.c.*540–*c.*510 BC) out of modesty called himself a 'philosopher' (a 'wisdom-lover'). A century later Protagoras of Abdera resumed the title, and the sophists became hostile to the philosophers. Their hypercritical attitudes eventually led to sophistry falling into contempt, as the less able increasingly appeared as a set of quibblers. Hence *sophos* and its derivatives came to be applied to 'wisdom falsely so called', and *philosophos* to the 'modest search after truth'. Current uses of sophisticated implying 'worldly-wise', 'refined' and 'technically advanced' reveal a further drift in meaning of what became a vogue word.

**Sophy, The.** An old title of the rulers of Persia, first given as an epithet to Sheik Junaid, whose grandson, Ismail I, founded the Safawid dynasty (1502–1736). It is derived from Arabic *Çafi-ud-din*, 'purity of religion'.

**Sorbonne.** The usual name for the University of Paris, which derives from the ancient college of this name, the *Collegium Pauperum Magistrorum* founded by Robert de Sorbon *c.*1257. He was confessor of St LOUIS and the college was for the advanced study of theology. It was suppressed in 1792, but re-established by NAPOLEON BONAPARTE in 1808 as a theological faculty which lasted until 1882.

**Sorites** (Greek *sōros*, 'heap'). A 'heaped-up' or cumulative SYLLOGISM, the predicate of one forming the subject of that which follows, the subject of the first being ultimately united with the predicate of the last. The following is an example:

All men who believe shall be saved.
All who are saved must be free from sin.
All who are free from sin are innocent in the sight of God.
All who are innocent in the sight of God are meet for heaven.
All who are meet for heaven will be admitted into heaven.
Therefore all who believe will be admitted into heaven.

**Famous Sorites of Themistocles, The.** *See under* FAMOUS.

**Sorrel.** The horse of William III was blind in one eye and 'mean of stature'. It stumbled over a molehill and the king's fall led to his death. Its name means 'reddish-brown', as the word used generally for a horse of this colour. *See also* LITTLE GENTLEMAN IN VELVET; SAVOY.

**Sorrow. Man of Sorrows.** *See under* MAN.

**Seven sorrows of Mary, The.** *See under* SEVEN.

**Sortes** (Latin *sors*, *sortis*, 'chance', 'lot'). A species of DIVINATION performed by selecting passages from a book haphazard. Virgil's *Aeneid* (1st century BC) was at one time the favourite work for the purpose (*Sortes Virgilianae*), but the Bible (*Sortes Biblicae*) has also been in common use.

The method is to open the book at random, and the passage touched by chance with one's finger is the oracular response. Severus consulted Virgil and read these words: 'Forget not thou, O Roman, to rule the people with royal sway.' Gordianus, who reigned only a few days, hit on this verse: 'Fate only showed him on this earth, and suffered him not to tarry.' Dr Wellwood gives an instance respecting CHARLES I and Lord Falkland. Falkland, to amuse the king, suggested this kind of AUGURY, and the king hit on IV, 615–20, the gist of which is that 'evil wars would break out, and the king lose his life'. Falkland, to laugh the matter off, said he would show his Majesty how ridiculously the 'lot' would foretell the next fate, and he hit on

XI, 152–81, the lament of Evander for the untimely death of his son Pallas. Soon after, King Charles mourned over his noble friend who was slain at Newbury (1643).

In Rabelais (*Pantagruel*, III, x (1532)), PANURGE consults the *Sortes Virgilianae et Homericae* on the burning question, whether or not he should marry.

**Sorts, Out of.** *See under* OUT.

**SOS.** The Morse code signal (3 dots, 3 dashes, 3 dots, · · · – – – · · ·) used by shipping and the like in distress to summon immediate aid, hence any urgent appeal for help.

The letters are simply a convenient and distinctive combination and are not an abbreviation, although they have been popularly held to stand for 'save our souls' or 'save our ship'.

**Soter.** PTOLEMY I of Egypt (d.283 BC) was given this Greek surname, meaning 'the Preserver', by the Rhodians because he compelled Demetrius to raise the siege of Rhodes (304 BC).

**Sothic period** or **year.** The Sothic year was the fixed year of the ancient Egyptians, the CANICULAR YEAR, determined from one heliacal rising of the DOG STAR Sirius (Sothis) to the next. Since Sothis rose one day later every four years, their CALENDAR did not accord with the solar year until after 1460 (365 × 4) solar years, when their first day of the year had worked through the seasons and come back into line. This was the Sothic or CANICULAR PERIOD.

**Soul.** The idea of the soul as the immaterial and immortal part of man surviving after death as a ghost or SPIRIT was an ancient and widespread belief. The ancient Egyptians represented it as a bird with a human head. With ARISTOTLE the soul is essentially the vital principle and the neo-Platonists held that it was located in the whole body and in every part. It has also been located in the blood, heart, brain, bowels, liver and kidneys, among other organs.

The Muslims say that the souls of the faithful assume the forms of snow-white birds, and nestle under the throne of ALLAH until the resurrection.

**Soul cakes.** Sweet cakes formerly distributed at the church door on ALL SOULS' DAY to the poor who went a-souling, i.e. begging for soul cakes. The words used were:

> Soul, soul, for soul-cake,
> Pray you, good mistress, a soul cake.

**Soul-destroying.** Deadly dull and monotonous; depressing and dreary.

> *Morell*: Candida: what dreadful! what soul-destroying cynicism! Are you jesting?
> GEORGE BERNARD SHAW: *Candida*, II (1895)

**Soulmate.** A person ideally suited to another.

**Soul papers.** Papers requesting prayers for the souls of the departed named thereon which were given away with SOUL CAKES.

**All Souls College.** *See under* ALL.

**All Souls' Day.** *See under* ALL.

**All Souls' Parish Magazine.** *See under* ALL.

**Iron entered his soul, The.** *See under* IRON.

**Keep body and soul together, To.** *See under* BODY.

**Life and soul of the party.** *See under* LIFE.

**Transmigration of souls.** *See under* TRANSMIGRATION.

**Upon my soul.** An exclamation of surprise.

**Sound. Sound all right on paper, To.** To seem workable in theory before being tested.

**Sound off, To.** To express one's views or feeling vehemently or forcibly

**As sound as a bell.** *See under* AS.

**Safe and sound.** *See under* SAFE.

**Soup. Bird's nest soup.** *See under* BIRD.

**Duck soup.** *See under* DUCK.

**In the soup.** In a mess; in trouble.

**Stone soup.** *See under* STONE .

**Sour grapes.** Something disparaged because it is beyond one's reach. The allusion is to AESOP's well-known fable of the fox who tried in vain to get at some grapes, but when he found they were beyond his reach went away saying, 'I see they are sour.'

**South. South Bank religion.** A journalistic label for the religious activities in the diocese of SOUTHWARK associated with Mervyn Stockwood, bishop of Southwark (1959–80), John Robinson, Suffragan Bishop of Woolwich (1959–69), author of *Honest to God* (1963), and some of their diocesan clergy. Characterized by outspokenness on moral and political issues, often from a socialist angle, and energetic attempts to bring the church into closer relation to contemporary society and its problems, South Bank religion was not without its critics and the label was often applied disparagingly by opponents. Dr Stockwood was appointed under Harold Macmillan's Conservative government and the appellation South Bank derives from the fact that the Southwark diocese borders on the south bank of the Thames.

> That is rather the new idea inside the Church. I should definitely say you were a South Banker.
> AUBERON WAUGH: *Consider the Lilies*, ch ix (1968)

**Southern gate of the sun, The.** The sign CAPRICORN or winter SOLSTICE, so called because it is the most southern limit of the sun's course in the ECLIPTIC.

**Southpaw.** In American usage, a left-handed baseball player, especially a pitcher or any left-handed person in general. In both American and British usage the term describes a boxer who leads with his right hand.

**South Sea Bubble, The** The speculative mania associated with South Sea Company and other stock in 1720, which ended disastrously in the ruin of many. The South Sea Company, founded in 1711, was given the monopoly of trade with Spanish America in return for an undertaking to convert part of the NATIONAL DEBT to a lower rate of interest. In 1720 the company's monopoly was extended to the South Seas and at the same time it offered to take over the whole National Debt. This led to gross over-speculation, and many other preposterous companies were floated. £100 shares of the company ran up to £890 and ultimately £1000, with the inevitable consequences. The South Sea Company continued its existence until 1856. *See also* MISSISSIPPI BUBBLE.

**Deep South, The.** *See under* DEEP.

**Solid South, The.** *See under* SOLID.

**Southcottians.** The followers of Joanna Southcott (1750–1814), one-time domestic servant at Exeter. Starting as a METHODIST, she became a prophetess and declared herself to be the 'woman clothed with the sun, and the moon under her feet, and upon her head a crown of twelve stars' (Revelation 12:1). At the age of 64 she announced that she was to be delivered of a son, the Shiloh of Genesis 49:10:

> The sceptre shall not depart from Judah, nor a lawgiver from between his feet, until Shiloh come; and unto him shall the gathering of the people be.

19 October 1814 was the date fixed for the birth, which did not take place, but the prophetess died in a trance soon afterwards and was buried in the churchyard of St John's Wood Chapel. She left a locked wooden box usually known as Joanna Southcott's Box, which was not to be opened until a time of national crisis, and then only in the presence of all the bishops in England. Attempts were made to persuade the episcopate to open it during the Crimean War (1854–6) and again in the First World War. It was opened in 1927 in the presence of one reluctant prelate, and found to contain a few oddments and papers, among which was a lottery ticket. It is claimed by some that the box opened was not the authentic one. *See also* NUNAWADING MESSIAH.

**Southwark.** The ancient suburb on the south bank of the Thames annexed to the City of London in 1327 and once known as 'the Borough'. It has a wealth of historical associations, including the site of the TABARD INN of Chaucer's *Canterbury Tales* (*c*.1387), the Globe Theatre on BANKSIDE, the CLINK, the MARSHALSEA PRISON and PARIS-GARDEN, as well as the church of St Mary OVERY, the George Inn and other sites. Southwark possessed two MINTS and held an annual fair (1550–1763), and it became an independent borough in 1899. As a diocese, it was formed out of Rochester in 1905. The name means 'southern fort' and is of Saxon origin. *See also* SOUTH BANK RELIGION; TABARD INN.

**Sovereign.** A strangely evolved word from Vulgar Latin *superanus*, 'supreme', the last syllable being assimilated to 'reign'. The French *souverain* is nearer the Latin.

The gold coin of this name valued at 20 shillings, first issued by Henry VII (r.1485–1509), was so called from its representation of the monarch enthroned and was replaced by the UNITE in the reign of James I (1603–25). A smaller sovereign was issued from 1817 until 1917.

**Sow** (noun). **As drunk as Davy's sow.** *See under* AS.

**Make a silk purse out of a sow's ear, To.** *See under* SILK.

**Sow** (verb). **Sow dragon's teeth, To.** To foment contentions; to stir up strife or war, or specifically to do something that is intended to put an end to strife but that actually brings it about. The PHILISTINES 'sowed dragons' teeth' when they took SAMSON, bound him and put out his eyes. Ethelred II did the same when in 1002 he ordered the massacre of the Danes on St Brice's Day (which brought such fierce reprisals that he was eventually forced to flee), as did the Germans when they took Alsace-Lorraine from France in 1871. The reference is to the classical story of CADMUS.

**Sow one's wild oats, To.** To indulge in youthful excesses and dissipations. The reference is to sowing bad grain, which is wild, instead of good, which is cultivated.

**Sow the wind and reap the whirlwind, To.** To provoke serious consequences through one's heedless actions. The saying is biblical in origin, and relates to Israel's impiety and idolatry:

> They have sown the wind, and they shall reap the whirlwind.
> Hosea 8:7

**Space, Deep.** *See under* DEEP.

**Spade.** The spade of playing cards is so called from Italian *spada*, 'sword', the suit in Italian packs being marked with short swords. In French and British cards the mark, largely through similarity in name, has been altered to the shape of a pointed spade.

**Spade guinea.** An English gold coin, value 21s, minted from 1787 to 1799, so called because its reverse bore a shield shaped like the spade on playing cards. The legend is MBF·ET·H·REX·FD·B·ET·LD·SRIAT·ET·E, referring to George III, and standing for *Magnae Britanniae, Franciae, et Hiberniae Rex; Fidei Defensor; Brunsvicensis et Lunenburgensis Dux; Sacri Romani Imperii Archi-Thesaurarius et Elector* ('King of Great Britain, France and Ireland,

Defender of the Faith, Duke of Brunswick-Lüneburg, Chief Treasurer and Elector of the Holy Roman Empire').

**Call a spade a spade, To.** *See under* CALL.

**Sam Spade.** The San Francisco-based private detective in Dashiell Hammett's *The Maltese Falcon* (1930) and a few other stories. He is the archetypal hero of the 'hardboiled' school of detective fiction, though he does not carry a gun.

**Spaghetti. Spaghetti bolognese.** Spaghetti with meat and tomato sauce, a favourite with children. The dish is popularly abbreviated as spag. bol.

**Spaghetti Junction.** The nickname of the Gravelly Hill Interchange, the junction between the M6, A38 and A5127 near Birmingham, where the many winding and intersecting roads, underpasses and overpasses bear a fanciful resemblance to spaghetti. It was opened in 1972.

**Spaghetti western.** A Western film (*see* WILD WEST) made cheaply by Italians (who eat spaghetti).

**Spagyric.** Pertaining to ALCHEMY. The term seems to have been invented by PARACELSUS. Alchemy is 'the spagyric art', and an alchemist is a 'spagyrist'.

**Spagyric food.** CAGLIOSTRO's name for the elixir of immortal youth.

**Spain** or **Spanish. Spanish fly.** The cantharis, a coleopterous insect used in medicine. Cantharides are dried and used externally as a blister and internally as a stimulant to the genito-urinary organs. They were formerly considered to act as an aphrodisiac.

**Spanish Fronde, The.** The war between France and Spain (1653–9), which was a sequel of the FRONDE and in which the *frondeur* Condé (1621–86) fought for Spain.

**Spanish Inquisition.** *See* INQUISITION.

**Spanish Main, The.** Properly, the northeast coast of South America from the mouth of the Orinoco to the Isthmus of Panama, or the mainland bordering the Caribbean Sea, called by the Spanish conquerors *Tierra Firme*. The term is often more loosely applied to the area of the Caribbean Sea and its islands.

> Then up and spake an old Sailor,
> Had sailed the Spanish Main.
>
> LONGFELLOW: 'The Wreck of the Hesperus' (1841)

**Spanish omelette.** An omelette made with green peppers, onions and tomatoes.

**Spanish practices** or **customs.** Irregular practices introduced by groups of workers with the aim of gaining certain advantages, such as more pay, shorter working hours and so on. The arranging of such a practice is also known as 'an old Spanish custom'. It is not clear why the Spanish are blamed for this.

**Spanish worm.** An old name for a nail concealed in a piece of wood, against which a carpenter blunts his saw or chisel.

**Castle in Spain** or **the air.** *See under* CASTLE.

**Old Spanish custom, An.** *See* SPANISH PRACTICES.

**Ride the Spanish mare, To.** *See under* RIDE.

**Singeing the king of Spain's beard.** *See* SINGEING.

**Span, Spick and.** *See under* SPICK.

**Spaniel.** Literally 'Spanish dog', from Old French *espaigneul*, ultimately from Latin *Hispaniolus*, 'Spanish'.

**King Charles spaniel.** *See under* KING.

**Spanker.** Said of a fast horse or person; also, colloquially, of something or someone that is an exceptionally fine specimen, a 'stunner'.

In nautical language the spanker is the fore-and-aft sail set upon the mizenmast of a three-masted vessel, and the jiggermast of a four-masted vessel. There is no spanker in a one- or two-masted vessel of any rig.

**Spanner. Box spanner.** *See under* BOX.

**Throw a spanner in the works, To.** *See under* THROW.

**Spare the rod and spoil the child.** An old saying drawing attention to the folly of allowing childish faults to go unreproved. The maxim is founded on Proverbs 13:24: 'He that spareth his rod hateth his son: but he that loveth him chasteneth him betimes.'

**Sparks.** A colloquial term for an electrician or a ship's radio operator.

**Marks and Sparks.** *See under* MARKS.

**Spartacists.** An extreme socialist group in Germany that flourished between 1916 and 1919. It was founded by Karl Liebknecht (1871–1919) who, with Rosa Luxemburg (1871–1919), led an attempted revolution in January of the latter year, in the suppression of which they were both killed. The movement was finally crushed by Friedrich Ebert's government in the April. It took its name from the Thracian GLADIATOR, Spartacus, who in 73 BC led a slave rebellion against Rome, which was not suppressed until 71 BC. During the uprising he defeated five Roman armies and devastated whole tracts of Italy.

**Spartans.** The inhabitants of ancient Sparta, one of the leading city-states of Greece, were noted for their frugality, courage and stern discipline. Hence someone who can bear pain unflinchingly is termed 'a Spartan', a very frugal diet is 'Spartan fare' and so on. It was a Spartan mother, who, on handing her son the shield he was to carry into battle, said that he was to come back either with it or on it. *See also* LACONIC.

**Spasmodic school, The.** A name applied in his parody *Firmilion* (1854) by the Scottish poet W.E. Aytoun to certain writers of the 19th century whose style was marked by sentimentality, extravagant imagery and a certain lack of taste. Among them were P.J. Bailey (1816–1902), Sydney Dobell (1824–74), Ernest Jones (1819–69), Ebenezer Jones (1820–60) and Alexander Smith (*c.*1830–67).

**Speak. Speakeasy.** A place where alcoholic liquors are sold illegally. An American term widely current in the years of prohibition (1920–34). 'Easy' here means 'softly', and the name refers either to the fact that such places were spoken about quietly or that people spoke quietly in them, to avoid attracting the attention of police or neighbours. *See also* BOOTLEGGER; CAPONE, AL.

**Speaker.** The title of the presiding officer and official spokesman of the British HOUSE OF COMMONS, the United States HOUSE OF REPRESENTATIVES and of some other legislative assemblies.

The Speaker of the House of Commons, who has autocratic power in the control of debates and internal arrangements of the House, is elected by the members irrespective of party and has no vote except in cases of a tie, when he or she can give a CASTING VOTE. Speakers hold office for the duration of that PARLIAMENT, but by custom (not law) are reappointed unless they wish to resign (in which case they go to the HOUSE OF LORDS). The name 'Speaker' derives from the fact that the office holder was originally the spokesman for the Commons, and would report the decisions of the House to the sovereign. Britain's first woman Speaker was elected in 1992.

The LORD CHANCELLOR is *ex officio* Speaker of the HOUSE OF LORDS.

**Speak for yourself.** Confine yourself to speaking about your own part in the matter or to expressing your own views; do not involve or compromise other people.

**Speaking heads.** Fables and romance tell of a variety of artificial heads that could speak. Among the best known are:

Statue of MEMNON (Amenophis III) at Thebes in Egypt: uttered musical sounds when the morning sun darted on it

Statue of ORPHEUS at Lesbos: said to have predicted the bloody death that terminated the expedition of Cyrus the Great into Scythia

Head of MINOS: fabled to have been brought by ODIN to Scandinavia, and to have uttered responses

BRAZEN HEADS: of Roger Bacon (*c.*1220–92) and of Gerbert, afterwards Pope Sylvester II (*c.*940–1003)

Earthen head: made by ALBERT THE GREAT or Albertus Magnus (c.1206–80), which both spoke and moved. THOMAS AQUINAS (c.1225–74) broke it, whereupon the mechanist exclaimed: 'There goes the labour of thirty years!'

Alexander's statue of AESCULAPIUS: this was supposed to speak, but Lucian says the sounds were uttered by a concealed man, and conveyed by tubes to the statue

**Speaking likeness, A.** A good and lifelike portrait; one that makes you imagine that the subject is about to speak to you.

**Speak one's mind, To.** To say clearly and emphatically what one thinks about the matter.

**Speak the same language, To.** To understand each other perfectly; to hold the same views.

**Speak volumes, To.** To be highly significant.

**Catch the Speaker's eye, To.** *See under* CATCH.

**It speaks for itself.** There is no need for further explanation, evidence or discussion; it is sufficiently clear in itself.

**Not on speaking terms.** Said of two people who have fallen out and are no longer friends.

**Strictly** or **properly speaking.** *See under* STRICTLY.

**Valley speak.** *See under* VALLEY.

**Spear.** If a KNIGHT kept the point of a spear forwards when he entered a strange land, it was a declaration of war, but if he carried it on his shoulder with the point behind him, it was a token of friendship. In Macpherson's OSSIAN (*Temora*, I (1763)), Cairbar asks if FINGAL comes in peace, to which Morannal replies: 'In peace he comes not, king of ERIN, I have seen his forward spear.'

**Spear of Achilles, The.** *See* ACHILLEA.

**Spear side, The.** The male line of descent, called by Anglo-Saxons *sperehealf*. *See also* DISTAFF SIDE; SPINDLE SIDE.

**Pass under the spear, To.** *See under* PASS.

**Special pleading.** Specious argument; making one's argument good by forcing certain words and phrases from their obvious and ordinary meaning. A pleading in law means a written statement of a cause PRO AND CON, and 'special pleaders' are people who have been CALLED TO THE BAR, but do not speak as advocates. They advise on evidence, draw up affidavits, state the merits and demerits of a cause and so on. After a time most special pleaders go to the bar and many get advanced to the BENCH.

**Specie** or **species.** The word means literally 'that which appears' (Latin *species*, 'appearance'). As things are distinguished by their visible forms, it has come to mean 'kind' or 'class'. As drugs and condiments at one time formed the most important articles of merchandise, they were called 'species', still retained in the French *épices* and English 'spices'. Again, as banknotes represent money, money itself is called 'specie', the thing represented.

**Spectre of the Brocken.** An optical illusion, first observed on the Brocken (the highest peak of the Hartz range in central Germany), in which shadows of the spectators, greatly magnified, are projected on the mists around the summit of the mountain opposite. In one of Thomas

De Quincey's (1785–1859) opium dreams, there is a powerful description of the Brocken spectre.

**Speculum Humanae Salvationis** (Latin, 'The Mirror of Human Salvation'). A book similar to the BIBLIA PAUPERUM but on a somewhat more extensive scale, pictorially telling the Bible story from the fall of LUCIFER to the Redemption of Man, with explanations of each picture in Latin rhymes. Its illustrations were copied in church sculptures, wall paintings, altarpieces and stained glass windows. Copies from the 13th century and earlier are extant, and it was one of the earliest of printed books (*c.*1467).

**Speech. Speech day.** The annual prizegiving day at a school when it is customary to invite a guest to make a speech and to distribute the prizes. The head also makes a report on the school's record for the preceding year, and sundry other worthies usually contribute votes of thanks and the like.

**Speech from the throne, The.** *See* KING'S SPEECH.

**Speech is silver, silence is golden.** An old proverb, said to be of oriental origin, pointing to the advantage of keeping one's own counsel. The Hebrew equivalent is: 'If a word be worth one shekel, silence is worth two.'

**Figure of speech.** *See under* FIGURE.

**Free speech.** *See under* FREE.

**King's** or **Queen's speech, The.** *See under* KING.

**Parts of speech.** *See under* PART.

**Speed. Speed the plough** or **God speed the plough.** A wish for success and prosperity in some undertaking. It is a very old phrase and occurs in the song sung by ploughmen on PLOUGH MONDAY. Thomas Morton's play *Speed the Plough* (1798) introduced Mrs Grundy to the English psyche. *See also* WHAT WILL MRS GRUNDY SAY?

**Christ's cross me speed.** *See under* CHRIST.

**Full speed ahead!** *See under* FULL.

**Speenhamland system.** The system of outdoor relief initiated by the magistrates of the parish of Speenhamland, at Speen, near Newbury, Berkshire, in 1795 to counter distress among the agricultural labourers. Wages were to be supplemented by rate aid according to a minimum wage scale related to the price of bread and the size of the family. Outdoor relief was not new, but the Speenhamland System spread rapidly, particularly in the south. It tended to depress wages and demoralize its beneficiaries and sharply increased the poor rate. The Poor Law Amendment Act (1834) sought to terminate outdoor relief, but never wholly succeeded.

**Speewah, The.** A mythical cattle station somewhere in Australia where everything is bigger and better than anywhere else in the world. A series of legends comparable only with the adventures of Baron MÜNCHAUSEN is associated with it. It is said to take its name from Speewa, an actual locality by the Murray River northwest of Swan Hill, Victoria.

**Spell** (Old English *spell*, 'speech'). Spells as charms and incantations are found the world over in folklore and superstition. They form part of the stock-in-trade of witches, WIZARDS, magicians, sorcerers, gypsies and the like, and many fairy stories centre on their use.

The component words of the spells used by medieval sorcerers were usually taken from Hebrew, Greek and Latin, but mere gibberish was often also employed. 'To spell', meaning to write or name the letters that make a word, is from Old French *espeller*, in turn from Frankish. *See also* ABRACADABRA; ABRAXAS.

**Spellbinders.** Orators who hold their audience spellbound, i.e. fascinated or charmed. The word came into use in America in the presidential election of 1888.

**Spelling bee.** A spelling competition, so called as the participants are socially active, like bees.

**Spencean philanthropists.** Followers of Thomas Spence (1750–1814), who in 1775 devised a system of land nationalization on socialist lines. They formed the Society of Spencean Philanthropists in 1812 and thought that their plan heralded the millennium. Spence denounced the landed aristocracy and was constantly in trouble for his views and pamphlets. It was the Spenceans who advocated seizing power by force. They addressed the Spa Fields meeting of 2 December 1816 which ended in the plundering of gunsmiths' shops, and they were prominent in the CATO STREET CONSPIRACY of 1820.

**Spencer.** The word is now applied to a type of knitted vest still worn by some women, but was formerly the name of a short outer coat worn by men. The name itself is that of the 2nd Earl Spencer (1758–1834).

**Spencerian handwriting.** The name given to a style of calligraphy introduced by Platt Rogers Spencer (1800–61), an American calligrapher. Written with a fine pen, with the downstrokes tapering from top to bottom and large loops, the writing has a forward slope and marked terminal flourishes. Spencer taught this style in many parts of USA and it is said to have had a marked influence on American calligraphy.

**Spend a penny, To.** To urinate. The allusion is to the door lock on a cubicle in a public lavatory, which in the pre-decimal era was opened by inserting a penny (1d). *See also* PENNY DROPPED.

**Spenserian stanza.** The stanza devised by Edmund Spenser for *The Faerie Queene* (1590, 1596). It may have been founded on the Italian *ottava rima*, or on Chaucer's stanza in 'The Monk's Tale' (*c.*1387). The Old French ballad has been suggested as another source. It is a stanza of nine IAMBIC lines, all of ten syllables except the last, which is an ALEXANDRINE. Only three different rhymes are admitted into a stanza and these are arranged: a b a b b c b c c.

Among those who used this stanza are Mark Akenside (1721–70), James Thomson (1700–48), Lord Byron (1788–1824), Percy Bysshe Shelley (1792–1822) and John Keats (1795–1821). The following is an example, from Keats' 'The Eve of St Agnes' (1820):

Full on this casement shone the wintry moon,
And threw warm gules on Madeline's fair breast,
As down she knelt for heaven's grace and boon;
Rose-bloom fell on her hands, together prest,
And on her silver cross soft amethyst,
And on her hair a glory, like a saint:
She seem'd a splendid angel, newly drest,
Save wings, for heaven: – Porphyro grew faint:
She knelt, so pure a thing, so free from mortal taint.

**Spheres.** In the PTOLEMAIC SYSTEM of astronomy the nine spheres were those carrying DIANA or the moon, MERCURY, VENUS, APOLLO or the sun, MARS, JUPITER, SATURN, the fixed stars (the Starry Sphere) and the CRYSTALLINE SPHERE, which was introduced by Hipparchus to account for the precession of the equinoxes. The PRIMUM MOBILE was added in the Middle Ages.

**Crystalline sphere.** *See under* CRYSTAL.

**Music of the spheres, The.** *See under* MUSIC.

**Sphinx.** The sphinx of Greek mythology, which was quite distinct from the Egyptian sphinx, was a monster with the head and breasts of a woman, the body of a dog or lion, the wings of a bird, a serpent's tail and lion's paws. It had a human voice and was said to be the daughter of ORTHOS (the two-headed dog of Geryon) or of TYPHOEUS or the CHIMERA. She inhabited the vicinity of THEBES, setting the inhabitants riddles and devouring those unable to find solutions. The Thebans were told by the oracles that she would kill herself if the following riddle was solved:

What goes on four feet, on two feet, and three,
But the more feet it goes on the weaker it be?

It was at length solved by OEDIPUS with the answer that it was a man, who as an infant crawls upon all fours, in manhood goes upright on two feet, and in old age supports his tottering legs with a staff. Thus were the Thebans delivered, and the Sphinx either threw herself to her death from a rock or, in some stories, was killed by Oedipus.

The Egyptian sphinx was a lion, usually with a pharaoh's head, symbolizing royal power, and it came to be associated with HORUS in the Horizon or Harmakhis. The Sphinx at Gizeh was hewn out of limestone rock by order of Khephren or Khafre (*c*.2620 BC) and is 60ft (18.3m) high and 180ft (55m) long.

**Spice. Spice Islands.** The Moluccas and most of the islands of the Malay Archipelago, whose chief products are spices of all kinds, much sought after by 15th- and 16th-century navigators and traders when spices were highly prized commodities in Europe.

**Variety is the spice of life.** *See under* VARIETY.

**Spick and span.** Very neat and clean. The phrase is a shortening of 'spick and span new', which was used of something new and fresh. A spick is a spike or nail, and a span is a chip. A spick and span new ship is one in which every nail and chip is new.

**Spider.** There are many OLD WIVES' TALES about spiders, the most widespread being that they are venomous.

But let thy spiders, that suck up thy venom,
And heavy-gaited toads lie in their way.
SHAKESPEARE: *Richard II*, III, ii (1595)

During the examination into the murder of Sir Thomas Overbury (1581–1613), one of the witnesses deposed 'that the countess wished him to get the strongest poison that he could'. Accordingly he brought seven great spiders. There are few spiders poisonous to man, but the American BLACK WIDOW spider is a notable exception.

Other tales were that fever could be cured by wearing a spider in a nutshell around the neck, and a common cure for jaundice was to swallow a large live house spider rolled up in butter. In Ireland this was a remedy for ague. A spider on one's clothes was a sign of good luck or that money was coming, and the very small spider is called a money spider. Yet another story was that spiders spin only on dark days. *See also* BRUCE, ROBERT; FREDERICK THE GREAT; MOHAMMED.

**Spiderman.** A comic strip hero of the 1960s, the creation of scriptwriter Stan Lee and artist Steve Ditko. His real name is Peter Parker, who as a youth had been bitten by a mutant spider and acquired its characteristics. He has great strength, can climb almost anything, especially New York skyscrapers, and pursues villains with a 'web-shooter'. His costume, which extends to a face mask, is a red and blue uniform decorated with black webbing.

**Spike.** Slang for the workhouse, so that 'to go on the spike' was to become a workhouse inmate. A spike is also a colloquialism for a HIGH CHURCH Anglican and the *Church Times* is colloquially known as 'Spiky Bits'.

**Spike a drink, To.** To add strong spirits to increase the alcoholic content.

**Spike someone's guns, To.** To render someone's plans abortive; to thwart someone's intention. The allusion is to the old way of making a gun useless by driving a spike into the touch hole.

**Spill. Spilling salt.** A mishap held to be an unlucky omen by the Romans, and the superstition remains. Evil may be averted, however, if whoever spills the salt throws a pinch of it over the left shoulder with the right hand. In Leonardo da Vinci's picture of the LAST SUPPER it is possible to identify JUDAS ISCARIOT by the salt cellar knocked over accidentally by his arm. Salt was used in sacrifice by the Jews, as well as by the Greeks and Romans. It was an emblem of purity and the sanctifying influence of a holy life on others because of its preservative quality. It was also a sign of incorruptibility. It is used for the preparation of HOLY WATER and it was not uncommon to put salt into a coffin, for it is said that SATAN hates salt. It was long customary to throw a handful of salt on the top of the mash when brewing to keep the witches from it. *See also* SIN-EATERS.

**Spill the beans, To.** To give away a secret; to LET THE CAT OUT OF THE BAG. The expression is variously explained. According to one account, it originated at the turn of the 20th century as a colourful American euphemism for vomiting, 'beans' representing basic food. It is thus on the same lines as 'cough it up' or SPIT IT OUT!

**Cry over spilt milk, To.** *See under* CRY.

**Spin. Spin a yarn, To.** To tell a story. A nautical expression, from the days when sailors whiled away the time telling stories while sitting on the deck making spun yarn and other rope work.

**Spin doctor.** The expression arose in the United States in the mid-1980s to refer to a politician or public relations expert employed to give a favourable interpretation of events to the media. Its origin is in baseball, from the spin put on the ball by a pitcher to make it go in the desired direction. The idiom later passed into British usage.

> The spin doctors, the PR [public relations] generals, argued after Reykjavik talks that Reagan still stands by Star Wars and within reach. The White House's primary target was opinion-makers in Washington and New York, but a special spin patrol will descend on 15 other cities this week.
> *Newsweek* (27 October 1986)

**Spin in one's grave, To.** *See* TURN OR SPIN IN ONE'S GRAVE *under* TURN.

**Flat spin.** *See under* FLAT.

**Spindle side.** The female line of descent. The spindle was the pin on which the thread was wound from the spinning wheel. *See also* DISTAFF SIDE; SPEAR SIDE; SPINSTER.

**Spinster.** An unmarried woman. In Saxon times, spinning was a routine winter occupation of the female members of the household. ALFRED THE GREAT, in his will, calls the female part of his family the SPINDLE SIDE, and it was formerly reckoned that no young woman was fit to be a wife until she had spun herself a set of body, table, and bed linen. Hence the maiden was termed a spinner or spinster.

It is said that the heraldic lozenge in which the armorial bearings of a woman are depicted originally represented a spindle. Among the Romans the bride carried a DISTAFF, and Homer writes that Chryseis was to spin and share the king's bed.

**Spires, The City of Dreaming.** *See under* CITY.

**Spirit.** Properly, the breath of life, from Latin *spiritus*, from *spirare*, 'to breathe', 'to blow':

> And the Lord God formed man of the dust of the ground, and breathed into his nostrils the breath of life; and man became a living soul.
> Genesis 2:7

Hence, life or the life principle, the SOUL, a disembodied soul (a ghost or apparition), or an immaterial being that was never believed to have had a body, as a GNOME, ELF OF FAIRY. Also, the temper or disposition of mind as animated by the breath of life, as in good spirits, high-spirited, a man of spirit.

The medieval physiological notion, adopted from Galen, the Greek physician and philosopher of the 2nd century AD, was that spirit existed in the body in three kinds:

(1) the natural spirit, the principle of the 'natural functions', growth, nutrition and generation, was said to be a vapour rising from the blood and having its seat in the liver
(2) the vital spirit, which arose in the heart by a mixture of the air breathed in with the natural spirit, supplied the body with heat and life
(3) the animal spirit, which was responsible for the power of motion and sensation and for the rational principle generally, was a modification of the vital spirit, effected in the brain

The elemental spirits of PARACELSUS and the ROSICRUCIANS, i.e. those which presided over the four ELEMENTS, were: the SALAMANDERS (or fire), GNOMES (earth), SYLPHS (air) and UNDINES (water).

'Spirit' also came to mean any volatile agent or essence, and hence, from the alchemists, is still used of solutions in alcohol and of any strong alcoholic liquor. The alchemists named four substances only as 'spirits': MERCURY, arsenic, sal ammoniac and sulphur.

> Among the spirits quicksilver came first
> And orpiment [arsenic] came second, then he passed
> To sal ammoniac and brimstone last.
> CHAUCER: 'The Canon's Yeoman's Tale' (*c.*1387) (modern translation by Nevill Coghill, 1951)

**Spirit away, To.** To kidnap; to abduct; to make away with speedily and secretly. The phrase first came into use in the 17th century, in connection with the kidnapping of boys and young men and their transportation to the West Indian plantations.

**Spiritualism.** The belief that communication between the living and the spirits of the departed can and does take place, usually through the agency of a specially qualified person (a medium) and often by means of TABLE-RAPPING, TABLE-TURNING or automatic writing. The term is also used for the system, doctrines and practice arising from this belief. *See also* OUIJA.

In philosophy, spiritualism, as the antithesis of materialism, is the doctrine that the spirit exists as distinct from matter, or as the only reality.

**Astral spirits.** *See under* ASTRAL.

**Free spirit.** *See under* FREE.

**High spirits.** *See under* HIGH.

**Holy Spirit.** *See* HOLY GHOST.

**If the spirit moves me.** If I feel so inclined. The expression derives from QUAKER use.

**Lords Spiritual.** *See under* LORD.

**Out of spirits.** *See under* OUT.

**Proof spirit.** *See under* PROOF.

**Raise someone's spirits, To.** *See under* RAISE.

**Sword of the Spirit, The.** *See under* SWORD.

**Spit. Spit and polish.** To give something 'a bit of spit and polish' is to clean it up, to make it shine. To spit on leather and the like and rub it to give it a shine was once common practice. The expression is of army origin, the army being properly concerned with the maintenance of smartness of equipment. *See also* BULL.

**Spit and rub collar.** A jocular term for the plastic collar worn by clerics, which does not need laundering but can be cleaned by rubbing with a damp cloth.

**Spit it out!** Say what it is! Let's have it! The idea is that the person is holding a piece of information in his mouth, ready to say, but reluctant to utter it. *See also* SPILL THE BEANS under SPILL.

**Spitting distance.** A very short distance, as: 'She lives within spitting distance of the shops.'

**Spitting for luck.** Spitting was a charm against enchantment among the ancient Greeks and Romans. Pliny says it averted WITCHCRAFT and helped in giving an enemy a shrewder blow. People sometimes spit for luck on a piece of money given to them or found, boxers spit on their hands, and traders were wont to spit on the first money taken in the day. There are numerous other instances of spitting for luck, and it was also common to spit for defiance or as a challenge.

**Spitting image.** An exact likeness or resemblance, just as if one person were to spit out of another's mouth.

**Cuckoo spit.** *See under* CUCKOO.

**Dead spit of someone, The.** *See under* DEAD.

**Spital** or **Spittle.** Contractions for 'hospital'. The London district of Spitalfields, which included parts of Bethnal Green, SHOREDITCH, WHITECHAPEL and Mile End, was named from its being the property of the Priory and hospital of St Mary Spittle founded by Walter Brune and his wife Rosia in 1197. HUGUENOT refugees settled there after the revocation of the EDICT OF NANTES in 1685, and it became a centre for silk and velvet manufacture.

**Spital sermons.** Sermons originally preached on GOOD FRIDAY and on the following Monday, Tuesday and Wednesday from the Pulpit Cross, Spitalfields, which were attended by the lord mayor and aldermen and the boys of Christ's Hospital. The pulpit was destroyed in the Civil Wars (1642–51) and at the RESTORATION the Spital Sermons were revived at St Bride's, Fleet Street. From 1797 they were delivered at Christ Church, Newgate Street and reduced to two. This church was destroyed by incendiary bombs in 1941. The one Spital Sermon is now given in the Corporation Church of St Lawrence Jewry. The pupils of Christ's Hospital, Horsham, now attend the St Matthew's Day service at the Church of the Holy Sepulchre without Newgate, which incorporates the former parish of Christ Church.

**Spleen.** The soft vascular organ placed to the left of the stomach and acting on the blood, once believed to be the seat of melancholy and ill humour. The fern spleenwort, of the genus *Asplenium*, was formerly used as a remedy for splenic disorders.

**Splice.** To marry; to join together. A phrase of nautical origin. Splice is related to German *spleissen*, 'to split', as ropes are split or unlayed before they are united or interwoven or 'spliced'.

**Splice the mainbrace, To.** A naval expression denoting an extra tot of GROG all round, a very rare occurrence. It probably alludes to the issue of an extra rum ration to those who performed the hard and difficult task of splicing the mainbrace, the brace attached to the main yard. It is also used more generally for celebrating and indulging in strong drink. The order to splice the mainbrace was given when Queen Elizabeth II reviewed the Fleet during the Silver Jubilee of 1977, and again on 30 July, 1981 to toast the Prince and Princess of Wales, married the day before.

**Split.** Colloquially, to give away one's accomplices; to betray secrets; to tell tales; to peach. Also to depart; to leave.

**Split an infinitive, To.** To interpose a word or words between 'to' and the verb, as: 'to thoroughly understand the subject'. This construction is branded as a SOLECISM by pedants and purists, but it is long established and has been used by many accomplished writers, such as Matthew Arnold and Robert Browning.

> These are the voyages of the Starship *Enterprise*. Its five-year mission: to explore strange new worlds, to seek out new life and new civilizations, to boldly go where no man has gone before.
>
> GENE RODDENBERRY: *Star Trek* (television series), Introduction (from 1966)

**Split hairs, To.** To argue over petty points; to make fine distinctions; to quibble over trifles.

**Split one's sides, To.** To laugh uproariously or unrestrainedly, as if one's sides were about to split.

**Split personality.** An alteration of personality occurring in some mental illnesses, especially schizophrenia (from Greek *skhizein*, 'to split' and *phren*, 'mind').

**Split second.** A very brief moment of time.

**Split the difference, To.** To settle a dispute by a compromise; to divide a remaining amount equally.

**Split ticket.** In American politics a vote for the candidates of more than one party. The opposite is a 'straight ticket', a vote for a single candidate.

**Spock, Mr.** The impassive, pointed-eared member of the Starship *Enterprise* played by Leonard Nimoy in the cult American television series STAR TREK. He became the most famous character of the series and featured prominently in the books that were subsequently based on it.

**Spoil. Spoiling for a fight, To be.** To seek one eagerly or aggressively. 'Spoiling' here implies that the aggressor has become stale or 'gone off' through long being deprived of a fight.

**Spoilsport.** One who spoils the pleasure or enjoyment of others.

**Spoils system.** The practice in the United States by which the victorious party in an election rewards its supporters by appointments to public office. It takes its name from the phrase 'to the victor belong the spoils', which was popularized by Senator Marcy in 1831. The 7th President, Andrew Jackson (1767–1845), was not the originator of the practice, nor did he noticeably extend it. It was first used by Thomas Jefferson (1743–1826), the 3rd President in 1801–9, and again on a big scale from 1841. The Pendleton Act of 1883 and subsequent legislation proved ineffective checks.

**Spoilt for choice.** Having so many choices that it is difficult to choose.

**Spoil the ship for a ha'porth o' tar, To.** To mar the final result by saving a small amount. 'Ship' here is a dialect version of 'sheep' and refers to the smearing of tar on sheep against various infections, a practice common in Shakespeare's day.

**Spare the rod and spoil the child.** *See under* SPARE.

**Spoke. Put a spoke in someone's wheel, To.** To thwart their plans. When solid wheels were used, the driver was provided with a pin or spoke, which was thrust into one of the three holes made to receive it, to skid the cart when it went downhill.

**Sponge. Sponge on** or **off someone, To.** To live on someone like a parasite, sucking up all they have as a dry sponge will suck up water.

**Sponger, A.** A person who is always accepting the hospitality of those who will give it and never makes any adequate return. *See also* CADGER.

**Sponging house, A.** A house where people arrested for debt were kept for 24 hours, before being sent to prison. They were generally kept by a bailiff, and the person lodged was 'sponged' of all his money before leaving.

**Throw up** or **in the sponge, To.** *See under* THROW.

**Spoon.** A simpleton used to be called a spoon because he was shallow, like the utensil. Hence the name came to be applied to anyone who indulged in foolish, sentimental amorous play. Such a person was said to be 'spoony' and to be 'spoons' on the girl and to 'spoon' was to kiss and cuddle.

**Apostle spoons.** *See under* APOSTLE.

**Born with a silver spoon in one's mouth, To be.** *See under* BORN.

**Love spoons.** *See under* LOVE.

**Runcible spoon.** *See* RUNCIBLE HAT.

**Wooden spoon, The.** *See under* WOOD.

**Spoonerism.** A form of METATHESIS that consists of transposing the initial sounds of words so as to form some ludicrous combination, often the accidental result of mental tiredness or absent-mindedness. It is so called from the Rev. W.A. Spooner (1844–1930), Warden of New College, Oxford. Some of the best (but possibly apocryphal) attributed to him are: 'We all know what it is to have a half-warmed fish within us' (for 'half-formed wish'). 'Yes, indeed; the Lord is a shoving leopard', and 'Kinkering Kongs their titles take'. Sometimes the term is applied to the accidental transposition of whole words, as when the teashop waitress was asked for 'a glass bun and a bath of milk'. This sort of spoonerism can lend itself to deliberate word play, as when Oscar Wilde said, 'Work is the curse of the drinking classes' (quoted in Hesketh Pearson, *Life of Oscar Wilde*, ch xii (1946)). *See also* MALAPROP.

**Sport. Sporting seasons in England.** The lawful season for venery, which began at Midsummer and lasted until HOLY CROSS DAY (14 September), used to be called the Time of Grace. The fox and wolf might be hunted from the NATIVITY to the ANNUNCIATION, the roebuck from EASTER to MICHAELMAS, the roe from Michaelmas to CANDLEMAS, the hare from Michaelmas to Midsummer, and the boar from the Nativity to the Purification.

The times for hunting and shooting are now fixed as follows:

Black game (blackcock and greyhen): from 20 August to 10 December (in Somerset, Devon and the New Forest, from 1 September to 10 December)
Grouse: 12 August to 10 December
Partridge: 1 September to 1 February
Pheasant: 1 October to 1 February
Ptarmigan (Scotland only): 12 August to 10 December

Despite the above, it is unlawful for grouse, partridge, pheasant or ptarmigan to be killed on a Sunday or on Christmas Day.

Deer have different dates depending on species (fallow, red, roe etc), sex and country (England and Wales or Scotland). Otters were also formerly hunted, but they are now a protected species.

There is no statutory close season for the hunting of foxes or hares or for the shooting of rabbits, but under an Act of 1892, still in force, it is illegal for shops to sell hares or leverets between 1 March and 31 July. The recognized date for the opening of the fox-hunting season is 1 November and it continues until the following April.

There are special permitted seasons for the taking of trout, salmon, oysters, carp etc.

**Sport one's oak, To.** An old university custom signifying that one is 'not at home' to visitors by closing the oak or outer door of one's rooms.

> Mr Verdant Green had for the first time 'sported his oak'. Under any circumstances it would have been a mere form, since his bashful politeness would have induced him to open it to any comer.
> 'CUTHBERT BEDE': *The Adventures of Mr Verdant Green*, ch viii (1853–7)

**Blood sport.** *See under* BLOOD.

**Spot. Spot cash.** READY MONEY or money down.

**Spot check.** A surprise check on the spot without notice being given; a random check to serve as a basis for conclusions on a wider basis.

**Spot dance.** A dance in which the couple focused in the spotlight when the music stops gain a prize or, when there is no spotlight, the couple are on a particular spot on the floor not previously revealed to the dancers.

**Spot on.** Exactly right; right on the mark.

**Spot price.** The price of goods or securities that are offered for immediate delivery and payment, 'on the spot'.

**Spotted dick.** A steamed or boiled suet pudding containing dried fruit. 'Dick' here probably represents a dialect term for 'pudding'. The dried fruit gives it a speckled appearance. Another name is SPOTTED DOG.

**Spotted dog.** A nickname for a Dalmatian, whose coat is covered in well-defined black or liver-coloured spots. *See also* SPOTTED DICK.

**Beauty spot.** *See under* BEAUTY.

**Black spot.** *See under* BLACK.

**Blind spot.** *See under* BLIND.

**Have a soft spot for, To.** *See under* SOFT.

**High spot, The.** *See under* HIGH.

**Hot spot.** *See under* HOT.

**In a tight spot.** *See under* TIGHT.

**Knock spots off someone, To.** *See under* KNOCK.

**Leopard cannot change its spots, A.** *See under* LEOPARD.

**On the spot.** Immediately; then and there; ready and able; without having time to move away or do anything else. Also, a difficult situation or predicament, as: 'He put me on the spot.'

**Running on the spot.** *See under* RUN.

**Weak spot.** *See under* WEAK.

**Spouse.** One who has promised (Latin *sponsus*, from *spondere*, 'to promise solemnly'). In ancient Rome the friends of the parties about to be married met at the house of the woman's father to settle the marriage contract. This contract was called *sponsalia* ('espousal'), the man *sponsus*, and the woman *sponsa*.

**Spouse of Jesus, The.** St TERESA OF AVILA (1515–82) was given this title by some of her contemporaries.

> All thy good works ... shall
> Weave a constellation
> Of Crowns with which the King thy spouse
> Shall build up thy triumphant brows.
> RICHARD CRASHAW: 'Hymn to the Name and Honour of the Admirable Saint Teresa' (1652)

**Spout. Spout, To.** To utter at length; to declaim.

**Up the spout.** *See under* UP.

**SPQR** (Latin *Senatus Populusque Romanus*, 'the Senate and People of Rome'). Letters inscribed on the standards of ancient Rome. Facetiously, 'small profits and quick returns'.

**Sprat. Jack Sprat.** *See under* JACK.

**Throw a sprat to catch a mackerel, To.** *See under* THROW.

**Spread. Spread-eagled.** A term originally used in the navy for the position of a man when he was lashed to the rigging for flogging, with outstretched arms and legs. The word is now used for anyone with arms and legs outstretched, whether lying or standing.

**Spread** or **stretch one's wings, To.** To make full use of one's talents and capabilities.

**Spree, On the.** Out for a frolic; on the binge; out partying. The origin of the word is unknown.

**Spring.** The season of young growth between winter and summer, which in the northern hemisphere is the months of March, April and May, or astronomically from 21 or 22 March to 21 or 22 June.

> Sweet spring, full of sweet days and roses,
> A box where sweets compacted lie;
> My music shows ye have your closes,
> And all must die.
> GEORGE HERBERT: 'Virtue' (1633)

**Spring a leak, To.** To start to admit water through a surface that is meant to be waterproof. The expression is nautical in origin and properly referred to timbers that had sprung out of position.

**Spring cleaning.** An annual thorough cleaning of a house, motivated by the lighter and warmer days of spring and serving to banish the dust and dirt of winter.

**Springers, The.** *See under* REGIMENTAL AND DIVISIONAL NICKNAMES.

**Spring fever.** A restless feeling that for some is associated with spring, when the sap rises.

**Spring tides.** The tides that spring or rise up higher than other tides. They occur just after new and full moon, when the gravitational attraction of both sun and moon acts in a direct line. *See also* NEAP TIDES.

**No spring chicken.** *See under* CHICKEN.

**Tom Spring.** One of the great pugilists of the English prize ring, Spring (1795–1851) claimed the title of English champion on the retirement of Tom Cribb (1781–1848). His real name was Winter, and on retiring (1828) he became landlord of the Castle Tavern, Holborn, London.

> Shall I name thee last? ay, why not? I believe that thou art the last of all that strong family still above the sod, where mayest thou long continue – true piece of English stuff, Tom of Bedford – sharp as winter, kind as spring. Hail to thee, Tom of Bedford, or by whatever name it may please thee to be called, Spring or Winter... 'Tis a treat to see thee, Tom of Bedford, in thy 'public' in Holborn way, whither thou hast retired with thy well-earned bays.
>
> GEORGE BORROW: *Lavengro*, ch xxvi (1851)

**Sprite.** *See* SPIRIT.

**Spruce.** Smart or dandified. The word is perhaps from Spruce leather, a fashionable leather imported in the 16th century from Spruce, otherwise Pruce, or Prussia.

> And after them came, syr Edward Haward, then admyral, and with him sir Thomas Parre, in doblettes of Crimosin velvet, voyded lowe on the backe, and before to the cannell bone, laced on the breastes with chaynes of silver, and over that shorte clokes of Crimosyn satyne, and on their heades hattes after dauncers fashion, with fesauntes fethers in theim; They were appareyled after the fashion of Prussia or Spruce.
>
> EDWARD HALL: *The Union of the Two Noble and Illustre Families of Lancastre and York*, Henry VII, year 1 (1542)

**Spruce beer.** A beer made of fermented molasses and flavoured with twigs and cones from the spruce tree.

**Spur. Spur money.** A small fine formerly imposed on those who entered a church wearing spurs, because of the interruption caused to divine service by their ringing. It was collected by the choirboys or the BEADLE.

**Battle of the Spurs, The.** *See under* BATTLE.

**On the spur of the moment.** Instantly; on impulse.

**Win one's spurs, To.** *See under* WIN.

**Sputnik** (Russian, 'fellow traveller'). A Russian artificial satellite. Sputnik 1, launched 4 October 1957, was the first satellite to be projected successfully into orbit around the earth.

**Spy. Spy Wednesday.** A name given in Ireland to the Wednesday before GOOD FRIDAY, when JUDAS ISCARIOT bargained to become the spy of the Jewish SANHEDRIN (Matthew 26:3–5, 14–16).

**I spy strangers!** The recognized form of words by which a Member of Parliament conveys to the SPEAKER the information that there is an unauthorized person in the HOUSE OF COMMONS.

**Welcome Stranger.** *See under* WELCOME.

**Squab.** Short and fat; plump. The word is used for a person or object like this (a fat woman is *sqvabba* in Swedish). A young pigeon, especially an unfledged one, is also called a squab.

**Squab pie.** Pigeon pie, or a pie of mutton, apples and onions.

> Cornwall squab-pie and Devon white-pot brings,
> And Leicester beans and bacon, fit for kings.
>
> WILLIAM KING: *Art of Cookery* (1708)

**Squad, Flying.** *See under* FLY.

**Squall. Look out for squalls.** *See under* LOOK.

**White squall, A.** *See under* WHITE.

**Square, A.** In modern slang, a person who likes orthodox music and not JAZZ and its derivatives; someone of 'bourgeois' tastes, who is not in with current trends, fashions, and is hence old-fashioned. There are several suggestions for the origin of these usages, none of which is particularly convincing, the most likely being associated with the patrons of the traditional square dance as opposed to the devotees of rock'n'rolling, jiving and twisting and the like.

**Square accounts with someone, To.** To get even with a person or take one's revenge on him or her. The expression derives from 'squaring accounts' in book-keeping, so that the debit balances the credit.

**Square-bashing.** A slang expression used by the armed services for parade-ground drill.

**Square deal, A.** A fair deal, one that is straight and above board.

**Square meal, A.** A substantial and satisying one. As for a SQUARE DEAL, square conveys the idea of 'solid' or 'right'.

**Square Mile, The.** The City of London, so called from its area (677 acres). A square mile consists of 640 acres (259 ha). *See also* MILE.

> Property groups and financial institutions in the Square Mile believe granting planning powers to the mayor of London will add an extra layer of bureaucracy to development.
>
> *The Times* (21 September 1998)

**Square peg in a round hole, A.** Someone who is doing (or trying to do) a job for which they are not suited.

> We shall generally find that the triangular person has got into the square hole, the oblong into the triangular, and a square person has squeezed himself into a round hole.
> SYDNEY SMITH: *Lectures* (1804–6)

**Square rig.** *See* FORE AND AFT.

**Square the circle, To.** To attempt an impossibility. The allusion is to the geometrical impossibility of exactly determining the precise ratio ($\pi$) between the diameter and the circumference of a circle, and thus constructing a square of the same area as a given circle. Approximately, $\pi$ is 3.14159, but the next five decimals are 26535 and the numbers go on *ad infinitum*. A solution to the problem was sought for hundreds of years by Euclidean means, using a straight-edge and compass, until in 1882 it was finally abandoned as impossible.

**Square up to a person, To.** To adopt a fighting attitude.

**Back to square one.** *See under* BACK.

**Fair and square.** *See under* FAIR.

**Printing House Square.** *See under* PRINT.

**Red Square.** *See under* RED.

**Smith Square.** *See under* SMITH.

**Squarson.** A 19th-century usage for a clergyman who was both squire and parson of the parish. The Rev. Sabine Baring-Gould (1834–1924), vicar of Lew Trenchard, Devon, was a classic example of this combination. He was also a novelist, investigator of prehistoric sites, collector of West Country songs and author of the hymn 'Onward Christian Soldiers' (1864), which he wrote for a group of Yorkshire village children marching in a procession with banners on Whit Monday. *See also* JACK RUSSELL.

**Squeak. Squeaky clean.** Completely clean; above criticism or reproach, free from taint. A floor that has been cleaned and polished will sometimes squeak when walked on.

**Bubble and squeak.** *See under* BUBBLE.

**Narrow squeak.** *See under* NARROW.

**Squeeze. Squeeze-box.** A colloquial name for a concertina, which is operated by opening and closing (squeezing) its bellows. It was invented in 1829 by Sir Charles Wheatstone (1802–75), a pioneer of the electric telegraph, and son of a musical instrument maker. *See also* HURDY-GURDY.

**Main squeeze.** *See under* MAIN.

**Put the squeeze on someone, To.** To coerce or pressurize them.

**Squib.** A small firework thrown by hand; also a LAMPOON or short SATIRE.

**Damp squib, A.** *See under* DAMP.

**Squire.** In medieval times, a youth of gentle birth attendant on a knight (*see* ESQUIRE). From the later 16th century the term was applied to country landowners who exercised sway, mostly paternal, over a district. The squirearchy as such has largely been extinguished by the rise of a more democratic urbanized society on the one hand and rapacious taxation on the other. Joseph Addison's benevolent Sir Roger de COVERLEY, Henry Fielding's Squire Western in *Tom Jones* (1749) and Squire Jawleyford, the creation of Robert Smith Surtees (1805–64), himself a Northumbrian squire, provide lively portraits of varying traditions.

**Squire of dames.** Any CAVALIER who is devoted to ladies. Edmund Spenser introduces 'the Squyre of Dames' in *The Faerie Queene* (III, vii (1590)).

**SS** (German *Schutzstaffel*, 'protection squad'). An armed force that originated as part of Hitler's bodyguard in 1925, two years after the formation of the SA, to which it was initially subordinate. In 1929 Heinrich Himmler took on the SS and, defining its duties as 'to find out, to fight and to destroy all open and secret enemies of the FÜHRER, the National Socialist Movement and our racial resurrection', raised it to a position of power and great numerical strength. During the Second World War, SS divisions fought with fanatical zeal. The sleek black uniforms of the SS men earned them the name BLACKSHIRTS and made them feel superior to the Brownshirts of the SA. *See also* NIGHT OF THE LONG KNIVES.

**Stabat Mater** (Latin, 'the mother was standing'). The Latin hymn reciting the SEVEN SORROWS OF MARY at the cross. So called from its opening words, it forms part of the service during Passion week in the ROMAN CATHOLIC CHURCH. It is of uncertain authorship, and in addition to its traditional plainsong, there are settings by Palestrina, Pergolesi, Haydn, Rossini and others.

> Stabat Mater dolorosa,
> Iuxta crucem lacrimosa,
> Dum pendebat filius.
> (At the cross her station keeping,
> Stood the mournful Mother weeping,
> Where he hung, the dying Lord.)
> JACOPONE DA TODI: 'Stabat Mater dolorosa' (13th century) (translation based on that of Edward Caswell (1849))

**Stable. Augean stables.** *See under* AUGEAN.

**Lock the stable door after the horse has bolted, To.** *See under* LOCK.

**Stadium.** This word is from Greek *stadion*, an altered form of *spadion*, 'racecourse', from *span*, 'to pull', referring to the drawing of chariots, while at the same time influenced by *stadios*, 'steady'. The *stade* (Greek *stadion*) was also measure of length, 600 Greek feet, the equivalent of about 607 English feet (185m). The

Olympic stadium had terraced seats along its length and the length of the course was traditionally said to have been fixed by HERCULES.

**Stadtholder** (Dutch, 'city holder'). Originally a provincial viceroy in the Netherlands, later the chief executive officer of the UNITED PROVINCES.

**Staff. Staff of life, The.** Bread, which is the support of life.

> 'Bread,' says he, 'dear brothers, is the staff of life.'
> JONATHAN SWIFT: *Tale of a Tub*, iv (1704)

*See also* BREAD IS THE STAFF OF LIFE.

**Bear and ragged staff, The.** *See under* BEAR.

**Jacob's staff.** *See under* JACOB.

**Stag.** A male deer or hart.

**Stag in Christian art, The.** The attribute of St JULIAN Hospitaller, St Felix of Valois and St AIDAN. When it has a crucifix between its horns it alludes to the legend of St HUBERT. When luminous it belongs to St Eustace (Eustachius).

**Stag line.** An American term for the line of men at the edge of the dance floor, without partners, who wait to claim one from among those dancing.

**Stag night.** A festive gathering of men only, especially on the eve of a wedding, the guest of honour then being the groom. *See also* HEN NIGHT.

> Stag nights have declined to such an extent that many grooms don't bother to have them at all. If they do, the nights are hardly worthy of the name. A typical stag night nowadays might involve a pleasant dinner, or some vaguely macho pursuit like climbing a mountain or firing paint-pellets.
> *The Times* (16 June 1993)

**Stags.** In Stock Exchange phraseology people who apply for an allotment of new shares, not because they wish to hold the shares, but because they hope to sell them for a quick profit when trading begins.

**Baldfaced Stag.** *See under* BALD.

**Royal stag.** *See under* ROYAL.

**Stage. Stage whisper.** A 'whisper' intended to be heard by other than those to whom it is addressed, as one on the stage is heard by the audience.

**Old stager.** *See under* OLD.

**Set the stage, To.** *See under* SET.

**Stagirite** or **Stagyrite, The.** ARISTOTLE, who was born at Stagira, in Macedon (4th century BC).

**Stairs. Below stairs.** *See under* BELOW.

**Giants' staircase.** *See under* GIANT.

**Stake. Ale stake.** *See under* ALE.

**Derby Stakes.** *See under* DERBY.

**Eclipse Stakes, The.** *See under* ECLIPSE.

**Grub stake.** *See under* GRUB.

**Stakhanovism.** In the former USSR, a movement for specially raising the output of labour on a basis of specialized efficiency, so called after Alexei Stakhanov (1906–77), a Donbass coalminer who substantially increased his daily output by rationalization. His record output was 102 tons of coal in a $5\frac{3}{4}$-hour night shift on 30 August 1935, 14 times the norm. That same year Stalin held a conference of Stakhanovites in which he extolled the working man.

**Stalemate.** A situation in which two opposing forces find that progress is impossible. The term is from CHESS, stalemate being the position in which the king is the only movable piece and, although not in check, cannot move without becoming so. 'Stale' in this word is probably from Old French *estal* (English 'stall'), a fixed position.

**Stalin.** The Soviet leader, who succeeded LENIN as head of the Communist Party, was born Iosif Vissarionovich Dzhugashvili (1879–1953), his surname being Georgian in origin. He adopted his well-known party name in 1913, from Russian *stal'*, 'steel', perhaps originally to indicate his unbroken spirit after repeated arrest, banishment and imprisonment. He had various other pseudonyms, including Soso, Koba (a short form of Yakoba, the name of a Georgian fictional patriotic hero), David, Nizheradze, Chizhikov and Ivanovich.

**Stalingrad.** Formerly Tsaritsyn, on the Volga, renamed in 1925 to commemorate its defence by Stalin, in 1917, against the WHITE RUSSIANS. Stalin died in 1953 and in 1961 the name was changed to Volgograd. In 1943 it was the scene of the decisive defeat of the German 6th Army.

**Stalking-horse.** A mask to conceal some design; a person put forward to mislead; a sham. Sportsmen would often conceal themselves behind horses, and go on stalking step by step until they got within shot of the game. In political parlance, a stalking-horse is a candidate put forward to mask the candidacy of another person, for whom the 'stalking-horse' would withdraw at the appropriate moment.

> He uses his folly like a stalking-horse, and under the presentation of that he shoots his wit.
> SHAKESPEARE: *As You Like It*, V, iv (1599)

**Stalky.** The leader of a gang of schoolboys in Rudyard Kipling's collection of short stories, *Stalky and Co.* (1899). His real name is Arthur Corkran, and his nickname represents a school slang word meaning 'clever', 'wily'. The gang have a healthy contempt for school discipline, organized sports and most of their teachers, and they indulge in ritual 'gloats' or vocalizations of victory on scoring a point over any of their enemies. Kipling based the story on contemporaries of his at the United Services College, Westward Ho!, Devon, and Stalky himself was modelled on Lionel Charles Dunsterville, in adult life an army major-general.

**Stammerer, The.** The following have been so called:

Louis II of France, le Bègue (846–879)
Michael II, emperor of the East (r.820–829)
Balbus Notker, monk of St Gall (surnamed Balbulus) (*c*.840–912)

**Stand. Stand a chance, To.** To have a real possibility of winning or succeeding.

**Stand and deliver!** The traditional command of a HIGHWAYMAN to those travelling in a coach to halt and hand over their valuables.

**Stand at ease!** A military command for a position less rigid than attention, with the feet apart and the hands joined behind the back (unless arms are being carried).

**Stand by, To.** To be ready to give assistance in case of need. A stand-by is a person or thing on which one can confidently rely.

**Stand easy!** In military drill, a position in which relaxation is permitted, short of moving away. In the Royal Navy a short break during working hours is called a stand easy.

**Stand-in, A.** A substitute.

**Standing committee.** A committee formed in the HOUSE OF COMMONS so as to represent the different parties according to their relative strength in the House. They are appointed for the session to deal with bills in the committee stage.

**Standing Fishes Bible, The.** *See under* BIBLE.

**Standing joke, A.** A permanent object of ridicule.

**Stand in good stead, To.** To be of benefit or advantage to.

**Standing orders.** Rules or instructions constantly in force, as those of a commanding officer or those rules of the Houses of Parliament for the conduct of proceedings, which stand in force until they are rescinded or superseded. The suspension of the latter is generally caused by a desire to hurry through a bill with unusual expedition.

**Standing ovation.** A period of prolonged applause during which the applauders rise to their feet.

**Standing Stones of Stenness, The.** In Orkney, some 4 miles (6.4km) from Stromness, stands a Neolithic stone circle 340ft (104m) in diameter of which only 13 stones of a probable 60 are still standing, the tallest being 14ft (4.3m) high. Sir Walter Scott in a note (*The Pirate*, ch xxxviii (1821)) writes: 'One of the pillars ... is perforated with a circular hole, through which loving couples are wont to join hands when they take the Promise of Odin.' The *Eyrbiggia Saga* gives an account of the setting apart of the Helga Fels, or Holy Rock, by the pontiff Thorolf for solemn meetings.

**Stand in someone's light, To.** Figuratively, to hinder someone's advancement.

**Stand mute, To.** An old legal term for a prisoner who, when arraigned for treason or felony, refused to plead or gave irrelevant answers.

**Stand-off.** An uneasy deadlock or impasse, when each of two sides 'stands off' the other.

> Trouble erupted across Northern Ireland last night after security forces blocked the biggest Drumcree parade in its 191-year history and hundreds of Orangemen embarked on a stand-off that could last weeks.
>
> *The Times* (6 July 1998)

**Stand off and on, To.** To sail away from the shore and then towards it repeatedly, usually in order to keep a particular mark in sight.

**Standoffish.** Unsociable; cold and reserved.

**Stand on ceremony, To.** To observe the necessary formalities, courtesies etc. The expression is mostly found in the negative, as: 'Please don't stand on ceremony.'

**Stand one's ground, To.** Not to yield or give way; to maintain one's stand.

**Stand on one's own two feet, To.** To be independent or self-supporting.

**Stand proud, To.** In engineering and the practical skills, said of something that protrudes further than it should or above a particular plane.

**Stand to reason, To.** To be logically manifest. This English expression reflects the Latin *constat*, from *constare*, 'to stand together'.

**Stand treat, To.** To pay the expenses of some entertainment, and especially to pay for drinks consumed by others.

**Stand up for, To.** To support; to uphold.

**Custer's Last Stand.** *See under* CUSTER.

**I stand corrected.** I accept that I was wrong.

**Leave someone standing, To.** *See under* LEAVE.

**One-night stand.** *See under* ONE.

**Without a leg to stand on.** *See under* WITHOUT.

**Standard.** Properly a large flag tapering towards the fly, slit at the end and flown by personages of rank. It bore the owner's badges and its length depended upon the owner's rank.

The personal Royal Standard of the British Sovereign is a banner in shape and quarterings. The word is from Old French *estandart*, 'gathering place', the place itself being marked by a flag. *See also* BATTLE OF THE STANDARD.

'Standard' is also applied to a measure of extent, weight, value or the like, which is established by law or custom as an example or criterion for others, also, in figurative use from this, to any criterion or principle, as, 'the standard of political rectitude'. The weights and measures were formerly known as 'the king's standard', as being official and recognized by royal authority.

In uses such as 'standard lamp' (one standing on its own support) and 'standard rose' (one standing on its own stem and not trained to a wall or espalier) the word is the result of confusion with 'stand'.

**Standard gauge.** A railway track with distances of 4ft 8½in (143.5cm) between the lines, used on most railways. This is based on the gauge of 4ft 8in (142cm) chosen by George Stephenson for the Stockton and Darlington railway (opened 1825), and was itself based on the gauge of the 'waggonways' that carried coal from pits to the 'staithes' on the Tyne. The extra ½in seems to have been added in the 1830s to allow extra play on the wheel flanges. The choice of this gauge was determined by a Royal Commission in 1845–6.

**Standard of living.** A conventional term to express the supposed degree of comfort or luxury usually enjoyed by a person, a family or a nation. The standard may be high or low according to circumstances.

> Within a generation, the economy has been transformed, standards of living have soared, manufacturing industry has declined, service industries have mushroomed, technology has made itself felt in every part of modern life.
>
> GREG HADFIELD and MARK SKIPWORTH: *Class*, ch i (1994)

**Standard time** or **zone time.** A system of timekeeping in most parts of the world based on 24 meridians, each 15° apart, starting from Greenwich, thus giving an exact difference of an hour between any two adjacent zones (certain countries have adopted zones involving half-hour differences). Such a system was first adopted by the chief railway companies of Canada and the USA in 1883 to overcome the obvious inconveniences caused by the differing local times on their routes. *See also* GREENWICH TIME; SUMMER TIME.

**Battle of the Standard, The.** *See under* BATTLE.

**Battle of the Standards, The.** *See under* BATTLE.

**Gold Standard, The.** *See under* GOLD.

**Stanhope. Stanhope lens.** A cylindrical lens with spherical ends of different radii.

**Stanhope press.** The first iron printing press to be used (1798). Both the lens and the press are so called from their inventor, Charles, 3rd Earl of Stanhope (1753–1816).

**Stannaries, The** (Latin *stannum*, 'tin'). The tin-mining areas of Devon and Cornwall, an appanage of the crown, and after 1337 of the Duchy of Cornwall. There were four in Cornwall and four in Devon (covering Dartmoor and surrounding areas). A warden was appointed in 1198, and in 1201 King John issued their first charter confirming the tinners' privileges and making the warden the only magistrate to have jurisdiction over them. The tinners had their own representative meetings or 'parliaments' as late as 1752 and were subject to special stannary courts, which were not finally abolished until 1897. The courts, under the lord warden, vice-warden and stewards, were also concerned with regulation of the trade. The miners were formerly called stannators. Their privileges arose from the king's aim to increase tin production.

**Stanza, Spenserian.** *See under* SPENSERIAN.

**Star.** In ecclesiastical art, a number of saints are depicted with a star. Thus, St Bruno bears one on his breast, and St DOMINIC, St Humbert, St Peter of Alcantara, one over the head or on the forehead. *See also* BLAZE.

A star of some form constitutes part of the insignia of every order of knighthood. The Star and Garter, a common PUBLIC HOUSE SIGN, refers to the MOST NOBLE ORDER OF THE GARTER.

'Star' is also figuratively applied to a noted performer, especially a film actor. Hence star part, the part taken by the leading actor or performer, who is the star turn.

The stars were said by the old astrologers to have almost omnipotent influence on the lives and destinies of man (*see* Judges 5:20: 'The stars in their courses fought against Sisera'), and to this belief is due a number of phrases, such as: 'thank your lucky stars', 'star-crossed' (not favoured by the stars, unfortunate), 'born under a lucky star' etc.

**Star Chamber.** A court of medieval origin, composed of the King's Council, reinforced by judges, which developed criminal jurisdiction. It was so named from its meeting place, the Star Chamber in the PALACE OF WESTMINSTER, the ceiling or roof of which was decorated with stars. The reputation it acquired for harshness was largely unjustified, and it was frequently attacked by the Common Lawyers who resented its jurisdiction. It was abolished by the LONG PARLIAMENT in 1641.

**Stargazy pie.** An old Cornish dish of pilchards baked in a pie with their heads poking through the crust. It is still made regularly in Mousehole each year just before Christmas.

**Star in the ascendant.** Said of a person to whom some good fortune has fallen and who is very prosperous, as: 'His star is in the ascendant.' According to ASTROLOGY, those leading stars which are above the horizon at a person's birth influence his life and fortune. When those stars are in the ASCENDANT, the person is strong, healthy and lucky, but when they are in the descendant below the horizon, his stars do not shine on him, so that he is in the shade and subject to ill fortune. *See also* ASTROLOGICAL HOUSES.

**Star of Bethlehem.** A bulbous plant of the lily family (*Ornithogalum umbellatum*), with star-shaped white flowers. The French call it *La dame d'onze heures* ('the eleven o'clock lady') for it opens at about this time. The English name alludes to the star that led the MAGI to Bethlehem to worship the newborn Christ.

**Star of David** or **Shield of David, The.** A symbol of obscure origin, also called SOLOMON'S SEAL, made up of two interlocking triangles thus: ✡. It was adopted by the first Zionist Conference in 1897 and is the symbol on the flag of Israel. It is found as early as the 3rd century but is not mentioned in the Bible or the TALMUD. Jews were made to wear such a cloth star under the NAZI regime and, to show his disapproval of this affront, King Christian X of Denmark (r.1912–47) wore a Star of David during the German occupation of his country.

**Star of India, The.** A British order of knighthood, the Most Exalted Order of the Star of India, instituted by Queen Victoria in 1861. Its motto is 'Heaven's Light our Guide', and it was a means of recognizing services to India and the loyalty of its princely rulers. No appointments have been made since 1947 and it is now obsolescent.

**Star of South Africa, The.** A pear-shaped DIAMOND discovered near the Orange River in 1869, also called the Dudley diamond after the Earl of Dudley, its first purchaser. It weighs 47.7 carats but was 85.75 carats when uncut.

**Stars and Bars, The.** The flag of the eleven CONFEDERATE STATES of America that broke away from the Union in 1861. It consisted of two horizontal red bars with a narrow white bar between them and, in the top left corner, a blue union bearing eleven white stars arranged in a circle.

**Stars and Stripes** or **Star-spangled Banner, The.** The flag of the United States of America. The stripes are emblematic of the original 13 states, and the stars, of which there are 50, of the states that now constitute the Union. It is also popularly called Old Glory, a name said to have been given by William Driver, a Salem skipper, in 1831.

At the outset of the American Revolution, each state adopted its own flag, that of Massachusetts bearing a pine tree and that of South Carolina a rattlesnake with the words 'Don't tread on me'. In 1776 a national flag of 13 red and white stripes with crosses of St GEORGE and St ANDREW in a canton was adopted.

By act of Congress, 14 June 1777, a flag of 13 alternate red and white stripes, with a union of 13 white stars on a blue field was adopted, the stars arranged in a circle representing 'a new constellation'. It was apparently designed by Francis Hopkinson and the story that it was first embroidered by Betsy ROSS is now discredited.

In 1794, after the admission of Vermont and Kentucky, the stripes and stars were increased to 15, but in 1818 it was decided that the original 13 stripes should be restored, and stars added to signify the number of states in the Union. The stars were also squared up for the first time.

'The Stars and Stripes Forever' is the name of Sousa's most popular military band tune, and 'The Star-spangled Banner' was adopted as the official anthem of the United States in 1931. The words were written by Francis Scott Key in 1814, the tune being that of 'Anacreon in Heaven', a popular drinking song composed by J.S. Smith for the Anacreontic Society of London.

**Star Trek.** The cult American space fiction television series, first screened in 1966 and set in the future, tells how the crew of the Starship *Enterprise* reconnoitre the universe, finding monsters and mysteries at every turn. The best known crew member is Mr SPOCK, the Starship's first officer (played by Leonard Nimoy), and others include Captain Kirk (William Shatner) and Captain Picard (Patrick Stewart). The creator of the whole series was Gene Roddenberry (1921–91). Its many fans, or 'Trekkers' (earlier 'Trekkies'), express their rapturous devotion in conventions in both America and Britain and eagerly await the latest Star Trek book, film or CD. In 1995 Paramount Pictures chose a fourth Star Trek series, *Voyager*, as the flagship programme of its new network, UPN, and in 1996 the eighth Star Trek movie, *First Contact*, was released.

> The five-year mission of the Enterprise has evolved into the 20th century's very own version of the quest myth – an epic story to rival the epic poetry of the Greeks.
>
> *Sunday Times* (12 February 1995)

**Star Wars.** The Strategic Defense Initiative (SDI) of the United States, conceived by President Reagan in 1983 as a means of defending the USA against attack from Soviet intercontinental ballistic missiles (ICBMs). Because parts of the system proposed by the president would be based in space, the SDI was dubbed Star Wars in allusion to the space weaponry of the popular SCIENCE FICTION film of this name (1977).

**Consenting stars.** *See under* CONSENTING.
**Dark star, A.** *See under* DARK.
**Dog star.** *See under* DOG.
**Falling star.** *See under* FALL.
**Fixed star.** *See under* FIX.
**Lone Star State.** *See under* LONE.
**Make someone see stars, To.** *See* SEE STARS.
**See stars, To.** *See under* SEE.
**Seven stars, The.** *See under* SEVEN.
**Shooting stars.** *See under* SHOOT.
**Silver Star.** *See under* SILVER.

**Starboard and larboard.** Star- is Old English *stēor*, 'steering paddle', and *-board*, 'side'. Larboard is probably from *laden*, 'to load'. *See also* PORT.

**Stare one in the face, To.** To be evident or obvious, as: 'The answer to the problem was staring me in the face all along.'

**Start. Start a hare, To.** To introduce or raise an irrelevant issue in an argument or discussion. To start a hare in the literal sense is to flush it from its form (nest).

**Starters.** The first course of a meal, as a homely English equivalent of the French HORS D'OEUVRE.

**Starting price.** The odds in force at the start of a horse race, as distinct from FIXED ODDS. The term is usually abbreviated SP.

**Start over, To.** To begin again.

**Start the ball rolling, To.** To begin or initiate an action.

**Start something, To.** To cause trouble, as: 'You certainly started something with your letter of complaint.'

**Start with a clean slate, To.** To be given another chance, one's past misdeeds having been forgiven and expunged, as writing is wiped from a slate.

**False start.** *See under* FALSE.

**For starters.** To start with; to begin with, as: 'I told him to tidy his room for starters.'

**Head start.** *See under* HEAD.

**Jump start.** *See under* JUMP.

**Under starter's orders.** *See under* UNDER.

**Starve. Starvation Dundas.** Henry Dundas, 1st Viscount Melville (1742–1811), was so called. He first used the word starvation or brought it to popular notice in a parliamentary speech (1775) concerned with the placing of restrictions on American colonial trade. The original meaning of the verb was 'to die', and it is related to German *sterben* in that sense.

**Starved of affection.** Deprived of it, or grudgingly granted it.

**State. States, The.** The UNITED STATES OF AMERICA.

**States General.** In France, the national consultative assembly; *see* ESTATES GENERAL.

The name is still applied to the parliament of the Netherlands, which consists of two chambers, the upper elected by members of the Provincial States and the second elected by the people.

**Buffer state.** *See under* BUFFER.

**In a state of nature.** Nude, naked.

**Lie in state, To.** *See under* LIE.

**Slave States, The.** *See under* STATE.

**Something is rotten in the state of Denmark.** *See under* SOMETHING.

**Welfare State.** *See under* WELFARE.

**Stately home.** A COUNTRY HOUSE or 'seat', especially one with historic associations owned by a member of the aristocracy and admired for its architecture and scenic setting. The phrase caught on from a poem by Felicia Hemans:

> The stately homes of England,
> How beautiful they stand!
> Amidst their tall ancestral trees,
> O'er all the pleasant land.
> FELICIA HEMANS: 'The Homes of England' (1849)

The first line of the above was further popularized by Noël Coward in his musical play *Operette* (1938):

> The Stately Homes of England,
> How beautiful they stand,
> To prove the upper classes
> Have still the upper hand.

**Station** (Latin *statio*, 'place of standing', 'station'). This word, with the meaning of a place where people assemble for a specific duty or purpose, has many applications, e.g. a railway station, police station, polling station and so on.

**Stations of the Cross, The.** Also known as the *Via Calvaria* or *Via Crucis*. Each station represents, by fresco, picture or otherwise, some incident in the passage of Christ from the judgement hall to CALVARY, and at each one prayers are offered up in memory of the event represented. They are as follows:

(1) The condemnation to death
(2) Christ is made to bear the cross
(3) His first fall under the cross
(4) The meeting with the Virgin
(5) Simon the Cyrenean helps to carry the cross
(6) Veronica wipes the sacred face
(7) The second fall
(8) Christ speaks to the daughters of Jerusalem
(9) The third fall
(10) Christ is stripped of his garments
(11) The nailing to the cross
(12) The giving up of the spirit
(13) Christ is taken down from the cross
(14) The deposition in the sepulchre

**Statistics, Vital.** *See under* VITAL.

**Stator** (Latin, 'stopper', 'arrester'). When the Romans fled from the SABINES, they stopped at a certain place and made terms with the victors. On this spot they afterwards built a temple to JUPITER, and called it the temple of Jupiter Stator, or Jupiter who caused them to stop in their flight.

**Statue of Liberty, The.** *See* LIBERTY ENLIGHTENING THE WORLD.

**Status. Status quo** (Latin, literally 'state in which'). The state in which the thing is; the existing state or condition.

**Status quo ante** (Latin, literally 'state in which before'). The previous position.

**Status symbol.** A possession, privilege or the like, which is a mark of one's social standing. The expression is generally used caustically of a fashionable, expensive, material object, the possession of which is designed to impress others and to flatter one's own self-esteem. *See also* KEEP UP WITH THE JONESES.

**Statute** (Late Latin *statutum*, from *statuere*, 'to cause to stand', related to English *statue*). A law enacted by a legislative body, an ACT OF PARLIAMENT, also laws enacted by the king and council before there were any regular Parliaments. Hence, a statute mile is the distance as established by law and not according to local custom.

**Statute cap.** A 'cap of wool knit', the wearing of which on holidays was enforced on all over six years of age (with certain exceptions for rank and sex) by a statute of Elizabeth I of 1571, for the benefit of the woollen trade. The fine for non-compliance was 3s 4d 'for each day's transgression'. The act was repealed in 1597. To a similar end, persons were at one time obliged to be buried in woollen shrouds. *See also* CAP AND STOCKING.

> Well, better wits have worn plain statute caps.
> SHAKESPEARE: *Love's Labour's Lost*, V, ii (1594)

**Statute fair.** A fair legalized by statute as opposed to custom or usage; a HIRING FAIR.

**Statute of Labourers, The.** An attempt made in 1351 to fix the rates of wages consequent upon the demand for labour after the BLACK DEATH. It attempted to hold them at their pre-plague levels, and the ensuing discontent helped to bring about the PEASANTS' REVOLT.

**On the statute book.** Included among the laws of the nation. The statute book is the whole body of the laws.

**Stay. Stay one's hand, To.** To refrain from action.

**Stay put, To.** To remain firmly in a position, literally or figuratively.

**Stay the course, To.** To persist or endure to the end.

**Come to stay, To.** *See under* COME.

**Stead, To stand in good.** *See under* STAND.

**Steady. Steady on!** Take care! WATCH IT!

**Steady state theory.** A theory explaining the origin of the universe, and contrasting with the more popular BIG BANG theory. It claims that the universe exists in time in a 'steady state', i.e. in such a way that the average density of matter does not vary with distance or time. Matter is thus continually being created in the space left by the receding stars and galaxies of the expanding universe. The theory was propounded in 1948 as the 'perfect cosmological principle' by three British scientists: Fred Hoyle, Hermann Bondi and Thomas Gold.

**Steady the Buffs!** Be careful! A cautionary phrase typically directed towards one whose physical coordination has become affected by alcohol, or even to oneself in such a state. The allusion is to The BUFFS. *See under* REGIMENTAL NICKNAMES.

**As steady as a rock.** *See under* AS.

**Go steady, To.** To have a regular boyfriend or girlfriend. The partner in turn is often known as 'a steady'.

**Steaks, The Sublime Society of the.** *See* BEEFSTEAK CLUB.

**Steal. Steal a march on someone, To.** To obtain an advantage on someone by stealth, as when an army appears unexpectedly before an enemy.

**Steal someone's thunder, To.** To forestall a person or to adopt another's own special methods as one's own. The phrase comes from the anecdote of John Dennis (1657–1734), the critic and playwright who invented an effective device for producing stage thunder for his play *Appius and Virginia* (1709). The play was a failure and was withdrawn, but shortly afterwards Dennis heard his thunder used in a performance of *Macbeth*. 'My God,' he exclaimed, 'the villains will play my thunder but not my plays!'

**Steal the show, To.** To win the greatest applause or acclamation; to surpass or outshine all other performers or players. An expression at first limited to performers in stage shows.

**Stolen sweets are always sweeter.** Things procured by stealth and game illicitly taken, have the charm of illegality to make them the more palatable. SOLOMON says: 'Stolen waters are sweet, and bread eaten in secret is pleasant' (Proverbs 9:17). In one of the songs in Act III, iv, of Thomas Randolph's *Amyntos* (1638) are the lines:

> Furto cuncta magis bella,
> Furto dulcior puella,
> Furto omnia decora,
> Furto poma dulciora

These were nicely translated by Leigh Hunt:

> Stolen sweets are always sweeter,
> Stolen kisses much completer,
> Stolen looks are nice in chapels,
> Stolen, stolen, be your apples.

**Steam. Steam age, The.** The era when trains were drawn by steam engines, nostalgically recalled by many. It is also known as the age of steam.

**Steam radio.** Sound broadcasting, as the original basic medium, by contrast with the later and more sophisticated television. The expression evokes the STEAM AGE of rail travel, preceding that of the diesel and electric train.

**Get up steam, To.** Figuratively, to work oneslf up into a state of anger. To be steamed up is similarly to be angry or 'worked up'.

**Let off steam, To.** *See under* LET.

**Run out of steam, To.** *See under* RUN.

**Under one's own steam.** *See under* UNDER.

**Steed, Barbed.** *See under* BARBED.

**Steel. Steelboys.** Bands of Ulster insurgents who committed agrarian outrages in protest against the system of TITHES in the early 1770s. They were probably named from their 'hearts of steel'. *See also* OAK BOYS; WHITEBOYS.

**Steelyard.** The London depot of the HANSEATIC LEAGUE from 1320 to 1597, occupying premises between Upper Thames Street and the river. The buildings were ultimately sold in 1853 and demolished ten years later to make way for Cannon Street Station. The name is a mistranslation of German *Stalhof*, 'a sample yard or hall'.

Also, the weighing machine with unequal arms, in which the article to be weighed is hung from the shorter arm and a weight moved along the other until they balance, is named from the metal and the measure, with 'yard' here in the old sense 'rod', 'pole'.

**Cold steel.** *See under* COLD.

**Steenie.** A nickname given by James I to his handsome favourite, George Villiers, Duke of Buckingham (1592–1628), with whom he was infatuated. 'Steenie' is a Scotticism for Stephen, the allusion being to Acts 6:15, where those who looked on Stephen the martyr 'saw his face as it had been the face of an angel'.

**Steeple. Steeplechase.** Originally a horse race across fields, hedges, ditches and other obstacles, now run over a prepared course. The term is said to have originated from the frolic of a party of fox-hunters in Ireland (1803) who decided to race in a straight line to a distant steeple. The term is also applied to a cross-country race of this kind on foot. *See also* RACES.

**Tenterden steeple was the cause of Goodwin Sands.** *See under* TENTERDEN.

**Steering committee.** A committee that decides the programme and order of business. A term of American origin.

**Sten gun.** The lightweight sub-machine gun takes its name from the initials of its designers, R.V. Shepherd and H.J. Turpin, with the -en from the name of the BREN GUN. It was first in use in the Second World War.

**Stenness, The Standing Stones of.** *See under* STAND.

**Stentor.** A person with a loud voice. Stentor was a Greek herald in the TROJAN WAR. According to HOMER (*Iliad*, v (8th century BC)), his voice was as loud as that of 50 men combined. He foolishly engaged HERMES in a shouting match and, on losing, was put to death. Hence 'stentorian', loud-voiced.

**Step. Break step, To.** *See under* BREAK.

**False step.** *See under* FALSE.

**Goose step.** *See under* GOOSE.

**Hop, step** or **skip and jump.** *See under* HOP.

**Watch one's step, To.** *See under* WATCH.

**Step-.** A prefix used before father, mother, brother, sister, son, daughter and so on to indicate that the person spoken of is a relative only by the marriage of a parent and not by blood. It is popularly thought to denote the 'step' in the relationship, but actually derives from Old English *stēop-*, 'orphan', cognate with *āstȳpan*, 'to bereave'. Thus, a man who marries a widow with children becomes stepfather to those children and, if she bears him children, these and the children of her earlier marriage are stepbrothers or stepsisters. The latter are sometimes also called half-brothers and half-sisters.

**Stephen. Crown of St Stephen, The.** *See under* CROWN.

**St Stephen.** The first Christian martyr or 'protomartyr'. He was accused of blasphemy and stoned to death *c.*35 (*see* Acts 6–8). He is commemorated on 26 December. The name means 'wreath' or 'crown' (Greek *stephanos*).

**St Stephen's.** Parliament is still sometimes so called, because for nearly 300 years prior to its destruction by fire in 1834, the House of Commons used to sit in the Chapel of St Stephen in the PALACE OF WESTMINSTER. *See also* BIG BEN.

**Sterling.** A term applied to British money and also to gold and silver plate denoting that they are of standard value or purity. Hence applied figuratively to anything of sound intrinsic worth, as 'a man of sterling qualities'. The word, first met with in the 12th century, has been held to be a corruption of *easterling*, a name given to the merchants of the HANSEATIC LEAGUE trading with England, but it is probably from late Old English *steorling*, an unrecorded word for a coin with a star, from the fact that some of the early Norman pennies had a small star on them.

**Stet** (Latin, 'let it stand'). A direction to cancel a correction or deletion previously made in a manuscript, proof or the like.

**Stetson.** A large-brimmed hat habitually worn by cattlemen in the USA, so called from the best known manufacturer, John B. Stetson (1830–1906).

**Stevengraphs.** Coloured silk pictures woven on a special JACQUARD LOOM, first made in 1879 by Thomas Stevens (1828–88), a Coventry silk weaver, who began by weaving bookmarks. Some 180 designs were produced on popular subjects including royalty, politicians, buildings, such as the CRYSTAL PALACE, Dick TURPIN ON BLACK BESS, and the London–York stagecoach. The factory continued to produce silk pictures until at least 1938, but was destroyed by bombing in 1940.

**Stevens, Even.** *See under* EVEN.

**Stew. Stew in one's own juice, To.** To suffer the natural consequences of one's own actions; to reap as one has sown. The expression is not peculiar to English and has its equivalent in French *cuire dans son jus*, German *im eigenen Saft schmoren* and Italian *cuocere nel proprio bodo*. The exact Russian counterpart, *varit'sya v sobstvennom soku*, means rather 'to keep oneself to oneself'.

**In a stew.** In an agitated or angry state; 'hot and bothered'.

**Irish stew.** *See under* IRELAND.

**Steward, Shop.** *See under* SHOP.

**Stewart, Walking.** *See under* WALK.

**Stick. Stick around, To.** To linger; to remain somewhere, especially when waiting for something or someone.

**Stick at it, To.** To persevere at a task.

**Stick at nothing, To.** To be heedless of all obstacles in accomplishing one's desire; to be utterly unscrupulous or ruthless.

**Stick 'em up!** *See* STICK UP.

**Sticking point, The.** The point where an obstacle arises in progress to an agreement or the like.

**Stick in one's gizzard, To.** To be distasteful. 'To stick in one's craw' is a similar expression. *See also* STICK IN ONE'S THROAT.

**Stick in one's throat, To.** To be against one's principles. *See also* STICK IN ONE'S GIZZARD.

**Stick-in-the-mud, A.** A conservative or old-fashioned person. *See also* SQUARE.

**Stick it out, To.** To put up with it; to see it through; to tolerate it to the end.

**Stick one's neck out, To.** To ask for trouble; to risk criticism. The reference is either to boxing, where to stick one's neck out is to expose one's head to a blow, or to beheading.

**Stick one's oar in, To.** *See* PUT OR STICK ONE'S OAR IN *under* OAR.

**Stick out a mile, To.** To be obvious; to be unmissable or unmistakable, as: 'Anyone can see he's a crook, it sticks out a mile.'

**Stick out for, To.** To persist in demanding.

**Stick out like a sore thumb, To.** To hit one in the eye; to look incongruous.

**Sticks, The.** An American colloquialism meaning countryside, rural area or wilds. A headline in *Variety* for 17 July 1935 ran: 'Sticks nix hick pix', meaning that rural residents gave the thumbs-down to films about farms. *See also* OUTBACK.

**Stick together, To.** To remain united; to be mutually loyal; to help one another.

**Stick to one's guns, To.** To maintain one's position or argument, in spite of opposition.

**Stick to one's last, To.** *See* COBBLER SHOULD STICK TO HIS LAST *under* COBBLER.

**Stick to someone's fingers, To.** To be stolen.

**Stick up, To.** To waylay and rob a coach or the like. The expression is familiar from accounts of an armed robbery, when the victims are covered with revolvers and told to 'stick 'em up', i.e. to hold their hands above their heads.

**Stick up for someone, To.** To support or champion them.

**Stick with, To.** To continue to accept; to be loyal to. *See also* STUCK WITH.

**Sticky wicket, A.** A difficult or awkward situation. The allusion is to CRICKET, when a pitch that is drying after rain causes difficulties for the batsman when the ball is bowled.

**Stuck on someone, To be.** To be infatuated with them.

**Stuck-up.** Said of pretentious people who give themselves airs, of nobodies who assume to be somebodies. The allusion is to the peacock, which sticks up its train allegedly to add to its 'importance' and overawe antagonists.

**Stuck with, To be.** To be unable to get rid of; to remain associated with. *See also* STICK WITH.

**Big stick diplomacy.** *See under* BIG.

**Come to a sticky end, To.** *See under* COME.

**Devil on two sticks.** *See under* DEVIL.

**Get hold of the wrong end of the stick, To.** *See under* HOLD.

**Get stuck in, To.** To set to in earnest.

**Give it some stick, To.** To use physical power or force.

**Gold Stick.** *See under* GOLD.

**In a cleft stick.** *See under* CLEFT.

**Over the sticks.** *See under* OVER.

**Swagger stick.** *See under* SWAG.

**White stick.** *See under* WHITE.

**Wrong end of the stick, The.** *See* GET HOLD OF THE WRONG END OF THE STICK.

**Stickit.** A Scotticism for 'stuck (sticked) half-way', as a 'stickit job', one that is unfinished or unsatisfactory. Hence the term is applied to persons who have given up their work through lack of means or capacity or some other reason, as a 'stickit minister', one who has failed to get a pastoral charge or to obtain preferment. S.R. Crockett wrote a novel called *The Stickit Minister* (1893).

**Stickler.** A person who insists on something, as: 'She's a real stickler for punctuality.' Sticklers were the umpires in tournaments, or seconds in single combats, very punctilious about the nice points of etiquette.

**Stiff.** Slang for a corpse, also for a horse that is sure to lose in a race.

**Stiff-necked.** Obstinate and self-willed. The allusion is to a wilful horse, ox or ass, which will not answer to the reins.

> And the Lord said unto Moses, I have seen this people, and, behold, it is a stiffnecked people.
> Exodus 32:9

**Stiff upper lip, A.** A firm resolve coupled with a

suppression of the emotions. A supposed traditional characteristic of the English. A trembling upper lip is often a sign of emotion.

**As stiff as a poker.** *See under* AS.

**Stigmata.** Marks developed on the body of certain persons, which correspond to some or all of the wounds received by Christ in his trial and crucifixion. It is a well-known psychological phenomenon and has been demonstrated in many modern instances. The word is the plural of Greek *stigma*, the brand with which slaves and criminals in ancient Greece and Rome were marked, from *stizein*, 'to tattoo'. Hence English 'stigmatize', to mark as with a brand of disgrace.

Among those, predominantly women, who are said to have been marked with the stigmata are:

Angelo del Paz: all the marks
Benedict of Reggio: the crown of thorns first appeared in 1602
Bianca de Gazeran
Carlo di Saeta: bore the lance-wound
Hieronyma Carvaglio: the spear mark, which bled every Friday
Catharine di Raconisco: the crown of thorns in 1538
Catherine of Genoa (1447–1510)
CATHERINE OF SIENNA
Cecilia di Nobili of Nocera (1655)
Clara di Pugny: the mark of the spear in 1514
Anna Katharina Emmerick of Dülmen, Westphalia (1774–1824)
'Estatica' of Caldaro: all the marks in 1842
Francesco Forgione (1887–1968): Capuchin friar from 1902, taking the name of Brother Pio, is said to have received stigmata on his hands in 1902
FRANCIS OF ASSISI (1181–1226): all the marks appeared on 15 September 1224
Gabriella da Piezolo of Aquila: the mark of the spear in 1472
Gemma Galgani (1878–1903), who received the stigmata and marks of scourging intermittently between 1899 and 1901
Mary Anne Girling (1827–86), founder of the English SHAKERS
Joanna Maria of the Cross
Louise Lateau in 1868
Maria Razzi of Chio: the marks of the crown of thorns
Maria Villani: the crown of thorns
Mary Magdalen di Pazzi
Mechthild von Stanz
Maria von Mörl in 1839
Nicholas of Ravenna
St PAUL: said 'I bear in my body the marks of the Lord Jesus' (Galatians 6:17)
Ursula of Valencia
Veronica Giuliani: all the marks in 1694
Vincenza Ferreri of Valencia

In addition to these, Theresa Neumann (1898–1962), of Konnersreuth, Germany, received her first stigmata on the tops of her hands and feet on GOOD FRIDAY 1926. In subsequent years more marks appeared, on her side, shoulders and brow. Stigmata, as studied in her case, never heal and never suppurate.

**Still life.** In artistic representation, inanimate objects such as books, furniture, fruit or flowers. The expression was originally used of living subjects at rest, i.e. humans or animals that were 'still'.

**Stilo novo** (Latin, 'in the new style'). Newfangled notions. When the CALENDAR was reformed by Pope Gregory XIII in 1582, letters used to be dated *stilo novo*, which grew in time to be a CANT phrase for any innovation. *See also* GREGORIAN CALENDAR; OLD STYLE.

**Sting. Sting Bible, The.** *See under* BIBLE.

**With a sting in its tail.** *See under* WITH.

**Stingo.** An old name for strong ale, so called because it stings the drinker. R.H. Barham's *Ingoldsby Legends* (1840) quotes the following 'primitive ballad' in Gothic print:

A Franklyn's dogge leped over a style,
And hys name was littel Byngo.
B with a Y—Y with an N,
N with a G—G with an O,
They call'd hym littel Byngo!

Thys Franklyn, Syrs, he brewed goode ayle,
And he called it Rare goode Styngo!
S, T, Y, N, G, O!
He called it rare good Styngo!

Nowe is notte thys a prettie song?
I thinke it is, bye Jyngo!
J withe a Y—N, G, O—
I sweare yt is, bye Jyngo!

**Stinkpot, Devil's.** *See under* DEVIL'S CANDLESTICK.

**Stir. Stir one's stumps, To.** To get a move on; to set about something expeditiously. Stumps here are one's legs. The word has been more obviously used for the wooden stump or peg leg once fastened to mutilated limbs, or for such limbs themselves.

**Stir-up Sunday.** The last Sunday after TRINITY SUNDAY, so called from the first two words of the collect: 'Stir up, we beseech thee, O Lord, the wills of thy faithful people.' It was an old custom to stir the Christmas plum pudding on this day, hence the old schoolboy rhyme: 'Stir up, we beseech thee, the pudding in the pot.'

**Stirrup.** Literally, a rope to step up by, from Old English *stigrāp*, from *stīg*, 'path', 'step', and *rāp*, 'rope'.

**Stirrup cup.** A 'parting cup' given to guests on leaving, originally when their feet were in the stirrups. *See also* DOCH-AN-DORIS.

Lord Marmion's bugles blew to horse;
Then came the stirrup-cup in course;
Between the baron and his host,
No point of courtesy was lost.
SIR WALTER SCOTT: *Marmion*, i (1808)

Among the ancient Romans a 'parting cup' was drunk to ensure sound sleep (*see* Ovid, *Fasti*, ii (1st century AD)).

**Stitch, To drop a.** *See under* DROP.

**Stiver, Not a.** Not a penny; not a cent. The stiver (*stuiver*) was a Dutch coin, equal to about a penny.

**Stock.** Originally a tree trunk or stem (connected with 'stick'), hence, in figurative use, something fixed. The word is also used for the 'stem' that is the origin of families, groups and the like, as 'He comes of a good stock', i.e. from a good stem, of good line of descent. The village stocks, in which petty offenders were confined by the wrists and ankles, are so called from the stakes or posts at the side. 'Stock' in the sense of a fund or capital derives from that part of the old wooden TALLY which the creditor took with him as evidence of the king's debt, the other portion, known as the counterstock, remaining in the EXCHEQUER. The word was then applied to the money that this tally represented, i.e. money lent to the government.

**Stockbroker** or **stockjobber.** A broker was formerly engaged in the purchase of stocks and shares for clients on commission, while a jobber speculated in stocks and shares so as to profit by market fluctuations, acting as an intermediary between buying and selling brokers. The jobber had to be a member of the STOCK EXCHANGE, but a broker not necessarily. If the latter was not, he was known as an 'outside broker' or 'kerbstone operator'. These differentiations were markedly changed by BIG BANG. *See also* BUCKET SHOP.

**Stockbroker belt.** A term for the areas outside a city, and especially London, where wealthy stockbrokers live.

> Macclesfield and its environs, in the heart of the Cheshire stockbroker belt, are among an élite few outside the southeast, with one in every 50 homes worth more than £320,000.
>
> GREG HADFIELD and MARK SKIPWORTH: *Class*, ch vii (1994)

**Stock car.** A car that has been specially strengthened and modified for a form of racing in which the cars deliberately collide. Such cars have a standard or stock chassis, hence the name.

**Stock dove.** Also called a blue rock, the stock dove (*Columba oenas*) is very similar to a ROCK DOVE, and so called from its nesting in old tree stumps or, less likely, from the (erroneous) idea that it was the ancestor of varieties of the domestic pigeon.

**Stock Exchange.** A market in which stocks and shares are bought and sold. Such markets had long existed in London (and elsewhere) and in the 18th century speculators and dealers met at JONATHAN'S and various other premises. In 1773 they formed an association or Stock Exchange meeting in Sweeting's Alley in what came to be known as the Stock Exchange coffee house or tavern. In 1801 it was decided that a more suitable building was needed, and the Stock Exchange in CAPEL COURT was opened in 1802, being considerably enlarged in 1853–4 and subsequently. The London Stock Exchange, known in the City as the House, is the oldest in the world and was not rivalled by that of New York (organized in 1817) until the 20th century. *See also* BACKWARDATION; BEAR; BIG BANG; CONTANGO; STOCKBROKER; WALL STREET.

**Stockfish.** Dried cod, cured without salt, said to be so called because dried on wooden racks. Until it was beaten it was very tough and was called buckhorn.

In Shakespeare's day the word was often used as abuse, so that Falstaff shouts at Prince Henry:

> 'Sblood, you starveling, you elf-skin, you dried neat's tongue, you bull's pizzle, you stock-fish!
>
> *Henry IV*, *Pt I*, II, iv (1590)

**Stock in trade.** The goods kept for sale by a shopkeeper; the tools or equipment used for a trade or profession.

**Stock still.** Absolutely still. The allusion is to a stock or log, which although once part of a living tree is now dead and motionless.

**Laughing stock.** *See under* LAUGH.

**Lock, stock and barrel.** *See under* LOCK.

**On the stocks, To be.** To be in hand, but not yet finished. The stocks is the frame in which a ship is placed during building, and so long as it is in hand it is said to be, or to lie, on the stocks.

**Rolling stock.** *See under* ROLL.

**Take stock, To.** To ascertain how one's business stands by taking an inventory of all goods and the like in hand, balancing one's books and so on. Hence, to survey one's position and prospects.

**Water stock, To.** *See under* WATER.

**Stockade, The Eureka.** *See under* EUREKA.

**Stocking.** A word sometimes used of a person's savings or NEST EGG, because formerly money used to be hoarded up in an old stocking, which was frequently hung up the chimney for safety.

**Stocking filler.** A small present suitable for a Christmas stocking.

**Blue stocking.** *See under* BLUE.

**Body stocking.** *See under* BODY.

**Cap and Stocking.** *See under* CAP.

**Stockwell ghost.** A supposed ghost that created a great sensation in Stockwell (London) in 1772, then a village. The author of the strange noises was Anne Robinson, a maidservant. *See also* COCK LANE GHOST; SAMPFORD GHOST.

**Stoic.** A school of Greek philosophers founded by ZENO OF CITIUM (334–262 BC), who held that virtue was the highest good, and that the passions and appetites should be rigidly subdued.

The later Stoic school of the Romans is represented by Seneca, Epictetus and Marcus Aurelius. *See also* PORCH.

The ancient Stoics in their porch
With fierce dispute maintained their church,
Beat out their brains in fight and study
To prove that virtue is a body,
That *bonum* is an animal,
Made good with stout polemic bawl.
SAMUEL BUTLER: *Hudibras*, II, ii (1663)

**Stole** (Latin *stola*). An ecclesiastical vestment, also called the orarium. Deacons wear the stole over the left shoulder like a sash. Priests normally wear it around the neck, both ends hanging loose in front. With Eucharistic vestments the ends are crossed over the chest.

**Groom of the Stole, The.** *See under* GROOM.

**Stomach.** Used figuratively of inclination, as: 'He had little stomach for the enterprise.'

**Stomach an insult, To.** To swallow it or put up with it.

**Army marches on its stomach, An.** *See under* ARMY.

**Butterflies in one's stomach, To have.** *See under* BUTTERFLY.

**Strong stomach, A.** *See under* STRONG.

**Stone.** Used figuratively when some characteristic of a stone is implied as: 'stone blind', 'stone cold', 'stone dead', 'stone deaf' and so on, meaning as blind, cold, dead or deaf as a stone.

In all parts of the world primitive peoples have set up stones, especially those of meteoric origin, fabled to have fallen from heaven, in connection with religious rites. Anaxagoras mentions a stone that fell from JUPITER in Thrace, a description of which is given by Pliny. The Ephesians asserted that their image of DIANA came from Jupiter. The stone at Emessa, in Syria, worshipped as a symbol of the sun, was a similar meteorite, and there were other stones at Abydos and Potidaea. At Corinth one was venerated as ZEUS, and Tacitus describes one in Cyprus dedicated to VENUS. The famous BLACK STONE set in the KAABA is also a meteorite.

The great stone circles of Avebury and STONEHENGE and the STANDING STONES OF STENNESS are particularly noteworthy examples of the industry and ingenuity of early man, each having their mythological and religious associations. *See also* AETITES; PHILOSOPHER'S STONE; PRECIOUS STONES; TOUCHSTONE.

**Stone Age.** The period when stone implements were used by primitive man, before the discovery of metals. Its dating varies considerably over the continents, with the use of bows and arrows, stone axes, bone tools and the like persisting in Papua New Guinea, for example, in the present century. *See also* NEOLITHIC AGE; PALAEOLITHIC AGE.

**Stone frigate.** A sailor's name for barracks or a shore establishment.

**Stone lilies.** St CUTHBERT'S BEADS.

**Stone of Destiny, The.** *See* STONE OF SCONE.

**Stone of Scone, The.** The great coronation stone, the Stone of Destiny, on which the Scottish kings were formerly crowned at Scone, near Perth. It was removed by Edward I in 1296 and brought to Westminster Abbey, where it was housed under the Chair of St Edward until 1996, when it was returned to Scotland. It was stolen on the night of 24–25 December 1950, but restored to its place in February 1952.

It is also, traditionally, called JACOB'S STONE. It is of reddish-grey sandstone and is fabled to have been once kept at Dunstaffnage in Argyll and brought to Scone by Kenneth MacAlpin in 843. *See also* TANIST STONE.

**Stone soup** or **St Bernard's soup.** The story goes that a beggar asked alms at a lordly mansion, but was told by the servants that they had nothing to give him. 'Sorry for it,' said the man, 'but will you let me boil a little water to make some soup of this stone?' This was so novel a proceeding, that the curiosity of the servants was aroused, and the man was readily furnished with a saucepan, water and a spoon. In he popped the stone and then begged for a little salt and pepper for flavouring. Stirring the water and tasting it, he said it would be the better for any fragments of meat and vegetables they might happen to have. These were supplied, and ultimately he asked for a little ketchup or other sauce. When ready, the servants tasted it, and declared that 'stone soup' was excellent.

This story, which was a great favourite in the 16th and 17th centuries, was told with many variations, and with horseshoes, nails, ram's horns and the like taking the place of the stone as narrated here.

**Stone the crows.** An exclamation of surprise, dismay, disgust or the like.

**Stonewall, To.** A cricketer's term for adopting purely defensive measures when at the wicket, blocking every ball and not attempting to score. It was originally Australian political slang and was used of obstructing business. In general usage, 'stonewalling' is employing obstructive or delaying tactics.

**Stonewall Jackson.** *See under* JACKSON.

**Alectorian stone.** *See under* ALECTORIAN.

**Bath stone.** *See under* BATH.

**Black Stone, The.** *See under* BLACK.

**Blarney Stone, The.** *See under* BLARNEY.

**Blowing Stone, The.** *See under* BLOW.

**Cast the first stone, To.** *See under* CAST.

**Coade stone.** *See under* COADE.

**Devil's stones.** *See under* DEVIL.

**Hagstones.** *See under* HAG.
**Heart of stone, A.** *See under* HEART.
**Hoarstone.** *See under* HOAR.
**Jacob's stone.** *See under* JACOB.
**Leave no stone unturned, To.** *See under* LEAVE.
**Logan stones.** *See under* LOGAN.
**London Stone.** *See under* LONDON.
**Lucky stone.** *See under* LUCK.
**Philosopher's stone.** *See under* PHILOSOPHER.
**Precious stones.** *See under* PRECIOUS.
**Rocking stones.** *See* LOGAN STONES.
**Rolling stone gathers no moss, A.** *See under* ROLL.
**Rollright Stones.** *See under* ROLLRIGHT.
**Rosetta Stone, The.** *See under* ROSETTA.
**Sarsen stones.** *See under* SARSEN.
**Snake stones.** *See under* SNAKE.
**St Radegonde's lifted stone.** *See under* RADEGONDE.
**Standing Stones of Stenness, The.** *See under* STAND.
**Tanist stone.** *See under* TANIST.

**Stonehenge.** The most famous prehistoric monument in Britain. It is situated on SALISBURY PLAIN about 8 miles (13km) north of Salisbury. The second half of the name is from Old English *hengen*, 'hanging place', so that the overall meaning is 'stone gallows', from its resemblance to such. At various times regarded as having been built by the DRUIDS, the Romans and the Danes, it was originally of Neolithic construction in *c*.3100 BC and was later reconstructed *c*.2100 BC and again *c*.1550 BC. It seems to have last been used *c*.1100 BC. It finally consisted of an outer circle of local SARSEN STONES and two inner circles of bluestones, apparently from the Preseli Mountains in southwest Wales. The first and third circles are capped with stone lintels. The whole is surrounded by a ditch, inside the bank of which are 56 shallow holes known as Aubrey Holes after their discoverer, the antiquary John Aubrey (1626–97). The Heel Stone, over which the sun approximately rises on Midsummer Day, stands in isolation outside the circles. It is probable that Stonehenge was a centre of worship, connected with the sun, but it was suggested in 1963 by the American astronomer, Gerald Hawkins, that it was a massive kind of astronomical clock. A more recent theory, proposed by the physicist Terence Meaden, is that the stones mark the site of a symbolic marriage between the sun god and the EARTH MOTHER, and that they are positioned so that the sun casts a phallic shadow which penetrates the monument's inner sanctum.

A report to the ROYAL SOCIETY in 1996 said that Stonehenge was probably 1000 years older than originally thought. RADIOCARBON DATING of bone fragments at the site showed that they were 5000 years old, thus dating from before the building of the PYRAMIDS.

> Intra lapidum structuram sepultus fuit, quae haud longe a Salesberia mira arte composita, Anglorum lingua Stanheng nuncupatur.
> ('He [King Constantine] was buried within the structure of the stones, which was set up with wonderful art not far from Salisbury, and called in the English tongue Stonehenge'.)
> GEOFFREY OF MONMOUTH: *Historia Regum Britanniae* XI, iv (*c*.1136)

**Stooges, The Three.** *See under* THREE.

**Stool. Stool of repentance.** The CUTTY STOOL, a low stool placed in front of the pulpit in Scottish churches, on which persons who had incurred ecclesiastical censure were placed during divine service. When the service was over, the penitent had to stand on the stool and receive the minister's rebuke.
**Stool pigeon.** A police spy or informer; a decoy. The name alludes to the former practice of tying or even nailing a pigeon to a stool to act as a decoy for other pigeons, which were then shot by the waiting hunters.
**Cucking stool.** *See under* CUCKING.
**Cutty stool.** *See under* CUTTY.
**Ducking stool.** *See under* DUCK.
**Fall between two stools, To.** *See under* FALL.

**Stop. Stop at nothing, To.** To be prepared to do anything.
**Stop-watch critics.**

> – And how did *Garrick* speak the soliloquy last night? – Oh, against all rule, my lord, – most ungrammatically! betwixt the substantive and the adjective, which should agree together in *number*, *case*, and *gender*, he made a breach thus, – stopping, as if the point wanted settling; – and betwixt the nominative case, which your lordship knows should govern the verb, he suspended his voice in the epilogue a dozen times three seconds and three-fifths by a stop-watch, my lord, each time, – Admirable grammarian! – But in suspending his voice – was the sense suspended likewise? Did no expression of attitude or countenance fill up the chasm? – Was the eye silent? Did you narrowly look? – I look'd only at the stop-watch, my lord. – Excellent observer!
> LAURENCE STERNE: *Tristram Shandy*, III, ch xii (1759–67)

**Pull out all the stops, To.** *See under* PULL.
**Show stopper.** *See under* SHOW.

**Store. Store cattle.** Beasts kept on a farm for breeding purposes, or lean cattle bought for fattening.
**Set store by, To.** *See under* SET.

**Stork.** According to Swedish legend, the stork received its name from flying around the cross of the crucified Redeemer, crying *Styrka! styrka!* ('Strengthen, strengthen!').

John Lyly in *Euphues* (1580) says of this bird:

Ladies use their lovers as the stork doth her young ones who pecketh them till they bleed with her bill, and then healeth them with her tongue.

It is an old tale to children that babies are brought by storks, and they still feature prominently on cards of congratulation to a baby's parents. It was also a belief that a stork will kill a snake 'on sight'. The name actually represents Old English *storc*, related to Old English *stearc*, 'stiff' (modern 'stark'). The allusion is to the bird's stiff-looking legs.

**King Stork.** A tyrant that devours his subjects, and makes them submissive with fear and trembling. The allusion is to the fable of 'The Frogs desiring a King' in which King Stork is contrasted with King LOG.

**Storm. Storm and Stress.** *See* STURM UND DRANG.

**Storm in a teacup, A.** A big fuss about a trifle; 'much ado about nothing'. The American equivalent is 'a tempest in a teapot'.

**Storm petrel.** A small seabird, *Hydrobates pelagicus*, traditionally so named from Italian *Petrello*, 'little Peter', because during storms these birds seem to be able to fly while patting the water with each foot alternately as though walking on it, reminiscent of St PETER, who walked on the lake of Gennesareth (Matthew 14:30). Sailors call them MOTHER CAREY'S CHICKENS. The term is occasionally used figuratively of someone whose coming always portends trouble.

**Any port in a storm.** *See under* ANY.

**Brainstorm, A.** *See under* BRAIN.

**Cape of Storms, The.** *See under* CAPE.

**Eye of the storm, The.** *See under* EYE.

**Gowk storm.** *See under* GOWK.

**Take by storm, To.** To seize by a sudden and irresistible attack. This military term is used figuratively of someone who becomes suddenly famous or popular or of a new performer who 'takes the town by storm'.

**Storting** or **Storthing.** The Norwegian Parliament, elected every fourth year, from *stor*, 'great', and *thing*, 'assembly'.

**Story. Shaggy dog story, A.** *See under* SHAGGY.

**Sob story.** *See under* SOB.

**Tall story.** *See under* TALL.

**Stout.** A dark beer made with roasted malt. Porter, a light stout, is still sold on draught in Ireland and stout derives its name from being a strong or stout porter. *See also* ALE.

**Stovepipe hat.** An old-fashioned tall, silk hat; a chimney-pot hat. The name is of American origin.

**Strad.** A colloquial name for a violin made by Antonio Stradivarius (1644–1737) of CREMONA, now much prized. His best violins were made between 1700 and 1723. *See also* AMATI.

**Strafe** (German *strafen*, 'to punish'). A word borrowed in amused contempt from the Germans during the First World War. One of their favourite slogans was *Gott strafe England!* The word was applied to any sharp and sudden bombardment, and also used by Americans in the Second World War for the machine-gunning of troops or civilians by low-flying aircraft.

**Straight. Straight and narrow, The.** Morally correct behaviour. The allusion is biblical.

Strait is the gate, and narrow is the way, which leadeth unto life.
Matthew 7:14

**Straight from the horse's mouth.** Direct from the highest source, which cannot be questioned. The only certain way of discovering the age of a horse is by examining its front teeth, the incisors.

**Straight from the shoulder.** With full force, physically, or verbally. A term from boxing.

**Straight up.** Truthfully; honestly.

**As straight as a die.** *See under* AS.

**Home straight, The.** *See under* HOME.

**Strain. Strain at a gnat and swallow a camel, To.** To make much fuss about minor misdeeds but commit offences of real magnitude. The expression comes from Matthew 23:24, which in Tyndale's, Coverdale's and other early versions of the Bible reads 'strain out', i.e. to filter out a gnat before drinking the wine. The Revised Version also adopts this form, but the Authorized Version's rendering is 'which strain at a gnat', which was not an error but established usage at the time.

**Strain at the leash, To.** To be eager to be off; to be impatient of restraint or delay. The reference is to the lead used to restrain hounds when coursing.

**Don't strain yourself.** Don't overdo it. A (usually) humorous recommendation to a person seen to make little effort.

**Strait of Magellan.** The strait between the mainland of South America and Tierra del Fuego is named after Fernão de Magelhães (Ferdinand Magellan) (1480–1521), the Portuguese navigator, who undertook the first expedition to circumnavigate the globe and who discovered it in 1520. He was killed in the Philippines.

**Strand, The.** One of the best known of London's thoroughfares, joining the City of London to WESTMINSTER along the riverside. Hence its name. Its many great inns or houses had riverside approaches (the Victoria Embankment was not begun until 1864). Its many historic buildings have almost entirely ceased to exist although names still survive as in Essex Street, the SAVOY Hotel and others. There is still a Roman bath in Strand Lane. Its boundary with FLEET STREET was formerly marked by the gateway at TEMPLE BAR.

Let's all go down the Strand!
Let's all go down the Strand!
I'll be leader, you can march behind
Come with me, and see what we can find
Let's all go down the Strand!

HARRY CASTLING and C.W. MURPHY: 'Let's All Go Down the Strand!' (song) (1909)

**Stranger.** Originally a foreigner, from Old French *estrangier* (modern French *étranger*), which is from Latin *extraneus*, 'person outside'.

It is said that BUSIRIS, king of Egypt, sacrificed to his gods all strangers who set foot on his territories. DIOMEDES gave strangers to his horses for food.

Floating tea leaves in one's cup, charred pieces of wick that make the candle gutter, little bits of soot hanging from the grate and similar objects, are called 'strangers', because they are said to foretell the coming of visitors.

**Stranger that is within thy gates, The.** *See* PROSELYTES.

**I spy strangers!** *See under* SPY.

**Little stranger.** *See under* LITTLE.

**Strangler, Boston.** *See under* BOSTON.

**Strap. Straphanger.** A passenger who stands in a bus or train when all the seats are taken, holding on to the strap hanging from the roof.

**Strap-oil.** Slang for a thrashing with a strap.

**Strapping young fellow, A.** A big sturdy chap. A vigorous young woman is similarly called a 'strapper'.

'To you I can talk of my lovely one: for now you have seen her and know her.'
'Yes, sir.'
'She's a rare one, is she not, Jane?'
'Yes, sir.'
'A strapper – a real strapper, Jane: big, brown, and buxom.'

CHARLOTTE BRONTË: *Jane Eyre*, ch xx (1847)

**Taste of the strap, A.** *See under* TASTE.

**Strappado** (Italian *strappare*, 'to tug'). A mode of torture formerly practised for extracting confessions, retractions and the like. The hands were tied behind the back, and the victim was pulled up to a beam by a rope tied to them and then let down suddenly. By this means a limb was not infrequently dislocated.

An I were at the strappado, or all the racks in the world, I would not tell you on compulsion.

SHAKESPEARE: *Henry IV, Pt I*, II, iv (1597)

**Straw.** Straw was proverbially regarded as worthless, something blown about by the wind. Hence the word is used in phrases as 'not worth a straw' for something quite valueless, or 'not to care a straw', meaning not to care at all.

**Straw in the wind, A.** A slight indication of the way things are going.

**Straw poll.** An early form of public opinion poll sponsored by the American press as early as 1824, when reporters of the *Harrisburg Pennsylvanian* were sent to inquire from the townsfolk of Wilmington which candidate they favoured for the presidency. Such polls were subsequently used on a much larger scale and postal voting came to be employed. The idea is of a straw 'showing which way the wind blows'. *See also* GALLUP POLL.

**Straw vote.** A n unofficial vote taken casually at a meeting as an indication of opinion.

**Bricks without straw.** *See under* BRICK.

**Draw the short straw, To.** *See under* DRAW.

**Drowning men clutch** or **catch at straws.** *See under* DROWN.

**Jack Straw.** One of the leaders of the riots in London during the PEASANTS' REVOLT of 1381, when he was captured and executed. Chaucer refers to his massacre of a number of Flemings.

Jack Straw and all his followers in their brawl
Were never half so shrill, for all their noise,
When they were murdering those Flemish boys.

CHAUCER: 'The Nun's Priest's Tale' (*c*.1387) (modern translation by Nevill Coghill, 1951)

**Last straw, The.** *See under* LAST.

**Man of straw, A.** *See under* MAN.

**Strawberry.** Izaak Walton (*Compleat Angler*, ch v (1653)) says of this fruit:

We may say of angling as Dr Boteler said of strawberries, 'doubtless God could have made a better berry, but doubtless God never did.'

**Strawberry leaves.** A dukedom, or the honour or rank of a duke. The ducal coronet is ornamented with eight strawberry leaves.

**Strawberry mark.** A birthmark something like a strawberry. In J.M. Morton's BOX AND COX (1847) the two heroes eventually recognize each other as long-lost brothers through one having a strawberry mark on his left arm.

**Crushed strawberry.** *See under* CRUSH.

**Streak. Streaking.** The act of running naked in a public place by way of a stunt, sometimes under the influence of a stimulant other than a bet or the buzz of bravado. The feat is usually staged out of doors, typically at a sporting venue, but may also be enacted in a public building such as a restaurant.

Abigail Saxon, 34, ... was challenged to streak twice around the fashionable Barca bar in Castlefield for £100.

*The Times* (22 December 1998)

**Silver Streak.** *See under* SILVER.

**Yellow streak.** *See under* YELLOW.

**Stream. Stream of consciousness.** A technique of novel writing, first deliberately employed by Dorothy Richardson (1873–1957) in *Pointed Roofs* (1915) and developed by James Joyce (1882–1941) and Virginia Woolf (1882–1941). By this technique the writer presents life as seen through impressions on the mind of one person.

The term itself was coined by William James in *Principles of Psychology* (1890).

**Golden Stream, The.** *See under* GOLDEN.

**Gulf Stream.** *See under* GULF.

**Swap horses in midstream, To.** *See under* SWAP.

**Swim with the stream, To.** *See under* SWIM.

**Street. Street Arab.** A homeless child, especially one who begs and steals. The reference is to the nomadic habits of the Arabs, who had no fixed abode.

> He strode on just in time to avoid a flight of street-arabs, who had seen the scuffle from a distance and were bearing down eagerly upon him.
>
> MRS HUMPHRY WARD: *The History of David Grieve*, Bk II, ch vii (1892).

**Street cred.** In full, street credibility, or the status of PERSONA GRATA among one's young and fashionable urban peers.

**Street jewellery.** A group term for enamelled advertising signs as collectors' items. The first such signs, with their memorable trade names and commercial slogans, began to appear in the mid-19th century, and were subsequently familiar features in towns and villages throughout the country. Their heyday was in the early 20th century. Their rapid demise came after the Second World War with the advent of the giant hoarding. Some signs are still to be found on back street corner shops.

**Streets ahead.** Well ahead; much in advance. The phrase conveys the idea of long distance.

**Street value.** The value of illicitly sold drugs.

**Carey Street.** *See under* CAREY.

**Carnaby Street.** *See under* CARNABY.

**Civvy Street.** *See under* CIVVIES.

**Easy street.** *See under* EASE.

**Ermine Street.** *See under* ERMINE.

**Fleet Street.** *See under* FLEET.

**Grub Street.** *See under* GRUB.

**Harley Street.** *See under* HARLEY.

**High Street.** *See under* HIGH.

**Main Street.** *See under* MAIN.

**Man in the street, The.** *See under* MAN.

**Monmouth Street.** *See under* MONMOUTH.

**Threadneedle Street.** *See under* THREADNEEDLE.

**Throgmorton Street.** *See under* THROGMORTON.

**Old Lady of Threadneedle Street, The.** *See under* OLD.

**Up one's street.** *See under* UP.

**Walk the streets, To.** *See under* WALK.

**Wall Street.** *See under* WALL.

**Watling Street.** *See under* WATLING.

**Woman of the streets.** *See under* WOMAN.

**Strenia.** A SABINE goddess identified with the Roman Salus (or Hygieia), to whom gifts (*strenae*) of figs, dates and honey were taken at the New Year. The custom is said to have been instituted by the Sabine King Titus Tatius, who entered Rome on New Year's Day and received from some augurs palms cut from the sacred grove that was dedicated to her. The French *étrenne*, a New Year's gift, is named from this goddess.

**Strephon.** A stock name for a rustic lover, from the languishing shepherd lover of that name in Sir Philip Sidney's *Arcadia* (1590).

**Stretch. Stretch a point, To.** To exceed or agree to what is not normally permissible. The expression may allude to the tagged laces called points formerly used in costume. To 'truss a point' was to tie the laces which fastened the garment, and to 'stretch a point' was to stretch these laces, so as to adjust for growth or temporary fullness after a meal.

**Stretch one's legs, To.** To take a walk for exercise after long sitting, as in a car journey. Also, euphemistically, to visit the lavatory.

**Stretch one's wings, To.** *See* SPREAD OR STRETCH ONE'S WINGS.

**At full stretch.** Working to capacity.

**Strictly. Strictly for the birds.** Unimportant; of no consequence. An expression of American origin. The allusion is to horse manure, which is good only for picking over by birds.

**Strictly** or **properly speaking.** Speaking in the strict and accurate meaning of the words; speaking without qualification.

**Stride, To take in one's.** *See under* TAKE.

**Strike.** This verb is now mainly used in the sense of to hit, to deliver a blow or to act swiftly. The noun 'strike' has numerous specialized meanings, e.g. an old grain measure varying locally from half a bushel to four bushels, or a wooden straight-edged implement for levelling off a measure of grain by 'striking it off', but it is most commonly used nowadays to denote a cessation of work by a body of employees for coercive purposes. Strikes over delayed payment were not unknown among the workmen employed on the royal tombs in ancient Egypt.

**Strike a balance, To.** To calculate the exact difference, if any, between the debit and credit sides of an account, or more generally, to compromise.

**Strike a bargain, To.** To make or conclude a transaction; to agree on terms.

**Strike-a-light.** The flint formerly used with tinderboxes for striking fire; also, the shaped piece of metal used to strike the flint. The latter's similarity with the links of the collar of the ORDER OF THE GOLDEN FLEECE gave the name 'the collar of strike-a-lights'. 'Strike a light' is also used as an exclamation of surprise.

**Strike an attitude, To.** To pose; to assume an exaggerated or theatrical attitude.

**Strike at the roots of, To.** To set about destroying; to aim at a radical demolition.

**Strikebreaker.** A BLACKLEG; a 'scab'; a worker induced by the employer to carry on working when the other employees are on strike.

**Strike, but hear me!** (Latin *verbera, sed audi*). Carry out your threats, if you must, but at least hear what I have to say. The phrase comes from Plutarch's life of Themistocles (1st century AD). He strongly opposed the proposal of Eurybiades to quit the Bay of Salamis. The hot-headed SPARTAN insultingly remarked that 'those who in the public games rise up before the proper signal are scourged'. 'True,' said Themistocles, 'but those who lag behind win no laurels.' On this, Eurybiades lifted up his staff to strike him, whereupon Themistocles exclaimed, 'Strike, but hear me!'

**Strike camp, To.** To take down the tents and move off.

**Strike hands, To.** To confirm a bargain by shaking or 'striking hands'.

**Strike home, To.** To achieve an intended effect by what one says or does.

**Strike it rich or lucky, To.** To have unexpected financial or good fortune. An allusion to oil or mineral mining. *See also* STRIKE OIL.

**Strike oil, To.** To make a lucky or valuable discovery; to come upon good fortune in some form or other. The phrase refers to the finding of mineral oil deposits, always a source of wealth.

**Strike out in another direction, To.** To open up a new way for oneself; to branch out into a new activity.

**Strike sail, To.** To acknowledge oneself beaten; to EAT HUMBLE PIE. When a ship in a fight or on meeting another ship, lowered her topsails at least half-mast high, she was said to strike, meaning that she submitted or paid respect to another.

**Strike the flag, To.** To lower it completely. To do so is a token of surrender, and when an admiral relinquishes his command he 'strikes his flag'.

**Strike the right note, To.** To say, write or do the appropriate thing to suit the occasion. The allusion is to a note in music.

**Strike up, To.** To begin or to start operations, as 'to strike up an acquaintance', meaning to set acquaintanceship going. The phrase was originally used of an orchestra or company of singers, who 'struck up' (began to play) the music.

**Strike while the iron is hot, To.** To act promptly when the opportunity arises. A metaphor from the blacksmith's shop, since iron cannot be bent once it has cooled. Similar expressions are 'Make hay while the sun shines' and 'Take time by the forelock.'

**Struck all of a heap, To be.** Struck with astonishment.

**Struck off the rolls, To be.** To be removed from the official list of qualified solicitors, and so prohibited from practising. This is done in cases of professional misconduct.

**Bird strike.** *See under* BIRD.

**First strike.** *See under* FIRST.

**General Strike, The.** *See under* GENERAL.

**Hunger strike.** *See under* HUNGER.

**It strikes me.** It seems to me; I think.

**Lightning never strikes the same place twice.** *See under* LIGHTNING.

**Lightning strike.** *See under* LIGHTNING.

**Sit-down strike.** *See under* SIT.

**Without striking a blow.** *See under* WITHOUT.

**String. String along with, To.** To accompany; to join up with, i.e. to join the line or 'string'. The allusion is to pack-mules in trains.

> You may not be an angel
> 'Cause angels are so few,
> But until the day that one comes along
> I'll string along with you.
> AL DUBIN: 'You May Not Be an Angel' (song) (1934)

**String someone along, To.** To deceive them by appearing to comply with them.

**String up, To.** To kill by hanging.

**First string.** *See under* FIRST.

**Have more than one string to one's bow, To.** To have an alternative available. The allusion is to the custom of archers carrying a reserve string for emergency.

**How long is a piece of string?** *See under* HOW.

**Leading strings.** *See under* LEAD.

**No strings attached.** No conditions; no complications.

**Pull strings, To.** *See under* PULL.

**Second string.** *See under* SECOND.

**Strip. Strip a cow, To.** To milk it to the last drop.

**Stripagram.** A form of 'greetings telegram' delivered by a messenger who performs a STRIPTEASE for the benefit of the recipient.

**Strip Jack naked.** Another name for BEGGAR-MY-NEIGHBOUR, a simple card game popular with children.

**Strip poker.** A game of poker in which a player with a losing hand removes an item of clothing as a penalty or forfeit.

**Strip search.** A search of a person involving the removal of all their clothes. The aim is to find drugs or the like concealed in body cavities.

**Striptease.** A club or cabaret performance in which a woman or, less often, a man, slowly and provocatively undresses, i.e. teases by stripping. The person who does this, usually to music, is a stripper. The entertainment dates from the 1930s.

**Comic strip or cartoon.** *See under* COMIC.

**Tear someone off a strip, To.** *See under* TEAR.

**Stripe. Forty stripes save one.** *See under* FORTY.

**Stars and Stripes, The.** *See under* STAR.

**Stroke.** The oarsman nearest the stern facing the COXSWAIN, who sets the time of the stroke for the rest.

> His blade struck the water a full second before any other... Nor did he flag as the race wore on: as the others tired, he seemed to grow more fresh, until at length, as the boats begin to near the winning-post, his oar was dipping into the water nearly twice as often as any other.
>
> 'BELINDA BLINDERS' (DESMOND COKE): *Sandford of Merton*, ch xii (1903) (often misquoted as 'All rowed fast, but none so fast as stroke')

**Stroke someone (up) the wrong way, To.** To annoy someone; to ruffle their temper. *See also* RUB SOMEONE UP THE WRONG WAY.

**Butterfly stroke.** *See under* BUTTERFLY.

**Strong. Strong language.** Forceful language; swearing.

**Strong meat.** Figuratively, something that arouses fear, repulsion or the like, such as a repressive regime or a gory crime novel.

**Strong point.** Something at which one excels, one's forte, as: 'Science was never his strong point.'

**Strong stomach, A.** One that is not easily upset, especially figuratively.

**Strong verb.** In grammar, a verb that changes its vowel on altering its tense, e.g. bind and bound, speak and spoke. The opposite is a weak verb, which simply adds a syllable or letter, e.g. love and loved, refund and refunded.

**As strong as a horse.** *See under* AS.

**Come it strong, To.** *See under* COME.

**God sides with the strongest.** *See under* GOD.

**Going strong.** Prospering; getting on famously; in an excellent state of health.

**Go it strong, To.** To go to great lengths; to exaggerate.

**Hot and strong.** *See under* HOT.

**Union is strength.** *See under* UNION.

**Struck.** *See* STRIKE.

**Struldbrugs.** Wretched inhabitants of Luggnagg in Swift's *Gulliver's Travels* who had the privilege of immortality without having eternal vigour, strength and intellect. Their name has been 'decoded' to mean 'stir dull blood', and they have been seen as a satirical reference to the French Academy, who are even now known as 'The Immortals'.

> I was asked by a Person of Quality, whether I had seen any of their Struldbrugs or Immortals. I said I had not; and desired he would explain to me what he meant by such an Appelation, applyed to a mortal Creature.
>
> JONATHAN SWIFT: *Gulliver's Travels*, Pt III, ch x (1726)

**Struwwelpeter.** 'Shock-headed Peter', the long-nailed boy who is the title character of a series of cautionary tales for children by Heinrich Hoffmann (1809–94), published in German in 1845 and first in English translation in 1848. Other memorable characters include JOHNNY-HEAD-IN-AIR, Augustus who would not have any soup, and Harriet who plays with matches. The most gruesome is the Scissor-man, who cuts the thumbs off thumb-suckers.

**Strymon.** (1) The father of Rhesus, who was famous on account of his horses. When Rhesus was slain at TROY he threw himself into the river that subsequently bore his name.

(2) The horse immolated by XERXES before he invaded Greece. It came from the vicinity of the River Strymon in Thrace.

**Stuart. All Stuarts are not sib.** *See under* ALL.

**Stuck.** *See* STICK.

**Study, Brown.** *See under* BROWN.

**Stuff. Stuffed shirt.** A pompous and vacuous person. The allusion is to a dummy displaying a dress-shirt in a menswear store. The figure is not only pompous-looking but hollow.

**Stuff gown.** A BARRISTER who has not yet taken SILK.

**Stuff it.** An expression of rejection or disdain. So also 'Stuff that', 'Stuff him' etc.

**Bit of stuff, A.** *See under* BIT.

**Do one's stuff, To.** To do what one has to do.

**Hard stuff.** *See under* HARD.

**Hot stuff.** *See under* HOT.

**Sob stuff.** *See under* SOB.

**That's the stuff!** That's what's wanted! Sometimes extended to: 'That's the stuff to give the troops!'

**Stumbling block, A.** An obstacle in the path of progress; a snag or cause of difficulty.

> Let us not therefore judge one another any more: but judge this rather, that no man put a stumblingblock or an occasion to fall in his brother's way.
>
> Romans 14:13

**Stumer.** A swindle or a swindler; a forged banknote or dud cheque; a fictitious bet recorded by bookmakers and published in the papers to deceive the public by increasing the odds on a horse that is not expected to win. In the First World War a dud shell was called a stumer. The word is of unknown origin.

**Stump. Stumped, To be.** To be outwitted; to be at a loss. A term borrowed from CRICKET.

**Stump speaker** or **orator, A.** A speaker who harangues all who will listen to him from some improvised vantage point, often with rant and bombast of the tub-thumping variety. The phrase is of American origin, where it does not necessarily have derogatory implications. It originates from the days when a tree stump was often the most readily available platform for political speeches. Hence such phrases as 'to stump the country' or 'on the stump' with regard to political speech-making or agitation.

**Stump up, To.** To pay one's reckoning; to

produce the money required. The expression is an Americanism, meaning money paid down on the spot, i.e. on the stump of a tree. *See also* ON THE NAIL *under* NAIL.

**Draw stumps, To.** *See under* DRAW.

**Stir one's stumps, To.** *See under* STIR.

**Stupid, Call me.** *See under* CALL.

**Stupor mundi** (Latin, 'wonder of the world'). Emperor Frederick II (1194–1250) was so called as being the greatest sovereign, soldier and patron of artists and scholars of his day.

**Sturm und Drang** (German, 'storm and stress'). The name given to the German literary movement of the late 18th century with which Johann von Goethe (1749–1832), Johann von Schiller (1759–1805) and Johann Gottfried Herder (1744–1803) were closely associated, from a tragedy of this title (1776) by Frederick Maximilian von Klinger. The dramas of the period are typified by the extravagant passion of the characters. The movement had a later influence on the ROMANTIC MOVEMENT.

**Stygian.** Infernal; gloomy; pertaining to the River STYX.

> Hence, loathèd Melancholy,
> Of Cerberus, and blackest Midnight born
> In Stygian cave forlorn
> 'Mongst horrid shapes, and shrieks, and sights
> unholy!
>
> MILTON: 'L'Allegro' (1645)

**Style.** The word goes back to Latin *stylus*, a metal pencil for writing on waxen tablets. The characteristic of someone's writing is thus called their style. Metaphorically, the term applies to composition and speech. Good writing is 'stylish', and, by extension, smartness of dress and deportment is so called.

> Style is the dress of thoughts, and well-dressed thought, like a well-dressed man, appears to great advantage.
>
> LORD CHESTERFIELD: *Letters*, clvi (1751)

**Style is the man, The.** A mistranslation of *Le style est l'homme même* ('Style is the man himself'), from the discourse of Georges Louis Leclerc, Comte de Buffon (1707–88) on his reception into the French Academy (1753).

**Do something in style, To.** *See under* DO.

**Empire style.** *See under* EMPIRE.

**New Style.** *See* STILO NOVO.

**Old Style.** *See under* OLD.

**Styles, Tom** or **John-A-Styles.** A name, like JOHN-A-NOKES, used as that of an imaginary plaintiff or defendant in a lawsuit, in the same way as John DOE and Richard Roe.

> And, like blind Fortune, with a sleight
> Convey men's interest and right
> From Stiles's pocket into Nokes's.
>
> SAMUEL BUTLER: *Hudibras*, III, iii (1680)

**Stylites** or **Pillar saints.** A class of ascetics found especially in Syria, Mesopotamia, Egypt and Greece between the 5th and 10th centuries. They established themselves on the tops of pillars, which were sometimes equipped with a small hut, from which they never descended. They take their name from St Simeon Stylites of Syria (390–459) who spent some 30 years on a pillar (Greek *stulos*) which was gradually raised to a height of 40 cubits. St Daniel, his best known disciple, was 33 years on a pillar near Constantinople. Tennyson has a poem on St Simeon Stylites.

> I, Simeon of the pillar, by surname
> Stylites, among men; I, Simeon,
> The watcher on the column to the end.
>
> ALFRED, LORD TENNYSON: 'St Simeon Stylites' (1842)

**Stymie.** A golfing term, officially obsolete since 1952. A player was laid a stymie if, on the putting green, the opponent's ball fell between the player and his path to the hole (providing the balls were not within 6in (15cm) of each other). To hole out could be achieved only by a difficult lofting stroke. Hence several still current expressions. A stymie is a frustrating situation or a discouragingly difficult position; to be stymied is to be in such a position; and to stymie is to hinder or thwart, also to oblige a person to negotiate. The origin of the word is unknown.

**Stymphalian Birds, The.** The long-legged, man-eating birds with bronze claws from Lake Stymphalus, ARCADIA, which were killed by HERCULES as his sixth labour.

**Styx.** The river of hate (Greek *stugein*, 'to hate'), called by Milton 'abhorred Styx, the flood of deadly hate' (*Paradise Lost*, ii (1667)). According to classical mythology, it flowed nine times around the infernal regions. Some say it was a river in ARCADIA whose waters were poisonous and dissolved any vessel put upon them. When a god swore falsely by the Styx, he was made to drink a draught of its water which made him lie speechless for a year. The river was said to take its name from Styx, the eldest daughter of OCEANUS and TETHYS, and wife of Pallas, by whom she had three daughters, Victory, Strength and Valour. *See also* ACHERON; CHARON.

**Sub** (Latin, 'under').

**Subfusc.** A term for formal academic dress at Oxford University, which students are required to wear at degree and matriculation ceremonies and examinations. For men it means a dark suit, dark socks and shoes, white shirt and white bow tie, and for women a white blouse, black tie, dark skirt or trousers, black stockings or tights and dark shoes. The word comes from Latin *suffuscus*, 'dark brown'.

**Sub hasta** (Latin, 'under the spear'). By auction. When an auction took place among the Romans, it was customary to stick a spear in the ground to give notice of it to the public.

**Sub Jove** (Latin, 'under Jove'). In the open air. JUPITER is the god of the upper regions of the air, as JUNO is of the lower regions, NEPTUNE of the waters of the sea, VESTA of the earth, CERES of the surface soil, and HADES of the invisible or underworld.

**Sub judice** (Latin, 'under a judge'). Under consideration; not yet decided in a court of law.

**Sub rosa** (Latin, 'under the rose'). In strict confidence. The origin of the phrase is obscure but the story is that CUPID gave HARPOCRATES (the god of silence) a rose to bribe him not to betray the amours of VENUS. Hence the flower became the emblem of silence and was sculptured on the ceilings of banquet rooms, to remind the guests that what was spoken *sub vino* was not to be repeated *sub divo* ('in the open air'). In the 16th century it was placed over confessionals.

**Subject. Broach a subject, To.** *See under* BROACH.

**Change the subject, To.** *See under* CHANGE.

**Sublapsarian** or **Infralapsarian.** A Calvinist who maintains that God devised the scheme of redemption after he had permitted the 'lapse' or fall of ADAM, when he elected some to salvation and left others to run their course. The Supralapsarian says that all this was ordained by God from the foundation of the world, and so before the 'lapse' of Adam.

**Sublime** (Latin *sublimis*, 'lofty', from *sub-* 'up to' and perhaps *limen*, 'lintel'). Noble or elevated in thought or tone.

**Sublime Porte, The.** *See* PORTE.

**From the sublime to the ridiculous.** *See under* FROM.

**Subpoena** (Latin, 'under penalty'). A writ commanding a person to appear in court, usually unwillingly, to bear witness or give evidence in a certain trial. It is so called because the party summoned is bound to appear *sub poena centum librorum* ('under a penalty of £100'). The verb is 'to subpoena'.

**Subsidy** (Latin *subsidere*, 'to sit down'). The *subsidii* of the Roman army were the troops held in reserve, the auxiliaries or supports, hence the word came to be applied to a support granted by Parliament to the king. It now usually applies to state aid in support of industries of public importance. 'Subsidiary', meaning auxiliary, is of the same origin.

**Subtle Doctor, The.** Duns Scotus. *See also* DUNCE.

**Subtopia.** A word coined (from 'suburb' and UTOPIA) by Ian Nairn to denote the sprawling suburban housing estates built to satisfy the town workers' yearning for country surroundings while clinging to the amenities of the town. The term includes all the paraphernalia of concrete posts, lamp standards, chain link fencing and other uglinesses associated with a disfigured landscape.

> There will be no real distinction between town and country. Both will consist of a limbo of shacks, bogus rusticities, wire and aerodromes, set in some fir-poled fields.... Upon this new Britain the *Review* bestows a name in the hope that it will stick – *Subtopia*.
>
> IAN NAIRN: *Architectural Review*, cxvii (1955)

**Suburb. Garden suburb.** *See under* GARDEN.

**Queen of the suburbs.** *See under* QUEEN.

**Succession, Apostolic.** *See under* APOSTOLIC.

**Succotash.** An American dish of green maize and beans boiled together. The name represents Narragansett *msiquatash*, literally 'broken pieces'.

**Succoth** or **Sukkoth** (Hebrew *sukkoth*, 'booths'). The Jewish name for the FEAST OF THE TABERNACLES.

**Succubus** (Medieval Latin masculine form of Late Latin *succuba*, 'harlot', from *succubare*, 'to lie under'). A female demon fabled to have sexual intercourse with sleeping men. *See also* INCUBUS.

**Suck. Sucked in, To be.** To be involved against one's will, as if drawn in by a whirlpool.

**Sucker.** An easy victim; a dupe, perhaps so called from the idea of an unweaned creature. But the allusion could equally be to the fish called a sucker as it easily caught, sucking up almost any bait offered to it.

**Sucking pig.** A pig not yet weaned, especially one fed on milk and suitable for roasting whole as a former delicacy. Such a pig was originally called a roasting pig.

**Suck it and see.** Said of anything experimental. The allusion is to a pill, which one has to suck to see if it will work.

**Sucks!** An exclamation of disappointment or defiance. In the latter case it is sometimes elaborated on the lines of 'Yah booh sucks to you'.

**Suck the monkey, To.** Among the Dutch drinking is called 'sucking the monkey', because the early morning appetizer of rum and salt was taken in a MONKEY SPOON. In sailor's slang 'to suck the monkey' is to suck liquor from a cask through a straw, and when milk has been taken from a coconut, and rum has been substituted, 'sucking the monkey' is drinking this rum.

> Besides, what the vulgar call 'sucking the monkey'
> Has much less effect on a man when he's funky.
>
> R.H. BARHAM: *Ingoldsby Legends*, 'The Black Mousquetaire', II (1840)

**Suck up, To.** To behave obsequiously; to be a TOADY or creep.

**Bear sucking his paws, A.** *See under* BEAR.

**Teach one's grandmother to suck eggs, To.** *See under* TEACH.

**Sudarium.** A cloth for wiping the face, from Latin *sudor*, 'sweat'. The word is an alternative term for the VERONICA and is applied also by some theologians to the napkin that had been on Christ's head in the tomb and that was found by the disciples 'not lying with the linen clothes, but wrapped together in a place by itself' (John 20:7).

The cathedral of Oviedo in northern Spain claims to hold the original. Accounts of its acquisition are varied, but it is known that when in 1075 a chest containing relics was opened by King Alfonso VI of León and Castile it contained an object listed as 'the holy sudarium of Our Lord Jesus Christ'. It has been subjected to scientific examination, and pollen samples confirm its Palestinian origins. More significantly, bloodstains on it coincide with the marks on the TURIN SHROUD (*see under* FAKES) and the blood comes from the same group, AB. If the conclusions on the bloodstains and the pollen are solid, they could thus cast doubt on the dating of the Shroud to between 1260 and 1390 and suggest that it could be substantially earlier.

**Suède.** Undressed kidskin, so called because the gloves made of this originally came from Sweden (French *gants de Suède*).

**Suffolk. Suffolk punch.** A short-legged, sturdy, thickset cart horse. The term was formerly applied to any short fat man, and is probably a dialect variant of 'bunch'.

> [I] did hear them call their fat child Punch, which pleased me mightily, that word being become a word of common use for everything that is thick and short.
>
> SAMUEL PEPYS: *Diary* (30 April 1669)

**Silly Suffolk.** *See under* SILLY.

**Suffragan.** An auxiliary bishop, one who has not a see of his own but is appointed to assist a bishop in a portion of his see. In relation to a METROPOLITAN or archbishop all bishops are suffragans. They were so called because they could be summoned to a synod to give their SUFFRAGE.

**Suffrage.** A person's vote, approval or consent, or right to vote, especially at parliamentary and municipal elections. The word is from Latin *suffragium*, 'voting tablet', perhaps from *suffrago*, the hock or anklebone of a horse, which may have been used by the Romans for balloting. *See also* BEANS; CALCULATE.

**Suffragettes.** Militant women who agitated for the parliamentary vote in the early years of the 20th century. *See also* CAT AND MOUSE ACT.

**Sugar. Sugar daddy.** A rich, middle-aged or elderly man who lavishes expensive gifts on a much younger woman. The expression is of American origin.

**Barley sugar.** *See under* SUGAR.

**Sui. Sui generis** (Latin, 'of its own kind'). Having a distinct character of its own; unlike anything else.

**Sui juris** (Latin, 'of one's own right'). Able to exercise one's legal rights, i.e. freed from legal disability.

**Suicide** (Latin *sui*, 'of oneself', and *-cidium*, from *caedere*, 'to kill'). Until 1823 a suicide was buried at the CROSSROADS with a stake thrust through the body.

**Suit.** A colloquial term for a business executive, who traditionally wears a suit.

> Suits uttering death threats if copy was lost worked alongside anoraks with the new skill of surfing the net.
>
> *The Times* (18 September 1998)

**Suit one down to the ground, To.** To be perfectly fitting, like a well-tailored garment.

**Birthday suit, To.** *See under* BIRTHDAY.

**Follow suit, To.** *See under* FOLLOW.

**Friendly suit.** *See under* FRIENDLY.

**Jump suit.** *See under* JUMP.

**Long suit.** *See under* LONG.

**Shell suit.** *See under* SHELL.

**Safari suit.** *See under* SAFARI.

**Siren suit.** *See under* SIREN.

**Sunday suit.** *See under* SUNDAY.

**Sukkoth.** *See* SUCCOTH.

**Sultan** (Arabic, 'rule'). Until 1923 the title of the ruler of the former Turkish Empire and, until 1957, of the king of Morocco. It is still in use in certain Islamic states, such as Oman and Brunei. The wife (also mother or daughter) of the sultan is called a sultana, a term also applied to a concubine.

> While Charles flirted with his three sultanas, Hortensia's French page, a handsome boy, whose vocal performances were the delight of Whitehall, ... warbled some amorous verses.
>
> LORD MACAULAY: *History of England*, ch iv (1849)

Sultana is also the name of a seedless raisin, a form of necklace worn by women in the latter half of the 18th century and an old musical instrument like a zither. Sultan also denotes a small white-crested variety of domestic hen, originally brought from Turkey.

**Summer.** The warmest season of the year, in Britain traditionally regarded as the months of June, July and August, but astronomically from the summer SOLSTICE to the autumn EQUINOX (about 22 September).

> Sumer is icumen in,
> Lhude sing cuccu!
> Groweth sed, and bloweth med [meadow]
> And springeth the wude nu.
>
> ANONYMOUS: 'Cuckoo Song' (*c*.1250)

St LUKE's summer is a period of mild weather around mid-October, St Luke's Day being 18 October. *See also* ALL HALLOWS SUMMER; INDIAN SUMMER; St MARTIN'S SUMMER.

**Summer pudding.** A sweet course of soft summer fruit encased in bread or sponge.

**Summer time.** The idea of making fuller use of the hours of daylight by advancing the clock originated with Benjamin Franklin (1706–90), but its introduction was due to its advocacy from 1907 by William Willett (1856–1915), a Chelsea builder. It was adopted in 1916 in Germany, then in Britain as a wartime measure, when clocks were advanced by one hour. In Britain it became permanent by an Act of 1925. Summer Time began on the day following the third Saturday in April, unless that was Easter Day, in which case it was the day following the second Saturday in April. It ended on the day following the first Saturday in October. In 1961 Summer Time was extended by six weeks, beginning March and ending in October, and similar extensions were made in 1962 and subsequent years. During the Second World War it ran from 25 February to 31 December in 1940 and from 1 January in the four years from 1941. In 1945 it ended in October. Double Summer Time (i.e. two hours in advance of GMT instead of one) was in force from 1941 to 1945 and in 1947 to save fuel. After the war Summer Time was in force in the years from 1948 to 1952 and 1961 to 1964. From 27 October 1968 until 31 October 1971 clocks were kept one hour ahead of GMT continuously. This was known as British Standard Time (BST). The most recent legislation is the Summer Time Act of 1972, which enacted that Summer Time should begin at 2 o'clock GMT in the morning of the day after the third Saturday in March or, if that is Easter Day, the day after the second Saturday in March, and that it should end at 2 o'clock GMT in the morning of the day after the fourth Saturday in October. Since the Second World War a number of other countries have adopted some form of Summer Time. *See also* GREENWICH TIME.

**Indian summer.** *See under* INDIAN.

**Long hot summer.** *See under* LONG.

**St Martin's summer.** *See under* MARTIN.

**Summum bonum** (Latin, 'the highest good'). The chief excellence; the highest attainable good. The STOIC school held that virtue and its attainment was the highest end. SOCRATES said knowledge is virtue, and ignorance is vice. ARISTOTLE said that happiness is the greatest good.

Bernard de Mandeville (1670–1733) and Claude-Adrien Helvétius (1715–71) contended that self-interest is the perfection of the ethical end. Jeremy Bentham (1748–1832) and John Stuart Mill (1806–73) were for the greatest happiness of the greatest number. Herbert Spencer (1820–1903) placed it in those actions that best tend to the survival of the individual and the race, and Robert Browning had a more personal realization:

> All the breath and bloom of the year in the bag of one bee:
> All the wonder and wealth of the mine in the heart of one gem:
> In the core of one pearl all the shade and the shine of the sea:
> Breath and bloom, shade and shine, – wonder, wealth, and – how far above them –
> Truth, that's brighter than gem,
> Truth, that's purer than pearl, –
> Brightest truth, purest trust in the universe – all were for me
> In the kiss of one girl.
>
> ROBERT BROWNING: *Asolando*, 'Summum Bonum' (1889)

**Sumptuary laws.** Laws to limit the expenses of food and dress or any luxury. The Romans had their *leges sumptuarii*, and they have been enacted in many states at various times. Those of England were all repealed by I James I, c.25, but during the two World Wars, with the rationing of food, coal and so on, and the compulsory lowering of the strength of beer and whisky, there was a temporary return to sumptuary legislation.

**Sun.** The source of light and heat, and consequently of life to the whole world, hence regarded as a deity and worshipped as such by all primitive peoples and having a leading place in their mythologies. Shamash was the principal sun god of the Assyrians and Babylonians, MITHRAS of the Persians, RA of the Egyptians, Tezcatlipoca ('smoking mirror') of the Aztecs, HELIOS of the Greeks, known to the Romans as SOL and usually identified with PHOEBUS and APOLLO.

**Sunbelt** or **Sun Belt, The.** The southern states of the USA, which have more sun than the northern. The name implies not merely a favourable climate, but a high standard of living, a high population density and generally conservative attitudes.

> That growth of small towns is distributed from region to region but national in scope: it is highest in the Sun Belt states of the West and South, lowest in the Middle West, but steady and substantial even in the Northeast, where the big cities are losing population.
>
> *Newsweek* (6 July 1981)

**Sundance Kid, The.** The byname of the American outlaw Harry Longabaugh or Longbaugh (1870–*c.*1909), famed as the best shot and fastest gun-slinger of the Wild Bunch, a group of robbers and rustlers who ranged through the Rocky Mountains in the late 19th century. He took his name from the town where he was imprisoned in 1887–9 for stealing a horse. He later teamed up with the outlaw Butch Cassidy, otherwise Robert LeRoy Parker (1866–*c.*1909). After a career robbing banks, trains and mine stations, with the law in full pursuit, the two lived mainly in South America, where (according to one theory) they were trapped and killed.

**Sundowner.** Old Australian slang for a tramp. In the early days the name was used for someone who went from one settlement to another arriving at sundown, so it is said, to be too late for work, but in time for food. In Africa and India, a sundowner denotes a drink taken just after sundown, and in the USA, an official who works late at the office.

**Sun is over the yardarm, The.** An expression among naval officers and others indicating that the time has come to have a drink. In home waters and northern latitudes the sun would be over the yardarm towards noon.

**Sun King, The** (French *Le Roi Soleil*). Louis XIV of France. The name alludes to the general 'brilliance' of his long reign (1643–1715), which saw a flowering of the arts and the building of VERSAILLES.

**Sunny side.** The more cheerful aspect of things; the optimistic side of one's nature. A fried egg served sunny side up is cooked on one side only, i.e. without being flipped over.

> Keep your sunny side up.
>
> LEW BROWN and BUDDY DE SYLVA: 'Sunny Side Up' (song title) (1929)

**Sun of Righteousness, The.** Jesus Christ (Malachi 4:2).

**Sunshine State.** A name for any of the US states California, Florida, New Mexico or South Dakota. *See also* UNITED STATES OF AMERICA.

**Catch the sun, To.** *See under* CATCH.

**City of the Sun, The.** *See under* CITY.

**Cycle of the sun.** *See under* CYCLE.

**Empire on which the sun never sets, The.** *See under* EMPIRE.

**Heaven cannot support two suns, nor earth two masters.** *See under* HEAVEN.

**Place in the sun, A.** *See under* PLACE.

**Shoot the sun, To.** *See under* SHOOT.

**Southern gate of the sun, The.** *See under* SOUTH.

**Under the sun.** *See under* UNDER.

**Sunday** (Old English *sunnandæg*). For centuries the first day of the week, anciently dedicated to the sun, but in many modern diaries and calendars, the seventh day. *See also* DAYS OF THE WEEK; SABBATH.

**Sunday best** or **suit.** One's best clothes, as worn on Sundays for churchgoing.

**Sunday driver.** A motorist who drives mainly at weekends, especially one going slowly or uncertainly.

**Sunday letters.** *See* DOMINICAL LETTERS.

**Sunday painter.** An amateur artist; a dilettante who paints only as a hobby.

**Sunday punch.** In boxing, a heavy blow, intended to knock out one's opponent.

**Sunday roast.** A traditional Sunday lunch, with roast beef, Yorkshire pudding, Brussels sprouts, roast potatoes, gravy and the like, with a decent pudding to follow.

**Sunday saint.** One who observes the ordinances of religion, and goes to church on a Sunday, but is worldly, grasping, 'indifferent honest', the other six days.

**Sunday school.** Classes for children organized by church and chapel for a fairly short time on Sundays for religious instruction. Actual schools were first established in the 18th century to teach working-class children their letters in order that they might learn to read the Bible, to improve their behaviour through moral instruction and to keep them off the streets all day. The movement gained considerable impetus when Robert Raikes (1735–1811) founded his school in Gloucester in 1780 and William Fox set up the Sunday School Society in 1785. Sunday schools became particularly strong in Wales.

**Advent Sunday.** *See under* ADVENT.

**Bloody Sunday.** *See under* BLOODY.

**Cantate Sunday.** *See under* CANTATE.

**Care Sunday.** *See under* CARE.

**Fig Sunday.** *See under* FIG.

**Hospital Sunday.** *See under* HOSPITAL.

**Jubilate Sunday.** *See under* JUBILATE.

**Judica Sunday.** *See under* JUDICA.

**Laetare Sunday.** *See under* LAETARE.

**Lost Sunday.** *See under* LOST.

**Low Sunday.** *See under* LOW.

**Mid-Lent Sunday.** *See under* MID-LENT.

**Month of Sundays, A.** *See under* MONTH.

**Orthodox Sunday.** *See under* ORTHODOX.

**Palm Sunday.** *See under* PALM.

**Refreshment Sunday.** *See* MID-LENT SUNDAY.

**Remembrance Sunday.** *See* REMEMBRANCE DAY.

**Rose Sunday.** *See under* ROSE.

**Rush-bearing Sunday.** *See under* RUSH.

**Septuagesima Sunday.** *See under* SEPTUAGESIMA.

**Sexagesima Sunday.** *See under* SEXAGESIMA.

**Stir-up Sunday.** *See under* STIR.

**Tap-up Sunday.** *See under* TAP.

**Trinity Sunday.** *See under* TRINITY.

**Week of Sundays.** *See under* WEEK.

**Whit Sunday.** *See under* WHITSUN.

**Sundial, The Shepherd's.** *See under* SHEPHERD.

**Sundry, All and.** *See under* ALL.

**Sunflower State, The.** Kansas, where these flowers grow in profusion. *See also* UNITED STATES OF AMERICA.

**Sunna** (Arabic, 'rule'). The traditional sayings and example of MOHAMMED and his immediate followers, as set forth in the HADITH.

**Sunnis** or **Sunnites.** Orthodox Muslims who consider the SUNNA as authentic as the KORAN itself and acknowledge the first four CALIPHS to be the rightful successors of MOHAMMED. They form by far the largest section of Muslims. *See also* SHI'ITES.

**Sunningdale.** The residential district in Berkshire, southwest of Staines, has long been associated with stockbrokers and similar City types, some of whom avail themselves of the pleasures of the golf course here. The Civil Service College here was the venue of the Sunningdale Agreement of 1973, signed between the British and Irish governments for the setting-up of a power-sharing executive in Northern Ireland.

**Sunset. Sunset Boulevard.** A broad and handsome street in downtown Los Angeles, so called as it runs from the city centre westward to the Pacific. The section of the street to the west of HOLLYWOOD is known as the Sunset Strip, and is the centre of the city's night life. *Sunset Boulevard* is also the name of a successful romantic film of 1950 and of Andrew Lloyd Webber's musical of 1993 based on it.

**Sunset gun.** *See* EVENING GUN.

**Supererogation, Works of.** *See under* WORK.

**Superman.** A hypothetical superior human being of high intellectual and moral attainment, fancied as evolved from the normally existing type. The term (*Übermensch*) was invented by the German philosopher Friedrich Nietzsche (1844–1900), and was popularized in England by George Bernard Shaw's play, *Man and Superman* (1903).

In the world of American comics, Superman is one of the most popular heroes. He can fly, he is invulnerable, he has X-ray vision, and he can move mountains single-handed. He is a refugee from the planet Krypton, and by day is the mild-mannered human newspaper reporter Clark Kent. When the occasion requires, however, he changes from his sober suit and spectacles into his blue tights and red cape and is 'up, up and away', soaring into the sky. He is the creation of two juvenile science fiction fans, Jerome Siegel and Joe Schuster, who first devised him in the 1930s. He has appeared in several films and a radio and television series, and there has even been a musical, *It's a Bird, It's a Plane, It's Superman* (a catchphrase from the radio series), turned into a television movie (1975).

The wide popularity of the term gave rise to many compounds, such as superwoman, superstar, supermodel and the like.

**Supernaculum.** The very best wine. The word is sham Latin for 'upon the nail' (German *auf den Nagel*), meaning that the wine is so good the drinker leaves only enough in his glass to make a bead on his nail. The French say of first-class wine, *Faire rubis sur l'ongle* ('to make a ruby on the nail'). Thomas Nashe, in *Pierce Penilesse* (1592), says that after a man had drunk his glass, it was usual, in the north, to turn the cup upside down, and let a drop fall on the thumbnail. If the drop rolled off, the drinker was obliged to fill and drink again. *See also* ON THE NAIL.

**Supper. Bump suppers.** *See under* BUMP.

**Last Supper, The.** *See under* LAST.

**Lord's Supper, The.** *See under* LORD.

**Supply. Supplies.** In parliamentary parlance, the various grants and moneys authorized annually by Parliament other than those paid out of the CONSOLIDATED FUND or permitted by an act during the session.

**Law of supply and demand, The.** *See under* LAW.

**Supralapsarian.** *See* SUBLAPSARIAN.

**Sure. As sure as eggs is eggs.** *See under* AS.

**As sure as God made little apples.** *See under* AS.

**As sure as God's in Gloucestershire.** *See under* AS.

**Slow but sure.** *See under* SLOW.

**Surface, To scratch the.** *See under* SCRATCH.

**Surfeit water.** An old name for a 'water' used to cure 'surfeits', i.e. the effects of gluttony. Hannah GLASSE's 18th-century recipe requires 4 gallons (18 litres) of brandy and 27 other ingredients, mostly herbs. This surfeit water was drunk from special tapering fluted glasses, and the dose of this highly alcoholic pick-me-up was two spoonfuls.

**Surgeon.** Literally a 'hand-worker', from Greek *kheir*, 'hand' and *ergon*, 'work'

**Surloin.** *See* SIRLOIN.

**Surly dog, A.** A sour-tempered fellow. 'Dog' is often used for 'chap' or 'fellow' as in a 'dull dog' and GAY DOG. Surly itself relates to 'sir', as a term for a haughty person.

**Surname.** The name added to, or given over and above, the Christian name (Old French *sur-*, from Latin *super-*, 'over', 'above'). Surnames, as names passed from father to son, were not widespread until the 13th century, and grew from the custom of adding the place of domicile or provenance, trade or some descriptive characteristic, to the Christian name to assist identification, e.g. York, Butcher, Large and Russell (red-haired). Yet another category derives from family relationship, e.g. Williamson, Fitzmaurice, Macgregor and O'Brien.

**Surplice.** A garment originally worn over the *pelisse* or fur robe, from Latin *superpellicium*, from *pellis*, 'skin'. The name passed to the white linen vestment worn by clergy, acolytes and choristers, so fashioned for its ease of wearing over fur dress in northern Europe in medieval times. The shorter cotta is a development from this.

**Surplice fees.** The fees for marriage and burials which are the right of the incumbent of a BENEFICE, whoever performs the service.

With tithes his barns replete he sees,
And chuckles o'er his surplice fees.
THOMAS WARTON: 'The Progress of Discontent' (1750)

**Surrealism.** A movement in art and the literary world that began in 1924 and that flourished between the two World Wars under the leadership of the poet André Breton (1896–1966). In painting it falls into two groups: hand-painted dream scenes as exemplified by Giorgio de Chirico (1888–1978), Salvador Dali (1904–89) and René Magritte (1898–1967), and the creation of abstract forms by the practice of complete spontaneity of technique as well as subject matter by the use of contrast as with Jean Arp (1888–1966), Man Ray (1890–1977), Joan Miró (1893–1983) and Dali. They sought to express thought uncontrolled by reason and aesthetic and moral concepts. *See also* CUBISM; DADAISM; FAUVISM; FUTURISM; IMPRESSIONISM; ORPHISM; SYNCHROMISM; VORTICISM.

**Surrey, White.** *See under* WHITE.

**Survey, Ordnance.** *See under* ORDNANCE.

**Susan, Lazy.** *See under* LAZY.

**Susanna and the Elders.** *See* DANIEL.

**Sutras** (Sanskrit *sutra*, 'a thread'). In Sanskrit literature, certain aphoristic writings giving the rules of systems of philosophy, grammar and the like, and in Brahmanic use, directions concerning religious ritual and ceremonial customs that are part of the VEDAS. *See also* KAMASUTRA.

**Suttee** (Sanskrit *satī*, 'virtuous wife'). The former Hindu custom of the widow immolating herself on the funeral pyre of her deceased husband; also, the widow so dying. Women with child and mothers of children not yet of age could not perform suttee. Suttee was prohibited in British India by Lord William Bentinck in 1829, but continued as late as 1877 in Nepal. *See also* THUG.

> After having bathed in the river, the widow lighted a brand, walked round the pile, set it on fire, and then mounted cheerfully: the flame caught and blazed up instantly; she sat down, placing the head of the corpse on her lap, and repeated several times the usual form, 'Ram, Ram, Suttee; Ram, Ram, Suttee'.
>
> FANNY PARKES: *Wanderings of a Pilgrim in Search of the Picturesque*, Bk I (1850)

**Sutton Hoo Treasure.** An Anglo-Saxon ship burial of the early 7th century, discovered at Sutton Hoo near Woodbridge, Suffolk, in 1939. It is one of the richest ever found and the treasure, consisting of a sword and sheath, helmet, bowls and other objects in precious metals, is now in the British Museum. The find is of considerable archaeological and historical importance.

**Svengali.** The villain of George du Maurier's bestselling novel *Trilby* (1894). He is a musician of purportedly Hungarian Jewish origin who exercises his sinister powers over the story's heroine, the young singer TRILBY.

**Swaddlers.** An early nickname for Wesleyans, and applied later by Roman Catholics to DISSENTERS and PROTESTANTS generally. Southey (*Life of Wesley*, ii (1820)) explains its origin as follows:

> It happened that Cennick, preaching on Christmas Day, took for his text these words from St Luke's Gospel: 'And this shall be a sign unto you; ye shall find the babe wrapped in swaddling clothes lying in a manger.' A Catholic who was present, and to whom the language of scripture was a novelty, thought this so ridiculous that he called the preacher a swaddler in derision, and this unmeaning word became a nickname for 'Protestant', and had all the effect of the most opprobrious appellation.

**Swag** (perhaps connected with Norwegian *svagga*, 'to sway'). One's goods carried in a pack or bundle, hence the booty obtained from a burglary, often carried away in a sack.

**Swagger** (probably from SWAG). To strut about with a superior air; to bluster, make oneself out a very important person; hence, ostentatiously smart or SWELL, as 'a swagger dinner', 'a swagger car' etc, although this adjectival use is now rare.

**Swagger stick.** The small cane a soldier was formerly obliged to carry when walking out, and now a similar stick carried on certain occasions by army officers.

**Swagman.** The Australian term for the numerous itinerant labourers who tramped from sheep station to sheep station in former times carrying their 'swag' (bundle of clothes, blankets etc), seeking employment from the squatters. *See also* SUNDOWNER.

> And you think of the days out on the track when you and Tom sat on your swags under a mulga at midday, and ate mutton and johnny-cake with clasp-knives, and drank by turns out of the old, battered, leaky billy.
>
> HENRY LAWSON: *On the Track*, 'Meeting Old Mates' (1900)

**Swallow** (noun). According to Scandinavian tradition, this bird hovered over the cross of Christ crying '*Svala! svala!*' ('Console! console!'), whence it was called *svalow* ('bird of consolation').

Aelian says that the swallow was sacred to the *penates* (*see* LARES AND PENATES) or household gods, and therefore to injure one would be to bring wrath upon your own house. It is still considered a sign of good luck if a swallow or martin builds under the eaves of one's house.

> Perhaps you fail'd in your fore-seeing skill,
> For *Swallows* are unlucky birds to kill.
>
> JOHN DRYDEN: *The Hind and the Panther*, Pt III (1687)

Longfellow refers to another old fable regarding this bird:

Oft in the barns they climbed to the populous nests on the rafters,
Seeking with eager eyes that wondrous stone, which the swallow
Brings from the shore of the sea to restore the sight of its fledglings;
Lucky was he who found that stone in the nest of the swallow!
*Evangeline*, Pt I (1849)

**One swallow does not make a summer.** *See under* ONE.

**Swallow** (verb). **Swallow the anchor, To.** A sailor is said to do so when he retires from the sea.

**Swan.** The fable that the swan sings beautifully just before it dies is very ancient, but baseless. The only one for which a song of any kind can be claimed is the whistling swan (*Cygnus musicus*). The superstition was credited by Plato, Aristotle, Euripides, Cicero, Seneca, Martial and others, and doubted by Pliny and Aelian. Shakespeare refers to it more than once. Emilia, just before she dies, says:

I will play the swan,
And die in music.
*Othello*, V, ii (1604)

Edmund Spenser speaks of the swan as a bird that sings:

He, were he not with loue so ill bedight [stricken]
Would mount as high, and sing as soote [sweetly] as Swanne.
*Shepheardes Calender*, 'October', (1579)

S.T. Coleridge ('Epigram on a Volunteer Singer' (1809)), referring to poetasters of the time, gives the old superstition an epigrammatic turn:

Swans sing before they die; 'twere no bad thing
Did certain persons die before they sing.

One Greek legend has it that the soul of APOLLO, the god of music, passed into a swan, hence the Pythagorean fable that the souls of all good poets passed into swans. *See also* SWAN OF AVON, SWAN OF MANTUA etc.

The male swan is called a cob, the female a pen and a young swan a cygnet. *See also* FIONNUALA; LEDA; LOHENGRIN.

**Swan about** or **around, To.** To move around aimlessly. A phrase popular among troops in the Second World War to describe a tank moving apparently aimlessly across the battlefield, like a swan swimming idly about the waters or meandering with others in an aimless convoy. The tank's long gun barrel additionally evokes the bird's long neck.

**Swan maidens.** Fairies of northern folklore, who can become maidens or swans at will by means of the swan shift, a magic garment of swan's feathers. Many stories are told of how the swan shift was stolen, and the FAIRY was obliged to remain in thrall to the thief until rescued by a knight.

**Swan of Avon, The.** Shakespeare was so called by Ben Jonson in allusion to his birthplace at Stratford-upon-Avon and the legend that APOLLO was changed into a swan.

**Swan of Lichfield, The.** The name given to the poet Anna Seward (1747–1809).

**Swan of Mantua, The.** VIRGIL, who was born at Mantua.

**Swan of Meander, The.** HOMER, who is said to have lived on the banks of the Meander.

**Swan of Usk, The.** Henry Vaughan, the SILURIST (1622–95), was so called, having given one of his volumes of verse this name: *Olor Iscanus* ('Swan of Usk' (1651)).

**Swan song.** The song fabled to be sung by a dying swan, so the last work or appearance of a poet, composer, actor or the like.

**Swan-upping.** A taking up of swans and placing the marks of ownership on their beaks. The term is specially applied to annual expeditions for this purpose up the River Thames, when the marks of the owners, i.e. the crown and the Dyers' and Vintners' Companies, are made. The royal swans are marked with five nicks, two lengthways and three across the bill, and the companies' swans with two nicks.

**Swan with Two Necks, The.** An old tavern sign, said to be a corruption of 'two nicks' with which the Vintners' Company mark the beaks of their swans. In coaching days, the Swan with Two Necks in Lad Lane (now Gresham Street) was the chief London departure point for the north. *See also* SWAN-UPPING.

**All one's swans are geese.** *See under* ALL.

**Dircaean Swan.** *See under* DIRCAEAN.

**Knight of the Swan, The.** LOHENGRIN.

**Order of the Swan, The.** *See under* ORDER.

**Swap** or **change horses in midstream, To.** To change leaders at the height of a crisis. Abraham Lincoln, in an address of 9 June 1864, referring to the fact that his fellow Republicans had renominated him for President, even though many were dissatisfied with his conduct of the Civil War (1861–5), said that the Convention had concluded 'that it is best not to swap horses while crossing the river'.

**Swashbuckler.** A ruffian; a swaggerer. 'From swashing,' says Thomas Fuller (*Worthies*, III (1662)), 'and making a noise on the buckler.' The sword players used to 'swash' or tap their shield as fencers rap their foot on the ground when they attack.

**Swastika.** The GAMMADION or FYLFOT, an elaborate cross-shaped design used as a charm to ward off evil and bring good luck. It was adopted by Hitler as the NAZI emblem about 1920, probably from the German Baltic Corps, who wore it on their helmets after service in Finland, where it was used as a distinguishing mark on Finnish aeroplanes. The word is from Sanskrit *svasti*, 'good fortune'.

> The swastika was used in such a way that it represented something more than itself: a relic of an Aryan culture, peculiarly German and Indian and possessing special and exclusive virtues.
>
> PETER CALVOCORESSI in *Times Literary Supplement* (review of Malcolm Quinn, *The Swastika*) (16 December 1994)

**Swear. Swear black and blue, To.** To assert vigorously and emphatically.

**Swear black is white, To.** To swear to any falsehood no matter how glaring.

**Swear blind, To.** To affirm emphatically.

**Swearing on the horns.** In public houses at Highgate it was once customary to administer an oath to travellers who called. A pair of horns mounted on a pole was brought in, the person to be sworn placed his right hand on one of the horns, and after a call for 'Silence!' the landlord proceeded to deliver his charge: 'You must not eat brown bread while you can get white, except you like brown the best. You must not drink small beer while you can get strong, except [etc]. You must not kiss the maid while you can kiss the mistress, except you like the maid the best, or have the chance to kiss them both.' Then finally: 'And now, my son, kiss the horns, or a pretty girl if you see one here, and so be free of Highgate'.

**Swear like a trooper, To.** To indulge in blasphemy or profanity, as a soldier sometimes does.

**Swear to.** Originally used only for solemn affirmations by the invocation of God or some sacred personage, hence to take an oath. The word was later extended to profanities and bad language through the use of sacred expressions as intensives and expletives.

**Sweat. Sweat a coin, To.** To shake up gold and silver coins to remove particles of metal from them without the diminution of weight being noticeable.

**Sweat blood, To.** To work very hard.

**Sweater girl, A.** A dated term for a young woman with a generous bust, which is made apparent by the wearing of a tight sweater.

**Sweating sickness.** A fatal disease characterized by its symptoms: the onset of shivers followed by intense sweating, which formerly brought death in a few hours. It first appeared in England in 1485, and the last outbreak was in 1551. Although infrequent in its occurrence (five visitations in all), the mortality was considerable. *See also* BLACK DEATH.

**Sweatshop.** A workshop where employees work long hours under poor conditions for low pay.

**Blood, toil, tears and sweat.** *See under* BLOOD.

**Cold sweat.** *See under* COLD.

**Old sweat, An.** *See under* OLD.

**Swedenborgians.** Followers of the Swedish scientist and mystic Emanuel Swedenborg (1688–1772), who in middle life came to hold himself appointed to reveal Christ's teachings to mankind. He taught that Christ is the one God and that the Divine Trinity was present in him. The New Jerusalem Church or New Church was set up in England in 1787 to propagate his teachings, which differ considerably from those of accepted Christianity. There are branches of the New Church in the USA, Australia, New Zealand as well as in Europe. Swedenborg wrote all his works in Latin and claimed to have witnessed the Last Judgement.

**Swedish Nightingale, The.** The operatic singer Jenny Lind (1820–87), afterwards Mme Goldschmidt. She was born in Stockholm.

**Sweep. Sweep the board, To.** In gaming, to win everything, to pocket all the stakes. Hence applied to someone who wins all the prizes.

**Sweep the deck, To.** To clear off all the stakes.

**Sweep under the carpet, To.** To conceal or put something out of sight so that it will not be noticed, to try and forget unpleasant difficulties or realities.

**Make a clean sweep, To.** *See under* CLEAN.

**New brooms sweep clean.** *See under* NEW.

**Sweepstakes.** A race in which stakes are made by the owners of horses engaged, to be awarded to the winner or other horse in the race. Entrance money has to be paid to the race fund. If the horse runs, the full stake must be paid, but if it is withdrawn, a forfeit only is imposed.

The term is also used for a gambling arrangement in which a number of persons stake money on some event (usually a horse race), each of whom draws a lot for every share bought, the total sum deposited being divided among the drawers of winners (or sometimes of starters). The allusion is to someone who sweeps or takes all the stakes in a game.

**Sweet. Sweet Fanny Adams, Sweet FA** or **SFA.** The phrase, meaning 'nothing at all' or 'sweet nothing', is of tragic origin. In 1867 eight-year-old Fanny Adams was raped and murdered in a hop garden at Alton, Hampshire, and her body dismembered. A 21-year-old solicitor's clerk, Frederick Baker, was tried soon after and hanged at Winchester. The Royal Navy, with grim humour, adopted her name as a synonym for tinned mutton, which was first issued at this time. Sweet Fanny Adams became, as a consequence, a phrase for anything worthless and then for 'nothing at all'. The 'F' of the initials is often taken as the 'F-word'. *See* FOUR-LETTER WORD.

**Sweetheart agreement** or **deal.** In industry, an agreement reached privately between employers and trade unions in their own interests.

**Sweetness and light.** A phrase much favoured by Matthew Arnold, particularly in his *Culture and Anarchy* (ch v (1869)):

> What we want is a fuller harmonious development of our humanity, a free play of thought upon our routine notions, spontaneity of consciousness, sweetness and light, and these are just what culture generates.

The phrase was used earlier by Jonathan Swift in BATTLE OF THE BOOKS (1704) in an imaginary fable by AESOP as to the merits of the bee (the ancients) and the spider (the moderns). The Preface concludes:

> The difference is that instead of dirt and poison, we have rather chosen to fill our hives with honey and wax, thus furnishing mankind with the two noblest of things, which are sweetness and light.

**Sweet on, To be.** To be in love with; to be infatuated by.

**Sweet singer of Israel, The.** King DAVID, traditional author of the PSALMS.

**Sweet william.** An old English garden flower, *Dianthus barbatus*, a member of the pink family. The name dates from the 16th century.

**Have a sweet tooth, To.** To be very fond of dainties and sweet things generally.

**Home, sweet home.** *See under* HOME.

**Keep someone sweet, To.** To ingratiate oneself in order ensure the other's cooperation.

**Short and sweet.** *See under* SHORT.

**Stolen sweets are always sweeter.** *See under* STEAL.

**Swell.** A somewhat dated term for a showily dressed person, one who puffs himself out beyond his proper dimensions, like the frog in the fable; hence, a fashionable person, one of high standing or importance. In American usage as an adjective, 'swell' means fine, stylish, first rate, just right. *See also* POSH.

**Swelled** or **swollen head.** An inflated sense of one's own dignity, usefulness, importance or the like.

**Swell out like the Mazikeen ass, To.** The allusion is to a Jewish tradition that a servant, whose task it was to rouse the neighbourhood to midnight prayer, one night mounted a stray ass and neglected his duty. As he rode along the ass grew bigger and bigger, until it finally towered as high as the tallest edifice, where it left the man, and there next morning he was found. *See also* MAZIKEEN.

**Ground swell.** *See under* GROUND.

**Swifties, Tom.** *See under* TOM.

**Swim. Swim with the stream** or **tide, To.** To allow one's actions and principles to be guided solely by the force of prevailing public opinion.

**In the swim.** In a favourable position in society of any kind; involved with what is going on. The phrase is from angling. A number of fish gathered together is called a swim, and when an angler can cast his line in such a place he is said to be 'in a good swim'.

**Sink or swim.** *See under* SINK.

**Swindle.** To cheat, defraud or gain a mean advantage by trickery. The verb is formed from the noun 'swindler', which was introduced into England by German Jews about 1760, from German *Schwindler*, a cheating company promoter (from *schwindeln*, 'to lie', 'to deceive').

**Swine, Gadarene.** *See under* GADARENE.

**Swing.** With reference to JAZZ, swing is solo or ensemble playing over a regular pulse beat in such a way as to give the impression of a 'swinging' (forward-moving) rhythmic momentum. 'To swing' is to play jazz music in this particular way and the term, although not new, gained a wide currency in the early 1930s from a popular number beginning: 'It don't mean a thing if it ain't got that swing.' *See also* BOOGIE-WOOGIE; RAGTIME.

**Swing a ship, To.** To check the compass deviation of a ship by swinging the vessel in as small a circle as possible through the points of the compass and taking bearings on suitable distant objects, and comparing the apparent with the true bearings. This is best done when the vessel is riding at a single anchor or at a buoy.

**Swing the lead, To.** To malinger or make up excuses. The allusion is to a lazy leadsman on a ship who idly swings the line and protracts the job of taking soundings.

**Captain Swing.** The name assumed (1830–3) by those who promoted the Swing Riots in the southern counties, resulting from the distressed condition of the agricultural labourers, and touched off by the introduction of new threshing machines, which threatened to aggravate their situation. Menacing letters were sent to farmers, the machines were smashed and ricks fired, and Captain Swing became the bogey of the propertied countryfolk. Although lives of Captain Swing appeared in 1830 and 1831, he seems to have been an imaginary character. *See also* LUDDITES.

> The neighbours thought all was not right,
> Scarcely one with him ventured to parley,
> And Captain Swing came in the night,
> And burnt all his beans and his barley.
>
> R.H. BARHAM: *Ingoldsby Legends*, 'The Babes in the Wood' (1840)

**Go with a swing, To.** *See under* GO.

**Have no room to swing a cat, To.** *See under* ROOM.

**In full swing.** *See under* FULL.

**What you lose on the swings you gain on the roundabouts.** *See under* WHAT.

**Swiss Guard.** The Bourbon kings of France maintained a Guard of Swiss mercenaries until the Revolution. Pope Julius II (1503–13) instituted a Swiss Guard supplied by the cantons of Lucerne and Zürich. Some 100 men are still maintained as a papal escort drawn from the various Swiss cantons. Their formal uniform is still of MICHELANGELO's design.

**Switch. Switched on.** AU FAIT with contemporary fashionable and popular cults; thoroughly up to date and responsive to current trends and tendencies. The expression is also applied to someone under the influence of drugs.

**Asleep at the switch, To be.** *See under* ASLEEP.

**Swithin, St.** According to the old adage, if it rains on St Swithin's Day (15 July), there will be rain for 40 days.

> St Swithin's day, gif ye do rain, for forty days it will remain;
> St Swithin's day an ye be fair, for forty days 'twill rain nae mair.

The legend is that St Swithin (or Swithun) (d.862), bishop of Winchester and adviser of Egbert of Wessex, desired to be buried in the churchyard of the minster, that the 'sweet rain of heaven might fall upon his grave'. At his canonization the monks thought to honour the saint by transferring his body into the cathedral choir and fixed 15 July 971 for the ceremony, but it rained day after day for 40 days, thereby, according to some, delaying the proceedings. His shrine was destroyed during the REFORMATION and a new one was dedicated in 1962. Those who hold to this superstition ignore the fact that it is based on the dating of the JULIAN CALENDAR and therefore could not hold for 40 days from the current 15 July which is based on the GREGORIAN YEAR.

The St Swithin of France is St Gervais (*see also* St MÉDARD). The rainy saint in Flanders is St Godeliève, while in Germany the SEVEN SLEEPERS have this attribute.

**Sword.** In the days of CHIVALRY and romance a knight's horse and sword were his two most carefully prized possessions and it was customary to give each a name. Among the most noted of such swords are:

ANGURVADEL
ARONDIGHT
AZOTH
Balisarda: ROGERO's sword, made by a sorceress
Balmung: one of the swords of SIEGFRIED made by Wieland
CALIBURN
Chrysaor ('sword as good as gold'): Artegal's sword in Spenser's *The Faerie Queene* (1590, 1596)
Corrouge: Otuel's sword
Courtain ('short sword'): one of the swords of OGIER THE DANE; Sauvagine was the other, and they both took Munifican three years to make
CURTANA
Durandal: ROLAND's sword
EXCALIBUR
Flamberge or Floberge ('flame cutter'): the name of one of CHARLEMAGNE's swords, and also of Rinaldo and Maugis
Frusberta: RINALDO's sword
Glorious: OLIVER's sword, which hacked to pieces the nine swords made by Ansias, Galasand Munifican
Gram ('grief'): one of the swords of SIEGFRIED
Greysteel: the sword of Koll the Thrall
Haute-claire ('very bright'): both Oliver's and Closamont's swords were so called
MERVEILLEUSE
Mimung: the sword that Wittich lent Siegfried
Morglay ('big blade'): Sir Bevis' sword
NAGELRING ('nail ring'): Dietrich of Bern's sword
Philippan: the sword of Marc Antony, one of the triumvirs
Quern-biter ('foot breadth'): both Haco I and Thoralf Skolinson had a sword of this name
ROSSE
Sanglamore ('big bloody blade'): Braggadochio's sword in Spenser's *The Faerie Queene* (1590, 1596)
Sauvagine ('relentless'): *see* COURTAIN
Tizona: the CID's sword

**Sword and buckler.** An old epithet for brag and bluster, as 'a sword and buckler voice', 'sword and buckler men'.

**Sword dance.** A Scottish dance performed over two swords laid crosswise on the floor, or sometimes danced among swords placed point downwards in the ground, also a dance in which the men brandish swords and clash them together, the women passing under them when crossed.

**Sword dollar.** A Scottish silver coin of James VI (king of Scotland from 1567) marked with a sword on the reverse. It was worth 30s Scots (2s 6d English) in contemporary coin.

**Sword of Damocles, The.** Impending danger or disaster. Damocles, a flatterer of Dionysius of Syracuse (4th century BC), was invited by the tyrant to test the felicity of which he boasted. Accepting, he was seated to a sumptuous banquet, but over his head a sword was suspended by a hair. Damocles was afraid to stir, and the banquet was a torment to him.

**Sword of Gideon.** The physical and spiritual weapon with which GIDEON vanquishes the Midianites and Amalekites. He and his three companies stage a surprise night attack in which his men blow trumpets, smash water jars, brandish burning torches, and shout the slogan, 'The sword of the Lord and of Gideon' (Judges 7:20), so routing the foe, who 'ran, and cried, and fled' (7:21).

**Sword of God, The.** Khalid-ibn-al-Walid (d.642), Muslim leader, was so called for his prowess at the Battle of Muta (629), when he defeated the Emperor Heraclius, after a fierce two days' engagement.

**Sword of Rome, The.** Marcellus, who opposed Hannibal (216–214 BC).

**Sword of the Spirit, The.** The Word of God (Ephesians 6:17). Also the name of a Roman Catholic social movement founded in 1940.

**Cross swords, To.** *See under* CROSS.

**Draw one's sword against, To.** *See under* DRAW.

**Flaming sword.** *See under* FLAME.

**Put to the sword, To.** To slay.

**Roland's sword.** *See under* ROLAND.

**Sheathe the sword, To.** *See under* SHEATHE.

**Sybarite.** A self-indulgent person; a sensualist. The inhabitants of Sybaris, in southern Italy, were proverbial for their luxurious living and self-indulgence. Seneca told a tale of a Sybarite who complained that he could not rest comfortably at night, and being asked why, replied that 'he found a rose-leaf doubled under him, and it hurt him'.

**Sybil.** A perverted spelling of SIBYL, in classical mythology a prophetess, especially the prophetesses of APOLLO (*see* SIBYLLINE BOOKS). George ELIOT was known to her friends as the Sybil.

**Sycophant.** A SPONGER, parasite or servile flatterer. The word comes from Greek *sukophantēs*, literally 'fig shower' (*sukon*, 'fig', and *phainein*, 'to show'), which is said to have meant someone who informed against those who exported figs contrary to law or who robbed the sacred fig trees, or else to someone who 'showed the fig' (made an insulting gesture) when making an accusation. Hence, by extension the sense from 'accuser' to 'informer', a tale-bearer or flatterer.

At Athens *sycophantes* were a class of professional prosecutors who often blackmailed the wealthy with threats of prosecution or litigation and thus their name may include the added allusion of 'shaking a fig tree' to expose the fruit, as a blackmailer might shake his wealthy victim to produce the cash. This has no direct connection with the modern use of the word.

**Syllables, Aretinian.** *See under* ARETINIAN.

**Syllepsis** (Greek, 'a taking together'). A figure of speech in which a word is applied to two others in different senses, as 'she caught the bus and a bad cold', or to two others when it grammatically suits only one, as 'neither he nor I am going'. *See also* ZEUGMA.

**Syllogism.** A form of argument consisting of three propositions, a major premise or general statement, a minor premise or instance, and the conclusion, which is deducted from these.

**Sylph.** An elemental spirit of air, probably so named from a combination of Latin *silva*, 'wood', and Greek *numphē*, NYMPH. Any mortal who has preserved inviolate chastity might enjoy intimate familiarity with these gentle spirits, and deceased coquettes were said to become sylphs, 'and sport and flutter in the fields of air'. *See also* SALAMANDER.

**Sylva, Carmen.** *See under* CARMEN.

**Sylvia, Rhea.** *See under* RHEA.

**Symbolists.** A group of French writers who, towards the end of the 19th century, revolted against Naturalism and the poets of the PARNASSIAN SCHOOL. Their aim was to suggest rather than to depict or transcribe, and their watchword was Paul Verlaine's, *Pas de couleur, rien que la nuance* ('No colour, nothing but light and shade'). Their precursors were Charles Baudelaire, Théodore Banville, Gérard de Nerval and Villiers de l'Isle-Adam. The chief Symbolists in verse were Verlaine, Arthur Rimbaud and Stéphane Mallarmé, and in prose, Joris Huysmans.

**Symbol. Symbols of saints.** *See under* SAINT.

**Status symbol.** *See under* STATUS.

**Sympathy, Tea and.** *See under* TEA.

**Symphony, Unfinished.** *See under* UNFINISHED.

**Symposium.** Properly, a drinking together (Greek *sun*, 'together', and *pinein*, 'to drink'), hence, a convivial meeting for social and intellectual entertainment. Hence also, a discussion on a subject, and the collected opinions of different authorities printed and published in a review or the like.

**Symposium, The.** The title given to a dialogue by Plato, and another by Xenophon, in which the conversation of Socrates and others is recorded.

**Synagogue** (Greek *sunagōgē*, 'assembly', 'gathering'). In Jewish communities, the institution for worship, the study of Judaism, and social life and service, which had its origins at the time of the BABYLONIAN CAPTIVITY. The most notable of its special symbols are the Ark, in which scrolls of the Law are kept, the ever-burning lamp and the reading desk, usually in the middle of the building. It is managed by a board of elders. *See also* TABERNACLE; TEMPLE OF SOLOMON.

**Great Synagogue, The.** *See under* GREAT.

**Synchromism** (Greek *sun*, 'with', and *khrōma*, 'colour'). A form of abstract art resembling ORPHISM begun in 1912 by two young American artists living in Paris, Morgan Russell (1886–1953) and Stanton Macdonald-Wright (1890–1973). It was characterized by movements of pure colour evolving by gradations or rhythms from the primaries to the intermediary colours. Russell's *Synchromy in Green* (1913) was the first painting to bear the name. *See also* CUBISM; DADAISM; FAUVISM; FUTURISM; IMPRESSIONISM; SURREALISM; VORTICISM.

**Syndicalism** (French *syndicalisme*, 'trade unionism'). A trade union movement originating in France about 1890 where it was known as *Syndicalisme révolutionnaire*. It was opposed to state socialism, the means of production being taken over by TRADES UNIONS and not by the state, and government was to be by a federation of trade union bodies. The syndicalists aimed at achieving their objectives by widespread STRIKES, GO SLOWS and so on. Syndicalism played an important part in fomenting trade union unrest in Britain immediately preceding the First World War, and syndicalists were a prominent element in Spain in the 1930s.

**Syndrome, False memory.** *See under* FAKES.

**Synecdoche** (Greek *sun*, 'with', and *ekdokhē*, 'interpretation'). A figure of speech that consists of putting a part for the whole, the whole for the part, a more comprehensive for a less comprehensive term, or vice versa. Thus, 'a hundred bayonets' (for 'a hundred soldiers'), 'the town was starving' (for 'the people in the town').

**Synod, General.** *See under* GENERAL.

**Synoptic. Synoptic Gospels.** Those of MATTHEW, MARK and LUKE, so called because, taken together and apart from that of JOHN, they form a synopsis (Greek, 'seeing together'), i.e. a general and harmonized account of the life of Christ.

**Synoptic problem.** The problems of the origin and relationship of the three SYNOPTIC GOSPELS arising from large sections of material, and often phrasing, being common to them. There is general agreement that MARK is the earliest of the Gospels and that it provides much of the material for MATTHEW and LUKE. The latter two contain material not found in Mark (*see* 'Q'). There are varying theories among biblical scholars to account for this parallelism.

**Syntax, Dr.** The pious, hen-pecked clergyman, very simple-minded, but of excellent taste and scholarship, created by William Combe (1741–1823) to accompany a series of coloured comic illustrations by Thomas Rowlandson. His adventures are told in eight-syllabled verse in the *Three Tours of Dr Syntax* (1812, 1820 and 1821). Syntax is properly the branch of linguistics that deals with the grammatical arrangement of words, from Greek *suntaxis*, literally 'ordering together'.

**Syrinx** (Greek, 'pipe'). An Arcadian NYMPH of Greek legend. On being pursued by PAN, she took refuge in the River Ladon and prayed to be changed into a reed. Her prayer was granted, and Pan made his pipes from the reed. Hence the name is given to the PANPIPE, or reed mouth organ, and also to the vocal organ of birds.

**Syrup, Golden.** *See under* GOLDEN.

**System. Block system.** *See under* BLOCK.

**Continental system.** *See under* CONTINENTAL.

**Copernican system.** *See under* COPERNICAN.

**Froebel system.** *See under* FROEBEL.

**Linnaean system.** *See under* LINNAEAN.

**Madras system.** *See under* MADRAS.

**Monitorial system.** *See under* MONITOR.

**Open-field system.** *See under* OPEN.

**Points system.** *See under* POINT.

**Ptolemaic system.** *See under* PTOLEMY.

**Pythagorean system.** *See under* PYTHAGORAS.

**Speenhamland system.** *See under* SPEENHAMLAND.

**Spoils system.** *See under* SPOIL.

**Three-field system.** *See under* THREE.

**Trachtenberg system.** *See under* TRACHTENBERG.

# T

**T.** The twentieth letter of the alphabet, representing Semitic and Greek *tau*, which meant 'a sign or a mark'. Roman T is a modification of the earlier form, X. *See also* TAU.

As a medieval numeral T represents 160, and T̄ 160,000.

**Dot the i's and cross the t's, To.** *See under* DOT.

**Marked with a T, To be.** *See under* MARK.

**To a T.** *See under* TO.

**Tab.** A flap; a tag; a tally.

**Keep tabs on, To.** To keep a record on; to keep a check or 'running watch' on.

**Pick up the tab, To.** *See under* PICK.

**Tabard.** An outer coat of rough, heavy material once worn by poor people; also a loose outer garment, with or without short sleeves, worn like a cloak by knights over their armour, what Chaucer called *cote-armour*, often emblazoned with heraldic devices. It survives in the tabard worn by Heralds and PURSUIVANTS.

**Tabardar** or **Taberder.** A scholar on the foundation of Queen's College, Oxford, so called because they wore gowns with tabard sleeves, i.e. loose and terminating a little below the elbow in a point.

**Tabard Inn, The.** The inn from which pilgrims from London used to set out on their journey to Canterbury. It was on the London estate of the abbots of Hyde (near Winchester) and lay in the SOUTHWARK (now Borough) High Street, a little to the south of LONDON BRIDGE. The site is marked by a commemorative plaque. The inn and its host Harry Baily are immortalized in Chaucer's *Canterbury Tales*.

> It happened in that season that one day
> In Southwark, at *The Tabard*, as I lay
> Ready to go on pilgrimage and start
> For Canterbury, most devout at heart,
> At night there came into that hostelry
> Some nine and twenty in a company.
> CHAUCER: *Canterbury Tales*, 'The Prologue' (*c*.1387) (modern translation by Nevill Coghill, 1951)

**Tabby.** Originally the name of a silk material with a 'watered' surface, giving an effect of wavy lines. This was later applied to the brownish cat with dark stripes, because its markings resemble this material. The ultimate source of the name is in Arabic *al-'attabiya*, literally 'quarter of (Prince) 'Attab', this being the district of Baghdad where the fabric was first made.

> Demurest of the tabby kind,
> The pensive Selima reclined.
> THOMAS GRAY: 'Ode on the Death of a Favourite Cat' (1747)

**Tabernacle** (Latin *tabernaculum*, 'tent'). The portable shrine instituted by MOSES during the wanderings of the Jews in the wilderness. It was divided by a veil or hanging, behind which, in the HOLY OF HOLIES, was the ARK OF THE COVENANT. The outer division was called the Holy Place. When set up in camp the whole was surrounded by an enclosure. (*See* Exodus 25–31, 33:7–10, 35–40.)

In Roman Catholic churches the tabernacle is the ornamental receptacle on the high altar, in which the vessels containing the Blessed Sacrament are reserved. The name derives from the application of the word 'tabernaculum' in church ornamentation to a variety of canopied forms.

**Feast of the Tabernacles, The.** *See under* FEAST.

**Tin tabernacles.** *See under* TIN.

**Tabitha.** A 'woman full of good works' who is raised from the dead by PETER (Acts 9:40). Her name is Aramaic for 'doe', and the other name by which she is known, Dorcas, represents Greek *dorkas*, 'gazelle', so is identical in meaning. Because of the similarity between Tabitha and TABBY, the name became a favourite one for cats, both real and fictional. An example of the latter is Tabitha Twitchett in the nursery tales by Beatrix Potter.

**Table. Table d'hôte** (French, 'host's table'). A meal at a hotel or restaurant for which one pays a fixed price whether one partakes of all the courses or not. In the Middle Ages and even down to the time of Louis XIV (r.1643–1715), the landlord's or host's table was the only public dining place known in Germany and France.

**Table money** or **charge.** A charge additional to that of the meal made at restaurants towards the cost of attendance or a small fee charged to players at bridge clubs. In the army and navy, the term is used for an allowance made to senior officers to assist in meeting the expenses of official entertaining.

**Table Mountain.** A flat-topped mountain, especially that overlooking Cape Town.

**Table-rapping.** The occurrence of knocking sounds on a table without apparent source but coming from the departed, according to spiritualists, who use them as a supposed means of contacting the dead. *See also* OUIJA; SPIRITUALISM.

**Table talk.** Small talk; chitchat; familiar conversation.

**Table-turning.** The turning of tables without the application of mechanical force, which in the early days of SPIRITUALISM was commonly practised at seances and sank to the level of a parlour trick. It was said by some to be the work of departed spirits, and by others to be due to a force akin to MESMERISM.

**Archbishop Parker's table.** *See under* ARCHBISHOP.

**Cards on the table.** *See under* CARD.

**Clear the table, To.** *See under* CLEAR.

**Credence table.** *See under* CREDENCE.

**Drink someone under the table, To.** *See under* DRINK.

**Eternal Tables, The.** *See under* ETERNAL.

**Gate-leg table.** *See under* GATE.

**High table.** *See under* HIGH.

**Keep a good table, To.** *See under* GOOD.

**Lay on the table, To.** *See under* LAY.

**Lord's Table, The.** An alternative name for an ALTAR.

**March table.** *See under* MARCH.

**On the table.** Offered for discussion, as: 'The union put a new proposal on the table.'

**Pythagoras' table.** *See under* PYTHAGORAS.

**Round Table** or **Table Round, The.** *See under* ROUND.

**Turn the tables, To.** *See under* TURN.

**Twelve tables, The.** *See under* TWELVE.

**Under the table.** *See under* UNDER.

**Tableaux vivants** (French, 'living pictures'). Representations of statuary groups by living persons, said to have been invented by Madame de Genlis (1746–1830) while she had charge of the children of the Duc d'Orléans.

**Tablets, Tel el Amarna.** *See under* TEL.

**Taboo or tabu.** A Polynesian word signifying that which is banned, the prohibition of the use of certain persons, animals or things, or the utterance of certain names and words. Thus a temple is taboo, and so is he who violates a temple and everyone and everything connected with what is taboo becomes taboo also. Captain Cook was made taboo when he tried to set up an observatory in the Sandwich Islands. The idea of taboo is not, of course, peculiar to the Polynesians and is found among the ancient Egyptians, Jews and others. Hence a person who is ostracized or an action or custom that is altogether forbidden by society, is said to be taboo or tabooed.

> For several days after entering the valley I had been saluted at least fifty times in twenty-four hours with the talismanic word 'Taboo' shrieked in my ears, at some gross violation of its provisions, of which I had unconsciously been guilty.
>
> HERMAN MELVILLE: *Typee*, ch xxx (1846)

**Tabouret, Right of.** *See under* RIGHT.

**Tabula rasa** (Latin, 'scraped tablet'). A clean slate, literally and figuratively, on which anything can be written. Thus, the mind of a person who has been badly taught must become a *tabula rasa* before they can learn anything properly.

**Tace is Latin for candle.** Silence is most discreet; MUM'S THE WORD. *Tace* is Latin for 'be silent', and a candle is symbolic of light. The phrase means 'keep it dark'; do not throw light upon it. Henry Fielding, in *Amelia* (ch x (1752)), has: '*Tace*, madam,' answered Murphy, 'is Latin for a candle.'

At one time it was customary to express disapproval of a play or an actor by throwing a candle on to the stage, thus sometimes causing the curtain to be drawn.

**Tachebrune** (French, 'brown patch'). The horse of OGIER THE DANE.

**Tack.** The use of the word, particularly by sailors and soldiers to denote food, is of unknown origin. It is used in such phrases as 'poor tack', 'hard tack' (especially ship's biscuit) as opposed to 'soft tack' (bread or other more palatable fare). 'Tack' as the word for the saddle, bridle etc of a horse is a shortening of 'tackle'.

**Tactics, Fabian.** *See under* FABIUS.

**Taffeta.** A material made of silk, one time watered. The word is from Persian *tāftan*, 'to twist' or 'to spin'. The fabric has often changed its character. At one time it was silk and linen, at another silk and wool. In the 18th century it was lustrous silk, sometimes striped with gold.

**Taffy.** A Welshman, from Davy (*Dafydd*, 'David'), a common name in Wales. Perhaps it is best known among the English from the (now derogatory) rhyme alluding to the days of border cattle raids.

> Taffy was a Welshman,
> Taffy was a thief,
> Taffy came to my house
> And stole a leg of beef.

**Tag.** A children's game of catch in which from the outset each person touched or 'caught' joins the line to catch those remaining.

**Tag day.** The American equivalent of the British FLAG DAY.

**Dog tags.** *See under* DOG.

**Tages.** In Etruscan mythology a mysterious boy with the wisdom of an old man who was ploughed up, or who sprang from the ground, at Tarquinii. He is said to have been the grandson (or son) of JUPITER and to have instructed the Etruscans in the art of AUGURY. The latter wrote down his teaching in 12 books, which were known as *Libri Tagetici* ('the books of Tages'), or 'the Acherontian books'.

**Tail.** According to an old fable, lions wipe out their footsteps with their tail, lest they be tracked.

**Tail a person, To.** To follow someone and not to lose sight of them.

**Tailback.** A long line of traffic extending back from an obstruction.

**Tailed men.** It was an old belief in medieval times that such creatures existed and among continental Europeans Englishmen were once reputed to have tails. It was long a saying that the men of Kent were born with tails, as a punishment for the murder of Thomas à Becket.

Peter Pindar (*Epistle to the Pope* (1793)) fastens the legend on the town of Strood:

> As Becket that good saint, sublimely rode,
> Thoughtless of insult, through the town of Strode,
> What did the mob? Attacked his horse's rump
> And cut the tail, so flowing, to the stump.
> What does the saint? Quoth he, 'For this vile trick
> The town of Strode shall heartily be sick'.
> And lo! by power divine, a curse prevails –
> The babes of Strode are born with horse's tails.

Jews and Cornishmen were also held to have tails, the appendage also being borne by the Devil. In the former case there was a confusion of 'rabbi' with 'raboin' or 'rabuino', the Devil, from Spanish *rabo*, 'a tail'.

**Tail-end Charlie.** An RAF phrase in the Second World War for the rear gunner in the tail of an aircraft; also for the aircraft at the rear of a group, or the last ship in a flotilla.

**Tail male or female.** *See* ENTAIL.

**Tail wags the dog, The.** The least or less important person or group has control.

**Fee tail.** *See under* FEE.

**Heads I win, tails you lose.** *See under* HEAD.

**Heads or tails.** *See under* HEAD.

**In two shakes of a lamb's tail.** *See under* TWO.

**Lamb's tails.** *See under* LAMB.

**On someone's tail.** Closely following them, as: 'The police were soon on his tail.'

**Salt on the tail.** *See under* SALT.

**Turn tail, To.** *See under* TURN.

**Venom is in the tail, The.** *See under* VENOM.

**With a sting in its tail.** *See under* WITH.

**With one's tail between one's legs.** *See under* WITH.

**Taillefer.** The Norman TROUVÈRE who accompanied William the Conqueror's army to England in 1066. He begged leave to strike the first blow and rode far ahead of the other horsemen, singing of CHARLEMAGNE and ROLAND and playing like a juggler with his sword. After overcoming his first two opponents he charged into the Saxon host and was cut to pieces.

**Tailor. Devil among the tailors, The.** *See under* DEVIL.

**Nine tailors make a man.** *See under* NINE.

**Taiping.** The name means 'great peace', and the Taipings were the Chinese followers of Hung Hsiu-ch'uan ('Heavenly Prince') in the rebellion of 1851–64 against the Manchu dynasty. Hung, a Christian of a kind, who claimed to be the younger brother of Christ, set out to establish the 'Great Peace' and captured Nanking in 1853. The rebellion was finally crushed, after millions had been killed by the emperor's forces aided by CHINESE GORDON and his force of Chinese soldiers known as the Ever-Victorious Army.

**Taj Mahal.** The mausoleum in Agra, India, was built in 1632 by Emperor Shah Jahan in memory of his favourite wife, Arjumand Banu Begam (1592–1631). She was known as Mumtaz Mahal, 'exalted one of the palace', and the name of the mausoleum is a corruption of this.

**Take.** For phrases beginning with 'take' that are not included here, look under the first main word of the expression.

**Take after, To.** To have a strong resemblance to; to be very similar to.

**Take against, To.** To begin to dislike.

**Takeaway.** Said of cooked food that one buys in a shop or (especially) CHINESE RESTAURANT to eat at home or elsewhere. The word is used for the shop itself as well as the food.

**Take back one's words, To.** To withdraw one's words; to recant.

**Take for granted, To.** To assume to be true or valid.

**Take God's name in vain, To.** *See under* GOD.

**Take heart, To.** *See under* HEART.

**Take-home pay.** That which is left to the wage earner after all income tax and other compulsory deductions, e.g. social security, have been made.

**Take in, To.** To deceive; to hoax.

**Take in one's stride, To.** To deal or cope effortlessly or unflurriedly, without disrupting one's normal activities or routine.

**Take it, To.** To withstand suffering, hardship, punishment, insult and the like. 'Britain can take it' was a popular slogan during the air raids of the Second World War.

**Take it easy, To.** To relax; to proceed gently or carefully.

**Take it into one's head, To.** *See* GET IT INTO ONE'S HEAD *under* HEAD.

**Take it lying down, To.** To submit to insult or oppression without protest or resistance, like a dog when it is cowed.

**Take it on oneself, To.** To make oneself responsible (perhaps unwarrantably); to assume control.

**Take it on the chin, To.** To endure bravely. The metaphor is from boxing, in which a blow to the chin may be a knock-out blow.

**Take it or leave it.** It is up to you to decide whether you want it or not. The implication is that I do not care whether you take it or not, or that you must make your decision one way or the other here and now.

**Take it out of someone, To.** To exact the utmost from someone; to give a person a real drubbing; to get one's own back. Also to tire or exhaust, as: 'Working nights does take it out of me.'

**Take it out on someone, To.** Colloquially, to work off one's irritation, frustration and the like by being unpleasant to someone else.

**Taken aback, To be.** *See under* ABACK.

**Take off, To.** To mimic or ridicule; to start, especially of an aircraft or of someone in an athletic contest, as jumping or racing.

**Take off one's hat to someone, To.** Figuratively, to express admiration for a person's achievements. The allusion is to the custom of removing the hat as a mark of deference.

**Take on, To.** To undertake to perform; to assume; to be upset or considerably affected as: 'Don't take on so' (i.e. don't distress yourself so); to make a fuss.

**Take one's breath away, To.** *See under* BREATH.

**Take oneself off, To.** To go away.

**Take over, To.** To assume the management, control or ownership.

**Take-over bid, A.** A favourable offer to the shareholders of a company by another company which wishes to secure control of it.

**Take someone at their word, To.** *See under* WORD.

**Take someone in hand, To.** *See under* HAND.

**Take someone out of themself.** To divert them so that they forget their worries.

**Take someone's name in vain, To.** *See under* NAME.

**Take someone to task, To.** *See under* TASK.

**Take someone up on, To.** To accept their offer; to challenge them verbally.

**Take stock, To.** *See under* STOCK.

**Take that!** Said when delivering a blow, a rebuff or the like.

**Take to, To.** To develop a liking for someone or something; to begin to develop a habit, as: 'He has taken to drink since his wife left him.'

**Take to one's heels, To.** *See under* HEEL.

**Take to pieces, To.** To dismantle or disassemble; to subject to detailed criticism.

**Take to the cleaners, To.** *See under* CLEAN.

**Take up, To.** To pick up; to raise; to begin to cultivate a hobby; to act as a patron to someone or to 'adopt' them, usually for their advancement in society, business or the like.

> 'Yes, Lady Rockminster has took us up,' said Lady Clavering.
>
> 'Taken us up, Mamma,' cried Blanche, in a shrill voice.
>
> 'Well, taken us up, then,' said my lady, 'it's very kind of her, and I dare say we shall like it when we get used to it, only at first one don't fancy being took – well, taken up, at all.'
>
> W.M. THACKERAY: *Pendennis*, ch xxxvii (1848–50)

**Take up the cudgels, To.** *See under* CUDGELS.

**Take up the gauntlet, To.** *See under* GAUNTLET.

**Take up with, To.** To commence to associate with.

**Double take.** *See under* DOUBLE.

**Give and take.** *See under* GIVE.

**You can take it from me.** I can assure you.

**You can't take it with you.** That is, with you to the grave, so make use of your resources, material and financial, while you have the chance. Moss Hart and George Kaufman have a comedy of this title (1936). The expression paraphrases the biblical truism:

> For we brought nothing into this world, and it is certain we can carry nothing out.
>
> 1 Timothy 6:7

**You must take us as you find us.** Said to an unexpected visitor before whose arrival there has been no time to make special preparations.

**Tale** (Old English *talu*, 'list'). A number; a reckoning; a story. Exodus 5:8 has a 'tale of bricks', a measure by number, as of a shepherd counting sheep:

> And every shepherd tells his tale
> Under the hawthorn in the dale.
>
> MILTON: 'L'Allegro' (1645)

**Tale of a tub, A.** A COCK AND BULL STORY; a RIGMAROLE; a nonsensical romance.

There is a comedy of this name by Ben Jonson (produced 1633), and a prose satire by Jonathan Swift (1704), which portrays allegorically the failings of the English, Roman Catholic and PRESBYTERIAN churches.

**Tale of Gamelyn, The.** A Middle English metrical romance, found among the Chaucer manuscripts and supposed to have been intended by him to form the basis of one of the unwritten *Canterbury Tales*, although the authorship is still in doubt. Gamelyn is a younger son to whom a large share of property has been bequeathed by his father. He is kept in servitude and tyrannically used by his elder brother until he is old enough to rebel. After many adventures, during which he becomes a leader of outlaws in the woods, he recovers his rightful position with the help of the king and justice is meted out to the elder brother. Thomas Lodge uses the story in his book, *Rosalynde, or Euphues' Golden Legacie* (1590), from which Shakespeare drew a large part of *As You Like It* (1599). The story also bears similarities to the legends of ROBIN HOOD.

**Tale of Sir Thopas, The.** A burlesque on contemporary metrical romances, told as Chaucer's own tale in the *Canterbury Tales*.

> Listen, lords, with all your might
> And I will tell you, honour bright,
> A tale of mirth and game,
> About a fair and gentle knight
> In battle, tournament and fight,
> Sir Topaz was his name.
> 'Chaucer's Tale of Sir Topaz' (*c*.1387) (modern translation by Nevill Coghill, 1951)

**And thereby hangs a tale.** *See under* AND.
**Canterbury Tales.** *See under* CANTERBURY.
**Fairy tale.** *See under* FAIRY.
**Old wives' tale, An.** *See under* OLD.
**Tell tales out of school, To.** *See under* TELL.
**Travellers' tales.** *See under* TRAVELLER.

**Taleban.** *See* TALIBAN.

**Talent.** An ability, aptitude or 'gift' for something or other. The word, which is borrowed from the parable in Matthew 25:14–30, was originally the name of a weight and piece of money in Assyria, Greece, Rome and elsewhere (Greek *talanton*, 'a balance'). The value varied, the later Attic talent weighing about 57lb troy (47lb/21kg) and worth about £250.

**Dutch talents.** *See under* DUTCH.
**Ministry of all the Talents, The.** *See* ALL THE TALENTS.

**Tales.** Persons in the vicinity of a court from whom selection is made to supply the place of jurors who have been empanelled, but are not in attendance. It is the first word of the Latin sentence providing for this contingency, *Tales de circumstantibus* ('from such (persons) as are standing about'). Those who supplement the jury are called 'talesmen', and their names are set down in the 'talesbook'.

**Pray a tales, To.** *See under* PRAY.

**Taliban** or **Taleban** (Persian, 'students'). A fundamentalist Muslim militia formed in Afghanistan in 1994 as a force of youthful fighters from religious schools in Pakistan. They pledged to replace with Islamic law the factionalism that had marked Afghan political life since the demise of the communist regime in 1992. Boosted by popular support and military success, they captured the capital, Kabul, within two years and by 1997 had come to control two-thirds of Afghanistan. They interpret Islamic law in the strictest terms, calling for public floggings and stoning to enforce social restrictions, banning music, television and even kite-flying, and prohibiting many activities by women, who may not attend school, work or appear in public unless accompanied by a male relative.

> Peace is not an option for Afghanistan, despite the near-conquest of the nation by Taleban, the strangest of many conquerors over the centuries.
> *The Times* (23 September 1998)

**Taliesin.** A Welsh BARD of the late 6th century about whom little is known. The so-called *Book of Taliesin* is of the 13th century, and its contents are the work of various authors. The village of Taliesin or Tre Taliesin in Cardiganshire (now Ceredigion) is named after him and his grave is reputedly there. The story is that Elphin, son of the king of Gwynedd, was given the right to net a certain weir near the mouth of the River Dovey once a year, and on this occasion his net was brought ashore without a single salmon in it. While bewailing his misfortune, he noticed a leather wallet suspended from the timber of the weir. Inside he found a youth of such lustrous brow that he named him Taliesin ('radiant brow'). Taliesin brought wonderful prosperity to Elphin and became the greatest of the British bards at the court of King ARTHUR at CAERLEON.

**Talisman.** A charm or magical figure or word, such as the ABRAXAS, which is cut on metal or stone under the influence of certain planets. It is said to be sympathetic and to communicate influence from the planets to the wearer.

> Know, then, that the medicine to which thou, Sir King and many one beside, owe their recovery, is a talisman, composed under certain aspects of the heavens, when the Divine Intelligences are most propitious. I am but the poor administrator of its virtues.
> SIR WALTER SCOTT: *The Talisman*, ch xviii (1825)

In order to free a place of vermin, a talisman consisting of the obnoxious creature was made in wax or consecrated metal, in a planetary hour.

The word is Arabic *tilsam*, from Medieval Greek *telesma*, 'ritual'.

**Talk. Talk big, To.** To boast or brag.

**Talking ring, The.** In Basque legend, this was given by Tartaro, the Basque CYCLOPS, to a girl whom he wished to marry. As soon as she put it on, it kept on saying, 'You there, and I here.' In order to get rid of the nuisance, the girl cut off her finger and threw it and the ring into a pond. The story is in John Francis Campbell's *Popular Tales of the West Highlands* (1860–2) and in Grimm's *Tales* ('The Robber and His Sons') (1812–15).

**Talk nineteen to the dozen, To.** To talk endlessly or at a great speed. The sense is literal: to say 19 words where most say 12.

**Talk of the Devil.** Said of a person who has been the subject of conversation and who unexpectedly makes an appearance.

> Forthwith the devil did appear,
> For name him, and he's always near.
> MATTHEW PRIOR: 'Hans Carvel' (1701)

**Talk of the town.** The object of general attention and interest; a CYNOSURE.

**Talk shop, To.** To talk about one's trade, occupation, business or the like. This is often regarded as an antisocial action, since it excludes those 'not in the know'.

**Talk someone down, To.** To silence them by talking more loudly or forcefully.

**Talk someone round, To.** To persuade them by talking.

**Talk the hind leg off a donkey, To.** To talk non-stop; to talk incessantly; less commonly, to wheedle. A donkey's hind legs are its source of strength, so to talk thus is to weary or enervate one's listener.

**Talk through one's hat, To.** To exaggerate; to bluff; to talk nonsensically. The allusion is perhaps to the piety feigned by men at prayer who hold their hats before their faces so as appear deep in reverent contemplation.

**Talk through the back of one's neck, To.** To be utterly wrong or inaccurate; to talk rubbish; to be hopelessly wide of the mark. The back of one's neck is the reverse of the front of one's face, where one normally speaks.

**Talk turkey, To.** To discuss frankly or seriously. The origin of the expression is uncertain, but it may have arisen from the efforts of turkey hunters to attract their prey by making gobbling noises. The stupid birds would then either emerge from their cover or return the call, so revealing their whereabouts.

**Chalk and talk.** *See under* CHALK.

**Fast talk.** *See under* FAST.

**Know what one is talking about, To.** *See under* KNOW.

**Now you're talking.** *See under* NOW.

**Small talk.** *See under* SMALL.

**Table talk.** *See under* TABLE.

**You can't** or **can talk.** You're equally guilty; the same could be said about you.

**Tall. Tall order, A.** An unreasonable demand.

**Tall story, A.** An unbelievable or unlikely tale. A tall story is one that is HIGH-FLOWN.

**Walk tall, To.** *See under* WALK.

**Tally, To.** To correspond. In England the tally, a notched piece of wood (French *taille*, 'notch', 'incision') used for reckoning, had a particular importance down to 1826 as an EXCHEQUER record and receipt (usually of money loaned to the Government). The notch on one side was an acknowledgement of the sum paid, two other sides were marked with the date, the name of the payer and so on, and the whole was split down the middle, so that each half contained one written side and half of every notch. One part was retained at the Exchequer (the counterstock) and the other (the stock) was issued. When payment was required the two parts were brought together. If they matched or 'tallied' all was in order.

In 1834 most of these valuable records were burnt in the stoves that heated the HOUSE OF LORDS. It was this action that caused the disastrous fire that destroyed the old parliament buildings. *See also* INDENTURE.

**Tally-ho!** The cry of fox hunters on catching sight of the fox. It is perhaps an English form of French *taïaut*, which was similarly used in deer hunting.

**Tallyman.** A travelling hawker who calls at private houses to sell wares on the tally system, i.e. part payment on account and other parts when he calls again, so called because he keeps a TALLY OR SCORE of his transactions.

**Talmud, The** (Hebrew, 'instruction'). The collection of Jewish civil and religious law, religious and moral doctrine and ritual founded on SCRIPTURE. It consists of the MISHNA and the GEMARA, and there are two recensions, the Babylonian and the Palestinian (or Jerusalem). The Babylonian Talmud, which is about three times the volume of the Palestinian, is held to be the more important, and it was completed towards the end of the 5th century AD. The Palestine Talmud was produced in the mid-4th century AD. After the BIBLE, the Talmud is the most important influence in Jewish life.

**Talus.** *See* MAN OF BRASS.

**Tamar.** In the Old Testament (Genesis 38), the wife of Er. After his death she was given to ONAN, but he aborted the coition rather than father children with her. Another Tamar (2 Samuel 13) is the beautiful and innocent daughter of DAVID who is raped by her half-brother Amnon. She is avenged by her brother ABSALOM, who kills Amnon.

**Tamberlane** or **Tamerlane.** Names under which the renowned Tartar conqueror Timur, or Timur Lenk, i.e. Timur the Lame (1336–1405), is commonly known. He subjugated most of Persia and India, Georgia and other Caucasian lands, routed the GOLDEN HORDE and had begun an expedition to conquer China when he died. The capital of his empire was at SAMARKAND. The story of his imprisonment of the Sultan BAJAZET in an iron cage is probably legendary. He is the hero of Christopher Marlowe's blank verse tragedy *Tamburlaine the Great* (acted 1587). In Nicholas Rowe's play *Tamerlane* (1702) the warrior appears as a calm, philosophical prince, out of compliment to William III, while Bajazet was intended to represent Louis XIV.

**Tammany Hall.** The headquarters (in 14th Street, New York) of the Democratic Party organization in New York City and State. In the 19th century, it became a powerful influence in the party as a whole, and in the 1870s, under William

M. 'Boss' Tweed (1823–78), it was associated with widespread corruption, and this and other incidents led to Tammany Hall being used figuratively for wholesale and widespread political or municipal malpractice.

Tammany Hall was the survivor of numerous Tammany societies, which sprang up at the time of the American Revolution as patriotic anti-British organizations, and 'St Tammany' became the patron of the SONS OF LIBERTY clubs. The name itself comes from that of Tamanend, a legendary Delaware chief. *See also* TWEED RING.

**Tammuz.** *See* THAMMUZ.

**Tam-o'-Shanter.** The hero of Robert Burns' poem (1791) of that name. The soft cloth head-dress is so called from him. His name means 'Tom of Shanter', the latter being a farm near Kirkoswald, Ayshire, with Tam himself based on its tenant, Douglas Graham. Burns regarded the poem as his finest, a judgement shared by Sir Walter Scott.

**Tancred.** One of the chief heroes of the First CRUSADE, and a leading character in Tasso's JERUSALEM DELIVERED. Tancred (*c*.1078–1112) was the son of Otho the Good and Emma (sister of Robert Guiscard). In the epic he was the greatest of all Christian warriors except RINALDO.

Boccaccio's *Decameron* (1349–51) includes the tale of Tancred, prince of Salerno, who, having killed the true love of his daughter SIGISMONDA, cut out the lover's heart and sent it to her. Sigismonda took poison, and Tancred buried the lovers in the same grave. This story formed the basis for the play *Tancred and Gismund* (1591) by Robert Wilmot. *Tancredi and Sigismunda* (1745), the play by James Thomson, was based on a story in Lesage's *Gil Blas* (1715–35).

Disraeli's strange romance *Tancred* (1847) tells of an early 19th-century heir to a dukedom who went on a 'New Crusade' to the HOLY LAND. The libretto for Rossini's opera *Tancredi* (1813) was based partly on Tasso's version of the tale and partly on Voltaire's *Tancrède* (1760).

> While Norman Tancred in Salerno reign'd,
> The Title of a Gracious Prince he gain'd;
> Till turn'd a Tyrant in his latter Days,
> He lost the Lustre of his former Praise,
> And from the bright Meridian where he stood
> Descending, dipp'd his Hands in Lovers Blood.
> JOHN DRYDEN: 'Sigismonda and Guiscardo' (1700)

**Tandoori.** The word is used for a method of cooking an Indian dish of meat or vegetables on a spit in a clay oven, and it simply represents the Urdu word *tandoor*, 'oven'.

**Tangerines, The.** *See* KIRKE'S LAMBS *under* REGIMENTAL AND DIVISIONAL NICKNAMES.

**Tangie.** A water spirit of the Orkneys appearing as a man covered with seaweed (Danish *tang*, 'seaweed') or as a little seahorse.

**Tangram** (Chinese *t'ang*, 'Chinese', and English parallelo*gram*). A type of Chinese puzzle containing seven pieces: five triangles, a square and a lozenge (parallelogram). The aim is to form these into a square and other prescribed figures.

**Tanist** (Irish *tánaiste*, literally 'second person'). The lord or chief of a territory or the elected heir. It was an ancient custom in Ireland and among Celtic peoples for the family or clan to elect a successor to the lands from among their number, usually the nearest male relative of the existing chieftain unless he were a minor or otherwise unsuitable. This mode of tenure is called 'tanistry'. The deputy prime minister of the Republic of Ireland has the title of Tánaiste.

**Tanist stone.** The monolith erected by the ancient Gaelic kings at their coronation, especially that called LIA FAIL, which, according to tradition, is identical with the STONE OF SCONE. It is said to have been set up at Icolmkil (Iona) for the coronation of Fergus I of Scotland, a contemporary of Alexander the Great and son of Ferchard, king of Ireland.

**Tank.** The heavy armoured combat vehicle running on caterpillar tracks was first introduced on the battlefield by the British in the Battle of the Somme (1916). It was called by the code name 'tank' in order not to arouse enemy suspicions. The term came about partly because the vehicle resembled a water tank, partly because it was supposedly designed for use in desert warfare.

> 'Tanks' is what these new machines are generally called, and the name has the evident official advantage of being quite undescriptive.
> *The Times* (18 September 1916)

**Tanner.** Slang for a sixpence, originally a silver coin, first minted in 1551. It survived after the introduction of DECIMAL CURRENCY with a value of $2\frac{1}{2}$p until its withdrawal in 1980. According to some, it got its nickname from John Sigismund Tanner (d.1775), an engraver at the MINT. Others claim a pun on the biblical 'Simon a tanner' (Acts 9:43) given that 'simon' was also a colloquial name for a sixpence. *See also* TESTER.

**Tannhäuser.** A lyrical poet or MINNESINGER of Germany, who flourished in the second half of the 13th century. He led a wandering life and is said even to have visited the Far East. This fact, together with his *Busslied* ('song of repentance') and the general character of his poems, probably gave rise to the legend about him, which first appeared in a 16th-century German ballad, the *Tannhäuserlied*. This related how he spends a voluptuous year with VENUS, in the VENUSBERG, a magic land reached through a subterranean cave. He eventually obtains leave to visit the upper world and goes to Pope Urban IV for absolution. 'No,' says His Holiness, 'you can no more hope for mercy than this dry staff can be expected to bud again.' Tannhäuser departs in despair, but on the third day the papal staff bursts into blossom. The pope sends in every direction for Tannhäuser, but the knight is nowhere to be found, for, mercy having been refused, he has returned to end his days in the arms of Venus.

Wagner's opera *Tannhäuser und der Sängerkrieg auf der Wartburg* ('Tannhäuser and the Singing Contest of the Wartburg') was first performed in 1845.

**Tans, Black and.** *See under* BLACK.

**Tantalus.** In Greek mythology the son of ZEUS and a NYMPH (or of the Titaness Pluto). He was a Lydian king, highly honoured and prosperous, but, because he offended the gods, he was plunged up to the chin in a river of HADES, a tree hung with clusters of fruit being just above his head. Because every time he tried to drink the waters receded from him, and because the fruit was just out of reach, he suffered agony from thirst, hunger and unfulfilled anticipation.

Hence 'to tantalize', to excite a hope and disappoint it, and hence also the name 'tantalus' applied to a lock-up spirit chest in which the bottles are visible but unobtainable without the key.

Accounts of the way in which Tantalus offended the gods vary. One version is that he invited the gods to dine with him and, to test their omniscience, offered them a dish containing his son PELOPS. Only DEMETER, mourning the loss of PROSERPINA, failed to realize what was in the dish and ate part of Pelops. Another version tells how Tantalus stole nectar and ambrosia from the gods to give to his friends. Yet another tells how Pandareus stole a guard-dog from Zeus and gave it to Tantalus but when, first, HERMES and later Pandareus asked for the dog back, Tanatalus denied possessing it. *See also* IVORY SHOULDER OF PELOPS.

**Tantony pig.** The smallest pig of a litter, which, according to the old proverb, will follow its owner anywhere. It is so called in honour of St ANTHONY OF EGYPT, who was the patron saint of swineherds and is frequently represented with a little pig at his side.

'Tantony' is also applied to a small church bell, or any hand bell, for there is usually a bell around the neck of St Anthony's pig or attached to the TAU CROSS he carries.

**Tantras, The.** Sanskrit religious books (6th and 7th century AD) of the Shaktas, a Hindu cult whose adherents worship the female principle, usually centring round SIVA's wife, Parvati. They are mostly in the form of a dialogue between Siva and his wife.

*Tantra* is Sanskrit for 'warp', and hence is used of groundwork, order or doctrine of religion.

**Taoism** (Chinese *dào*, 'way'). One of the three religious systems of China along with Confucianism and BUDDHISM. It derives from the philosophical system of Lao Zi (6th century BC).

**Tap. Tap-up Sunday.** An old local name for the Sunday preceding 2 October, when a fair was held on St Catherine's Hill, near Guildford. It is so called because any person, with or without a licence, might open a 'tap', or sell beer of his own brew on the hill for that one day.

**On tap.** Available; ready for use, as liquor is from a cask when it has been tapped.

**Tape. Taped.** Fully appraised or summed up; completely 'weighed up' or assessed, as if measured with a tape. When one has a person or a situation 'taped' it can also imply having everything under control.

**Red tape.** *See under* RED.

**Ticker tape.** *See under* TICKER.

**Tapestry. Bayeux Tapestry.** *See under* BAYEUX.

**Gobelin tapestry.** *See under* GOBELIN.

**Tapis, On the.** Literally, 'on the tablecloth'; hence, under consideration. An English-French phrase.

> My business comes now upon the tapis.
>
> GEORGE FARQUHAR: *The Beaux' Stratagem*, III, iii (1707)

**Tapley, Mark.** Martin's servant and companion in Dickens' *Martin Chuzzlewit* (1843–4), sometimes taken to typify anyone who is cheerful under all circumstances.

**Tappit-hen.** A Scots term, properly for a hen with a crest or tuft on its head, but generally used for a large beer or wine measure. Sir Walter Scott's *Waverley* (1814) has (in ch xi) Baron Bradwardine's tappit-hen of claret 'containing at least three English quarts'. 'Tappit' means 'topped', i.e. crested. *See also* JEROBOAM; JORUM; MAGNUM; REHOBOAM.

**Tar. Tar Heel.** The colloquial name for a native of North Carolina, the Tar Heel State, so called from the early production of rosin, turpentine and tar from its pine woods.

**Tarpaulin** (probably from 'tar', 'pall', and '-ing'). Properly, canvas sheeting made waterproof with tar; also, in former days, a sailor's hat made of tarred cloth (as were the waterproof jacket and trousers). Hence a colloquial term for a sailor, often abbreviated to tar and so to Jack Tar.

**Tarred and feathered.** Stripped naked, daubed with tar and then rolled in feathers so that the feathers adhere. This was a common popular punishment in primitive communities, and it is still occasionally resorted to. The first record of this punishment is in 1189 when it was ordered by Richard I for theft in the navy. A statute was made that any robber voyaging with the crusaders 'shall be first shaved, then boiling pitch shall be poured on his head and a cushion of feathers shook over it'. The wretch was then to be put ashore at the first place the ship came to. *See also* WITCHCRAFT.

**All tarred with the same brush.** *See under* ALL.

**Jack Tar.** *See* TARPAULIN.

**Spoil a ship for a ha'porth o' tar, To.** *See under* SPOIL.

**Tara, The Hill of.** *See under* HILL.

**Tarantella.** A very quick Neapolitan dance (or its music) in 6/8 time for one couple, said to have been based on the gyrations carried out by those whom the TARANTULA had bitten, either as a result of the poisoning or because the poison was thought to be curable by dancing.

**Tarantula.** A large and hairy spider (so called from Taranto, Latin *Tarentum*, a town in Apulia, Italy, where they once abounded), whose bite was formerly supposed to be the cause of the dancing mania hence known as 'tarantism'. This was a hysterical disease, common as an epidemic in southern Europe from the 15th to the 17th centuries. The wolf spider found in southern Europe, *Lycosa narbonensis* (*Lycosa tarentula*) is not the same as the spider, also known as the tarantula, found in the southwestern USA and tropical South America, which is of the family Theraphosidae. *See also* TARANTELLA.

**Ta-ra-ra-boom-de-ay!** This song, with a refrain redolent of the Victorian music hall, was the hallmark of the comedienne Lottie Collins (1866–1910), a blackface minstrel's daughter, who first performed it at the Tivoli Music Hall in 1891 and who could never subsequently appear without singing it. It was of American origin and had words by Richard Morton. The song was all the rage in London and soon became popular in Europe, where Anton Chekhov heard it and incorporated it in his play *The Three Sisters* (1901).

**Targums** (Aramaic, 'interpretations'). The name given to the various Aramaic (Chaldean) interpretations and translations of the Old Testament, made in Babylon and Palestine when Hebrew was ceasing to be the everyday speech of the Jews. They were transmitted orally and the oldest, that of Onkelos on the PENTATEUCH, is probably of the 2nd century AD.

**Tarnkappe** (German, 'secret cap'). The cap that rendered SIEGFRIED invisible. In some versions of the story he wears a cloak or cape of invisibility. 'Cap' and 'cape' are related words.

**Tarot** (Italian *tarocchi*, of unknown origin). A pack of Italian playing cards, first used in the 14th century and still occasionally employed in fortune-telling. The pack originally contained 78 cards: the Minor Arcana, consisting of four suits of numeral cards with four COURT CARDS, i.e. king, queen, knight and page, and the Major Arcana of 22 cards. These have individual figures as follows:

| | |
|---|---|
| 0 | The Fool |
| I | The Magician |
| II | The High Priestess |
| III | The Empress |
| IV | The Emperor |
| V | The Pope |
| VI | The Lovers |
| VII | The Chariot |
| VIII | Justice |
| IX | The Hermit |
| X | The Wheel of Fortune |
| XI | Strength |
| XII | The Hanged Man |
| XIII | Death |
| XIV | Temperance |
| XV | The Devil |
| XVI | The House of God |
| XVII | The Star |
| XVIII | The Moon |
| XIX | The Sun |
| XX | Judgement |
| XXI | The World |

**Tarpeian rock.** An ancient rock or peak (no longer in existence) of the Capitoline Hill, Rome, so called from Tarpeia, the faithless daughter of the governor of the citadel, who was flung from this rock by the SABINES. It became the traditional place from which traitors were hurled.

> Bear him to the rock Tarpeian, and from thence
> Into destruction cast him.
>
> SHAKESPEARE: *Coriolanus*, III, i (1607)

**Tarquin.** The family name of a legendary line of early Roman kings. Tarquinius Priscus, the fifth king of Rome, is dated 617–578 BC. His son, Tarquinius Superbus, was the seventh (and last) king of Rome, and it was his son, Tarquinius Sextus, who violated LUCRETIA, in revenge for which the Tarquins were expelled from Rome and a republic established.

Tarquin is also the name of a 'recreant knight' figuring in the ARTHURIAN ROMANCES.

**Tarroo-Ushtey.** An amphibious bull of Manx folklore, which frequented the curraghs (fens) and sometimes mingled with the cattle in the fields to lure the finest heifer to death. The name represents the Manx for 'water bull'.

**Tart.** As applied to a woman of loose sexual morals this word, probably a contraction of 'sweetheart', came into use in the later Victorian period.

**Tartan army, The.** Scottish football supporters, famed for following their team's fortunes wherever they play and for visibly and audibly advertising their national allegiance. A typical contingent will wear tartan costumes or bonnets, sport ginger wigs, paint blue St Andrew's saltires on their faces and fearlessly flaunt the Scottish flag in the territory of the enemy. *See also* BARMY ARMY.

> The good-natured tartan army, in kilts and with bagpipes, is giving the canny Scots the edge over the Brazilians.
>
> *Evening Standard* (9 June 1998)

**Tartar** or **Tatar.** The Asiatic tribes of this name are properly called Tatars, the form Tartar probably deriving from association with TARTARUS or hell, the Tatars being part of the Asiatic host under GENGHIS KHAN that threatened 13th-century Europe. Hence a savage, irritable or excessively severe person is called a 'tartar'. When the word is applied to a woman it denoes a VIXEN or shrew.

**Tartarus.** The infernal regions of classical mythology, used as equivalent to HADES by later writers, but by Homer placed as far beneath Hades as Hades is beneath the earth. It was here that ZEUS confined the TITANS. *See also* HELL.

**Tartuffe.** The quintessential religious hypocrite who is the central character of Molière's play of the same name (1664). He uses his guile to obtain the property of the sincere but wealthy Orgon and even tries to purloin his wife Elmire. His name was apparently borrowed from that of Tartufo, a character in an Italian pamphlet of 1609. This means 'truffle', and is appropriate for a hypocrite, whose true nature lies concealed beneath the surface, like a truffle hidden in the earth.

**Tarzan.** The foundling who was reared by apes in the African jungle was created in 1912 by the American writer Edgar Rice Burroughs (1875–1950). He has countless adventures in novels and films, in which he communes with animals, rescues DAMSELS IN DISTRESS and discovers long-lost civilizations. The first novel of 24 in which he appears is *Tarzan of the Apes* (1914). In the 'monkey language' that Burroughs invented for him, his name means 'white skin', from *tar*, 'white', and *zan*, 'skin'. He is given this name by his foster-mother, Kala the ape. *See also* SHEENA.

**Task, To take someone to.** To rebuke them; to call them to account. The idea is of challenging them to a task that one could have taken upon oneself.

**Tassel-gentle.** The male goshawk trained for falconry, tassel being a corruption of 'tiercel', a male hawk, which is a third (*tierce*) less in size than the female, and called gentle because of its tractable disposition. Shakespeare uses the term figuratively for a sweetheart:

> O for a falconer's voice
> To lure this tassel-gentle back again!
>
> *Romeo and Juliet*, II, ii (1594)

*See also* HAWK.

**Tassies.** Tasmanians. *See also* APPLE ISLANDERS.

**Tasso, Torquato.** The celebrated Italian poet (1544–95), author of RINALDO (1562) and JERUSALEM DELIVERED (1575). He became the idol of the brilliant court of Ferrara, but his exhausting literary labours and the excitement and stresses of court life caused mental breakdown, and he spent most of the rest of his life in confinement, exile and poverty. His *Jerusalem Delivered* was pirated in 1580, and he received no payment for his masterpiece. He died as a pensioner of Pope Clement VIII.

Lord Byron's poem *The Lament of Tasso* (1817) tells of the imprisoned poet's love for Leonora d'Este and the writing of *Jerusalem Delivered.*

**Taste. Taste of the rope's end, A.** A flogging. A nautical expression, where it was formerly a routine punishment to administer a flogging with the end of a rope.

**Taste of the strap, A.** A strapping or flogging, properly with a leather strap.

**Leave a bad** or **nasty taste in the mouth, To.** *See under* LEAVE.

**Tatar.** *See* TARTAR.

**Tattersall's.** A name synonymous with horse-racing and betting. It is that of the horseman Richard Tattersall (1724–95) who founded a firm of race horse auctioneers in 1766. It was originally based in London, but later moved to Newmarket, Suffolk.

The betting associations come from Tattersall's Committee, unrelated except in name to the auctioneers. It is an authority set up to settle questions relating to bets on horse races. It has the power to report defaulters to the JOCKEY CLUB, which although itself not directly involved in betting disputes, will bar such defaulters until the report is withdrawn.

**Tattoo.** The beat of the drum at night to recall soldiers to barracks is from Dutch *taptoe*, from the command *tap toe!* ('turn off the taps'), meaning to close the barrels of beer.

Tattoo, as the indelible marking of the skin, represents Tahitian *tatau*, 'mark'. The word was introduced by Captain Cook in 1769.

**Beat the Devil's tattoo, To.** *See under* BEAT.

**Searchlight tattoo.** *See under* SEARCHLIGHT.

**Tau.** The letter T in Greek and the SEMITIC languages. Originally it was the last letter of the Greek alphabet (as it still is of the Hebrew), and in Middle English literature the phrase 'Alpha to Omega' was not infrequently rendered 'Alpha to Tau'.

**Tau cross.** A T-shaped cross, especially St ANTHONY OF EGYPT's cross.

**Tauchnitz.** The library of 'British and American authors' in English, bound in paper for circulation in continental Europe, was founded in 1841 at Leipzig by Christian Bernhard Tauchnitz (1816–95). He came of a family that had been in the publishing business for several generations.

The library eventually included more than 5000 titles.

**Taurus** (Latin, 'bull'). The second zodiacal constellation and the second sign of the ZODIAC, which the sun enters about 21 April.

**Taverner's Bible.** *See under* BIBLE.

**Tawdry.** A corruption of St Audrey. At the annual fair of St Audrey, in the Isle of Ely, cheap jewellery and showy lace called St Audrey's lace were sold. Hence 'tawdry', which is applied to anything gaudy, in bad taste and of little value. The story is that St Audrey, otherwise Etheldreda or Æthelthryth (*c*.630–679), queen of Northumbria and abbess of Ely, died of a throat tumour as a punishment for her girlish fondness for showy necklaces.

> Come, you promised me a tawdry lace and a pair of sweet gloves.
>
> SHAKESPEARE: *The Winter's Tale*, IV, iv (1610)

**Tax. Tax on beards.** Peter the Great (1672–1725) encouraged shaving in Russia by imposing a tax on beards. Clerks were stationed at the gate of every town to collect the tax. He personally cut off the beards of his chief boyars.

**Direct tax.** *See under* DIRECT.

**Indirect taxation.** *See under* INDIRECT.

**Nose tax.** *See under* NOSE.

**Poll tax.** *See under* POLL.

**Window tax.** *See under* WINDOW.

**Taxi.** The word, shortened from taximeter, is the accepted term for a motor cab, and originally referred to the meter that was installed on French horse-drawn cabs or *fiacres* long before motor cabs appeared on the road. In Britain it became common only with the introduction of motor cabs and was thus associated with them.

**Hail a taxi, To.** *See under* HAIL.

**Te. Te Deum, The.** So called from the opening words *Te Deum laudamus* ('We praise Thee, O God'). This Latin hymn was traditionally assigned to St AMBROSE and St AUGUSTINE and is said to have been improvised by St Ambrose while baptizing St Augustine (386). Hence it is sometimes called 'the Ambrosian Hymn' and in some early psalters it is entitled *Canticum Ambrosii et Augustini*. It is now generally thought to have been written by Niceta, bishop of Remesiana (d.*c*.414). It is used in various offices and at MATINS.

**Te igitur** (Latin, 'Thee therefore'). In the ROMAN CATHOLIC CHURCH, the first words of the old form of the CANONS OF THE MASS and consequently the name for the first section of the canon.

**Tea. Tea and sympathy.** Caring and hospitable behaviour towards a troubled person.

> All you're supposed to do is every once in a while give the boys a little tea and sympathy.
>
> ROBERT ANDERSON: *Tea and Sympathy*, I (1957)

**Teapoy.** A small, three- or four-legged occasional table. Though largely used for standing a tea tray on, the teapoy has nothing to do with tea, the name coming from Sanskrit *tri*, 'three', and *pāda*, 'foot'.

**Boston Tea Party, The.** *See under* BOSTON.

**Brick tea.** *See under* BRICK.

**High tea.** *See under* HIGH.

**New Jersey tea.** *See under* NEW.

**Not for all the tea in China.** Under no circumstances; not for any consideration.

**Not my cup of tea.** *See under* CUP.

**Storm in a teacup, A.** *See under* STORM.

**Teach. Teach-in.** An American term for a series of lectures and discussions on a particular theme led by experts. The expression became current in England in the 1960s.

**Teach one's grandmother to suck eggs, To.** To tell somebody how to do something that they already know.

**Teach someone a lesson, To.** To punish them as a deterrent.

**You can't teach an old dog new tricks.** An elderly person is not adaptable and does not readily take to new ways.

**Tear** (verb). **Tear Christ's body, To.** Formerly, to use imprecations. The common oaths of medieval times were by different parts of Christ's body, hence the preachers used to talk of 'tearing God's body by imprecations'.

> With oaths so damnable in blasphemy
> That it's a grisly thing to hear them swear.
> Our dear Lord's body they will rend and tear
> As if the Jews had rent Him not enough.
>
> CHAUCER: 'The Pardoner's Tale' (*c*.1387) (modern translation by Nevill Coghill, 1951)

**Tear oneself away, To.** To force oneself to leave, although keenly wishing to stay.

**Tear one's hair, To.** To show signs of extreme vexation, anxiety, anguish or grief. Tearing the hair was anciently a sign of mourning.

**Tear someone apart, To.** Figuratively, to criticize them severely.

**Tear someone off a strip, To.** To give them a severe castigation; to reprimand them sternly. The allusion is to 'skinning' a person.

**That's torn it.** That's spoiled things; that's caused a problem.

**Torn between, To be.** To have difficulty choosing between, as: 'She was torn between the yellow dress and the green'.

**Tear** (noun). **Tear-jerker.** A novel, play, film or the like with a very sad or sentimental theme.

**Tears of Eos, The.** The dewdrops of the morning were so called by the Greeks. EOS (Dawn) was the mother of MEMNON and wept for him every morning.

**Blood, toil, tears and sweat.** *See under* BLOOD.

**Burst into tears, To.** *See under* BURST.

**Crocodile tears.** *See under* CROCODILE.

**Gate of Tears, The.** *See under* GATE.

**St Lawrence's tears.** *See* SHOOTING STARS.

**Trail of Tears.** *See under* TRAIL.

**Without tears.** Painlessly. Said of something learned or done easily, as 'Cookery without tears'.

> TERENCE RATTIGAN: *French Without Tears* (play title) (1936)

**Teazle, The Ram and.** *See under* RAM.

**Technogamia.** The title of a curious play by Barten Holyday (1593–1661), an Oxford cleric and noted translator of Juvenal. Subtitled 'The Marriage of the Arts', it was published in 1618 and has the arts themselves as the *dramatis personae*, among them the magistrate Polites, the matron Physica, Physica's daughter Astronomia, the traveller and courtier Geographus, in love with Astronomia, Poeta, in love with Historia, the schoolmaster Grammaticus and so on. In 1621 the work was acted at Woodstock before James I, who found the performance tedious in the extreme and made several times to leave after sitting out the first two acts. In the course of the action, such as it is, Poeta capriciously falls in love with Astronomia and, in a passage quoted in Isaac D'Israeli's *Curiosities of Literature* (1791–1834), compares his mistress to Historia as follows:

> Her brow is like a brave heroic line
> That does a sacred majestie inshrine;
> Her nose, Phaleuciake-like, in comely sort,
> Ends in a Trochie, or a long and short.
> Her mouth is like a pretty Dimeter;
> Her eie-brows like a little-longer Trimeter.
> Her chinne is an adonicke, and her tongue
> Is an Hypermeter, somewhat too long.
> Her eies I may compare them unto two
> Quick-turning dactyles, for their nimble view.
> Her ribs like staues of Sapphicks doe descend
> Thither, which but to name were to offend.
> Her arms like two Iambics raised on hie,
> Doe with her brow bear equal majestie;
> Her legs like two straight spondees keep apace
> Slow as two scazons, but with stately grace.

**Ted** or **Teddy.** A pet form of Edward.

**Ted, teddy boy** and **girl.** *See* EDWARDIAN.

**Teddy bear.** A child's toy bear, named after Theodore (Teddy) ROOSEVELT (1858–1919), who was fond of bear-hunting.

**Teenybopper.** An American colloquialism, formerly applied to girls in their early teens who adopted current fashions in dress and were devotees of pop music and the latest crazes generally.

**Teeth.** *See* TOOTH.

**Teetotal.** A word expressive of total abstinence from alcoholic liquors. The origin of the word has two explanations. According to one, Dick Turner, a Lancashire artisan of Preston, coined it in 1833, and his tombstone bears the inscription:

> Beneath this stone are deposited the remains of Richard Turner, author of the word *Teetotal* as applied to abstinence from all intoxicating liquors, who departed this life on the 27th day of October, 1846, aged 56 years.

However, it is the other explanation that is the more likely. This derives it from T-total, the initial T probably originating as the mark of someone who had 'signed the pledge' of total abstinence in an American temperance society. There is evidence that this use of the word predates 1833 in any case.

**Teian muse, The.** ANACREON, who was born at Teos, Asia Minor.

> The Scian and the Teian muse,
> The hero's heart, the lover's lute,
> Have found the fame your shores refuse.
> LORD BYRON: *Don Juan*, III, lxxxvi, 'The Isles of Greece', ii (1819–24)

**Telamones.** Large, sculptured male figures serving as architectural columns or pilasters. They are so called from the Greek legendary hero Telamon (father of AJAX) who took part in the hunt for the CALYDONIAN BOAR and the expedition of the ARGONAUTS. *See also* ATLANTES; CARYATIDES.

**Telegonus.** The son of ULYSSES and CIRCE (or CALYPSO) who was sent to find his father. On coming to Ithaca, he began to plunder the fields when Ulysses and TELEMACHUS appeared in arms to prevent him. Telegonus killed his father, who was unknown to him, with a lance pointed with the spine of a trygon, or stingray, which Circe had given him. He subsequently married PENELOPE.

**Telegram, Kruger.** *See under* KRUGER.

**Telegraph, Bush.** *See under* BUSH.

**Tel el Amarna tablets.** Cuneiform tablets found in 1887 at Tel el Amarna, the modern name for the abandoned site of Akhetaten, the short-lived capital built (*c*.1360 BC) by Akhenaten (AMENHOTEP) in place of THEBES. These important sources of historical evidence concern a period before the exodus of the Israelites from Egypt and consist of letters from Egyptian governors in Syria and Palestine, from the kings of Assyria and Babylon and others. About two-thirds of the 230 or so tablets went to the Berlin Museum, the remainder to the British Museum.

**Telemachus.** The only son of ULYSSES and PENELOPE. After the fall of TROY he went in quest of his father, attended by ATHENE in the guise of MENTOR. He ultimately found him, and the two returned to Ithaca and slew Penelope's suitors.

**Telepathy.** The word was invented in 1882 by the writer and psychic researcher F.W.H. Myers (1843–1901) to describe 'the communication of impressions of any kind from one mind to another independently of the recognized channels of sense'. The term 'thought-transference' is often used for this phenomenon and more accurately expresses its implications, for it indicates the communication of thought from one person to another without the medium of speech. Myers was one of the founders the Society for Psychical Research in 1882.

**Telephus.** *See* ACHILLEA.

**Telescope, Gregorian.** *See under* GREGORIAN.

**Tell. Tell it not in Gath.** Do not let your enemies hear it. Gath was famed as the birthplace of the giant GOLIATH.

> Tell it not in Gath, publish it not in the streets of Askelon; lest the daughters of the Philistines rejoice, lest the daughters of the uncircumcised triumph.
>
> 2 Samuel 1:20

**Tell tales out of school, To.** To talk publicly about matters not meant for the public ear; to reveal confidences. The application was originally to schoolchildren, who let slip at home items of gossip they had heard from classmates.

**Tell that to the Marines!** I don't believe you! The phrase was current by 1806 and apparently originated among sailors, who regarded the marines as gullible. In 1904 Colonel W.P. Drury published a book, *The Tadpole of an Archangel*, in which he derived the expression from an occasion in 1664 when Samuel Pepys regaled Charles II with a tale in which an officer of the Maritime Regiment of Foot supported a sighting of flying fish. 'Mr Pepys,' said the monarch, laughing, 'Henceforward, ere ever We cast doubts upon a tale that lacketh likelihood, We will first *tell it to the Marines!*' The colonel later admitted the leg-pull.

**Tell the truth and shame the Devil.** Do the right thing and be honest.

**That would be telling.** That would be to say too much; that would be to reveal the secret.

**You're telling me.** I agree entirely with what you say.

**Tell, William.** The legendary national hero of Switzerland, whose deeds appear to be an invention of the 15th century and are paralleled in numerous European myths and legends.

The story goes that Tell was the champion of the Swiss in the struggle against Albert II, Duke of Austria (d.1308). Tell refused to salute the cap of Gessler, Albert's tyrannical steward and bailiff of Uri, and for this act of independence was sentenced to shoot with his bow and arrow an apple on the head of his own son. He achieved this feat and Gessler demanded what his second arrow was for, whereupon Tell boldly replied: 'To shoot you with, had I killed my son.' Gessler had him conveyed to Küssnacht castle, but he escaped on the way and later killed Gessler in ambush. A rising followed which established the independence of Switzerland.

The story has been systematically exposed as having no foundation in fact, and similar feats are recorded in the Norse legend of Toki. The popularity of tales of the 'master shot' is evidence by the stories of Adam Bell, CLYM OF THE CLOUGH, EGIL and WILLIAM OF CLOUDESLIE.

Schiller's play *Wilhelm Tell* (1804), which is based on the legend, was the inspiration for Rossini's opera *Guillaume Tell* (1829).

**Teller.** Originally, someone who kept the tallies (Anglo-French *talier*) and counted the money, but now a bank clerk who receives and pays out money at the counter.

Up to 1834 there were four officers of the EXCHEQUER known as Tellers of the Exchequer, whose duty was to receive and pay out moneys. *See also* TALLY.

**Telstar.** The name given to the satellite launched by the USA in 1962 for relaying transatlantic telephone messages and television pictures. It was something of a pioneer of its time.

**Temper, To lose one's.** *See under* LOSE.

**Temperance, The Apostle of.** *See under* APOSTLE.

**Templars** or **Knights Templar.** In 1119 nine French knights bound themselves to protect pilgrims on their way to the HOLY PLACES and took monastic vows. They received the name Templars because they had their headquarters in a building on the site of the old TEMPLE OF SOLOMON at JERUSALEM.

Their habit was a long white mantle ornamented with a red cross on the left shoulder. Their seal showed two knights riding on one horse, the story being that the first Master was so poor that he had to share a horse with one of his followers. Their banner, called *Le Beauseant* or *Bauceant* (an old French name for a piebald horse), was half black, half white, and charged with a red cross.

Their bravery in the field was unquestionable, as was in due course the wealth and power of the Order, which had houses throughout Europe, but the fall of Acre (1291) marked the ultimate failure of their efforts. Jealousy of their power and wealth rather than the internal corruption of the Order resulted in 1312 in their suppression and extinction throughout Europe, events which in France were accompanied by particular cruelties.

In England the Order had its first house (*c.*1121) near Holborn Bars, London, but it later settled on the site still called the TEMPLE.

At Paris the stronghold of the Knights Templar was taken over by the Knights of St John. The old tower later became a prison where, in 1792, the royal family of France was incarcerated prior to execution. The DAUPHIN (Louis XVII) probably died within its walls.

**Temple.** This word is Latin *templum*, from Greek *temenos*, a sacred enclosure, i.e. a space cut off from its surroundings (Greek *temnein*, 'to cut'). The Latin *templum* originally denoted the space marked out by the augurs within which the sign was to occur.

**Temple, The.** The site between FLEET STREET and the THAMES formerly occupied by the building of the TEMPLARS (*c*.1160–1312) of which the Temple Church, one of the four circular churches built in England by them, is the only portion remaining. On the suppression of the Order, the site was granted to the Knights HOSPITALLERS and, from 1346, it has been occupied by practitioners and students of law who, since 1609, have formed two separate INNS OF COURT known as the INNER TEMPLE and MIDDLE TEMPLE. The badge of the former is the Winged Horse (PEGASUS), that of the latter the Lamb (AGNUS DEI).

**Temple** or **Society of the Temple, The.** At Paris in the early 18th century, a lively and dissipated côterie at the Temple presided over by the Duke of Vendôme and his brother Philippe, Grand Prior of the Knights of Malta in France. The Abbé de Chaulieu was a prominent member and VOLTAIRE was introduced to it in his youth. *See also* TEMPLARS.

**Temple Bar.** The old FLEET STREET gateway into the City of London, formerly situated close to the entrance into the TEMPLE on the spot since 1880 occupied by the monument known as the 'Griffin'. The old 'bar' was destroyed in the GREAT FIRE OF LONDON and a new one erected (1670–2) by Sir Christopher Wren. This was removed in 1878 to ease traffic jams and re-erected in Theobalds Park, Cheshunt, Hertfordshire. It has survived there, but it is in a very dilapidated condition, and in the early 1990s there were plans to restore it and replace it in the City as part of a new development. Until 1746, heads of rebels and conspirators were displayed on iron spikes above the original pediment. The last shrivelled head apparently fell off *c*.1772.

**Temple of Fame.** A PANTHEON where monuments to the famous dead of a nation are erected and their memories honoured. Hence, 'he will have a niche in the Temple of Fame' means his achievements will cause his people to honour him and keep his memory green.

**Temple of Reason, The.** During the REIGN OF TERROR (1793–4), the Paris Commune enthroned a dancer on the high altar of Notre-Dame Cathedral as the GODDESS OF REASON. She was draped in a tricolour flag and the cathedral became the Temple of Reason. There was much desecration and plundering of Notre-Dame by the Paris mob.

**Temple of Solomon, The.** The national shrine of the Jews at JERUSALEM, erected by SOLOMON and his Tyrian workmen on Mount Moriah in the 10th century BC. It was destroyed in the siege of Jerusalem by NEBUCHADNEZZAR (558 BC), and some 70 years later the new Temple of Zerubbabel was completed on its site. The third building, the Temple of Herod begun in 20 BC, was the grandest and was that of NEW TESTAMENT times. It is said to have covered 19 acres (7.7 ha). In the holy place were kept the golden candlestick, the altar of incense and the table of the SHEWBREAD, while within were the HOLY OF HOLIES, the ARK OF THE COVENANT and the mercy seat. It was destroyed by fire by the Romans under Titus, AD 70. The site has long been covered by a Muslim shrine. *See also* JACHIN AND BOAZ.

**Anacreon of the Temple.** *See under* ANACREON.

**Golden Temple.** *See under* GOLDEN.

**Inner Temple.** *See under* INNER.

**Temporal, Lords.** *See under* LORD.

**Tempora mutantur** (Latin, 'the times are changed'). The tag is founded on *Omnia mutantur, nos et mutamur in illis* ('All things change, and we change with them'), attributed to Lothair (795–855), emperor of the HOLY ROMAN EMPIRE.

**Tempus fugit** (Latin, 'time flies'). The Latin tag is based on a line in Virgil's *Georgics* (iii (1st century BC)): *Sed fugit interea, fugit inreparabile tempus* ('But meanwhile it is flying, irretrievable time is flying').

**Ten. Ten-cent Jimmy.** James Buchanan (1791–1868), 15th President of the USA (1857–61), was so nicknamed on account of his advocacy of low tariffs and low wages.

**Ten Commandments.** The commandments summarizing the obligations of human beings to God and to others, as delivered to MOSES on Mount Sinai, when they were engraved on two stone tablets (Exodus 20:1–17). They are known collectively as the DECALOGUE and state:

(1) I am the Lord thy God ... thou shalt have no other gods before me;
(2) Thou shalt not make unto thee any graven image;
(3) Thou shalt not take the name of the Lord thy God in vain;
(4) Remember the sabbath day, to keep it holy;
(5) Honour thy father and thy mother;
(6) Thou shalt not kill;
(7) Thou shalt not commit adultery;
(8) Thou shalt not steal;
(9) Thou shalt not bear false witness against thy neighbour;
(10) Thou shalt not covet.

Modern versions of the Commandments have been devised for all audiences. One for young black Americans has 'Don't waste nobody' for the Sixth Commandment, while the Seventh is paraphrased: 'Don't mess around with somebody else's ol' man or ol' lady.'

**Ten commandments, The.** A common expression in Elizabethan days for the ten fingers and nails, especially when used by an angry woman for scratching her opponent's face.

> Could I come near your beauty with my nails
> I'd set my ten commandments in your face.
> SHAKESPEARE: *Henry VI, Pt II*, I, iii (1590)

**Ten-gallon hat.** The original tall-crowned, wide-brimmed hat worn by cowboys. The name is a jocular allusion to its capacity.

**Ten Great Persecutions, The.** According to Orosius they were those that occurred under

(1) Nero, AD 64
(2) Domitian, 95
(3) Trajan, 98–117
(4) Marcus Aurelius, 177
(5) Septimius Severus, 193–211
(6) Maximinus Thrax, 235
(7) Decius, 250
(8) Valerian, 258
(9) Aurelian, 272
(10) Diocletian, 303–305

In fact, neither Trajan nor Severus was an active persecutor. These were all persecutions of Christians, but Christians persecuted each other before they slowly learned toleration.

Jews in particular have suffered persecution for religious and other reasons, the worst of all being perpetrated by the NAZI regime, when possibly as many as 6 million were exterminated. Political persecutions have been common through the ages and in modern times totalitarian and Communist countries have relied on this weapon.

*See also* ALBIGENSES; BARTHOLOMEW'S DAY MASSACRE; DRAGONNADES; HOLOCAUST; HUGUENOTS; INQUISITION; WALDENSIANS.

**Tenner.** A £10 note, as 'fiver' is a £5 note. In the USA a 'tenner' is a $10 note or bill.

**Tenpenny nails.** Large nails, originally so called because they were sold at 10d a hundred. Smaller nails used to be known as eightpenny, sixpenny or fourpenny nails.

**Tenth muse, The.** A name given originally to SAPPHO, there being nine true MUSES, and afterwards applied to literary women, including Mme de la Garde Deshoulières (1638–94), Mlle de Scudéry (1607–1701), Queen Christina of Sweden (1626–89) and the English novelist and essay writer, Hannah More (1745–1833).

**Tenths.** In English ecclesiastical usage, the tenth part of the annual profit of every living originally paid to the pope and transferred to the crown after the breach with Rome, later to Queen ANNE'S BOUNTY. Also, in former days, a tax levied by the crown of one-tenth of every man's personal property. *See also* ANNATES; TITHES.

**Tenth wave, The.** A notion prevails that the waves keep increasing in regular series until the maximum arrives, and then the series begins again. No doubt when two waves coalesce they form a large one, but this does not occur at fixed intervals.

The most common theory is that the tenth wave is the largest, but Tennyson says the ninth:

> And then the two
> Dropt to the cove, and watch'd the great sea fall,
> Wave after wave, each mightier than the last,
> Till last, a ninth one, gathering half the deep
> And full of voices, slowly rose and plunged
> Roaring, and all the wave was in a flame.
> *Idylls of the King*, 'The Coming of Arthur' (1869)

**Ten to one.** The chances are very much in favour of something happening; there is a very strong probability, as: 'Ten to one it'll rain today,' i.e. it is ten times more likely to rain than not.

**Council of Ten, The.** *See under* COUNCIL.

**Nine times out of ten.** *See under* NINE.

**Upper Ten, The.** *See under* UP.

**Tenant** (French *tenant*, 'holding', from *tenir*, 'to hold'). Someone who holds property or premises.

**Tenant at will.** A person who at any moment can be dispossessed of his tenancy at the will of the landlord or lessor.

**Tenant-in-chief.** A person who held land direct from the king. By the 10th century the western Franks had established a feudal system by which a few dukes and counts were the direct vassals of the king. These tenants had their own tenants, and so on down the pyramid to the peasants, who worked the land. *See also* FEUDALISM; VASSAL.

**Tenant-right.** The right of an outgoing tenant to claim compensation from an incoming tenant for improvements, manuring, crops left in the ground and the like. In earlier times, the term denoted the right of passing on a tenancy, at decease, to the eldest surviving issue. It is also applied to the right of a well-behaved tenant to compensation if deprived of his tenancy. The right is now generally superseded by the provisions of the Agricultural Holdings Act of 1986.

**Tender.** *See* LEGAL TENDER.

**Tendon of Achilles.** *See* ACHILLES' TENDON.

**Tène, La** (Swiss French dialect, 'the shallows', from Latin *tenuis*, 'shallow'). A site at the eastern end of the Lake of Neuchâtel, Switzerland, where extensive remains of the late IRON AGE have been found. The term covers a period of CELTIC culture from the 5th century BC to about the beginning of the Christian era.

**Tenebrae** (Latin, 'darkness', 'gloom'). In the Western Church, the MATINS and LAUDS of the following day sung on the Wednesday, Thursday and Friday of HOLY WEEK. The lights of 15 candles are extinguished one by one at the end of each psalm, the last after the *Benedictus*. The MISERERE is then sung in darkness. This ritual goes back to the 8th century and symbolizes dramatically Christ's PASSION and Death.

**Ténébreux, Le Beau.** *See under* BEAU.

**Tennis. Tennis-court Oath, The.** The oath taken on 20 June 1789 by the THIRD ESTATE in the Tennis Court at VERSAILLES: never to separate and to meet wherever circumstances might make it necessary for it to meet, until the Constitution had been established and set on a firm foundation. The occasion was when Louis XVI (r.1774–93) excluded the deputies from their assembly hall and they met in the neighbouring building, the royal tennis court. It was another step towards revolution.

**Little old ladies in tennis shoes.** *See under* LITTLE.

**Tenson** (Latin *tensio*, 'struggle'). A contention in verse between rival TROUBADOURS before a court of love, as a metrical dialogue consisting of smart repartees, usually on women and love, but also on politics and literature. The term was also used for a subdivision of the troubadours' love lyrics.

**Tenterden steeple was the cause of Goodwin Sands.** A former satirical riposte when some ridiculous reason is given for a thing. The story, according to one of Hugh Latimer's sermons, is that Sir Thomas More, being sent to Kent to ascertain the cause of the GOODWIN SANDS, called together the oldest inhabitants to ask their opinion. A very old man said, 'I believe Tenterden steeple is the cause,' and went on to explain that in his early days there was no Tenterden steeple and there were no complaints about the sands. This reason seems absurd enough, but the fact seems to be that the bishops of Rochester applied to the building of Tenterden steeple moneys raised in the county for the purpose of keeping Sandwich haven clear, so that when they found the harbour was becoming blocked up there was no money for the drainage work.

**Tenterhooks, To be on.** To be in suspense; to await an outcome anxiously. The allusion is to newly woven cloth being stretched or 'tentered' on hooks passed through the selvages (Latin *tentus*, 'stretched', hence 'tent', canvas stretched).

**Tenth.** *See* TEN.

**Tenure, Base.** *See under* BASE.

**Teocalli** (Mexican, 'house of a god'). A temple of earth and stone or brick used by the aborigines of Mexico, built like a four-sided truncated pyramid on a platform at the top of terraces. The best known is the pyramid of Cholula which is 177ft (54m) high.

**Terabil, Castle.** *See under* CASTLE.

**Teraphim.** The idols or images of the ancient Hebrews and other Semitic peoples, worshipped by them as household gods or individual protecting deities (*see* Judges 18:5, Hosea 3:4). It was her father LABAN's teraphim that RACHEL stole and hid in the camel's saddle in Genesis 31:17–35. It seems likely that they were also used for DIVINATION and soothsaying (*see* Ezekiel 21:21, Zechariah 10:2). The word itself is of uncertain origin. A derivation from Hittite *tarpi*, meaning some sort of benevolent (or malevolent) spirit, has been proposed. *See also* LARES AND PENATES.

**Teresa** or **Theresa.** The name of two CARMELITE nuns of remarkable qualities, the first Spanish, the second French.

**St Teresa of Avila.** Also known as St Teresa of Jesus, St Teresa's life (1515–82) combined great practical achievement with continual prayer and religious sanctity in which she reached a state of 'spiritual marriage'. She was responsible for the reform of the Carmelite Order and founded 32 convents as well as writing outstanding works on prayer and meditation. She was canonized in 1622 and in 1970 became the first woman to be made a DOCTOR OF THE CHURCH. Her day is 15 October. *See also* JOHN OF THE CROSS.

**St Teresa of Lisieux.** A Carmelite nun (1873–97), professed in 1890, who died of tuberculosis and who is associated with miracles of healing and prophecy. Her autobiography, *L'Histoire d'une âme* ('The Story of a Soul') (1899) made her famous, and she was canonized in 1925. She was associated with JOAN OF ARC as patroness of France in 1947 and in England she is known, somewhat sentimentally, as the Little Flower of Jesus. Her day is 1 October.

**Term. Come to terms, To.** *See under* COME.

**Full term.** *See under* FULL.

**Hilary Term.** *See under* HILARY.

**Keep a term, To.** To attend a term of study at a college or university.

**Inkhorn term.** *See under* INK.

**Keep one's terms, To.** To reside in college, attend INNS OF COURT and so on during the recognized term times.

**On good** or **bad terms, To be.** To be on a good or bad footing with a person.

**Trinity Term.** *See under* TRINITY.

**Termagant.** The name given by the Crusaders, and in medieval romances, to a Muslim idol or deity that the SARACENS were popularly said to worship. He was introduced into the MORALITY PLAYS as a most violent and turbulent person in long, flowing eastern robes, a dress that led to his acceptance as a woman, whence the name came to be applied to a shrewish, violently abusive VIRAGO. The word comes from Old French *Tervagan*, a form of Italian *Trivigante*, the original name of the character in the morality plays.

**Termination, Addisonian.** *See under* ADDISON.

**Terminer.** *See* OYER AND TERMINER.

**Terminological inexactitude, A.** A mock-pompous euphemism for a downright lie, sometimes resorted to in Parliament for this purpose. It was first so used in a speech about labour contracts by Winston Churchill:

> It cannot in the opinion of His Majesty's Government be classified as slavery in the extreme acceptance of the word without some risk of terminological inexactitude.
>
> *Hansard* (22 February 1906)

**Terpsichore.** One of the nine MUSES of ancient Greece, the Muse of dancing and the dramatic chorus and later of lyric poetry. Hence Terpsichorean, pertaining to dancing. She is usually represented seated and holding a lyre. Her name means 'delighting in the dance', from Greek *terpein*, 'to delight', and *khoros*, 'dance' (English 'chorus'). She was said by some to be the mother of the SIRENS.

**Terra firma** (Latin). Dry land, as opposed to water; the continents as distinguished from islands. The Venetians so called the mainland of Italy under their sway and the continental parts of America belonging to Spain were called by the same term.

**Terrapin War.** An American name for the war with Britain of 1812–14, so called because, through the blockade, the USA was shut up in its shell like a terrapin (a tide-water turtle).

**Terrible, The.** *See* IVAN THE TERRIBLE.

**Terrier.** (1) A dog that 'takes the earth', or unearths its prey (Latin *terra*, 'earth').

(2) A register or list of lands belonging to an individual or corporation, especially the latter, is also called a terrier (Old French *papier terrier*, 'register of the lord's tenants').

(3) Terrier is also the popular name for a member of the Territorial Army, which under the Territorial and Reserve Forces Act (1907) superseded the old Militia, Yeomanry and Volunteers on a territorial basis until it was absorbed into the newly created Territorial and Army Volunteer Reserve in 1967. The strength of the Territorial Army itself has diminished in recent years, with an establishment of 74,000 in the early 1980s declining to about 59,000 in the late 1990s.

**Border terrier.** *See under* BORDER.

**Terror. Terror** or **Reign of Terror, The.** *See under* REIGN.

**Balance of terror.** *See under* BALANCE.

**Terry Alts.** One of the numerous secret societies of Irish insurrectionists similar to the Blackfeet, Lady Clares and MOLLY MAGUIRES. It was active in County Clare in the early 19th century. According to a diary extract of 1831 quoted in the *Times Literary Supplement* of 29 September 1932, Terry Alts was the name of an innocent bystander accused of assaulting a man. *See also* WHITEBOYS.

**Ter-sanctus.** *See* TRISAGION.

**Tertiaries.** Members of 'a third order', an institution that began with the FRANCISCANS in the 13th century for lay folk who wished to strive for Christian perfection in their day-to-day life in accordance with the spirit and teaching of St FRANCIS OF ASSISI. The system spread to other Orders such as the DOMINICANS, AUGUSTINIANS and CARMELITES. Tertiaries are obedient to a rule and take a solemn promise. There are also Regular Tertiaries who live in communities under vows and are fully 'religious' in the technical sense. The name Third Order arises from friars and nuns being classed as the First and Second Orders.

**Tertium quid** (Latin). A third party which shall be nameless; a third thing resulting from the combination of two things, but different from both. Fable has it that the expression originated with PYTHAGORAS, who, defining bipeds, said:

> Sunt bipes homo, et avis, et tertium quid.
> ('A man is a biped, so is a bird, and a third thing (which shall be nameless).')

Iamblichus said this third thing was Pythagoras himself.

In chemistry, when two substances chemically unite, the new substance is called a *tertium quid*, as a neutral salt produced by the mixture of an acid and an alkali.

**Terza rima** (Italian, 'third rhyme'). An Italian verse form in triplets, the second line rhyming with the first and third of the succeeding triplet. In the first triplet lines 1 and 3 rhyme, and in the last there is an extra line, rhyming with its second.

Dante's *Divine Comedy* (*c*.1309–*c*.1320) is in this metre, and it was introduced into England by Sir Thomas Wyatt in the 16th century. It was much used by P.B. Shelley, and also by Lord Byron in *The Prophecy of Dante* (1821). The following is an example from Shelley's *Ode to the West Wind* (1819):

> O wild West Wind, thou breath of Autumn's being,
> Thou, from whose unseen presence the leaves dead
> Are driven, like ghosts from an enchanter fleeing,
> Yellow, and black, and pale, and hectic red,
> Pestilence-stricken multitudes: O thou,
> Who chariotest to their dark wintry bed
> The winged seeds, where they lie cold and low,
> Each like a corpse within its grave …

**Tessie, Two-ton.** *See under* TWO.

**Test. Test Acts.** A name given to the various Acts of Parliament designed to exclude Roman Catholics, Protestant NONCONFORMISTS and 'disaffected persons' from public offices and the like. They include Acts of Abjuration, Allegiance and Supremacy, the Corporation Act, 1661, the Act of Uniformity, 1662, as well as those specifically named Test Acts. Those named 'Test Acts' were those of:

(1) 1673 which insisted that all holders of civil and military office must be communicants of the CHURCH OF ENGLAND as well as taking the oaths of Allegiance and Supremacy
(2) 1678 which excluded all Roman Catholics, other than the Duke of York, from Parliament
(3) 1681 for Scotland, which made all state and municipal officials affirm their belief in the PROTESTANT faith

These Acts were repealed in 1828. *See also* UNIVERSITY TESTS ACT.

**Test Match.** In CRICKET one of the matches between selected national teams arranged by the International Conference, which replaced the Imperial Cricket Conference (1909–65) after South Africa left the COMMONWEALTH (1961). *See also* ASHES.

England *v* Australia: first played 1877
England *v* South Africa: first played 1889
England *v* West Indies: first played 1928
England *v* New Zealand: first played 1930
England *v* India: first played 1932
England *v* Pakistan: first played 1952
England *v* Sri Lanka: first played 1982

**Acid test.** *See under* ACID.

**Ink-blot test.** *See* RORSCHACH TEST.

**Rorschach test.** *See under* RORSCHACH.

**Testament. New Testament, The.** *See under* NEW.

**New Testament in Modern English, The.** *See under* BIBLE.

**New Testament in Modern Speech, The.** *See under* BIBLE.

**Old Testament, The.** *See under* OLD.

**Tester.** A sixpence, so called from the teston or testoon (SHILLING) first introduced by Henry VII (r.1485–1509). As the coinage depreciated, it later came to be applied to a sixpence. The teston took its name from the sovereign's head (Italian *testa*) stamped on one side. Similarly the head canopy of a bed is called its tester. *See also* TANNER.

**Testudo.** *See* TORTOISE.

**Tête. Tête-à-tête** (French, 'head to head'). A confidential conversation; a heart-to-heart talk. A tête-à-tête is also an S-shaped sofa on which two people can sit face to face.

**Tête-bêche** (French, from obsolete *béchevet*, 'double-headed', originally applied to a bed). In philately, an unseparated pair of stamps printed in such a way that one is inverted with regard to the other.

> Tête-bêche stamps must, of course, be collected in pairs as, when separated, the stamps show no peculiarity.
>
> B.W.H. POOLE and WILLARD O. WYLIE: *The Standard Philatelic Dictionary* (1922)

**Tête-de-mouton** (French, 'sheep's head'). A 17th-century head-dress, the hair being arranged in short, thick curls.

**Tether, At the end of one's.** *See under* AT.

**Tethys.** A sea goddess, the wife of OCEANUS, hence, the sea itself. She was the daughter of URANUS and GAIA and mother of the OCEANIDS.

**Tetragrammaton.** A word of four letters (Greek *tetra-*, 'four', and *gramma*, 'letter'), especially the Jewish name of the Deity JHVH, which the Jews never pronounced but substituted the word ADONAI instead (usually rendered in the Bible as 'Lord'). Its probable pronunciation was Yahweh and from the 16th century it was corrupted into JEHOVAH by combining the vowels of Adonai with JHVH.

PYTHAGORAS called Deity a Tetrad or Tetracys, meaning the 'four sacred letters'. Greek Ζευς (*Zeus*) and Θεος (*Theos*, 'God'), Latin *Jove* and *Deus*, French *Dieu*, German *Gott*, Sanskrit *Deva*, Spanish *Dios*, Russian *Bog"*, Scandinavian *Odin* and English 'Lord' are all tetragrams.

**Tetrarch** (Greek *tetrarkhēs*, 'one of four rulers'). Originally meaning the ruler of one of four parts of a region, under the Roman Empire the term came to be applied to minor rulers, especially to the princes of Syria subject to the Roman emperor.

**Teucer.** (1) In the ILIAD the son of Telamon and Hesione and the stepbrother of AJAX. He went with the allied Greeks to the siege of TROY, and on his return was banished by his father for not avenging on Odysseus (ULYSSES) the death of his brother. He eventually settled in Cyprus.

(2) The son of the river-god Scamander and the NYMPH Idaea. The first mythical founder of the house of TROY.

**Teutons.** The name of an ancient tribe of northern Europe, called by the Romans *Teutones* or *Teutoni*. The adjective Teutonic has also been applied to the Germanic peoples generally and in the widest sense includes both Scandinavians and Anglo-Saxons.

**Teutonic cross.** A CROSS POTENT, the badge of the order of TEUTONIC KNIGHTS.

**Teutonic Knights.** The third great military crusading order, which has its origin in the time of the Third CRUSADE (1188–92). It developed from the provision of a hospital service by Germans at the siege of Acre (1190), which became the German Hospital of St Mary at Jerusalem. It was made a Knightly Order in 1198, thenceforward confined to those of noble birth. In 1229 the Knights began the conquest of heathen Prussia, and after 1291 their contact with the East ceased. They survived as a powerful and wealthy body until their disastrous defeat by the Poles and Lithuanians at the Battle of Tannenberg in 1410. The order lingered on until its suppression in 1809 but was revived in

Austria in 1840 although with HABSBURG associations.

**Texas Rangers.** A constabulary force first organized in Texas in 1835 and much developed by General Sam Houston (1793–1863) a few years later. They wore no uniform and especially proved their worth in 1870 against rustlers and raiders. Their resourcefulness in the saddle, their toughness and their colourful exploits have given them legendary fame.

**Thais.** The Athenian courtesan of the 4th century BC who, it is said, induced Alexander the Great, when inflamed with wine, to set fire to the palace of the Persian kings at Persepolis. After Alexander's death, she married Ptolemy Lagus, king of Egypt, by whom she had seven children.

> And the King seized a Flambeau with Zeal to destroy;
> *Thais* led the Way,
> To light him to his Prey,
> And, like another *Hellen*, fir'd another *Troy*.
> JOHN DRYDEN: *Alexander's Feast*, vi (1697)

*Thaïs* is also the title of an historico-political novel (1890) by Anatole France and of an opera by Massenet (1894) based on it.

**Thalestris.** A queen of the AMAZONS who went with 300 women to meet Alexander the Great in the hope of raising a race of Alexanders.

**Thalia** (Greek *thaleia*, 'blooming').

(1) One of the MUSES, who presided over comedy and pastoral poetry. She also favoured rural pursuits and is represented holding a comic mask and a shepherd's crook. By APOLLO she was mother of the CORYBANTES.

(2) One of the THREE GRACES or *Charites* and the daughter of ZEUS and Eurynome or HERA.

(3) One of the NEREIDS, the daughter of NEREUS and Doris.

**Thames.** The second longest river in Britain (the longest being the Severn), called Tamesis by the Romans, who based the name on the existing British name. At Oxford and upstream it is often called Isis, an artificial development from Tamesis.

**Set the Thames on fire, To.** *See under* SET.

**Thammuz** or **Tammuz.** A Sumerian, Babylonian and Assyrian god who died annually, rising again in the spring. He is identified with the Babylonian MARDUK and the Greek ADONIS. In Ezekiel 8:14 reference is made to the heathen 'women weeping for Tammuz'.

His name derives ultimately from Sumerian *Dumu-zi*, a shortened form of *Dumu-zi-abzu*, 'true son of the circumterrestrial ocean'. His festival was in June and July, in the fourth month of the Jewish year (tenth month of the civil year), which accordingly is named Tammuz after him. He was born of a virgin and his return to life took place three days after his death.

> Thammuz came next behind,
> Whose annual wound in Lebanon allured
> The Syrian damsels to lament his fate
> In amorous ditties all a summer's day,
> While smooth Adonis from his native rock
> Ran purple to the sea, supposed with blood
> Of Thammuz yearly wounded.
> MILTON: *Paradise Lost*, i (1667)

**Thamyris.** A Thracian bard mentioned by Homer (*Iliad*, ii (8th century BC)). He challenged the MUSES to a trial of skill and, being overcome in the contest, was deprived by them of his sight and powers of song. He is represented with a broken lyre in his hand.

> Blind Thamyris and blind Maeonides [Homer]
> And Tiresias and Phineus, prophets old.
> MILTON: *Paradise Lost*, iii (1667)

**Thanatos.** The Greek personification of death, twin brother of Sleep (*Hypnos*). Hesiod says he was born of Night with no father.

**Thane.** The name given in Anglo-Saxon England to a class of soldiers and landholders ranking between the earl and the churl. The rank of thane could be obtained by a man of lower degree. After the Norman Conquest the word disappeared in England, giving place to knight. In Scotland, a thane ranked with an earl's son, holding his land direct from the king. The title was given also to the chief of a clan who became one of the king's barons.

**Thanksgiving Day.** An annual holiday in the USA, usually held on the last Thursday in November and observed as an acknowledgement of the divine favours received during the year. It was first celebrated by the Plymouth Colony in 1621. After the Revolution its observance became general, and from 1863 it was annually recommended by the President. In 1941 it was fixed as a public holiday for the fourth Thursday in November. Pumpkin pies and turkey are part of the traditional fare.

**That.** Seven 'thats' may follow one other and make sense, as in the following verse:

> For be it known that we may safely write
> Or say that 'that *that*' that that man wrote was right;
> Nay, e'en that that *that*, that 'that THAT' has followed,
> Through six repeats, the grammar's rule has hallowed;
> And that that *that* that *that* 'that THAT' began
> Repeated seven times is right, deny't who can.

Or this, in prose:

> 'My Lords, with humble submission, *that* that I say is this: that that that 'that that' that that gentleman has advanced is not *that* that he should have proved to your lordships.'
> *Spectator*, No. 86 (1714)

**That's more like it.** *See under* MORE.

**That's that.** There is no more to be said; the matter is closed.

**That will do.** No more is needed or wanted.

**Thatcherism.** A term for the policies and style of government of Margaret Thatcher (b.1925) as Conservative Prime Minister (1979–90). It involved an emphasis on monetarism as a means of controlling the economy, the privatization of nationalized industries and trade union legislation. In a broader sense Thatcherism implied a stress on individual responsibility and enterprise.

**Thaumaturgus** (Greek, 'wonder-working'). A miracle worker, a name applied to saints and others who are reputed to have performed miracles, and especially Gregory, bishop of Neocaesarea, called Thaumaturgus (*c.*213–*c.*270), whose miracles included the moving of a mountain. St BERNARD of Clairvaux (1090–1153) was called the Thaumaturgus of the West.

**Theatre. Globe Theatre.** *See under* GLOBE.

**Mermaid Theatre.** *See under* MERMAID.

**Sheldonian Theatre.** *See under* SHELDONIAN.

**Windmill Theatre.** *See under* WINDMILL.

**Thebes.** The Thebes that was called the Hundred-Gated was not Thebes of Boeotia, but the chief town of the Thebaid, on the Nile in Upper Egypt, said to have extended over 23 miles (37km) of land. Homer says that out of each gate the Thebans could send forth 200 war chariots.

> The world's great empress on the Egyptian plain,
> That spreads her conquests o'er a thousand states,
> And pours her heroes through a hundred gates,
> Two hundred horsemen and two hundred cars
> From each wide portal issuing to the wars.
> ALEXANDER POPE: *Iliad*, i (1715–20)

It is here that the vocal statue of MEMNON stood. The sound was caused by internal vibrations resulting from a split in the statue after an earthquake. Here too is the VALLEY OF THE KINGS, including the tomb of TUTANKHAMUN, the Temples of Luxor and Karnak. It is now a popular tourist centre. *See also* SPEAKING HEADS; SPHINX.

**Theban Bard** or **Eagle, The.** PINDAR, born at Thebes (*c.*522–443 BC).

**Theban Legion, The.** Another name for the THUNDERING LEGION, which was raised in the Thebaid of Egypt, led by St Maurice.

**Theban Sphinx.** *See* SPHINX.

**Seven against Thebes, The.** *See under* SEVEN.

**Thecla.** One of the best known saints of the 1st century, the first woman martyr. All that is known of her is from the Acts of Paul and Thecla, pronounced APOCRYPHAL by Pope Gelasius. According to the legend, she was born of a noble family at Iconium and was converted by St PAUL. She is of dubious authenticity, and her cult was suppressed by the Roman Catholic Church in 1969.

> While Paul was preaching this sermon in the church which was in the house of Onesiphorus, a certain virgin, named Thecla ... sat at a certain window in her house.
> Paul and Thecla 2:1

**Thé dansant** (French). An afternoon tea party with dancing. Such genteel entertainments were popular in the 1920s and 1930s.

> How restful to putt, when the strains of a band
> Announced a *thé dansant* was on at the Grand.
> JOHN BETJEMAN: *New Bats in Old Belfries*, 'Margate, 1940' (1945)

**Theist, deist, atheist** and **agnostic.** Theists believe there is a God who made and governs all creation. Christians, Jews and Muslims are included among theists.

Deists believe there is a God who created all things, but do not believe in his superintendence and government. They think the Creator implanted in all things certain immutable laws, called the Laws of Nature, which act *per se*, as a clock acts without the supervision of its maker. They do not believe in the doctrine of the TRINITY nor in a divine revelation.

Atheists disbelieve even the existence of a god. They think matter is eternal, and that 'creation' is the result of natural laws.

Agnostics believe only what is knowable. They reject revelation and the doctrine of the Trinity as 'past human understanding'. They are neither theist nor deist nor atheist, as these all subscribe to doctrines that are incapable of scientific proof. *See also* AGNOSTIC; GNOSTICS.

**Thellusson Act.** An Act (1800) to prevent testators from leaving their property to accumulate for more than 21 years. It was passed in reference to the will of Peter Thellusson (1737–97), a London banker who left £600,000 and £4500 a year to accumulate for the benefit of his eldest great-grandson after the death of all his sons and grandsons. The last grandson died in 1856, and the expense of the legal actions that followed swallowed up all the accumulated interest, so that Thellusson's eldest son's eldest grandson received barely the amount of the original legacy. It was better known as the Accumulations Act and was replaced by the Law of Property Act 1925.

**Theme song.** A song that recurs during the course of a musical play or film and that generally reflects the mood or theme of the production.

**Themis.** A daughter of URANUS and GAIA and a wife of ZEUS (JUPITER), mother of the HORAE, the Moirai or Parcae (*see* FATES), Astraea (the personification of justice) and of the NYMPHS of the River Eridanus. Some sources say that the HESPERIDES were born of Themis and Zeus. With Zeus she presides over law and order. She also is protector of hospitality and the oppressed and has oracular powers.

**Themistocles, The Famous Sorites of.** *See under* FAMOUS.

**Theocritus.** A Greek poet of Syracuse (3rd century BC), the creator of pastoral poetry, whose verse was imitated by VIRGIL.

**Theodora.** A courtesan (*c*.500–548), the daughter of a bear-tamer, who in 525 married the future East Roman emperor Justinian and who was empress from 527. Her influence over government was considerable.

**Theodoric.** King of the Ostrogoths (*c*.454–526), who became celebrated in German legend as Dietrich of Bern and also has a place in the Norse romances and the NIBELUNGENLIED. He invaded Italy, slew Odoacer (493) and became sole ruler.

**Theophany.** *See* TIFFANY.

**Theorem, Pythagoras'.** *See under* PYTHAGORAS.

**Theosophy** (Greek, 'wisdom of God'). The name adopted by the Theosophical Society (founded in 1875 by Helena Petrovna Blavatsky (1831–91), Henry Steel Olcott (1832–1907), William Q. Judge and others) to define their religious or philosophical system, which aims at the knowledge of God by means of intuition and contemplative illumination or by direct communion. Esoteric Buddhism is another name for it, and its adherents claim that the doctrines of the great world religions are merely the exoteric expressions of their own esoteric traditions.

> The Theosophist is a man who, whatever be his race, creed, or condition, aspires to reach this height of wisdom and beatitude by self-development.
> H.S. OLCOTT: *Theosophy* (1885)

**Théot, Catherine.** A French visionary (*c*.1725–94) like the English Joanna Southcott, calling herself the Mother of God and changing her name to *Theos* (Greek, 'God'). At the height of the Revolution she preached the worship of the Supreme Being and announced that Robespierre was the forerunner of 'The Word'. She called him her well-beloved son and chief prophet. She died in prison.

> This Théot mystery they affect to regard as a Plot; but have evidently introduced a vein of satire, of irreverent banter, not against the Spinster alone but obliquely against her Regenerative Man!
> THOMAS CARLYLE: *The French Revolution*, Pt III, Bk VI, ch vi (1837)

*See also* SOUTHCOTTIANS.

**Theramenes.** *See* WEAR THE SANDALS OF THERAMENES.

**Therapeutae** (Greek, 'servants', 'ministers'). A sect of Jewish ascetics in Egypt described in Philo's *De Vita Contemplativa* (1st century AD). They lived in a community near Alexandria run on monastic lines, which was developed long before the rise of Christianity. *See also* ESSENES.

**Therapy, Deep.** *See under* DEEP.

**Thermidor.** The eleventh month of the FRENCH REVOLUTIONARY CALENDAR, corresponding to the period from 20 July to 18 August. Its name means 'gift of heat', from Greek *thermē*, 'heat', and *dōron*, 'gift'.

**Thermidorians.** The French Revolutionaries who took part in the *coup d'état* that effected the fall of Robespierre, on 9th Thermidor of the second Republican year (27 July 1794), thus ending the REIGN OF TERROR.

**Thermopylae.** The pass from Thessaly to Locris, only 25ft (7.6m) wide at its narrowest part, celebrated for its heroic defence (480 BC) by LEONIDAS, with some 6000 or 7000 Greeks, against XERXES and the Persians. Eventually, treachery by a local Greek allowed the Persians to get to the rear of the Greeks and the Spartan king and his band were all slain, though fighting to the last. The pass took its name from the hot sulphur springs nearby, from Greek *thermos*, 'hot', and *pulai*, 'gates'.

**Thermopylae of America.** *See* ALAMO.

**Thersites.** A deformed, scurrilous and cowardly officer in the Greek army at the siege of TROY. He was always railing at the chiefs, hence the name is applied to any dastardly, malevolent, impudent railer against the powers that be. ACHILLES felled him to the earth with his fist and killed him when Thersites taunted and put out the eyes of the dying Amazon, PENTHESILEA, whom Achilles had just mortally wounded.

In Shakespeare's *Troilus and Cressida* (I, iii (1601)) he is: 'A slave whose gall coins slanders like a mint.'

**Thesaurus, Roget's.** *See under* ROGET.

**Theseus.** (1) The chief hero of Attica in ancient Greek legend, the son of AEGEUS and the centre of countless exploits. Among them are the capture of the Marathonian bull, the slaying of the MINOTAUR, his war against the AMAZONS and the hunting of the CALYDONIAN BOAR. He was eventually murdered by Lycomedes in Scyros. *See also* SINIS.

(2) Theseus is also the name of the Duke of Athens in Chaucer's 'The Knight's Tale' (*c*.1387). He married Hippolita, and as he returned home with his bride and Emily her sister, was accosted by a crowd of female suppliants who complained of Creon, king of Thebes. The duke forthwith set out for Thebes, slew Creon and took the city by assault. Many captives fell into his hands, among whom were the two knights, Palamon and ARCITE.

Shakespeare gives the same name to the Duke of Athens in *A Midsummer Night's Dream* (1595).

**Thespians.** Actors, so called from Thespis, an Attic poet of the 6th century BC, reputed to be the FATHER OF GREEK TRAGEDY.

*Thespis*, the first Professor of our Art,
At Country Wakes, Sung Ballads in a Cart.
JOHN DRYDEN: 'Prologue' to Nathaniel Lee's *Sophonisba* (1676)

**Thestylis.** A stock poetic name for a rustic maiden, from a young female slave of that name in the *Idylls* (3rd century BC) of THEOCRITUS.

And then in haste her bower she leaves,
With Thestylis to bind the sheaves.
MILTON: 'L'Allegro' (1645)

**Thetis.** The chief of the NEREIDS of Greek legend and one of the daughters of NEREUS and Doris. She was a divinity of the sea and was brought up by HERA. By PELEUS she was the mother of ACHILLES, whom she tried to prevent from going to TROY, because she knew he would die there, by concealing him among the daughters of Lycomedes of Scyros. *See also* MOMUS.

**Thick. Thick, To be.** To be not very bright or intelligent; to be slow on the uptake.

**Thick and fast.** Abundantly; following one another in quick succession. The allusion is probably to heavy archery fire, with the arrows descending in great numbers and at rapid intervals.

**Thick ear, A.** A blow on the ear as a punishment or in anger.

**Thick-skinned.** Not sensitive; not irritated by rebukes or slanders. To have a thick skin is to be insensitive or indifferent to jibes, criticism or even insults; 'to have a hide like a rhinoceros'. To have a thin skin, on the contrary, is to be hypersensitive about such things; to be impatient of reproof or censure; having skin so thin that it is an annoyance to be touched.

**As thick as thieves.** *See under* AS.

**As thick as two short planks.** *See under* AS.

**In the thick of it.** In the midst of it; in the most intense or active part of it.

Poirot, of course, was in the thick of things.
AGATHA CHRISTIE: *The ABC Murders*, ch xvii (1935)

**It's a bit thick.** It's unreasonable; it's more than one should be expected to tolerate.

**Lay it on thick, To.** *See under* LAY.

**Those two are very thick.** They are very good friends; they are on excellent terms with one another.

**Through thick and thin.** *See under* THROUGH.

**Thief. Thieves' Latin.** Slang, cant or jargon employed as a secret language by rogues and vagabonds.

**As thick as thieves.** *See under* AS.

**Penitent Thief, The.** *See* DISMAS.

**Thimble.** From Old English *thȳmel*, 'thumbstall', so called because it was originally worn on the thumb, as is the 'thimble' of a sailmaker's palm.

**Thimble-rigging.** A form of cheating, carried on with three thimbles and a pea, formerly mainly practised on or about racecourses. A pea is put on a table, and the manipulator places three thimbles over it in succession and then, setting them on the table, asks you to say under which thimble the pea is. You are sure to guess wrong. The modern equivalent is the THREE-CARD TRICK. The term thimble-rigging is used allusively of any kind of mean cheating or JIGGERY-POKERY.

**Thin. Thin end of the wedge, The.** An action of apparently small consequence that may lead to major, undesirable developments. The reference is to wedges used for splitting blocks of stone or wood.

**Thin on the ground.** Few in number; scarce.

**Thin on top.** Going bald.

**Thin red line, The.** Red-uniformed British infantrymen in action. The old 93rd Highlanders were so described at the Battle of Balaclava (1854) by W.H. Russell, because they did not take the trouble to form into a square. Their regimental magazine was later called *The Thin Red Line*.

**Thin-skinned.** *See* THICK-SKINNED.

**Thin time, A.** A wretched or uncomfortable time, as: 'The team had a thin time last season, not winning a single game.'

**As thin as a rake.** *See under* AS.

**Skate on thin ice, To.** *See under* SKATE.

**Vanish into thin air, To.** *See under* VANISH.

**Thing.** The Old Norse word for the assembly of the people, otherwise a parliament. It is etymologically the same word as English 'thing' (an object), the original meaning of which was a discussion (from *thingian*, 'to discuss'), hence a cause or an object.

The Parliament of Norway is still called the STORTING, which divides itself into the *Lagting* ('law assembly') and the *Odelsting* ('allodium assembly').

**Thing, The.** The latest fashion, as: 'Split skirts are now all the thing.'

**Thingummy.** A person or thing whose name one has forgotten or does not know or does not wish to mention. An extended form is thingamabob or thingamajig. *See also* WHAT'S-HIS-NAME.

He would answer to 'Hi!' or to any loud cry,
Such as 'Fry me!' or 'Fritter my wig!'
To 'What-you-may-call-um!' or 'What-was-his-name!'
But especially to 'Thing-um-a-jig!'
LEWIS CARROLL: *The Hunting of the Snark*, Fit 1 (1876)

**Done thing, The.** *See under* DO.

**Do one's own thing, To.** *See under* DO.

**First thing.** *See under* FIRST.

**First things first.** *See under* FIRST.

**Four Last Things.** *See under* FOUR.

**Have a thing about, To.** To have a prejudice or obsession about, as: 'She's got a thing about fresh air.'
**Just the thing** or **very thing.** *See under* JUST.
**Know a thing or two, To.** *See under* KNOW.
**Last thing.** *See under* LAST.
**Make a thing of, To.** To make a fuss about or to exaggerate the importance of, as: 'There's no need to make a thing of it: I came as soon as I could.'
**Old thing.** *See under* OLD.
**One of those things.** Something one has to accept; something unavoidable or inevitable.
**One's things.** One's belongings, especially what one takes with one, as clothes or luggage.
**On to a good thing, To be.** To be in a profitable position; to enjoy a rewarding situation.
**Poor thing, A.** *See under* POOR.
**Real thing.** *See under* REAL.
**See things, To.** *See under* SEE.
**See things in their true colours, To.** *See under* SEE.
**Young thing.** *See under* YOUNG.

**Think. Think better of, To.** To reconsider; to revise one's opinion on second thoughts.
**Thinking cap.** To put on one's thinking cap is to consider carefully before giving a final answer. The allusion is to the official cap of the judge, formerly donned when passing sentence, later reserved for passing the death sentence.
**Think nothing of, To.** To regard as unimportant or easy.
**Think-tank.** A popular term for a group of people with specialized knowledge and ability, set up to carry out research into particular problems (usually social, political and technological) and to provide ideas and possible solutions. The expression is of American origin and arose in the mid-20th century.
**Think twice, To.** To consider carefully; to avoid any hasty decision. The phrase is mostly used in the negative, as: 'I didn't think twice about accepting the invitation'.
**Wishful thinking.** *See under* WISH.
**You think of Parmenio and I of Alexander.** You think of what you ought to receive, and I of what I ought to give; you think of those castigated or rewarded, but I of my position, and what reward is consistent with my rank. The allusion is to the tale that Alexander the Great said to Parmenio: 'I consider not what Parmenio should receive, but what Alexander should give.'

**Third.** *See also* THREE.
**Third age.** Old age, regarded positively as an opportunity for travel, further education and the like.
**Third degree.** The highest degree, that of MASTER MASON, in British FREEMASONRY. In the USA the term is applied to the use of exhaustive questioning and cross-questioning by the police in an endeavour to extort a confession of compromising information from a suspect, criminal, accomplice or witness.
**Third-degree burn.** The most severe kind of burn, with destruction of both the epidermis, or outer layer of the skin, and the dermis, the deep inner layer of the skin. A second-degree burn produces blisters on the skin. A first-degree burn makes the skin painful and red.
**Third estate, The.** The HOUSE OF COMMONS. Historically the term usually refers to the third chamber (*Tiers État*) of the French ESTATES GENERAL at the time of the Revolution. *See also* ESTATES OF THE REALM.
**Third eye.** In Hinduism and Buddhism, the 'eye of wisdom' in the forehead of a deity's image, especially that of the god Siva.

The following five kinds of 'eyes' are mentioned and explained in the Cula Niddesa: (1) the physical eye (*mamsa-cakkhu*), (2) the divine eye (*dibba-cakkhu*), (3) the eye of wisdom (*pañña-cakkhu*), (4) the eye of a Buddha (*Buddha-cakkhu*), (5) the eye of all-round knowledge (*samanta-cakkhu*). This last is a frequent appellation of the BUDDHA.
**Third man.** In CRICKET a fielder on the off side near the boundary, behind the batsman's wicket. This is the hardest area to hit the ball to, so that a fielder there is apt to be isolated or even forgotten about. There may be an allusion to this situation in the title of Graham Greene's film script (later novelized) for the romantic thriller *The Third Man* (1949), in which the title character is a shadowy figure.
**Third Order.** *See* TERTIARIES.
**Third party.** A person involved by chance in a legal proceeding, especially one against whom indemnity is claimed. Third party insurance for motor vehicle owners is obligatory.
**Third reading.** In parliamentary parlance, the final stage of discussion on a bill. This is usually a formality, and the bill is rarely defeated at this stage.
**Third Reich.** The German state under the rule of Hitler and the NAZI party (1933–45). The term was adopted from the title of Arthur Moeller van den Bruck's cultural study of Germany, *Das Dritte Reich* ('The Third Empire') (1923). In terms of German history the 'First Reich' was the HOLY ROMAN EMPIRE and the 'Second Reich' that under the Hohenzollern emperors (1871–1918).
**Third Republic.** The French Republic established in 1870 after the capitulation of NAPOLEON III at Sedan (4 September). It came to an end with another French capitulation to Germany in 1940, when a collaborationist government was set up under Marshal Pétain at VICHY. The

FOURTH REPUBLIC came into being in 1946 following the resignation of General de Gaulle, and the Fifth Republic followed in 1958 on his re-election as president.

**Third Romulus, The.** Caius Marius, who saved Rome from the Teutons and Cimbri in 101 BC.

**Third wave.** A term coined in the early 1980s by the American futurist Alvin Toffler (b.1928) to denote the age of information technology, as a development of the agrarian first wave and the industrial second wave.

**Third way.** A VIA MEDIA or 'middle way' between the political left and right, especially as evolving through the moral, social or economic failure of either of these. The expression came to be particularly associated with the 'New Labour' policies of Tony Blair after the GENERAL ELECTION of 1997. However, there were many 'third ways' long before this. Examples may be found in the Fascism of the 1920s, in Harold Macmillan's 'capitalism with a human face' in the 1930s, in the path between capitalism and COMMUNISM sought by the Socialist International in the 1950s, in the German GREEN PARTY in the 1970s, and in the Swedish Social Democrats in the 1980s. Tony Blair's 'third way' followed two decades of THATCHERISM on the one hand and the collapse of communism on the other.

**Third World** (French, *tiers monde*). An expression coined in 1952 by the French demographer Alfred Sauvy (1898–1990), when he compared the developing countries of Asia, Africa and Latin America to the pre-Revolutionary third estate in France. The term was subsequently applied to these same countries regarded as distinct from the capitalist ('first') world and communist ('second') world. Sauvy's thesis was that 'the third world is nothing, but wants to be something'.

**Thirteen.** Thirteen was regarded as an unlucky number even among the Romans, who held it as a sign of death and destruction. The origin of the idea that sitting down 13 at a table is unlucky is said to be that, at a banquet in VALHALLA, LOKI once intruded, making 13 guests, and BALDER was slain. The superstition was confirmed in Christian countries by the LAST SUPPER of Christ and the 12 APOSTLES. In the Middle Ages witch covens were believed always to have 13 members. Addison writes:

> I remember I was once in a mixed assembly that was full of noise and mirth, when on a sudden an old woman unluckily observed there were thirteen of us in company. This remark struck a panic terror into several who were present, insomuch that one or two of the Ladies were going to leave the room: but a friend of mine, taking notice that one of our female companions was big with child, affirmed there were fourteen in the room, and that, instead of portending one of the company should die, it plainly foretold one of them should be born. Had not my friend found this expedient to break the omen, I question not but half the women in the company would have fallen sick that night.
>
> 'On popular superstitions', *Spectator* (8 March 1711)

The 13th of any month is widely regarded as an inauspicious day on which to undertake any new enterprise, and it is traditionally thought to be unlucky for a ship to begin a voyage on the 13th, especially if it happens to be FRIDAY THE THIRTEENTH.

**Thirty. Thirty-nine Articles, The.** The Articles of Religion in the BOOK OF COMMON PRAYER largely defining the CHURCH OF ENGLAND's position in certain matters of dogma which were in dispute at the time. They were first issued in 1563, based on the Forty-two Articles of 1553 and revised in 1571. Clergy had to subscribe to them, but since 1865 a more general affirmation has been substituted.

**Thirty pieces of silver.** The sum of money that JUDAS ISCARIOT received from the chief priests for the betrayal of Christ (Matthew 26:5). Hence the expression is used proverbially of a bribe or BLOOD MONEY.

**Thirty-six-line Bible, The.** *See under* BIBLE.

**Thirty-something.** In one's thirties, an age when aims and ambitions crystallize and relationships 'make or break'. The expression was popularized by the American television series so titled, which from 1987 recounted the stories of the family lives of those born in the postwar BABY BOOM. The second part of the term is freely attached to any age decade.

> I suspect a generation gap has opened up between twentysomethings and the middle-aged baby-boomers who thought *they* had created the sexual revolution.
>
> *The Times* (19 September 1998)

**Thirty Tyrants, The.** The 30 magistrates appointed by Sparta over Athens, at the termination of the Peloponnesian War. This 'reign of terror', after one year's continuance, was overthrown by Thrasybulus (403 BC).

In Roman history, those military leaders who endeavoured in the reigns of Valerian and Gallienus (AD 253–268) to make themselves independent princes are also known as the Thirty Tyrants, although the number is loosely applied.

**Thirty-year rule.** The rule that public records may be open to public inspection after a lapse of 30 years. The rule, introduced by the Public Records Act 1967, allows a fresh batch of material to become available at the Public Record Office on the first working day in each January. Some papers, however, are regarded as too sensitive even for this delay and have a longer restriction placed on them.

**Thirty Years' War, The.** The wars in Germany that began in Bohemia in 1618 and were terminated by the Peace of Westphalia in 1648. Traditionally regarded as a struggle initially between German Protestants and Catholics, which was exploited by foreign powers, it was more essentially part of a contest between BOURBON and HABSBURG dynastic interests combined with constitutional struggles inside the Habsburg Empire waged under the cloak of religion. The idea that 'Germany' was universally devastated is largely a myth.

**Thisbe.** *See* PYRAMUS.

**Thistle.** The heraldic emblem of Scotland, which seems to have been adopted by James III (r.1460–88), possibly as a symbol of defence. The motto NEMO ME IMPUNE LACESSIT ('Nobody touches (or provokes) me with impunity') first appeared on the coinage of James VI (r.1567–1625).

Thistles, especially Our Lady's thistle or the Marian or milk thistle, are said to be a cure for stitch in the side. According to the doctrine of signatures, Nature has labelled every plant, and the prickles of the thistle tell that the plant is efficacious for prickles or the stitch. The species called *Silybum marianum*, similarly, owes the white markings on its leaves to milk from MARY's breast, some of which fell on them and left a white mark behind.

**Most Ancient Order of the Thistle, The.** *See under* MOST.

**Thomas. Thomasing.** Collecting small sums of money or obtaining drink from employers on St Thomas' Day. In the City of London, every one of the Common Council has to be elected or re-elected on St Thomas' Day, which was formerly observed on 21 December.

**Thomas Ingoldsby.** *See under* INGOLDSBY.

**Thomas Parr.** *See under* PARR.

**Thomas the Rhymer.** Thomas Ercildoune or Thomas Rymour of Erceldoune (*c*.1220–*c*.1297), border poet and seer, also called Thomas Learmont. He is the reputed author of a number of poems, including one on TRISTRAM (which Sir Walter Scott believed to be genuine), and is fabled to have predicted the death of Alexander III of Scotland, the Battle of Bannockburn, the accession of James VI to the English throne and other events. Erceldoune is the present town of Earlston, about 30 miles southwest of BERWICK. Thomas the Rhymer is not to be confused with Thomas Rymer (1641–1713), historiographer royal to William III.

**Thomists.** Followers of St THOMAS AQUINAS. They were opponents of the SCOTISTS or followers of Duns Scotus. *See also* DUNCE.

**Gospel of Thomas, The.** *See under* GOSPEL.

**St Thomas.** The Apostle who doubted (John 20:25); hence the phrase, 'a doubting Thomas', applied to a sceptic. The story told of him in the APOCRYPHAL Acts of St Thomas is that he was deputed to go as a missionary to India and, on refusing, Christ appeared and sold him as a slave to an Indian prince who was visiting JERUSALEM. He was taken to India, where he baptized the prince and many others and was finally martyred at Mylapore, near Madras.

Another legend has it that Gundaphorus, an Indian king, gave him a large sum of money to build a palace. St Thomas spent it on the poor, 'thus creating a superb palace in heaven'. Through this he is the patron saint of masons and architects, and his symbol is a builder's square.

Another story is that he once saw a huge beam of timber floating on the sea near the coast, and the king unsuccessfully endeavouring, with men and elephants, to haul it ashore. St Thomas desired leave to use it in building a church, and, his request granted, he dragged it easily ashore with a piece of packthread.

His feast-day is 3 July (formerly 21 December). His relics are now said to be at Ortona in the Abruzzi.

**St Thomas Aquinas.** A DOMINICAN scholastic philosopher and theologian (*c*.1225–74) of outstanding authority and intellectual distinction among his contemporaries, whose teachings have been a major influence on the doctrines of the ROMAN CATHOLIC CHURCH. He was the youngest son of Count Landulf of Aquino (midway between Rome and Naples) and became a Dominican in the face of strong family opposition. He was a pupil of ALBERT THE GREAT (Albertus Magnus) and subsequently taught at Paris, Rome, Bologna and Pisa. First nicknamed the DUMB OX, he became Doctor Angelicus and the Fifth DOCTOR OF THE CHURCH. Among his many writings *Summa Theologiae* (*c*.1266) is his classic work. He drew a clear distinction between faith and reason and was considerably influenced by the philosophy of ARISTOTLE. He was canonized in 1323 and his feast-day is 28 January.

**Sir Thomas Gresham.** *See* CLEOPATRA AND HER PEARL; GRASSHOPPER.

**Thone** or **Thonis.** In Greek mythology the governor of a province of Egypt to which, it is said by post-Homeric poets, PARIS took HELEN, who was given by Polydamnia, wife to Thone, the drug NEPENTHES, to make her forget her sorrows.

**Thopas, Tale of Sir.** *See under* TALE.

**Thor.** Son of WODEN, god of war and the second god in the PANTHEON of the ancient Scandinavians, as their VULCAN and god of thunder. He had three principal possessions, a hammer (*Mjöllnir*), typifying thunder and lightning and having the virtue of returning to him after it was thrown, a belt (*Meginjardir*), which doubled his strength, and iron gloves to aid him in throwing his hammer.

He was a god of the household and of peasants and was married to Sif, a typical peasant woman. His name is perpetuated in THURSDAY.

**Thorn. Thorn in one's flesh** or **side, A.** A source of constant irritation, annoyance or affliction, said of objectionable and parasitical acquaintances, obnoxious conditions and the like. There was a sect of the PHARISEES which used to insert thorns in the borders of their gabardines to prick their legs in walking and make them bleed. The phrase is taken from St PAUL'S reference to some physical complaint or misfortune.

> And lest I should be exalted above measure through the abundance of the revelations, there was given to me a thorn in the flesh, the messenger of Satan to buffet me.
>
> 2 Corinthians 12:7

**Crown of Thorns, The.** *See under* CROWN.

**Glastonbury thorn.** *See* GLASTONBURY.

**Rose between two thorns, A.** *See under* ROSE.

**Thorough.** The name given to the methods of government in the reign of CHARLES I associated with Strafford and Laud, especially Strafford's policy in Ireland (1632–9). It was characterized by firm, efficient and orderly government, but was also associated with corruption and tyrannical methods. 'Through' and 'thorough' were then interchangeable terms.

**Thoroughbred.** Of pure or unmixed breed, especially said of horses and cattle. A thoroughbred is a race horse of English breed remotely derived by crossing with Arab and other strains.

**Thoth.** The Egyptian lunar god, usually with the head of an IBIS but sometimes that of a baboon. His chief centre was Hermopolis Magna (modern El-Ashmunein), and he was identified with HERMES by the Greeks. He was the master over writing, languages, laws, annals, calculations and the like and was patron of scribes and magicians. He made the CALENDAR and his control over HIEROGLYPHICS and divine words enhanced his magical powers. He acted as secretary of the gods. At the judgement after death he weighed the heart.

**Thought. Food for thought.** *See under* FOOD.

**New Thought.** *See under* NEW.

**On second thoughts.** *See under* SECOND.

**Penny for your thoughts.** *See under* PENNY.

**Perish the thought!** *See under* PERISH.

**Thousand. Thousand and One Nights, The.** *See* ARABIAN NIGHTS ENTERTAINMENTS.

**Hundreds and thousands.** *See under* HUNDRED.

**One in a thousand.** *See under* ONE.

**Thrash out, To.** To decide and settle by discussion and argument the points at issue. A metaphor from the threshing of corn to separate the grain from the chaff.

**Thread. Thread and thrum.** Everything; good and bad together.

> O Fates, come, come, cut thread and thrum;
> Quail, crush, conclude and quell!
>
> SHAKESPEARE: *A Midsummer Night's Dream*, V, i (1595)

*See also* THRUMS.

**Thread of destiny, The.** That on which destiny depends, the imaginary thread or span of life provided by the FATES.

**Hang by a thread, To.** *See under* HANG.

**Lose the thread, To.** *See under* LOSE.

**Pick up the threads, To.** *See under* PICK.

**Triple thread, The.** *See under* TRIPLE.

**Threadneedle Street.** The street in the City of London leading from Bishopsgate to the Bank of England. The name first appears as Three Needle Street in 1598, and previously it seems to have been called Broad Street, forming part of the present Old Broad Street. The name is usually said to derive from a signboard with three needles on it, or from the arms of the Needlemakers' Company, but it may derive from the children's game of thread-the-needle having been played there.

**Old Lady of Threadneedle Street, The.** *See under* OLD.

**Three.** PYTHAGORAS calls three the perfect number, expressive of 'beginning, middle and end', wherefore he makes it a symbol of deity.

A TRINITY is by no means confined to the CHRISTIAN creed. The BRAHMANS represent their god with three heads, and the world was supposed by the ancients to be under the rule of three gods, i.e. JUPITER (heaven), NEPTUNE (sea) and PLUTO (HADES or hell). Jupiter is represented with three-forked lightning, Neptune with a trident and Pluto with a three-headed dog. There are three FATES, three FURIES, THREE GRACES and three Harpies (*see* HARPY). The SIBYLLINE BOOKS were originally three times three (of which only three survived), the fountain from which HYLAS drew water was presided over by three NYMPHS and the MUSES were three times three. Scandinavian mythology tells of 'the Mysterious Three', i.e. 'Har' ('High'), 'Jafenhar' ('Equally High') and 'Thridi' ('the third'), who sat on three thrones in ASGARD.

Man is threefold (body, mind and spirit), the world is threefold (earth, sea and air), the enemies of man are threefold (the world, the flesh and the DEVIL), the Christian graces are threefold (Faith, Hope and Charity), the kingdoms of Nature are threefold (animal, vegetable and mineral), the cardinal or primary colours are three in number (red, yellow and blue) and so on. *See also* NINE which is three times three.

**Three acres and a cow.** A phrase particularly associated with the English politician Jesse Collings (1831–1920) and his advocacy of radical agrarian policies in the 1880s and the smallholdings and allotments movement in general.

**Three bells, five bells.** At sea a bell is rung at half-hourly intervals to mark the passing of time in the WATCH. Five of the seven watches last four hours. Thus 'three bells' (three strokes on the bell) denotes the third half-hour of the watch, 'five bells' the fifth and so on. 'Eight bells' marks the ending of a watch. The two dog watches are each of two hours duration (4–6 pm and 6–8 pm). The passing of the first DOGWATCH is marked by four bells and that of the second by eight.

**Three-card trick.** A game, also known as 'Find the Lady', in which bets are placed on which is the queen of three cards lying face downwards. The swindle is traditionally worked by grafters on London's Oxford Street and the gullible punter never wins. *See also* THIMBLE-RIGGING.

**Three cheers.** Three successive hurrahs (preceded by 'hip, hip') for the person or thing honoured.

> Then give three cheers, and one cheer more,
> For the hardy Captain of the *Pinafore*!
> W.S. GILBERT: *H.M.S. Pinafore*, I (1878)

**Three Choirs Festival.** A festival for the performance of sacred music given since 1724 by the choirs of the cathedrals of Gloucester, Worcester and Hereford, held in each of the three cities in rotation.

**Three-cornered fight, A.** A parliamentary (or other) contest in which there are three participants.

**Three-day event.** A horse-riding contest held over three days, originating at BADMINTON in 1949. The first day is devoted to dressage, the second to cross-country riding and the third to show-jumping. The major annual contests are the European Championships at Burghley, near Stamford, Lincolnshire, the Badminton Horse Trials, and the British Open Horse Trials at Gatcombe Park, near Stroud, Gloucestershire.

**Three-decker, A.** Properly, in the days of sail, a warship having three gun decks. The term is applied to other triplicates arranged in tiers, such as the old-fashioned pulpit, reading desk and clerk's desk arranged one above the other, and to the three-volume novel, as the usual way of publishing the 19th-century novel. The custom had virtually become extinct by the end of the century.

> Of an average novel the libraries buy as few as they possibly can, frequently not as many as they used to buy in the three-volume form ... In the three-volume days the risk of producing an average novel was reduced to a minimum. Now it can hardly be produced at all.
> EDWARD MARSTON in *The Literary Year-Book* (1901)

The name is also given to a sandwich with three slices of bread.

**Three Estates of the Realm, The.** *See* ESTATES OF THE REALM.

**Three-field system.** The system of crop rotation under the old OPEN-FIELD SYSTEM of agriculture that persisted from manorial times until well into the time of George III (r.1760–1820). The three open arable fields were successively used for wheat or rye, then peas, beans, barley, oats and the like, and left fallow for the third season.

**Threefold man, The.** According to Diogenes Laertius, the body was composed of (1) a mortal part, (2) a divine and ethereal part, called the *phren*, and (3) an ethereal and vaporous part, called the *thumos*.

According to the Romans, man has a threefold soul, which at the dissolution of the body resolves itself into (1) the *manes*, (2) the *anima* or spirit, (3) the *umbra*. The *manes* went either to ELYSIUM OR TARTARUS, the *anima* returned to the gods, but the *umbra* hovered about the body as unwilling to quit it.

According to the Jews, man consists of body, SOUL and spirit.

**Three Fs, The.** Fair rent, free sale and fixity of tenure, which were demanded by the Irish LAND LEAGUE and conceded by Gladstone's Land Act of 1881.

**Three golden balls.** The once familiar pawnbroker's sign is said to have been taken from the coat of arms of the MEDICI family and first introduced to London by the LOMBARD bankers and moneylenders. The positioning of the balls was popularly explained in that there were two chances to one that what was brought to UNCLE would be redeemed.

Three golden balls are also the emblem of St NICHOLAS of Bari, who is said to have given three purses of gold to three virgin sisters to enable them to marry.

> I say to myself each day
> In definitely Marble Halls,
> Today it may be three white feathers,
> But yesterday it was three brass balls.
> NOËL COWARD: *Set to Music* (1938)

**Three Graces, The.** In classical mythology the *Charites* or *Gratiae*, goddesses who bestowed beauty and charm and were themselves the embodiment of both. They were the sisters AGLAIA, THALIA and Euphrosyne, the daughters of ZEUS and Eurynome or, according to some, HERA. *See also* MUSES.

Andrea Appiani (1754–1817), the Italian fresco artist, was known as the 'Painter of the Graces'. Antonio Canova's sculpture *The Three Graces* (1813–16) was the subject of an unseemly legal wrangle in 1994 when plans to export it from Britain to the Getty Museum in California were thwarted by the Court of Appeal.

**Three greater mysteries, The.** The TRINITY, ORIGINAL SIN and the INCARNATION.

**Three great saints of Ireland, The.** St PATRICK, St Columba and St BRIDGET.

**Three Kings, The.** The MAGI.

**Three Kings' Day.** EPIPHANY or Twelfth Day, designed to commemorate the visit of the 'three kings' or Wise Men of the East to the infant Jesus. *See also* MAGI.

**Three Kings of Cologne, The.** The three Wise Men of the East, the MAGI, whose bones, according to medieval legend, were deposited in Cologne Cathedral.

**Three-legged race.** A race between pairs, the left ankle of one pair member being tied to the right of the other to form the third 'leg'. It is popular with children, but coordination is essential for measurable progress.

**Three-line whip.** In politics a written notice, underlined three times to denote urgency, requiring party members to attend a parliamentary vote. As its name suggests, the notice is issued by the party WHIP. A one-line whip means that the matter in question is not contentious, but a two-line whip means that the government expects opposition and that most BACKBENCHERS are expected to vote.

**Three-mile limit.** The usual limit of territorial waters around their coasts claimed by maritime states, including Great Britain and the USA. Some states claim much wider jurisdiction and disputes over territorial waters are not infrequent.

**Three Musketeers, The.** Athos, Porthos and Aramis, the three heroes of Dumas' novels *The Three Musketeers* (1844), *Twenty Years After* (1845) and *Vicomte de Bragelonne* (1848–50). The Musketeers were a mounted guard of gentlemen in the service of the kings of France from 1661 until the Revolution caused their abolition in 1791. They formed two companies, called the Grey and the Black from the colour of their horses. The uniform was scarlet, hence their quarters were known as *La Maison Rouge*. In peace time the Musketeers formed the king's bodyguard, but in war they fought on foot or on horseback with the army. Their ranks included many Scots, either JACOBITE exiles or mere soldiers of fortune.

**Three primitive languages, The.** The Persians say that Arabic, Persian and Turkish are three primitive languages. Legend has it that the serpent that seduced EVE spoke Arabic, the most persuasive language in the world, that ADAM and Eve spoke Persian, the most poetic of all languages, and that the angel GABRIEL spoke Turkish, the most menacing.

**Three-ring circus.** Originally, in American usage, a circus having three rings for simultaneous performances. Hence the figurative sense of an extravagant display

**Three Rs, The.** Reading, writing and arithmetic. The phrase is said to have been originated by Sir William Curtis (1752–1829), an illiterate alderman and lord mayor of London, who gave this as a toast, i.e. 'Riting, Reading and Rithmetic'. In 1998 the home secretary, Jack Straw, proposed three Rs for young offenders: restoration and apology to the victim, reintegration into the community and responsibility on the part of offenders and their parents.

**Three score years and ten.** A ripe old age, not necessarily (in allusive use) exactly 70 years. The reference is to Psalm 90:10:

> The days of our years are three score years and ten; and if by reason of strength they be fourscore years, yet is their strength labour and sorrow; for it is soon cut off, and we fly away.

**Three sheets in the wind.** Very drunk. The sheet is the rope attached to the clew of a sail used for trimming sail. If the sheet is quite free, leaving the sail free to flap without restraint, the sheet is said to be 'in the wind', and 'a sheet in the wind' is a colloquial nautical expression for being tipsy. Thus to have 'three sheets in the wind' is to be very drunk.

> Captain Cuttle looking, candle in hand, at Bunsby more attentively, perceived that he was three sheets in the wind, or, in plain words, drunk.
>
> DICKENS: *Dombey and Son*, ch xxxix (1847–8)

**Three Stooges, The.** Three American knockabout comedians who appeared in hundreds of short films from the 1930s. They were Larry Fine (1911–75), Moe Howard (1895–1975) and Moe's brother, Jerry (Curly) Howard (1906–52). In 1947 Curly was replaced by another brother, Shemp Howard (Samuel Howard) (1891–1955). Their form of slapstick was peculiarly violent.

**Three tongues, The.** Those in which the inscription on the cross was written, i.e. Hebrew, Greek and Latin. In the Middle Ages it was considered that a thorough knowledge of these was necessary before one could begin to understand theology.

**Three Wise Monkeys, The.** Images of three monkeys carved over the door of the Sacred Stable, Nikko, Japan, in the 17th century. They have their paws respectively over their ears, eyes and mouth, representing their motto: 'Hear no evil, see no evil, speak no evil.' The Latin motto of the United Grand Lodge of Freemasons is similar: *Audi, Vide, Tace*, literally, 'Hear, see, keep silent'. This in turn is reminiscent of the traditional Yorkshire rhyme:

Hear all, see all, say nowt,
Aight all, sup all, pay nowt,
And if ever tha does owt for nowt
Do it for thisen.
(Hear everything, see everything, say nothing,
Eat everything, drink everything, pay nothing,
And if ever you do something for nothing,
Do it for yourself.)

**Battle of the Three Emperors, The.** *See under* BATTLE.

**Give someone three times three, To.** To give them a rousing ovation, cheer after cheer.

**League of the Three Emperors, The.** *See under* LEAGUE.

**Page Three.** *See under* PAGE.

**Rule of three, The.** *See under* RULE.

**Song of the Three Holy Children, The.** *See under* SONG.

**We three.** *See under* WE.

**Throat. Clear one's throat, To.** *See under* CLEAR.

**Clergyman's throat.** *See under* CLERGYMAN.

**Cut one's own throat, To.** *See under* CUT.

**Devil's Throat, The.** *See under* DEVIL.

**Frog in the throat, A.** *See under* FROG.

**Have a bone in one's throat, To.** *See under* BONE.

**Jump down someone's throat, To.** *See under* JUMP.

**Lie in one's throat, To.** *See under* LIE.

**Ram** or **force something down someone's throat, To.** *See under* RAM.

**Stick in one's throat, To.** *See under* STICK.

**Words stuck in my throat, The.** *See under* WORD.

**Throgmorton Street.** The financial world at large, or the STOCK EXCHANGE, which is situated in this narrow London street. It is so named from Sir Nicholas Throckmorton (1515–71), head of the ancient Warwickshire family and ambassador to France in the reign of Elizabeth I.

**Throne, The.** A comprehensive name for the office of queen or king, as: 'The throne is above party politics.'

**Thrones, Principalities and Powers.** According to Dionysius the Areopagite these are three of the nine orders of ANGELS. These names or their linguistic counterparts occur frequently in Jewish-Christian writings around New Testament times.

**Speech from the throne, The.** *See* KING'S SPEECH.

**Through.** *See* THOROUGH.

**Through thick and thin.** Despite all difficulties; under any conditions; in good times and bad.

Lo where a griesly Foster [grim forester] forth did rush,
Breathing out beastly lust her to defile:
His tyreling iade [tired horse] he fiercely forth did push,
Through thicke and thin, both ouer banke and bush
In hope her to attaine by hooke or crooke,
That from his gorie sides the bloud did gush.

EDMUND SPENSER: *The Faerie Queene*, III, i (1590)

**Throw. Throw a spanner in the works, To.** To sabotage deliberately a plan or enterprise or to spoil a scheme by creating difficulties or obstructions designed to promote failure, as some machinery can be wrecked by literally throwing a spanner or a piece of metal into moving parts.

**Throw a sprat to catch a mackerel, To.** To give a trifle or make a concession, in the hope of a bigger return.

**Throw away one's money, To.** To spend it carelessly or extravagantly.

**Throw back, To.** To revert to ancestral traits. Someone who does this is a throwback. 'To throw back at someone' is to retort.

**Throw** or **pour cold water on a scheme, To.** To discourage a proposal; to dwell upon its weaknesses and disadvantages and perceived shortcomings; to speak slightingly of it; to dampen the ardour of enthusiasm.

**Throw down the gauntlet, To.** To challenge. In medieval times, when one knight challenged another, the custom was for the challenger to throw his gauntlet on the ground, and if the challenge were accepted the person to whom it was thrown picked it up. Such a challenge was used by the CHAMPION OF ENGLAND.

**Throw dust in someone's eyes, To.** To mislead, dupe or trick them. The allusion is to 'the swiftest runner in a sandy race, who to make his fellows aloofe, casteth dust with his heeles into their envious eyes' (Cotgrave's *Dictionary* (1611)).

The Muslims had a practice of casting dust into the air for the sake of confounding the enemies of the Faith. This was done by the Prophet on two or three occasions, as in the Battle of Honein, and the Koran refers to it when it says: 'Neither didst thou, O Mahomet, cast dust into their eyes; but it was God who confounded them.'

**Throw good money after bad, To.** Having already lost money on a scheme, investment or project, to continue to spend more on what is bound to result in loss.

**Throwing the hammer.** An athletic contest involving the throwing of a 16lb (7.3kg) hammer. The original hammer used was a blacksmith's sledgehammer.

**Throw in one's hand, To.** To abandon a project; to concede defeat. A metaphor from card playing, especially poker.

**Throw in one's lot with someone, To.** To decide to share one's fortune with them.

**Throw in the towel, To.** To concede defeat. The allusion is to boxing, in which a second or trainer would throw the towel in the ring to admit that his man had lost. *See also* THROW UP THE SPONGE.

**Throw it to the dogs.** Throw it away, it is useless and worthless.

> Throw physic to the dogs, I'll none of it.
> SHAKESPEARE: *Macbeth*, V, iii (1605)

**Throw** or **shed light on, To.** To elucidate; to explain.

**Throw oneself at someone, To.** To offer oneself openly to them as a sexual partner.

**Throw oneself into, To.** To involve oneself enthusiastically.

**Throw oneself on someone, To.** To commit oneself to another's mercy or protection.

**Throw one's hat into the ring, To.** To enter a contest or to become a candidate for office. There was a custom of throwing one's hat into the ring as the sign of accepting a pugilist's challenge.

**Throw one's weight about, To.** To behave assertively; to act authoritatively.

**Throw the baby out with the bath water, To.** To reform or alter something so radically or indiscriminately that the essentials are lost.

**Throw the book at, To.** To charge a person with a particular offence; to inflict a severe punishment on someone. The 'book' is imaginary but is based on books that list crimes and their punishments.

**Throw the helve after the hatchet, To.** To be reckless; to throw away what remains because what has already been lost has been so great. The allusion is to the fable of the woodcutter who lost the head of his axe in a river and threw the helve (handle) in after it. By confusion, the expression is sometimes inverted as: 'to send the axe after the helve'.

**Throw to the wolves, To.** To sacrifice someone, such as a colleague or subordinate, usually to divert criticism from the 'thrower', or to abandon a person to their downfall or destruction. A pack of hungry wolves will spring eagerly on anything they see as food and tear it to pieces.

**Throw up one's hands, To.** To give up in despair.

**Throw up** or **in the sponge, To.** To give up; to confess oneself beaten. The metaphor is from boxing matches, for when a second tossed a sponge (used to refresh a contestant) into the air it was a sign that his man was beaten.

**Thrums.** The fringe of warp threads left when the web (woven fabric) has been cut off the loom; weaver's ends of carpet, used for common rugs.

The town featured by Sir James Barrie in *A Window in Thrums* (1889) is Kirriemuir, Forfarshire, his birthplace, a town whose staple industry was linen weaving. At the time of his writing this book, Kirriemuir was one of the few places in which the handloom still existed.

**Thread and thrum.** *See under* THREAD.

**Thurst, Cut and.** *See under* CUT.

**Thug.** A worshipper of KALI, who practised 'thuggee', the strangling of human victims in the name of religion. Robbery of the victim provided the means of livelihood. They were also called *Phansigars* (Hindi, 'noose operators') from the method employed. Vigorous suppression was begun by Lord William Bentinck, the first governor general of India, in 1828, but the fraternity did not become completely extinct for another 50 years or so. In common parlance the word is used for any violent 'tough'. *See also* SUTTEE.

**Thule.** The name given by the ancients to an island, or point of land, six days' sail north of Britain, and considered by them to be the extreme northern limit of the world. The name is first found in the account by Polybius (*c.*150 BC) of the voyage made by Pytheas in the late 4th century BC. Pliny says: 'It is an island in the Northern Ocean discovered by Pytheas, after sailing six days from the Orcades.' Others, like Camden, consider it to be Shetland, in which opinion they agree with Marinus and the descriptions of Ptolemy and Tacitus, and still others that it was some part of the coast of Norway. The etymology of the word is uncertain, although attempts have been made to derive it from Greek *tholos*, 'mud', or *tēle*, 'far'.

**Ultima Thule.** *See under* ULTIMA.

**Thumb.** In the ancient Roman combats, when a GLADIATOR was vanquished, it rested with the spectators to decide whether he should be slain or not. If they wished him to live, they enclosed their thumbs in their fists (*pollice compresso favor judicabatur*). If they wished him to be slain, they turned their thumbs out. The popular saying 'thumbs up', expressive of pleasure or approval, is probably a development from this custom, as is its opposite, 'thumbs down'.

**Thumb a lift, To.** To ask for or to 'scrounge' a ride from a passing vehicle by holding out the hand with the thumb pointing in the direction of intended travel.

**Thumb index.** A series of rounded notches or indentations, cut in the pages of a book showing initial letters or other particulars to enable the reader to find a reference easily.

**Thumbnail.** Used attributively of various things, especially sketches, portraits and so on, that are on a very small scale.

**Thumbscrew.** An instrument of torture used largely by the INQUISITION, whereby the thumbs are compressed between two bars of iron, by means of a screw. The Scottish clergyman William Carstares (1649–1715) was a noted victim. Because the law of England did not permit torture, in 1683 he was sent by the PRIVY COUNCIL for examination in Edinburgh, to elicit the names of the accomplices in the RYE HOUSE PLOT. He remained eighteen months in prison, when he was released for lack of evidence. He later demonstrated the thumbscrews to William III (r.1689–1702), who insisted on trying them and admitted that they would have made him confess to anything.

**Thumb the nose, To.** To COCK A SNOOK.

**All thumbs.** *See under* ALL.

**Bite one's thumb at, To.** *See under* BITE.

**Pricking of one's thumb, The.** *See under* PRICK.

**Rule of thumb.** *See under* RULE.

**Stick out like a sore thumb, To.** *See under* STICK.

**Tom Thumb.** *See under* TOM.

**Twiddle one's thumbs, To.** *See under* TWIDDLE.

**Under someone's thumb.** *See under* UNDER.

**Thummin, Urim and.** *See under* URIM.

**Thunder.** Used figuratively of any loud noise, also of vehement denunciations or threats, as: 'the thunders of the VATICAN', meaning the anathemas and denunciations of the pope.

THOR was the Scandinavian god of thunder and JUPITER in Roman mythology. Hence Dryden's allusion to the inactivity of Louis XIV:

> And threatning *France*, plac'd like a painted *Jove*,
> Kept idle Thunder in his lifted hand.
> *Annus Mirabilis*, xxxix (1667)

**Thunderbolt.** A missile or mass of heated matter that was formerly supposed to be discharged from thunderclouds during a storm, used figuratively of an irresistible blow, a sudden and overwhelming shock. *See also* BOLT FROM THE BLUE.

JUPITER was depicted by the ancients as a man seated on a throne, holding a sceptre in his left hand and thunderbolts in his right.

> Be ready, gods, with all your thunderbolts;
> Dash him to pieces!
> SHAKESPEARE: *Julius Caesar*, IV, iii (1599)

**Thunderer, The.** A name facetiously applied to *The Times* newspaper in the mid-19th century, in allusion to an article by the assistant editor, Edward Sterling (1773–1847), which began: 'We thundered forth the other day an article on the subject of social and political reform.' *See also* PRINTING HOUSE SQUARE.

**Thundering Legion, The.** The XIIth Legion of the Roman army, probably so called because its ensign was a representation of *Jupiter tonans* ('the thundering Jupiter').

The name *Fulminata* dates from the time of Augustus (31 BC–AD 14), but fable relates it to the time of Marcus Aurelius. The story is that in this emperor's expedition against the Marcomanni, Quadi and others (AD 170–174), the XIIth Legion, consisting of Christians, saved the whole army from a disastrous drought by praying for rain. A terrible thunderstorm burst and not only provided abundance of water but dispersed the enemy with lightning and THUNDERBOLTS. Hence the legion's name.

**Blood and thunder.** *See under* BLOOD.

**Sons of Thunder.** *See* BOANERGES.

**Steal someone's thunder, To.** *See under* STEAL.

**Thursday.** The fifth day of the week, or commonly now the fourth. The day of the god THOR, called by the French *jeudi*, i.e. 'JOVE's day'. Both JUPITER (Jove) and Thor were gods of THUNDER and formerly Thursday was sometimes called Thunderday.

**Black Thursday.** *See under* BLACK.

**Holy Thursday.** *See under* HOLY.

**Maundy Thursday.** *See under* MAUNDY.

**Sheer Thursday.** *See under* SHEER.

**Thyestes.** The brother (some sources say the twin) of ATREUS and son of PELOPS and Hippodamia (*see* BRISEIS). He raped his brother's wife and also contrived a situation that led to Atreus slaying his own son. By way of revenge, Atreus invited Thyestes to a banquet in which the limbs of two of his sons, slain by Atreus, were served as a dish. Hence a Thyestean feast means one at which human flesh is served. When AGAMEMNON and MENELAUS, Atreus' sons, who had fled from Mycenae on their father's death, returned with an army to reclaim their father's throne, Thyestes fled to Cytherea, where he died. His son AEGISTHUS later killed Agamemnon and took the throne of Mycenae.

**Thyrsus.** The staff carried by Dionysus (BACCHUS) and his attendants, topped with a pine cone and decorated with vine and ivy leaves. *See also* TORSO.

**Ti.** *See* ARETINIAN SYLLABLES.

**Tiara.** Originally the turban-like head-dress worn erect by the Persian kings and turned down by lords and priests, but now applied to a coronet-like head ornament, especially to the triple crown of the pope. The latter resembles the old-style beehive in shape and until the death of Paul VI (1978) was worn on extra-liturgical occasions. It typifies the temporal or sovereign power of the papacy and is composed of gold cloth encircled by three crowns and surmounted by a golden globe and cross. It is first mentioned in the early 8th century and was a kind of white LIBERTY CAP called *camelaucum*. By the 11th century a coronet had been added to the rim, to which were added in the 13th century two lappets hanging down at the back. The second circlet was added by Boniface VIII (r.1294–1303), perhaps to symbolize both temporal and spiritual powers, and the third coronet was added either by Benedict XI (r.1303–4) or Clement V (r.1305–14).

**Tib. St Tib's Eve.** Never. There is no such saint in the calendar, and her eve is thus non-existent, like the GREEK CALENDS.

**Tiberius.** Tiberius Julius Caesar Augustus (42 BC–AD 37), second emperor of Rome, appears in several historical works as the instigator of a brutal reign of terror. His sexual proclivities are graphically described by Suetonius in his *Lives of the Caesars* (2nd century AD).

**Tich** or **Titch.** A diminutive person, from the celebrated dwarfish music hall comedian Harry Relph (1868–1928), known as Little Tich. As a podgy infant at the time of the TICHBORNE CASE, he was nicknamed 'Tichborne' or 'Tich' in allusion to the Tichborne claimant, who was very corpulent. As he remained a TOM THUMB he came to be called 'Little Tich', a name he used professionally. He first appeared at ROSHERVILLE GARDENS playing a tin whistle and then as a NIGGER MINSTREL. He became renowned for his stage pranks and satirical humour and in due course appeared at the DRURY LANE with Dan Leno and Marie Lloyd. His popularity in Paris gained him the LEGION OF HONOUR.

**Tichborne. Tichborne case.** The most celebrated impersonation case in English law. In March 1853 Roger Charles Tichborne, heir to an ancient Hampshire baronetcy, sailed for Valparaiso, Chile, and after travelling a while in South America embarked on 20 April 1854 in a sailing ship named the *Bella*, bound for Jamaica. The ship went down and nothing more was heard or seen of Roger Tichborne. In October 1865 'R.C. Richborne' turned up at Wagga Wagga, in Australia, in the person of a man locally known as Tom Castro. On Christmas Day 1866 he landed in England as a claimant to the Tichborne baronetcy, asserting that he was the lost Roger. Lady Tichborne, the real Roger's mother, professed to recognize him, but the family could not be deceived. The case came into the courts, where the fellow's claims were proved to be false and he himself identified as Arthur Orton (1834–98), the son of a Wapping butcher. A further trial for perjury, lasting 188 days, ended in his being sentenced to 14 years' penal servitude. Orton confessed in 1884. *See also* B OF BK.

**Tichborne dole.** An ancient charity maintained by the Tichborne family said to have been instituted by Lady Mabel Tichborne in 1150. The legend is that, when dying, she begged her husband to provide for the poor from the produce of the estate, and he promised to give the value of the land she could encircle while holding a burning torch. She rose from her deathbed, encompassed 23 acres and prophesied that if the charity were allowed to lapse, seven sons would be born to the family, followed by seven daughters, and the title would lapse. The dole was stopped after 644 years and the then baronet had seven sons and his heir seven daughters. The third son changed his name to Doughty and revived the dole and escaped the full consequences of the curse. The title became extinct in 1968 with the death of Sir Anthony Doughty-Tichborne, the 14th baronet, who had three daughters but no son.

**Tick. Tick someone off, To.** To rebuke a person or 'tell someone off' sharply. Both 'tick off' and 'tell off' involve the idea of enumerating or checking off a list of complaints or offences.

**Get something on tick, To.** To get it on credit. In the 17th century, 'ticket' was the ordinary term for the written acknowledgement of a debt, and someone living on credit was said to be living on ticket or tick.

**What makes it tick?** *See under* WHAT.

**Ticker tape.** The paper strip on which a telegraphic ticker prints off its information. New York's ticker-tape parades, honouring heroes, athletes, soldiers and statesmen, sprang from the occasion on 29 October 1886 when office workers spontaneously threw ticker tape during a parade for the dedication of the STATUE OF LIBERTY (*see* LIBERTY ENLIGHTENING THE WORLD). Confetti and shredded paper are now added to the ticker tape.

**Ticket.** In American politics, the party list of candidates in an election, as: 'I intend to vote for the straight Republican ticket.'

**Ticket of leave.** A warrant given to convicts to have their liberty on condition of good behaviour, hence, 'ticket-of-leave man', a convict freed from prison but obliged to report himself to the police from to time until his sentence was completed. The system no longer exists and has been superseded by that of parole.

> The lady patroness of Michaelis, the ticket-of-leave apostle of humanitarian hopes, was one of the most influential and distinguished connections of the Assistant Commissioner's wife.
>
> JOSEPH CONRAD: *The Secret Agent*, ch vi (1907)

**All tickety-boo.** *See under* ALL.

**Book a ticket, To.** *See under* BOOK.

**Get one's ticket, To.** In the Merchant Service the expression denotes becoming a qualified mate or master of a ship, i.e. to get one's certificate as such. Thus 'to lose one's ticket' is to have one's certificate withdrawn as a result of incompetence causing the hazarding of a ship.

**Season ticket.** *See under* SEASON.

**Single ticket.** *See under* SINGLE.

**Split ticket.** *See under* SPLIT.

**That's the ticket.** That's the right thing; that's what's wanted. The allusion is to the custom among 19th-century charities of issuing tickets to the needy that could be exchanged for soup, clothing, coal and the like.

**Tyburn ticket.** *See under* TYBURN.

**Work one's ticket, To.** *See under* WORK.

**Tickle. Tickled pink** or **to death.** Very amused or pleased. A tickled person will often be red in the face from laughing.

**Tickle one's fancy, To.** To appeal to one's imagination; to excite one's interest pleasurably.

**Slap and tickle.** *See under* SLAP.

**Tiddy-oggie.** The local name for the Cornish pasty of meat and potato. 'Tiddy' is the dialect word for potato (compare 'tater') and 'oggie' is a pasty. The Cornish miner's lunch usually consisted of a pasty, and its crust was formerly supposed to be sufficiently hard to be dropped down the mine shaft to the man below.

**Tide** (Old English *tīd*, 'time', 'season', 'tide'). The word is cognate with 'time' and with modern German *Zeit*, 'time'. It is used figuratively of a tendency, a current or flow of events or the like, as in a tide of feeling, and in Shakespeare's:

> There is a tide in the affairs of men,
> Which, taken at the flood, leads on to fortune.
> *Julius Caesar*, IV, iii (1599)

*See also* TIDY.

**Tide one over, To.** To help one through a difficult time.

**Tidewaiter.** Formerly, a customs officer who boarded ships entering port to ensure that the customs regulations were observed. The term came to be figuratively applied to someone who waits to see the trend of events before taking action, or which way the 'tide of opinion is flowing'.

**Lee tide.** *See under* LEE.

**Neap tides.** *See under* NEAP.

**Spring tides.** *See under* SPRING.

**Time and tide wait for no man.** *See under* TIME.

**Turn the tide, To.** *See under* TURN.

**Tidy.** The word means in TIDE, in season, in time, as in eventide, springtide and the like. Thomas Tusser (*c*.1524–80) has the phrase, 'If the weather be fair and tidy', meaning seasonable. Things done in their proper season are sure to be done orderly and properly. Hence, by association, tidy came to imply methodical, neat or well arranged.

The word is also used in the sense of a thing being worth consideration: 'a tidy penny' is thus quite a good sum, and 'a tidy fortune' is an inheritance worth having.

**Tie. Tied house.** A retail business, especially a public house, that is tied by agreement to obtain its supplies from a particular firm.

**Tied to one's mother's apron strings, To be.** Completely under one's mother's thumb, particularly of a young man dominated by his mother.

> Even at his age, he ought not to be always tied to his mother's apron string.
> ANNE BRONTË: *The Tenant of Wildfell Hall*, I, ch iii (1848)

**Tie-wig.** The small wig as worn by barristers.

**Black tie.** *See under* BLACK.

**Ride and tie, To.** *See under* RIDE.

**White tie affair, A.** *See under* WHITE.

**Tiercel.** *See* TASSEL-GENTLE.

**Tiffany.** A kind of thin silk-like gauze. The word is related to theophany (Greek *theos*, 'god', and *phainein*, 'to show'), the manifestation of God to man, the EPIPHANY, and the material was so called because it used to be worn at the TWELFTH NIGHT (Epiphany) revels. The first name Tiffany was formerly given to girls born about the time of the Epiphany (6 January), and this in turn gave the surname, as that of Charles L. Tiffany (1812–1902), founder in 1837 of the noted New York firm of jewellers.

**Tiffin.** An old north of England provincialism for a small draught of liquor; also a lunch or slight repast between breakfast and dinner. In Anglo-Indian usage it denoted a light meal or lunch, especially of curried dishes, chutney and fruit.

> 'I bought a pineapple at the same time, which I gave to Sambo. Let's have it for tiffin; very cool and nice this hot weather.'
> W.M. THACKERAY: *Vanity Fair*, ch iv (1847–8)

**Tiger.** The nickname was given to the following:

- Georges Clemenceau (1841–1929), the French statesman
- Tipu Sahib, Sultan of Mysore (1750–99), who was ruthless and warlike

A liveried servant who rides out with his master used to be called a tiger, and the name is also applied to a boy in buttons, a page. In America the word is applied to a final yell in a round of cheering.

In poker, tiger is the lowest hand that can be drawn: six high, ace low, without pair, straight or flush. Great nerve is required to hold and bluff on such a hand, and the expression is responsible for the title of the Original Dixieland Jazz Band hit *Tiger Rag* (1918). *See also* YARBOROUGH.

**Tiger Tim.** The mild little cartoon tiger, leader of the Bruin Boys, first appeared in the *Daily Mirror* in 1904 as the creation of the artist Julius Stafford Baker. For many years he and his chums appeared in the children's weekly comic *Rainbow*.

**Paper tiger.** *See under* PAPER.

**Tigger.** The toy tiger who, with WINNIE-THE-POOH, is

one of the animal friends of CHRISTOPHER ROBIN in the children's stories by A.A. Milne. He makes his first appearance in *The House at Pooh Corner* (1928), in which three of the ten stories concern him. He suddenly shows up in the forest as 'a Very Bouncy Animal, with a way of saying How-do-you-do, which always left your ears full of sand'.

**Tight.** In colloquial usage, 'intoxicated'.

**Tighten one's belt, To.** To economize. Tightening the belt reduces the size of the stomach, so that the pangs of hunger are lessened.

**Blow me tight!** *See under* BLOW.

**In a tight spot** or **corner.** In a jam or difficulty; up against it.

**Keep a tight rein on, To.** To control carefully or to limit, as: 'We must keep a tight rein on expenses this year.'

**Sit tight, To.** *See under* SIT.

**Tike** or **tyke.** A provincial word (from Old Norse) for a dog or cur, hence used of a low or rough-mannered fellow, as in the contemptuous insults, 'you dirty tike', 'you measly tyke'.

**Yorkshire tike, A.** *See under* YORK.

**Tilbury.** A once fashionable well-sprung, two-wheeled horse carriage or gig, without top or cover, designed by John Tilbury of London in the early 19th century. He was a horse dealer and later a job master, and both NIMROD (Major Charles Apperley) and Apperley's fictional creation, John Mytton, used his mounts.

**Tile.** Old slang for a hat, this being to the head what tiles are to a house.

> Where did you get that hat?
> Where did you get that tile?
> Isn't it a nobby one
> And just the proper style?
>
> JAMES ROLMAZ: 'Where Did You Get That Hat?' (1888)

**Tile a lodge, To.** In FREEMASONRY to close and guard the doors to prevent anyone uninitiated from entering, the officer who does this being called the tiler, sometimes spelled tyler.

**Have a tile** or **slate loose, To.** To be not quite *compos mentis*; to be 'not all there'.

**Night on the tiles.** *See under* NIGHT.

**On the tiles.** On a spree; on the loose; on a drinking bout. *See also* NIGHT ON THE TILES.

**Till.** Now a less formal equivalent of 'until'.

**Till the cows come home.** For an indefinitely long time. Dairy herds formerly worked on a more natural cycle than they do today when cows are milked daily, and under normal conditions in a dry spell they would not come in from pasture for some time.

**Till the pips squeak.** Said of anything that exerts extreme pressure on someone, literally or metaphorically. It is an allusion to the squeezing of such fruits as oranges and lemons.

> The Germans, if this Government is returned, are going to pay every penny; they are going to be squeezed as a lemon – until the pips squeak. My only doubt is not whether we can squeeze hard enough, but whether there is enough juice.
>
> SIR ERIC GEDDES: Speech at Cambridge, 10 December 1918, *Cambridge Daily News* (11 December 1918)

**Till Eulenspiegel.** *See under* EULENSPIEGEL.

**Tilt. Tilt at windmills, To.** To face imaginary adversaries. The allusion is to *Don* QUIXOTE (I, viii (1605)) when the crazy knight imagines them to be giants and gives battle.

**Tilting at the quintain.** An ancient military exercise and pastime, particularly practised by medieval knights. A dummy figure or just a head, often representing a Turk or Saracen, was fastened to pivot or swing horizontally from an upright stake fixed in the ground. The knight tilted at the figure, and if he did not strike it in the right place with his lance it moved round at speed and struck him in the back before he could pass on. There were various forms of quintain, and in the 14th century Londoners used to tilt from boats, the quintain being fixed to a mast erected in the Thames. Tilting at the quintain remained a rustic sport, associated particularly with wedding festivities, until the outbreak of the English Civil Wars (1642–51). The word is probably from Latin *quintana*, 'fifth', a street in a Roman camp between the fifth and sixth maniples where the camp market was situated, supposedly a place for martial exercise.

**At full tilt.** *See under* AT.

**Tim, Tiger.** *See under* TIGER.

**Timber. Jack timbers.** *See under* JACK.

**Shiver my timbers.** *See under* SHIVER.

**Timbuctoo** or **Timbuktu.** An ancient African city on the southern edge of the Sahara, 'the part of the Sudan in the Sahara', which first began as a settlement in the 11th century and subsequently developed as a mart for gold and achieved legendary repute. It was the last great goal of 19th-century European travellers searching for fabulous wealth and splendour. Major Alexander Gordon Laing (1793–1826) reached it from Tripoli only to be murdered by Arabs in his bivouac, but René Caillé of Bordeaux (1799–1838), to whom its then ruinous condition became apparent, made a safe return in 1828. It was occupied by the French in 1894 and is now in the Republic of Mali.

**From here to Timbuctoo.** *See under* FROM.

**Time. Time and tide wait for no man.** One of many sayings denoting the folly of procrastination.

**Time-expired.** Applied to soldiers whose term of service is completed. Also used of convicts who have served their sentences.

**Time, gentlemen, please!** The traditional announcement for closing time in bars and public houses.

**Time-honoured Lancaster.** Old John of Gaunt, Duke of Lancaster (*c*.1340–99), so called by Shakespeare (*Richard II*, I, i (1595)) because his memory had been honoured by Time. His father was Edward III, his son Henry IV and his nephew Richard II, and through his great-granddaughter, Margaret Beaufort, he is the ancestor of all British sovereigns from Henry VII, Margaret's son. Shakespeare calls him 'old', but he was only 59 at his death.

**Time lag.** The term given to the pause that elapses between a cause and its effect.

**Time of grace.** *See* SPORTING SEASONS IN ENGLAND.

**Time of one's life, The.** A memorably pleasant or highly enjoyable time.

**Time of Troubles** (Russian *Smutnoye vremya*). In Russian history, the years 1584–1613, a period of monarchical instability, foreign intervention, social disorder and economic crises. It began with the accession of Ivan IV's son Feodor, who was incapable of exercising his office, with resultant intrigues among the boyars, and did not end until the accession of Michael Romanov in 1613. Boris Godunov was proclaimed Tsar in 1598 and ruled until his death in 1605, but from 1604 various pretenders intrigued for the throne. In 1609 King Sigismund of Poland intervened until Patriarch Hermogen stimulated national resistance, which led to the election of Michael by the Zemsky Sobor and the expulsion of the Poles.

**Time out of mind.** Time longer than anyone can remember. *See also* FROM TIME IMMEMORIAL.

**Time-sharing.** A system of part ownership whereby each participant buys the right to use a holiday home for the same fixed period annually. The scheme has drawn criticism for its irresponsible and even fraudulent management by some firms.

**Time was.** There was a time, as: 'Time was when I went for a swim every morning.'

**Time zone.** *See* STANDARD TIME.

**Ahead of one's time.** *See under* AHEAD.

**All in good time.** *See under* ALL.

**At the best of times.** *See under* AT.

**At this moment in time.** *See under* AT.

**Beat time, To.** *See under* BEAT.

**Behind the times.** *See under* BEHIND.

**Big time.** *See under* BIG.

**Borrowed time.** *See under* BORROW.

**Buy time, To.** *See under* BUY.

**Closing time.** *See under* CLOSE.

**Double time.** *See under* DOUBLE.

**Down time.** *See under* DOWN.

**Drinking-up time.** *See under* DRINK.

**Father Time.** *See under* FATHER.

**From time immemorial.** *See under* FROM.

**From time to time.** *See under* FROM.

**Gain time, To.** *See under* GAIN.

**Good times.** *See under* GOOD.

**Good time was had by all.** *See under* GOOD.

**Greenwich Time.** *See under* GREENWICH.

**Half the time.** *See under* HALF.

**Have a time of it, To.** To experience problems or difficulties.

**Have had one's time, To.** In the Second World War a British soldier's expression for being ripe for death; to expect imminent disaster. In the Royal Navy, part of the traditional 'Wakey, wakey' chant when calling the hands is, 'You've had your time', i.e. your allotted period of rest.

**Have no time for someone, To.** To be intolerant of them or impatient with them.

**High time.** *See under* HIGH.

**In no time** or **less than no time.** Very quickly; almost instantly.

**In one's own good time.** At a time and rate decided by oneself.

**In one's own time.** Outside working hours.

**In the nick of time.** *See under* NICK.

**Know the time of day, To.** *See under* KNOW.

**Long time no see.** *See under* LONG.

**Make time, To.** To set aside time for a person or thing when one is otherwise busy.

**Mark time, To.** *See under* MARK.

**Needle time.** *See under* NEEDLE.

**Not before time.** Not too soon; timely.

**Old-time dancing.** *See under* OLD.

**Old time.** *See under* OLD.

**Pass the time of day, To.** *See under* PASS.

**Peace in our time.** *See under* PEACE.

**Play for time.** *See under* PLAY.

**Second of time, A.** *See under* SECOND.

**Serve one's time, To.** *See under* SERVE.

**Standard time.** *See under* STANDARD.

**Summer Time.** *See under* SUMMER.

**Take one's time, To.** To use as much time as one needs.

**Take time by the forelock.** Seize the present moment; CARPE DIEM. Time, called by Shakespeare 'that bald sexton' (*King John*, III, i (1596)), is represented with a lock of hair on his forehead but none on the rest of his head, to signify that time past cannot be used, but time present may be seized by the forelock. The saying is attributed to Pittacus of Mitylene, one of the WISE MEN OF GREECE. It is also suggested that the statue of Opportunity by Lysippus inspired the phrase.

**Thin time.** *See under* THIN.

**Timeo Danaos.** *See* GREEK GIFT.

**Times Square.** The garish heart of Manhattan, New York City, famous (and infamous) for its lurid neon advertisements, its theatres and cinemas, and its prostitutes and pickpockets. It evolved as a commercial centre in the 19th century and was originally known as Long Acre Square. It gained its present name early in the 20th century when the *New York Times* erected a building nearby on 43rd Street.

**Timoleon.** The Greek general and statesman (d.*c*.336 BC) who so hated tyranny that he voted for the death (*c*.364) of his own brother Timophanes when the latter made himself tyrant in Corinth.

**Timon of Athens.** An Athenian misanthrope of the late 5th century BC and the principal figure in Shakespeare's play of this name (1607).

**Timothy.** In the New Testament a faithful friend of PAUL, a minister at Ephesus, and the recipient of the two epistles addressed to him.

> O Timothy, keep that which is committed to thy trust, avoiding profane and vain babblings, and oppositions of science falsely so called.
> 1 Timothy 6:20

**Timur.** *See* TAMBERLANE.

**Tin.** Money. A deprecatory synonym for silver, called JUPITER by alchemists.

**Tin fish.** Naval slang for a torpedo.

**Tin god.** A self-important person. *See also* TINPOT.

**Tin hat.** A soldier's name for his protective metal helmet. To 'put the tin hat' on something is to bring it to an abrupt and conclusive end.

**Tin lizzie, A.** An old car; a jalopy or 'banger'. The name was originally an American nickname for a Model T Ford, itself probably so called as it was sturdy, dependable and black, like the traditional Southern servant, called Elizabeth.

**Tinny.** Australian slang for a can of beer.

> While Sydneysiders are used to celebrating the festive season quietly with a turkey and a few 'tinnies' on the beach, their northern hemisphere cousins suffer an immediate metamorphosis when enveloped by the temptations of the Australian Christmas.
> *The Times* (21 December 1994)

**Tin Pan Alley.** The district of New York City, originally in the area of BROADWAY and 14th Street, where popular music is published. In London, Denmark Street, off Charing Cross Road, was so called as the centre of the popular music industry. The name probably derives from the 19th-century jazz musician's nickname 'tin pan' for a cheap tinny piano. The 'Alley' is now largely deserted by song writers and music publishers who have moved to bigger premises. *See also* OLD GREY WHISTLE TEST.

**Tinpot.** Cheap; inferior; puny, as: 'A tinpot dictator.' *See also* TIN GOD.

**Tin soldier.** A miniature soldier, usually made of lead rather than tin. Also, a name for someone who enjoys 'playing at soldiers'.

**Tin tabernacles.** The name given to the corrugated iron Nonconformist chapels and other churches, which were erected in the 19th and early 20th centuries to meet the needs of developing or scattered Christian communities.

**Tincture.** In HERALDRY, the hues or colours of the shield and its charges. It include metals, colours and furs.

**White tincture.** *See under* WHITE.

**Tinderbox, The Pig and the.** *See under* PIG.

**Tinker. Immortal Tinker, The.** *See under* IMMORTAL.

**Not to give a tinker's curse** or **cuss.** Not to care in the least.

**Not worth a tinker's damn** or **cuss.** *See under* WORTH.

**Tintagel.** The castle on the north coast of Cornwall fabled as King ARTHUR's Castle and, according to Geoffrey of Monmouth (*Historia Regum Britanniae*, xix (*c*.1136)), the birthplace of King Arthur. The present ruin upon the cliff is of mid-12th-century origin.

**Tintin.** A cub reporter who is the main character of the comic strip stories by the Belgian artist Hergé (Georges Rémi). He has a constantly worried expression beneath his quiff of hair, and is accompanied everywhere by his faithful dog, Milou (Snowy, in the English versions). He first appeared in 1929. His name relates to French slang *tintin*, 'nothing at all'.

**Tip.** A small present of money, such as that given to a waiter or porter, from the CANT verb (common in the 16th and 17th centuries) 'to tip', meaning 'to hand over', which also gives rise to the other signification of the verb, i.e. private warning, such secret information as may guide the person tipped to make successful bets or gain some other advantage. A 'straight tip' comes straight or direct from the owner or trainer of a horse, or from one in a position to know.

**Tip and run raid.** A phrase used in the Second World War to denote a hurried and often indiscriminate air raid when the enemy sped homeward after jettisoning their bombs. So called from the light-hearted form of CRICKET in which the batsman is forced to run every time he hits the ball.

**Tip-off.** A warning, especially a timely one, as of a police raid.

**Tip of the iceberg, The.** That which is merely on the surface; a small or superficial manifestation of something, with the implication that there is much more or worse to follow of which the present is only a beginning. Ninety per cent of a real iceberg is submerged.

**Tip one's hat or cap, To.** To touch or raise it in greeting or acknowledgement.

**Tip someone the wink, To.** To signal information to someone by a wink; to tip a person off, i.e. to give them a hint or warning.

**Tip the balance, To.** To make the critical difference.

**Tip the scales, To.** *See* TURN THE SCALES.

**Tip-top.** First rate; capital; splendid.

**On the tip of one's tongue, To be.** To be just about to utter something or to have it on the verge of one's memory but to be unable to say it because one cannot finally recall it.

**Tiphys.** The pilot of the ARGONAUTS, hence a generic name for pilots.

**Tipperary.** The song, 'It's a long way to Tipperary', is inseparably associated with the First World War. It was composed by Jack Judge (1878–1938), of Oldbury, Birmingham, and the words were by Harry J. Williams (1874–1924) of Temple Balsall, Warwickshire (now Solihull). The first line of the refrain was engraved on his tombstone. It was composed in 1912 and was already popular in the MUSIC HALL by 1914. It was sung by troops embarking for France and on the front.

It's a long way to Tipperary,
It's a long way to go;
It's a long way to Tipperary,
To the sweetest girl I know!
Goodbye, Piccadilly,
Farewell, Leicester Square;
It's a long, long way to Tipperary,
But my heart's right there!

**Tippling house.** A contemptuous name for a tavern or public house. A tippler was formerly a tavern-keeper or tapster, and the tavern was called a tippling house. At Boston, Lincolnshire, in 1577, five people were appointed 'tipplers of Lincoln beer', and no 'other tippler [might] draw or sell beer' under penalties.

**Tipstaff.** A constable, bailiff or SHERIFF'S officer, so called because he carried a staff tipped with a bull's horn or with metal. In the documents of Edward III (r.1327–77) allusion is often made to his staff.

**Tirant lo Blanch.** A romance of CHIVALRY by Joanot Martorell and Martí Joan de Galba, written in Catalan and produced at Valencia in 1490. It was a favourite book of Cervantes and one that figures in Don QUIXOTE'S library. It to some extent parallels the story of GUY OF WARWICK, which Martorell had seen in London. The title is the name of the central character, Tirant the White, a type of WHITE KNIGHT. The first English translation to appear was that of David H. Rosenthal in 1984 under the title *Tirant lo Blanc*.

**Tired, Sick and.** *See under* SICK.

**Tiresias.** A Theban of Greek legend, who by accident saw ATHENE bathing and was therefore struck with blindness by her splashing water in his face. She afterwards repented and, as she could not restore his sight, conferred on him the power of soothsaying and of understanding the language of birds, giving him a staff with which he could walk as safely as if he had his sight. He found death at last by drinking from the well of Tilphusa.

Another story is that he had been temporarily changed into a woman (for seven years) and was therefore called upon by JUPITER and JUNO to settle an argument as to which of the sexes derived the greatest pleasure from making love. Tiresias, speaking from experience, declared in favour of the female, whereupon Juno struck him blind.

It was Tiresias who revealed to OEDIPUS that he had killed his father and married his mother, and it was Tiresias who during the attack of the SEVEN AGAINST THEBES advised CREON that the city could be saved only by the sacrifice of an unmarried noble, advice that led to Creon's son Menoeceus throwing himself from the city walls.

**Tirl.** A Scottish variant of 'twirl'

**Tirl at the pin, To.** To twiddle or rattle the latch before opening the door. The pin was part of the door latch and it was a signal that one wished to enter.

**Tironian.** Pertaining to a system of shorthand said to have been invented by Tiro, the freedman and amanuensis of CICERO. The symbol '&' (*see* AMPERSAND) has been called the Tironian sign, for it represents the contraction of Latin *et* introduced by Tiro.

**Tisiphone.** *See* FURIES.

**Titania.** The wife of OBERON and queen of the fairies. Shakespeare uses the name in *A Midsummer Night's Dream* (1595).

**Titans.** In Greek mythology the offspring of URANUS and GAIA, of enormous size and strength and typical of lawlessness and the power of force. There were twelve: six male (Coeus, Crius, HYPERION, IAPETUS or Japetus, KRONUS and OCEANUS) and six female (MNEMOSYNE, PHOEBE, RHEA, TETHYS, Theia and THEMIS). This is according to Hesiod, but the number is variously given by other writers.

Incited by their mother, they overthrew Uranus and castrated him and set up Kronus as king. Kronus was in turn overthrown by his son ZEUS. After the long struggle that some of the Titans carried on against Zeus, they were finally hurled down into TARTARUS. *See also* GIANTS' WAR WITH ZEUS.

Virgil and Ovid sometimes surnamed the sun as Titan, hence Shakespeare's:

And flecked Darkness like a drunkard reels
From forth Day's path and Titan's fiery wheels.
*Romeo and Juliet*, II, iii (1594)

**Titch.** *See* TICH.

**Tit for tat.** Retaliation. The phrase probably represents 'tip for tap', i.e. blow for blow, although some authorities favour an origin in Dutch *dit* *vor dat* ('this for that'), corresponding to Latin QUID PRO QUO or the LEX TALIONIS. *See also* EYE FOR AN EYE AND A TOOTH FOR A TOOTH.

**Tithes.** One-tenth of the produce of the land given to the church, at first voluntarily but made compulsory by the end of the 8th century. The great tithes were those of the major crops, the small consisting of lesser produce. With the growth of the parochial system, they became an important item in the income of the parson and source of friction between clergy and their parishioners. With the rise of the PURITANS and later Nonconformity, a new grievance arose. Commutation of tithes began before 1600 and an attempt to commute tithes to a single rent charge was begun by an Act of 1836. The Tithe Act of 1936 extinguished all tithe rent-charges and replaced them by an annuity payable for 60 years by the landowner to the Crown. The Finance Act of 1977 finally ended payment of this annuity, and in 1988 all the remaining stock created under the 1936 Act was redeemed from the beneficiaries by the Treasury. Tithes have therefore ceased to exist in England altogether. *See also* TENTHS *under* TEN; VICAR.

**Saladin tithe.** *See under* SALADIN.

**Tithing.** King CANUTE provided that all free men and boys over the age of 12 should be put in a tithing, a group of ten upon which rested the responsibility of securing the good behaviour of the group.

**Tithonus.** A handsome Trojan of Greek legend, brother or son of Laomedon and beloved by EOS (Dawn). At his prayer, the goddess granted him immortality, but as he had forgotten to ask for youth and vigour he grew old, and life became insupportable. He now prayed Eos to remove him from the world. This, however, she could not do, but she changed him into a GRASSHOPPER, so that he could change his aged skin each year. Tithonus and Eos had two sons, Emathion and MEMNON.

**Titi, Prince.** The nickname of Frederick, PRINCE OF WALES (1707–51), eldest son of George II. In constant opposition to his father, he wrote the *Histoire du Prince Titi* (1735), which contained gross and unmanly caricatures of his father and mother, Caroline of Anspach. Two English translations of this offensive work appeared in 1736. *Titi* suggests French *petit*, 'little', 'tiny'.

**Titivil.** *See* TUTIVILLUS.

**Title. Titled trains.** A number of passenger trains on mainline routes have borne titles since the early 20th century. Most are now extinct, but some have been revived in more recent times. Below is a selection of some of the best known, with their routes (omitted when given in the cross-referred entry).

Atlantic Coast Express (London–Padstow)
BON ACCORD (Glasgow–Aberdeen)
Bournemouth Belle (London–Bournemouth)
Brighton Belle (London–Brighton)
Bristolian (London–Bristol)
Broadsman (London–Norfolk) (*see* BROADS)
Caledonian (London–Glasgow) (*see* CALEDONIA)
Cathedrals Express (London–Oxford–Worcester–Hereford)
Cheltenham Flyer (London–Cheltenham)
Clansman (London–Inverness) (*see* CLAN)
Cornish Riviera Express (*see* RIVIERA)
Coronation Scot (London–Glasgow) (introduced to mark the coronation of George VI in 1937)
Devon Belle (London–Plymouth)
Elizabethan (London–Edinburgh) (introduced to mark the coronation of Elizabeth II in 1953)
Emerald Isle Express (London–Holyhead) (*see* EMERALD ISLE)
Fair Maid (London–Edinburgh–Perth) (*see* FAIR MAID OF PERTH)
Fenman (London–Hunstanton) (*see* FENS)
FLYING SCOTSMAN
GOLDEN ARROW
GOLDEN HIND
GRANITE CITY (London–Aberdeen)
HEART OF MIDLOTHIAN (London–Edinburgh)
Highlandman (London–Inverness) (*see* HIGHLANDS)
HIGHWAYMAN (*see under* HIGHWAY)
Kentish Belle (London–Canterbury) (the name partly puns on CANTERBURY BELL)
Lakes Express (London–Windermere) (*see* LAKE DISTRICT)
LANCASTRIAN (London–Manchester)
Mancunian (London–Manchester) (*see* MANCHESTER)
Master Cutler (London–Sheffield) (*see* SHEFFIELD PLATE)
MAYFLOWER (London–Plymouth)
Merchant Venturer (London–Bristol) (*see* MERCHANT ADVENTURERS)
Palatine (London–Manchester) (*see* COUNTY PALATINE)
Pines Express (Manchester–Bournemouth) (named for Bournemouth's prolific pines)
Queen of Scots (London–Edinburgh–Glasgow) (*see* MARY, QUEEN OF SCOTS)
RED DRAGON (London–Carmarthen)
RED ROSE (London–Liverpool)
ROBIN HOOD (London–Nottingham)
Royal Duchy (London–Penzance) (*see* DUKE)
Royal Scot (London–Glasgow)
Royal Wessex (London–Bournemouth) (*see* WESSEX)
St Mungo (Glasgow–Aberdeen) (*see* KENTIGERN)
Scandinavian (London–Harwich)
Silver Jubilee (London–Newcastle) (introduced 1935; *see* JUBILEE)
TALISMAN (London–Edinburgh)
Waverley (London–Edinburgh) (*see* WAVERLEY NOVELS)
WHITE ROSE (London–Leeds–Bradford)

**Title role.** In a play, opera or film, the part or role from which the title is taken, e.g. HAMLET, CARMEN, KING KONG.

**Titles of kings.** *See* RULERS.

**Abstract of title.** *See under* ABSTRACT.

**Clerical titles.** *See under* CLERGY.

**Courtesy titles.** *See under* COURTESY.

**Titmouse.** *See* MISNOMERS.

**Tittle, Jot or.** *See under* JOT.

**Titular bishops.** Roman Catholic bishops without a diocese, who take their title from a place where there is no longer a bishop's see. Until 1882 they were known as bishops *in partibus infidelium* ('in the regions of the faithless').

**Titus.** An alternative name for DISMAS. Also the name of one of St PAUL'S disciples to whom he wrote one of his Epistles. This latter Titus is traditionally regarded as the first bishop of Crete, where he died. His head was eventually carried off by the Venetians and the skull was returned to the ORTHODOX CHURCH in Crete in 1964.

**Arch of Titus, The.** *See under* ARCH.

**Tityre-tus.** Dissolute young scapegraces of the late 17th century whose delight was to annoy the watchmen, upset SEDAN CHAIRS, wrench knockers off doors and insult pretty women. The name comes from the first line of Virgil's first *Eclogue* (1st century BC), *Tityre, tu patulae recubans sub tegmine fagi* ('Tityrus, thou lying at ease under the shade of the spreading beech tree'), because the Tityre-tus loved to lurk in the dark night looking for mischief. *See also* MOHOCKS.

**Tityrus.** A poetic name for a shepherd, from its use in Greek idylls and Virgil's first *Eclogue* (1st century BC). *See also* TITYRE-TUS.

In *The Shepheardes Calender*, 'February', 'June' and 'December' (1579), Edmund Spenser calls Chaucer by this name.

> But shall I tel thee a tale of truth,
> Which I cond [learned] of *Tityrus* in my youth,
> Keeping his sheepe on the hils of Kent?
> *The Shepheardes Calender*, 'February'

**Tityus.** In Greek mythology a gigantic son of ZEUS and GAIA (or of Elara) whose body covered 9 acres (3.6 ha) of land. He tried to rape LATONA (LETO), the mother of APOLLO and ARTEMIS, but Apollo cast him into TARTARUS, where a vulture fed on his liver which grew as fast as it was devoured. *See also* PROMETHEUS.

**Tiu, Tiw or Tyr.** In Scandinavian mythology the son of ODIN and a younger brother of THOR. He had his hand bitten off when chaining up the wolf FENRIR. He was identified with MARS, the Roman god of war, and his name is found in 'Tuesday' (French *mardi*). Philologists have generally equated the name with Greek ZEUS, Latin *Deus*, Sanskrit *devas*.

**Tizona.** The CID's sword.

**Tizzy.** A sixpence, a variant of TESTER. *See also* TANNER.

**Tmesis** (Greek, 'cutting'). The grammatical term for the separation of the parts of a compound word by inserting other words between them, or the rearrangement thus of the words of a phrase, e.g. 'A large meal and rich', instead of, 'A large, rich meal', or 'The greatness of his power to usward' (Ephesians 1:19) instead of 'The greatness of his power toward us.'

**To. To a fault.** Excessively, as: 'generous to a fault'. Excess of every kind is almost a defect. A similar idea is expressed in the phrase KILL BY KINDNESS.

**To a man.** Without exception; all together; everyone; unanimously, as: 'The audience applauded to a man.'

**To arms!** Arm yourselves! Prepare for battle!

**To a T.** Exactly. The allusion is to the use of a T-square for the accurate drawing of right-angles, parallel lines and so on.

**To Birmingham by way of Beachy Head.** Metaphorically, a roundabout approach. It is a quotation from G.K. Chesterton's poem 'The Rolling English Road' (1914):

> A merry road, a mazy road, and such as we did tread
> The night we went to Birmingham by way of Beachy Head.

**To boot.** In addition, from Old English *bōt*, 'compensation'.

**To date.** As yet; up to now.

**'To remain' Bible, The.** *See under* BIBLE.

**To the bad.** On the wrong side of the account; in arrears.

**To the bitter end.** Until the present hard time or task is over, or until final defeat or death. In nautical parlance, the bitter end is the end of a rope or chain secured in a vessel's chain locker, or tied to one of the bitts, the strong posts on the deck to which mooring lines are attached. The association with bitter in the sense 'sharp', 'unpleasant', may have been aided by the biblical words: 'But her end is bitter as wormwood' (Proverbs 5:4).

**To the fore.** In the front rank; eminent.

**To the full.** To the utmost extent; as completely as possible.

**To the life.** In exact imitation; representing an original in every detail.

**To the manner born.** Naturally suited to a particular thing. The expression comes from Shakespeare's *Hamlet*, I, iv (1600), where it means 'subject to the custom from birth'. Hamlet explains to Horatio and Marcellus why a flourish of trumpets and the sound of guns has been heard. He says it means that the king 'doth wake tonight and ... keeps wassail'. Horatio asks if this is a custom:

> Ay, marry, is't:
> But to my mind,—though I am native here
> And to the manner born,—it is a custom
> More honour'd in the breach than the observance.

The expression is frequently given as 'to the manor born', apparently from the belief that the allusion is to one born to wealth or luxury. This misapprehension was reinforced by the popular television series *To the Manor Born* (1979–81), starring Penelope Keith as Audrey fforbes-Hamilton, an upper-class lady forced to move out of her STATELY HOME.

**To the tune of.** To the amount of, as: 'I had to pay up to the tune of £500.'

**To wit.** Namely; that is to say.

**Toad. Toad-eater or toady.** A cringing parasite; an obsequious lickspittle. The old MOUNTEBANKS used to take around with them a boy who ate, or pretended to eat, toads, then believed to be poisonous. This gave the master the chance to exhibit his skill in expelling poison.

> Be the most scorn'd Jack-Pudding of the pack,
> And turn toad-eater to some foreign quack.
>
> THOMAS BROWN: 'Satire on an Ignorant Quack', *Works*, i (1704)

**Toad-in-the-hole.** A dish of sausages baked in batter.

**Toads.** The device of CLOVIS was three toads (or *botes*, as they were called in Old French). Legend relates that after his conversion and baptism, the ARIANS assembled a large army under King Candat against him. While he was on his way to meet the heretics, Clovis saw in the heavens his device miraculously changed into three lilies or on a blue banner. He instantly had such a banner made and called it his ORIFLAMME, and even before his army came in sight of King Candat, the host of the HERETIC lay dead, slain, like the army of SENNACHERIB, by a blast from the God of Battles. *See also* FLEUR-DE-LIS.

**Toads unknown in Ireland.** It is said that St PATRICK cleared the island of all vermin by his malediction.

**Toad, ugly and venomous, wears yet a precious jewel in its head, The.** Thomas Nashe (*Anatomie of Absurditie* (1589)) says, 'It fareth with finer wits as it doth with the pearl, which is affirmed to be in the head of the toad', and Shakespeare says:

> Sweet are the uses of adversity,
> Which, like the toad, ugly and venomous,
> Wears yet a precious jewel in its head.
>
> *As You Like It*, II, i (1599)

Thomas Lupton, in his *One Thousand Notable Things* (1579), speaks of the virtues of the toadstone, which the toad carried inside its head. 'A toad-stone (*crapaudina*) touching any part envenomed, hurt, or stung with rat, spider, wasp, or any other venomous beast, ceaseth the pain or swelling thereof.' Such stones, toad-like in shape or colour, believed to have come from the toad, were used as amulets and set in rings. Toads were also generally held to be poisonous.

**Toast.** The person or thing to which guests are invited to drink in compliment, as well as the drink itself. The word is taken from the piece of toast that used at one time to be put into the tankard and that still floats in the LOVING CUPS at the old universities.

The story goes that in the reign of Charles II, a certain beau pledged a noted beauty in a glass of water taken from her bath, whereupon another roysterer cried out he would have nothing to do with the liquor, but would have the toast, i.e. the lady herself.

**Toastmaster.** The official who announces the after-dinner speakers at a formal banquet. He must be a man of stentorian voice and enjoy a nice knowledge of precedence.

**As warm as toast.** *See under* AS.

**French toast.** *See under* FRENCH.

**Loyal Toast, The.** *See under* LOYAL.

**Yorkshireman's toast.** *See under* YORK.

**Tobacco baron.** In prison slang, a 'baron' is a prisoner who traffics in various items such as sweets, cigarettes, tobacco and the like. Tobacco is the most sought-after commodity, and rations are often mortgaged for a smoke. The term 'Tobacco baron', for one who wields power by trading in tobacco, or 'snout', is a term more commonly used by journalists than the prisoners themselves.

**Tobias.** *See* TOBIT.

**Tobit.** The central character of the popular story in the Book of Tobit in the APOCRYPHA. Tobit is a scrupulous and pious Jew who practised good works, but, while sleeping in his courtyard, being unclean from burying a Jew found strangled in the street, he was blinded by sparrows, which 'muted warm dung in his eyes'. His son Tobias was attacked on the Tigris by a fish, which leapt out of the water and which he caught at the bidding of the angel RAPHAEL, his mentor. Tobit's blindness was cured by applying the gall of the fish to his eyes. Father and son prepared to reward Azarias (Raphael), whereupon the angel revealed his identity and returned to heaven.

**Tobit's dog.** *See* CAMEL.

**Toby.** The dog in the puppet show of PUNCH AND JUDY. He wears a frill garnished with bells to frighten away the Devil from his master.

**Toby jug.** A small jug in the form of a squat old man in 18th-century dress, wearing a three-cornered hat, one corner of which forms the lip. The name comes from a poem (1761) about one 'Toby Philpot', adapted from the Latin by Francis Fawkes (1720–77), and the design of the jug from a print sold by Carrington Bowles, a London print seller, to Ralph Wood, the potter, who turned out a great number of Toby jugs.

**Sir Toby Belch.** *See under* BELCH.

**Toc H.** The old telegraphy code for the letters TH, the initials of Talbot House. The term was used in the First World War, when the first Talbot House was founded, in December 1915, at Poperinghe, Belgium, in memory of Gilbert Talbot, son of the bishop of Winchester, who had been killed at Hooge in the preceding July. The Rev. P.T.B. 'Tubby' Clayton, MC, made it a famous rest and recreation centre. In 1920 he founded a similar centre in London, also known as Toc H, which developed into an inter-denominational association for Christian social service. *See also* PIP EMMA.

**Tod, To be on one's.** To be alone, a contraction of Tod Sloan in cockney RHYMING SLANG. James Forman 'Tod' Sloan (1874–1933) was a famous American jockey.

**Today a man, tomorrow a mouse.** Fortune is so fickle that one day we may be at the top of the wheel, and the next day at the bottom. The French equivalent is: *Aujourd'hui roi, demain rien* ('Today king, tomorrow nothing'). *See also* WHEEL OF FORTUNE.

**Toddy.** Properly the juice obtained by tapping certain palms, fermented so as to become intoxicating. It is also applied to a beverage made of spirits, hot water and sugar, a kind of PUNCH. The word comes from Hindi *tārī*, the juice of the palmyra palm, from *tār*, the name of the tree itself.

**Toe. Toe-curling.** Embarrassing; 'cringe-making'; such as to make one squirm.

**Toehold.** An initial grasp or gain of something. The allusion is to a hold in wrestling, in which one's opponent's toe is grasped.

**Toerag.** A slang term for a despicable person. The name was originally used for a tramp or beggar, who wrapped pieces of rag around their feet instead of socks.

**Toe the line, To.** To submit to discipline or regulations; to come into line with the rest. In foot races the runners are made to assemble with toes up to the start line.

**Toe the party line, To.** To follow or be coerced into following party policy.

**Dip one's toe in, To.** *See under* DIP.

**From top to toe.** *See under* FROM.

**On one's toes.** Alert and eager. Young children often stand or dance on tiptoe when excited or eager.

**Tread on someone's toes, To.** *See under* TREAD.

**Turn up one's toes, To.** *See under* TURN.

**Tofana.** *See* AQUA TOFANA.

**Toffee-nosed.** In its sense of 'supercilious', the word is a pun on 'toff', this being a 'superior' person who looks down his nose at others.

**Toga.** The distinctive public garb of the Roman citizen, consisting of a single semicircular piece of white woollen cloth worn in a flowing fashion round the shoulders and body. The Romans were hence the *Gens togata*, the 'togaed people'. It was also worn by freed women and prostitutes (respectable women wore the *stola*). *See also* GALLIA BRACATA; GENS BRACATA; PALLIUM.

**Toga candida.** A new toga whitened with chalk, worn by candidates for public office when they appeared before the people.

**Toga picta.** The toga embroidered with golden stars that was worn by the emperor on special occasions, or by a victorious general at his TRIUMPH.

**Toga praetexta.** The toga bordered (*praetexta*) with purple that was worn by children, by those engaged in sacred rites, magistrates on duty and others.

**Toga virilis.** The toga worn by men (*virilis*, 'manly'), assumed at the age of 15.

**Together, To get it.** To achieve one's full potential. 'To get one's act together' is to organize oneself; to make an effort, especially when one has not previously been doing so.

**Togs.** Slang for clothes, hence 'togged out', dressed in one's best clothes, and toggery, finery. The word is probably connected with TOGA. It is also the source of the 'tog' as a unit of thermal resistance used to express the insulating properties of clothes and quilts. This was itself based on the earlier American equivalent, 'clo'.

**Toil. Blood, toil, tears and sweat.** *See under* BLOOD.

**Token payment.** A small payment made as a formal and binding acknowledgment of indebtedness. The word 'token' is often used to describe some action or phrase used in lieu of, but acknowledging, a greater obligation.

**Tokyo Rose.** The name given by US servicemen to a woman broadcaster of propaganda from Japan during the Second World War. Several American-born Japanese ('Nisei', literally 'second generation') girls were suspected of taking part in these broadcasts but only one was found guilty. *See also* HAW-HAW, LORD.

**Tolbooth** or **tollbooth.** Originally a booth or stall where taxes were collected.

> And whanne Jesus passide fro thennis, he saw a man,
> Matheu bi name, sittingge in a tolbothe.
> JOHN WYCLIF, Matthew 9:9 (*c*.1388)

In Scotland the term was applied to the town jail, from the custom of confining offenders against the laws of a fair or market in the booth where market dues were collected. The old Edinburgh tolbooth was the HEART OF MIDLOTHIAN.

**Toledo.** A sword made at Toledo in Spain, which place, long before and after the Middle Ages, was specially famous for them. *See also* ANDREA FERRARA; BILBO.

> I give him three years and a day to match my
> Toledo,
> And then we'll fight like dragons.
> PHILIP MASSINGER: *The Maid of Honour*, II, ii
> (1621–2)

**Toll, Charon's.** *See under* CHARON.

**Tolpuddle Martyrs.** Six agricultural labourers of Tolpuddle, Dorset, who formed a TRADE UNION to resist wage cuts. They were sentenced to seven years' transportation to Australia in 1834 on a concocted charge of administering illegal oaths. After continuous protests they were pardoned in 1836, returning home two years later.

**Tom** or **Tommy.** Short for Thomas, used for the male of certain animals (especially the cat), and generically, like JACK, for a man or boy. It sometimes has a somewhat contemptuous implication, as in TOMFOOL; TOM O'BEDLAM.

> The man that hails you Tom or Jack,
> And proves by thumps upon your back
> How he esteems your merit,
> Is such a friend, that one had need
> Be very much his friend indeed
> To pardon or to bear it.
>
> WILLIAM COWPER: 'Friendship' (1782)

**Tom and Jerry.** Names formerly used for roystering young men about town, from Pierce Egan's *Life in London; or, The Day and Night Scenes of Jerry Hawthorn, Esq, and his Elegant Friend Corinthian Tom* (1821). In modern times the names are familiar from the cat and mouse cartoon characters. They first appeared in an animated cartoon called *Puss Gets the Boot* in 1940. Their names were chosen from hundreds of suggestions submitted by studio employees in a contest held at MGM, the film company that launched them. The characters themselves were created by the veteran animators, William Hanna and Joseph Barbera.

Tom and Jerry is also the name of a hot mixed drink containing rum, brandy, egg, nutmeg and sometimes milk.

**Tomboy.** A boyish girl, especially one who enjoys outdoor activities. The word was also used of a loose or immodest woman, whence the slang name, Tom, for a prostitute. A famous literary tomboy is Jo March, in Louisa M. Alcott's novels *Little Women* (1868) and *Good Wives* (1869). The word was first applied to a boisterous boy before settling to the opposite gender.

> Of such short-haired Gentlewomen I find not one example either in Scripture or elsewhere. And what shall I say of such poled rigs, ramps and Tomboyes?
>
> THOMAS STOUGHTON: *The Christian's Sacrifice*, ch xii (1622)

**Tom Collins.** *See* JOHN COLLINS.

**Tom, Dick and Harry.** A Victorian term for the MAN IN THE STREET, more particularly people of no note or people unworthy of notice. 'Brown, Jones and Robinson' are for the vulgar rich, who give themselves airs, especially abroad, and look with scorn on all foreign manners and customs that differ from their own.

**Tomfool.** A clumsy, witless fool, fond of stupid practical jokes. Hence 'tomfoolery'.

**Tom Gate.** The great gate of Christ Church, Oxford, begun by Wolsey and completed (1682) by Christopher Wren. In its tower is GREAT TOM.

**Tom Hickathrift.** *See under* HICKATHRIFT.

**Tommy** or **Tommy Atkins.** A British army private soldier, as a JACK TAR is a British sailor. From 1815 and throughout the 19th century Thomas Atkins was the name used in the specimen form accompanying the official manual issued to all army recruits, supplied to show them how details of name, age, date of enlistment and the like should be filled in on their own form.

> O it's Tommy this, an' Tommy that, an' 'Tommy, go away';
> But it's 'Thank you, Mister Atkins', when the band begins to play.
>
> RUDYARD KIPLING: *Barrack Room Ballads*, 'Tommy' (1892)

**Tommy bar.** This is a small bar of rounded metal used for inserting into and turning box spanners and similar tools.

**Tommy gun.** A Thompson short-barrelled submachine-gun, so named after its co-inventor, the American army officer John T. Thompson (1860–1940).

**Tommyrot.** Utter nonsense; rubbish; otherwise TOMFOOL behaviour.

**Tom Noddy, A.** *See under* NOD.

**Tom o'Bedlam.** A wandering beggar who levies charity on the plea of insanity. In the 16th and 17th centuries many harmless inmates of BEDLAM were let out to beg and such a mendicant was called an ABRAHAM MAN. A famous anonymous Elizabethan poem is called 'Tom of Bedlam's Song'. *See also* BESS O'BEDLAM.

**Tom Piper.** The name of the piper in the MORRIS DANCE.

**Tom Quad.** The great quadrangle of Christ Church, Oxford. *See also* GREAT TOM.

**Tom's.** A noted COFFEE house of the late 18th century, that was in existence in Russell Street, COVENT GARDEN, as late as 1865. It was owned and named after Thomas West, and here in 1764 was founded Tom's Club, which included most of the literary and social notables of the day.

**Tom Spring.** *See under* SPRING.

**Tom Styles.** *See under* STYLES.

**Tom Swifties.** A development of the WELLERISM, in which an adverb relates both properly and punningly to a sentence of reported speech. An example is: '"What can I get you?" asked the waitress fetchingly.' The quip takes its name from Tom Swift, a boy's adventure hero created by the prolific American writer Edward L. Stratemeyer in the early 20th century. Tom Swift rarely passed a remark without a qualifying adverb, as 'Tom added eagerly' or 'Tom smiled ruefully', and the wordplay arose as a pastiche of this.

**Tom Thumb.** Any dwarfish or insignificant person is so called from the tiny hero of the old nursery tale, popular in the 16th century. *The History of Tom Thumb* was published by Richard Johnson in 1621, and there was a similar tale by Perrault, *Le Petit Poucet* (1697).

Henry Fielding wrote a burlesque (acted 1730) entitled *Tom Thumb the Great*. The American DWARF Charles Sherwood Stratton (1838–83) was called General Tom Thumb when he was first exhibited by Phineas T. Barnum. The 'General' was then under 5 years of age and less than 24in (61cm) in height but eventually grew to 40in (102cm). When at London he was summoned to Buckingham Palace by Queen Victoria and subsequently visited King Louis Philippe in France. He married another American dwarf, Lavinia Warren, in 1863. *See also* BOAST OF ENGLAND; DWARF.

**Tom Tiddler's ground.** A place where it is easy to pick up a fortune or make a place in the world for oneself. The name comes from the old children's game in which a base keeper, who is called Tom Tiddler, tries to keep the other children from crossing the boundary into his base. As he does so, they sing:

> Here we are on Tom Tiddler's ground
> Picking up gold and silver.

**Black Tom.** *See under* BLACK.
**Great Tom of Lincoln.** *See under* GREAT.
**Great Tom of Oxford.** *See under* GREAT.
**Long Tom.** *See under* LONG.
**Old Tom.** *See under* OLD.
**Uncle Tom.** *See* UNCLE TOM'S CABIN.

**Tomahawk.** The war axe of the Native Americans, prehistorically made of stone or deer horn, but after the coming of the white man, of iron or steel with a wooden handle. Sometimes the blunt end of the head was hollowed into a pipe bowl, the handle being bored to form a stem. *See also* BURY THE HATCHET.

**Tombola.** A type of lottery or raffle, especially at a fête, in which winning tickets or numbers are drawn from a revolving drum. The word comes from Italian *tombolare*, 'to somersault', a word related to English 'tumble'.

**Tommy.** *See under* TOM.

**Tomorrow. Jam tomorrow.** *See under* JAM.
**Today a man, tomorrow a mouse.** *See under* TODAY.

**Tongs. Hammer and tongs.** *See under* HAMMER.
**Lazy tongs.** *See under* LAZY.

**Tongue. Tongues are wagging.** There is talk; there are rumours; people are gossiping.

**Tongue-twister.** A sequence of words difficult to pronounce quickly and correctly. There are many classic examples, not all of which actually 'twist the tongue'. The following is more likely to trick the lips:

> Peter Piper picked a peck of pickled peppers;
> A peck of pickled peppers Peter Piper picked;
> If Peter Piper picked a peck of pickled peppers,
> Where's the peck of pickled peppers Peter Piper
> picked?

**Bite one's tongue, To.** *See under* BITE.
**Confusion of tongues.** *See under* CONFUSION.
**Devil's tongue.** *See under* DEVIL.
**Find one's tongue, To.** *See under* FIND.
**Gift of tongues, The.** *See under* GIFT.
**Haven't you got a tongue in your head?** Why didn't you say something at the time? It is no good complaining now that the opportunity has been missed.
**Hold one's tongue, To.** *See under* HOLD.
**Keep a civil tongue in one's head, To.** *See under* CIVIL.
**Keep a clean tongue, To.** *See under* CLEAN.
**Lose one's tongue, To.** *See under* LOSE.
**Mother tongue.** *See under* MOTHER.
**On the tip of one's tongue, To be.** *See under* TIP.
**Three tongues, The.** *See under* THREE.
**With one's tongue hanging out.** *See under* WITH.
**With one's tongue in one's cheek.** *See under* WITH.

**Tonic sol-fa.** A system of musical notation and sight singing in which diatonic scales are written always in one way (the keynote being indicated), the tones being represented by syllables or initials, and time and accents by dashes and colons. Tonic is a musical term denoting pertaining to, or founded on, the keynote; sol and fa are two of the ARETINIAN SYLLABLES. The system was developed in the 1840s by the Rev. John Curwen (1816–60), a CONGREGATIONALIST minister who made use of the earlier work of Miss Sarah Anna Glover (1786–1867). *See also* DOH; GAMUT.

**Tonnage** or **tunnage.** From the 12th century English imports of Bordeaux wine increased steadily and the ships carried it in huge casks or tuns containing 252 gallons (1145.6 litres), occupying some 60 cubic feet (1.7 cu m) in the holds. In due course this became the unit of measurement of the stowage or tonnage of a ship.

Today tonnage is either displacement tonnage, the weight of water displaced by the ship, gross tonnage, the internal capacity of the vessel in tons of 100 cubic feet (2.8 cu m), or net or register tonnage, which is essentially its carrying capacity as recorded in *Lloyd's Register of Shipping* (now independent of LLOYD'S). Many measures are now made in the tonne or metric ton.

**Tonnage and poundage.** Customs duties levied from the early years of the 14th century and granted to the sovereign by Parliament from 1373 until their abolition in 1787 (except during the reign of CHARLES I, when they were levied without parliamentary consent). Tonnage came to be fixed at 3 shillings on a cask or tun of wine and poundage a 5 per cent duty on all imports and exports.

**Tonsure** (Latin *tonsura*, 'shearing'). The shaving of part of the head among Roman Catholic clergy became customary in the 6th and 7th centuries as a mark of the clerical state. It is not retained in such countries as Britain and the USA, where it is not in accordance with custom. The western form of tonsure leaving a circle of hair around the head is said to symbolize the CROWN OF THORNS. The Celtic tonsure consisted of shaving off all the hair in front of a line extending over the head from ear to ear. In the East the whole head was shorn. The modern Roman Catholic tonsure varies among the different orders and that of the secular clergy is a small circle on the crown of the head.

**Tontine.** A form of annuity shared by several subscribers, in which the shares of those who die are added to the holdings of the survivors until the last survivor inherits all. It is so named from Lorenzo Tonti (1620–90), a Neapolitan banker who introduced the system into France in 1653. In 1765 the HOUSE OF COMMONS raised £300,000 by way of tontine annuities at 3 per cent, and as late as 1871 the *Daily News* announced a proposed tontine to raise £650,000 to purchase the Alexandra Palace (ALLY PALLY) and 100 acres (40.5 ha) of land.

**Too. Too big for one's boots, To be.** To be unduly self-confident; to be above oneself, conceited, COCKSURE.

**Too big for one's breeches, To be.** To be TOO BIG FOR ONE'S BOOTS.

**Too funny for words.** Too amusing to be adequately described. The adjective is variable, as: 'His speech was too pathetic for words.'

**Have too much of a good thing, To.** 'Enough is as good as a feast.'

> 'Too much of a good thing' suggests that the Nemesis on departures from the golden mean applies to good things as well as bad.
>
> R.G. MOULTON: *Shakespeare as a Dramatic Artist* (1885)

**Tooley Street.** A corruption of St Olaf Street. Similarly, Sise Lane is St Osyth's Lane.

**Tools, To down.** *See under* DOWN.

**Tooth** or **teeth. Teeth are drawn.** When one's teeth are drawn, one's power of doing mischief is taken away. The phrase comes from the fable of the lion in love, who consented to have his teeth drawn and his claws cut, in order that a fair damsel might marry him. When this was done the girl's father attacked the lion and slew him.

**Armed to the teeth.** *See under* ARM.

**As scarce as hen's teeth.** *See under* AS.

**Bit between one's teeth, The.** *See under* BIT.

**Buck tooth.** *See under* BUCK.

**By the skin of one's teeth.** *See under* BY.

**Cast in someone's teeth, To.** *See under* CAST.

**Cut one's eye-teeth on, To.** *See under* CUT.

**Cut one's teeth, To.** *See under* CUT.

**Cut one's wisdom teeth, To.** *See under* CUT.

**Dragon's teeth.** *See under* DRAGON.

**Eye teeth.** *See under* EYE.

**Fight tooth and nail, To.** *See under* FIGHT.

**Get one's teeth into something, To.** To get to grips with something; to set to work with energy and determination.

**Have a sweet tooth, To.** *See under* SWEET.

**In the teeth of the wind.** With the wind dead against one, blowing in or against one's teeth.

**Kick in the teeth.** *See under* KICK.

**Lie in one's teeth, To.** *See under* LIE.

**Long in the tooth.** *See under* LONG.

**Milk** or **baby teeth.** *See under* MILK.

**Put teeth into something, To.** Said of a law, regulation or the like, when steps are taken to make it effective.

**Set one's teeth, To.** *See under* SET.

**Set one's teeth on edge, To.** *See under* SET.

**Show one's teeth, To.** *See under* SHOW.

**Sow dragon's teeth, To.** *See under* SOW.

**Take the bear by the tooth, To.** *See under* BEAR.

**Wisdom tooth.** *See under* WISDOM.

**Top. Top banana.** The top comedian in a show, or the top person or leader generally. The expression originated from an old skit involving the sharing of a banana. *See also* SECOND BANANA.

**Top brass.** The most important officials or leaders, as in industry or politics.

**Top dog.** The one who by skill, personality or violence obtains the mastery, as the dog who is on top of his adversary in a fight.

**Top drawer.** Upper class; of top grade socially. The expression probably derives from the fact that the top drawers of a chest often contain the more valued of one's personal effects. *See also* BOTTOM DRAWER.

**Top-heavy.** Liable to tip over because the centre of gravity is too high.

**Top-hole.** Excellent; splendid; TOP-NOTCH. A rather dated term.

**Top-notch.** Excellent. The reference is probably to the notch cut in a board to record the score in a game. TOP-HOLE is similar.

**Top o' the morning to ye!** A cheery greeting on a fine day, regarded as typical of the Irish. It is about the same as: 'All the best to you!'

**Topping out.** A traditional drinking ceremony

when the framework of a building is completed and the highest stone put in place.

**Tops, The.** The best.

**Top secret.** Service or governmental information about which the greatest secrecy is to be observed. *See also* HUSH-HUSH.

**At the top of the tree.** *See under* AT.

**Big top, The.** *See under* BIG.

**Blow one's top, To.** *See under* BLOW.

**Can you top that?** Can you beat or surpass that? An American phrase, especially in the telling of outlandish stories.

**Flat top.** *See under* FLAT.

**From top to toe.** *See under* FROM.

**Off the top of one's head.** *See under* OFF.

**On top of the world.** Exuberant; in excellent health and with one's affairs flourishing.

**Over the top.** *See under* OVER.

**Sleep like a log or top, To.** *See under* SLEEP.

**Thin on top.** *See under* THIN.

**Tophet.** The valley of the children of Hinnom through which children were made 'to pass through the fire of Moloch' (2 Kings 23:10). Isaiah (30:31), in prophesying the destruction of the Assyrians, foretold that their king would be destroyed by fire in Tophet. It is a loathsome place associated with horror and defilement, a place of human sacrifice, but its location is a matter of surmise. The name is taken as symbolic of hell, and it may mean 'place of burning'.

> The pleasant Vally of Hinnom, Tophet thence
> And black Gehenna call'd, the Type of Hell.
> MILTON: *Paradise Lost*, i (1667)

**Toplady ring.** A ring set with stones in the form of the pips on the ten of diamonds, named after Augustus Montague Toplady (1740–78), in allusion to the story of his beginning to write the ROCK OF AGES on this playing card.

**Topsy.** The little black slave-girl in Harriet Beecher Stowe's UNCLE TOM'S CABIN (1852), chiefly remembered because when asked by 'Aunt Ophelia' about her parents, she maintained that she had neither father nor mother, her solution of her existence being: 'I 'spect I growed. Don't think nobody never made me.'

**Topsy-turvy.** Upside down, in a state of confusion. The term probably comes from 'tops' and obsolete 'terve', a verb meaning to turn upside down, itself perhaps related to Old English *tearflian*, 'to roll over'.

**Torah** (Hebrew, 'precept'). The Jewish term for the PENTATEUCH, which contains the Mosaic Law, otherwise the revealed will of God as contained in the Jewish SCRIPTURES.

**Torch.** The code name for the Allied plan for the North African landings which began on 8 November 1942.

**Torch or put to the torch, To.** To set fire to; to burn down, especially deliberately.

**Carry a torch for someone, To.** *See under* CARRY.

**Hand on the torch, To.** *See under* HAND.

**Torpids.** The name given to the spring (Hilary Term) boat races at Oxford, between the college eights. The races were originally held between the college second eights and were not always taken seriously. The crews were consequently considered lethargic or 'torpid'.

> The torpids being filled with the refuse of the rowing men – generally awkward or very young oarsmen.
> THOMAS HUGHES: *Tom Brown at Oxford*, Pt II, ch iv (1861)

**Torquemada, Tomás de.** An infamous Inquisitor-General of Spain (1420–98), whose zeal in torturing Jews and heretics, among others, made his name a byword for cruelty and persecution. It is purely a coincidence that his name evokes Latin *torquere*, 'to torture'. It actually comes from the village so called in Old Castile, its own name meaning 'burnt tower', from *torre*, 'tower', and *quemada*, 'burnt'. This name also happens to have appropriate overtones for an inquisitor. *See also* INQUISITION.

**Torricelli, Evangelista.** An Italian mathematician and physicist (1608–47), noted for the discovery of atmospheric pressure and his explanation of the rise of mercury in a common barometer. The phenomenon is explained by Spinoza's words: NATURE ABHORS A VACUUM.

**Torso.** A statue or human body devoid of head and limbs. The word is Italian for a trunk or stalk, from Latin THYRSUS, the staff borne by BACCHUS.

**Torso Belvedere, The.** The famous torso of HERCULES in the VATICAN, discovered in the 15th century. It is said that MICHELANGELO greatly admired it.

**Tortoise.** This animal is frequently taken as typifying plodding persistence, 'slow but sure'.

In Hindu myth, the tortoise Chukwa supports the elephant Maha-padma, which in its turn supports the world.

The name 'tortoise' (Latin *testudo*) is also given to the ancient Roman protective shelter formed by soldiers with shields overlapping above their heads when attacking a fort.

**Achilles and the tortoise.** *See under* ACHILLES.

**Hare and the tortoise, The.** *See under* HARE.

**Torture. Chinese water torture.** *See under* CHINESE.

**Water Torture.** *See under* WATER.

**Tory** (Irish *tóraighe*, 'pursuer'). The name applied in the 17th century to Irish Roman Catholic outlaws and bandits who harassed the English in Ireland. In the reign of Charles II (1660–85), the name came to be used as an abusive term for the supporters of the crown and its prerogatives at the time of the struggle over the Exclusion Bills.

As supporters of the CHURCH OF ENGLAND they opposed NONCONFORMIST and Roman Catholic alike, but most of them acquiesced in the Revolution of 1688. Tory extremists remained JACOBITES at the time of the Hanoverian succession, which led to a WHIG monopoly of political power during the reigns of George I and George II, after which they regained office under Pitt the Younger and remained dominant throughout the period of the French Revolutionary and Napoleonic Wars. From about 1830 the Tory party under the leadership of Sir Robert Peel came to be called CONSERVATIVE, the older name being associated with reaction. Nowadays Tory and Conservative are essentially interchangeable terms, with Tory preferred in newspaper headlines for its brevity. *See also* DIEHARD; LIBERAL; UNIONIST.

> Tory MPs fail to deliver party cash.
> *The Times* (headline) (23 September 1998)

**Tosca.** The self-centred heroine of Puccini's opera that bears her name (1900), itself based on Victorien Sardou's play *La Tosca* (1887). Her jealousy causes her lover, Cavaradossi, to be arrested for treason. Given an opportunity to trade her sexual favours in return for his release, she agrees, only to stab the villain, Scarpia, before it is consummated. She finally throws herself into the Tiber.

**Toss. Toss off, To.** To drink off in a single draught; to dispatch a task easily or effortlessly.

**Toss the oars, To.** To raise them vertically, resting on the handles. This is a form of salute.

**Toss-up, A.** An even chance; a matter of HEADS OR TAILS, as in the spinning of a coin.

**Argue the toss, To.** *See under* ARGUE.

**Pitch and toss.** *See under* PITCH.

**Totem.** A Native American (Ojibwa) word for some natural object, usually an animal, taken as the EMBLEM of a person or clan on account of a supposed relationship. Persons bearing the same totem were not allowed to marry, thus totemism prevented intermarriage between near relations. The animal borne as one's totem must neither be killed nor eaten. Totemism is common among primitive peoples.

**Totem pole.** A post standing before a dwelling on which grotesque and frequently brilliantly coloured representations of the TOTEM were carved or hung. It is often of great size, and sometimes so broad at the base that an archway is cut through it.

**Tottenham, The Tournament of.** *See under* TOURNAMENT.

**Touch. Touch and go.** A very narrow escape, a metaphor derived, perhaps, from driving, when the wheel of one vehicle touches that of another without damaging it. It was a touch, but because neither vehicle was stopped, each could go on.

**Touch bottom, To.** To run aground.

**Touch down, To.** In rugby and American football, to score by touching the ball on the ground within a certain defined area behind the opponent's goal posts. When an aircraft lands it is also said to touch down.

**Touch not the cat** or, in full, **touch not the cat but a glove.** The punning motto of the Mackintosh clan, whose crest is a 'cat-a-mountain salient guardant proper', with 'two cats proper' for supporters. Their clan was the clan Cattan or Chattan, thus 'touch not the clan Cattan'. The meaning of 'but' here is 'without'. The saying is quoted by Sir Walter Scott in *The Fair Maid of Perth* (1828), and *Touch Not the Cat* (1976) is the title of a romantic thriller by Mary Stewart.

**Touch pieces.** *See* KING'S EVIL.

**Touch someone on the raw, To.** To mention something that makes them wince, like touching a horse on a raw place in combing or brushing him.

**Touchstone.** A dark, flinty schist, jasper or basanite (the *Lapis Lydius* of the ancients), so called because gold was assayed by comparing the streak made on it by the sample of gold with those made by touch needles of known gold content, after all the streaks had been treated with nitric acid. The needles were made of varying proportions of gold and silver, gold and copper, or of all three metals. Hence the use of touchstone as any criterion or standard.

Ovid (*Metamorphoses*, Bk II, xi (1st century AD)) tells that Battus saw MERCURY steal APOLLO'S oxen, and Mercury gave him a cow to secure his silence, but, being distrustful of the man, changed himself into a peasant, and offered him a cow and an ox if he would tell him where he got the cow. Battus, caught in the trap, told the secret, and Mercury changed him into a touchstone.

> Men have a touchstone whereby to try gold; but gold is the touchstone whereby to try men.
> THOMAS FULLER: *The Holy State and the Profane State*, 'The Good Judge' (1642)

Touchstone is the name given to the clown in Shakespeare's *As You Like It* (1599).

**Touch with a bargepole, To.** An expression usually found in the negative, as 'I wouldn't touch it with a bargepole', meaning I don't want anything to do with it or I do not wish to be even remotely involved with it. A bargepole, as a long pole used for propelling a barge, is figuratively not long enough to keep one from touching something undesirable or unpleasant.

**Touch wood, To.** An old superstition to avert bad luck or misfortune or to make sure of something good; also when feeling pleased with one's achievement or when bragging. Traditionally, certain trees, such as the oak, ash, hazel, hawthorn and willow, had a sacred significance and thus protective powers. Properly these should be the ones touched, but this detail has largely passed into oblivion and any wood to hand is now used. Often, jocularly, the head is touched. *See also* KNOCK ON WOOD.

**Touchy-feely.** Expressing one's emotions openly and through physical contact. The phrase implies both senses of 'touch' (make physical contact, affect emotionally) and of 'feel' (perceive by touch, be emotionally affected)

> I [MP Helen Brinton] am very touchy-feely with my constituents. If people break down during my surgery, I give them a hug.
> *The Times* (19 September 1998)

**Easy touch.** *See under* EASE.

**In touch, To be** or **keep.** To maintain contact with someone, either in person or by correspondence, telephone or the like.

**Out of touch.** *See under* OUT.

**Soft touch, A.** *See under* SOFT.

**Touché** (French, 'touched'). An acknowledgment of a telling remark or rejoinder by one's opponent in an argument. It is the fencing term denoting a hit or touch.

**Touchstone.** *See under* TOUCH.

**Tough. Tough nut to crack, A.** *See* HARD NUT TO CRACK.

**As tough as old boots.** *See under* AS.

**Toulouse, The Sappho of.** *See under* SAPPHO.

**Tour. Tour de force** (French). A feat of strength or skill.

**Cook's tour.** *See under* COOK.

**Grand Tour, The.** *See under* GRAND.

**Mystery tour.** *See under* MYSTERY.

**Whistle-stop tour.** *See under* WHISTLE.

**Tournament** (Old French *torneiement*, ultimately from Latin *tornare*, 'to turn'). In the days of CHIVALRY, a martial sport or contest among knights of jousting or tilting, the chief art being to manoeuvre or turn one's horse away to avoid the adversary's blow. Blunted weapons were mostly used and the contests came to be associated with elaborate pageantry. *See also* TILTING AT THE QUINTAIN.

**Tournament of Tottenham, The.** A comic romance, given in PERCY'S RELIQUES (1765). A number of clowns are introduced, practising warlike games and making vows like knights of high degree. They tilt on carthorses, fight with ploughshares and flails, and wear wooden bowls and saucepan lids for armour.

**Tours.** Geoffrey of Monmouth (*Historia Regum Britanniae*, xvi (*c.*1136)) says that BRUTUS had a nephew called Turonus who slew 600 men before being overwhelmed by the Gauls. 'From him the city of Tours derived its name, because he was buried there.' The name, in fact, derives from the Turones, a people of Gallia Lugdunensis.

**St Martin of Tours.** *See under* MARTIN.

**Tout ensemble** (French). The whole massed together; the general effect.

**Towel, To throw in the.** *See under* THROW.

**Tower. Tower Liberty.** The TOWER OF LONDON with the fortifications and Tower Hill. This formed part of the ancient demesne of the crown, with jurisdiction and privileges distinct from and independent of the City of London. Its bounds are still beaten triennially by choirboys and children after a service in the Royal Chapel of St PETER AD VINCULA. Governor, Chaplain, Warders and residents accompany them and at each of the 31 boundary stones the Chaplain exclaims, 'Cursed is he who removeth his neighbours' landmark.' The Chief Warder then says, 'Whack it, boys, whack it.'

**Tower of Babel, The.** *See* BABEL; CONFUSION OF TONGUES.

**Tower of London, The.** The oldest part of the Tower is the great keep known as the WHITE TOWER built by WILLIAM THE CONQUEROR, traditionally on the site of a fort erected by Julius CAESAR.

As well as being a fortress, it has a special place in English history, both as a royal residence down to the time of James I (r.1603–25), and as a state prison. It has also housed the Royal MINT (until 1810), a menagerie and the Public Records, and is still the home of the CROWN JEWELS. Among those buried in its chapel are Edward Seymour, 1st Duke of Somerset, Protector Somerset (*c.*1506–52), Henry, 8th Earl of Northumberland (d.1585), Anne Boleyn (*c.*1504–36), Catherine Howard (d.1542), Lord Guildford Dudley (d.1554), Lady Jane Grey (1537–54), the Duke of Monmouth (1649–85), and Lords Kilmarnock, Balmerino and Lovat (supporters of the FORTY-FIVE rebellion). State prisoners confined there range from Ralf Flambard to Sir Walter Raleigh, Sir Roger Casement, and Rudolf Hess. W. Harrison Ainsworth's novel *The Tower of London* was first published in 1840. *See also* BEEFEATERS; CEREMONY OF THE KEYS; TRAITORS' GATE.

**Tower pound.** The legal pound of 5400 grains (11¼oz TROY WEIGHT), used in England until the adoption of the Troy pound in 1526. It was so called from the standard pound kept in the TOWER OF LONDON. *See also* PENNYWEIGHT.

**Towers of Silence.** The small towers on which the PARSEES and ZOROASTRIANS place their dead to be consumed by birds of prey. The bones are picked clean in the course of a day, and are then thrown into a receptacle covered with charcoal.

Parsees do not burn or bury their dead, because they consider a corpse impure, and they will not defile any of the elements. They carry it on a bier to the tower. At the entrance they look their last on the body, and the corpse bearers carry it within the precincts and lay it down to be devoured by vultures which are constantly on the watch as they circle overhead.

**Bloody Tower, The.** *See under* BLOODY.

**City of a Hundred Towers, The.** *See under* CITY.

**Devil's Tower, The.** *See under* DEVIL.

**Ivory tower.** *See under* IVORY.

**Leaning tower.** *See under* LEANING.

**Martello towers.** *See under* MARTELLO.

**Mouse Tower, The.** *See under* MOUSE.

**Princes in the Tower, The.** *See under* PRINCE.

**Rolandseck Tower.** *See under* ROLAND.

**White Tower, The.** *See under* WHITE.

**Town** (Old English *tūn*, German *Zaun*, 'hedge', 'enclosure'). Originally a group of dwellings surrounded by a hedge or wall.

**Town and Gown.** The two sections of a university town, composed of those not connected with the university and those who are members of it, hence 'a town and gown row', a collision or brawl between the students and non-gownsmen.

> Here another Town and Gown party had fought their way from the Corn-market; and the Gown getting considerably the worse of the conflict, had taken refuge within Exeter College by the express order of the Senior Proctor, the Rev. Thomas Tozer, more familiarly known as 'old Towser'.
>
> 'CUTHBERT BEDE': *The Adventures of Mr Verdant Green*, II, iv (1853–7)

**Town crier.** Also called a bellman, a town official, usually in a robe, ringing a bell and crying OYEZ! OYEZ! to attract attention to his public announcements and proclamations. The earlier bellman was a night watchman whose duty was to parade the streets at night and call out the hours.

**Five Towns, The.** *See under* FIVE.

**Ghost town.** *See under* GHOST.

**Go to town, To.** To let oneself go in a light-hearted fashion. To go to town on something is to GO THE WHOLE HOG (*see under* HOG); to exploit the situation to the full. The expression is of American origin, probably originating among country folk who went to town for a spree.

**Maiden town.** *See under* MAIDEN.

**Man about town, A.** *See under* MAN.

**New town.** *See under* NEW.

**One-horse town.** *See under* ONE.

**Paint the town red, To.** *See under* PAINT.

**Talk of the town.** *See under* TALK.

**Toyshop of Europe, The.** Edmund Burke called Birmingham thus. Here the word 'toy' does not refer to playthings for children, but to trinkets, knick-knacks and similar articles.

**Traces, To kick over the.** *See under* KICK.

**Trachtenberg system.** A system of speedy mathematical calculations based upon simple counting according to prescribed keys or formulae, which need to be memorized. There is no division or multiplication as such, and complicated calculations can be more easily and rapidly handled than by normal processes. The system was devised by Jakow Trachtenberg (1888–*c*.1960) during his seven long years in a NAZI concentration camp. He was born at Odessa and trained as an engineer and became a refugee in Germany after the Russian Revolution. *See also* CALCULATOR.

**Track. Cover one's tracks, To.** *See under* COVER.

**Fast track.** *See under* FAST.

**In one's tracks.** Where one is; there and then. 'He was stopped in his tracks' means that he was brought suddenly to a standstill.

**Make tracks, To.** To hurry away; to depart.

**On the right** or **wrong track.** Having the right (or wrong) idea; following the right (or wrong) line of enquiry.

**On the wrong side of the tracks.** Socially inferior. The expression is of American origin and refers to the fact that poor and industrial areas were formerly often located to one side of the railroad tracks, partly because the prevailing wind would carry smoke into them, away from the better-off neighbourhoods. The poorer districts of British cities are often east of the city centre for this reason, since the prevailing wind is usually west or southwest. *See also* EAST END; WEST END.

**Tractarians.** *See* OXFORD MOVEMENT.

**Tracy.** William de Tracy (d.1173) was the most active of the knights who slew Archbishop Thomas à Becket in Canterbury Cathedral in 1170, and for this misdeed all who bore the name were saddled by the church with this ban:

> Wherever by the sea or land they go
> For ever the wind in their face shall blow.

Tracy (Tracey) as a female forename, highly popular in the 1960s and 1970s, evolved from the Norman surname, itself from a place in France. It was at one time a male forename, as were the surnames of other English noble families. As a female name it later gained something of the connotation of a 'bimbo' or AIRHEAD, and when coupled with SHARON served subsequently to personify an ESSEX GIRL type.

**Trade. Trade, The.** Usually the liquor trade, especially those engaged in brewing and distilling; also applied to those engaged in the particular trade under consideration.

**Trade board.** A committee representing workers and management set up under Act of Parliament to regulate conditions of labour in a particular industry.

**Trade dollar.** A United States silver dollar formerly coined specially for Oriental trade. It weighed 420g, instead of the 412.5g of the ordinary dollar, and has not been coined since 1887.

**Trade follows the flag.** Wherever the flag flies, trade with the mother country develops and prospers; where the flag is established trade will grow up.

**Trademark.** The name or distinctive device for an article made for sale indicating that it was made by the holder of that device. Trademarks are usually registered and protected by law.

**Trade on, To.** To make use of so as to gain some advantage, as in making unscrupulous use of private knowledge, or using a personal affliction to arouse sympathy, other people's kindness and generosity or the like.

**Trade secret.** Originally a secret formula or process known only to a particular manufacturer. Hence generally any secret, especially knowledge of something that gives an advantage.

**Trade something in, To.** To hand over a used article such as a cooker or car in part payment for a new one.

**Trade something off, To.** To barter or exchange something; to sell it as a JOB LOT.

**Trade union.** An association of employees formed for the promotion and protection of their working conditions, wages and the like by collective bargaining, and sometimes also acting as Friendly Societies to their members. Until recently they constituted powerful pressure groups. They are essentially a by-product of the INDUSTRIAL REVOLUTION. *See also* TOLPUDDLE MARTYRS.

**Trade winds.** Winds that blow trade, i.e. regularly in one track or direction (Low German *Trade*, 'track', modern English 'tread'). In the northern hemisphere they blow from the northeast, and in the southern hemisphere from the southeast, about 30° each side of the equator. In some places they blow six months in one direction, and six months in the opposite.

**Balance of trade, The.** *See under* BALANCE.

**Board of Trade, The.** *See under* BOARD.

**Carriage trade.** *See under* CARRIAGE.

**Floor traders.** *See under* FLOOR.

**Free trade.** *See under* FREE.

**Horse trading.** *See under* HORSE.

**Rag trade.** *See under* RAG.

**Roaring trade.** *See under* ROAR.

**Stock in trade.** *See under* STOCK.

**Two of a trade did never agree.** *See under* TWO.

**Traditional nicknames.** Those associated with a particular surname are numerous. Among them are: BLANCO WHITE, Ding-Dong Bell, Dicky Bird, NOBBY Clark, Shady Lane, DUSTY MILLER, Spud Murphy, Smudger Smith, Chalky White, Tug Wilson.

In Australia fair-haired people are called Snowy and red-haired people Bluey. *See also* NICKNAME.

**Tragedy.** Literally, a goat song (Greek *tragos*, 'goat', and *ōdē*, 'song'), though why so called is not clear. Horace (*Ars Poetica* (1st century BC)) says, because the winner at choral competitions received a goat as a prize, but the explanation has no authority. The actual allusion may be to the goat-satyrs of Peloponnesian plays. *See also* COMEDY.

**Father of Greek Tragedy** or **Tragedy, The.** *See under* FATHER.

**Trahison des clercs** (French, 'treason of the intellectuals'). The incursion of the intelligentsia, who should be concerned with the pursuit of truth and guided by abstract principle, into the field of partisan politics and propaganda.

**Trail. Trail of Tears.** The name of the forced migration of Cherokee Indians in 1838–9. Their passage from Georgia to the wastelands of Oklahoma was strewn with the bodies of those who had perished from cold and hunger.

**Trail one's coat, To.** To try to pick a deliberate quarrel. The reference is to an old Irish custom of trailing one's coat along the ground as a sign that the owner was prepared to fight anyone daring to tread on his coat-tails.

**Freedom Trail, The.** *See under* FREE.

**Oregon Trail.** *See under* OREGON.

**Santa Fe Trail, The.** *See under* SANTA.

**Train. Train names.** *See* TITLED TRAINS.

**Down train, The.** *See under* DOWN.

**Ghost train.** *See under* GHOST.

**Omnibus train.** *See under* OMNIBUS.

**Parliamentary train.** *See under* PARLIAMENT.

**Trainbands.** Local bodies of citizen soldiers or MILITIA of little military value, with the exception of those of London. They derived from an order of Elizabeth I (1573) that a 'convenient number' in every county were to be organized in bands and trained. They were not willing to leave their districts and were seldom suitably trained.

> John Gilpin was a citizen
> Of credit and renown,
> A train-band captain eke [also] was he
> Of famous London town.
> WILLIAM COWPER: 'John Gilpin' (1785)

**Traitors' Gate.** The old water gate under St Thomas' Tower to the River Thames under which many state prisoners were brought to imprisonment or death in the TOWER OF LONDON. An old proverb says:

> A loyal heart may be landed at the Traitors' Gate.

**Trajan.** Marcus Ulpius Trajanus, Roman emperor (*c.*53–117), notable for his campaigns against the

Dacians and Parthians, and for his buildings and public works.

**Trajan's Arch.** There are two arches known by this name, commemorating the triumphs of TRAJAN. One, the finest ancient arch in existence, was erected in AD 114 over the APPIAN WAY at Benevento, and the other in 112 at Ancona. Both are of white marble.

**Trajan's Column.** A famous column in Rome. It was built of marble in AD 114 by Apollodorus of Damascus, and is a Roman DORIC column 127ft 6in (38.9m) high, on a square pedestal with a spiral staircase inside lighted by 40 windows. It was surmounted by a statue of the Emperor TRAJAN but Pope Sixtus V (r.1521–90) substituted one of St Peter. The outside spiral represents the emperor's battles in bas-relief.

**Trajan's Wall.** A line of fortifications in eastern Romania stretching across the Dobrudja from Cernavoda to the BLACK SEA.

**Tram.** The former popular derivation of this word from the name of Benjamin Outram, who ran vehicles on stone rails at Little Eaton, Derbyshire, in 1800, is discredited. The word is connected with Low German *traam*, 'baulk', 'beam', and was applied as early as the 16th century to trucks used in coal mines, and run on long wooden beams as rails.

**Tramontana.** The north wind, so called by the Italians, because to them it comes from over the mountains (Latin *trans*, 'across', and *montem*, 'mountain').

**Tramontane.** Beyond the mountain, i.e. on the other side of the Alps from Rome; hence, barbarous, foreign. *See also* ULTRAMONTANE PARTY.

**Transcendental Meditation.** A movement based on special techniques of meditation. TM, as it is usually known, was founded in India in the late 1950s by the Maharishi Mahesh Yogi and became popular in the West soon after. It uses one of a number of Sanskrit mantras, each being a short word or phrase that is repeated in the mind to help the user quiet the activity of thought and so attain a deeper level of consciousness. This process, it is claimed, gives the practitioner deep relaxation, leading to inner joy, vitality and creativity. TM became particularly popular when the BEATLES embraced it for a few months in 1967.

**Transept.** An architectural term (from Latin *trans*, 'across', and *saeptum*, 'enclosure') for the transverse portion of any building lying across the main body of that building. The transept became common in ecclesiastical architecture in the Middle Ages and almost universal in the Gothic period. The cross is often surmounted by a tower, spire or dome. In a BASILICA church the transept is the transverse portion in front of the choir. *See also* GOTHIC ARCHITECTURE.

**Transfiguration.** The word applied to the miraculous transformation of Christ's appearance, which occurred on a mountain where he was praying. It was witnessed by PETER, JAMES and JOHN and is celebrated on 6 August. It is described in Mark 9:2–8, Matthew 17: 1–8 and Luke 9:28–36.

**Translator-General.** Thomas Fuller, in his *Worthies* (1662), thus called Philemon Holland (1552–1637), who translated works by Pliny, Livy, Plutarch and a large number of other Greek and Latin classics.

**Transmigration of souls.** An ancient belief concerning the transition of the soul after death to another body or substance, usually human or animal, also known as metempsychosis. BRAHMANS and Buddhists accept human descent into plants as well as animals, and the BUDDHA underwent 550 births in different forms. The ancient Egyptians held to a form of transmigration in which the soul could inhabit another form to allow temporary revisiting the earth. *See also* PYTHAGORAS.

**Transubstantiation.** A change from one substance into another. Theologically, the change of the whole substance of the bread and wine in the EUCHARIST to the body and blood of Christ, only their outward form or ACCIDENTS remaining.

**Transylvania.** A region of forests and mountains in Romania that has come to be darkly associated with VAMPIRES and the occult, thanks to Bram Stoker's novel *Dracula* (1897), in which it is Count Dracula's homeland.

**Trap.** Slang for the mouth. Hence, 'shut your trap', meaning 'be quiet'.

**Booby trap.** *See under* BOOBY.

**Death trap.** *See under* DEATH.

**Trappists.** Properly, the CISTERCIANS of the French abbey at Soligny La Trappe (founded 1122) after their reform and reorganization in 1664. They were absorbed by the Cistercian Order of the Strict Observance in 1893, to whom the name is now applied. They are noted for extreme austerity, their rule including absolute silence, a common dormitory and no recreation.

**Traps.** A somewhat dated colloquial term for luggage or one's personal belongings, in origin short for 'trappings', bits of additional finery for decoration, especially the ornamental harness or caparison of a horse (French *drap*, 'cloth').

**Traveller. Traveller's joy** (*Clematis vitalba*). A plant with rope-like stems found in hedgerows in southern England, the Midlands and Wales. It has greenish flowers with feathery fruit. It was so called by the botanist John Gerard in *The Herball* (1597) as a plant 'decking and adorning waies and hedges, where people travell, and thereupon I have named it the Traveller's Ioie'.

**Travellers' tale.** A tall yarn; an incredible and probably untrue story of wonderful adventures and sights. The tales told by Baron MÜNCHAUSEN are a classic example.

**Fellow traveller.** *See under* FELLOW.

**Travelogue.** A film or illustrated lecture about travel. The word suggests a blend of 'travel' and 'monologue'.

**Tre, Pol, Pen.** *See* CORNISH NAMES.

**Treacle.** The word, which properly means an antidote against the bite of wild beasts, is from Greek *thēriakē*, ultimately from *thēr*, 'wild beast'. The ancients gave the name to several sorts of antidotes, but it was applied chiefly to Venice treacle (*Theriaca androchi*), a compound of some 64 drugs in honey.

**Treacle Bible, The.** *See under* BIBLE.

**Tread. Tread a measure, To.** A poetic and archaic expression meaning 'to dance', especially a slow stately dance.

> 'Now tread we a measure!' said young Lochinvar.
> SIR WALTER SCOTT: *Marmion*, V, xii (1808)

**Tread on someone's corns, To.** To offend someone by disregarding their sensitivities or encroaching on their rights.

**Tread on someone's neck, To.** To oppress or bully a person.

**Tread on someone's toes, To.** To upset someone; to offend a person, especially by encroaching on their area of responsibility or authority.

**Tread the boards, To.** To be an actor.

**Tread the light fantastic, To.** To dance.

> Come and trip it as ye go
> On the light fantastic toe.
> MILTON: 'L'Allegro' (1645)

**Tread** or **trample under foot, To.** To oppress; to treat with great contempt and discourtesy.

**Tread upon eggs, To.** To walk gingerly or warily, as if over eggs, which are easily broken.

**Tread water, To.** In swimming, to keep the body erect moving the hands and feet up and down, thus keeping one's head above water.

**Treason.** Betrayal of a trust or of a person.

**High treason.** *See under* HIGH.

**Misprision of treason.** *See under* MISPRISION.

**Petty treason.** *See under* PETTY.

**Treasure. Treasure trove** (Old French *trove*, 'found'). The term applied to coins and other valuables of gold and silver found in the ground or other place of concealment. Gold ornaments and the like found in tombs where there is no purpose of concealment are not treasure trove. Treasure trove belongs to the crown unless the owner appears to claim it, with the British Museum given the first refusal. If the treasure goes to a museum, the finder is usually given its full market value.

**Sutton Hoo Treasure.** *See under* SUTTON.

**These are my treasures.** The sick and the poor. So said St LAWRENCE when the Roman praetor commanded him to deliver up his treasures. *See also* CORNELIA.

**Treasury. Treasury bills.** A form of British government security issued in multiples of £1000 and repayable in (usually) three or six months.

**Treasury bonds.** Bonds for money borrowed for a number of years.

**Treasury notes.** Issued by the Treasury from 1924 to 1928 for £1 and 10 shillings. Their place was taken by notes issued by the Bank of England. *See also* BRADBURY.

**Treat. Treat someone like dirt, To.** To show little or no respect for someone.

**Dutch treat.** *See under* DUTCH.

**Stand treat, To.** *See under* STAND.

**Trick or treat.** *See under* TRICK.

**Treaty. City of the Violated Treaty, The.** *See under* CITY.

**Lateran Treaty.** *See under* LATERAN.

**Trebizond.** The grey horse of Guarinos, one of the French Knights taken at Roncesvalles. It is named after the ancient Greek colony of Trebizond, now the Turkish port of Trabzon. *See also* SONG OF ROLAND.

**Tree.** For particulars of some famous and patriarchal trees *see* OAK *and* YEW.

In the Natural History Museum, London, is the section of a *Sequoiadendron giganteum* (formerly *Sequoia gigantea*) with 1335 rings, representing that number of years, and the Jardin des Plantes at Paris has a similar section. There are yet older trees still in full life in the forests of America.

The cross on which Christ was crucified is frequently spoken of in hymns and poetry as 'the tree'. See Acts 5:30: 'Jesus, whom ye slew and hanged on a tree'; and 1 Peter 2:24: 'Who his own self bare our sins in his own body on the tree.'

The gallows is also called the tree, or the fatal tree. *See also* TYBURN.

One proverb says, 'If on the trees the leaves still hold, the coming winter will be cold,' and another, 'When caught by the tempest, wherever it be, if it lightens and thunders beware of a tree.'

Some trees have mystical or superstitious associations, depending on their species.

> Ash is benign and a healer
> Birch protects babies from the fairies
> Elder guards against disease and cures it
> Monkey puzzle can bring bad luck
> Oak is strong and healing; it is unlucky to harm it
> Rowan protects from harm
> Willow can bring bad luck if its branches are used for fuel
> Wych elm protects and heals
> Yew is unlucky and symbolizes the underworld and death

*See also* FLOWERS AND TREES.

**Tree is known by its fruit, The.** One is judged by what one does, not by what one says. The saying is from Matthew 12:33.

**Tree must be bent while it is young, A.** It is not possible to TEACH AN OLD DOG NEW TRICKS. The Scots say: 'Thraw the wand while it is green.'

**Treeness of the tree, The.** The essential qualities that compose a tree, in the absence of which the tree would cease to be a tree. Hence, the absolute essentials of anything. The phrase is perhaps modelled on Sterne's 'Correggiosity of Correggio' (*Tristram Shandy*, III, xii (1759–67)).

**Tree of Diana, The.** PHILOSOPHER'S TREE.

**Tree of Knowledge, The.** The tree which God planted, together with the Tree of Life, in the Garden of EDEN. 'But of the tree of the knowledge of good and evil, thou shalt not eat of it: for in the day that thou eatest thereof thou shalt surely die' (Genesis 2:17). EVE partook of the forbidden fruit and gave some to ADAM: 'And the Lord God said, Behold, the man is become as one of us, to know good and evil: and now, lest he put forth his hand, and take also of the tree of life, and eat, and live for ever' (Genesis 3:22); and so the first man and the first woman were driven from the garden and the woes of mankind began.

**Tree of Liberty, The.** A post or tree set up by the people, hung with flags and devices and crowned with a LIBERTY CAP. In the United States, poplars and other trees were planted during the War of Independence 'as growing symbols of growing freedom'. The JACOBINS in Paris planted their first trees of liberty in 1790, and used to decorate them with tricoloured ribbons, circles to indicate unity, triangles to signify equality and Liberty Caps. Trees of liberty were also planted by the Italians in the revolution of 1848.

**Tree of Life, The.** *See* TREE OF KNOWLEDGE.

**Tree of the Universe, The.** YGGDRASIL.

**At the top of the tree.** *See under* AT.

**Bark up the wrong tree, To.** *See under* BARK.

**Elder tree.** *See under* ELDER.

**Fig tree.** *See under* FIG.

**Flourish like a green bay tree, To.** *See under* FLOURISH.

**Grow on trees, To.** *See under* GROW.

**Jesse tree.** *See* JESSE.

**Judas tree.** *See under* JUDAS.

**Not to see the wood for the trees.** *See under* SEE.

**Philosopher's tree.** *See under* PHILOSOPHER.

**Rain tree.** *See under* RAIN.

**Saturn's tree.** *See under* SATURN.

**Up a gum tree.** *See under* UP.

**Upas tree.** *See under* UPAS.

**Up a tree.** *See under* UP.

**Tregeagle.** A kind of Cornish BLUEBEARD who sold his soul to the Devil and married and murdered numerous rich heiresses, and whose ghost haunts various parts of Cornwall. His allotted task is to bale out Dozmary Pool on Bodmin Moor with a leaky limpet shell. When the wintry blast howls over the moor, local people say it is Tregeagle roaring, and a child crying lustily is said to be 'roaring worse than Tregeagle'.

**Trek. Great Trek, The.** *See under* GREAT.

**Star Trek.** *See under* STAR.

**Trembling poplar.** *See* ASPEN.

**Trencher. Trencher cap.** A cap with a square board on top, generally covered with black cloth, and with a tassel, worn with academic dress, otherwise a COLLEGE CAP or MORTARBOARD. So called from the trenchered or split boards which form the top.

**Good trencherman, A.** *See under* GOOD.

**Trench fever.** A remittent or relapsing fever affecting men living in trenches, dugouts and the like, and transmitted by the excrement of lice. It first appeared in the First World War, in the static warfare on the Western Front.

**Trente-et-quarante.** *See* ROUGE ET NOIR.

**Tressure** (Old French *tressour*, from *trecier*, 'to plait'). A border within an heraldic shield and surrounding the bearings. The origin of the 'double-tressure flory-counterflory gules' in the royal arms of Scotland is traced by old heralds to the 9th century. They assert that CHARLEMAGNE granted it to King Achaius of Scotland in token of alliance, and as an assurance that 'the lilies of France should be a defence to the lion of Scotland'.

**Triads.** Three subjects more or less connected, treated as a group, as the Creation, Redemption and Resurrection; BRAHMA, VISHNU and SIVA; Alexander the Great, Julius CAESAR and NAPOLEON BONAPARTE; Law, Physic and Divinity.

The Welsh Triads are collections of historic facts, mythological traditions, moral maxims or rules of poetry disposed in groups of three for mnemonic purposes.

The anciently established Chinese secret society known as the Hung or the Society of Heaven and Earth, is also called the Triad from the trinity of heaven, earth and man, and the use of the triangle in its ritual.

**Tria juncta in uno** (Latin, 'three combined in one'). The motto of the Order of the Bath. It refers to the three classes of which the order consists: the Knights Grand Cross, the Knights Commander and the Companions. *See also* KNIGHTS OF THE BATH.

**Trial. Trial at bar.** Trial by a full court of judges in the KING'S BENCH division. These trials are for very difficult causes, before special juries, and occupy the attention of the four judges in the superior court, instead of at NISI PRIUS.

**Trial of the Pyx.** In England out of every 15lb TROY WEIGHT of gold and every 60lb of 'silver' minted a coin was put into the pyx or box for annual testing at Goldsmiths' Hall in the City of London. The trial of the pyx is conducted in the presence of the KING'S REMEMBRANCER and a jury of goldsmiths. Their verdict is delivered in the presence of the CHANCELLOR OF THE EXCHEQUER. The trial was initiated in the reign of Edward I (r.1272–1307) and formerly took place in the Chapel of the Pyx in Westminster Abbey. Samples are now taken and coins are not assayed separately. Silver was replaced by cupronickel in 1947.

**Nuremberg trials.** *See under* NUREMBERG.

**Triangle. Bermuda triangle.** *See under* BERMUDA.

**Big triangle.** *See under* BIG.

**Eternal triangle, The.** *See under* ETERNAL.

**Golden Triangle.** *See under* GOLDEN.

**Tribe. City of the Tribes, The.** *See under* CITY.

**Indian tribes.** *See under* INDIAN.

**Lost Tribes of Israel, The.** *See under* LOST.

**Tribune.** A chief magistrate and very powerful official among the ancient Romans. During the revolt of the plebs in 494 BC they appointed two tribunes as protectors against the PATRICIANS' oppression. Later the number was increased to ten and their office put on a proper footing. They were personally inviolable, and could separately veto measures and proceedings.

As a military title tribune denoted the commander of a cohort.

**Tribune of the people, A.** A democratic leader.

**Last of the Tribunes, The.** *See under* LAST.

**Trice, In a.** In an instant; in a twinkling. The origin is probably 'trice', to haul or to tie up, the idea being 'at a single tug'. The older expression was 'at a trice'.

**Trick. Trick or treat.** A HALLOWEEN custom of American origin, in which children in FANCY DRESS call at houses and threaten to play a prank ('trick') if they are not given sweets or a small gift ('treat'). In most cases the latter is usually proffered and the former rarely realized. A good example of the practice can be seen in the musical film *Meet Me in St Louis* (1944).

> This year the first group thump on the door at 6pm and we open it to an assorted bunch of mini-Supermans, a Pocahontas, two non-specific princesses and Po, the Teletubby, eagerly waving their plastic pumpkin buckets in expectation of sugar booty. 'Trick or treat', they chorus, as I produce the basket full of candycorn.
> *The Times* (4 November 1998)

**Bag of tricks.** *See under* BAG.

**Confidence trick.** *See under* CONFIDENCE.

**Davenport trick.** *See under* DAVENPORT.

**Dirty trick.** *See under* DIRTY.

**Do the trick, To.** *See under* DO.

**Hat trick.** *See under* HAT.

**Nose trick.** *See under* NOSE.

**Parlour tricks.** *See under* PARLOUR.

**Three-card trick.** *See under* THREE.

**Up to one's tricks.** *See under* UP.

**You can't teach an old dog new tricks.** *See under* TEACH.

**Tricolour.** A flag of three different colours, often in horizontal or vertical stripes, and especially the national standard of France, with three vertical bands of blue, white, and red. The first flag of the Republicans was green. The tricolour was adopted on 11 July 1789, when the people were disgusted with the king for dismissing Jacques Necker. The popular tale is that the insurgents had adopted for their flag the two colours, red and blue (the colour of the city of Paris), but that Lafayette persuaded them to add the BOURBON white, to show that they bore no hostility to the king. Other tricolours are:

Afghanistan: horizontal green, white, black*
Andorra: vertical blue, yellow, red*
Armenia: horizontal red, blue, orange
Azerbaijan: horizontal blue, red, green*
Belgium: vertical black, yellow, red
Benin: vertical green in hoist, then horizontal yellow, red
Bolivia: horizontal red, yellow, green
Bulgaria: horizontal white, green, red*
Cameroon: vertical green, red, yellow*
Chad: vertical blue, yellow, red
Colombia: horizontal yellow, blue, red*
Congo: diagonal green, yellow, red
Côte d'Ivoire: vertical orange, white, green
Croatia: horizontal red, white, blue*
Czech Republic: triangular white in hoist, then horizontal white, red
Djibouti: triangular white in hoist, then horizontal blue, green*
Ecuador: horizontal yellow, blue, red*
Egypt: horizontal red, white, black*
Eritrea: triangular red in hoist, then triangular green, blue*
Estonia: horizontal blue, black, white
Ethiopia: horizontal green, yellow, red
Gabon: horizontal green, gold, blue
Germany: horizontal black, red, gold
Ghana: horizontal red, gold, green*
Guinea: vertical red, yellow, green
Guinea-Bissau: vertical red in hoist, then horizontal yellow, green*
Hungary: horizontal red, white, green
India: horizontal saffron, white, green*
Iran: horizontal green, white, red*
Iraq: horizontal red, white, black*
Ireland: vertical green, white, orange
Italy: vertical green, white, red
Lesotho: diagonal white, blue, green*
Lithuania: horizontal yellow, green, red
Luxembourg: horizontal red, white, blue
Madagascar: vertical white in hoist, then horizontal red, green
Malawi: horizontal black, red, green*
Mali: vertical green, gold, red
Mexico: vertical green, white, red*
Moldova: vertical blue, yellow, red*
Netherlands: horizontal red, white, blue
Niger: horizontal orange, white, green*

Paraguay: horizontal red, white, blue*
Philippines: triangular white in hoist, then horizontal blue, red*
Romania: vertical blue, yellow, red*
Russia: horizontal white, blue, red
Rwanda: vertical red, yellow, green*
Senegal: vertical green, gold, red*
Sierra Leone: horizontal green, white, blue
Slovakia: horizontal white, blue, red*
Slovenia: horizontal white, blue, red*
St Vincent: vertical blue, yellow, green*
Syria: horizontal red, white, black*
Tajikistan: horizontal red, white, green*
Venezuela: horizontal yellow, blue, red*
Yemen: horizontal red, white, black
Yugoslavia: horizontal blue, white, red

Flags divided vertically have the colour given from the hoist outwards, while for those divided horizontally the first colour given is at the top. While most tricolours have bands, a few have triangles. Flags bearing devices and emblems are marked with an asterisk (*).

**Tricoteuses** (French, 'knitters'). Parisian women who, during the French Revolution, used to attend the meetings of the National Convention and, while they went on with their *tricotage*, encouraged the leaders in their bloodthirsty excesses. They gained for themselves the additional title, Furies of the Guillotine.

**Trident.** In Greek mythology the three-pronged spear which POSEIDON (Roman NEPTUNE), the god of the sea, bore as the symbol of his sovereignty. It has come to be regarded as the emblem of sea power and as such is borne by BRITANNIA. In gladiatorial combats in Rome, the trident was used by the RETIARIUS, whose skill lay in entangling his opponent in a net, and then despatching him with his trident.

**Trigger, Hair.** *See under* HAIR.

**Trigon.** In ASTROLOGY the junction of three signs. The ZODIAC is partitioned into four trigons, named respectively after the four elements: the watery trigon includes CANCER, SCORPIO and PISCES; the fiery, ARIES, LEO and SAGITTARIUS; the earthly, TAURUS, VIRGO and CAPRICORN; and the airy, GEMINI, LIBRA and AQUARIUS.

**Trilby.** Trilby O'Ferrall, the heroine of George du Maurier's novel *Trilby* (1894). She is an artist's model with pretty feet who cannot sing unless hypnotized by SVENGALI. She becomes a famous performer under his influence but loses her voice when he dies. The trilby hat is so named from its being worn by Little Billee in one of du Maurier's own illustrations for the book.

> Never call a soft hat a 'trilby', unless you are a detective—which you are not.
> GUY EGMONT: *The Art of Egmontese*, ch vi (1961)

**Trilogy.** A group of three tragedies. Everyone in Greece who took part in the poetic contest had to produce a trilogy and a satiric drama. The only complete specimen extant, the *Oresteia* (5th century BC) by AESCHYLUS, contains the *Agamemnon*, the *Choephoroi* and the *Eumenides*.

Hence, any literary, dramatic or operatic work consisting of three self-contained parts but related to a central theme, such as Shakespeare's *Henry VI* (1590) or Schiller's *Wallenstein* (1799).

**Trim.** The general set and appearance of a vessel.

**Trim one's sails, To.** To modify or reshape one's policy or opinion to meet the circumstances, as the sails of a ship are 'trimmed' or adjusted according to the wind.

**Trimalchio.** The vulgar, ostentatious and fabulously rich parvenu of Book 15 of Petronius Arbiter's *Satyricon* (1st century AD). He is a subject of allusion on account of the *Cena Trimalchionis* ('dinner of Trimalchio'), the absurdly extravagant banquet that he gave.

**Trimmer.** One who RUNS WITH THE HARE AND HUNTS WITH THE HOUNDS. George Savile, Marquis of Halifax (1633–95), circulated a pamphlet in 1688 called *On the Character of a Trimmer* in which he defended his policy of 'trimming' or avoiding party extremes and excesses. Owing to his frequent changes of side he was called Halifax the Trimmer, although fundamentally he strove for a policy of moderation.

**Trimurti** (Sanskrit *tri*, 'three', and *mūrti*, 'form'). The Hindu TRIAD of BRAHMA, VISHNU and SIVA as a unity, represented as one body with three heads. It bears only a forced resemblance to the idea of a TRINITY.

**Trine** (Latin *trinus*, 'threefold'). In ASTROLOGY a planet distant from another one-third of the circle is said to be in trine, one-fourth, it is in square, one-sixth or two signs, it is in sextile, but when one-half distant, it is said to be 'opposite'.

> In sextile, square, and trine, and opposite
> Of noxious efficacy.
> MILTON: *Paradise Lost*, x (1667)

Planets distant from each other six signs or half a circle have opposite influences, and are therefore opposed to each other.

**Trinitarians.** Believers in the doctrine of the Holy TRINITY as distinct from UNITARIANS. Also, members of the Order of the Most Holy Trinity, or Mathurins, founded by St John of Matha and St Felix of Valois in 1198, concerned with the ransoming of captives and slaves and sometimes known as REDEMPTIONISTS. Their rule is an austere form of the AUGUSTINIAN.

**Trinity, The.** The three Persons in one God: God the Father, God the Son, and God the HOLY GHOST. *See also* THREE.

The term TRIAD was first used by Theophilus of Antioch (*c*.180) for this concept, while the term Trinity was introduced by Tertullian about 217 in his treatise *Adversus Praxean* ('Against Praxeas').

**Trinity** or **Trinity Sunday.** The Sunday next after WHITSUNDAY, widely observed as a feast in honour of the Trinity since the Middle Ages. Its general observance was enjoined by Pope John XXII (r.1316–34) in 1334. The epistle and gospel used in the CHURCH OF ENGLAND on this day are the same as those in the Lectionary of St JEROME, and the collect comes from the Sacramentary of St GREGORY. The Church of England followed the Sarum Use in reckoning Sundays after Trinity, the ROMAN CATHOLIC CHURCH reckons them after PENTECOST, but this latter reckoning is now adopted in the Alternative Services Book (*see* BOOK OF COMMON PRAYER).

**Trinity Term.** The period of law sittings in England from the first Tuesday after TRINITY SUNDAY to the end of July.

**Corporation of Trinity House.** *See under* CORPORATION.

**Trinovantes.** A tribe, referred to in Caesar's *Gallic Wars* (1st century BC), inhabiting the area of Essex and the southern part of Suffolk. Their capital was probably at *Caesaromagus* (Chelmsford). *See also* TROYNOVANT.

**Trip, Ego.** *See under* EGO.

**Tripitaka** (Pali, 'threefold basket'). The three classes into which the sacred writings of the Buddhists are divided, i.e. the *Vinayapitaka* ('Basket of Disciplinary Directions' for the monks), the *Sutrapitaka* ('Basket of Aphorisms or Discourses'), and the *Abhidhammapitaka* ('Basket of Metaphysics').

**Triple thread, The.** Brahminism. The ancient BRAHMANS wore a symbol of three threads, reaching from the right shoulder to the left. João de Faria says that their religion sprang from fishermen, who left the charge of the temples to their successors on the condition of their wearing some threads of their nets in remembrance of their vocation.

**Tripos** (Latin *tripus*, 'three-footed stool'). A Cambridge term, meaning the three honour classes in which candidates are grouped at the final examination, whether of Mathematics, Law, Theology or Natural Science, among others. It is so called because the Bachelor of Arts who disputed with the 'Father' in the Philosophy School on ASH WEDNESDAY sat on a three-legged stool and was called 'Mr Tripos'.

**Triptolemus.** A Greek hero and demigod who was born at Eleusis and was taught the arts of agriculture by DEMETER. He established the ELEUSINIAN MYSTERIES and festivals, and some sources say he invented the wheel. He became one of the judges of the dead in the Underworld.

**Trisagion** (Greek, 'thrice holy'). A hymn in the liturgies of the Greek and Eastern Churches in which (after Isaiah 5:3) a threefold invocation to the Deity is the refrain: 'Holy God, Holy and Mighty, Holy and Immortal, have mercy on us.'

The name is sometimes applied to Bishop Heber's hymn for Trinity Sunday (1826):

> Holy, Holy, Holy! Lord God Almighty!
> Early in the morning our song shall rise to Thee;

which is more properly called the Ter-sanctus.

**Triskelion** (Greek, 'three-legged'). The emblem of the ISLE OF MAN and of Sicily: three human legs, bent at the knee and joined at the thigh.

**Trismegistus.** *See* HERMES TRISMEGISTUS.

**Tristram, Sir.** A hero of medieval romance whose exploits, though originally unconnected with it, became attached to the ARTHURIAN ROMANCES, he himself being named as one of the KNIGHTS OF THE ROUND TABLE. There are many versions of his story, which is, roughly, that he was cured of a wound by YSOLDE OR Iseult, daughter of the king of Ireland, and on his return to Cornwall told his uncle, King MARK, of the beautiful princess. Mark sent him to solicit her hand in marriage, and was accepted. Tristram escorted her to England, but on the way they both unknowingly partook of a magic potion and became irretrievably enamoured of each other. Ysolde married the king, and on Mark's discovering their liaison Tristram fled to Brittany and married Iseult, daughter of the Duke of Brittany. Wounded by a poisoned weapon, he sent for Ysolde of Ireland to come and heal him. The vessel in which she was to come had orders to hoist a white sail if she was on board, otherwise a black sail. Tristram's wife, seeing the vessel approach, told her husband, from jealousy, that it bore a black sail. In despair Tristram died. Ysolde of Ireland, arriving too late, killed herself.

The name was originally Drystan, from the Pictish name *Drustan*, and the initial was changed so that the name began with T apparently to connect it with Latin *tristis*, 'sad'. Wagner's opera *Tristan und Isolde* was first performed in 1865. Wagner based his libretto on *Tristan* (*c*.1210) by Gottfried von Strassburg. The legend also inspired Matthew Arnold's three-part 'Tristram and Iseult' (1852), and A.C. Swinburne's poem *Tristram of Lyonnesse* was published in 1882.

**Tristram Shandy.** *See* SHANDEAN.

**Triton.** The son of POSEIDON and AMPHITRITE, represented as a fish with a human head. It is this sea-god that makes the roaring of the ocean by blowing through his shell.

**Triton among the minnows, A.** A great man among a host of inferiors.

**Triumph.** A word formed from Greek *thriambos*, the Bacchic hymn, *Triumphe* being an exclamation used in the solemn processions of the ARVAL BROTHERS.

The old Roman *triumphus* was the solemn and magnificent entrance of a general into Rome after having obtained a great or decisive victory. *See also* OVATION.

**Church Triumphant.** *See under* CHURCH.

**Triumvir.** In ancient Rome one of a group of three men (Latin *trium*, genitive of *tres*, 'three', and *vir*, 'man') acting as joint magistrates for some special purpose or function. In Roman history the best known triumvirate was that of Octavian, Antony and Lepidus (43 BC), which was known as the Second Triumvirate to distinguish it from the combination of CAESAR, Pompey and Crassus in 60 BC, which is known as the First Triumvirate.

**Trivet, As right as a.** *See under* AS.

**Trivia.** John Gay's name for his invented goddess of streets and ways (Latin *trivius*, 'of three roads'). His burlesque in three books entitled *Trivia, or The Art of Walking the Streets of London* (1716) is a mine of information on the outdoor life of Queen ANNE's time.

**Trivium** (Latin, 'place where three ways meet', from *tres*, 'three', and *via*, 'road'). In the Middle Ages, the three roads to learning, i.e. grammar, rhetoric and logic, forming the lower division of the seven liberal arts. *See also* QUADRIVIUM.

**Trochilus.** (1) A small Egyptian bird said by the ancients to enter the mouth of the CROCODILE with impunity and to pick its teeth, especially of a leech which greatly tormented the creature.

It is known as the crocodile bird (*Pluvianus aegyptius*), a species of plover, which not only picks the crocodile's teeth but by its cry gives warning of an approaching foe.

(2) In Greek mythology a priest of DEMETER, who is said to have been translated into the constellation of the Charioteer.

**Troglodytes** (Greek *trōglē*, 'cave', and *duein*, 'to enter'). A name given by the ancient Greeks to races of uncivilized men who dwelt in caves or holes in the ground. Strabo mentions troglodytes in Syria and Arabia, and Pliny asserts that they fed on serpents. The best known were those of southern Egypt and Ethiopia. The term is applied to other cave dwellers, and, figuratively, to those who dwell in seclusion.

In ornithology, the wren, which mostly builds its nests in holes, is named a troglodyte (*Troglodytes troglodytes*).

**Troilus.** The prince of CHIVALRY, one of the sons of PRIAM, killed by ACHILLES in the TROJAN WAR.

The loves of Troilus and CRESSIDA, celebrated by Chaucer and Shakespeare, form no part of the old classic tale. This story appears for the first time in the *Roman de Troie* by the 12th-century TROUVÈRE Benoît de Sainte Maure. Guido delle Colonne included it in his *Historia Trojana* (1287), it thence passed to Boccaccio, whose *Il Filostrato* (1338), where Pandarus first appears, was the basis of Chaucer's *Troilus and Criseyde* (*c.*1385).

**As true as Troilus.** *See under* AS.

**Trojan. Trojan Horse.** *See* WOODEN HORSE OF TROY.

**Trojan horse, A.** A deception; a concealed danger. *See also* WOODEN HORSE OF TROY.

**Trojan War.** The legendary war sung by HOMER in the ILIAD as having been waged for ten years by the confederated Greeks against the men of TROY and their allies, as a result of PARIS, son of PRIAM, the Trojan king, having carried off HELEN, wife of MENELAUS. The last year of the siege is the subject of the *Iliad* (8th century BC), and the burning of Troy and the flight of AENEAS is told by VIRGIL in his AENEID (1st century BC).

It is known that the story of the siege of Troy, much doubted in the 19th century, has a historical basis and probably took place during the 13th and 12th centuries BC.

**Trolls.** In Icelandic myth malignant one-eyed giants, and in Scandinavian folklore mischievous DWARFS, some cunning and treacherous, some fair and good to men, akin to the Scottish BROWNIE. They lived in hills and were wonderfully skilled in working metals, and they had a propensity for stealing, even carrying off women and children. They were especially averse to noise, from a recollection of the time when THOR used to be forever flinging his hammer after them. Their name is Old Norse for 'demon'.

**Trompe l'oeil** (French, 'deception of the eye'). A trick of the eye; a visual deception. It is applied to art that gives a distinct impression of reality, as, for example, perspective art, which can give a sense of distance, solidity and space. The apparent dimensions of an interior can be magnified by such decorative effects.

**Troop. Trooping the Colour.** The annual ceremony on Horse Guards Parade, WHITEHALL, in which the colour or regimental flag is carried between files of troops and received by the sovereign. It takes place on the sovereign's official birthday.

The ceremony dates from the early 18th century and was originally a guard-mounting parade, the battalion providing the guards for the day 'trooping' the colour to be carried on king's guard. In 1748 it was ordered that this parade would mark the official birthday of the sovereign.

**Household Troops.** *See under* HOUSEHOLD.

**Light troops.** *See under* LIGHT.

**Swear like a trooper, To.** *See under* SWEAR.

**Trophonius.** An architect, celebrated in Greek legend as the builder of the Temple of APOLLO at DELPHI. After his death he was deified and had an ORACLE in a cave near Lebadeia, Boeotia, which was so awe-inspiring that those who entered and consulted the oracle never smiled again. Hence a melancholy or habitually terrified man was said to have visited the cave of Trophonius.

**Trophy.** Originally the arms of a vanquished foe, collected and set up by the victors on the field of battle. The captured standards were hung from the branches of an oak tree, a portion of the booty being laid at the foot of the tree and dedicated to the tutelary deity. The Romans frequently bore their trophies to Rome. Under the empire, the triumphs of the victorious generals were also celebrated with arches and columns. The word relates to Greek *tropē*, 'turning', referring to the act of turning back an enemy.

**Troth, To plight one's.** *See under* PLIGHT.

**Troubadours.** Poets of the south of France in the 11th to 14th centuries whose works were often performed and sung by wandering minstrels or JONGLEURS. They are so called from the Old Provençal verb *trobar*, 'to find' or 'to invent' (compare 'poet', which means 'maker'). They wrote in the LANGUE D'OC or Provençal, principally on the subjects of love and CHIVALRY. *See also* TROUVÈRES.

**Last of the Troubadours, The.** *See under* LAST.

**Trouble. Troubleshooter.** An American coinage for someone expert in locating and mending 'trouble', mechanical or otherwise. Hence its application to those brought into industry to mend relations between employer and employee.

**Finger trouble.** *See under* FINGER.

**Pack up your troubles in your old kit-bag.** *See under* PACK.

**Time of Troubles.** *See under* TIME.

**Trousers. Catch someone with their trousers down, To.** *See under* CATCH.

**Wear the trousers, To.** *See under* WEAR.

**Trouvères.** Court poets in central and northern France in the 12th to 14th centuries, writing chiefly of love. They are so called from Old French *trover*, 'to compose'. They wrote in the *langue d'oïl* (*see* LANGUE D'OC). *See also* TROUBADOURS.

**Trove, Treasure.** *See under* TREASURE.

**Trowel, To lay it on with a.** *See under* LAY.

**Troy.** The fortress city of HOMER's ILIAD in the extreme northwest corner of Asia Minor overlooking the strait of the Dardanelles; also the land of Troy or the Troad, with Ilium as its chief city.

**Troy town.** A Cornish expression for a labyrinth of streets; a regular maze. Sir Arthur Quiller-Couch (*see* Q) in his writings uses the name as a disguise for Fowey (pronounced 'Foy'). Troy was formerly used figuratively of any scene of disorder or confusion, so that a room in disarray would be called a Troy fair.

**Troy weight.** The system of weights used in weighing precious metals and gems, the pound of 12 ounces weighing 5760 grains as compared with the pound avoirdupois, which weighs 7000 grains and is divided into 16 ounces. It is so named as it was the system used at the great fairs at Troyes, in France. 1lb troy = 0.822861 lb avoirdupois, rather over four-fifths. *See also* TOWER POUND.

**Siege of Troy, The.** *See* ACHILLES; HELEN; ILIAD; TROJAN WAR; ULYSSES; WOODEN HORSE OF TROY.

**Troynovant.** The name given by the early chroniclers to LONDON, originally the city of the TRINOVANTES. It is a corruption of Trinovant, and was assumed to mean the New Troy, which Geoffrey of Monmouth (*Historia Regum Britanniae*, Bk I, ch xvii (*c*.1136)) tells was built by BRUTUS, a Trojan refugee, from whom the name Britain was said to have derived Later LUD surrounded it with walls and called it Caer-Lud, or the City of Lud (London).

> For noble *Britons* sprong from *Troians* bold,
> And *Troynouant* was built of old *Troyes* ashes cold.
> EDMUND SPENSER: *The Faerie Queene*, III, ix (1590)

**Truce of God.** In the Middle Ages a suspension of private warfare decreed by the church on certain days or for certain seasons such as ADVENT and LENT. In 1027 hostilities between Saturday night and Monday morning were forbidden, and the Truce of God was reaffirmed and extended by various councils, including the LATERAN COUNCIL of 1179. It was only partly effective and was eventually superseded by the king's peace.

**Trucking, To keep on.** *See under* KEEP.

**True. True blue.** A lasting blue, hence a type of constancy. A true blue is one who is constant, steadfast, loyal and faithful, probably from the idea of such qualities being characteristic of BLUE BLOOD. Also, a loyal or DYED-IN-THE-WOOL Conservative.

**Truelove** or **true-lovers' knot.** A complicated double knot with two interlacing bows on each side and two ends, used as a symbol of love. Sir Thomas Browne (1605–82) maintained in *Pseudodoxia Epidemica* (V, xxii (1646)) that the knot owes its origin to the *nodus Herculanus*, a snaky device in the CADUCEUS or rod of MERCURY, as this was the form in which the woollen girdle of Greek brides was fastened. This interlacing knot is a symbol of interwoven affection.

> Three times a true-love's knot I tie secure;
> Firm be the knot, firm may his love endure.
> JOHN GAY: *Pastorals*, 'The Spell' (1714)

**True to one's salt.** Faithful to one's employers. Here salt means SALARY.

**As true as Troilus.** *See under* AS.

**Ring true, To.** *See under* RING.

**Trump.** This word, in such phrases as 'a trumped-up affair' (falsely concocted), 'trumpery' (showy finery, worthless stuff) and the like, is the same word as 'trumpet', from French *trompe*, 'a trumpet', whence *tromper*, which, originally meaning 'to play on a trumpet', came to mean to beguile, deceive, impose on.

In cards, the word is from French *triomphe* ('triumph'), the name of an old variant of *écarté*.

**Trump card.** A decisive or advantageous move; a winning stroke or ploy.

**Jew's trump.** A JEW'S HARP.

**Last trump, The.** *See under* LAST.

**Play one's trump card, To.** *See under* PLAY.

**Turn up trumps, To.** *See under* TURN.

**Trumpet.** *See* TRUMP.

**Blow one's own trumpet, To.** *See under* BLOW.

**Feast of Trumpets, The.** *See under* FEAST.

**Flourish of trumpets, A.** *See under* FLOURISH.

**Trunk.** In its sense of denominating the main body as opposed to the roots and branches, the word is used to describe the main lines of railway, postal, and telephone systems, from which branch lines radiate.

**Trunk call, A.** The old name for a telephone call on a trunk line from one town to another; now usually called a long-distance call or, officially, a national call.

**Trunk hose.** A style of breeches worn in the 16th and 17th centuries, reaching from the waist to mid-thigh.

**Trunk road, A.** A main highway between two principal towns.

**Trunks.** The name is used for three types of menswear: (1) swimming trunks; (2) shorts worn for some sports; (3) underpants with legs reaching mid-thigh.

**Saratoga trunk, A.** *See under* SARATOGA.

**Trust.** A combination of a number of companies or businesses doing similar trade, for the purpose of defeating competition or creating a monopoly, under one general control. It is so called because each member is on trust not to undersell the others, but to remain faithful to the terms agreed.

**Brains Trust.** *See under* BRAIN.

**Truth.** PILATE said: 'What is truth?' (John 18:38). This was the great question of the Platonists. PLATO said we could know truth if we could sublimate our minds to their original purity. Arcesilaus said that man's understanding is not capable of knowing what truth is. Carneades maintained that not only could our understanding not comprehend it, but even our senses are wholly inadequate to help us in the investigation. Gorgias the SOPHIST said: 'What is right but what we prove to be right? and what is truth but what we believe to be truth?'

> 'What is truth?' said jesting Pilate, and would not stay for an answer.
>
> FRANCIS BACON: *Essayes*, 'Of Truth' (1625)

**Truth drug.** A drug claimed to make a person tell the truth under questioning. An American doctor, R.E. House (1875–1930), used alkaloid scopolamine to induce a state of lethargic intoxication in which the patient lost many of his defences and spoke the truth concerning matters about which he would normally have lied or prevaricated. The value of this and other drugs in penology has by no means been established.

**Act of truth.** *See under* ACT.

**Home truth.** *See under* HOME.

**Naked truth.** *See under* NAKED.

**Tell the truth and shame the Devil.** *See under* TELL.

**Try. Try it on, To.** To attempt to dupe or outwit.

**Try one's hand, To.** To attempt something; to 'have a go'.

**Try one's luck, To.** To attempt something that is uncertain.

**Try something for size, To.** To test it for suitability, as one tries on a garment to judge its fit.

**Trygon.** *See* TELEGONUS.

**Tsar** or **Czar.** The common title of the former emperors of Russia, first assumed by IVAN THE TERRIBLE in 1547 (from Latin *Caesar*). His wife was the Tsarina (not a Russian form, which is *Tsaritsa*), his son the Tsarevitch, and his daughter the Tsarevna. The latter titles were eventually reserved for the eldest son and his wife respectively. From 1721 the tsars took the title of EMPEROR.

The title was adopted in the late 1990s as a catchword for the British government overseer dealing with the homeless, drugs and similar matters. It was already then in use in the USA as the term for the leader of an official task force. Earlier still, it was a nickname of the American House of Representatives speaker Thomas B. Reed (1839–1902), dubbed 'Czar Reed' for his iron control of the House.

**Tu. Tu autem** (Latin, 'But thou'). A hint to leave off; 'hurry up and come to the last clause'. In the long Latin grace at St John's College, Cambridge, the last clause used to be *Tu autem miserere mei, Domine, Amen* ('But thou, Lord, have mercy upon me, Amen'), and it was not unusual, when a scholar read slowly, for the senior fellow to whisper *Tu autem*, i.e. skip all the rest and give us only the last sentence. The grace itself reflects the words that traditionally concluded every lesson from the scriptures or the Fathers of the Church read during the daily office in the Roman Church. This was *Tu autem, Domine, miserere nobis* ('But thou, Lord, have mercy upon us'), to which the response was *Deo Gratias* ('Thanks be to God'). Where this conclusion occurred, it was sometimes printed in the service books as simply *Tu autem*.

**Tu quoque** (Latin, 'Thou also'). A retort implying that the one addressed is in the same case as the speaker, no better and no worse.

**Tuatha Dé Danann** (Irish, 'people of the goddess Dana'). A legendary race of superhuman heroes, which invaded Ireland, overthrew the Firbolgs and Fomors, and were themselves overthrown by the MILESIANS, who later worshipped them as gods.

**Tub. Tub of naked children, A.** An emblematic representation in religious paintings of St NICHOLAS.

**Tubs.** In college rowing slang, 'tubs' are gig pairs of college boat clubs, who practise for the term's races, and 'tubbing' is taking out pairs under the supervision of a coach for training.

**Tub-thumper.** A ranter; a SOAPBOX ORATOR or STUMP ORATOR, the term alluding to the upturned tub formerly used as a platform at open-air meetings.

**Devil's Beef Tub.** *See under* DEVIL.

**Cynic tub.** *See under* CYNIC.

**Dolly tub.** *See under* DOLLY.

**Tale of a tub, A.** *See under* TALE.

**Tube, The twopenny.** *See under* TWO.

**Tuck.** In the sense of eatables, 'tuck' is a mid-18th-century slang word, especially used by boys in boarding schools whose tuck box, supplied from home, supplemented the school fare.

**Tuck in, To.** To eat heartily and with relish. In Australia the word became 'tucker' for any kind of food, especially that carried on journeys in one's tucker bag.

**Tuck in your twopenny!** Mind your head! A schoolboy's warning to the boy over whose back the leap is to be made in leapfrog. 'Twopenny' here is short for 'twopenny loaf'. *See* USE YOUR LOAF.

**Friar Tuck.** Chaplain and steward of ROBIN HOOD.

**Nip and tuck.** *See under* NIP.

**Tuckahoe.** An inhabitant of that part of the state of Virginia that lies east of the Blue Ridge Mountains. The word represents Algonquian *tockawhoughe*, 'it is round', originally referring to a plant whose round rootstocks were used by the Native Americans for food.

**Tucker.** The ornamental frill of lace or muslin worn by women in the 17th and 18th centuries round the top of their dresses to cover the neck and shoulders. Hence, 'in one's best bib and tucker', dressed in one's best, looking fresh and spruce.

**Tudor Rose, The.** Henry of Richmond (1457–1509), son of Edmund Tudor, Earl of Richmond, and head of the House of Lancaster after the death of Henry VI in 1471, adopted the RED ROSE to emphasize his LANCASTRIAN claims. After his victory at Bosworth (1485), he became king as Henry VII and in 1486 married Princess Elizabeth of York. The union of the two Houses gave rise to the Tudor Rose, a superimposition of the WHITE ROSE on the red. *See also* WARS OF THE ROSES.

**Tuesday.** The third day of the week, or popularly the second, named after TIU. *See also* SUNDAY.

**Hock Tuesday.** *See* HOCKTIDE.

**Shrove Tuesday.** *See under* SHROVE.

**Tuffet.** A dialect variant of 'tuft', which was formerly used of a small, grassy mound or hillock.

> Little Miss Muffet
> Sat on a tuffet
> Eating her curds and whey.
> Nursery rhyme

**Tug.** A name by which Collegers are known at Eton, from the 'tog' (i.e. toga) worn by them to distinguish them from the rest of the school.

> My interlocutor was a red-headed freckled little boy of eleven, who had come from Aberdeen 'to try for Tuggery' – that is, to try and pass on to the foundation as a King's Scholar.
>
> JAMES BRINSLEY-RICHARDS: *Seven Years at Eton*, ch xii (1883)

**Tug of love.** A dispute over the custody of a child, who is thus torn between his or her parents, or between each of the adults who claims custody.

**Tug of war.** A sporting activity in which a number of contestants, divided into two teams, lay hold of a strong rope and pull against each other until one side has tugged the other over the dividing line.

**Tuileries.** A former palace in Paris, so named from the tileyards (*tuileries*) once on the site. It stood between the LOUVRE and the Place de la Concorde. The palace was designed in 1564 by Philibert de l'Orme or Philibert Delorme (*c.*1510–70) for Catherine de Medici, and it long served as a residence for the sovereigns of France. In 1871 it was burned down by the COMMUNARDS, but the gardens remain as a pleasant public open space.

**Tulchan bishops.** Certain titular Scottish bishops introduced by the PRESBYTERIANS in 1572 and whose office had ceased by 1580. A tulchan, from Gaelic *tulachan*, 'little hillock', is a stuffed calfskin placed under a cow to deceive her into giving milk. The bishops were contemptuously so called because their title was an empty one, their revenues being mainly absorbed by nobles as lay patrons.

**Tulip mania.** A reckless mania for the purchase of tulip bulbs that arose in Holland in the 17th century and was at its greatest height about 1633–7. A bulb of the tulip called Viceroy sold for £250, and one called Semper Augustus more than double that sum. The mania spread all over Europe, and became a mere stockjobbing speculation. *La Tulipe Noire* (1850) by Alexandre Dumas *père*, centres around the black tulip and a tulip fancier, Cornelius van Baerle, of the period of the 'tulipomania'. He succeeded in growing a black tulip, thereby winning a prize of one hundred thousand florins.

**Tumbledown Dick.** Anything that will not stand firmly. 'Dick' is King DICK, who was a tottering wall at best.

**Tumbler.** The flat-bottomed stemless glass derives its name from the fact that it was originally made with a rounded bottom, which made it tumble over if placed on a table. This meant that it should be held until it was emptied.

**Tun, Bolt in.** *See under* BOLT.

**Tunbridge Wells.** The worthy and respectable Kent town, with its spa and royal seal of approval, has popularly come to be regarded as an old-fogeyish bastion of morality and decency. Its residents are supposed to express their dismay at the way standards are falling by penning anonymous letters to the editors of *The Times*, the *Daily Telegraph* and other newspapers, signed with the pen-name 'Disgusted, Tunbridge Wells'. It is uncertain when and where the expression originated, but it is hardly likely to have been Tunbridge Wells itself.

**Tune. Tuneful Nine, The.** The nine MUSES.

**Tune the old cow died of, The.** Advice instead of relief; remonstrance instead of help. The reference is to the song:

> There was an old man, and he had an old cow,
> But he had no fodder to give her,
> So he took up his fiddle and played her the tune;
> 'Consider, good cow, consider,
> This isn't the time for the grass to grow,
> Consider, good cow, consider.'

**Change one's tune, To.** *See under* CHANGE.

**He who pays the piper calls the tune.** *See under* PAY.

**Make someone sing another tune, To.** *See under* SING.

**Signature tune.** *See under* SIGNATURE.

**To the tune of.** *See under* TO.

**Tunkers, Dunkers** or **Dunkards** (German, 'dippers'). A religious sect, also known as the German Baptists, which was founded in Germany in 1708 by Alexander Mack (1679–1735). In the decade from 1719 they emigrated to Pennsylvania and spread westwards and into Canada. They reject infant baptism, the taking of oaths and the bearing of arms, and practise total immersion, the AGAPE and so on. They are now called the Church of the Brethren. The SEVENTH-DAY BAPTISTS (1728) are an offshoot.

**Tunnage.** *See* TONNAGE.

**Turandot.** The opera by Giacomo Puccini of this name (1926) has a story that can be traced back to a tale given by Antoine Galland as part of his translation of *The Arabian Nights* (1704–8), but Puccini's libretto (written by Giuseppe Adami and Renato Simoni) was based on the play (1762) by the Italian dramatist Carlo Gozzi. The central character of the title is a Chinese princess who vows vengeance on all men for some past grievance but offers to marry any nobleman who can solve three riddles. If he cannot, she will kill him. A prince does solve them, but she refuses to marry him after all. A final change of heart, however, is also a change of mind. The opera is unpopular with many, who point to the torture and death of the loyal slave-girl Liu, the only genuinely good character. The princess's name is of Persian origin and means 'daughter of the Turanians', i.e. of the northern people (to the Arabians) who inhabit ancient Turkestan. The final *-dot* is related to English 'daughter'. Ferruccio Busoni also wrote an opera (1917) with this title, which was similarly based on Gozzi's play.

**Turf. Turf, The.** The racecourse, horse-racing and the racing world, in allusion to the turf or grass of the course. A turfite is (or was) a devotee of horse-racing or one who gets his living from it, otherwise generally a supporter of the turf.

**Turf war.** An acrimonious dispute between rival groups over territory. The concept is of an area of turf as personal property. The phrase arose among American street gangs.

> Police called in to keep the rival sides apart said: 'This is not so much a neighbourhood watch any more as a turf war.'
> *The Times* (2 December 1998)

**Turin Shroud, The.** *See under* FAKES.

**Turk.** A name formerly applied to those who were barbarous, savage and cruel, from the European association of the old Ottoman Empire with barbaric practices, from medieval times until the early years of the 20th century. More recently the name came to be applied to mischievous and unruly children, as: 'You little Turk!' or 'You young Turk!'

> Fierce revolt against intolerable misrule slowly blazed upon Bosnia and Herzegovina, and a rising in Bulgaria, not dangerous in itself, was put down by Turkish troops despatched for the purpose from Constantinople, with deeds described by the British agent who investigated them on the spot, as the most heinous crimes that had stained the history of the century.
> JOHN MORLEY: *Life of Gladstone*, VII, iv (1903)

**Turkish bath.** This is a MISNOMER, for the bath is not of Turkish origin, although it was introduced from the Near East, which was associated with Turkish rule. The correct term of hammam was commonly used in 17th-century England. Hummum's Hotel in COVENT GARDEN was on the site of a 17th-century hammam.

**Turkish delight.** A confection of flavoured gelatin cubes coated in powdered sugar. It is of Turkish origin but in Turkish itself is known as *rahat lokum*, from Arabic *rahat al-hulqum*, literally 'ease of the throat'.

**Turn Turk, To.** *See under* TURN.

**Young Turks, The.** *See under* YOUNG.

**Turkey.** *See* MISNOMERS.

**Turkeycock.** A pompous person. *See also* GOBBLEDYGOOK.

**Cape Cod turkey.** *See under* CAPE.

**Cold turkey.** *See under* COLD.

**Talk turkey, To.** *See under* TALK.

**Turn. Turn a blind eye, To.** To pretend tactfully not to see; to overlook, in order to avoid embarrassment to all concerned. At the Battle of Copenhagen (1801) Admiral Nelson reputedly disregarded an order to disengage by putting his telescope to his blind eye and averring that he saw no signal from Admiral Sir Hyde Parker's ship. In reality Parker had arranged with Nelson that the latter could use his discretion if such a signal were hoisted.

**Turn a deaf ear, To.** To refuse to listen; to refuse to accede to a request.

**Turn and turn about.** Taking turns; alternating.

**Turn an honest penny, To.** To earn money honestly by working for it.

**Turncoat.** A renegade, one who deserts his principles or party.

Fable has it that a certain Duke of Saxony, whose dominions were bounded in part by France, hit upon the device of a coat blue one side and white the other. When he wished to be thought in the French interest he wore the white outside, otherwise the blue. Hence a SAXON was nicknamed Emmanuel Turncoat.

**Turn down, To.** To reject, as: 'She turned down his offer' or 'His application for the post was turned down.'

In Eastern countries a glass is turned down at convivial gatherings as a memento of a recently departed companion.

> And when thyself with shining feet shalt pass
> Among the guests star-scattered on the grass
> And in the joyous errand reach the spot
> Where I made one – turn down an empty glass!
> EDWARD FITZGERALD: *Rubáiyát of Omar Khayyám* (1859)

**Turn in, To.** Colloquially, to go to bed.

**Turn** or **spin in one's grave, To.** Said of a deceased person who, if still living, would be shocked or angry at something they felt strongly about or were connected with in some way. The image is of a corpse expressing its reaction by sudden movement.

> J.M.W. Turner would be spinning in his grave at the thought of his name being used even remotely in connection with Ofili's complete lack of taste.
> *The Times* (Letter to the Editor) (19 December 1998)

**Turn one's back on, To.** To have nothing more to do with; to abandon.

**Turn one's hand to, To.** To undertake as a new activity.

**Turn on one's heel, To.** To turn round sharply.

**Turn on the heat, To.** To increase the pace or pitch of activity.

**Turn on the waterworks, To.** To cry; to blubber.

**Turn over a new leaf, To.** To amend one's ways; to start afresh. The allusion is to the old school copybook. If the pupil spoilt a page, he was required to turn over and start the writing exercise all over again.

**Turn someone's head, To.** To make them vain or conceited by flattery or the like.

**Turn tail, To.** To turn one's back and make off.

**Turn the corner, To.** To be over the worst; to be on the mend after an illness. In nautical parlance 'turning the corner' implied sailing on, either to port or starboard, after reaching either the CAPE of Good Hope or CAPE HORN.

**Turn the other cheek, To.** To refuse to retaliate when attacked or provoked.

> Whosoever shall smite thee on the right cheek, turn to him the other also.
> Matthew 5:39

**Turn** or **tip the scales, To.** To outweigh the other side by just a small amount.

**Turn the tables, To.** To reverse the conditions or relations, as, for instance, to rebut a charge by bringing forth a countercharge. The phrase comes from the old custom of reversing the table or board, in games such as CHESS and draughts, so that the opponent's relative position is altogether changed.

**Turn the tide, To.** To reverse the course of events; to alter the way things are going.

**Turn to, To.** To carry on with one's work; to get to work.

**Turn Turk, To.** To become a Muslim; to turn renegade; to change for the worse.

**Turn turtle, To.** To turn over completely; to land upside down. The term is usually said of boats, from the fact that a turtle, when turned on its back, is quite helpless.

**Turn up, To.** To arrive, often unexpectedly; to appear.

**Turn-up for the books, A.** A bit of good luck; a surprise. The reference is to a contestant who turned up at the last minute for a sporting event and had to be added to the bookmaker's books.

**Turn up like a bad penny, To.** To appear. Said of an unwelcome person or thing.

**Turn up one's nose, To.** To express contempt. When one sneers, one turns up the nose by curling the upper lip.

**Turn up one's toes, To.** To die.

**Turn up trumps, To.** To prove very friendly and helpful unexpectedly; to be much better than anticipated. An allusion to card playing.

**Buggins' turn.** *See under* BUGGINS.

**Done to a turn.** *See under* DO.

**Hand's turn.** *See under* HAND.

**It's a long lane that has no turning.** *See under* LONG.

**Not to know which way to turn.** *See under* KNOW.

**Not to turn a hair.** To remain quite calm and unruffled.

**One good turn deserves another.** *See under* ONE.

**Serve its turn, To.** *See under* SERVE.

**Wait for something to turn up, To.** *See under* WAIT.

**World turned upside down, The.** *See under* WORLD.

**Turnip.** Former slang for a large, old-fashioned silver watch, so called from its shape.

**Turpin.** Archbishop of Rheims, who appears in several CHANSONS DE GESTE as a friend and companion of CHARLEMAGNE. He was formerly supposed to be the writer of the *Historia de vita Caroli et Rolandi*. In the *Chanson de Roland* Turpin dies with the hero and is buried with him. He is most likely the same as Tilpin, archbishop of Rheims in the 8th century (*c.*753–*c.*800).

**Dick Turpin.** The 'King of the Road' (1705–39) was born at the Bell Inn, Hempstead, Essex, and apprenticed to a butcher at WHITECHAPEL at the age of 16. He soon became a footpad to supplement his earnings and, after his marriage in 1728, set up as a butcher in Essex. He took to stocking his shop with stolen cattle and sheep and, on discovery, joined a gang of smugglers near Canvey Island and there turned to housebreaking with Gregory's Gang in Epping Forest. In 1735 he became a highwayman, working around the south of London, and in 1736 began his partnership with Tom King. His boldness became a public legend, as did his activities in Epping Forest and Hounslow Heath. After the death of King in 1737, he shifted to Lincolnshire and thence to Yorkshire, where he was finally apprehended and hanged at the Mount, outside the walls of York. The legend of BLACK BESS and the ride to York derives from Harrison Ainsworth's *Rookwood* (1834). The ride was in fact probably carried out by 'Swift' John Nevison (1639–84), who in 1676 is said to have robbed a sailor at Gadshill at 4 am and to have established an 'alibi' by reaching York at 7.45 pm.

**Turret-ship.** *See* INVENTORS.

**Turtle, To turn.** *See under* TURN.

**Tuscan order.** In architecture, essentially a simplified form of Roman DORIC, plain and lacking in ornament. The columns are never fluted. *See also* CORINTHIAN ORDER; IONIC ORDER.

**Tusitala.** Teller of tales, the name given by the Samoans to Robert Louis Stevenson (1850–94), who lived on Samoa from 1889 until his death.

**Tussaud's, Madame.** *See under* MADAME.

**Tutankhamun.** King of Egypt from 1333 to 1323 BC, the son-in-law of the great King AKHENATEN (AMENHOTEP). He came to the throne as a young boy and died prematurely, aged about 18. He is famous not for his reign but for his tomb at Luxor, which when excavated in 1922 by the English Egyptologist Howard Carter proved to be virtually intact and piled high with magnificent treasures, including the solid gold coffin.

The king's original name was Tutankhaten, 'living image of ATEN', but when this god fell from favour he changed it to Tutankhamun, 'living image of Amon'. The middle part of his name contains the Egyptian word that gave ANKH. *See also* AMEN-RA; VALLEY OF THE KINGS.

**Curse of Tutankhamun.** *See under* CURSE.

**Tutivillus** or **Titivil.** The demon of medieval legend who collects all the words skipped over or mutilated by priests in the celebration of the MASS. These scraps or shreds he deposits in that pit that is said to be paved with 'good intentions' never brought to effect.

**Tutors, Achilles'.** *See under* ACHILLES.

**Tuxedo.** The American name for a dinner jacket, so called because it was first taken to the USA from England by Griswold Lorillard, in 1886, and introduced by him at the Tuxedo Club, Tuxedo, New York.

**TV, As seen on.** *See under* AS.

**Twain, Mark.** The pen name of Samuel Langhorne Clemens (1835–1910), the novelist and humorist, creator of Tom Sawyer and Huckleberry FINN. The name 'Mark Twain' is from the calls used by Mississippi pilots when taking sounds, in this case the two-fathom mark on the leadline.

**Tweed.** The origin of this name of a woollen cloth used for garments is to be found in a blunder. It should have been 'tweel', the Scots form of 'twill', but when the Scottish manufacturer sent a consignment to James Locke of London, in 1826, the name was badly written and misread, and as the cloth was made on the banks of the Tweed, 'tweed' was accordingly adopted. 'Twill', like DIMITY, means 'two-threaded'.

**Tweed ring, The.** In American history, the political ring under William M. 'Boss' Tweed (1823–78), which by wholesale graft and corruption controlled the New York Democratic party and municipal finances (1869–71). Boss Tweed died in prison. *See also* TAMMANY HALL.

**Tweedledum and Tweedledee.** Names invented by John Byrom (1692–1763) to satirize two quarrelling schools of musicians between whom the real difference was negligible, although Tweedledum's name suggests low notes and

Tweedledee's high. Hence used of people whose persons or opinions are 'as like as two peas'.

Some say, that Signor Bononcini
Compar'd to Handel's a mere ninny;
Others aver, to him, that Handel
Is scarcely fit to hold a candle.
Strange! That such high dispute should be
'Twixt Tweedledum and Tweedledee.
JOHN BYROM: 'On the Feuds between Handel and Bononcini' (1727)

The Duke of Marlborough and most of the nobility took the side of Giovanni Bononcini (or Buononcini) (1670–1747), but the Prince of Wales, with Pope and Arbuthnot, was for Handel. *See also* GLUCKISTS.

Lewis Carroll used the names for two little fat men in *Through the Looking-Glass* (1871).

**Twelve** and **twelfth. Twelfth man.** The reserve chosen for a team of eleven, especially in CRICKET; hence, anyone who just misses distinction.

**Twelfth Night.** 5 January, the eve of the Twelfth Day after CHRISTMAS or Feast of the EPIPHANY. Formerly this was a time of great merrymaking, when the BEAN KING was appointed, and the celebrations and festivities seemingly derive from the SATURNALIA of old Roman times, which were held at the same season. By the JULIAN CALENDAR Twelfth Day is Old Christmas Day.

Shakespeare's play of this name (1599) was so called because it was written for acting at the Twelfth Night revels.

**Twelve good rules.** (1) Urge no healths, (2) Profane no divine ordinances, (3) Touch no state matters, (4) Reveal no secrets, (5) Pick no quarrels, (6) Make no comparisons, (7) Maintain no ill opinions, (8) Keep no bad company, (9) Encourage no vice, (10) Make no long meals, (11) Repeat no grievances, (12) Lay no wagers.

The rules were framed and displayed in many taverns in the 18th century and derived from a broadside showing a rough-cut of the execution of CHARLES I, and were said to have been 'found in the study of King Charles the First, of Blessed Memory'. Goldsmith refers to them in *The Deserted Village* (1770).

**Twelve labours of Hercules, The.** *See* HERCULES.

**Twelve Peers of Charlemagne, The.** *See* PALADIN.

**Twelvers, The.** A sect of SHI'ITES who accept 12 of the descendants of ALI as Imams. The 12th IMAM, MOHAMMED, it is held, disappeared (*c.*874) but is still alive and will return at the end to set up the Shi'ite faith through the world.

**Twelve tables, The.** The earliest code of Roman law, engraved on brass and brought from Athens to Rome by the decemvirs. They were compiled by the Decemviri (451–450 BC), and engraved on 12 tablets. Originally ten, to which two were added, they were supposed to comprise the basis of all Roman law. In CICERO's boyhood it was still customary for them to be learned by heart.

**Twelve Tribes of Israel, The.** The tribes whose eponymous ancestors were the 12 sons of JACOB. Ten of them held territory in the PROMISED LAND, but the LEVITES did not as they were scattered among the other tribes. The name of Joseph, too, as that of the eleventh son, is not associated with a particular territory but with Israel as a whole. His sons, Ephraim and Manasseh, were regarded as founders of tribes in their own right. The ten remaining tribal heads held territory in the Promised Land as follows, in order of seniority:

(1) Reuben: east of the Dead Sea
(2) Simeon: in the south
(3) JUDAH: west of the Dead Sea
(4) ISSACHAR: southwest of the Sea of Galilee in the north
(5) Zebulun: west of the Sea of Galilee in the north
(6) Dan: in the extreme north
(7) Naphtali: between the Sea of Galilee and the Mediterranean
(8) Gad: east of the Jordan
(9) Asher: along the Mediterranean coast north of Mount Carmel
(10) Benjamin: to the north of Judah's territory in Hebron

Ephraim held territory in the centre of the Promised Land, while Manasseh had territory divided, part east and part west of the Jordan. *See also* ISRAEL; KINGS OF ISRAEL; LOST TRIBES OF ISRAEL.

**Glorious Twelfth, The.** *See under* GLORIOUS. *See also* SPORTING SEASONS IN ENGLAND.

**Twice, To think.** *See under* THINK.

**Twickenham** or **Twickers.** *See* BILLY WILLIAMS' CABBAGE PATCH.

**Bard of Twickenham, The.** *See under* BARD.

**Twiddle one's thumbs, To.** To sit in a state of bored inactivity, often against one's inclination; to be wasting time or to have to waste one's time. An allusion to the habit at such times of sitting with the hands clasped in one's lap idly rotating the thumbs round each other.

**Twig. I twig you.** I catch your meaning; I understand (perhaps from Scottish Gaelic *tuig*, 'I understand').

**Hop the twig, To.** *See under* HOP.

**Twilight. Twilight of the Gods, The.** *See* RAGNAROK.

**Twilight sleep.** A state of semi-consciousness produced by injection of scopolamine and morphia in which a woman can undergo childbirth with comparatively little pain. *See also* TRUTH DRUG.

**Twilight zone.** The run-down area that sometimes develops around the central business district of a city.

**Celtic twilight.** *See under* CELTIC.

**Twinkling of an eye, In the.** Immediately; in a very short time.

> In a moment, in the twinkling of an eye, at the last trump: for the trumpet shall sound, and the dead shall be raised incorruptible, and we shall be changed.
> 1 Corinthians 15:52

**Twins, The.** *See* GEMINI.

**Siamese twins.** *See under* SIAMESE.

**Twirl.** In prison parlance, the same as a SCREW, and for a similar reason.

**Twist. Twist, The.** A dance popular in the 1960s, so called from the contortions performed.

**Twist** or **wrap someone round one's little finger, To.** To be able to influence a person at will; to have someone do exactly what one wants.

**Twist someone's arm, To.** To coerce or persuade a person to do something against their inclination. The phrase is sometimes used facetiously, as: 'Can I twist your arm?', said when offering another drink.

**Twist the lion's tail, To.** To insult or impose humiliating treatment on Britain when she is unable to retaliate, the lion being a British national emblem.

**Double and twist, To.** *See under* DOUBLE.

**Oliver Twist.** The foundling who is the central character in Dickens's novel named after him (1838–9). He is raised in a workhouse, where he is mistreated for asking for more food. His subsequent adventures and misadventures involve him with FAGIN and his gang of thieves but he is subsequently rescued and adopted by the benevolent Mr Brownlow.

**Round the twist.** *See under* ROUND.

**Twitcher, Jemmy.** A cunning, treacherous highwayman in John Gay's *Beggar's Opera* (1728). The name was given about 1765, in a poem by Thomas Gray, to John Montagu, Lord SANDWICH (1718–92), who was noted for his liaison with Margaret Ray, his mistress, with whom he had been living for some 16 years when she was shot by the Rev. 'Captain' Hackman out of jealousy.

**Twm Shon Catti.** A kind of Welsh ROBIN HOOD (*c.*1530–1609). Tales of his exploits are told in George Borrow's *Wild Wales*, ch xcii (1862). He is said to have eventually married an heiress and ended up as a squire and magistrate. His name means 'Thomas (son of) John (and) Catherine'.

**Two.** The evil principle of PYTHAGORAS. The second day of the second month of the year was, accordingly, sacred to PLUTO and was esteemed unlucky.

**Two bites at a cherry.** Two sessions spent on a piece of work that should be done in one.

**Two bits.** American term for 25 cents, otherwise known as a quarter. The origin of the term is in British slang 'bit' (e.g. threepenny bit), which was adopted in the south and west of the USA for the old Mexican *real* worth 12½ cents.

**Two can play at that game.** A person's deeds or behaviour can be copied to their disadvantage.

**Two cultures, The.** The existence in England, and to a great extent in western Europe, of two separate cultures with few points of contact between them, one based on the humanities and the other on the sciences. The phrase gained immediate popularity after C.P. Snow's Rede Lecture, subsequently published as *The Two Cultures and the Scientific Revolution* (1959). A comparison may be made with the ideas expressed in Matthew Arnold's *Culture and Anarchy* (1869) and his Rede Lecture entitled *Literature and Science* (1882).

> I believe the intellectual life of the whole of western society is increasingly being split into two polar groups ... Literary intellectuals at one pole – at the other scientists, and as the most representative, the physical scientists. Between the two a gulf of mutual incomprehension.
> C.P. SNOW: *The Two Cultures and the Scientific Revolution* (1959)

**Two-faced, To be.** *See* DOUBLE-FACED.

**Two-headed eagle.** The German eagle has its head turned to the left (as one looks at it) and the Roman eagle to the right. CHARLEMAGNE, as successor to the Roman emperors, is said to have adopted the eagle as a badge, but the two-headed eagle, reputedly symbolizing the eastern and western divisions of the empire, did not appear on the arms of the HOLY ROMAN EMPIRE until the early 15th century. It was retained by the Austrian emperors as successors to the Holy Roman Emperors. In 1472 Ivan III of Russia assumed the two-headed eagle after his marriage to Sophia, daughter of Thomas Palaeologus, and niece of Constantine XIV.

**Two heads are better than one.** Another's advice is often very useful.

**Two-legged mare, The.** The gallows.

**Two-minute silence.** The cessation of traffic and all other activities for two minutes at 11 am on 11 November to commemorate those who died in the First World War. First observed in 1919, it remained a central feature of REMEMBRANCE DAY. A special nationwide two-minute silence began at 8.38 pm (sunset) on 8 May 1995 to mark the 50th anniversary of VE DAY.

> At the going down of the sun and in the morning
> We will remember them.
> LAURENCE BINYON: 'For the Fallen' (1914)

**Two more, and up goes the donkey.** An old cry at fairs, the showman having promised his credulous hearers that as soon as enough pennies are collected his donkey will balance on the top of a pole or ladder. Always a matter of 'two more pennies', the trick is never performed.

**Two of a trade did never agree.** A very old proverb (it occurs in Hesiod's *Works and Days* (7th century BC)).

In every age and clime we see
Two of a trade can ne'er agree.
JOHN GAY: *Fables*, I, xxi (1727)

**Twopenny.** Often used slightingly of things of little value.

**Twopenny-halfpenny.** Said of something cheap or tawdry.

**Twopenny Tube, The.** The Central London Railway was so called, because for some years after its opening (1900) the fare between any two stations was 2d.

**Two sacraments, The.** Within the Protestant churches they are BAPTISM and the LORD'S SUPPER.

**Two's company, three's a crowd.** An old saying, much used by lovers.

**Two Sicilies, The.** The old name for the Spanish Bourbon kingdom of Naples and Sicily formerly united under their Angevin rulers in the 13th century. The Two Sicilies were annexed to the Kingdom of Italy in 1860.

**Two-time, To.** To swindle; to DOUBLE-CROSS.

The expression originally applied to a deceitful lover, who tried to persuade the other that they were 'the one and only'.

**Two-ton Tessie.** Tessie O'Shea (1917–95), an amply proportioned British music hall singer of the mid-20th century.

**Ass with two panniers, An.** *See under* ASS.

**Goody Two-Shoes.** *See under* GOODY.

**In two minds, To be.** To be in doubt over a matter.

**In two shakes of a lamb's tail.** In a moment. An expression originating in the USA in the early 19th century.

**Penny plain, twopence coloured.** *See under* PENNY.

**Put two and two together, To.** To come to an inference or conclusion (usually fairly obvious) from the facts of the matter. Two and two make four, hence the suggestion of a simple and obvious deduction.

**That makes two of us.** That applies to me too.

**Tuck in your twopenny!** *See under* TUCK.

**Tyana, Apollonius of.** *See under* APOLLONIUS.

**Tybalt.** An old name given to a cat. Hence the allusions to cats in connection with Tybalt, one of the CAPULET family in Shakespeare's ROMEO AND JULIET (III, i (1594)). Mercutio says, 'Tybalt, you rat-catcher, will you walk?', and again, when Tybalt asks, 'What wouldst thou have with me?', Mercutio answers, 'Good King of Cats! nothing but one of your nine lives.' *See also* GIB CAT.

**Tyburn.** A tributary of the River Thames rising at Hampstead, which gave its name to the village that was later called MARYLEBONE and to a place of execution. Hence, formerly, 'Tyburn tree', the gallows (at Tyburn), 'to take a ride to Tyburn', to go to one's hanging, 'Lord of the Manor of Tyburn', the common hangman, and the like.

The site of the gallows is marked by three brass triangles let into the pavement at the corner of Edgware Road and Bayswater Road. The last criminal to be hanged there was John Austin in 1783. After that, executions were carried out at NEWGATE until its demolition.

**Tyburnia.** A district of London near the old TYBURN gallows was so called. It consisted approximately of the area between what is now Paddington Station and MARBLE ARCH.

**Tyburn ticket.** A certificate that, under a statute of William III (10 W III, c12), 1698, was granted to prosecutors who had secured a capital conviction against a criminal, exempting them from all parish and ward offices within the parish in which the felony had been committed. This, with the privilege it conferred, might be sold once, and once only, and the *Stamford Mercury* for 27 March 1818 announced the sale of one for £280. The Act was repealed in 1818, but as late as 1856 Mr Pratt of Bond Street claimed exemption from serving on an OLD BAILEY jury on the strength of the possession of a Tyburn ticket and was successful.

**Tycoon.** A title of the SHOGUN, also applied to an industrial or business magnate. The word derives from Japanese *taikun*, itself from Chinese *dà*, 'great', and *jūn*, 'monarch'.

**Tyke.** *See* TIKE.

**Tylwyth Teg** (Welsh *tylwyth*, 'family', and *teg*, 'fair'). The fairies of Welsh folklore, friendly but mischievous, who live in caves and on the mountains, who communicate by signs and never speak. They are versed in country lore, but if they touch iron, they vanish away.

**Tyndale's Bible.** *See under* BIBLE.

**Tynwald.** The Court of Tynwald constitutes the governing body of the ISLE OF MAN. It claims to be the oldest parliament in the world in continuous existence and has two branches: the Legislative Council and the House of Keys. The Council consists of the president of Tynwald, the bishop of Sodor and Man, the Attorney-General, and eight members elected by the House of Keys, itself composed of 24 members elected by universal adult suffrage. The Lieutenant-Governor is the sovereign's personal representative in the island, to which no British Act of Parliament applies unless specifically stated. The House of Keys was self-elected until 1866. 'Tyn-' is from THING and '-wald' from Old Norse *völlr*, 'field', meaning the hill on which it originally assembled. The origin of 'Keys' is a matter of conjecture. In the 15th century the 24 keys are referred to as Keys of Man and Keys of the Law.

**Type. Clarendon type.** *See under* CLARENDON.

**Italic type.** *See under* ITALIC.

**Roman type.** *See under* ROMAN.

**Typhoeus** or **Typhon.** A monster of Greek mythology, the son of GAIA and TARTARUS, with a hundred heads, each with a terrible voice. He made war on ZEUS, who killed him with a THUNDERBOLT. According to one legend, he lies buried under Mount ETNA. By ECHIDNA he is said to have fathered ORTHOS, CERBERUS, the Lernaean HYDRA, the CHIMERA, the Theban SPHINX and the NEMEAN LION. *See also* SET.

**Typhoid Mary.** The nickname of Mary Mallon (*c*.1870–1938), a carrier of typhoid fever in the New York area. Her case first arose in 1904, when an epidemic of typhoid spread over Oyster Bay and nearby towns on Long Island. The sources were traced to households where Mary had been a cook. She was apprehended but escaped. She was eventually committed to an isolation centre and released only in 1910 on condition that she never worked with food again. But she resumed her occupation, and in 1914 a further epidemic broke out at Newfoundland, New Jersey, and at a Manhattan maternity hospital, both places where Mary had worked. Altogether 51 cases of typhoid, including three deaths, were directly attributed to her, although she herself was immune to the typhoid bacillus.

**Typhon.** *Seer* TYPHOEUS.

**Typhoon** (Chinese *tai fung*, 'great wind', influenced by Greek *tuphōn*, 'whirlwind'). A violent tropical storm or cyclone commonly associated with the China seas and the southwest Pacific. Typhoons are formed by converging masses of air, blowing from right to left in the northern hemisphere, but left to right in the southern.

> My coursers are fed with the lightning,
> They drink of the whirlwind's stream,
> And when the red morning is bright'ning
> They bathe in the fresh sunbeam ...
> I desire: and their speed makes night kindle;
> I fear: they outstrip the Typhoon;
> Ere the cloud piled on Atlas can dwindle
> We encircle the earth and the moon.
>
> PERCY BYSSHE SHELLEY: *Prometheus Unbound*, II, iv (1819)

**Tyr.** *See* TIU.

**Tyranny, The Eleven Years'.** *See under* ELEVEN.

**Tyrant.** In ancient Greece the tyrant was merely the absolute ruler, the despot, of a state, and at first the word had no implication of cruelty or what is now known as tyranny. Many of the Greek tyrants were model rulers, as Pisistratus and Pericles of Athens, Periander of Corinth, Dionysius the Younger, Gelon and his brother Hieron of Syracuse, Pheidon of Argos, Polycrates of Samos (*see* RING OF AMASIS) and others. Soon, however, the word (*turannos*) acquired much the same meaning as it has today.

**Thirty Tyrants, The.** *See under* THIRTY.

**Violet on the tyrant's grave, The.** *See under* VIOLET.

**Tyrian purple.** *See* PURPLE.

**Tyrtaeus.** A lame schoolmaster and elegiac poet of Athens, who is said to have so inspired the Spartans by his songs that they defeated the Messenians (7th century BC). The name has hence been given to many martial poets who have urged on their countrymen to deeds of arms and victory.

# U

**U.** The twenty-first letter of the English alphabet, in form a modification of V, with which for many centuries it was interchangeable. Words beginning with U and V were (like those beginning with I and J) not separated in English dictionaries until about 1800 and later. *A Dictionary of the English Language* published in London by Henry Washbourne (1847) adhered to the old practice. In 16th- and early 17th-century books spellings such as 'vpon' and 'haue' are the rule rather than the exception. The following extract from Edmund Spenser's *The Faerie Queene* (II, viii (1590)) is typical of the situation:

> How oft do they, their siluer bowers leaue,
> To come to succour vs, that succour want?
> How oft do they with golden pineons, cleaue
> The flitting skyes, like flying Pursuiuant,
> Against foule feends to aide vs millitant?
> They for vs fight, they watch and dewly ward,
> And their bright Squadrons round about vs plant,
> And all for loue, and nothing for reward:
> O why should heauenly God to men haue such regard?

**U and Non-U.** A former semi-humorous mark of distinction between social classes in England based on the usage of certain words. 'U' is Upper Class and 'Non-U' is non-Upper Class. It is 'U' to say 'luncheon' for what 'Non-U' folk call 'lunch', 'U' to say 'napkin' instead of 'serviette', and 'U' to prefer 'cycle' to 'bike'. The terms owe their popularity to Nancy Mitford (1904–73), who quoted them in an article in the magazine *Encounter* in September 1955, but they were invented by Professor Alan Ross in 1954 and appeared in his article 'Linguistic class-indicators in present-day English' in the Finnish philological journal *Neuphilologische Mitteilungen.* A simplified and condensed version of this, entitled 'U and Non-U: An Essay in Sociological Linguistics', was later included in *Noblesse Oblige* (1956), edited by Nancy Mitford. *See also* NOBLESSE OBLIGE.

> No wonder show-jumping had recently attracted so many enthusiasts: it is the gypsy life of modern times, nomadic, transitory and glamorous, in which the gentry can take part as legitimately as the professional, where it is just as 'U' to sleep on straw in a horse-box as it is in the smartest hotel.
>
> MOYRA WILLIAMS: *Adventures Unbridled*, ch xi (1960)

**Uberrimae fidei** (Latin, 'of the fullest confidence'). A legal expression used of contracts in which the fullest and frankest information must be disclosed by the applicant or promisee. All insurance contracts are governed by this principle in order that the insurers may judge whether or not to accept the proposal.

**U-boat.** A German submarine. The term is adapted from German *Unterseeboot* ('underwater vessel'). *See also* E-BOAT.

**Udolpho, The Mysteries of.** *See under* MYSTERY.

**UFO.** Unidentified flying object, the name given to objects claimed to have been sighted in the sky such as FLYING SAUCERS, or picked up on radar screens, the exact nature of which is uncertain. Study and observation of UFOs is termed ufology by enthusiasts. The peak of interest in such phenomena was in the 1950s and 1960s.

**Ugly. Ugly customer, An.** A threatening and easily provoked person, so one who is best handled carefully.

**Ugly duckling.** An unpromising child who develops into a beautiful or handsome adult; also anything of an unprepossessing character that may change with time into something attractive. The expression is taken from Hans Christian Andersen's story of the 'Ugly Duckling' (1835), a cygnet raised in a brood of ducks to grow into a beautiful swan.

**As ugly as sin.** *See under* AS.

**Plug ugly.** *See under* PLUG.

**Uisnech.** *See* SONS OF USNECH.

**Uitlander.** The Boer term for a foreigner (Outlander), and especially those Europeans resident in the Transvaal and Orange Free State (mostly British subjects) after the discoveries of gold, who were not given political rights.

Their situation led to the JAMESON RAID of 1895 and the subsequent Boer War of 1899–1902. *See also* KRUGER TELEGRAM.

**Ulema.** The learned classes in Muslim countries, interpreters of the KORAN and the law, from whose numbers came the MULLAHS, MUFTIS, IMAMS, cadis and others (teachers of religion and law, and administrators of justice). The word represents Arabic *'ulamā'*, 'scholars'.

**Ullage** (Old French *ouillage*, noun of *ouiller*, 'to fill a cask'). The difference between the amount of liquid a vessel can contain and what it actually does contain. The term is applied to a bottle of wine of which part of the contents have evaporated. Colloquially it is applied to dregs or rubbish generally.

**Ulloa, Circle of.** *See under* CIRCLE.

**Ulster.** The northernmost province of Ireland, administratively divided in the 16th century into nine counties, of which those in the Republic of Ireland (Cavan, Donegal and Monaghan) still exist. Ulster was forfeited to the crown in the time of James I (r.1603–25) in consequence of the rebellions of Richard Talbot, 1st Earl of Tyrconnell and Hugh O'Neill, 2nd Earl of Tyrone and planted by English and Scottish settlers (1609–12). In 1920 the remaining SIX COUNTIES were formed into the state of Northern Ireland. The name Ulster is now commonly but strictly speaking inaccurately used for Northern Ireland, especially for brevity in newspaper headlines. *See also* IRA; ORANGEMEN; SINN FÉIN.

**Ulster King of Arms.** Formerly the chief heraldic officer for Ireland and Registrar to the ORDER OF ST PATRICK, created by Edward VI in 1553. The office was united with that of the NORROY King of Arms in 1943. His present jurisdiction is restricted to the SIX COUNTIES. Eire appointed its own Chief Herald of Ireland in 1943 who occupies the former office of the Ulster King in Dublin Castle. *See also* HERALD.

**Red** or **Bloody Hand of Ulster, The.** *See* RED HAND.

**Ultima Thule.** The end of the world, the last extremity. *See also* THULE.

**Ultimus Romanorum** (Latin). The LAST OF THE ROMANS.

**Ultor** (Latin, 'avenger'). A title given to MARS when, after defeating the murderers of Julius CAESAR at Philippi, Augustus built a temple to him in the Forum at Rome.

**Ultra. Ultra vires** (Latin *ultra*, 'beyond', and *vires*, 'the powers'). In excess of the authority given by law, hence invalid in the legal sense. Thus if the Bank of England were to set up a MINT on its premises it would be acting *ultra vires*.

**Plus ultra.** *See under* PLUS.

**Ultramontane party.** The extreme party in the Church of Rome. Ultramontane opinions or tendencies are those that favour the high 'Catholic' party. Ultramontane (beyond the mountains, i.e. the Alps) means Italy or the old Papal States. The term was first used by the French, to distinguish those who look upon the pope as the fountain of all power in the church, from the Gallican school, which maintained the right of self-government by national churches. *See also* TRAMONTANE.

**Ulysses** or **Odysseus.** A mythical king of Ithaca, a small rocky island off Greece, one of the leading chieftains of the Greeks in HOMER'S ILIAD, and the hero of his ODYSSEY, represented by Homer as wise, eloquent and full of guile.

He was the son of LAERTES, ruler of Ithaca. His wife was PENELOPE, by whom he had a son, TELEMACHUS. After some initial unwillingness, he sailed with the Greeks to TROY, his courage proving more than worthy of him in the siege of that city. The *Odyssey* recounts his ten years of wanderings after the fall of Troy. According to VIRGIL, it was Ulysses who suggested the device of the WOODEN HORSE OF TROY through which Troy was ultimately taken. *See also* TELEGONUS.

The *Odyssey* interprets the name as meaning 'child of hatred', but this is simply a popular etymology. The true origin is unknown.

**Ulysses' bow.** Only ULYSSES could draw his own bow, and he could shoot an arrow through 12 rings. By this sign PENELOPE recognized her husband after an absence of 20 years. He was also recognized by his dog, Argus. The bow was prophetic, and belonged at one time to Eurytus of Oechalia.

**Umble pie.** *See* EAT HUMBLE PIE.

**Umbrage, To take** (Latin *umbra*, 'shade'). Originally to feel overshadowed or slighted and hence to take offence.

**Umbrella** (Latin *umbra*, 'shade'). The device was used in ancient China, Babylon, Egypt and elsewhere, but it was not commonly found in England until after Jonas Hanway (1712–86), the philanthropist, publicized it from about 1750 by carrying one regularly in the streets of London to keep off the rain. He incurred a good deal of ridicule in the process.

Francis Quarles in his *Emblems* (1635) used the word to signify the Deity hidden in the manhood of Christ: 'Nature is made th'umbrella of the Deity' (iv). There are further mentions in Jonathan Swift's *City Shower* (1710) and in John Gay's *Trivia* (1716), and *The Female Tatler* (12 December 1709) contains this notice:

> The young gentleman belonging to the Custom House, that for fear of rain, borrowed the Umbrella at Will's Coffee House in Cornhill of the Mistress, is hereby advertised that to be dry from head to foot on the like occasion he shall be welcome to the Maid's pattens.

**Under the umbrella of someone.** *See under* UNDER.

**Umlaut.** The change or modification of sound characteristic of certain Germanic languages occasioned when a vowel is influenced by a following vowel. It is typically found in related verb forms, as *ich trage*, 'I carry', *er trägt*, 'he carries', in comparatives, as *alt*, 'old', *älter*, 'older', and in plurals, as *der Bruder*, 'the brother', *die Brüder*, 'the brothers'. The modifying vowel may appear, especially in older forms or proper names, as Roentgen, Röntgen (*see* X-RAYS), but it is usually replaced by an umlaut sign, as exemplified above. The word, which literally means 'around sound', i.e. 'sound that changes places', was invented by the philologist Jakob Grimm (1785–1863).

**Umpire.** *See* APRON.

**Unam sanctam** (Latin, 'One holy'). The opening words of Boniface VIII's BULL of 1302 declaring that there was 'One holy Catholic and Apostolic Church', membership of which was necessary for salvation. It is notable for its assertion of papal claims and of the authority of the spiritual power over the temporal.

**Uncials.** A form of majuscule (large) script used in manuscripts dating from about the 4th century AD to the 8th century. It is so called from Latin *uncia*, twelfth part, inch, because the letters were about an inch (2.5cm) high. There were also half-uncials.

**Uncle.** Slang for a pawnbroker, in use as early as 1756. Its origin is unknown. An article that has 'gone to uncle's' is in pawn. *See also* THREE GOLDEN BALLS.

**Uncle George.** King George III (1738, r.1760–1820); he was also called FARMER GEORGE.

**Uncle Joe.** A British nickname, dating from the Second World War, for Joseph Stalin, head of the government of the USSR (1941–53).

**Uncle Remus.** The old plantation Negro whose quaint and proverbial wisdom and stories of BRER RABBIT AND BRER FOX, were related by Joel Chandler Harris (1848–1908) in *Uncle Remus, his Songs and Sayings* (1880) and *Nights with Uncle Remus* (1883).

**Uncle Sam.** A nickname for the collective citizens of the USA. It arose in the neighbourhood of Troy, New York, in about 1812, partly from the frequent appearance of the initials US on government supplies to the army and others. The other contributory factor to the derivation is puzzling, but some have maintained that there was a local resident who had a connection with army supplies and who was actually known as Uncle Sam.

**Uncle Tom's Cabin.** A story by Harriet Beecher Stowe (1811–96) that appeared in 1852. It tells of the sale of a pious and faithful old Negro slave to a bad owner. By its emphasis on the worst sides of Negro slavery, the book helped in no small degree to arouse the American nation to an understanding of the iniquities of the system. The original of Uncle Tom is popularly identified as Josiah Henson (1789–1883), a black slave who was subsequently ordained as a Methodist preacher and who came to London in 1876 to be presented to Queen Victoria. 'Uncle Tom' is now used by black nationalists to denote blacks who are over-subservient to the white ESTABLISHMENT.

**Bob's your uncle.** *See under* BOB.

**Dutch uncle.** *See under* DUTCH.

**Old Uncle Tom Cobbleigh.** *See under* OLD.

**Unclubable** or **unclubbable.** 'A very unclubable man' is one who is very unsocial; one lacking in urbanity. A word coined by Dr Johnson and applied by him to Sir John Hawkins (1719–89), one of the original members of the Literary CLUB founded in 1763, which met at the Turk's Head, Gerrard Street, SOHO, London.

**Unco.** A Scottish variant of 'uncouth' ('unknown', hence, 'strange', 'extraordinary'). It has two meanings. As an adjective it means 'unknown', 'strange', 'unusual', but as an adverb it means 'very', as 'unco good', 'unco glad'. The 'unco guid' are the PINCHBECK saints, those who are too good by half.

**Unction, Extreme.** *See under* EXTREME.

**Uncumber, St.** The Portuguese saint Wilgefortis, about whom little is known with any accuracy and who was so called according to Sir Thomas More 'because they [women] reken that for a pecke of oats she will not faile to uncumber them of their husbondys'. Traditionally, she was one of seven beautiful princesses, who, wishing to lead a single life, prayed that she might have a beard. The prayer was granted and she was no more cumbered with suitors, but one of them, a prince of Sicily, was so enraged that he had her crucified. The legend of Wilgefortis is explained by some as an attempt to explain the clothed and bearded figure of Christ on the cross.

**Undecimilla.** *See* URSULA.

**Under. Under a cloud.** Under suspicion; in a bad temper.

**Under arms.** Prepared for battle; in battle array.

**Under canvas.** In camp; in a tent.

**Under colour of.** Under pretence of; under the alleged authority of.

**Under cover.** Working out of sight or in secret. An undercover agent is one who pursues his inquiries or work unknown to any but his employer.

**Underground.** A political or military movement carried on in secret against an oppressor government of an occupying enemy administration, especially in the Second World War.

**Underground railroad.** In the USA the name given (*c.*1830) to the secret and changing system of hiding places and routes organized for helping runaway slaves to escape to the northern states and Canada. An 'underground road' was its forerunner.

**Under hatches.** Down in the world; out of sight; dead. The hatches of a ship are the coverings over the hatchways, and to be 'under hatches' is to be below deck.

For, though his body's under hatches,
His soul is gone aloft.
CHARLES DIBDIN: 'Tom Bowling' (1790)

These lines were inscribed on Dibdin's tombstone at St Martin-in-the-Fields.

**Under my hand and seal.** A legal phrase indicating that the document in question is both signed and sealed by the person on whose behalf it has been drawn up.

**Under one's belt.** Eaten; accomplished. The figurative use is common in describing achievements, as: 'She has ten years' sailing experience under her belt.'

**Under one's breath.** In a whisper or quiet voice; *sotto voce*.

**Under one's feet.** In the way, as: 'The dog would not settle but was always under my feet.'

**Under one's own steam.** Availing oneself of one's own resources; without assistance.

**Under one's very nose.** Right in front of one; without one's noticing it.

**Under someone's thumb.** Under the influence or power of a person.

**Under starter's orders.** Of racehorses or other runners, awaiting the starter's signal to depart. *See also* READY, STEADY, GO!

**Undertaker.** Originally any contractor. The application of this word to one who carries out funerals (in the USA termed a mortician) dates from the 17th century. The principal English and Scottish grantees of land during the plantation of ULSTER (1609–12) were called Undertakers, as were those who undertook to secure the return to Parliament of members favourable to the policies of James I in 1614. The term was also applied to the 18th-century magnates who monopolized political power in Ireland and who controlled the Irish Parliament.

> 'There's a Providence in it all,' said Sam. 'O' course there is,' replied his father with a nod of grave approval. 'Wot 'ud become of the undertakers without it, Sammy?'
> DICKENS: *Pickwick Papers*, ch lii (1836–7)

**Under the counter.** A phrase first current in the Second World War in connection with an illegal practice in some shops. Articles in short supply were kept out of sight, under the counter, for sale to favoured customers, often at inflated prices. *See also* BLACK MARKET.

> Chief goods to 'go under the counter' are fully fashioned silk stockings, watches and silk handkerchiefs.
> *Evening Standard* (20 December 1945)

**Under the knife.** Undergoing a surgical operation.

**Under the lee of a ship.** On the side away from the wind, so that the ship provides shelter and breaks the force of the wind.

**Under the lee of the land.** Under the shelter of the land.

**Under the rose.** *See* SUB ROSA.

**Under the sun.** Anywhere in the world. 'There is nothing new under the sun' is a saying commonly used to mean that whatever may seem new or original will probably already have occurred or been found elsewhere.

**Under the table.** Very drunk, as: 'Some of the guests were already under the table.'

**Under the umbrella of someone.** Under someone's dominion, influence, patronage or the like. The allusion is to the umbrella carried over certain African potentates as an emblem of sovereignty. In 1876 the sacred umbrella of King Koffee of the Ashantis was captured and placed in the South Kensington Museum.

In the Second World War the term 'umbrella' was used to denote air cover to ground or sea operations.

**Under the weather.** Unwell or out of sorts; intoxicated, as if affected by the weather.

**Under way.** Said of a ship making headway. 'To lose way' is to lose speed when sailing, and 'to gather way' is to pick up speed. Hence generally, making progress, as: 'The project is now well under way.'

**Underwriter.** A person who engages to buy at a certain prearranged price all the stock in a new company, of a new issue or the like, that is not taken up by the public. An underwriter at LLOYD'S is one who insures a ship or its merchandise and undertakes other insurance to a stated amount. He is so called because he writes his name under the policy.

**Down under.** *See under* DOWN.

**Get under someone's skin, To.** To irritate them; to annoy or 'bug' them. The allusion is probably to the activities of such larvae as harvest bugs, which cause intense irritation 'under the skin'.

**Keep it under one's hat, To.** To keep something to oneself; to keep it secret. The expression may allude to urchin messenger boys in Victorian times, who lacking pockets in their garments would convey a letter or message under their cloth cap.

**Undine.** One of the elemental spirits of PARACELSUS, the spirit of the waters. She was created without a soul, but had this privilege, that by marrying a mortal and bearing him a child she obtained a soul, and with it all the pains and penalties of the human race. She is the subject of the tale *Undine* (1811) by Friedrich de la Motte Fouqué (1777–1843). *See also* SYLPH.

**Unfinished Symphony.** A name for Franz Schubert's Symphony No. 8 in B Minor (1822), of which only two movements were completed. The phrase is applied figuratively and humorously to various unfinished compositions.

**Unguent, Promethean.** *See under* PROMETHEUS.

**Unhinged.** With one's nerves badly shaken; with one's balance of mind disturbed, like a door that has lost one of its hinges.

**Uniat** or **Uniate Churches** (Latin *unus*, 'one'). Churches of Eastern Christendom that are in communion with Rome but that retain their own rights, languages and canon law.

**Unicorn** (Latin *unus*, 'one', and *cornu*, 'horn'). A mythical and heraldic animal, represented by medieval writers as having the legs of a buck, the tail of a lion, the head and body of a horse, and a single horn, white at the base, black in the middle and red at the tip, in the middle of its forehead. The body is white, the head red, and the eyes blue. The earliest author that describes it is Ctesias (400 BC). The medieval concept of it is encapsulated in the following extract:

> The unicorn has but one horn in the middle of its forehead. It is the only animal that ventures to attack the elephant; and so sharp is the nail of its foot, that with one blow it can rip the belly of the beast. Hunters can catch the unicorn only by placing a young virgin in his haunts. No sooner does he see the damsel, than he runs towards her, and lies down at her feet, and so suffers himself to be captured by the hunters. The unicorn represents Jesus Christ, who took on Him our nature in the virgin's womb, was betrayed by the Jews and delivered into the hands of Pontius Pilate. Its one horn signifies the Gospel of Truth.
>
> *Le Bestiaire Divin de Guillaume, Clerc de Normandie* (13th century)

Another popular belief was that the unicorn, by dipping its horn into a liquid, could detect whether or not it contained poison. In the designs for gold and silver plate made for the Austrian emperor Rudolph II by Ottavio Strada (1550–1612) is a cup on which a unicorn stands as if to assay or test the liquid.

The supporters of the old royal arms of Scotland are two unicorns. When James VI of Scotland came to reign over England as James I (1603) he brought one of the unicorns with him, and with it supplanted the RED DRAGON, which, as representing Wales, was one of the supporters of the English shield, the other being the lion.

The animosity that existed between the lion and the unicorn referred to by Edmund Spenser in *The Faerie Queene* (II, v (1590)) is allegorical of that which once existed between England and Scotland:

> Like as a Lyon, whose imperiall powre
> A prowd rebellious Vnicorne defies.

Hence also the words of the familiar nursery rhyme:

> The lion and the unicorn
> Were fighting for the crown;
> The lion beat the unicorn
> All round the town.

**Unigenitus** (Latin, 'the only-begotten'). A PAPAL BULL, so called from its opening sentence *Unigenitus, Dei Filius*, issued in 1713 by Clement XI (r.1700–21) in condemnation of Pasquier Quesnel's *Réflexions morales sur le Nouveau Testament* (1692), which favoured JANSENISTS. It was a *damnatio in globo*, i.e. a condemnation of the whole book without exception. It was confirmed in 1725, but in 1730 the bull was condemned by the civil authorities of Paris, and this clerical controversy died out.

**Union, The.** A short term for the United States of America. In England the phrase was a once familiar colloquialism for the workhouse, from its being maintained by a group of parishes formed into a 'union' in accordance with the Poor Law Amendment Act of 1834.

**Union is strength** (Latin *unitate fortior*). The wise saw of Periander, tyrant of Corinth between *c*.627 and 586 BC.

**Unionists.** In 1886, when W.E. Gladstone introduced his first Home Rule Bill for Ireland, 78 LIBERALS under Joseph Chamberlain and Lord Hartington allied with the CONSERVATIVES as LIBERAL UNIONISTS to uphold the union with Ireland. From 1886, the Conservative Party was also called the Unionist Party. It adopted the official name of Conservative and Unionist Party in 1909. *See also* ACT OF UNION.

**Union Jack.** The national banner of the United Kingdom. It consists of three united crosses: that of St GEORGE for England, the saltire of St ANDREW for Scotland (added by James I), and the cross of St PATRICK for Ireland (added at the Union in 1801).

The white edging of St George's cross shows the white field. In the saltire the cross is reversed on each side, showing that the other half of the cross is covered over. The broad white band is the St Andrew's cross and should be uppermost at the top left-hand corner of the flag (i.e. the hoist). The narrow white edge is the white field of St Patrick's cross.

The Union Jack is technically described thus:

> The Union Flag shall be azure, the Crosses saltire of St Andrew and St Patrick quarterly per saltire, counter-changed, argent and gules, the latter fimbriated of the second, surmounted by the Cross of St George of the third fimbriated as the saltire. – *By order of the Council*.

*See also* JACK (4).

**Union of South Africa.** The union of the former self-governing colonies of the Cape of Good Hope, Natal, the Transvaal and the Orange River Colony, with its Parliament at Cape Town. The title was changed to the Republic of South Africa in 1961, when South Africa left the British COMMONWEALTH. It rejoined it, however, in 1994.

**Union rose, The.** The TUDOR ROSE.
**Act of Union, The.** *See under* ACT.
**Art Union.** *See under* ART.
**Hypostatic union.** *See under* HYPOSTATIC.
**Peace Pledge Union.** *See under* PEACE.
**Trade union.** *See under* TRADE.

**Unitarians.** Originally Christians who denied the existence of the TRINITY, maintaining that God existed in one person only. Many of the early heretical sects were unitarian in belief if not in name, and at the time of the REFORMATION unitarianism had numerous exponents who may be regarded as the founders of the modern movement.

In England John Biddle (1615–62) is generally regarded as the founding father, and among the famous men who have been Unitarians are the philosopher Dr Samuel Clarke (1675–1729), the chemist Joseph Priestley (1733–1804), the scholar and clergyman Nathaniel Lardner (1684–1768), the theologian James Martineau (1805–1900) and the politician Joseph Chamberlain (1836–1914). Modern Unitarianism is not based on scriptural authority, but on reason and conscience and includes AGNOSTICS and humanists among its members. There is no formal dogma or creed.

**Unite.** A gold coin worth 20s, also called a 'broad', from its size. It was first minted by James I in 1604 in place of the SOVEREIGN, named from the union of the crowns of England and Scotland (1603), and bore the motto *Faciam eos in gentem unam* ('I will make them one people', from Ezekiel 37:22). It was replaced by the GUINEA in 1663. *See also* JACOBUS.

**United. United Ancient Order of Druids, The.** A secret benefit society, akin to FREEMASONRY, founded in London in 1781 and introduced into the USA in 1833. It now has lodges, or 'groves', in many parts of the world.

**United Empire Loyalists.** Many of those American colonists who remained loyal to the mother country during the American War of Independence subsequently migrated to Ontario and the Maritime Provinces. They formed the nucleus of British Canada and were given the honourable title of United Empire Loyalists.

**United Irishmen.** A society formed by Theobald Wolfe Tone (1763–98) in 1791 after the publication of his pamphlet *An Argument on Behalf of the Catholics of Ireland*. Its first headquarters was at Belfast, and its objects were to secure a representative national Parliament and to unite all Irishmen against British influence. Membership included both Protestants and Roman Catholics, but it soon became revolutionary and was largely responsible for the rebellion of 1798. *See also* VINEGAR HILL.

**United Kingdom.** The name adopted on 1 January 1801, when Great Britain and Ireland were united. *See also* ACT OF UNION.

**United Nations.** The successor to the LEAGUE OF NATIONS as a world organization primarily concerned with the maintenance of peace but with numerous other functions and agencies. It sprang from the Dumbarton Oaks talks (1944) between the United States, Great Britain and Soviet Russia, and was formally inaugurated in 1945. Its headquarters is in New York City.

**United Provinces.** Guelderland, Utrecht, Friesland, Overijssel, Groningen, Zeeland and Holland, the seven provinces whose independence was recognized by Spain in 1648 and which first came together in the Union of Utrecht (1579), thus laying the foundation of the United Kingdom of the Netherlands. They became the Batavian Republic in 1795 and the Kingdom of Holland under Louis Bonaparte in 1806. At the end of the Napoleonic Wars (1814), the Kingdom of the Netherlands was reconstituted with the addition of the Southern Netherlands. Belgium secured its independence after the revolt in 1830 and was formally recognized in 1839.

The United Provinces of Agra and Oudh (1902) were renamed the United Provinces in 1935, and Uttar Pradesh in 1950.

**United Reformed Church.** The church formed in 1972 from the union of the Congregational Church of England and Wales with the English PRESBYTERIAN Church. *See also* CONGREGATIONALISTS.

**United States of America.** The federal republic of 50 states and one federal district that has developed from the original 13 states (marked with an asterisk in the list below) which secured their independence from Britain in 1783. Its government is based on the Constitution of 1787. *See also* UNCLE SAM; YANK.

All states except three have official abbreviations and nicknames which are shown below, together with the state capital and the date of admission to the UNION. The two-letter abbreviations are those drawn up by the US Post Office when it instituted the ZIP CODE for mail in 1963.

Alabama (AL): Montgomery; Camellia State, Heart of Dixie, Yellowhammer State (1819: 22nd)
Alaska (AK): Juneau; Land of the Midnight Sun, Last Frontier, Mainland State (1959: 49th)
Arizona (AZ): Phoenix; Apache State, Aztec State, Grand Canyon State, Valentine State (1912: 48th)
Arkansas (AR): Little Rock; Bear State, Land of Opportunity (1836: 25th)
California (CA): Sacramento; Golden State, Sunshine State (1850: 31st)
Colorado (CO): Denver; Centennial State (1876: 38th)

Connecticut (CT): Hartford; Constitution State, Nutmeg State (1788: 5th)*
Delaware (DE): Dover; Diamond State, First State, Small Wonder (1787: 1st)*
District of Columbia (DC): Washington, D.C. (1791)
Florida (FL): Tallahassee; Everglade State, Sunshine State (1845: 27th)
Georgia (GA): Atlanta; Empire State of the South, Peach State (1788: 4th)*
Hawaii (HI): Honolulu; Aloha State (1959:50th)
Idaho (ID): Boise; Gem State, Panhandle State, Spud State (1890: 43rd)
Illinois (IL): Springfield; Land of Lincoln, Prairie State (1818: 21st)
Indiana (IN): Indianapolis; Hoosier State (1816: 19th)
Iowa (IA): Des Moines; Corn State, Hawkeye State (1846: 29th)
Kansas (KS): Topeka; Jayhawker State, Sunflower State (1861: 34th)
Kentucky (KY): Frankfort; Bluegrass State (1792: 15th)
Louisiana (LA): Baton Rouge; Creole State, Pelican State, Sportsman's Paradise, Sugar State (1812: 18th)
Maine (ME): Augusta; Pine Tree State (1820: 23rd)
Maryland (MD): Annapolis; Free State, Old Line State (1788: 7th)*
Massachusetts (MA): Boston; Bay State, Old Colony State (1788: 6th)*
Michigan (MI): Lansing; Auto State, Great Lake State, Wolverine State (1837: 26th)
Minnesota (MN): St Paul; Gopher State, Land of 10,000 Lakes, North Star State (1858: 32nd)
Mississippi (MS): Jackson; Bayou State, Magnolia State (1817: 20th)
Missouri (MO): Jefferson City; Bullion State, Show-me State (1821: 24th)
Montana (MT): Helena; Big Sky Country, Treasure State (1889: 41st)
Nebraska (NE): Lincoln; Beef State, Cornhusker State, Tree Planter State (1867:37th)
Nevada (NV): Carson City; Battle-born State, Sagebrush State, Silver State (1864: 36th)
New Hampshire (NH): Concord; Granite State (1788: 9th)*
New Jersey (NJ): Trenton; Garden State (1787: 3rd)*
New Mexico (NM): Santa Fe; Land of Enchantment, Sunshine State (1912: 47th)
New York (NY): Albany; Empire State (1788: 11th)*
North Carolina (NC): Raleigh; Old North State, Tar Heel State (1789: 12th)*
North Dakota (ND): Bismarck; Flickertail State, Peace Garden State, Sioux State (1889: 39th)
Ohio (OH): Columbus; Buckeye State (1803: 17th)
Oklahoma (OK): Oklahoma City; Sooner State (1907: 46th)
Oregon (OR): Salem; Beaver State, Sunset State (1859: 33rd)
Pennsylvania (PA): Harrisburg; Keystone State (1787: 2nd)*
Rhode Island (RI): Providence; Little Rhody, Ocean State, Plantation State (1790: 13th)*
South Carolina (SC): Columbia; Gamecock State, Palmetto State (1788: 8th)*
South Dakota (SD): Pierre; Artesian State, Coyote State, Mount Rushmore State, Sunshine State (1889: 40th)
Tennessee (TN): Nashville; Volunteer State (1796: 16th)
Texas (TX): Austin; Lone Star State (1845: 28th)
Utah (UT): Salt Lake City; Beehive State, Mormon State (1896: 45th)
Vermont (VT): Montpelier; Green Mountain State (1791: 14th)
Virginia (VA): Richmond; Mother of Presidents, Old Dominion State (1788: 10th)*
Washington (WA): Olympia; Chinook State, Evergreen State (1889: 42nd)
West Virginia (WV): Charlestown; Mountain State, Panhandle State (1863: 35th)
Wisconsin (WI): Madison; America's Dairyland, Badger State (1848: 30th)
Wyoming (WY): Cheyenne; Equality State (1890: 44th)

There are other outlying territories.

**Unities, The Dramatic.** *See under* DRAMA.

**Universal. Universal Declaration of Human Rights, The.** A document adopted by the General Assembly of the UNITED NATIONS in 1948 setting forth basic rights and fundamental freedoms to which all are entitled. They include the right to life, liberty, freedom from servitude, fair trial, marriage, ownership of property, freedom of thought and conscience, freedom of expression and the right to vote, work and education.

**Universal Doctor.** Alain de Lille (*c.*1128–1202), French theologian, so called for his varied learning.

ALBERT THE GREAT or Albertus Magnus (*c.*1206–80), the scholastic philosopher, was also called 'doctor universalis'.

**University.** The word was generally applied to collegiate societies of learning from the 14th century, from Medieval Latin *universitas*, a community or corporation, in this case a corporation of teachers and scholars. Oxford University has its origins in the 12th century and that of Cambridge early in the 13th century. The more common and earlier term was *studium* or *studium generale*, a place of instruction of general resort, i.e. for students from all parts. They were essentially ecclesiastical institutions.

**University colours.** Traditionally, light blue for Cambridge, dark blue for Oxford, purple for London, and so on. Such colours are used as distinguishing dress in all sports, so that Oxford and Cambridge teams are referred to as the Dark Blues and the Light Blues. *See also* GET ONE'S COLOURS *under* COLOUR.

**University Tests Act, The.** An Act passed in 1871 abolishing in the Universities of Oxford, Cambridge and Durham subscriptions to the THIRTY-NINE ARTICLES of Religion, all declarations and oaths concerning religious belief, and all compulsory attendance at public worship except for those taking divinity degrees. The Act also applied to all holders of lay posts. *See also* TEST ACTS.

**Harvard University.** *See under* HARVARD.

**Unkindest cut of all, Most.** *See under* MOST.

**Unknown. Unknown country** or **territory.** An unfamiliar place or topic; an unfamiliar area of research.

**Unknown Prime Minister, The.** A name given to A. Bonar Law (1858–1923), who held office as CONSERVATIVE leader in 1922–3.

**Unknown Warrior, The.** The body of an unknown British soldier of the First World War brought home from one of the battlefields of the Western Front and 'buried among the kings' in Westminster Abbey (11 November 1920). The inscription, in capital letters, begins: 'Beneath this stone rests the body of a British warrior unknown by name or rank brought from France to lie among the most illustrious of the land and buried here on Armistice Day'. Similar tombs were set up in the Arlington National Cemetery, Virginia, beneath the Arc de Triomphe at Paris, in the Unter den Linden at Berlin, and by the walls of the Kremlin in Moscow. In 1958 the bodies of two more unknown American servicemen were placed in the Tomb of the Unknown Soldier at Arlington, one who died in the Second World War and one in the Korean War. Casualties of later conflicts have also been housed there. DNA testing has confirmed that the Vietnam 'Unknown' is US Air Force Lieutenant Michael J. Blassie, killed in action in 1972.

**Great Unknown, The.** *See under* GREAT.

**Unlearned Parliament, The.** *See* PARLIAMENT OF DUNCES.

**Unlucky. It is unlucky to break a mirror.** The nature of the ill luck varies. If the person who breaks the glass is a maiden, she will never marry; if she is married, there will soon be a death. The superstition arose from the use made of mirrors in former times by magicians. If in their operations the mirror used was broken, the unlucky inquirer could receive no answer.

**Unmentionables.** One of the 19th-century humorous colloquialisms for trousers. They were also known as INEXPRESSIBLES.

**Unmerciful Parliament, The.** The MERCILESS PARLIAMENT; also called the WONDERFUL PARLIAMENT.

**Unready, The.** Ethelred II, king of England (968, r.978–1016), called the 'redeless', or lacking in counsel. 'Unready' is a modern corruption. Ethelred means 'noble-counsel'. His nickname is first found in the 13th century.

**Unrighteous Bible, The.** *See under* BIBLE.

**Unrighteousness, The Mammon of.** *See under* MAMMON.

**Untouchables.** The lowest CASTE in India, excluded from social and religious contact with HINDUISM and subjected to many indignities. Their touch was supposed to sully the higher castes. Largely through the teaching of Mahatma Gandhi, untouchability was legally ended in 1949 in India and in 1953 in Pakistan. The preferred term is now Harijan, from the Sanskrit word for a person dedicated to VISHNU (from *Hari*, 'Vishnu', and *jana*, 'person'). *See also* PARIAH.

**Unwashed, The Great.** *See under* GREAT.

**Unwritten law.** Uncodified custom that rests for its authority on the supposed right of the individual to take into his or her hands the avenging of personal wrongs. The term is also applied to understood and long-standing custom or convention. COMMON LAW, which rests upon judicial decision as opposed to written statute, is sometimes so called.

**Up. Up against it.** In great difficulties.

**Up a gum tree.** Faced with a serious problem; in a highly awkward situation. The allusion may be to the gum tree as a refuge for the opossum. *See also* PLAY POSSUM.

**Up and about.** Having risen from one's bed.

**Up-and-coming.** Making good progress; showing promise.

**Up and running.** In operation; functioning.

**Up a tree.** In a difficulty; in a mess; nonplussed. An American phrase, from racoon hunting. As soon as the racoon is driven up a tree he is helpless.

It is said that the Baptist preacher Charles Spurgeon (1834–92) used to exercise his students in extempore preaching, and that one of his young men, on reaching the desk and opening the note containing his text, read the single word 'Zacchaeus'. He thought for a minute or two, and then delivered himself thus:

> Zacchaeus was a little man, so am I; Zacchaeus was up a tree, so am I; Zacchaeus made haste and came down, and so do I.

**Up country.** In the interior; away from the coast; inland. The term is sometimes used in America and Australia with slighting implications, meaning 'unsophisticated' or 'rustic'.

**'Up, Guards, and at 'em!'** The somewhat apocryphal order attributed to the Duke of Wellington as his order to the Guards at the Battle of Waterloo (18 June 1815).

**Up hill and down dale.** Literally, up and down hills. Figuratively, confronting many obstacles, as on an arduous journey or mission.

**Up in arms.** In open rebellion, or figuratively, indignant.

**Up one's street.** In one's particular province or field; in 'one's line of country'. The allusion is to something as familiar as one's own street.

**Upper case.** The printer's name for the large letters of a FONT or fount of type, as opposed to the small letters. *See also* LOWER CASE.

**Upper crust, The.** The aristocracy; the cream of society. The phrase was first used in Thomas Haliburton's *Sayings and Doings of Samuel Slick* (1836). The upper crust was at one time the part of the loaf placed before the most honoured guests.

**Upper House, The.** The HOUSE OF LORDS, in the 15th century termed the 'higher house'. It developed from the GREAT COUNCIL of magnates. The term is also used in the USA for the Senate.

**Upper Ten, The.** The aristocracy, the cream of society. The expression is short for 'the upper ten thousand'. The term was first used by the American editor Nathaniel P. Willis (1806–67) in speaking of the fashionable folk of New York.

**Ups and downs.** The twists and turns of fortune; one's successes and failures.

> Fraudulent transactions have their downs as well as their ups.
> DICKENS: *Martin Chuzzlewit*, ch xvi (1843–4)

**Upstage.** As a technical theatrical direction this means 'at the back of the stage', which in many theatres slopes down slightly to the footlights. Colloquially, the term 'upstage' means aloof; putting on airs of consequence or superiority. An actor upstage of another has the advantage, the latter having to act with his back to the audience.

**Upstate.** In the USA, the part of a state farthest north or distant from the coast. The term is used more particularly of the northern parts of New York State.

**Up the pole.** Slightly mad; in difficulties. The pole is probably a ship's mast, which sailors were popularly judged crazy to climb.

**Up the spout.** At the pawnbroker's, or more usually now 'down the drain', gone, lost, ruined. The allusion is to the 'spout' up which brokers sent the articles ticketed. When redeemed they returned down the spout, i.e. from the storeroom to the shop. The phrase is also a vulgarism meaning 'pregnant', especially when outside marriage. The reference here may be to a loaded rifle with a round in its breech ready to fire.

**Up to a point.** Not entirely; only so far. A phrase used when politely disagreeing with someone.

> Mr Salter's side of the conversation was limited to expressions of assent. When Lord Copper was right he said, 'Definitely, Lord Copper'; when he was wrong, 'Up to a point'.
> EVELYN WAUGH: *Scoop*, ch i (1938)

**Up to date.** Modern; current; fashionable; contemporary.

**Up to here.** More than enough. A phrase usually accompanied by a gesture of the hand to the chin, as if almost drowning. 'I've had it up to here with him' means that he has tried my patience to the limit and I am sick of him.

**Up to one's ears** or **eyes.** Wholly, completely or desperately; said of work, debt and so forth. Someone who is 'up to their eyes in work' is very busy or fully occupied, and a person who is 'up to their eyes in debt' is seriously in debt. *See also* UP TO HERE.

**Up to one's elbows.** Very busy, with work piled up to one's elbows.

**Up to one's neck.** Deeply involved; having much, or too much, work or many responsibilities.

**Up to one's tricks.** Misbehaving; 'playing up'.

**Up to snuff.** In good condition; in good health. An allusion to the tobacco preparation.

**Up to the mark.** Generally used in the negative as: 'Not quite up to the mark', not good enough. The original allusion was to metal that was not up to the standard fixed by the ASSAY office for gold and silver articles.

**Uptown.** In the USA the part of a town that is away from the centre and that is typically residential. *See also* DOWNTOWN *under* DOWN.

**Up with!** An expression of support for person or thing, as: 'Up with the Rovers!' *See also* DOWN WITH!

**Get** or **gain the upper hand, To.** To obtain mastery.

**It's all up with him.** It is hopeless for him; he is finished.

**It's up to him.** It is for him to take the initiative or to decide what is to be done.

**On the up and up.** Steadily improving.

**Something's up.** Something unusual or undesirable is afoot.

**Upanishads.** Part of the oldest speculative literature of the Hindus, a collection of treatises on the nature of the universe, the deity and man. They form the VEDANTA, or last part of the VEDAS, and date from about 500 BC. The name is Sanskrit, and means 'a sitting down' (at another's feet), hence 'a confidential talk' or 'esoteric doctrine'.

**Upas tree.** The Javanese tree *Antiaris toxicaria*, the milky juice of which contains a virulent poison and is used for tipping arrows.

Fable has it that a putrid steam rises from it, and that whatever the vapour touches dies. A Dutch physician by the name of Foersch is said to have written in 1783: 'Not a tree, nor blade of grass is to be found in the valley or surrounding mountains. Not a beast or bird, reptile or living thing, lives in the vicinity.' He adds that on 'one occasion 1600 refugees encamped within 14 miles of it, and all but 300 died within two months'. This 'traveller's tale' has given rise to the figurative use of upas for a corrupting or pernicious influence. *Upas* itself is a Malay word meaning 'poison'.

**Upper.** *See* UP.

**Upset. Upset price.** The price at which goods sold by auction are first offered for competition. If no advance is made they fall to the person who offered the upset price. 'Reserve price' is virtually the same thing.

**Upset the applecart, To.** To spoil carefully made plans or arrangements. The imagery is of the overturning of a farmer's laboriously loaded cartful of apples. The phrase is recorded in use as early as 1788. G.B. Shaw's play *The Apple Cart* (1930) turns on the phrase.

**Upstairs, Kicked.** *See under* KICK.

**Urania.** One of the MUSES in Greek mythology. She presides over ASTROLOGY and is usually represented pointing at a celestial globe with a staff. Her name, also an epithet of APHRODITE or VENUS, means 'heavenly' or 'celestial'. Milton (*Paradise Lost*, vii (1667)) makes her the spirit of the loftiest poetry, and calls her 'heavenly born' and the sister of Wisdom.

**Uranus.** In Greek mythology, the personification of heaven, the son and husband of GAIA (Earth), and father of the TITANS and the CYCLOPS, among others. He hated his children and confined them in the body of Earth who begged them to avenge her, and his son KRONUS castrated him with a sickle and dethroned him.

The planet Uranus was discovered in 1781 by Sir William Herschel (1738–1822), and named by him 'Georgium Sidus' in honour of George III. Except for Umbriel and Belinda, its 15 satellites are all named after characters in Shakespeare: Ariel, Umbriel, Titania, Oberon, Miranda, Cordelia, Ophelia, Bianca, Cressida, Desdemona, Juliet, Portia, Rosalind, Belinda, Puck. The last 10 of these are much smaller than the first five, and were discovered by the space probe *Voyager 2* in 1986.

**Urbanists.** *See* FRANCISCANS.

**Urbi et orbi** (Latin, 'to the city and the world'). A phrase applied to the solemn blessing given from time to time by the pope from the balcony of St Peter's. The custom fell into abeyance after 1870 but was revived by Pius XI after his election in 1922. The 'city' is of course Rome.

**Urdu.** The form of Hindustani spoken by Muslims and Hindus in contact with them. From *urdu zabani*, 'the language of the camp', which grew up as the means of communication between the Muslim conquerors and their subject population.

**Uriah. Uriah Heep.** *See under* HEEP.

**Uriah the Hittite.** In the Old Testament, the husband of BATHSHEBA. He is sent into the front line of battle by DAVID so that he gets killed, thus freeing Bathsheba to become David's wife. The story is told in 2 Samuel 11.

**Letter of Uriah.** *See under* LETTER.

**Uriel.** One of the seven ARCHANGELS of rabbinical angelology, sent by God to answer the questions of Esdras (1 Esdras 4). In Milton's *Paradise Lost* (iii (1667)) he is the 'Regent of the Sun' and 'sharpest-sighted spirit of all in HEAVEN'.

**Urim and Thummim.** Sacred lots of unknown nature used for DIVINATION by the ancient Hebrews as a means of ascertaining the will of God. They are mentioned in various Old Testament verses, e.g. Exodus 28:30, Deuteronomy 33:8, 1 Samuel 28:6 and Ezra 2:63, but fell out of use as more spiritual conceptions of the Deity developed and there is no mention of them after the time of DAVID.

**Ursa. Ursa Major.** The GREAT BEAR, or CHARLES'S WAIN, the most conspicuous of the northern constellations.

Boswell's father, Lord Auchinleck, used to call Dr Johnson 'Ursa Major'.

**Ursa Minor.** The Little Bear, the northern constellation known also as Cynosura or Dog's tail, from its circular sweep. The Pole star is in the tail. *See also* CYNOSURE; GREAT BEAR.

**Ursula. Ursulines.** An order of nuns founded by St Angela Merici of Brescia in 1535, from their patron saint, URSULA. They were primarily concerned with the education of girls.

**St Ursula.** A 5th-century British princess, according to legend, who went with 11,000 virgins on a pilgrimage to Rome and was massacred with all her companions by the Huns at Cologne. One explanation of the story is that Undecimilla (mistaken for *undecim millia*, 11,000) was one of Ursula's companions. Her feast-day is 21 October.

**Use. Use a sledgehammer to crack a nut, To.** To take quite disproportionate steps to settle what is really a very small matter. Virtually the same as TO BREAK A BUTTERFLY ON A WHEEL.

**Use someone's name, To.** To mention it as a reference or authority.

**Use your loaf.** A slang expression meaning 'use your brains', 'use your head'. Loaf (of bread) is here RHYMING SLANG for 'head'.

**I could use a drink.** I would love a drink.

**Useless Parliament, The.** The Parliament convened by CHARLES I on 8 June 1625, adjourned to Oxford on 1 August and dissolved on 12 August, having done nothing but quarrel with the king.

**Usher.** The word comes from Old French *huissier*, 'doorkeeper', ultimately from Latin *ostium*, 'door'.

**Usher of the Green Rod.** An officer in attendance on the Knights of the Thistle at their chapters. *See also* MOST ANCIENT ORDER OF THE THISTLE.

**Gentlemen Ushers.** *See under* GENTLEMAN.

**Usk, The Swan of.** *See under* SWAN.

**Usnech** or **Uisnech, The Sons of.** *See under* SON.

**Usquebaugh.** Whisky, from Irish and Gaelic *uisge beatha*, 'water of life'. *See also* AQUA VITAE; EAU DE VIE.

**Utgard.** In Scandinavian mythology, the abode of the giants, where LOKI had his castle. The name means 'outer enclosure', from Old Norse *út*, 'out', and *garthr*, 'enclosure'.

**Uther.** According to Geoffrey of Monmouth (*Historia Regum Britanniae* (*c*.1136)), king of Britain and father of King ARTHUR by an adulterous liaison with Igerna, wife of Gorlois, Duke of Cornwall, at TINTAGEL. *See also* ARTHURIAN ROMANCES; PENDRAGON.

**Utility.** The official name given during and after the Second World War to clothing, furniture and the like made according to government specification and sold at controlled prices. The name was a sign of the austerity of the times, practical qualities being more important than ornamentation.

**Utilitarianism.** The ethical doctrine that actions are right in proportion to their usefulness or as they tend to promote happiness. The doctrine holds that the end and criterion of public action is 'the greatest happiness of the greatest number'.

The term originated with Jeremy Bentham (1748–1832), whose ideas were expounded by his disciple James Mill (1773–1836) and by the latter's son John Stuart Mill (1806–73), in his *Utilitarianism* (1869), who also introduced quantitative and qualitative distinctions in pleasures. *See also* PANOPTICON.

**Uti possidetis** (Latin, 'as you possess'). The principle that the property remains with its present possessor, or in international law that the belligerents retain possession of their acquisitions in war.

**Utnapishtim.** The Babylonian counterpart of NOAH, whose story is told in the GILGAMESH EPIC, and which has many notable resemblances to the Bible story. The Hebrews almost certainly derived their account from Babylonia. His name may derive from Sumerian *utu*, 'sun', and Akkadian *napishtu*, 'soul', although it has also been popularly interpreted as 'he who has found everlasting life'.

**Utopia.** A name for Nowhere, from Greek *ou*, 'not', and *topos*, 'place'. It was given by Sir Thomas More to the imaginary island in his political romance of the same name (1516), where everything, including laws, morals and politics, is perfect, and in which the evils of existing laws and the like are shown by contrast. Hence 'Utopian' is applied to any idealistic but impractical scheme. *See also* IDEAL COMMONWEALTHS.

The opposite of a Utopia is a 'dystopia', an imaginary world which is much worse than our own. *See also* SUBTOPIA.

**Utter. Utter** and **inner barristers.** An utter or outer BARRISTER is one who has not taken silk. An inner barrister is a student.

**Delphic utterance.** *See under* DELPHI.

**Uzziah.** In the Old Testament (2 Kings 15), a king of JUDAH made a leper by God because he allowed incense to be burned in the temple.

**Uzziel.** One of the principal angels of rabbinical angelology, the name meaning 'Strength of God'. He was next in command to GABRIEL, and in Milton's *Paradise Lost* (iv (1667)) is commanded by Gabriel to 'coast the south with strictest watch'.

# V

**V.** The twenty-second letter of the alphabet, formerly sharing its form with U.

In the Roman notation it stands for 5 and represents ideographically the four fingers and thumb with the latter extended. $\bar{V}$ represents 5000.

**V for Victory.** On 14 January 1941 Victor de Lavaleye, a member of the exiled Belgian government in London, proposed in a broadcast to Belgium that the letter V, standing for Victory in many European languages, be substituted for the letters RAF which were being chalked up on walls and other places in Belgium. The plan was immediately adopted, and the Morse code V (· · · –) was featured in every BBC broadcast to Europe, followed by the opening bar of Beethoven's 5th Symphony, which has the same rhythm. 'Colonel Britton' (D.E. Ritchie), director of the BBC European news service, was responsible for the diffusion of the V-sign propaganda, which gave hope to those under the NAZI yoke. Sir Winston Churchill greatly popularized the sign of two upraised fingers in the form of a V. *See also* V-SIGN.

**V-1.** A jet-propelled ROBOT plane bomb sent against Britain by the Germans, June to August 1944, and subsequently sent against Antwerp. V stood for *Vergeltungswaffe* ('reprisal weapon').

**V-2.** A long-range rocket with an explosive warhead, projected against Britain by the Germans in the autumn of 1944. V had the same origin as for the V-1.

**V-sign.** A sign of the letter V made with the first two fingers pointing up and the back of the hand facing outwards. It is a crude gesture of abuse or contempt, and is not to be confused with the V FOR VICTORY sign, which is made with the palm of the hand facing outwards. *See also* HARVEY SMITH.

**Vacuum** (Latin *vacare*, 'to be empty'). The word is commonly used for a vacuum cleaner and 'to vacuum' is to clean up with this instrument. *See also* HOOVER.

**Nature abhors a vacuum.** *See under* NATURE.

**Vade mecum** (Latin, 'go-with-me'). A pocket book, memorandum book, pocket cyclopedia, lady's pocket companion or anything else that contains many things of daily use in a small compass.

**Vae victis!** (Latin). Woe to the vanquished! So much the worse for the conquered! This was the exclamation of Brennus, the Gaulish chief, on throwing his sword into the balance as a makeweight, when determining the price of peace with Rome (390 BC).

**Vagitanus.** *See* DEITIES PROTECTING BABIES.

**Vain. Take God's name in vain, To.** *See under* GOD.

**Take someone's name in vain, To.** *See under* NAME.

**Vaivode.** *See* VOIVODE.

**Vale!** Farewell! The second person singular imperative of Latin *valere*, 'to be worth', 'to fare well'.

> I thought once agayne here to have made an ende, with a heartie *Vale*, of the best fashion.
>
> EDMUND SPENSER: letter to Gabriel Harvey (1580)

**Ave atque vale!** *See under* AVE.

**Vale. Vale of Tears, The.** This world. *See also* VALLEY OF BACA.

**Vale of White Horse.** *See* WHITE HORSE.

**Golden Vale.** *See under* GOLDEN.

**Maida Vale.** *See under* MAIDA.

**Valentine. Valentine and Orson.** An old French romance connected with the CAROLINGIAN cycle. The heroes, from whom it is named, were the twin sons of Bellisant, sister of King Pepin, and Alexander, and were born in a forest near Orleans. Orson (French *ourson*, 'little bear') was carried off by a bear and became a wild man and the terror of France. While the mother was searching for him, Valentine was carried off by his uncle, the king. The brothers had many adventures and Orson was reclaimed by Valentine. Orson married Fezon, daughter of Duke Savary of Aquitaine, and Valentine married Clerimond, sister of the Green Knight.

**St Valentine.** A priest of Rome who was imprisoned for succouring persecuted Christians. He became a convert and, although he is supposed to have restored the sight of the gaoler's blind daughter, he was clubbed to death (*c*.270). His day is 14 February, as is that of St Valentine, bishop of Terni, who was martyred a few years later. There are several other saints of this name.

The ancient custom of choosing Valentines has only accidental relation to either saint, being essentially a relic of the old Roman Lupercalia (*see* LUPERCAL), or from association with the mating season of birds. It was marked by the giving of presents and nowadays by the sending of a card on which CUPIDS, transfixed hearts, and similar amorous attributes are depicted.

Chaucer refers to this in his *Parliament of Fowls* (*c*.1381):

For this was on seynt Volantynys day
Whan euery bryd comyth there to chese his make
[match].

and Shakespeare (*A Midsummer Night's Dream*, IV, i (1595)) has:

Good morrow, friends. Saint Valentine is past;
Begin these wood-birds but to couple now?

**Valerian.** According to Christian legend Valerian was the husband of the virgin martyr St CECILIA. Chaucer, in the *Canterbury Tales*, 'The Second Nun's Tale' (*c*.1397), relates how Cecilia refused her husband admittance to her bedchamber because she was meeting an angel there. Valerian thereupon became baptized by the pope in order to gain entry to the room, and the angel granted him and his brother the chance to be holy martyrs.

**Valhalla.** In Scandinavian mythology the hall in the celestial regions where the souls of heroes slain in battle were carried by the VALKYRIES, to spend eternity in joy and feasting (Old Norse *valr*, 'slain warriors', and *höll*, 'hall'). Hence the name is sometimes applied to buildings, such as Westminster Abbey, used as the last resting place of a nation's great men.

**Vali** (Turkish, 'governor'). The title of the governors of Egypt prior to their holding of the style KHEDIVE.

**Valiant, Reproof.** *See under* REPROOF.

**Valkyries** (Old Norse *valr*, 'slain warriors', and *köri*, 'to choose'). The 'choosers of the slain', as the nine (or seven or twelve) handmaidens of ODIN, who, mounted on swift horses and holding drawn swords, rushed into the thick of battle and selected those destined to die. These heroes they conducted to VALHALLA, where they waited upon them and served them with mead and ale in the skulls of the vanquished.

**Valley. Valley of Baca, The.** An unidentified place mentioned in Psalm 84:6, meaning the 'Valley of Weeping', and so translated in the Revised Version of the Bible.

**Valley of Ten Thousand Smokes, The.** A volcanic valley in the region of Mount Katmai, Alaska. Shortly before Mount Katmai blew up on 6 June 1912 there were many bursts of molten matter in the valley, and these fissures have since discharged hot gases, hence the name of the valley. It has been a National Monument since 1918.

**Valley of the Kings, The.** A site in the Theban Hills, northwest of THEBES, Egypt, containing the tombs of PHARAOHS of the New Kingdom. Thutmosis I (1530–20 BC) was the first to build his tomb there. The wadi was guarded by small forts and the tombs were walled up with rubble, but pillaging began as the New Kingdom declined. The many tombs uncovered include that of TUTANKHAMUN, revealed with its remarkable treasures in 1922–3 by Howard Carter (1874–1939) who, with Lord Carnarvon (1866–1923), had been engaged in excavations there since 1906. *See also* CURSE OF TUTANKHAMUN.

**Valley of the Queens, The.** The less spectacular cemetery of the wives and daughters of pharaohs of the 20th Dynasty. It lies to the south of the VALLEY OF THE KINGS.

**Valley speak.** Valley speak or Valspeak arose in the early 1980s as the jargon adopted by well-to-do teenagers in the San Fernando Valley near Los Angeles. It was specifically popularized by the rock musician Frank Zappa and his daughter Moon Unit in the song 'Valley Girl' (1982), and its words and turns of phrase were characterized by sarcasm and exaggeration, as well as by an underlying ironic tone in expressions such as 'for sure' and 'as if'. Much of its content consisted of 'filler' words, such as 'like' and 'totally', and it employed set phrases such as 'grody to the max' (grotty in the extreme). It was typically heard in the speech of the 'valley girl', with her disenchanted view of the world, and has been preserved in the dialogue of several novels and films. A good example of the latter is *Clueless* (1995), in which a Beverly Hills teenager worries about losing her status as the most popular girl in the school and about winning the boy of her dreams.

**Death Valley.** *See under* DEATH.

**Happy Valley.** *See under* HAPPY.

**Valois.** The reigning dynasty in France from 1328 to 1589, taking its name from Philip, Duke of Valois, the first of the line. They were a branch of the CAPET family and were succeeded by the BOURBON line when Henry of Navarre, husband of Marguerite of Valois, became king as Henry IV in 1589.

**Valois head-dress.** A mid-19th-century women's hair style, the hair being pulled back from the forehead to form a roll on the crown of the head.

**Value, Face.** *See under* FACE.

**Vamana.** *See* AVATAR.

**Vamp, To.** Properly, the word means to put new uppers to old boots, and vamps were short hose covering the feet and ankles (French *avant-pied*, 'forepart of the foot').

'To vamp up' an old story is to refurbish it, and 'to vamp an accompaniment' to a song is to improvise as one goes along. Another verb 'to vamp', derived from VAMPIRE, means to flirt outrageously or allure with the intent of gaining some predatory end, and a 'vamp' is a woman who flirts and preys thus.

> The innocent heroine of the serial was soon supplanted in public favour by the 'Vamp', and the film gained in sophistication what it lost in simple morality. Billed as the 'wickedest face in the world', Theda Bara not only symbolized this new siren, she played her to the hilt.
>
> FREDERIC THRASHER: *Okay for Sound* (1946)

**Vampire.** A fabulous being, supposed to be the ghost of a heretic, criminal or the like, who returned from the grave in the guise of a monstrous bat to suck the blood of sleeping persons who usually became vampires themselves. The only way to destroy them was to drive a stake through their body. The superstition is essentially Slavonic, from a word related to Russian *upyr'*, 'vampire'.

> But first, on earth as Vampire sent,
> Thy corse shall from its tomb be rent:
> Then ghastly haunt thy native place
> And suck the blood of all thy race.
>
> LORD BYRON: *The Giaour* (1813)

The word is also applied to someone who preys on their fellows, a 'bloodsucker'.

One of the classic horror stories, Bram Stoker's *Dracula* (1897), centres on vampirism. The Dracula of Transylvanian legend appears to originate from Vlad IV of Wallachia (1430–76), known as Vlad the Impaler, although he was not a vampire. It is suggested that Stoker's Count Dracula was a composite figure derived from Vlad the Impaler and the Countess Báthori (d.1614), who was arrested in 1610 for murdering some 650 girls. It was her habit to wash in the blood of her young victims in order to maintain her skin in a youthful condition. The name comes from Vlad's membership of the Order of the Dragon, although *dracul* in Romanian strictly speaking means 'the Devil'.

**Vandals.** A Teutonic race first recorded in northeast Germany, which in the 5th century ravaged GAUL, Spain and North Africa, and in 455 Rome itself, when they despoiled it of its treasures of art and literature.

The name is hence applied to those who wilfully or ignorantly indulge in destruction of works of art and the like. Vandalism is now applied to most forms of wanton damage.

**Van Diemen's Land.** The former name for Tasmania, given in 1642 by its Dutch discoverer Abel Jans Tasman (1603–*c*.1659) in honour of his patron, the Dutch Governor General of Batavia. It became a British settlement in 1803, and its name was changed to Tasmania in 1853, to obliterate memories of its associations with BUSHRANGERS and convicts, transportation having ceased at that time.

**Vandyke beard.** A pointed beard such as those frequently shown in Sir Anthony Van Dyck's portraits, especially of CHARLES I.

**Vanessa.** Jonathan Swift's name for his friend and correspondent, Esther Vanhomrigh (1690–1723), made by compounding Van, the first syllable of her surname, with Essa, the pet form of Esther. Swift called himself Cadenus, an anagram of *Decanus* (Latin for 'dean'; Swift was appointed Dean of St Patrick's Cathedral, Dublin, in 1713). Swift's poem *Cadenus and Vanessa* was written in 1713.

**Vanguard.** *See* AVANT-GARDE.

**Vanir.** A Scandinavian race of gods of peaceful and benevolent functions, in contrast to the AESIR, who were essentially warriors. Among them were NIORD, FREYR and FREYJA. Their name comes from that of Vanr, a Norse fertility god.

**Vanish into thin air, To.** To disappear completely; to leave no trace of one's existence.

**Vanity Fair.** In Bunyan's PILGRIM'S PROGRESS (1678, 1684), a fair established by BEELZEBUB, APOLLYON and LEGION, in the town of Vanity, and lasting all the year round. Here were sold houses, lands, trades, places, honours, preferments, titles, countries, kingdoms, lusts, pleasures and delights of all sorts.

W.M. Thackeray adopted the name for the title of his novel (1847–8) satirizing the weaknesses and follies of human nature.

**Vantage loaf.** The thirteenth loaf of a BAKER'S DOZEN.

**Varaha.** *See* AVATAR.

**Varden, Dolly.** *See under* DOLLY.

**Variety is the spice of life.** It is variety in all its aspects that makes life interesting. The saying is an established aphorism, which tends to be forgotten by modern politicians, civil servants, and those who favour conformity at the expense of originality.

> Variety's the very spice of life,
> That gives it all its flavour.
>
> WILLIAM COWPER: *The Task*, ii (1785)

**Variorum edition** (Latin *variorum*, 'of various persons'). An edition of a literary text giving the variant readings, notes and comments of different scholars.

**'Varsity.** A shortened form of 'university', formerly used only of Oxford or Cambridge. The word survives in the annual Rugby League Varsity Match between Oxford and Cambridge at Twickenham.

**Varuna.** In Hindu mythology, the brother of Mitra, one of the ADITYAS. Varuna shines at night and is linked with the moon. He is represented as a white man riding on a sea monster, is the witness of everything, orders the seasons and controls the rains. Mitra is linked with the sun and shines or sees by day. Varuna's name may be linked with Greek *ouranos*, 'sky', in which case he is also linked with URANUS.

**Vase, Portland.** *See under* PORTLAND.

**Vashti.** In the Old Testament (Esther 1), the beautiful queen of Persia who held her own women's banquet and refused to attend that given by her husband, AHASUERUS. He thereupon divorced her lest other Persian women be tempted to follow her example of wifely disobedience. *See also* ESTHER.

**Vassal.** A feudal tenant with military obligations to his superior, hence, a dependant, retainer or servant. The word is ultimately of Celtic origin, and is related to Welsh *gwas*, 'boy', and Old Irish *foss*, 'servant'. *See also* FEUDALISM; TENANT-IN-CHIEF.

**VAT.** Value added tax, as essentially a sales tax on various goods and services. In practice it means that a tax is levied on a product each time it changes hands on its route to the point of sale. It was introduced in 1973 and in the late 1990s stood at 17½ per cent. There are inconsistencies. Newspapers and books are not subject to VAT, although the processes involved in their production are. Food and drink are generally not subject to VAT, but again there are anomalies. For example, a pie sold cold is not subject to VAT but the same pie, heated by the vendor and sold as TAKEAWAY food, is subject to the tax. Ice creams, chocolates, sweets, potato crisps and alcoholic drinks are also taxable. Further, while public transport in general is not subject to VAT, public transport designed to carry less than 12 persons is. This means that standard bus and train journeys are zero-rated for VAT but public minibus trips are not.

**Vathek.** The hero of the acclaimed oriental novel of this name by William Beckford (1760–1844) of Fonthill (*see* FOLLY). It was written in French and first appeared in English in 1786. Vathek, the ninth caliph of the ABBASSID dynasty, is a haughty, effeminate monarch, induced by a malignant genius to commit all sorts of crimes. He abjured faith and offered allegiance to EBLIS, under the hope of obtaining the throne of the pre-Adamite sultans. This he gained, only to find that it was a place of torture and that he was doomed to remain in it for ever.

**Vatican.** The palace of the pope, so called because it stands on the *Vaticanus Mons* (Vatican Hill) of ancient Rome, which got its name through being the headquarters of the *vaticinatores* ('soothsayers').

**Vatican City State, The.** The area of Rome occupied by the city of the VATICAN, recognized by the LATERAN TREATY (1929) as constituting the territorial extent of the temporal power of the HOLY SEE. It consists of the papal palace, the LIBRARY, archives and museums, St Peter's Square and contiguous buildings including a radio station and railway station, in all an area of just under a square mile (2.6 sq km). It has about 850 inhabitants and its own coinage. Certain other buildings outside the Vatican enjoy extraterritorial rights.

**Vatican Council, The.** The twentieth ECUMENICAL COUNCIL of the ROMAN CATHOLIC CHURCH (1869–70), summoned by Pius IX (r.1846–78) and suspended when the Italians occupied Rome after the withdrawal of the French garrison. It was notable for its definition of papal INFALLIBILITY, which was limited to when the pope speaks EX CATHEDRA regarding faith or morals.

A second Vatican Council was opened by John XXIII (r.1958–63) in October 1962 and concluded by Paul VI (r.1963–78) in December 1965. Among numerous controversial proposals for change, it was notably concerned with the need for Christian unity, liturgical reforms and matters of church government. One special feature was the presence of observers from non-Roman Catholic Churches.

**Prisoner of the Vatican, The.** *See under* PRISONER.

**Vaudeville.** A corruption of French *val de Vire* or Old French *vau de Vire*, 'valley of the Vire', the native valley of Olivier Basselin, a Norman poet (d.1418) and author of convivial songs, which were so named from the place where he composed them. It is now applied to variety entertainment made of songs, dances, sketches and the like.

**Vaudois.** *See* VOODOO; WALDENSIANS.

**Vauxhall.** A part of LAMBETH, London, so called from Falkes de Bréauté who was lord of the manor in the early 13th century.

**Vauxhall Gardens.** A highly popular pleasure resort for Londoners, first laid out in 1661 as Spring Gardens and finally closed in 1859. Samuel Pepys refers to it as Fox Hall. It finds mention in the *Spectator*, Dickens' *Sketches by Boz* (1836–7), W.M. Thackeray's *Vanity Fair* (1847–8) and elsewhere. It provided ample refreshments, musical entertainment, fireworks, displays of pictures and statuary and the like, and at night was lit by over 1000 lamps. *See also* CREMORNE GARDENS; ROSHERVILLE GARDENS.

**VDMIAE.** Latin *Verbum Dei manet in aeternum* ('the word of God endureth for ever'). The inscription was found on the liveries of the servants of the Duke of Saxony and Landgrave of Hesse, the Lutheran princes, at the Diet of Spires (Speier) in 1526.

**Vedanta** (Sanskrit, 'end of the Veda'). The UPANISHADS or philosophy of the Upanishads, the system of Hindu philosophy based on the VEDAS.

**Vedas.** The four sacred books of the BRAHMANS, consisting of the *Rigveda*, the *Samaveda*, the *Yajurveda* and the *Atharvaveda*. The first consists of hymns, the second of chants, the third mainly of sacrificial prayers in prose and verse, and the fourth largely of hymns and spells concerned with superstitious practices. The word *Veda* means knowledge.

**VE Day.** 'Victory in Europe' Day. The end of hostilities in Europe after the Second World War, 8 May 1945. *See also* TWO-MINUTE SILENCE; VJ DAY.

**Veep.** *See* VP.

**Veer cable, To.** To pay or ease out cable.

**Vegliantino** (Italian, 'little vigilant one'). ORLANDO's steed, called Veillantif in French romance, while Orlando appears as ROLAND.

**Vehmgerichte** (obsolete German, 'judgement courts'). Also *Fehmgerichte*. Courts or tribunals conducted by groups of free men under the presidency of a *Freigraf* (free count), which flourished in Germany (especially in Westphalia) between the 12th and 16th centuries. They were restricted to Westphalia in the 16th century, and their last vestiges abolished in 1811. They dealt with serious crimes (punishable by death), heresy and witchcraft. Although generally portrayed as sinister institutions, for the most part they did not abuse their power. In secret session the only punishment awarded was the death sentence, which was carried out on the guilty forthwith.

> 'And was that opinion', said the presiding Judge, 'favourable or otherwise to the Holy and Secret Vehmegericht? Let truth rule your tongue – remember, life is short, Judgement is eternal.'
>
> SIR WALTER SCOTT: *Anne of Geierstein*, ch xx (1829)

**Veil. Beyond the veil.** *See under* BEYOND.

**Draw a veil over, To.** *See under* DRAW.

**Take the veil, To.** To become a nun, from the traditional head-dress of women in religious orders.

**Vein-openers, The.** *See under* REGIMENTAL AND DIVISIONAL NICKNAMES.

**Velvet. Black velvet.** *See under* BLACK.

**Iron fist** or **hand in the velvet glove, The.** *See under* IRON.

**Little gentleman in velvet, The.** The MOLE. *See also* LITTLE.

**Velveteens.** An old nickname for a gamekeeper, from his once common velveteen jacket, velveteen being a sort of FUSTIAN or twilled cotton with a pile.

> 'I'm the new under-keeper, and master's told me to keep a sharp look-out on all o' you young chaps. And I tells 'ee I means business, and you'd better keep on your own side, or we shall fall out.'
>
> 'Well, that's right, Velveteens – speak out, and let's know your mind at once.'
>
> THOMAS HUGHES: *Tom Brown's Schooldays*, Pt I, ch ix (1857)

**Vendémiaire.** The first month in the FRENCH REVOLUTIONARY CALENDAR, corresponding to the period from 23 September to 22 October. The word means 'vintage month', literally 'wine-taking', from Latin *vinum*, 'wine', and *demere*, 'to take away'.

**Vendôme, The Column of the Place.** *See under* COLUMN.

**Vendue.** A word of obvious French origin for a public auction sale, in American use from about the mid-18th century to the mid-19th century.

> We'd better take maysures for shettin' up shop,
> An' put off our stock by a vendoo or swop.
>
> JAMES RUSSELL LOWELL: *Biglow Papers, Series 2*, v (1848, 1867)

**Venerable** (Latin *venerabilis*, 'worthy of honour'). The title applied to archdeacons in formal address ('The Venerable the Archdeacon of Barset', or 'The Venerable E.L. Brown'), and in the ROMAN CATHOLIC CHURCH, the title of one who has attained the first of the three degrees of CANONIZATION.

In addition to the VENERABLE BEDE, the title is bestowed on William of Champeaux (d.1121), the French scholastic philosopher and opponent of ABELARD.

**Venerable Bede, The.** This most renowned of early English scholars (*c*.673–735) became a monk at Jarrow (now in Tyne and Wear) and devoted his life to religion and learning. His industry, output and range were remarkable, but he is best known for his Latin *Historia ecclesiastica gentis anglorum* ('Ecclesiastical History of the English People') (731), a work of unusual interest and importance, which has led him to be called the Father of English History. The title 'Venerable' was added to Bede's name in the 9th century. It means 'worthy to be revered', and does not refer to great age.

**Veni. Veni, Creator Spiritus** (Latin, 'Come, begetter spirit'). A hymn to the HOLY GHOST in the Roman Catholic BREVIARY, probably of the 9th century and often attributed to Rhabanus Maurus (d.856), archbishop of Mainz. It is sung at VESPERS and Terce during PENTECOST and on other occasions, such as the consecration of a church or of a bishop. The popular English version, beginning 'Come, Holy Ghost, our souls inspire', is by John Cosin (1594–1672), bishop of Durham.

**Veni, Sancte Spiritus** (Latin, 'Come, Holy Spirit'). A medieval Latin hymn, used as a sequence at PENTECOST in the ROMAN CATHOLIC CHURCH.

**Veni, vidi, vici** (Latin, 'I came, I saw, I conquered'). According to Plutarch, it was thus that Julius CAESAR announced to his friend Amintius his victory at Zela (47 BC), in Asia Minor, over

Pharnaces, son of Mithridates, who had rendered aid to Pompey.

**Venial sin.** One that does not forfeit grace. In the ROMAN CATHOLIC CHURCH sins are of two sorts, MORTAL SINS and venial sins (Latin *venia*, 'grace', 'pardon').

> Wherefore I say unto you, All manner of sin and blasphemy shall be forgiven unto men: but the blasphemy against the Holy Ghost shall not be forgiven unto men.
> Matthew 12:31

**Venice. Venice glass.** The drinking glasses of the Middle Ages, made at Venice, were said to break into shivers if poison were put into them.

> *Doge*: 'Tis said that our Venetian crystal has
> Such pure antipathy to poisons as
> To burst, if aught of venom touches it.
> LORD BYRON: *The Two Foscari*, V, i (1821)

**Little Venice.** *See under* LITTLE.

**Venire facias** (Latin, 'cause to come'). An ancient writ directing a SHERIFF to assemble a jury.

**Venison.** Anything taken in hunting or by the chase. Hence ISAAC bids ESAU to go and get venison such as he loved (Genesis 27:3), meaning the wild kid. The word is the Latin *venatio*, 'hunting', but is now restricted to the flesh of deer.

**Venite.** Psalm 95, from its opening words *Venite, exultemus Domino* ('O come, let us sing unto the Lord'). It is said or sung at MATTINS.

**Venner's rising.** The last futile attempt of some 80 men under the wine cooper Thomas Venner to set up the Fifth Monarchy in January 1661. They fought desperately, and Venner and 16 of his accomplices were executed. *See also* FIFTH-MONARCHY MEN.

**Venom is in the tail, The.** The real difficulty is the conclusion. A similar expression is WITH A STING IN ITS TAIL.

**Ventôse** (French, from Latin *ventosus*, 'full of wind'). The sixth month of the FRENCH REVOLUTIONARY CALENDAR, corresponding to the period from 20 February to 21 March.

**Ventre-saint-Gris.** The usual oath of Henry IV of France, *Gris* being a euphemism for 'Christ', and *ventre*, 'stomach'. Oaths not infrequently took this form of blasphemy, and 'God's nails', 'God's teeth' and so on were common in England.

A similar oath is *Par le ventre de Dieu*. Rabelais has *Par sainct Gris*, and the suggestion has been made that the allusion was to St FRANCIS OF ASSISI, who was *ceint* (girdled) and clad in *gris* (grey).

**Ventriloquism.** The trick of producing vocal sounds so that they appear to come, not from the person producing them, but from some other quarter. The art is so called from Latin *venter*, 'belly', and *loqui*, 'to speak' (speaking from the belly), from the erroneous notion that the voice of the ventriloquist proceeded from his stomach.

**Venture. Nothing venture, nothing win.** *See under* NOTHING.

**Venus.** The Roman goddess of beauty and sensual love, identified with APHRODITE, in some accounts said to have sprung from the foam of the sea, in others to have been the daughter of JUPITER and DIONE, a NYMPH. VULCAN was her husband, but she had amours with MARS and many other gods and demigods. By MERCURY she was the mother of CUPID, and by the hero ANCHISES, the mother of AENEAS, through whom she was regarded by the Romans as the foundress of their race. Her chief festival is 1 April. *See also* VENUS VERTICORDIA.

Her name is given to the second planet from the sun. *See also* HESPERUS.

> Mercury stands for wisdom, thrift and science,
> Venus for revel, squandering and defiance.
> CHAUCER: Prologue to 'The Wife of Bath's Tale' (*c*.1387) (modern translation by Nevill Coghill, 1951)

By the alchemists copper was designated Venus, probably because mirrors were originally made of copper. A mirror is still the astronomical symbol of the planet Venus.

The best cast at dice (three sixes) used to be called Venus, and the worst (three aces), Canis (dog). Hence the phrase, 'His Venus has turned out a whelp', equivalent to ALL ONE'S SWANS ARE GEESE.

**Venusberg.** The Hörselberg, or mountain of delight and love, situated between Eisenach and Gotha, in the caverns of which, according to medieval German legend, the Lady Venus held her court. Human visitors were sometimes allowed in, such as THOMAS THE RHYMER (Thomas Ercildoune) and TANNHÄUSER, but they ran the risk of eternal perdition. Eckhardt the Faithful sat outside to warn them against entering.

**Venus de Medici.** A famous statue, since 1860 in the Uffizi Gallery, Florence, ranking as a model of female beauty. It is believed to date from the 4th century BC, and was dug up in the 17th century in the villa of Hadrian, near Tivoli, in 11 pieces. It was kept in the Medici Palace at Rome until its removal to Florence by Cosimo III.

**Venus' fly-trap.** *Dionaea muscipula*, a plant with hinged leaves that close on and digest insects. It is found in the southeastern USA. Its botanical name alludes to DIONE, the mother of Venus.

**Venus Genetrix** (Latin, 'she that has borne'). VENUS worshipped as a symbol of marriage and motherhood. CAESAR erected a temple to Venus Genetrix in the Forum at Rome, and there are several statues of this name. She is represented as raising her light drapery and holding an apple, the emblem of fecundity.

**Venus' girdle.** The CESTUS.

**Venus' hair.** The maidenhair fern, *Adiantum capillus-veneris.*

**Venus' looking-glass.** The rare small plant, *Legousia speculum-veneris*, which grows in the south and east of England on chalky soil. It has blue or purple flowers.

**Venus of Cnidus.** The exquisite nude statue by Praxiteles, purchased by the ancient Cnidians and placed in the temple of Venus at Cnidus. The Cnidians refused to part with it, although Nicomedes, king of Bithynia, offered to pay off their national debt as its price. It was subsequently removed to Constantinople, and perished in the great fire during the reign of Justinian (AD 532), but a historic copy is in the Vatican. It was the first lifesize statue to show Venus completely nude.

**Venus of Milo** or **Melos.** This statue, with three of HERMES, was discovered by the French admiral Dumont d'Urville in Milo or Melos, one of the Greek islands. It dates from the 2nd century BC and is probably the finest single work of ancient art extant. It is now in the LOUVRE.

**Venus on the Half Shell.** The popular name of Sandro Botticelli's painting *The Birth of Venus* (*c.*1483–4), in the Uffizi, Florence. *See also* APHRODITE ANADYOMENE.

**Venus Verticordia.** One of the bynames of VENUS, because she was invoked to 'turn the hearts' of women to virtue and chastity (Latin *vertere*, 'to turn', and *cor*, *cordis*, 'heart'). Dante Gabriel Rossetti has a painting of this title (1864–8) in which a nude model holds an arrow in one hand and an apple in the other, a butterfly resting on each.

**Venus Victrix.** Venus, as goddess of victory, represented on numerous Roman coins.

**Vera causa** (Latin, 'true cause'). A cause in harmony with other causes already known. A fairy godmother may be assigned in a story as the cause of certain marvellous effects, but is not a *vera causa*. The revolution of the earth round the sun may be assigned as the cause of the four seasons, and is a *vera causa*.

**Verb, Strong.** *See under* STRONG.

**Verbatim et literatim** (Latin). 'Word for word and letter for letter.' Text that is accurately rendered.

**Verbena.** *See* VERVAIN.

**Verb sap** or **Verb sat.** The abbreviations of the Latin *verbum sapienti sat est* ('a word to the wise is enough'), i.e. a hint is sufficient to any intelligent person.

**Vercingetorix.** Probably the best known Gaulish chieftain, born in 72 BC. He led a revolt against the Romans with some initial success but was captured and delivered to Caesar in 52 BC on the surrender of Alesia. He was then taken to Rome and paraded for Caesar's triumph. In 46 BC he was put to death by being strangled in prison. His name means 'great king of a hundred heads', from Gaulish *ver*, 'great', *cenn geto*, 'hundred heads', and *rix*, 'king'.

**Verdant Green.** An excessively 'green' or unsophisticated young man. The character was epitomized in *The Adventures of Mr Verdant Green* (1853) by 'Cuthbert Bede, BA' (Rev. Edward Bradley). Verdant's adventures at Oxford, where he goes as a very green freshman, the victim of endless practical jokes and impostures, make an entertaining and enlightening commentary on life at the university in the mid-19th century.

**Verderer.** In English forest law an official having jurisdiction in the royal forests with especial charge of trees and undergrowth. *See also* FOREST COURTS.

**Verdict, Open.** *See under* OPEN.

**Vere adeptus** (Latin, 'one who has truly attained'). A title assumed by a person admitted to the fraternity of the ROSICRUCIANS.

> In Rosicrucian lore as learned
> As he the vere-adeptus earned.
>
> SAMUEL BUTLER: *Hudibras*, I, i (1662)

**Verger.** The BEADLE in a church who carries the rod or staff, which was formerly called the verge (Latin *virga*, 'rod').

**Vergil.** *See* VIRGIL.

**Verlan.** A French form of PIG LATIN or BACK SLANG, in the late 20th century a highly popular type of talk among young people. It is formed by inverting the syllables or letters of a word and incorporating any spelling changes to facilitate pronunciation. Thus *pourri*, 'rotten' becomes *ripou*, *femme*, 'woman', is *meuf* and *chaud*, 'hot' is *auch*. The name itself is the inverted form of *l'envers*, 'the other way round'.

**Vermeer forgeries, The.** *See under* FAKES.

**Veronica.** According to late medieval legend, a woman of Jerusalem who handed her headcloth to Jesus on his way to CALVARY. He wiped his brow and returned it to the giver, when it was found to bear a perfect likeness of Christ impressed upon it and was called *vera icona* ('true image'), the woman becoming St Veronica. It is one of the relics at St Peter's, Rome. In Spanish bull fighting the most classic movement with the cape is called the Veronica, the cape being swung so slowly before the face of the charging bull that it resembles St Veronica's wiping of Christ's face. *See also* SUDARIUM.

**Vers. Vers de société** (French, 'society verse'). Light poetry of a witty or fanciful kind, generally with a vein of social satire running through it.

**Vers libre.** *See* FREE VERSE.

**Versailles.** The great palace built by Louis XIV in the town of that name to the southwest of Paris. It was begun by Louis XIII, but in 1661 the enlargement was started that made it the greatest palace in Europe. Louis XIV's architect was Jules Hardouin Mansart (1646–1708), and his work was continued under Louis XV by Jacques Ange Gabriel (1698–1782). The gardens were planned by André Le Nôtre (1613–1700), and the original park contained the Grand Trianon and the Petit Trianon. Its fountains, water courses, statuary and shrubberies were all executed on a grand scale.

The palace was the scene of many historic occasions, including the signing of the armistice between Great Britain and the United States with their French allies in 1783, and the taking of the TENNIS-COURT OATH by the STATES GENERAL in 1789. Here, too, in the Galerie des Glaces (HALL OF MIRRORS), William I of Prussia was crowned first German emperor, and the Treaty of Versailles between the Allied Powers and Germany was signed after the First World War. *See also* OEIL-DE-BOEUF.

**Verse. Alcaic verse.** *See under* ALCAIC.

**Blank verse.** *See under* BLANK.

**Cap verses, To.** *See under* CAP.

**Chapter and verse.** *See under* CHAPTER.

**Father of Iambic Verse, The.** *See under* FATHER.

**Free verse.** *See under* FREE.

**Gnomic verse.** *See under* GNOMIC.

**Golden verses.** *See under* GOLDEN.

**Heroic verse.** *See under* HEROIC.

**Leonine verses.** *See under* LEONINE.

**Macaronic verse.** *See under* MACARONI.

**Neck verse.** *See under* NECK.

**Pindaric verse.** *See under* PINDAR.

**Rhopalic verse.** *See under* RHOPALIC.

**Saturnian verses.** *See under* SATURN.

**Serpentine verses.** *See under* SERPENT.

**Society verse.** *See* VERS DE SOCIÉTÉ.

**Versi Berneschi.** *See* BERNESQUE POETRY.

**Version. Cover version.** See under COVER.

**Italic version.** *See under* ITALIC.

**Vert.** The heraldic term (from French) for green, said to signify love, joy and abundance. In engravings it is indicated by lines running diagonally across the shield from right to left.

**Verticordia, Venus.** *See under* VENUS.

**Vertumnus.** The ancient Roman god of the seasons, and the deity presiding over gardens and orchards. He was the husband of POMONA, and his festival was held on 12 August.

**Vervain.** The plant called 'holy herb', from its use in ancient rites. It is also known as pigeons' grass, Juno's tears and simpler's joy. Its botanical name is *Verbena officinalis*. *See also* HERBA SACRA.

**Vesica piscis** (Latin, 'fish bladder'). The ovoid frame or glory, which, in the 12th century, was much used, especially in painted windows, to surround pictures of the Virgin MARY and of Christ. It is intended to represent a fish, from the acronym *ichthus*. *See also* ICHTHYS.

**Vespers.** The sixth of the canonical hours in the Greek and Roman Churches, with the name sometimes also used of the evening service in the English Church. The word comes from Latin *vesperus*, 'evening', cognate with HESPERUS, Greek *Hesperos*, the evening star.

**Fatal Vespers, The.** *See under* FATAL.

**Sicilian Vespers, The.** *See under* SICILY.

**Vessel, To burst a blood.** *See under* BURST.

**Vesta.** The virgin goddess of the hearth in Roman mythology, corresponding to the Greek Hestia, one of the 12 great Olympians. She was custodian of the sacred fire brought by AENEAS from TROY, which was never permitted to go out lest a national calamity should follow. Wax matches were named from her.

**Vestal Virgins.** The six spotless virgins who tended the sacred fire brought by AENEAS from TROY, and preserved by the state in a sanctuary in the Forum at Rome. They were chosen by lot from young girls between the ages of six and ten and served under strict discipline for 30 years, after which they were free to marry, although few took this step. In the event of their losing their virginity they were buried alive.

The word 'vestal' has been figuratively applied by poets to any woman of spotless chastity, and Shakespeare bestowed the epithet on Elizabeth I.

**Vestiarian controversy.** The name given to the dispute about the wearing of clerical vestments raised by puritanically minded clergy in the reign of Edward VI and again in the reign of Elizabeth I. The simplest vestments such as the surplice and gown were described as the livery of ANTICHRIST. Matthew Parker, archbishop of Canterbury, sought to enforce conformity by his 'Advertisements' of 1566, which ordered the wearing of the four-cornered cap, scholar's gown and surplice, but many refused and deprivations followed. Diversity of practice remained, and the controversy became merged with the puritan agitation against EPISCOPACY.

**Vestments, Clerical.** *See under* CLERGY.

**Vestry** (Latin *vestiarium*, 'robing room'). A room in a church in which the vestments, registers, altar vessels and the like are kept and which is used as a robing room by the clergy. Some larger churches contain a priests' vestry, wardens' vestry and choir vestry. From the habit of parishioners meeting to conduct parish business in the vestry, both the body of parishioners and the meeting were called the vestry.

Up to 1894 the vestry was the final authority in all parish matters, civil and ecclesiastical. The parish priest presided over the meeting, which elected churchwardens and other parish officers, and the property of the parish was usually vested in the churchwardens. The common vestry consisted of the general assembly of rate-payers, and the select vestry of a body of vestrymen was elected to represent the parish, the usual procedure in many of the larger parishes. With the passing of the Local Government Act of 1894, secular parish councils were elected to take over the civil administrative functions of the rural parishes, and in the towns such work was subsequently transferred to urban councils. In 1921 ecclesiastical administration passed to the newly created parochial church councils, although the meeting that elects the churchwardens is still called a vestry meeting.

**Veteran.** In Britain this word is applied only to soldiers with long experience under arms, but in the USA it is bestowed on one who has had any service, however brief, in some field of warfare.

In the USA the abbreviation 'vet' stands for 'veteran' and 'veterinarian', but in Britain it is an abbreviation for veterinary surgeon.

**Veteran's Day.** *See* ARMISTICE DAY.

**Veto** (Latin, 'I forbid'). Louis XVI and Marie Antoinette were called Monsieur and Madame Veto by the Republicans, because the CONSTITUENT ASSEMBLY (1791) allowed the king to have the power, which he abused, of putting his veto upon any decree submitted to him. *See also* CARMAGNOLE.

**Pocket veto.** *See under* POCKET.

**Vexillum** (Latin, 'standard'). The standard borne by troops of the Roman army. In particular it was the red flag flown on the general's tent as a signal for marching or for battle.

**Via** (Latin, 'way'). The English use of the word, in 'I'll go via Chester', i.e. 'by way of Chester', is the ablative case of Latin *via*.

**Via Appia.** The APPIAN WAY.

**Via Dolorosa** (Latin, 'sorrowful way'). The route taken by Christ from the place of judgement to CALVARY, now marked by the 14 STATIONS OF THE CROSS.

**Via Flaminia.** The FLAMINIAN WAY.

**Via Lactea** (Latin). The Milky Way. *See also* GALAXY.

**Via media** (Latin, 'middle way'). The mean between two extremes. The Elizabethan church settlement of the 16th century is often so called, the CHURCH OF ENGLAND being regarded as the mean between extreme Protestantism and Roman Catholicism.

**Sacra Via.** *See under* SACRA.

**Vials of wrath.** Vengeance; the execution of wrath on the wicked. The allusion is to the seven angels who pour out upon the earth their vials full of wrath (Revelation 16).

**Viaticum** (Latin). The EUCHARIST administered to the dying. The word means 'provision for a journey', and its application is obvious.

**Vic, Old.** *See under* OLD.

**Vicar** (Latin *vicarius*, 'a substitute'). The priest of a parish where the TITHES were appropriated in pre-REFORMATION times, usually to monasteries. The monastery retained the rectorial or great tithes and reserved the small tithes (vicarial tithes) for the incumbent. After the Dissolution, such rectorial tithes were granted to CHAPTERS, COLLEGES, laymen and others, known as impropriators (*see* IMPROPRIATION), who were under obligation to appoint vicars to carry out the ecclesiastical duties. The title is also given to perpetual curates. *See also* CLERICAL TITLES.

In the US Episcopal Church a vicar is head of a chapel dependent on a parish church. In the ROMAN CATHOLIC CHURCH he is an ecclesiastic representing a bishop.

**Vicar apostolic.** In the ROMAN CATHOLIC CHURCH a titular bishop appointed to a place where no episcopate has been established or where the succession has been interrupted. In 1585 the English hierarchy came to an end, and until 1594 Catholics came under the jurisdiction of William Allen (1532–94), who was appointed cardinal in 1587, then that of archpriests from 1599 until 1621, but from 1623 until 1850 the Roman Catholic Church in England was governed by vicars apostolic. The term formerly denoted a bishop to whom the pope delegated some part of his jurisdiction.

**Vicar choral.** One of the minor clergy, or a layman, attached to a cathedral for singing certain portions of the service.

**Vicar forane.** A priest appointed by a Roman Catholic bishop to exercise limited (usually disciplinary) jurisdiction in a particular part of his diocese. The office is similar to that of RURAL DEAN. 'Forane' is a form of 'foreign', hence outlying or rural.

**Vicar general.** An ecclesiastical functionary assisting a bishop or archbishop in the exercise of his jurisdiction. In 1535 Thomas Cromwell (*c.*1485–1540) was appointed vicar general to carry out Henry VIII's ecclesiastical policies.

**Vicar of Bray, The.** This popular, probably early 18th-century, song depicting a time-serving vicar of the 17th and 18th centuries is based on a 16th-century vicar of Bray in Berkshire, who managed to retain his living during the religious changes of the reigns of Henry VIII, Edward VI, Mary and Elizabeth.

> And this is the law, I will maintain,
> Unto my dying day, Sir,
> That whatsoever King shall reign,
> I will be the Vicar of Bray, sir!
>
> ANONYMOUS: 'The Vicar of Bray', in *British Musical Miscellany*, vol i (1734)

**Vicar of Christ, The.** A title given to the pope, in allusion to his claim to be the representative of Christ on earth.

**Vicar of Hell, The.** A name playfully given by Henry VIII to John Skelton, his 'poet laureate', perhaps because Skelton was rector of Diss, in Norfolk, the pun being on Dis (PLUTO). Milton refers to the story in his *Areopagitica* (1644):

> I name not him for posterity's sake, whom Henry the Eighth named in merriment his vicar of hell.

**Lay vicar.** *See under* LAY.

**Vice.** The buffoon in the old English MORALITY PLAYS. He wore a cap with ass's ears and was generally named after some particular vice, such as gluttony, pride and the like.

**Vice versa** (Latin *vicis*, 'change', and *versa*, 'turned'). The reverse; the other way round. A humorous fantasy of this title (1882) by 'F. Anstey' (Thomas Anstey Guthrie) tells how a father changes place with his son at school while the son, by the working of the same charm, assumes his father's role at home, each retaining their original age.

**Vichy.** A town in the department of Allier, in central France, formerly fashionable on account of its thermal and medicinal springs, Vichy water being a considerable export and taken for various forms of indigestion, catarrh and other complaints.

Vichy acquired a new significance during the Second World War as the seat of Marshal Pétain's collaborationist government (1940–4), after the German occupation.

**Vichyssoise.** A thick soup made from leeks, potatoes, cream and the like, and usually served cold. Its name is short for French *crème Vichyssoise glacée* ('ice-cold cream from Vichy').

**Vicious circle.** A chain of circumstances, in which the solving of a problem creates a new problem, which makes the original problem more difficult of solution.

In logic a vicious circle is the fallacy of proving one statement by another that itself rests on the first for proof.

**Vicisti, Galilaee.** *See* GALILEAN *under* GALILEE.

**Victim, Fashion.** *See under* FASHION.

**Victoria Cross.** The premier British award for conspicuous bravery in the presence of the enemy, instituted by Queen Victoria in 1856. The ribbon is now crimson coloured, but was formerly blue for the Royal Navy and red for the Army. It is a bronze MALTESE CROSS with the royal crown surmounted by a lion in its centre under which is the inscription 'For Valour'. It is worn on the left breast and takes precedence over all other decorations. The crosses were made from the metal of guns captured in the Crimean War at Sebastopol (1855).

**Victory. Victory Medal.** A bronze medal with a winged figure of Victory on the obverse, awarded in 1919 to all allied service personnel who had served in a theatre of war in the First World War, also to certain women's formations.

**Cadmean victory.** *See under* CADMUS.

**Hallelujah victory.** *See under* HALLELUJAH.

**Pyrrhic victory.** *See under* PYRRHIC.

**V for Victory.** *See under* V.

**Victrix, Venus.** *See under* VENUS.

**Vidar.** In Scandinavian mythology, a son of ODIN, noted for his taciturnity and fearless destruction of FENRIR.

**Videlicet** (Latin *videre licet*, 'it is permitted to see'). To wit; that is to say; namely. The term is more familiar in its abbreviated form, VIZ.

**View. Bird's-eye view.** *See under* BIRD.

**Order to view.** *See under* ORDER.

**Point of view.** *See under* POINT.

**Vigilance committee.** A privately formed group of citizens who take it upon themselves to assist in the maintenance of law and order. They are sometimes found in the southern states of the USA as a body intimidating Negroes. During the Civil War (1861–5) they also strove to suppress the activities of loyalists to the northern cause. Members of such committees are called vigilantes.

**Vigiliae.** *See* MATINS.

**Village, Greenwich.** *See under* GREENWICH.

**Villain** or **villein** (Late Latin *villanus*, 'farm worker', from *villa*, 'a farm'). Originally the unfree peasant of feudal times was called a villein. He was bound to the MANOR and owed service to its lord. As the latter's personal chattel, he could be sold or transferred, but he had shares in the village fields. From the time of the BLACK DEATH the shortage of labour led to an improvement in the villein's status under the system of COPYHOLD tenure. *See also* OPEN-FIELD SYSTEM; WEEKWORK.

The notion of rascality, wickedness and worthlessness now associated with the word villain is a result of aristocratic condescension and sense of superiority.

> I am no villain; I am the youngest son of Sir Rowland de Boys; he was my father, and he is thrice a villain that says such a father begot villains.
>
> SHAKESPEARE: *As You Like It*, I, i (1599)

**Villain of the deepest dye, A.** One steeped in villainy; a villain of the worst kind.

**Vim.** Slang for energy, force or 'go', usually in the phrase 'vim and vigour'. It is the accusative of Latin *vis*, 'strength'.

**Vin** (French, 'wine').

**Vin ordinaire.** The French name for inexpensive table wine of no particular regional origin. It is often a blend of different regional wines and not usually of any particular VINTAGE. It is generally a red wine, but not necessarily so.

**Vin rosé.** Pink wine, usually made by leaving the black skins of the grape in the juice long enough to produce the required colour, but sometimes from a mixture of red and white wine or by the addition of artificial colouring. In certain parts of France this is called *vin gris*.

**Vinalia.** Roman wine festivals in honour of JUPITER and also associated with VENUS as a goddess of vineyards. The first such festival was held on 23 April, when the wine of the previous season was broached and the second on 19 August, when the VINTAGE began (Latin *vinalis*, 'pertaining to wine').

**Vinayapitaka.** *See* TRIPITAKA.

**Vincent.** A deacon of Saragossa, martyred *c.*304 during the persecution under Diocletian. He is the most celebrated of Spanish martyrs and was put to death, following other tortures, by being roasted on a grid. His day is 22 January. He is a patron saint of drunkards for no apparent reason, but possibly from an association with Latin *vinum*, 'wine'. An old rhyme says:

> If on St Vincent's Day the sky is clear
> More wine than water will crown the year.

**Vincentian.** A Lazarist or Lazarite, a member of the Congregation of Priests of the Mission founded (1625) by St Vincent de Paul.

**Vincula, St Peter ad.** *See under* PETER.

**Vinculo matrimonii, A.** *See under* A.

**Vindaloo.** An Indian dish similar to curry but differing from it in that the meat is marinated and cooked in a vinegar sauce rather than one that is water-based. The name is used loosely to mean almost any hot and spicy meat dish, and it has become popular as a TAKEAWAY. For some young stalwarts, the hotter and spicier the vindaloo, the better. Perversely, the word itself is not Indian in origin but Portuguese, from *vin d'alho* ('wine with garlic sauce').

**Vine.** The Rabbis say that the Devil buried a lion, a lamb and a hog at the foot of the first vine planted by NOAH, and that hence men receive from wine ferocity, mildness or wallowing in the mire.

**Martha's Vineyard.** *See under* MARTHA.

**Naboth's vineyard.** *See under* NABOTH.

**Vinegar.** Livy writes that when Hannibal led his army over the Alps from Spain into Italy in 218 BC he splintered the rocks with fire and vinegar to create a zigzag road for the descent. The vinegar or sour wine may have been used because water was scarce.

**Vinegar Bible, The.** *See under* BIBLE.

**Vinegar Hill.** A hill in Ireland some 389ft (119m) high near Enniscorthy, County Wexford. An insurrection organized by the UNITED IRISHMEN in the spring of 1798 was soon suppressed after General Lake's victory over the rebels at the Battle of Vinegar Hill on 21 June. The name of the hill is an English corruption of Irish *Cnoc Fiodh na gCaor* ('hill of the wood of the berries').

**Vinegar Joe.** The Second World War nickname of General Joseph W. Stilwell (1883–1946), US commander of troops in China. The allusion is to his sour temperament.

**Vingt-et-un** (French, 'twenty-one'). A card game in which the object is to get as near as possible to 21 without exceeding it. The court cards count as 10 and the ace as one or 11. The name of the English card game pontoon probably derives from the French.

**Vinland.** The name ('Wineland') given to that portion of North America known to the Norsemen and first discovered by Leif Ericsson about AD 1000. Its location is uncertain, but it is generally held to have been in the region of Newfoundland, and its estimated position ranges from Labrador to VIRGINIA. Some account for much of the discrepancy in Scandinavian writings by positing a Vinland I and Vinland II. Vinland may well refer to pasture land, thus obviating the difficulties presented by the association of the name with the vine.

**Vinland Map, The.** *See under* FAKES.

**Vintage** (French *vendange*). The gathering of the grapes, or the year in which a certain wine was made. The wine of a good vintage year is known as vintage wine and hence 'a vintage year' is a memorable and notable year in any context.

**Vintry ward.** One of the 25 electoral WARDS of the City of London. They are so called, according to John Stow, from the site occupied by the wine merchants from Bordeaux, who settled on this part of the bank of the THAMES around QUEENHITHE. The Vintners built large houses with vaults, and the great house built by Sir John Stodie (mayor in 1357) was called the Vintry.

**Vinum theologicum** (Latin). An old term for the best wine obtainable. Raphael Holinshed (d.*c.*1580) says it was so called because religious men would be sure 'neither to drinke nor be served of the worst, or such as was anie wais vined by the vintner; naie, the merchant would have thought that his soule would have gone streightwaie to the devil if he would have served them with other than the best.'

**Viola.** In Shakespeare's *Twelfth Night* (1599) a young woman who is shipwrecked, disguises herself as a man, falls in love with the lord Orsino and then finds that Olivia, the woman to whom she carries Orsino's declarations of love, has fallen in love with her male *alter ego*.

**Violet.** A flower usually taken as symbolizing modesty, and fabled by the ancients to have sprung from the blood of the boaster AJAX.

The colour indicates the love of truth and the truth of love. In the language of flowers the white violet is emblematic of innocence, and the blue violet of faithful love. For ecclesiastical and symbolical uses *see* COLOURS.

**Violet on the tyrant's grave, The.** The reference, from Tennyson's 'Aylmer's Field' (1864), is to NERO. It is said that some unknown hand went by night and strewed violets over his grave. At his death his statues are said to have been 'crowned with garlands of flowers'.

**City of the Violet Crown, The.** *See under* CITY.

**Corporal Violet.** NAPOLEON BONAPARTE, so nicknamed because when banished to Elba in 1814 he told his friends he would return with the violets. 'Corporal Violet' became a favourite toast of his partisans, and when he reached Fréjus a gang of women assembled with violets, which were freely sold. The SHIBBOLETH was, 'Do you like violets?' If the answer given was 'Oui', the person was known not to be a confederate, but if the answer was 'Eh bien', the respondent was recognized as an adherent. *See also* LITTLE CORPORAL.

**Violin.** *See* AMATI; CREMONA; FIDDLE; FIRST FIDDLE; STRAD.

**VIP.** Very Important Person. This well-established abbreviation was popularized by a station commander of Transport Command in 1944 who was responsible for the movement of a plane-load of important individuals, including Lord Mountbatten, to the Middle East. He so described them in his movement orders to avoid disclosing their identity.

**Viper.** An American slang term for a smoker of marijuana.

**Viper and file.** The biter bit. AESOP says a viper found a file, and tried to bite it, under the supposition that it was good food, but the file said that its province was to bite others, and not to be bitten.

**Virago.** Literally, a manlike maiden, but a term usually employed to designate a loud-mouthed or ill-tempered woman, otherwise a scold or shrew. *See also* TERMAGANT.

**Viraj.** *See* MANU.

**Virgate** (Latin *virga*, 'rod'). An old English measure of land, usually about 30 acres (12 ha), i.e. about one-quarter of a HIDE, but differing considerably in different districts. It is also sometimes called 'yardland'.

**Virgil.** The greatest poet of ancient Rome, Publius Virgilius Maro (70–19 BC), born near Mantua (hence called the Mantuan Swan), a master of epic, didactic and idyllic poetry. His chief works are the AENEID, the *Eclogues* or *Bucolics*, and the *Georgics*. From the *Aeneid*, grammarians illustrated their rules and rhetoricians selected the subjects of their declamations, and even Christians looked on the poet as half-inspired. Hence the use of his poems in DIVINATION. *See also* SORTES.

In the Middle Ages Virgil came to be represented as a magician and enchanter, hence Dante's conception in his *Divina Commedia* (*c.*1309–*c.*1320) of making Virgil, as the personification of human wisdom, his guide through the infernal regions.

Virgil was wise, and as craft was considered a part of wisdom, especially overreaching the spirit of evil, he is thus represented by medieval writers as outwitting the demon. Much of this legend grew out of Neapolitan folklore, and one story says that he beguiled the Devil into a glass bottle and kept him there until he had learned the Devil's magic arts. The tale has much in common with that of 'The Fisherman and the Genie' in the ARABIAN NIGHTS ENTERTAINMENTS. Virgil's magical exploits are recounted in numerous medieval romances and poems, and there is an account of Virgil's NECROMANCY in the GESTA ROMANORUM (13th century).

**Virgin. Virgin Birth, The.** The belief that Christ had no human father and that his miraculous birth did not impair the virginity of his mother, the Virgin MARY (*see* Matthew 1:18, Luke 1:27–35). It is generally held that Christ himself was a virgin.

> Christ was a virgin, fashioned as a man,
> And many of his saints since time began
> Were ever perfect in their chastity.
>
> CHAUCER: *Canterbury Tales*, Prologue to 'The Wife of Bath's Tale' (*c.*1387) (modern translation by Nevill Coghill, 1951)

**Virgin Mary's Bodyguard, The.** *See under* REGIMENTAL AND DIVISIONAL NICKNAMES.

**Virgin Queen, The.** Elizabeth I (1533, r.1558–1603), also called by Shakespeare 'the fair Vestal'. How actually virginal Elizabeth was is uncertain, despite her neither having married nor borne children.

**Eleven thousand virgins, The.** *See* URSULA.

**Vestal Virgins.** *See under* VESTA.

**Virginal.** A quilled keyboard instrument of the harpsichord family in use in the 16th and early 17th century, often referred to as a pair of virginals. It has been suggested that it was so called because it was used in convents to lead the virginals or hymns to the Virgin, but its name probably arises from the fact that it was mostly played by young ladies. Support for the latter origin is lent by the fact that the first collection of keyboard pieces printed for the instrument was entitled *Parthenia, or the Maydenhead of the First Musicke that ever was printed for the Virginalls*. It was presented to Princess Elizabeth and Prince Frederick on the occasion of their marriage in 1613.

**Virginia.** The first securely established English colony in North America, founded at Jamestown in 1607. It took its name from the earlier attempt (1584–7) of Sir Walter Raleigh to found a colony on Roanoke Island (now in North Carolina), which was named after the VIRGIN QUEEN. In the early days of settlement, the name Virginia was applied to the whole coast between FLORIDA and Nova Scotia. *See also* ACADIA.

**Virginia Water.** This residential district of Surrey takes its name from Virginia Water Lake, in the southeast corner of Windsor Great Park. The park was laid out in 1746 by William Augustus, Duke of Cumberland (1721–65), victor at CULLODEN, and the artificial lake named to commemorate the pioneers who founded and settled the American colony in 1607.

> Virginia Water: the name was a forecast of the forest wilds, the broad waters, and tranquil solitudes that were to be called forth by the waving of the magician's wand.
>
> JAMES THORNE: *Handbook to the Environs of London* (1876)

**Virgo** (Latin, 'Virgin'). One of the ancient constellations and the sixth sign of the ZODIAC (23 August to 22 September). The constellation is the metamorphosis of ASTRAEA. *See also* ICARIUS.

**Virtue. Cardinal virtues.** *See under* CARDINAL.

**Lady of easy virtue, A.** *See under* LADY.

**Make a virtue of necessity, To.** To grin and bear it; 'what can't be cured must be endured'.

**Moral virtue.** *See under* MORAL.

**Seven virtues, The.** *See under* SEVEN.

**Virtuoso.** An Italian word meaning one who excels. It is applied to those with expert knowledge or appreciation for works of art or *virtu* and is especially used for instrumental performers of the highest ability. A 'virtuoso performance' is thus one given with exceptional skill.

**Vis à vis** (French, 'face to face'). The term is properly applied to persons facing one another, as in a railway carriage. It is also an old name for a carriage or coach that enables the occupants to face one another. The phrase is now often used in the sense of 'in relation to', 'as regards'.

**Viscount** (Old French *visconte*, from Medieval Latin *vicecomes*, 'deputy of a count'). In Britain, a peer ranking next below an EARL and above a BARON. The title was first granted to John, Lord Beaumont in 1440. The CORONET of a viscount bears 16 pearls set around the rim. He is styled 'Right Honourable' and is addressed by the sovereign as 'Our right trusty and well-beloved Cousin'. *See also* COURTESY TITLES; PEERS OF THE REALM.

**Vishnu.** The Preserver or Pervader, the second deity in the Hindu TRIMURTI, although worshipped by many Hindus as the supreme. He originally appears as the sun-god. He is beneficent to man and has made numerous incarnations or 'descents', ten being the number most generally reckoned. He is usually represented as four-armed and carrying a mace, a conch-shell, a disc and a LOTUS, and often riding the eagle Garuda. His wife is LAKSHMI, born from the sea. His name is Sanskrit in origin, literally meaning 'he who works everywhere'. *See also* AVATAR.

**Visible, Church.** *See under* CHURCH.

**Vis inertiae** (Latin, 'the power of inactivity'). It is a common mistake to imagine that 'inertia' means absence of motion, since it is actually that property of matter that makes it resist any change. Thus it is hard to set in motion what is still, or to stop what is in motion. Figuratively, it applies to that unwillingness to change that makes people choose to bear the ills they have rather than turn to others of which they are ignorant.

**Vision. Vision of Piers Plowman, The.** A long allegorical poem in Middle English alliterative verse, written by William Langland (*c.*1332–*c.*1400), who was probably born in the West Midlands. The poet's dream or vision gives a vivid insight into 14th-century conditions and the current social and religious evils. The full title is *The Vision of William concerning Piers the Plowman*. In the earlier part Piers typifies the simple, pious English labourer, and in the latter, Christ himself. Piers is the subject, not the author of the poem. There are several texts in three widely varying versions, known as the A, B and C texts. The Prologue of the B text has as its opening line: 'In a somer seson, whan softe was the sonne'.

**Beatific Vision.** *See under* BEATIFIC.

**Field of vision.** *See under* FIELD.

**Visits, Angel.** *See under* ANGEL.

**Visitation** or **Visitation of Our Lady, The.** The Blessed Virgin's visit to her cousin St ELIZABETH before the birth of St JOHN THE BAPTIST (Luke 1:39–56). It is celebrated on 2 July.

**Order of the Visitation** or **Visitandines, The.** *See under* ORDER.

**Vital statistics.** Properly, population statistics concerned with births, marriages, deaths, divorces and the like (Latin *vita*, 'life'). The phrase is now applied semi-seriously to a woman's bust, waist and hip measurements, usually given in inches.

> We are now privy to Ms Bailey's vital statistics (34–24–35), and the knowledge that she is a model aged 22, five foot seven, and buys her underwear from Marks and Spencer.
>
> *The Times* (4 December 1994)

**Vitamin.** The word as proposed in 1912 by the American biochemist Casimir Funk was originally 'vitamine', from Latin *vita*, 'life', and English amine, the latter referring to the amino acid that the substance was believed to contain. When it was found this was not the case, the term was modified to its present spelling in 1920.

Vitamins are generally classified as water-soluble (B and C) or fat-soluble (A, D, E and K), and each of the letter-names has its chemical equivalent. Thus vitamin A is another name for retinol, vitamin $B_1$ is thiamine, vitamin $B_2$ is riboflavin, vitamin C is ascorbic acid, vitamin $D_3$ is cholecalciferol and so on.

**Vitex** (Latin *vitis*, 'vine', from *viere*, 'to twist'). A genus of plants of the family Verbenaceae, more familiar from its specific name *Vitex agnus-castus* (Latin, 'chaste lamb') or chaste tree, also called Abraham's balm, monk's pepper tree and hemp tree. In the language of flowers it means 'insensibility to love'. Dioscorides, Pliny and Galen mention the plant as a mild anaphrodisiac and say that Grecian ladies used to strew their couches with its leaves as a guard against impure thoughts. A syrup concocted from its fruits was also used in convents for similar reasons.

> And Wreaths of *Agnus castus* others bore:
> These last, who with those Virgin Crowns were dress'd,
> Appear'd in higher Honour than the rest.
>
> JOHN DRYDEN: *Fables, Ancient and Modern*, 'The Flower and the Leaf; or, The Lady in the Arbour' (1700)

**Vitus.** A Sicilian youth who was martyred with Modestus, his tutor, and Crescentia, his nurse, during the Diocletian persecution, *c.*303. He is sometimes regarded as the patron saint of dancers and comedians.

**St Vitus' dance.** In Germany in the 17th century it was believed that good health for the year could be secured by anyone who danced before a statue of St VITUS on his feast-day, 15 June. Such dancing to excess is said to have come to be confused with chorea, hence its name, St Vitus' dance, the saint being invoked against it.

**Viva!** An exclamation of applause or joy, from the Italian, meaning '(long) live'. A VIVA VOCE examination is usually called a 'viva'. *See also* VIVAT REX OR REGINA!

**Viva voce** (Latin, 'with the living voice'). Orally; by word of mouth. A viva voce examination is one in which the respondent gives spoken answers.

**Vivandière.** A woman formerly officially attached to a French (and other continental) regiment for the purpose of selling liquor and food to the soldiers. OUIDA portrays the vivandière, Cigarette, in *Under Two Flags* (1866).

**Vivat rex** or **regina!** (Latin, 'Long live the King or Queen!'). At the coronation of British sovereigns the boys of Westminster School have the privilege of acclaiming the king or queen with shouts of *Vivat rex* or *Vivat regina!*

**Vivien.** An enchantress of ARTHURIAN ROMANCES and the mistress of MERLIN; the LADY OF THE LAKE. *See also* LANCELOT OF THE LAKE.

**Vixen** (Old English *fyxen*). A female fox. Metaphorically, a shrewish woman, one of villainous and ungovernable temper.

**Viz.** A contraction of VIDELICET. The z represents ʒ, a common mark of contraction in writing in the Middle Ages, as om̄ibʒ, omnibus.

**Vizier** (Arabic *wazīr*, 'bearer of the burden'). A name given to the chief minister of the ABBASSID caliphs and to officials serving other Muslim rulers. The title was also formerly given to Turkish ministers and governors. Until 1878 the chief minister was called the Grand Vizier.

**VJ Day.** 'Victory in Japan' Day. The end of hostilities in the Far East, 15 August 1945. *See also* VE DAY.

**Vobis, Pax.** *See under* PAX.

**Vogue.** A loan word from the French. 'In vogue' means in fashion; in popular favour. The verb *voguer* means to be carried forward on the water by oar or by sail, hence the idea of sailing with the tide.

**Vogue la galère** (French, 'let the galley be rowed'). Let's get on with it; let's give it a go.

**Voice. Voice crying in the wilderness, A.** An unheeded advocate of reform. The reference is to John the Baptist, who preached in the wilderness of Judaea and whose preaching was foretold by the prophet Isaiah.

> For this is he that was spoken of by the prophet Esaias, saying, The voice of one crying in the wilderness, Prepare ye the way of the Lord, make his paths straight.
>
> Matthew 3:3

**Lift up one's voice, To.** *See under* LIFT.

**Void, Null and.** *See under* NULL.

**Voivode** or **Vaivode** (Slavic, 'leader of an army', Russian *voyevoda*). A title once used by the princes of Moldavia and Wallachia, later called HOSPODARS.

**Volapük.** An artificial language invented in 1879 by a German pastor, Johann M. Schleyer. It was based on European languages, about one-third from English and the remainder from Latin, German and the ROMANCE LANGUAGES. The words were cut down so that no original is recognizable. The LORD'S PRAYER in Volapük begins thus: '*O Fat obas, kel binol in süls, paisaludomöz nem ola; kömomöd monargän ola; janomöz vil olik, äs in sül, i su tal*'. The language takes its name from *vol*, based on 'world', and *pük*, based on 'speak'. After about ten years its place was taken by ESPERANTO. *See also* INTERLINGUA.

**Vol-au-vent** (French, 'flight in the wind'). A small case of very light puff pastry with a savoury filling.

**Volpone** (Italian, 'Fox'). The devious and rapacious Venetian who is the hero of Ben Jonson's play that bears his name (1605). He pretends to be dying to trick his even greedier neighbours into giving him outrageously costly gifts in the hope of being named in his will. He is devious and cynical, but he attacks his schemes with an enviable enthusiasm.

**Volsungs.** A dynasty of fierce Scandinavian heroes whose exploits are recounted in the 13th-century *Volsunga* saga. The Volsungs descend from Volsung himself, a great-grandson of ODIN and grandfather of SIGURD, the slayer of FAFNIR. The tales are linked to the saga of Ragnar Lodbrok, the semi-legendary ancestor of the kings of Norway and Denmark.

**Voltaire.** The assumed name of François Marie Arouet (1694–1778), the great French philosopher, poet, dramatist and author. He began to use the name on his release from imprisonment in the Bastille in 1718. It is popularly said to be an anagram of *Arouet l(e) j(eune)*, 'Arouet the Young', with the u giving the initial V and the j serving as i. However, there is evidence that he actually based it on *Veauterre* ('valley land'), the name of an estate that he had bought near Asnières-sur-Oise, with the first syllable respelled for reasons of euphony. *See also* CANDIDE.

**Volte-face** (French, from Italian *volta-faccia*, from *volta*, 'turn', and *faccia*, 'face'). A term used of a complete about-face or change of front in argument, opinions, views or the like.

**Volume.** The word shows its ancestry, for it comes from Latin *volvere*, 'to roll'. The ancient form of books was of written sheets fastened together and rolled up on a stick or roller.

**Omnibus volumne.** *See under* OMNIBUS.

**Volund.** *See* WAYLAND SMITH .

**Voluntary schools.** The name for schools established by the voluntary societies such as the NATIONAL SOCIETY and the British and Foreign Schools Society, religious bodies and so on, as opposed to those established by local public authorities which were formerly called council schools, and until 1902, board schools (*see* SCHOOLBOARDS). All primary and secondary schools maintained by a local education authority are still classified as county (the majority) or voluntary schools according to their origins, although the voluntary principle in education has largely been submerged.

**Voodoo** or **voodooism.** A mixture of superstition, magic, WITCHCRAFT, serpent worship and the like, derived from African rites and some Christian beliefs. It still survives among some Negro groups in Haiti, and other parts of the West Indies and the Americas.

The name is said to have been first given to it by missionaries, from French *Vaudois*, a WALDENSIAN, as these were accused of sorcery, but Sir Richard Burton derived it from *vodun*, a dialect form of Ashanti *obosum*, a fetish or tutelary spirit. *See also* OBEAH.

**Vorticism.** An artistic movement that began in Britain in 1914, somewhat akin to CUBISM and FUTURISM and embracing art and literature. It was iconoclastic and regarded the question of representation as irrelevant. Its designs are in straight lines and angular patterns. Concern with machinery was also a feature. Among its representatives, Percy Wyndham Lewis (1882–1957) and Edward Wadsworth (1889–1949) were the most notable. The name was bestowed by the US poet Ezra Pound (1885–1972) and alludes to the 'vortices' of human life on which the movement was based. *See also* DADAISM; FAUVISM; IMPRESSIONISM; ORPHISM; SURREALISM; SYNCHROMISM.

**Vortigern.** The British ruler (*fl*.425–*c*.450 AD) who is said to have invited the Saxons, led by HENGIST and Horsa, into Britain to render aid against the PICTS. He married Hengist's daughter, ROWENA. *See also* HEALTHS.

**Vote. Block vote.** *See under* BLOCK.

**Casting vote.** *See under* CAST.

**Flapper vote, The.** *See under* FLAPPER.

**Snap vote.** *See under* SNAP.

**Straw vote.** *See under* STRAW.

**Votive offerings.** *See* ANATHEMA.

**Vow. Vow a candle to the Devil, To.** To seek to bribe or propitiate the Devil.

**Vow of Odin, The.** A matrimonial or other vow made before the Stone of Odin in the Orkneys. This was an oval stone, with a hole in it large enough to admit a man's hand. Anyone who violated a vow made before this stone was held infamous. *See also* STANDING STONES OF STENNESS.

**Cup of vows, The.** *See under* CUP.

**Vox. Vox et praeterea nihil** (Latin, 'a voice, and nothing more'). Empty words, 'full of sound and fury, signifying nothing'; a threat not followed out. When the Lacedaemonian plucked the nightingale, on seeing so little substance he exclaimed, *Vox tu es, et nihil praeterea* (Plutarch, *Apophthegmata Laconica* (2nd century AD)).

**Vox pop.** A term for interviews with members of the public conducted by radio or television reporters. The expression is a shortening of Latin *vox populi*, 'voice of the people'.

> A few days ago, a BBC camera crew went round Washington collecting vox pops – close-ups of men in the street saying pithily what they think of things.
> *Listener* (8 February 1968)

**Vox populi, vox Dei** (Latin, 'the voice of the people is the voice of God'). This does not mean that the voice of the many is wise and good, but only that it is irresistible. After Edward II had been dethroned in 1327 by the people in favour of his son (Edward III), Walter Reynolds (d.1327), archbishop of Canterbury, preached at the coronation of Edward III with these words as his text. The words themselves come from a text by the 8th-century scholar Alcuin.

> Nec audiendi qui solent dicere, Vox populi, vox Dei, quum tumultuositas vulgi semper insaniae proxima sit.
> (And those people who keep saying the voice of the people is the voice of God should not be listened to, since the clangour of the crowd is always very close to insanity.)
> ALCUIN: *Works*, Vol i, Letter 164

**Voyage of Maelduin** or **Maeldune, The.** In early Irish romance, Maelduin was the son of Ailill, who had been killed by a robber from Leix. As a young man, he set sail to seek the murderer and voyaged for three years and seven months, visiting many islands and seeing marvels hitherto unknown. He eventually found the culprit but took no vengeance, out of gratitude to God for his deliverance from such a variety of great dangers. The story has much in common with the voyage of St BRENDAN.

**Voyageur.** A French Canadian or half-breed, accustomed to portage his canoe when necessary; formerly employed by the Hudson's Bay Company and Northwest Company to maintain supplies and communications between their trading stations.

**VP.** Vice President. In the USA, the abbreviation has given the word 'Veep'.

**Vulcan.** In Roman mythology a son of JUPITER and JUNO, and god of fire and metal working; also the patron of handicraftsmen in metals, identified with the Greek Hephaestus. He is sometimes called MULCIBER, i.e. the softener.

His workshops were under Mount ETNA and other volcanoes, where the CYCLOPS assisted him in forging thunderbolts for Jupiter. It is said that he took the part of Juno against Jupiter who hurled him out of heaven. He was nine days in falling and was saved by the people of LEMNOS from crashing to earth, but one leg was broken, hence his lameness. VENUS was his wife and, in consequence of her amour with MARS, he came to be regarded as the special patron of cuckolds. He was the father of CUPID and, according to some, of Cecrops (a mythical king of Attica), and he created PANDORA from clay.

**Vulcanist.** A supporter of the Vulcanian or Plutonian theory, which ascribes the changes on the earth's surface to the agency of fire. These theorists say the earth was once in a state of igneous fusion and that the crust has gradually cooled down to its present temperature.

**Vulcan's mirror.** It showed the past, the present and the future. Sir John Davies (1569–1626) says that CUPID gave it to ANTINOUS and Antinous gave it to PENELOPE, who saw therein 'the court of Queen Elizabeth'.

**Vulgar Latin.** Any of the dialects of CLASSICAL LATIN spoken by the ancient Romans. The ROMANCE LANGUAGES developed from them.

**Vulgate, The.** The Latin translation of the Bible, made about 384–404 by St JEROME at the request of Pope Damasus I, originally to establish a standard text. It was not an instant success, and in some parts of Europe, e.g. Spain, was never in general use. The first printed edition was the MAZARIN BIBLE (1456) (*see under* BIBLE). A revised edition was issued by Clement VIII in 1592, and in 1965 a commission was appointed by the Second Vatican Council to produce a new revision. The name, which is much later than the text, comes from Late Latin *vulgata editio*, 'popular version', as the common edition sanctioned by the ROMAN CATHOLIC CHURCH.

**VXL.** A punning monogram on lockets and the like, standing for UXL (you excel). U and V were formerly interchangeable.

# W

**W.** The twenty-third letter of the English alphabet. The form is simply a ligature of two Vs (VV). Hence the name, for v was formerly the symbol of U as well as of V.

**Waac.** The familiar name of a member of the Women's Army Auxiliary Corps, a body of women raised for non-combatant army service in the First World War. In the Second World War they were termed the Auxiliary Territorial Service (ATS). This became the Women's Royal Army Corps (WRAC) in 1949. The WRAC was disbanded in 1992, when women wishing to enlist joined the regular army.

**Waaf.** The familiar name of a member of the Women's Auxiliary Air Force, or the force itself, which was originally set up in 1918 as the Women's Royal Air Force (WRAF). It was disbanded in 1920, but re-formed in 1939 as the WAAF. It once again became the WRAF in 1949, and was finally disbanded in 1994. Women are now able to enlist in the regular RAF.

**WAC.** In the Second World War the Women's Army Corps, the American equivalent of the British ATS. *See also* WAVES.

**Wad.** A roll of paper money, and hence the money itself.

**Wade. Wade's boat.**

> They are as tricky as the Boat of Wade
> With so much trouble breaking when they please
> To fight, I should not have a moment's ease.
> CHAUCER: 'The Merchant's Tale' (*c*.1387) (modern translation by Nevill Coghill, 1951)

Wade was a hero of medieval romance, whose adventures were a favourite theme in the 16th century. Nothing is known about his boat except that it was called *Guingelot*.

**General Wade.** The old rhyme:

> Had you seen but these roads before they were made,
> You would hold up your hands and bless General Wade,

refers to Field-Marshal George Wade (1673–1748), famous for his construction of many military roads in the Highlands of Scotland (*c*.1724–30) as a precaution against JACOBITE insurrection.

> Soon afterwards we came to the *General's Hut*, so called because it was the temporary abode of Wade, while he superintended the works upon the road.
> SAMUEL JOHNSON: *A Journey to the Western Islands of Scotland*, 'Lough Ness' (1775)

**Wafer.** Ecclesiastically, a thin disc of unleavened bread used in the EUCHARIST.

Before the device of gummed envelope flaps was introduced, thin round discs of dried paste or gelatin were inserted between the flap and the envelope or, earlier still, between the outer sides of the folded letter, and having been moistened and pressed with a seal served the same purpose of keeping the paper closed.

**Wag.** As used of a humorous person, one given to jest, the word is Old English *wagge*, perhaps from the facetious use of *waghalter*, a droll, a rascal, one who 'wags' or shakes a 'halter'.

**Tail wags the dog, The.** *See under* TAIL.

**Tongues are wagging.** *See under* TONGUE.

**Wage. Earn the wages of sin, To.** *See under* EARN.

**Wager.** Anything staked or hazarded on the event of a contest. The word is connected with gage and wage (Old Northern French *wagier*, to pledge).

**Wager of battle.** *See* ORDEAL OF BATTLE.

**Waggoner.** An old name for a volume of sea charts, Dalrymple's charts of the late 18th century being known as the 'English Waggoner'. The word is a corruption of 'Wagenaar', from a collection of such charts published at Leyden in 1584 by Lukas Wagenaar.

**Wagon. Wagoner.** *See* BOÖTES.

**Hitch your wagon to a star.** *See under* HITCH.

**Northern Wagoner.** *See under* NORTH.

**On the wagon.** Abstaining from alcoholic drink. The allusion is probably to American logging and mining camps, some of which were formerly in such a remote location that fresh water had to be brought in by wagon.

**Wahabis** or **Wahabites.** Adherents of a Muslim movement seeking to purify ISLAM and restore it to its primitive simplicity. They are so called from the founder, Muhammad ibn-Abd-ul-Wahab (1703–92), who began his activities about 1760. The sect centres on Saudi Arabia.

**Wailing Wall.** The length of high stone wall at Jerusalem, said to be a relic of the Temple of Herod (*see* TEMPLE OF SOLOMON), which was destroyed in AD 70. After the Jews returned, it eventually became a tradition to gather there every Friday for prayer and lamentations for the Dispersion and lost glories of Israel.

**Wain, Charles's.** *See under* CHARLES.

**Wait. Wait and see.** A phrase at one time humorously used with reference to the Liberal politician H.H. Asquith, 1st Earl of Oxford and Asquith (1852–1928); thus, 'What did Asquith say?' was formerly another way of saying 'Wait and see.' Asquith used the phrase in answer to a question in the House of Commons on 4 April 1910, and he took to repeating it subsequently when faced with an awkward question. Eventually the OPPOSITION took it up and chanted it back at him when questions were put to him. The same phrase was associated with the stalling policy of John Major when prime minister (1990–97) with regard to Britain's joining the SINGLE CURRENCY.

**Wait for it!** Don't start yet! Hold on! A phrase heard on the parade-ground when a movement begins before the command that orders it has been completed, as: 'Parade, parade – wait for it! – *'shun*!' The expression also creates suspense in a narrative or explanation, as: 'We get paid this week and – wait for it! – they're giving us a bonus!'

**Wait for something to turn up, To.** To expect that one's luck will change and that good fortune will arrive without much effort on one's own part. Mr MICAWBER's philosophy of life:

> 'And then', said Mr Micawber, who was present, 'I have no doubt I shall, please Heaven, begin to be beforehand with the world, and to live in a perfectly new manner, if – in short, if anything turns up.'
>
> DICKENS: *David Copperfield*, ch xi (1849–50)

**Waiting in the wings.** Holding oneself in readiness, like an actor about to go on stage.

**Wait on someone hand and foot, To.** To be at someone's constant beck and call; to be someone's slave.

**Accident waiting to happen, An.** *See under* ACCIDENT.

**I can't wait.** I'm very impatient, as: 'I can't wait to see his face when he opens his card.'

**Lords in Waiting.** *See under* LORD.

**Watchful waiting.** *See under* WATCH.

**Waitangi Day.** Since 1960 6 February has been celebrated as New Zealand's national day. It is a public holiday and commemorates the day on which the Treaty of Waitangi was made in 1840 by the British governor, William Hobson, with the Maori chiefs. They recognized British sovereignty in return for the tribes being guaranteed possession of their lands.

**Waits.** A name given to parties of singers and musicians who perform outside people's houses at CHRISTMAS. They derive their name from those watchmen of former times called 'waits' who sounded a horn or played a tune to mark the passing hours. Waits were employed at the royal court 'to pipe the watch' and also by town corporations. The household expenses of Edward IV (r.1461–83) provide for 'A *wayte*, that nightelye from Mychelmas to Shreve Thorsdaye pipe the watche withen this courte fower tymes in the somere nightes three tymes' (Thomas Rymer, *Foedera* (1704–35)).

Waits duly came to provide a uniformed band for their town for civic occasions, and played to the public at Christmas time, hence the current usage. The hautboy (oboe) was also called a 'wayte' or 'wait', from its being their chief instrument.

> I had scarcely got into bed when a strain of music seemed to break forth in the air just below the window. I listened, and found it proceeded from a band which I concluded to be the waits from some neighboring village.
>
> WASHINGTON IRVING: *The Sketch Book*, 'Christmas Eve' (1819–20)

**Wake.** A watch or vigil. The name was early applied to the all-night watch kept in church before certain holy days and to the festival kept at the annual commemoration of the dedication of a church. In due course the festive element predominated and the name came to be associated with annual fairs and revelries held at such times. Some towns in the north of England still observe local holidays called wakes.

In Ireland the term denotes the watching of the body of the deceased before the funeral, and the feasting that follows, a custom formerly also common in Wales and Scotland.

**Wake-robin.** In Britain an arum (*Arum maculatum*), usually called cuckoo pint or lords and ladies. In the USA the name is that of the trillium or jack-in-the-pulpit.

**Waking a witch.** If a witch was obdurate, the most effective way of obtaining a confession was by what was termed 'waking' her. An iron bridle or hoop was bound across her face with prongs thrust into her mouth. This was then fastened to the wall by a chain in such a manner that the victim was unable to lie down, and men were constantly at hand to keep her awake, sometimes for several days. *See also* WITCHCRAFT.

**Waldensians** or **Waldenses.** Also known by their French name as the Vaudois. Followers of Peter Waldo (or Valdes) of Lyons (*fl.*1175), who sought to govern their lives by the teaching of the Gospels and who came to be known as the Poor Men of Lyons or the Holy Paupers. The movement began about 1170, and papal prohibition of their preaching culminated in Waldo's EXCOMMUNICATION. Various heretical teachings followed and papal authority was completely rejected. Active persecution scattered them to other parts of France, Italy, Spain and elsewhere, and the movement continued until the late 17th century. Their doctrinal descendants still exist, principally in the Alpine valleys of Piedmont.

> Avenge, O Lord, thy slaughtered Saints, whose bones
> Lie scatter'd on the Alpine mountains cold.
> MILTON: 'On the Late Massacre in Piedmont' (1655)

**Wales.** From Old English *wealas*, plural of *wealh*, 'foreigner', applied to the Britons by the Anglo-Saxons. The Old English name for CORNWALL was similarly *Cornwalas*, 'Corn-foreigners'. The Welsh call their own land Cymru, 'compatriots'.

The names of many Welsh towns differ from the English and appear in their indigenous forms in official literature, at railway stations and the like. Thus Newport is Casnewydd, Swansea is Abertawe, Carmarthen is Caerfyrddin and Tenby is Dinbych-y-Pysgod. Most such names approximate in meaning, although Abertawe is 'mouth of the Tawe'. Train timetables with services running to towns in England give the Welsh names for those towns, where they exist, so that one can travel from Caerdydd (Cardiff) to Amwythig (Shrewsbury), Henffordd (Hereford), Lerpwl (Liverpool), Manceinion (Manchester) and ultimately Llundain (London). *See also* BELLS OF ABERDOVEY.

**Church in Wales.** *See under* CHURCH.

**Prince of Wales, The.** *See under* PRINCE.

**Prince of Wales's feathers, The.** *See* ICH DIEN.

**Walhalla.** *See* VALHALLA.

**Walk.** This word comes from Old English *wealcan*, 'to roll', whence *wealcare*, 'a fuller of cloth', which gave the surname Walker, as an equivalent to Fuller.

**Walk all over someone, To.** To defeat someone easily; to take advantage of them.

**Walk away from, To.** To have nothing to do with; to refuse to be involved with.

**Walk away with, To.** To win or achieve easily; to WALK OFF WITH.

**Walkies!** A verbal intimation to a dog (or a fellow human) that it is time for a walk.

**Walkie-talkie.** A small portable short-range radio containing receiver and transmitter, as used by the fighting services, the police and others.

**Walking dictionary, A.** A person with wide-ranging knowledge.

**Walking-out dress.** Uniform, smarter than that used on duty, worn by British soldiers when out of barracks.

**Walking papers.** A person's dismissal from work, as: 'He was given his walking papers.'

**Walking Stewart.** The nickname of John Stewart (1749–1822). The son of a London linen draper, he secured a post in the East India Company and went to Madras. After serious quarrels with his superiors, he resigned and started out on his travels. During the following years he went on foot through Hindustan, Persia, Nubia, Abyssinia, across the Arabian Desert, and through Europe from Constantinople to England, passing through most of the continental countries. In 1791 he crossed to America and walked through what was then known of Canada and the United States.

**Walk off with, To.** To filch and decamp with; to win a prize or contest easily.

**Walk on air, To.** To feel elated; to be exhilarated.

**Walk-on part, A.** A part in a play in which the actor has only to walk about on the stage, sometimes with a word or two to say.

**Walk on water, To.** To perform, or seem to perform, miracles; to survive failure or misfortune repeatedly. The reference is to the miracle of Christ's walking on the sea (Matthew 14:15, Mark 6:48–51, John 6:19–21).

> Tony Blair walks on water. To the frustration of the Tories, the Prime Minister and Labour continue to dominate the political scene.
> *The Times* (21 December 1998)

**Walk-out, A.** A downing of tools preparatory to a strike. *See also* INDUSTRIAL ACTION.

**Walk out with, To.** To court, as a preliminary to marriage. The expression is now dated.

**Walkover, A.** Properly, an uncontested race, won by the only competitor perambulating the course. Hence, a very easy victory with little serious competition.

**Walk someone off their feet, To.** To exhaust them with walking.

**Walk tall, To.** To hold one's head high; to maintain one's proper sense of pride and self-respect.

**Walk the boards, To.** To be an actor.

**Walk the chalk, To.** An old-established method of testing sobriety by making the suspected inebriate walk between two parallel lines chalked on the floor without stepping on either line. Hence, figuratively, to keep on the straight and narrow path of rectitude.

**Walk the plank, To.** To be put to the supreme test. Also, to be about to die. Walking the plank was a mode of disposing of prisoners at sea among pirates in the 17th century. The practice is more familiar in fiction than in fact, however, since pirates would be unlikely to kill off captives, who could be useful to them. In Robert Louis Stevenson's novel *The Master of Ballantrae* (1889), James Durie and Colonel Francis Burke enlist with the pirates who capture their ship but the brigands make their other prisoners walk the plank.

**Walk the streets, To.** To be a prostitute; to look for work in a town or city.

**Walk the wards, To.** To attend hospitals as a medical student, from the practice of accompanying the doctors when visiting patients in the wards.

**Walk through one's part, To.** To repeat one's part at rehearsal verbally, but without dressing for it or acting it.

**Walk your chalk.** Be gone. Lodgings wanted for the royal retinue were formerly requisitioned by the marshal and sergeant chamberlain, and the occupants of houses marked with chalk were turned out without further ado. The full phrase is 'Walk, you're chalked', corrupted to 'Walk your chalk'. When Marie de Medici came to England in 1638, Sieur de Labat was employed to mark 'all sorts of houses commodious for her retinue in Colchester'.

At one time it was customary for a landlord to give the tenant notice to quit by chalking the door.

> The prisoner has cut his stick, and walked his chalk, and is off to London.
>
> CHARLES KINGSLEY: *Two Years Ago*, ch i (1857)

**Birdcage Walk.** *See under* BIRD.
**Cock of the walk.** *See under* COCK.
**Devil's walking-stick.** *See under* DEVIL.
**Ghost walks, The.** *See under* GHOST.
**Lambeth walk.** *See under* LAMBETH.

**Wall. Wall-eyed.** The word comes from Old Norse *vagleygr*, from *vage*, probably 'film (over the eye)', and *auga*, 'eye'. A person is wall-eyed when the white is unusually large, and the sight defective, due to opacity of the cornea, or when there is a squint. The term is particularly used of horses.

> To this proposal I objected that walking would be twenty times more genteel than such a paltry conveyance, as Blackberry was wall-eyed, and the colt wanted a tail.
>
> OLIVER GOLDSMITH: *The Vicar of Wakefield*, ch x (1766)

**Wallflower.** The spring-flowering garden plant (*Erisymum cheiri*) is so called because it grows on old walls. Young women who sit by the wall during a dance, either because they have no partner or because they are shy, are also called wallflowers.

**Wall game, The.** A version of football at Eton, so called because it is played against the wall that divides the Slough Road from the Lower Playing Fields. Three players on each side act as 'walls', forming a line against the bricks. The game is started with a 'bully' in the centre of the wall. One 'wall' forms down with his shoulder against the wall while the two other 'walls' back him. The ball is placed between the feet of the two first opposing 'walls' and the game begins.

**Wall of death.** A fairground attraction consisting of a giant cylinder, around the inside walls of which a motorcyclist rides, often blindfolded. *See also* WHEEL OF DEATH.

**Wall of Severus, The.** The Emperor Severus (146–211), who spent the last three years of his life in Britain, thoroughly strengthened the fortified line between the Tyne and Solway originally constructed by Hadrian. His work was so extensive that some ancient authorities speak of him as its original builder. *See also* ANTONINE WALL; HADRIAN'S WALL.

**Walls have ears.** Things uttered in secret get rumoured abroad; there are listeners everywhere, and you'd better be careful. Certain rooms in the LOUVRE were said to be so constructed in the time of Catherine de Medici (1519–89) that what was said in one room could be heard distinctly in another. It was by this contrivance that the suspicious queen became acquainted with state secrets and plots. The tubes of communication were called the *auriculaires*. *See also* DIONYSIUS' EAR.

**Wall Street.** The street in lower Manhattan, New York City, that contains the STOCK EXCHANGE and offices of major banking and insurance concerns. It is the financial centre of the USA, hence the name is a synonym for the American stock market and 'big business' generally. The street is on the site of a wooden wall built by the Dutch *c*.1653 against a possible Indian or English attack. It was never tested in battle before the English demolished it in 1699.

**Wall-to-wall.** Literally, running from one wall to another in a room, as a fited carpet. Figuratively, continuous; endless, as wall-to-wall sports coverage on a television channel.

**Antonine Wall.** *See under* ANTONINE.
**Atlantic Wall.** *See under* ATLANTIC.
**Back to the wall.** *See under* BACK.
**Bang** or **run one's head against a brick** or **stone wall, To.** *See under* BANG.
**Chinese wall.** *See under* CHINESE.
**Drive someone up the wall, To.** *See under* DRIVE.
**Drive to the wall, To.** *See under* DRIVE.
**Fly on the wall, A.** *See under* FLY.
**Garlic Wall.** *See under* GARLIC.
**Go to the wall, To.** To be ruined; collapse financially. This is in allusion to another phrase, 'laid by the wall', i.e. dead but not buried.
**Go up the wall, To.** To become crazy or furious.
**Great Wall of China.** *See under* GREAT.
**Hadrian's Wall.** *See under* HADRIAN.
**Hole in the wall.** *See under* HOLE.
**Off the wall.** *See under* OFF.
**Party wall.** *See under* PARTY.
**Trajan's Wall.** *See under* TRAJAN.
**Wailing Wall.** *See under* WAILING.
**Weakest go to the wall, The.** *See under* WEAK.

**Wooden walls, The.** *See under* WOOD.

**Writing on the wall, The.** *See under* WRITE.

**Wallace. Wallace's larder.** Similar to the DOUGLAS LARDER. It consisted of the dead bodies of the garrison of Ardrossan, in Ayrshire, cast into the dungeon keep. The castle was surprised by William WALLACE in his campaigns against Edward I of England (r.1272–1307).

**Wallace's line.** A line of demarcation in Indonesia running from the Indian Ocean northwards between Bali and Lombok, through the Makassar Straits (between Borneo and the Celebes), then northeastward, south of Mindanao, into the Philippine Sea. It separates the fauna of the Indo-Malayan region from the widely divergent species of the Australian region, which includes New Guinea and the islands to the eastward. It is named after Alfred Russel Wallace (1823–1913), the English naturalist who defined it.

**Sir William Wallace.** The Scottish hero (*c*.1274–1305) who won a victory over the English at Stirling Bridge in 1297 but was hanged, disembowelled, beheaded and quartered at West SMITHFIELD, the quarters being sent to Newcastle, BERWICK, Stirling and Perth.

**Wallah.** Anglo-Indian for a man of specified attributes or duties, as 'dhobi-wallah', the Indian washerman, 'bathroom-wallah', the man who looks after the bathrooms in a hotel, 'punkawallah', the man who waves a fan, and so on. A 'competition wallah' was a successful competitor in the Indian Civil Service examinations introduced in 1856, as distinct from one who obtained his appointment under the old system of influence. The MERCHANT-IVORY FILM *Shakespeare Wallah* (1965) is based on the experiences of the actor Geoffrey Kendal and his family as they toured India staging Shakespeare's plays in the 1940s and 1950s. *Wallah* is a Hindi suffix denoting an agent, as '-er' in English.

**Wallbanger, Harvey.** *See under* HARVEY.

**Wallop.** To thrash; properly, to boil with a noisy bubbling sound. 'Gallop' is a variant of 'wallop'. It is also a slang term for ALE.

**Walnut.** The foreign nut, called in Middle English *walnote*, from Old English *wealh*, 'foreign', since it came from Persia.

> Some difficulty there is in cracking the name thereof: why Wall-nuts, having no affinity with a Wall, whose substantial Trees need to borrow nothing thence for their support. Nor are they so called because walled with Shells, which is common to all other Nuts. The truth is *Gual* or *Wall* in the old Dutch signifieth strange or exotick (whence *Welsh* that is Foreigners); these Nuts being no Natives of England or Europe.
>
> THOMAS FULLER: *Worthies of England*, ii (1662)

**Walpurgis. Walpurgis Night** (German *Walpurgisnacht*). The eve of MAY DAY, when the witch world was supposed to hold high revelry under its chief, the Devil, on high places, such as the Brocken, the highest point of the Harz Mountains. Walpurga was an English nun (*c*.710–*c*.779) who went as a missionary to Germany and became abbess of Heidenheim. The date of the transfer of her remains to Eichstätt – 1 May – led to her coincidental association with the rites of an earlier pagan festival. Her feast-day is 25 February. *See also* SPECTRE OF THE BROCKEN.

**Walpurgis oil.** A bituminous kind of oil exuding from the rock at Eichstätt in which the relics of St Walpurga were deposited. It was supposed to have miraculous healing and curative properties.

**Walstan, St.** In England the patron saint of husbandmen. He worked as a farm labourer in Norfolk and was noted for the austerity and piety of his life and for his charity. He died in 1016 and is usually depicted with a scythe in his hand and cattle in the background.

**Walter. Walter Mitty.** A fantasist who daydreams of achievements he could never realise in ordinary life. He was the creation of the American writer James Thurber and appears in his short story *The Secret Life of Walter Mitty* (1939).

> 'From that moment he was in a fantasy world of Walter Mitty. He claimed he was Lady Rendlesham's son and soon even believed it himself,' Mr Lewis said.
>
> *The Times* (16 April 1983)

**Sir Walter Raleigh.** *See under* RALEIGH.

**Waltzing Matilda.** An Australian phrase made famous by the Australian poet A.B. (Banjo) Paterson (1864–1941). It means carrying or humping one's bag or pack as a tramp does. Henry Lawson (*The Romance of Song*) says: 'Travelling with SWAG in Australia is variously and picturesquely described as "humping bluey", "walking Matilda", "humping Matilda", "humping your drum", "being on the wallaby".'

The reason for the tramp's roll being called a 'Matilda' is obscure. To 'waltz' conveys the impression of tramping along with one's pack jogging up and down. *See also* BILLABONG.

> Once a jolly swagman camped by a billabong,
> Under the shade of a coolibah tree;
> And he sang as he watched and waited till his 'Billy' boiled:
> 'You'll come a-waltzing, Matilda, with me.'

**Wampum.** Shell beads made and strung for ornament, currency, ceremonial gift belts and the like, by Native American tribes. They were used as money as late as the 19th century, but machine-made, mass-produced 'wampum' with resultant inflation first caused its obsolescence in the eastern states. The name comes from Narraganset *wampumpeag*, from *wampan*, 'light', and *api*, 'string', with *-ag* the plural suffix.

When he came in triumph homeward
With the sacred Belt of Wampum.

H.W. LONGFELLOW: *The Song of Hiawatha*, ii (1858)

**Wandering Jew, The.** The central figure of the widespread later medieval legend, which tells of a JEW who insulted or spurned Christ when he was bearing the cross to CALVARY and was condemned to wander over the face of the earth until Judgement Day.

The usual form of the legend says that he was Ahasuerus, a cobbler, who refused to allow Christ to rest at his door, saying, 'Get off! Away with you, away!' Christ replied, 'Truly I go away, and that quickly, but tarry thou till I come.'

An earlier tradition, related in the *Chronicle of St Alban's Abbey* (1228), has it that the Wandering Jew was Cartaphilus, the doorkeeper of the judgement hall in the service of Pontius PILATE. He struck Christ as he led him forth, saying, 'Go on faster, Jesus', whereupon the latter replied: 'I am going, but thou shalt tarry till I come again.' The same *Chronicle*, continued by Matthew Paris (*c*.1200–59), tells that Cartaphilus was baptized by Ananias, and received the name of Joseph. At the end of every hundred years he falls into a trance, and wakes up as a young man of about 30.

In German legend he is associated with John Buttadaeus, seen at Antwerp in the 13th century, again in the 15th, and the third time in the 16th. His last appearance was in 1868 at Salt Lake City. In the French version he is named Isaac Laquedom or Lakedion. Another story has it that he was Salathiel ben-Sadi, who appeared and disappeared towards the close of the 16th century at Venice, in so sudden a manner as to attract the notice of all Europe. Yet another legend connects him with the WILD HUNTSMAN.

There are various creeping or trailing plants called wandering Jew, the name most often being applied to species of *Tradescantia* and to *Zebrina pendula*.

**Wansdyke.** WODEN's dike. A system of dikes, perhaps built by the Romano-Britons, stretching some 60 miles (96.5km) from Inkpen in Berkshire to Portishead in Somerset. It was probably a defence against the English invaders. *See also* GRIMSDYKE; OFFA'S DYKE.

**Wantley, The Dragon of.** *See under* DRAGON.

**Wapentake.** A subdivision of a county similar to a HUNDRED, found in Yorkshire and other areas of once strong Danish influence, such as Derbyshire, Leicestershire, Lincolnshire, Nottinghamshire and Rutland. The word is of Scandinavian origin meaning literally 'weapon-taking', probably signifying a show of arms when voting in an assembly.

**Wappenshaw.** A 'weapon show', the early spelling being 'wappinschaw'. This was formerly the Scottish term for the review of men under arms to check that they were properly equipped according to rank. It is now sometimes used of a rifle-shooting competition.

**War. War baby.** A baby born in wartime, especially the illegitimate offspring of a serviceman.

**War bride.** A soldier's foreign bride, met as a result of wartime postings or operations.

**War cloud.** A threatening international situation, literally a cloud of dust and smoke rising from a battlefield. The phrase (Greek *polemioi nephros*) occurs in the ILIAD.

**War cry.** A phrase or name shouted to rally one's troops in batle; a SLOGAN.

**War dance.** A ceremonial dance traditionally performed by Native Americans either before going into battle or after a victory.

**War game.** Originally known by its German name *Kriegsspiel*, it was introduced in 1824 by a Prussian officer, Lieutenant von Reiswitz, who completed and improved on his father's design. It depends on the use of maps as battlefields in miniature and blocks or counters representing troops and the like, for the purpose of instructing officers in military tactics. In modern times the computer is used to this end.

**Warhead.** The explosive head of a torpedo or bomb.

**Warhorse.** A veteran or old warrior. An allusion to the charger formerly used in battle.

**Warlord.** A military commander or commander-in-chief.

**War of attrition.** A war in which each side seeks to wear the other out. The expression dates from the First World War. Fabius CUNCTATOR employed tactics of this type.

**War of nerves.** Tactics to undermine morale by threats, rumours, sabotage and similar psychological means.

**War of the Brown Bull, The.** Also known as the 'cattle raid of Cooley' or 'Cuailnge'. In Irish legend, the struggle provoked by Queen MAEVE (Medb) of Connaught who led the forces of four provinces to capture the great bull Donn, the Brown One of Cuailnge, belonging to Duaire, an Ulster chief. Her husband Ailill had a great bull called Finnbhenach ('white-horned'), and she wished to equal his possessions. The Brown Bull was taken by stratagem, but Maeve's forces were driven into retreat by CUCHULAIN and the men of Ulster. The Brown One fought the White Bull all over Ireland until the latter was slain, and the Brown Bull then rushed northwards until its heart burst.

**War of the elements.** A storm or natural catastrophe.

**War paint.** The paint applied to their faces by Native Americans and other peoples to make their appearance terrifying before going out on the warpath. 'Putting on one's war paint' is a phrase applied figuratively to getting ready to enter energetically into a dispute or, of a woman, to putting on elaborate make-up in order to overcome her rivals.

**Wars of the Roses, The.** The usual name given to the civil wars in England (1455–85) between LANCASTRIANS and YORKISTS, which ended in the triumph of Henry Tudor (Henry VII) at Bosworth. The wars were partly dynastic and partly private wars of the nobility, occasioned by the weakness of government under Henry VI (r.1422–61, 1470–1) and the collapse of law and order. The name is not really historical and appears to derive from Sir Walter Scott.

> He now turned his eyes to the regaining of those rich and valuable foreign possessions which had been lost during the administration of the feeble Henry VI, and the civil discords so dreadfully prosecuted in the wars of the White and Red Roses.
>
> *Anne of Geierstein*, ch vii (1829)

There is no contemporary record of the use of the term for these struggles for political control. *See also* RED ROSE; TUDOR ROSE; WHITE ROSE.

**Barons' War, The.** *See under* BARON.
**Bishops' Wars, The.** *See under* BISHOP.
**Civil war.** *See under* CIVIL.
**Cold war.** *See under* COLD.
**Council of war.** *See under* COUNCIL.
**Dogs of war, The.** *See under* DOG.
**Great War, The.** *See under* WAR.
**Guerrilla war.** *See under* GUERRILLA.
**Holy War, A.** *See under* HOLY.
**Honours of war.** *See under* HONOURS.
**Hundred Years' War, The.** *See under* HUNDRED.

**In the wars, To be.** To be, or appear to be, injured or a victim of rough treatment. One might thus say to a normally neatly dressed person, seeing them the worse for wear: 'You look as if you've been in the wars.'

**On the warpath.** Bent on some hostile course; out looking for trouble. In its proper sense a warpath is a warlike expedition of American Indians.

**Opium War.** *See under* OPIUM.
**Potato War.** *See under* POTATO.
**Sacred war, The.** *See under* SACRED.
**Seven Weeks' War, The.** *See under* SEVEN.
**Seven Years' War, The.** *See under* SEVEN.
**Shooting war.** *See under* SHOOT.
**Star Wars.** *See under* STAR.
**Terrapin War.** *See under* TERRAPIN.
**Thirty Years' War, The.** *See under* THIRTY.
**Trojan War.** *See under* TROJAN.
**Tug of war.** *See under* TUG.
**Turf war.** *See under* TURF.

**Ward** (Old English *weard*, 'guard', 'protector'). A district under the charge of a warden. The word is the equivalent of HUNDRED in some northern counties of England, and also in parts of Scotland. In medieval times, the wardens were appointed by the English and Scottish governments to watch over the border districts.

The word is also applied to administrative divisions of a town or city, a large room or division of a hospital, a part of a lock or key that prevents the door being opened by the wrong key, a minor placed under the care of a guardian and so on. *See also* WATCH AND WARD.

**Wardroom.** In British warships, a mess shared by the officers (except the captain). The name is not found before the 18th century and derives from the compartment known as the Ward Robe, which was used as a store for valuables captured from prizes. It came to be used for officers of the rank of lieutenant upwards. *See also* GUN ROOM.

**Artemus Ward.** The name of an imaginary showman and writer, the guise adopted by the American humorist, Charles Farrer Browne (1834–67), for a series of books that became popular in both America and England. Browne is said to have adopted the name from that of an actual showman known to him.

**Portsoken ward.** *See under* PORTSOKEN.
**Vintry ward.** *See under* WARD.
**Walk the wards, To.** *See under* WALK.
**Watch and ward.** *See under* WARD.

**Warden pear.** A pear said to be so called from Warden in Bedfordshire, but quite probably from Old French *wardant* ('keeping'), because it is a type that keep well.

**Wardour Street English.** The affected use of archaic words and phrases. A term first applied by William Morris (1834–96) in 1888 to a translation of the ODYSSEY, couched in language that reminded him of the pseudo-antique furniture that in those days was sold in Wardour Street, London. This thoroughfare in the present century came to be associated with the film industry.

**Ware. Great Bed of Ware, The.** *See under* GREAT.
**Palissy ware.** *See under* PALISSY.
**Queen's ware.** *See under* QUEEN.
**Sèvres ware.** *See under* SÈVRES.

**Warkworth, The Hermit of.** *See under* HERMIT.

**Warlock.** An evil spirit; a WIZARD. The word represents Old English *wǣrloga*, 'traitor', literally 'oath liar'.

**Warm.** The word is used colloquially with much the same force as 'hot', so that 'warm thanks' are hearty thanks, 'warm support' is ardent support, and 'warm praise' is high praise.

**Warming-pan baby, The.** The OLD PRETENDER, so nicknamed from the widely circulated story that he was introduced into the lying-in chamber of Mary of Modena, queen of James II, in a warming pan and that her own child was stillborn. Hence 'warming pans' as a nickname for JACOBITES.

**Warm the bell, To.** In nautical parlance, to do something before the proper time, e.g. to prepare to leave early. The idea seems to be that if a bell is warmed, it will move faster or strike sooner.

**Warm the cockles of one's heart, To.** To warm and gratify one's deepest feelings. The cockles of the heart are its ventricles, named by some in Latin as *cochleae cordis*, from *cochlea*, 'snail', alluding to their shape.

**As warm as toast.** *See under* AS.

**British warm, A.** *See under* BRITISH.

**House-warming, A.** *See under* HOUSE.

**Warning. Early warning.** *See under* EARLY.

**Scarborough warning.** *See under* SCARBOROUGH.

**Shepherd's warning.** *See under* SHEPHERD.

**Warrant. Death warrant.** *See under* DEATH.

**General warrants.** *See under* GENERAL.

**Warrior. Warrior Queen, The.** BOADICEA.

**Unknown Warrior, The.** *See under* UNKNOWN.

**Wart.** An army name for a second lieutenant, from the single 'pip' or badge of rank on his shoulders. *See also* SNOTTY.

**Warts and all.** Said of a description, biography or the like that seeks to give the rounded portrait, including the blemishes and defects. Oliver Cromwell, whose face was not without blemishes, when having his portrait painted by Sir Peter Lely (1618–80), apparently told him to 'Remark all these roughnesses, pimples, warts, and everything as you see me.'

**Wartburg, Contest of.** *See under* CONTEST.

**Warwick. Warwick, Guy of.** *See under* GUY.

**Warwick shakes his bells.** Beware of danger, for Warwick is in the field: 'Trojans beware, ACHILLES has donned his armour.' A metaphor from falconry, the bells being those of a HAWK.

> Neither the king, nor he that loves him best,
> The proudest he that holds up Lancaster,
> Dares stir a wing if Warwick shake his bells.
> SHAKESPEARE: *Henry VI, Pt III*, I, i (1590)

**Warwick the Kingmaker.** *See* KINGMAKER.

**Wash. Washed out** or **up.** Exhausted; done up; with no strength or spirit left.

**Wash one's dirty linen in public, To.** To expose the family skeleton to the public gaze; to discuss openly private affairs that are more or less discreditable.

**Wash one's hands, To.** To go to the lavatory. One of many euphemisms. A lavatory was at one time simply a room with washing facilities. Hence the word's ultimate origin in Latin *lavare*, 'to wash'.

**Wash one's hands of something, To.** To have nothing to do with a matter after having been concerned with it; to abandon or 'drop' it. The allusion is to PILATE's washing his hands at the trial of Jesus.

> When Pilate saw that he could prevail nothing, but that rather a tumult was made, he took water, and washed his hands before the multitude, saying, I am innocent of the blood of this just person: see ye to it.
> Matthew 27:24

**Washout, A.** A fiasco; a failure. To wash out as a verb is to cancel, to disregard, from the times when naval signal messages were taken down on a slate, which was washed clean when the message had been transmitted to the proper quarters.

**It got lost in the wash.** It just disappeared, as items sometimes get lost in the laundry. The expression is also sometimes punningly used with reference to King John's loss of royal treasure and baggage when his convoy of horses and wagons was caught and swallowed up by the incoming tide on the sands of the Wash in 1216.

**It will all come out in the wash.** It will all be ultimately clarified or resolved, as dirt and stains are removed by washing.

**That won't wash.** That story or excuse won't do at all; you'll have to think of a better tale than that. Said of an explanation or excuse that is palpably false, far-fetched or exaggerated.

**Washington, The Bird of.** *See* BIRD OF FREEDOM.

**Wassail** (Old Norse *ves heill*, 'be in health', related to Middle English *wœs hœil* in the same sense). A salutation, especially over the spiced ale cup at the New Year, hence called the 'wassail bowl'.

Joseph Strutt (*Sports and Pastimes of the People of England*, III, iv (1801)) says: 'Wassail, or rather the wassail bowl, which was a bowl of spiced ale, formerly carried about by young women on New-year's eve, who went from door to door in their several parishes singing a few couplets of homely verses composed for the purpose, and presented the liquor to the inhabitants of the house where they called, expecting a small gratuity in return.' *See also* HEALTHS.

**Waste. Waste words, To.** To talk in vain. The phrase is mostly used negatively, as: 'I won't waste any more words talking to you'.

**Natural wastage.** *See under* NATURAL.

**Wat.** An old name for a hare, short for Walter. Compare NEDDY for a donkey, TOM for cat, Jenny wren and so on.

> By this poor Wat, far off upon a hill,
> Stands on his hinder legs, with listening ear.
> SHAKESPEARE: *Venus and Adonis* (1593)

**Watch.** In nautical usage, the time during which part of a ship's complement is on duty, usually four hours except during the DOGWATCHES of two hours each, by which the variation in the watches kept by any individual is effected. Ship's companies are arranged in two watches, port and starboard, each of which is usually subdivided thus providing four groups for normal watch-keeping duties. The day is regulated according to the following watches:

1200–1600: afternoon watch (12 noon to 4 pm)
1600–1800: first dogwatch (4 to 6 pm)
1800–2000: second dogwatch (6 to 8 pm)
2000–2400: first watch (8 pm to 12 midnight)
2400–0400: middle watch (12 midnight to 4 am)
0400–0800: morning watch (4 am to 8 am)
0800–1200: forenoon watch (8 am to 12 noon)

Formerly the First Watch was usually called the 'First night watch'. Sometimes duties are arranged in three watches but this does not, of course, affect the time-keeping system shown above. *See also* ONE BELL IN THE LAST DOGWATCH; THREE BELLS.

Historically, the Watch refers to the body of men in towns who patrolled the streets at night before the introduction of police forces, which, in the boroughs, were under the control of the Watch Committee until their amalgamation with the County Police in 1967. *See also* COCKCROW; WAKE; WATCH AND WARD.

**Watch and ward.** Continuous vigilance, 'watch' and 'ward' being the terms formerly used to denote a look-out for rioters and robbers by night and by day respectively. Townships were made responsible for appointing watchmen in the 13th century.

**Watchdog.** In the figurative sense, a person or body, such as a financial regulator, that monitors the rights and procedures of others.

> Watchdog orders new pensions inquiry.
> *The Times* (headline) (20 October 1998)

**Watched pot never boils, A.** Said as a mild reproof to someone who is impatient. Watching and anxiety will not make things happen any faster.

**Watchful waiting.** The phrase used by Woodrow Wilson (President 1913–21) in 1913 to describe his policy of non-recognition of the Mexican Government of General Huerta. It did not last long as, in 1914, the Americans occupied Vera Cruz. The phrase was previously used by President Jackson (OLD HICKORY) in 1836.

**Watching brief, A.** A state of interest in a matter which does not directly concern one. In the legal sense a watching brief is one held by a barrister following a case for a client not directly involved.

**Watch it!** Look out! Take care!

**Watch Night.** 31 December, to see the Old Year out and the New Year in by a religious service. John Wesley (1703–91) introduced it among the METHODISTS, and it has been adopted by other Christian denominations.

**Watch one's step, To.** Literally, to take care where one walks. Figuratively, to proceed cautiously. A person taking liberties may be warned: 'You'd better watch your step.'

**Watch on the Rhine, The** (German *Die Wacht am Rhein*). A German national song, which achieved a place of honour with *Deutschland über Alles* ('Germany over All') in the former German Empire. It was written by Max Schneckenburger in 1840 at a time when French policies were suspect.

**Watch the birdie, To.** To be attentive. Photographers formerly held up a model bird for young children to look at when having their picture taken. When it was time to click the shutter, they would say, 'Watch the birdie!'

**Watchword.** A word given to sentries as a signal that one has the right of admission; a password. Hence, a motto, word or phrase symbolizing or epitomizing the principles of a party or the like. *See also* SHIBBOLETH.

**Anchor watch.** *See under* ANCHOR.

**Black Watch.** *See under* BLACK.

**Fire watcher.** *See under* FIRE.

**Marching watch.** *See under* MARCH.

**Neighbourhood Watch.** *See under* NEIGHBOURHOOD.

**Water.** It was once believed that no enchantment could survive running water. Robert Burns' poem 'Tam o' Shanter' (1791), for example, tells the story of a farmer, Tam, who is able to escape the witches pursuing him only once he is halfway over the bridge across the Doon.

**Watergate.** In the USA an area of flats and offices beside the River Potomac, Washington, D.C., which gave its name to a major political scandal. An illegal bugging attempt was made by Republicans at the Watergate headquarters of the Democratic Party during the 1972 elections followed by attempts to cover up the affair. The subsequent resignation and prosecution of senior WHITE HOUSE officials and further evidence of corruption eventually led to the resignation of the Republican President Richard Nixon (1913–94, President 1968–74) when threatened with impeachment. *See also* -GATE *under* GATE.

**Watering hole.** A pool where animals drink, or, in human terms, a favourite pub or bar.

> The 'Jampot' [Jamaica Wine House], one of the City's best-known watering-holes.
> *The Times* (29 December 1994)

**Watering place.** A now dated term for a spa or seaside resort, where one can drink the water or bathe in it.

> Brighton, which stands in the first rank among English watering-places.
> *The National Gazetteer of Great Britain and Ireland* (1868)

**Waterman.** A boatman, especially one who rows a boat for hire. The Thames watermen were a feature of old London. *See also* DOGGET'S COAT AND BADGE.

Hackney coach stands and cab ranks were each supplied with a licensed waterman, whose duty it was to water the cab horses, among other things.

**Watermark.** A design impressed into paper by fine wire during manufacture and while the paper is still wet. Watermarks were used as early as 1282 and served to identify the products of each paper mill.

The watermark has in many instances been the origin of paper trade nomenclature. Thus the mark of the cap and bells gave foolscap, the posthorn gave post, the pot gave pott, and the crown and elephant similarly came to denote sizes of paper.

**Water of jealousy, The.** According to Mosaic law, if a woman was known to have committed adultery, she was to be put to death (Deuteronomy 22:22). If, however, the husband only suspected his wife of infidelity but had no proof of it, he might take her before the SANHEDRIN to be examined, and 'bitter water' was prepared from holy water and the dust of the floor of the tabernacle. The priest then said to the woman: 'If thou hast not gone aside to uncleanness with another instead of thy husband, be thou free from this bitter water that causeth the curse.' If she had 'gone aside', the priest wrote the curses on a roll, sprinkled it with water and gave the woman the 'water of jealousy' to drink (Numbers 5:11–29).

**Water Poet, The.** John Taylor (1580–1654), the witty and sometimes scurrilous Thames WATERMAN, who early left Gloucester Grammar School for London, having failed at Latin accidence (grammar). He wrote many books and verse pamphlets and in his closing days kept an alehouse in Long Acre.

> Taylor, their better Charon, lends an oar,
> (Once swan of Thames, tho' now he sings no more).
>
> ALEXANDER POPE: *The Dunciad*, iii (1728)

**Water sky.** The term used by Arctic navigators to denote a dark or brown sky, indicating an open sea. An ice sky is a white one, or a sky tinted with orange or rose colour, indicative of a frozen sea.

**Water stock, To.** To add extra shares. Say a trust consists of 1000 shares of £50 each, and the profit available for dividend is 40 per cent. The managers 'water the stock', i.e. add another 1000 fully paid-up shares to the original 1000. There are now 2000 shares, and the dividend, instead of £40, is reduced to £20, but the shares are more easily sold, and the shareholders are increased in number.

**Water torture.** A form of torture in which the victim is exposed to the incessant dripping of water on the forehead or, in a psychological variant, to the sound of water dripping. *See also* CHINESE WATER TORTURE.

**Water under the bridge.** Events that are over and done with; past history.

**Water witch.** Another name for a dowser. *See also* DIVINING ROD.

**Angel water.** *See under* ANGEL.

**As weak as water.** *See under* AS.

**Barley water.** *See under* BARLEY.

**Back water, To.** *See under* BACK.

**Bilge water.** *See under* BILGE.

**Blood is thicker than water.** *See under* BLOOD.

**Carry water to the river, To.** *See under* CARRY.

**Cast one's bread upon the waters, To.** *See under* CAST.

**Chinese water torture.** *See under* CHINESE.

**Clary water.** *See under* CLARY.

**Come hell or high water.** *See under* COME.

**Dancing water.** *See under* DANCE.

**Dead water.** *See under* DEAD.

**Diamond of the first water.** *See under* DIAMOND.

**Father of the waters, The.** *See under* FATHER.

**Fish in troubled water, To.** *See under* FISH.

**Fish out of water.** *See under* FISH.

**Hold water, To.** *See under* HOLD.

**Holy water.** *See under* HOLY.

**In deep water.** *See under* DEEP.

**In hot water, To be.** *See under* HOT.

**Keep one's head above water, To.** *See under* HEAD.

**King of waters, The.** *See under* KING.

**King over the Water, The.** *See under* KING.

**Like water off a duck's back.** *See under* LIKE.

**Make one's mouth water, To.** *See under* MOUTH.

**Make water, To.** To urinate.

**Milk and water.** *See under* MILK.

**Of the first water.** *See under* OF.

**Ordeal by cold water.** *See under* ORDEAL.

**Ordeal of boiling water.** *See under* ORDEAL.

**Pass water, To.** *See under* PASS.

**Pour oil on troubled waters, To.** *See under* POUR.

**Rag water.** *See under* RAG.

**Smooth** or **still waters run deep.** *See under* SMOOTH.

**Surfeit water.** *See under* SURFEIT.

**Take the waters, To.** To visit a spa for health reasons, a common routine among fashionable folk in the 18th and 19th centuries. Spas take their name from the town of Spa in Belgium.

**Territorial waters.** *See* THREE-MILE LIMIT.

**Throw** or **pour cold water on a scheme, To.** *See under* THROW.

**Tread water, To.** *See under* TREAD.

**Turn on the waterworks, To.** *See under* TURN.

**Virginia Water.** *See under* VIRGINIA.

**Walk on water, To.** *See under* WALK.

**Waterloo. Waterloo Cup, The.** The 'Derby' (*see* DERBY STAKES) of the coursing fraternity, the great dog race held annually at Altcar during three days in February. It was founded in 1836 by William Lynn, the sporting owner of the

Waterloo Hotel in Liverpool (whence its name). Lynn was also the founder of the GRAND NATIONAL, run at Aintree.

**Waterloo Handicap, The.** The principal event in crown green bowling, held annually (since 1907) at the Waterloo Hotel, Blackpool.

**Meet one's Waterloo, To.** *See under* MEET.

**Watford.** The Hertfordshire town, 16 miles (26km) northwest of London, is popularly reckoned to mark the outer limit of urban-based civilization, so that everything and everybody 'north of Watford' are in a supposed cultural wilderness. Watford was itself presumably chosen for this key role as it lies on the M1, the main thoroughfare to London. This Watford is sometimes confused, especially by non-motorists, with the Watford Gap, which is a service station, also on the M1, but north of Daventry in Northamptonshire. It lies in a broad valley at the northern end of the Cotswolds at the point where road, rail and canal routes run close together through the hills. It also has a 'marker' role, and is sometimes regarded as the southern boundary of the Midlands.

**Watling Street.** The great Roman road, beginning at Dover and running through Canterbury to London, thence through St Albans and Dunstable, along the boundary of Leicestershire and Warwickshire to Wroxeter on the Severn. In the late 9th century it became the boundary between English and Danish territory. There are several other sections of road so called.

The name is from Old English *Wæclinga stræt*, the road leading to *Wæclingaceaster* (now St Albans).

**Watson. Watson's Plot.** Also known as the Bye Plot because of its supposed connection with the MAIN PLOT or Cobham's Plot. In 1603 William Watson, a Roman Catholic priest, and others plotted to capture James I and to secure religious toleration from him. Some PURITANS collaborated, but the plans were revealed by a Jesuit and Watson was beheaded.

**Dr Watson.** *See* HOLMES, SHERLOCK.

**Wattle.** Australian settlers built wattle-and-daub huts after the English manner from twigs of the abundant acacia trees, which hence became known as wattles. Wattle Day is a national festival in Australia, held on 1 August or 1 September, according to the peak of the flowering of the wattle in each state.

**Wave. Waves.** In the USA the women's section of the Naval Reserve. The name is formed by the initial letters of Women Accepted for Voluntary Emergency Service.

**Wavy Navy.** The popular name for the former Royal Naval Volunteer Reserve (RNVR), whose officers wore gold distinction lace made in wavy lines instead of straight, as worn on the sleeves of regular officers belonging to the 'Straight Navy'. The RNVR lost its separate existence, after a fine wartime record, in 1957, when it was combined with the Royal Naval Reserve (RNR). *See also* WAVES; WRENS.

**Brain wave.** *See under* BRAIN.

**Mexican wave.** *See* MEXICAN WAVE.

**New Wave.** *See under* NEW.

**Tenth wave, The.** *See under* TEN.

**Third wave.** *See under* THIRD.

**Waverley Novels.** The novels of Sir Walter Scott (1771–1832), which took their name from the first of the series, the title of which was derived from the ruined Waverley Abbey, near Farnham, Surrey. *See also* GREAT UNKNOWN.

**Wax.** Somewhat dated slang for temper, anger, as 'he's in an awful wax', he's in a regular rage. Hence 'waxy', irritated, vexed, angry. The term may derive from 'to wax angry', 'wax' here meaning 'grow'.

**Wax in someone's hands, To be.** To be easily influenced by them; to let them do with one what they will.

**Man of wax, A.** *See under* MAN.

**Way. Way of all flesh, The.** Death. Samuel Butler (1835–1902) had a novel of this title published posthumously in 1903.

**Way of the Cross, The.** *See* STATIONS OF THE CROSS.

**Way of the world, The.** The customary way of proceeding; the usual way of doing things. William Congreve has a play of this title (1700).

**Way out.** Said of something unusual, excellent or eccentric. It is so remarkable that it deviates by far from the norm.

**Ways and means.** Methods and means of accomplishing one's purposes, resources, facilities.

**Appian Way.** *See under* APPIAN.

**Clear the way, To.** *See under* CLEAR.

**Committee of Ways and Means, The.** *See under* COMMITTEE.

**Cut both ways, To.** *See under* CUT.

**Fall by the wayside, To.** *See under* FALL.

**Feel one's way, To.** *See under* FEEL.

**Find one's way, To.** *See under* FIND.

**Flaminian Way.** *See under* FLAMINIAN.

**Fosse Way.** *See under* FOSSE.

**Get** or **have one's own way, To.** To achieve what one wants or needs. To have it both ways, by contrast, is to benefit by two things that would otherwise contradict each other. The expression is usually negative, as: 'You can't have it both ways: either you come with me or you stay here.'

**Go down the wrong way, To.** Said of food that enters the windpipe instead of the gullet.

**Go out of one's way, To.** To take special trouble; to experience inconvenience (in doing something).

**Have a way with, To.** To have a special skill or 'knack', as: 'She has a way with horses.'

**Icknield Way.** *See under* ICKNIELD.

**In no way.** By no means; on no account; not at all.

**Look the other way, To.** *See under* LOOK.

**Milky Way, The.** The GALAXY.

**No way.** *See under* NO.

**On the way out.** Diminishing; becoming antiquated or obsolete.

**Parting of the ways, The.** *See under* PART.

**Pay one's way, To.** *See under* PAY.

**Pilgrims' Way.** *See under* PILGRIM.

**Right of way.** *See under* RIGHT.

**See one's way, To.** *See under* SEE.

**Six-foot way, The.** *See under* SIX.

**Third way.** *See under* THIRD.

**Under way.** *See under* UNDER.

**Wayland Smith.** The English form of the Scandinavian *Volund* (German *Wieland*), a wonderful and supernatural smith and lord of the elves (*see* ELF), a kind of VULCAN. The legend is found in the EDDA and is alluded to in BEOWULF. He was bound apprentice to Mimir, the smith. King Nidung cut the sinews in his feet in order to retain his services, but he eventually flew away in a feather robe which had been first tested out by his brother EGIL. The legend has much in common with that of DAEDALUS.

Tradition has placed his forge in a megalithic monument known as Wayland's Smithy near the WHITE HORSE in Berkshire (now Oxfordshire), where it was said that if a traveller tied up his horse, left sixpence for fee and retired from sight, he would find the horse shod on his return.

> Neither the tradition of Alfred's Victory, or of the celebrated Pusey Horn, are better preserved in Berkshire than the wild legend of Wayland Smith.
>
> SIR WALTER SCOTT: *Kenilworth*, ch xiii (1821)

**Wayzgoose.** An annual dinner, picnic or BEANFEAST especially one given to, or held by, those employed in a printing house. 'Wayz' ('wase') is an obsolete word for a bundle of hay, straw or stubble, hence a harvest goose or fat goose, which is the crowning dish of the entertainment.

**We.** Used of himself or herself by a sovereign, the ROYAL 'WE' is said to have been used first by Richard I (r.1189–99). His Charter to Winchester (1190) reads: *'Sciatis nos concessisse civibus nostris Wintoniae ...'* ('Know ye that we have granted our citizens of Winchester ...'), while an earlier charter of his father, Henry II (r.1154–89), reads: *'Sciatis me concessisse civibus meis Wyntoniae ...'* ('Know ye that I have granted my citizens of Winchester ...').

'We' is also used by the editor of a newspaper or the writer of unsigned articles, as representing the journal for which he or she is writing and to avoid the appearance of egotism.

**'We are not amused!'** A reproof attributed to Queen Victoria when a groom-in-waiting, Alexander Grantham Yorke, allegedly imitated her, and frequently used as an ironical rebuke. There appears to be no evidence that Queen Victoria ever used the expression.

**We three.** 'Did you never see the picture of We Three?' asks Sir Andrew Aguecheek (Shakespeare, *Twelfth Night*, II, iii (1599)), not meaning himself, Sir Toby Belch and the clown, but referring to a PUBLIC HOUSE SIGN of Two Loggerheads with the inscription, 'We three loggerheads be,' the third being the spectator. 'When shall we three meet again?', the title of a picture of two asses, is a similar 'joke'.

**Royal 'we', The.** *See under* ROYAL.

**Weak. Weakest go to the wall, The.** The saying is explained by the literary scholar James Halliwell-Phillipps (1820–89) as deriving from the placing of beds along the side of the room and putting the youngest or feeblest in the safest place, i.e. against the wall. Another explanation is that, in the days when few churches had pews, except maybe for the gentry, there were benches along the walls for the aged. Pews were not installed generally until the late 17th century and subsequently.

**Weak-kneed.** Irresolute, infirm of purpose or conviction, as a 'weak-kneed Christian', a LAODICEAN, neither hot nor cold.

**Weak spot** or **point.** The aspect of a person's character or knowledge that is lower than the norm or less than it should be, as: 'Overambition is his weak spot' or 'Latin is my weak point.'

**As weak as water.** *See under* AS.

**In a weak moment.** On an occasion when one was unusually compliant or easily tempted.

**Wealth, The gospel of.** *See under* GOSPEL.

**Weapon salve.** A salve said to cure wounds by sympathy, applied not to the wound, but to the instrument that gave the wound. The advice 'Bind the wound and grease the nail' is similar. Sir Kenelm Digby (1603–65) says the salve is sympathetic, and quotes several instances to prove that: 'as the sword is treated the wound inflicted by it feels. Thus, if the instrument is kept wet, the wound will feel cool, and if it is held to the fire, it will feel hot.'

> But she has ta'en the broken lance,
> And wash'd it from the clotted gore,
> And salved the splinter o'er and o'er.
>
> SIR WALTER SCOTT: *The Lay of the Last Minstrel*, III, xxiii (1805)

**Wear. Wearing of the green, The.** An anonymous Irish patriotic and revolutionary song dating from about 1795. Green was the emblematic colour of Irish patriots. *See also* EMERALD ISLE.

I met wid Napper Tandy, and he took me by the hand,
And he said, 'How's poor ould Ireland, and how does she stand?'
She's the most disthressful country that iver yet was seen,
For they're hangin' men an' women there for wearin' o' the Green.

**Wear one's heart on one's sleeve, To.** To reveal one's secret thoughts or intentions to others; to show one's feelings plainly. The reference is to the custom of tying one's lady's favour to one's sleeve and thus revealing the secret of one's heart.

But I will wear my heart upon my sleeve
For daws to peck at: I am not what I am.
SHAKESPEARE: *Othello*, I, i (1604)

**Wear one's years well, To.** To remain youthful-looking.

**Wear sackcloth and ashes, To.** Metaphorically, to express one's contrition and penitence. The expression is an allusion to the Hebrew custom of wearing sackcloth and ashes as suitably humble attire for religious ceremonies, mourning, penitence and the like. The sackcloth in question was a coarse dark haircloth from which sacks were made.

And I set my face unto the Lord God, to seek by prayer and supplications, with fasting, and sackcloth, and ashes.
Daniel 9:3

**Wear someone's colours, To.** To side with someone or support them; to be attached to a person. The concept is from livery. Football supporters sport the colours of their team in similar manner.

**Wear the cap and bells, To.** To be a source of amusement; to make jokes at one's own expense. The reference is to jesters, formerly attached to noblemen's establishments, who wore the CAP AND BELLS.

**Wear the horns, To.** To be a CUCKOLD. This old term is connected with the hunt. In the rutting season, one stag selects several females for his mates. If challenged and beaten by another stag he is without associates unless he defeats another stag in turn. As stags are horned and have their mates taken from them by their fellows, the application is obvious. *See also* ACTAEON.

**Wear the sandals of Theramenes, To.** Said of a TRIMMER, an opportunist. Theramenes (put to death *c.*404 BC) was one of the Athenian oligarchy, and was nicknamed Cothurnus (i.e. a sandal or boot which might be worn on either foot), because he could not be depended upon. He 'blew hot and cold with the same breath'.

**Wear the trousers, To.** Said of a married woman who dominates her husband, from the days when only men normally wore trousers and more usually 'ruled the roost'. In recent decades, women having largely become a GENS BRACATA, the phrase has become somewhat less expressive.

**Wear the willow, To.** To go into mourning, especially for a sweetheart or bride; to bewail a lost lover.

The willow, especially the weeping willow, has long been associated with sorrow and ever since the BABYLONIAN CAPTIVITY the latter is said to have drooped its branches.

By the rivers of Babylon, there we sat down, yea, we wept, when we remembered Zion.
We hanged our harps upon the willows in the midst thereof.
Psalm 137:1, 2

The refrain of the well-known song 'There is a Tavern in the Town' has the line, 'I'll hang my harp on a weeping willow-tree.'

In Shakespeare's *Othello* (IV, iii (1604)), Desdemona says:

My mother had a maid call'd Barbara;
She was in love, and he she lov'd prov'd mad
And did forsake her; she had a song of 'willow';
An old thing 'twas, but it express'd her fortune,
And she died singing it.

And then she sings the song:

The poor soul sat sighing by a sycamore tree,
Sing all a green willow;
Her hand on her bosom, her head on her knee,
Sing willow, willow, willow;
The fresh streams ran by her, and murmur'd her moans;
Sing willow, willow, willow;
Her salt tears fell from her, and soften'd the stones;
Sing willow, willow, willow.

This in turn evokes the song sung by Ko-Ko in Act II of Gilbert and Sullivan's *The Mikado* (1885):

On a tree by a river a little tom-tit
Sang 'Willow, titwillow, titwillow!'
And I said to him, 'Dicky-bird, why do you sit
Singing 'Willow, titwillow, titwillow?'

**Worn to a frazzle.** Reduced to a state of nervous exhaustion.

**Weasel. Weasel words.** Words of convenient ambiguity, or a statement from which the original meaning has been sucked or retracted. Theodore Roosevelt popularized the term by using it in a speech in 1916 when criticizing President Wilson. A quotation from the speech provides a good example: 'You can have universal training, or you can have voluntary training, but when you use the word *voluntary* to qualify the word *universal*, you are using a weasel word; it has sucked all the meaning out of *universal*. The two words flatly contradict one another.'

Roosevelt was indebted to a story by Stewart Chaplin, 'Stained-glass Political Platform', which appeared in the *Century Magazine* in

June 1900, and in which occurs the sentence: 'Why, weasel words are words that suck the life out of the words next to them, just as a weasel sucks the egg and leaves the shell.'

**Pop goes the weasel.** *See under* POP.

**Weather. Weathercock.** By a papal enactment made in the middle of the 9th century, the figure of a cock was set up on every church steeple as the emblem of St PETER. The emblem is in allusion to his denial of Christ three times before the cock crew twice. On the second crowing of the cock the warning of Jesus flashed across his memory, and the repentant apostle 'went out and wept bitterly'.

A person who is always changing his mind is, figuratively, a weathercock.

> Ther is no feith that may your herte embrace;
> But, as a wedercock, that turneth his face
> With every wind, ye fare.
> CHAUCER: *Balade Against Women Unconstant* (*c*.1400)

**Bird walking weather.** *See under* BIRD.

**Buchan's weather periods.** *See under* BUCHAN.

**Clerk of the weather.** *See under* CLERK.

**Dirty weather.** *See under* DIRTY.

**Fair-weather friends.** *See under* FAIR.

**Foul-weather Jack.** *See under* FOUL.

**Keep one's weather eye open, To.** To remain alert. The weather eye is towards the wind, supposedly to observe the weather and to be on the look out for squalls.

**Make heavy weather of, To.** *See under* HEAVY.

**Under the weather.** *See under* UNDER.

**Weave. Bottom the Weaver.** *See under* BOTTOM.

**Get weaving, To.** To set about a task briskly. A colloquial expression in the armed services in the Second World War. Weaving implies dextrous movement, as when aircraft make rapid directional changes to escape enemy fire.

**Web. Web of life, The.** The destiny of an individual from the cradle to the grave. An allusion to the three FATES who, according to Roman mythology, spin the thread of life, the pattern being the events that are to occur.

**Web of Penelope, The.** A work 'never ending, still beginning', never done, but ever ongoing. PENELOPE, according to HOMER, was pestered with suitors at Ithaca while ULYSSES was absent at the siege of TROY. To relieve herself of their importunities, she promised to make a choice of one as soon as she had finished a shroud for her father-in-law. Every night she unravelled what she had woven in the day, and so deferred making any choice until Ulysses returned and slew the suitors.

**Wed** or **wedding.** The word 'wed' is Old English, and means a pledge. The ring is the pledge given by the man to confirm that he will perform his part of the contract. *See also* MARRIAGE.

**Wedding anniversaries.** Fanciful names have been given to many wedding anniversaries, the popular idea being that they designate the nature of the gifts suitable for the occasion. The following includes variants for the lesser anniversaries. Many of them are not observed, with the exception of the twenty-fifth and fiftieth.

First: Cotton
Second: Paper
Third: Leather
Fourth: Flower or fruit
Fifth: Wooden
Sixth: Iron or sugar-candy
Seventh: Woollen
Eighth: Bronze or electrical appliances
Ninth: Copper or pottery
Tenth: Tin
Eleventh: Steel
Twelfth: Silk and fine linen
Thirteenth: Lace
Fourteenth: Ivory
Fifteenth: Crystal
Twentieth: China
Twenty-fifth: Silver
Thirtieth: Pearl
Thirty-fifth: Coral
Fortieth: Ruby
Forty-fifth: Sapphire
Fiftieth: Golden
Fifty-fifth: Emerald
Sixtieth: Diamond
Seventieth: Platinum
Seventy-fifth: Diamond

The sixtieth anniversary is often reckoned the Diamond wedding in place of the seventy-fifth, as the sixtieth anniversary of Queen Victoria's accession was her 'Diamond Jubilee'. *See also* JUBILEE.

**Wedding breakfast.** The meal (not actually breakfast) that is traditionally served at the reception after a wedding ceremony or just before the married couple leave for their honeymoon. Weddings now usually take place in the early afternoon, but the expression dates from the time when they were held in the morning.

**Wedding finger.** The fourth finger of the left hand. Macrobius says that the thumb is too busy to be set apart, the forefinger and little finger are only half-protected, the middle finger is called *medicus*, and is too opprobrious for the purpose of honour, so the only finger left is the *pronubus*.

Aulus Gellius tells how Appianus asserts in his Egyptian books that a very delicate nerve runs from the fourth finger on the left hand to the heart, on which account this finger is used for the marriage ring.

> The finger on which the [wedding] ring is to be worn is the fourth finger on the left hand, next unto the little finger; because by the received opinion of the learned ... in ripping up and anatomising men's bodies, there is a vein of blood, called *vena amoris*, which passeth from that finger to the heart.
> HENRY SWINBURNE: *Treaties of Spousals* (1680)

In the ROMAN CATHOLIC CHURCH, the thumb and next two fingers represent the TRINITY. The bridegroom says, 'In the name of the Father' and touches the thumb, 'in the name of the Son' and touches the index finger, and 'in the name of the Holy Ghost' and touches the long or third finger. With the word 'Amen' he then puts it on the fourth finger and leaves it there. In some countries the wedding ring is worn on the right hand. This was the custom generally in England until the end of the 16th century, and among Roman Catholics until much later.

In the Hereford, York and Salisbury missals, the ring is directed to be put first on the thumb, then on the index finger, then on the long finger and lastly on the ring finger, *quia in illo digito est quaedam vena procedens usque ad cor* ('because in this finger there is a certain vein running to the heart').

**Wedlock.** This word comes from Old English *wed*, 'pledge', and *-lāc*, a suffix indicating activity, the whole meaning the marriage vow and hence the married state. It does not imply the unopenable lock of marriage, as has sometimes been supposed.

**Blood-red wedding, The.** *See under* BLOOD.

**Golden wedding.** *See under* GOLDEN.

**No herring, no wedding.** *See under* HERRING.

**Parisian wedding.** *See under* PARIS.

**Penny weddings.** *See under* PENNY.

**Shotgun wedding.** *See under* SHOT.

**Silver wedding.** *See under* SILVER.

**White wedding.** *See under* WHITE.

**Wedge. Thin end of the wedge, The.** *See under* THIN.

**Wooden wedge, The.** *See under* WOOD.

**Wednesday.** The fourth day of the week, or popularly the third (*see* SUNDAY). Its name marks it as WODEN's day, but it is called by the French *mercredi*, 'Mercury's day'. The Persians regard it as a RED-LETTER DAY because the moon was created on the fourth day (Genesis 1:14–19).

**Ash Wednesday.** *See under* ASH.

**Black Wednesday.** *See under* BLACK.

**Spy Wednesday.** *See under* SPY.

**Wee. Wee drappie, A.** A nip of Scotch whisky.

**Wee Frees.** The minority of the FREE CHURCH OF SCOTLAND, which refused to join the United Free Church in 1900.

**Weed. Sacred weed, The.** *See under* SACRED.

**Widow's weeds.** *See under* WIDOW.

**Week. Week of Sundays, A.** A long time; an indefinite period. *See also* MONTH OF SUNDAYS.

**Weekwork.** Under FEUDALISM compulsory work by the unfree tenant on his lord's land for a specific number of days, usually three, each week. It was the chief mark of serfdom or villeinage. *See also* COMMON; COPYHOLD; MANOR; OPEN-FIELD SYSTEM; VILLAIN.

**Bob-a-Job Week.** *See under* BOB.

**Days of the week.** *See under* DAY.

**Dirty weekend.** *See under* DIRTY.

**Eights Week.** *See under* EIGHT.

**Ember weeks.** *See under* EMBER.

**Holy Week.** *See under* HOLY.

**Weep. Weeper.** In the more elaborate and formal funeral ceremonial of the 19th century, undertakers attending (called 'mutes') and the principal male mourners wore long black streamers hanging from the hatband. These were commonly known as weepers, as was also the widow's long black veil. In humorous allusion to the former, the long side whiskers in fashion in the 1860s were called Piccadilly weepers.

**Weeping.** A notion long prevailed in this country that it augured ill for future married happiness if the bride did not weep profusely at the wedding. Because no witch could shed more than three tears, and those from her left eye only, a copious flow of tears gave assurance to the husband that the lady had not 'plighted her troth' to Satan and was no witch.

**Weeping cross.** A cross set up by the roadside, perhaps for penitential devotions. The name appears on Ordnance Survey maps at various crossroads, for example 2 miles (3km) southeast of Shrewsbury, 2 miles (3km) southeast of Banbury, and also near Bury St Edmunds and Ludlow.

> Various conjectures have been made as to the significance of the name – that acts of devotion at these crosses were enjoined on penitents, that the cross marked the place where bodies carried to interment were set down for the bearers to rest – but there is no evidence to support them.
>
> MARGARET GELLING: *The Place-Names of Oxfordshire* (1954)

**Weeping Philosopher, The.** The Greek philosopher Heraclitus (d.*c*.475 BC), so called because he grieved at the folly of man.

**Weeping Saint, The.** St SWITHIN, because of the tradition of 40 days' rain if it rains on his day (15 July).

**Weeping willow.** A Chinese willow tree, *Salix babylonica*, whose long branches hang low as if weeping.

**Weigh** (Old English *wegan*, 'to carry').

**Weigh anchor, To.** To haul up the anchor preparatory to sailing. When broken out of the ground it is 'aweigh'.

**Weighed in the balance and found wanting.** Tested and proved to be at fault, or a failure. The phrase is from DANIEL's interpretation of the vision of BELSHAZZAR (Daniel 5:27). *See also* WRITING ON THE WALL.

**Weight-for-age race, A.** A sort of handicap in which the weights carried are apportioned according to certain conditions. Horses of the same age carry similar weights.

**Carry weight, To.** *See under* CARRY.

**Dead weight.** *See under* DEAD.

**Makeweight.** *See under* MAKE.

**Pull one's weight, To.** *See under* PULL.

**Throw one's weight about, To.** *See under* THROW.

**Troy weight.** *See under* TROY.

**Weimar Republic, The.** The German federal republic established under the Constitution of 1919, which lasted until it was overthrown by Hitler in 1933. It was so called from the Thuringian town, particularly associated with Goethe, where the constitution was adopted by the National Assembly.

**Welch.** An old spelling of 'Welsh', surviving in such names as the Royal Welch Fusiliers (who became the Royal Welsh Fusiliers in 1881 but reverted to the old spelling in 1920).

**Welcome. Welcome Nugget.** One of the largest nuggets of gold ever discovered. It was found at Baker's Hill, Ballarat, Victoria, Australia, on 11 June 1858 and weighed 2217oz (62,850g).

**Welcome Stranger.** The largest gold nugget found to date. It weighed 2520oz (71,440g) and was found in Victoria, Australia, in 1869.

**You're welcome.** A polite response to an expression of thanks, the English equivalent of the French *De rien*, the German *Bitte schön*, the Italian *Prego* and the Russian *Pozhaluysta*.

**Welfare State, The.** A term applied to Britain after the implementation of the Beveridge Report (1942) providing for nationwide social security services for sickness, unemployment, retirement and the like, and essentially based on the National Insurance Act of 1946. The system depends on compulsory contributions and taxation and was built up on the less sweeping Liberal legislation of 1908–14.

**Well** (noun).

**Sadler's Wells.** *See under* SADLER.

**Wishing well.** *See under* WISH.

**Well** (adjective and adverb).

**Well-beloved.** Charles VI of France, le Bien-aimé (r.1380–1422), was known also as Charles the Foolish. The name was also applied to Louis XV (r.1715–74).

**Well-heeled.** Materially prosperous as indicated by one's being well shod, the reverse of DOWN AT HEEL.

**Well-meaning.** Well-intentioned but ineffective.

**Well-oiled.** Fairly drunk.

**Well-to-do.** In good circumstances; comfortably off.

**Wellerism.** Sam Weller in Charles Dickens's *Pickwick Papers* (1836–7) was prone to producing punning sentences such as: 'Out with it, as the father said to the child, when he swallowed a farden [farthing]'. This type of verbal play, involving a metaphorical and a punningly literal sense, soon gained popularity under the name of wellerism, and a craze for devising such expressions rapidly sprang up on both sides of the Atlantic. A crude example familiar to children is: 'I see, said the blind man, when he couldn't see at all.' In the 20th century TOM SWIFTIES evolved as a variation on the wellerism, while innocent remarks suffixed by AS THE BISHOP SAID TO THE ACTRESS may be instanced as quips of a similar colour.

**Wellies, Green.** *See under* GREEN.

**Wellington.** Arthur Wellesley, 1st Duke of Wellington (1769–1852) is commemorated in the name of a type of boots; in a tree, the Wellingtonia or giant redwood (*Sequoiadendron giganteum*); and as a term in cards. Thus in NAP a call of Wellington doubles Napoleon, i.e. the caller has to take all five tricks and wins (or loses) double stakes. Wellington College (opened 1853, as a public school for the sons of officers) was also named after him (but not Wellington School), as were Wellington, the capital of New Zealand, and many streets and public houses in Britain.

**Wells Fargo.** The American company founded by William George Fargo (1818–81) and Henry Wells (1805–78) in 1852. It carried on the stage express business between New York and San Francisco via the isthmus of Panama. It absorbed the PONY EXPRESS and took over the Overland Mail Company in 1866, and was also an agency for the transport of bullion. It amalgamated with the Adams Express in 1918 as the American Railway Express Company. *See also* COBB & CO.

**Welsh.** *See* TAFFY; WALES.

**Welsh, To.** To decamp from a racecourse without settling one's debts; to avoid settling a debt. Hence, a 'welsher' is one who does this. The origin of the term is uncertain.

**Welsh cake.** A small, flat cake or GIRDLECAKE cooked on a bakestone or in an iron pan. It is made from flour, fat, currants, egg, milk, salt and sugar.

**Welsh harp.** The musical instrument of the ancient Welsh bards. It is a large harp with three rows of strings, two tuned diatonically in unison, the third supplying the chromatic sharps and flats. The name is also applied loosely to the Brent Reservoir, in Middlesex, from the inn of that name in the vicinity.

**Welsh main.** In COCKFIGHTING a form of BATTLE ROYAL in which eight pairs were matched, next the eight winners, then four, and finally the last two, until only one was left alive.

**Welsh mortgage.** A pledge of land in which no day is fixed for redemption.

**Welsh rabbit.** Cheese melted with butter, milk, Worcester sauce and the like, spread on buttered toast. 'Rabbit' is not a corruption of 'rarebit', since the term is on a par with MOCK TURTLE SOUP, BOMBAY DUCK and so on, indicating a dish that is the substitute for 'the real thing'. *See also* SCOTCH WOODCOCK *under* SCOTCH.

**Welterweight.** A boxer between light and middle weight, professionally not more than 147 pounds (67kg). In racing the term is applied to any extra heavy weight.

**Weltpolitik.** The German phrase ('world politics') for the policy a nation pursues in its relations with the world at large.

**Wen** or **Great Wen, The.** London. A name used by William Cobbett in his *Rural Rides* (1830), meaning that it was an abnormal growth or blot on the landscape. To him the sprawl and growth of any town was 'a wen'. Thus he says, 'Chatham has had some monstrous wens stuck on to it by the lavish expenditure of the war' (4 December 1821) and 'Croydon is a good market-town; but is, by the funds, swelled out into a wen' (8 January 1822).

**Wenceslas, St.** The Bohemian martyr prince (*c.*907–929), made famous in England by J.M. Neale's 19th-century carol 'Good King Wenceslas'. He was noted for his piety and was murdered by Boleslav, his brother. He became recognized as the patron of Bohemia (Czech Republic), and his day is 28 September.

**Werewolf.** A 'man-wolf' (Old English *wer*, 'man'), i.e. a man who, according to ancient superstition, was turned, or could at will turn himself, into a WOLF (the *loupgarou* of France). It had the appetite of a wolf and roamed about at night devouring infants and sometimes exhuming corpses. Its skin was proof against shot or steel, unless the weapon had been blessed in a chapel dedicated to St HUBERT.

Ovid tells the story of LYCAON, king of ARCADIA and, by some accounts, father of CALLISTO, who was turned into a wolf because he tested the divinity of ZEUS by serving up to him a 'hash of human flesh' (either one of his own sons or the child of a hostage or even Callisto's son, Arcas). Another version of the tale relates how Lycaon offended Zeus by sacrificing a child on the altar to Zeus that Lycaon had founded. From that time, each time a sacrifice was made on the altar of Lycaean Zeus, a man was turned into a wolf but if, after eight years, he had not eaten human flesh he became a human again. Herodotus describes the Neuri as having the power of assuming once a year the shape of wolves. Pliny relates that one of the family of ANTAEUS was chosen annually, by lot, to be transformed into a wolf, in which shape he continued for nine years, and St PATRICK, it is said, converted Vereticus, king of Wales, into a wolf.

Hence the term 'lycanthropy' (Greek *lukos*, 'wolf', and *anthropos*, 'man') for this supposed transformation and for the form of insanity in which the subject exhibits depraved animal traits.

Tigers, hyenas and leopards had the same associations in other parts of the world, and after the disappearance of the wolf in England witches were commonly 'transformed' into cats.

**Wergild.** The BLOOD MONEY (*wer*, 'man', and *gield*, 'tribute') paid in Anglo-Saxon times by the kindred of the slayer to the kindred of the slain to avoid a blood feud in cases of murder or manslaughter. There was a fixed scale, as 1200 shillings for a thegn, 200 shillings for a ceorl and so on.

**Werwolf.** *See* WEREWOLF.

**Wesleyan.** A member of the NONCONFORMIST church which grew out of the evangelical movement started by John Wesley (1703–91) and his associates, although there was no real break with the CHURCH OF ENGLAND until 1795. *See also* METHODISTS.

**Wessex.** The ancient kingdom of the West Saxons, founded by the Saxon Cerdic (d.534) in the 6th century. Its nucleus was modern Berkshire and Hampshire, and it later spread to Cornwall in the west and to Kent and Essex in the east. The Danish invasions of the 9th century destroyed the other English kingdoms and ALFRED THE GREAT came to be recognized as king of all the English outside the Danish areas. The subsequent reconquest of the DANELAW resulted in the king of Wessex becoming king of England.

**Novelist of Wessex, The.** *See under* NOVEL.

**West. West Country, The.** The southwestern counties of England, especially Cornwall, Devon and Somerset.

**West End, The.** The western district of inner London, noted for its fashionable shopping, theatres, clubs, hotels, restaurants, the expensive residential district of MAYFAIR, SOHO and so on. It includes largely the area between Hyde Park and CHARING CROSS Road. *See also* CLUBLAND; EAST END.

**Western Church, The.** The ROMAN CATHOLIC CHURCH.

**Western Empire, The.** The western division of the ROMAN EMPIRE with Rome as its capital, after the division in 395 into the Eastern and Western Empires after the death of Theodosius I (*c.*346–395).

**Westerns.** *See* WILD WEST.

**West Side.** Contrary to popular perception, New York's West Side is not the fashionable counterpart to the somewhat seedy EAST SIDE. It is certainly more scenically attractive, with several luxury apartment blocks, but has its dangerous neighbourhoods like anywhere else in Manhattan, and is overall more déclassé than its name suggests. Leonard Bernstein's musical play *West Side Story* (1957), with lyrics by Stephen Sondheim, was based on Shakespeare's *Romeo and Juliet* (1594).

**East is East and West is West.** *See under* EAST.

**Go west, To.** To die (of persons); to be lost; to become useless (of things), as: 'My chance of promotion has gone west.' The reference is to the setting sun, which 'goes west' and then sinks or expires.

**Mae West.** *See under* MAE.

**Spaghetti western.** *See under* SPAGHETTI.

**Wild West.** *See under* WILD.

**Westminster.** The seat of government in England since the time of Canute (1016–35). From the time of WILLIAM THE CONQUEROR (r.1066–87) the sovereign has been crowned in Westminster Abbey, and it later became the home of Parliament. Hence, like WHITEHALL and DOWNING STREET, it is sometimes used as a synonym for government or Parliament itself.

**Westminster Assembly, The.** The assembly appointed by the LONG PARLIAMENT to reform the English Church. It consisted of 30 laymen and 120 clergy and met in Westminster Abbey precincts (1643–53). Its most important achievement was the WESTMINSTER CONFESSION. *See also* ERASTIANISM.

**Westminster Confession, The.** The PRESBYTERIAN Confession of faith adopted by the WESTMINSTER ASSEMBLY in 1646 and approved by Parliament in 1648. It became a standard definition of Presbyterian doctrine.

**Long Meg of Westminster.** *See under* LONG.

**Palace of Westminster, The.** *See under* PALACE.

**Wet.** Slang for a drink. In the USA, 'wet states' were those which did not support the prohibition of the sale of alcoholic drinks.

In colloquial speech 'wet' also denotes stupidity, foolishness; thus, 'he is pretty wet' means he is fairly stupid and 'don't talk wet' means don't talk such nonsense, don't be silly. The more liberal element in the TORY party, which did not favour all the policies of Margaret Thatcher (prime minister 1979–90), were called 'wets'.

**Wetback.** An illegal immigrant to the USA from Mexico. The term originates in the fact that such interlopers usually had to swim the Rio Grande.

**Wet behind the ears.** Inexperienced; naive; as innocent as a newborn child. When young animals are born, the last place to become dry after birth is the small depression behind each ear.

**Wet blanket, A.** A person whose low spirits or lack of enthusiasm depresses others or discourages a proposed scheme. A wet blanket smothers fire.

**Wet bob.** At Eton, a wet bob is a boy who goes in for boating, while a DRY BOB is one who chooses CRICKET.

**Wet nurse.** A woman employed to suckle the babies of others.

**Wet one's whistle, To.** To have a drink, one's whistle being one's lips. Chaucer has, 'So was hir joly whistle wel y-wet' ('The Reeve's Tale' (*c.*1387)).

**Wet the baby's head, To.** To celebrate a baptism with a social gathering to drink to the health of the newborn baby.

**W.H., Mr.** When Shakespeare's Sonnets appeared in 1609 they were dedicated to a Mr W.H., called their 'onlie begetter'. The identity of Shakespeare's friend is uncertain. Various names have been put forward, and for long the most favoured were William Herbert, 3rd Earl of Pembroke, to whom (with his brother) the First Folio Shakespeare was dedicated, and Henry Wriothesley, 3rd Earl of Southampton, to whom *Venus and Adonis* (1593) and *The Rape of Lucrece* (1594) were dedicated. In 1964 Dr Leslie Hotson put forward a case for William Hatcliffe of Lincolnshire, 'Prince of Purpoole' in the GRAY'S INN revels of 1588. According to Dr A.L. Rowse, Master W.H is Sir William Harvey, the Earl of Southampton's stepfather.

**Whale. Whalebone.** *See* MISNOMERS.

**Whale of a lot, A.** A great amount. Colloquially 'whale' is used of something very fine or big as 'we had a whale of a time', a fine time, or 'a whale of a job', a very considerable task.

**Whammy, Double.** *See under* DOUBLE.

**What. What are you driving at?** What do you mean? What are you implying?

**What a way to run a railway!** What an inefficient, chaotic or disorderly way of doing things. The expression is probably of American origin.

**What did your last servant die of?** An expression sometimes said to someone who is expecting you to help and work like a galley slave, doing one thing after another. It goes back to the days when household servants were often grossly overworked from morning till night.

**What-d'you-call-it or what's-its-name.** A substitute for a name one cannot recall. *See also* WHAT'S-HIS-NAME.

**Whatever are you at?** So the cricketer Dr W.G. Grace (1848–1915) is reported to have called out when, in 1896, Ernest Jones, the Australian fast bowler, bowled through W.G.'s beard.

**What is sauce for the goose is sauce for the gander.** The same principle applies in both cases; what is fitting for the husband should also be fitting for the wife.

**What makes it tick?** The child's question, asked about a watch or clock, has given rise to a figurative use: 'What makes him (her or it) tick?' meaning, 'What keeps him on the go?' Sometimes the question is asked with wider implications, such as, what are a person's beliefs and interests?

**Whatnot.** A small stand with shelves for photographs, knick-knacks, china ornaments and 'whatnot', i.e. other trinkets, popular in Victorian and Edwardian times.

**What on earth?** An emphatic question. So also Where on earth?, How on earth?, Why on earth? and so forth.

**What's cooking?** What's up? What's doing?

**What's eating you?** What's bothering you? What's the problem?

**What's-his-name.** A substitute for a name one has forgotten. The feminine equivalent is 'What's-her-name'. *See also* THINGUMMY; WHAT-D'YOU-CALL-IT.

> *I'll Never Forget Whatshisname* (film title) (1967)

**What's the matter?** What's wrong?

**What's your poison?** What would you like to drink? Alcohol actually is a poison, so the expression is not quite the euphemism it appears to be.

**What the dickens.** What the Devil. 'Dickens' here is a euphemism for Devil, adopted from the surname.

> I cannot tell what the dickens his name is.
> SHAKESPEARE: *The Merry Wives of Windsor*, III, ii (1600)

**What the hell?** What on earth? So also, for emphasis, 'who the hell?', 'where the hell?', 'why the hell?' and the like.

> but wotthehell
> archy wotthehell
> it s cheerio
> my deario that
> pulls a lady through.
> DON MARQUIS: *archy and mehitabel* (1927)

**What we gave we have.** The epitaph on 'the Good Earl of Courtenay' (*see* Gibbon's *Decline and Fall*, VI, ch lxi (1788)):

> What wee gave, wee have;
> What wee spent, wee had;
> What wee left, wee lost.

This was a free rendering of Martial's:

> Extra fortunam est quidquid donatur amicis
> Quas dederis, solas semper habebis opes.

There are similar epitaphs in many churches. One in St George's, Doncaster, runs thus:

> How now, who is here?
> I, Robin of Doncastere
> And Margaret, my feere [companion].
> That I spent, that I had;
> That I gave, that I have;
> That I left, that I lost.

**What will Mrs Grundy say?** What will the prim neighbours say? The phrase is from Thomas Morton's *Speed the Plough* (1798). In the first scene Mrs Ashfield shows herself very jealous of her neighbour Mrs Grundy, and Farmer Ashfield says to her: 'Be quiet, wool ye? Always ding dinging Dame Grundy into my ears – What will Mrs Grundy zay? What will Mrs Grundy think?' Mrs Grundy has ever since served as an embodiment of conventional propriety and prudery.

> At last we are free, –
> All hail, Hymenaeus!
> From C., and from D., –
> *At last*! – we are free.
> What a comfort 'twill be
> 'Mrs. Grundy' can't see us!
> AUSTIN DOBSON: 'Notes of a Honeymoon' (1878)

**What you lose on the swings you gain on the roundabouts.** What you lose on one venture you recoup on another. A way of stating the law of averages.

**Give someone what for, To.** *See under* GIVE.

**Know what's what, To.** *See under* KNOW.

**Wheat. Separate the wheat from the chaff, To.** *See under* SEPARATE.

**Wheatear.** A bird (*Oenanthe oenanthe*) with a white rump and base of tail, one of the thrush family. The name has no connection with either wheat or ear, but represents Old English *hwit*, 'white', and *ears*, 'arse'. The French name of the bird, *culblanc*, signifies exactly the same thing.

**Wheel.** The emblem of St CATHERINE, who was reputedly broken on a spiked wheel and after whom the firework known as the Catherine wheel is named. Other saints associated with wheels include:

> St Donatus: bears a wheel set round with lights
> St Euphemia and St Willigis: both carry wheels
> St Quintin: sometimes represented with a broken wheel at his feet

**Wheeler-dealer.** A person who 'wheels and deals'. 'Wheel' in American slang signifies an important person or leader, a BIG WHEEL. Hence one of great influence in a particular field (usually business or politics), a shrewd and influential operator and manipulator.

**Wheelie.** A stunt whereby the front wheel of a bicycle or motorcycle is lifted off the ground while being ridden.

**Wheel is come full circle, The.** Just retribution has followed. The line is from Shakespeare's *King Lear* (V, iii (1605)), where the reference is to the WHEEL OF FORTUNE.

**Wheel of death.** A hazardous circus act, in which a performer spins in and on a large 'hamster wheel' as it is gradually lowered to the ground from a 50ft (15m) high wire. *See also* WALL OF DEATH.

> The circus acrobat who fell to his death in front of hundreds of spectators was killed performing the same 'wheel of death' act that crippled his brother 18 months ago.
> *The Times* (28 December 1994)

**Wheel of fortune, The.** Fortuna, the goddess, is represented on ancient monuments with a wheel in her hand, emblematic of her inconstancy.

> Though Fortune's malice overthrow my state,
> My mind exceeds the compass of her wheel.
> SHAKESPEARE: *Henry VI, Pt III*, IV, iii (1590)

*See also* PRAYER WHEEL; TODAY A MAN, TOMORROW A MOUSE.

**Wheels within wheels.** A complex of motives and influences and circumstances at work that are not always apparent. The allusion is to Ezekiel 1:16:

> The appearance of the wheels and their work was like unto the colour of a beryl: and they four had one likeness: and their appearance and their work was as it were a wheel in the middle of a wheel.

**Big wheel.** *See under* BIG.
**Break a butterfly on a wheel, To.** *See under* BREAK.
**Catherine wheel.** *See under* CATHERINE.
**Break on the wheel, To.** *See under* BREAK.
**Ferris wheel.** *See under* FERRIS.
**Fifth wheel.** *See under* FIFTH.
**Oil the wheels, To.** *See under* OIL.
**Prayer wheel.** *See under* PRAYER.
**Put a spoke in someone's wheel, To.** *See under* SPOKE.
**Put one's shoulder to the wheel, To.** *See under* SHOULDER.

**When. When Adam delved.**

> When Adam delved and Eve span,
> Who was then the gentleman?

This, according to the *Historia Anglicana* of Thomas Walsingham (d.1422), was the text of John Ball's speech at Blackheath, London, to the rebels in the PEASANTS' REVOLT (1381). The lines were doubtless adapted from those of the hermit and mystical writer Richard Rolle of Hampole (*c*.1300–49):

> When Adam dalfe and Eue spane
> Go spire if thou may spede [ask if you can],
> Where was than the pride of man,
> That now merres his meed? [spoils his reward]

*See also* JACK'S AS GOOD AS HIS MASTER.
**When Dover and Calais meet.** *See* NEVER.
**When good Americans die they go to Paris.** Not an original witticism of Oscar Wilde, who used it in *A Woman of No Importance* (1893), but attributed by Oliver Wendell Holmes to Thomas Gold Appleton (1812–84).

**When Greek meets Greek.** When two men or armies of undoubted courage fight, the contest will be very severe. The phrase is slightly altered from a 17th-century play, and the reference is to the obstinate resistance of the Greek cities to Philip and Alexander, the Macedonian kings.

> When Greeks joined Greeks, then was the tug of war!
> NATHANIEL LEE: *The Rival Queens*, IV, ii (1677)

**When in Rome, do as the Romans do.** Conform to the manners and customs of those among whom you live. St Monica and her son St AUGUSTINE of Hippo said to St AMBROSE: 'At Rome they fast on Saturday, but not at Milan. Which practice ought to be observed?' St Ambrose replied: 'When I am at Milan, I do as they do at Milan, but when I go to Rome, I do as Rome does!' (*Epistle* xxxvi). The saying is found in that great storehouse of proverbs, *Two Angry Women of Abingdon* (1597).

> On the 'when in Rome' principle Boyd strips off himself and invites his reluctant production team to do likewise.
> *The Times* (2 January 1999)

**When one's ship comes in** or **home.** When one's fortune is made. The allusion is to the ARGOSY returning from foreign parts laden with rich freight, and so enriching the merchant who sent it forth.

> And I have better news in store for you
> Than you expect: unseal this letter soon;
> There you shall find three of your argosies
> Are richly come to harbour suddenly.
> SHAKESPEARE: *The Merchant of Venice*, V, i (1596)

**When poverty comes in at the door, love flies out at the window.** An old proverb, given in John Ray's *Collection of English Proverbs* (1670), and appearing in many languages. *See also* LOVE IN A COTTAGE.
**When push comes to shove.** When action must be taken; when a decision has to be made.
**When the balloon goes up.** When the action starts; when the trouble begins. The expression dates from the First World War.
**When the cat's away the mice will play.** Advantage will be taken of the absence of the person in authority. A proverb found in many languages, as French *Quand le chat n'est pas là, les souris dansent*, German *Wenn die Katze aus dem Haus ist, tanzen die Mäuse*, and Russian *Bez kota mysham razdol'ye*.
**When the chips are down.** At a time of crisis or trial. The phrase may have the same derivation as TO CHIP IN.
**When the Devil is blind.** NEVER.
**When the dust settles.** When things have quietened down.
**When the fat lady sings.** When everything is

finally over. The expression implies that further action is still possible. The full expression runs: 'The opera's never over till the fat lady sings.' The reference is to the final act of the opera, in which the heroine often appears. Opera singers are sometimes endowed with figures as full as their voices.

**Say when.** *See under* SAY.

**Where. Where it's at.** The 'scene of the action'; the place where something interesting or exciting is happening.

**Where's the beef?** Where is the substance in what you say? The phrase has its origin in a television commercial screened in 1984 by the Wendy International hamburger chain. In this, an outraged old lady, patronizing a non-Wendy establishment that served buns with salad and little else, demanded of the manager: 'Where's the beef?'

**Where's the fire?** A humorous remark addressed to someone in a hurry.

> 'Where's the fire, dear boy?' he drawled. 'Do we really have to run for it?'
>
> J.F. STRAKER: *Final Witness*, ch xvi (1963)

**Where there's a will there's a way.** You will succeed in your aim if you are sufficiently determined; perseverance brings results.

**Where there's muck, there's brass.** Where there is dirt, there is money. Feeding the soil and harvesting the crops can make one rich. The saying has come to be associated with the grimy mining and manufacturing industries of the north of England, many of which brought their owners substantial wealth.

**Where the shoe pinches.** 'No one knows where the shoe pinches like the wearer' is the reputed saying of a Roman sage who was blamed for divorcing his wife, with whom he seemed to live happily. The cause of the trouble, or where the difficulty lies, is called 'the place where the shoe pinches'.

**Wherewithal.** In older writings this is a form of 'wherewith' as in:

> Wherewithal shall a young man cleanse his way?
>
> Psalm 119:9

'The wherewithal' is now used with the sense of 'means' or 'money'.

**Whetstone.** *See* ACCIUS NAEVIUS.

**Whetstone of Witte, The.** A treatise on algebra (1557) by the English mathematician Robert Recorde (*c*.1510–58) . The old name for algebra was the 'Cossic Art', and *Cos ingenii* rendered into English is 'the Whetstone of Wit'. In Sir Walter Scott's *Fortunes of Nigel* (ch xxiv (1822)), the servant told Nigel that she knew of no other books in the house 'than her mistress's Bible ...; and her Master's Whetstone of Witte, being the second part of Arithmetic, by Robert Record, with the Cossike Practice and Rule of Equation'.

**Whig.** A name applied to Scottish cattle rustlers and horse thieves, then to the Presbyterian COVENANTERS and later, in the reign of Charles II (1660–85), to those seeking to exclude the Duke of York from succession to the throne. The name was used abusively by their TORY opponents. From the time of the GLORIOUS REVOLUTION in 1688 the Whigs were upholders of parliamentary supremacy and toleration for NONCONFORMISTS. They supported the Hanoverian succession and enjoyed a monopoly of political power until the reign of George III, when they were superseded by the Tories after 1783 and did not recover the ascendancy until the 1830s, the time of the Reform Bill. By 1868 the name LIBERAL had largely replaced that of Whig.

The origin of the word is obscure, but it is probably a shortened form of 'whiggamore', a horse drover, allegedly one who in the 17th century took part in an attack on Edinburgh known as 'the whiggamore raid'.

In American usage, 'Whig' denotes a supporter of the American Revolution, also a member of the American Whig party, which was formed in 1834 from the old National Republican Party against President Andrew Jackson and 'executive tyranny'. The party disintegrated by 1854 over the question of 'free soil' and slavery.

**Whig Bible, The.** *See under* BIBLE.

**Whip.** In British parliamentary usage, MPs appointed by a party, whose duty it is to see that the members of their party vote at important divisions and to discipline them if they do not attend or vote against the party. The name derives from the whipper-in at a fox hunt. *See also* THREE-LINE WHIP.

**Whip-dog Day.** St LUKE's day, 18 October. John Brand (*Observations on Popular Antiquities*, ii (1777)) says that it is so called because a priest about to celebrate Mass on St Luke's Day happened to drop the PYX, which was snatched up by a dog.

**Whippersnapper.** An inexperienced, insignificant and often intrusive young person. The word probably derives from 'whipsnapper', one who has nothing to do but snap (i.e. crack) a whip.

**Whipping boy.** A boy educated with a prince and whipped when the latter deserved chastisement. Thomas Fuller (*Church History*, ii (1655)) says Barnaby Fitzpatrick so stood for Edward VI, and Mungo Murray for CHARLES I. When Henry IV of France abjured Protestantism and was received into the Roman Catholic Church in 1593, Bishop Duperron and Cardinal d'Ossat were sent to Rome to obtain the king's absolution. They knelt in the portico of St Peter's singing the MISERERE. At each verse a blow with a switch was dealt to their shoulders.

**Whipping post.** A post set up for public punishment by whipping. Many parishes had such a post to which offenders, particularly women, were manacled for this purpose. The name of York's Whip-ma Whop-ma Gate is thought to commemorate the whipping post and pillory that stood at the end of this street.

**Whip-round, A.** An impromptu collection of money, often for some benevolent object, such as a colleague's birthday or leaving present.

**Whipsaw, To.** To have or take the advantage over an opponent; especially in faro, to win two different bets at one turn. 'Whipsawing' is also an American term for accepting bribes from two opposing interests at the same time. The whip-saw is a long narrow frame saw with a handle at either end so that it cuts both ways.

**Dog whipper.** *See under* DOG.

**Fair crack of the whip, A.** *See under* FAIR.

**Six-stringed whip, The.** *See* SIX ARTICLES.

**Three-line whip.** *See under* THREE.

**Whirling** or **dancing dervishes.** Dervishes are Islamic monks who have rejected the material world for the spiritual love of God. Whirling dervishes belong to a particular order, the Mevlevi, founded in the 14th century. Their ecstatic whirling dance, which is performed to the music of the reed flute, began as a form of worship but is now performed as public entertainment. Dervish is a word of Turkish origin meaning 'beggar'.

**Whisker. Cat's whisker.** *See under* CAT.

**Dundreary whiskers.** *See under* DUNDREARY.

**Whisky.** SCOTCH. In Ireland and the USA the spirit is spelt 'whiskey'. *See also* USQUEBAUGH.

**Whiskey Insurrection.** An outbreak in western Pennsylvania in 1794, when the federal government tried to enforce the excise tax of 1791, which was opposed by farmers in the area who distilled whiskey to make use of surplus grain. It culminated in a riot and the destruction of private property. Some federal excise officers were TARRED AND FEATHERED, and the rising was eventually suppressed by the militia.

**Whisky money.** The name given to the money diverted to county and county borough councils in 1890, for the development of technical education in accordance with the Technical Instruction Act, 1889. It was derived from the extra duty (6d per gallon) levied on spirits in 1890 as part of an abortive scheme to compensate licensees of redundant public houses, but was used instead for technical and secondary education. As a consequence, temperance did not help education.

**Nip of whisky, A.** *See under* NIP.

**Whisper. Whispering campaign.** The deliberate spreading of rumours by word of mouth with the aim of discrediting a particular person or group.

**Whispering gallery.** A gallery under a dome whose acoustic properties are such that a whisper may be heard round its entire circumference. St Paul's cathedral in London is famous for this feature.

**Chinese whispers.** *See under* CHINESE.

**Stage whisper.** *See under* STAGE.

**Whist.** The card game originated in England (16th century). It was first called 'triumph' (whence 'trump'), then 'ruff' or 'honours', and then, early in the 17th century, 'whisk', in allusion to the sweeping up of the cards. 'Whist', the later name, appears in Samuel Butler's *Hudibras* (1662–80), and was adopted through confusion with 'Whisht!' meaning Hush! Silence!

> Let nice Piquette the boast of France remain,
> And studious Ombre be the pride of Spain!
> Invention's praise shall England yield to none,
> While she can call delightful Whist her own.
> ALEXANDER THOMAS: *Whist* (1792)

*See also* WHITECHAPEL.

**Whistle.** RHYMING SLANG for a suit, from 'whistle and flute'.

**Whistle down the wind, To.** To abandon; to talk or argue purposelessly. The allusion is to the releasing of a HAWK downwind.

**Whistle for it, To.** It was an old superstition among sailors that when a ship was becalmed a wind could be raised by whistling, but to many seamen whistling was 'the Devil's music', which could raise a gale. It was not tolerated, therefore. The phrase 'you can whistle for it' now means 'you won't get it'.

**Whistle in the dark, To.** To strive to keep one's spirits up.

**Whistle-stop tour.** In the USA a brief campaign, usually political, conducted by travelling the country visiting the smaller communities, often talking from the rear platform of a train. A 'whistle stop' is a small town on a railroad where the train only stopped on a given signal. *See also* JERKWATER.

**Whistle up, To.** To call or summon as if by whistling.

**As clean as a whistle.** *See under* AS.

**Bells and whistles.** *See under* BELL.

**Blow the whistle on, To.** *See under* BLOW.

**Kist of whistles.** *See under* KIST.

**Penny whistle.** *See under* PENNY.

**Pig and Whistle.** *See under* PUBLIC HOUSE SIGNS.

**Wet one's whistle, To.** *See under* WET.

**Wolf whistle.** *See under* WOLF.

**White.** The colour denotes purity, virginity, simplicity, innocence, truth and hope. For its ecclesiastical use and symbolism *see* COLOURS.

Generally, the priests of antiquity wore white

vestments, and bardic costume, supposedly derived from the DRUIDS, is always white. OSIRIS, the ancient Egyptian god, wore a white crown, the priests of JUPITER were clad in white, and at the death of a CAESAR the national mourning was white. The Persians affirm that the divinities are clothed in white.

**White** or **pale about the gills.** Showing signs of fear or terror or sickness.

**White admiral.** The butterfly *Limenitis camilla*, which has brown wings with white markings.

**White bird, The.** Conscience, or the SOUL of man. The Muslims have preserved the old idea that the souls of the just lie under the throne of God, like white birds, till the resurrection morn. *See also* DOVE.

**Whiteboys.** Irish Catholic peasant organizations first appearing in Munster in the 1760s, whose outrages were a protest against RACK-RENTS, TITHES, enclosures and the like. They again terrorized southern Ireland from the late 1780s until the end of the century. They were so called because they wore white frocks over their clothing. In the ISLE OF MAN, Christmas mummers were known as White Boys.

**White Canons.** *See* PREMONSTRATENSIAN.

**Whitechapel.** A district of Stepney in the EAST END of London, east of Aldgate, and a noted Jewish quarter. It contains part of PETTICOAT LANE and was the scene of the notorious Whitechapel murders, committed by JACK THE RIPPER. It is also notable for its bell foundry. It takes its name from the colour of the original chapel-of-ease to Stepney built there.

In WHIST, Whitechapel denotes unskilful play such as leading out with winning cards, or leading from a one-card suit in order to trump.

**White Christmas.** A Christmas with snow on the ground, the latter being a nostalgically or romantically desirable ingredient of the festival but in practice an often unwelcome addition.

> I'm dreaming of a white Christmas,
> Just like the ones I used to know,
> Where the tree-tops glisten
> And children listen
> To hear sleigh bells in the snow.
> IRVING BERLIN: 'White Christmas' (song) (1942)

**White cliffs of Dover, The.** The chalk cliffs near Dover, Kent, serving as a patriotic or nostalgic landmark for those returning home from abroad. They were popularized from a morale-boosting song sung by Vera Lynn in the Second World War:

> There'll be bluebirds over
> The white cliffs of Dover,
> Tomorrow, just you wait and see.
> NAT BURTON: 'The White Cliffs of Dover' (1941)

**White coal.** Water, especially when regarded as a source of power.

**White Cockade, The.** The badge worn by the followers of Charles Edward, the YOUNG PRETENDER.

**White-collar worker.** The professional or clerical worker, whose calling demands a certain nicety of attire typified by the wearing of a white shirt and collar. *See also* BLUE-COLLAR WORKER.

**White Company, The.** In 13th-century France a band of cut-throats organized by Folquet, bishop of Toulouse, to extirpate heretics in his diocese. The name is better known for its association with the FREE COMPANIES of the late 14th century, especially those that Bertrand du Guesclin (*c.*1320–80) led against Pedro the Cruel of Castile in 1367, whose members wore a white cross on the shoulder, and that under Sir John Hawkwood (d.1394) in Italy. Sir Arthur Conan Doyle's notable story, *The White Company*, was first published in 1891. *See also* CONDOTTIERI; FREELANCE.

**White Devil, The.** Vittoria Corombona, an Italian murderess whose story was dramatized (1608) by John Webster under this name. 'White devils' was a slang term for prostitutes in the 16th and 17th centuries.

**White Devil of Wallachia, The.** SCANDERBEG or George Castriota (1403–68), the Albanian leader, was so called by the Turks.

**Whited sepulchre, A.** A hypocrite, especially one who conceals wickedness under a cloak of virtue.

In biblical times Jewish sepulchres were whitened to make them conspicuous so that passers-by might avoid ritual defilement by close approach. Thus Jesus (Matthew 23:27) says: 'Ye are like unto whited sepulchres, which indeed appear beautiful outward, but are within full of dead men's bones, and of all uncleanness.'

**White elephant, A.** A possession that is of little use and that is costly to maintain. The allusion is to the story of a king of Siam who used to make a present of a white elephant to courtiers he wished to ruin.

**White Ensign.** A St George's cross on a white ground with the UNION JACK in a canton, since 1864 the ensign of the Royal Navy but also used by members of the Royal Yacht Squadron who have the requisite warrant.

**Whiteface.** A nickname for a man from Herefordshire, from the white faces of Herefordshire cattle.

**White Fathers.** Members of the French Society of Missionaries of Africa, which was established at Algiers in 1868 and so called from the white tunic worn by the fathers.

**White flag.** An all white flag is universally used as the signal of surrender or desiring to parley and its bearer is by international custom immune from harm.

**White Friars.** *See* CARMELITES.

**White goods.** A commercial term for large electric appliances such as refrigerators and cookers, which were formerly mostly white. The expression was at one time also current for household linen.

**White-haired** or **white-headed boy.** A nickname for a favourite or darling.

**Whitehall.** This thoroughfare takes its name from the royal palace sited there, which was in use from the time of Henry VIII (r.1509–47) to William III (r.1689–1702). It was mostly destroyed by fire in 1698 and only the Banqueting Hall, built 1619–22 by Inigo Jones (1573–1652), still stands. The palace was formerly Cardinal Wolsey's mansion called York Place, but was named White Hall after its confiscation by Henry VIII.

> You must no more call it York-place, that's past:
> For, since the cardinal fell, that title's lost:
> 'Tis now the king's, and call'd Whitehall.
>
> SHAKESPEARE: *King Henry VIII*, IV, i (1612)

From its being the site of the major government offices, the name is often used as a synonym for the British government.

**White Hart, The.** A white hart with a golden chain in PUBLIC HOUSE SIGNS is the badge of Richard II (r.1377–99), which was worn by his adherents. It was adopted by his mother, Joan of Kent, whose cognizance it was.

**White harvest.** A late harvest, when the ground is white of a morning with hoar frost.

**White heat.** Figuratively, a state of intense excitement or emotion.

> We are redefining and we are restating our socialism in terms of the scientific revolution ... the Britain that is going to be forged in the white heat of this revolution will be no place for restrictive practices or outdated methods on either side of industry.
>
> HAROLD WILSON: addressing the Labour Party Conference (1 October 1963)

**White Horse, The.** The standard of the ancient Saxons, hence the emblem of Kent.

The name is also given to the hillside figures formed by removing the turf, thus revealing the underlying chalk. The most famous of these is at Uffington, Oxfordshire, traditionally said to commemorate ALFRED THE GREAT's victory over the Danes in 871 but probably dating from much earlier than this. The strangely elongated figure measures some 350ft (107m) from nose to tail and bears little resemblance to the traditional representation of a horse. It has been suggested, by the archaeologist Jacquetta Hawkes and others, that the figure may actually be that of a dragon, so that the site is associated with DRAGON HILL, which lies just below it. Whatever the case, it gives its name to the Vale of White Horse, to the west of Abingdon. The scouring of the White Horse was once a local ceremony.

> And then what a hill is the White Horse Hill! There it stands right up above all the rest, nine hundred feet above the sea, and the boldest, bravest shape for a chalk hill that you ever saw.
>
> THOMAS HUGHES: *Tom Brown's Schooldays*, Pt I, ch i (1857)

Among other white horses that at Westbury, Wiltshire, is also well known.

A galloping white horse is the device of the House of Hanover, and during the reigns of George I (1714–27) and George II (1727–60) the White Horse replaced the Royal Oak of Stuart fame on many PUBLIC HOUSE SIGNS.

**White horses.** A poetic phrase for the white-capped waves as they race in from the sea.

**White House, The.** The presidential mansion at Washington, D.C. The cornerstone was laid in 1792 and President John Adams and his wife, Abigail, became the first occupants in 1800. It was already known as the White House by 1809, the name referring to its white-grey sandstone, which contrasted with the red brick of the buildings nearby. Its official name from 1818 to 1902 was the Executive Mansion, but in the latter year Theodore Roosevelt adopted White House as the official name, which now figuratively denotes the Presidency of the USA.

**White knight.** A champion or rescuer, especially one who comes to the aid of a company in financial difficulties. *See also* TIRANT LO BLANCH.

**White-knuckle ride.** A fairground ride aiming to give a 'thrill of a lifetime' to its intrepid travellers, who so tightly grasp the rail before them that their knuckles turn white.

**White Ladies.** A popular name for the CISTERCIAN nuns in medieval England, from the colour of their habit, and for the Magdalenes. The name is also applied to the French Order of the Sisters of the Presentation of Mary (1796).

**White lady.** A kind of spectre, the appearance of which generally forebodes death in the house. It is a relic of Teutonic mythology, representing HULDA OR BERCHTA, the goddess who received the souls of maidens and young children. She is dressed in white and carries a bunch of keys at her side.

The first recorded instance of this apparition was in the 15th century, and the name given to the lady is Bertha von Rosenberg. She last appeared, it is said, in 1879. German legend says that when the castle of Neuhaus, Bohemia, was being built a white lady appeared and promised the workmen a sweet soup and a carp on the completion of the castle. In remembrance, these dainties were for long given to the poor on MAUNDY THURSDAY.

In Normandy the white ladies lurk in ravines, fords, bridges and the like, and ask wayfarers to dance. If the travellers refuse, the spirits fling them into a ditch. The best known of these ladies are La Dame d'Aprigny, who used to occupy the site of the Rue St Quentin, at Bayeux, and La Dame Abonde.

The White Lady of Avenel, in Sir Walter Scott's *The Monastery* (1820), is based on these legends.

A white lady is also a cocktail made from gin, Cointreau and lemon juice.

**White League, The.** A name for the KU KLUX KLAN, from the white robes and hoods worn by the members.

**White lie, A.** A harmless or trivial lie; an untruth in a positive or good cause. Such a lie is light or mild, qualities associated with white.

**White-livered.** Cowardly, from the old notion that the LIVERS of cowards were bloodless.

> How many cowards, whose hearts are all as false
> As stairs of sand, wear yet upon their chins
> The beards of Hercules and frowning Mars,
> Who, inward search'd, have livers white as milk.
> SHAKESPEARE: *The Merchant of Venice*, III, ii (1596)

**White magic.** Sorcery in which the Devil is not invoked and plays no part, as distinct from BLACK MAGIC.

**White man, A.** A thoroughly straightforward and honourable man.

**White man's burden, The.** In the days of imperialism, the duty supposed to be imposed upon the white races, especially the British, to govern and to educate the more 'backward' coloured peoples.

> Take up the White Man's burden –
> Send forth the best ye breed –
> Go bind your sons to exile
> To serve your captives' need.
> RUDYARD KIPLING: 'The White Man's Burden' (1899)

**White man's grave, The.** The unhealthy areas of equatorial West Africa, especially Sierra Leone.

**White man speak with forked tongue.** A phrase used humorously of an untruth. It may have originated in a Western film, although it has the genuine ring of a translated Native American saying.

**White meat.** Poultry, veal, rabbit or pork, with a low blood content, as distinct from beef or lamb, which are red with blood when raw.

**White Monks.** The CISTERCIAN monks, whose habits were made from white wool.

**White night, A.** A sleepless night. The French have the phrase, *passer une nuit blanche*.

To the Russians, white nights are those in northern regions when the sky never properly darkens in the summer months. In St Petersburg the white nights last from 11 June to 2 July, and in Archangel, further north, from 13 May to 30 July.

**White Paper.** A government publication printed for the information of Parliament. Such a report or statement of policy is not bulky enough to warrant the protective covers of a BLUEBOOK. White Papers are available to the public through HM Stationery Office.

**White poplar, The.** The tree is fabled to have originally been the NYMPH Leuce, daughter of OCEANUS and TETHYS and beloved by PLUTO, who changed her into a tree at death so that she should be immortal.

**White Queen, The.** Mary, Queen of Scots (1542–87), so called because she dressed in white mourning for her French husband, Francis II (1544–60).

**White Rose, The.** Used as a badge by Richard, Duke of York (1411–60), and derived from his Mortimer ancestors. It was one of the numerous badges used by his son Edward IV and was adopted by his descendants, but Richard III's badge was the white boar. It was also adopted by the JACOBITES as an emblem of the OLD PRETENDER, because his adherents were obliged to abet him SUB ROSA. Cecily Neville, wife of Richard, Duke of York, and granddaughter of John of Gaunt, was known as the White Rose of Raby. *See also* RED ROSE; TUDOR ROSE; WARS OF THE ROSES.

**Whiter than white.** Free from taint; beyond reproach; absolutely pure and innocent.

**White Russian.** An inhabitant of White Russia or Belorussia (now Belarus) (Russian *bely*, 'white'), a former republic of the USSR. White Russian is also a term for a counter-revolutionary or *émigré* at the time of the BOLSHEVIK revolution, and their army was known as the White Army, in direct contrast to the Communist RED ARMY.

**White's.** A chocolate house and later a fashionable CLUB, first opened by Francis White (d.1711) on the east side of St James's Street in London in 1693, moving across the street to larger premises in 1697. The fashionable fraternity soon congregated upstairs to avoid the general company of the chocolate house, which, after 1711, was in the hands of the Arthur family. Early on it earned notoriety as a gaming house. It also gained fame for the exclusiveness of its upstairs clientele, from which in due course White's Club developed. The transition was virtually complete by the mid-18th century, and it can with some justification be regarded as the first of the London clubs, moving to larger premises in 1755. Gambling and gaming excesses continued until the accession of George III (1760), when they were reduced to more modest proportions in keeping with the changed tone of the court. At this juncture a group of the more extravagant younger men from White's became the patrons of ALMACK'S.

**White satin.** An old nickname for GIN.

**White sheep.** *See* BLACK SHEEP.

**White Ship, The.** The ship carrying Henry I of England's 17-year-old son William from Normandy to England, which struck a rock off Barfleur (25 November 1120) and sank. William was drowned, and his death led to the conflict for the crown between Stephen (*c*.1097–1154), who was the grandson of WILLIAM THE CONQUEROR, and Matilda or Maud (1102–67), the daughter of Henry I and the wife of Geoffrey Plantagenet, Count of Anjou. The disaster was due to the drunken laxity of the crew.

**White Sisters.** The Congregation of the Daughters of the Holy Ghost, founded in Brittany in 1706, so called from the colour of their habit. Also the Congregation of the Missionary Sisters of Our Lady of Africa (1869), the counterpart of the WHITE FATHERS.

**White slave.** A woman who is sold or forced into prostitution, especially when taken abroad.

**White squall, A.** One that produces no diminution of light, as distinct from a black squall, in which the clouds are black and heavy.

**White stick.** A white-painted stick used by a blind person when out walking.

**White supremacy.** The doctrine that White people are innately superior to those of other races.

**White Surrey.** Richard III's favourite horse, presumably named for the Earl of Surrey, son of the Duke of Norfolk, who appears in Shakespeare's play.

> Saddle White Surrey for the field to-morrow.
> SHAKESPEARE: *Richard III*, V, iii (1592)

**White tie affair, A.** A social function at which the men wear formal evening dress with a white bow tie and a coat with tails. Invitations to such functions are usually printed simply 'White tie'. *See also* BLACK TIE *under* BLACK.

> Full evening dress, or 'white tie', is rarely required except on the most formal occasions.
> *Debrett's Etiquette and Modern Manners* (1981)

**White tincture.** The alchemist's name for a preparation that was supposed to convert any base metal into silver. It is also called the Stone of the Second Order, the Little Elixir and the Little Magisterium. *See also* RED.

**White Tower, The.** The approximately square keep of the TOWER OF LONDON, the oldest part of the fortress begun by WILLIAM THE CONQUEROR. There is a turret at each corner and the sides are over 100ft (30m) wide, the walls being 15ft (4.5m) thick in the lower parts and 11ft (3.4m) thick in the upper storey. It has housed many notable prisoners. *See also* PRINCES IN THE TOWER.

**Whitewash.** Figuratively, excuses made in palliation of bad conduct, otherwise a false colouring given to a person's character or memory, or to their tarnished reputation.

The term is also applied to the clearance by a bankrupt of his debts, not by paying them but by judicial process. In sport, a whitewash is a defeat in which the losing side or person scores no points at all.

**White wedding.** A wedding in which the bride wears the traditional white wedding dress and veil, white symbolizing purity and virginity. For the same reason, grey horses were formerly used for the wedding carriage and the postboys wore white hats. Wedding cake is coated with white icing and invitations are usually printed in silver. It is said to be unlucky to be married in anything but white.

**White wine.** Any wine of a light colour as distinct from red wine, e.g. champagne, hock, Sauternes, Moselle, Graves, Chablis and so on.

**White witch.** One who practises WHITE MAGIC only.

**As white as a sheet.** *See under* AS.

**Big white chief.** *See under* BIG.

**Blanco White.** *See under* BLANCO.

**Bleed someone white, To.** *See under* BLEED.

**Days marked with a white stone.** *See under* DAY.

**Great White Way, The.** *See under* GREAT.

**Hit the white, To.** *See under* HIT.

**In black and white.** *See under* BLACK.

**Poor white.** *See under* POOR.

**Show the white feather, To.** *See under* SHOW.

**Snow White.** *See under* SNOW.

**Whitsun. Whitsun ale.** The most important CHURCH-ALE, formerly celebrated with much revelry.

**Whit Sunday.** 'White Sunday'. The seventh Sunday after EASTER, commemorating the descent of the HOLY GHOST on the day of PENTECOST. It was one of the great seasons for baptism and the candidates wore white garments, hence the name.

**Whitsun farthings.** *See* PENTECOSTALS.

**Whitsuntide.** The whole week following WHIT SUNDAY.

**Whittington, Dick.** According to the popular legend and PANTOMIME story, a poor boy who made his way to London when he heard that the streets were paved with gold and silver. He found shelter as a scullion in the house of a rich merchant who permitted each of his servants to partake in sending a cargo of merchandise to Barbary. Dick sent his cat, but subsequently ran away because of the ill treatment meted out to the servants. He was recalled by Bow Bells seeming to say:

Turn again Whittington
Thrice Lord Mayor of London.

He returned to find his cat had been purchased for a vast sum by the king of Barbary, who was much plagued by rats and mice. He married his master's daughter Alice, prospered exceedingly, and became lord mayor three times.

Richard Whittington (*c*.1358–1423) was, in fact, the youngest son of Sir William Whittington of Pauntley in Gloucestershire and duly became a mercer of London, having married Alice, the daughter of Sir Ivo Fitzwaryn. He became very wealthy, the richest merchant of his day, and was made lord mayor of London in 1397–8, 1406–7 and 1419–20. When he died he left his vast wealth for charitable and public purposes.

The part of the cat in the story has been explained as follows: he traded in coals brought to London in 'cats' (a type of sailing vessel), or that the word is a confusion with French *achat*, 'purchase' (a term then used for trading at a profit). Whatever the case, Dick Whittington and his cat are now inseparable and form the subject of many Christmas pantomimes.

**Whizz** or **whiz kid.** A highly intelligent young person, one who achieves rapid success, the onomatopoeic word 'whizz' being the sound of something moving through the air with great rapidity. No doubt the term has also been influenced by 'wizard'.

**Who. Whodunit.** A colloquialism originating in the USA for a detective story (in American usage, a mystery).

**Who goes home?** When the HOUSE OF COMMONS adjourns at night the doorkeeper asks this question of the members. In bygone days, when danger lurked in the unlit streets from cutthroats and thieves, the cry was raised to enable them to depart in groups and to escort the SPEAKER to his residence.

**Whom God would destroy He first makes mad.** A translation of the Latin version (*Quos Deus vult perdere, prius dementat*) of one of the *Fragments* of Euripides (5th century BC).

**Whom the gods love die young.** A translation of the Latin *Quem Di diligunt adolescens moritur* (Plautus, *Bacchides*, IV, vii, 18 (3rd century BC)), or more properly of the Greek line in this work's source, *Hon oi theoi philousin apothneskei neos* (Menander, *Dis Exapaton*, Fragment 4 (4th century BC)). Lord Byron quotes the saying (among many others) in *Don Juan* (IV, xii (1819–24)): '"Whom the gods love die young", was said of yore. And many deaths do they escape by this.' Compare the popular saying ONLY THE GOOD DIE YOUNG.

**Who stole the donkey?** An old gibe against policemen. The story is that in the early days of the force a donkey was stolen but the police failed to discover the thief, and this made them an object of mockery. The correct answer is 'The man with the white hat', because white hats were made from the skins of donkeys, many of which were stolen and sold to hatters.

**Who's Who.** The annual biographical dictionary of 'people of influence' was first issued in 1849 but took its present form in 1897, when it incorporated material from an earlier work, *Men and Women of the Time*. The entries are compiled with the assistance of the entrants themselves, leading occasionally to some subjectivity, for example in the matter of personal relationships and dates of birth. The freest section is that labelled 'Recreations', which may be purely prosaic, such as 'Reading, gardening', or else idiosyncratic, as the following for the writer Jack Rosenthal (b.1931) in the 1991 edition:

Work, frying fish, polishing almost anything tarnished, playing the violin in enforced privacy, remembering how Manchester United used to play, collecting models of rhinoceri and tortoisi.

**Doctor Who.** The Time Lord hero of the children's television SCIENCE FICTION series first shown in 1963. He travels through time and space in a vehicle called the 'Tardis', disguised on the outside to resemble a London police telephone box, and he is invariably accompanied by a winsome female assistant. The first actor to play the part was William Hartnell, who portrayed him as a testy elderly academic. One of the most memorable depictions was by Tom Baker, whose Doctor was a tousle-headed eccentric sporting a long scarf. The series was created by Sydney Newman and Donald Wilson.

**Whole. Whole bag of tricks, A.** *See* BAG OF TRICKS.

**Whole ball of wax, The.** The lot; everything. The origin of the expression is uncertain. It may derive from a former method of distributing the land of an estate to heirs, in which the amount of each portion was concealed in a wax ball to be drawn out of a hat at random.

**Whole bang shoot** or **whole shooting match, The.** The lot; everything. *See also* SHEBANG.

**Whole Booke of Psalmes, The.** *See* BAY PSALM BOOK.

**Whole caboodle, The.** The whole lot; the whole collection. The word has long been a common term among New England longshoremen to mean possessions or property, and it probably originates from a shortened form of the more general American phrase 'kit and boodle', having the same meaning.

**Half is more than the whole, The.** *See under* HALF.

**Whoopee. Whoopee cushion.** A joke cushion that makes a sound like the breaking of wind when someone sits on it.

**Make whoopee, To.** To enjoy oneself uproariously; to go 'on the razzle' or spree.

**Whore of Babylon, The.** A PURITAN epithet for the ROMAN CATHOLIC CHURCH. The allusion is to Revelation 17–19, where Babylon stands for Rome, the embodiment of luxury, vice, splendour, tyranny and all that the early church held was against the spirit of Christ. *See also* SCARLET WOMAN.

**Why. Why did the chicken cross the road?** An appropriate reply to an unanswerable question. *See also* HOW LONG IS A PIECE OF STRING? *under* HOW.

**Why should the Devil have all the good tunes?** A saying allegedly popularized by Charles Wesley in about 1740, when he adapted the music of current popular songs to promote the use of his hymns.

> He did not see any reason why the devil should have all the good tunes.
>
> E.W. BROOME: *The Reverend Rowland Hill*, ch vii (1881)

**Wick, To get on someone's.** *See under* GET.

**Wicked.** The word is probably connected with Old English *wicca*, a WIZARD.

**Wicked Bible, The.** *See under* BIBLE.

**Wicked Prayer Book, The.** Printed 1686. In the Epistle for the 14th Sunday after Trinity the following passage occurs:

> Now the works of the flesh are manifest, which are these, adultery, fornication, uncleanness, idolatry ... they who do such things shall inherit the kingdom of God.

('shall inherit' should be 'shall not inherit'.)

**Wicket. Leg before wicket.** *See under* LEG.

**Sticky wicket.** *See under* STICK.

**Widdershins.** *See* WITHERSHINS.

**Wide.** Slang for cunning, artful, or for one who is very wide awake. Hence formerly 'wide boy', a plebeian type of SMART ALEC who needs watching.

**Wide-awake.** Types of felt hat, with a low crown and wide brim, common in Victorian times. They were punningly so called because they never had a 'nap'.

**Wide of the mark.** Not to the point; inaccurate; irrelevant. The metaphor is from archery. *See also* BESIDE THE MARK.

**Wide world, The.** The whole world in all its greatness. *The Wide, Wide World* (1850) by 'Elizabeth Wetherell' (Susan B. Warner) was one of the most popular novels of the 19th century. Its heroine suffers a series of misfortunes, including the loss of her mother and of a close friend, but learns to love the God who inflicts these tragedies upon her.

**Give a wide berth to, To.** To avoid; to keep at a distance from. The reference is to giving a ship plenty of room to swing when at anchor. The place where a ship is anchored or tied up is its berth.

**Widecombe Fair.** The fair held annually on the second Tuesday of September at Widecombe-in-the-Moor, Devon. The long-established sheep and pony fair in this DARTMOOR parish became widely known from the old folk song telling the story of OLD UNCLE TOM COBBLEIGH. He still appears in the modern carnival dressed in an old linen smock astride an old grey mare that gives rides to children.

**Widow, The.** Old slang for the gallows. Also Victorian slang for champagne, in allusion to the well-known brand Veuve Clicquot, so called from 'Widow' Clicquot who, at the age of 27, took over the firm in 1806 on the death of her husband François, and with her associates made it an outstanding success. The House of Clicquot was founded by Philippe Clicquot in 1772 and eventually renamed Veuve Clicquot-Ponsardin in 1810.

**Widow at Windsor, The.** A name applied to Queen Victoria whose husband Albert, the PRINCE CONSORT, died at the end of 1861. Her remaining 39 years were largely spent in seclusion, and she never ceased to mourn her loss. The name 'The Widow at Windsor' was applied by Rudyard Kipling in his *Barrack-Room Ballad* of that name (1892).

> Then 'ere's to the Widow at Windsor,
> An' 'ere's to the stores an' the guns,
> The men an' the 'orses what makes up the forces
> O' Missis Victorier's sons.

**Widow's cruse, The.** A small supply of anything which, by good management, is made to go a long way and to be apparently inexhaustible. The allusion is to the miracle of the cruse of oil in 1 Kings 17:10–16.

**Widow's mite.** An offering, small in itself but representing self-sacrifice on the part of the giver; otherwise a small contribution from one who cannot give much. The allusion is biblical.

> And there came a certain poor widow, and she threw in two mites, which make a farthing.
>
> Mark 12:42

**Widow's peak.** A V-shaped point of hair over the forehead, reminiscent of the front cusp of the cap formerly worn by widows.

**Widow's weeds.** The mourning worn by a widow, from Old English *wǣd*, 'garment'. Edmund Spenser (*The Faerie Queene*, II, iii (1590)) tells of 'A goodly Ladie clad in hunters weed'. Shakespeare in *A Midsummer Night's Dream* (II, i (1595)) has:

> And there the snake throws her enamell'd skin,
> Weed wide enough to wrap a fairy in.

**Black widow.** *See under* BLACK.

**Grass widow.** *See under* GRASS.

**Wife.** Old English *wīf*, 'woman'. The ultimate source of the word is obscure. It is related to German *Weib* (Old High German *wīb*) but 'cannot be allied to Anglo-Saxon *wefan*, to weave' (W.W. Skeat, *An Etymological Dictionary of the English Language* (1909)). The original meaning may have been 'the veiled one', i.e. the bride, in allusion to the marriage custom.

The old meaning, 'woman', still appears in such combinations as fishwife, housewife and so on, and old wives' tales for unconvincing stories or proverbial legend.

**Bachelor's wife.** *See under* BACHELOR.

**Caesar's wife must be above suspicion.** *See under* CAESAR.

**Common-law wife.** *See under* COMMON.

**Dutch wife.** *See under* DUTCH.

**Noah's wife.** *See under* NOAH.

**Old wives' tale.** *See under* OLD.

**Wife-hater Bible, The.** *See under* BIBLE.

**Wig.** A shortened form of 'periwig' (earlier, 'perwig'), from French *perruque*. The long flowing wig of Louis XIV's reign (1643–1715) was called the *allonge* ('lengthening'), and in the 18th century there were 30 or 40 different styles and names, including the artichoke, bag, barrister's, bishop's, Blenheim, brush, buckle, busby, bush (buzz), campaigning, cauliflower, chain, chancellor's corded, Count Saxe's mode, crutch, cut bob, Dalmahoy (a bob wig worn by tradesmen), detached buckle, drop, Dutch, full, half natural, Jansenist bob, judge's, ladder, long bob, Louis, pigeon's wing, rhinoceros, rose, she-dragon, small back, spinach seed, staircase, wild boar's back, wolf's paw. *See also* MIND ONE'S PS AND QS.

**Wigging.** A scolding or reprimand. The reference may be to the idea of dislodging or ruffling someone's wig, or from a reproof by a BIGWIG or a wigged superior.

**Wigs on the green.** A serious disagreement likely to lead to a scrimmage or rumpus. The expression is of Irish origin. Wigs are liable to be pulled off or fall on the grass in a tussle.

**Wiggentree.** *See* ROWAN.

**Wight.** An Old English word (originally *wiht*) meaning a person or human being. It chiefly survives in the phrase 'wretched wight', one for whom everything goes wrong.

**Wild. Wild and woolly.** Said of an unkempt or ferocious-looking person. The allusion is to a wild, long-haired animal such as a yak.

**Wild Bill Hickok.** *See under* HICKOK.

**Wild boar of the Ardennes, The.** Guillaume, Comte de la Marck (1446–85), Flemish adventurer, was so called from his ferocity. He features in Sir Walter Scott's *Quentin Durward* (1823). The Countess de Croye falls into his hands as a result of the scheme by which she hoped to escape with Quentin Durward from Schonwaldt Castle, and his head becomes the price by which her hand is won.

**Wild boy of Aveyron, The.** An 11-year-old boy found running naked and wild in a wood near Aveyron in the south of France. In 1801–5 the French physician Jean Itard tried to train and educate him, describing the results of his endeavours in *Rapports sur le Sauvage d'Aveyron* (1807). *See also* NOBLE SAVAGE; WILD CHILD.

**Wild card.** A playing card that has any rank chosen for it by the player holding it. The JOKER in many games is wild. In computing jargon a wild card is a character that will match any character or sequence of characters in a file name or the like, while a wild card in sport is an extra player chosen to enter a game at the selector's discretion.

**Wildcat.** A female of fierce and uncontrolled temper is often called a wildcat for obvious reasons, and the expression is variously applied to reckless, uncontrolled and unsound activities and ventures. Thus a wildcat strike is an impromptu or unofficial strike, and a wild-cat scheme is a rash and hazardous scheme, especially a financial one. The usage is of colloquial American origin, and in the USA a prospective well for oil or natural gas is also called a wildcat.

**Wild child.** A general term for any of the children found wandering wild in woods or deserts from the 18th century and held up as the pure offspring of nature, free from any taint, good or bad, of civilization. In some cases they are said to have been raised by animals. Famous examples are the GAZELLE BOY, PETER THE WILD BOY and the WILD BOY OF AVEYRON. Noted literary types are MOWGLI and TARZAN. *See also* NOBLE SAVAGE.

**Wildfire.** An old term for a composition of inflammable materials that catch fire quickly. It is now used figuratively in the phrase 'to spread like wildfire', meaning to be disseminated quickly.

**Wild-goose chase, A.** An impracticable or useless pursuit of something; a hopeless enterprise. A wild goose is very difficult to catch. *See also* WILDCAT.

**Wild horse.** An undomesticated horse, one that has not been broken in. The phrase is mostly found in an expression such as: 'Wild horses would not drag your secret from me.'

**Wild Huntsman, The.** A spectral hunter of medieval legend who, with his pack of spectral dogs, frequents certain forests and occasionally appears to mortals. The legend takes numerous forms in Germany, France and England, and the wild huntsman is often identified with various heroes of national legend. In England there is notably Herne the Hunter, one-time keeper in Windsor Forest. Shakespeare says he 'walks' in winter, about midnight, blasts trees and takes cattle. He wears horns and rattles a chain (*Merry Wives of Windsor*, IV, iv (1600)). Herne is also featured in Harrison Ainsworth's *Windsor Castle* (1843). *See also* HERNE'S OAK *under* OAK.

There is a Midnight Hunter of Dartmoor accompanied by the WISH HOUNDS. *See also* GABRIEL'S HOUNDS; MODDEY DHOO.

**Wild man of the woods.** A name sometimes used for an orang-utan, translating the Malay original, from *orang*, 'person', 'man' and *utan*, 'woods', 'forest'.

**Wild silk.** Silk from wild silkworms, or an imitation of this.

**Wild West.** In 19th-century America, the unstable western frontier, before orderly settlement was established under governmental control. It was an area of action and adventure, of desperadoes and cattle rustlers, noted for hard drinking, gambling, violence and crime generally. It has since been romanticized in stories and films called Westerns, and has its own folk heroes varying from the LONE RANGER to Deadwood Dick.

**Peter the Wild Boy.** *See under* PETER.

**Run wild, To.** *See under* RUN.

**Sow one's wild oats, To.** *See under* SOW.

**Wilderness. Go into the wilderness, To.** *See under* GO.

**Voice crying in the wilderness, A.** *See under* VOICE.

**Wilfrid.** A Northumbrian, educated at Lindisfarne, St Wilfrid (*c*.634–709) subsequently visited Canterbury and Rome, learning the Roman liturgy. He became abbot of Ripon and was largely responsible for the adoption of Roman usages in preference to Celtic ones at the Synod of Whitby in 664. Soon afterwards he became bishop of York and finally of Hexham. His day is 12 October.

**St Wilfrid's needle.** A narrow passage in the crypt of Ripon cathedral, built by Odo, archbishop of Canterbury, and said to have been used to test a woman's chastity, as none but a virgin was able to squeeze through.

**Wilgefortis.** *See* UNCUMBER.

**Wilhelmstrasse.** A street in Berlin where the principal government offices, including the Foreign Office, were situated. Hence used figuratively for the German Foreign Office and its policies. Much of the street was destroyed by Allied bombing in the Second World War.

**Will. At will.** *See under* AT.

**Living will.** *See under* LIVE.

**Free will.** *See under* FREE.

**Tenant at will.** *See under* TENANT.

**Where there's a will there's a way.** *See under* WHERE.

**With the best will in the world.** However good one's intentions.

**William.** One of the most popular of Christian names (French *Guillaume*, German *Wilhelm*), it means a protector, literally, a 'determined helmet' (Germanic *wil* and *helm*).

**William Caxton.** *See under* CAXTON.

**William Longsword.** Longsword (*Longespée, Longepée, Longspée* etc) was the surname of William, the first Duke of Normandy (d.943). He was the great-great-grandfather of WILLIAM THE CONQUEROR. The name was also given to William, 3rd Earl of Salisbury (d.1226), a natural son of Henry II and (according to late tradition) of FAIR ROSAMOND.

**William of Cloudeslie.** A noted outlaw and archer of the 'north country'. *See also* CLYM OF THE CLOUGH.

**William of Malmesbury.** A monk and librarian of Malmesbury Abbey and noted chronicler and historian (*c*.1080–1143). Among his numerous works the two most important are his *De gestis regum Anglorum* ('Chronicle of the Kings of England', to 1125) and *De gestis pontificum Anglorum* ('The History of the Prelates of England', to 1122).

**William of Occam.** The famous NOMINALIST philosopher (1285–1349). He was a native of Ockham, Surrey, and was also called *Doctor Invincibilis* or the INVINCIBLE DOCTOR. *See also* OCCAM'S RAZOR.

**William of Orange.** The territorial name of William III (r.1689–1702) originally came from Orange (anciently Arausio), a town on the Rhône, north of Avignon in the south of France, which his ancestors acquired through marriage. The House of Orange still reigns in the Netherlands.

**William of Wykeham.** *See* WYKEHAMIST.

**William pear, The.** Properly the Williams' pear or Bon Chrétien, so called after the name of its introducer to England from France. It is known in the USA as the Bartlett pear, from the name of its importer.

**William Rufus.** King William II of England (*c*.1056–1100), so called from his ruddy complexion.

**William Shakespeare.** *See under* SHAKESPEARE.

**William Tell.** *See under* TELL.

**William the Conqueror.** King William I of England (*c*.1027–87), who as Duke of Normandy invaded and conquered the English in 1066. He is also called William the Bastard, from his parentage.

**William the Lyon.** King of Scotland (1143–1214). The reason for this appellation is not known, but it is popularly supposed that he was the first Scottish king to adopt the LION as his achievement.

**William the Silent.** Prince William of Orange (1533–84), so called because when (1559) Henry II of France, thinking that he would be a ready accomplice, revealed to him the plans for a general massacre of Protestants:

> the Prince, although horror-struck and indignant at the Royal revelations, held his peace, and kept his countenance ... William of Orange earned the name of 'the Silent', from the manner in which he received the communications of Henry without revealing to the monarch by word or look, the enormous blunder which he had committed.
>
> JOHN MOTLEY: *The Rise of the Dutch Republic*, II, i (1856)

**St William of Maleval.** A Frenchman of the 12th century who died in Tuscany in 1157. He went as a pilgrim to the HOLY LAND and on his return adopted the religious life. He was noted for his piety and asceticism and for his gifts of prayer and prophecy. His day is 10 February.

**St William of Montevergine.** A 12th-century hermit of Piedmont who built himself a cell on Montevergine and subsequently founded several monasteries. He died in 1142 and his day is 25 June.

**St William of Norwich.** A 12-year-old skinner's apprentice of Norwich (1132–44). According to Thomas of Monmouth, a monk of Norwich, he was abducted by a strange man who promised he would become kitchen-boy to the archdeacon. Instead he was gagged, shaved, lacerated with a crown of thorns and crucified by Jews during the PASSOVER. It was said at the time that it was part of Jewish ritual to sacrifice a Christian every year. St HUGH OF LINCOLN underwent a similar fate.

**St William of York.** William Fitzherbert, chaplain to King Stephen and archbishop of York (1142). He died in 1154 and was canonized by Honorius III in 1227, largely on account of the miracles reported to have been performed at his tomb.

**Sir William Wallace.** *See under* WALLACE.

**Sweet william.** *See under* SWEET.

**Will Scarlet.** *See under* SCARLET.

**Willie. Willie wastle.** This old children's game is said to be named from William Wastle, governor of Hume Castle, Haddington, Scotland. When Cromwell summoned him to surrender, he is said to have replied:

> I, Wullie Wastle,
> Stand here in ma castle,
> An' a' the dogs o' your toon
> Will never drive Wullie Wastle doon!

For Scottish children, this is the equivalent of the English KING OF THE CASTLE.

**Holy Willie.** *See under* HOLY.

**Woodbine Willie.** *See under* WOOD.

**Willis's rooms.** *See* ALMACK'S.

**Will-o'-the-wisp.** *See* IGNIS FATUUS.

**Willow. Willow pattern.** This celebrated design for porcelain in blue and white was introduced by Thomas Turner of Caughley, Shropshire, in 1779. It imitated the Chinese style of decoration but was not an exact copy of any Chinese original. It is so called from the weeping willow in the design.

**Weeping willow.** *See under* WEEP.

**Wear the willow, To.** *See under* WEAR.

**Will's Coffee House.** A famous resort in the time of John Dryden (1631–1700), who added much to its popularity. It stood on the corner of Bow Street and Russell Street, COVENT GARDEN. Originally called the Red Cow, then the Rose, it took its name from Will Urwin, who was its proprietor at the time of the RESTORATION in 1660. Known as the 'Wits Coffee House', it was the headquarters of TORY men of letters but from 1714 was rivalled by Button's COFFEE house, the home of the WHIG literati. In his *Diary* for 3 February 1664 Samuel Pepys notes meeting 'Dryden, the poet I knew at Cambridge, and all the wits of the town'. Confusion sometimes arises from the coexistence of five or more coffee houses of this name, but this is undoubtedly the Will's associated with the *Spectator*. It closed some time before the middle years of the 18th century.

**Willy-nilly** (Latin *nolens volens*, 'willing or not'). The expression represents Old English *wile hē, nyle hē*, literally 'will he or will he not', with *nyle* from *ne*, 'not', and *willan*, 'to will'.

**Willy-willy.** The Australian Aboriginal term for the sudden whirlwinds that are common on the northwest coast. They can be seen approaching in a high circular column of leaves and dust from a great distance.

**Wilshire Boulevard.** A broad street that passes through the centre of Los Angeles and leads to the Pacific coast in the region of Santa Monica. It is famous for its Miracle Mile, close to HOLLYWOOD, a glamorously glittering stretch of stores, boutiques, hotels, restaurants and night-clubs. It takes its name from a local developer, H.G. Wilshire (1861–1927).

**Wimbledon.** A name synonymous with tennis and tennis championships, as the London suburb that is the location of the All England Croquet Club. In the middle of the 1870s the club, being in low water, added 'Lawn Tennis' to its title, this being then a new game increasing in popularity. On the club's courts, the first lawn tennis championship in the world was held in 1877. The annual tournament run by the All England Club at Wimbledon ranks as the premier championship.

**Wimp.** A weak or ineffectual person, especially a

male. The word may have originated in an Oxford University slang term for a female student, and derive from a blend of 'woman' and 'whimperer'.

**Wimsey, Lord Peter.** The aristocratic private detective is the central character of the crime novels of Dorothy L. Sayers (1893–1957). He first appears in *Whose Body?* (1923), and in many of his manners is similar to Bertie WOOSTER. He has a manservant, Mervyn Bunter, a private income, and a number of acquaintances among the idle rich. He is said to be based on the travel writer Eric Whelpton (1894–1981).

**Win. Win by a head or by a short head, To.** To win narrowly; only just to outdistance one's competitors; to win with practically nothing to spare. The phrase is from horse-racing, in which a rider wins by a distance shorter than that of a horse's head.

**Win hands down, To.** To win easily. A jockey rides with hands down when he is winning comfortably and easily.

**Win one's spurs, To.** To gain the rank of knighthood, hence to win entitlement to recognition by one's efforts. When a man was knighted, the person who dubbed him presented him with a pair of gilt spurs.

**Win on points, To.** In boxing, to win a contest by scoring more points, not by a knockout.

**Win the day, To.** To be victorious or successful.

**Win the field, To.** To win the battle.

**Win the mare or lose the halter, To.** To play DOUBLE OR QUITS; to stake all or nothing.

**Clear winner.** *See under* WINNER.

**You can't win.** There is no way of succeeding; you lose either way.

**You can't win them all.** An expression of resignation, or of consolation, on failure. A similar phrase is 'Win some, lose some'.

**Winchester.** Identified by Sir Thomas Malory (d.1471) and other old writers with the CAMELOT of ARTHURIAN ROMANCES. It was King Alfred's capital. *See also* SWITHIN; WYKEHAMIST.

**Wind.** According to classical mythology, the north, south, east and west winds (BOREAS, Notus, EURUS and ZEPHYRUS) were under the rule of AEOLUS, who kept them confined in a cave on Mount Haemus, Thrace. Other strong winds of a more destructive nature were the brood of TYPHOEUS.

The story says that Aeolus gave Odysseus (ULYSSES) a bag tied with a silver string, in which were all the hurtful and unfavourable winds, so that he might arrive home without being delayed by tempests. His crew, however, opened the bag in the belief that it contained treasure, the winds escaped, and a terrible storm at once arose, driving the vessel out of its course and back to the island of Aeolus.

Aquilo is another Latin name for the north wind, as AUSTER is of the south and FAVONIUS of the west. Thrascias is a north-northwest wind and Libs a west-southwest wind, CAURUS or Corus a northwest wind (also personified as Argestes), Volturnus a southeast wind, and Africus and Afer ventus a southwest wind. *See also* ETESIAN WIND; TRADE WINDS; WILLY-WILLY.

**Windbag.** A long-winded speaker, who uses inflated phrases and promises far more than he can perform.

**Windcheater.** A warm, more or less weather-proof jacket with close-fitting neck, cuffs and waist to keep out ('cheat') the wind.

**Wind egg, A.** An egg without a shell, or with a soft shell, or an unfertilized one, from the old superstition that the hen that lays it was impregnated by the wind.

**Windfall.** An unexpected piece of good luck, especially an unexpected legacy, or something worth having that comes to one without any personal exertion, like fruit that has fallen from the tree and so does not have to be picked.

**Windjammer.** A sailing ship or one of its crew. The term is a modern one, born since steam superseded sail.

**Wind of change.** A new current of opinion; reformist trend. The phrase was popularized by Harold Macmillan (1894–1986) in his speech to the South African Parliament (3 February 1960), with reference to the social and political ferment in the African continent.

> The wind of change is blowing through this continent, and, whether we like it or not, this growth of national consciousness is a political fact.

**Windy City.** Chicago, so nicknamed not because of its meteorological characteristics but because of its blustering self-confidence.

**Between wind and water.** *See under* BETWEEN.

**Break wind, To.** *See under* BREAK.

**Capful of wind.** *See under* CAP.

**Etesian wind.** *See under* ETESIAN.

**Eye of the wind.** *See under* EYE.

**Get one's second wind, To.** *See under* SECOND.

**Get the wind up, To.** To become thoroughly alarmed, nervous, over-anxious and frightened.

**Get wind of something, To.** To get advance knowledge of something that has not yet happened. The allusion is to an animal's ability to detect the approach of others by their scent on the wind.

**Gone with the wind.** A phrase said of events or persons that have left no trace by which to be remembered. It is also the title of what long remained America's most widely read novel, a story of the American Civil War (1861–5) as seen through Southern eyes. It was written by Margaret Mitchell and published in 1936. The words themselves come from Ernest Dowson's poem

'Non Sum Qualis Eram', also known as 'Cynara' (1896):

> I have forgot much, Cynara! gone with the wind,
> Flung roses, roses, riotously, with the throng.

**Hug the wind, To.** *See under* HUG.

**In the teeth of the wind.** *See under* TOOTH.

**It's an ill wind that blows nobody any good.** *See under* ILL.

**Raise the wind, To.** *See under* RAISE.

**Reed shaken by the wind, A.** *See under* REED.

**Robin Hood wind.** *See under* ROBIN.

**Sail against the wind, To.** *See under* SAIL.

**Sail before the wind, To.** *See under* SAIL.

**Sail close to the wind, To.** *See under* SAIL.

**See which way the wind blows, To.** *See under* SEE.

**Sow the wind and reap the whirlwind, To.** *See under* SOW.

**Straw in the wind, The.** *See under* STRAW.

**Take the wind out of someone's sails, To.** To forestall someone; to frustrate a person by utilizing their own material or methods. Literally, it is to sail to windward of a ship and so rob its sails of the wind. *See also* STEAL SOMEONE'S THUNDER.

**There's something in the wind.** There are signs that something is about to happen; something is being prepared or concocted without one's knowledge.

**Three sheets in the wind.** *See under* THREE.

**Trade winds.** *See under* TRADE.

**Whistle down the wind, To.** *See under* WHISTLE.

**Windmill. Windmill Theatre.** A theatre in Soho that was famous in the 1930s and the Second World War for its shows with nude women, who were allowed to appear so long as they remained still. The logic behind this was that movement would have given them a sexual import, whereas if they posed stationary they were regarded as artistic displays. The Wind-mill remained open right through the war, leading it to boast the proud slogan, 'We never closed'. In 1964 it was converted into a cinema and casino and at the turn of the 21st century was a lap-dancing club. *See also* MOULIN ROUGE.

**Tilt at windmills, To.** *See under* TILT.

**Window. Window dressing.** Properly the display of goods in a shop window for the purpose of attracting customers. Figuratively, a specious display presenting oneself or one's case in a favourable light.

**Window shopping.** The pastime (in the literal sense) of looking at wares displayed in shop windows without actually buying any of them.

**Window tax.** A tax first imposed in 1691 and abolished in 1851, which accounts for the blocked-up window spaces in many old houses. It took the place of the Hearth Tax and was greatly increased in 1782 and 1797 but reduced in 1823. Houses with fewer than seven windows were exempt in 1782 and those with fewer than eight in 1825.

**Bay window.** *See under* BAY.

**Catherine wheel window.** *See under* CATHERINE.

**Judas window.** *See under* JUDAS.

**Picture window.** *See under* PICTURE.

**Windsor. Windsor Herald.** One of six heralds of the College of Arms, the others being Chester, Lancaster, Richmond, Somerset and York. *See also* HERALDRY.

**House of Windsor, The.** *See under* HOUSE.

**Knights of Windsor, The.** *See under* KNIGHT.

**Widow at Windsor, The.** *See under* WIDOW.

**Wine. Dry wine.** *See under* DRY.

**Good wine needs no bush.** *See under* GOOD.

**New wine in old bottles.** *See under* NEW.

**White wine.** *See under* WHITE.

**Wing.** In the RAF, a group of several squadrons.

**Winged words.** Highly apposite words. Homer has the expression as *epea pteroenta*.

**Wings of Azrael, The.** The approach of death; the signs of death coming on the dying. *See also* AZRAEL.

**Clip someone's wings, To.** *See under* CLIP.

**On a wing and a prayer.** With only a small hope or chance of success. The phrase comes from a Second World War song based on the words that the pilot of a damaged aircraft radioed to ground control as he prepared to come in to land:

> Tho' there's one motor gone, we can still carry on
> Comin' in on a wing and pray'r.
> HAROLD ADAMSON: 'Comin' in on a wing and a Pray'r' (1943)

**On the wing.** Flying; in motion; about to depart or take flight.

**Spread** or **stretch one's wings, To.** *See under* SPREAD.

**Take someone under one's wing, To.** To assume patronage of a person in order to protect them. The allusion is to a hen gathering her chicks under her wing.

**Take wing, To.** To fly away; to depart without warning.

> Oh, God! it is a fearful thing
> To see the human soul take wing.
> LORD BYRON: *The Prisoner of Chillon* (1816)

**Waiting in the wings.** *See under* WAIT.

**Winifred** or **Winefride.** The patron saint of north Wales and a virgin martyr. According to the story, she was the daughter of a Welsh chieftain and was instructed by St Beuno. Prince Caradoc made violent advances to her, and she fled to the church for safety. Caradoc pursued her and struck off her head, but it was replaced on her body by St Beuno who breathed life into her again. She died a second time *c*.660. The miraculous healing spring of Holywell, Flintshire, gushed forth where her head had come to rest, and it became a regular resort of pilgrims.

**Wink. Wink at, To.** To connive at, or to affect not to notice.

> He knows not how to wink at human frailty
> Or pardon weakness that he never felt.
> JOSEPH ADDISON: *Cato* (1713)

**Forty winks.** *See under* FORTY.

**Nod is as good as a wink to a blind horse, A.** *See under* NOD.

**Tip someone the wink, To.** *See under* TIP.

**Winkle. Winkle-pickers.** Shoes with very elongated and pointed toes, affected by some in the early 1960s. The allusion is to the use of a pin for picking winkles out of their shells.

**Rip Van Winkle.** A character whose fabled adventures are recounted in Washington Irving's *Sketch Book* (1819). The tale is represented as being found among the papers of one Diedrich Knickerbocker, a Dutch antiquary of New York. Rip Van Winkle was a happy-go-lucky, henpecked husband with a fondness for the bottle. During a ramble on the Catskill Mountains he met some quaint personages dressed in the old Flemish style playing at ninepins. Unobserved, he took a draught of their Hollands and soon fell asleep. He awoke to find himself alone. Even his dog had disappeared and his firearm was heavy with rust. He set off for home in alarm only to find his house deserted and none of his former companions about. He had apparently slept for 20 years and after establishing his identity became a village patriarch. He had set out as a subject of George III and returned as a free citizen of the United States.

**Winnie-the-Pooh.** The 'Bear of Very Little Brain' who appears in the nursery verses and children's stories by A.A. Milne (1882–1956). He made his bow in 1924 and has gained near cult status since. He had his genesis in an actual teddy bear of the name owned by Milne's young son, CHRISTOPHER ROBIN Milne, who also appears in the various narratives.

> Pooh woke up suddenly with a sinking feeling. He had had that sinking feeling before, and he knew what it was. *He was hungry.*
> A.A. MILNE: *Winnie-the-Pooh*, ch v (1926)

*See also* TIGGER.

**Winter.** The coldest part of the year. In the northern hemisphere traditionally the months of December, January and February, and astronomically from 21–22 December to 21–22 March.

**Winter for shoeing, peascod for wooing.** The allusion in the latter half of the saying is to the custom of placing a peascod containing nine peas on the door lintel, under the notion that the first man who came through the door would be the husband of the person who placed the peascod. Another custom is alluded to by William Browne of Tavistock:

> The peascod greene oft with no little toyle
> Hee'd seeke for in the fattest, fertil'st soile,
> And rend it from the stalke to bring it to her
> And in her bosome for acceptance woo her.
> WILLIAM BROWNE: *Britannia's Pastorals*, ii (1616)

**Blackthorn winter.** *See under* BLACK.

**Wipe. Wiped out.** Destroyed; annihilated; quite obliterated.

**Wipe someone's eye, To.** To get the better of them.

**Wipe the floor with someone, To.** To inflict a humiliating defeat on them; to demolish all their arguments; to floor them absolutely.

**Wipe the slate clean, To.** To cancel past debts or offences; to START WITH A CLEAN SLATE.

**Wire. Wireless.** Applied to radio transmission or broadcasting, because the signals are not transmitted along wires. The word is old- fashioned but is still heard.

**Get one's wires crossed, To.** To become confused; to have a misunderstanding, as: 'I think we've got our wires crossed.'

**Live wire, A.** *See under* LIVE.

**Pull wires, To.** *See* PULL STRINGS.

**Wisden.** The 'bible' of cricket, as an annual ALMANAC issued since 1864. They contain full match scores and much cumulative cricketing history and take their name from John Wisden (1826–84), a fast bowler and leading cricketer of his day.

**Wisdom. Wisdom of many and the wit of one, The.** Lord John Russell (1792–1878) thus defined a proverb.

**Wisdom of Solomon, The.** A book of the APOCRYPHA, probably written by an Alexandrian Jew in the latter part of the 1st century BC or the early part of the 1st century AD. It seems to be a reply to the STOICISM and EPICUREANISM reflected in the Book of Ecclesiastes, and it is designed to reawaken loyalty and zeal for the old Jewish faith among apostates and waverers.

**Wisdom tooth.** The popular name for the third molar in each jaw. Wisdom teeth usually appear between the ages of 17 and 25, hence the name from an association with the years of discretion.

**Cut one's wisdom teeth, To.** *See under* CUT.

**In his** etc. **wisdom.** As he etc. judges best. The expression is usually ironic, as: 'The government in its wisdom decided otherwise.'

**Wise. Wise, The.** The following have been thus named:

> Albert II, Duke of Austria, called the Lame and Wise (1293–1358)

Alfonso X of Leon, and IV of Castile, called the Wise and the Astronomer (1202–84)
Charles V of France, called le Sage (1337–80)
Frederick II, elector Palatine (1482–1556)
Frederick III, elector of Saxony (1463–1525)

**Wiseacre** (Middle Dutch *wijssegghher*, related to German *Weissager*, 'soothsayer'). This word, like SOPHIST, has lost its original meaning and is applied to dunces, who are wise only in their own opinion.

A tale tells that Ben Jonson, at the Devil, in FLEET STREET, said to a country gentleman who boasted of his estates, 'What care we for your dirt and clods? Where you have an acre of land, I have ten acres of wit.' The landowner retorted by calling Jonson 'Good Mr Wiseacre'.

**Wise after the event.** Knowing what should have been done to prevent something happening.

**Wisecrack.** A colloquialism for a facetious or witty remark.

**Wise men of Gotham.** Fools; wiseacres. The village of Gotham just south of Nottingham was proverbial for the stupidity of its inhabitants, and many tales have been told about them. One tells how they joined hands round a thorn bush to prevent a cuckoo flying away. The Cuckoo Bush public house in the village commemorates the legend.

It is said that King John intended to visit the place with the aim of establishing a hunting lodge, but the villagers had no wish to be saddled with the cost of supporting the court. Wherever the royal messengers went, they saw the people engaged in some idiotic pursuit, and the king, when told, abandoned his intention. The 'wise men' cunningly remarked: 'We ween there are more fools pass through Gotham than remain in it.' The nursery rhyme runs:

Three wise men of Gotham,
They went to sea in a bowl,
And if the bowl had been stronger
My song had been longer.

*See also* COGGESHALL JOB.

**Wise Men of Greece, The.** Also known as the Philosophical Pleiad or the Seven Sages, all of whom flourished in the 6th century BC:

Bias of Priene: 'Most men are bad.'
Chilo of Sparta: 'Consider the end.' *See also* DE MORTUIS NIL NISI BONUM.
Cleobulus of Lindos: 'The golden mean' or 'Avoid extremes.'
Periander of Corinth: 'Nothing is impossible to industry.'
Pittacus of Mitylene: 'Seize or TAKE TIME BY THE FORELOCK.'
Solon of Athens (*c*.640–*c*.558 BC): 'Know thyself.'
Thales of Miletus: 'Who hateth suretyship is sure.'

**Wise Men of the East.** *See* MAGI.

**Wisest fool in Christendom, The.** James VI of Scotland (r.1567–1625) and I of England (r.1603–25) was so called by Henry IV of France, who learned the phrase from Sully. The identity of the original Frenchman so named is unknown.

**Wisest man of Greece, The.** So the Delphic ORACLE pronounced SOCRATES to be. Socrates modestly replied: 'It is because I alone of all the Greeks know that I know nothing.'

**Word to the wise, A.** *See under* WORD.

**Wish. Wishbone.** The forked bone (furcula) between the neck and breast of a bird. When taken at table from a cooked bird such as a chicken or turkey, the bone is held between between two people and broken as each makes a wish. The person holding the longer portion will have their wish granted. *See also* MERRYTHOUGHT.

**Wishful thinking.** A popular psychoanalytical term used to describe the unconscious expression of one's desire in accordance with one's wishes; otherwise the thinking of a thing to be true because one wishes it to be.

**Wish hounds** or **yell hounds.** Ghostly hounds that hunt the wildest parts of Dartmoor on moonless nights, urged on by the Midnight Hunter on the Moor on his huge horse, which breathes fire and flame. If it is heard, the baying of these hounds, which some hold to be headless, spells death to the hearer within the year. *See also* WILD HUNTSMAN.

**Wishing bone.** *See* MERRYTHOUGHT.

**Wishing cap.** *See* FORTUNATUS.

**Wishing well.** A well into which coins are dropped and a wish made. The modern custom springs from the holy wells of medieval times, many of which were held to contain healing waters. These in turn go back to wells supposedly inhabited by pagan water gods. The dropping of coins ultimately evolves from the neolithic practice of casting precious and sacrificial objects into rivers and meres.

**Wish is father to the thought, The.** We are always ready to believe what we most wish to believe. When the Prince says to his dying father, 'I never thought to hear you speak again,' Henry IV replies:

Thy wish was father, Harry, to that thought.
I stay too long for thee, I weary thee.
SHAKESPEARE: *Henry IV, Pt II*, IV, iv (1597)

**Wish me luck.** Said when one is about to embark on a risky or difficult enterprise. The expression was popularized by Gracie Fields' song (written by Phil Park and Harry Parr Davies), 'Wish me luck as you wave me goodbye', which she first sang in the film *Shipyard Sally* (1939) and which went well into the years of the Second World War.

**Death wish.** *See under* DEATH.

**Wit. At one's wits' end.** *See under* AT.

**Have** or **keep one's wits about one, To.** To be wide awake; to be observant of all that is going on and prepared to take advantage of any opportunity that offers itself.

**Live on one's wits, To.** *See under* LIVE.

**To wit.** *See under* TO.

**Witch. Witch balls.** The popular name for the lustred glass globes in use since the 16th century as domestic ornaments. They mirror in miniature the contents of a room, and the name is probably a fanciful corruption of 'watch ball'. The inside of the ball was usually coated with a preparation largely made up of mercury.

**Witchcraft.** Belief in witchcraft, prevalent into the 18th century and later, was a legacy from pagan times and is found in the Bible (*see* WITCH OF ENDOR). DIVINATION of all kinds was a fundamental aspect of witchcraft. Even St AUGUSTINE believed in it. In 1258 Pope Alexander IV (r.1254–61) instructed the INQUISITION to deal with witchcraft when allied to heresy, and Innocent VIII's celebrated bull *Summis desiderantes affectibus* ('Desiring with the most profound anxiety') (1484) encouraged the Inquisition to take severe measures against witches. Countless people suffered death from this persecution, especially old women. Witchcraft was made a felony in England in 1542 and causing death by witchcraft became a capital offence in 1563. In the same year witchcraft became subject to the death penalty in Scotland. The last person to be executed for witchcraft in England was Alice Molland, hanged at Exeter in 1684, while the last trial for witchcraft took place in 1712. The last judicial execution for witchcraft in Scotland was in 1727, when Janet Horne was TARRED AND FEATHERED and roasted at Dornoch, Sutherland, accused of having turned her daughter into a pony and having her shod by the Devil. English and Scottish laws against witchcraft were repealed in 1736.

**Witches of Salem, The.** The women accused of witchcraft in Salem, Massachusetts, in 1692. The trials began when a West Indian slave named Tituba told VOODOO tales. Some teenage girls claimed they had been possessed by the Devil and accused four Salem women, including the slave, of witchcraft. Public hysteria followed, and a special civil court was set up to try those accused. A total of 19 'witches' were executed, six of them men, and hundreds imprisoned. The trials lasted from May to October, when the court was dissolved and the remaining prisoners released. Indemnities were subsequently granted to the families of those who had been executed. Arthur Miller's play *The Crucible* (1952) draws parallels between the persecution of the Salem witches and MCCARTHYISM. *See also* SALEM.

**Witches' Sabbath.** A midnight meeting of witches, demons and the like, said to have been held annually. Medieval devotees of the witchcraft cult held sabbaths at CANDLEMAS, Roodmas (14 September), LAMMAS and ALL HALLOWS EVE, and their celebrations lasted until dawn. The rites were led by the 'Coven', a group of 12 members and one Devil.

**Witch-hunting.** A particular pastime of 17th-century PRESBYTERIANS until after the RESTORATION. The notorious self-appointed 'Witch-Finder General' Matthew Hopkins (*c.*1621–47) travelled through the East Anglia in the 1640s to hunt out witches, and he is said to have hanged over 100 in a little more than a year in Essex alone. His victims were typically old, impoverished and physically unattractive. His prime method of extracting confessions was the 'swimming' of witches, a procedure that involved tying the right thumb to the left big toe and immersing the witch in water. If she floated, she was guilty. If she sank, she very likely drowned. In 1647 he is said to have been tested by his own methods, so that he was cast into the river, floated and was hanged as a WIZARD. This is a fabrication, however, and he actually died 'of a consumption' at his home in Manningtree, near Ipswich.

In political usage, the term denotes the searching out and exposure of opponents alleged to be disloyal to the state, often amounting to persecution. *See also* MCCARTHYISM.

**Witch of Endor, The.** The woman who had 'a familiar spirit' through whom SAUL sought communication with the dead SAMUEL. She brought Samuel up 'out of the earth' (a classic case of NECROMANCY) having first secured a promise from Saul that he would take no action against her as a witch. The account is in 1 Samuel 28.

**Witch of Wookey, The.** *See* WOOKEY HOLE.

**City of Witches, The.** *See under* CITY.

**Waking a witch.** *See under* WAKE.

**Water witch.** *See under* WATER.

**White witch.** *See under* WHITE.

**Witenagemot.** The Anglo-Saxon national assembly of higher clerics and laymen (ealdormen, thegns and so on), which gave advice and consent on legislation, taxation, important judicial matters and the like, and which formally elected a new king. The word represents Old English *witena*, the genitive plural of *wita*, 'councillor', and *gemōt*, 'meeting' (modern 'moot'), so that the sense is 'meeting of councillors'.

**With. With a capital A.** Emphatically so, the letter varying for what is mentioned, such as 'art with a capital A', 'jealous with a capital J'.

**With a good** or **bad grace.** Gracefully or ungracefully; willingly or unwillingly. To do something 'with a good grace' often implies a forced acquiescence in some action.

**With a heavy hand.** Oppressively; without sparing.

> It is a damned and a bloody work;
> The graceless action of a heavy hand
> If that it be the work of any hand.
> SHAKESPEARE, *King John*, IV, iii (1596)

**With all one's heart.** With all the energy and enthusiasm of which one is capable.

**With a pinch** or **grain of salt** (Latin *cum grano salis*). With great reservations, allowing it a mere grain of truth. A pinch of salt with something may help one to swallow it.

**With a sting in its tail.** With an unexpectedly unpleasant ending. The bee has a sting in its tail, as have the stingray and the scorpion. *See also* TELEGONUS.

**With egg on one's face.** Made to look ridiculous, as after some gaffe. The reference is to someone who has eaten a runny egg and not wiped their mouth.

**With flying colours.** Triumphantly; easily. The allusion is to a victorious fleet sailing into port with flags still flying at the mastheads.

**With it, To be.** A formerly popular phrase meaning to be completely conversant with current fads, fashions, music and so on, especially of the kind popular with young people.

**With knobs** or **brass knobs on.** Whatever you say and more. The allusion is to the brass fittings that formerly adorned some types of furniture and that are still found on some ornate metal bedsteads.

**With one foot in the grave.** Dying or so old as to seem to have only a little time to live.

**With one's eyes open.** Fully aware of the situation; knowing of any risks or dangers.

**With one's eyes shut.** With ease. Said of something with which one is thoroughly familiar, as: 'I could do that with my eyes shut.'

**With one's head in the clouds.** Immersed in thought or imaginings, as when daydreaming.

**With one's nose in the air.** Haughtily; arrogantly.

**With one's tail between one's legs.** Very dejected; downcast. The allusion is to certain dogs, which slink off thus when scolded.

**With one's tongue hanging out.** Eagerly or expectantly, like a panting dog.

**With one's tongue in one's cheek.** Said of something spoken insincerely or ironically, when one says one thing but means another. In the early 19th century the forcing of the tongue into the left cheek served as a secret signal of disbelief for the speaker at the time. The expression OVER THE LEFT has its origin in a similar clandestine signal.

**With open arms.** Cordially, as a dear friend is received, with arms open for an embrace.

**With the best of them.** As well as anyone; on a par with the experts or professionals.

**With the colours.** On the active strength of a regiment, as opposed to being in the reserve.

**With the gloves off.** Mercilessly; without compassion or compunction. An allusion to the old pugilists who fought with bare fists.

**Withershins** or **widdershins** (Middle High German *wider*, 'against', and *sinnes*, genitive of *sin*, 'course'). An old English word, still in use in Scotland and in north country dialects, denoting a movement in a contrary direction to that of the sun, i.e. anticlockwise. Witches and warlocks were believed to approach the Devil withershins.

The opposite of withershins is 'deasil', meaning sunwise or clockwise (Scottish Gaelic *deiseil*).

**Within. Within an inch.** Almost at the point, as: 'I was within an inch of winning.'

**Within arm's reach.** Close at hand.

**Within earshot.** Within hearing; audible. The opposite is 'out of earshot'.

**Within hail.** Within calling distance; near enough to attract a person's attention.

**Within one's grasp.** Capable of being grasped, literally or figuratively, in the latter case thus capable of being comprehended.

**Within reason.** Within certain bounds; up to a point.

**Without. Without a leg to stand on.** Having no excuse; without a chance to get away with it.

**Without batting an eyelid.** Without the involuntary lowering or flicker of the eyelids that betrays surprise. Here 'batting' is derived from the now obsolete *bate* (Old French *batre*, 'to beat'), meaning to beat the wings or to flutter.

**Without striking a blow.** Without coming to an actual contest.

**Witnesses, Jehovah's.** *See under* JEHOVAH.

**Witte, The Whetstone of.** *See under* WHETSTONE.

**Wivern.** *See* WYVERN.

**Wizard.** A magician, one adept in the black arts, the male counterpart of a witch. The word is derived from 'wise'. *See also* WITCHCRAFT.

'Wizard' is popularly (but now rather datedly) used to mean superb, excellent, as, 'a wizard performance' or 'absolutely wizard'. Modern 'magic' (or 'magical') has the same colloquial sense.

**Wizard of Oz, The.** The central figure in the popular children's book, *The Wonderful Wizard of Oz* (1900), by L. Frank Baum, an American journalist. The musical comedy of the same name (1901) was a great success, which was repeated in the film of 1939.

> We're off to see the Wizard,
> The wonderful Wizard of Oz.
> We hear he is a whiz of a wiz
> If ever a wiz there was.
> Song sung in film by Dorothy, the Cowardly Lion, the Scarecrow and the Tin Man on the 'Yellow Brick Road'

**Wizard of the North, The.** A nickname given to Sir Walter Scott (1771–1832). *See also* WAVERLEY NOVELS.

**Carpathian Wizard, The.** *See under* CARPATHIAN.

**Wobblies, The.** The Industrial Workers of the World or IWW were so nicknamed. This American revolutionary labour organization was formed in 1905 and reached its peak before the First World War, but largely petered out after the war. They drew their main support from migratory farmers, textile workers and dockers. Noted for their songs, the best known are 'Pie in the Sky' and 'Hallelujah, I'm a Bum.' They were also known as the Bummery.

Wobbly may be from a Chinese-American pronunciation of 'w' in IWW, as 'wobble'.

**Woden.** The greatest Anglo-Saxon god, the equivalent of the Germanic WOTAN and Norse ODIN. *See also* WANSDYKE; WEDNESDAY.

**Woebegone.** Overwhelmed by woe, especially applied to the appearance, as 'a woebegone countenance'. The word does not mean 'woe, be gone' but comes from a phrase such as 'Me is wo begon' ('Woe has beset me').

**Wog.** A derogatory colloquial name applied to blacks, Arabs, Egyptians and other non-whites. It is possibly a contraction of 'golliwog', but in popular naval parlance is held to stand for 'wily oriental gentleman'. Another assertion is that it was formerly applied by the British army to its Egyptian labourers and is an abbreviation of 'workers on government service'.

**Wolf.** WILLIAM OF MALMESBURY (*Gesta regum Anglorum*, Bk II, ch viii (12th century)) says that the tribute of 300 wolves payable yearly by the king of Wales to Edgar the Peaceful (r.959–975) ceased after the third year because 'he could find no more', but they are recorded in England as late as the 15th century and in Ireland and Scotland apparently lingered on until the 18th century.

In music a harsh or grating sound resulting from the system of tuning or temperament in certain keyboard instruments was called a wolf, as also was the jarring note sometimes heard from bowed instruments. In the case of a harp it was said to be caused by the use of a string made from the entrails of a wolf. The squeak made in reed instruments by unskilled players is termed a 'goose'.

**Wolf Cub.** The long-established and original name for a member of the junior branch of the SCOUT Movement, now called Cub Scouts (age range 8–11 years). The conception owes much to Rudyard Kipling's *Jungle Books* (1894, 1895).

**Wolf in sheep's clothing, A.** An enemy posing as a friend. The phrase is taken from the well-known fable of AESOP.

**Wolf pack, A.** A term applied in the Second World War to German submarines in a group.

**Wolf whistle.** A whistle made by a male at the sight of a female, expressing sexual admiration. It usually consists of two notes, one rising, the other falling. The name implies that the male is 'hungry', like a wolf.

> Kingston upon Thames Crown Court echoed with laughter when the caged Red Lored Amazon [parrot] let out a wolf-whistle as he saw Miss Morgans in the witness box.
> *The Times* (16 February 1995)

**Cry wolf, To.** *See under* CRY.

**Keep the wolf from the door, To.** To ward off starvation. The allusion is to the pangs of hunger, like those of a ravening wolf. Someone who eats voraciously is said 'to wolf' their food, and French *manger comme un loup* is to eat greedily.

**Lone wolf, A.** *See under* LONE.

**Put one's head into the wolf's mouth, To.** *See under* HEAD.

**She-wolf of France, The.** *See under* SHE.

**Throw to the wolves, To.** *See under* THROW.

**Wolfe's Own.** *See under* REGIMENTAL AND DIVISIONAL NICKNAMES.

**Woman or women. Woman of the streets, A.** A prostitute.

**Fancy woman.** *See under* FANCY.

**Hell hath no fury like a woman scorned.** *See under* HELL.

**Little woman.** *See under* LITTLE.

**New woman, The.** *See under* NEW.

**Old woman.** *See under* OLD.

**Scarlet woman.** *See under* SCARLET.

**Seal women.** *See under* SEAL.

**Wonder. Wonderful Doctor, The.** Roger Bacon (*c.*1220–92), also called the ADMIRABLE DOCTOR.

**Wonder of the World, The.** The title given to Otto III, Holy Roman Emperor (980–1002), because of his brilliant intellect. The title was also applied to Frederick II (1194–1250). *See also* STUPOR MUNDI.

**Wonderful** or **Wondermaking Parliament, The.** Also called the MERCILESS PARLIAMENT (1388), when Richard II's favourites were condemned for treason.

**Wonder-worker.** *See* THAUMATURGUS.

**Alice in Wonderland.** *See under* ALICE.

**Cornish Wonder, The.** *See under* CORNISH.
**Nine days's wonder.** *See under* NINE.
**No wonder.** *See under* NO.
**Seven wonders of the world, The.** *See under* SEVEN.

**Wonky.** This slang word, meaning unsteady, unsound or unstable, comes from Old English *wancol*, of the same meaning.

**Wood** or **wooden. Woodbine.** A common name for the wild honeysuckle (*Lonicera periclymenum*), also applied to other plants that bind or wind themselves around trees.

**Woodbine Willie.** The Rev. G.A. Studdert-Kennedy (1883–1929) was so called from the well-liked brand of small cigarettes named Woodbines, which he gave to the men in the trenches in the First World War when serving as chaplain to the forces (1916–19).

**Wooden.** A word used of someone who is awkward or ungainly, or of a spiritless, emotionless person.

**Wooden Horse, The.** Called Clavileno el Aligero in *Don* QUIXOTE, the horse is governed by a peg in its forehead and has the same magical qualities as the BRAZEN HORSE given to CAMBUSCAN. Its name means 'Wooden-Peg the Swift', with Clavileno from Spanish *clavija*, 'peg', and *leña*, 'wood', and *alígero*, 'swift'. The similar Magic Horse in the ARABIAN NIGHTS ENTERTAINMENTS was of ivory and ebony.

A former instrument of military punishment was called a wooden horse. The victim was seated on the horse's back, a sharply ridged beam of oak, with his hands tied behind his back and weights attached to his feet. He was then compelled to remain in this painful position for hours at a time. This was known as 'riding the wooden horse'.

Eric Williams' bestseller *The Wooden Horse* (1949) tells how the author, an RAF navigator captured by the Germans in the Second World War, made a daring escape from Stalag-Luft III in Silesia by digging a tunnel beneath a wooden vaulting-horse that his fellow prisoners used daily for exercise by way of a decoy. The title of the book, and that of the film based on it (1950), alludes both to the horse and to the WOODEN HORSE OF TROY, serving similarly for military concealment.

**Wooden Horse of Troy, The.** VIRGIL recounts that, after the death of HECTOR, ULYSSES had a monster wooden horse made by Epios and gave out that it was an offering to the gods to secure a prosperous voyage back to Greece. The Trojans dragged the horse within their city, but it was packed full of Grecian soldiers, including MENELAUS, who stole out at night, slew the guards, opened the city gates and set fire to the city.

**Wooden nickels.** Like WOODEN NUTMEGS, these were said to have been made in the USA by those unwilling to earn an honest living. As the nickel piece of 1857 was only worth a cent it was an unrewarding enterprise, but it gave rise to the phrase 'Don't take any wooden nickels' as a friendly warning to the unsuspecting or easily duped.

**Wooden nutmegs.** In the early 19th century Connecticut, the Nutmeg State, was referred to derisively as the land of wooden nutmegs because certain dishonest merchants were said to have exported nutmegs made of wood.

**Wooden spoon, The.** A booby prize gained by the student last in the mathematical TRIPOS list at Cambridge. Hence a booby prize generally. *See also* WOODEN WEDGE.

**Wooden walls.** The wooden warships of the Royal Navy were so called before the days of IRONCLADS, and it is said that some 3500 oak trees were used in the construction of the big THREE-DECKERS. The *Victory*, now at Portsmouth, is perhaps the best known of these vessels. The screw wood ship HMS *Duncan* was launched in 1869 and the well-known training ship *Mercury*, associated with C.B. Fry (1872–1956), was built as late as 1878.

When the Greeks consulted the Delphic ORACLE to ask how they were to defend themselves against XERXES, who had invaded their country, the evasive answer was to this effect:

> Pallas hath urged, and Zeus, the sire of all,
> Hath safety promised in a wooden wall;
> Seed-time and harvest, weeping sires shall tell
> How thousands fought at Salamis and fell.

Themistocles interpreted 'wooden wall' to mean the Greek ships in the Bay of Salamis and so won a decisive victory over the Persians.

**Wooden wedge, The.** Last in the classical TRIPOS. When the classical Tripos was instituted at Cambridge in 1824, it was debated by what name to call the last on the list. It so happened that the last on the list was Wedgwood (a famous Cambridge name) and the name was adopted in this slightly modified form. *See also* WOODEN SPOON.

**Wood's Halfpence.** The copper coinage that the iron-founder William Wood (1671–1744) began to introduce into Ireland (1723) under a patent purchased from the Duchess of Kendal, George I's mistress, to whom it had been granted. The outcry against Wood's Halfpence, supported by Jonathan Swift in his DRAPIER'S LETTERS, led to the withdrawal of the patent in 1725. The Irish Parliament and government were not informed of the scheme in advance, and it was feared that the flood of copper coins would drive out the existing small stocks of gold and silver.

**Babes in the wood.** *See under* BABE.
**Children in the wood.** *See under* CHILD.
**Dead wood.** *See under* DEAD.
**Don't cry** or **halloo till you are out of the wood.** *See under* CRY.
**Drawn from the wood.** *See under* DRAW.
**Gopher wood.** *See under* GOPHER.
**Grovely Wood.** *See under* GROVELY.
**Neck of the woods.** *See under* NECK.
**Nigger in the woodpile, A.** *See under* NIGGER.
**Not to see the wood for the trees.** *See under* SEE.
**Out of the woods.** *See under* OUT.
**Touch wood, To.** *See under* TOUCH.

**Woodbines, The Packet of.** *See under* PACKET.

**Woodcock, Scotch.** *See under* SCOTCH.

**Woodfall, Memory.** William Woodfall (1746–1803), brother of the Woodfall who controlled the *Public Advertiser* in which the LETTERS OF JUNIUS appeared. He established *The Diary* (1789), the first journal to report parliamentary proceedings the morning after the occurrence. He would attend a debate, then, without notes, report it accurately. *See also* HANSARD.

**Wookey Hole.** A cavern near Wells in Somerset, which has given rise to numerous legends. 'As wicked as the Witch of Wookey' is an old local simile. Her repulsiveness led to her directing her spells against 'the youth of either sex' as well as blasting every plant and blistering every flock. She was turned into a stone by a 'lerned wight' from 'Glaston' (Glastonbury) but left her curse behind, since the girls of Wookey found 'that men are wondrous scant'.

> Here's beauty, wit and sense combin'd,
> With all that's good and virtuous join'd
> Yet hardly one gallant.
> PERCY: *Reliques*, 'The Witch of Wookey' (1765)

**Wool. Wool-gathering, To be.** To let one's mind wander from the matter in hand; to be absent-minded. The allusion is perhaps to children sent to gather wool from hedges, who wander hither and thither, apparently aimlessly.

**Woolsack, The.** The official seat of the LORD CHANCELLOR as SPEAKER of the HOUSE OF LORDS. It is a large red square bag of wool, rather like an enlarged hassock. There were originally four, probably introduced in the reign of Edward III (1327–77) as symbols of England's staple trade, on which sat the Judges, the Barons of the EXCHEQUER, the SERJEANTS-AT-LAW and the Masters in CHANCERY. The woolsacks were technically outside the precincts of the House, because these officials had no voice in the proceedings. Thus, when the Lord Chancellor wishes to speak as a peer he goes to his place in the House.

**Botany wool.** *See under* BOTANY.
**Burial in woollen.** *See under* BURY.
**Dyed-in-the-wool.** *See under* DYE.
**Great cry and little wool.** *See under* GREAT.
**Pull the wool over someone's eyes, To.** *See under* PULL.
**Wild and woolly.** *See under* WILD.

**Woolworth Building.** A 60-storey neo-Gothic office building on New York's BROADWAY, erected in 1911 by the chain-store magnate F.W. Woolworth (1852–1919), effectively as a monument to himself. It was the tallest building in the world until it was surpassed by the Chrysler Building in 1926. It is popularly known as the Cathedral of Commerce, a term used of it at the time of its dedication.

**Woomera.** The name of the rocket testing range in south Australia, appropriately an Aborigine word for a spear-throwing stick.

**Wooster, Bertie.** The amiable young man-about-town who, with his manservant JEEVES, has various comic and amorous adventures in the stories and novels by P.G. Wodehouse (1881–1975), of which he is the narrator. He is as dull-witted as Jeeves is clever, and his speech is a goldmine of fashionable pre-First World War slang. His indolent existence is marred chiefly by his fearsome aunts. He made his literary début in the short story 'The Artistic Career of Corky' (1916), and is said to be based on John Wodehouse Kimberley, 3rd Earl of Kimberley (1883–1941), Wodehouse's cousin.

> It is no use telling me that there are bad aunts and good aunts. At the core they are all alike. Sooner or later, out pops the cloven hoof.
> P.G. WODEHOUSE: *The Code of the Woosters*, ch ii (1938).

**Wop.** In the original American slang usage this meant an uncouth or aggressive person. The term was later used as a derogatory name for Italians and those of similar complexion. It is probably from southern Italian dialect *guappo*, 'braggart', 'dandy', itself from Spanish *guapo*.

**Word. Word, The.** The SCRIPTURES, Christ as the Logos or the word of God, i.e. his revelation or his meaning.

> In the beginning was the Word, and the Word was with God, and the Word was God.
> John 1:1

*See also* TETRAGRAMMATON.

**Word of honour.** A pledge that cannot be broken without disgrace.
**Word of mouth.** Spoken communication between two people as a means of imparting information.
**Words fail me.** I don't believe it; I am speechless with emotion.
**Words italicized in the Bible.** Such words have no corresponding words in the originals but were supplied by the translators to make the sense of the passage clearer, e.g. 'All *the things* that *are* in mine house have they seen' (2 Kings 20:15).

**Words stuck in my throat, The.** I was unable to speak owing to nervousness or great reluctance.
**Word to the wise, A.** Said when giving advice as a hint that it would be well for the recipient to follow it. *See also* VERB SAP.
**As good as one's word.** *See under* AS.
**At a loss for words, To be.** *See under* AT.
**Bandy words.** *See under* BANDY.
**Better than one's word.** *See under* BETTER.
**Book of words.** *See under* BOOK.
**Break one's word, To.** *See under* BREAK.
**By word of mouth.** *See under* BY.
**Eat one's words, To.** *See under* EAT.
**Dirty word.** *See under* DIRTY.
**Fighting words.** *See under* FIGHT.
**Fine** or **fair words butter no parsnips.** *See under* FINE.
**Four-letter word.** *See under* FOUR.
**From the word go.** *See under* FROM.
**Frozen words.** *See under* FROZEN.
**Gender words.** *See under* GENDER.
**Ghost word.** *See under* GHOST.
**Give one's word, To.** To give a definite undertaking; to make a binding promise.
**Have a word with someone, To.** To have a brief conversation with them, often a 'meaningful' one.
**Have words with someone, To.** To quarrel with them.
**In a word.** Briefly, as: 'He's not the keenest of workers; in a word, he's bone idle'.
**Keep one's word, To.** *See under* KEEP.
**Last word, The.** *See under* LAST.
**Long words.** *See under* LONG.
**My word!** or **upon my word!** An exclamation of surprise, annoyance or irritation.
**Nonce word.** *See under* NONCE.
**Not the word for it.** Inadequate to describe, as: '"Warm" is not the word for it: it's absolutely sweltering.'
**Of one's word.** Reliable in keeping promises, as: 'He's a man of his word'.
**On one's word of honour.** An affirmation of the speaker as to the truth of what he asserts.
**Play on words.** *See under* PLAY.
**Portmanteau word.** *See under* PORTMANTEAU.
**Put in a word** or **good word for someone, To.** To speak on someone else's behalf; to support a person's claim to something.
**Put into words, To.** To express in speech or writing, as: 'I can't put into words how grateful I am.'
**Put words into someone's mouth, To.** To misrepresent what someone actually said.
**Reduplicated words.** *See under* REDUPLICATED.
**Say the word, To.** *See under* SAY.
**Seven words from the cross, The.** *See under* SEVEN.
**Sharp's the word!** *See under* SHARP.
**Take back one's words, To.** *See under* TAKE.
**Take someone at their word** or **take someone's word for something, To.** To regard what they say as trustworthy; to accept or rely on what they say.
**Take the words out of someone's mouth, To.** To say what someone else is about to say.
**Too funny for words.** *See under* TOO.
**Waste words, To.** *See under* WASTE.
**Weasel words.** *See under* WEASEL.
**Winged words.** *See under* WING.

**Work. Work one's fingers to the bone, To.** To work very hard, usually without thanks or appreciation.
**Work one's ticket, To.** An army expression meaning to secure one's discharge before the contract of service has expired.
**Workshop of the World, The.** England in its 19th-century heyday as the leading industrial nation was so called. In the days of CHARTISM F.D. Maurice (1805–72) and Charles Kingsley (1819–75) produced a poster in 1848 that addressed the workers: 'Englishmen! Saxons! Workers of the great cool-headed, strong-headed nation of England, the workshop of the world.'
**Works of supererogation.** A theological expression for good works that are not enjoined or of obligation and therefore 'better' (Latin *super*, 'over', 'above', and *erogare*, 'to pay out'). The phrase is commonly applied to acts performed beyond the bounds of duty.

> Voluntary Works besides, over and above, God's Commandments, which they call Works of Supererogation, cannot be taught without arrogancy and impiety: for by them men do declare, that they do not only render unto God as much as they are bound to do, but that they do more for his sake, than of bounden duty is required: whereas Christ saith plainly, When ye have done all that are commanded to you, say, We are unprofitable servants.
>
> Book of Common Prayer, Articles of Religion, XIV 'Of Works of Supererogation' (1662)

**Work the oracle, To.** To succeed in persuading someone to favour some plan or to join in a project or undertaking when the chances seemed slender. Also, in slang, to raise money.
**Work to rule, To.** In trade union parlance, to fulfil all the regulations relating to one's work literally and pedantically, in order to bring about delays in working, and frustration generally, as another form of GO SLOW tactics.
**American workhouse.** *See under* AMERICA.
**Christmas Day in the Workhouse.** *See under* CHRISTMAS.
**Clerk of the works.** *See under* CLERK.
**Field work.** *See under* FIELD.
**Field works.** *See under* FIELD.

**Give someone the works, To.** To subject someone to rigorous or extreme treatment, either verbally or physically, even to the point of murder.

**Good works.** *See under* GOOD.

**Gum up the works, To.** *See under* GUM.

**Have one's work cut out, To.** To have difficulty in completing or carrying out a task.

**Maid of all work.** *See under* MAID.

**Make light work of, To.** *See under* LIGHT.

**Make short work of, To.** *See under* SHORT.

**Seven works of mercy.** *See* SEVEN CORPORAL WORKS OF MERCY; SEVEN SPIRITUAL WORKS OF MERCY.

**Worker. Blue-collar worker.** *See under* BLUE.

**Fast worker.** *See under* FAST.

**White-collar worker.** *See under* WHITE.

**World. World is his oyster, The.** The world is the place from which he can extract success and profit, as a pearl can be extracted from an oyster.

> *Falstaff*: I will not lend thee a penny.
> *Pistol*: Why, then the world's mine oyster,
> Which I with sword will open.
> SHAKESPEARE: *The Merry Wives of Windsor*, II, ii (1600)

**World, the flesh and the Devil, The.** 'The world' is the material things of this world as opposed to the things of the spirit, 'the flesh' is sensual pleasures, and 'the Devil' is evil of every kind.

> From all the deceits of the world, the flesh, and the devil, Good Lord, deliver us.
> The Litany (Book of Common Prayer)

**World turned upside down, The.** An inn sign illustrating an unnatural state of affairs, and also an allusion to the antipodes. It often took the form of a man walking at the South Pole.

It was also the name of the tune played by the military band when General Cornwallis surrendered to the Americans at Yorktown in 1781.

**All the world and his wife.** *See under* ALL.

**Best of both worlds, The.** *See under* BEST.

**Citizen of the world, A.** *See under* CITIZEN.

**Dead to the world.** *See under* DEAD.

**End of the world, The.** *See under* END.

**For all the world.** Precisely; as: 'The pearls looked for all the world as if they were real.'

**In a world of one's own.** Mentally detached; absorbed in one's own preoccupations.

**King of the World, The.** *See under* KING.

**Light of the World, The.** *See under* LIGHT.

**Man of the world, A.** *See under* MAN.

**New World.** *See under* NEW.

**Not for the world.** Not for any inducement, as: 'I wouldn't go there for the world.'

**Not long for this world.** *See under* LONG.

**Olde worlde.** *See under* OLD.

**Old World.** *See under* OLD.

**On top of the world, To be.** *See under* TOP.

**Out of this world.** *See under* OUT.

**Rise in the world, To.** *See under* RISE.

**Roof of the world.** *See under* ROOF.

**See the world, To.** *See under* SEE.

**Seven wonders of the world, The.** *See under* SEVEN.

**Third World, The.** *See under* THIRD.

**Way of the world, The.** *See under* WAY.

**Wide world, The.** *See under* WIDE.

**Wonder of the World, The.** *See under* WONDER.

**Workshop of the World, The.** *See under* WORK.

**Worm.** The word was formerly used of DRAGONS and great SERPENTS, especially those of Teutonic and old Norse legend. It is now figuratively applied to miserable or grovelling creatures, and also to the ligament under a dog's tongue.

**Worm oneself into another's favour, To.** To insinuate oneself into the good graces of another.

**Worm out information, To.** To extract it piecemeal or indirectly.

**Worm's eye view, A.** A view from below or from a more humble position.

**Wormwood.** The common name for the aromatic herbs of the genus *Artemisia*, especially *A. absinthium*, from which ABSINTHE and vermouth are concocted. Nicholas Culpeper (1616–54) recommends it as a specific against worms. It is said to have been so called because this plant, according to legend, sprang up in the track of the SERPENT as it writhed along the ground when driven out of Paradise. The word in fact comes from Old English *wormod* and has no connection, except in folk etymology, with 'worm' or 'wood'. 'Vermouth' is directly related.

**Wormwood Scrubs.** The well-known prison in the Hammersmith area of London was built by prison labour between 1874 and 1890 and is the largest prison in Britain, able to accommodate over 1000 inmates. It takes its unattractive name from the locality. 'Wormwood' is actually a corruption of Old English *wyrmholt*, 'wood of snakes', while 'Scrubs' refers to the former scrubland or brushwood here.

**Can of worms.** *See under* CAN.

**Even the worm will turn.** *See under* EVEN.

**Food for worms, To be.** *See under* FOOD.

**Spanish worm.** *See under* SPAIN.

**Worn.** *See* WEAR.

**Worse luck.** Unfortunately.

**Worship.** Literally 'worth-ship', honour, dignity, reverence. In its highest and now usual sense, the respect and reverence man pays to God.

At one time the word carried a sense of personal respect, as in: 'Thou shalt have worship in the presence of them that sit at meat with thee' (Luke 14:10), and in the marriage service (Book of Common Prayer), the man says to the woman: 'With my body I thee worship, and with all my worldly goods I thee endow.'

Magistrates and mayors are addressed as 'Your Worship' and referred to as 'the Worshipful Mayor of [such-and-such a town]'.

**Worship the golden calf, To.** To bow down to money; to abandon one's principles for the sake of gain. The reference is to the golden calf made by AARON when MOSES was absent on Mount Sinai. The Israelites paid dearly for their sin in worshipping the calf (Exodus 32).

**Fire worship.** *See under* FIRE.

**Worst. Do your worst.** An expression of defiance.

> 'You threaten us, fellow? Do your worst,
> Blow your pipe there till you burst!'
> ROBERT BROWNING: 'The Pied Piper of Hamelin', xi (1842)

**Get the worst of it, To.** To be beaten; to be defeated; to come off second best.

**If the worst comes to the worst.** *See under* IF.

**Worsted.** This variety of woollen thread formed of regular parallel strands takes its name from Worsted (now Worstead), a village near Norwich, once an important woollen centre. The name occurs as early as the 13th century.

**Worth. Worth its weight in gold.** Of great value or use. The phrase is applied both literally and metaphorically to people and things

**Worth one's salt.** Efficient and worth one's pay. The reference is to the SALARY issued to Roman soldiers.

**Worth one's while.** Worth the time or effort spent. To say 'I'll make it worth your while' is to offer to pay for someone's services.

**Not worth a bean.** Worthless.

**Not worth a brass farthing.** Virtually worthless. Erasmus, when Professor of Greek at Cambridge, described his profits as 'not worth a brass farthing', a phrase that is possibly an allusion to the Nuremberg monastic token. The expression probably gained further use from the 17th-century farthing tokens or HARRINGTONS, or from GUN MONEY, or it may date from the 18th century, when farthings were minted in bronze rather than silver.

**Not worth a continental.** Worthless, like the paper money issued by the American Continental Congress during the War of Independence, which became valueless by the end of 1780.

**Not worth a damn.** Worthless; of no value. Oliver Goldsmith, in his *Citizen of the World* (1762), uses the expression 'Not that I care three damns' and a common expression of the Duke of Wellington was 'Not a twopenny damn'. The derivation of these phrases from the 'dam', a former Indian coin of small value, is without foundation.

**Not worth a maravedi.** Worthless. *See also* MARAVEDI.

**Not worth a pin.** Wholly worthless.

**Not worth a rap.** Worth nothing at all. The rap was a base halfpenny, intrinsically worth about half a FARTHING, circulated in Ireland in 1721, because small coin was so very scarce. The word is probably from Irish *ropaire*, 'robber', 'scoundrel'. *See also* RAPPAREE.

**Not worth a rush.** Worthless; not worth a STRAW. When floors used to be strewn with rushes, distinguished guests were given clean rushes, but those of inferior standing were left with used rushes or none at all, being considered 'not worth a rush'.

**Not worth a tinker's damn or cuss.** Absolutely worthless. It has been suggested that the term derives from the old-time tinker's custom of blocking up the hole in the article he was mending with a pellet of bread, thus making a dam that would prevent the solder from escaping. This pellet was discarded as useless when the job was finished.

**Not worth the candle.** To be not worth the trouble involved. The full form is often heard: 'the game is not worth the candle.' The saying is of French origin, and translates *Le jeu n'en vaut pas la chandelle*. The reference is to a bad play or bad acting, which is not worth the lighting.

**Not worth the paper it is written on.** Said of a worthless statement, promise or the like.

**Worthies. Nine Worthies, The.** *See under* NINE.

**Nine Worthies of London, The.** *See under* NINE.

**Wotan.** The Germanic equivalent of ODIN. In Wagner's RING OF THE NIBELUNG Wotan is the god who steals the ring of the Nibelung from ALBERICH. Wotan's Anglo-Saxon equivalent is WODEN, who gave the name of WEDNESDAY. *See also* NIBELUNGENLIED.

**Wounded Knee.** Two unhappy conflicts are associated with this South Dakota village. On 29 December 1890 more than 200 Sioux men, women and children were massacred by US troops following the death of Chief SITTING BULL, who had been killed by reservation police while being arrested two weeks earlier. The event is usually known as the 'Battle' of Wounded Knee, although the only weapons carried by the fleeing Indians were clubs and knives hidden in blankets.

On 27 February 1973 some 200 members of the American Indian Movement took the reservation village by force, declaring it the Independent Oglala Sioux Nation. The Indians were surrounded by federal marshals and a ten-week siege began, during which two Indians were killed and one marshal seriously wounded.

**Wounds, To lick one's.** *See under* LICK.

**Wove.** Applied to papers made on an ordinary dandy roll or mould in which the wires are woven. Used by contrast with LAID PAPER.

**Wraith.** The phantom or spectral appearance of someone still living, usually taken as a warning that the person's death is imminent. It appears to people at a distance and forewarns them of the event. In general, a spectre or ghost.

**Wrangle. Wrangle for an ass's shadow, To.** To contend about trifles. The tale told by Demosthenes is that a man hired an ass to take him to Megara. At noon, when the sun was very hot, the traveller dismounted, and sat down in the shadow of the animal. Just then the owner came up and claimed the right of sitting in this shady spot, saying that although he let out the ass for hire, there was no bargain made about the ass's shade. The two men then fell to blows to settle the point. While they were arguing the ass took to its heels and ran off, leaving them both in the glare of the sun.

**Wrangler.** The Cambridge term for one who has obtained a place in the highest class of the mathematical TRIPOS. The first man was (until 1909) called the Senior Wrangler. A wrangler is a disputant and the name arises from the former public disputations in which candidates were required to take part. *See also* OPTIME.

> 'Senior Wrangler, indeed; that's at the other shop.'
> 'What is the other shop, my dear child?' said the lady.
> 'Senior Wrangler's at Cambridge, not Oxford,' said the scholar, with a knowing air.
> W.M. THACKERAY: *Vanity Fair*, ch xxxiv (1847–8)

In the western USA, a wrangler is a herder of saddle horses.

**Wrath, Vials of.** *See under* VIAL.

**Wreck of the Hesperus, The.** An episode made famous by H.W. Longfellow's ballad of 1840, formerly widely learned by schoolchildren. The *Hesperus* was wrecked on Norman's Woe, near Gloucester, Massachusetts, in 1839.

> It was the schooner Hesperus,
> That sailed the wintry sea;
> And the skipper had taken his little daughtèr,
> To bear him company.

**Wren.** A member of the Women's Royal Naval Service, which was formed in 1917. It was temporarily disbanded between the wars, then finally disbanded in 1993, when women were able to enlist in the regular Royal Navy. *See also* WAAC; WAAF.

**Wrenning Day.** St STEPHEN's Day (26 December) used to be so called, because it was a local custom among villagers to stone a wren to death on that day in commemoration of the stoning of St Stephen.

**Writ. Serve a writ on someone, To.** *See under* SERVE.

**Write.** Old English *wrītan*, originally meaning to scratch runes into bark.

**Write down, To.** To commit to writing; to criticize unfavourably or to depreciate.

**Write off, To.** To cancel a debt; to damage something beyond repair.

**Write off a debt, To.** To cancel it.

**Write oneself out, To.** To exhaust one's powers of literary production.

**Writer.** In Scotland a legal practitioner in a small town. In the Royal Navy a writer is a rating engaged for clerical duties.

**Writer's block.** A periodic lack of inspiration that can descend on the most experienced of writers and that results in an almost pathological inability to put pen to paper.

**Writer's cramp.** A muscular spasm caused by excessive writing, resulting in the sufferer's being unable to write at all. It is a purely physical condition and does not respond to psychotherapy.

**Writer to the Signet, A.** A member of an anciently established society of solicitors in Scotland who still have the sole right of preparing crown writs.

**Write up, To.** To promote; to bring into public notice or estimation by favourable criticism or accounts.

**Writing on the wall, The.** Said of something foreshadowing trouble or disaster. The reference is to Daniel 5:5–31, when a mysterious hand appeared writing on the wall while BELSHAZZAR was feasting. DANIEL interpreted the words ('mene, mene, tekel, upharsin') to him as portending his downfall and that of his kingdom. Belshazzar was slain that night. *See also* WEIGHED IN THE BALANCE AND FOUND WANTING.

**Ghost writer.** *See under* GHOST.

**Nothing to write home about.** *See under* NOTHING.

**Wrong. Wrong end of the stick, The.** *See* GET HOLD OF THE WRONG END OF THE STICK.

**Wrong'un.** A swindler, cheat or palpably dishonest person. The word has also been applied to false coin and other fakes, as well as to a horse that has run in any flat race meeting not recognized by the JOCKEY CLUB and so boycotted by the Club.

In CRICKET a wrong'un is a GOOGLY.

**Absent are always wrong, The.** *See under* ABSENT.

**Back the wrong horse.** *See under* BACK.

**Bark up the wrong tree, To.** *See under* BARK.

**Born on the wrong side of the blanket, To be.** *See under* BORN.

**Get out of bed on the wrong side, To.** *See under* GET.

**Go down the wrong way, To.** *See under* GO.

**In the wrong box.** In the wrong place; not where the thing or person normally belongs.

**King or Queen can do no wrong, The.** *See under* KING.

**On the right** or **wrong tracks.** *See under* TRACK.

**On the wrong side of someone.** Out of favour with them.

**On the wrong side of the tracks.** *See under* TRACK.

**Rub someone up the wrong way, To.** *See under* RUB.

**Wry face, A.** An expression with the features distorted, showing distaste.

**Wulfstan** or **Wulstan.** There are two English saints of this name:

(1) Archbishop of York (d.1023), and formerly bishop of Worcester, best known for his homily in Old English prose *Sermo Lupi ad Anglos* ('Sermon of Lupus [Wolf] to the English'), portraying the miseries of the year 1014 during the Danish onslaught.

(2) Bishop of Worcester (*c*.1008–95), reputed author of part of the ANGLO-SAXON CHRONICLE, who was noted, in association with Lanfranc, for suppression of the slave trade between England and Ireland.

**Wuyck's Bible.** *See under* BIBLE.

**WVS.** The Women's Voluntary Service, set up in 1938, primarily to help with air raid precautions. It became the WRVS (Women's Royal Voluntary Service) in 1949. It continues to do valuable social and welfare work with the aged and infirm and gives help in emergencies. It is particularly noted for its 'meals on wheels' service.

**Wycliffite.** A LOLLARD, a follower of John Wyclif or Wycliffe (*c*.1320–84), who was called the Morning Star of the REFORMATION. He condemned TRANSUBSTANTIATION and monasticism, and held that only the righteous have the right to dominion and property. He attacked the papacy and the bishops, and advocated the use of the Bible in English.

**Wyclif's Bible.** *See under* BIBLE.

**Wykehamist.** A member of Winchester College, past or present, which was founded in 1378 by William of Wykeham (1324–1404), bishop of Winchester and chancellor of England, who was born at Wickham in Hampshire. He also founded New College, Oxford.

> Broad of Church and broad of mind,
> Broad before and broad behind,
> A keen ecclesiologist,
> A rather dirty Wykehamist.
>
> JOHN BETJEMAN: *Mount Zion*, 'The Wykehamist' (1931)

**Wysiwyg.** Computer slang for 'What you see is what you get', i.e. what you see on the screen is exactly what will appear in computer-printed form. The acronym is pronounced 'wiziwig'.

**Wyvern** or **wivern.** A fabulous creature of HERALDRY consisting of a winged DRAGON ending in a barbed, serpent's tail. The word ultimately comes from Latin *vipera*, 'viper'.

# X

**X.** The twenty-fourth letter of the alphabet, representing the twenty-second letter of the Greek alphabet (*chi*), and denoting in Roman numeration 10, or, on its side (⋈) 1000, and with a dash over it ($\overline{\text{X}}$) 10,000.

In algebra and mathematics generally *x* denotes an unknown quantity. The reason for this is that algebra came into use in Europe from Arabia and that Arabic *shei*, 'a thing', 'a something', used to designate the mathematically 'unknown', was transcribed as 'xei'. *See also* CROSS.

X as an abbreviation stands for Christ as in 'Xmas'.

X on beer casks formerly indicated beer that had paid the old 10s duty, and hence it came to mean beer of a given quality. Two or three crosses are mere trademarks, intended to convey an impression of its extra strength.

X was at one time a classification for 'adult' films, meaning in the main those of a specifically sexual or violent nature. The designation was replaced in Britain in 1983 by '18', the legal age of majority, and in the USA in 1990 by 'NC–17', i.e. 'no children under 17'.

**X-rated.** Indecent; pornographic, as 'X-rated humour'. The allusion is to the former X film classification.

**X-rays.** The uniquely-propertied rays were discovered almost incidentally on 8 November 1895 by the German chemist Wilhelm Roentgen (1845–1923) while investigating the effects of cathode rays produced by electrical discharges through gases at low pressures. He called the strange new rays *X-Strahlen*, from *X* as an unknown quantity (*see* X) and *Strahlen*, the plural of *Strahl*, 'ray'. The English name thus translates the German. The nonce designation has persisted, although some languages now know the rays by the name of their discoverer, as German *Röntgenstrahlen*, Russian *rentgenovskiye luchi* and Japanese *rentogen*.

**Xanadu.** The summer residence of KUBLAI KHAN, about 180 miles (290km) north of Peking. The name is a corruption of *Shang-du*, 'imperial capital'. It was made famous by S.T. Coleridge's poem 'Kubla Khan' (1816), with its opening lines:

In Xanadu did Kubla Khan
A stately pleasure-dome decree.

Coleridge was inspired by a sentence in Samuel Purchas' *Purchas his Pilgrimage* (1613):

In Xamdu did Cublai Can build a stately Palace, encompassing sixteene miles of plaine ground with a wall, wherein are fertile Meddowes, pleasant Springs, delightfull Streames, and all sorts of beasts of chase and game, and in the middest thereof a sumptuous house of pleasure.

**Xanthian marbles, The.** A collection of ancient sculptures and friezes discovered in 1838 by the English archaeologist Sir Charles Fellows (1799–1860) at Xanthus, a Greek city of Lycia, Asia Minor, and now in the BRITISH MUSEUM.

**Xanthippe** or **Xantippe.** The wife of the philosopher SOCRATES. Her bad temper shown towards her husband has rendered her name proverbial for a conjugal scold.

Be she as foul as was Florentius' love,
As old as Sibyl, and as curst and shrewd
As Socrates' Xanthippe, or a worse,
She moves me not.

SHAKESPEARE: *The Taming of the Shrew*, I, ii (1593)

**Xanthus** or **Xanthos** (Greek, 'reddish-yellow').

(1) ACHILLES' wonderful horse, the brother of BALIOS, Achilles' other horse, and offspring of ZEPHYR and the HARPY, Podarge. On being chided by his master for leaving PATROCLUS on the field of battle, Xanthus turned his head reproachfully, and told Achilles that he also would soon be numbered with the dead, not from any fault of his horse, but by the decree of inexorable destiny (*Iliad*, XIX (8th century BC)).

(2) Xanthus is also the ancient name of the River Scamander, now the Menderes in northwest Turkey, and of a city on its banks. Aelian and Pliny say that Homer called the Scamander 'Xanthus', or the 'Gold-red river', because it coloured the fleeces of sheep washed in its waters with this tinge. Others maintain that it was so called because a Greek hero of this name defeated a body of TROJANS on its banks, and pushed half of them into the stream.

**Xavier. Xaverian Brothers, The.** A Roman Catholic congregation founded at Bruges in 1839, concerned chiefly with the education of youth.

It was founded by Theodore Jacob Ryken (1797–1871) who took the name Brother Francis Xavier after St FRANCIS XAVIER.

**St Francis Xavier.** *See under* FRANCIS.

**X-craft.** A code name for the Royal Navy's midget submarines that were in action against the German battleship *Tirpitz* in 1943. Each submarine was designated 'X' followed by a distinguishing number.

> Of the six attacking craft X9 was lost on passage and X8 ... had to be scuttled. X10 found that *Scharnhorst* had left the fiord and X5 was sunk by gunfire, leaving X6 ... and X7 to make their way up Altenfiord.
>
> *The Times*, obituary of Rear-Admiral Godfrey Place (30 December 1994)

**Xenocratic.** Pertaining to the doctrine of Xenocrates (396–314 BC), a disciple of PLATO, and noted for his chastity and fidelity and contempt of wealth. He combined Pythagoreanism with Platonism. Even the courtesan LAIS failed to tempt him from the path of virtue.

> Warmed by such youthful beauty, the severe
> Xenocrates would not have more been chaste.
>
> L. ARIOSTO: *Orlando Furioso*, xi (1532)

**Xerxes.** A Greek way of writing the Persian *Khshayarsha*, meaning 'great ruler'. Xerxes I, the great Xerxes, king of Persia (510–465 BC), is identical with the AHASUERUS of the Bible (Esther, *passim*).

When Xerxes invaded Greece he constructed a pontoon bridge across the Dardanelles, which was swept away by the force of the waves. This so enraged the Persian despot that he 'inflicted 300 lashes on the rebellious sea, and cast chains of iron across it'. This story is a Greek myth, founded on the peculiar construction of Xerxes' second bridge, which consisted of 300 boats, lashed by iron chains to two ships serving as supporters.

Another story tells that when he reviewed his enormous army before starting for Greece, he wept at the thought of the slaughter about to take place: 'Of all this multitude, who shall say how many will return?'

**Ximena.** The CID's bride.

**Xiphias** (Greek *xiphos*, 'sword'). The name used in medieval times for a sword-shaped comet, also for the southern constellation now called Dorado. It is also a poetic name given to the swordfish (genus *Xiphias*).

> Strong is the horse upon his speed;
> Strong in pursuit the rapid glede [kite]
> Which makes at once his game:
> Strong the tall ostrich on the ground;
> Strong through the turbulent profound
> Shoots xiphias to his aim.
>
> CHRISTOPHER SMART: *A Song to David*, lxxv (1763)

**Xylomancy.** A form of DIVINATION using twigs, rods and the like (Greek *xulon*, 'wood', and *manteia*, 'prophecy').

**XYZ Affair.** In 1797 the American President, John Adams (1735–1826), sent his commissioners, Charles Pinckney, John Marshall and Elbridge Gerry, to France to negotiate on maritime differences. From Paris they reported that three French agents had intercepted them and demanded a large sum of money and an American loan before the DIRECTORY would receive them. The Americans refused, and the whole correspondence with the three French agents, designated X, Y and Z, was published at Washington. This led to undeclared maritime hostility with France (1798–1800).

# Y

**Y.** The twenty-fifth letter of the alphabet, derived from the Greek Y (upsilon), added by the Greeks to the Phoenician alphabet. It is used to represent both consonantal and vowel sounds, as respectively in 'yew' and 'fly'. *See also* SAMIAN LETTER.

As a medieval numeral Y represents 150 and $\overline{Y}$, 150,000.

In algebra it denotes the second unknown quantity. *See also* X; YE.

**Y-fronts.** The registered trade name of a make of boys' or men's underpants, with a front opening within an inverted Y-shape.

**Y-gun.** A Y-shaped gun mounted in ships for firing a pair of depth charges.

**Yachtsman, The Noble.** *See under* NOBLE.

**Yaga, Baba.** *See under* BABA.

**Yahoo.** Jonathan Swift's name, in *Gulliver's Travels* (1726), for brutes with human forms and vicious propensities. They are subject to the HOUYHNHNMS, the horses with human reason. Hence the use of the word for coarse, brutish or degraded persons. Swift doubtless based the word on a blend of the two exclamations of disgust, 'yah!' and 'ugh!', although some see the influence of 'whinny'.

**Yahweh.** *See* JEHOVAH.

**Elohistic and Yahwistic sources.** *See under* ELOHIM.

**Yama.** In Hindu mythology the first of the dead, born from the sun, the judge of men and king of the dead. His kingdom is the Paradise for the worthy where friends and relations are reunited. His twin sister is called Yami, and he is usually represented as having four arms and riding a buffalo.

**Yang.** *See* YIN AND YANG.

**Yank** or **Yankee.** A citizen of the USA, properly a New Englander. The derivation is uncertain but is perhaps from Dutch *Jan Kees*, 'John Cheese', a nickname used derisively by Dutch settlers in New York (then New Amsterdam) for English colonialists in Connecticut. The word was popularized by the song YANKEE DOODLE.

**Yankee Doodle.** A popular mid-18th-century song, perhaps first introduced by British troops during the Anglo-French war (1755–63). It is now a quasi-national air of the United States.

There are several suggested origins of the tune, which was first printed in England in 1778 and in America in 1794, but none is conclusive.

> Yankee Doodle came to town
> Riding on a pony;
> Stuck a feather in his cap
> And called it Macaroni.

**Yarborough.** A hand at bridge in which there is no card higher than a nine. It is so called because the 2nd Lord Yarborough (1809–62) used to lay 1000 to 1 against such an occurrence in any named hand. The actual mathematical odds are 1827 to 1 against. *See also* TIGER.

**Yard, Scotland.** *See under* SCOTLAND.

**Yardarm, The sun is over the.** *See under* SUN.

**Yarmouth capon, A.** A RED HERRING.

**Yarn. Rogue's yarn.** *See under* ROGUE.

**Spin a yarn, To.** *See under* SPIN.

**Yclept.** An old English word meaning 'called', 'named'. It is now used only in the sort of arch facetiousness that FOWLER calls 'worn-out humour'.

> The Associated South London Extended Gold Mines Corporation, Limited, yclept in the market Suds.
>
> *Westminster Gazette* (23 February 1900)

**Ye.** An archaic way of writing 'the', the 'y' representing Old English ʒ. Early printers used y as a substitute for the letter Þ, the character representing modern 'th', hence the use of 'ye' for 'the' and 'yt' as an abbreviation for 'that'. It was always pronounced 'the'. It is found in modern pseudo-historical use in some quaint contexts, such as 'Ye Old Tea Shoppe'.

'Ye' is also, of course, the archaic nominative plural of the second person.

**Year** (connected with Greek *horos*, 'season', and Latin *hora*, 'hour'). The period of time occupied by the revolution of the earth round the sun.

The astronomical, equinoctial, natural, solar or tropical year is the time taken by the sun in returning to the same equinox, in mean length, 365 days 5 hours 48 minutes and 46 seconds.

The astral or sidereal year is the time in which the sun returns from a given star to the same star again: 365 days 6 hours 9 minutes and 9.6 seconds.

The Platonic, great or perfect year (*Annus magnus*), is a great cycle of years (estimated by early Greek astronomers at about 26,000 years) at the end of which all the heavenly bodies were imagined to return to the same places as they occupied at the Creation. *See also* CALENDAR; CANICULAR PERIOD; LEAP YEAR; LUNAR YEAR; SABBATICAL YEAR; SOTHIC PERIOD.

**Yearbooks.** The name given to annual publications summarizing the events, changes and so on, of the preceding year in the world at large, or in some particular subject, profession, trade, industry and the like, e.g. *The Statesman's Yearbook*, *Whitaker's Almanack*, *The Mining Annual Review*, *The Writers' & Artists' Year Book*, *Wisden Cricketers' Almanack*.

Historically, the term denotes the unique series of reports of cases decided in the courts of COMMON LAW, written in Norman French, and covering the period 1292–1534.

**Year dot, The.** A time long ago. The dot implies that the date of the year is too old to be stated with any certainty.

**Year in, year out.** Continuously; all the time. The expression has a nuance of monotony.

**Year of Confusion.** The year AD 46, when the JULIAN CALENDAR was introduced, a year of 445 days.

**Year of Grace.** The year of our Lord, ANNO DOMINI. Also the favour of benefiting from a year's delay in resigning an appointment, submitting a doctoral thesis or the like. *See also* DAYS OF GRACE.

**Year of Our Lord.** A year of the Christian era.

**Academic year.** *See under* ACADEMY.

**Canicular year.** *See under* CANICULAR.

**Donkey's years.** *See under* DONKEY.

**Financial year.** *See under* FINANCIAL.

**For a year and a day.** *See under* FOR.

**Forty Years On.** *See under* FORTY.

**Gap year.** *See under* GAP.

**Gregorian year.** *See under* GREGORIAN.

**Julian year.** *See under* JULIAN.

**Leap year.** *See under* LEAP.

**Light year.** *See under* LIGHT.

**Lunar year.** *See under* LUNAR.

**Marian year.** *See under* MARIAN.

**Regnal year.** *See under* REGNAL.

**Sabbatical year.** *See under* SABBATICAL.

**Sothic year.** *See under* SOTHIC.

**Wear one's years well, To.** *See under* WEAR.

**Yell Hounds.** *See* WISH HOUNDS.

**Yellow** (Old English *geolu*, related to Greek *khloros*, 'green', and to 'gall', the yellowish fluid secreted by the liver). In symbolism the colour indicates jealousy, inconstancy, adultery, perfidy and cowardice. In France the doors of traitors used to be daubed with yellow, and in some countries the laws ordained that Jews must be clothed in yellow, because they betrayed Jesus, so that in medieval pictures JUDAS ISCARIOT is arrayed in yellow. In Spain at an AUTO-DA-FÉ, the victims wore yellow, to denote heresy and treason. *See also* COLOURS.

In HERALDRY and ecclesiastical symbolism yellow is frequently used in place of gold.

**Yellowback.** A now dated term for a cheap novel, especially of the sensational kind, so called from the yellow board binding familiar on the railway bookstalls of Victorian days.

**Yellow-bellies.** A name given to natives of Lincolnshire, in humorous allusion to the frogs found in the fenland districts. The Mexicans are also so called.

**Yellow Book, The.** A yellow-covered quarterly magazine published between 1894 and 1897 by John Lane (1854–1925), the title being chosen to suggest certain qualities of the 'yellowback' French novel. It was edited by Henry Harland (1861–1905) and its contributors included Arnold Bennett, A.C. Benson, Edmund Gosse, Henry James, George Moore, Arthur Symons and Oscar Wilde. Aubrey Beardsley and Max Beerbohm contributed drawings, Beardsley's work having erotic overtones. The Yellow Book became the AVANT-GARDE reading of the NAUGHTY NINETIES.

**Yellow books.** Official documents, government reports and the like in France, corresponding to British BLUEBOOKS. They are so called (*livres jaunes*) from the colour of their covers.

**Yellow boy.** Old slang for a golden SOVEREIGN, once fairly common in Britain.

> John did not starve the cause: there wanted not yellow-boys to fee counsel.
>
> JOHN ARBUTHNOT: *History of John Bull* (1712)

**Yellow card.** A card shown by a football referee to a player being cautioned. The use of yellow here is analogous to that of the traffic light. If the player repeats the offence he will be shown a RED CARD.

**Yellow dog contracts.** An American name for agreements made by the employers with employees to prevent the latter from joining labour unions. Such contracts became invalid under an Act of 1932.

**Yellow fever.** A tropical fever accompanied by jaundice and black vomit, also called YELLOW JACK. In Australia the name was given to the gold-prospecting mania of colonial days.

**Yellow flag.** One of the three QUARANTINE flags. *See also* YELLOW JACK.

**Yellowhammer.** A bunting (*Emberiza citrinella*) with yellowish head, neck and breast (Old English *amore*, German *Ammer*, 'bunting'). The tradition is that, at Christ's crucifixion, the bird fluttered about the cross and got its plumage stained with blood. By way of punishment its eggs were doomed ever after to bear marks of blood. Because the bird was 'cursed', boys were taught that it was right and proper to destroy its eggs.

**Yellow jack.** The YELLOW FEVER, also the yellow flag displayed from lazarettos (plague hospitals) and commonly, but somewhat inaccurately, called the QUARANTINE flag, probably because it was the flag usually flown by vessels liable to the performance of quarantine. By an Act of 1825 the yellow flag was adopted as one of three quarantine flags, and when it was flown signified a clean bill of health. A yellow flag with a black ball in the centre signified the converse, and the yellow and black quartered flag meant dangerous plague or disease on board. In the International Code of Signals (1931), the yellow (Q) flag, when flown by a ship entering territorial waters from abroad, still has the same meaning: 'My ship is healthy and I request free PRATIQUE.' Flag Q flown over the first substitute (QQ) means, in short, 'My ship is suspect', and Flag Q flown over L (QL) means 'My ship is infected'.

**Yellow jersey.** The jersey worn by the overall leader of a cycle race at the end of a day's stage and presented to the final winner. The best known is the French *maillot jaune* of the Tour de France.

**Yellow Pages.** The registered trade name of a classified telephone directory, printed on yellow paper. It lists subscribers alphabetically by their product, occupation or service, e.g. (under B) Baby goods, Background music, Bags, Bailiffs, Bait merchants, Ballet shoes.

**Yellow peril, The.** A scare, originally raised in Germany in the late 1890s, that the yellow races of China and Japan would rapidly increase in population and overrun the territories occupied by the white races with fearful consequences.

**Yellow press, The.** The sensationalist newspapers. The name arose in the United States when William Randolph Hearst's *Journal*, during the circulation battle with Pulitzer's *World*, introduced a comic picture feature called 'The Yellow Kid'. This rivalry was dubbed 'yellow journalism' and came to be characterized by scare headlines, sensational articles, lavish illustrations, comic features, Sunday supplements and the like.

**Yellow River, The.** The Hwang-Ho in China, so called from the yellow earth or loess that it carries in suspension.

**Yellow streak.** A cowardly or weak trait in a person's character.

**Yen. Have a yen for, To.** An expression of American origin, meaning to have an intense desire or longing for. The word comes from Chinese *yan*, 'craving'.

**Yeoman.** Historically, a middle class of small freeholders, variously defined at different periods and later applied to the class of 'forty-shilling freeholders'.

**Yeoman of the Guard.** *See* BEEFEATERS.

**Yeomanry.** British volunteer cavalry units were so called from 1761, although not effectively formed until 1794. In the 19th century they were largely used for suppressing riots and were essentially maintained by private benevolence and voluntary efforts. Most of them were former members of the regular cavalry. The Yeomanry were absorbed in the Territorial Army in 1907. *See also* TERRIER.

**Yeoman service.** Effectual service, characterized by hard and steady work. The reference is to the service of yeomen in the English armies of former days.

**Yes-man.** An expressive colloquialism for someone who always expresses agreement with a superior, irrespective of any privately held opinions.

**Yeti.** The Tibetan name for the ABOMINABLE SNOWMAN.

**Yeux, Beaux.** *See under* BEAUX.

**Yew.** The yew is a native British tree (*Taxus baccata*) and is commonly planted in churchyards because, as an evergreen, it is a symbol of immortality. The practice was also encouraged to provide a supply of bow staves from the hard, elastic wood resulting from the slow growth of this tree, which lives to a great age. To decorate the house with yew was held to lead to a death in the family. Yew leaves and berries are poisonous.

Some well-known yews are at the following sites:

- Brabourne, Kent: in Evelyn's time was reputed to have a girth of nearly 59ft (18m)
- Darley churchyard, Derbyshire: claimed to be well over 2000 years old and to have a girth of 33ft (10m)
- Fortingall, Glen Lyon, Perthshire: now a relic but claimed to have been between 2000 and 3000 years old.
- Fountains Abbey, Yorkshire: three yews are said to have existed before the abbey was built in the 12th century
- St Mary's, Painswick, Gloucestershire: the churchyard contains a collection of neatly clipped yews dating from *c.*1779, and just under, or just over, but never exactly, 100 in number

Dr John Lowe's *The Yew Trees of Great Britain and Ireland* (1897) lists the oldest and biggest yew trees and of the 211 given with girths of over 10ft (3m), 36 were in Wales. The largest tree in the grove at Mamhilad, Monmouthshire, has a girth of over 31ft (9.4m). Given that a yew tree grows about 1ft (30cm) in girth every 30 years, it is possible to date them reasonably accurately. Thus yew trees planted in monasteries in the 12th century now have a girth of between 20ft (6.1m) and 30ft (9.1m).

**Yggdrasil.** The world tree of Scandinavian mythology that, with its roots and branches, binds together heaven, earth and hell. It is an ash, but it is evergreen, and at its root is MIMIR's fountain of wonderful virtues. In the tree, which drops honey, sit an eagle, a squirrel and four stags. It is the tree of time and space, life and knowledge, and ODIN is said to have hanged himself from its branches in order to learn the secret of the runes. Close to its roots live the three sisters, the NORNS, who, representing past, present and future, brought time from the land of the Giants and so ended the great age of the gods.

Its name probably means 'Uggr's horse', from Old Norse *Uggr*, a name of Odin (from *uggr*, 'frightful'), and *drasill*, 'horse'.

**Yiddish** (German *jüdisch*, 'Jewish'). A Middle German dialect developed in Poland under Hebrew and Slavonic influence, written in Hebrew characters, and used as a language by east European Jews. As a result of the latter's widespread dispersal, Yiddish became the LINGUA FRANCA of world Jewry. Hence Yid as a derogatory term for a Jew.

**Yield the palm, To.** To yield the palm of victory; to admit another's superiority in a given field. *See also* BEAR THE PALM.

**Yin and yang.** The two complementary forces, or principles, that in eastern thought are believed to make up all aspects of life. Yin ('dark') is regarded as being earth, female, dark, passive and absorbing. It is present in even numbers and in valleys and streams, and it is represented by the tiger, the colour orange and a broken line. Yang ('bright') is heaven, male, light, active and penetrating. It is present in odd numbers and in mountains, and it is represented by the dragon, the colour azure and an unbroken line.

Chinese thought associates the yin–yang concept with that of the five agents or elements: metal, wood, water, fire and earth.

**Ymir.** The primeval being of Scandinavian mythology, father of all the giants. He was nourished by the four milky streams, which flowed from the cow Audhumla. ODIN, Vili and Ve, the sons of Bor, slew Ymir and all the frost giants were drowned in his blood, which formed the world's lakes and seas. His bones and flesh became the mountains and the land, and his skull the vault of heaven. A race of dwarfs grew within his carcass.

**Yob.** *See* BACK SLANG.

**Yodel.** To sing with frequent alternations between the ordinary voice and falsetto. It is properly peculiar to Switzerland and is a development of Switzerland and the Tyrolese. It may have derived from, or at any rate been based on, the RANZ DES VACHES.

**Yoga.** A practice of Hindu philosophy, involving the withdrawal of the physical senses from external objects. Adepts in yoga are able to hold their breath for protracted periods and to do other things in apparent contravention of natural requirements. Hypnotism and self-mortification are part of the cult. Union with the deity became its object (Sanskrit *yoga*, 'yoking', 'devotion'). A yogi is someone who practises yoga.

**Yogi Bear.** The cartoon bear who starred in the American animated television series named after him, broadcast from 1958 to 1963 and produced by the Hanna-Barbera team. He lives in Jellystone Park and has a little friend in Boo-Boo.

**Yoke, To pass under the.** *See under* PASS.

**Yom Kippur.** *See* DAY OF ATONEMENT.

**Yonks.** The slang word meaning 'a long time', especially in the phrase 'for yonks', first emerged in general use in the 1960s. Its origin is uncertain, though it may be a shortened form of DONKEY'S YEARS.

**Yorick.** In Shakespeare's *Hamlet* (1600) the dead jester whose skull is exhumed, leading to HAMLET's reflection, 'Alas, poor Yorick', and his meditation on the transience of life. In Laurence Sterne's novel *Tristram Shandy* (1759–67) Yorick is an eccentric parson noted for his spavined nag, his inability to lie and his tombstone, which similarly reads, 'Alas, poor Yorick'. *See also* SHANDEAN.

**York. Yorker.** In CRICKET a deceptive ball delivered so that it pitches directly beneath the bat and is thus likely to be missed by the batsman. It is perhaps so called from its first being developed by a Yorkshire bowler.

**Yorkist.** A partisan of the House of York in the WARS OF THE ROSES. *See also* WHITE ROSE.

**Yorkshireman's toast, The.** 'Here's tiv us, all on us; may we never want nowt, noan on us; nor me nawther,' i.e. 'Here's to us, all of us; may we never want anything, any of us; nor I either.'

**Yorkshire tike, A.** An long-established nickname for a Yorkshireman, now without any derogatory implications. It formerly specially denoted a clownish rustic of that county. *See also* TIKE.

**Duke of York's Column, The.** *See under* DUKE.

**Grand Old Duke of York, The.** *See under* GRAND.

**Noble Duke of York, The.** *See under* NOBLE.

**St William of York.** *See under* WILLIAM.

**Young.** Apart from its general use to designate a young or junior person of some kind, the word is characteristically found as an epithet in the names of political parties which aim to bring about sweeping political changes or to reawaken the national spirit.

**Young blood.** *See* NEW, FRESH OR YOUNG BLOOD.

**Young Chevalier, The.** Charles Edward Stuart, the YOUNG PRETENDER.

**Young England.** A group of young TORY politicians of the early 1840s who sought to revive a somewhat romantic concept of paternal feudalism and to idealize the functions of the territorial aristocracy. They saw their movement as a safeguard against revolution and the triumph of the LAISSEZ FAIRE doctrines of the MANCHESTER SCHOOL. Their leaders were John Manners, 7th Duke of Rutland (1818–1906) and George Smythe, 7th Viscount Strangford (1818–57). Benjamin Disraeli, 1st Earl of Beaconsfield (1804–81) also joined their ranks.

**Young Europe.** An Italian political organization (*Giovine Europa*) founded by Giuseppe Mazzini (1805–72) in 1834 with the aim of coordinating the democratic forces of Europe, and embracing YOUNG ITALY, YOUNG GERMANY, Young Poland and Young Switzerland. It was wound up by the Swiss authorities in 1836.

**Young fogey** or **fogy.** A young person of conservative tastes and attitude. The expression copies the traditional 'old fogey', or dull and old-fashioned middle-aged or elderly person. *See also* OLD FOGEY.

**Young Germany.** A German school of the 1830s (*Junges Deutschland*) whose aim was to liberate politics, religion and manners from the old conventional trammels. Heinrich Heine (1797–1856) was its most prominent representative.

**Young hopeful, A.** A young or at any rate youngish person who is likely to succeed.

**Young Ireland.** An Irish nationalist movement of the 1840s taking its name in imitation of Mazzini's YOUNG ITALY. Their aims included the revival of Irish language and literature and national independence. The members included both Protestants and Catholics, and they were responsible for the futile rising of 1848. Their leaders included William Smith O'Brien (1803–64), Sir Charles Gavan Duffy (1816–1903), John Mitchel (1815–75) and Thomas Francis Meagher (1822–67).

**Young Italy.** A republican nationalist movement (*Giovine Italia*) inspired by the exiled Giuseppe Mazzini and seeking to promote an Italian revolution. Founded in 1831 and imbued by its leader with fervent idealism, it never gained the support of the masses, but it did much to develop the spirit of nationalism in the 1830s and 1840s. *See also* CARBONARI; YOUNG EUROPE.

**Young lady.** A young single woman; a girl; a girlfriend.

> 'This here young lady,' said the Gryphon, 'she wants for to know your history, she do.'
>
> LEWIS CARROLL: *Alice in Wonderland*, ch ix (1865)

**Young Pretender, The.** Charles Edward Stuart (1720–88), son of the OLD PRETENDER, and popularly known as Bonnie Prince Charlie or the Young Chevalier. *See also* FORTY-FIVE.

**Young Russia.** A left-wing proclamation (*Molodaya Rossiya*) published secretly in Ryazan in 1862 by the Russian revolutionary P.G. Zaichnevsky (1842–96) and distributed in St Petersburg, Moscow and the provinces. It called for the abolition of the monarchy and the death of the Romanovs, and was the most extreme of the revolutionary publications of the 1860s.

**Young thing, A.** A young person, especially one seen to possess any or all of the positive characteristics of youth, as flair, enthusiasm, good looks, physical prowess and the like. The 'bright young things' or FLAPPERS of the 1920s and 1930s were prominent on the social scene for their exuberance and often outrageous behaviour.

**Young Turks, The.** A Turkish reforming party seeking to transform the decadent Turkish Empire into a modern European state and to give it a parliamentary constitution. It had its origins in a committee formed at Geneva in 1891, and the party, considerably supported by students, raised the standard of revolt at Salonika in 1908, deposed Sultan Abdul Hamid, and replaced him by his brother as Mohammed V (1909). Their 'liberalism' was not dominant, but they remained the major force in Turkish politics until the end of the First World War, when the party was dissolved. Turkey was proclaimed a republic in 1923.

**Angry Young Men.** *See under* ANGRY.

**Tree must be bent while it is young, A.** *See under* TREE.

**Yours truly.** This conventional ending to letters is sometimes humorously used to indicate the speaker, as: 'Yours truly was left to do the washing up.'

**Youth. Fountain of Youth.** *See under* FOUNTAIN.

**Gilded youth.** *See under* GILD.

**If youth knew; if age could.** *See under* IF.

**Thy youth is renewed like the eagle's.** Biblical words from Psalm 103:5. They refer to the ancient superstition that every ten years the eagle soars into the 'fiery region', and plunges into the sea, where, moulting its feathers, it acquires new life. *See also* PHOENIX.

> At last she saw, where he vpstarted braue
> Out of the well, wherein he drenched lay:
> As Eagle fresh out of the Ocean waue,
> Where he hath left his plumes all hoary gray,
> And deckt himselfe with feathers youthly gay.
>
> EDMUND SPENSER: *The Faerie Queene*, I, xi (1590)

**Ysolde, Yseult, Iseult** or **Isolde.** The name of two heroines of ARTHURIAN ROMANCES: Ysolde the Fair, daughter of the king of Ireland, wife of King MARK and lover of TRISTRAM; the other Ysolde or Iseult of the White Hands or Ysolde of Brittany.

**Yuga.** One of the four ages of the world into which, according to Hindu cosmogony, mundane time is divided.

**Yule** or **Yuletide.** The CHRISTMAS season, from Old English *geōla*, related to Old Norse *jōl*, the name of a pagan festival at the winter SOLSTICE.

**Yule log.** A great log of wood formerly laid across the hearth with great ceremony on Christmas Eve and lit with a brand from the previous year's log. There followed drinking and merriment. The name is now used for a chocolate iced cake in the shape of such a log.

And the Yule-log cracked in the chimney,
And the Abbot bowed his head,
And the flamelets flapped and flickered,
But the Abbot was stark and dead.

H.W. LONGFELLOW: 'King Witlaf's Drinking-Horn' (1848)

**Yuppie.** A young urban (or upwardly mobile) professional person. A popular acronym from the 1980s, and of American origin.

'The Yuppie Handbook' [1984] defined the yuppie as a fast-track baby-boomer between 25 and 46 residing in or near a major city and living on aspirations of glory and power or 'anyone who brunches on the weekend or works out after work'.
*International Herald Tribune* (March 1986)

**Yusupov.** The Russian princely family of this name traces its origins back to the Nogay prince Yusuf (Joseph) (d.1555), whose sons lived in Russia from 1563. Among the more important members of the clan are Grigory Dmitrievich Yusupov (1676–1730), head of the Military College under Peter II; Boris Grigorievich Yusupov (1695–1759), president of the College of Commerce and the owner of several manufacturing concerns; and Nikolay Borisovich Yusupov (1750–1831), an art lover, composer and writer on music, who in 1810 converted the Arkhangelskoye estate outside Moscow into the family's palatial parkland home. The male princely line ceased on the death in 1891 of his identically named grandson, Nikolay Borisovich Yusupov, but by royal order of Nicholas II the title and name of Yusupov passed to Count Feliks Feliksovich Sumarokov-Elston (1856–1928), who had married Nikolay Borisovich's daughter, Zinaida Nikolaevna Yusupova (1861–1939). In 1914 their son, Feliks Feliksovich Yusupov (1887–1967), married Nicholas II's niece, Grand Princess Irina Aleksandrovna (1895–1970). It was this last Yusupov and his associates who in 1916 murdered RASPUTIN.

**Yves** or **Yvo.** The patron saint of lawyers, being himself a lawyer. St Yves (1253–1303) became an ecclesiastical judge at Rennes and in 1285 entered the priesthood. His work for orphans and widows earned him the title of Advocate of the Poor. He was canonized in 1347 and his day is 19 May.

**Yvetot, The King of.** A man of great pretensions but little merit. Yvetot is a town in Normandy. The 'King' was the lord of the town, and the title was in use from the 14th to the 16th century. *Le Roi d'Yvetot*, the ballad by Pierre-Jean de Béranger (1780–1857), which contains satirical allusions to NAPOLEON BONAPARTE, appeared in 1813.

[Il] n'agrandit point ses États,
Fut un voisin commode,
Et, modèle des potentats,
Prit le plaisir pour code.
([He] did not enlarge his estates,
Was a genial neighbour,
And, as a model potentate,
Took pleasure as his code.)

# Z

**Z.** The last letter of the alphabet, called 'zed' in England, but in America 'zee'. Its older English name was 'izzard'. It was the sixth letter of the Greek alphabet, zeta, ζ.

> Thou whoreson zed! thou unnecessary letter!
> SHAKESPEARE: *King Lear*, II, ii (1605)

In mathematics it denotes the third unknown quantity, and as a medieval numeral it represents 2000. It is also used as a contraction mark as in VIZ (for videlicet) and oz (for ounce).

**Zacchaeus.** In the New Testament (Luke 19) a tax collector who being 'little of stature' climbs a tree to see Jesus and with whom Jesus stays, despite complaints that he is a sinner. He is redeemed by the experience.

**Zacharias.** Two men of this name appear in the New Testament. In Matthew 23:35 and Luke 11:51 Zacharias is mentioned as a prophet stoned 'between the temple and the altar' for his prophecies. He is probably the same as the Zechariah of 2 Chronicles 24:20–23, described as being slain in this way, and distinct from the identically named ZECHARIAH. Better known is the Zacharias of Luke 1 who is the father of JOHN THE BAPTIST.

**Zadkiel.** In rabbinical angelology the angel of the planet JUPITER. The name was adopted as a pseudonym by the astrologer Richard James Morrison (1795–1874), a naval lieutenant, author of the *Herald of Astrology* (1831), which continued to appear as *Zadkiel's Almanack*.

**Zadok.** In the Old Testament, the priest who with NATHAN the prophet plays a decisive role in securing the throne for SOLOMON after the death of DAVID (1 Kings 1–2, 1 Chronicles 15–16, 18). His name is familiar to music lovers from Handel's anthem 'Zadok the Priest', which was composed for the coronation of George II in Westminster Abbey in 1727.

**Zany.** The buffoon who mimicked the CLOWN in the Commedia dell'Arte, hence, a simpleton or one who 'acts the goat'. The name comes from Italian *zanni*, a buffoon, a familiar form of Giovanni (i.e. John). Horace Walpole famously described James Boswell's *Tour of the Hebrides* (1785), chronicling the journey that he undertook with Dr Johnson, as 'the story of a mountebank and his zany' (letter to Hon. Henry Conway, 6 October 1785).

**Zarathustra.** *See* ZOROASTRIANS.

**Zealots.** A Jewish sect founded by Judas of Gamala in the early years of the 1st century AD, who fiercely opposed Roman domination. They fought fanatically during the great rebellion, which ended in the destruction of Jerusalem in AD 70. *See also* MASADA.

**Zebi.** *See* SABBATAEANS.

**Zechariah.** An Old Testament prophet who had visions of a new world order and of a nameless MESSIAH who would bring universal peace. The book named after him contains many less conventional prophecies and some strange imagery. *See also* ZACHARIAS.

> And I took my staff, even Beauty, and cut it asunder, that I might break my covenant which I had made with the people.
> Zechariah 11:10

**Zeitgeist** (German *Zeit*, 'time', and *Geist*, 'spirit'). The spirit of the time; the moral or intellectual tendency characteristic of a period.

**Zemindar** (Persian, 'landholder'). Under the MOGUL emperors of India, one of a class of tax farmers, responsible for the revenues of land held in common. They were treated as landlords by the British and made into proprietors who paid a fixed annual tax. This change, introduced by Lord Cornwallis in Bengal in 1793, did not prevent RACK-RENTING of the peasantry by the zemindars.

**Zemstvo** (Russian *zemlya*, 'land'). The name given to the elected district assemblies and provincial councils (elected by the district assemblies) in Russia, introduced by Alexander II in 1864. They dealt with local taxation, primary education, famine precautions, roads and bridges and the like.

**Zem Zem.** The sacred well near the KAABA at MECCA. According to Arab tradition, this is the very well that was shown to HAGAR when ISHMAEL was perishing of thirst.

**Zen.** A Japanese Buddhist sect that believes that the ultimate truth is greater than words and is therefore not to be wholly found in the sacred writings, but must be sought through the 'inner light' and self-mastery. It originated in the 6th century in China.

**Zend-Avesta.** The sacred writings of Zoroaster that formed the basis of the religion that prevailed in Persia from the 6th century BC to the 7th century AD. AVESTA means the lore, or sacred writings, and *Zend*, the commentary. Hence the application of *Zend* to the ancient Iranian language in which the *Zend-Avesta* is written. *See also* ZOROASTRIANS.

**Zenith** (Arabic). Zenith is the point of the heavens immediately over the head of the spectator. NADIR is the opposite point immediately beneath the spectator's feet. Hence, to go from the zenith of one's fortunes to the nadir is to fall from the height of fortune to the depths of poverty. Zenith is based on Arabic *samt*, 'way', extracted from the full phrase *samt ar-rās*, literally 'path over the head', from *samt*, 'way', 'path', *al*, 'the', and *rās*, 'head'.

**Zeno.** The name of several philosophers.

**Zeno of Citium.** The founder of the STOIC school at Athens (*c*.335–*c*.263 BC). One of his maxims was that humans are given two ears, but only one mouth, to indicate that they should listen more than they should speak. Citium, the biblical Kittim (Genesis 10:4 etc) is an ancient city of Cyprus, now merged into Larnaka.

**Zeno of Elea.** A mathematician as well as a philosopher (*c*.495–*c*.430 BC). He was a disciple of Parmenides and one of the Eleatic school. He is said to have been the inventor of DIALECTIC. When tortured for conspiring against the tyrant Nearchus he bit off his tongue and spat it in the tyrant's face. Elea is now Velia, Italy.

**Zeno of Sidon.** The leader (*c*.150–*c*.70 BC) of the Epicurean (*see* EPICURUS) school in Athens.

**Zeno of Tarsus.** A STOIC who lived in the 3rd century BC.

**Zephaniah.** The prophet and probably great-grandson of King HEZEKIAH. In the Old Testament book named after him, he attacks the ruling class of JUDAH, the PHILISTINES and the Assyrians, and his prophecies are of the wrath to come.

**Zephyr** or **Zephyrus.** In classical mythology the west wind, the son of Astraeus and AURORA (EOS) and the brother of BOREAS. He loved HYACINTH, but because the youth preferred APOLLO, Zephyr caused the god's quoit or discus to strike Hyacinth, causing his death. Zephyr was the father of ACHILLES' immortal horses XANTHUS and BALIOS, which he fathered on the HARPY Podarge. His wife was said by some to be IRIS, but he was also said to be the lover of FLORA. He was identified with the Roman FAVONIUS, and his name is used for any soft, gentle wind.

> Fair laughs the morn, and soft the zephyr blows,
> While proudly riding o'er the azure realm
> In gallant trim the gilded vessel goes;
> Youth on the prow, and Pleasure at the helm.
>
> THOMAS GRAY: *The Bard* (1757)

**Zero** (Arabic *sifr*, 'empty', giving English 'cipher' and French *chiffre*, 'number'). The figure 0, nothing, especially the point on a scale (such as that of a thermometer) from which positive and negative quantities are measured. On the Centigrade or Celsius thermometer this is fixed at the freezing point of water, and on the Fahrenheit at 32° below freezing point.

**Zero hour.** A military term, first used in the First World War, for the exact time at which an attack or operation is to be begun. From this are timed the subsequent operations, e.g. zero + 3 means 3 minutes after zero hour. The term was succeeded in the Second World War by H-hour.

**Absolute zero.** *See under* ABSOLUTE.

**Ceiling zero.** *See under* CEILING.

**Hero from zero.** *See under* HERO.

**Zeugma** (Greek *zeugnunai*, 'to yoke'). In grammar and logic a term for a phrase in which one word modifies or governs two or more not connected in meaning. A well-known example is the following, in which the third and fifth lines are zeugmas:

> Whether the nymph shall break Diana's law,
> Or some frail china-jar receive a flaw;
> Or stain her honour or her new brocade;
> Forget her prayers, or miss a masquerade;
> Or lose her heart, or necklace, at a ball.
>
> ALEXANDER POPE: *The Rape of the Lock*, ii (1712)

**Zeus.** The most powerful of the Greek gods, the ruler of heaven and earth, and known to the Romans as JUPITER. He obtains his power by overthrowing the TITANS and rules from OLYMPUS. He is usually depicted as a great bearded figure carrying a thunderbolt. He is notorious for his affairs with human women, often changing his appearance to seduce them, despite his marriage to HERA. He fathers many other gods with the Titans or other goddesses. The root meaning of the name is perhaps 'life' (Greek *zēn*, 'to live') or, from the genitive form, *Dios*, 'sky', 'day' (Sanskrit *dyaus*, itself related to Latin *deus*, 'god'). *See also* GIANTS' WAR WITH ZEUS.

**Bacchus sprang from the thigh of Zeus.** *See under* BACCHUS.

**Giants' War with Zeus.** *See under* GIANT.

**Olympian Zeus.** *See under* OLYMPIA.

**Zigger-zagger.** The onomatopoeic nickname of the large rattle that football fans formerly brandished at matches. As it was swung round a handle it made a loud rasping or clacking sound. Peter Terson's play *Zigger Zagger* (1967) is about a football fan named Zigger and a football crowd.

**Zimri.** The name given by John Dryden in *Absalom and Achitophel* (1681) to George Villiers, 2nd Duke of Buckingham (1628–87), in allusion to the king of Israel who 'slew his master' and was himself overthrown (1 Kings 16).

**Zingari.** Gypsies, so called in Italy. The name is thought to derive from Byzantine Greek *Tsiganos*, the name of an oriental people, itself perhaps meaning 'not touching', from *atsigganos*, popularly pronounced *athigannos* (from *a-*, 'not', and *thigganō*, 'I touch').

> Zingaro is Sanscrit, and signifies a man of mixed race, a mongrel.
>
> GEORGE BORROW: *Lavengro*, Preface (1872 edition)

*See also* ROMANY.

**I Zingari** (Italian, 'the gypsies'). An exclusive nomadic CRICKET club, founded in 1845 by William Bolland. The club has no ground of its own, no subscription is payable, and Bolland is its perpetual president.

**Zinoviev Letter, The.** *See under* FAKES.

**Zion** (Hebrew *tsīyōn*, 'hill'). Figuratively, the chosen people, the Israelites, otherwise the church of God, the kingdom of heaven. The city of David stood on Mount Zion.

In PILGRIM'S PROGRESS (1678, 1684) John Bunyan calls the Celestial City (i.e. heaven) Mount Zion.

**Zionism.** The Jewish movement for the establishment of the 'national home' in Palestine. The Zionist movement was founded in 1895 by the Austrian Theodor Herzl (1860–1904), and the Balfour Declaration of 1917 recognized Zionist aspirations. From 1920 to 1948 Palestine was a British mandate, administered under great difficulties arising from the friction between Jews and Arabs. The independent state of Israel was established in 1948. The Palestine Liberation Organization (PLO), founded in 1964, has fought constantly, often at bitter cost, to regain some kind of Palestinian representation in what it regards as Israeli-occupied territory.

**Daughter of Zion.** *See under* DAUGHTER.

**Protocols of the Elders of Zion, The.** *See under* FAKES.

**Zip code.** In the USA the system used to differentiate the mail delivery zones, based on five-digit (or, since the late 1970s, nine-digit) numbers. The word 'Zip', while suggesting speed, is actually derived from the initial letters of the name of the system, Zone Improvement Plan. The British postcode composed of letters and numbers is a similar system. *See also* UNITED STATES OF AMERICA.

**Zodiac** (Greek *zōidiakos*, 'pertaining to animals', from *zōion*, 'animal'). The imaginary belt or zone of the heavens, extending about eight degrees each side of the ECLIPTIC, which the sun traverses annually.

The zodiac was divided by the ancients into 12 equal parts, proceeding from west to east, each part of 30 degrees and distinguished by a sign. These originally corresponded to the zodiacal constellations bearing the same names, but now, because of the precession of the equinoxes, they coincide with the constellations bearing the names next in order.

Beginning with ARIES, there are six signs on the north side and six on the south side of the Equator, while beginning with CAPRICORN, there are six ascending and then six descending signs, i.e. six that ascend higher and higher towards the north, and six that descend lower and lower towards the south. The six northern signs are: Aries (the ram), TAURUS (the bull) and GEMINI (the twins) as the spring signs, then CANCER (the crab), LEO (the lion) and VIRGO (the virgin) as the summer signs. The six southern signs are: LIBRA (the balance), SCORPIO (the scorpion) and SAGITTARIUS (the archer) as the autumn signs, then Capricorn (the goat), AQUARIUS (the water carrier) and PISCES (the fishes) as the winter signs.

> Our vernal signs the RAM begins,
> Then comes the BULL, in May the TWINS;
> The CRAB in June, next LEO shines,
> And VIRGO ends the northern signs.
> The BALANCE brings autumnal fruits,
> The SCORPION stings, the ARCHER shoots;
> December's GOAT brings wintry blast,
> AQUARIUS rain, the FISH come last.

*See also* ASCENDANT; ASTROLOGY; ASTROLOGICAL HOUSES; HOROSCOPE.

**Ram of the Zodiac, The.** *See under* RAM.

**Zoilus.** A Greek rhetorician of the 4th century BC, a literary THERSITES, shrewd, witty and spiteful, nicknamed Homeromastix ('Homer's scourge'), because he mercilessly assailed the epics of HOMER, and called the companions of Odysseus (ULYSSES) in the island of CIRCE 'weeping porkers'. He also attacked PLATO and ISOCRATES. His name has been applied to a spiteful and carping critic.

**Zollverein** (German *Zoll*, 'duty', and *Verein*, 'union'). A customs union. In German history the Prussian Zollverein, which developed from 1819, is of particular importance. By 1852 it included practically the whole of Germany, with the notable exclusion of Austria. Attempts to form rival unions were stillborn and the Zollverein was used by Prussia as an economic prelude to the struggle with Austria.

**Zombie.** The python god of certain West African tribes. Its worship was carried to the West Indies with the slave trade and still somewhat covertly survives in VOODOO ceremonies in Haiti and some of the southern states of the USA.

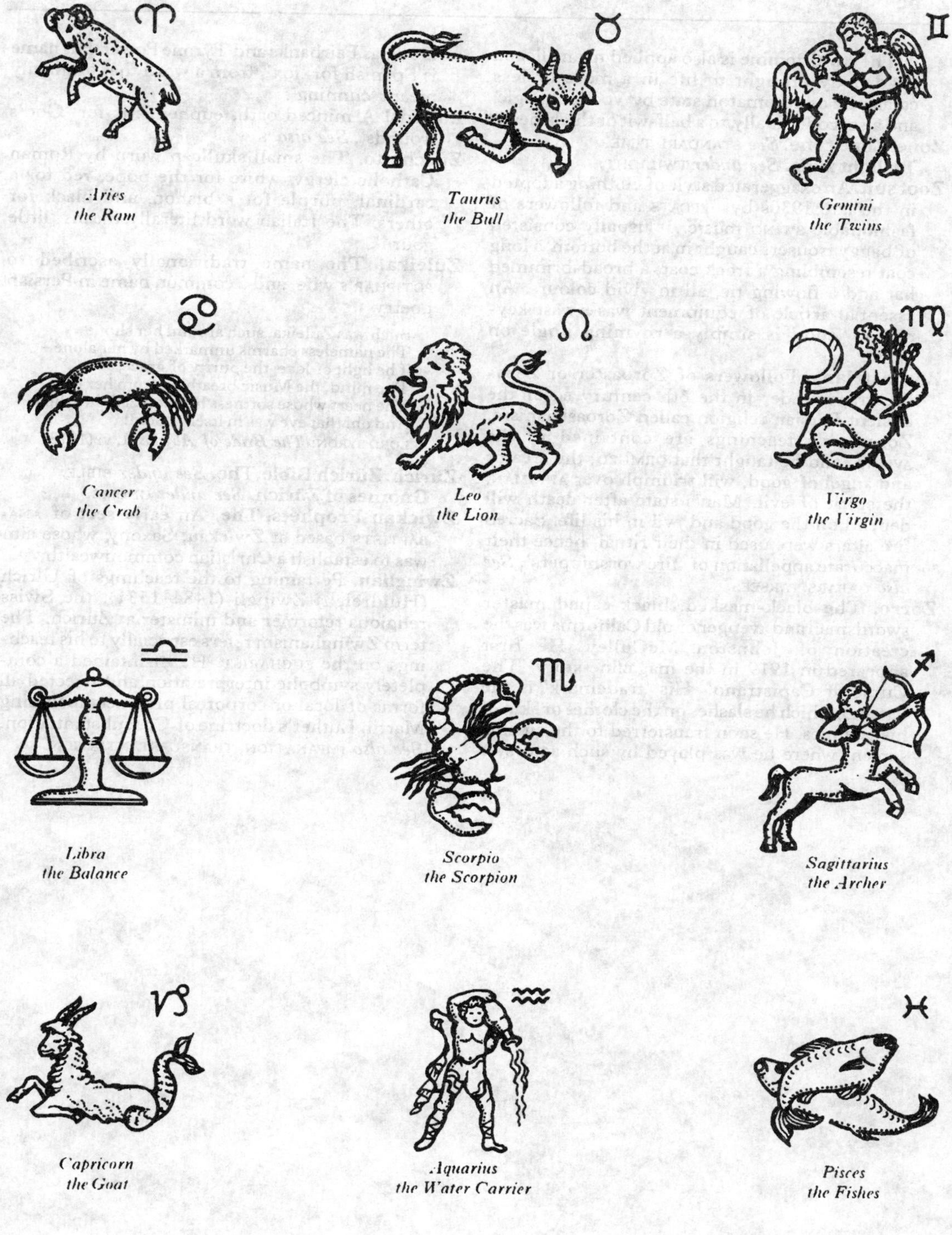
Aries
the Ram
Taurus
the Bull
Gemini
the Twins
Cancer
the Crab
Leo
the Lion
Virgo
the Virgin
Libra
the Balance
Scorpio
the Scorpion
Sagittarius
the Archer
Capricorn
the Goat
Aquarius
the Water Carrier
Pisces
the Fishes

**Zodiac**

The word zombie is also applied to an alleged dead body brought to life in a more or less cataleptic or automaton state by Voodoo magic, and also, colloquially, to a half-wit or thick-head.

**Zone. Zone time.** *See* STANDARD TIME.

**Twilight zone.** *See under* TWILIGHT.

**Zoot suit.** An exaggerated style of clothing adopted in the late 1930s by HEPCATS and followers of fashionable SWING music. It usually consisted of baggy trousers caught in at the bottom, a long coat resembling a frock coat, a broad-brimmed hat and a flowing tie, all in vivid colours. An essential article of equipment was a vast key-chain. 'Zoot' is simply a rhyming jingle on 'suit'.

**Zoroastrians.** Followers of Zoroaster or Zarathustra, founder in the 6th century BC of the ancient Persian religion called Zoroastrianism. Zoroaster's teachings are contained in the AVESTA, and he taught that ORMUZD, the creator and angel of good, will triumph over AHRIMAN, the spirit of evil. Man's state after death will depend on the good and evil in his life. Sacred fire altars were used in their ritual, hence their inaccurate appellation of 'fire worshippers'. *See also* GABARS; PARSEES.

**Zorro.** The black-masked, black-caped master swordsman and avenger of old California was the creation of Johnston McCulley. He first appeared in 1919 in the magazine story 'The Curse of Capistrano'. His 'trademark' is the letter Z, which he slashes on the clothes or skin of his enemies. He soon transferred to the cinema screen, where he was played by such actors as Douglas Fairbanks and Tyrone Power. His name is Spanish for 'fox', from a word that originally meant 'cunning'.

**Zounds!** A minced oath, euphemistic for 'God's wounds'. *See also* 'S.

**Zucchetto.** The small skullcap worn by Roman Catholic clergy, white for the pope, red for a cardinal, purple for a bishop, and black for others. The Italian word literally means 'little gourd'.

**Zuleika.** The name traditionally ascribed to POTIPHAR's wife, and a common name in Persian poetry.

> Such was Zuleika, such around her shone
> The nameless charms unmarked by her alone –
> The light of love, the purity of grace,
> The mind, the Music breathing from her face,
> The heart whose softness harmonized the whole,
> And oh! that eye was in itself a Soul!
>
> LORD BYRON: *The Bride of Abydos*, I, vi (1813)

**Zürich. Zürich Bible, The.** *See under* BIBLE.

**Gnomes of Zürich.** *See under* GNOME.

**Zwickau Prophets, The.** An early sect of ANABAPTISTS based at Zwickau, Saxony, whose aim was to establish a Christian commonwealth.

**Zwinglian.** Pertaining to the teachings of Ulrich (Huldreich) Zwingli (1484–1531), the Swiss religious reformer and minister at Zürich. The term Zwinglianism refers especially to his teachings on the EUCHARIST. He maintained a completely symbolic interpretation and rejected all forms of local or corporeal presence, including Martin Luther's doctrine of Consubstantiation. *See also* IMPANATION; TRANSUBSTANTIATION.